Hebrew Bible / Old Testament
The History of Its Interpretation

Volume II

V&R

Hebrew Bible / Old Testament
The History of Its Interpretation

Edited by
Magne Sæbø

VOLUME II
From the Renaissance to the Enlightenment

Göttingen · Vandenhoeck & Ruprecht · 2008

Hebrew Bible / Old Testament
The History of Its Interpretation

VOLUME II
From the Renaissance to the Enlightenment

In Co-operation with
Michael Fishbane and Jean Louis Ska, SJ

Edited by
Magne Sæbø

Göttingen · Vandenhoeck & Ruprecht · 2008

Mit 3 Abbildungen

Bibliografische Information der Deutschen Nationalbibliothek
Die Deutsche Nationalbibliothek verzeichnet diese Publikation in
der Deutschen Nationalbibliografie; detaillierte bibliografische Daten
sind im Internet über http://dnb.d-nb.de abrufbar.

ISBN 978-3-525-53982-8

Gesamtherstellung: ⊕ Hubert & Co, Göttingen

Gedruckt auf alterungsbeständigem Papier

Contents

A. Scriptural Interpretation
in the Context of the Renaissance

B. Scriptural Interpretation in
Church Reforms and in the Reformation

C. Scriptural Interpretation between Orthodoxy and Rationalism and the Establishing of a Historical-Critical Study of the Hebrew Bible / Old Testament in the Seventeenth and Eighteenth Centuries

Preface

When the planning of the Hebrew Bible / Old Testament Project (HBOT) started, around 1980, the general interest in the reception-history of the interpretation of the Bible – the Old as well as the New Testament – was surprisingly low and stood at the fringe of Bible studies and Church History. Since then there has been an awakening of interest in this field, with a related demand, and various publications have appeared.[1] In this context, it has been most encouraging that the two parts of the first HBOT volume (I/1, *Antiquity*, 1996, and I/2, *The Middle Ages*, 2000) have generally been well received. The progress of the project as a whole, on the other hand, has regrettably not proceeded according to the original plan and timetable. This is especially the case with the publication of the present HBOT volume which, for various reasons, has been greatly delayed. I can only ask for the readers' kind understanding and forbearance.

Unlike the division of the first volume into two parts, the second volume has not been divided in the same way, although it covers a very long and widely diverse period of time, *From the Renaissance to the Enlightenment*. Quite apart from some technical difficulties, this *modus procedendi* may at least be justified by the subject matter itself. Despite the fact that this long period of time includes very different historical epochs which display a diverse and varied character, it exhibits nonetheless a certain consistency with many connecting lines and interwoven threads continuing throughout the duration of the period. As will be shown, this can to a large extent be associated with the influence of a pronounced humanism and individualism, which forms a bridge between the Renaissance and the Enlightenment, taking into account the particular character of both. With this spread across such a complex period due consideration has had to be given both to its diversity and its unitary character.

The time of completion is also a time for acknowledgements. First of all, I should like to thank the colleagues and experts of various disciplines and different scholarly milieux who have contributed to the presentation of this part of the history of biblical interpretation in general and of the Hebrew Bible / Old Testament in particular. Throughout the period from the Renaissance to the Enlightenment there appears a very distinctive and many-sided web of intellectual history. Without drawing any sharp borderlines, there are two main types of contribution to the present HBOT volume. Some authors have set out the 'non-theological' factors which form the wider institutional, cultural and ideological context of biblical interpretation, on which it was, in varying de-

---

[1] See further by the present author: "Zur neueren Interpretationsgeschichte des Alten Testaments", *ThLZ* 130 (2005) 1033–44.

grees, dependent. In contrast, however, most of the contributors have treated in closer detail the more specific history of biblical interpretation. It may be affirmed throughout that the essays represent new personal research, often grounded on the individual author's original investigation. As in the preceding HBOT volumes it has been important to preserve the authors' presentation, even in respect of cases where a subject has also been treated elsewhere in the volume, since this may contribute to the completeness of a many-sided picture. Cases of obvious overlapping have been avoided.

Furthermore, it is a pleasure to express my deep gratitude to the distinguished Coeditors of this volume, Professor Michael Fishbane, of Chicago, on the Jewish side, and Professor Jean Louis Ska SJ, of Rome, on the Catholic side, in acknowledgement of their excellent advice and help. Likewise, I feel deeply obliged to Professor Ronald E. Clements, of Cambridge, who has given HBOT a required and valuable help by correcting the English of essays written by non native-speaking authors. In addition, I would also like to pay tribute to colleagues who most generously have assisted me in various ways, especially the HBOT authors John W. Rogerson, of Sheffield, Bertram E. Schwarzbach, of Paris, Lesley Smith, of Oxford, and Arjo Vanderjagt, of Groningen, and, outside the HBOT authors, my Oslo colleagues, Professor Ivar Asheim, and Professor Ingun Montgomery (now Uppsala).

Like the preceding HBOT volumes also this volume has received financial support and I am deeply indebted to the *Norwegian Research Council* as well as to the *Norwegian Academy of Science and Letters*, and especially to the *Fridtjof Nansen Fond*, for their generous support of the editorial work and the linguistic control. I also remain indebted to my own faculty, the *Norwegian School of Theology*, in Oslo, and in particular to its Library staff, for their great practical support of the Project. Finally, I would like to thank Dr. theol. Øystein Lund and M. theol. Rune Vik for their invaluable assistance in the work on the Indexes.

Oslo, in November 2006/October 2007   Magne Sæbø

From the Renaissance to the Enlightenment – Aspects of the Cultural and Ideological Framework of Scriptural Interpretation

By MAGNE SÆBØ, Oslo

General works: Bible de tous les temps [BTT] (ed. C. Kannengiesser; Paris: Beauchesne), 5. *Le temps des Réformes et la Bible* (ed. G. Bedouelle / B. Roussel; 1989); 6. *Le Grand Siècle et la Bible* (ed. J.-R. Armogathe; 1989); 7. *Le siècle des Lumières et la Bible* (ed. Y. Belaval / D. Bourel; 1986); *The Cambridge Companion to Renaissance Humanism* (ed. J. Kraye; Cambridge: Cambridge UP 1996); *The Cambridge History of the Bible* [CHB] (Cambridge: Cambridge UP), 2. *The West from the Fathers to the Reformation* (ed. G. W. H. Lampe; 1969; repr. 1980); 3. *The West from the Reformation to the Present Day* (ed. S. L. Greenslade; 1963, repr. 1978); *The Cambridge History of Renaissance Philosophy* (ed. C. B. Schmitt e.a.; Cambridge: Cambridge UP 1988; repr. 1996); *The Cambridge Illustrated History of the Middle Ages* III. *1250–1520* (ed. R. Fossier; Cambridge: Cambridge UP 1986); L. DIESTEL, *Die Geschichte des Alten Testamentes in der christlichen Kirche* (Jena 1869; repr. Leipzig 1981); F. W. FARRAR, *History of Interpretation* (London: Macmillan / New York: Duton 1886; repr. Grand Rapids, MI 1961, 1979); R. M. GRANT / D. TRACY, *A Short History of the Interpretation of the Bible* (Sec. edn., rev. and enlarged; London: SCM Press 1984); E. McQUEEN GRAY, *Old Testament Criticism, Its Rise and Progress: From the Second Century to the End of the Eighteenth. A Historical Sketch* (New York / London cr. 1923); *Handbook of European History 1400–1600. Late Middle Ages, Renaissance and Reformation* I–II (ed. Th. A. Brady / H. A. Oberman / J. D. Tracy; Leiden e.a. 1994–95); *Handbuch der Dogmen- und Theologiegeschichte* [HDTG] (ed. C. Andresen; Göttingen: Vandenhoeck & Ruprecht), 2. *Die Lehrentwicklung im Rahmen der Konfessionalität* (1980); 3. *Die Lehrentwicklung im Rahmen der Ökumenizität* (1984) 1–146; E. HIRSCH, *Geschichte der neuern evangelischen Theologie im Zusammenhang mit den allgemeinen Bewegungen des europäischen Denkens* I–IV (Gütersloh: Gerd Mohn ²1960); H. KARPP, *Schrift, Geist und Wort Gottes. Geltung und Wirkung der Bibel in der Geschichte der Kirche von der Alten Kirche bis zum Ausgang der Reformationszeit* (Darmstadt: Wiss. Buchgesellschaft 1992); E. G. KRAELING, *The Old Testament since the Reformation* (London 1955; New York 1969); H.-J. KRAUS, *Geschichte der historisch-kritischen Erforschung des Alten Testaments* ([1956] 3. erw. Aufl., Neukirchen-Vluyn: Neukirchener 1982); H.-W. KRUMWIEDE, *Geschichte des Christentums* III. *Neuzeit: 17. bis 20. Jahrhundert* (Theol. Wiss. 8; Stuttgart: Kohlhammer 1977); H. DE LUBAC, *Exégèse médiévale: les quatre sens de l'écriture* I/1–2, II/1–2 (Paris: Aubier 1959–64); A. E. McGRATH, *Reformation Thought. An Introduction* (Oxford: Blackwell [1988] ³1999); *The Oxford Illustrated History of the Bible* (ed. J. Rogerson; Oxford: Oxford UP 2001); H. GRAF REVENTLOW, *Epochen der Bibelauslegung* III. *Renaissance, Reformation, Humanismus* (München: Beck 1997); IV. *Von der Aufklärung bis zum 20. Jahrhundert* (2001); J. ROGERSON / CHR. ROWLAND / B. LINDARS, *The Study and Use of the Bible* (Basingstoke: Pickering / Grand Rapids: Eerdmans 1988); J. ROHLS, *Protestantische Theologie der Neuzeit* I. *Die Voraussetzungen und das 19. Jahrhundert* (Tübingen: Mohr Siebeck 1997); J. SANDYS-WUNSCH, *What Have They Done to the Bible? A History of Modern Biblical Interpretation* (Collegeville, MN: Liturgical Press 2005); R. SCHÄFER, *Die Bibelauslegung in der Geschichte der Kirche* (Gütersloh: Gerd Mohn 1980).

Reference and bibliographical works: U. BARTH, "Säkularisierung", TRE XXIX (1998) 603–34 (I. Systematisch-theologisch); A. BAUM / G. BADER, "Skepsis / Skeptizismus", TRE XXXI (2000) 349–61 (I. Philosophisch), 361–67 (II. Systematisch-theologisch); A. BEUTEL, "Aufklärung" I–II,

RGG⁴ 1 (1998) 929–51; H.-O. Binder, "Säkularisation", TRE XXIX (1998) 597–602; *A Dictionary of Biblical Interpretation* [DBI] (ed. R. J. Coggins / J. L. Houlden; London: SCM Press / Philadelphia: Trinity Press International 1990); *Dictionary of Biblical Interpretation* A-J, K-Z [DBInt] (ed. J. H. Hayes; Nashville: Abingdon 1999); *The Dante Encyclopedia* (ed. R. Lansing; New York / London 2000); *Encyclopedia of the Renaissance* 1–6 [EncRen] (ed. P. F. Grendler; New York: Charles Scribner's Sons 1999; esp. the main entry "Renaissance", 5 [1999] 259–305, with five subentries, first, P. F. Grendler, "The Renaissance in Historical Thought", 259–68, later, "Renaissance Studies", where various modern scholars are presented [by various authors] 283–305); *Historical Handbook of Major Biblical Interpreters* (ed. D. K. McKim; Downers Grove, IL / Leicester: InterVarsity Press 1998); U. Köpf, "Renaissance" I, II.2, RGG⁴ 7 (2004) 431–32, 434–40; B. G. Kohl, *Renaissance Humanism, 1300–1550. A Bibliography of Materials in English* (New York / London: Garland Publ. 1985); M. Landfester / H. Scheible, "Humanismus" I-IV, RGG⁴ 3 (2000) 1938–46; H. Lehmann / F. W. Graf, "Säkularisation / Säkularisierung II. Geschichtlich", RGG⁴ 7 (2004) 775–82; J.-C. Margolin, "Renaissance", TRE XXIX (1998) 74–87; R. Piepmeier / M. Schmidt / H. Greive, "Aufklärung", TRE IV (1979) 575–615 (I, Philosophisch, 575–94; II. Theologisch, 594–608; III. Jüdische Aufklärung, 608–15); *Reformation Europe: A Guide to Research* (ed. S. Ozment; St. Louis, MO cr. 1982); M. Sæbø, "Zur neueren Interpretationsgeschichte des Alten Testaments", *ThLZ* 130 (2005) 1033–44; L. W. Spitz, "Humanismus / Humanismusforschung", TRE XV (1986) 639–61; G. Stemberger / D.-A. Koch / E. Mühlenberg, "Schriftauslegung" I-III, TRE XXX (1999) 442–88; F. Wagner, "Erleuchtung", TRE X (1982) 164–74; F. Watson, "Enlightenment", DBI (1990) 191–94 ; Th. Zippert / S. Andersen, "Humanität (Menschlichkeit)", RGG⁴ 3 (2000) 1938–46.

Special studies: H. Baron, "Burckhardt's 'Civilization of the Renaissance'. A Century after its Publication", *Renaissance News* 13 (1960) 207–22; idem, *The Crisis of the Early Italian Renaissance. Civic Humanism and Republican Liberty in an Age of Classicism and Tyranny* (rev. edn. with an Epilogue; Princeton, NJ: Princeton UP 1966); C. Bartholomew e.a. (eds.), *"Behind" the Text: History and Biblical Interpretation* (Scripture and Hermeneutics Series 4; Carlisle: Paternoster Press / Grand Rapids, MI: Zondervan 2003); [Pierre Bayle:] *The Great Contest of Faith and Reason: Selections from the Writings of Pierre Bayle* (tr. and ed. with an introduction by K. C. Sandberg; Milestones of Thought; New York: Frederick Ungar 1963); G. Bedouelle, "L'humanisme et la Bible", BTT 5 (1989) 53–121; G. von Below, *Über historische Periodisierungen* (Berlin 1925); J. H. Bentley, *Humanists and Holy Writ. New Testament Scholarship in the Renaissance* (Princeton, NJ: Princeton UP 1983); J. Berlinerblau, *The Secular Bible. Why Nonbelievers Must Take Religion Seriously* (Cambridge: Cambridge UP 2005); R. Black, *Humanism and education in medieval and Renaissance Italy: tradition and innovation in Latin schools from the twelfth to the fifteenth century* (Cambridge: Cambridge UP 2001); H. Blumenberg, "Licht als Metapher der Wahrheit", StGen 10 (1957) 432–47; R. Bonfil, *Jewish Life in Renaissance Italy* (Berkeley, CA: University of California Press 1994); E. Breisach (ed.), *Classical Rhetoric & Medieval Historiography* (Studies in Medieval Culture XIX; Kalamazoo, MI 1985); A. Buck (ed.), *Zu Begriff und Problem der Renaissance* (WdF CCIV; Darmstadt: Wiss. Buchgesellschaft 1969); J. Burckhardt, *Die Kultur der Renaissance in Italien. Ein Versuch* ([orig. *Die Cultur der Renaissance...*, Basel 1860], *Jacob Burckhardt-Gesamtausgabe* 5; ed. W. Kaegi; Stuttgart e.a.: Deutsche Verlags-Anstalt 1930; Mikrofice 18914/18915, München: Saur [1994]), ET: *The Civilisation of the Period of the Renaissance in Italy* 1–2 (tr. S. G. C. Middlemore; London 1878), also *The Civilization of the Renaissance in Italy* 1–2 (edn. Harper Torchbooks / The Cloister Library; New York ⁸1965), and *The Civilization of the Renaissance. An Essay* (tr. S. G. C. Middlemore; 3ʳᵈ edn.; Oxford / London: Phaidon 1995); P. Burke, *The Renaissance Sense of the Past* (New York: St. Martin's 1970); idem, "The Spread of Italian Humanism", in [see below]: Goodman / MacKay, The Impact of Humanism (1993) 1–22; J. B. Bullen, *The Myth of the Renaissance in Nineteenth-Century Writing* (Oxford: Clarendon Press 1994); A. Chastel, *The Crisis of the Renaissance 1520–1600* (tr. from French by P. Price; Geneva 1968); T. K. Cheyne, *Founders of Old Testament Criticism. Biographical, Descriptive, and Critical Studies* (London: Methuen 1893); B. Cohen, "The Many Faces of the History of Science", in: C. F. Delzell (ed.), *The Future of History: Essays in the Vanderbilt University Centennial Symposium* (Nashville: Vanderbilt UP 1977) 65–110; J. F. D'Amico, *Theory and Practice in Renaissance Textual Criticism: Beatus Rhenanus between Conjecture and History* (Berkeley, CA: University of California Press 1988); H. Daniel-Rops, *L'Eglise de la Renaissance et de la Réforme* I-II (Paris 1955); K. H. Dannenfeldt (ed.), *The Renaissance. Basic Interpretations* (Problems in European Civilization; sec. edn., Lexington, MA: D. C. Heath 1974); G. EBELING, *Wort und Glaube* (Tübingen: Mohr 1960, ³1967), ET: *Word and Faith* (Philadelphia: Fortress Press 1963); idem, "Kirchengeschichte als Geschichte der Auslegung der Heiligen Schrift", in: idem, *Wort Gottes und Tradition* (Göttingen: Vandenhoeck & Ruprecht 1964) 9–27; O. FATIO / P. FRAENKEL, *Histoire de l'exégèse au XVIe siècle. Textes du colloque international tenu à Genève en 1976* (Genève: Droz 1978); H. FELD, *Die Anfänge der modernen biblischen Hermeneutik in der spätmittelalterlichen Theologie* (Wiesbaden: Franz Steiner 1977); J. FELLERMEIER, "Die Illuminationstheorie bei Augustinus und Bonaventura und die aprioristische Begründung der Erkenntnis durch Kant", PhJ 60 (1950) 296–305; W. K. FERGUSON, "Humanist Views of the Renaissance", *AHR* 45 (1939) 1–28; idem, *The Renaissance in Historical Thought. Five Centuries of Interpretation* (Boston: Houghton Mifflin 1948; repr. New York: AMS Press 1981); idem, "The Reinterpretations of the Renaissance", in: W. H. WERKMEISTER (ed.), *Facets of the Renaissance* (Los Angeles 1959, repr. 1971) 1–17 (also repr. in: Dannenfeldt, The Renaissance [1974] 200–14); idem e.a., *The Renaissance. Six Essays* (New York / Evanston: Harper & Row 1962); K. FLASCH / U. R. JECK (eds.), *Das Licht der Vernunft: die Anfänge der Aufklärung im Mittelalter* (München: Beck 1997); J. E. FORCE / R. H. POPKIN (eds.), *The Books of Nature and Scripture: Recent Essays on Natural Philosophy, Theology, and Biblical Criticism in the Netherlands of Spinoza's Time and the British Isles of Newton's Time* (Archives internationales d'histoire des idées 139; Dordrecht: Kluwer Academics cr. 1994); H. FREI, *The Eclipse of Biblical Narrative: A Study in Eighteenth and Nineteenth Century Hermeneutics* (New Haven / London: Yale UP 1974); idem, *Theology and Narrative: Selected Essays* (ed. G. Hunsinger / W. C. Placher; New York: Oxford UP 1993); J. FRIEDMAN, *The Most Ancient Testimony. Sixteenth-Century Christian-Hebraica in the Age of Renaissance Nostalgia* (Athens, OH: Ohio UP cr. 1983); E. B. FRYDE, *Humanism and Renaissance Historiography* (London: Hambledon 1983); A. FUNKENSTEIN, *Perceptions of Jewish History* (Berkeley / Los Angeles: University of California Press 1993; German tr. *Jüdische Geschichte und ihre Deutungen*, Frankfurt/M: Jüdischer Verlag 1995); H.-G. GADAMER, *Wahrheit und Methode* (Tübingen: Mohr 1960, ⁴1975; ET: *Truth and Method*; sec. edn.; London: Sheed and Ward 1979); E. GARIN, *Italian Humanism: Philosophy and Civic Life in the Renaissance* (tr. P. Munz; New York 1965); P. GAY, *The Enlightenment: an Interpretation. The Rise of Modern Paganism* (The Norton Library 870; New York: Norton 1977); idem, *The Enlightenment: an Interpretation. The Science of Freedom* (The Norton Library 875; New York: Norton 1977); D. GERHARD, "Periodization in European History", *AHR* 61 (1955/56) 900–13; M. P. GILMORE, *The World of Humanism, 1453–1517* (New York: Harper & Row 1952, 1962); A. GOODMAN / A. MACKAY (eds.), *The Impact of Humanism on Western Europe* (London / New York: Longman 1990, repr. 1993); E. GÖLLER, *Die Periodisierung der Kirchengeschichte und die epochale Stellung des Mittelalters zwischen dem christlichen Altertum und der Neuzeit* [Freiburg / Br. 1919] (together with [see below]; K. HEUSSI, *Altertum, Mittelalter und Neuzeit in der Kirchengeschichte* [Tübingen 1921]; repr. in: Reihe "Libelli", CCLXIII; Darmstadt: Wiss. Buchgesellschaft [1969] 7–73); A. GRAFTON, *Defenders of the Text: The Traditions of Scholarship in an Age of Science, 1450–1800* (Cambridge, MA 1991); idem, "The new science and the traditions of humanism", in: *The Cambridge Companion to Renaissance Humanism* (1996) 203–23; A. HAMILTON, "Humanists and the Bible", in: *The Cambridge Companion to Renaissance Humanism* (1996) 100–17; R. A. HARRISVILLE / W. SUNDBERG, *The Bible in Modern Culture: Baruch Spinoza to Brevard Childs* (sec. edn.; Grand Rapids, MI: Eerdmans 2002); C. H. HASKINS, *The Renaissance of the Twelfth Century* ([1927] Cleveland, OH: Meridian 1957); E. HASSINGER, *Das Werden des neuzeitlichen Europa. 1300–1600* (Geschichte der Neuzeit; Braunschweig 1959); D. HAY, *Europe. The Emergence of an Idea* (Edinburgh 1957; New York: Harper & Row 1966); idem, *The Italian Renaissance in Its Historical Background* (Cambridge 1961, ²1977); idem (ed.), *The Age of the Renaissance* (London: Thames and Hudson 1967; amply ill.); idem (ed.), *The Renaissance Debate* (New York e.a.: Holt, Rinehart and Winston 1965); P. HAZARD, *The European Mind: The Critical Years 1680–1715* (orig.: *La crise de la conscience européenne*; tr. J. Lewis May; New Haven 1953); T. HELTON (ed.), *The Renaissance. A Reconsideration of the Theories and Interpretations of the Age* (Madison, WI: Univ. of Wisconsin Press 1961; repr. 1964); K. HEUSSI, *Altertum, Mittelalter und Neuzeit in der Kirchengeschichte. Ein Beitrag zum Problem der historischen Periodisierung* (1921/1969; together with [see above]; E. GÖLLER, *Die Periodisierung der Kirchengeschichte*) 74–146; G. A. HOLMES, *The Florentine Enlightenment, 1400–1450* (New York 1969); G. HORNIG, *Die Anfänge der historisch-kritischen Theologie: Johann Salomo Semlers Schriftverständnis und seine Stellung zu Luther* (FSThR 8; Göttingen: Vandenhoeck & Ruprecht 1961); W. HÜBENER, "Descartes, René (1596–1650)", TRE VIII (1981) 499–510; J. HUIZINGA, *The Autumn of the Middle*

Ages (orig.: *Herfsttij der Middeleeuwen* [1921]; tr. R. Payton / U. Mammitzsch; Chicago: Univ. of Chicago Press 1996); J. I. ISRAEL, *Radical Enlightenment. Philosophy and the Making of Modernity 1650–1750* (Oxford: Oxford UP 2001); A. KLEMPT, *Die Säkularisierung der universalhistorischen Auffassung. Zum Wandel des Geschichtsdenkens im 16. und 17. Jahrhundert* (Göttinger Bausteine zur Geschichtswissenschaft 31; Göttingen: Musterschmidt 1960); P. KONDYLIS, *Die Aufklärung im Rahmen des neuzeitlichen Rationalismus* (Stuttgart: Klett-Cotta 1981); P. O. KRISTELLER, *The Classics and Renaissance Thought* (Martin Classical Lectures XV; Cambridge, MA 1955); idem, *Studies in Renaissance Thought and Letters* (Roma: Edizioni di storia e letteratura 1956); idem, "Renaissanceforschung und Altertumswissenschaft", *FuF* 33 (1959) 363–69; idem, *Renaissance Thought: The Classic, Scholastic, and Humanist Strains* (rev. edn. of *The Classics and Renaissance Thought*; Harper Torchbooks 1048; New York: Harper & Row 1961); idem, "Changing Views of the Intellectual History of the Renaissance since Jacob Burckhardt", in: Helton, The Renaissance (1964) 27–52; idem, "The Place of Classical Humanism in Renaissance Thought", in: Dannenfeldt (ed.), The Renaissance (1974) 141–47; idem, *Humanismus und Renaissance* I-II (UTB 914/915; München: Wilhelm Fink 1974/1976); idem, "Humanism", in: *The Cambridge History of Renaissance Philosophy* (ed. C. B. Schmitt e.a.; Cambridge: Cambridge UP 1988) 113–37; idem, "Renaissance Humanism and Classical Antiquity", in: Rabil, Renaissance Humanism 1 (1988) 5–16; idem, "The Cultural Heritage of Humanism: An Overview", in: Rabil, Renaissance Humanism 3 (1988) 515–28; J. L. KUGEL, "The Bible in the University", in: *The Hebrew Bible and Its Interpreters* (ed. W. H. Propp e.a.; Winona Lake, IN: Eisenbrauns 1990) 143–65; R. E. LERNER / E. MÜLLER-LUCKNER (eds.), *Neue Richtungen in der hoch- und spätmittelalterlichen Bibelexegese* (Schriften des Historischen Kollegs 32; München: Oldenbourg 1996); W. MCKANE, *Selected Christian Hebraists* (Cambridge: Cambridge UP 1989); J. MICHELET, *OEuvres complètes* (ed. P. Viallaneix), 7. *Histoire de France au seizième siècle: Renaissance, Reforme* ([1855], ed. R. Casanova; Paris: Flammarion 1978); W. D. MIGNOLO, *The Darker Side of the Renaissance: Literacy, Territoriality, and Colonization* (Ann Arbor: Univ. of Michigan Press 1995); E. MINER (ed.), *Literary Uses of Typology from the Late Middle Ages to the Present* (Princeton: Princeton UP 1977); J. MITTELSTRASS, *Neuzeit und Aufklärung: Studien zur Entstehung der neuzeitlichen Wissenschaft und Philosophie* (Berlin: de Gruyter 1970); B. MOELLER, "Vom Mittelalter zur Neuzeit. Neue Meinungen und Einsichten zu Renaissance und Humanismus", *VuF* 21 (1976) 32–46; H. MÖLLER, *Vernunft und Kritik: Deutsche Aufklärung im 17. und 18. Jahrhundert* (Edition Suhrkamp 1269; Frankfurt / M: Suhrkamp 1997); TH. E. MOMMSEN, *Medieval and Renaissance Studies* (ed. E. F. Rice, Jr.; Ithaca, NY: Cornell UP 1959, repr. 1966); C. G. NAUERT, JR., *Humanism and the Culture of Renaissance Europe* (New Approaches to European History 6; Cambridge: Cambridge UP 1995, repr. 1998); idem, "Humanism / The Definition of Humanism", EncRen 3 (1999) 209–10; U. NEDDERMEYER, *Das Mittelalter in der deutschen Historiographie vom 15. bis zum 18. Jahrhundert. Geschichtsgliederung und Epochenverständnis in der frühen Neuzeit* (Phil. Diss. Univ. Köln; Kölner hist. Abhandlungen 34; Köln / Wien: Böhlau 1988); S. OZMENT, *The Age of Reform, 1250–1550* (New Haven / London 1980); W. PHILIPP, *Das Werden der Aufklärung in theologiegeschichtlicher Sicht* (FSThR 3; Göttingen: Vandenhoeck & Ruprecht 1957); R. POMEAU, *L'Europe des Lumières: Cosmopolitisme et unité européenne au XVIIIe siècle* (Nouv. éd.; Paris: Stock 1991); R. H. POPKIN, *The History of Scepticism from Erasmus to Descartes* (Wijsgerige Teksten en Studies IV; Assen: Van Gorcum 1960; Berkely / Los Angeles 1979); G. R. POTTER, *The Renaissance, 1493–1520* (The New Cambridge Modern History 1; Cambridge: Cambridge UP 1957); J. S. PREUS, *From Shadow to Promise: Old Testament Interpretation from Augustine to the Young Luther* (Cambridge, MA: Harvard UP 1969); P. PÜTZ (ed.), *Die deutsche Aufklärung* (EdF 81; Darmstadt: Wiss. Buchgesellschaft 1978); A. RABIL, JR. (ed.), *Renaissance Humanism: Foundations, Forms, and Legacy* 1-3 (Philadelphia: Univ. of Pennsylvania Press 1988); J. RATZINGER, "Licht und Erleuchtung", *StGen* 13 (1960) 368–78; T. RENDTORFF (ed.), *Religion als Problem der Aufklärung: eine Bilanz aus der religionstheoretischen Forschung* (Göttingen: Vandenhoeck & Ruprecht 1980); H. GRAF REVENTLOW, *Bibelautorität und Geist der Moderne* (Göttingen: Vandenhoeck & Ruprecht 1980; ET: *The Authority of the Bible and the Rise of the Modern World;* tr. J. Bowden; London: SCM 1984); idem, "Computing Times, Ages and the Millennium: An Astronomer Defends the Bible. William Whiston (1667–1752) and Biblical Chronology", in: *The Bible in Human Society. Essays in Honour of John Rogerson* (JSOTSup 200; ed. M. D. Carroll e.a.; Sheffield: Sheffield Academic Press 1995) 411–21; J. B. ROGERS / D. K. MCKIM, *The Authority and Interpretation of the Bible. An Historical Approach* (San Francisco: Harper & Row 1979); D. B. RUDERMAN, *The World of a Renaissance Jew. The Life and Thought of Abraham ben Mordecai Far-*

issol (Cincinnati: Hebrew Union College Press 1981); idem, *Jewish Thought and Scientific Discovery in Early Modern Europe* (New Haven / London: Yale UP 1995); E. SANFORD, "The Twelfth Century – Renaissance or Proto-Renaissance?", *Spec.* 26 (1951) 635–42; G. SARTON, *Six Wings. Men of Science in the Renaissance* (Bloomington: Indiana UP 1957); P. SCHAEFFER, "The Emergence of the Concept 'Medieval' in Central European Humanism", *Sixteenth Century Journal* 7 (1973) 19–30; C. SCHMID, *Die Mittelalterrezeption des 18. Jahrhunderts zwischen Aufklärung und Romantik* (EHS, R. 1: Deutsche Literatur und Germanistik 278; Frankfurt/M: Peter Lang 1979); W. SCHNEIDERS, *Die wahre Aufklärung: Zum Selbstverständnis der deutschen Aufklärung* (Freiburg / Br.: Karl Alber 1974); K. SCHOLDER, *Ursprünge und Probleme der Bibelkritik im 17. Jahrhundert. Ein Beitrag zur Entstehung der historisch-kritischen Theologie* (FGLP 10/XXXIII; München: Kaiser 1966); B. E. SCHWARZBACH (ed.), *La Bible imprimée dans l'Europe moderne* (Paris: BNF 1999); J. E. SEIGEL, *Rhetoric and Philosophy in Renaissance Humanism. The Union of Eloquence and Wisdom, Petrarch to Valla* (Princeton, NJ: Princeton UP 1968); J. SHEEHAN, *The Enlightenment Bible: Translation, Scholarship, Culture* (Princeton: Princeton UP 2005); S. SKALWEIT, *Der Beginn der Neuzeit. Epochengrenze und Epochenbegriff* (EdF 178; Darmstadt: Wiss. Buchgesellschaft 1982); R. SMEND, *Deutsche Alttestamentler in drei Jahrhunderten* (Göttingen: Vandenhoeck & Ruprecht 1989); idem, *Epochen der Bibelkritik* (BevT 109; München: Kaiser 1991); idem (ed.), *Das Alte Testament im Protestantismus* (Neukirchen-Vluyn: Neukirchener 1995); idem, *Bibel und Wissenschaft* (Tübingen: Mohr Siebeck 2004); L. W. SPITZ, *The Religious Renaissance of the German Humanists* (Cambridge, MA: Harvard UP 1963); idem, "Periodization in History: Renaissance and Reformation", in: C. F. DELZELL (ed.), *The Future of History: Essays in the Vanderbilt University Centennial Symposium* (Nashville: Vanderbilt UP 1977) 189–218; idem, *The Renaissance and Reformation Movements* 1–2 (St. Louis, MO: Concordia 1980, rev. edn. 1987); D. C. STEINMETZ (ed.), *The Bible in the Sixteenth Century* (Duke Monographs in Medieval and Renaissance Studies 11; Durham, NC: Duke UP 1990); R. N. STROMBERG, *Religious Liberalism in Eighteenth Century England* (London: Oxford UP 1954); N. STRUEVER (ed.), *Language and the History of Thought* (Library of the History of Ideas XIII; Rochester: Univ. of Rochester Press 1995); B. THOMPSON, *Humanists and Reformers. A History of the Renaissance and Reformation* (Grand Rapids, MI / Cambridge: Eerdmans 1996); L. THORNDIKE, "Renaissance or Prerenaissance?", *JHI* 4 (1943) 65–74; G. TOFFANIN, *Geschichte des Humanismus* (orig.: Storia dell'Umanesimo; s.l. [Amsterdam]: Akademische Verlagsanstalt Pantheon 1941); C. TRINKAUS, *In Our Image and Likeness: Humanity and Divinity in Italian Humanist Thought* 1–2 ([Chicago 1970] Notre Dame, IN: Univ. of Notre Dame Press 1995); idem, *The Scope of Renaissance Humanism* (Ann Arbor: Univ. of Michigan Press cr. 1983); E. TROELTSCH, "Die Aufklärung" (1897), in: idem, *Ges. Schriften* IV (Tübingen: Mohr 1925) 338–74; B. UFFENHEIMER / H. GRAF REVENTLOW (eds.), *Creative Biblical Exegesis. Christian and Jewish Hermeneutics through the Centuries* (JSOTSup 59; Sheffield 1988); B. L. ULLMAN, *Studies in the Italian Renaissance* (Roma: Edizioni di storia e letteratura 1955); G. VOIGT, *Die Wiederbelebung des classischen Alterthums, oder Das erste Jahrhundert des Humanismus* 1–2 ([1859], unveränd. Nachdruck der im 1895 ersch. 3. Aufl.; Berlin: De Gruyter 1960); R. WEISS, *The Spread of Italian Humanism* (London: Hutchinson 1964); W. H. WERKMEISTER (ed.), *Facets of the Renaissance* (Los Angeles 1959, repr. 1971); H. ZABEL, *Verweltlichung/Säkularisierung. Zur Geschichte einer Interpretationskategorie* (Diss. Phil. Münster 1968).

> *Geschichtsdarstellung kann nicht*
> *Gerichtsverkündigung sein.*
> Karl Barth[1]

The present HBOT volume, *From the Renaissance to the Enlightenment*, covers a relatively long span of time, from about 1300 to about 1800, which has not been chosen as if it comprised just one 'coherent' historical epoch. In this period there are many intertwining trends and features, as will be shown, and it includes different historical periods of radically shifting character. The actual

---

[1] K. BARTH, *Die protestantische Theologie im 19. Jahrhundert* (Zürich: Evang. Verlag ³1960) 9; ET: *Protestant Theology in the Nineteenth Century* (New Edition; London: SCM 2001) 9: "History writing cannot be a proclamation of judgment".

period begins with the era usually called Renaissance and ends with the Enlightenment – with the multi-faceted Protestant Reformation and the Roman-Catholic 'Counter-Reformation' as well as *le Grand Siècle* wedged in between them.

The entire age has generated many historiographical problems, both general and specific. Of special importance here are the questions of historical periodization and terminology. These questions were also discussed in the introduction to the preceding HBOT volume on *The Middle Ages*.[2] There, the subject was the general problem of historical periodization as well as the more specific one of the 'Middle Ages' as a historiographical term for a unique epoch. The discussion of this term was related to its characteristic content and also to the chronological limitation of the age; in addition, it referred to the historical transition from the Middle Ages to the Renaissance, which for quite some time has been subject of a considerable debate among historians.[3]

1. On the Renaissance

In this context, first, the content of the Renaissance claims special attention but the term itself obviously needs further consideration and clarification. As is well demonstrated in modern historical research, the senses of the term 'Renaissance' are remarkably diverse, and scholars have been far from reaching any consensus on the content and limitation of a specific Renaissance period – if this term is to be used at all.[4] Some historians have used the term for cultural phenomena of the twelfth century as well as of some other temporal intervals during the Middle Ages,[5] whereas most historians simply use the term 'Renaissance' to designate the latter part of the Middle Ages and the succeeding centuries, i. e., from the fourteenth to the sixteenth century;[6] still others seem to prefer the term 'Late Middle Ages'.[7]

---

[2] See M. Sæbø, "The Problem of Periodization of the 'the Middle Ages'", HBOT I/2 (2000) 19–27.

[3] On 'periodization' see i.a. von Below, Über historische Periodisierungen (1925); Göller, Die Periodisierung der Kirchengeschichte (1919/1969); Heussi, Altertum, Mittelalter und Neuzeit in der Kirchengeschichte (1921/1969); Gerhard, Periodization in European History (1955/56) 900–13; Moeller, Vom Mittelalter zur Neuzeit (1976) 32–46; Spitz, Periodization in History: Renaissance and Reformation, in: Delzell, The Future of History (1977) 189–218; recently esp. Neddermeyer, Das Mittelalter in der deutschen Historiographie (1988).

[4] See i.a. Helton, The Renaissance. A Reconsideration of the Theories and Interpretations of the Age (1964); Buck, Zu Begriff und Problem der Renaissance (1969); Dannenfeldt, The Renaissance. Basic Interpretations (1974), with its presentation of "Conflict of opinion"; Ferguson, The Renaissance in Historical Thought. Five Centuries of Interpretation (1981); Bullen, The Myth of the Renaissance in the Nineteenth-century Writing (1994).

[5] In addition to the general works referred to in the preceding note, see for an early dating especially Haskins, The Renaissance of the Twelfth Century (1927/1957); Sanford, The Twelfth Century (1951) 635–42; Thorndike, Renaissance or Prerenaissance? (1943); cf. Thompson, Humanists and Refomers (1996) 34–39.

[6] These centuries are often in historical research referred to by their Italian terms: *trecènto*, the 1300s, *quattrocènto*, the 1400s, and *cinquecènto*, the 1500s. Cf. n. 14 below.

[7] In the present volume, cf. U. Köpf, who – like other historians – prefers the term 'Late Middle

In this terminological and methodical quandary it is essential, in any case, to make clear in what sense the term 'Renaissance' is used here, not least because it has been employed by some authors in a general way to indicate a fresh start, and by others in a strictly limited sense as referring to a specific historical phenomenon and period[8] – as will be the case in the present volume, too. With regard to the historically specific use of the term, it may further be worth remarking that just as any historical periodization is dependent, to some extent, on how the actual epoch is defined materially, what the specific content of the 'Renaissance' appeared to be will also be relevant in this context. Thus, the basic questions to be asked on this occasion will first apply to why the 'Renaissance' was so called; further, what has been regarded as its ideological content or its inner structure; and, finally, when did the 'Renaissance', as a distinct historical period, commence and how long did it last? However, due to the disagreements among historians about these questions,[9] entering into the complex problem of defining the Renaissance is like walk into a minefield. It calls for great caution.

The term 'Renaissance' is a conventional and widely used historical designation, and presumably it will remain so.[10] Despite some criticism of the term *per se* in modern research, it seems unlikely that there will be strong arguments against its continued use. In addition, it may be useful to recall that the term has roots that go back to the fifteenth century, when Italian humanists characterized their own time and, in particular, their art and literature as a *rinascità* in relation to the old Roman and Greek culture. Yet, there arises at this point a seemingly simple but actually quite complex question, how the metaphor *rinascità* may be understood adequately.[11] Traditionally, the word has been translated as 'rebirth', but recent studies of relevant sources of the time seem to make it more plausible that it should be understood as 'revival' or 'awakening',[12] or as an organic metaphor like 'new growth' (*Wiederwuchs*).[13] Be this as it may, it testifies to the fact that a new, self-conscious cultural movement came into existence, which was remarkably heterogeneous. A new general history of the age starts by simply stating: "Scholars since the eighteenth century have agreed that some sort of major change took place in Western European

---

Ages' and may say: "the Renaissance in the Late Middle Ages itself" (see below Chap. 6 in this vol.), or, "spätmittelalterliche Renaissance", see idem, Renaissance (2004) 431–32, 434 ff.

[8] See i.a. Buck, Zu Begriff und Problem der Renaissance (1969), esp. 1–95; cf. nn. 10–11 below.

[9] Cf. the introductory words of H. Baron in his essay "Articulation and Unity in the Italian Renaissance and in the Modern West", *Annual Report of the American Historical Association* III (1942) 123–38, 123: "Concepts of Italian Renaissance have changed so often that one must overcome a disinclination to seek a fresh perspective of this breeding-place of historical relativity".

[10] In much of the literature it has retained its French form; as for the – relatively late – date of this French term see B. L. Ullman, "Renaissance – the Word and the Underlying Concept", in: idem, Studies (1955) 11–25, 12 and 23f (German tr. in: Buck, Zu Begriff und Problem der Renaissance (1969) 263–79, 264 and 277f).

[11] See the general survey by D. Cantimori, "Zur Geschichte des Begriffes 'Renaissance'" (1932), in: Buck, Zu Begriff und Problem der Renaissance (1969) 37–95.

[12] Cf. Ullman, Renaissance, ibid. 13, 18f, 23, where he adds: "The idea of rebirth came into use very slowly" (in the German version: 266f, 271, 276).

[13] Cf. J. Trier, "Wiederwuchs", *AKuG* 43 (1961) 177–87; Köpf, Renaissance I (2004) 431 f.

civilization in the period from 1300 to 1600".[14] One may, however, ask: what did constitute that "major change"? Attempts at answering this question in an appropriate way reflect a core of ardent debates in current historical research. The answers have differed considerably – as they still do.

In this state of affairs, a suitable point of departure for further discussion may simply be the fact that in fourteenth-century Italy there was a growing sense of living in a time of a 'new beginning'. This sense – perhaps the most idiosyncratic aspect of the *Trecento* – found an impressive manifestation in the work of "the first modern man",[15] Petrarch / Francesco Petrarca (1304–74), who has been characterized as "the crucial innovator, responsible for the emergence of a new Renaissance culture".[16] Primarily a poet, he also contributed to the "new Renaissance culture" in many other ways. Among his main concerns like those of other early humanists were matters of *philology* and *history*, both of which may be best understood in a quite practical way.[17] At this time there were also various philosophical concerns and tensions, such as, first of all, the 'rivalry' between Aristotelianism – primarily represented by medieval Scholasticism but still considered to be pertinent in the Renaissance – and Platonism and Neoplatonism which came to play a more prominent role in the Renaissance. These aspects, however, will not be commented upon here though they will be discussed in subsequent chapters of the present volume.[18]

As for *philology*, humanist concerns were, in the first place, addressed to the fostering and improvement of the usage of Latin, especially in relation – and also reaction – to its general use and standard in the learning of the Middle Ages. The model for this new endeavour was taken to be the Latin of Antiquity, particularly in its Ciceronian form.

The new linguistic and literary activities were, moreover, closely related to the broader ideal of classical education, the very nerve of the 'new culture', as it was realized in the old *studia humanitatis/humaniora* (including five subjects:

---

[14] Thompson, Humanists and Reformers (1996) 3; cf. Kristeller, Renaissance Thought (1961) 3f; also Nauert, Humanism (1998) ix: "Whether historians like the concepts of 'Renaissance' and 'humanism' or not, the centuries to which those terms are conventionally applied really did exist and must be faced, since they contributed in important ways to the subsequant development of Western society and civilization".

[15] B. L. ULLMAN, "Some Aspects of the Origin of Italian Humanism", in: idem, Studies (1955) 27–40; 30: "… Petrarch, the most remarkable figure among the early humanists, a man far ahead of his time and one who, in spite of all reservations, may still fittingly be called the first modern man".

[16] So, Nauert, Humanism (1998) 11; cf. Voigt, Wiederbelebung I (1893/1960) 20–156 ("Erstes Buch Francesco Petrarca, die Genealität und ihre zündende Kraft"); Mommsen, Studies (1966), Part II ("Petrarchan Studies"), 73–261; also EncRen 3 (1999) 213.

[17] Cf. P. O. KRISTELLER, "Humanism and Scholasticism in the Italian Renaissance", in: idem, Studies (1956) 553–83.

[18] Cf. i.a. P. O. KRISTELLER, "Introductory Essays" and "Marsilio Ficino and his Circle", in: idem, Studies (1956) 1–31 and 35–257; idem, "The Aristotelian Tradition" and "Renaissance Platonism", in: idem, Renaissance Thought (1961) 24–47 and 48–69 (German tr. in: idem, Humanismus und Renaissance I [1974] 30–49, 50–68; cf. also 177–94). In the present volume see esp. chap. 5, by JEREMY CATTO, who has a general view of the matter as well as a special discussion of Nicholas of Cusa, Marsilio Ficino and Pico della Mirandola as prominent figures of Renaissance philosophy.

grammatica, rhetorica, poetica, historia and *philosophia moralis*).[19] These *studia* had their roots in Roman Antiquity, and, as adopted in the Middle Ages, they had a pronounced theological framework (also including logic and *quadrivium*).[20] But Petrarch and, somewhat later, Coluccio Salutati (1331–1406), the decisive figure "in establishing the cultural hegemony of Florence" and its literary circle and also in "reviving the Greek classical heritage",[21] strengthened the significance of the *studia humanitatis* in a new and successful way. A basic issue of the 'new culture' was the promotion of rhetoric and eloquence, as referring to classical culture.[22] An important pedagogical subject was the old *ars dictaminis.* The students had not only an academic activity in mind, but more often 'practical' ones such as their service as notaries, secretaries or diplomats.

Another substantial part of the work of wealthy humanists, higher churchmen and nobles – a work of special significance in this context – was the new and extensive collecting of classical manuscripts and also the establishment of libraries open to scholars.[23] The great importance of this activity, enhanced in the middle of the fifteenth century by the invention of printing by Johann Gutenberg of Mainz (c. 1397–1468),[24] was above all related to the desire of having complete and reliable texts of classical and theological works at hand, not only the manuscript fragments that all but the richest libraries contained. This new situation lent a crucial impulse to the critical comparison and examination of the ancient texts, which again generated a fresh text-critical approach, in which the 'weighing' of the manuscripts and their readings became more important than the 'counting' of them.[25] Not less important in this connection was the fact that such textual study generated new historical perspectives, which not only referred to the age and history of the texts and manuscripts but also, in a general way, with respect to a new hermeneutical and methodical state of affairs; thus, in the theological context a shift gradually came about in the Church's traditional practice of the four senses, the *quadriga*, of the biblical interpretation – and in the *pardes* that in the Jewish tradition represented

---

[19] See i.a. Kristeller, Studies (1956) 571–74; idem, Humanism (1988) 113f; Nauert, Humanism (1998) 12–14.

[20] Cf. Kristeller, Humanism (1988) 113f.

[21] Ullman, Studies (1955) 12.

[22] Cf. J. E. Seigel, "Rhetoric and Philosophy: The Ciceronian Model", and "The Intellectual and Social Setting of the Humanist Movement", in: idem, Rhetoric and Philosophy in Renaissance Humanism (1968) 3–30 and 173–99; see further Rabil, Renaissance Humanism, 1 (1988) xi-xii, on the studies of P. O. Kristeller in this respect: "Kristeller has effectively established the claim that humanism is part of a rhetorical tradition that has been a continuous aspect of western civilization since classical antiquty" (xi); cf. also R. Black, *Humanism and Education*, Cambridge: Cambridge UP 2001.

[23] See i.a. J. F. D'Amico, "Manuscripts", in: *The Cambridge History of Renaissance Philosophy* (1988/1996) 11–24; cf. Gilmore, The World of Humanism (1962) 182–86; P. O. Kristeller, "Aufgaben und Probleme der Handschriftenforschung", in: idem, Humanismus und Renaissance I (1974) 210–21; Fryde, Humanism and Renaissance Historiography (1983) 159–214, 215–34; Grafton, The new science and the traditions of humanism (1996) 214f; Nauert, Humanism (1998) 34–36 (and 36–41 on Lorenzo Valla).

[24] See further, in this volume, Chap. 4.5, by T. Berg Eriksen.

[25] Cf. the well-known text-critical rule: *non numerantur sed ponderantur manuscripta.*

four types of exegesis;[26] by all this, the *literal sense* (*peshat* in Hebrew) as the *sensus historicus* of the texts began to appear to be the most cogent of the four.[27] In sum, text-critical activities of the early Renaissance as well as a concentration on the literal and historical sense of the texts led to general cultural and special hermeneutical attitudes that had profound consequences for theology and, in particular, for the further development of biblical interpretation. Somewhat later the same concern was expressed by the famous humanist invitation: *Ad fontes!*[28]

As a result of this development *history* - the other main subject in this context - was introduced into many facets of Renaissance thought. In the cases above, as in other parts of the rich Renaissance tradition of culture and the arts, a sense of a fresh beginning established direct contact - bridging the Middle Ages - with Roman and Greek Antiquity as the unique standard of excellence. This gave rise to a new sense of historical distance,[29] exhibited already by the very notion of *rinascità*. Closer examination of the Renaissance understanding of history, however, demonstrates another new beginning as well: unlike medieval historians - especially the ecclesiastical historians, whose concept of history was universal, and who "made the birth of Christ a major turning point in history"[30] - Renaissance historians had comparatively shorter and more local historical perspectives, despite their many references to Antiquity. When historical lines were drawn in this new way, a more distinct sequence of shifting periods emerged, and a critical historiography, which included a concern for causal relations, was launched. This approach was already visible in the work of Petrarch, and more so later in the work of Leonardo Bruni (c. 1370–1444) and Flavio Biondo (1392–1463) as well as in the critical scrutiny of the philologist and rhetorician Lorenzo Valla (1405–57).[31] The further development of critical historiography extended over the following centuries.[32]

The new historiography created a tripartite *periodization*: Antiquity, the Middle Ages and contemporary, 'modern', time.[33] The appreciation of these

---

[26] See, further, HBOT I/2 (2000) 54, 56, 457–59, 464, 583; cf. also *The Oxford Handbook of Jewish Studies* (ed. M. Goodman; Oxford 2002) 698.

[27] Cf. Hamilton, Humanists and the Bible (1996) 112f; see also HBOT I/2 (2000) 132–33; 512 pass.; in this volume, cf. Chap. 2.1, on Nicholas of Lyra, by LESLEY SMITH.

[28] See esp. the essay by ARJO VANDERJAGT, Chap. 7 in this volume.

[29] Cf. Gilmore, The World of Humanism (1962) 201–03.

[30] So, Grendler, The Renaissance in Historical Thought, EncRen 5 (1999) 259; cf. Mommsen, Medieval and Renaissance Studies (1966) 265–98 (on Augustine and "Early Christian Historiography").

[31] Cf. i.a. B. L. ULLMAN, "Leonardi Bruni and Humanistic Historiography", in: idem, Studies (1955) 321–44; Seigel, Rhetoric and Philosophy (1968), esp. 99–169; Fryde, Humanism and Renaissance Historiography (1983); Neddermeyer, Das Mittelalter in der deutschen Historiographie (1988) 12–32; Thompson, Humanists and Reformers (1996) 29–32; 207–13; Nauert, Humanism (1998) 19–41.

[32] Cf. i.a. Voigt, Wiederbelebung II (1893/1960) 488–505; E. GARIN, "Der Begriff der Geschichte in der Philosophie der Renaissance", in: Buck, Zu Begriff und Problem der Renaissance (1969) 245–62.

[33] Cf. TH. E. MOMMSEN, "Petrarch's Conception of the 'Dark Ages'", *Spec.* XVII (1942) 226–42, repr. in: idem, Medieval and Renaissance Studies (1966) 106–29; also in: Buck, Zu Begriff und Problem der Renaissance (1969) 151–79, esp. (1966) 125–29, resp. (1969) 175–79. An elaborated tripartite concept of history, combined with a universal outlook, has traditionally been connected

parts varied with the first and the last parts becoming the favoured periods that were brought into focus, whereas the long 'middle' part, eventually called the 'Middle Ages', was definitely the weak link, possibly due to the Renaissance scholars' lack of interest in it. Petrarch's characterization of the Middle Ages as a "dark age" – an often cited phrase that may not be his[34] – should probably not be understood as a general criticism, or even a disparagement, of the Middle Ages, although it was an expression of superiority in some sense. It is more likely that, besides referring to the "barbarous" status of Latin at the time, it should be understood as "a protest against medieval Scholasticism, with its Aristotelian base, which Petrarch deem[ed] too speculative, too sterile, too unproductive of religious imagination and ethical fervor".[35] As a metaphor for the Middle Ages, the "dark age" may also have been used in contrast to positive metaphorical characterizations of the Renaissance itself, such as "new light" and "brightness" that were applied to the contemporary learning and culture that was understood as a "revival" of the bright and ideal antiquity.

However this may be, the critical views of certain humanists regarding various elements of medieval culture and learning seem to have led some modern historians to construct a needlessly sharp contrast between the Middle Ages and the Renaissance.[36] This is evident in the first major description of Renaissance culture, *Die Cultur der Renaissance in Italien. Ein Versuch*, published by JACOB BURCKHARDT in 1860,[37] which was to become a classical work that had an immense impact on the future study of the Renaissance by emphasizing the specificity of the Renaissance and by postulating a sharp discontinuity with the preceding Middle Ages. Although BURCKHARDT's interpretation of the Renaissance was widely accepted for many years, it was also received with strong opposition, particularly with regard to its formulation of the relationship between the Renaissance and the Middle Ages.[38] The criticism of BURCKHARDT's neglect of the medieval culture in its broadest sense (including also economics), was first of all expressed by medievalists like C. H. HASKINS[39] and TH. THORN-

---

to Christoph Cellarius, *Historia universalis in antiquam et medii aevi ac novam divisa* (1685–96), cf. Ferguson, Renaissance (1981) 73–77; Sæbø, HBOT I/2 (2000) 21f; but it may better be moved forward to Joachim Vadian (1483/84–1551), so, Neddermeyer, Das Mittelalter in der deutschen Historiographie (1988) 101–28 ("Die Trias Antike – Mittelalter – Neuzeit").

[34] See esp. Mommsen, Petrarch's Conception of the 'Dark Ages' (1966) 107–10, resp. (1969) 153–56, referring to L. VARGA, *Das Schlagwort vom 'finsteren Mittelalter'* (Vienna / Leipzig 1932) 41; further, on Petrarch's use of *tenebrae*, see Mommsen, ibid. (1966) 118 ff. resp. (1969) 166 ff; Neddermeyer, Das Mittelalter in der deutschen Historiographie (1988) 202–07.

[35] So, Thompson, Humanists and Reformers (1996) 210; cf. ibid. 13; 207–11.

[36] Cf. Grendler, The Renaissance in Historical Thought, EncRen 5 (1999) 262.

[37] On the various (German and English) editions of Burckhardt, Die Cultur der Renaissance in Italien (1860), see the Bibliography above. Cf. the presentation of the Burckhardtian view and its impact by Ferguson, The Renaissance in Historical Thought (1981), Chaps. VII and VIII, 179–252.

[38] See esp. P. O. KRISTELLER, "Changing views of the Intellectual History of the Renaissance since Jacob Burkhardt", in: Helton, Renaissance (1964) 27–52; Ferguson, ibid., Chaps. X–XI, 290–385; cf. Nauert, Humanism (1995) 2–4.

[39] Haskins, The Renaissance of the Twelfth Century (1927/1957).

DIKE,[40] as well as by others.[41] In recent times, though no replacement has been produced, there seems to have arisen what may be called a kind of synthesis between the thesis of BURCKHARDT and the antithesis of his critics.[42] Among outstanding recent Renaissance scholars,[43] PAUL OSKAR KRISTELLER, in a very extensive scholarly *oeuvre*, has balanced many elements of the very complex phenomenon of the Renaissance in a comprehensive view.[44] He has also expressed a methodically sharp criticism of modern historical studies in this respect:

> Modern scholarship has been far too much influenced by all kinds of prejudices, against the use of Latin, against scholasticism, against the medieval church, and also by the unwarranted effort to read later developments, such as … nineteenth-century liberalism and nationalism, back into the Renaissance. The only way to understand the Renaissance is a direct and, possibly, an objective study of the original sources. … we should try to develop a kind of historical pluralism.[45]

BURCKHARDT was not without precursors,[46] which is not least evident in his focus on the concept of *individualism* as a characteristic of the Renaissance.[47] Thus, five years earlier, JULES MICHELET had, in his *Renaissance, Réforme*, pointed out that some earlier modern writers had simply forgotten "two things, although small, that belong to this age [i.e., the Renaissance] more than to any of its predecessors: the discovery of the world, the discovery of man";[48] BURCKHARDT, in a similar way, entitled the Fourth Part of his great work: "The discovery of the world and of man" (*Die Entdeckung der Welt und des Menschen*).[49] It may, however, be preferable here to discuss Renaissance individualism as well as other of its elements in context of the narrower phenomenon of humanism that is so intertwined with the Renaissance.

But before proceeding to the concept of humanism, the question of periodization of the Renaissance may be dealt with briefly.

As far as the *terminus a quo* of the Renaissance as a specific historical period

---

[40] Thorndike, Renaissance or Prerenaissance? (1943).

[41] Cf. i.a. E. PATZELT, *Die karolingische Renaissance* (Vienna 1924); H. NAUMANN, *Karolingische und Ottonische Renaissance* (Frankfurt/M 1926); Huizinga, The Autumn of the Middle Ages (1921 / 1996) 73f, also 382f.

[42] On 'synthesis', cf. esp. Ferguson, The Renaissance in Historical Thought (1981) 394–97.

[43] Cf. i.a. Ullman, Studies in the Italian Renaissance (1955); Baron, Burckhardt's Civilization (1960); idem, The Crisis of the Early Italian Renaissance (1966); Garin, Italian Humanism (1965); esp. Ferguson, The Renaissance in Historical Thought (1981), Chap. VIII, 195–252 ("The Burckhardtian Tradition in the Interpretation of the Italian Renaissance").

[44] See, e.g., Kristeller, The Classics and Renaissance Thought (1955); Studies (1956); Changing Views of the Intellectual History of the Renaissance (1964) [see n. 37 above]; Humanismus und Renaissance I-II (1974/76).

[45] KRISTELLER, "Humanism and Scholasticism in the Italian Renaissance", in: idem, Studies (1956) 553–83, 582.

[46] First of all, JULES MICHELET (see nn. 48 and 50 below), and Voigt, Wiederbelebung I-II (1859/1893; 1960).

[47] Burckhardt, Die Kultur der Renaissance (1860/1930) 95–123 (*Zweiter Abschnitt: Entwicklung des Individuums*); The Civilisation of the Period of the Renaissance I (1878) 181–235 ("Part II. The Development of the Individual").

[48] Michelet, Renaissance, Réforme (1855/1978) 51: "Ces esprits trop prévenus ont seulement oublié deux choses, petites en effet, qui appartiennent à cet âge plus qu'à tous ses prédécesseurs: la découverte du monde, la découverte de l'homme".

[49] Burckhardt, Kultur (1860/1930) 202–56; Civilisation II (1878) 1–105 (Part IV).

is concerned, it may now be taken as relatively obvious that this began with the first part of the *Trecento*,[50] although without any sharp discontinuity with the Middle Ages. This is notably the case in view of the unique achievements of Petrarch[51] and other early humanists as recent scholarship has sufficiently shown. But it is more difficult to define adequately its *terminus ad quem*, especially because some elements of the Renaissance, in particular its individualism and partly its humanism, were still identifiable in the Enlightenment. There appears to be, however, a significant shift of many interests, not to say a creation of new paradigms, at the beginning of the seventeenth century, *le Grand Siècle*, which above all was an age of revolution in physics and the other natural sciences, of new philosophies,[52] of baroque art and culture, of new trends in critical biblical studies, and of a doctrinal Protestant orthodoxy.

The period of the Renaissance, then, may be delimited to the three centuries that traditionally, by old Italian terms, have been indicated as *Trecento, Quattrocento* and *Cinquecento*.

2. On Humanism

'Humanism' was a historical phenomenon closely connected with and characteristic of the Renaissance; it has most aptly been called "the principal intellectual movement of the European Renaissance".[53] As for the rise of this movement, Petrarch, though not a *humanista* in the strict sense of the word, was its leading figure and has often been called the "Father of Humanism".[54] As the development and history of the phenomenon of humanism clearly demonstrates, no more than the Renaissance did it constitute a homogeneous movement, and, in addition, it extended beyond the Renaissance proper. An unbiased discussion of humanism should not exaggerate any of its aspects or periods, however great their importance, but rather be conscious of its considerable complexity.[55]

Like the term 'Renaissance', 'humanism' is also a modern designation – the German word *Humanismus* was coined in 1808 (by F. J. Niethammer), but it was first used for a historical movement in 1841/43 (by K. Hagen). In England

---

[50] Cf. Michelet, Renaissance, Réforme (1855/1978) 52–54; 250–53; esp. Ferguson, The Renaissance in Historical Thought (1981) 329ff, Chap. 11: "… The Renaissance Interpreted as Continuation of the Middle Ages".

[51] Cf. EncRen 3 (1999) 213.

[52] Cf. Kristeller, Renaissance Thought (1961) 88: "With the seventeenth century, there begins a new period in the history of Western science and philosophy, and the traditions of the Renaissance begin to recede into the background".

[53] So, C. G. NAUERT, "The Definition of Humanism", EncRen 3 (1999) 210; cf. Grendler, The Renaissance in Historical Thought, EncRen 5 (1999) 263: "The most important contribution that historians of the Renaissance have made since the 1940s has been to identify humanism as the unifying force of the Renaissance across Europe, and to see it as the major intellectual and cultural movement that stimulated Renaissance men and women to express new ideas".

[54] Cf. Mommsen, Petrarch's Conception of the 'Dark Ages' (1966) 129; Spitz, Humanismus (1986) 642.

[55] Cf. Kristeller, Renaissance Thought (1961) 4f.

the word 'humanism' was initially used in 1812 (by S. C. Taylor) and "in its cultural sense in 1832".[56] Though the abstract term 'humanism' is modern and its use can be variegated and at times ambiguous,[57] the matter itself is old. The concept, again like Renaissance, has long roots back into time, first, to the Renaissance institution of the *studia humanitatis,*[58] and also, in the *Quattrocento*, to the personal designation of *humanista/umanista,* originally for a person teaching the subjects of the *studia humanitatis,* and only later in a broader sense. As for the Latin concept of *humanitas*, it was likewise variously applied and reaches back to Antiquity.[59]

With regard to the content and inner structure of humanism as a historical movement and a concept, much of what has just been said about the Renaissance is valid here, too. However, some aspects of its inner structure are of special pertinence to the history of Bible study and deserve to be mentioned. For brevity's sake, only three of its major facets will be discussed.

First, the aspect of *individualism* – to which we have already referred – has generally been considered to be one of the most distinctive features of Renaissance humanism; it has even been called the "spirit" of the Renaissance.[60] Returning to MICHELET's definition of the essence of the Renaissance as "the discovery of the world, the discovery of man", this dual formulation seems not only to be a unique expression of the general inclination of the cultural interests of the Renaissance period but also an appropriate description of its humanism; the two parts of this statement converge upon the very concept of humanism with its focus on the individual human being and how he is culturally surrounded and conditioned by the world. Furthermore, regarding the concepts of man and world in the Renaissance and its humanism, they are first of all to be taken concretely, not in some philosophically or theologically speculative sense, their subject being human culture in its broadest sense.

BURCKHARDT did not treat individualism primarily as an abstract concept but as a concrete description of the position of the individual in his various relations to the world. He underscored, in phrases typical of the time, the "development of the individual" and the "awakening of the personality",[61] and he began his presentation by contrasting "the mediæval man", who "was conscious of himself only as a member of a race, people, party, family, or corporation", to the new man of the Renaissance who removed the medieval "veil" that "was woven of faith, illusion, and childish prepossession" and "became a spritual *individual,* and recognised himself as such".[62] However, this contrast,

---

[56] See Kristeller, ibid. 8–10; McGrath, Reformation Thought (1999) 41; cf. Spitz, Humanismus (1986) 639.

[57] Not to speak of the disparate modern use of the word; cf. the comment in Kristeller, Studies (1956) 261 f.

[58] See i.a. Rabil, Renaissance Humanism, 3 (1988) 67–309.

[59] Cf. Kohl, Renaissance Humanism (1985) xv: "Since antiquity the term *humanitas* has had a double meaning: it espresses the idea of kindness ..., a basic humaneness, and it also has the meaning of literary culture...".

[60] Cf. Grendler, The Renaissance in Historical Thought, EncRen 5 (1999) 262b: "The spirit of the age of the Renaissance was individualism manifested through all aspects of life".

[61] Kultur (1860/1930) xi; Civilisation I (1878) x.

[62] Ibid. 95 resp. 181.

so much to the disadvantage of the Middle Ages, was to be considered by later historians as unduly sharp and one-sided.[63] On the other hand, with due respect to all connecting lines and overlapping trends and traits between the Middle Ages and the Renaissance and its humanism, which rightly have been emphasized in research since Huizinga, there was, nevertheless, a genuine shift in the Italian *Trecento* from an earlier, mainly collective consciousness to an individual way of thinking and way of living, a "change of mentality",[64] to a definitely broader focus on the individual's creativity, particularly in art and literature, and to a relatively greater degree of individual independence and freedom. Two issues, among many, may be mentioned as examples of the greater importance that was attached to the individual in the Renaissance, and to which Burckhardt and later historians paid particular attention: first, personal fame and honour, and, secondly, the biography of individual persons – reflected, in art, by the increasing popularity of portraits.[65] In these and many other ways individual man and woman stepped forward, with a new self-consciousness.

Secondly, the contrast of *Paganism* and *Christianity* became a specific problem in Renaissance humanism when Christian humanists exhibited a sincere interest in the pagan culture of Roman and Greek Antiquity. This problem has been treated by many modern scholars, from Burckhardt, in the last part of *Die Cultur der Renaissance in Italien*, where he focussed on the mainly secular character and "worldliness" of the Renaissance, in contrast to the piety as well as the forms of superstition in the Middle Ages,[66] to recent historians like Toffanin,[67] Kristeller,[68] Trinkaus[69] and Stinger,[70] among others,[71] who have also emphasized the religious aspects of Renaissance humanism and even the cohabitation of Christian faith and ancient culture.[72] This problem and the tension it generated seem to have already been materialized in Petrarch who, on the one hand, was a Christian who had taken holy orders, who combatted Aristotelianism and Averroism and gave preference to a 'dialogue' with the theology of Augustine, especially in the *Confessions*, but who, on the other hand, was also deeply engaged with classical pagan learning as well, and held

---

[63] See i.a. P. O. Kristeller, "Changing views of the Intellectual History of the Renaissance since Jacob Burkhardt", in: Helton, Renaissance (1964) 27–52; cf. idem, "The Philosophy of Man in the Italian Renaissance", in: idem, Studies (1956) 261–78 (also in: idem, Renaissance Thought [1961] 120–39); Ferguson, The Renaissance in Historical Thought (1981), esp. Chaps. X–XI, 290–385; see also nn. 38–40 above.

[64] So, Nauert, Humanism (1998) 10–12.

[65] Cf. Burckhardt, Kultur (1860/1930) 100–11; 236–44; Civilisation I (1878) 197–214; ibid. II (1878) 65–79; Voigt, Wiederbelebung II (1893/1960) 501–04.

[66] Kultur (1860/1930) 308–406 (*Sitte und Religion*); Civilisation II (1878) 211–383 ("Morality and Religion").

[67] Toffanin, Geschichte des Humanismus (1941).

[68] Se esp. his "Paganism and Christianity", in: idem, Renaissance Thought (1961) 70–91.

[69] Trinkaus, In Our Image and Likeness (1995), esp. II, 553ff; cf. idem, The Scope of Renaissance Humanism (1983).

[70] C. L. Stinger, *Humanism and the Church Fathers. Ambrogio Traversari (1386–1439) and Christian Antiquity in the Italian Renaissance* (Albany: State University of New York Press 1977).

[71] Cf. i.a. Gay, The Enlightenment: The Rise of Modern Paganism (1977).

[72] Cf. also Spitz, The Religious Renaissance (1963).

Cicero and his work in the highest esteem. It has been argued that Petrarch represented "the union of classicism and Western Christianity that is the foundation of Renaissance humanism".[73] However, this dual attitude of Petrarch has been assessed very differently by other historians, and Voigt, for example, characterized both Augustine and Petrarch as "Janus-figures".[74] Be this as it may, the position of Petrarch – like later that of Lorenzo Valla – seems to be difficult to determine precisely, although at the same time it shows clearly the complexity of early Renaissance humanism, especially in Italy.

Later, and particularly outside of Italy and north of the Alps, there were other humanists who brought their faith and traditions more strongly into focus when they aimed at balancing the legacy of Athens and Rome, in particular their philological and literary traditions, with the Jewish and Christian heritage. From a Christian perspective, they have been called "Christian humanists", although the utility of such a designation has been widely debated.[75] First among these Christian humanists were excellent scholars like Erasmus of Rotterdam[76] and Jacques Lefèvre d'Étaples / Faber Stapulensis,[77] who both promoted and advanced the philological and interpretative study of the Bible.[78] Increasing contact between Christian and Jewish scholars constituted a further broadening of the humanist sphere of interest, not least as it was expressed by early Christian hebraists, like Johannes Reuchlin.[79] Spain, too, deserves to be mentioned, not only because many Iberian Bible commentators were influenced by humanism,[80] but in particular with reference to the remarkable work of Cardinal Jiménez de Cisneros, who in 1498 founded the University of Alcalá / *Complutum* (later Madrid), established a *collegium trilingue* in 1508 – a decade and more before those of Louvain (1518) and Paris (1530) – and who also commissioned the first polyglot Bible, the Complutensian Polyglot of 1514–17, which was a great scholarly and administrative achievement for its time and had an extensive impact on the later polyglot Bibles of Antwerp, Paris and London.[81]

The Reformation and other historical circumstances brought about fundamental innovations. The old *Corpus christianum* fell apart and confessional and national churches gained influence.[82] Most significant theologically was the so-called 'formal principle' of the Reformation, that is, the new centrality

---

[73] Cf. Thompson, Humanists and Reformers (1996) 207–11; citation: 211.

[74] Voigt, Wiederbelebung I (1893/1960) 85 (*Janusgestalten*).

[75] Cf. i.a. Kristeller, "Paganism and Christianity", in: idem, Renaissance Thought (1961), esp. 86–87; Gilmore, World of Humanism (1962) 204–28.

[76] Cf. the essay on Erasmus by Erika Rummel, Chap. 9 in this volume.

[77] Cf. Sect. 4 of Chap. 7 in this volume, by Arjo Vanderjagt.

[78] Cf. Hamilton, Humanists and the Bible (1996) 100–17; also Bentley, Humanists and Holy Writ (1983).

[79] See, in this volume, Sect. 1 of Chap.11 on the "Early Christian Hebraists", by Sophie Kessler Mesguich. Cf. further Friedman, The Most Ancient Testimony (1983); Ruderman, The World of a Renaissance Jew (1981); idem, Jewish Thought and Scientific Discovery (1995).

[80] As for the Jewish side, see, in this volume, esp. Eric Lawee's essay on Abarbanel, Chap. 8, and for the Christian side, Chap. 10, by Emilia Fernández Tejero and Natalio Fernández Marcos.

[81] Cf. Sect. 2 of Chap. 12 in this volume, by Adrian Schenker.

[82] See i.a. HDTG 2 (1980); Rohls, Protestantische Theologie, I (1997) 1, 12 ff.

of holy Scripture, expressed by the formula *sola scriptura*, which was widely influential, also beyond the Lutheran sphere, especially in Calvinism.[83] On the
other hand, the Reformers diverged in their hermeneutics, as in their varying
evaluation of the Old Testament in relation to the New.[84] The Reformation
was not, in its essence, an outcome of Renaissance humanism, nor can it be explained by it. Nevertheless, the Reformation was deeply influenced by humanism, as is especially evident in Calvin and Zwingli but also in Luther, despite
his controversy with Erasmus. In particular, Philipp Melanchthon of Wittenberg was an outstanding representative of the Christian humanists, above all,
due to his philological and paedagogical achievements.[85] On the whole, it may
be fair to say that the Reformation, under the impact of Renaissance humanism, made some of the more decisive steps in the history of biblical interpretation and hermeneutics.

Thirdly, toward the end of the Renaissance a specific part of the so-called
Late Humanism (*Späthumanismus*)[86] developed into Radical Humanism. Humanism did not end with the Renaissance – around the end of the sixteenth
century – but continued, to some degree, into the seventeenth century.[87] Due
to that period's radically new interests, humanism transformed itself and became more complex than ever before. On the one hand, humanist culture and
education – and the old humanist curriculum – continued as previously for a
relatively long time, as did the ancient tradition of rhetoric. An "active command of elegant Latin ... [still] gave those who possessed it an entrée to the international Republic of Letters", and "Latin eloquence, the core skill and mental discipline of the Renaissance humanist, lived".[88] On the other hand, however, other factors led increasingly to a new view of the world and of man – to
retain these Renaissance concepts – and fostered, to some extent, a radical humanism. This was especially the case in two respects: first, there was a distinct
empirical factor with regard to numerous new experiments made by various
natural sciences, both old and new; and, secondly, there was a substantially
new and critical *philosophical* aspect, particularly in the form of what has been

---

[83] When Kraus, Geschichte ([1956] 1982) 3ff, begins his historical discussion of the modern
historical-critical study of the Old Testament by a presentation of the principle of *sola scriptura* under the heading "The Protestant Principle of Scripture and the Beginnings of Bible Criticism", this
may be judged an undue simplification, cf. the criticism by G. FOHRER, *ThLZ* 82 (1957) 682–84,
and W. BAUMGARTNER, "Eine alttestamentliche Forschungsgeschichte", *ThR* NF 25 (1959) 93–110.
Otherwise, cf. Kraeling, The Old Testament (1969) 9–32; Grant / Tracy, A Short History (1984)
92–99 ("10. The Bible and the Reformation").

[84] See, in this volume, the Chaps. 17, by SIEGFRIED RAEDER, 18, by PETER OPITZ, and 19, by R.
GERALD HOBBS; and cf. i.a. McGrath, Reformation Thought (1999).

[85] See i.a. Spitz, Humanismus (1986) 658; McGrath, Reformation Thought (1999) 39ff; 145ff.

[86] Cf. Grafton, The new science and the traditions of humanism (1996) 215f; also, Schmidt,
TRE IV (1981) 596.

[87] Grafton, ibid. 207: "During the last generation, intellectual historians have come to see more
and more clearly that late sixteenth- and seventeenth-century announcements of the death of humanism were a considerable exaggeration. Characteristic humanist enterpries, both philological
and philosophical, continued to be carried out, sometimes on a grande scale, throughout the age
of the new science".

[88] Ibid. 204.

called the New Philosophy, which marked a greater independence, or emancipation, after a long period of serving as *ancilla theologiae*.

With regard to the *empirical* factor it goes without saying that it was not
new in the seventeenth century but its significance was considerably enhanced
when voyages of discovery increased and new experimental insights in physics,
astronomy and other fields of science became more telling, and mathematical
precision came to be an ideal.[89] Then, in many ways, it became overwhelmingly clear that a new world view was emerging. As for the old tradition of
'the two books', it was apparent that now the Book of Nature was read and interpreted with an abundance of new insights, which, in turn, had a great impact on the interpretation of the Bible, the Book of Revelation.[90] As in Renaissance humanism, also in this new situation a distinct individualism prevailed
and it appeared to be even more strongly expressed – and in a new way: man
was not only at the centre of interest but was increasingly seen as the autonomous subject of an expanding scientific research that created a new world.

The *philosophical* aspect – closely related to the comprehensive and multi-faceted empiricism of natural science as well as to mathematics – also represented a remarkable individualism and in this respect continued the tradition
of Renaissance humanism, although in a fundamentally new way, not least
with regard to epistemology. In particular, this was evident in the philosophy
of René Descartes / Cartesius (1596–1650) as well as in the work of his somewhat older contemporary, the great scholar of jurisprudence Hugo Grotius
(1583–1645). Obviously, these pre-eminent thinkers, who had such great influence on the subsequent development of ideas in Europe, considered themselves to be part of the Christian humanist tradition. In an epoch of confessional antagonism and wars of religion (especially in 1618–48), Grotius focused on peace among Christians. In his Bible interpretation (as in *Annotata ad
Vetus Testamentum*, 1644), he was mainly occupied with its historical background and he commented on philological and historical matters. Despite his
great achievements Grotius met with opposition.

Descartes was brought up at the Jesuit college of La Flèche and may have intended to promote a theologically positive relationship to the Church, even
more so as he remained silent and neutral in the bitter struggle about the validity of the work of Galileo Galilei (1564–1642). He favoured, with some reserve, "a scientific explanation of the literal text of the Bible".[91] He was, however, more concerned about his liberty of philosophical inquiry. In his epistemology, with its famous *cogito ergo sum*, Descartes attributed new authority to
the individual man's reason and established methods for a critical philosophy
(*Discours de la méthode*, 1637; *Meditationes*, 1641), by which he not only radicalized humanist individualism considerably but also advanced a new scepti-

---

[89] See in this volume, Chap. 27, by CHARLOTTE METHUEN.
[90] Cf. Force / Popkin, The Books of Nature and Scripture (1994); A. VANDERJAGT / K. VAN
BERKEL (eds.), *The Book of Nature in Antiquity and the Middle Ages* (Leuven: Peeters 2005), and
VAN BERKEL / VANDERJAGT (eds.), *The Book of Nature in Early Modern and Modern History* (Leuven:
Peeters 2006).
[91] For both Grotius and Descartes, see HENK J. M. NELLEN's essay in this volume, Chap. 32,
sect. 3 and 5.

cism, howbeit with roots into the past.[92] On the whole, he had a manifold and far-reaching *Wirkungsgeschichte* in European intellectual life.

Between the new science and philosophical criticism and scepticism, on the one hand, and the Church and its many-faceted theology, both Catholic and Protestant, as well as the Jewish community, on the other, there was in the first part of the seventeenth century – to put it mildly – an increasing tension which, in its broad extention, seems not yet to have received sufficient attention in modern historical research.[93]

3. On the Enlightenment

Like Renaissance and humanism, 'Enlightenment' as well is a modern term (Germ. *Aufklärung*, Fr. *les Lumières / le Siècle des Lumières*, Ital. *illuminismo*); the period is sometimes called the 'Age of Reason'. Its terminological emergence exhibits a relatively late and complex history.[94] Again like the earlier two terms, 'Enlightenment' is a conventional and broadly used historical designation. Contrary to the general impression, however, it did not constitute a homogeneous but rather a multifarious movement, and the historical period it describes which seems to have begun around 1650 and lasted to the end of the eighteenth century, was even more complex, presenting a cluster of various trends and ideas, currents and countercurrents. Therefore, any discussion of the Enlightenment can only profit from recognizing its great complexity, historically and ideologically.

As for the primary question of what the Enlightenment really was about,[95] three main aspects of this complicated phenomenon will be dealt with, partly in connection with the preceding discussion of similar issues in the Renaissance and humanism. However, before proceeding to the discussion of these aspects, two other issues may be mentioned, the problem of determining the Enlightenment's historical position and the question of the metaphorical character of the term 'Enlightenment'.

Significant for an understanding of the Enlightenment's special character is its relationship to the past, in particular to the preceding Renaissance humanism and its pronounced individualism. Whereas some historians, especially in

---

[92] On the complex issue of the emerging scepticism, cf. i.a. Popkin, The History of Scepticism (1960 / 1979); also Baum / Bader, Skepsis / Skeptizismus (2000).

[93] For instance, with regard to the field of Protestant Orthodoxy, see, in the present volume, STEIGER, Chap. 28, esp. sect. 1.1: "Observations on the History of Research".

[94] See references in Pütz, Die deutsche Aufklärung (1978) 10–25 (*I. Aufklärung wird Begriff*), esp. 12–15; cf. Schmidt, TRE IV (1979) 594–96; Beutel, RGG⁴ I (1998) 929f.

[95] The question: *Was ist Aufklärung?* was first formulated by J. F. Zöllner, BerMS II (1783) 516, extensively discussed by M. Mendelssohn, BerMS IV (1784) 193f, and by I. Kant, BerMS IV (1784), where he starts, ibid. 481, with a well known and often cited definition of 'Enlightenment', saying: *Aufklärung ist der Ausgang des Menschen aus seiner selbst verschuldeten Unmündigkeit. ... Sapere aude! Habe Muth dich deines eingenen Verstandes zu bedienen! ist also der Wahlspruch der Aufklärung.* See Pütz, Die deutsche Aufklärung (1978), esp. 10–25; further 26–40; cf. also Diestel, Geschichte (1869/1981) 555–63; Kraus, Geschichte (1982) 77.

earlier research, let the history of humanism end with the Renaissance,[96] currently, it seems to be more accepted that the Enlightenment, in some way or
another, represented a further development of Renaissance humanism. Similarly to the relationship of the Middle Ages and the Renaissance there were in
fact various connecting lines and no abrupt historical break between Renaissance humanism and the Enlightenment. Both transitions were combinations
of continuity and discontinuity, an interplay of tradition and innovation. From
this perspective, it is essential to recognize that a significant shift in paradigm
took place during the middle of *le Grand Siècle*, after "the 'Barock' period",[97]
and initiated the Enlightenment proper.[98]

Further, it may be instructive for the understanding of the term 'Enlightenment' to take a quick look at the metaphor of 'light'. This metaphor has a long
and complex history,[99] both as regards the *lumen naturale*, by which Descartes, for instance, referred to human reason,[100] and especially with regard to
the widely used concept of *illuminatio*, which reaches back to Greek philosophy, in particular to Plato, and is found both in Augustine and in Christian
mysticism as well as in eighteenth-century Pietism; in secular modernity the
concept became radically rationalized.[101] To take a single example, there is indeed a great distance between the old and scripturally inspired device of Oxford University: *Dominus illuminatio mea*[102] and the entirely secular understanding of *illuminatio* in the Age of Reason, now related to the rational individual alone. This illustrates a part of the fundamental change that took place
in the usage and meaning of this metaphor. In addition, *illuminatio* may correspond to other metaphors that were used in the characterization of the Renaissance, such as "new light" and "brightness", whereas the preceding Middle
Ages were also called in Enlightenment historiography, in a somewhat condescending way, a "dark age".[103]

The first aspect of the Enlightenment to be dealt with is its distinctive concept of *individualism*, the centrality of man in the world, that had been so prominent in Renaissance humanism. Individualism and individualistic thought
continued into the Enlightenment where it not only became dominant but
where it also became radicalized as focus was increasingly applied to man's
reason. There are, further, fairly good reasons to maintain that individualism

---

[96] Cf. i.a. Toffanin, Geschichte des Humanismus (1941).

[97] Cf. Sandys-Wunsch, What Have They Done to the Bible (2005) 75–117, where Chap. 3 is
entitled: "the 'Barock' period (1600–1660)".

[98] Cf. Israel, Radical Enlightenment (2001) 3f: "During the later Middle Ages and the early
modern age down to around 1650, western civilization was based on a largely shared core of faith,
tradition, and authority. By contrast, after 1650, everything, no matter how fundamental or deeply
rooted, was questioned in the light of philosophical reason and frequently challenged or replaced
by startlingly different concepts generated by the New Philosophy and what may still usefully be
termed the Scientific Revolution"; cf. also Beutel, RGG⁴ I (1998) 932.

[99] See i.a. Blumenberg, Licht als Metapher (1957); Wagner, Erleuchtung (1982).

[100] Cf. Pütz, ibid. 15, see also 30; 32.

[101] See i.a. Fellermeier, Die Illuminationstheorie (1950); Ratzinger, Licht und Erleuchtung
(1960); Wagner, Erleuchtung (1982); cf. also C. Elsas / M. Mühling-Schlapkohl / M. Mar-
quardt, "Erleuchtung", RGG⁴ II (1999) 1430f.

[102] Ps 26 (27):1.

[103] See above, sect. 1 of this essay.

was the most significant connecting line from the early Renaissance to the Enlightenment, and beyond. However, not least in the interplay of tradition and innovation, individualism itself changed character, to some degree, as it developed into an escalating anthropocentrism, buttressed by similar ideas, such as the revival of the ancient idea of Protagoras: *homo mensura*, "man as the measure (of all things)". In general, it seems that through the entire period of Enlightenment individualism was like a 'common denominator' among the diverse trends of the time, being part of various intellectual currents, while, at the same time, it was increasingly realized that man played a very modest role in the universe.

The second aspect of the Enlightenment that deserves specific attention is its great complexity, not least when viewed against the background of the period as a whole, and particularly as for the broader cultural situation in the last half of the eighteenth century where there were competing currents like Pietism and the so-called "counter-Enlightenment".

Compared to the broad field of interest and activity characteristic of Renaissance humanism, the rationalism of the Enlightenment seems to represent some narrowing of the field: first of all, earlier humanism's concern for philology and text studies, rhetoric and classical culture receded more into the background in the Enlightenment whose driving force was an empiricism that initiated in late humanism and was grounded in a multitude of new discoveries and wide-ranging physical insights, which, in all their abundance, fascinated modern man. To a large extent, rationalism became an *empirical* rationalism: scholars' eyes were not so much directed towards the past as to the nature and world around them.

Besides this increasing commitment to empiricism, the influence of a new critical philosophy was of basic significance for the making of the Enlightenment, in particular with regard to its rationalist character. Enlightenment rationalism was not only empirical but also essentially philosophical. The new philosophical criticism and scepticism initiated by Descartes became further radicalized by the philosophy of Baruch de Spinoza (1632–77). Like Descartes he was raised in a religious community, namely the Jewish community of Amsterdam that was to excommunicate him in 1656. This expulsion occurred years before the publication of his great works, among which the *Tractatus Theologico-Politicus* (1670) must be mentioned here because of its bearing on biblical hermeneutics.[104] The critical philosophy of Spinoza – and of the subsequent Spinozism – not only encouraged rationalization and secularization but promoted even a shift of authority, from theology to philosophy, from biblical revelation-based faith and ecclesiastical tradition to the scepticism of critical minds. In his recent discussion of "Philosophy and the Making of Modernity 1650–1750", JONATHAN ISRAEL, concentrating on "the radical Wing" of the Enlightenment that he calls the *Radical Enlightenment*, has fo-

---

[104] On Spinoza, see further the essay by S. NADLER, Chap. 33 of the present volume. Among recent publications special attention should be paid to Israel, Radical Enlightenment (2001) 159–74 and passim; J. SANDYS-WUNSCH, "Spinoza – The First Biblical Theologian", *ZAW* 93 (1981) 327–41; idem, What Have They Done to the Bible? (2005) 148–53.

cused attention upon the central role and great impact of Spinoza and Spinoz-ism, among many other philosophical tendencies of the period.[105]

Another distinction that ISRAEL makes is significant as well. There seem to be two conflicting tendencies in the assessment and presentation of the Enlightenment. Generally, attention has been paid to diverse, most often national, forms of Enlightenment in a way that may be called "fragmentation" of the movement. ISRAEL questions "the validity of such an approach", holding that a discussion of the Enlightenment should not "concentrate on developments in only one or two countries, particularly England and France", because "the intellectual scenario of the age was extremely wide-ranging and was never confined to just one or two regions". Instead, he speaks of a "drama played out from the depths of Spain to Russia and from Scandinavia to Sicily".[106] In other words, ISRAEL favours what may be called a holistic approach that primarily regards the Enlightenment as a European phenomenon of great unitary character. Both aspects, however, should be recognized, and in view of the broad and complex character of the Enlightenment as a whole, an either-or approach here seems inappropriate. Rather, one should take into account the basic relation of totality and part.[107] Therefore, both the Enlightenment's individual historical forms, on the one hand, in particular the Deism in England,[108] the French *philosophes* and *encyclopédistes*,[109] the broad and mani-faceted *deutsche Aufklärung*,[110] including their interplay across the national borders, and, on the other hand, the recognition of the Enlightenment as a comprehensive European phenomenon should equally receive attention and be examined, as also ISRAEL does in his *oeuvre*, despite his primary focus on Spinozism as "the intellectual backbone" of the Radical Enlightenment.

When, in this connection, ISRAEL speaks of a "drama", he refers to the historically broad and variegated scale of different fronts. Enlightenment was more than rationalism. The scale of the Enlightenment's ideological rainbow ranged from the extreme left, "the radical Wing", to the multiple "mainstream moderate Enlightenment", with many inner tensions and competing "camps",[111] and, on the right wing, to the various opponents of the new and liberal thoughts and trends, whom ISRAEL calls "traditionalists", and who in-

---

[105] To those who may be "surprised by the prominence given here to the role of Spinoza and Spinozism...", ISRAEL says in the Preface (vi): "Yet a close reading of the primary materials strongly suggests, at least to me, that Spinoza and Spinozism were in fact the intellectual backbone of the European Radical Enlightenment ...".

[106] Israel, ibid. 7; cf. also his expression, in the Preface (v): "a whole family of Enlightenments".

[107] Cf. also the methodologically close theory of a 'hermeneutical circle'; see Gadamer, Wahrheit und Methode (1975) 250ff (resp. idem, Truth and Method, 1979, 265ff).

[108] Cf. in this volume, Chap. 35, by H. GRAF REVENTLOW; cf. also idem, Bibelautorität und Geist der Moderne (1980; resp. idem, The Authority of the Bible, 1984).

[109] Cf. in this volume, Chap. 36, by CHR. BULTMANN.

[110] Cf. i.a. Mittelstrass, Neuzeit und Aufklärung (1970); Schneiders, Die wahre Aufklärung (1974): Pütz, Die deutsche Aufklärung (1978); Kondylis, Die Aufklärung (1981); also Piepmeier / Schmidt / Greive, Aufklärung, TRE IV (1979) 575–615, and Beutel, Aufklärung, RGG⁴ 1 (1998) 929–51.

[111] Israel, Radical Enlightenment (2001) 9–13.

cited "a veritable 'Counter-Enlightenment'".[112] In this ideological turmoil, moreover, Pierre Bayle (1647–1706), a Huguenot from the south of France, occupied a very special position. With his dual attitude, in life and work, he has remained an enigma to the historians – like Petrarch before him. He may, nevertheless, be regarded as an impressive personification of the complex ideological situation of the time: on the one hand, he was connected to the new empiricism and critical philosophy, and, on the other, he had religious commitments, without being a "traditionalist". Toward the end of his life he characterized himself as one who had taken part in the "great contest of faith and reason".[113] In addition, finally, to make the whole picture of this time even more complex, Johann Gottfried Herder (1744–1803) and the up-coming Romanticism at the end of the eighteenth century also deserve attention.[114] With the romanticists, the philogical and aesthetic concerns of earlier Renaissance humanism, again, came to the fore. But most important to them was: Man is more than his reason.

With Herder, we have reached the third aspect of the Enlightenment to be dealt with here. It refers to a diversity of religious questions that were closely associated with the Enlightenment's ideological character. In the broad intellectual and cultural drama the philosophy was indeed a motor in the process of rationalization and secularization, as already indicated; but in this complex process the question of God and religion, or, 'natural religion', was a driving force as well. Yet, the main point seemed to be that religion *per se* did not constitute the real issue, even for most of the rationalists, but in which form religion was to be held and practised. The quintessence of the ardent disputes of the time can be expressed by the famous and often cited dictum in *Le Mémorial* (1654) of Blaise Pascal (1623–62): *"Dieu d'Abraham, Dieu d'Isaac, Dieu de Jacob" / non des philosophes et des savants.*[115] For, in sum, the question of a history-related faith in a biblically revealed God versus a philosophically argumented faith, or, traditional, i.e., revealed religion versus 'natural religion', constituted actually a key problem around which many of the confrontations in the time of the Enlightenment revolved.

In Renaissance humanism the issue of Paganism and Christianity,[116] was an

---

[112] Ibid. 7: "Its [i.e., the drama's] complexity and awesome dynamic force sprang not only from the diversity and incompatibility of the new philosophical and scientific systems themselves but also from the tremendous power of the traditionalist counter-offensive, a veritable 'Counter-Enlightenment' which, as with the Counter-Reformation of the sixteenth century, generated a major reorganization and revitalization of traditional structures of authority, thought, and belief"; cf. further 445–560: "Part IV: The Intellectual Counter-Offensive".

[113] Among Bayle's works especially his *Dictionnaire historique et critique* I-III (Amsterdam 1692–95) has attracted great attention; otherwise, see Sandberg, The Great Contest of Faith and Reason: Selections from the Writings of Pierre Bayle (1963); cf. Israel, Radical Enlightenment (2001), Chap. 18, 331ff; also R. H. POPKIN, "Bayle, Pierre", EncPh 1 (1972) 257–62; E. BEYREUTHER, "Bayle, Pierre (1647–1706)", TRE V (1979) 387–89.

[114] On Herder, see in this volume Chap. 44, sect. 3, by H. GRAF REVENTLOW. The Romanticism that was so dominant in the nineteenth century will be discussed further in the next volume of HBOT, Vol. III/1.

[115] Cf. Blaise Pascal, *Pensées et opuscules* (ed. L. Brunschvicg; Classiques Hachette 1961) 142–44.

[116] See above, sect. 1 of this introductory essay.

important subject. In the Enlightenment, however, the classical paganism was scarcely a primary concern, although there could well be "wellsprings of ancient pagan tradition" in the Spinozism, with special reference to ethically interesting philosophers like Epicurus (341–270 BCE) or Lucretius (94–55 BCE).[117] But a possible Enlightenment 'paganism' may rather – to remain in the idiolect of BURCKHARDT – be related to the Renaissance "worldliness" and, with an eye to the Enlightenment's secularism and strong sense of immanence, be regarded as a new and more complete 'worldliness'; and, likewise, the Renaissance relation of man and world may readily be rephrased to man *in* the world.

In this context, then, it is evident that the new cultural climate easily generated a growing tension between the Enlightenment, especially its radical humanism, and organized religion. In the Age of Reason – and unlike the situation in early Renaissance humanism – not only the common cultural life, the world of man, but also the relations between the radicalized cultural life and the Judeo-Christian world[118] became increasingly polarized. There was an extensive *interaction of challenge and response.* Responses from the Christian or the Jewish side varied to a great extent; just as J. ISRAEL distinguished between three main fronts regarding the Enlightenment, recent historical studies have usually differentiated "between three general groups among Protestant theologians: the orthodox, the neologians and the rationalists";[119] but at this point J. SANDYS-WUNSCH has critically and rightly commented that such a classification "obscures differences among members of various groups even as it obscures connections between those within and those without".[120] The actual situation was much more complicated.

Finally, also another distinction may be made, namely regarding the character of the theologians' reactions to the Enlightenment's empirical and philosophical challenges, whether they were made on mainly dogmatic or doctrinal grounds, or in the realm of biblical studies. In the latter case, there was, for the most part, greater openness towards empirical and historical aspects. Gradually, especially after the middle of the eighteenth century, a historical-critical study of the Old and New Testament emerged.[121] With Johann Gottfried Eichhorn (1752–1827),[122] the historical criticism of the biblical books was further divided into 'lower' and 'higher' criticism, and, succeedingly, biblical studies became more and more specialized. Whether the historical-critical study of the Bible meant a "dethronement of the Bible", as has been main-

---

[117] Harrisville / Sundberg, The Bible in Modern Culture (2002) 42f; cf. Gay, The Enlightenment, vol. 1, The Rise of Modern Paganism (1966).

[118] Cf. in this volume, Chaps. 39, by M. IDEL, and 43, by E. BREUER.

[119] Sandys-Wunsch, What Have They Done to the Bible? (2005) 230. Similar statements might presumably be made on Jewish side.

[120] Ibid. 231, and SANDYS-WUNSCH remarks: "Therefore, while the distinction between orthodox, neologians, and rationalists is useful for understanding history, it is not itself historical".

[121] Cf. in this volume Chaps. 29, by P. GIBERT, 34, by J. W. ROGERSON, 40, by W. McKANE, 41, by J. SANDYS-WUNSCH, and 42, by J. H. HAYES; see also above nn. 91 (Ch. 32), 104 (Ch. 33), 108 (Ch. 35), 109 (Ch. 36), 114 as also below 122 and 124 (Ch. 44).

[122] On Eichhorn, see in this volume Chap. 44, sect. 4, by H. GRAF REVENTLOW.

tained,[123] will remain a matter of discussion, for there were also countercurrents. Various endeavours were made to discuss and present biblical questions of lasting value, so, among other matters, the new attempts at describing a 'biblical theology', as proposed by Johann Philipp Gabler (1753–1826) and others.[124]

In conclusion, it may be said that despite many historical and ideological changes and differences, there was a certain consistency throughout the long and variegated period of time that is covered by the present volume. This seems, above all, to be due to the phenomenon of humanism, at the core of which there was an increasingly strong individualism; thus the triad of Renaissance, Humanism and Enlightenment, in all their diversity, may lend a considerable degree of unity to the compound period "from the Renaissance to the Enlightenment". In the cultural and ideological framework of this multi-faceted and complex period of time traditional biblical interpretation, facing numerous challenges, became to some extent transformed and the foundations of modern biblical interpretation were established.

---

[123] Cf. Sandys-Wunsch, What Have They Done to the Bible? (2005) 80, with reference to Chr. Hill, *The English Bible and the Seventeenth-century Revolution* (London 1993), who "coined the perspective term".
[124] On Gabler, see in this volume Chap. 44, sect. 5, by H. Graf Reventlow.

A.

Scriptural Interpretation
in the Context of the Renaissance

CHAPTER TWO

The Exegetical and Hermeneutical Legacy
of the Middle Ages: Christian and Jewish Perspectives

2.1. Nicholas of Lyra and Old Testament Interpretation

By LESLEY SMITH, Oxford

Sources: Nicolaus de Lyra. Postilla super totam bibliam (Strassburg 1492; facsimile repr., Frankfurt am Main: Minerva 1971); *Biblia Latina cum Glossa ordinaria* (Adolph Rusch; Strassburg 1480/81; facsimile repr. ed. K. Froehlich / M. T. Gibson; Turnhout: Brepols 1992); *Biblia latina cum postillis Nicolai de Lyra...* (Nuremberg: Anton Koberger 1487); *Biblia cum glosa ordinaria et expositione Lyre litterali et morali...*(Basel: Johannes Petri, Johannes Froben 1498); *Biblia Sacra cum glossis interlineari et ordinaria, Nicolai Lyrani Postilla, ac Moralitatibus, Burgensis Additionibus, et Thoringi* [= Matthias Doering] *Replicis* 1–6 (Basel 1506–08); *Domini Hugonis de Sancto Caro. Postilla in totam bibliam...*, 4 vols. in 3 (Paris 1533–39).

Bibliographies and reference works: M. A. SCHMIDT, "Nikolaus von Lyra", TRE 24 (1994) 564–66; K. FROEHLICH, "Nicholas of Lyra (c. 1270-1349)", DBI, K-Z (1999) 206–08; H. LABROSSE, "Sources de la biographie de Nicolas de Lyre", Etudes Franciscaines 16 (1906) 383–404; idem, "Biographie de Nicolas de Lyre", ibid. 17 (1907) 489–505, 593–608; idem, "Oeuvres de Nicolas de Lyre. Sources bibliographiques", ibid. 19 (1908) 41–52; idem, "Oeuvres de Nicolas de Lyre. Catalogue des oeuvres", ibid. 19 (1908) 153–75, 368–79 and 35 (1923) 171–87, 400–32; C. L. PATTON, "Nicholas of Lyra (c. 1270-1349)", HHMBI (1998) 116–22.

General works: P. D. W. KREY, "Many Readers but Few Followers: The Fate of Nicholas of Lyra's Apocalypse Commentary in the Hands of his Late-Medieval Admirers", *CH* 64 (1995) 185–201; P. D. W. KREY / L. SMITH (eds.), *Nicholas of Lyra: The Senses of Scripture* (Leiden e.a.: Brill 2000); A. J. MINNIS, *Medieval Theory of Authorship: Scholastic literary attitudes in the later Middle Ages* (2nd edn.; Aldershot: Wildwood House 1988); A. J. MINNIS / A. B. SCOTT, with the assistance of D. WALLACE, *Medieval Literary Theory and Criticism c. 1100-c. 1375* (rev. edn.; Oxford: Clarendon Press 1998); B. SMALLEY, *The Study of the Bible in the Middle Ages* (2nd edn.; Notre Dame, IN: UP 1978).

1. Introduction

The Franciscan exegete Nicholas of Lyra (c. 1270–1349), was the author of a massive, and massively circulated, commentary on the entire Bible, known as his *Postillae*,[1] easily the most widely-copied commentary of his generation.

---

[1] Although I have used the plural *Postillae* for the title of Nicholas' work, saving the singular *Postilla* to be used to refer to a commentary on an individual biblical book, there is no consistency among either medieval or modern authors or cataloguers with regard to this usage, and readers may find *postilla* or *postillae* used almost interchangeably.

The *Postillae* were written (and often circulated) in two parts: the *Postillae* on the literal sense of Scripture were composed between about 1322 and 1333; and the much slighter *Postillae* on the moral senses of Scripture date from about 1333 to 1339. It is hard to overstate the success, measured in terms of distribution, that the work achieved. Over 800 manuscripts of the *Postillae* still survive in libraries all over Europe; they range from workmanlike reference editions to large-format sets, decorated with coloured initials and diagrams. In addition, there are around fifty early printed editions of all or parts of the *Postillae*, beginning with the 1471–72 Rome edition in five volumes, printed by Sweynheym and Pannartz. This was the first biblical commentary to be printed, even though it was already more than a century old.[2]

Born at Lyra, near Evreux, Nicholas was a Norman, and joined his local Franciscan convent in Verneuil only when he was about thirty years of age. His scholarly talents seem to have been recognised quickly, and he was sent to study in Paris, where he became a Franciscan regent master at the end of the first decade of the fourteenth century. He was elected to various administrative posts in the Order, whilst continuing to write. In 1330, he attempted, with somewhat limited success, to retire from administration to write full-time, with the aim of finishing his *Postillae*; but he was nonetheless enlisted for various special administrative duties. A complete list of his works is still uncertain, in part because the *Postillae* outshone everything else. He became as synonymous with them as Peter Lombard with the *Sentences*, and the fame of *this* Nicholas caused confusion in the minds of copyists, cataloguers and scholars with other writers such as Nicholas Gorran.

The origins of the term *postilla(e)* are unknown, as, indeed, is the exact nature of a set of postills and their difference from works called 'commentaries', 'expositions' or, the most common title in medieval catalogues, simply "On…" (*In* or *Super* in Latin). The usual modern definition is that postills are expositions of a text which move word-by-word or phrase-by-phrase, covering everything. Following this, BERYL SMALLEY suggested that the term comes from the phrase *post illa verba*, "after these words", which would introduce an interpretation of a biblical lemma.[3] Although this seems a commonsense proposition, nevertheless I know of no place where the phrase is actually to be found in a commentary. It may be that the phrase was used only orally, by a master teaching in class, a verbal tic to introduce the next interpretation. Though it is not always clear in what way the technique of *postillae* differed from the technique of previous glossing, the word *postillae*, as applied to this activity, gained popularity with the circulation of the *Postillae in totam bibliam* by the Dominican scholar, Hugh of St Cher, written probably between 1230 and 1235 at the Order's Paris house of study, St Jacques, where Hugh was a regent master. Lyra's *Postillae* take their place in a short but important line of what might be called 'pandect' commentaries on Scripture, by which I mean those covering the entire Bible systematically, following the same format, intended to be seen as an intelligible whole, and forming a reference work for scholars

---

[2] The little we know about Nicholas' life and works, together with a comprehensive bibliography may be found in Krey / Smith, Nicholas of Lyra (2000). For this essay, I used *Nicolaus de Lyra. Postilla super totam bibliam* (ed. 1492; repr. 1971).

[3] Smalley, Study of the Bible (1978) 270. Cf. also K. FROEHLICH in: HBOT I/2 (2000) 517, n. 86.

and preachers. The medieval line begins with the so-called *Glossa ordinaria*, the Ordinary Gloss on the Bible, a compilation of excerpts from patristic and early medieval exegesis, probably made in Laon and complete by about 1130. Hugh of St Cher's *Postillae* hold the field throughout the thirteenth century, with occasional rivals; but Hugh's work is not really replaced until Nicholas' *Postillae*, which all scholarly libraries seem to have wished to own.[4]

Yet, despite the wide circulation of the *Postillae*, Nicholas' work did not inspire other exegetes to work in similar ways. Rather, as PHILIP KREY has said, he had "many readers but few followers".[5] Nonetheless, his work is often credited with taking a decisive step towards the Reformation:

> *Si Lyra non lyrasset*
> *Lutherus non saltasset*

– "If Lyra had never played his harp, Luther would never have danced".

Certainly, Luther, Wyclif and the editors of the Lollard Bible specifically mention Nicholas' *Postillae* as influencing their exegesis. But he was both criticised and defended in the fifteenth century, and some of the printed editions of his works include the *Additiones* of Paul of Burgos, attacking Lyra's hebraism, and the *Replicationes* by Matthias Doering, written in his support. If his work was not a model for others, what caused it to be so widely circulated?

Two characteristics in particular make Nicholas interesting to other scholars: his fascination with Jewish interpretations of the Bible; and his absorption in working with the literal sense of the biblical text, which links to his concern for the theoretical aspect of an exegete's task. In neither of these interests was he unique; but the combination of them, alongside his scholarly attention to detail and the *Postillae*'s coverage of the whole Bible, added to the historical serendipity of a work and a man which appear in the right place at the right time.

In what follows, I shall look at each of these characteristics, illustrating them with examples from the *Postillae*, and making comparisons between Nicholas' treatment of some biblical pericopes and those of the *Glossa* and Hugh of St Cher. We may then see what each of these pandect commentaries brought to their scholarly milieu, and what Nicholas especially had to offer. Readers may then judge for themselves whether Nicholas' reputation as a hinge between the medieval approach to exegesis and that of the Reformers is well-earned.

2. Jewish Exegesis

Research into Jewish biblical scholarship by Christians had been known, on and off, since the work of Andrew of St Victor in the twelfth century; but for

---

[4] *Biblia Latina cum Glossa ordinaria*, with bibliography. There is little bibliography for Hugh; see Smalley, Study of the Bible (1978), Ch. 6, 264–355; for this essay I used a sixteenth-century edition, *Domini Hugonis de Sancto Caro*.

[5] Krey, Many Readers but Few Followers (1995).

Nicholas, his knowledge of, and respect for, Jewish scriptural interpretation is his most conspicuous interpretative characteristic. Why and how Nicholas became interested in Jewish exegesis is unknown; neither do we know whether the chicken of his interest in the literal interpretation of Scripture came before or after the egg of his fascination with Jewish biblical scholarship. What is clear, however, is his acquisition of some degree of proficiency in Hebrew (how much is disputed); his thorough knowledge of the work of the eleventh-century French Rabbi Solomon ben Isaac (known, from his initials, as Rashi), which included a familiarity with the arguments Jewish biblical interpreters had amongst themselves about the text and its meaning; and his sympathy with and respect for the Jewish exegetical point of view. Constantly, in the *Postillae*, Nicholas compares the opinions of "catholic doctors" or "our doctors" with those of "the Hebrews" or "Rabbi Solomon". In the majority of cases, he prefers the Jewish reading of the text, using phrases such as "the Jews, however, understand better here", or simply giving Rashi's exposition of the lemma. He never treats the arguments of the Hebrews (as he tends to address the scholarly interpreters, as opposed to using "Judaei", which he rather reserves for ordinary, contemporary Jews) with anything less than seriousness, and at times, as we shall see, he frames his exposition of the biblical text around points and questions that the Jewish interpreters consider important.

What is it that Nicholas finds in the Jewish interpreters that attracts him so much? Unfortunately, he never tells us directly. The Jewish exegetes provide him with two things that might appeal, the one appealing to him as a Franciscan, the other to his scholarly self as well. Many of the interpretations that Nicholas bases on Rashi take the biblical text and, in a manner of speaking, 'humanise' it; they shift the focus of the narrative to the portrayal of the characters as real people with comprehensible motives and desires, and they ask and answer straightforward, unlearned questions that ordinary people might ask about the text. The Bible comes vividly alive in their hands, and the characters seem very present to the reader.

For example, in the Genesis story of Abraham receiving the three visitors at the oaks of Mamre (Genesis 18), Nicholas notes that the tale shows how useful Abraham was to his neighbour (conceived of in the widest sense), carrying out works of temporal mercy with his generous hospitality. Nicholas notes that the "catholic doctors" and the "Hebrews" explain this passage differently, but that both are consonant with the Christian faith, and so he will give both, beginning with the views of the Jews, though he will "cut out certain frivolities". The portrait of Abraham that Nicholas proceeds to paint with his Hebrew palette instantly conjures up an old but convivial man, longing for company as he sits at the door of his tent waiting for travellers to pass. He is genuinely hospitable and wants to show all strangers charity, but he is also eager for news and talk from the passers-by. He is waiting at the tent in the heat of the day, because that is when journeyers would most want to turn aside for refreshment.

Two short verses of the chapter are opened up and brought to life by the combined talents of Nicholas and Rashi. We know this old man; and this solid base of human empathy makes the rest of the remarkable, indeed miraculous, story – of Sara's conceiving, of the men as angels, of Lot and Sodom – somehow more believable, because it starts with a character we know. And Nicholas adds some details that add to our feeling for the scene. Firstly, he notes that the Hebrews say that this happened three days after Abraham had been circumcised, and that one of the strangers was the angel Raphael, sent to heal him. Secondly, Nicholas reports that the Hebrews take the first words of the chapter literally, so that "God [as well as the three angels in the guise of men] appeared to Abraham at the oaks of Mamre". How then could Abraham remain seated when God was in front of him? "A certain Hebrew gloss" supplies the answer: that Abraham *wanted* to get up and worship God, but that God said "Sit!", for Abraham was there as a sign of what his sons would be in the future: they will sit as judges, while God stands. This everyday detail, with Abraham struggling to his feet in the heat, and God crying "Sit!" (we hear the sympathetic tone of voice and see the restraining gesture of the hand) is a perfect preacher's tool. It takes us directly to the tent by the trees; we see ourselves in the story; we are gripped.

Nicholas does add Christian interpretation to this gloss: Christ did indeed stand before the seated Caiaphas, in order to save those who believed in him, the true sons of Abraham. In his short *moraliter* treatment of the verses, he states that the angels signify preachers, who proclaim the faith of the Trinity, and who should be received with humility and devoutly invited into one's life. However, in comparison with the *Glossa*'s purely spiritual interpretation of these verses, and even with Hugh's longer and more varied approach, Nicholas concentrates much more on the story *per se*, without an automatic leap to the Trinitarian theology that the three men (agreed to be angels by both Christians and Jews) generally represent. Hugh uses this pericope to discuss nuances of the theology of the Son's appearance before the Incarnation, and the kind of worship that would have been appropriate in the circumstances. But Nicholas stays away from these considerations, and makes the narrative, with its example of charity and of recognition of the stranger as a gift from God, all of a moral that any Christian might need.

In a similar vein, we see Nicholas take over one of Rashi's interpretative expansions, when he expounds the passage in the book of Ruth (1:16–17) when Ruth tells Naomi that she will not leave her and go home. Rashi turns Ruth's monologue: "I shall go wherever you go. I shall lodge wherever you lodge. Your people are my people, and your God my God", into a teaching dialogue. Realising that Ruth wished to convert to Judaism, her mother-in-law, Naomi, was obliged to tell her about the most difficult parts of the Law. Naomi lists the things that Jews can and cannot do, and her words are intercut with Ruth's biblically reported replies: "And she told her that it was not lawful for Jews to go outside the land of Israel, except in great necessity. And Ruth answered her, 'Wherever you go, I shall go', and nowhere else... Again she said, 'It is forbidden to us to worship any other gods'. And she answered, 'Your God is my God'...".

This approach must have appealed very strongly to Nicholas as a Franciscan, because it is so easily translated into popular preaching terms. Reading Nicholas re-telling the story as the rabbinical interpreters have taught him, it is impossible not to be drawn into the fascinating human dramas of the Old

Testament. For a member of an Order which was especially fond of using stories and capsule *exempla* to communicate the Gospel, and where the founding history of the Order was enshrined in an authoritative set of *stories* of the life of Francis, Rashi's expositions must have had immediate allure. Nicholas' Franciscan sensibilities must have recognised the didactic qualities of these Jewish readings; they could teach God's purpose effectively in their literal meaning, without any need to resort to complicated, and sometimes belaboured, allegorical or moral senses of Scripture.

Jewish scholarship can at times provide more than simply grist for Nicholas' interpretative mill; it can provide the structure, too. In his exegesis of Exod 20:13 ("You shall not kill"), Hugh of St Cher considers the common question why there are two commandments to prohibit stealing and the desire to steal, and two prohibiting adultery and the desire of it, whereas there is only one prohibition of killing – even though, as Christians know from the Sermon on the Mount, the desire to kill is as heinous a sin as the deed itself. Hugh answers this problem in *questio* form, including amongst the arguments points made by "Hebrews" and points drawn from Aristotle's four causes. As is generally true of exegesis of this point, his solution is rather weak. Indeed, he must know that the solution is not strong; and it may be for this reason that he utilises the *questio* form to argue for it, intending the authority of the *questio*-method to bolster the inherent implausibility of the arguments.

Lyra at this pericope simply does not consider the issue of the double prohibition, even though, in the discussion of the two commandments against covetousness (Exod 20:17), he is at pains to defend the Christian division of them into two, opposing the Jewish treatment of them as one. His argument is that a guilty will is necessary for there to be sin as an evil deed (which is why children and the insane cannot be thought of as guilty of sin). Yet this approach is as valid for killing and homicide as it is for adultery, so why does Nicholas not consider it? In his exposition of the commandments in Exodus 20, Nicholas repeatedly sets out the Jewish understanding of the text together with the Christian view, letting the two traditions stand alongside one another with little or no comment, even when they disagree – until he reaches the two final precepts, against covetousness. Here there is a direct confrontation, since the Christian division of the two areas of covertousness into two commandments is at odds with the Jewish understanding of them as one. Nicholas comes down on the side of the traditional Christian partition of the precepts, and we should not expect him to do anything else: his scholarship is always at the service of correct doctrine. Nevertheless, at the commandment against killing, Rashi divides what is prohibited according to the penalty involved, and this is what Nicholas duly reports. Whereas Christian teachers use this commandment to ban all harm done to another person's body, Rashi says that only homicide merits the death penalty, and so only homicide is prohibited in this precept. Other crimes against the person, such as mutilation or flogging, are dealt with elsewhere. Since Rashi does not consider the question of intention versus deed, nor does Nicholas.

There is a further use that Nicholas finds for Jewish exegesis, which is a very practical one. Christian commentators had long found many of the names,

places and customs described in the Bible baffling. Jerome's glossaries of Hebrew proper names were an attempt to deal with this problem. Nicholas went
further, realising that Jewish scholars could provide him with, if not complete
solutions, then at least their own traditional understanding of their own words
and customs, a guide to the landscape of the Holy Land, and their view of
their own history and its chronology. In some manuscripts and editions of the
Postillae some of this material is codified into maps, diagrams (for instance, of
the Temple and its vessels and vestments), and genealogies, which make excellent aids to reading. His acquaintance with Jewish sources and linguistic skills
was able to gratify Nicholas' very scholarly interest in the detail of the text. It
is part and parcel of his second interpretative characteristic, to which we shall
now turn.

3. The Literal Sense of Scripture and Exegetical Theory

Nicholas' late-medieval soubriquet describes him as the "plain and useful doctor". Compared to the 'angelic' Aquinas and 'seraphic' Bonaventure, or even
the 'undefeatable' Alexander of Hales, the name seems something of a back-
handed compliment. Yet Nicholas would approve; for in 'useful' it recognises
his scholarly purpose, in which no aim can be higher than that of collecting
and passing on previously-neglected interpretative material; whilst in 'plain' it
sites the success of his endeavour in his constant re-examination of the literal
sense of Scripture.

Standard high-medieval theory of interpretation held that the biblical text
might hold four sorts of meaning, called *quadriga* or the four *sensus* (senses) of
Scripture: literal (or historical), allegorical, moral (or tropological), and the
anagogical. Deriving ultimately from John Cassian, the range of each sense
was summed up in a commonly repeated rhyme, probably attributable to the
thirteenth-century scholar Augustine of Dacia:

> *Littera gesta docet, quid credas allegoria,*
> *Moralis quid agas, quo tendas anagogia.*

The literal sense teaches about historical deeds; allegory is about what to believe; the moral sense teaches how to behave; the anagogical about where we
are headed, that is, to heaven.[6]

The four senses were divided into two groups, the literal sense standing on
its own as the meaning in plain sight, and the other three joined together as
the 'spiritual' senses, which encompass the hidden meanings of the text. Crudely put, patristic and early medieval exegesis (such as we find excerpted in the
Glossa) favoured the spiritual meanings, as those which were more useful for

---

[6] For discussions of medieval literary and exegetical theory, see Minnis, Medieval Theory of
Authorship (1988); and for translation of excerpts from Nicholas' prologues, Minnis / Scott, with
Wallace, Medieval Literary Theory (1998).

instructing the faithful Christian in what to do to win eternal life. They were the golden hoard contained in the silver casket of the literal. Twelfth-century scholars, such as Hugh of St Victor, were, however, adamant that spiritual senses were no use if they lost touch with their literal roots: they used the analogy of a house in which the spiritual senses formed the walls and roof, but the literal sense was the foundation. Some spiritual interpretations, for example those typological exegeses which turned human sinners such as David and Solomon into types of Christ, could seem at odds with the plain text of the story; and pastorally-concerned theologians, like the master-turned-bishop, William of Auvergne, were aware that these rarified interpretations, which needed to be explained before they could be understood, could appear to ordinary believers as either laughable or scandalous.

On top of this concern came a growing recognition of the importance of the human author in the making of any biblical text. Accordingly, thirteenth-century interpreters began to widen the scope of the literal sense to include the historical facts of the story and the author's meaning, using author here to mean both the human writer and God. Sometimes the literal sense of a text came to include both an historical meaning and a figurative, spiritual interpretation, when that was deemed to be a primary understanding of the text. This expansion of the historical reading of the text came to be known as the *duplex sensus litteralis*, the double literal sense. Nicholas not only uses the double literal, but is fond of explaining how it works. His favourite image, which we find (among other places) in his exegesis of Dan 11:21, tells us something both about medieval shop signs and Nicholas' acute preacher's sense of what sort of example would appeal to students; for the image is that of a circle hanging outside a tavern. This can be 'read' simply as a circle, or it can be seen to signify the wine that will be found in the cellar within; and it can be understood simultaneously to be both. "Similarly in sacred Scripture, if something is said in relation to another thing only as a figure of that other thing, then there is only one literal sense... But when something is said in relation to another thing both in its own right *and* as a figure of that other thing, then both are the literal sense [that is, there is a double literal sense], although the principal literal sense is that of which it is a figure". To illustrate this, Nicholas gives two examples of the use of the word Solomon. In Psalm 71 (72), Solomon is invoked, but only to be a figure of Christ in the text; in 1 Chronicles 22, however, Solomon is used in a double sense, to represent both the man himself, David's son, and as a figure of Christ, the son of God, although of these two meanings priority should be given to the figuration of Christ.

Nicholas is explaining the theory of the double literal sense at this point in his exposition of Daniel in order to illuminate the meaning of "the vilest man", which is understood to refer both to Antiochus Epiphanes and to the Antichrist. He is characteristically careful in his analysis of the text, pointing out that in part of the text Antiochus appears merely as a figure of Antichrist (a single literal sense, but not referring to the historical person), but that the beginning of the text refers both to Antiochus *per se* and to the Antichrist, although what is said is a closer match for the Antichrist than for Antiochus (a double literal sense).

Nicholas' distinction here is not new to him. We can find it in Hugh of St Cher's *Postillae* at the same pericope, even using the same biblical examples to make his points. However, there are two differences between their discussions. Firstly, although Hugh states what each of the parts of the text signifies at which point (even noting that expositors vary in their views on this passage), he has no theoretical treatment of how this comes about. Hugh is first and foremost interested in providing a useful reference tool for his brother Dominicans, and other preachers, to use in their ministry. His treatment is clear, unambiguous, and concise. Secondly, Hugh uses his literal interpretation to provide an historical and syntactical explanation of the text, quoting a chronology established in Peter Comestor's *Historia scholastica*. The double understanding of the text, as figurative of Antichrist, is part of his spiritual exegesis. Nicholas has adopted the same solutions (which indeed date back to the Fathers), but he regards them as belonging to the literal sense of the text, and he sets out his understanding of the letter that makes this possible.

Why is Nicholas so intent on the literal sense? Obviously, he seems to have regarded the other senses as otiose. One of his more common phrases is "as is clear in the letter", or some variation on it. It suggests that all that needs to be understood can be found in a reading of the text in its literal sense, even though the lesson may be something traditionally thought of as residing in the spiritual senses. His exposition of Psalm 138 (139), for example, is all under the literal heading, with no associated spiritual reading. Yet he ends with a simple description of the *moralitas* of the Psalm: that anyone who follows David's example and notices the ubiquitous presence of God in the world will grow in awe of God and the saints, and in his detestation of injustice. Nicholas sees no need to find this lesson in a special sense; it comes to him as part of the plain and useful reading of the letter.

Another reason for Nicholas' concentration on the literal may be, as we saw earlier, that he regularly seems to construct the framework of his commentary following Jewish interests, and especially those of Rashi. This means that the *Postillae* can take its own tack, leaving untouched passages that generations of earlier Christian exegetes considered important. For example, on Gen 27:24, when Isaac appears to be tricked into blessing Jacob instead of Esau, Nicholas simply does not ask the question of whether Jacob lied. But the story involves a breaking of a commandment (even though they had not yet been given) by a Patriarch (though he was not yet of this status), and so generations of Christian interpreters had struggled over this most difficult of pericopes, acquitting Jacob of any lie so that ordinary readers would not do likewise.

Nicholas' treatment of this passage contrasts with that of the *Glossa*. The patristic opinions gathered there prefer to emphasise the spiritual reading of the text: here, the Jews are the technically elder but in truth less worthy son, Esau, preoccupied with doing good works; Jacob represents the Gentile Church, led into his father's presence by the grace of his mother, Rebecca, who represents Christ. Thus Jacob did not secretly steal the blessing rightly due to Esau, but received that which had been prepared for him all along. The line taken by the compilers of the *Glossa* certainly depends on the text in all its particulars, carefully allegorised to reassure Christians of the rightness of their choice. Nicholas of Lyra comes to the same conclusion (that the blessing was rightly Jacob's: how could he not?), but he does so by using the text in a different way. His approach, unsurprising in someone with linguistic interests and Hebrew skills (or with access to scholars who knew Hebrew), is to see the problem as one of syntax. His treatment of the section is very short, and relies on his reading of the phrase, *Tu es filius meus Esau.* This is not, he says, a question ("as if there were doubt"), but an order: Isaac tells the man in front of him that he is his son Esau, so that he is commanded to comply with the blessing. And so, Nicholas says, the literal sense is clear: there is no issue of duplicity. Jacob is simply doing what he is told; and with this reading, all other problems disappear.

Hugh of St Cher had tried a similar syntactical approach. Asking, perhaps sheepishly, "But surely Jacob lied here?", he says that he did not, because he meant his answer metaphorically (*transumptive*), in the same way that Jesus called John the Baptist Elijah (Matt 11:14). Being less sweeping (and admitting that a problem exists), Hugh's attempt seems to come off rather less well than Nicholas' flatly positive statement. And his apparent uncertainty is compounded when he follows up the literal exegesis with expositions according to the allegorical and moral senses. Allegorically, Isaac is read as God the Father seeming not to know his Son at the Passion ("My God, My God, why have you forsaken me?", Psalm 21 [22]); the name Esau depends on its meaning 'red', for Christ was red with the blood of the Crucifixion. In the moral sense, the Father acknowledges every penitent soul ("rough and hairy", like Esau's hand), even though the sinner, like the prodigal son, claims not to be worthy to be called God's son. Nicholas gives no *moraliter* interpretation here; he notes only, giving both "Hebrew" and "catholic" reasons, that Isaac knew the blessing to be the will of God, and so confirmed it.

But perhaps the most interesting – and paradoxical – reason that Nicholas concentrates so much on the literal sense is his use of it as a polemical weapon against the Jews. Admiring though Nicholas generally seems to be of Rashi and his Jewish interpretations, and useful as he finds them, yet as an orthodox friar he necessarily regards the faith of the Jews as fundamentally wrong. Though in their time the Jews were the chosen people of God, most of them nevertheless failed to recognise the Messiah when he came. In their stubborn blindness, they stuck fast by their old ways and failed to see the light that God had sent to redeem them. Since God gave everyone the capacity to recognise the truth, only wilful ignorance prevents anyone from doing so. Such was the medieval Christian view, and Nicholas held to it as strongly as his vocation might suggest. At the conclusion to his postill on Ruth, for instance, he is unambiguous: "…they who are created from Christ and the Church in faith, *and no others*, will reign in heavenly glory" (my italics). Coming from another commentator, one less appreciative of and indebted to Jewish scholarship, this unbending opinion would not surprise us; but our modern sensibilities cannot help feeling it to be at the very least ungrateful, if not downright schizophrenic.

Nicholas, however, realises that it is only by arguing with the Jews over the literal sense that he can successfully prove the rightness of the Gospel. He must beat them on their own ground, and show that certain Old Testament passages, as he says in his exegesis of Isa 11:1-2, "*even in the Hebrew*, are understood as being about Christ". At theologically contested passages, Nicholas understands that the letter of the Hebrew text can make him sharper in defending the Christian reading and in attacking that of the Jews. Because he never relies on an interpretation from the spiritual senses to make his point, he sees himself on much firmer ground against his Jewish opponents.

Isa 7:14 ("Therefore the Lord himself shall give you a sign. Behold, the virgin shall conceive, and bear a son, and shall call his name Emmanuel") was a contested passage even among Jews. For Christians, it was the key to the Incarnation, since Matthew's Gospel (1:22-23) was clear that Jesus' birth happened as it did, "so that what the Lord said through the prophet might be fulfilled". Necessarily, the pericope contained several difficult problems: what was to be expected as a sign? what did the Hebrew word *alma*, which Christians translated 'virgin', really mean? how could someone who had been named Jesus be the same as one who was to be called Emmanuel?

The problems are acknowledged in the *Glossa* text, which uses Jerome's argument that unless *alma* refers to a virgin, rather than simply to a young girl, then there was no miraculous sign. It swiftly notes arguments against other Jewish interpretations of the text, and interprets the name Emmanuel in real and allegorical types.

Hugh of St Cher has a characteristically long and thorough treatment, entirely concentrating on the literal sense. Under the *mystice* heading he simply writes: "we could not find a sweeter mystery here than the sense of the letter"! He opens up the *Glossa* reading, making it easier to see what the *Glossa* extracts intended, including the refutation of various Jewish interpretations of the text. He gives short glosses of the words of the verse, and he also reports two alternative, slightly different Latin texts, one of which he glosses, the other of which he dismisses as incorrect. He considers the meanings of *alma*, and makes an interesting observation that the Jews may here be using not a Hebrew word but a 'Punic' one, for *alma* in Punic means 'virgo'. It is not unusual, he says, for the Jews to employ a non-Hebrew word, since they are used to nearly all other languages. In the end, he concludes, "Let us dismiss the Jews in their blindness, and follow our own [literal] reading".

Nicholas of Lyra here is more polemical than Hugh. The Jews, he says, have "perverted" this part of Scripture, so he must deal with it at length. As good as his word, he produces a comprehensive, argumentative, textually detailed response, including an implicit statement of the theory of the double literal sense. It is almost a scholastic question: considering the opinions of those who say the prophecy cannot have been intended to mean Christ; looking at other false expositions (by Jews) and excluding them; giving the true catholic exposition of the text; and finally, disposing of the Jewish objections. Most interestingly, he employs Rashi's refutation of some Jewish interpretations of the passage, but then proceeds to refute Rashi's own solution himself, although, as ever in his dealings with Rashi, treating him with great respect. Nicholas' argument for accepting the Christian reading of the passage is ultimately completely circular – it is true because Matthew's Gospel says it is true, and Matthew was filled with the Holy Spirit – but, crucially, it is based on a literal reading of the text.

4. Conclusions

All Christian biblical interpreters are ultimately concerned with the spiritual gold that can be mined by the faithful believer from the rough ore of the text; but each approaches the text with different expectations of what can be hewn from it.

This brief sample of exegesis from three great 'pandect' commentaries, the *Glossa ordinaria*, Hugh of St Cher's *Postillae* and the *Postillae* of Nicholas of Lyra, is instructive, illuminating some of the characteristics distinctive to each. The *Glossa* chooses its patristic excerpts so as virtually to ignore the literal meaning of the text; it moves directly to the spiritual senses and presents the Bible as a puzzle in which the true meaning is hidden in an outward shell of words. The reader must look *through* the casing of the letter to the veiled truths within. The *Glossa* reads the letter of the biblical text with allegory and moral interpretations to point the faithful reader to belief and action that will build and strengthen faith. The *Glossa* is difficult to read, as the extracts are introduced without context and their syntax can be hard to make out. The reader is dropped into complicated theological or textual arguments with no warning. Yet some of the short glosses are self-evident, and this uneasy mixture makes it difficult to imagine how it was really used. Hugh of St Cher takes a more varied line, presenting as many meanings as possible, and reading literal, moral and allegorical truths as existing simultaneously in the biblical text. The reader is not to choose just one of these, but to see that they co-exist and should all be understood as true and equally valid.

Nicholas of Lyra, however, has little space for the spiritual senses, separately explained. He sees the letter of the text as the proving ground for interpretation; meaning can be wrung from the syntax and grammar of the words themselves. Reading *with* the letter, with the help of native Hebrew guides, rather than reading *through* the letter to a secret interpretation, is his approach to the biblical text.

Nevertheless, even Nicholas of Lyra cannot rely on the literal sense for every biblical text. The Song of Songs has always been regarded as a text whose literal meaning cannot be the human love poem it appears to be. Lyra explains at Cant 1:1 that he intends, "as far as I am able", to expound the Song literally, but that the literal sense in this case is what the Hebrews call the parabolic, or figurative, meaning of the words. The primary understanding then is "not that which is signified through the words of the text, but what is signified by the things (*res*) in it". Using this technique, the Hebrews consider the Song to be about the love of God for the Israelites, from the time of their wedding at Sinai; catholic doctors take the book to be about the love of Christ and the Church, from the time that the Church and the Synagogue divide, when Christ's side was opened up on the cross.

Even when he must resort to this parabolic literal sense, Nicholas still tries his hardest to discuss the letter of the text, for he begins his exegesis with a discussion of the translation difficulties which result in Jews and Christians using slightly different versions. Further, even in these tricky conditions he does not address the spiritual senses; all the spiritual meanings are enclosed within his readings of the literal sense.

In comparison, the *Glossa* and Hugh use very different approaches. The *Glossa* presents only a spiritual reading of the text, using the image of the kiss to link the human and divine natures of the incarnate Son. At the other extreme, Hugh of St Cher uses his very long exposition of Cant 1:1 as a practical aid for preachers. Although he briefly includes the *Glossa*'s reading in his allegorical sense, Hugh's real energy is directed elsewhere, making sure that any preacher can deliver an elevating sermon, without coming to grief in the ambiguities of the words. He begins with short glosses reading the verse as God the Father sending the Son to instruct humanity with his own mouth. This allows Hugh a perfect opportunity to dilate on four types of mouth and four types of kisses, and, in the moral sense, on four lips (two each for the bride and groom, signifying pity, truth, love, and fear, and joined in various partnerships!), and three more sorts of kisses, this time kissing three different parts of the body (feet, hands, and lips) in confession, devotion, and contemplation. These in turn show the three conditions a sinner must meet in order to kiss Christ: penitence, purity, and spiritual fervour. Again, in comparison with Nicholas, Hugh does not deal with the theoretical basis of parabolic interpretation, steering firmly away from anything that might lead the reader to view the letter of the text as more than a signifier. What he does instead, and which Nicholas lacks, is a strong sense of his intended audience and their needs. Hugh writes always with preachers in mind, whether to tell them how to behave or to tell them what to preach. For example, understanding *celi* to mean 'preachers' in his exegesis of Psalm 18 (19), *Celi enarrant gloriam dei*, Hugh uses the text as an opportunity to list nine properties which good preachers ought to have, from subtlety of understanding to cleanliness in intention, and rotundity caused by their simplicity – for they should have no sharp corners formed by falseness. Then, understanding *celi* to mean ordinary 'faithful men', he uses the signs of the zodiac (known by every congregation, and often painted on the walls of medieval churches) to show six ways of ascending to God and six ways of removing oneself from sin. In a further, wonderfully practical aside, as part of his moral exegesis, he berates those "preachers or hearers" in the cloister who, knowing there to be many simple folk present, nevertheless insist on preaching (or on only listening to) a sermon in Latin, rather than French, even though most of the congregation will not understand! As he states in his general prologue to the *Postillae*, all Scripture exists to drag men away from evil and lead them to good. Hugh's work is highly focussed to allow his Dominican audience to do just that. Clear and comprehensive, Hugh's *Postillae* is the answer to a preacher's prayer, and it is obvious why the work was so popular.

Nicholas of Lyra's work is much more complex. Although he covers most of the text, nevertheless Nicholas' Hebrew focus can mean that he neglects passages that most Christian commentators feel obliged to address. Moreover, his obviously – sometimes relentlessly – scholarly approach can prevent him from achieving Hugh's clarity. His evident desire to understand every inch of the letter of the biblical text can result in him losing his way in detail. But he has other virtues. He is full of information, much of it new to his readers, who knew nothing of the Jewish traditions of scholarship. Nicholas carefully lays out his arguments and shows his working, so that readers can come to conclusions on their own, rather than simply having to accept what he says. Indeed, he often gives varying interpretations of the text and allows readers to decide for themselves.

Although there is a spiritual side to his work, it is clear that this kind of interpretation is not where his expertise (or perhaps his heart) lies. The moral postils are usually short, if not non-existent. This is not to say that he does not make spiritual points, but rather that he makes them arising from the letter of the text, rather than from a spiritual reading of it. As we have seen, there may not be one simple reason why Nicholas is so eager to concentrate on the literal sense of the text; but his use of it in polemical arguments against the Jewish interpretation of the Bible and the Jewish faith are striking. Rightly, the Jews would not accept Christian reasoning based on a spiritual reading of the text; but Nicholas believes that if he can turn their own sense – the letter – against them, then they will have no defence against the Gospel message.

Why, finally, does Nicholas seem to have had "many readers but few followers"? And why did the Reformers find his work attractive? The reason for the first must lie in the question of audience. Fascinating though Nicholas is to read, his text is not one that a busy preacher could keep at his elbow. Nicholas is too idiosyncratic and too 'modern' in his interests, and too scholarly in his presentation. Hugh's old-fashioned but crisply practical *Postillae* would find a much clearer natural readership.

For the modern scholars of the late Middle Ages, eager to address questions of exegetical theory and literal understanding, Nicholas' *Postillae* were a goldmine of material. They could admire his scholarly attitude and his Hebrew knowledge, whilst working out their exegesis in their own way. For although the Reforming commentators, for whom doctrine was entirely derived from the biblical text, and who accepted vernacular reading of the Bible, believed like Nicholas that interpretation must be rooted in the literal sense, nevertheless they and he had their differences. Nicholas would not, I think, encourage non-learned readings of the text. He worked hard with his Jewish sources to understand the literal sense; it was not something that merely reading the letter could accomplish. As any medieval commentator would, Nicholas is careful to note, in his second prologue to the *Postillae*, that his exegesis is subject to correction by the authority of the Church. It might be argued that this is a merely conventional disclaimer on his part, yet Nicholas shows no sign of wishing to argue with doctrine in any way. Moreover, the purpose of his desire to know the literal meaning, in all its fullness, was not to declare that understanding the literal sense is clear and available to all, outside of the decisions of the councils of the Church. On the contrary, he reads the letter in order to argue in detail and on their own ground, as one scholar to another, against the faith of the Jews.

"Plain and useful" is, in the end, a rather ill-fitting description of Nicholas' work, for his "plain" reading of the letter of the text proved to be anything but simple, and his usefulness was not perceived in the evangelical way he might have desired. Although he is a constant user of the exegesis of his Christian predecessors, both his employment of Jewish sources and his quirky incorporation of spiritual meanings into the literal sense mean that Nicholas is not simply a summing-up of the medieval tradition. Neither does he clearly fit in the Reforming mould. Instead, his academic interests set him slightly apart from both, and perhaps explain why he was read but not imitated. Nevertheless, reading Nicholas today one can recognise a scholarly mind at work, in a way that is not always true of other medieval writers, whose leaps to the spiritual senses can leave a twenty-first-century reader stuck on the other side of the interpretative ravine. Distant though Nicholas remains from us, yet his textual and linguistic awareness, his pursuit of answers in the exegesis of the Jews, and his concern with matters of theory make it impossible not to admire the achievement of the *Postillae*.

2.2. Levi ben Gershom / Gersonides

By Seymour Feldman, New Brunswick, NJ

Sources: Gersonides: *Perush al ha-Torah / Commentary on the Pentateuch* (Venice 1547; repr. New York 1958; ed. J. L. Levy, *Genesis*, Jerusalem 1992; *Exodus*, ibid. 1994; *Leviticus*, ibid. 1997; *Numbers*, ibid. 1998; *Deuteronomy*, ibid. 2000); *Commentary on the Book of Job* (tr. by A. Lassen; New York: Bloch Publishing House 1946); *Commentaries on Joshua and Proverbs* (included in most editions of Rabbinic Bibles); *Commentary on Song of Songs* (tr. by M. Kellner; New Haven: Yale UP 1998); *Milhamoth Adonai / The Wars of the Lord* 1-3 (tr. S. Feldman; Philadelphia: Jewish Publication Society 1984, 1987, 1999); Hasdai Crescas: *Or Adonai / The Light of the Lord* (ed. S. Fischer; Jerusalem: Sifrei Ramot 1990); Moses b. Maimon / Maimonides: *The Guide of the Perplexed* (tr. S. Pines; Chicago: University of Chicago Press 1963); Philo of Alexandria: *Works* (LCL; vol. 1, *Allegorical Interpretation of the Law*, 1956; 3, *That God is Immutable*, 1930; 7-8, *The Special Laws*, 1950, 1968).

Bibliographies: S. Feldman, "Bibliography", in: *The Wars of the Lord* 3 (1999) 520-32; M. Kellner, "Bibliographia Gersonideana: An Annotated List of Writings by and about R. Levi ben Gershom", in: *Studies on Gersonides: A Fourteenth Century Philosopher-Scientist* (ed. G. Freudenthal; Leiden: Brill 1992) 367-414.

General works: R. Eisen, *Gersonides on Providence, Covenant and the Chosen People*, (Albany: State of New York UP 1995); idem, "Gersonides' Commentary on the Book of Job", *JJTP* 10 (2001) 239-88; S. Feldman, "The Binding of Isaac: A Test-case of Divine Foreknowledge", in: *Divine Omniscience and Omnipotence* (ed. T. Rudavsky; 1985) 105-33; idem, "Gersonides and Biblical Exegesis", in: *The Wars of the Lord* 2 (1987) Appendix, 213-47; idem, "The Wisdom of Solomon: A Gersonidean Interpretation", in: *Gersonide en son temps* (ed. G. Dahan; Louvain / Paris: E. Peeters 1991) 61-80; E. Freiman, "Le commentaire de Gersonide sur le Pentateuque", in: *Gersonide en son temps* (1991) 117-32; E. Freiman / B. Brenner, "Gersonides' Commentary on the Pentateuch" (Hebr.), *Mahanaim* 4 (1992) 224-41; G. Freudenthal, "Cosmogonie et physique chez Gersonide", *REJ* 145 (1986) 294-314; A. Funkenstein, "Gersonides' Biblical Commentary: Science, History and Providence", in: *Studies on Gersonides: A Fourteenth Century Philosopher-Scientist* (ed. G. Freudenthal; Leiden 1992) 305-16; B. R. Goldstein, "Preliminary Remarks on Levi ben Gerson's Contributions to Astronomy", PIASH 3 (1969) 239-54; R. Glasner, "The Early Stages in the Evolution of Gersonides' The Wars of the Lord", *JQR* 87 (1996) 1-47; idem, "On Gersonides' Knowledge of Languages", *Aleph* 2 (2002) 235-57; M. Kellner, "Gersonides' Commentary on Song of Songs", in: *Gersonide en son temps* (1991) 81-107; S. Klein-Braslavy, "Prophecy, Clairvoyance and Dreams and the Concept of 'Hitbodedut' in Gersonides' Thought", *Da'at* 39 (1997) 23-68 (Hebr.); C. Manekin, "Preliminary Observations on Gersonides' Logical Writings", PAAJR 52 (1985) 85-113; idem, "Conservative tendencies in Gersonides' religious philosophy", in: *The Cambridge Companion to Medieval Jewish Philosophy* (eds. D. H. Frank / O. Leaman; Cambridge 2003) 304-44; T. Rudavsky (ed.), *Divine Omniscience and Omnipotence in Medieval Philosophy* (ed. T. Rudavsky; Dordrecht: D. Reidel 1985); idem, "Divine Omniscience, Contingency and Prophecy in Gersonides", in idem: *Divine Omniscience and Divine Omnipotence* (1985) 161-81; N. Samuelson, "Gersonides' Account of God's Knowledge of Particulars", *JHP* 10 (1972) 399-416; C. Sirat / S. Klein-Braslavy / O. Weijers (eds.), *Les Methodes de travail de Gersonide et le maniement du savoir chez les scolastiques* (Paris: Vrin 2003); C. Touati, "Les idées philosophiques et théologiques de Gersonide (1288-1344) dans ses commentaires bibliques", *RevSR* 28 (1954) 335-67; idem, "La lumière de l'intellect, création du premier jour: L'exégèse de Genèse 1,1-3 chez Gersonide", *In Principio: Interprétations des premiers versets de la Genèse* (Paris: Centre des Religions du Livre 1973) 37-45; idem, *La pensée philosophique et théologique de Gersonide* (Paris: Les Editions de Minuit 1973).

1. Introduction

Levi ben Gershom, generally known by the Latin form of his name: *Gersonides* (known also by the Hebrew acronym RaLBaG), was born in 1288 in the Provence (at Bagnols-sur-Cèze); he died in 1344. He was also called Magister Leo Hebraeus. Gersonides made important contributions to astronomy, mathematics, philosophy and biblical exegesis. He wrote in Hebrew, and there is no hard evidence that he had adequate knowledge of any other language except Provencal.[1] His scientific work elicited the attention of the Papal court in Avignon, and some of his astronomical and mathematical writings were commissioned by Church authorities.[2] His philosophical corpus includes supercommentaries on Averroes' commentaries upon Aristotle and a major independent philosophical treatise *The Wars of the Lord*, consisting of six books discussing the more controversial and significant issues in medieval philosophy and science (the first part of Book 5 is entirely devoted to astronomy and mathematics).[3] While working on his philosophical books, Gersonides was also engaged in biblical exegesis; often the former refer to the latter and conversely. The biblical commentaries cover the Pentateuch, the Former Prophets, the books of Job, Proverbs, Ecclesiastes, Song of Songs, Ruth, Esther, Daniel, Ezra, Nehemiah, Chronicles and Daniel. He appears to have commented on Isaiah, but the commentary is no longer extant.[4] Many of these commentaries have been quite popular and have been included in the standard editions of the Hebrew Bible along with the other almost canonical medieval commentators Solomon Isaac of Troyes (Rashi), Abraham ibn Ezra and Moses ben Nahman (Nahmanides). Before we examine these commentaries it will be useful to note Gersonides' general philosophical orientation and tendencies, since they will both shape and appear in the exegesis of the biblical texts.

2. Philosophy and Exegesis

Gersonides' philosophy and exegesis were shaped by the twin influences of Maimonides (1135/40–1204) and Averroes (1126–98), the two giants of medieval Jewish and Muslim Aristotelian philosophy. Yet, despite their deep impact upon his thinking, Gersonides often reached different results. For example, on the extremely controversial question of creation or eternity of the universe, Gersonides rejected Aristotle's and Averroes' claim that the world is eternal in duration; on the other hand, he rejected the traditional view of *creatio ex nihilo*, the view apparently adopted by Maimonides and most medieval

---

[1] Touati, La pensée (1973) 33–48; Glasner, Gersonides' Knowledge of Languages (2002) 235–57.

[2] Goldstein, Preliminary Remarks (1969) 239–54; K. CHEMLA / S. PAHAUT, "Remarques sur les ouvrages mathématiques de Gersonide", in: Studies on Gersonides (1992) 149–94.

[3] Gersonides, *The Wars* 1.17–30.

[4] Touati, La pensée (1973) 49–72; idem, Les idées philosophiques et théologiques (1954) 335–67; Freiman, Le commentaire de Gersonide sur le Pentateuque (1991) 117–32.

Jewish, Muslim and Christian thinkers. According to Gersonides, the universe is indeed created, i.e., it is finite in duration *a parte ante*, but is created from some independent eternal material stuff that is without shape or stability. His treatment of this subject is philosophical throughout, consisting of rigorous arguments that cover the whole range of issues in medieval cosmology.[5]

Yet, like Maimonides and Averroes, Gersonides believes that the *summum bonum*, the attainment of which results in human happiness, consists in intellectual perfection. This is to be achieved by moral excellence, religious piety and rigorous studies, especially in philosophy and in the sciences. The fruit of this arduous discipline is, as we shall see, immortality, which like anything of value, has to be earned, not just given gratuitously. This philosophical 'bias' leads Gersonides to view the Torah as a philosophical book, or a text that teaches philosophical truths as well as practical moral and religious precepts. Indeed, the Torah is especially important and valuable since it leads the attentive and prepared reader to appreciate and recognize philosophical truths that would be very difficult to learn if left to his own devices. This does not mean for Gersonides, as it did for many medieval thinkers, especially among the Christian Scholastics, that the Bible teaches doctrines that are 'beyond' reason, as mysteries that surpass the domain of ordinary logic. Rather, the Torah provides us with data for knowing metaphysical propositions that are perfectly rational but difficult to grasp without the clues given us by Scripture. The Bible is then a kind of philosophical tutor who stimulates us to open and study the books of the philosophers, especially Aristotle and his commentators, which will enable us to prove philosophically what we have learned through prophetic revelation. In this enterprise there is no need to fear that philosophy will contradict prophecy since the author of both is the same; indeed, it will turn out that one confirms what the other teaches. Of course, the assumption here is that we have determined what philosophy truly teaches and what the Bible truly says. And the latter is what Gersonides' exegesis is aimed to accomplish, as his *Wars of the Lord* is intended to do for the former. If Maimonides' *Guide of the Perplexed* was written to clear up biblical difficulties for the philosophically initiated reader, the Bible is for Gersonides intended to guide us in our pursuit of philosophical, as well as moral, perfection.[6]

3. Gersonides' Biblical Interpretation

Now, if Holy Scripture aids and leads us to our ultimate felicity, which is intellectual perfection involving the pursuit of philosophical and scientific truths, *how* does it do this? The biblical text is *prima facie* a collection of narratives, poems and laws. Even when it raises or suggests philosophical problems, which is not often, the language is non-philosophical. Accordingly, it is incumbent upon the philosophically minded exegete to justify a philosophical reading of

---

[5] Gersonides, *The Wars* 3, Bk. 6, Part 1, Chs. 17–18.
[6] Gersonides, *Commentary on the Torah, Genesis*, 2a (Venice), 1–2 (Jerusalem).

the biblical text, especially since by the time of Gersonides such readings were often suspected of heterodox doctrines.[7] The most common route taken by advocates of philosophical exegesis was to appeal to the polyvalent character of the Bible, a doctrine that had already been well-established in traditional rabbinic literature.[8] If the biblical text could be interpreted aggadically or mystically, why not read it philosophically? But even if we allow and accept this mode of exegesis, we still have to determine how the philosophical meaning enters the text and to whom this meaning is addressed. In short, a theory of philosophical biblical hermeneutics is needed.

In the Introduction to his Pentateuch commentary Gersonides immediately tells the reader not to expect from him citations from rabbinic Aggadah, which, although edifying and quite popular, depart from the literal meaning of the text. For the most part, Gersonides aims to give us the plain meaning of the Bible, or the *peshat*.[9] However, there will be exceptions to this general rule, and we shall have to examine when and why deviations from the apparent meaning of the text need to be adopted. Unlike those philosophically-minded exegetes, such as Philo of Alexandria and perhaps also Maimonides, who were inclined to insinuate non-literal readings into the text freely, Gersonides is not so liberal. Although he does not mention the earlier exegete and theologian Saadiah ben Joseph (882–942), Gersonides suscribes to the latter's general hermeneutical principle that the plain meaning of the biblical text is to be accepted unless there is a good reason not to. The good reasons are if the text is inconsistent with logic, sense-experience or the clear meaning of another biblical text.[10] Hence, the burden of proof is upon the exegete to show that a non-literal reading is required; otherwise, the text stands as is.

Nevertheless, Gersonides' professed fidelity to the *peshat* is more complicated than it seems. In the first place, he believes that the philosophical meaning he finds in a particular passage *is* its literal meaning. It is not as if the philosophical content is intentionally hidden, waiting to be uncovered by the skilled reader, who should be wary of divulging this meaning to the unqualified. This was Maimonides' obsession.[11] Thus, Gersonides is not afraid to express in his commentaries the same philosophical doctrines that he propounded in his purely philosophical works. Indeed, with one exception – The Song of Songs, which we shall discuss later – Gersonides explicitly disavows the 'esoteric' mode of discourse, which was so favored by Maimonides.[12] This implies that for Gersonides the 'exoteric' meaning of the Bible is often a philosophy lesson, which should be accessible to all.

This is most evident at the outset of his commentary upon the opening verses of Genesis. Before he begins his explication of the key terms in biblical account

---

[7] Touati, La pensée (1973) 15–30; Gersonides, *The Wars* 1.31–34.

[8] *Song of Songs, Rabbah*, 2.4.

[9] Gersonides, *Commentary on the Torah, Genesis*, Introduction, 2c (Venice), 3 (Jerusalem).

[10] Saadiah b. Joseph, *The Book of Beliefs and Opinions* (tr. S. Rosenblatt; New Haven: Yale UP 1948), Treatise 7, 265–66; Gersonides, *Commentary on the Torah, Genesis*, 16d, 28b (Venice), 67, 133 (Jerusalem).

[11] Maimonides, *The Guide of the Perplexed*, Introduction to the First Part.

[12] Gersonides, *The Wars* 1, Introductory Remarks, 97, 100–01.

of creation, Gersonides lays down several fundamental principles guiding his understanding of creation. The first principle states that although Scripture describes the creation in temporal language, we are not to understand the sequence chronologically, such that the land animals were created 24 hours after the fish. Rather, the sequence is one of causal or natural priority, whereby the prior entity is a cause of the posterior or occupies a higher place, or level, in the natural hierarchy of substances. For Gersonides the whole universe was created by God in one instant according to a definite order of rank and causal interdependence. Accordingly, when we read that on the "first day" light was created, we need to understand this passage as referring not to the visible, or sensible, light, but to the domain of the separate, incorporeal intellects, or angels. After all, the heavenly bodies themselves were created on the "fourth day"; so the "light" on the "first day" must have some other referent. Now, some of these separate intellects are the movers of the heavenly bodies, and as the causes of celestial movement they "precede" the creation of the bodies. One of these intellects, the Agent Intellect, is a cause of human intellection, and hence precedes the creation of man, whose ultimate happiness lies in intellectual perfection. Gersonides' exegesis of this passage also enables him to answer easily a question that vexed many ancient and medieval exegetes, when were the angels created? Obviously, the "first day"![13] All of this is for Gersonides the *plain* meaning of the biblical text.

In some cases, however, there will be a need to provide a non-literal interpretation of the text. At this point we shall need to distinguish different degrees of 'parabolic' (*mashal*) readings. The most limited or minimal resort to a non-literal reading is one already recognized by the Rabbis in their exegesis: here a word or phrase is interpreted metaphorically; such readings are justified by the rabbinic hermeneutical principle that the Torah speaks the language of men.[14] In many cases this rule was used to avoid anthropomorphisms, and was frequently employed by Philo and Maimonides.[15] Gersonides too often appeals to this kind of exegesis. For example, in Gen 6:6, God is depicted as "regretting" his creation of the human species. Now, for the Aristotelian philosophers God is not subject to human passions, such as regret; hence, this phrase requires interpretation, but only a modest and minor one: the Torah speaks in ordinary human terms using a metaphor to bring out the point that at this juncture in human history man departed from the path that God had intended him to follow.[16]

Nevertheless, there will be some places where a more extensive use of parable is required. Here the literal meaning of the text is almost obliterated or relegated to the background to the point of disappearance. Consider now the story of Adam and Eve in the Garden of Eden. Many readers of the Bible read this story literally: for them every detail of the story is a historical fact; and for some believers crucial theological doctrines are based upon these details (e.g.

---

[13] Gersonides, *Commentary on the Torah, Genesis,* 9d–10a (Venice), 26 (Jerusalem).
[14] *b. Yebam.* 71a; *B. Meṣ* 31b.
[15] Philo, *That God is Immutable,* 51–69; Maimonides, *Guide,* 1.1 and pass.
[16] Gersonides, *Commentary on the Torah, Genesis,* 6:6, 18d (Venice), 77 (Jerusalem).

original sin). Others construe it as an extended parable devoid of any historical implications albeit having philosophical content. Such were the readings of Philo and Maimonides.[17] Here Gersonides forges a middle path. Some elements of the story are indeed parabolic; others, however, are real. For example, the episode of the serpent's dialogue with Eve is parabolic. After all, snakes do not speak. And it is not acceptable to introduce here a miracle to account for the serpent's speech. In general, one should be very parsimonious in resorting to miracles, especially in this case where we would have to say that the snake's nature, just created on the fifth day, was annulled on the sixth day. No, claims Gersonides: this part of the story is just that – a story teaching a philosophical lesson, not relating historical information. The serpent is a symbol of the seductive power of the imagination, especially in the domain of moral concepts and practice, where rigorous philosophical proof is almost impossible to attain. Yet, there is some historical truth in the story. Eve, for example, did give birth to three sons. Moreover, there was a place called Eden and four rivers flowed from it.[18]

Indeed, Gersonides maintains, good parables contain a mixture of factual truth and philosophical instruction conveyed parabolically. This is quite true in King Solomon's book *Proverbs*, where often the surface meaning makes very good practical sense, while at the same time teaches us some philosophy. For example, at the end of this treatise in moral instruction, we read about the woman of valor, the perfect wife. The surface meaning of the text is straightforward and raises no philosophical or theological problems. But for Gersonides there is more here than just praise for a virtuous woman. The woman of valor is a symbol for the role of sense-perception in the cognitive enterprise. As Aristotle had maintained, matter is feminine and form is masculine. Moreover, knowledge requires sensory imputs; or in Aristotle's own language, sensation is the material cause of knowledge. Solomon teaches us this piece of epistemology by having the virtuous woman symbolize material sensory data to be used in the acquisition of knowledge. This is her contribution to intellectual perfection. Indeed, for Gersonides the Book of Proverbs is in general a treatise in epistemology.[19]

The sole example where the biblical text has to be read entirely as a parable, or allegory, is Solomon's *Song of Songs*. Of course, here Gersonides was not unique: rabbinic exegesis of this book mandated an allegorical reading, according to which the male character in this love poem is God and the female character is the People of Israel; and a similar interpretation was adopted by the medieval Church, with the People of Christ replacing Israel. Although adopting the allegorical mode of interpretation for this book, Gersonides goes his own way. For him the allegory is purely philosophical: it depicts the epistemological relationship between the human intellect and the transcendent immaterial Agent Intellect, which, as we have already learned, is the efficient

[17] Philo, *Allegorical Interpretation of the Law*, 1.43–108; Maimonides, *Guide*, 1.2 and 2.30.

[18] Gersonides, *Commentary on the Torah*, Genesis, 14b–16d (Venice), 53–67 (Jerusalem).

[19] Gersonides, *Commentary on Proverbs*, end; Feldman, The Wisdom of Solomon (1991) 61–80.

cause of human cognition. This is nicely illustrated in Gersonides' reading of
the opening verse: "Let him kiss me with kisses of his mouth". Gersonides interprets this passage as follows:

> "Would that God kiss me with the kisses of His mouth!", that is, that it [the human intellect]
> cleave to Him so far as possible...He [Solomon] said "Let him kiss me" and not "I will kiss him"
> because in truth God is the Actor in this matter; for what we know is an emanation emanating upon
> us from God, through the intermediation of the Active Intellect.[20]

Not only is Song of Songs not about erotic love; it is not even about the love
between God and man or Israel. It is a treatise in psychology and epistemology
written in such a way as to impart its message to those who are qualified to receive it without harm. For the unqualified it is, as the Rabbis have said, a love
song between God and Israel; this is an acceptable reading for most believers.
Here we have one of those many cases where the aggadic Midrash is useful,
even though not the exact truth.

One of the more unusual stylistic devices adopted by Gersonides in many of
his commentaries is the tri-parte analysis of the biblical pericope. He first provides the reader with an explanation of the more difficult words; then he
moves on to the explication of the "story"; and he concludes with "Useful Lessons". The latter are frequently subdivided into three parts: philosophical or
theological doctrines; moral or political precepts; and legal commandments.
The doctrinal lessons and legal discussions are especially interesting, since the
former afford Gersonides the opportunity to present his philosophical views as
the intended meaning of the biblical text, whereas the latter allow him to exhibit not only his legal expertise but the opportunity to show how the Oral Law
is included in the Written Law.

A striking example of a philosophical reading of a biblical narrative that results in a radical innovation in biblical theology is Gersonides' interpretation
of God's dialogue with Abraham about Sodom and Gomorrah. Already in his
philosophical work *The Wars of the Lord* Gersonides had demonstrated that
the standard doctrine of divine omniscience has to be understood differently
from the way it is usually construed. Instead of saying that God knows everything, we should say that God knows everything that is knowable. Now, some
things are not knowable to anyone; for example, no one knows how to square
the circle, since this is logically impossible. Gersonides believes, as did Aristotle and some of his commentators, that knowing future contingent events is logically impossible. For to know such events is to fix their truth-value and thus
to annul their contingency. In so far as they are contingent, they are "open-
ended", or "free-floating". Like Aristotle Gersonides wants to preserve the
genuine contingency of the future in order to safeguard human freedom.[21]

This is at issue in the story of Abraham and his intervention on behalf of the
people of Sodom and Gomorrah (Gen 18:16–33). The story begins with God
saying: "I shall go down and see whether their deeds warrant the outcry which
has reached me. I am resolved to know the truth". Now, the text raises at least

---

[20] Gersonides, *Commentary on Song of Songs*, 24. See KELLNER's Introduction for a fine analysis
of Gersonides' hermeneutical strategy in Song of Songs.
[21] Gersonides, *The Wars* 2, Bk. 3; Aristotle, *On Interpretation*, Ch. 9.

two problems: first, can we read the verbs 'go down' and 'see' literally? Second, is God ignorant that He needs to undertake a on-site investigation of the moral behavior of the people? The first issue is easily handled: it is just another example of Scripture using language adapted to the ordinary mode of human speech. The second problem is far more serious; for if we read the passage literally, we shall have to say that God is not omniscient and that like us He has to do research and accumulate information. Gersonides solves the second problem by reading the story according to his philosophical theory of divine knowledge. God knows what the people of Sodom and Gomorrah generally do; for He knows their natural dispositions and their moral consequences. He knows them because these tendencies are nomological patterns determined by the heavenly bodies and the laws governing their movements. But God does not know what any given individual in Sodom or Gomorrah will do on any given occasion; for that is an open question, even for God. If a particular person has free-will, then his future actions are, if contingent, undetermined, and hence unknowable to everyone, including God. Accordingly, when God says to Abraham that He needs further information about Sodom and Gomorrah, He is saying something significant: "In so far as the people have free-will, they have the capacity to go against what their naturally determined dispositions have dictated. True, I know what they would ordinarily do; but I don't know what some individual in Sodom will do or if some individual has acted righteously, contrary to what as a resident of Sodom I should have expected him to do. If it turns out that they have acted differently from what I had expected, then I shall treat them accordingly; if not, then they will suffer the consequences of their evil actions".[22] Thus, the biblical story illustrates Gersonides' theory of divine knowledge, which one recent writer has labelled a theory of "limited omniscience".[23] The 'heterodox' implications of Gersonides' interpretation of this story and his general account of divine omniscience did not escape the notice and criticism of later medieval exegetes, who objected to his "limiting" God's knowledge.[24]

Gersonides' philosophical reading of Scripture is also evident in his account of biblical miracles. Unlike those exegetes who attempted to eliminate the miraculous element entirely or those who accentuate it,[25] Gersonides wanted to preserve divine intervention but without abolishing the natural course of events altogether. For example, the transformation of Moses' staff into a snake in Exod 4:2–4 was indeed a miracle, something that was not ordinary. But it did not violate the laws of logic, although it was not what nature usually does. What we have here is a case of a natural process being accelerated to such a de-

---

[22] Gersonides, *Commentary on the Torah, Genesis,* 18:16–33, 27a, 28d (Venice), 130, 136–37 (Jerusalem); *The Wars* 2, Appendix, 228.

[23] C. Manekin, "On the Limited-Omniscience Interpretation of Gersonides' Theory of Divine Cognition", *Perspectives on Jewish Thought and Mysticism* (ed. A. Ivry / E. Wolfson / A. Arkush; Amsterdam: Harwood Academic Publishers 1998) 135–70.

[24] Hasdai Crescas, *Or Adonai / The Light of the Lord,* Second Treatise, First Principle. See Feldman, "Crescas' Theological Determinism", *Da'at* 9 (1982) 3–28.

[25] Maimonides, *Guide,* 2.29; *Commentary on Avot,* 5.6; *Eight Chapters,* Ch. 8; Isaac Abravanel, *Mif'alot Elohim,* Treatise, 10.

gree that it appears to be utterly impossible. If nature runs its course, the wooden staff will decompose and ultimately its matter will take on a different form – after all, matter is conserved –, say a snake. In Moses' case, however, the natural course of events was truncated to such an extent that it took place almost instantaneously. This was the miracle.[26]

Perhaps Gersonides' most radical reading of a biblical miracle is his account of the miracle in Joshua 10. According to the usual reading of the story, Joshua asked God to stop the sun from moving while he battles the Amorites. For the moment we need to adopt a Ptolemaic astronomical model according to which the sun rotates around the earth. Yet, even on this view there is a serious scientific problem for the medieval philosophical reader of the Bible: how can the movements of the heavenly bodies be interrupted or changed, even just for a moment, without the whole universe being utterly thrown into disorder? Since the Bible does not record any such catastrophic events, it is unlikely that the sun stopped moving. Moreover, according to Aristotle, the heavenly domain is immutable and unchangeable.[27] So, for Gersonides, the miracle had to have occurred in the earthly domain. It had to do with the rapidity with which Joshua defeated the enemies of Israel and took place in about an hour, the period during which the sun reaches its zenith in the horizon and appears to have halted before it begins to set. Nothing unusual happened to the sun; what was unusual was the quick dispatch of the Amorites.[28]

Nevertheless, one must note one important, indeed crucial, topic where Gersonides' attempt to find complete congruence between true philosophy and the Torah appears to break down; and surprisingly it is found right at the very beginning of everything: Genesis. As we mentioned at the outset of this essay, Gersonides departed from the standard medieval cosmological model of *creatio ex nihilo* interpreted in the strong sense as creation from absolutely nothing. In his *The Wars of the Lord* he argued vigorously in favor of a revised version of Plato's thesis that God created the physical universe out of some kind of formless matter that is itself eternal. Realizing that he was advocating a 'heterodox' position, Gersonides claimed that this view was consistent with Scripture, and in particular with biblical accounts of miracles.[29] Moreover, he also maintained that not only is this world unique, but that it is indestructible: one God, one world forever. Here too Gersonides deviated from some rabbinic doctrines wherein God is depicted as having created many worlds before the present one and as having the ability to destroy it if He wills.[30]

None of this, however, appears in his *Commentary on Genesis*! What is especially puzzling is that in the introductory remarks to his commentary he explicitly states as one of his fundamental cosmological principles the thesis

---

[26] Gersonides, *Commentary on the Torah, Genesis,* 16:30–33, 188d, 191a (Venice), 71, 90 (Jerusalem); *The Wars* 3, Bk. 6, Part 2, Ch. 12.

[27] Aristotle, *On the Heavens,* 1.10–12.

[28] Gersonides, *Commentary on Joshua,* ch. 10; *The Wars* 3, Bk. 6, Part 2, Ch. 12. See FELDMAN, "'Sun Stand Still': A Philosophical-Astronomical Midrash", Proceedings of the Ninth World Congress of Jewish Studies. Division C (Jerusalem: World Union of Jewish Studies 1986) 77–84.

[29] Gersonides, *The Wars* 3, Bk. 6, Part 1, Chs. 17–18; Part 2, Ch. 1.

[30] Gersonides, *The Wars* 3, Bk. 6, Part 1, Chs. 16 and 19.

that there is "a body that does not keep its shape" distributed between the various celestial spheres, preventing them from colliding, which would result in complete disorder. He identifies this body with the scriptural "waters" of Gen 1:2, since like water this body has no inherent form, or shape.[31] Now, in *The Wars of the Lord* Gersonides argues that this body is the very stuff from which the whole physical world was made. It is the analogue to Plato's "receptacle" in the *Timaeus*. But about this crucial cosmological role Gersonides is silent in the Torah Commentary.[32] As far as we can tell, there is no mention at all in his biblical commentaries of the doctrine of creation from eternal formless matter. Nor is there any allusion in the commentaries to the doctrines of the unicity of this world and its indestructibility. It would seem that Gersonides was aware of his innovative cosmology and reluctant to disturb or confuse the readers of his biblical commentaries, who although somewhat philosophically literate would not be wholly competent to appreciate the philosophical issues involved in the doctrine of *creatio ex nihilo* or plural worlds. So why create problems if it is not necessary to do so? Since the doctrine of creation from eternal formless matter does not undermine belief in the Torah, there is no compelling reason even to mention the issue in the commentary. Yet, it is somewhat surprising to find this lacuna while at the same time realizing that on some other controversial issues, as we have indicated, Gersonides was not hesitant to read the Bible according to his philosophical theories, indeed even to say that it was the Bible that suggested to him these views.

The Pentateuch is of course not only an introductory treatise in cosmology and a series of historical narratives. Many of its chapters are replete with legal matters and prescriptions, and hence constitute the scriptural basis for the whole legal structure of Judaism. In this part of his commentary on the Pentateuch Gersonides is both detailed and systematic in his treatment of the commandments. He sets for himself two general objectives: first, to show that the rabbinic Oral Law is derived directly from the Written Law; second, to demonstrate that the commandments, each and every one of them, has some philosophical significance. In undertaking the first goal Gersonides explicitly abandons the rabbinic practice of justifying a rabbinic ordinance either by attaching it to a biblical verse or by employing a particular set of thirteen legal hermeneutical rules from which the law can be inferred. In the first case, he claims the attachment is either artificial or arbitrary, or both; in the second, the rule is often illogical, since by the same rule the opposite law can be inferred. Accordingly, a new legal hermeneutics is needed that avoids these pitfalls. This new logic will show that the rabbinic ordinances are already implicit in the Written Law and can be derived therefrom by means of a more rational set of legal rules. Realizing that the latter undertaking cannot be included in the biblical commentary itself because of the vastness of rabbinic law, Gersonides contents himself with just laying out his new rules and sketching its fu-

---

[31] Gersonides, *Commentary on the Torah, Genesis*, 9c (Venice), 22 (Jerusalem).
[32] Gersonides, *The Wars* 3, Bk. 5, Part 2, Ch. 2; Bk. 6, Part 1, Ch. 17; Plato, *Timaeus*, 49A, 50B–C.

ture applications. He promises to write a legal treatise dealing with this question in detail; unfortunately, it does not seem that he did write such a work.[33]

However, he is more than generous in executing his second objective. His
discussion of particular commandments is most comprehensive and detailed.
He is not only concerned to lay out the various legal principles underlying and
inherent in the biblical precepts, but to demonstrate their moral and metaphysical meaning. In doing the latter Gersonides is following the tradition of Philo
and Maimonides, both of whom were committed to the enterprise of providing
"reasons for the commandments".[34] Whereas the Rabbis were satisfied to distinguish between those commandments that have some obvious point (*mishpa-
tim*) and those that do not (*chuqqim*), Gersonides, as well as Philo and Maimonides, believed that all the commandments have some rationale that com-
mends itself to sound philosophy. This is true not only in those precepts that
have an evident moral or social benefit (e.g., adultery), but also in the cultic
and ritual commandments (e.g., dietary laws) that do not seem to have any
significance at all.

As CHARLES TOUATI has emphasized, the pervasive principle throughout
Gersonides' rationalization of the commandments is the Aristotelian form-
matter dichotomy.[35] Consider, for example, his account of the biblical prohibition against combining wool and linen in the same garment (Lev 19:19; Deut
22:11). This prohibition is one of several commandments that preclude the
mixing of species, or forms. These combinations violate the biblical concept of
creation according to kind stated quite explicitly in Gen 1:12 and 1:21, which
agrees nicely with the Aristotelian biological theory of natural kinds. Now in
the case of the wool-linen garment, we have a combination that brings together two different genera, a plant and an animal. Indeed, the wool itself is
not really the form of the sheep but just a necessary excrescence of its matter.
Whereas the linen comes from flax, a specific form in its own right, wool is just
surplus matter. The former is clearly more perfect than the latter. A sport jack-
et made of wool and linen is then a mixture of a form (flax) and something that
is just an offshoot of a generically different form (the sheep). Nature and
God's plan have been overturned.[36]

This principle of the existence and primacy of form is most evident in Gersonides' interpretation of the Tabernacle and its ritual appurtenances (Exodus
25–28). However, here this principle is exhibited in a different manner.
Whereas in the previous case, the commandment is literally about forms and
their 'unnatural' mixing, in the many precepts concerning the construction, arrangement and use of the Tabernacle the concept of form is expressed, or sym-
bolized, through the various components of the physical structure. Although
Scripture is quite detailed in prescribing how and where each material element
of the Tabernacle is to be made and arranged, what is really significant, for

---

[33] Gersonides, *Commentary on the Torah, Genesis*, Introduction.
[34] Philo, *The Special Laws*, Bks. 1–4; Maimonides, *Guide*, 3.31–50.
[35] Touati, La pensée (1973) 496–98.
[36] Gersonides, *Commentary on the Torah, Leviticus*, 19:19, 162a–c (Venice), 299–301 (Jerusalem).

Gersonides, is the philosophical import of the sanctuary and its equipment. And again, it is form over matter.

Perhaps the most important of the cultic objects in the Tabernacle is the Ark of the Covenant (Exod 25:10–22). The Israelites were commanded to place two Cherubim, made out of gold and with wings reaching upwards, on the cover of the Ark. At first sight we may not be especially surprised by or attentive to this feature, since we expect important ritual objects to be nicely ornamented. But for Gersonides these two aesthetic objects have profound philosophical meaning. They represent the Agent Intellect and the material, or human, intellect: the Agent Intellect is a separate, or immaterial, form, whereas the material intellect is a disposition to receive and know the generic and specific forms embedded in material objects. If perfected through proper and continuous study the material intellect is separable and can become immortal. The wings of the Cherubim stretch upwards to convey the idea that they, especially the one representing the Agent Intellect, are created by and hence subordinate to God, the "Form of forms", or First Form. The two figurines are placed face to face to teach us that human intellection is the outcome of a cognitive relation between the Agent Intellect and the material intellect. In short, the Ark is not just a wooden box but the visible expression of a cosmological and epistemological theory about the formal structure of the universe and man's place in it.[37] The philosophically untrained reader of Gersonides' biblical commentaries may be both overwhelmed and shocked by them: overwhelmed because of their extensive philosophical content, shocked by their striking and often radical theological implications. Nevertheless, they are still studied by traditional Jews, and some of them have been recently published in critical editions, with supercommentaries. Perhaps their appeal is precisely the 'openness' with which Gersonides expresses his understanding of the biblical text and his ability to impart in relatively clear language the philosophical dimension of Scripture. Assuming that true philosophy and prophetic truth are one, Gersonides could not but give us a commentary that would demonstrate their identity. To some modern readers this assumption is either naive or erroneous. But to those who believe that there are many 'faces' to the Torah, it is not too far-fetched to recognize one of these faces as philosophical.

---

[37] Gersonides, *Commentary on the Torah, Exodus*, 25:10–22, 104b–105d (Venice), 361–65 (Jerusalem).

CHAPTER THREE

Bridging the Middle Ages and the Renaissance:
Biblia Pauperum, their Genre
and Hermeneutical Significance

By Tarald Rasmussen, Oslo

Sources: Biblia Pauperum. Billedbibelen fra Middelalderen (Introd. and transl. from Latin to Danish by K. Banning; Copenhagen: Gad 1991); J. K. Elliott, *The Apocryphal New Testament. A Collection of Apocryphal Christian Literature in an English Translation* (Oxford 1993); H. von Gabelentz (ed.), *Die Biblia Pauperum und Apokalypse der grossherzoglichen Bibliothek zu Weimar* (Strassburg 1912); A. Henry, *Biblia Pauperum: A Facsimile and Edition* (Ithaca, NY: Cornell UP 1987); *The Bible of the Poor. A Facsimile and Edition of the British Library Blockbook C.9d.2* (Tr. and comm. by A. C. Labriola / J. W. Smelz; Pittsburg 1990); E. Soltész / H. Th. Musper, *Biblia Pauperum. Die vierzigblättrige Armenbibel in der Bibliothek der Erzdiözese Esztergom* (Hanau/Main 1961).

Studies: K. Banning, "Biblia Pauperum and the Wall-paintings in the Church of Bellinge", in: *Medieval Iconography and Narrative. A Symposium* (Odense 1980) 124–34; H. Belting, *Bild und Kult* (München 1996); M. Berve, *Die Armenbibel. Herkunft – Gestalt – Typologie* (Beuron 1969); U. von Bloch, *Die illustrierten Historienbibeln* (Vestigia Bibliae 13/14 [1991/92]; Bern 1993); M. Camille, "Reading the Printed Image: Illuminations and Woodcuts of the Pèlerinage de la vie humaine in the Fifteenth Century", in: S. L. Hindman (ed.), *Printing the Written Word: The Social History of Books circa 1450–1520* (Ithaca / London 1991) 259–91; D. R. Cartlidge / J. K. Elliott, *Art and the Christian Apocrypha* (London / New York 2001); J. Cohen, *The Friars and the Jews: the Evolution of Medieval Anti-Judaism* (Ithaca, NY 1982); H. Cornell, *Biblia Pauperum* (Stockholm 1925); H. Cornell / S. Wallin, *Albertus Pictor: Sten Stures och Jacob Ulvssons målare* (Stockholm 1972); J. M. Lenhart, "The Biblia Pauperum or Medieval Biblical Mnemonics", *EcR* 73 (1925) 359–72, 502–18; J. Lowden, *The Making of the Bibles Moralisées* 1–2 (University Park, PA; Pennsylvania State UP 2000); R. Kroll, *Blockbücher des Mittelalters* (Mainz 1991); T. Nellhaus, "Mementos of Things to Come. Orality, Literacy, and Typology in the Biblia Pauperum", in: Hindman, Printing the Written Word (1991) 292–321; W. J. Ong, *Orality & Literacy. The Technologizing of the Word* (London / New York 1982); F. P. Pickering, *Literature and Art in the Middle Ages* (London 1970); G. Schmidt, *Die Armenbibeln des XIV. Jahrhunderts* (Veröffentlichungen des Instituts für Österreichische Geschichtsforschung, 19; Graz: Boehlau 1959); A. Weckwerth, "Der Name 'Biblia Pauperum'", *ZKG* 83 (1972) 1–33.

1. Introductory

Biblia Pauperum, "the Bible of the poor",[1] is the most common name used to label a group of Bible commentaries created on the European continent from

---

[1] The title is misleading in several respects. "Biblia Pauperum is a dull title with which to encumber a good book. It ... is inaccurate, as well as being uninviting in its Latin. The Biblia Pauperum is not a Bible (or a substitute for one); clearly it was not for the simple poor, who did not buy books, let alone read Latin – especially heavily abbreviated Latin printed in black letter of peculiar

the thirteenth to the fifteenth century. We have to do with a rather significant group of books, with several identifying characteristics:

Firstly, from a technical point of view, the most well-known and widest distributed editions of the Biblia Pauperum were so-called blockbooks – which means that the pages are carved out in wood like a series of woodcuts. The first blockbook print was made in the Netherlands around 1460. In the history of book production, they belong to the transition period just prior to the revolution of bookprint. When modern printing tehniques flourished throughout the sixteenth century, the blockbooks – and with them the production of Bibliae Pauperum – also vanished. Prior to the blockbook-editions, however, the Biblia Pauperum had also for a long period been produced as manuscripts. The first manuscripts date from the time around 1200, and totally about 40 Biblia Pauperum manuscripts from the thirteenth throughout the fifteenth centuries are preserved. They all seem to have been produced in Germany and Central Europe (the Netherlands, Austria, Hungary).[2]

Secondly, the pictures play an essential role on every page of these commentaries. The pages always include both biblical texts – in Latin – and pictures with biblical motives, and these elements refer to one another in a quite intricate way which makes them both indispensible. Any interpretation of the Biblia Pauperum has to pay attention both to text and to pictures, and to the interrelationship between them. The pictures sometimes are in black and white, sometimes in colour; colour copies exist both in manuscript and in blockbook version.

Thirdly, the canon of text elements as well as of pictural motives to be found in the Biblia Pauperum is rather restricted. There are few variations between the different editions. Texts and pictures are combined to form quite invariable theme groups on each page of the book. The number of pages vary between 34 and 47; the blockbook editions normally have 40 pages; and here the pages are numbered from a through v, and then start over again with .a. through .v. as the 40th page.[3]

Fourthly, a typological reasoning is essential to the interpretation of these books. Each page brings in themes both from the Old and the New Testaments. From a quantitative point of view, there is no doubt that the Old Testament elements dominate. But throughout the book it is a main objective to demonstrate how the Old Testament is a shadow of what is fulfilled in the New Testament.

Fifthly, the Biblia Pauperum – both as manuscript and as blockbook – seems to have been rather influential in its time. This influence can be inferred from the distribution of the book through a wide geographical area over 300 years,

---

illegibility", Henry, Biblia Pauperum (1987) 3. The title can be found on two medieval copies of the book, but other titles were also used. However, since the end of the eighteenth century, the title has been accepted and in general use, and it has become difficult to replace.

[2] For a general survey of the tradition of Biblia Pauperum manuscripts and blockbook editions, see Cornell, Biblia Pauperum (1925).

[3] When we in this text refer to specific pages in the Biblia Pauperum, we refer to the blockbook edition. This system of pagination is found in the facsimile editions of Banning, Biblia Pauperum (1991), and Henry, Biblia Pauperum (1987).

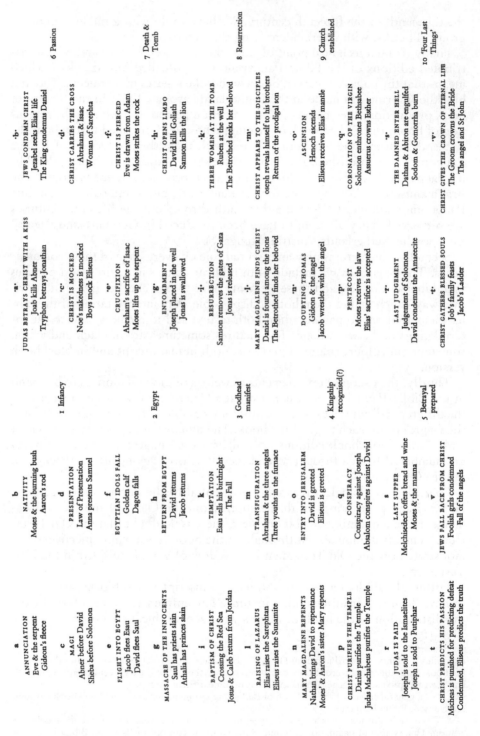

Tables of Pairs and 'Chapters', Fig. 4 in: Henry, Biblia Pauperum (1987) 7.

but it can also, more concretely, be traced in late medieval art, where the typological combinations specific to the Biblia Pauperum tradition are reflected in the combination of biblical themes in the interior decoration of churches in different parts of Europe.[4]

Historical research up to the 1960s tended to focus on questions such as the historical genesis of the genre, source criticism and classification of prevailing manuscripts into different subgroups. In addition, a great deal of work was done in order to clarify the typological structure of the Biblia Pauperum – both with regard to the details on the single pages and with regard to the overruling composition of the book.[5] In later research focus has at least partly shifted to questions about cultural and religious functions.[6]

2. Contents and Structure of the Biblia Pauperum

For the purpose of evaluating the Biblia Pauperum as a contribution to Old Testament interpretation, it is important to start out with a closer look at the contents and structure of the book. One could as a first observation say that what is presented throughout the pages of the Biblia Pauperum is a Christian theological summary of the Old Testament in its function as pointing towards and supporting the New Testament story of Christ. The Biblia Pauperum contributes with a systematic arrangement of central Old Testament stories and sayings which in terms of typology, allegory or prophecy verify the main images and themes in the story of Christ. The central focus of the Biblia Pauperum, then, is not to tell the story of Christ on its own, but to show the Old Testament support for or context of this story. And the Old Testament context in which the story of Christ is integrated, is not a traditional medieval Augustinian context of salvation history, where the temporal continuity from the beginning of time with the creation of the world and the covenant with Abraham is the major focus. Rather, we seem to have to do with a theologically argumentative context, where the main focus is – by the methods of typology, allegory or prophecy – to point to roots of the New Testament story in the Old Testament.

This, again, means that a systematic rather than a narrative reasoning seems to dominate in Biblia Pauperum's exposition of the Old Testament. This can be maintained both with regard to the single pages and the total structure of the Biblia Pauperum. Looking at a typical Biblia Pauperum page, there always is a picture in the middle as the central theme to which everything else is re-

---

[4] See, for instance, Cornell / Wallin, Albertus Pictor (1972), and Banning, Biblia Pauperum (1980), on the influence of Biblia Pauperum on chalice paintings in late medieval Danish churches. See also the introduction in Henry, Biblia Pauperum (1987), which contains several interesting observations on the interrelationship between the Biblia Pauperum tradition and Medieval Christian art.

[5] Classical studies are still Cornell, Biblia Pauperum (1925), and Schmidt, Die Armenbibeln (1959). See also, as a modern example, Henry, ibid.

[6] See for instance Henry, ibid., and Nellhaus, Mementos (1990).

lated. With three exceptions,[7] this central picture takes its theme from the New Testament, which is stated in a short *titulus* at the bottom of the page. The rest of the page – pictures as well as texts – deal with the Old Testament and the relationship between the Old Testament and the New.

Most prominent among these Old Testament elements on a page are the two pictures on each side of the central theme. Here, we have to do with typological, or in some cases also an allegorical, attribution. Above each of these side pictures there is a so-called *lectio*, which explains hermeneutically, at some length, the attribution of the Old Testament picture to the New Testament theme in the centre. Beneath each of the three pictures, there is a *titulus*, a small verse in hexameter, commenting on each picture. Both the *lectio* and the *titulus* are explanatory texts; they do not contain Old Testament quotations.

These two Old Testament pictures accompanying the central New Testament scene sometimes represent two different levels of the Old Testament: namely before and after the Law of Moses (*ante legem / sub lege*). In addition, the prophets are always present both with texts and pictures on a Biblia Pauperum page. They are placed at the top and at the bottom: two prophets at the top and two at the bottom. They are represented with a small picture (sometimes with a relevant attribute) of the specific prophet, and with a quotation of the prophetic saying attributed to the New Testament scene at the centre of the page. The number of prophets appearing here – as is natural in the perspective of medieval Old Testament hermeneutics – also includes figures like David, Solomon and Job.

In this way, a Biblia Pauperum page often presents to the reader three levels of Old Testament tradition (the tradition prior to the covenant at Sinai, Mosaic tradition and the rest of the Old Testament under the label of prophetic tradition) attributed to the New Testament fulfillment by means of up to three different hermeneutical strategies: typology, prophecy, and, in some cases, also allegory. This rather complex structure indicates that these pages must have been composed by learned persons, and also that the primary user of a Biblia Pauperum in the later Middle Ages would have belonged to the educated section of society.

In order to understand the hermeneutical and theological logic of a Biblia Pauperum page, it is necessary to look at a concrete example. We choose one of the compositions which appears in almost the same form in most editions of the Biblia Pauperum: the page dealing with the birth of Christ.

In the middle, we see Mary in her bed, Joseph sitting by her side, and the child Jesus lying in the crib, which looks more like a table[8] than a crib. Above the child are the ox and the donkey looking down on him. This central picture

---

[7] The exceptions are Christ destroying idols in Egypt (f), the coronation of Mary (.q.) and the coronation of the soul (.u.).

[8] It is easy to associate this way of arranging the child with the sacramental significance of the body of Christ. Christ's body is present to the believers on the altar, and the way in which the body of the child is represented here could very well be interpreted as a way of pointing to the sacramental function of the body of Christ. See Banning, Billedbibelen (1991) 11. In late medieval and early modern pictures of the deposition of the body of Christ from the cross, a similar tendency can be observed.

*Page b from a blockbook printed c. 1450, Ex. Paris, Bibliothèque Nationale, Xylogr. 2 and
5, reprinted in: Banning, Biblia Pauperum (1991) 19.*

is surrounded by two Old Testament themes: To the left we see Moses in a scene from Exodus 3 – *ante legem* – sitting with his herd and looking up on the Lord who appears to him in the burning bush. Moses holds his hand before his face by the sight of God, who looks more like Christ than like the Father. The Old Testament text says nothing about the appearance of a person in the burning bush: this is part of the spiritual interpretation of the story. In the *lectio* in the upper left corner, it is explained: "We can read in the book of Exodus, chapter III, that Moses saw a burning bush which did not burn after all, and he heard the voice of the Lord speaking to him from the bush: The burning bush which is not consumed signifies the blessed virgin Mary, who gave birth without having corrupted her perfect body because she gave birth as a virgin and remained untouched".[9] Below the picture we find the little hexameter verse: "It is shining and burning, but the fire does not consume the bush".

To the right we see a picture from the Old Testament period *sub lege*: from the story in Numeri about the rod of Aaron. The corresponding *lectio* in the upper right corner reads: "We can read in the book of Numeri, chapter xvii, that the rod of Aaron one night became green and flowered. This rod (Latin: *virga*) was a figure of the childless virgin (Latin: *virgo*) Mary, who without the seed from a man was to give birth to a son, that is to Jesus Christ, who is blessed forever". Below this picture we find a similar hexameter verse: "Here, contrary to what is usual, the rod produces a flower".

It is interesting to notice, now, that the Aaron episode is commented on in terms of typological interpretation: "*virga figurabat virginem*". The wonder that happened to the rod of Aaron, which produced life in a miraculous way, against nature, is seen as a *figura* pointing forwards to the much greater miracle which happened to Mary by the birth of Christ. The linguistic similarity between the two key-words *virga* and *virgo* supports the typological argument in a very nice way, but is not the main point.

The Moses episode, on the other hand, is interpreted in terms of allegorical hermeneutics: "*rubus ardens ... significat beatam virginem*". Here, the text of the *lectio* does not speak of a *figura* pointing towards a fulfillment in Christ, but of a *signum*, pointing to a different meaning in addition to the meaning the episode has within its Old Testament context. This seems to be an indication of an allegorical instead of a typological way of thinking. The allegorical interpretation is more general and also easier to apply, because it is not restricted to a logic of fulfillment. The burning bush, then, is not seen as an episode pointing towards a fulfillment in the birth of Christ. Rather, one specific point in the story: the burning without being consumed, is applied to Mary and compared to her bearing without being corrupted. Mary's body and the bush were both scenes of a divine presence, and they were both in a miraculous way left undamaged or uncorrupted afterwards.[10]

---

[9] In transcription: *Legitur in libro Exodi iiio capitulo quod moyses vidit rubum ardentem et non ardebat et dominum audiuit de rubo sibi loquentem: Rubus ardens qui non consumitur significat beatam virginem mariam parientem sine corruptione integritatis corporis quae virgo peperit et incorrupta permansit.*

[10] One could add, though, that the difference between a typological and an allegorical inter-

So far, we have commented on the Old Testament *ante legem* and *sub lege*, interpreted in terms of allegory and typology. In addition, the Old Testament prophets also have their part to play. They can be seen in the four small pictures above and beneath the central picture of Mary, with one biblical saying attributed to each of them. Above, Daniel is on the left hand and Isaiah on the right. Daniel says: "The corner stone has been torn away from the mountain without hands" (Dan 2:45), and from Isaiah the quotation is: "To us a child is born, a son is given" (Isa 9:6). Beneath we have Habakkuk to the left: "Lord, I listened to what I could hear from you, and I was frightened" (Hab 3:2), and Micah to the right: "Bethlehem of the land of Juda, you shall not be the smallest among the princes of Juda" (Mic 5:2). The sayings comment on different aspects of the birth of Christ: Isaiah on the birth itself, Micah on the place of the birth, and Daniel and Habakkuk on the miraculous aspects of what has happened through the birth of Christ.

All the pictures on the page are placed within frames, and make us look through the frames into the pictorial themes inside. The frames underline the dignity of each picture and each prophetic authority. The biblical qoutations are placed on ribbons, giving these words, too, a special dignity.

We have been looking at a typical Biblia Pauperum page, but it is important to note that the structure we have seen here is not present in all details on every page of a Biblia Pauperum. One type of irregularity is for instance that sometimes both the Old Testament episodes supporting the central New Testament scene are taken from the period *sub lege*. Also, the typological interpretation dominates over the allegorical as hermeneutical logic of connecting Old and New Testament themes.

If we proceed from this more detailed investigation of one page of a Biblia Pauperum belonging to the blockbook tradition to a description of the total structure of the book, it first has to be noted that the pages were placed two by two, with double blank pages between. This means that from a formal compositional point of view, we do not only have to deal with single pages on the one hand and the whole book on the other. We also have the double page composition where two pages – most often thematically related – are put together.

The Jesus story appearing in the total composition has one focus on the birth and childhood of Jesus and another on the passion story. The first eight of a total of 40 scenes of the blockbook edition from Esztergom deal with the story of Jesus from Annunciation to the return from Egypt. The pages are arranged in the following pairs: The annunciation and the birth of Christ; the

---

pretation suggested through the difference between *figura* and *signum* is not altogether clear: even though the story of the burning bush is commented on in terms of allegory, we have to do with a theme which throughout the story of patristic and medieval Old Testament exegesis has also been subject to typological interpretation, see Berve, Armenbibel (1969) 39f. According to Berve, this story was in the Early Church typologically applied partly to point to the double nature of Christ (Justin, Clemens), but then more often to point to Mary, who should also be able to carry God inside herself without being destructed. This interpretation was developed among others by Cyril of Alexandria, and also applied in medieval liturgical texts and by medieval theologians like Bernhard of Clairveaux and Rupert of Deutz. A reasonable conclusion seems to be that it is quite difficult to maintain a consequent distinction between allegorical and typological interpretation of a text like this.

Magi and Jesus as child in the temple; the flight to Egypt and the destruction of idols in Egypt (the only non-biblical scene among the 40 illustrating the story of Jesus); the slaughter of children in Bethlehem and the return from Egypt. We see from this listing that a chronological order is not followed strictly. For instance, in the New Testament storyline the slaughter of children in Bethlehem occured long before the return of Jesus and his parents from Egypt, just as the flight to Egypt occured long before the presentation of Jesus in the temple. This is because in the Biblia Pauperum the logic of chronology is partly overruled by the logic of thematic pairs. It is, however, often impossible to see this latter logic without looking more closely at the total composition of the paired pages, both at texts and at pictures.

More important than the story of the birth and childhood is the story of the passion. After a short intermezzo of four pages (i – m) dealing with some central episodes in the life of Christ,[11] the scenes from n to .h. deal with different aspects of the passion story, and the scenes from .i. to .o. with the resurrection. In the sequence dealing with the passion, special attention is paid to the story of Judas and his betrayal of Christ. One scene is devoted to Judas offering himself to betray Jesus (r), one to Judas and the 30 silver coins (r), and one to Judas betraying Christ (.a.).

The six final scenes deal with themes pertaining to Christianity more in general: in the first pair we see the pouring out of the Holy Spirit to the left and the coronation of Mary to the right, in the second pair we first see Judgement day and then hell, and in the third we see Christ with the souls of the blessed to the left and the crown of eternal life to the right. These six scenes – and especially the final four – have a direct spiritual appeal to the late medieval reader. The biblical story of Christ has come to an end and has to be applied to the believer. But this application does not go through the institution of the Church, as one could expect.[12] In fact, the institution of the Church does not seem to be present at all in the Biblia Pauperum pictures and texts. Instead, the final scenes of the book deal directly with heaven and hell and the soul. On the last double page to the left, salvation is represented by the bosom af Abraham (Luk 16:19ff) where the souls find their rest. To the right, on the final page of the book, the soul represented as a woman, is crowned by Christ himself, and the coming together of the two is interpreted as a marriage through the accompanying texts and pictures surrounding the central motif.

---

[11] First with Baptism and Christ being tempted by the Devil, then with the waking up of Lazarus and the transfiguration of Christ on Mount Tabor with Moses and Elijah.

[12] This was often the case in pictorial sequences in medieval decoration of churches and monasteries. The *communio sanctorum* in heaven and on earth play a major role in medieval Christian art. The coronation of Mary is one such theme where accompanying saints could be expected to be present according to iconographical tradition. But in the Biblia Pauperum illustrations – also in the illustration of the coronation of Mary (.q.) – neither saints nor bishops are to be seen.

3. The Hermeneutical Function of the Old Testament

Having now established an overview of the sequence and distribution of New Testament scenes in the central pictures throughout the book, one could ask a similar question with regard to the Old Testament themes and sayings present in the Biblia Pauperum. If the New Testament is primarily represented through scenes from the childhood history and the passion and resurrection of Christ, how is the Old Testament represented? What parts of it are primarily activated as context for supporting and validating this *summa* of Christian belief?

If one first concentrates on the side pictures with the accompanying *lectiones*, it may be observed that the references to the historical books of the Old Testament dominate. Of a total of 80 pictures – two pictures on each side – 29 refer to scenes from the historical books: to Judges, the books of Samuel and the books of Kings. 24 pictures refer to Old Testament history *ante legem* (mostly to the book of Genesis), whereas only 8 pictures refer to the books of Moses from Exodus 19 on. Looking at the prophetic references, the most striking observation is that 34 of the 40 pages have one prophetic reference to the Psalms and its author David, most often put on the top to the left – so to speak where the page starts. In view of the central role of Psalm exegesis both in monastic and scholastic circles in the later Middle Ages, it is not very surprising that David plays a central role. But it is nevertheless noteworthy that he here is supposed to have had a prophetic knowledge covering nearly every central aspect of the story of Christ.

In order to come beyond general observations like these, it is necessary to look at the Old Testament elements in the Biblia Pauperum not in general and *per se*, but in their supportive and validating function with regard to the central elements of the Biblia Pauperum – dominated by the story of Christ. In what way are the Old Testament scenes and sayings used to support, identify and validate the story of Christ? Why is the story of Christ in the Biblia Pauperum dominated by Old Testament sayings and pictures, rather than by a further elaboration of the Gospel narrratives?

It goes without saying that the Biblia Pauperum depends heavily on a long Christian tradition of typological and allegorical interpretation. There is an exegetical tradition behind most of the Old Testament pictures and texts introduced in the Biblia Pauperum. The majority of the links between the testaments presupposed in the Biblia Pauperum are commented on in Nicholas of Lyra's *Postilla super totam bibliam*; a lot of them have roots back to Old Testament interpretation by the Fathers of the Early Church, and many of them also are well established in pictural programmes of medieval churches and monasteries.[13]

The general hermeneutical strategy of the Biblia Pauperum, however, is quite different from Lyra's in his *Postilla*. Lyra relies heavily on the literal sense, within the framework of the *quadriga*, which implies that a plurality of

---

[13] Berve, Armenbibel (1969), offers a number of observations on the exegetical traditions behind some of the typological combinations in the Biblia Pauperum. Cf. also Schmidt, Die Armenbibeln (1959).

meanings are presupposed to be present in any Old Testament text. It is up to the reader to explore the different layers of meaning inherent in the sacred text: a text is related to Christ and to the Church both in terms of literal, allegorical, tropological and anagogical meaning.

The Biblia Pauperum also establishes a plurality of meanings on every page, but the hermeneutical strategy could be said to be quite the opposite of Lyra's. Whereas Lyra in accordance with the *quadriga* tradition establishes his plurality of meaning by opening up an Old Testament text or episode for Christian interpretation on three different levels, the Biblia Pauperum most often establishes its plurality of meaning by relating the New Testament theme to six different Old Testament elements. These Old Testament texts and pictures establish the primary context for understanding the central theme, and – different as they are – they convey a quite complex framework for interpreting this.

If we pursue this comparison with the hermeneutical tradition represented by Lyra and the method of *quadriga* one step further, it may be said that whereas Lyra's method depends on the interpretative principle of multiple meaning of the biblical text, the Biblia Pauperum method rather tends to presuppose that a biblical text has only one meaning – which is, of course, spiritual. The texture of multiple meaning on a Biblia Pauperum page is established through the reciprocal interrelation between the six elements of the Old Testament and the one of the New Testament. But as against Lyra, only one spiritual meaning is attributed to each of these elements. This could be regarded as a 'modern' tendency in the Biblia Pauperum, parallel to the hermeneutical change brought about in Protestant hermeneutics: There, too, the guiding principle for biblical interpretation both of the Old and the New Testament was that the text has one, and only one, spiritual meaning.

In modern theoretical terms, one might speak of a specific kind of intertextuality in the Biblia Pauperum. The textual fragments and pictural representations of texts here depend very heavily on other textual and pictorial traditions for their interpretation: first of all on the complete biblical text, then on exegetical tradition of the Early Church and the Middle Ages, on medieval legend and on medieval Christian art. The Biblia Pauperum is impossible to use and to understand without this intertextual framework. But in addition to this, the elements of the Biblia Pauperum make up a new composition. And one important characteristic of this new composition is that the Old Testament elements are brought into a particularly close connection with the New Testament.

This point might be illustrated by an example from one of the three pages in the Biblia Pauperum where the central theme is not taken from the Old Testament. The first place where this occurs is in the group of pages dealing with the childhood of Christ. On the third double page (e and f) to the left the central theme is the flight to Egypt, and it is accompanied on the right side by a page with the *titulus*: "In the presence of Christ the idols suddenly have fallen down". This is a theme from medieval legend, with no support in the New Testament text.[14] Nevertheless, it belongs to the canon of central topics in the Bib-

---

[14] See Nellhaus, Mementos (1991) 315 f. – In the early medieval Gospel of Pseudo-Matthew – often referred to as the *Liber de infantia* – chapter 23, one can read the following story: "And it

lia Pauperum. How is that to be explained? How can a theme with absolutely no textual support in the New Testament defend this place as a central picture, and how can the six Old Testament elements be arranged to support the truth about Christ which is not verified in the New Testament text itself?

What seems to be the case here, is the following: The theme of idols and the destruction of idols has an important place throughout the Old Testament, both in the Pentateuch, in the historical books and in the prophets. This central position within the Old Testament seems to constitute a context which is so powerful that the theme is introduced as a main event in the story of Christ regardless of the lack of New Testament textual support. It is not sufficient for the Biblia Pauperum to deal with the somehow similar theme of Jesus driving out the merchants from the temple a few pages later. The specific motif of Jesus and the destruction of the idols also has to be there.

On the page – of the next illustration – dealing with the idols, then, it is definitely not the case that the Old Testament elements are introduced in order to verify and explain a New Testament motif. Instead, the elements from the Old Testament on their own create and constitute the central theme from the story of Christ. Here, intertextuality not only means that the Old Testament is used as the context for interpreting and understanding the New, but also as a context for creating a New Testament text where it fails. We are not dealing with the sacred text of the Old Testament functioning as verification of the even more sacred text of the New Testament. Rather, the two testaments, together with legend and the tradition of interpretation, seem to constitute a whole, where it is no longer the case that one part is more important than the other. One might add that this logic of reciprocal intertextual correlation is a logic somewhat different from the logic of typology, where a crucial point is the difference between the levels of type and antitype. In the intertextual discourse which seems to underly this page – and maybe the whole Biblia Pauperum – the different texts and pictures tend to be integrated and correlated on one and the same level. The increasing hermeneutical power of the Old Testament context tends to reduce the power of the typological logic.

Which are the Old Testament themes, then, that constitute this context which has the power to create a central scene not present in the New Testament? To the left of this central scene, we see Moses and the golden calf (Exodus 31f), and to the right we see the Philistine idol Dagon being destroyed in the presence of the Ark of the Covenant (1 Samuel 5). The prophets quoted are Hosea (10:2), Nahum (1:14), Zechariah (13:2) and Zephaniah (2:11) – all speaking of how the Lord is going to sweep away and crush the idols from his house or from the earth.

Avril Henry has suggested[15] that one link of importance for the composi-

---

came to pass, when Mary went into the temple with the child, all the idols prostrated themselves on the ground, so that all of them were lying on their faces shattered and broken to pieces; and thus they plainly showed that they were nothing. Then was fulfilled that which was said by the prophet Isaiah, 'Behold, the Lord will come upon a swift cloud and will enter Egypt, and all the handiwork of the Egyptians shall be moved before his face'"; Elliott, The Apocryphal New Testament (1993) 96. See also Cartlidge/Elliott, Art and the Christian Apocrypha (2001) 104.

[15] Cf. Henry, Biblia Pauperum (1987) 58.

Page f from a blockbook printed ca. 1450, Ex. Paris, Bibliothèque Nationale, Xylogr. 2 and 5, reprinted in: Banning, Biblia Pauperum (1991) 27.

tion of this page of the Biblia Pauperum was one of the prophetic sayings on the accompanying page (on the left side of the double page) dealing with the flight to Egypt. Here, Isaiah is quoted saying: "See, the Lord will enter Egypt, and the idols shall be dislodged" (19:1). This saying talks about the flight to Egypt, also referred to in the New Testament. But in addition, Isaiah suggests that something more happened when the Lord was in Egypt – which he was on only this one occasion: he destroyed idols. This future destruction of idols by the Lord, in its turn, is also documented in several other Old Testament texts. Therefore, it must have taken place, and it must have taken place in Egypt. The Old Testament foretold what was going to happen, and constitutes a sufficient context for understanding it. Then, one does not need the New Testament text to verify the story; it is evident enough without.

On the central picture of the destruction of idols in Egypt, it is interesting to see that the destruction happens through the power present in the small child Jesus. He can be seen in the picture on his mother's arm, doing nothing else than being present in order to obtain the effect on the idols. Thus, the Old Testament scene with Dagon being destroyed just by the presence of the Ark of the Covenant is a better parallel than the scene with Moses, actively destroying the golden calf. But in view of the prominent position of Moses in the history of idol destruction, it is easy to understand why he is here, too.

Before we leave this page, two more observations deserve to be mentioned. Firstly, here again the *lectio* text above the Old Testament scenes apply the distinction between *signum / significat* and *figura*. The story of Moses and Aaron and the golden calf *significat* "the fall of the idols when Christ went into Egypt", whereas the story of the Ark of the Covenant and the idol Dagon is "fulfilled in a figurative way"[16] when the blessed virgin with her son Christ came to Egypt, then the idols of Egypt fell together". This distinction between *signum* and *figura* might have to do with the point mentioned above: The Dagon story is a closer parallel than the Moses story, and therefore a better *figura*. But this example also supports the conclusion that the difference between typological and allegorical interpretation is not very clearly defined at all.

In the *lectio* about the Ark of the Covenant, however, a more general application of the Old Testament episode is also added: "…and in a nice way this signifies (*significat*) that when Christ comes to the miseries, that is to the errors of the infidels, they fall together". Here – a rare case in the Biblia Pauperum – the *lectio* text moves close to an interpretation of the episode in terms of the *quadriga*, adding a moral explication to the first typological one.

The other observation has to do with the picture of Moses. If one looks closely, it appears that two different stages of the Moses story are included in the picture: In the upper part, one can see Moses receiving the tablets of the Law at Mount Sinai, underneath the tablets can be seen crushed on the ground and Moses is about to destroy the calf. This is a technique quite common in religious art in the later Middle Ages, before panels with sequential scenes take over more and more, when the aim is to illustrate a biblical story.

---

[16] *figurative completum est* . . . .

4. The Religious Function of the Biblia Pauperum

After this hermeneutical discussion of the interrelationship between the two testaments in the Biblia Pauperum, we proceed to a further discussion of the religious function of the book. If Nicholas of Lyra's *Postilla super totam bibliam* was the medieval standard Bible exposition representing academic and monastic literacy, the Biblia Pauperum had a quite different function and addressed itself to a different audience. To be sure, this audience was not just the common uneducated people. The hermeneutical complexity of the book suggests that it is produced by intellectuals and also addressed to a sophisticated audience.

Also, it is not primarily a book for reading; rather, it presents itself as a book for meditation and piety, comparable for instance to the Books of Hours. But whereas the Books of Hours as a genre were closely connected to monastic culture and to the monastic hours, the Biblia Pauperum shows no trace of this connection. It seems more reasonable to assume that it has served a piety which held a certain distance both to monastic and to clerical culture.[17]

The religious setting for the book may very well have been the educated laity, familiar with books, but not extensive users of them. The lay piety fostered by the friars in the late Middle Ages could be one possible setting. Among the friars, maybe especially among the Franciscans, personal meditation, often also mystical experience, was an important part of religious life. This fits in rather well with the concluding pages of the Biblia Pauperum, devoted to personal, mystically coloured, experience of the soul.[18] It also fits in well with the devotional theme of the the wounds of Christ, which is the central theme on page .f. of the Biblia Pauperum.[19]

It may also help interpretation of another remarkable aspect of the Biblia Pauperum: the predominant occupation with the betrayal of Judas and with the Jews as the enemies of Christ. On three different pages, the betrayal of Judas is the central theme, and in acccordance with late medieval anti-Judaism, the Jews are focused on as the enemies and killers of Christ in the interpretation of the passion.[20] One could here see a connection to the well documented

---

[17] Compare the remarks about the concluding section of Biblia Pauperum at the end of Sect. 2 above (p. 84).

[18] On the last page, dealing with the non-biblical theme of the coronation of the soul, the main theme is the spiritual wedding between the individual soul and Christ: a theme very typical of late medieval mysticism, and often developed within a mendicant context.

[19] Subordinate Old Testament themes here contribute to a mystical interpretation of the wounds of Christ, connecting the wounds of Christ on the right to the life-giving water from the rock (Exodus 17). The rock is Christ and the water signifies the sacraments. To the left, the wounds of Christ are connected to the creation of the woman from Adam's rib. Adam here signifies the dead Christ, "…and from his side the sacraments flowed out for our sake…".

[20] This is evident on several of the pages dealing with the passion, for instance on p. v (Jesus being captured), p. .b. (Jesus for Pilate) and p. .c. (the crown of thorns). On p. v, one of the side themes is the fall of Lucifer and all his adherants, with biblical reference to Revelation 12 and to Isaiah 14. And in the *lectio* on this picture, the superbia of the Jews, similar to the superbia of Lucifer and his adherants, is described: " … they were afraid to lose their home and their country, and therefore they killed and crucified the humble and pious Jesus, and so they fell into the grave, which they had dug themselves: that is to say, they came to hell, as is written in the psalm". On the

development of a new and radical anti-Judaism, especially among the friars in the later Middle Ages.[21]

Discussing questions about religious milieu and religious function of the Biblia Pauperum, the most important evidence is the book itself. We know very little about concrete circumstances of production, reception and use of the book. Accordingly, we primarily have to guess and draw conclusions on the basis of the evidence given in the book itself. It is important to bear this in mind as a background of the suggestions made here.

Also with regard to the actual usage of the book, many issues remain open in spite of important new research during the last generation. The hermeneutical complexity of each page of the Biblia Pauperum indicates that not only the artists and intellectuals who created and produced it, but also the people who bought it and used it must have had an extensive knowledge of the Bible, and not least of the Old Testament. But one does not have to presuppose that the users had a biblical text at hand. In the later Middle Ages, orality played a major role in transmitting biblical knowledge to the laity and among lay people. Oral transmission is closely connected to memory: Knowledge which is not written down in books has to be transmitted so that it can be easily remembered. And an important mnemotechnical divice was the principle of similarity: Elements were combined through some kind of resemblance which made it easy to remember them.[22]

From this point of view, the typological logic of the Biblia Pauperum could very well be influenced by this aspect of oral culture. The book belongs not only to a transitional period in Europe between manuscript and print, but also to a transitional period between a predominantly oral and an increasingly literal culture. In a quite complex and interesting way, it is part of both these changes. Pictures were also devices supporting memory. In the Biblia Pauperum, the main principle for composing a page is the principle of similarity, functioning on more than one level, and often comprising not only one, but two pages (a double page) at the time. The picture of the New Testament central theme and the pictures of the Old Testament side motifs are combined because they are similar, they tell us about the same thing. This impression of similarity between the one New Testament and the two Old Testament themes in the middle of the page is often supported and increased through the composition of the pictures. Sometimes, the persons and actions are arranged in such a way that they look more or less like three variations on the same main theme.[23]

---

other side picture, which in this case is taken from the New Testament, the story of the foolish virgins is interpreted as a story about the Jews, and on the accompanying picture, the devil himself appears, pushing the foolish Jews down to hell.

[21] See Cohen, The Friars and the Jews (1982), esp. ch. 10.

[22] Ong, Orality & Literacy (1982) 33ff, 142ff ("Oral memory and the story line"). According to ONG, it is typical of oral narrative to move very quickly to the central theme, and organize the narrative around this centre, instead of following a story line from the beginning to the end.

[23] The blockbook, p. d: The presentation of Jesus in the temple, is one example of this. Parallel themes: Leviticus 12 (about women having born their first son, being obliged to buy him free in the temple) and 1 Samuel 1 (about Hannah offering Samuel to Eli). Other examples: The holy kings, p. c, with 2 Samuel 3 (Abner came to David) and 1 Kings 10 (the queen of Sheba came to Solomon)

Also, the blockbook technique itself adds to the same impression of similarity. Whereas the contrast between text and illumination often was quite remarkable in the manuscript tradition, including the manuscript tradition of the Biblia Pauperum, the blockbook technique brought illustration and text down to the same level, with the same colours, the same print and the same layout.[24] The similarity is stated briefly in the *tituli*, which are very short, written in verse, and easy to remember. In addition, the same logic of similarity is validated through the short prophetic sayings. The impression is conveyed, that all these elements deal with the same theme.

As the last element, up in the corners, we find the most typically literary part of the composition: the *lectiones*. The *lectio* explains in theological terms the logic of the similarity underlying the combination of the main pictures of the page. In addition, it sometimes introduces themes for meditation and personal devotion. If we look at a page like this, then, from the centre and out, we could say that essential strategies of oral communication are in function in presenting the main themes through pictures and short text elements throughout most of the page. But the page also introduces the user to the more specific world of religious and biblical literacy through the *lectio* at the top. In this way, each page of the book might be said to mediate between the world of orality and the world of literacy – corresponding to the preferences and needs of the users of the book.

We made some short comments earlier in this chapter about the quantitative distribution of Old Testament references in the Biblia Pauperum, and stated that from a quantitative point of view, pictures and texts from the Old Testament by far dominate the pages of the Biblia Pauperum. We could now add some more fundamental observations on the reception of the Old Testament in the Biblia Pauperum: The Old Testament which emerges through the pages of the Biblia Pauperum is fragmented. The fragments are introduced into the book by means of a logic of similarity dominated by the central New Testament themes in the book. Whereas these New Testament themes, put together, can be said to form a narrative, concentrated on the birth, childhood, passion and resurrection of Christ, the Old Testament here tends to disappear as a narrative.

One must add that the different elements of the Old Testament depend on their narrative context in order to convey their intended meaning in the Biblia Pauperum. The relevant associations and the whole logic of similarity presuppose at least part of the narrative context of the different Old Testament stories introduced on the pages. One could guess, then, that the devotional use of the book must have included the meditation also on the Old Testament themes within their respective context – but certainly with the spiritual, and not the historical, meaning in view.

---

as side themes; the ascension of Christ, p. .o., with Enoch (Genesis 5) and Elijah (2 Kings 2) as side themes, and the coronation of Mary, p. .q., with 1 Kings 2 about Bathsheba, the mother of Solomon, and Esther 2 about Esther and Ahasuerus as side theme. In all these cases, the compositional similarity between the three pictures is quite striking.

[24] See Camille, Reading the Printed Image (1991) 283.

The general logic of similarity seems to have been the dominant hermeneutical and religious principle underlying both the composition and use of the book. Here, the differences between typology and allegory are of little impact, and consequently, one should not try too hard to define the sharp difference between these two hermeneutical strategies in the Biblia Pauperum. More important is to note that the fundamental logic of similarity contributes to a hermeneutical practice where the Old Testament themes function on the same level as the New Testament themes. The two testaments form a context for each other in a quite radical way.

CHAPTER FOUR

Some Sociopolitical and Cultural Aspects of the Renaissance

By TROND BERG ERIKSEN, Oslo

Sources: DANTE ALIGHIERI: *Le opere di Dante. Testo critico della Società Dantesca Italiana* (Florence [1921] ²1960); "Opere di Dante", in: *Enciclopedia Dantesca.* Appendice (Rome 1978 / 1984) 619–996.

Reference works: Enciclopedia Dantesca I-V. Appendice (ed. U. Bosco; Rome: Istituto della Enciclopedia Italiana 1970–78); *The Dante Encyclopedia* (ed. R. Lansing; New York / London 2000); *The Cambridge History of the Bible* [CHB] (2. *The West from the Fathers to the Reformation*; ed. G. W. H. Lampe; Cambridge 1969; repr. 1980; 3. *The West from the Reformation to the Present Day*; ed. S. L. Greenslade; ibid. 1963, repr. 1978); *Encyclopedia of the Renaissance* 1–6 (ed. P. F. Grendler; New York 1999).

Studies: D. W. AMRAM, *Makers of Hebrew Books in Italy* (Philadelphia 1909); A. W. ASTELL, *The Song of Songs in the Middle Ages* (Ithaca 1990); H. BARON, *The Crisis of the Early Italian Renaissance. Civic Humanism and Republican Liberty in an Age of Classicism and Tyranny* (Princeton [1955] 1966); J. L. BLAU, *The Christian Interpretation of the Cabala in the Renaissance* (New York 1944); G. A. BRUCKER, *The Civic World of Early Renaissance Florence* (Princeton 1977); A. BUCK, "Dante Alighieri (1265–1321)", TRE VIII (1981) 349–53; J. BURCKHARDT, *Die Kultur der Renaissance in Italien. Ein Versuch* (orig. 1860/1869; repr. Darmstadt 1962); ET: *The Civilization of the Renaissance. An Essay by Jacob Burckhardt* (tr. S. G. C. Middlemore; Oxford / London: Phaidon Press 1945), and *The Civilization of the Renaissance in Italy* 1–2 (Introd. by B. Nelson / Ch. Trinkaus; New York [1958] ⁸1965); A. C. CHARITY, *Events and their Afterlife. The Dialectic of Christian Typology in the Bible and Dante* (London 1966); N. COHN, *Noah's Flood. The Genesis Story in Western Thought* (New Haven / London 1996); R. G. COLLINGWOOD, *The Idea of History* (Oxford 1946); L. DIESTEL, *Geschichte des Alten Testamentes in der christlichen Kirche* (Jena 1869; repr. Leipzig 1981); E. L. EISENSTEIN, *The Printing Press as an Agent of Change. Communications and Cultural Transformations in Early-modern Europe* 1–2 (Cambridge 1979); eadem, *The Printing Revolution in Early Modern Europe* (Cambridge / New York 1983); L. FEBVRE / H.-J. MARTIN, *The Coming of the Book. The Impact of Printing 1450–1800* (London / New York 1976); W. K. FERGUSON, *Renaissance Studies* (London / Ontario 1963); idem, *The Renaissance in Historical Thought: Five Centuries of Interpretation* (Boston 1948); H. F. FLETCHER, *Milton's Semitic Studies and Some Manifestations of Them in His Poetry* (Chicago 1926); N. FRYE, *The Great Code. The Bible and Literature* (London 1983); J. M. GELLRICH, *The Idea of the Book in the Middle Ages* (Ithaca / London 1985); F. GILBERT, *Machiavelli and Guicciardini. Politics and History in Sixteenth Century Florence* ([1965] New York / London 1984); M. GISECKE, *Der Buchdruck in der frühen Neuzeit* (Frankfurt / Main 1991); idem, *Sinnenwandel, Sprachwandel, Kulturwandel. Studien zur Vorgeschichte der Informationsgesellschaft* (Frankfurt / Main 1992); O. GRAF, *Die Divina Comedia als Zeugnis des Glaubens* (Freiburg 1965); A. GRAFTON (ed.), *Rome Reborn. The Vatican Library and Renaissance Culture* (Washington / New Haven 1993); J. HALE, *The Civilization of Europe in the Renaissance* (New York 1994); J. HALL, *A History of Ideas and Images in Italian Art* (New York 1983); F. HARTT, *History of Italian Renaissance Art* (London ⁴1994); S. L. HINDMAN (ed.), *Printing the Written Word. The Social History of Books, circa 1450–1520* (Ithaca / London 1991); R. HIRSCH, *Printing, Selling and Reading 1450–1550* (Wiesbaden 1967); P. O. KRISTELLER, *The Classics and Renaissance Thought* (Martin Classical Lectures XV; Cambridge, MA 1955); idem, *Renaissance Thought. The*

Classic, Scholastic and Humanist Strains (New York 1961); idem, *Humanismus und Renaissance* 1–2 (München 1974–76); J. L. KUGEL, *The Bible as it was* (Cambridge, MA 1997); J. LARNER, *Culture and Society in Italy 1290–1420* (London 1971); H. D. LASSWELL / D. LERNER / H. SPEIER (eds.), *Propaganda and Communication in World History* 1–3 (Honolulu 1979–80); E. A. MATTER, *The Voice of My Beloved. The Song of Songs in Western Medieval Christianity* (Philadephia 1990); CH. G. NAUERT Jr., *Humanism and the Culture of Renaissance Europe* (Cambridge 1995; repr. 1998); J. PELIKAN, *The Reformation of the Bible. The Bible of the Reformation* (New Haven / London 1996); A. PENNA, "Bibbia", *Enciclopedia Dantesca* I (ed. U. Bosco; Roma 1970); G. POLETTO, *La Santa Scrittura nelle opere e nel pensiero di Dante Aleghieri* (Siena 1909); M. E. REEVES, *The Influence of Prophecy in the Later Middle Ages* (Oxford 1970); E. F. RICE Jr., *Saint Jerome in the Renaissance* (Baltimore 1985); H. SCHNEIDER, *Der Text der Gutenbergbibel* (BBB 7; Bonn: Hanstein 1954); J. T. SHOTWELL, *The History of History* (New York 1939); D. KULLER SHUGER, *The Renaissance Bible. Scholarship, Sacrifice and Subjectivity* (Berkeley 1994); B. SMALLEY, *The Study of the Bible in the Middle Ages* (Oxford ³1983, repr. 1984); eadem, *Historians in the Middle Ages* (London 1994); J. A. SYMONDS, *The Renaissance in Italy* 1–7 (London 1904–09). B. THOMPSON, *Humanists and Reformers. A History of the Renaissance and the Reformation* (Grand Rapids 1996); J. W. THOMPSON / B. J. HOLM, *A History of Historical Writing* 1–2 (New York 1942); K. VOSSLER, *Medieval Culture. An Introduction to Dante and his Times* 1–2 ([1929] New York 1958); A. D. WHITE, *A History of the Warfare of Science with Theology in Christendom* 1–2 (New York 1903).

1. Sociopolitical Changes in the Fourteenth and Fifteenth Centuries in Italy and North of the Alps

The transitions from the commonly called Middle Ages to the Renaissance are fluent. Many aspects of the social and cultural changes that are regarded as characteristic to the Renaissance, and that we unifyingly describe by the word 'Renaissance', were already in existence in the Middle Ages and had made great progress before the catastrophy of the Great Plague of 1348. These changes never reached any final conclusion because they initiated the development of the modern world that became a never ending series of transformations. Already by the High Middle Ages the city cultures of both northern and southern Europe had established a marked independence relative to the feudal order of the countryside. The town communes and the princely courts played a progressively more prominent part as protectors of art and learning.

Cities were perceived as breading grounds of a new freedom. A range of Italian Renaissance cities carried *libertas* in their arms and devises. The 'freedom' that was presupposed was precisely that of the towns relative to the feudal hierarchy and its legal culture. City life put a premium on new qualities and skills. It represented a new form of social coexistence where dialogue, argument, individual creativity and intellectual curiosity found new outlets.

As a special mark of the Italian Renaissance of the fourteenth and fifteenth centuries one usually thinks of the development of a new culture of personality stressing individualism. Collective identities like family and clan played a less prominent role than before. It was the great epoch of biography and autobiography, portrait and selfportrait. In particular JACOB BURCKHARDT contributed to this way of delimiting and characterizing Renaissance culture in Italy in his classical work *Die Kultur der Renaissance in Italien. Ein Versuch* (1860, reprinted in 1962).[1] We may note some of his characterizations.

Learning and education were changed by the ideal of all-roundedness. Individuals emerged who by their intellect sought after knowledge and exceptional skills. Communities built great libraries, collected manuscripts and crowned their poets with laurel. People travelled more, further and in other ways than earlier. Both the natural sciences and the artistic appreciation of landscape were fed by travel. At the outset, however, the typical Renaissance experience provided a lifestyle and a set of ambitions found only in a few.

The yearning for immortality became in leading circles a dream of glory and eternal fame. Many religious motives acquired similar secular substitutes. A new scepticism showed itself in the mockery that coloured social intercourse in the streets and markets. People dreamt of resurrecting the greatness of life that echoed that of the ancient ruins of Italian cities. They became interested in human nature, studying its psychological qualities, temperaments and physiognomies.

Together with a fashionable paganism among the upper classes there emerged with great vigour among the lower classes revivalist preachers who could set whole cities on fire. It was the moment of birth of early modern science, but it was also the most energetic period of astrology, alchemy, witch-hunts and belief in demons. The cult of beauty promoted not only pictorial art and literature, but also the art of war and dress fashions. Both war and the state became works of art, according to BURCKHARDT.

Great princely courts in Italy had from the thirteenth century on adorned themselves with representatives of learning and art. Already the poet Dante served the Scala family in Verona. The Viscontis and Sforzas in Milano, the Malatestas in Rimini, Gonzagas in Mantova, Montefeltros in Urbino, Estes in Ferrara and Medicis in Florence were examples of politically leading families that were also patrons of the arts and learning. Merchant economy was developing into money economy, especially along the pilgrim routes. This resulted in new forms of social mobility and thus new demands for legitimizing social privileges. Florins and ducats were already common European currencies by the fourteenth century.

City culture and its economy promoted a lay learning that was no longer under the complete control of the Church. The so-called humanism of the notaries sprang from precisely the type of learning and command of Latin that served the needs of princes and city administrations rather than of the Church. For the greater part of the Middle Ages classical Latin texts had been studied the way one studied the Bible. There now occurred a change in the study of the classics that over time was to spread also to biblical studies.[2] In both cases there arose a search for the most original text. Both required comment on the

---

[1] Cf. also the English editions of his monumental work: The Civilization of the Renaissance. An Essay by Jacob Burckhardt (1945); The Civilization of the Renaissance in Italy,1–2, with Introduction by B. NELSON and CH. TRINKAUS (1958 / [8]1965).

[2] Cf. Kristeller, The Classics and Renaissance Thought (1955) 3–23.

major authorities. Neither classical nor biblical texts were regarded primarily as historical documents but as sources of truth.

The complete depiction of the Renaissance as an epoch of European history is often influenced by the ideological standpoint of the historian, how she or he personally relates to phenomena like classical humanism, western individualism, secularisation of the world-view, the protestant Reformation or the rise of modernity. The detailed knowledge of the culture of the Renaissance, its authors and its texts has grown enormously since the time of JACOB BURCKHARDT. Broad synthetic pictures of the epoch are, however, still discussing his ideas as well as the perspectives of J. A. SYMONDS (1904–09) and his monumental work on the Renaissance in Italy.[3] The dependency on the monumental expositions is particularly obvious among the authors who set out to correct them. WALLACE K. FERGUSON (1948) has traced the development of the picture of the Renaissance as a study in historiography.[4] Among the last synthetic pictures which deserve to be mentioned here, are the books of JOHN HALE (1994)[5] and BARD THOMPSON (1996).[6]

2. The General Character of Renaissance Art and Literature

The Renaissance was first and foremost an Italian phenomenon that over time was exported to the rest of Europe. When the English speak of 'Renaissance' they think primarily of their own Renaissance at the time of Elizabeth I, which occurred more than a hundred years after the Italian experience. The only country north of the Alps that can be said to have experienced a religious and artistic Renaissance comparable to the Italian, was the Netherlands. In its core the Renaissance was a rebirth, or revival, of the ethical, aesthetical and political ideals of Antiquity. In Italy the movement was associated with a revival of the most glorious period of national history.

The Italian Renaissance never regarded itself as a European event. By invoking the rebirth of ancient culture there was a desire to reestablish the roots of local, regional and national history. To many writers of the Renaissance the texts of the early Church formed an integral part of ancient literature. The Church Fathers — especially Augustine and Jerome — were fêted as much as Cicero, Seneca and Livy. The Renaissance humanists saw themselves as "the legitimate heirs of Jerome".[7] Like some protohumanist Jerome had commanded all three languages of sacred philology: Hebrew, Greek and Latin. His example gave the Renaissance a model for a complete education that also included Hebrew. The humanism of this period did not yet draw a sharp distinction between ancient heathen and ancient Christian traditions.

The ideological conception of Rome as the centre of the world was the common property of many political and Christian writers. The removal of the papacy from Rome to Avignon (1307) and finally back again (1427) created a longing for a reunion of what was, or had been, separated. All the way from

---

[3] The Renaissance in Italy, 1–7 (1904–09).
[4] The Renaissance in Historical Thought: Five Centuries of Interpretation (1948); cf. also his Renaissance Studies (1963).
[5] The Civilization of Europe in the Renaissance (1994).
[6] Humanists and Reformers. A History of the Renaissance and the Reformation (1996).
[7] Pelikan, Reformation (1996) 11.

the time of Dante Alighieri to the papacy of Enea Silvio Piccolomini the re-es-
tablishing of Rome as a political and religious centre was a major concern of
Renaissance protagonists.

Often the religious history of the Middle Ages has been seen to end with the
Reformation and the artistic history of the same period with the Renaissance.
But the Reformation was clearly also an important event in art history, and the
Renaissance likewise had great significance for religious history, especially
that part of the Renaissance that had to do with textual scholarship and inter-
pretation.

In contrast to Greek and classical Latin, which in many ways were rediscovered during the fourteenth and fifteenth centuries, there had always existed an
expert knowledge of Hebrew in Jewish circles throughout the Middle Ages.[8]
The new Hebrew learning in some Christian circles, that especially blossomed
with Johannes Reuchlin's *De rudimentis hebraicis* (1506) and *De arte cabalistica*
(1517),[9] was to some degree a double-edged sword because through it Christian learning acquired the traditions of a religious minority and trained itself
in textual criticism on a material that for this minority had the most eminent
religious status.

The freedom to practise textual criticism as research was possibly greater
within Hebrew than in Greek or Latin philology. The controversies around all
proposed changes in the Vulgate text show that many considered the Latin text
an original version of the Bible which therefore had its own specific value.
Something of the same applied to the Greek versions of the Bible and the
authority of the Septuagint stood to some degree in the way of Hebrew studies. The tradition of a miraculous translation from Hebrew to Greek by the
seventy-two translators made it difficult to criticize the Greek version and rendered it superfluous to check it. Most of the New Testament authors had already adopted the Septuagint as *their* Bible and this applied even to St Paul.
On the other hand, the Septuagint created problems because it included other
texts than those of the Hebrew Bible so that discussion of it also entailed discussion of the canon. Whether there existed a Hebrew original text contributed
to determining the limitations of the new scriptural canon.

Christians had somewhat greater freedom relative to the Old Testament
than the New. Only through convoluted typological interpretations could the
Old Testament stories be made relevant to belief in Christ. In pictorial art too
there was usually greater freedom in regard to Old Testament themes than to
those of the New. Everything that was of central and immediate relevance for
Christian faith, could only be schematically and stereotypically represented.
Here art was under strict ecclesiastic control, while already in the High Middle Ages Old Testament themes could be treated somewhat more resourcefully.
Michelangelo's *David* shows how closely Old Testament stories were tied in
with the artistic renewal of the Renaissance.

What is usually called "sacred philology" was the common property of the

---

[8] See HBOT I/2 (2000) pass.
[9] See Chap. 11 in the present volume on "Early Christian Hebraists", by Sophie Kessler Mesguich.

Renaissance and the Reformation.[10] Both movements wanted to renew culture by turning away from an uncertain future toward a supposed perfect past. Much research of the last century has exaggerated the difference between Renaissance and Reformation. Philology, however, was a concern central to both movements so that the reforming movement north of the Alps and the Renaissance in the south were in close and frequent contact with each other.

Marsilio Ficino's translation of Plato into Latin in Florence became in many ways a model for Erasmus of Rotterdam's various editions of the Church Fathers. Augustine and the others were treated like classical authors by the humanist tradition. Critically revised texts and commentaries on Augustine and Jerome were published in the same way one commented on Cicero. Johannes Reuchlin and his grand nephew Philip Melanchthon were both humanists, though on opposite sides in the confessional controversy. Erasmus was and remained a Catholic, whereas Huldrych Zwingli (1484–1531) became a reformer primarily inspired by Erasmus. The humanist tradition was the common property and the common inspiration of both the Catholic and the Protestant wings of the religious disputes.

As early as the fourteenth century jurisprudence was considered paradigmatic for many of the modern tendencies in scientific development. This was especially true of textual interpretation, analyses of texts and argumentation. The needs of the city communes favoured argumentative resolutions based on common sense rather than ostentatious use of force based on authority. In this way there arose new ideals of intelligibility in relation to biblical texts. Johannes Marchesinus' *Mammotrectus super Bibliam*, printed by Schöffer in Mainz as early as 1470, was a popular book for use by clerics who were confronted with new explanatory demands among curious citizens not afraid to question moot points in Holy Writ. Incomprehensibility was no longer seen as a sign of the existence of unfathomable mysteries, but rather as a pointer to intellectual difficulties that had to be resolved.

3. Biblical Interpretation in the Work of Dante Alighieri

The political ideal of the poet and diplomat Dante Alighieri (1265–1321) was king David who was at the same time singer, ruler and priest. After Dante's time the political and the religious dimensions became separated, and between the time of Marsilio of Padua and that of Machiavelli there arose an idea of political order that was no longer grounded in theology. Society came to regard the political field as one governed by its own laws. But in Dante the political domain and theological speculation were still interwoven.

Dante had taught himself Latin through close study of the Psalms of David. His *Divina Commedia* derived important aspects of its prophet-and-psalmist style from the Old Testament. The lyrical subjectivity of the psalmist and the

---

[10] White, A History of the Warfare of Science with Theology in Christendom (1903), Chap. XVII.

forceful, objective warnings of the prophet were both different aspects of
Dante's repertoire. It is David as king, priest and singer that furnishes Dante
with his conception of the poet's comprehensive mandate. In the *Commedia*
Dante tries to reproduce the encyclopedic completeness of the Bible by touch-
ing upon all important contingencies of human life and at the same time he endeavours to write the work in such a way that it can be interpreted both literally, allegorically, morally and anagogically.[11]

In Dante's time the Bible was the obvious point of reference for all questions
of right and wrong, good and evil, and the meanings and absurdities of life.
Dante quotes the Bible more often than any other source. He derives both
scenes, tales and personalities from Holy Writ, but still wants to believe that
his art is independent and self-contained. He refers to themes from both the
Old and the New Testament on the assumption that the whole Bible — in all
its details — was known to his readers. He uses a number of parables from
Scripture to elaborate and illuminate his poetic descriptions.

His total works include in all 575 direct biblical quotations, but the presence
of the Bible is much more comprehensive than this. From the Bible Dante had
his conception of what a book should be, what an authority could be and what
a complete repertoire of forms of expression must encompass. In addition to
the many features taken from the Bible the prayers, hymns and liturgical texts
of divine service were used as prototypes for his work. Not only stories and
figures, but also styles and literary forms drew their models from the Bible. In
addition, the genres and stories of Roman literature undoubtedly influenced
Dante's poetic creativity. A poet of his stature could draw upon the vast variety
of the whole of tradition when searching for forms of expression.

References to the Bible are unequally distributed between *Inferno, Purgatorio* and *Paradiso*. In *Inferno* the biblical references are few, as one could expect.
Here the figures of Roman mythology are more strongly present. It is in *Purgatorio* that the Bible really comes to the fore, since the Bible is a book for people on a journey like the figures of *Purgatorio*. In *Paradiso* it is the liturgical
texts and hymns that furnish the most important references and examples.
Dante himself saw his work as inspired by the same spirit that brought forth
the Old and the New Testament.[12] He uses Ps 113 (114): *In exitu Isra[h]el de
Aegypto* ... as an example to illustrate the fourfold reading of Scripture[13] in his
Letter to Cangrande. The story of Israel's exodus from Egypt in fact provides
one of the basic structures for the whole of Dante's poem. To Dante more than
any other poet the figures, metaphors and stories of Scripture were 'the great
code', to use an expression of NORTHROP FRYE.

In reality, Dante had to use a range of artistic means to develop his poetic
authority. He had personally to create a position that gave him the right to
speak within the community of language represented by Scripture and the ecclesiastical tradition. To Dante Scripture was "infallible truth" and "divine
authority", as he expressly says in *De Monarchia* (I, 5 and 2,1). Dante himself

---

[11] *Conv.* II, 1; cf *Par.* IV, 40 ff.
[12] *Par.* XXV, 64–78.
[13] Cf. *Purg.* II, 43–48.

wanted to shout like the voice on the mountain (Isa 40:9). He wanted to be a singer with both a religious and a political mission like David — "he who instilled it first into my heart, who was the great songman of the Great King"[14] — and a prophet of doom for his hometown Florence that had rejected him and sent him into exile. As PETER S. HAWKINS concludes: "In all these ways the poet rewrites Scripture precisely by continuing to write it — not as the third testament, but as a sacred poem that is fully aware of itself as a work of literature".[15]

In his fundamental placing of the Old Testament in relation to the New Dante made use of the most widespread interpretative key of his own time. As St Paul said, the Old Testament too speaks of Christ as soon as one removes the veil. But to Dante this was true also of Vergil's *Aeneid*. Vergil's poem too speaks of Christ, when read in the right manner. Dante used the position of the Old Testament relative to the New to explain the deeper meaning of both Roman literature and ancient, heathen philosophy, especially Platonism. The thoughts of pre-Christian philosophy were anticipations and omens whose deepest meaning could only be grasped with hindsight — in light of the Christ event.

4. The Renaissance Concept of 'History'

Actual historical research is not found in the Renaissance. The humanists did change the writing of history, but in the main it stayed a literary and rhetorical activity. The ancient exemplars determined both what should be written about and how it should be written. When historiography was discussed, the discussion usually had to do with which ancient historians that were exemplary. Caesar, Sallust and Livy are the shining stars. Because treatises on historical method were unknown in ancient literature, systematic reflections were lacking in the Renaissance too.

The humanist and poet Francesco Petrarca (1304–74) had carried classical Latin language back to its homeland; others had brought ancient literary genres including historiography back to life. In the Middle Ages local chronicles and accounts of universal history became common. The Renaissance pursued the history of city states, wars and ruling families since there were good ancient models for all of these. Historiography was a literary genre that could often sit lightly to the documentation of facts. Fictional tales were composed that allegedly accounted for the motives of persons in the way ancient historiography had previously done, using Homer as a model. The incidents of history were related for inspiration and warning, not to trace the real course of events. The purpose of the telling was to give concrete form to some moral idea or to support a political ideology.

The stylistic ideal was to write in such a way that one could imagine some

---

[14] *Par.* XXV, 72.
[15] In his major article in The Dante Encyclopedia (2000) 103.

ancient author behind the text. The truth of the story did not so much depend on its capacity to report actual happenings as on its power to promote moral or political understanding. Positive models, however, had more force than admonitory warnings, which is to say that many regarded strictures on human weakness to be incompatible with the dignity of historiography.

Historical research as a critical and scientific activity was still far beyond the horizon. Only with a philological quest for the original wording of texts was the sensitivity to facts sharpened. Even for a philologist like Erasmus of Rotterdam textual accuracy was primarily an avenue to a new and purified piety. Erasmus wished to intensify the meditation on the words of Scripture by improving the texts and making them credible.

Erasmus seems to know little of medieval Bible studies and in developing his textual criticism he actually began something entirely new. *Devotio moderna* sought to meditate on a pure and improved Bible. He was a follower of the new form of piety north of the Alps, but he was also an enthusiastic admirer of what was going on in Italy in the way of the arts and the sciences. Lorenzo Valla's *Adnotationes in Nov. Test.* was the work that turned Erasmus to Bible studies of a wholly new kind when he lightened upon it in 1504. In Erasmus' opinion real guidance was only to be found in the original and unadulterated text. His scientific studies were meant to support a rejuvenation of Christian piety and his idea of a Christian humanism was fastened to a dream of reliving and reviving the culture and education of the Church Fathers. However, acquaintance with Hebrew he had none, no more than Augustine had had.

Among humanists of the fifteenth century the disdain for monastic chronicles became tied to a reverence for the ancient exemplars. However, the latter seldom represented any scientific advance over the former. Adornments had become more important than the factual contents of humanist writing, as FELIX GILBERT says: "Not factual completeness and accuracy, but moral guidance was expected".[16]

Only with Francesco Guicciardini (1483–1540) and Niccolò Machiavelli (1469–1527) do we encounter a more modern form of historiography that concerns itself with how causes work together to produce historical events. To Guicciardini the goal of historical research was to detect the criteria and conditions for the development of benevolent government. In Machiavelli the study of history was motivated by an interest in the natural regularities that steer social and political processes. If factual accounts did not accord with a basic standard of accuracy, then one could not learn anything from history. Writers did not use history to exemplify wisdom they already possessed, but to find still hidden causal connections.

In the Middle Ages the idea of universal history drawn from biblical inspiration had its foremost representative in Joachim di Fiore (d. 1202). He speculated on how the epochs of Father and Son were in the process of being replaced by the epoch of the Holy Spirit before Antichrist and Judgement Day. The histories of Jews and Gentiles had been brought together in the incarna-

---

[16] Gilbert, Machiavelli and Guicciardini (1984) 225.

tion of the Son of God and were superseded by a Christian history that furnished the only valid key to a universal history subsequent to the incarnation. Only because the world was created by one will and governed through one providence could its history be told in one coherent story. To Joachim as to other Christian readers of the Bible in the twelfth century the truth and meaning of the Old Testament was something that only became manifest in the New. In the same way, he thought, only the reign of the Spirit would give full enlightenment as to the meaning of the kingdoms of the Father and the Son.

As medieval preachers had sought to find paradigms in Scripture and the history of the Church, the first humanists probed profane history for moral or political insight. In the works on universal history conclusions were general and vague: God punishes pride; the wheel of Fortune spares no one; and so on. Those who wrote about history in the Middle Ages seem not to have had any strong idea of historical distance and difference. Historical figures were mainly treated as contemporary and were judged by the same standard. In pictorial art Old Testament figures were represented in contemporary clothing, for both we and they lived by the same rules of universal history. The genealogies of the ruling houses gave a first tentative conception of causal continuity in historical events. But only the historical relativism of a later stage opened the possibility of detecting historical relativity and discovering historical diversity.

With Giotto di Bondone (1267–1367) in pictorial art and Francesco Petrarca in literature we meet for the first time an inkling of historical distance. Yet they were exceptions in their own time, and BERYL SMALLEY underlines the modernity of the humanists in saying: "The humanists did not 'rediscover the past'. It belonged to the medieval inheritance from antiquity. What they did was to discover the past *as* past. History was seen in perspective, not as a painting on a flat surface".[17] She may be exaggerating, but she is right in that this was in fact the direction taken by modern development.

5. From Manuscripts to Books:
the Significance of the Printing Invention of Johann Gutenberg

Both Judaism and Christianity were literate religions; their holy texts were the chief authority, and the transmission and interpretation of texts were central parts of religious practice. Therefore, the art of printing as it was invented by Johann Gutenberg (c. 1397–1468) in the mid-fifteenth century deeply influenced the range of practices and ideas that governed the transmission of the religious tradition. The change from manuscript culture and oral transmission to a religious practice that primarily related to the printed page engendered a series of changes in religious culture.

The Bible was the masterpiece of the first printers, beginning with Johann Gutenberg's 42-line Bible, *Biblia Latina Vulgata*, produced in Mainz 1452–

---

[17] Smalley, Historians in the Middle Ages (1994) 193.

55.[18] Shortly afterwards Johann Fust and Peter Schöffer printed their 36-line version in the same place (1462). A remarkable achievement was the new Vulgate of Robert Estienne published in Paris 1527–28. The boldness and skill of Estienne's publishing activities were striking since he had never held Church office nor had its approval. Both as printer, biblical scholar and humanist he influenced the ecclesiastical tradition with his research. The historical outcome of a veritable flood of Bible editions was the new Vulgate of 1592–93 approved by the Church.

The priestly monopoly on literacy was broken. Ideas and interpretations could no longer be as easily controlled by a central ecclesiastical authority. The Reformation was throughout a movement that exploited the potential created by the new technique and printed books hastened the development of reading skills in general. There had been no point in learning to read as long as one could not afford books. The printed book led to deep changes within both the political, literary, scientific and religious spheres. Renaissance and Reformation were therefore periods of fundamental shifts in the forms of social communication.

The first printed books belonged to ancient and medieval culture. We might therefore imagine the art of printing to be a conservative or reactionary instrument, but texts became cheaper and had a wider dissemination. They carried with them a standardization, or rather a demand for standardization, that encouraged philological science. In the fifteenth century book collections were of quite a different order compared with those of the Middle Ages. Among other things one could more easily compare the older texts. It soon became easier to note disagreements since texts no longer spoke with one voice. Simultaneous access to the received texts gave rise to a new form of critical engagement with them.

The first time that the Western art of printing attempted a complete Greek text was with the publication of Constantinos Lasaris in 1476. Aldus reprinted it in an inexpensive edition in Venice in 1495. In 1488 Homer's *Iliad* and *Odyssey* were printed in Greek in Florence. The Complutensian *Biblia Polyglotta* (1514–17) of the Spanish Renaissance utilized printing skills in a work of enormous, and previously unheard of, editorial complexity, marking a *tour de force* among all activities within the field of sacred philology. The comparisons of philologists between different textual variants inspired in their turn historians to compare different versions of the course of events. In humanist historiography before Erasmus the rhetorical masterpieces most often were based on a single source only.

Learning itself had to change as a result of the change in communication technology. It no longer consisted in a knowledge immediately gleaned from authorities, but became over time the investigation of what these authorities really had intended to say. Medieval students had spent their time making copies by dictation. They could now instead spend it in sorting out the contradictions and clearing up the controversial passages of tradition. The community

---

[18] See further the essay by A. SCHENKER, Chap. 12, Sect. 1, in the present volume.

of readers of identical texts became also a community of research. This could hardly have happened within a manuscript culture for the simple reason that all text editions were then different.

Scholars no longer had to worry that the old books would disappear and it was no longer possible to expunge texts when they were printed in large numbers and spread across an entire continent. The *index expurgatorius* therefore became quite futile as an instrument of controlling the new art of printing. The flaws in the technology of transmission had up till then protected political and religious institutions by permitting oblivion. Now all controversies developed a tendency to escalate because contested words and attacks no longer could be forgotten. They were there in print. Black on white.

The phenomenon of renaissances was well known in earlier European history, but even these flowerings of culture and their programmes could again be forgotten when transmission took place through manuscripts. The Italian Renaissance and the German Reformation carried with them a great number of changes on a wide front and of an irreversible character, because all utterances became spread and documented for future times. The art of printing and the community of bookreaders soon raised wholly new demands for standardization and accuracy in all fields, demands different from those of a manuscript culture. Even the idea of a fact changed from the level of personal experience to that which was documented or documentable in writing.

The authority of priests as carriers of tradition was weakened. They had been the privileged literates, but now learned men not in holy orders could by their knowledge of texts and their philology instruct priests and bishops in controversial religious questions. An author gained a new type of authority transmitted from his public rather than an authority granted him through institutional connections or office.

The isolated reader created new, individualistic ideals of piety. The reader's dialogue with his soul over the meaning of a text became as important for the pious life as the community in celebrating Mass. The printing art took over the management of collective memory including the religious tradition insofar as it was coupled to available texts. The printed book favoured religious self-help and the orientation toward public needs rather than institutional legitimacy encouraged the use of everyday language at the cost of Latin.

The transformations that we call 'Renaissance' had no simple historical cause. Economic, social, technical, political and intellectual changes working together hastened the larger change in the direction of the early modern world. Changes occurred in all these fields, and no part of cultural life was left untouched. Nevertheless, to far greater degree than the Reformation the Renaissance was an élitist phenomenon. A relatively few culture bearers in the fields of finance, literature and science created innovations that in their turn had the widest consequences. This is not to say that the Reformation was a result of the Renaissance. The forerunners of the Reformation and the Renaissance appear nearly simultaneously. John Wyclif's *De Veritate Sacrae Scripturae* made the Bible the sole ecclesiastical source of truth nearly a hundred years before the art of printing realised the material possibility for such a type of Christianity.

CHAPTER FIVE

The Philosophical Context of the Renaissance Interpretation of the Bible

By Jeremy Catto, Oxford

Sources: BLASIUS OF PARMA: *Quaestiones de Anima* (ed. G. Federici-Vescovini; Florence: Olschki 1974). – JOHANNES CAPREOLUS: *In libros sententiarum amplissimae quaestiones* (Venice 1588–89). – PETRUS CROCKAERT: *Quaestiones in singulos Aristotelis libros logicales* (Paris 1509). – NICHOLAUS CUSANUS: *Opera Omnia* (ed. R. Klibansky e.a.; Leipzig: F. Meiner 1932-); *Trialogus de Possest* (ET by J. Hopkins; in: idem, *A Concise Introduction to the Philosophy of Nicholas of Cusa*, 1986 ; see below). – DIONYSIUS CARTHUSIENSIS: *Opera Omnia* (Montreuil-sur-Mer: Patres Carthusiani 1896–1935). – MARSILIO FICINO: *Opera Omnia* (Basel 1576; repr. Turin: Bottega d'Erasmo 1959); *Theologia platonica de immortalitate animae* (ed. J. Hankins / M. J. B. Allen; Cambridge, MA: Harvard UP 2001-). – GAETANO DE THIENE: *Expositio super libros de anima* (Vicenza 1486). – GEORGIUS BRUXELLENSIS: *Cursus quaestionum super philosophiam Aristotelis* (Lyons 1504). – JEAN GERSON: *Opera Omnia* (ed. P. Glorieux; Paris: Desclée 1960–73). – HEYMERIC DE CAMPO: *Opera Selecta* (ed. R. Imbach / P. Ladner; Spicilegium Friburgense; Freiburg: Universitätsverlag 2001). – JACQUES LE-FÈVRE D'ETAPLES / FABER STAPULENSIS: *The prefacing Epistles and related Texts* (ed. E. F. Rice; New York: Columbia UP 1972). – JOHN MAIR: *Quaestiones logicales cum expositione in veterem Aristotelis dialecticen* (Paris 1528). – PAULUS VENETUS: *Logica Magna* (ed. N. Kretzmann; Oxford: Oxford UP 1978–91); *Super libros de anima* (Venice 1481). – GIOVANNI PICO DELLA MIRANDOLA: *Opera Omnia* (Basel 1572; repr. Turin: Bottega d'Erasmo 1971); *De dignitate hominis* (ed. L. Valcke / R. Galibois; in: *Le periple intellectuel de Jean Pic de la Mirandole*; Sainte Foy and Sherbrooke, Quebec: Presses de l'Université Laval 1994). – PIETRO POMPONAZZI: *Tractatus de immortalitate animae* (ed. G. Morra; Bologna: Nenni e Fiammenghi 1954). – GIROLAMO SAVONAROLA: *Compendium totius philosophiae* (Venice 1542); *Trattato circa el reggimento e governo della città di Firenze* (ed. L. Firpo; in: *Savonarola, Opere: Prediche super Aggeo*; Rome: A. Belardetti 1965). – JOHN SHARPE: *Quaestio de Universalibus* (ed. A. D. Conti; Florence: Olschki 1990). – PIERRE TARTARET: *Commentarii in libros phylosophiae naturalis et metaphysiciae Aristotelis* (Paris 1520). – NICOLETTO VERNIA: *Quaestio an ens mobile sit totius philosophiae naturalis subiectum* (Padua 1480). – JOHANNES VERSORIS: *In Aristotelis philosophiae libros quaestiones* (Lyons 1496). – GUILELMUS VORRILLON: *Super quattuor libros sententiarum* (Venice 1496). – JOHANNES WENCK: *De ignota litteratura* (ed. J. Hopkins; Minneapolis: A. J. Banning Press 1981). – JOHN WYCLIF: *Tractatus de logica* (ed. M. H. Dziewicki; London: Wyclif Society 1893–99); *De statu innocentiae* (ed. F. D. Matthew; London: Wyclif Society 1922); *Tractatus de universalibus* (ed. J. Mueller; Oxford: Oxford UP 1985).

General works: M. J. B. ALLEN, *The Platonism of Marsilio Ficino* (Berkeley: Berkely UP 1984); A. BROADIE, *The Circle of John Mair* (Oxford: Oxford UP 1985); *The Cambridge History of Renaissance Philosophy* [CHRP] (ed. C. B. Schmitt / Quentin Skinner; Cambridge: Cambridge UP 1988; bibliography: 805–930); A. J. FESTUGIÈRE, *La Revélation d'Hermes Trismegiste* (Paris: Lecoffre 1944–54); *Marsilio Ficino e il Ritorno di Platone* (ed. S. Gentile e.a.; Florence: Le Lettere 1984); *Marsilio Ficino: his Theology, his Philosophy, his Legacy* (ed. M. J. B. Allen / G. Rees; Leiden: Brill 2002); E. GARIN, *La cultura filosofica del Rinascimento italiano* (Florence: Sansoni 1961); J. HOP-KINS, *A Concise Introduction to the Philosophy of Nicholas of Cusa* (Minneapolis: A. J. Banning Press 1978); idem, *Nicholas of Cusa's Metaphysic of Contraction* (Minneapolis: A. J. Banning Press 1983); R. KLIBANSKY, *The Continuity of the Platonic Tradition during the Middle Ages* (Munich: Kraus International 1981); K. KREMER, Praegustatio naturalis sapientiae. *Gott suchen mit Nikolaus von Kues* (Münster: Aschendorff 2004); P. O. KRISTELLER, *The Philosophy of Marsilio Ficino* (New

York 1943); idem, *Studies in Renaissance Thought and Letters* (Rome: Edizioni di Storia 1969); J. OVERFIELD, *Humanism and Scholasticism in Late Medieval Germany* (Princeton, NJ: Princeton UP 1984); *Pico della Mirandola, Convegno internazionale de studi nel cinquecentesimo* (ed. G. C. Garfagnini; Florence: Olschki 1997); M. L. PINE, *Pietro Pomponazzi: Radical Philosopher of the Renaisssance* (Padua: Antenore 1986); G. RITTER, *Studien zur Spätscholastik* (SHAW 13; Heidelberg 1922); *Scienza e filosofia all' Università di Padova nel' 400* (ed. A. Poppi; Trieste: Edizioni Lint 1983); G. WEINSTEIN, *Savonarola and Florence* (Princeton, NJ: Princeton UP 1970).

1. New Theological Developments

Commentators on the Bible in the fifteenth and sixteenth centuries, whether they approached the text in the traditional course of fulfilling the requirements for the degree of Doctor of Theology, or as an essentially historical document susceptible to scholarly inquiry and critical principles, shared an education in which Aristotle's empirical approach and critical method was fundamental. This was as much the case in Lorenzo Valla's Florentine schooldays as at the Augustinian nuns' establishment at Avila where St Theresa went to school, or in the gentlemanly formation of Guillaume Budé in late fifteenth-century Paris; it applied equally to the early training in friars' schools of Juan de Torquemada OP, the young Sebastian Münster, then OFM, or Cipriano de la Huerga OC. Writers on the sacred text were familiar, even if they rejected it, with the ancient distinction of literal, spiritual, allegorical and anagogical levels of meaning in Scripture; the empirical method of Aristotle had sharpened commentators' investigation of the literal sense of Scripture since the thirteenth century, and had given an impetus to the discussion of natural phenomena in biblical lectures, especially in the English universities. William Woodford OFM, for instance, had discussed the properties of salt in his comment on the text *Vos estis sal terrae* (Matt 5:13), lecturing on Matthew at Oxford in 1373–74.[1] The same method underpinned the critical and historical approach to the biblical text, already foreshadowed by both Woodford and his opponent John Wyclif in argument in the Oxford schools over the status of Scripture and tradition, and carried forward in the scholarly work of Valla, Erasmus and Ximenes.

Equally, however, serious students of the Bible were aware of the spiritual exercise of meditation on the Gospels or the Psalms, which had been made more or less universally popular by the proponents of the *devotio moderna* and its analogues during the fifteenth century. The proliferation of versions of the Bible in vernacular languages must have sharpened their sense that the sacred text was not to be corralled within the ambit of professional theological study. Nor could they ignore the opportunities which arose in the fifteenth century for wider and closer reading of the Latin fathers, for direct access to the Greek patristic tradition and for textual criticism of Scripture in its Hebrew and Greek original and in the light of ancient manuscripts. Wider knowledge posed no challenge to their inherited principles of empirical criticism, but gave them

---

[1] Cambridge University Library MS Add. 3571, fols. 171r–172r.

new material to consider. A broader awareness of the world beyond Christendom, and of the historical era which had preceded the Incarnation had induced some scholars of the later fourteenth and early fifteenth centuries to speculate on the state of innocence before the Fall, and the salvation of unbaptized children and pagans untouched by Christianity.[2] These new developments were part of a more general repositioning of philosophical and theological debate. Before the middle of the fourteenth century the discussion of the great issues of theology and natural philosophy had generally taken place within the schools of universities, and in the schools of the friars which followed the pattern of university education. Lectures on the Bible had equally been given in the schools, usually by bachelors and doctors of theology who had taken part in philosophical disputation. The same questions, therefore, were often discussed in biblical lectures and in lectures on the Sentences of Peter Lombard or even on Aristotle; they were couched in technical terms, and addressed to a select audience or circulated to a limited readership. After 1350, as the scope of both theology and natural philosophy broadened, formal commentaries on the Sentences gave way to books and tracts directed to a wider audience in less technical language: for example, John Wyclif's polemic on the civil dominion of the clergy or on the Eucharist, which partly turned on philosophical points, addressed a readership not of students but of graduate careerists and educated laymen, and much of Jean Gerson's work on mystical theology had similar readers in mind. In the fifteenth century, the writers who contributed to philosophical debate tended to be older and to have more worldly experience than their predecessors in the high scholastic age: some were university professors, like John Versor (Jean le Tourneur) in mid-fifteenth-century Paris or Pietro Pomponazzi in early sixteenth-century Padua and Bologna, while others had passed from university to active or leisured life like Nicholas of Cusa and Marsilio Ficino. Their works were the product not only of the lecture hall but of the study; if they reflected debate, it was of a literary kind such as Nicholas of Cusa conducted with John Wenck; more often, they were prompted by wider reading and the discovery of new texts whether antique or recent. Generally they had at their disposal considerable libraries, in which the standard texts, Aristotle and his mediaeval commentators together with the Fathers and the main commentators on the Sentences could be consulted in turn; this encouraged a critical attitude to received authorities and a sharper awareness of the history of philosophy.

Much of this broader and more critical reading simply deepened fifteenth-century thinkers' understanding of familiar texts. Among them was the *Mystical Theology* then attributed to Dionysius the Areopagite the disciple of St. Paul, which had fundamentally affected the theological underpinning of the practice of contemplation in the fourteenth century. From 1400, when Jean Gerson first lectured on mystical theology at Paris, the pseudo-Dionysius began to attract the careful study of philosophers and theologians: of Gerson himself, in the commentary which occupied his last years; of the Carthusian

---

[2] See Wyclif, *De statu innocentiae* (1922) 475–524.

Denys Ryckel (Dionysius Carthusiensis, d. 1471), who also commented on his namesake; of the Camaldolese humanist Ambrogio Traversari, whose new translations of the *Mystical Theology* and other works in 1436–37 were familiar to Ficino; of Lorenzo Valla who first pointed out, in 1457, that the works of Pseudo-Dionysius must have been written by a neoplatonic philosopher of about 500 A.D.; and of Erasmus, who gave Valla's observation general circulation. The writings of Augustine were even more widely and carefully studied: his profound influence on the unorthodox ideas of John Wyclif and Jan Hus was matched by the Augustinian learning of their opponent Thomas Netter, whose knowledge of the range of Augustine's writings was wider than that of any earlier scholar. Augustine's psychological orientation and sense of the subconscious mind inspired the *devotio moderna*, the contemplative movement among whose devotees were the theologians Wessel Gansfort and Gabriel Biel, as well as the young Erasmus. He was equally influential on the scholars of the early Renaissance: Petrarch's religious personality was thoroughly Augustinian, while for Ficino his authority justified the synthesis of Christianity and Platonism.[3] Augustine's intellectual odyssey, as he had set it out in the *Confessions* and other works, delineated a landscape of ancient philosophies and religions which acquired added significance for Ficino, Pico della Mirandola and others from the newly available texts of Greek authors. Erasmus published the first great critical edition of Augustine, in 1528–29, though his ineradicable disrespect for all established authorities embraced even the greatest of the Latin Fathers, and earned the sharp strictures of both Luther and his Catholic opponent John Eck. But the deep critical reading Erasmus devoted to Augustine was only an extension of the Augustinian learning of a century and more of his predecessors.

2. Aspects of a New Philosophical Climate

Next to these Christian authorities in the libraries of fifteenth-century scholars, a growing body of classical philosophical texts would soon appear. Greek texts caught their sharpest attention, but the *De rerum natura* of Lucretius, unearthed by Poggio in 1417, and Cicero's *De oratore*, discovered at Lodi in 1421, afforded them other insights into ancient moral philosophy. Ambrogio Traversari's Latin translation of the *Lives of the Philosophers* of Diogenes Laertius showed scholars that neither Aristotle nor Plato commanded philosophical opinion in the ancient world; they merely contributed to more wide-ranging debates. Leonardo Bruni's more accurate translations of Aristotle's *Ethics* and *Politics*, while they helped to make the philosopher's ideas more generally known, gave him an historical context which corroded his status as an authority; the diffusion of his Greek commentators' work in the sixteenth century confirmed his reduced standing and more accurate assessment. But by far the most influential new author was Plato, with Plotinus and other neoplatonist

---

[3] P. O. KRISTELLER, "Augustine and the early Renaissance", in: idem, Studies (1969) 355–72.

philosophers in his wake. Plato's influence before 1450 had largely been indirect, through Augustine and the Greek Fathers; a few of his dialogues were translated into Latin in the first decade of the century. It was the achievement of Ficino to translate the whole corpus, together with the *Enneads* of Plotinus and Iamblichus's *De Mysteriis*, neoplatonist works which he believed to embody the true spirit of Plato, and to accompany it with an extensive commentary. The Latin Plato had an immediate and widespread impact, especially on the philosophy of religion: many of its readers had already been influenced by Augustine and the neoplatonist pseudo-Dionysius, and touched by the spirit of the *devotio moderna*. If its force was initially clouded by Ficino's belief that Plato's ideas were derived from the mythical Hermes Trismegistus, the access it afforded to one of the greatest minds of Antiquity was perhaps the most important achievement of all Renaissance philosophy. These new developments did not however diminish and indeed may have contributed to the continued ascendancy of the University of Paris in the study of philosophy, both as the most important centre for the transmission and informed discussion of ideas and as the model of other universities in Germany, in Italy (especially at Padua) and in the sixteenth century in Spain. Most if not all of the ideas which preoccupied humanist thinkers, the nature and immortality of the soul, the mathematical foundation of logic and the metaphysical basis of the empirical sciences for instance, had long been debated in a more sophisticated manner in the schools, and it is clear that in Paris they were among topics disputed throughout the fifteenth century, argued with renewed vigour by John Mair, Peter Tartaret and Jacques Lefèvre d'Etaples in the early sixteenth century and transmitted to the Spanish neo-scholastic philosophers (and to Calvin) in the following generation. The period is characterized, in Paris as in Oxford and the new German universities, by a eclecticism made up of all the traditions of the past: Thomism, Scotism, the various Augustinian schools and the radical scepticism about the knowability of God and the limitations of philosophical enquiry which were associated, though not exclusively, with the name of William of Ockham. The contributions of all these schools were brought to bear on the philosophical work of theologians such as Peter of Candia, Wyclif and Gerson, who, living or recently dead, dominated debate about 1400. It might seem on the evidence of the *Wegestreit* in German universities that fifteenth-century Thomists, Albertists and Nominalists flourished separately and in competition: but apart from the original stimulus given by the general German reaction against the Wycliffite or realist view of universals taught by the Hussites in Prague about 1410, the difference between the parties concerned merely the method of teaching. So-called Scotists, Thomists and Albertists favoured the "way of exposition", lecturing on an authoritative text, while the nominalists preferred the "way of questions", raising speculative issues.[4] In practice the original thinkers in German universities, above all Nicholas of Cusa and Gabriel Biel, while they read extensively the works of their predecessors ignored the controversies of the *Wegestreit*. The consequence of well-read

---

[4] Ritter, Studien zur Spätscholastik II (1922); Overfield, Humanism and Scholasticism (1984) 49–60.

eclecticism was the rise of the philosophical text-book, in which the views of all the main protagonists were summarized. New text-books became the most influential means of transmitting the ideas of the schools both in the theology and the arts faculties of Paris; they usually took one tradition as their ground, but absorbed ideas from many writings, including newly available ancient works. In the theology faculty this led to the revival of commentaries on the Sentences of Peter Lombard, which reverted to comprehensive coverage of the ground: the Thomist commentary of John Capreolus OP, delivered as lectures in Paris about 1435, provided an up-to-date textbook for Dominican convents, while the Scotist commentary of Guillaume de Vorillon OFM (about 1455) filled the same function for the Franciscan schools. Both were frequently printed. In the arts faculty the Aristotelian commentaries of Johannes Versor, especially on the *Metaphysics*, written in Paris in the mid-fifteenth century, had much the same effect, summarizing Aristotle's teaching on the natural world from a Thomist perspective. They were supplemented by the compendia of Thomas Bricot (d. 1516) and Peter Tartaret (died c. 1522), and by the *Introductiones* of Jacques Lefèvre d'Etaples to the set philosophical texts; in the latter works much of the recent Italian scholarship on Aristotle and other ancient authors was distilled and circulated. Lefèvre d'Etaples was a theologian as well as a master of arts; his contemporaries in the theology schools were equally broad in their reading, notably Petrus Crockaert OP (d. 1514), in whose Thomist school Francisco de Vitoria OP, the progenitor of the neo-Thomist philosophy of Salamanca and the Jesuit neo-scholastics was formed.[5] The vitality of Parisian Aristotelianism and its capacity to generate powerful new philosophical schools as late as the sixteenth century was due both to the professional rigour of its traditional training, rooted in the schools of the thirteenth and fourteenth centuries, and to its capacity to absorb new intellectual stimuli, whether Oxford logic in the fourteenth century or rediscovered texts in the fifteenth.

The vigour of the Paris schools was transmitted to the new universities of Germany and to the burgeoning schools of Padua, where the effect of developments in logic, mathematics and natural philosophy was also felt. The great theological debates of the fourteenth century on the relation between the principle of God's omnipotence and the inescapable observed reality of time and contingency had increasingly been subjected to the analysis of an increasingly rigorous and abstract mathematical "terminist" logic, developed by William of Ockham, Thomas Bradwardine, William Heytesbury and Richard Billingham and taken forward by Marsilius of Inghen and Paul of Venice. This led to surprisingly free debates, in Paris towards the end of the century, on such subjects as the existence of God.[6] But increasingly it focussed attention on the nature and limits of human knowledge of God and revealed truth: as logic was applied with ever-increasing rigour, the body of theological propositions open to

---

[5] C. B. SCHMITT, "The rise of the philosophical textbook", CHRP (1988) 792–804; Q. SKINNER, "Political Philosophy", CHRP (1988) 405.

[6] Z. KALUZA, "Le problème du 'Deum non esse' chez Etienne de Chaumont, Nicolas Aston et Thomas Bradwardine", *Mediaevalia Philosophica Polonorum* 24 (1979) 3–19.

rational demonstration diminished, leaving a chasm between a theology dependent on revelation and a natural order determined by human reason. The
dual prevalence of fideism in theology and scepticism in respect of the natural
order threatened the overarching metaphysical concept of being which for
both Aquinas and Scotus had joined God and creatures together: Scotus especially had taken the notion of *ens sub ratione entis* to its furthest limit, including everything the existence of which is not contradictory. Many philosophers
tried to bridge the chasm. In Oxford, John Wyclif rejected terminist logic, asserting the reality of universal ideas present in the mind of God, on which the
reality of particular entities depended. His solution, though it anticipated
some of the neoplatonist notions prevalent in fifteenth-century Italy, found little favour beyond his disciples in the University of Prague, being associated
with his call to radical action against established cults and ecclesiastical institutions. For Gerson, who was influenced by the contemplative writers of the Rhineland and who first lectured on mystical theology in Paris in 1400, revealed
truth was itself the basis for metaphysics and therefore of all the physical
sciences; being itself, the *conceptus entis*, was beyond purely human understanding. Any attempt to apply to God principles derived from the created
world would limit his absolute freedom. His appeal to an infused rather than a
reasoned understanding of theological truths would also look forward to Ficino's Platonism. Later theologians, such as the Heidelberg professor Johannes
Wenck, the opponent of Nicholas of Cusa, and Johannes Versor in mid-century Paris, would fall back on the Thomist idea that human knowledge was
grounded in sense-perception, and permitted some degree of knowledge of
God, or natural theology; but they would reach their position in full awareness
of the alternative solutions to the problem of essence and existence, and of the
relation of possible to actual worlds. Underlying the more or less unsatisfactory solutions to these problems posed in the century from 1350 to 1450 was a
slow change in the *conceptus entis*, the concept of 'being' itself. Scotus had
adumbrated a more dynamic notion of 'being' by grounding it in the causal
principle of the divine will: God imparted to creation a vestige of his own creativity and freedom. A notion of *ens* which embraced both creator and creation
must imply some hierarchy or scale of 'being', which in turn opened the possibility of applying to it the measure language of intension and remission developed in the course of the century by Thomas Bradwardine, Nicolas Oresme
and others to describe variations of heat, velocity and other qualities. The
Paris theologian Johannes de Ripa OFM was the first to apply these terms to
variability in substantial forms, in attempting to define the conditions for the
union of God and creatures in the beatific vision. For Ripa, in the words of
Lohr, "forms are accordingly not static, immutable essences, but include an
ontological intensity which can be measured as a distance between the relative
nothingness of finite reality and a supreme terminus to which it tends as to its
own unattainable perfection".[7] This idea of a *latitudo formarum* was much discussed in Paris about 1400, and was transmitted to Padua and developed by

---

[7] C. LOHR, "Metaphysics", CHRP (1988) 593.

Paul of Venice and other philosophers. In this context the development of many branches of natural philosophy in the course of the fourteenth century, notably physics, biology and geology, provoked a return to the writings of Albertus Magnus, including his metaphysics which addressed many problems of elemental and compound forms to which the notion of the *latitudo formarum* could be applied. Johannes de Nova Domo, a Parisian master of arts active in the first years of the fifteenth century, summed up the dynamic notion of 'being' in his image of a river of existing things flowing from its source in their essence; his student Heimeric de Campo went on to teach similar ideas at Cologne, where he in turn influenced Nicholas of Cusa.[8]

The development of terminist logic and the measure languages of physics also permitted the study of natural philosophy in a new and more dynamic way, though still on the basis of Aristotle's treatises, both in Paris and elsewhere. Commentaries on the *Physics* and other texts of the master multiplied, supplemented in Paris by "questionaries" on disputed points, some by original thinkers such as George of Brussels and Petrus Crockaert in the early sixteenth century; their approach was adopted by Domingo de Soto and followed at Salamanca. The Aristotelians of Paris and especially Padua turned in the sixteenth century to experimental verification of such points as the comparative velocity of bodies, and founded permanent institutions of empirical data such as botanical gardens, natural history museums and anatomical theatres: they, rather than their humanist or platonist critics, laid the foundations of modern science. Terminist logic and mathematical physics were introduced to Padua by Paul of Venice at the beginning of the fifteenth century, giving the essential stimulus to the growth of the Paduan Aristotelian school (which in practice included masters teaching at Bologna and Pavia) in which Pietro Pomponazzi was probably the most distinguished philosopher. Padua had originally had no theology faculty, and Aristotle was accordingly read there in the arts and medical faculties with a more naturalistic and Averroist bias; the masters were open to the newly translated Greek commentaries on the text, and were able to discuss ideas such as the eternity of the world and the mortality of the soul which were not reconcileable with Christian doctrine. In particular they developed a notion of the intellective soul and its manner of knowing universal ideas. Consideration of this difficult topic lasted from the final years of the fourteenth century to the second decade of the sixteenth, in commentaries on Aristotle's *De anima* and treatises on the unity of the intellect and the immortality of the soul. On Aristotle's principles, if the mind existed only as a form of the material body, it must be mortal; if it existed as an immaterial being independently of the body, it could be immortal but could not be individual, as eternal beings cannot differ one from another merely numerically; individuals must therefore share a single intellect. Blasius of Parma writing about 1395 took a purely material view of the process of intellection, and appeared to endorse the mortality of the soul, an unacceptable conclusion on religious grounds. Paul of Venice about 1408 accepted the unity of the intellect, but de-

---

[8] Ibid. 594–95.

fined it as the *forma informans* of individual minds, which (following Ockham) could only grasp universal ideas in the particulars which gave them actual being. His student Gaetano da Thiene, writing in 1436–43, resolved the dilemma by positing that the one intellect was multiplied and infused into individual bodies by a series of separate divine acts of creation. Gaetano's student and successor Nicoletto Vernia, writing in the 1480s and 1490s found this solution incompatible with Aristotelian principles, but after some tergiversations concluded that it could only be understood by revelation and was beyond the sphere of the philosopher. His own successor Pomponazzi, in his *De immortalitate animae* of 1516, was equally concerned to defend the principles of natural philosophy, which he had refined by reading the ancient commentaries on Aristotle as well as Plato and Stoic writers, and on those grounds reverted to the materialistic interpretation of the Philosopher put forward by Blasius; but he asserted that only by revelation could the truth of the immortality of the soul be understood. The fideism of both Blasius of Parma and Pietro Pomponazzi seems to have represented their real view, in spite of modern suspicions that Pomponazzi at least merely pretended to disbelieve Aristotle; both philosophers satisfied the Church authorities who challenged their assertions. The real significance of the question lay in its gradually recognized insolubility in Aristotelian terms. The question could at least be formulated clearly in the language of the schools, to which platonic opponents of the Paduans like Marsilio Ficino did not contribute.

3. Nicholas of Cusa

It was characteristic of the age that one of its most original philosophers, Nicholas of Cusa (1401–64), developed his ideas neither in the course of university debate nor, like Ficino, in the subsidized calm of a Tuscan villa, but in the interstices of a life in the service of archbishops, cardinals and popes. In the course of a university education at Heidelberg, Padua (where he attained the degree of Doctor of Canon Law) and Cologne (1416–27), he became familiar with the philosophical issues debated in faculties of arts and theology, the Scotist notion of 'being' encompassing both Creator and creatures, the limits of possible worlds and their relation to the actual world, and the extent to which created minds could know God; and with terminist logic and mathematics and the measure languages associated with it. These were the issues which he strove to resolve in his own way in the many philosophical works, beginning with *De docta ignorantia* in 1440, which he produced until his death in 1464. But if the subjects of his thinking were those of the schools, his approach to them was Ciceronian, often employing the dialogue form; and his intended readership was the educated world in general rather than students in the schools. His open mind and broad interests were constantly stimulated by the books which he collected on every subject, many of which survive in the library of the hospital of St. Nicholas which he founded at Cues, and in other places. To the end of his life he continued to acquire and read new texts, notably Plato's *Par-*

menides, a copy of which, obtained about 1460, survives with his annotations. He had therefore the instincts of a scholar, and his developing thought must be followed in his annotations as much as in his circulated works. His broad interests stretched from the ecclesiological concerns which arose from his professional career and involvement in the Council of Basel to the nature of Islam and the place of the earth in a universe no longer conceived only in Ptolemaic terms. The philosophical ideas which he developed informed all these interests, but they seem to have been dormant before the climacteric of his intellectual life in 1437–38. Undoubtedly he had been influenced at Cologne by his master Heimeric de Campo, the leader of the Albertists and the chief purveyor of Parisian realist ideas there, and Heimeric may well have refined the questions to which he devoted his mind in his later years, though Nicholas must have encountered them in some form as an arts student. There is no real hint of them in his earlier ecclesiological work which culminated in his eirenic *De concordantia catholica* (1436); they arose from a sudden enlightenment "while I was at sea en route back from Greece; I was led by, as I believe, a heavenly gift from the Father of lights...to embrace in learned ignorance...incomprehensible things incomprehensibly".[9] As this incident inaugurated a new direction in Nicholas's thinking which proved to be permanent, it was probably more than a rhetorical device. But the language and imagery both of this passage and of *De docta ignorantia* in general look back to the mystical theology of Gerson, and to the great contemplative writers of the fourteenth century: to Meister Eckart, Henry Suso and Jan Ruysbroeck, whose spiritual experience had turned on the inward enlightenment of God upon minds swept clean of the feeble constructs of the human intellect; and of course to the pseudo-Dionysius, their guide, who would be Nicholas's constant inspiration.

The essential features of Nicholas of Cusa's developing philosophy from 1440 to his death in 1464 are perhaps best summed up in his *Trialogus de Possest* (1460). Its starting point was the question addressed by Henry of Ghent and Scotus: how is God known by men? Nicholas began conventionally enough with the words of St. Paul: *For the invisible things of him from the creation of the world are clearly seen, being understood by the things that are made*, which he glossed with the comment that the intellect "invisibly sees the invisible truth which is hidden behind the writing (of what it reads)".[10] The power of perception itself was derived from a higher power: it was a gift of God to human minds which were in a state of "necessary ignorance", a state following from the absolute disproportion of the infinity of God to the limited capacity of the human intellect. God, in the language of the schools, is absolute activity and absolute potentiality; in creatures, potentiality and actuality are distinct. As God contains in himself the absolute maximum of all qualities, he must reconcile opposites in himself (*coincidentia oppositorum*), a conclusion which he illustrated with the image of a spinning top: the faster it spins, the more it appears to be motionless, and a top which span at the absolute maximum velocity would not move at all. God even emcompasses non-being: "for since not-being

[9] *De docta ignorantia* (tr. J. Hopkins; Minneapolis: A. J. Banning Press 1981) 158.
[10] *Trialogus de Possest* (Hopkins, Introduction, 1986) 67–163; cf. 67.

is able to exist through the Almighty, assuredly it is actual, since absolute possibility is actual in the Almighty. For if some thing is able to be made from not-being by some power, assuredly this thing is enfolded within Infinite Power".[11] He is therefore "actualized possibility" or *posse est* (*possest*).

Like Eckhart, Nicholas was in danger in these conjectures of the accusation of pantheism, and an early opponent, Dr. Johannes Wenck of Heidelberg, was already so accusing him in his *De ignota litteratura* of 1441. It was an easy charge to make against this most boldly speculative of philosophers. Nicholas was no pantheist however: he remained firm in his principle that no proportionality could exist between God and creatures, the infinite and the finite.[12] Even the terms which are commonly used to characterize God, such as 'justice' or 'creator' are derived from human experience.[13] In considering the Scotist principle of individuation, how created things differed from one another, he asserted that creatures had individual substances. God was the essence of the respective essences of creatures: 'being' (*entitas*) but not 'beings' (*entes*). In his speculation on possible and actual existence, Nicholas' notion of concepts innate in the mind seems to have varied between rejection of the view that anything could be in the mind unless it derived from sensory experience, and an admission that there were mental constructs independent of such experience. Underlying his hesitation was the belief that no human mind could know the precise quiddity of any creature, though it could know creatures approximately through the medium of the senses and conceptual forms.

He did however make an exception of mathematical concepts, which he maintained were known precisely by the intellect independently of sensory perception, a line of reasoning which may been provoked by his reading of Ramon Lull / Raimundus Lullus (1235–1316).[14] Numbers, he was tempted to think, were images of the ideas of God, and he addressed his speculative mind particularly to the problem of squaring the circle. The perfection of numbers, and the approximation at best of actual physical objects to perfect geometrical shapes continued to exercise his imagination, and provoked much speculation not only on abstract mathematical themes but on the shape of the world and its position in a universe the nature of which was no longer satisfactorily explained either by Ptolemy or by Aristotle. The lack of exact proportions encountered in the problem of the circle was repeated in the empirical observation that the world was not perfectly spherical. Nor, he speculated, was the universe: the question of its finitude particularly exercised him. It could not be limited, by definition, by anything outside itself; nor could it as a created entity share the infinity of God. His somewhat provisional conclusion was that it had a definite magnitude, which God alone knew. He was more imaginative in his conjectures that the earth moved, though its motion was imperceptible, and that stars might be inhabited worlds of their own.[15] These

---

[11] Ibid. 93.
[12] *De docta ignorantia* (ed. Hopkins) ii.2.
[13] Hopkins, Introduction (1986) 19.
[14] *Trialogus de Possest* (Hopkins, Introduction, 1986) 43–44.
[15] *De docta ignorantia* (ed. Hopkins) ii.1, 11–12.

ideas, which were based on no elaborate calculations of his own, only looked forward to the astronomy of the following century insofar as he was willing to speculate beyond the bounds set by Aristotle and Ptolemy. Nicholas's cosmology, like his mathematics, had both the virtues and the drawbacks of his untrammelled speculative mind: it rode on flights of imagination which passed over established concepts of astronomy; by the same token, it could offer no probable reason for any particular idea.

The philosophical books of Nicholas of Cusa were soon printed.[16] They bestowed an authoritative variety of more or less neoplatonic ideas on minds predisposed by the contemplative literature of Northern Europe to absorb the notion of "learned ignorance". There is significantly little evidence however that any particular speculation of his had much influence on later thinkers. Developed in the agreeable atmosphere of the study and in the company of respectful friends, they had not been subjected to the healthy criticism of the schools. He did not expound either Aristotle or the Bible and probably had no profound knowledge of either. But his work represented the escape of philosophy into the hands of a wider readership influenced by contemplative writers to embrace an unformed Platonism.

4. Marsilio Ficino and Pico della Mirandola

In that broader milieu, the need for authoritative guidance in this general direction was widely recognized: it was at length supplied by a sound and accessible translation of Plato, undertaken at the behest of Cosimo de' Medici by the young scholar *Marsilio Ficino* (1433–99). Ficino had several qualifications for the task. Like Nicholas, he was steeped in the works of the pseudo-Dionysius, though in his case mediated by the Italian spirituality of the Camaldolese order and read together with Greek patristic writers, John Climacus and the Cappadocian fathers.[17] He also shared with the Cardinal a basic training in Aristotelian philosophy, and had read the *De Anima* and the *Metaphysics* in his youth.[18] The philosophical ideas he discerned in Plato and in neoplatonic writings were essentially religious: he saw Platonism as the *pia philosophia* which would refute the materialism and 'Averroism' of the Paduan Aristotelians. But unlike Nicholas he was a scholar by temperament, versed in Greek beyond any contemporary, and his greatest achievement was his Latin translation of the platonic corpus (1463–84) with his further rendering of neoplatonic writings and commentaries on Plato's most important dialogues. Ficino came

---

[16] At Strasbourg 1489, and by Lefèvre d'Etaples (Paris 1514).

[17] See D. F. LACKNER, "The Camaldolese Academy: Ambrosio Traversari, Marsilio Ficino and the Christian platonic tradition", in: Marsilio Ficino: his Theology, his Philosophy, his Legacy (2001) 15–44.

[18] See P. O. KRISTELLER, "The Scholastic Background of Marsilio Ficino", in: idem, Studies (1969) 46–47.

to see Plato as the vindicator of religious truth, whose work reflected an ancient wisdom going back to Mosaic times. He soon became aware of other apparent sources of "ancient theology": above all, the body of writings then attributed to Hermes Trismegistos, a collection of philosophical tracts and occult wisdom written in Egypt in the early Christian period, but believed by Ficino and his contemporaries to have originated long before. Their mixture of
platonic and gnostic elements served to confirm his belief that Plato had
merely transmitted a much older wisdom, a natural theology or *prisca theologia*, which was implanted as a seed in human consciousness at the creation.
With the further help of other apparent fragments of ancient wisdom such as
the orphic hymns (in reality a product of late Antiquity), Ficino created a framework for the history of philosophy: a group of sages, headed by Zoroaster,
taught ancient theology to worthy initiates, whence it was transmitted to
Pythagoras and Plato. While a few ancient writers, such as Heraclitus, Mani-
lius and Varro, had made some headway in the ascent to truth, only the revelation of Christian doctrine could complete the journey.

Though Ficino had enjoyed the patronage of the Medici, who provided him
with the leisure and means to complete his Latin Plato, he came to lecture regularly in the Studio Fiorentino and was prepared to defend his platonizing interpretation of the Christian religion against the Averroist or Aristotelian
school of thought dominant in the Italian universities, "the irreligious men
who divorce the study of philosophy from sacred religion".[19] The central question which occupied his attention was the doctrine of the immortality of the
soul, which the Paduans would only allow either as a single "world-soul" or
by divine revelation in defiance of Aristotelian reasoning. In his *Theologia Platonica* of 1474, Ficino did not engage with Gaetano da Thiene or any other
master of the school on their own logical terms, but proposed a series of arguments the basis of which is individual experience of the divine through contemplation: like the readers of Eckhart in Northern Europe, and independently of
his life's work on Plato, he was as an heir of Camaldolese spirituality under
the influence of the pseudo-Dionysius and his neoplatonist forbears. He proposed a new ontological hierarchy, ascending from body through quality,
soul, and angel to God; the inclusion of quality appears to be an idea original
to Ficino, but the general scheme is that of Proclus. On that basis he argued
that there were two opposing tendencies in the soul: one, to ascend towards
the light of God, was rooted in the soul's higher faculties, and the other, to
descend to the needs of the body, originated in its lower powers. It was characteristic of platonizing philosophies that Ficino did not easily incorporate into
his system a strong idea of human freedom or of the capacity to sin: the Ploti-
nian idea of the return of the soul to the One perhaps lent to his notion of the
soul an impersonal note. Though his view seems to have varied, he generally
explained the soul as an independent substance, following Plato's general line,
rather than as the form of the body. He was more open to criticism in his at-

---

[19] Ficino, *Theologia platonica de animorum immortalitate* (ed. and tr. Hankins / Allen; 2001-)
i.11; (ed. R. Marcel, 1–3; Paris: Société d'édition "belles lettres" 1964–70) i.36.

tempt to gloss Plato's supposed notion of the transmigration of souls from one body to another. This was an idea which Plotinus had understood Plato to hold, and Plotinus had been followed in this particular by Augustine and the generality of opinion in the west. Ficino attempted to show that Plato did not maintain that souls could migrate from body to body; for this, he was criticized himself, and had to endure the condemnation of the idea of transmigration by the Inquisition in 1490. Nevertheless his *Theologia Platonica* was immensely popular. It effectively brought to bear on the so-called Averroists the authority not only of Plato but of the less suspect contemplative writers of the past three centuries, buttressed by their inspirer, the platonizing pseudo-Dionysius.

Ficino's work of translation and interpretation brought Plato into the mainstream of philosophical debate, focussing attention on the idea of a *prisca theologia* taught not only by Plato but by his supposed predecessors, Zoroaster, Hermes and other ancient sages. The idea of a natural theology as he developed it would be potent into the eighteenth century, influencing for instance the missionary Jesuits' reaction to Confucius. More immediately, it provoked further attempts to achieve a concord between different religious traditions and philosophical schools of which the most far-reaching was that of *Pico della Mirandola* (1463–94). Ficino liked to regard Pico as his pupil and protagonist, but Pico, a youthful prodigy, was more eclectic, having attended lectures at Padua (1480) before coming to Ficino (1484–85) and studying afterwards in Paris (1485–86), as well as learning Hebrew and absorbing Jewish theology. His specific contribution to *prisca theologia* was knowledge of the writings of the Jewish Kabbalah, a body of mystical interpretations of the Scriptures which he saw as the key to ancient wisdom, but which in reality were written in stages from about 200 to 900 and were influenced, like the Hermetic corpus, by neo-Platonism. They therefore bore some resemblance to platonic doctrines as interpreted by Ficino. Pico's writings between 1486 and his early death in 1494 are only fragments of his project to create a more critical and more far-reaching concord of Plato, Aristotle and the Kabbalah. More aware than Ficino of the profound differences between the various schools of philosophy and theology, he proposed to isolate and debate them rather than attempt a false accord. To that end he planned to hold a series of disputations in Rome in 1487 on points at issue in developing his universal theology, summed up in 900 "theses" drawn from many theological traditions. The project ended in the wholesale condemnation of his theses by Innocent VIII (1487), and in a charge of heresy. His inaugural oration for the series, miscalled *De dignitate hominis*, sums up his approach. Like Ficino, he defended the interest of non-professionals in the truths of theology, and approached the subject as an ascent to truth of a generally platonic kind. But his notion of the metaphysical order allowed a much larger and more integral place for human free will. It was the prerogative of the individual to choose his place in the ontological hierarchy, living either like angels or like beasts; he was not subject to the ineluctable process of emanation and return to the One which seems to have attracted the older philosopher. Pico's emphasis on human free will showed how much he had absorbed from the theology schools of Padua and Paris; he had in particular learnt from Aquinas, whom together with other scholastic authors he defended against the critique of his contemporaries.[20]

After the fiasco of his Roman disputations, Pico settled down to work out the concord of the various natural theologies and philosophical schools step by step in a few highly original works. In his study of the first chapter of Genesis, his *Heptaplus* (1489), he interpreted the story of the creation as a coded cosmology which could be decrypted through the Kabbalah; in that light it could be seen as concordant with Aristotle and other ancient writers; man, created on the sixth day, was not only a microcosm of the universe but the object of creation itself.[21] Two years later he turned to the old problem of essence and existence in *De ente et uno*, a problem which had acquired a new character through Ficino's exposition of Plato and especially, perhaps, his recent translation of the Enneads of Plotinus. But Pico had moved away from Plotinus, and now intended to show that Plato was effectively in agreement with Aristotle. His understanding was once again Thomist: essence, or *esse ipsum*, he identified with the One, while distinguishing it from the existence of particular entities (*ens*).[22] Here and in other works, he took issue with Ficino in his interpretation of Plato, rejecting Ficino's neoplatonist exposition; for Pico, Aristotle's metaphysics were another witness to the *prisca theologia* whose nature he, like Ficino, constantly sought. Taken together, Pico's several treatises had the boldness and energy of a young mind; his great work of synthesis was never written. As they stand, they are witness to the transforming effect of reading Plato, and neoplatonic texts in various traditions such as the Kabbalah, on fifteenth-century intellectuals; but they also reveal the continuing power of ideas current in the theology schools of Paris and Padua to attract intelligent thinkers prepared to learn their specialist vocabulary.

The speculations of both Pico and Ficino were halted by the fall of the Medici in 1494 and by the brief but stormy predominance of the Dominican prophet *Girolamo Savonarola* (1452–98). Savonarola had a profound effect on the Florentine intellectual world: with a humanist education, a Thomist training in the schools of Bologna and a terrifying command of the art of penitential preaching, together with, as he claimed, a gift of prophecy, he seemed a source of purifying light to many intellectuals made expectant of a final revelation by the heady mixture of Plato, Hermes and the Kabbalah. Ficino himself was only, as he later claimed, "briefly deceived", but his disciples Giovanni Nesi and Girolamo Benivieni saw Savonarola as an embodiment of platonic wisdom. Pico had come under the influence of Savonarola in the last years of his life; the preacher had – in stark contradiction of Nesi's praise of him – discouraged the philosopher's residual Platonism and fostered his growing admiration for Aristotle and Aquinas. Savonarola was no fanatic: his gift of prophecy allowed him no specific vision of Florence's future and he did not embroider it

---

[20] Pico, *De dignitate hominis* (tr. L. Valcke / R. Galibois; in: *Le périple intellectuel*, 1994) 185–225.
[21] *Heptaplus* (ed. in: *Opera Omnia Johannis Pici Mirandulae;* Basel 1572; repr. Turin 1971) i.1–62, cf. 41.
[22] *De ente et uno* (tr. Valcke / Galibois; in: *Le périple intellectuel*, 1994) 273–316.

with the apocalyptic trappings of Joachim of Fiore or other systematic prophets. His *Compendium totius philosophiae*, written for the Dominican novices
about 1484, was a textbook comparable with those of Peter Tartaret or Thomas Bricot, repeating Thomist teaching much as Capreolus had in his Sentences commentary.[23] His *Trattato circa el reggimento e governo della città di
Firenze* was an equally Thomist tract, based on the *De regno* of St. Thomas
but within the long Florentine tradition of recognizing republican liberty.[24]
His four years of dominance showed both the power and the limitations of
philosophy in its impact on government and politics. In the long run it merely
confirmed what Pico's later work implied: platonic speculation and other ideas
could flourish in protected circumstances without the discipline of the strict logic still taught in universities, but it could only develop so far without confronting either its own logical inconsistencies or the brutal dialectic of events.

5. Summing up

In retrospect, the backbone of the study of philosophy between the last decades of the fourteenth century and the first of the sixteenth was still Aristotle's
scheme of education, on which all students of the Bible were nurtured. Paris,
together with Padua, Salamanca, Oxford and the German universities still
provided the critical sinews which had been hardened by the rules of fourteenth-century logic. Lectures on Scripture as much as on Aristotle were given
within the bounds set by the new logic. But many in the second half of the
fourteenth century had become more broadly aware of the world outside, and
the world before Christendom, and with this new perspective had come the desire to learn the languages which held the key to access to pagan, Hebrew and
early Christian writings. The works of Ramon Lull, written on the borders of
the Christian world with a solid knowledge of Islamic and Jewish theology,
began to be widely read, notably by Nicholas of Cusa. Greek texts in Latin
translation reached an even larger readership and brought a new critical approach to several books of the Bible, including the writings of St. Paul. They
appealed to an educated cadre, university graduates largely but often immersed in affairs or in a position to cultivate private scholarship, who had been
marked by the influence of the contemplative writers of the fourteenth century,
by Meister Eckhart or Walter Hilton in Northern Europe or by Catherine of
Siena in Italy – authors whose works had been circulated through Carthusian
or Camaldolese channels. For them the Greek and especially the Cappadocian
fathers, the works of Plato, and the corpus of neoplatonic writings whether
openly recognized like those of Plotinus and Iamblichus or disguised in a false
antiquity like the Hermetic or kabbalistic texts, could appear as a revelation of

---

[23] *Compendium totius philosophiae* (Venice 1542).
[24] The *Trattato* is ed. by L. FIRPO, in: *Savonarola: Opere: Prediche super Aggeo* (Rome: A. Belardetti 1965) 435–87. On Savonarola's ideas and their relation to those of Pico and Ficino see Weinstein, *Savonarola and Florence* (1970), esp. 185–226, and G. C. GARFAGNINI, "Savonarola tra Giovanni e Gianfrancesco Pico", in: *Pico della Mirandola: Convegno* (1997) 237–79.

truths familiar from, but half-hidden in modern contemplative writings in the tradition of the pseudo-Dionysius. Plato's appeal to the non-professional philosopher in the fifteenth-century educated world was not confined to Italian humanists. Only for those few, like Pico, strong-minded enough to absorb the logic and theology of the universities did the influence of Plato begin to pall. For them, the Aristotle long taught in the schools would ultimately have as much to offer at the end of the century as he had had at the beginning.

Chapter Six

The Institutional Framework of Theological Studies in the Late Middle Ages

By Ulrich Köpf, Tübingen

1. Theological Erudition and Education under the Predominance of Scholasticism

Sources: Chartularium Universitatis Parisiensis 1–4 (ed. H. Denifle / Ae. Chatelain; Paris 1889–97; quoted: CUP); *Les statuts et privilèges des universités françaises depuis leur fondation jusqu'en 1789* (ed. M. Fournier), 1. *Moyen-Âge* (Paris 1890); *Statuta antiqua Universitatis Oxoniensis* (ed. S. Gibson; Oxford 1931).

General studies (in chronological order): H. Denifle, *Die Entstehung der Universitäten des Mittelalters bis 1400* <I> (Berlin 1885; repr. Graz 1956); H. Rashdall, *The Universities of Europe in the Middle Ages* 1–3 (New edn. by F. M. Powicke / A. B. Emden; Oxford 1936; repr. Oxford 1988); P. Kibre, *The Nations in the Mediaeval Universities* (Mediaeval Academy of America, Publication 49; Cambridge, MA 1948); F. W. Oediger, *Über die Bildung der Geistlichen im späten Mittelalter* (STGMA 2; Leiden / Köln 1953); *Los monjes y los estudios. IV Semana de estudios monasticos Poblet 1961* (Poblet 1963); W. A. Hinnebusch, *The History of the Dominican Order* 1–2 (New York 1966/73); G. Leff, *Paris and Oxford Universities in the Thirteenth and Fourteenth Centuries* (New York / London / Sydney 1968); J. Moorman, *A History of the Franciscan Order from its Origins to the Year 1517* (Oxford 1968; repr. Chicago 1988); J. Verger, *Les universités au Moyen Age* (Collection SUP – L'historien 14; Paris 1973); *The Cultural Context of Medieval Learning* (ed. J. E. Murdoch / E. D. Sylla; Boston Studies in the Philosophy of Science 26; Dordrecht / Boston 1975); A. B. Cobban, *The Medieval Universities* (London 1975); K. Rückbrod, *Universität und Kollegium, Baugeschichte und Bautyp* (Darmstadt 1977); *Stadt und Universität im Mittelalter und in der frühen Neuzeit* (ed. E. Maschke / J. Sydow; Stadt in der Geschichte 3; Sigmaringen 1977); *The Universities in the Late Middle Ages* (ed. J. Ijsewijn / J. Paquet; Mediaevalia Lovaniensia 1,6 = Université Catholique de Louvain. Publications de l'Institut d'études médiévales 2,2; Louvain 1978); *Università e società nei secoli XII–XVI* (ed. Centro Italiano di Studi di Storia e d'Arte Pistoia; Nono Convegno Internazionale; Pistoia 1982); *The History of the University of Oxford* 1–8 (Gen. ed. T. H. Aston; Oxford 1984–2000), 1. *The Early Oxford Schools* (ed. J. I. Catto; 1984), 2. *Late Medieval Oxford* (ed. J. I. Catto / R. Evans; 1992); *Rebirth, Reform and Resilience. Universities in Transition 1300–1700* (ed. J. M. Kittelson / P. J. Transue; Columbus, OH 1984); *Schulen und Studium im sozialen Wandel des hohen und späten Mittelalters* (ed. J. Fried; Vorträge und Forschungen 30; Sigmaringen 1986); O. Weijers, *Terminologie des universités au XIIIe siècle* (Lessico Intellettuale Europeo 39; Roma 1987); W. J. Courtenay, *Schools and Scholars in Fourteenth-Century England* (Princeton, NJ 1987); idem, *Teaching Careers at the University of Paris in the thirteenth and fourteenth centuries* (Texts and Studies in the History of Mediaeval Education 8; Notre Dame, IN 1988); *A History of the University of Cambridge* 1–4 (Gen. ed. C. Brooke; Cambridge 1988–2004), 1. *The University to 1546* (ed. D. Riehl Leader; 1988); A. B. Cobban, *The Medieval English Universities: Oxford and Cambridge to c. 1500* (Aldershot 1988); M. Bellomo, *Saggio sull'università nell'età del diritto comune* (Roma 1992); *A History of the University in Europe* 1–4 (Gen. ed. W.

Rüegg; Cambridge 1992-), 1. *Universities in the Middle Ages* (ed. H. de Ridder-Symoens; 1992); *Stadt und Universität* (ed. H. Duchhardt; Städteforschung A/33; Köln e.a. 1993); *Die Universität in Alteuropa* (ed. A. Patschovsky / H. Rabe; Konstanzer Bibliothek 22; Konstanz 1994); *Gelehrte im Reich. Zur Sozial- und Wirkungsgeschichte akademischer Eliten des 14. bis 16. Jahrhunderts* (ed. R. C. Schwinges; Zeitschrift für historische Forschung. Beiheft 18; Berlin 1996); O. PEDERSEN, *The First Universities* (Cambridge 1997); *La storia delle università italiane: Archivi, fonti, indirizzi di ricerca* (Atti del Convegno Padova, 27–29 settembre 1994; Trieste 1997); J. VERGER, *Les gens de savoir dans l'Europe de la fin du Moyen Age* (Paris 1997); *Attempto – oder wie stiftet man eine Universität? Die Universitätsgründungen der sogenannten zweiten Gründungswelle im Vergleich* (ed. S. Lorenz; Contubernium 50; Stuttgart 1999); *Stätten des Geistes. Grosse Universitäten Europas von der Antike bis zur Gegenwart* (ed. A. Demandt; Köln / Weimar / Wien 1999); W. J. COURTENAY, *Parisian Scholars in the Early Fourteenth Century. A Social Portrait* (Cambridge 1999); *Learning Institutionalized. Teaching in the Medieval University* (ed. J. Van Engen; Notre Dame Conferences in Medieval Studies 9; Notre Dame, IN 2000); W. E. J. WEBER, *Geschichte der europäischen Universität* (Stuttgart 2002); L. PELLEGRINI, *L'incontro tra due "invenzioni" medievali: Università e Ordini Mendicanti* (Scienze storiche 13; Napoli 2003); *Stiftsschulen in der Region* (ed. S. Lorenz e.a.; Schriften zur südwestdeutschen Landeskunde 50; Ostfildern 2005); *Formation intellectuelle et culture du clergé dans les territoires angevins (milieu du XIIIe – fin du XVe siècle)* (ed. M.-M. de Cevins / J.-M. Matz; Collection de l'École française de Rome 349; Roma 2005).

Special abbreviation:
CUP = *Chartularium Universitatis Parisiensis* (see above).

The history of learning and education in the western Middle Ages was divided into two periods by the rise of universities. This new institution was destined to dominate the future. Of course, all universities differed more or less with regard to the local situation, the time and the circumstances of their beginning. But they had many common characteristics, too. First of all, the new institution was so successful as a place of studies and higher education that before long it replaced the different types of learning, by whose variety the twelfth century was distinguished. Monasteries and canons' houses, cathedral schools and schools of free teachers therefore did not disappear totally, but quickly lost their importance for the maintenance of erudition and higher education. Where they remained, they mainly served the purpose of providing students with elementary education, but as places of higher education they had only a limited area of influence. The higher education of *religiosi* and secular clergy was extensively integrated into the institution of the university, which brought about a high degree of standardization. Especially in theology the scholastic type of learning with its uniform methods, its homogeneous kinds of teaching and its stereotype literary forms resulting thereof was most successful. The former type of monastic theology gradually fell into decline, but survived in some monasteries and in the work of some scholastic theologians until its re-establishment in the fifteenth century.[1]

---

[1] U. KÖPF, "Monastische Theologie im 15. Jahrhundert", Rottenburger Jahrbuch für Kirchengeschichte 11 (1992) 117–35; idem, "Monastische und scholastische Theologie", in: *Bernhard von Clairvaux und der Beginn der Moderne* (ed. D. R. Bauer / G. Fuchs; Innsbruck 1995) 96–135; A. SIMÓN, "'Teología monástica': la recepción y el debate en torno a un concepto innovador", *Studia monastica* 44 (2002) 313–71; 45 (2003) 189–233.

1.1. The Institutional Character of the University

The scholastic institution appearing for the first time during the twelfth century at Bologna, about 1200 at Paris and some years later at Oxford was called *universitas* – a term which at the time generally meant a corporation, e.g., a company or guild, but also a community of religious persons.[2] Its character as an institution of education was expressed by additions to its name: The universities dominated by students, like the ones in Bologna and in other Italian cities, were called *universitas scholarium*, the ones directed by professors in Paris and Oxford *universitas magistrorum et scholarium.*[3] The formation of these corporations was accompanied by privileges written by temporal sovereigns and ecclesiastical authorities (popes, bishops): They guaranteed protection, liberation of secular and assignment to ecclesiastical jurisdiction, tax-exemption, and above all the privilege of teaching everywhere *(licentia ubique docendi).* The constitution of the universities was regulated by statutes. Their observance was guaranteed by oaths, which played a central part in the *universitas* as a sworn community *(coniuratio)*;[4] it can also be characterized as a kind of fraternity. Its internal unity was demonstrated by many symbolic acts and signs (common services, processions, other festive celebrations, graduations, robes, sceptres, seals etc.). On the other hand, for a long time universities did not possess their own buildings. Their educational work was performed in private rooms or in religious houses; festive acts (graduations included) were celebrated in the choir of churches.

The organizing structure of universities was based on two principles: according to the students' geographical origin, they were divided into nations *(nationes)*, according to the subjects of erudition in faculties *(facultates)*. At the top of the faculty was the dean *(decanus)*, at the top of the whole university the rector *(rector)*, who was a student at the student universities and a member of the council of teachers (mostly a member of the staff of the greatest faculty, the *facultas artium*) at the master-ruled universities. The chancellor (either the bishop himself or his representative) officiated as ecclesiastical supervisor over the correctness of the teaching. Whereas in Bologna (and, for a long time, in other Italian universities as well) at first only the *artes liberales* and both laws (canon and civil law) were taught, in Paris the first full university with four faculties came into being about 1200: with the faculty of arts, of theology, of medicine and of jurisprudence (which in Paris embraced only canon law). Most of the older universities were restricted to a part of the disciplines; theology was at first taught only in Paris, Oxford, Cambridge, Toulouse and at the universities of the Iberian peninsula. The old university of law at Bologna obtained a theological faculty not before 1364, other Italian universities even

---

[2] P. MICHAUD-QUANTIN, *Universitas. Expressions du mouvement communautaire dans le moyen âge latin* (Paris 1970); cf. C. WIELAND, "Universitas als Sodalitas", *Saec.* 47 (1996) 120–35.
[3] The manifold formulations are presented by Weijers, Terminologie (1987) 15–45.
[4] J. MIETHKE, "Der Eid an der mittelalterlichen Universität", in: *Glaube und Eid* (ed. P. Prodi; Schriften des Historischen Kollegs. Kolloquien 28; München 1993; 49–67).

later. Only the sovereign's foundations since the fourteenth century were from the outset full universities with all four faculties.

1.2. Rise and Development of the Universities

Especially among the older universities there were many different ways of coming into being and growing; nevertheless, according to their origins, we can distinguish roughly between two types: 1. Universities spontaneously grown, and 2. Universities founded.

1.2.1. Universities Spontaneously Grown

The first universities came into existence by spontaneous fusion of already existing particular schools to a *studium generale*,[5] mostly caused by extern motives (e.g., the wish for protection from infringements of a city's population). Thus a bloody conflict between students and citizens of Paris induced the masters and students of different Paris schools to join into a *universitas magistrorum et scholarium*, which obtained a privilege by the French king Philippe II Augustus that became effective in 1200.[6] In 1215 the first preserved statutes of Robert de Courçon were confirmed by Pope Innocent III.[7] In Oxford, where a see was erected not before 1542, at the beginnings of the thirteenth century the existing schools for *artes liberales*, jurisprudence and theology conjoined as a university, into which the office of the chancellor – differing from Paris – was integrated early and by this means was withdrawn from the influence of the proper Bishop of Lincoln.[8] It is impossible to give exact dates of the foundations of these universities, which spontaneously came into existence; we are accustomed to use the dates of their earliest privileges and statutes.

Some new universities were the result of a spontaneous separation from an existing university. After a conflict with the township in 1209 most masters and students left Oxford university; a part of them founded the new university of Cambridge, which was consolidated about 1225.[9] The Padova university originated in 1222[10] as a descendant of Bologna,[11] and the Angers and Toulouse universities in one way or the other were the result of the Paris university strike in 1229.[12] In 1409 in Prague disagreements about the Great Schism[13] and a change of the proportion of votes by king

---

[5] Cf. Weijers, Terminologie (1987) 34–45; P. Nardi, "Le origini del concetto di 'Studium Generale'", *Rivista internazionale di diritto comune* 3 (1992) 47–78.

[6] CUP 1, 59–61, no. 1.

[7] CUP 1, 78–80, no. 20. For the growing and formation of the University of Paris cf. S. C. Ferruolo, *The Origins of the University. The Schools of Paris and their Critics* (Stanford 1985), esp. 279–315.

[8] R. W. Southern, "From Schools to University", in: History of the University of Oxford 1 (1984) 1–36; M. B. Hackett, "The University as a Corporate Body", ibid. 37–95.

[9] Rashdall, Universities 3 (1936) 33f, 276–78; Riehl Leader, Cambridge 1 (1988) 16–34.

[10] Rashdall, Universities 2 (1936) 10f; G. Arnaldi, "Le origini dello Studio di Padova. Dalla migrazione universitaria del 1222 alla fine del periodo Ezzeliniano", *La Cultura* 15 (1977) 388–431; N. G. Siraisi, *Arts and Sciences at Padua: The "Studium" of Padua before 1350* (Toronto 1973).

[11] Cf. the list of Secessions from Bologna given by Rashdall, Universities 1 (1936) 589.

[12] Cf. ibid. 2 (1936) 151–53, 161–65.

[13] Different political opinions between the rival obediences during the Schism from 1378 unto 1418 were also a cause for founding new universities. Cf. R. N. Swanson, *Universities, Academics*

Wenceslas (Václav)[14] in favour of the Bohemian nation caused the great majority of the foreign masters and students to emigrate – the Germans mainly[15] to the margravate Meissen, where they soon founded a new university at Leipzig, supported by both the city and the sovereign.[16]

1.2.2. Universities Founded

Another type of university dominating in the later Middle Ages was brought forth by the formal act of foundation by an authority – secular (sovereign, city) or ecclesiastical (pope, bishop). Some of the older foundations cannot be dated precisely; for in founded universities, too, existing schools were often integrated.[17] The first examples of a foundation by a sovereign are Salamanca, erected in 1218 by Alfonso IX of León (and refounded by Fernando III of Castilia in 1243),[18] and Napoli, founded in 1224 by the emperor Frederick II.[19] Further universities followed in France, Italy and on the Iberian peninsula.[20] The main intention of the founders was to guarantee a university training of future clergymen, lawyers and other officials for their territory. This intention is especially proved by foundations which are competing with existing universities (e. g., Vienna versus Prague). Hence, they were usually founded with all four faculties. Perhaps the first foundation by a papal Bull (by Gregory IX) was Toulouse in 1229/33, endowed with all four faculties.[21] Innocent IV founded the university of the Roman Court (Studium curiae Romanae) in

---

and the Great Schism (Cambridge studies in medieval life and thought III 12; Cambridge e.a. 1979).

[14] The Kuttenberg Decree from 18.1.1409 promised to the Bohemian nation three votes, to the 'German' nation (i. e., the hitherto separately voting Bavarian, Saxonian and Polish nations) only one.

[15] Cf. F. Šmahel, "The Kuttenberg Decree and the withdrawal of the German students from Prague in 1409: a discussion", History of Universities 4 (1984) 153–66.

[16] S. Hoyer, "Die Gründung der Leipziger Universität und Probleme ihrer Frühgeschichte", in: Karl-Marx-Universität Leipzig 1409–1959 1 (Leipzig 1959) 1–32.

[17] Cf. Stiftsschulen in der Region (2005). An important example is Erfurt: G. C. Boyce, "Erfurt schools and scholars in the thirteenth century", Spec. 24 (1949) 1–18; E. Kleineidam, Universitas Studii Erffordensis 1 (Erfurter Theologische Studien 14; Leipzig ²1985); S. Lorenz, Studium generale Erfordense (MGMA 34; Stuttgart 1989); idem, "'Studium generale Erfordense': Neue Forschungen zum Erfurter Schulleben", Traditio 46 (1991) 261–89; idem, "Das Erfurter 'Studium generale artium' – Deutschlands älteste Hochschule", in: Erfurt 742–1992 (ed. U. Weiß; Weimar 1992) 123–34; idem, "Erfurt – die älteste Hochschule Mitteleuropas?", in: Aspekte thüringisch-hessischer Geschichte (ed. M. Gockel; Marburg/L. 1992) 139–46.

[18] Rashdall, Universities 2 (1936) 74–90. It is doubtful whether the studium of Palencia, founded 1208/09 by King Alfonso VIII of Castilia, had the character of a university (cf. Rashdall, ibid. 65–69).

[19] F. Torraca, "Le origini. L'età sveva", in: Storia della Università di Napoli (Napoli 1924) 1–16.

[20] The (until 1911) sole university of Portugal was founded in 1288/90 by King Dinis at Lisbon and transferred in 1308 to Coimbra. In the time to come its site again and again changed between the two cities. Cf. Rashdall, ibid. 2, 108–14; M. A. Rodrigues, Chronologia Historiae Vniversitatis Conimbrigensis (Coimbra 1998).

[21] Rashdall, ibid. 2, 161–66.

1244/45,[22] which perhaps was the same as the University of Rome *(Studium urbis)*.[23]

Whereas in the last two centuries of the Middle Ages in France, Castilia-Aragon and the small states of Northern and Middle Italy the number of new foundations gradually grew,[24] in the Holy Roman Empire universities were founded not before the middle of the fourteenth century.[25] The first of them was the Prague university established in 1348 by Emperor Charles IV,[26] which was followed by Vienna (1365) and Heidelberg (1386), by the municipal foundations of Cologne (1388) and Erfurt (1392) and again by the princely foundations of Rostock (1419), Dole (1423) and Louvain (1425). After the middle of the fifteenth century a second great wave of foundations started: Greifswald (1456), Freiburg im Breisgau (1457), Basel (1459), Ingolstadt (1472), Trier (1473), Mainz (1477), Tübingen (1477), Wittenberg (1502) and Frankfurt/Oder (1506).[27] In the second half of the fourteenth century the basic idea of the university also spread to territories in Eastern and Northern Europe: Poland got its first university in Cracow (1364), Hungary in Pécs (Fünfkirchen; 1367), followed by Buda (1389/95), Scotland in St. Andrews (1411), followed by Glasgow (1451), and Scandinavia in Copenhagen (1475/78) and Uppsala (1477). Some of the late mediaeval foundations (especially in Italy) were only a revival of older *studia generalia*, others (e. g., Cracow or Ferrara) came to an end after a few years already and were only later on reactivated for a longer time. In England the monopoly of Oxford and Cambridge prevented new foundations until modern times. At the end of the fifteenth century more than 70 universities of very different structure, size and importance existed.

1.3. The collegia

General studies (in chronological order): Rashdall, Universities 1–3 (1936) passim; A. L. GABRIEL, *The College System in the fourteenth-century Universities* (Baltimore, MD s.a. [1962]); A. SEIFERT, "Die Universitätskollegien – eine historisch-typologische Übersicht", in: *Stiftungen aus Vergangenheit und Gegenwart* [2] (ed. F. Rüth / R. Hauer / W. Frhr. v. Pölnitz-Egloffstein; Lebensbilder deutscher Stiftungen 3; Tübingen 1974) 355–78; idem, "Sozialgeschichtliche Aspekte spätmittelalterlicher Studentenbursen in Deutschland", in: Schulen und Studium (1986) 527–64; *I Collegi universitari in Europa tra il XIV e il XVIII secolo* (ed. D. Maffei / H. de Ridder-Symoens; Milano 1991); *Vocabulaire des collèges universitaires (XIIIᵉ–XVIᵉ siècles)* (ed. O. Weijers; Turnhout 1993).

Among the buildings erected for the university were foremost the lodging and boarding houses for poor students. In Paris the existence of a *domus pauperum*

---

[22] Rashdall, ibid. 2, 28–31; R. CREYTENS, "Le 'Studium Romanae Curiae' et le maître du sacré palais", *AFP* 12 (1942) 5–83.

[23] According to G. ADORNI, "L'Università di Roma e i suoi archivi", in: *La storia delle università italiane* (1997) 109–31.

[24] For Italy cf. the survey of 'the second wave' in P. F. GRENDLER, *The Universities of the Italian Renaissance* (Baltimore / London 2002) 70–108: Pisa (1343), Florence (1348), Pavia (1361), Torino (1411/13), Ferrara (1442), Catania (1445).

[25] G. KAUFMANN, *Geschichte der deutschen Universitäten* 1–2 (Stuttgart 1888/96; repr. 1958); Rashdall, Universities 2 (1936) 211–88; *Universitäten und Hochschulen in Deutschland, Österreich und der Schweiz* (ed. L. Boehm / R. A. Müller; Düsseldorf / Wien 1983); F. REXROTH, *Deutsche Universitätsstiftungen von Prag bis Köln* (Beiheft zum AKuG 34; Köln / Weimar / Wien 1992).

[26] P. MORAW, "Die Universität Prag im Mittelalter", in: *Die Universität zu Prag* (Schriften der Sudetendeutschen Akademie der Wissenschaften und Künste 7; München 1986) 9–134; *A History of Charles University* (Gen. ed. F. Kavka / J. Petráň), 1. *1348–1802* (ed. I. Čornejová / M. Svatoš; Prague 2001).

[27] Attempto (1999).

scolarium S. Thome martyris is verified in 1210.[28] In the second half of the thirteenth century both in Paris and in Oxford the ambiguous term *collegium*[29]
came into use. Robert de Sorbon (1201–74), chaplain of King Louis IX, the
Saint, created in 1257 for poor *magistri artium*, who were studying theology
while teaching in the faculty of arts, a *collegium pauperum magistrorum Parisius
studentium in theologica facultate*[30] etc. Here as in other cases *collegia* were
houses for *clerici saeculares*.

With respect to the *religiosi*,[31] the word *collegium* initially merely meant *conventus*.[32] The Benedictine Cluniac monasteries, the Cistercian and Premonstrate orders as well as the mendicant orders, which came into existence in the thirteenth century, and other religious communities had
houses in the university cities at their disposal, where their teaching and studying members lived.[33]
What in historical literature is called "Collège S. Bernard", "Collège de Cluny" or the like, in the
sources is simply called *domus, locus, conventus* or *studium*.[34] Only much later the word *collegium*
was applied to those houses, too. Further names were *bursa, contubernium, hospicium*, and others.[35]

All these houses which at first were established for the dwelling and boarding of students and
masters soon turned into sites of teaching for the diverse communities. Since the university itself
did not possess buildings of its own, many lectures were given in the large rooms of the *collegia*,
the *bursae* and the religious houses. This corresponded to the desire of the communities for their
own study places (cf. below 1.5).

During the Middle Ages a large number of *collegia* came into existence at
the various universities in very different forms, for different groups, and was
organized in different ways. It contributed to their variety that they were without exception charitable foundations of quite different size and financial endowment. Originally founded for poor students and masters, in the fourteenth
and fifteenth centuries they increasingly admitted noble and rich students, too.

---

[28] CUP 1, 69, no. 10.
[29] O. WEIJERS, "Collège, une institution avant la lettre", *Vivarium* 21 (1983) 73–82; eadem,
Terminologie (1987) 70–75, 80–84.
[30] P. GLORIEUX, *Aux origines de la Sorbonne* 1. *Robert de Sorbon* (EPhM 53; Paris 1966); 2. *Le
Cartulaire* (EPhM 54; Paris 1965); the quotation: 2, 265 no. 235.
[31] Alexander IV calls the growing group of mendicants in 1256 a *regulare collegium* (CUP 1,
344 no. 296).
[32] A letter of the Paris university after having mentioned *diversarum religionum vj collegia* [i.e.,
conventus] (CUP 1, 253 no. 230) decides that *nullus regularium conventus in collegio* [i.e., *in universitate*] *nostro duas simul sollempnes cathedras habere valeat actu regentium magistrorum* (ibid. 254).
[33] For the monks cf. e.g., Los monjes y los estudios (1963); C. H. LAWRENCE, "Stephen of Lexington and Cistercian University Studies in the Thirteenth Century", *JEH* 11 (1960) 164–78; C. H.
TALBOT, "The English Cistercians and the Universities", *Studia Monastica* 4 (1962) 197–220; L. J.
LEKAI, "Introduction à l'étude des collèges cisterciens en France avant la Révolution", *ACi* 25
(1969) 145–79; J. E. SULLIVAN, 'Studia monastica': Benedictine and Cluniac Monks at the University
of Paris, 1229–1500 (Diss. University of Wisconsin; Madison 1982); R. SCHNEIDER, "Studium und
Zisterzienserorden", in: Schulen und Studium (1986) 321–50; T. SULLIVAN, "Benedictine Masters
of the University of Paris in the Late Middle Ages. Patterns of Recruitment", *Vivarium* 31 (1993)
226–40; for the Regular Canons: J. J. JOHN, "The College of Prémontré in mediaeval Paris", *Analecta Praemonstratensia* 28 (1952) 137–71; 30 (1954) 161–77; S. FORDE, "The Educational Organization of the Augustinian Canons in England and Wales, and their University Life at Oxford",
1325–1448, History of Universities 13 (1994) 21–60; for all the *religiosi*: L. BOEHM, "Papst Benedikt XII. (1334–1342) als Förderer der Ordensstudien. Restaurator – Reformator – oder Deforma-
tor regularer Lebensform?", in: *Secundum Regulam vivere* (ed. G. Melville; Windberg 1978) 281–
310.
[34] Weijers, Collège (cf. n. 29) 78f; eadem, Terminologie (1987) 84.
[35] Weijers, Terminologie (1987) 76–78, 85f, 93–99.

The *Collegium Carolinum* at Prague, in 1366 founded by Emperor Charles IV for twelve masters, gave a pattern for the German *collegia* "in being intended from the first as colleges for teachers, and only secondarily (if at all) for students".[36] The relation between students' houses and the university as a whole differed likewise. Whereas in Paris and on the Continent the *collegia* generally were more or less associated with, or incorporated into, a university, the *colleges* and *halls*[37] in Oxford and Cambridge were independent from the university's organs.[38]

1.4. The Position of the Theological Faculty within the University[39]

For master-ruled universities the statutes, organization and curricula of the university of Paris were exemplary from the beginning. This concerns especially the faculty of theology and its cooperation with the faculty of arts. In the course of the twelfth century Paris already had developed into the most important school site for occidental theologians. The theological faculty of the university maintained this central position until the end of the Middle Ages. The connection with the Church – represented by the bishop or the chancellor – was of momentous significance for its importance.[40] The Roman *curia* controlled and supported the Paris faculty to such a degree, that in a way Paris became the doctrinal authority of Western Christianity. Oxford, on the contrary, was not a see during the Middle Ages; neither the proper bishop of Lincoln nor the pope were able to influence the initial development here to the

---

[36] Rashdall, Universities 2 (1936) 221; about Prague as model for the German universities cf. F. Seibt, "Von Prag bis Rostock", in: *Festschrift für Walter Schlesinger* 1 (ed. H. Beumann; Köln / Wien 1973) 406–26; repr. in: idem, *Mittelalter und Gegenwart* (ed. W. Eberhard / H.-D. Heimann; Sigmaringen 1987) 197–217, about the *Collegium Carolinum* 423–25.

[37] The *colleges* originally were destinated for graduates, the *halls* for undergraduates. Cf. W. A. Pantin, "The Halls and Schools of Medieval Oxford: An Attempt at Reconstruction", in: *Oxford Studies presented to Daniel Callus* (Oxford Historical Society. NS 16; Oxford 1964) 31–100.

[38] Rashdall, Universities 3 (1936) 169–235, 293–324; "The Colleges and Halls", in: *The Victoria History of the County of Oxford 3. The University of Oxford* (ed. H. E. Salter / M. D. Lobel; The Victoria History of the Counties of England [29:] Oxfordshire; Oxford 1954) 61–354; R. L. Highfield, "The Early Colleges", in: History of the University of Oxford 1 (1984) 225–63; T. H. Aston / R. Faith, "The Endowments of the University and Colleges to *circa* 1348", ibid. 265–309; T. H. Aston, "The External Administration and Ressources of Merton College to *circa* 1348", ibid. 311–68; Riehl Leader, Cambridge 1 (1988) 58–88; Cobban, English Universities (1988) 111–60; cf. J. Twigg, "Evolution, Obstacles and Aims: the Writing of Oxford and Cambridge College Histories", History of Universities 8 (1989) 179–99.

[39] Survey: M. Asztalos, "The Faculty of Theology", in: History of the University 1 (1992) 409–41.

[40] For the relations between universities and ecclesiastical authorities cf. W. J. Courtenay, "Inquiry and Inquisition: Academic Freedom in Medieval Universities", *CH* 58 (1989) 168–81; J. Miethke, "Gelehrte Ketzerei und kirchliche Disziplinierung", in: *Recht und Verfassung im Übergang vom Mittelalter zur Neuzeit* 2 (ed. H. Boockmann / L. Grenzmann / B. Moeller / M. Staehelin; Göttingen 2001) 9–45; U. Köpf, "Theologie und Kirchenleitung von der Alten Kirche zum Mittelalter. Einleitende Bemerkungen", in: *Wissenschaftliche Theologie und Kirchenleitung* (ed. U. Köpf; Tübingen 2001) 1–27; idem, "Die Ausübung kirchlicher Lehrgewalt im 13. und frühen 14. Jahrhundert", in: *Gewalt und ihre Legitimation im Mittelalter* (ed. G. Mensching; Contradictio 1; Würzburg 2003) 138–55.

same degree as they did in Paris. For this reason the theological faculty as well as the university in general could develop much more independently. Thereby Oxford university became the pioneer of the complete reception of Aristotle in the first half of the thirteenth century. For a long time, however, close connections existed between the two theological faculties of Paris and Oxford, brought forth especially by Englishmen studying and teaching at Paris. Apart from Paris and the two English universities until the middle of the fourteenth century only the pontificial foundation Toulouse and the universities of the Iberian peninsula had the right to give theological degrees. Only during the last one and a half centuries of the Middle Ages some older and many newly founded universities gained limited importance for the development of theology. Due to the establishment of a theological faculty at the university of Prague (founded in 1348) the former predominance of Paris and Oxford theologians came to an end. After the middle of the fourteenth century theological faculties were established at many older universities, especially in Italy.[41] But by that time the gaps existing so long in Italy already had been filled by the mendicants' *studia* – they, too, being of geographically limited importance.

1.5. The studia *of the Mendicants*

General studies (in chronological order): D. BERG, *Armut und Wissenschaft. Beiträge zur Geschichte des Studienwesens der Bettelorden im 13. Jahrhundert* (GuG 15; Düsseldorf 1977); *Le scuole degli ordini mendicanti (secoli XIII-XIV)* (Convegni del Centro di Studi sulla spiritualità medievale 17; Todi 1978); G. BARONE, "Università e scuole degli ordini mendicanti: Parigi alla metà del XIII secolo", in: idem e.a., *Il concetto di "sapientia" in San Bonaventura e San Tommaso* (Palermo 1983) 1–11; K. ELM, "Mendikantenstudium, Laienbildung und Klerikerschulung im spätmittelalterlichen Westfalen", in: *Studien zum städtischen Bildungswesen des späten Mittelalters und der frühen Neuzeit* (ed. B. Moeller / H. Patze / K. Stackmann; AAWG.PH 3. Folge, 137; Göttingen 1983) 586–617; Courtenay, Schools and Scholars (1987), esp. 56–117; I. W. FRANK, *Die Bettelordensstudia im Gefüge des spätmittelalterlichen Universitätswesens* (Institut für europäische Geschichte Mainz. Vorträge 83; Stuttgart 1988); K. ELM, "Studien und Studienwesen der Bettelorden", in: Stätten des Geistes (1999) 111–26; *Le vocabulaire des écoles des Mendiants au moyen âge. Actes du colloque Porto (Portugal) 11–12 octobre 1996* (ed. M. C. Pacheco; Études sur le vocabulaire intellectuel du moyen âge 9; Turnhout 1999); *Studio et studia: le scuole degli ordini mendicanti tra XIII e XIV secolo* (Atti dei Convegni della Società internazionale di studi francescani e del Centro interuniversitario di studi francescani 29 = NS 12; Spoleto 2002).

By the rise of the mendicant orders in the thirteenth century a third group of persons was added to the secular clergy and the older monks.

The mendicants had a particular suitability for academic work due to their mobility, their preference for cities, their duties as preachers, pastors, persecutors of heretics etc. The *Ordo praedicatorum* of the Dominicans, at first a community of Augustinian Canons, which was admitted as an order in 1216, became a main representative of university scholasticism.[42] It soon was followed by

---

[41] In Bologna 1364: F. EHRLE, *I più antichi statuti della Facoltà teologica dell' Università di Bologna* (Universitatis Bononiensis Monumenta 1; Bologna 1932).

[42] A. DUVAL, "L'étude dans la législation religieuse de saint Dominique", in: *Mélanges offerts à M.-D. Chenu* (BiblThom 37; Paris 1967); I. W. FRANK, "Die Spannung zwischen Ordensleben und wissenschaftlicher Arbeit im frühen Dominikanerorden", *AKuG* 49 (1967) 164–207; idem, *Hausstudium und Universitätsstudium der Wiener Dominikaner bis 1500* (AÖG 127; Wien 1968); L. GAR-

the *Ordo fratrum minorum* of the Franciscans inspired by Francis of Assisi, whose rule was approved 1223 by Pope Honorius III,[43] by the Order of the Hermits of St. Augustine in 1256,[44] the Order of the Carmelites, which was definitively authorized in 1286,[45] and the Servites acknowledged as a mendicant order in 1304 by Pope Benedict XI.[46]

All these and other orders created proper institutions of studies, which had very much in common. The basic idea, which was especially observed by the Dominican order, was that each *conventus* should have its own study *(studium particulare)* including a *doctor (lector)*. The education of these masters was carried out methodically at the *studia generalia* of the provinces. The *studia generalia* of the orders in Paris had a central function within this educational system and were favoured by the popes. They inevitably developed close relations to Paris university. At first, the secular clergy predominating at the university tried to impede the newly appearing rivals. The mendicant struggle from 1252 to 1257 was settled by the fact, that Paris university acknowledged the activities of the mendicant orders and admitted the friars as *magistri* to its staff – without hurting the autonomy of the proper mendicant studies, which were independent outside of university cities, anyway. The English Carmelites even avoided establishing their *studium generale* in Oxford or Cambridge and pre-

---

GAN, *Lo studio teologico e la biblioteca dei Domenicani a Padova nel tre e quattrocento* (Contributi alla storia dell'Università di Padova 6; Padova 1971); Hinnebusch, Dominican Order 2 (1973), esp. chaps. 1–3; J.-P. RENARD, *La formation et la désignation des prédicateurs au début de l'Ordre des Prêcheurs (1215–1237)* (Diss. Fribourg/Suisse 1977); M. O'CARROLL, "The educational organisation of the Dominicans in England and Wales 1221–1348: a multidisciplinary approach", *AFP* 50 (1980) 23–62; M. M. MULCHAHEY, "The Dominican *studium* system and the universities of Europe in the thirteenth century", in: *Manuels, programmes de cours et techniques d'enseignement dans les universités médiévales* (Ed. J. Hamesse; PIEM 16; Louvain-la-neuve 1994); eadem, *"First the Bow is Bent in Study...". Dominican Education before 1350* (STPIMS 132; Toronto 1998); eadem, "Societas studii: Dominic's conception of pastoral care as collaborative study and teaching", in: *Domenico di Caleruega e la nascità dell' Ordine dei Frati Predicatori. Atti del XLI Convegno storico internazionale Todi, 10–12 ottobre 2004* (Atti dei Convegni del Centro italiano di studi sul basso medioevo. NS 18; Spoleto 2005) 441–65.
    [43] H. FELDER, *Geschichte der wissenschaftlichen Studien im Franziskanerorden um die Mitte des 13. Jahrhunderts* (Freiburg 1904); L. DI FONZO, "Studi, studenti e maestri nell'Ordine dei francescani conventuali dal 1223 al 1517", *MF* 44 (1944) 167–95; Moorman, Franciscan Order (1968), esp. chaps. 13, 28, 40; D. BERG, "Das Studienproblem im Spiegel der franziskanischen Historiographie des 13. und beginnenden 14. Jahrhunderts", *Wissenschaft und Weisheit* 42 (1979) 11–33, 106–56; P. IANNELLI, *Lo Studio Teologico OFMConv nel San Lorenzo Maggiore di Napoli* (I Maestri francescani 3; Roma 1994); B. ROEST, *A History of Franciscan Education (c. 1210–1517)* (Education and Society in the Middle Ages and Renaissance 11; Leiden e.a. 2000).
    [44] E. YPMA, *La formation des professeurs chez les Ermites de Saint-Augustin de 1256 à 1354* (Paris 1956); D. GUTIÉRREZ, "Los estudios en la Orden Agustiniana desde la edad media hasta la contemporánea", *AAug* 33 (1970) 75–149; idem, *Los Agustinos en la edad media 1357–1517* (Historia de la Orden de San Agustin I/2; Roma 1977) 141–76; idem, *Los Agustinos en la edad media* (Historia de la Orden de San Agustin I/1; Roma 1980) 166–99.
    [45] B. F. M. XIBERTA, "De institutis ordinis Carmelitarum quae ad doctrinas philosophorum et theologorum sequendas pertinent", Analecta Ordinis Carmelitarum 6 (1927[-29]) 337–79; B.-M. de la Croix, "Les Carmes aux Universités du Moyen âge", *Études Carmélitaines* 17/1 (1932) 82–112; H. G. J. LANSINK, *Studie en Onderwijs in de Nederduitse Provincie van de Karmelieten gedurende de Middeleeuwen* (Nijmegen 1967); F.-B. LICKTEIG, *The German Carmelites at the Medieval Universities* (Textus et studia historica Carmelitana 13; Roma 1981).
    [46] A.-M. ROSSI, "Prospectus Historicus Studiorum in Ordine Servorum B. Mariae Virginis", *Studi storici dell'Ordine dei Servi di Maria* 16 (1966) 153–71.

ferred London as the site of their studies.[47] Even before the foundation of universities in Central Europe, in many places there existed important *studia generalia* of the mendicants, some of which had received the pontifical privilege of graduation. In the early fourteenth century the Franciscans held about 30, the Dominicans and the Augustine Friars both about 20, and the Carmelites about 16 *studia generalia* across Europe.[48] Along with the foundation of universities these *studia* were integrated into the new institution; theological faculties often resulted from a fusion of existing mendicant *studia*.[49] They could as well be created by *religiosi*, who came from different places.[50] In such cases the secular clergy was of minor importance within the theological faculty. In other places according to the Paris model the mendicant *studia generalia* were incorporated into the new university. Thereby the support of a professor's chair was guaranteed without financial burden for the founder. Because the mediaeval universities as a rule did not possess any buildings, the mendicant's houses generally played an important part within the organizational framework of universities.[51] The education of mendicants in the *artes*, however, was usually reserved to their own *studia*. In this case, their proper studies and degrees in the *artes* were acknowledged as a premise for studying theology at a university. This arrangement did not clash with the fact that friars studying theology often had to teach at the faculty of *artes* (like, e.g., the Augustine Friars in Wittenberg).

1.6. The Organization of Theological Studies

For the organization of theological studies and the career of theologians the pattern, which was developed in Paris in the first half of the thirteenth century, remained a standard until the Reformation.[52] The aim of university studies always was the graduation conferring the *licentia (ubique) docendi*. Studying theology did not necessarily lead to an ecclesiastical office; the layman became a priest not by study, but by ordination. Studying theology, however, was useful and even necessary for all those, who aspired, or were destined, to

---

[47] Lickteig, German Carmelites (1981) 25f, 29, 79f.

[48] P. AMARGIER / M. D'ALATRI / C. RIBAUCOURT / J. CANNON / J. KŁOCZOWSKI, "Panorama geografico, cronologico e statistico sulla distribuzione degli *studia* degli ordini mendicanti", in: Le scuole (1978) 33–149.

[49] For the beginnings cf., e.g., A. G. LITTLE, "The Friars and the foundation of the Faculty of Theology in the University of Cambridge", in: *Mélanges Mandonnet* 2 (BiblThom 14; Paris 1930) 389–401. – In 1363 the theological faculty of the university of Padova was established by association of the four existing mendicant studies of the Domenicans, Franciscans, Augustinian Friars and Carmelites (cf. G. BROTTO / G. ZONTA, *La facoltà teologica dell'Università di Padova* 1. secoli XIV e XV [Padova 1922]).

[50] One Dominican Friar, three Franciscan Friars, two Carmelites, two Augustinian Friars and a Cluniacense monk took part in establishing the theological faculty of Bologna in 1364 (Ehrle, I più antichi statuti [n. 41 above] 5f).

[51] Cf., e.g., the contract between the university of Tübingen and the Augustinian Friars for using a room in the Friars monastery as *lectorium theologorum ipsius facultatis*, cf. *Urkunden zur Geschichte der Universität Tübingen aus den Jahren 1476–1550* (ed. R. v. Roth; Tübingen 1877, repr. 1973) 80–82.

[52] For more information and special literature see U. KÖPF, HBOT I/2, Ch. 27, esp. 170–79.

become ecclesiastical teachers – especially as members of the higher clergy or as preachers.

The condition for being admitted to studies at the faculty of theology were previous studies of the *artes* finished with the degree of a *magister*, which friars often obtained at their own *studia*. While the *magister artium* was still teaching for some years at the faculty of arts, he already was studying at the faculty of theology. After some years as participant of theological lectures, disputations and exercises he was graduated *baccalarius*[53] *biblicus*. Now, for one or two years he had to interpret one book of the Old and one of the New Testament *cursorie* (i.e., successively and hastily, without discussion of single, difficult questions; hence the title *cursor*). After this, he had to give lectures on the sentences as *baccalarius sententiarius* for one or two years, i.e., he had to comment on the four books *Sententiae* of Petrus Lombardus, the dogmatic text-book of the Middle Ages. At the beginning of the third part (i.e., of the lecture on the third book) he usually received the degree of a *baccalarius formatus*. When he had accomplished the Sentence lecture and some further work (especially assistance in disputations), he could be graduated *licentiatus*, i.e., obtain the *licentia ubique docendi*. The bestowal of the degree of *doctor (master) theologiae* on the *licentiatus* required high payments, which prevented especially many mendicants from acquiring this highest degree. The full right of teaching, however, was already conferred by the *licentia*. The duration of the several stages of the study could be different in diverse universities, especially in the Later Middle Ages. The educational work of the *licentiatus, magister* or *doctor theologiae* consisted in giving lectures about the Holy Scripture, which surpassed the lectures of the *baccalarius biblicus* by length and profoundness, in directing disputations (i.e., in setting up questions [*quaestiones*] or theses [*propositiones*] and in formulating the solutions, moreover in supervising the whole procedure) as well as in delivering sermons on biblical texts.

Exegesis thus always obtained a central position in theological education. Because in the Middle Ages there were no other theological disciplines, strictly speaking the lectures of the masters were not restricted to exegesis, but increasingly referred to historical subjects and theological problems, too, making use of all the means of dialectics and philosophical knowledge, which were provided by the artists and were known to theologians from their studies of the *artes*. At some universities of the Late Middle Ages the professors of theology were obliged, too, to give *resumptiones (repetitiones)* of works (*Summae, Sententiae, Quodlibeta* e.a.) of important theological authorities.[54]

1.7. Universities and their Schools in the Late Middle Ages

Teaching and learning always resulted in "schools" in the sense of a close relation between teacher and students, which frequently becomes a community of mind. In the mediaeval world founded on authority, the university with its unifying tendencies brought forth schools with a distinct doctrinal conformity (*Lehrrichtung*), whose existence to some extent was even fixed in statutes.

This phenomenon was particularly remarkable in the faculty of arts.[55] Here

---

[53] There were different spellings, in the Late Middle Ages usually *baccalaureus*, which could be associated with *laurea* (the laurel of the *poeta laureatus*, the crowned poet or scholar). For the thirteenth century cf. Weijers, Terminologie (1987) 178–80.

[54] E.g., at Tübingen, cf. Ordinatio Facultatis theologicae 1496 (Urkunden [above n. 51] 264–69).

[55] Cf. *The Cambridge History of Later Medieval Philosophy* (ed. N. Kretzmann / A. Kenny / J. Pinborg; Cambridge 1982); A. DE LIBERA, *La querelle des universaux* (Paris 1996).

the different opinions on the logical-ontological problem of the *universalia*, i.e., the problem of the reality of universal notions, became a criterion for the separation of schools (*viae*, 'ways'). The problem of the universals was discussed intensely since the eleventh century; it lived on in the debates of the faculty of arts. Since the rise of the universities a moderate realism in the line of Aristotle (*universalia in re*) had developed, whereas the older, platonizing realism of Anselm of Canterbury and William of Champeaux had only few adherents. Because the moderate realism was taught in the thirteenth century by Thomas Aquinas and in the early fourteenth century by Johannes Duns Scotus in different ways, the faculty of arts distinguished between two main trends: *via Thomae* and *via Scoti*. When a new conception introduced by William of Ockham, which can be characterized roughly as nominalism or terminism,[56] found followers, this school was named, according to its leader, *via Guillelmi*. Not before the early fifteenth century Ockham's and his partisans' opinion was contrasted as *via moderna* with the *via antiqua* of Thomas Aquinas and Duns Scotus.[57] The faculties of arts at the various universities were organized in different ways. Whereas, e.g., in Cologne and Leipzig the *via antiqua* reigned durably, in Vienna and Erfurt the *via moderna* prevailed. Some universities, as Prague about 1400, were deeply affected by conflicts between the opposite ways. In some universities at first dominated by nominalism after violent controversies the *via antiqua* later on was admitted, too, as in Heidelberg 1452 and in Basel 1464. At some newly founded universities, as in Tübingen and Wittenberg, from the beginnings both *viae* were established in the statutes. Each *via* often had its own *bursa* or its own area within the same building. The adherence to the *viae*, which was crucial for the faculty of arts, was not essential for the faculty of theology. But, of course, theologians who had formerly studied and taught as artists in accordance with a distinct *via*, took over ideas of this philosophical doctrine into their theology.[58] Therefore also some theological faculties were organized in *viae* (e.g., Tübingen). The formation of theological schools, however, which was established in the statutes, was much more determined by the membership of a religious community.[59] In addition to the secular clergy, the single communities had a fixed number of theological chairs at their disposal,[60] and in universities founded in the Late Middle Ages the chairs to be occupied by *religiosi* were often included in the

---

[56] Its adherents later were called *nominales* in contrast to *reales*.

[57] Cf. N. W. GILBERT, "Ockham, Wyclif, and the 'via moderna'", in: *Antiqui und Moderni* (ed. A. Zimmermann; Miscellanea mediaevalia 9; Berlin / New York 1974) 85–125; W. J. COURTENAY, "*Antiqui* and *moderni* in Late Medieval Thought", *JHI* 48 (1987) 3–10.

[58] In the introducing parts of Sentence commentaries of the fourteenth and fifteenth centuries there are often extensive discussions about human cognition, about the universals and about similar subjects.

[59] Cf., e.g., P. GLORIEUX, *Répertoire des maîtres en théologie de Paris au XIIIe siècle* 1–2 (EPhM 17–18; Paris 1933); V. DOUCET, "Maîtres franciscains de Paris. Supplément au 'Répertoire des maîtres en théologie de Paris au XIIIᵉ siècle' de M. le Chan. P.Glorieux", *AFH* 27 (1934) 531–64; Courtenay, Schools and Scholars (1987) 56–87.

[60] About 1300 there existed in Paris eleven chairs for secular masters, two for Dominicans, and one for Franciscans, Augustinian Friars, Carmelites, Augustinian Canons (*Ordo Vallis Scolarium*), Benedictines and Cistercians (cf. the schema in CUP 1).

planning of resources from the beginning. Best developed were the theological schools of the Dominicans, at first influenced by Albertus Magnus, later on by Thomas Aquinas, whose authority in his order was consolidated by many general chapters and confirmed definitively by his canonization in 1323. The Franciscan school in the thirteenth century was above all formed by Bonaventure; since the early fourteenth century Duns Scotus and later on William of Ockham became the heads of schools. Other communities took over ideas from these teachers, like the Augustinian friars since Aegidius Romanus joined the school of Thomas Aquinas. Since the end of the thirteenth century Aegidius himself became the main authority in his Order. Thus the theological doctrines of important masters durably influenced the teaching in the theological faculties without being as prevailing as the *viae* at the faculty of arts.

2. Modifications of the Educational System in the Late Mediaeval Renaissance

General studies (in chronological order): E. GARIN, *Medioevo e Rinascimento* (Bari 1954); P. O. KRISTELLER, *Studies in Renaissance Thought and Letters* 1–4 (Storia e letteratura 54, 166, 178, 193; Roma 1956, 1985, 1993, 1996); W. F. SCHIRMER, *Der englische Frühhumanismus* (Tübingen ²1963); R. WEISS, *The Spread of Italian Humanism* (London 1964); E. GARIN, *La cultura filosofica del Rinascimento italiano* (Firenze 1961); P. O. KRISTELLER, *Eight Philosophers of the Italian Renaissance* (London 1965); idem, *Renaissance Philosophy and the Medieval Tradition* (Wimmer Lecture 15; Latrobe, PA 1966); R. WEISS, *Humanism in England During the Fifteenth Century* (Oxford ³1967); *Zu Begriff und Problem der Renaissance* (ed. A. Buck; WdF 204; Darmstadt 1969); L. W. SPITZ, *The Renaissance and Reformation Mouvements* 1. *The Renaissance* (St. Louis 1971; ²1987); A. G. DICKENS e.a., *Background to the English Renaissance* (London 1974); P. O. KRISTELLER, *Humanismus und Renaissance* 1–2 (Humanistische Bibliothek I/21–22; München 1974 / 1976); idem, *Medieval Aspects of Renaissance Learning* (Duke Monographs in Medieval and Renaissance Studies 1; Durham, NC 1974); E. GARIN, *Italian Humanism* (Westport, CT 1975); *Itinerarium Italicum. The Profile of the Italian Renaissance in the Mirror of its European Transformations* (ed. H. A. Oberman / Th. A. Brady, Jr.; Studies in Medieval and Reformation Thought 14; Leiden 1975); *Die Humanisten in ihrer politischen und sozialen Umwelt* (ed. O. Herding / R. Stupperich; Kommission für Humanismusforschung. Mitteilung 3; Boppard 1976); *Ethik im Humanismus* (Beiträge zur Humanismusforschung 5; Boppard 1979); P. O. KRISTELLER, *Renaissance Thought and its Sources* (New York 1979); A. BUCK, *Studia humanitatis* (Wiesbaden 1981); *Università, Accademie e Società scientifiche in Italia e in Germania dal Cinquecento al Settecento* (ed. L. Boehm / E. Raimondi; Annali dell'Istituto storico italo-germanico Quaderno 9; Bologna 1981); J. F. D'AMICO, *Renaissance Humanism in Papal Rome* (The Johns Hopkins University Studies in Historical and Political Science, 101st Series 1; Baltimore / London 1983); *Humanismus im Bildungswesen des 15. und 16. Jahrhunderts* (ed. W. Reinhard; Mitteilung 12 der Kommission für Humanismusforschung; Weinheim 1984); *Der Humanismus und die oberen Fakultäten* (ed. G. Keil / B. Moeller / W. Trusen; Mitteilung 14 der Kommission für Humanismusforschung; Weinheim 1987); *Renaissance Humanism* 1–3 (ed. A. Rabil Jr.; Philadelphia 1988); *The Cambridge History of Renaissance Philosophy* (ed. Ch. B. Schmitt; Cambridge 1988); P. F. GRENDLER, *Schooling in Renaissance Italy. Literacy and Learning, 1300–1600* (The Johns Hopkins University Studies in Historical and Political Science, 107th Series 1; Baltimore / London 1989); *Christianity and the Renaissance* (ed. T. Verdon / J. Henderson; Syracuse, NY 1990); A. BUCK, *Studien zu Humanismus und Renaissance* (Wolfenbütteler Abhandlungen zur Renaissanceforschung 11; Wiesbaden 1991); W. RÜEGG, "The Rise of Humanism", in: *A History of the University in Europe* 1. *Universities in the Middle Ages* (ed. H. de Ridder-Symoens; Cambridge etc. 1992) 442–68; A. NOE, *Der Einfluss des italienischen Humanismus auf die deutsche Literatur vor 1600* (Internationales Archiv für Sozialgeschichte der deutschen Literatur, 5, Sonderheft;

Tübingen 1993); P. F. GRENDLER, *Books and Schools in the Italian Renaissance* (Aldershot 1995); CH. G. NAUERT JR., *Humanism and the Culture of Renaissance Europe* (Cambridge 1995); *Storia della Teologia* 3. *Età della* Rinascita (ed. G. d'Onofrio; Casale Monferrato 1995); *The Cambridge Companion to Renaissance Humanism* (ed. J. Kraye; Cambridge 1996); A. BUCK, "Der italienische Humanismus", in: *Handbuch der deutschen Bildungsgeschichte 1. 15. bis 17. Jahrhundert* (ed. N. Hammerstein; München 1996) 1–56; *Europäische Sozietätsbewegung und demokratische Tradition. Die europäischen Akademien der Frühen Neuzeit zwischen Frührenaissance und Spätaufklärung 1–2* (ed. K. Garber / H. Wismann; Frühe Neuzeit 26–27; Tübingen 1996); P. BURKE, *The European Renaissance* (Oxford 1998); P. F. GRENDLER, *The Universities of the Italian Renaissance* (Baltimore / London 2002); C. AUGUSTIJN, *Humanismus* (Die Kirche in ihrer Geschichte 2/H2; Göttingen 2003); J. HANKINS, *Humanism and Platonism in the Italian Renaissance 1–2* (Storia e letteratura 215, 220; Roma 2003–04); *Humanisme et église en Italie et en France méridionale (XV^{e}siècle – milieu du XVIe siècle)* (ed. P. Gilli; Collection de l'École française de Rome 330; Roma 2004); *Il Rinascimento italiano e l'Europa* (ed. G. L. Fontana / L. Molà) 1. *Storia e storiografia* (ed. M. Fantoni; s.l. 2005).

2.1. Idea and Extent of the Late Mediaeval Renaissance

The Renaissance of the Late Middle Ages brought up a decisive change in the concept and practice of scholarship and education, which in some aspects led to modern times. Recent research has shown, however, that its contrast to the Middle Ages and to scholasticism, which was often accentuated formerly, must not be stressed in every area. Undoubtedly, the humanists of the time again and again criticized religious customs, clerical persons and the traditional system of education. The scholastic sophistries were just as much ridiculed by humanists as the bondage of ecclesiastical authority and religious superstition. But the Renaissance in the Late Middle Ages itself was deeply founded in the mediaeval world, especially in mediaeval piety. Its representatives questioned neither the ecclesiastical system nor its dogmas and used to participate in the religious life of their time. When they brought up elements from pagan antiquity, they did not play them off against Christian traditions, but linked them together. It is significant that the great translator and mediator of the pagan Platonic tradition, Marsilio Ficino of Florence (1433–99), not only tried to mediate between Plato and St. Paul, but also was ordained priest still at an age of forty years.

The late mediaeval Renaissance, being a great cultural emergence, was the last and most important of a sequence of intellectual movements, which since Carolingian times again and again gave highly important impulses to mediaeval thought and work. 'Renaissance'[61] is a metaphor taken from the organic world, which originally refers to trees or bushes sprouting again after they had been cut off. In Christian usage it was connected with the conception of rebirth (according to Joh 3:4f, 7; Tit 3:5 and others). It means a renewal and revival of the past connected with better circumstances in the field of politics and of culture in particular. The Florentine humanist Matteo Palmieri (1406–75) seems to have been the first who ca. 1436 spoke of such regrowth of the lost arts.[62] The related noun, however, does not occur before the sixteenth century.[63] In the concept of 'revival' the resumption of antique – pagan and Christian – traditions plays a central part – abridged in

---

[61] Cf. U. KÖPF, "Renaissance I. Zum Begriff", RGG⁴ 7 (2004) 431 f.

[62] *Vita civile* 1, 155 (ed. G. Belloni; Studi e Testi 7; Firenze 1982; 46): *rinascere l'arti perdute*.

[63] At first German (Albrecht Dürer 1523: *widererwaxsung*), afterwards Italian (Giorgio Vasari 1550: *rinascità*) and French (Pierre Belon 1553: *renaissance*).

the parole: *ad fontes!* Whenever such traditions were discovered and explored again in the Middle Ages since Carolingian times, they gave a strong impulse to cultural life, especially to theology.

It is only adequate to speak of an age of Renaissance, if the phenomena we call 'Renaissance' play a fundamental part in the cultural life and if the consciousness of a historical distance between present time and antiquity has awakened. Both facts – despite some former signs – can be observed for the first time in the life and work of Francesco Petrarca (1304–74). The beginning of the late mediaeval Renaissance therefore has to be fixed in the second third of the fourteenth century. The movement began with a reconsideration of the language and literature of ancient Rome (especially of Cicero), embraced – beginning with architecture – all the arts, but affected other areas of public life, too. The knowledge of Greek in Italy revived since the end of the fourteenth century, whereas Hebrew was made accessible not before the beginning of the sixteenth century by Johannes Reuchlin. We are accustomed to call the study of language, of literature and of other subjects connected with language (from *trivium* to theology) Humanism according to the contemporary notion of *studia humanitatis* and to our understanding of scholars as humanists (according to the contemporary word *humanista*).

The age of late mediaeval Renaissance, however, cannot be exactly limited; for its chronological extension depends on its geographical coverage. Starting from Italy in the second third of the fourteenth century, the movement of the Renaissance had its centre in Florence and Tuscany until the middle of the fifteenth century. Afterwards it expanded more to Northern and Middle Italy with its centre at Rome and lasted until the end of the sixteenth century. It was extended beyond Italy during the fifteenth century partly by Italian humanists travelling abroad, partly by foreign visitors of Italy (especially students of Law at Italian universities). After the connections of Emperor Charles IV and his Prague court with Italian humanists, humanist influences were present north of the Alps at first during the Council of Constance (1414–18). Poggio Bracciolini (1380–1459), who was secretary at the Council, detected numerous manuscripts of Roman authors in monasteries; during his stay at England (1418–23) he introduced humanistic ideas in this country. In Germany the Renaissance as an intellectual movement got a firm footing by personal contacts at the Council of Basel (1431–48) and by the activity of Enea Silvio Piccolomini (1405–64; since 1458 Pope Pius II) at the court of Emperor Frederick III in Vienna (since 1443). There, it had an effect on the arts since about 1500. Before this, the residence of the Hungarian king at Buda was already open to influences from Italy, most considerably under Matthias Corvinus (king 1458–90). Despite early contacts with Italy (by Petrarca and the papal court at Avignon) the Renaissance did not reach France (Paris university) before the middle of the fifteenth century, less effectively the Burgundian empire, and the Iberian peninsula not before the later fifteenth century. From France and the Netherlands there were connections with England by the end of the fifteenth century. Since the early fifteenth century influences of the Italian Renaissance could also be perceived in Slavonic countries; but not before the late fifteenth and early sixteenth century in Bohemia, Poland and in Croatic Dalmatia (especially in the aristocratic republic of Ragusa) a Renaissance Humanism could develop. – A clear date for the end of the age of Renaissance also cannot be determined. Whereas in the arts the late Renaissance, mainly characterized by mannerism (about 1520 until about 1600, in some parts of Europe until the middle of seventeenth century) merged into the baroque, in education and learning in general as well as in theology humanist ideas survived until modern times.

2.2. The Social and Cultural Background of Late Mediaeval Humanism

The late mediaeval Humanism came into being outside the existing institutions of education (schools, universities, religious houses) and at first was a matter of learned individuals. From its beginnings it was also associated with a certain distance towards the scholastic system of education and it often criticized scholasticism, whereas the scholastics vice versa criticized the humanists.[64]

---

[64] C. G. NAUERT, "The Clash of Humanists and Scholastics: an Approach to Pre-Reformation Controversies", *Sixteenth Century Journal* 4 (1973) 1–18; J. H. OVERFIELD, "Scholastic Opposition

Humanism, however, never created an alternative system of education, which could compete with the scholastic system with regard to its uniformity and effectiveness. In Humanism we can find different conceptions; during the fifteenth century it was even adapted to the institutional framework of the universities, and since the Reformation it penetrated the latter with its ideas.

The political and social background of the late mediaeval Humanism was established by the manifold world of the cities and city-states of Central and Northern Italy: Florence, Pisa, Siena, Lucca, Ferrara, Modena, Genua, Milan, Mantua, Venice etc. The republican communities, which were a result of the communal movement of the twelfth century, often were ruled by a group of families, out of whom some did rise to monarchical government. Because they were usurpers, they struggled intensely for legitimation by furthering the community, especially its culture. This way they often became great benefactors, their courts turned into centres of humanistic and artistic activities. An important example is the rise of the Medici family at Florence,[65] the homeland of the early Renaissance in Italy. Cosimo il Vecchio (1389-1464) had become great as financier; his grandson Lorenzo il Magnifico (1449-92) was a humanist himself and the most enthusiastic promoter of Humanism. In the fifteenth century the popes since Nicolaus V (1447-55)[66] turned Rome into the basis of the Italian High Renaissance. At that point, also courts of secular princes outside of Italy attracted humanists: from the Emperor's court at Vienna to the little seat of the court of archduchess Mechthild (1419-82; mother of count Eberhard im Bart of Württemberg, who founded the university of Tübingen), which existed from 1455 to her death at the town of Rottenburg am Neckar, belonging to *Vorderösterreich*.[67]

2.3. Humanism and the Institutions of Education

Learned humanists first had passed the conventional institutions of education, but often did not find the possibility of working within this traditional system and therefore frequently were active as individuals. This is the case from Petrarca onward, including the many travelling teachers of the late fifteenth century and continuing to scholars like Erasmus of Rotterdam, who never had a permanent position, and still beyond his time. Because the humanistic aspirations at first were missing an institutional framework with its obvious contacts, the humanists tried to find other opportunities for an exchange of ideas. Since

---

to Humanism in Pre-Reformation Germany", *Viator* 7 (1976) 391-420; idem, *Humanism and Scholasticism in Late Medieval Germany* (Princeton, NJ 1984); J. HELMRATH, "'Humanismus und Scholastik' und die deutschen Universitäten um 1500", *Zeitschrift für historische Forschung* 15 (1988) 187-203; J. HANKINS, "Marsilio Ficino as a Critic of Scholasticism", *Vivens homo* 5 (1994) 325-34; E. RUMMEL, *The Humanist-Scholastic Debate in the Renaissance and Reformation* (Cambridge, MA / London 1995); C. G. NAUERT, "Humanism as Method: Roots of Conflict with the Scholastics", *Sixteenth Century Journal* 29 (1998) 427-38. For the institutional aspect cf. L. BOEHM, "Humanistische Bildungsbewegung und mittelalterliche Universitätsverfassung. Aspekte zur frühneuzeitlichen Reformgeschichte der deutschen Universitäten", in: *Grundwissenschaften und Geschichte. Festschrift für Peter Acht* (Münchener historische Studien. Abt. Geschichtliche Hilfswissenschaften 15; Kallmünz 1976) 311-33.

[65] J. R. HALE, *Florence and the Medici* (London 1977); D. KENT, *The Rise of the Medici. Faction in Florence 1426-1434* (Oxford 1978); M. VANNUCCI, *I Medici* (Roma ²2000).

[66] Nicolaus and its followers Calixtus III (1455-58), Pius II (1458-64), Paul II (1464-71), Sixtus IV (1471-84), Innocentius VIII (1484-92), Alexander VI (1492-1503), Pius III (1503), Julius II (1503-13), and Leo X (1513-21) form the group of the Renaissance popes.

[67] Cf. B.THEIL, "Literatur und Literaten am Hof der Erzherzogin Mechthild in Rottenburg", *Zeitschrift für württembergische Landesgeschichte* 42 (1983) 125-44.

Petrarca, who had rediscovered the letters of Cicero about 1345, they entertained an intense and amicable interchange of ideas and of newly found texts (manuscripts) by their letters. If there were several humanistic scholars living at one place, they formed a circle of friends which combined learned discourses with sociability (feasts, banquets etc.).[68] Following the pattern of the *collegia* of ancient Rome these circles liked to call themselves *sodalitates*. In 1495 under the leadership of Konrad Celtis (1459–1508) and of John of Dalberg, bishop of Worms and chancellor of the university, at Heidelberg a circle came into existence, which was called *academia, coetus*, and *sodalitas*.[69] In the following years Celtis became the moving force of the *sodalitates*-movement, particularly after he had been appointed professor of rhetoric and poetic at the university of Vienna in 1497. Here he became at the same time the centre of a *sodalitas litteraria Danubiana*, which spread all over Germany and encouraged the foundation of local *sodalitates*. Several humanistic *sodalitates* looked more like religious convents than like a *universitas magistrorum et studentium*, even more so because also religious persons in leading positions participated in them. In the development of Humanism in Italy and beyond, religious houses with their effective scriptoria and rich libraries played a distinguished role, anyway.[70] For good reasons the notion of a conventual Humanism (*Klosterhumanismus*) has been introduced.[71] In Florence, the house of Augustinian Friars S. Spirito under its Prior Luigi Marsili became a centre of civic Humanism already in the second half of the fourteenth century, and similar circles arose in the Augustinian houses at Padova and Napoli.[72] In the Nuremberg house of Augustinian Friars in 1515/16 a *Sodalitas Augustiniana* or *Staupitiana* came into existence.[73] Humanistic influences grew, and a monastic Humanism developed already during the fifteenth century in Benedictine monasteries as Tegernsee, Sponheim and others. Here, as in other places of the Holy Roman Empire (at Strasbourg, Schlettstadt, Basel, Augsburg, Nuremberg, and others), the political situation and the society of the German Imperial City provided the ground on which a humanistic culture could prosper.

---

[68] Cf. V. DE CAPRIO, "I cenacoli umanistici", in: *Letteratura italiana* 1. *Il letterato e le istituzioni* (ed. A. Asor Rosa; Torino 1982) 799–822.

[69] T. KLANICZAY, "Celtis und die sodalitas litteraria per Germaniam", in: *Republica Guelpherbytana. Wolfenbütteler Beiträge zur Renaissance- und Barockforschung. Festschrift für Paul Raabe* (ed. A. Buck / M. Bircher; Chloe 6; Amsterdam 1987) 79–105; C. TREML, *Humanistische Gemeinschaftsbildung* (Historische Texte und Studien 12; Hildesheim e.a. 1989); H. ENTNER, "Was steckt hinter dem Wort 'sodalitas litteraria'? Ein Diskussionsbeitrag zu Conrad Celtis und seinen Freundeskreisen", in: *Europäische Sozietätsbewegung* 2 (1996), 1069–1101; H. DICKERHOF, "Der deutsche Erzhumanist Conrad Celtis und seine Sodalen", ibid. 1102–1123.

[70] It is significant that the printing of books in Italy had its beginning at a monastery: in 1464/65 in Santa Scolastica of Subiaco the first printing-office of Italy was established; cf. G. P. CAROSI, *I monasteri di Subiaco* (Subiaco 1987) 127–45.

[71] 1926, by R. NEWALD, "Beiträge zur Geschichte des Humanismus in Oberösterreich", in: idem, *Probleme und Gestalten des deutschen Humanismus* (Berlin 1963) 67–112, esp. 82 and 102; F. MACHILEK, "Klosterhumanismus in Nürnberg um 1500", in: Mitteilungen des Vereins für Geschichte der Stadt Nürnberg 64 (1977) 10–45.

[72] P. O. KRISTELLER, "The Contribution of Religious Orders to Renaissance Thought and Learning", in: Medieval Aspects (1974) 93–158; K. ELM, "Mendikanten und Humanisten im Florenz des Tre- und Quattrocento", in: Die Humanisten (1976) 51–85.

[73] Machilek, Klosterhumanismus (1977) 41–43.

In fifteenth century Florence[74] the typical form of a humanistic circle of scholars was established.[75] Since 1454 in the residence of Alamanno Rinuccini (1426-99) a group of persons met regularly in order to study ancient authors and to deliver Latin speeches. This circle derived its name from the Platonic school as transmitted by Cicero: *Achademia* (later on *Achademia nova*, *Achademia Florentina* or *Chorus Achademiae Florentinae*). Most important was the *Accademia Platonica* under the guidance of Marsilio Ficino (1433-99), whose efforts were concentrated on the regeneration of Platonism and its reconciliation with Christianity.[76] His eminent promoter Cosimo de'-Medici (1389-1464) had encouraged him to study Plato; in 1462 he gave him a country-house at Careggi near Florence.[77] Later on, Lorenzo il Magnifico (1449-92), educated by Marsilio,[78] supported the work of his teacher and of other humanists.[79] Whether Marsilio really met his circle of statesmen, clergymen, poets, and students of different subjects at this or at another place, is radically questioned by James Hankins.[80] The *Accademia Platonica* possessed neither statutes nor an institutional framework; its members, however, strove to observe a set of rules, which were attributed to Plato's school. It is improbable, that after Marsilio's death the *Accademia* continued to exist under the direction of Marsilio's pupil Francesco Cattani da Diacceto (1466-1522), professor at the university of Pisa-Florence.[81] He was a member, too, of another Florentine circle, which met in the patrician Bernardo Ruccellai's Gardens; from that circle the *Accademia degli Orti Oricellari* originated, whose members discussed political and literary themes.[82] In imitation of the Florentine patterns and independent from them many academies came to existence in other parts of Italy as

---

[74] Since about 1349 in Florence there existed a university of little importance. This first university in Italy with a theological faculty merged in the university of Pisa in 1472 – a city, which had been conquered by Florence in 1406. Cf. A. F. Verde, *Lo Studio Fiorentino: 1473-1503* 1-5 (Firenze 1973-94); S. I. Camporeale, "Lo Studio Fiorentino e la vita universitaria 1473-1503", *Memorie Dominicane* NS 18 (1987) 347-67; A. Field, The Origins (1988; see below n. 76) 77-106; J. Davies, *Florence and its University during the Early Renaissance* (Education and Society in the Middle Ages and Renaissance 8; Leiden 1998); idem, "The *Studio pisano* under Florentine Domination, 1406-1472", *History of Universities* 16 (2000) 197-235.

[75] For the following cf. M. Maylender, *Storia delle Accademie d'Italia* 1-6 (Bologna 1926-1930); A. Buck, "Die humanistischen Akademien in Italien" (1977), in: idem, *Studia humanitatis* (Wiesbaden 1981) 216-24; A. Quondam, "L'Accademia", in: *Letteratura italiana* 1. *Il letterato e le istituzioni* (ed. A. Asor Rosa; Torino 1982) 823-98; T. Klaniczay, "Die Akademie als die Organisation der intellektuellen Elite in der Renaissance", in: *Sozialgeschichtliche Fragestellungen in der Renaissanceforschung* (ed. A. Buck / T. Klaniczay; Wolfenbütteler Abhandlungen zur Renaissanceforschung 13; Wiesbaden 1992) 1-16; M. Lentzen, "Die humanistische Akademiebewegung des Quattrocento und die Accademia Platonica in Florenz", in: *Europäische Sozietätsbewegung* 1 (1996) 190-213.

[76] A. della Torre, *Storia dell'Accademia Platonica di Firenze* (Pubblicazioni del R. Istituto di Studi Superiori Pratici e di Perfezionamento in Firenze. [A.] Sezione di Filosofia e Filologia [28.]; Firenze 1902); P. O. Kristeller, "Die platonische Akademie von Florenz", in: idem, Humanismus und Renaissance 2 (1976) 101-14; A. Field, *The Origins of the Platonic Academy of Florence* (Princeton, NJ 1988).

[77] R. Fubini, "Ficino e i Medici all'avvento di Lorenzo il Magnifico", *Rinascimento* 2, 24 (1984) 3-52; idem, "Ancora su Ficino e i Medici", ibid. 2, 27 (1987) 275-91; M. Meriam Bullard, "Marsilio Ficino and the Medici. The Inner Dimension of Patronage", in: Christianity and the Renaissance (1990) 467-92.

[78] J. Hankins, "Lorenzo de'Medici as a Student of Ficino: The *De summo bono*", in: idem, Humanism and Platonism 2 (2004) 317-50.

[79] Idem, "Lorenzo de'Medici as a Patron of Philosophy" (1994), in: idem, Humanism and Platonism 2 (2004) 273-316.

[80] See esp. J. Hankins, "Cosimo de'Medici and the 'Platonic Academy'" (1990), in: idem, Humanism and Platonism 2 (2004) 187-217; idem, "The Myth of the Platonic Academy of Florence" (1991), ibid. 219-72; idem, "The Invention of the Platonic Academy of Florence" (2002), ibid. 351-95; but cf. A. Field, "The Platonic Academy of Florence", in: *Marsilio Ficino: his philosophy, his legacy* (ed. M. J. B. Allen e.a.; SIH 108; Leiden e.a.: Brill 2002) 359-76.

[81] P. O. Kristeller, "Francesco da Diacceto and Florentine Platonism in the Sixteenth Century" (1946), in: idem, Studies 1 (1984) 287-336.

[82] A. L. de Gaetano, "The Florentine Academy and the Advancement of Learning through the

well since the fifteenth century.[83] The interests of all these academies[84] became increasingly narrowed to the field of Italian language and literature.[85] Besides, these circles were often very short-lived.

Despite all reservations on the part of the traditional educational system's representatives, the Humanism of the Late Middle Ages was still connected with their traditions as well. Humanists, however, felt an aversion against the institutional proceedings of scholastic graduations structured by obligatory disputations, that constituted a central part of the mediaeval university. The custom of crowning poets did not offer full compensation. In 1315 the judge, historian and poet Albertino Mussato (1261–1329) on the initiative of the university of Padua received the laurel crown in the city hall. The most famous example is the coronation performed on Petrarca in 1341 on the Capitolium Romanum by the Roman senator Orso dell'Anguillara.[86] By this act the title of *magister* and the privilege of teaching the *artes liberales* were bestowed on Petrarca. But he refused the chair that Florence offered to him as a consequence of this bestowal. Later on the Roman Emperor claimed the conferring of the laurel.[87] The first poet's coronation in Germany took place in 1442 at Frankfurt am Main: Emperor Frederick III decorated Enea Silvio Piccolomini, who made use of his privilege of teaching by only two lectures at the university of Vienna. In contrast, the coronation performed for the first time on a German, Conrad Celtis, by Frederick III in 1487 at Nuremberg, constituted the basis of Celtis' teaching at the Vienna university.

Apart from that, Humanism entered the existing universities in different ways – at first in Italy, but in the course of the fifteenth century outside of Italy, too.[88] The payment of humanistic professors constituted a fundamental problem, which could not always be solved by prebends. Another problem was the mobility of many humanists, who often moved from place to place as wan-

---

Vernacular: the Orti Oricellari and the Sacra Accademia", in: *Bibliothèque d'Humanisme et Renaissance* 30 (1968) 19–52.

[83] For the different model of the academies of Rome cf. J. D'AMICO, *Renaissance Humanism in Papal Rome. Humanists and Churchmen on the Eve of the Reformation* (The Johns Hopkins University Studies in Historical and Political Science 101; Baltimore / London 1983) 89–112.

[84] Cf. also B. GUTHMÜLLER, "Die Akademiebewegung im Cinquecento", in: Europäische Sozietätsbewegung 1 (1996) 238–70.

[85] Cf., e. g., A. L. DE GAETANO, *Giambattista Gelli and the Florentine Academy. The Rebellion against Latin* (Biblioteca dell'«Archivum Romanum» 1, 119; Firenze 1976).

[86] U. DOTTI, *Vita di Petrarca* (Bari 2004) 86–89; E. H. WILKINS, "The Coronation of Petrarch", in: idem, *The Making of the "Canzoniere" and other Petrarchan Studies* (Storia e letteratura 38; Roma 1951) 9–69.

[87] K. SCHOTTENLOHER, "Kaiserliche Dichterkrönungen im Heiligen Römischen Reiche Deutscher Nation", in: *Papsttum und Kaisertum. Forschungen zur politischen Geschichte und Geisteskultur des Mittelalters Paul Kehr zum 65. Geburtstag dargebracht* (ed. A. Brackmann; München 1926) 648–73; A. SCHIRRMEISTER, *Triumph des Dichters. Gekrönte Intellektuelle im 16. Jahrhundert* (Frühneuzeitstudien NF 4; Köln / Weimar / Wien 2003); J. L. FLOOD, "'Viridibus lauri ramis et foliis decoratus': zur Geschichte der kaiserlichen Dichterkrönungen", in: *Reichspersonal: Funktionsträger für Kaiser und Reich* (ed. A. Baumann e.a.; Quellen und Forschungen zur höchsten Gerichtsbarkeit im Alten Reich 46; Köln / Weimar / Wien 2003) 353–77; D. MERTENS, "Die Dichterkrönung des Konrad Celtis. Ritual und Programm", in: *Konrad Celtis und Nürnberg* (ed. F. Fuchs; Pirckheimer Jahrbuch für Renaissance- und Humanismusforschung 19; Wiesbaden 2004) 31–50.

[88] For Germany cf. A. SEIFERT, "L'integrazione dell'Umanesimo nelle università tedesche", Annali dell'Istituto storico italo-germanico in Trento 5 (1979) 25–41.

dering teachers and who were teaching only for one year or a couple of years at one distinct university. In this way a continuous teaching and the formation of a tradition could not be established.

2.4. The Curriculum of Humanism

Due to its central interest in language and literature, Humanism found its place first and foremost in the Curriculum of the faculty of arts, where it fitted nicely in with the *Trivium*, whereas it had less interest in the *Quadrivium*. In most cases, however, the humanists were not really integrated in the faculty of arts, but appointed immediately by the Senate.

As the humanists aspired to reduce the broad scholastic treatment of logic and were interested more in linguistic problems, they paid special attention to grammar and, even more, to rhetoric. On the other hand, they extended the canon of the *artes* to include poetics, history and ethics. Therefore, from the fourteenth century five subjects were mentioned again and again in programmatic utterings. These subjects constituted the *studia humanitatis:* grammar, rhetoric, poetics, history and moral philosophy. Moral philosophy in the form of commenting the Aristotelian *Ethica Nicomachea*, *Oeconomica* and *Politica* (i. e., individual, family and political ethics) was already established as part of the philosophical curriculum of the scholastics, along with logic, metaphysics, psychology and natural philosophy. It was just that part of the program developed out of the Aristotelian writings, which the humanists estimated most. Among the humanistic commentaries of Aristotle the commentaries of the Nicomachean Ethics are the most important.

A new part of the humanistic curriculum consisted in the study of the biblical languages, first of Greek.[89] As suggested by the learned poet Giovanni Boccaccio (1313-75), the *Comune* of Florence established a chair for the Greek Lorenzo Pilato (1360-62), which, however, did not result in a continuity of Greek studies. Not before the teachings of the Byzantine scholar Manuel Chrysoloras (ca. 1350-1415) – first at Florence (1397-1400), later at Pavia and Milano (1400-03) – knowledge of the Greek language became familiar in Italy. Leonardo Bruni of Arezzo (1370-1444), a student of Chrysoloras, was the first and the most popular of the fifteenth century's translators from Greek into Latin.[90] Guarino da Verona (d. 1460) and Vittorino da Feltre (d. 1446) continued to teach Greek. Thereby they created a basis for the great translation works of Marsilio Ficino, Ambrogio Traversari, Angelo Poliziano and others. Teachers of Greek were active at Paris from 1430 onwards, in England (after a short visit of Manuel Chrysoloras in 1408) not until the end of the fifteenth century – fighting in both places against resistances concerning the alleged language of the eastern heretics. Since 1497 Erasmus of Rotterdam (1466/69-1536) studied Greek with his friends at Oxford, where a first teacher of Greek in 1516 was appointed at Corpus Christi College. In 1518 the first lectorship for Greek was established here as well. In Germany, too, the knowledge of Greek acquired abroad was not transmitted before about 1500. The first ordinary chair for Greek was established 1518 at Wittenberg university for Philipp Melanchthon.

Much later than Greek, Hebrew became a subject of public teaching. In the second half of the fifteenth century Hebrew studies especially in Florence were

---

[89] K. M. Setton, "The Byzantine Background to the Italian Renaissance", Proceedings of the American Philosophical Society 100 (1956) 1-76; R. Weiss, *Medieval and Humanist Greek* (Padova 1977); W. Berschin, *Griechisch-lateinisches Mittelalter* (Bern / München 1980); N. G. Wilson, *From Byzantium to Italy. Greek Studies in the Italian Renaissance* (London 1992); J. Hankins, "The Study of Greek in the Latin West" (2001), in: idem, Humanism and Platonism 1 (2003) 273-91.

[90] J. Hankins, "Translation Practice in the Renaissance: The Case of Leonardo Bruni" (1994), in: idem, Humanism and Platonism 1 (2003) 177-92; idem, "Manuel Chrysoloras and the Greek Studies of Leonardo Bruni" (2002), ibid. 243-71.

connected with a marked interest in the Kabbalah, that had not yet been translated. Giovanni Pico della Mirandola (1463–94), e. g., apart from his commentary of the Psalms in the *Heptaplus* (1489), wrote an allegoric exposition of the
first verses of Genesis, which contained kabbalistic doctrines. At that time anyone who wished to learn Hebrew could neither attend suitable educational institutions nor use school-books, but depended on individual teaching by Jews,
like Giovanni Pico's teachers Elia del Medigo, Flavio Mitridate and Yohanan
Alemanno.[91] Even the founder of Hebrew studies as a learned discipline, Johannes Reuchlin (1455–1522), still resorted to this kind of help in Linz 1492
and later on during his studies in Italy. His *Rudimenta hebraica* (1506) rendered a regular teaching of Hebrew possible for the first time. Since 1518 Erasmus pursued the foundation of a *Collegium trilingue* at Louvain which was financed by the legacy of the Burgundian councillor and scholar Hieronymus
Busleiden (d. 1517).[92] At this Collegium were employed three professors, who
had to teach Hebrew, Greek and Latin *publice et gratis*. Wittenberg university
adopted this pattern in 1518,[93] and soon other universities followed as well by
establishing lecturerships or ordinary chairs for Hebrew, which often at first
were occupied by converted Jews.

Although the representatives of Humanism were chiefly interested in the
Platonic tradition, that had been mostly neglected by the scholastics, and
although Marsilio Ficino made this tradition in a new way accessible for his
contemporaries by his Latin translations and his commentaries, especially of
Plato and Plotinus, broad and intensive studies of Aristotle were going on as
well, as mentioned above. This concerns especially fifteenth-century Italy,
where the Aristotelian tradition was primarily not taught according to the Parisian model in the context of theology but instead mainly in connection with
medicine. The common interest in Aristotle could bring together humanists
and scholastics (esp. in Padova: Pietro Pomponazzi, 1462–1525).[94] But a humanistic philologian like Jacques Lefèvre d'Étaples, could take a lively interest
in Aristotle, too, whose writings he edited since 1494 in a sequence of learned
editions. His work differed from the scholastic study of Aristotle insofar as he
explicitly took care of the philosopher's original text and rejected the whole
mediaeval commenting.

---

[91] B. C. NOVAK, "Giovanni Pico della Mirandola and Jochanan Alemanno", *Journal of the War-burg and Courtauld Institutes* 45 (1982) 125–47; F. LELLI, "Un collaboratore ebreo di Giovanni Pico della Mirandola: Yohanan Alemanno", *Vivens homo* 5 (1994) 401–30.

[92] H. DE VOCHT, *History of the Foundation and the Rise of the Collegium Trilingue Lovaniense 1517–1550*, 1–4 (Humanistica Lovaniensia 10–13; Louvain 1951/53/54/55).

[93] The Faculty of Arts was enlarged in spring 1518 by the foundation of a *pedagogium* for the learning of the three most distinguished languages Latin, Greek and Hebrew and by establishing chairs for Greek and Hebrew (*Urkundenbuch der Universität Wittenberg* 1 *[1502–1611]*; ed. W. Friedensburg; Geschichtsquellen der Provinz Sachsen und des Freistaates Anhalt NS 3; Magde-burg 1926) 85f, no. 64.

[94] B. NARDI, *Saggi sull'Aristotelismo padovano del secolo XIV al XVI* (Università degli Studi di Padova. Studi sulla tradizione Aristotelica nel Veneto 1; Firenze 1958); idem, *Studi su Pietro Pom-ponazzi* (Firenze 1965); *Platon et Aristote à la Renaissance. XVIᵉ Colloque International de Tours* (De Pétrarque à Descartes 32; Paris 1976); L. BIANCHI, *Studi sull'Aristotelismo del Rinascimento* (Padova 2003).

2.5. Humanistic Learning and its Literary Outcome

At university Humanism took advantage of the existing scholastic institutions, the conventional methods of instruction and the current literary forms. Many humanistic school-books and commentaries came into existence, at the faculty of theology even Sentence commentaries.[95] Apart from university teaching the humanists, however, did not use so much scholastic methods of working and teaching, but developed their own forms of studying and conveying which were expressed in appropriate old and new literary *genera*. Their aversion against the scholastic hypertrophy of logic made the humanists mostly avoid the method of the *quaestio*; instead they resorted to the literary forms of classical Antiquity and emphasized the role of rhetoric. The humanists, too, trusted in commentary as a fundamental form of learned working. But they did not acknowledge the traditional commentary of the scholastics, that was excessively filled with *quaestiones* and in which the discussion of problems was often separated from the text. They prefered a type of commentary explaining the text with philological and historical methods – also in vernacular language (in Italy especially in commenting poetry, above all regarding the works of Dante Alighieri).[96] Instead of the scholastic *lectio* rich in questions and digressions, the humanists liked speeches and orations (and series of speeches). Already in the fourteenth century in Florence and other cities they gave public lectures on Dante. Lectures and commentaries on poetry originated especially from academies that were established for the study of language and literature. Speeches could be written down in the form of the learned Latin treatise (later in vernacular, as well), i.e., in the *tractatus*. Humanists liked the form of the dialogue, which was composed according to literary patterns (first according to Cicero, later on to Plato, too) and which, for the most part, was fictional. Treatises could turn into large works, e.g., Marsilio Ficino's *Theologia Platonica*. As a matter of fact, humanists mostly gave up the *disputatio* and the *quaestio* so important for the scholastics. But when Giovanni Pico della Mirandola published a series of 900 theses *(conclusiones)* on different subjects in 1486 and invited scholars from universities all over Europe for a public debate to Rome, he wished to use the traditional form of the disputation; anyhow, this meeting could not be realized. One of the most characteristic literary forms of humanistic communication was last but not least the letter and the letter collection

---

[95] E.g., Aegidius of Viterbo OESA (1470–1532), *In sententias ad mentem Platonis* (F. STEGMÜLLER, *Repertorium commentariorum in Sententias Petri Lombardi* 1 [Würzburg 1947] 22f); cf. A. ZUMKELLER, "Die Augustinerschule des Mittelalters. Vertreter und philosophisch-theologische Lehre (Übersicht nach dem heutigen Stand der Forschung)", *Analecta Augustiniana* 27 (1964)167–262; 254f; Kristeller, Studies 2 (1985) 80f.

[96] B. SANDKÜHLER, *Die frühen Dantekommentare und ihr Verhältnis zur mittelalterlichen Kommentartradition* (Regensburg 1966); *Der Kommentar in der Renaissance* (ed. A. Buck / O. Herding; Deutsche Forschungsgemeinschaft – Kommission für Humanismusforschung, Mitteilung 1; Boppard 1975); B. SANDKÜHLER, "Die Kommentare zur Commedia bis zur Mitte des 15. Jahrhunderts", in: *Die italienische Literatur im Zeitalter Dantes und am Übergang vom Mittelalter zur Renaissance* (ed. A. Buck; Grundriss der romanischen Literaturen des Mittelalters X/1; Heidelberg 1987) 166–208.

following the pattern of Cicero's *Epistolae*, which were discovered anew by Petrarca. This form corresponded with the sociable or learned exchange of thoughts – the private letter as well as the letter-treatise destined for publication (esp. the political letter).[97]

3. New Developments in the Fifteenth Century and their Influence on Learning and Education

In the fifteenth century trends appeared that had originated independent of Humanism, but displayed a certain congeniality to it and, in fact, often interacted with Humanism. These tendencies influenced the system of learning and education, too.

3.1. Religious Reforming Ideas and Reforming Movements

In many fields the period from late fourteenth to early sixteenth century was a period of reform ideas and – usually fruitless – reforming efforts. They were inspired by notorious and massive grievances *(gravamina)*. Since 1378 the Great Schism not only had created the need to deal with the separation of occidental Christianity pragmatically, but moreover, to overcome it by appropriate fundamental reforming measures. To that purpose Reform Councils were convoked at Pisa (1409), Constance (1414–18), Basel (1431–49, 1437 transferred to Ferrara, 1439 to Florence) and Rome (Lateranum V, 1512–17).

Representatives of the conciliar idea, the conciliarists, embraced reforming ideas, whereas their opponents, the papalists or curialists, refused these ideas. A mediation between these two positions failed. In the discussions between the opponents, however, both in the Holy German Empire and in Imperial Italy other issues were stressed than in those countries, in which strong efforts for a national church already had been developed and realized (esp. in France and England). Therefore the German reforming claims *(Gravamina nationis Germanicae* e.a.) necessarily had to have an effect that would be breaking up the ecclesiastical system – if they really came into effect.

Especially marked was the reforming movement at the end of the Middle Ages. It became particularly prominent within the area, which had been a supporter of reforming ideas and impulses during the whole Middle Ages: in monasticism (including the mendicant orders).[98] The Council of Constance urged the need for monastic reforms, which were already discussed before the council's closing in 1417 at the Benedictine provincial chapter in the monastery of Petershausen situated close to the city.[99] The longing for reformation in Benedictine monasticism brought about reform-

---

[97] C. H. CLOUGH, "The Cult of Antiquity: Letters and Letter Collections", in: *Cultural Aspects of the Italian Renaissance. Essays in Honour of Paul Oskar Kristeller* (ed. C. H. Clough; Manchester / New York, NY. 1976) 33–67.

[98] *Reformbemühungen und Observanzbestrebungen im spätmittelalterlichen Ordenswesen* (ed. K. Elm; Berliner historische Studien 14 = Ordensstudien 6; Berlin 1989).

[99] J. ZELLER, "Das Provinzialkapitel im Stifte Petershausen im Jahre 1417. Ein Beitrag zur

ing congregations, which influenced even monasteries, that were not associated with them.[100] In the reforming congregations of Bursfelde, Kastl, Melk and other central places a religious renewal joined in with an improvement of intellectual life. The congregation of Melk, moreover, was closely connected with the university of Vienna and also wide open for influences of Humanism. Other Benedictine congregations and monasteries, too, provided a framework, within which theological and other learned activities could flourish, often under humanistic influences.

Very important for the monastic scholarship of the fifteenth century were the Carthusian monasteries. In the era of a monastic awakening in the fifteenth century the Carthusian order experienced a new rise, although its motto claims the opposite: *Cartusia numquam reformata, quia numquam deformata.*[101] Surely, also the Carthusians were representatives of the strong reforming efforts at the end of the Middle Ages.[102] Following about 100 foundations of Charterhouses in the fourteenth century, the fifteenth century saw about 40 more communities. Many monasteries were built immediately outside city walls, so that – despite the isolation inherent in the Carthusian existence – an active intellectual interchange was possible by all means.[103] It is striking, how many professors at that time retired at an advanced age from their university into a Chartusian monastery, taking their libraries with them in order to lead there a *vita contemplativa* and to write learned books,[104] among them voluminous Bible commentaries.[105] E.g., the secular clergyman Johannes Heynlin von Stein (before 1433–1496) retired after working as professor at Paris, Basel and Tübingen and after pursuing a new activity as preacher at the Münster of Basel in 1487, moving together with his comprehensive library to the Basel Charterhouse.[106] The intensive work of writers in the order as well as legacies of such scholars, who entered the community later in their lives, resulted in large book collections in many monasteries.[107]

Geschichte der Reformen im Benediktinerorden zur Zeit des Konstanzer Konzils", Studien und Mitteilungen zur Geschichte des Benediktinerordens und seiner Zweige 41 (1921/22) 1–73.

[100] *Die Reformverbände und Kongregationen der Benediktiner im deutschen Sprachraum* (ed. U. Faust / F. Quarthal; Germania Benedictina 1; St. Ottilien 1999) esp. 195–418.

[101] "On a dit: *Cartusia numquam reformata, quia numquam deformata* [...]. En fait, on n'a jamais toléré qu'un abus s'installe. Il y a eu, comme partout, des faiblesses humaines qu'il a été nécessaire de corriger, mais le Chapitre Géneral a toujours réagi à temps, pour qu'aucune déviation ne s'enracine ou ne se généralise" (Un Chartreux, *La Grande Chartreuse*; Bellegarde; 1976) 219f.

[102] H. RÜTHING, "Die Kartäuser und die spätmittelalterlichen Ordensreformen", in: Reformbemühungen (1989; above n. 98) 35–58.

[103] F. KLOS-BUZEK, "Kartause und mittelalterliche Stadt", in: *Stadt und Kirche* (ed. F.-H. Hye; Beiträge zur Geschichte der Städte Mitteleuropas 13; Linz 1995) 301–12.

[104] Cf. D. MERTENS, "Kartäuser-Professoren", in: *Die Kartäuser in Österreich* 3 (Analecta Cartusiana 83/3; Salzburg 1981) 75–87; G.-R. TEWES, "Die Kölner Universität und das Kartäuserkloster im 15. Jahrhundert – eine fruchtbare Beziehung", in: *Die Kölner Kartause um 1500* (ed. W. Schäfke; Köln 1991) 154–68.

[105] Esp. Dionysius the Carthusian (1402/03–71), who commented the whole Bible. Cf. F. STEGMÜLLER, *Repertorium biblicum medii aevi* 2 (Madrid 1950) 263–80; D. WASSERMANN, *Dionysius der Kartäuser. Einführung in Werk und Gedankenwelt* (Analecta Cartusiana 133; Salzburg 1996).

[106] M. HOSSFELD, "Johannes Heynlin aus Stein", *Basler Zeitschrift für Geschichte und Altertumskunde* 6 (1907) 309–56; 7 (1908) 79–219, 235–431; M. STEINMANN, "Basler Büchersammler I. Johannes Heynlin de Lapide (1430–1496)", *Librarium* 20 (1977) 22–27.

[107] *Bücher, Bibliotheken und Schriftkultur der Kartäuser* (ed. S. Lorenz; Contubernium 59; Stuttgart 2002).

The reforming idea played an important part also in the Franciscan order, divided in different sections since the thirteenth century, for the Dominican friars and for the Augustinian hermits. The division into an observant and a more conformist line affected their educational systems and became part of the institutional framework of their theological efforts. The form of life of regular canons, too, constituted an important religious movement, which had come into existence in the Netherlands and, above all, influenced the religious life in Germany: the *devotio moderna*.[108] From its very beginnings it was connected with the Carthusians; their founder Geert Grote had lived as guest in the Charterhouse of Monnikhuizen from the end of 1374 until 1377. Like him his adherents, the Brethren of the Common Life, devoted themselves above all to the study of the Bible and to meditation. As a means of earning their living, Grote had recommended education and the copying of books. This kind of work was so characteristic for them, that a sovereign, who aspired to improve the religious and intellectual life, as count (since 1495 duke) Eberhard im Bart of Württemberg did, invited them deliberately to come into his country and favoured them.[109] Single brethren were also teaching at universities, like Gabriel Biel, who held a theological chair in Tübingen from 1484 until his death in 1495. Due to the reforming efforts in monasticism in the fifteenth century the monastery became a centre of theological activity again. It is significant that scholars at that point again paid attention to the religious – especially to the monastic – literature of the twelfth century.[110] Besides, a renewal of the monastic theology, which had culminated before in the twelfth century, seems to have become obvious. In monasteries also the new humanistic ideas were adopted (as mentioned above).

Various ideas both of the monastic reformers and the humanistic spirit united again and again in the reforming efforts of universities. Although having mostly indirect effects, the suggestions made by the secular clergyman Jean Gerson (1363–1429) became influential.[111] Gerson, professor of theology and chancellor of Paris university, Church reformer and representative of conciliarism, committed himself since 1399/1400 for the reform of the university of Paris and in 1402 for the reform of the study of theology in his *Lectiones contra curiositatem studentium*.[112] He, too, had close relations to the Carthusians and to the *devotio moderna*. By his comprehensive work he influenced the thought of the fifteenth century up to the Reformation of the sixteenth century.

---

[108] R. R. Post, *The Modern Devotion* (Studies in Medieval and Reformation Thought 3; Leiden 1968); A. G. Weiler, *Volgens de norm van de vroege kerk: de geschiedenis van de huizen van de broeders van het Gemene leven in Nederland* (Middeleeuwse studies 13; Nijmegen 1997).

[109] W. Schöntag, "Die Anfänge der Brüder vom gemeinsamen Leben in Württemberg. Ein Beitrag zur vorreformatorischen Kirchen- und Bildungsgeschichte", in: *Archiv für Diplomatik* 23 (1977) 459–85; *Gabriel Biel und die Brüder vom gemeinsamen Leben* (ed. U. Köpf / S. Lorenz; Contubernium 47; Stuttgart 1998); G. Faix, *Gabriel Biel und die Brüder vom Gemeinsamen Leben* (Spätmittelalter und Reformation 11; Tübingen 1999).

[110] G. Constable, "Twelfth-Century Spirituality and the Late Middle Ages", in: Medieval and Renaissance Studies 5 (1971) 27–60; idem, "The Popularity of Twelfth-Century Spiritual Writers in the Late Middle Ages", in: *Renaissance Studies in Honor of Hans Baron* (Dekalb, IL 1971) 3–28.

[111] P. Glorieux, "Le Chancelier Gerson et la réforme de l'enseignement", in: *Mélanges offerts à Étienne Gilson de l'Académie française* (EphM. Hors série; Toronto 1959) 285–98; S. E. Ozment, "The University and the Church. Patterns of Reform in Jean Gerson", MeH (Boulder, Col.) NS 1 (1970) 111–26; L. B. Pascoe, *Jean Gerson: Principles of Church Reform* (Studies in Medieval and Reformation Thought 7; Leiden 1973) 80–109; H. Smolinsky, "Johannes Gerson (1363–1429), Kanzler der Universität Paris, und seine Vorschläge zur Reform der theologischen Studien", Historisches Jahrbuch 96 (1976) 270–95; cf. idem, "Kirchenreform als Bildungsreform im Spätmittelalter und in der frühen Neuzeit", in: *Bildungs- und schulgeschichtliche Studien zu Spätmittelalter, Reformation und konfessionellem Zeitalter* (ed. H. Dickerhof; Wissensliteratur im Mittelalter 19 ; Wiesbaden 1994) 35–51.

[112] Jean Gerson, *Œuvres complètes* 3 (ed. P. Glorieux; Paris e.a. 1962) 224–49.

3.2. Transformation and Popularization

A new form of theological work, which had been initiated already in the thirteenth century, flourished in the fifteenth century. It was advanced by the growing longing for the transmission of learned knowledge to a wider group of people. The resulting literature was, on the one hand, a help for clergymen, who had not received a theological education, on the other hand, a religious and theological information for people who did not know Latin, i.e., for such male laymen, who had not studied, and for women.

Already in the thirteenth century a growing amount of religious and theological literature was written in the vernacular languages, which at that time were developing. The production of religious literature was especially connected with the boom in the religious women's movement, which was partly concentrated and organized by the new mendicant orders and partly resulted in a new group of 'semireligious' women and men *(beginae, beghardi)*. Their religious instruction did not take place in the forms of academic education, but first of all by preaching and ministry, and, apart from that, by treatises in vernacular languages. Already in the thirteenth century examples of a learned theological vernacular literature occurred (as a 'vernacular scholastic').[113] This literature was growing until the end of the Middle Ages and continued to flourish without interruption in the Reformation of the early sixteenth century (e.g., in Martin Luther's German treatises known as "Sermons"). This development was supported by the humanists' interest in language and literature.

A basic medium of religious and theological education was the translation of the Bible into vernacular languages.[114] It was especially supported by religious reforming movements, partly in cooperation with those academic theologians, who wished for a reformation of the Church. Already the Waldensian movement in the twelfth century promoted the translation of parts of the Bible into French; from it depended Italian translations, which are not preserved. John Wyclif pursued the project of a complete translation of the Vulgate into English. But it is not sure whether he contributed to the first version of the Lollard Bible from 1380/84. It seems, that the Old Testament was translated by Nicholas of Hereford, the New Testament by John Purvey. A first extensive Dutch translation was created in the last years of the fourteenth century by Jan Scutken. Whereas from the fourteenth century onward a growing number of Middle High German translations of parts of the Bible had been accomplished, during the fifteenth century several complete German Bibles came into existence. The first of these was printed in Upper German language by the Strasbourg printer Johannes Mentelin according to a translation which had been made in the middle of the fourteenth century.

---

[113] For the German scholastic cf. esp. W. STAMMLER, "Deutsche Scholastik", *Zeitschrift für deutsche Philologie* 72 (1953) 1–23; K. RUH, "Die trinitarische Spekulation in deutscher Mystik und Scholastik", ibid. 24–53; G. STEER, "Germanistische Scholastikforschung", *ThPh* 45 (1970) 204–26; 46 (1971) 195–222; 48 (1973) 65–106. The German literature now is completely recorded in an extremely valuable work: *Die deutsche Literatur des Mittelalters. Verfasserlexikon* (2nd edn. by K. Ruh e.a.; 11 vols., Berlin 1978–2004).

[114] Cf. the survey in the art. *Bibelübersetzungen* (parts X–XVII) by D. KARTSCHOKE e.a., LM 2 (1983) 96–106.

Among the many religious-theological treatises that were used as a means of religious people's education by catechizing,[115] the explanation of the Decalogue must be marked out especially. This kind of popular biblical exposition formed an important literary genus in the Late Middle Ages. Its most important representative in German language was written by Marquard of Lindau, a Franciscan in the second half of the fourteenth century, who had received a scholastic education.[116] His essential source was a Latin treatise of the Augustinian friar Heinrich of Friemar (about 1245–1340): *De decem praeceptis*, a manual for the preacher and father confessor.[117] Marquard's explanation of the Decalogue, on the contrary, was destined for penitents (esp. for secular people and *religiosae*).

4. Books and Libraries

Studies (in chronological order): V. SCHOLDERER, "Der Buchdruck Italiens im fünfzehnten Jahrhundert", *Beiträge zur Inkunabelkunde* NF 2 (1938) 17–61; E. P. GOLDSCHMIDT, *Medieval Texts and their First Appearance in Print* (London 1943); G. ABATE, "Manoscritti e biblioteche francescane del medio evo", in: *Il libro e le biblioteche. Atti del Primo Congresso Bibliologico Francescano Internazionale 20–27 febbraio 1949* 2 (Bibliotheca Pontificii Athenaei 6; Roma 1950) 77–126; A. BÖMER e.a., *Geschichte der Bibliotheken* 1–2 (Handbuch der Bibliothekswissenschaft 3,1–2; Leipzig ²1955/57); C. F. BÜHLER, *The Fifteenth-Century Book. The Scribes, the Printers, the Decorators* (Philadelphia 1960); J. W. THOMPSON, *The Medieval Library* (New York ³1967); V. SCHOLDERER, *Fifty Essays in Fifteenth- and Sixteenth-Century Bibliography* (Amsterdam 1966); L. BUZÁS, *Deutsche Bibliotheksgeschichte des Mittelalters* (Elemente des Buch- und Bibliothekswesens 1; Wiesbaden 1975); G. S. POLICA, "Libro, lettura, 'lezione' negli studia degli ordini mendicanti (sec. XIII)", in: *Le scuole degli ordini mendicanti (secoli XIII-XIV)* (Convegni del Centro di studi sulla spiritualità medievale 17; Todi 1978) 373–413; *Libri, scrittura e pubblico nel Rinascimento. Guida storica e critica* (ed. A. Petrucci; Bari 1979); W. SCHMITZ, *Deutsche Bibliotheksgeschichte* (Germanistische Lehrbuchsammlung 52; Bern 1984); A. LABARRE, *Histoire du livre* (Paris ⁴1985); J. FEATHER, *A Dictionary of Book History* (London 1986); *La production du livre universitaire au moyen âge* (ed. L. Baillon e.a.; Paris 1988); *Histoire des bibliothèques françaises* 1. *Les bibliothèques médiévales* (ed. A. Vernet; Paris 1989); *Vocabulaire du livre et de l'écriture au moyen âge* (ed. O. Weijers; Études sur le vocabulaire intellectuel du moyen âge 2; Turnhout 1989); *Livres et bibliothèques (XIIIᵉ -XVᵉ siècle)*, Cahiers de Fanjeaux 31 (1996); *Der Codex im Gebrauch* (ed. C. Meier e.a.; Münstersche Mittelalter-Schriften 70; München 1996); *L'Europa del libro nell'età dell'umanesimo. Atti del XIV Convegno Internazionale (Chianciano, Firenze, Pienza 16–19 luglio 2002)* (ed. L. Secchi Tarugi; Quaderni della Rassegna 36; Firenze 2004); *Libri, biblioteche e letture dei frati mendicanti (secoli XIII-XIV)* (Atti dei Convegni della Società internazionale di studi francescani e del Centro interuniversitario di studi francescani 32 = NS 15; Spoleto 2005).

Books are of fundamental importance for education and learning. Before the invention of printed books, the university and school lectures had the purpose of providing the students with books – textbooks and commentaries – by making them write down what was dictated by their teachers. But when the number

---

[115] E. WEIDENHILLER, *Untersuchungen zur deutschsprachigen katechetischen Literatur des späten Mittelalters* (Münchener Texte und Untersuchungen zur deutschen Literatur des Mittelalters 10; München 1965).

[116] N. F. PALMER, "Marquard von Lindau", in: Die deutsche Literatur [see n.113 above] 6 (1987) 81–126.

[117] R. G. WARNOCK, "Heinrich von Friemar", ibid. 3 (1981) 730–37.

of students increased, this procedure no longer sufficed for providing teachers and students completely with the books they needed. Therefore at the universities the production and trade in books by *stationarii* (also *librarii*[118]) developed soon and even in a business-like fashion. A distinction between two kinds of book-traders existed already in the first half of the thirteenth century: a) The *stationarii peciarum (stationarii exemplaria tenentes* or, shortly, *stationarii)* – rather publishers than booksellers – had the texts which were to be published by the teachers as well as other books acknowledged for education *(exemplaria)*. From these manuscripts they made copies in their workshops *(stationes)*, which they sold or lent to single persons for making individual copies. b) The *stationarii librorum* or *venditores librorum* were the true booksellers, but they, too, could have copies made at their own expense. All publishing and selling of books at the universities was organized by them; publishers and booksellers as well as the books were controlled, and the prices of books were determined by the universities.[119] In order to facilitate the copying and the controlling of the copies at the universities soon a system was developed, which looked after the division and distribution of the texts destined for publication in the form of quires *(peciae)*, i.e., loose (unbound) lots of parchment or paper sheets.[120] Thus it was possible, e.g., that several scribes were copying the same obligatory text (the *exemplar*) simultaneously. Like other persons occupied with producing books *(correctores, rasores, miniatores, ligatores* and others) they were subordinated to the university authorities (rector, chancellor).

Books were also written outside universities. In religious houses of monks or friars the composition and the copying of texts was continued throughout the Middle Ages.[121] In the fifteenth century the production of books was especially enforced by the Carthusians who had since their beginning in the thirteenth century a predilection for writing and preserving books,[122] as well as by the Augustinian canons of the Windesheim congregation and by the Brethren of the Common Life who considered the writing of manuscripts and later the printing of books as their most important work.[123] Besides universities and re-

---

[118] Paris university statutes from 1275 (CUP 1, 533,1f. no. 462): *stacionarii, qui vulgo librarii appellantur.*

[119] The first preserved Paris price-list dates from about 1275/1286 (CUP 1, 644–50 no. 530).

[120] J. DESTREZ, *La Pecia dans les manuscrits universitaires du XIIIe et du XIVe siècle* (Paris 1935); K. CHRIST, "Petia", *Zentralblatt für Bibliothekswesen* 55 (1938) 1–44; C. A. ROBSON, "The *pecia* of the Twelfth-Century Paris School", *Dominican Studies* 2 (1949) 267–79; M.-D. CHENU / J. DESTREZ, "*Exemplaria* universitaires des XIIIe et XIVe siècles", *Vivarium* 7 (1953) 68–80; G. POLLARD, "The *pecia* system in the medieval universities", in: *Medieval scribes, manuscripts & libraries. Essays presented to N. R. Ker* (ed. M. B. Parkes / A. G. Watson; London 1978) 145–61; A. J. PIPER / M. R. FOSTER, "Evidence of the Oxford Booktrade, about 1300", *Viator* 20 (1989) 155–60.

[121] Cf. HBOT I/2 (2000) 154–56.

[122] Guigo I, Consuetudines 28,3f. (Guiges Ier, *Coutumes de Chartreuse*; ed. par un Chartreux; SC 313; Paris 1984) 224. Cf. *Bücher, Bibliotheken und Schriftkultur der Kartäuser* (above n.107); specimen of a monograph: J. P. GUMBERT, *Die Utrechter Kartäuser und ihre Bücher im frühen fünfzehnten Jahrhundert* (Leiden 1974).

[123] W. LOURDAUX, "Het boekenbezit en het boekengebruik bij de Moderne Devoten", in: *Studies over het boekenbezit en boekengebruik in de Nederlanden vóór 1600* (Archiefen Bibliotheekwezen in Belgie, special no. 11; Bruxelles 1974) 247–325; J. VAN ENGEN, "The Virtues, the Brothers, and the Schools", *RBén* 98 (1988) 178–217; N. STAUBACH, "Pragmatische Schriftlichkeit im Bereich der Devotio moderna", in: *Frühmittelalterliche Studien* 25 (1991) 418–61; idem, "Der Codex

ligious houses there was a growing production of books and book trade, too, especially in Later Middle Ages.[124]

For the preservation of books libraries were established, which often reflected the intellectual interests of their owners.[125] For a long time autonomous university libraries did not exist, because the universities in general did not get their own buildings before the fifteenth century. Collections of books larger than the private properties of masters and students existed above all in the colleges and in the houses of *religiosi*. In most cases they were desk libraries, which served both as a storage of books and as reading-rooms. The books were kept on desks; they often were chained to them (chain libraries). This form of library, however, was appropriate only for the stocks of manuscripts common in the Middle Ages. Some hundred books already made up a large library. An important English scholar of the thirteenth century, bishop Robert Grosseteste, had perhaps about 90 books;[126] his younger contemporary Gérard d'Abbeville, professor of theology in Paris, seems to have possessed about 460, of which he bequeathed about 300 to the library of the Sorbonne.[127] The Sorbonne had at its disposal 1017 volumes in 1289, 1722 volumes in 1338.[128]

During the twelfth century the production of paper, which had been invented in China, was introduced to the Christian West via the Arabian Near East and Arabian Spain. Since 1144 paper was produced in Spain, since the thirteenth century in Middle and North Italy. The introduction of this material, which was much cheaper than the hitherto exclusively used parchment, led to a remarkable increase in scholarly books. Yet even more decisive was the invention of books printed by movable types, introduced by Johannes Gutenberg (d. 1468) in Mainz about the middle of the fifteenth century.[129] This new practice of printing made it possible to produce a great number of identical copies of the same book. Up to 1500 about 30000 printed books can be identified, which are called incunables *(incunabula)*. About 7000 of them were printed in German speaking countries. Centres of early printing were Paris, London, Oxford and Venice, in Germany Cologne, Strasbourg, Basel, Augsburg and Nuremberg.

Book collections in universities were enlarged not so much by purchase as by donations and legacies of complete private libraries, especially of libraries of scholars and princes, who possessed the most important secular collections of the Late Middle Ages, e. g., the Count Palatin (Pfalzgraf bei Rhein) at Heidelberg. Apart from the collections used by universities, of course, there still existed the libraries of monasteries.[130] With the rise of universities during the

---

als Ware. Wirtschaftliche Aspekte der Handschriftenproduktion im Bereich der Devotio moderna", in: Der Codex im Gebrauch (1996) 143–62; Faix, *Gabriel Biel* (above n. 109) 167–75; T. KOCK, *Die Buchkultur der Devotio moderna. Handschriftenproduktion, Literaturversorgung und Bibliotheksaufbau im Zeitalter des Medienwechsels* (Tradition – Reform – Innovation 2; Frankfurt a. M. ²2002).

[124] Cf., e. g., C. P. CHRISTIANSON, "A Century of the Manuscript-Book Trade in Late Medieval London", *MeH* (Boulder) NS 12 (1984) 143–65.

[125] P. KIBRE, "The Intellectual Interests Reflected in Libraries of the Fourteenth and Fifteenth Centuries", *JHI* 7 (1946) 257–97.

[126] R. W. HUNT, "The Library of Robert Grosseteste", in: *Robert Grosseteste. Scholar and Bishop* (ed. D. A. Callus; Oxford 1955) 127–29.

[127] P. GLORIEUX, "Bibliothèques de Maîtres parisiens: Gérard d'Abbeville", *RThAM* 36 (1969) 148–83.

[128] J. DE GHELLINCK, "Un bibliophile au XIVᵉ siècle. Richard Aungerville de Bury (1345)", *RHE* 28 (1922) 271–312, 482–508; 29 (1923) 157–200, here: 176.

[129] S. FÜSSEL, *Johannes Gutenberg* (Reinbek bei Hamburg 1999); idem, *Gutenberg und seine Wirkung* (Frankfurt a. M. / Leipzig 1999); *Gutenberg – aventur und kunst. Vom Geheimunternehmen zur ersten Medienrevolution* (Catalogue; ed. Stadt Mainz; Mainz 2000).

[130] One of the largest was that of Cîteaux, which contained about 1200 volumes in 1480 (Ghellinck [see n. 128] 29 [1923] 176). – For the mendicants cf., e. g., S. ORLANDI, *La biblioteca di S. Maria Novella in Firenze dal sec. XIV al sec. XIX* (Firenze 1952); D. GUTIÉRREZ, "De antiquis Ordinis Eremitarum Sancti Augustini bibliothecis", *Analecta Augustiniana* 23 (1954) 164–372; F. MATTESINI, "La biblioteca francescana di S. Croce e Fra Tedaldo Della Casa", *Studi francescani* 57

fourteenth century they had diminished at first, but due to the reforming movement of the fifteenth century they flourished again.

Late mediaeval Humanism brought about a vigorous revival of making and collecting books. The libraries of the humanists Francesco Petrarca and Coluccio Salutati were among the largest mediaeval private book collections, and the Nuremberg patrician family Pirckheimer collected books for several generations. In German speaking countries – apart from the Vadiana in St. Gallen – only the library of the humanist Beatus Rhenanus at Schlettstadt (Sélestat) in Alsace containing about 670 volumes is completely preserved.[131] The library of the Medici family contained more than 1000 volumes according to the inventory, which was made 1495, when the library was received by the Dominicans of S. Marco in October 1495 after Piero's de'Medici flight from Florence in 1494.[132] Only a tenth is saved of the largest princely collection of books in the late Middle Ages and the largest but one in the Occident beside the Vatican library: that of the Hungarian king Matthias Corvinus, which in 1490 contained about 2000 to 2500 volumes.[133] During the fifteenth century also the tendency to open libraries for external users increased. Public libraries, however, did only gradually come into existence, at first in Italy: e. g., the Biblioteca di S. Marco of Florence dating back to 1441, or the Biblioteca di S. Marco of Venice from 1468. Book collections of the urban councils served primarily for official use and did not become public libraries before the Reformation.

(1960) 254–316; Ch. T. Davis, "The Earlier Collection of Books of S. Croce in Florence", *Proceedings of the American Philosophical Society* 107 (1963) 399–414; D. Gutiérrez, "La biblioteca di Santo Spirito in Firenze nella metà del secolo XV", *Analecta Augustiniana* 25 (1962) 5–88.

[131] P. Adam, *Der Humanismus zu Schlettstadt* (Obernai s. a.) 83–90.

[132] E. S. Piccolomini, "Delle condizioni e delle vicende della libreria Medicea dal 1494 al 1508 privata compilato nel 1495", *Archivio Storico Italiano* 3, 19 (1874) 101–29; "Documenti intorno alle vicende della libreria Medicea privata dal 1494 al 1508", ibid. 254–91; idem, "Inventario della libreria Medicea privata compilato nel 1495"; ibid. 3, 20 (1874) 51–94.

[133] C. Csapodi, *Bibliotheca Corviniana: the Library of King Matthias Corvinus of Hungary* (Budapest ²1981); E. Gamillscheg e.a., *Matthias Corvinus und die Bildung der Renaissance* (Catalogue; Wien 1994); *Nel segno del Corvo – libri e miniature della biblioteca di Mattia Corvino re d'Ungheria (1443–1490)* (ed. N. Bono e.a.; Modena 2002).

CHAPTER SEVEN

Ad fontes!
The Early Humanist Concern for the *Hebraica veritas*

By Arjo Vanderjagt, Groningen

Bibliographies: Early Printed Bibles. Printed Bibles and Bible Translations in the Fifteenth and Six-teenth Centuries on Microfiche (ed. F. Büsser; Leiden: University Library 1988). Literature on hu-manism, the Renaissance and the Reformation is enormous but the study of Hebrew and the Old Testament is usually only sporadically mentioned. The best bibliographical instruments are inter-net search engines such as *Google*; also valuable is the electronic bibliography of the Renaissance Society of America: ITER <http://iter.library.utoronto.ca/iter/iter1a3.htm>. For humanists in the Low Countries mentioned in this chapter (often not found in more general bibliographies): A. Gerlo / H. D. L. Vervliet, *Bibliographie de l'Humanisme des Anciens Pays-Bas avec un répertoire bibliographique des humanistes et poètes néo-latins* (Brussels: Presses Universitaires de Bruxelles 1972), and its Supplément 1970–1985 (ed. M. de Schepper / C. L. Heesakkers; Brussels: Konink-lijke Academie 1988).

General works: BTT IV (1984); BTT V (1989); I. Backus / G. Bedouelle / R. G. Hobbs, "Bi-ble", *The Oxford Encyclopedia of the Reformation* 1 (ed. H. J. Hillerbrand; Oxford: Oxford UP 1996) 152–71; G. Bedouelle / I. Backus / K. Bland / D. Price / D. Danielle, "Bible", *Encyclo-pedia of the Renaissance* 1 (ed. P. F. Grendler; New York: Scribner's 1999) 209–25; J. H. Bentley, *Humanists and Holy Writ* (Princeton: Princeton UP 1983); CHB II ([1969] repr.1980); CHB III ([1963] repr.1978); *The Cambridge History of Later Medieval Philosophy* (ed. N. Kretzmann / A. Kenny / J. Pinborg; Cambridge: Cambridge UP 1982); *The Cambridge History of Renaissance Phi-losophy* (ed. C. B. Schmitt / Q. Skinner; Cambridge: Cambridge UP 1988); J. Friedman, *The Most Ancient Testimony. Sixteenth-Century Christian-Hebraica in the Age of Renaissance Nostalgia* (Athens, OH: Ohio UP 1983); A. Grabois, "The Hebraica veritas and Jewish-Christian intellec-tual relations in the twelfth century", *Spec.* 50 (1975) 613–34; idem, "Bible", *Dictionary of the Mid-dle Ages* 3 (ed. J. R. Strayer; New York: Scribner's 1983) 210–17; idem, "Political and Cultural Changes from the Fifth to the Eleventh Century", HBOT I/2 (2000) 28–55; *Histoire de l'exégèse au 16e siècle: Texts du colloque international tenu à Genève en 1976* (ed. O. Fatio / P. Fraenkel; Gene-va: Droz 1978); A. Morisi Guerra, "Cultura ebraica ed esegesi biblica cristiana tra Umanesimo e Riforma", *Ebrei e Cristiani nell'Italia Medievale e Moderna: Conversioni, scambi, contrasti* (Rome: Carucci 1988) 209–23; A. Hamilton, "Humanists and the Bible", *The Cambridge Companion to Renaissance Humanism* (ed. J. Kraye; Cambridge: Cambridge UP 1996); HBOT I/1 (1996); HBOT I/2 (2000); H. A. Oberman, "Discovery of Hebrew and Discrimination against the Jews: The *Veritas Hebraica* as Double-Edged Sword in Renaissance and Reformation", *Germania Illus-trata. Essays on Early Modern Germany Presented to Gerald Strauss* (ed. A. C. Fix / S. C. Karant-Nunn; Kirksville, MO: Northeast Missouri State University 1992) 19–34; J. S. Preus, *From Sha-dow to Promise. Old Testament Interpretation from Augustine to the Young Luther* (Cambridge, MA: Belknap 1969); S. Rebenich, "Jerome: The 'vir trilinguis' and the 'hebraica veritas'", *VC* 47 (1993), 50–77; *Renaissance Humanism. Foundations, Forms, and Legacy* 1–3 (ed. A. Rabil, Jr.; Phila-delphia: University of Pennsylvania Press 1988); A. Saltman, *Stephen Langton. Commentary on the Book of Chronicles* (Ramat-Gan: Bar-Ilan UP 1978); B. Smalley, *The Study of the Bible in the Mid-dle Ages* (Oxford: Blackwell 1952, ³1983); *The Bible in the Sixteenth Century* (ed. D. C. Steinmetz; Durham / London: Duke UP 1990); *Théorie et pratique de l'exégèse. Actes du troisième colloque in-ternational sur l'histoire de l'exégèse biblique au XVe siècle en 1988* (ed. I. Backus / F. Higman; Gen-eva: Droz 1990); A. J. Vanderjagt, "Mediating the Bible: Three approaches. The cases of Gian-

nozzo Manetti (1396–1459), Wessel Gansfort (1419–1489) and Sanctes Pagninus (1470–1536)",
*Cultural Mediators. Artists and Writers at the Crossroads of Tradition, Innovation and Reception in
the Low Countries and Italy 1450–1650* (ed. A. de Vries; Leuven: Peeters 2007) 23–40; J. VERGER,
"L'exégèse de l'Université", BTT IV (1984) 199–232.

1. Introduction

Sources: JEAN GERSON: *Propositiones de sensu litterali sacrae Scripturae* (Jean Gerson, *Oeuvres Complètes*, ed. M. Glorieux; Paris: Desclée 1962), vol. 3, 333–40. Many of the sources mentioned in
this section have not been edited and are available only in manuscripts; often they are quoted at
length in the general works listed here.

General works: P. ARNADE, *Realms of Ritual. Burgundian Ceremony and Civic Life in Late Medieval Ghent* (Ithaca / London: Cornell UP 1996); D. BELL, "*Agrestis et infatua interpretatio*: The
Background and Purpose of John of Forde's condemnation of Jewish Exegesis", *A Gathering of
Friends. The Learning and Spirituality of John of Forde* (ed. H. Costello / C. Holdsworth: Kalamazoo: Cistercian Publications 1996) 131–51; C. C. DE BRUIN, *De Delftse Bijbel in het lichte der historie. Inleiding bij de heruitgave A.D. 1477* (Amsterdam / Alphen aan de Rijn: Buijten en Schipper-
heijn 1977); A. COMBES, *Essai sur la critique de Ruysbroeck par Gerson* 1–3 (Paris: Vrin 1945-59);
H. DE LUBAC, *Exégèse médiévale. Les quatre sens de l'Ecriture* 4 (2 vols. in 4; Paris: Aubier 1959–
64); K. FROEHLICH, "Christian Interpretation of the Old Testament in the High Middle Ages",
HBOT I/2 (2000) 496–558; D. GALLET-GUERNE, *Vasque de Lucène et la Cyropédie à la cour de
Bourgogne (1470). Le traité de Xénophon mis en français d'après la version latine du Pogge* (Genève:
Droz 1974); *Geert Grote en Moderne Devotie* (ed. J. Andriesen / P. Bange / A. G. Weiler; Nijme-
gen: Katholieke Universiteit / "Ons Geestelijke Erf" 59: 2–3 [1985] 1985); A. Gow, "Challenging
the Protestant paradigm: Bible reading in lay and urban contexts of the Later Middle Ages", in:
*Scripture and Pluralism. Reading the Bible in the Religiously Plural Worlds of the Middle Ages and Re-
naissance* (ed. T. J. Hefferman / T. E. Burman; Leiden: Brill 2005) 161–91; N. GREITEMANN, *De
Windesheimsche Vulgaatrevisie in de vijftiende eeuw* (Hilversum: Paul Brand 1937); B. HAGGH,
"The Virgin Mary and the Order of the Golden Fleece", *Le Banquet du Faisan 1454: l'Occident face
au défi de l'Empire ottoman* (ed. M.-T. Caron / D. Clauzel; Arras: Artois PU 1997) 273–87; B.
HALL, "Biblical scholarship: editions and commentaries", CHB II (1980) 38–93; J. G. HEYMANS,
Psalters der moderne devotie (Leiden: Brill 1978); G. KIPLING, *Enter the king. Theatre, Liturgy, and
Ritual in the Medieval Civic Triumph* (Oxford: Clarendon 1998); K. KOCK, *Die Buchkultur der De-
votio moderna. Handschriftenproduktion, Literaturversorgung und Bibliothekaufbau im Zeitalter des
Medienwechsels* (Frankfurt am Main: Peter Lang 1999); V. LEROQUAIS, *Les psautiers manuscrits la-
tins des bibliothèques de France* 1–3 (Macon: Protat 1940–41); *Literary Uses of Typology from the
Late Middle Ages to the Present* (ed. E. Miner; Princeton: Princeton UP 1977); *L'ordre de la Toison
d'or de Philippe le Bon à Philippe le Beau (1430–1505). Idéal ou reflet d'une société?* (ed. C. Van den
Bergen-Pantens; Brussels: Bibliothèque royale 1996); *The Place of the Psalms in the Intellectual Culture of the Middle Ages* (ed. N. Van Deusen; Albany: SUNY Press 1999); R. R. POST, *The Modern
Devotion. Confrontation with Reformation and Humanism* (Leiden: Brill 1968); M. PRIETZEL, *Guillaume Fillastre der Jüngere (1400/1407–1473). Kirchenfürst und herzoglich-burgundischer Rat* (Stuttgart: Thorbecke 2001); *Time Sanctified. The Book of Hours in Medieval Art and Life* (ed. R. S.
Wieck; New York: Braziller 1988); P. VAN GEEST, *Thomas a Kempis (1379/80–1471). Een studie
van zijn mens-en godsbeeld* (Kampen: Kok 1996).

At the very end of the thirteenth century, Roger Bacon (c. 1214/15 – c. 1292)
complained bitterly that young mendicants were preaching and teaching
Christian doctrine without the solid liberal arts background that is necessary
for a fruitful study and interpretation of the Bible.[1] Instead of steeping them-

---

[1] Froehlich, Christian Interpretation (2000) 556f; cf. Smalley, The Study of the Bible (1983)
329ff.

selves in the "sapiential languages", Greek, Hebrew, Aramaic and Arabic, theologians became consumed by the grammatical and logical intricacies of scholastic philosophy. They neglected preaching the biblical message which ought to have been at the apex of their duties. Still, Bacon's focus was not really on the use of the ancient text of the Bible, but he emphasised that an understanding of the vices and virtues, penalties and rewards implicit in Christian doctrine "is written in the hearts through the Church's *liturgical* practice". This was a far cry from any desire to find meaning for the Scriptures in either the Greek or the Aramaic and Hebrew sources. It has been argued by JEROME FRIEDMAN that the ideal of the *Hebraica veritas* was surely one of the "most overstated ideals of the Christian Middle Ages. [...] The fact is that probably no more than a few dozen Christians from 500–1500 could read Hebrew at all and perhaps a quarter of that number could use Hebrew in any constructive sense. Indeed, knowledge of Hebrew may have been an ideal precisely because no one knew any".[2] This is all the more remarkable because much as the Greek sources were far away in distance and in time for Latin Europeans, the Hebrew texts were directly available to them in any city or town with a Jewish community in the degree to which periodical expulsions were not effective. Furthermore, copies of the Bible of the twelfth and thirteenth centuries often have Hebrew-Latin glossaries as an appendix.[3]

Scholarly exegesis, however, of a textual, literal sort such as that of Stephen Langton declined in the Latin West through the fourteenth century, and not until the rise of the spiritual and mystical movements at the end of that century was there a revival of allegorical and anagogical interpretations of Scripture, notably of the Psalms, in direct relation to the Gospels.[4] This renewed interest in the Bible was primarily a practical one, geared to providing guidelines for an "imitation" by the simple and devout faithful of Christ's life, as in *De imitatione Christi* by Thomas a Kempis (1379/80–1471), or to establishing methods of mystical fulfillment in the contemplation of God, outlined earlier by Jan van Ruusbroec (1293–1381) in, for example, *Die geestelike brulocht.* This is part of the programme of Jean Gerson (1363–1429) at Paris when he explains the literal sense of Scripture in terms of what has been called "une religion plus sensible au coeur".[5] The Scriptures do not follow academic logic or the rhetoric of scholasticism, they possess their own spiritual rhetoric. Gerson recognizes the traditional fourfold interpretation of Scripture but his higher regard for the literal sense is evident. However, the literal sense of the Old Testament as he understands it has no meaning or use in or of itself. In *De sensu litterali sacrae*

---

[2] Friedman, The Most Ancient Testimony (1983) 12f, 49, n.1; see also Bell, *Agrestis et infatua interpretatio* (1996); cf. the discussion by Froehlich, Christian Interpretation (2000) 555, of SMALLEY's definition of 'biblical scholarship' (Smalley, The Study of the Bible); he quotes SALTMAN (Stephen Langton, 1978, 30) to the effect that it is even doubtful whether Nicholas of Lyra, "the most 'Jewish' of the medieval Christian exegetes", could have passed an examination in elementary Hebrew; but see Grabois, The 'Hebraica veritas' (1975) and De Lubac, Exégèse médiévale, II/1 (1963), chs. 3 and 4.

[3] Bell, *Agrestis et infatua interpretatio* (1996) 137–38.

[4] Grabois, Bible (1983) 214; on the style of exegesis by Grote, Ruusbroec and Gerson see De Lubac, Exégèse médiévale, II/2 (1964) 487–94.

[5] Verger, L'exégèse de l'Université (1984) 226–27; cf. Vanderjagt, Mediating the Bible (2007).

Scripturae, Gerson writes that the literal meaning of the Old and New Testaments is revealed by Christ and his Apostles and clarified by their miracles, and that it has subsequently been confirmed by the blood of the martyrs.[6] Casting aside the subtleties of scholastic theology and of solipsistic mysticism, he points the way to the literal text of the Bible as it was known at the end of the fourteenth century. Furthermore, he insists on a kind of 'common sense' interpretation to discover the meaning of that literal text.[7] Regardless, there is here no clamor of *ad fontes!* and no return to the ancient sources. Gerson's emphasis on the literal text has to do with the dangers inherent in allegorical, anagogical and mystical interpretations – especially of a Platonist kind – which in his eyes all too easily lead to subjectivity, even to pantheism and thus to heterodoxy, as in the case of Ruusbroec.[8] Moreover, the almost exclusive emphasis of these theologians on the New Testament is abundantly clear. The Old Testament is not studied except within the interpretative framework of the New. By and large, the majority of Old Testament quotations in the works of these 'spiritual' authors are from the Psalms and the Canticle of Canticles, and all are applied directly to Christ.[9]

Geert Grote (1340–84), often called the founder of the Modern Devotion, was the first to translate seven Psalms from the Vulgate into Netherlandish, and his book of hours for laymen, which contains the vernacular texts of 54 Psalms completely and of 6 partially, was widely distributed.[10] Through the influence of the Modern Devouts, the Dutch vernacular *Eerste Historiebijbel* (translated by the Carthusians of Herne in South Brabant) had a greater readership in the northern Low Countries than in the south. Yet, the many richly illuminated copies made of it around Utrecht in the middle of the fifteenth century lacked the Old Testament Chronicles and the Prophets, and instead of the individual Gospels of Matthew, Mark, Luke and John they contained only the old Gospel harmony. Similarly, the first printed book in Dutch, the so-called *Delft Bible* (1477) – which published the text of the Bible without any commentary – lacked the Psalms and the New Testament. Both these Bibles were thus heavily weighted towards the Old Testament. This must not, however, be interpreted as a sign of disinterest in the New. Rather, it shows to the contrary that there were many copies of the Psalms already in circulation "both as a complete book and – more commonly – in the Books of Hours ... The so-called Epistles and Gospels, which contained selections from the New Testament – as well as several from the Old Testament – and were widely read as a translation of the Scripture lessons of the Missal, could serve to take the place of the New Testament".[11] Apparently publishing these parts of Scripture in a printed book did not make economic good sense in such a surplus market. In fact, it is surprising that the *Old* Testament was printed at all.

---

[6] Gerson, *Propositiones de sensu litterali sacrae Scripturae* (1962) 335.
[7] Froehlich, 'Always to Keep the Literal Sense in Holy Scripture Means to Kill One's Soul', in: Literary Uses of Typology (1977) 20–48. Gerson's discussion is part of his vivid debate with Jean Petit, the defender of John the Fearless, duke of Burgundy, against charges of having illicitly (!) assassinated the duke of Orleans, the brother of the king of France, in 1407. On Gerson's version of the common-sense argument, especially 39 ff. Gerson's 'common sense' attitude has been characterised by De Lubac, Exégèse médiévale, II/2 (1963) 491–92, as "un procédé pédagogique souvent tout artificiel". Gerson himself defends the rhetorical figures *quas communis usus committit, cum consideratione circumstantiarum litterae ex praecedentibus et posterius appositas*, ibid. 334.
[8] Combes, Essai sur la critique de Ruysbroeck (1945–1959).
[9] See, for example, the analysis of Thomas a Kempis by Van Geest, Thomas a Kempis (1996).
[10] Heymans, Psalters der moderne devotie (1978).
[11] De Bruin, De Delftse Bijbel (1977) *45-*46.

Among the followers of the Modern Devotion, Gerhard Zerbolt (1367–98), for example, stipulates that large parts of the Bible, the Apocalypse of the New Testament and the Prophets of the Old, in particular Isaiah and Jeremiah, were not to be made accessible to laymen in translation because they might easily be misled by the figures and parables (*figure parabolen unde gelykenissen*) contained therein.[12] But here again there is the very highest regard for the New Testament, in particular for the Gospels, and for the pious works of Augustine, Gregory, Bernard of Clairvaux and Anselm of Canterbury. Curiously, the works of these teachers of the Church are seen as less difficult than much of the Bible. This does not mean that the Modern Devotion was completely uninterested in having a good Latin text of the Bible. Grote and even Zerbolt remark not infrequently on their desire for uncorrupted texts. In the fifteenth century, the Windesheimers attempted to revise the heterogeneous Vulgate on the basis of randomly selected texts from the Alcuinian tradition. Their ambitious but deeply flawed version does not stand comparison to critical humanist revisions and it had no practical influence on translators at all.[13] REGNERUS POST sums up this painstaking but methodologically unsound undertaking: "They were not interested in the correct text of the Bible or in its meaning, but in uniformity at the choir service and in reading aloud".[14] Thus piety and spirituality took precedence over interest in the original meaning of the texts.

It is difficult to overestimate the emotional and spiritual power which the book of Psalms exercised throughout the Middle Ages and far into modern times.[15] It stood central in the liturgical practices governing everyone's life and death, at first in medieval Christianity and later also in Evangelical or Reformed circles as it continued to do so in Catholic faith. Through breviary readings at the appointed hours, their hundred- and even thousandfold repetition at funerals and in memory of the dead, the inclusion of crucial passages in various confessions of faith and by memorisation, the Psalms were second nature to much sacred and secular speech. Allegorical and anagogical interpretations transformed them virtually into a part of the New Testament even to the extent that their literal sense is regarded as the voice of Jesus himself. Editions of the Gospels and Epistles through the centuries down to our own accordingly often include the book of Psalms. It is not by coincidence that the first attempt to print a book of the Bible in Hebrew was that of the Psalms at Bologna in 1477.[16] Without doubt, the humanist cry *ad fontes!* resonated immediately with Ps 41 (42): *Quemadmodum desiderat cervus ad fontes aquarum, ita desiderat anima mea ad te, Deus.*

This is not to say that the other books of the Old Testament were not being used in the Late Middle Ages and the early Modern Era. They often served as mixed collections for didactic and pedagogical examples. Learned clerics serving kings and dukes frequently worked hand in glove with the ideologues and masters of ceremonies of princely courts to illustrate the ideas and ideals of sacred kingship. As in earlier centuries, prime examples in these theocratic the-

---

[12] Kock, Die Buchkultur der Devotio moderna (1999) 186–87; for a thorough analysis see Gow, Challenging the Protestant paradigm (2005).

[13] Greitemann, De Windesheimsche Vulgaatrevisie (1937); Post, The Modern Devotion (1968) 304–08.

[14] Ibid. 307.

[15] Leroquais, Les psautiers manuscrits latins (1940–41); Time Sanctified (1988); The Place of the Psalms (1999).

[16] Hall, Biblical scholarship (1980) 49. The very first Hebrew book printed anywhere was Qimhi's great dictionary, the so-called 'Book of Roots' (1469–73, Rome).

ories are drawn from the Old Testament: David, Solomon and the nebulous Melchizedek.[17]

In the fourteenth, fifteenth and sixteenth centuries, an entire body of 'secular' exegesis and of multi-media events arose from Isa 11:1–10, popularly known as the "Jesse Tree". GORDON KIPLING has pointed out how this tree, which is interpreted throughout the Middle Ages in the terms of Christ's ancestry, is allegorized twice over in the socio-political context of late-medieval civic ritual.[18] In the first civic triumph or "entry" of the Burgundian duke, Philip the Good, into Bruges in Flanders on December 11, 1440, it is not Christ who buds forth from the topmost branch of the Jesse Tree. Philip's "presence before the tree defines the duke himself as its promised flower. A spiritual son of David sprung from the house of Jesse, his coming illustrates Isaiah's prophecy of messianic advent". Thus the Old Testament Jesse Tree and the New Testament entry of Christ into Jerusalem are fused into one to sacralise the power of the duke. Again the Old Testament is fully christianised.

Vasco da Lucena (c. 1435–1512) of Portugal, working at the Burgundian court, employs the Old Testament independently from the New in the prologue to his Frenched version (1470) of Poggio Bracciolini's Latin rendition of Xenophon's *Cyropedia*. He provides an exegesis of Isaiah 64 and 65 and Ezra 1, applied to the aspirations of Charles the Bold, duke of Burgundy. The latter is compared to Cyrus the Great, who was directly appointed by God to be the shepherd of the people of Israel on their return to Jerusalem.[19] The Old Testament had been even more extensively mined a few decades earlier in the context of the Burgundian ideology of the Golden Fleece. On the occasion of his marriage to Isabella of Portugal in 1430, duke Philip the Good instituted the Order of the Golden Fleece.[20] The patron of that order was Jason, the famous ancient hero who had sailed from Greece to the land of Colchis to steal the Golden Fleece; Philip, then, was to emulate his virtues. The first chancellor of the order, Jean Germain (c.1400-61), bishop of Chalon-sur Saône, had little time for this pagan theme and he set out to make it religiously acceptable by adding to Jason's fleece that of Old Testament Gideon as a symbol of prudence from Judg 6:37–40. Soon four other fleeces were culled from the Old Testament: those of Jacob or justice from Gen 30:31ff, Mesa, king of Moab, or faithfulness from 2 Kgs 3:4, Job or patience from Job 31:2, and finally of David or clemency from Ps 71:6. An extremely lengthy and learned multi-part exegesis of each of these passages was provided for in a projected set of six massive volumes authored by the proto-humanist Guillaume Fillastre (1400/1407–73), bishop of Tournai and second chancellor of the Order, from 1468 onwards, but only the first three volumes were completed.[21] Yet here too, in a further leap, there is a christianisation of this material: the political theology of the fleeces is connected directly to the virginal state of St. Mary by the musicians of the court.[22]

The uses to which the Old Testament was put in the late Middle Ages described above demonstrate neither a sense of the sources as sources nor a methodology for attaining to a critical editon of the Old Testament on the basis of the Hebrew text. The humanists' urge *ad fontes!* suggests that they are conscious of a distance from a more pure or original past, but this feeling is not found either in theological discussions such as those of Gerson and Grote nor in the learned, secularised use of the Old Testament for political purposes of the Burgundians. Data-bytes from the past are assigned their own places in a single present-day continuum. With regard to the secular use of the Old and New Testaments together with classical Antiquity, PETER ARNADE understatedly observes that "Hercules, Jason, Old Testament prophets such as Isaiah

---

[17] Grabois, Political and Cultural Changes (2000) 44–49
[18] Kipling, Enter the king (1998) 55–56.
[19] Gallet-Guerne, Vasque de Lucène et la Cyropédie (1974) 185.
[20] See for all of this: L'ordre de la Toison d'or de Philippe le Bon (1996).
[21] On Fillastre see Prietzel, Guillaume Fillastre der Jüngere (2001).
[22] Haggh, The Virgin Mary and the Order of the Golden Fleece (1997).

and Ezekiel, and pietistic images of Christ met in street pageantry and banquet tableaux".[23]

2. *Hebraica veritas* and Piety: Northern Humanism

Sources: ALBERT HARDENBERG: *Vita Wesseli Groningensis*, in: Wessel Gansfort, *Opera*, **[1r]-***2v; *Humanismus und Renaissance in den deutschen Städten und an den Universitäten* (ed. H. Rupprich; Leipzig: Philipp Reclam 1932; repr. Darmstadt: Wiss. Buchgesellschaft 1964, in 2 vols.); JOHANNES VON PLENINGEN: *Commentarii seu index vite Rhodolphi Agricole*: W. STRAUBE, "Die Agricola-Bibliographie des Johannes von Plieningen", *Rudolf Agricola 1444-1485* (see below under *General works*) 11-48; E. W. MILLER / J. W. SCUDDER, *Wessel Gansfort. Life and Writings. Principal Works* 1-2 (New York / London: Putnam's / Knickerbocker 1917); RODOLPHUS AGRICOLA: *De inventione dialectica. Lucubrationes* (ed. Alardus of Amsterdam; Cologne: Gymnich 1539; facsimile, Nieuwkoop: De Graaf 1967); RUDOLPH AGRICOLA, *Letters* (ed. A. H. van der Laan / F. Akkerman; Assen: Van Gorcum 2002); L. W. SPITZ / A. BENJAMIN, "Rudolph Agricola's *Exhortatio ad Clerum Wormatiensem*", *ARefG* 54:1/2 (1963) 1-15; WESSEL GANSFORT: *Opera* (facsimile of the edition Groningen 1614; Nieuwkoop: De Graaf 1966).

General works: F. AKKERMAN / C. G. SANTING, "Rudolf Agricola en de Aduarder academie", *Groningse Volksalmanak* 1987, 7-28; F. AKKERMAN, *Six Lives and Erasmus on Rudolph Agricola* (Assen: Van Gorcum, forthcoming); J. LINDEBOOM, *Het bijbelsch humanisme in Nederland. Erasmus en de vroege reformatie* (Leiden 1913; repr. with critical introduction by C. Augustijn: Leeuwarden: Dijkstra 1982); M. VAN RHIJN, *Wessel Gansfort* (The Hague: Nijhoff 1917); *Rodolphus Agricola Phrisius (1444-1485). Proceedings of the International Conference at the University of Groningen 28-30 October 1985* (ed. F. Akkerman /A. J. Vanderjagt; Leiden: Brill 1988); C. AUGUSTIJN, "Erasmus en de Moderne Devotie", *De doorwerking van de Moderne Devotie. Windesheim 1387-1987. Voordrachten gehouden tijdens het Windesheim Symposium Zwolle / Windesheim 15-17 oktober 1987* (ed. P. Bange / C. Graafland / A. J. Jelsma / A. G. Weiler; Hilversum: Verloren 1988) 71-80; G. BEDOUELLE, "L'humanisme et la Bible", *BTT* V (1989) 53-121; B. P. COPENHAVER, "Lefèvre d'Étaples, Symporien Champier, and the secret names of God", *Journal of the Warburg and Courtauld Institutes* 40 (1977) 189-211; J. FRIEDMAN, *The Most Ancient Testimony. Sixteenth-Century Christian-Hebraica in the Age of Renaissance Nostalgia* (Athens, OH: Ohio UP 1983); *Northern Humanism in European Context, 1469-1625. From the 'Adwert Academy' to Ubbo Emmius* (ed. F. Akkerman / A. J. Vanderjagt / A. H. van der Laan; Leiden: Brill 1999) 307-32; H. A. OBERMAN, "Discovery of Hebrew and Discrimination against the Jews" (see above under *General bibliography*); *RudolfAgricola 1444-1485. Protagonist des nordeuropäischen Humanismus zum 550. Geburtstag* (ed. W. Kühlmann; Bern: Lang 1994); A. J. VANDERJAGT, "Wessel Gansfort (1419-1489) and Rudolph Agricola (1443?-1485): Piety and Hebrew", *Frömmigkeit - Theologie - Frömmigkeitstheologie: Contributions to European Church History* (ed. R. Liebenberg / H. Munzert / G. Litz; Leiden: Brill 2005) 159-72; idem, Mediating the Bible (2007; see above under General bibliography); A. H. VAN DER LAAN, "Humanism in the Low Countries before Erasmus: Rodolphus Agricola's address to the clergy at Worms", *Antiquity Renewed* (ed. Z. R. W. M. von Martels / V. Schmidt; Louvain: Peeters 2003) 127-66; H. E. J. M. VAN DER VELDEN, *Rodolphus Agricola (Roelof Huusman). Een nederlandsch humanist der vijftiende eeuw* (Leiden: A. W. Sijthoff 1911); H. DE VOCHT, *History of the Foundation and the Rise of the Collegium Trilingue Lovaniense 1517-1550* 1 (Louvain: Publications Universitaires 1951); *Wessel Gansfort (1419-1489) and Northern Humanism* (ed. F. Akkerman / G. C. Huisman / A. J. Vanderjagt; Leiden: Brill 1993).

Desiderius Erasmus and Johannes Reuchlin gloriously put down the agenda for the North-European humanist movement *ad fontes*.[24] Their light has tended to leave in the shadows the work of two northern scholars from an ear-

---

[23] Arnade, Realms of Ritual (1996) 29-30.
[24] See the relevant chapters in the present volume.

lier generation who each had a high regard for the *Hebraica veritas* and acquired Hebrew with enough skill to interpret Old Testament passages in an often suprisingly new light. Although their impact on the study of the Hebrew
Bible by later sixteenth-century humanists, reformers and academics was not
great, their work is part of the backdrop against which such scholarship can
be appreciated. They are *Wessel Gansfort* and *Rudolph Agricola*, both from
Groningen in the northernmost regions of the Low Countries.[25] Since the pioneering work of JOHANNES LINDEBOOM on what he has called "Bible or biblical
Humanism", Gansfort and Agricola have featured as forerunners of Erasmus
and the early Reformation.[26] LINDEBOOM was sceptical about their connections
to the Modern Devotion and to the spiritual movements of Geert Grote and
Thomas a Kempis, in which he could find no humanist attitudes. Recently,
however, it has been demonstrated that the scholarly intent of the work of
Gansfort and Agricola may even be seen as a culmination of the piety of the
Brethren of the Common Life.[27] HEIKO OBERMAN goes so far as to call Gansfort the *Doctor Devotionis Modernae* precisely because he had set his sights on
the essentials of the *praxis pietatis*. However this may be, it is in this context of
pious devotion that Gansfort's and Agricola's desire to learn Hebrew and their
way of putting their newly acquired knowledge into immediate practice must
be understood.

2.1. Wessel Gansfort

Wessel Gansfort was born at Groningen in 1419.[28] After an initial schooling probably at the local
St Maarten's Latin school, he went to study at Zwolle, where he stayed with the Brethren and
befriended Thomas a Kempis. Leaving Zwolle around 1449, he continued his studies at Cologne
(MA in 1452) and travelled on learning and teaching to Louvain and Paris (1454/1455), Cologne
again (1455/1456), Heidelberg (1456/1457), and Paris once more (1459-c.1473/4). The young
Reuchlin befriended the much older Gansfort at Paris around 1472, long before he had learned
Hebrew himself. In fact, Gansfort is said to have dissuaded him from the study of that language
possibly so the gifted student would devote all his energies to learning Greek.[29] At Paris, too,

---

[25] Recent collections of studies on Agricola, Gansfort and their circles are: Rodolphus Agricola
Phrisius (1988); Rudolf Agricola (1994); Wessel Gansfort (1993); Northern Humanism in European Context (1999). DE VOCHT (History of the Collegium Trilingue Lovaniense, 1951, 139–61)
considers that these "First Heralds of the Renascence" profited from the proto-humanist "spirit
that was at work in Louvain from the middle of the fifteenth century". On the establishment of the
Collegium Trilingue Lovaniense, see below, 181–85.

[26] Lindeboom, Het bijbels humanisme (1913) 39–111, for the idea of 'Bible humanism', 1–38,
but see the introduction by Augustijn of the repr. 1982 and his scepticism on Gansfort's relation
with Erasmus.

[27] H. OBERMAN, "Wessel Gansfort", in: Wessel Gansfort (1993) 97–121; A. G. WEILER, "The
Dutch Brethren of the Common Life", in: Northern Humanism in European Context (1999) 307–
32, contradicting POST (The Modern Devotion, 1968), and AUGUSTIJN (Erasmus en de Moderne
Devotie, 1988; and also his introduction to the reprint of Lindeboom, 1982), connects Gansfort
closely to the Brethren as well as to Erasmus, 322 ff.

[28] The standard account of Gansfort's life is still Van Rhijn, Wessel Gansfort (1917); cf. Wessel
Gansfort (1993).

[29] Van Rhijn, Wessel Gansfort (1917) 94–95 and Bijlage A, ix–x; cf. Agricola's letter of November 9, 1484, in reply to Reuchlin: Agricola, Letters (2002) 231; apparently Gansfort himself did
not know Greek as well as he did Hebrew, if we may conclude this from his well-known mistake in

around 1473, Gansfort became embroiled in the controversies between the *via antiqua* and the *via moderna* about the epistemological status of 'reality' and 'language' and the theological issues to which this gave rise.[30] He did not choose for one school or the other but went his own way, selecting those points of view that suited his reading of the Bible, thus quickly earning for himself the epithet *magister contradictionis*.[31]

Gansfort insisted that he would not agree with any teaching which he saw as contrary to the "canonical Scriptures", that is to say: the Gospels, and what had been handed down by the Apostles.[32] The Gospel is the first and only rule of faith for everyone, for popes as well as for common believers, and the Gospel and its wise interpreters should be obeyed rather than the pope. Gansfort himself contests a number of teachings stipulated by the pope and the Church.[33] Given Gansfort's insistance on personally reading and interpreting the Gospel, it can come as no surprise that he set great store as well by the Hebrew text of the Old Testament. According to one of his earliest biographers in the middle of the sixteenth century, Albert Hardenberg, Gansfort sought out the Greek – and by extension – the Hebrew sources (*sed quaesivit fontes quantum omnino potuit pro tempore illo*) so as not to be misled with regard to the meaning of the original texts.[34]

Gansfort's interest in Hebrew is aptly demonstrated during a visit he made to Rome around 1473, where he was reunited with his old Parisian friend Francesco della Rovere, once general of the Franciscan Order and now elected Pope as Sixtus IV. He found the formerly devout Franciscan to have become a prince of the Church who would have appointed him to a bishopric. Yet instead Wessel requested that he be given a Hebrew Bible from the Vatican Library.[35] This Bible he took with him when he returned to Groningen around 1477, where he avidly studied it, apparently sometimes out loud to the bemusement of bystanders. Pieces of it were apparently still extant in the mid-seventeenth century. Until his death at Groningen in 1489, Gansfort was a member of the circle of humanist scholars who met regularly in the Cistercian abbey of St Bernard at Aduard.[36]

No facts have been discovered about where and how Gansfort learned to read Hebrew, but that he was good at it is clear not only from the frequent quotations of the text of the Old Testament in his works but also from his cri-

---

the Greek superlative form in his *Scala meditationis*, Exemplum I, in: Gansfort, Opera (1614) 331; Melanchthon reports that Reuchlin had told him that Gansfort's knowledge of Greek was at most mediocre; cf. Van Rhijn, Wessel Gansfort (1917) 65.

[30] Hoenen, Albertistae, Thomistae und Nominales, in: Wessel Gansfort (1993) 71–96.

[31] OBERMAN (Wessel Gansfort, 1993) broadens this title out to encompass his entire intellectual activity.

[32] Gansfort, Opera, 877–79, in a letter to Jacobus Hoeck, dean of Naaldwijk.

[33] For example, in the cited letter to Jacobus Hoeck.

[34] Hardenberg, *Vita Wesseli Groningensis* (1614) **[1v]; also published in English translation in Miller / Scudder, Wessel Gansfort 2 (1917) 317 ff.

[35] Hardenberg, *Vita Wesseli Groningensis*, **3r-v; cf. Van Rhijn, Wessel Gansfort (1917) 103–04, with further details.

[36] On the relations of Gansfort to this so-called 'Adwert Academy' and on the activities of these humanists see Hardenberg, *Vita Wesseli Groningensis*; the only modern translation is in Dutch, published by Akkerman / Santing, Rudolf Agricola en de Aduarder Academie (1987).

ticism of the Vulgate in the light of that knowledge.[37] Two examples out of many may suffice to illustrate this here.

The first is a comment on Ps 25:6 in the context of Gansfort's reappraisal of the Lord's Prayer.[38] The Vulgate reads: *reminiscere miserationum tuarum Domine et misericordiarum tuarum*; the Hebrew reads: זכר־רחמיך יהוה וחסדיך. Gansfort introduces his novel exegesis by stating that the Psalmist joins maternal and paternal love in this verse. He then proceeds to explain that contrary to the traditional Latin interpreters who use a single word, namely *miserationes/misericordiae*, to explain God's mercy, the Hebrew uses two different terms: *Ubi loco miserationum habet Hebraeus* Rahem [רחם] *quod maternum affectum a matrice significare diximus; et loco misericordiarum* Hased [חסד], *quod paternum affectum in filios signat*. Having appealed to the Proverbs and to the Canticles that a child should not forget either his mother or his father, Wessel gives a long list of verbs which demonstrate first maternal and then paternal care. He impresses upon his reader that the text of the Bible enjoins us to pray to God as Mother and as Father. In a passage almost too physical in its reference for modern sensibilites in a devotional context, he writes: *Et haec paterna pietas et materna viscera sunt de principalibus operativis nostrae salutis ex parte Dei.*[39] That this exegesis stands central in much of his thought and experience is illustrated by the fact that he returns to it in the middle of a schooled discussion and criticism of Aristotle's theory of the active intellect (*intellectus agens*) as well as in his instructions on meditation.[40] Of course, there is a medieval devotional tradition in which God is described in terms of maternity as in the meditations of Anselm of Canterbury (1033–1109), based upon the exegesis of texts such as Matt 23:37. Gansfort's exercise, however, is different because his exegesis is based not on the face-value of the Latin text – which in the case of Matthew is unambiguously a comparison of a hen and her chicks to God's care of the faithful – but upon an analysis of the meanings of the Psalm's Hebrew words themselves behind the synonymous Latin. In this sense, his is a humanist approach to the text of the Bible.

A second example demonstrating that Gansfort's acute knowledge of Hebrew is fundamentally important for him in understanding the very keystone of Christian doctrine properly and that it is no mere posturing can be taken from his treatise on the sacrament of the Eucharist.[41] In chapter 14 of that work he discusses how Jesus' body is food for salvation for the faithful and food for condemnation to the unfaithful – in Gansfort's eyes in first instance the Jews.[42]

As often in his writings, he departs from a Psalm text, in this case Ps 111:4–5: *Memoriam fecit mirabilium suorum misericors et miserator Dominus escam dedit timentibus se*, which Gansfort, showing his Hebrew, summarises as *Memoriam fecit mirabilium suorum, Thereph dedit timentibus se*; the Hebrew has:

זכר עשה לנפלאתיו חנון ורחום יהוה: טרף נתן ליראיו יזכר לעולם בריתו.

But how is it possible, asks Gansfort, that according to the Psalmist, God gives *Thereph* (טרף), that is to say: unclean flesh which must be put outside the city, to those who fear him? Obviously,

---

[37] Van Rhijn (Wessel Gansfort, 1917, 76) gives a listing of the many instances where Gansfort takes recourse to the Hebrew text. See the important observations by Oberman, Discovery of Hebrew and Discrimination against the Jews (1992) 26–30, and idem, Wessel Gansfort (1993) 114–16, who points out several instances of textual criticism by Gansfort, and Vanderjagt, Wessel Gansfort and Rudolph Agricola (2005); cf. Vanderjagt, Mediating the Bible (2007); Hardenberg, *Vita Wesseli Groningensis*, vaguely mentions mendicants from overseas who taught him Hebrew.

[38] Gansfort, *De oratione et modo orandi*, in: Gansfort, Opera, 59–61; cf. Oberman as cited in the preceding note.

[39] Gansfort, ibid. 61.

[40] Gansfort, *De providentia Dei*, in: Opera, 721; *Scala meditationis*, in: Gansfort, Opera, 403.

[41] Gansfort, *De sacramento Eucharistiae*, in: Gansfort, Opera, 655–708; for this example 684–89.

[42] On Wessel Gansfort's characterisation of the Jews as 'enemies of our faith', see Oberman, Discovery of Hebrew and Discrimination against the Jews (1994) 32.

the Latin word *esca* (food for nourishment) is incorrect for the Hebrew. Referring then to Lev 6:30 (Vg): *hostia enim quae caeditur pro peccato cuius sanguis infertur in tabernaculum testimonii ad expiandum in sanctuario non comedetur sed conburetur igni* (=6:23 HT:

‮(וכל-חטאת אשר יובא מדמה אל-אהל מועד לכפר בקדש לא תאכל באש תשרף‬),

Gansfort explains that for *hostia* – clearly an important liturgical word for any medieval Christian – Moses at Exod 22:12 also has "*Thereph jetareph* (‮טרף יטרף‬, to be read as *taroph yittareph*), that is to say: food (unclean flesh) which must be eaten, [A.V.], without congruence of the first and the second letter of the two words but *without diverging in their meaning at all* [ital. A.V.]". Thus the Hebrew *yittareph* (‮יטרף‬) at the end of the sentence is of utmost importance. In fact, it is the Christian injunction *par excellence*: partake and you shall be saved. He then quotes the explanation in Heb 13:11–12, where Lev 6:23 is glossed: it is Jesus who has suffered outside the city gates as unclean in order to expiate the sins of those who will have faith in him. Gansfort summarises Christ as *Thereph* "to those who persist in their unbelief; but to those who fear God, he serves as a remembrance of His marvelous works", namely his death outside the gates on their behalf. Gansfort reaches back to the Hebrew behind the Latin *esca* and *hostia*, and he uses it to establish a far more profound, even alarming interpretation – at least with regard to unbelievers – than that which the Vulgate offers at first and second reading.

As throughout the Middle Ages, the Psalms are read entirely in a christological way, but the sophistication of Gansfort's exegesis and his philological recourse to the Hebrew text place him foursquare at the beginning of the humanist tradition.

2.2. Rudolph Agricola

In the Autumn of 1485, Johannes Reuchlin pronounced the eulogy for his older contemporary and fellow humanist Rudolph Agricola, who had died on October 27 at Heidelberg.[43] Regrettably his oration has not survived. Doubtless he waxed eloquent in the purest of humanist Latin over the learning and European reputation which Agricola had acquired in Latin, Greek and also, late in life, in Hebrew, and over his untiring pursuit of classical texts and unstinting pedagogical and didactic advice. Attention will also have been given to Agricola's piety, which was evident from the fact that he was buried in the habit of the third-order Franciscans in the church of St. Francis. This would have been especially fitting because it was precisely for religious and spiritual reasons that only five or six years earlier Agricola had commenced Hebrew studies, directing his attention first of all to translating the Psalms.[44]

Rudolph Agricola was born at Baflo near Groningen in 1443 / 1444 to Zycka Huusman ("Agricola" is the Latinised form of "Huusman", which in the Groningen language of the period signifies an independent farmer) as probably the 'natural' son of Hinrick Vries, abbot of Siloë.[45] He was first taught at the St. Maarten's Latin school in Groningen which Gansfort had attended earlier. A young and excellent scholar, he matriculated in the university of Erfurt in 1456 and was awarded

---

[43] The standard account of Agricola's life is still Van der Velden, Rodolphus Agricola (1911); cf. Rodolphus Agricola Phrisius (1444–1485) (1988).

[44] Van der Velden, Rodolphus Agricola (1911) 226–31, and the sources cited there; cf. Rodolphus Agricola Phrisius (1988) 326; Agricola's love of the Psalms is clear, e.g. from his oration to the clergy of Worms where he quotes them almost as often (7 times) as he does the New Testament (10 times); see Spitz / Benjamin, Rudolph Agricola's Exhortatio (1963), and for a philologically sound edition of this oration, Van der Laan, Humanism in the Low Countries (2003).

[45] Bakker, Roeloff Huusman, in: Rodolphus Agricola Phrisius (1988) 99–111.

his MA in 1460. Further studies followed perhaps at Cologne and at Louvain, and he acquired another MA with highest honors. A literary man, an avid reader of Plato, Aristotle and Cicero, a mathematician and a gifted musician, even an organ builder, Agricola disdained contemporary scholastic debate. He was drawn to Italy where he began to study law at Pavia. Increasingly in the thrall of Cicero and Quintilian, especially for their Latin style, he immersed himself in the study of classical Latin and Greek. In the summer of 1475, Agricola moved on to the university of Ferrara where his teachers in Greek were Battista Guarino and Ludovico Carbone. Meanwhile his reputation was steadily growing and he was honorably appointed to deliver the inaugural lecture for 1476 / 1477 in the presence of Ercole d'Este, the duke of Ferrara himself. This oration is entitled *Oratio in laudem philosophiae et reliquarum artium*; it is a typical humanist exercise praising the literary arts and that kind of philosophy and science that is beneficial to humankind.[46] In this period, too, he wrote his main work on rhetoric and logic, *De inventione dialectica*, meant to counteract scholasticism and put down the methodology for humanist studies. It was to become an important textbook, in use throughout Europe in the sixteenth century. Once again in Groningen in 1479, Agricola was an active member together with Wessel Gansfort of the "Aduard circle". Soon he was appointed secretary and ambassador of the city, while his fame as a humanist and teacher continued to spread. He was invited to the court at Heidelberg of Johannes Kämmerer von Dalberg, bishop of Worms, for the sole purpose of furthering his own studies as he instructed the bishop. Among the humanists whom he met here was Johannes Reuchlin. In the Spring of 1485, Dalberg and Agricola traveled to Rome to pay their respects to the newly elected Pope Innocent VIII on behalf of the Palatinate. On the voyage home, Agricola fell ill and shortly after his return to Heidelberg, he died in the arms of his patron Dalberg.

In a letter of November 9, 1484, Agricola dissuades Reuchlin rhetorically from the study of Hebrew:[47] great men such as Reuchlin "have acquired a famous and illustrious reputation through more distinguished studies" and they do not need Hebrew to augment it. He himself, however, must "try my hand at something more impressive than [the studies] of the common herd" in order to excel. He continues that he has mastered his languages in order to be of benefit to others in "the Republic of Learning of my fatherland". Hebrew he is learning for himself; "for I have decided to spend the leisure of my old age (if I reach it, that is) in the examination of Holy Writ ... and simultaneously [to] get to really know the peculiar nature of that language, full of so many mysteries". Concluding, Agricola remarks that Wessel Gansfort has spurred him on to undertake these studies.

It is unknown how Agricola exactly acquired his knowledge of and perhaps even versatility in Hebrew. The court of bishop Dalberg was accessible to Jews; the bishop had taken in a recently converted Jew, who served as a kind of intellectual sparring partner in learned disputes involving matters of faith. In a letter to Jacob Barbireau of June 7, 1484, Agricola mentions this man as his Hebrew teacher. Apparently he had other friendly relations with Jews as well. On April 13, 1485, Agricola writes his friend the publisher Adolf Rusch at Strasbourg that his letter will be delivered to the latter by the hand of Flavius Wilhelmus Raimundus Mithridates de Moncata, a converted Jew from the environs of Barcelona.[48] In a kind of jealous irony, Agricola writes that this man is "an expert in all languages (Latin, Greek, Hebrew, Syriac, Arabic – I may have forgotten some-

---

[46] Agricola, *Oratio in laudem philosophiae*, in: Humanismus und Renaissance (1932) 164–83; cf. Vanderjagt, Rudolph Agricola, in: Rodolphus Agricola Phrisius (1988) 219–28.

[47] Agricola, Letters, 227–31; see also Vanderjagt, Wessel Gansort and Rudolph Agricola (2005).

[48] For his Hebrew teacher: Agricola, Letters, 216; for Flavius: Agricola, Letters, 245–47; 376. Styling himself Flavius Mithridates when he moved to Italy, he was closely connected to Christian Kabbalism; among his students was Pico della Mirandola; BEDOUELLE (L'humanisme et la Bible, 1989, 64) calls him "le célèbre Flavius Mithridate, personnage étrange"; cf. De Vocht, History of the Collegium Trilingue Lovaniense (1951) 160–61; some say that his origins were in Agrigento.

thing)". Agricola regrets that he has not been able to spend more time with someone who is at once a theologian, a philosopher and a poet, "in short, one man in all disciplines and all disciplines in one man". Wilhelmus Raimundus had studied theology at Tübingen; he also taught Hebrew there and at Louvain, and now he was studying arts and theology at Cologne. Doubtless, there were other Jews or converts whom Agricola with the approbation of Dalberg might have enlisted to teach him.

He must have been a quick student because already late in 1484 or in early 1485 Reuchlin is seeking his advice on a translation problem with regard to the names of God in Pss 53:3 (54) and 39:5 (40). By which name are Christians saved: by *JOSHUA* [יהושע] that is to say: Jesus, transposed back to Hebrew by Reuchlin from his reading of Acts 4:12, or rather by *YHWH* [יהוה]. Apparently, Reuchlin at this time did not yet have enough Hebrew and Greek to phrase his question more precisely, nor had he apparently read Nicholas of Cusa on this matter. Cusa thought that the name *IHSUH* [יהשוה] might be written as *YHWH* [יהוה] with the consonant *shin* [ש] in the middle.[49] Thus God and Jesus could be joined grammatically, even alphabetically, and the unity of the Old and the New Testament proved through the conjunction of Psalms and Acts. Regrettably, Agricola's answer has either been lost or for some reason he was unable to write one.[50] Although he found the going hard, Agricola writes to Hegius in the winter of 1485, alluding to the Vulgate, that he intends to persist because he "cannot stand the barbarism, the impurity, the crudeness of those who have a firm grip on everything [regarding religious studies] in our times".[51] But death put an end to his plans.

What then of the influence of Gansfort and Agricola? Little of it can be traced. Martin Luther and his ardent supporter in the middle of the sixteenth century, Matthias Flacius Illyricus, consider the work of Wessel Gansfort as a tributary to their own. In a letter, Luther writes that "If I had read his [= Gansfort's, A.V.] works earlier, my enemies might think that Luther had absorbed everything from Wessel, his spirit is so in accord with mine".[52] Illyricus considers Wessel and Luther to be true prophets, called by God, even if he uses Greek and not Hebrew to designate them.[53] Erasmus praised Agricola in several letters, and he is known to have purchased some of Agricola's works for his personal use. He seems also to have used Agricola's translations from

---

[49] FRIEDMAN (The Most Ancient Testimony, 1983, 80–81) has pointed out that this is, of course, philologically impossible.

[50] Agricola, Letters, 257; this problem went on to plague Reuchlin for the next quarter of a century. FRIEDMAN (ibid.), for whom Agricola comes too early, gives a detailed analysis of it to show the limits of both Reuchlin's and Lefèvre d'Étaples's technical knowledge of Hebrew. On the history of this problem see Copenhaver, Lefèvre d'Étaples, Symphorien Champier, and the secret names of God (1977), esp. 198–206. See also below, 174–79.

[51] Agricola, Letters, 236–39; Van der Velden, Rodolphus Agricola (1911) 229–30. This and other activities (orations and poems on religious subjects) make clear that the assessment of LINDEBOOM (Het bijbels humanisme, 1913 / 1982, 62) is off the mark; he writes that Agricola's humanism is "rich in form but poor in ideas" and contrasts him with Wessel Gansfort "to whom religious humanism owes much". See also the analysis by Van der Laan, Humanism in the Low Countries (2003).

[52] For this letter: Gansfort, Opera, 854.

[53] For quotes and references see Augustijn, Wessel Gansfort's rise to celebrity, in: Wessel Gansfort (1993) 15.

the Greek.[54] But neither Luther nor Erasmus nor their successors show any sign of having consulted Gansfort's and Agricola's knowledge of Hebrew, even though for modern eyes especially Gansfort's insights are remarkable. This all-important second generation of humanists and reformers may have regarded Gansfort and Agricola as too closely related for their purposes to medieval piety such as that of the Modern Devotion. Moreover, very soon after the deaths of these forerunners from Groningen there was a veritable deluge of Hebrew scholarship by Pico della Mirandola and Reuchlin which inundated their small cultivation.

3. *Hebraica veritas* and Humanism: Giannozzo Manetti and the Debate on Hebrew and the Jews

Sources: GIANNOZZO MANETTI: *Apologeticus* (ed. A. De Petris; Roma: Storia e Letteratura 1981); *De dignitate et excellentia hominis* (ed. E. R. Leonard; Padua: Antenore 1975); *Vite di uomini illustri del secolo XV* (ed. P. d'Ancona / E. Aeschlimann; Milan: Hoepli 1951). Manetti's other studies on Hebrew and his translations have not been edited. GAROFALO, TRINKAUS, DRÖGE and BOTLEY (see below) publish long quotations from the manuscripts.

General works: P. BOTLEY, *Latin Translation in the Renaissance. The Theory and Practice of Leonardo Bruni, Giannozzo Manetti, Erasmus* (Cambridge: Cambridge UP 2004); U. CASSUTO, *Gli ebrei a Firenze nell'età del Rinascimento* (Firenze: Galletti e Cocci 1918); idem, *I manoscritti palatini ebraici della Biblioteca Apostolica Vaticana e la loro storia* (StT 66; Vatican City 1935); C. DRÖGE, *Giannozzo Manetti als Denker und Hebraist* (Frankfurt a. M.: Lang 1987); S. GAROFALO, "Gli umanisti italiani del secolo XV e la Bibbia", *Bib.* 27 (1946) 338–75; A. DE PETRIS, "Le teorie umanistiche del tradurre e l'*Apologeticus* di Giannozzo Manetti", *Bibliothèque d'humanisme et renaissance. Travaux et documents* 37 (1975) 15–32; idem, "*L'Adversus Judeos et Gentes* di Giannozzo Manetti", *Rinascimento* 16 (1976) 193–205; G. FIORAVANTI, "L'apologetica anti-giudaica di Giannozzo Manetti", *Rinascimento* 23 (1983) 3–32; O. GLAAP, *Untersuchungen zu Giannozzo Manetti, "De dignitate et excellentia hominis". Ein Renaissance-Humanist und sein Menschenbild* (Stuttgart / Leipzig: Teubner 1994); A. HAMILTON, "Humanists and the Bible", *The Cambridge Companion to Renaissance Humanism* (see above under *General bibliography*) 100–17; R. G. HAMILTON, "*Hebraica Veritas* and *Traditio Apostolica*: Saint Paul and the Interpretation of the Psalms in the Sixteenth Century", *The Bible in the Sixteenth Century* (ed. D. C. Steinmetz; Durham / London: Duke UP 1990) 83–99; A. MORISI GUERRA, "Cultura ebraica ed esegesi biblica cristiana tra Umanesimo et Riforma", *Ebrei e Cristiani nell'Italia Medievale e Moderna. Atti del VI Congresso internazionale dell'AISG, S. Miniato, 4–6 novembre 1986* (Rome: Carucci 1988) 209–23; H. A. OBERMAN, "Discovery of Hebrew and Discrimination against the Jews" (see above under *General bibliography*); C. L. STINGER, *Humanism and the Church Fathers. Ambrogio Traversari (1386–1439) and Christian Antiquity in the Italian Renaissance* (Albany: SUNY Press 1977); C. TRINKAUS, *In Our Image and Likeness. Humanity and Divinity in Italian Humanist Thought* ([1970]; repr. in 2 vols.: Notre Dame: University of Notre Dame 1995); A. J. VANDERJAGT, "Mediating the Bible" (see above under General bibliography); W. Wittschier, *Giannozzo Manetti. Das Corpus der Orationes* (Cologne / Graz: Böhlau 1968).

Neither the Modern Devouts nor early humanists such as Gansfort and Agricola saw the Bible, whether the Old or the New Testament, as a repository of concepts and truths to be used in building gothic systems aspiring to the theo-

---

[54] Schoeck, Agricola and Erasmus, in: Rodolphus Agricola Phrisius (1988) 181–88; for a full discussion: Akkerman, Six Lives (forthcoming).

logical coherence of Christian doctrine; hence their scepticism, often even aversion toward scholasticism. Although sometimes troubled by seeming logical contradictions, their main objective was to understand the Bible as the Word of God pointing to the salvific sacrifice of Jesus, which could be used to meditate on that mystery. The *trait d'union* between the two testaments was the book of Psalms, the voice of which was Jesus'.[55] For the humanist tradition of Italy in the fifteenth century, too, the Psalms have a central interpretative place besides having a merit of their own. Hence it is easy to understand how, in the words of ALASTAIR HAMILTON, "humanists approached the Bible as a work of literature, an example of inspired poetry", for it was by poetry that the soul could be uplifted.[56] If the Bible is literature even of a divinely inspired kind, it should be studied in the same way as other literary works. It is a very different thing to extricate from a text central concepts which can be used in a theological or philosophical system than to study it from an aesthetic and inspirational or spiritual point of view. For the first approach, the text as a text in the original language is at most secondary; it is dialectic, even logic that counts. For the latter pathway, the original text is fundamental, and the instruments for understanding and especially for following, imitating or even emulating it are to be grammar and rhetoric. Yet, early humanists such as Petrarch and Salutati did not have the linguistic skills in Hebrew, Aramaic and Greek that are needed to interpret the original text of the Bible in a literary manner. One way, however, to approach the sources of the Bible more closely was to take recourse to the Church Fathers, and there was a veritable explosion of interest in them from around 1400 onwards.[57] Of course, this was the path taken by Lorenzo Valla (1407–57), whose primary focus in biblical studies was on the New Testament. He recognized theoretically that it is necessary to know Hebrew even in order to understand the terms and grammatical constructions of the Greek of the New Testament if not the Old, but in practice he never tried to acquire that knowledge.[58] This does not mean, however, that Valla's work was unimportant for the study of the Old Testament. JERRY BENTLEY has pointed out that Valla's approach is based upon the conviction "that scholars properly versed in linguistic and philological matters could produce a translation of the Latin scriptures much more accurate and meaningful than the Vulgate".[59] This idea informed the work of most Renaissance biblical scholars, indeed it may even be seen as defining their work.

Others, however, were almost magnetically drawn especially to the Hebrew Bible. Around 1430, Ambrogio Traversari (1386–1439) attempted to add Hebrew to his proficiency in Greek. Hearing of his project, the wealthy young Roman nobleman Mariano Porcari – brother of the ill-fated Stefano, would-be assassin of Pope Nicolas V in 1453 – presented him with a Hebrew manu-

---

[55] Hobbs, Hebraica Veritas and Traditio Apostolica (1990) [see Bibl. of Sect. 5, below].

[56] Garofalo, Gli umanisti italiani (1946) 343ff; Hamilton, Humanists and the Bible (1996) 100; Vanderjagt, Mediating the Bible (2007).

[57] Stinger, Humanism and the Church Fathers (1977).

[58] Garofalo, Gli umanisti italiani (1946) 350: Valla "dimostra scarsa sensibilità per i semitismi", with examples in the footnotes.

[59] Bentley, Humanists and Holy Writ (1983) 59.

script including the Psalms, Job, Daniel, the Lamentations of Jeremiah and Esther.[60] Still, Traversari and interested humanists such as Poggio Bracciolini (1380–1459), hard as they tried, made little or no progress themselves, but they did stimulate others to follow the difficult road of learning Hebrew.

Giannozzo Manetti (1396–1459), Traversari's brilliant pupil, immersed himself in Greek and Hebrew alike and was the first Christian in the Latin West since Patristic times to penetrate *ad fontes Scripturae*. Indeed, SALVATORE GAROFALO writes that he was the first of the humanists who had *una completa cultura ebraica*.[61] However great though his insight into Hebrew literature – the Bible and its rabbinical commentaries – and his ability to speak the language fluently, Manetti remained a declared enemy of Judaism and Jews, as had been the case with scholars in Paris in the late twelfth century who yet claimed a love for the *Hebraica veritas*.[62]

3.1. Giannozzo Manetti

Giannozzo Manetti was born in 1396 into a rich merchant family of Florence, allowing him to become an independent scholar around 1420.[63] Little is known about his early, private studies. He went public around 1430 to fulfil minor political duties for his sestiere. More importantly for scholarly purposes, he became a member of the circle of learned men whom Traversari collected around himself after 1431. Here he came into contact with humanists such as Niccolò Niccoli, Carlo Marsuppini and Agnolo Acciaiuoli. Meanwhile, Traversari taught Manetti Greek. Soon after 1437, Manetti entered diplomatic service on behalf of Florence under Cosimo de'Medici, and in the following decade or so he travelled on missions to Genoa, Naples, Venice, Urbino, Rome and Rimini. Closely connected to the highest governing circles of Florence, it fell to him to deliver a funeral oration for the famous humanist chancellor of the city, Leonardo Bruni, in 1444, the famous castigator of Judaism, Jews themselves and even Hebrew as a language.[64] Manetti fell out of Cosimo's grace in the early 1450s and he spent the last six years of his life in exile at Rome and Naples, becoming a secretary successively of the Popes Nicholas V, Calixtus III and Pius II Piccolomini but spending much of his time on humanist studies at the court of king Alfonso V of Naples. He died in 1459.

Perhaps the most important date in the history of humanist Hebrew scholarship of the Renaissance is November 11, 1442. On this Sunday Manetti began to read the Hebrew text of the Bible, coached by one "Emanuel Hebreo", identified as Immanuel ben Abraham da San Miniato, a member of the Jewish

---

[60] Stinger, Humanism and the Church Fathers (1977) 51 ff.

[61] Garofalo, Gli umanisti italiani (1946) 356; see also the remarks by DE PETRIS in: Manetti, *Apologeticus* (1981) xiii. Manetti collected a library of Hebrew manuscripts that later became the nucleus of the Fondo Palatino of the Vatican Library; Cassuto, I manoscritti palatini ebraica (1935) 44–47, 79–90.

[62] Manetti's fluency is attested to by his near contemporary Vespasiano da Bisticci, see Cassuto, Gli ebrei a Firenze (1918) 276–77; see also Botley, Latin Translation (2004) 108–09.

[63] For Vespasiano da Bisticci's biography see *Vite di uomini illustri* (1951) 259–91. For a short but clear analysis: Wittschier, Giannozzo Manetti (1968) 7–18; the best analyses of Manetti and his works are Trinkaus, In Our Image and Likeness (1970) passim (refer to the full indices), who meticulously discusses his role in the history of ideas, Dröge, Giannozzo Manetti (1987), who concentrates on Manetti's work in Hebrew, and Botley, Latin Translation (2004).

[64] On Bruni's anti-Judaism see Oberman, Discovery of Hebrew and discrimination against the Jews (1992) 23; Morisi Guerra, Cultura ebraica ed esegesi biblica cristiana (1988) 213, and the sources and literature cited there.

community of Florence.[65] Using rabbinic commentaries, Manetti read through
the Bible twice, not apparently, as SALVATORE GARAFOLO observes, for the humanist desire to know everything and to be able to do everything but in order
to enjoy the Bible in its literary sources and to glean from it material that
would help in defending the Christian faith against the Jews. For Manetti the
Bible was the rational basis of life, scholarship and knowledge. Vespasiano da
Bisticci reports that in a debate with an English prelate at Florence, Manetti
exclaimed that all things contained in the canonical Scriptures are as true as
the fact that a triangle by definition has two lines and a hypotenuse. In his
Apologeticus, written as a defense against those who objected to his translation
of the Psalms from the Hebrew, he adds to this the idea that there is not a single syllable in the original Scripture that is without the grandest mystery.[66]
Thus he connects biblical aesthetics and faith with geometrical knowledge in a
way that half a century later will be developed further in the (neo-)platonic
and magical traditions associated with Ficino and Pico della Mirandola.

In 1455, Manetti entered the service of King Alfonso, who besides making
him one of his councillors also gave him a palace and as much secretarial assis-
tence as he needed.[67] In the three years till his death, Manetti amazingly made
accomplished Latin translations not only of the New Testament but also of
Aristotle's ethical treatises. Meanwhile, on the king's request he wrote a book
on earthquakes – Naples, after all, is near Mount Vesuvius – and he revised his
book *Contra Iudeos et Gentes*, which he had written in the late 1440s, probably
based upon a discussion in 1447 with learned Jewish scholars at the Rimini
court of Sigismond Malatesta. It discusses the value of Hebrew culture for understanding the Bible but at the same time broadly condemns Jews of the past
and present and also Greek and Latin pagan learning, albeit cursorily and less
vehemently.[68] More importantly for our purposes, Manetti began to translate

---

[65] Garofalo, Gli umanisti italiani del secolo XV e la Bibbia (1946) 357 ff. It seems that Immanuel was not a convert to Christianity in the way of many teachers of Hebrew later in the century.
Manetti had already begun Hebrew studies around 1435 under the tutelage of a young Jewish man
whom he took into his house and converted to Christianity: *Apologeticus*, xiii, where the manuscript passage is printed. Manetti's colleague for a time as papal secretary was Lorenzo Valla who
noted the importance of grasping the *Hebraica veritas* of the Psalms, in particular in order to
achieve true devotion in church services; but he himself does not seem to have known Hebrew. For
Manetti's theory of translation from the Hebrew but especially the Greek, see Botley, Latin Translation (2004) 63–114; he importantly prints Manetti's preface to his version of the Psalter as an Appendix, cf. 178–81.

[66] Manetti, *Apologeticus*, 48–49, and passim; see also the remarks by GAROFALO (n. 61, above).
This idea of a 'mysterious' Scripture is found in many humanists, for example also in Rudolph Agricola (see above, 164–67), in Lefèvre (see below, 174–79) and in Pagninus (see below, 185–89), and it
may be directly related to an awareness and perhaps even reading of Kabbalah. Without doubt,
there is a connection here to their reading of biblical passages such as Matt 5:18 and 2 Tim 3:16.

[67] See on this Trinkaus, In Our Image and Likeness 2 (1970) 581ff, who cites the sources.

[68] There is no edition of this important work *Adversus Iudeos et Gentes*, as it is called in the final
version; see De Petris, L'Adversus Judeos et Gentes (1976), who also discusses the analysis by
Trinkaus, In Our Image and Likeness 2 (1970) 726–34. For Manetti's translation of the New Testament and a comparison of it with Valla's adnotations, see Bentley, Humanists and Holy Writ
(1983) 45–49, 57–59; although the two men – both secretaries at the court of Pope Nicholas V –
must have known each other, they did not collaborate in their translation work, possibly because
they espoused rather different methods. On this see also the valuable comments by Botley, Latin
Translation (2004) 87–98.

the Old Testament from the Hebrew, commencing with the Psalms, in the end the only book which he completed. CHRISTOPH DRÖGE has given a lengthy and lucid analysis of this translation, comparing it closely to Jerome's *Iuxta Septuaginta* and *De Hebraica Veritate*, the Latin version of Immanuel ben Abraham di San Miniato and, of course, the Hebrew text.[69] A confrontation with these texts shows that Manetti's rendition is fundamentally a renewal. He eliminates grecisms and late-latinisations. Against Valla's general approach of translating as literally as possible, Manetti insists on giving a version that is meaningful if not always literal, and besides one that is supported by the best classical Latin style.[70] In fact, DRÖGE observes that at those places where Manetti departs from the Vulgate he does so more in order to write elegant Ciceronian Latin than on the basis of his knowledge of rabbinic sources and commentaries. Nonetheless, his version of the Psalms is often closer to the Hebrew than those either of his predecessors or of his teacher Immanuel ben Abraham, although it is stylistically freer.

An illustrative example of Manetti's translation style is his rendition of the first two verses of Psalm 40 (39):[71]

HEBREW

קוה קויתי יהוה ויט אלי וישמע שועתי: ויעלני | מבור שאון מטיט היון ויקם על־סלע רגלי כונן אשרי:

IUXTA SEPTUAGINTA

2. *Expectans expectavi Dominum et intendit mihi. 3. Et exaudivit preces meas et eduxit me de lacu miseriae et de luto fecis et statuit super petram pedes meos et direxit gressus meos.*

DE HEBRAICA VERITATE

2. *Expectans expectavi Dominum et inclinatus est ad me 3. et audivit clamorem meum et eduxit me de lacu famoso de luto caeni et statuit super petram pedes meos stabilivit gressus meos.*

IMMANUEL BEN ABRAHAM[72]

1. *Expectando expectavi dominum, et inclinatus est ad me, et audivit clamorem meum, et eduxit me de lacu clamoris, a luto fecis, et statuit super petram pedes meos. 2. Direxit gressos meos, ...*

GIANNOZZO MANETTI

1. *Dum sperarem speravi in dominum et inclinavit ad me et exaudivit clamorem meum. 2. Et eduxit me de puteo profundo, et de luto fecis, et statuit super petram pedes meos, dirigens gressus meos.*

These few lines are sufficient to show something of Manetti's procedure. Comparing his text to the other Latin versions, attention must first be called to his hypotactic procedure, initiated with *Dum*, and ending the second verse with the syntactic use of the participle, *dirigens gressus meos*. At the same time he constructs his phrases rhythmically. This clearly demonstrates that Manetti is styling his translation on the model of Cicero, favorite of humanist Latinity; syntactically, however, the latter would most probably have used the imperfect indicative *sperabam* instead of the imperfect subjunctive *sperarem*. Manetti's translation of *kavvo kivviti* [קוה קויתי] as *Dum sperarem speravi* is closer to the literal Hebrew than the earlier translations, although there is also the second meaning that accords with 'expectation'. Something similar is true in v. 2, where he translates *mibbor sha'on* [מבור שאון] as *de puteo profundo*. DRÖGE remarks that Manetti ignores the alarm that is implicit in *sha'on* [שאון], but it would seem that the word *clamavi* from Psalm 130 (129), *De pro-*

---

[69] Dröge, Giannozzo Manetti (1987); cf. De Petris, Le teorie umanistiche del tradurre (1975) and Vanderjagt, Mediating the Bible (2007).

[70] On Valla as a New Testament exegete see Margolin, The Epistle to the Romans (1990) 140–51.

[71] DRÖGE (Giannozzo Manetti, 1987) transcribes and discusses a number of Manetti's Psalm translations and compares them to the two versions reported as Jerome's and that of Manetti's teacher, Immanuel ben Abraham; some of the remarks here are indebted to him.

[72] For Immanuel's and Manetti's versions see Dröge, Giannozzo Manetti (1987) 159–61.

fundis clamavi, is echoing in the humanist translator's ear as he uses *profundo* here and that it is thus implicit in the Latin he gives for *sha'on* [שאון].[73]

Both GAROFALO and DRÖGE agree that in his translation of the Psalms, Manetti is an unambiguous forerunner of Erasmus and of modern Latin versions of the Bible.[74] Yet, it must be remembered that Manetti's desire is not, in fact, to go *ad fontes* to discover the best text. Rather, by making available a trustworthy translation from the Hebrew, Jews will no longer have anything to complain about with regard to the translated, christianised Bible and nothing then stands in the way of their conversion to Christianity. The faithful rendition of the Bible into the aesthetically acceptable Ciceronian Latin of the humanists leaves them no rational excuse to make another choice.[75]

Close though Manetti's translation of the Psalms is to the Hebrew text, it remains a fundamentally Christian text, but this Christianity must be seen in the light of his eulogy on the dignity of man and not in the terms of medieval ideas on his misery.[76] Given the energy Manetti put into the study of Hebrew and his translation of the Psalms, it is remarkable that his efforts do not show in his political orations or his humanist work on the dignity of man, even if these are especially geared to demonstrate his knowledge of Latin and Greek language and literature and not of Hebrew culture. On the other hand, his *Apologeticus* for translating the Psalms flows over with information and insights gleaned from the pagan classical tradition, as does the *Adversus Judeos et Gentes*. Again, an explanation may be that Manetti's primary objective is not to follow the river back in order to read the Psalms as springing from the Hebrew fount, but, on the contrary, to move them forward from that wellspring in order to accommodate them entirely to the amalgam of Christianity and the Classical tradition of Renaissance humanism. In this light his polemic must be seen against on the one side those Christians who saw no merit in studying Hebrew such as Bruni Aretino and on the other Jews and pagans.[77]

3.2. Giannozzo Manetti and the Jews

Whatever the origins of Manetti's dislike of the Jews and Judaism even in the face of his close relationship with his Jewish teachers, he constructs his aversion on the basis of his exegesis of the Old Testament, as is particularly evident

---

[73] Dröge, ibid. 47; see also 187–88, below, for Pagninus's rendering of this passage.

[74] Garofalo, Gli umanisti italiani (1946) 364; Dröge, Giannozzo Manetti (1987) 50; for example, DRÖGE explains that Manetti's subdivision of the Psalms is rabbinical, as indeed he himself writes in the *Apologeticus*; in that work, Manetti gives a precise and blow by blow account of the methodological problems with which he was confronted as he was translating the Psalms; cf. Hamilton, Humanists and the Bible (1996) 103–04, and in particular De Petris, Le teorie umanistiche del tradurre (1975) 23.

[75] Cf. Dröge, Giannozzo Manetti (1987) 55 ff.

[76] Trinkaus, In Our Image and Likeness 1 (1970) 230–70; but esp. the analysis by Dröge, ibid. 94–142.

[77] For Bruni's attitudes – which even go so far as to allow him to make disparaging remarks about the aesthetics of the letter forms themselves of Hebrew – see especially Trinkaus, In Our Image and Likeness (1970) 578–81, and the literature cited there.

in the *Adversus Judeos et Gentes*. CHARLES TRINKAUS has cogently observed that "that much of Manetti's purpose in writing is to address contemporary Jews and convince them that their ancestors had made a colossal mistake".[78]

The central issue at the heart of Manetti's ideas on Judaism is his conviction that *prisci illi Hebrei* were the true and pious worshippers of God, long before the advent either of the Greeks or even of Moses. From the time of Moses, Jews were named from Judah, but the Hebrews were named from Heber, the ancestor of Abraham.[79] Moses he considers the Lawgiver – that is: of the Ten Commandments – and the founder of Judaism. But Jewish law in general – for example, the dietary injunctions – is no more than a foreshadowing of Christ, and it has been abolished by him.[80] Hence those ancient Hebrews, who have continued to follow the Ten Commandments, are the forebears of the Christians who have accepted the teachings of the New Testament that fulfils the Old. In this sense, too, Manetti casts the prophecies of the Old and the miracles related in the New Testament along the same line.[81] In fact, the *Adversus Judeos et Gentes* systematically interprets all passages from the Old Testament entirely in the light of the New.[82] In this kind of exegesis, humanist scholars with a vengeance also followed the Church Fathers. Chrysostom, a great favorite of the humanists, in his *Homilies against the Jews* casts a dark eye on Christians who maintain relations with Jews, visiting synagogues and celebrating Jewish feastdays.[83] He goes on to argue that the Jews are rightly punished for their treatment of Christ. CHARLES STINGER in what reads like an understatement writes about Traversari's love for Chrystostom: "The rhetorical nature of the homilies again seems the most plausible reason for Traversari's decision to translate them, but Renaissance humanism was not marked by an end of animosity towards Judaism".[84] HEIKO OBERMAN has remarked that in the Renaissance Jews were increasingly typecast as *voluntary* agents of evil precisely because they would not conform to Christian doctrine.[85] This not only made Jews the victims of a 'conservative' movement which saw them as instruments of God's wrath, but they also drew the fire of 'progressive' humanists who interpreted social evils as a matter of individual human responsibility. Since the Jews would not choose for the *rational* continuation of the Old Testament by the New which would lead to societal renovation, they could not be regarded as excellent and dignified human beings. Thus in a terrible turn-

---

[78] Trinkaus, In Our Image and Likeness 2 (1970) 726–27; a thorough analysis is given by Fioravanti, L'apologetica anti-giudaica di Giannozzo Manetti (1983).

[79] For the Latin text see Trinkaus, In Our Image and Likeness 2 (1970), notes on 877.

[80] Interestingly, Manetti's problems with Jewish law are formulated in terms derived from the vision of the dignity of man which he developed in his *De dignitate et excellentia hominis libri* IV; cf. Manetti, *De dignitate et excellentia hominis* (1975); Glaap, Untersuchungen zu Giannozzo Manetti (1994). Jewish law, according to Manetti, undermines the high position of man in the universe.

[81] De Petris, L'*Adversus Judeos et Gentes* di Giannozzo Manetti (1976) 204–05.

[82] Fioravanti, L'apologetica anti-giudaica di Giannozzo Manetti (1983) 10–11 and passim.

[83] This is pointed out by Stinger, Humanism and the Church Fathers (1977) 132–33.

[84] Ibid. 132.

[85] Oberman, Discovery of Hebrew and Discrimination against the Jews (1992) 34.

about, the *Hebraica veritas* of fifteenth-century humanists such as Manetti condemned the descendants of the writers and first audience of the Psalms.

4. *Hebraica veritas* and Mysticism: Jacques Lefèvre d'Étaples

Sources: G. BEDOUELLE / F. GIACONE, *Lefèvre d'Étaples et ses disciples. Épistres et Évangiles pour les cinquante et deux dimenches de l'an* (Leiden: Brill 1976); G. BEDOUELLE, *Le "Quincuplex Psalterium" de Lefèvre d'Étaples. Un guide de lecture* (Genève: Droz 1979); E. F. RICE, Jr., *The Prefatory Epistles of Jacques Lefèvre d'Étaples and Related Texts* (New York / London: Columbia UP 1972); for a bibliography of the medieval mystical works which Lefèvre edited with Josse Clichtove: idem, "Appendix" to his "Jacques Lefèvre d'Étaples and the medieval Christian mystics" (see below); for Lefèvre's occult/Kabbalist work, especially the six books of *De magia naturali*, which were never printed: B. P. COPENHAVER, "Lefèvre d'Étaples" (see below).

General works: G. BEDOUELLE, "La lecture christologique du Psautier dans le *Quincuplex Psalterium* de Lefèvre d'Étaples", *Histoire de l'exégèse au XVIe siècle* (ed. O. Fatio / P. Fraenkel; Genève: Droz 1978) 133–43; idem, *Lefèvre d'Étaples et l'Intelligence des Ecritures* (Genève: Droz 1976); idem, "L'humanisme et la Bible", BTT V (1989) 53–121; S. CAVAZZA, "Platonismo e riforma religiosa. La *Theologia vivificans* di Jacques Lefèvre d'Étaples", *Rinascimento* 22 (1982) 98–149; C. S. CELENZA, "The search for ancient wisdom in early modern Europe: Reuchlin and the late ancient esoteric paradigm", *JRH* 25:2 (2001) 115–33; B. P. COPENHAVER, "Lefèvre d'Étaples, Symporien Champier, and the secret names of God", *Journal of the Warburg and Courtauld Institutes* 40 (1977) 189–211; J. FRIEDMAN, *The Most Ancient Testimony* (see above under *General bibliography*); E. A. GOSSELIN, *The King's Progress to Jerusalem: Some Interpretations of David during the Reformation Period and their Patristic and Medieval Background* (Malibu: Undena 1976); B. HALL, "Biblical scholarship: editions and commentaries", CHB III (1978) 38–93; P. E. HUGHES, *Lefèvre. Pioneer of Ecclesiastical Renewal in France* (Grand Rapids: Eerdmans 1984); *Jacques Lefèvre d'Étaples (1450?-1536). Actes du colloque d'Étaples les 7 et 8 novembre 1992* (ed. F. Pernot; Paris: Champion 1995); J.-C. MARGOLIN, "The Epistle to the Romans (Chapter 11) according to the versions and / or commentaries of Valla, Colet, Lefèvre, and Erasmus", *The Bible in the Sixteenth Century* (ed. D. C. Steinmetz; Durham / London: Duke UP 1990) 136–66; H. A. OBERMAN, *Forerunners of the Reformation. The Shape of Late Medieval Thought* (London: Lutterworth 1967); idem, *Wurzeln des Antisemitismus. Christenangst und Judenplage im Zeitalter von Humanismus und Reformation* (Berlin: Siedler 1981); J. S. PREUS, *From Shadow to Promise* (see above under *General bibliography*); A. RENAUDET, *Préréforme et humanisme à Paris pendant les premières guerres d'Italie (1494–1517)* (Paris: [1916] Librairie d'Argences ²1953); E. F. RICE, Jr., "The humanist idea of Christian Antiquity: Lefèvre d'Étaples and his circle", *Studies in the Renaissance* 9 (1962) 126–60; idem, "Jacques Lefèvre d'Etaples and the medieval Christian mystics", *Florilegium Historiale. Essays presented to Wallace K. Ferguson* (ed. J. G. Rowe / W. H. Stockdale; Toronto / Buffalo: University of Toronto 1971) 90–124; idem, "The *De Magia Naturali* of Jacques Lefèvre d'Étaples", *Philosophy and Humanism. Renaissance Essays in Honor of Paul Oskar Kristeller* (ed. E. P. Mahoney; Leiden: Brill 1976) 19–29; idem, "Humanism in France", *Renaissance Humanism. Foundations, Forms, and Legacy* 1–3 (ed. A. Rabil, Jr.; Philadelphia: University of Pennsylvania 1988), vol. 2, 108–22.

Jacques Lefèvre d'Étaples (Jacobus Faber Stapulensis) was born in the middle of the fifteenth century, around 1460, in Étaples, a town in Picardy ruled by Charles the Bold of Burgundy until the latter's death in 1477; he died in 1536 at the court of Marguerite d'Angoulême, queen of Navarre, in Nérac. Matriculating at the university of Paris around 1474, he must have been aware both of the power struggle between the king of France, Louis XI, and his rival Charles the Bold and also of the intellectual contest between various forms of realism and nominalism so much castigated by Wessel Gansfort.[86] Lefèvre took his BA and MA degrees in 1479 and

---

[86] See above, 161–64.

1480.[87] He lived in the Collège du Cardinal Lemoine and taught philosophy in the faculty of arts until 1508.

Initially Lefèvre immersed himself in peripatetic philosophy, translating, paraphrasing and commenting on Aristotle's *Physics, Metaphysics, Ethics* and *Politics*. Also interested in mathematics and neoplatonism, he was drawn to magic, occultism and Kabbalah,[88] especially after he travelled to Italy in 1491–92 to meet Pico della Mirandola and Ermolao Barbaro.[89] The result of all of this was his *De magia naturali* (c. 1493). Gradually repudiating his earlier praise of magi as philosophers and of natural magic as the way to ascend to the Christian mystic vision, he turned to patristic neoplatonism and medieval Christian mysticism.[90] After his retirement from active teaching, he gained the support of Guillaume Briçonnet, abbot of Saint Germain des Prés, later to become bishop of Meaux, and began work on the Psalms and on his commented translation of Paul's letters. His famous *Quincuplex Psalterium* was published by Henri Estienne at Paris in 1509 with a new edition appearing in 1513. Meanwhile, Briçonnet had begun an educational and religious reform of Meaux, and in 1521 Lefèvre was called upon to render his services to that project, especially by translating the Bible into French. Vigilant against the incipient Lutheranism in France, the faculty of theology at Paris in 1523 found doctrinal errors in his commentary on the Gospels. Lefèvre fled to Strasbourg in 1525 but was soon recalled by King Francis I, who appointed him royal librarian and tutor to his children. He completed his translation of the Bible and it was printed at Antwerp in 1530, just as the King was establishing regius chairs in the oriental languages.[91] EUGENE RICE has noted that an astonishing number of more than 350 editions or printings of works written or edited by Lefèvre were published between his first publication in 1492 and the 1540s.

4.1. Jacques Lefèvre's Programme

This enormous activity was not haphazard. Lefèvre had a clear programme in mind, which he described in his commentary in 1506 on Aristotle's *Politics*:[92]

> For knowledge of natural philosophy, for knowledge of ethics, politics, and economics, drink from the fountain of a purified Aristotle [...] Those who wish to set themselves a higher end and a happier leisure will prepare themselves by studying Aristotle's *Metaphysics*, which deals with first and supramundane philosophy. Turn from this to a reverent reading of Scripture, guided by Cyprian, Hilary, Origen, Jerome, Augustine, Chrysostom, Athanasius, Nazianzus, John of Damas-

---

[87] There are many versions of Lefèvre's life; particularly lively and informative accounts are those by Bedouelle, Lefèvre d'Étaples (1976) and Rice, Jr., Humanism in France (1988) 110–15; a full account in English placing him in the Reformed tradition is Hughes, Lefèvre (1984).

[88] See HBOT I/2 (2000) 676, and passim.

[89] Cf. Copenhaver, Lefèvre d'Étaples, Symphorien Champier, and the secret names of God (1977), and Rice, Jr., The De magia naturali of Jacques Lefèvre d'Étaples (1976), who both analyse Lefèvre's unpublished *De magia naturali*; for a recent overview of magic and esoteric wisdom in early modern Europe, see Celenza, The search for ancient wisdom (2001).

[90] Rice, Jr., Jacques Lefèvre d'Étaples and the medieval Christian mystics (1971).

[91] See below, 183–85.

[92] For this translation see Rice, Jr., The humanist idea of Christian antiquity (1962) 126–27.

cus, and other fathers. Once these studies have purified the mind and disciplined the senses (and provided one has extirpated vice and leads a becoming and upright life), then the generous mind may aspire to scale gradually the heights of contemplation, instructed by Nicholas of Cusa and the divine Dionysius and others like them.

Although Lefèvre taught at a 'traditional' university in which the scholastic method of the Middle Ages reigned supreme, he kept distance from the prevalent speculations on Aristotelian metaphysics and natural philosophy. He judged the study of the Philosopher's moral works to be more important because they put down a solid basis from which to climb from the world of sensible experience to the contemplation of God. Still, each of Aristotle's works must be taken seriously on the face value of the Greek text, and undue and complicated digressions must not be allowed. In this vein he published commented editions of Aristotle for the use of his students. Although Lefèvre tried to approach the text of the Bible in the same way, his results were not very satisfactory. With regard to his Pauline scholarship, JERRY BENTLEY notes that he "possessed the right instincts, but lacked the mental toughness required to act properly on them".[93] He often made erratic and arbitrary textual decisions, allowing his ideas of tradition and legend and his theological interests to supersede philological correctness. Erasmus was not loathe to point this out, and he was especially indignant when Lefèvre published the infamous Seneca-Paul correspondence and the *Epistle to the Laodiceans* as authentic writings by Paul. But Lefèvre reached the nadir of wrong, even blasphemous exegesis in his discussion of Heb 2:7 in connection with Ps 8:6: Erasmus accused him of degrading Jesus to a place lower than the angels, allowing himself to be misled by his faulty knowledge of the texts, his sloppy exegesis and weak logic.[94]

In the course of his long, changeable life, Lefèvre came to believe that the ultimate goal of philosophy is to attain to wisdom and that true wisdom can be reached only by imitating the simple and eloquent piety taught by the Jesus of the Gospels, his disciples and the Church Fathers, especially as they were spiritually interpreted by Modern Devouts such as Thomas a Kempis and the earlier medieval mystical tradition.[95] Thus the ancient sources of Christianity, first the Bible and especially the New Testament and then its patristic interpreters, are valuable indeed. Yet, their authentic meaning has been obscured by the intricacies of scholastic philosophy and the misleading literal-historical exegesis of medieval theologians – in particular that of Nicholas of Lyra – and preachers bent on allegory and tropology. At first intrigued by magic and Kabbalah, Lefèvre learned to put these aside as dangerous except for those few elements that can be of help in biblical exegesis. Hebrew, as long as it did not advance Judaism, but especially Greek are the instruments with which the fount of all knowledge, the Bible, can be reopened.[96] This stricture on Hebrew does not mean that the cry *ad fontes!* is not taken seriously by Lefèvre and other humanists and reformers. The prevailing idea is that the Jews have no entrance to the real meaning of the Hebrew of the Old Testament because they reject the interpretative key to it that the New provides, particularly in its use of the

---

[93] Bentley, Humanists and Holy Writ (1983) 177.

[94] Bentley, ibid. 177–79; but see Bedouelle, La lecture christologique (1978) 138–41; in connection with his commentary on the Epistle to the Romans, MARGOLIN (The Epistle to the Romans, 1990, 160–64) points out that Lefèvre's exegetical procedure is less intellectual and more spiritual and homilectic in character than that of Erasmus; this is true, too, for the Psalms. The affair with regard to Heb 2:7 nearly ended the friendship between the two men; on Erasmus see E. RUMMEL, Chap. 9 of the present volume.

[95] Rice, Jr., Humanism in France, and his many other writings.

[96] FRIEDMAN (The Most Ancient Testimony, 1983, 80–81) has pointed out in connection with the spelling of the name 'Jesus' in Hebrew, that neither Lefèvre nor Reuchlin were very good scholars in that language; see nn. 106–07 below.

Psalms. Such a theory of interpretation in principle thus chillingly locks out Judaism from access to the sources while heralding those same sources for the sole parochial purposes of Christian humanists.

This entire programme demonstrates clearly how it was possible for biblical humanists like Erasmus – regardless of the sometimes violent disagreements of the two scholars – and for evangelicals and reformers as well, to see in Lefèvre a compatriot in the Christian republic of learning with its banner of *ad fontes!* Lefèvre, however, did not abandon the Catholic Church.

4.2. Jacques Lefèvre's Kabbalah and Psalms

Lefèvre wrote his above-mentioned programme for Christian, humanist studies in 1506, just three years before he published the *Quincuplex Psalterium*.[97] In it he gives five Latin versions of the Psalms: 1. The *Psalterium vetus*, 2. The *Psalterium Romanum*, 3. The *Psalterium Gallicanum*, 4. The *Psalterium Hebraicum*, and 5. The *Psalterium Conciliatum*, his own revision of the Latin based upon a comparison with the original Hebrew text. The edition was met with wide acclaim. Luther, for example, possessed his own copy and annotated it profusely; he was taken especially by two aspects of Lefèvre's work: its vindication of the literal text and its christological approach. But others were not so sure, and Lefèvre's knowledge of Hebrew was at best spotty. Mutianus Rufus in a letter of June 21, 1514, is rather staccato about his effort: *Porro habeo Psalterium Stapulensis. Legi cursim. Nescit hebraicas literas. Sequitur Hieronymum;* and to drive in the nail even further, the arch-humanist also faults Lefèvre's Latin in another letter a week later, pointing him to Quintilian.[98] Nonetheless, the *Quincuplex Psalterium* was regarded by humanists and reformers alike as an important triumph of the literal interpretation of the Bible over allegory.

In his Psalter, Lefèvre does not mention his great interest in magic and the occult, especially in Kabbalah, of the late 1480s and early 1490s. Indeed, by the time of its publication he had abandoned natural magic as a dangerous delusion and he never published his *De magia naturali*.[99] Still he retained elements of his former learning in the works of Hermes Trismegistus, Pythagoras and in the Platonists, including their revival by Marsilio Ficino and his circle, in his biblical works. EUGENE RICE writes that they "seemed as admirable as ever when he found them in the Dionysian corpus, the Fathers of the Church,

---

[97] The most important and wide-ranging studies of Lefèvre's *Quincuplex Psalterium* are those by BEDOUELLE, especially Lefèvre d'Étaples et l'intelligence des Écritures (1976) and Le "Quincuplex Psalterium" de Lefèvre d'Étaples (1979). See also Oberman, Forerunners of the Reformation (1967) 279–307; Preus, From Shadow to Promise (1969) 137–42; and Hughes, Lefèvre, Chapter *4 "The assertion of biblical authority", 53–64.

[98] Cited by Bedouelle, Lefèvre d'Étaples et l'intelligence des Écritures (1976) 88, who also comes to the defense of his intentions but not of the facts themselves.

[99] Rice, Jr., The *De magia naturali* (1976) 28–29; cf. idem, Lefèvre (1971) 15–25. His friend Erasmus, too, saw both Judaism and the love for the writings of Italian humanists, who were enthralled by pagan writers, as dangerous to the Christian humanist cause; cf. Oberman, Wurzeln des Antisemitismus (1981) 51 ff.

Ramon Lull or Cusanus".[100] Lefèvre also used the Kabbalah to uncover what he regarded as the very heart of the Psalms.

In the preface to his Psalter, Lefèvre puts forward his way of interpreting Scripture.[101] Given the various contradictory explanations of what it means to understand the Psalms – or for that matter, any part of the Bible – Lefèvre explains his idea of the *sensus literalis* of a biblical text. For one, it is not the *sensus historicus*. The historical meaning might seem at first sight to be the literal one, but on the testimony of no less an authority than David it is not. In the Psalms it is not the historical David who is singing or weeping and praising: according to 2 Sam 23:2, David himself testifies that it is the spirit of the Lord who speaks through him.[102] To those who might object that such a literal sense is in fact a kind of interpretative allegory or tropology, Lefèvre replies that his literal sense coincides with the spiritual sense, and that it is this sense which the Holy Spirit intends when he speaks through the prophet, in this case David. The Old Testament has no usable literal sense in the ordinary meaning of that word. It is the task of the present reader of the Psalms to uncover that meaning. JAMES PREUS sums this up neatly: "The divine author meant one thing, the Old Testament writer meant the same thing, the New Testament authors discerned that thing, and the interpreter must discover it".[103] Thus the meaning of the Old Testament is entirely revealed by the New, by Jesus himself and the Apostles. Of course, this is the position taken by Jean Gerson, the Modern Devotion, by Wessel Gansfort, Rudolph Agricola and other humanists and reformers as well, and by philologists such as Sanctes Pagninus, although they may have quibbled over the exact terminology of *literal* or *spiritual*. It is up to the spiritually endowed reader who has a good knowledge of the New Testament and whose eyes have been enlightened by the Holy Spirit to uncover the meaning of the Hebrew Bible.

For Lefèvre the meaning of Scripture is manifest above all in the Psalms. There is no place in the Scriptures where God's voice is more clearly present. In a letter of 1524 to Jean de Selve, first president of the Parlement of Paris, which Lefèvre used as a preface to an edition of the Psalms, he insists: *Et nescio an usquam magis sit Dei loquela et non fluxae sed consubstantiabilis loquelae eius (quae Christus dominus est) expressio quam in psalmis Davidicis.*[104] In fact, the Psalms are a compendium of all Christian truth, in effect "a small Bible". These words in a letter of 1532 summarise his views:[105]

> Et oultre ce que le Psaultier contient excellentes doctrines et preceptes de pieté, nous le debvons aymer principalement pource qu'il comprent tant manifestes propheties de la mort et resurrection de Christ et nous exhibe tant nobles promesses du regne du Christ, du cours de l'Evangile et de l'estat de toute l'eglise. Parquoy droicturement pourrois tu appeller le Psaultier la Petite

---

[100] Rice, Jr., The *De magia naturali* (1976) 29.
[101] Rice, Jr., The Prefatory Epistles (1972) 470–77.
[102] Ibid. 473.
[103] Preus, From Shadow to Promise (1969) 140–41.
[104] Rice, Jr., The Prefatory Epistles (1972) 471.
[105] Ibid. 517–23; for an extended analysis see also Bedouelle, Lefèvre d'Étaples et l'intelligence des Ecritures (1976), Ch. 7 "Le sens de l'Écriture", who also gives a translation of the preface of Lefèvre's Psalter.

Bible, car en luy toutes choses plus amplement exposees en toute la Bible sont par merveilleuse et tresdelectable brevité serrez en ung tresbeau Manuel.

Generally both biblical humanists and reformers had a very high regard for the Psalms, but in Lefèvre's case there is an additional element. Luther also loved the Psalms but had not taken the trouble to learn Hebrew when he was composing his influential lectures on the Psalms. JEROME FRIEDMAN has pointed out that Luther condemned the application of the Hebrew by the very people whom he himself consulted, the medieval scholars Nicholas of Lyra and Paul of Burgos.[106] Although he had left magic, numerology and Kabbalah behind him, Lefèvre did use the doctrine of the secret names of God when he was composing his *Quincuplex Psalterium*. BRIAN COPENHAVER thinks that Lefèvre may have retained his love for Christian Kabbalah even after he had publicly denounced it: "a psalter was a safer place than a tract on magic for allusions to the Kabbalist understanding of God's secret names".[107] In the end it seems that the key to the interpretation of the Psalms for Lefèvre is not really the Hebrew text, but rather his spiritual reading of the New Testament made mystical by those elements of Kabbalist numerology which he could safely use within the confines of his renewed Latin text. His was not a quest for the original sources of the Latin text of the Bible but for the meaning that allegorising interpetations had obscured.

5. *Hebraica veritas* and Formal Philology

Sources: JEROME BUSLEYDEN's last will and testament is published in H. DE VOCHT, *History of the Foundation and the Rise of the Collegium Trilingue Lovaniense* (see above), 20–46; VIENNE: the text of the decree / canon calling for the establishment of chairs in oriental languages is published in *Histoire des Conciles d'après les documents originaux*, vol. VI/2 (ed. C. J. Hefele / H. Leclercq; Paris: Letouzey et Ané 1915) 688ff; JACOBUS LATOMUS, *De trium linguarum, et studii Theologici ratione Dialogus* (1519), *Biblioteca Reformatoria Neerlandica. Geschriften uit den tijd der Hervorming in de Nederlanden* 3 (ed. S. Cramer / E. Pijper; The Hague: Nijhoff 1905) 41–84; MATTHEW ADRIANUS, *Oratio* is published as Appendix I of H. De Vocht, *History of the Foundation and the Rise of the Collegium Trilingue Lovaniense* (see above) 533–43; SANCTES PAGNINUS: אוצר לשון הקדש [*Osar lashon haqodesh*], hoc est, *Thesaurus linguae sanctae. Sic enim inscribere placuit lexicon hoc hebraicum* ... (Lyon: Gryphius 1529); *Isagoge ad sacras literas Liber unicus. Eiusdem Isagoge ad mysticos sacrae scripturae sensus Libri xviii* (Cologne: Soter 1540); [Sanctes Pagninus] *Liber Psalmorum Hebraice cum versione Latina Sanctis Pagnini* (Basle: Brandmüller 1705).

General works: B. ALTANER, "Raymundus Lullus und der Sprachkanon (can.11) des Konzils von Vienne (1312)", HJ 1932:2; idem, "Die Durchführung des Vienner Konzilbeschlusses über die Errichtung von Lehrstühlen für orientalische Sprachen", ZKG 52 (1933) 226–36; D. BARTHÉLEMY, "Origine et rayonnement de la 'Bible de Vatable'", in: *Théorie et pratique de l'exégèse. Actes du troisième colloque international sur l'histoire de l'exégèse Biblique au XVe siècle (Genève, 31 août – 3 septembre 1988)* (ed. I. Backus / F. Higman; Genève: Droz 1990) 385–401; G. BEDOUELLE, "L'humanisme et la Bible", BTT V (1989) 53–121; M. H. BLACK, "The Printed Bible", CHB III (1978) 408–75; T. M. CENTI, "L'attività letteraria di Santi Pagnini (1470-1536) nel campo delle scienze bib-

---

[106] Friedman, The Most Ancient Testimony (1983) 132ff.

[107] Copenhaver, Lefèvre d'Étaples, Symphorien Champier, and the secret names of God (1977) 210; for a discussion of the significance of the magical number 300 and the letter shin (ש) see the quoted article by Copenhaver, 198–99, and also Hughes, Lefèvre, 18–20; cf. the remarks on Agricola and Reuchlin, above, 164–67.

liche", *AFP* 15 (1945) 5–51; C. COPPENS, "Matthaeus Adrianus", *Ex officina* 1 (1984) 50–52; H.
DE VOCHT, *Jérôme de Busleyden, founder of the Louvain Collegium Trilingue. His life and writings*
(Humanistica Lovaniensia 9, Louvain 1950); idem, *History of the Foundation and the Rise of the
Collegium Trilingue Lovaniense 1517–1550* (see above); J. FRIEDMAN, *The Most Ancient Testimony.
Sixteenth-Century Christian-Hebraica in the Age of Renaissance Nostalgia* (Athens, OH: Ohio UP
1983); G. GADOFFRE, *La Révolution Culturelle dans la France des humanistes. Guillaume Budé et
François Ier* (Genève: Droz 1997); J. GARCÍA ORO, *El Cardinal Cisneros. Vida y empresas* 1–2 (Ma-
drid: BAC 1992-93); J. D. GAUTHIER, "Sanctes Pagninus, O.P.", *CBQ* 7 (1939) 175–90; B. HALL,
"Biblical Scholarship: Editions and Commentaries", CHB III (1978) 38–93; A. HAMILTON, "Humanists and the Bible", *The Cambridge Companion to Renaissance Humanism* (ed. J. Kraye; Cambridge: Cambridge UP 1996) 100–17; J. N. HILLGARTH, *Ramon Lull and Lullism in Fourteenth-
Century France* (Oxford: Clarendon 1971); R. G. HOBBS, "*Hebraica Veritas* and *Traditio Apostolica*", *The Bible in the Sixteenth Century* (ed. D. G. Steinmetz; Durham / London: Duke UP 1990)
83–99; A. P. HUBBARD, "'The Bible of Vatable'", *JBL* 66 (1947) 197–209; A. LEFRANC, *Histoire du
Collège de France depuis ses origines jusqu'à la fin du premier empire* (Paris: Hachette 1893); R.
LOEWE, "The medieval history of the Latin Vulgate", CHB II (1980) 102–54; N. FERNÁNDEZ MAR-
COS / E. FERNÁNDEZ TEJERO, "Pagnino, Servet y Arias Montano. Avatares de una traducción latina
de Biblia Hebrea", *Sef.* 63 (2003) 283–329; A. MORISI GUERRA, "Santi Pagnini, traducteur de la Bible", in: *Théorie et pratique de l'exégèse. Actes du troisième colloque international sur l'histoire de l'exégèse Biblique au XVe siècle (Genève, 31 août – 3 septembre 1988)* (ed. I. Backus / F. Higman; Genève: Droz 1990) 191–98; D. O. MCNEIL, *Guillaume Budé and Humanism in the Reign of Francis I*
(Genève: Droz 1975); E. F. RICE, Jr., "Humanism in France", in: *Renaissance Humanism. Foundations, Forms, and Legacy* 1–3 (ed. A. Rabil, Jr.; Philadelphia: University of Pennsylvania Press
1988) 2, 108–22; C. ROTH, *The Jews in the Renaissance* (Philadelphia: Jewish Publication Society
1959); G. SANDY, "Guillaume Budé: Philologist and Polymath. A Preliminary Study", *The Classical
Heritage in France* (ed. G. Sandy; Leiden: Brill 2002) 79–108; B. SMALLEY, "The Bible in the Medieval Schools", CHB II (1980) 197–219; A. J. VANDERJAGT, "Mediating the Bible" (see above under
General bibliography).

By 1300 several generations of scholastics had turned *ad fontes*, translating the
works of the great Greek philosophers and scientists of Antiquity from the
Greek and the Arabic. It is impossible to imagine the development of the various philosophical and scientifc systems and traditions of scholasticism without taking into account the circulation of these texts and the use that was made
of them. To be sure, sometimes the resulting works showed apologetic or almost missionary zeal as in the case of Thomas Aquinas's *Summa contra gentiles*.
Mostly, however, material from Antiquity or from Arabic Muslim-Jewish civilisation was used merely to shore up the philosophical and theological systems
of Latin Christendom. A different approach towards the East and even to "the
East around the corner" – the Jewish neighbors who might under the right circumstances be encountered in almost any larger town in Europe and many
small ones – evolved at the end of the thirteenth century. What has been called
"an incipient Orientalism" is especially evident in the mendicant orders.[108]
Two rather different motives gave rise to this renewed interest in Greek, Hebrew and Arabic. The first was the wish to evangelise the Jews and to convert
the Muslims, the second the desire to recreate the spiritual background of Jesus for purposes of contemplation on his life, in order to prepare a way to heaven for the faithful soul.

---

[108] Loewe, The medieval history of the Latin Vulgate (1969) 152.

The untiring champion at this time of the study of oriental languages as a way both to gain entry to the great mysteries of spirituality and to convert the Muslims – and to a lesser degree, the Jews – to the truth of Christianity was the Catalan knight, theologian, philosopher and missionary Ramon Lull (1232/33 – c. 1316).[109] It was mainly due to his persuasive powers that the Council of Vienne in 1312 adopted the decree *Inter sollicitudines* which enjoined the authorities to create two chairs in Greek, Hebrew, Syriac and Arabic at each of five universities: Paris, Bologna, Oxford, Salamanca and at the papal court.[110] The entire undertaking failed because there was a lack of teachers particularly in Hebrew, who were considered responsible Christians of a non-Judaising sort. But the desire of the Council survived two centuries and its decree was explicitly cited by the Castilian Cardinal Francisco Jiménez de Cisneros (1436–1517) when he was establishing his university of Alcalá de Henares (1498–1508).[111] Here the monumentally important Complutensian Polyglot edition of the Bible was prepared, which has the Hebrew, Aramaic and Greek texts complemented by the Latin; it was published in 1520.[112] ALASTAIR HAMILTON has described this book as the first great product of biblical scholarship of the Renaissance because it fruitfully combines the various new philological methods of the Renaissance and is based on solid Hebrew scholarship.[113] Startlingly, Cisneros's biblical project stands in the context of Queen Isabella's policy after 1499 of a forced conversion of the Muslim population, which had remained immune to gradual evangelisation, and her decision to banish the Jews from her territories in 1492, of which the Cardinal was one of the major architects. He is at once also the Spanish heir of the Modern Devotion of the Low Countries, with which Wessel Gansfort had held close relations.[114] Through Cisneros's efforts this movement was to play a major role in sixteenth-century Spanish spirituality. None of this – however intellectually astute – shows any sense of appreciation of or even respect for the Old Testament and its Hebrew text on its own terms nor for the Jews, who are its direct heirs. Neither does this philology of the sources surpass the needs of evangelism, missionary activity or of Christian spirituality.

5.1. Hebrew at the Foundation of the Collegium Trilingue Lovaniense and the Collège de France

While the editors of the Complutensian Polyglot were working in Spain, the Flemish humanist and public servant Jerome Busleyden (c. 1470–1517) was writing his last will and testament.[115] In it he provided for the foundation of a

---

[109] The standard work on Lull is Hillgarth, Ramon Lull and Lullism (1971).

[110] The most informative studies are still those of ALTANER (Raymundus Lullus und der Sprachkanon, 1932, and Die Durchführung des Vienner Konzilsbeschlusses, 1933); for the text of the decree see Histoire des Conciles (1915) 699 ff.

[111] On Cisneros: García Oro, El Cardinal Cisneros (1992–93).

[112] See A. SCHENKER, Chap. 12, below.

[113] Hamilton, Humanists and the Bible (1996) 106.

[114] See above, 161–64.

college at the university of Leuven, based upon the premise that a sure knowledge of the languages of its sources would open up the message of the Bible,
so that theologians would be able to preach it to the faithful truly and without
scholastic accretions. Busleyden died quite suddenly of pleurisy at Bordeaux
on August 17, 1517, and immediately his friends and advisers, first and foremost Erasmus, fearful that the will would not be executed and that procrasti-
nation would lead to dissolution, began to implement his wishes. A professor
of Hebrew – Matthew Adrianus, a Jewish physician from Spain who had converted to Christianity and was just then visiting Leuven – was engaged as early
as the first days of November, even before Busleyden's will had been settled.[116]
On September 1, 1518, the new professors of Hebrew, Greek and Latin were
officially inaugurated. The *Collegium Trilingue Lovaniense* had been born,
although it was not to be officially recognised until March 1520.

Immediately problems arose. Himself a convert, Adrianus published Hebrew translations of the *Pater Noster*, the *Ave Maria* and the *Credo*, thus demonstrating the Christian apologetics vis-à-vis the Jews to which he inclined,
possibly along the lines of a Johannes Pfefferkorn. Regrettably, however, humanists found his Latin wanting, and Erasmus soon became suspicious about
his moral character, especially about his lack of hospitality and what HENRY
DE VOCHT interprets as "sheer stinginess". This accords with rumors that he
was interested in alchemy and magic and possibly numerology and Kabbalah
as well, and this *pertinaciter*, as his colleague in Greek, Amerot, alleged.[117] No
doubt, interests like these required that he kept a closed house. More importantly, at the same time, open hostility broke out between Jacobus Latomus
(Jacques Masson; 1475–1544) and the newly founded college, especially with
Erasmus.[118]

Latomus was a theologian who taught in the faculty of arts of the Leuven
university. He was a defender of the scholastic method against the broad trilingual *studia humanitatis*. Much like Leonardi Bruni, he argued vehemently
that Hebrew is not necessary for the study of the Bible; less assertively and
quite differently, of course, than Bruni, he also condemned Greek. Indeed,
Augustine himself, who knew no Hebrew, wrote commentaries on the Old
Testament. In an allusion to Hebrew, Latomus ironically claims that an understanding of the Bible does not hinge on a knowledge of characters or points.
For Latomus, it is enough to have Jerome's Latin versions of the Bible at hand.
The correct interpretation of the Bible does not rest upon a knowledge of its
languages but only on the spiritual insight afforded by authors such as Peter
Lombard. The scholastic method saves readers from errors and besides it gives
a philosophical explanation of what must be believed, which neither Paul nor
even the Apostles can offer.[119] The study of Greek and Hebrew was thought

---

[115] De Vocht, Jérôme de Busleyden (1950); for Busleyden's will see idem, History of the Collegium Trilingue Lovaniense (1951) 20–46.
[116] On Adrianus see De Vocht, History of the Collegium Trilingue Lovaniense (1951) 241–55,
369–75, 534–42; also, summarising, Coppens, Matthaeus Adrianus (1984).
[117] De Vocht, ibid. 255.
[118] On Erasmus see E. RUMMEL, Chap. 9, below.
[119] Latomus, *De Trium Linguarum...Dialogus* (1519) 66–73; cf. De Vocht, ibid. 330–31.

to lead directly to heresy, a charge very much in the air, of course, so soon after 1517.

Even before Erasmus could write a reply, Adrianus interrupted his own lectures on March 21, 1519, to give a public *Oratio* taking Latomus's *Dialogus* to task.[120] Central to his argument is the fact that Jerome himself had been dissatisfied with his own translating work. Moreover, if Greek is honorable because Plato, Aristotle and Theophrastus wrote in it, how much more should we not honor Hebrew as the oldest human language, the language of the greater part of the Bible, and even the source of Greek philosophy.[121] The Council of Vienne was quite aware of the need to study the oriental languages when it passed its decree for the establishment of chairs for their advancement. As for Latomus's sneer at the specific linguistic characteristics of Hebrew – a snide remark, too, of Leonardo Bruni[122] – Adrianus replies that the "mystery" of the meaning of the text is often hidden precisely in these syllables, letters and points (*ac mysterium saepenumero in syllabis latet, ac literis & punctis in ipsis linguae idiomatibus seu proprietatibus*).[123] Possibly, he is here covertly alluding as well to Kabbalah. Adrianus insists that a theologian should not be led by the knowledge of others but that if he wants to understand matters from Antiquity itself, he must begin by learning Hebrew, the primordial language of the world. The status of Hebrew as a prime interpretative instrument for Jesus is proved by the fact that it is the first of the three languages on the titulus of the Cross. Thus Adrianus – the converted Jew – follows the Christian tradition of coupling the Old Testament directly to Jesus and of finding in this conjunction the prime reason to study Hebrew. He closes his oration in a fashion typical for pedagogical humanism: now that these matters have been clarified and put into proper perspective, it is the duty of the listening students to learn and of himself to teach what really matters.[124] And that of course is Hebrew as the *fons et origo* of the Old Testament and therefore the New.

Adrianus departed from Leuven precipitously in July 1519, leaving his many debtors unpaid. He never published the Hebrew grammar which he wished to edit nor his study of Jerome. Yet, on the authority of no less a Hebrew master than Reuchlin, DE VOCHT is able to write that through the work of this curious professor "to Louvain is due the honour of having shown the example to all the Universities, of securing an organized and stable instruction" in Hebrew.[125] Here, then, a beginning was made in formal philological instruction, even though Adrianus's instruction book was not published.

About ten years after these events at Leuven, King Francis I of France established four royal professorial chairs, two in Greek and two in Hebrew, at the university of Paris, in a move that has often been interpreted as initiating the *Collège de France*. He had been prompted to take this step much earlier, in

---

[120] It was printed at Wittenberg in 1520 by John Grunenberg; a modern edition is given by De Vocht, ibid. 533–43.

[121] Adrianus, *Oratio*, in: De Vocht, ibid. 539.

[122] See above, 172.

[123] Adrianus, *Oratio*, 540.

[124] Adrianus, *Oratio*, 541.

[125] De Vocht, ibid. 375.

1517, by a group of humanist courtiers among whom Guillaume Budé (c. 1467–1540), a close friend of Jacques Lefèvre d'Étaples.[126] At that time Erasmus had been invited to put these plans into practice, but he was soon busy at Leuven and unable to accept. More delays were caused by the war between the King and the Emperor Charles V, and it was not until after the Treaty of Cambrai in 1529, that Francis could implement his plans. Thus four chairs were established in 1530 and four *lecteurs royaux* duly appointed: Pierre Danès and Jacques Toussaint were to teach Greek and François Vatable and Agathias Guidacerius Hebrew.[127] As at Leuven, here, too, problems arose quickly. The university of Paris, the Sorbonne, already in April 1530 denounced the new courses of the royal lectures as scandalous, daring, heretical, and tainted by Lutheranism.[128] No action, however, was brought against the new regius professors, presumably because it was assumed that the king would have any prosecution of them cancelled.

Things were different in 1533. The *lecteurs royaux* publicly posted a listing of their courses: on Monday at seven, Guidacerius would be reading Psalm 20, while on Tuesday at two, one of his students would study the Hebrew alphabet and the grammar of Moses Rinitius; on Monday at one, Vatable would be continuing his interpretation of the Psalms; Danès planned to teach Aristotle on Monday at two; and, finally, Paul Paradis would be teaching Sanctes Pagninus's newly published Hebrew grammar and giving a commentary on Proverbs on Monday at ten.[129] Without delay, the Faculty of Theology brought suit. "Son farouche syndic, l'éternel Noël Béda, le mauvais génie de la vieille école" – as LEFRANC designates him – demanded that the professors desist from lecturing until they were authorised to do so after an examination by the Faculty. More importantly, he wanted to know what good this Greek and Hebrew would do. The Church had used the Vulgate Latin for 1100 years, so why change? Moreover, the editions which the *lecteurs* prescribed had all been printed in Germany, sure proof that they were infected by heresy, whether of the Jewish or the Lutheran kind. And everyone knows that these people – the Hebrews –can easily change the text of the Bible itself. In short, he demanded strict adherence to the Vulgate. Béda lost. After the hearings before the Parlement of Paris in 1534, the King's professors were not condemned: they were defended as a royal institution independent of the Faculty of Theology and as experts in linguistics not in theology. Nonetheless, they were strictly advised by the royal commissioners, among whom the humanist Guillaume Budé, against commenting unfavorably on the Latin Vulgate.

From the publicly posted listing of courses, it is clear that Hebrew and the Old Testament were being taught in formal settings with a clear philological, grammatical emphasis. With regard to Guidacerius's work, JEROME FRIEDMAN has pointed out that it was notable on two counts. He was the first true Hebrew scholar in France and set a high standard for accurate publication. Sec-

---

[126] For this and the cultural environment at the time cf. McNeil, Guillaume Budé and Humanism (1975); Gadoffre, La Révolution Culturelle (1997); on Budé see also Sandy, Guillaume Budé (2002).

[127] For the history of the Collège de France: Lefranc, Histoire du Collège de France (1893), and for these first four professors, esp. 125–67; individual discussions of them, 169–201; Bedouelle, L'humanisme et la Bible (1989) 68. It must be noted here that although François Vatable probably published nothing during his lifetime, his notes and lecture commentary on the Bible were printed by Robert Estienne at Paris in 1545, soon after the former's death; for this: Hubbard, 'The Bible of Vatable' (1947); Barthélemy, Origine et rayonnement de la 'Bible de Vatable' (1990); cf. Hobbs, Hebraica Veritas and Tradition Apostolica (1990) 88 ff.

[128] McNeil, Guillaume Budé and Humanism (1975) 122f; see also the relevant, colorfully written chapters in Lefranc, Histoire du Collège de France (1893).

[129] The entire text of this poster in: Lefranc, ibid. 144–45.

ond, his work demonstrates a divide between Catholic and Protestant Hebrew scholarship in the early sixteenth century: the former mostly adhered strictly to only the study of the Hebrew text of the Bible but the latter "were as devoted to rabbinic exegesis as they were to retrieving the text itself".[130] After the Council of Trent had established the position of the Vulgate as the only religiously valid translation, Catholic interest in the Hebrew Scriptures diminished. Catholic Hebraica increasingly inclined towards kabbalistic studies, while Protestant efforts concentrated on reading rabbinic commentaries to seek help for new exegeses of the Old Testament that were necessary in formulating new doctrinal points against the rival theology of Catholicism. Returning again to the *lecteurs royaux* and the announcement of their lectures: a strong emphasis was still on the Psalms and there is little doubt that this had to do with their perceived 'Christianity'.[131] Still it was in this royal humanist setting and the trilingual one at Leuven that the roots were sunk of future Hebrew and biblical philological scholarship.

5.2. Sanctes Pagninus, O.P.

In 1536 the Dominican preacher, scholar and practical humanist, Sanctes Pagninus (Santi Pagnini) died at Lyon. He had been born as Antonio at Lucca around 1470; entering the Dominican house at Fiesole near Florence as Sanctes (Santi) in 1487, he was instructed by Girolamo Savonarola.[132] Probably inspired by a Rabbi converted to Christianity, Clemente Abramo, Pagnini was enthralled by the Hebrew Bible and he was also an excellent Greek scholar. He befriended the De Medici cardinals, later to become Pope Leo X and Pope Clement VII. After a series of monastic functions – prior of the Dominican house at Pistoia in 1502, of San Marco at Florence in 1504 and the Vicar General of its houses in 1508, prior of San Domenico at Fiesole in 1510 and of San Marco again from 1511 to 1513 and then of San Romano of Lucca – Pagninus was invited by the Pope in 1513 to teach Greek and Hebrew at the new school of oriental languages which had opened at Rome. Leaving the then fashionable Christian Kabbalism aside and also discarding the subtleties of scholastic academic philosophy, he systematically concentrated his attention on the text and grammar of the Bible. At Rome he was for a time the prefect of the Vatican Library during its unprecented expansion under Leo X.[133] Pagninus worked in papal diplomacy under the cardinal legate to Avignon from 1521 to 1524. Soon he moved to Lyon as a preacher against Lutheranism and Waldensianism. The struggle against heresy was regarded as a political and public duty, and the success booked by Pagninus earned him the honorary citizenship of Lyon. A humanist of general

---

[130] Friedman, The Most Ancient Testimony (1983) 30–31.

[131] This 'Christianity' hinged on the conviction that the Psalms were written by David, speaking with the voice of Christ. However, a caveat must be sounded here: although aware of the Jewish tradition that attributes Psalms 91–100 to Moses, some Christian exegetes make no mention of it (Bucer, Münster and Pellican), but others, as good philologists, hesitate and hedge (Calvin); Vatable in 1546 notes the Jewish insight but also says that Paul in Hebrews claims David as the author of Psalm 95. Interestingly, in his edition of Vatable's commentary in 1556, Robert Estienne omits this note thus staying in line with Christian anti-Jewish feelings; on this see Hobbs, Hebraica Veritas and Tradition Apostolica (1990) 89.

[132] On his life and works, see Centi, L'attività letteraria di Santi Pagnini (1945); cf. Gauthier, Sanctes Pagninus (1939); Roth, The Jews in the Renaissance (1959) 146f; Bedouelle, L'humanisme et la Bible (1989) 77f; Morisi Guerra, Santi Pagnini, traducteur de la Bible (1990); and especially Marcos / Tejero, Pagnino, Servet y Arias Montano (2003). On Savonarola's interpretations of the Old Testament see, in this volume, J. Catto, Chap. 5, the end of Sect. 4.

[133] Gauthier, Sanctes Pagninus (1939) 177–78.

civic zeal, he was heralded for his services to the poor and also for public works such as the establishment of a lepers and plague asylum.[134]

Meanwhile, Pagninus was hard at work on his biblical studies. In 1528, he published his translation of the Bible from the Hebrew and the Greek texts: *Veteris et Novi Testamenti Nova Translatio*, which appeared at Lyon at Du Ry's publishing house.[135] This massive work was followed in 1529 by his greatly influential dictionary: אוצר לשון הקדש [*Osar lashon haqodesh*], hoc est, *Thesaurus linguae sanctae*. He also published a large study manual on the interpretation of Scripture: [*Pagnini*] *Isagogae ad sacras literas liber unicus. Eiusdem Isagogae ad mysticos sacrae scripturae sensus, libri xviii* (1536). Remarks by Pagninus on the Pentateuch are said to have appeared in the year of his death: *Catena Argentea in Pentateuchum*.[136] He also wrote a great many other works.

Pagninus's translation of the Bible is a milestone in humanist philology. He is careful and astute, and, most importantly, his version is literal, even to the extreme. It differed radically – the term is ALASTAIR HAMILTON's and it characterises Pagnini's work in a single word as going to the roots themselves of the text of the Bible[137] – from the Vulgate because Pagninus's Old Testament owed a great deal to rabbinic commentaries and especially to David Qimhi (= Radak; France / Spain, c.1160-c.1235) but also to Solomon Yishaqi (= Rashi; Germany / France, 1040–1105) and Abraham ibn Ezra (= Avenares; Spain / Italy / France / England, 1089–1164) and a host of others.[138] His version of the Bible, too, is the first to divide the entire text into verses. In fact, it was precisely this that raised the scepticism of men like Luther; the latter criticized Pagnini for being overly dependent on Jewish scholarship and for following the Targums in his edition of the Hebrew text.[139] On the other hand, his edition appears to have been the only Latin Christian version which the Jews respected. It was also acceptable to many humanists and Reformers because Pagninus relegated the apocryphal books to a place between the two testaments, thus removing them from the Hebrew 'canon', or the real sources of the Bible.

Obviously, for Pagninus the Hebrew as the source of the Biblical text is of the utmost importance. At the beginning of his *Isagoge*, he writes at length about the clear meanings of Hebrew and Greek words in the original, which they lose in translations because these are always interpretative. Some of his

---

[134] One important desideratum for the study of Hebrew scholarship in the Renaissance is an intellectual biography of this intriguing man, especially, too, because so much use was made of his works by humanists, Catholics and Reformers alike.

[135] See Hall, Biblical Scholarship: Editions and Commentaries (1963) 69–70; Black, The Printed Bible (1963) 436–37, and the magnificent plate 17. GAUTHIER (Sanctes Pagninus, 1939, 179–81) discusses at length the reception of Pagninus's Bible in the middle of the sixteenth century and the use to which it was put by the Council of Trent (1536).

[136] CENTI (L'attività letteraria di Santi Pagnini, 1945, 43–45) is sceptical about this publication and says that only ÉCHARD (*Scriptores Ordinis Praedicatorum* 1-2; ed. J. Quétif / J. Échard; Paris 1719-1721) and a few others seem to have seen it in the late seventeenth century. CENTI gives a full discussion about the publication history of Pagnini's works.

[137] Hamilton, Humanists and the Bible (1996) 113–15.

[138] Pagninus lists his sources at the beginning of his *Thesaurus Linguae sanctae*; cf. on these Jewish scholars HBOT I/2 (2000) 332–46 (Chap.32.5 on Rashi), 377–87 (Chap.33.2 on Abraham ibn Ezra) and 396–415 (Chap. 33.3.3 on David Qimhi = Radak).

[139] Hall, Biblical scholarship, 70, and the literature quoted in this chapter.

examples are 'Amen', 'Alleluia' and 'Hosanna'.[140] For this reason, too, he usually gives the Hebrew versions of biblical names: Chavvah for Eve, Jahacob, Jehudah, and "Jesuah, qui dicitur Massiach". Still, Pagninus's understanding of the meaning of returning *ad fontes* in connection with the biblical text would seem not to have the historical sense which this expression carries today. In the same fashion as many other scholars of the Bible in the late Middle Ages and the Early Modern Era – for example, Lefèvre d'Étaples or Jean Gerson[141] – Pagninus's idea of the sources is not based upon the conviction that historical insight into the development of the text is necessary for a full understanding of it, but it is related directly to finding the linguistically 'purest' text, which, in this case, also happens to be the oldest. As Pagninus has it in a prefatory letter to his *Isagoge*: *Cortex est historia, mysticus vero sensus, nucleus suavissimus*. This mystical sense can be retrieved only from the original text itself. In a sense, the Greek, but especially the Hebrew, has a magical, spiritual quality because they reveal the "real", single primal language of man. Hence also Pagninus's extended discussion at the beginnning of the *Isagoge* on Hebrew as the language of Heber before the confusion of tongues in the time of the tower of Babel; here people were put at one remove from the meaning of God's Word. It is through learning this original language of Hebrew that universal knowledge of man, the universe and God can be acquired. There is possibly here a connection with the mystical neoplatonism of Giovanni Pico della Mirandola, although Pagninus carefully negotiated the straight and narrow of Catholic orthodoxy.[142]

Pagninus's edition of the Bible is preceded by the Psalms, again a clear indication of the overwhelming popularity of the Psalms in the Christian tradition. As generally, he gives the most important rabbinic commentaries. A case in point is his rendition of Ps 40 (39).[143] He translates the first two verses as follows:[144]

> 2. *Expectandum expectavi Jehovam, et inclinavit aurem suam mihi, et audivit clamorem meum. 3. Et ascendere fecit me e cisterna sonitus, a luto coeni, et statuit super petram pedes meos, direxit gressus meos.*

In this translation, Pagninus begins by straightforwardly following the *Iuxta Septuaginta* and the *De Hebraica veritate*: *Expectandum expectavi*, but using the gerund instead of the participle. He then departs from both earlier versions by giving *Jehovah* as a direct transcription of יהוה instead of the customary *Dominus*. He expands *ad sententiam* by adding *aurem suam*, as a slight embroidery of the Hebrew. The *ascendere fecit me a* is a somewhat 'hebraistic' way of saying the same as *eduxit me de* of the Vulgate. More interesting is his translation of *mibbor sha'on* [מבור שאון] as *e cisterna sonitus*. Pagninus is quite aware

---

[140] Pagninus, Isagoge (1540) 2.

[141] See above, 175–79 and 156.

[142] Roth, The Jews in the Renaissance (1959) 147, points to the close personal relationship of Pagninus to contemporary neoplatonists.

[143] Compare the discussion on Manetti, above, 169–74.

[144] *Liber Psalmorum Hebraice cum versione Latina Sanctis Pagnini* (1705), Psalmus 40 (39); quoted from the edition published by Johan Brandmüller (Basle 1705).

that he is here departing from the *de lacu miseriae* and the *de lacu famoso* of the Vulgate versions. In his *Thesaurus Linguae sanctae*, he follows David Qimhi glossing [מבור] *mibbor* as *e cisterna*; he remarks that בור *est cisterna, cuius aquae non scaturiunt ut in fonte, sed colliguntur* (as in a well which might also be dry).[145] He then shows how the term in fact means *in domum carceris*, known from Joseph's plight in Gen 37:21 and 41:17. Quoting Ps 28:1, *cum descendentibus in sepulchrum*, Pagninus again improves on the Vulgate which has *qui descendunt / descendentibus in lacum.* Thus this is not an infamous lake of misery (as in the Septuagint), but a dry cistern with an added *sonitus*, translated from שאון [*sha'on*] quite literally as "echoingly, alarmingly noisy".[146] It must be conceded that the Latin is not very elegant, but the closeness to the Hebrew is what counts for Pagninus and also what made his work so valuable to others across Europe.[147] Thus, in this way, too, the christological inference of the Psalm – the Lord's sepulchre – is clearer to him in this translation than in the Vulgate.

Pagninus's use of Qimhi and the Targum and also his engaging and somewhat eccentric commentary and translation can be illustrated from the opening lines of his version of Psalm 42 (41):[148]
Quemadmodum cerva clamat ad torrentes aquarum, ita anima mea clamat ad te, Deus.
The Iuxta Septuaginta has:[149]
Quemadmodum desiderat cervus ad fontes aquarum, ita desiderat anima mea ad te, Deus...
and the Hebrew:
כאיל תערג על־אפיקי־מים כן נפשי תערג אליך אלהים:
It must first be noted that Pagninus gives the correct gender (*cerva*), according to the commentaries, but more importantly he discusses the word תערג [*ta'rog*] in this Psalm in his *Thesaurus* as follows:[150] ערג *Sicut hinnire est proprium equorum, quum vocem emittunt, et mugire boum et rudere asinorum, et rugire leonum, ita* ערג *proprium est cervorum.* Stating that this Hebrew word cannot be expressed correctly in Latin and referring to Qimhi, he arrives at his translation of *clamavit, tumultum fecit, aut sonuit.* He notes that the Targum uses the equivalent of *desiderare*, and then he translates the verse in the *Thesaurus* as *Quemadmodum cerva (vel anima cervi)* תערג *id est, clamabit (pro clamat, aut desiderat) ad torrentes aquarum, ita anima mea* תערג *id est, clamabit (pro clamat, aut desiderat) ad te deus.* In the version made for more general use, the *Liber Psalmorum Hebraice*, he uses *clamat*, as can be seen above.[151]

Pagninus's edition of the Bible and the *Thesaurus* were frequently reprinted, and they were widely used by scholars of all Christian persuasions in the six-

---

[145] Pagninus, *Thesaurus Linguae sanctae* (1529) q.v.

[146] Pagninus's translation is quite similar in this respect, of course, to that of Immanuel ben Abraham (*de lacu clamoris*), see above, 171. It is improbable that Pagninus was aware of this version.

[147] On the other hand, he had many detractors as well. As late as 1895, König was still complaining in his lemma on Pagninus in the *Wetzer-Welte Kirchenlexikon* (vol. 9, 1270–71), that "sein Bestreben treu zu übersetzen, verleitete ihn vielfach zu ängstlicher, ja sklavischer Genauigkeit, und er wird manchmal geradezu dunkel und unverständlich, abgesehen von den vielen unlateinischen Ausdrücken"; this is a clear echo of Richard Simons's view in 1685 (*Histoire critique au Vieux Testament*, Rotterdam, 314): "Pagnino a trop négligé les anciens interprètes de l'Ecriture, pour s'attacher aux sentiments des rabbins... Bien loin d'exprimer son original dans le même pureté qu'il est écrit, il le défigure et le depouille de tous ses ornemens".

[148] Liber Psalmorum Hebraice cum versione Latina Sanctis Pagnini (1705) Psalmus 42 (41).

[149] The version of the *De Hebraica veritate* is quite different so it is best to leave it aside here.

[150] Pagninus, *Thesaurus linguae sanctae* (1529), col. 1821.

[151] At least with regard to this verse, Luther is not correct in his criticism that Pagninus prefers the Targum.

teenth century, Catholics and Reformers alike, in their own editions and translations. Both works were the result of his systematic and formal approach to the philology of the languages of the Bible. Pagninus's Bible and his grammatical endeavors demonstrate the very best philological research and exegesis that the humanist movement *ad fontes!* engendered. From his editions, translations, grammar and dictionary and their numerous reprints and reworkings issued a veritable torrent of scriptural studies in the sixteenth and seventeenth centuries. Much further study must still be done on Pagninus's endeavors so that a better understanding may be gained of the precise agreements and divisions between Catholic and Reformed humanist scholarship on the Bible in the late Renaissance and Early Modern era.[152]

---

[152] I am grateful to my colleagues Professor Wout van Bekkum for his advice on matters of Hebrew exegesis and edition, and Professor Jan Ziolkowski for his careful perusal of and commentary on the entire text. Rector Wim Blockmans of the Netherlands Institute for Advanced Study (Wassenaar) of the Royal Academy provided shelter for the final version of this chapter.

CHAPTER EIGHT

Isaac Abarbanel:
From Medieval to Renaissance Jewish Biblical
Scholarship

By Eric Lawee, Toronto

Sources: (A) ABARBANEL's biblical commentaries: *Perush 'al ha-torah* 1–3 (on the Pentateuch; Jerusalem: Benei Arabel 1964); *Perush ha-torah le-rabbenu Yiṣḥaq 'Abarbanel* (on the Pentateuch; 5 vols. [vols. 1, 4 forthcoming]; ed. A. Shotland; Jerusalem: Horev 1997–); S. REGEV, "Nusaḥ rishon shel perush 'Abarbanel le-sefer devarim", *Kobez 'al-yad* NS 15 (2000) 306–80 (fragment of draft of the Deuteronomy commentary); *Perush 'al nevi'im rishonim* (on Joshua, Judges, 1–2 Samuel, 1–2 Kings; Jerusalem: Torah Wa-Daat 1955); *Perush 'al nevi'im 'aharonim* (on Isaiah, Jeremiah, Ezekiel; Jerusalem: Benei Arabel 1979); *Perush 'al nevi'im u-khetuvim* (on 'Minor Prophets'; Tel Aviv: Sefarim Abarbanel 1961); *Ma'ayenei ha-yeshu'ah* (on Daniel; in: *Perush 'al nevi'im u-khetuvim*, 268–421); *Mashmia' yeshu'ah* (on prophecies of redemption outside of Daniel; in: *Perush 'al nevi'im u-khetuvim*, 425–606); *'Aṭeret zeqenim* (on Exod 23:20–24:18; photo-offset Jerusalem 1967); *Ṭa'anot lequhot mi-ṭeva' ha-ketuvim* (on Ezekiel's theophany; in: *Moreh nevukhim* [photo-offset Jerusalem 1960] 71v-73r).
(B) Modern translations of the biblical commentaries of ABARBANEL: G. RUIZ, *Don Isaac Abrabanel y su commentario al libro de Amos* (Madrid: Universidad Pontificia Comillas Madrid 1984); J. C. ATTIAS, *Isaac Abravanel: La Mémoire et l'Espérance* (Paris: Cerf 1992) 77–156, 189–276 (selections from *Ma'ayenei ha-yeshu'ah* and *Mashmia' yeshu'ah*); *The Fifty-Third Chapter of Isaiah According to the Jewish Interpreters* 1–2 (ed. S. R. Driver / A. Neubauer; photo-offset New York: KTAV 1969), 2, 153–97; A. BERLIN, *Biblical Poetry Through Medieval Jewish Eyes* (Bloomington, IN: Indiana UP 1991) 121–32 (extracts from commentaries on Exodus 15 and Isaiah 5); E. LAWEE, "Don Isaac Abarbanel: Who Wrote the Books of the Bible?", *Tradition* 30 (1996) 65–73 (from the prologue to Abarbanel's commentary on the Former Prophets).
(C) Other writings of ABARBANEL: *Naḥalat 'avot* in: *Pirqei 'avot 'im perush Moshe ben Maimon ve- 'im perush naḥalat 'avot* (New York 1953); *Perush 'al moreh nevukhim*, in: *Moreh nevukhim; Rosh 'amanah* (ed. M. Kellner; Ramat-Gan: Bar-Ilan University 1993); *Shamayim ḥadashim* (Rödelheim 1828); *Ṣurot ha-yesodot*, in: *'Aṭeret zeqenim* 107–17; *Yeshu'ot meshiḥo* (Königsberg 1861); *Zevaḥ pesaḥ*, in: *Seder haggadah shel pesaḥ* (repr. Jerusalem: Sefarim Toraniyim 1985); *She'elot le-he-ḥakham Sha'ul ha-Kohen* (Venice 1574); *Don Isaac Abravanel: Opera Minora* (Westmead 1972); letters in: *'Oṣar neḥmad* 2 (1857) 67–68; addendum to Abraham ibn Ezra, *Sefer ha-'aṣamim* (ed. M. Grossberg; London: A. Z. Rabinovitsh 1901).
Reference work: Encyclopedia of the Renaissance 1–6 (ed. P. F. Grendler; New York: Charles Scribner's Sons 1999) [EncRen].
Studies: (A) of versions of the biblical commentaries of ABARBANEL: S. Z. LEIMAN, "Abarbanel and the Censor", *JJS* 19 (1968) 49–61; B. RICHLER, "Isaac Abravanel's 'Lost' Commentary on Deuteronomy", *Jewish Social Studies at the Turn of the Twentieth Century* 1–2 (ed. Judit Targonna e.a.; Leiden: Brill 1999), 1, 199–204.
(B) on the biblical exegesis of ABARBANEL: B. CASPER, *An Introduction to Jewish Bible Commentary* (New York 1960) 90–98; Y. ELMAN, "The Book of Deuteronomy as Revelation: Nahmanides and Abarbanel", in: *Ḥazon Naḥum* (ed. Y. Elman e.a.; New York: Yeshiva UP 1997) 229–50; S. GAON, *The Influence of the Catholic Theologian Alfonso Tostado on the Pentateuch Commentary of Isaac Abravanel* (Hoboken, NJ: KTAV 1993); A. GROSSMAN, "Biblical Exegesis in Spain During the

13th-15th Centuries", in: *Moreshet Sepharad: The Sephardi Legacy* 1-2 (ed. H. Beinart; Jerusalem 1992), 1, 144-46; S. GRUNBERG, "Eine Leuchte der Bibelexegese um die Wende des Mittelalters", *Jeschurun* 15 (1928) 21-32, 213-25, 297-312; E. GUTWIRTH, "Don Ishaq Abravanel and Vernacular Humanism in Fifteenth Century Iberia", *Bibliotheque d'Humanisme et Renaissance* 60 (1998) 641-71; Y. HAS, "Stiyot metodologiyot shel 'Abarbanel be-ferusho la-torah, le-'or tefisato 'el mahut ha-torah" (MA thesis, Bar-Ilan University, 2001); S. LEIMAN, "Don Isaac Abravanel", in: *Parshanut ha-miqra' ha-yehudit: pirkei mavo'* (ed. M. Greenberg; Jerusalem: Mosad Biyalik 1983) 96-98; E. LAWEE, "Isaac Abarbanel's 'Stance Towards Tradition': the case of '*Ateret Zeqenim*", *AJS Review* 22 (1997) 165-98; idem, "On the Threshold of the Renaissance: New Methods and Sensibilities in the Biblical Commentaries of Isaac Abarbanel", *Viator* 26 (1995) 283-319; idem, "The 'Ways of Midrash' in the Biblical Commentaries of Isaac Abarbanel", *HUCA* 67 (1996) 107-42; A. LIPSHITZ, "Ha-gishah ha-parshanit shel R. 'Avraham ibn 'Ezra ve-R. Yishaq 'Abravanel 'el ha-nevu'ot she-ne'emeru le-'atid", *Proceedings of the the Sixth World Congress of Jewish Studies* 1-2 (Division A; Jerusalem 1977), 1, 133-39; idem, *Pirqei 'iyyun be-mishnat raba'* (Jerusalem: Mosad ha-rav Kuk 1982) 93-217; H.-G. V. MUTIUS, *Der Kainiterstambaum Genesis 4/17-24 in der jüdischen und christlichen Exegese: Von den Anfängen bis zum Ende des Mittelalters nach dem Zeugnis des Don Isaak Ben Jehuda Abravanel* (Judaistische Texte und Studien 7; Hildesheim: Georg Olms 1978); L. RABINOWITZ, "Abravanel as Exegete", in: *Isaac Abravanel: Six Lectures* (ed. J. B. Trend / H. Loewe; Cambridge: Cambridge UP 1937) 77-92; S. REGEV, "Ha-shitah ha-parshanit shel ha-'Abarbanel", *Mahanayim* 4 (1992) 242-49; E. I. J. ROSENTHAL, "The Study of the Bible in Medieval Judaism", in: CHB 2 (repr. 1980) 272-74; G. RUIZ, "Actualidad de la exegesis de Don Isaac Abrabanel", in: *Identitad y Testimonio* (Madrid: Centro de Estudios Judeo-Christianos 1979) 131-40; idem, "Las introducciones y cuestiones de Don Isaac Abrabanel", in: *Simposio Biblico Español* (ed. N. Fernandez Marcos e.a.; Madrid: Universidad Complutense 1984) 707-22; A. SAENZ-BADILLOS / J. TARGARONA BORRAS, *Los judios de sefarad ante la Biblia: la interpretación de la Biblia en el Medievo* (Estudios de Cultura Hebrea 13; Cordoba: Ediciones El Almendro 1996) 242-47; M. S. SEGAL, "R. Yishaq 'Abravanel be-tor parshan ha-miqra'", *Tarbiz* 8 (1937) 260-99; J. WIESNER, "Abravanels Thorakommentar, namentlich in seinem Verhältnisse zur Halacha", Beilage zu *Ben Chananja* 12, 14, 17, 18, 22 (1867) 237-39, 254-56, 174-75, 197-200, 209-12.

(C) on other aspects of the scholarship and writings of ABARBANEL: ATTIAS, *Isaac Abravanel* (see above under 'Sources', B); M. AWERBUCH, *Zwischen Hoffnung und Vernunft: Geschichtsdeutung der Juden in Spanien vor der Vertreibung am Beispiel Abravanels und Ibn Vergas* (Berlin: Institut Kirche und Judentum 1985); Y. BAER, "Don Yishaq 'Abravanel we-yehaso 'el be'ayot ha-historiyah we-ha-medinah", *Tarbiz* 8 (1937) 241-59; idem, *Galut* (New York: Schocken 1947) 60-68; J. BERGMANN, "Abrabanels Stellung zur Agada", *MGWJ* 81 (1937) 270-80; A. F. BORODOWSKY, *Isaac Abravanel on Miracles, Creation, Prophecy, and Evil: The Tension Between Medieval Jewish Philosophy and Biblical Commentary* (Studies in Biblical Literature 53; New York: Peter Lang 2003); F. CANTERA BURGOS, "Don Isaac Abravanel: Estadista y Filosofo", *Sef.* 30 (1970) 53-59; S. FELDMAN, "Abravanel on Maimonides' Critique of the Kalam Arguments for Creation", *Maimonidean Studies* 1 (1990) 5-25; idem, *Philosophy in a Time of Crisis: Isaac Abravanel, Defender of the Faith* (London: Routledge Curzon 2003); idem, "Prophecy and Perception in Isaac Abravanel", in: *Perspectives on Jewish Thought and Mysticism* (ed. Alfred Ivry e.a.; London: Harwood Academic Publishers 1998) 223-35; idem, "R. Isaac Abravanel's Defense of Creation *Ex Nihilo*", in: *Proceedings of the Eleventh World Congress of Jewish Studies* 1-2 (Division C; Jerusalem: World Union of Jewish Studies 1994), 2, 33-40; S. GAON, "Don Isaac Abravanel and the Christian Scholars", *The American Sephardi* 6 (1973) 17-21; J. GENOT-BISMUTH, "L'argument de l'histoire dans la tradition espagnole de polémique judéo-chrétienne d'Isidore de Seville à Isaac Abravanel, et Abraham Zacuto", in: *From Iberia to Diaspora* (ed. Y. K. Stillman / N. A. Stillman; Leiden: Brill 1999) 197-213; eadem, "La replica ideologica degli ebrei della penisola iberica all'antisemitismo dei re cattolica: la tesi di Isaac Abravanel sulle origini del cristianesimo e del cattolicesimo romano", *La Rassegna Mensile di Israel* 58 (1992) 23-46; R. GOETSCHEL, *Isaac Abravanel: conseiller des princes et philosophe* (Paris: Albin Michel 1996); A. GROSS, "R. Yosef Hayyun ve-r[abbi] Yishaq 'Abarbanel - yehasim 'inteleqtu'a-liyim", *Michael* 11 (1989) 23-33; J. GUTTMANN, *Die religionsphilosophischen Lehren des Isaak Abravanel* (Breslau: M. & H. Marcus 1916); E. GUTWIRTH, "Consolatio: Don Ishaq Abravanel and the Classical Tradition", *MeH* NS 27 (2000) 79-98; I. HEINEMANN, "Abravanels Lehre vom Niedergang des Menschheit", *MGWJ* 82 (1938) 381-400; A. J. HESCHEL, *Don Jizchak Abravanel* (Berlin: E. Reiss 1937); M. IDEL, "Qabbalah u-filosofiyah qedumah 'esel R. Yishaq we-Yehudah 'Abravanel", in: *Filosofiyat ha-'ahavah shel Yehudah 'Abravanel* (ed. M. Dorman / Z. Levi; Haifa: Haifa UP 1985) 73–112; M. KELLNER, *Dogma in Medieval Jewish Thought* (Oxford: Oxford UP 1986) 179–95; idem, "Gersonides and His Cultured Despisers: Arama and Abravanel", *JMRS* 6 (1976) 269–92; idem, "Jewish Dogmatics After the Spanish Expulsion: Rabbis Isaac Abravanel and Joseph Yabes on Belief in Creation as an Article of Faith", *JQR* 72 (1982) 178–87; idem, "Kefirah be-sho-geg be-hagut yehudit bi-yemei ha-benayim: ha-Rambam ve-'Abravanel mul Rashbaz ve-Raḥaq?", *Meḥqerei yerushalayim be-maḥashevet yisra'el* 3 (1984) 393–403; idem, "Maimonides, Crescas, and Abravanel on Exodus 20:2: A Medieval Exegetical Debate", *JQR* 69 (1979) 129–57; idem, "R. Isaac Abravanel on Maimonides' Principles of Faith", *Tradition* 18 (1980) 343–56; E. LAWEE, "Abravanel, Isaac", in: EncRen 1 (1999) 1–2; idem, "Abravanel, Isaac", in: *Reader's Guide to Juda-ism* (ed. M. Terry; Chicago: Fitzroy Dearborn 2000) 2–3; idem, "'The Good We Accept and the Bad We Do Not': Aspects of Isaac Abarbanel's Stance towards Maimonides", in: *Be'erot Yitzhak: Studies in Memory of Isadore Twersky* (ed. J. M. Harris; Cambridge, MA: Harvard UP 2005) 119–60; idem, "Isaac Abarbanel's Intellectual Achievement and Literary Legacy in Modern Scholarship: A Retrospective and Opportunity", in: *Studies in Medieval Jewish History and Literature* III (ed. I. Twersky / J. M. Harris; Cambridge, MA: Harvard University Center for Jewish Studies 2000) 213–47; idem, *Isaac Abarbanel's Stance Toward Tradition: Defense, Dissent, and Dialogue* (Albany: State University of New York Press 2001); idem, "The Messianism of Isaac Abarbanel, 'Father of the [Jewish] Messianic Movements of the Sixteenth and Seventeenth Centuries'", in: *Jewish Mes-sianism in the Early Modern Period* (ed. R. H. Popkin / M. Goldish; Dordrecht: Kluwer 2001) 1–39; A. MELAMED, "R. Yiṣḥaq 'Abravanel ve-ha-politiqah le-'Aristo – deramah shel ta'uyot", *Da'at* 29 (1992) 69–81; idem, "Torat ha-'iqqarim shel 'Abravanel", *Pe'amim* 57 (1994) 137–41; Y. NAVO, "Galut u-ge'ulah be-haguto shel Don Yiṣḥaq 'Abravanel", *Sinai* 110 (1993) 36–57; B. NETANYAHU, *Don Isaac Abravanel: Statesman and Philosopher* (Ithaca: Cornell UP [5]1998); M. NISSAN, "Yesodot be-mishnato ha-medinit shel ha-rav Yiṣḥaq 'Abarbanel legabei yeḥasei yisra'el we-'umot ha-'olam", *Kiwwunim* 37 (1987) 61–69; B. OGREN, "Circularity, the Soul-Vehicle and the Renais-sance Rebirth of Reincarnation: Marsilio Ficino and Isaac Abarbanel on the Possibility of Trans-migration", *Accademia* 6 (2004) 63–94; U. PIPERNO, "Abravanel e le istituzioni politiche della re-pubblica de Venezia", *La Rassegna Mensile di Israel* 59 (1993) 154–70; A. RAVITZKY, "'Al melakhim u-mishpatim be-hagut ha-yehudit bi-yemei ha-benayim (ben R. Nissim Gerondi le-R. Yiṣḥaq 'Abarbanel)", in: *Tarbut we-ḥevrah be-toldot yisra'el bi-yemei ha-benayim* (ed. R. Bonfil e.a.; Jeru-salem: Merkaz Zalman Shazar 1989) 469–91; S. REGEV, "Beḥirat 'am yisra'el be-haguto shel Rabbi Yiṣḥaq 'Abravanel", *'Asufot* 2 (1989) 271–83; idem, "Meshiḥiyut ve-'astrologiyah be-haguto shel rabbi Yiṣḥaq 'Abravanel", *'Asufot* 1 (1987) 169–87; A. REINES, *Maimonides and Abrabanel on Pro-phecy* (Cincinnati: HUC Press 1970); E. I. J. ROSENTHAL, "Don Isaac Abravanel: Financier, States-man and Scholar, 1437–1937", BJRL 24 (1937) 445–78; G. RUIZ, "Modernidad de la profetologia de Maimonides y de la critica de don Isaac Abrabanel", in: *Sobre la vida y obra de Maimonides* (ed. J. Pelaez del Rosal; Cordoba: Ediciones El Almendio 1991) 473–82; Y. SAFRAN, "Mishnato ha-ḥi-nukhit shel r[abbi] Yiṣḥaq 'Abarbanel", *Sinai* 68 (1972) 55–86; E. SHEMUELI, *Don Yiṣḥaq 'Abrava-nel we-gerush sefarad* (Jerusalem: Mosad Biyalik 1963); J. B. TREND / H. LOEWE (eds.), *Isaac Abra-vanel: Six Lectures* (Cambridge: Cambridge UP 1937); R. SIRAT, "Leshon sippur gerush yehudei sefarad shel don Yiṣḥaq 'Abarbanel (mavo' le-ferush le-sefer melakhim)", in: *Divrei ha-kenes ha-'ivri ha-mada'i ha-shemini be-'eropah* (Jerusalem: Berit Ivrit Olamit 1991) 39–54; E. URBACH, "Die Staatsauffassung des Don Isaak Abravanel", *MGWJ* 81 (1937) 270–77; M. WAXMAN, "Don Yiṣḥaq 'Abravanel", *Sefer ha-shanah li-yehudei 'ameriqah* 3 (1939) 68–101.

Additional studies cited below: C. ALONSO FONTELA, "Anotaciones de Alfonso de Zamora en un comentario a los profetas posteriores de don Isaac Abravanel", *Sef.* 47 (1987) 227–43; R. BEN-SHA-LOM, "Mitos u-mitologiyah shel yavan va-roma' be-toda'ah ha-hisṭorit shel yehudei sefarad bi-ye-mei ha-benayim", *Zion* 66 (2001) 451–94; J. H. BENTLEY, *Humanists and Holy Writ: New Testa-ment Scholarship in the Renaissance* (Princeton: Princeton UP 1983); K. P. BLAND, "Issues in Six-teenth-Century Jewish Exegesis", in: *The Bible in the Sixteenth Century* (ed. D. Steinmetz; Dur-ham, NC: Duke UP 1990) 50–67; R. BONFIL, *Jewish Life in Renaissance Italy* (Berkeley, CA: Uni-versity of California Press 1994); J. F. BOYLE, "The Theological Character of the Scholastic 'Divi-sion of the Text' with Particular Reference to the Commentaries of Saint Thomas Aquinas", in: *With Reverence for the Word* (ed. J. D. McAuliffe e.a.; New York: Oxford UP 2002) 276–83; R. BRODY, "The Geonim of Babylonia as Biblical Exegetes", in: HBOT I/2 (2000) 74–88; P. BURKE, *The Renaissance Sense of the Past* (New York: St. Martin's 1970); G. DAHAN, "Genres, Forms and

Various Methods in Christian Exegesis of the Middle Ages", in: HBOT I/2 (2000) 196–236; J. F. D'AMICO, *Theory and Practice in Renaissance Textual Criticism: Beatus Rhenanus between Conjecture and History* (Berkeley, CA: University of California Press 1988); Y. ELMAN, "'It Is No Empty Thing': Nahmanides and the Search for Omnisignificance", *The Torah U-Madda Journal* 4 (1993) 1–83; idem, "Moses ben Nahman / Nahmanides (Ramban)", in: HBOT I/2 (2000) 416–32; K. FROEHLICH, "'Always to Keep the Literal Sense in Holy Scripture Means to Kill One's Soul': The State of Biblical Hermeneutics at the Beginning of the Fifteenth Century", in: *Literary Uses of Typology from the Late Middle Ages to the Present* (ed. E. Miner; Princeton: Princeton UP 1977) 20–48; C. D. GINSBURG, *Jacob ben Chajim ibn Adonijah's Introduction to the Rabbinic Bible / The Massoreth Ha-Massoreth of Elias Levita* (New York: KTAV 1968); A. GOMEZ MORENO, *España y la Italia de los humanistas* (Madrid: Gredos 1994); D. GONZOLO MAESO, "Alonso de Madrigal (Tostado) y su labor escrituraria", *Miscelánea de Estudios Árabes y Hebráicos* 4 (1955) 143–85; M. H. GOSHEN-GOTTSTEIN, "Christianity, Judaism and Modern Bible Study", VTSup 28 (1974) 69–88; M. GREENBERG, "Ha-biqoret ve-ha-'emunah", in: *'Al ha-miqra' ve-'al ha-yahadut: koveṣ ketavim* (ed. A. Shapira; Tel Aviv: Am Oved 1984) 275–80; idem, "Jewish Conceptions of the Human Factor in Biblical Prophecy", in: *Justice and the Holy: Essays in Honor of Walter Harrelson* (ed. D. A. Knight / P. J. Paris; Atlanta: Scholars 1989) 145–62; A. GROSS, *R[abbi] Yosef ben 'Avraham Ḥayyun: manhig qehilat lisbon ve-yeṣirato* (Ramat-Gan: Bar-Ilan UP 1993); idem, "Rashi u-mesoret limmud ha-torah she-bi-ketav bi-sefarad", *in Rashi: 'iyyunim be-yeṣirato* (ed. Z. A. Steinfeld; Ramat-Gan: Bar-Ilan UP 1993) 27–55; A. GROSSMAN, "The School of Literal Jewish Exegesis in Northern France", in: HBOT I/2 (2000) 321–71; J. HANKINS, *Plato in the Italian Renaissance* 1–2 (Leiden: Brill 1991); M. IDEL, "Ha-perush ha-magi ve-ha-te'urgi shel ha-musiqah be-teqsṭim yehudiyim mi-tequfat ha-renesans ve-'ad ha-ḥasidut", *Yuval* 4 (1982) 33–63; idem, "The Magical and Neoplatonic Interpretations of the Kabbalah in the Renaissance", in: *Jewish Thought in the Sixteenth Century* (ed. B. D. Cooperman; Cambridge, MA: Harvard UP 1983) 186–242; S. JAPHET, *The Ideology of the Book of Chronicles and Its Place in Biblical Thought* (Frankfurt am Main: Peter Lang 1989); eadem, *I & II Chronicles: A Commentary* (Louisville, KY: Westminster 1993); I. HEINEMANN, "Die wissenschaftliche Allegoristik des jüdischen Mittelalters", HUCA 23 (1950–51) 611–43; English: "Scientific Allegorization During the Jewish Middle Ages", in: *Studies in Jewish Thought: An Anthology of German Jewish Scholarship* (ed. A. Jospe; Detroit: Wayne State UP 1981) 247–69; S. KLEIN-BRASLAVY, "The Philosophical Exegesis", in: HBOT I/2 (2000) 302–20; J. L. KUGEL, "The Bible in the University", in: *The Hebrew Bible and Its Interpreters* (Biblical and Judaic Studies from the University of California, San Diego 1; ed. W. H. Propp e.a.; Winona Lake, IN: Eisenbrauns 1990) 143–65; E. LAWEE, "Introducing Scripture: the *accessus ad auctores* in Medieval Hebrew Exegetical Literature from the 13th to 15th Centuries", in: *With Reverence for the Word* (2002) 157–79; J. N. H. LAWRANCE, "Humanism in the Iberian Peninsula", in: *The Impact of Humanism on Western Europe* (ed. A. Goodman / A. MacKay; London: Longman 1990) 220–58; B. LEVY, *Fixing God's Torah: The Accuracy of the Hebrew Bible Text in Jewish Law* (New York: Oxford UP 2001); D. LOMAX / R. J. OAKLEY, *Fernão Lopes: The English in Portugal 1367–87* (Warminster: Aris and Phillips 1988); H. MACK, "Shiv'im panim la-torah – le-mehalekho shel biṭṭui", in: *Sefer ha-yovel la-rav Mordekhai Breuer* 1–2 (ed. Moshe Bar-Asher; Jerusalem: Akademon 1992), 2, 449–62; A. MELAMED, "'Al yithallel: perushim filosofiyim le-yirmiyahu 9:22-23 be-maḥashavah ha-yehudit bi-yemei ha-benayim ve-ha-renesans", *Meḥqerei yerushalayim ba-maḥashevet yisra'el* 4 (1984) 31–82; A. J. MINNIS, *Medieval Theory of Authorship: Scholastic Literary Attitudes in the Later Middle Ages* (Aldershot: Scolar ²1988); H. NADER, *The Mendoza Family in the Spanish Renaissance, 1350–1550* (New Brunswick, NJ: Rutgers UP 1979); J. S. PENKOWER, "'Iyyun meḥudash be-s[efer] mesoret ha-masoret le-'Eliyahu Baḥur", *Italia* 8 (1989) 7–77 (Hebrew section); J. T. ROBINSON, "Samuel ibn Tibbon's *Commentary on Ecclesiastes* and the Philosopher's Prooemium", in: *Studies in Medieval Jewish History and Literature* III (ed. I. Twersky / J. M. Harris; Cambridge, MA: Harvard University Center for Jewish Studies 2000) 83–146; E. RUMMEL, *The Humanist-Scholastic Debate in the Renaissance and Reformation* (HHS 120; Cambridge, MA: Harvard UP 1995); M. SAPERSTEIN, *Jewish Preaching 1200–1800: An Anthology* (Yale Judaica Series 26; New Haven: Yale UP 1989); idem, "The Method of Doubts: Problematizing of the Bible in Late Medieval Jewish Exegesis", in: *With Reverence for the Word* (2002) 133–56; U. SIMON, *'Arba' gishot le-sefer tehillim* (Ramat-Gan: Bar-Ilan UP 1982); C. COHEN SKALLI, "The Dual Humanism of Don Isaac Abravanel", *Leituras* 14–15 (2004–05) 151–71; B. SMALLEY, *The Study of the Bible in The Middle Ages* (Notre Dame, IN: University of Notre Dame Press ²1964); F. E. TALMAGE, "Apples of

Gold: The Inner Meaning of Sacred Texts in Medieval Judaism", in: *Jewish Spirituality: From the Bible Through the Middle Ages* 1–2 (ed. A. Green; New York: Crossroad 1988), 1, 313–55; idem, *David Kimhi: The Man and the Commentaries* (Cambridge, MA: Harvard UP 1975); G. E. WEIL, *Elie Lévita: Humaniste et Massorète (1469–1549)* (Leiden: Brill 1963); B. D. WALFISH, *Esther in Medieval Garb: Jewish Interpretation of the Book of Esther in the Middle Ages* (Albany, NY: State University of New York Press 1993); H. A. WOLFSON, *Crescas' Critique of Aristotle* (Cambridge, MA: Harvard UP 1929).

1. Biographical Outline

Born in Lisbon in 1437 into a distinguished Ibero-Jewish family, Isaac Abarbanel spent most of his life in Portugal where he served as a leader in the Jewish community and important figure at the court of Afonso V. Implicated in a plot against Afonso's son João II (unjustly, he claimed), Abarbanel fled to Castile in 1483 where he quickly regained prominence as chief tax collector for Spain's senior prelate, Cardinal Mendoza, and as a financier to Spain's dual monarchs, Ferdinand and Isabella. When, however, the Crown issued an edict of expulsion against Spanish Jewry in 1492, Abarbanel and family (including son Judah, later to win fame as Leone Hebreo, author of the Renaissance neoplatonic tract *Dialogues of Love*) chose exile over conversion to Christianity.

Abarbanel passed the rest of his years in Italy, mostly pursuing scholarly projects. He first resided in Naples, but fled following the French invasion of Italy in 1494. After possibly spending time in Sicily, traveling to Corfu, and aborting a planned move to Salonika (a major Ottoman center of Hispano-Jewish refugee settlement), he passed a significant interval in the Adriatic seaport of Monopoli, a Venetian holding that stood under the shadow of French military superiority. In 1503, he headed for Venice proper, where he intervened in a spice-trade dispute between the Venetian republic and his native Portugal. Abarbanel died in the winter of 1508–09 and was buried in Padua, mourned by Jewish and Venetian eminences alike.[1]

2. Overview of the Commentaries

2.1. Contents and Chronology

Abarbanel authored one of the largest Hebrew literary corpora of medieval and early modern times. Though his writings traverse many fields, they mainly comprise works of scriptural interpretation (with one estimate putting his total output at "12000 pages of biblical commentary").[2] Abarbanel's other works, exegetical (e.g., his commentary on the Passover Haggadah) and theological, contain significant quantities of biblical interpretation as well.

Abarbanel's exegesis found its earliest literary expression in the 1460s with the beginnings of a commentary on Deuteronomy (*Mirkevet ha-mishneh / Second Chariot*) and his completion of a monograph on a challenging pericope in Exodus (*'Aṭeret zeqenim / Crown of the Elders*).[3] A recently discovered manuscript seemingly reflects a Portuguese draft of the former work, which was

---

[1] For a fuller biography, see Lawee, Isaac Abarbanel's Stance (2001) 9–25.
[2] Ruiz, Don Isaac Abrabanel (1984) xxii; reprised in Saenz-Badillos / Targarona Borras, Los judios (1996) 242.
[3] For the latter, see Lawee, Isaac Abarbanel's Stance (2001) 59–82.

finished only decades later in Italy.[4] Though a plan to interpret the Former Prophets did not come to fruition in the land of his birth, Abarbanel lectured on these books soon after arriving in Castile and, in amazingly short order, completed ample commentaries on Joshua, Judges, and Samuel.[5] Before leaving Spain, he composed a litany of exegetical objections to Maimonides' philosophic interpretation of the theophany of Ezekiel 1 and 10 (*Ṭa'anot lequḥot mi-ṭeva' ha-ketuvim / Objections Derived from the Nature of the Verses*).

After landing in Naples in 1492, Abarbanel wrote the concluding segment of his commentary on the Former Prophets, on Kings. He returned to biblical commentary during a dauntingly prolific literary period passed mainly in Monopoli. After completing the long-deferred Deuteronomy commentary, he produced a prodigious messianic compendium in which, among other things, he interpreted the Hebrew Bible's eschatological *locus classicus*, Daniel (*Ma'ayenei ha-yeshu'ah / Wells of Salvation*), and prophecies of redemption in other biblical books (*Mashmia' yeshu'ah / Announcer of Salvation*). Commentaries on Isaiah and the Minor Prophets followed and, after his move to Venice, ones on Jeremiah and Ezekiel.[6] Beginning in 1505, Abarbanel revived a long-standing dream to interpret the whole of the Torah, writing extended commentaries on Genesis, Exodus, Leviticus, and Numbers and, it would seem, revising the already extant Deuteronomy commentary.[7] In a list of his writings that he compiled soon thereafter, Abarbanel described the Torah commentary as his "preeminent" work comprising all his "perceptions and learning".[8]

2.2. Format, Relation to Predecessors, Exegetical Aims

In a statement in the "general prologue" to his commentaries on the Former Prophets, Abarbanel clarified some of his exegetical procedures and his vision of the interpretive enterprise.[9] To ease the demanding task of explaining the whole of the Former Prophets and to enhance "comprehensiveness" in his coverage of "their narratives", Abarbanel would "divide each of the books into pericopes". These would be smaller than the units devised by Abarbanel's fourteenth-century Jewish predecessor, Gersonides, but larger than the ones fashioned by "the scholar Jerome, who translated Holy Writ for the Christians". At the outset of each book, Abarbanel would outline its pericopae and indicate each pericope's theme as well as the verses marking its beginning and end. This venture would abet "the recollection of matters and their retention in [our] hearts, since it behooves us to strive for retention of matters and their recollection".

Before explaining a pericope, Abarbanel would raise questions or "doubts" about it in order to "highlight issues, spark debate, and broaden the inquiry". The expectation was that this method would trigger a "more intense scrutiny of the verses" that would in turn yield new insight. In his

---

[4] Richler, Isaac Abravanel's 'Lost' Commentary (1999); Regev, Nusaḥ rishon (2000).

[5] *Perush 'al nevi'im rishonim* (1955) 422 (for the plan to interpret the Former Prophets in Lisbon); 3, 91 (for the lectures); 91, 161, 421 (for the completion dates of the commentaries on Joshua, Judges, and Samuel).

[6] Inaccurate surmises as to the correct chronology of these commentaries have been replaced by clarification of the correct chronology on the basis of the colophon to Escorial MS G-I-11; see Ruiz, Don Isaac Abrabanel y su commentario (1984) 246.

[7] For evidence of revisions to the Deuteronomy commentary, see Lawee, Retrospective and Opportunity (2000) 242, n.70.

[8] *She'elot le-he-ḥakham Sha'ul ha-Kohen* (1574) 8r (actual as opposed to printed foliation).

[9] *Perush 'al nevi'im rishonim* (1955) 13.

commentaries on the Prophets, Abarbanel detailed six queries for each pericope,[10] granting the ar-
tificiality of this number but justifying his consistent adherence to it on the grounds that a fixed tally would ease understanding and facilitate the reader's ability to retain findings. In his Torah commentaries, Abarbanel abandoned this approach, at times posing two dozen queries or more before
a new pericope prior to setting out on his running commentary. Abarbanel's adoption of the ques-
tion-based approach – which has been linked with a novel method of talmudic study advanced by
the mid-fifteenth century Sefardic scholar, Isaac Canpanton – was not unique. His Catalonian contemporary, Isaac Arama, and ostensible Lisbon mentor, Joseph Hayyun, and yet other exegetes
and preachers associated with the "Spanish Expulsion generation" used it as well.[11] Still, the length
and involved nature of Abarbanel's queries (which often extensively survey earlier rabbinic and
medieval opinion) mark a novelty in Hebrew exegetical literature. Lying behind this innovation,
possibly, is Abarbanel's awareness of the commentaries of his older Hispano-Christian contemporary, Alfonso de Madrigal Tostado, who often posed extremely detailed questions in great number.[12] At any rate, Abarbanel's use of the "method of doubts" popularized it among sixteenth-century Hebrew exegetes[13] who shared Abarbanel's conviction that Bible study should entail a "process of active intellectual inquiry, as opposed to the more passive reception of mere information".[14]

   With respect to forerunners, Abarbanel would "at times derive a bit of assistance from the words of the [earlier medieval] commentators and the ways of
the [classical rabbinic] *midrashot*" and "at times incline away from them". As
regards his stance towards the rabbinic inheritance, he affirmed his intention
to adduce the midrashim "most pleasing" to him, implying the existence of
others that he viewed less kindly or, as is clear in some circumstances, found
downright disagreeable. He would not hesitate to expose the "weakness" of
rabbinic views that reflected ultimately fallible rabbinic "interpretation" rather
than an indubitably true "received tradition" in rabbinic hands. The distinction
was not a new one. Stretching back through earlier southern Mediterranean
centers to the Babylonian Geonim of the Muslim east, some schools of Jewish
biblical exegesis had sanctioned the rejection of nonlegal rabbinic interpretations under some circumstances.[15]

   Abarbanel would deviate from assorted emphases and practices of his medieval predecessors. He would forego reiteration of their "grammatical observations" – this, supposedly, "for the sake of brevity", though he clearly lacked
any special interest or competence in this area. He would not "try" his reader
with cryptic exegetical prose of the sort cultivated at times by his main Spanish
predecessors, Abraham ibn Ezra and Moses ben Nahman / Nahmanides, who
had sought to conceal certain esoteric teachings from ordinary readers. He

---

   [10] See, e.g., for the six questions on Isaiah 5 in English translation, Berlin, Biblical Poetry
(1991) 128–31.
   [11] See Saperstein, The Method of Doubts (2003), where the theory of possible (albeit, in the
event, elusive) scholastic origins is also discussed (and at 147, n. 5, for those who connect Ababa-
nel's technique with Canpanton).
   [12] For questions in Tostado's commentaries, see Gonzolo Maeso, Alonso de Madrigal (1955)
179. For Abarbanel's relationship to Tostado, see Gaon, The Influence of the Catholic Theologian
(1993).
   [13] Saperstein, Jewish Preaching (1989) 74.
   [14] Bland, Sixteenth-Century Jewish Exegesis (1990) 52–63. Or as Abarbanel expressed it in one
place, "[positing] doubts at the outset of an inquiry arouses the mind to find 'words of delight'
[Qoh 12:10]". See *Ma'ayenei ha-yeshu'ah* (1961) 351.
   [15] For gaonic origins, see Brody, The Geonim of Babylonia (2000) 86–87. For a brief overview
of high and late medieval developments, see Lawee, Isaac Abarbanel's Stance (2001) 83–92.

would also eschew a consistent feature of Gersonides' biblical commentaries, the derivation of "lessons from the narratives", this being "a pointless activity" since "all of the words of the prophets are themselves lessons concerning ethical matters and [correct] opinions". While, in practice, Abarbanel would not forgo the extraction of lessons entirely, what he apparently wished to stress by his condemnation of Gersonides' passage-by-passage culling of legal, moral, and philosophic precepts was any implication that the divine word's depths were exhausted through such an enumeration.[16] Alternatively or additionally, Abarbanel may have detected in Gersonides' approach an invidious view of Scripture as a mere vehicle for communicating teachings known independently of it.[17]

Overall, Abarbanel's interpretive aim would be twofold: explanation of the verses "in the most satisfactory way possible" and exploration of "the conceptual problems (*derushim*) embedded therein to their very end".[18] In short, he would explore both Scripture's exegetical and doctrinal-theological dimensions. Abarbanel warns that such interpretation yields lengthy commentary. He seeks to forestall criticism of this outcome by claiming that extended exposition reflects "the extensiveness of the inquiry" that Holy Writ demands. Far from being a symptom of "prolixity" or "extraneousness", exegetical expansiveness is a natural outcome of any attempt to achieve "understanding of the truth of [scriptural] matters and their depth".[19]

On this note, Abarbanel takes to task his exegetical forerunners, grouping them into what he presents as the two main streams of post-rabbinic Jewish exegesis. The first Abarbanel associates with Rashi, eleventh-century dean of northern French interpretation, and the second with Abraham ibn Ezra, capstone of the Andalusi-Jewish exegetical school. He pronounces it "an evil and bitter thing to me" that Rashi "contented himself in his commentaries on the Holy Scriptures in most matters with that which the rabbinic sages expounded" while Ibn Ezra focussed on "[explanations of] the grammar of the words and the superficial meaning of the text's simple sense (such that, he adds caustically, Ibn Ezra's exegetical works are more concise than the texts that they purport to unpack). These commentators' epigons "imitated their [interpretive] modes, [expounding] either in a midrashic vein [in the manner of Rashi] or according to the superficial meaning of the [text's] contextual sense [in the manner of Ibn Ezra's commentaries]". Abarbanel finds embedded

---

[16] Comparable in this regard from a theological point of view is Abarbanel's denial of the existence of Jewish dogmatic principles on the grounds that "the Torah is true" and hence "no belief or narrative in it has any advantage over any other"; *Rosh 'amanah* (1993) 147. Exegetically speaking, Abarbanel's criticism of Gersonides' elicitation of lessons from Scripture made on the grounds that *all* prophetic words offer revelatory enlightenment echoes a standard rabbinic assumption regarding Scripture's maximal meaningfulness.

[17] Cf. Walfish, Esther in Medieval Garb (1993) 169: "In his Esther commentary, the fifty-one lessons he [Gersonides] lists make up more than half the commentary. Most of these pertain to court etiquette and when compiled and classified comprise a veritable manual of behavior and etiquette for the courtier, and not necessarily a Jewish one at that".

[18] As used by Abarbanel here and similarly by other late medieval Jewish writers, *derush* ('conceptual problem') traces back to the medieval Latin *quaesitum*; see Wolfson, Crescas' Critique of Aristotle (1929) 336.

[19] Reading *'omqam* for *'amaqim* on the basis of the first printed edition (Pesaro? 1511?) [5v]. Abarbanel did not escape the charge of prolixity. For a long list of his detractors on this score, see Ruiz, Don Isaac Abrabanel y su commentario (1984) cxx nn. 451–56. These critics invariably fail to note Abarbanel's defense of expansive exposition when condemning his exegetical longwindedness.

in both approaches an inexcusably narrow definition of the exegetical discipline. Building on a re-proach coined by Maimonides, he castigates his forerunners for reading Scripture "as if skimming a historical work or piece of poetry, with great brevity". As appended to the original Maimonidean formulation, Abarbanel's gloss – "with great brevity" – communicates his view that what might seem admirably pithy commentary is actually an outward manifestation of a misguided perception of Scripture.[20] Did his predecessors "really not know nor understand that the Torah has seventy faces" and that Scripture comprehends "the secrets of existence and of divine science in wondrous measure?"[21] If so, they should have gone beyond the cardinal requirement to explicate the logic and language of Scripture's phrases and verses to supply exegesis that penetrated Scripture in its full dimension. For his part, Abarbanel would not forebear to explicate Scripture's contextual sense. Indeed, he elsewhere stresses his primary occupation with this sense – that is, *peshuṭo shel miqra*.[22] But while operating with what, drawing on Ibn Ezra's exegetical lexicon, he called "the method of *peshaṭ*", Abarbanel would insist on exposing Scripture's many other "faces". Regarding the profuse commentary engendered by this definition of the exegetical task he states: "where it is fitting to expatiate I am not entitled to curtail".

Some of Abarbanel's techniques of biblical interpretation and his broad definition of the exe-gete's task were, it would seem, partially shaped by developments in the Latin commentary tradi-tion and Ibero-Jewish perceptions of Christian achievements in the exegetical sphere. In its basic operations of interpretation, Abarbanel's interpretive program mirrors the one carried out in the Christian university which involved *divisio* (Abarbanel's division into pericopes, however rudimen-tary his execution thereof may seem when compared to the highly elaborate use of this interpretive tool by Christian counterparts); *expositio* (Abarbanel's explanation of verses "in the most satisfac-tory way possible"), and *dubia / quaestiones* (investigation of "conceptual problems").[23] Abarba-nel's critique of Ibn Ezra – which amounts to an attack on Andalusi-Jewish exegetical aspirations generally for their overly constricted focus on grammar and the "superficial meaning of the [text's] contextual sense" – points to a larger Christian context by invoking a catch-phrase of Latin ori-gin.[24]

More to the point, it recalls comments of one of Abarbanel's colleagues who revealed late med-ieval Hispano-Jewish awareness of Christian virtuosity in scripturally-based homiletical preaching. In particular, this colleague, the Aragonese preacher Isaac Arama, related his parishioners' com-plaint that while Christian preachers search "enthusiastically for religious and ethical content" in their biblical interpretation "using all appropriate hermeneutical techniques", their Jewish counter-parts limit themselves to the "grammatical forms of words and the simple meaning of the stories

---

[20] For the original coinage, see Moses ben Maimon, *Guide of the Perplexed* I.2, where this alle-gation is directed at an anonymous interlocutor. One of Maimonides' thirteenth-century followers applied it to Jewish communities in his day (Jacob Anatoli, *Malmad ha-talmidim* [Lyck 1866] [10]), but it was left to Abarbanel to turn the Maimonidean formula against the Jewish Middle Ages' leading exegetes!

[21] For the image of the Torah's faces, see Mack, Shiv'im panim la-torah (1992). For the same metaphor in Quranic interpretation, see Talmage, Apples (1988) 348, n. 37. For additional sources on Abarbanel's conception of scriptural polysemy in relation to other Jewish and Christian writers, see Lawee, Isaac Abarbanel's Stance (2001) 255, n. 34.

[22] Lawee, Isaac Abarbanel's Stance (2001) 93–125.

[23] For the threefold Christian approach, see Dahan, Genres (2000) 213–14. For comprehensive and intricate division of the text by scholastics (e. g. Thomas' division of the Gospel according to John, which fills some 37 pages in its modern edition), see Boyle, The Theological Character (2003) 276.

[24] "According to the superficial meaning" / *ke-fi shiṭhiyut ha-peshaṭ = iuxta superficiem littere*. Abarbanel imbues this formula with a negative valence attested in some later medieval Christian texts as well. Though the quest for the *superficiem littere* could be a goal of exegesis in earlier medi-eval times (as in the case of Andrew of St. Victor; see Smalley, Study of the Bible [1964] 169), the probing of this textual plane was denigrated in Christian circles closer to Abarbanel's day (Froeh-lich, 'Always to Keep the Literal Sense' [1977] 32–33). For what is apparently the earliest Hebrew usage of the equivalent of the Latin *iuxta superficiem littere*, see Hillel ben Samuel, *Sefer tagmulei ha-nefesh* (ed. J. Sermoneta; Jerusalem: The Israel Academy of Sciences and Humanities 1981, 146).

and commandments".[25] Abarbanel wrote his biblical commentaries as if responding to this indictment, not only explaining verses according to "the method of *peshaṭ*" but seeking also to explore seminal theological issues as they arose from Scripture and to provide interpretation rich in religious edification and spiritual food for thought.

3. Medieval Characteristics of the Commentaries

Abarbanel has often been considered the "last great representative exegete" of the Jewish Middle Ages, and with reason: his commentaries reflect a predominantly medieval ambience.[26]

To begin with, these commentaries evince their author's running dialogue with a wide panoply of remote and immediate medieval predecessors. To a degree unprecedented in earlier Jewish biblical exegesis, this dialogue also embraces medieval Christian theologians and exegetes.[27] Abarbanel naturally relates to Jewish interlocutors more frequently, among whom three stand out. Abarbanel evinces strong awareness of Rashi, pioneering purveyor of what he took to be Scripture's contextual sense who, more often than not, selected from an endlessly abundant inventory of rabbinic interpretation in relaying what he considered Scripture's contextual sense. Abarbanel's encounter with Rashi's Torah commentary reflects a new development: the rise to prominence of Rashi's exegesis in late medieval Iberia.[28] Abarbanel also frequently interacts with his two most influential Iberian predecessors, Abraham ibn Ezra and Nahmanides. His recourse to the former, transmitter to the Jewries of Christian Europe of the grammatically oriented and rationalist exegesis of al-Andalus, is more episodic than his engagement with the latter, the most important Jewish exegete to emerge from Christian Spain and one whom Abarbanel viewed as kabbalistic biblical interpretation's outstanding representative.[29]

Nahmanides was the medieval predecessor who most shaped Abarbanel's exegetical program.[30] Abarbanel's amplification of trends prominent in Nahmanidean exegesis is evident in the attention that he gives to issues of scriptural narrative style (e.g., the issue of resumptive repetition) and literary structure (up to and including the structure of the whole of the Bible and the structural coherence of particular biblical books).[31] Like Nahmanides, but still more adamantly, Abarbanel argues for the biblical text's chronological sequentiality against those, like Ibn Ezra, who had resorted to asequential interpretation.[32] Though not inclined to follow Nahmanides in finding resumptive repetitions in the Torah, Abarbanel is alert to the textual quandaries that triggered his

---

[25] For Arama, see ʿAqedat yiṣḥaq 1 (ed. H. J. Pollak; 5 vols.; Pressburg, Czechoslovakia [1849]) [1v], here cited according to the translation of Saperstein (Jewish Preaching [1989] 393).

[26] For the cited formulation, see Rosenthal, The Study of the Bible (1969) 272. Cf. Ruiz, Las introducciones (1984) 707 ("el último exégeta del judaísmo español medieval") and the title of Grünberg (1928).

[27] Guttmann, Die religionsphilosophischen Lehren (1916) 45–47; Lawee, Isaac Abarbanel's Stance (2001), in the index under Aquinas, Saint Thomas; Nicholas of Lyre; Paul of Burgos.

[28] On this development, see, briefly, Grossman, The School of Literal Jewish Exegesis (2000) 245–46; and, in greater detail, Gross, Rashi u-mesoret limmud ha-torah (1993).

[29] For Abarbanel and Ibn Ezra, see Lipshitz, Pirqei ʿiyyun (1982). For Abarbanel's perception of Nahmanides as the leading kabbalistic exegete, see Lawee, Isaac Abarbanel's Stance (2001) 79–81.

[30] ELMAN speaks, with some hyperbole one should think, of Abarbanel's "consuming engagement with Nahmanides' commentary" (The Book of Deuteronomy [1997] 231).

[31] For Nahmanides on these scores, see Elman, Moses ben Nahman (2000) 420–31. For Abarbanel, see Has, Sṭiyot metodologiyot (2001).

[32] Lawee, Isaac Abarbanel's Stance (2001) 187; Has, Sṭiyot metodologiyot (2001) 32–35, 92–93.

predecessor's recourse to this interpretive mechanism (Abarbanel's own predilection is to see such repetitions as explanatory in nature).[33] Like Nahmanides, Abarbanel assumes the thematic unity of individual books of the Torah.[34] Abarbanel's yen for topically coherent interpretation of larger biblical units surpasses Nahmanides' such that structurally guided approaches at times yield forced interpretations of adjacent texts and contextual readings of biblical laws at odds with legally binding rabbinic interpretation.[35] Other aspects of apparent Nahmanidean influence on Abarbanel – such as interest in typological prefiguration (an exegetical approach with rabbinic roots turned to effective use by Nahmanides in his Torah commentary) – could be adduced.[36]

Beyond his regular invocations of the fruits of medieval exegesis and frequent role as a "harvester" of earlier biblical scholarship, Abarbanel regularly exhibits embeddedness in the mentality and techniques of medieval Jewish biblical interpretation.[37] A case in point mentioned already is his allegiance to a gaonic-Spanish tradition that distinguished between binding rabbinic scriptural interpretations, especially in the legal realm, and a large segment of nonlegal rabbinic exegesis that could be rejected. In addition, Abarbanel's utilization of numerous medieval *modi interpretandi* (like the just-mentioned example of typology) is evident on every page of his commentaries. Abarbanel also meets intra- and interreligious exegetical challenges in a manner essentially continuous with medieval models, be it the Karaite assault on Rabbanite interpretation or the Christian attempt to read parts of the Hebrew Bible to christological purpose.[38] Even some of the prologues to Abarbanel's biblical commentaries – those parts of his corpus which attest the greatest concentration of novelties born of Abarbanel's Renaissance exegetical turn – follow a well-known medieval exordial format, the Latin *accessus ad auctores*. Modifying earlier versions of this format in light of methods of thinking derived from Aristotle, high and late medieval Christian writers introduced sacred and secular books using prologue-headings derived from Aristotelian causal theory (the book's author was its "efficient cause", its subject-matter its "material cause", and so on). Abarbanel follows suit. Though his introductions have often been cast as the inception of a Hebrew '*Einleitungswissenschaft*', Abarbanel's considerable exordial achievements rest in part on medieval accomplishments, both Jewish and Christian, in the field.[39]

Abarbanel's medievalism also emerges from his handling of larger hermeneutic issues – for instance, the power and hazards of allegorical interpretation.

---

[33] Elman, 'No Empty Thing' (1993) 23–29; Has, Sṭiyot metodologiyot (2001) 76–83.

[34] Elman, 'No Empty Thing' (1993) 21–24.

[35] See, e.g., for forced interpretation, *Perush 'al ha-torah* 3 (1964) 155–56: Abarbanel explains the three worship prohibitions in Deut 16:21–17:1 in terms of the appointment of judges treated in the larger context. For contra-halakhic exegesis abetted by imposition of a larger structural framework, see ibid. 217: following Isaac Arama (albeit without attribution), Abarbanel views the series of largely miscellaneous laws recorded in Deuteronomy 23 as connected topically to "wartime and its affairs". In keeping with this view, his contextual reading of the restricted permission to eat of one's neighbor's crops (Deut 23:25–26) is not limited to harvest workers in accordance with the dominant rabbinic interpretation but includes "any man", since hungry soldiers trespassing fields and vineyards will need to eat their fill. Having set forth this understanding, Abarbanel cites the legally binding rabbinic tradition regarding the matter as well, distinguishing it from his contextual interpretation more sharply than does Arama (for which see *'Aqedat yiṣḥaq* 5 [1849] 89r).

[36] Lawee, Isaac Abarbanel's Stance (2001) 102, 256, n. 42 (where the nature of Abarbanel's reservations regarding a famous instance of Nahmanidean typological interpretation is analyzed).

[37] For the role as harvester, see Lawee, Isaac Abarbanel's Stance (2001) 203–05.

[38] For Karaites, see Lipshitz, Pirqei 'iyyun (1982) 197–203. For a representative sample of Abarbanel's anti-Christian exegesis, see the interpretation of the "suffering servant" poems (Isaiah 52–53) aimed, as Abarbanel says, "at disencumbering us from the murmurings of the learned men of Edom [Christendom] with their spurious interpretations"; *Perush 'al nevi'im 'aḥaronim* (1979) 241–53 (English in Driver / Neubauer, The Fifty-Third Chapter of Isaiah [1969]).

[39] For generally overstated claims of Abarbanel's originality in this area, see the sources in Ruiz, Las introducciones (1984) 708, nn. 3, 4, 5 and, more recently, Saenz-Badillos / Targarona Borras, Los judios (1996) 243. For the prologue-tradition in medieval Jewish exegetical literature prior to Abarbanel, see Robinson, Samuel ibn Tibbon (2000); Lawee, Introducing Scripture (2002). For the "Aristotelian prologue" in Christian literature, see Minnis, Medieval Theory of Authorship (1988) 28–33.

Abarbanel was especially ambivalent about philosophically oriented allegorization of Scripture as practiced and promoted by his most revered medieval predecessor, Maimonides. On the basis of this hermeneutic, Jewish rationalists had located philosophic concepts in Holy Writ by identifying Scripture's "internal meaning" with teachings known from the discursive inquiries of human reason.[40] Though fluent in the ways of philosophic-allegorical interpretation, Abarbanel often inclined away from them, his already mentioned exegetical "objections" to Maimonides' Aristotelian-metaphysical reading of Ezekiel 1 and 10 being the most significant case in point. Called the "Account of the Chariot" in rabbinic literature, this prophetic vision had long been viewed as the acme of Jewish esoteric wisdom. For his part, Abarbanel was at pains to disprove Maimonides' reading of its bizarre details in terms of Greco-Arabic philosophy. Yet Abarbanel's rejection of rationalistic allegorization was far from total. For another biblical narrative deemed by rabbinic tradition to be replete with profundities, the paradise story, Abarbanel offers a contextual interpretation and an allegorical one cast in the Maimonidean mode.[41] Whatever was his final holding regarding rationalistic allegorical interpretation and other philosophically informed modes of exegesis (e.g., naturalistic interpretation of biblical miracles), Abarbanel's main frame of reference for considering the whole issue was essentially the legacy of Jewish theology bequeathed to him from the Middle Ages.[42]

4. Renaissance Departures in the Commentaries

4.1. Contextual Elements

Oft seen as the last in the line of medieval Jewish biblical exegetes (or even "last spokesman" of the Jewish Middle Ages simply), Abarbanel has also been viewed as "the first among the Jews to join Renaissance views to traditional Judaism" or, in his role an exegete, as a medieval who, stimulated by incipient Renaissance humanism, set forth ideas that adumbrated "the scientific and critical exegesis developed over time by non-Jewish scholars in particular".[43]

---

[40] On Maimonidean exegesis, see Klein-Braslavy, The Philosophical Exegesis (2000) 311–20. For medieval Jewish philosophic-allegorical interpretation more generally, see Talmage, Apples of Gold (1988).

[41] For summaries of Maimonides' and Abarbanel's allegorizations of the paradise story, see Heinemann, Scientific Allegorization (1981) 257–59. For discussion, see Lawee, The Good We Accept (2005) 146–49.

[42] For Abarbanel's immersion in Maimonidean and Gersonidean philosophic exegesis, see Borodowski, Isaac Abravanel on Miracles (2003).

[43] For the cited passages, see respectively Netanyahu, Abravanel (1998) ix; Baer, Don Yiṣḥaq 'Abravanel (1937) 245; Segal, R. Yiṣḥaq 'Abravanel (1937) 261. For other assessments of Abarbanel as an exegete who straddles traditional/medieval and critical/modern interpretive modes, see Ruiz, Don Isaac Abrabanel y su commentario (1984) xxxvii–xxxviii; Regev, Ha-shiṭah ha-parshanit (1992) 242; Saenz-Badillos / Targarona Borras, Los judios (1996) 243. For stress on the thoroughgoing medieval character of Abarbanel's theology, as opposed to his exegesis, see Feldman, Philosophy in a Time of Crisis (2003) 150–60.

While one can easily overstate the dichotomy between ostensibly pre-critical medieval interpretation and purportedly critical post-medieval exegesis (especially as regards the Jewish commentary tradition), the claim of a novel turn in Abarbanel's biblical hermeneutic has much to ground it.[44] Before spotlighting aspects of this turn, though, it seems necessary to sketch a few of its biographical and intellectual contexts to buttress the plausibility of the claim that Abarbanel's exegetical profile possesses a Renaissance dimension.

Abarbanel spent most of his years in Iberia at a time when Renaissance trends were in the ascendant. The dominant intellectual force to emerge during the Renaissance was Humanism, a classicizing literary and educational movement which transformed literature, art, and scholarship in Italy beginning in the fourteenth century and which arrived in Spain around the turn of the fifteenth century, first in Aragon and then in Castile and Portugal. Spanish literature was transformed through the exertions of Iñigo López de Mendoza who, among other things, sponsored translations of classical authors such as Virgil, Ovid, and Seneca into Castilian. Santillana disdained those who lacked a knowledge of history, one of the *studia humanitatis*, and he was drawn to classical mythology, which held a significant place in Renaissance consciousness due to the humanist revival of classical literature. In the decades prior to Abarbanel's arrival in Castile, Santillana's sons patronized Spanish Renaissance architecture and humanism, with Abarbanel's employer Cardinal Mendoza himself producing Castilian translations of classical works like Ovid's *Metamorphoses*, a central text in the transmission of pagan myth to Renaissance readers. Humanist historiography was practiced during this period by Alfonso de Palencia and Cardinal Joan Margarit. The Latin and vernacular writings of Alfonso Tostado also signal a humanist turn in Iberian learning and letters.[45]

That Abarbanel was familiar with Iberian Renaissance currents seems clear, though the precise conduits for his awareness of them are hard to determine. In Lisbon, he may have known the first and greatest of the Portuguese royal chroniclers, Fernão Lopes, secretary to his father's 'client' Prince Ferdinand. He certainly would have encountered humanist trends at the court of Afonso V where Abarbanel's royal employer was tutored by Italian humanists and whence emanated a fifteenth-century revival of Portuguese letters. Abarbanel's only surviving vernacular composition, a letter of consolation sent to a member of Portugal's leading noble house, displays nascent humanist predilections.[46]

Abarbanel's brushes with the Castilian Renaissance are most evidently suggested by his links with the Mendoza, but other Spanish figures and trends known to him should not be overlooked. With Alfonso Tostado, whose biblical commentaries he knew, Abarbanel shared an enriched knowledge of history and classical myth that he, like Tostado, deployed in understanding Holy Writ.[47] Abarbanel served at the Spanish court at a time when great importance was attached there to the posts of royal historian and secretary of Latin letters, offices established earlier in the fifteenth century under the influence of huma-

---

[44] In the case of Jewish exegetical tradition, models of progressively 'critical' interpretation over the course of the Middle Ages fail in part in consequence of the sophisticated early and high medieval Judeo-Arabic literary-critical stratum of Rabbanite and Karaite interpretation. For samplings, see Simon, 'Arba' gishot (1982).

[45] On Spanish Humanism, see Lawrance, Humanism (1990); Gomez Marino, España (1994). On the Mendoza in particular, see Nader, The Mendoza Family (1979).

[46] Gutwirth, Consolatio (2000); Cohen Skalli, Dual Humanism (2005).

[47] Ben-Shalom, Mitos u-mitologiyah (2001) 464–80.

nist pedagogy. One might therefore partially ascribe his interest in the Hebrew Bible's oft neglected historical books – an interest he shared with Tostado, whose Old Testament commentaries focussed on these books – to the stimulus of a humanist *paideia*. Little wonder, at any rate, that ideas and concerns attested in Spanish humanist literature appear in Abarbanel's Spanish biblical commentaries, making these the earliest witnesses to Renaissance stimuli on Jewish exegetical literature produced outside of Italy.

Of course, Abarbanel composed most of his works in Renaissance Italy. His sojourn there began in Naples, an important Renaissance center where the leading fifteenth-century humanist biblicists, Giannozzo Manetti and Lorenzo Valla, had worked.[48] At the time of Abarbanel's arrival there, Naples was home to Giovanni Pontano, head of the city's famed humanist academy, and Judah Messer Leon, Italy's foremost native Jewish scholar, whose eclectic intellectual interests included rhetoric, a discipline at humanism's core. Yohanan Alemanno, a student of Judah affiliated with the Florentine Neoplatonist Pico della Mirandola, apparently played an important role in making Abarbanel aware of distinctively Italian Renaissance notions. Characteristic Alemanno adaptations of Renaissance ideas regarding magic, music, and king Solomon as the ideal Renaissance sage already appear in the commentary on Kings that Abarbanel composed shortly after his arrival in Italy. Other views championed by Pico, and by the most influential representative of Renaissance Neoplatonism, Marsilio Ficino, including the idea that a single universal truth pervaded the writings of "the ancient theologians", arise in suitably judaized form in Abarbanel's later Italian works along with elements of Neoplatonism and "civic humanism" prominent on the fifteenth-century Italian Renaissance scene.[49]

As it transformed disciplines from art to political theory, Humanism profoundly reoriented biblical scholarship. Humanist biblicists like Valla, whose philologically oriented exegesis later inspired Erasmus of Rotterdam, have been credited with laying "the foundations for characteristically modern scholarship on the New Testament".[50] Similar claims have been made for Renaissance biblicism's impact on Hebrew Bible study.[51] Applied to biblical interpretation, the term 'humanism' suggests the new Renaissance focus "on the human (as opposed to the divine) side of biblical texts", but the Renaissance reexamination of Scripture was wide-ranging, embracing everything from the "minutely philological" to questions concerning the authorship and unity of biblical books.[52] Whatever the role assigned to it in the rise of modern biblical criticism, Renaissance exegesis set Christian biblical interpretation on a dramatically new course.

Turning to fifteenth- and sixteenth-century Hebrew biblical interpretation, one finds no radical alteration of the medieval landscape born of encounters with the Renaissance and, in fact, few Jewish exegetes who viewed Scripture through one or another Renaissance lens. In Abarbanel's time, there was the aforementioned Judah Messer, who wrote *Nofet ṣufim*, a "marvelous synthesis

---

[48] See Chap. 7.3, by A. VANDERJAGT, in this volume.

[49] Cf. Ogren, Circularity (2004); Idel, Qabbalah u-filosofiyah qedumah (1985); idem, The Magical and Neoplatonic Interpretations (1983) 213–15, 226–27; idem, Ha-perush ha-magi ve-ha-te'urgi (1982) 42–45; Melamed, 'Al yithallel (1984) 60–75. For Solomon as Renaissance sage, see *Perush 'al nevi'im rishonim* (1955) 466–78.

[50] Bentley, Humanists (1983) ix.

[51] Kugel, The Bible in the University (1990).

[52] Ibid. 143–51.

of the humanist sensibility", in which he tried to demonstrate the oratorical superiority of the Hebrew prophets by analyzing their words in terms of rhetorical categories known to him from writings of Cicero, Quintillian, and other classical authors.[53] Several decades later, Abarbanel's younger contemporary, Eliyahu / Elias Levita, resident in Padua during Abarbanel's final years in neighboring Venice, investigated the textual tradition of the Hebrew Bible (Masorah) in a manner that bespoke his humanist sensibilities. The most startling discovery of this teacher and friend of several leading "Christian Hebraists" was that the Tiberian Masoretes had added the Hebrew Bible's vowel points in post-talmudic times. If Valla had exposed the New Testament as a text "subject to the same laws of decay as any other literary artifact", Levita, while in no way intending to undermine the biblical text's authority, provided a benchmark in revealing the Hebrew Bible as "a book with a history".[54]

With Judah Messer Leon's exegetical researches focussed on rhetoric and Levita's centered on textual criticism and lexicography, one must seek elsewhere for stirrings of a Jewish *via exegetica moderna* concerning the sorts of larger questions pursued by Renaissance biblicists as alluded to above. To be sure, it has been asserted that the fifteenth and sixteenth centuries saw no such stirrings, only the flourishing of "the last Jewish Bible scholars of the traditional kind", with Abarbanel a prime example.[55] But Abarbanel's commentaries suggest otherwise. While continuities between them and the exegetical works of his traditional forerunners are undeniably plentiful, these commentaries attest innovative tendencies that belie the impress of Renaissance and especially humanist ideas on their author's exegetical inclinations and thought-processes. One of the best places to see signs of the Renaissance turn in Abarbanel's biblical scholarship is his accounts of the origins and authorship of the Former Prophets and Chronicles.

4.2. Authorship and Formation of Biblical Books

Pondering questions of biblical authorship already in his youth, Abarbanel asked one of his Lisbon mentors whether Deuteronomy was "from God ... like the rest of the words of the Torah" or "was written by Moses on his own".[56] In elaborating his uncertainty, he noted that if the Torah's last book was intended as a clarification of earlier ones, then there was a problem since "an author (*meḥabber*) should not obscure his meaning and then explain himself". Then too, he was alert to the first-person references in Deuteronomy's Mosaic

[53] Bonfil, Jewish Life in Renaissance Italy (1994) 164–67.

[54] For these assessments of Valla's and Levita's work, see respectively D'Amico, Theory and Practice (1988) 16; Preus, The Bible and Religion (1998) 17. On Levita generally, see Weil, Elie Levita (1963), and Chap. 11.3, by S. Kessler Mesguich, in this volume. On his late dating of vowel points, see Penkower, 'Iyyun meḥudash (1989).

[55] Goshen-Gottstein, Christianity (1974) 76.

[56] Gross, R[abbi] Yosef ben 'Avraham (1993) 31–32. The apparently daring phrase "Moses on his own" actually reflects a well-known rabbinic locution. See *Meg.* 31b and parallels.

speeches over and against the invariable third-person references to Moses in
the Torah's three previous books. In interpreting Deuteronomy, Abarbanel
elucidated Moses' contribution to the book in a manner essentially consistent
with earlier medieval ruminations on the topic (such as they existed), those
of Nahmanides especially.[57] By contrast, Abarbanel's consideration of the
authorship and formation of the Former Prophets is replete with new questions and unprecedented insights. As these appear in works written less than a
year after Abarbanel's departure from Portugal, it seems evident that his
plunge beneath Scripture's surface to explore the historical processes and literary sources that shaped the Former Prophets occurred during his Lisbon
period, though the larger Portuguese background from which his new departures sprang is mostly occluded from view.

In an essay on Joshua's and Samuel's "efficient causes", Abarbanel explains why time-honored
rabbinic ascriptions of authorship for these books are wanting.[58] With respect to Joshua, his decisive objection is that verses therein contain the expression "unto this day", a formula that bespeaks
a long interval between an event and its recording. How could Joshua, who lacked the requisite
historical distance, have employed this locution? Abarbanel therefore concludes that Samuel
authored the book. At the same time, Abarbanel denies Samuel's authorship of the sections of the
book bearing this prophet's name since they also contain the historically revealing expression "unto
this day" and, what is more, a telling apposition: "'Come and let us go to the seer'; for he that is
now called a prophet was beforetime called a seer (1 Sam 9:9)". On the basis of this verse's clarification of archaic language, some earlier Jewish exegetes had indicated that Samuel could not have
been written "in the days of Samuel" while others, like David Qimhi, had struggled to uphold what
they took to be an authoritative tradition of Samuel's authorship despite the difficulty posed by the
verse. Both approaches put into relief Abarbanel's more concrete formulation born of his heightened sense of temporal perspective. He takes the objection to be "decisive proof" that Samuel did
not compose the book bearing his name in its biblical version since such an elucidative interpola-
tion would have been required only "a long time" after his death when "[linguistic] habits had
changed".[59]

Abarbanel further parts company with the world of medieval exegesis when he speculatively re-
constructs Samuel's textual prehistory. His point of departure is Scripture's saying that the acts of
King David were "written in the words of Samuel the seer and in the words of Nathan the prophet
and in the words of Gad the seer" (1 Chr 29:29), a verse which suggests that the book bearing Samuel's name is a composite of writings originally produced by Samuel, Nathan, and Gad. These independent documents Jeremiah "collected and joined together, editing the book as a whole on
their basis". While fusing his sources, Jeremiah added explanatory notes "as he saw fit". Abarbanel
illuminates the gradual coming-into-being of a canonical text in a way that stands at a far remove
from his medieval predecessors.[60]

Abarbanel's break with tradition reaches a high point when he pierces the
Former Prophets' compositional history while investigating these books' "formal cause". He takes the "form" of a biblical book to be "pure prophecy" if it
meets a threefold criterion: it must have been written by a prophet, have issued
from "a divine command come to the prophet", and contain information that
otherwise would have remained "unknown in Israel", be it regarding "the

---

[57] Elman, Book of Deuteronomy (1997).
[58] For this essay in English translation, see Lawee, Don Isaac Abarbanel: Who Wrote the
Books of the Bible? (1996).
[59] Perush 'al nevi'im rishonim (1955) 7.
[60] Ibid. 8.

thoughts of the nations and their kings, what they said, the sins of the children of Israel and their acts of repentance", or the like. Elaborating on this last point, Abarbanel posits that the Former Prophets derived from "scattered and disparate" documents composed in earlier times by "judges, kings, the rest of the righteous people of those generations, or chroniclers". He assumes the need for later sifting of these annalistic sources since they contained "things written according to wish rather than the truth" and in some cases "extraneous matters". The sources' limitations reflect the fact that "it is the way of chroniclers and narrators" to "praise or blame more than is fitting in accordance with what they venerate or despise such that in them [the prebiblical records] truth was mixed with falsehood and the extraneous with the essential". Precisely for these reasons, prophets were required to reconstruct the past "fully and accurately" in accordance with the divine will. With the relevant documents (*ketavim*) "gathered to" them, God informed these prophets "of the completion of these events, their truth, their justification", and the manner by which to distinguish "the true from the false and the essential from the extraneous" in the sources. The "form" of the Former Prophets is, then, prophetic strictly speaking. Written by prophets at divine behest, these books do indeed contain information that could only have been known by way of divine revelation – this, in the form of accurate accounts of thoughts, words, and deeds that otherwise would have been comprehended imperfectly on the basis of dispersed unreliable sources composed by anonymous writers.[61]

Elsewhere, Abarbanel is not deterred from ascribing superfluity and tendentiousness of the sort that he associates with generic chronicles to the work of the Chronicler par excellence. The context for this assertion is his concerted effort to explain why Samuel and Kings contains material omitted from Chronicles and vice-versa, despite the largely overlapping historical coverage of these two sets of sources. Abarbanel explains that the author of Samuel and Kings did not record past events for purely antiquarian purposes "as with the histories produced by all of the nations regarding their affairs", but rather to impart lessons concerning "service of the Lord". For this reason, "unnecessary" material was omitted from Samuel and Kings in contrast to Chronicles, a "history pure and simple" that, as such, includes extraneous material.[62] Abarbanel does not even shrink from asserting as a further likeness between Chronicles and the "histories of the nations" their subordination of truth to their authors' purposes. In the case of Chronicles, Ezra the Scribe, writing in postexilic times, was inspired by the conviction that God has chosen David and his descendants in Judah as the true leaders of Israel (and that "the rest of the kings who ruled in Israel from the rest of the tribes did not do so in accordance with the will of God"). Politically, he wished to burnish the reputation of Zerubbabel, the principal Jewish leader at the time of the Temple's restoration, whose status would have been diminished were uncomplimentary details in his Davidic ancestors' lives to be highlighted. As the goal of his epideictic narrative was to extol "King David's excellence and recount his genealogy ... and all of his story and deeds which attest to his perfection" and to carry forward this idea through "the chain of kings who descended from his [David's] seed until Zerubbabel son of Shealtiel", Ezra suppressed, for instance, "the matter of Bathsheba and Uriah the Hittite" since "through his sin of illicit sexual relations and murder it contained a great disgrace to King David". Similarly, seeking to "recount Solomon's praises and not to deprecate him", he disregarded "anything which was blameworthy" in Solomon's career. If earlier Jewish exegetes could have recognized editorial activity in the production of Chronicles, notions of editorial bias

---

[61] Ibid.
[62] Ibid. 163–65.

were well beyond their ken.[63] Not so Abarbanel, who presages modern evaluations of the Chronicler's work by exposing his special interests and clear point of view.[64]

Abarbanel's reflections on the Former Prophets and Chronicles reveal, in several dimensions, his transition to a humanist exegetical stance. Abarbanel's willingness – nay eagerness – to depict Israel's ancient prophets as divinely inspired historians ratifies history's high standing in the new humanist dispensation. Elsewhere in the general prologue to the Former Prophets, Abarbanel speaks of the imperative to understand "the unfolding of the generations from the beginning of creation up to the dispersion from Jerusalem and 'until Shiloh comes' (Gen 49:10)" – that is, to study biblical and post-biblical history. In Italy, he commenced a chronicle of the sufferings of the Jewish people "from the birth of Adam until today", attesting an innovative rise in the production of Hebrew historical literature.[65]

More significant than the valorization of history which they evince, Abarbanel's accounts of the Former Prophets and Chronicles reflect the sort of "historical thinking" and "critical reading" that propelled humanist historiography. A key feature of Renaissance historical thinking was an appreciation of temporal perspective. Renaissance critical reading included a view of earlier sources as *fontes* and a comparative approach to variant versions of the past with the aim of constructing a true account.[66] Abarbanel's assumptions about and inferences concerning the authorship and source documents of the Former Prophets bespeak these traits and others of a similar stamp. For example, Abarbanel's resolve to address the "plethora of doubts" surrounding the "great question" of Chronicles' relationship to Samuel-Kings is a noteworthy example of his comparative orientation. In this case, he stresses his cultivation of exegetical terra incognita, lamenting that among earlier rabbinic and medieval commentators "not even one alluded to the difficulty at all and not one among them suggested a path towards its resolution".[67] The minor dissertations in which Abarbanel presents his findings point towards critical reading's "natural genre", the short study or monograph.[68]

Having been penned at the beginning of the heyday of humanist activity in Spain, one would expect Abarbanel's accounts of the genesis of the Former Prophets and Chronicles to show points of contact with the burgeoning Iberian historiographic and humanist literature of his day – and they do. Abarbanel's supposition that the vocation of historian was one available to an Israelite prophet and, more so, the manner in which he depicts ancient chroniclers seem

---

[63] See Talmage, David Kimhi (1975) 113, who states that while Kimhi recognized editorial involvement in Chronicles "it would be too much to expect him to speak of editorial bias".

[64] See, e.g., the literature cited in Japhet, The Ideology of the Book of Chronicles (1989) 468, n.61.

[65] The work has not survived. For Abarbanel's plan to write it, see *Perush 'al nevi'im rishonim* (1955) 425. For his description of it, see *Ma'ayenei ha-yeshu'ah* (1961) 288.

[66] For definitions of Renaissance historical thinking and critical reading, see, respectively, Burke, Renaissance (1970) 1; Hankins, Plato in the Italian Renaissance 1 (1991) 24–25.

[67] *Perush 'al nevi'im rishonim* (1955) 163–64. Abarbanel slightly overstates the case as David Qimhi had at least recognized the "many obscurities and discrepancies" between Chronicles on one hand and Samuel-Kings on the other; see Talmage, David Kimhi (1975) 108–09.

[68] Hankins, Plato in the Italian Renaissance 1 (1991) 24–25.

indebted to his experience with chroniclers at the Portuguese and Spanish courts where he worked. A Portuguese point of reference for his ascription of bias to ancient "chroniclers and narrators" is Fernão Lopes, who singles out attachment to one's land as a prime cause of historiographic distortion.[69] Spanish parallels are forthcoming from Fernando del Pulgar, historian to the "Catholic Monarchs" during the period that Abarbanel found himself in their employ. For example, Pulgar asserted that lies were occasionally required in accounts of the past in order to demonstrate Isabella's legitimate right to the succession of the Castilian throne.[70] In general, notions found in fifteenth-century Iberian vernacular humanist literature such as "the distinction between history for praise or *fama*; history as reliable record of the past and even history as product of labours of research" make more than a fleeting appearance in Abarbanel's Spanish biblical commentaries.[71]

The commentaries of Alfonso Tostado provide another Renaissance-inflected Spanish point of reference, this one exegetical, for Abarbanel's exploration of the authorship and origins of biblical books. Tostado also sought to clarify what Abarbanel called the "form" of the Former Prophets, a task made more pressing in Tostado's case by the quadripartite structure of the Christian canon with its distinction between "prophetic" and "historical" books. Like Abarbanel, Tostado attempted to define the "prophetic" genre, concluding, for instance, that a book composed by a prophet was not necessarily prophetic *per se* (hence Job's inclusion among the Old Testament's "poetical and wisdom" books rather than "prophetic" writings).[72] It is likely that Tostado's ruminations on scriptural genres and content-categories stimulated Abarbanel's thinking about such topics, though the extent of Abarbanel's interaction with these remains to be researched.

4.3. Scripture's Human Dimension

If Humanism suggests the new focus in the Renaissance on the human side of biblical texts, Abarbanel's at times trailblazing discernments concerning Scripture's human dimension accord with this exegetical trend.

Prophetological subtleties intersect with literary sensibilities when Abarbanel distinguishes the divine and human components in biblical texts. He notes, for instance, that full-fledged prophets at times expressed themselves in language of their own devising when speaking through the Holy Spirit, a truth which explains the appearance of such books as Ruth and Lamentations as authored by the prophets Samuel and Jeremiah respectively (according to rabbinic tradition) in the Writings rather than Prophets, where the main expressions of these prophets are found.[73] Developing a rabbinic dictum in an unpre-

---

[69] Lomax / Oakley, Fernão Lopes (1988) 157–59.

[70] Nader, The Mendoza Family (1979) 33–34.

[71] Gutwirth, Don Ishaq Abravanel and Vernacular Humanism (1998) 667.

[72] *Commentaria in primam partem Iosue et Commentaria in secundam partem Iosue* (Venice 1530) 1r–1v.

[73] *Perush 'al ha-torah* 2 (1964) 125. For a translation of the larger essay containing this observation, see Berlin, Biblical Poetry (1991) 121–28. In the case of Ruth, additional factors are at play: Samuel wrote the book on his own initiative "in honour of David ... without a divine command", meaning the book is not prophetic simply speaking; when Samuel composed the scroll he had already completed his writing of the book of Judges, so "he made the book of Ruth into a scroll on

cedented way, Abarbanel explains why it "frequently" occurs that "one prophet says what another prophet already said in the very same words". The divine effluence bestowed upon non-Mosaic prophets being of a general sort, these prophets were responsible for the arrangement and verbal formulation of their prophecies and naturally "couched them in the language of verses [uttered by earlier prophets] with which they were familiar". Thus Micah "received from God ... the matter of the prophecy [in Micah 4] while the wording of the communication he took from Isaiah" and Jeremiah (Jer 49:16) expressed himself in the language of Obadiah (Obad 3).[74] In explaining the matter thus, Abarbanel has "virtually anticipated the modern notion of the literary education of prophets, and on the same ground: evidence within the oracles of familiarity with antecedent Israelite traditions".[75]

More audaciously, Abarbanel finds defects in the oral and written expression of Jeremiah and Ezekiel, which he explains in terms of the *Sitz-im-Leben* of these biblical prophets. Though exceptional in their ability to impress truths on their souls, this being the first power of "figurative representation" which a human being might perfect, Jeremiah and Ezekiel were inferior when it came to the other powers, the expression of truth correctly and eloquently orally and in writing.[76] A consequence of these oratorical and literary shortcomings is the multitude of grammatical and structural irregularities in their prophecies and the numerous "written (*ketiv*)" and "read (*qere*)" forms (words left unvocalized in the text of the Bible over and against the vocalized versions found in the margin that were to be read) in their books. But one should not expect it to be otherwise. After all, unlike Isaiah, the product of the court whose eloquence was assured by his circumstances, Jeremiah grew up among village priests and received the prophetic call at a young age. In light of his background, he was "forced to express that which God commanded him in the language to which he was accustomed". Jeremiah's larger milieu explain the preponderance of anomalous forms that appear in his book, for even where "irregularities occur also in the rest of the prophets there is a great difference in proportion – that is, in the rest you find that this is the exception whereas with Jeremiah it is the rule".[77] In focussing on the grammatical and rhetorical mastery of the prophets, Abarbanel seemingly shares in the humanist concern for correct and powerful speech. In erecting arguments from historical circumstance in this regard, he stands at one with those Christian humanists who urged that biblical language reflected "the humble social status of the writers" and hence "admitted of improvement".[78]

Discoursing more generally on the origins of the "written" forms and their "read" variants, Abarbanel advances two hypotheses. Denying the views of two of his predecessors that it traces to the corruption of the biblical text in antiquity ("how can I believe in my soul and bring forth on my lips that Ezra the Scribe found the book of the law of God and the books of His prophets and all others who spoke through the Holy Spirit to be doubtful due to omission and confusion?"), Abarbanel surmises that the substituted "read" forms emerged at a later date for other reasons. On one view, Ezra discerned that

---

its own"; due to Ruth's specific focus, it was not proper that it should be included in Judges, which was reserved for more general narratives. See *Perush 'al nevi'im rishonim* (1955) 9.

[74] *Perush 'al nevi'im 'aharonim* (1979) 422. For the translations cited here, see Greenberg, Jewish Conceptions (1989) 157–58.

[75] Greenberg, Jewish Conceptions (1989) 158.

[76] *Perush 'al nevi'im 'aharonim* (1979) 298–99, 382, 534, 514, 571. Abarbanel's usage of *ḥiqqui* for figurative representation reflects an Arabic critical term that in turn renders Greek 'mimesis'; see Robinson, Samuel ibn Tibbon (2000) 139, n.202.

[77] *Perush 'al nevi'im 'aharonim* (1979) 298.

[78] Rummel, The Humanist-Scholastic Debate (1995) 125.

"anomalous expressions" found in the written text required elucidation, which he provided in marginal glosses to be read in their place. An example that Abarbanel supplies highlights his sense of change over time: Ezra, understanding that the simple purport of a place-name in Genesis was no longer meaningful to Jews in Second Temple times, explained it in modern terms. According to a second hypothesis – which Abarbanel characteristically stresses is in no way applicable to the Torah – Ezra believed that certain scriptural expressions "lacked precision", either on account of the carelessness of their speakers or deficiencies in these figures' knowledge of correct writing. Reticent to correct even flawed words when they derived from inspired speakers, Ezra explicated the problematic passages in marginal *qere* notations.[79]

The possibility of prophetic imprecision, or even outright error, crops up with greater frequency than one would expect in Abarbanel's commentaries. According to his general explanation for the more than seventy variants that Abarbanel finds between the two versions of the song of thanksgiving found in 2 Samuel 22 and Psalm 18, the former text reflects a private outpouring of gratitude after the Lord saved David "from the hands of all his enemies" whereas the latter version reflects his effort late in life to compile a compendium of prayers for use by others. In a few cases, however, in accounting for particular variants between the versions, Abarbanel "all but admits that something approaching outright error" appears in 2 Samuel which was subsequently "corrected in the later text".[80]

In an exceptional instance, Abarbanel does not think it amiss to impute to Ezra a misunderstanding of an earlier sacred text. Commenting on references to "ships of Tarshish", he observes that the verse that relates that "Jehoshaphat made ships of Tarshish to go to Ophir" (1 Kgs 22:49) presents only a slight difficulty since it only seems to posit the impossibility that ships went from the Mediterranean port of Tarshish ("the city known in earlier times as Carthage and today called Tunis") to the eastern port of Ophir. A close reading reveals that the verse does not explicitly affirm that the ships initiated their voyage from Tarshish. Intractable, by contrast, is the formulation in Chronicles wherein Jehoshaphat is said to have joined Ahaziah in making ships in Ezion-geber which were "broken" with the result that they were unable "to go" to Tarshish (2 Chr 20:36–37). To Abarbanel it is patent that no such voyage could have taken place at any rate since "the Sea of Reeds does not connect with the Mediterranean". He postulates that upon examining the report in Kings that Jehoshaphat made "ships of Tarshish", Ezra mistook it to mean that the ships in questions were intended *to go* to Tarshish in which case, he adds, "this was an error on the part of Ezra the Scribe".[81] This verdict, as well as Abarbanel's claim that the designation "ships of Tarshish" refers not to the origins or destination of the vessels in question but their mode of construction, anticipates modern biblical scholarship's findings in detail.[82]

---

[79] *Perush 'al nevi'im 'aharonim* (1979) 299–300.

[80] Elman, The Book of Deuteronomy (1997) 244.

[81] *Perush 'al nevi'im rishonim* (1955) 543–44. For an earlier example of imputation of error to Chronicles, see the commentary of Abraham ibn Ezra on Exod 25:29.

[82] Japhet, I & II Chronicles (1993) 802: "'the ships of Tarshish' ... are clearly a type of vessel; the destination of the expedition was to be 'Ophir' ... [Whereas] for the Chronicler, 'ships of Tarshish' denotes a fleet sailing to Tarshish ...; this explains the Chronicler's omission of 'to go to Ophir', which is replaced by 'to go to Tarshish'."

4.4. Chronological Sensibilities

If a heightened awareness of chronology was a key component of the Renaissance "sense of the past", Abarbanel's special keenness for chronological issues in his biblical commentaries is striking. He periodically treats matters of chronology in long excurses rather than passing remarks in his running commentary. For example, he invests much energy in an attempt to unravel chronological difficulties appertaining to Judges and Samuel's lifespan, in both cases arriving at final holdings at variance with long-standing rabbinic views. He wonders how his predecessors could have remained indifferent to vital chronological issues: "I am amazed that the commentators did not ... exert themselves to determine whether these wars occurred before the affairs concerning Absalom and the Gibionites as they appear in Scripture or before. Certainly, this is something crucial to know!" In the medieval manner, Abarbanel's chronological analyses usually issue from some exegetical concern but he is not content with mere textual reconciliation. Gersonides' solution to the problem posed by the report that Saul ruled over Israel for two years (1 Sam 13:1) is deemed "of no avail if it does not accord with the [actual] chronology of the judges and kings" while Abarbanel's resolve, in turn, to "dilate" on this topic is grounded in a conviction that "knowledge of the chronology of the judges and kings" is "significant per se".[83]

Illustrative of Abarbanel's chronological orientation in another way is his division of the "Holy Scriptures according to the time in which they were written and compiled". In addition to the threefold rabbinic division of the canon into Torah, Prophets, and Writings which he accepts, and the fourfold Christian arrangement into legal, historical, prophetic, and wisdom books which he rejects, Abarbanel advances a tripartite canonical division into books written prior to the conquest of Canaan, ones composed after it but prior to the exile, and post-exilic works.[84] In a later version of this approach, he accepts the Masoretes' placement of Isaiah before Jeremiah and Ezekiel over the divergent rabbinic arrangement since "it is appropriate for the temporally prior be mentioned first ... and it is well-known that Isaiah prophesied ... long before Jeremiah and Ezekiel".[85] Given the chronological principal which governs Abarbanel's classification, the placement of the book of Job depends on which of several views of its temporal origins one accepts, ranging from the age of the Patriarchs through the Persian period. Like Tostado, Abarbanel feels compelled to raise if not resolve the question of Job's place in the broader chronological scheme of things.[86]

---

[83] *Perush 'al nevi'im rishonim* (1955) 141–42, 201–02, 230, 386.
[84] Ibid. 4–5.
[85] *Perush 'al nevi'im 'aharonim* (1979) 3.
[86] *Perush 'al nevi'im rishonim* (1955) 5. Cf. Tostado, Commentaria in primam partem Iosue (1530) 1r–1v. While Abarbanel remains agnostic on Job's temporal frame of reference, Tostado, assuming an early date for both figure and book, poses the question of Job's place in the canon accordingly.

5. Legacy

By provisioning his readers with fresh insights into Scripture's authors, the origins of biblical books, Holy Writ's human dimensions, and more, Abarbanel believed he had performed a signal service to future generations. He summoned Proverbs to the effect that Jews should carry forward his accomplishment. He invoked Aristotle to the effect that gratitude was due to "early scholars" such as himself who "initiated investigations" even if their views were later invalidated since their disclosure of hitherto unperceived questions paved the way for conclusive findings by "latter-day scholars".[87] By way of conclusion, it seems well to sample some "latter-day" scholarly reactions to Abarbanel's rich endowment of novel biblical insights, focusing on some of the several negative responses to some of his boldest conclusions.

Several figures in the century after Abarbanel's death were exercised by his understanding of the origin of "written" and "read" forms. Jacob ben Hayyim ibn Adoniyah, editor of the famous rabbinic Bible of 1524, expressed pained amazement at Abarbanel's second suggestion in particular, that *ketiv* forms might reflect deficiencies in their authors' linguistic skills. Ibn Adoniyah was aghast at Abarbanel's hubris in seemingly assuming that his own mastery of Hebrew exceeded that of Israel's ancient prophets. Ibn Adoniyah's colleague, Eliyahu / Elias Levita, also found Abarbanel's analysis of *qere/ketiv* forms "null and void". Unlike Ibn Adoniyah, he forbore even to discuss it.[88] The Egyptian legist, David ben Solomon ibn Zimra, without naming names, roundly condemned Abarbanel on this score as well.[89] From the evidence of the Talmud, Ibn Adoniyah and Ibn Zimra affirmed that "words read but not written and words written but omitted in reading are all a law given to Moses at Sinai".[90] So did the leading central European rabbinic figure of the second half of the sixteenth century, Judah Loew of Prague. To Judah, Abarbanel stood among a number of scholars who should better have had "their tongues lick dust" than impart their corrupt pronouncements concerning *qere/ketiv* forms. Abarbanel's "wholly unprecedented" suggestion that "the prophets were ignorant of [proper] language" especially evoked his ire. This utterly foolish notion could only be held by a sheer ignoramus. As such, it defied any response.[91]

From the sixteenth through eighteenth centuries, Abarbanel was studied by an impressive array of Christian thinkers, some of whom translated excerpts from his biblical commentaries into Latin.[92] The most prominent Christian biblicist

---

[87]   *Perush 'al nevi'im rishonim* (1955) 13.

[88]   Ginsburg, Jacob ben Chajim ibn Adonijah's Introduction / The Massoreth Ha-Massoreth of Elias Levita (1968) 48–52, 107.

[89]   Levy, Fixing God's Torah (2001) 80–81, 143–44.

[90]   *Ned.* 37b.

[91]   *Tiferet yisra'el* Chap. 66, in: *Sifrei maharal* (Benei Berak: Yahadut 1980) 198–99.

[92]   For the latter, see Steinschneider, Catalogus Librorum (1852–1860) 1077–83; Ruiz, Isaac Abrabanel y su commentario (1984) cxlviii–cl. The fullest account of Christian interest in Abarbanel through the early eighteenth century occurs in Henricus Johannes Majus' *Vita Don Isaaci Abrabanelis*, found at the back of his Latin translation of *Mashmia' yeshu'ah* (*Praeco salutis* [Frankfurt am Main 1711] 20–34). See also Gaon, Don Isaac Abravanel and the Christian Scholars (1973).
A subject in need of further study is *converso* awareness of Abarbanel's biblical commentaries. Evidence of such in his native Iberia is forthcoming from a manuscript of Abarbanel's commentary on Latter Prophets copied by Alfonso de Zamora; see Alonso Fontela, Anotaciones de Alfonso de Zamora (1987). Zamora was a member of the editorial team that produced the Old Testament component of the Complutensian Polyglot Bible executed at the University of Alcalá in the early sixteenth century under the direction of Cardinal Jimenez Cisneros, on which see Chap. 12.2, by A. SCHENKER, in this volume.

to accord Abarbanel attention during this period was the seventeenth-century Catholic savant, Richard Simon.[93] For Simon, Abarbanel was of "all the Rabbis" the one from whom one could "derive the greatest benefit in attaining knowledge of Scripture".[94] Simon found Abarbanel's arguments against Joshua's and Samuel's authorship of the books bearing their names "convincing", albeit Abarbanel's case for Samuel's authorship of Joshua and Jeremiah's composition of Samuel less so. Simon also astutely alluded to the manner in which Abarbanel's theology at times preempted his critical stance. Had Abarbanel applied the same principles of textual analysis to the Torah as other prophetic books, observed Simon, he would have been forced to deny the Torah's Mosaic authorship.[95]

If Simon deemed Abarbanel insufficiently thoroughgoing in his biblical criticism, two early modern Jewish exegetes reproached him for venturing too far along the critical path. The Syrian exegete of the turn of the seventeenth century, Samuel Laniado, having resolved to his satisfaction the questions raised by Abarbanel concerning the "ships of Tarshish" built by Jehoshophat, chided Abarbanel for ascribing error to Ezra, a "prophet of the Lord" from whom all "fallacy and error" was absent.[96] Writing in the same vein, Solomon Zalman Hanau, an early eighteenth-century grammarian eager to focus Jewish attention on Bible study at a time of nascent Jewish Enlightenment, denounced Abarbanel's critique of the Hebrew of Jeremiah, "a prophet to whom God's word was transmitted" whose powers of "linguistic embellishment" were "flawless". Hanau sought to confute Abarbanel in detail, in part on the basis of Abarbanel's own exegesis, explaining all alleged "irregularities" in Jeremiah's discourse, including its many "written" and "read" variants.[97]

Though the prolific nineteenth-century biblical interpreter, Meir Loeb ben Yehiel Michael (Malbim), singled out Abarbanel as the leading commentator since high medieval times "to breathe life into the biblical verses using the method of *peshaṭ*",[98] he took umbrage at a number of Abarbanel's critical views. Abarbanel's ascription of error to Ezra evoked Malbim's appeal for divine protection from any opinion that would "have us say Chronicles' author erred and was ignorant of the simple meaning of the verse in Kings".[99] Abarbanel's critique of Jeremiah's prophetic expressions elicited similar outrage, both for its substance and, as slowly emerges over the course of Malbim's extended refutation of it, for its potential validation of the sorts of perfidious notions spread by the large cadre of modern Bible critics active in Malbim's day.[100]

What remains of the exegetical innovations that Abarbanel believed would

---

[93] See Chap. 34.1, by J. W. ROGERSON, in this volume.

[94] *Histoire critique du Vieux Testament* (Rotterdam 1685) 380.

[95] Ibid. 26, 45.

[96] *Keli yaqar: perush nevi'im rishonim, Melakhim* 1–2 (Jerusalem: Mekhon ha-Ketav 1988), 1, 422–24.

[97] *Binyan shelomo* (Frankfurt am Main 1708) [viii–x].

[98] See the introduction to his commentary on Joshua.

[99] Commentary on 1 Kgs 10:22.

[100] See the introduction to his commentary on Jeremiah. Malbim begins by lambasting Abarbanel but eventually speaks in the plural of "critics who seek to slander our prophets".

win him a share of destiny? If his specific findings on matters of biblical authorship may nowadays look little more than quaint, having been refined or surpassed by those of "latter-day scholars" (as Abarbanel surmised they might be), one might nevertheless find in Abarbanel's approach a model of abiding significance. Thus did a leading contemporary biblicist, when queried about the challenge of reconciling religious faith and critical scholarship, invoke Abarbanel as one who exemplified an allegiance to Scripture's ultimately divine origins that did not preclude critical engagement with the scriptural word.[101] Seen from this perspective, Abarbanel's exegesis, though born of a combination of medieval learning and incipient Renaissance sensibilities (whatever the precise interlacings), transcends historical periods.

Acknowledgement:
This article was written in conjunction with a larger project supported by a UCLA Center for Jewish Studies, Maurice Amado Foundation Research Grant in Sephardic Studies and a grant from the Faculty of Arts at York University, Toronto, Canada. It was completed during my tenure as a Visiting Fellow at the Pontifical Institute of Mediaeval Studies. I wish to express my thanks to all of these institutions for their support.

---

[101] Greenberg, Ha-biqoret ve-ha-'emunah (1984) 275–76.

CHAPTER NINE

The Textual and Hermeneutic Work of Desiderius Erasmus of Rotterdam

By ERIKA RUMMEL, Toronto

Sources: ERASMUS: *Opus epistolarum Des. Erasmi Roterodami* (ed. P. S. Allen; Oxford 1906–58) [quoted Allen]; *Opera Omnia Desiderii Erasmi Roterodami* (no editor; Amsterdam 1969–) [quoted ASD]; *The Collected Works of Erasmus* (no editor; Toronto 1974–) [quoted CWE]; *Opuscula Erasmi* (ed. W. K. Ferguson; The Hague 1933); *Desiderius Erasmus Roterodamus: Ausgewählte Werke* (ed. H. Holborn; Munich 1933) [quoted Holborn]; *Desiderii Erasmi Roterodami opera omnia* (ed. J. Leclerc; Leiden 1703–06) [quoted LB]; *Ratio seu compendium verae theologiae* (1519), in: *Ausgewählte Schriften* 3 (ed. W. Welzig; Darmstadt: Wiss. Buchgesellschaft 1967); A. REEVE / M. A. SCREECH (eds.), *Erasmus' Annotations on the New Testament: The Gospels* (London 1986), *Acts-Romans-I and II Corinthians* (Leiden 1990), *Galatians to Apocalypse* (Leiden 1993).

Bibliographical and reference works: C. AUGUSTIJN, "Erasmus, Desiderius (1466/69–1536)", TRE 10 (1982) 1–18 (Lit.); J.-C. MARGOLIN, Douze années de bibliographie Érasmienne (1950–1961) (Paris 1963); idem, Quatorze années de bibliographie Érasmienne (1936–1949) (Paris 1969); idem, Neuf années de bibliographie Érasmienne (1962–1970) (Paris / Toronto / Buffalo 1977).

General works: J. W. ALDRIDGE, *The Hermeneutic of Erasmus* (Zurich 1966); J. J. BATEMAN, "From Soul to Soul: Persuasion in Erasmus' Paraphrases on the New Testament", ERSY 15 (1987/88) 7–16; C. AUGUSTIJN, *Erasmus: His Life, Works and Influence* (Toronto 1991); R. BAINTON, *Erasmus of Christendom* (New York 1969); J. J. BENTLEY, *Humanists and Holy Writ: New Testament Scholarship in the Renaissance* (Princeton 1983); C. BENE, "L'exégèse des Psaumes chez Erasme", *Histoire de l'exégèse au XVIe siècle* (ed. O. Fatio / P. Fraenkel; Geneva 1978) 118–32; L. BOUYER, "Erasmus in Relation to the Medieval Biblical Tradition", CHB 2 (1969) 492–505; M. BOYLE, *Rhetoric and Reform: Erasmus' Civil Dispute with Luther* (Cambridge, MA 1983); eadem, *Erasmus on Language and Method in Theology* (Toronto 1977); G. CHANTRAINE, "Erasme, lecteur des psaumes", *Colloquia Erasmiana Turonensia* 2 (no editor; Paris 1972) 691–713; J. CHOMARAT, *Grammaire et rhetorique chez Erasme* (Paris 1981); K. EDEN, "Rhetoric in the Hermeneutics of Erasmus' Later Works", ERSY 11 (1991) 88–104; A. GODIN, *Erasme, lecteur d'Origène* (Paris 1982); idem, "La Bible et la 'philosophie chrètienne'", *Le temps des Réformes et la Bible* (BTT 5, ed. G. Bedouelle / B. Roussel; Paris 1989) 563–86; K. HAGEN, "What Did the Term Commentarius Mean to Sixteenth-century Theologians?", *Théorie et pratique de l'exégèse* (ed. I. Backus / F. Higman; Geneva 1990) 13–38; L.-E. HALKIN, *Erasmus: A Critical Biography* (Oxford 1993); M. HEATH, "Allegory, Rhetoric and Spirituality: Erasmus' Early Psalm Commentaries", *Acta Conventus Neo-Latini Torontoniensis* (ed. A. Dalzell / C. Fantazzi / R. Schoeck; Binghamton, NY 1991) 363–70; H. HOLECZEK, *Humanistische Bibelphilologie als Reformproblem bei Erasmus von Rotterdam, Thomas More und William Tyndale* (Leiden 1975); M. HOFFMAN, *Rhetoric and Theology: The Hermeneutic of Erasmus* (Toronto 1994); H. J. DE JONGE, "Novum Testamentum a nobis versum: The Essence of Erasmus' Edition of the New Testament", *JTS* 35 (1984) 394–413; G. KISCH, *Erasmus' Stellung zu Juden und Judentum* (Tübingen 1969); F. KRÜGER, *Humanistische Evangelienauslegung. Desiderius Erasmus von Rotterdam als Ausleger der Evangelien in seinen Paraphrasen* (Tübingen 1986); H. DE LUBAC, *Exégèse mèdiévale. Les quatre sens de l'Écriture* II/2 (Paris 1964) 427–53; S. MARKISH, *Erasmus and the Jews* (Chicago 1986); J. K. MCCONICA, "Erasmus and the Grammar of Consent", Scrinium Erasmianum 2 (ed. J. Coppens; Leiden 1969) 77–99; J. O'MALLEY, "Erasmus and the History of Sacred Rhetoric: The Ecclesiastes of 1535", ERSY 5 (1985) 14–22; H. PABEL, "Erasmus of Rotterdam and Judaism: A Reexamination in the Light of New Evidence", *ARefG* 81 (1996) 9–37; J. B.

Payne, "Toward the Hermeneutics of Erasmus", *Scrinium Erasmianum* 2 (ed. J. Coppens; Leiden 1969) 13–49; idem, "Erasmus and Lefèvre d'Etaples as Interpreters of Paul", *ARefG* 65 (1974) 54–83; J. Phillips, "Food and Drink in Erasmus' Gospel Paraphrases", ERSY 14 (1994) 24–45; A. Rabil, *Erasmus and the New Testament: The Mind of a Christian Humanist* (San Antonio 1972); E. Rummel, *Erasmus' Annotations on the New Testament: From Philologist to Theologian* (Toronto 1986); eadem, *Erasmus and His Catholic Critics* (Nieuwkoop 1989); eadem, *The Humanist-Scholastic Debate in the Renaissance and Reformation* (Cambridge, MA 1995); eadem, *Erasmus* (Outstanding Christian Thinkers; London 2004); T. F. Torrance, "The Hermeneutics of Erasmus", *Probing the Reformed Tradition, Historical Studies in Honor of Edward A. Dowey Jr.* (ed. E. A. McKee / B. G. Armstrong; Louisville 1989) 48–76; J. Tracy, *Erasmus of the Low Countries* (Berkeley 1996); C. Trinkaus, "Erasmus, Augustine and the Nominalists", *ARefG* 67 (1976) 1–32; G. Winkler, *Erasmus von Rotterdam und die Einleitungsschriften zum Neuen Testament* (Münster 1974).

Special abbreviations (see above):
Allen = *Opus epistolarum Des. Erasmi Roterodami* (1906–58)
ASD = *Opera Omnia Desiderii Erasmi Roterodami* (1969-)
CWE = *The Collected Works of Erasmus* (1974-)
Holborn = *Desiderius Erasmus Roterodamus: Ausgewählte Werke* (1933)
LB = *Desiderii Erasmi Roterodami opera omnia* (1703–06)

1. Introduction

Desiderius Erasmus is one of the pioneers of biblical humanism. His *magnum opus*, an edition of the New Testament containing a revised Vulgate and the *editio princeps* of the Greek text, appeared in 1516. A year earlier he had published the first in a series of Psalm commentaries. Both works were the fruit of a decade of biblical studies.

Erasmus (1466?-1536) was born in Rotterdam as the illegitimate son of a priest. Orphaned as a boy, he was pressured by his guardians into entering an Augustinian monastery and taking religious vows. He was ordained priest in 1492 and served for a while as secretary to the Bishop of Cambrai. In 1495, the Bishop sent him to the Collège de Montaigu in Paris to study theology, but according to Erasmus, he received little financial support and was obliged to make a living as best he could by tutoring. He remained in Paris, with some interruptions, for almost five years, but expressed great distaste for the scholastic theology, tutored private pupils there and departed without a degree. In 1506 the University of Turin conferred a doctorate of theology on him *per saltum*, that is, without the normal requirements. It was an acknowledgment of the expertise Erasmus had acquired in the field. He was, however, largely self-taught and, unlike most biblical scholars of his generation, stayed away from an academic career. With the exception of a short stint at the University of Cambridge and a tempestuous three years in Louvain, marked by quarrels with the theological faculty into which he had been "coopted",[1] Erasmus avoided affiliation with academic institutions and declined invitations to teach at universities.

Erasmus' first publications – an anthology of proverbs, the satirical *Praise of Folly*, a panegyric on Philip the Handsome, and a handbook of style – were typical productions of a humanist. Yet Erasmus turned his attention to biblical studies as early as 1499 during the first of several sojourns in England, when he made the acquaintance of John Colet and heard his lectures on the Pauline epistles. Colet was instrumental in focusing Erasmus' interest on the scriptural text and in shaping his *philosophia Christi*, a philosophy that called for the imi-

---

[1] *Cooptatus* is Erasmus' term (Allen *Ep.* 843.315). It is unclear what functions or duties, if any, are implied by this term.

tation of Christ in one's life. It was Colet who urged Erasmus to study the Old Testament and write a commentary "on the ancient Moses or the eloquent Isaiah", but the humanist felt inadequate and unprepared for the task.[2] He did not have the requisite language skills to read the biblical texts in the original and, unlike Colet, was not content with using the Vulgate. "It is almost sacrilege to rush into these studies with unwashed hands and feet", he wrote.[3] Over the next years Erasmus made a concerted effort to learn Greek. He published translations of Euripides, Plutarch, Lucian, and other classical authors, but emphasized that he regarded this work as preparatory to biblical studies. He wished "to avoid risking the potter's skills on a big jar", as he put it.[4] In 1504, he sent Colet a copy of the *Handbook of the Christian Soldier*, his manifesto of the philosophy of Christ. He reported that he had been busy with Pauline and patristic studies, but that he was still hampered by a lack of Greek. He had also begun to study Hebrew, but abandoned the effort, "deterred by the strangeness of the idiom and because the shortness of life and the limitations of our intellect do not allow a man to master many things at once".[5] When he undertook to expound the Psalms, he was uneasy on that count. One could hardly do the subject justice, he said, if one "did not know the Hebrew language and traditions".[6]

2. Erasmus' General Approach to Biblical Studies

By the time he published the first fruits of his scriptural studies, Erasmus had formulated the twin hermeneutical principles governing his biblical scholarship: an emphasis on the tropological sense and an appreciation for the supporting role philology played in the interpretation of a text. His first purpose in writing devotional or exegetical works, he stated in the *Handbook of the Christian Soldier*, was the conversion of his readers to a truly Christian life. He wanted to make them receptive to the divine word and motivate them to "grow up and become perfect in Christ".[7] He repeated this message in his commentary on Psalm 1 ("Blessed is the man"). That man, he says, is blessed who is "transfigured and, so to speak, made one with Christ". To aid in that process, the exegete must adopt the tropological method "which is more conducive to reforming a man's life".[8]

In his textual and exegetical work, Erasmus applied humanistic philology to Holy Writ. Adopting the slogan *ad fontes*, he consulted and collated scriptural and patristic manuscripts in the original language and studied the manuscript traditions. Erasmus' edition of Jerome appeared in the same year as his New

---

[2] Allen *Ep.* 108.77–78
[3] Holborn 32.14–15
[4] Allen *Ep.* 188.4–5
[5] Allen *Ep.* 181.36–8
[6] Allen *Ep.* 2315.175
[7] Introductory letter to the *Handbook of the Christian Soldier*, Allen *Ep.* 164.58
[8] ASD V-2, 31.20 and 36.87.

Testament and was followed by editions or translations of other major patristic writers, among them, Augustine, Ambrose, Hilary, Origen, Chrysostom, and Theophylactus. His work on the Psalm commentaries benefited from that research.[9] In 1501 he asked a friend to obtain for him a Psalter in Greek and in a contemporary letter he likewise speaks of being engaged in studying the Psalms, but his biblical scholarship remained focused on the New Testament.[10]

Erasmus' biblical studies received a new impetus in 1504, when he discovered (and a year later published) a manuscript of Lorenzo Valla's annotations on the Gospels. The prefaces he added to the edition of Valla and to his own New Testament best explain and defend his method against the objections of conservative theologians. Valla and Erasmus based their textual criticism on the collation of manuscripts and interpreted the meaning of individual words and phrases in light of classical usage and the historical context. The theologians criticized them for three reasons. To begin with, they did not consider philologists qualified to comment on Scripture. Secondly, they insisted that the Vulgate was the authoritative version, and the translator, Jerome, had worked under divine inspiration. It was therefore blasphemous, not to say, heretical to change or correct the Vulgate. Thirdly, to correct the Latin text on the basis of Greek manuscripts was especially dangerous because the Greeks were schismatics and likely to corrupt the texts to suit their interpretation. We find these arguments, for example, in Pierre Cousturier's *On translating the Bible*. The French theologian insisted that the Vulgate was flawless, that "Jerome himself undertook the emendation not only taking prudent counsel but also being guided in a mysterious way by the Holy Spirit".[11] Similarly, Noël Beda scoffed at biblical humanists: "Who are those scholars who deny Jerome's authorship? You mean perhaps to say 'We who speak Greek, who add the charm of human wisdom to God's Word, are the only scholars, the only men of sound judgment'".[12] The Louvain scholar Martin van Dorp likewise questioned the wisdom of consulting Greek manuscripts: "What! Are the Greek books more correct than the Latin ones? Did they take greater care in preserving Holy Writ intact than the Latins, when the Christian religion was so often shaken up by them?"[13] In his own and in Valla's defense, Erasmus pointed out that textual criticism and translation were philological rather than theological tasks. "Theology, the queen of sciences", did not reject the services of her "humble maid, Grammar".[14] The Vulgate version, he noted, had never been formally authorized, and Jerome was not its author. After all, the biblical quotations in his works were often at variance with the Vulgate. It was clear therefore that he merely corrected the text in circulation at the time. Nor had Jer-

---

[9] He published his Psalm 2 together with an edition of Arnobius' Psalm commentaries (see below, n. 29); in 1533 he published Haymo's *In omnes psalmos explanatio*.
[10] Allen *Epp.* 160.7–8, 149.26–41.
[11] *De tralatione Bibliae* (Paris 1525) 49 r.
[12] *Annotationum…in Des. Erasmum liber* (Paris 1526) a3 r. The book was directed against Jacques Lefèvre and Erasmus.
[13] Allen *Ep.* 304.110–113.
[14] Allen *Ep.* 182.113–131.

ome acted under divine guidance. On the contrary, he clearly distinguished his work from that of the inspired prophet, stating that the translator drew on human skills. Indeed Jerome had faced many of the criticisms now faced by Valla and Erasmus and had answered them all.[15] Turning the tables on the theologians, Erasmus boldly declared that they were poorly qualified to interpret the Bible. When dealing with the biblical text, he said, they were acting in the capacity of philologists, and it was madness to engage in that task without a knowledge of the three biblical languages.

Erasmus' application of humanistic philology to biblical texts and his divergence from traditional methods of exegesis involved him in numerous controversies with Catholic theologians, notably from the Universities of Louvain and Paris. His works were also investigated by the Spanish Inquisition, but Erasmus had powerful friends at court and the proceedings were adjourned indefinitely. In 1531, however, the Faculty of Theology at Paris issued a formal condemnation of passages in Erasmus' work and, in a strongly worded conclusion, censured the activities of biblical humanists in general: "Those who think that a knowledge of Greek and Hebrew is the equivalent of consummate theology should take note that those who know languages but have not received instruction in the discipline of theology are to be considered philologists (*grammatici*), not theologians".[16]

Erasmus continued to defend his New Testament edition and in the four revisions published during his lifetime shored up his editorial decisions and the exegesis offered in his annotations by adding numerous proof texts, primarily from classical authors and from the Fathers. He emphasized throughout that he was merely proffering suggestions and submitted all his findings to the verdict of the Church. Such disclaimers, however, did not prevent the Church from placing his works on the Index of Forbidden Books.

3. Erasmus' Old Testament Scholarship:
his Attitude toward Hebrew and the Jews

A study of Erasmus' Old Testament scholarship must first address his attitude toward the Hebrew language and tradition. Erasmus never acquired proficiency in Hebrew. He "merely tasted it with the top of [his] lips", as he put it.[17] In preparing the edition of Jerome he therefore consulted with the Amerbach brothers and for his New Testament edition he relied on the advice of John Oecolampadius and Wolfgang Capito for questions involving Hebrew.[18] Although he was instrumental in establishing the trilingual college at Louvain and recommended the study of Hebrew in his *Method of Theology*, Erasmus ranked it below the study of Latin and Greek.[19] Privately he disparaged the ef-

---

[15] Ibid., lines 140–57.
[16] LB IX.922 B-C.
[17] Allen *Ep.* 334.128.
[18] Allen *Epp.* 373.74–75, 396.274.
[19] Holborn 151.25–28, cf. *Ecclesiastes* LB V 855 B.

forts of Wolfgang Capito. "I wish you were more intent on Greek rather than on those Hebrew studies, although I do not reprehend them. I see that that race is full of the most inane fables and succeeds only in bringing forth a kind of fog. Talmud, Kabbalah, Tetragrammaton, Gates of Light: what inane titles! I would rather have Christ tainted by [the scholastic] Scotus than by that nonsense. Italy has many Jews, Spain has hardly any Christians. I fear that this will be an opportunity for the long-suppressed plague to rise up again. I wish the Christian Church did not give such weight to the Old Testament! It was given for a time only and consists of shadows, yet it is almost preferred to Christian writings".[20] He repeats this assessment in his commentary on Psalm 2, where he claims that the Jewish commentaries are full of "smoke and old wives' tales".[21] On another occasion he explained his misgivings to Capito. He was concerned that the study of ancient literature might inspire readers with pagan thoughts and, more specifically, that the study of Hebrew might revive Judaism, and "there is no pestilence more adverse and hostile to the doctrine of Christ... I see how Paul exerted himself to free Christ from Judaism, and I sense that some people secretly slip back into it". In his commentary on Psalm 2, he likewise deprecated the writings of Hebrew authors because of "their hatred of Christ".[22]

Such remarks grate on the ears of modern readers. In exploring Erasmus' attitude toward the Jewish tradition, we must, however, distinguish between anti-Semitism, that is, racial discrimination which was pervasive in Erasmus' time, and anti-Judaism, that is, religious discrimination. Erasmus shared the prejudices of his contemporaries or at any rate was ambivalent about ethnic Jews. While he had enthusiastic praise for the scholarship of Paolo Ricci, the personal physician of Charles V, and was on good terms with Matthaeus Adrianus, professor of Hebrew at Louvain, he clearly wished to denigrate the papal legate Girolamo Aleandro, when he suggested that he was an ethnic Jew,[23] and his comments on the Reuchlin affair are blatantly anti-semitic. On the instigation of the Jewish convert Johann Pfefferkorn, the celebrated Hebraist Johann Reuchlin had been charged with Judaism and was obliged to defend his cause in the inquisitorial court. Many humanists considered the trial an attack on language studies and, more generally, the New Learning. They rallied around Reuchlin, reviling Pfefferkorn and his Dominican mentors. In a notorious letter commenting on the case, Erasmus described Pfefferkorn in terms that have clear racial overtones. Pfefferkorn, he said, was "infecting the entire population with his Jewish poison"; he was a true Jew, that is, "true to his race" in slandering Christians.[24] In a self-critical moment, however, Erasmus mocks the anti-semitism of his contemporaries: "If it is Christian to hate the Jews, we are all sufficiently good Christians!"[25]

---

[20] Allen *Ep.* 298.19–28.
[21] ASD V-2, 104.242.
[22] Allen *Ep.* 541.138–39, 148–49; ASD V-2, 104.243
[23] On Ricci, see Allen *Ep.* 549.36–40; on Adrianus, *Ep.* 686.5–7; on Aleandro's ethnic background, *Ep.* 1166.84–85.
[24] Allen *Ep.* 694.47, 50.
[25] Allen *Ep.* 1006.142–43.

The majority of Erasmus' negative remarks about Jews are motivated by religious and doctrinal considerations. He principally objected to the legalism he identified with the Jewish tradition. He often used the term "Jews" in a metaphorical sense. When he says, for example, that some monks "are not Christians but Jews" or exclaims: "Where has this new race of Jews sprung from?" he refers to the rigid observance of external rites which is at odds with the inner piety taught by Saint Paul.[26] In these and in other passages, his objection to Jews and the Jewish tradition is based on doctrinal rather than racial considerations. In the Psalm commentaries he repeatedly censures Jewish exegesis as too literal. He notes for example that the whole of Psalm 2 "is a prophecy of Christ" with David foreshadowing the Saviour. He therefore criticizes Rashi / Solomon Yishaqi, the eleventh-century Jewish exegete, calling his remarks on the historical context irrelevant: "I shall not waste any time in considering how individual parts of the psalm may be applied to history; let us investigate instead the extent to which it applies to our 'David', that is, to Jesus Christ".[27]

4. The Publication History of the Psalm Commentaries and their Reception

In spite of reservations concerning his qualifications and the respective merits of the Old and New Testaments, Erasmus undertook to write commentaries on the entire Psalter. He abandoned the plan after the first four Psalms, however, and chose instead to comment only on selected Psalms. By the time of his death, he had written expositions on eleven of them. In the dedicatory letter to *An Exposition of Psalm 1* (1515) he playfully explains his immediate purpose: to give an appropriate gift to Beatus Rhenanus, whose name matched the beginning of the Psalm, "Beatus vir".[28] The work was a publishing success. It was reprinted seven times over the following ten years and was translated into German and Spanish. *A Commentary on Psalm 2* (1522) first appeared as an appendix to the Psalm commentaries of Arnobius.[29] In a letter to the reader, ghost-written by Erasmus himself, the printer, Johann Froben, announces Erasmus' plan of writing commentaries on the whole Psalter and calls Psalm 2 a "specimen" to test readership reaction. In the dedicatory letter to *A Paraphrase on Psalm 3* (1524) Erasmus again alludes to such a plan. Melchior Vianden, to whom he dedicated the work, was trying to persuade him to do "for the mystical psalms what [he] had done for the New Testament".[30] Like the preceding commentary, the paraphrase on Psalm 3 appeared as an appendix to a larger work, *Exomologesis or The Method of Confessing*. *A Sermon on Psalm 4* was published in 1525 in a volume that also contained reprints of the first three

---

[26] Allen *Ep.* 1211.240; CWE 27, 132.

[27] ASD V-2, 104.244–46.

[28] *Enarratio allegorica in primum Psalmum, Beatus Vir* (Strasbourg 1515).

[29] *Commentarius in Psalmum II, Quare fremuerunt gentes* (Basel 1522).

[30] *Paraphrasis in tertium Psalmum, Domine quid multiplicati* (Basel 1524). Cf. Allen *Ep.* 1427.5–6.

Psalm commentaries.[31] The collection was reprinted twice within a year. Three years later Erasmus published the next commentary, which he says was written desultorily in the space of seven days. It is the *Sermon on Psalm 85*,[32] dedicated like Psalm 4 to John Longlond, Bishop of Lincoln. Erasmus does not explain why he abandoned the sequence. Unlike the preceding commentaries, Psalm 85 does not seem to have aroused sufficient interest to warrant a reprint. The *Three-fold exposition of Psalm 22*, published in 1530, was written on the request of Thomas Boleyn, father of Anne Boleyn and a man of learning. Erasmus hesitated at first to comply with Boleyn's wish, sensing that there were political reasons behind it. He had dedicated his handbook of marriage to Catherine of Aragon in 1526 before becoming aware that a divorce was being contemplated by King Henry VIII. Erasmus therefore speculated concerning Boleyn's motives: "It could be that the other party requested this work from me in a competitive spirit".[33] In the end he did oblige Boleyn since, as he explained, he did not think the affairs of the King concerned him. "What is beyond us is nothing to us", he wrote blithely. "Now at any rate I have both parties favourably inclined toward me. I only wish the best of kings and the holiest of queens might show the same agreement in other matters!"[34] The commentary on Psalm 28, published the same year, served a double purpose, as the title indicates: *Most useful advice on the war against the Turks, and by the way, an exposition of Psalm 28*.[35] The battle of Mohacz (1526), in which the Hungarian troops were defeated and Louis II, King of Hungary and Bohemia, was killed, brought the Ottoman Turks very close to the border of the German Empire. No concerted effort was made to halt their advance, however, because the German estates were locked in a battle over the Luther affair. By 1529 the Turks were laying siege to Vienna, the principal city of Ferdinand, the successor of Louis and brother of Emperor Charles V. The proximity of the Turkish danger brought about a change of priorities. Luther had earlier on written against a Turkish campaign and had called papal efforts to finance it a ploy to extract money from German believers. He now abandoned his opposition to war, but insisted that the Turks represented divine retribution and that spiritual renewal must therefore precede military action. The siege was raised with great difficulty, and the Turkish question remained on the agenda of the Diet of Augsburg in 1530. It is possible that Erasmus, who had been appointed councilor by Charles in 1515, was aiming his advice at the members of the Diet.[36] Like Luther, however, he spoke of the Turks as the scourge of God, and offered spiritual rather than political or strategic counsel. Psalm 28 spoke of the "voice

---

[31] *In Psalmum quartum concio* (Basel 1525).
[32] *Concionalis Interpretatio in Psalmum LXXXV* (Basel 1528). Cf. the dedicatory letter, Allen *Ep.* 2017.18 ("*utcunque tractatum*").
[33] *Enarratio triplex in Psalmum XXII* was published in Basel, 1530. The rather candid words concerning Boleyn's motives contained in a letter to Jacopo Sadoleto (Allen *Ep.* 2315.139–40) were removed when it was published in the *Epistolae palaeonaeoi* (Freiburg 1532).
[34] Allen *Ep.* 2315.144–46.
[35] *Utilissima consultatio de bello Turcis inferendo, et obiter enarratus Psalmus XXVIII* (Basel 1531).
[36] The dedicatory letter, *Ep.* 2285, is dated 15 March 1530. The Diet took place in the early summer.

of God", and the Turks were the mouthpiece of God calling his people to moral reform and Christian princes to concord. The Turks, Erasmus explained, "gained power, not through their own piety, not through their own bravery, but because of our discord".[37] The work, dedicated to the jurist Johann Rinck, was popular and saw five reprints in the year of publication. In 1531 Erasmus published the *Exposition of Psalm 33*, dedicating it to Konrad von Thüngen, Bishop of Würzburg.[38] Unlike its predecessor, it lacked topical significance and received correspondingly less attention. It was not reprinted during Erasmus' lifetime. It is, however, significant for our understanding of Erasmus' hermeneutics, which are briefly recapitulated here. Anyone who doubts the historical meaning of the text lacks piety, Erasmus says, but anyone "who denies a more sublime meaning equally lacks piety". Indeed "the writings of the entire Old Testament were a prophecy of Christ" and "the whole of Scripture was mystical".[39] In 1532 Erasmus published the *Exposition of Psalm 38*, which he dedicated to the Bishop of Olmütz, Stanislaus Turzo, a great patron of learning.[40] Although Erasmus claimed that he had given relevance to his comments, it received no more attention from his contemporaries than Psalm 33.[41] His next effort, however, a commentary on Psalm 83, addressed a question of great urgency and prompted a great deal of critical reaction. *On Mending the peace of the Church* was published in 1533 and dedicated to Julius Pflug, later Bishop of Naumburg. As the title indicates, it contains advice on healing the schism of the Church. At the time Erasmus was regarded as the chief representative of moderate Catholics willing to work toward a compromise. Erasmus' plea for peace and the proposals contained in the psalm commentary met with sharp criticism from both Catholics and Reformers. Erasmus distinguished between articles of faith and human laws and customs. He advocated flexibility and a measure of tolerance with respect to human laws and proposed that disputes involving articles of faith be determined by a universal council. Erasmus' advice was hardly practicable. The categories themselves were subject to dispute. Efforts to arrange for a universal council had so far been unsuccessful and were not destined to succeed in the near future. The Christian world had to wait another decade before the Council of Trent began its sessions and another generation before its conclusions were published. Erasmus' proposals were immediately attacked by the Catholic theologian Jacques Masson, who protested that Erasmus was treating the confessional debate like a squabble over a piece of land. Religious principles, he said, allowed no compromise and must be defended with one's life. The Lutheran Antonius Corvinus took a similar stand: one might be flexible on the issue of abuses, but could not bend on doctrinal issues.[42] The commentary on Psalm 83 was reprinted no less than six

---

[37] ASD V-3, 38.215–16.
[38] *Enarratio Psalmi XXXIII* (Basel 1531).
[39] ASD V-3, 99.157–58, 162.
[40] *Enarratio Psalmi Trigesimi Octavi multum ab enarratione veterum differens* (Basel 1532).
[41] *Videbis obiter nonnullam horum temporum imaginem* (Allen *Ep.* 2608.44).
[42] *Iacobi Latomi...Opera* (Louvain 1550) 172r–175r; *Quatenus expediat...Erasmi...rationem sequi* (Wittenberg 1534) D3r–v.

times in the year of publication. It was, moreover, translated into Dutch, German (twice), and Danish within a year of its first appearance.

The last of Erasmus' commentaries, titled *On the purity of the tabernacle or the Christian Church*, was an exposition of Psalm 14. Published in 1536, the year of Erasmus' death, it was written on the request of the customs official Christopher Eschenfelder, a long-standing admirer. Apparently, Eschenfelder had asked for an exposition of Psalm 114, but was presented instead with Psalm 14 because, as Erasmus explained, he had forgotten which Psalm his friend had requested.[43] It was concerned with the nature of the Church and indeed with all Christians, for they were the living Church, "having been through baptism and through their faith been coopted into the mystical body of Christ".[44] Fittingly, the commentary was reprinted the following year together with *Mending the Peace of the Church*, Erasmus' appeal for unity.

5. The Genre of the Psalm Commentaries

It is clear even from the titles of the Psalm commentaries that they represent distinct literary genres appropriate to distinct purposes. They are variously designated as sermons (*concio, concionalis interpretatio*), commentaries (*commentarius, enarratio*),[45] or paraphrases (*paraphrasis*). In Erasmus' view the last two genres were closely related. "The paraphrase", he said, "is a kind of commentary".[46] Although it did not deal in the same measure with text critical and exegetical problems, it shared with the commentary the purpose of elucidating the meaning of a difficult text. The purpose of a paraphrase was to "fill gaps, smooth rough passages, impose order on confusion, make the complex simple, resolve knotty problems, throw light on dark passages, and turn Hebrew idiom into Latin".[47] Nor did Erasmus strictly distinguish between sermon and *enarratio*, for he refers to his interpretation of Psalm 22 in the title as an *enarratio* and in the preface as a "sermon".[48] Although he attributed a great deal of importance to preaching and saw the sermon as one of the central duties of the cleric, he hinted that he adopted what amounts to a hybrid genre here for the sake of novelty: "In such a heap of [psalm] commentaries, the reader must be attracted by some novelty in the treatment".[49] The title of his exposition of Psalm 85 again points out the vagueness of the designation "sermon" and Erasmus' reluctance to make a strict distinction between the homiletic and exegetical genres. Accordingly he calls the work an "interpretative sermon", a *concionalis interpretatio*.

---

[43] See the introductory letter, Allen *Ep.* 3086.22.
[44] ASD V-2 300.444.
[45] Quintilian employed the term enarratio to denote a commentary, *Inst. or.* 1.4.2.
[46] Allen *Ep.* 1255.38–39, similarly *Epp.* 1333.395–97 and 1381.421–22.
[47] In the prefatory letter to the *Paraphrase on Romans*, Allen *Ep.* 710.26–28.
[48] Allen *Ep.* 2261.42.
[49] Allen *Ep.* 1535.14–15.

Erasmus' mixed approach may have been determined by a wish to conciliate the reader. When he published his first New Testament paraphrase in 1517, Erasmus was clearly looking for relief from the text critical and editorial work he had done and from the hostile response his annotations on the New Testament had generated. "What if I had explained all the sacred books by paraphrasing them so that they could be read with the sense intact, yet give less trouble and be understood more easily – would [those critics] indict me then?" The Psalms, he noted, were sung by the choir in a version different from that found in the liturgy, and no one complained. The Augustinian friar Felix Pratensis had published a paraphrase of the Psalter in 1515, and no one attacked him or "made a tragedy out of it".[50] The blurring of distinctions between commentary, paraphrase, and sermon in Erasmus' usage and in the titles he chose for his Psalm commentaries would therefore suggest a desire to escape the close scrutiny invited by the genre 'commentary' and take cover under another designation, which might qualify as literature rather than theology. No doubt, Erasmus also decided on a mixed genre because it allowed him to treat individual parts of a Psalm in the most suitable fashion and permitted him to muse on the text and comment on it as a social historian and observer of the world rather than a theologian.[51] He may have abandoned the task of writing a commentary on the entire Psalter, not only because of the vast scope of the undertaking, but also because he found that only a few Psalms were suitable for his more general purpose. Echoing the description of Psalm 2 as a "specimen" to test the waters and discover the readers' reaction, he described his commentary on Psalm 3 as a "specimen of the frustration an author will necessarily experience in the attempt...to deal with intractable material", that is, material unsuited to his purpose.[52]

6. Erasmian Hermeneutics in the Psalm Commentaries

Traditionally, medieval exegetes, following Augustine's lead, examined Scripture according to its four senses.[53] Erasmus was aware of this tradition and discusses it in the *Methodus*: "It is not enough to consider the various ways – historical, tropological, allegorical, and anagogical – in which the eternal truth shines forth. We must also consider the gradations, distinctions, and rationale behind the treatment... If anyone wanted to explain these various senses through examples, it would take more than a volume".[54] Like other biblical humanists, Erasmus often reduced the four senses to two, the literal and the spiritual. He uses this dichotomy when he counsels readers of the Bible:

---

[50] Allen *Ep.* 456.83–94.

[51] In a paraphrase, as he noted, it was permitted "to add something of your own" (Allen *Ep.* 1274.34–36.

[52] The Psalm presented problems of internal chronology and of interpretation. It was, moreover, difficult to shift and change the assumed persona of the narrator (cf. Allen *Epp.* 1427.40–51; 1274.39).

[53] *De utilitate credendi* (PL 42 68–69).

[54] Holborn pp. 157–58.

"Break though the shell and extract the nut".[55] The title of his commentary on Psalm 22 alludes to a three-fold sense, that is, the three mystical senses, but in the text Erasmus once again simplifies the interpretation, opposing the 'allegorical' to the 'literal' sense.[56] Among the three mystical senses, Erasmus preferred the tropological sense. He makes this preference clear in the commentary on Psalm 14, where he talks about the grammatical, mystical, anagogical, and tropological senses, but gives as much space to the last than to the first three combined, explaining: "I prefer to deal with the moral sense, which may appear to be humbler, but in my opinionis is more useful".[57] This preference follows from his advocacy of the *philosophia Christi*, which is concerned with the application of biblical precepts to an individual's conduct. Clinging to the literal sense of the Bible diminished the faith, he said, while contemplation of the spiritual sense kindled devotion. At the same time he warned of departing too far from the words and allowing oneself to be carried away by imagination. He explains in the *Handbook of the Christian Soldier*: "In expounding mysteries you must not follow the conjectures of your mind; rather you must know the method, which is a kind of skill...in which Origen holds the principal place". In Psalm 38, however, he criticizes Origen on this point: "Origen sometimes exceeds due measure, drawing out the allegorical and rejecting the literal meaning". The Jewish interpretation, he said, was on the other end of the spectrum. It was barren, because it considered only the historical sense. Saint Paul had the right approach, when he said: "I shall sing the psalm in my spirit, I shall sing it in my mind".[58] Here Erasmus advocates a balance. The historical sense was the foundation on which the exegete must build and advance to a higher level of interpretation: "You must not reject the historical sense in a passage that admits of an allegorical explanation, but the historical sense should be the base and foundation, and building on that one may properly deal with the more obscure and mystical meaning". Yet one must avoid speculation and *curiositas*, undue inquisitiveness. If the sense of a passage was not clear, it was preferable "not to say every single thing that could be said on the occasion, but only those things which seem closest to the truth when compared with other scriptural passages and which are appropriate to the context of the argument as a whole".[59] The purpose of meditating on Scripture was not to ferret out what God meant to be hidden from the knowledge of human beings, but to believe and worship his words as divine mysteries and to exemplify his teachings in every day life.

Explaining how best to imitate Christ, Erasmus often uses the image of "digesting" the biblical message. We find this metaphor in Erasmus' writings both as a moral and stylistic precept, to guide readers how to live and to speak in a manner appropriate to Christians. Thus a Christian author "imitates" pagan writers, not by regurgitating their phrases, but by adapting their style to the

---

[55] Holborn 34.23.
[56] ASD V-2 330.29–30; the same bipartition also appears at ASD V-3, 172.35–39.
[57] ASD V-2 300.436–37.
[58] Holborn 71.25–26, ASD V-3, 185.523–27; cf. *Ecclesiastes* LB V 1038E.
[59] ASD V-3 259.48–50, 243.752–53.

Christian world in which he lives. He "transmits [the features] to the mind for inward digestion, so that becoming part of your own system, it gives the impression not of something begged from someone else, but of something that springs from your own mental processes... a river welling out from your inmost being". If Cicero had "studied the philosophy of Christ, he would... have been numbered among those who are now honoured as saints for their blameless and spiritual lives". Thus Erasmus links his literary theory with the practical philosophy of Christ and asserts that the purpose of studying eloquence is "to know Christ, to celebrate the glory of Christ".[60] Similarly, he recommends the study of the Psalms as food for thought and for further digestion: "There is no more effective food for the soul than spiritual precepts". Christ's flock feeds on his words, which they "commit to their upper stomach, that is, their memory". Later they "chew the cud... and finally pass it down into the stomach, and from there it is distributed throughout the body and becomes the substance of the mind".[61] Explaining the metaphor, Erasmus writes: "What I have here described as digestion, Psalm 1 calls meditation". Meditation in turn has both an intellectual and a practical ingredient, for in Latin 'meditari' means not 'to meditate' but 'to practise'.[62] Thus meditation leads to a transformation.

Transformation or metamorphosis is another important image in Erasmus' Psalm commentaries. In Psalm 1 he connects the ideas of nourishment with meditation and transformation. Reading Holy Scripture, he says, and "being transformed into Christ, drinking in his spirit...truly means meditating on the law of the Lord".[63] Just as baptism transforms us and restores us to innocence, the word transforms us through its persuasive powers. In his *Paraclesis* Erasmus prays for that transforming rhetorical power, which only the Spirit can supply, "which leaves tenacious hooks in the minds of the hearers, which carries them away and transforms them". Scriptural allegories have that power. "No other kind of teaching is more familiar or more effective than comparison through similarity".[64]

Erasmus often describes the spiritual meaning of the scriptural text as a hidden treasure. In that context he uses the metaphor of the Sileni figures found in Plato's *Symposium*. The Sileni are outwardly plain but conceal beautiful images within. Similarly, the allegories in Scripture are common and ordinary, using features of everyday life, but they convey the beauty of virtue.[65] In the Psalm commentaries Erasmus refers to the Silenus image to describe the process of discovering the hidden spiritual meaning of God's words, "when you open up the Silenus figure, your minds will enjoy spiritual delights, feed on salutary food, and marvel as you contemplate God's wisdom".[66] Here, then, Erasmus combines images of digestion and meditation with finding a hidden

---

[60] CWE 28, 441, 447; cp. ASD V-2, 206–07.
[61] ASD V-2, 372.444–49.
[62] ASD V-2, 51.542.
[63] ASD V-2, 52.581–83.
[64] Holborn 139.23–25. In using allegory, Christ "accommodates" familiar things to his philosophy (*Ratio*, Holborn 283.3–9; cf. ASD V-2 124.844–45).
[65] Cf. *Adages* 3.3.1; Holborn 70.17–19.
[66] ASD V-3, 97.98–101.

treasure. He also applies the Silenus image to David. The historical David is a Silenus figure, which the reader must open up to penetrate to the spiritual meaning. "It is good, if we leave David behind and come to Christ, if we leave the letter that kills and find the life-giving spirit".[67]

Whereas the philological principle dominates Erasmus' annotations on the New Testament, it occupies only a subordinate position in his Psalm commentaries. The reason for staying away from etymological or text critical remarks might be found either in Erasmus' reluctance to add to the burden of unpopularity which the humanistic principle had brought him or in his lack of Hebrew language skills. His rudimentary knowledge of Hebrew did not allow him to inspect the original text of the Old Testament and naturally made him reluctant to comment on variant readings. The Psalm commentaries are not, however, completely devoid of textual criticism. There are occasional references to the Greek version[68] and isolated comments on the Hebrew text.[69] A comment on a difficult passage in Psalm 4 is reminiscent of the apologetic prefaces to Erasmus' New Testament edition, where he explains that he is not faulting the biblical author for the ambiguities but rather careless scribes or an inattentive translator. What the psalmist wrote under divine inspiration was no doubt clear and simple, he says. The variants were introduced by copyists and translators, and God permitted them "so that these difficulties would rouse us from our lethargy and inattention".[70] He declines, however, to give preference to any one variant. In Psalm 33, Erasmus again discusses textual problems, explaining that they may be the result of scribal error. Alternatively, he says, they may be an indication of the impotence of the human intellect, for "that celestial spirit, under whose inspiration Holy Writ has been handed down to us, cannot err." The "semblance of absurdity" in a text indicates a sacred mystery, he adds, and we must pray for enlightenment.[71]

Although the text-critical element is comparatively insignificant in Erasmus' Psalm commentaries, the typically humanistic emphasis on the word provides a continuous subtext. Words are to the meaning what the body is to the soul, Erasmus explains in his introduction to the New Testament.[72] Placing his philosophy of language into a theological context, he writes: "As God the Father begets from himself his Son, so our mind begets our thoughts and speech; and as the Son proceeds from the Father, so our speech proceeds from our mind".[73] Heeding the biblical warning against the letter that kills, Erasmus nevertheless recognizes the power of the word as a bearer and medium of thought, which facilitates the transit from the visible and the invisible world.

---

[67] ASD V-3 112.645–49.

[68] E.g. ASD V-3, 346.446–53, 370.131–136, 388.611–13.

[69] ASD V-2 46.378, 60.793, 830, etc.

[70] ASD V-2 246.720–24.

[71] ASD V-3, 108.486–87.

[72] See also *Ecclesiastes* LB V 1043D, where he likens the historical sense to the body, and the mystical sense to the soul.

[73] Cf. *Lingua*, CWE 29, 326.

7. Erasmus' Use of Sources

Erasmus' Psalm commentaries are not produced in a cultural vacuum. They reflect the exegetical tradition of the Church. Nevertheless they are imprinted with an Erasmian stamp. There is a lesser degree of direct dependence on patristic writings than one might expect from the editor and translator of numerous patristic works. Psalm 14 may serve as a representative example, illustrating Erasmus' use of sources. Most of references are to the biblical sources themselves. Allusions to the prophets and the Pauline epistles are ubiquitous. Erasmus knew the Psalm commentaries of Augustine, Pseudo-Jerome, and Arnobius, and may have been familiar with the work of Cassiodorus, but there is only one passage echoing Jerome's words and two that might be construed as allusions to Augustine.[74] Indeed, references to classical authors (Lucretius, Virgil, Terence, Livy, Seneca) outnumber those to patristic sources. As CHARLES BÉNÉ rightly observes: *on retrouve enfin dans ce commentaire, l'Erasme de toujours*.[75] He means the Christian humanist, the critical observer of his own time. Not surprisingly, then, the most prominent theme in the commentary is one familiar from Erasmus' devotional writings and a central issue of the Reformation debate: the respective value of faith and works.[76] Denouncing legalism and rejecting undue emphasis on ritual and external manifestations of faith, Erasmus pursues a theme characteristic of his writings. One might therefore say that, apart from Scripture, the source he quotes most often is himself.

Being true to himself was Erasmus' recipe for success. He never strikes the reader as derivative. He always seems to address his audience directly, from the heart. Indeed, he displays a surprising ability to inject a personal note into works normally regarded as academic and by their very nature dry and impersonal. Interposing himself between the reader and the subject matter, adopting the role of the preacher, moral counselor, or social critic, bringing the world into the scholar's study is a typical feature of Erasmus' writings. It is clear that his purpose was never purely academic or purely rhetorical. He always pursued a practical moral aim, whether he was putting together a commentary or an anthology or a manual. It is for this reason that Erasmus has been labeled a "Christian humanist". He represents a humanism that is not merely an aesthetic or a pedagogical programme, but a *Weltanschauung*. Thus his *Adages* are not merely an anthology of proverbs but contain a plea for peace. His *Education of a Christian Prince* is not merely a manual of statecraft but an appeal to rulers to serve as vicars of God. Similarly, his Psalm commentaries are not merely a vehicle to explain the text, but commentaries on the questions of the day: legalism, the Turkish threat, the schism of the Church. No doubt, Erasmus had a knack of liberating the text "from the restrictions of its original cul-

---

[74] ASD V-3, 299.424, an allusion to either Jerome or Augustine; 303.506–511 and 309.715, perhaps allusions to Augustine; 316.998–1000, echoing Jerome.

[75] ASD V-2, 281.

[76] For that theme in his commentary on Psalm 14, see for example ASD V-2, 291.131, 301.432–33; 307.688–91, 313.881–83, 889–891.

tural matrix".[77] It was one of the charms of his writing, but also its most controversial feature. The topical Psalm commentaries were read eagerly, though
not always with approval. That caused Jacopo Sadoleto to muse on Erasmus'
choice of subject matter: "When the field of sacred letters stretches so far on
every side...why not choose a subject that will make men admire you rather
than pick a quarrel with you?"[78] In his reply Erasmus acknowledged that his
candor had landed him "between a rock and a hard place". He sounded a note
of regret ("I wish I could rework everything and start over!"), but he could not
help being who he was and continued in the same vein to the end of his life,
courting controversy.[79]

---

[77] D. BAKER-SMITH in his introduction to CWE 63, xxv.
[78] Allen *Ep.* 2272.47–50.
[79] Allen *Ep.* 2315.288, 299–300.

CHAPTER TEN

Scriptural Interpretation in Renaissance Spain

By Emilia Fernández Tejero /
Natalio Fernández Marcos, Madrid

Sources and general works: K. Reinhardt, *Bibelkommentare spanischer Autoren (1500–1700)* I-II (Madrid: CSIC 1990, 1999). Since this work brings together both the sources and the bibliography relevant to the principal Spanish biblical writers of the sixteenth century, references will be made to it in the different sections of this chapter in order to avoid unnecessary repetition; when the information is of special significance works in the *Bibelkommentare* will be cited. - Further: A. Alcalá e.a., *Inquisición española y mentalidad inquisitorial* (Barcelona: Editorial Ariel 1984); Q. Aldea Vaquero / T. Martín Martínez / J. Vives Gatell, *Diccionario de Historia Eclesiástica de España* (Madrid: CSIC 1972–75) [DHEE]; ibid., Suplemento I (Madrid 1987); M. Andrés, *La teología española en el siglo XVI*, I-II (Madrid: BAC 1976–77); E. Asensio, *El erasmismo y las corrientes espirituales afines* (Salamanca: Seminario de Estudios Medievales y Renacentistas 2000), new edition of the study published in *RFE* 36 (1952) 31–99; V. Baroni, *La Contre-Réforme devant la Bible* (Lausanne: Imprimerie La Concorde 1943); M. Bataillon, *Érasme et l'Espagne* (nouvelle édition en trois volumes; Genève: Librairie Droz 1991); J. H. Bently, *Humanists and Holy Writ: New Testament Scholarship in the Renaissance* (Princeton, NJ: Princeton UP 1983); *Septuaginta* I-II (ed. A. Rahlfs; Stuttgart: Privil. Württembergische Bibelanstalt 1935, [3]1949); *Biblia Sacra iuxta Vulgatam versionem* I-II (ed. R. Weber; Stuttgart: Württembergische Bibelanstalt 1969); *Biblia Hebraica Stuttgartensia* (ed. K. Elliger / W. Rudolph; Stuttgart: Deutsche Bibelgesellschaft 1967–77); J. M. de Bujanda, "Índices de libros prohibidos", DHEE. Suplemento I (Madrid: CSIC 1987) 399–409; idem (ed.), *Index des livres interdits* I-IX (Québec: Éditions de l'Université de Sherbrooke / Genève: Droz 1984–94); *Enciclopedia Cattolica* (Firenze: Casa Editrice G. C. Sansoni 1948–54); *Encyclopaedia Judaica* 1–16 (Jerusalem 1971); N. Fernández Marcos / E. Fernández Tejero, *Biblia y Humanismo.* Textos, talantes y controversias del siglo XVI español (Madrid: FUE 1997); J. Goñi, "Erasmismo en España", DHEE. Suplemento I (Madrid: CSIC 1987) 272–81; A. Hamilton, *Heresy and Mysticism in Sixteenth Century Spain. The Alumbrados* (Cambridge: Clarke 1992); J. Kraye, *Introducción al humanismo renacentista* (Cambridge: Cambridge UP 1998); H. de Lubac, *Medieval Exegesis.* The Four Senses of Scripture 1–2 (ET by E. M. Macierowski; Edinburgh: T&T Clark 1998–2000); J. C. Nieto, *El Renacimiento y la otra España. Visión Cultural Socioespiritual* (Genève: Droz 1997); K. Reinhardt / H. Santiago-Otero, *Biblioteca bíblica ibérica medieval* (Madrid: CSIC 1986); J. Rodríguez de Castro, *Biblioteca española de los escritores rabinos españoles* I (Madrid 1781); H. Santiago-Otero / K. Reinhardt, *La Biblia en la península ibérica durante la edad media (siglos XII-XV): el texto y su interpretación* (Coimbra: Arquivo da Universidade de Coimbra 2001); P. Sáinz Rodríguez, *Antología de la literatura espiritual española.* I. *Edad Media* (Madrid: FUE 1980); II-III. *Siglo XVI* (1983–84); IV. *Siglo XVII* (1985); D. C. Steinmetz (ed.), *The Bible in the Sixteenth Century* (Durham / London: Duke UP 1990).

1. The Early Humanist Interpreters

Sources and studies: K. Reinhardt / H. Santiago-Otero, *Biblioteca bíblica ibérica medieval* (Madrid: CSIC 1986) 240–49 (Pablo de Burgos); 64–79 (Fernández de Madrigal); 213–19 (Juan de Torquemada); 172–79 (Pérez de Valencia).

Other studies: J. Conde, *La creación de un discurso historiográfico en el cuatrocientos castellano: Las siete edades del mundo de Pablo de Santa María.* Estudio y edición crítica (Salamanca: Universidad de Salamanca 1999); J. Formentín Ibáñez / M. J. Villegas Sanz, *Tratado contra los judíos* (Madrid: Aben Ezra Ediciones 1998); M. Morreale, "Vernacular Scriptures in Spain", CHB 2 (1969) 465–91; M. Peinado-Muñoz, "Criterios hermenéuticos de Jaime Pérez de Valencia", in: J. Carreira das Neves / V. Collado Bertomeu / J. Vilar Hueso (eds.), *III Simposio Bíblico Español (I Luso-Espanhol)* (Valencia / Lisboa 1991) 667–72; H. Santiago-Otero / K. Reinhardt, *La Biblia en la península ibérica durante la edad media (siglos XII-XV): el texto y su interpretación* (Coimbra: Arquivo da Universidade de Coimbra 2001); M. J. Sconza, *History and literature in fifteenth-century Spain: an edition and study of Pablo de Santa Maria's Siete edades del mundo* (Madison: The Hispanic Seminary of Medieval Studies 1991); M. Sæbø (ed.), *Hebrew Bible / Old Testament: The History of Its Interpretation* [HBOT] I/2. *The Middle Ages* (Göttingen: Vandenhoeck & Ruprecht 2000); P. Saquero Suárez-Somonte / T. González Rolán, *Sobre los dioses de los gentiles. Alonso Fernández de Madrigal (El Tostado).* Edición y estudio preliminar (Madrid: Clásicas 1995).

The humanist interpretation of Scripture in Spain brought together two specific phenomena which were to determine both its content and its form: the Christian coexistence in the Middle Ages with the Jewish communities and the contribution of the *conversos* ('converts'), who gave access to the interpretations of the Spanish Rabbis, in particular Moses Maimonides, Abraham ibn Ezra and Moses Nahmanides[1] as well as to the Rabbinic Bibles of Felix Pratensis (1517) and Jacob ben Hayyim (1525). At another level, several translations from the original Hebrew and Latin into the vernacular Castillian, Catalan and Valencian appeared in the Iberian Peninsula at a very early period. The best example of both phenonema is to be found in the work known as the *Biblia de Alba* translated from the Hebrew to Castillian by Mosés Arragel de Guadalajara (1422–1433?).[2] However, it was not until the sixteenth century that the interpretation of Scripture in Spain had recourse to the original languages. That said, there were a few authors in the previous century who attempted an approach to the original texts and as such could be considered as precursors of the humanist interpreters.

– *Pablo de Burgos* (c. 1355–1435), or de Santamaría, a name he adopted after his conversion to Christianity, came from a noble Jewish family of Burgos. In his *Additiones ad postillam Nicolai de Lira* (1429–31), he tried to get close to the *hebraica veritas*. The work comprises one thousand one hundred glosses, of different lengths, on passages from the Old Testament and reached such renown that the *Postillae* of Nicholas of Lyra[3] were rarely reprinted without the *Additiones* of Pablo de Burgos. He agreed with the use that Nicholas of Lyra had made of the Jewish exegesis to arrive at a literal interpretation of the Bible in the Christian sense, and he was to take this method to its limit, since his knowledge of Hebrew and rabbinic writings were far superior to those of the author of the *Postillae*. In his *Scrutinium scripturarum contra perfidiam iudaeorum* (1434) he presented, in the form of a dialogue, the truths of the Christian faith, based on the literal sense of the Scripture and with reference to the Talmud and other Jewish sources.

– *Alfonso Fernández de Madrigal* (1410–55), also called the Tostado, was probably the most prolific of the Spanish interpreters in the fifteenth century. His works, which included the *Postillae* to the historical books of the Old Testament and the Gospel according to Saint Matthew, took up thirteen volumes *in-folio* in the *editio princeps*; he was, however, not able to complete his task of glossing the whole Bible. Despite his ties to the scholastic four senses of Scripture (the literal, the

---

[1] Cf. HBOT I/2: The Middle Ages (2000) 311–20, 377–87, 416–32.
[2] Cf. Morreale, Vernacular Scriptures in Spain (1969) 465–91.
[3] Cf. Chap. 2.1 of the present volume.

allegorical, the moral and the anagogic), he showed a leaning towards the literal interpretation, considering that it was the immediate sense of the holy books, but without neglecting the spiritual and metaphoric meanings. He distinguished, as had Nicholas of Lyra, a double literal meaning in the prophecies: one coeval to the writings themselves, and another applicable to the New Testament which could only be apprehended on the basis of the faith in Jesus Christ. His *Postillae* were considered to be the response of Spanish exegesis to the works of Nicholas of Lyra.

– *Juan de Torquemada* (c. 1388–1468), in his *Expositio brevis et utilis super toto psalterio* (1463), followed the traditional exegesis by gathering together quotations from the Fathers, in the style of the *catenae*, and applied the meaning of the Psalms to Christ and to the Church.

– *Jaime Pérez de Valencia* (c. 1408–90) attempted to renew biblical exegesis, as is apparent in his most important work: *Commentum in psalmos David (Centum et quinquaginta psalmi Davidici cum…expositione)*; it was completed around 1478 and was so successful that thirty-two editions were printed in the sixteenth century. The introduction to this commentary constituted a synthesis of medieval biblical hermeneutics. His starting point was the four senses of Scripture; he concentrated, however, mainly on the literal as well as the spiritual or allegorical sense; in this way he was a forerunner of the model of interpretation to be used later by such humanists as Erasmus of Rotterdam and Jacques Lefèvre d'Étaples. Although using his knowledge of Jewish exegesis (albeit to a lesser extent than Pablo de Burgos or Alfonso de Madrigal) he justified his Christian interpretation of the Psalms in his *Tractatus contra iudaeos*; and to go beyond the Jewish interpretation of the Old Testament he had to have recourse to the allegorical sense, following the Christological exegesis of the Psalms in the Patristic tradition.

With some justification one can refer to these exegetes as Early Humanist Interpreters. They had at their command much greater knowledge of the Hebrew language and rabbinic exegesis than did Nicholas of Lyra, and without their legacy the sixteenth century in Spain would not have reached the brilliant heights of biblical science that it attained.

2. The Sixteenth Century in Spain: Hermeneutics and Philology

The major themes at the centre of biblical debate in the sixteenth century were the following: philological – the search for the authentic text of the Scriptures, given the fact that there were differences between the Hebrew and Greek texts and between them and the Latin of the Vulgate; determining the accuracy of the different versions in relation to the original; appraising the value of the Vulgate itself as a translation and the authority of Jerome as a translator; hermeneutic – the plurality of the meanings of Scripture and their hierarchy in the practice of exegesis.

A result was the philological renaissance, the study of the original languages and a return to the sources which found its most important exponent in the Polyglot Bibles. The response to the second question led to the introductions and annotations or keys to the reading of Holy Scripture.

2.1. Introductions to Scripture

Sources and studies: K. REINHARDT, *Bibelkommentare spanischer Autoren (1500–1700)* I-II (Madrid: CSIC 1990, 1999): I, 68–72 (Pedro Antonio Beuter); II, 51–55 (Martín Martínez de Cantalapiedra).

Introductions to Scripture had a long history in the Christian tradition, dating back to the *Liber Regularum Tyconii* (380 CE). During the sixteenth century in Spain, several books in this vein were edited: in 1546 Francisco Ruiz published *Regulae intelligendi Scripturas sacras*; and a *Praeludia in universam Sacram doctrinam et Scripturam*[4] is attributed to Pedro Irurozqui; Ignacio Fermín de Ibero, the first editor of Cipriano de la Huerga, made reference to a lost work of this author, *Isagogue in totam divinam scripturam.*[5] We shall concentrate here on two of the most important introductions in chronological order of their publication: those of Pedro Antonio Beuter and Martín Martínez de Cantalapiedra.

2.1.1. Pedro Antonio Beuter

Pedro Antonio Beuter (1490/95–c. 1555) published his *Annotationes decem in Sacram Scripturam*[6] in Valencia in 1547. In the hermeneutic tradition of Jaime Pérez de Valencia, he approached the principal themes of biblical introduction on a philological level and defended recourse to the original Hebrew and Greek when the Latin text presented certain doubts. He distinguished three senses of Scripture: literal, mystical and allegorical, although he maintained that the latter was not always to be followed systematically. The principal issues in his *Annotationes* are: the order of the books in the Church and the Synagogue; the canonical and apocryphal books; lost books; authorship and chronology; the various meanings of Scripture and keys for their comprehension; the principal translations of the Bible and in particular that of St. Jerome. For each treatise he adduced the testimonies of the Fathers, of councils, ancient and modern authors. The name of Erasmus took pride of place together with those of Pico della Mirandola and Cardinal Cisneros – one of the few references of the age to the Polyglot of Alcalá that passed virtually unnoticed by the theologians of the time. He also cited Alfonso de Zamora, whose legacy was to have a very strong influence on the later Spanish Hebrew scholars,[7] as well as Johannes Reuchlin, with whom he shared a Christian kabbalistic interest.

2.1.2. Martín Martínez de Cantalapiedra

Martín Martínez de Cantalapiedra (1518–79) published his work *Libri decem hypotyposeon theologicarum, sive regularum ad intelligendum scripturas divinas*[8] in 1565, a year before Sixtus of Siena edited his *Bibliotheca Sancta*, and two

---

[4] Mss. 372, 429, Seminario Conciliar of Barcelona (cf. Andrés, La teología española II [1977] 632–33).

[5] Cipriano de la Huerga, *Obras completas* VI/I (1990) 106.

[6] Cf. F. Secret, "Les Annotationes decem in sacram Scripturam de Petrus Antonius Beuter", *Sef.* 29 (1969) 319–32; F. Jordán Gallego Salvadores, "Los estudios bíblicos en la Universidad de Valencia durante la primera mitad del siglo XVI", *Anales Valentinos* (1975) 307–41, esp. 333–35.

[7] Asensio, El erasmismo (2000) 51–52.

[8] Cf. N. Fernández Marcos, "Censura y exégesis: las *Hypotyposeis* de Martín Martínez de Cantalapiedra", in: Fernández Marcos / Fernández Tejero, Biblia y Humanismo (1997) 27–34.

years before Matthias Flacius Illyricus was to publish his *Clavis Scripturae Sacrae*. The first part of the *Libri decem* is comprised of eight books and is a systematic reflection on biblical and extra-biblical texts: reasons for the obscure nature of the Scriptures, literary figures, the benefits of the knowledge of ancient languages, the importance of geography, history and the humanities, names of God, symbolic and allegorical theology, the Psalms, the figures of prophetic language and hebraisms. In the second part (books IX and X) he set out one hundred rules to help theologians interpret the Bible. The *Index* of sacred and profane writers, which appears at the beginning of the book, is a proof of the erudition of this Hebraic scholar from Salamanca. The work was denounced to the Inquisition[9] and placed on the Index of prohibited books in 1583. The passages censured by the Inquisition, texts concerning Christology, angelology, anthropology, certain discrepancies with the doctrines of St. Thomas and the attacks on the scholastics and the dialecticals had already been removed from the second edition (1582). This probably explains why the work of Sixtus of Siena had greater diffusion and influence among Catholics. The *Libri decem* of Cantalapiedra were not reedited until 1771.

2.2. Philological Exegesis

Sources and studies: K. REINHARDT, *Bibelkommentare spanischer Autoren (1500–1700)* I-II (Madrid: CSIC 1990, 1999): I, 214–17 (Huerga); I, 193–94 (Grajal); I, 243–61 (Luis de León); I, 29–42 (Montano).

From the middle of the fifteenth century Lorenzo Valla[10] began to criticize the New Testament text of the Vulgate which had been adopted by the Church as a *textus receptus*. The proliferation of medieval Bibles, with their glosses, historical and moralising annotations, had become so monotonous that it incited the sixteenth-century humanists to propose a return to the original sources. Valla's attacks were followed by those of Erasmus.[11] The major innovation in his bilingual edition of the New Testament (1516) was his new translation of the Greek text into Latin. Any innovation in the canonical terminology used by ecclesiastics during a millenium, any attempt to replace the translation of the Vulgate by a new version, became not only a theological problem but also caused political malaise that threatened the very basis of society.[12] In Spain, Pedro Martínez de Osma (c. 1430–80) had already begun a correction of the text of the Vulgate based on codices preserved in the Cathedral of Salamanca. We also know that the main reason for Nebrija's being removed from the pro-

---

[9] M. DE LA PINTA LLORENTE, *Proceso criminal contra el hebraísta salmantino Martín Martínez de Cantalapiedra* (Madrid: CSIC 1946).

[10] *In Novum Testamentum ex diversorum utriusque linguae codicum collatione adnotationes* (1449?).

[11] Cf. Chap. 9 of this volume.

[12] H. J. DE JONGE, "Novum Testamentum a nobis versum: the essence of Erasmus' edition of the New Testament", *JTS* 35 (1984) 394–413.

ject of the Polyglot of Alcalá was his differences with Cardinal Cisneros regarding the critical treatment of the Latin version.

The return to the original sources began in Spain with the founding of the Trilingual College of St. Idelfonso (University of Alcalá, 1512), the creation of Chairs of Biblical Studies in the universities of Salamanca and Alcalá, 1532,[13] and, its most important manifestation, the publication in the same century of two polyglot Bibles, the Complutensian (1514–17) and the Regia or Antwerp Polyglot (1569–73).[14] Antwerp was at that time a part of the Spanish kingdom.

It must be stressed here that, apart from the philological importance and the interest in the text of the polyglots, the preliminary work demanded a great deal of effort at the level of interpretation: the prologues – which affected both the form and the content of the work, the interlineal translations, the grammars, the lexica and the treatises that complemented them.[15] Moreover, these polyglots were not a mere elitist display of knowledge of sources, or a superb demonstration of typography, there existed a definite pedagogical objective in disclosing the original texts, making them understandable with interlineal Latin translations, the aforementioned grammars and lexica, and notes in the margins of the Hebrew column identifying the roots of the Hebrew words.

As for the plurality of the sense of the biblical text, there was also a change in the hermeneutics. Compared to the four classical senses of medieval exegesis,[16] adopted by the theologians, in the Renaissance the literal sense was preferred by the philologists. The humanists were especially critical of the abuse of the allegory. In the words of Erasmus: "Can you imagine their [the theologians'] delight as they mould and re-mould at whim the most obscure passages of the Scriptures as if they were wax, expecting that their conclusions… be taken more seriously than the laws of Solon…".[17]

Many are the Spaniards who are representative of the literal exegesis during the Golden Age. We shall mention here just the four most significant who use principally the literal interpretation based on the analysis of the original texts.[18]

2.2.1. Cipriano de la Huerga

CIPRIANO DE LA HUERGA: *Obras completas* I–IX (ed. by G. Morocho Gayo; León: Universidad de León 1990–96), esp. IX. *Estudio monográfico colectivo.*

---

[13] V. BELTRÁN DE HEREDIA, "Catedráticos de Sagrada Escritura en la Universidad de Alcalá durante el siglo XVI", *Ciencia Tomista* 18 (1918) 140–55; 19 (1919) 45–55; 144–56; J. JUAN GARCÍA, *Los estudios bíblicos en el siglo de oro de la universidad salmantina* (Salamanca 1921).

[14] For the history and content of the Polyglots see Chaps. 12 and 30 of this volume.

[15] Cf. A. SÁENZ-BADILLOS, *La Filología bíblica en los primeros helenistas de Alcalá* (Estella 1990); idem, *Anejo a la edición facsímile de la Biblia Políglota Complutense* (Valencia 1987) 15–20; Fernández Marcos / Fernández Tejero, Biblia y Humanismo (1997) 155–238.

[16] De Lubac, Medieval Exegesis 1–2 (1998–2000).

[17] Desiderius Erasmus, *Elogio de la locura* (Barcelona: Ediciones Orbis/Origen 1982) 117.

[18] The representatives of theology in the polemic between the theologians and the philologists may be disregarded here; among the theologians were León de Castro and Bartolomé de Medina. As for León de Castro cf. Reinhardt, Bibelkommentare I (1990) 110–14; for Bartolomé de Medina cf. G. FRAILE, DHEE III, 1453.

Cipriano de la Huerga (c. 1509–60), professor of Biblical Studies at Alcalá and rector of the Cistercian College in the same city,[19] was part of the privileged age of Spanish Humanism and, among Spanish biblical scholars in the sixteenth century, can be considered to be a 'hinge' joining two generations of philologists, those who collaborated on the Polyglot of Alcalá, and those who worked on the Biblia Regia. His biographers stress his new technique for explaining Scripture, not using the routine method of the traditional four senses, but examining the original texts. This can be seen in his biblical commentaries, notably those on the Song of Songs, the book of Job, the prophet Nahum and the Psalms 38 and 130.[20]

The exegesis of Cipriano de la Huerga was moved by two intellectual motives: the *arcanae litterae* and the *prophana philosophia*. The search for the literal sense led him to investigate the secrets of the Hebrew text and to compare it to the Greek, Latin and Aramaic versions, rather than to repeat the trite options put forward by his predecessors: "We must be very cautious and have a critical mind when interpreting the Holy Scriptures, otherwise, as do other commentators, we shall, like beasts of burden, always follow in the tracks of others".[21] His remarks on the Hebrew language, the wealth of its meanings and the symbolism in the figures of speech were a precursor of Arias Montano's treatise on Hebrew idioms. One translation alone cannot do justice to all the meanings of the original; it is essential to recover them all; in the words of Cipriano de la Huerga: "we must be very familiar with the Hebrew language, pregnant with parables and with sentences full of curls".[22]

The list of Greco-Latin authors that appeared in the commentaries to the book of Job and the Song of Songs was so long that it aroused the admiration of E. Asensio.[23] It mentioned pre-Socratic philosophers, Homer, Hesiod, Plato, Orpheus, the Chaldean Oracles, Hermes Trismegistos, the ancient Egyptian theologians and the ancient Kabbalah. Cipriano de la Huerga, as well as his contemporaries, had an imprecise understanding of the Kabbalah, but it was as if his profane knowledge emerged at times with the force of a revelation similar to that of the Old and New Testaments. At other times it manifested itself as a trail of wisdom going right back to Moses from whom both the Egyptian and Greek *prisci theologi* had been inspired. The connecting thread between these two approaches to the interpretation of the biblical text holds – with regard to fundamental issues concerning God, man, the spirits or the world – that there is a basic concordance between the Scriptures and the profane philosophies which he considered to be of fabulous antiquity. Cipriano de la Huerga believed that there were secret traditions handed down from God to Moses on Sinai and which were subsequently passed on by oral tradition to an unbroken chain of chosen men, one of whom was Esdras. Huerga identified these traditions with the contents of the apocryphal books edited at the time of Esdras and referred to in IV Esdras.[24]

The passion for the tradition of wisdom in Antiquity was shared by all the humanists. It may not be ignored that Marsilio Ficino[25] made the wisdom of Hermes Trismegistos popular in the Florentine Academy when he translated

---

[19] Cf. Fernández Marcos / Fernández Tejero, Biblia y humanismo (1997) 47–82.

[20] *Comentario al Cantar de los Cantares* V, VI; *Comentarios al libro de Job* II, III; *Comentario al Profeta Nahum* VII; *Comentario a los Salmos XXXVIII y CXXX* IV.

[21] *Comentario al Cantar* V, 267.

[22] *Comentario a Nahum* VII, 254.

[23] E. Asensio, "Cipriano de la Huerga, Maestro de Fray Luis de León", *Homenaje a Pedro Sainz Rodríguez* III: *Estudios históricos* (Madrid: FUE 1986) 57–71.

[24] 4 Ezra 14:26: *Quaedam palam facies, quaedam sapientibus absconse trades... Novissimos autem LXX conservabis, ut tradas eos sapientibus de populo tuo*; cf. Cipriano de la Huerga, *Comentario a Nahum*, VII, 22.

[25] Cf. Chap. 5, Sect. 4, of this volume.

the work of this author – being brought to the West by a Byzantine monk – from the original Greek into Latin.[26]

The mention of the ancient Kabbalists brings together Cipriano de la Huerga and Luis de León. According to Cipriano de la Huerga, the etymology and the true form of proper names in relation to their meaning were respected in the whole of the Old Testament up to the coming of Jesus; this was reflected in the ancient Kabbalah, given that one of the main features of the kabbalistic tradition was its concern with the etymology of names, in particular those that refer to God. He claimed that the Platonists, the Pythagorists and Dionysius the Areopagite,[27] were all influenced by the teaching of the Kabbalists.

2.2.2. Gaspar de Grajal

F. DOMÍNGUEZ REBOIRAS, *Gaspar de Grajal (1530–1575)* (Münster: Aschendorff 1998); C. MIGUÉLEZ BAÑOS, *Gaspar de Grajar: Obras completas* I (León: Universidad de León 2002), II (León: Universidad de León 2004); M. DE LA PINTA LLORENTE, *Procesos inquisitoriales contra los catedráticos hebraístas de Salamanca: Gaspar de Grajal, Martínez de Cantalapiedra y Fray Luis de León*, I: *Gaspar de Grajal* (Madrid: Monasterio de El Escorial 1935).

Gaspar de Grajal (c. 1530–75), son of a convert family, educated in Salamanca, Paris and Louvain, gave lessons on Bible in Salamanca. Together with Luis de León and Martínez de Cantalapiedra he was part of the group of Hebraists who insisted on the literal exegesis of Scripture in opposition to the conservative theologians who defended the allegorical interpretation and the supremacy of the Vulgate and the Septuagint over the Hebrew text. In 1572, he was imprisoned by the Inquisition; in 1577, following a trial, the court of Valladolid vindicated him but, unfortunately, he had died in prison two years earlier.

He participated in the commission that had been appointed to correct the Vatable's Bible; this was the name given to the edition published in Paris by Robert d'Estienne in 1545 with two translations from the Hebrew to the Latin, one being the Vulgate, and another new version incorporating notes from the teaching of Vatable. It had been included in the Spanish Index of prohibited books in 1559. In 1569, the Salamanca printer Gaspar de Portonariis wanted to reprint that Bible with commission's corrections. When the deliberations of the commission came to an end, three of its members – Grajal, Martínez de Cantalapiedra and Luis de León – were denounced to the Inquisition by several of their colleagues.[28]

The only published work of Grajal is his *In Michaeam prophetam commentaria* (Salamanca 1570). Some handwritten pages of his commentaries on Hos-

---

[26] Asensio, Cipriano de la Huerga (1986) 67, and G. Morocho, "Cipriano de la Huerga, maestro de humanistas", in: V. GARCÍA DE LA CONCHA / J. SAN JOSÉ LERA (eds.), *Fray Luis de León. Historia, Humanismo y Letras* (Salamanca: Universidad 1996) 173–93.

[27] *Comentario al Cantar*, VI, 222: *Kabalaei, qui inter hebraeos principes habentur theologi, inter reliquas partes artis kabalisticae hanc unam praecipuam magisque illustrem statuunt, quae circa vocum etymologias versatur; quorum libris et platonici et pythagorici, quicquid de nominum etymologiis literis commissere, accepere mutuo. Divus etiam Dionisius totam rationem theologiae ab ipsis nominibus divinis conquisivit, quasi arcana quaedam eximia divinis appellationibus lateant.*

[28] D. BARTHÉLEMY, *Critique textuelle de l'Ancien Testament 2: Isaïe, Jérémie, Lamentations* (OBO 50/2; Fribourg: Editions Universitaires / Göttingen: Vandenhoeck & Ruprecht 1986) *34-*43.

ea, Amos and Jeremiah as well as some writings on the authority of the Vulgate and some letters from his prison cell have also survived.

He was an accomplished philologist, a true representative of the school that insisted upon literal exegesis based on the Hebrew text; he was also well acquainted with the Targum and other ancient versions. He explained some of the differences between the text of the Septuagint and the Hebrew as a confusion among similar Hebrew consonants; he accepted the existence of variant readings in the codices without blaming them for Jewish introducing errors; he followed Jerome in his commentary on Micah, but had constant recourse to Pagninus' and Vatable's translations for his interpretations, and to the commentaries of Jewish authors such as Qimhi and Ibn Ezra, and to humanists like Jaime Pérez de Valencia, Pedro Antonio Beuter, Johannes Reuchlin and Petrus Galatinus. His good knowledge of Hebrew meant that he was able to appreciate the plays on words, the alliterations and other forms of figures of speech which were beyond the reach of those who did not know the original language of the Bible. In his commentary on Jeremiah, and in line with other humanists, he would introduce the vernacular –in this case Castillian– translations. The linguistic interest of these passages is undeniable: they are hidden translations spread through the commentaries, published during a period and in an environment in which vernacular renderings were under suspicion.

2.2.3. Luis de León

A. ALCALÁ, *El proceso inquisitorial de Fray Luis de León* (Valladolid: Junta de Castilla y León 1991); L. G. ALONSO GETINO, *Vida y procesos del Maestro Fr. Luis de León* (Salamanca: Calatrava 1907); J. BARRIENTOS GARCÍA, *Fray Luis de León. Escritos desde la cárcel*. Autógrafos del primer proceso inquisitorial (Madrid: Ediciones Escurialenses 1991); A. F. G. BELL, *Luis de León. Un estudio del Renacimiento español* (Barcelona: Araluce [s. a.], Preface 1923); J. M. BLECUA (ed.), *Cantar de cantares de Salomón* (Madrid: Gredos 1994); G. DÍAZ GARCÍA, *Fray Luis de León. Opera X. In Epistolam ad Romanos Expositio* (El Escorial 1993); N. FERNÁNDEZ MARCOS / E. FERNÁNDEZ TEJERO, *Biblia y Humanismo*. Textos, talantes y controversias del siglo XVI español (Madrid: FUE 1997) 83–152; E. FERNÁNDEZ TEJERO, *El cantar más bello* (Madrid: Trotta ³1998); *Fray Luis de León 1591/1991* (*La ciudad de Dios* CCIV/1-3; volume of homage; El Escorial 1991); F. GARCÍA, *Obras completas castellanas de Fray Luis de León* (Madrid: BAC ³1959); V. GARCÍA DE LA CONCHA / J. SAN JOSÉ LERA (eds.), *Fray Luis de León. Historia, Humanismo y Letras* (Salamanca 1996); R. LAZCANO GONZÁLEZ, *Fray Luis de León. Bibliografía* (Madrid: Editorial Revista Agustiniana ²1994); *Magistri Luysii Legionensis Augustiniani… opera nunc primum ex manuscriptis eiusdem omnibus patrum Augustiniensium studio edita* I-VII (Salamanca 1891–95); C. MORÓN ARROYO / M. REVUELTA SAÑUDO, *Fray Luis de León. Aproximaciones a su vida y su obra* (Santander: Sociedad Menéndez Pelayo 1989); J. M. NIETO IBÁÑEZ, *Espiritualidad y patrística en "De los nombres de Cristo" de Fray Luis de León* (El Escorial: Ediciones Escurialenses 2001); J. RODRÍGUEZ DÍEZ (ed.), *Fray Luis de León, Opera VIII, Quaestiones Variae* (El Escorial: Ediciones Escurialenses 1992); J. SAN JOSÉ LERA, *Fray Luis de León. Exposición al Libro de Job* (Salamanca 1992); C. P. THOMPSON, *The Strife of Tongues. Fray Luis de León and the Golden Age of Spain* (Cambridge: Cambridge UP 1988); T. VIÑAS ROMÁN (coord.), *Fray Luis de León. IV Centenario (1591–1991). Congreso Interdisciplinar. Madrid, 16–19 de octubre de 1991. Actas* (Madrid: Ediciones Escurialenses 1992), esp. S. SABUGAL, "Exégesis y hermenéutica bíblica de Fray Luis de León", ibid. 117-28.

Luis de León (1527–91) studied theology in the universities of Salamanca and Alcalá and held various chairs in the former (that of St Thomas, 1561, then that of Durando, 1565); but his main interest was always concentrated on the Bible, whose texts he commented in all his lessons. After his trial and imprisonment by the Inquisition in Valladolid (1572-77) he finally returned to teaching in Salamanca, and in 1579 his dream came true when he was awarded the Chair of Bible, after a tight contest with the Dominican, Domingo de Guzmán.[29]

Several commentaries on Holy Scripture among the writings of Luis de León are worth mentioning (in Spanish, on the Book of Job, the Song of Songs, on the Names of Christ; and in Latin, the commentary on the first three chapters of Genesis, on Ecclesiastes, the Song of Songs, various Psalms, the prophet Obadiah and a number of Paul's letters). The principles guiding the exegesis which made up the work of Luis de León were: the recourse to the original texts -Hebrew and Greek – in order to achieve a more comprehensive interpretation of Scripture because, in his opinion, there were passages in the Vulgate which were not well translated, and failed to transmit the real meaning of the Hebrew; the plurality of the senses of the original, which were not always fully reflected in the Vulgate. Consequently, his first approach to the biblical text was through the Hebrew and the Greek texts. The Bible, as a work inspired by God, includes passages which contain arcane and hidden senses associated to the meaning and signification of the original Hebrew; these go beyond the literal sense and point to future events which could be applied to the coming of Christ, the history of the world or the history of the Church.

He made a clear distinction between philology and exegesis, a methodology which was already used by Jewish writers such as Abraham ibn Ezra who, like Luis de León in his Latin *Explanationes*, structured his interpretation of the Song of Songs into three parallel commentaries: the literal interpretation, the external plot, and the spiritual sense. In the Preface to his Spanish translation of the Song of Songs,[30] Luis de León clearly explains his aims and his methodology: to state *la corteza de la letra* ("the bark of the word") and to leave the spiritual interpretation to "those great books written by holy and learned people".

In a first instance, he criticised the text of the Vulgate, to the point that the Inquisitorial trial was to accuse him of advocating that certain of the biblical texts could be translated *melius, aptius, clarius, significantius*. He also maintained that the Jewish interpretations could be right, since their texts had neither been corrupted or falsified, that there could be other interpretations, not opposed to, but certainly with a broader significance than those of the Fathers, that Scripture could be understood from the point of view of grammar, without taking theology into account. However, like Arias Montano, he was against correcting the Vulgate because: "We could get it right once, but we could be mistaken in our understanding of the interpreter who, as we know, often read the Hebrew text in a different form from that in which we read it now; at other times, he followed the Greek translators, rather than the original

---

[29] As E. ASENSIO, "Fray Luis de León y la Biblia", *Edad de Oro* 4 (1985) 5–13, points out, these chairs, which were awarded for life, were decided by votes of students, doctors and professors, and provoked heated debates among the colleges, or in the most powerful convents, if the chairs in question were of theology.

[30] F. García, *Obras completas castellanas* (1959) 61–66.

Hebrew; in our attempt to render a more accurate Vulgate, we may, in fact, produce an even more corrupt version than we have at present".[31]

There is no doubt that the methodology followed by Luis de León in his biblical exegesis was positive or philological, based on the knowledge of the biblical languages, in particular the Hebrew, as well as other fields of learning and related sciences ("it is important to know everything"[32]), taking into account both the classical and the Christian authors. For Luis de León, all the sciences were at the service of hermeneutics. This position is confirmed in his writings: in the second and third *Explanationes* of the Song of Songs, in the *Exposición del libro de Job*, in the treatise *De los nombres de Cristo*, in his commentaries on certain Psalms (in particular Psalms 28, 57 and 67), and more especially in his *Commentaria in epistolam Pauli ad Galatas*.

It is also interesting to note the sober use that Luis de León made of the Christian Kabbalah and the Jewish exegetic techniques such as the *notariqon* (system of abbreviations), the *gematria* (numeric value of the letters), and the *temurah* (permutation of the letters). The allusions to the Kabbalah are scarce, but he does retain, at least, one of the typical lucubrations of the Christian Kabbalah concerning the name of Jesus, in Hebrew *Iehosuach*. This is the same ineffable name for God or Tetragrammaton, that became pronounced with the addition of two letters[33].

The Spanish humanists lived in their time and were not insensitive to such important events as the discovery of America. Given that Scripture was an inspired text, that all truths could be found there, and that God was the architect of the world, it was natural to believe that the New World had to be integrated therein in one form or another. Guided by the opinions of many Rabbis, the Targum and Arias Montano in his commentary on the Twelve Prophets, Luis de León interpreted the passage of Obad 20[34] as referring to Spain (Sefarad). There would be a third preaching of the Gospel: the first, was addressed to the Jews; the second, to the gentiles of the Roman Empire; and the third, to the people of the New World. The Bible was also studied as a source for toponyms found in the New World (Peru was identified as the *Parwayim* in 2 Chr 3:6; Yucatán as the *Yoqtan* in Gen 10:26).[35]

---

[31] E. Fernández Tejero, "Luis de León, hebraísta", in: Fernández Marcos / Fernández Tejero, Biblia y humanismo (1997) 101–18.

[32] M. Salvá / P. Sáinz de Baranda, *Colección de documentos inéditos para la historia de España* (Madrid 1847) X, 361: *Dije que para el entero entendimiento de la Escritura era menester sabello todo, y principalmente tres cosas: la theulogia escolástica: lo que escribieron los sanctos: las lenguas griega y hebrea.*

[33] N. Fernández Marcos, "De los nombres de Cristo", in: Fernández Marcos / Fernández Tejero, Biblia y humanismo (1997) 133–52.

[34] *Transmigratio Hierusalem quae in Bosforo est, possidebit civitates Austri.* Cf. *Magistri Luysii Legionensis*, III (Salamanca 1892) 172–73. The original Hebrew (בספרד) probably refers to Sardes in Asia Minor, and not to Spain as in the Targum Jonathan, or to the Bosphorus, as it is translated in the Vulgate.

[35] Treatise *Phaleg, sive de gentium sedibus primis...* and the map joined to the volume of *Apparatus* in the Biblia Regia; cf. N. Fernández Marcos, "El nuevo mundo en la exégesis española del siglo XVI", in: Fernández Marcos / Fernández Tejero, Biblia y humanismo (1997) 35–44.

Luis de León was not a biblical scholar in the strict sense of the term, so he has not been studied by the historians of biblical exegesis.[36] E. Asensio quite rightly reserves that title for Arias Montano and some of his disciples, who based their work on the Hebrew text with practically no reference to the Christian tradition of the Fathers. On the contrary, Luis de León, although making use of the original texts, incorporated into his commentaries all the Christian tradition: the Fathers, the scholastic theology, and the medieval commentaries, as well as those of his time. In the words of Asensio, "Fray Luis de León personifies, better than any other writer in the Castillian language, the confluence of Bible and Greco-Roman culture, of Poetry and Theology".[37]

2.2.4. Benito Arias Montano

Arias Montano (volume of homage; *Revista de Estudios Extremeños* LII/3; Badajoz 1996); V. Bécares Botas, *Arias Montano y Plantino* (León: Universidad de León 1999); *Benito Arias Montano* (volume of homage; *Cuadernos de Pensamiento* 12; Madrid 1998); *Benito Arias Montano* (volume of homage; *La Ciudad de Dios* CCXI/1; El Escorial 1998); *Benito Arias Montano* (volume of homage; *Revista Agustiniana* XXXIX; El Escorial 1998), esp. the articles by R. Lazcano ("Bibliografía", 1157-93) and E. Fernández Tejero / N. Fernández Marcos ("De Hebraicis Idiotismis", 997-1016); N. Fernández Marcos, "La Biblia Regia de Arias Montano: ¿Biblia de la concordia o Biblia de la discordia?", *El Humanismo Extremeño. II Jornadas 1997* (Trujillo: Real Academia de Extremadura 1998) 89-103; idem, "Lenguaje arcano y lenguaje del cuerpo: la hermenéutica bíblica de Arias Montano", *Sefarad* 62 (2002) 57-83; N. Fernández Marcos / E. Fernández Tejero, *Biblia y Humanismo*. Textos, talantes y controversias del siglo XVI español (Madrid: FUE 1997) 155-206; idem / eadem, "De 'Elteqeh a Hita. Arias Montano traductor de topónimos", in: E. Romero (ed.), *Judaísmo hispano. Estudios en memoria de José Luis Lacave Riaño* I-II (Madrid: CSIC 2002), I, 255-64; L. Gómez Canseco (ed.), *Anatomía del Humanismo. Benito Arias Montano 1598-1998* (Huelva: Servicio de Publicaciones de la Universidad de Huelva 1998); L. Gómez Canseco / M. A. Márquez (eds.), *Tractatus de figuris rhetoricis cum exemplis ex sacra scriptura petitis* (Huelva: Universidad de Huelva 1995); L. Gómez Canseco / V. Núñez Rivera, *Arias Montano y el Cantar de los cantares* (Kassel: Edition Reichenberger 2001); J. A. Jones, "Pedro de Valencia's defence of Arias Montano: a note on the Spanish Indexes of 1632, 1640 and 1667", *Bibliothèque d' Humanisme et Renaissance* 57 (1995) 83-88; idem, "The Censor censored: the case of Benito Arias Montano", *Romance Studies* 25 (1995) 19-29; B. Macías Rosendo, *La Biblia Políglota de Amberes en la correspondencia de Benito Arias Montano* (Huelva: Universidad de Huelva 1998); G. Morocho Gayo, "Trayectoria humanística de Benito Arias Montano I. Sus cuarenta primeros años (c. 1525/27-1567)", *El Humanismo Extremeño. II Jornadas 1997* (Trujillo: Real Academia de Extremadura 1998) 157-210; idem, "Trayectoria humanística de Benito Arias Montano II. Años de plenitud (1568-1598)", *El Humanismo Extremeño. III Jornadas 1998* (Trujillo: Real Academia de Extremadura 1999) 227-304; F. Pérez Castro / L. Voet, *La Biblia Políglota de Amberes* (Madrid: FUE 1973); B. Rekers, *Benito Arias Montano* (London / Leiden 1972); M. A. Sánchez Manzano, *Benito Arias Montano. Comentarios a los treinta y un primeros Salmos de David*. Estudio introductorio, edición crítica, versión española y notas; Vocabulario hebreo E. Fernández Tejero, 1-2 (León: Universidad de León 1999).

Benito Arias Montano (1527-98) studied in the universities of Sevilla and Alcalá where he graduated in Arts in 1549. From 1550 to 1552 he studied theology in Alcalá and began to study Oriental languages. One of his teachers was Cipriano de la Huerga. In 1560, he entered the order of Santiago in the convent of St. Marcos of León; he took part in the Council of Trent in 1562-1563, as an adviser to bishop Martín Pérez de Ayala. In 1566 he was appointed Royal Chaplain by Philip II;

---

[36] J. San Pedro García, "Principios exegéticos del Mtro. Fr. Luis de León", *Salmanticensis* IV (1957) 51-74.

[37] Asensio, Fray Luis de León (1985) 6 and 18.

in 1568 he was entrusted with the edition of the Antwerp Polyglot or Biblia Regia, and in 1571 he prepared an *Index expurgatorius librorum* which brought him much praise for his capacity of judgement and tolerance. Interestingly enough, his works were included in the Index of prohibited books drawn up by Juan de Pineda in 1607. Arias Montano was also active on the political scene of his time[38] as an adviser to the Duke of Alba, governor in the Netherlands, and on a diplomatic mission to Portugal for the King of Spain. He assembled a collection of books and manuscripts for the library of El Escorial and was its first librarian. He spent the last years of his life between the retreat of La Peña de Aracena and the convent of Santiago de Sevilla, where he was Prior until his death.[39]

The most important work of Arias Montano was the edition of the *Biblia sacra hebraice, chaldaice, graece, latine* (Biblia Polyglotta Regia) in eight volumes (Antwerp 1569–73), published by Plantin.[40] For the history of interpretation, of particular interest are the volume of *Apparatus*, in which he proposed in several treatises his philological and hermeneutic conception of the biblical text, and his commentaries, especially the following ones: *De optimo Imperio sive in librum Iosuae commentarium, De varia Republica sive commentaria in librum Iudicum, In XXXI Davidis psalmos priores commentaria, Commentaria in Isaiae Prophetae sermones, Commentaria in duodecim prophetas, Elucidationes in quatuor Evangelia…Quibus accedunt eiusdem Elucidationes in Acta Apostolorum,* and *Elucidationes in omnia sanctorum apostolorum scripta.*

He systematized his principles of biblical hermeneutics in three of the treatises of the *Apparatus: Communes et familiares hebraice linguae idiotismi,*[41] *Liber Ioseph sive de arcano sermone* and *Liber Ieremiae sive de actione.* The first is devoted to the description of the major semitisms or idiomatic features of the Hebrew language, with occasional references to comparisons with the figures of classical rhetoric; the second is a treatise on biblical semantics, while the third deals with exemplary gestures of the prophetic actions (*quasi corporis sermonem*).

Arias Montano was a fervent defender of the need to know biblical languages, and in particular Hebrew, for a correct understanding of Scripture. Hebrew was the primordial language, born with the creation of the world, the sacred language of paradise, taught by God to the first humans on Earth, and consequently, whose every detail is replete with meanings. That is how it is expressed in his Preface to the Biblia Regia, *De divinae scripturae dignitate, linguarum usu et Catholici regis consilio*, and in the *Praefatio ad Christianae doctrinae studiosos*, which introduced his edition of the Hebrew Bible with the interlineal version by Sanctes Pagninus, corrected by Arias Montano and his collaborators. Subsequently, Arias Montano did not hesitate to make use of the Hebrew text in his exegetical commentaries. He goes even further when trying to explain a passage from the book of Judges, where he affirms that it would be more worthwhile to learn the holy language than to try to disentangle the

---

[38] L. MORALES OLIVER, *Arias Montano y la política de Felipe II en Flandes* (Madrid: Volvntad 1927).

[39] Cf. Morocho Gayo, Trayectoria humanística, I-II (1997–99).

[40] Cf. Chap. 30 of this volume.

[41] E. Fernández Tejero / N. Fernández Marcos, De Hebraicis Idiotismis (1998).

interminable controversies surrounding the interpretations of the different versions.[42]

Arias Montano was more than a Hebraist, he was also one of the most accomplished Orientalists of his time. His knowledge of Hebrew was so deep, that he was able to include in the *Apparatus* a treatise in defence of its value and authenticity, and even to analyse specific masoretic features such as the description and listings of ketib/qere/yattir readings.[43] He was certainly at the same level as Reuchlin[44] and his disciples.

The treatise *De arcano sermone* deals with semantics, refers to the symbolic sense of the Hebrew Scriptures. It is the longest treatise of the *Apparatus*, 122 pages in-folio, and explanes several thousand passages of the Bible. To judge from the cover page, this treatise, together with the next one, *De Actione*, would make up a complete commentary on Scripture. The arcane meaning is not as accessible to everyone as is the literal; it embraces a whole range of nuances from the poetic and stylistic dimensions of Scripture to the symbolic, oneiric, mystical and secret or kabbalistic senses. For this reason *De arcano semone* is also known as the Liber Ioseph, after the biblical hero famous for his skill in interpretation of dreams. These meanings are hidden in enigmatic passages and prophecies of the Old Testament, in particular in Ezekiel, Jeremiah, Kings, and Revelation. Arias Montano envisaged several levels of comprehension, and he mentioned both an arcane and even more arcane (*magis arcanum*) significances, reserving the latter, more secret and profound, for the events and types of the Old Testament which point to the person of Jesus or the mysteries of the New Testament. Since he was also a partisan of the literal sense, he used this arcane sense to make the connections between the Old and New Testaments. The third treatise of the *Apparatus*, entitled *Liber Ieremiae sive de actione*, is dedicated to the rhetorical uses of action and gesture. Arias Montano was convinced of the importance of body language both in profane literature and the Holy books. Languages can be and are, in fact, different, but the language of gesture is more universal (*quasi corporis sermonem universo fere hominum generi communem*).[45] The treatise is named after Jeremiah, since no other book makes such wide use of the so-called "prophetic actions", or techniques of non-verbal communication, in which the image and the action play a fundamental role in the transmission of the message.[46]

A wealth of encyclopaedic knowledge (biblical commentaries, treatises, dictionaries, lexica and translations) was thus developed by Arias Montano in the context of the Biblia Regia and more especially in the volume of the *Apparatus*,

---

[42] *De varia Repvblica, sive commentaria in librvm Ivdicvm* (Antverpiae: Ex officina Plantiniana, Apud Viduam, & Ioannem Moretum 1592) 680: *quam quidem ob rem longe minore labore linguam sacram discere consulerem, quam de huiusmodi versionum varietate quotidie controversias ad invidiam vsque et inimicitias persequi.*

[43] E. FERNÁNDEZ TEJERO, "De Mazzoreth ratione atqve vsv", in: Fernández Marcos / Fernández Tejero, Biblia y humanismo (1997) 155–60; M. T. ORTEGA MONASTERIO, "Ariae Montani List of Qere-Ketiv-Yattir Readings", in: A. DOTAN (ed.), *Proceedings of the Ninth International Congress of the International Organization for Masoretic Studies* (SBLMS 7; 1992) 71–84.

[44] Cf. Chap. 11 of this volume.

[45] *Liber Ieremiae sive de actione, Praefatio*, a2b.

[46] N. FERNÁNDEZ MARCOS, "Lenguaje arcano y lenguaje del cuerpo", *Sef.* 62 (2002) 57–83.

where all the auxiliary sciences are treated: philology, hermeneutics, geography, history, archaeology, numismatics... Even his biblical commentaries, which are not included in the polyglot, constantly refer back to the *Apparatus*.

This Biblia Regia, however, was a source of problems and misfortunes: Arias Montano had to struggle in Rome for Papal approval, while in Spain, his Bible was a battle-ground for the two fractions that had already appeared during the trial of the Hebraists of Salamanca, in particular with reference to the novelties it included, compared to the Complutensian Polyglot. Not even the printer Plantin could defray all the costs the edition had caused, but he was more than compensated by the privilege conferred on him by the Crown for the printing of liturgical books (missals and breviaries).[47]

Although Arias Montano never went to prison, the trial inchoated against him for the denunciations against the Biblia Regia lasted until 1577, when finally, Juan de Mariana, who had been entrusted by the Inquisition to make a report, rendered a verdict favourable to him. We know of the principal accusations with regard to the Biblia Regia from a letter sent to Arias Montano by his friend Luis de Estrada, the Cistercian abbot of Santa María de Huerta.[48] These were the use in the Polyglot of Hebrew and Aramaic originals that were full of errors and corrupted, the inclusion of Pagninus's Latin version, the publication of an Aramaic version of the Prophets and Writings plagued with mistakes, the inclusion of the Syriac version of the New Testament, and, the correction of the Vulgate text of the New Testament. There were also certain complaints about some of the treatises in the *Apparatus*; the Papal commission was, in particular, suspicious of the treatise *De arcano sermone*, which it considered to be kabbalistic.

The polemic which surrounded the Biblia Regia continued after the death of Arias Montano in 1598, and is documented in two large dossiers in the National Library in Madrid.[49] Some of the works of Arias Montano were included in the Indices of prohibited books of 1607 (Rome) and 1612 (Madrid).[50] In the latter it was ordered that the annotation *caute legatur* appear next to the Chaldean paraphrase.

Arias Montano was undoubtedly the foremost Biblical and Oriental scholar in Spanish sixteenth century, a Spain which, at that time included all the territories ruled over by Philip II, that is, other parts of Europe and stretching out to the New World.

As we have seen, it was the literal sense that dominated the interpretation of the great biblical scholars in sixteenth-century Spain. The most frequent accusations made against the Hebraists of Salamanca to be found in the Inquisitorial trials were[51] the use of Hebrew and Jewish commentaries in their exegesis,

---

[47] Bécares Botas, Arias Montano y Plantino (1999) 98–99.

[48] E. FERNÁNDEZ TEJERO / N. FERNÁNDEZ MARCOS, "Luis de Estrada y Arias Montano", in eadem/idem, Biblia y Humanismo (1997) 193–206.

[49] E. FERNÁNDEZ TEJERO / N. FERNÁNDEZ MARCOS, "La polémica en torno a la Biblia Regia de Arias Montano", in eadem/idem, Biblia y Humanismo (1997) 229–38.

[50] Jones, Pedro de Valencia's Defence of Arias Montano (1987) 121–30.

[51] Cf. M. de la Pinta Llorente, Proceso criminal (1946) 244–50; idem, *Causa criminal contra el biblista Alonso Gudiel, Catedrático de la Universidad de Osuna* (Madrid: CSIC 1942); Alcalá, El

the preference for Vatable, Pagninus, and the Rabbis at the expense of the translation of the Vulgate and the interpretations of the Fathers and the doctors of the Church, who were accused by the Hebraists of arbitrary and formalistic use of the Scriptures, the depreciation of the authority and veracity of the Vulgate, affirming that it contained many errors and could have been better translated, the admission that Christian interpretations of the Old Testament and those of the Jews could have the same value though proposing different meanings, the criticism of the Septuagint translators, and the accusation that their knowledge of Hebrew was deficient,[52] the encouragement of translations into the vernacular languages, the affirmation that the allegorical sense of Scripture was not the only or principal one, the belief that scholastic doctrine was prejudicial to the understanding of the Holy Text, and that the Old Testament did not promise eternal life.

But, with the passing of time, these humanists began to regret the plenitude lost through their critical stance, which had led them to exclude other approaches to Scripture that they regarded as less scientific. They came to recognise the unifying role of hermeneutics which allowed them to apply the message of the Old Testament to the New: Valdés achieved this by moving from the consideration of Scripture as an alphabet to that of Scripture as a conversation. Cipriano de la Huerga, Luis de León and Arias Montano took the route of the arcane sense.[53]

3. The Sixteenth Century in Spain: Mysticism and Reformation

The Golden Age in Spain is full of writers who, from different points of view, considered Scripture to be their source of inspiration, the object of their commentaries and even their life-long preoccupation. Until now we have focused on the authors who really contributed to scientific knowledge in the history of biblical interpretation.[54]

Below, we set out as a guide two areas which are worthy of a more detailed study but go beyond the scope of this work: The Bible and mysticism, and the exegesis of the Spanish Reformers. Nor can we ignore the contribution brought to the exegesis in sixteenth-century Spain by the commentators who came after the Council of Trent; but these authors will also have their place in another chapter of this volume.[55]

---

proceso inquisitorial (1991) 3–24; Barrientos García, Escritos desde la cárcel (1991) 445–47; Miguélez Baños, Gaspar de Grajar II (2004) 553–65.

[52] Barthélemy, Critique textuelle 2 (1986) *37-*38.

[53] N. FERNÁNDEZ MARCOS, "La exégesis bíblica de Cipriano de la Huerga", in: Fernández Marcos / E. Fernández Tejero, Biblia y Humanismo (1997) 65–82.

[54] We know from personal experience that significant writers like Luis de León and Arias Montano, mentioned in the previous section, are practically unknown outside of Spain, even in the circles of prestigious biblical scholars and humanists.

[55] Cf. Chap. 25 of this volume.

3.1. Bible and Mysticism

Sources and Studies: K. REINHARDT, *Bibelkommentare spanischer Autoren (1500–1700)* I-II (Madrid: CSIC 1990–1999); II, 153–55 (Francisco de Osuna), II, 337–39 (Teresa de Jesús), I, 131–32 (Juan de la Cruz).

Other publications: M. ANDRÉS, *Historia de la mística de la edad de oro en España y América* (Madrid: BAC 1994); idem, *Los Recogidos. Nueva visión de la mística española* (Madrid: FUE 1976); P. M. CÁTEDRA e.a., *Místicos franciscanos españoles* (Madrid: BAC 1998); U. DOBHAN, "Teresa von Avila", TRE 33 (2002) 76–78; P. ELIA / M. J. MANCHO, *Cántico espiritual y poesía completa.* Edición, prólogo y notas, con un estudio preliminar de D. Ynduráin (Barcelona: Crítica 2002); A. HAMILTON, *Heresy and Mysticism in Sixteenth-century Spain: The Alumbrados* (Cambridge: James Clarke & Co 1992); A. HUERGA, *Historia de los Alumbrados* I-V (Madrid: FUE 1978–1994); S. LóPEZ SANTIDRIÁN, *Místicos franciscanos españoles*, II. *Tercer abecedario espiritual de Francisco de Osuna.* Introducción y edición preparada por ... (Madrid: BAC 1998); E. DE LA MADRE DE DIOS / O. STEGGINK, *Obras completas de santa Teresa de Jesús* (Madrid: BAC ⁹1997); M. J. MANCHO DUQUE (ed.), *Teresa de Jesús. Camino de perfección* (Madrid: Espasa Calpe 2000); T. O'REILLY, "El Cántico espiritual y la interpretación mística del Cantar de los Cantares", in: *Hermenéutica y mística: San Juan de la Cruz* (ed. J. A. Valente e.a.; Madrid: Tecnos 1995) 271–80; L. RUANO DE LA IGLESIA, *San Juan de la Cruz. Obras completas.* Edición crítica, notas y apéndices por... (Madrid: BAC ¹⁴1994); C. SWIETLICKI, *Spanish Christian Cabala. The work of Luis de León, Santa Teresa de Jesús and San Juan de la Cruz* (Columbia University of Missouri Press 1986); C. THOMPSON, *Canciones en la noche. Traducción de M. Balcells* (Madrid: Trotta 2002).

– *Francisco de Osuna* (c. 1492 – c. 1540) was born in Sevilla, where he later studied and in 1513 entered the Franciscan order. He studied philosophy in Torrelaguna and then theology for four years in the convent of Alcalá and in the university as an extra-mural student. He was a disciple of Pedro Ciruelo, Alfonso de Castro and Antonio de Nebrija. In 1523 he was sent to the hermitage of La Salceda (Guadalajara), the centre of affective mysticism. Between 1532 and 1536 he travelled through Europe.

Francisco de Osuna wrote several biblical commentaries, but his most significant work was the *Abecedario espiritual* (1527, with several subsequent editions); he even became the most widely read spiritual author in Spain between 1527 and 1559. He was the first to set out the way of devotion (*recogimiento*) and was the forerunner of the major traits of the Spanish mysticism in the Golden Age. Osuna defended the doctrine of *recogimiento* in the belief that it was possible to enter into communication with God,[56] in contrast to the doctrine of the *Alumbrados* who were originally devout laymen but became a heretical sect, criticized from various points of view because they did not formulate a definite system of religious thinking.

The *recogimiento* was more a method of prayer than a method of exegesis; it was a mystical theology which took the negative way rather than the positive one used by the scholastics. The exegetic methodology used in the work of Osuna is the symbolic one, but his recourse to the biblical quotations is constant.[57]

– *Teresa de Jesús* (1515–82) was born in Avila and died in Alba de Tormes (Salamanca). She entered the Carmelite Convent of the Incarnation of Avila in 1535. In her youth she read Osuna's

---

[56] On his life and works as well as his notion of *recogimiento*, cf. López Santidrián, Tercer abecedario espiritual (1998) 5–78.

[57] Some significant examples in López Sanchidrián, Tercer abecedario (1998) 168 (on Ezek 10:16), 169 (on Judg 15:5), 412 (on Judg 18:27–28).

Tercer abedecedario which was to have a considerable influence on her life: *holguéme mucho con él y determinéme a seguir aquel camino con todas mis fuerzas... tiniendo aquel libro por maestro.*[58] Despite many obstacles, some of which were created by her own order, she founded the first Reform Convent of the Discalced Carmelites of San José in 1562.

In this first Reform Convent Teresa de Jesús wrote *El camino de perfección*; she rewrote her *Vida* and composed the *Meditaciones sobre los Cantares*. Over a period of time she founded numerous convents throughout Spain; her reform reached the male branch of the Carmelites as well. Further, she wrote the *Moradas del castillo interior*. Her works are among the most representative of the Spanish school of mysticism, but from the point of view of biblical interpretation, we need only analyse her *Meditaciones sobre los Cantares* or *Conceptos del amor de Dios*.[59] Around 1580 she burned all the copies of this work, on the advice of her confessor; some, however, survived and were edited by her friend and spiritual adviser Jerónimo Gracián de la Madre de Dios, in Brussels in 1611. The *Meditaciones* are not a commentary on the Song of Songs, but personal, pious thoughts, destined for her nuns; they are based on the text of the Vulgate as it was used in the Liturgy of the Hours, according to the Roman Breviary. The commentaries only cover the Cant 1:1 – 2:5. Specialists in the work seem more interested in the fact that it is the first commentary of the Song of Songs written by a woman than in its exegetic value; from a philological point of view the work has nothing to offer. Her interpretation is purely spiritual; the text of the Song of Songs finds its meaning in an intimate relationship of the soul with God, in the path towards mystical union. Critics have underlined the audacity of her language, since she, in the first person, addresses God as her beloved and friend: *¿Qué mejor cosa podemos pedir que lo que yo os pido, Señor mío, que me deis esta paz con beso de vuestra boca?; ... que me beséis con el beso de la boca, que sin Vos ¿qué soy yo?*[60] The spiritual freedom with which she affronts the biblical text is that of the Renaissance, a freedom similar to that which we find in Juan de la Cruz, but the poetry of the latter attained a sublimity she did not equal. Teresa de Jesús was much more interested in the spiritual interpretation which she believed that God had destined for uneducated woman, than in the intellectual exegesis of the theologians.[61]

– *Juan de la Cruz* (1542–91) was born in Fontiveros (Avila) and died in Úbeda (Jaén). He studied Arts and Holy Sciences in Salamanca, and founded the first Discalced Carmelite convent in Duruelo (Avila), on the inspiration of Teresa de Jesús. Between 1572 and 1577 he was the confessor, vicar and reformer of the Convent of the Incarnation in Avila where Teresa de Jesús was the prioress. Due to conflicts with his superiors in the Calced Carmelite order, he was imprisoned in Toledo from November 1577 to August 1578; there he wrote *Las Noches*.

---

[58] "I was entranced by it and decided that it was the path to follow with all my might... with that book to guide me", *Obras completas*, 42–43.

[59] *Obras completas*, 421–68.

[60] "What better can I ask than that I plead thee, my Lord, That thou give me peace with a kiss from thy mouth?"; "...that thou give me a kiss from thy mouth, for without thee, What am I?", *Obras completas*, 428 and 453.

[61] K. REINHARDT, "Erfahrung und Theologie der Liebe Gottes. Die Auslegung des Hohenliedes bei Teresa von Avila und Jerónimo Gracián", in: M. SCHMIDT / F. DOMÍNGUEZ REBOIRAS (eds.), *Von der Suche nach Gott* (Stuttgart 1998) 109–29, esp. 120.

Other works of Juan de la Cruz were *Subida al monte Carmelo, Llama de amor viva,* and more especially, the *Cántico espiritual,* inspired by the Song of Songs. In the words of L. Ruano, he had "a very strong imagination, a sensitivity beyond bounds, a prodigious memory at all levels, a wonderful intuition and talent for synthesis, a creative genius, a perfect command of the Holy Scriptures, of their vocabulary and their subject matter, and an excellent knowledge of humanistic culture".[62] In Juan de la Cruz reality and spiritual experience of the Bible converge in a poetic sensitivity. In Salamanca, he was a pupil of Gaspar de Grajal, a remarkable exponent of the literal exegesis of Scripture. He would, at times, call on this literal sense to help demonstrate the spiritual sense, but most of his explanations did not contribute to clarify the literal meaning. His use of the Bible was pure adaptation and allegory; he was not an exegete, but rather a spiritual writer. He made great use of the characters of the Old Testament, frequently citing texts from Job, Jeremiah and the Psalms to describe the tribulations the soul has to undergo in its itinerary towards the union with God. He also took a broad view of the texts of the New Testament to give them an extreme and Christ-centred interpretation which would be in line with his spiritual doctrine.[63] The relationship between the Old and New Testaments presented no problem for Juan de la Cruz; the New Testament was the fulfilment of the Old, and the Scripture was a process centred on the historical Jesus.[64]

The exegesis of the mystical writers is quite different from that of the Hebraists mentioned in the previous section. Just one example to prove the point: the Song of Songs was the object of all sorts of commentaries, yet it was only with the translation and Spanish commentary by Luis de León that it managed to open the doors to a modern interpretation as a profane song (poetic philology). Juan de la Cruz converted it into a poetic mysticism. In her short and pious pages Teresa de Jesús gave it a free and spiritual interpretation that was a result of her own mystical experience.

The Hebraists based their philological and literal exegesis on the ancient languages. The mystical writers, on the other hand, had no interest in these languages, nor had they any knowledge of them; they used the allegorical and spiritual sense to express their spirituality. We have included them here because of the repercussions their works had and continued to have, even to this day.

---

[62] "Juan de la Cruz", in: DHEE II, 1246–48.

[63] Cf. J. Vilnet, *Bible et Mystique chez S. Jean de la Croix* (Paris: Desclée de Brouwer 1949); B. M. Ahern, "The Use of Scripture in the Spiritual Theology of St. John of the Cross", *CBQ* XIV (1952) 6–17; A. Colunga, "San Juan de la Cruz, intérprete de la Sagrada Escritura", *Ciencia Tomista* 63 (1942) 257–76.

[64] J. C. Nieto, "Mystical Theology and 'Salvation-History' in John of the Cross: Two conflicting Methods of Biblical Interpretation", *Bibliothèque d'Humanisme et Renaissance* 36 (1974) 17–32.

3.2. The Exegesis of the Spanish Reformers

Sources and studies: K. Reinhardt, *Bibelkommentare spanischer Autoren (1500–1700)* I–II (Madrid: CSIC 1990–99): II, 365–67 (Juan de Valdés); I, 144–46 (Francisco de Enzinas); II, 233–34 (Casiodoro de Reina); II, 374–75 (Cipriano de Valera).

Other publications: N. Fernández Marcos, "La Biblia de Ferrara y sus efectos en las traducciones bíblicas al español", in: N. Fernández Marcos / E. Fernández Tejero, *Biblia y Humanismo* (1997) 239–60; I. J. García Pinilla (ed.), *Francisco de Enzinas, Epistolario* (Geneva: Droz 1995); C. Gilly, *Spanien und der Basler Buchdruck bis 1600* (Basel / Frankfurt am Main: Helbing & Lichtenhahn 1985) 274–441; P. J. Hauben, *Three Spanish Heretics and the Reformation* (Geneva: Droz 1967); A. G. Kinder, *Spanish Protestants and Reformers in the Sixteenth Century* (London 1983), Supplement 1 (London 1995); A. Márquez, "Reforma protestante (Período clásico)", DHEE III, 2059–63; J. C. Nieto, *El Renacimiento y la otra España. Visión cultural socioespiritual* (Geneva: Droz 1997).

The subject of the Reformation in Spain has been widely covered in the classical works of B. B. Wiffen and L. de Usoz y Río, *Reformistas Antiguos Españoles*,[65] and in the later work by E. Boehmer, *Bibliotheca Wiffeniana: Spanish Reformers of Two Centuries from 1520.*[66] It may be appropriate to devote some lines to these Reformers, not only for their importance as exegetes but also for the fact that any so-called dissidents should not be historiographically ignored, whatever the dominant ideology may be. They all published their translations and their biblical commentaries outside the Iberian Peninsula for fear of the Spanish Inquisition.

– *Juan de Valdés* (c. 1505–41) came from a family of converts. He was in Rome in 1531 at the court of Pope Clement VII, in the service of Charles V. He soon came into contact with the theses of Luther and became familiar with the thinking of the Alumbrados and the ideas of Erasmus and the Erasmians. He was the object of two trials before the Inquisitors and certain of his disciples were considered to be heterodox, the orthodoxy of some of his writings is still a subject of controversy. His major works were the *Diálogo de la Lengua* (c. 1535) and the *Alfabeto cristiano* (1536). From the point of view of exegesis, his *Diálogo de doctrina christiana* (1529) which, in the final part, includes his *Traducción de los capítulos quinto, sexto y sétimo del evangelio de sant Matheo de griego en nuestro romance castellano*, is of special interest, as are also *El Salterio traducido del hebreo en romance castellano* and the *Comentario a los Salmos* (Psalms 1–41), both published in 1537.[67] His translation of the Psalms was very literal, to the point that he decided to add some words of his own: *á fin que la letra lleve más lustre, vaya más clara y más sabrosa*;[68] he wrote them in red ink so that they could not be confused with the original. The purpose of his exegesis was to capture and understand the spirit and feelings that were at work in the redaction of the Hebrew originals. The same can be said for his com-

---

[65] 1–20 (London / San Sebastián / Madrid 1848–1870).

[66] 1–3 (Strassburg: Karl Trubner 1874; repr. New York: Burt Franklin 1962).

[67] Cf. D. Ricart, *Juan de Valdés. Diálogo de Doctrina Cristiana y El Salterio traducido del hebreo en romance castellano* (México: Universidad Nacional Autónoma 1964).

[68] Ibid. 135: "in order to give a bit more lustre to the words, to make them clearer and more attractive".

mentaries on the New Testament[69] in relation to the Greek text. He was the first to write biblical commentaries in Castillian; and despite his attempt to be as faithful as possible to the original languages, his style is still unequalled in modern translations. His version of the Psalms is one of the jewels of Spanish literature. His exegesis was not limited to the literal sense, to Scripture as an alphabet, which might satisfy the novices; the perfect Christian has to search for the spiritual sense that makes the Bible the path towards direct conversation with God.[70] Some critics consider his commentaries to be devotional or pious literature; but one has to be mindful of Valdés's view: "devotion and piety were not divorced from learned scholarship, objectivity in method, or honest and sincere pursuit of truth, and that he did not attempt to fill the gaps with pious explanations. These are qualities which are not always present in the so-called devotional literature".[71]

There were also other important Spanish translators, like *Francisco de Enzinas* (c. 1520–52), who translated the New Testament into Castillian in 1543, and *Juan Pérez de Pineda* (? --1566), who also translated the New Testament, published in 1556. It is said that Francisco de Enzinas had the intention of translating the whole Bible into Castillian,[72] but his early death prevented him from doing so.

– *Casiodoro de Reina* (c. 1520–94) was to complete this task. He was the leading representative of the circle of Sevillian Reformers that included Antonio del Corro and Cipriano de Valera, monks in the Hieronymite monastery of San Isidro del Campo, but also of other ecclesiastics such as the priest and preacher of the Cathedral of Sevilla, Constantino Ponce de la Fuente, or Juan Gil (Egidio), high canon in the same cathedral.[73]

Casiodoro de Reina was of Morisco origin, had studied at the University of Sevilla and entered the Hieronymite order. Together with several members of his order, who also were in favour of the Reform, he moved to Geneva in 1557 to flee the Inquisition. There he adopted Calvinism. Reina next moved to Frankfurt and later to London where he was pastor of a small Spanish community of Reformers.

His most important work is the full translation of the Bible into Castillian, published in Basel in 1569, known as *La Biblia del Oso*, after his ex-libris. This Bible was later revised by Cipriano de Valera and published in Amsterdam in 1602. Through its successive revisions it became the official Bible of the Spanish-speaking Protestants, and has remained so until this day.[74] From the: *Amonestacion del interprete de los sacros libros al lector ...*, we know some of the

---

[69] *El evangelio según San Mateo* (1539); *Comentario... sobre la epístola de San Pablo a los Romanos...* (1538–39); *Comentario... sobre la primera epístola de San Pablo apóstol a los Corinthios...* (1538–39).

[70] J. C. Nieto, *Juan de Valdes and the Origins of the Spanish and Italian Reformation* (Geneva: Droz 1970) 239–45.

[71] Idem, Juan de Valdes (1970) 195.

[72] Cf. Gilly, Spanien und der Basler Buchdruck (1985) 326–53.

[73] On Antonio del Corro cf. Reinhardt, Bibelkommentare I (1990) 127–29, and Hauben, Three Spanish heretics (1967) 1–82; on Valera cf. Reinhardt, Bibelkommentare II (1999) 374–75; on Ponce de la Fuente, ibid., 200–02; on Juan Gil cf. Reinhardt, Bibelkommentare I (1990) 183–84.

[74] Reina's Bible was edited in a facsimile edition in 1986, published by the Sociedades Bíblicas Unidas; a facsimile edition of Valera's Bible was published in 1990.

principles that Casiodoro de Reina followed in his version. He consulted the Latin translation of the Vulgate, but also referred to the Hebrew text whenever possible: *lo qual hezimos siguiendo comunmente la translacion de Santes Pagninus, que al voto de todos los doctos en la lengua Hebraica es tenida por la mas pura que hasta aora ay.*[75] When there were differences in the translations he noted, in the margin, the interpretations he could not include in the text. He also had recourse to the *Biblia de Ferrara* (1553),[76] "to give us the natural and original meaning of the Hebrew words as well as the differences in the tenses of the verbs as they were in the text itself".

De Reina's search for the literal meaning is reflected in his method, as is his interest in bringing together all the possible interpretations of the most difficult passages. Like Juan de Valdés, he made a point of distinguishing his explanatory additions from the original text, even in the typography, "because our additions are not additions to the text, but free commentaries, which will only have a value if they are in conformity with the text". He consulted "most of the extant versions and commentaries". There is still no detailed study of his methodology or of the sources he used. His literal translation, his notes in the margins and final annotations on the most difficult passages are his most important contribution to the exegesis of the Bible.

4. A Retrospective View

The first Spanish humanists, the precursors of the Golden Age, built their exegesis on two pillars which were particular to the Iberian Peninsula: the Jewish tradition, and the so-called *Biblias romanceadas*, many of which were translations from the Hebrew into the vernacular. Those who wrote the commentaries of that period had some knowledge of Hebrew and the rabbinic exegesis.

But when we arrive in the sixteenth century, the fundamental factors that determined the intellectual talent of the principal authors and their form of exegesis were philology and the return to the original texts. The polyglot Bibles with their editions of texts in different ancient languages, interlineal versions, prologues and treatises with grammars and lexica included are the best examples of these tendencies. From an exegetical point of view, the authors who based their interpretation on philology gave priority to the literal sense; as a result, they became aware of the failings of the Vulgate as a translation, which put them at odds with the Spanish Inquisition.

Together with this philological exegesis, the strength of the mystical movements should not be ignored. But these writers, for the most part, did not know the original texts and their works moved towards a spiritual interpretation of the Bible, and in their writings they were trying to reach God through

---

[75] "Thus we did, following the translation of Sanctes Pagninus, who in the opinion of Hebrew scholars is considered to be the most pure that exists", Reina's Bible, *Amonestacion... al lector.*

[76] I. M. Hassán (ed.), with the collaboration of A. Berenguer Amador, *Introducción a la Biblia de Ferrara. Actas del simposio internacional.* Sevilla, November 1991 (Madrid: Siruela 1994); facsimile edition, introduction and notes by I. M. Hassán and U. Macías Kapón (Madrid 1992).

different ways of prayer. Their exegesis had nothing of the scientific, nor did they pretend that it had; but their spiritual works made a great impression on the time, an influence which has lasted up to the present day; for that reason Teresa de Jesús and Juan de la Cruz are far better known in academic circles today than Benito Arias Montano.

The Spanish Reformers followed the original texts to the letter, but they also appreciated the Spirit which helped to interpret that letter. Thanks to the spiritual sense, authors like Juan de Valdés, could bring together the Old and New Testaments and understand Scripture as a conversation with God. For a complete overview of the sixteenth century in Spain, the writers of the Counter-Reformation should also be included.[77] Although their knowledge of philology was not lacking, they preferred to retain the ecclesiastical orthodoxy that placed the Vulgate at the centre of their biblical commentaries.

Throughout the sixteenth century in Spain, we find both a multiple and varied approach to exegesis, a philological one, on the one hand, and a mystical and spiritual one, on the other. Methodologies stood side by side, from the scientific analysis of texts in the different ancient languages to the most sublime biblical spirituality. In contrast to the authentic philologists of the century (above all, Arias Montano), the authors who used other forms of interpretation were to turn their writings towards a more personal spirituality and a direct relationship with God. But whether they were in one field or another, they all contributed with their works to the fact that the sixteenth century is rightly known as the Golden Age of Spanish exegesis.

---

[77] Cf. Chap. 25 of this volume.

CHAPTER ELEVEN

Early Christian Hebraists

By Sophie Kessler Mesguich, Paris

Sources: J. Böschenstain: *Hebraicae Grammaticae Institutiones* (Wittenberg: J. Grünenberg 1518).
– W. F. Capito: *Hebraicarum Institutionum libri duo* (Basel: Froben 1518). – E. Levita / Ashkenazi:
Sefer ha-Baḥur (Rome 1518); *Sefer ha-Harkava* (Rome 1518); *Pirqei Eliyahu* (Pesaro: G. Soncino
1520); *Sefer Massoreth ha-Massoreth* (Venice: D. Bomberg s. a. [1538]; ed. Chr. Ginsburg; London
1867); *Tishbi* (Isny: P. Fagius 1541); *Meturgeman* (Isny: P. Fagius 1541); *Shemot Devarim* (Isny: P.
Fagius 1542); (ed.), *Diqduqim* (Venice: D. Bomberg 1546). – S. Münster: (tr. and ed.) *Sefer ha-
Diqduq. Grammatica hebraea absolutissima Eliae Levitae Germani... per S. Munsterum donata*
(Basel: Froben 1525); *Qiṣur ha-Diqduq. Compendium Hebraicae Grammaticae...* (Basel: Froben
1527); *Melekhet ha-Diqduq ha-Shalem, Opus grammaticum consummatum...* (Basel: H. Petrus
1542); *Dictionarium hebraicum* (Basel: Froben & Episcopius 1535). – *Shillush Leshonot, Dictionarium trilingue* (Basel: H. Petrus 1530); (ed.), *Ioannis Reuchlini Phorcensis Lexicon hebraicum...*
(Basel: H. Petrus 1537); *Messias Christianorum et Iudaeorum: Hebraicè & Latinè...* (Basel: H. Petrus 1539). – C. Pellican: *De modo legendi et intelligendi Hebraeum*, in: G. Reisch, *Margarita philosophica* (Strasburg 1504); *Das Chronikon des Konrad Pellikan* (ed. B. Riggenbach; Basel 1877). – J.
Reuchlin: *Sämtliche Werke* 1–12 (ed. K. Kahlenberg / H. Scheible / H. Greive; Berlin: de Gruyter
1981-); *Sämtliche Werke* I,1– (ed. W.-W. Ehlers e.a.; Stuttgart: Frommann-Holzboog 1996-); *De
Verbo mirifico* (Basel: J. Amerbach 1494; new edn. with Germ. tr. in: *Sämtliche Werke* I,1; ed. Ehlers; 1996); *De arte cabalistica* (Haguenau: Th. Anshelm 1517; facs. edn., with French tr., *La Kab-
bale*; tr. F. Secret; Milan: Archè 1995); *De rudimentis hebraicis* [abbr. *RH*] (Pforzheim: Th. Anshelm 1506; repr. Hildesheim: Olms 1974); *Johannes Reuchlins Briefwechsel* (ed. L. Geiger; Tübingen 1875; repr. Hildesheim: Olms 1962); *Briefwechsel* I: *1477-1505* (ed. S. Rhein / M. Dall'Asta /
G. Dörner; Stuttgart: Frommann-Holzboog 1999); *De accentibus et orthographia linguae hebraicae*
(Haguenau: Th. Anshelm 1518).

Bibliographies: J. Benzing, *Bibliographie der Schriften Johannes Reuchlins im 15. und. 16. Jahrhundert* (Bad Bocklet: W. Krieg 1955); K. H. Burmeister, *Sebastian Münster, eine Bibliographie mit 22
Abbildungen* (Wiesbaden: G. Pressler 1964); idem, Art."Münster, Sebastian (1488–1552)", TRE
23 (1994) 407–09; M. Steinschneider, *Bibliographisches Handbuch über die theoretische und prak-
tische Literatur für hebräische Sprachkunde* (Leipzig 1859; repr. Hildesheim: Olms 1976).

Studies: S. W. Baron, *A Social and Religious History of the Jews* XIII. *Inquisition, Renaissance,
and Reformation* (New York / Philadelphia: Columbia UP 1969); J. L. Blau, *The Christian Interpretation of the Cabala in the Renaissance* (New York: Columbia UP 1944); K. H. Burmeister, *Sebastian Münster. Versuch eines biographischen Gesamtbildes* (Basler Beiträge zur Geschichtswissenschaft 91; Basel: Helbing / Lichtenhahn 1963, ²1969); S. Burnett, "Reassessing the Basel-Wittenberg Conflict: Dimensions of the Reformation-Era Discussion of Hebrew Scholarship", in:
Hebraica Veritas? Christian Hebraists and the Study of Judaism in Early Modern Europe (ed. A. D.
Coudert / J. S. Shoulson; Philadelphia: University of Pennsylvania Press 2004) 181–201; K.
Christ, "Die Bibliothek Reuchlins in Pforzheim", *Zentralblatt für Bibliothekswesen*, Suppl. no. 52
(Leipzig 1924) 1–96; J. Friedman, *The Most Ancient Testimony: Sixteenth Century Christian-Hebraica in the Age of Renaissance Nostalgia* (Athens, OH: Ohio UP c. 1983); L. Geiger, *Johann Reu-
chlin, sein Leben und seine Werke* (Nieuwkoop: B. de Graaf 1964); idem, *Das Studium der Hebräischen Sprache in Deutschland vom Ende des XV. bis zur Mitte des XVI. Jahrhunderts* (Breslau:
Schletter 1870); H. Greive, "Die hebräische Grammatik Johannes Reuchlins: *De rudimentis hebraicis*", *ZAW* 90 (1978) 395–409; V. Hantzsch, *Sebastian Münster. Leben, Werk, wissenschaftliche Be-*

deutung (ASGW.PH 18,3; Leipzig: Teubner 1898; repr. 1965); S. KESSLER MESGUICH, "Grammaires de l'hébreu", *Corpus représentatif des grammaires et des traditions linguistiques* 2 (Hors-série n° 3 *d'Histoire Epistémologie Langage*; ed. B. Colombat; Paris 2000) 185–210; L. KUKENHEIM, *Contributions à l'histoire de la grammaire grecque, latine et hébraïque à l'époque de la Renaissance* (Leiden: Brill 1951); W. MAURER, "Reuchlin und das Judentum", *Kirche und Geschichte* 2 (Göttingen: Vandenhoeck & Ruprecht 1970) 333–46; E. NESTLE, "Nigri, Böhm und Pellikan", *Marginalien und Materialien* (Tübingen 1893) 1–35; H. A. OBERMAN, "Three Sixteenth-Century Attitudes to Judaism: Reuchlin, Erasmus and Luther", *Jewish Thought in the Sixteenth Century* (ed. B. D. Coperman; Cambridge, MA: Harvard UP 1983) 326–64; J. H. OVERFIELD, "A new look at the Reuchlin affair", *Studies in Medieval and Renaissance History* VIII (1971) 167–207; H. PETERSE, *Jacobus Hoogstraeten gegen Johannes Reuchlin, ein Beitrag zur Geschichte des Antijudaismus im 16. Jahrhundert* (Mainz: Philipp von Zabern 1995); J. PRIJS, *Die Basler hebräischen Drucke (1492-1866)* (Olten / Freiburg: Graf 1964); S. RAEDER, "Johannes Reuchlin", in: *Gestalten der Kirchengeschichte* (ed. M. Greschat), 5. *Die Reformationszeit* I (Stuttgart 1981) 33–51; E. I. J. ROSENTHAL, "Sebastian Münster's Knowledge and Use of Jewish Exegesis", *Essays in Honor of J. H. Hertz* (ed. I. Epstein e.a.; London: Goldston 1943) 351–69; H. RUPPRICH, "Johannes Reuchlin und seine Bedeutung im europäischen Humanismus", *Johannes Reuchlin 1455-1522. Festgabe seiner Vaterstadt Pforzheim zur 500. Wiederkehr seines Geburtstages* (ed. M. Krebs; Pforzheim 1955) 10–34; F. SECRET, *Les Kabbalistes chrétiens de la Renaissance* (Paris: Dunod 1964; repr. Milan: Archè 1985); E. SILBERSTEIN, *Conrad Pellicanus, ein Beitrag zur Studiums der hebräischen Sprache in der ersten Hälfte des XVI. Jahrhunderts* (Diss. Univ. Erlangen 1900); L. W. SPITZ, "Reuchlin, Pythagoras reborn", *The Religious Renaissance of the German Humanists* (Cambridge, MA: Harvard UP 1963) 61–80; B. WALDE, *Christliche Hebraisten Deutschlands am Ausgang des Mittelalters* (Münster 1916); G. E. WEIL, *Elie Lévita, humaniste et massorète (1469-1549)* (Leiden: Brill 1963); T. WILLI, "Christliche Hebraistik aus jüdischen Quellen. Beobachtungen zu den Anfängen einer christlichen Hebraistik", in: G. VELTRI (ed.), *Gottes Sprache in der philologischen Werkstatt. Hebraistik vom 15. bis zum 19. Jahrhundert* (Studies in European Judaism 11; Leiden: Brill 2004) 25–48; CH. WIRSZUBSKI, *Pico della Mirandola's Encounter with Jewish Mysticism* (Jerusalem: The Israel Academy of Sciences and Humanities 1989); idem, *Three studies in Christian Kabbala* (Jerusalem: Bialik Institute 1975); C. ZÜRCHER, *Konrad Pellikans Wirken in Zurich 1526-1556* (Zürich: Theol. Verlag 1975).

Special abbreviation:
RH = Johannes Reuchlin, *De rudimentis hebraicis*

In J. FRIEDMAN's definition, Christian Hebraism was "the use of Hebrew, rabbinic or Cabbalistic sources for Christian religious purposes".[1] In fact, there had been prominent Christian seekers of the *Hebraica veritas* throughout the Middle Ages,[2] but they were individuals who had some knowledge of Hebrew and stood out from their contemporaries who disliked Jews and, as a result, distrusted their language. Despite the general mistrust of the Jews, by the end of the fifteenth and throughout the sixteenth century, a knowledge of their language and a familiarity with their classical sources became respected elements in the new intellectual scene. Some persons wanted to read the Old Testament in its original language for any of several reasons; others sought techniques in the Jewish medieval commentators to create a more modern biblical exegesis, while others thought that they could discover in the Jews' own texts arguments to support the truth of the Christian faith.[3] Still others sought to give

---

[1] Friedman, The Most Ancient Testimony (1983) 1.

[2] Cf. HBOT I/2 (2000), Chapters 43 and 37; and see H. HAILPERIN, *Rashi and the Christian scholars* (Pittsburgh: University of Pittsburgh Press 1963), and B. SMALLEY, *The Study of the Bible in the Middle Ages* (Oxford: Blackwell 1952, rev. edn. 1983).

[3] The same kind of argument was used by Christian Arabists of Reuchlin's time, such as N. Clénard (1495–1543) who thought that Arabic learning could lead to a "pacific crusade" against Islam.

grammatical descriptions of all the languages, classical and vernacular, including Hebrew, in terms of the Greco-Latin model.[4]

This paper will deal with the main features of the first works published by Christian scholars for a Christian public, from Johannes Reuchlin (1455–1522) and Conrad Pellican (1478–1556) to Sebastian Münster (1489–1552): grammars, lexicons, Bible commentaries and expositions of Kabbalah, all using Hebrew or explaining it. In addition, the work of the influential Jewish scholar Eliyahu (Elias) Levita / Ashkenazi (1469–1549), who taught a lot of Christian Hebraists, will be paid due attention.

1. Johannes Reuchlin

1.1. Reuchlin's Life and Works

The life of Johannes Reuchlin (1455–1522) has been well-known since LUDWIG GEIGER published a detailed biography which has been enriched by subsequent studies on specific aspects of his career. Those studies have added, as might be expected, much information about Reuchlin's career, but none of them has yet superseded GEIGER's work. All biographical sketches of Reuchlin, including this one, are thus necessarily based upon his research.

Johannes Reuchlin, who, in his books and correspondence, sometimes hellenized his name to Capnion, i.e., 'smoke', was born in Pforzheim, Baden, 22 February 1455. Both his parents were natives of that city, which was at the time the second residence of the Margrave of Baden. Reuchlin's father was a steward of the local Dominican monastery. Throughout his life, Reuchlin displayed an attachment to his native town, signing his books and most of his letters *Iohannis Reuchlin Phorcensis*, 'of Pforzheim'. At the age of fifteen he matriculated at Freiburg University; in 1473, he interrupted his study there to accompany the margrave's third son for a year of study in Paris where he studied the Medieval cursus, rhetoric under Guillaume Tardif (1440–92) and Robert Gaguin (c. 1434–1501), and grammar under the 'realist', Johann Heynlin (Johannes a Lapide, c. 1430–96);[5] and he made the acquaintance of some of the early French humanists including his future printer, Johann Amerbach (c. 1440–1513), and the philosopher Rudolf Agricola (1444–85), a disciple of Nicholas of Cusa (1401–64) whose neoplatonic philosophy would have a lasting influence upon Reuchlin.[6] We know from a letter to J. Lefèvre d'Étaples that Reuchlin began to learn Greek in Paris in 1473.[7] While he could surely have continued his studies in Freiburg, Paris was the city in Northern Europe where Renaissance trends and aspirations were already visible in 1473, and where a desire to learn ancient languages could be satisfied, in sum, a city where a gifted and ambitious student could participate in these movements.

From 1474 to 1477 Reuchlin studied in Basel where, in 1477, he obtained the degree of *magister artium*, took Greek lessons from Andronicus Contoblakas and, at Amerbach's request, wrote his first book, a Latin dictionary, *Vocabularius Breviloquus*, which was published anonymously in 1478 and reprinted more than twenty times before 1504. Back in Paris, he improved his Greek un-

---

[4] For that last point, see S. AUROUX, *Histoire des idées linguistiques* II (Bruxelles: Mardaga 1989), esp. the Introduction.

[5] Reuchlins Briefwechsel (1875) 199.

[6] Reuchlin possessed manuscript copies of his works; see K. PREISENDANZ, "Die Bibliothek Johannes Reuchlins", in: Johannes Reuchlin 1455–1522 (1955) 42.

[7] Reuchlins Briefwechsel (1875) 199: *[…] graeca elementa […] quae ipse ego quondam in vestra Gallia ex discipulis Gregorii Tiphernatis adulescens Parisii acceperam anno Domini 1473.*

der Georgius Hermonymus of Sparta. Having to choose a career, he decided to study civil law at Orleans and then in Poitiers. In July 1481 he received the diploma of a licentiate in Roman law and returned to Germany to matriculate in Tübingen University which had recently been founded by Count Eberhard V of Württemberg. Though still a young university, it counted such eminent men among its professors as the theologian Conrad Summerhart (d. 1502); though his knowledge of Hebrew was scanty, Summerhart would influence the development of Hebrew learning in Germany both by lending his copy of Peter Nigri's *Stella Messiae* (1475), which contained a few Hebrew texts and their transliteration and translation, to the young Conrad Pellican who was trying to decipher Hebrew without a teacher, and by introducing him to Reuchlin who had already learnt to read Hebrew.[8]

Reuchlin first took active interest in the Hebrew language in the 1480s but, for lack of competent Christian teachers, it was quite difficult for him, as it would still be for Pellican a few years later, to learn Hebrew in Germany. Whoever really wanted to learn Hebrew had to learn it by himself or had to turn to Jews or Jewish converts. Contrary to his own testimony,[9] Reuchlin did not begin his study in 1492 with the Emperor's personal physician, Jacob Yehiel Loans, as is often claimed. A note he added to his copy of Menaḥem ben Saruq's *Maḥberet*, a dictionary of biblical Hebrew, shows that he had been introduced to Hebrew six years earlier by an otherwise unknown *melammed*, a teacher of children, named Calman.[10]

Thanks to his talent for speaking and writing Latin, Reuchlin entered the service of Count Eberhard as a secretary and interpreter and remained in his service until the count's death in 1496. Reuchlin's duties took him to Italy twice. This is of more than anecdotal interest since at the end of the fifteenth century, it was much easier to find Hebrew or Greek teachers, manuscripts and printed books in Italy than in the Northern countries from which the Jews had been banished and to which few refugee scholars from Byzantium were attracted; so it is not surprising that Reuchlin bought almost all his books in Italy.[11] During his first journey to Florence and Rome (1482) he had the opportunity of hearing the Greek lectures of Johannes Argyropulos, and of meeting Pope Sixtus IV who had commissioned Latin translations of certain kabbalistic works. Even more fruitful for Reuchlin's intellectual development was his second journey (1490), when he became acquainted with the Platonists, Marsilio Ficino (1433–99)[12] and Pico della Mirandola (1463–94) who introduced him to the kabbalistic literature. A successful diplomatic mission to the imperial court in Linz (1492) had two happy outcomes: Reuchlin was ennobled by Emperor Frederick III[13] with the title of Count Palatine, and he made further progress in his Hebrew studies in Linz with Loans, whose learning and open-mindedness he would praise on several occasions.[14] As a result of

---

[8] Walde, Christliche Hebraisten (1916) 156.

[9] In the Preface of *RH*, 3: *Is me (...) primus edocuit.*

[10] See Walde, Christliche Hebraisten (1916) 36: *Calman Judaeus, Elementarius praeceptor – Joannis Reuchlin phorcensis In alphabetho hebraico, haec Vocabula scripsit eidem suo discipulo mercede conductus. Anno 1486* ("Calman the Jew, elementary teacher [who taught] J. Reuchlin from Pforzheim the Hebrew alphabet, made a copy of this Lexicon for his student in exchange for a fee, in the year 1486").

[11] Except for 30 titles printed in Spain, before the expulsion of the Jews in 1492, and 24 in Portugal, before the forced baptisms of 1498, all Hebrew incunabula were printed in Italy and surely more easily purchased there than in France or Germany.

[12] "Who brought Greece into Latium", *De arte cabalistica*, fol. A.

[13] In 1492, Frederick III offered Reuchlin a twelfth-century manuscript containing the entire Hebrew Bible, with the Onqelos Targum and masoretic notes, which is now known as the Codex Reuchlinianus. Cf. Christ, Bibliothek (1924) 37.

[14] He calls him *doctus*, *literatus* and *humanissimus*; see Geiger, Johann Reuchlin (1964) 106, n. 3.

his studies in Italy and in Linz, Reuchlin was able to compose and publish 1494 a work of kabbalistic inspiration, *De Verbo mirifico* ("the wonder-working word").[15]

After Count Eberhard's death, Reuchlin was forced to leave Stuttgart and take up residence in Heidelberg. During this exile he found himself in contact with the circle of intellectuals around Johann von Dalberg, Bishop of Worms, that included Conrad Leontorius and Jacob Wimpfeling.[16] There Reuchlin wrote two Latin comedies: *Sergius vel capita capitis*, a satire against monastic ignorance and stubborness (1496, but only printed in 1504), and *Scaenica progymnasmata*[17] (1498, and subsequently reprinted many times).

A diplomatic mission for the Elector Palatine in 1498 brought Reuchlin to Italy for a third and last time. There he pursued his Hebrew studies with the Jewish physician and eminent Bible commentator, Ovadiah Sforno (c. 1470 – c. 1550), and bought more books.[18] When he returned to Germany in 1500 the political situation in Stuttgart had once more become favorable to him, and in 1502 he was appointed to a three-member tribunal created by the Swabian League; he fulfilled his juridical functions in that tribunal until 1512, when he retired to live near Stuttgart. He seems to have married a second time in those years – a first marriage had been contracted around 1490 – but this wife died childless a few years later.

This last period of Reuchlin's life was very productive. In 1506 he published his Hebrew grammar, *De rudimentis hebraicis*; in 1517 a major kabbalistic work, *De arte cabalistica*; in 1518 a treatise on Hebrew grammar and on the cantillations of the Bible, *De accentibus et orthographia linguae hebraicae*, and in 1529 an annotated translation of the seven penitential Psalms. Unfortunately much of his energy during this period had to be dissipated in a controversy with a converted Jew, Johannes Pfefferkorn, concerning the advisability of burning of Jewish books and especially the Talmud.

In 1519, a conflict between the Swabian League and Duke Ulrich of Württemberg forced Reuchlin to move to Ingolstadt, where the University engaged him to teach Greek and Hebrew. His lessons achieved great success, attracting more than three hundred students. Fear of contagion when an epidemic struck Ingolstadt in 1521 led him to move to Tübingen where he continued teaching Greek and Hebrew. He died 30 June 1522.

1.2. Hebrew Philology

For Reuchlin, Hebrew knowledge was not only essential for a correct understanding of the Old Testament, but also provided access to God's secrets, since Hebrew was the very language of God, as he says: "The Word has been the interface between God and man, as we read in the Pentateuch, but not any

---

[15] It was reprinted five times in the sixteenth century and appears, with a German translation, in: Sämtliche Werke I,1 (1996).

[16] A letter from Leontorius to Reuchlin, a glowing account of *De Verbo mirifico* and its author, who is qualified as "most eloquent and most skillful in the three languages" (*in laudem disertissimi atque trium linguarum peritissimi viri Ioannis Reuchlin Phorcensis*), is printed at the beginning of that work. Leontorius even claims that Reuchlin mastered Hebrew literature more thoroughly than the Jews themselves, surely a polite exaggeration, since Reuchlin's knowledge was not yet very thorough. This may be confirmed by a comparison of *De Verbo mirifico* with the later *De arte cabalistica*, by which Reuchlin's progress in Hebrew is evident.

[17] Also called *Henno*. Some elements in that play might have been borrowed from the French *Farce de Maître Pathelin* (1485).

[18] For instance, he wrote inside his exemplar of David Qimhi's *Sefer ha-Shorashim* (Naples: Soncino 1491): "I, Johann Reuchlin of Pforzheim, Doctor of Laws, bought this book [...] in 1498"; cf. Christ, Bibliothek (1924) 40 f.

word, only the Hebrew word, by which God wanted to reveal His secrets to the mortals".[19] That this public declaration was his private opinion as well is confirmed by his correspondence with Agricola.[20]

When Reuchlin came to compose his dictionary of Hebrew, contained in *De rudimentis hebraicis* (1506), he did not take as his model the tenth-century's *Mahberet* of Menahem ben Saruq, from which he himself had studied, but rather the *Sefer ha-Shorashim*, the lexical part of the *Mikhlol*, composed by David Qimhi (c. 1160 – c. 1235) in the early thirteenth century.[21] Because the *Mikhlol* was more of a synthesis than an original work – it drew heavily upon Qimhi's eleventh-century predecessors – it demonstrates a pedagogical preoccupation which may be seen, for instance, in his arrangement of the vowel signs and the systematic presentation of verbal morphology, and it became extremely popular in Jewish circles and subsequently, in the Latin translation by Sanctes Pagninus (Lyon 1526; Paris 1549), also among Christians trying to learn Hebrew without Jewish masters. Reuchlin also used the shorter and easier manual of Hebrew grammar composed at the end of the twelfth century by David Qimhi's brother, Moses, *Mahalakh Shevilei ha-Da'at*, "A walk along the paths of learning", which was the first grammar to present the verb conjugations (*binyanim*) in the form of a limited number of paradigms, making it easier for Christians unfamiliar with the language to identify the characteristics of the various *binyanim*.[22] Most of the Latin sixteenth-century Hebrew grammars were, like Reuchlin's, to be adaptations of the Qimhis' grammars to the more familiar Latin grammatical tradition.

In the preface to that grammatical and lexicographic work, Reuchlin claimed that he was the first to attempt such a program, "No one among Latin [speakers] seems to have done such a thing".[23] This was something of an exaggeration since Aldus Manutius's *Introductio* (1501), and Pellican's *De modo legendi et intelligendi Hebraeum* (1504), had each attempted some measure of adaptation of Hebrew grammar to Latin models. However, both were sketchy works, neither of which exceeded 45 pages, and they focused on reading and pronunciation, while Reuchlin's *RH* was a massive tome of 621 pages[24] whose grammatical part occupies a bit more than 100 pages. It has no title on the first page which begins as *principium libri*, so that the Latin readers would under-

---

[19] Briefwechsel (1875), letter no. CII (Oct. 1508), 105: *Vox enim fuit mediatrix Dei et hominum, ut in Pentateucho legimus, at non quaelibet vox, sed tantum Hebraica, per quam Deus voluit arcana sua mortalibus innotescere.* See also letter no. CXV (March 1510), ibid. 123.

[20] See letters 12 and 13, Briefwechsel I: 1477–1505 (1999), and the notes therein.

[21] For Menahem ben Saruq, see HBOT I/2 (2000) 96–109, and for David Qimhi, see ibid. 396–415.

[22] Reuchlin calls them *conjugationes* and recognizes four of them: *pa'al, pi'el, hif'il, hitpa'el*, and each of them with a relative passive – which obliged him, for the sake of symmetry, to count the very rare *hotpa'al* as the relative passive of *hitpa'el*. He also includes the *po'el*, called *quadrata*.

[23] *RH*, Preface, 3: *Quod cum ante me inter latinos nemo fecisse appareat...* And again in 1517, *Liber de accent.*, fol. a2: *Ego primus omnium quos terra sustinet, Libros de Accentibus & Orthographia Iudaeorum, sermone latino edidi* ("I am the first one on Earth to publish in Latin the Jewish books about the accents and orthography").

[24] Reuchlin's last words (p. 621) are a quotation of Horatio: *Exegi monumentum aere perennius* ("I completed a monument that is stronger than bronze").

stand that the book was to be read like Hebrew, from right to left! The first twenty pages are very close to what would be called later in the century an *alphabetum hebraicum*. Such an *alphabetum* is, of course, never found in grammars written for Jews. Any Jew who could read a grammar written in Hebrew, which he would have learned in his childhood, no longer needed rules of pronunciation. But for Christians, a grammar of Hebrew was first of all an initiation into an unknown alphabet. The practical exercise Reuchlin proposed to the readers was a Hebrew genealogy of the Virgin Mary accompanied by an interlinear transliteration. He then interrupts his presentation of Hebrew grammar with a 510-page lexicon, after which he continues with a study of the flexion of nouns and particles, an organization of his treatise which corresponds to the Jewish grammatical tradition which also emphasizes morphology. In the grammatical part of the *RH*, Reuchlin merges the Hebrew linguistic tradition with the Latin one. For instance, he asserts that there are three parts of speech (noun, verb and particle), which corresponds to the analysis of the language by the Jewish grammarians but was surely rather strange to readers accustomed to the design of the Latin grammarians, Donatus and Priscian, who organized their studies around eight parts of speech. So Reuchlin writes: "In the noun are included the pronoun and the participle; in the particle are contained the adverb, the conjunction, the preposition and the interjection" (p. 551). A pedagogical ambition is visible throughout the book. Like Priscian, whom he cites several times, his grammar begins with the elements of language, letters and sounds, and then proceeds to words and expressions – the lexicographic part of his grammar is its most fully developed part – before analyzing the parts of speech and their modifications: plurals, genders of nouns and the morphology of nouns and verbs. Finally, the last pages of the book concern the "constructions", i.e., what is now called syntax. Here, once more, Reuchlin mixes the analyses of Priscian with those to be found in Jewish sources. Drawing upon Priscian's *Institutiones grammaticae* XVII, he argues that syntax must be related to the comprehensibility of expression which, in turn, depends upon a correct interpretation of the qualities of words, such as their tense, their gender and number, and of the invariant words, which constituted the third class of discourse in the analyses of the Jewish grammarians.[25]

Often Reuchlin proposes parallels between Latin and Greek structures and Hebrew ones. Thus, when he observes that Hebrew lacks cases and thus declensions for nouns, he does not hesitate to use the different particles, which he calls *articuli*, to create Hebrew declensions on the model of those in Latin and Greek.[26] A devotion to pedagogy is again visible in his explanation of the structure of Hebrew words. So that a reader who knows Latin might understand how to find a Hebrew stem, Reuchlin adopts the metaphor of undressing a word, stripping away the clothing that covers its most primitive form, and he

---

[25] *RH*, 615.
[26] *RH*, 557. This procedure was widely used in the sixteenth century for other languages as well that have no declensions. In some French grammars one can find "le maître, du maître, au maître", etc., explained as corresponding to the Latin nominative, genitive and dative cases.

invents a Latin word, *hae inhonorificabilitudines*, to serve as an example. Once all the prefixes and suffixes that are its derivative morphemes have been stripped away, one confronts its "primitive form", which is how Reuchlin designated the stem.[27] As for terminology, Reuchlin always uses the terms of the Latin tradition, whether in their usual sense, for instance *consignificativum* to translate *milla*, 'particle', or in a sense that differs from the Latin usage as, for instance, when he uses *gerundivum* to designate the construct infinitive, but he also, occasionally, coins new terms, the most remarkable of which being *affixa*, which has entered general metalinguistic terminology.

What were the reception and the influence of Reuchlin's grammatical and lexicographic work? If we may believe certain contemporary witnesses, the *RH* sold badly when it first appeared,[28] but demand eventually justified a new edition, prepared by Sebastian Münster in 1537,[29] with its grammar separated from the dictionary proper, the three parts of the *RH* reduced to two, and the introduction of section titles to facilitate its reading and to highlight explanations based upon the teaching of Levita / Ashkenazi that Münster introduced. In any event, certain Hebrew primers, like the *Alphabeta hebraica* that Robert Estienne was to publish in Paris in 1528 and reissue in subsequent editions and Johann Böschenstain's *Hebraicae grammaticae institutiones* (Wittenberg 1518) were directly inspired by the *RH*, parts of which they copy nearly word for word, while an anonymous *Rudimenta hebraicae* published in Basel by Froben in 1522[30] is actually an abridgement of Reuchlin's *RH*, retaining only its phonetics, some elements of its morphology and a few of its exercises.

In conclusion, it should be noted that sixteenth- and seventeenth-century Hebraists were not very generous to Reuchlin. They praised him more often for being the first Christian Hebraist and for initiating the study of Hebrew than for the quality of his grammar. His works dealing with the Kabbalah had a greater impact and were cited more often than the *RH*.[31] Reuchlin never published a Bible commentary though he did publish a translation of seven psalms, *In Septem Psalmos poenitentiales hebraicos cum grammatica tralactone*

---

[27] *RH*, 582: *Cum omnis dictio aut primitiva sit aut derivativa, exuere nomen derivativum singulis vestibus ad nuditatem quousque appareat primitivum latine prius tecum agam [...] quid facies? decorticabis illud omnibus tunicis quousque absolutum appendiciis appareat primitivum.*

[28] This may be deduced from a passage in his translation of the *Septem Psalmos poenitentialos* (fol. A 4 v°) which alludes to the money he had to spend on the printing of his grammar (*feci rudimenta hebraicae linguae [...] aere non parvo publicitus imprimi*). It seems that few of the 1500 copies that had been printed were sold, and that he had to reimburse Anshelm, his publisher. When Amerbach asked Reuchlin to contribute to his edition of Jerome's *Opera omnia*, he replied (March 1510) that he would agree if Amerbach bought some of the unsold exemplars of the *RH*. See B. C. Halporn, *The Correspondence of Johann Amerbach* (Ann Arbor, MI: University of Michigan Press 2000) 346–47.

[29] *J. Reuchlini Phorcensis ... Lexicon hebraicum et in Hebraeorum grammaticen* (Basel: Heinrich Petrus 1537).

[30] See Prijs, Die Basler hebräischen Drucke (1964) 23, no. 12. Steinschneider, Bibliographisches Handbuch (1859) 12, no. 97, proposed attributing this abridgement to Münster, but Prijs argues that Froben was its author as well as its publisher. An abridgement of this abridgement was published in Paris by J. Chéradame (s. a., but surely in 1523) under the title *Rudimenta quaedam Hebraicae Grammaticae.*

[31] See Secret, Les Kabbalistes chrétiens (1964) pass.

[sic] *latina* (Wittenberg: Iosephum Clugum 1529), whose second part is dated 1512, but it is only an exercise with notes that refer to the *RH.*

1.3. Reuchlin and Jewish Books

Since this "thrice-told story"[32] is so well known, it needs only be sketched here, though the main lines of the different interpretations that it has occasioned[33] must be mentioned. In 1507, Johannes Pfefferkorn, a Moravian Jew who had converted and entered the Dominican order, published a virulently antisemitic pamphlet in which he urged the confiscation and destruction of Jewish books in order to facilitate the conversion of their possessors. After having given Pfefferkorn a sympathetic hearing, the Emperor Maximilian solicited the opinions of three specialists, a priest of Jewish birth, Victor Karben, a Dominican theologian, Jacob van Hoogstraeten, and Reuchlin. Reuchlin defended the Jewish books first on legal grounds,[34] arguing that the Jews enjoyed the same rights as their Christian fellow citizens (*concives*), so an expropriation of their books was juridically indefensible, then, on religious grounds, arguing that the study of Hebrew, of the Jewish Bible commentaries and of the Kabbalah were useful to both humanists and Christians because the Talmud contained passages which confirm Christian doctrines. He further argued that the Jews should not be induced to convert by violence, or by burning their texts, but by persuasion. It was suspected that Reuchlin's knowledge of Hebrew and his contact with Jewish scholars had rendered him favourable to their interests, while Hoogstraeten feared that humanists' reading of the biblical texts in their original language might weaken the authority of the Vulgate. But as the controversy developed it became clear that Pfefferkorn and Hoogstraeten were as motivated by anti-Judaism as they were by anti-humanism.[35] Reuchlin's defence of the Jews' rights occasioned a pamphlet against him by Pfefferkorn, and he defended himself in a pamphlet entitled *Augenspiegel* (1511) which antagonized the theologians of Cologne to the point of condemning him. The ensuing controversy attracted attention throughout Germany and was the occasion for the publication of many pamphlets defending or attacking Reuchlin[36] who was finally acquitted by the Archbishop of Speyer in 1520.

Reuchlin's biographers have proposed contrasting explanations of his position in this controversy. Analysing his *De Verbo mirifico* (1494) and his *Tutsch Missive* (1505), H. OBERMAN thinks that even though Reuchlin assented to the

---

[32] The expression of Baron, A Social and Religious History XIII (1969) 184.

[33] See in particular, Peterse, Jacobus Hoogstraeten (1995), and the articles by W. MAURER, H. OBERMAN and J. OVERFIELD cited in the Bibliography above.

[34] See G. KISCH, *Zasius und Reuchlin: eine rechtsgeschichtlich-vergleichende Studie zum Toleranzproblem im 16. Jahrhundert* (Konstanz / Stuttgart: Thorbecke 1961).

[35] See in particular Overfield, A New Look at the Reuchlin Affair (1971) 191, and the criticism of his position by Peterse, Jacobus Hoogstraeten (1995) 147 f.

[36] In particular, the *Defensio*, drawn up in support of Reuchlin by Giorgius Benignus and published in 1517 by Hermann von Neuenar, a leader of the humanists of Cologne.

anti-Jewish clichés of Catholic theology, that the Jews still bore collective guilt for Jesus' crucifixion and that their misfortunes were a sign of divine punishment,[37] he "combine[d] the plea for civil emancipation of the Jews with social discrimination and religious ostracism".[38] A similar ambivalence towards the Jews would be typical of other Christian Hebraists of the fifteenth and sixteenth centuries whose enthusiasm for Jewish sources was an inseparable mixture of fascination and mistrust. Because a Christian who had acquired any Hebraic learning was always suspected being of Jewish descent, he had occasionally to show, by a public display of hostility to Jews, that he was not disposed to "Judaize", an offence that could be tried by the Inquisition. Just as he was the first, and, for many years, the only humanist to defend the books of the Jews and their civil rights, Reuchlin was also the first Renaissance scholar to coordinate such a defence with vigorous criticism of Judaism, real or feigned, in his *De Verbo mirifico*, which ends with the conversion of its two non-Christian interlocutors, and in his other studies of Jewish sources which were oriented towards a search for the confirmation of Christian doctrines. Thus, a generation later, Sebastian Münster would write in 1539, or had to write to save his reputation from calumny, that, "while having definitively devoted my name and all my strength to Hebrew studies, I have always distanced myself from Jews and their blindness".[39] Reuchlin could not escape that same ambivalence and, even if *De Verbo mirifico* ends with the conversion of its two non-Christian interlocutors, and even if his own study of Jewish sources was oriented towards a search for the confirmation of Christian doctrines, he was still the first, and for many years the only humanist, as jurist and as a Hebrew scholar, to defend the books of the Jews.

1.4. *Reuchlin and the Kabbalah*

Reuchlin's two kabbalistic works have been frequently described and adequately analyzed.[40] As J. FRIEDMAN has shown, Reuchlin is one of the first Renaissance figures who might be considered a syncretist because he thought that ancient non-Christian traditions also contained truths which might be exploited to reinforce the Christian truth.[41] In particular, he argued that the Hebrew language itself was pure and sacred, a vector of communication be-

---

[37] See Oberman, Three Sixteenth-century Attitudes (1983) 332.

[38] Ibid. 335.

[39] *Messias Christianorum*, Preface (1539) 3: *Postquam semel nomen dedi hebraismo (…) eidemque totis viribus incumbere coepi, perpetuum mihi fuit cum ex coecatis Judaeis dissidium.*

[40] See FRIEDMAN, SECRET, WIRSZUBSKI and the Bibliography above.

[41] Pico della Mirandola was thinking along these lines when he wrote in 1486: "When I had procured these books at no small expense and had read them through with the greatest diligence and unwearied labor, I saw in them (God is my witness) a religion not so much Mosaic as Christian. There is the mystery of the Trinity, there the incarnation of the Word, there the divinity of the Messiah; [...] In those matters that regard philosophy, you may really hear Pythagoras and Plato, whose doctrines are so akin to Christian faith that our Augustine gives great thanks to God that the books of the Platonists came into his hands", *De hominis dignitate* (tr. by C. G. Wallis, *On the Dignity of Man*, Cambridge: Hackett 1998) 32.

tween God and man, and between man and the angels, but that only those who have studied that language thoroughly could obtain access to the truths that it hid since it was in the form and numerical value of the Hebrew letters rather than in the most direct sense of the texts that God revealed his most precious secrets.[42] Some of those truths could only be discovered by kabbalistic techniques, in particular numerology, which he regarded as very ancient traditions.[43]

The chronology of Reuchlin's works is important in permitting an understanding of his kabbalism. Between *De Verbo mirifico* (1494), whose references to Jewish texts are relatively few and imprecise despite the translations of kabbalistic texts that a converted Jew, Flavius Mithridates, prepared for him in the summer of 1486, and the more learned *De arte cabalistica* (1517), Reuchlin had produced his *De rudimentis hebraicis* and had mastered many more Jewish texts, as can be seen from his list of about twenty kabbalistic treatises that *De arte cabalistica* cites, a 'bibliography' which inspired several of his successors like Levita's student, Cardinal Egidio da Viterbo. J. FRIEDMAN claims, on the basis of these two works, that Reuchlin "must be ranked among the great mystics of his age", but he may be confusing exposition of (Jewish) mystical doctrine with mystical experience and with innovation in mystical techniques and theory, none of which are prominent in Reuchlin's treatises.

2. Christian Hebraists in Basel

2.1. Conrad Pellican, "who opened the way"[44]

While Reuchlin left his mark upon the creation of Hebrew philology and the study of Kabbalah, his younger contemporary, Conrad Pellican (Konrad Kürschner, 1478–1556) left his on the Bible studies of the first half of the sixteenth century.[45] Although he actually published only a small part of his translations of Jewish source-texts, Pellican led what B. ROUSSEL has called the

---

[42] See J. SANDYS-WUNSCH, "The influence of Jewish Mysticism on Renaissance Biblical Interpretation", *Mysticism: Select essays. Essays in honour of John Sahadat* (ed. M. Mbonimpa / G. Bonneau / K-R. Bonin; Ontario, Can.: Editions Glopro Sudbury 2002) 47–69.

[43] See Secret, Les Kabbalistes chrétiens (1964) 47. Secret calls *De arte cabalistica* "The Bible of Christian Kabbala", ibid. 57.

[44] R. G. HOBBS used this expression (*celui qui fraie la voie*) in a lecture he gave in 1997 in Paris, Ecole pratique des hautes études (B. Roussel's seminar): "Réformes et renaissance des lettres hébraïques dans 'l'Ecole rhénane d'exégèse' (1520–1540)". See HOBBS's essay in this volume, Chap. 19, sect. 1.

[45] Pellican was somewhat interested by the Christian Kabbalah. He knew the works of the Christian Kabbalists, Paul Rici, Jacques Lefèvre d'Étaples, whom he met in 1516, and the Orientalist, Guillaume Postel, whose *Candelabrum typici in Mosis interpretatio* he copied in Hebrew and then translated into Latin in 1549, a translation that has never been published; see F. SECRET, *G. Postel et son interprétation du Candélabre de Moïse* (Nieuwkoop 1966) 67–84. Through Reuchlin Pellican came into contact with the writings of the latter's master, Pico della Mirandola who initiated the Christian Kabbalah; see Secret, Les Kabbalistes chrétiens (1964) 142–43; Zürcher, Konrad Pellikans Wirken (1975) 182–89, and Wirszubski, Three studies in Christian Kabbala (1975).

"Rhineland school of exegesis",[46] a humanistic approach to Scripture inspired by the writings of Erasmus whom Pellican had helped in the preparation of his edition of the works of St. Jerome. The members of the Rhineland school were the biblically oriented theologians and humanists of Strasbourg, Basel and Zurich: Wolfgang Fabricius (Köpfel) Capito (1478–1541), Johannes Häusgen Oecolampadius (1482–1531), Huldrych Zwingli (1484–1531), Sebastian Münster (1488–1552), and Martin Bucer (1491–1551). Most of them, unlike Reuchlin, had evangelical sympathies or would eventually join the Reform movement. Together they formed an intellectual network which left its mark on their individual contributions to Bible study, on their correspondence and on the prefaces to their works. They differed with Luther concerning the status of the biblical text and the status of the Jews. For them the philological study of the Old Testament was fundamental, both from an intellectual and a spiritual point of view, while Luther more emphasized the study of the New Testament, especially for theological reasons. Both Pellican and Oecolampadius taught theology at Basel between 1523 and 1526, alternating, from week to week, lectures on the Old Testament with lectures on the New. Their Bible commentaries were based on modern Latin translations of the Hebrew Bible rather than on the Vulgate. When, in 1526, Pellican accepted Zwingli's invitation to come to Zurich, he taught both Greek and Hebrew and contributed to the editing of the "Zurich Bible", *Biblia sacrosancta Testamenti Veteris & Novi* (Zurich: Christoph Froschauer 1543). His principle was that interpretation was necessarily based upon a precise knowledge of the letter of the biblical text. As he wrote in the preface to his *Commentaria bibliorum* (Zurich, 1532–39), "the soul of Scripture is contained within the letter of the texts".[47]

Pellican was an autodidact in Hebrew; he read and translated much but published relatively little. In 1518 the printer Froben, who would subsequently specialize in Hebrew texts, published his *Quadruplex Psalterium* which contained the Hebrew text, a Greek text and two Latin translations.[48] Pellican also collaborated with his student, Sebastian Münster, to bring out an edition of Proverbs (1524) whose Hebrew text is accompanied by a new Latin translation "closer to the Hebrew truth", i. e., the literal sense, than was the Vulgate, as its Preface, signed by Pellican and Münster, claims and as its grammatical annotations demonstrate.[49]

It has often been argued that Reuchlin's claim to have been the first Christian author to have written a Hebrew grammar was spurious because, in fact, Pellican's *De modo legendi et intelligendi hebraeum* had preceded it by two

---

[46] B. ROUSSEL, "De Strasbourg à Bâle et Zurich: une 'école rhénane d'exégèse' (ca 1525–ca 1540)", *RHPhR* 68 (1988) 19–39. Also see G. BEDOUELLE / B. ROUSSEL (eds.), *Le temps des Réformes et la Bible* (BTT 5; Paris 1989) 215–33.

[47] This commentary has been published and analysed in Zürcher, Konrad Pellikans Wirken (1975) 85–134.

[48] This Psalter does not bear Pellican's name. The same year, Bishop Agostino Giustiniani's polyglot Psalter with Coptic appeared in Genoa, and two years later the Cologne polyglot Psalter with an Aramaic translation would appear.

[49] Thus, in Prov 31:10 Pellican and Münster retain the flavor of the Hebrew construct state: *mulierem fortitudinis qui inveniet?*, "a woman of valor, who can find such a one?", where Jerome had translated more simply: *mulierem fortem*, "a valiant woman".

years, appearing in the *Margarita philosophica*, an encyclopedia compiled by G. Reisch in 1504.[50] Actually, however, Pellican's grammar is much more limited than Reuchlin's. This may be explained by the fact that Pellican had great difficulty in obtaining a variety of Hebrew texts without which his self-instruction in Hebrew, which had begun in 1499, was necessarily laborious and prone to error. For lack of a longer and better text, he used the *Stella Messiae* of P. Nigri (Schwartz)[51] in which passages from Isaiah had been transliterated into Latin characters. By comparing the transliterations with the Hebrew characters he learnt the Hebrew alphabet.[52] It is not astonishing that, with these handicaps, Pellican should have soon been blocked in his study. He then called upon Reuchlin who explained to him that the stem of a Hebrew verb is to be found in its third-person masculine singular form in the past tense, and who furnished him with a German translation of Moses Qimhi's *Mahalakh Shevilei ha-Da'at*.[53] Pellican subsequently became the disciple of Matthias Adrianus, a Jewish convert.[54]

De modo legendi ..., like certain medieval Latin grammars, took the form of questions and answers. The transcriptions from Hebrew reflect the ashkenazic pronunciation: *bets* (the letter /b/), *patsah* (the vowel /a/), *cometz* (the name of the vowel sign representing, like its transcription, an open *o*), *dogesch* (note the first vowel, an open *o* instead of the *a* in sefardic pronunciation). One also finds in this introduction to Hebrew many elements which were to appear in other elementary works of the same type in the early years of the century (notably those of Matthias Adrianus[55] and Reuchlin): the presentation of consonants according to their point of articulation, as labials, dentals, etc., the distinction between consonants that are part of a stem and those that are prefixed to it, the pronunciation of vowels,[56] and the rules concerning the *dagesh* and the *rafeh*. These phonetic explanations, which can also be found in Abraham ibn Ezra's Bible commentaries, though for other reasons, are an innovation in the teaching of Hebrew because, as remarked above, rabbinic grammars had no need to teach pronunciation, though David Qimhi's *Sefer ha-Shorashim*, exceptionally does precisely that. However, Pellican did take from the Rabbis

---

[50] The Strasbourg edition published in the same year by Johann Grünninger is a pirate edition. For the other editions of the *Margarita philosophica*, see Prijs, Die Basler hebräischen Drucke (1964) 14.

[51] See Nestle, Nigri, Böhm, Pellikan (1893).

[52] See *Das Chronikon des Konrad Pellikan* (1877) 16–18.

[53] Ibid. 19: *Tunc subridens humanissimus Doctor Reuchlin dicebat, apud Hebraeos thema verborum non esse primam personam, nec Indicativi, sed tertiam singularem praeteriti perfecti*, and p. 21: *Annuit Capnion, et me vicissim exaudivit, petentem ab eo exemplar manuscriptum grammaticae R. Mosse Kimhi, quod ab eodem Judæo germanice translatum habebat....*

[54] Unlike Reuchlin, Pellican does not seem to have had contacts with non-converted Jews. Concerning his relations with Jews, see Zürcher, Konrad Pellikans Wirken (1975) 179.

[55] He wrote an *Introductio utilissima hebraice discere cupientibus* (Basel: Froben 1518 and 1520), and influenced several Christian Hebraists by his oral teaching, see GEIGER, Das Studium der hebräischen Sprache in Deutschland (1870) 41–48; and H. DE VOCHT, *History of the Foundation and the Rise of the Collegium Trilingue Lovaniense* 1 (Louvain 1951) 241–55.

[56] It should be noted that the *qamets* is transcribed a, but that Pellican describes its pronunciation very precisely as being *inter a clarum et o medium* and proposes to transcribe it by *å* (fol. F XI v°), a transcription that is still retained in some scholarly publications on biblical Hebrew.

their explanations of the "servile" consonants (conjunctions and the definite article). Thus he indicates (Fol. F XIIII v°) that a *h*, at the beginning of a word, is the equivalent of the definite article, while at the end of a word it is the sign of the feminine. His description of the pronunciation of Hebrew "letters" (*litterae*) is not exclusively phonetic but includes an introduction of their morphological and syntactic functions. The same organisation of the presentation of Hebrew reading was to appear in subsequent authors like Capito and Pagninus. Pellican then outlines, very briefly, the flexion of nouns and the conjugation of verbs, for the latter using Moses Qimhi's paradigm, *paqad*. His examples are not exempt from error; he writes *paqadtem* ("you have commanded") for *peqadtem*, and *'ishot* for *nashim* ("women"), among many others. Even though Hebrew does not have a case structure, Pellican reconstitutes one for the pronouns with the use of prepositions, as Reuchlin was to do. This comparison with Latin was surely for pedagogical purposes.[57] *De modo legendi...* ends with several extracts from Isaiah and Psalms and a Hebrew / Latin / Greek glossary.

Pellican played a rôle in the history of Christian Hebraism that was more important than his sketchy and often grossly incorrect grammar might suggest because he encouraged his disciples to turn to the letter of the text of the Old Testament, to read Hebrew with the aid of the Jewish commentators, and to translate it as literally as possible. He also played an important rôle in the diffusion of the knowledge of Hebrew among Christians because, as his 1544 autobiography shows,[58] he served as a dealer in the Hebrew books being printed by Robert Estienne in Paris and, in particular, in those, more complete and precise than his own, written by Pagninus and published in Lyon. He also furnished Estienne with Latin translations of the medieval Hebrew Bible commentaries.[59] After Zwingli's death in 1531 Pellican devoted himself to developing the library of the Grossmünster in Zurich which eventually comprised a thousand books and manuscripts including around ten in Hebrew, books and manuscripts that Protestant scholars would have found useful.[60]

---

[57] For certain authors, like Münster and Pagninus, the distinction between morphology (flexion) and the syntactic value of the case is clearly established. The Renaissance grammarians had difficulty in describing the morphology of nouns without recourse to the idea or at least the terminology of a declensional system because the other languages that they knew (for instance German and even Medieval French) retain elaborate or vestigial declensions.

[58] This autobiography, *Das Chronikon des Konrad Pellikan* (ed. Riggenbach; 1877), is of great value for understanding the education of Pellican and his rôle in the diffusion of Hebrew among Christians. Few authors of the period described their studies, travels and encounters in equal detail.

[59] See ibid. 178–79. Among other rabbinical works, Pellican translated Abraham ibn Ezra's commentary on the Pentateuch and Rashi's commentary to Genesis and Exodus, but they remain unpublished. See Zürcher, Konrad Pellikans Wirken (1975) 155–65.

[60] See M. GERMANN, *Die reformierte Stiftsbibliothek am Großmünster im 16. Jahrhundert* (Wiesbaden: Otto Harrassowitz 1994). In that library one could find the 1517 Bomberg (Venice) and the 1536 Froben (Basel) editions of the Bible, polyglot Psalters, including Pellican's. There were also manuals of grammar, Reuchlin's, Tissard's and Levita's, and Münster's and Pagninus's dictionaries as well as the concordance of Isaac Nathan ben Kalonymos ([Pesaro] 1517).

2.2. Wolfgang Fabricius Capito

Wolfgang Fabricius (Köpfel) Capito (1478–1541) was born in Haguenau and studied medecine, law and theology. In 1515 he was appointed preacher in the Basel cathedral and professor of theology at the university. His tendencies as a Bible interpreter were close to those of Pellican and Zwingli. In a letter to Erasmus he criticized the medieval schemes of biblical interpretation.[61] Like the other members of 'the Rhineland school', he accepted typological interpretation, but he had even less respect than Pellican for the Kabbalah.[62] His students included Paul Fagius (1504–50), who was to publish in Isny several of the most important works of Levita / Ashkenazi and of Pierre-Robert Olivétan, whose translation of the Bible into French ([Neufchâtel] 1535) would become the standard for the Reformed community.

Capito published a Hebrew grammar in Basel, *Hebraicarum Institutionum libri duo* (Froben 1518), in which the influence of Pellican is visible and indeed the latter claimed, in 1520, to have collaborated in its composition. This grammar is more complete than Pellican's *De modo legendi* …, but it follows that work's general lines. Among other differences, Capito shows that he is aware of different pronunciations of Hebrew among Jews, which Pellican had not recognized.[63] He sometimes digresses for pages, for instance on the *aleph* in Aramaic, or on the correct reading, *ka'ari / ka'aru*, in Ps 22:17.[64] The language he describes is, as it was for Pellican, Reuchlin and would still be for Pagninus (*Hebraicarum institutionum libri IIII*; Paris: Robert Estienne 1549), biblical Hebrew,[65] but his chapter 20 lists abbreviations that are frequent in the rabbinic literature, which shows that Capito recognized the interest in reading Jewish Bible commentaries and maybe other rabbinic texts. His presentation of Hebrew morphology shows the very strong influence of the grammars of Abraham ibn Ezra, who is cited occasionally, and of Moses and David Qimhi.

2.3. Sebastian Münster

Sebastian Münster[66] was born in Ingelheim, a small town near Mainz, in January 1488. He came from what would nowadays be termed a middle-class family, as his father was hospital administrator. In 1505, Münster entered the Franciscan order at Heidelberg where he studied arithmetics, geometry, music and astronomy (the *Quadrivium* subjects), as well as philosophy and theology. A brilliant student, he was particularly interested in astronomy. Therefore, in the year 1509, he was

---

[61] Erasmus, *Opus epistolarum* … (*recognitum et auctum per* P. S. Allen) II (Oxford: Clarendon Press 1910), letter 459.

[62] See Secret, Les Kabbalistes chrétiens (1964) 145–46.

[63] Fol. B 2. Capito explains that "the Jews of our country" pronounce *s, z, t,* and *sh* in the same manner, by the equivalent of a *s* in Latin, but that his informant, of Spanish descent, pronounced the suffix of the feminine -*oth* rather than -*os*, *blesulum*, which suggests an interdental pronunciation which Capito prefers because it permits distinguishing the two sounds, dental *s* and interdental ϑ.

[64] The reading *ka'aru* corresponds to the Vulgate, *foderunt*, which permits interpreting the verse as a prophecy of Jesus' crucifixion.

[65] However, on fol. Gg 3 v°, he uses the word *'atsmi*, 'myself', which is post-biblical Hebrew.

[66] On Sebastian Münster, in addition to publications listed in the Bibliography above, see also K. H. BURMEISTER / E. EMMERLING, "Neue Forschungen zu Sebastian Münster", *Beiträge zur Ingelheimer Geschichte* 21 (1971) 42–57. In that paper is included a bibliography containing almost 300 items on Münster.

sent to Rufach (Upper Alsace), where he completed his astronomy studies under the guidance of Conrad Pellican. It was also with Pellican as his teacher that Münster began studying Hebrew. The works that he composed at that time – which remained unpublished – show how quickly he mastered the Hebrew language. Münster subsequently studied other biblical languages of the Semitic family, such as Aramaic and Ethiopian.[67] Münster was ordained in 1512; and he taught theology and philosophy at the Tübingen Franciscan Monastery, where he was appointed Lecturer in 1514. In addition, he developed his knowledge in the fields of geography and astronomy under the supervision of Johann Stöffler (1452–1531).

From 1518 to 1520, Münster taught philosophy at Basel and collaborated with his master Pellican to publish an edition of the Book of Proverbs, preceded by an *Epitome hebraicae grammaticae* written by Münster himself. It should be noted that in the Hebrew colophon Münster referred to grammar as *sefer 'otiyot* (i.e. "book of the letters"), which is a new phrase, based on Hebrew, for "grammatica": he did not use the standard word *diqduq* until he read the works of Levita / Ashkenazi. Just as Pellican who, after publishing the works of Luther (1519), left the Franciscan order (1523) and embraced the Protestant faith, so too Münster – though he had been ordained in 1512 – felt evangelical sympathies: in 1520 he undertook to translate Luther's *Decem praecepta Wittenbergensi praedicta populo* into German. In 1521, he moved to Heidelberg, where he taught Hebrew until 1529. Those were particularly fruitful years with regard to his intellectual activity in the fields of Hebrew and Aramaic; the numerous books of that decade – nearly all of which were published by Froben in Basel – represent tools necessary for the readers of the Bible and of the rabbinic commentaries, whether they be beginners or advanced students. A few of Münster's publications of that time may be mentioned:[68]

– Biblical books: Proverbs (1524), Ecclesiastes (1525), Song of Songs (1525), and the Decalogue, published with Abraham ibn Ezra's commentary (1527);
– A philosophical text: the Latin translation of Maimonides' *Millot ha-Higgayon* (1527);
– A treatise on the Hebrew calendar (1527);
– Grammatical and lexicographic works: *'Arukh ha-Shorashim, Dictionarium hebraicum* (1523); *Melekhet ha-Diqduq, Institutiones Grammaticae in Hebraicam linguam* (1524); *Compendium Hebraicae Grammaticae, ex Eliae Iudaei... libris* (1527); *Tabula omnium hebraicarum conjugationum* (1525).[69] In addition to these works, Münster's Latin translations of Levita / Ashkenazi's works deserve special mention. They allowed Christian Hebraists to come into contact with the writings of that author, whom Münster considered his master though they probably never met: *Grammatica hebraica absolutissima* (1525, translation of *Sefer ha-Baḥur*); *Composita verborum et nominum Hebraicorum* (1525, translation of *Sefer ha-Harkava*) and *Capitula cantici* (1527, translation of *Pirqei Eliyahu*).
– Münster was the first Christian Hebraist who wrote specific books on biblical and rabbinical

---

[67] The first Ethiopian text of the Psalms was published by J. Potken in 1513: *Psalterium Davidis, aethiopice...* (Roma: M. Silber alias Franck 1513). In his Aramaic Grammar (1527), Münster devoted two pages (14–16) to the Ethiopian language, presenting its alphabet and quoting a verse from the Book of Psalms. He also made comparisons between Hebrew, Aramaic and Ethiopian words. However, his study was not in the field of comparative linguistics. What mattered to him was to define Chaldean and contrast it to the languages that were akin to it. This Aramaic grammar – as well as a large number of other works by Münster is available on the website: gallica.bnf.fr.

[68] We refer only to the *editio princeps*. For a more complete list and editions, see Burmeister, Sebastian Münster, eine Bibliographie (1964).

[69] Münster integrated this table of Hebrew verbs to his Latin edition of Levita / Ashkenazi's *Sefer ha-Baḥur*.

Aramaic: he published a dictionary (*Dictionarium chaldaicum*, 1527) and a grammar (*Chaldaica grammatica, antehac a nemine attentata...*, 1527).

Besides such strenuous activity in Hebrew studies, Münster also published works in geography. He was influenced by Beatus Rhenanus (1485–1547) who believed that geography leads to a better understanding of the Bible, and is therefore of paramount importance in the field of theology. Münster's *Cosmographia* met with vast success: after the first German edition (1544), forty-five new editions were published, in Latin and in a number of vernacular languages.[70]

In 1529, Münster moved to Basel, where he had been offered a chair of Hebrew at the University – Jean Calvin was to be one of his students – and where he stayed until his death in 1552. Living in a place where Protestant views were fully accepted, Münster definitively left the Franciscan order and joined the Protestant camp. He subsequently married the widow of Adam Petrus, a printer for whom he had worked as press corrector in the years 1519–1520.[71] He continued to publish works that testify to his devotion to pedagogy: *Isagoge elementalis ... in Hebraicam linguam* (Basel: Froben 1535), *Hebraicae grammaticae... pars... quae est de verborum conjugationibus* (Basel: H. Petrus 1536), *Opus grammaticum consummatum*, (Basel: H. Petrus 1542), which is a synthesis of Münster's own grammatical teaching based upon Levita's works. In the years 1534–35, Münster published an entire Old Testament in Hebrew and Latin (reissued as *Biblia sacra*, Zurich 1539), with philological comments following each chapter. The new translation[72] was somewhat reminiscent of Pagninus' work.[73] Münster followed closely the Hebrew text, as had Pagninus done before him. He did not hesitate to use loan translations from Hebrew and thus translated Hebrew structures literally. Münster's annotated translation was criticized by Luther on theological grounds, and by P. Melanchthon on linguistic grounds. A century later, Richard Simon wrote that Münster "was the most accurate and the most faithful of all Protestants in his Bible translation"; however, he reproached Münster with his tendency to resort to the Jewish source-texts in both the translation and the annotations: "This version is very close to a translation of the Rabbis, whose commentaries Münster had studied (...) It might have been advisable for him to follow his master in the Hebrew language, Conrad Pellican, who was opposed to borrowing anything from the Rabbis but grammar".[74]

This brings us to the question of the relationship of Münster to Jewish sources. The quotations from rabbinic literature that are to be found in his biblical commentaries, in his Hebrew writings and in his correspondence led K. H. BURMEISTER to try and appraise what the German Hebraist's "rabbinic li-

---

[70] For Münster's geographical works, see JEAN BERGEVIN, "La Cosmographie universelle de Sebastian Münster", *Déterminisme et géographie* (Sainte-Foy, Québec: Presses de l'Université Laval 1992) 115–63; M. BÜTTNER / K. H. BURMEISTER, "Sebastian Münster 1488–1552", *Geographers, Biobibliographical Studies* 3 (ed. T. W. Freeman / P. Pinchemel; London: Mansell 1979) 99–106.

[71] Adam's son, Heinrich Petrus, published the Hebrew works that Münster wrote in those years.

[72] *En tibi lector Hebraica Biblia Latina planeque nova Sebast. Munsteri tralatione...* (Basileae, ex officina Bebeliana, impendiis Michaëlis Isingrinii et Henrici Petri).

[73] *Biblia... Habes in hoc libro prudens lector utriusque instrumenti novam tranlationem [sic]...* (Lyon: A. du Ry 1528). On Pagninus, see also, in the present volume, Chap. 7, sect. 5.2, by ARJO VANDERJAGT.

[74] Richard Simon, *Histoire critique du Vieux Testament* (Rotterdam: R. Leers 1685) 322.

brary" might have been. BURMEISTER's conclusions command respect.[75] His list contains books about philosophy, theology, grammar, history, astronomy and science. Münster read the source-texts in the original language, and quoted from them accurately. The Jewish authors to whom he referred most frequently were Rashi, David Qimhi, Abraham ibn Ezra and Nahmanides.[76] Besides, he often resorted to the Targum. His position was ambivalent: from a scientific point of view he extensively drew upon the rabbinic texts; from a theological point of view, however, he was constantly trying to prove that the Christian doctrines were to be read in the Old Testament. In Münster's opinion, the only reason why the Jews refused to recognize Christ as the Messiah was that they did not read their own texts – i.e. the Old Testament – correctly.

Whenever Münster quoted a lengthy passage from the Midrash, he would apologize for doing so, and justify himself from a linguistic point of view, writing that he had to read such texts in order to master the Hebrew language. In addition, he never failed to remark upon the absurdity of the Jewish interpretations. On the one hand, he gave all the necessary information that permitted a correct reading of rabbinic literature: for example, at the end of his Aramaic grammar-book, he included a list of abbreviations and initials which cannot be dispensed with if the texts are to be understood. On the other hand, he cautioned his readers against reading the Jewish sources. Among Münster's polemical and apologetic works, his Hebrew translation of the Gospel according to Matthew and his *Messias Christianorum and Iudaeorum, hebraice et latine* (Basel: H. Petrus 1539) deserve special mention.

Owing to his extensive reading of Hebrew texts, Münster – unlike many of his Christian contemporaries – had a superb command of the Hebrew language, as testified in his prefaces. The Hebrew he wrote was fluent, correct, and rich in rabbinical phrases derived from the Midrash, from Rashi, or from David Qimhi. It is known that Münster corresponded in Hebrew with fellow-scholars, and in particular with Levita / Ashkenazi.

A follower of the *ad fontes* ("back to the sources") principle, which was dear to the Humanists, Münster published numerous teaching books. His teaching method is clearly visible in his *Opus grammaticum consummatum* (Basel: Heinrich Petrus 1542).[77] In his preface, he gave a survey of the state of Hebrew studies at his time.[78] Then he highly praised Eliyahu Levita for his scientific qualities and the clarity of his pedagogy. This 290-page book perfectly illustrates the state of knowledge and the teaching methods in the field of Hebrew studies in the first half of the century. Following Reuchlin and Pagninus, Münster based his own research on the works of the Qimhis, who were not referred to

---

[75] Burmeister, Sebastian Münster (1969) 200. See also, in the same book, "Verhältnis zum Judentum", 72–85.

[76] Rosenthal, Sebastian Münster's Knowledge (1942), cites several instances of Münster's quotations from these and other Jewish authors.

[77] Reprinted in 1544, 1549, 1556, 1563, 1570.

[78] He mentions Reuchlin and Pellican – and himself – as pioneers in the field. Then he cites W. F. Capito and M. Adrianus, and finally gives a list of the Hebraists of different countries: J. Oecolampadius, C. Ammonius, H. Zwingli, M. Aurogallus, J. Campensis (Germany); P. Galatinus, S. Pagninus, A. Giustiniani (Italy) and D. Lopez de Stunica (Spain).

by name, but simply called *veteres*, i.e. the grammarians from ancient times, as opposed to Levita / Ashkenazi who was Münster's contemporary. To begin with, he explained how to read and pronounce Hebrew. All his explanations are to be found in a number of similar textbooks, like those we presented above. Münster's original contribution, however, was his two-page discussion of the part played by the Masoretes: a faithful disciple of Levita, Münster summed up his master's analyses as presented in the preface to the *Masoret ha-Masoret*. Besides, Münster follows Levita's opinion on the question of dating the first appearance of the vowel-signs.

He was again following the Hebrew grammar tradition when he presented the parts of speech (noun, verb, particle). He described the verb and noun from a solely morphological point of view. With regard to the third part of speech (invariant words), Münster merely gave a list of conjunctions and adverbs presented in alphabetical order, as David Qimhi did.

This book clearly shows Münster's pedagogical preoccupation. He did not use many technical terms, and he tried – as Reuchlin did – to make his Latin readers feel at home with Hebrew. The grammar-book closes with three chapters on abbreviations, accents and meter – the last two of which being largely derived from Levita's works.

3. Eliyahu (Elias) Levita / Ashkenazi

R. *Eliyahu ben Asher ha-Levi* (the Levite) *ha-Ashkenazi* (the German) (1469–1549), known among Jews as Eliyahu Baḥur and among Christians as Elias Levita,[79] was born in Germany (probably in a little village near Neustadt), migrated to Padua from whence he fled a plague to Venice (1509) and subsequently migrated to Rome (1516). Because of the sack of the city in 1527 by the Imperial forces and the subsequent plague, he returned to Venice.

In Rome Levita wrote several grammars and taught Hebrew to Christians. Anticipating the criticism of his Jewish contemporaries or reacting to it, he assured the readers of his masterpiece, the *Masoret ha-Masoret*[80], that they were all upright men to whom it was licit to teach Hebrew, and besides, he needed their fees to provide dowries for his daughters. In Venice he continued to write and participated in the printing of Hebrew books at the presses of Daniel Bomberg, apparently as the successor to Yaʻakov ben Ḥayyim ibn Adoniah who first edited the *Masora parva* and *magna*, the rabbinical critical apparatus that accompanied manuscripts of the Bible and, since 1524, printed Bibles, and who created for that edition the *Masora finalis*, an index to the *Masora magna*. Levita left Venice briefly in 1541 to work in Isny (Bavaria) with Paul Fagius, who published a number of his books in Hebrew and in translation and where, one may assume, Levita advised the choice of certain if not all of the Hebrew books that Fagius published there.[81] In 1542, Levita returned to

---

[79] See esp. WEIL's extensive biography, *Elie Levita, humaniste et massorète* (1963).

[80] According to Ginsburg's transcription (see Bibliography above), *Massoreth ha-Massoreth*.

[81] In particular, David Qimhi's commentary on the Psalms with the refutations of the Christian apologetic interpretations of Psalms 2, 22, and 110 that construe them as referring to Jesus re-

Venice and participated in the editing of Bomberg's third rabbinical Bible (1548). Since he was an expert in the Masorah, possibly the only real expert at the time, one would like to know in what ways the Masorah of the books of that Bible for which he was responsible as well as the texts of the rabbinical commentaries that accompanied them differed from those of the Ya'akov ben Hayyim's rabbinical Bible, but that question remains open.

The heritage of Levita for biblical studies can be described under four headings, since he worked as a teacher, a philologist, a publisher and a Masorete – teaching Christians, publishing his own grammars and dictionaries as well as works of others with annotations, and writing the first (and still) valuable essay on the Masorah. He had amicable relations with several Christian students in Italy – Cardinal Egidio da Viterbo and the French ambassadors, Lazare de Baïf and Bishop Georges de Selve – and subsequently with Fagius in Isny and possibly Münster[82] in Basel. Fagius and Münster, without initiating new approaches to Bible study, certainly disseminated to a Christian public what they had learnt from Levita, so he was the source for generations of Christian Hebraists,[83] even if he could have taken little pleasure in their polemical dimensions.

Levita was a poet, lexicographer and grammarian.[84] He composed four dictionaries: *Tishbi*[85] (two editions, one in Hebrew and one with a Latin translation by Fagius, Isny 1541) of rabbinic Hebrew, words and even concepts; *Meturgeman* (Isny 1541) of Aramaic, *Shemot devarim* (Isny 1542) of proper nouns, and *Sefer Zikhronot*, a concordance to the Bible with references to the masora.[86] Levita also wrote grammars: the *Sefer ha-Bahur* (Rome 1517; Isny 1542; Mantua 1556[87]), *Pirqei Eliyahu* (Pesaro: G. Soncino 1520), a versified treatise on pronunciation and vocalization, and the *Sefer ha-Harkava* (Basel 1525, 1536, Venice 1541, Prague 1793). He also annotated David Qimhi's *Sefer ha-Shorashim* (Venice: Giustiniani 1547, Mantua, s.a.). These grammars and dictionaries were composed and published for Jews, to judge from the Venice editions and the omission of elementary material that would have been

---

moved from their normal place, at the end of each of these Psalms, and collected in a sort of four-page appendix (*Teshuvot la-noṣrim*), which was not included or at least has not survived in all exemplars of this Psalter.

[82] They probably never met, but they did correspond. Only one of their letters remains; cf. G. WEIL, "Une leçon de l'humaniste hébreu Elias Lévita à son élève Sébastien Münster", *Revue d'Alsace* 95 (1956) 30–40.

[83] He strongly influenced the grammatical works of J. Van Campen (d. 1538) and his pupil N. Clenardus (1495–1543). Van Campen's grammar, first printed in Louvain (1528), then reprinted in Paris (1539, 1543, 1545), is the first in Europe to refer explicitly to Levita's teaching, and in fact refers to Levita in its title: *Ex variis libellis Eliae grammaticorum omnium doctissimi (…) quidquid ad absolutam grammaticen Hebraicam est necessarium.* See S. KESSLER MESGUICH, "Deux hébraïsants à Louvain: J. Campensis et N. Clénard", *Helmantica* 154 (2000) 59–73.

[84] In *Pirqei Eliyahu*, he paraphrases Amos 7:14 and says: "I am neither a philosopher, nor am I a philosopher's son; but I am a grammarian".

[85] So called because his homonym, the prophet Elijah, is identified in 1 Kgs 17:1 etc. as the Tishbite, i.e., born or brought up in a city or village Tishbeh.

[86] This work remained unpublished until 1875, when a small part was published by B. GOLDBERG (Frankfurt) It is described and analysed by Weil, Elie Lévita (1963) 292–297.

[87] For later editions, see Steinschneider, Bibliographisches Handbuch (1859).

useful to non-Hebraists proposing to learn Hebrew from them, but they were nevertheless subsequently published for Christians in Isny and Basel, which suggests that Fagius and Münster recognized their great value for advanced students. In particular, the latter published in 1525 (Basel, Froben) a Latin version of the *Sefer ha-Baḥur* to which he added an *introductio elementalis* about Hebrew reading and pronunciation, clearly intended to bridge the gap for Christian beginners between complete ignorance and Levita's advanced presentation.[88]

Clearly Levita was the Hebrew master of generations of serious Christian Hebraists, and at least one, Richard Simon, often expressed his admiration for him, especially for his *Masoret ha-Masoret* which can only be described as a critical history of the *masoret* and of the *qere/ketiv* problem. Here his legacy is doubtful, not because of any failure on his part, but because Jews and Christians, except Simon, were equally obtuse and did not really understand his analysis. He first tried to determine the age of the vocalization, not on dogmatic grounds, as all previous scholars had done and most of his successors would continue to do, but on the basis of their earliest attestations, and when he could not find any references in the Talmud to the names of the vowel-points or the cantilations, he concluded that they had to be post-talmudic. Only Simon understood that Levita's analysis did not imply that the readings of the biblical texts preserved in the relatively recently invented vocalizations were themselves recent and thus inauthentic or even tendentious, as Louis Cappel and Jean Morin were to assert, and as many Protestants were to fear, only that the vowel-points were a recent graphic system invented to formalize a much older reading tradition. In a still more daring statistical analysis, Levita remarked that the frequency of *qere'in/ketivin* did not correspond to the relative age of the biblical books. The Pentateuch has relatively few of them while Daniel, Jeremiah, certain of the later prophets and the Aramaic parts of Ezra / Nehemiah[89] – the duration of whose transmission was, by hypothesis, briefer than that of the older books – show relatively many *qere'in/ketivin*. He concluded that the *qere/ketiv* phenomenon did not depend upon the age of biblical book but coded esoteric meanings. Here, despite a promising methodology, Levita regressed from the solution to the problem that had been proposed by Isaac Abarbanel / Abravanel,[90] that the *qere'in* were linguistic corrections, to a more gnostic solution which is not subject to verification. In fact, the *qere'in* are not always better, i. e., more modern, readings, as Abravanel had argued and as Levita probably recognized – he remarks that they never concern *plenum* of defective spelling – nor are they always palaeographic corrections, as Levita may also have understood. He was a thoroughly traditional Jew and so not yet ready to accept an analysis of the *qere'in/ketivin* like Abra-

---

[88] *Sefer ha-diqduq* [in Hebrew characters], *Grammatica hebraica absolutissima, Eliae Levitae Germani: nuper per S. Munsterum juxta Hebraismum Latinitate donata* (Basel: Froben 1525, repr. 1532, 1537, 1543, 1552). See Prijs, Die Basler hebräischen Drucke (1964) 33, and above sect. 2.3.

[89] Relying upon traditional chronology, Levita assumed that the authors of those late books survived the exile and should have been well placed to correct any errors that David Qimhi had supposed were introduced during that troubled interregnum.

[90] See the essay above, Chap. 8, on Isaac Abarbanel, by ERIC LAWEE.

vanel's which weakened the claims for the inspiration of every letter of the bib-lical texts, much less the explanations that Richard Simon in 1678 and ALEXAN-DER SPERBER in our own time[91] would propose.

It has been claimed that there is nothing new in Levita's grammars, and that seems to be the case, but they are well written and organized. The clarity of his pedagogy is clear from his *nimmuqim*, the explicative and critical notes that he added to his editions of the grammars of Moses and David Qimhi.[92] Although his grammatical works were composed for Jews, he sometimes uses, for the sake of clarity, the Latin metalanguage. For instance, in *Pirqei Eliyahu*, he refers to the Latin syntax when explaining the function of certain preposi-tions: *we-ha-romiyim qor'im le-zeh ha-shimmush dativu leshon netina*, "the La-tins call this use 'dative', which means to give".[93] In his own grammatical works he distinguishes between transitive and intransitive verbs (including sta-tive verbs like *'ahev*) and shows that all verbs that occur in the *nif'al* are not passive in their meaning. He does not admit the vestigial *po'el* whose existence David Qimhi had recognized, but instead he includes the *po'el* and *pa'ul* (a *pa'al* past participle) with the *nif'al*. All told, his analyses of tense and the *waw*-conversive are quite subtle without being dogmatic, recognizing that de-viations from his rules occur, especially in the use of tenses, but that they are rare and tend to occur in prophetic books, in Psalms, Proverbs and Job, which is to say that in this context he already entertains a notion of the stratification of biblical Hebrew, even if he was not ready to revise the traditional order of the biblical books to accommodate a historicizing theory of *qere* and *ketiv*.

In conclusion, because of his independence, his distinctions between attesta-tion and dogmatic formulations, and his notions of frequency of linguistic phenomena, Levita / Ashkenazi clearly initiated modern methods of study of the language of the Bible.

---

[91] A. SPERBER, *A Historical Grammar of Biblical Hebrew* (Leiden: Brill 1966).

[92] Printed in Venice (D. Bomberg 1546), the volume *Diqduqim* ("grammars") gathers several grammatical Jewish texts, in Hebrew by, among others, Moses Qimhi and Abraham ibn Ezra.

[93] *Pirqei Eliyahu* (ed. and tr. by S. Münster; Basel: s.n. [Froben] 1527) p. [186] of the numer-ized edition, available on the Bibliothèque Nationale de France website (gallica.bnf.fr). S. Münster translates: *Romani vocant hoc officium dativum, a vocabulo dare.*

CHAPTER TWELVE

From the First Printed Hebrew, Greek and Latin Bibles to the First Polyglot Bible, the Complutensian Polyglot: 1477–1517

By ADRIAN SCHENKER, Fribourg, CH

General works: The Cambridge History of the Bible [CHB] (2. *The West from the Fathers to the Reformation*, ed. G. W. H. Lampe; Cambridge: Cambridge UP 1969; repr. 1980; 3. *The West From the Reformation to the Present Day*, ed. S. L. Greenslade; 1963; repr. 1978); W. A. COPINGER, *The Bible and Its Transmission* (London: Henry Sotheran 1897; repr. Leipzig 1972); C. D. GINSBURG, *Introduction to the Massoretico-Critical Edition of the Hebrew Bible* (London: Trinitarian Bible Society 1897; repr. New York: Ktav 1966); M. J. MULDER, "The Transmission of the Biblical Text", idem (ed.), *Mikra. Text, Translation, Reading and Interpretation of the Hebrew Bible in Ancient Judaism and Early Christianity* (Assen / Maastricht: van Gorcum / Philadelphia: Fortress 1988).

1. Early Printings of the Hebrew Bible

Sources and studies: C. BERNHEIMER, "Prophetae Posteriores (1487 [1486]). Eine neue, hebräische Inkunabel", *Zeitschrift für hebräische Bibliographie* 23 (1920) 36–40; J. BLOCH, "Early Hebrew Printing in Spain and Portugal", *BNYPL* 42 (1938) v, 371–420 (= *Hebrew Printing and Bibliography. Studies by Joshua Bloch and Others ... Selected and with a Preface by* CH. BERLIN; New York: The New York Public Library / Ktav 1976, 5–54 [second pag. 7–56; the first pag. is quoted]); idem, "Incunabula", *UJE* 5 (1941) 548–53; idem, "Hebrew Printing in Naples", *BNYPL* 46/vi (1942) 489–514 (= *Hebrew Printing and Bibliography*, New York 1976, 1–28 [second pag. 111–37; the first pag. is quoted]); idem, *The People and the Book. The Background of Three Hundred Years of Jewish Life in America* (A tricentennial exhibition at the New York Public Library ... October-December, 1954) 1–134 (= *Hebrew Printing and Bibliography*, 1976, 343–475); *Die Bibelsammlung der Württembergischen Landesbibliothek Stuttgart* (Stuttgart-Bad Cannstatt: Frommann-Holzboog 1984-): Abt. 1. *Polyglotte Bibeldrucke und Drucke in den Grundsprachen*, 1. *Polyglotte Bibeldrucke* (in prep.); 2. *Hebräische Bibeldrucke* (in prep.); 3. *Griechische Bibeldrucke* (beschrieben von St. Strohm unter Mitarbeit von P. Amelung / I. Schauffler / E. Zwink; 1984); 4. *Lateinische Bibeldrucke* (beschrieben von Ch. Heitzmann / M. Santos Noya unter Mitarbeit von I. Schauffler / E. Zwink; 2002); T. H. DARLOW / H. F. MOULE, *Historical Catalogue of the Printed Editions of Holy Scripture in the Library of the British and Foreign Bible Society*, II. *Polyglots and Languages other than English* (London: British and Foreign Bible Society 1903–09; repr. Cambridge, MA: Maurizio Martino Publisher, s.a.); I. B. DE-ROSSI, *De Hebraicae Typographiae origine ac primitiis...*, 2nd edn. (Erlangae: Schleich 1778); idem, *De typographia Hebraeo-Ferrariensi commentarius historicus quo Ferrarienses Iudaeorum editiones Hebraicae Hispanicae Lusitanae recensentur...*, ed. altera, accessit cel. Auctoris epistola ... (Erlangae: Palm 1781); idem, *Variae Lectiones Veteris Testamenti* 1 (Parmae: ex Regio Typographeo 1786; repr. Amsterdam: Philo Press 1970); idem, *Annales Hebraeo-Typographici sec. XV et ab anno 1501 ad 1540* (Parmae: ex Regio Typographeo 1795; repr. Amsterdam: Philo Press 1969); idem, *Scholia critica in V. T. Libros seu Supplementa ad varias Sacri Textus lectiones* (Parmae: ex Regio Typographeo 1798; repr. Amsterdam: Philo Press 1970); idem, *Libri stampati di letteratura sacra, ebraica ed orientale della biblioteca del dottore G. Bernardo De-Rossi* (printed catalogue written by De-Rossi of the books of his collection; Parma s.a.); A. FREIMANN, "A Gazetteer of Hebrew Printing. With a Foreword by J. Bloch", *BNYPL* 49 (1945) v, 355–74; vi, 456–68; vii, 530–40; xii, 913–39 (repr. with rev. and add. 1946 = *Hebrew Printing and Bibliography*, 1976, 1–86 [second pag. 255–340; the first pag. is quoted]); A. FREIMANN / M. MARX (eds.), *Thesaurus Typographiae Hebraicae Saeculi XV - Hebrew Printing in the Fifteenth Century* (A Facsimile Reproduction of the Edition 1924–1931; Jerusalem: Universitas-Booksellers 1968); F. R. GOFF, *Incunabula in American Libraries. A Third Census of Fifteenth-Century Books Recorded in North-American Collections* (Reproduced from the annotated copy maintained by Frederick R. Goff, Compiler and Editor; Millwood, NY: Kraus Reprint 1973) 317–19; B. HALL, "Biblical Scholarship: Editions and Commentaries", CHB 3 (1978) 38–93; B. G. MANZONI, *Annali tipografici dei Soncino* 1–4 (Bologna: presso Gaetano Romagnoli 1883–86; repr. Westmead, Farnborough: Gregg International 1969); H. M. Z. MEYER, *A Short-Title Catalogue of the Hebrew Incunables and Other Books Illustrated in the "Thesaurus" with some Bibliographical References. Supplement to Part I of A. Freimann - M. Marx, Thesaurus Typographiae Hebraicae Saeculi XV...* (Jerusalem: Universitas-Booksellers 1968); H. M. Z. MEYER, "Incunabula", EncJud 8 (1972) 1319–44; A. K. OFFENBERG, *Hebrew Incunabula in Public Collections. A First International Census* (BHRef 47; Nieuwkoop: De Graaf 1990); idem, "Hebräischer Buchdruck", in: S. CORSTEN e.a. (eds.), *Lexikon des gesamten Buchwesens* 3 (Stuttgart: Hiersemann ²1991) 408–10; idem, *A Choice of Corals. Facets of Fifteenth-Century Hebrew Printing* (BHRef 52; Nieuwkoop: De Graaf 1992); idem, "Hebrew Printing of the Bible in the XVth Century", in: P. SAENGER / K. VAN KAMPEN (eds.), *The Bible as Book. The First Printed Editions* (London: The British Library & Oak Knoll Press 1999) 71–78; J. QUETIF / J. ECHARD, *Scriptores Ordinis Praedicatorum recensiti...* 1 (Lutetiae Parisiorum 1719); K. REINHARDT / H. SANTIAGO OTERO, *Biblioteca bíblica Ibérica medieval* (MeH(M) 1; Madrid: CSIC 1986); M. SCHWOB, *Les incunables orientaux et les impressions orientales au commencement du XVIe siècle* (Paris: Techener 1883; repr. Nieuwkoop: B. de Graaf 1964); idem, "Deux singuliers éléments de bibliographie orientale", *JA* 6 (1915) 311–20; M. STEINSCHNEIDER, *Catalogus Librorum Hebraeorum in Bibliotheca Bodleiana* (Berolini: Friedlaender 1852–1860 = repr. s.a.); G. TAMANI, *Gli incunaboli ebraici delle biblioteche d'Italia, Indici e cataloghi*, NS. Ministero per i beni culturali e ambientali, *Indice generale degli incunaboli delle biblioteche d'Italia* VI (Roma: Istituto poligrafico e zecca dello Stato 1981) 281–304; C. UGOLOTTI, "Incunaboli ebraici", *Indice generale degli incunaboli delle biblioteche d'Italia. Incunaboli della biblioteca Palatina di Parma*, 1. *Aggiornamento dati corredati delle segnature relativi agli incunaboli della biblioteca Palatina di Parma* (Parma: Biblioteca Palatina, s.a.); R. WEBER, "Der Text der Gutenbergbibel und seine Stellung in der Geschichte der Vulgata", *Johannes Gutenbergs zweiundvierzigzeilige Bibel* (Faksimile Ausgabe nach dem Exemplar der Staatsbibliothek Preussischer Kulturbesitz Berlin. Kommentarband; München: Idion Verlag s.a. [1979]); H. C. ZAFREN, "Bible Editions, Bible Study and the Early History of Hebrew Printing", *Eretz-Israel* 16 (H. M. Orlinsky Volume; Jerusalem: Israel Exploration Society 1982).

Soon after Gutenberg's Latin Bibles[1] the printing of Hebrew Bibles, in their entirety or in portions, started. The earliest dated printed Bible text is the book of Psalms. Its date is 20 Elul 5237 (29 August 1477). This book is in a small folio size. Apparently it was printed in Bologna. The printers were Jews from Germany: Joseph Neriah, Chayyim Mordekai, Hezekiah Montero de Venturo.[2] They used 'Rashi' or rabbinic characters for it. The first four Psalms

---

[1] *Editio princeps* of *Biblia Latina Vulgata* (Mainz 1455; Bible with 42 lines). In the following notes, it should be noted that in most cases De-Rossi, *Libri stampati*, with a number, will be indicated. This work corresponds to De-Rossi's personal catalogue of his library, and today the numbers are the signatures of De-Rossi's book collection (*Raccolta De-Rossi*) in the Biblioteca Palatina of Parma. Some incunabula do not appear in De-Rossi, *Libri stampati*. For these the signature of the Biblioteca Palatina will be given as well. As for Freimann, Thesaurus (1968), the numbers within parentheses refer to incunabula which were to be reproduced in the 2nd volume of the Thesaurus which was never published. Meyer, Catalogue (1969), has no pagination.

[2] De-Rossi, *Annales*, no. 5 (1795) 14–19; Ginsburg, Introduction, no. 1 (1897) 780–94; Darlow / Moule, Catalogue, no. 5071 (1903/11) 701; Freimann, Thesaurus, no. A13, 1–4 (1968) 30–

only have vowel-points, but no accents. Two other editions of the Psalms without accents and vowel-points are known, again in 'Rashi' or semi-cursive characters.[3] Their format is in *sexdecimo*. Offenberg makes a case that these supposedly two editions are in fact a unique edition of the Psalms. He lists five still existing copies in Parma (two), London, Oxford and Karlsruhe. On grounds of printing technique and of the paper used he comes to the conclusion that this pocket Psalter was printed around 1474–77 in the region of Parma, Mantua and Ferrara, and that it is thus the first printed Hebrew Bible text outside of a commentary.[4] Only twenty five years later the preparation of the first printed edition of a polyglot Bible began in Alcalá de Henares in Spain![5]

In this short interval an intense printing activity of Hebrew books shot up in the Jewish communities of Italy, Spain and Portugal.[6] These were the only countries where the printing of Hebrew books and Bibles flourished before 1500, while no Christian printers before the Complutensian Polyglot tried to print either Bibles or other books in Hebrew characters.[7] It is remarkable that Spain until 1492 and Portugal until about 1497 were, besides Italy, the homelands for Hebrew printing. The *incunabula* of the Iberian peninsula are of even better printing quality than those of Italy. The first Jewish printers in Italy, however, seem to have immigrated there from Germany. The Hebrew biblical incunables were often printed on vellum, but also on paper. Thus the polyglot of Alcalá takes up and continues a flourishing Jewish printing tradition abruptly cut off by the expulsion of Jews from Spain 1492 and from Portugal 1496.

Before the dated *editio princeps* of the whole Hebrew Bible in 1488 (see be-

---

33; Meyer, Catalogue, no. 24 (1969); Goff, Incunabula, no. Heb-28 (1973) 318; Tamani, Incunaboli, no. E24 (1981) 288; Mulder, Biblical Text (1988) 116–17; De-Rossi, *Libri stampati*, no. 1253, p. 17. The first dated printed Hebrew book, Rashi's commentary on the *Torah*, left the printer's press on February 5 or 18, 1475 in Reggio di Calabria, cf. Freimann, Gazetteer (1945/46) 61, 82. Meyer, Catalogue no. 1–9 (1969), however, assigns to the first Hebrew printed books dates between 1463 and 1475; Offenberg, Hebrew printing (1999) 72, mentions six undated books printed in square characters produced in Rome at about 1469–73.

[3] De-Rossi, *Annales*, no. 16 and 17 (1795) 128–30; De-Rossi, *Scholia critica*, no. 320 (1798) XII; Ginsburg, Introduction (1897) 794; Freimann, Thesaurus, no. A14, 1–3 (1968) 34–36; Meyer, Catalogue, no. 25 and 26 (1969); Tamani, Incunaboli, no. E26 and E27 (1981) 289; De-Rossi, *Libri stampati*, no. 122 and 123, p. 17.

[4] Meyer, Catalogue, no. 25, 26: in *duodecimo*; Offenberg, Hebrew Printing (1999) 73–77.

[5] Sáenz-Badillos, Filología (1990) 204; Bloch, Hebrew Printing in Spain (1938) 45; Darlow / Moule, Catalogue (1903/11) 2. Bataillon, Erasme (1991) 41, however, considers the date of 1510 to be more likely.

[6] Cf. the list of Hebrew incunabula in Meyer, Catalogue (1969); Meyer, Incunabula (1972) 1335–38; Hall, Scholarship (1963) 48–50. According to Offenberg, Hebrew Printing (1999) 73, the first known Hebrew book in Spain is Rashi's commentary on the Pentateuch, printed by Solomon b. Moses Alkabiz Halevi in Guadalajara.

[7] According to Quétif-Echard, Scriptores (1719) 861–63, the Dominican Petrus Niger (Schwarz) composed a *Tractatus ad Judaeorum perfidiam extirpandam* (wich is sometimes given the title *Stella Messiae*) which was printed by Conrad Finer in Esslingen on 6 July 1475. The table of contents reproduced by Quétif-Echard, p. 862, shows that this book contained an alphabet and the Decalogue printed in Hebrew characters while the rest of the Hebrew terms quoted by Schwarz were given in transliteration in Latin characters. Cf. Bedouelle, L'humanisme (1989) 64. – At the end of the fifteenth century, Hebrew printing presses were established in Constantinople and Saloniki; cf. Offenberg, Hebrew printing (1999) 72–73.

low) many partial editions of biblical books had been printed. These editions will be described here as far as they are dated or can be given a date with some likelihood.[8]

The Jewish Theological Seminary of America, New York, owns 27 leaves of Leviticus and Numeri, printed in Spain, perhaps around 1480.[9] These fragments of the Pentateuch might form part of a whole Bible to which possibly belongs the fragment of Hosea 8–11 in the *Raccolta De-Rossi* of the Biblioteca Palatina in Parma.[10] The Parma fragment is in folio size and has neither vowel-points nor accents. De-Rossi observes that it is full of textual variants. He calls it *amasorethica editio*. If the New York and Parma fragments belong indeed together they could represent the *editio princeps* of the whole Bible.[11] Printer, place and date however of these fragments are unknown.

Around 1480 a Pentateuch with the Five Scrolls and the *Haphtaroth*, together with Targum Onkelos, was printed at some unknown place in Italy in folio format. It has vowel-points and accents. The printers possibly were Isaac b. Aaron of Este and Moses b. Eliezer Raphael.[12] Another Pentateuch, with Targum Onkelos and the commentary of Rashi, in folio size, was printed in Bologna in 1482. It bears the date 5 Adar 5242 (25 Jan. 1482). The printer was Abraham b. Chayyim dei Tintori of Pesaro. He printed this Torah for Joseph Caravita.[13] This is the *editio princeps* of the Pentateuch with a date.

In the same year 1482, or a year later, the *Five Scrolls* were printed, probably in Bologna. They might be the *editio princeps* of that biblical book. The printer was again Abraham b. Chayyim dei Tintori, just mentioned. The text is provided with vowel-points and accents. It is a folio volume. Together with the Bible text, the commentaries of Rashi on Ruth, Ecclesiastes, Canticles, Lamentations and of Ibn Ezra on Esther appear on the top and at the bottom of the page. The biblical text is in square characters while the commentaries are printed in the so-called 'Rashi' or semi-cursive types. The sequence of the scrolls is the 'historic' one: Ruth, Ecclesiastes, Canticles, Lamentations, Esther.[14] It consists of 27 leaves and is printed on vellum like most of the Pentateuch incunables. According to De-Rossi it was to belong as a second volume to the Bologna Torah of 1482 just mentioned.[15]

In 1487 (or 1486) an edition of the *Latter prophets* was to appear in Spain, in a small town of the province of Teruel in Aragón, Híjar (or Hixar). Printed in two columns it has no vowel-points. Only the Bible text has been reproduced, no commentary. Its printer was Eliezer b. Alantansi. The

---

[8] Meyer, Catalogue (1969) no. 109, 110, 229, 230, 244, 247, 249, 253, 257–268, gives the list of mainly fragmentary Bible incunabula which cannot be dated with certainty.

[9] Freimann, Thesaurus, no. (B50); Meyer, Catalogue (1969) no. 256; Goff, Incunabula, no. Heb-12 (1973) 317.

[10] De-Rossi, *Annales*, no. 28 (1795) 145–46; Freimann, Thesaurus (1969), no. (B50); Meyer, Catalogue (1969) no. 256; Tamani, Incunaboli, no. E19 (1981) 288; De-Rossi, *Libri stampati*, no. 1463/1.

[11] The relation between these incunabula needs to be studied further (unless this has been done in a study which I ignore).

[12] Freimann, Thesaurus, no. B40,1–2 (1968) 321–22; Meyer, Catalogue (1969) no. 27; Goff, Incunabula, no. Heb-13 (1973) 317. Freimann and Marx give no date and consider this Pentateuch to be printed in Spain or Portugal while Meyer identifies names of the printers and correctors. Meyer dates it between 1480 and 1490.

[13] De-Rossi, *Annales*, no. 7 (1795) 22–28; Ginsburg, Introduction, no. 2 (1897) 794–802; Darlow / Moule, Catalogue, no. 5072 (1903/11) 701; Freimann, Thesaurus, no. A15,1–2 (1968) 37–38; Meyer, Catalogue (1969) no. 22; Goff, Incunabula, no. Heb-18 (1973) 317; Tamani, Incunaboli, no. E12 (1981) 286; De-Rossi, *Libri stampati*, no. 1299 and 1300, p.13.

[14] De-Rossi, *Annales*, no. 18 (1795) 130–31; De-Rossi, *Variae Lectiones* (1786) 151–52; Freimann, Thesaurus, no. (A16); Meyer, Catalogue (1969) no. 23; Tamani, Incunaboli, no. E34 (1981) 290; De-Rossi, *Libri stampati*, no. 1362, p.21. Cf. Ginsburg, Introduction, no. 2* (1897) 802.

[15] De-Rossi, *Annales* (1795) 130–31. Meyer, Catalogue (1969) no. 241, assigns a book of Proverbs with Radak's commentary to the year 1482 and to the printer Toledano in Lisbon (with a question mark).

book, in quarto, does indicate neither place nor printer but it offers the date.[16] The *Former Prophets* were issued in a printed edition at about the same time in Italy. Joshua Solomon Soncino, originating from Speyer, printed them in a small folio format on the 6 Marcheshwan 5246 (10 or 15 October 1485).[17] The biblical text occupies one column of the page while the second column and the bottom of the page contains the commentary of Radak. Only the consonantic text is printed. A year later, the same printer issued in a second volume of the same size the *Latter Prophets*.[18] The layout and the types (square characters for the Bible text and semi-cursive ones for Radak) are identical with the *Former Prophets*. In the mind of the printer, this edition of the two parts of the prophetical books was the continuation of the Bologna Pentateuch of 1482. Obviously, these three incunabula taken together were to prepare an edition of the whole Hebrew Bible in the planning of the printer.

In 1487 another Psalter in small folio was published in Naples by the printer of Bavarian origin, Joseph b. Jacob Ashkenazi Gunzenhauser. The book is dated from 4 Nisan 5247 = 28 March 1487.[19] The biblical text has vowel-points. The layout of the page is in two columns, one of which displays Radak's commentary. Soon after the Psalms, the rest of the *Ketuvim* was issued in the same format. The Proverbs were printed with the commentary of Immanuel b. Solomon Yekutiel of Rome (a friend of Dante).[20] The third part of *Ketuvim* is dated from 9 Tishri 5247 (26 September 1487), or perhaps 5248.[21] It is arranged in layout and printing similar to the Psalms and Proverbs. Job, with the commentary of Levi b. Gershom (Ralbag), is followed by Canticles, Ecclesiastes with Rashi's commentary, then Lamentations with the commentary of Joseph Kara, followed by Ruth, Esther, Daniel, Ezra-Nehemiah with the commentary of Rashi, and 1–2 Chronicles with a Pseudo-Rashi commentary.

In the same year 1487 a Pentateuch was printed under the date of 9 Tammuz 5247 (30 June 1487).[22] Its printing place was Faro on the south coast of Portugal (province of Algave). It is the first dated printed portion of the Bible on the Iberian peninsula. Its format is a small folio. It has (sometimes incorrect) vowel-points, but no accents. It offers the biblical text without commentary or Targum. This Hebrew *Torah* is the first book ever printed in Portugal.[23] In Híjar another Pen-

---

[16] Meyer, Catalogue (1969) no. 223 (with two errors in his note); Tamani, Incunaboli, no. E21 (1981) 288. Signature: Parma, Biblioteca Palatina, Libri stampati De-Rossi 1463/1. It is not mentioned by De-Rossi, *Annales*, and it is not reproduced by Freimann, Thesaurus, where it has the number (B10). Bernheimer, Prophetae posteriores (1920) 38 (not 1930 as indicated in Meyer, Catalogue) gives the date 5247 which corresponds to 1487 (or 1486) and which allows to identify the printer Eliezer ibn Alantansi who dated another of his books exactly in the same way.

[17] De-Rossi, *Annales*, no. 12 (1795) 40–44; Ginsburg, Introduction, no. 3 (1897) 803–07; Darlow / Moule, Catalogue, no. 5073 (1903/11) 702; Freimann, Thesaurus, no. A31,1–4 (1968) 65–69; Goff, Incunabula, no. Heb-22 (1973) 318; Tamani, Incunaboli, no. E17 (1981) 287; De-Rossi, *Libri stampati*, no. 1252, p. 16. Origin of the Soncino family: Offenberg, Hebrew Printing (1999) 72.

[18] De-Rossi, *Annales*, no. 20 (1795) 131–33; Freimann, Thesaurus, no. A39,1–2 (1967/9) 82–83; Goff, Incunabula, no. Heb-24 (1973) 318; Tamani, Incunaboli, no. E 20 (1981) 288; De-Rossi, Libri stampati, no. 1173, p. 16. Cf. n. 17.

[19] De-Rossi, *Annales*, no. 15 (1795) 48–51; Ginsburg, Introduction, no. 4 (1897) 807–10; Darlow / Moule, Catalogue, no. 5074 (1903/11) 702; Freimann, Thesaurus, no. A57,1–2 (1968) 128–29; Goff, Incunabula, no. Heb-29 (1973) 318; Tamani, Incunaboli, no. E25 (1981) 288; De-Rossi, *Libri stampati*, no. 1046/1, p. 18. See notes 20 and 21.

[20] De-Rossi, *Annales*, no. 21 (1795) 133–35; Ginsburg, Introduction, no. 4 (1897) 810–11; Freimann, Thesaurus, no. A58,1–2 (1968) 128–29; Goff, Incunabula, no. Heb-34 (1973) 318–19; Tamani, Incunaboli, no. E32 (1981) 289; De-Rossi, *Libri stampati*, no. 1046/2, p. 20. See notes 19 and 21.

[21] De-Rossi, *Annales*, no. 44 (1795) 92; Ginsburg, Introduction, no. 4 (1897) 811–14; Freimann, Thesaurus, no. A59,1–2 (1968) 130–31; Goff, Incunabula, no. Heb-26 (1973) 318; Tamani, Incunaboli, no. E23 (1981) 288; De-Rossi, *Libri stampati*, no. 1046/3–11, p. 20. See notes 19 and 21.

[22] Ginsburg, Introduction, no. 5 (1897) 815–20; Freimann, Thesaurus, no. B14,1–3 (1968) 260–62; Meyer, Catalogue (1969) no. 233.

[23] Bloch, Hebrew Printing in Spain (1938) 27–32, esp. 28.

tateuch in folio with *Haphtarot* and Canticles, Ruth, Ecclesiastes, Lamentations, Esther appeared at about the same time (1487–88).[24] Its text is printed without vowels and accents. The printer probably was the same who had published shortly before the *Latter Prophets*.[25]

In 1488 Joshua Solomon Soncino published a whole Bible in the small town of Soncino. It bears the date 11 Iyyar 5248 (22 April 1488). This is the (dated) *editio princeps* of the full Hebrew Bible.[26] In small folio size this Bible offers a vocalized and accentuated text in two columns without Targums and commentaries. No edition is signalled for 1489 while the following year saw the publication of a Pentateuch, the *Three Poetical Books* (תא״ם) and perhaps still other parts of the Bible: a *Torah* was printed in Híjar in the month of Av (19 July – 17 August 5250) by the printer Eliezer ibn Alantansi.[27] It is a small folio with Targum Onkelos and the commentary of Rashi, both printed in semi-cursive character. Between them the Bible text, in square character, lacks accents and vowel-points. An edition of Psalms, Job, Proverbs is dated from the same year (29 Kislev 5251 = 12 Dec. 1490). It is a quarto volume, printed in Naples by the Soncino press.[28] It shows accents and vowel-points. In the years 1490–92 several biblical books or groups of books left the press of Joshua Soncino in Naples; they have survived only in fragments.[29] In 1491 the same printer, or his sons according to FREIMANN, GOFF, produced a *Pentateuch* with the commentary of Rashi, *Haphtarot* and the *Five Scrolls* as well as the *Megillat Antiochos.*[30] The order of the *Megillot* is liturgical (Canticles, Ruth, Lamentations, Ecclesiastes, Esther). It is in folio size and has vowel-points and accents in the

---

[24] De-Rossi, *Annales*, no. 27 (1795) 143–45; Freimann, Thesaurus, no. B12,1–3 (1968) 254–56 (between 1486–89); Meyer, Catalogue (1969) no. 227 (between 1487–88); Goff, Incunabula, no. Heb-14 (1973) 317; Tamani no. E9 (1981) 286; De-Rossi, *Libri stampati*, no. 1045, p. 14.

[25] Cf. n. 16.

[26] De-Rossi, *Annales*, no. 20 (1795) 54–58; Ginsburg, Introduction, no. 6 (1897) 820–31; Darlow / Moule, Catalogue, no. 5075 (1903/11) 702; Freimann, Thesaurus, no. A45,1–4 (1968) 96–99; Meyer, Catalogue (1969) no. 49; Goff, Incunabula, no. Heb-8 (1973) 317; Tamani, Incunaboli, no. E4 (1981) 285; De-Rossi, *Libri stampati*, no. 1244–1246, p. 10. (Ginsburg identifies the date as 13 Febr. following Steinschneider, Catalogus [1852] 2, but Steinschneider read the month *Adar* while it is clearly *Iyyar*, cf. Freimann, Thesaurus [1968] 98.)

[27] De-Rossi, *Annales*, no. 32 (1795) 73–76; Ginsburg, Introduction, no. 7 (1897) 831–36; Freimann, Thesaurus, no. B11,1–4 (1968) 250–52; Meyer, Catalogue (1969) no. 228; Goff, Incunabula, no. Heb-19 (1973) 317; Tamani, Incunaboli, no. E13 (1981) 287; De-Rossi, *Libri stampati*, no. 1250, p. 13.

[28] De-Rossi, *Annales*, no. 25 (1795) 79–80; Freimann, Thesaurus, no. A68,1–4 (1968) 152–55; Meyer, Catalogue (1969) no. 60; Goff, Incunabula, no. Heb-32 (1973) 318; Tamani, Incunaboli, no. E30 (1981) 289; De-Rossi, *Libri stampati*, no. 1463/3. Meyer, Catalogue (1969) no. 58 adscribes a fragmentary Psalter, reproduced by Freimann, Thesaurus no. A91 (1968) 220, printed probably in Naples, to the same year 1490. According to Freimann it would be a product of the Soncino, according to Meyer, one of the Gunzenhausen press.

[29] *Pentateuch* in *octavo* with vowel-points and accents: De-Rossi, *Annales*, no. 32 (1795) 148 (date: 1483–92); Freimann, Thesaurus, no. A99,1–2 (1968) 233–34; Meyer, Catalogue (1969) no. 65; Goff, Incunabula, no. Heb-16 (1973) 317; Tamani, Incunaboli, no. E7 (1981) 286; De-Rossi, *Libri stampati*, no. 1463/9; *Pentateuch* with *Haphtarot*, vowel-points, accents, in folio: Freimann, Thesaurus, A98,1–2 (1968) 231–32; Meyer, Catalogue (1969) no. 64; Goff, Incunabula, no. Heb-17 (1973) 317; *Psalms*, vowel-points, accents, in *duodecimo*: Freimann, Thesaurus, no. A100 (1968) 235; Meyer, Catalogue (1969) no. 66; Goff, Incunabula, no. Heb-31.1–2 (1973) 318.

[30] De-Rossi, *Annales*, no. 38 (1995) 82–84; Freimann, Thesaurus, no. A70,2–3 (1968) 160–61; Meyer, Catalogue (1969) no. 63; Goff, Incunabula, No. Heb-21 (1973) 318; Tamani, Incunaboli, no. E15 (1981) 287; De-Rossi, *Libri stampati*, no. 1238, p. 13 (copy of vellum).

Bible text. In the month of Av 5251 (8 July-6 Aug. 1491) another *Torah* with Targum Onkelos and the commentary of Rashi was published in Lisbon by the printer Eliezer Toledano.[31] It is a beautiful small folio in two volumes. While Rashi's commentary in the upper and lower margin is printed in rabbinic character, the Hebrew and Aramaic Bible texts are vocalized and accentuated. The editors of the Complutensian Polyglot made use of this edition.[32]

Before summer 1492 Joshua Soncino published the second full Hebrew Bible in Naples.[33] It is a small folio, giving the Bible text only, displayed in two columns and provided with vowel-points and accents. The *Megillot*, arranged according to the festival order (Canticles, Ruth, Lamentations, Ecclesiastes, Esther), immediately follow the Pentateuch. The book is adorned with fine woodcuts. The *Three Poetical Books* are laid out on the full breadth of the page in a hemistichal division which does not correspond to the hemistichs of the verses.[34] A list of the *Haphtarot* concludes the volume. This Bible was sold in copies of vellum and of paper. It served for the translators of the Zurich Bible of 1535 (Conrad Pellican and the "Prophezey") as their Hebrew text.[35] Meanwhile the printer Gershom (Menzlein) Soncino in Brescia produced under the date of 24 Shevat 5252 (23 Jan. 1492) a Pentateuch with *Haphtarot* and the *Five Scrolls* in the liturgical order, in a quarto format.[36] This Pentateuch was to be reprinted in a slightly modified form for the edition of the whole Bible in Brescia 1494.

On the 1 Av 5252 (25 July 1492) Don Samuel d'Ortas printed the Proverbs in a folio edition, probably in Leiria, some 120 km north of Lisbon.[37] He care-

---

[31] De-Rossi, *Annales*, no. 37 (1795) 81–82; Ginsburg, Introduction, no. 8 (1897) 836–47; Freimann, Thesaurus, no. B20,1–6 (1968) 274–79; Meyer, Catalogue (1969) no. 240; Goff, Incunabula, no. Heb-20 (1973) 318; Tamani, Incunaboli, no. E14 (1981) 287; De-Rossi, *Libri stampati*, no. 1359, 1360, 1361, p. 13 (copy on vellum). Meyer, Catalogue (1969) no. 245 attributes the fragment of one leaf of a Torah at the Jewish National and University Library, Jerusalem, to Toledano before 1492. A small Psalter (32° format), Freimann, Thesaurus (B32 A), may be dated from 1491 and stem from Spain, Meyer, Catalogue (1969) no. 268.

[32] Bloch, Hebrew Printing in Spain (1938) 42–45.

[33] De-Rossi, *Annales*, no. 25 (1795) 139–42; Ginsburg, Introduction, no. 9 (1897) 847–55; Darlow / Moule, Catalogue, no. 5076 (1903/11) 702; Freimann, Thesaurus, no. 75,1–5 (1968) 179–83; Meyer, Catalogue (1969) no. 69; Goff, Incunabula, no. Heb-9 (1973) 317; Tamani, Incunaboli, no. E5 (1981) 285; De-Rossi, *Libri stampati*, no. 1297, 1298, p. 10. Meyer, referring to M. Marx, states as *terminus ad quem* for this Bible 3 July 1492, probably sometimes in 1491.

[34] Freimann, Thesaurus, no. 75,2 (1968) 180.

[35] Hall, Scholarship (1963) 49; Bedouelle, L'humanisme (1989) 70. – Meyer, Catalogue (1969) no. 61, mentions another fragment of a *Torah* which he considers to be a product of the Soncino press in Naples of 1491; he refers to Freimann, Thesaurus, no. (A70 A). In the colophon of an edition of Rashi's commentary on the Pentateuch printed at Zamora in 1492 (or 1487), cf. Freimann, Thesaurus, no. B13,1–3 (1968) 257–59, here p. 259, Meyer, Catalogue (1969) no. 251, there is a mention of a Pentateuch printed at Zamora of which no copy seems to be known.

[36] De-Rossi, *Annales*, no. 41 (1795) 88–89; Ginsburg, Introduction, no. 12 (1897) 865–71; Darlow / Moule, Catalogue, no. 5077 (1903/11) 702; Freimann, Thesaurus, no. A78,1–3 (1968) 198–200; Meyer, Catalogue (1969) no. 84; Goff, Incunabula, no. Heb-15 (1973) 317; Tamani, Incunaboli, no. E10 (1981) 286; De-Rossi, *Libri stampati*, no. 288, p. 14.

[37] De-Rossi, *Annales*, no. 44 (1795) 92–93; Ginsburg, Introduction, no. 11 (1897) 859–65; Bloch, Hebrew Printing in Spain (1938) 36–37; Freimann, Thesaurus, no. B26,1–3 (1968) 290–92; Meyer, Catalogue (1969) no. 252; Goff, Incunabula, no. Heb-33 (1973) 318; Tamani, Incunaboli, no. E31 (1981) 289; De-Rossi, *Libri stampati*, no. 1176, p. 20. (Freimann's legends to the facsimiles erroneously mention Radak instead of Ralbag.)

fully vocalized and accentuated both the Masoretic text and the Targum, while the side and lower margins of the page were occupied by the commentaries of Meïri and Levi ben Gershom (Ralbag) in semi-cursive characters. In Lisbon, Eliezer Toledano produced in the same year 5252 (1492) an edition of Isaiah and Jeremiah with Radak's commentary.[38] It is the companion volume of the *Torah* printed a year earlier by the same printer in the same small folio size. It lacks the Targum.[39] Radak is displayed in the upper, lower and side margins. In both books the vowels are not always perfectly placed. Probably in the same year, Toledano published the Proverbs with the commentary *Kav w-Naki* of David b. Solomon ibn Yachya.[40] The size, the characters of the Bible text and the commentary, and the layout of the page are the same as in the Pentateuch of 1491 and Isaiah and Jeremiah just mentioned. These three portions of the Bible obviously belong together. The Hebrew prints of Eliezer Toledano of Lisbon especially might have served as the models for the Complutensian Polyglot because of the printing quality and the vocalization of both their Hebrew and Aramaic texts.

At the end of the following year 1493 Gershom Soncino published in Brescia a new Pentateuch with *Haphtarot* and *Megillot*, dated from 15 Kislev 5254 (24 November 1493).[41] In fact this was a second, hardly modified edition of his Pentateuch of January 1492 (see above the Bible editions of that year). A month later, 7 Tevet 5254 (16 December 1493) the same printer produced a Psalter in *duodecimo*.[42] These two editions of the Soncino press restricted themselves to the vocalized, accentuated biblical text without commentaries. The date of 19–25 Sivan 5254 (24–30 May 1494) marks the edition of the new full Bible in two *octavo* volumes which Gershom (Menzlein) Soncino realized at Brescia.[43] The Torah was a new issue of the 1492 and 1493 editions. It offers the mere vocalized and accentuated Bible text without commentaries. The

---

[38] De-Rossi, *Annales*, no. 45 (1795) 94–96; Ginsburg, Introduction, no. 10 (1897) 855–59; Freimann, Thesaurus, no. B21,1–3 (1968) 282–84; Meyer, Catalogue (1969) no. 242; Goff, Incunabula, no. Heb-25 (1973) 318; Tamani, Incunaboli, no. E22 (1981) 288; De-Rossi, *Libri stampati*, no. 1174, p. 17.

[39] The Complutensian Polyglot will print likewise the vocalized Targum Onkelos but restrain itself from printing the Targum in the Prophets and the Writings.

[40] De-Rossi, *Annales*, no. 26 (1795) 143; Freimann, Thesaurus, no. B23,1–3 (1968) 286–88; Meyer, Catalogue (1969) no. 244; Goff, Incunabula, no. Heb-35 (1973) 319; Tamani, Incunaboli, no. E33 (1981) 290; De-Rossi, *Libri stampati*, no. 1176, p. 20. David ibn Yachya flourished in the fifteenth century. De-Rossi, *Annales*, p. 143, translates the title: *cabus et purus* ("a little, but pure and solid"), title of a rabbinical treatise.

[41] De-Rossi, *Annales*, no. 46 (1795) 96–98; Meyer, Catalogue, no. 85; Tamani, Incunaboli, no. E11 (1981) 286; De-Rossi, *Libri stampati*, no. 289, p. 14; cf. Ginsburg, Introduction, no. 12 (1897) 865–71; Darlow / Moule, Catalogue, no. 5077–5078 (1903/11) 702–03; Freimann, Thesaurus, no. (A79). Ginsburg, Darlow / Moule, Freimann, Thesaurus, no. A78,1–3, describe the first edition of this *Torah*, printed in 1492 (14 Shevat 5242) by Soncino in Brescia, see above. This edition was reissued in a slightly modified form at the end of 1493 for Soncino's third full Bible.

[42] De-Rossi, *Annales*, no. 47 (1795) 98–99; Freimann, Thesaurus, no. A80 (1960) 201; Meyer, Catalogue (1969) no. 87; Goff, Incunabula, no. Heb-30 (1973) 318; Tamani, Incunaboli, no. 28 (1981) 289; De-Rossi, *Libri stampati*, no. 1463/6,10. According to De-Rossi, Tamani the format is 16° or 32°.

[43] De-Rossi, *Annales*, no. 48 (1795) 99–104 (he proposes for the Hebrew date two equivalences: either 24 April-1 May or 24–31 May 1494); Ginsburg, Introduction, no. 13 (1897) 871–880; Darlow / Moule, Catalogue, no. 5078 (1903/11) 703; Freimann, Thesaurus, no. A81,1–2

Megillot, in liturgical order, immediately follow the Pentateuch. The text is printed in one column, except for the Psalms laid out in two columns. The printer explains in the colophon the reason for the small format: it was to be an affordable edition enabling many to carry the Bible with them as they carry the phylacteries, and to study day and night in it.[44] It is well known that Luther used this edition for his Bible translation.

Four months earlier, Samuel d'Ortas and his three sons had edited in Leiria the *Former Prophets* with the Targum and the commentaries of Radak and Ralbag. The date was 19–21 Shevat 5254 (26–28 January 1494).[45] Both Hebrew and Aramaic texts are vocalized and accentuated. It is a beautiful in-folio volume with the Bible text in square characters while the commentaries are printed in semi-cursive types.[46]

In the years after 1494 the expulsion of the Jews from Spain (30 March 1492) and later from Portugal and, as a consequence, the difficult economic conditions of the Jewish communities in Italy, which had to harbour thousands of refugees, brought the Hebrew printing to a standstill in Italy, Spain and Portugal for some years (until 1510).[47]

All Hebrew incunables restrain themselves from masoretic notes. However, the totals of letters and words at the end of books sometimes are given. Neither do they print the *qere* readings in the margin. Sometimes they combine the vowels of the *qere* with the consonants of the *ketiv* reading in the Bible text. It happens also that the *qere* reading is introduced into the text both with its vowels and its consonants; in other cases the *ketiv* is written and vocalized as such. Other masoretic features, like the twenty-six large and nineteen small letters in the *Torah*, the fifteen words with dots, the inverted *nun*'s (Num 10:35–36), the suspended *ain*'s, often are neglected. The fifty-four pericopes of the *Torah* usually are laid out and marked with their headings while sometimes the *setumot* and *petuhot* are not distinguished according to the masoretic rules; they often are characterized with *samek*'s and *pe*'s.[48] The layout, however, of the traditional songs and lists (Exodus 15, Deuteronomy 32, Judges 5, Joshua 12 etc.) is generally observed. The quality of the texts used depends on the manuscripts the printers had at their disposal. These were not outstanding

---

(1968) 202–203; Meyer, Catalogue (1969) no. 89; Goff, Incunabula, no. Heb-10 (1973) 317; Tamani, Incunaboli, no. E6 (1981) 286; De-Rossi, *Libri stampati*, no. 293, 290, 1463/6, p. 10.

[44] Freimann, Thesaurus (1968) 203, cf. De-Rossi, *Annales* (1795) 99–100. – Meyer, Catalogue (1969) no. 110 signals another possible complete Bible, of which fragments of the Prophets and Hagiographa are known. He assigns them a date around 1495 and Naples as place, but with question marks.

[45] De-Rossi, *Annales*, no. 49 (1795) 104–06; Schwob, Eléments (1915) 311–16; Bloch, Hebrew Printing in Spain (1938) 36–37; Freimann, Thesaurus, no. 27,1–5 (facsimile 4 missing!) (1968) 293–96; Meyer, Catalogue (1969) no. 254; Goff, Incunabula, no. Heb-23 (1973) 318; Tamani, Incunaboli, no. E18 (1981) 287; De-Rossi, *Libri stampati*, no. 1172, p. 16.

[46] Meyer, Catalogue (1969) nos. 256–67, Freimann, Thesaurus, no. B30,1–3 (1968) 302–04, no. B38,1–2, pp. 317–18, mention twelve other fragments of Bible incunables from Spain and Portugal which cannot be identified as to their place of production and date.

[47] Ginsburg, Introduction (1897) 880–81; Offenberg, Hebrew Printing (1999) 72–73.

[48] Ginsburg, Introduction (1897), Chap. XIII describes the textual features for each of the incunables he discusses.

masoretic manuscripts.[49] The Pentateuch is most often printed on vellum, the other books on paper. The number of copies of one edition is not known. When Cisneros projected his polyglot Bible before 1502 there were no more Jewish printers active in Spain, Portugal and Italy publishing new Bibles. On the other hand, especially in Portugal, but in Spain and Italy too, there existed fine, beautifully printed Hebrew and Aramaic vocalized (and accentuated) Bible texts which had paved the way for the first non Jewish Hebrew Bible printed in the Polyglot of Alcalá. OFFENBERG counts for the fifteenth century thirty-six full or partial Bible editions, twenty-four of them from Italy, twelve from Spain and Portugal. Two thirds of these editions offer the Bible text without commentaries. From these thirty-six biblical editions thirteen are Pentateuchs.[50]

As for the *Greek Old Testament*, the first complete editon in print, the *editio princeps*, is the Complutensian Polyglot as well, as far as the date of the printing is concerned.[51] Its publication, however, was delayed until 1520, and in the meantime, in February 1518 appeared in Venice a complete Bible with the Old Testament and the New Testament in Greek.[52] Before these complete editions of the Greek Old Testament, at least three incunables of the Septuagint Psalter were published in Milan and Venice.[53] The liturgical Psalter with the *Magnificat* and *Benedictus*, printed as a quarto volume on 20 September 1481 in Milan is the first Bible book to be printed in Greek, and the two hymns of the Gospel of Luke are the two first portions of the New Testament printed in Greek. The second liturgical Psalter appeared in Venice 1486 while Aldo Manuzio (Manutius) produced a third one before 1498 in Venice. This last Psalter was used again by Manuzio for his edition of the Greek Bible of 1518.

This complete Bible, Old Testament and New Testament, in Greek was the work of the printers Manuzio (the elder) and of his father-in-law Andrea Asulano. They based their edition mainly on three manuscripts of Cardinal Bessarion which exist still today in the Biblioteca Marciana in Venice.[54] The complete Latin Bible was printed between the first Gutenberg Bible of 42 lines from 1455 and 1500 about a hundred times,[55] while the book of Psalms exists in about 230 incunable editions. In addition there were also some special publications of the penitential Psalms alone.[56] From Spain a complete Bible incunable seems to have been published in Sevilla, printed in 1491.[57]

The Gutenberg Bible of 1455 reproduced a text of the recension of the University of Paris of average quality. Since the following printed Bible editions

---

[49] Ginsburg, Hebrew Old Testament (1926), collated the readings of twelve incunables.

[50] Offenberg, Hebrew Printing (1999) 73.

[51] The Greek OT was printed between 1515 and 10 July 1517, Darlow / Moule, Catalogue (1903/11) 3.

[52] Nestle, Bibelübersetzungen (1897) 4; Darlow / Moule, Catalogue (1903/11) 574.

[53] Nestle, Bibelübersetzungen (1897) 5; Darlow / Moule, Catalogue (1903/11) 576–77.

[54] Rahlfs, Verzeichnis (1914) 306–07: mss 29, 121, 68; Swete, Introduction (1914) 173–74.

[55] Copinger, Bible (1897) 220; Fritzsche / Nestle, Bibelübersetzungen (1897) 42; Rost, Bibel (1939) 367–72. Copinger mentions 124 editions; according to Rost's list, the number is 94.

[56] Pss 6; 31; 37; 50; 101; 129; 142 (numbering of Vulg). Rost, Bibel (1939) 386–92, 395, 418.

[57] Kaulen, Vulgata (1868) 305; Copinger, Bible (1897) 224. Reinhardt / Santiago Otero, Biblioteca Bíblica (1986) 13, however, affirm that no copy of this incunable is known.

took as their *Vorlage* this printed Gutenberg text, it became the standard Vulgate text of the second half of the fifteenth century, with but a few exceptions.[58] The number of copies of the single Latin Bible editions may have oscillated between 200 and 1000.[59] There ought to be added the Bibles published in the national languages between the Gutenberg Bible and the Complutensian Polyglot in order to get the full picture of the publishing of the Bible.[60]

2. The Polyglot Bible of Alcalá 1514–17

Sources and studies: *Anejo a la edición facsimile de la Biblia Políglota Complutense* (Valencia: Fundación Bíblica Española y Universidad Complutense de Madrid 1987); *Biblia Polyglotta Complutensis*: 1. *Vetus Testamentum multiplici lingua nunc primum impressum. Et imprimis Pentateuchus Hebraico Greco et Chaldaico Idiomate. Adiuncta unicuique sua latina interpretatione*; 2–4. *Secunda-Quarta Pars Veteris Testamenti* (colophon 10 July 1517); 5. *Novum Testamentum grece et latine in accademia complutensi noviter impressum* (colophon 10 January 1514); 6. *Vocabularium hebraicum atque chaldaicum totius veteris testamenti cum aliis tractatibus* ... (two colophons 17 March 1515 and 31 May 1515; facsimile repr. Rome: Gregoriana 1983–84).

V. BARON, *La contre-réforme devant la Bible. La question biblique* (Lausanne 1943; repr. Genève: Slatkine 1986); M. BATAILLON, *Erasme et l'Espagne* (Nouvelle éd. en 3 vol.; Genève: Droz 1991); D. BARTHÉLEMY, "Les relations de la Complutensis avec le papyrus 967 pour Ez 40,42 à 46,24", in: D. FRAENKEL / U. QUAST (eds.), *Studien zur Septuaginta* (FS R. Hanhart; MSU 20; Göttingen: Vandenhoeck & Ruprecht 1990) 253–61; idem, "La polyglotte d'Alcalá", *Critique textuelle de l'Ancien Testament* 3 (Fribourg, CH: Ed. Universitaires / Göttingen: Vandenhoeck & Ruprecht 1992) cxxxix–clx, cxciii; G.-TH. BEDOUELLE, *Le Quincuplex Psalterium de Lefèvre d'Etaples. Un guide de lecture* (Genève: Droz 1979); idem, "L'humanisme et la Bible", *Le temps des Réformes et la Bible* (BTT 5; Paris: Beauchesne 1989) 53–121; J. H. BENTLEY, "New Light on the Editing of the Complutensian New Testament", *Bibliothèque d'humanisme et de renaissance* (Travaux et documents XLII; Genève: Droz 1980); FRANZ DELITZSCH, *Complutensische Varianten zu dem alttestamentlichen Texte* (Feier des Reformationsfestes; Leipzig: Edelmann 1878); idem, *Fortgesetzte Studien zur Entstehungsgeschichte der Complutensischen Polyglotte* (Feier des Reformationsfestes; Leipzig: Edelmann 1886); F. FALK, *Die Bibel am Ausgang des Mittelalters, ihre Kenntnis und ihre Verbreitung* (Köln: Bachem 1905); E. FERNÁNDEZ TEJERO, "El texto hebreo de la Biblia políglota Complutense", and N. FERNÁNDEZ MARCOS, "El texto griego de la Biblia políglota Complutense", in: eadem / idem, *Biblia y humanismo* (Madrid: FUE 1997) 209–27; E. FERNÁNDEZ TEJERO, *La tradición textual española de la Biblia hebrea. El manuscrito 118-Z-42 (M 1) de la Biblioteca de la Universidad Complutense de Madrid* (Textos y estudios "Cardenal Cisneros" 14; Madrid: CSIC 1976); D. FRAENKEL, "Die Quellen der asterisierten Zusätze im zweiten Tabernakelbericht Exod 35–40", in: D. FRAENKEL / U. QUAST, *Studien zur Septuaginta* (FS R. Hanhart; MSU 20; Göttingen: Vandenhoeck & Ruprecht 1990) 140–86; J. GARCÍA ORO, *El cardenal Cisneros: vida y empresas* 1–2 (Madrid: Biblioteca de Autores Cristianos 1993) 492–502; A. GÓMEZ DE CASTRO, *De rebus gestis a Francisco Ximenio Cisnerio, Archiepiscopo Toletano libri octo*, Alvaro Gomecio Toletano authore, Alcalá 1569, ed. J. Oroz Reta, *De las hazañas de Francisco Jiménez de Cisneros* (Madrid: Fundación universitaria española 1984); C. J. HEFELE, *Der Cardinal Ximenes und die kirchlichen Zustände Spaniens am Ende des 15. und Anfang des 16. Jahrhunderts* (Tübingen: Laupp [2]1851) 94–147; P. KAHLE, "Die Complutensische Polyglotte", in: idem, *Die Kairoer Genisa. Untersuchungen zur Geschichte des hebräischen Bibeltextes und seiner Übersetzungen* (Berlin: Akademie-Verlag 1962) 134–38; F. KAULEN, *Geschichte der Vulgata* (Mainz: Kirchheim 1868); J. E. MANGENOT, "Polyglottes", DB 5 (1912) 513–29; J. MARTÍN ABAD, *La imprenta en Alcalá de Henares (1502–1600)* 1–3 (Madrid: Arco Libros 1991); idem., "The Printing Press at Alcalá de Henares. The Complutensian Polyglot Bible", in: P.

---

[58] Schneider, Gutenbergbibel (1954) 109–17.
[59] Rost, Bibel (1939) 417.
[60] Copinger, Bible (1897); Rost, Bibel (1939); Darlow / Moule, Catalogue (1903/11) etc.

Saenger / K. Van Kampen (eds.), *The Bible as Book. The First Printed Editions* (London: The British Library & Oak Knoll Press 1999) 101–15; E. Nestle, "Bibelübersetzungen, griechische", RE 3 (^{3}1897) 1–24; E. Nestle (E. Reuss), "Polyglottenbibeln", RE 15 (^{3}1904) 528–35; S. O'Connell, *From Most Ancient Sources. The Nature and Text-Critical Use of the Greek Old Testament Text of the Complutensian Polyglot Bible* (OBO 215; Fribourg: Academic Press / Göttingen: Vandenhoeck & Ruprecht 2006); F. Perez Castro, "Bíblias políglotas", Gran Enciclopedia Rialp 2 (Madrid: FUE 1979) 178–85; A. Rahlfs, *Verzeichnis der griechischen Handschriften des Alten Testaments* (MSU 2; Berlin: Weidmannsche Buchhandlung 1914); K. Reinhardt, *Bibelkommentare spanischer Autoren (1500–1700)* I–II (MeH(M) 5; Madrid: CSIC 1990, 1999); M. Revilla rico, *La políglota de Alcalá. Estúdio histórico-crítico* (Madrid: Imprenta helénica 1917); H. Rost, *Die Bibel im Mittelalter. Beiträge zur Geschichte und Bibliographie der Bibel* (Augsburg: Kommissions-Verlag 1939); A. Sáenz-Badillos, *La filología bíblica en los primeros helenistas de Alcalá* (Institución San Jerónimo 18; Estella: ed. Verbo divino 1990); A. Sáenz-Badillos / J. Targarona Borras, *Diccionario de autores Judios* (Sefarad. Siglos X–XV) (Cordoba: ed. El Almendro 1988); A. Schenker, "Der alttestamentliche Text in den vier grossen Polyglottenbibeln nach dem heutigen Stand der Forschung", *ThRv* 90 (1994) 177–88; idem, "Polyglotten", TRE 27 (1997) 22–25; H. Schneider, *Der Text der Gutenbergbibel* (BBB 7; Bonn: Hanstein 1954); M. V. Spottorno, "The Textual Significance of Spanish Polyglot Bibles", *Sef.* 62 (2002) 375–92; H. B. Swete, *An Introduction to the Old Testament in Greek.* (Rev. by R. R. Ottley; Cambridge: UP 1914; repr. Peabody, MA: Hendrickson 1989) 171–73 (this edition is identical with the first, Cambridge 1900, as far as the Polyglots are concerned); J. de Vallejo, *Memorial de la vida de Fray Francisco de Jiménez de Cisneros* (ed. A. de la Torre y del Cerro; Madrid: Bailly-Baillere 1913); M. Welte, "The Problem of the Manuscript Basis for the Earliest Printed Editions of the Greek New Testament", in: P. Saenger / K. van Kampen (eds.), *The Bible as Book. The First Printed Editions* (London: The British Library & Oak Knoll Press 1999) 117–24.

The originality of the Polyglot Bible of Alcalá appears against the background of the fifty years of Bible printing which preceded it. Indeed, for the first time an attempt of a critical edition in print of the Hebrew (and Aramaic), Greek and Latin Bible texts is made. The circumstances which surrounded this famous Bible were often described.[61] The accent here shall be laid on the choice of the texts which were to be printed.

Francisco (Gonzalo) Jiménez (Ximénez) de Cisneros (1436–1517),[62] first secular priest, then franciscan of the (strict) observance, 1495 archbishop of Toledo, chancelor of the kingdom of Castile, since 1507 Cardinal and Great Inquisitor, founded 1498 the University of Alcalá de Henares (with its Latin name *Complutum*). In this University – which later became the University of Madrid where it was to be transferred in the nineteenth century – he established a *collegium trilingue* that opened its doors on 26 July 1508, many years earlier than the *collegia trilinguia* of Louvain (1518) and Paris (1530)[63] and the teaching of Greek and Hebrew in Wittenberg.

The institution of a school of Latin, Greek and Hebrew within the Univer-

---

[61] See esp. Gómez, *De rebus gestis* (1569); Hefele, Ximenes (1851); Revilla Rico, Políglota (1917); Ginsburg, Introduction, no. 19 (1897) 906–25; Darlow / Moule, Catalogue, no. 1412; 5082 (1903/11) 2–6; 703; Mangenot, Polyglottes (1912) 513–29; Bloch, Hebrew Printing in Spain (1938) 41–48; Hall, Scholarship (1963) 50–52; Perez Castro, Bíblias (1979); Bedouelle, L'humanisme (1989) 80–83; Sáenz Badillos, Filología (1990); Bataillon, Erasme 1 (1991) 24–47; 781–93; 2, 28–31; García Oro, Cisneros 2 (1993); Schenker, Text (1994); idem, Polyglotten (1997).

[62] The main source for the life of Cisneros is Gómez, *De rebus gestis* (1569), ed. Oroz Reta, Hazañas.

[63] Bedouelle, L'humanisme (1989) 66–68. The *collegium* in Paris, established by Francis I, later became the *Collège de France*.

sity itself was at that time the sign of a modern, humanistic mind. In such an intellectual and spiritual climate the idea of an edition of a pure text of the Bible in the original Hebrew, Aramaic and Greek languages and of a genuine Latin Vulgate text lay at hand. But the technical side of the production of such a complex work in print, hardly fifty years after the invention of this new art and technique, needed audacity, an enterprising genius and important economic means. Cardinal Cisneros united these advantages with his humanist ideals – he had learned Greek and Hebrew himself. He was the very inspirator and realizer of this enormous venture, not only financing the editing and printing costs with his own means, but by actively framing the conception of the whole work.

He succeeded to win excellent collaborators for his edition. The printer, Arnaldo Guillén de Brocar, working in Logroño, realized the printing of the six volumes from 1514 until July 1517 in Alcalá.[64] His work is of outstanding, unrivalled perfection and beauty, especially in the New Testament.

The group of editors (*junta*) consisted of three converted Jews, Alfonso of Alcalá, Alfonso (Alonso) of Zamora (or Arcos) (ca. 1474–1544), Paul Coronel of Segovia (1480–1534), and of the two most famous Spanish humanists Antonio Martínez de Cala y Jaraba, known with his scholarly name as Antonio de Nebrija (or Lebrija, Lebrixa), in Latin Aelius Antonius Nebrissensis (1441 or 1444–1522), and Hernán Nuñez de Guzman, commander of the knightly order of Santiago and thus bearing the name *Comendador griego* or also *el Pinciano*. Besides these there were other scholars: Diego López de Zúñiga (Stunica or Astuniga, d. 1531), Juan de Vergara of Toledo (d. 1557), Demetrios Dukas of Crete and the two professors of the university of Alcalá, Gonzalo Gil and Bartholomé de Castro. All these scholars did not work simultaneously during the years 1502–1517, but they all were under the guiding of Jiménez, not without some tensions.[65]

The Polyglot was issued in six volumes and in 600 copies, some printed on vellum. The estimated costs were more than 50.000 ducats.[66] It was not published until 1520 although the printing was completed on 10 July 1517.

The conception of the Complutensian Polyglot was more than the simple simultaneous layout of the original texts and of the Vulgate. Such polyglots were popular at the beginning of the sixteenth century as is shown e.g. by the *Quincuplex Psalterium* by Faber Stapulensis or the Polyglot Psalter of Bishop Augustin Giustiniani OP (1470–1536).[67] But these (and similar editions) are not marked by the critical search for the best available texts. Jiménez had the am-

---

[64] Bloch, Hebrew Printing in Spain (1938) 45–48; Martín Abad, Imprenta de Alcalá (1991); idem, Printing Press (1999).

[65] For these editors cf. García Oro, Cisneros (1993); Sáenz Badillos, Filología (1990).

[66] Hefele, Ximénez (1851) 116.

[67] *Quincuplex Psalterium. Gallicum. Romanum. Hebraicum. Vetus. Conciliatum*, printed by Henri Stephanus (Etienne) in Paris 1509. It was a Psalter of five Latin translations (the Gallican, the Roman Psalters, Psalter of Jerome iuxta Hebraicum, a Psalter close to that of Augustine, a corrected Gallican Psalter) in synoptic fivefold display by Faber Stapulensis / Jacques Lefèvre d'Etaples (ca. 1455–1536; see Chap. 7.4, by A. Vanderjagt, in the present volume); cf. Bedouelle, Quincuplex Psalterium (1979); *Psalterium, Hebreum, Grecum, Arabicum, & Chaldeum, cum tribus latinis interpretationibus & glossis. Autore Augustino Justiniani. Genuae per Petrum Paulum Porrum. Anno 1516*. In the dedicatory letter to Pope Leo X Giustiniani refers to Origen's Hexapla and to his plan to publish the Old Testament and the New Testament in an eightfold polyglot edition. Cf. Bedouelle, L'humanisme (1989) 61; Darlow / Moule, Catalogue (1903/11) 1–2 mention the plans of Aldo Manuzio for a triglot Old Testament already at the end of the fifteenth century.

bition to edit the Bible in Latin and in its original languages in the most original textual forms. Therefore he made great efforts to establish a critical text, in
the measure of the possibilities afforded by his time. The previous Hebrew,
Aramaic, Greek and Latin editions had not aimed at this goal with the same
methodological and critical thoroughness. Beside this humanist ideal of establishing a text coming close to the original, with the help of the best manuscripts, the second leading idea was didactic.[68] Readers should be taught to
use the Bible text in the best way by making use of the original languages.
Therefore, to the edition itself didactic tools were added which by no means
were less important than the texts. The sixth volume contains thus a Hebrew
and Aramaic thesaurus (dictionary with the biblical occurrences of the words),
filling 122 folios, followed by a Latin index which allows the reader to find the
corresponding Hebrew equivalents. Then all the proper names in Hebrew,
Aramaic and Greek are explained. At the end of this list of all personal, topo-
graphical and other proper names another list of the Latin names is appended
which occur in the 'modern' Latin Bibles while the original texts and the old
Latin editions give them in another form, e. g. "Nabuchodonosor. in toto hier-
emia excepto. cap. 27. &. 28. &. 29.a. & 34. &. 39b. & in Ezech. 26. &. 29. &.
30. pro. nabuchodorosor". A Hebrew grammar concludes the volume.[69] In vol.
V, containing the New Testament, several didactic treatises in Greek accompany the Bible text, in addition to the prologues of Jerome: on the journeys
and the chronology of Paul, several résumés (*argumenta*) of the writings of the
New Testament and especially an explanation of all proper names occurring in
the New Testament and a Greek-Latin glossary of the vocabulary of the New
Testament and the Greek wisdom books of the Old Testament. This is the first
dictionary of New Testament Greek ever published.

Another most important feature of the Complutensian Polyglot resulting
from the pedagogical orientation of the editors, and of Cisneros himself, is the
rigorous system of cross references between each Hebrew, Aramaic and Greek
word and its equivalent in the Latin translation as well as the simplification of
the Hebrew vowels (no composite shewa) and the omission of the *te'amim* (accents) except *sof pasuq* and *atnach*, parallel to the abandonment of the accents
and spirits in the Greek of the New Testament, not however in the Septuagint.
This they did in both the Hebrew of the Old Testament and the Greek of the
New Testament because they estimated that the oldest Hebrew and Greek
texts were without the *te'amim*, Greek accents and spirits. Instead the editors
placed signs of their own invention in order to mark phonetic stress and linguistic differences, e. g. between the *he* of the article and of the interrogative
particle, and as distinctive sign for non-radical letters.[70]

---

[68] The humanists were spurned by pedagogical intentions, cf. Bedouelle, L'humanisme (1989)
54–58; Fernández Tejero, Biblia políglota (1997).

[69] Thesaurus and Grammar are the work of Alonso de Zamora, cf. Sáenz-Badillos, Targarona
Borrás, Diccionario (1988) 30; García Oro, Cisneros (1993).

[70] Ginsburg, Introduction, no. 19 (1897) 906–25; Fernández Tejero, Biblia Políglota (1997)
210–12.

Moreover they suppressed the *makkef* and gave the *atnach* another function than it has in the *masorah* (thus a verse may have more than one *atnach*). They omitted the special masoretic passages (suspended *nun*'s and *ain*'s, inverted *nun*'s etc.) and introduced the vowels of the *qere* readings into the consonants of the *ketiv* in the Bible text. In this they followed the practice of the Jewish printed incunable Bibles. It was not before the first rabbinic Bible of Felix of Prato (Pratensis), published in Venice 1516–17 (the Complutensian Polyglot having been printed between 1514 and July 1517) that the printed Hebrew Bibles began to reproduce at least some of all five constitutive elements of the masoretic text (consonants, vowel-points, accents, masoretic notes, layout). This was a progress beyond the Hebrew Bible incunables and the Complutensian Polyglot.[71] Another important didactic means of the editors of Alcalá is the overall interlinear translation of the Septuagint and the Latin version of Targum Onkelos.

As for the choice of their texts, the editors selected for the Hebrew columns two excellent Spanish manuscripts from 1280 and 1482.[72] Moreover they made use of the Soncino Bible of Naples (1491–93) and of the Pentateuch printed in Lisbon 1491.[73] PAUL KAHLE suggested an additional use of manuscripts with babylonian vocalization because this could explain some of the peculiarities of the vocalization in the Polyglot.[74] The textcritical value of the Hebrew Text of the Polyglot rests on the value of the source manuscripts used by the editors of Alcalá. The Targum Onkelos was printed on the base of a manuscript in the Biblioteca de la Universidad Complutense, of the thirteenth century, annotated by Alfonso de Zamora.[75]

For the Septuagint the editors used several manuscripts for the different parts of the Old Testament. They usually followed one principal manuscript which they corrected with the help of another, secondary textual witness. The Greek text therefore is not uniform. It changes from book to book or even from one part of the book to another, in dependence of the selected manuscripts. The character of the Greek text of the Old Testament varies also in function of the several editors at work who did not apply the general method in exactly the same way. Despite some influence played by the Vulgate, Jerome's commentaries and the Hebrew text of the Complutensian Septuagint, the Greek sources were faithfully edited. This is proven by the very old Septuagint text forms of the Complutensian Polyglot, e.g. in the Twelve, in Ezechiel and elsewhere. Because the source manuscripts of the Complutensian editors in these sections are no longer extant the Complutensian Septuagint remains

---

[71] Ginsburg, Introduction, no. 20 (1897) 925–48.

[72] Delitzsch, Complutensische Varianten (1878) 4–5; Ginsburg, Introduction, no. 59 (1897) 771–76, 918–22; Revilla Rico, Políglota (1917) 82–84; Schenker, Der alttestamentliche Text (1994); Fernández Tejero, Biblia Políglota (1997) 212–14; Biblia Hebrea Complutense No. 1: Cat. Villa-Amil 118-Z-24; Biblia Hebrea Complutense No. 2: Cat. Villa-Amil 118-Z-38.

[73] Ginsburg, Introduction (1897) 921–25. Revilla Rico, Políglota (1917) 84–85 adds two other Spanish Bible manuscripts: Biblia Hebrea Complutense No. 3: Cat. Villa-Amil 116-Z-38 (12th c.); Biblia Hebrea Complutense No. 4: Cat. Villa-Amil 116-Z-24 (12th-13th c.).

[74] Kahle, Complutensische Polyglotte (1962) 136–38; Fernández Tejero, Biblia Políglota (1997) 214–15.

[75] Revilla Rico, Políglota (1917) 91–92: Cat. Villa-Amil 117-Z-15.

sometimes an important textual witness of old readings.[76] The Septuagint manuscripts of the Complutensian editors have been identified in a large measure by FRANZ DELITZSCH and others. For the Pentateuch a Lucianic witness, RAHLFS, Verzeichnis, no. 108, and for the Hagiographa the manuscript RAHLFS, Verzeichnis no. 248, were of foremost importance.[77] The source manuscripts for the New Testament, however, have not yet been identified.[78] The value of the text (or texts!) in the Polyglot of Alcalá stays with the value of its source manuscripts, and this is in several cases outstanding, in the Old Testament and the New Testament. The Vulgate was mainly based on three known manuscripts, but also on some others unknown.[79]

Except for the Psalter where the editors prepared a Latin recension of their own, they tried to prefer the authentic Vulgate text although in the choice of variant readings they tended to select those more close to the Hebrew. On the whole they refused to alter the authentic Vulgate text in order to bring it into closer conformity with the Hebrew or Greek original texts. This seems to have been the policy of Nebrija, editor of the Vulgate in the Alcalá Polyglot. Since Cisneros decidedly precluded it Nebrija left the editorial *junta* of the Polyglot.[80] On the other hand, they refrained from changing the original texts in order to assimilate them to the Vulgate,[81] contrary to what is often claimed.[82]

The publication and diffusion of the Complutensian Polyglot was delayed until 1520 when the papal approval arrived (22 March 1520). Its influence was considerable on the later large polyglot Bibles of Antwerp (1568–1572), Paris (1628–1645) and London (1653–1657/8).

[76] Barthélemy, Complutensis (1990); Barthélemy, La polyglotte (1992); O'Connell, Ancient Sources (2006); Fernández Marcos, Texto griego (1997) 223–24.

[77] Delitzsch, Entstehungsgeschichte (1886); Revilla Rico, Políglota (1917) 95–111; 113–35; Schenker, Der alttestamentliche Text (1994) 181; Fernández Marcos, Texto griego (1997) 220–25. The second Tabernacle section, Ex 35–40, corresponds to a text which the editors of the Complutensian Polyglot edited without the direct base of a Greek manuscript: Fraenkel, Quellen (1990); O'Connel, Ancient Sources (2006) 37–73.

[78] Revilla Rico, Políglota (1917) 137–35; Bataillon, Erasme vol. 1 (1991) 44–46; Welte, Problem (1999).

[79] Revilla Rico, Políglota (1917) 137–48, esp. 145f; Schenker, Der alttestamentliche Text (1994) 181.

[80] Bataillon, Erasme 1 (1991) 38–46.

[81] Welte, Problem (1999).

[82] E.g. Bataillon, Erasme 1 (1991) 44–45; cf. Revilla Rico, Políglota (1917) 86–88 (Hebrew manuscripts), 118–26 (New Testament, history of the debate of the eighteenth century).

B.

Scriptural Interpretation in Church Reforms
and in the Reformation

CHAPTER THIRTEEN

Scriptural Interpretation in Pre-Reformation Dissident Movements

By G. R. EVANS, Cambridge

General sources: BERNARD GUI: *Manuel de l'Inquisiteur* I-II (ed. G. Mollat; Paris 1926–27); *Omnis apostolica et evangelica institutio huiusmodi fine claudatur*, PL 142, 1271–1312. – N. P. TANNER, *Decrees of the Ecumenical Councils* I-II (Georgetown 1990).
    General works: M. LAMBERT, *Medieval Heresy* (Oxford: Blackwell 1977; repr. 1992); W. L. WAKEFIELD / A. P. EVANS, *Heresies of the High Middle Ages* (New York: Columbia UP 1991).

1. Introduction

A number of the attitudes to the study of Scripture found in the pre-Reformation dissident movements eventually emerged as core questions in the Reformation debates of the sixteenth century. The most crucial of these was the setting of the authority of the Bible against the authority of the Church. This was a result of disillusion with the Church of the day, and also a response to the Church's repeated official condemnations of what had begun as a desire to simply to follow Christ and preach the Gospel. With some help from supportive clerics, even popular dissidents found that they could make use of Scripture for themselves and they could quote it to defend their position against the Church's apologists. Some of those dissidents who were themselves clerics developed a hermeneutic accordingly. This is the story to be told in this chapter.

Numerous individuals and 'movements' arose in the period from the tenth to the fifteenth century, of which we can examine only a few. Some were of brief appearance. Others had a protracted aftermath. There was a broad division into 'dualist' heretics, the heirs of the Gnostics and Manichees of the patristic period, and what may loosely be called 'anti-establishment' dissidents. The first group were preoccupied with the paradox of the existence of evil in a world whose God is good; the second with the return to the 'apostolic' ideal of the life which they believed Jesus had sent out his disciples to spread. The extreme dualists held beliefs which were ultimately incompatible with those of the Christian faith, for they postulated that evil was a deity. Not all dualists were of the 'absolute' persuasion which held that there were 'two gods' in this way. Bogomils seem to have held views which were at least partially compatible with the Christian faith. They said that there was one God, but that he was not responsible for the creation of matter and evil. That was the work of a fallen angel. So they retained the core dualist idea that matter is evil and spirit good without going as far as maintaining that there are *duo principia*.

The second broad division of dissidents seemed on the face of it to be doing nothing wrong. They encouraged their adherents to follow Christ in the ways he himself had taught. They became categorized as 'heretics' only as they found themselves in opposition to the Church's authorities, and then in separation from the Church. Augustine had regarded schism as the worst of heresies because it divided the body of Christ; and that now became a contemporary reality as such 'schisms' created classes of 'heretic' in the Church's eyes.

Both these big categories of mediaeval heretic turned to the Bible for support for their respective positions and became skilled in its interpretation. They took away the monopoly of the Church as 'official' interpreter. They used Scripture in apologetic and in debate with the Church's own 'official' apologists, so that it became the bedrock on which any definitive position could be adopted.

Moreover, all these dissidents were returning to another practice of the early Church. They all emphasised the importance of preaching and made homiletic the natural vehicle of exegesis.

2. Petrus Waldes and the Waldensians

Sources and translations: GILBERT CRISPIN: *Works* (ed. A. Abulafia / G. R. Evans; London 1986). – DURANDUS DE HUESCA: *Une Somme anti-Cathare: le* Liber contra Manicheos (ed. C. Thouzellier; SSL 32; 1964, 33ff). – A. POTTHAST: *Regesta* I (Berlin 1874). – WALTER MAP: *De Nugis Curialium* (ed. M. James / C. Brooke / R. Mynors; Oxford 1983).
   Special studies: G. AUDISIO, *The Waldensian Dissent, Persecution and Survival c. 1170 – c. 1570* (ET by C. Davison; Cambridge: Cambridge UP 1999); M. BARBER, *The Cathars* (Harlow: Longman 2000); A. DONDAINE, "Aux origins de Valdéisme: une profession de foi de Valdès", *AFP* 16 (1946) 191–235; E. MONTET, *Histoire littéraire des Vaudois du Piémont* (Paris 1885); R. I. MOORE, *The Birth of Popular Heresy* (London: Edward Arnold 1975); P. STEPHENS, *The Waldensian Story* (Lewes: Book Guild 1998); M. LAMBERT, *Medieval heresy* (Oxford: Blackwell 1977; repr. 1992).

2.1. *The Return to the Apostolic Life*

Heresy was popular in the tenth century,[1] but the Synod of Orléans in 1022 was the first instance of a burning for heresy in the mediaeval West. To the Synod of Arras in 1025 were brought some heretics from Italy. It was said that they were claiming that they alone had the key to the truth; that only in their 'way' could sinners be cleansed of their sin.

The surviving description of the manner in which they were examined suggests that to begin with it was possible for issues to be debated publicly and without undue acrimony. It was admitted that they did not accept the sacraments. They were asked how, in that case, they answered the words of Jesus to Nicodemus, when he told him that no one could enter the Kingdom of Heaven

---

[1] See the list in Wakefield / Evans, Heresies (1991) 20.

unless he had been born again of water and the Spirit (John 3:5). They answered that their "law and discipline" did not seem to them to be contrary to the Gospel or to "apostolic sanctions". They explained that they tried to follow the apostolic way of life, abandoning the "world"; restraining fleshly appetites; harming no one and loving their neighbours. They said that those who lived in that way had no need of baptism; for those who did not, baptism could be of no avail. They described this as their *justificationis summa*, the essence of their doctrine of justification, so that baptism can add nothing to it. Baptism had served its purpose and was no longer needed.[2] There is much in this exchange about which we should like to know more, for example, the degree of "writing up" to which it has been subjected by the clerks who made the record of the proceedings of the synod. It is a repeating problem in the case of popular heresies where there is no leader, such as Wyclif or Hus who left some account of himself with his own pen, that the record is subject to the tidying up of the views of alleged heretics by those not in sympathy with their views. Nevertheless, even in the form in which we have it, this is a helpful indicator of the ideal at the heart of the dissident movement which emerged more than a century later under the leadership of Waldes.

We need such a pointer. One of the results of the heightening of talk of heresy was that those groups which came under suspicion might be labelled almost at random, and gossip flourished, so that rumours of secret meetings and devil worship and magical practices and sexual misbehaviour and assorted forms of Satanism ran about, linked to various individuals and groups.[3] Little reliance can be placed on such descriptions as a basis for the classification of these early mediaeval movements. But almost all those of the 'anti-establishment' type seem to have had in common a desire to live the apostolic life, to follow the Jesus of the New Testament.

2.2. *The Life of Waldes and the Beginning of the Movement*

The members of the early mediaeval bourgeoisie began to be able to make themselves heard, as a class, from the eleventh and twelfth centuries, even though they were not clerics and lacked formal education. Waldes (d. 1217?) is an example. A transforming moment of insight showed him the way to live as a Christian and he set about acting upon it. At first he did not meet opposition. Étienne de Bourbon says that he turned to two priests for guidance, one of whom, Stephen d'Anse, translated some portions (now lost) of the Bible, notably the Gospels and the Psalms, into Lyonnais, a dialect of Provençal. Waldes preached, especially on passages from the New Testament. He founded a lay community, who read the Bible and prayed together and confessed to one another.[4] They went about in pairs, of mixed sexes, preaching the Gospel.

---

[2] *Omnis apostolica et evangelica institutio*, PL 142, 1271–1312 , cols. 1271–72.
[3] Wakefield / Evans, Heresies (1991) 20.
[4] On attitudes to penance, see Montet, Histoire littéraire des Vaudois (1885) 192.

In 1179 Waldes sought approval from the Third Lateran Council. Lateran III made a series of pronouncements designed to discourage corruption in the Church and especially among its clergy. It condemned Publicani and Patarenes and Cathars (Canon 27). The contemporary commentator Walter Map described the way the Waldensians were made to look foolish when questioned on theological points.[5] Nevertheless, they escaped condemnation. The Pope gave them authority to preach so long as they did so with the approval of local clergy. Waldes obediently came before the diocesan synod at Lyons in 1180, and signed a profession of faith so that he and his followers might continue to preach with formal local approval.[6] They even foreshadowed the mendicant orders in preaching as 'wanderers', and living on alms.

But these genial permissive circumstances abruptly changed. John Bellesmains became archbishop and in 1182 Waldes and his followers were told to stop preaching. This was a defining moment. Faced with challenge, Waldes said that he must obey God not man. In continuing to preach when permission had been withdrawn, he did the one thing which would in the end make him unacceptable to the Church, however well he preached and however helpful the content of his preaching to the salvation of the faithful. The archbishop expelled him from the diocese. At the Council of Verona 1184, Pope Lucius III condemned the Waldensians, along with others who preached without licence. The Waldensians scattered and especially in the areas where Cathars were already numerous.

The Church remained open for a short time yet to the notion that the 'apostolic life' movements were a potential influence for good in the Church. The clergy were being censured by Councils for their failure to follow Christ's example. Here were preachers with the right priorities. But it was important that the Church should be in control of such 'movements'. The Fourth Lateran Council, as late as 1215, was prepared to give official sanction to Dominicans and Franciscans, but that was on the understanding that they were being 'sent'. In its third Canon it takes a firm line on heretics in general and especially on those who "holding to the form of religion but denying its power" (2 Tim 3:5) take it upon themselves to preach (*auctoritatem sibi vendicant praedicandi*) against the stricture of the same Paul, who asks "How shall they preach unless they are sent ?" (Rom 10:15).[7] The 'sending' was essential.

This structure of Lateran IV describes with great economy what had now become the nub of the problem. Heresy successfully resisting the Church's censure and carrying on regardless, became schism. Groups such as the Waldensians and the Humiliati, north Italian wool workers living lives of charitable work (and also condemned at Verona), ceased to set a good example when they continued with their work without the Church's official support and against its orders. By contrast, in supporting the Dominicans, Innocent III saw the possibility of a world-wide order of preachers, who would work for the Church and under its authority.[8] The reasons for the Church's shift to disapproval of the Waldensians were perhaps much the same as those which prompted its resistance to the similar 'call to be Christlike' on the part of those Franciscans who wanted to go on after St. Francis' death in the life of poverty and simplicity he had led in such an exemplary way. For it was also a direct

[5] Tanner, Decrees (1990) 206, and see Map, *De Nugis Curialium* 1,31 (1983) 125–29.
[6] Dondaine, Aux origins de Valdéisme (1946) 191–235.
[7] Tanner, Decrees I (1990) 234.
[8] See for example, S. Tugwell, "Notes on the Life of St. Dominic", *AFP* 178 (1998) 1–116, 66.

challenge to what had become, with the contemporary aggrandisment to papal claims to plenitude of power, a considerable ecclesial power-structure.

When Alan of Lille wrote his fourfold treatise *Against the heretics* in the late twelfth century, he made a point of this aspect of the Waldensian error. Waldes was "led by his own spirit, not sent by God" *(suo spiritu ductus, non a Deo missus)*. "He invented a new sect which presumed to preach without the authority of a prelate, without divine inspiration, without knowledge *(sine scientia)*, without education *(sine littera)*". He and his followers say that no-one is to be obeyed except God, in particular that only good priests ought to be obeyed. They say that powers to consecrate or bless are not bestowed with ordination; that the faithful may confess to the laity; and they say that salvation does not lie in the Church but in living the apostolic life.[9]

2.3. *The Waldensian Ideal Matures*

The Waldensians dispersed into the areas in which the Cathars were to be found, south-west France, northern Italy.[10] There were fears in ecclesiastical circles that they would become infected with Cathar views.[11] It is not surprising that there was indeed a resulting degree of overlap in the thinking of the Waldensians and the dualists, heightened by this relegation of the Waldensians to the category of 'outlaw'. Waldensians continued to be active in preaching against the Cathars in the late twelfth century, even after they themselves were banned from preaching.[12] Yet they could not but recognise that they had, in important respects, a common objective with the dualists. They were both striving after 'perfection'. The Waldensians were trying to live perfectly in imitation of Christ; the Cathars had a class of the *perfecti* among their members. There was also a certain parallelism of ascetic practice and ideal.

Durandus of Huesca was himself once a Waldensian. He wrote an *Antiheresis* at that time in which he argued against both Cathars and Catholics. Durandus was converted back to orthodoxy at Pamiers in 1207, and then became Prior of the Poor Catholics, an order which was, perhaps surprisingly, in view of his 'history', able to obtain papal approval for its members to engage in preaching without diocesan control.[13] Innocent III laid down careful rules. The group was to remain *sub magisterio et regimine Romani pontificis*. It was to take neither silver nor gold in payment for its preaching; its members were to undergo instruction by those who had a knowledge of Scripture and the points to be made in arguing with heretics so as to bring them back to the Faith and into the bosom of the Holy Roman Church. Those members not equipped to take part in this work were to stay quietly at home, living holy lives.[14] Durandus became, in effect, a professional controversialist and his writings afford an unusual depth of insight into the development of the ideas of the Waldensians. From this time we have in Durandus a former Waldensian who is writing against the Cathars, a writer who was once an anti-Establishment heretic taking issue with the dualists with the zeal of a convert.[15] Nevertheless, many of his points remained much as he had made them in his earlier work.

---

[9] PL 210, 377–88.
[10] Audisio, The Waldensian Dissent (1999) 33.
[11] Dondaine, Aux origins du Valdéisme (1946) 197.
[12] Audisio, The Waldensian Dissent (1999) 28.
[13] Innocent III, *Letters*, XI,196, December 18, 1208, PL 215, 1512, and Durandus, *Une Somme anti-Cathare* (1964) 33 ff.
[14] PL 216, 1512–13.
[15] C. Thouzellier, "La profession trinitaire du Vaudois Durand de Huesca", *RTAM* 27 (1960) 267–89.

The modern scholar needs all the help he can get. The oldest surviving documentary evidence from within the movement may be as late as 1230, by which time Waldensian ideas were different and more 'politically' radical than those which had first fired Waldes.[16] There is a 'confession', preserved in the Decretals of Gregory IX (V, Tit. vii, c. 9). This may give a picture of the position of the early Waldes, though to judge from the evidence of a remark of Ermengaud, it may represent what he found he 'had' to say rather than what he may have wished to say. Ermengaud says that Waldes swore before a cardinal of the Roman Church that he had never held the views of this sect nor associated with its members.[17] The 'confession', together with a list of points condemned, reappears in a letter of Innocent III in 1208, in which he writes to the Bishop of Tarragon asking him to receive the newly-converted Durandus.[18]

Durandus' confession is an expanded creed, with particular emphases in areas where the Waldensians were being asked to make it clear that they were not dualists. For example, "we believe that the Old and the New Testament had the same author, who created all things, and who sent John the Baptist". There are also elements to which Waldes and his followers could be expected to find it more difficult to assent in later years. The confession asserts that no one can be saved (*extra quam neminem salvari credimus*) outside the one holy, catholic and immaculate church; it accepts baptism for the remission of sins, confession to a priest as *secundum scripturas*, the real presence in the consecrated elements of the eucharist. It promises obedience to the precepts of the evangelical councils.[19] Resistance on a number of these points became issues of principle for the Waldensians in later years, after they had been excluded from the Church.

2.4. *The Waldensian Bible*

Much of the Waldensian 'archive' of two hundred or so manuscripts consists of a preponderance of collections of biblical extracts.[20] The Waldensians had access to translations of Scripture into the vernacular. Bernard Gui describes how Waldes "had written for him Gospels and various other books of the Bible in the common gallic tongue and also some authorities".[21] The obvious area of concern in the climate of thought we are concerned with was the danger that such 'do-it-yourself' study of Scripture might encourage the faithful to regard themselves as free of the control of the Church.

There is some disagreement as to whether Innocent III wished to suppress such vernacular versions of Scripture (there seems to have been no formal condemnation of the use of translations by a Pope or a Council).[22] Correspondence from early in Innocent's pontificate tells us that there was a problem in Metz. The first of these letters was important enough to find a place in the Decretals

---

[16] Dondaine, Aux origines du Valdéisme (1946) 191.

[17] Quoted from MS Troyes 1068, fol. 130va, in: Dondaine, ibid. 196.

[18] PL 215, 1510–13, Potthast, *Regesta* I (Berlin 1874) nn. 3571–72; Dondaine, ibid. 198.

[19] Dondaine, ibid. 231–32.

[20] Divided by Montet, Histoire littéraire des Vaudois (1885), into four historical stages, the 'catholic' phase of the twelfth to early thirteenth centuries, the 'vaudoise' stage, the Taborite period, when the influence of the Hussites was strong, and the 'Protestant' stage of the sixteenth century.

[21] Gui, *Manuel de l'Inquisiteur* I (1926) 35.

[22] L. E. BOYLE, "Innocent III and vernacular versions of Scripture", *The Bible in the Mediaeval World: Essays in Honour of Beryl Smalley* (ed. K. Walsh / D. Wood; Studies in Church History, Subsidia 4; Oxford 1985) 97.

of Gregory IX. The local bishop alleged that a "multitude" of lay people, men and women, were gathering in secret and studying a French translation of the Gospels. Innocent's questions suggest where his anxiety lay. The questions which needed to be raised were whose translation was being used (was the text reliable?). What was the purpose for which the translation had been made? How sound was the faith of those who are using it? Why were they teaching by this means? What was their attitude to the Apostolic See and the Church?

The use to which vernacular versions of Scripture were put was of concern beyond their use by the heretics themselves for their own private edification and for arguing back when challenged by the Church's apologists. They preached on them. Bernard Gui complained that "half-understanding, puffed up with their own opinion, when they were barely literate, they took to themselves the office of the apostles and presumed to preach the Gospel in the streets", not only men but women.[23] The Waldensians were called "barbes" (*barbari*) because they did not do their exegesis in the Latin language but in the vernacular, but the Latin was not far in the background. Some of them, Gui admits, are literate, and some even have a knowledge of Latin and can compare the text in the vernacular with the Vulgate.[24]

2.5. *Exegetical Methods*

There are clues as to the exegetical methods of heretics and dissidents. Waldensians and Albigensians alike in the late twelfth century famously sometimes threw the Cistercians who first preached against them off balance by the adroitness with which they could deploy Scripture in defence of their positions. They proved hard to examine because they knew Scripture so well and were so cunning with it in argument. They were said to be able to deploy fallacies and equivocations adroitly: *propter fallacies et dupplicitates verborum quibus se contegunt in responsionibus suis.*[25] Sometimes they even mislead those who seek to set them back on the right road, suggests Bernard Gui, by pretending to a simplicity they do not have.[26]

As Durandus of Huesca sums it up, now in principle classifying dualists and Waldensians together, the heretics are not merely bad and dangerous as individuals of twisted mind (*homines corrupti mente, ...incurabiliter fermentantes*). They are also *corruptores* of Holy Scripture, and that endangers the faithful.[27] He calls the dualist exegete "apostate", "adulterer",[28] *corruptor Scripture.*[29] The latter-day "Manichees" have made a compilation which is an "Anti-Scripture".[30] The temptation to draw an analogy with the newly-emerging 'Anti-Christ' vocabulary of the period is irresistible.[31] The Christian should take ex-

---

[23] Gui, ibid. 35.
[24] Idem, 62.
[25] Idem, 64.
[26] Idem, 74.
[27] Durandus, Une Somme anti-Cathare (1964) 160.
[28] Idem, 92–94.
[29] Ibid.
[30] Idem, 87.
[31] Thouzellier, La profession trinitaire du Vaudois Durand (1960) 284.

ception to the heretics' twisting of the evidence of the text of Scripture: *Sed obiciendum est. ... perverso sensui eorum*, says Durandus. *Hii auctoritatibus abutendo dementant instabiles et incautos.*[32] The dualists are not only insane; they are hypocrites: *suam dementem energiam ypocrisantes.*[33] Christians who want to succeed in an argument against them have to reverse this, taking the testimonia and rejecting only the twisted constructions put upon them (*perverso sensui eorum solummodo renitamur*).[34] They must oppose each interpretation with argument or put text against text. "To this first testimony we object that they do not believe that God is telling the truth when he says, 'I am the first and the last', for they believe in an eternal Devil".[35] The Christian's best defence against being led astray is to concentrate on understanding what Scripture is actually saying, as the texts "ought to be understood in the truth (*sicut debent intelligi in veritate*)".[36] Like others in these pages advocating a return to Scripture in its wholeness, Durandus did not rule out figurative interpretation. For example, he said that the mystical sense does not exclude the literal: *misticus intellectus, quia non destruit historicum, non est tamen praetermittendus.*[37] The mystical sense derives from the literal, but the literal remains. *Et quia ab historico sensu manente misticus derivatur.*[38]

2.6. Old Testament and New

One of the crucial difficulties for defenders of the faith against a range of dissident views was to know what texts to rely on in rebutting the body of opinion of a given group. There was no point in using argument texts which they would dismiss as having no authority. This was a problem already familiar at the beginning of the twelfth century, when Gilbert Crispin chose to use mainly the Old Testament in his *Disputation with a Jew* and to concentrate on arguments from reason in debating the Christian faith with a 'pagan'.[39] Bernard of Fontcaud wrote an account of the way in which the local heretics of Narbonne were confuted in another of the public debates referred to earlier. There were various opinions to be dealt with, and Bernard gives the biblical texts relied on. "The dispute went backwards and forwards for a long time (*hinc inde diu disputatum est*) and both sides produced many authorities".[40] The issues are seen as ecclesiological, since heretics of various complexions tend to argue that there is not need to obey the Pope or that there is no need to obey priests.[41] Bonacursus gives a list of beliefs of the Pasagii, dissidents who took a quite op-

---

[32] Durandus, *Une Somme anti-Cathare* (1964) 98.
[33] Idem, 147.
[34] Idem, 88–89.
[35] Idem, 137.
[36] Idem, 92–94.
[37] Idem, 150.
[38] Idem, 159.
[39] Crispin, *Works* (1986).
[40] PL 204, 795.
[41] PL 204, 795 and 798.

posite view of the reliance to be placed on the Old Testament from the Cathars. "First, they say that the Law of Moses is to be observed to the letter, and
that the force of the rules about the Sabbath and circumcision and other legal
observances is still as it was.[42] They say that Christ is not the equal of the
Father and that the three persons of the Trinity are not one substance".[43] In response to these, Bonacursus argues that the law of Moses is to be observed
spiritually. Elsewhere, we find him bringing in against the Arnaldists Old Testament and New, the Fathers and other "authorities".

The balance of the use of Old Testament and New seems to depend on the
purpose of a given collection. In a survey of five Provençal and Waldensian 'Bibles', or collections of texts, BERGER found a preponderance of New Testament
material, with a selection of Old Testament texts (Wisdom literature from Ecclesiasticus, Ecclesiastes, the Song of Songs, Wisdom) and 'Exemplary tales'
(from Tobit, Job, 2 Maccabees), together with apocryphal texts from the Pastor of Hermes, Manasses, Esdras, and extracts from the Fathers (Augustine,
Jerome, Ambrose, Gregory the Great).[44] Elsewhere, in the prologue to Durandus' treatise against the Manichees, the emphasis is consistently on Old Testament support for Durandus' arguments. He reuses a good deal of his earlier
Prologue to the *Antiheresis* for this purpose. A close look at a passage of the
text may give the flavour. Durandus explains how God has disposed everything (Gen 6:5) according to rule and 'weight and measure' (Wis 11:21), loving
justice and hating iniquity (Ps 44:8), and how he brought a flood upon the
earth, seeing that as a result of the work of Satan that there was evil in the
earth and that every thought in the hearts of men was prone to evil (Gen 6:5,
12 and cf. Sir 40:10).

On the subject of Lucifer, Durandus has a lengthy list of Old Testament allusions and citations.[45] These Old Testament references and episodes are designed to be striking to the dualists,
apparently on the rather perverse principle that the evil god, as author of the Old Testament, is
bearing witness to himself there just as God speaks of himself in his Word in the New Testament.
The view of the Cathars was that the Old Testament which describes the creation of a material
world was the work of an evil 'god' or a fallen angel. That is underlined by Bonacursus in his *Libellus contra Catharos*. These heretics say that everything done by Abraham, Isaac and Jacob was done
by the Devil. They say that it was the Devil who appeared to Moses in the burning bush and spoke
to him; they say that the miracles done by Moses and the crossing of the Red Sea are all the work
of the Devil; they say that all the stars are demons.[46] Against this it is necessary for the apologist
for orthodoxy to argue that the omnipotent God created Adam and Eve; that he is responsible for
the Law of Moses; that John the Baptist, Isaac, Jacob and Moses are elect and "friends of God"
(*amici Dei*); that Son of God assumed real flesh.[47]

---

[42] PL 204, 784.
[43] Ibid.
[44] S. BERGER, "Les bibles provençales et vaudoises", *Romania* 18 (1889) 353–424.
[45] Durandus, *Une Somme anti-Cathare* (1964) 70 ff.
[46] PL 204, 777.
[47] PL 204, 779–82.

2.7. Nulla salus extra ecclesiam *and the Salvific Effect of the Bible*

Durandus was already pointing to the danger of losing sight of the authority of the Bible when he wrote his *Antiheresis* against the Cathars from – at that time – the view-point of a Waldensian. "It seems to us that your teaching is unscriptural", he says, "and that you have almost forgotten the apostolic way of life".[48]

The heretics, far from being brought to salvation by the Word of God, are led to their perdition by even the best *testimonia* when they interpret them perversely, says Durandus in his later book *Against the Manichees*, now written as a former Waldensian turned Catholic.[49] It is not the text but the construction placed upon it which does the spiritual harm.[50] This appears to establish an important principle and to place the interpreter in a position of high responsibility, if he can thus stand between text and reader and interfere with the salvific effect of the Scriptures. The heretics seem to accept the same principle, from their own mirror-image standpoint. The saving power of the Bible works, in the view of the Church, as mediated through its teaching authority by its ordained and therefore authorized ministers. The dissidents who were arguing that they could read and understand the Bible for themselves were, in effect, challenging the doctrine that there is no salvation outside the (Roman) Church. These heretics, characteristically of the schismatics they really are, say that it is they not the Catholic Church who are the true Church. "They say that they have the faith of God", for "they believe their blasphemous error to be the faith of God". For our present purposes, the important point here is that this happens because "they do not understand the Scriptures according to the voice of truth": *quia iuxta vocem veritatis non intelligent Scripturas.*[51] The theme of the unworthy minister recurs a good deal in the reports of the beliefs of anti-Establishment heretics. For example, the heretics say to the Church's apologists: "Your assertion cannot be correct because the clergy of the Roman Church, on whose behalf you speak, are perverse and live against God and when they speak of God their speech is blasphemy".[52] For the Church's apologists the important question is how far the laity may be allowed to go in running their own religious affairs. It is for priests to decide religious questions, says Bernard of Fontcaud.[53] Moses said to the elders of Israel when he went up alone to speak with God: "Wait here until I return to you. You have Aaron and Hur with you. If any question arises, refer it to them" (Exod 24:14). Bernard says that it is not proper for the laity to preach. They do not have the authority; they may lead the faithful astray. He is clear that women cannot preach.[54]

There lingers in Durandus' text still a Waldensian confidence in Scripture as its own illumination: *ad sentenciam Danihelis prophete dicimus quod luculentissima est et nulla indiget responsione.*[55] "That opinion of the Apostle is clear and needs no exposition".[56] Waldensian poems reflect the same idea. "Mai l'ecriture dit et c'est très manifeste".[57] This theory of 'self-evidency' implicitly assumes that the faithful reading the Bible for themselves will have the guidance of the Holy Spirit to ensure that they do not go astray.

---

[48] Dondaine, Aux origins du Valdéisme (1946) 233.
[49] Durandus, *Une Somme anti-Cathare* (1964) 106.
[50] Idem, 107.
[51] Idem, 104–05.
[52] Idem, 95.
[53] PL 204, 801.
[54] PL 204, 805, 806, 822, 825.
[55] Durandus, *Une Somme anti-Cathare* (1964) 137.
[56] Idem, 141.
[57] On attitudes to penance, see Montet, Histoire littéraire des Vaudois (1885) 129.

2.8. Conclusion

The Waldensian movement, then, set the scene for much of what followed in the movements we turn to next. Whether or not direct influence can be established, it is easy to show that certain ideas became pervasive in groups where there was disaffection with the Church.

3. John Wyclif and the Lollards

Sources and translations: Wyclif's works are available in the nineteenth century Wyclif Society editions. JOHN WYCLIF: *Polemical Works* I-II (ed. R. Buddensieg; London: Wyclif Society 1883); *Sermones, Super Evangelia Dominicalia* I (ed. J. Loserth; London: Wyclif Society 1887); *Opus Evangelicum* I-IV (ed. J. Loserth; London: Wyclif Society 1895); *De Veritate Sacrae Scripturae* 1-2 (ed. R. Buddensieg; London 1905-07); *English Wycliffite Sermons* I-V (ed. A. Hudson / P. Gradon; Oxford 1983-96). – JOHN KENNINGHAM: *Ingressus. Fr. J. Kynyngham Carmelita contra Wicclyff. Fasciculi Zizaniorum* (ed. W. Waddington Shirley; Rolls Series 1857); *Acta ... contra ideas Magistri Johannis Wyclif. Fasciculi Zizaniorum* (ed. W. Waddington Shirley; Rolls Series 1858).

  Special studies: J. M. FLETCHER, "Inter-faculty Disputes in Late Mediaeval Oxford", *From Ockham to Wyclif* (ed. A. Hudson / M. Wilks; Studies in Church History, Subsidia 5; Oxford: Blackwell 1987) 331-42; A. HUDSON, *English Wycliffite Writings* (Cambridge 1978); eadem, *The Premature Reformation* (Oxford 1988); J. GUY, "Perceptions of heresy, 1200-1550", in: *Reformation, Humanism and "Revolution"* (ed. G. J. Schocher; Washington 1990); A. K. McHARDY, "The Dissemination of Wyclif's Ideas", in: *From Ockham to Wyclif* (Oxford 1987, see above) 361-68; A. KENNY, *Wyclif* (Oxford 1985); idem, *Wyclif in his Times* (Oxford 1986); J. A. ROBSON, *Wyclif and the Oxford Schools* (Cambridge 1961); E. H. ROBERTSON, *John Wyclif: Morning Star of the Reformation* (Basingstoke: Marshall 1984); K. WALSH, *Richard Fitzralph in Oxford, Avignon and Armagh* (Oxford 1981).

John Wyclif (c. 1320-84) was an academic whose contentious views[58] had an impact outside the world of the university. Wyclif himself was something of a populariser, and he had friends who saw to it that the ideas he had developed by the end of his life were disseminated. The result was the 'movement' known as Lollardy. Lollardy included ideas familiar from the Waldensians and similar groups of the earlier Middle Ages, not all of which were prominent in Wyclif's own writing, especially at first. But by the end of his life, Wyclif was calling, in the same way as the Waldensians, for a return to the simple apostolic ideals, to a simple following of Christ. His *Postilla super totam bibliam*, which he probably finished in 1375-76, pointed to the poverty and humility of the early Church. The *De Civili Dominio* (1376-78) also included an emphasis on poverty. Wyclif resembled Waldes in being led to his conclusions by the Church's own reactions, and they were in several respects the same conclusions, though Wyclif's emphasis was different.

  Wyclif probably began to teach at Oxford in the 1350s. His first writings on logic survive from 1361-71, when he was already making a name. The university world was by now accustomed to public controversy. Oxford itself had long been something of a centre of discontents and challenges. Richard Fitzralph (at Oxford from about 1315, a Fellow of Balliol before 1325 and Chan-

---

  [58] Fletcher, Inter-faculty Disputes in Late Mediaeval Oxford (1987) 331-42.

cellor of the University of Oxford 1332–34 before becoming Dean of Lichfield in 1335) and Brad-wardine and Thomas Buckingham had all been involved in controversy in their day. Richard Fitz-ralph, who came to be thought of as a 'Lollard Saint', left a collection of sermons and anti-mendi-cant writings and something approaching a cult formed. Wyclif was certainly influenced by his thinking on the poverty of Christ, in the *De pauperie salvatoris* (c. 1350–56).

There were heightened debates in English politics too. Wyclif entered the royal service in 1371 or 1372 and allowed himself to be drawn into partisan preaching. He escaped royal wrath because the king died, Richard II succeeded him and attention turned to other matters. The Great Schism (1378–1417), and the politically important questions about the future of the divided papacy were preoccupying the Church.

Nevertheless, the Church's concerted opposition was eventually aroused. 1377–78 was a defin-ing moment for Wyclif. His objections to papal claims to secular power; the heightening of ten-sions within the political situation in England; combined with his attempt to set out definitively his 'position' on Scripture. In 1377 Bulls of Pope Gregory IX reached London, in which 19 errors of Wyclif were listed; there were attempts in England to get him condemned. In 1378 he published his *De Veritate Scripturae Sacrae* (*On the Truth of Holy Scripture*) and his *De Ecclesia*; in 1379 the *De Officio Regis* and the *De Potestate Papae* appeared, considering respectively the powers of King and Pope. These were accompanied by numerous other increasingly polemical works as a 'cor-nered' Wyclif defended his position. Wyclif went further than many of the Waldensians and ques-tioning the legitimacy of the actions and legislation of 'authorities', whether civil or religious. He argued that Christ had forbidden his followers to exercise civil dominion, so that all ecclesiastical exercise of civil power becomes improper. He saw such exercise as corrupting. It was in the contro-versy on the Eucharist of 1380–81, that William Barton, one of Wyclif's enemies, contrived a means of getting the University to make a public condemnation of Wyclif's teaching on the Euchar-ist. He brought together a 'commission' of twelve doctors for the purpose (1380), and this brought about Wyclif's downfall.

Wyclif was finally driven out of Oxford in 1380, at the age of about 50, and he lived out his life in retirement at Lutterworth parsonage from 1381. In 1382 a Council at Blackfriars condemned ten propositions of Wyclif and some of his followers thought it politic to flee the country. Wyclif car-ried on writing. In 1382 his *Trialogus* was completed and in 1384, the year of his death, the *Opus Evangelicum*.

3.1. The Eternal Truth of Scripture: Wyclif's First Controversial Position on Scripture

One of the first areas in which Wyclif attracted criticism concerned the Bible. As early as 1371–73 he was attacked by John Kenningham, who was then a Carmelite master of theology at Oxford. He accused Wyclif of saying that Scripture's authority rests on its antiquity (with other writings less reliable be-cause they are more recent). Kenningham pointed out that this was inconsis-tent. Many famous poets lived about the date of the book of Judges while So-crates, Plato, Aristotle, Pythagoras lived after the captivity in Babylon; yet these poets are now of no moment while the philosophers are. So antiquity af-fords no guarantee: *ergo antiquitas non auctenticat*, he concluded.[59] The fla-vour of this peculiarly scholastic argument becomes clear when Kenningham gives the example of a charter (for a monastery) or notary's *instrumentum*, where an older document would have more authority in the eyes of lawyers than a more recent one.[60] Wyclif said that Kenningham's argument from char-

---

[59] *Ingressus*, 4–5.
[60] *Acta... contra ideas Magistri Johannis Wyclif*, 17.

ters proceeds from an analogy which will not bear the weight he wants to place on it (*ab insufficienti similitudine*).[61] Wyclif did not really want to be side-tracked into this debate. He said that it is "not a theologian's job to get into the habit of defending charters; he should rather be studying how the Word of God lives and reigns through all ages".[62] He said that it is not antiquity but eternity which is the warrant of the Bible's truth.[63] Wyclif regretted the modern habit of taking the Bible too lightly, with *impertinencia*. He began from the principle that God perceives past, present and future as though they were equally 'present' to him. He argued that what God perceives must exist. So what 'was' and what 'will be' also 'is', in the sight of God.[64] For Wyclif the Bible as the Word of God is a divine exemplar which existed before the actual writing of the words which make up the Scriptures we know.

3.2. Does the Bible Mean What It Says?

The dispute with Kenningham threw up another question which prompted Wyclif to clarify his position. If the Bible is always 'true' it ought to be possible to be sure what it is saying.[65] It was no straightforward matter to claim that the text of Scripture should be taken at its face value. The claim of the prophet Amos that he was not a prophet: *non sum propheta* (Amos 7:14) was a familiar puzzle to mediaeval commentators. Gregory the Great said that Amos bears truthful testimony to himself when he says he is not a prophet. Otherwise he would not be a prophet, for as a prophet he must be telling the truth.[66]

Wyclif did not insist upon a crude literal interpretation.[67] He was happy like other mediaeval commentators to accept that Scripture has figurative interpretations. Indeed, Wyclif asked Kenningham to explain why Scripture so often employs tropes and the figurative mode of speech. Kenningham conceded that this is sometimes *ad designando aeternitatem* ("before Abraham was I am" John 8:58), sometimes to imply certainty (John 3:18), sometimes just at the whim of the translator: *solum placitum translatorum vel interpretem*.[68] Wyclif's exegesis is in many respects extremely conventional in mediaeval terms, as his handling of the two disciples and the *castellani* shows (Matt 21:1). He was happy here, too, to use the system of mutiple senses. He made remarks such as: "Christ prophesies in the mystical sense", *ad sensum autem mysticum prophetizat Christus*.[69]

---

[61] Ibid. 18.
[62] *Non pertinet at theologum induere habitum defendentis cartas, sed magis studuere quomodo verbum vivit et regnat per omnia secula seculorum sicut erat in principio, et nunc, et semper*, ibid. 15.
[63] Ibid. 15.
[64] *Ingressus*, 9.
[65] *Acta*, 20.
[66] Ibid. 24.
[67] Ibid. 28.
[68] Ibid. 31.
[69] Wyclif, *Sermones, Super Evangelia Dominicalia*, 12.

3.3. Bible and a Church Gone Astray

Wyclif's *De ecclesia* (1378) set forth a revolutionary doctrine of the Church of the same broad type as we saw emerging in the Waldensian sect. The rejection of the visible Church of the day as authoritative in its teaching and ministry encouraged him to take 'Scripture alone' to be the locus and source of all authority. Legislation promulgated by Popes is "mannis law".

Wyclif began to question the rightful authority of a Church which seemed to be setting itself against the principles Jesus laid down for his disciples and whose ordained ministry – the 'authorised' officers – were frequently unworthy. It is not in dispute that there was widespread disquiet on this point. The very twelfth and early thirteenth century councils we saw condemning heretics also made extensive comment on the unacceptable behaviour of many of the clergy. The 'unworthy minister' question had been resolved in the patristic period in favour of an acceptance that divine grace can work through even the most corrupt of ministers. But it was becoming difficult not to return to it. Wyclif writes that no-one can hold true 'dominion' over others, or over possessions, while in a state of mortal sin. He said that some think that if a priest leads an evil life that may take from him the power to administer the sacraments.[70] Wycliffites wanted to see ministers chosen according to God's law and not at the behest of princes or for money.[71] The wrong people, chosen for the wrong reasons, may be subject to avarice, worldly love, given to simony, and above all, eager for power.[72]

While defect in an unworthy minister might be supplied by grace with reference to his sacramental functions, it did not follow, to the thinking of many of the dissident groups, that a corrupt priest could be an adequate Minister of the Word. Wyclif, like the Waldensians, saw ministry as an office, in which the ministry of the Word is the most important thing. The minister is the vicar of Christ in that he feeds the people with the Word which is Christ. So the preaching office is primary.

It is ironic that Wyclif particularly disliked what he called the "sects", by which he meant the religious orders, particularly the Mendicants; for their very *raison d'être* was preaching. His reason is that he saw them as claiming to be a superior order of Christians. The *De perfectione statuum* is an attack on the claim of the "sects" to a status which "exceeds even that of the popes and bishops".[73] Wyclif said there are really only two "sects", that of Christ and that of worldly men, but he subdivides the class of the wordly into monks, canons, friars. The encouragement of diversity in the religious life is also an encouragement to quarrelling and division, he says. The "sects" divide the Christian community and thus the unity of Christ's order. Christ wanted his people to be one. The divine purpose was that there was to be one faith and one baptism. The "sects", with their claims to a special entry requirement which is like a second baptism, are dividing Christians into the superior and the inferior.[74] In his discussion in the *De solutione Satanae* of the date when Satan was released to take over the Church as Antichrist the "sects" are in Wyclif's mind as much as the Pope.[75] In his 'two kinds of heretics' Wyclif distinguished the simoniacal, among whom he included Pope, bishops and curates, and the apostates, among whom he included all priests, who refuse to follow the humble example of Christ.[76]

Another feature of the "sects" which the Wycliffites mistrusted was their novelty. They are

---

[70] *English Wycliffite Sermons* IV (1994) 114.
[71] Ibid. 115.
[72] Ibid. 115–17.
[73] Wyclif, *De Perfectione Statuum, Polemical Works* II (1883) 449.
[74] Wyclif, *De detectione perfidiarum Antichristi*, ibid. 380.
[75] Wyclif, *De solutione Satane*, ibid.
[76] Wyclif, *De duobus generibus hereticorum*, ibid. 431–32.

"newe mannys orders", and therefore of human invention. That means that people are following human leaders instead of following Christ. It means they are adding to the teaching of Christ new 'requirements' for salvation. They also bring in a form of slavery, for they keep some out of orders to which others may belong. They require unnecessary 'observances' of human origin, such as the wearing of habits.

3.4. Spirit-led Exegesis and Private Interpretation

Wyclif gives a further definition of heresy in his *De fundatione sectarum* which contains an important additional element: "Anyone who pertinaciously expounds the faith of Scripture other than as the Holy Spirit directs, is a heretic".[77] He touched here on a theme which was to prove important in the Reformation debates. Once the *magisterium* of the Church is denied, it is necessary to identify an authority which can keep the private reader of Scripture on the right path. Anything else is mere personal opinion. Wyclif explained, speaking for himself, that "as far as those parts of Scripture are concerned of whose meaning we have a [mere] opinion or are humbly uncertain, we regard our sense as held *opinative* and we are always prepared to concede the 'catholic meaning', whether it is expressed by the Pope or by some friar or by a lay person or by a learned man".[78] But where Scripture seems to him to give a clear lead, Wyclif will not submit to the Church's teaching.

In his *De Veritate Sacrae Scripturae*[79] Wyclif regarded the Bible as the repository of all truth and as inerrant. He urged Christians "to believe steadily in the faith of Scripture, and not to believe any other source on any subject unless what it says is based on Scripture".[80] Equally, it follows from the presumption that the ecclesiastical authorities are now fallible that they cannot be relied upon as interpreters of Scripture, so each person may be his own interpreter.[81] Both these lines of argument need to be qualified by an awareness that Wyclif was not hostile to the Church of earlier times. In fact, it is one of his objections to the "sects" that they expound the Scripture in ways which have no precedent in the Fathers.[82] Nor, as we have just seen, would he necessarily resist the Church's teaching on matters of mere opinion. Wyclif also asserted that the Bible ought to be in the hands of all Christians, for in an age where the 'official' Church has gone astray, that is where they must look for confirmation of and guidance on their faith. If they cannot rely on the Church's official teaching they will need to know for themselves what the Bible says. One of the ramifications of the debate about the place of the commandments of the Old Law in the new Christian dispensation is picked up by Wyclif in his *De Nova Prevaricancia Mandatorum*.[83] Does Scripture teach that it is necessary to obey the law

---

[77] Wyclif, *De fundatione sectarum*, ibid. 74.
[78] Ibid. 75.
[79] Wyclif, *De Veritate SS* 2 (1906).
[80] Ibid. 382.
[81] Ibid. 384.
[82] Wyclif, *De fundatione sectarum*, *Polemical Works*, II (1883) 74.
[83] Wyclif, *De Nova Prevaricancia Mandatorum* 1, ibid. 116.

in order to be saved?, he asks. *Recentes heretici,* claimed Wyclif, say that no one can obey the law perfectly, and if that is so, none can be saved. That must mean that there is no need to obey the law. Wyclif's own view was that there is an obligation on Christians to obey the law, and that it is possible for everyone who is predestinate to do so.[84] This is an argument in favour of the provision of vernacular versions, for everyone will need to know what the law is.[85]

He examines the same question in his *De Veritate Sacrae Scripturae* (1378). There was a contemporary view that it was right and necessary for at least the Ten Commandments to be available in English as well as in Latin. There had been some 'progress' on this front in the provision of manuals for the less well-educated clergy to use. Archbishop Pecham had held a Provincial Council at Lambeth in 1281 at which a plan of "instruction for the laity" was drawn up. This was turned into verse for use in the Province of York in 1357, on the orders of Archbishop Thoresby. In 1425 it was translated into English at the instigation of the Bishop of Bath and Wells. He had it put in every church in the diocese. Wyclif speaks strongly about the duty to preach on Scripture and the neglect of that duty by the clergy and religious of his day. "The false brothers and dumb priests ought to be ashamed to omit to defend the Law of God". Their failure to do so brings ruin to the faithful.[86]

The evidence is strong that it was his dislike of the "sects" of the religious orders and others in the Church whom he did not like as a class, that was sometimes driving his exegesis on the subject of popular access to the Bible. Preaching *ad populum* on Matt 21:1 (*Iesus misit duos discipulos*), Wyclif explains that the two disciples are *presbyteri et seculares*, priests and seculars, and that it is their duty to speak out against the *castellani*, the keepers of the *castellum* which appears later in this passage. The *castellani* are the beneficed clergy who are, says Wyclif "always" against the disciples of Christ (*semper contra Christi discipulos*).[87] It is possible to identify "side-swipes" at his enemies again and again. In his third sermon on the Sunday Gospels he mentions John the Baptist's notable unconcern for soft raiment (*mollia vestimenta*) and he does not resist adding "unlike the Friars!".[88] Addressing the question of the definition of 'prophet' he remarks in passing on the *rancosa* and *inutilis* definition of "many in the sects" (*multi de sectis*).[89] Again, "the disciples of Antichrist" falsely say that the building of rich buildings (Churches) is "necessary to the Christian religion", basing their argument on the fallacy that since God cannot have too splendid a house, it is incumbent on the laity to build him the best they can so as to honour him.[90] In his *De fundatione sectae* (V-XV) he gives biblical proofs for his assertions that the *sectae* were not only superfluous but also harmful, and others. The sixteenth chapter takes him to methodological questions of exegesis, but again with an irritability on the subject of the "sects" which frequently gets in the ways of his reflection on Scripture.[91]

Wyclif made a distinction between the mode of preaching appropriate for an academic audience and the way sermons should be preached to the ordinary people. The preface to his collected sermons on the Sunday Gospels sets out the principles.[92] He says he has brought them together so that God's teaching shall be clearer and he himself may be of use as God's servant (*ut sentencia Dei sit planior et servus suus inutilis excusabilior*). These are *sermones rudes ad populum*, simple sermons for the people. In them Wyclif can be expected to know

---

[84] Idem, *De Nova Prevaricancia Mandatorum* 3, ibid. 122–24.
[85] Idem, *De Nova Prevaricancia Mandatorum* 1, ibid. 116.
[86] Wyclif, *Sermones, Super Evangelia Dominicalia, Sermo* VI, I (1887) 42.
[87] Ibid. *Sermo* I, I (1887) 2.
[88] Ibid. *Sermo* III, I (1887) 17.
[89] Ibid. *Sermo* III, I (1887), Vol. I, 18.
[90] Ibid. *Sermo* III, I (1887), Vol. I, 20.
[91] Wyclif, *De fundatione Sectarum, Polemical Works* I (1883) 74.
[92] Wyclif, *Sermones, Super Evangelia Dominicalia,* Preface, I (1887) V.

when he is deliberately influencing popular opinion, and here, too, his hatred of the 'sects' is to the fore.

3.5. Sola Scriptura *and the* Opus Evangelicum

Towards the end of his life, Wyclif came close to embracing a doctrine of *sola scriptura*. It seems to him, in the end, to follow that what is not in Scripture directly or by inference is *ipso facto* the teaching of Antichrist. Wyclif's *Opus Evangelicum* is his statement that the faith found in Scripture is sufficient for the regulation of the whole Church in the world (*Fides...scripture est sufficiens ad regendum ecclesiam militantem*).[93] Indeed, even the faith as set out in the Sermon on the Mount contains all that is needful to govern everyone in this life, without the addition of any "human tradition" (*sic sufficeret eciam sermo Domini in Monte regulare perfecte sine tradicione humana quotlibet viatores*).[94] No other law has force unless it conforms to this. In the days of the first beginnings of the Church, that was understood, and indeed the Apostles and their followers were "ruled by the pure law of the Gospel" (*pura lege evangelii regulati*).[95]

The 'biblical ecclesiology" Wyclif expounds in this work rests on Matthew 5–7; 23–25 and John 13–17. It still bears all the characteristic marks of his polemic, in its repeated sideswipes at his enemies. For example, in I.vi he gives Robert Grosseteste's list of the signs of humility. He argues that the Pope lacks them all, and that enables him to move on to the theme of the Pope as usurper.[96] This he readily couples with the accusation that the Curia neglects the study of Scripture. Those working at the Curia, he says elsewhere,[97] can see for themselves that they are in the abomination of desolation and hear blasphemy and lies, but they do not respond by setting out the *sensus scripturae* and nothing they say is directed to the salvation of the soul (*pertinens ad salutem anime*).

In his description of the proper motivation for preaching Wyclif criticizes the Mendicants for preaching only in order to get rich and to despoil their listeners. "No one should preach in the name of Jesus except for the pure motive of saving souls".[98] This kind of thing is noticeable even when Wyclif is at his most positive, explaining how Christ's ascent to the mountain to preach teaches us that the preacher ought to "teach the words of the Gospel" from on high downwards (*ab alto descendentia*), that is with a proper respect for their dignity. That means avoiding *apocrypha* and fables, and especially falsehood and greed. He does not believe the *sects* are really capable of understanding that.[99]

---

[93] Wyclif, *Opus Evangelicum*, I-II (1895) 37.
[94] Ibid. 368.
[95] Ibid. 368.
[96] Ibid. 18–19.
[97] Wyclif, *De citationibus frivolis*, *Polemical Works* I (1883) 74 and 2 (1883) 552.
[98] Wyclif, *Opus Evangelicum*, I-II (1895) 2.
[99] Ibid. 3.

3.6. The Lollards: the Movement

How did Wyclif come to be regarded as the instigator of a popular movement on the scale of Lollardy?[100] For Wyclif's name became associated with an increasingly popular movement, probably during his last years at Lutterworth. John Purvey, Nicholas Hereford, Philip Repington and John Aston were important in spreading Wyclif's ideas. Repington was an Augustinian canon, the others secular clerks. All except John Purvey had been attracted to Wyclif at Oxford and had become fired by him with reforming zeal.

Wyclif was probably not himself the driving force behind the translations of the Bible into English which came to be associated with the Lollards. Nicholas of Hereford, a fellow academic who helped to lead the 'Wyclif party' in Oxford in the early 1380s, and John Purvey, who lived in Wyclif's parish and assisted him at the end of his life, have been linked with this translation in its different versions.[101]

4. Jan Hus and the Hussites

Sources and translations: JAN HUS: *Opera Omnia* I– (1959–); *Expositio Decalogi* (ed. V. Flajshans; Prague 1903); *Tractatus de Corpore Christi* (ed. V. Flajshans; Prague 1903); *In Sententias* (ed. V. Flajshans; Prague 1904); *De libris hereticorum legendis, Polemica* (ed. J. Ersil; *Opera Omnia* 22, 19–37; Prague 1966); *The Letters of John Hus* (tr. by Matthew Spinka, from: V. NOVOTNY [ed.], *M. Jana Husi Korespondence a dokumenty* [1920]; Manchester 1972); V. NOVOTNY (ed.), *Historické spisy Petra z Mladonovic a jine z právy a mameti o M. Janovi Husovi a M. Jeronymovi z prahy* (Fontes rerum Bohemicarum; Praha 1932).

Special studies: H. KAMINSKY, *A History of the Hussite Revolution* (Berkeley / Los Angeles 1967); M. SPINKA, *John Hus, a Biography* (Princeton: Princeton UP 1968; repr. 1979); idem, *John Hus at the Council of Constance* (New York / London: Columbia UP 1965); idem, *John Hus' Concept of the Church* (Princeton 1966).

4.1. Jan Hus from Dedicated Priest to Dissident

From the beginning the letters of Jan Hus evince a steady honesty. "Have the most just Judge before your eyes, so that you would neither knowingly cause suffering to a just man, nor flatter an unjust man".[102] He cites Old Testament support (Isa 33:15 and Ecclus 42:1). He was at first no dissident but a dedicated priest and preacher.

Hus was born in the early 1370s in Bohemia.[103] He was ordained priest in 1400, and was teaching at the University of Prague in the first decade of the fifteenth century. Even in 1402 he was evidently a 'coming man', for he was appointed preacher at the Bethlehem Chapel, which was in the gift of the masters of the University. Most of the sermons he preached there survive in Latin

---

[100] McHardy, The Dissemination of Wyclif's ideas (1987) 361–68.
[101] Kenny, Wyclif (1985) 65.
[102] *Letter 1*, The Letters (1972) 2.
[103] On all this, see Spinka, John Hus' Concept of the Church (1966).

(rather than in the Czech in which Hus originally preached them), and they show an able preacher, giving good and evidently popular sermons on conventional subjects such as the Virgin Mary. They are exercises in practical theology, whose purpose is to encourage people who hear them to lead a good Christian life. They use familiar mediaeval methods. Like Wyclif, Hus had no objection to citing Fathers such as Chrysostom, Augustine, Gregory, Bernard, and discussing the figurative meanings of passages of Scripture.

The echoes of the Wycliffite controversy quickly reached Hus's Prague. There were links between England and Bohemia, cemented by the marriage of Anne of Bohemia with Richard II in 1382. A number of Czechs had been studying in Oxford and events there were known in Prague. There is evidence that Wyclif's own works were reaching Prague by 1390.[104]

In 1403 the question of Wyclif ceased to be of mere academic interest in Prague. A list of already-condemned "articles of Wyclif" was sent to the office of the Archbishop by a disturbed German Master, together with twenty-one 'articles' he had added. He asked for an opinion on these. The Czech Masters at Prague (which was divided into 'parties' or 'nations' like many mediaeval universities), saw this as a direct challenge to themselves, for some of them were known to be interested in, even sympathetic to, what Wyclif had been saying. In May 1403 the University of Prague met to consider and condemn as heretical 45 articles said to be derived from the writings of Wyclif.[105] The argument was advanced, as so often in mediaeval academic defences against charges of heresy, that the alleged "articles of Wyclif" misrepresented what he had been teaching, but, as was also becoming common in such situations, the politics not the pursuit of truth appear to have been in the driving seat.

It is by no means clear that Hus was involved in the support of Wycliffite positions at all at first, but he was soon attacked by influential men whose own conduct he had been impugning in his sermons. He had criticised the rich living of some of the pastors in Prague. There was a Wycliffite ring to that. The Archbishop received a complaint. Hus protested. "I am accused by my adversaries before your Paternity's Grace as if I were a scandalous and erroneous preacher, contrary to the Holy Mother Church, and thus wandering from the faith....With God's help, I wish to refute the scandalous accusations of my enemies laid before your most gracious Paternity, humbly and faithfully to give reason for my faith and hope....For the immediate vicar of Christ [Peter] says (1 Pet 3:15–16)...'Be ready always to give an answer to every man that asks you for a reason for the faith and hope that is in you, but with meekness and fear, having a good conscience; that, whereas they slander you, as if you were evildoers, they would be shamed that calumniate your good conversation in Christ'."[106]

When the Archbishop ordered that copies of Wyclif's writings which were in the hands of his clergy should be brought to him for "examination", Hus duly delivered up his own copies. He soon found himself under accusation as a Wycliffite heretic. Hus was not without support in the University. The Rector of the University of Prague, Christian of Prachatice, tried to comfort Hus. He cited the assurance in Prov 12:21 that nothing which happens to a just man will cause him sadnes. In reply, Hus reminded him of 2 Tim 3:12, which promises that those who try to live a godly life will suffer persecution. He invited Christian to join the battle.

Hus was now caught in the familiar trap of mediaeval 'heretics', from which he could escape neither by 'proving his innocence' nor by 'recantation'. The more vigorously and publicly he defended himself and his orthodoxy the more insistent became the accusations. And, as he attempted to 'explain himself' he was gradually drawn into clearer and clearer statements of positions which began to look very like Wycliffite heresies. He said that God ordered the preaching of his Word throughout the world (Heb 13:17); that if the Pope and prelates forbid that they are false witnesses; that it is disobedience to God's will which ought to be punished, not the carrying out of his wishes for the ministry of his Word.

---

[104] Kaminsky, History (1967) 23.
[105] Spinka, John Hus, a Biography (1979) 63–65.
[106] Letter 7, to Archbishop Zbynek, The Letters (1972) 22.

In 1411 Hus was excommunicated by the Pope. At the Council of Constance in 1415, Hus was brought to trial. He went there under a promised safe-conduct, but he soon found that again he was naïve in expecting that he would be given a fair hearing, or a hearing at all (there was an attempt to try him in his absence).[107] An extended account survives of "the trial and condemnation of Master Hus in Constance", by Peter of Mladonovice, who was an eye-witness and author of some of the documents in play. He was a loyal follower of Hus, who shared lodgings with him at Constance.[108] It was he who outwitted the attempt to try Hus in his absence by alerting the Czech nobility and who says he overheard a conversation in which it was proposed that even if he did recant, Hus should be burned as a heretic.

Hus was condemned and died at the stake in 1415. The Czech nobility was now involved; the battle over Hus had become entangled with high politics and the power-struggle between Church and state. A martyr can be extremely influential after his death and Hus became a national hero. His writings, especially those of the later period when he had been working out under challenge and threat a body of now quite radical teaching on the nature of the Church, gained a lasting influence. There was now a Hussite 'movement', fighting for big things, and also for small ones which came to loom disproportionately large, such as the Utraquist controversy, over allowing the ordinary faithful to receive both bread and wine at the Mass, instead of just bread as had become the custom in recent centuries. Utraquism became an issue when the Hussites began to offer wine, and, perhaps because it was a distinctive mark and easy to fix on, it became the 'badge' of the 'movement'.[109]

4.2. Hus's Theological Position

A repeating feature of the thinking of the anti-establishment dissidents discussed in this chapter is the way in which the Ministry of the Word comes to stand in opposition to the claims of the Church in its contemporary visible manifestation. Hus began by criticizing priests he knew for living lives which were, as he saw it, unbiblical. He thought he was doing no more than his duty, that he was indeed obeying his Archbishop. Indeed, Hus had written to the Archbishop of Prague towards the end of 1408 protesting his canonical obedience and reproving the Archbishop for having believed the accusations against him without testing them and writing fiercely to condemn him.[110] He pointed out that his duty of obedience does not extend to "perverse" but only to "lawful" commands. "Very often I repeat to myself that not long ago after your enthronement Your Paternity had set up the rule that whenever I should observe some defect in the administration, that I should instantly report such de-

---

[107] Spinka, John Hus at the Council of Constance (1965).
[108] *Historické spisy* (1932) VIII, 25–120.
[109] Kaminsky, History (1967) 97–98.
[110] *Letter 9*, The Letters (1972) 35–36.

fect."[111] Straightforward obedience of this sort was, it turned out, not only not 'received' in a constructive spirit; it brought down retribution on his head, so that he was prompted to complain: "This rule now compels me to express myself: how is it that fornicating and otherwise criminal priests walk about freely and without rigorous correction …while humble priests…who fulfil the duties of your administration with proper devotion, are not avaricious, but offer themselves freely for God's sake to the labour of proclaiming the Gospel – these are jailed as heretics and suffer exile for the very proclamation of the Gospel?".[112] "What poor priests will dare to fight against criminal conduct? Who will dare to make known vices?".[113] In 1414 Stephan Pálec was trying to make a distinction between preaching against clerical faults (which was proper), and preaching in the same way in conjunction with "the errors of Wyclif's 45 articles".

Hus's ecclesiology like that of Waldes and Wyclif was perforce drawn together into a system during the period when he found himself in a position where the enmity of those in power in Church and state alike made it impossible for him to continue to work in Prague. Hus's motivation as a preacher was in the end two-fold, on the positive side, to preach the Word and on the negative, to preach against "the malice of Antichrist". Hus thus saw himself as defending the truth as well as spreading it.[114] In exile he was writing De ecclesia, a book on the Church, which he finished in June 1413.[115] In it he crystallized his doctrine of the Church. If the Church is the congregatio fidelium, the community of the baptized, it is visible; and Hus had come to believe as a result of his experiences that the visible Church had been brought under the control of Antichrist, acting in the persons of the Pope and cardinals. He was concerned not to 'set aside' the Church but to make it clear where the 'true Church' was to be found. If the true Church is the universitas praedestinatorum, it is made up only of the elect; it is the mystical body of Christ; it is without spot or wrinkle; it is invisible. The Pope is head of a Church which has ceased to be the true Church. The Church of the elect recognizes the Headship of Christ. Hus wrote to Master Christian of Prachatice from exile sometime before April 1413, citing Acts 17:28. It is in Christ that his people live and move and have their being.[116]

For Hus, to say that the Church is the Body of which Christ is the Head meant that it was the whole people of God; it could not consist solely of the cardinals. "O, if the disciples of Antichrist were content to hold that the holy Roman Church consists of all the faithful, saintly Christians, militant in the faith of Christ."[117] As it is, he pointed out, "it follows that whatsoever the holy Roman Church determines – namely the Pope with the cardinals – that is to be held as the faith".[118] Hus's teaching thus had much the same ecclesiological implications as that of others identified as 'anti-establishment dissidents'.

Despite the vigour of his determination that the Word of God must be brought to the people, Hus's exegetical methods remained on the whole the conventional ones of his age. His Sermones de sanctis are full of the familiar and uncontroversial themes of preachers of his age. He approached the Decalogue (c. 1407), by dividing the commandments between the two Tables of the Law. In the first he places the first three precepts "which teach us the contem-

---

[111] Letter 7, to Archbishop Zbynek. The Letters (1972) 22.
[112] Ibid.
[113] Ibid.
[114] Letter 27, to the people of Prague, The Letters (1972) 84.
[115] Kaminsky, History (1967) 95.
[116] Letter 34, to Christian of Prachatice, The Letters (1972) 96.
[117] Ibid. 99.
[118] Ibid. 96.

plative life in God", with the first referring to the power of the Father, the second to the Wisdom of the Son, the third to the goodness of the Holy Spirit. The second group of seven commandments are placed in the second Table, with the note that they instruct us in the way to live the active life for the good of our neighbour.[119] When he comes to the commandment against swearing, he does not launch into the familiar debate about the taking of oaths. Similarly, when Hus discusses transubstantiation (c. 1408), it is to uphold the doctrine against those who deny that the bread really becomes the body of Christ. He takes the warrant of Scripture to be clear. On the *Sentences*, too, he is conventional enough, exclaiming: "How clear and wholesome is this medicine of Holy Scripture!", and describing how the uncreated Trinity freely gave Holy Scripture, which is "most worthy in wisdom and knowledge" for the salvation of mankind.[120] "The Church bases itself on the words of its head Christ" and also the views of the *sancti doctores* of the Church, Augustine, Jerome, Ambrose, Gregory, and so on.[121]

4.3. Countenancing Dissidence

Hus was robust in his attitude to teachings which seemed 'risky'. He thought there was value in reading and discussing heretical ideas, for something was often to be learned from them. In his *De libris hereticorum legendis*, a work which made the Archbishop angry and still more determined to bring him to justice, Hus cited *oportet hereses esse* (1 Cor 11:19). The Church needs to encounter such tests in order to learn where the truth lay. "The books of the heretics are to be read not burned, so long as there is truth in what they say" (*dum in ipsis veritas continetur*). They can, he pointed out, often be supported by the authority of the Fathers, by canon law or by reason.[122] The books of the heretics, he said, have the capacity to stir up spirituality, to clarify the truth, and, paradoxically, to encourage the reader to seek the truth so as to avoid falling into the same errors. He cites Augustine on this point.[123]

Hus did not hesitate to point out that Church itself over the centuries had had to "correct", or "expressly revoke" many things which it had allowed to appear in its teaching. Similarly, the most respected authors had had their periods of condemnation. Peter Lombard's *Sentences* was criticized at first on many points, but far from being burned it had now become a standard work.[124] He extended this argument even to the study of Scripture. A common subject of dispute in debates with mediaeval dissidents was the place of the ritual requirements of the Old Testament. Hus argues that "with reference to the *ceremonialia*", the Old Law is buried by the New, so that as Augustine says, if anyone submitted to circumcision in the Jewish way he would be

---

[119] Hus, *Expositio Decalogi* I, 2 and 8.
[120] Hus, *In Sententias* 4–6, 8 and 12.
[121] Hus, *Tractatus* 3, 2.
[122] Hus, *De libris hereticorum legendis* 19–37 and 21.
[123] Ibid. 19–37 and 30.
[124] Ibid. 19–37 and 30–31.

counted a heretic. Nevertheless, the parts of the Old Testament which contain the *ceremonialia* are not burned.[125] This line of argument seems to place Hus outside the 'fundamentalist' stream. It is not his position that everything in the Bible must be taken as it stands. He sees the Bible as a whole, in which the New Testament alters for the Christian some of what is taught in the Old.

Nevertheless, Hus gave a definition of a heretic which takes Scripture to be the only secure test. "A heretic, properly speaking and strictly (*proprie et solum*) is someone who insistently contradicts the word of Holy Scripture, in writing or in deed". There are three essential elements in this definition. There must be an error in understanding (*error in intellectu*); a falsehood which is contrary to Holy Scripture (*falsitas sacre Scripture contraria*); persistence in the wrong opinion.[126] Dissent from the teaching of an institutional Church on which Hus no longer felt able to rely is no indicator of heresy; it therefore does not enter into this definition.

Hus wrote to the people of Louny (after March 1411) to warn them against allowing themselves to give rise to schisms, which he couples with "treacheries, envies, angers etc.". He seems to have in mind chiefly the kinds of internal disagreements which arise in a local community: "If anyone among you is intractable and disseminates discords, admonish him as a brother among yourselves".[127] Yet when it came to the great issues of the day, Hus came to believe that "the schism among the people" was not to be helped, for Paul had prophesied that "the son of iniquity shall not be revealed until the schism comes first" (2 Thess 2:3, much adapted).[128] These are indicators of a thinker driven from a starting-point to a conclusion by events which made it increasingly difficult for him to withdraw from his initial position.

Another natural consequence of the ecclesiology Hus forged in the heat of the controversy which began to surround his teaching was the view that the Word of God itself must be made freely available to all the people of God, and that there must also be freedom for those engaged in the Ministry of the Word. He wrote to the lords "gathered at the supreme court of the Kingdom of Bohemia" exhorting them to "strive to stop" the abuses to which he was drawing attention, "in order that the Word of God may enjoy freedom among the people of God". "I am grieved, he says, that I cannot preach the Word of God, not wishing to have the divine service stopped and the people distressed".[129] There is little doubt that Hus's driving interest in exegesis lay in preaching.

4.4. The Hussite 'Movement'

When a leader of reform dies his followers are confronted with the difficulty of deciding whether to carry on, and if they are to carry on, how they are to do it. The history of the Church is full of these moments of decision. They often lead to division and sub-division of the 'movement'. The Franciscans di-

---

[125] Ibid. 19–37 and 31.
[126] Ibid. 19–37 and 35.
[127] *Letter 16*, to the people of Louny, The Letters (1972) 49.
[128] *Letter 33*, to Christian of Prachatice, The Letters (1972) 94.
[129] *Letter 31*, to The lords gathered at the supreme court of the Kingdom of Bohemia, The Letters (1972) 90.

vided after Francis into those who became 'institutionalised' and those who tried to keep alive the flame of the extreme call to poverty they believed to be his legacy. Hus died a martyr, and in those heightened circumstances there were heightened reactions, even a sense that the end of the world was at hand. There was also fragmentation and adoption of extreme positions by some of those who had been, however loosely, of his 'party'. The Taborites, for example, were preaching the Second Coming of Christ, and making their own interpretations of the prophetical books of the Old Testament. They spoke of a flight from Babylon, of a gathering of the Elect, of active resistance to the forces of Antichrist. The expected Day of Wrath when an angry God would descend, failed to materialize.[130] This millenarianism or chiliasm led in the direction of the practices of the Brethren of the Free Spirit. It also encouraged people to hand over their worldly goods, in the expectation that they would not be needing them much longer. Taborite priests behaved in a 'Lollard' way, holding services in the open air, without benefit of church buildings or vestments or conventional liturgy. They led worship in the vernacular, and they used rough pieces of bread and any vessel which came to hand instead of a chalice. The Lollard heresy had begun with academic controversy, and it did not prove difficult for the personal supporters of Wyclif to spread his ideas in a form which caught on very widely among people with no academic pretensions. Something similar happened in the expansion of the Hussite movement; and in the same way a cluster of ideas already associated with Waldes and Wyclif seem to have won ready popular support in the Hussite movement. The authorities responded with a 'witch-hunt' against those thought to be Hus's followers.

---

[130] On the Taborites and other manifestations of the Hussite movement, see Kaminsky, History (1967) 311 ff.

CHAPTER FOURTEEN

From the Reform Councils to the Counter-Reformation – the Council as Interpreter of Scripture

By OSKAR SKARSAUNE, Oslo

Primary sources: The now current edition of the acts of the so-called ecumenical councils is G. AL-BERIGO e.a. (eds.), *Conciliorum Oecumenicorum Decreta* (3rd edn.; Bologna: Istituto per le scienze religiose 1973). The same critical text is printed, with English translation, in: N. P. TANNER, *Decrees of the Ecumenical Councils* I-II (London: Sheed & Ward / Washington DC: Georgetown UP 1990). For the councils of Constance (1414–18) and Basel-Ferrara-Florence-Rome (1431–45), see ibid. I, 403–592; for the council of Trent, see ibid. II, 657–799.

General works: On the epoch of the reform councils in general: for quick and easy orientation, see H. JEDIN, *Kleine Konziliengeschichte* (Herder-Bücherei 51; Freiburg e.a. 81969). Further, C. M. D. CROWDER, *Unity, Heresy and Reform, 1378–1460: The Conciliar Response to the Great Schism* (Documents of Medieval History; London: Edward Arnold 1977); E. F. JACOB, *Essays in the Conciliar Epoch* (Publications of the University of Manchester, Historical Series 80; Manchester: UP 1943); H. JEDIN, *Bischöfliches Konzil oder Kirchenparlament? Ein Beitrag zur Ekklesiologie der Konzilien von Konstanz und Basel* (Vorträge der Aeneas Silvius Stiftung an der Universität Basel 2; Basel / Stuttgart: Helbing & Lichtenhahn 21965); J. WOHLMUTH, "Die Konzilien von Konstanz (1414–1418) und Basel (1431–1449)", in: G. ALBERIGO (ed.), *Geschichte der Konzilien: Vom Nicaenum bis zum Vaticanum II* (Düsseldorf: Patmos Verlag 1993) 235–90; U. PROCH, "Die Unionskonzilien von Lyon (1274) und Florenz (1438–1445)", in: G. ALBERIGO (ed.), *Geschichte der Konzilien* (1993) 292–329.

The Council of Constance: R. BÄUMER (ed.), *Das Konstanzer Konzil* (WdF 415; Darmstadt: Wiss. Buchgesellschaft 1977); P. H. STUMP, *The Reforms of the Council of Constance (1414–1418)* (SHCT 53; Leiden: Brill 1994); P. DE VOOGHT, *Les pouvoirs du concile et l'autorité du Pape au concile de Constance: Le décret Haec Sancta Synodus du 6 avril 1415* (Unam Sanctam 56; Paris: Cerf 1965).

Jan Hus and the Council: M. SPINKA, *John Hus at the Council of Constance: Translated from the Latin and the Czech with Notes and Introduction* (RoC 73; New York: Columbia UP 1965); idem, *John Hus: A Biography* (Westport, CT: Greenwood Press 1968).

The Council of Basel-Ferrara-Florence-Rome: W. KRÄMER, *Konsens und Rezeption. Verfassungsprinzipien der Kirche im Basler Konziliarismus* (BGPhMA NF 19; Münster: Aschendorff 1980); E. MEUTHEN, *Das Basler Konzil als Forschungsproblem der europäischen Geschichte* (Vorträge / Rheinisch-Westfälische Akademie der Wissenschaften: Geisteswissenschaften G 274; Opladen: Westdeutscher Verlag 1985); J. W. STIEBER, *Pope Eugenius IV, the Council of Basel, and the Secular and Ecclesiastical Authorities in the Empire: The Conflict over Supreme Authority and Power in the Church* (SHCT 13; Leiden: Brill 1978); A. VAGEDES, *Das Konzil über dem Papst? Die Stellungnahmen des Nikolaus von Kues und des Panormitanus zum Streit zwischen dem Konzil von Basel und Eugen IV* (PaThSt 11; Paderborn e.a.: Ferdinand Schöningh 1981).

1. Introduction: Church Councils as Interpreters of Scripture

The subject of this chapter is not directly relevant to a history of the interpretation of the Old Testament. But its indirect relevance is considerable. The boost to biblical science which came from the dramatic events in the century of the Reformation, with a blossoming of biblical studies on all sides of the confessional divides as a result, is not unrelated to processes that took place at the highest levels of doctrinal authority within the Church (or the Churches), at councils and diets. This resulted in something quite new: In the dogmatic decrees of the Council of Trent (1545–63), the reader familiar with the decrees and canons of medieval councils notices a novelty: the Catholic Church quotes Scripture, and quotes it quite profusely, to establish important points of doctrine. The scriptural quotes are not just embellishments or edifying phrases interspersed in the otherwise quite scholastic formulations of the decrees. They serve an argumentative purpose; they are quoted as final arguments because taken from the ultimate authority: Scripture.

This is all the more striking when one compares the decrees on justification, the sacraments, holy mass, etc., with the articles of the Augsburg Confession (1530). The Augsburg Confession sometimes has brief scriptural quotations, but more often the quotations are patristic: Augustine, Ambrose, etc. In the doctrinal decrees of Trent, one looks in vain for explicit patristic quotations, whereas the quotes from Scripture abound. The same council which elevated tradition as a source of revelation to be received with the same pious reverence as Scripture, is almost over-scrupulous in only quoting Scripture, not Fathers or councils, when it comes to authenticating Church doctrine.

This state of affairs may not be as paradoxical as it seems at first sight. The protestant participants at the Diet of Augsburg had not been accused of neglecting the authority of Scripture. They were accused, however, of advancing their own and novel interpretations of Scripture, at variance with established interpretations in the Church Fathers. Therefore the authors of the Augsburg Confession were particularly scrupulous in producing patristic support for their interpretations of Scripture, and for their Church reforms in general. As it is said, e.g. in article 20.12–14: "So that no one should quarrel about us introducing a new interpretation of Paul: this whole matter has the witness of the Fathers in its favour. Augustine asserts in several books ... and Ambrose likewise in *De vocatione gentium* and elsewhere ...".[1] It is therefore no accident that the Augsburg Confession so frequently adduces the testimony of the Fathers. It is easily explained from the polemical situation in which the document was produced. And it is very much the same with the Council of Trent. The Catholics had been accused of setting aside or neglecting the authority of Scripture, and only being able to establish their positions from Church tradition, not clear scriptural testimonies. The decrees of Trent are a vigorous re-

---

[1] Latin text to be found in *Die Bekenntnisschriften der evangelisch-lutherischen Kirche* (Göttingen: Vandenhoeck & Ruprecht ⁶1967) 77; author's translation.

joinder to this: point by point they produce scriptural basis for each and every point argued in the decrees.

It was said above that this was a novelty in this kind of documents. But was it? Or could it be that the Council is here not merely, maybe not even primarily, taking up a challenge from the Protestants. Could it be that the precedent of this practice was set by the great reform councils of the preceding century. One could mention *a priori* considerations that would point to the probability of such being the case. The two reform councils, Constance and Basel-Ferrara-Florence-Rome, were councils called forth by a great crisis of authority within the Church: where was the ultimate authority to be found, when several contestants claimed it? Should not this prompt a recourse to the one authority recognized by all: Scripture? Specifically with regard to Constance one could also ask: since John Wyclif and Jan Hus had based their challenge to Church practice and doctrine on Scriptural arguments – would it not be necessary for the Council to respond in kind, with scriptural counter-arguments? One could further argue that some of the main proponents of the theories behind the conciliar movement – men like William of Ockham (d. 1349) and his pupil Pierre d'Ailly (1350–1420) – were also promoters of the idea that Church doctrine should always be verified by Scripture.[2]

This makes one curious to investigate which, if any, role the interpretation of Scripture played in the deliberations of these councils.

2. The Council of Constance (1414–1418)

A few words are in place concerning the historical circumstances that called forth the council in the first place. Since 1378 there had been two popes of Western Christendom, one in Rome and one in Avignon. The scandal caused by this unhappy state of affairs is not difficult to understand. In 1409 the collegia of cardinals of both popes together called a council to convene in Pisa. It deposed the two popes, and elected a third in their place. The deposition of the two did not prove effective, however, with the unhappy result that after the council, the Church had three popes. This, of course, did little to improve the situation, which was perceived as unbearable by many, not least the Roman-German Emperor, King Sigismund of Hungary (elected 1411). He prevailed on the reluctant Pope John 23 – the successor of the 'third' pope elected in Pisa – to convene a council on German territory, to get rid of the triple schism once and for all, and to reform the Church "in head and members". There was also a *causa fidei* to be looked into: the alleged heresy of Jan Hus. The council convened in October/November 1414, but the real convener, Emperor Sigismund, did not arrive until two hours past midnight on Christmas Eve. After his arrival, the forces wanting the deposal of John 23 got the upper hand, and in the night of 20/21 March 1415 the Pope fled from Constance in disguise. This did little to improve his standing with the council, which or-

---

[2] See e.g., Crowder, Unity, Heresy (1977) 4–5 and 41–54.

dered his arrest, and in the meantime issued a series of texts affirming the supreme authority of the council. The council claimed this authority was given it directly from Christ, and that every believer was obliged to obey, be he the Pope himself. During sessions in May the council conducted a 'show process' against the Pope, and formally deposed him on 29 May. The council also decreed that no new pope be elected without the participation and consent of the council. None of the three present popes were eligible in the future election.

There is no doubt that we here see a council in action, which clearly regards itself as the supreme authority within the Church. In our context the interesting question would be: did the council in any way *argue* this point, and if so, did it appeal to the authority of Scripture? The answer is: it did neither.

> First it declares that, legitimately assembled in the Holy Spirit, constituting a general council and representing the catholic Church militant, it has power immediately from Christ; and that everyone of whatever state or dignity, even papal, is bound to obey it in those matters which pertain to the faith, the eradication of the said schism and the general reform of the said Church of God in head and members.[3]

One may discern, however, an implicit argument for the authority of the council in the way it presents itself as *representative* of the Catholic Church. And it was indeed more representative of all different orders within the Church than most previous councils. Secular princes and other lay people took part, not to forget a new group at such councils: the professors of the most distinguished universities, first and foremost that of Paris. When it came to matters of faith, the last mentioned group had an important say. The superiority of such a council over against the pope was not explicitly argued by the council, it was simply taken for granted. The arguments for this position had been presented during the preceding period by the spokesmen of the conciliar theory.[4] What carried the day, however, in favour of the council's supreme authority, was not theoretical considerations, but the simple fact that the papal authority had eliminated itself by the very fact of there being three popes, not one.

The Council of Constance is often called a 'reform council', and indeed it was. But the reform often spoken of in its acts – "reform in head and members" – was a reform of moral and mores within the Church, not anything like a reform of doctrine. In the latter respect, this council was quite conservative. That came to the fore in its treatment of three *causae fidei*: the case of Wyclif, the case of Hus, and the case of Jerome of Prague.

Before dealing with Hus, the council had to deal with Wyclif, although he had been dead for 30 years. Everyone realized that Hus was in many ways a follower of Wyclif. As long as Wyclif's doctrine had not been condemned by an authority the council could recognize as final,[5] anyone was free to claim that Wyclif's ideas were permissible opinions. Now, how did the council go

---

[3] Session 5, 6 April 1415; Tanner, Decrees I (1990) 409.
[4] See i.a. Stump, The Reforms (1994) 173–231; and in general BRIAN TIERNEY, *Foundations of the Conciliar Theory* (SHCT 81; Leiden: Brill 1998).
[5] Sentences of Wyclif had been condemned by the Faculty of divinity at Oxford (see below), and by a council convened at Rome by Pope John 23 in 1412–13. But the Council of Constance did not regard council convened by this problematic Pope as authoritative.

about treating the affair of Wyclif? He had challenged current doctrine on several points, not least concerning the idea of transubstantiation in the Eucharist, and he had done so basing himself on a double authority: reason and *clear statements of Scripture.* Would the council meet this challenge with counter-arguments based on the same two authorities? It did not. Doing so would have amounted to an implicit admission that the authoritative tradition of interpretation, administered by the teaching office of the Church, was no final authority; that it could in principle be overturned by each and every private interpreter thinking he had seen in Scripture something the Church had not.

What the council did, was to quote several "articles" of Wyclif collected by a commission at Oxford University in 1380. This commission of twelve members had found these articles – short quotes from several of Wyclif's writings – to be at variance with established Church doctrines, e.g., the doctrine of transubstantiation as authorized by the Fourth Lateran Council (1215). The Council at Constance found it sufficient to quote a selection of these articles (forty-five) – they were supposed to prove to anyone who could read that Wyclif was a notorious heretic. The council stated that learned men had subjected these articles to renewed scrutiny, and had found some of them to be "notoriously heretical …, others … not catholic but erroneous, others scandalous and blasphemous, some offensive to the ears of the devout, and some rash and seditious".[6] In conclusion, the council "anathematises him and condemns his memory. It decrees and orders that his body and bones are to be exhumed, if they can be identified among the corpses of the faithful, and to be scattered far from a burial place of the church, in accordance with canonical and lawful sanctions". This post mortem execution did not bode well for Jan Hus.

Hus had been summoned to the council under promise of safe-conduct by Emperor Sigismund. He also thought he had been promised the opportunity to defend himself at free hearings at the council, free from any threats. He soon learned, however, that all this was illusion, and that leading ecclesiastics at the council had entirely different ideas about his status. They argued that Hus had already been convicted of heresy by three cardinals prior to the council, and that all the council had to do, was to confirm these condemnations. As a convicted heretic, Hus had no right to address the council and defend himself. Sigismund was only able to force the council to let Hus himself make a public defence on the 5, 7 and 8 June 1415, but he was already condemned as a liar who tried to sneak away from his true opinions; his defence was therefore dismissed as irrelevant. The only option offered Hus by the council fathers was that he could save himself by abjuring the "articles" collected from his writings – meaning he no longer held them. Hus found this unacceptable; it would mean admitting that the articles correctly rendered his opinions, which they did not. He refused to abjure *as his opinions* something he had never held. Having refused to save his life by perjury, he was convicted of heresy at the council's fifteenth session, 6 July. The council first repeated the condemnation of Wyclif, quoting this time a selection of 58 articles from the 260 condemned

----

6 Session 8, 4 May 1415; Tanner, Decrees I (1990) 414.

by the commission at Oxford University. Next, Hus is condemned as a follower of Wyclif, teaching the same abominable heresy as he. And even worse:
He has shown disobedience with regard to the sanctions imposed upon him on
earlier occasions. "He has persisted in these things for many years with a hardened h[e]art. He has greatly scandalised Christ's faithful by his obstinacy
since, bypassing the Church's intermediaries, he has made appeal directly to
our Lord Jesus Christ, as to the supreme judge, in which he has introduced
many false, harmful and scandalous things to the contempt of the apostolic
see, ecclesiastical censures and the keys".[7] In fact, the council was hitting the
nail on its head here, as far as the real disagreement with Hus was concerned.
For Hus, the true Church was a hidden entity, identical with the number of
the predetermined elect ones, and Christ, not the Pope, was their real head.
For the council, the true Church was identical with the visible corporation of
which the council itself was the representative. Hus's ecclesiology would effectively undermine the authority of any council, not to mention the Pope, to
speak on behalf of the true Church.[8] – The same day, Hus was handed over to
the secular arm and burned at the stake. One year later he was followed in this
fate by Jerome of Prague. He was condemned in session 21, 30 May 1416, as a
follower of Wyclif and Hus, and immediately burned at the stake.

Having dealt with the three *causae fidei* in this way, the council was able to
depose effectively all three reigning Popes, and elect a new one. In this regard
the council was successful: it restored Church unity, but at a price. The task of
reforming the Church in head and members came to little more than nothing;
the newly elected Pope soon saw to it that the council lost impetus and energy,
and it gradually dissolved.

At Constance we see two men addressing the institutional Church – one
posthumously – with basically the same challenge: The present Church is not
living up to biblical ideals – its putative shepherds least of all. The challenge
from Wyclif and Hus could be summarized like this: "I can prove it from
Scripture, I can prove it from the Fathers, I can prove it from reason. And I
beg anyone who wants to refute me, to do so from these authorities, and first
and foremost from Scripture." The institutional Church refused to meet this
challenge. For the Church to do so, would have meant suspending its authority
as the supreme interpreter of Scripture.

3. The Council(s) of Basel-Ferrara-Florence-Rome (1431–1445/49)

Before dissolving, the Council of Constance had decreed that a new council
was to be convened in five years, then again seven years after that, and then

---

[7] Tanner, Decrees I (1990) 428. The condemnation of Hus is followed by 30 condemned "articles" of his. One can here observe a supposedly infallible council gravely misquoting sources that
are preserved elsewhere in their authentic text. For details, see Spinka, John Hus (1965) 76–79.
[8] For this analysis, see Spinka, John Hus (1965) 68–70.

regularly every 10 years. This was an attempt by the conciliar movement to make the sort of council convened at Constance a regular institution, thereby controlling the papacy. No wonder, therefore, that the papacy boycotted these initiatives to the best of its ability. After five years, the Pope convened a council in Pavia, then moved it to Siena, and was happy soon to dissolve it because too few delegates showed up. After the next seven years a council convened in Basel on 23 July 1431. Again there was minimal attendance, not a single bishop turned up, and the Pope, Eugenius IV, was again happy to dissolve the council on 18 December. This time, however, the council delegates refused to obey, and continued with the council, supported by the royal authority of Sigismund, and the theological authority of Nicholas of Cusa. For two years the council spent most of its time and energy on a protracted power-struggle with the Pope, until the latter gave in and recognized the legitimacy of the council. Under his recognition, the council proceeded with hammering out the practical consequences of the conciliar theory, to such an extent and with such consequence that the Pope again began protesting several of its decrees. In the summer of 1437 there was a new schism between Pope and Council. The Pope convened a new council in Ferrara, and ordered the delegates at Basel to transfer to Ferrara. This order was obeyed only by a minority (Nicholas of Cusa being among them), the majority refused to comply, and in 1439 made the schism final by deposing Eugenius IV as being a heretic, and electing a new Pope of their own. Thus the conciliar movement, which so successfully had ended schism in Constance, ended tragically by creating a new schism only twenty years later. The council dragged on for another ten years, and was finally ended on 25 April 1449. In none of the many decrees of this Basel Council did interpretation of Scripture play any significant role – as one would expect.

One would expect, however, that the question of the right interpretation of Scripture would arise at the papal council of Ferrara, due to the main theme of this council: negotiations with representatives of Constantinople to create unity with the Greek Church. The Emperor of Constantinople, John VIII Paleologos, was in dire straits, being hard pressed by the Osman Turks. In order to get assistance from the West, the Emperor induced his prelates to open negotiations about Church unity with the Westerners. It was a triumph as well for him as for Pope Eugenius, when the council of Ferrara was solemnly opened on 9 April 1438 in the presence of Pope, Emperor, 70 Western bishops, and from the East by the Patriarch of Constantinople, and the archbishops of Ephesus, Nicaea, Kiev, and representatives of the patriarchs of Alexandria, Antioch and Jerusalem. Within less than a year, the council was transferred to Florence. There the council could book its first success: a bull of union between the Roman and the Greek Church of 6 July 1439. The Latin version was read out by cardinal Caesarini, the Greek version by the archbishop of Nicaea, Bessarion. What lay behind this stunning ecumenical achievement?[9]

---

[9] It was to a very great extent prepared by the previous "Council of Union" at Lyons, 1274. See UMBERTO PROCH, "Das Zweite Konzil von Lyon (1274)", in: Alberigo, Geschichte der Konzilien (1993) 292–307.

The order of negotiations had been this: the Greeks were first allowed to state their objections against the controversial points in Roman doctrine, the Latins then responded. The first difficult question to tackle was the addition of the famous *filioque* in the Latin text of the Nicene Creed. Whereas the original Greek of the third article states that the Holy Spirit proceeds from the Father, the Latin text here adds "and the Son" (Latin: *filioque*). Since the days of the Old Church, both parties had argued that their version was in better agreement with Scripture. Accordingly, and since the creed was anyway regarded by both sides as a summary of the doctrine of Scripture, one would expect questions of exegesis to come on the table in this bull. The crucial passage reads like this:

> Texts were produced from divine Scriptures and many authorities of Eastern and Western holy doctors, some saying the Holy Spirit proceeds from the Father and the Son, others saying the procession is from the Father through the Son. All were aiming at the same meaning in different words. The Greeks asserted that when they claim that the Holy Spirit proceeds from the Father, they do not intend to exclude the Son; but because it seemed to them that the Latins assert that the holy Spirit proceeds from the Father and the Son as from two principles and two spirations, they refrain from saying that the Holy Spirit proceeds from the Father and the Son. The Latins asserted that they say the Holy Spirit proceeds from the Father and the Son not with the intention of excluding the Father from being the source and principle of all deity, that is of the Son and of the Holy Spirit, nor to imply that the Son does not receive from the Father, because the Holy Spirit proceeds from the Son, nor that they posit two principles or two spirations; but they assert that there is only one principle and a single spiration of the Holy Spirit, as they have asserted hitherto. Since, then, one and the same meaning resulted from all this, they unanimously agreed and consented to the following holy and God-pleasing union, in the same sense and with one mind: ...[10]

In its wording and methodology this statement sounds strikingly modern; it recurs in a striking way in the modern Joint Declaration on Justification – except for one important point. The modern statement begins with an extensive section on relevant biblical doctrine, comprising a whole compendium of Pauline and other New Testament texts on the issue. In Florence, they were satisfied to report that extensive exegetical and patristic arguments had been exchanged, but none of the biblical arguments are incorporated into the final text of the bull. This probably has to do with the genre of the text: it consciously aligns itself with the wording of the creed, presenting itself more as a dogmatic comment on the meaning of the Nicene Creed than as a piece of biblical theology. It could hardly be otherwise. That the text of the Creed faithfully rendered biblical doctrine, was a conviction shared by both sides. As soon as they agreed that their different wording of the creed meant the same, adducing additional biblical testimonies might sooner bring remaining differences to the surface than bolster the achieved unity.

After having achieved this unity with the Greeks, the council followed up by bulls of unity with the Armenians and the Copts. These bulls, however, were clearly more imposed upon these churches than genuine results of negotiated consensus. In 1443 the council was transferred to Rome, where it was concluded, probably in 1445. Bulls of union with the Syrian Orthodox, with the

---

[10] Session 6, 6 July 1439; Tanner, Decrees I (1990) 525 f.

Chaldeans and the Maronites of Cyprus were hastily issued – one can sense how Western and Eastern Christendom is making a last desperate effort to unite before the threatening onslaught of the Osman Turks. There are less than 10 years to the fall of Constantinople in 1453.

4. Concluding Remarks

The protestant Reformers of the sixteenth century had many precursors, and different precursors for different aspects of their efforts. To varying degrees, their efforts to establish Scripture alone as the one and only authority of Church doctrine and Church practice were anticipated by men like Wyclif and Hus. But these were not the only ones who called for "reform in head and members" – this was a standing slogan for the conciliar movement, too. Two of the several councils that seriously tried to put this programme into practice during the fifteenth century were later recognized as authoritative, ecumenical councils. These councils of reform, however, were not interested in making relative the authority of the Church as such; their main concern was to redefine what and who the Church was, and then to *assert* the authority of this redefined Church, not to argue in its favour.

The big difference concerning the *effect* that men like Wyclif and Hus on the one hand, and Luther and the other Reformers contemporary with him on the other, had on the Catholic Church is easily seen when one compares the decrees of the two reform councils of the fifteenth century with the decrees of the council of Trent in the sixteenth century. The difference is almost dramatic. The reform councils refused to enter any discussion about the teaching of Scripture; the Church does not discuss with heretics. In Trent, the Catholic Church itself put forward quite extensive and detailed expositions of doctrine, based on crucial Scriptural testimonies, and in constant polemical dialogue with the Scriptural expositions of the Reformers. This was a novelty, indeed a radical novelty, as far as conciliar statements are concerned. And the dialogue is not always polemical. When defining the main categories of causes of justification, the council states the following: "Finally, the one formal cause is the justness of God; *not that by which he himself is just, but that by which he makes us just*[11] and endowed with which we are renewed in the spirit of our mind ...". Anyone familiar with the language of Luther will recognize his peculiar way of speaking here, as e. g., in his preface to his Latin works of 1545 (two years earlier).[12] I discovered, he says here, that the justness of God does not consist in his giving each what he deserves (God himself being just), but in his declaring *us* just because of faith. Having discovered this, "I ran through the Scriptures by memory, and collected other concepts having a similar meaning, e. g., God's work: what he works in us; God's power: by which he makes us strong; God's

---

[11] Session 6, 13 January 1547; decree on justification, ch. 7: ... iustitia Dei, *non qua ipse iustus est, sed qua nos iustos facit*...; Tanner, Decrees II (1990) 673.
[12] Latin text conveniently found in O. CLEMEN (ed.), *Luthers Werke in Auswahl* 4 (Berlin: Walter de Gruyter, ⁵1959) 421–28. Translations in the following are my own.

wisdom: by which he makes us wise; God's strength... etc. ... I had great pleasure in teaching *God's justice, by which we are justified*.[13] In this way Luther's
discovery of the dynamic-communicative quality of the Hebrew concept of
God's *zedaka* ('justice') found its way into the text of the Tridentine decree on
justification. That the borrowing from Luther is quite conscious, is shown by
the continuation of the passage quoted above – here the decree follows up with
a passage clearly corrective and polemical against Luther: "and we are not
merely considered to be just but we are truly named and are just".

In Trent the Roman Catholic Church, for the first time, met challenges to
its doctrine by meeting the challengers on common ground: the interpretation
of Scripture. Another chapter in this volume deals with the different pronouncements of Trent on the biblical text and canon, and the significance of
these. But it should be noticed carefully that Trent not only said important
things about the Bible. The Council illustrated its principles by its own practice
in the main decrees. Trent is the first council to fix doctrine by expounding the
Bible, Old and New Testaments indiscriminately.

---

[13] "... placuit ... iustitiam Dei doceri, *qua nos iustificemur*". The whole passage in Clemen,
Luthers Werke 4 (1959) 427.35–428.16.

CHAPTER FIFTEEN

The Cultural and Sociopolitical Context of the Reformation

By Euan Cameron, New York

General works: J. Bossy, Christianity in the West 1400–1700 (Oxford / New York: Oxford UP 1985); E. Cameron, The European Reformation (Oxford: Clarendon 1991); A. Cunningham / O. P. Grell, The Four Horsemen of the Apocalypse: Religion, War, Famine and Death in Reformation Europe (Cambridge: Cambridge UP 2000); E. J. Dempsey Douglass, Justification in late medieval preaching: a study of John Geiler of Keisersberg (2nd edn.; Leiden / New York: Brill 1989); E. Duffy, The Stripping of the Altars: Traditional Religion in England, 1400–1580 (New Haven, CT: Yale UP 1992); P. A. Dykema / H. A. Oberman (eds.), Anticlericalism in late medieval and early modern Europe (SMRT 51; Leiden / New York: Brill 1992); G. R. Evans (ed.), The Medieval Theologians (Oxford / Malden, MA: Blackwell 2001); J. N. Galpern, The Religions of the People in sixteenth-century Champagne (Cambridge, MA: Harvard UP 1976); B. Hamilton, Religion in the Medieval West (London / Baltimore, MD: Edward Arnold 1986); M. Lambert, Medieval Heresy: Popular Movements from the Gregorian Reform to the Reformation (Cambridge, MA: Blackwell 1992); F. Oakley, The Western Church in the Later Middle Ages (Ithaca, NY / London 1979); H. A. Oberman, The Harvest of Medieval Theology: Gabriel Biel and Late Medieval Nominalism (Cambridge, MA: Harvard UP 1963); J. H. Overfield, Humanism and Scholasticism in Late Medieval Germany (Princeton, NJ: Princeton UP 1984); S. Ozment, The Age of Reform, 1250–1550: an intellectual and religious history of late Medieval and Reformation Europe (New Haven / London: Yale UP 1980); idem (ed.), Reformation Europe: A Guide to Research (St. Louis: Center for Reformation Research 1982); R. R. Post, The Modern Devotion: Confrontation with Reformation and Humanism (Leiden: Brill 1968); M. Rubin, Corpus Christi: The Eucharist in Late Medieval Culture (Cambridge / New York: Cambridge UP 1991); R. W. Scribner / T. Johnson (eds.), Popular religion in Germany and Central Europe, 1400–1800 (New York: St. Martin's Press 1996); R. N. Swanson, Religion and Devotion in Europe, c. 1215 – c. 1515 (Cambridge / New York: Cambridge UP 1995); J. A. F. Thomson, Popes and princes, 1417–1517: Politics and Polity in the Late Medieval Church (London / Boston: Allen & Unwin 1980); Ch. Trinkaus / H. A. Oberman (eds.), The Pursuit of Holiness in Late Medieval and Renaissance Religion: Papers from the University of Michigan Conference (Leiden: Brill 1974); A. Vauchez, Sainthood in the later Middle Ages (tr. by J. Birrell; Cambridge 1997); S. Wilson, The Magical Universe: Everyday Ritual and Magic in Pre-Modern Europe (London: Hambledon and London 2000).

1. Introduction

The social and cultural background to the Reformation, as reflected in historical writing over the past few decades, presents a more complex and nuanced appearance than formerly. Generations of scholars had grown used to reading and writing about a morbid, overblown and materialistic piety; a corrupt, venal, and ill-trained clergy; a fractious, fragmented and pharisaical tribe of mendicants and other religious; and a morally discredited and corrupt papacy, reduced to brokering between the squabbling princes of Europe. The present risk is that, if anything, too much may be said on the opposing side. Historical revisionism lays so much stress on vigorously reformed observant orders, on zealous pastoral bishops, and on vibrant and generous lay piety, that the Reformation appears as nothing more than illogical and ungrateful iconoclasm. Finding a way out of this historiographical *impasse* requires a more subtle assessment of both the positive and negative factors in the western European religious context. Not all criticism is destructive or morbid; not all enthusiasm and zeal is directed towards ultimately productive ends. From the paradoxical and contrary trends in late medieval society it may be possible, with some interpretation, to discern a certain crisis of authority, a need for a secure criterion of truth, which would soon thrust the issue of biblical exegesis to the forefront.

If one had the good fortune to stay healthy, the fifteenth century was not an entirely unattractive time to be alive in Western Europe. For reasons including but not confined to visitations of plague, the population declined to a half or, in some areas, even as low as one third of its previous maxima by around 1440.[1] Staple foods became abundant; prices fell, and a healthy market opened up in non-essential foods. Specialist zones emerged for the production of wine, fruits, wool, or dyestuffs.[2] As structural poverty diminished, surplus wealth became available for, amongst other things, the reconstruction of churches, the adorning of shrines and pilgrimage sites, and the production of works of art. The late Gothic grew into one of the most extravagantly ornate phases in Latin Christian culture, and the scale of its surviving legacy is almost overpowering.[3]

However, signs of strain appeared in the last quarter of the fifteenth century. After a century of stagnation Europe's population began to grow from around 1470, although the claim that it had already recovered to its pre-plague levels by 1500 seems excessive.[4] It is more likely that, after a century of realignment in the agrarian economy, a relatively small increase in population caused it to rub against a lowered ceiling in the production of basic foods. Prices rose, and expectations of a continued rise in standards of living were disappointed. In various parts of Europe, but most noticeably in Germany, tenants expressed their grievances as landlords tried to re-impose servile status, to require additional services from their subjects, and to restrict access to

---

[1] For population estimates of this period see esp. T. H. HOLLINGSWORTH, *Historical Demography* (Sources of History, Studies in the uses of historical evidence; Cambridge: Cambridge UP 1976).

[2] For the agrarian history of later medieval Europe see G. DUBY, *L'économie rurale et la vie des campagnes dans l'occident médiéval (France, Angleterre, Empire, IXe-XVe siècles): essais de synthèse et perspectives de recherches* (Collection historique; Paris: Aubier 1962).

[3] For the religious art of the later Gothic see e.g. M. BAXANDALL, *The Limewood Sculptors of Renaissance Germany* (New Haven / London: Yale UP 1980).

[4] Estimates of such an early recovery in population numbers are made in Ozment, Age of Reform (1980) 190–92, and in Cunningham / Grell, Four Horsemen of the Apocalypse (2000) 14–16; but compare e.g. E. A. WRIGLEY / R. S. SCHOFIELD, *The Population History of England, 1541–1871: a Reconstruction* (Edward Arnold for the Cambridge Group for the History of Population and Social Structure 1981).

woods, rivers and waste lands.[5] To these problems was added, from the 1490s onwards, the disruption caused by the presence of ever-larger armies. The mainland of Europe had seen little serious campaigning between the 1450s and the early 1490s. After 1494 huge mercenary armies tramped across Europe to the battlegrounds in northern and central Italy, in an increasingly destructive and futile duel between the Habsburg and Valois dynasties that lasted until 1559.[6] The professional soldier became a stock figure of woodblock illustrations and moral tales. The morality of soldiers fell under deeper scrutiny when French soldiers at Naples in the 1490s produced the first documented signs of what soon became known as the 'French pox'.[7]

2. The Religious Experience of the Majority

The overwhelming majority of Western Europe's people lived within the structures of the Catholic Church. Even the tiny minority of Europeans who belonged to dissenting movements such as the Lollard or Waldensian heresies continued, in the main, to attend Church as well.[8] The Church's frameworks were, however, supple and adaptable, and in some areas ill defined. The keynote of late medieval Christianity was the belief that the infinite merits of Christ's sacrifice on the cross were transmitted and mediated through the masses said by priests at every altar in Christendom, apart from and independent of any congregational communion. In each mass, it was argued, a certain quantum of divine grace was secured through the sacrificial offering whereby Christ, personated by the priest, offered himself again on the altar. As a fifteenth-century English canon law collection put it: "God doth work in such mysteries under a certain distribution of his fullness, which He hath knit unto them with a law that cannot be expressed".[9] This statement reflects the mixture of awe and mathematics that characterized the age. It justified the multiplication, sometimes to prodigious numbers, of masses said for the souls of quite ordinary believers, and the even more copious service performed for dead aristocrats and royalty.[10]

---

[5] On these grievances and their outcome see P. BLICKLE, *The revolution of 1525: the German Peasants' War from a new perspective* (tr. by T. A. Brady, Jr. / H. C. E. Midelfort; Baltimore, MD / London: Johns Hopkins UP 1981); T. SCOTT / B. SCRIBNER (eds.), *The German Peasants' War: a History in Documents* (Atlantic Highlands, NJ / London: Humanities Press 1991).

[6] On the wars see R. BONNEY, *The European Dynastic States, 1494–1660* (Oxford: Oxford UP 1991) 79–130.

[7] On soldiers see K. MOXEY, *Peasants Warriors and Wives: Popular Imagery in the Reformation* (Chicago / London: University of Chicago Press 1989) 67–100; on syphilis, Cunningham / Grell, *Four Horsemen of the Apocalypse* (2000) 247–70.

[8] See E. CAMERON, "Dissent and Heresy", in: R. Po-Chia Hsia (ed.), *A Companion to the Reformation World* (Oxford: Blackwell 2004) 3–21, and esp. 10–11.

[9] This extract comes from the canon *Sacerdotes caveant* of Archbishop John Pecham, as edited in J. V. BULLARD / H. CHALMER BELL (eds.), *Lyndwood's Provinciale: the text of the canons therein contained, reprinted from the translation made in 1534* (London: The Faith Press 1929) 95.

[10] For the multiplying of masses for the dead see J. CHIFFOLEAU, *La Comptabilité de l'au-delà: les hommes, la mort et la religion dans la région d'Avignon à la fin du Moyen Age, vers 1320-vers 1480* (Collection de l'École française de Rome 47; Rome: École française de Rome / Paris: Diffusion de

Equally typical of later medieval piety was an acute sense of the presence of Christ in the Eucharistic elements, especially the consecrated wafer. The *Dialogues* of Gregory the Great had contained a story of the avaricious monk Justus, who was only released from punishment after death when Gregory had commanded thirty masses to be said for his soul on consecutive days.[11] To this was added, in late medieval folklore and many pictorial representations, the story that a sceptical young priest had sought from Pope Gregory confirmation of the real presence. On Gregory's praying for some miraculous sign, the crucified Christ had suddenly appeared on the altar as the Pope said mass, surrounded by the attributes of the passion.[12] This fable illustrated and accompanied a growing collective preoccupation with Christ as physically present in the consecrated Host. The annual observance of Corpus Christi day on the Thursday after Trinity, according to a rite popularly attributed to St Thomas Aquinas, spread from the Low Countries to become general across western Europe.[13] It was accompanied by public processions, sometimes organized by confraternities created for the purpose, where the host was paraded under a canopy in a manner more appropriate to a living sovereign.[14]

The feast of Corpus Christi was in a sense an 'official' creation of the Church. However, Eucharistic devotion also produced voluntary, spontaneous and somewhat unofficial cults, even more dynamically popular. Across central and southern Germany, new devotions and centres of pilgrimage sprang up, many of them centred on some aspect of the Eucharist. When some consecrated Hosts were found to have survived a fire at a field-chapel at Wilsnack in northern Germany in 1383, and shortly afterwards appeared to shed small drops of blood at intervals, great crowds flocked there on pilgrimage; soon rival shrines with similar miraculous relics were founded at Sternberg and elsewhere.[15] Although the Fourth Lateran Council of 1215 had attempted to stem the growth in new relics to be venerated, this edict appears to have had little effect.[16] Christ's seamless robe exhibited at Trier, or Christ's shroud shown at Chambéry (now at Turin) came into vogue in the fourteenth and fifteenth centuries. Even images could become quasi-relics, surrounded by an aura of spiritual power: those of the Virgin at Grimmenthal and Regensburg (the latter discovered as late as 1518) were believed to have been miraculously formed, and attracted fervent devotion for some decades.[17]

Boccard 1980); and the description of early sixteenth-century religion as "a cult of the living in the service of the dead", in: Galpern, Religions of the People (1976) 20, and 16–29 for the overall point.

[11] The story occurs in Gregory I, *Dialogues*, bk. 4, ch. 55; it was probably best known through the summary in Jacobus de Voragine: *The Golden Legend of Jacobus de Voragine* (tr. and ed. by Granger Ryan / H. Ripperger; London; Longmans 1941) 653f.

[12] Typical representations of the Mass of St Gregory were painted around 1510 by Adrien Ysenbrandt, now in the J. Paul Getty Museum (The Getty Center, Los Angeles, CA); and in 1511 by Hans Baldung Grien (1484/85–1545), now in the Cleveland Museum of Art (Cleveland, OH) as well as a famous woodcut engraving by Albrecht Dürer from around the same period.

[13] On the Corpus Christi festival see Rubin, Corpus Christi (1991) 164–212, and for Thomas Aquinas's role in composing the rite, ibid. 185–96.

[14] C. ZIKA, "Hosts, Processions and Pilgrimages: Controlling the Sacred in Fifteenth-Century Germany", *Past and Present* 118 (1988) 25–64.

[15] Luther's comments on the field-shrines occur in his *Address to the Christian Nobility* in: *Luther's Works* (ed. J. Pelikan; St. Louis, MT: Concordia 1955–86), vol. 44 (1966) 185–87; *Luthers Werke: kritische Gesamtausgabe* (Weimar: Böhlaus Nachfolger 1883–1948), vol. 6 (1888) 447f. On Wilsnack see also R. DAMERAU, *Das Gutachten der Theologischen Fakultät Erfurt 1452 über 'Das heilige Blut von Wilsnak'* (Studien zu den Grundlagen der Reformation 13; Marburg: im Selbstverlag 1976); C. LICHTE, *Die Inszenierung einer Wallfahrt: der Lettner im Havelberger Dom und das Wilsnacker Wunderblut* (Worms: Wernersche Verlagsgesellschaft 1990); C. W. BYNUM, "Bleeding Hosts and their Contact Relics in Late Medieval Northern Germany", *The Medieval History Journal* 7/2 (2004) 227–41.

[16] For constitution 62 of the Fourth Lateran Council of 1215, see N. P. TANNER (ed.), *Decrees of the Ecumenical Councils...*(London: Sheed & Ward / Georgetown UP 1990) 263.

[17] For the Schöne Maria at Regensburg see e.g. Michael Ostendorfer's depiction in S. MICHALSKI, *The Reformation and the visual arts: the Protestant image question in Western and Eastern Europe* (London: Routledge 1993), plate 3; for the legend of the Virgin of Grimmenthal see L. BECHSTEIN, *Deutsches Sagenbuch* (Leipzig: Wigand 1853) 605f.

Devotion to the Blessed Virgin Mary consumed vast spiritual energy and material resources. Most of the new shrines created in southern Germany on the eve of the Reformation were dedicated to her. Countless images, prayers, and lives of the saint attest to her popularity, as much as do the sarcastic remarks of humanists like Erasmus.[18] In some of the iconography, but also in some of the preaching of the period, the Virgin all but supplanted Christ as the mediator and intercessor to whom sinners fled for security and relief. She became the 'co-redeemer', the 'Virgin of Mercy' who covered her devotees from the rigours of her judgmental son.[19] However, for the many challenges and threatening circumstances of everyday life, a more specialized intercessor was called for. The cult of the 'auxiliary saints' or 'holy helpers' enlisted a pantheon of minor saints to assist with everyday problems. More serious issues, like plague, had several specialists assigned, St Roche, St Sebastian, and others. Renaissance humanists, and later Reformers, would lose no time in parodying a culture in which different aspects of one's life and one's household were commended to a different saint: "Every man, as his superstition leadeth him, he commendeth his riches to God and St Erasmus; his ox to God and St Luke; his horse to God and St Loye; for every disease he hath a diverse patron ...".[20] It must be underscored, therefore, that these devotions were not merely the product of the overflowing effluent of uneducated religious enthusiasm. The Church actively encouraged them, through the liturgies and calendars at its heart.

Intractable semantic and conceptual problems surround the analysis and definition of so-called 'popular religion'.[21] It is widely recognized–and observers remarked at the time–that many people had recourse to the saints, and to the rituals of religion in general, in the search for material assistance and protection in the everyday business of life. As Jean Gerson (1363–1429) complained, "too many people ... for whatsoever thing, howsoever profane and mean, seek from God and the saints some supernatural working, although the opposite of

---

[18] On Marian shrines see L. ROTHKRUG, "Popular religion and holy shrines: their influence on the origins of the German Reformation and their role in German cultural development", in: J. OBELKEVICH (ed.), Religion and the people, 800–1700 (Princeton University, Shelby Cullom Davis Center for Historical Studies; Chapel Hill: University of North Carolina Press 1979) 20–86, esp. 64–76; for some sign of the popularity of the Marian legend see Albrecht Dürer's series of engravings, The Life of Mary, executed in the 1500s. The excesses of Marian piety are pilloried in Erasmus's Colloquies "A Pilgrimage for Religion's Sake" and "The Shipwreck": see Desiderius Erasmus: Collected works of Erasmus, vols. 39–40: Colloquies (tr. and annotated by C. R. Thompson; Toronto e.a.: University of Toronto Press 1997), vol. 39, 351–67; vol. 40, 619–74.

[19] On Marian theology in popular preaching see e.g. Oberman, Harvest of Medieval Theology (1963) 281–322.

[20] For the Holy Helpers, and for Saints Roch and Sebastian see D. H. FARMER, The Oxford Dictionary of Saints (3rd edn.; Oxford / New York: Oxford UP 1992) 185, 420f, 429 and refs.; for the quotation see Early writings of John Hooper, D.D., Lord Bishop of Gloucester and Worcester (ed. Samuel Carr; Parker Society; Cambridge: Cambridge UP 1843) 309f.

[21] For some discussions see R. MANSELLI, La Religion populaire au Moyen Age: problèmes de méthode et d'histoire (Montréal: Institut d'études médiévales Albert-le-Grand 1975), esp. 11–41; N. Z. DAVIS, "From 'Popular Religion' to Religious Cultures", in: Ozment, Reformation Europe (1982) 321–41.

what they seek might work often for their spiritual good".[22] There was no simple dualistic or polarized state of affairs, in which the Church hierarchy exhorted people to seek only for spiritual benefits, while the uneducated vulgar looked for material advantage. The Church, even in the shape of its most intelligent pastoral theologians, took a complex and paradoxical view. On one hand, countless expositions of the Book of Job explained how a provident God sent adversity to people to test and prove their faith. On the other hand, an ultimately benign deity from time to time allowed evil forces, demons and sorcerers, to cause physical harm and misfortune. To address such harm God provided remedies and defences, above all the sign of the cross and Holy Water, valid against all sorts of assaults. The two attitudes, the providentialist and the ritualist, could coincide in the same text, as in the sermons on sorcery preached by the theologian Martin Plantsch of Tübingen in 1505. These ascribed all evil occurrences to the specific permission of God, but also encouraged the use of lawful exorcisms, holy water, other consecrated objects, relics, and other aids against them.[23]

Thus encouraged by the Church, less educated clergy and most laity could not resist discovering a panoply of other, less officially approved means to address their needs. Contemporary writers all report that unauthorized amulets, charms and spells made free use of the names of God (real or imaginary) and of fragments of the liturgy or Scripture to try to harness supernatural power for human benefit.[24] It was also believed that the same power could be used to harm. All kinds of misfortune could be blamed on sorcery performed with demonic assistance. Even theoretically 'good' magic, it was argued, would invariably cause harm to the soul and might even cause physical ills rather than curing them.[25] By a curious sort of transference of ideas, even saints and images could cause as well as cure illness or misfortune, if their devotees behaved in the wrong way.[26]

This rich diversity of layers of belief did not originate from an ill-educated clergy and laity, deprived of pastoral advice or of suitably presented theology. On the contrary, the decades before the Reformation saw an explosion in the publication of all sorts of religious literature, much of it accessible in the vernacular. Manuals on hearing confessions, which set out the Church's moral

---

[22] Jean [Charlier de] Gerson: *Oeuvres Complètes* 1–9 (ed. P. Glorieux; Paris: Desclée et Cie 1960–73), vol. 8, 110.

[23] See the edition of these sermons as Martinus Plantsch, *Opusculum de sagis maleficis* (Phorce [i.e. Pforzheim]: in aedibus Thomae Anshelmi [1507]), pass.

[24] For the abuse of the liturgy in charms see Johann Nider OP, *Preceptorium divine legis* (s.l. 1470?), precept 1, ch. 11, qq. 26–27; Jacob von Hochstraten, *Tractatus magistralis declarans quam graviter peccent querentes auxilium a maleficis* (Cologne 1510), ch. 3.

[25] Johann Nider illustrated this point through the story of the devout folk-healer called 'Seriosa' who blamed the illnesses of her patients on their use of unauthorized charms; see Johann Nider OP, *Formicarius*, as edited in: *Malleorum quorundam maleficarum, tam veterum quàm recentiorum authorum, tomi duo* (Francofurti: ... sumptibus Nicolai Bassæi 1582) 725 f.

[26] On diseases believed to be caused by saints see e.g. M. P. CARROLL, *Madonnas that maim: popular Catholicism in Italy since the fifteenth century* (Baltimore / London: Johns Hopkins UP 1992); Wilson, Magical Universe (2000) 322–32.

rules, were published in literally dozens of editions.[27] Literate priests had a be-wildering array of vocational guidebooks available. Primers, almanacs, and devotional treatises circulated freely, as did printed collections of sermons.[28] The keynote of the majority religious culture before the Reformation era is its diversity and abundance, not its decay or corruption.

Not everyone responded to this diversity with the complacent acceptance shown by some recent historians. The lack of an agreed universal criterion of good Christian teaching and practice was deplored, not welcomed. Ultimately, the supreme source of authority was, naturally enough, Holy Scripture as in-terpreted within the ongoing tradition of the Church. However, even here there was room for divergence. Was the *sole* source of authority Scripture properly interpreted, or might the traditions of the Church also generate rites and customs, or even beliefs, which were not explicitly foreshadowed in Scrip-ture?[29] The late medieval period fostered a number of 'new' doctrines, most notably that Mary had been conceived immaculate from original sin, and that she had been bodily taken up into heaven after her death. These beliefs were vigorously promoted long before (sometimes centuries before) the Roman hierarchy decided for or against them. The doctrine of the Immaculate Con-ception caused virtual civil war in the Church between the rival orders of men-dicant friars who took opposed views, Franciscans in its favour and Domini-cans against it.[30]

The spectacular and notorious case of the Immaculate Conception seems to have been repeated, on a much smaller scale, all across pre-Reformation Europe. Cults developed more or less sponta-neously, receiving belated and contradictory verdicts from the hierarchy. In 1400s England the custom developed of observing a "Lady Fast", i.e. fasting for seven years on the day of the week that the Feast of the Annunciation happened to fall: this was supposed to guarantee freedom from sudden death, therefore, in principle, eventual access to paradise. The author of the pastoral tract *Dives and Pauper* inveighed ineffectually against this setting of limits and rules for the divine dis-pensation.[31] The Dominican Johannes Nider's *Formicarius* set up an imaginary debate between a layman who questioned the allegedly 'guaranteed' rewards for those who devoted themselves to certain saints, and a theologian who defended them: the copious examples quoted by the theolo-gian suggest strongly that Nider sympathized with the latter.[32] Even the rational Gerson admitted

---

[27] On confessional manuals see above all T. N. Tentler, *Sin and Confession on the Eve of the Reformation* (Princeton, NJ: Princeton UP 1977); leading examples of the confessors' manual in-clude Angelo Carletti, *Summa angelica de casibus conscientiae* (Chivasso: Jacobinus Suigus, de Suico 1486, and many subsequent editions); Silvestro Mazzolini da Prierio, *Summa Summarum, que Syl-vestrina dicitur* (Bologna 1515, and many subsequent editions).

[28] For typical pastoral manuals see e.g. Guido, de Monte Rocherii, *Manipulus curatorum* ([Augsburg]: C. Heyny 14[8]1, and numerous subsequent editions). For one of the most popular almanacs, see *Le Compost et kalendrier des bergiers: reproduction en fac-simile de l'édition de Guy Marchant (Paris 1493)* (ed. by Pierre Champion; Paris: Éditions des quatre chemins [1926]).

[29] The ambiguities of medieval theology on the issue of Scripture and tradition are discussed in H. A. Oberman, *Forerunners of the Reformation: the shape of late medieval thought* (Philadelphia: Fortress 1981) 53–120.

[30] For the Immaculate Conception see Oberman, Harvest of Medieval Theology (1963) 283–85; J. J. Pelikan, *Reformation of Church and Dogma (1300–1700)* (Chicago: University of Chicago Press 1984) 45–50.

[31] See P. Heath Barnum (ed.), *Dives and pauper* (Early English Text Society, vols. 275, 280; London: Oxford UP 1976–80), vol. 1, 172–74.

[32] Johann Nider OP, [*Formicarius*=]: *Johannis Nideri … de Visionibus ac Revelationibus opus, … anno 1517 Argentinæ editum … luci et integritati restitutum* (Helmestadii 1692) 417 ff.

that it would be impractical for a relatively junior priest to dissuade a large congregation from its entrenched, albeit 'superstitious' local observances.[33]

3. A Crisis in the Spiritual Leadership of the Church?

The label 'anticlerical' is an anachronism at the end of the Middle Ages.[34] Yet many historians long used to argue that at least some clergy earned the contempt of their peers and the laity; and that some probably deserved that contempt. More recent scholars, especially of the traditional Church in England, insist that almost to a man the clergy were respected, admired, even beloved spiritual fathers of their communities. Such contemporary criticisms as exist, these revisionists blame on the ambition of clerical would-be-reformers, the sectional self-interest of lawyers, or on theological heresy masquerading as attacks on clerical vice.[35] Notwithstanding those reservations, if one discards the idea of a single uniform entity, 'anticlericalism', and does not claim that problems were everywhere the same, one can discern a series of image problems affecting those who wielded spiritual authority in the western Church.

First, European culture sent out decidedly mixed messages about the role of the preacher and theologian as spiritual guide to the people. On one hand, the prestige of the preachers had rarely been higher. In fifteenth-century France preachers like Jean Raulin, Olivier Maillard, or Michel Menot preached to often vast audiences, and enjoyed considerable esteem and even charisma.[36] The Strasbourg theologian and popular preacher Johann Geiler von Kaisersberg wrote a series of sermon-cycles, often drawing on fashionable literary genres of the age, which found their way into print as readily accessible transmissions of academic theology.[37] Early printer-publishers issued multiple editions of the sermons of eminent preachers such as St Vincent Ferrer, Johannes Herolt, Johannes Nider, Johannes von Werden, or Michael of Hungary.[38] Many Ger-

---

[33] Gerson, *Oeuvres Complètes* (see n. 22 above), vol. 8, 108 f.

[34] J. VAN ENGEN, "Late Medieval Anticlericalism: the Case of the New Devout", in: Dykema / Oberman, Anticlericalism (1992) 19.

[35] For such sceptical views of 'anticlericalism' see C. HAIGH, "Anticlericalism and the English Reformation", *History* 68 (1973) 391–407; also idem, *English Reformations: Religion, Politics, and Society under the Tudors* (Oxford: Oxford UP 1993) 40–55, 72–87.

[36] On these preachers see L. J. TAYLOR, *Soldiers of Christ: Preaching in Late Medieval and Reformation France* (Oxford: Oxford UP 1992), pass.

[37] On Geiler see Douglass, Justification in Late Medieval Preaching (1989); examples of Geiler's printed works include Johann Geiler von Kaisersberg, *Das buch granatapfel, im latin genant Malogranatus* (Augsburg 1510); idem, *Des hocwirdigen doctor Kaiserspergs Narrenschiff* (Strassburg: J. Gruninger 1520); idem, *Doctor Keiserspegrs [sic] Passion Des Here Jesu* (Strassburg: [Johann Grüninger 1513]); idem, *Die Emeis. Dis ist das büch von der Omeissen* (Strassburg 1516). See however TH. A. BRADY, JR., "'You Hate us Priests': Anticlericalism, Communalism and the Control of Women at Strasbourg in the Age of the Reformation", in: Dykema / Oberman, Anticlericalism (1992) 167ff and refs.

[38] See for instance Saint Vincent [Ferrer], *Sermones quadragesimales sancti vincentii sacre theologie professoris cum thematibus [&] introductionibus per totum annum feliciter incipient* ([Cologne]: [Johann Koelhoff] 1482); idem, *Diuini verbi preconis interpretis [&] professoris subtillissimi sancti Vincentij Ferrarij ... sermones vberrimi estiuales de tempore incipiunt feliciter ...* ([Lyons]: Diligentia

man towns in the pre-Reformation era established civic preacherships to attract talented clerics and supply a steady flow of the spoken word.[39] Careful exploration of the texts of these sermons has shown them to be liberally supplied with scriptural references, while their authors' moral conduct seems to have been largely blameless.[40]

On the other hand, the theologian-preacher entered the Reformation era as a figure of fun in many quarters. Erasmus of Rotterdam depicted the mendicant scholastic preacher to devastating effect in *Praise of Folly*. This was someone who would launch a sermon with obscure scholarly references of unimaginable relevance to his topic, would wander around a subject without form, sense, or proportion, and would vary his diction with meaningless, inept theatricality.[41] One could dismiss this as gross satirical exaggeration, were it not that another Dutchman, Geert Groote, had said something similar over a century earlier. In one of his letters Groote complained of contemporary sermons as useless, full of unnecessary subdivisions and recapitulations, in short "earthly, beastly, diabolical".[42] Some of the surviving outlines of sermons, organized according to the 'modern' method of multiple layers of scholastic subdivision, do at times appear bizarrely over-wrought.[43] Erasmus wrote his critique of the preacher into a section of *Praise of Folly* where he lampooned friars and monks, and the whole works-righteous business of late medieval formal religion. Even satirical exaggerations have to bear some relationship to truth, or they cease to be amusing.

Worse was to come. An essentially local and arcane scholarly dispute led to a serious assault on the image of theologians in general. The Cologne theology faculty took the side of the convert ex-Jew Johannes Pfefferkorn when he argued for the destruction of all Hebrew books save Scripture. On the other side of the argument was the reclusive Christian Hebraist Johannes Reuchlin, author of one of the earliest printed Hebrew grammars for the use of Christian Latin scholars. Reuchlin vigorously defended the conservation and study of non-Biblical Hebrew literature.[44] Most of the controversy, it now appears, re-

---

et impensis Simonis Vincent 1509); Joannes Herolt OP, *Sermones discipuli* ([Lyons]: [Johannes Trechsel] 1489; Strasbourg 1490; Nuremberg 1492, and many further editions); Johann Nider OP, *Aurei Sermones, tocius anni de tem[per]e et de sanctis cum quadragesimali. pluribus[que] extrauagantibus sermonibus* (Ulm: Per Johanem Zainer [1475?]); Johannes von Werden, *Sermones d[o]m[i-ni]cales cu[m] expositionib[us] euangelioru[m] p[er] annu[m] satis notabiles [et] vtiles o[mn]ibus sacerdotib[us] pastorib[us] [et] capellanis* ([Cologne]: [Conrad Winters de Homborch; before 20 Sept. 1479?]); Michael de Hungaria: *Sermones Michaelis de ungaria praedicabiles per totum annum licet breves* (Strasbourg: [Georg Husner] 24 Mar. 1487, and subsequent editions).

[39] On late medieval urban preacherships see S. E. OZMENT, *The Reformation in the Cities: the appeal of Protestantism to sixteenth-century Germany and Switzerland* (New Haven: Yale UP 1975) 38–42.

[40] J. W. DAHMUS, "A medieval preacher and his sources: Johannes Nider's use of Jacobus de Voragine", *AFP* 58 (1988); idem, "Preaching the laity in fifteenth-century Germany: Johannes Nider's 'harps'", *JEH* 24 (1983); Taylor, Soldiers of Christ (1992) 49.

[41] See Desiderius Erasmus, *Praise of Folly*, in: *Collected Works of Erasmus*, vol. 27: *Literary and Educational Writings* 5 (ed. A. H. T. Levi; Toronto e.a.: University of Toronto Press 1986) 132–35.

[42] Van Engen, Late Medieval Anticlericalism (1992) 25.

[43] Taylor, Soldiers of Christ (1992) 63–66.

[44] Johann Reuchlin, *De rudimentis hebraicis* (Phorce: in aedib. Tho. Anshelmi 1506); cf. Ch. 11 above.

mained confined to the views of the Cologne theologians and Reuchlin himself.[45] Unfortunately, the one contribution that broadened, trivialized, and polarized the debate over Reuchlin and the scholastics was also the one work that was amusingly written and widely read. The *Letters of Obscure Men* were purportedly written by imaginary caricatures of scholastic drunkenness, lechery, and vainglorious pseudo-scholarship to the (real) conservative theologian Ortuinus Gratius in support of the anti-Reuchlin campaign. They mingled burlesque depictions of the gross self-satisfied ignorance of the theologian ideal-type with individual barbed accusations of scandal.[46] This piece of satire struck at remarkably similar targets to those of *Praise of Folly* some years before. When the Reformation controversies broke out, traditional scholastic theologians, who aspired to be regarded as paragons of biblical authority, suddenly found themselves merely ludicrous. *Eccius Dedolatus*, a satire against Johannes Eck, one of Luther's most cogent opponents, drew on many levels of intellectual and popular invective.[47] Early Reformation pamphlets applied the German proverb *die Gelehrten die Verkehrten*, "the learned are the perverted", to Luther's enemies.[48]

The moral leadership of the clergy fell under no less hostile scrutiny than its intellectual and spiritual leadership. Any religious elite that claimed greater sanctity than the average faced the accusation of moral failings and hypocrisy. Whether the charge was deserved or not is a separate issue. Even as the observant movement was bringing the better of the friars back to something like their primitive rigour by the late fifteenth century, the accusations against them continued and if anything intensified. Erasmus and other Renaissance humanists took over the tropes that accused these self-proclaimed godly of all manner of vices, and the abuse of power in all the forms in which they held it.[49] At Bern, Niklaus Manuel brought the humanist scepticism over the spiritual claims of the clergy to a lay audience, through his satirical dramas *The Indulgence-Seller* and *The Devourers of the Dead*.[50] It is noteworthy that the *Re-*

---

[45] See the discussion in Overfield, Humanism and Scholasticism (1984) 253–97.

[46] The *Letters of Obscure Men* is probably the only tract from the Reuchlin controversy that survived it. The text went through at least 3 editions in 1515–17 and was re-issued in 1556, 1557, 1570, 1581, 1599, 1624, and subsequently. A modern edition is *Epistolae obscurorum virorum / Briefe der Dunkelmänner* (ed. and tr. W. Binder; Editiones neolatinae 16; Wien: Eigenverlag Sommer 2001).

[47] See ['Joannefranciscus Cottalembergius',] *Eccius dedolatus: a Reformation satire* (tr. and ed. by Th. W. Best; Lexington: University Press of Kentucky 1971); P. Matheson, *The Rhetoric of the Reformation* (Edinburgh: T&T Clark 1998) 157 f.

[48] The phrase is used e.g. in Hans Schwalb: *Beclagung eines Leyens genant Hanns Schwalb*, as repr. in: O. Clemen (ed.), *Flugschriften aus den ersten Jahren der Reformation* 1–4 (Leipzig / New York: Haupt 1907–11), vol. 1, 348. See also Luther's casual use of the phrase, in: Luther's Works 46, 232.

[49] See for instance Ulrich von Hutten: *Hulderichi Hutteni eq. germ. Dialogi. Fortuna. Febris prima. Febris secunda. Trias Romana. Inspicientes* (Moguntiae: Joannis Scheffer 1520); Erasmus, "the Funeral", in *Colloquies*, in: Collected Works 40, 767–70; G. Dipple, *Antifraternalism and anticlericalism in the German Reformation: Johann Eberlin von Günzburg and the campaign against the friars* (Aldershot / Brookfield, VT: Scolar Press 1996) 29–36; B. Scribner, "Anticlericalism and the Cities", in: Dykema / Oberman, Anticlericalism (1992) 147.

[50] Niklaus Manuel: *Werke und Briefe* ("Vollständige Neuedition"; ed. Paul Zinsli / Thomas Hengartner, with the assistance of Barbara Freiburghaus; Bern: Stämpfli 1999); see also B. Gor-

formation of Kaiser Sigismund, a visionary pamphlet probably written in the 1430s but reprinted many times in the decades just before the Reformation, contained repeated abrasive attacks against the regular orders, and recommended they be totally excluded from positions of trust.[51]

The *Reformation of Kaiser Sigismund*, which was probably written by a secular priest, draws attention to an important aspect of the unease over the spiritual authority of the elite. Many of the most potent charges, and those that stuck most effectively, originated from the clergy themselves. If the priestly status was injured on the eve of the Reformation, it was to some extent from self-inflicted wounds. One of the most notorious abuses of some of the south-German and Swiss bishops was the custom of levying a tax, in lieu of any other punishment, from priests whose housekeepers bore children to them (the so-called 'cradle tax'). The Council of Basel first drew attention to this practice.[52] Some of the best guides to the alleged sins of the English clergy are the sermons preached by the would-be-reformers of the clergy William Melton and John Colet in 1510 and 1512 respectively.[53] Recent reviews of these broadsides have focused on whether, if at all, they were justified by the facts. It may be just as important that the criticisms were made, and made repeatedly, whether the facts justified them or not.

4. The Age of the Layperson?

Was this, then, an age in which the lay person was promoted ahead of the cleric in spiritual esteem? Here, as in so much else, the answer is complex. In this atmosphere the learned theologian and preacher both had high expectations thrust upon him, and was simultaneously not quite trusted. Many people seem to have looked for devout laypeople, who either by the exercise of their innate good sense and spirituality, or by some special miraculous revelation, were qualified to act as the vectors of the divine message. Yet the opportunities for wishful thinking and risks of disillusionment were even more extreme in the case of the lay visionary than in that of the scholastically trained preacher and theologian. Hans Boheim, 'the Drummer of Niklashausen', generated an ephemeral frenzy of popular enthusiasm with his visionary and anticlerical preaching in 1476. Even his clothing was reputed to have miraculous curative properties. Yet the chronicle that describes his preaching also reports that a Franciscan friar was rumoured to hover close by and prompt him as he

---

DON, "Toleration in the Early Swiss Reformation: the art and politics of Niklaus Manuel of Berne", in: O. P. GRELL / R. W. SCRIBNER (eds.), *Tolerance and Intolerance in the European Reformation* (Cambridge / New York: Cambridge UP 1996) 128–44.

[51] [Anon.], *Reformatio Sigismundi* (Augsburg: Lukas Zeissenmair 1497); for a modern edn. see H. KOLLER (ed.), *Reformation Kaiser Siegmunds* (MGH, scriptores 10: Staatsschriften des späteren Mittelalters 6; Stuttgart: Hiersemann 1964); see partial translation and discussion in G. STRAUSS (ed.), *Manifestations of Discontent in Germany on the Eve of the Reformation: a collection of documents* (Bloomington / London: Indiana UP 1971) 3–19.

[52] See the "Decree on Concubinaries" from the Council of Basel in 1435, as in: Tanner (ed.), Decrees of the Ecumenical Councils (1990) 485–86; see also the *Reformatio Sigismundi*, as in: Strauss, Manifestations of Discontent (1971) 14.

[53] For William Melton's sermon see A. G. DICKENS / D. CARR (eds.), *The Reformation in England to the Accession of Elizabeth I* (London: Edward Arnold 1967) 15–16; on Colet, C. HARPER-BILL, "Dean Colet's Convocation Sermon and the Pre-Reformation Church in England", *History* 73/238 (1988) 192 ff.

spoke.[54] Diepold Peringer, 'the Peasant of Wöhrd', who preached around Franconia in 1523–24, went one degree worse. He presented himself as a divinely inspired layman whose knowledge of patristics and scholastic theology came by a miracle. He appears in fact to have been a renegade priest with a good conventional clerical education. Most interesting is his assumption that by adopting the garb and demeanour of a layman he would attract audiences more readily.[55] Some of his sermons were printed in the early 1520s, that era when laypeople, men and women alike, were given the opportunity as never before to air their religious views in public.[56] In the same climate Sebastian Lotzer, the furrier of Memmingen, could write a pamphlet with the title *That the lay person has the power and the right to teach, learn and write about the Holy Word of God.*[57] Perhaps the most influential of these 'holy layperson' pieces, however, the dialogue *Karsthans*, made a slightly more modest claim. It represented the idealized layman as an honest open-minded soul, ready to be persuaded by an effective and honest expositor of Scripture. Promoting the evangelical cause was reserved to a young student.[58]

In this climate the inspired layperson seems to have been as much of an elusive ideal as a practical reality. One may wonder whether the era just before the Reformation was really any more receptive to the spiritual role of the real layperson than, say, a century earlier. Many of the characteristic currents of the so-called 'lay spirit' movement had either died down or become, as it were, clericalized into ordinariness.[59] The Brethren of the Common Life, who had begun with such hostility to the pretensions of the conventional religious and deliberately sought a low-key, non-priestly vocation, had by the eve of the Reformation come to think of themselves as like another religious order. So far from rejecting the erudite theology of the academy, the brother-houses held within them some of the best theological minds of the later fifteenth century.[60]

---

[54] See the report from Georg Widman's *Chronika* as trans. in: Strauss, Manifestations of Discontent (1971) 218–22; R. M. WUNDERLI, *Peasant Fires: the Drummer of Niklashausen* (Bloomington: Indiana UP 1992).

[55] See [Diepold Peringer], *Ain Schön Ausslegung vber das Gotlich gebet, Uater vnser: das vnns Got selbs gelernet hat. Das hat betracht eyn Armer Bawr der weder lessen noch schreyben kan. gar hupsch vnd nutzlich allen christgläubigen menschen tzü güt, auch auss Brüderlicher Trew* ([Erfurt: Wolfgang Stürmer 1522]); idem, *Ain Sermon geprediget vom Pawren zu Werdt bey Nürmberg, am Sontag vor Fassnacht, von dem freyen willen des menschen, auch von anruffung der hailigen* (Eylenburgk: N. Widemar 1524; also [Nuremberg], [1524.]); idem, *Ein Sermon von der Abgötterey durch den Pawern der weder schreyben noch lesen kann, gepredigt* (1524); on the 'Peasant of Wöhrd' see also Ozment, Reformation in the Cities (1975) 66f; D. DEMANDT / H.-C. RUBLACK, *Stadt und Kirche in Kitzingen: Darstellungen und Quellen zu Spätmittelalter und Reformation* (Stuttgart: Klett-Cotta 1978) 68–73.

[56] For the period in which 'lay theology' became possible, see Matheson, Rhetoric of the Reformation (1998) pass.; P. A. RUSSELL, *Lay Theology in the Reformation: Popular Pamphleteers in Southwest Germany, 1521–1525* (Cambridge: Cambridge UP 1986).

[57] Sebastian Lotzer, *Ain christlicher sendbrief darin angetzaigt wirt, dz die layen macht und recht haben von dem hailigen wort gots reden, lern, un schreiben, etc.* ([Memmingen?] 1523).

[58] [Anon.], *Karsthans* ([s.l. 1520?]); on 'Karsthans' see A. G. DICKENS, *The German Nation and Martin Luther* (London: Edward Arnold 1974) 118–20; Moxey, Peasants warriors and wives (1989) 58 f.

[59] For the so-called 'lay spirit' of the later Middle Ages see Cameron, European Reformation (1991) 61–64.

[60] On the original values of the Brethren of the Common Life see Van Engen, Late Medieval

The reception-history of the *Imitation of Christ*, traditionally regarded (quite mistakenly) as subversive of sacramental or formal piety in its search for personal discipleship, suggests that it found its most enthusiastic readers around 1500 among the devout elite of the regular orders.[61] Even mystical theology, the preserve of women as much as men, so apparently pregnant with potential threats to orthodoxy, offered few real challenges to the hierarchy by the end of the Middle Ages. The jargon and intellectual complexity of many mystical schemes made them inherently most suitable for leisured clerics and religious anyway. One of the last followers of Jan van Ruysbroeck was a Franciscan friar, Heinrich Herp.[62] When Martin Luther edited *Ein deutsch Theologia* in 1518, his action could be interpreted, with hindsight, not as a further blow struck against scholasticism by the prophet-reformer, but rather as a sign that a career theologian and regular priest now found the German mystical tradition harmless and even beneficial.[63]

5. A Quest for Charismatic or Miraculous Authority?

Some pamphleteers in the Reformation era sought confirmation or legitimation of supernatural authority through prophecies, portents, astrological observations, or any other events where the Divine appeared to send messages directly or indirectly into this lower world. The later Middle Ages had long been under the spell of twelfth-century predictions of the end-time of history. Since the time of Joachim of Fiore (c. 1130–1202) it had been quite conventional to sketch out the details of the apocalypse, and the roles of the Antichrist, the pope and the emperor in preparing for the second coming of Christ. In many versions of such prophecies there was an expectation that a messianic emperor would appear, who would chastise the clergy and papacy for their failings and reform the Church.[64] In the first tract published in his pamphlet *The Fifteen Confederates*, Johannes Eberlin von Günzburg, like others in the early Reformation, drew upon but also modified this tradition to give legitimacy to the acts and reputation of Luther.[65] In due course the expectation of the messianic

---

Anticlericalism (1992) 22–50; but for their later outlook see esp. Post, Modern Devotion (1968) 442ff, 470ff, 552–631; E. F. JACOB, *Essays in the Conciliar Epoch* (Manchester: Manchester UP 1943) 134–36.

[61] See e.g. the reception of the *Imitation* in England, as in: R. LOVATT, "The *Imitation of Christ* in Late Medieval England", in: *Transactions of the Royal Historical Society*, 5th series, 18 (1968) 100; J. CATTO, "Religious Change under Henry V", in: G. L. HARRISS (ed.), *Henry V: the Practice of Kingship* (Oxford: Oxford UP 1985) 110ff; F. RAPP, *L'Église et la vie religieuse en occident à la fin du moyen âge* (Paris: Presses universitaires de France 1971) 312–14.

[62] Rapp, ibid. 242f.

[63] See Luther's Preface to his edition of *A German Theology*, in: *Luther's Works* 31, 73–76; *Luthers Werke* 1, 375–79.

[64] A particularly classic but abbreviated version of this prophecy is incorporated in the last chapter of the *Reformatio Sigismundi*.

[65] For medieval apocalypticism see e.g. B. McGINN, *Visions of the End: Apocalyptic Traditions in the Middle Ages* (New York: Columbia UP 1979); R. K. EMMERSON, *Antichrist in the Middle Ages: a study of medieval apocalypticism, art, and literature* (Seattle: University of Washington Press 1981).

emperor would prove an embarrassment rather than an aid to the Reformers. Its early adoption, despite the behaviour of Charles V, seems instinctive, and suggests that such expectations were very widespread.[66]

The study of astrology and of portents entailed some ambiguities or contradictions. If extraordinary events were foretold by astrological calculation (such as the notorious conjunction in Pisces in 1524, which generated nearly 160 almanacs and other tracts) then they formed part of a predictable natural order. If, on the other hand, they were announced by exceptional and erratic manifestations in nature, such as comets in the sky, or notorious misbirths or prodigies appearing on earth, then these were direct signs placed by God in the creation, which no natural law could explain.[67] The tension between these two interpretative schemes helps to explain the ambivalence that many theologians, before and during the Reformation, felt towards astrology. Nevertheless, Philipp Melanchthon (whose own horoscope was cast at his birth in 1497 by the German astrologer Johannes Virdung von Hasfurt) had no hesitation in including astrological principles in his lectures on Aristotle's *Physics*.[68]

Special signs and portents were less controversial. Nearly every writer on the subject cited two misborn or composite animals, the 'papal ass' found dead in the Tiber in 1496, and the 'monk calf' born in Freiberg in Saxony in 1522, though the interpretation of these prodigies was always controversial.[69] Collectors of such prodigies continued to relate tales of monstrous misbirths or conjoined births; of visions seen in the sky, especially of multiple suns or armies fighting; and of abnormal showers of rain, especially those that contained blood, stones, fire, or small animals.[70] From time to time the normal order of nature could be spectacularly disrupted, when a provident but justly angry God sent dire and frightening signs to the people to repent and change their ways. Or at least, that was how preachers and publicists presented such portents. It would be dangerous to speculate as to how seriously they were taken; even more dangerous to think that such things altered people's usual patterns of behaviour.

---

[66] See R. B. BARNES, *Prophecy and gnosis: apocalypticism in the wake of the Lutheran Reformation* (Stanford, CA: Stanford UP 1988).

[67] The tension between natural and divine interpretations of prodigies is discussed in W.-E. PEUCKERT, *Die grosse Wende: Das apokalyptische Saeculum und Luther* ([1948] Darmstadt: Wiss. Buchgesellschaft 1966); for contemporary analysis of the meaning of prodigies see C. Peucer, *Commentarius, de Praecipuis Divinationum generibus, in quo a prophetiis, authoritate divine traditis, et a Physicis conjecturis, discernuntur artes et imposturae diabolicae, atque observationes natae ex superstitione, et cum hac conjunctae* (Frankfurt 1607) 720–35; on the Pisces conjunction see Cunningham / Grell, Four Horsemen of the Apocalypse (2000) 77; also R. W. SCRIBNER, *For the Sake of Simple Folk: Popular Propaganda for the German Reformation* (Cambridge Studies in oral and literate culture 2: Cambridge: Cambridge UP 1981) 124.

[68] For Melanchthon's horoscope see H. SCHEIBLE (ed.), *Melanchthons Briefwechsel: Kritische und kommentierte Gesamtausgabe* (Stuttgart / Bad Cannstatt: Frommann-Holzboog 1977-), vol. 8 (1995) 95, 98; for his *Initia Doctrinae Physicae*, see C. G. BRETSCHNEIDER e.a. (eds.), *Philippi Melanchthonis Opera quae supersunt Omnia*, CR 1–28 (Halle 1834–60), vol. 13 (1846) cols. 179–412.

[69] Scribner, For the Sake of Simple Folk (1981) 127–32.

[70] Cunningham / Grell, Four Horsemen of the Apocalypse (2000) 80–86 and refs.; Peucer, *Commentarius, de Praecipuis Divinationum generibus* (1607) 727–38; Scribner, For the Sake of Simple Folk (1981) 125–27.

6. The Church and Political Power

Though there were challenges to the *spiritual* standing, authority, and cred-ibility of the Church and its clergy on the eve of the Reformation, it would be hard to demonstrate that they added up to any single powerful or concentrated assault. In so far as resentment or resistance was focused on anything, it was on the role of the Roman hierarchy as an administrative and as a *political* en-tity. Late medieval people were quite subtle enough to distinguish between Rome as the 'well of grace' from which spiritual benefits and priestly authority flowed, and the sink of iniquity staffed by dubious politicians and overfed ad-ministrators that resided there. Yet even here it is open to question whether things were as bad in around 1500 as they had been a century earlier. It may have seemed to the curia, as the Fifth Lateran Council of 1512–17 carried through its mostly routine and unspectacular business[71], that the storm had been well and truly weathered.

Two political threats confronted the papacy during the fifteenth century. The first threat came from the claims made in Church councils, during the Great Schism and afterwards, that the Church was a corporate body whose monarch held only delegated rather than absolute power; and that a Council of the Church might remove even a duly elected pope. The second came from the less ideological but more practical challenge posed by the demands of secu-lar rulers, especially territorial monarchs, for more effective control over the personnel of the Church in their domains. Neither of these problems was by any means resolved by the eve of the Reformation, yet in each case a sort of accommodation had been reached. The appeal from the Pope to a Church Council, theoretically forbidden under the papal bull *Execrabilis* of 1460, had become a rhetorical ploy, used by prelates or monarchs who found themselves at odds with Rome. The behaviour of the schismatic councillors who gathered at Pisa in 1511 was not markedly more holy or disinterested than that of the Pope, Julius II, whom they challenged.[72] Conciliar theory was not dead, as the fears of the Roman hierarchy around the calling of the Council of Trent amply demonstrated. However, the academic theory espoused by a scholastic like Jacques Almain had grown apart from the complex, messy realities of church government.[73]

Similarly, the relationship between papacy and secular rulers had long ceased to be a matter of the clash of titanic, grandiose claims, as it had been in the era of Boniface VIII and Philip IV of France. Nothing proves more convin-cingly that secular rulers did not 'need' the Reformation simply to achieve their political aims with Rome, than the history of the pre-Reformation concordats.

---

[71] For the acts of the Fifth Lateran Council see Tanner (ed.), Decrees of the Ecumenical Coun-cils (1990) 593–655.

[72] CHR. SHAW, *Julius II: the warrior pope* (Oxford: Blackwell 1993) 279–99; Thomson, Popes and Princes (1980) 16–23.

[73] For late Conciliarism see Thomson, ibid. 21–24; Q. SKINNER, *The Foundations of Modern Po-litical Thought* I–II (Cambridge: Cambridge UP 1978) II, 117–23; F. OAKLEY, "Almain and Conci-liar Theory on the Eve of the Reformation", *AHR* 70 (1965) 673–90.

Under these arrangements, most territorial sovereigns struck deals with the papacy. They ensured that those clerics appointed to major benefices would, on the whole, be natives and loyal subjects of the realms where they served. Concordats also allowed for some measure of taxation of the clergy in those realms.[74] However, the strength or weakness of a ruler vis-à-vis the papacy reflected that ruler's overall constitutional strength or weakness. An emperor of Germany, especially the chronically weak Friedrich III, could only strike the relatively poor bargain of the Concordat of Vienna of 1448. This arrangement left the papacy with the right to provide for benefices in six months of the year, and under a range of other special circumstances.[75] The defects of this concordat prompted the issuing of lists of 'grievances' by the German *Reichstag* against the papacy for some sixty years before the Reformation broke out.[76] German nobles and bourgeois were convinced that German money was 'flying over the Alps to Rome' long before Martin Luther pointed it out to them.[77]

Perhaps more damaging was the widespread perception of Rome as the head of a bloated, overgrown bureaucracy, which sold dispensations from every article of the canon law for money. In such matters as the issuing of dispensations, the spiritual and worldly aspects of the Church clashed more blatantly than anywhere else. As the first of the list of grievances issued at the Nuremberg *Reichstag* of 1523 put it:

> Many things are forbidden or commanded by human constitutions, that are not prohibited or commanded by any divine precept ... the innumerable invented obstacles to marriage, arising from public honesty, spiritual and legal affinity, and so many degrees of consanguinity. Also, the forbidding of the uses of foods ... These things, and other numberless human constitutions like them, bind people until with money they obtain relief of those laws from those who established them; such that money makes it lawful to the rich to do what is forbidden to those of slender means. By these unlawful filaments of nets a great deal of money is fished from the Germans, and carried out of Germany and across the Alps ... .[78]

German observers seemed unaware of–or unimpressed by–the fact that Rome had multiplied administrative business partly because of the demands of the petitioners themselves; and partly because Rome had sold additional venal offices in its administration to raise cash. Even a centralized monarchy like England, with a generally good working relationship with the papacy, generated a huge volume of routine correspondence with the curia, which is only now beginning to be comprehensively edited.[79] For those who took the law of the

---

[74] See the discussion in Cameron, European Reformation (1991) 52–55 and refs.

[75] For the German concordats see F. R. H. Du Boulay, *Germany in the Later Middle Ages* (London: Athlone 1983) 196–200; Ozment, Age of Reform (1980) 188f.

[76] The classic work on the 'Gravamina' is B. Gebhardt, *Die Gravamina der Deutschen Nation gegen den römischen Hof: Ein Beitrag zur Vorgeschichte der Reformation* (2nd edn.; Breslau 1895); see also Strauss, Manifestations of Discontent (1971) 52–63.

[77] See the denunciation of the avarice of the papal court in Luther, *Address to the Christian Nobility*, in: Luther's Works 44, 141–56; Luthers Werke 6, 416–27.

[78] Extract translated from B. J. Kidd (ed.), *Documents Illustrative of the Continental Reformation* (Oxford: Oxford UP 1911) 113.

[79] See J. A. F. Thomson, "'The Well of Grace': Englishmen and Rome in the Fifteenth Century", in: R. B. Dobson (ed.), *Church, Politics and Patronage in Later Medieval England* (Gloucester: Sutton / New York: St. Martin's Press 1984) 102ff; for continuing editorial work on this corpus see M. J. Haren (ed.), *Calendar of entries in the Papal registers relating to Great Britain and Ire-*

Church seriously, like Martin Luther, the very idea of buying and selling one's way out of the terms of the law was utterly repugnant. In a striking conflation of two originally quite separate cultural themes, Luther argued that the tangled web of canon law, its apparent lack of interest in moral right and wrong, its readiness to legalize the unlawful for cash, all proved that, in truth, the papacy was the Antichrist.[80]

In one other significant area the claims of clergy and leading laity came into unresolved conflict on the eve of the Reformation. In Christian late Antiquity, bishops and clergy had formed the leadership, the soul, in many cases the *raison d'être*, of corporate towns and cities. By the end of the Middle Ages many cities had long since forced their bishops to live outside the walls; while the privileges and immunities claimed by the clergy, especially houses of mendicant friars, grated on lay sensibilities that no longer took for granted the intellectual and cultural superiority, never mind the moral superiority, of the priesthood. Here, as in other disputes, late medieval people found a way of negotiation that did not closely anticipate the Reformation clashes. In several of the largest and most sophisticated of German corporate towns, the city authorities coaxed their clergy into accepting lay protection and guardianship of their property and institutions. They acquired, often at great cost, limited rights of presentment to clerical posts within the city, as well as appointing their own salaried preachers.[81] However, such arrangements did not end the frustration caused by clergy privileges, above all in the area of commerce and trade, which had no evident spiritual rationale. Ironically, it has been observed that Erfurt's ordinary citizens would willingly buy cheap beer even if it were brewed in clerical breweries.[82]

7. Conclusion

In all of these disputes, it is more appropriate to speak of clashes over the wielding of power and authority, than of a simple hostility between two artificially homogenized groups called 'clergy' and 'laity'. The problem consisted in deciding exactly where the proper authority to resolve spiritual questions truly lay. It is appropriate to end this survey with the climactic expression of this dilemma. In the early 1520s, as rival preachers excoriated each other from the pulpits of the churches of Germany and the Swiss Confederation, town after

---

land 15. Innocent VIII: Lateran registers 1484–1492 (Great Britain: Public Record Office / Dublin: Stationery Office for the Irish Manuscripts Commission 1978).

[80] Luther, *Address to the Christian Nobility*, in: Luther's Works 44, 193–94; Luthers Werke 6, 452–54.

[81] See Cameron, European Reformation (1991) 58–61 and refs.; see the classic article of B. MOELLER, "Kleriker als Bürger", in: *Festschrift für Hermann Heimpel zum 70. Geburtstag am 19. September 1971* (Veröffentlichungen des Max-Planck-Instituts für Geschichte 36; Göttingen: Vandenhoeck & Ruprecht 1971–72) II, 195–210.

[82] On clergy's brewing rights see S. C. KARANT-NUNN, *Zwickau in Transition 1500–1547: The Reformation as an agent of change* (Columbus: Ohio State UP 1987) 33–43; also Scribner, Anticlericalism and the Cities (1992) 151.

town issued what became known as 'scripture-mandates'. These edicts commanded that clergy in preaching positions cease attacking each other or the church hierarchy, or disputing about contentious dogmas or ceremonies. Instead they were to preach only what was based on Scripture and consistent with it. These mandates were not intended, as was once thought, to give covert support to the Reformers. Rather, the magistrates who issued them hoped that preachers might return to expounding the unquestioned authoritative text, and end their disruptive and dangerous wrangling.[83] However, the city magistrates soon found that they had impaled themselves on a dilemma. Now that ecclesiastical authority was hopelessly divided, the authority to decide *whose* exegesis of Scripture was correct had devolved to the lay congregation. The crisis of spiritual authority now resided, for the time being, in citizens' own council chambers and in their own hearts.

---

[83] See Cameron, European Reformation (1991) 235ff and refs.

CHAPTER SIXTEEN

The Reformation as an Epoch of the History of Theological Education

By ULRICH KÖPF, Tübingen

Sources: Corpus Reformatorum 1– (Halle / Braunschweig e.a. 1834–; quoted: CR); *Die evangelischen Schulordnungen des sechszehnten Jahrhunderts* (ed. R. Vormbaum; Gütersloh 1860); *Die evangelischen Kirchenordnungen des XVI. Jahrhunderts* (ed. E. Sehling e.a.; 1–5: Leipzig 1902–13; 6–: Tübingen 1955–; quoted: Sehling). – J. CALVIN: *Opera quae supersunt omnia* 1–59 (ed. G. Baum e.a.; CR 29–87; Braunschweig / Berlin 1863–1900). – M. LUTHER: *Werke. Kritische Gesamtausgabe* 1– (Weimar 1883–; quoted: WA); *Briefwechsel* 1–13 (Weimar 1930–68; quoted: WA.B); *Deutsche Bibel* 1–12 (Weimar 1906–61; quoted: WA.DB); *Tischreden* 1–6 (Weimar 1912–21; quoted: WA.TR). – PH. MELANCHTHON: *Opera quae supersunt omnia* 1–28 (ed. C. G. Bretschneider / H. E. Bindseil; CR 1–28; Halle / Braunschweig 1834–60); *Briefwechsel* 1– (ed. H. Scheible; Stuttgart-Bad Cannstatt 1977–; quoted: MBW). – U. ZWINGLI, *Sämtliche Werke* (ed. E. Egli e.a.; CR 88–101; Berlin e.a. 1905–63).

General studies (in chronological order): F. EULENBURG, *Die Frequenz der deutschen Universitäten von ihrer Gründung bis zur Gegenwart* (ASGW.PH 24,2; Leipzig 1906); J. K. MCCONICA, *English Humanists and Reformation Politics under Henry VIII and Edward VI* (Oxford 1965); *Beiträge zu Problemen deutscher Universitätsgründungen der frühen Neuzeit* (ed. P. Baumgart / N. Hammerstein; Wolfenbütteler Forschungen 4; Nendeln 1978); *A History of the University in Europe* (Gen. ed. W. Rüegg), II. *Universities in Early Modern Europe (1500–1800)* (ed. H. de Ridder-Symoens; Cambridge e.a. 1992); *Handbuch der Geschichte des Bayerischen Bildungswesens 1. Geschichte der Schule in Bayern. Von den Anfängen bis 1800* (ed. M. Liedtke, Bad Heilbrunn/Obb. 1991); *Handbuch der deutschen Bildungsgeschichte 1. 15. bis 17. Jahrhundert* (ed. N. Hammerstein; München 1996); H. SCHEIBLE, *Melanchthon und die Reformation* (Veröffentlichungen des Instituts für Europäische Geschichte Mainz, Beiheft 41; Mainz 1996); *Attempto – oder wie stiftet man eine Universität? Die Universitätsgründungen der sogenannten zweiten Gründungswelle im Vergleich* (ed. S. Lorenz; Contubernium 50; Stuttgart 1999).

Special abbreviations (see above):
CR = *Corpus Reformatorum*
MBW = Melanchthon, *Briefwechsel*
Sehling = *Die evangelischen Kirchenordnungen des XVI. Jahrhunderts* (ed. E. Sehling e.a.)
Urk. = *Urkundenbuch der Universität Wittenberg* (see Sect. 3)
WA = M. Luther, *Werke. Kritische Gesamtausgabe* (Weimarana)
WA.B = ibid. *Briefwechsel*
WA.DB = ibid. *Deutsche Bibel*
WA.TR = ibid. *Tischreden*

1. The Importance of the Reformation for the History of Education

If we consider the Reformation as an epoch in the history of education, at first sight it does not seem to have had an innovative character. It did not create

really new institutions and methods of education, but has basically maintained
the traditional educational institutions – from elementary school to university.
In those areas where the Reformation did introduce substantial innovations,
this helped first and foremost old and new humanistic demands and proposals
to succeed. In the field of education Humanism and Reformation mutually fer-
tilized and supported their effects. If we, nevertheless, can claim an epochal
importance of the Reformation for the development of Christian education, at
first this is due to the substantial religious and theological arguments and opinions, by which the Reformers entered into the discussion. It was these ideas
also, which, in a deeper sense, gave the impulse for decisive consequences in
the history of education. First of all, the traditional hierarchy of authorities
was profoundly disturbed: The Reformation abandoned ecclesiastical authority and even more the Church's monopoly of doctrine; instead, on diverse levels the early modern state, the university, especially the theological faculty,
and the single Christian (without distinction between clergy and laymen)
gained the dignity of educational authorities.

2. The Criticism of the Traditional System of Education by the Reformation

Special studies (in chronological order): I. Asheim, *Glaube und Erziehung bei Luther. Ein Beitrag
zur Geschichte des Verhältnisses von Theologie und Pädagogik* (Pädagogische Forschungen. Veröffentlichungen des Comenius-Instituts 17; Heidelberg 1961); G. Strauss, *Luther's House of Learning* (Baltimore / London 1978); U. Köpf, "Der Anspruch der Kirchen auf die Schule im 16. Jahrhundert", in: *Handbuch der Geschichte des Bayerischen Bildungswesens* 1 (ed. M. Liedtke; Bad Heil-
brunn/Obb. 1991) 491–503; M. Wriedt, "Continuity and competition: Luther's call for educational reform in the light of medieval precedents", in: *Reformations Old and New* (ed. B. A. Kümin;
Aldershot / Brookfield 1996) 171–84; idem, "Erneuerung der Frömmigkeit durch Ausbildung: Zur
theologischen Begründung der evangelischen Bildungsreform bei Luther und Melanchthon", in:
Frömmigkeit und Spiritualität / Piété et Spiritualité (ed. M. Arnold / R. Decot; Veröffentlichungen
des Instituts für europäische Geschichte Mainz. Beiheft 54; Mainz 2002) 59–71.

To begin with, the Reformers criticized the traditional system of education in
a way that displayed a marked distance from humanistic positions, resulting
even in an opposition to many humanists. The reason for Martin Luther's refusal of scholastic theology was, after all, his theologically founded rejection of
the traditional scholastic use of Aristotelian philosophy in theology. First of
all, this rejection referred to those doctrines, which Luther had to refuse because of his new religious and theological insights: especially the aristotelian-
scholastic conception of *iustitia activa (iustitia distributiva)*, which was fundamental for the traditional doctrine of *merita* from good works. By his new understanding of God's justice, which he started to set forth already in the First
Lecture on the Psalms (1513/15), Luther perceived, that the Aristotelian
Ethics was not useful for a theology based on the letters of St. Paul. From this
refusal of a certain doctrine he developed a criticism of scholastic thought arguing by using Aristotelian notions and axioms. Already in his disputations of

the years 1516 to 1518 he developed his position in opposition to scholastic theology.[1]

In 1520 Luther conveyed his concrete – critical and constructive – considerations on education for the first time. In his German manifesto *An den christlichen Adel deutscher Nation von des christlichen Standes Besserung* he set out his ideas concerning the reformation of schools and universities. In this treatise he asked that the dominance of Aristotle[2] at the universities should be ended and that his writings on Physics and Metaphysics, *De anima* and *Ethica Nicomachea*, should be abolished as text-books, whereas Luther wanted to retain the logical writings, *Rhetorica* and *Poetica*, or further use them in a modified, shorter form as manuals.[3] Moreover, he demanded that the commentaries and scholastic treatises should be done away with.[4] In theology he criticized (in an exaggerated manner, however[5]) the neglect of Holy Scripture in comparison with the attention given to the Sentences of Peter Lombard and asked for concentration on the study of the Bible – in accordance with the humanistic parole *Ad fontes!*[6] The most important and fundamental subject of religious and theological education should be the Gospel, already in elementary instruction. In every town Luther thought it necessary to establish a school for girls, too, where they could hear the Gospel an hour every day – either in German or in Latin.[7]

This demand for informing the general public about the Gospel led as well to the new reforming motivation of education. For every Christian the knowledge of the Gospel is necessary for his personal salvation. The common priesthood of the faithful, which abolished the traditional distinction between clergy and laymen, qualifies every Christian to read and to explain the Holy Scripture adequately.[8] A necessary condition for this is, however, that all Christians, not only the clergy and the educated persons, at least can read and have a basic knowledge for a correct understanding of Scripture. Luther explained this religious motivation for general education more comprehensively and deeply in his later programmatic writings about schools: *An die Ratherren aller Städte deutsches Lands, daß sie christliche Schulen aufrichten [...] und halten sollen* (1524),[9] and *Eine Predigt, daß man Kinder zur Schulen halten solle* (1530).[10] Luther's demands were taken up and propagated by Philipp Melanchthon, the

---

[1] *Quaestio de viribus et voluntate hominis sine gratia disputata* (graduation thesis of Bartholomaeus Bernhardi), 1516 (WA 1, 145–51); *Disputatio contra scholasticam theologiam* (graduation of Franz Günther), 1517 (WA 1, 224–28).
[2] Here he calls Aristotle "der blind, heydnischer meyster" (WA 6, 457,34) and "der vordampter, hochmutiger, schalckhafftiger heide" (ibid. 458,4f).
[3] Ibid. 458,26–28.
[4] Ibid. 458,28. 31.
[5] Because exposition of the Holy Scripture, too, was the main work of the teachers of theology (of the *Baccalaureus biblicus* and of the *Magister theologiae*) at the mediaeval university. See above Ch. 6; 1.6.
[6] WA 6, 460,6–462,11.
[7] Ibid. 461,13–15.
[8] Ibid. 407–12.
[9] WA 15, 9–53.
[10] WA 30II, 508–88.

most important teacher and writer on pedagogy of the Reformation.[11] He stressed this point in his expertise for the town Soest from 15 June 1543.[12] Huldrych Zwingli in his only work on education *Quo pacto ingenui adolescentes formandi sint* (1523)[13] also justified the necessity of education by pointing out its religious aim: that youth should follow Christ and the truth personified by him as purely as possible.[14] To reach this aim, a profound knowledge of biblical languages is required.[15] Calvin's thoughts on education are determined by the religious idea that every Christian must be able to render an account of his faith.[16] This theological motivation of education was introduced to reforming school regulations *(Schulordnungen)*.[17]

3. The Wittenberg Reformation of Studies

Sources: Liber decanorum facultatis theologicae academiae Vitebergensis (ed. C. E. Förstemann; Leipzig 1838); *Urkundenbuch der Universität Wittenberg* 1 *(1502–1611)* (ed. W. Friedensburg; Geschichtsquellen der Provinz Sachsen und des Freistaates Anhalt NS 3; Magdeburg 1926; quoted: Urk.)

Special studies (in chronological order): W. FRIEDENSBURG, *Geschichte der Universität Wittenberg* (Halle 1917); *450 Jahre Martin-Luther-Universität Halle-Wittenberg,* 1. *Wittenberg 1502–1817* (Halle 1952); I. LUDOLPHY, *Friedrich der Weise, Kurfürst von Sachsen 1463–1525* (Göttingen 1984); I. HÖSS, *Georg Spalatin 1484–1545* (Weimar 1989); D. STIEVERMANN, "Friedrich der Weise und seine Universität Wittenberg", in: Attempto (1999) 175–207; *Die Theologische Fakultät Wittenberg 1502 bis 1602* (ed. I. Dingel / G. Wartenberg; Leucorea-Studien 5; Leipzig 2002); H. KATHE, *Die Wittenberger philosophische Fakultät 1502–1817* (Mitteldeutsche Forschungen 117; Köln / Weimar / Wien 2002); J.-M. KRUSE, *Universitätstheologie und Kirchenreform. Die Anfänge der Reformation in Wittenberg 1516–1522* (Veröffentlichungen des Instituts für Europäische Geschichte Mainz 187; Mainz 2002).

Since the University of Wittenberg *(Leucorea)* was the starting-point of the Reformation in the German Empire and since the renewal of the institutions of education was strongly influenced from that place, it is necessary to describe the Wittenberg reformation of university and studies in some detail.

The success of this reformation derived not only from the genius of Luther and the other Reformers, but also from the fact, that the young university of Wittenberg was open to reforming ideas from its beginning. The Elector Frederick the Wise had founded it in 1502 at his residential city Wittenberg with-

---

[11] K. HARTFELDER, *Philipp Melanchthon als Praeceptor Germaniae* (Monumenta Germaniae Paedagogica 7; Berlin 1889); H. SCHEIBLE, "Melanchthons Bildungsprogramm", in: idem, Melanchthon und die Reformation (1996) 99–114.

[12] MBW III no. 3262 = CR 5, 125–37, here 126: *Denn zur ewigen Seligkeit gehört Erkenntniß des Evangelii, davon menschliche Vernunft von ihr selbst nichts weiß.*

[13] Zwingli, Sämtliche Werke 2 (1908) = CR 89, 526–51. German version: *Wie man die jugendt in gůten sitten und christenlicher zucht uferziehen unnd leeren sölle,* Sämtliche Werke 5 (1934) = CR 92, 430–47.

[14] Ibid. CR 92, 550 f.

[15] CR 92, 437,3–9.

[16] On the periodical examinations cf. Calvin to Olevianus (1536): Opera 18 = CR 46, 236; Beza in his *Vita Calvini* Opera 21 = CR 49,142: *decretum est, ut ministri... ab unoquoque fidei rationem summatim exposcerent.*

[17] Cf. Köpf, Anspruch (1991) 497–99.

out cooperation of the Church or the states and without building it up from existing schools, but with a privilege of Emperor Maximilian I.[18] Twelve chairs were financed by prebends of the Wittenberg All Saints Chapter, three were maintained freely by mendicant friars (one at the faculty of arts by an Augustinian friar, two at the faculty of theology by an Augustinian and a Franciscan). For the remaining chairs the Elector had initiated a new kind of salary from a specific monetary stock. The constitution was installed by the statutes of 1508 for the university and the four faculties. Nevertheless, the full number of lectures was not yet accomplished at that time. For that reason the reforming-humanistic criticism did not attack a well-established and proved curriculum, but a scholastic system with open structures. Luther's lectures, too, followed the mediaeval teaching system. Luther was not, as biographers like to phrase it, "Professor of biblical exegesis" or even "Professor of Old Testament", but "Professor of theology".[19] He had, as it was the duty of a *magister* since the beginning of the theological faculties, to comment on biblical books in his lectures and to preside over the discussion of questions in the disputations.[20] While giving his lectures, however, he followed his own ideas, which resulted in a growing alienation from scholastic thought by taking up elements of monastic theology and Humanism. From 1516 onwards he openly expressed his criticism of the scholastic system of education. During the winter semester 1517/18 staff and subjects of teaching were considerably expanded. In philosophy close reading and commentary on Aristotle according to new translations were introduced and the group of Latin authors, which had to be read, was enlarged by Quintilian, Plinius and Priscianus. In addition, two new chairs for Greek and Hebrew were established. Moreover, a *paedagogium* for beginners was founded for the instruction of Latin, Greek and Hebrew.[21] After several changes of staff the chair for Hebrew finally was filled constantly only in 1521 by Matthaeus Aurogallus (Goldhahn, about 1490–1543). Compared to that, the choice of the professor of Greek was definitely advantageous: Philipp Melanchthon, who was to become the most important reformer of education at Wittenberg, forcibly called for a reformation of studies born out of the spirit of Humanism already on the 28 August 1518 in his innovative inaugural lecture *De corrigendis adulescentiae studiis.*[22]

The reforming criticism, however, raised a twofold danger: On the one hand, it threatened the financing of the educational institutions. Already at the eve of the Reformation it had become obvious that the maintenance of chairs by prebends was very insecure.[23] Luther's criticism of Church and clergy de-

---

[18] Urk. 1, 1–4 (no. 1f); cf. A. BLASCHKA, "Der Stiftsbrief Maximilians I. und das Patent Friedrichs des Weisen zur Gründung der Wittenberger Universität", in: 450 Jahre Martin-Luther-Universität (1952) 69–85; H. SCHEIBLE, "Gründung und Ausbau der Universität Wittenberg", in: idem: Melanchthon und die Reformation (1996) 131–369.

[19] This is the exact meaning of the title *doctor sacrae scripture* or *Doktor der Heiligen Schrift.*

[20] For more details about the refutation of the *communis opinio* cf. U. KÖPF, "Martin Luthers theologischer Lehrstuhl", in: Die Theologische Fakultät Wittenberg 1502 bis 1602 (2002) 71–86.

[21] Urk. 1, 85f (no. 64).

[22] CR 11, 15–25.

[23] As clearly pointed out by the University of Wittenberg in the following writing to Elector Frederick (Urk. 1, 74f [no. 55]): *Aber der grost und recht mangel und gebrechen ist, das kein lection*

prived the financing of tutorships by prebends of its base; in turn, the majority of the canons of the Wittenberg All Saints Chapter were not willing to support reforming-minded professors. On the 1 October 1525 Georg Spalatin informed Elector John about Luther's proposal, to confiscate all prebends in order to maintain the clergy from that source.[24] At this point, Elector John newly regulated the salary of the professors.[25] But not until the reign of his son John Frederick the university was put on a solid financial base. On the 6 September 1532 the new Elector announced his intention to guarantee the teacher's salaries,[26] and on the 5 May 1536 he signed the document of foundation, that would be basic for the university's future.[27]

On the other hand, the routine of teaching got into a crisis despite all reforming efforts. The reforming criticism of the Church and the treatment of ecclesiastical property resulting from it diminished the professional career perspectives and thereby also the motivation of students up to the point when a new, evangelical church was established and a corresponding conception of ecclesiastical ministry was developed. This revolutionary change coincided with a general reduction of the number of students at the German universities in the twenties of the sixteenth century. After a summit in 1520/21, the number dropped down for years.[28] It would be too simple to trace back this fact to the reforming criticism; for universities adherent to the old creed as Leipzig and Cologne underwent the same change.[29] But, without doubt, in its beginning the Reformation caused uncertainty for students and teachers for years.

The Wittenberg reformation of studies proceeded only gradually. On the 9 December 1518 Luther proposed to Georg Spalatin, the counsellor of the Elector, in accordance with Bartholomaeus Bernhardi, the Rector of the university, to give up the Thomistic commenting of the Aristotelian Physics and works on logics, and to establish instead of this a lecture on Ovidius' *Metamorphoses*.[30] He repeated this proposal on the 7 February 1519[31] and uttered it

---

gefundirt und ewiglich also zu bleiben gestift, ausgenommen was auf die geistlikeit geordent ist. […]
Auf das E. chf. g. universitet nicht als Gribswalde, Mentz, Trier, Bassel und ander universiteten, die
auch allein auf die geistlikeit fundirt sein, desolirt, wust und zu nicht werde, darumb wolde E. chf. g.
sulche berumpte leuthe stiften, die des dinges warten und den der hauf der studenten nachzeuchet; sunst
wirt E. chf. g. universitet unsers bedunkens kein bleiblichen bestand behalten. …

[24] Urk. 1, 136–38 (no. 141).
[25] Urk. 1, 142f (no. 145).
[26] Urk. 1, 153 (no. 169).
[27] Urk. 1, 172–84 (no. 193).
[28] Cf. F. EULENBURG, *Die Frequenz der deutschen Universitäten* (ASGW.PH 24,2; Leipzig 1906) 288 f. In Wittenberg the numbers of students increased from 162 (1516) over 273 (1518) and 458 (1519) to 579 (1520), were halved to 245 (1521), ascended at first again to 285 (1522), but during a few years sunk over 198 (1523) to 73 (1527). After that lowest mark they increased anew. Despite of this decline Wittenberg held a top position among the German universities until the end of the sixteenth century, even 1544 reached a maximum of 814 students. – Cf. M. ASCHE, "Frequenzeinbrüche und Reformen – Die deutschen Universitäten in den 1520er bis 1560er Jahren zwischen Reformation und humanistischem Neuanfang", in: *Die Musen im Reformationszeitalter* (ed. W. Ludwig; Schriften der Stiftung Luthergedenkstätten in Sachsen-Anhalt 1; Leipzig 2001) 53–96.
[29] Eulenburg, ibid. 288: Leipzig sunk from 417 (1520) over 339 (1521) and 285 (1522) to 90 (1524) and 81 (1526), Cologne with a slight retardation from 251 (1521) over 218 (1522) to 65 (1527).
[30] WA.B 1, 262 (no. 117).

again together with several colleagues on the 23 February addressing the Elector directly.[32] The Scotists should be tolerated in the meantime; their representative Johann Dölsch, however, himself was looking for another task. This was welcomed by the Elector.[33]

Two forms of teaching especially attracted the reforming criticism: Firstly, the Sentence lecture. Luther, in an earlier phase, had read on the Sentences, but never elaborated a Sentence commentary. Yet in a letter to Spalatin from 8 May 1519 he still stressed the use of this lecture. Melanchthon being a *magister artium*, as usual in the mediaeval system of education, at the same time was a student at the faculty of theology. On the 19 September 1519 he acquired the degree of a *baccalaureus biblicus*, which conferred on him the license to give biblical lectures at the theological faculty. When in the following period he deliberately renounced the promotion to *baccalaureus sententiarius*, he draw conclusions from Luther's reservations against the Sentences.[34] During Luther's stay at the Wartburg (4 May 1521–1 March 1522) Melanchthon created a new kind of school book based on the Epistle to the Romans, on which he had given lectures over a long period: the *Loci communes rerum theologicarum seu hypotyposes theologicae*. The book was published in a series of parts from August to December 1521,[35] and later on repeatedly revised by the author. This first systematic delineation of the Wittenberg theology replaced the Sentences as a systematic text-book in Protestantism for a long time.[36]

Another essential type of systematic teaching had been criticized at the same time: the disputations.[37] Under the decanate of Karlstadt, the theological faculty decided in the summer semester of 1521 to restrain disputations to two forms: to the periodical disputations during the week *(disputationes ordinariae*, also called *Zirkulardisputationen*[38]), and the disputations at the graduations.[39] But at that point, the disputations in general went to ruins. In the beginning of 1522 – without doubt under the influence of Karlstadt – Matt 23:8 was used as an argument against the title of *magister*.[40] Karlstadt's aversion against the university was reinforced by the Wittenberg measures of censorship against him,

---

[31] WA.B 1, 325 (no. 144).

[32] WA.B 1, 349f (no. 155).

[33] Urk. 1, 90f (no. 73), here: 90.

[34] That Melanchthon at this time intensively was engaged in reflections on the Sentences, shows his announcement of critical remarks on this theme *(obelisci sententiarum;* to J. Heß, 27.4.1520; MBW 1 no. 84,3).

[35] CR 21, 59–230.

[36] U. Köpf, "Melanchthon als systematischer Theologe neben Luther", in: *Der Theologe Melanchthon* (ed. G. Frank; Melanchthon-Schriften der Stadt Bretten 5; Stuttgart 2000) 103–27.

[37] E. Wolf, "Zur wissenschaftsgeschichtlichen Bedeutung der Disputationen an der Wittenberger Universität im 16. Jahrhundert", in: *450 Jahre Martin-Luther-Universität* (1952) 335–44; again in: idem, *Peregrinatio* 2 (München 1965) 38–51.

[38] Urk. 1, 63 (no. 35; 22.1.1512): *respondentibus in disputacionibus circularibus facultatum majorum;* 1, 42 (no. 24; 15.11.1508): *baccalaureandus tres circulos teneat;* 1, 45 (ibid.): *in quindecim diebus procurent aliquem scholasticum tenere circulum.*

[39] Urk. 1, 110 (no. 101).

[40] Cf. a letter of the student Arsacius Seehofer from 4.1.1522 (Th. Kolde, "Arsacius Seehofer und Argula von Grumbach", in: Beiträge zur bayerischen Kirchengeschichte 11, 1905, 49–188, esp. 73).

which were supported by Luther, who had returned from the Wartburg. On the 3 February 1523 dean Karlstadt used the occasion of the graduation of two Augustinian friars for declaring that he would furthermore not participate in graduations, because Christ (Matt 23:8–10) had forbidden to call anyone on earth father or master (e.g., *magister*).[41] Soon after that event he abandoned his teaching, received the ministry of Orlamünde and disputed against clerical dignities as well as against the academic establishment.[42] Later on he took up again an academic office (since 1534 at Basel as professor for Old Testament); but his attitude in Wittenberg had temporarily diminished the position of the university in the Reformation movement.

Melanchthon now took even more pains for improving the teaching of the artists and the theologians.[43] An expert opinion of the university from 19 March 1523 written by him asked for replacing the disputations at the faculty of arts, which in the meantime had come to a stop, by periodical *declamationes*.[44] When he was *Rector*, in winter semester 1523/24 he could realize this counsel.[45] But the decline of the theological disputations and graduations influenced by Karlstadt's polemics could not be stopped. Until 1525 the *Liber decanorum* records five further graduations; afterwards they were interrupted until 1533.

The reorganization of the university according to the reforming aims began in 1533 with Melanchthon's statutes for the faculty of theology.[46] They assign a *collegium* of four permanent professors,[47] who had to expound the books of the Old and the New Testament (esp. Romans, John, Psalms, Genesis and Isaiah) alternating. At times, one of the professors should comment on Augustine's *De spiritu et littera*.[48] Moreover, once in a quarter of a year a regular disputation should again take place.[49] For the first steps to the doctorate the old titles were retained. The *baccalaureus biblicus* had to comment on the letter to the Romans, because it contains the *summa doctrinae christianae* and presents together with the doctrine of Trinity founded in the Gospel of John the whole *corpus doctrinae ecclesiasticae*. The *sententiarius* and *formatus* had to explain some Psalms and sections of the Prophets on the basis of the doctrine received from St. Paul.[50] The theological *curriculum* now was totally orientated towards the Bible, and completed by occasional recourse to Augustine, the most important ecclesiastical authority.

---

[41] *Liber decanorum* (1838) 28 with Luther's contradiction (n. 1).

[42] E.g., *Was gesagt ist: Sich gelassen* (1523); cf. H. BARGE, *Andreas Bodenstein von Karlstadt* 2 (Leipzig 1905) 80.

[43] Cf. also his letters to Spalatin MBW 1, no. 268f, 272, 279, 282.

[44] G. BAUCH, *Die Einführung der Melanchthonischen Deklamationen und andere gleichzeitige Reformen an der Universität zu Wittenberg* (Breslau 1900) 10–14.

[45] Urk. 1, 128–30 (no. 131), here: 129.

[46] Urk. 1, 154–58 (no. 171).

[47] Ch. II.

[48] Ch. III.

[49] Ch. V.

[50] Ch. VIII.

The main features of Melanchthon's statutes were taken over in the foundation charter of Elector John Frederick from 5 May 1536.[51] In the three superior faculties the quarterly disputations were to be retained besides the graduation disputations.[52] The statutes laid down that the staff of the theological faculty had to consist of three professors and a lecturer, whose teaching tasks were exactly defined: The first professor should read on Romans, Galatians and John, the second on Genesis, Psalms, Isaiah and at times on Augustine, *De spiritue et littera*, the third on the remaining letters of St. Paul and the letters of Peter and John. Moreover, a graduated Wittenberg clergyman was to read on Matthew, Deuteronomy and one or other of the Minor Prophets.[53] Again, the *curriculum* contained almost only biblical books – by the way, those which had formed the nucleus of the mediaeval lectures – without clearly distinguishing between the Old and the New Testament. Melanchthon made this distinction in his statutes from 1545 for the theological faculty,[54] when he decided that two teachers at a time should comment on books of the New and of the Old Testament. For the sake of showing the conformity of the Churches of the Reformation with ecclesiastical tradition, he decided, that lectures should be given not only on Augustine, but also on the *Symbolum Nicaenum*.[55] By this measure the beginning of a Protestant discipline of dogmatics apart from exegesis were widened.

It became important for the development of a Protestant system of education, that the Wittenberg Reformation established a close connection between erudition and ecclesiastical practice. It was a decisive innovation, that the vocation to an ecclesiastical office became dependent on an examination.[56] Already in 1525 in the Reformed duchy of Prussia an obligatory examination of the clergy was introduced before their investiture by the bishops of Samland and Riesenburg.[57] The *Reformatio Ecclesiarum Hassiae (Homberger Kirchenordnung)* of 1526 established an evaluation of the elected clergy by visitors.[58] In the electoral-Saxonian *Unterricht der Visitatoren* (1528) the monitoring of correct Christian doctrine, evangelical preaching and manner of life by supervisors was introduced.[59] This kind of examination was performed from 1528 to 1535. At the same time the possibility existed of having preachers examined by the Wittenberg professors of theology before their appointment.[60] Moreover, the presentation to the Elector by the Wittenberg theologians without a formal examination was valid as a sufficient acknowledgement of the necessary quali-

---

[51] Urk. 1, 172–84 (no. 193), here: 174.

[52] Ibid. 177.

[53] Ibid. 174 f.

[54] Ibid. 261–65 (no. 279).

[55] Ibid. 263.

[56] P. Drews, "Die Ordination, Prüfung und Lehrverpflichtung der Ordinanden in Wittenberg 1535", in: *Deutsche Zeitschrift für Kirchenrecht* 15 (1905) 66–90, 273–321; idem, "Das Ordinationsformular. Einleitung" (1912), in: WA 38, 401–22.

[57] Sehling 4 (1911) 38.

[58] Cap. 22: Sehling 8 (1965) 59.

[59] *Unterricht der visitatoren an die pfarrherrn im kurfürstenthum zu Sachsen*, in: Sehling 1 (1902) 149–74, here: 171.

[60] *Kirchen-Ordnung für die Stadt Schlieben* (1529), in: Sehling 1, 659–61, here: 660.

fications.[61] But after the introduction of an ordination for evangelical clergymen in electoral Saxonia by an edict from 12 May 1535, this action was connected with an examination by the Wittenberg theological faculty since summer 1535.[62] The examination focused on theological erudition and at the same time on orthodoxy.

An additional revaluation of the theological faculty was caused by its integration into the direction of the new churches. In the electoral-Saxonian foundation charter of 1536 it was already made obligatory to give counsels in questions concerning marriage and ecclesiastical affairs.[63] In this way the current practice was legally determined. For the visitations and later on for the permanent ruling of the Church apart from lawyers, academic theologians were also permanently recruited. Especially the Wittenberg theologians were responsible for the monitoring of correct teaching.

4. The Organization of Protestant Educational Institutions in the Area under the Influence of Wittenberg

Sources: *Die evangelischen Schulordnungen des sechszehnten Jahrhunderts* (ed. R. Vormbaum; Gütersloh 1860); *Die evangelischen Kirchenordnungen des XVI. Jahrhunderts* (ed. E. Sehling e.a.; 1–5: Leipzig 1902–1913; 6–: Tübingen 1955–; quoted: Sehling); *Vor- und frühreformatorische Schulordnungen und Schulverträge in deutscher und niederländischer Sprache* 1–2 (ed. J. Müller; Zschopau 1885–86).
  Special study: H. Hettwer, *Herkunft und Zusammenhang der Schulordnungen* (Mainz 1965).

The Reformers' epoch-making criticism of the old doctrinal authorities and of the traditional form of studies brought the need for a reform of the system of education in churches, that were open to the Reformation. In this process Wittenberg played a leading role: The university, where at that time many students were enrolled, served as a model, and several professors were actively involved. Melanchthon exercised the greatest influence. He was consulted by means of letters from all over Germany and, soon, the whole of Europe; he was asked for the formulation of statutes and *curricula*, and was invited to visit a number of cities and courts.[64] At many places his statutes for the university of Wittenberg were taken as a pattern.

In the area under the influence of the Wittenberg Reformation, especially in the German Empire, the institutions of higher education were renewed in two ways: by reformation of existing universities and by foundation of new universities.

---

[61] E.g., Luther, letter from 30.10.1529 (WA.B 5, 172 no. 1489).
[62] Text of the electoral edict: Drews, Die Ordination (1905) 288 f.
[63] Urk. 1, 175 (no. 193): *auch sollen sie uber die berurten burden des lesens und predigens in ehe- und gaistlichen sachen, so wir ader unsere erben und nachkommen an sie gelangen, zu raten und ire urtail und bedenken dorinnen mitzutailen vorpflicht sein.*
[64] Cf., e.g., *Melanchthon und Europa* 1. *Skandinavien und Mittelosteuropa* (ed. G. Frank / M. Treu; Melanchthon-Schriften der Stadt Bretten 6/1; Stuttgart 2001), 2. *Westeuropa* (ed. G. Frank / K. Meerhoff; Melanchthon-Schriften der Stadt Bretten 6/2; Stuttgart 2002).

4.1. Foundation of New Universities

During the reformation of the Wittenberg University already the first Protestant university came into existence in 1527 at Marburg.[65] The *Reformatio Ecclesiarum Hassiae* already planned an *universale studium* at Marburg.[66] At this place, besides theologians and lawyers, it was necessary to have at least one professor of medicine and in addition to that several professors of the *artes liberales* and languages. The canon law was explicitly excluded. In 1527 Landgrave Philipp of Hesse founded the university with the traditional four faculties, but without canon law, furthermore without papal and imperial privileges. Its economic consolidation by monastic property was made sure in 1540. Marburg received a privilege by Emperor Charles V not before 1541, which conferred on the theological faculty the full right of graduation. In 1529, when the *Homberger Kirchenordnung* had already arranged the support of poor students,[67] the *Stipendium* was established, which was to guarantee both regular attendance at the university and the continual education of future officials. It became a model for other Protestant universities like Tübingen, Wittenberg and Jena.[68] The second Protestant university was founded in 1541 at Königsberg by duke Albrecht of Prussia and was opened in 1544 with four faculties.[69] Melanchthon took part in establishing this university; its first statutes from 1546 followed the pattern of Wittenberg. It could not acquire papal and imperial privileges; but in 1560 King Sigismund II of Poland, as feudal lord of the duke of Prussia, transferred the privileges of the Cracow University with graduation rights to Königsberg.

4.2. Reformation of Existing Universities

At the University of Basel[70] since 1523 the reforming minded professors of theology, John Oecolampadius (until his death in 1531) and Conrad Pellican (until his departure to Zurich in 1526), were working against a majority of professors adhering to the Roman Church. When in 1529 the city decided to introduce the Reformation, many teachers and students went away, especially

---

[65] H. HERMELINK / S. A. KAEHLER, *Die Philipps-Universität zu Marburg 1527–1927* (Marburg 1927); *Academia Marburgensis* (ed. W. Heinemeyer / T. Klein / H. Seier; Marburg 1977); H. SCHNEIDER, "Marburg, Universität", TRE 22 (1991) 68–75.

[66] Sehling 8 (1965) 43–65, esp. Ch. 29, ibid. 63.

[67] Ch. 32, ibid. 63 f.

[68] Hermelink / Kaehler, Die Philipps-Universität (1927) 13f, 71–81.

[69] G. VON SELLE, *Geschichte der Albertus-Universität zu Königsberg in Preußen* (Würzburg ²1956); K. LAWRYNOWICZ, *Albertina. Zur Geschichte der Albertus-Universität zu Königsberg in Preußen* (ed. D. Rauschning; Abhandlungen des Göttinger Arbeitskreises 13; Berlin 1999); *Kulturgeschichte Ostpreußens in der Frühen Neuzeit* (ed. K. Garber / M. Komorowski / A. E. Walter; Tübingen 2001).

[70] E. VISCHER, "Die Lehrstühle und der Unterricht an der theolog. Fakultät Basels seit der Reformation", in: *Festschrift zur Feier des 450jährigen Bestehens der Universität Basel* (ed. Rektor and Regenz; Basel 1910) 115–242; E. BONJOUR, *Die Universität Basel von den Anfängen bis zur Gegenwart* (Basel ²1971).

to Freiburg im Breisgau. The reformation of the university, which had become necessary, was initiated in 1532 by the enactment of new statutes by the town council; it took several years. The new statutes were considerably influenced by humanistic ideals; in the *facultas artium* the ancient languages were prominent. They also formed the basis of the study of theology which was first of all conceived as the study of the Bible. However now with the demand for exercises in preaching, as in the education of lawyers and of physicians, the connection with practice was stressed. For a hundred years there were only two ordinary chairs of theology: one for the New and one for the Old Testament, which was also responsible for Practical theology. Besides that lecturers read sections of dogmatics.

Two years after Basel the reformation of the university arrived at Tübingen.[71] When after an exile lasting from 1519 Duke Ulrich had reconquered Württemberg in 1534 and at once introduced the Reformation, the sole university of the country was concerned from the very beginning. Already on 30 January 1535 the duke published a new order, which was renewed in 1536; but the reform was accomplished by Johannes Brenz against the opposition of the majority of professors not until 1537/38. Following the Marburg model, in 1536 the duke founded a *Stipendium* for the supply of ecclesiastical personal: the Tübingen *Stift*,[72] which since 1547 was placed in the former house of the Augustinian friars, where already since 1490 the lectures of the theological faculty had taken place. The faculty had three chairs at its disposal (focal points: Pentateuch, Prophets, New Testament. The professor responsible for the New Testament in addition had to give a systematic survey of Protestant doctrine); in 1561 an extraordinary chair especially for disputations and declamations was added.

The reformation of other German universities was closely connected with the consolidation of the Protestant confessions. The university of Greifswald, where since 1527 educational work was interrupted, in 1539 was newly opened by Duke Philipp I.[73] The university of Frankfurt / Oder (*Viadrina*) was reformed 1537/41,[74] Leipzig 1539/44,[75] Rostock in a procedure lasting for three decades and ending by the *Formula Concordiae* 1563.[76]

In the course of the Reformation, not only the universities, but after a temporary short interruption, the system of school education was reorganized as

---

[71] U. Köpf, "Johannes Brenz in Tübingen oder Wie reformiert man eine Universität?", *Blätter für württembergische Kirchengeschichte* 100 (2000) 282–96.

[72] M. Leube, *Die Geschichte des Tübinger Stifts. 1. 16. und 17. Jahrhundert* (Stuttgart 1921).

[73] F. Schubel, *Universität Greifswald* (Mitteldeutsche Hochschulen 4; Frankfurt/M. 1960).

[74] M. Höhle, *Universität und Reformation. Die Universität Frankfurt (Oder) von 1506 bis 1550* (Bonner Beiträge zur Kirchengeschichte 25; Köln e.a. 2002).

[75] H. Helbig, *Universität Leipzig* (Mitteldeutsche Hochschulen 2; Frankfurt/M. 1961).

[76] P. Kretschmann, *Universität Rostock* (Mitteldeutsche Hochschulen 3; Köln / Wien 1969); T. Kaufmann, *Universität und lutherische Konfessionalisierung. Die Rostocker Theologieprofessoren und ihr Beitrag zur theologischen Bildung und kirchlichen Gestaltung im Herzogtum Mecklenburg zwischen 1550 und 1675* (Quellen und Forschungen zur Reformationsgeschichte 66; Gütersloh 1997); M. Asche, *Von der reichen hansischen Bürgeruniversität zur armen mecklenburgischen Landeshochschule. Das regionale und soziale Besucherprofil der Universitäten Rostock und Bützow in der Frühen Neuzeit (1500–1800)* (Contubernium 52; Stuttgart 2000).

well, which provided the basis for studies at the university. Autonomous school regulations *(Schulordnungen)* or sections in church regulations *(Kirchenordnungen)* that concerned school affairs were of fundamental importance in this process.[77] The first printed, separate school regulation was drafted in 1523 for the electorial Saxony town Zwickau, and already at the end of the thirties the municipal regulations were completed by Johannes Bugenhagen's drafts. For the electorate Saxony and the territories influenced by Wittenberg, Melanchthon's *Unterricht der Visitatoren*[78] became a guideline; the sovereign's regulations were not completed before the eighties. Especially in Protestant imperial, residential and university cities schools for the preparation of university studies were established above the level of the Latin schools, e.g., under the influence of Melanchthon the 'Superior school' at Nuremberg, which was inaugurated in 1526. These institutions were called *Gymnasium* or *Paedagogium* or had a similar name. Furthermore, Protestant monastery schools in secularized monasteries were established, especially in Württemberg and Saxony.[79] In these schools, which were founded out of a humanistic and evangelical spirit, students learned not only the ancient languages, but received a training in the exegesis of the Old and the New Testament as well. Several of their teachers were important exegetes; some of these schools became first steps towards a university. At other places they were even regarded as a surrogate for a university.

5. Alternative Institutions of Education

Another system of higher education completely different from Wittenberg and the area under its influence emerged in the territories and the cities, where no universities existed that could be at the Reformation's service. In these places it was necessary to build upon existing Latin schools (i.e., monastery and clerical

---

[77] See Vormbaum, Die evangelischen Schulordnungen des sechszehnten Jahrhunderts (1860); Sehling; Müller, Vor- und frühreformatorische Schulordnungen und Schulverträge (1885–86). Cf. Hettwer, Herkunft (1965).

[78] See *Unterricht der visitatoren*, in: Sehling 1 (1902) 149–74, here: 171; school regulations therein: 171–74.

[79] G. LANG, *Geschichte der württembergischen Klosterschulen von ihrer Stiftung bis zu ihrer endgültigen Verwandlung in evangelisch-theologische Seminare* (Stuttgart 1938); H. EHMER, "Vom Kloster zur Klosterschule. Die Reformation in Maulbronn", in: *Maulbronn: zur 850jährigen Geschichte des Zisterzienserklosters* (ed. Landesdenkmalamt Baden-Württemberg; Forschungen und Berichte der Bau- und Kunstdenkmalpflege in Baden-Württemberg 7; Stuttgart 1997) 59–82; idem, "Die Maulbronner Klosterschule. Zur Bewahrung zisterziensischen Erbes durch die Reformation", in: *Anfänge der Zisterzienser in Südwestdeutschland* (ed. P. Rückert / D. Planck; Oberrheinische Studien 16; Stuttgart 1997) 233–46; idem, "Die Klosterschule 1556–1595", in: *Alpirsbach. Zur Geschichte von Kloster und Stadt* (ed. Landesdenkmalamt Baden-Württemberg; Forschungen und Berichte der Bau- und Kunstdenkmalpflege in Baden-Württemberg 10; Stuttgart 2001) 677–707. – Duke Christoph of Württemberg's regulation for monasteries from 1556 is now available in Sehling 16 (2004) 296–303. – P. FLEMMING, *Briefe und Aktenstücke zur ältesten Geschichte von Schulpforta* (Jahresbericht der Königlichen Landesschule Pforta 357 [1899/1900] Beigabe; Naumburg 1900); H. HEUMANN, *Schulpforta* (Erfurt 1994); M. PERNET, *Religion und Bildung: eine Untersuchung zur Geschichte von Schulpforta* (Mittelstädt 2000).

schools). This happened in the greater part of the Reformed Churches – in Switzerland, France, the Netherlands and in some regions of the Empire. Here, especially in the domain of the Reformed confession, a peculiar type of institution of education developed, which was called *High School (Hohe Schule), Academy, Academic Gymnasium.*[80]

The development in Zurich was exemplary for the Reformed domain.[81] Here at the Grossmünster a school for canons (*Schola Turicensi* or *Tigurina*) had been in existence for a long time, and according to the tradition went back to Charlemagne. When under the influence of Huldrych Zwingli after the First Zurich Disputation on 29 January 1523 the mayor and council of the city had decided to carry through the Reformation, on 29 September 1523 they decreed a mandate on the reformation of the Grossmünster. This document declared that a part of the income from the prebends should be invested in the improvement of the educational system. Learned persons had to be appointed, who had to expound the Holy Scripture in Hebrew and Greek and in the Latin version every day in public for one hour per language.[82] On 19 June 1525 the new school was inaugurated, which, in conformity with Zwingli's conception of exegesis as prophecy (according to 1 Cor 14:26–29), was called *Prophezey.* In the morning the studies until noon concentrated on the Old Testament, which was read to the participants from the Vulgate, commented according to the Hebrew text, compared with the Septuagint and finally interpreted; the outcome was delivered in a German sermon. In the afternoon the New Testament was – at first at the Zurich Fraumünster with Zwingli's participation – translated and explained.[83] Even though the Zurich school was not a university, it attracted important humanistic scholars, who developed an outstanding work of translation and interpretation of the Bible at this institution.

Zurich became the model for other Reformed schools. Already in 1528 a High School was opened at Bern with three teachers coming from Zurich. Since 1535 it was located in the former Franciscan friary (therefore called *Collegium zun Barfüssen*). Its first school regulation, which was written in 1548 especially by Johannes Haller, contained three chairs for theology, the biblical languages (two since 1574, divided into Greek and Hebrew), and the *artes* lo-

---

[80] U. Im Hof, "Die Entstehung der reformierten Hohen Schule. Zürich (1525) – Bern (1528) – Lausanne (1537) – Genf (1559)", in: Beiträge zu Problemen (1978) 243–62; U. M. Zahnd, "Lateinschule – Universität – Prophezey. Zu den Wandlungen im Schulwesen eidgenössischer Städte in der ersten Hälfte des 16. Jahrhunderts", in: *Bildungs- und schulgeschichtliche Studien zu Spätmittelalter, Reformation und konfessionellem Zeitalter* (ed. H. Dickerhof; Wissensliteratur im Mittelalter 19; Wiesbaden 1994) 91–115.

[81] H. Nabholz, "Zürichs Höhere Schulen von der Reformation bis zur Gründung der Universität 1525–1833", in: *Die Universität Zürich 1833–1933 und ihre Vorläufer* (ed. E. Gagliardi e.a.; Zürich 1938) 1–164, 923–30; K. Spillmann, "Zwingli und die Zürcher Schulverhältnisse", *Zwingliana* 11 (1959–63) 427–48; *Schola Tigurina. Die Zürcher Hohe Schule und ihre Gelehrten um 1550* (ed. Institut für Schweizerische Reformationsgeschichte, Zürich; Zürich / Freiburg im Br. 1999).

[82] *Actensammlung zur Geschichte der Zürcher Reformation in den Jahren 1519–1533* (ed. E. Egli; Zürich 1879) 169.

[83] The situation thirty years later is described by Ludwig Lavater, *De ritibus institutis Ecclesiae Tigurinae* (Zürich 1559; new edn. by J. B. Ott; Zürich 1702, Ch. 18; German tr.: *Die Gebräuche und Einrichtungen der Zürcher Kirche*; übersetzt und erläutert von G. A. Keller; Zürich 1987).

gic and rhetoric.[84] In 1536 a similar school in Lausanne was established, which in 1548 was organized definitively likewise with four chairs,[85] and in 1559 the Geneva Academy, whose nucleus consisted of three professors from Lausanne.[86] It became the prototype for many other foundations in Reformed congregations of France, the Netherlands, the Empire and Hungary. The first institution called *Hohe Schule* was opened in 1584 at Herborn by Count John VI of Nassau-Dillenburg.[87]

Most German imperial cities (e.g., Augsburg, Ulm, Frankfurt/M) and the Hanseatic cities abstained from the efforts necessary to found a university, which always was connected with the difficulty of receiving imperial privileges for a Protestant institution of education. In most cases the establishment of municipal *gymnasia illustria* was regarded as sufficient. Only two Protestant imperial cities finally managed to develop universities out of such *gymnasia* by turning them first into partly privileged *academiae* and extending their status later on: Strasbourg and Nuremberg.[88] In Strasbourg[89] since 1525 intense efforts for the educational system were undertaken. Soon biblical instruction was made available; in 1534 a *Collegium praedicatorum* was established, i.e., a school for the supply of ecclesiastical personnel in the Protestant cities of South Germany and German speaking Switzerland. In 1538/39 the existing Latin schools of Strasbourg were united to form one single school (*gymnasium illustre*) under the direction of the humanist Johann Sturm (1507–89), who had been invited from Paris. At this school important theologians as Martin Bucer, Wolfgang Capito and Caspar Hedio taught as well. When its number of students decreased, the magistrate procured the privilege for graduating from emperor Maximilian II in 1566. They had decided on purpose to aspire only to the partial privilege for the graduation in arts. Not before 1621 the Strasbourg "Academy" became a university in the proper sense by receiving the full right of graduation.

Nuremberg already in 1526 obtained a "Superior school" (*Obere Schule*), supported by Melanchthon, which, however, was deprived not only of a con-

---

[84] F. HAAG, *Die Hohen Schulen zu Bern in ihrer geschichtlichen Entwicklung von 1528 bis 1834* (Bern 1903) esp. 18–32; U. IM HOF, "Die reformierte Hohe Schule zu Bern, vom Gründungsjahr 1528 bis in die zweite Hälfte des 16. Jahrhunderts", in: Archiv des Historischen Vereins des Kantons Bern 64/65 (1980/81) 194–224; idem, "Hohe Schule – Akademie – Universität 1528–1805 – 1834–1984", in: idem e.a., *Hochschulgeschichte Berns 1528–1984* (Bern 1984) 23–127, esp. 25–36.

[85] H. MEYLAN, *La Haute École de Lausanne 1537–1937* (Études et documents pour servir à l'histoire de l'Université de Lausanne 11; Lausanne 1937, ²1986).

[86] C. BORGEAUD, *Histoire de l'Université de Genève* 1 (Genève 1900); P.-F. GEISENDORF, *L'Université de Genève 1559–1959* (Genève 1959); K. MAAG, *Seminary or University? The Genevan Academy and Reformed Higher Education, 1560–1620* (Aldershot / Brookfield 1995); W. G. NAPHY, "The Reformation and the evolution of Geneva's schools", in: *Reformations Old and New* (ed. B. A. Kümin; Aldershot / Brookfield 1996) 185–202.

[87] G. MENK, *Die Hohe Schule Herborn in ihrer Frühzeit (1584–1660)* (Veröffentlichungen der Historischen Kommission für Nassau 30; Wiesbaden 1981).

[88] A. SCHINDLING, "Straßburg und Altdorf – Zwei humanistische Hochschulgründungen von evangelischen freien Reichsstädten", in: Beiträge zu Problemen (1978) 149–89.

[89] A. SCHINDLING, *Humanistische Hochschule und Freie Reichsstadt. Gymnasium und Akademie in Straßburg 1538–1621* (Veröffentlichungen des Instituts für Europäische Geschichte Mainz 77; Wiesbaden 1977).

tinuous direction, but also of a sufficient financial basis. Therefore it was not successful, whilst the Strasbourg Gymnasium in 1545 had already far more than 600 students. As a substitute for the failing Nuremberg High School, the Senate, advised by Joachim Camerarius (then professor in Leipzig), projected a *gymnasium illustre* in the small Nuremberg country town of Altdorf from 1565: an institution for which an imperial partial privilege, following the Strasbourg model, was issued. In 1575 the school opened; as early as 1577 it also offered *lectiones publicae* of the higher faculties. The right to juridical and medical graduations was conferred on this institute in 1622, but the right for theological graduations not until 1696.[90]

---

[90] S. FREIHERR VON SCHEURL, *Die theologische Fakultät Altdorf im Rahmen der werdenden Universität 1575–1623* (Einzelarbeiten aus der Kirchengeschichte Bayerns 23; Nürnberg 1949).

CHAPTER SEVENTEEN

The Exegetical and Hermeneutical Work of Martin Luther

By SIEGFRIED RAEDER †

(University of Tübingen)

Sources: I. Works of MARTIN LUTHER: *Werke. Kritische Gesamtausgabe* [WA] 1– (Weimar 1883–); *Briefwechsel* [WA.B] 1– (1930-); *Deutsche Bibel* [WA.DB] 1– (1906–); *Tischreden* [WA.TR] 1– (1912–); *Luthers Werke in Auswahl* 1–8 (Bonner Ausgabe [BoA]; ed. O. Clemen; Bonn 1912-13); here: 5. *Der junge Luther* (ed. E. Vogelsang; Berlin ²1955); 6. *Luthers Briefe* (ed. H. Rückert; Berlin ²1955); *Archiv zur Weimarer Ausgabe der Werke Martin Luthers. Texte und Untersuchungen* [AWA] ("Im Auftrag der Kommission zur Herausgabe der Werke Martin Luthers", ed. G. Ebeling / U. Köpf / B. Moeller / H. A. Oberman) 1 (Köln /Wien 1991), 2 (1981), 5 (1984); *Die gantze Heilige Schrifft Deudsch* (Wittenberg 1545; ed. H. Volz, together with H. Blanke; ed. of text F. Kur; München 1972; last edition in the lifetime of Luther); *Dokumente zu Luthers Entwicklung (bis 1519)* (ed. O. Scheel; Tübingen ²1929); *Luthers Vorreden zur Bibel* (ed. H. Bornkamm; Hamburg 1967; the Prefaces are to be found also in *Die gantze Heilige Schrifft* 1-2, Anhang, 238*-41*, and, distributed, in WA.DB 1–12). II. Works of other authors: AUGUSTINE: *De civitate Dei* (CCL 47-48); GABRIEL BIEL: *Collectorium circa quattuor libros Sententiarum. Prologus et Liber primus* (ed. W. Werbeck / U. Hofmann; Tübingen 1973); *Enchiridion symbolorum definitionum et declarationum de rebus fidei et morum* [DS] (ed. H. Denzinger ... retractavit ... A. Schönmetzer; Freiburg/Br. ³⁴1967). – DESIDERIUS ERASMUS ROTERODAMUS: *Ausgewählte Werke* (Latin-German edn. by Annemarie / Hajo Holborn; Munich 1933); *Opera omnia* (ed. P. S. Allan; t. 3, Lugduni Batavorum [Leuven] 1913). – FABER STAPULENSIS / J. LEFÈVRE D'ÉTAPLES: *Quincuplex Psalterium. Gallicum. Romanum. Hebraicum. Vetus. Conciliatum* (Paris 1509). – HUGO CARDINALIS: *Textus Bibliae cum Postilla domini Hugonis Cardinalis* 1-6 (Basel 1503-04). – JEROME: *Epistulae* (CSEL 54, 55); *The New English Bible* [NEB] (Oxford / Cambridge ²³1994). – NICHOLAS OF LYRA: *Biblia Sacra cum glossis interlineari et ordinaria, Nicolai Lyrani Postilla, ac Moralitatibus, Burgensis Additionibus, et Thoringi* [= Matthias Doering] *Replicis* 1-6 (Basel 1506-08); *Quellen zur Geschichte des Papsttums und des römischen Katholizismus* [QGPRK] (1-5th edn. by C. Mirbt; 6th new and rev. edn. by K. Aland), 1. *Von den Anfängen bis zum Tridentinum* (Tübingen 1967); *Renaissance, Glaubenskämpfe, Absolutismus* (*Geschichte in Quellen*, ed. W. Lautemann / M. Schlenker; 3, rev. by F. Dickmann; Munich ²1976). – JOHANNES REUCHLIN: *De rudimentis hebraicis* (Pforzheim 1506); *De verbo mirifico* (1494) and *De arte cabalistica* (1517), facsimile repr. in one volume (Stuttgart / Bad Cannstatt 1964); *In septem psalmos poenitentiales hebraicos interpretatio de verbo ad verbum, et super eisdem commentarioli sui, ad discendum linguam hebraicam ex rudimentis* (Tübingen 1512). – THOMAS AQUINAS: *Summa Theologiae* II/1 (BAC; Madrid ³1962); *Vom Spätmittelhochdeutschen zum Frühneuhochdeutschen. Synoptischer Text des Propheten Daniel in sechs deutschen Übersetzungen des 14. bis 16. Jahrhunderts* (ed. H. Volz; Tübingen 1963).

Bibliographies: K. ALAND, *Hilfsbuch zum Lutherstudium* (rev. together with E. O. Reichert and G. Jordan; Witten ³1970); B. ALTANER / A. STUIBER, *Patrologie. Leben, Schriften und Lehre der Kirchenväter* (Freiburg / Basel / Wien ⁸1978); R. SCHWARZ, *Luther* (*Die Kirche in ihrer Geschichte* 3/I; Göttingen 1986) 1-13; M. BRECHT / K.-H. ZUR MÜHLEN, Art. "Luther, Martin (1483-1546)" I-II, TRE 21 (1991) 524-30, 561-67 (Bibl.).

Studies: I. Concerning Luther: H. BEINTKER, "Luthers Bemühungen um die Erarbeitung eines Psalmenkommentars zwischen 1513 und 1523", AWA 5, 193–218; A. BEUTEL, *In dem Anfang war das Wort: Studien zu Luthers Sprachverständnis* (HUTh 27; Tübingen 1991); M. BIERSACK, "Die Unschuld Davids. Zur Auslegung von Psalm 7 in Luthers Operationes in Psalmos", AWA 5, 245–268; H. BORNKAMM, *Luther und das Alte Testament* (Tübingen 1948); idem, *Das Jahrhundert der Reformation. Gestalten und Kräfte* (Göttingen ²1966; 11–36: "Martin Luther. Chronik seines Lebens"); idem, *Martin Luther in der Mitte seines Lebens. Das Jahrzehnt zwischen dem Wormser und dem Augsburger Reichstag* (ed. K. Bornkamm; Göttingen 1979); M. BRECHT, *Martin Luther* 1–3 (Stuttgart ²1983; Berlin ³1986–87); M. BRECHT / K.-H. ZUR MÜHLEN, Art. "Luther, Martin (1483–1546)" I-II, TRE 21 (1991) 513–67; G. EBELING, "Die Anfänge von Luthers Hermeneutik", *Lutherstudien* I (Tübingen 1971) 1–68; idem, "Luthers Psalterdruck vom Jahre 1513", ibid. 69–131; idem, "Luthers Auslegung des 14. (15.) Psalms in der ersten Psalmenvorlesung im Vergleich mit der exegetischen Tradition", ibid. 132–95; idem, "Luthers Auslegung des 44. (45.) Psalms", ibid. 196–220; H. GAESE, "Psalm 1 der Operationes in psalmos im Spiegel der späteren Auslegung Luthers", AWA 5, 219–28; A. HAMEL, *Der junge Luther und Augustin, ihre Beziehungen in der Rechtfertigungslehre nach Luthers ersten Vorlesungen 1509-1518 untersucht* (Gütersloh 1934; repr. Hildesheim 1980); H. CHR. KNUTH, *Zur Auslegungsgeschichte von Psalm 6* (Tübingen 1971; 134–274: "Luthers Auslegung zu Ps 6"); J. KÖSTLIN / G. KAWERAU, *Martin Luther. Sein Leben und seine Schriften* (Berlin ⁵1903); G. KRAUSE, *Studien zu Luthers Auslegung der Kleinen Propheten* (Tübingen 1962); W. MAASER, *Die schöpferische Kraft des Wortes: die Bedeutung der Rhetorik für Luthers Schöpfungs- und Ethikverständnis* (Neukirchener theol. Diss. u. Hab. 22; Neukirchen-Vluyn 1999); P. MEINHOLD, *Die Genesisvorlesung Luthers und ihre Herausgeber* (Stuttgart 1936); idem, *Luthers Sprachphilosophie* (Berlin 1958); K. A. MEISSINGER, *Luthers Exegese in der Frühzeit* (Leipzig 1911); W. MOSTERT, "'Scriptura sacra sui ipsius interpres'. Bemerkungen zum Verständnis der Heiligen Schrift durch Luther", LuJ 46 (1979) 60–96; TH. PAHL, *Quellenstudien zu Luthers Psalmenübersetzung* (Weimar 1931); J. PELLIKAN, *Luther the Expositor* (*Luther's Works.* Companion Volume to the American Edition of Luther's Works; St. Louis, MO 1959); J. S. PREUSS, *From Shadow to Promise: Old Testament Interpretation from Augustine to the Young Luther* (Cambridge, MA 1969); S. RAEDER, *Das Hebräische bei Luther untersucht bis zum Ende der ersten Psalmenvorlesung* (Tübingen 1961); idem, *Die Benutzung des masoretischen Textes bei Luther in der Zeit zwischen der ersten und der zweiten Psalmenvorlesung (1515-1518)* (Tübingen 1967); idem, *Grammatica Theologica. Studien zu Luthers Operationes in Psalmos* (Tübingen 1977); idem, "Voraussetzungen und Methode von Luthers Bibelübersetzung", *Geist und Geschichte der Reformation* (FS Hanns Rückert; ed. H. Liebing / K. Scholder; Berlin 1966) 152–78; idem, "Die Auslegung des 50. (51.) Psalms in Augustins Enarrationes in psalmos und in Luthers Dictata super Psalterium", AWA 5, 153–92; idem, "Luther als Ausleger und Übersetzer der Heiligen Schrift", *Leben und Werk Martin Luthers* 1–2 (Festgabe zu seinem 500. Geburtstag; ed. H. Junghans; Berlin ²1985), 1, 253–78; 2, 800–05; R. SAARINEN, "The Word of God in Luther's Theology", LuthQ NS 4 (1990) 31–44; H. VON SCHUBERT / K. MEISSINGER, *Zu Luthers Vorlesungstätigkeit* (Heidelberg 1920); R. SCHWARZ, "Prophetische Rede vom messianischen Heil. Jes 9,1–6 in Luthers Auslegung von 1525/26", in: *Schriftprophetie* (FS Jörg Jeremias zum 65. Geburtstag, ed. F. Hartenstein / J. Krispenz / A. Schart; Neukirchen-Vluyn 2004) 431–58; E. SEEBERG, *Studien zu Luthers Genesisvorlesung. Zugleich ein Beitrag zu der Frage nach dem alten Luther* (Gütersloh [1932]); U. STOCK, "'Spes exercens conscientiam'. Sprache und Affekt in Luthers Auslegung des 6. Psalms in den Operationes in Psalmos", AWA 5, 229–44; B. STOLT, "Luthers Übersetzungstheorie und Übersetzungspraxis", *Leben und Werk Martin Luthers* 1–2 (Festgabe zu seinem 500. Geburtstag; ed. H. Junghans; Berlin ²1985), 1, 241–52; 2, 797–800; D. THYEN, *Untersuchungen zu Luthers Jesaja-Vorlesung* (theol. Diss. Heidelberg 1964); idem, "Martin Luthers Hohelied-Vorlesung von 1530/31", *Siegener Pädagogische Studien* 23 (1977/78) 62–77; E. VOGELSANG, *Die Anfänge von Luthers Christologie nach der ersten Psalmenvorlesung, insbesondere in ihren exegetischen und systematischen Zusammenhängen mit Augustin und der Scholastik dargestellt* (Berlin 1929). II. Studies concerning other topics: C. AUGUSTIJN, *Erasmus von Rotterdam. Leben – Werk – Wirkung* (Munich 1986); TH. BOMAN, *Das hebräische Denken im Vergleich mit dem Griechischen* (Göttingen ³1959; ⁷1983. ET: Hebrew Thought Compared with Greek [London 1960; New York 1970]); D. J. GOLDHAGEN, *Hitlers willige Vollstrecker. Ganz gewöhnliche Deutsche und der Holocaust* (tr. by K. Kochmann; Berlin 1996); A. VON HARNACK, *Marcion. Das Evangelium vom fremden Gott* (Leipzig 1921; ²1924); S. RAEDER, "Johannes Reuchlin", in: *Gestalten der Kirchengeschichte* (ed. M. Greschat), 5. *Die Reformationszeit* I (Stuttgart 1981) 33–51; R. SCHLIEBEN,

Christliche Theologie und Philologie in der Spätantike (Berlin / New York 1974); C. Tresmontant, *Biblisches Denken und hellenische Überlieferung. Ein Versuch* (Düsseldorf 1956); L. Weisgerber, *Das Menschheitsgesetz der Sprache* (Heidelberg ^{2}1964).

Special abbreviations:

AWA= *Archiv zur Weimarer Ausgabe der Werke Martin Luthers*

BoA= Bonner Ausgabe [der Werke Luthers]

WA= Weimarana – *Kritische Gesamtausgabe* [der Werke Luthers]

WA.B= Weimarana – *Briefwechsel*

WA.DB = Weimarana – *Deutsche Bibel*

WA.TR = Weimarana – *Tischreden*

1. Luther as a Theologian Concentrating on the Bible

Luther's entire work can be understood as a comprehensive, many-faceted interpretation of the Bible. There is exegesis of the Holy Scriptures not only in his lectures on biblical books, but also in his sermons and postillae, in his numerous expositions of particular biblical texts, in his disputations, his scriptures, dealing with crucial aspects of theological, ecclesiastical, social and economical life, in his catechisms, his hymns, his letters, his after-dinner speeches, and, last not least, it is correct to recognize his German Bible as the most concentrated form of Luther's biblical exegesis. He refused to translate only words from one language into another; his intention was to render the meaning and matter of the text comprehensible to the readers of his *Die ganze Heilige Schrift Deutsch*. In order to achieve this he supplemented his translation with introductions into the biblical Scriptures, along with marginal notes and references to biblical parallels. Additionally, illustrations drawn according to Luthers stipulations, were to help the reader to grasp the sense of the text.

On 19th October 1512 Luther received a doctorate in theology from the University of Wittenberg. Swearing the oath he promised "to teach Holy Scripture faithfully and in purity". The doctorate being the highest possible academic title, Luther held the same teaching position which Albert the Great (d. 1280), Thomas Aquinas (d. 1274) and Bonaventure (d. 1274) had held before him. In the Middle Ages the chair of theology was defined as *lectura in Biblia*. However, this did not mean that necessarily all doctors of theology restricted themselves to the exegesis of the Bible in their lectures. They also examined other texts, philosophical as well as theological, they gave lectures in a systematic form and, of course, they disputed all sorts of issues. But Luther, having received his doctorate in theology, lectured on biblical Scriptures exclusively. His disputations likewise served the understanding of the Bible. In other words, for Martin Luther, theological work was to be aimed exclusively at the exposition of Holy Scripture.

This was anything but the norm for a man educated in scholastic traditions. Gabriel Biel (d. 1495), for example, taught as a doctor of theology at the University of Tübingen, but never gave one exegetical lecture on the Bible. His main work was a long commentary on the *Four Books of Sentences* by Peter Lombard (d. 1160). A vast number of commentaries was written on Peter's work; until the sixteenth century it was the fundamental textbook for students of theology.[1] In his preface Biel explains, why he felt it necessary to write a commentary on Peter's famous work: "The way of the Scriptures, which leads us to the knowledge of God, is very broad. Therefore it is detrimental, difficult and almost futile to send out especially the beginners and the newborne children in theology on this vast, wide ocean. Because of that for the glory of the catholic faith and for promoting students Magister Petrus Lombardus ... like a hard-working bee edited a helpful work, [extracted] from the beehives of the holy Fathers, the Books of Sentences, in which he summarizes and unifies theological doctrines together with their testimonies in exquisite and praised order".[2] Biel, no doubt, warned beginners in theology about the dangers of studying the Holy Scriptures, because the Church had, after all, taken a beating with the so-called heretics, like John Wyclif (d. 1384) and Jan Hus (d. 1415) who used to cite the Bible to defend their doctrines.

2. Luther as Successor of the Ancient and Medieval Interpreters of the Old Testament

From 1513 to 1515, having been awarded his *doctor sacrae scripturae*, Luther lectured on the Psalms.[3] The Psalter was an excellent means for cultivating Christian devotion. For monks and clergymen it formed the essential element of prayer, recited at the canonical hours. The Psalms were the most widely examined texts of the Old Testament, due to the tradition that the famous king and prophet David had spoken about the mysteries of Christ and the Church in the Psalms.[4] It is therefore no surprise that Luther, soon after he had received his doctorate in theology, turned to the exposition of the Psalter.

He had many commentaries at his disposal, written between the fourth and the sixteenth century. Besides these commentaries, which Luther made use of mainly for his lectures, there were many other scriptures of theological, liturgical, canonical, philosophical, philological, historical, poetic, mystical and devotional character, which he used to expound the Psalms. More detailed information can be taken from the source index for Luther's *Dictata super Psalterium*.[5]

As far as the Ancient Christian tradition was concerned, three authors in

---

[1] As a Sententiarius also Luther, being very familiar with Biel's commentary, dealt with Peter's *Sentences* in a series of lectures held from 1509 to 1511.

[2] *Et quoniam scriptura, qua ad cognoscendum Deum ducimur, latissima est, est denique dispensiosum, difficile et fere inutile incipientes praesertim et in sacra theologia primogenitos infantes in mare tam magnum quam spatiosum mittere. Eapropter ad catholicae fidei exaltationem et studentium profectum magister Petrus Lombardus ... opus utile velut apis argumentosa ex sanctorum patrum alveariis edidit, libros scilicet Sententiarum, in quibus ordine exquisito pariter et laudato theologica dogmata appositis eorundem testimoniis congessit et in unum redegit* (Biel, Collectorium, Prologus et Liber primus, p. 6,5–12).

[3] WA 55I (1993), II (2000).

[4] Cf. e. g., Matt 22:43, 45.

[5] WA 55I, XXXIX–XLVII; 55II, X–XIV.

particular were of great significance for Luther's exegesis: Jerome, Augustine and Cassiodorus.

Luther was acquainted not only with the Psalter of the Vulgate (a revised Latin translation of the Psalms based on the Septuagint), but also with a version of the Psalms translated directly from the Hebrew text into Latin by Jerome (d. 420).[6] In addition, he knew those letters of Jerome, which contained philological and exegetical declarations on the Psalms. Finally, the Church Father's scriptures dealing with Hebrew names and sites were very helpful for Luther.

While Jerome, especially in the role of a philologist, had a great influence on later exegesis, Augustine (d. 430)[7] was the eminent theological authority. Using the method of spiritual exposition he related the Psalms to Christ: both to Christ as the Head of the Church, and to Christ as living in his members. Augustine drew Luther's attention also to the problems of sin, grace and justification, dealt with in the Psalms.[8]

Cassiodorus (d. around 580)[9] followed for the most part in Augustine's footsteps; in a certain sense, however, he opened a new door when he used the canon of ancient sciences as an instrument of exegesis more consistently and systematically than Augustine had done, mainly by applying the rules and figures of the ancient rhetoric to the Psalms. In this respect he might be regarded as a predecessor of scholastic exegesis. Cassiodorus made Luther investigate the forms of poetry and rhetoric in the Psalter.[10]

In the early Middle Ages interpreters of the Bible mainly excerpted and combined the exegesis of the ancient Fathers. The *Glossa ordinaria*,[11] written in the twelfth century, is a widely recognized result of these efforts. But later there was also a certain modification of medieval traditionalism. Scholastic theologians were accustomed to dealing with the texts by analysing their dispositions, by investigating conceptual differences of words and by attempting to solve problems or *quaestiones*, arising from contrary traditions, and so forth.

In the Middle Ages the distinction between literal and spiritual exposition, dating back to Origen (d. 254), was pursued further and developed into the doctrine of the fourfold sense (*quadriga*) of Holy Scripture. This method was elucidated in the verse:

Littera gesta docet, quid credas allegoria,
moralis quid agas, quo tendas anagogia

The letter teaches, what happened,
the allegory what you have to believe,
the morality, how you have to act,
and the anagogia, what you have to strive to.

---

[6] See Altaner / Stuiber, Patrologie (1978) 394–404, 632–34; esp. 397–400, 633.
[7] See ibid. 412–49, 636–46; esp. 429–32, 640f.
[8] See Hamel, Der junge Luther und Augustin (1934 / 1980).
[9] Altaner / Stuiber, Patrologie (1978) 486–88, 654–55; Schlieben, Christliche Theologie und Philologie in der Spätantike (1974).
[10] Raeder, Das Hebräische (1961) 281–310.
[11] *Biblia Sacra cum glossis* etc.

The postills of Hugh of St. Cher (d. 1263)[12] are a monumental opus of scholastic exegesis, which Luther also consulted. Hugh dealt with both the Old and the New Testament according to the doctrine of the fourfold sense of the Bible. He also drew up the first concordance to Holy Scripture.

A real progress was made by two interpreters in the late Middle Ages: Nicholas of Lyra (d. 1349)[13] and Paul (Pablo) of Burgos (d. 1435).[14] Both were acquainted with the Hebrew language, Burgensis more so than Lyranus. Paul – originally Salomon ben Levi – was converted from Judaism to Christianity at the age of about forty. Both interpreters used the Hebrew text of the Old Testament and were familiar with Jewish commentaries. In his *additiones* Paul supplemented and corrected Lyra's interpretations, whom he reproached for being sometimes uncritical with regard to Jewish commentators. Paul valued the interpretations of the Fathers more than Nicholas had done. One monumental work, *Biblia cum glossa ordinaria* [...], printed time and again since the fifteenth century, contained not only the Latin text of the Bible according to the Vulgate, but additionally the *Glossa interlinearis* and *Glossa ordinaria*, Lyra's *postilla litteralis* together with his explanations on morality, Paul's *additiones* and the unimportant *replicae* of Matthias Doering (OFM), in which he tried to defend Nicholas of Lyra, his brother monk, from Paul's *additiones*. Luther also made use of this large Bible work.

3. Luther and the Humanistic Exegesis

The motto of the humanists was: *Ad fontes!* ("Back to the sources!"). They regarded the Bible and the scriptures of the ancient Fathers as the sources of Christianity. Three great representatives of the humanistic movement in particular were important for Martin Luther: Johannes Reuchlin, Jacques Lefèvre d'Étaples / Faber Stapulensis and Erasmus of Rotterdam, the latter with regard to the New Testament.

Johannes Reuchlin (d. 1522)[15] was very familiar with the Old Testament, the Hebrew language and Jewish scriptures. He was the author of the first extensive textbook dealing with the Hebrew language: *De rudimentis hebraicis* (The rudiments of Hebrew, 1506). Well aware of his extraordinary achievement, he concluded his work by quoting Horace (*Liber carminum* III 30): *Exegi monumentum aere perennius* ("I have erected a monument, more durable than bronze").[16] The Rudimenta cover 621 pages, dealing with the letters (consonants and vowels) and their pronounciation, the grammar and the vocabulary of the Hebrew language. The most extensive part of this work is the Hebrew lexicon, arranged according to the order of the Hebrew radicals. Here we find not only the Hebrew words and their Latin meanings, but also the places and contexts in which they are used. When there are different translations, Reuchlin often offers critical remarks. This book was extremely heplful to Luther as an interpreter of the Old Testament. He already had it at his disposal in 1509, perhaps even as early as 1506. When in the role of a Sententiarius he lectured to his monastic brethren (1509–1511) on the handbook of Peter Lombard, he had already taken great pains to work through the *Rudimenta Hebraica*.[17] His copy of the Vulgate, which is no longer preserved, contained many references to the Rudimenta, written by his hand. In the Preface of his Ru-

---

[12] *Textus Bibliae*. On Hugh of St. Cher, see also HBOT I/2 (2000), Chaps. 29, by G. DAHAN, and 35, by K. FROEHLICH.

[13] *Biblia Sacra*. On Nicholas of Lyra, see also Chap. 2.1. in this volume, by L. SMITH.

[14] Ibid. On Paul of Burgos, see also Chap. 10.1. in this volume, by E. FERNÁNDEZ TEJERO and N. FERNÁNDEZ MARCOS.

[15] Raeder, Johannes Reuchlin (1981). On Reuchlin, see also Chap. 11.1. in this volume, by S. KESSLER MESGUICH.

[16] Reuchlin, *Rudimenta* [621].

[17] Raeder, Das Hebräische (1961) 62 f.

dimenta Reuchlin speaks about "the general decline in the study of the Holy Scriptures".[18] In order to encourage theologians to pay attention to the original texts of the Old Testament, he published the *Septem Psalmi poenitentiales* (Tübingen 1512). This edition contained the Hebrew text, translated word for word into Latin, and commentaries, strictly confined to grammatical explanations: Reuchlin did not wish to be regarded as a theologian, but only as a philologist (*grammaticus*).[19] Although he made no comments on the Bible as a theologian, nevertheless he investigated the mysteries of the Kabbalah, deeply hidden in the Hebrew language of the Old Testament. As a result of his kabbalistic investigations he published two works: *De verbo mirifico* (The Miracle-working Word), and *De arte cabalistica* (The kabbalistic Art). While Pico della Mirandola investigated Platonism, and Lefèvre d'Étaples Aristotelism, Reuchlin devoted himself to Kabbalism, which he regarded as the oldest philosophy of mankind, elaborated on in the school of Pythagoras.

In 1509, Jacques Lefèvre d'Étaples / Jacobus Faber Stapulensis (d. 1536) edited the *Quincuplex Psalterium* (sec. edn. 1513). It contained five translations of the Psalter (Psalterium Gallicum, Romanum, Hebraicum, Vetus, Conciliatum), along with expositions of the titles of the Psalms, summeries of their contents, continuous expositions and specific interpretations of difficult passages. Lefèvre commented on the Psalms according to their *sensus literalis propheticus* ("literal prophetical meaning"). He rejected the false literal sense, which would have lead Jewish interpreters and their Christian emulators to relate the Psalms to particular events in Old Testament history.[20]

Erasmus of Rotterdam (d. 1536), "the king of the humanists", also wished to lead the Christians, especially theologians and heads of the Church, back to the sources. Whereas Reuchlin turned to the Hebrew language and the Old Testament, Erasmus preferred the New Testament. His own edition of it (Basel 1516) contained the Greek text, three introductions, a literal translation into Latin and numerous notes, some of them concerning Old Testament quotations in the New Testament. Erasmus made a plea for the study of theology on the basis of the Bible in its original languages.[21]

Although Luther approved the humanists' refusal to align themselves with scholastic "sophists", and emphasized the humanistic demand that the Bible should be studied in its original texts, his conviction diverged in regard to one essential point: From the very beginning Luther was moved by the question: "What is at the centre of the biblical message?" This question can be found as far back as 1509, when Luther wrote a letter dated 17th March to his friend Braun: "The study of philosophy is difficult", he says. "From the very beginning I would have preferred to exchange it for theology, I mean [that kind of] theology, which examines the medulla of the wheat and the medulla of the bones".[22] In other words, the Bible is not merely a collection of many true doctrines, on the contrary, the Bible gives witness to the one truth in its different forms. Later Luther discovered that the fundamental issue of the Bible is the dialectic relationship of Law and Gospel.

The great humanistic authorities understood the Bible differently from Luther. What Erasmus believed he had discovered in the New Testament was "the philosophy of Christ". In his opinion Christ was teaching nothing other

---

[18] Reuchlin, *Rudimenta*, 1.

[19] *Sed ego non de sententia ut theologus, sed de vocabulis ut grammaticus disputo* (*Rudimenta*, 123).

[20] *Quincuplex Psalterium* a. On Lefèvre, see also Chap. 7.4. in this volume, by A. VANDERJAGT.

[21] *Prima cura debetur perdiscendis tribus linguis Latinae, Graecae, Hebraicae, quod constet omnem scripturam mysticam hisce proditam esse*, *Methodus* (1516; ed. Holborn) 151,26–28; 152,1–28. On Erasmus, see also Chap. 9 in this volume, by E. RUMMEL.

[22] Latin text in: Dokumente zu Luthers Entwicklung (1929) 218,7–10.

than "the renewel of the well created human nature".[23] For Erasmus, therefore, the doctrine of the Gospel was more or less clearly expressed in the lives and scriptures of famous ancient philosophers, poets and heroes. The interpretation of the New Testament from the viewpoint of ancient culture prevented Erasmus from listening to the message of the Old Testament. He thought that Christians could manage very well without the Old Testament. In a letter, dated 15th March 1518, Erasmus tells Wolfgang Capito, an expert on the Hebrew language: "Oh, [I wish] that the Church of the Christians would not value the Old Testament so highly. It is almost preferred to the Christian scriptures, although it has been given only for a limited time and consists of nothing but darkness".[24] Nevertheless, Erasmus did not deny that the Old Testament could be helpful with regard to Christ and to moral doctrines, but only through allegorical interpretation.

Although Reuchlin, in contrast to Erasmus, was very familiar with the Old Testament, he scrutinized only the secret mysteries of the Kabbalah in it, deeply hidden in the Hebrew letters, and not, as Luther did, a clear message.

Lefèvre d'Étaples strove to recognize the message of the Psalms, and by that he was near to Luther. But the strictly christological interpretation of the Psalter prevented Lefèvre from investigating the historical forms of faith, love und hope in the Old Testament.

4. Luther's Hermeneutics or Method of Interpreting the Bible

For Luther the method of interpreting the Bible is much more than a mere application of certain scientific rules to the Bible. For him method is a path leading the interpreter to a personal encounter with the text saying to him: *Tua res agitur.*

4.1. The Findings in the Dictata super Psalterium

At first sight Luther's *Dictata super Psalterium* (1513–15) seem to be very traditional. The lectures have the form of continuous short glosses (*glossae*) and of detailed explanations concerning particular passages (*scholae*). As for the glosses, Luther caused a special Psalter to be printed (1513) having broad borders and a large distance between its lines, so that he himself and his students could add his interpretations as interlinear or marginal glosses to the printed text by hand.

---

[23] *Methodus* (1516; ed. Holborn) 145.
[24] *Opera omnia* 3 (1913; ed. Allen) 253.

4.2. The Fourfold Sense of the Scriptures

As was usual in the Middle Ages, Luther expounded the Psalms according to "the fourfold sense" (*quadriga*). This method had made many commentators lapse into a wilderness of incoherent expositions, so that it was impossible to say, what the text meant really and properly. Luther recognized this danger. Therefore he strove to retain a coherent meaning of the text, when he explained it according to the fourfold sense. We can find this in his introduction[25] to the special copy of the already mentioned Psalter, printed 1513. Its headline reads: *Praefatio Ihesu Christi, filii dei et domini nostri, in Psalterium David* ("Preface of Jesus Christ, the Son of God and our Lord, to the Psalter of David").[26] Usually prefaces preceded biblical scriptures. The authors of such introductory texts were human beings, e.g. Jerome or anonymous persons. But Jesus Christ never appears in the role of an author of a biblical preface. Luther intends to say this: It is not any man, who teaches the reader to understand the Psalms, it is Christ himself, the son of God, who is speaking in the Psalter. Luther proves it: first, by quoting words of Christ himself, second, by quoting words of an Old Testament witness, namely Moses, and two New Testament witnesses, namely Peter and Paul.[27] Thereupon Luther declares this christological composition of quotations. As Lefèvre does, he rejects the Jewish exegesis and its influence upon ecclesiastic commentators. By this he seems to have in mind Nicholas of Lyra and Paul of Burgos, but he does not mention any name. Luther says: "We have to understand every prophecy and every prophet with reference to the Lord Christ, except when he seems to speak about another person with clear words ... Some [commentators] explain too many Psalms not in a prophetical, but in a historical sense, because they follow certain Hebrew Rabbis writing false things, and [follow] those who invent Jewish vanities".[28]

But differently from Lefèvre, Luther has the conception that it is Christ, about whom the Psalms speak according to the fourfold sense. Explicitly Luther only mentions the literal, the allegorical and the tropological sense in his preface: "Whatever is said about the Lord Jesus Christ in his own person according to the letter (*litera*), just this (*hoc ipsum*) is to be understood allegorically about ... the Church, being in every respect conformed to him, and simultaneously (*simul*) the same (*idemque*) is to be understood tropologically about every spiritual and inward man, [fighting] against his flesh and the outward man".[29] It seems that Luther may not be original in affirming the doctrine of the fourfold sense of Scripture. But on looking more carefully we recognize that he is using this method in order to overcome it. For the literal, allegorical and tropological expositions deal with the same matter (*hoc ipsum, idemque, simul*), though they do it from different viewpoints. The unity of the

---

[25] WA 55I, 6,1–11, 13.
[26] Ibid. 6,1–3.
[27] Ibid. 6,4–21.
[28] Ibid. 6,25–8,5.
[29] Ibid. 8,8–11.

four senses prevails over their variety. The centre of the unity is Christ in his person; but the effective reality of Christ transcends his existence as a person and embraces both: his Church and the inward man in Christ. Luther, therefore, interprets the Psalms in christocentric wholeness, not in christological restriction, as Lefèvre does.

4.3. The Relation of Tropology to Faith

In his *Dictata super Psalterium* Luther is occupied with the question: "How does Christ become effective in man?" His answer is that this happens through faith in Christ, and he explains it by means of the tropological interpretation. According to Luther's understanding the moral sense, being also traditionally called the tropological sense, does not only deal with moral prescriptions, as the medieval commentators thought, primarily it concerns faith in Christ. Luther says: "Who wants to understand the Apostle and the other Scriptures reasonably, has to understand all this tropologically, [namely] truth, wisdom, virtue (*virtus*), salvation, justice, that is by which God makes us strong [in virtue], saved, just[ified], wise etc., also the 'works of God', the 'ways of God'. All that is Christ literally, and the faith in Christ is all that in the moral sense". "In the tropological sense justice is the faith in Christ. Rom. 1 (17)".[30] The central issue in Luther's first lectures on the Psalms is: Christ himself (*in persona sua*) and faith in Christ.

4.4. Letter and Spirit[31]

Besides the tropology and its relation to faith the distinction between spirit and letter (*spiritus et littera*) is very important in the *Dictata super Psalterium*. This distinction goes back to Paul, especially to his sentence: *Littera occidit, spiritus autem vivificat* ("the letter kills, but the Spirit gives life", 2 Cor 3:6). Origen interpreted the words 'letter' and 'spirit' in a Platonic way: 'letter' being the world of the material, visible, perishable things, 'spirit' the world of the intellectual, invisible, eternal things. In his later years, Augustine approached to Paul's conception, identifying 'spirit' with the power of life-giving grace and 'letter' with the Law, which condemns everybody to death, who is not renewed by grace. In the Middle Ages the understanding of Origen had more influence than that of Augustine. Allegory, tropology and anagogy were related to the sphere of unvisible, spiritual and eternal things, elevated above the sphere of the historic, visible and perishable things. Luther followed in the footsteps of Paul and Augustine in regard to the conception of 'spirit' and 'letter'. For the Reformer 'letter' is the false, mortal understanding of texts, 'spirit' the true, life-giving understanding. The method of the fourfold sense, being not sufficient to grant a true understanding of the Bible, may lead man either to death

---

[30] WA 55II, 440,184–88.
[31] Cf. G. EBELING, "Geist und Buchstabe", RGG³ 2 (1958) 1290–96.

or to life. Luther explaines this by the expression "Mount Zion" (*Mons Zion*).[32] In relation to the mortal 'letter' "Mount Zion" means "the land Canaan" literally or historically, "the synagogue or an eminent person in the same" allegorically, "the Pharisaic or legal justice" tropologically and "the future glory according to the flesh" anagogically. On the other hand, in relation to the life-giving 'spirit' "mount Zion" means "the people existing in Zion" literally or historically, "the Church or whoever is an eminent teacher or bishop" allegorically, "the justice of faith or another excellent virtue" tropologically and "the eternal glory in the heavens" anagogically. The 'letter' which brings death, therefore, may become effective by the so-called 'spiritual' interpretations, namely allegory, tropology and anagogy, and, on the other hand, the life-giving 'spirit' may become effective by the right literal or historical interpretation. Therefore, the exegesis of the Psalms is not a matter of hermeneutic ontology, not a matter of intellectual rising from lower to higher spheres; the truth is that the interpreter of the Psalms has to choose between the death-bringing 'letter' and the life-bringing 'spirit', that is to say: between belief and unbelief.

4.5. Was Luther an Anti-semitic Interpreter of the Old Testament?

Luther may seem to prove himself to be an anti-Semite and intellectual predecessor of the holocaust[33] saying that the letter which brings death is effective in the Synagogue. But we should not apply terms to Luther, which were unknown in the sixteenth century. The truth is that Luther, like the Apostle Paul (cf. Rom 9:1–5), was terrified deeply, whenever he realized the destiny of the Jewish people: They have Moses and the prophets in their Hebrew Bible, they have clear prophecies about the Messiah, and yet they do not believe in the Gospel. For Luther this seemed to be a terrible judgement of God. Until his end he feared more and more that the same judgement would come down upon the German people, if they continued despising the Gospel.

4.6. Beginnings of Philological Exegesis[34]

The hermeneutic of the young Luther does not glide over the problems of the texts. He did not develop his hermeneutic from his own head, but worked it out, carefully investigating the texts themselves. Because, as a rule, in literary perspective the Psalms speak about Christ in his person, for Luther it was necessary to have knowledge of the original text, as far as possible. Therefore he was not content with the version of the Psalter in the Vulgate, since it was a secondary translation. He made use of all scriptures, which could inform him

---

[32] WA 55I, 4,7–18.
[33] Goldhagen, Hitlers willige Vollstrecker (1996) 75.
[34] Raeder, Das Hebräische (1961); idem, Die Benutzung des masoretischen Textes (1967); idem, Grammatica Theologica (1977).

about the Hebrew text; primarily he used the *Psalterium Hebraicum* of Jerome, contained in Lefèvre's *Quincuplex Psalterium*, furthermore the translations and interpretations of Nicholas of Lyra and Paul of Burgos, and last not least Reuchlin's work *De rudimentis hebraicis* and his edition of the *Septem Psalmi poenitentiales*. In a few cases Luther seems also to have used the Hebrew text of the Psalms.

5. The New Testament Intermezzo

In the following years Luther lectured on the Epistles to the Romans (1515–16), to the Galatians (1516–17) and to the Hebrews (1517–18). Studying these texts he made essential progress, especially in the understanding of Paul's theology.

In Gal 4:21–27 Paul interprets the story of Sarah and Hagar allegorically (v. 24): "This is an allegory. The two women stand for two covenants". These words give Luther an occasion, to refuse the traditional doctrine of the four-fold sense (*quadriga*): "Properly speaking according to the Apostle neither 'letter' is the same as history nor 'spirit' the same as tropology or allegory, more-over, as Augustine says in his scripture *De spiritu et littera*, really the 'letter' is every doctrine or law, which lacks grace. Therefore it is clear that history as well as tropology, allegory and anagogy are 'letter' according to the Apostle, but 'spirit' is grace itself, signified by the the law or that, which the law de-mands."[35]

In the years from 1515 to 1518/19 Luther came to realize that the dialectic relationship between Law and Gospel is the central problem of the Bible. So with better understanding he turned to the Psalms a second time. He lectured on them from 1518/19 to 1521.

6. The Findings in the *Operationes in Psalmos*

6.1. Allegory as a Spiritual Game

Principally, Luther reached beyond the method of the fourfold sense. Never-theless, sometimes, especially in sermons, he made use of it as a kind of 'spiri-tual play'.[36] But always he was careful to apply the allegory to faith in Christ. Since the years 1524/25 and still more after 1529 allegorical interpretation was pushed into the background. No doubt, this was Luther's reaction to radi-cal reformers, for example Thomas Müntzer and Andreas Bodenstein von

---

[35] BoA 5, 340,12-19 (= WA 57, 96).
[36] Luther says in regard to Bernard of Clairvaux: "Aber siehe, wie er mit der Schrift so oft (wie-wohl geistlich) spielt und sie führet außer dem rechten Sinn" (*An die Ratsherrn aller Städte deutsches Landes, daß sie christliche Schulen aufrichten und halten sollen*, 1524. BoA 2, 454,7-8 = WA 15, 40-41).

Karlstadt. They blamed Luther for sticking to the letter of the Bible and neglecting the spirit, which would inspire man's mind directly. Luther called
these enthusiasts *Schwarmgeister*. Unknowingly they made him recognize the
danger of 'spiritual' exegesis more clearly.

6.2. Allegory and Metaphorical Speech[37]

Luther made a distinction between allegorical interpretation, which introduces
a foreign sense into the text, and allegory as a rhetorical form, when the
author speaks metaphorically. Luther accuses former commentators of not observing this distinction. So Luther thinks, erroneously, that Psalm 19 has to be
understood in literary perspective as metaphorical speech. He believes that the
prophet himself does not speak about the material cosmos, but about "the
preachers of the new law". By the words "heavens", "firmament", "sun",
"days", "nights" the prophetic "spirit raises us from this visible world to the aspect of a certain new world, where are other heavens, days and nights, of
which we only see a figure and a shadow in this material world". Luther was
convinced that he interpreted Psalm 19 according to the author's intention.
For Paul, Luther says, also understood this text as metaphorical speech describing the proclamation of the Gospel (cf. Rom 10:18). In addition to the
Apostle's authority Luther refers to "the evident context of the words" in
Psalm 19.[38]

6.3. The Single Sense of Holy Scripture[39]

In his second series of lectures on the Psalms, edited as *Operationes in Psalmos*
(1519–1521), Luther emphasizes that Holy Scripture has only one (*unus*[40]),
literal (*literalis*[41]), legitimate (*legitimus*[42]), proper (*proprius*[43]), genuine (*ger-
manus*[44]), pure (*purus*[45]), simple (*simplex*[46]) and constant (*constans*[47]) sense,
and this one sense is both literal and spiritual simultaneously. For it is always
directed to "faith, love and hope". In the Psalms the prophet David speaks "in
spirit", and what he demands, is "faith".[48]

---

[37] Raeder, Grammatica Theologica (1977) 28 f.
[38] WA 5, 541,6–17.
[39] Raeder, Grammatica Theologica (1977) 26–31.
[40] WA 5, 280,36 f.
[41] Ibid. 384,20 f.
[42] Ibid. 22,26–28 (= AWA 2II, 4–5).
[43] Ibid. 75,3 (= AWA 2II, 119,9).
[44] Ibid. 75,3; 281,11 (= AWA II, 119,10).
[45] Ibid. 281,11 (= AWA 2II, 500,6).
[46] WA 5, 609,1.
[47] Ibid. 280,37 (= AWA 2II, 499,15).
[48] Ibid. 320,33f (= AWA 2II, 561,4).

6.4. Typological Interpretation

Ecclesiastical commentators of the Bible also made use of typological interpretation. Especially in the ancient Church theologians of the Antiochene School preferred typology to allegory. According to typology certain historical phenomena in the Old Testament have the character of pointing to future salvation in Christ. This may be said about Levitic laws concerning cultic forms of worship. Luther recommends interpreting such texts in regard to Christ, as the Letter to the Hebrews does.[49]

6.5. Grammatica theologica[50]

Because in his *Operationes in Psalmos* Luther is concentrating all his energies on the one sense, being literal and spiritual simultanously, philological work is yet more important, than it was in the *Dictata super Psalterium*. Now, regularily he goes back from the Vulgate to the Masoretic text, though he said later, that in the *Operationes in Psalmos* he was still not familiar enough with the Hebrew language.[51]

For Luther philology is not a matter altogether distinct from theology, on the contrary, biblical philology has a theological quality. Therefore Luther begins his exposition of Psalm 1 saying: "First let us look at the linguistic [findings], but [so that we regard them] as theological" (*Primum grammatica videamus, verum ea theologica*).[52] Thereupon he explains the exact meaning of the individual Hebrew words in Psalm 1. After that he offers an interpretation of the coherent text, based on the words, previously analysed. Luther recognized that a right understanding of the Bible is based on the understanding of biblical words. Their meaning differs from the philosophical conceptions of Aristotle. As Luther knew, scholastic interpreters often accepted words, occuring in their Latin Bible, in an Aristotelian sense. So, for instance, they understood the words *voluntas* (will), *intellectus* (intellect) or *iustitia* (justice, rightesness) falsely.[53]

In a writing of the year 1524 Luther speaks about the influence of the biblical languages on his theology: "Although the spirit does all things alone, nevertheless I could not have succeeded, if the languages had not helped me in making me sure in regard to Scripture. Possibly, I may have been devout and preaching rightly in quietness; but certainly, I had tolerated the Pope and the sophists [the scholastics] together with their endchristian [antichristian] power".[54]

---

[49] See infra n. 127 with text.
[50] Raeder, Grammatica Theologica (1977) 34–36.
[51] WA 5, 2.
[52] Ibid. 27,8 (= AWA 2II, 29,4).
[53] Raeder, Grammatica Theologica (1977) 121–28; 262–302.
[54] BoA 2, 455,20–25 (WA 15, 42f).

As the knowledge of the Hebrew language, so also history, geography and other sciences were important for Luther's exegesis of the Old Testament.

6.6. The Gospel as the Centre of Interpretation

Luther's interpretation is 'evangelio-centric' rather than christological. The unusual expression 'evangelio-centric' will say that Luther interprets the Psalms in his *Operationes in Psalmos* more in regard to the Gospel of Christ than in regard to the person of Christ. It is obvious that in the *Operationes* less Psalms are related to the person of Christ than in the *Dictata super Psalterium*.[55] But despite of the fact that Luther understands certain Psalms not prophetically about Christ, he explains them in the light of faith. For he presupposes belief and unbelief in all times. "Although the customs, persons, localities and rites change in the course of time, nevertheless the same godliness (*pietas*) and the same godlessness (*impietas*) go through all the centuries".[56] In this way Luther came to a new understanding of history. Now he can turn uninhibited to the historical interpretation of the Old Testament. He must not fear to forget Christ, because Christ sheds some light on the prophets, who fought against unbelief, idolatry and sin.

6.7. The Limits of Grammar. Words and Reality.
Old Testament and New Testament

For Luther the hermeneutical key to open the door to the Old Testament is the fact that God has revealed himself in Christ. Therefore linguistic findings are subordinated to the Gospel of Christ. Luther will not hurt the grammatical rules, but he knows that they have their limits. His interpretation of Ps 22:17 is an informative example of that.[57] Luther finds that here the Masoretic text is not comprehensible without the New Testament. The Jews translate: "As the lion (כָּאֲרִי) my hands and my feet". But, supposing, that אֲרִי is a word for 'lion', what does it mean, even if we supplement the incomplete sentence by its context as follows: "As the lion [they besieged] my hands and my feet"? There is no lion doing so. The Vulgate, following the Septuagint, makes a clear sense: *Foderunt*[58] *manus meas et pedes meos* ("They pierced my hands and my feet"). Luther is convinced that this is the right sense: The prophet wished to hint at Christ's crucifixion by the mysterious word כָּאֲרִי. From this example Luther draws the general conclusion: "We do not illuminate the history (*rem gestam*) by the mysteries of the Scripture, but [we illuminate] the mysteries of Scripture by history, that means: [we illuminate] the Old Testament by the Gospel and

---

[55] Raeder, Grammatica Theologica (1977) 31–34; 310–20.
[56] WA 5, 29,27–33 (= AWA II2, 34,19–35,3).
[57] Raeder, Grammatica Theologica (1977) 51–59.
[58] According to this translation we have to read: כָּרוּ or כָּארוּ.

not vice versa".[59] Further he says: "It is proper, that the grammar gives way to theology. For reality (*res*) does not submit to words, but words submit to reality and give way to it. Rightly the expression follows the sense and the letter [follows] the spirit".[60] Nevertheless, Luther tries to harmonize the consonants of the Hebrew expression *ka'ari* (כָּאֲרִי) with the Vulgate-version *foderunt* by changing the punctation, so that we can read *ka'are* (כָּאֲרֵי), which is the status constructus of *ka'arim* (כָּאֲרִים). Therefore, whithout changing the sentence we may keep the original text and translate as follows: "The council of the malicious has besieged me, [the council of those] who pierce (*fodientes vel fodientum*) my hands and my feet". But there is yet an obstacle: Luther knows that the Hebrew participle differs from the verbum finitum by *waw* and *cholem* (וֹ) behind the first consonant, so that the grammatically correct form would be כּוֹרִים. But the prophet made use of his freedom, choosing א instead of וֹ. By that he wanted to give a hint of an extraordinary event: the crucifixion of Christ.[61]

7. A Chronological Survey of Luther's Lectures on the Old Testament[62]

Luther began his lectures on the Old Testament with the *Dictata super Psalterium* (August 1513 to Eastern 1515).[63] His preparations, that means glosses and scholia, written by his own hand, have been preserved almost completely. As for form, method and terminology Luther goes on in the old way of scholastic exegesis. But if we compare his interpretations with their historical sources, we discover the first shoots of a new theology. They become more visible in his lectures on the Epistles to the Romans (Easter 1515 to September 1516),[64] to the Galatians (October 1516 to March 1517)[65] and to the Hebrews (April 1515 to March 1518).[66]

Having gained more profound theological knowledge by lecturing on these New Testament scriptures he returned to the Psalms, probably in 1518. But he had to break off his lectures 29th March 1521, because Emperor Charles V had ordered him to come to Worms, where he should give account for his writ-

---

[59] WA 5, 632,39–633,14.

[60] Ibid. 634,14–16.

[61] Ibid. 634,16–20.

[62] Von Schubert / Meissinger, Zu Luthers Vorlesungstätigkeit (1920); Bornkamm, Luther und das Alte Testament (1948) 229–34; idem, Das Jahrhundert der Reformation (1966), 11–36: "Martin Luther. Chronik seines Lebens"; idem, Martin Luther in der Mitte seines Lebens (1979); Brecht, Martin Luther (1986–87); Aland, Hilfsbuch zum Lutherstudium (1970). In the following the numbers in Aland's *Hilfsbuch* are indicated, which gives more informations about the edition of Luther's works here mentioned.

[63] WA 55I Glossen), II (Scholien); Aland, no. 593.

[64] WA 56, 3–154 (Glossen), 157–528 (Scholien); WA 57, 5–127 (Glossen), 131–232 (Scholien); Aland, no. 646.

[65] WA 57, 5–49 (Glossen), 53–108 (Scholien); Aland, no. 230.

[66] WA 56, 3–91 (Glossen), 97–238 (Scholien); Aland, no. 274.

ings on the Imperial Diet. Declared an outlaw, he was taken to the Wartburg, where he finished his exposition of Psalm 22. His second series of lectures on the Psalms (1-22), the *Operationes in Psalmos*,[67] were published from 1519 to 1521 successively. Later Luther said about this commentary: "The Hebrew grammar is not in there completely" and the theology is "still immature". But "the article of the justification and [the polemics] against the Pope are carried out faithfully". Luther thought that his second series of lectures on the Psalms was different from his first "at great length" (*longe lateque*).[68]

In the first stormy years after his exile in the Wartburg (4. 4. 1521-1. 3. 1522) Luther was occupied with a lot of new tasks, so that he could not perform his official teaching at the university. But privately he lectured a small circle of hearers on the Deuteronomy (1523-1524).[69] His teaching was joined with discussions. On the basis of these lectures he edited his commentary on the Deuteronomy, connected with a Latin translation (1525). The preface of this publication was directed to Georg von Polentz, being the bishop of Samland, who was an adherent of the reformation, working in Prussia.

Melanchthon, being a master of arts (*magister artium liberalium*), refused to carry on giving theological lectures, but he also did not wish to do a doctorate in theology, which was connected with the official obligation to give theological lectures. Luther, therefore, was forced to conclude that he should revert to his official teaching profession, and he did so by giving lectures on the Twelve Prophets from May 1524 to spring 1526.[70] On the basis of these lectures he published his translation and exposition of the scriptures Jonah,[71] Habakkuk (1526)[72] and Zechariah (1527)[73] in German. He interpreted the texts of these prophets in regard to the situation of their times as in relation to Christ. From 30th July to 7th November 1526 Luther lectured on the book of Ecclesiastes.[74] He had a great deal trouble with it. Though he was not satisfied with his work, he allowed his friends to send the text, written up afterwards, to be printed (1532). In his preface he proposed to call Ecclesiastes "The policy or economics of Solomon", because this scripture would comfort the statesman in all sorts of misfortune.[75] In the late summer 1527 plague arrived at Wittenberg, already having raged at other places. Therefore the university was transferred to Jena 1527 for a period of eight months. Luther remained at Wittenberg. After the teachers and students had returned gradually, he put into effect his plan of lecturing on the book of Isaiah. He started his course on 18th May

---

[67] WA 5. AWA 1I, Historisch-theologische Einleitung (1991); 2II, Psalm 1-10 (1981); Aland, no. 594.

[68] WA 5,2.

[69] WA 14, 545-744; Aland, no. 523.

[70] WA 13; Aland, no. 22 (Amos); 265 (Habakkuk); 269 (Haggai); 294 (Hosea); 312 (Joel); 347 (Jonah); 449 (Malachi); 505 (Micah); 529 (Nahum); 539 (Obadiah); 653 (Zechariah); 783 (Zephaniah).

[71] WA 19, 169-251; Aland, no. 348.

[72] WA 19, 337-435; Aland, no. 266.

[73] WA 23, 485-664; Aland, no. 654.

[74] WA 20, 1-203; Aland, no. 172.

[75] WA 20, 7,29ff; 8,19ff. Bornkamm, Martin Luther in der Mitte seines Lebens (1979) 500.

1528 and finished it on 22nd February 1530.[76] In the book of Isaiah Luther found more detailed prophecies about Christ and his kingdom than in any other scripture of the Old Testament. Nevertheless, besides the christological exposition, he did not neglect the historical interpretation. From 7th March 1530 to 22nd June 1531 Luther delivered lectures on "The Song of the Songs".[77] His course was interrupted from 3rd April to 8th November 1530, when Luther stayed at the Coburg. Here he was nearer to his theological and political adherents, who were present at the Imperial Diet at Augsburg. Being a heretic and outlaw, though protected by his sovereign, the elector of Saxony, Luther himself was not allowed to visit the Diet.

From 6th December 1530 to 15th May 1531 he was forced again to interrupt his lectures on the Canticum, presumably because he was ill. 1539 his disciple Veit Dietrich published an excerpt of Luther's exposition of "The Songs of the Songs", to which the Reformer had written a preface. He did not apply the Canticum to the earthly love between a husband and his wife, he applied it to obedience as a gift from God. After his lectures on the Epistle to the Galatians (3rd July to 12th December 1531)[78] Luther delivered a series of lectures on several Psalms from 5th March 1532 to 31st May 1535: on Psalm 2 (to 5th May),[79] on Psalm 51 (to 6th August),[80] on Psalm 45 (to 4th November),[81] on Psalms 120–134 (from 5th November 1532 to 27th October 1533)[82] and on Psalm 90 (with interruptions, from 26th October 1534 to 31st May 1535).[83] The exposition of the fifteen Psalms of Ascents (Psalms 120–134) was published 1540. Luther's last and most voluminous series of lectures was given on Genesis.[84] Soon after he had begun it, on 18th July 1535, the University was transferred again to Jena because of the plague. Also this time Luther remained at Wittenberg. From 3rd June 1535 to Advent 1543 he lectured on Genesis 1–37. From about the middle of January 1544 to Lent 1544 he continued his lectures, and from spring 1544 to 17th November 1545 he finished them. In his last lecture he said: "I cannot go on. I am feeble. Orate Deum pro me ["pray God for me"], that he may give me a good, blessed last hour".[85]

It is nearly impossible to characterize Luther's lectures on the book of Genesis in a few words. "They are an especially rich treasure of his theology as a whole and of his philosophy of life."[86] He does his philological work thoroughly, he has a critical look at Jewish exegesis, as far he is acquinted with it, and he is very interested in history. ERICH SEEBERG said that there is a strong "ecclesiastical positivism", being Luther's nominalistic heirloom, in the lectures on Genesis.[87] – In the years 1543 and 1544 Luther delivered two small lectures: from Advent 1543 to the middle of January 1544 on Isaiah 9,[88] and in Lent 1544 on Isaiah 53.[89]

---

[76] WA 31II, 1–585 (Nachschrift); WA 25, 79–401 (Bearbeitung); Aland, no. 306. Thyen, Untersuchungen zu Luthers Jesaja-Vorlesung (1964).

[77] WA 31II, 586–769 (771); Aland, no. 291; Thyen, Martin Luthers Hohelied-Vorlesung von 1530/31 (1977–78).

[78] WA 40I (1) 15–32, 33–688 (691); 40II, 1–48; Aland, no. 229.

[79] WA 40II (185) 193–312; Aland, no. 600.

[80] WA 40II, 313–470; Aland, no. 607.

[81] WA 40II, 471–610; Aland, no. 606.

[82] WA 40III, 15–475; Aland, no. 599.

[83] WA 40III, 476–594; Aland, no. 612.

[84] WA 42–44; Aland, no. 517.

[85] WA 44, 825,11 f.

[86] Köstlin / Kawerau, Martin Luther 2 (1903) 425.

[87] Seeberg, Studien zu Luthers Genesisvorlesung (1932) 106.

[88] WA 40III, 592–682; Aland, no. 206.

[89] WA 40III, 683–746; Aland, no. 207.

Luther never lectured more than two or three times weekly. Until the year 1518 he dictated his expositions to students on the basis of extensive preparations. Later he made only short notes, which are preserved partly, whereupon he extemporized in the lecture room, while the hearers wrote down his speech, according to their ability. Roerer's stenographic transcripts are the most reliable. They are recorded since 1526, when Luther lectured on the book of Ecclesiastes.

The Old Testament was the main object and by far the greatest part of Luther's exegetical work.[90] Only in the years from 1515 to 1518 was the New Testament to the fore. Luther owed essential features of his theology to the Old Testament: the strict conception of God, God's elevation above all human thinking, the severity of God's commandments, God's faithfulness in regard to his promises, the eminent importance of faith and trust in God, the affirmative answer to creation, the refusal of all forms of ascetic flight from reality, the realism of religious life, the theological character of history etc. Luther's exegesis of the Old Testament shows clearly, that only the bond with this part of our Canon can preserve the Christian faith from humanistic-idealistic misinterpretations of the New Testament, as we find them in the work of Erasmus and later in the work of ADOLF VON HARNACK.[91]

Further, it is worth mentioning that Luther does not make an essential distinction when he interpreted the Old Testament on the one hand in lectures and on the other hand in sermons and popular scriptures. Of course, Latin was the language of sciences, and naturally Luther presupposed certain special knowledge in the lecture room; but also his expositions, suitable for the general public, are founded on a reliable basis. Already in his first publication, the translation and interpretation of the Seven Penitential Psalms (1517), written in German, Luther referred to the Hebrew text in several cases and explained the different Hebrew words, used for the conception of 'sin'.[92] In whatever form he interpreted the Bible, always it was his intention, to enforce the word of God in the hearts of people. "So for Luther the pulpit ... became a sort of lectern in the presence of the laity, and the lectern a sort of pulpit in the presence of students."[93]

Finally, it should be mentioned that Luther preached very often on Old Testament texts. ALAND's *Hilfsbuch zum Lutherstudium* gives precise information.[94] The Pentateuch was a preferred subject. So he delivered 62 sermons on Genesis (1523–1524), 65 on Exodus (1523–1524), 32 on Leviticus and Numbers (1527–1528) and 17 on Deuteronomy (1529).

---

[90] Bornkamm, Luther und das Alte Testament (1948) 229–34.

[91] Von Harnack, Marcion (1924) 243: "Das A. T. im 2. Jahrhundert zu verwerfen, war ein Fehler, den die große Kirche mit Recht abgelehnt hat; es im 16. Jahrhundert beizubehalten, war ein Schicksal, dem sich die Reformation noch nicht zu entziehen vermochte; es aber seit dem 19. Jh. als kanonische Urkunde im Protestantismus zu konservieren, ist die Folge einer religiösen und kirchlichen Lähmung".

[92] Raeder, Die Benutzung des masoretischen Textes (1967) 62–68.

[93] Von Schubert / Meissinger, Zu Luthers Vorlesungstätigkeit (1920) 3.

[94] Aland, no. 683.

8. Luther's Views on the Old Testament

Luther's prefaces, contained in his German Bible, offer an excellent overview of his understanding the Old Testament, both as a whole and its parts.[95]

8.1. The General Importance of the Old Testament for Christians

In his "Preface on the Old Testament" (1523)[96] Luther begins by noting that certain people neglect the Old Testament, because they think that it deals only with bygone stories. They suppose that the New Testament is sufficient for Christians. As for the Old Testament, they are interested only in its spiritual or allegorical meaning. Luther names Origen and Jerome as authors of that opinion. As for his contemporaries, Luther seems to think of Erasmus, but he does not mention him. Erasmus regarded Origen as the best and most famous interpreter of the Bible.[97] Luther confronts the false opinion about the Old Testament, he has described, with the evidence of the New Testament, which refers to the promises of the Old Testament again and again. In the Old Testament, he says, "you will find the swaddling-clothes and the manger, wherein Christ is. They are simple swaddling-clothes, but the treasure, Christ, who is in there, is dear".[98]

But there is a difference between the Old Testament and the New Testament. As a whole the Old Testament is a "book of Law" (*Gesetzbuch*), whereas the New Testament is "a Gospel or a book of grace" (*Evangelium oder Gnadenbuch*).[99] However, there are in the New Testament also commandments, "in order to rule the flesh".[100]

8.2. Summary of the Pentateuch

After Luther has characterized the Old Testament as a whole, he gives a summery of the Pentateuch. The book Genesis tells about the creation and the origin of sin and death. Still before Moses had received the Law at Mount Sinai, the "seed of the wife" (cf. Gen 3:15) was promised to Adam and Eve. It is a prophecy of Christ, who will overcome sin and death. Luther assesses Genesis as "a nearly evangelical book".[101] In the book Exodus the Law of God is given to one nation only. Israel's destination is to enlighten the world and to reveal

---

[95] In the following Luther's prefaces will be quoted according to: *Luthers Vorreden zur Bibel* (ed. Bornkamm; 1967). They are to be found distributed in WA.DB 1–12. See also Luther, *Die gantze Heilige Schrifft Deudsch* (1545; ed. Volz), Anhang (p. 238*-41*): "Seit der Wittenberger Bibel von 1534 fortgefallene Luthertexte".

[96] *Vorreden* (1967) 31–46.

[97] Augustijn, Erasmus von Rotterdam (1986) 92.

[98] *Vorreden* (1967) 32.

[99] Ibid.

[100] Ibid.

[101] Ibid. 33.

the Law. The book Leviticus deals with priesthood. The office of the priests is "to make sin known and to expiate it in the presence of God".[102] The book Numbers shows that it is impossible to make people right and good by laws. The Law brings about only the sin and the wrath of God, as Paul says. After the sin of people has been punished, Moses repeats and explains the Law in the book Deuteronomy. Properly speaking, the Law "teaches nothing but faith in God and brotherly love".[103]

8.3. The Law of Moses

8.3.1. Content and Intention of the Mosaic Law

Luther gives detailed information about the Law, which Moses received from God.

First, Moses regulates Israel's entire life, even going into details. What is his intention? Evidently it is to prevent human reason from "choosing any [especial] work or inventing its own private devotions".[104] "Obedience, hanging on God's word, is the nobility and goodness of all activity."[105]

Second, Luther names three parts of the Law: Some prescriptions deal only with "worldly goods", some others with "external worship". They are transcended by "the precepts of faith and love". "Faith and love shall be the measure" of all the other commandments. Luther mentions several examples from the Old Testament, which show "that often kings, priests and chiefs put their hands into the Law, when faith and love demanded that they do so". Therefore Luther blames the Jews for keeping so strictly the letter of the Law. "They let perish peace and love rather than eating and drinking with Christians."[106]

Third, Luther asks the question, "why Moses mixes up the laws so untidily". The answer is: The Law of Moses is a figure of life, in which matters and duties are also mixed up. Further, whenever you find repetitions in the Law, you can conclude "that the works of Law are forced works".[107]

The main intention of Moses is "to reveal sin by Law and to ruin all the presumption of human ability". Therefore Luther calls the task of Moses an "office of sin and death" (*Sündenamt und Todesamt*). For Moses reveals what nobody knows of himself. "Man does not know by reason that unbelief and despairing of God is sin, moreover, he does not know that he has to believe in God and to trust him." Further, man does not know by reason "that evil inclination of the flesh and hatred of the enemies is sin". Those stirrings are taken as being natural. People believe "that it is sufficient to omit only externally evil

---

[102] Ibid.
[103] Ibid. 34.
[104] Ibid. 34 f.
[105] Ibid. 35.
[106] Ibid. 36.
[107] Ibid. 37.

actions".[108] But when man recognizes sin in his heart, he must despair of himself "and sigh and strive for the divine grace in Christ".[109]

At this point, when Christ comes, the Law, even the Decalogue, comes to an end, which does not mean that the Ten Commandments should not be fulfilled, rather it means that the "office of sin and death" comes to an end.[110] "For sin has been forgiven by Christ, God has been reconciled and the heart has begun to love the Law."[111] Thereupon Luther describes three classes of disciples of the Law.[112] The disciples of the first class despise the Law and lead a bad life. Those of the second try to fulfill the Law by their own ability, without the grace of God. They cannot endure that Moses reveals their sin. Therefore they put a veil over the Law. Finally, the disciples of the third class "see Moses clearly without any veil ... They understand the true meaning of the Law, [namely] that it demands impossible things" (cf. 2 Cor 3:3–5).[113] Therefore Moses himself says that his office of sin and death shall only last until Christ comes: "The Lord your God will raise up a prophet from among you like myself, and you shall listen to him" (Deut 18:15). According to Luther the promised prophet is Christ.[114]

8.3.2. Luthers' Understanding of the Old Testament Law in Relation to Scholasticism and to Radical Reformation

Luther differs in his understandig of the Old Testament Law both from the scholastic tradition and from the radical reformation. The scholastic theologians summarized the Old and the New Testaments under the general conception of 'law', speaking about "the old and the new Law". In contrast, for Luther the very nature of the Old Testament is Law, and the very nature of the New Testament is Gospel, that means: Good Tidings. The scholastic theologians regarded the "new Law" or the "evangelical Law", given by Jesus, as the "perfect Law", unlike the incomplete or imperfect "old Law", given by Moses. Thomas Aquinas says about that: "In the new Law [evil] stirrings are forbidden, whereas in the old Law they were not forbidden without any exception and explicitly, and also in such cases, in which they were to be forbidden, they were not to be punished."[115] According to Thomas the "old Law" is similar to "disciplinary rules for boys", whereas the "new Law" is like a law for the adult and "perfect men" of a polity.[116] Because the "new Law" is nearer to the supernatural goal of man, it can be fulfilled only by the power of supernatural grace,

---

[108] Ibid. 38.
[109] Ibid. 40.
[110] Ibid.
[111] Ibid. 41.
[112] Ibid. 41 f.
[113] Ibid. 42.
[114] Ibid.
[115] *Summa Theologiae*, II/1, q. 107 a. 4 (*Respondeo*): *In nova lege prohibentur interiores motus animi, qui expresse in veteri lege non prohibebantur in omnibus, etsi in aliquibus prohiberentur, in quibus tamen prohibendis poena non apponebatur.*
[116] *Summa Theologiae*, II/1, q. 107 a. 1 (*Respondeo*).

as Thomas often says. In contrast to Thomas, Luther emphasizes that the Law of Moses, demanding "faith in God and brotherly love", does not need to be perfected. In the Sermon on the Mount Christ himself explains the intention of Moses very clearly.[117]

But Luther also differs from radical groups in his own camp. In the first stormy years of the Reformation the ruin of old structures made many people look out for new forms, suitable for organizing public life. What seemed to be better in this situation, than going back to the commandments of Moses, as far as it was possible in a Christian community? That seemed to be a practical consequence of the reforming slogan *sola Scriptura*. Jakob Strauß, a preacher at Eisenach, and Wolfgang Stein, a court chaplain at Weimar, demanded to organize civil life according Holy Scripture. Specially they called for abolishing usury, because it is forbidden by the Law of Moses. The insurgent peasants also justified their program, referring both to the Old and to the New Testament in their *Twelve Articles* (1525). They would give only "the right tithe", which is demanded in the Law of Moses and confirmed by the Gospel, whereas they refused other taxes and services, not based on the Bible.[118] Luther's former colleague and fellow-worker, Andreas Bodenstein von Karlstadt, called for the abolition of images, because God says in the Decalogue: "You shall not make a carved image for yourself nor likeness of anything ... " (Exod 20:4).

8.3.3. The Law of Moses as the Sachsenspiegel of the Jews

Luther dealt with this urgent question preaching about Exodus 19–20 in August 1525. His sermon was published in 1526 under the title *Eine Unterrichtung, wie sich Christen in Mose sollen schicken* ("An instruction how Christians should prepare for [unterstanding] Moses").[119] Luther maintains: "The Law of Moses is not binding on Gentiles, it only applies to Jews".[120] For Luther the expression "Law of Moses" not only means the Old Testament prescriptions concerning worship, but means the entire Old Testament legislation, including the Decalogue. He proves it by the introductory words of the Ten Commandments: "'I am the LORD your God who brought you out of Egypt, out of the house of slavery' (Exod 20:2). The text shows us clearly that also the Ten Commandments do not concern us, because God did not bring us out of Egypt, he only brought the Jews out of Egypt".[121] In 1525 Luther published his book *Wider die himmlischen Propheten, von Bildern und Sakrament* ("Against the heavenly prophets, about images and sacrament").[122] It concerned Karlstadt primarily. Here we find the well-known words: "Therefore let Moses be the 'Sachsenspiegel' of the Jews, and do not disturb us Gentiles by Moses".[123] The *Sachsenspiegel* was an important collection of German

---

[117] WA 10III, 401,1; 400,22.
[118] Article 2, in: Renaissance, Glaubenskämpfe, Absolutismus (1976) 145f.
[119] WA 16, 363–93. 651; WA 24, 2–16, 739; 17 II, 516; Aland, no. 520.
[120] WA 16, 371,13.
[121] WA 16, 373,15–18.
[122] WA 18, 62–125, 792; Aland, no. 588.
[123] WA 18, 81,14f.

Laws, written around 1221/24. Nevertheless, Christians keep the Ten Commandments; but they do not do so, "because it was Moses, who enacted
them". The Ten Commandments are to be kept, "because they are implanted
into me and because Moses [that means: the Decalogue] agrees with nature.
The other statutes in [the Law of] Moses, which are not from nature, are not
kept by Gentiles and do not concern them".[124]

Thereupon Luther summarizes the threefold importance of Moses for
Christians:

1. It would be desirable that political leaders should rule "according to the
example of Moses"; but they are not obliged to do so. They have all the freedom to learn from Moses or not to learn in the field of political order.

2. Moses offers what nature cannot give, namely "God's promise and pledge
about Christ".

3. We read Moses "because of the fine examples of faith, love and the
cross". On the other hand, there are in [the books of] Moses "also examples
of ungodly people".[125]

For Luther the rest of the Old Testament Scriptures is nothing but an explanation and illustration of the Law of Moses. "They all together execute the office of Moses and repel the false prophets." They prevent people from [trust-
ing] in works and "make them stay in the right office and knowledge of the
Law", so that they bring people to Christ, as Moses does.[126]

At last, Luther mentions the "spiritual interpretation" of the Levitical laws.
All cultic activities and persons must be related to Christ, as the Epistle to the
Hebrews shows.[127]

8.4. The Poetic Books

Luther thinks that the book of Job[128] is very difficult, not because of its content but because of its style. The speech of this book is so powerful and marvellous, that it exceeds the style of all the other Old Testament scriptures. The
author of this work comes to the conclusion "that only God is righteous".[129]
Nevertheless, Job's friends are mistaken in affirming that God punishes him
because of his sin. On the contrary, Job led a blameless life in the presence of
God and among people. But the poet comforts us by showing that God makes
even his great saints suffer, especially when they are in heavy temptation. The
devout Job praises God, after he has heard about the loss of his goods and
about the death of his children. But when he himself is in mortal agony, he
thinks "that God is not God, but only a judge and an angry tyrant, who is acting by force and does not care about anybody's good life. This is the highest
matter in this book, which only those understand, who also experience and

---

[124] WA 16, 380,10–13.
[125] WA 16, 376,13; 381,9; 391,7–8. 10.
[126] *Vorreden* (1967) 43.
[127] Ibid. 43 f.
[128] Ibid. 47 f.
[129] Ibid. 47.

feel, what it means to suffer the wrath and judgement of God and [to feel] that his grace is hidden".[130]

Presumably the Psalms had the greatest influence on Luther's faith and prayer, more than any other text of the Old Testament. In his Preface to the Psalter (1528)[131] he opposes the Psalms to the medieval legends of saints. The legends make much noise about the deeds of the saints, whereas they say almost nothing about their words. The character of the Psalms is otherwise. Here the saints, and Christ in front of them, meet us, using words, which are the noblest expression of human life. Further, the Psalter does not speak about worthless things, it speaks about "the most important matters".[132] In the Psalms the saints talk with God himself. Luther says:

> There you [may] look into the heart of all the saints as into beautiful, joyful gardens, moreover, as into the heaven, [you see] fine, heartly, joyful flowers, blooming from all kinds of beautiful, happy thoughts about God and his favour. On the other hand, where do you find deeper, more lamenting, more pitiful words of sadness than in the Psalms of lamentation? There once again you look into the heart of the saints as into death, moreover, as into hell. How dark and gloomy is it there from seeing all forms of God's wrath! Likewise, when the saints speak about fear and hope, they use such words, that neither any painter could paint fear and hope with such [words] nor Cicero or any orator could illustrate them in that way.[133]

Luther felt joined together especially with the 118th Psalm, "the beautiful Confitemini", as he called it. He explained it at the Saxon fortress Coburg in 1530,[134] when the Imperial Diet was gathered at Augsburg. He writes in his Preface, addressed to Friedrich Pistorius: "It is my Psalm, which I love. Although the entire Psalter and Holy Scripture as a whole is beloved to me, because it is my only consolation and life, I have got into this Psalm especially, so that it must be called and [must] be my [own] Psalm. For often it rendered outstanding services to me and helped me out of a good many troubles, whereas emperors, kings, wise, prudent and saints not had been able to help me".[135]

In his scripture *Summarien über die Psalmen und Ursachen des Dolmetschens* ("Summaries about the Psalms and reasons of translating"),[136] published from 1531 to 1533, Luther divides the Psalter into five genres: Psalms of 1. prophecy, 2. teaching, 3. consolation, 4. prayer and 5. thanks. He regards the last genre as the noblest. "Therefore the Psalter is called 'Sepher Thehillim', that means: 'Book of praising or book of thanks'."[137]

In his Preface to the books of Solomon (1531)[138] Luther says about the Proverbs that they could be entitled "A book about good works". Here especially "the dear youth are educated to [keep] the commands of God".[139]

---

[130] Ibid. 47 f.
[131] Ibid. 51–55.
[132] Ibid. 52.
[133] Ibid. 53 f.
[134] WA 31I, 65–182. 588; Aland, no. 141.
[135] WA 31I, 66,17–22.
[136] WA 38, 8–69. 668; Aland, no. 595.
[137] WA 38, 17,24–18,6.
[138] *Vorreden* (1967) 59–62.
[139] Ibid. 59.

Ecclesiastes is "a book of consolation", because whenever man wants to live according to the doctrine of this book, "devil, world and the flesh balk, so one becomes tired". Therefore the "Preacher" teaches "to be patient and constant in obedience, against reluctance and affliction",[140] and to expect the last hour "in peace and happiness".[141]

The Song of Songs praises obedience as a gift from God. Luther does not understand this poetic work as praising sexual love, moreover, he explains it allegorically, saying: "At those places where obedience and good government are, exactly there God kisses and hugs his dear bride by his word, and this is the 'kiss of his mouth'" (cf. Cant 1:2).[142]

8.5. The Old Testament Prophets

8.5.1. The Old Testament Prophets are Helpful for Christians

Luther devoted his attention to the Old Testament prophets for a great part of his lectures. In his general Preface to the prophets (1532)[143] he, at first, assesses that certain people, regarding themselves as clever, do not know what to do with the prophetical books. That is because "the history and work" of the prophets are no longer known to us.[144]

The prophets are of great help for Christians. First, they proclaim "the kingdom of Christ".[145] Before entering it man has a great deal to bear.

Second, the prophets show "many and great examples concerning the First Commandment".[146] They lead people to the fear of God and to faith. They threaten the ungodly with terrible punishments, and they comfort the godfearing in all their vexations. More threats than promises can be found in the prophetical scriptures. That is because always the number of the ungodly is greater than the number of the godly.

Third, the prophets preach against idolatry. They do not mean that Israelites would have worshipped things of "simple wood and stone",[147] moreover, they take idolatry for the fact that the true God of Israel is worshipped without God's commandment according to one's own discretion by an invented service. Jeroboam I introduced such a high-handed service, having put up two golden calves, the one at Bethel, the other at Dan. The king did not say: "Behold, Israel, this is a calf"; rather he said: "This is your God, who brought you out of Egypt". By these words he professed the true God of Israel. Nevertheless, he did not wish that God should be worshipped at Jerusalem, at the Ark

---

[140] Ibid. 61.
[141] Ibid. 62.
[142] Ibid.
[143] Ibid. 66–74.
[144] Ibid. 66.
[145] Ibid.
[146] Ibid. 67.
[147] Ibid. 70.

of the Covenant, God should be worshipped at Bethel and Dan, at the golden calves.[148]

Thereupon Luther speaks of present idolatry. Idolatrous people refer to their "good intention" (*bona intentio*), as the scholastics use to say. In that manner, surely, they direct their confidence to their works, which they have chosen, and not to Jesus Christ exclusively. The prophets call this sort of people "adulteresses", because "they do not feel satisfied with their husband Christ, so that they run after other [lovers], too, as if Christ alone could not help [them]".[149] Luther allows also the Turks that they mean the true God, "who has created heaven and earth";[150] but they worship him in a manner which they themselves have chosen.

8.5.2. The Great Prophets

Who wants to understand the book of Isaiah[151] at first has to pay attention to its introduction (Isa 1:1) and in addition, to read the second book of the Kings and the second book of Chronicles, which give explicit information about the kings mentioned in Isa 1:1. Thereupon Luther offers a survey on the political geography of the Near East in the time presupposed in the book of Isaiah.

The content of this scripture consists of three parts, mingled with each other. In the first part sinful and idolatrous Israel is threatened with punishment from God, further, the kingdom of Christ is foretold. Isaiah prophesies the coming of Christ more clearly than any other of the prophets, telling in which way his mother Mary "should conceive and bear him with unhurt virginity" (cf. Isa 7:14), and how Christ should suffer and rise from the dead (cf. Isaiah 53).[152] The second part deals with Assyria and the emperor Sennacherib. When Sennacherib besieged Jerusalem, Isaiah proved to be a rock. He promised that Jerusalem was to be defended and saved from the threats of the mighty emperor. The fact that people believed Isaiah was a greater wonder than the deliverance of the city itself. The third part of the book deals with the Babylonian captivity. Isaiah consoles the exiles prophesying the end of the captivity and their returning to Jerusalem under the rule of Cyrus, king of Persia. Moreover, Isaiah keeps alive faith in the coming of Christ's kingdom. For Isaiah "Christ is the main point". The prophet aims at this "that the coming of Christ and [the coming] of the promised kingdom of grace and beatitude should not be neglected or lost by people and [nor become] futile because of great misfortune and impatience".[153]

Luther asks the question whether Isaiah himself or any other person compiled the prophetical speeches of his book, but he feels incapable of giving an answer.[154] Concerning the actual importance of this scripture Luther says:

---

[148] Ibid. 70f.
[149] Ibid. 71.
[150] Ibid. 72.
[151] Ibid. 75–80.
[152] Ibid. 77.
[153] Ibid. 78.
[154] Ibid.

"Really, it is full of comfort, reassuring sayings for every poor conscience and saddened heart. Likewise, there are sufficient sayings threatening the obstinate, arrogant and harsh minds of the ungodly, if they could be helped".[155]

Isaiah was a man despised by his nation. "For there was a habit with his people of deriding prophets and regarding them as mad." Luther thinks so concluding from 2 Kgs 21: 9–11. According to Jewish tradition he assumes that king Manasseh ordered Isaiah to be killed cruelly by means of a saw dividing his body.[156]

Luther says that the book of Jeremiah[157] can be understood easily, if attention is payed to the historical situation and the time of the prophet. There are three main issues dealt with in this scripture, but they are not separated strictly each from the other. First, Jeremiah preaches against the vices and idolatry of the Jews (to chap. 20). Second, he prophesies the destruction of Jerusalem and the Babylonian captivity. But in addition, he comforts people promising that the exile will return to Judah. "This is a main point [in the book] of Jeremiah."[158] The third important issue is the prophecy of Christ and his kingdom (especially Jeremiah 23 and 31). Jeremiah teaches the lesson "that people become the worse the nearer the punishment is".[159] Like Isaiah, so Jeremiah "was a pitiful, saddened man". He is told to be stoned by Jews in Egypt.[160]

Luther's first introduction to the book of Ezekiel[161] was written in 1532, his second[162] in 1542. The first introduction concerns the Babylonian captivity mainly, the second, being longer, deals with the kingdom of Christ. According to the text written in 1532, Ezekiel went into captivity voluntarily. He was called by God to comfort the captives, to preach against the false prophets and to prophesy the return of Jews to their land (chaps. 1–25). Chaps. 26–34 refer "to the other countries all around".[163] After that the prophet speaks "about the spirit and kingdom of Christ" (chaps. 35–38) and about Gog and Magog (chap. 39). In the rest of his book Ezekiel "rebuilds Jerusalem and comforts people by the promise that they will return home. But in spirit he means the eternal city, the heavenly Jerusalem, which the Revelation [of John] also speaks about".[164] In his second preface (1542) Luther has a critical look at the Jewish interpretation of Ezekiel's book. He understands the vision of the prophet (cf. chap. 1) as a "revelation of Christ's kingdom".[165] At the same time this vision gives to understand "the end and the destruction of synagogue and Judaism",[166] according to chaps. 8–9.

---

[155] Ibid. 79.
[156] Ibid. 79–80.
[157] Ibid. 80–83.
[158] Ibid. 81.
[159] Ibid. 82.
[160] Ibid. 81.
[161] Ibid. 83 f.
[162] Ibid. 84–91.
[163] Ibid. 84.
[164] Ibid.
[165] Ibid. 85.
[166] Ibid. 86.

Luther distinguishes two issues in Ezekiel's prophecy: first, the return of the Jews to Judaea under the rule of Cyrus, king of Persia; second, the foundation of the New Covenant by Christ in exactly this country. The Jews are mistaken, if they hope that after their return, which happened already under the rule of Cyrus, in a second time all the people will return to Canaan and restore the Mosaic order. The prophecy of Ezekiel has been fulfilled already by Christ. According to the promises of God Christ founded the New Covenant "in the same earthly Canaan and in the same earthly Jerusalem …, to which the Jews were brought back".[167] The spiritual and eternal kingdom of Christ does not abolish the transitory realms of the world, moreover, the kingdom of Christ exists "under them and within them".[168] The Jews harm themselves: Instead of desiring the New Kingdom, founded by Jesus, the Messiah, they desire their old realm to be restored.

In 1530 Luther published his preface to the book of Daniel.[169] He enlarged this introductory text in 1541. For Luther the book of Daniel was very important, because it gave him clear knowledge about the history of the world and of the Church.

At first Luther says that Daniel went to Babel some years before the destruction of Jerusalem; more information may be found about Daniel's life-time in 2 Kings 24 and 2 Chronicles 36. In the following Luther deals with the content of the book of Daniel in detail. In chap. 1 the godly life of the prophet is told. Chap. 2: Daniel is honoured highly, because he has interpreted the dream of the ruler. Luther relates the king's vision to four kingdoms, namely 1. of the Assyrians and Babylonians, 2. of the Medes and Persians, 3. of Alexander and the Greeks, 4. of the Romans. By the divided toes (Dan 2:41) the division of the Roman Empire is indicated. It was transferred from the Greeks to the Germans under the rule of Charlemagne in the year 800. Here Luther refers to the medieval idea of the 'translatio imperii'. The Roman Empire will be the last of all. "Nobody but Christ shall it break."[170] In chap. 3 "a great miraculous sign of faith" is told: "Three men were kept alive in a blazing furnace".[171] In chap. 4 is shown, how badly tyrants fare. They should not simply be endured, however, since it is necessary to intercede with God on their behalf, as Daniel did. In chap. 5 a tyrant refusing repentance is shown. Chap. 6: Daniel is thrown into the lions' pit. Here we may see "the fight and victory of faith by God's grace against all the devils and men".[172] Chap. 7 deals with the four kingdoms, mentioned already. In chap. 8 the history of the Jews is told during the time of the Diadochi until the death of Antiochus Epiphanes. Luther, following former interpreters, regards Antiochus as "a figure of the Antichrist".[173] According to chap. 9 the time, extending from the second year of the reign of king Darius Longimanus to the coming of Christ, is equal to seventy "weeks", each of them containing seven years, so that the total is 490 years. In addition, Luther refers to historians, who calculate a total of 483 years. Chap. 10 is a kind of preface to chap. 11 and gives detailed information about angels. Such reports cannot be found in other scriptures. In chap. 12 the Antichrist and the final age are described under the name of Antiochus. In 1541 Luther inserted an interpretation of Dan 11:36–12:12 in his preface. The passage he added concerns the Pope as the Antichrist and the signs of the last days. On the basis of Daniel's prophecy Luther is convinced "that the last day must be just around the corner, because now nearly all the signs announced by Christ and the Apostles Peter and Paul have already happened".[174]

---

[167] Ibid. 87.
[168] Ibid. 89.
[169] Ibid. 91–104.
[170] Ibid. 93.
[171] Ibid. 94.
[172] Ibid. 96.
[173] Ibid. 98.
[174] Ibid. 101.

Concluding his preface Luther says that "Daniel was an excellent, great man ... before God and [before] the world".[175] He was great before God, because he did not prophesy Christ more generally, as other prophets did, moreover he determined the time of Christ's coming exactly; and before the world Daniel was a great man, because nobody of Abraham's children was raised so highly as Daniel was.

8.5.3. The Twelve Prophets

Hosea,[176] living in the time of Jeroboam II, preached against idolatry and prophesied the kingdom of Christ, especially in chaps. 2, 13 and 14. Luther affirms that Hosea did not marry a prostitute. The truth is that he had both a legitimate wife and legitimate children. But "his wife and his children had to bear such a shameful name [i.e. "prostitute" and "children of a prostitute"] as a sign and punishment of the adulterous people, being full of spiritual adultery, that is idolatry".[177] Only some of Hosea's sayings and sermons are composed in his book.

Luther regards the prophet Joel[178] as a "kind and peaceful man". He is shown to be "highly famous" in the New Testament (cf. Acts 2:16–17). Chap. 1 of this scripture is directed against the Assyrians. Starting with chap. 2 Joel prophesies "the kingdom of Christ and the [coming of] the Holy Spirit". The expression "Valley of Jehoshaphat" (4:2) means "that all the world is called [to come] to the Christian Church, where they are [to be] judged and punished by the preaching that they all are sinners in the presence of God".[179]

Amos,[180] a contemporary of Hosea and Isaiah, announced the Assyrian captivity. His preaching is almost nothing but threatening. Because of that rightly his name is Amos, i.e. "who bears a burden".[181] Only in the last chapter he prophesies Christ and his kingdom.

Obadiah's[182] prophesying concerns the Babylonian Captivity. He comforts Judah, saying that people will return to Zion. The kingdom of Christ will not be only at Jerusalem, it will be everywhere.

Jonah,[183] son of Amittai, lived in the time of Jeroboam II. Preaching penitence among the Assyrians, he succeeded more than among his own people. He is an example "that all, who have the word [of God] amply, nevertheless despise it highly, and that those, who cannot have it, accept it willingly".[184]

Micah,[185] a contemporary of Isaiah, preaches about Christ using almost the same words in chap. 4:1–3 as Isaiah in 2:2–4. It seems as if "they had held

---

[175] Ibid.
[176] Ibid. 104 f.
[177] Ibid. 105.
[178] Ibid. 105–07.
[179] Ibid. 106.
[180] Ibid. 107 f.
[181] Ibid. 107.
[182] Ibid. 108 f.
[183] Ibid. 110 f.
[184] Ibid. 111.
[185] Ibid. 111 f.

talks about this [issue]".[186] Micah is the only one of the prophets, who names Bethlehem as the town, where Christ should be born. Because of that Micah was very famous in the time of the Old Testament, as the quotation in Matt 2:6 enables us to understand.

Nahum[187] prophesies the devastation of Israel and Judah by the Assyrians and the destruction of the Assyrian Empire after that. This prophet seems to have lived before Isaiah or in the time of Isaiah. The name Nahum means 'Comforter',[188] because this prophet announces that the enemies of God's people are to be destroyed. Nah 2:1 can be understood about the time of Hezekiah, after Sennacherib had withdrawn; nevertheless it is also "a general prophecy about Christ [by which is promised] that the Good News and joyful worship will remain in Judah".[189] The name of Nahum goes with that very well.

The name Habakkuk[190] means "'Herzer', or who hugs somebody to himself". Probably Habakkuk lived in the Babylonian Captivity, "perhaps about the time of Jeremiah".[191] He was a prophet of consolation, who comforted people foretelling Christ.

Zephaniah[192] lived in the time of Jeremiah. He prophesies the destruction of Judah and Jerusalem and foretells that people will be led away to Babylon and that also the surrounding nations are doomed to such a disaster. In chap. 3 he announces the "joyful and blessed kingdom of Christ", which will be spread "all over the world". Zephaniah "speaks about Christ more than many other great prophet".[193]

Haggai[194] is the first prophet living after the Babylonian Captivity. He scolds people, because they care for their goods and houses more than for rebuilding the temple and restoring worship. In chap. 2 Haggai prophesies the coming of Christ, "the consolation of the Gentiles". He indicates "that the kingdom and law of the Jews will come to an end and that all the kingdoms in the world will be destroyed and subjugated to Christ".[195]

Zechariah[196] helped Haggai to rebuild the temple and to gather the dispersed people. He is "one of the most comforting prophets".[197] In chap. 9 he foretells that Christ as a king, mounted on an ass, will move into Jerusalem, and in chap. 11 is prophesied that he will be sold for thirty pieces of silver and that Jerusalem will be ruined.

According to the opinion of the Jews Malachi[198] lived in the time of Ezra.

---

[186] Ibid. 111.
[187] Ibid. 112 f.
[188] Ibid. 112.
[189] Ibid. 113.
[190] Ibid. 113 f.
[191] Ibid. 114.
[192] Ibid. 114 f.
[193] Ibid. 115.
[194] Ibid. 116 f.
[195] Ibid. 117.
[196] Ibid. 117 f.
[197] Ibid. 117.
[198] Ibid. 118 f.

But Luther thinks that he preached "not a long time before Christ was born",[199] which he concludes from 3:1. He was the last of the prophets. He speaks about "Christ and the Gospel, which he calls a pure sacrifice in all the world" (cf. 1:11).[200] Further, he announces the coming of John the Baptist. People are blamed, because they refuse to give the tithe, and the priests, because they distort the word of God and pollute sacrifices and worship by repudiating their wives. Doing so, falsely they refer to the example of Abraham and Hagar.

8.6. A Critical Acknowledgement of Luther as an Interpreter of the Old Testament

We are separated from Luther's way of interpreting the Old Testament by the broad trench of historic-critical science, which came into being in the time of the Enlightenment and has proceeded until now. Modern interpreters have come to understand the scriptures of Old Israel against the background of their historical contexts. Because of this it is no longer possible to find texts in the Old Testament, which must be related to Christ directly as prophecies. Nowadays the Old Testament is comprehended as a collection of scriptures, reflecting the history, which Israel had with God; and this was a history which proceeded through centuries to the expectation of a great future: the kingdom of God. All the scriptures of the New Testament are based on the conviction that the great future to which the Old Testament is directed has begun already in Christ and will be completed by the coming of the kingdom of God. From this New Testament viewpoint we may say: As we cannot prove by reason that the Old Testament is fulfilled in the New Testament, so we cannot disprove it by reason. For this is not a matter of logical demonstration, as it was supposed in former times, moreover it is a matter of faith, given by the Holy Spirit. Therefore we have to make a distinction in regard to Luther's interpretation of the Old Testament: The Reformer's understanding of certain texts as explicit prophecies about Christ is no longer acceptable; but his principal standpoint cannot be given up, namely that the Old Testament is focused towards the New Testament. This principle is grounded on the very centre of Christian faith. With regard to this question we should not fail to see that Luther does not interpret the Old Testament solely within the narrow limits of prophetic christology; more and more in the course of the years he endeavoured to understand the Hebrew Bible also in the context of its own history.

Luther's exegesis of Psalm 111, written in 1530,[201] is an instructive example for that. As he thinks, this Psalm was composed, "so that the Jews could sing, when they were together or came together, in order to [eat] the paschal lamb".[202] But – so we may ask – if this Psalm has its place in the cultic customs of Old Israel, how can it be of any importance for Christians? Luther is con-

---

[199] Ibid. 118.
[200] Ibid.
[201] WA 31I, 384–426; Aland, no. 617.
[202] WA 31I, 396,24 f.

vinced that the historical interpretation of Old Testament texts does not exclude the Christian interpretation, moreover, the former demands the latter. Therefore Christians are allowed to relate this Psalm to their own pascha or Easter. According to the ecclesiastical year Easter is bound to a determined time, but according to its true nature, "it is not limited to that time, but it may be celebrated every day".[203]

Consequently, Luther's interpretation of Psalm 111 consists of two parts: First, he understands the Psalm historically as a ritual hymn of Old Israel; second, he applies the Psalm "to our Easter, that is to the Lord's Supper or the Holy Mass".[204] The Christian interpretation of the Psalm ist not only possible, moreover, it is necessary. "For even if the [modern] Jews would comprehend this Psalm, they would not be able to sing it, because they are deprived of nearly all the favours, which are praised in it."[205]

In the first interpretation, according to the historical meaning, Christ is not mentioned at all. But if both expositions are compared, a threefold result may be found:

1. It is the same merciful God, who reveals his grace, both in the Old and in the New Testament.

2. It is the same spirit of godliness, both in the Old Testament and in the Church of Christ.

3. Because the grace, revealed by Christ to mankind, is infinitely greater than all that God has done for Israel, Christians are under greater obligation to praise, serve and thank God, than Old Israel was.

9. Luther as a Translator of the Old Testament[206]

9.1. Translations of the Bible into German in the Time before Luther

Luther was not the first to translate the Bible into the German language. There was an old tradition the beginnings of which go back to the eighth and early ninth century. At that time Charlemagne caused parts of the Psalter and of the Gospels to be translated into the Franconian vernacular. The first complete translations of the Bible into German, being only a few, were made in the fourteenth century. Without any exception they are based on the Vulgate. They differ in regard to their linguistic quality.

The art of printing, invented by Johannes Gutenberg, made it possible for the first complete printed German Bible to be published by Johann Mentelin, a former assistant of Johannes Gutenberg, in Strasbourg in 1466. This Bible was based on an antiquated translation into German, made by an anonymous person in the region of Nuremberg about a hundred years before. Until 1518 Mentelin's German Bible was reprinted thirteen times.

The relatively large number of these printed German Bibles shows that there

---

[203] WA 31I, 397,23.
[204] WA 31I, 404,4f.
[205] WA 31I, 404,11–14.
[206] Luther, *Die gantze Heilige Schrifft Deudsch* (1545; ed. Volz) 33*-144* (introduction).

was a strong piety among laymen in Germany before the Reformation. But the high dignitaries of the Church looked with distrust on the translation of the Bible into the vernacular. Berthold von Henneberg, Archbishop of Mainz, and the highest ecclesiastical dignitary in Germany, enacted an edict about censorship on 22nd March 1485, wherein it is said that "the lack" of the German language does not permit the rendering of "the highest ideas of the Christian religion" without distortion and falsification. He regarded it as very dangerous that translations of the Bible into the vernacular were printed, so that everybody could buy them. "Who will make laymen, not learned people and the female sex, who have the books of Holy Scripture in their hands, find out the true understanding?" Therefore the archbishop forbad "to translate works of any science from the Greek, Latin oder another language into the German vernacular ... and to sell or to buy them" without an ecclesiastical licence.[207]

Erasmus of Rotterdam thought about the translation of the Bible into the vernacular differently from Berthold von Henneberg, Archishop of Mainz. But Erasmus was only interested in the New Testament, whereas he supposed the Old Testament to be obsolete in the Christian age. "I want", he says, "that all the women read the Gospel, that they read Paul's epistles, that [these scriptures] should be translated into all the languages".[208] But Erasmus himself did not translate any one text of the New Testament into the vernacular, never mind the Old Testament. The great humanist esteemed the classic Latin language more highly. Nevertheless, his edition of the New Testament in Greek (1516; [2]1519) was a work of great merit, which enabled Luther's translation from the original text into German.

All the German Bibles, printed before Luther's translation, are based on the Vulgate. Unlike his predecessors, Luther went back to the Hebrew and Greek texts; unlike Luther, the adherents of papacy preferred the traditional Latin text. Johann Eck, a determined adversary of the Reformer, being a professor of theology in Ingolstadt, was ordered by the dukes of Bavaria, Wilhelm IV and Ludwig X, to translate the Vulgate into German. His translation was published at Augsburg 1537. In his preface, dedicated to Cardinal Matthaeus Lang, Archbishop of Salzburg, Eck says, because "falsified Bibles" are used and read everywhere, he was ordered by the dukes of Bavaria "to translate the Bible according to the literal sense afresh, [in such a way] as the Bible is chanted, read, used and accepted by the holy Latin Church". Eck "should not care for the Jewish, Greek or Aramaic texts". According to the order of the dukes he had "to stay with our Latin Church. Doubtless this Church has the true, right text from the infallible master, [that is to say from] the Holy Spirit".[209] A few years later, in 1546, the Council of Trent declared the Latin text of the Vulgate to be a norm of ecclesiastical doctrine.[210]

---

[207] QGPRK 1, no. 781.

[208] Erasmus, Ausgewählte Werke (ed. Holborn; 1933) 142.

[209] Vom Spätmittelhochdeutschen (1963) XXI.

[210] Sessio IV, 8. Apr. 1546: Decretum de vulgata editione Bibliorum et de modo interpretandi s. Scripturam: sacrosancta Synodus ... statuit et declarat, ut haec ipsa vetus et vulgata editio, quae longo tot saeculorum usu in ipsa Ecclesia probata est, in publicis lectionibus, praedicationibus et expositionibus

9.2. The Time of Preparation

When Luther began to translate the Old Testament in 1522, he looked back upon some years of studying the Hebrew language. He had the textbook *De rudimentis hebraicis* by Johannes Reuchlin very early in his hands, not later than 1509. Luther's marginal notes to the *Four Books of Sentences* by Peter Lombard, written from 1509 to 1511, bear witness of his using the Rudimenta. When Luther lectured on the Psalms (1513–1515), he had already worked through the Rudimenta carefully. In the copy of a liturgical Psalter that he in 1513 caused to be printed for his lectures the titles of the Psalms differ from the Vulgate. They are "translated" by Luther "from more reliable sources": ... *titulis electissime translatis.*[211] The division of the verses, too, is reduced by Luther "to the old order".[212] Interpreting the Psalms in the *Dictata* he very often indicated that the Vulgate differs from the Hebrew text, to which he referred on the basis of different sources, both primary and secondary. The first work Luther published was his translation of the Seven Penitential Psalms into German, together with a commentary. Generally his translation was based on the Vulgate, but several times on the Masoretic text and on Latin word-for-word translations, mostly by Jerome and Reuchlin. Luther paid special attention to the consistant rendering of important Hebrew terms.

The first suggestion to translate the complete Bible into German was made by Melanchthon in 1521. In September 1522 *Das Neue Testament Deutsch* was published at Wittenberg. Translator, printer and year of publication were not named.

9.3. The Chronology of Luther's Translation of the Old Testament

Because the Old Testament is much more voluminous than the New Testament and its rendering from Hebrew into German is more difficult, Luther, at first, planned to publish his translation of the Hebrew Bible successively in three parts: First, the books of Moses, second, the historical books, third, the poetic and prophetic books.

The translation of the first part came on very well. Luther revised his manuscript together with Philipp Melanchthon and Matthaeus Aurogallus. The last-named was a teacher of the Hebrew language at the University of Wittenberg since the year 1521. The translation of the Pentateuch was published under the title of *Das Alte Testament Deutsch* by Melchior Lotter junior at Wittenberg around July 1523. In his preface Luther says: "Although I may not boast of having been successful in every respect, yet I dare say that this German Bible is clearer and more reliable in many passages than the Latin Bible".[213]

---

pro authentica habeatur, et quod nemo illam reicere quovis praetextu audeat vel praesumat (DS, no. 1506).

[211] WA 55I, 1,11 f.

[212] WA 55I, 1,7–11: *Versiculis singulis in numerum et ordinem veterem reductis.*

[213] *Vorreden* (1967) 45.

The second part of the Old Testament, containing the historical books from Joshua to Esther, was brought out by Lucas Cranach senior and Christian Doering at Wittenberg in January 1524.

The translation of the third part proved to be very difficult and went on for a longer time. The book of Job took a great deal of trouble, because of the author's ambitious and excellent style. Luther wrote to Spalatin on 23rd February 1524 that Job suffered from the attempts of the translators yet more than from the unsuitable consolations of his friends.[214] Six years later the Reformer remembered: "We, [that is to say] Philipp [Melanchthon], Aurogallus and I myself, struggled away with [the book of] Job, so that we hardly could complete three lines in four days".[215] The difficulties of translating this scripture forced Luther to change his timetable. He edited the poetic books (from Job to the Song of Songs) separately first. They were brought out by Cranach and Doering at Wittenberg in October 1524. A separate edition of the Psalter, translated by Luther, was published also by Cranach and Doering in September 1524.

Luther's lectures on the Twelve Prophets came in useful for his translation of these texts. So he edited his translation and interpretation of the books of Jonah (about March 1526) and Habakkuk (in January 1528), both published by Michael Lotter at Wittenberg. The translation of the book of Isaiah, which had begun in February 1527, was interrupted, because Luther was taken ill in the summer of that year, and, in addition, the plague forced the University of Wittenberg to move to Jena for eight months. By that Luther, remaining at Wittenberg, was bereft of his fellow workers Melanchthon and Aurogallus, who had fled from the threat. Because there was no way of foretelling how long the work of translating all prophetic scriptures would last, Luther edited the book of Isaiah for the time being separately in October (published by Hans Lufft, Wittenberg).

The book of Daniel followed about April 1530 (by Hans Lufft, Wittenberg). Luther wrote a detailed introduction to this scripture. He had felt the desire to translate the book of Daniel, because the Turks besieged Vienna in September and October 1529. Luther found a prophecy about Muhammad and the Turkish Empire in Dan 7:8 and a description of the Pope, being the Antichrist, and of the last days in Dan 11:36–12:12. In June 1530 Luther edited his translation and interpretation of Ezekiel 38–39 (by Klaus Schirlentz, Wittenberg). Also this publication was suggested by the threatened danger from the Turks. Finally, in 1532, the complete edition of the prophetic scriptures was brought out by Hans Lufft at Wittenberg.

Another edition of the prophetic books had been printed by Peter Schoeffer at Worms already in April 1527. The translation was made by Ludwig Haetzer and Hans Denck, living in Upper Germany. They felt in a direct manner inspired by God. On the one hand, the so-called "prophets of Worms" were influenced by Luther's translations, while, on the other hand, Luther corrected his own translation by the work of Haetzer and Denck.

---

[214] WA.DB 3, 249,15–17.
[215] WA 30II, 636,18–20 (*Sendbrief vom Dolmetschen*, 1530).

Now only the Apocrypha had to be translated. Luther's translation of the book The Wisdom of Solomon was published by Hans Lufft at Wittenberg in June 1529. Philipp Melanchthon and Caspar Cruciger assisted Luther with translating the Book of Sirach. This scripture was published by Hans Lufft at Wittenberg around the end of the year 1530. Because Luther was not in the best of health, the rest of the Apocrypha was translated by Melanchthon and Justus Jonas, the last of whom was professor of theology at Wittenberg. They finished their work in spring 1534.

But the first printed edition of Luther's complete German Bible was not in the original High German form, but in a Low German form. Luther's colleague Johannes Bugenhagen played an essential part in this version; according to the country of his origin he was called 'Doctor Pommeranus'. This edition was published by Ludwig Dietz at Luebeck in April 1534. It was not until September 1534 that Luther's original High German Bible left the press of Hans Lufft at Wittenberg. The translation of the Old Testament had lasted twelve years.

A complete German Bible was published by Peter Schoeffer at Worms already in 1529. It is called the "combined" Bible, because it contains texts of different translators. The New Testament and the first three parts of the Old Testament came from Luther, the prophetic books from preachers, working at Zurich, and the Apocrypha from Leo Jud of Zurich. The "combined" Bible was almost identical with the *Ganze Bibel*, published by Christopher Froschauer at Zurich in 1530.

Luther defined the *canon* of the Old Testament according to the Hebrew Bible, not according to the Septuagint and the Vulgate. He separated the Apocrypha from the Old Testament canon, remarking in the headline that "they should not be considered as equal to the Holy Scripture, although it is useful and well done to read them". Though Luther took over the conception of the Hebrew canon, he did not follow this in regard to the order of scriptures. There is the sequence in the Hebrew Bible: *Torah, Nebi'im, Kethubim* (Law, Prophets, Scriptures). The Vulgate, following the Septuagint, adds at the end of the Old Testament canon the prophetic scriptures (before 1–2 Maccabees) and Luther kept this order. It shows that the Old Testament reaches its high-point in prophecy, which announces the kingdom of God. Later, the New Testament affirms that the promises of the Old Testament are fulfilled in Jesus Christ.

As the preceding parts of Luther's translation, so his complete German Bible contained useful additions to the biblical texts: prefaces, marginal notes, references to parallel places and many pictures. Luther himself had given suggestions, as to how the Holy Scripture may be illustrated. At no time did the Reformer regard his translation of the Bible as finished. He was continuously active to improve it. More than the New Testament the Old Testament provided opportunity to improve the translation again and again. The emendations concerned not only typographical errors, but also choice of words, grammar, style, and – last but not least – questions of interpretation.

In October 1528 Luther edited the emended Psalter, published by Hans Lufft at Wittenberg. After a new, far-reaching revision, which lasted from January to March 1531 the Psalter took its final form. In his epilogue to this edition (published by Hans Lufft at Wittenberg, 1531) Luther says: "The preceding German Psalter [edited 1524, emended 1528] is nearer to the Hebrew language at many places. This [Psalter of 1531] is nearer to the German [language] and more far-off from the Hebrew [language]".[216]

There was a revision of the Bible from January to March 1534. It served the preparation of the first print of the complete German Bible at Wittenberg, 1534. This revision concerned the older parts of translation, especially Genesis. The last revision of the Bible – with the exception of the Apocrypha – went on from 17th July 1539 to September 1541. Johann Matthesius, living in Luther's house in summer 1540, tells about this work:

> Luther appointed the best men, who were available. They came together in the Doctor's house once a week for some hours before supper, namely D. Johann Bugenhagen, D. Justus Jonas, D. Creutziger [Cruciger], Magister Philipp Malanchthon and Matthaeus Aurogallus. Also Georg Roerer was present. He was a corrector [i.e. writing down the corrections]. Often foreign doctors and learned men came to this high work … When Doctor [Luther] had checked the [printed] German Bible … , he came into the consistorium, having his old [Latin] and his new German Bible and in addition the Hebrew text [with him]. Master [Herr] Philippus brought the Greek text with him, Doctor Creutziger the Hebrew Bible and the Chaldean text [i.e. the Aramaic paraphrases in the rabbinic Bible, published by Jacob ben Chajjim at Venice, 1524–1525]. The professors had with them their Rabbis [i.e. Jewish commentaries], D. Pommer [i.e. Bugenhagen] had before his eyes also the Latin text, he was very familiar with it. At first everybody had prepared for the text to be discussed and had looked into Greek, Latin and Jewish interpretations. Thereupon this president [i.e. Luther] proposed a text and asked one after the other, what each of them wanted to say about it, according to the nature of the language or according to the interpretation of old doctors. Wonderful and informative speeches were given about this work. M[agister] Georg [Roerer] has some of them written down.[217]

Roerer's records of revision, undertaken from 1539 to 1541, are still preserved.[218] The results of this revision had some influence already on the Bible, printed in spring 1541; in their completeness they were adopted into the Median-Bible of September 1541.

Luther's translation of the Holy Scripture is his own work, with the exception of the major part of the Apocrypha. Admittedly, his learned friends helped him, especially with revising his translation. Nevertheless, it was Luther, who decided on all questions of translation.

9.4. Luther's Method of Translating the Bible

Luther gave his views on translating the Bible in his scriptures *Ein Sendbrief vom Dolmetschen und Fürbitte der Heiligen* (1530)[219] and *Summarien über die Psalmen und Ursachen des Dolmetschens* (1531–1533).[220]

In his *Sendbrief vom Dolmetschen* Luther shows by examples that he follows three principles of translating:

---

[216] *Vorreden* (1967) 57.
[217] *Die gantze Heilige Schrifft Deudsch* (1545; ed. Volz) 105*.
[218] WA.DB 3, 167–577. 578–80; WA.DB 4, 1–278.
[219] WA 30II, 632–46. 694. See Aland, no. 161.
[220] WA 38, 8–69; Aland, no. 595.

1. In contrast to those, whom he calls *Buchstabilisten* (slavish adherents of the letter), Luther intends to render the original text in the best possible German.

2. If that is not possible without shortening the full meaning of the original text, Luther retains the unusual and foreign style of biblical speech.

3. Luther's dominant principle is not to render words, but to express the "meaning" and "matter"[221] of a text. Therefore Luther's translation of the Bible is its interpretation.

9.4.1. Free Translation

There are many places in Luther's translation of the Old Testament, which might give the impression to the German reader, as though the biblical authors were persons speaking German.

For instance, Jer 17:9 reads: עָקֹב הַלֵּב מִכֹּל וְאָנֻשׁ הוּא מִי יֵדָעֶנּוּ, translated from word to word: "The heart is most deceitful and sick, who will know it?" The Vulgate gives the version: *Pravum est cor omnium, et inscrutabile; quis cognoscet illud?* Luther renders the vers: *Es ist das Herz ein trotzig und verzagt Ding. Wer kann es ergründen?* ("The heart is a contrary and despondent thing. Who can fathom it?"). Luther interprets these words in a marginal note: *In German we would say: "Es ist ein verzweifelt und bös Ding um ein Herz. Es kann weder Gutes noch Böses ertragen"* ("A heart is a desperate and bad thing. It can endure neither goodness nor badness"). Luther describes the instability of the human heart.

Luther translates Ps 23:5 as follows: *Du salbest mein Haupt mit Oel, und schenkest mir voll ein.* This verse has a rhythm, which sounds like music: *Du sálbest mein Háupt mit Óel, und schénkest mir vóll eín.* Luther's translation of the Bible, especially of the Psalms, appeals more to hearing ears than to seeing eyes. The Hebrew text reads: דִּשַּׁנְתָּ בַשֶּׁמֶן רֹאשִׁי כּוֹסִי רְוָיָה, and Jerome translates in his *Psalterium Hebraicum*: *Impinguasti oleo caput meum: calix meus inebrians.* He renders the Hebrew word דִּשַּׁנְתָּ into the perfect time. Reuchlin affirms in his Rudimenta, that there are three tempora in the Hebrew language: "Praesens [פּוֹעֵל], praeteritum [פָּעַל] et futurum [יִפְעַל]".[222] But that is the Latin conception of time, not the Hebrew. Why does not Luther follow Jerome, all the other Latin translators and Reuchlin by translating: *Du salbtest* or *Du hast gesalbt?* In contrast to them he renders the verb in the present. By that he will say that the grace of God that the Psalm describes, is not a matter of past time, moreover God's grace is definitely present. Luther emphasizes the actuality of the word of God in his translation.

The second part of the verse reads translated word-for-word: "My cup [is] saturation". Here Luther detaches himself from the Hebrew letter completely: *(Du) schenkest mir voll ein.* The grammatical subject is not a 'cup', but God, addressed by the psalmist in the second person: *Du*, and the predicate is not the abstract noun 'saturation', it is a verb, expressing God's merciful doing, who gives his abundant grace to the psalmist.

9.4.2. Literal Translation

For the most part Luther's translation of the Bible is looked at by linguists from the viewpoint of his masterly German. But it is not less remarkable that he also retains the strange features of Hebrew style, whenever he considers it necessary. This is an important matter for both theologians and linguists. Each of the languages implies a sort of petrified philosophy, analysing the structures

---

[221] BoA 4, 187,35–188,1.15–16. (WA 30II, 640f.).
[222] Reuchlin, *De rudimentis*, 585.

of reality in its own way. For instance, the conception of time is different in the Semitic languages from the Indo-European. By that every language has its limits in interpreting reality. Therefore a language may be enriched and enlarged by adopting elements of another.[223] Luther was convinced that certain things could not be expressed in German as completely as in Hebrew.

For instance, the Hebrew language uses the word בָּשָׂר 'flesh' in order to name the totality of living things on the earth, both animals and human beings. Originally, the German word *Fleisch* cannot be used with that wide meaning; usually we understand 'flesh' only as a material element. But Luther loved the Hebrew word בָּשָׂר. Man is hungry, thirsty, in one word: pitiful, and "flesh is the most common ... form in all of us".[224] This is a humble anthropology. In contrast to Aristotle, Luther calls 'flesh' the form of man. Aristotle would say that the soul is the essential form of man and that 'flesh' is only the matter to be formed. Luther retained the word 'flesh' in his translation, differing from the German (and English) mode of speaking: Ps 56:5: *Was sollte mir Fleisch tun?* (NEB: "What can mortal men do to me?"); Ps 65:3: *Darum kommt alles Fleisch zu dir* (NEB: "All men shall lay their guilt before thee"); Isa 40:10: *Alles Fleisch miteinander wird es sehen* (NEB: "all mankind together shall see it"); Isa 49:26: *Alles Fleisch soll erfahren, daß ich bin der HErr* (NEB: "all mankind shall know that it is I, the Lord").

Often the Hebrew language names a thing or an organ in order to describe its effect or function. The reason seems to be that the vocabulary of the Hebrew language mostly focuses on radicals of verbs, so that we may say: The genius of the Hebrew language does not ask: "What is this thing?" Rather he asks: "What does this thing do?" In Hebrew there seems to be an integral and 'dynamic' view of reality.[225] Luther retains this peculiarity of the Hebrew style in his translating.

German *Same* ("sperm") means descendants: Ps 55:13: *Sein Same wird das Land besitzen* (NEB: "his children after him inherit the land"); Ps 37:28: *Der Gottlosen Same wird ausgerottet* (NEB: "the children of the wicked [are] destroyed"). *Arm* means powerful doing: Isa 51:5: *Die Inseln ... warten auf meinen Arm* (NEB: "for me ... islands shall wait"); Jer 17:5: *(Verflucht sei der Mann, der Fleisch für seinen Arm hält* (NEB: "the man ... who leans for support on human kind"). Likewise, the word 'hand' describes the action and power of the hand: Ps 95:4: *Wir sind Schafe seiner Hand* (NEB: "we are ... the flock he shepherds"); Dan 8:7 speaks of the he-goat's hand: *Niemand konnte den Widder aus seiner Hand erretten.* Here the contemporary translators Claus Cranc (1530), the "Prophets of Worms" (1527) and the preachers of Zurich (1529) say *Gewalt* instead of *Hand*[226] (NEB: "there was no one to save the ram").

---

[223] Weisgerber, Das Menschheitsgesetz der Sprache (1964) 174: "Gegenüber der unvermeidlichen Einseitigkeit einer einzigen Sprache bringt die Vielheit der Sprachen sowohl eine Bereicherung durch eine Vielheit von Sehweisen, wie eine Abwehr der Überbewertung einer Teilerkenntnis als der einzig möglichen".

[224] WA 5, 270,36–38 (= AWA 2II, 482,13–15). Cf. Tresmontant, Biblisches Denken (1956) 99–130 ("Grundzüge der biblischen Anthropologie"), esp. 99–100, 103 f.

[225] Cf. Boman, Das hebräische Denken (1959) 18–103; for critical assessment of his views see i.a. J. BARR, *The Semantics of Biblical Language* (Oxford 1961) 72–82; idem, *Biblical Words for Time* (2nd rev. edn.; London 1969) 136f, 144–47; cf. further BOMAN's response: *Sprache und Denken. Eine Auseinandersetzung* (Göttingen 1968; offprint, at the same time, of the 5th edn. of *Das hebräische Denken*, pp. 194–231). Luther says "that it is necessary to observe verbs more than nouns in the Holy Scriptures in order to understand the spirit" (*in sacris letteris oportere magis observari verba quam nomina pro intelligendo spiritu*), AWA 2II, 529,2–4.

[226] Vom Spätmittelhochdeutschen (1963) 104–05.

9.4.3. Translation as a Form of Interpretation

As we are taught by old and new grammar books, the Hebrew language has no comparative and superlative forms. The comparative is, as linguists say, "paraphrased" by the preposition מִן ('from'). Let us see how translators proceed with comparisons in Hebrew. The original text of Ps 118:8 reads: טוֹב לַחֲסוֹת בַּיהוָה מִבְּטֹחַ בָּאָדָם. The Septuagint (117:8) reads: ἀγαθὸν πεποιθέναι ἐπὶ κύριον ἢ πεποιθέναι επ' ἄνθρωπον. The Vulgate follows the Septuagint: *Bonum est confidere domino quam confidere in homine*. This is a barbaric word-for-word translation. In the *Psalterium Hebraicum* Jerome renders the sentence into good Latin using the comparative form: *Melius est sperare in domino quam sperare in homine*. The New English Bible reads likewise: "It is better to find refuge in the Lord than to trust in man". In contrast to that Luther does not use the comparative form. He renders the verse as an antithesis: *Es ist gut auf den HErrn vertrauen und nicht sich verlassen auf Menschen*. This is not only a translation, moreover it is an interpretation. But is it grammatically correct? I think so. The scheme of positive, comparative and superlative forms is based on the distinction between the categories of quality and quantity. For instance, the degrees of comparison 'good', 'better', 'best' presuppose the identity of quality and the difference of quantity. But this is not the Hebrew conception of comparison. The Hebrew language does not know a constant quality in degrees of different quantity, morever it demands a decision on two things: which of them is really good: trusting in man or seeking refuge in God? From the standpoint of trusting in man there cannot be any doubt that only seeking refuge in God is really good. In addition, it should be mentioned that unlike Jerome and according to the Hebrew text Luther uses two different verbs: *vertrauen* ('to trust') and *sich verlassen* ('to depend on'). Also by that he emphasizes that 'trusting in God' and 'depending on man' are quite different things.

9.4.4. Luther's Scepticism about Rabbinical Philology

Luther was not willing to trust the Rabbis in all questions of grammar. He doubted that they had kept the original understanding of the Hebrew language and text. Therefore he often started with the subject of the text and then tried to prove his interpretation philologically. When the German Bible was revised, Johann Forster, an expert on the Hebrew language, sometimes tried to disprove Luther's translation saying that the Rabbis understood the text in another sense, whereupon Luther answered: "Well, can you make the text by grammar and characters of vowels so that it agrees with the New Testament?" Then usually Forster had to realize that Luther's translation was acceptable by vocalizing the consonants differently from the Masoretic text.[227] In the autumn of his life Luther regretted that in his role of a translator he had not resisted rabbinical exegesis enough. Therefore he sought to express the Old Tes-

---

[227] BoA 8 (*Tischreden*), 320,26–30 (no. 5533).

tament witness about Christ yet more clearly in his scripture (1543) *Von den letzten Worten Davids* (2 Sam 23:1–7).[228]

> Gen 4:1 may be cited here as an example of Luther's anti-rabbinical way of translation. According to the Masoretic text the New English Bible renders the words of Eve as follows: "With the help of the LORD I have brought a man into being". The Hebrew text reads: קָנִיתִי אִישׁ אֶת־יְהוָה. Luther translates: *Ich habe den Mann des Herrn*. He understands these words as a testimony of Eve's belief into the coming saviour, being God and Man. Luther comprehends the preposition אֶת as a nota accusativi, as his marginal note shows: *Da hab ich den HERRN, den Mann,* [...] *der dem Satan oder [der] Schlange den Kopf zertreten soll* ("There I have the LORD, the man, who shall strike Satan's or the Serpent's head"). Nobody had translated Eve's words in this way before Luther.

9.4.5. Philosophical and Theological Conditions of Luther's Bible Translation[229]

The characteristic of Luther's translation of the Old Testament may be recognized more clearly if we have a look at Jerome, his famous predecessor in this work. This Father of the Church wrote to Pammachius in the year 396: "I confess frankly that I translate Greek texts according to their meaning, and not word for word, unlike my translating the Holy Scriptures. For in these even the order of words is a mystery".[230] For his method of translating non-canonical Greek texts Jerome refers to Cicero. After he had gained a deeper experience by translating the Bible (391–406), in the year 403, Jerome wrote to Sunnia and Fretela, two eager students of the Holy Scriptures, men of Gothic origin, that he payed attention to the melodious sound and the peculiarity of the Latin language, into which he had rendered the Bible. But always he was careful not to damage the meaning of a text.[231] It is evident that to a certain degree Luther followed in the footsteps of Jerome, whenever he strove to render the meaning of biblical texts without clinging to their letter. But it seems that more than Jerome Luther took into account the peculiarity of the language into which he translated the Bible, and there are two reasons for that.

First, Jerome as well as Origen and Augustine regarded the Hebrew language as holy, because it is the original language of mankind, taught by God himself,[232] used already in paradise and later by the Patriarchs, Moses, the prophets and the Son of God. In consequence other languages must be infer-

---

[228] Aland, no. 151. WA 54,28–100. *Darumb hab ich zum Exempel fur mich genommen* [mir vorgenommen], *die letzten wort David auszulegen, nicht wie sie verdeudscht sind, da ich den anderen allen gefolget habe, damit ich nicht allein klug wäre. Itzt* [Jetzt] *will ich eigensinnig sein und niemand folgen, denn* [als] *meinem geist* (31,2–5. "Therefore I will give an example by interpreting David's last words, not as they have been translated, when I did as all others, so that not I alone should be wise. Now, I will be stubborn and follow nobody except my own spirit").

[229] Meinhold, Luthers Sprachphilosophie (1958).

[230] CSEL 54, 508,9–13 (ep. 57, ch. 5, *Ad Pammachium de optimo genere interpretandi*).

[231] CSEL 55, 275,19–21 (ep. 106, ch. 55).

[232] Reuchlin, *Septem psalmi poenitentiales* (preface to Jacob Lemp) 7: The Psalter is given in the Hebrew language, *in illa ipsa lingua omnium linguarum matrice, ut scribit Hieromymus, quam sanctam vocat, quam Origenes divinitus esse traditam asserit, quae sola est ante confusionem linguarum orta, quae nihil impuritatis continet, ut Moses Aegyptius dilucide tractavit.* See also Augustine, *De civitate Dei*, 16, 11; 18, 39.

ior, compared with the Hebrew. For this reason it is difficult to translate the Old Testament into another language in a spirit of freedom.

For Luther only the word of God is holy, and not a language in its own right. Moreover, it is the word of God which sanctifies languages to be its "vessel".[233] The German language is a sanctified language, and therefore it is of the same dignity as the Hebrew and the Greek languages, since it has also become a vessel of God's word. Luther understands his translation of the Bible as a sanctification of the German language by the word of God. The freedom, Luther uses as a translator of the Holy Scriptures, is based on his theology of God's word in languages of mankind.

Second, there is yet another reason, why Luther translated the Bible in a spirit of freedom. Jerome did not know an "inner canon" of the Bible, that is to say: the word within the words. For Luther this "inner canon" is the Gospel of Jesus Christ as a criterion or *lydicus lapis*, in order to examine and scrutinize all scriptures. Therefore, at the same time Luther's translation was an interpretation having the Gospel of Christ as its centre.

9.4.6. Did Luther 'Christianize' the Old Testament?

In his book *Luther und das Alte Testament* H. Bornkamm deals with the issue: *Luthers Übersetzung des Alten Testaments ins Christliche* ("Luther's translation of the Old Testament into a Christian [understanding]").[234] Bornkamm speaks of a "*Verchristlichung* [Christianization] *des Alten Testaments*".[235] He explains it by many examples, showing that for Luther faith, justification, God, Christ, salvation, grace, beatitude, holiness, God's word, preaching etc. have the same meaning, both in the Old and in the New Testament. Nevertheless, Bornkamm thinks that it is almost impossible to describe the process of the *Verchristlichung* exactly: "So to speak, Luther injected the blood-stream of the Old Testament with the Gospel, so that it spread out into its finest branchings almost by itself".[236] These words might be understood just as if the Christian feature of Luther's translation of the Old Testament would be something foreign to it, introduced artificially by Luther. Admittedly, Luther translated and interpreted certain passages of the Old Testament in a christological sense, which was not the original. But apart from that we are allowed to ask the question, whether it is right – so to speak – to lock up the message of the Old Testament in the limits of its original meaning, scrutinized by historians. The Old Testament ist not a museum, but a living thing, going through centuries and winning new horizons of meaning and understanding. For example, we do not know, who was the first to pray: "My God, my God, why hast thou forsaken me?" (Ps 22:1). But there were many, who followed in his footsteps, and the greatest of them was Jesus (if the critical historians would permit him to have prayed so).

---

[233] WA 15, 37,27–38,6 (*An die Ratsherrn*).
[234] Luther und das Alte Testament (1948) 185–208.
[235] Ibid. VIII.
[236] Ibid. 185.

Therefore, Luther's translation (and likewise his exegesis) may be looked at from two perspectives: On the one hand, it is qualified and limited by conditions of a time, when the method of investigating the Bible in a historical and critical way had not yet arisen. On the other hand, his translation of the Bible is based on the principal conviction, being as old as Christianity itself, that the Old Testament comes to its fulfilment in Jesus Christ.

Chapter Eighteen

The Exegetical and Hermeneutical Work of John Oecolampadius, Huldrych Zwingli and John Calvin

By Peter Opitz, Zurich

I. John Oecolampadius

Sources: There is no criticial edition of the works of Oecolampadius. Old editions are available on IDC-Mikrofiche: *Reformed Protestantism. Sources of the 16th and 17th centuries on microfiche.* 1. *Switzerland. A. Heinrich Bullinger and the Zurich Reformation* (ed. by F. Büsser. EPBU 346/1–389/1; Zug: Inter Documentation Company); *Briefe und Akten zum Leben Oekolampads: zum 400jährigen Jubiläum der Basler Reformation* 1–2 (ed. by E. Staehelin; Leipzig 1927–34; repr. New York: Johnson 1971). – Erasmus: *Ratio seu compendium verae theologiae* (1519) (*Ausgewählte Schriften* 3; ed. W. Welzig; Darmstadt: Wissenschaftliche Buchgesellschaft 1967).

Bibliographic and reference works: E. Staehelin, *Oecolampad-Bibliographie. Verzeichnis der im 16. Jahrhundert erschienenen Oekolampaddrucke* (2nd edn.; Nieuwkoop: B. De Graaf 1963); U. Gäbler, "Oekolampad, Johannes (1482–1531)", TRE 25 (1995) 29–36; W. Troxler, "Oekolampad, Johannes", BBKL VI (1993) 1133–50.

General works: H. R. Guggisberg, "Johannes Oekolampad", *Gestalten der Kirchengeschichte* 5. *Die Reformationszeit* 1 (ed. M. Greschat; Stuttgart: W. Kohlhammer 1981) 117–28; K. Hammer, "Der Reformator Oekolampad (1482–1531)", *Reformiertes Erbe* 1 (FS for Gottfried W. Locher; *Zwing.* 19/1; ed. H. A. Oberman / W. Saxer / A. Schindler / H. Stucki; Zürich: Theol. Verlag Zürich 1992) 157–70; G. Nordholt, *Via regia. Die Theologie Oekolampads als Lehre von der Kirche* (Diss. Maschinenschrift; Münster: Westfälische Wilhelmsuniversität 1954); E. G. Rupp, "Johannes Oecolompadius: The Reformer as Scholar", *Patterns of Reformation* (London: Epworth press 1969) 3–46; E. Staehelin, *Das thelogische Lebenwerk Johannes Oekolampads* (QFRG 21; Leipzig: Heinsius 1939).

1. Oecolampadius in the Context of the Renaissance

Studies: H. R. Guggisberg, *Basel in the Sixteenth Century. Aspects of the City Republic before, during, and after the Reformation* (St. Louis, MO: Center for Reformation Research 1982); K. R. Hagenbach, *Johann Oekolampad und Oswald Myconius die Reformatoren Basels* (Elberfeld: R. L. Friderichs 1859); K. Hammer, "Oekolampads Reformprogramm", *ThZ* 37 (1981) 149–63; O. Kuhr, *"Die Macht des Bannes und der Busse". Kirchenzucht und Erneuerung der Kirche bei Johannes Oekolampad (1482–1531)* (Berner und Basler Studien zur historischen und systematischen Theologie 68; Bern e.a.: Peter Lang 1999); E. L. Miller, "Oecolampadius: the unsung hero of the Basel Reformation", *IliffRev* 39 (1982) 5–25; A. Moser, "Die Anfänge der Freundschaft zwischen Zwingli und Oekolampad", *Zwing.* 10 (1958) 614–20; E. Staehelin, *Das Buch der Basler Reformation* (Basel: Helbing 1929); idem, "Erasmus und Oekolampad in ihrem Ringen um die Kirche Jesu Christi", in: *Gedenkschrift zum 400. Todestag des Erasmus von Rotterdam* (ed. die Historische und Antiquarische Gesellschaft zu Basel; Basel: Braus-Riggenbach 1936) 166–82.

John Oecolampadius (1482–1531), born in Weinsberg, is generally regarded as the Reformer of Basel. As pastor at St. Martin and since 1529 at the Cathedral, he was as preacher and organizer of the Church decisively involved in carrying out and securing the Reformation in Basel. His influence in church politics was felt beyond Basel through his participation at the Disputations of Baden (May 1526) and, together with Zwingli, of Berne (January 1528), at the Marburg Colloquy (1529) and, together with Martin Bucer and Ambrosius Blarer, on the draft of the Church Order for Ulm (1531).[1] Nevertheless, Oecolampadius was no agitator of reform, rather he remained a scholar throughout his life; on the basis of his knowledge of the Biblical languages and the Church Fathers he was widely respected.

He began his theological studies after earning his master's degree at the University of Heidelberg. Consecrated to the priesthood, he became preacher in his home town. From 1513, however, he resumed his university studies and devoted himself to studies of Greek and Hebrew at Tübingen, Stuttgart and Heidelberg. During that time he came into contact with Melanchthon and Reuchlin, and began a friendship with his first biographer, Wolfgang Capito. Oecolampadius's first printed works reflected the deep roots of this humanist scholar in a 'devout', ethical and ecclesiastically accentuated Christ mysticism,[2] which also left traces in his later reformation writings.[3] After his friend Capito was called to become cathedral preacher in Basel, he followed him there in 1515 and worked on the printing of Erasmus's *Novum instrumentum*.[4] He composed an afterword to this monumental work, and was also active as advisor to Erasmus in the Hebraistic explanations.[5] In the subsequent years he continued his theological studies which resulted in the obtaining of his doctorate in theology in Basel in 1518 and worked on the production of the indexes of Erasmus's nine-volume edition of Jerome. Moreover, he worked to deepen his linguistic knowledge and continued his translations of the Church Fathers. In December 1518 he became preacher at the cathedral of Augsburg. After a period of self-examination and reading of Luther's writings, culminating in a stay in the Brigittine monastery at Altomünster (1520 until January 1522), Oecolampadius decided for the Reformation.[6] He worked from November 1522 to his death, 24 November 1531, in Basel, where he held lectures at the university, as he was entitled to do on the basis of the doctorate he had earned there. In addition to the continuation of his translation of Chrysostom, Oecolampadius began in April 1523 a series of lectures on the Book of Isaiah, which he continued after being named professor for Old Testament in June, along with Conrad Pellican.

2. Oecolampadius's Exegesis of the Old Testament

Studies: W. De Greef, "Johannes Oecolampadius (1482–1531)", *"De ware Uitleg". Hervormers en hun verklaring van de Bijbel* (Leiden: J. J. Groen en Zoon 1995) 117–34; A. Demura, "Two Commentaries on The Epistle to the Romans: Calvin and Oecolampadius", *Calvinus Sincerioris Religio-*

---

[1] See Briefe und Akten 2 (1971) 650f.652–62 [Nr. 920.922].

[2] On this, see Staehelin, Oekolampad (1939) 20–93 (still the classical biography).

[3] See *Declamationes de passione et ultimo sermone … domini nostri Jesu Christi*, Staehelin, Oekolampad-Bibliographie (1963) Nr. 2; and Staehelin, Oekolampad (1939) 43–54. What Staehelin calls "Wimpfelingsche Reformbewegung" is not definitely distinguishible from a "christian humanism", see Staehelin, Oekolampad (1939) 15–93; also: Briefe und Akten 1 (1971) 17–22 [Nr. 10–14].

[4] See Briefe und Akten 1 (1971) 114 [Nr. 76]; concerning his relationship to Erasmus, see Briefe und Akten 1 (1971) 32–34 [Nr. 27].

[5] Staehelin, Oekolampad (1939) 65f. See Briefe und Akten 1 (1971) 24f. 26–28 [Nr. 17; 21].

[6] On this, see his letter to Rhenanus (?) from February 1522 (Briefe und Akten 1 (1971) 168 [Nr. 119]).

nis Vindex. Calvin as Protector of the Purer Religion (ed. W. H. Neuser; SCES 36; Kirkville, MO: Sixteen Century Journal Publishers 1997) 123–37; H. O. OLD, "The Homiletics of John Oecolampadius and the Sermons of the Greek Fathers", *Communio Sanctorum: Mélanges offerts à Jean-Jacques von Allmen* (ed. I. Congar e.a.; Geneva: Labor et Fides 1982) 239–50; D. M. POYTHRESS, *Johannes Oecolampadius' Exposition of Isaiah, Chapters 36–37* (PhD Westminster Theological Seminary 1992 [UMI 9224636]; Ann Arbor, MI 1993); E. STAEHELIN, "Die Väterübersetzungen Oekolampads", *SThZ* 33 (1916) 57–91; T. WILLI, "Der Beitrag des Hebräischen zum Werden der Reformation in Basel", *ThZ* 35 (1979) 139–54.

Oecolampadius's Isaiah lectures drew attention far beyond Basel and university circles. By focusing resolutely on the meaning of the Hebrew text, on the one hand, while on the other supplementing his Latin exposition with words directed in German to the broad circle of his listeners,[7] he placed himself in a paradigmatic way in the service of the divine word, which without official ecclesiastical legitimation or sacramental linkage could speak to the present as biblical word of a prophet and gain a hearing for itself.

Oecolampadius reworked the lectures into a commentary, which appeared in the spring of 1525. Although he expounded on a series of other Old Testament books, with emphasis on the prophets, in a series of lectures, which were in part published posthumously on the basis of listeners' notes,[8] it is the extensive Isaiah commentary, with a complete index compiled by his Basel colleague Conrad Pellican, that is worthy of special attention. Luther, Zwingli and Calvin profited from it, even if they did not always follow his interpretation,[9] and Bullinger's foreword to the complete edition of Oecolampadius's exegetical works on the Old Testament, which appeared in Geneva in the fifties, underlines its importance.[10]

If Oecolampadius here places his humanistic education in the service of a reformed-prophetic interpretation of the book of Isaiah,[11] it means initially that he is striving to remain as close as possible to the Hebrew text as solely authoritative.[12] For this reason, Hebrew names for persons and places are purposely not latinized, in order to retain the meaning of the Hebrew root words. He attempts to sketch the semantic domains of important Hebrew texts through inner-biblical comparisons. Oecolampadius further compares the Hebrew text constantly with the Septuagint. He draws frequently on Nicholas of Lyra, the

---

[7] See Staehelin, Oekolampad (1939) 189f.

[8] Haggai, Zechariah and Malachi (1525/26), Jeremiah and Lamentations (1527), Ezekiel (1527/28), Daniel (1528) – see the correnspondance with Zwingli (Briefe und Akten 2 [1971] 426–28 [Nr.730]; ibid. 420–26 [Nr.729]; further, Job (1528–30), the rest of the minor Prophets (1530/31) and Genesis (1531), until chap. 16, at the time of his death. During his lifetime, besides the commentary on Isaiah, as real commentaries only the commentary on the three minor Prophets (Oekolampad-Bibliographie [1963] Nr.137) and on Daniel (ibid. Nr.162) have appeared in print. In addition, there exist some sermons on single texts.

[9] For Luther, see WA 31.2, 2,15; WA 25, 88,41f; 152,26; 160,7f. For Zwingli, see Briefe und Akten 2 (1971) 342f. [Nr.679]; also Zwinglis commentaries on Isaiah from 1529 (cf. Z XIV 103,15). For Calvin: ...*nemo ergo adhuc diligentius Oecolampadio in hoc opere versatus est, qui tamen etiam scopum non semper attingit*, Letter to Viret of 19 May 1540 (CO 11,36).

[10] Oekolampad-Bibliographie 2 [1963] Nr.1014.

[11] See Briefe und Akten 1 (1971) 219–23 [Nr.151; 153; 154; 157].

[12] See the preface (Briefe und Akten 1 [1971] 348 [Nr.241]).

Isaiah commentary of Jerome, and other patristic works, as well as rabbinic interpreters. The Biblia Rabbinica of Felix Pratensis from 1517/18, which contains, in addition to the Targum Jonathan and the commentary of David Qimhi, further textual variants, was already among his possessions in Augsburg. Through the connection with Pellican and Sebastian Münster, he had access to further rabbinic works.[13]

The goal of Oecolampadius's interpretation, however, is to let the prophet Isaiah speak in the present. Guidelines for his interpretation are the conviction that Christ is the goal of all Scripture, on the one hand,[14] and at the same time that, according to 1 Cor 10:6–11, everything written in the Old Testament is written "for our instruction", and that its aim is not only to transmit knowledge but in an extensive sense to mould our lives in a salutary and guiding way.[15] Only the one who seeks Christ and Christian life in the prophets will understand them. In the Foreword this is explained with reference to Luke 4:16–20 and Acts 8:26–35.[16]

The application of biblical texts to contemporary Christians was performed in the medieval tradition of the fourfold sense of Scripture (quadriga), especially with the investigation of the three 'spiritual' senses, tropology, allegory and anagogy. Erasmus could still refer to them in the Preface to his Novum Testamentum,[17] and he was fully convinced of the necessity of spiritual interpretation, but via the literal meaning, and not from a rigid application of the medieval scheme to biblical texts. In particular, the differentiations within the spiritual exegesis seemed artificial to him and often not appropriate for the biblical text in question.[18] Oecolampadius builds on this and identifies the concept of 'allegorical' interpretation in a general sense with the sensus mysticus of Scripture.[19] This is necessary in his eyes because it makes it possible, while drawing on the insights of Jewish exegetes, to hold to a christological and ecclesiastical sense of the text of the Old Testament. Nevertheless, according to Oecolampadius, allegorizing can only avoid arbitrariness and Jewish derision, if it builds on a foundation of the literal sense and the historical events reported there, in accordance with 'apostolic' example, indeed, the example of Jesus himself. Oecolampadius recalls the allusion to Numeri 21 in John 3:14–15: The 'real' historical events carry in themselves an 'allegorical' meaning that points 'figuratively' to Christ and his mystical body, the Church.[20] Thus Oecolampadius strives first to apply Isaiah's discourses to the political and religious

---

[13] See Stahelin, Oekolampad (1939) 193.

[14] Nam scriptura omnis ad Christum tanquam ad scopum spectat, In Ies 22v.

[15] Neque enim negari potest, omnis quae scripta ad nostram doctrinam scripta 1. Cor. 10 non ut tantum discamus, sed et ut inde accipiamus aliquid commodi, non scientiae duntaxat, quod vanitatis foret, sed vitae, In Ies 5v.

[16] In Ies praefatio b2.

[17] Erasmus, Ratio seu compendium verae theologiae (1519; ed. Welzig, 1967) 428f.

[18] See Erasmus, Ecclesiastes (LB V 1034 F to 1036 F). See F. KRÜGER, Humanistische Evangelienauslegung: Desiderius Erasmus von Rotterdam als Ausleger der Evangelien in seinen Paraphrasen (Tübingen: Mohr 1986) 80–86.

[19] In Ies 5r; vgl. ibid. 168v. See Staehelin, Oekolampad (1939) 196.

[20] Ibid. 5r-v.

situation of Jerusalem and the Jewish people of his time.[21] The orientation toward Christ and his 'mystical body' had the consequence that the traditional
'anagogic', ecclesiologic-eschatological sense, as well as the traditional tropo-
logic sense, which points to morals and life in general,[22] are integrated by Oecolampadius in the 'allegorical', 'spiritual' sense, which is directed to Christ
and his kingdom.[23] In view of the interpretation of historical events then typology comes into the foreground. At the same time, the aim is not to provide
philosophical or moral instruction through certain pictures.[24] Instead the
'types' are interpreted salvation-historically, eschatologically and christologically. Personalites such as the prophet Isaiah himself,[25] or the Persian king
Cyrus,[26] but also events such as the liberation from the Babylonian captivity,[27]
point as 'types' to Christ and his kingdom. Accordingly Sennacherib (Isa 36:1)
is a type of the "Antichrist".[28] Typology can also refer to a collective. Thus,
the earthly Jerusalem in the time of Isaiah can be interpreted typologically to
apply to the situation of the Church,[29] yet, at the same time, the prophetic
word has to be understood as pointing to the 'spiritual' Jerusalem, which
comes to fulfillment in the eschatological reign of Christ or God.[30] For Oecolampadius this manner of interpretation is based in the book of Isaiah itself:
beginning with the inhabitants of Jerusalem and Judah, the prophet's view is
expanded to take in Tyre, Babylon, even the entire world, whereby with increasing clarity the subject is Christ and his kingdom[31] as well as the calling of
the nations.[32]

The Christological sense of Scripture includes in itself not only an anagogic-
eschatological, but also a tropologic-moral sense. This becomes clear when
Oecolampadius formulates, in the Foreword to his Romans commentary: "The
goal of the entirety of Scripture is the vindication of the glory of God, that
God would be sovereign in all, but above all in the human heart".[33] Even before his time as a Reformer, Oecolampadius had been very interested in the
question of repentance and the consequent renewal of life through the Spirit;[34]
in Isaiah he found a great deal on this topic. The concept of *humiliatio*,[35] already important in Pre-Reformation Christ-mysticism, takes on new meaning
through the newly recovered truth of the Gospel, and the pair of terms 'lex'

---

[21] See *In Ies* 4v. For other Prophets accordingly, for example, *In Danielem* 2v to 5v.
[22] See Erasmus, *Ratio* (1967) 432f.
[23] See *In Ies* 22[b].
[24] See Erasmus, *Ratio* (1967) 426f.
[25] *In Ies* 198[b].
[26] Ibid. 234[b].
[27] Ibid. 99[b].
[28] Ibid. 194[a].
[29] E.g., *In Ies* 25[a-b].
[30] Ibid. 22[b] – 28[a], etc.
[31] See ibid. 4[b].
[32] Ibid. 4[a].
[33] *Scopus enim totius scripturae est vindicare gloriam Dei, ut regnet Deus in omnibus, maxime autem in cordibus hominum* (Preface to the commentary on Romans 1525 [Briefe und Akten 1 (1971)
380, Nr. 268]).
[34] See Kuhr, Die Macht des Bannes und der Busse (1999) 43–78.
[35] See e.g., *In Ies* 11r; 32v; 168v; 193r; 218v; 279r; and *In Dan* 2v. 7r; *In Gen* 4r. 5r.

and 'evangelium' appear repeatedly.[36] Oecolampadius can, however, only understand this repentance in connection with the entire Church – a conviction
he also found confirmed in the book of Isaiah. Its renewal and increased 'sanctification', the desire that its form of existence would correspond to its pneumatic being as the body of Christ, is a recurrent theme throughout Oecolampadius's interpretation of Isaiah. Oecolampadius makes it unmistakably clear,
however, that the striving for the heavenly Jerusalem, or 'sanctification', consists in heeding the word of God.[37] When the Law of God goes out from Zion
according to Isaiah 2, this means: it goes out from neither Rome nor Constantinople; instead: wherever the unadulterated word of God is, there and there
alone is the Church.[38] It is for this reason that the first task is to differentiate
the word of God from the human tradition, followed by the worship of God
"in spirit and in truth",[39] which means: not in external splendor and honorary
titles, but in faith and love.[40] The latter should also take form in concrete organized congregations.[41] In this Isaiah's original audience, the inhabitants of
Jerusalem und Judah, and the concrete Basel *christiana respublica*, are joined
together,[42] for God's righteousness (*iusticia*) and mercy (*misericordia*) remain
for all time the same.[43]

Oecolampadius's dedication of his Isaiah commentary to the Basel municipal council is programmatic and consists in a clearly audible summons to a
"Reformation" of the city according to God's word.[44] Accordingly, sin remains unchanged: the turning away from God as a turning away from life or,
what is substantially equivalent, apostasy from the covenant.[45] The Jews in the
Old Covenant and the Christians in Basel stand together before the same eternal God. Jerusalem points typologically to the Church of Christ,[46] so that
Isaiah utters the will of God for the latter as well. The criticism of cult and society in the book of Isaiah, the threats as well as the promises of salvation, are
for Oecolampadius a mirror for his own time. At issue is the restoration of the
true worship of God in the fullest sense: true *pietas*. The ceremonies must re-
gain the place that is appropriate for them, righteous and care for the poor
must be restored and the entire city cleansed from human tradition and re-

---

[36] See e.g., 127v; 193r; 210v; 211v.

[37] *Studium praecipuum civitatis Hierusalem est occupari in verbo dei. Ideo venitur ad ecclesiam, ut
in verbo dei discamus quae sit voluntas deo beneplacita, In Ies* 25ᵃ.

[38] *ubi inadulteratum verbum dei, ibi esse ecclesiam, ubi autem non verbum dei, ibi non essse ecclesiam, In Ies* 25ᵇ.

[39] Ibid. 24ᵃ.

[40] See ibid. 24ᵃ; 25ᵃ; etc.

[41] *Ubi enim christianus principatus est, ibi et christianae vigent leges, quae in uno charitatis praecep-
to recapitulantur* (Briefe und Akten 1 (1971) 350 [Nr. 241]).

[42] *Et quid ad nos illa? Eadem iusticia dei est omnibus seculis, eadem et misericordia, In Ies* 5v.

[43] E.g., *In Ies* 5ᵇ.

[44] Briefe und Akten 1 (1971) 346–52 [Nr. 241].

[45] *... vitam derelinquentes et mortem eligentes, ab amico discendentes et inimico adhaerentes. Haec
haec est apostasia, et derelicto gravissima, foedus cum deo in circuncisione, vel baptismo initum violare,
In Ies* 9v (recte: 8v).

[46] Ibid. 23v. Kuhr, Die Macht des Bannes und der Busse (1999) 96.

formed according to the word of God.[47] To accomplish this, the word of God, both in the interpretation of Isaiah as well as in discipleship to the prophets, must be spoken clearly and unashamedly to the politically powerful ones, even if one gains thereby the accusation of imprudence and presumptuousness.[48] Oecolampadius's Isaiah commentary, in common with his theology in general, found little recognition so far. Nevertheless, it represented without doubt a pioneering effort in 'reformed' or 'upper German' exposition of Scripture.

II. Huldrych Zwingli

Sources: HULDREICH ZWINGLI: *Sämtliche Werke* [quoted: Z] (CR 88–101; Berlin / Leipzig / Zürich 1905–; incomplete); *Werke* 1–8 [quoted: S] (ed. M. Schuler / J. Schulthess; Zürich 1828–42); *Huldrych Zwingli Schriften* 1–4 (ed. Th. Brunschweiler / S. Lutz; Zürich: Theol. Verlag Zürich 1995); *Huldrych Zwingli Writings* 1–2 (vol. 1 tr. by E. J. Furcha; vol. 2 tr. by H. W. Pipkin; Allison Park, PA: Pickwick Publications 1984).

Bibliographies: An extensive bibliography is published annually in: *Zwingliana. Beiträge zur Geschichte Zwinglis, der Reformation und des Protestantismus in der Schweiz* [quoted: Zwing.] (ed. Zwingliverein, in co-operation with Institut für Schweizerische Reformationsgeschichte; Zürich: Theol. Verlag Zürich, since 1897); U. GÄBLER, *Huldrych Zwingli im 20. Jahrhundert. Forschungsbericht und annotierte Bibliographie 1897–1972* (Zürich: Theol. Verlag Zürich 1975; T. HIMMIGHÖFER, *Die Zürcher Bibel bis zum Tode Zwinglis (1531). Darstellung und Bibliographie* (VIEG 154; Mainz: von Zabern 1995); H. W. PIPKIN, *A Zwingli Bibliography* (Pittsburgh, PN: Barbour Library 1972); J. POLLET, "Huldrych Zwingli. Biographie Theologie d'après les recherches récentes", *Huldrych Zwingli et le Zwinglianisme. Essai de synthèse historique et théologique mis à jour d'après les recherches récentes* (De Pétrarque à Descartes 52; Paris: Librairie Philosophique J. Vrin 1988) 217–415.

General works: Zwingli und Europa. *Referate und Protokoll des Internationalen Kongresses aus Anlass des 500. Geburtstages von Huldrych Zwingli vom 26. bis 30. März 1984* (ed. P. Blickle / A. Lindt / A. Schindler; Zürich: Vandenhoeck & Ruprecht 1985); *Die Zürcher Reformation. Ausstrahlungen und Rückwirkungen. Wissenschaftliche Tagung zum hundertjährigen Bestehen des Zwinglivereins 1997* (ed. A. Schindler / H. Stickelberger; Bern / New York: Peter Lang 2001); *Prophet, Pastor, Protestant. The Work of Huldrych Zwingli after Five Hundred Years* (ed. E. J. Furcha / H. W. Pipkin; Allison Park, PA: Pickwick Publications 1984); U. GÄBLER, *Huldrych Zwingli. Eine Einführung in sein Leben und sein Werk* (3rd edition; Zürich: Theologischer Verlag Zürich 2004) ET: U. Gäbler, *Huldrych Zwingli: his life and work* (transl. by R. C. L. Gritsch; Philadelphia: Fortress Press 1986 and Edinburgh: T. & T. Clark 1987); B. GORDON, *The Swiss Reformation* (Manchester e.a.: Manchester UP / New York: distrib. Palgrave e.a. 2003); B. HAMM, *Zwinglis Reformation der Freiheit* (Neukirchen-Vluyn: Neukirchener 1988); G. W. LOCHER, *Huldrych Zwingli in neuer Sicht. Zehn Beiträge zur Theologie der Zürcher Reformation* (Zürich: Zwingli Verlag 1969); idem, *Die Zwinglische Reformation im Rahmen der europäischen Kirchengeschichte* (Göttingen / Zürich: Vandenhoeck & Ruprecht 1979); W. E. MEYER, *Huldrych Zwinglis Eschatologie. Reformatorische Wende, Theologie und Geschichtsbild des Zürcher Reformators im Lichte seines eschatologischen Ansatzes* (Zürich: Theologischer Verlag Zürich 1987); J. POLLET, "Art. Zwinglianismus", Huldrych Zwingli et le Zwinglianisme (see above; 1988) 1–216; W. P. STEPHENS, *The Theology of Huldrych Zwingli* (Oxford: Oxford UP; repr. 1995).

Special abbreviations (see above):
S = Zwingli, *Werke* 1–8 (1828–42)
Z = Zwingli, *Sämtliche Werke* (1905-)
Zwing. = *Zwingliana. Beiträge zur Geschichte Zwinglis* etc. (1897-)

---

[47] See the preface to the council of Basel (*Clarissimis ac omnis iusticiae amantissimis viris Senatoribus inclytae urbis Basiliensis...* α2 – α6).
[48] See ibid. 11r.

1. Zwingli in the Context of the Renaissance

Sources: E. EGLI, *Analecta Reformatoria* I. *Dokumente und Abhandlungen zur Geschichte Zwinglis und seiner Zeit* (Zürich 1899); idem, *Actensammlung zur Geschichte der Zürcher Reformation in den Jahren 1529–1533* (Zürich: Schabelitz 1879; repr. Aalen 1973).

Studies: F. BÜSSER, *Die Prophezei. Humanismus und Reformation in Zürich* (Bern: Peter Lang 1994); E. CAMPI, *Zwingli und Maria. Eine reformationsgeschichtliche Studie* (Zürich: Theol. Verlag Zürich 1997) 24–34; W. KETTLER, *Die Zürcher Bibel von 1531: philologische Studien zu ihrer Übersetzungstechnik und den Beziehungen zu ihren Vorlagen* (Bern: Peter Lang 2001); G. W. LOCHER, "Zwingli und Erasmus", *Zwing.* 13 (1969) 37–61; A. RICH, *Die Anfänge der Theologie Huldrych Zwinglis* (Zürich: Zwingli-Verlag 1949); M. SALLMANN, *Zwischen Gott und Mensch. Huldrych Zwinglis theologischer Denkweg im 'De vera et falsa religione commentarius' (1525)* (BHTh 108; Tübingen: Mohr Siebeck 1999); A. SCHINDLER, *Zwingli und die Kirchenväter* (147. Neujahrsblatt zum Besten des Waisenhauses; Zürich: Beer 1984).

1.1. *His Career*

Huldrych Zwingli, born 1 January 1484 in Toggenburg, studied in Vienna and Basel; then he became a priest in Glarus, later in Einsiedeln, where he served until his call to Zurich's Grossmünster at the beginning of 1519. Influenced by Erasmus, he increasingly studied the Bible itself,[49] and pursued studies in the Greek language from about 1513.[50] Even the basics of his knowledge of Hebrew seem to have been self-taught at an early date.[51] Reuchlin's *De rudimentis hebraicis* served Zwingli both as textbook and source of his Hebrew vocabulary.[52]

According to Zwingli's own testimony he began to preach "the gospel" in 1516, but he does not go into detail concerning its content, giving but a reference to the principle of the sufficiency of Scripture.[53] Zwingli emphasizes his independence from Luther,[54] and points to a poem of Erasmus which gave him an important impetus to make headway to a consistent christological reading of the whole Bible with all its practical consequences.[55] Instead of a "reformatory turning point", one may rather speak of a process that began in 1516 and led in 1522 to the programmatic emphasis on the "liberating" divine word and then in 1523 to the "theses" of the first Zurich disputation and their "exposition", in which Luther certainly does play a role, but hardly as the sole decisive

---

[49] See Gäbler, Huldrych Zwingli (1983) 33–43; Locher, Zwinglische Reformation (1979) 55–82; idem, Zwingli und Erasmus (1969) 37–61; CHR. CHRIST-VON WEDEL, "Das Schriftverständnis von Zwingli und Erasmus im Jahre 1522", *Zwing.* 16 (1983) 111–25. On the Scotistic influence see D. BOLLIGER, *Infinitis contemplatio: Grundzüge der Skotus- und Skotismusrezeption im Werk Huldrych Zwinglis, mit ausführlicher Edition bisher unpublizierter Annotationen Zwinglis* (Leiden e.a.: Brill 2003).

[50] Z VII 22,8–12.

[51] See E. EGLI, "Zwingli als Ausleger des Alten Testaments", Z XIV 878–880; idem, "Zwingli als Hebräer", *Zwing.* 1/2 (1900) 153–58; L. I. NEWMAN, *Jewish Influence on Christian Reform Movements* (New York 1925; repr. New York: AMS Press 1966) 454–510; R. G. HOBBS, "Zwingli and the Study of the Old Testament", *Huldrych Zwingli (1484–1531). Legacy of a Radical Reform. Papers from the 1984 International Zwingli Symposium, McGill University* (ed. E. J. Furcha; ARC Suppl. 2; Montreal: McGill University 1985) 159 f.

[52] Cf. Egli, Zwingli als Ausleger des Alten Testaments, Z XIV 886.

[53] Z II 144,17–145,4; 149,33–36.

[54] Z II 144,32–145,4.

[55] Cf. Z II 217,5–218,3; cf. Z V 712,24–715,1.

factor.[56] Aware of the profound ecclesiastic, moral, and political abuses of his time, and not without inner conflicts and the conscience of personal sin, Zwingli arrives at insights which, on the one hand, place the Erasmian emphasis on Scripture and on listening to the authentic voice of Christ on a new foundation, which lead to the break with Rome. On the other hand, he retains important humanist elements and applies them to theology.[57] Thus Christ remains an example, teacher and impulse for human behavior. All this, however, on the sole basis of his work as mediator, and under the sign of his accomplished work of atonement, which liberates humanity. Putting one's trust in him and not in anything else is the only appropriate Christian "deed", identical with answering to Christ's words in Matt 11:28.

In contrast to Erasmus, Zwingli saw a categorical difference between the human spirit and the spirit of God, rather than a mere difference of degree with no fixed boundary. This difference could only be overcome through the sovereign activity of God.

1.2. The Meaning of Scripture

Beginning with his defense of the breaking of the Lenten fast in 1522[58] Zwingli started a series of writings in which he consistently put forward the Bible as the sole source of the divine "word" and as the only measure of that which deserves to be called "Christian", in opposition to all human traditions and inventions.[59] The sufficiency of Scripture is all the while understood as liberation: The "hearing of the word of God"[60] is identical with liberation not only from "self-love",[61] but also from all enslaving human ordinances, from ecclesiastic sovereignty over the human conscience, as in the fasting ordinances, for example,[62] and from political and social enslavement, as his position against mercenary service and on the question of interest make clear.[63] As early as in *Archeteles* (1522) Zwingli outlines the ideal of a scripturally based reform of the Church: through the sufficiency of Scripture the presumptuous sovereignty of the papacy would be replaced by the genuine sovereignty of God.[64] The fundamental differentiation between the truth of the divine word that makes

---

[56] Cf. Schindler, Zwingli und die Kirchenväter (1984) 28–41; Rich, Die Anfänge der Theologie Huldrych Zwinglis (1949).

[57] See for example his *The Education of the Youth* (Quo pacto ingenui adolescentes formandi sint, Z II 526–551); on this, see P. Opitz, "Zwingli, Huldrych", *Lexikon der Religionspädagogik* (ed. N. Mette / F. Rickers; Neukirchen-Vluyn: Neukirchener 2000) 2272–75; and the *Praefatio* and *Epistola* to Pindar (Z IV 863–879).

[58] *Von erkiesen und fryheit der spysen* (1522), Z I 74–136.

[59] *Controversia est divinis obtemperare an oportet an humanis* (*Archeteles*), Z I 314,27 f. Zwingli's emphasis on the freedom of the spirit and its independence from every kind of created means does not weaken the crucial role of Scripture. On this, see W. P. Stephens, *The Theology of Huldrych Zwingli* (Oxford: Oxford UP repr. 1995) 127–38.

[60] See e.g., Z II 494,5–24; Z III 113,16.

[61] E.g., Z III 712,4–715,8

[62] Cf. *Von erkiesen und fryheit der spysen* (1522), Z I 74–136.

[63] Cf. *Eine treue und ernstliche Vermahnung an die frommen Eidgenossen*, Z III 103–113.

[64] E.g., Z I 295,8,17–309,15.

free and certain as only "way of salvation"[65] and the (self-) deceiving and enslaving human word is found by Zwingli in the entire Bible, also essentially in
the Old Testament.[66] Thus he puts forward texts from both the Old and New
Testaments to demonstrate the "certitude" and "power" of the word of God,
but also its "perspicacity".[67] He urges that all of his teachings be put to the test
"on the basis of the Scriptures of the New and Old Testaments".[68]

1.3. The Meaning of the Old Testament

Zwingli's entire career, including his theological argumentation, is strongly
embedded in the political, social and intellectual situation of his time. It is in
dialogue with this that he seeks to make his influence felt. Accordingly he left
no writing that worked out in detail the question of the status and exposition
of the Old Testament. Instead, relevant statements must be gathered from
scattered remarks in diverse argumentative contexts. Nevertheless, the guiding
principles in his dealings with the Old Testament can be laid open in this way,
even if it remains incomplete in some points. Zwingli's point of departure is undoubtedly the basic unity of the Old and New Testaments, which is based in
the unity of God and his word, and which possesses in Christ its center, but
also its critical principle.[69]

Just as Scripture as a whole witnesses to Christ and his work of atonement,[70]
thus seeking to win human trust, at the same time it claims, on the basis of this,
to guide human behavior.[71] The hearing of this "guiding" word is for Zwingli
an integral component of true faith as love to God and Christ.[72] He can compare the relationship between the spirit of God and the word of Scripture with
the interplay of a horse and a bridle.[73] Admittedly, words of command, prohibition, and promise are to be distinguished.[74] They only diverge, however,
when they meet humans as sinners. In and of itself, the entire Bible is "Gospel", a salutory word of God pointing to Christ, not only as promise, but also
as helpful "instruction", as "doctrine" and "preservation": "everything that

---

[65] Cf. Z I 372f; Z I 259-261 (*Archeteles* 1522). See G. W. LOCHER, "Grundzüge der Theologie
Zwinglis", in: idem, Huldrych Zwingli in neuer Sicht (1969) 190-99. For this fundamental aspect
of Zwingli's thought, see Meyer, Huldrych Zwinglis Eschatologie (1987).

[66] Zwingli's first important writing as a reformer in Zurich deals with "Choice and Liberty Respecting Food", and compares the proclamation of the Gospel with the liberation from the slavery
in Egypt, a way into evangelical freedom, Z I 89,2-20. On this, see Hamm, Zwinglis Reformation
der Freiheit (1988).

[67] Z I 353,7; Z I 358,11.

[68] Z I 133,13f.

[69] *Videmus ergo iam ab initio patrum fidem et nostram unam eandemque fuisse. Omnes enim hoc
testamento et foedere salvantur, quod cum fideli Abram et semine eius pepigit deus. Quod capita singula
singulis capitibus e regione opponit, significat, quod omnes in unam eandemque fidem (quam habuit
Abram) aliquando essent converturi per caput Christum*, Commentary on Gen 15:10 (Z XIII 89,18-
24). Cf. the argumentation in Z III 269-87.

[70] E.g., Z I 286,17-20.

[71] Z I 315,7-9. Z V 13,1-8.

[72] Z I 133,5-9.

[73] *Scriptura ergo regula et finis est, iuxta quam omnia dirigenda sunt*, S VI/1 680.

[74] Z II 78,17-82,14.

God reveals to humans and demands from them" is Gospel, for "whenever God shows humans his will, then those who love him rejoice; for it is for them a faithful, good message".[75] When for instance the eschatological word of Isaiah promises the proclamation of Torah to all nations from Zion (Isa 2:3), it speaks of the entire will of God as revealed in the Old Testament, a saving will that passes from Israel to the "nations", nothing other than the proclamation of Christ.[76] Thus every divine word, even those of the Old Testament, have as their aim the faith and trust of humans and are in that way liberating, for wherever there is true faith, there is freedom.[77] For the one who has faith in Christ, Christ is reason, righteousness and innocence, for Christ lives in him.[78]

Within a basic unity, the Old and the New Testament, however, are to be differentiated. First and foremost as an increase of divine revelation from a shadow-like indication to a bright light. Zwingli brings here the traditional proofs, Heb 10:1 and Col 2:17, to demonstrate the christological connection of Old and New Testaments.[79] Whereas the Old Testament looks ahead prophetically to Christ's work of atonement and even partakes of it proleptically, the apostolic proclamation reminds us of the *ephapax* of atonement. The clearer witness of the New Testament is therefore the light in which the Old Testament "figures" must be understood.[80] Against this hermeneutical background it is inadmissible to use Old Testament texts to argue for the Roman sacrifice of the mass.[81]

Conversely, it is Christ himself who points to the Old Testament as that which witnesses to him, so that to despise the Old Testament would be to despise Christ, since in it God revealed his power, wisdom, goodness and righteousness. Although it is the New Testament that fulfills the Old and makes it "true",[82] in a certain sense the Old Testament throws light upon the New.

---

[75] Cf. Z II 79,11–15. See the commentary on Luke 16:16, where the threefold biblical use of *lex* is explained: ...*vocem legis varie poni. Aliquando pro omni scriptura sacra in genere. Aliquando pro ceremoniis legis: nam in lege et ceremoniae continentur simulque spiritualia, ad quae ducunt, et ob quae instituta sunt, ut agnus, circumcisio, sacrificia. ... Tertio lex capitur pro mente legi spirituali, ut deum super omnia diligere, et proximum ut te ipsum. Hic enim nucleus est legis. ... "Lex et prophetae usque ad Ioannem". Intelligens per legem et prophetas quidquid est ceremoniale, typicum et propheticum in lege. Interim non vult quod spiritus legis, scripturae ac veritatis abolitus sit aut cessarit*, S VI/1 680.

[76] *Accipiunt autem Hebraei legem non tantum pro decretis et sanctionibus: sed pro omnibus divinis oraculis carminibus, et rebus in gente sua gestis: quae nos Canonicos veteris Testamenti libros vocamus. Quae omnia quid aliud sunt quam coelestis disciplina? Haec autem quando alias, quam quum Christus per orbem praedicaretur, publica gentibus facta est? Potest igitur hic sermo, de Zion profectura est lex; perinde ac si tu iactes: Religio nostra, leges, mores, et constitutiones, apud exteras quoque gentes colentur. Et caute observa ut legem sive coelestem disciplinam synecdochice capias pro gratia et amicitia, quam deus erga genus humanum gerit: quam tamen praecipue genti Hebraicae, atque ante omnes alias, impartitus est, ac tandem misso filio suo in omnes Gentes propagavit*, Z XIV 130,35–131,8.

[77] Z II 80,19f.

[78] Z II 82,9–11.

[79] Cf. Z III 187,5; 193,24; 194,1.

[80] Z III 193,32–194,3; 195,1–3.

[81] Z III 187,1–195,27.

[82] *Uñ wirt also das neuw im alten angezeiget uñ vfschlossen: das alt im neuwen erfüllt unnd waar gemachet*, Preface (*Vorred*) to the Zürcher Bibel 1532, *Die Zürcher Bibel von 1531* (facsimile edn.; Zürich: Theol. Verlag Zürich 1983) (without pagination). Obviously, a try to take into consideration John 5:39 as well as Rom 10:4.

Thus in the question of infant baptism, which on the basis of the New Testament alone can be neither sufficiently substantiated nor refuted, Zwingli can find in the Old, in the horizon of the unified revelation of God an analogy in the form of circumcision as sign of the covenant.[83] But also for other "external" matters in view of the conduct of life, where the New Testament is silent, appeal must be made to the Old, as for example in the question of marriage of relatives (Lev 18:6–18), or the institution of restitution (Exod 22:1–15).[84] In doing this, Zwingli in no way simply puts Old Testament institutions and customs on the same level without any distinction, but regards them as confirmation or concretization of that for which the New Testament supplies the framework. This becomes clear in the hermeneutic points that he lists in *Wer Ursache zur Aufruhr gibt*, in which theological and humanistic motifs combine. In dealing with cases, in which two disputing parties each argue by appeal to Scripture, he advises giving greater weight to clear words of Scripture than to an indirect argumentation from Scripture. Where two clear statements of Scripture are set in opposition, the one placing confidence in God rather than in humans is to be preferred; where the New Testament is ambiguous, then we must, in accordance with the instruction of Jesus, hold to "Moses and the prophets". In doing so, however, one must consider circumstances of the time.[85]

Correspondingly, Zwingli holds with regard to Old Testament Law, in accordance with the hermeneutical principle of Jesus, that the dual love command, as the perpetual will of God, is the criterion of what remains of the Old Testament Law:

> Whatever reveals itself, when investigated on the basis of this rule of the perpetual will of God, to fall under this, can never be abolished. Whatever does not fall under this, is already abolished and made obsolete through Christ. "For Christ is the end of the law", Rom 10:4, and "the end of the law is love", 1 Tim 1:5. Therefore Christ and love are the same thing ... Whoever serves Christ is obligated to that which love prescribes; whatever is not prescribed by it or derives from it is either not commanded or useless, 1 Cor 13:3.[86]

When Zwingli refers primarily to the New Testament in dispute with his Roman opponents[87] and then stresses the continuity of the one covenant against the Baptists,[88] this represents no change in his basic position. If Christ is "mediator of a better testament",[89] which possesses perpetual and universal validity, this is not something alien compared to the "old", but its improvement, extension, and fulfillment.[90] Zwingli's basic theological differentiation remains that between word of God and human word, between divine worship and the worship of idols. This is found equally, however, in both testaments.[91]

---

[83] Cf. Z IV 325,17–326,30; Z IV 631,6–639,31.

[84] Z III 326,4–11.

[85] Z III 409,1–8.

[86] Z III 707,36–708,8.

[87] E.g., in: *Von Erkiesen und Freiheit der Speisen* (1522), Z I 134–136.

[88] Z IV 629–639 (Antwort über Balthasar Hubmaiers Taufbüchlein); cf. Z III 629–639. Cf. P. A. LILLIBACK, *The Binding of God. Calvin's Role in the Development of Covenant Theology* (Grand Rapids, MI: Baker Academic 2001) 81–109.

[89] Z II 165,15 (with reference to Heb 8:6).

[90] Z II 131,9–13.

[91] Cf. e.g., Z II 218–222.

2. Zwingli's Exegesis of the Old Testament

Sources: Exegetische Schriften 1–9 (1–4: OT; 5–9: NT) = *Huldreich Zwinglis Sämtliche Werke* XIII–XXI (CR 101–109; Zürich 1959, 1963; vols. 1–2 (Z XIII and Z XIV) have appeared, vols. 3–9 in preparation); *Opera. Completa Editio Prima. Latinorum Scripta pars quinta* (ed. M Schuler / J. Schulthess; vols. 5 and 6/1: OT, vols. 6/1 and 6/2: NT; Zürich 1835 [5].1838 [6]); *Aus Zwinglis Predigten zu Jesaja und Jeremia. Unbekannte Nachschriften,* ausgewählt und sprachlich bearbeitet von OSKAR FARNER (Veröffentlichungen der Rosa Ritter-Zweifel-Stiftung, Religiöse Reihe; Zürich: Berichthaus 1957).

Studies: P. BARTH, "Zwinglis Beitrag zum Verständnis der biblischen Botschaft", *RKZ* 81 (1931) 220f, 260f, 267f, 298–300; D. BOLLIGER, "Dramatisches Symbol konfessioneller Grundhaltungen zwischen Glaube und Politik: Die Opferung Isaaks in frühen reformierten Auslegungen von Huldrych Zwingli bis Jean Crespin", *Die Opferung Isaaks (Genesis 22) in den Konfessionen und Medien der Frühen Neuzeit* (ed. J. A. Steiger and U. Heinen ; Berlin/New York: Walter De Gruyter 2006) 15–66; F. BÜSSER, "Schrift und Dienst bei Zwingli", *Wurzeln der Reformation in Zürich. Zum 500. Geburtstag des Reformators Huldrych Zwingli* (ed. F. Büsser; SMRT 31; Leiden: Brill 1985); idem, "Zwingli, the Exegete. A Contribution to the 450th Anniversary of the Death of Erasmus", *Probing the Reformed tradition. Historical studies in honor of Edward A Dowey* (ed. E. A. McKee / B. G. Armstrong; Louisville, KY: Westminster 1989) 175–96; H. BYLAND, *Der Wortschatz des Zürcher Alten Testaments von 1525 und 1531, verglichen mit dem Wortschatz Luthers* (Diss. Basel; Naumburg a/S: von Lippert 1903); A. DETMERS, *Reformation und Judentum. Israel-Lehren und Einstellungen zum Judentum von Luther bis zum frühen Calvin* (Stuttgart: Kohlhammer 2001); E. EGLI, "Zwingli als Hebraer", *Zwing.* 1 (1900) 153–58; O. FARNER, "Huldrych Zwingli und seine Sprache", *Zwing.* 10/2 (1954) 70–97; idem, *Nachwort zu den Erläuterungen zur Genesis,* Z XIII, 289f; idem, *Nachwort zu den Jeremia-Erläuterungen,* Z XIV, 680f; idem, *Nachwort zu den Jesaja-Erläuterungen,* Z XIV, 411f; *idem, Nachwort zu den Übersetzungen und Erläuterungen der Psalmen,* Z XIII, 829–36; idem, *Nachwort zur Übersetzung des Buches Hiob,* Z XIII, 466; idem, "Zwinglis lateinische Bibel", *Zwing.* 1 (1900), 116–20; R. G. HOBBS, "Exegetical Projects and Problems: a new Look at an undated Letter from Bucer to Zwingli", *Prophet, Pastor, Protestant: the Work of Huldrych Zwingli after 500 years* (ed. E. J. Furcha / H. W. Pipkin; Allison Park, PA: Pickwick Publ. 1984) 89–108; idem, "Zwingli and the Study of the Old Testament", *Huldrych Zwingli (1484–1531), Legacy of a Radical Reform. Papers from the 1984 International Zwingli Symposium, McGill University* (ed. E. J. Furcha; ARC Suppl. 2; Montreal: McGill University 1985) 144–78; H.-J. KRAUS, "Charisma Prophetikon. Eine Studie zum Verständnis der neutestamentlichen Geistesgabe bei Zwingli und Calvin", *Wort und Gemeinde. Probleme und Aufgaben der Praktischen Theologie. Eduard Thurneysen zum 80. Geburtstag* (ed. R. Bohren / M. Geiger; Zürich: Evang. Verlag Zürich 1968) 80–103; G. KRAUSE, "Zwinglis Auslegung der Propheten", *Zwing.* 11 (1960) 257–65; E. KÜNZLI, *Zwingli als Ausleger von Genesis und Exodus* (Zürich: Berichthaus 1950); idem, "Zwingli als Ausleger des Alten Testamentes", Z XIV, 869–99; idem, "Zwinglis Jesaja-Erklärungen", *Zwing.* 10 (1957) 488–91; idem, "Zwinglis theologische Wertung des Alten Testaments", *Der Kirchenfreund* 83 (1949) 244–48; 276–84; idem, "Antwort an Paul Marti", *Zwing.* 9/6 (1951) 375–77; idem, "Quellenproblem und mystischer Schriftsinn in Zwinglis Genesis und Exoduskommentar", *Zwing.* 9/2 (1950) 185–207; 10 (1951) 253–307; idem, "Register der grammatisch-rhetorischen Ausdrücke", Z XIII, 837–54; idem, "Vorwort zur Vorrede zur Prophetenbibel", Z VI/II, 283–88; M. LIENHARD, "Aus der Arbeiten an Zwinglis Exegetica zum Neuen Testament. Zu den Quellen der Schriftauslegung", *Zwing.* 18 (1990–1991) 310–28; P. MARTI, "Mystischer Schriftsinn und wissenschaftliche Auslegung des Alten Testaments. Bemerkungen zu Edwin Künzli: Quellenproblem (etc.)", *Zwing.* 9/6 (1951) 365–74; L. VON MURALT, "Aus Zwinglis Predigten", *Zwing.* 10 (1957) 473–87; E. NAGEL, *Zwinglis Stellung zur Schrift* (Freiburg / Leipzig: Mohr 1896); L. I. NEWMAN, *Jewish Influence on Christian Reform Movements* (New York 1925; repr. New York: AMS Press 1966); J.-V. POLLET, "Zwingli comme Exégète", *Huldrych Zwingli et le Zwinglianisme. Essai de synthèse historique et théologique mis à jour d'après les recherches récentes* (J.-V. POLLET; Paris: De Pétrarque à Descartes 52; Paris: Librairie Philosophique J. Vrin 1988) 321–27; G. R. POTTER, "Zwingli and the Book of Psalms", *SCJ* 10,2 (1979) 43–50; J. QUACK, *Evangelische Bibelvorreden von der Reformation bis zur Aufklärung* (QFRG 43; Gütersloh: Mohn 1975); H. GRAF REVENTLOW, "Nach der Bibel die Kirche gestalten: Huldrych Zwingli", in: idem, *Renaissance, Reformation, Hu-*

manismus (*Epochen der Bibelauslegung* III; München: Beck 1997) 97–118; W. SCHENKER, *Die Sprache Huldrych Zwinglis im Kontrast zur Sprache Luthers* (Studia Linguistica Germanica 14; Berlin e.a.: de Gruyter 1977); B. STIERLE, "Schriftauslegung der Reformationszeit", *VF* 16 (1971) 55–88; J. L. THOMPSON, "The Survival of Allegorical Argumentation in Peter Martyr Vermigli's Old Testament Exegesis" *Biblical Interpretation in the Era of the Reformation. Essays Presented to David C. Steinmetz in Honor of His Sixtieth Birthday* (ed. R. A. Muller / John L. Thompson; Grand Rapids MI / Cambridge: Eerdmans 1996) 255–271; K. P. Voss, *Der Gedanke des allgemeinen Priester- und Prophetentums. Seine gemeindetheologische Aktualisierung in der Reformationszeit* (Wuppertal e.a.; Brockhaus 1990); H. WANNER, "Zu Zwinglis Psalmenübersetzung", *Zwing.* 13 (1970) 231–33; T. WENGERT, "Dating Zwingli's Lectures on the Gospel of John", *Zwing.* 17 (1986) 6–10.

2.1. *The* Prophezei

The place to begin any discussion of Zwingli's exegesis of the Old Testament is the Zurich *lectorium* (*Letzgen*), known as *Prophezei*, which took up its work 19 June 1525 in the choir of the Grossmünster in Zurich.[92] With the primary aim of equipping the Zurich clergy to read the Scriptures in the original languages and to expound them, the convent of the Great Minster was transformed into a theological seminary.[93] After the Latin chant was suspended, it was replaced, with reference to 1 Corinthians 14, by exegesis of the Hebrew and Greek Scriptures each morning, five days a week.[94] This procedure reflected the theological intention to inquire after the original word of God, in order to let it speak in the present: After the reading of the Bible text in the Vulgate, a Hebrew scholar read the Hebrew text and made philological observation. This duty was first performed by Ceporin,[95] who had studied under Reuchlin and had already begun to give Zwingli Hebrew instruction in 1522. After his untimely death in 1526, this task was taken over by Conrad Pellican,[96] who had already published a Hebrew grammar in 1501, and was called to Zurich as Ceporin's successor. Zwingli then commented on the text on the basis of the Septuagint, after which Leo Jud[97] summarized the exegetical results, which had been spoken in Latin, in the language of the people in a manner similar to a sermon.[98] Only Old Testament texts were expounded in the *Prophezei*, the New Testament was handled in afternoon sessions in the neighboring Fraumünster church. Beginning with Genesis 1 and proceeding in a

---

[92] Cf. H. BULLINGER, *Reformationsgeschichte* I (ed. J. J. Hottinger / H. H. Vögeli; Frauenfeld 1838; repr. Zürich: Nova-Buchhandlung 1984) 289–91; H. R. LAVATER, "Die Froschauer Bibel 1531 – Das Buch der Zürcher Reformation", in: *Die Zürcher Bibel von 1531* (facsimile edn.; Zürich: Theol. Verlag Zürich 1983) 1360–1421.

[93] The 29 September 1523; see Egli, Actensammlung (1879; repr. 1973) Nr. 426.

[94] Cf. Locher, Zwinglische Reformation (1979) 161–63; Lavater, Froschauer Bibel (1983) 1383.

[95] Cf. Locher, ibid. 581.

[96] Cf. Locher, ibid. 605f. *Schola Tigurina. Die Zürcher Hohe Schule und ihre Gelehrten um 1550. Katalog zur Ausstellung vom 25. Mai bis 10. Juni 1999 in der Zentralbibliothek Zürich* (ed. by Institut für Schweizerische Reformationsgeschichte, Zürich: Pano Verlag 1999).

[97] Locher, Zwinglische Reformation (1979) 568–75.

[98] Lavater, Froschauer Bibel (1983) 1384. Cf. J. KESSLER, *Sabbata mit kleineren Schriften und Briefen* (ed. E. Egli / R. Schoch; St. Gallen 1902) 203f; Bullinger, Reformationsgeschichte I (1984) 290f.

chronological-salvation history order, the series had reached 2 Chronicles 20 by the time of Zwingli's death in 1531.[99] The opening prayer spoken by Zwingli at the inauguration of the *Prophezei* on 19 Juni 1525 is characteristic of his theological intention: Whoever does not understand the Old Testament and treasure it as the place in which God reveals himself to humans in his wisdom, goodness, and righteousness, despises Christ himself. The philological work on the biblical text stands wholly in service of the "transformation" of humans through the divine word:

> Almighty, eternal and merciful God, whose word is a lamp to our feet and a light to our path [Ps 119:105], open and enlighten our minds, that we may understand your secrets in a pure and holy way, and through that, which we have rightly understood, be transformed, that we may in no way displease your majesty, through Jesus Christ, our Lord. Amen.[100]

The 'practical' meaning of the *Prophezei* is underlined by the fact that Zwingli organized his preaching according to the texts expounded there.[101]

2.2. Scriptural Exposition as 'Prophecy'

As the name *Prophezei* already suggests, the exposition of Scripture was understood as 'prophecy'. In the foreword to the Prophet's Bible of 1529,[102] which perhaps was not written by Zwingli himself, although it no doubt reflects his opinion,[103] three functions of the "office of prophet" are distinguished. The "prophesying" of 1 Corinthians 14, the responsibility entrusted to Old Testament prophets Isaiah, Jeremiah, and Amos, as well as the expository transmission of the tradition according to 1 Corinthians 11 and Luke 2 are thus joined together: the purpose is to expound Scripture, to announce God's work of salvation and to transmit divine warnings and threats.[104] This corresponds in content to the description of the office of prophet given by Zwingli in other writings. In *Von dem Predigtamt* from 1525 he names two aspects that converge in the office of prophet: Based on Jer 1:9–10 it concerns resisting evil and planting good, and based on 1 Corinthians 14 it concerns the public exposition of Scripture, which primarily means the Old Testament.[105] In the explanation of 1 Cor 14:26–33 found there, Zwingli outlines the biblical basis and the order of what takes place in the *Prophezei*, whereby the recourse to the Hebrew

---

[99] Lavater, Froschauer Bibel (1983) 1385.

[100] *Omnipotens sempiterne et misericors deus, cuius verbum est lucerna pedibus nostris et lumen semitarum nostrarum, aperi et illumina mentes nostras, ut oraculas tua pure et sancte intelligamus et in illud, quod recte intellexerimus, transformemur, quo maiestati tuae nulla ex parte displiceamus, per Jesum Christum, dominum nostrum. Amen!*, Z IV 365,1-6. See *Vorrede zur Prophetenbibel*, Z VI/II 295,29–32.

[101] Cf. Künzli, Zwingli als Ausleger des Alten Testaments, Z XIV 872f.

[102] Cf. J. QUACK, *Evangelische Bibelvorreden von der Reformation bis zur Aufklärung* (Gütersloh: Gütersloher Verlagshaus; Verein für Reformationsgeschichte 1975) 47–60.

[103] Cf. the introduction by Künzli, Vorwort zu *Vorrede zur Prophetenbibel*, Z VI/II 283–312.

[104] Z VI/II 295f.

[105] Z IV 397,33–398,5.

text is justified by 1 Cor 14:26 but also there is reference to the hearing congregation, which is to "spiritually" judge what is spoken.[106]

2.3. Zwingli's Exegetical Works

The Old Testament translations and expositions of Zwingli that have come down to us should be seen against this background. Zwingli himself published Latin translations and exegetical explanations of Isaiah, Jeremiah and Lamentations.[107] Explanations of Genesis and Exodus were published during Zwingli's lifetime by Leo Jud and Kaspar Megander with the intention of reproducing Zwingli's own exegesis.[108] Even if they cannot be seen as Zwingli's own work in the strict sense,[109] it would be mistaken not to see here Zwingli's exegesis, at least in its essentials.[110] Zwingli checked them in part and gave permission to place his name on them. The context of the *Prophezei* doubtlessly flowed into these expositions, which of course is also true for the expositions of Isaiah and Jeremiah. The other works on the Old Testament were either first published after Zwingli's death (the Latin translation of the Psalms), or have been preserved in manuscript, either as autographs (the German translation of the Psalms[111]) or in copies (the translation of Job,[112] the explanations of the Psalms, Ezekiel, Daniel, and the Minor Prophets[113]). The various forewords also witness, as should not be forgotten, to Zwingli's leading role in a collective effort to understand the word of God.[114] The foreword to the *Zürcher Bibel of 1531* has no indication of authorship, as is also the case with the Prophet's Bible of 1529. Yet the connections to Zwingli's writings, for instance to the foreword to Isaiah, are so strong that in view of its content it can be considered a work of Zwingli.[115]

Zwingli's 'exegetical' Old Testament writings can only be characterized as genuine commentaries in a limited sense, however, since the explanations take various forms. Often they consist merely of explanations of words that draw on comparisons of usage in other passages, as well as on the Septuagint and

---

[106] Z IV 395 f. The main goal of the translation of the Bible is to give the hearer of the sermons the means to examine them, cf. *Die Zürcher Bibel von 1531* (*Vorred*), no pagination.

[107] *Complanationis Isaiae prophetae, foetura prima, cum apologia qur quidque sic versum sit*, Tiguri 1529 (Z XIV, 2–412); *Complanationis Jeremiae prophetae, foetura prima, cum Apologia quur quidque sic versum sit*, Tiguri 1531 (Z XIV, 417–681). There exist several copies of Zwingli's work on Isaiah and on Jeremiah, see: *Aus Zwinglis Predigten zu Jesaja und Jeremia* (1957).

[108] *Farrago Annotationum in Genesim ex ore Huldrychi Zuinglii per Leonem Judae et Casparem Megandrum exceptarum*, (Z XIII 1,290).

[109] See Hobbs, Zwingli and the Study of the Old Testament (1985) 146.

[110] Cf. Künzli, Zwingli als Ausleger des Alten Testaments, Z XIV, 876.

[111] See Z XIII 468–827. Cf. O. Farner, Nachwort zu den Übersetzungen und Erläuterungen der Psalmen, Z XIII, 829–36.

[112] *Übersetzung des Buches Hiob*, 4 February 1530 (Z XIII, 430–466).

[113] *Scholia H[uldrici] Z[winglii] in Ezechielem, Danielem et in 12 prophetas minores*, 1533 (Z XIV, 687–867). Künzli, Zwingli als Ausleger des Alten Testaments, Z XIV, 871.

[114] Cf. Lavater, Froschauer Bibel 1531 (1983) 1382.

[115] Cf. the introduction by Künzli (Z VI / II 283–288) and the proofs in the footnotes; see also Kettler, Die Zürcher Bibel von 1531 (2001) 80–86, 99–112.

the Vulgate. Zwingli's goal is evidently to avoid standing between the text and its audience with his exegetical comments, but rather to let the text itself speak. Since the ultimate goal is to enable all Christians to read and understand the Bible,[116] the work of translation receives great importance. This explains not only Zwingli's own translations into German and Latin, but also his decision to give precedence to making the meaning of the text understandable and even to endow it with a certain linguistic elegance over the most literal translation. Thus the *Jesajakommentar* consists of a Latin translation of the book and, as a second part, a commentary, entitled "First Witness of a Leveling of the Prophet Isaiah, with an Apology, Why Everything Is Translated the Way It Is".[117] To put it pointedly, the goal of exegetical or translation work on a Biblical book is not an *Enarratio* but the *Zürcher Bibel.*

2.4. *Zwingli's Exegetical Procedure*

Zwingli's concrete procedure for the exegesis of Old Testament texts can be analyzed in three steps: establishment of the 'literal sense', the explanation of its meaning for the congregation in the present, and the 'allegorical' exegesis, which in a hidden way points to Christ.[118]

The establishment of the literal sense usually begins with word studies. Here the effort is made to determine the sense of the Hebrew term with the help of etymological derivation, drawing on the Septuagint and with consideration of its biblical and general usage, with the result either of a more precise meaning, or, in view of its many-faceted use, expanded meaning. This can happen briefly, but in the case of central theological concepts it can occupy an entire excursus. Following this, the exact grammatical construction is examined, the rhetorical genre is determined, and figurative language and metaphors are identified as such, for which Zwingli richly employs his humanistic-rhetorical apparatus.[119] It corresponds to Zwingli's task in the framework of the *Prophezei* to always bring in the Septuagint, but also his intensive use of his Greek *Hausbibel*, which his notations in the margin attest, show that the Septuagint text carried great weight for him.[120] In the introduction to his Isaiah commentary he admittedly demythologizes the account of its origin according to the Letter of Aristeas through stylistic observations. He goes on to make critical remarks on the quality of its translation, especially with regard to Isaiah, yet nevertheless emphasizes that, on the basis of its antiquity, it is at times to be preferred to the rabbinic Masoretic text.[121] An important example for him as

---

[116] See the end of the preface (*Vorred*) of *Die Zürcher Bibel von 1531* (no pagination).

[117] *Complanationis Isaiae Prophetae foetura prima cum Apologia cur quidque sic versum sit* (Z XIV 2); cf. Z XIV 88,3–8; see Hobbs, Zwingli and the Study of the Old Testament (1985) 162–65.

[118] In the preface to the commentaries on Exodus, these three levels are mentioned by Jud and Megander as rules applied in the *Prophezei*, Z XIII 294,4–295,10; cf. Künzli, Zwingli als Ausleger des Alten Testaments, Z XIV 882f.

[119] Cf. the list Z XIII 839–54.

[120] Cf. Künzli, Zwingli als Ausleger des Alten Testaments, Z XIV 874–78.

[121] Z XIV 95–98. Cf. Hobbs, Zwingli and the Study of the Old Testament (1985) 154–61.

an exegete from the period of the Early Church is Jerome, even though he had already recognized the latter's limits in his pre-Zurich time.[122]

The fact that Zwingli's exegesis always points to the utterance of the divine word in the present means that after referring back to the original languages the next step moves in the opposite direction. The interpretation of historical events leads to the question of what we can learn from the example;[123] the explanation of prophetic texts moves from explanations of words to the meaning of the complete text.[124] The application to the reader's own situation as the core of the 'prophetic' act in exegesis is for Zwingli not the result of a departure from the *simplex litera*. In the contrary, it is following this principle by finding parallels to present times in the text.[125] The 'pedagogical' nature of the Old Testament (cf. 1 Cor 10:6, 11) is already supported through the humanistic understanding that he learned from Erasmus of the *historia vitae magistra*.[126] A broad range of application for both individual and communal Christian life is thereby opened up, but is also limited by the basic unity of the divine will and word. This points in diverse ways to Christ, on the one hand, and to the unity of the people of God, on the other. It involves obedience and innocence, faithfulness, thanksgiving, love and trust in God, who has accepted us as his people in Christ, as he had done with Israel.[127] So in the exegesis of historical texts both lines of questioning must be taken into account: "in sacred history we must always go back to the source, to the beginning of the divine promises, and consider its examples for life".[128] The Old Testament stories speak of the faith and tribulation of the fathers, und thus serve to strengthen our faith.[129] They also serve as an example for our behavior. Thus Zwingli answers the question, with regard to Gen 18:1-6, why Moses describes everyday matters in such detail by saying that Scripture also gives instruction for our "external" life, and that Abraham's hospitality can serve the selfish and divided Swiss as an example.[130] At the same time it is always important to consider the different times and customs, so that not all Old Testament stories can serve as moral "exempla",[131] and texts concerning warfare must be interpreted as applying to the spiritual warfare.[132] It is not a hidden 'allegorical' meaning, but the clear, literal meaning, applied to one's own time and existence that is for Zwingli the 'spiritual' meaning of Scripture, namely, that which leads humans

---

[122] Cf. Künzli, Zwingli als Ausleger des Alten Testaments, Z XIV 884; cf. Z II 144,8–17.

[123] *hoc exemplo discimus...*, Z XIII 319,36.

[124] *Hactenus de verborum complanatione. Nunc de sententia prophetae...*, Z XIV 128,35 f.

[125] E.g., *incidit in tumultuosa tempora Isaias, qualia ferme haec nostra sunt*, Z XIV 107,18 f. Cf. Z XIII 209,8–12; Künzli, Zwingli als Ausleger des Alten Testaments, Z XIV 889.

[126] *Quod ad finem et mores attinet, plena est historia exemplis ac typis, quae nos decent mansuetudinem, charitatem, tolerantiam*, Z XIII 264,8 f.

[127] *Vorrede zur Prophetenbibel*, Z VI/II 311 f. Cf. the epilogue of Jud and Megander to the explanations on Genesis, Z XIII 287,29; 288,14–16.

[128] *In historiis ergo sacris semper ad fontem, ad initium promissionis divinae nobis recurrendum est et ad exempla vitae spectanda*, Z XIII 266,5–7.

[129] *Sic enim legendae sunt sacrarum scripturarum historiae, ut etiam sentiamus adfectus eorum, quibuscum operatus deus, sed ita, ut in nobis quoque fidem excitent*, Z XIII 146,12–15.

[130] Z XIII 112,1–26.

[131] *Aliud iam tempus alios mores postulat*, Z XIII 189,33 f.

[132] See e. g., Z I 177,21–178,4; Z XIII 420,16–422,24.

to God.[133] Scripture is understood as *spiritus*, not as mere *littera*, when it is understood as witness to Christ, and when this is understood as an address by God that seeks to gain trust and introduce us to true liberty.[134]

This does not simply abolish allegorical interpretation. Even the determination of the *sensus literalis* is for Zwingli also the recognition that Scripture is full of "tropes" und "figures".[135] Christ himself (e. g., in John 10), but also the Apostles (e. g., Acts 20:28) repeatedly use figurative language, which must be recognized as such. Zwingli strives to name various kinds of figurative speech, yet recognizes at the same time the limits set to such clear differentiation by the biblical texts themselves. As a basic difference to a parable, for instance, he can observe concerning allegory that it possesses no *tertium comparationis* nor does it refer to anything proximate, but in a mysterious way to something more distant.[136] Through the adoption of a definition of Plutarch, however, Zwingli's concept of allegory becomes very broad.[137] He establishes some rules for handling allegorical biblical texts,[138] yet also believes that allegorical exegesis is not only permitted where a Biblical author consciously uses allegory.[139] New Testament passages that had already been important for traditional allegorical interpretation, such as 1 Cor 10:6, 11; Col 2:17; Gal 4:22–31, give him, as Oecolampadius before him, the direction, since he seeks to interpret the often puzzling Old Testament texts in light of the clearer New Testament texts as witness to Christ.[140]

The essential traits of Zwingli's use of allegories (*Allegorese*) are thoroughly consistent with his basic remarks on the Old Testament. They go in the direction of their scriptural limitation and standardization and at the same time of a christological orientation, two traits that blend however in Zwingli's exegesis. Scriptural standardization is given for Zwingli first through the not only relative, but absolute preference for the literal sense. The clarity and certitude of the divine word is the clear and convincing literal sense of Scripture. Where Zwingli comes to speak of 'allegorical' exegesis, he warns first of all against it, since he sees the authority of Scripture endangered through the possibility it opens of an arbitrary exposition.[141] This warning against allegorical interpretation generally stands against the background of distinguishing God's own word from human traditions and inventions.[142] It is precisely the study of the

---

[133] *Hoc docet nos simplex litera, ut scilicet mox in necessitatibus et angustiis ad deum curramus, auxilium eius implorantes, et hic est spiritualis intellectus seu sensus literae et historiae. Nam figurae seu mysteria aliud sunt et ad allegoriam pertinent*, Z XIII 209,8–12; cf. Z III 205,28–206,6.

[134] Cf. Z I 358,8–13; 365,14–21; Z II 111,9–11; Z III 900,6f; Z XIV 391,1–7. See Stephens, Theology of Huldrych Zwingli (1995) 59–64, 135–38.

[135] Cf. Z XIV 89,5–92,21.

[136] Z XIV 148,22–149,25; *Vorrede zur Prophetenbibel* Z VI/II 308,15–309,4.

[137] Z XIV 148,7 f. STEPHENS (Theology of Huldrych Zwingli, 1995, 78) is clearly right against KÜNZLI (Zwingli als Ausleger des Alten Testaments, Z XIV 892).

[138] Z XIV 149,25–150,11.

[139] Z XIV 151,13–15.

[140] E.g., Z I 176,19–178,4; Z II 399,6–400,6. Cf. *Vorrede zur Prophetenbibel*, Z VI/II 308,15–309,3; 311,19–23.

[141] Cf. Z VI/II 305,6–27.

[142] E.g., Z XIII 151,19f.

original languages and the inner-biblical comparison of words and passages that should make it possible to find the "natural sense" of the Biblical text without recourse to the old commentaries that overflowed with allegory.[143] Where the natural sense of Scripture yields a clear sense that is fruitful for us, then playing with allegories[144] is not only superfluous, but even a sign of pride that despises Scripture and God's condescension.[145] Only where this is not the case is allegorical interpretation permitted, and in part mandatory, since its total abolition would be the same as a "Jewish-fleshly" exegesis and would thus deny the prophetic witness to Christ of the entire Bible.[146] The condition, however, is that it must not say anything beyond the clear sense of Scripture. Only in this way does it possess the character of theological proof.[147] Since the point of scriptural interpretation is this clear divine word, which for believers should be, according to John 6, "food for the soul",[148] then allegorical interpretation can only be a "spicy sauce as an added ingredient to the meal", which of itself cannot satisfy hunger, but can make the food tastier.[149] Such spices only have their effect, however, when they are sparingly used, and can also bring aversion instead of edification.[150] Thus it is clear: allegorical interpretation that goes beyond the exegesis of the figurative language of a given pericope belongs for Zwingli on the level of a means to edification. It only convinces those listeners who already for other reasons have been convinced of the theological truth expressed therein. In addition, it should clearly be labeled as allegorical interpretation as a sign of a clear subordination of the exegete to Scripture.[151] As a rule of legitimate allegorical interpretation, Zwingli names the *analogia fidei.*[152] By this he means not so much the rule of faith of the Early Church as the christologically understood Scripture principle. The allegories of Scripture must also be opened with the key of Scripture.[153] Zwingli can thus even go beyond explicit New Testament typologies such as Gal 4:22–31: The two wives of Jacob, Leah and Rachel, symbolize Jews and Gentiles united in Christ, since the New Testament witnesses to this union without carrying out this typology.[154]

Since Zwingli's early discussion of allegorical interpretation already stands in the context of the examination of theological content,[155] its standardization according to Scripture is inseparable from his christological orientation of all scriptural exposition, and thus allegorical interpretation as well. Whilst Luke 17:14 and John 11:44 were adduced in the scholastic tradition to justify the

---

[143] *In apologiam complanationis Isaiae,* Z XIV 103,9–17.
[144] Z XIII 310,32f.
[145] Cf. Z III 860,20–22; Z XIII 14,20–26; 361,27–35; Z XIV 151,15–152,1.
[146] Cf. *Vorrede zur Prophetenbibel,* Z VI/II 305,28–306,5.
[147] Z II 396,4–6; 399,8.
[148] E.g., Z II 141,17; 412,2f; Z III 776,27–777,36.
[149] Z II 398,20–399,6; cf. Z XIII 294,11–16. Zwingli has in mind Col 4:6.
[150] Z XIII 152,6–32. To this kind of "playing", see Erasmus, *Ratio* (1967) 418f.
[151] Z XIII 152,8–15; cf. Z XIII 151,15–20.
[152] Cf. Z XIII 310,32–311,9; 373,2–4.
[153] Z XIII 152,23f.
[154] Z II 399,8–400,6.
[155] Z II 437–42.

function of confession in the context of the question of the ecclesiastical power to bind and loose,[156] Zwingli contests the legitimacy of these passages as *dicta probantia* and uses them in their theological sense: we do not learn from Luke 17:11-19 that oral confession to a priest authorizes or guarantees the forgiveness of sins, but that God alone forgives sins through Christ.[157] Zwingli even considers his own exegesis of this text as allegorization.[158] But its criterion is clearly *solus Christus*, for it is decisive that even allegorical exposition of Scripture is oriented to Christ. What Zwingli observes in the figurative speech of Christ in John 6, he applies hermeneutically to the entire Bible: There Christ speaks alternately directly of himself and faith (*credere*) in him (John 6:40), at the same time however figuratively (*edere*) as well (John 6:51).

If all of Scripture, even the Old Testament, is witness to Christ (cf. John 5:39), then it can be so in a direct way as prophetic messianic oracle, but also in an indirect way. Therefore it must be expounded in another way christologically. This is true also for those texts, above all in the Old Testament, that do not speak openly of Christ. Thereby two methods of exegesis come to the foreground for Zwingli, who in addition to the hermeneutical instructions of 1 Cor 10:6, 11 and Gal 4:21-24 also pays attention to further texts such as Matt 3:3:[159] concerning 'typology' and 'anagogy'. Through 'typology' the narrative texts of the Old Testament can be expounded "prophetically" to point to Christ, while 'anagogy' fundamentally takes into account the Old Testament history leading up to Christ, including the prophetic texts.

In contrast to the neglect of the prophets in the medieval tradition, Zwingli places them in the foreground on the basis of his understanding of the word of God. Thus Zwingli focuses on the 'anagogical' exegesis in the foreword to his explanation of Isaiah, without emphasizing the term.[160] In this he builds on thoughts that Oecolampadius had expressed at the beginning of his exegesis of Isaiah. Three types of texts that are expounded 'anagogically' are to be distinguished: First, Old Testament words of prophets that directly predict the coming of Christ, such as Isa 7:14-15 or Isaiah 53.[161] Secondly, words of prophets that relate initially to a historical event in the Old Testament, and find an additional fulfillment in another way in the history of Christ, such as the announcement of the return from the Babylonian exile (Isa 40:3), which is claimed for Christ in the Gospel of Matthew (Matt 3:3). Thirdly, events of Old Testament time that point in advance to Christ. Inasmuch as the last two are real events, they point to Christ as 'types'.

With typology, which comes into play especially in the exegesis of the stories of Genesis and Exodus, certain persons or events - sometimes only in individual traits - prefigure above all Christ in his person and work. Thus Noah,

---

[156] See Z II 394,8-398,20; cf. Petrus Lombardus, *sent.* IV 17,3; 18,6.

[157] Z II 393,15 -394,5; 394,15-17.

[158] Z II 396,4-6.

[159] Z XIV 94,31.

[160] See Z XIV 94,16-95,16. Cf. *Vorrede zur Prophetenbibel*, Z VI/II 306,6-9.

[161] In a more explicit or in a more hidden, figurative way. Ezekiel 40 to 46, for example, is to be understood "allegorically", because the prophet predicts something, that never has become a reality in the history of Israel, cf. Z XIV 739,23-26.

Melchizedek, Isaac, Jacob, Joseph, Moses, Joshua etc. are 'types' of Christ, who in advance and imperfectly "portray" what in Christ will be perfectly fulfilled.[162] Christ's role as mediator and his atoning work stand in the center. But also the Church as his body or "bride" is prefigured in the Old Testament. "Carnal" and "spiritual" Israel in the form of Hagar and Sarah according to Gal 4:21–14,[163] and correspondingly, but without clear New Testament suggestion, Rachel and Leah, who Jacob takes with him from Mesopotamia (Gen 31:17–18), as the two brides of Christ, Church and Synagogue.[164] In addition, indications of the two "natures" of Christ are found in Old Testament texts,[165] comparable to the portrayal of the struggle between flesh and spirit in individual believers.[166] Doubtless, the medieval "typological teaching", classically formulated for example by Isidore of Seville,[167] exercises a certain influence on Zwingli's exegesis. It is, however, subject to Zwingli's selection and interpretation.

III. John Calvin

Sources: JOHN CALVIN: *Ioannis Calvini Opera quae supersunt omnia* [quoted: CO] (= CR 28–87; ed. G. Baum / E. Cunitz / E. Reuss; Braunschweig 1863–1900); *Joannis Calvini Opera Selecta* I–V [quoted: OS] (ed. P. Barth / W. Niesel; München: Kaiser 1938; vols. III–V: *Institutio Christianae Religionis* [quoted: Inst.]); *Calvin Studienausgabe* (ed. E. Busch / M. Freudenberg / A. Heron / Chr. Link / P. Opitz / E. Saxer / H. Scholl; Neukirchen-Vluyn: Neukirchener 1994-); *Ioannis Calvini opera omnia* [quoted: COR] Series II. *Opera exegetica Veteris et Novi Testamenti* (vol. XIII: *Commentarius in epistolam Pauli ad Romanos;* ed. T. H. L. Parker / D. C. Parker; Geneva: Droz 1999); *Supplementa Calviniana. Sermons inédits* (Neukirchen-Vluyn; Neukirchener 1961-). – HEINRICH BULLINGER: *Heinrich Bullinger. Theologische Schriften 2. Unveröffentlichte Werke der Kappeler Zeit. Theologica* (bearb. von H.-G. vom Berg / B. Schneider / E. Zsindely; Zürich: Theol. Verlag Zürich 1991); *Heinrich Bullinger Briefwechsel 4. Briefe des Jahres 1534* (bearb. von E. Zsindely / M. Senn / K. J. Rüetschi / H. U. Bächtold; Zürich: Theol. Verlag Zürich 1989).

Bibliographies: Calvin Bibliography (by P. Fields) annually in: *Calvin Theological Journal* [*CTJ*] (ed. L. Bierma, for the Faculty of Calvin Theological Seminary, Grand Rapids, MI); *Heinrich Bullinger Bibliographie. Beschreibendes Verzeichnis der gedruckten Werke von Heinrich Bullinger* 1 (bearb. von J. Staedtke; Zürich: Theol. Verlag 1972).

General works: W. BALKE, "Calvins Auslegung von Genesis 22", *Théorie et pratique de l'exégèse. Actes du troisième colloque international sur l'histoire de l'exégèse biblique au XVIe siècle (Genève, 31 août – 2 septembre 1988* (ed. I. Backus / F. Higman; Geneva: Droz 1990) 211–29; E. M. FABER, *Symphonie von Gott und Mensch. Die responsorische Struktur von Vermittlung in der Theologie Johannes Calvins* (Neukirchen-Vluyn: Neukirchener 1999); O. FATIO / P. FRAENKEL, *Histoire de l'exégèse au XVIe siècle. Textes du colloque international tenue à Genève en 1976* (Geneva: Droz 1978); *Le temps des Réformes et la Bible* (BTT 5; ed. G. Bedouelle / B. Roussel; Paris: Beauchesne 1989); R. C. GAMBLE, "Calvin as Theologian and Exegete: Is there anything new?", *CTJ* 23/2 (1988) 178–94; A. GANOCZY / S. SCHELD, *Die Hermeneutik Calvins* (Wiesbaden: Franz Steiner Verlag 1983); G. R. HOBBS, "Hebraica Veritas and Traditio Apostolica. Saint Paul and the Interpretation of the Psalms in the Sixteenth Century", *The Bible in the Sixteenth Century* (ed. D. C. Steinmetz;

---

[162] See his commentary on the corresponding passages in Genesis (Z XIII).
[163] Z XIII 137.
[164] *Vorrede zur Prophetenbibel,* Z VI/II 311,15–19; Z XIII 188.225.
[165] E.g., Z XIII 148,23f.
[166] Künzli, Zwingli als Ausleger des Alten Testaments, Z XIV 891.
[167] See e.g., for Leah and Rachel: *Allegoriae quaedam scripturae sacrae,* PL 83,105.

Durham, NC e.a.: Duke UP 1990) 83–118; A. E. McGRATH, *A Life of John Calvin. A Study in the Shaping of Western Culture* (Oxford: Blackwell 1990); R. A. MULLER, *The Unaccommodated Calvin: Studies in the Foundation of a Theological Tradition* (New York / Oxford: Oxford UP 2000); P. OPITZ, *Calvins theologische Hermeneutik* (Neukirchen-Vluyn: Neukirchener 1994); T. H. L. PARKER, *John Calvin* (London: Dent & Sons 1975); idem, *Calvin's Old Testament Commentaries* (Edinburgh: T&T Clark 1986); H. J. SELDERHUIS, *Gott in der Mitte. Calvins Theologie der Psalmen* (Leipzig: Evangelische Verlagsanstalt 2004); T. F. TORRANCE, *The Hermeneutics of John Calvin* (Edinburgh: Scottish Academic Press 1988); W. VAN'T SPIJKER, *Calvin: Biographie und Theologie* (Göttingen: Vandenhoeck & Ruprecht 2001); F. WENDEL, *Calvin. Sources et évolution de sa pensée religieuse* (2ème éd. rev. et complétée; Genève: Labor et fides 1985).

Special abbreviations (see above)*:*
CO = *Ioannis Calvini Opera quae supersunt omnia*
COR = *Ioannis Calvini Opera omnia [recognita]*
Inst. = *Institutio Christianae Religionis*
OS = *Ioannis Calvini Opera Selecta*

1. Calvin in the Context of the Renaissance

Studies: G. BABELOTZKY, *Platonische Bilder und Gedankengänge in Calvins Lehre vom Menschen* (Wiesbaden: Franz Steiner Verlag 1977); CH. PARTEE, *Calvin and Classical Philosophy* (Leiden: Brill 1977); W. J. BOUWSMA, *John Calvin. A Sixteenth Century Portrait* (New York / Oxford: Oxford UP 1988); B. COTTRET, *Calvin: Biographie* (Paris: Ed. Jean -Claude Lattès 1995); A. GANOCZY, *Le jeune Calvin* (Wiesbaden: Franz Steiner Verlag 1966) 23–196; A. N. S. LANE, *John Calvin. Student of the Church Fathers* (Edinburgh: T&T Clark 1999); P. OPITZ (ed.), *Calvin im Kontext der Schweizer Reformation: Historische und theologische Beiträge zur Calvinforschung* (Zürich: Theol. Verlag Zürich 2003); K. REUTER, *Das Grundverständnis der Theologie Calvins* (Neukirchen: Neukirchener 1963) 55–124; E. SAXER, *Aberglaube, Heuchelei und Frömmigkeit. Eine Untersuchung zu Calvins reformatorischer Eigenart* (Zürich: Zwingli Verlag 1970); B. J. VAN DER WALT, "Renaissance and Reformation: Contemporaries but not allies", *Calvinus Reformator* (Wetenskaplike Bydraes of the PU for CHE Series F: Institute for Reformational Studies F 3 Collections Number 17; Potchefstroom 1982) 85–92.

1.1. Calvin's Education in the humanae artes

John Calvin (1509–64), after attending the faculty of arts at the Collège de Montaigu in Paris, studied law between 1528 and 1531 in Orléans and Bourges. While the basic course contents can be reconstructed with a degree of certainty, the decisive question of the manner and interpretation with which the material commonly offered there was presented to Calvin cannot be described so accurately. It can be assumed, however, that the tension that was typical for the time between a nominalistically oriented theory of knowledge and logic that critically developed the Aristotelian foundations of logic and physics, on the one hand,[168] and the increasingly strong 'humanistic' influences that orientated themselves on Cicero's ideal of education,[169] on the other, may

---

[168] Cf. K. Reuter, Grundverständnis (1963) 31–55; Torrance, Hermeneutics (1988) 3–95.

[169] Calvin's relationship to the contemporary 'humanism' cannot be treated fruitfully in general. As an introduction see C. AUGUSTIJN, "Calvin und der Humanismus", *Calvinus Servus Christi. Die Referate des Internationalen Kongresses für Calvinforschung vom 25. Bis 28. August 1986 in Debrecen* (ed. W. H. Neuser; Budapest: Presseabteilung des Ráday-Kollegiums 1988) 127–42.

already have been felt during the time of his master studies. However this tension undoubtedly marked a decisive point during the time of his legal studies. Setting the tone as opposing authorities were Pierre de l'Etoile, who taught in the 'old' manner, and the humanist legal scholar Andreas Alciat. It must be remembered, however, that when it came to the interpretation of ancient legal texts, a certain cross-fertilization of the two elements influences/schools of thought can be observed.

With his commentary on Seneca's *De clementia* in 1532, completed shortly after the conclusion of his legal studies, Calvin places himself clearly in the early French humanist movement. In his extensive commentary on this text, which had reappeared in 1529 as part of Erasmus's complete edition of Seneca's writings, Calvin obviously strives to demonstrate his skills as an erudite humanist exegete. He not only makes direct reference to the two "pillars"[170] Erasmus and Budé, he comments on Seneca's text following all the rules of the arts of 'philology' and 'rhetoric'.[171]

Already in this work, however, the sobriety with which Calvin uses the philological-grammatical and rhetorical methods is remarkable. For Erasmus, and even more clearly for Budé, *philologia* as an approach to ancient texts is a step in a comprehensive process of refinement that leads from the occupation with the *bonae litterae* to philosophy, theology and mysticism and includes an ethical 'education', in other words, it was seen against the background of a Platonic-Neoplatonic understanding of 'education' and 'wisdom'.[172] Hardly any of this can be felt in Calvin's Seneca commentary. He maintains the standpoint of the analyzing exegete who places the text in the life and time of Seneca, clarifies concepts and allusions, and identifies the figures of speech that are used. The goal of interpretation as the placing of the text in its historical and linguistic context is simply to reveal clearly the meaning of the statements Seneca makes as well as the intention that he had pursued with this 'discourse'.[173]

1.2. The artes liberales *in the Service of the Exposition of Scripture*

With his commentary on *De clementia*, Calvin prefigured the path of text interpretation that he would later follow in his Bible exposition. The philological and rhetorical methods are again put at the service of the interpretation of text, this time on a theological basis. In the exegesis of biblical texts, too, what matters is the sober understanding of the *mens scriptoris* and to grasp the rhetorical-kerygmatic movement of the text, without thereby immediately transporting the text to one's own day.

---

[170] CO 5,54; CO 5,6.

[171] Cf. Erasmus, *Ratio* (1967) 117–495.

[172] Cf. G. Budé, *De studio literarum recte et commode instituendo* (new facsimile-edn. of the edn. of Paris 1532, with introduction by A. Buck; Stuttgart-Bad Cannstatt 1964). Erasmus is generally more cautious and more christologically orientated, but points in the same direction, see *Ratio* (1967) 120–26. On Erasmus, see further Chap. 9, by E. RUMMEL, in the present volume.

[173] Cf. CO 5,54.

This presumes an understanding of the biblical writings derived from the Reformation conviction of the 'perspicuity' of Scripture, which sees Scripture as no divine means of transporting the reader mystagogically from an exoteric to an esoteric meaning and thus to knowledge and contemplation of eternal things.[174] Instead, its movement goes in the other direction. It is, as Calvin formulates it in the foreword to the French Geneva Bible translation, "the key that opens the kingdom of God to us, to introduce us there, with the goal that we may know which God we worship, and what he calls us to" and "the means of the covenant that he has concluded with us".[175] It is God's word, addressed and accommodated to us[176] in the form of human transmission and speech.

It is precisely for this reason that the understanding of the biblical text requires rational thinking, and begins with the determination of the *mens scriptoris* in each particular context; therefore the particular rhetorical dimension of the text is also to be taken into account for its interpretation. It is only with this that its intention can be fully disclosed, since these texts are to be understood against the background of the movement of God's address to humans. The goal is, in this way, to draw from them a "useful teaching".

This assumes a theological understanding of the *artes liberales*, according to which they are understood as divine gifts to be used by humans. Calvin praised them in his *Institutio*, without thereby weakening his doctrine of sin.[177] The *bonae litterae* in and of themselves do not bring humans to the path of wisdom, but are meant for and limited to earthly life. There, they are to be exercised, however,[178] for the "unfree will" with regard to God does not exclude the appreciation and use of human mental capacities as gifts of creation.[179]

1.2.1. *The Question of the* mens scriptoris

Even though Calvin did not compose a work devoted to the hermeneutical problem,[180] he did concern himself thoroughly with the problem of an adequate interpretation of Scripture. For the second generation of Reformers the necessity of dealing with this question had become evident for both internal

---

[174] Cf. Budé, *De studio* (1964) XXVI-XXVII.

[175] ... *la clef qui nous ouvre le Royaume de Dieu, pour nous y introduire, à fin que nous sachions quel Dieu nous devons adorer, et à quoy il nous appelle*, CO 9,823; cf. OS III 7,21; OS IV 13,18f; CO 7,540; CO 26,286.

[176] Cf. Inst. I 13.1 (OS III 109,13–18); Inst. II 6.4 (OS III 326,1–3); *scriptura loquitur humano more* (CO 43,161); *balbutire* (CO 8,15). Cf. E. A. Dowey, *The Knowledge of God in Calvin's Theology* (New York: Columbia UP 1952) 3–17; F. L. Battles, "God Was Accommodating Himself to Human Capacity", *Int* 31 (1977) 19–38; repr. in: *Calvin and Hermeneutics* (vol. 6 of: *Articles on Calvin and Calvinism. A fourteen-volume Anthology of Scholarly Articles*, ed. R. C. Gamble; New York / London: Garland 1992) 13–32.

[177] Inst. II 2.14–17 (OS III 257,20–260,26).

[178] Cf. CO 7,516.

[179] ... *in huius vitae constitutione, nullum destitui luce rationis hominem*, OS III 257, 18 [Inst. II 2.13]. Concerning things, which ... *cum vita praesenti rationem relationemque habent, et quodammodo intra eius fines continentur*, OS III 256,25 ff. [Inst. II 2.13]; cf. Inst. II 2.15 (OS III 258, 18–27).

[180] A thoroughly possible thing at his time, see Bullinger's *Studiorum ratio* from 1528: Heinrich Bullinger, *Studiorum ratio – Studienanleitung* 1–2 (ed. P. Stotz; Zürich: Theol. Verlag Zürich 1987).

and external reasons. On the one hand, the confrontation with the Anabaptists, who appealed to the Scripture principle, as well as the experience of various interpretations of Scripture within the Reformation movement required this; on the other hand, the attempt and the necessity of a 'didactic' presentation of the content of the faith on the basis of *sola scriptura* made this necessary. Calvin's famous preface to the commentary on Romans of 15 November 1539, written in Strasbourg, sheds light on the context in which his exegesis developed. The addressee and the interpreters of Romans mentioned in it – Bucer, Bullinger, and Melanchthon – allow us to see that Calvin already concerned himself with the proper exegesis of Scripture in Basel, but then intensively in Strasbourg, and that he received decisive impulses from the circle of interpreters characterized by scholars as the "Ecole Rhénane", the "Upper Rhine School".[181] He reminds Simon Grynäus, for instance, to whom the preface is dedicated, of their agreement in their conversations on the proper manner of scriptural exegesis.[182] Grynäus, though a respected humanist and Greek scholar, experienced hostility in Heidelberg as a 'Zwinglian' and in 1529 followed a call from Oecolampadius to Basel. There he took part in the theological discussions of the time between Strasbourg, Basel und Zurich, as his collaboration in the composition of the *Confessio helvetica prior* shows.[183] It is evident that with this dedication Calvin shows the debt he feels to this circle of exegetes, while at the same time he seeks to introduce himself into it as an interpreter of Romans.[184] When Calvin names *perspicuitas* and *brevitas* as the two principles that guide his own exegetical intent,[185] he presumes a basic consensus that the aim of interpretation is to reflect adequately the *mens scriptoris*. To open this up is the primary duty of exegesis.[186]

From this follows Calvin's specific concern. Although he praises the interpreters of Romans who preceded him, Bucer, Bullinger and Melanchthon, his brief characterization of their exegesis reflects his implicit criticism. Whereas Melanchthon is content to name the chief points of each section, and thereby overlooks much that is worth mentioning,[187] Bucer instead, in his great learn-

---

[181] B. Roussel, "De Strasbourg à Bâle et Zurich: une 'Ecole Rhénane' d'exégèse (ca. 1525 – ca. 1540)", *RHPhR* 68 (1988) 19–39. Cf. H.-J. Kraus, "Calvins exegetische Prinzipien", *ZKG* 79 (1968) 329–41; ET in: R. C. Gamble, Calvin and hermeneutics (1992) 2–12. The "Upper Rhine School" is also treated by R. G. Hobbs, in the next chapter (19.1).

[182] CO 10/2,402.

[183] Cf. J. V. Pollet, *Martin Bucer. Etudes sur la correspondance avec de nombreux textes inédits* 2 (Paris: Presses Universitaires de France 1962) 370–400; Locher, Zwinglische Reformation (1979) 342.

[184] See N. Kuropka, "Calvins Römerbriefwidmung und der Consensus piorum", in: Opitz, Calvin im Kontext der Schweizer Reformation (2003) 147–68.

[185] *Sentiebat enim uterque nostrum, praecipuam interpretis virtutem in perspicua brevitate esse positam*, CO 10/2,402. Cf. R. C. Gamble, "Brevitas et Facilitas: Toward an Understanding of Calvin's Hermeneutic", *WTJ* 47 (1985) 1–17.

[186] *Et sane quum hoc sit prope unicum illius officium, mentem scriptoris, quem explicandum sumpsit, patefacere: quantum ab ea lectores abducit, tantundem a scopo suo aberrat, vel certe a suis finibus quodammodo evagatur*, CO 10/2,403.

[187] *Philippus enim quod voluit adeptus est, ut maxime necessaria capita illustraret. Multa quae negligenda non sunt, dum in illis primis occupatus praetermisit, noluit alios impedire quin ea quoque excuterent*, CO 10/2,404.

ing gathers so much material that his readers risk missing the point.[188] This characterization can be combined with Calvin's opinion of the Isaiah interpretations of Zwingli, Luther and Oecolampadius expressed in a letter to Viret on 19 May 1540. Though he concedes that Zwingli has exegetical "skill", he often takes "too much freedom" and strays "far from the meaning of the prophet".[189] His judgment of Luther as interpreter is even more critical: he is "not too careful with regard to the characteristics of the wording and the historical circumstances", he "contents himself with carving out a fruitful teaching".[190] Less severe is the assessment of Oecolampadius, to whom great industry as interpreter is ascribed, though not always accompanied by accuracy.[191] This clarifies what Calvin means when he says that *perspicuitas* and *brevitas* are the guiding principles of his exegesis: While it is self-evident that exegesis is done to uncover a "useful teaching", this can never weaken the effort to recover the original "meaning" of the biblical text, and this sense in turn is found by understanding the text in its grammatical and historical context and the intention followed by its author,[192] which is formally expressed in certain rhetorical figures.[193] Calvin's assessment of the quality of the exegesis of the Church Fathers corresponds to his emphasis and interpretation of the concept of *perspicua brevitas*. Above all, Chrysostom seems to be exemplary for him, while all exegetes who use allegorical interpretation, especially Origen, but also Augustine, because of their own inventions, obscure the sense of a text more than they illuminate it.[194]

Calvin's rule of *perspicua brevitas* is totally at the service of the question of the sense of the text, the *mens scriptoris*. This assumes that all exposition remains subordinate to the truth that finds expression in the text. As explication of the statement of the text, exegesis remains subordinate to the self-explication of the truth of the text. It should create a space in which this truth can reveal itself. For this purpose, the *artes liberales* serve as helps. Not only are they legitimated, their help is demanded. They must be used appropriately, however, and not for their own sake. Their task consists solely in removing hindrances to understanding that they point to the context and the aim of a statement. The interpreter fulfills his task by clearly distinguishing between the text and the argumentative unfolding of the interpretation he makes by drawing on

---

[188] *Bucerus et prolixior est quam ut ab hominibus aliis occupationibus districtis raptim legi: et sublimior quam ut ab humilibus et non valde attentis intelligi facile queat*, CO 10/2,404.

[189] CO 11,36.

[190] Ibid.

[191] Ibid.

[192] When Calvin in the preface to the *Institutio* 1539 sees it as an aim to prepare the candidates of theology to read the Scriptures, and at the same time speaks of his commentaries, it is clear, that the task of the *Institutio* is to deal with the theological loci and "problems", so that he in his exegesis can concentrate on the biblical text, without being urged to make thematical disgressions (cf. OS III 6,18–28).

[193] On the rhetorical tradition of *perspicua brevitas*, cf. QUINTILIAN, *Inst. orat.* 8.2.22; 4.2.36; 4.2.40, 4.2.45; 4.2.52. See further F. L. BATTLES / A. M. HUGO, *Calvin's Commentary on Seneca's De clementia. With Introduction, Translation, and Notes* (Leiden: E. J. Brill 1969) 82*; 435–36.

[194] CO 9, 834 f.

grammar and rhetoric. In this way, he seeks to recede as far as possible behind the opinion of the author.

1.2.2. *Drawing out the "Use" as Goal of Exegesis*

The goal of all scriptural exegesis however is to draw out its "use". Calvin fills this rhetorical category with theological meaning[195] and allows himself to be led by the biblical statement itself. In stating that scriptural exegesis has to occur according to the *analogia fidei* according to Rom 12:6, Calvin agrees with the rule of the early Church Fathers,[196] but interprets it in the sense that, in addition to the Apostles' Creed as traditional *regula fidei*, the ultimate witness is Scripture itself, which is understood as the soteriologically oriented witness to Christ.[197]

In the foreword of the French Bible translation, he summarizes the "use" of Scripture as that which "instructs us in sound doctrine, comforts us, exhorts us, and makes us perfect in all good works",[198] combining thereby 1 Cor 14:3, Rom 15:4 and 2 Tim 3:16–17, which complement and mutually interpret each other. "Edification", which scriptural exegesis should serve, according to 1 Cor 14:3, consists "in one word, in this, that we learn through it to place our trust in God and to go our way in fear of him", and that we recognize Christ, the end and goal of the Law and the prophets and the "substance" of the Gospel.[199] The explanation of the "use" of Scripture thus goes beyond the proper application of philological methods; it is a "prophetic" task, which he understands in connection with Old Testament prophecy.[200]

2. The Relationship of the Testaments

Studies: W. DE GREEF, *Calvijn en het Oude Testament* (Groningen: T. Bolland 1984). On the question of Calvin's "covenant theology": J. HESSELINK, *Calvin's Concept of the Law* (Allison Park, PA: Pickwick Publications 1992); A. A. HOEKEMA, "The Covenant of Grace in Calvin's Teaching", *CTJ* 2/2 (1967) 133–61; P. A. LILLIBACK, *The Binding of God. Calvin's Role in the Development of Covenant Theology* (Grand Rapids, MI: Baker Academic 2001); T. H. L. PARKER, *Calvin's Old Testament Commentaries* (Edinburgh: T&T Clark 1986); J. B. TORRANCE, "The Concept of Federal Theology – Was Calvin a Federal Theologian?", *Calvinus Sacrae Scripturae Professor. Die Referate des Internationalen Kongresses für Calvinforschung vom 20. bis 23. August 1990 in Grand Rapids* (ed.

---

[195] Cf. B. GIRARDIN, *Rhétorique et Théologique. Calvin: Le Commentaire de l'Épître aux Romains* (Paris: Beauchesne 1979) 207; O. MILLET, *Calvin et la dynamique de la Parole. Etudes de rhétorique réformée* (Paris: Librairie Honoré Champion 1992).

[196] Cf. Tertullian, *Praescr.* 13 (CChr.SL I 197–198).

[197] Cf. the preface to the *Institutio*, OS III 12,25–13,28.

[198] CO 9,825.

[199] CO 9,825.

[200] Cf. on Rom 12:6: CO 49, 239; (new edition COR [see Bibliography above]: Series 2; Vol. XIII [1999] 261). Cf. Heinrich Bullinger, *De prophetae officio* (Tiguri: Christoph Froschauer 1532 [Heinrich Bullinger Bibliographie, 1972, Nr.33]; german translation: "Das Amt des Propheten", *Heinrich Bullinger Schriften I* (ed. E. Campi / D. Roth / P. Stotz; Zürich: Theologischer Verlag Zürich 2004) 11–48.

W. H. Neuser; Grand Rapids: Eerdmans 1994) 15–40; H. H. WOLF, *Die Einheit des Bundes. Das Verhältnis von Altem und Neuem Testament bei Calvin* (Neukirchen: Neukirchener 1958).

In addition to exegetical methods, the determination of the theological relation between the two testaments is decisive for Calvin's interpretation of Old Testament texts. Calvin grappled with the relation of the Old and New Testaments intensively in his time in Strasbourg. The fruit of these studies is found in an extensive chapter of the *Institutio* of 1539, where both testaments are explained as unity which is in itself differentiated and dynamic.[201] In this regard, the influence of Martin Bucer was doubtlessly decisive, beyond this, however, the entire circle of Upper German Reformers with humanist background and Zwinglian influences. Bucer, who had already championed the idea of the unity of the two testaments in his commentary on the Gospels,[202] not only was in lively correspondence with his Strasbourg colleagues, Capito, the Hebrew scholar, and Hedio, but also with Heinrich Bullinger. By drawing further on a thesis brought up by Zwingli,[203] Bullinger had already claimed the one covenant as the aim of Scripture since the twenties[204] and had received Bucer's endorsement for his work *De testamento*,[205] 1532.[206] As had Zwingli, Bullinger and Bucer before him, Calvin regarded the Anabaptists, but then Servet as well, as the chief opponents, against whom the unity of the covenant and with it the validity of the Old Testament was to be maintained.[207] In the *Institutio* of 1559, which will be quoted in the following, Calvin integrated the teaching of one covenant fully in his soteriology. In addition, the 'covenant' concept became a decisive connecting element between Calvin's theology, especially his Christology, and his exegesis.[208] Book Two of the *Institutio* was entitled "The Knowledge of God the Redeemer in Christ, First Disclosed to the Fathers under the Law, and Then to Us in the Gospel".[209] Whereas Calvin's first *Institutio* of 1536 was still too reminiscent of Luther's *Smaller Catechism*, the teaching on the Law in *Institutio* II 7 was now headed by the title: "The Law Was Given, Not to Restrain the Folk of the Old Covenant Under Itself, but to Foster Hope of Salvation in Christ until His Coming".[210] The Law is expressly defined in the sense of Old Testament Torah understanding: "I understand by the word 'law' not only the Ten Commandments, which set forth a godly and

---

[201] *Cap. VII. De similitudine et differentia Veteris et Novi Testamenti* CO 1, 225–44.

[202] Cf. A. LANG, *Der Evangelienkommentar Martin Bucers und die Grundzüge seiner Theologie* (Leipzig 1900; repr. Aalen: Scientia Verlag 1972) 329–35.

[203] Cf. *Von der Taufe, von der Wiedertaufe und von der Kindertaufe* (Z IV 292–295); and the *Antwort über Balthasar Hubmaiers Taufbüchlein* (Z IV 634–639).

[204] Cf. Heinrich Bullinger, *Von dem Touff* (1525); see Heinrich Bullinger, Theologische Schriften 2 (1991) 71–85.

[205] Heinrich Bullinger, *De testamento seu foedere dei unico et aeterno*, Tiguri 1534 (No critical edition existing; see: *Heinrich Bullinger Bibliographie*, 1972, Nr. 54).

[206] *Heinrich Bullinger Briefwechsel 4. Briefe des Jahres 1534* (1989) 325–26.

[207] Inst. II 10.1 (OS III 403,19–404,4).

[208] About the connection between theology and exegesis, see Opitz, Calvins theologische Hermeneutik (1994).

[209] Inst. II (OS III 228,3–5). Translations here and subsequently by Ford Lewis Battles in the Libary of Christian Classics edition [LCC], Philadelphia: Westminster 1960.

[210] Inst. II 7 (OS III 326,19–21).

righteous rule of living, but the form of religion (*formam religionis*) handed down by God through Moses".[211] Since this Law is based however on God's elective grace, Christ is already present: even though the mediatorship of Christ "in Moses' writings was not yet expressed in clear words",[212] nevertheless, "apart from the Mediator, God never showed favor toward the ancient people, nor ever gave hope of grace to them".[213] For "the blessed and happy state of the church always had its foundation in the person of Christ".[214] For the relation of the Old and New Testaments this means: "The covenant made with all the Patriarchs is so much like ours in substance and reality that the two are actually one and the same. Yet they differ in the mode of dispensation".[215]

The similarity (*similitudo*) or unity (*unitas*)[216] of the two Testaments is treated in Inst. II 10, the differences (*differentia*) in the following chapter, Chap. 11. For Calvin, the unity of the covenant is constituted by three factors: First the election to "the hope of immortality", which was already the goal for the Jews in the time of the Old Testament, no less than it is for Christians.[217] The Old Testament promises were not aimed merely at earthly happiness. Rather, the covenant God made with the people of Israel was, despite the inclusion of the promise of land and the ceremonial law, a "spiritual" covenant.[218] Secondly, the covenant is purely a covenant of grace, and was so already in Old Testament times. The continuity of *sola gratia* spans both Testaments.[219] Thirdly, fellowship with God and participation in the divine promises was based on the mediation of Christ, no less in the Old Testament than in the New. The Patriarchs, too, "had and knew Christ as Mediator".[220]

Calvin deals with the differences in Inst. II 11. They arise from the way in which God had accommodated his word for pedagogical reasons, in the service of salvation. The first difference is that promises, which rest on Christ as their only foundation, and which, in accordance with the word of God as elective word contain the "grace of future life",[221] were mediated in the Old Testament "under earthly benefits", for instance in the promise of the land of Canaan. In the New Testament, in contrast, they are spoken more plainly and clearly.[222] The second difference also concerns the increasing clarity of revelation, especially with regard to the Old Testament ceremonies, which are abolished for the Christian community and replaced by the New Testament sacra-

---

[211] Inst. II 7.1 (OS III 326,27–30).
[212] Inst. II 6.2 (OS III 322,13).
[213] Ibid. (OS III 321,31f).
[214] Ibid. (OS III 321,35–37).
[215] Inst. II 10.2 (OS III 404,5–7).
[216] Ibid. (OS III 404,10f).
[217] Ibid. (OS III 404,15–18).
[218] Ibid. (OS III 405, 15–19).
[219] Ibid. (OS III 404,18–20).
[220] Ibid. (OS III 404, 20–22).
[221] Cf. Inst. II 11.1 (OS III 423,13–23).
[222] Inst. II 11.2 (OS III 424,16–21). Because of the connection of the promise with the spirit, it must contain more than earthly goods even in Old Testament times, see Inst. II 10.3 (OS III 405,15–19).

ments. Here Calvin recalls above all the differentiation in Heb 10:1 between the "shadow of good things to come" and the "true form of these realities" and on the distinction of Col 2:17 between the "shadow of what is to come" and the "substance", identified with Christ.[223] The fifth difference runs along these lines as well. It consists in the calling of the nations, through the Gospel going beyond the boundaries of Israel (Inst. II 11.11).[224] Both the third difference, that between 'letter' and 'spirit', and the fourth, between 'bondage' and 'freedom', are seen against the background of the one divine saving activity as merely relative differences.[225]

The antithetical contrast of Law and Gospel as presented by Luther and Melanchthon does not have a hermeneutically fundamental character in Calvin's view. It has its place where "Law" is not the "whole Law", but used in a narrower sense and restricted to a path to salvation for sinful humanity by keeping moral or religious rules.[226] "But the gospel did not so supplant the entire law as to bring forward a different way of salvation. Rather, it confirmed and satisfied whatever the law had promised, and gave substance to the shadows".[227] In accordance with this, the teaching on the Law is entitled: "Christ, Although He Was Known to the Jews Under the Law, Was at Length Clearly Revealed Only in the Gospel".[228]

Calvin illustrates this history of the covenant as the history of revelation with the image of the progressive increase of light. The history of God's covenant of grace with humankind is the history of how God "meted out the light of his Word",[229] until in Christ the previously hidden source of all light appears, and God now not only speaks to humans, but has become a human and thereby reached the summit of his accommodation.[230] The old promises are thereby fulfilled and in this fulfillment surpassed.[231]

> The Lord held to this orderly plan in administering the covenant of his mercy: as the day of full revelation approached with the passing of time, the more he increased each day the brightness of its manifestation. Accordingly, at the beginning when the first promise of salvation was given to Adam it glowed like a feeble spark. Then, as it was added to, the light grew in fullness, breaking forth increasingly and shedding its radiance more widely. At last – when all the clouds were dispersed – Christ, the Sun of Righteousness, fully illumined the whole earth.[232]

The image of increasing light, which expresses the character of God's activity, of the administration in his covenant of grace, corresponds, with regard to humans, to the image of the education pedagogy of God, who as "a householder instructs, rules, and guides, his children one way in infancy, another way in youth, and still another in young manhood", and who should not on this ac-

---

[223] Cf. Inst. II 11.4–5; Inst. II 7.16; Inst. IV 14.25. Cf. Parker, Calvin's Old Testament Commentaries (1986) 56–62.
[224] Cf. Inst. II 11.11 (OS III 433,24–434,9).
[225] Inst. II 11.9 (OS III 430,23ff.; 432,2–12); cf. Inst. II 11.8–9 (OS III 430,4–432,12).
[226] Inst. II 9.4 (OS III 401,22–26).
[227] Ibid. (OS III 401,31–35).
[228] Inst. II 9 (OS III 398,8f).
[229] Inst. II 11.5 (OS III 428,1–17).
[230] Cf. Battles, God Was Accommodating Himself to Human Capacity (1977) 19–38.
[231] Inst. II 9.2 (OS III 400,10f); see on Heb 7:19f (CO 55,92f).
[232] Inst. II 10.20 (OS III 420,3–13).

count be considered fickle, as someone who lightly changes his mind. Rather, "he has accommodated himself to men's capacity, which is varied and changeable".[233] It is precisely the immutable will of God that demands it to be communicated in different ways. The Law, according to Calvin, is essentially determined by this pedagogical context. It is the time of "rudiments"[234] and this points beyond itself to the time of the Gospel.

With this Calvin sets a boundary on two opposite sides: Although the Law is, with regard to humans as sinners, a "mirror of sin", it is in itself good and not a "deadly" or "crushing" divine word.[235] On the other hand, the time before Christ, as time "under the law", is clearly characterized by hope and expectation and may not, despite the fundamental unity of the covenant, be simply equated with the time of the New Testament. This would abolish the historical dynamic of the covenant.

3. Calvin's Exegesis of the Old Testament

Studies: The scope of this study does not allow for an overview of the large number of monographs and articles on Calvin's exposition of various Old Testament texts; see the annual Calvin bibliography in *CTJ*; a few selected titles must suffice. Various articles on the question of Calvin's hermeneutics and his exposition of Scripture, which also reflect the diverse perceptions of Calvin are collected in: *Calvin and Hermeneutics* (vol. 6 of *Articles on Calvin and Calvinism.* A fourteen-volume Anthology of Scholarly Articles, ed. by R. C. Gamble; New York / London: Garland 1992); E. A. DE BOER, *Calvin on the Visions of Ezechiel: Studies in His Sermons With a Critical Edition of the Sermons on Ezechiel 36–48* 1–2 (PhD diss. University of Geneva 1999); J. FRIEDMAN, *The Most Ancient Testimony: Sixteenth-Century Christian-Hebraica in the Age of Renaissance Nostalgia* (Athens, OH: Ohio State UP 1983); K. E. GREENE-McCREIGHT, *How Augustine, Calvin, and Barth read the 'plain sense' of Genesis 1–3* (New York e.a.: Peter Lang 1999) 95–173; W. DE GREEF, *Calvijn en zijn uitleg van de Psalmen. Een onderzoek naar zijn exegetische methode* (Kampen: Uitgeverij Kok 2006); B. HALL, "Calvin and Biblical Humanism", *Huguenot Society Proceedings* 20 (1959–1964) 195–309; H.-J. KRAUS, "Calvins exegetische Prinzipien", *ZKG* 79 (1968) 329–41; R. MARTIN-ACHARD, "Aperçus sur l'enseignement de l'Ancien Testament à l'Académie et à l'Université de Genève", *RThPh* 118 (1986) 373–88; O. MILLET, *Calvin et la dynamique de la Parole. Etudes de rhétorique réformée* (Paris: Librairie Honoré Champion 1992); M. L. MONHEIT, "Young Calvin, Textual Interpretation and Roman Law", *BHR* 59 (1997) 263–82; R. A. MULLER, "The Hermeneutic of Promise and Fulfillment in Calvin's Exegesis of the Old Testament Prophecies of the Kingdom", *The Bible in the Sixteenth Century* (ed. David C. Steinmetz; Durham and London: Duke University Press 1990) 68–82; W. H. NEUSER, "Calvins Verständnis der Heiligen Schrift", *Calvinus Sacrae Scripturae Professor. Die Referate des Internationalen Kongresses für Calvinforschung vom 20. bis 23. August 1990 in Grand Rapids* (ed. W. H. Neuser; Grand Rapids: Eerdmans 1994) 41–71; P. OPITZ, "'Asperges me Domine hyssopo, et mundabor'. Beobachtungen zu Sadolets und Calvins Exegesen von Psalm 51 als Frage nach dem 'proprium' reformierter Schriftauslegung", *Reformiertes Erbe* 2 (FS for Gottfried W. Locher; ed. H. A. Obermann / E. Saxer / A. Schindler / H. Stucki; Zürich: Theol. Verlag Zürich 1993) 297–313; idem, "Ein Thorapsalm als ABC des christlichen Glaubens. Beobachtungen zu Calvins Predigten über Psalm 119", *Calvin's Books* (FS for Peter De Klerk; ed. W. H. Neuser / H. J. Selderhuis / W. van't Spijker; Heerenveen: J. J. Groen 1997) 117–31; T. H. L. PARKER, *Calvin's Preaching* (Edinburgh: T&T Clark 1992); D. L. PUCKETT, *John Calvin's Exe-*

---

[233] Inst. II 11.13 (OS III 435,22–27); see Inst. II 11.5 (OS III 427,34–428,4). Cf. Irenäus, *Adversus haereses* IV 4,2.
[234] Cf. Inst. II 9.4 (OS III 401,35–402,3).
[235] See Luther, *Die Schmalkaldischen Artikel*, WA 50,225,25–226,5.

gesis of the Old Testament (Louisville, KY: Westminster John Knox 1995); B. Roussel, "De Strasbourg à Bâle et Zurich: une 'Ecole Rhénane' d'exégèse (ca. 1525 – ca. 1540)", *RHPhR* 68 (1988) 19–39; R. Stauffer, "L'exégèse de Genèse 1/1–3 chez Luther et Calvin", *Interprètes de la Bible. Études sur les Réformateurs du XVIe siècle* (ed. R. Stauffer; Paris: Beauchesne 1982) 59–85; D. Steinmetz, *Calvin in Context* (New York: Oxford UP 1995); J. L. Thompson, "Calvin's Exegetical Legacy: His Reception and Transmission of Text and Tradition", *The Legacy of John Calvin: Calvin Studies Society Papers 1999* (ed. D. L. Foxgrover; Grand Rapids: Calvin Studies Society 2000) 31–56.

3.1. *The Exposition of Old Testament Books in Sermons, Lectures, and Commentaries*[236]

In the late 1540s, Calvin turned increasingly to the exposition of the Old Testament in his sermons and lectures, in the *Congrégations,* and finally in his written commentaries. But only the commentaries on Psalms (1552), the books of Moses (1563) and Joshua (1565) can be considered works that he completed for publication. All three grew out of the *Congrégations*, the gatherings of the Geneva clergy that took place each Friday. The commentary on Genesis was begun by Calvin,[237] but then completed by Nicolas des Gallars on the basis of lecture notes.[238] Other commentaries were produced in a similar way. The Isaiah commentary came entirely from Gallard's notes of lectures Calvin held in the "school".[239] These were, however, largely authorized by Calvin.[240] Apart from the Old Testament lectures Calvin devoted his weekly sermons to the Old Testament. In addition to the Sunday sermons, which with exception of the Psalms were devoted to New Testament texts, Calvin generally preached daily every other week. Despite some uncertainty,[241] the number of Calvin's Old Testament sermons reach an estimated two thousand.[242] From 1549 on these sermons, held more or less extemporaneously and with reference to the Hebrew text,[243] were recorded stenographically by Denis Raguenier,[244] a labor that was continued by others after Raguenier's death in 1560.[245]

Calvin's efforts to provide an Old Testament exegesis of the highest level is underlined by his attempts to bring the best Hebrew scholars to the newly founded (1559) Geneva Academy. One example is his unsuccessful attempt to attract Jewish convert Immanuel Tremellius in 1558.[246] Calvin left no record of how he himself acquired Hebrew. Colladon's remark that Calvin visited lec-

---

[236] Cf. CO 23 X–IVX.
[237] CO 13,606.
[238] Cf. Parker, Commentaries (1986) 25–26.
[239] Cf. Parker, ibid. 16.
[240] Cf. CO 36 *Prolegomena*; see Parker, Commentaries (1986) 24.
[241] This concerns also the indications of Colladon (CO 21,66.88f).
[242] Cf. Parker, ibid. 10.
[243] Cf. M. Engammare, "Johannes Calvinus trium linguarum peritus?", *BHR* 58 (1996) 35–60.
[244] Cf. CO 25,587 f.
[245] Cf. B. Gagnebin, "L'Histoire des Manuscrits des Sermons de Calvin", *Supplementa Calviniana* II (ed. E. A. Barrois; Neukirchen: Neukirchener 1961) XIV–XXVIII.
[246] Cf. Calvin's letter to Tremellius (4 September 1558) (CO 17,309f).

tures by Sebastian Münster during his stay in Basel 1535–1536 and that he later deepened his knowledge of Hebrew during his stay in Strasbourg, where
the recognized Hebrew scholars Bucer and Capito were active,[247] seems plausible and is supported by indications in Calvin's own writings.[248] Calvin doubtlessly continued his studies of the language on his own in his later years.

In his exegesis of Old Testament texts the *Biblia hebraica* of Sebastian Münster (1535 / 1546) together with his *Dictionarium hebraicum* (1535) were essential aids. Equally important are the printings of Robert Estienne, his 1548
reprint of the *Thesaurus linguae sanctae* of Sanctes Pagninus (1529), and his Bibles: the 1545 Biblia sacra with the 1543 Latin translation of the Old Testament by Leo Jud, Theodor Bibliander and Conrad Pellican and the Biblia sacra latina of 1556/57 with the translation of the Old Testament by Pagninus,
both with numerous annotations by the French humanist and Hebraist scholar
François Vatable.[249] Following Bucer's assessment expressed for example in
his Commentary on the Psalms, Calvin recommends David Qimhi as the most
reliable rabbinic scholar.[250] The consultation of text variants and translations
formed an important part of his exegetical work, as well as the use of available
commentaries. Although Calvin does not belong to the circle of the leading
Hebraist scholars of his time, he is able to provide his own translations.[251]

3.2. Principles in the Exposition of Old Testament Texts

The consequences of Calvin's concrete exposition of Old Testament texts shall
now be briefly sketched and illustrated with a few examples.

3.2.1. Sensus literalis *and* mens scriptoris

The main duty of exegesis, as formulated by Calvin in the foreword to his Romans commentary, is to reveal the sense of the biblical text and the intent of its
author.[252] This was true for Calvin's Old Testament exposition as well. In
pursuit of this goal, he identifies the genre of the text to be explained, its historical situation and the circumstances of its production, its author and addressees.[253] In addition, he explores the meaning of important Hebrew expres-

---

[247] Calvin has attended Capito's lectures on Isaiah (cf. his letter to Viret, 19 May 1540) (CO
11,36).
[248] Cf. Calvin's hints in his writing against Caroli (CO 7,306). See Engammare, Johannes Calvinus (1996) 35–60.
[249] On Sanctes Pagninus, see also Chap. 5.2, by A. VANDERJAGT, in this volume. Greene-
McCreight, How Augustine, Calvin, and Barth read the 'plain sense' of Genesis 1–3 (1999) 155;
Thompson, Calvin's Exegetical Legacy (2000) 31–56; P. A. VERHOEF, "Luther's and Calvin's Exegetical Library", *CTJ* 3 (1968) 5–20 (repr. in: Gamble, Calvin and Hermeneutics, 1992, 467–82).
[250] *fidelissimus est inter Rabbinos* (on Ps 112:5, CO 32,174).
[251] See P. OPITZ, "Calvin als Übersetzer der Psalmen", *Calvinus Sacrarum Litterarum Interpres.
Papers from the International Congress on Calvin Research Emden, 2006* (forthcoming).
[252] *mentem prophetae* (on Ps 132:10, CO 32, 347); *Ad Mosis consilium redeo, Argumentum in
Genesim* (CO 23,8).
[253] Cf. the *argumenta* on individual Psalms, e.g., on Psalm 120 (CO 32,295) and on Psalm 55
(CO 32,535).

sions.[254] By determining the *circumstantia* and the historical and linguistic con-text,[255] Calvin advances to the *sensus* of the text.[256] The prophets speak in their time to their contemporaries; even Moses in his books is first to be taken seriously as the "teacher for Israel".[257] In accordance with his criticism of "wandering" exegesis that departs from the text basis, Calvin repeatedly criti-cizes baseless "allegorization". This expression, when used by Calvin, goes be-yond the traditional *sensus allegoricus* to cover any baseless departure from the literal meaning of the text, although Calvin is at the same time conscious that this meaning can also be expressed in figurative language or metaphor. Calvin can work with biblical texts on this level as with historical documents, in which some things can only be suspected and at any rate remain in the area of prob-ability. Very often he discusses various possible interpretations, often drawing on diverse versions of the text, translations, and commentaries, without how-ever naming names, in order to leave the final decision with the reader.[258]

In accordance with this procedure, Calvin, compared to other exegetes of the time, generally interprets cautiously; just as unclear statements are often commented with what he admits is a guess, so images, for example from apoc-alyptic texts, are very cautiously interpreted with historical-theological specu-lation.[259] In a similar manner, cultic details or the description of the individual elements of the tabernacle are not generally subjected to a christological inter-pretation, which would necessarily be "allegorical". Instead, he restricted him-self to the general remark of the sign character of the Old Testament cult, which points to Christ.[260]

3.2.2. Situation Analogy in One Covenant and Pneumatic Body of Christ

Goal of scriptural exposition however is to draw a "useful teaching" out of the *mens scriptoris*.[261] For Calvin, this unfolds through an analogy of situation in the framework of the one covenant. It can appear in many different ways, ex-tending from individual fate[262] to political[263] and economic[264] themes. By pla-

---

[254] E.g., *Ideo interponitur particula* גם, *quae amplificat apud Hebraeos* (CO 23,424); *Quamquam Hebraei interdum* תרפים *vocat imagines* ... (CO 23,425); *Hebraica loquutio*... (CO 23,426) etc.

[255] *ex circumstantia temporis*, on Ps 32:1 (CO 32,316); *ex contextu melius patebit*, on Ps 33:1 (CO 32,324).

[256] *Sensus ergo huius loci est*..., on Ps 73:11 (CO 32,680).

[257] *Quum Moses Israelitis ordinatus esset doctor, non dubium est quin proprie eos respexerit*... , *Argumentum in Genesim* (CO 23,12).

[258] Typical is the sequence: *Multi putant*..., *Et fateor*..., *Sed huius loci mihi videtur diversa esse ratio*...; *Sensus est igitur*...; on Ps 54:5 (CO 32,533). *Quia tamen ad rei summam nihil fere interest, sequantur lectores utrum malint*, on Ps 68:15 (CO 32,625).

[259] Cf. E. DE BOER, *"Hermeneutische Schlüssel zur alttestamentlichen Prophetie in Calvins Hese-kielpredigten"*, in: *Calvinus Sacrae Scripturae Professor. Die Referate des Internationalen Kongresses für Calvinforschung vom 20. Bis 23. August 1990 in Grand Rapids* (ed. W.H. Neuser; Grand Rapids (MI): Eerdmans 1994) 199–208.

[260] With a few exceptions. Cf. Parker, Commentaries (1986) 75–77.

[261] He often uses formulations as: *Videtur in speciem levis et puerilis esse narratio* ... *Continet tamen utilem doctrinam*... (CO 23,411).

[262] Cf. e.g., on Psalm 56 (CO 31,546–554).

[263] E.g., on Psalm 72 (CO 31, 663. 673); on Psalm 101 (CO 32,56–60).

[264] E.g., Ps 15:5 (CO 31,147 f.).

cing the question of the *mens scriptoris* in the framework of the one covenant that changes over time, it always concerns in various ways the relation of the Old Covenant community and the individual to God, and thus the proper manner of the knowledge of God and of human self-knowledge, which Calvin formulated as the basic constituents of his theology at the beginning of the *Institutio*.[265]

In the previously cited foreword to the Geneva Bible, Calvin defines the "use" of Scripture by saying "that we learn through it to place our trust in God and to go our way in fear of him", and finally to recognize Christ as the "end" and "goal" of the Law and the prophets and as the "substance" of the Gospel.[266] Thereby "faith", in the sense of *fiducia* based completedly on God's *promissio*, is connected to praise of the Law, as expressed for example in Psalm 119. At the same time, with allusion to Rom 10:4, everything points to and is rooted in Christ. These are the basic elements of Calvin's exposition of the Old Testament with a view to its "use".

3.2.3. History of Education

The Old Testament witnesses, first of all, to a pedagogical process, to the history of the education of the chosen people by God. This is clear in the narrative texts, but also in the legal texts and the writings of the prophets.

3.2.3.1. *The Historical Texts.* As a history book,[267] the Old Testament narrates – against the background of the one covenant – the history of Israel as a history of God's "bringing up" of the Church in the time of its youth. Calvin repeatedly reminds his listeners or readers of this basic insight.

> For that age, we know, was the infancy of the Church; wherefore the Lord retained the faithful, who then lived, under the teaching of the schoolmaster. And now, though, since the coming of Christ, our condition is more free; the memory of the fact ought to be retained among us, that God disciplined his people of old by external ceremonies.[268]

The historical texts serve us as "mirror" of God's teaching and care, active in the history of the covenant. They show us the "singular Providence of God in governing and preserving the Church",[269] from which we can learn trust and reverence.[270]

---

[265] Cf. Inst. I 1.1 (OS III 31,5–8).

[266] ...*c'est en un mot que nous apprenions par icelle de mettre nostre fiance en Dieu et de cheminer en sa crainte. Et d'autant que Iesus Christ est la fin de la Loy et des Prophetes, et la substance de l'Evangile, que nous ne tendions à autre but que de le cogniostre* (CO 9,825).

[267] Cf. M. H. WOUDSTRA, "Calvin interprets what 'Moses reports': Observations on Calvin's Commentary on Exodus 1–19", *CTJ* 21 (1986) 151–74 (repr. in: Gamble, Calvin and Hermeneutics, 1992, 189–212); D. F. WRIGHT, "Calvin's Pentateuchal Criticism: Equity, hardnes of Heart, and Divine Accommodation in the Mosaic Harmony Commentary", *CTJ* 21 (1986) 33–50 (repr. in: Gamble, Calvin and Hermeneutics, 1992, 213–30).

[268] *Scimus enim illud saeculum fuisse ecclesiae pueritiam. Quare Dominus fideles qui tunc vixerunt, sub paedagogia continuit. Nunc quamvis post Christi adventum liberior sit nostra conditio, vigere apud nos debet eius rei memoria, in qua Deus veterem populum sub externo ritu exercuit* (CO 23,447; tr. J. King, Calvin Translation Societies edition).

[269] CO 23,11/12 (tr. J. King).

From the unity of the covenant and with it the unity of the people of God follows the continuity of the Church as *ecclesia militans*. This is ultimately grounded in the consideration of the one God, who has chosen his people, remains faithful to them, and gives them an eschatological hope. In this way, Calvin can interweave the orientation of the Old and the New Testament people of God, in that he has the Old Testament community look forward to the coming Christ, that of the New Testament however look back to the God of election. For the Patriarchs,

> since they possessed Christ as the pledge of their salvation when he had not yet appeared, so we retain the God who formerly manifested himself to them. ... Further, the Governance of the Church is to be considered, that the reader may come to the conclusion that God has been its perpetual guard and ruler, yet in such a way as to exercise it in the warfare of the cross. Here, truly, the peculiar conflicts of the Church present themselves to view ... it behooves us, with the holy Fathers to press towards the mask of a happy immortality.[271]

The eschatologically-oriented implementation of the divine will, which leads the chosen community through all external battles and inner contradictions, and thereby the topic of providence, is a basic characteristic throughout Calvin's Old Testament exegesis. Even God's "wrath" and his periodic "chastisement" are aligned with this educational program. In this way, the Geneva congregation, the threatened evangelical contemporaries of Calvin, can be instructed in their Christian lives, in their *militia*, "warfare", through past historical events and examples.[272] This Christian "militia" encompasses for Calvin the entire spectrum of Christian and ecclesiastical life. It bases itself on the promise of God, recognized in faith (cf. Inst. III 2), out of which the Old Testament community had lived as well,[273] and realizes itself thereby essentially as *tolerantia crucis* (cf. Inst. III 8) and as *meditatio vitae futurae* (Inst. III 9)[274] under the sovereignty of Christ, who reigns in the midst of his enemies.[275] In his sermons, Calvin can clearly draw the connection between the suffering of those who feared God in the Old Testament and those of the Reformed community, and in the process achieve a very 'existential' dimension of the "use" of Old Testament texts.

> Whoever truly knows his God will be steadfast. And when? Not when we are at repose, when we can talk at our ease. No, but rather, when we are in the power of tyrants, when we see the pyres lighted, when we see the most horrible persecutions in the world, that is when we will be steadfast. In this we will be approved, that we know God.[276]

---

[270] Cf. CO 24,5/6f.

[271] *Praefatio in Genesim*, CO 23,11/12 (tr. J. King).

[272] Cf. CO 23,11/12. See e.g., on Psalm 10 (CO 31,108); on Ps 123:4 (CO 32,309f.); on Ps 137:4 (CO 32,369f). Cf. Selderhuis, Gott in der Mitte. Calvins Theologie der Psalmen (2004).

[273] Cf. CO 23,11/12.

[274] *Videmum enim quasi in speculo, vel in pictura, Deum fuisse sollicitum de ecclesia sua, etiam quum visus est eius curam abiiecisse (Praelectiones in Danielem, CO 40,532). Tandem hoc etiam notandum est, quod sicuti veterem populum ad tolerantiam crucis instruxerat, sic etiam admonet, non fore tranquillum ecclesiae statum, ubi Christus fuerit exhibitus: sed militandum esse filiis Dei usque ad finem, nec fructum victoriae sperandum esse, donec resurgent mortui, et Christus ipse colliget nos in regnum suum coeleste. Nunc paucis comprehendimus, vel saltem gustamus quam utilis sit nobis hic liber et fructuosus, Praelectiones in Danielem*, CO 40,533.

[275] Cf. Inst. II 15.4 (OS III 475,30–476,10); cf. CO 36,247f.

[276] *Quiconques connoist vrayement son Dieu il tiendra bon: et en quel temps? ce ne sera pas quand*

3.2.3.2. *The Law.* Calvin's treatment of Old Testament legal texts occurs on the basis of his nuanced understanding of the Law. The Law, in the sense of the moral law, the unchangeable will of God recorded in the Decalogue, belongs to God's education of the Church. It is not viewed in isolation, but against the horizon of the "whole law", the Torah, as it unfolds in the Pentateuch as the good instruction of God, but containing as well the message of his elective love and grace.[277] To that extent, even the Decalogue is to be appreciated as God's helpful, "instructive" word. At the beginning of his compilation and explanation of the various introductory words to the Law out of Exodus and Deuteronomy, in which God explains the meaning of the Law he has given to his people Israel, Calvin quotes Ps 119:103. In spite of all "terror" of the people at God's majesty, as reported in the revelation at Sinai, the point is to taste the "sweetness" of the Law and thus submit themselves "voluntarily" to it, since it is, as "rules of life", part of God's Word.[278]

Calvin's foreword to his *Harmony* of the books from Exodus to Deuteronomy is revealing for his exposition of Old Testament legal texts. As in his commentary on the Gospels, Calvin attempts a "harmony" in his exposition of the books Exodus to Deuteronomy. It consists, on the one hand, in ordering the "story" reported in these books in chronological order and, on the other hand, the "teaching", all the legal texts contained in them, grouped around the Decalogue as their center and point of departure. In his foreword he justifies this procedure, defusing potential criticism of his radical reordering of the original text;[279] the aim is "to assist the unpracticed readers, so that they might more easily, more commodiously, and more profitably acquaint themselves with the writings of Moses".[280]

The legal texts are divided into four parts: Firstly, texts that emphasize the importance and dignity of the law as a whole. Secondly, the Decalogue, as "short, but complete instruction", "how to live in a pious and holy manner". Thirdly, the "appendices". In relation to the first table these are all the concrete instructions about ceremonial customs (cultic ceremonies), in relation to the second table they concern dealings of human beings with each other (civil laws). As "appendix" their authority is clearly lesser; they are merely "helps" for the fulfillment of the Decalogue, in the exposition of which care must be taken that they remain thus. The fourth part, finally, deals with the "aim and use" of the Law, that is, with its application: Included in this are all the "promises" and "curses" that are connected with the Law. Their purpose is to lead to the "covenant of grace" and to "Christ", the aim of the Law in general.[281]

---

nous serons à repos, quand nous pourrons parler à nostre aise, nenni non, mais quand nous serons entre les mains des tirans, que nous verrons les feux allumés, que nous verrons les persecutions les plus horribles du monde, quand alors nous tiendrons bon. Voila comme nous serons approuvés, que nous connoistrons Dieu, Homily on Dan 11:30–32 (CO 42,54).

[277] Cf. Inst. II 7.1 (OS III 326,27–33).

[278] CO 24,210. On Calvin's exposition of the law as Torah, see Opitz, Ein Thorapsalm (1997) 117–31.

[279] *Praefatio* on First to Fifth Book of Moses (CO 24,5/6).

[280] Ibid. (tr. C. W. Bingham, Calvin Translation Societies edition).

[281] Cf. Parker, Commentaries (1986) 93 ff.

Against this background Calvin's "ethical" exposition of the Law occurs in a nuanced handling of the legal texts, which have for the Christian congregation widely diverse importance.[282]

3.2.3.3. *The Prophets*. The prophets also are part of the divine activities of education.[283] Their task is briefly summarized by Calvin in the foreword to his commentary on Isaiah. The prophets are interpreters of the Law in its widest sense: As moral precepts, by which the moral law is meant, as warnings and promises that are connected to it in the Pentateuch and which the prophets in their individual contexts validate, and as covenant of grace, founded in Christ, and containing all promises within itself.[284]

From this "prophetic" task proceeds an instruction for contemporary proclaimers and thus expositors of the Old Testament: In accordance with the example of the prophets they should "draw from it advises, reproofs, threatenings, and consolations, which they applied to the present condition of the people".[285] Through this Calvin has a broad room for interpretation that enables him to investigate the concrete political situation in which the various prophets speak,[286] and to apply their words to his own situation.[287]

3.2.4. History of Liberation

The analogy of situation must be understood, however, as an analogy of situation of salvation history. Scripture is not the mirror of timeless truths. On the basis of the identical substance of the covenant there are of course always analogies to discover, which enable us to learn from Scripture. Through the various, progressive "administration" of the covenant, however, these analogies are organized in the development of salvation history. The exposition of Scripture, according to Calvin, has to pattern itself on the inner-biblical prophetic interpretation process, which consists in understanding one's own situation in light of past events of salvation history and thus interpret them in the framework of progressive revelation of salvation. When David points back to the

---

[282] On this, see A. THIEL, *In der Schule Gottes. Die Ethik Calvins im Spiegel seiner Predigten über das Deuteronomium* (Neukirchen-Vluyn: Neukirchener 1999).

[283] N. N. PALUKU RUBINGA, Calvin Commentateur du Prophète Isaie (Thèse de doctorat, Université de Strasbourg 1978).

[284] *Doctrinam igitur latius explicant prophetae: et quae duae tabulae paucis comprehendunt, plenius interpretantur. Minas vero et promissiones quas in genere Moses promulgaverat ipsi accommodant suo tempori, easque in specie designant. Postremo, quae obscurius apud Mosem de Christo et gratia eius habentur, declarant apertius, plenioraque gratuiti foederis et uberiora testimonia afferunt", In Isaiam prophetam praefatio* (CO 36,19).

[285] *Hinc colligere licet quomodo tractanda sit doctrina verbi: atque imitandos esse prophetas, qui sic legis doctrinam administrarunt, ut ex ea monitiones, reprehensiones, minas, consolationes peterent, quas populo accommodarent pro status praesentis ratione", In Isaiam prophetam praefatio* (CO 36,22; tr. W. Pringle, Calvin Translation Societies edition).

[286] Cf. the *praefatio* on Hosea (CO 42,197f).

[287] *Tametsi enim non reveletur nobis quotidie quod pro vaticinia proferamus tamen mores nostrorum hominum conferre operae pretium est cum prisci illius populi moribus: atque ex historiis et exemplis patefacienda iudicia Dei. Ideo quae olim ultus est, non minus hodie etiam esse ulturum quia sit perpetuo similis sibi. Hanc igitur prudentiam adhibeant pii doctores, si cum aliquo fructu prophetarum doctrinam tractare velint, In Isaiam prophetam praefatio* (CO 36,22). Cf. on Isa 9:2–3 (CO 36,189–192).

passage through the Red Sea in Ps 18:16 in order to express his own deliverance in personal need, this is exemplary for Calvin of how to use Scripture.

> David fitly conjoins with that ancient deliverance of the Church the assistance which God had sent from heaven to him in particular. As the grace which he declares God had shown towards him was not to be separated from that first deliverance, since it was, so to speak, a part and an appendage of it, he beholds, as it were at a glance, or in an instant, both the ancient miracle of the drying up of the Red Sea, and the assistance which God granted to himself. In short, God, who once opened up for his people a way through the Red Sea, and then showed himself to be their protector upon this condition, that they should assure themselves of being always maintained and preserved under his keeping, now again displayed his wonderful power in the defense and preservation of one man, to renew the remembrance of that ancient history. From this it appears the more evidently, that David, in using these apparently strange and exaggerated hyperboles, does not recite to us the mere creations of romance to please the fancy, after the manner of the heathen poets, but observes the style and manner which God had, as it were, prescribed to his people.[288]

With the appearance of Christ the time of "worship under the Law" (*legalis cultus*)[289] is at an end, but that does not terminate the entire history of the covenant. Even the Christian community has Christ only in the form of promise,[290] so that Christians too can understand biblical salvation history as liberation history, in which they themselves are included. In this history, early events of salvation point to later ones, while the later are to be understood as their fulfillment in such a way that they contain these in themselves and now bring them to their full truth. The Christian community understands them however in light of Christ, but not in such a way that Christ is so to speak set in contrast to them externally, but remains their immanent criterion. It can thus be strengthened in its own faith by looking back to the Exodus and at the same time look forward. It is more or less in this way that Calvin understands Exod 6:7 ("And I will take you for my people, and I will be your God; and you shall know that I am the Lord your God, who has brought you out from the burdens of the Egyptians") as a statement of the beginning of the history of salvation that has its goal in Christ and is already determined by him.[291] In the same way, the prophets presume this salvation history as an unfolding history of liberation. When Isaiah looks back to the exodus out of Egypt in order to announce the return out of the Babylonian captivity (Isa 11:15–16), he does this so that the people may recognize that nothing can hinder God in the liberation of his people, but rather that "it will be the same with that which they formerly enjoyed".[292] The remembrance of the earlier exodus should confirm the hope of liberation from the Babylonian exile, a liberation, for which, apart from the mere promise through Isaiah, there was yet no sign. This promise bases itself, however, on the faithfulness of the covenant God, on the fact that the God who freed the people out of Egypt, "is always like himself".[293] The people

---

[288] On Ps 18:16 [English Bible: v. 15] (CO 31,177f; tr. J. Anderson, Calvin Translation Societies edition).

[289] OS III 326,38 [Inst. II 7.1].

[290] Cf. OS III 401,12 f. [Inst. II 9.3].

[291] Cf. CO 24,80.

[292] CO 36,250 (tr. W. Pringle, Calvin Translation Societies edition).

would perceive the same power of God in the deliverance from Babylon as they had perceived in the deliverance from Egypt. He had opened up a way through the seas, through untrodden deserts, and through Jordan. In like manner, Isaiah says, that by an unexpected and astonishing method he will again open up a way for his people to go out.[294]

In this tradition of liberation histories the Christian community, too, reads the Scripture and recognizes its own future in light of this: "What the Lord has once performed let us also expect for the future; and for that purpose let us ponder the ancient histories".[295]

In the process, these liberation histories themselves must be understood, according to Calvin, as part of the one, increasing, liberation history of God that climaxes in eschatological salvation. So Calvin can cite Isa 11:15–16 in connection with the "final deliverance of the Church",

by which we shall all be delivered from all troubles and distresses, so that, though what we are told about a resurrection and immortal life may appear to be incredible, and the means of accomplishing them are not seen by us, still the Lord will easily find a way.[296]

3.2.5. Christological Interpretation: Christ as Aim and Substance of the Law

Calvin emphasises the knowledge of Christ as goal of Scripture exposition in the foreword to the Geneva edition of the Bible: Since Christ is the "end of the law and the prophets", so the aim of reading Scripture is "that we have no other goal than to know him in the knowledge that we go astray in the moment when we turn just a little from him".[297]

3.2.5.1. *Christ as Goal and "Soul" of the Law.* Since Christ as source of all revelation[298] is the "sole light of truth",[299] Calvin can also say of the Law, as the "entire teaching of Moses", that "every doctrine of the law, every command, every promise, always points to Christ".[300]

---

[293] *Praefatio in Isaiam* CO 36,22 (tr. W. Pringle).

[294] CO 36,250 (tr. W. Pringle).

[295] Ibid. (tr. W. Pringle).

[296] Ibid. (tr. W. Pringle). Cf. CO 36,247. Eschatologically orientated exposition means for Calvin first looking at the eschatological *communio* of the saints, and aims then at the creation as a whole, cf. CO 27,428ff. 433f. See H. QUISTORP, *Die letzten Dinge im Zeugnis Calvins* (Gütersloh: Bertelsmann 1941) 182–92; D. E. HOLWERDA, "Eschatology and History: A Look at Calvin's Eschatological Vision", *Exploring the Heritage of John Calvin* (ed. idem; Grand Rapids, MI: Baker Book House 1976) 110–39. Cf. de Boer, Calvin on the Visions of Ezechiel (1999).

[297] CO 9,825 [own translation]; cf. CO 9,815/6. After naming the two essential points of the exposition of Scripture, *docilitas* and Christ as scopus, he continues: *Ce qui me fait pour le present deporter de traicter plus au long ces deux articles, est que ce n'est pas matière d'une seule preface, mais d'un livre entier, pour donner suffisante declaration*, CO 9,825. This book is his *Institutio*.

[298] Cf. Inst. I 13.7 (OS III 118,11–16).

[299] CO 36,492 [own translation].

[300] On Rom 10:4 (CO 49,196; tr. Ross Mackenzie).

For Calvin's precision of the way in which Christ is the aim of the Law, his combination of two Pauline texts is decisive. Christ is both the "end" (Rom 10:4) and the "soul" [sic] (2 Cor 3:16–17) of the Law.[301] When Calvin illustrates the history of the one covenant with the image of the increase of light, this ultimately has Christological reasons. Christ himself is the sun of righteousness,[302] which previously cast its light in Old Testament times. To the extent that the Law points to him, he is its goal, to the extent that the mere outline is filled by the matter itself, he is its living spirit.[303]

All promises of the Old Testament discourse of God and covenant of grace itself, but also the cultic law, which points to atonement, contains in Christ its solid "foundation", becomes in him "Yea and Amen".[304] In the same way, the Decalogue finds its fulfillment in Christ. As "faithful interpreter" Christ explains "the nature of the Law, its object, and its scope".[305] Thus he confirms, in the exercise of his earthly office of prophet, its validity and opens its true meaning and purpose,[306] which he summarizes in the double law of love.[307] But also the "warnings and promises" that were conditional on the observance of the Decalogue and with them the judging character of the Law, which brought the knowledge of sin, points pedagogically to Christ.[308] Christ is thus the "end", the object, to which the Law in its various functions points. He is this at the same time as the "spirit" of the Law, as the one who is its foundation and who supports this Law in all its dimensions through his spirit, thereby determining it from the inside. So the Law has its sense only as Law of the covenant and is outside of this covenant, that is, separated from Christ and his spirit, dead letter.[309] As foundation of the covenant Christ determines and comprises the Law and takes it in his service, just as the soul enlivens a lifeless body and determines it and at the same time takes shape in it.

3.2.5.2. Prophetic-typological Interpretation as Christological Interpretation. The meaning of the context, constitutive of the understanding of a text, forbids Calvin to make a "christological" interpretation that ignores the context of a text and jumps to a higher, "spiritual" level, whether this is mediated by allegorization, or the discovering of "christological" prophecies out of context that do not have their own Sitz im Leben. Compared with most of his contemporary Christian exegetes, including Bucer, Calvin is for that reason very re-

---

[301] Cf. Inst. II 7.2 (OS III 328,26–29); Christ as the "soul" of the Law is what Calvin reads in 2 Cor 3:16f. (CO 50,45). *Car il est dit au troisieme de la seconde aux Corinthiens, que Iesus Christ est l'ame de la Loy …* (CO 54,280). Cf. on 2 Cor 1:19 (CO 50,21f); on John 5:39 (CO 47,125); on Luke 24:46 (CO 45,817).

[302] Cf. on 2 Cor 3:15 (CO 50,45).

[303] Cf. e.g., CO 36,492.

[304] Calvin often points to 2 Cor 1:20 (see CO 50,22f) as his main scriptural proof for Christ as the basis of the covenant, cf. Inst. II 9.2 (OS III 400,12ff).

[305] On Matt 5:21 (CO 45,175; tr. A. W. Morrison).

[306] On Matt 5:21 (CO 45,175).

[307] Cf. Inst. II 8.11 (OS III 352,38–353,2); CO 24,721ff.

[308] Cf. Inst. II 7.8 (OS III 334,9–25).

[309] Cf. on 2 Cor 3:17 (CO 50,45f).

served in christological exposition and opposes "forced"[310] interpretations that fail to take the context into consideration. Christian exegetes must not expose themselves to the accusation that they "as sophists apply to Christ that which strictly speaking does not speak of him".[311] In his rejection of christological interpretations that rip individual Old Testament verses out of their historical and grammatical context Calvin can also oppose a long tradition of interpretation. For example, the passage Gen 3:15, traditionally interpreted christologically, the so-called "Protevangelium", is for Calvin on grammatical grounds not a direct promise of Christ.[312]

By reading all biblical history against the background of the one covenant, however, and at the same time as a liberation history that is grounded in and points to Christ, in which even the present Christian community is included, Calvin interprets biblical history in its entirety from the perspective of the sovereignty (*regnum*) of Christ that is taking place in time. In this sense his interpretation of Old Testament texts is materially fully christological, but there is no need to claim that the Old Testament witnesses refer explicitly to Christ. At the same time this gives him the possibility to integrate hermeneutically the use that the New Testament writings make of the Old Testament without being unfaithful to his demand for a "contextual" interpretation of Old Testament texts. Matthew sees in the murder of the innocents commanded by Herod the fulfillment of Jer 31:15: "A voice was heard in Ramah, wailing and loud lamentation, Rachel weeping for her children; she refused to be consoled, because they were no more" (Matt 2:18). According to Calvin, Matthew does not mean that Jeremiah had prophesied this in such a way that he informed his contemporaries of an event that would happen centuries later and had nothing to do with his own time. Instead, Matthew wants to say that by the time of the appearance of Christ it was as if that murder had been renewed. Likewise, Calvin points to the context of the words of Jeremiah quoted by Matthew, namely, that these words led to a word of comfort ("Thus says the Lord: 'Keep your voice from weeping, and your eyes from tears, for your work shall be rewarded...'", Jer 31:16). Thus, it is an analogy: "the comparison between the earlier disaster for the tribe of Benjamin, and this other, is made because both were preliminary to salvation soon to be restored".[313] The entire fulfillment in Christ both includes the original prophecy, referring to the tribe of Benjamin, and surpasses it. Liberation in its full and actual sense takes place in the appearance of Christ. The Church, as his body, already takes part in this process during the time of the Law. In this way, the history of the Church is a history pointing to him, and is grounded in him at the same time.[314]

In the course of the unfolding salvation history there are not only certain

---

[310] *habere aliquid coactum* occurs repeatedly with regard to an inappropriate christological exegesis, cf. on Rom 9:25 f. (CO 49,189f).

[311] *Qui simpliciter vaticinium esse volunt de regno Christi, videntur nimis violenter torquere verba. Deinde semper cavendum est ne Iudaeis obstrependi detur occasio, ac si nobis propositum esse sophistice ad Christum trahere quae directe in eum non competunt*, on Ps 72:1 (CO 32,664) [own translation].

[312] Cf. on Gen 3:15 (CO 23,71), and on Ps 132:10 (CO 32,347).

[313] On Matt 2:18 (CO 45,100; trans. A. W. Morrison).

[314] See Calvin's exegesis of Matt 2:15, where Hos 11:1 is quoted (CO 45,98f).

basic events, such as the exodus from Egypt or the Babylonian captivity, there are also certain "types" that point to the coming Christ in a special way. David is in this regard an important figure for Calvin. As special carrier of promises, David points in a particular way to Christ, as he combines in himself the prophetic and kingly offices.[315] He points to Christ in his words, in his whole being, in the rule God gave to him, and in his sufferings. As can be seen from David's statements, which go far beyond earthly reality, he knew that the promises given to him went beyond his time and that he and his kingdom, compared with the coming of Christ, were only a sketchy preliminary image.[316] Calvin recognizes this kind of prophetic-typological exposition in the New Testament interpretation of the Old Testament itself. So David says in Psalm 2: "Why do the nations conspire, and the peoples plot in vain? The kings of the earth set themselves, and the rulers take counsel together, against the Lord and his anointed ..." (Ps 2:1–2). It is for Calvin self-evident that he says this in his time and situation in view of the enemies who fought against his royal office at the time. Subsequently, this passage is used by the Apostles as comfort (Acts 4:25) and thereby ultimately understood christologically and placed in their own situation.[317] This is legitimate, however, according to Calvin, and a model for Christian scriptural exposition. David was after all a type[318] of the coming Christ, and so, that which was said applied to him, yet received its full fulfillment in Christ. At the same time what is said is not to be limited to the person of Christ, but is valid for the entire course of the Gospel. By this the Christian community of Calvin's day is united with David and with the primitive Christian community in the framework of the reign (*regnum*) of Christ.

David is, however, not only a type of the coming Christ. In his position as king and head of the community he represents these – and is in this position, too, an image of Christ. Since he as special carrier of promises remains at the same time a fallible believer,[319] believers can recognize themselves in his behavior and fate. Not only in his reign and his successes, which he sings of in some Psalms, but also in his sufferings, as they find expression in his laments over personally experienced injustice, David represents Christ, the head of the Church, and at the same time the entire body of the Church.[320]

Therefore, what happens to David does not only point typologically to Christ,[321] it serves simultaneously as a model for the Christian *militia*, "warfare", of the individual believer. Calvin himself repeatedly understood and interpreted his personal fate in the mirror of the fate of David, as he confesses in the foreword of his Psalms commentary, one of his most personal texts. In

---

[315] Cf. Inst. II 10.15 (OS III 415,26–31); Inst. II 7.1; 10.17.

[316] Cf. on Psalm 2 (CO 31,41); cf. e.g., on Ps 22:28 (CO 31,234f).

[317] Cf. on Acts 4:25 (CO 48,91).

[318] Calvin develops further in his own way, what Erasmus has explained, Erasmus, *Ratio* (1967) 182–84.

[319] Cf. on Ps 22:15 (CO 31,228f).

[320] *Ita memoria tenendum est quod dixi, de privatis quas patiebatur iniuriis sic eum conqueri, ut in sua persona Christum et totum ecclesiae corpus repraesentet*, on Ps 109:1 (CO 32,147).

[321] Cf. S. H. RUSSELL, "Calvin and the Messianic Interpretation of the Psalms", *SJT* 21 (1968) 37–47 (repr. in: Gamble, Calvin and Hermeneutics, 1992, 261–72).

Calvin's love of the Psalter, the only Old Testament book on which he preached even on Sunday, can be seen essential elements of his spirituality,[322] since the Psalter is an "Anatomy of all Parts of the Soul".[323] The similarity of Calvin's own experiences with those of David gives Calvin in his own eyes a certain competence in the exposition of these texts.[324]

Obviously, Calvin follows the direction in which, more than two decades ago, the pioneers Oecolampadius and Zwingli had already pointed in their undertaking of transforming the traditional ways of dealing with the Old Testament into a "reformed" exegesis; and there is some evidence for the claim, that he consistently and resolutely makes a big step further.

---

[322] On the Psalms as a mirror for "individual" spirituality, see J. A. DE JONG, "'An Anatomy of All Parts of the Soul': Insights into Calvin's Spirituality from His Psalms Commentary", in: *Calvinus Sacrae Scripturae Professor* (1994) 1–14; on the Psalms as a mirror for the Church, see H. SELDERHUIJS, "Kirche im Theater: Die Dynamik der Ekklesiologie Calvins", in: Opitz, Calvin im Kontext der Schweizer Reformation (2003) 195–214.

[323] ἀνατομήν *omnium animae partium* (CO 31,15; tr. J. Anderson).

[324] *experientia me non mediocriter fuisse adiutum, non modo accommodarem ad praesentem usum … sed ut ad consilium scriptoris cuiusque psalmorum intelligendum familiarior pateret via* (CO 31,19).

CHAPTER NINETEEN

Pluriformity of Early Reformation Scriptural Interpretation

By R. GERALD HOBBS, Vancouver, BC

1. Martin Bucer and the Upper Rhine School

Sources: MARTIN BUCER: A critical edition of the complete works of Martin Bucer is in course of publication: *Martin Bucers Deutsche Schriften* [BDS] (Gütersloh: Gerd Mohn 1960-); *Martini Buceri Opera Omnia* [BOL] (Paris: Presses Universitaires de France 1954-55), vols. 15, 15b; (SMRT 30, 40–42,83; Leiden: Brill 1982-); "Quomodo S. literae pro concionibus tractandae sint instructio", in: *RHPhR* 26 (1946) 32–75; *Correspondance de Martin Bucer* [BCorr] (SMRT 25, 43, 56, 78, Leiden: Brill 1979-); [George Joye], *The Psalter of David in Englishe...*([Antwerp] 1530, also 1534, 1541?; photo repr. of 1530; Appleford: Sutton Courtenay 1971). – PETER MARTYR VERMIGLI: The complete works of Peter Martyr Vermigli are appearing in English translation in: *The Peter Martyr Library* (ed. J. P. Donnelly / J. C. McLelland; SCES; Kirksville, MI 1994-). – OECOLAMPADIUS: *Briefe und Akten zum Leben Oekolampads: zum 400jährigen Jubiläum der Basler Reformation* 1–2 (ed. by E. Staehelin; Leipzig 1927–34; repr. New York: Johnson 1971); further on Oecolampadius, see supra Chap. 18, sect. 1; on Zwingli, Chap. 18, sect. 2. – The exegetical works of Wolfgang Capito, François Lambert, Conrad Pellican and Sebastian Münster are available in IDC microfiche, Leiden: Brill; further on Pellican, see supra Chap. 11, sect. 2 (cf. esp. *Das Chronikon des Konrad Pellikan;* ed. B. Riggenbach; Basel 1877).

Bibliographies: R. STUPPERICH, *Bibliographia Bucerana* (SVRG 169/2 1952) 37–96; M. KÖHN, "Bucer-Bibliographie", in: *Bucer und seine Zeit* (ed. M. de Kroon / F. Krüger; VIEG 80; Wiesbaden: Franz Steiner 1976); G. SEEBASS e.a., *Martin Bucer (1491-1551) Bibliographie* (Gütersloh 2005); I. BACKUS, *Martin Borrhaus (Cellarius)* (Bibliotheca Dissidentium 2; Baden-Baden 1981); R. BODENMANN, "Bibliotheca Lambertiana", in: *Pour retrouver François Lambert. Bio-bibliographie et études* (ed. P. Fraenkel; BBAur 108; Baden-Baden 1987) 9–213; P. ROMANE-MUSCULUS, "Catalogue des oeuvres imprimées du théologien Wolfgang Musculus", *RHPhR* 43 (1963) 260–78.

General works and studies: M. W. ANDERSON, *Peter Martyr. A Reformer in exile (1542-1562). A chronology of biblical writings in England and Europe* (BHRef 10; Nieuwkoop: De Graaf 1975); R. BODENMANN, *Wolfgang Musculus (1497-1563). Destin d'un autodidacte lorrain* (THR 343; Geneva: Droz 2000); M. U. CHRISMAN, *Strasbourg and the Reform* (New Haven, CN: Yale UP 1967); PH. DENIS, "La prophétie dans les Églises de la Réforme au XVIᵉ siècle", *RHE* 72 (1977) 289–316; J. FRIEDMAN, *The most ancient testimony. Sixteenth-century Christian Hebraica in the age of Renaissance nostalgia* (Athens, OH: Ohio UP 1983); M. GRESCHAT, *Martin Bucer. Ein Reformator und seine Zeit 1491-1551* (Munich: Beck 1990; French tr. EHPhR 80; Paris: Presses Universitaires de France 2002; ET: Louisville, KY / London: Westminster John Knox 2004); R. G. HOBBS, "Martin Bucer on Psalm 22: a study in the application of rabbinic exegesis by a Christian Hebraist", in: *Histoire de l'exégèse au XVIᵉ siècle* (EPH 34; Geneva 1978) 144–63; idem, "Monitio amica: Pellican et Capiton sur le danger des lectures rabbiniques", in: *Horizons Européens. De la Réforme en Alsace* (ed. M. de Kroon / M. Lienhard; Strasbourg 1980) 81–93; idem, "Exegetical projects and problems: a new look at an undated letter from Bucer to Zwingli", in: *Prophet, Pastor, Protestant: the work of Huldrych Zwingli after Five Hundred Years* (ed. E. J. Furcha / H. Wayne Pipkin; Allison Park, PA 1984) 89–107; idem, *"How firm a foundation*: Martin Bucer's historical exegesis of the Psalms", *CH* 53 (1984) 477–91; idem, "Le félin et le dauphin: Martin Bucer dédie ses commentaires sur le psautier au fils de François Ier", *Revue Française d'Histoire du Livre*, 54, n. 50 n. s. (1986) 217–34; idem, "François Lambert sur les langues et la prophétie", in: *Pour retrouver François Lambert. Bio-bibliographie et études* (ed. P. Fraenkel; BBAur 108; Baden-Baden 1987) 273–301; idem, "*Hebraica veritas* and *traditio apostolica*: St. Paul and the interpretation of the Psalms in the Sixteenth century", in: *The Bible in the Sixteenth Century* (ed. D. C. Steinmetz; Durham / London 1990) 83–99, 221–31; idem, "Conrad Pellican and the Psalms: the ambivalent legacy of a pioneer Hebraist", *RRRev* 1 (1999) 72–99; idem, "Bucer's use of King David as mirror of the Christian prince", *RRRev* 5/1 (2003) 102–28; idem, "<Quam apposita religioni sit musica> Martin Bucer and music in the liturgy", *RRRev* 6/2 (2004) 155–78; idem, "Martin Bucer, the Jews and Judaism", in: *Jews, Judaism and the Reformation in Sixteenth-Century Germany* (ed. S. Burnett / D. Bell; Leiden: Brill 2006) 137–69; also in: *Le Livre et la Réforme*, ed. R. Peter / B. Roussel; Bordeaux 1987); J. KITTELSON, *Wolfgang Capito. From humanist to reformer* (SMRT 17; Leiden: Brill 1975); J. MÜLLER, *Martin Bucers Hermeneutik* (QFRG 32; Gütersloh: Gerd Mohn 1965); R. RAUBENHEIMER, *Paul Fagius aus Rheinzabern* (VVPfKG 6; Grünstadt: Emil Sommer 1957); B. ROUSSEL, "De Strasbourg à Bâle et Zurich: une <école rhénane> d'exégèse (ca 1525–ca 1540)", *RHPhR* 68 (1988) 19–39; idem, "Martin Bucer exégète", in: *Strasbourg au coeur religieux du XVIe Siècle* (ed. G. Livet / F. Rapp; Strasbourg: Istra 1977) 153–66; idem / G. BEDOUELLE, *Le temps des Réformes et la Bible* (BTT 5; Paris: Beauchesne 1989); idem / G. HOBBS, "Strasbourg et l <'ecole rhénane> d'exégèse", BSHPF 135 (1989) 36–53; W. P. STEPHENS, *The Holy Spirit in the Theology of Martin Bucer* (Cambridge: Cambridge UP 1970); G. WEIL, *Elie Lévita. Humaniste et Massorète (1469–1549)* (StPB 7; Leiden: Brill 1963); C. ZÜRCHER, *Konrad Pellikans Wirken in Zürich 1526–1556* (ZBRG 4; Zurich: Theologischer Verlag 1975).

Special abbreviations (see above):
BCorr = *Correspondance de Martin Bucer* (SMRT)
BDS = *Martin Bucers Deutsche Schriften*
BOL = *Martini Buceri Opera Omnia*
CWE = *Collected Works of Erasmus*

1.1. Strasbourg and the Upper Rhine School

The imperial free city of Strasbourg, situated at the heart of the fertile Alsatian plain astride an important juncture of trade and transport routes on the Upper Rhine, assumed for several decades a significant role in the study of the Hebrew Bible. Lacking a university, the city of 20,000 had nonetheless been home at the beginning of the sixteenth century to a *sodalitas* of conservative humanists whose membership included Sebastian Brant and Jakob Wimpheling. Although never in the first rank amongst German cities, Strasbourg early had a flourishing print trade. Primary schools for both sexes educated at least a portion of the citizenry, strengthening their ability to participate in the magistracy. And Luther's call for evangelical reform of the Church found early resonance amongst a laity that had a generation earlier followed attentively the cathedral preaching of Johann Geiler of Kaysersberg. But while an independent city state within the Empire, Strasbourg was integrated culturally within a wider Upper Rhine region, a factor that is directly germane to the theme of this chapter. Nearby Sélestat was justly renowned for its Latin school, led by Beatus Rhenanus. The future clergy and lay leaders of Strasbourg attended in particular the universities of Heidelberg, Freiburg and Basel. Capito was for some years an associate of Erasmus in Basel, and many Strasbourgers considered themselves disciples of the Rotterdamer. Leo Jud, an Alsatian whose evangelical career was largely in Zurich, published several German translations of Erasmus, whilst Conrad Pellican of Rouffach, who prepared the polyglot

Psalter for Erasmus' 1516 edition of Jerome, taught first in Basel alongside Johannes Oecolampadius, then for his last three decades in Zurich. Basel, Zurich and Strasbourg were all city-states with rural hinterland, and this common social pattern,[1] added to these intellectual and religious ties, will have played some part in the development of an Upper Rhine evangelical school of biblical interpretation. As recent studies have demonstrated, in the first half of the sixteenth century this school is rightly understood as one of the leading centres of biblical interpretation in Europe.[2]

The recognition of a school involves identifying the existence of several elements: a body of interpreters consciously working along similar lines with analogous methods in the use of common tools, employing a mutually agreed hermeneutic in pursuit of goals at least tacitly identified. Perusal of the regular exchanges in the voluminous correspondence of these evangelical exegetes makes all of these elements visible, and careful reading of their published translations and commentaries confirms this analysis. This said, however, three qualifying remarks need to be added. In the first place, it must not be assumed that there was consensus on all questions. As will be shown (in section 1.5), while proceeding with a sense of common task along a number of recognized parameters, the interpreters of the three cities differed amongst themselves on several issues. These will receive particular discussion below, for the differences are sometimes as revealing as the agreements. The second concerns the relationship of these evangelical interpreters with Luther and the Wittenberg exegetes, notably Johannes Bugenhagen, Phillip Melanchthon, and Johannes Brenz. Early in the period under study, relationships were cordial, and when public disagreement over the understanding of the Eucharist, or Lord's Supper, emerged, in the case of Bucer this came ironically in his very translations of exegetical writings of Luther and Bugenhagen, published with the authors' encouragement. The Supper-strife opened, of course, a breach between most south-German/Swiss evangelicals and the Wittenbergers, which in the case notably of Luther and Zwingli, was never reconciled. In Bucer's case, later editions of his larger commentaries saw the revision of a number of passages in the service of such a reconciliation.[3] There were also significant differences in their respective approaches to the Old Testament, and in Zurich at least, linguistic differences led to the production of a different Bible translation. These should not be permitted, however, to obscure the genuine respect shown by the Upper Rhine evangelicals for the exegetical accomplishments of Luther and associates, and significant elements of commonalty in their methods and interpretations, and in the case of Strasbourg, in the general use of the Luther Bible.[4] Many of Brenz' Old Testament commentaries were first published in

---

[1] In contrast, Freiburg was firmly integrated within the Hapsburg domains, and played no part in this development.

[2] The most complete chart of its publications: Bedouelle / Roussel, Le temps des Réformes (1989) 226–32.

[3] For example, his criticism of the Wittenberg Law-Gospel hermeneutic in the 1529 Psalms is attenuated in the 1532 edition. See below n. 228.

[4] Pellican actively promoted the publication of Luther and Bugenhagen in Basel in the early 1520's; cf. Hobbs, Conrad Pellican (1999) 84–85. In Strasbourg, in addition to the publication of

Hagenau in northern Alsace. Thirdly, the matter of localities and personalities. The origins of the school undoubtedly lay in Basel, in the text editions, notes and philological tools of Pellican and Sebastian Münster, which anticipated and in turn facilitated the appearance of the first of the large commentaries, Oecolampadius' *Isaiah* of 1525, and Bucer's German *Psalter* of January 1526.[5] The first of Zwingli's Old Testament publications – notes on Genesis and part of Exodus, the fruit of the *Prophezei* studies – appeared in 1527, his own *Isaiah* in 1529. Except for Bucer, these interpreters have been given attention in preceding chapters, and I shall try to avoid unnecessary repetition here. Strasbourg, where Capito's *Habakuk* appeared in 1526, is the primary focus of attention in this chapter, although given the nature of the school, there will be periodic cross-references to Basel and Zurich. Moreover, as will be seen, although first on the ground, Capito would be eclipsed by the rising career of his younger colleague, Bucer. The latter will therefore be the more central figure of this chapter, while Capito's accomplishment and concerns will appear in relation to the former.

1.2. *Capito, Bucer and the Reform in Strasbourg*

From 1521, Matthis Zell of Kaysersberg was sounding distinctly evangelical notes from his prominent Strasbourg pulpit in the Cathedral parish of St. Laurence. Wolfgang Capito of Hagenau, provost of St. Thomas and later dean of St. Peter-the-Younger, was more cautious, but by early 1523 had also moved into the evangelical camp. The arrival of Martin Bucer, a native of Sélestat, in 1523 – a refugee because of his evangelical preaching in the diocese of Speyer as well as his marriage to a former nun – and their decision to welcome him as a potential colleague and to encourage the city authorities to grant him citizenship, were early steps in a series of events that would finally bring the Strasbourg magistrates to the abolition of celebration of the Latin Mass in 1529, and formally to identify the city with the "protesting" members of the Diet of Speyer that same year. Central to this development was a programme of biblical lectures offered to the general public. These will initially have had a less formal character; Bucer began lecturing in a room in Zell's rectory, and a cautious city magistrate at first refused him permission for other than Latin lectures. This restriction was soon lifted, however, and growing popularity forced the move to more spacious quarters in the cathedral's St. Laurence parish. The lectures also became increasingly institutionalized, being held in various ecclesiastical venues, notably the Dominican church, before settling at St. Thomas' church into a regular pattern intended to replace the daily Office. In response to regular memoranda from the clergy, the Senior School was es-

various Luther editions, his hymns and psalms were sung in the liturgy, see Hobbs, Music in the Liturgy (2004) 161.
   [5] On Oecolampadius' commentary, see supra Chap. 18. Bucer's *Psalter wol verteutscht* was a free adaptation into German of Bugenhagen's *In librum Psalmorum interpretatio* (Basel 1524), accompanying Luther's new German translation of the Psalms.

tablished by the city in 1538. Although this latter was intended for the advanced education of youth, including the training of evangelical clergy, its formal teaching of biblical languages and interpretation means that it must be understood as the institutional perpetuation of this earlier biblical work. This school, with an international faculty and student body, would in time be transformed into the university of Strasbourg.

Writing in 1528, Bucer underlined the centrality of the study of the Hebrew Scriptures for the Strasbourg evangelicals.

> If we believe that to know God aright is eternal life, ... all we who bear the name children of God, but above all we who have been set as eyes and guides for others to attain this knowledge of God, ought to be ashamed that so many things in all the holy books of the Old Testament, but especially of the prophets... have until now not yet been presented in their own light, not yet rescued from the fog of differing interpretations, and, with the veil of the diction and tropes of the Hebrew tongue removed, clearly set forth for the contemplation of all believers.[6]

It was of course a commonplace for all would-be reformers that the Church's life and teaching must be directed in accordance with Scripture. On this even the divided Diet of Nuremberg could agree in 1523, its famous Recess calling, in the interest of public order, for the restriction of public preaching and teaching to Scripture, with the rider (generally overlooked by evangelicals) that this be according to the Church's received interpretation.[7] But from the beginning for the Strasbourg evangelicals this Scriptural exposition had to include the Hebrew Bible, not merely the New Testament, let alone the Church's slim annual lectionary of epistle and gospel excerpts for the mass. The Old Testament, as Bucer reminded his readers later in this same passage, was after all the sole Scripture known to Christ and the Apostles and is, according to their testimony, amply sufficient unto salvation.

In the initial phase of the Strasbourg lectures, Capito and Bucer agreed to divide the Testaments respectively, with Capito, the published Hebraist, lecturing successively and seriatim on the prophets Habakkuk, Malachi, Hosea and then Genesis and Jonah. Bucer meanwhile lectured on the Gospels and Epistles, albeit also on the Psalms. Some of the lectures were in German, some in Latin, and they drew an enthusiastic crowd of laity as well as clergy, to the displeasure of more conservative authorities, suspicious of the popular impact of such activity.[8] It became quickly apparent, however, that such lectures could

---

[6] Bucer, *Tzephaniah* (Strasbourg 1528; repr. Geneva 1554), dedicatory epistle, p. 523 (1554 ed.): *Si ergo credimus aeternam vitam esse, Deum recte cognovisse...pudere profecto debet quicunque inter filios Dei nomen dedimus, maxime autem eos qui oculorum vice et duces ad istam Dei scientiam perveniendi aliis constituti sunt, tam multa adhuc in omnibus sacris Veteris instrumenti libris, praecipue autem Prophetarum... sua nondum esse luce donata, nondum e caligine variarum interpretationum eruta, remotoque phraseos et troporum Hebraeae linguae velamento contemplanda, clare credentibus omnibus exposita.*

[7] *Tantummodo sacrum Evangelium, iuxta interpretationem Scripturae ab Ecclesia Christiana iam approbatae et receptae, praedicetur ac doceatur*: B. J. Kidd, *Documents Illustrative of the Continental Reformation* (Oxford 1911; repr. 1967) # 62.

[8] Bucer, *Evangelia* (Strasbourg 1527) Sign. 3r; cf. Capito, *Habakuk* (Strasbourg 1526) fol. 2v. Nicholas Gerbel reported these lectures, and noted the discomfort of the Catholic apologist Thomas Mürner (also lecturing on Paul) at the presence of laity in the audience; they should have been at their daily work instead, cf. N. Gerbel, *Centuria Epistolarum Theologicarum* (ed. J. Schwebel; Zweibrücken 1597) 67.

serve only those close enough and able for physical attendance. The clergy of Strasbourg's rural hinterland, who were now being required to preach each Sunday, needed, in the eyes of Reformers, guides to Scripture with an evangelical bent. Moreover Bucer in particular was from the beginning conscious of a potential Europe-wide audience.[9] It was therefore a natural step in Strasbourg as it was in Zurich and Basel, to polish some at least of these lecture notes for publication. A reluctant Capito was pushed to this by the warning that, if he were not to prepare an edition himself, he might expect to have to endure the publication elsewhere of an unauthorized set of student notes. This was no empty threat, as others could testify to their rue.[10]

So Bucer's *Psalms* appeared in German edition early in 1526; Capito's *Habakuk* in Latin later that same year, his German *Hosea* in 1527, and a much more extensive Latin edition in 1528. Later that year came Bucer's *Zephaniah*, and one year later the first edition of his magisterial Latin *Psalms*, subsequently revised and expanded in 1532. All these, save Bucer's German *Psalter* of 1526, were Strasbourg imprints. After 1532, however, only Capito's *Hexaemeron* (1539), a commentary on the first six days of Creation, would be added to this list of their published Hebrew exegetica, although the two Reformers seem to have continued lecture activity.[11] Bucer returned to the New Testament for a time, but essentially his interest and energies seem to have shifted to leadership of the evangelical reform in other German centres. For his part, Capito may have been deterred by the 1527–28 quarrel with Bucer over the hermeneutic of the prophets, an issue that will be discussed later. He did nonetheless edit and see through the press in Strasbourg lecture notes on Jeremiah and Lamentations (1533) and Ezekiel (1534) by Oecolampadius of Basel, who had died in 1531. Capito himself died in the return of the plague in 1541. His place as Hebraist in the Senior School was taken by his onetime student, Paul Fagius, who had been till then situated in Isny, working in close collaboration with his teacher and friend, the great Massoretic scholar Elias Levita. Fagius' interest, like that of Münster, lay less in commentary itself (although amongst other books, he did lecture on Job) than in providing tools for Christian students of the Hebrew Bible and Jewish thought. He published a close guide, with excerpts from rabbinic commentators, to the first four chapters of Genesis (1542, 1543), an edition with his own Latin translation, of David Qimhi on the first ten Psalms (1544) and various translations of post-biblical Jewish texts, including a collection of contemporary prayers, and the *Pirke Avot*.[12]

The coming of the Italian refugee, Peter Martyr Vermigli, to Strasbourg meant yet another lecturer on Hebrew Scriptures in the Senior School, but the work of his two Strasbourg periods (1542–47; 1553–56) was only published much later, in particular by Christopher Froschauer in Zurich, where Vermigli established himself as successor to Pellican.[13] Thereafter the on-going work of Upper Rhine evangelical exegetes of the Old Testament would be centred in Basel and Zurich. To these must be added, over the next three decades, the massive commentaries of Wolfgang Musculus in Berne, as well as the impressive extension and polishing of the school's work in the numerous commentaries of Calvin, who had spent three years teaching at the Strasbourg Senior

---

[9] See his dedications of his 1524–26 Latin translations of Luther, to would-be evangelicals in France and Italy: BCorr 1, # 68; 2, ## 88, 135. Concern for untrammelled circulation in France led him to publish his Latin Psalms in 1529 and 1532 under a French pseudonym: BCorr 3, # 240; cf. Hobbs, *Le félin et le dauphin* (1986).

[10] Capito, *Habakuk*, fol. 2v. Conrad Pellican's 1527 Psalter was printed in Strasbourg without his consent, necessitating a 1532 Zurich edition corrected by the author.

[11] A set of Bucer lecture notes on Judges, undated, was published by Robert Estienne in his 1553–54 folio of Bucer exegetica. Other Bucer manuscripts perished in the 1870 burning of the Strasbourg library.

[12] Fagius' Genesis notes were included in the great compendium, *Critici Sacri* (London 1660). See Raubenheimer, *Paul Fagius* (1957) 129–33.

[13] Commentaries on Judges (1561), the books of Samuel (1564), Kings (1566), Genesis (1569); and the much later Lamentations, also in Zurich, 1629.

School (1538–41). But the heart of the particular Strasbourg contribution to evangelical exegesis of the Old Testament lies in the period 1526–1534.

Bucer's call, cited above, to remove the obstacles posed by the strangeness of Hebrew idiom to European readers is a prescription at least as old as St. Augustine's *De doctrina christiana*.[14] But unlike the bishop of Hippo, Capito and Bucer practiced a method shaped by Renaissance humanism, which insisted on the centrality of linguistic and historical studies. Before discussing the specifics of the Strasbourg exegesis, it is appropriate to ask what training and tools Capito and Bucer possessed which will have equipped them for, and even shaped their direction.

Born in the imperial free city of Hagenau, Wolfgang Capito studied at the Latin school in Pforzheim, then in Ingolstadt, Heidelberg and Freiburg universities. His beginnings in Hebrew apparently belong to the period of his doctoral studies. He had some limited tutoring from the Spanish convert from Judaism, Matthaeus Adrianus, although he claimed in 1518 to have found the latter expensive and relatively unhelpful, leaving him to acquire most of his knowledge from books.[15] His disparaging reference to that "resentful Jew" not surprisingly drew a snide comment from Adrianus on the inadequacies of Capito's Hebrew.[16] From 1515–1520 Capito was cathedral preacher in Basel, where he moved in the circles of Erasmus and the printer Johann Froben, while building friendships with Oecolampadius and Pellican, and corresponding with Bucer. His enthusiasm for the Hebrew language drew a cautionary response from Erasmus already in 1517, but also praise for an unusual *homo trilinguis*.[17]

Capito contributed an elementary Hebrew grammar to Pellican's pocket edition of the Hebrew Psalter (1516); although he assembled it in haste, he claimed that from it the beginner could acquire a reading knowledge of Hebrew without the aid of any other teacher.[18] This grammar would be re-issued in more substantial form in 1518 and 1525.[19] Capito's correspondence gives the occasional tantalizing hint of the gradual acquisition of a substantial library of Hebraica, although most of his tools must be deduced from their use in his commentaries.[20] He will undoubtedly have purchased the 1517 and 1524–25 editions of the rabbinic Bible, with their Hebrew and Aramaic biblical text, framed by commentaries by David Qimhi, Abraham ibn Ezra and Rashi, amongst others.[21] Thus, when Capito arrived in Strasbourg in 1523, it was as a recognized contributor to the renaissance of Hebrew letters, although to that point he had yet to publish any interpretation of the biblical text.

The beginnings of Bucer's Hebraism are more obscure. Born into an artisan family without citizenship in Sélestat, Bucer probably attended the renowned Latin school there. At age sixteen he

---

[14] See esp. from Bk 2,11, CCSL 32, p. 42.

[15] Capito, *Hebraicarum Institutionum libri duo* (Basel 1518), A 4r.

[16] Erasmus, *Opus Epistolarum* (ed. Allen; Oxford 1906–58) 3, # 798; CWE 2, # 798.

[17] Erasmus, *Opus Epistolarum* (ed. Allen) 2, 491; CWE 4, Ep. 541; cf. CWE 5, # 798.

[18] Pellican, *Hebraicum Psalterium* (Basel 1516); preface in E. Rummel, Ep. 3. Capito informed the reader that it had been assembled in nine days.

[19] *Institutionum Hebraicarum libri duo* (Basel 1518; Strasbourg 1525).

[20] Capito to Bruno Amerbach, March 1518; see A. HARTMANN / B. R. JENNY (eds.), *Die Amerbachkorrespondenz* (Basel 1942–) # 605.

[21] The *Miqraoth gedoloth*, published by Daniel Bomberg in Venice. Oecolampadius' order in 1519 of the 1517 edition appears in his correspondence, see *Briefe und Akten* 1 (ed. E. Staehelin, 1927) # 56. Pellican purchased the much superior 1524–25 edition in 1527, see his *Chronikon* (1877) 114–16.

entered the Dominican order as a means of pursuing the higher education his family could not afford him. Sent eventually to Heidelberg in 1517, Bucer seems by that time to have begun Hebrew studies, to judge from the presence of an unidentified Hebrew grammar and Psalter in a booklist he sent to his superior in Sélestat.[22] He worked on Greek alongside Brenz in Heidelberg, but there is no indication that he encountered Adrianus as Hebrew teacher there. Bucer's correspondence shows him to have been an avid reader of Luther on the Psalms, and to have incurred the animus of the Dominican inquisitor, Jakob van Hoogstraten (the foe of Reuchlin).

Beyond this there are no hints of the developing Hebraist until 1525, when as we have seen he lectured on the Psalms in Strasbourg, undoubtedly as part of his preparation of the German commentary noted above. It is within this text that the reader discovers early, but significant traces of readings in rabbinic Jewish commentators, a pattern that he would expand greatly over the next six years, in his *Zephaniah*, and above all, in the two editions of the Latin *Psalms*. Now upon his arrival in Strasbourg in 1523, the rumour circulated that Bucer was of Jewish descent. He denied this as a slander all his life; this is not beyond the realm of the possible, but more likely it simply attests to the presence of Hebrew books amongst his possessions.[23] He would not be the first Christian Hebraist to be the object of that accusation. As for his working library, on the Psalms Bucer's standard version of the Massoretic Hebrew and Septuagint, as well as Jerome's Latin translations of these, was the *Quadruplex Psalterium* from the Basel 1516 edition of Jerome, a volume whose Hebrew was overseen by Pellican, although Bucer was probably using the second edition of 1525.[24] That he owned both editions of the Bomberg rabbinic Bibles can be established on internal evidence in his Psalms commentary. Similarly, it can be shown that he made use of the splendid Hebrew concordances of Ibn Qalonymos, likewise from Bomberg; they were an indispensable tool for decoding the tightly written commentaries of the mediaeval rabbis, and Fagius seems to have been at work on a Strasbourg edition of such a concordance when he was forced into exile in 1548.[25] Bucer probably also possessed the *Sefer ha-Shorashim*, David Qimhi's definitive Hebrew dictionary. Agostino Giustiniani's so-called *Octuplex Psalterium* was regularly consulted for the Targum and its Latin translation, and we may therefore assume several of the philological texts of Sebastian Münster, notably his guides to Aramaic and to rabbinic Hebrew.[26]

---

[22] BCorr 1, p. 45, 60.

[23] See Hobbs, Bucer, Jews and Judaism (2006) 155.

[24] *Appendici huic inest Quadruplex Psalterium, videlicet Hebraeum, et Hebraica veritas divo Hieronymo interprete, Graecum et aeditio ultima Latina autore incerto* (Basel 1516; 1525; etc.). As the title suggests, this fine edition was appended to tome 8 of Erasmus' edition of Jerome; it also was sold as a separate volume. Erasmus' scepticism concerning Jerome's authorship of the Gallican Psalter (sometimes termed the Vulgata) is evident on the title page. This volume is not to be confused with Pellican's 16° student edition, referred to above.

[25] Isaac Nathan ben Qalonymos, *Meir Nathiv – Concordantiae* (Venice 1523). Raubenheimer, Paul Fagius (1957) 133, # A 21.

[26] Qimhi's dictionary was available in several editions from about 1470; Giustiniani, *Psalterium Hebraeum, Graecum, Arabicum et Chaldaeum cum tribus latinis interpretationibus et glossis* (Genoa 1516); Münster, *Chaldaica Grammatica*, and *Perusch seu Biur Haperuschim* (Basel 1527), and *Dictionarium Chaldaicum* (Basel 1527).

Thus both Capito and Bucer came to the task well equipped by the standards of their generation. Confirmation that these were the tools generally employed within the Upper Rhine school comes too from the records that have survived of the libraries of Martin Cellarius and Peter Martyr Vermigli, who both moved within the circles of the school for a time.[27]

1.3. Interpreting the Old Testament

The distinctive characteristics of both Capito's and Bucer's approach to the Old Testament were set forth explicitly in a *ratio enarrandi prophetas*, prefaced to Capito's *Habakuk*. "Whoever undertakes commentary upon the prophets must have, I believe, precise knowledge of the histories of that time, at least a passable learning in languages, especially Hebrew, and acquaintance with Christ, with most certain experiences of faith".[28] Three things, then, Capito required of a sound interpreter of the prophetic writings: serious heed to the historical context of the writing, linguistic tools adequate to decode the ancient text, and a personal engagement in the Christian faith. Now the Strasbourgers would subsequently give this formula greater elaboration, and it would become apparent that there were significant questions that it left unresolved. Nonetheless, it does point to the central thrust of the Strasbourg interpreters, and as such, it is a good starting point in our examination of their work on the Old Testament.

First, contextuality: it is necessary to take with absolute seriousness the historical setting of the text. Now respect for the *fundamentum historiae* as the base upon which all spiritual interpretation must be built had been enshrined by Aquinas at the heart of his affirmation of the polyvalence of the biblical text, and acknowledged by virtually all interpreters, although opinions on what constituted the historical sense could differ significantly. In the late 1520's the Strasbourg exegetes were certain that this meant locating the primary sense in the life of ancient Israel, although admittedly they also identified passages in the prophetic writings where the seer was gifted with a vision that allowed a direct speaking of Christ and his kingdom.

Here they parted ways with an important late mediaeval tradition that had recently been vigorously reaffirmed by the French humanist, Jacques Lefèvre d'Etaples in his *Quincuplex Psalterium*. Lefèvre had been faced with a distaste for the Psalms amongst the monks in his charge at St. Germain-des-Prés in Paris. He argued in his edition of the several Latin Psalter texts that one cause of the decline in the celebration of the monastic office was certainly the tendency of some more recent interpreters to situate the historical sense in the life

---

[27] Cellarius, or Borrhaus, was active in Strasbourg exegetical circles in 1526–27 (see below), and he later taught Old Testament in Basel. The inventory of his library has been published by Backus, *Martin Borrhaus* (1981). On the remains of Vermigli's library, see A. GANOCZY, *La bibliothèque de l'Académie de Calvin* (Geneva 1969).

[28] Capito, *In Habakuk prophetam*, fol. 4r: *Qui sibi sumit enarrandos prophetas, huic esse opus puto, historiarum illius temporis exacta scientia, linguarum praesertim Hebraeae vel mediocri eruditione, et cognitione Christi fideique certissimis experientiis.*

of David, as if he were "an historian rather than a prophet".[29] For Lefèvre, the true literal sense of the Psalms is christological. Now Lefèvre came to Strasbourg as a temporary refugee in the winter of 1525–26, and living in Capito's spacious deanery, he worked away on his translation of the Old Testament into French. Subsequent relations between the Strasbourgers and their honoured guest were excellent; it may be that they agreed to disagree on this point. In any event, Bucer would not publicly take his stance on the historical reading of the Psalter until long after Lefèvre's return to France.

A corollary of this contextual principle was the refusal to practice the allegorical method. Allegory, however widespread amongst older and even some contemporary Christian interpreters, they denounced as a misguided, fanciful flight from the literal into the pursuit of edifying spiritual senses, a hermeneutical practice to be eschewed. Here Capito and Bucer parted company with another great humanist interpreter, Erasmus, whose Psalms treatises regularly employed that method. Already in 1516, Capito had respectfully expressed to Erasmus his reservations concerning the practice of the traditional four-fold sense (*quadriga*).[30] The early Luther was to a lesser degree vulnerable to the same strictures. To the Strasbourgers' mind, in the absence of a proper historical foundation, the interpreter is delivered by his own uncertainties to the playing of allegorical games. In the preface to his Gospels, Bucer derided such interpretation as an absurdly permissive elasticity that gave justification to the popular adage: "Scripture is a wax nose that can be twisted in any direction". The more adventuresome of these interpretations he called "unnatural" and "monstrous", but to his mind the method itself was at fault, in authorizing the interpreter to find anything anywhere, thereby effectively undermining the confidence of the hearers or readers in the certainty of the sense of Scripture.[31] He expressed it less polemically, but with no less firmness in his Psalms: "I have kept myself from anagogical interpretations, because if done rashly, these are not introduced without the danger of undermining the authority of Scripture". Enlightened readers, once confident of the historical sense, can develop spiritual applications for themselves; besides, "there is nothing pertaining to godliness which the historical does not abundantly teach". Therefore "those who fancy allegorical interpretations can find them in others".[32]

It followed, then, that for interpretation of a particular text those sources that shed light upon its setting in the biblical period would be prized, at the expense of "the others", those authors who, however godly, were ignorant of the history of Israel. Just as commentators of Homer must be familiar with the

---

[29] *Quincuplex Psalterium* (Paris 1509, 1513), Sign. Aii v: *absit igitur nobis credere hunc litteralem sensum, quem litterae sensum appellant, et David historicum potius facere quam prophetam.* Following the late mediaeval current represented by Jacob Pérez of Valencia, Lefèvre argued that David, author of the Psalms, thanks to his prophetic gift, intended Christ as the literal sense of the text; see H. A. Oberman, *Forerunners of the Reformation* (New York 1966) 286–88.

[30] CWE # 459.

[31] *Enarrationum in Evangelia* (1527), Sign. 3–7.

[32] *Sacrorum Psalmorum* (1529), preface, Sign. 7v: *Ab anagogicis interpretationibus mihi temperavi, quod illae non sine labefactandae Scripturarum authoritatis periculo ingerantur, si id temere fiat...praesertim cum nihil pietatis sit quod historia non abunde doceat*; on Ps 19:1, fol. 109v: *Quibus allegorica horum interpretatio arriserit, habent illam apud alios.*

events of the Trojan period, so the properly equipped interpreter of the prophets should turn to sources that elucidate the realities of the ancient world. Josephus would be a prized guide to Jewish history. But Aristotle, Strabo and Pliny would also be essential for understanding details of various aspects of the ancient world. The historical setting is to be discerned with exactitude; that effort is "unfortunate" that flattens all historical particularities and tries to make everything fit into every period.[33] Presumably to underline this principle, Capito prefaced his commentary on Habakkuk with a sketch of the history of the Babylonian empire, drawing explicitly upon Josephus.[34]

If the first principle was historical, Capito's second was linguistic. Study of the Hebrew language would enable the interpreter to decode the ancient text, and reveal the mysteries of the *lingua sacra*, the language of the Holy Spirit. Capito anticipated and rebutted as inadequate the solution to this issue proposed by Augustine in the *De doctrina christiana*, namely the recourse to a variety of reliable interpreters. He argued that no translator is capable of capturing the full nuance of another language, let alone that of Hebrew, a language so distant in time, and so concise in contrast with the prolixity of Latin. Then there are the particular tropes, the different style of the Hebrew tongue. Here, as on the previous point, Capito drew a similar conclusion with respect to most earlier Christian exegesis. The failure to read Hebrew vitiates the interpretations of even the most godly commentators of previous centuries, like Rupert of Teutz, while the widely consulted *Glossa ordinaria* is of no practical value for this very reason.[35] Capito was willing to allow that a good translation can be useful; he was too much an Erasmian to wish to discourage the unlearned from the reading of Scripture. But for commentators the rule is different; anyone wishing to come correctly to the mind of an entire prophet must have knowledge of Hebrew.

This principle set the Strasbourgers firmly on the side of the humanist linguistic agenda. So committed, indeed, were they in their early enthusiasm for Hebrew and Greek studies, so effusive in their public rhetoric, that they found themselves impelled to write to Luther and to Beatus Rhenanus, defending themselves from the accusation of contempt for Latin and classical literature.[36] They seem to have been able to reassure most critics on this score, but their enthusiasm for the teaching of Hebrew was undiminished. In 1529, Bucer even expressed the extraordinary hope that the day was approaching when, in fulfilment of the prophecy of Isaiah, Hebrew would be universally spoken in

---

[33] Capito, *Habakuk*, fol. 5v: *Adeo infoelix diligentia est, quae quidvis ad quamlibet periodi caesuram exaggerat.*

[34] Ibid. fol. 9–11. In his 1528 Hosea, the historical background was integrated into the body of his commentary.

[35] Here, too, a rupture with the older humanist tradition: see its prominent place, together with the Postils of Nicholas of Lyra, in the multi-volume edition of the Latin Bible, the *Biblia cum Glossa ordinaria*... printed by the Amerbachs in Basel, 1506–08, under the editorship of Sebastian Brant.

[36] Bucer, BCorr 1, # 83; 2, ## 100, 106. Bucer was widely, and correctly, quoted as having referred disparagingly to Latin, in the liturgical context, as a language of servility; cf. Hobbs, Bucer and music (2004) 164–65.

Christian cities, and there would be much less need for commentators![37] A similar, if less idealistic note was sounded by Zwingli that same year: translation serves beginners, until the day when they can swim without a cork.[38] This naturally allied the Strasbourgers with the humanist critics of the Church's Latin Bible. The so-called Vulgate itself – and therefore the various late mediaeval vernacular translations of it – quite apart from its lamentable state of textual transmission – suffered from the fatal defect of failing to grasp the full sense of the *Hebraica veritas*, and therefore the teachings of the Church drawn or buttressed from it suffered for this defect. The time had come for all commentators to work from the Hebrew original, from the source, not from a pool downstream. There would be differences, as we shall see, with colleagues over the precise manner in which this was to be accomplished; but Capito and Bucer were unyielding on this point.

A necessary corollary to this conviction was the task of translation. Despite the growing Christian familiarity with Hebrew, there would still have to be translations, destined for a general public increasingly literate in their mother tongue, as well as for a generation of priests of limited education now become evangelical pastors, who were obliged in the new order to preach weekly to their rural flock. For the reasons named, it was imperative that these translations must likewise be made from the Hebrew. In the words of George Joye, translator of Bucer's Latin Psalter into English, "God hath sente ye his Psalter in Englisshe, faithfully and purely translated, which ye may not mesure and juge aftir the comen texte [i.e. the Vulgate]. For the trowth of the Psalmes muste be fetched more nyghe the Ebrue verite...".[39] Now this was not an uncontested principle, even in Strasbourg. While Capito prepared his *Habakuk* with its manifesto for Hebrew-based commentary, his venerable house-guest, Lefèvre was at work on his French translation of the Old Testament, from the Vulgate. Admittedly, one of his own companions found this persistence regrettable, in view of his lack of Hebrew.[40] In this instance, Lefèvre may have begged indulgence on grounds of his age. François Lambert, the former Franciscan *praedicator apostolicus*, who was in Strasbourg from 1524–26, was another matter. Lambert, who spoke no German and had only a smattering of Hebrew, if any, published in these years a series of commentaries on all the minor prophets as well as the Song of Songs. It is not difficult to imagine him as the unnamed object of Capito's strictures on commentators without the Hebrew language. For in a treatise tellingly entitled *On Prophecy, Learning and Languages, and on the Letter and the Spirit*, Lambert positioned himself vigorously on the side of Spirit inspiration, and cautioned against all human erudition that would quench it. Accordingly, knowledge of Hebrew, while useful

---

[37] Bucer, *Sacrorum Psalmorum*, fol. 269v: *ut non quinque tantum sed universae urbes quae Christo nomen dederunt, lingua Cenaan, id est Ebraea, loquantur, habeantque hanc familiorem, quam ut tantis opus sit explanationibus.* The reference is Isa 19:18.

[38] Zwingli, *Complanationis Isaiae*, CR 101, p. 103. For the expression, see Erasmus, *Adagia*, LB 2, 313C.

[39] *The Psalter of David* ... [Antwerp ?] 1530; photo reprint, Appleford 1971, Sign. A v.

[40] Gerard Roussel, December 1525, in Herminjard, *Correspondance*, vol. 1, 415: *nec a nobis terreri potuit, ob rei difficultatem et linguarum imperitiam, ut desisteret....*

for the production of a good translation in the vernacular, is not at all essential for preaching; it is indeed to this extent dangerous, that it tempts the preacher to have confidence in his own learning, rather than the direct inspiration of the Spirit. Consistent with this view, Lambert encouraged the preaching of lay-men and women as equally susceptible to divine inspiration, although he added a warning here too against pride.[41] In a Strasbourg where a more radi-cal faction claimed precisely this right, the evangelical clergy could not have been pleased. Bucer responded, without naming the colleague, at a number of points in his commentary on the Gospels (1527). Notably, he asserted firmly that the apostolic gift of Acts 2 was indeed the knowledge of biblical lan-guages, but that while this may have been an instantaneous charism on that one occasion, in sixteenth-century Strasbourg God's gift was transmitted through the equally miraculous revival of Hebrew studies in their day. Com-menting upon Matt 4:7, he argued that

> they *tempt the Lord*, who have been appointed in order to teach the people to search the Scrip-tures with utmost diligence, and yet that they may do this better, they neglect to learn lan-guages, meanwhile quoting that the letter kills, that knowledge puffs up, that it is the Spirit who speaks, that the Lord will give them what they are say in that hour when they have to speak for the faith.[42]

Capito's *Habakuk* preface again: although the Christian faith of such older in-terpreters was not in doubt, these two defects – ignorance of history and of languages – vitiated hopelessly their efforts, encouraging recourse to that alle-gorical development of spiritual senses, which amounted frequently to the sub-stitution of their own religious ideas for the actual message of the text.

Both Capito and Bucer set a new Latin translation at the head of their pub-lished commentaries. The character of translation will be discussed in the next section; but the question that is immediately posed is this: If the translator is obliged to work directly from the original Hebrew, how will he gain in-depth access to the sense of more complex passages? Capito says nothing explicit on this score in the *Habakuk* preface. The answer, however, had already been an-ticipated in Oecolampadius' prefaces to his 1525 *Isaiah*: "Had I not been able to read Hebrew, and consult the commentaries of the Jews, I would never have dared engage this task".[43] If one took as starting premise the failure of all La-tin and Greek translations to capture accurately the sense of the prophet, for a Christian interpreter the recourse to mediaeval Jewish commentary on the text was indispensable. In the following section, we shall see how this was applied in Bucer's *Psalms*, the most mature work of the Strasbourg exegetes. Here Ca-pito's silence on the need for these sources is curious, given that he in fact cited

---

[41] *Commentarii de prophetia, eruditione, et linguis, deque litera et Spiritu* (Strasbourg 1526).

[42] *Enarrationum in Evangelia*, I, fol. 100rv: *Ita profecto tentant Dominum, qui constituti ut doc-eant plebem, Scripturam diligentissime excutere, atque ut id melius possint, linguas discere negligunt, in-terim iactantes literam occidere, scientiam inflare, Spiritum esse qui loquatur...*; see Hobbs, Lambert (1987) 285–88.

[43] Oecolampadius, *In Iesaiam prophetam*, Sign. α 3v: *Hoc ipse fateri cogor, me neque ex graeca ne-que latina tralatione mentem prophetae in multis locis potuisse deprehendere, et nisi hebraice legere va-luissem, Hebraeorumque consuluissem commentario, ne ausum quidem fuisse illum attingere*; cf. *Briefe und Akten* 1 (ed. E. Staehelin, 1927) 348.

Jewish commentary by name on a number of occasions in the text. On the first verse of Habakuk, he refers to a book called "Sidor Olam" to locate the prophet in the history of ancient Israel; this is a reference to the *Seder Olam Rabbah* taken, uncredited, from David Qimhi. Subsequently, explicit references are made to Qimhi and others, and in particular to the Targum. Was Capito assuming the reader's awareness of this, or was he proceeding cautiously, even defensively, perhaps mindful of Erasmus' concern about judaizing the Scriptures that was noted earlier? That the latter is the more likely is confirmed by the exposition of his last rule, that personal commitment to the Christian faith is the third essential for interpreting the prophets correctly. Here Capito made it quickly apparent that his remarks under this head do not refer primarily to Christian, but to Jewish commentators. If earlier he had accused many of the former of substituting their own thoughts for the mind of Scripture due to their ignorance of history and languages, now it is the Rabbis who are handicapped, if not altogether excluded, because they read the prophets without the prophetic spirit, which looked to Christ. Admittedly, Jews are persistent scholars, yet they are in bondage to their Rabbis' opinions; they go scrupulously to great lengths to reverence the written page and the divine name, yet miss the mind of Christ, and so wander in an interpretive dreamland: "Beyond the thread of the historical they seek nothing".[44] True, much of this is the conventional rhetoric of polemic. Between the lines, however, we must read a concern for the inner Christian debate, where a deep suspicion of a judaizing exegesis seemed to many justified by the exegetical practices of the Upper Rhine evangelicals.

This concern for the opinion of the wider community points to one final element raised by Capito in his dedicatory epistle addressed to the Strasbourg magistrate, Jacob Sturm. Traditionalist opponents saw in the Scripture-centredness of the evangelicals and their preoccupation with the development of new commentary faithful to linguistic and historical principles, a dangerous individualism, the substitution of private judgement in place of the historic doctrinal consensus of the Church especially as articulated in its councils. Anticipating this objection, Capito began by reminding Sturm that although individualist arrogance has done harm to the faith, Scripture teaches a principle intended precisely to obviate this danger: "According to the apostolic text, let there be judgement by those seated. Let two or three speak, and let the others exercise judgement. Moreover, if a revelation comes to another who is seated, let the first one be silent." The words are St. Paul's (1 Cor 14:29-32), the context the regulation of disorderly public worship in first-century Corinth. The text took on a dramatic new life, however, in the first decades of the sixteenth century. In the *Paraclesis* (1516) Erasmus had suggested, alluding to a portion of this text, that his contemporaries exercise their own judgement, on whether the biblical authors are not superior to all later theologians.[45] Four years later, in the *Address to the Christian Nobility of the German Nation*, Luther took a

---

[44] Capito, *Habakuk*, fol. 7rv: *Supra historiae filum nihil explorant.*
[45] Erasmus, *Paraclesis*, LB 5, 143; tr. in: JOHN OLIN, *Christian Humanism and the Reformation* (New York: Fordham 1975) 103.

further significant step. Citing the same verses used here by Capito, Luther claimed them as Pauline authority in rebuttal of the claim for the primacy of papal teaching. All Christians, Luther argued, are taught by God, and given spiritual judgement; all are therefore called to judge the truth of teachings, with no priority assigned to the pope.[46] In urging the noble and well-educated Sturm to read the commentary at his leisure and form his own judgement, in welcoming this critique, Capito is reminiscent of the Luther passage. He would also, however, have been well aware of the remarkable use to which this passage had recently been put in Zurich, where the action of "prophesying" as biblical interpretation, accompanied by the manifestation of "tongues" as literacy in the biblical languages, was set into a communal process of discernment in the institution of the *Prophezei*.[47] In Strasbourg, Bucer and Capito were appealing to the Magistrate to establish a comparable institution as replacement for the celebration of the Daily Office, on occasion citing the Zurich model.[48] But they were also in their written commentary consciously claiming a modest exercise of the prophetic office; and in submitting their Spirit-guided interpretations to the judgment of a wider public, in calling for judgment to be exercised by each reader, they were giving to the hermeneutical circle of discernment a larger than geographic situation. Moreover, that discernment was to be exercised "according to the Scriptures, and the analogy of faith".[49] In invoking the latter, the circle of the assembly was made wider still, to include the discernment of earlier generations, of the historic faith community, in particular, of the Patristic era. The most mature statement of this principle comes in the preface to Bucer's *Psalms*. It is the duty of all Christian interpreters, he argued, to submit the results of the gifts and graces received, to the general judgment of the community. Then, seeking to steer evangelical exegesis between the equally unacceptable alternatives of individualism and a papal magisterium, he wrote:

> Lest I should thus be peddling my own comments for gifts of God, I wish to have affirmed nothing at all that the common consensus of the orthodox does not receive...Accordingly I submit whatever I have written in this work to the judgement and censure not only of the leaders of the church, not only of the professors of sacred theology, but precisely of all Christians... Whatever is such that it conflicts with the Word of God, with the decrees of the holy Church of God, and with the opinions of the orthodox Fathers, I wish, I command, I require be taken as condemned and withdrawn.[50]

This Strasbourg exegetical method would receive its most mature expression in

---

[46] Luther, *An den christlichen Adel*, WA 6, 411; *Luther's Works* 44 (Philadelphia: Fortress 1966) 134.

[47] See supra Chap.18, sect. II, 2.1.

[48] Bucer, BDS 2, 466–67; 519–23.

[49] Bucer, *Tzephaniah* (1554 edn.) 584; cf. Bucer, *In Evangelion Iohannis* (ed. I. Backus; BOL 2, SMRT 40; Leiden: Brill 1987) 546.

[50] Bucer, *Sacrorum Psalmorum* (1529) Sign. 4rv: *Ne autem mea commenta ita pro donis Dei venditarem, nihil omnium quae communis orthodoxorum consensus non recipit, adfirmasse volo.... Proinde quicquid in hoc opera scripsi, non solum procerum ecclesiae, non solum S. theologiam professorum, sed omnium omnino Christianorum iudicio et censurae subiicio...Quicquid tale est, quod Verbo Dei, quod placitis Ecclesiae sanctae Dei orthodoxorumque patrum sententiis adversetur, pro indicto proque recantato haberi volo, iubeo, postulo.*

these same Latin Psalms commentaries of Bucer (1529, 1532). Some comment upon their salient features will provide concrete illustration of its application to the Old Testament.

Bucer had already published in German an extensive revision of Bugenhagen's Latin commentary (1526). This may have whetted his appetite for a more original effort. In spring-summer 1528, he advertised his work on the minor prophet Zephaniah as a trial set-piece for the Psalter.[51] The completed work was impressively large, more than 400 folios in-quarto; revised and expanded in 1532, it was lightly retouched in the Basel 1547 edition, an in-folio of some 628 pages; here as in his Gospels and Romans commentaries, Bucer was already anticipating the ponderous tomes of later sixteenth-century exegetes, like Wolfgang Musculus, his sometime assistant.[52] A brief description of the form: the work was introduced first by a dedication to the dauphin of France,[53] then by a substantial programmatic preface, which discussed in some detail issues of base text, translation, sources and technical Psalter terms. There followed a psalm-by-psalm treatment of the whole: each psalm was prefaced by an *argumentum*, a succinct statement of the Psalm's theme and development; there followed a new translation of the Hebrew, whereupon the Psalm was divided for commentary into units of one or more verses. Each of these units was introduced by *ad verbum* notes in those instances where Bucer felt that his new translation might require some more literal justification.[54] The commentary sections could be extensive, although they were significantly shortened in the later Psalms, both because Bucer could cross-reference earlier discussion, and under pressure from his printer. Finally, he appended the occasional theological essay at the end of particular Psalms, a dozen of these "loci communes" in all, on themes like law and faith, but also on ethical matters like usury, and liturgical, like prayer and music in worship.

At the heart of the project lay a radically new translation of the Psalter. Already in his *Ephesians* and *Zephaniah*, Bucer had experimented with translation; now he was prepared fully to offer a rationale for his "version which is a little freer, and thereby I trust also somewhat clearer".[55] His guiding principles for what he would in subsequent editions advertise as "a natural, (or authentic) rendering"[56] began with an expansion of the arguments earlier cited from Capito. But he was in particular concerned to justify his practice of free, or paraphrastic translation, rather than following the erstwhile canons of biblical translation in a tradition of literal, or word-for-word renderings. To do so, he re-engaged the question posed by Jerome, of what characterizes "fidelity" in the translator.[57] Jerome had defended translation by sense rather than an at-

---

[51] Bucer, *Sophoniam* (1554), preface, 527.

[52] Bodenmann, *Wolfgang Musculus* (2000) 146–47: Musculus boarded in Bucer's home, and prepared a fair copy of his Zephaniah and Psalms notes for the printer, 1528–29.

[53] The work appeared under the pseudonym "Aretius Felinus theologus", signed in Lyons, but actually printed in Strasbourg. Bucer hoped by this subterfuge to gain a hearing for his irenical exegesis amongst reform-minded Catholics in France and elsewhere. See Hobbs, Le félin et le dauphin (1986) 217–34.

[54] Bucer, *Sacrorum Psalmorum* (1529), Table of contents: *Ubi a verbis Psaltis nonnihil recedendum fuit, reddendi sensus gratia, id ab initio explanationis cuiusque psalmi indicator, posita versione eorum locorum ad verbum.*

[55] Bucer, *Sacrorum Psalmorum* (1529) Sign. 4v – 6v: *Iam versionis, et ut paulo liberioris, ita spero nonnihil quoque planioris, reddenda ratio est.* His views are sketched in *Ephesios*, fol. [5]rv, and alluded to briefly in *Sophoniam*, 527.

[56] Titlepage in 1532 ad 1547 (although not in 1554): *Sacrorum Psalmorum libri quinque, ad Ebraicam veritatem genuine versione in Latinum traducti....*

[57] *Epistulae*, 57/5, *Ad Pammachium de optimo genere interpretandi*, CSEL 54, 508; PL 22, 571. On the mediaeval discussion and practice, see W. Schwarz, "The meaning of <fidus interpres> in mediaeval translation", *JThS* 45 (1944) 73–78.

tempt at literal equivalence, but added one fatal exception, "save in holy Scripture, where the word order also contains a mystery".[58] To this exception, lamentable in his eyes, Bucer posed two responses. In the first place, Jerome himself often abandoned literalism for a freer rendering that reproduced the meaning of the original. Secondly, not to do so is to deliver the reader and eventually the Church to the worst perils of arbitrary individualism:

> I know that some people fear that if we allow everyone the possibility of pulling away from the words [themselves], many will introduce their own comments as the oracles of Scripture. For my part I really fear that wishing to avoid Scylla they are falling upon Charybdis. For when one works word-for-word, in a great many places no meaning is given at all; and therefore not just the occasion, but the necessity intrudes both for readers and for commentators, of each introducing his own. In this way Scripture is torn into as many meanings as there are readers; whereas the freer translator, even if in a few places he will mingle his own for the sense of Scripture, will not however do so lightly, save in passages where there is no danger for sound doctrine. Besides, he will express many passages – and especially those that teach godliness – with corresponding appropriateness and clarity, and thereby with sure benefit for those who will read what has been translated. It is to this splendid counsel that one cannot draw away from the words, that we owe that four-wheeled chariot of the interpreters, the allegorical as they call it, the anagogical, the moral and the historical. From this it has also come about that for many years now not a few of those who have undertaken the explication of Scripture have said whatever they wanted wherever they wanted.[59]

In the end, it is widespread familiarity with the biblical languages that will deliver the Church from this ill, and underline the solemn authority of Scripture. Here Bucer underlines evangelical continuity with the best of the mediaeval tradition, by evoking the decree of the Council of Vienne (1311) that had called for the establishment of five chairs of Hebrew study in western Europe.[60] But this should now become the practice in all Christian cities! Meanwhile, let translations give their readers the sense of the original, rather than the often incomprehensible stew served up by those overly scrupulous translators who slavishly follow a word-for-word method. "It flies in the face of common sense that what ought to be especially set forth for everyone, be so translated as to be understood by none".[61] In this lengthy apologia for paraphrastic translation, Bucer knew that even if he had allies in Luther and Zwingli, he was challenging not only the centuries-old tradition, but the practice of some fellow Christian Hebraists of his day, even within the circle of his evangelical

---

[58] *absque Scripturis sanctis, ubi et verborum ordo mysterium est.*

[59] Bucer, *Sacrorum Psalmorum*, Sign. 5v – 6r: *Scio timent quidam, si a verbis recedendi facultas omnibus fiat, multos sua commenta pro oraculis Scripurae allaturos. Istos vero ego plane vereor, volentes vitare Scyllam incidere in Charybdim. Dum enim verbum e verbo exprimitur, plurimis in locis prorsus nullus sensus redditur; et ideo non occasio sed necessitas obiicitur tam legentibus quam enarrantibus, ut quisque inferat suum. Sic discerpitur Scriptura in tot sensus quot eam legerint; cum interpres liberior, etiamsi aliquot in locis suum pro Scripturae sensu admiscebit, id tamen non facile admittet, quam in locis ubi est nullum sanae doctrinae periculum. Praeterea plurimos, et eos praecipue pietatem docentes exprimet proprie iuxta et plane, eoque certo cum fructu qui versa legerint. Huic profecto consilio, non esse a verbis recendendum, debemus quadrigam illam enarrationum: allegoricam quam ipsi vocant, anagogicam, moralem et historicam.*

[60] The decree of Pope Clement V, which Bucer quotes from the *Corpus Iuris Canonici*, CIC(L) 2, 1179. The decree was cited as warrant by other Christian Hebraists as well: Sanctes Pagninus, *Biblia* (Lyon 1528), pref.; Pietro Galatini, *De arcanis Catholicae veritatis* (1518) I,7, fol. 23.

[61] Ibid.

colleagues, as we shall see. He argued, however – specifically against Oeco-lampadius (albeit without naming him) – that it is not the primary function of biblical translation to teach Hebrew to beginners, but rather to expound the Word of God in such a manner that true doctrine and godliness be advanced amongst its readers.

Bucer's "versio" did indeed employ that liberty, although unevenly, and at times with signs of evident haste. The most daring of his renderings involved the handling of the divine name, the Tetragrammaton. Since pre-Christian times, convention had substituted *Adonai* for the pronunciation of the original Hebrew name. Bucer was uninterested in the speculations of Christian Kabba-lists like Reuchlin on the mysteries of the ineffable name. Convinced from his reading of Exodus 3 that this traditional reverence was misplaced – he termed it a Jewish superstition – and that on the contrary it was the divine will that the name be known and understood as widely as possible, he introduced in 1529 the Greek epithet *Autophyes*, i.e. the self-existent one, as his rendering of the Tetragrammaton.[62] In this instance, however, he found himself forced to re-treat; in the second edition he admitted that he had gradually allowed himself to be convinced that this was too radical an innovation, and thereafter he em-ployed instead *Jehovah*, giving him the dubious distinction of being the first Old Testament translator to bring this hybrid form into regular usage in a pub-lished translation. Other efforts met with more success. He argued – as did other Hebraists – that in Hebrew poetry singular and plural were employed in-discriminately, and that the usage of perfect and imperfect verb forms in no way corresponded consistently to Latin tenses. These canons gave him larger freedom than his predecessors had permitted themselves in the Psalms. Simi-larly, where he judged Hebrew idioms too harsh for European ears, he some-times Latinized. An example or two must suffice. At Ps 10:4, the Hebrew *kego-va appo*, "as the lifting up of his nose", was rendered in 1529 *attollens superci-lium*, a nicely comparable Latin metaphor, but sadly the image was dissolved in 1532 into *prae fastu suo*. At Ps 51:6, *vehara be'eneka 'asithi*, "I have done what is evil in your eyes", was translated *quod molestum tibi est* in 1529, and *quod displicet tibi* in 1532. These examples enable us to make two points, first, that his free rendering tended to flatten metaphors, losing in poetic quality what he hoped to gain in clarity. Secondly, his translation was clearly a work in progress. It was frequently, not always happily, revised for the 1532 edition. And this points to a further observation. There were undoubtedly a number of readers, almost certainly some of his colleagues, who demanded consistent justification for his paraphrastic renderings. As a result, in 1532, he standar-dized his occasional practice in 1529, setting an "ad verbum" rendering of his own making at the head of every unit of text, thereby encouraging the reader of his commentary to make his own comparison of the "versio" with the "ad verbum".

---

[62] Ibid. Sign. 8v and passim. The term was borrowed from the Christian apologist, Lactantius, who quoted it approvingly from the oracle of Apollo: *Divinae Institutiones* 1,7,1 (CSEL 19).

Bucer was well known for prolixity. Since he did not shrink from the title of paraphrast, one might expect that his rendering would tend to imitate the style of the greatly admired Erasmus in the New Testament, and expand the text significantly. There are certainly instances of this, as for example, where the Hebrew *qavvam* in Ps 19:5 in 1529 appeared as *indicium eorum*, but in 1532 as *eorum ad certam exactam regulam compositio et motus*![63] But such explanatory glosses in the translation are limited in number. When one compares word-count in the traditional Latin of the Gallican Psalter with Bucer's *versio*, the two are similar in length; and if Bucer sometimes exceeds Jerome's *Hebraicum* in length, the margin is generally less than ten percent. In comparison, the 1532 Psalter paraphrase of Joannes Campensis is consistently 40–50 percent greater in length than Jerome.

The bulk of the commentary is occupied by Bucer's *familiaris explanatio*, a commentary intended, as the name suggests, closely to accompany and elucidate the biblical translation. Here too we begin with Bucer's preface.

> Herein I have striven with all my natural powers to this end, that I might expound the details soundly and above all, in accord with the history, such namely that there be no occasion left the Jews for mocking our work, nor the dealers in subtleties among our own people for sneering at it, let alone calling it into question. Then those things which are interpreted concerning Christ our Saviour and the Church, may stand correspondingly more firmly upon the foundation of the historical.[64]

A Christian reading of the Old Testament that is at last defensible to Jewish critics, an interpretation that can also withstand the objections or scorn of scholastic Christian theologians: this would be accomplished through a thorough grounding in the historical, yet without losing sight of applications to Christ and the Church. One hears echoes of Capito's three points, elaborated much more fully. Bucer began by a text-critical survey. If he would make little use of the Greek version of the Psalms, this was for two reasons – its significant variance from the Hebrew, and secondly, its unreliable state of transmission. The two versions of the text available to him (he seems not to have had the Complutensian) – that of Aldo Manutius[65] and the Basel edition (that he would in fact use as his referent) – differed both from one another, and from readings in the Fathers; he concluded that the text available to him was almost certainly not the original Septuagint, but a conflation of several ancient versions. Finally, whatever vestigial authority clung to the "Septuagint" could not apply to the Psalter, since Josephus had made clear that only the Torah could properly claim that title. On the other hand, his admiration for the dependability of the massoretic Hebrew text tradition was without reservation: "As often as I consider that incredible care and diligence whereby these [manuscripts] have been preserved by the Jews...I am compelled to admire and embrace God's immense goodness toward us, despite our lack of gratitude".[66]

---

[63] The accompanying *ad verbum* gave *amussis eorum*.

[64] Bucer, *Sacrorum Psalmorum*, Sign. 6v: *In hac totos ingenii nervos huc intendi, ut germane singular, et ante omnia iuxta historiam enarrarem, ne scilicet Iudaeis occasion esset nostra ridendi, et argutulis quoque ex nostris ea fastidiendi, ne dicam de eis subdubitandi. Tum quae de Christo servatore atque ecclesia interpretantur fundamento historiae iuxta perstarent firmius.*

[65] The *editio princeps* of the Greek Bible, Venice 1518; reprinted in Strasbourg 1526–28; and the Pellican edition, see above n. 24.

[66] Bucer, *Sacrorum Psalmorum*, Sign. 7r: *Quoties siquidem considero incredibilem curam et diligentiam, qua illa per Iudaeos servata sunt...admirari et exosculari cogor immensam Dei in nos ingratos adeo bonitatem.*

Not that all Jewish resources were to be received with equal enthusiasm. To his mind, most Jewish interpretation was hopelessly distorted by talmudic traditions that sought to fortify co-religionaries against Christianity; and they found a thousand ways to evade the proper, christological sense of so many prophecies, especially in maintaining the promise of a restored earthly Zion. Even their revered Rashi was often unreliable, if not ludicrous, in his interpretations. However, Bucer found in two mediaeval commentators, David Qimhi and Abraham ibn Ezra, an extraordinarily helpful resource, on account of their steadfast commitment through lexicographical and grammatical studies, to the literal sense of the text. Naturally, he had to make exception with them as well in passages where they failed to interpret christological prophecies aright, "but I confess to the glory of God, the giver of all that is beneficial, that I have been greatly assisted by these men in expounding the Psalms, as I have indicated throughout the work".[67] Mindful, one assumes, of Capito's third point, Bucer added that his trust was never entire and without caution. He employed his own word studies to verify the rabbinic observations, he tested their proposals against the larger context of the psalm as a whole, and finally, brought his interpretations to the test of the analogy of faith in Christ. Let the whole Church be the judge of his success.

Bucer's praise for Radak and Ibn Ezra was not mere humanist window-dressing. A detailed analysis of his commentary reveals an endebtedness that is methodological and that goes well beyond the numerous explicit references to them. *Peshat* interpretation of the Psalter, as practiced by Radak in particular, placed a premium upon the determination of the *historia* of a particular psalm, the circumstances in the life of ancient Israel that led to its creation. Already within the canonical text are found traces of such interpretive lenses included as psalm titles, e. g. associating Psalm 3 with David's flight from Absalom. Bucer found the extensive practice of this interpretive method in the interpreters of *peshat* attractive; he regularly consulted their proposals, and where his three rabbinic sources (Radak, Ibn Eza and Rashi) did not agree, debated their relative merits. Moreover, having learned the value of the method, he could also advance his own hypotheses.[68] One discerns a similar development of the lexicographical method. Bucer frequently cites one or more parallel usages of a word proposed by Radak; but he has also sufficiently internalized the method that he will add examples of his own gleaning, or in other instances create a new word study, with, it must be said, uneven results.[69]

So central and thorough a role for his rabbinic sources was the consequence of Bucer's conviction that Christian reading of the Old Testament must be firmly grounded in an accurate understanding of the Hebrew original. Cer-

---

[67] Ibid. Sign. 7v: *Ab his in gloriam Dei, cuius donum est quicquid utile, fateor me in enarratione Psalmorum plurimum esse adiutum, quod et passim indicavi.* On the nuances of Bucer's evaluation of Jewish interpretation, see Hobbs, Bucer, the Jews (2006) 149–53.

[68] For example, while recognizing the Jewish tradition that made Ezra the general editor of the Psalter, he presumed later additions, and so assigned the authorship of Psalms 74, 79 and 80 to the Maccabean period.

[69] It is on the basis of these that one can deduce his ownership of Qalonymos' Hebrew concordance, and most probably also Radak's *Sefer ha-Shorashim*.

tainly this had a polemical dimension with respect to the Jewish community. It is true that Bucer's reference above to Jewish ridicule of Christian interpretations may be a conventional reminiscence of his own Dominican heritage. But that Christian debaters could be bested even in his own day by Jews due to the formers' ignorance of Hebrew is attested by Bucer's older colleague, Conrad Pellican; he attributed his passion to acquire Hebrew to his witnessing the discomfiture of a priest by a Jewish man and woman.[70] Christians must be properly equipped to defend their reading of the Old Testament. The Hebraizing of Christian theology could mean formally, for Bucer, the re-writing of proper names from a Latinized to a Hebraic form: as Iaacob for Iacob, or Hizkiiah for Ezechias. This practice he did justify as removing an object of Jewish mockery, but more positively also as a restoration from depravity of the pure sounds of the Spirit's voice.[71] More substantial was his commitment to recover the original Hebraic coloring of the varied elements of theological vocabulary. Here the most controversial result came when he addressed in his 1527 Gospels commentary the term *infernus*, as in the article of the Creed traditionally rendered "he [Christ] descended into hell". Bucer raised the issue, because the passion narratives are silent on this claim of the Creed. However, when one recognized that the term *infernus* renders the Hebrew *sheol*, and one examined the content of this word from its usages in the Old Testament, it became evident to Bucer at least that the term meant simply the resting place of the dead. He quoted the use of Ps 16:10 in Acts 2:31 and 13:35 as demonstrating this clearly, an argument he would repeat – and even buttress with a claim for Radak's lexical support! – in the Psalms commentary. The Gospels are clear that Jesus really did die; that is what the creed should be taken to mean. Therefore, he argued, all the misguided fancies of mediaeval theologians on the subject of limbo and purgatory are to be dismissed, let alone the "blasphemous claim" that popes, monks or theologians can establish articles of faith such as this without explicit Scriptural warrant![72] This exegesis and consequent re-interpretation of an article of the Apostles Creed, maintained in each of his subsequent commentaries, would provoke the accusation of Judaizing from a Silesian evangelical, Valentin Crautwald.[73] Others will certainly have suspected 'heresy', where Bucer insisted upon a primary historical interpretation in the life of King David or others of ancient Israel, for Psalms whose literal christological sense seemed to Christian tradition to have been clearly and indisputably established by their quotation in the New Testament as messianic prooftexts.[74]

---

[70] Pellican, *Chronikon* (1877) 14–15.

[71] Bucer, *Evangelia*, fol. 11r.

[72] Ibid. vol. 2, fol. 361r – 362v; *Sacrorum Psalmorum*, fol. 92v – 93r.

[73] Crautwald to Capito, *Täuferakten Elsaß* 1 (ed. H. G. Rott / M. Krebs; QFRG 26; Gütersloh: Gerd Mohn 1959) 170–71; to Bucer, BCorr 3, 178–79; see Hobbs, Bucer, the Jews (2006) 154–55.

[74] The most egregious example will have been Psalm 22, which Bucer assigned to two moments in David's career, before and after his coronation; see Hobbs, Martin Bucer on Psalm 22 (1978) 153–55. Theodore of Mopsuestia was condemned by the Second Council of Constantinople for ascribing it to a Davidic setting; and thereafter Christian interpreters frequently repeated this condemnation at the outset of their commentary.

1.4. The Hermeneutic of the Old Testament

That his manner of reading the Old Testament might be deemed heretical may seem at first an unlikely concern for Bucer. The quest for an historical setting for the composition of individual Psalms was, after all, not new; amongst others Nicholas of Lyra had practiced this, and in the Basel 1506 Bible Paul of Burgos' rebuttals were printed alongside Lyra, allowing the reader to choose. Interpreters like Lyra found themselves constrained, however, where a particular text had been given a christological or allegorical reading in the Christian New Testament. For example, Lyra's *Literal Postil* on Psalm 19 initially presented the whole as a text celebrating the glory of God in creation and in the giving of the Law. He then argued, however, that this could not be the literal sense, due to Paul's application of 19:5 to the preaching of Christ's apostles in Rom 10:18; in effect the former was an unacceptable Jewish reading. Bucer, on the other hand, argued that the primary sense for the same text really is such a celebration; the Pauline application is not the literal meaning, but is an entirely appropriate extension of the first:

> It is generally agreed amongst all the Hebrews, and the very words of the psalm attest the same, that the Seer preaches in the first seven verses God's power that is so strikingly declared in the fabric of the heavens. I shall interpret them thus, and as it will be shown, with the agreement of St. Paul in Romans 10. Those desirous of an allegorical interpretation will find it elsewhere.[75]

Having expounded this literal sense, Bucer felt compelled to return to the issue, in order to demonstrate his claim that St. Paul would obviously have understood the text exactly as Bucer presented it, and that out of this literal, creation sense the Apostle had made an allegorical application to the preaching of the Gospel. From the lesser to the greater sense, *a minore ad maius*,[76] "Paul understood that just as the heavens celebrate the power of God throughout the whole planet, so the apostles had already at that time divulged God's glory to the ends of the earth".[77] Given, however, that Bucer's *argumentum* at the head of the Psalm makes no mention of this canonical allegorical application, a sixteenth-century reader might be pardoned for drawing the conclusion: St. Paul agrees with Bucer, not Bucer with St. Paul.[78]

The issue, of course, was Judaizing, the age-old fear of surrendering the reading of the Hebrew Scriptures to the Jewish rival. Bucer clearly did not believe that his extensive use of rabbinic sources, not only for lexicographical detail, but also for an interpretive framework, led necessarily to that end. That

---

[75] Bucer, *Sacrorum Psalmorum*, fol. 109r – 111v: *Inconfesso est apud omnes Ebraeos, et ipsa verba Psalmi idem testantur, vatem versibus septem prioribus Dei potentiam in coelorum machina tam insigniter declaratam praedicare; de hac eos interpretabor, et ut videtur, consentente d. Paulo ad Rom. 10. Quibus allegorica horum interpretatio arriserit, habent illam apud alios.*

[76] To my knowledge, however, Bucer never names this Pauline exegesis as the rabbinic principle of *kal vahomer*.

[77] Ibid. fol. 111r: *Nihil obstat quin alligoricos dictum hos citasse dicamus, historiae simplicitate haudquaquam negata, atque intellixisse, sicut coeli in universo orbe Dei potentiam celebrant, ita iam tum apostolos gloriam Dei ad fines usque terrae, per praecipuas silicet orbis regions divulgasse.*

[78] On the fascinating question of the weight assigned to apostolic quotation for sixteenth century exegetes of the Hebrew, see Hobbs, *Hebraica veritas* and *apostolica tradition* (1990).

possibility did exist, however, and the case of Miguel Servetus, who apparently completed the manuscript of his *De erroribus trinitatis* in Strasbourg in this same period, illustrated the danger.[79] We have seen that Lefèvre d'Etaples had warned that a concentration upon a Davidic historical sense in the Psalter was precisely that. We recall too that Capito's third principle enunciated in the preface to his *Habakuk* excluded Jews from a right understanding of the prophets. How did Bucer address and satisfy this concern?

The starting point is with the events leading up to the publication in March 1528 of two Strasbourg commentaries, Capito on Hosea and Bucer on John. As we have suggested earlier, these two volumes had their origins in biblical lectures by their respective authors in 1526–28 in the Strasbourg *prophezei* and the passionate exegetical debate which they engendered. Bucer's Zephaniah commentary of late summer 1528 carries significant hermeneutical overtones from that debate. Now the fundamental difference did not lie in their understanding of election. Each believed that by the divine will, the elect people of God existed from all time, both before and after the coming of Christ. This one elect people, of Jews and Gentiles, would come to completion in Christ in the future kingdom of God. What did, it emerged, divide them was the question of the place of the contemporary Jewish people in the divine economy of salvation; and related to this, therefore, the reliability of Jewish commentators who pointed their readers to an as-yet-to-dawn Messianic future in a restored Jewish nation in Palestine. The question was initially posed by another Hebraist, Martin Cellarius (Borrhaus), who had recently arrived in Strasbourg, fresh from controversial sojourns in both Wittenberg and Zurich.[80] He was for a time house-guest in Capito's spacious deanery of St. Thomas. The controversy involving Cellarius' stay in Strasbourg has usually been explained by the Anabaptist sympathies he manifested at a time when Bucer and the other leadership of the Strasbourg evangelical clergy were under special stress from this quarter. This was undoubtedly a significant factor, but another argument would introduce division within the *prophezei*, and alienate him profoundly from Bucer. Cellarius was an advocate of the view that many of the prophetic promises for a restored Israel had never been fulfilled; as word of God, their accomplishment must therefore form part of the divinely willed end of history. He introduced "his own tenets" promptly into the discussions in the Strasbourg *prophezei*, to Capito's initial bemusement.[81] But Cellarius also included

---

[79] Servetus was in Strasbourg for a time during 1528–31. He published *De erroribus* in Hagenau, some 25 miles north of Strasbourg, in 1531. For a time, it was feared he had infected Capito with his ideas; see Bucer to A. Blaurer, in: T. SCHIESS, *Briefwechsel der Brüder Blaurer* I (Freiburg: Fehsenfeld 1908) 306–07; and Friedman, The most ancient testimony (1983), Chap. 7.

[80] R. L. WILLIAMS, "Martin Cellarius and the Reformation in Strasbourg", *JEH* 32 (1981) 477–97, mentions this matter in passing, but does not explore it. Kittelson, Capito (1975) 177–81, attributed the whole conflict to the Anabaptists.

[81] Capito praised Cellarius to Zwingli, who mistrusted him, but added with respect precisely to this question: *habet tamen sua dogmata: Illustrandam totam gentem Israelitarum ac terram Chananaeorum hic possessuram, in terrena etiam potestate praesignes, si rite hominem assequor*, so 14 November 1526; CR Z 8, # 551.

this argument in the third part of a 1527 Strasbourg publication, the *De operibus Dei*, to which Capito contributed a highly complimentary preface. If therefore initially skeptical on this subject, as Capito moved through his Hosea lectures, he was evidently fully won over to Cellarius' position, and this interpretation – that the Jews must be restored to their homeland in Palestine before the fulfillment of God's kingdom – became a central leitmotif in his reading of the prophet. Cellarius had elaborated the argument in the *De operibus Dei* as a commentary upon the apocalyptic seventy weeks in Daniel 9. If ancient Israel prefigured the reign of the Spirit in Christ, for many centuries now the time of the seventy weeks – a spiritual captivity of the Jews in bondage to materialism and to the human traditions of the Talmud – has prefigured the similar captivity of Christians to the errors of the anti-Christ that have long bound the Church. Christians have therefore no reproach to make to their Jewish contemporaries, for they are held captive in similar ways. But now there are signs of the dawn of the final stage, when Jewish restoration will prefigure the final in-gathering of the whole people of God: "when the holy land, long devastated and utterly deserted, shall be restored through God's blessing to its fertility after such sterility, and will then represent the kingdom of glory which resides in all the elect....Then Israel will be brought back into its own land, in order that in this way it may prefigure the resurrection of the elect".[82]

In his *Hosea*, Capito repeated this scenario of a three-stage typological reading of Israel "according to the flesh", in relation to the spiritual Israel, anchoring it likewise in an interpretation of Daniel 9 that is undoubtedly borrowed from Cellarius.[83] He also quoted frequently, and favorably, from rabbinic sources on the interpretation of his text, at one point inviting the reader to marvel at "how close the Jews are to the truth".[84] They err simply in not understanding the distinction between outer and inner, and therefore fail to apply the heart of the promises not to Jews as such, but to God's elect people, a people composed without discrimination of Jews and Gentiles. Yet this latter ultimate truth does not exclude the material blessing that is to come for all Jews as prefiguration of the final glory of all God's people. Commenting upon Hos 2:24, and again in his summation of the book, in terms that are repeated throughout the commentary:

> We too, with the Jews, expect with utmost certitude that these things are going to be materially fulfilled. For all things have been created to God's glory and the use of the elect. It is therefore going to happen, so that when all the material blessings have been displayed, this may be a prelude to the eternal blessing being displayed. Moreover the blessing of the Lord will especially be abundant in the land of Canaan.

---

[82] Cellarius, *De operibus Dei*, fol. 72–86: *terra sancta, sicut hactenus...vastata ac tota deserta...solitudinem ac desolationem regni Dei ...deliniavit, sic...ipsa per benedictionem Dei, foecunditati suae post tantam sterilitatem restitute... regnum gloriae, „quod omnibus electis sedet, representabit. Sicque fiet ut Israel... in terram suam reducatur, ut hoc modo electorum resurrectionem...praefiguret* (fol. 85–86).

[83] Capito, *Hoseam*, fol. 66–68; for a statement of the three stages of the type that has the merit of being much clearer than in Cellarius' prose, fol. 79v. The reader is referred to Cellarius' book on occasion: fol. 74, 284.

[84] *Vide optime lectore quam Hebraei sint vicini vero"*; ibid. fol. 65–66.

When Christ the king has been perfectly revealed, Israel will possess its own land without hindrance and with great splendour ... for the spiritual kingdom of Christ does not exclude a physical one, which will in this type-people shed light upon the future glory.[85]

Despite a theology of election common to his colleagues, and his employment of a typological hermeneutic for relating the Old and New Testaments, Capito cannot have been unaware that his colleague Bucer was in serious disagreement with him. Indeed, to the first passage just quoted Capito added a paragraph that is without doubt a summary of Bucer's objections raised in the *prophezei*. He could not, he said, understand why some might oppose what he believed conformed to "the simplicity of the Spirit". However, "we speak these things according to the analogy of faith and the tenor of Scripture; let those sitting by judge by the same standard".[86]

It is apparent that Bucer found any notion of a restored Jewish state in an earthly Palestine repugnant; it was fundamentally in conflict with his understanding of the essentially spiritual character of the kingdom of God, and had unacceptable implications for Christology, as we shall see. But he was unsuccessful in convincing Capito within the *prophezei*; the latter informed him he could not see how the prophet could be interpreted differently.[87] The Hosea commentary appeared at Easter, Bucer's commentary on the Gospel of John the same fortnight. Into the early chapters of the latter, Bucer inserted several discussions of the nature of typology, most notably at John 3:14, intended implicitly to refute Cellarius' and Capito's position.[88] The disagreement was now effectively in the public record. In considerable distress, Bucer wrote to Oecolampadius and to Zwingli, appealing for support.[89] He accused Capito of attacking his own colleague Bucer's views, without however naming him. Meanwhile Capito, as was the custom amongst the colleagues of the school, had already sent off a copy of his *Hosea* for Zwingli's approbation, as he hoped, although he admitted there might be "some minor points" on which they would disagree.[90] The decisive response came in fact from Pellican, who here as on some other occasions read and wrote on Zwingli's behalf. God's kingdom, Pellican argued, is purely spiritual; the Jews, "that miserable race of mortals", are sadly mistaken when they look for glory in an earthly kingdom. They will know a glorious future in this world and the next, only if and when they accept Christ as their Messiah. Pellican cautioned Capito that he was allowing too much authority to the rabbinic sources he quoted so abundantly; he evidently presumed that Capito's views were influenced by these. He ended by

---

[85] *Haec nos cum Iudaeis corporaliter quoque praestanda certissime expectamus. Omnia enim creata sunt ad gloriam Dei et usum electorum. Futurum est igitur, ut omnibus benedictionibus corporalibus exhibitis exhibendae aeternae benedictioni praeludatur. Maxime autem in terra Chananeorum benedictio Domini abundabit;* ibid. fol. 63r. *Israel Christo rege perfecte revelato terram suam libere possidebit cum magno splendore... Neque enim spirituale regnum Christi carnale excludit, quod futurae gloriae in typico populo praelucebit;* fol. 269–70.

[86] Ibid. fol. [63]rv: *Cur haec aversantur quidam non video, nisi alienum rationibus Conditoris et Patris consent, per corporalia quae sunt Spiritus adumbrari, aut nisi existimant cum regno Spiritus (quod est Christi) pugnare corporales benedictiones. Simplicitas enim, sic loqui et verbis ita prae se ferre Spiritus est... Neque crux deerit electis tamen, quamvis extra maledictionem et absque persecutione de gentibus, quia caro mortificanda supererit.... Haec iuxta fidei analogiam et Scripturarum tenorem nos dicimus; ad eandem regulam sedentes diiudicent.*

[87] Bucer to Zwingli, 15 April 1528; CR Z 9, # 713, and BCorr 3, # 186: *Respondit sic se habere fidem suam, nec videre quomodo prophetae enarrari possint, suis – imo nugis Cellarii – non receptis.*

[88] Bucer, *In Evangelion Iohannis*, SMRT 40, BOL 2, 81–83 (directed against Cellarius), 120–21, and especially 142–54 (where he noted that he could have written more, but had only a month to complete his manuscript for the Frankfurt fair).

[89] Bucer to Oecolampadius is lost; to Zwingli, supra n. 86. See also Bucer to Zwingli, 26 September 1528; CR Z 9 # 762, BCorr 3, # 206.

[90] Capito to Zwingli, 29 March 1528; CR Z 9, # 705. This copy is preserved in the Zürich Zentralbibliothek, bearing Capito's inscription to Zwingli.

sending a somewhat caustic greeting to Cellarius, warning against the perils of Judaizing, as well as of spiritual arrogance.[91] Capito replied directly to Zwingli, vigorously defending his views, and urging the value of the Hebrew text; but he recognized a lost cause when he saw it. Some months later, in commenting upon Zwingli's own Isaiah commentary, he urged the Zuricher not to neglect rabbinic commentaries, which reflect so well "the simplicity of the Spirit" (again!); the suggestion seems however not to have been appreciated, to judge from the apologetic tone of Capito's subsequent letter.[92] Capito suggested in a letter a few years later that he had learned to keep such views to himself, knowing that "time will teach the more inward understanding of all scriptures".[93]

The disagreement amongst close colleagues and friends had an immediate impact. In rejecting Capito's plea for an agreement to disagree on matters non-essential, Bucer felt himself obliged to refine and set forth clearly his own hermeneutic of the Old Testament, one that would permit him, like Capito, to consult rabbinic sources regularly, but satisfy his own concern – and that of colleagues as well as critics – to show consistently that all things pointed to Christ and his spiritual kingdom, without any notion of a Jewish restoration.[94]

This brings us to his Zephaniah commentary. Earlier it was noted that Bucer had seen this work as an opportunity to hone his skills as interpreter of the Old Testament on a text of modest dimensions, before re-engaging the Psalms. Certainly he would use this task as an opportunity for sharpening his ability in rabbinic commentaries; but Bucer now intended a demonstration of a sound, as opposed to an erroneous hermeneutic, viz. the reading of a Hebrew prophet using the Hebrew original and rabbinic commentaries, in a truly Christian manner. The epithet he gave the prophetic volume is suggestive: *prophetarum epitomographus*, an epitome or abridged version of the prophets.[95] With this commentary Bucer proposed to establish an evangelical model for interpreting all Old Testament prophetic writings. The importance Bucer attached to this is underlined in the letters he wrote several colleagues, including Zwingli, forwarding his book, and inviting their criticism.[96]

The demonstration was continuous throughout the Zephaniah commentary; but the specific argument was propounded in two passages. In the first, at Zeph 2:11, he paused to expound: "How one may arrive at the proper meaning of the prophets".[97] Here the three points clearly reflect his consensus with the earlier Capito in his *Habakuk*. One must have the Hebrew language, and one must dispense with all manner of allegorical game-playing. Once this was agreed, Bucer argued, it would be easy to discern the "universal practice" of all the prophets. One finds in them a consistent pattern of foreshadowing: in the punishment of the ungodly and simultaneous purging of the elect among God's people, and in the eventual liberation from their likewise typical oppressors, anticipating that full reign of God that would come once Christ had been

---

[91] *Cellarium... admonitum cupio, ut pax in Christo servetur, et ne nimium iudaissare videamur, et spiritui nostro arrogemus divinitatem, quem toties humanum deprehendimus.* For details of the debate, including the full text of Pellican's letter, see Hobbs, Monitio amica (1980).

[92] Capito to Zwingli, 31 July 1528, 15 March 1529 and 29 March 1529, CR Z 9, # 743; 10, ## 821, 827a.

[93] To Martianus Lucanius [= Calvin], late 1534: *Tempus etiam docebit Scripturarum omnium penitiorem intelligentiam*; see A.-L. HERMINJARD, *Correspondance des réformateurs dans les pays de langue française* 3 (Geneva-Paris 1870; Nieuwkoop: De Graaf 1965) 244.

[94] Amongst the exegetes of the school Capito and Cellarius found themselves isolated on this question. In addition to the critics already cited here, see the notes by Sebastian Münster on Hos 3:5 in: *Biblia* (Basel 1534–35) and Pellican, *Commentaria* (Zurich 1532–39) on Hos 1:11 and 3:5, also in preface, Sign. A 4v.

[95] Bucer, *Tzephaniah, quem Sophoniam vulgo vocant, prophetarum epitomographus, ad ebraicam veritatem versus et commentario explanatus* (Strasbourg 1528); *qui epitomen omnium scriptorium propheticorum composuisse videtur*, to Ambrose Blaurer, 23 September 1528; BCorr 3, # 205.

[96] To Zwingli, 26 September 1528; CR Z 9, # 762; and to Blaurer, see previous note.

[97] Bucer, *Sophoniam* (1554) 550–51.

exalted. The alert reader will observe that "there is nothing written by the pro-phets which does not square most authentically with Christ and the church".[98] Already in his Ephesians commentary of the previous year, commenting on the last verses of chapter 5, Bucer had outlined his understanding of the relation of the Testaments through typology. Using the Augustinian distinction of *res* and *verba*, he argued that God had concealed the mysteries of Christ under the cover of words describing events whose typological relation to Christ would be made clear to the elect by the Spirit, although the ungodly, the non-elect, would see nothing but the historical pre-figuration. To illustrate his point, he used the promise of an eternal throne succession made to David in 2 Samuel 7 and elsewhere. While all Christians agree that this was directly ful-filled in Christ, it is also obvious that there were real points of application in many aspects to Solomon, David's son and immediate successor. "What then? Would you surrender so significant a prophecy to the Jews? Not at all!" Divine providence has made this unnecessary, in that however well Solomon's reign began, it degenerated disastrously toward the end of his life, and this disap-pointment thereby has revealed that one must look to the "heavenly Solomon" for the fullest sense of the text: "Christ it is in whom all that is truly magnifi-cent comes together, and through whom all that is truly felicitous is ful-filled".[99]

This argument Bucer refined in the excursus on typology in his John commentary. There he ar-gued notably that while there are many biblical prophecies that must be referred directly to Christ and his kingdom, there are others which only can be understood as operating through the type. But again the interpreter needs wisdom to make this discernment. Bucer was in fact addressing what he understood to be two fundamental misapprehensions in the understanding and use of a ty-pological relation of the Testaments, views which could lead to either an under-valuing or an over-valuing of the typological. On the one hand, one might argue that the era of ancient Israel had in-deed been gifted with various external, or carnal elements of religion, which certainly prefigured or foreshadowed the spiritual religion of Christ; but that these had now served their typological purpose, they have no longer any authority in the practice of religion in a spiritual age. This was in fact the argument put forward by Cellarius against Bucer's invocation of Israel's rite of circumci-sion as warrant for the baptism of infants.[100] The other error, in Bucer's judgement, was to give too much authority to the typological role of Israel, notably as we have seen by extending it sym-metrically, as Capito following Cellarius had done, until the arrival of the eschaton.

First, on the under-valuing of the typological. The distinction between ex-ternals and internals in religion, with the belief that the true worship of God was in the end a spiritual one needing no external supports , was central to Bu-cer's theology. Jesus' words to the Samaritan woman, "God is spirit, and those who worship must worship in spirit and in truth" (John 4:23) anchored this be-

---

[98] Ibid. *His observandis, si recte animum adverteris, perfacile videbis, nihil a prophetis scriptum quod non verissime in Christum et ecclesiam eius quadret.*

[99] Bucer, *Ad Ephesios* (Strasbourg 1527) fol. [101]rv: *Canon observandus interpretandi Scrip-turas: Quid igitur facies, concedes tam insignem prophetiam Iudaeis? Absit... Is Christus est in hunc, quae vere magnifica sunt quadrant, et per eum quae vere felicia perficiuntur.* Bucer would certainly have recalled as he wrote the magnificent thirteenth-century sculptures of Church and Synagogue, with a typological representation of the two Solomons occupying the central doorpost, at the south door of Strasbourg cathedral.

[100] See Bucer in *In Evangelion Iohannis*, SMRT 40, BOL 2, 81–85, and BACKUS' notes ad loc.

lief. This being so, "why did God give so many ceremonies to the ancients, given that the Spirit was present then, and that even then God only recognized worship in the spirit?" Bucer's reply invoked the Pauline (and Augustinian) notion of an infantile state of religion: "because the people was more unformed and like a child... he gave them many ceremonies whereby they might be prompted to meditate his benefits toward them". The heart of this practice of religion was however the demand for reverence and obedience from the heart, and "here you see worship in spirit and truth".[101] This last is an important statement. For Bucer, such true religion did exist in ancient Israel. He would allow no simplistic opposition of old and new peoples, characterized to an absolute degree by external versus spiritual worship. To this end he often employed a hermeneutical schema of the human life cycle. Again in Zephaniah, he described the spiritual life of God's people in terms of three, or sometimes four stages: infancy, childhood, adolescence and adulthood.[102] The general state of religion in ancient Israel under the Torah was puerile, "it was a time in which they were committed to the pedagogy of so many ceremonies"; the spirit in them was weaker (*infirmior*). Nonetheless, there were among them great souls living the spiritual heights. "You often find some children wiser than their elders...so he gave to them some leaders endued with a more powerful Spirit than are many even in Christianity". Moses, Joshua, Samuel, David, the prophets lived in a spirit more ample than in the time of the Apostles, or even today, although this did not exempt them altogether from behaving at times like spiritual children, or invalidate the general principle.[103]

Such an understanding makes clear why Bucer took seriously the historical sense of the Old Testament. Even if called to a form of religion less marked by external rites, many of Bucer's contemporaries would find in its pages exemplary exhortations and warnings suited to their actual spiritual state, while there sparkled throughout, thanks to the David's and Isaiah's, incentives to a spirituality most Christians had not yet lived into. This mindset had practical consequences for Bucer's leadership of evangelical reform as well. As seen, it enabled him, with Zwingli, to urge that "we embrace as it were this kernel of the rite of circumcision, the offering of our children to God from their very infancy, as useful for godliness and pleasing to God" as the still authoritative mandate for the baptism of infants, while noting that the requirements for practice on the seventh day and involving males alone had been superseded in the Christian era.[104]

---

[101] Ibid. 186.

[102] He had little interest in the first, which he used on occasion for the pre-Mosaic world.

[103] Bucer, *Sophoniam*, 569–71: *Nam etsi paucos quosdam, ut Moscheh, Iehosua, Schmuelem atque Davidem aliosque prophetas aliquot spiritu ampliore donatos legimus, quam vel tempore apostolorum ac hodie multos videmus, id publicum tamen ordinem Dei non invertit. Saepe in puerili aetate invenias qui plus senibus aliquot sapient; ita dum omnno ducibus illi populo, et tanto spiritu potentioribus quanto ipse erat spiritu infirmior, opus esset, dedit ei qui de mandato muneri pares esse possent, eoque spiritu potentiore quam multi etiam in Christianismo praediti. Quanquam et in his ipsis puerilis spiritus se non raro prodiderit.*

[104] *In Evangelion Iohannis*, 85: *Sic in circuncisione quod octava die et maribus tantum adhibebatur missum facimus. Illud quia indignum esset libero Spiritu alligari certo tempori; hoc, quia convenit signo initiative testari in Christo neque marem neque foeminam sed tantum novam creaturam aestimari.*

His views and practice of church music are also a useful illustration. If early in his reforming career (1524), Bucer gave hints of a tendency to prize the spiritual at the expense of externals, we trace in his commentaries – and especially in his Latin Psalms – the development of the views that made him one of the most prominent of evangelical liturgiologists. He did not follow Zwingli here into liturgical silence (the banning of all song in public worship) as the proper form of prayer in the spirit, precisely because he had recognized the need of his contemporaries for strong outward forms to aid the growth of godliness. And unlike Calvin, he welcomed the contribution of musical instruments in worship, concluding that wise spiritual leaders like David, although needing no such prompting themselves, knew the value, indeed necessity of attention to the externals of religion, the importance of the beautiful and the majestic for the stimulation of inner devotion in those under their spiritual charge. "The godly prince gave attention that the external symbol be as majestic as possible, so that from it the interior worship of God would also gain in strength". Indeed, the reverse is also observable: "when true godliness is neglected, ceremonies also suffer".[105]

The type, then, was and would remain of significance for Christians in this world. But Bucer was not prepared to extend this to a future historical role for the Jewish people as such. Expounding the last verses of Zephaniah, he engaged a lengthy debate with the position taken by Cellarius and Capito, which he associated at several points with interpretations advanced both by Jews and by the Christian radicals of his own day (whom he termed at this point Catabaptists), marked by a like error.[106] His detailed arguments and textual interpretations may be summarized as follows. To look for a restored earthly kingdom with the Jews is fundamentally to misapprehend the significance of the Christ event in human history: "it seems to me thoroughly to obscure the redemption brought to birth through Christ and thus Christ's glory".[107] That is the primordial event that determines entirely the character of the history of salvation. As he would put it in the Psalms a year later, if Hosea can rightly call his contemporaries children of God, it is *propter Christum*.[108] Test this claim by the *analogia fidei*, by the articles of Christian faith. There can be no saving future outside Christ. But the relationship established in Christ has distinct, essential characteristics. One, it is spiritual, as we have seen, but second, it is, in this world, life under the cross. So, on the one hand, the elect children of God, Jewish and Gentile, live here and now in anticipation of a future life in God that is purely spiritual, they know their citizenship is in heaven, not on this earth, and material blessings would seem a poor substitute, indeed, an unwanted distraction from the glory toward which they tend. Meanwhile, however, they know the sufferings of an existence not set free from sin, suffering and death, and this will cease only in the fullness of the kingdom. To take Old Testament prophecies otherwise (and Bucer deals seriatim with a series of

---

Quia autem experti sumus ut utile sit ad pietatem, ita et Deo gratum ab incunabulis ipsi nostros liberos offerre, hoc tanquam nucleum in observatione circuncisionis nobis desumimus.

[105] Cf. Hobbs, Quam apposita (2004), and Bucer, *Sacrorum Psalmorum*, fol. 137rv on Psalm 24: *Psaltes ... consideravit, cultu Dei etiam externo sarto tecto et iuxta verbum Domini instituto, fidem, timorem et observantiam Dei in populo obtinere. Nam simulatque fides et observantia Dei in populo labascit, et externa ista negliguntur.*

[106] *Sophoniam*, 573–78.

[107] Ibid. 573: *Valde enim redemptionem per Christum partam atque adeo gloriam Christi obscurare videtur, terrenam adhuc cum Iudaeis rerum foelicitatem expectare.*

[108] Bucer, *Sacrorum Psalmorum*, ad Ps 19:1–7, fol. 111.

these) is to read in literalist, materialist fashion the glorious images and hyperbole of Scripture which point to a spiritual fulfillment, it is to overlook their accomplishment already at various points in history, it is also to argue for a pre-millenial reign of Christ on earth, and a material blessing in a state of sinless living for which Bucer can find no evidence in Scripture. Finally there are no specially privileged members of God's elect people: Jerusalem takes no precedence over Rome, Canaan over any other land, nor will the last generation of God's elect escape the sufferings of this world common to Christ and all their predecessors in the faith. The full promised glory will come "when after the sin of all has been overcome, Christ hands over the kingdom to his God and Father. Until then, death has a certain power over the saints and they are oppressed by other ills".[109]

This typological hermeneutic of the Old Testament was the lens through which Bucer deployed his skills as Hebraist in his magisterial Latin Psalms commentary. Now there is a sense in which little here is new or startling. But Bucer would have wanted, indeed did claim that he stood with the mainstream of the tradition. What there was new in Strasbourg in a typological schema was rather the scenario advanced by Cellarius and Capito, and discredited by Bucer. What Bucer does represent in a significant way is a confident appropriation of the mediaeval Jewish tradition of *peshat* in particular, and its extensive deployment in the service of Christian interpretation. His conclusions were in the end insufficiently venturesome for a few colleagues like Capito, and they certainly did not tempt the vast majority of contemporary Jews to convert, although such may well have been the hope in the mid-20's.[110] But then, he himself was clear; he wrote for Christians, not for Jews,[111] and even his point-by-point attempts at rebuttal of Qimhi's polemic in the Psalms must be seen in this light. His accomplishment, attested by the extensive circulation of his *Psalms*, was the demonstration that the Hebrew text, elucidated by solid Jewish lexicography, was serviceable and even desirable (he would say essential) for an orthodox, if evangelical Christian reading of the Old Testament.

1.5. The Upper Rhine School

The preceding chapter has addressed the work of three contemporaries of Bucer and Capito. As their correspondence and mutual cross-references show, Zwingli in Zurich and Oecolampadius in Basel worked in close association with the Strasbourgers until their deaths, both in 1531. Calvin was recruited by Bucer in 1538 for several tasks, among them teaching in the newly founded Strasbourg Senior School. His publications on the Old Testament date from

---

[109] Bucer, *Sophoniam*, 576–77: *tum consummabitur, quando Christus, expugnato omnium peccato, regnum tradiderit Deo et Patri. Interea, ut mors in sanctos imperium aliquatenus habet, ita et aliis malis premuntur.*

[110] Rabbi Josel of Rosheim did report attending the *prophezei* on occasion: S. STERN, *Josel of Rosheim* (New York: Jewish Publication Society 1965) 178; Hobbs, Bucer and the Jews (2006) 160–64.

[111] Ibid. 574; *Sacrorum Psalmorum*, fol. 124v (on Ps 22:17).

his return to Geneva (1541); in many ways these, together with the Genevan French and Latin Bible translations, should be understood as the culmination of the work of the Upper Rhine School. There is no question of repeating here what has already been well said in a previous chapter. This section will attempt instead a synthesis, noting briefly the workers and their accomplishments, and identifying the common elements that define the school as well as the areas of disagreement or nuanced differences.

From June 1525, Zurich biblical activity took place around the framework of the *prophezei*, an institution that would give fundamental direction and shape to several generations of Reformed exegetes, beginning with the Strasbourgers.[112] Within that setting there gathered around Zwingli several others with exegetical tools and interest. Notably, the Alsatian Leo Jud, pastor of St. Peter from 1523, was modestly competent in Hebrew, and would contribute to the Zurich Bibles.[113] Jacob Ceporinus was briefly considered the specialist in both Greek and Hebrew; upon his death in 1526, the Hebraist Conrad Pellican was persuaded to leave the Franciscans and his teaching position in Basel, and join the Zurich team. After Zwingli's death in 1531, Theodore Bibliander taught Old Testament, contributing to the Latin Bible, in particular after the death of Jud, and producing a controversial edition of an older Latin translation of the Koran.[114] Until Zwingli's death, the exegetical publications of the group appeared under his name. The collective produced two monumental Bible translations, the German in 1530-31, the Latin in 1543. OPITZ is certainly correct when he states in the previous chapter that the paramount goal of this work was the production of the German Bible.[115] But we must also understand that although trusting that in time all preachers would work directly from the biblical original texts – "swim without a cork", as Zwingli put it[116] – the commentaries in their various forms intended also to enable a solid evangelical preaching. The most ambitious exegetical project was Pellican's, who between 1532-38 issued a Latin commentary on the entire Scriptures.[117] Although himself a skilled Hebraist who left manuscript notebooks filled with translations from mediaeval rabbinic commentaries, Pellican understood his objective in this last publication to be the furnishing for simple country pastors with limited or no skill in the biblical languages, of homiletical notes enabling them to preach from all parts of the Bible.[118] Upon Pellican's death in 1556, Vermigli took his place, and published commentaries notably on Genesis and the historical books of the Old Testament. In Basel, Pellican and Sebastian Münster furnished early, useful text editions, and grammatical and lexical tools, including the latter's guides to Aramaic and rabbinic Hebrew.[119] As in Zurich, it was one figure, Oecolampadius, who dominated the exegetical scene until his death (1531). As we saw above, his unpublished lecture notes were turned by his successor Oswald Myconius, as well as by Capito, into commentaries. In 1534-5, Sebastian Münster produced a Latin Bible with concise exegetical notes largely gleaned from rabbinic sources; it was several times reprinted.[120] In Berne, Wolfgang Musculus should also be understood as carrying forward and complementing the work of the older members of the Upper Rhine School, with exhaustive commentaries notably on Psalms (1551), Exodus (1553), Genesis (1554), and Isaiah (1557). He is a transitional figure, however, into the second generation; all his

---

[112] See supra, Chap. 18, sect. 2.1, and Denis, La prophétie (1977).

[113] On Jude, cf. P. BIETENHOLZ, in: *Contemporaries of Erasmus* 2 (Toronto: Univ. of Toronto Press 1985) 248-50; LEO WEISS, *Leo Jud. Ulrich Zwinglis Kampfgenosse 1482-1542* (Zurich 1942).

[114] Bedouelle / Roussel, Le Temps des Réformes (1989) 247-49.

[115] See supra, Chap.18, end of sect. 2.3.

[116] See above n. 38.

[117] The *Commentaria Bibliorum* (Zurich 1532-39; re-edited 1536-46; 1582); cf. Zürcher, Pellikans Wirken (1975) 85-145.

[118] Cf. Zürcher, Pellikans Wirken (1975) 87-88; Hobbs, Pellican (1999) 87; Pellican, *Commentaria*, vol. 1, Sign. B v: *Simplicioribus in hoc opere inservitum.*

[119] See above n. 26.

[120] *Hebraica Biblia Latina planeque nova tralatione...adiectis insuper e Rabinorum commentariis annotationibus* (Basel 1543-35).

commentaries on the Old Testament repeat, expand, improve upon, even as they utilize commentaries of the first generation.

The demonstration of a school requires identification of significant commonalty, but also a community of scholarship and finally, a concertation of effort in the pursuit of a common goal. A comparison of this and the preceding chapter will reveal the strong congruence of exegetical methods and interpretive patterns that existed in the Upper Rhine valley. The argument that these interpreters of the Old Testament constituted a school is buttressed by several further arguments. In the first place, there is the regular exchange of information, ideas and even of emerging books that is witnessed in and through their abundant correspondence. We saw in the previous section how this functioned in 1528, as Capito and Bucer disagreed, and each submitted his case to the colleagues of the sodalitas. The next year Bucer sent early portions of his Latin Psalms up-river, requesting a quick reading and judgement; to Zwingli he pled ignorance of the latter's plans for the Psalter, had he known he would not have intruded there.[121] Meanwhile, Oecolampadius was reading and praising Zwingli's work on Isaiah, while Capito, although complimenting his associate, reserved the right to wish Zwingli had used the Rabbis more.[122] In these same years, Oecolampadius, preparing his Daniel commentary, sought Zwingli's advice on the seventy weeks that likewise figured in the Bucer-Capito debate, suggesting to the Zuricher that he found neither Strasbourger's published interpretation altogether satisfactory. To judge from the correspondence, Zwingli seems rarely to have replied to such requests, and Oecolampadius apparently worked out a solution without his aid.[123] These are but samplings from an instructive and regular exchange, only portions of which have survived, but which abundantly attest the close and conscious degree of collaboration.

Formal evidence may also be deduced from the list of publications. From the first, there was evidently a concerted effort to furnish an evangelical interpretation of the entire Old Testament, and manifestly without unnecessary overlap. Oecolampadius, Capito and Bucer published on almost all the prophets, without duplicating the others' effort, save that Hosea appeared in Myconius' posthumous edition of Oecolampadius' treatment of nine of the twelve minor prophets.[124] Oecolampadius had expressed himself very discreetly in the 1528 Bucer-Capito argument; the repetition of Hosea here may, however, suggest his dissatisfaction with Capito's commentary.[125] Bucer published the Psalms, from Oecolampadius posthumously came Job and Genesis. When Vermigli picked up the project in Zurich in the 1560's, there was another Genesis, but he seems to have given particular attention to the as yet uncommented histories, Judges, Samuel and Kings. The striking exception to this division of labour is the work of Zwingli. His 1529 *Isaiah*, in particular, although praising the work of Oecolampadius in the preface, clearly represents a revisiting of the prophet. Oecolampadius' and later Vermigli's Genesis commentaries undoubtedly attest the insufficiency, to their minds, of the early Zwingli notes; and although Bucer professed embarrassment at finding himself paralleling Zwingli's work on the Psalter, he would not likely have found the latter satisfactory from his point of view, even had Zwingli lived to write a commentary to accompany his new Latin translation. The reasons for these apparent exceptions to the rule will be discussed in what follows.

That the Strasbourg church considered the work of Oecolampadius complementary to that of their own chiefs is attested in a 1534 *Kirchenordnung*, which prescribed for each parish the purchase of the commentaries of all three, adding prudently that these volumes should be inventoried, inscribed and remain the property of the parish, not the pastor![126] The absence of two names here

---

[121] BCorr 3, ## 223, 228, 230, 239.

[122] Zwingli, CR 97, ## 821, 827a, 883.

[123] Zwingli, CR 96, ## 774, 786.

[124] *Briefe und Akten* 2/2 (ed. E. Staehelin, 1934) # 977. The prophets Nahum and Habakuk had not been treated by him. The omission of Zephaniah may be a tribute to Bucer's commentary; and of Habakuk to Capito.

[125] Oecolampadius to Zwingli, 6 August 1528; CR 96, # 747.

[126] T. RÖHRICH, *Mittheilungen aus der Geschichte der evangelischen Kirche des Elsasses* 2 (Paris-Strasbourg 1855) 27: *Item was von Oecolampadio und hie über die heilige Schrift ausgegangen, als über Esajam, Jeremiam [etc.]…und was sonst mag nützlich und jeder Pfarr zu kaufen träglich sein. Und die Bücher so also gekaufet, sollen auch inventirt und uffgeschrieben, und nit von der Pfarr genommen werden.*

invites comment. François Lambert of Avignon, while living in Strasbourg 1524–26, had published a host of commentaries, on the Song of Songs and all twelve minor prophets. We noted earlier his dismissal of erudition in the biblical languages as non-essential and even an impediment to the work of the Spirit. His omission from the 1534 list underlines how central to the Upper Rhine vision was work from the originals; however passionate the evangelical theology, it could not remedy this defect.

The case of Zwingli is more complex; it needs to be understood in the light of the differences that can be observed within the workings of the sodalitas. Our interpreters were all disciples of Erasmus, and firmly committed to placing the Scriptures in the hands of the ordinary Christian, both in vernacular translations, and through the learned expositions of parish preachers. It would, however, be naïve to conclude from their confidence in the clarity of Scripture and the sufficiency of the Spirit to direct the emerging consensus on its meaning that there were no disagreements amongst them. We have seen earlier that there were occasional fundamental challenges to interpretive consensus, and that these could lead to a silencing or even to exile.[127] More typically, and less threateningly, their differences focused around the questions of base text, of translation style, and of the value of rabbinic sources. The first two of these matters were identified succinctly by the translators of the Zurich 1543 Bible, with reference to their immediate predecessors:

> Now in truth we must not regret the work performed by certain scholarly and holy men in translating from Hebrew, this is to be lauded above all by all the godly and learned. However, some of them were so devoted to the Greek translation, others so hemmed in by scrupulous regard for the old interpreter, and others on the other hand so committed and fixed upon the Hebrew style, that the resulting Latin translation either was not sufficiently corrected with reference to the Hebrew truth, or it became too Hebrew, i.e., was impeded and quite obscured by remaining Hebraisms that were never translated into Latin.[128]

Although these were matters debated across the range of sixteenth-century interpreters, there is no need to look outside the school itself for instances of each of Heinrich Bullinger's categories here, and this will explain the sensitivity with which he dismisses their work. The first group, those whose translation was characterized by what the 1543 translators (notably Leo Jud and after his death Theodore Bibliander) considered too great a fondness for the Septuagint, is represented above all by Zwingli. The latter professed respect for the Hebrew, but argued in the preface to his 1529 *Isaiah* that the Greek translation was a more reliable guide than was the massoretic text, whose vowel points represented a deformation of the original by Jewish scribes.[129] A decade after his death, his Zurich colleagues and disciples no longer accepted this option, and we may moreover take it as certain that it was this (and the concomi-

---

[127] Ludwig Haetzer and Miguel Servetus both became *personae non gratae* in Strasbourg.

[128] *Biblia sacrosancta testamenti veteris et novi e sacra Hebraeorum lingua Graecorumque fontibus...translate* (Zurich 1543), Heinrich Bullinger in the *praefatio ad lectorem*, sign. 2v: *Iam vero praestitisse quosdam viros doctos et sanctos operam in vertendis sacris ex Hebraeo libris non poenitendam, maximeque ab omnibus piis et doctis laudandam. Horum tamen alios ita Graecae versioni addictos, alios Veteris interpretis religione sic obstrictos, et alios rursus Hebraicae phrasi adeo fuisse deditos et affixos, ut versio Latina vel non usquequaquam ad Hebraicam veritatem sit emendata, vel nimis Hebraica facta, id est propter Hebraismos relictos impedita et in ea lingua nunquam versatis, obscurissima.*

[129] CR 101, 97–105; see supra Chap. 18, sect. 2.4.

tant decision respecting rabbinic sources) which also caused the Strasbourgers to leave his *Isaiah* off their pastoral library list.

Respect for the "old interpreter", by which is meant Jerome and those anonymous others whose work was preserved in the Church's Latin Bible, the so-called Vulgate, is more surprising in these circles, but was likewise found in Zurich in particular. Despite his abilities in Hebrew, Conrad Pellican was cautious in his use of new translation. His twice-issued Psalter (1527, 1532) was a revision of Jerome's Hebraicum, and when he came to issue his multi-volume homiletical commentary (destined for clergy of limited education), he would have preferred simply to have it accompany the Vulgate text, because of the latter's familiarity. Pressed by colleagues and by his printer, Froschauer, Pellican reluctantly agreed to issue a modestly revised version of the Vulgate, but added, "please God the popular translation continue in venerable authority amongst the Christian people, and that this one we have done be compared with it".[130] This paralleling of the new with the Vulgate was the pattern he also succeeded in having adopted for the 1529 edition of Zwingli's *Isaiah*.

The third translation style Bullinger disparaged was not uncommon amongst early sixteenth-century Hebraists – for example, Sanctes Pagninus – and in our instance, was that followed by Oecolampadius in his 1525 *Isaiah*. He justified his word-for-word translation of the prophet on the grounds of his hearers' ignorance of Hebrew. His work would be a tool for beginners in Hebrew; for despite the harshness of Hebrew idiom rendered this way, it would permit them more easily to decipher the original.[131] He may have been influenced in this direction by Pellican, at that time still his colleague in Basel; Pellican was proud of having initially acquired Hebrew through use of an interlinear text.[132] Here, however, Zwingli and Bucer concurred in a stance that profoundly disagreed with their Basel colleague, although again they are careful to leave him unnamed.[133] Such so-called translation, the word-for-word, was too often merely incomprehensible in the host language, leaving the reader to invent meaning where none was apparent. The title chosen for Zwingli's translation, *complanatio*, a rendering smooth or plain, of the prophet is probably to be understood as an implicit contrast to Oecolampadius' version. In place of the older attempt at literalist renderings, both Zwingli and Bucer gave eloquent defenses for their regular practice of sense-for-sense translation.[134]

---

[130] Pellican, *Commentaria*, 1, Sign. B 2v – 3r: *placeat autem venerandae authoritatis habere translationem vulgarem in populo Christiano, et nostrum hanc ei conferri.* See Hobbs, Pellican (1999) 86–87.

[131] Oecolampadius, *In Iesaiam*, Sign. a 3v – 4r: *Igitur alicubi idiotismi Hebraeae gentis in lingua nostra durius sonantes servati sunt, idque consulto, habita scholasticorum ratione, qui sic facilius Hebraicari poterunt, et sicubi anxie verborum quaeratur pensiculatio, habeatur in promptu verborum proprietas.*

[132] Pellican, *Chronikon*, 17–18; Hobbs, Pellican (1999) 76.

[133] Zwingli, *Isaiae*, CR 101, 89–91; Bucer, *Sacrorum Psalmorum*, Sign. 5r – 6v. See the latter: *His autem nemo putet me voluisse quorundam diligentiam et eruditionem, quam ecclesiae iura suspiciunt, qui verbum e verbo exprimere studuerunt, traducere. Scio enim illos partim non suo iudicio, sed volentes cum divo Paulo et insipientium debitores esse fecisse... quare etiam commentariis pulchre illustrarunt, quod verterunt obscurius, et complanarunt quod reddiderunt asperius.*

[134] In addition to the passages cited earlier in this chapter, n. 59, and in the previous note, see

Theirs was the direction of humanist translation theory and practice. Luther, likewise, thought and acted similarly. This was also, clearly, the position of the translators of the 1543 Zurich Latin Bible. The highwater mark in Bible translation of this nature came with the work of Sebastian Castellio;[135] by mid-century, however, it was apparent that the principal Protestant vernacular translations were in cautious retreat even from the degree of freedom that Bucer and Zwingli claimed, to say nothing of the Ciceronian elegance of Castellio.[136] Only a later century would reclaim this liberty.

The third methodological issue that saw differences amongst the Upper Rhine Reformers was the question of the value and appropriateness of rabbinic sources for understanding and interpreting the Old Testament. Here, too, there were shades and nuances in attitude, but Zwingli markedly distanced himself from the majority of his colleagues. As we have seen, in sharp contrast to Bucer,[137] he considered the work of the massoretic scribes to have come too late to do anything but deform, if not corrupt the original Hebrew, and the commentaries of the Rabbis to be so recent, and vitiated both by their blindness (to Christ) and their general ignorance of wider culture, as to be virtually useless. He repeated this judgement in the preface to the 1531 German Bible.[138] As we saw earlier, Capito clearly understood he had offended Zwingli by urging him to give greater heed to these sources.[139] In this decision, Zwingli was probably reinforced by the views of Pellican, his resident Hebraist. Correspondence from the latter urges both Capito and Bucer to greater caution in their use of Jewish sources. Pellican argued that his years of extensive readings in rabbinic commentaries had gleaned only a few flowers from amongst the many thorns.[140]

These were not insignificant differences. They make comprehensible the exclusion of both Pellican and Zwingli from the Strasbourg 1534 parish book list, despite the long friendship with them. Seen from our perspective, it would not be difficult to argue that neither properly belongs within the Upper Rhine School, that at best they can be seen as ancillary. Yet this judgement leaves us with the dilemma of understanding the next Zurich generation, where the work of Jud, Bibliander, Bullinger and Vermigli, like the 1543 Latin Bible itself, understands itself as a continuation of the endeavours of the first Reformers, at the same time as in intimate association with Strasbourg and

---

the preface to the 1531 Zurich *Die gantze Bibel*, Sign. 4r: *wir nit so vil auff den buchstaben als auff den sinn unnd meynung achtend. Denn eigenschafft der spraach mag niemants mit nutz in ein andere spraach bringen, deshalb es wager ist man behalte einer yeden spraach ir eigenschafft unverseert. Die toerchte supersticion etlicher, die für ein grosse sünd habend vonn den silben unnd worten zeweychen, bedunckt unns mer ein eigenrichtiger kyb weder ein vernünfftig ermuessen unnd urteyl.*

[135] *Biblia interprete Sebastiano Castalione* (Basel 1551).

[136] This becomes apparent in studying the influence of Bucer's Psalms in English (in 1530 the first published version) upon the evolving English Bible; see R. G. Hobbs, "Martin Bucer and the Englishing of the Psalms: pseudonymity in the service of early English Protestant piety", in: D. F. Wright (ed.), *Martin Bucer. Reforming Church and Community* (Cambridge 1994) 161–75.

[137] Above n. 66.

[138] Sign. 3v – 4r: *Nun wöllend wir hie nit verhalten, das in unser translation wenig der puncten acht gehebt ist, dann die selben auch neüwlich von der Rabinen der Juden erdacht, von anfang nit gewesen sind. Es bekümmert unns auch wenig was die Rabinen in iren commentieren schreybend, welche auch innerthalb etlich hundert jaren aufgestanden, die offt ungetympte unnd torächte ding fabulierend... mögend sie zu erklärung unnd verstand der gschrifft wenig fürderlich sein.*

[139] Above n. 92.

[140] Hobbs, Pellican (1999) 91–93.

Basel. In effect, to exclude Zwingli and Pellican would place too much weight on the methodological. We are on surer ground in accepting their own evident self-understanding, their clear sense of being a company of interpreters in pursuit, directed by the Spirit, of an exegetical good, an evangelical global interpretation of the Scriptures grounded in a renewed commitment to their fundamental authority for the Church.[141]

In years to come, the naivete of some elements of the vision would become apparent, as for example, the utopian expectation of a Hebrew-speaking Christian public, and more significantly, the assumption that communal consensus would resolve all issues of authority. The distinctiveness of the *prophezei* would gradually dissolve itself into one-person biblical lectures, and enthusiasm for frequent attendance upon these would wane. Musculus, who knew Strasbourg well in the early, glory days, could lament in 1554:

> where once the Holy Books were in every hand, and there was no pause in writing, reading, discussing and singing,... today some seek gold, others honours, and some simply want to earn their bread. They drop biblical studies in favour of chairs in secular literature. Even in the evangelical academies, how few there are who follow the biblical classes.[142]

Put otherwise, with the passage of decades the school experienced the general evolution of the evangelical Reform. This does not surprise, nor should it detract from its remarkable accomplishment, in laying the groundwork for ongoing commitments and methods in Reformed biblical interpretation.

2. Philipp Melanchthon and the Wittenbergers

Sources: JOHANNES BUGENHAGEN: There is no critical modern edition of the works of Bugenhagen; see those available in microform in IDC, "The Lutheran Reformation: Sources 1500-1650". – PHILIPP MELANCHTHON: There is no full critical edition of the works of Melanchthon; see the IDC microform collection, "Philipp Melanchthon, theologian and humanist". *Philippi Melanthonis Opera quae supersunt omnia* (ed. C. G. Bretschneider / H. E. Bindseil, CR 1-28; Halle / Braunschweig 1834-1860 = Frankfurt 1963; cited CR); *Supplementa Melanchthoniana* (Leipzig 1910-1929 = Frankfurt 1968, cited SM); *Melanchthons Werke in Auswahl* 1-7 (ed. R Stupperich; Gütersloh: Bertelsmann 1951f; vol. 4 *Frühe Exegetische Schriften*, ed. P. F. Barton; Gütersloh: Gerd Mohn 1963; cited StA); *Melanchthons Briefwechsel* (MBW, in progress, ed. H. Scheible; Stuttgart-Bad Cannstatt: Frommann-Holzboog, 1977-); *Loci Communes Theologici 1521* (ET by L. J. Satre) in: *Melanchthon and Bucer* (ed. W. Pauck, LCC 19; London: SCM / Philadelphia: Westminster 1969) 1-152; *The Loci Communes of Philip Melanchthon with a critical introduction* (1521; tr. C. L. Hill; Boston: Meador cr. 1944); *Melanchthon on Christian Doctrine. Loci Communes 1555* (tr. C. L. Manschreck; New York: Oxford UP 1965); C. L. HILL, *Melanchthon. Selected Writings* (Minneapolis: Augsburg 1962; repr. Westport CN: Greenwood 1978).

Bibliographies: G. GEISENHOF, *Bibliotheca Bugenhagiana. Bibliographie der Druckschriften des D. Johannes Bugenhagens* (QDGR 6, 1908, repr. De Graaf 1963); W. HAMMER, *Die Melanchthonforschung im Wandel der Jahrhunderte. Ein beschreibendes Verz.*, 3 vols. (QFRG 35f.49); R. KEEN, *A Checklist of Melanchthon Imprints through 1560* (St. Louis: Center for Reformation Research 1988); H. SCHEIBLE, in: TRE 22 (1992) 395-410.

General works and studies: P. F. BARTON, "Die exegetische Arbeit des jungen Melanchthon 1518/ 19 bis 1528/29", *ARefG* 54 (1963) 52-89; G. BEDOUELLE / B. ROUSSEL, *Le Temps des Réformes et la Bible* (BTT 5; Paris: Beauchesne 1989); D. BELLUCCI, "Genèse 1,14 et astrologie dans l'exégèse de Philippe Melanchthon", in: *Théorie et Pratique de l'Exégèse* (ed. I. Backus / F. Higman; EPH 43;

---

[141] Ibid. 95-97.
[142] Musculus, *In Mosis Genesim* (Basel 1554) Sign. 2r.

Geneva: Droz 1990) 177–90; D. Buzogany, "Melanchthon as a Humanist and a Reformer", in: *Melanchthon in Europe. His work and influence beyond Wittenberg* (ed. K. Maag; Texts & Studies in Reformation & Post-Reformation Thought; Grand Rapids MI, Carlise: Baker / Paternoster 1999) 87–101; A. Detmers, *Reformation und Judentum: Israel-Lehren und Einstellungen zum Judentum von Luther bis zum frühen Calvin* (Stuttgart: Kohlhammer 2001) 119–43; E. Gosselin, *The King's Progress to Jerusalem. Some Interpretations of David during the Reformation Period and their Patristic and Medieval Background* (Humana Civilitas 2; Malibu 1976); L. Green, "Formgeschichtliche und inhaltliche Probleme in den Werken des jungen Melanchthon. Ein neuer Zugang zu seinen Bibelarbeiten und Disputationsthesen", *ZKG* 84 (1973) 30–48; W.-D. Hauschild, "Johannes Bugenhagen", OEncRef 1 (1996) 226–27; H. Holfelder, "Johannes Bugenhagen", TRE 7 (1981) 354–63; idem, *Tentatio et Consolatio. Studien zu Bugenhagens <Interpretatio in librum Psalmorum>* (AKG 45; Berlin / New York: De Gruyter 1974); E. Kruse, "Bugenhagens plattdeutsche Bibel", *Luther* 29 (1958) 73–80, 135–40; S. Kusukawa, "Melanchthon", in: *The Cambridge Companion to Reformation Theology* (ed. D. Bagchi / D. C. Steinmetz; Cambridge UP 2004) 57–67; C. L. Manschreck, *Melanchthon, the Quiet Reformer* (New York: Abingdon 1958; 1975); W. Maurer, *Der junge Melanchthon zwischen Humanismus und Reformation* (Göttingen: Vandenhoeck & Ruprecht 1967); M. Rogness, *Philip Melanchthon. Reformer without honour* (Minneapolis, MN: Augsburg 1969); H. Scheible, "Melanchthon", TRE 22 (1992) 371–95; idem, "Melanchthon, Philipp", in: OEncRef 2 (New York / Oxford: Oxford UP 1996) 41–45; idem, *Melanchthon: eine Biographie* (Munich: Beck 1997); idem, "Reuchlins Einfluß auf Melanchthon", H. Scheible, *Reuchlin und die Juden* (ed. A. Herzig e.a.; Sigmaringen 1993); and *Melanchthon und die Reformation. Forschungsbeiträge* (ed. G. May / R. Decot; VIEG 41; Mainz: Philipp von Zabern 1996) 71–97 [123–49]; J. R. Schneider, "The hermeneutics of commentary: origins of Melanchthon's integration of dialectic into rhetoric", in: *Philip Melanchthon (1497–1560) and the Commentary* (ed. T. J. Wengert / M. P. Graham; Sheffield: Academic Press 1997) 20–47; idem, "Melanchthon's Rhetoric as a context for understanding his theology", in: *Melanchthon in Europe. His work and influence beyond Wittenberg* (ed. K. Maag; Texts & Studies in Reformation & Post-Reformation Thought; Grand Rapids MI, Carlise: Baker / Paternoster 1999) 141–59; idem, *Philip Melanchthon's Rhetorical Construal of Biblical Authority. Oratio Sacra* (Lewiston / Queenston / Lampeter: Edwin Mellen 1990); H. Sick, *Melanchthon als Ausleger des Alten Testaments* (BGBH, 2, Tübingen: Mohr 1959); R. Stupperich, *Melanchthon* (Berlin: De Gruyter 1960; ET: London: Lutterworth 1966); idem, "Melanchthon's Proverbien-Kommentare", in: *Der Kommentar in der Renaissance* (ed. A. Buck / O. Herding; Kommission für Humanismusforschung 1; Boppard: Deutsche Forschungsgemeinschaft 1975) 21–34; H. Volz, "Beiträge zu Melanchthons und Calvins Auslegungen des Propheten Daniels", *ZKG* 67 (1955–56) 93–118; T. Wengert, "Caspar Cruciger (1504–1548): the case of the disappearing reformer", *SCJ* 20 (1989) 417–41; idem, "The Biblical commentaries of Philip Melanchthon", in: *Philip Melanchthon (1497–1560) and the Commentary* (ed. T. J. Wengert / M. P. Graham; Sheffield: Academic Press 1997) 106–48; idem, *Human freedom, Christian righteousness, Philip Melanchthon's exegetical dispute with Erasmus of Rotterdam* (New York: Oxford UP 1998); idem, "Philip Melanchthon and the Jews: a reappraisal", in: *Jews, Judaism and the Reformation in Sixteenth-Century Germany* (ed. D. Bell / S. Burnett; Leiden: Brill 2006) 105–35.

   Special abbreviations (see above):
MBW = *Melanchthons Briefwechsel* (ed. H. Scheible)
SM = *Supplementa Melanchthoniana*
StA = *Melanchthons Werke in Auswahl* 1–7 (ed. R. Stupperich)

The presence and dynamic biblical interpretation of Martin Luther in Wittenberg drew attention out of all proportion to the size and importance of the fledging university (founded in 1502). Around Luther there gathered a cadre of exegetes, some for a shorter time, others to be part of the group that would bring to fulfillment the project launched by Luther in 1522, the new German Bible. Of these the most prolific interpreter of the Old Testament was Johannes Bugenhagen (1485–1558), nicknamed "Pomeranus" for his country of origin, who arrived in Wittenberg in 1521, became town pastor in 1525, and eventually a full member of the theological faculty (1535). His immensely popular 1524 Latin commentary on the Psalms[143] with prefaces by Luther and Melanchthon, was the first in a series of commentaries; if editions alone be counted, he is correctly described as "one of the most noted exegetes of his day".[144] There followed, often in pirate editions, volumes on Deuteronomy, the books of Samuel and Kings, and Job, as well as numerous commentaries on New Testament books. His Old Testament commentaries are of limited interest, due to his deficient knowledge of Hebrew. But they were very influential for their presentation of Wittenberg theology in an exegetical framework, for the first generation of evangelical pastors. Throughout his long career, divided between Wittenberg and various projects of ecclesiastical reorganization in northern Germany, he remained close to Luther and to his younger colleague, Philipp Melanchthon. This chapter-section on Wittenberg exegesis will focus upon Melanchthon in particular.

2.1. Philipp Melanchthon

The appointment of the 21-year old Philipp Melanchthon as professor of Greek in the faculty of arts at the University of Wittenberg would have major impact both upon the small, recently founded university, and upon the development of evangelical biblical interpretation itself. Melanchthon was recommended for the post by Germany's well-known, if highly controversial senior humanist, Johannes Reuchlin. This was in itself enough to draw attention to the youthful scholar. In his inaugural address of August 28, 1518, delivered within a few days of his arrival in Wittenberg, Melanchthon signaled that he situated himself firmly within the camp of humanists that was bringing radical reform to German institutions of education. He called for the adoption of an educational programme that would form youth by the study of mathematics, history and Greek.[145] Despite his unprepossessing presence, Melanchthon impressed his colleagues, including Martin Luther in the theological faculty, and he quickly became a magnet for students. Upon arrival Melanchthon was certainly not yet publicly identified with Luther's theology, but he addressed himself quickly to the study of Scripture. The publication in 1521 of the first of the several recensions of his *Loci communes* that would accompany his entire theological career, showed him clearly to have become an evangelical, who was already making significant contributions to the elaboration of the Wittenberg theology. This development did put severe strain upon his relations with Reuchlin. In the months of Luther's absence from Wittenberg, in protective custody in the Wartburg after the Diet of Worms, Melanchthon assumed responsibility for Luther's biblical lectures.

The wave of iconoclasm and radical liturgical reforms advanced by the "Zwickau prophets" in the name of the Spirit in mid-winter 1521–22, Me-

---

[143] The *In librum Psalmorum interpretatio* (Basel 1524). It was quickly reprinted in Basel, Nuremberg, Strasbourg and Wittenberg, and translated into high German and Dutch.
[144] Holfelder, *Tentatio et Consolatio* (1974) 3.
[145] *De corrigendis adulescentiae studiis*, CR 11, 15–25.

lanchthon found confusing. But he rallied promptly and vigorously to Luther's side upon the latter's return and resumption of leadership in Lent 1522. With the consequent unhappy departure of Andreas Bodenstein von Karlstadt, Melanchthon gradually emerged in the role of Luther's closest colleague and second leader of the evangelical reform in Wittenberg, a role that would be his until his death in 1560. As principal author of the Augsburg Confession (*Confessio Augustana* 1530) and its defence, the *Apologia Confessionis Augustanae*, his theological formulations would become fundamental for all Lutheran Churches until the present. Although the preponderance of his biblical work was in the New Testament, his work (in the *Loci*) on Law and Gospel, and the relation of the Testaments was seminal, and he published a number of commentaries on the first Testament. At the same time, his on-going teaching and publications made him the unchallenged leader of humanist education in the German world, the *praeceptor Germaniae*. Throughout the lifetime of Luther, the theological nuances and differences of strategy that characterized the relationship of the two men were never able to open a fundamental breach between them. On the other hand, the years following Luther's death were clouded by intra-Lutheran theological controversies, in particular with Flacius Illyricus, who argued that Melanchthon's irenical temperament, his willingness to explore accommodation with both Rome and Geneva, was placing the integrity of Evangelical (i.e., Lutheran) theology at grave risk. Recent studies have tended to vindicate Melanchthon's reputation, and restore his honour as the second theologian of Lutheranism.

Philipp was born in 1497 in the small city of Bretten in the Palatinate,[146] the oldest child of Georg Schwartzerdt, armourer to the Palatine court, and Barbara Reuter, daughter of a comfortable merchant. The Hellenized name Melanchthon would be bestowed upon him by Johannes Reuchlin, a relation of his mother's parents, who, after the early death of his father (1508), took an interest in his education. The talented youth was sent to complete his Latin schooling in nearby Pforzheim; here too he began his Greek studies. After a year, he attended university in Heidelberg (1509–11) and then Tübingen (1512–14), taking a bachelor's and master's in arts respectively. During these university years he was formed in both major scholastic traditions, with the *via moderna* of nominalism remaining his preference.[147] At Heidelberg, he was certainly influenced by the views on rhetoric and its place in education of Jacob Wimpfeling, the Alsatian humanist and sometime professor of rhetoric. During these years he formed numerous acquaintances with fellow-students who would likewise become leaders in evangelical reform, in particular in the upper Rhine territories: amongst others Caspar Hedio, Berthold Haller and Simon Grynaeus in Pforzheim, Johannes Brenz and Theobald Billican in Heidelberg, Ambrosius Blarer and Johannes Oecolampadius in Tübingen. These friendships would subsequently strengthen Melanchthon's personal impulse to irenicism in the intra-evangelical doctrinal conflicts. Throughout these years he developed his great mastery of the Greek language, and acquired, too, a firm knowledge of Hebrew, although his skill in this language never matched that in the former. It was Oecolampadius who introduced him to the *Dialectics* of Rudolf Agricola, a text "that not only educated but excited me".[148]

These Tübingen years strengthened Melanchthon's development as a humanist, and began to draw attention to the young man. If the precise nature of his

---

[146] In the mountains some 50 km. south of Heidelberg, today in the state of Baden-Württemberg.
[147] Scheible, Melanchthon (1992) 371.
[148] CR 4, 716: *horum lectione non erudiebar tantum, sed etiam excitabar...*

endebtedness to Erasmus remains a debate,[149] he certainly moved in Erasmian circles, and attracted the master's recognition,[150] for which he reciprocated with a tribute to Erasmus in Greek. He worked as corrector for the well-known printer Thomas Anshelmus. The project of a full Aristotle edition was discussed with friends, although never undertaken. His first book appeared, an edition of Terence' Comedies which enjoyed many reprintings. Next, in spring 1518, came a Greek grammar. Meanwhile, he had entered the fray of the great scholastic-humanist controversy surrounding Reuchlin, identifying himself with the cause of his family patron against the attempt of the Cologne Dominicans to have Jewish literature destroyed. He thereby merited a brief mention in the *Letters of Obscure Men*.[151] Thus the young man whom Reuchlin recommended to Elector Frederick of Saxony for the new chair in Greek at Wittenberg was already making a name for himself in the world of the new learning.

2.2. Exegetical Activity

As we have seen, Melanchthon brought significant linguistic tools and a profound commitment to the humanist agenda to his new role in the arts faculty. He found himself, however, also rapidly drawn into the excitement surrounding his theologian colleague, Luther. Hitherto he had shown relatively little interest for the world of theology. The ideas of Luther, on the other hand, he found gripping. With his linguistic abilities, he was able alongside his classical lectures, to begin a class on Titus, and perhaps other of the pastoral epistles in Greek. He turned himself also to the more formal study of theology. In scarcely more than a year, he received the biblical bachelor's degree (September 1519). One month before, he had accompanied Luther to the Leipzig disputation with Johannes Eck, where the evangelical position on the supremacy of Scripture over the Church was first clearly articulated. Not surprisingly, then, the final authority of Scripture was affirmed in Melanchthon's baccalaureate disputation (September 9, 1519). Articles 16 and 17 asserted the sufficiency of Scripture alone for articles of saving, Catholic faith, and the supremacy of Scripture over the authority of church councils.[152]

Given Melanchthon's mastery of Greek and his newly awakened excitement for theology as taught by Luther in Wittenberg, we are not surprised to find that he moved quickly into regular lecturing on the New Testament. "We are completely in the sacred texts", he wrote to Johann Schwebel, adding that he could wish the same for his correspondent. Specifically he refers to his work on Romans and Matthew.[153] This work continued, moreover, at an augmented level when he stepped into the role of the absent Luther after the Diet of

---

[149] See Schneider, *Oratio Sacra* (1990) 17,34–36.
[150] CR 1, CXLVI: ...*Quae sermonis puritas et elegantia! Quanta reconditarum rerum memoria....*
[151] CR 10, 475: of Gratius' Tübingen foes, Melanchthon is *vilissimus.*
[152] StA 1,23–25; *Melanchthon: selected writings* (1962/1978) 18.
[153] MBW 68, CR 1,128: *Toti in sacris literis sumus....*

Worms, with lectures sequentially on the two Corinthian epistles and the Gospel of John. With Luther's return in Lent 1522, this pace would not be maintained, but the task of New Testament lecturing and printed commentary would be a central part of his Wittenberg ministry henceforth. Amongst numerous volumes on Gospels and epistles, we may observe that at least four commentaries on Romans would bear his name. Luther was instrumental in having the 1521 lectures published in 1522; new commentaries followed in 1530, 1532, 1540 (a revision of 1532) and 1556. Here and on other biblical books, Melanchthon was a frequent victim of pirate editions. Where he was reluctant to publish a not-yet polished set of annotations, others, including Luther himself, saw the contribution they might make to the cause of evangelical exegesis. Printers, needless to say, could also discern commercial advantages!

It is, however, Melanchthon's work in the Old Testament that concerns us here. In a seminal article PETER BARTON has underlined the complexities entailed in any interpretation of Melanchthon's early exegetical work, where questions of exegetical substance mingle with his own intellectual and doctrinal development, the whole bedeviled by issues of dating and publication history, in particular the challenge of working with pirate editions.[154] We have seen that Melanchthon began the study of Hebrew while still a university student. In a letter to Spalatin in September 1518, Melanchthon reported that he had acquired two Hebrew Bibles, the one simple, the second an expensive volume accompanied by commentaries, i.e., mediaeval rabbinic texts.[155] This latter will most likely have been a copy of the first edition of the Bomberg so-called Rabbinic Bible.[156] At the time of Melanchthon's appointment, there had been hope of also establishing a permanent Hebrew chair in Wittenberg, although this did not immediately happen. In the letter just cited Melanchthon indicated that he was at work in Hebrew, diligently occupied with the preparation of a new Latin translation of the book of Proverbs from the Hebrew. He expressed the hope that with the coming to Wittenberg of Johannes Böschenstein as teacher of Hebrew, they might together produce an annotated edition of Proverbs in Hebrew, Greek and Latin. In the event, this was not to be. Although Böschenstein published there a Hebrew grammar that autumn, he abandoned Wittenberg definitively in mid-winter.[157] In consequence Melanchthon found himself drafted to teach beginners' Hebrew. This may have continued for a time, as Wittenberg sought with difficulty a capable Hebraist. He expressed his frustration with one candidate who refused to take over the Psalms class

---

[154] Barton, Die exegetische Arbeit (1963) 56–58.

[155] MBW 24, CR 1,43: *Habemus Hebraica Biblia, quae feci ex Lipsia afferri. Libri duo sunt, alter cum commentariis aureorum XIIII pretio aestimatus, alter sine commentario.*

[156] The *Miqraoth gedoloth* (Venice 1517); suspect for prejudicial editing by the convert, Felix of Prato / Pratensis, it was followed by the 1524–25 edition which established the definitive model for subsequent editions.

[157] Böschenstein (1472–1540) had taught Hebrew for some years in Ingolstadt. His abrupt departure from Wittenberg after so brief a sojourn turned Melanchthon's admiration for him to intense dislike; see Scheible, Reuchlins Einfluß (1993) 132–133.

from him, apparently deeming it beyond his competence.[158] The situation was resolved to general satisfaction in 1521 with the appointment of Matthaeus Aurogallus as Hebrew lecturer.[159] Melanchthon no longer taught Hebrew grammar; but continued to offer classes on Old Testament exegesis, notably on Proverbs and Psalms.

The Psalms class to which Melanchthon alluded figures in several of his letters of 1519. He seems to have found the pressures of this teaching demanding, and at this stage, hoped for relief from this duty with the new appointee.[160] No published volume came directly from this class, nor has a student set of notes survived. It is possible, indeed likely, that the lectures will have left traces in the volume of translation and annotations published in Hagenau in 1528.[161] This volume was, however, the immediate consequence of a set of lectures, perhaps incomplete, given by Melanchthon in Jena in 1527, whither the university had temporarily migrated during an outbreak of plague. The text is a curious combination of translation and notes. A little more than half of the fifty leaves is given over to a Latin rendering of selected Psalms (1–4, 19, 32, 110, 111, 115–116, 119–133, MT numbering); neither the traditional Gallican nor Jerome's Hebraicum, it is apparently Melanchthon's own. The remainder of the volume is an *Interpretatio aliquot Psalmorum*, largely but not fully coinciding with those included in the translations (1–4, 110–133), and generally the notes are very sparse. BARTON is probably correct in concluding that we have certainly to do with a pirate edition, probably gathering together a variety of student manuscripts from both 1519 and 1527.[162]

BARTON's caution about the complicated state of Melanchthon's exegetica remains valid, moreover, for the later period of his career. Within the Psalms texts of the *Corpus Reformatorum* are materials already identified there as not coming from Melanchthon himself. The researches of WENGERT have confirmed the ascription in CR of much of these to Caspar Cruciger, from his 1546 commentary.[163] This confusion dates from their mistaken inclusion in the sixteenth century Peucer edition of Melanchthon's *Opera*.[164] Accordingly, we will consider, in the next section, only those materials that are genuinely from Melanchthon, a treatment of Psalms 1–60 and 110–133, identified in CR as 1555, but to be dated, again from WENGERT's research, to a lecture series in 1547–48.[165]

Lastly, we must not leave the Psalms without noting that Melanchthon contributed prefaces to both Luther's and Johannes Bugenhagen's Psalms commentaries in the early Wittenberg years. The

---

[158] CR 13,759; 1,104–05
[159] Aurogallus (Goldhahn) c. 1490–1543, came to Wittenberg as student in 1519. He would be a central member of the German Bible translation project.
[160] CR 1,76–77; 80–81; 104–05 = MBW 50,58,60.
[161] *In Psalmos aliquot Davidicos, Ph'I Mel'is enarrationes doctissimae* (Hagenau: Setzer 1528).
[162] Barton, Die exegetische Arbeit (1963) 64–65, 84–85.
[163] CR 13,1245–1472. Cruciger (1504–48) was first a student, then a close associate of Melanchthon, who worked at various points on the Wittenberg Bible project; after 1533 he was a regular teacher in the Wittenberg faculty; OEncRef 1, 456–57; Wengert, Caspar Cruciger (1989).
[164] Caspar Peucer, Melanchthon's son-in-law, who issued a collected works in Wittenberg, 1562f.
[165] Wengert, The Biblical Commentaries (1997) 119–21.

former were the *Operationes in Psalmos*, Luther's magisterial and at the same time intensely personal lectures on the first twenty-two Psalms, delivered throughout the critical years 1518–21, and
appearing in a series of fascicles first in Wittenberg, then in Basel through the instrumentality of
Conrad Pellican.[166] The preface to Luther took the form of a letter addressed "To students of
theology".[167] SCHNEIDER has argued that the character of this preface, when considered in the light
of development in Luther's Psalms exegesis since the 1513–15 Psalms, suggests that the Melanch-
thon-Luther relationship was not a one-way street. Given in addition that Melanchthon was lecturing on the Hebrew Psalms at the same time as Luther was delivering the lectures that would become the *Operationes*, it is a reasonable conjecture that "Luther found in Melanchthon exactly the
right linguistic discipline (not merely in grammar and languages but in linguistic theory) for a final
push into a systematic control over [the] literal sense [of Scripture]".[168] That one can identify passages in the *Operationes* where Luther was not altogether consistent in this abandon of the older,
allegorical interpretation should not vitiate the general thesis.[169] The second Psalms preface was
for Bugenhagen's *In librum Psalmorum Interpretatio*.[170] Melanchthon's support for the publication
of this commentary should be understood as recognition of the need for an evangelical commentary on the entire Psalter, Luther having abandoned, after 1521, proceeding in any systematic
fashion beyond the 22nd Psalm.[171]

The other Old Testament book that was central, as we have seen, to Melanchthon's work in Hebrew exegesis in his early years in Wittenberg was Proverbs. Even more than the Psalms, this was an interest that would be maintained
throughout his lifetime, resulting in a series of publications over three decades
from 1524–25 on. The first printing was an unfortunate beginning. There appeared in Hagenau (initially in late 1524 or early 1525) an unauthorized edition entitled the ΠΑΡΟΙΜΙΑΙ *sive Proverbia Solomonis filii Davidis, cum adno-
tationibus Philippi Melanchthonis*, apparently the gleaning by the printer Setzer
of student notes from Melanchthon's 1523–5 lectures. Angered on this occasion by the poor quality of the materials, Melanchthon required the same printer to issue his new translation of the book from the Hebrew, this appearing in
1525 as *Solomonis Sententiae, versae ad Hebraicam veritatem*. A German edition
also appeared in 1526.[172] Within two years he was lecturing again on Proverbs,
and preparing a new edition of his commentary.[173] This would appear as the
Nova Scholia in 1529, still with Setzer, and would be reprinted several times.
In the dedication to the duke of Mecklenburg, Melanchthon discussed his dissatisfaction with the previous effort, and set forth the hermeneutic he now was
employing.[174] We shall have occasion to refer to this in discussing his exegesis
in the following section. But Melanchthon was not yet done in Proverbs. In
1548 he lectured again on this book, and in spring 1550, published his com-

---

[166] Hobbs, Conrad Pellican and the Psalms, RRRev 1 (1999) 84.

[167] *Theologiae studiosis Philippus Melanchthon*, in: *D. Martin Luther. Operationes in Psal-
mos.1519–21*, v. 2 (ed. G. Hammer & M. Biersack; AzWA 2; Cologne / Vienna: Böhlau 1981) 16–
22; = MBW 47; CR 1, 70–76.

[168] Schneider, *Oratio Sacra* (1990) 99–100.

[169] For example, Ps 3 is expounded, with Augustine, as an allegory of Christ; but at the end is
appended an interpretation of David, exemplar of Christ and every Christian: *Operationes*, 119–
20; 154–56.

[170] First published in its entirety in Basel, early 1524, with Pellican's encouragement, and reprinted several times in the next few years. Above n. 143.

[171] *Lectoribus S.*, CR 1, 665; MBW 299.

[172] Barton, Die exegetische Arbeit (1963) 80–81; Wengert, Biblical commentaries (1997) 122.

[173] CR 1, 983; MBW 693.

[174] CR 1, 1089–92; MBW 750.

mentary as the *Explicatio Proverbiorum Salomonis.*[175] This effort was revised and republished, the definitive form coming in 1555.[176] Melanchthon's work on Ecclesiastes (Qoheleth) can be understood as a natural, if late-appearing complement to his fascination as a pedagogue with Hebrew wisdom literature. He seems to have lectured on it for the first time in 1548–9, after completing his series on Proverbs. The commentary appeared as *Enarratio brevis concionum libri Salomonis cui titulus est Ecclesiastes* in 1550; it was revised and printed in 1551, and again in 1556, with a German edition the year after his death.[177]

With the exception of the book of Daniel, Melanchthon published little of substantial commentary on the other books of the Old Testament. There are notes on the earliest chapters of Genesis, which break off at 6:8, the beginning of the Noah narrative. Although the source has been debated, in BARTON's view they stem from a lecture series in spring 1522, which was published without the author's consent, again by Setzer in Hagenau.[178] They were reprinted several times, and apparently translated into German; to Melanchthon, however, they felt unsatisfactory and unworthy of the book.[179] A brief set of lecture notes on Exodus 20 is apparently from the same period.[180] There are brief treatments of the themes (*argumenta*) of Isaiah, Jeremiah and Lamentations, in their present state of preservation all from the 1540's.[181] There were also notes on the final three minor prophets – Haggai, Zechariah and Malachi – printed in one or other of the sixteenth century editions of the collected works, and thence included in the *Corpus Reformatorum*. They were probably all delivered in sequence in 1553.[182] With the exception of an excursus at Mal 1:7 on the profanation of the Lord's Supper, these are again notes on the general themes, with in the case of Zechariah, notes to introduce each chapter of the book.

Melanchthon's interest in the book of Daniel was lively, and spanned decades of his career. He first published in 1529 (with Setzer of Hagenau) a preface intended to accompany a commentary, in which he expounded the imagery and visions of the prophet in relation to the contemporary Turkish threat. The announced commentary itself seems not to have been written, but the preface enjoyed wide circulation.[183] In 1542 Melanchthon lectured on Daniel, and in early 1543 this came to press as a full-fledged commentary; VOLZ suggests that the earlier lectures probably contributed the foundation to this work.[184] Again, Melanchthon's interest in making application of the apocalyptic materials to the renewed Turkish menace doubtless contributed to the work's popularity. It was also marked by what WENGERT has termed "some of the strongest statements by Melanchthon against the papacy and the Mass". These were the years following the failure of the Worms and Regensburg

---

[175] Frankfurt 1550, see CR 14,1.

[176] This is the text printed in CR 14, 1–88.

[177] CR 14, 89–160.

[178] *In obscuriora aliquot capita Geneseos Ph'l Mel'is annotations* (Hagenau 1523; again 1524). Barton, Die exegetische Arbeit (1963) 77–78.

[179] In the preface to the 1541 Basel edition of his works, which included the Genesis lectures, Melanchthon states he would not have included them, had he had the say: They are *inchoatae* annotations; their distinguishing of Law and Gospel pleased the elders (read Luther), but they are too brief for what is needed; CR 4, 718.

[180] So Barton, Die exegetische Arbeit (1963) 79.

[181] CR 13, 793–822; see Wengert, Biblical commentaries (1997) 124–25.

[182] CR 13, 981–1016; Wengert, op. cit. 128–29.

[183] *Danielis enarratio. Praefatio ad regem Ferdinandum.* CR 1, 1051–56; see Volz, "Beiträge" (1955/56) 97, n. 10, for corrections of a faulty text.

[184] Volz, ibid. 109–10.

inter-confessional colloquies (1540–41) that brought leading Roman and Evangelical theologians together in an ultimately futile attempt to re-unite German Christianity. In these efforts Melanchthon played a key role representing Wittenberg. Following their collapse, he and Bucer of Strasbourg – the other key Protestant theologian – were invited by its Prince Elector to undertake a moderate reform of the Cologne archdiocese. This effort too ultimately foundered on the rock of conservative Catholic opposition, and in the increasingly acrimonious debates of these years, Melanchthon's anti-Roman commentary in Daniel was cited against him.[185]

2.3. Interpreting the Old Testament

In 1556, Melanchthon reflected upon his work as Scriptural interpreter:

> I can truly affirm from the heart that, since God called me to this labour of teaching, I have taken great care to seek out simple explanations and to avoid those labyrinths in which others show off their talent. In effect I daily pray to God with frequent groans that he would teach me. I know, therefore, that my commentaries are despised by some, and admittedly they are more slender than adequately expound the breadth of divine wisdom. I do this chiefly so that the youth may consider the manner of expression and order of the argument, and afterwards draw the meaning from the sources. But whatever the quality of my writings, I always subject myself and all of my advice and actions to this one thing, to the judgement of the church, and I beg you, should ever you feel I am off in dreamland, do admonish me.[186]

Within this self-analysis as interpreter of Scripture Melanchthon makes some crucial observations that are helpful as we move into a survey of his method. In the first place, he underlines his quest for simplicity in exposition. Certainly this is grounded in the evangelical conviction that the essential message of Scripture can be stated with clarity and without obfuscation. As he wrote against the traditional quest for a multi-layered interpretation of Scripture in his 1529 dedication of Proverbs, "the meaning of Scripture is single and simple".[187] The quest for that central insight made of him a man of prayer. But it also relates directly to a second point. His work was always profoundly shaped by his role as pedagogue, as a teacher of university youth. His concern was to inculcate and therefore also to model a style of interpreting Scripture that proceeded along a clear path, from the establishment of the nature of the text and its form of argumentation, to illustration through details of the text itself. Now from earliest years he had been convinced of the value of rhetoric and

---

[185] Wengert, Biblical commentaries (1997) 127–28. The work is printed in CR 13, 823–980.
[186] *Vere hoc possum affirmare de mea conscientia, cum Deus ad hos docendi labores me vocaverit, magna me cura quaesivisse simplices explicationes, et vitasse quosdam labyrinthos in quibus alii ostentant ingenia. Quotidie enim crebris gemitibus Deum oro, ut me doceat. Ideo scio, despici a quibusdam meas enarrationes, quas, fateor esse tenuiores, quam ut amplitudinem sapientiae divinae satis exponent. Illud praecipue ago, ut adolescentes considerent phrasin et ordinem disputationis, postea sententiam sumant ex fontibus. Sed qualiacunque sunt scripta mea, uno quidquid est meorum consiliorum et actionum, omnia illa et me ipsum et iudicio Ecclesiae subieci semper, teque oro ut, sicubi hallucinari me senties, me admoneas.* I am grateful to Wengert (Biblical commentaries, 1997, 148) for drawing my attention to this letter of Oct 29, 1556; CR 8,893–94; MBW 8009.
[187] *una et simplex est Scripturae sententia*; CR 1, 1090.

dialectic for the exposition of the sacred text. His students were taught how to proceed in this manner, not only by theoretical discourse, but by his own practice. Melanchthon acknowledges here that his relatively consistent use of such an approach left him open to the accusation of treating the Scriptures too lightly, that those whose large commentaries exposed to the reader the grammatical complexities of many passages, might well accuse him of unfortunate brevity, if not superficiality. On this difference, as on his particular interpretations, he appealed to the judgement of the Church. That the approbation of evangelical readership did matter to him is evidenced by many references to his biblical work in his voluminous correspondence. It is also appropriate to observe that the pirating of his lectures, their premature (in his judgement) hastening to the printer, is a good indication that students and colleagues alike found profundity in his very simplicity of style.

The starting point for a discussion of Melanchthon's Old Testament interpretation is not the commentaries themselves, but his 1521 guide to the reading of Scripture, the *Loci Communes rerum theologicarum*. In the introduction to this work he wrote:

> Here are indicated the principal subjects of Christian teaching, so that our youth may understand both what things are most to be sought in Scripture, and how scandalously they have daydreamed at all points in theology who produced for us Aristotelian subtleties in place of Christ's teaching.We have, in truth, treated everything sparingly and with few words, because we are providing more an index than a commentary, when we simply make a list of the themes to which someone wandering through the divine books should, as it were, be pointed.[188]

Commentary he disparaged, including those of most Fathers of the early Church, because their very prolixity, to say nothing of interpretive method, distracted the reader from the Scriptures themselves. For his part, "we are not writing a commentary, but rather delineating a kind of popular form of the themes (*loci*) which you may follow in studying Scripture".[189] Now the complexity of the layering of the versions of the *Loci*, as Melanchthon worked and reworked his chef d'oeuvre throughout his long career, is not our concern here.[190] What is significant, however, is the methodology made explicit in the *Loci* and retained *mutatis mutandis* throughout his exegetical career, and, secondly, particular thematic discussions that would continue fundamentally to impact his interpretation of the Old Testament, however they might be expanded and nuanced differently in the successive editions. Melanchthon approached Scripture with all the tools of his humanist training and mindset, but unlike Bucer and the evangelicals of the Upper Rhine, he deemed the initial

---

[188] CR 21, 81–82: *indicantur hic Christianae disciplinae praecipui loci, ut intelligat iuventus, et quae sint in Scripturis potissimum requirenda, et quam foede hallucinati sint ubique in re theological qui nobis pro Christi doctrina Aristotelicas argutias prodidere. Parce vero ac breviter omnia tractamus, quod indicis magis quam commentarii vice fungimur, dum nomenclaturam tantum facimus locorum, ad quos veluti divertendum est erranti per divina volumina.*

[189] CR 21,139: *De Evangelio: non enim commentarium scribimus, sed vulgarem quondam locorum formam adumbramus, quos in discendis sacris literis sequaris.* This and the passage cited in the previous note are identified by Pauck, Melanchthon and Bucer (1969) 9. I am endebted to his introduction in what follows here; the translations are my own.

[190] Vol. 21 of the CR contains four versions, from preliminary notes to the 1543 ff. edition. The Stupperich StA has a version of 1521.

task to be the application of dialectics, not grammar. We have noted earlier[191] his excitement at discovering in Tübingen the dialectics of Agricola. In his own career as educator, he would press upon his students the acquisition and pursuit of a systematic theological method. From 1520–1547, he issued three editions of his own guide to dialectics. The dialectical method involved the identification of an author's central concepts in a work, those master ideas which determined the shape and flow of thought. In biblical interpretation, then, the first responsibility of the interpreter was to find and name the key themes of the text under study. PAUCK argues convincingly that the young Melanchthon was certainly influenced by the counsels of Erasmus, who in particular in his methodological preface to the New Testament, the *Ratio seu Methodus perveniendi ad veram theologiam* of 1518–19 had urged his readers to "organize for yourselves collections of *loci theologici… Loci* are little nests in which you place the fruit of your readings". For the Scriptures as a whole, several hundred of these little "nests" could be readily identified, and within them appropriate biblical references stored.[192] Obviously a particular biblical book would be likely to favour a smaller number of central *loci*; all the more reason for being aware what precisely were those which the work emphasized. In this, SCHEIBLE has argued that Melanchthon distinguishes himself from the Erasmian method, because the Rotterdamer was inclined to the employment of a more universalized list of *topoi* or *loci*.[193] For Melanchthon, at least in principle, one should arrive at the list of *loci* through examination of the particular text.

In fact one can observe Melanchthon employ both methods side by side. The short preface to the prophet Haggai, apparently from 1553 lectures, began with a discussion of the general history of the people of God, and how this people has been miraculously preserved by God throughout history. Despite their having been afflicted with many unlearned priests and others who even corrupted good teaching, God raised up also a sequence of outstanding teachers from Samuel through Isaiah and to the Apostles. Into this sequence fell the post-exilic prophets, of whom in this instance Haggai. Now Melanchthon's exposition concerns initially the history of Israel, but he understands that the primary interest lies in the Christian Church. "This history is first to be considered in the prophets, but in the details of the history the Church of all ages is to be contemplated".[194] Melanchthon's hearers and readers were therefore to read in the two chapters of this short prophetic book, with its exhortation to the re-building of the temple destroyed by the Babylonians in 587 BCE, the divine truth that enemies have never been finally able to destroy the Church, thanks to divine protection, and take heart for their own day. Having absorbed this historical lesson (*haec historia*), they are then to turn to "the signi-

---

[191] Above, n. 148.
[192] Quoted in Pauck, Melanchthon and Bucer (1969) 12.
[193] Scheible, Melanchthon, OEncRef 2 (1996) 42.
[194] *Haec historia in prophetis primum consideranda sunt[!], in partibus historiae tamen Ecclesia omnium temporum intuenda est… Eluctatur tamen divinitus Ecclesia*; CR 13, 984.

ficant *loci* specific to each prophet".[195] He identified three to be observed in Haggai. The first was that God blesses those who support the ministry of the Gospel in maintaining the clergy, building schools, etc. This benediction could be vividly seen in the manner in which "God preserved our devout prince John Frederick of Saxony unharmed in war and in captivity and afterwards restored him to wife and children". Melanchthon admitted that this last application of the prophetic message might seem farfetched and awkward; "it is nonetheless the genuine meaning of the prophet", and most necessary for the contemporary situation.[196] The second of the *loci* concerned the coming of Messiah, prophesied here in the verse "in a little while, I will shake the heavens and the earth" (2:6–7). While God is the architect of all the natural order, Melanchthon wrote, nothing can match the union of the human and divine in Christ, signaled here by the shaking of the *heavens* – "God's Son will assume human nature", and the *earth* – "human nature will be united with the divine, and this son will be born of a virgin and will gather the eternal church".[197] The final *locus* was likewise of christological import. The glory of the re-built temple named in Haggai (2:8) could only refer to the days of Jesus Christ, whose preaching of the Gospel and calling of the Gentiles to the Church in the temple of his day was precisely a splendour quite denied the post-exilic Jerusalem temple.

Because the Haggai text contains no actual commentary on the two chapters themselves, it is not possible here to assess the manner in which, as he suggested above, he would subsequently "draw this meaning from the sources" themselves.[198] His preface does conclude with a brief historical note, that attempted to situate the text in Persian as well as Jewish history. What is readily apparent, however, is that the definition of the *loci* that govern the interpretation of the text was external, driven by a set of Christian theological convictions. Melanchthon situated himself, as we would expect, within a traditional Christian orthodoxy that understood that the Old Testament must be read in the light of the New, and in particular of the Christ-event itself. There were, of course, a variety of ways in which this conviction expressed itself and was worked out hermeneutically, and these were receiving new nuances, even distinctly new expression, in the early sixteenth century. Within the 1521 *Loci*, Melanchthon specifically addressed this issue in the section, "On the difference between the Old and New Testaments, and the Abrogation of the Law".[199] In contrast to other schemata which employed notions of covenant, of typology, or of pre-figuring, Melanchthon employed as his central tool the theological concepts of Law and Gospel, as he linked these to an evangelical understanding of justification by grace through faith.

From the things we have said concerning Law and Gospel and their respective functions one can easily ascertain the difference between the Old and New Testaments. The Schools fail just as miserably in this area as in their distinction between Law and Gospel; they call the Old Testament a kind of Law which demands external works only, and the New Testament a law which demands the heart in addition to external works. From this kind of reasoning the majesty and

---

[195] *qui sint insignes et proprii loci in quolibet propheta;* CR 13, 985.

[196] *Etsi autem videri potest haec accommodatio in hoc propheta ad nostras ecclesias et scholas rustica, et requirit aliquis sublimem allegoriam, tamen haec native prophetae sententia est et de re maxima concionatur;* ibid.

[197] *Movebo coelum, videlicet, quia Filius Dei assumet humanam naturam, et movebo terram, humana natura copulabitur divinae, et hic Filius ex virgine nascetur et colliget aeternam ecclesiam;* CR 13, 986.

[198] See above n. 186.

[199] CR 21, 192–206.

fullness of grace are obfuscated. But grace ought to be placed in the spotlight where it is perfectly obvious for all to see from every direction, and it alone should be preached.[200]

At heart, then, was the preservation of the centrality of grace, that "veritable prodigality of divine mercy".[201] That the distinction of Law and Gospel should be this vital hermeneutical key for Melanchthon certainly owes greatly to his older colleague Luther. In 1520 Luther had written that "the entire Scripture of God is divided into two parts: commandments and promises". The commandments reveal what God requires of us, but also that we cannot accomplish this, and hence bring us to despair of ourselves: so the commandments "are called the Old Testament and constitute the Old Testament". To human aid comes however the second part of Scripture, the promises that offer all good spiritual gifts to those who believe, although only to faith. "The promises of God...fulfil what the law prescribes, so that all things may be God's alone...Therefore the promises of God belong to the New Testament. Indeed they are the New Testament".[202] Luther himself quickly qualified the apparent equation Law-Gospel with the two Testaments as such, but the distinction of commandment and promise as the two essential words of God found in both Testaments was henceforth central. It is this that Melanchthon presents in the *Loci* as the key that maintains the centrality of grace. In the Old Testament, one finds "a promise of material things linked up with the demands of the law"; the New Testament, on the other hand, "is the promise of all good things without regard to the law... promised unconditionally, since nothing is demanded of us in turn". Now this promise is anchored in Christ, the Son of God, whose coming has abrogated all the Law, for Melanchthon surprisingly even the *moral* law, and inaugurated the era of Christian freedom. The Spirit of Christ leads all who live in this Christ faith to live in freedom. They are likely to act according to God's revealed will, at least most of the time in this as yet imperfect state, but spontaneously, not under any obligation or condemnation. Now this freedom of the Spirit was equally available to Moses and David; the prophets and Psalms make clear that they understood that they lived out of God's immense mercy, not their faltering attempts at obedience of law. In their day, however, "that freedom had not yet been revealed and the gospel of freedom had not yet been spread abroad". They therefore continued to rule their lives by the moral, judicial and ceremonial law, even as "they realized that they were justified by faith".[203]

Scholars like ROGNESS have pointed out that in 1521 Melanchthon's thought on law was yet imperfectly formulated, even antinomian, and would receive

---

[200] *Ex iis quae de lege ac evangelio, deque legis et evangelii officio diximus, colligi facile potest, quid intersit inter vetus testamentum ac novum. Qua in re non aliter atque in discrimine legis ac evangelii misere loborant scholae, cum vetus testamentum vocant legem quondam, quae externa tantum opera exigat. Novum, legem quae praeter externa opera etiam adfectus exigat. Quo fit ut obscuretur gratiae maiestas et amplitudo, quam oportuit velut in illustri positam loco undique omnibus conspicuam ostendi et vel solam praedicari;* CR 21, 192; Pauck, LCC 19, 120.

[201] *quae sit misericordiae divinae prodigalitas;* CR 21, 193; Pauck, LCC 19, 121.

[202] *De libertate Christiana,* WA 7, 53–4; quoted from LW 31, 348–49.

[203] Pauck, LCC 19, 120–30.

considerable refinement in years to come.[204] Yet the Law-Gospel hermeneutic would remain fundamental to his interpretation of the Old Testament. In the 1555 *Loci*, in this same section: "Here once more it is necessary to know the difference between law and gospel".[205] And, introducing his Psalms commentaries of 1547–8 (1555) he wrote:

> Just as the whole doctrine of the Church is separated into two parts, namely law and gospel, so let the Psalms too be distinguished. Some contain more teaching of the law, that is, precepts and exhortations; others interpret more the promise of Christ proper to the Gospel. Some pertain precisely to the didactic or demonstrative genus, as Psalm [110]*Dixit Dominus*, which is an interpretation of the promise of Christ. For this was the principal office of the prophets, to be witnesses of the Messiah who was to come, and interpreters of the promises; other [psalms] are of the hortatory genus, as those which preach of good works, or console the godly in afflictions, or contain petitions, as Psalm 51 *Miserere mei Deus.*[206]

This distinction is moreover one which God has kept down through the ages, in the teachings of all great series of leaders and prophets. "God has in this way granted in his church both his word and the gift of interpretation".[207] When readers respect this distinction, they gain access to the goal of the Holy Spirit in individual Psalms, and are able to benefit thereby. Much later in the commentary he reminded his readers that it is vital that he repeat this admonition from time to time; keeping the Law-Gospel distinction diligently before ourselves, "we may be able both to discover the one simple and self-congruent meaning, and also come to know to what use for ourselves each psalm is to be applied".[208]

Such a hermeneutic, with its assumption of "one simple" reading, did not encourage Melanchthon to explore the possible layers of meaning of a text. He had, of course, as we have seen, eschewed the traditional four-fold reading. But since at least the fourteenth century Christian interpreters had been fascinated by the witness of rabbinic interpreters to *peshat*, a literal reading of the text in the life of ancient Israel, and the challenge of employing this, then turning it to Christian ends. In the Psalms, with the widespread assumption of Davidic authorship of many, if not all the Psalms, this meant seeking incidents and moments in the life of David that might have stimulated the composition of the text, reminiscences of which would be found within the phrasing, the vocabulary, the images. Now Melanchthon was not wholly oblivious to this style of reading. A few examples from the Psalms will illustrate the range of his hermeneutic.

---

[204] Rogness, Melanchthon (1969) 20–21.

[205] Manschreck, *On Christian Doctrine*, 1555, 193.

[206] *Ut universa doctrina Ecclesiae in duas partes distribuitur, videlicet legem et evangelium, ita discernantur et psalmi. Alii magis continent doctrinam legis, id est praecepta et adhortationes; alii magis interpretantur promissionem de Christo propriam evangelii; alii prorsus pertinent ad genus* διδασκαλικον *seu demonstrativum, ut Psalmus Dixit Dominus. Id enim praecipuum est prophetarum officium, testes esse de venturo Messia et interpretes promissionum; alii sunt generis suasorii, ut qui concionantur de bonis operibus, aut consolantur pios in afflictionibus, aut continent petitiones, ut Psalmus 51,* Miserere mei Deus; CR 13, 1018.

[207] *Ita Deus in ecclesia et suum verbum et donum interpretationis largitus est*; CR 13, 1017.

[208] Ad Ps 111: *Prodest autem haec diligentia, et ut una simplex et secum congruens sententia inveniri possit, et ut ipsi agnoscamus ad quem usum nostrum singuli Psalmi transferendi sint*; CR 13, 1166.

First, there are places where a Davidic interpretation serves his ends. At Psalm 7, he observed – as had Luther in the *Operationes*[209] – that the interpreters differed widely on its reading, and that he would give his readers "the simplest one". He concluded (again with Luther) using the canonical title of the psalm (which he rendered as *ignorantia David quam cecinit Domino de verbis Cus filii Iemini*),[210] that David was here rightly protesting his innocence against the imprecations of Shimei (2 Sam 16:5–8). He allegorized the origins of the name Cus, using the etymology "black" to refer to the enemies of Israelites – and therefore of the true Church. In a nice contemporary touch, "this is as if someone had called the ungodly Eck black, and an enemy of the true church".[211] Thus in this Psalm it is easily apparent that David furnishes Christians of Melanchthon's day with a model for denial of slander and prayer for liberation, thereby teaching by his example that these defences for the true community of faith will come from God.[212] A similar attention to the original context of composition comes at the beginning of the fifteen "Songs of Ascent" (Psalms 120–134). To those who would dispute the sense of this title Melanchthon gave a "simple response": priests sang these Psalms, the *cantica graduum*, from such an elevation in front of the temple, in order that they might be heard.[213]

In contrast, there are many Psalms where Melanchthon insisted that the primary, simple sense is the one that came into focus through Christ. A striking illustration is found in his interpretation of Psalm 19, "The heavens are telling the glory of God". The first and longer portion of the Psalm is the narration and prophecy of the Gospel spreading through the whole world, of the coming of Christ and his glorious victories, and the efficacy of the word whereby God is revealed and the eternal Church is collected.[214]

Melanchthon admitted that the Jewish interpretation of verses 1–6, referring them to the evidence of God displayed within the created order, has some justification in the testimonies to God, the great architect. Yet the addition (in verses 7–9) of the praise of the word, as well as of "preaching" means this can only be properly understood "of the propagation of the Gospel". The knowledge of God in creation is incapable of birthing the Church; philosophical knowledge errs in many ways in understanding God. This reading is confirmed, moreover, by the ending of the Psalm, which speaks of the forgiveness of sins. Philosophy gives some knowledge of God, to be sure, but never embraces the Gospel of the forgiveness of sins; "nor does the law of Moses alone show the forgiveness of sins". Melanchthon was therefore confident in holding fast to his christological interpretation as the right reading of the Psalm. There are a couple of observations to make. First, Melanchthon was not alone in making this judgement, even among contemporaries, but it was a contested reading. Very specifically, Lefèvre d'Etaples denounced in his *Five-fold Psalter* those Christian interpreters who were following the opinions of Rabbis rather than the prophetic word; he gave this Psalm as a specific instance of where a supposed literal sense proposed by Jewish interpreters was in fact a fiction and a lie.[215] On the other hand, Melanchthon will certainly have known Bucer's commentary, which claimed that sense as primary. Secondly, the reference Melanchthon made to "preaching of the Gospel" introduces, without however making it explicit, the Pauline allegorical application of Ps 19:4 in Rom 10:18. In his 1528 commentary, he had harmonized the two texts, in favour of St. Paul. Here we must understand the same hermeneutic, and be

---

[209] AWA 2, 394–95

[210] A reading he may have taken from Jerome's *Hebraicum* (as it was given in Lefèvre d'Etaples' *Psalterium Quincuplex*, Paris 1513).

[211] CR 13, 1028. Johann Eck had entitled his highly effective polemic against Luther and the evangelicals, *Enchiridion locorum communium adversus Lutherum et alios hostes Ecclesiae* (1525)!

[212] *Nunc facile est videre sententias et ordinem Psalmi, considerate hac argumenti expositione et applicatione ad nostra pericula. Ut David titulum fecit, ita nos inscribamus nobis hunc titulum...*; CR 13, 1029.

[213] CR 13, 1200.

[214] *Prior et longior pars psalmi est narratio ac prophetia de Evangelio spargendo per totum orbem terrarum, de adventu Christi et gloriosis eius victoriis, de efficacia verbi, quo Deus patefit et colligitur aeterna ecclesia*; CR 13, 1045–47.

[215] *Psalterium Quincuplex* (Paris 1508, 1513, repr. Geneva 1979) Sign. A ii rv: *Et longe esset per singulos psalmos ostendere quem Hebraei astruunt litteralem sensum nequaquam illum litteram velle, sed figmentum esse et mendacium.* ET in: H. A. OBERMAN, *Forerunners of the Reformation* (New York / Chicago / San Francisco: Holt, Rinehart and Winston 1966) 297–301.

only surprised that the Romans use is not named, since it certainly was for him decisive.[216] Lastly, it is apparent that the Law-Gospel dialectic was operative here for Melanchthon; since the Psalm spoke both of law and of forgiveness of sins, to preserve this essential distinction, "law" here must refer to the word of the Gospel!

It is not difficult to multiply examples of this sort. Psalm 2, which some interpreters (as Lefèvre noted caustically, in the text just cited) took to originate in a revolt of surrounding territories upon David's accession to the throne, was treated by Melanchthon as a simple "prophecy of the coming Messiah"; David is not even mentioned by name. "This psalm states exactly what the Baptist says in John 3 [36]: the one who believes in the Son has eternal life".[217] This is consistent with his treatment of the Psalm in the *Loci*: the Psalm is about the new freedom in Christ, and the decree of the Lord named in Ps 2:7 must be a new preaching, not that of the Law, whose message is "abrogated by the new preaching".[218] Psalm 118, because of its citation in Matt 21:42, "we shall interpret as if Messiah himself recites his passion and victory. And at the beginning the Lord addresses the church universal, ordering everyone to give thanks to God for this immense benefit, that he constituted the Son the Mediator".[219]

It is all the more surprising, then, to encounter Melanchthon's treatment of Psalm 22. The presence of fragments of this Psalm on the lips of Christ on the cross, the application of others to the narrative of his passion, would lead one to expect a thoroughly christological application. Augustine had described it as a gospel recitation, the Ordinary Gloss as "rather a history than a prophecy" of Christ, and Luther in the *Operationes* stated simply: "the psalm is to be totally understood of Christ".[220] In his brief commentary, Melanchthon preferred to play on two registers. Certainly Christ is the speaker, but so also is David. In effect, David knew that in his own sufferings, he was presenting images of those of Christ, and if many elements of the Psalm fit Christ's experience more closely than David's, the latter had some comparable experiences, "therefore I don't argue too anxiously about individual expressions. It is enough to hold this as the main point, that Christ's passion and victories are described here, but David is not to be excluded, because he was the type of Christ". This reading of the Psalm is, at least in its general hermeneutic, very reminiscent of that given by Bucer in 1529-32.[221] Another illustration of this David-Christ typological hermeneutic is found in his notes on Psalm 3. In this instance the Psalm is prefaced by a canonical note, or title, suggesting a setting

---

[216] See Hobbs, "*Hebraica Veritas* and *Traditio Apostolica*: St. Paul and the interpretation of the Psalms in the sixteenth century", in: *The Bible in the Sixteenth Century* (ed. D. Steinmetz; Durham, NC / London: Duke UP 1990) 94–97.

[217] CR 13, 1019–21.

[218] CR 21, 195; Pauck, LCC 19, 122–23.

[219] CR 13, 1183.

[220] Augustine, CChr 38, 123; Glossa marginalis *quasi sit historia, non prophetia*; Luther, WA 5, 601.

[221] *Nec nimis anxie de singulorum verborum accomodatione disputo. Satis est in summa hoc tenere, describi hic passionem Christi et victorias. Nec excludendum esse Davidem, quia typus sit Christi*; CR 13, 1050. Cf. R. G. HOBBS, "Martin Bucer on Psalm 22", in: *Histoire de l'exégèse au XVIe siècle* (ed. O. Fatio / P. Fraenkel; EPH 34; Geneva: Deoz 1978) 144–63.

in David's flight from his son Absalom (2 Samuel 15). Melanchthon made no direct reference to the Davidic supposed *historia*. On the words of v. 5, "I was lulled to sleep and rose up" (in his rendering), he wrote: "I do not disapprove that they be applied to Christ's death and resurrection; for the prophet also prayed it of his own peril and deliverance, yet he signifies that Christ would suffer similar things, indeed he teaches that we are set free because of that Lord". Thus in the Psalms, "observe this rule, that often the voice of David is at the same time the voice of Christ, and conversely the voice is David's or our own".[222]

In the Psalms, then, Melanchthon played with both a prophetic and a typological hermeneutic alongside the Law-Gospel distinction, in his endeavour to present a fully Christian reading of the Old Testament. Law-Gospel plays an equally vital role in his presentation of his beloved book of Proverbs. Already in 1529 he showed awareness of the challenge of presenting a Christian reading of this collection of the wisdom sayings of ancient Israel. In his dedicatory epistle to the Duke of Mecklenburg, he indicated that in contrast to both his earlier effort and to traditional four-fold reading that could allegorize Christ into the texts, he would seek to present "the one and simple meaning of Scripture, namely that opened up by a grammatical method".[223] This method enabled him to identify at their simplest the four themes at the core of Proverbs: the inculcation of the fear of God, the building-up of faith and trust in God's goodness, the teaching of endurance in affliction, and finally the ordering of custom and actions. These four *loci*, he stated, should never be lost sight of, and in fact, in a time of religious disorder and doctrinal conflict such as German evangelicals were experiencing, they are particularly to be held onto.

The 1555 preface picks up the definition of this sense. Melanchthon was aware of older skepticism about the worth for the Christian Church of Hebrew wisdom. The challenge of the emperor Julian, for example, who argued the superiority of Phoclydes to Solomon, had been rebutted by Cyril of Alexandria on the grounds of Solomon's greater antiquity. Melanchthon found this quite unsatisfactory: "this puerile response does not correspond to the seriousness of the challenge".[224] Instead, Cyril ought to have spoken of "the true sources of doctrine – law and gospel". Phoclydes, like all ancient pagan philosophers, understood a good part of the Law, but it belongs only to the Church to know the Gospel of the forgiveness of sins, the gift of eternal life through the Son, and the consolation of the cross. It is true that much of Proverbs concerns the second table of the Law; but there are also teachings on "the true knowledge and worship of God and other virtues pertaining to the first table". For example in Prov 1:7, we learn that "the fear of the Lord is the beginning of wisdom". The cross is taught in Prov 3:12, "whom the Lord loves, he chas-

---

[222] Ego sopitus sum et surrexi *ideo accommodatur ad Christi mortem et resurrectionem, id non improbo. Nam propheta etiam eum de suo periculo et sua liberatione precatur, tamen significat Christum similia passurum, imo docet nos propter illum Dominum liberari....Haec regula in Psalmis observetur, ut sciamus saepe vocem Davidis simul esse vocem Christi, et econtra vocem esse Davidis seu nostrum vocem*; CR 13, 1022.

[223] *una et simplex sit Scripturae sententia, videlicet quam aperit ratio grammatica*; CR 1, 1090.

[224] *Haec puerilis responsio non satisfacit magnitudini huius disputationis*; CR 14, 5.

tens"; and, to a modern reader even more dubiously than the previous, salvation in the after life in Prov 14:32. More convincingly, perhaps, he added that where Proverbs speaks of the figure of God's wisdom preaching to the human race, we must understand this of the Son sent to the Church. Beyond this reaching for convincing examples, however, Melanchthon developped a fundamental argument. Proverbs was a book written in the Church, i.e., the faithful community of God's people, all of whom were for him saved through faith, trust in the promise of the Christ who was yet to come. This promise, the Gospel, was known to them; therefore one must understand that this faith is *implicit* throughout the book. "The doctrine of the Messiah was admittedly more clearly transmitted in the psalms and the prophets." But as Solomon commanded regularly that the teaching given by God be known among the people, we must understand this to mean the promises that at first appearance are less visible than the Law. Melanchthon illustrated his point with reference to Prov 5:18, "rejoice in the wife of your youth". Where mention is made of faith (*fides*), presumably as fidelity in this case, one must understand that the promises of God are implicit, and that this divinely required work is acceptable and pleasing to God, "because of the Mediator".[225]

Melanchthon's work on Ecclesiastes (Qoheleth) came late in his career. In the preface he indicated his awareness of interpreters who read the book differently, but he found that "the entire sermon is doctrine, viz. the vigorous assertion of providence and a rebuttal [of skeptics] in which are both consolations and warnings".[226] Here, as in Proverbs, his strong caution to the reader was to understand that the Christian reader must begin from the canonical position.

> These sermons are recited in the Church of God, where the doctrine of calling upon the true God and of the redeemer, God's Son, must be known. Recognition of God's Son and our redeemer must shine forth by these *labours* of which this sermon speaks; so that Solomon himself commands here that the entire doctrine of the Church be known and heard, and he censures worship that is worthless saying: *you who enter God's house, approach in order to hear!* [Eccl 5:1]... We must hear in the house of God, i.e., in the true Church, doctrine speaking, which embraces the whole foundational doctrine.[227]

Melanchthon, then, employed with remarkable consistency a hermeneutic which found the dialectic of Law and Gospel in all corners of the Old Testament. A contemporary like Bucer, in his commentary on Psalm 19, could criticize this practice, although even at the height of the strife over the Eucharist

---

[225] *Sic ubique simul complectenda est doctrina de Messia, quae in Psalmis et prophetis magis perspicue tradita est*; CR 14, 5–6.

[226] *Quanquam autem de argumento huius libri alii aliter locuti sunt, tamen in hac sententia acquiesco, et iudico summam operis hoc modo recte distribui: totam concionem esse doctrinam, videlicet adseverationem de providentia ac refutationem in qua consolationes sunt et comminationes*; CR 14, 90–1.

[227] *Sciat autem lector et hoc, has conciones in ecclesia Dei recitari, ubi notam esse oportet doctrinam de veri Dei invocatione et de redemptore Filio Dei. Praelucere agnitionem Filii Dei et redemptoris oportet his* laboribus, *de quibus haec concio loquitur. Ut ipse Salomon hic universam doctrinam Ecclesiae cognosci et audiri praecipit, et cultus inutiles taxat inquiens:* ingrediens domum Dei accede ut audias. *Ut doctrinam in domo Dei, id est, in vera Ecclesia sonantem audiamus, quae totam fundamenti doctrinam complectitur*; CR 14, 92.

he named this discretely as the work of "certain recent authors". Bucer argued that such a distinction did not correspond to either prophetic or Pauline usage of the terms.[228] His attenuation of the criticism in a subsequent edition had more to do with Bucer's pursuit of evangelical concord than with any change of heart on his part; nor as we have seen in Melanchthon's practice. In assessing the latter's writings, one must always keep in mind Melanchthon's pedagogical interest. Again and again, he expressed his concern that his work teach youth a proper theology and manner of reading Scripture; this is explicit in his stated goal in the 1521 *Loci*;[229] and so for example at Psalm 132, he invites his young students (*iuniores*) to pay attention to a peculiarity of Hebrew style, or again at Ps 118:25, to the Hebrew words lying behind the Christian acclamation "Hosanna".[230] The end of Scripture's teaching is "to nourish and confirm faith".[231] This is in particular directed to his youthful students, as in the preface to his *Ecclesiastes*: "a book that is beneficial to be known intimately by all who are learning their letters".[232] Melanchthon's frequent identification of Greek rhetorical figures is to be understood precisely in this pedagogical context.

We saw earlier that Melanchthon had sufficient Hebrew to teach the rudiments of the language, and that his library included texts giving him access to rabbinic literature. What can be said of his Hebrew scholarship as it is evidenced in his commentaries? In the first place, like the large majority of contemporary Hebraists, it is apparent that he was committed at a basic level to the authority and therefore the use of the Hebrew original in preference to the Septuagint-Vulgate text tradition. An examination of selected samples from his translation in the fragmentary 1528 Psalms reveals that the base text is generally the Massoretic. So at 1:4 and 4:8, he reads with the shorter MT; at 2:7 and 3:8 he has the MT reading, not that of the Vulgate. The same is true at 132:4–5, where Septuagint and Vulgate have an additional clause: *et requiem temporibus meis*. An unusual exception is 19:5, where his rendering of the *qavvam* of the MT as *sonus eorum* has been shaped by the Septuagint tradition as it is present in Rom 10:18. Although admittedly a complex case – Jerome's *Hebraicum* also gave *sonus* – his thoroughly christological interpretation of the Psalm referred to above, suggests that here this consideration trumped the more natural sense of the MT, which a number of Melanchthon's contemporaries endeavored to respect.[233] At 2:12 his *osculamini filium* was the preference of most Hebraists (over Jerome's *adorate pure*), but as it also served well his christological interpretation of the Psalm, it is not conclusive here.

---

[228] Bucer, *Sacrorum Psalmorum libri quinque* (Strasbourg 1529), fol. 111v–112r. He softened the passage in the 1532 edition, suggesting that despite the validity of his critique, the unnamed contemporaries taught rightly the heart of the matter. It is unlikely his opinon of the hermeneutic had changed.
[229] CR 21, 81; LCC 19, 19.
[230] CR 13, 1218; 1186: *sciant iuniores*....
[231] CR 13, 1018.
[232] CR 14, 93.
[233] Hobbs, *Hebraica veritas* (1990) 94–97.

Commentary on text-critical issues apparently did not interest Melanchthon. No published commentary survives on any of the textual variants noted in the previous paragraph. His commentary on Psalm 22, as we have seen, leaves a space that surprises the modern reader – in the light of other Christological readings in Psalms 2, 19 and 118 for example – for what has been called a double literal sense.[234] But at Ps 22:17 a famous *crux interpretum* left Christian interpreters able to argue that Jewish scribes had altered a text that once read "they have pierced my hands and my feet", a reading obviously well adapted to the crucifixion of Jesus.[235] Luther had devoted several pages to an affirmation of the preferred traditional Christian reading, drawing upon the arguments of Paul of Burgos and Felix Pratensis[236]. For him, the change had been deliberate, *pertinaciter*. Now Bucer, as we have seen earlier, read the psalm much as did Melanchthon. In the process of noting this text issue, Bucer had corrected some of Luther's inexpert reasoning, before somewhat surprisingly recommending to his Christian readers the translation "they have pierced". On this verse Melanchthon is completely silent in his commentary. Is this indicative of a more general disinterest in details of text readings? Or was Melanchthon influenced by Bucer in this regard, to conclude that there had been both in Luther and in Bucer "much ado about nothing"? I have not found evidence that indicates decisively that he had read Bucer, although this is highly likely, given the substantial qualities of the latter's commentaries, and the fact that the two reformers found themselves increasingly working together from the mid–1530's.

As has been shown in the first section of this chapter (19.1), the exegetes of the upper Rhine found much that was invaluable in mediaeval Jewish commentary on the Hebrew text. In particular they drew upon these sources for insight into the presumed historical setting of composition, and for philological detail. Now we have seen that Melanchthon possessed some access to these commentaries.[237] Did he consult one or other as he read the Hebrew? Only a close examination of both his *Psalms* and *Proverbs* will allow a definitive answer; but the extensive samplings undertaken for this study suggest not. Philological comments are uncommon, and such as those noted earlier a commonplace in dictionaries like that of Reuchlin.[238] He simply does not engage, in pursuit of the nuance of a usage, in the sort of study of comparative passages that is so common in Bucer (learned from his rabbinic sources). Thus, when he did offer comment upon *tamim* at Ps 15:2, his rejection of some traditional Christian renderings was in the interest of showing its application to the holding of a true understanding of God.[239] In this respect Melanchthon's commentary is the diametric opposite of the sort of philological pursuit found in Reuchlin's study of the Penitential Psalms.[240] That Reuchlin's commentary was reprinted in Wittenberg in 1529 suggests that such works were valued in their own place by the Wittenbergers; but Melanchthon's work was of a different order, con-

---

[234] Oberman, Forerunners (1966) 286–89.

[235] The polemical accusation of Raymond Martin in the *Pugio Fidei* (Leipzig 1687, repr. Farnborough 1967) fol. 222 (= p. 278), etc.

[236] Burgos, *Additiones* to the *Postilla Litteralis* of Nicholas of Lyra, printed in the great *Biblia* of Basel, 1506–08; Felix Pratensis, *Psalterium ex Hebraeo diligentissime ad verbum fere tralatum* (Venice 1515; Hagenau 1522), ad loc.; Luther, *Operationes*, WA 7, 632–35.

[237] Above, at n. 13.

[238] *De rudimentis hebraicis* (Pforzheim 1506; repr. Hildesheim / New York: Olms 1974) 231 (Hosanna).

[239] *Nec significant* perfectum...*nec* immaculatum, *ut multi intelligunt, sed* incorruptum, *non contaminatum cultu idolorum, aut falsis aut fanaticis opinionibus de Deo*; CR 13, 1039–40.

[240] Reuchlin, *In septem psalmos poenitentiales...interpretatio* (Tübingen 1512, and reprinted in Wittenberg 1529).

cerned with the broad sweep of the interpretation, the over-all theme of the whole.

What then of this dimension of the rabbinic commentaries? One finds the occasional use of a supposed *historia* as interpretive lens. Earlier we noted the Shimei incident from 2 Samuel 16 which gives some flavour to the reading of Psalm 7.[241] This lens was not taken, however, from the commentators found in the rabbinic Bibles – all of these consider the Psalm to refer to David's troubles under king Saul – but from Paul of Burgos (who admittedly may be transmitting an earlier Jewish interpretation), either directly or through Luther. At Psalm 22, where he allowed a Davidic as well as christological sense, Melanchthon offered no specific setting (as had Bucer). In Psalm 24, where David Qimhi and Abraham ibn Ezra proposed David's purchase of the threshing floor as future site for the ark (2 Samuel 24), Melanchthon saw a pure prophecy of the gathering of the Church. The Rabbis proposed the same setting for Psalm 132. There Melanchthon proposed in 1528 that the Psalm was apparently written with a view to Solomon's construction of the temple, while in the later commentary he offered an interpretation that was generally "according to the history", but remained at the level of Davidic generalities, with no evidence he was familiar with the rabbinic lens.[242] At Psalm 19, he explicitly opposed what he saw as the Jewish sense promoted by the Rabbis.[243] Finally, to complete this survey, at Psalm 118 he argued that while it was true that some interpreters wished to make David the speaker of the Psalm, "even the old synagogue" understood the voice as that of Messiah, as Jesus himself claimed at Matt 21:42, "so let us therefore interpret the psalm as if Messiah himself recites his passion and victory". Melanchthon may have been reading Burgos here, from his reference to what looks like *midrash* and possibly Rashi; David Qimhi presented a double interpretation, of David upon his full accession to the throne, and of the future Messianic age. Again here, there is no evidence Melanchthon read him. While needing confirmation by a systematic reading of all the Psalms commentary, it seems already safe to conclude that while Melanchthon was aware, thanks to his reading of Lyra, Burgos and Bucer, that other options were presented by rabbinic commentators, he did not himself pursue this avenue.

2.4. Melanchthon and the Jews

Any inquiry into the interpretation of the Old Testament by a Christian scholar will be incomplete if it fails to address the question of the interpreter's attitude toward the Jewish people. Yet remarkably little attention has been paid to Melanchthon in this regard. The contribution by WENGERT to the 2006 volume by BELL and BURNETT on the Reformers and the Jews has drawn together and

---

[241] Above at n. 155.
[242] CR 13, 1052–54; *iuxta historiam*, 1217–19.
[243] CR 13, 1045.

expanded the earlier researches by SCHEIBLE and DETMERS, and here we shall draw upon WENGERT's helpful findings, with a few complementary observations of our own.[244]

Melanchthon's attitude toward Jews and Judaism was marked by the ambivalence and even contradictory stances unfortunately all too characteristic of the age. This is true for his public positions and attitudes as well as for his written comment. On the one hand, he was a participant in the remarkable renaissance of Hebrew letters amongst Christians that was a hallmark of his age, a religio-cultural movement whose public symbol was Johannes Reuchlin, his family relative and early scholarly patron. As a young student deeply imbued with the values of humanism and its ideal of the *homo trilinguis*, Melanchthon acquired some Hebrew as a matter of course, purchased Hebrew books, and from this beginning taught at least for a time the rudiments of Hebrew and, much more importantly, continued the practice of translating and interpreting the Hebrew Bible throughout his career, including his significant on-going contribution to the final production of the so-called Luther German Bible. He allowed himself to be identified with the humanist scholars supporting Reuchlin, in the academic conflict of the early sixteenth century, against the attempt to destroy Jewish literature. It would seem that Melanchthon himself made little use of such potentially helpful tools for his biblical interpretation as rabbinic commentaries, although he was respectful of at least some Christian colleagues who differed on this point, notably Capito, Osiander and I would add Bucer.[245] His condemnation of Jewish interpretation of the Hebrew Scriptures was based of course upon their denial that Jesus Christ, as God's future Messiah, was the heart and goal of the prophetic message.[246] Unlike some of his contemporaries, however, who were able to identify useful aids to interpretation, and even to thank God for them, while bracketing the Messianic question, for him "these terrible errors" vitiated altogether what might have been useful in their commentaries. His praise of Eobanus Hessus' Latin versification of the Psalms for its avoidance of "judaizing" the Psalter is, I judge, a fair indication of Melanchthon's low esteem for rabbinic interpretation, and his profound reticence with respect to that aspect of the work of some contemporaries, of Sebastian Münster, if not Bucer himself.[247] His denunciation as misguided of on-going contemporary Jewish hopes for a return to the land of Israel in a Messianic age is hardly surprising; rare indeed were colleagues like

---

[244] Scheible, Reuchlins Einfluß (1993) 135–40; Detmers, Reformation und Judentum (2001) 119–43; Wengert, Melanchthon and the Jews (2006) 104–35.

[245] Wengert, Melanchthon and the Jews (2006) 114–15; his condemnation of Bucer observed by Wengert (121) was certainly tied directly to the issue of images, and did not interfere with future collaboration.

[246] For a fuller set of quotations, see Wengert, ibid. 119–25.

[247] Münster, *Hebraica Biblia Latina planeque Nova* (Basel 1534–35), a translation with notes purporting to give Christian readers the fruits of rabbinic interpretation in an acceptable form. CR 3, 394: *Ineptissimum genus est illorum, qui quadam Iudaica superstitione addicti glossematis Iudaeorum, cum figuras non intelligant nec sententiarum ordinem animadvertant, saepe absurdas interpretationes... affingunt.*

Capito who endeavored to accommodate this vision to a Christian view of the End Times.[248] But by using the term "pertinacious" for such interpretations Melanchthon was drifting toward the rhetoric of anti-Jewish polemic.[249] It is therefore initially somewhat surprising to find him declining to repeat the traditional accusation of willful text corruption, which he most certainly read in Luther and others, at Ps 22:17.[250] This may, on the other hand, simply confirm that he was reading Bucer at that point, and had decided to avoid entering a complicated, and from his point of view, pointless discussion.

Several incidents suggest that Melanchthon could at moments be capable of an intellectual honesty, what WENGERT has termed "fairness", in refusing assent to blanket denunciations of Jews.[251] The most striking is certainly the role he took at the Frankfurt consultation where he impressed Rabbi Josel of Rosheim with his demonstration to the elector Joachim II of Brandenburg that the accusations of host-desecration against the thirty-eight Jews burned in 1510 as prelude to the expulsion of all Jews from the electoral territory, were false.[252] SCHEIBLE argues, however, that Melanchthon was addressing a theoretical question as theologian, and was unconcerned with the re-entry of Jews to Brandenburg; WENGERT concurs, in the light of his subsequent opposition to the toleration of Jews in Hesse.[253] In 1543 he wrote the prince, commending Luther's *On the Jews and their Lies* to his perusal, as containing "much more useful teaching". Granted it is unclear precisely what Melanchthon meant by this, it accords only too well with the instances of his recourse to scurrilous anti-Jewish diatribe, and employment of stereotypes.

Hope for the conversion of Jews never faded altogether, but WENGERT has shown that through successive editions of the Romans commentary, Melanchthon placed less and less emphasis upon an eschatological in-gathering.[254] They were more fittingly ranked for him amongst the enemies of an embattled Church. It would be too charitable, however, to excuse his anti-Jewish expression and stance as primarily theological in motivation. Whether as the result of a shared cultural antipathy or as the consequence of long years exposure to views of Luther that he lacked the courage openly to oppose, or both, Melanchthon's position on Jews and Judaism is a sad blot on the reputation of this brilliant humanist and teacher, from whom one might have expected something better.

---

[248] See nn. 82–83 above, and R. G. HOBBS, "Bucer, the Jews and Judaism", in: *Jews, Judaism and the Reformation* (ed. D. Bell / S. Burnett; Leiden 2006) 156–57.

[249] CR 24, 895, quoted in Wengert, Melanchthon and the Jews (2006) 120.

[250] A specific instance, the accusation of Jewish falsification of the text of Ps 22:17; see above, ad n. 92.

[251] Melanchthon and the Jews (2006) 113.

[252] S. STERN, *Josel of Rosheim* (New York: Jewish Publication Society 1965) 171.

[253] Scheible, Reuchlins Einfluß (1993) 137–38; Wengert, Melanchthon and the Jews (2006) 112 and n. 22.

[254] Wengert, ibid. 131–35.

2.5. Conclusion

At the conclusion of his useful survey of Melanchthon's activity as biblical commentator, WENGERT characterized him as "one of the premier biblical exegetes of the sixteenth century. Few can match his output in either scope or popularity. None can match his clarity of style or simplicity of method".[255]

This encomium is a judgement on the merits of Melanchthon's complete oeuvre on the two Testaments. It requires some qualification when we confine our consideration to Melanchthon's Old Testament work. In the first place, Melanchthon seems not to have been of more than average ability amongst the second generation of Christian Hebraists. There is little evidence in his commentaries that he pressed beyond the dictionary equivalences available to him. Where he did (as in Ps 15:2) he was in pursuit of a theological argument, not a greater insight into the secrets of the language. A number of his contemporaries developed the skill necessary to explore the resources of rabbinic commentary. There is again no evidence that he did so; it is likely that his dismissal of these was based not upon personal familiarity, but was a theological *a priori*.

A Greek scholar of deserved repute, Melanchthon devoted his greater effort to the New Testament. In the Old, only his *Daniel*, *Proverbs* and *Ecclesiastes* offer a commentary on the complete book, and even in these the text is in places very sparsely handled. His *Psalms* treats only a little more than half the Psalter, while the remaining texts are for the most part thematic prolegomena to the biblical work. Given Melanchthon's reluctance to publish, and the corresponding frequency with which student manuscripts found their way to the publisher, the modern reader is left wondering what is missing from the corpus. Did he in fact comment more extensively than these remains suggest? In style, his writing is indeed limpid, refreshing after the turgid prose of some of his contemporaries. Their clarity and ease of reading will certainly have contributed to the popularity of their author.

One must be careful not to judge Melanchthon by a standard to which he did not subscribe. His own self-appraisal quoted earlier (n. 186) suggests that his principal preoccupation was to furnish an accurate lens through which youthful readers might then proceed themselves to "draw the meaning from the sources". Judged by this standard, and not by the weighty tomes of the south Germans and Swiss, Melanchthon can be praised for the manner in which he opened the text to his readers, and the consistency with which he adhered to the theological principles he articulated from his earliest Wittenberg days. Judgement upon these, and in particular whether his Law-Gospel hermeneutic was appropriate to the materials under consideration, lies outside the purview of this volume, a discernment, he would argue, by his confessional community to which he was pleased to submit.

---

[255] Wengert, Melanchthon and the Jews (2006) 148.

CHAPTER TWENTY

Humanism and Reformation in England and Scotland

By RICHARD REX, Cambridge

Sources: JOHN BALE: *Scriptorum illustrium maioris Brytanniae ... catalogus* 1–2 (Basel: Oporinus 1557–59). – JOHN CAPGRAVE: *The Chronicle of England* (ed. F. C. Hingeston; Rolls Series; London 1858); *Johannis Capgrave Liber de illustribus Henricis* (ed. F. C. Hingeston; Rolls Series; London 1869). – *Letters and Papers, Foreign and Domestic, of the Reign of Henry VIII* 1–21 (ed. J. S. Brewer e.a.; London: HMSO 1862–1910). – WILLIAM CHILLINGWORTH: *The Religion of Protestants* (London: John Clark 1638). – *The Divorce Tracts of Henry VIII* (ed. E. Surtz / V. Murphy; Angers: Moreana 1988). – JOHN FISHER: *The English Works of John Fisher* (ed. J. E. B. Mayor; Early English Text Society, extra series, 27; London 1976). – JOHN HOOPER: *Early Writings of John Hooper* (ed. S. Carr; Cambridge: Parker Society 1843). – *Records of Early English Drama* (Manchester e.a. 1979–); *Religious Lyrics of the XVth Century* (ed. C. Brown; Oxford: Clarendon 1939). – ROBERT WAKEFIELD: *On the Three Languages* ([1524] ed. and tr. G. Lloyd Jones; MRTS 68; Binghamton, NY 1989). – WILLIAM TYNDALE: *The Obedience of a Christen Man* (Marlborow: H. Luft [i. e. Antwerp: J. Hoochstraten] 1528).

Bibliographies: A. W. POLLARD / G. R. REDGRAVE, *A Short-Title Catalogue of Books Printed in England, Scotland & Ireland and of English Books Printed Abroad, 1475–1640* (2nd edn. rev. & enl., 1–3; London: Bibliographical Society 1976–91[cited STC]).

General works and studies: *The Bible as Book: the First Printed Editions* (ed. P. Saenger / K. van Kampen; London: British Library 1999); *The Bible as Book: the Reformation* (ed. O. O'Sullivan; London: British Library 2000); *The Cambridge History of the Book in Britain* III. *1400–1557* (ed. L. Hellinga / J. B. Trapp; Cambridge: Cambridge UP 1999); *The Bible in the Middle Ages: its Influence on Literature and Art* (ed. B. S. Levy; MRTS 89; Binghamton, NY 1992); I. B. COWAN, *The Scottish Reformation* (London: Weidenfeld & Nicolson 1982); *Le divorce du roi Henry VIII* (ed. G. Bedouelle / Patrick Le Gal; Travaux d'humanisme et renaissance, 221; Geneva: Droz 1987); M. DOWLING, *Humanism in the Age of Henry VIII* (London: Croom Helm 1986); E. DUFFY, *The Stripping of the Altars* (New Haven / London: Yale UP 1992); E. EISENSTEIN, *The Printing Press as an Agent of Change: Communications and Cultural Transformations in Early-modern Europe* 1–2 (Cambridge: Cambridge UP 1979); A. Fox / J. Guy, *Reassessing the Henrician Age* (Oxford: Blackwell 1986); J. B. GLEASON, *John Colet* (Berkeley: University of California Press 1989); I. GREEN, *Print and Protestantism in Early Modern England* (Oxford: Oxford UP 2000); J. GUY, *Tudor England* (Oxford: Oxford UP 1988); C. HAIGH, *English Reformations* (Oxford: Oxford UP 1993); W. HALLER, *Foxe's Book of Martyrs and the Elect Nation* (London: Jonathan Cape 1963); F. HEAL, *Reformation in Britain and Ireland* (Oxford: Oxford UP 2003); *The History of Scottish Literature* 1. *Origins to 1660* (ed. R. D. S. Jack; Aberdeen: Aberdeen UP 1988); *The History of the University of Oxford* II. *Late Medieval Oxford* (ed. J. I. Catto / R. Evans; Oxford: Oxford UP 1992); *The History of the University of Oxford* III. *The Collegiate University* (ed. J. K. McConica; Oxford: Oxford UP 1986); *Humanism in Renaissance Scotland* (ed. J. MacQueen; Edinburgh: Edinburgh UP 1990); H. LEITH SPENCER, *English Preaching in the Late Middle Ages* (Oxford: Oxford UP 1993); J. M. LEVINE, *Humanism and History: the Origins of Modern English Historiography* (Ithaca: Cornell UP 1987); G. LLOYD JONES, *The Discovery of Hebrew in Tudor England* (Manchester: Manchester UP 1983); J. A. LÖWE, *Richard Smyth and the Language of Orthodoxy: Re-imagining Tudor Catholic Polemicism* (SMRT 96; Leiden: Brill 2003); J. K. McCONICA, *English Humanists and Reformation Politics* (Oxford: Oxford UP 1965); M.-R. McLAREN, *The London Chronicles of the Fifteenth Century* (Cambridge: Brewer 2002); *The Reign of Henry VIII* (ed. D. MacCulloch; London: Macmillan

1995); *The Renaissance in Scotland* (ed. A. A. MacDonald / M. Lynch / I. B. Cowan; Leiden: Brill 1994); H. Graf Reventlow, *The Authority of the Bible and the Rise of the Modern World* (London: SCM 1984); R. Rex, *The Theology of John Fisher* (Cambridge: Cambridge UP 1991); idem, "St John Fisher's Treatise on the Authority of the Septuagint", *JTS* NS 43 (1992) 55–116; idem, "Lady Margaret Beaufort and her Professorship: 1502–1559", in: P. Collinson / R. Rex / G. Stanton, *Lady Margaret Beaufort and her Professors of Divinity at Cambridge, 1502–1649* (Cambridge: Cambridge UP 2003); idem, *Henry VIII and the English Reformation* (Basingstoke: Macmillan 1993); J. Simpson, *Reform and Cultural Revolution*, The Oxford English Literary History 2 (Oxford: Oxford UP 2002); A. Walsham, *Providence in Early Modern England* (Oxford: Oxford UP 1999); R. Weiss, *Humanism in Fifteenth-Century England* (3rd edn.; Oxford: Oxford UP 1965); G. Wiedermann, *Der Reformator Alexander Alesius als Ausleger der Psalmen* (Diss. Universität Erlangen-Nürnberg; Erlangen 1988); J. Wormald, *Court, Kirk and Community: Scotland, 1470–1625* (Edinburgh: Edinburgh UP 1981).

Special abbreviations (see above):
HMSO = Her Majesty's Stationery Office
STC = *A Short-Title Catalogue of Books Printed in England etc.*

1. Bible and Theology

1.1. Bible – a Closed Book?

As far as most of the people of England and Scotland were concerned, the Bible was a closed book in the later Middle Ages. A Middle English carol referred to the story of the Fall as something that *clerkis fyndyn wretyn in here book*. For the laity, the Bible was *here book* ("their book"), the special possession of the *clerkis*.[1] Few beyond the ranks of the clergy (and in fact by no means all within) were equipped with the knowledge of Latin necessary to read the Vulgate, which was *the* Bible of Western Christendom. The so-called 'Lollard Bible', the English version of the Vulgate produced by disciples of John Wyclif at the end of the fourteenth century, was generally prohibited. Yet by the end of the sixteenth century, the Bible, in the guise of the Geneva Bible, stood at the intellectual, devotional, and cultural heart of religion in the English-speaking world – which at that time did not entirely occupy the island of Britain (which contained substantial Welsh and Gaelic minorities), but which would soon begin its expansion into the continent of North America. By the 1630s, it was possible for an English theologian to exclaim, in defending his religion against a resurgent Roman Catholicism, "The Bible, the Bible only, I say, is the Religion of Protestants!".[2]

The massive cultural transformation of which the English Bible was both the driving force and the most potent symbol was a complex process comprising not simply the Protestant Reformation, gradually and hesitantly introduced, but also the reception of Renaissance Humanism, the advent of the new technology of print, and the consequent increase in literacy (which,

---

[1] For the carol *Adam lay I-bowndyn*, see *Religious Lyrics of the XVth Century* (1939) 120. I owe this point to my colleague, Professor Eamon Duffy. – I am particularly grateful to James P. Carley of York University, Toronto, and Andrew W. Taylor, of Churchill College, Cambridge, for their comments on an earlier version of this chapter, and for their advice in improving it.

[2] Chillingworth, *The Religion of Protestants* (1638) 375.

though far from universal, was much higher at the end of the Tudor era than at the start). While the emergence of the English Bible itself is the subject of the next chapter in the present volume, the exploration of the context for that process, with particular reference to the Old Testament, is the subject of this one.

Although the Bible was largely a closed book around 1500, people were by no means entirely ignorant of its contents.[3] England and Scotland were semi-literate societies whose culture remained predominantly oral and visual. In both countries, scenes and stories derived from the Old Testament (often via secondary sources) were widely represented in the visual arts and drama. The quality and quantity of such provision varied widely. There was more and finer decoration in England than in Scotland, more in towns than in the country, more in the castles and houses of the wealthy than in the hovels and huts of the rural poor. Nor was all religious art scriptural, much less Old Testament. In windows and wall-paintings, votive depictions of Christ, Our Lady, and the saints predominated.[4] Nevertheless, scriptural scenes were to be found. At their finest, as in the programme of parallel Old and New Testament scenes which fill the early Tudor stained glass windows in the chapel of King's College, Cambridge, these representations could be theologically sophisticated as well as aesthetically brilliant. Nor were such media confined to churches or clerical establishments. The tapestries and hangings with which the wealthy decorated their walls were as likely to depict scriptural scenes as mythical and historical ones. Lady Margaret Beaufort's hangings included depictions of Saul, Samson, and Nebuchadnezzar's Feast.[5] Nicholas West, Bishop of Ely (1515–33), possessed a fine collection of biblical, classical, and historical tapestries, including some telling the stories of Moses and Solomon.[6] The best collection was of course that of Henry VIII, whose dozens of arrases, hangings, and tapestries (some of which had previously belonged to Cardinal Wolsey) depicted Old Testament scenes and figures ranging from Abraham to Zacharias.[7]

Religious drama was one of the highlights of fifteenth-century English culture. Though based mainly in the towns and organised by their guilds, especially in the large and wealthy towns such as York and Chester, it had a far wider reach, both because players took drama into the villages and because

---

[3] As D. DANIELL notes in his article, "William Tyndale, the English Bible, and the English Language", in: The Bible as Book (2000) 39–50, at 41. His subsequent comment that before Tyndale "the darkness was almost total" presumably refers to the interpretation of Paul pioneered by Luther and popularised in English by Tyndale, which DANIELL, following Luther and Tyndale, describes as "the whole Bible".

[4] For some useful comments on windows, see M. H. CAVINESS, "Biblical stories in windows: were they Bibles for the poor?", The Bible in the Middle Ages (1992) 103–47.

[5] M. K. JONES / M. G. UNDERWOOD, The King's Mother: Lady Margaret Beaufort, Countess of Richmond and Derby (Cambridge: Cambridge UP 1992) 189.

[6] Letters and Papers 6, no. 625, inventory of Nicholas West, 11 June 1533.

[7] See The Inventory of King Henry VIII (ed. D. Starkey; London: Society of Antiquaries 1998) in the index under the headings arras (p. 448), pictures: religious (p. 491), tapestry: religious (p. 502), and textiles: linen diaper (p. 505).

towns acted as centres for the people of the surrounding countryside. The evidence amassed in the *Records of Early English Drama* shows us how widely and how often these plays were performed. Many of them retold biblical stories and were an important vehicle for knowledge of religion in general and of the Old Testament in particular. The Chester mystery cycle, for example, covered the Creation and Fall, Cain and Abel, Noah, Abraham and Isaac, Moses, and Balaam.[8] And the Cornish play *The Origin of the World* (or *Gwyrans an bys* in the Celtic language then still spoken in Cornwall) covers much the same ground. Even late in Elizabeth's reign it was reported that "The country people flock from all sides, many miles off, to hear and see it",[9] although by that time most such plays had fallen victim to the iconoclastic zeal of Protestant Reformers, which not only ended the performance tradition but destroyed countless texts. Nevertheless, in the surviving plays, the same biblical stories crop up again and again. Though often taken from secondary sources (such as the *Historia scholastica* of Peter Comestor, or the fourteenth-century vernacular poem *Cursor mundi*), and embroidered with pious imagination or dramatic business, these plays gave some sense of the course of salvation history. Scotland, like England, had a flourishing tradition of religious drama in the fifteenth century, and this presumably included biblical plays, as the Church of Scotland's General Assembly of 1574 specifically forbade vernacular plays on scriptural subjects. But no texts survive, as the Scottish Reformers apparently eliminated them all when they stamped out that medieval dramatic tradition in the reign of James VI.[10]

For the literate minority of the laity, the English Bible was not in any case completely inaccessible. The 'Lollard Bible' was available in restricted circles despite its official prohibition early in the fifteenth century. For that prohibition was not absolute, but left some limited scope for the possession and reading of the Scriptures in English subject to the approval of the bishop. The extraordinarily large number (around 250) of surviving manuscripts of the English Scriptures suggests that such approval could indeed be granted. However, most of these manuscripts are individual books or groups of books rather than complete Bibles, and New Testament books predominate over Old Testament in those that survive. Such evidence as we have for the ownership of these manuscripts indicates that their owners were usually pious Catholics (including, for example, Henry VI), and also that authorised possession of the Scriptures was confined to the learned clergy and privileged sectors of lay society.[11] Thus only a very small minority of the people of England, whether Catholics or Lollards, had direct access to the Old Testament in the vernacular. In Scotland, the 'Lollard Bible' was all but unknown. It was not until the early six-

---

[8] *The Chester Mystery Cycle* 1–2 (ed. R. M. Lumiansky / D. Mills; Early English Text Society, suppl. series, 3 and 9; Oxford 1974–86).

[9] The Legend of the Rood (done into English verse with an introduction by F. E. Halliday; London: Duckworth 1955) 29.

[10] S. CARPENTER, "Early Scottish Drama", History of Scottish Literature 1 (1988) 199–212, esp. 201–02.

[11] Rex, Henry VIII and the English Reformation (1993) 108.

teenth century that Murdoch Nisbet made a Scots version of the Lollard Bible.[12]

There were other routes, however, by which literate layfolk might legitimately become acquainted with the outlines of the great stories of the Old Testament. The most obvious source was the chronicle. There were two main families of vernacular chronicle in late medieval Britain. One family, now known as the Middle English *Brut* (of which there are over 170 manuscripts extant), took as its starting point the mythical history of Britain, which was traced in sub-Virgilian fashion to Brutus, an exiled Trojan prince (the Scottish variant on this invoked a Greek prince and an Egyptian princess).[13] The other, following the aspirations to universal history often seen in ecclesiastical chronicles, took as its starting-point the creation of the world.[14] The leading instance of this was Ranulph Higden's fourteenth-century *Polychronicon* (translated into English in Chaucer's time), which drew together sacred, ancient, and mythical history with medieval English and French chronicles. Like many medieval texts, it struggled to draw the line between fact and fiction, between history and myth, a line which in any case Christian chroniclers would in principle have drawn in a different place from modern historians.[15] But it provided its readers with an adequate summary of the historical or mythical contents of the Old Testament. The fifteenth-century Scots chronicle, *The Sex Werkdays According to the Sex Agis*, was a text of similar scope.[16]

Thus the broad outlines of salvation history were available in a wide variety of late medieval texts. One of the most popular works of the fifteenth-century poet John Lydgate (a monk of Bury St Edmunds) was his *Fall of Princes* (a version of Boccaccio's *De casibus virorum illustrium*). A lengthy poem moralising on pride, fortune, and the vanity of human ambition through a series of biographical narratives, it intersperses biblical figures with mythical, classical, and historical subjects. Besides Adam and Eve we find Deborah, Gideon, Samson, Saul, Rehoboam, Jeroboam and the kings of Israel. The fourteenth-century devotional epic *Cursor mundi* (a vernacular work despite its Latin title), another widely-read text, was to a large extent a summary of the Bible.[17] In short, notwithstanding the limitations on access to the Bible as such, late medieval preachers were able to assume a fair degree of general knowledge

---

[12] The surviving manuscripts of the Lollard Bible are uniformly in southern dialects of English, and would have been difficult for northern English readers, let alone for the Scots, whose own language was at that time different in many respects from Chaucerian English. For Nisbet, see H. H. Meier, "A Pre-Reformation Biblical Paraphrase", *The Innes Review* 17 (1966) 11–23, at 19.

[13] For the Middle English *Brut*, see L. M. Matheson, The Prose Brut: the Development of a Middle English Chronicle (Tempe, AZ: Medieval & Renaissance Texts & Studies 1998). For Scotland, see M. P. McDiarmid, "The Metrical Chronicles and the Non-alliterative Romances", History of Scottish Literature 1 (1988) 27–38 at 27–30.

[14] There was a third class, the 'London chronicles', which were late medieval accounts of late medieval events from the metropolitan perspective. See McLaren, The London Chronicles (2002) for a thorough introduction to this third, essentially secular and vernacular, genre. Individual chronicles often in fact straddle these rather simplified boundaries.

[15] Levine, Humanism and History (1987), ch. 1, offers some penetrating insights into what is from our point of view the blurring of fact and fiction in much medieval historical writing. For a particular instance of this blurring in practice, see J. P. Carley, "A Glastonbury Translator at Work", *Glastonbury Abbey and the Arthurian Tradition* (ed. J. P. Carley; Cambridge: Brewer 2001) 337–45.

[16] R. J. Lyall, "Vernacular Prose before the Reformation", History of Scottish Literature 1 (1988) 163–81, at 170.

[17] *Lydgate's Fall of Princes* 1–4 (ed. H. Bergen; Early English Text Society, extra series, 121–24; London 1924–27); *Cursor mundi* (3 vols. in 7, ed. R. Morris; Early English Text Society, original series, 57, 59, 62, 66, 68, 99, 101; London 1874–93).

among their audiences. While there are hazards in seeking to use works of fiction as historical sources, perhaps one of Chaucer's greatest comic creations,
the Wife of Bath, can legitimately be adduced in evidence here. In the lengthy
prologue to her tale, she deploys a ready knowledge of women in the Old Testament to good comic effect. And although this can only testify properly to the
learning of Chaucer himself, it may nevertheless be fair to conclude that for
the Wife of Bath's character to ring true to his readers, the level of knowledge
she evinces must have been plausible to them.[18]

1.2. Theology

The creative and speculative theology which had flourished at Oxford in the
fourteenth century culminated in what was, from the point of view of the
church authorities, the spectacular disaster of John Wyclif. The determined
censorship with which the hierarchy responded to this threat not only kept the
vernacular Scriptures under tight control but also led to the abrupt termination
of that creative and speculative tradition both at Oxford and elsewhere. NI-
CHOLAS WATSON has documented this in the field of devotional literature,
where the great age of Rolle and Hilton gives way in the early fifteenth century
to the copying of established spiritual classics and the importation of foreign
works such as the *Imitatio Christi*. And J. I. CATTO has shown how academic
theology retreated into the safer domain of pastoral theology and preaching.[19]
Lectures on Peter Lombard's Sentences and on certain books of the Bible (predominantly the New Testament and the Psalms) remained the basis of the curriculum, but the lectures ran down familiar grooves, following the commentaries of Thomas and Scotus, or of Hugh of Vienne and Nicholas of Lyra. Original thought was no longer at a premium. The Cambridge Augustinian John
Capgrave was the most zealous expositor of Scripture in England after Wyclif
himself, commenting on most of the Old Testament.[20] Yet his own account of
his methods shows the limits of his ambition. He drew his literal exposition,
he tells us, largely from Augustine, Jerome, and Lyra, and his allegorical exposition from various ancient Fathers, adding occasional moral interpretation to
the mixture – all of this in Latin, even if some of his commentaries were dedicated to a layman, Duke Humphrey of Gloucester.[21] But both Duke Humphrey (Henry VI's uncle) and Capgrave were by way of being exceptions in the
chilly post-Wycliffite climate: Capgrave in even aspiring to sustained biblical
commentary; and Duke Humphrey (1391–1447), one of the earliest English

---

[18] I owe this observation to JAMES P. CARLEY.

[19] N. WATSON, "Censorship and Cultural Change in Late Medieval England: Vernacular
Theology, the Oxford Translation Debate, and Arundel's Constitutions of 1409", *Spec.* 70 (1995)
822–64; J. I. CATTO, "Theology after Wycliffism", History of the University of Oxford II (1992)
264–80.

[20] Bale, *Scriptorum ... catalogus* (1557–59), 660–61. For comment, see John Capgrave, The
Chronicle of England (1858) 323–27.

[21] *Johannis Capgrave Liber de illustribus Henricis* (1869) 231. For Duke Humphrey's role in
early English humanism see J. B. TRAPP, "The Humanist Book", The Cambridge History of the
Book III (1999) 285–315, at 293–96.

patrons of humanist scholars and scholarship (he bestowed his important collection of manuscripts upon the University of Oxford), in showing an interest in him. Most theologians confined themselves to compiling sermons or auxiliary works such as indexes, handbooks, and florilegia, while most laymen were happy to leave all such matters to the theologians.

The purpose of theology was identified in fifteenth-century England as the training of preachers.[22] As H. Leith Spencer has shown so compellingly, there was much more preaching going on in late medieval England than was formerly acknowledged in a historiographical tradition still dominated in part by echoes of Reformation controversies.[23] But while preaching was increasingly common in the fifteenth century, the parish ministry would not be a preaching ministry until at least 1600. A sermon was neither a compulsory nor even a common feature of a High Mass, and while there was also more Scripture in late medieval preaching than has previously been acknowledged, preaching was by no means confined to scriptural subjects, let alone to the Old Testament. The main occasions for preaching on Old Testament subjects were the eight Sundays from Septuagesima until Passion Sunday. Surviving sermons indicate that this would have been a means for many people to have gained some knowledge of the Old Testament. Two of the sermon collections most frequently found in the hands of clergymen, John Mirk's *Festial*, and Jacobus de Voragine's *Golden Legend*, provide very detailed summaries of Old Testament history in their sermons for those Sundays.[24]

The Tudor era unquestionably saw a significant increase in knowledge of the Old Testament in England and Scotland at both the popular and the academic level. Underlying this growth were two interdependent material causes – the advent of print and the diffusion of literacy. Both Renaissance Humanism and Reformation theology were to a considerable extent dependent on print and literacy for their character and their impact.[25] But for print, the philological advances of Lorenzo Valla might soon have been forgotten; nor would the radical liturgical changes imposed upon England in 1549 by the *Book of Common Prayer* have been feasible. Although the Bible itself was not printed in English until the 1530s, in the new political and cultural context afforded by Henry VIII's Reformation, nevertheless print had already done much to diffuse Old Testament knowledge. In 1484, William Caxton printed the *Polychronicon* in English, and he followed this in 1485 with the *Golden Legend*, both of them works which considerably increased the possibilities for knowledge of salvation history in the households of the literate.

---

[22] Catto, Theology after Wycliffism (1992) 264–67, esp. 264: "The duty of divines beyond the confines of the universities, in English practice, was primarily to preach and hear confessions". Catto sets this in the perspective of the post-Wycliffite reaction against speculative theology.

[23] Leith Spencer, English Preaching (1993) 60.

[24] *Mirk's Festial* (ed. Th. Erbe; Early English Text Society, extra series, 96; London 1905); *The Golden Legend* [from Caxton's edition] 1–3 (Hammersmith: William Morris 1892), I, 105 onwards.

[25] Eisenstein, The Printing Press 1–2 (1979), is excellent on the technical and intellectual implications of the rise of print, although in her enthusiasm for its revolutionary impact she overlooks its powerful conservative tendencies: the most frequently printed books in the later fifteenth century were liturgical texts. See also L. Jardine, *Worldly Goods* (London: Macmillan 1996), for a discussion of the place of print in the material as well as the intellectual culture of the Renaissance.

2. Renaissance Humanism

One of the consequences of the new intellectual stimulation brought about by humanism and by the advent of print was the re-emergence, after nearly a hundred years, of a native school of devotional writing in England. This did not fundamentally change the way that the Old Testament was used in such literature, but it did increase its diffusion. John Fisher's *Treatyse Concerninge the Fruytful Saynges of Dauyd*, published towards the end of Henry VII's reign, was the first sustained vernacular exposition of any part of Scripture in England since Wycliffite times. However, his treatise consisted of sermons rather than of academic commentary, and these sermons were rooted in the devotional framework of medieval Catholicism. The seven 'Penitential Psalms' which he took as his subject were a medieval devotional construct, not a natural division of the text, and Fisher did not even provide a complete English rendering of them, let alone a close one – he gave a partial paraphrase.[26] His interpretation was equally rooted in medieval devotion. These Psalms had been defined as "penitential", and Fisher's exposition played variations on this theme. His emphasis on human sinfulness and the need for repentance was far from the mechanistic ritualism which Protestant polemic subsequently – and falsely – attributed to Catholic theology and devotion. His call to conversion and a change of heart was as urgent as that of any Reformer. But his account of conversion presupposed the threefold framework of sacramental penance (contrition, confession, and satisfaction), and he frequently gave allegorical or 'tropological' readings of the texts in order to connect the world of the Psalms with that of the late medieval Church. The Old Testament figured in similar fashion in the writings of the devotional authors associated with Syon Priory near London. Many of these authors, like Fisher, had studied at Cambridge in the decades around 1500, and they were bookish men, familiar with the initial stirrings of humanism.[27]

Oxford, like Cambridge, was experiencing the first stirrings of humanism in the later fifteenth century. Having imbibed the doctrines and atmosphere of humanism in its Italian homeland, John Colet (whose earlier studies had been in Cambridge) proceeded to study theology at Oxford in the later 1490s. Although his lectures there were on Romans, and his later scriptural work concentrated on the Pauline Epistles, at some point he wrote a commentary on the first four chapters of Genesis, inspired by Pico and Ficino.[28] Burgeoning aca-

---

[26] For the sermons, see The English Works of John Fisher (1976) 1–267. For comment, see Rex, The Theology of John Fisher (1991) 34–39; and K. VAN KAMPEN, "Biblical Books and the Circulation of the Psalms in Late-Medieval England", in: The Bible as Book: the First Printed Editions (1999) 79–94, at 86–87.

[27] Catto, Theology after Wycliffism, 266 and 274 f. See also *Syon Abbey* (ed. V. Gillespie; Corpus of British Medieval Library Catalogues 9; London: British Library 2001), liii-liv, lviiii, and lxii.

[28] GLEASON suggests that this should be dated between 1512 and 1516, but while his arguments for the dating of surviving manuscripts of Colet's work are very strong, his arguments for the dating of the works in those manuscripts are not conclusive; Gleason, John Colet (1989) 67–92, esp. 90.

demic interest in the Old Testament was probably also part of what lay behind
Thomas More's lectures on Augustine's *City of God*, given in London in the
early sixteenth century. His later writings show a good knowledge of the Old
Testament, with More assuming his readers' acquaintance with the major stories, but taking the trouble to explain less familiar episodes.[29] John Longland,
an Oxford theology graduate, has left us a several sermons on various of the
Penitential Psalms preached at Henry VIII's Court in his capacity as the king's
confessor.[30] In short, the main impact of humanism in England at this time
was concentrated within the triangle formed by Oxford, Cambridge, and London – an intellectual topography which was to become very familiar over the
following centuries – and all three of those centres were home to increasing
numbers of humanist scholars.[31]

2.1. The Study of Hebrew

The most obvious change which the advent of humanism brought about in attitudes to the Old Testament was the stimulation of a new interest in Hebrew itself. Neither Greek nor Hebrew was widely studied in medieval Latin Christendom, and if anything it had probably been easier for scholars to acquire
Hebrew than Greek, thanks to the communities of Jews which were still to be
found in Spain, Germany, and Italy (though not in England and France,
whence they had been expelled in 1290 and 1394 respectively). The humanist
recourse *ad fontes*, when applied to the Scriptures, inevitably led students to
Hebrew as well as to the Greek which was integral to the programme of classical humanism. Although Erasmus showed little personal interest in the Old
Testament,[32] he insisted on the value of Hebrew to the theologian. The notion
of the *collegium trilingue* (the trilingual college, specialising in Latin, Greek,
and Hebrew) originated with his friend Jerome Busleiden, who founded such a
college at Louvain. It was certainly thanks to Erasmus's influence that the trilingual ideal was embodied in two new colleges founded in England in the
reign of Henry VIII: St John's College, Cambridge (1511) and Corpus Christi
College, Oxford (1515–16). Bishop Richard Foxe's statutes for Corpus Christi, issued in 1517, struck a mildly Erasmian note in requiring theology lectures

---

[29] G. MARC'HADOUR, "Scripture in the *Dialogue*", in: Thomas More, *A Dialogue Concerning Heresies* I-II (ed. Th. M. C. Lawler / G. Marc'hadour / R. C. Marius; *The Complete Works of St Thomas More* 6; New Haven: Yale UP 1981), II, 494–526, esp. 524.

[30] John Longland, *Psalmus centesi. pri. Expositio concionalis quinti psalmi poenitentialis prefati Ioannis Longlondi, coram maiestate regia. Annis do. 1523. 1524. 1525. 1526. 1527. 1528. 1529* (London: R. Redman? 1532. STC 16792). See also STC 16971, 16971.5, 16973, and 16973.5, for his sermons on Psalms 6, 31, 37, and 50. Longland's presentation copy for the king still survives. See *The Libraries of King Henry VIII* (ed. J. P. Carley; Corpus of British Medieval Library Catalogues 7; London: British Library 2000) 101.

[31] There is a vast literature on English Renaissance humanism. Useful points of departure are Weiss, Humanism in Fifteenth-Century England (1965); McConica, English Humanists and Re-formation Politics (1965); Fox and Guy, Reassessing the Henrician Age (1986); and Dowling, Humanism in the Age of Henry VIII (1986).

[32] Reventlow, The Authority of the Bible (1984) 44.

upon the New Testament and the Old Testament in alternate years, with the lectures following "ancient doctors" rather than medieval authorities such as Nicholas of Lyra.[33] But it was at St John's, founded by Lady Margaret Beaufort (Henry VIII's grandmother), and guided in its early years by John Fisher, a friend of Erasmus, that the trilingual programme was first set out in England. Fisher's statutes for St John's, promulgated in 1516, declared that some of the fellows should set about learning Hebrew and Greek as soon as possible.[34]

It was the scholar who first set about fulfilling Fisher's injunction who was to be the fountainhead of Hebraic scholarship in England. Robert Wakefield, initially self-taught, departed to further his studies at Louvain in 1518–19, and ended up teaching there briefly. After returning for a while to Cambridge, he set off for Tübingen to sit at the feet of Reuchlin himself. Arriving shortly after Reuchlin died (June 1523), Wakefield was asked to stay on and take his place. Meanwhile, Fisher persuaded Henry VIII to fund a lecture in Hebrew at Cambridge University, and with royal help Wakefield was persuaded to return to take up that post in 1524. His inaugural lecture, delivered that year but published a few years later, was a bold manifesto for the study of Hebrew, couched in that mixture of genuine scholarship with boasting and bombast which was to characterise all Wakefield's writings.[35] In its attempt to sell its subject to listeners and readers, the lecture gives the names of several influential Englishmen who had already studied Hebrew under Wakefield's tuition. They included John Stokesley (later Bishop of London), Thomas Hurskey (Master General of the Order of St Giles of Sempringham, an English monastic order), James Boleyn (a clerical uncle of Anne Boleyn), and Reginald Pole (later Cardinal Archbishop of Canterbury). Elsewhere, Wakefield also informs us that he had taught John Fisher.[36]

Part of the fascination of Hebrew for these early enthusiasts lay in the concept of the Kabbalah, the oral tradition of scriptural interpretation said in some schools of Judaism to hand on wisdom from the age of the Patriarchs and prophets, and expounded by Reuchlin in his De arte cabbalistica. Both Colet and Fisher were intrigued by the Kabbalah, and read Reuchlin's work.[37] Fisher went so far as to adduce the concept of the Kabbalah as part of his justification of ecclesiastical tradition against Luther's insistence on the authority of Scripture alone, and in addition cited a few rabbinical authorities in the course of his polemics.[38]

Among the sacred Scriptures, it was the Psalms and the Wisdom books that held a particular fascination for this first generation of Christian Hebraists. Perhaps the Wisdom literature provided a bridge between the philosophical learning of the ancient world, so dear to the humanists of the Renaissance,

---

[33] S. L. Greenslade, "The Faculty of Theology", in: The History of the University of Oxford, III (1986) 295–334, at 313.

[34] Early Statutes of St John's College, Cambridge (ed. J. E. B. Mayor; Cambridge: Cambridge UP 1859) 375.

[35] R. Rex, "The earliest use of Hebrew in books printed in England: dating some works of Richard Pace and Robert Wakefield", TCBS 9 (1990) 517–25.

[36] Wakefield, On the Three Languages (1989) 46f, 64f; and Syntagma de hebraeorum codicum incorruptione (London: W. de Worde s. a. [1534?]; STC 24946), sig. A3v.

[37] Gleason, John Colet (1989) 144–51.

[38] Rex, The Theology of John Fisher (1991) 59f.

and the world of the Old Testament. Certainly one can detect affinities between this trait among the Christian Hebraists and the huge popularity in the
sixteenth century of Erasmus's *Adages*, his ever expanding books of essays expounding proverbial wisdom. New translations and paraphrases of the Wisdom texts were produced in remarkable numbers in the early sixteenth century, both in England and abroad. After the Psalms, Ecclesiastes was an espe-
cial favourite. When the English humanist Richard Pace was studying Hebrew
at Syon Priory under Robert Wakefield in 1526–27, he cut his teeth on a new
version of Ecclesiastes. Pace had been anticipated in this by another English
Hebraist, Robert Shirwood, who had published his *Liber hebraeorum concionatoris, seu Ecclesiasten* at Antwerp in January 1523.[39]

Pace, with the bravado of the tyro, first produced a manifesto for his project, the *Praefatio in Ecclesiasten ad hebraicam veritatem recognitum.* This immediately, and perhaps unexpectedly, got him into trouble with none other than
John Fisher, for the arguments with which Pace sought to justify his own efforts to improve on Jerome's Vulgate proved far too much for the Bishop of
Rochester, who, though quite possibly a patron of Shirwood's earlier effort in
this line, was now acutely sensitive to the danger of heresy. In his enthusiasm
for Hebrew, Pace accused not only the Vulgate but even the Septuagint of inaccuracy. Fisher interpreted this as an implicit threat to the entire teaching
authority of the Catholic Church. It was not criticism of the Vulgate that both-
ered him – he had been vocal in his support for Erasmus's *Novum instrumentum* (1516), despite the outcry raised against it by ultra-conservative Catholics
such as Peter Sutor and Noel Beda. Nor was he an obscurantist: like many
others, he had written an open letter in support of Reuchlin in the controversy
over Hebrew books. Fisher, however, was aware that the "Old Testament of
the New Testament" was not the Massoretic but the Septuagint. In an elegant
but, as it turned out, unpublished treatise, Fisher argued against Pace that the
Greek text of the Septuagint was, as much as the Hebrew original, the product
of divine inspiration. This argument was bolstered with the legend of the seventy translators, drawn from the so-called *Letter of Aristeas* and corroborated
from an impressive range of patristic testimonies. Adding a theological argument to this historical case, he urged that, since the New Testament authors
almost always cited the Old Testament in a Septuagint rendering, to impugn
the inspiration and accuracy of the Septuagint was in fact to undermine the inspiration and authority of the Apostles and Evangelists.[40]

---

[39] It is interesting to note that two books by John Fisher, his *Convulsio calumniaru*m and his
Assertionis lutheranae confutatio, were both being seen through the press in Antwerp at this same
time, printed respectively by Vorsterman (November 1522) and Hillenius (January 1523), under
the supervision of Fisher's chaplain, John Addison. Shirwood may perhaps have been in Addison's
entourage.

[40] Rex, John Fisher's Treatise on the Septuagint (1992).

2.2. The 'King's Great Matter'

As with so much else in the history of Tudor England, so with the study of Hebrew and the Old Testament, the 'king's great matter' – Henry VIII's first divorce, from Catherine of Aragon – was a turning-point.

Disappointed by his first wife's failure to deliver him a son, Henry began to consider a divorce
in the mid-1520s, and sought grounds in the nature of his relationship to Catherine, formerly his
elder brother's wife. After Prince Arthur had died in 1502, a papal dispensation was obtained to
enable her to marry Henry, although this second marriage did not take place until 1509. Yet Leviticus stipulated at two points that a man should not marry his brother's wife (Lev 18:16 and 20:21),
and Henry now argued that the Pope had no authority to dispense anyone from such a clear scriptural prohibition. Catherine's advisers, however, drew attention to the contrary passage in Deuteronomy which positively enjoined such unions when a dying husband left behind a childless widow
(Deut 25:5). Since, for political reasons, the Pope was unable to deliver a prompt verdict, the exegesis and reconciliation of these apparently contradictory texts became a matter of the highest political moment.

Knowledge of Hebrew now became a career asset. Robert Wakefield found
himself catapulted from relative obscurity to a central role in the king's service.
He fell out with his former patron, John Fisher, who became the queen's chief
adviser, and abandoned his position at Cambridge for something very similar
at Oxford. When Henry restructured Wolsey's Cardinal College as King
Henry VIII's College in 1532, Wakefield was one of the founding fellows. In
the meantime, Wakefield was also busy at Court, not only teaching elementary
Hebrew to royal advisers, but also furnishing the royal case with valuable arguments from the original Hebrew, and writing treatises and opinions on the
king's side.

Wakefield was to publish four books over the next few years. The first was his inaugural lecture
as the king's reader in Hebrew at Cambridge. Then, probably in 1534, he issued a portion of a major treatise he wrote for the king against John Fisher in the matter of the divorce. And perhaps that
same year he put out a collection of little pieces which included his inaugural lecture at Oxford, a
polemic affirming the purity of the Hebrew Scriptures (which may have been originally designed as
a contribution to the abortive controversy between Fisher and Pace), and another tract on the divorce. These were followed in 1536 by his own contribution to the Hebraists' genre, paraphrases
of Ecclesiastes.[41]

The controversy over the divorce expanded well beyond the pages of Leviticus and Deuteronomy. The account of the marriages of Thamar to the sons of
Jacob (Genesis 38), which of course represents the implementation of the marriage custom of the levirate prescribed by Deuteronomy, became one bone of
contention. Another was the story of Ruth and Boaz (Ruth 3). In addition, the
case of Abraham and Sarah was invoked, on the grounds that, if Abraham had
lawfully married his own sister, then a fortiori marriage to a sister-in-law must
also be permissible under certain circumstances. It is unlikely that any question
of Old Testament interpretation had ever before aroused such sustained and
detailed critical scrutiny. The irony was that while the greatest expertise in He-

---

[41] For his inaugural lectures, see above, note 36. See also his *Kotser codicis* (London: T. Berthe-
let s. a. [1534?]; STC 24943); and *Paraphrasis in librum Koheleth* (London?: T. Gybson 1536; STC
24945).

brew lay on the king's side, in the person of Wakefield, his shameless prostitu-
tion of his skills to a dubious cause left the best exegesis on the queen's side.
For all Wakefield's ingenuity in arguing otherwise, the marital situation envisaged in Deuteronomy was precisely that in which Henry VIII found himself,
and the relevant stories in Genesis and elsewhere were instances of it. Henry's
case depended on identifying marriages such as his to Catherine as incestuous
and absolutely forbidden under divine and natural law: and the evidence of the
Old Testament simply did not bear this out. Fisher's treatises (among many
others) laid this out in remorseless detail, and his interpretation of the texts
was much the same as that which was worked out independently from the opposite end of the theological spectrum by William Tyndale.[42] There can be no
doubt that the queen's side won the argument.

2.3. Hebrew in the English and Scottish Universities

Regardless of the rights and wrongs of the case, however, the controversy over
the divorce put the Old Testament and Hebrew on the English political map.
As Wakefield recorded, Henry VIII now realised that Hebrew would henceforth be "absolutely necessary for future theologians".[43] Robert Wakefield
held his unestablished position as the 'king's reader' in Hebrew, first at Cambridge from about 1524, then at the king's Court, and finally, probably from
1532, at Oxford. It was not long after Wakefield's death in 1538 that Henry
decided to endow, among the 'Regius Professorships' which he founded at
both Oxford and Cambridge, a professorship in Hebrew at each. The first
professor at Cambridge was Robert Wakefield's younger brother, Thomas,
who inherited his brother's library as well as his talents and interests. At Oxford the first professor was John Shepreve (or Shepreth). Probably both of
them had been Robert's pupils, and both were anxious to convince Henry that
his money was being well-spent, and therefore sought to impress him with
samples of their work, presented, like many such offerings, as New Year's
gifts. Shepreth's effort was a rendering of the epistles of James and Jude into
Hebrew.[44] Thomas Wakefield's was a more substantial and adventurous piece
of scholarship, an analysis of Hebraisms discernible in the Greek of the New
Testament.[45] The books which survive from the library of the Wakefields include many Hebrew and Oriental texts, and the copious annotations which
both of them (especially Thomas) scrawled in the margins testify to their immense facility and familiarity with the languages. Though Robert, in particu-

---

[42] For an introduction to the controversy over Henry's marriage, see Le divorce du roi Henry
VIII (1987); The Divorce Tracts of Henry VIII (1988); Rex, Theology of John Fisher (1991) 162–
83; and V. Murphy, "The Literature and Propaganda of Henry VIII's First Divorce", in: The
Reign of Henry VIII (1995) 135–58.

[43] Wakefield, On the Three Languages (1989) 46 f.

[44] British Library Royal Manuscripts 7 C xvi (item 37) and 16 A ii are respectively the covering
letter of dedication to Henry VIII and the Hebrew version itself.

[45] Locutiones seu phrases que reperiuntur in novo testamento, British Library Additional Manuscript 5663, with a dedication to Henry VIII dated Christmas Day 1544.

lar, was extraordinarily arrogant (his inaugural lecture at Cambridge sneers at Luther's Hebrew scholarship with Olympian disdain, while in the controversy over the divorce he brushed aside Fisher's arguments with a tart reminder that he himself had taught the bishop what little Hebrew the latter actually knew), it seems that both men had plenty to be arrogant about.

Thomas Wakefield was a still more substantial scholar than his brother Robert, although he published nothing. But his Bomberg Bible, now in the library of Trinity College, Cambridge, contains a wealth of marginal annotations which testify to the range and solidity of his learning.[46] Cross-references to the 'Cotton Genesis' (now badly damaged, but once a fine Greek manuscript of Genesis) show that he was a master of textual collation.[47] The fact that he not only remained a layman but married and had numerous children serves as a salutary rebuke to many preconceptions about sixteenth-century scholarship and religion. For although a humanist of the first rank, and despite the vista of stellar promotion in the Church which would have been open to him had he followed the religious path of so many of his contemporaries, he remained a lifelong Catholic – prepared to accept the royal supremacy under Henry VIII, but not to abandon the Mass under Edward VI or Elizabeth I. If the history of English biblical study in the Tudor era tells us anything, it is that neither Catholics nor Protestants had a monopoly on scholarship.

The traditions of Hebrew scholarship which, thanks to Henry VIII's patronage, Robert Wakefield inaugurated in both the English universities were to prove enduring. At Oxford, Shepreve (d. 1542) was succeeded by Thomas Harding, who was followed in 1547 by Richard Bruerne. The revised statutes for the university issued in 1549 formally made Hebrew part of the curriculum for students of theology.[48] At Cambridge, Thomas Wakefield remained Regius Professor in name until the 1570s. But his profoundly Catholic religious sympathies saw him suspended from the exercise of his office under the Protestant regimes of Edward VI and Elizabeth I, during which times he was replaced by foreign Protestant Hebraists seeking a safe haven in England: Paulus Fagius, Immanuel Tremellius, and Antoine Chevalier.[49] Such movements were not all one way. Ralph Baynes, Robert Wakefield's successor as Hebrew lecturer in St John's College, Cambridge, was more loyal than his teacher to the guiding star of the college, John Fisher. Baynes fled the country in 1534 rather than accept Henry VIII's break with Rome, and his expertise was such that within a few years he was lecturing in Hebrew at the prestigious Collège du Roi in Paris – a position comparable to a Regius Professorship in England. Like his English counterparts, he was anxious to show that he was worth his salt, and in due course published a commentary on Proverbs as well as a Hebrew grammar.[50]

The evidence furnished by the inventories of scholars who died at Oxford and Cambridge confirms that Hebrew established a genuine place in the university curriculum in the Tudor era. The accounts of the Oxford bookseller John Dorne for the year 1520 record but a single sale of a Hebrew book. At Cambridge, Brian Rowe, a fellow of King's College who died in 1521, already pos-

---

[46] *Biblia rabbinica* (Venice: Bomberg 1521), Library of Trinity College, Cambridge, Adv. C.1.18. See J. P. CARLEY, "Religious controversy and marginalia: Pierfrancesco di Piero Bardi, Thomas Wakefield, and their books", TCBS 12 (2002) 206–45, at 241.

[47] J. P. CARLEY, "Thomas Wakefield, Robert Wakefield and the Cotton Genesis", TCBS 12 (2002) 246–65. The 'Cotton Genesis' itself is British Library MS Cotton Otho B vi.

[48] Greenslade, The Faculty of Theology (1986) 297, 316.

[49] Our knowledge of Tremellius has been considerably advanced by the recent dissertation of K. R. G. AUSTIN, "From Judaism to Calvinism: the Life and Writings of Immanuel Tremellius (1510–1580)" (St Andrews PhD diss., 2003).

[50] R. BAYNES, *In Prouerbia Salomonis tres libri commentariorum ex ipsis hebraeorum fontibus manantium* (Paris 1555) and *Prima rudimenta in linguam hebraeam* (Paris 1550).

sessed a copy of Reuchlin's Hebrew grammar. And one or two sales of Hebrew grammars and dictionaries are recorded in the fragmentary accounts of the Cambridge bookseller, Garrett Godfrey, in the later 1520s, once Wakefield had begun teaching there. Personal inventories at both Oxford and Cambridge show scholars owning such texts in the 1530s, and by the latter stages of the century this had become common. The evidence also shows that – perhaps because of the successive impact of Robert and Thomas Wakefield – enthusiasm for Hebrew took off more rapidly at Cambridge. Only three Oxford scholars before 1560 had Hebrew books (seven books in total) listed in their inventories, whereas in the same period about 30 Cambridge inventories listed Hebrew books numbering well over a hundred.[51]

The course of events in Scotland was somewhat different. The impact of humanism was later there, and coincided more closely with the advent of the Protestant Reformation. Moreover, because England took the lead in rejecting first the Papacy and then the Mass, the cause of the Reformation in Scotland tended to be associated with English political and cultural influence. It was not for nothing that dissent in Scotland in the 1540s was linked with what the hierarchy saw as the problem of 'English books'. There is no firm evidence for the study of Hebrew in Scotland prior to the onset of the Reformation. The changes in the cultural significance of the Old Testament there were entirely driven by Protestantism. Although the Catholic humanist Archibald Hay, appointed Principal of St Andrews University in 1546, aspired to make St Andrews a trilingual college, his hopes died with him at the Battle of Pinkie in 1547.[52] Similar aspirations towards the study of Hebrew were voiced, increasingly by Protestants, in the 1550s and 1560s, but it was not until Andrew Melville returned in the 1570s from years of study first at Paris and then at Geneva that this aspiration could become a reality. Appointed Principal of Glasgow University in 1574, Melville set about teaching Hebrew, and, like Robert Wakefield before him in England, personally inaugurated an enduring tradition. His nephews, James and Philip, took up the language as though it was a family trade, and when he himself moved from Glasgow to St Andrews in 1580, he introduced the subject there as well. Marischal College at Aberdeen, founded in 1593, was governed by statutes modelled on those Melville drafted for Glasgow and St Andrews, as was Edinburgh, and by 1600 Hebrew was available at all four Scottish universities.[53] And the evidence of book ownership in the later sixteenth century shows that the clerical elite were availing themselves of this opportunity.[54]

Thus, by the end of the sixteenth century, the scholarly culture of scriptural study in both England and Scotland was dominated by a conception of the primacy of the original scriptural languages. For Andrew Melville, the presiding

---

[51] Lloyd Jones, Discovery of Hebrew, Appendix III. See below, n. 76, for an edition of the Cambridge inventories. See also *Garrett Godfrey's Accounts, c. 1527–1533* (ed. E. Leedham-Green / D. E. Rhodes / F. H. Stubbings; Cambridge: Cambridge University Library 1992), esp. 76f.

[52] J. Durkan, "Education: the Laying of Fresh Foundations", in: Humanism in Renaissance Scotland (1990) 123–60, at 154f.

[53] J. Durkan / J. Kirk, *The University of Glasgow 1451–1577* (Glasgow: University of Glasgow Press 1977) 267–77, 290–91, 311, 320, and 333. See also J. Kirk, "Melvillian reform in the Scottish Universities", in: The Renaissance in Scotland (1994) 276–300.

[54] J. Durkan / A. Ross, "Early Scottish libraries", *The Innes Review* 9 (1958) 5–167, esp. 54, 85, 89, 115, 138, 140, and 160.

genius of Scottish university education, theology had to be based on the study of Scripture in the original Hebrew and Greek, "from which to resort to Latin or vernacular editions in controversies is practically foolish and impious".[55] For Laurence Chaderton, a central figure in late Tudor Cambridge, the first of the gifts necessary for the student of divinity was "the knowledge of tongues especially of the Hebrew and Greek wherein God hath revealed and written his will and Testament by his prophets and Apostles".[56]

2.4. The Old Testament in Politics

While Henry VIII's divorce gave a lasting stimulus to the study of Hebrew, his break with Rome sharpened the perceived relevance of the Old Testament. Much of the intellectual foundation and popular propaganda for the royal supremacy was derived from the histories and Wisdom literature of the Old Testament. In seeking to justify the overthrow of papal jurisdiction which was a prerequisite of the sentence annulling his marriage to Catherine of Aragon, the evident authority over their priests of such Old Testament kings as Josiah, Hezekiah, and Solomon was an invaluable model. As Cardinal Reginald Pole was assured by two of Henry's bishops, John Stokesley and Cuthbert Tunstall, Henry's status as supreme head of the Church of England simply allowed him to act "as the chiefe and best of the kinges of Israll did, and as all good Christian kings ought to doe".[57] Henry himself came to identify very strongly with King David. A manuscript psalter produced for his private use actually depicts David in Henry's likeness, and Henry expressed a particular interest in commentaries on the Psalms, commissioning them from, among others, Erasmus, John Fisher, John Longland, and Richard Sampson.[58]

The political earthquake of Henry's divorce, with its recurrent aftershocks through the 1530s and 1540s, brought a particular new pressure to bear on life at Court. This is reflected in the Court culture of the mid-Tudor years, and especially in the role played by the literature of the Old Testament in enabling courtiers and others to cope with the hazards of their life.[59] Sir Thomas More's 'Tower works' from the years 1534–35 already strike some of these

---

[55] Kirk, Melvillian reform (1994) 298, citing Melville's *Scholastica diatriba de rebus divinis* (Edinburgh: R. Waldegrave 1599).

[56] P. Lake, *Moderate Puritans and the Elizabethan Church* (Cambridge: Cambridge UP 1982) 36, citing Chaderton. See also 94 for the similar views of William Whitaker.

[57] "A Letter written by Cutbert Tunstall, late Bishop of Duresme, and Iohn Stokesley, sometime Bishop of London ... to Reginald Pole Cardinall", in: *A Newyeares Gifte* (ed. B. G.; London: H. Bynneman 1579), sigs. A1r-C4r, at C2v.

[58] See P. Tudor-Craig, "Henry VIII and King David", in: *Early Tudor England: Proceedings of the 1987 Harlaxton Symposium* (ed. D. Williams; Woodbridge: Boydell 1989) 183–205, esp. 192–93 and 195–98; and J. N. King, "Henry VIII as David: the King's Image and Reformation Politics", in: *Rethinking the Henrician Era* (ed. P. C. Herman; Urbana: University of Illinois Press 1994) 78–92, at 83–85. The psalter itself is British Library Royal MS 2 A xvi, and the picture is conveniently available on the cover of Haigh, English Reformations (1993).

[59] I owe the ideas in this paragraph to the kindness of Andrew W. Taylor of Churchill College, Cambridge, who is engaged on a study of the cultural role of the Psalms in early Tudor England, with particular attention to their place in Court culture and poetry.

new notes. His *Dialogue of Comfort against Tribulation*, a work of political as well as of devotional reflection and consolation, is in part a commentary on Psalm 90. The Psalms and the Wisdom literature, already growing in vogue before the break with Rome, were appropriated in new ways by the mid-Tudor generation of Sir Thomas Wyatt and Henry Howard (Earl of Surrey). Wyatt's verse paraphrases of the seven Penitential Psalms derive recognisably from the medieval tradition represented by Fisher and Longland, yet also evince a still more subjective personal response to the text, characteristic of the humanist sensibilities of the Renaissance. The intensity of Court life in the 1530s brought home to many courtiers their peculiar vulnerability before the extension and withdrawal of the grace of their unpredictable and often implacable sovereign, and the biblical paraphrases of Wyatt and Howard served to capture this sense of danger.[60] Recitation of and meditation on the Psalms became a favourite way of emotionally and intellectually negotiating the political rapids. Savonarola's exposition of the *Miserere mei* (Psalm 50[51]), already widely read in academic circles, became still more popular from 1535, translated into English and included in several devotional compilations.[61]

The early Tudor Court was becoming, in a way that the medieval Court had never been, the cultural crucible of England, and, like the Reformation itself, cultural appropriations and uses of the Old Testament spread to a wider audience thanks to their prominence at Court. For example, Sternhold's metrical Psalms, having started life at the Court in the 1540s, became one of the great monuments of English popular culture over the following two centuries, and were printed more often than any other book in the following 150 years.[62] By a similar process, Clément Marot's vernacular Psalms inspired the Huguenot metrical Psalms which rapidly became a characteristic feature of French Protestant culture.

The relentless invocation of Old Testament kingship in justification of the royal supremacy played a large part in the momentous decision to authorise the publication of the Bible in English. Given that the Old Testament provided models of godly kingship and that the New Testament inculcated obedience to the civil power, the utility of the vernacular Bible in promoting civil order and social discipline appeared undeniable. It was of course evangelical theologians who were especially keen on recommending this policy to the king. John Hooper summed up the case in dedicating his sermons on Jonah to the young Edward VI in 1550:

Nor ever had God in heaven, or king upon the earth, such a friend as is the holy Bible; for it teacheth the people and subjects of the realm fear of God, obedience to the king's majesty and his magistrates, and all mutual and fraternal love.[63]

In Scotland, the Old Testament was not harnessed in the same way to a monarchical ideology. Politically, the Scottish Reformation was driven by the nobles and lairds rather than by the crown, against which it was ranged during the regency of Mary of Guise and the reign of Mary Stewart, and of which it

---

[60] J. SIMPSON, *Reform and Cultural Revolution*, The Oxford English Literary History 2, *1350–1547* (Oxford: Oxford UP 2002) 322–29, 499–501.

[61] C. C. BUTTERWORTH, *The English Primers (1529–1545)* (Philadephia: University of Pennsylvania Press 1953), 66–69, 80, 131–32, 149, 172–73.

[62] King, Henry VIII as David (1989) 84; Green, Print and Protestantism (2000) 503.

[63] Hooper, Early Writings (1843) 441.

needed to take little account during the long minority of James VI. James himself, despite his education at the hands of George Buchanan, was much taken with the Old Testament vision of kingship worked out in the English context, and adopted it wholeheartedly on his move to England.[64] But Calvinism of a distinctly republican or at least aristocratic variety dominated Scottish theology, where, following the example of John Knox, attention was focussed more on the prophets who admonished kings than on the kings themselves. While Old Testament kingship predominated in the English context, it was the concept of the 'covenant', as originally worked out by Swiss exegetes in their reading of salvation history, which struck particularly resonant chords in Scottish culture. It harmonised with the traditional political instrument of the 'bond' (or 'band'), by which nobles contracted with each other to pursue political goals (which could vary widely in legality and still more in morality). The idea of the chosen people covenanted with God underlay the National League and Covenant with which the Scots withstood what they saw as the rising tide of popery and idolatry advancing towards them under the guidance of Archbishop William Laud of Canterbury during the reign of Charles I. In both England and Scotland, in different ways, readings of the Old Testament helped form a sense of the Christian people as a new Israel, in short, as an "elect nation".[65]

3. The Protestant Reformation

Both England and Scotland felt the impact of the way in which Protestant theology changed the understanding of the Old Testament. Before the Reformation, the uses of the Old Testament were essentially moral and allegorical. Indeed, as JOSEPH LEVINE has argued, it was precisely because analysis and argument were focussed upon allegory and moralising that fact and fiction were used so indiscriminately by preachers and commentators.[66] Preachers and devotional writers drew upon the stories of the Old Testament, just as they drew upon saints' lives, history, legend, and fiction, to illustrate their accounts of virtue and vice. Richard Whytford, for example, inevitably put forward Job as "one great champion & syngular exeample of pacience" in his treatise on that virtue.[67] More esoterically to modern eyes (though perfectly ordinarily in the context of late medieval culture), the Old Testament was drawn upon to illuminate the power and wisdom of God, who had literally adumbrated or foreshadowed in the events and words of the Old Testament the mysteries of salvation embodied in Jesus Christ and communicated to the faithful through his

---

[64] A. STEWART, *The Cradle King: a Life of James VI and I* (London: Chatto & Windus 2003) 147–49, 187 f.

[65] Haller, Foxe's Book of Martyrs (1963).

[66] Levine, Humanism and History (1987), ch. 1.

[67] Richard Whytford, *The Boke of Pacience* ([1541] facsim. edn.; Salzburg Studies in English Literature. Elizabethan & Renaissance Studies 92:18; Salzburg: Institut für Anglistik und Amerikanistik, Universität Salzburg / Lewiston, NY: Edwin Mellen Press 1991) fol. 31r.

mystical body, the Church. John Colet presented the Synagogue of the Old
Testament as the shadow cast back by the Church, which herself stood in the
full sunlight of Christ.[68] In similar fashion John Fisher felt able to call upon
the Old as well as the New Testament in defending papal primacy against
Martin Luther. Explaining that the Old Testament stood in relation to the
New much as the shadow in relation to the tree which cast it, he foreshadowed
the relationship of Jesus and Peter in the ancient relationship of Moses and
Aaron.[69] In his unfinished Latin paraphrase of the Psalms, Fisher found reason in the text to address most major aspects of Catholic doctrine.[70] Thus the
early Tudor Catholic humanists saw no need to abandon the heritage of scholasticism in their enthusiasm for humanism. John Longland, preaching in 1525
at the opening of Cardinal's College, Oxford (designed as a showpiece of humanist learning and education), took as his text Prov 9:1-2, and identified the
traditional four senses of Scripture as the four courses of the feast with which
Wisdom had furnished her table.[71] Such modes of argument became increasingly alien in the context of the Protestant Reformation. William Tyndale was
scathing in his assault on Fisher's Old Testament parallel for papal primacy in
his *Obedience of a Christen Man* (1528), insisting more generally that doctrinal
argument could be based only on the literal sense of the Scriptures.[72]

The most dramatic impact of the Protestant Reformation in Old Testament scholarship was
quite simply the explosion in biblical commentary. Until the early sixteenth century, few commentaries on Old Testament books had been printed, and fewer still were being newly written. Nicholas of Lyra, Hugh of Vienne, and the *Glossa ordinaria* were of course widely available. And the
massive revival of the early Christian Fathers which set in from about the time of Amerbach's landmark edition of Augustine's *Opera omnia* (1-10; Basel 1490-1506) made patristic commentaries
more widely available. Erasmus's main contribution to Old Testament scholarship lay here, at second-hand, in the publication of the commentaries of men such as Jerome, Hilary, and Origen. But
Erasmus, like John Fisher and indeed the ancient Fathers, remained wedded to the moral and allegorical methods of reading the Old Testament.[73]

It was Luther's revolutionary approach to the Scriptures, summed up in his
dichotomy between 'Law' and 'Gospel', that set exegesis on a new footing.
Starting with his early efforts on Galatians and Psalms, he and his successors
poured out innovative commentaries on book after book of the Bible, and
these works were soon being bought in England. The development of 'covenant' theology by the theologians of Zurich and their followers put another
powerful exegetical tool into the hands of young scholars. The new hermeneutics of Protestant theology were an integral element in its overall appeal, espe-

---

[68] John Colet, *Two Treatises on the Hierarchies of Dionysius* (ed. J. H. Lupton; London: Bell &
Daldy 1869) 7, 169. For more on Colet's use of allegory, see Gleason, John Colet (1989) 154-57.
[69] *English Works of John Fisher, Bishop of Rochester (1469-1535): Sermons and Other Writings,
1520-1535* (ed. C. A. Hatt; Oxford: Oxford UP 2002) 79-81.
[70] London, Public Record Office, SP2/R, fols. 28-272. See also Rex, Theology of John Fisher
(1991) 81f.
[71] John Longland, *Tres conciones* (London: Pynson c. 1529) fol. 33v, a reference I owe to Colet,
Two Treatises on the Hierarchies (1869) 106.
[72] Tyndale, Obedience (1528), fols. LVIr-LVIIv, LXr, and LXIv.
[73] Reventlow, Authority of the Bible (1984) 43f.

cially in the heady early days of the Reformation, when the new ideas were still liberating concepts rather than dogmatic straitjackets. Nor was the appeal of the new hermeneutics confined to the academic world. It was soon evident also at the royal Court, where George Boleyn presented his sister, Queen Anne Boleyn, with a French commentary on Ecclesiastes which derived ultimately from the labours of Johannes Brenz.[74]

One of the earliest presentations of the Law/Gospel dichotomy to an English audience was in the frontispiece of the Coverdale Bible, the first complete Bible printed in English. The frontispiece, modelled on a German design, matches a sketch of Moses handing down the Law with a sketch of Jesus preaching his Gospel of healing and forgiveness. Interestingly, while Henry VIII's Great Bible followed the Coverdale Bible in showing the king handing out the Scriptures to his people, it replaced the Law/Gospel motif with a less than subtle depiction of ministers preaching to the people a Gospel of obedience, enforced by the secular magistrates.[75] The Lutheran doctrine of political obedience to the prince was far more welcome to Henry than the Lutheran doctrine of justification by faith alone, which he never accepted. Lutheran hermeneutics infiltrated English culture by other routes, such as Tyndale's *Obedience*, which instructs readers on how to read the Bible, and the unpublished *Tropes and Figures of Scripture* written in the 1530s by the evangelical preacher Thomas Swynnerton. Tyndale's prologues to those books of the Bible which he had managed to translate before his arrest in 1535 were derived largely from the prologues of Luther. However, while both Tyndale and Swynnerton had studied at Wittenberg in the 1520s, neither was an unswerving Lutheran along the lines of Robert Barnes or Alexander Alesius (see below).

The evangelicalism of the early English Reformation was in fact eclectic rather than narrowly confessional. The books which the evangelical activist Thomas Garrett was offering for sale at Oxford in 1527–28 show how wide a range of evangelical polemic and commentary was available, with authors including Luther, Bugenhagen, Jonas, Lambert, Zwingli, and Melanchthon. Subsequent Oxford inventories reveal rather less of this material, perhaps because the arrest of Garrett and his clients made Oxford students more cautious if not over what they read, then at least over whom they told about it. But the inventories of Cambridge scholars in the 1530s and 1540s show much the same pattern as Garrett's sales records. For example, John Chekyn (d. 1535) owned Luther on Deuteronomy and Melanchthon on Proverbs, while John Johnson (d. 1541) owned Brenz on Job and Ecclesiastes, and James Townley (d. 1543) owned Bucer on Zephaniah and Bugenhagen on the Psalms.[76]

---

[74] J. P. CARLEY, "Early Her moost lovyng and fryndely brother sendeth gretyng: Anne Boleyn's manuscripts and their sources", *Illuminating the Book: Makers and Interpreters: Essays in Honour of Janet Backhouse* (ed. M. P. Brown / S. McKendrick; London: British Library 1998) 261–80, esp. 263–66.

[75] The two pictures can be compared in M. ASTON, *The King's Bedpost* (Cambridge: Cambridge UP 1993), at 156f. See also King, Henry VIII as David (1989) 78–82; and T. C. STRING, "Henry VIII's Illuminated Great Bible", *Journal of the Warburg and Courtauld Institutes* 59 (1996) 315–24.

[76] Greenslade, The Faculty of Theology (1986) 314. For the Oxford inventories, see *Private Libraries in Renaissance England* II (ed. R. J. Fehrenbach / E. S. Leedham-Green; MRTS 105; Binghamton, NY 1993). For those from Cambridge, see Books in Cambridge Inventories 1–2 (ed. E. S. Leedham-Green; Cambridge: Cambridge UP 1986). For further comment on this material, see R. REX, "The Early Impact of Reformation Theology at Cambridge University, 1521–1547", *Reformation & Renaissance Review* 2 (1999) 38–71, esp. 39f, 60–62.

In terms of the scholarship actually done in England, it is not surprising to record that the Reformation initially stimulated work on the New Testament. It was not for nothing that the new movement called itself 'evangelical'. Thus George Stafford was lecturing on Romans in Cambridge as early as 1527. What broke the mould of theological instruction in the English universities were the "injunctions" (i.e. instructions) issued by agents acting under the authority of Thomas Cromwell (Henry VIII's 'vicegerent' or vicar-general in spirituals) during their visitations of the two universities in 1535. Their main objective was to ensure that the newly enacted royal supremacy of Henry VIII over the Church of England was accepted, and that its implications were clearly laid out and understood in the universities, the nursery of that church's hierarchy. Besides exacting personal oaths to the royal supremacy from both teachers and students, the visitors laid down some guidelines for teaching. The most significant of these for our purposes were the prohibition of the teaching of canon law (which embodied the authority of the papacy) and the requirement that henceforth all theology lectures were to be based on the Bible rather than on the Sentences of Peter Lombard.[77]

Shortly after the injunctions were issued, new lectureships at the two universities were introduced as standard-bearers for the new kind of theology. The two 'king's readers' in theology were Richard Smyth at Oxford and Alexander Alesius at Cambridge. Smyth was renowned throughout his career as an exponent of the 'old learning', Alesius (a Scot who had taken refuge in England) as an exponent of the 'new learning'.[78] Both ended their lives as refugees abroad, Alesius as Professor of Theology at Lutheran Leipzig, Smyth as Professor of Theology at the new Catholic University of Douai. Alesius resigned his post at Cambridge in 1536, disillusioned by the conservative aspects of Henry VIII's Ten Articles of religion, and discouraged by the frosty reception accorded to his teachings. During his brief tenure (1535–36), he had chosen to lecture on the Psalms, and a polished version of his lectures survives, showing that he was thoroughly versed in the expositions of Luther and Melanchthon. His commentary on the first 25 Psalms was the fullest presentation of Lutheran theology thus far produced in England – albeit in Latin, by a Scot, and unpublished.[79] Smyth's tenure at Oxford was rather longer. He retained the post when it was established on a permanent basis in 1540 as the Regius Professorship of Divinity, but he was eventually dispossessed in favour of Peter Martyr Vermigli in 1549 under the Protestant regime of Edward VI. We have no evidence about the content of his lectures at Oxford, but it is overwhelmingly likely that he fulfilled the royal injunctions by lecturing on Scripture. We know from his later work at Douai that, notwithstanding his reputation as a scholastic, he lectured on Scripture – but he probably concentrated on the New Testament, and his theology was unequivocally traditional in content, usually with a sharp polemical edge against the Reformation.[80]

When the Protestant Reformation suddenly became 'official' under Edward VI, there was a further surge in scriptural exegesis at the universities and elsewhere. The New Testament, of course, was the initial focus, in particular the Epistles of Paul. Peter Martyr lectured on Corinthians in Oxford, while at

---

[77] F. DONALD LOGAN, "The First Royal Visitation of the English Universities, 1535", *English Historical Review* 106 (1991) 861–88, esp. 882f. 'Injunctions' is the technical term for the binding instructions issued by duly accredited agents during formal visitations of ecclesiastical institutions.

[78] This kind of balancing act between the old learning and the new was a recurrent feature of Henry VIII's policy after the break with Rome. See D. MacCulloch, "Henry VIII and the Reform of the Church", in: The Reign of Henry VIII (1995) 159–80, at 174–77.

[79] Wiedermann, Der Reformator Alexander Alesius (1988) includes a critical edition of the text.

[80] Löwe, Richard Smyth (2003).

Cambridge Martin Bucer lectured on Ephesians. However, the Old Testament was not neglected. Bucer also lectured on Micah outside term.[81] John Hooper's sermons on Jonah, preached before Edward VI at Court in Lent 1550 and published later that year, were the first sustained piece of original vernacular commentary on the Old Testament to be published in Reformation England. Hooper was not alone. Anthony Gilby published vernacular commentaries on Malachi and Micah in the early 1550s, and English Protestant interest in the Old Testament intensified during the reign of Mary Tudor, as the parallels between the Babylonian captivity and their own experience struck the exiles with irresistible force. As a refugee in Geneva, James Pilkington extended his interests from the New Testament (on which he had lectured in Cambridge as Lady Margaret's Professor) to the Old Testament, expounding to the English community there not only the Epistles of Peter but also Proverbs and Ecclesiastes. On his return to England, he served briefly as Regius Professor of Divinity at Cambridge before becoming Bishop of Durham. Despite his diocesan commitments, he found the time to publish English commentaries on Haggai (1560) and Obadiah (1562), and a further commentary on Nehemiah appeared posthumously (1585). These texts are predictably Protestant in their theological tendencies, vigorous presentations of law and gospel, faith and predestination, with liberal helpings of antipapal polemic.[82] Elizabeth's reign saw the translation of massive biblical commentaries and sermon-cycles such as Calvin on Genesis, Deuteronomy, and Isaiah, and Beza on Job, as the Protestantism of the Church of England aligned itself with the Reformed Churches of Europe.

Although the Protestant Reformation had undoubtedly sparked off the widening and deepening of interest in the Old Testament, and had added a powerful stimulus to the humanistic interest in Hebrew, neither Old Testament scholarship nor Hebrew were the exclusive preserve of Protestant theologians and writers in sixteenth-century Britain. At the popular level, Catholics were inspired to attempt vernacular verse paraphrases of the Scriptures, such as William Forrest's account of Joseph, or George Makeson's version of Genesis.[83] John Young, the driving force of the restoration of Roman Catholicism in Cambridge under Mary Tudor, presented a commentary on the prophet Joel to Cardinal Reginald Pole during the latter's visitation of the university during the winter of 1556–57.[84] Educated as he had been in a theology school whose curriculum had been shaped by the injunctions of 1535, it may be that this commentary derived in some way from lectures he gave while serving at Cambridge as the Regius Professor of Divinity. The Regius Professor of Hebrew, Thomas Wakefield, was able once more to discharge his duties during the Catholic interlude of Mary's reign, and the Hebraist Ralph Baynes returned to England under Mary to become Bishop of Coventry and Lichfield. George Bullock, another Cambridge Catholic humanist, made a life's work of the compilation of a massive concordance to the entire Bible. Although the work which he finally published at Antwerp in 1572 was almost certainly begun afresh after he lost everything to pirates during his flight from England in 1559, the impulse to the study of Scripture which it represented was certainly something which he owed to his education at Cambridge, and it is equally certain that Scripture will have remained the basis of his teaching in the last years of his life, which he

[81] N. Scott Amos, "The Alsatian among the Athenians: Martin Bucer, Mid-Tudor Cambridge, and the Edwardian Reformation", *Reformation & Renaissance Review* 4 (2002) 94–124, at 100.

[82] *The Works of James Pilkington* (ed. J. Scholefield; Cambridge: Parker Society 1842).

[83] Forrest's history of Joseph is British Library Royal MS 18 C xiii. For Makeson's Genesis see Meier, A Pre-Reformation biblical paraphrase (1966).

[84] Bodleian Library, Rawlinson MS C 45, *Enarrationes Joelis prophetae*, with the dedication dated 13 November 1556.

spent as theology lecturer at the monastery of Ninove.[85] The Catholic refugees included many men whose interest in the Scriptures had been nourished in the mid-Tudor universities. Thomas Harding, the second Regius Professor of Hebrew at Oxford, having abandoned his earlier evangelical commitments in the reign of Mary, was the most illustrious of those who fled Oxford for Louvain rather than subscribe to the Elizabethan Settlement. Another Oxford theologian, Gregory Martin, was to lead the project which resulted in an official Catholic translation of the Bible into English. He himself worked on the New Testament (1582), and by 1609 the Old Testament was also officially available to English Catholics in their own tongue. Post-Reformation English Catholicism, in short, showed few signs of that outright hostility to the vernacular Bible which was voiced (though not endorsed) at the Council of Trent.

That said, the impact upon British hebraic scholarship of the political and theological divisions fomented by the Reformation was not entirely positive. While both Protestants and Catholics, in their different ways, developed a far deeper interest in Hebrew and the Old Testament, this interest was channelled into doctrinal theology, theological polemic, and biblical translation (and the editorial annotations in, for example, the Geneva Bible and the Douai Bible showed how much even translation could be driven by a polemical agenda). The Wakefield brothers had blazed a trail towards serious and original philological scholarship on the Hebrew Bible, but as theological and scholarly energies were directed towards more pressing issues, their lead would not really be followed in Britain until well into the seventeenth century.

In the reigns of Queen Elizabeth and King James, nevertheless, the Old Testament entered into the marrow of the British bodies politic, penetrating both popular and elite culture. At the private level, it can be seen in the christening of children with Old Testament names (and at times even with words or phrases used as names), a custom that had become fashionable by the end of the sixteenth century and would be famously satirised by Ben Jonson. At the public level, ALEXANDRA WALSHAM has documented the readiness with which Elizabethan and Jacobean preachers identified England with Israel, and were thus able to apply the prophetic rhetoric of the Old Testament almost without mediation to their own times and their own audiences.[86] The anti-catholicism which pervaded politics and culture at every level in both England and Scotland was shot through with a horror of idolatry – with which 'popery' was automatically associated – a horror that was conceived and expressed in entirely Old Testament terms. The sabbatarianism which was to be a unique feature of British religious culture until within living memory was a direct fruit of that close engagement with the Old Testament. Only in the English-speaking world did the traditional Christian analogy of Sunday and Sabbath collapse into an identification so literal that the word 'sabbath' came to refer primarily to Sunday rather than to Saturday. Indeed, in the late sixteenth and early seventeenth centuries the fringes of the English religious scene saw the first stirrings of eccentric religious developments which included a movement for the observance of Saturday as the Christian day of rest. Such eccentricities briefly ran riot in the false dawn which followed the dismantling of the Church of

---

[85] Rex, Lady Margaret Beaufort and her Professorship (2003) 51–56.
[86] Walsham, Providence in Early Modern England (1999) 281–325. See also Haller, Foxe's Book of Martyrs (1963).

England after Charles I's defeat in the English Civil War. While the mid-seventeenth-century proliferation of sects lies beyond the scope of this paper, it is worth noting that many of them were founded upon a familiarity with the words and concepts of the Old Testament, and upon a ready identification of England or Scotland with Israel, which would have made them all but unthinkable during the Middle Ages.

Such eccentricities, which were periodically to resurface later in British history (one thinks in particular of the bizarre 'British Israel' theory), were, as much as mainstream scholarly study of the Hebrew Bible, a testimony to that profound engagement with the Old Testament which was the fruit of Christian Humanism and the Protestant Reformation in early modern Britain. The Bible was printed more frequently in England than in any other country during the early modern period.[87] In England and Scotland, at least, there really was some justification for Chillingworth's claim that the Bible was "the Religion of Protestants" – even if we must allow the qualification upon which their Catholic adversaries insisted, namely that it did not mean the same religion to all Protestants.

---

[87] Green, Print and Protestantism (2000) 42–100 on English Bibles.

CHAPTER TWENTY-ONE

History and Impact of English Bible Translations

By Henry Wansbrough, Oxford

Sources: Aelfric: *Lives of the Saints* (Early English Text Society; Oxford: Oxford UP 1966). –
Chronicon Henrici Knighton (ed J. R. Lumby; London: Eyre & Spottiswode 1889 and 1895). –
Myles Coverdale: *The Holy Scriptures, faithfully and truly translated by Myles Coverdale* (1535;
repr. from the copy in the library of HRH the Duke of Sussex; London: Bagster 1838). – *The Gospels: Gothic, Anglo-Saxon, Wycliffe and Tyndale versions arranged in parallel columns* (by Joseph
Bosworth; London: Gibbings & Co 1907). – Nicholas de Hereford: *The Books of Job, Psalms,
Proverbs, Ecclesiastes and the Song of Songs, according to the version made by Nicholas de Hereford and
revised by J. Purvey* (Oxford: Clarendon Press 1881). – John Wyclif: *Iohannis Wyclif Opus Evangelicum* (ed. Iohann Loserth; London: Trübner & Co 1895–96). – *Lindisfarne and Rushworth Gospels* (Surtees Society, vols. 28, 39, 43, 48; London 1854–65). – Gregory Martin: *The holie Bible
faithfully translated into English* (Doway: Laurence Kellam 1609–10); *The New Testament of Iesus
Christ* (Rhemes: Iohn Fogny 1582). – Thomas Mathewe: *The Byble...translated into Englishe by
Thomas Matthewe* (London: Thomas Raynalde 1537). – *The Old English Version of the Heptateuch*
(ed. S. J. Crawford; Oxford: Oxford UP 1922). – Sanctes Pagninus: *Biblia Veteris ac Novi Testamenti, summa fide ac studio singulari...ex Hebraeis Graecisque fontibus expressa* (Basileae per Tho-
mam Guarinum MDLXIIII). – *Paris Psalter* (ed. Bertram Colgrave; Copenhagen: Rosenkilde and
Bagger 1958); Th. Wright, *Reliquiae Antiquae* (London: Pickering 1845). – *Surtees Psalter* (Surtees Society, vols. 16, 19; London 1845 / 1847). – William Tyndale: *Tyndale's New Testament,
translated from the Greek by William Tyndale in 1534: in a modern-spelling edition...*(by David Daniell; New Haven: Yale UP 1989); *Tyndale's Old Testament, being the Pentateuch of 1530...trans-
lated by William Tyndale in a modern edition* (by D. Daniell; New Haven: Yale UP 1992). – William Whittingham: *The Geneva Bible, a facsimile of the 1560 edition* (London: University of Wisconsin Press 1969).

General works and studies: M. Aston, *Lollards and Reformers* (London: Hambledon Press 1984);
F. F. Bruce, *The English Bible* (London: Lutterworth Press 1963); *The Cambridge History of the Bi-
ble* [CHB] (Cambridge: Cambridge UP), 2. *The West from the Fathers to the Reformation* (ed. G.
W. H. Lampe; 1969, repr. 1980), 3. *The West from the Reformation to the Present Day* (ed. S. L.
Greenslade; 1963, repr. 1978); D. Daniell, *William Tyndale, a Biography* ([1994] New Haven:
Yale Nota Bene 2001); M. Deanesly, *The Lollard Bible* (Cambridge: Cambridge UP 1920); I.
Green, *Print and Protestantism in Early Modern England* (Oxford: Oxford UP 2000); R. Griffiths
(ed.), *The Bible in the Renaissance* (Aldershot: Ashgate 2001); Chr. Hill, *The English Bible and the
Seventeenth Century Revolution* (London: Allen Lane 1993); G. Lloyd Jones, "People of the Book.
King James' Men", *Scripture Bulletin* 35 (2005) 31–41; L. Long, *Translating the Bible* (Aldershot:
Ashgate 2001); A. McGrath, *In the Beginning* (New York: Doubleday 2001); J. F. Mozley, *Cov-
erdale and his Bibles* (London: Lutterworth Press 1953); A. Nicholson, *Power and Glory* (London:
HarperCollins 2003).

The genesis and consequences of English Bible translations during the five centuries from 1300 to 1800 are intimately interwoven with English political and
social history. In the first half of the period there were three important moments, each leading to a landmark translation, the Wycliffite Bible, the translations made during the reign of Henry VIII and the King James Version, com-

monly known as the 'Authorized Version'. Not to be neglected, and equally representative of political and social history, is the Catholic Rheims-Douai Version.

1. Anglo-Saxon Bible Translations

The translations of the Bible associated with John Wyclif were not without precedent. The first biblical translation into English is said to have been the Venerable Bede's translation of the Gospel of John from the beginning up to John 6:9, which his disciple and biographer Cuthbert says he completed on his deathbed. This translation has certainly not survived, and may have died with him – perhaps Bede's literary executors considered it unready for dissemination. In the following centuries, however, tentative beginnings were made, centred on the most-used books of the Bible, the Psalter and the Gospels. Notable are the Lindisfarne and Rushworth Gospels,[1] not true translations but more in the nature of glosses or aids to a reader who needs guidance through the Latin text: the vernacular words are written, one for one, over the top of the Latin text. The Lindisfarne gloss, in Old Northumbrian dialect, was added to the manuscript about 950, the Rushworth gloss, in Old Mercian, about 1000. A similar work is the Surtees Psalter,[2] an eighth-century manuscript with words in the Northumbrian dialect written over the Latin. To this was later added a metrical version of the Psalms, dating from around 1300; the beginning of Psalm 66 reads:

> Haf merci of me, God, haf merci of me,
> for my saule traistes in thee,
> and in schadw of thine wenges hope I sal.

Of the same genre is the magnificent Paris Psalter.[3] This contains a prose version of the Psalms in the West Saxon dialect, made possibly under the leadership of King Alfred (the style is more similar to his translation of Boethius than to any work of the other near-contemporary great translator Aelfric or Wulfstan). To this is added a mid-tenth century metrical version, in non-standard West Saxon, and of little literary merit.

The most important figure in translation into the vernacular before the Conquest was undoubtedly Aelfric (monk of Winchester, Abbot of Eynsham in 1005). Not only did he include large portions of translated Scripture in his *Catholic Homilies* and his *Lives of the Saints*, but he also provided an excerpted and abbreviated form of the Pentateuch and most of the historical books of the Old Testament.[4] The crown of pre-Conquest vernacular translation is, however, the West-Saxon Gospels, a powerful translation of all the Gospels. This exists in at least six manuscripts of varying date,[5] evidence that

---

[1] *Surtees Society*, vol. xxviii (1854).
[2] *Surtees Society*, vols. xvi, xix (1845 / 1847).
[3] Edn. Colgrave (1958).
[4] Available in *Old English Version of the Heptateuch* (ed. Crawford; 1922).
[5] Detailed in *The Gospels* (ed. Bosworth; 1907) xiii-xvi.

the version continued to be used for some centuries. One of these manuscripts claims Aelfric as author (*ego Aelfricus scripsi hunc librum*). An attractive and significant feature of these Gospels is the use of straightforward compound forms where no single English word yet exists, e. g. *mild-heortnesse* for 'mercy' (Matt 9:13), *blod-ryne* for 'haemorrhage' (Matt 9:20).

2. The Wycliffite Bible

2.1. Context

These promising developments were abruptly halted in the eleventh century. The Norman Conquest of England in 1066 effected a major setback in the development of vernacular literature in England.

French became the language of the literary classes. Robert of Gloucester, in his Chronicle,[6] describes how it dominated the upper echelons of society. William of Malmesbury, sixty years after the Conquest laments: "At the present time there is neither duke, bishop nor abbot who is English. Foreigners are corroding the guts of England, and there is no hope of an end to this misery". Only the French-speaking aristocracy could afford books. Norman French remained their language until, in the mid-fourteenth century, the Hundred Years War began to give French the *allure* of being the language of the enemy. Henry V (1387–1422) is the first king of England since the Conquest from whom we possess a letter written in English. Shakespeare is probably right in showing that the young king knew little French. The English language seems to have suddenly acquired confidence in the second half of the fourteenth century. So the speech for the opening of Parliament was in English in 1362, 1363 and 1364. From 1362 lawsuits were to be conducted in English. The first wills in English date from 1387. While in 1330 Higden's *Polichronicon* claims that French was the language for the education of children, in his English translation of 1385 John Trevisa notes that English has taken its place.

Latin was, of course, the language of the Church, of theology and of learned discussion. It had long been felt that the Bible was too abstruse and too liable to misunderstanding to be laid before the laity. Prohibition of translations of the Bible meant that knowledge of the Bible was confined to the clergy and more educated laity. Even Aelfric had written: "I do not promise to write very many in this tongue because it is not fitting, lest peradventure the pearls of Christ be had in disrespect", and that such things "ought not to be laid open to the laity".[7] Knighton complains that by translation "the jewel of the clergy is turned into the sport of the laity".[8] With the specialisation of university studies, theology was becoming more and more abstruse, more and more the preserve of the learned clergy. By contrast the educational standards of parish clergy were declining. In 1199 the Welshman Giraldus Cambrensis presented to Pope Innocent III his *Gemma Ecclesiastica*, containing a ludicrous list of clerical 'howlers' (e. g. "St Barnabas had been a robber", by confusion with Barabbas). In 1222 the Council of Oxford required that priests should be able at least to understand the Latin formula of eucharistic consecration, but

---

[6] *Gesta Regum*, RS. 90.i.278.
[7] Preface to his *Lives of the Saints*.
[8] *Chronicon Henrici Knighton* (ed. Lumby) 1 (1889) 152.

in the same year a Visitation of Salisbury shows that five in seventeen parish clergy were incapable of this.[9] In 1300 a copy of the Vulgate was so expensive that few individuals apart from higher clergy possessed one. It is no surprise that the only books bequeathed by parish clergy in England before 1400 are service-books, apart from one bequest of a Vulgate.[10] Such clergy can hardly have been in a position to expound the Bible to their flocks.

There were, of course, other means even of biblical instruction, available to those who could read. Outstanding among these was the early fourteenth-century *Psalter* of Richard Rolle, the North Yorkshire hermit. This is a translation (e. g. *thou that makes gostis thin aungels and thine minystres fire brennand*, for Ps 103:5) and verse-by-verse commentary on the Psalms and certain Old Testament canticles used in the Office, written for the recluse Margaret Kirkby, who presumably knew no Latin. Biblical knowledge was also spread by a host of other paraphrases, meditations, after the model of *Piers Plowman*. At least as influential as these – and available to those who could not read – were the visual meditations on the walls of churches. These were often as dependent on the apocryphal as on the canonical Gospels, as is shown by the confession of the ploughman to the priest: "Sir, I believe in Jesu Christ, which suffered death and harrowed hell, as I have heard mine olders tell", though the poem goes on to say that the ploughman had not heard of the *Pater Noster*.[11]

2.2. *The Translation*

John Wyclif (c. 1320–84) is often portrayed as the first of the Protestants, the founder of Lollardy, and the first translator of the whole Bible into English. All of these are misconceptions; he was primarily a philosopher. A contemporary, Henry Knighton, describes him as "a doctor of theology most eminent in his day. In philosophy he was considered second to none, in scholarly learning incomparable".[12] At Oxford he was Master of Balliol and later Warden of Canterbury Hall, and was sufficiently respected there for the Oxford establishment to close ranks in his defence (the Chancellor refused to publish his condemnation, and the university suspended an Irish Cistercian who preached against his views). He had always grounded his teaching on the Bible, and, unusually, gave lectures on the whole of the Bible. However, translation of the Bible seems to have been almost an afterthought, for Archbishop Arundel wrote to the Pope in 1412, "to fill up the measure of his malice he devised the expedient of a new translation of the Scriptures",[13] though it was indeed the logical outcome of his theological position and his continual appeal to the Bible as the only source of true doctrine. The chief animus against Wyclif was

[9] Deanesly, The Lollard Bible (1920) 193.
[10] Ibid. 203.
[11] Wright, *Reliquiae Antiquae* (1845) vol. 1.43, (representations of the punishments of hell, and the harrowing of hell were particularly popular, and dependent on the Gospel of Nicodemus).
[12] *Chronicon Henrici Knighton* (ed. Lumby) 2 (1895) 151. Further on Wyclif, see Chap. 13, Sect. 3, by G. R. EVANS, in the present volume.
[13] Quoted by Deanesly, The Lollard Bible (1920) 238.

aroused by his theological contention that both secular and ecclesiastical jurisdiction depended on being in a state of grace, with its consequence that unworthy office-holders deserved no obedience. It was only after this doctrine
was condemned by the Pope in 1377 that he became more extreme and began
to teach that neither papal authority nor the vowed religious life had adequate
foundation in Scripture, and to teach also against the philosophical basis of
the doctrine of transsubstantiation. A match was put to the tinder by the frightening but ultimately unsuccessful Peasants' Revolt of 1382, which appealed to
his theological position. This led to his condemnation in the same year at the
"Earthquake Synod" (so called because an earthquake occurred in London in
the course of its sittings). Wyclif withdrew to his living of Lutterworth, under
the nearby protection of his patron, John of Gaunt, the powerful Duke of Lan-
caster, in Leicester Castle, who was sufficiently committed to him and his
ideals to speak in the House of Lords against the bill to suppress the English
Bible: "We will not be the dregs of all, seeing that other nations have the Law
of God, which is the Law of our faith, written in their own language".[14]

The work of translation is attributed to him by the continuator of Knighton's *Chronicle*: "This Master John Wyclif translated from Latin into English
the Gospel that Christ gave to the clergy and doctors of the Church... and so
the pearl of the Gospel is scattered abroad and trodden underfoot by swine".
Jan Hus, the contemporary Czech reformer, had also heard this: "It is said by
the English that Wyclif translated the whole Bible from Latin into English". In
fact the translations appear to be two, one a development of the other. They
are preserved in two distinct sets of manuscripts, amounting in all to some 200
exemplars, of which the larger group is consistently more developed and therefore presumably later. The smaller group is almost touchingly anxious to preserve literally the forms of the Vulgate (*but in the face he blesse to thee* becomes
if he curseth not thee in the face at Job 1:11), the word-order (*ther schul gon
many peplis* becomes *many puplis schulen go*), the distinctively Latin participial
phrase (*Jesus clepinge hem seith* becomes *Jesus clepide hem and seyde*), latinate
omission of the verb 'to be' (*I bounden at Ierusalem am bitaken* becomes *I was
bounden at Ierusalem and was bitaken*). In each of these cases the former version is more timid, the latter bolder and more experienced.

Two manuscripts suggest that the earlier translation is the work of Nicholas Hereford. The
Bodleian Douce MS 369 breaks off at Baruch 3:20 with the Latin note in a later hand: "Here ends
the translation of Nicholas of Herford". This is partly confirmed by the note in Cambridge University Library MS Ee 1.10 at the same place: *Here endith the translacioun of N and now bigynnth
the translacioun of J and of othere men.* Who the "J and othere men" were we do not know, but Nicholas Hereford was one of Wyclif's most fiery supporters. After the Condemnation at Oxford in
1382 he hied himself to Rome, where he was again condemned and imprisoned, though he soon escaped and returned to minister in England. Denounced again in 1387, he recanted under extreme
pressure, perhaps threat of torture[15] and returned to favour, finally retiring to a Carthusian monastery in 1417. Among the candidates for the 'J' of the Cambridge note are John Trevisa, a well-
known translator, and John Purvey, Wyclif's own secretary; but no clarity is possible.

---

[14] Quoted in ABD 6, 818.
[15] See A. W. Pollard, *Fifteenth Century Prose and Verse* (Westminster: Constable 1903) 1651.

2.3. *Aftermath*

Wyclif himself died in 1384, but Lollardy continued, merging seamlessly into the Lutheran Reformation. The persecution of Lollardy also continued, and perhaps Wyclif's most striking biblical legacy was the resultant blockage on translating the Scriptures. In 1401 the statute *De Heretico Comburendo* introduced the death penalty, soon after put into effect on the Lollard William Sawtry and others. A turning-point was reached with the Constitutions of Oxford in 1407, when Archbishop Arundel finally forbade all unauthorized translation:

> We therefore resolve and ordain that no one henceforth on his own authority translate any text of holy Scripture into the English or any other language by way of book, pamphlet or tract, and that no book, pamphlet or tract of this kind, whether already recently composed in the time of the said John Wyclif or since, or to be composed in the future, be read in part or in whole… until the translation shall have been approved by the diocesan of the place.

It is notable that this same Archbishop Arundel had, in his funeral oration in 1394 for Anne of Bohemia, wife of Henry II, complimented her piety for using an English version of the Gospels which he himself had licensed. Thomas More also indicated that some individuals possessed authorized translations. However, the taint of heresy attaching to English translation and the prohibition of 1407 remained among the significant factors in delaying further efforts at rendering the Scriptures into the vernacular. Lollardy was continually felt to remain a danger, and the witchhunt against it continued. The term seems to have been used in general for any heterodox opinions. In 1458 the statutes of King's and Queens' Colleges, Cambridge, were modified to require an oath against the heresies of Wyclif and Pecock, and in 1476 the University of Oxford assured the king that a search for Pecock's and Wyclif's books had been made and that a few had been burnt. As late as 1523 Tunstall wrote of the current unorthodox tendencies: "It is no question of pernicious novelty; it is only that new arms are being added to the great crowd of Wycliffite heresies".[16] It was into this atmosphere that William Tyndale was born and would struggle to produce the translation which would be the progenitor of all future attempts to English the Bible.

3. Tyndale's Translation

3.1. *Literary Context*

Two other factors, one real and one possibly imaginary, were also at work to delay any further translation into English. The real factor was the tardy development of printing in England, the possibly imaginary one the undeveloped state of the English language. Already in 1455 Aeneas Sylvius, the later Pope

---

[16] Letter to Erasmus, *The Collected Works of Erasmus* 10 (Toronto: University of Toronto Press 1992) 26.

Pius II, was delighted to come across at Frankfurt a Bible which might be read without spectacles and in many copies – presumably the Gutenberg Bible. In England, by contrast, the first working printer was William Caxton.

Caxton learnt printing as late as 1471/72 in Cologne, and it was not until 1477 that he published at Westminster the first book to be printed in England. For another contrast we may compare the printing of biblical translations on the continent. Before Caxton's first English book there were already Bibles printed in Italian (1471), French (1474) and Dutch (1477), to be closely followed by printed versions in Catalan (1478) and Czech (1488). The sophistication of Greek printing, which had long been common on the continent in Italy and Switzerland, and certainly the magnificent Complutensian Polyglot Bible, now virtually ready for publication in Spain, was light-years ahead of English standards. The market for printed books remained small in England, and before he embarked on a book Caxton, shrewd businessman that he was, was always careful to ensure that he would be able to cover his costs, securing patrons to cover the costs for 23 of his 77 printed books. After Caxton's death in 1491 there remained only two printers of any note, Richard Pynson and Wynkyn de Worde, who were responsible for 70 percent of the English output. There was, therefore, hardly the market-opening for a printed English Bible.

A second factor in the delay of translation was the current estimate of the English language. This seems to have been used as an excuse for not challenging the 1407 prohibition of translation.

The academic language was still Latin. Scholars all over Europe corresponded with each other in Latin. More's *Utopia* was written in Latin, and Tunstall thought it necessary to ask More explicitly to write in English when he was writing against Tyndale. As late as 1605 of the 60,000 volumes listed in the *First Printed Catalogue of the Bodleian Library*[17] only 60 are in English. Similarly, of the 1,830 books listed as sold by the Oxford bookseller John Dorne in 1520, the overwhelming majority was in Latin, with only the occasional intrusion of such works as 'Robin Hod' or 'balets' (ballads). This is perhaps not so surprising for a university city. However, even a popular manual of etiquette for children in the dining-room is written in Latin, *Stans Puer ad Mensam*, of which he sold several copies.

English was not yet considered a literary language; as a prose medium it was still characterised as "rude" and "barbarous". Sir Thomas Elyot in 1531 in the Preface to *The Boke named the Governour* complains of the difficulty made by the poverty of the language. He in fact invented in that book such terms as 'modesty', 'mediocrity', 'industrious', 'frugality', 'beneficence', but the complaint has all the marks of a literary convention. It is possible to quote contemporary casual figures about illiteracy, but it is important to remember that these testimonies are suspect because their authors have an axe to grind. Thus Thomas More in his *Apology* (1523) is arguing that there is no point in Englishing the Bible when he makes the estimate that "people far more than four parts of all the whole divided into ten could never read english yet, and many now too old to go to school". A quarter of a century later Bishop Stephen Gardiner of Winchester's estimate is still more pessimistic when he writes (*Letter*, May 1547) that "not one in a hundredth part of the realm" could read. These are not serious estimates, let alone reliable statistics, and evidence to the contrary may be garnered from the numerous heresy trials where possession and use of heretical books forms a regular part of the accusation, even among the artisan classes. There were plenty of good plain works, manuals of instruction

---

[17] Oxford: Clarendon Press 1986.

on medicine, hawking, cooking, behaviour. There were letters, such as the Paston and Stonor letters, which are often playful and merry. There was the English Chronicle, which Tyndale claims to have read as a child (*The Obedience of a Christian Man*, preface), and which may well have had no small influence on his purposeful, episodic style. There were devotional works, such as Walter Hilton's *Scale of Perfection*, or Nicholas Love's popular *Mirror of the Life of Christ*. This is full of warm and memorable passages which make its popularity in English still easy to appreciate. The field was clearly open and ready for some major works in English.

3.2. William Tyndale

William Tyndale (c. 1490/91–1536) was the beneficiary of two great personal influences, Wyclif and Erasmus. His formal education took place at Oxford.

The beginning of Greek in Oxford seems to have been at the hands of Emmanuel of Constantinople, who already taught Greek there in 1462. It was slow to catch on. In the 1490s both Grocyn and William Lily found it necessary to go to Florence to gain an adequate knowledge of Greek. Cambridge seems to have been more advanced than Oxford. In 1518 the first Reader in Greek was appointed at Cambridge, while Thomas More was encouraging Oxford to emulate its sister university. Erasmus wrote to the President of the newly-founded Corpus Christi College (Letter 990): he numbered the College *inter praecipua decora Britanniae* on account of its *bibliotheca trilinguis*, though in fact in 1537 the only Hebrew book in the library catalogue was that classic Hebrew grammar, Reuchlin's *De rudimentis hebraicis.* The real revival of learning is, however, shown by the invaluable list of sales for the year 1520 by the book-seller of John Dorne, which inevitably gives a picture of what people in Oxford were reading in that year. A lot of Latin classical texts were being read. Many copies of Tully, especially *De Officiis*, were sold, but also a good number of other authors, such as Ovid, Vergil, Lucan, Sallust, Terence. There is, however, quite a clutch of Greek texts: Aesop, Aristophanes' *Plutus*, Lucian, Dionysius Areopagita (uncertain whether in Greek or Latin), and a big Greek dictionary for the price of 6/4. There is even an *Alphabetum Ebraicum*, though at a price of 2d this cannot have been a very extensive work. There are two valuable indications of the buzz-interests of the day. First, the clutch of indications already of Lutheran controversy: several copies of Luther's *De Potestate Papae* were sold for 3d each. One investigative purchaser got to the heart of the controversy by buying (for a shilling) this work, plus the *Resolutio*, plus the *Responsio Lutheri*. More important, a large number of books by Erasmus sold. DAVID DANIELL calculates that one in every seven customers bought a book by Erasmus.[18] Besides his theoretical works, the *Adagia*, the *Colloquia* and the *Enchiridion*, interest centres on the extraordinary hunger for his grammatico-rhetorical works; these will have been important in training any rhetorician or translator; chief among them are two. *De utraque verborum ac rerum copia* has some valuable writing on the use of synonyms, advising the user to observe the difference of nuance between them (Lib. I, fol. VII), giving lists of synonyms, e.g. near-synonyms for the negative, *non, haud, neque, haudquaqaum, neutiquam, minime, minus, parum* (Lib. I, fol. XXVI). Of this book, *De Copia*, John Dorne sold 16 copies in the year. Of another grammatical work by Erasmus, *De Constructione Verborum* (actually by William Lily, first High Master of St Paul's School, and revised by Erasmus) he sold a staggering 30 copies in the year. These must have been text-books in the hands of every student, showing the importance of such literary exercises, an invaluable propaedeutic for any translator. Practice in saying the same thing in several different ways is an essential training for a translator.

It was into this atmosphere that young William Tyndale – admittedly, just a decade earlier – arrived from the borders of Wales in the early years of the

---

[18] William Tyndale, a biography (1994) 396, n. 31.

century, taking his BA in 1512 and MA in 1515. In the Preface to *The Obedience of a Christian Man* (1529) Tyndale has some hard remarks to make about
scholastic disputations which were presumably the staple fare in Oxford. One
complaint is that Scripture may be studied only after several years of previous
study: "Ye drive them [students] from God's word and will let no man come
thereto until he have been two years master of arts".[19] What he thought of that
study may be gathered from another comment: "Of what text thou provest
hell, another limbo patrum and another the assumption of our lady, and another shall prove of the same that an ape hath a tail" (158f). His basic complaint is that this is putting the cart before the horse, or as he put it, measuring
the meteyard by the cloth (153). The Scripture should provide the yardstick
for understanding of the Fathers, not vice versa, as was so often the case.

After his time at university (and Foxe's *Book of Martyrs*[20] mysteriously claims that he spent some
months also in Cambridge) Tyndale secured a place as tutor to the children of a Gloucestershire
squire, Sir John Walsh. Two stories about Tyndale during this period illustrate his passionate concern to provide the text of the Bible to every man. The first relates a confrontation between Tyndale and a learned country cleric who held that Canon Law was more important than Scripture.
Master Tyndale happened to be in the company of a certain divine, recounted for a learned man,
and in communing and disputing with him he drave him to that issue, that the said great doctor
burst out into these blasphemous words, and said: "We were better to be without God's laws than
the pope's". Master Tyndale, hearing this, full of godly zeal and not bearing that blasphemous saying, replied again and said: "I defy the pope and all his laws", and further added that, if God
spared him life, ere many years he would cause the boy that driveth the plough to know more of
scripture than he did. Tyndale's mention of the ploughboy must surely be a reminiscence of Erasmus' preface to his 1516 first printed edition of the Greek New Testament: "I could wish that all
women should read the Gospel and St Paul's Epistles. I wish the farm worker might sing parts of
them at the plough and the weaver might hum them at the shuttle, and the traveller might beguile
the weariness of the way by reciting them".

Tyndale expresses the same idea, but with his own customary vigour and
clarity. This brings us to the second profound influence on Tyndale at this
time. His employer, Sir John, kept a good table, so that "there resorted to him
many times sundry abbots, deans, archdeacons with divers other doctors and
beneficed men". Master Tyndale "spared not to show unto them simply and
plainly his judgement in matters, and lay plainly before them the open and
manifest places of the Scriptures, to confute their errors and confirm his sayings" to such good effect that "at length they waxed weary, and bare a secret
grudge in their hearts against him". The secret of Tyndale's devastating effectiveness was surely Erasmus. During this period Tyndale translated Erasmus'
Enchiridion Militis Christiani and presented it to his master and lady – with
significant effect on the Walshes' social life! "After they had read well and per-
used the same, the doctorly prelates were no more so often called to the house,
neither had they the cheer and countenance when they came as before they
had." Erasmus, already the intellectual guru of Europe,[21] provided the academic backbone for the varied yearnings of Lollardy. Tyndale's programme is
strikingly similar. He was in one of the heartlands of Lollardy, giving regular

---

[19] Parker edition, 156f, echoing the similar complaint of Wyclif, *Opus Evangelicum*, 3.38.
[20] 1838 edition, vol. 5.
[21] Further on Erasmus, see Chap. 9, by ERIKA RUMMEL, in the present volume.

open-air sermons in Bristol, less than a dozen miles from his position in Little Sodbury. The secret of Tyndale is that he was the combination of the rural dissatisfaction of Lollardy with the academic dissatisfaction of Erasmus and the Renaissance.

It was after this time that came the decisive move to break the jinx on translations of the Bible into the vernacular. Tyndale offered himself in 1520 as a translator to that noted humanist and friend of Erasmus, Cuthbert Tunstall, Bishop of London. It is striking that as his sample submission to Tunstall Tyndale chose so luxuriantly and artificial a rhetorical author as Isocrates. Tyndale had clearly already given thought to the requirements of biblical translation. In *The Obedience of a Christian Man* he writes:

> The Greek tongue agreeth a thousand times more with the English than with the Latin. The manner of speaking is both one, so that in a thousand places thou needest not but to translate it into the English word for word, when thou must seek a compass in the Latin, and yet shall have much work to translate it well favouredly, so that it have the same grace and sweetness, sense and pure understanding with it in the Latin, and as it hath in the Hebrew. A thousand parts better may it be translated into the English than into the Latin.

Tunstall, however, refused his request, on the grounds that he had no room for him in his household. The subsequent history makes it quite clear that Tunstall was a dedicated opponent of Bible translation. Having been cold-shouldered by Tunstall, Tyndale went abroad to Flanders in April 1524, to pursue his objectives in the more tolerant air of the continent. He first set about translating the New Testament, and by the summer of 1525 he had got as far as printing the middle of Matthew chapter 22 at Cologne, when the authorities set out to arrest him. However, he fled to Worms, where he finished and published the New Testament, complete with copious notes which were heavily indebted to Luther.

As soon as this translation began arriving in England Tunstall mounted a virulent campaign against it. On the physical level he had the books burnt as they arrived at the docks. Finding this to be insufficiently effective, he arranged that his agent Packyngton should buy up Tyndale's entire stock, thus effectively clearing Tyndale's considerable debt, "so the bishop had the books, Packyngton the thanks and Tyndale had the money".[22] On the intellectual level Tunstall commissioned Thomas More, one of the greatest of Renaissance scholars and soon to become Lord Chancellor, to attack the translation. More's violent, not to say scatological, attack pilloried it as "Luther's Testament". Linguistically, the translation was of course indebted to Luther, though certainly independent, and in places correcting Luther, for Tyndale was a better Greek scholar than Luther (even though Luther had help from Melanchthon). Similarly later, in his Old Testament translation, Tyndale clearly had correct and alert access to the Hebrew text. Theologically, however, the Lutheran tendencies protrude even in the translation. More's attack focussed on three translation options in which Tyndale, exercising his Lollard or Lutheran legacy, had deliberately set about avoiding the overtones of eccle-

---

[22] E. HALL, *Hall's Chronicle* (London: J. Johnson 1809) 763.

siastical tradition. For the traditional 'priest' Tyndale used 'senior' or 'elder',
for 'church' he used 'congregation' and for 'charity' he used 'love' – all thoroughly defensible but theologically explosive options.

Uncowed, Tyndale set about translating the Old Testament. His Pentateuch
was published in 1530 in five distinct books, probably to make it more portable (I have in fact carried the original edition around in my back pocket) and
the book of Jonah in 1531. At his death he left a translation of Joshua to
Chronicles which was later used in the Matthew Bible. However, in 1536 he
was, at the instigation of the English authorities, kidnapped in Vilvorde, in-
carcerated and eventually garrotted, his body being burnt at the same stake.
His undaunted spirit and his continuing passion for language and translation
is shown in his letter to the prison governor:

> I suffer greatly from cold in the head and am afflicted with perpetual catarrh. I ask to have a
> lamp in the evening; it is indeed wearisome sitting alone in the dark. Most of all I beg and be-
> seech Your Clemency to urge the Commissary that he will kindly permit me to have the Hebrew
> Bible, Hebrew grammar and Hebrew dictionary, that I may pass the time in that study.

Tyndale's achievement is sufficiently proved by the fact that his translation
has formed the basis of every subsequent English version. In the King James
Version some 80 percent of those books which Tyndale translated has been
adopted word for word. The number of phrases which have become proverbial
and unnoticed current coin in the English language is countless ('the powers
that be', 'the fat of the land', 'not unto us, O Lord, not unto us'), the number
of words felicitously invented by Tyndale remarkable ('passover', 'long-suffer-
ing', 'scapegoat'). Three qualities which show his genius as a translator are
rhythm, directness and a witty gaiety ("Tush, ye shall not die", says the tempting serpent to the woman). Changes made by subsequent versions may improve
on details of accuracy and steadiness (particularly in restraining Tyndale's passion for *variatio*), but always, even in the case of the King James Version, at
the cost of vigour and boldness.

3.3. Subsequent Sixteenth Century Translations

After the nationalisation of the English Church an English Bible was felt by
many to be needed. The three principal sponsored Bible versions which resulted were all secondary to other translations. Their principal interest is not
the translation but the politico-religious situation which they illustrate. Henry
VIII was no reformer, but wanted only independence from Rome, whose
authorities had refused to legitimize his divorce, and whose interference limited his autocratic rule. In matters of doctrine he remained orthodox, conservative and determined to retain control of religious developments. Although
his early *Assertio Septem Sacramentorum* (1521) received substantial help from
Thomas More, he retained enough personal interest in theology to argue extensively about the interpretation of Origen in a letter to Tunstall late in his
reign. He recognised that the English Church required an English Bible, and
that this was desired by many – the Convocation of Canterbury petitioned the
king in 1534 that "the whole Bible might be translated into English". Cover-

dale's Bible was dedicated to the king, and its title-page shows the king delivering the Bible to his bishops, but the king insisted that the reading of the Bible be strictly controlled. He did indeed order that a Bible should be placed in every parish church, but an Act of 1543 forbade the reading of the Bible by women (except noblewomen), merchants, artificers, journeymen, yeomen and labourers. In his last address to parliament he warned against the use of the Bible "to dispute and make scripture a railing and taunting stock against priests and preachers. I am very sorry to know and hear how irreverently that most precious jewel the word of God is disputed, rimed, sung and jangled in every ale-house and tavern".[23] The story of the different Bible versions during Henry's reign is intimately linked with his passionate and difficult task of both drawing the people with him and achieving uniformity and peace in religion.[24]

Under these conditions three Bibles were produced during the reign of Henry VIII. The first of these is Miles Coverdale's (1535), not authorized by, but dedicated to the king. It was the first complete Bible to be printed in English, and printed in Zurich! However, apart from Coverdale's melodious rendering of the Psalms, which has become beloved by its adoption into the Book of Common Prayer, it is not in itself an important version, though J. F. MozLEY maintains that "in the line of scholars who made our king James' bible the name of Coverdale stands second only to Tyndale".[25] Coverdale had no pretensions to being an original scholar. He was ignorant of both Greek and Hebrew, translating from the Latin, and admitting in his preface that he relied on five interpreters: these have been discerned as the Vulgate, Pagninus's Latin of 1528 (a meticulously mechanical translation of the Hebrew, retaining even the Hebrew spelling of names, e.g. "Somron" for Samaria, "Selomoh" for Solomon),[26] Luther's German (from which Coverdale derived such monster forms as "overbodycoat", Exod 25:7, for Luther's *leibrock*,[27] "morningshine", Isa 59:9, and "winesupper" for Luther's *weinseuffer*, Joel 1:5), the Zürich Bible of 1531 and Tyndale (revised version of the Pentateuch and the New Testament, but not including his Joshua to Chronicles).

Coverdale was closely followed by the so-called Matthew's Bible (1537); this was in fact the work not of Thomas Matthew, but of John Rogers. Cranmer, the Archbishop of Canterbury, had long before attempted to enlist the help of his bishops in authorizing a translation, but had met only opposition, at any rate from the Bishop of London.[28] He now recognized that the bishops would not authorize a translation "till a day after domesday" and submitted this version to the king. The fact that it was not a bare text, but had some 2,000 notes will have pleased the king, though the content of the notes less, since many of them were by Luther, Tyndale and other Reformers. The trans-

---

[23] *Letters of Henry VIII* (ed. M. St. Clare Byrne; London: Cassell 1968) 421.

[24] See E. DUFFY, *The Stripping of the Altars* (New Haven: Yale UP 1992), chaps. 11 and 12.

[25] Mozley, Coverdale and his Bibles (1953) 109.

[26] Further on Sanctes Pagninus, see Chap. 7, Sect. 5.2, by ARJO VANDERJAGT, in the present volume.

[27] Sic. The 1534 edition of Luther does not, of course, use capitals for nouns.

[28] A. POLLARD, *Records of the English Bible* (Oxford: Oxford UP 1911) 196.

lation drew heavily on Tyndale (including the first publication of his Joshua to Chronicles) and lightly on Coverdale.

In 1538 Thomas Cromwell, the king's Vicar General, re-iterated to the bishops the royal wish that a Bible in English be "openly laid forth in every parish church at the charges and costs of the parson and vicars". For this purpose Cranmer found neither of the two previous publications satisfactory: the text of Coverdale was insufficiently authentic and the notes of Matthew too inflammatory. Accordingly he entrusted to Coverdale the task of editing a third Bible, which from its parish-lectern size (38cm x 23cm) became known as 'The Great Bible'. Again, the importance of the royal patronage and control is shown by the title-page woodcut of Henry handing the Bible to Cromwell and Cranmer, amid cheering populace. The conservative temper of the time is shown by the respect paid to Latin and to the Vulgate. The version is founded on Matthew's Bible, but the Old Testament corrected according to Münster's Hebrew-Latin diglot of 1535 and the New Testament according to Erasmus's Latin version. Where the Vulgate differs from these, its version is included – for the sake of the firm conservatives – in small type. A set of end-notes was planned, and the hand-symbol L inserted in the text at appropriate places, but no notes (apart from minimal marginal cross-references) were ever included; was the task of composing them too delicate, or was the revision simply too rushed? This Bible, the first to be widely available, proved hugely popular, despite its price of 12 shillings bound (a labourer's wage for two weeks): an estimated 20,000 copies were printed by 1541,[29] and the crowds who gathered round to read the six copies placed in St Paul's Cathedral were so noisy that the Bishop of London had to forbid such reading during the service.

Apart from these versions presented to the English people under royal patronage, two sixteenth-century translations deserve mention, the Geneva Bible and the Rheims-Douai version. The Geneva Bible was the child of Protestant exiles in Calvin's Geneva, under the leadership of William Whittingham, a Marian exile who returned under Elizabeth to become Dean of Durham in 1563. It was a sort of study-bible equipped with illustrations and with copious maps, tables and notes, the notes being heavily dependent on Calvin himself and his theological orientation.[30] This was the first English Bible to be printed in Roman type and to have divisions into chapters and verses, thus making both reading and reference incomparably easier. The text was scholarly and thoughtful, a thorough and responsible revision of the Great Bible in the light of the important scholarship of the previous half-century. It was the first Bible to be printed in Scotland. In England it was given a cautious royal licence, subject to the approval of the Bishops of Canterbury and London. The Great Bible remained, however, the official version for parish churches. The popularity of the Geneva Bible is easy to understand. With its helpful apparatus it is attractive and easy to use even today. For the Bible-reading conventicles for which it was intended (and in which it was copiously used) some sort of notes

---

[29] F. Fry, *A Description of the Great Bible 1539* (London [no publisher given] 1865).
[30] The notes of subsequent editions become progressively more Calvinistic and anti-Catholic: the note on Rev 11:2 applies it directly to the accession of Pope Boniface VIII!

are essential. It was printed in every size: folio, quarto, octave, duodecimo and even sextodecimo.

Before long, however, the Calvinistic tone of the apparatus was seen to threaten the delicate balance of retention and reform which Queen Elizabeth and her ministers were intent on forging in the Church of England. In 1566 Archbishop Parker instructed a new team, mostly bishops, to prepare a new version, removing the "bitter notes". This compromise version, 'the Bishops' Bible' was ready in three years, but it never won the enthusiastic success enjoyed by the Geneva Bible. As a whole its production is a throw-back from the Geneva Bible, making it far less attractive to handle and to use. In addition, Parker's Protestant successor as archbishop, Grindal, encouraged the use of the Geneva Bible, and during his archiepiscopate there were no editions of the Bishops' Bible. In the years 1583–1603 there were only seven editions of the latter as against 51 of the former. The Geneva Bible is the version principally used by Shakespeare, and is even the text quoted (14 times) in the preface to the King James Bible.

Another group of exiles also produced their Bible. Cardinal William Allen set up a College at Rheims for the education of Catholic clergy, who would later return to the English Mission, working for the return of England to the traditional Catholic faith and practice. It was felt essential that they should have their own English version of the Bible to counter the Protestant Bibles now available, as is explained frankly in the preface. This version was prepared by the Oxford scholar and teacher at Rheims, Gregory Martin, with the help of Richard Bristow. It was based primarily on the Vulgate, which had been declared the official Bible of the Church at the Council of Trent in 1546, though marginal notes also refer to the Greek. The translation is marked by the deliberate retention of latinisms, sometimes to bizarre effect, such as "our supersubstantial bread" in the Lord's Prayer (Matt 6:11), or "every knee shall bow, of celestials, terrestrials and infernals" (Phil 2:10). This literal fidelity to the Vulgate sometimes produced meaningless phrases, e.g. "A vineyard was made to my beloved in horn, the son of oil" (Isa 5:1). Particularly vulnerable were the Psalms, where the translation was based on the Gallican Psalter, whose reverence for the Hebraisms mirrored in the Septuagint already often had produced an unintelligible rendering. The Bible was copiously equipped with notes, naturally concentrating especially on specifically Catholic doctrines, such as the virgin birth (Matt 1:25) and the Petrine primacy (Matt 16:18). The New Testament appeared in 1582 and the Old Testament – after the transfer of the College to Douai – in 1609/10. This Rheims-Douai version (in a 1772 revision by Bishop Richard Challoner) remained the Bible of English Catholics until well into the twentieth century.

4. The King James Bible

4.1. The Genesis of the Version

King James VI of Scotland came to the throne of England as James I with the determination of reconciling the Puritan tendencies he knew too well from Scotland with the traditionalism of the Church of England. This he set about doing at a conference in Hampton Court the year after his accession. As part of the deal, the Reformed Protestant President of Corpus Christi College, Oxford, John Rainolds, suggested a new translation of the Bible, and the method by which it should be done: six panels of translators, two at Oxford, Cambridge and Westminster respectively, each charged with a set section of the Bible. This should be submitted for revision and approval in turn to the Bishops, the royal Privy Council and the King himself. The King seems to have jumped at this idea, for the most widespread of the current Bibles was the Geneva Bible, which he considered "the worst" of all. He found the notes "very partiell, untrue, seditious and savouring too much of daungerous and trayterous conceits". The notes were indeed not favourable to kingship. For example, the notes on Dan 6:22 and 11:36 question the king's authority, and suggest that some "tyrants" (a word significantly never even used in the King James Version) are imposed by God for a time to punish the people. Futhermore, the note to Ps 105:15 applies the expression "mine anointed" to the people of God, when King James would certainly consider it to refer to the royalty. James made clear in *Basilikon Doron*, written as guidance of his son and would-be successor, that the right of kings is God-given and that this can be proved by the Scriptures. In his zeal to replace the Geneva Bible and its notes he was perfectly right. Since the common availability of Bibles in translation, by the end of the sixteenth century "the Bible was the source of virtually all ideas; it supplied the idiom in which men and women discussed them".[31] It was the source not only for geology, astronomy and medicine, but also for heady political discussion. In a world before the invention of the distractions of the novel it was so well known that subversive ideas could be expressed vividly by allusion. The puritan notes to the Geneva Bible gave a consistent and powerful impetus to such subversion.

However, keeping rigorously to the principle of compromise, the king did not demand notes to set things right, but insisted that any new translation should merely be devoid of notes. Rules for translators were firmly laid down. The new Bible should follow the Bishops' Bible as closely as possible, avoiding some recent idiosyncracies like the hebraizing spelling of names. The Bishops' Bible had spelt the son of Abraham as "Izhàc" and the Geneva Bible as "Isahac". One instance of fidelity to the Bishops' Bible has had immense consequences for all ecclesiastical and biblical language in England, namely the retention of the second person singular, "thou" and "thee", which have been regularly used in hymns and prayers until very recently. There is strong evidence

---

[31] Hill, The English Bible (1993) 34.

that this usage was waning (the court records of Durham in 1575 show that the singular was now being used only rather aggressively to social inferiors).[32] The translation-decision taken here may well have influenced the arrested development of the language on this point, so that the usage still continues in the North of England.

The new translation was to draw on the best of previous translations, mentioned in the careful instructions being Tyndale, Matthew's Bible, Coverdale, the Geneva Bible. In fact in at least one place (Hebr 11:1) the Rheims-Douai version was also pillaged. Not only words but principles were invoked, for example, there was to be no attempt to standardize translation of one Greek word by the same English word. This imparts a certain liveliness but has disadvantages; thus in Rom 5:2–11 καύχωμαι is translated by three different words within nine verses. Similarly, since the panels worked independently of one another, quotations of the Old Testament in the New often differ from the version in their original position (e. g. Luke 3:4, 5).

Too strong a Puritan bias was to be avoided, in that the familiar traditional forms of words were to be retained rather than the Puritan equivalents, so 'church' not 'congregation', 'baptism' not 'washing'. Even-handedly, however, the final preface was written jointly by the Puritan sympathizer Miles Smith and the learned High Church bishop Thomas Bilson. Although this version, completed in 1611, has frequently been termed 'the Authorized Version' there is in fact no record that when it appeared it had ever been finally authorized either by king or parliament or bishops. The title-page carries the note: "appointed to be read in churches". It is perhaps best called the 'King James Version', after "the principle mover and author of the work" (as said in the Preface).

4.2. The Impact of the King James Version

Within a generation this version had superseded all others, though Roman Catholics clung tenaciously to the Rheims-Douai version. The King James Version was, of course, much cheaper to produce than the Geneva Bible, with its notes, tables and illustrations. In the Fast Sermons (i. e. sermons preached before parliament on days of fasting) during the 1640s it was already this Bible which supplied the texts for penetrating political satire and persuasion. In the closing years of the reign of Charles I and at his trial in 1649, he was powerfully excoriated at "the man of blood" (Num 35:33), whose blood-guilt was defiling the land. In that Bible-dominated age, and throughout the Puritan revolution, the opportunities for making political capital by biblical symbol and allusion were endless.

It has retained this dominant position even to this day, despite the subsequent advance of language and of scholarship. Partly unintelligible to modern ears though it may be, the nobility and dignity of the language ensures that it

---

[32] Cited by McGrath, In the Beginning (2001) 266.

is still read on formal and traditional occasions. Perhaps its most serious limitation is the Greek text from which it is derived. Erasmus's Greek text on which it is founded was at the time a rushed piece of editing, and was anyway based on rather late manuscripts, now known as the 'Byzantine' text-type, (for example, it includes 1 John 5:7–8, a fourth-century gloss found in no original Greek manuscript before the sixteenth century, though sometimes in manuscripts of the Vulgate from the sixth century). This text has now been well superseded through the wider availability and more careful evaluation of manuscripts since the sixteenth century, especially the revaluation of the three great manuscripts Vaticanus, Alexandrinus and Sinaiticus. Already at that time, however, the progress in Greek and Hebrew scholarship in nearly a century since Tyndale's version had prepared a much more solid basis for translation.

The climate was right for a great translation. During the years in which this version was being created an astonishing constellation of great writers was at work. Poets like John Donne (1572–1631), dramatists like William Shakespeare (1564–1625), Ben Jonson (1573–1637), essayists like Francis Bacon (1561–1626), homilists like Launcelot Andrewes (1555–1626) were at the height of their powers, writing with vigour, drama and confidence. There was also a vigorous tradition behind it, stretching back uninterruptedly to Tyndale. The Preface freely grants that "we, building upon their foundation that went before us, and being holpen by their labours, do endeavour to make better that which they left us so good", and indeed it has been estimated that in 80 percent of those books which Tyndale translated his version is retained. Departures from it are often less bold and imaginative, though perhaps more sober. Tyndale was a young and bold translator, deliberately setting out to reproduce the cragginess of the Hebrew. The King James Version is more polished, more rhetorical and even more baroque, sometimes reminiscent of the ornate style of the decorative visual arts of the period. The speech rhythms of the King James Version have entered into any elevated prose in the English language, and the expressions which have become proverbial, used by those who have no familiarity with the Bible and are quite unaware of their origin (e.g. sports commentators), are numberless: "sour grapes", "go from strength to strength", "the salt of the earth", "a thorn in the flesh".

It remains to mention only two developments during the remainder of the seventeenth and the eighteenth century, though neither of them made more than a minor ripple on the surface to rock the stable superiority of the King James Version. The first development is a couple of attempts to make use of the advances in textual criticism. In 1745 William Whiston, best known as the translator of Josephus, published a *Primitive New Testament* for which he used the fifth/sixth century Cambridge *Codex Bezae*, which he considered to be early second-century. Its principal value is, however, as chief representative of the Western Text. In 1755 the Methodist John Wesley published another New Testament, containing some 12,000 changes from the King James Version, making valuable use of new Greek texts to depart from 'Byzantine' readings. The second notable development is the first indigenous American version of the Bible, by Robert Aitken of Philadelphia in 1782.

Chapter Twenty-two

Three French Bible Translations

By Bertram Eugene Schwarzbach, Paris

Sources: Sébastien Chateillon: *La Bible / nouvellement / translatee, / Avec la suite de l'histoire depuis le tems d'Esdras iusqu'aux / Maccabées: e depuis les Maccabées iusqu'à Christ* (Basel: Iehan Hervage 1555). – Pierre-Robert Olivétan: *La Bible / qui est toute la saincte escriture. / En laquelle sont contenus le Vieil Testament / & le Nouveau translatez en Francoys. Le Vieil de Lebrieu; / & le Nouveau / du Grec* (s.l. [Neufchâtel] s.a. [1535]). – Louis-Isaac Le Maistre de Sacy: (in canonical order) *Genèse* (Paris: Roulland 1682); *L'Exode et le Lévitique* (Lyon: Plaignard 1683); *Les Nombres* (Paris: Desprez 1685); *Le Deutéronome* (Paris: Roulland 1685); *Josué, les Juges et Ruth* (Paris: Desprez 1687); *Les deux premiers livres des Rois* (Paris: Roulland 1674); *Les deux derniers livres des Rois* (Paris: Desprez 1686); *Isaïe* (Paris: Desprez 1673); *Jérémie* (Paris: Desprez 1690); *Ezéchiel* (Paris: Desprez 1692); *Les douze petits prophètes* (Paris: Desprez 1679); *Pseaumes de David* (Paris: Pierre Le Petit 1665); *Les Proverbes de Salomon* (Paris: la Veuve de Ch. Savreux 1672); *Job* (Paris: Desprez 1688); *Daniel* (Paris: Desprez 1691); *Esdras et Néhémie* (Paris: Desprez 1693); *Le Cantique des cantiques* (Paris: Desprez 1694); *L'Ecclésiastique* (Paris: Pierre Le Petit 1684); *Tobie, Judith et Esther* (Paris: Desprez 1688); *Les Paralipomènes* (Paris: Desprez 1693); *L'Ecclésiaste de Salomon* (Paris: la Veuve de Ch. Savreux 1673); *Le Livre de la Sagesse* (Paris: la Veuve de Ch. Savreux 1673). – R. Simon, *Histoire critique du Vieux Testament* ([1678] Rotterdam: Reinier Leers 1685), Bk. II, Chaps. 24, 25. – Augustin Calmet, *Commentaire littéral de tous les livres de l'Ancien et du Nouveau Testament* (Paris 1707–1716).

Bibliography: B. Th. Chambers, *Bibliography of French Bibles. XVth and XVIth century French language editions of Scripture* (Geneva: Droz 1983).

General works and studies: Bible de tous les temps [BTT] 1–8 (ed. Ch. Kannengiesser; Paris: Beauchesne 1984–89), esp. BTT 5, *Le temps des Réformes et la Bible* (ed. G. Bedouelle / B. Roussel; 1989); BTT 6, *Le grand siècle et la Bible* (ed. J.-R. Armogathe; 1989); *The Cambridge History of the Bible* [CHB] 3. *The West from the Reformation to the Present Day* (ed. S. L. Greenslade; Cambridge: Cambridge UP 1976), esp. Chap. III, "Continental Versions to c. 1600", Sect. 3, "French Versions", by R. A. Sayce, 113–22, and Chap. IX, "Continental Versions from c. 1600 to the Present Day", Sect. 2. "French Versions", by R. A. Sayce, 347–52 [both quoted Sayce, French Versions (1976)]; F. Delforge, *La Bible en France et dans la francophonie: Histoire, traduction, diffusion* (Paris, Villiers-le-Bel: Publisud / Société biblique française 1991) 65–74, 85–87; P. M. Bogaert (ed.), *Les Bibles en français. Histoire illustrée du Moyen-Âge à nos jours* (s.l., Brepols 1991) 66–70, 82–86, 134–50; G. Bedouelle / B. Roussel, "L'Ecriture et ses traductions. Eloge et réticences", BTT 5 (1989) 463–85; B. E. Schwarzbach (ed.), *La Bible imprimée dans l'Europe moderne* (Paris: BNF 1999).

1. General Introduction

Huguenots in France and Switzerland needed a translation of the Bible that would be accurate, inspiring and that would avoid lending authority to what they considered to be Roman distortions of biblical doctrine. One must conclude from the papal prohibition on reading the Bible in the vernacular

(1559),[1] anticipated in France by a royal edict (Edict of Châteaubriant, June 1551) prohibiting the printing and even the possession of a Bible in the vernacular,[2] that Catholics as well wanted a Bible in a language that spoke to them. The results were, first the Pierre-Robert Olivétan translation for Huguenots, *La Bible* (of 1535). The first modern French Catholic translation was actually a revision of Olivétan's translation by theologians of the most Catholic university of Louvain, first published in 1578. It was frequently reprinted until the publication of the *Version de Mons*, so-called because of the address of the New Testament translation, *Mons, chez Gaspard Migeot* (1667), actually published in Amsterdam by Daniel Elzevier; it was also known as the *Version de Port-Royal* because it was executed by a group of Jansenist *solitaires* associated with the Cistercian convent of Port-Royal des Champs, and as *La Bible de Sacy* because the principal translator was Louis-Isaac Le Maistre de Sacy.

Olivétan's Bible was adopted by French-speaking Protestant communities but never achieved the almost canonical status of Luther's Bible. It is unhistorical to speak of its scholarly failures and weaknesses, which were already evident in 1678 to the pioneering Bible critic, Richard Simon, who was, unusually for him, quite indulgent.[3] The French language, as Montaigne testified,[4] was changing very rapidly. Since the Huguenots were a minority community, Olivétan's French, however influential within that community, could not succeed in arresting that development by imposing itself upon the wider French nation, as Luther's German was to do in Germany,[5] so it was inevitable that the language of his translation should soon have become archaic and should soon have required revision. Olivétan is said to have studied Hebrew "with", or more likely under, Martin Bucer and Wolfgang Capito in Strasbourg. His references to rabbinical commentaries are almost all drawn from secondary (Christian) sources, mostly the Latin translations of the Hebrew Bible by two of the best Christian Hebraists of the time, Sebastian Münster and Sanctes Pagninus. ENGAMMARE[6] and ROUSSEL[7] demonstrate that Olivétan's knowledge of rabbinical commentaries comes from the comments that accompany their translations, but some of his marginal references to variants in, or with regard

---

[1] Cited by G. FRAGNITO, "La bible en italien et l'enquête de la congrégation de l'index dans les bibliothèques des couvents italiens à la fin du XVIᵉ siècle", in: Schwarzbach, La Bible imprimée (1999) 288, n. 2.

[2] Cited by Sayce, French Versions (1976) 113. See E. DROZ, "Bibles françaises après le Concile de Trente (1546)", *Journal of the Warburg and Courtauld Institutes* XVIII (1965) 209–22.

[3] *Histoire critique* (1685) 342–44. Simon had a score to settle with the Genevan theologians of his own day, and that may have induced his indulgence towards Olivétan and severity towards their predecessors who, without knowing any Hebrew, dared to revise a fellow Hebraist's translation.

[4] Michel de Montaigne, *Essais* III.ix, cited by Sayce, French Versions (1976) 114.

[5] Actually Luther's German was revised and adapted to the dialects of several regions of Germany and even discreetly modernized. See S. STROHM, "Évolution du texte de la Bible de Luther. Réflexion sur les problèmes rencontrés dans l'histoire de son édition de la Réforme à nos jours ", in: Schwarzbach, La Bible imprimée (1999) 166–88.

[6] See M. ENGAMMARE, "Olivétan et les commentaires rabbiniques", in: I. ZINGUER, *L'hébreu au temps de la Renaissance* (Leiden: Brill 1992) 27–61.

[7] B. ROUSSEL, "La Bible d'Olivétan. La traduction du livre du prophète Habaquq", *ETR* 57 (1982) 537–57.

to, the massoretic text are independent of them, which would demonstrate that he had actually learned some Hebrew. But Hebrew studies among Christians were still in their earliest and crudest stages. Eliyahu Ashkenazi's ספר הדקדוק (1525), by far the best Hebrew grammar available in the sixteenth century, had already appeared when Olivétan set to work, but Ashkenazi's two dictionaries of biblical Hebrew and Aramaic, התשבי and the מתורגמן, that were equally fundamental, were yet to be published. They would appear in Isny in 1541. Ashkenazi's grammar was not, of course, the only one available in the early sixteenth century, but it was more sophisticated than the first Hebrew primers, Conrad Pellican's *De modo legendi et intelligendi Hebræum* (1504), Johannes Reuchlin's *De rudimentis hebraicis* (1506), and Capito's *Hebraicæ institutiones* (1518) that Olivétan is likely to have used, and his dictionaries were also more complete and sophisticated than the early Hebrew-Latin dictionaries, Münster's *Dictionarium hebraicum* (1525) and Pagninus's *Thesaurus linguæ sanctæ* (1529), which were the only ones that Olivétan could have used. Another ingredient that was lacking in the equipment of any Christian trying to translate the Old Testament in 1535 was Ashkenazi's מסורת המסורת (1538) which defined the *massorah* of the Hebrew Bible and reflected on the transmission of the biblical texts. Olivétan claims in his preface [3v°] what Ashkenazi was to show magisterially, that the vowel points and the *massorah* were relatively late accretions to the biblical texts because the names of the vowels do not appear in the Talmud. He could not have known that himself so he must have borrowed it from a good scholar in rabbinics, almost necessarily a Jew or a Christian who had that information from such a Jew, since none of the early Christian Hebraists had yet explored the Talmud thoroughly. Olivétan was thus a Hebraist who had to exploit the secondary sources, as yet inadequately developed, for lack of a thorough knowledge of the primary Hebrew texts.

Despite Olivétan's good intentions, it was soon felt necessary to revise his translation for both linguistic and scholarly reasons. In addition his translation was typographically dense, in heavy gothic letters, which were already going out of style, and had not sold well despite the public's "thirst for the Bible".[8] He himself revised his translation of the Psalter, *Les psalmes de David*, by "Belisem de Belimakom" [בלי שם בלי מקום] (1537) and finally *Les livres de Salomoh*, by the same modest person, in 1538, the year of his death.[9] A subsequent revision was produced by Calvin himself (1540, the *Bible de l'épée*, after the handsome printer's mark), and another by Théodore de Bèze, who was no Hebraist (1588, the "Geneva Bible"), still another by Jean Diodati (1644), then another by David Martin (1707), and a final revision by Jean-Frédéric Ostervald (1711). In 1676–1677 the consistory of Charenton wanted to engage Richard Simon, then a young and still nearly unknown Hebraist, to revise the Old Testament part of the Diodati translation or possibly even his entire Bible, but the Genevans refused to pay for his work, which went no further than the Pentateuch which Simon had executed as a sample.[10] It is not clear whether the refusal of the Genevan consistory to fund the project was based entirely upon whom Simon was, a Catholic priest, or reflected their opinion that he had strayed too far from Olivétan, either in the direction of Catholic orthodoxy or even, possibly, in the direction that his *Histoire critique du Vieux Testament* would

---

[8] The expression is due to J.-R. ARMOGATHE, "Introduction: La soif des Écritures", BTT 6 (1989) 15–16.

[9] We have never seen either of these books and know no more about them than what BOGAERT published (Les Bibles, 1991) 70.

[10] This most interesting text was discovered in manuscript in Germany and identified in 1985; it should appear shortly in an edition by JACQUES LE BRUN and JOHN WOODBRIDGE.

take in 1678. Of course the Genevans may have refused out of conservatism, being unwilling to participate in a radical modernization of the language of Diodati's familiar and revered text.

The de Sacy translation, from the Vulgate and not from the Hebrew, first appeared in a bilingual edition, Latin and French, book by book, 18 volumes in-8° and 2 in-12°, between 1665 (Psalms) and 1693 (Chronicles and Song of Songs), the later volumes appearing after de Sacy's death in 1684. De Sacy was responsible for the complete translation even though the extensive *explications* for the post-1684 volumes were written by his collaborators, notably Thomas Du Fossé. This translation, written in the language of the French *classiques* can, with modernized spelling, still pass as conservative but entirely comprehensible French, so it is hardly surprising that it should have been reissued many times in the course of the eighteenth, nineteenth and twentieth centuries. It was last reissued in 1990, in a grossly deformed edition – the notes and *explications* were omitted – with a laudatory preface by a Sorbonne professor, PH. SELLIERS, and then again in 1998. In a trenchant analysis, H. MESCHONIC[11] argues that it was reissued because of its ideological position rather than for its literary qualities, which is not implausible since the impeccably orthodox and much sounder *Bible de Jérusalem*, which is remarkably open to modern Bible scholarship and criticism, had been available since 1955 to satisfy any scrupulous Catholic's need for an accurate and idiomatic French translation. Despite its association with the Jansenist movement whose orthodoxy had been denied by the bulls *In eminenti* (1642), *Cum occasione* (1653), *Ad sacram* (1656) and would be denied again by *Unigenitus* (1713), and the fact that it had a predecessor and worthy competitor unburdened with doubts about its orthodoxy in Denis Amelote's *Le Nouveau Testament* (1666–1670), in 3 volumes, de Sacy's translation, in various revisions, some produced by his Jansenist heirs very soon after his death, became standard among French Catholics. Subsequent Catholic attempts to translate Bible into French, like Richard Simon's *Version de Trévoux* (*Le Nouveau Testament*, 1701), the revision of de Sacy by the quietist, Mme Guyon (1714–15), and a second revision, by Nicolas Le Gros (1739), both for the complete Bible, never replaced it.

There were other French Protestant translations, notably New Testaments by Jean Le Clerc (Amsterdam 1703), and Jacques Lenfant and Isaac de Beausobre (Amsterdam 1718, with an additional volume of learned notes and commentaries in 1742), and the very interesting, complete Bible by Charles Le Cène (Amsterdam 1741); but the Huguenot community never adopted the Le Clerc translation, possibly because he was close to the Arminians, nor the Le Cène translation, because it was (justly) suspected of Socinian leanings. Unlike the Olivétan translation and its revisions, none of these translations was ever reprinted except for the Lenfant/Beausobre New Testament, which was reissued once, in Lausanne in 1735.

The third Bible to be discussed here is another complete Huguenot translation that was never reprinted and had no influence at all despite its remarkable qualities, *La Bible nouvellement translatee*, by Sébastien Châteillon, published in 1555. While Olivétan is little known as a person and actor in the drama of the second wave of the Reformation, much is known about Châteillon or Cas-

---

[11] H. MESCHONIC, "Traduire le goût, c'est la guerre du rythme", *L'Infini* 76 (2001) 25–60, here 43.

tallion (1515–1563), as he signed his Latin works. He was a Hebrew, Greek, and Latin scholar who had first translated the Bible from Hebrew into Latin: *Moses latinus*, in 1546, the *Psalterium* in 1547, and the complete Old Testament in 1551 with a second edition in 1553, and had defended the rights of conscience, for which reason he had to flee Geneva to Basel. The twenty years that separate his translation from Olivétan's made a great difference in language. It has been claimed and has been often repeated that Châteillon wrote a Rabelaisian French which suggests that his is a linguistically inventive text, but often vulgar and difficult to read. Simon[12] cites Henri Estienne's opinion that Châteillon's translation was in the language of the *gueux* and contained *argot*. In particular, his translation of the Song of Songs acquired the reputation of being pornographic, and its pages were cut out of the exemplar in the American Bible Society Library, New York, by a reader more sensitive to literary indelicacy than ourselves or Simon, who complained on the contrary that Châteillon's style was too polished and elegant! The alleged pornography of his translation seems to be an uncritically repeated slander. Our impression is that Châteillon's French, despite an occasionally picturesque vocabulary, is surprisingly close to modern usage, much closer than Olivétan's language. He uses the apostrophe, cedilla, circumflex and acute accents and especially possessive pronouns which obviate the profusion of archaic relative pronouns that encumbers Olivétan's prose.[13] The typography of this translation is also more spacious than that of Olivétan's first edition which contributes as well to this translation's comprehensibility and even its charm. Because of Châteillon's differences with Calvin it was not accepted by the Reformed community of his day,[14] and because it issued from a Reformed source it was not acceptable to Catholic readers. Its literary reputation fell victim to Counter-Reformation respectability which also penetrated Huguenot circles. Rather than compare these three translations with each other on small but representative samples of Old Testament prose or poetry, as B. Roussel has done so well for the successive revisions of the Olivétan New Testament translation,[15] we shall try to take a broad sampling of each in the hope of answering certain questions: 1) how are the names of God handled, because the choices could betray rationalistic or deistic sensitivities? 2) are there any hesitations about the authenticity of any biblical verses, which is to ask whether there are any intimations of the Bible criticism to be created by Louis Cappel, Baruch Spinoza and Richard Simon in the 1650s, 60s and 70s? 3) are miracles ever reduced to natural phenomena, which would betray a measure of rationalism and a disposition towards natural science trying to coexist with faith in the letter of the texts, which would be still another anticipation of Spinoza? 4) are the vestigial

---

[12] *Histoire critique* (1685) 349.

[13] See P. M. Bogaert and J. F. Gilmont, in: Bogaert, Les Bibles (1991) 84.

[14] Sayce, French Versions (1976) 120, cites a description of Châteillon from the introduction to the 1560 Geneva New Testament as an "homme si bien cogneu en ceste Eglise tant pour son ingratitude & impudence … instrument choisi de Satan pour amuser les esprits volages & indiscrets".

[15] B. Roussel, "Après Olivétan (1535): neuf années de révisions du Nouveau Testament (1536–1544)", in: Schwarzbach, La Bible imprimée (1999) 189–212.

mythological elements ("older, darker shapes"[16]) and distant memories of cruel rites preserved in the Old Testament recognized as such, and are any of them demythologized? 5) are there any traces of unease in passages that could offend ethical sensitivity, which would suggest a consciousness of changes in values from biblical times to those of the translator? 6) to what extent is the Old Testament forced to bear Christian witness? and 7) how are sexually frank passages translated? This is a very eighteenth-century way of looking at Bible translations and exegesis, one that seeks the diversity within Bible and suspects harmonizers of the Bible with itself or with a corpus of doctrine of insufficient respect for Bible; other students of Bible surely have other priorities, feminist perspectives, gay perspectives, liberation perspectives, etc. whose presence or absence they would emphasize. We shall not be concerned with the way each of these translations deals with passages that were subjects of doctrinal differences among Catholics, Lutherans and Calvinists because that is more theology than Bible study.

As ROUSSEL astutely pointed out, Bible translations are created incrementally.[17] Olivétan used the French translation (from the Vulgate) of the humanist, Jacques Lefèvre d'Étaples, the Old Testament appearing in 1523 and the New Testament in 1528, Châteillon used Olivétan's translation, and the King James is reputed to have taken many of its most eloquent passages from Tyndale's translation. In a longer study it would have been possible to isolate the strands of the translations and to discuss each one separately. But here we shall deal only with the original Olivétan translation as it appeared in 1535, without reference to Lefèvre d'Étaples or to its various subsequent revisions, even though it was through these revisions that it dominated Huguenot thought and religious conscience. Nor shall we systematically distinguish in Châteillon's translation those expressions that come from neither Lefèvre d'Étaples nor Olivétan in order to discuss his personal contribution to Bible translation. Analogously, we shall not deal with the revisions of the de Sacy translation that appeared after 1700, nor the *Commentaire littéral*[18] of Augustin Calmet (1707–16), that revises it again and casts it in a very different context, nor with Mme Guyon's or Le Gros's revisions. There is not much point in comparing any of these translations with the best of modern biblical scholarship, though their position relative to the best Bible scholarship of their day is pertinent.

2. Pierre-Robert Olivétan

Special studies: I. BACKUS / F. HIGMAN (eds.), *Théorie et pratique de l'exégète. Actes du troisième colloque sur l'histoire de l'exégèse biblique au XVIe siècle (Genève, 31 août-2 sept. 1988)* (Geneva: Droz 1990); M. ENGAMMARE, "Cinquante ans de révision de la traduction biblique d'Olivétan: Les Bibles réformées genevoises en français au XVIe siècle", *Bibliothèque d'humanisme et de renaissance* 53 (1991) 347–77; idem, "Olivétan et les commentaires rabbiniques ...", I. ZINGUER, *L'hébreu au temps de la Renaissance* (Leiden: Brill 1992) 27–61; H. KUNZE, *Die Bibelübersetzungen von Lefèvre d'Eta-*

---

[16] An expression attributed to JANE HARRISON.
[17] Roussel, Après Olivétan (1999) 190.
[18] Calmet, *Commentaire littéral* (Paris: 1707–1716) 23v.

ples und von P. R. Olivétan verglichen in ihrem Wortschatz (Leipzig: Selbstverlag des Romanischen Seminars 1935); B. ROUSSEL / G. CASSALIS (eds.), *Olivétan traducteur de la Bible. Actes du colloque Olivétan (Noyon, mai 1985)* (Paris: Éd. du Cerf 1987), and particularly S. AMSLER, "L'Ancien testament d'Olivétan à la lumière de sa traduction d'Esaïe 35", in: ibid. 107–13; B. ROUSSEL, "La Bible d'Olivétan. La traduction du livre du prophète Habaquq", *Études théologiques et religieuses* 57 (1982) 537–57; idem, "Après Olivétan (1535): neuf années de révisions du Nouveau Testament (1536–1544)", in: Schwarzbach, *La Bible imprimée* (1999) 189–212.

Pierre-Robert Olivétan (c. 1500/06–1535/38) follows the *massoretic* numbering of the Psalms, omits the Latin chapters after Esth 10:3 and the Canticle of Shadrach, Meshach and Abednego in Daniel 3, but he follows the Vulgate for the order of books and, at the end of the canon, he adds III and IV Ezra, Tobit, Judith, Wisdom, Ben-Sira, Baruch and the Epistle of Jeremiah, I and II Maccabees, the Latin chapters of Esther, the Canticle of Shadrach, Meshach and Abednego, the story of Susanna, the story of Bel and the Dragon (the latter three from Daniel) from the Catholic canon of Scripture and the Prayer of Manasseh that everyone considered to be non-canonical.

Although Olivétan is concerned about the authenticity of Hebrew pronunciation, we have found no hesitations or comments regarding the authenticity of the biblical texts.

This is clear from the lack of a marginal note for 2 Chron 36:21, which cites a prophecy of Jeremiah which in fact appears in Lev 26:43, which obviously implies that the author of that chapter of Chronicles did not know that that prophecy had already been integrated into Leviticus, if he even knew that such a book existed. However Olivétan translated בעבר הירדן in Deut 1:1 honestly as *oultre le Iordan*, surely aware of the problems it posed because he had read, as ENGAMMARE demonstrates, the notes of Münster, ׳יר מקדש *Hebraica Biblia* (Basel 1534), who knew the standard rabbinical commentaries that were aware of a number of verses in the Pentateuch, including this one, which, at first glance, appear to be post-Mosaic (curiously, Münster does not mention Ibn Ezra on Deut 1:2). Olivétan cites Hebrew texts in the margins when the readings are not sure, for instance three in Genesis 49 which are not mentioned by Münster, or when they are disputed, for instance ילדתך / ילדותך, "she who bore you / your childhood" of Ps 110:3 and כרו / כארי, "like a lion" [the standard but not unanimous *massoretic* reading] / "they cut or dug", of Ps 22:17, where he translates כרו, following Jerome and the Christian apologetic tradition, *ils ont p[er]ce mes maïs & mes piedz*. He could have found many of his textual variants in the Venice 1517 Hebrew Bible, which is a primitive critical edition, but not the כארי / כרו variant which he could have found through Münster. Elsewhere he uses the margins to list translations that differ from the ones he adopted.

The effect was not necessarily to relativize the Hebrew text, as polyglot Bibles since the Complutensian of 1514–1517 and the polyglot Psalters of 1517 and 1518 are supposed to have done, but at least to suggest that authentic texts and accurate translations were still to be sought, and that the reader could, democratically, take his pick among the plausible alternatives to the texts and translations that Olivétan considered. In a contrary sense, when Olivétan found it necessary to add an explicative word or two, for instance when he wanted to make Gen 3:15 more explicit by replacing a pronoun by its antecedent *Ceste semence te poindra la teste*, or Ps 110:3, *Tõ peuple viendra volũtiers au iour que tu auras ton exercite en saincte põpe: ta nativite sera depuis sa matrice comme du matin vient la rosee*, he scrupulously printed his insertions (here in Roman) in a smaller character, which suggests that it is each word, as well as the sense of the text, which is sacred. For Gen 38:21 he is terribly literal, to the point of being incomprehensible: he refers to Tamar as the *paillarde* who *sassit en lieu patent es yeulx qui est sur le chemin de Thimnath* in preference to the more comprehensible *a la porte de la fontaine* ..., probably because the primary sense of עין is 'eye'. As ENGAMMARE says, Olivétan was fundamentally a philologist seeking the precise meanings of words and passages.[19]

---

[19] *Olivétan et les commentaires rabbiniques* [1992] 50–51.

Olivétan translates אלהים as the singular, *Dieu*, even in Gen 20:13 and 35:7, *Or quand Dieu me feit departir de la maison de mon pere* and *car Dieu lui fut la revele quãd il sen fuyoit de devant son frere*, respectively, although the accompanying verbs' agreement is in the plural, which is to say that he was not sensitive to a vestige of polytheism in the Old Testament despite the fact that the Medieval Jewish commentators dealt with the problem, or he intentionally suppressed it.

However in Gen 1:26, he does not hide the plural, *faisons lhomme a nostre image*, and in 1 Sam 28:13 אלהים ראיתי עלים מן הארץ, where the plural was also ineluctible, he comments, *Iay veu [chald. lãge de Dieu. Ra. Kim: grãd p[er]sonnage] des dieux montans de la terre*, which shows that at least in these two verses he realized that there was a real problem. The יהוה אלהים of Genesis 2 comes out *le Seigneur Dieu*, and the אל שדי of Gen 48:3 and Exod 6:3 is rendered *Tout puissant*, following the Vulgate translation, *Deus omnipotens*. Where יהוה appears alone it can be transliterated as *Jehovah*, as in Exod 6:3, *Mais ie ne leur ay point manifeste mõ nom Iehovah [cest Eternel ...]*, or *Eternel*, as he glosses Exod 3:14, *Et Dieu dist a Moseh: Ie suis [selon le grec ... Ie seray qui seray. De ce mot est dict Eternel ...] qui suis.*[20]

Olivétan can be quite independent of the Vulgate.

This is the case in Gen 36:24, where he follows the Palestinian Targum[21] to translate the mysterious ימם *mulets* instead of *eaux chaudes* (Vulgate, *aquas calidas*) – Münster mentions Qimhi's interpretation in this sense, but not the Targum! – and in Gen 49:10–11, translating (and transliterating) *Le sceptre ne sera point oste de Iehudah, ne le legistateur dẽtre ses piedz iusque a ce que [ou le paisible ayãt p[ro]sperite. Chald. Le Mesiah. Grec lisant* שלח *pour* שלה, *celuy q[ui] doit estre envoye] Siloh viẽne, & a luy sassembleront les peuples. Liant a la vigne son asnon, & au sep le petit de son asnesse ...*, where the Vulgate has *...donec veniat qui mittendus est ... Ligans ad vineam pullum suum, et ad vitem, o fili mi, asinam suam*, which is at best a misunderstanding of an archaic Hebrew genitive, בני אתנו, or an intentional christological distortion. Luther, too, had refused Jerome's invocation of "my son" in this verse. Engammare has found another example of Olivétan's independence: Zach 4:14, where he prefers Qimhi's non-Christian identification of the שני בני היצהר with Joshua, the high priest, and Zorobabel,[22] rather than with Saints Peter and Paul,[23] and he adds that in such a passage we see the influence of Olivétan's master, Capito.

Olivétan's translation tends to reduce mythology, but quite erratically.

In Gen 6:2, he translates בני אלהים by an entirely mythological singular, *les filz de Dieu*, possibly because he had already translated אלהים as a singular in the Genesis 1 narrative, and he explains in the margin here, *c'est hões notables & puissans. Aucũs cõgnoissans Dieu*, an interpretation that follows Rashi and a Jewish tradition which sought at any price to avoid the anthropomorphism of a God having sons. The offspring of these unions, the נפילים, are rendered "geans": *En ce temps la estoiẽt les geans sur la terre & aussi apres que ainsi les filz de Dieu convindrent avec les filles des hõmes: lors elles engendrerent. Iceulx sont les puissans qui iadis furẽt gens de renom*, which sacrifices the etymology of נפילים, from נפל, 'to fall', and thus support for the legend of the revolt of Satan and the fall of the angels in Jude 6. The marine beasts of Gen 1:21, התנינם הגדלים, are rendered *les grandes baleines*. But there is also a contrary impulse which embraces the most marvelous elements in the Bible. The תנים of Isa 34:13, apparently jackals or similar terrestrial creatures (cf. Jer 9:10; 10:22; 49:33; 51:37, etc.), are identified, following the Vulgate, as "dragons". *Behemoth* and *leviathan* of Job 40:15 and 25 are not translated, as though they were proper nouns, the names of unique beasts (שם בהמה גדולה, Ibn Ezra), just like the untranslated *ziim*, *ohim* and *iim* of Isa 13:21 and 34:14 which, on the contrary, are probably banal beasts of desolate landscapes, even if

---

[20] Cf. Preface [4v°].
[21] See his Preface [5r°]: *en suivant la translation chaldee et doctes Ebrieux.*
[22] Münster, [*Hebraica Biblia* (1534)], ad loc.
[23] See de Sacy, *Les douze petits prophètes* (1679), Zech 4, "Sens spirituel", ad vv. 2 and 3.

they can no longer be identified precisely,[24] while, in Ps 74:13–14, *leviathan* is translated "whale": *Tu as enfondre la mer par ta force & as casse les testes des baleines sur les eaues*. For Isa 27:1,

על לויתן נחש ברח ועל לויתן נחש עקלתון והרג את התנין אשר בים

Olivétan rather inconsistently identifies *leviathan* with a "snake" and *tanin* with a "whale": *Leviathan le serpent grãd & Leviathan le serpẽt tortu: et occira la Baleine qui est en la mer*, taking the first two to be marvelous and unique beasts and the third, again, to be a banal whale. Sometimes he mythologizes more than necessary. The שעירים, probably "hairy demons" (Th. Gaster's translation, Vulgate: *dæmones*) of Lev 17:7 are rendered "diables", while in Isa 13:21 they are merely "luittons" (malicious but not nefarious night spirits). Rather than Adam's first wife (see *Alphabeta de Ben-Sira*) or the child-killing demon that she is in other *midrashim*, the לילית of the same verse is a less menacing *faee*. The שטן of Job 2 and 1:6 is transliterated, "Satan", rather than identified with the Devil who revolted against God and would tempt Jesus. Olivétan consistently misses the mythological nuance of רפאים (Isa 26:14; Prov 2:18; 9:18; 21:16, Ps 88:11 and Job 26:5) translating *les trespasses, les morts, les choses mortes, les geans* and *les invités*.

We conclude that mythology in the Bible was not yet enough of a problem to oblige him to seek consistency in his translations, though he seems to avoid introducing the devil and the reification of evil so prominent in the Gospels but de-emphasized in Calvinist theology.

The translation of Isa 45:6 is rather weak, possibly intentionally so, when Olivétan renders רע, in the prophet's vigorous denial of dualism, as adversity, *Ie suis le Seigneur et nen y a dautre: formant la lumiere & creant les tenebres: faisant la paix et creant ladversité. Ie suis le Seigneur faisant toutes ces choses la*. He misses the fusion of sacred and sexual elements in קדשה and קדש, translating the former in Gen 38:21, *Ou est ceste putain?*, but cannot miss it entirely in 2 Kgs 23:7, *Et aussi ceulx qui faisoient les encẽsemens a Baal, au soleil, a la lune, aux planettes, et a tout lexercite du ciel*, but *Apres il [le roi Josiah] demolit les maisons des paillards qui estoient en la maison du Seigneur*. He translates אשרה as just plain *bois*.

Olivétan's translation and especially his marginal notes identify Jesus as the subject of a limited number of Old Testament passages.

Isa 7:14 comes out, as in the Vulgate: *Voicy la vierge concevra & enfãtera ung filz & appeleras son nom Emanu-el*. The same word, עלמה, occurs in Gen 24:43, Exod 2:8 and Cant 1:3, and in all three verses Olivétan translates *pucelle* which, to judge from Prov 30:19, where it is translated by the same word, did not imply virginity in his Picard French, *la voye de lhomme apres la pucelle. Telle est aussi la voye de la femme adultere qui mange et torche sa bouche et dist: Ie nay point faict liniquite*. The child of Isa 9:5 is not identified with Jesus, possibly because it would have been superfluous for Christian readers, but Olivétan does identify the subject of Isaiah 11 as *De la paix & felicite au regne de Christ*, and that of Psalm 22 as *Oraison de David figure de Christ*, while Isaiah 53 is summarized as *De lestat et condition de Christ*, followed by New Testament references. Nothing surprising here except the non-identification of the 'virgin' of Isa 7:14 with Mary, whose role in the economy of salvation is more prominent in sixteenth-century Catholic thought than in Calvinist theology. Or it may have been too obvious to belabor.

Olivétan is rather direct about sexual matters.

A זונה is *une paillarde* (Gen 38:15), and in the story of Dinah and her brothers' vengeance upon the town of Shechem in Genesis 34, *Et Dinah ... issit pour veoir les filles du pays. Lors la veit Sichem filz de Hemor.... [il] la ravist et dormit avec elle et [ou viola] et lhumilia et appliqua son courage a Dinah fille de Iakob e ayma la fille et parloit cordialement avec la fille* (vv. 1–3). When the men of Sodom learn that Loth has guests, they demand, Gen 19:5, that he turn them over *affin [cest que no[ous] ayõs compaignie charnelle de eulx] que nous les congnoissions*, while *Onan congnoissant quil nauroit point lignee quãd il entroit a la fẽme de son frere: il se corrompoit sur la terre, affin quil ne don-*

---

[24] HAL translates אחים as "eagle owls" and איים as "jackals", but ציים as "demon dwellers of ציה".

nast semence a son frere (Gen 38:9), and the midwives of Exod 1:16 are instructed to observe על האבנים, *sur les fesses*, to determine whether the child is male or female. The place to look for a translator's scruples in rendering sex related prose is the Song of Songs which Olivétan construes as a dialogue between *lespouse, lespoux* and then *les pucelles ou lespouse*. He translates דדי (Cant 1:2, etc.) as *amours* and שדי (Cant 1:13) as *mes mamelles*. Cant 4:3, which seems to refer to the beloved's charming sex and *mons veneris*, comes out quite chastely, *Tes levres sont cõme une bẽde de couleur de graine: & est ta parolle* (מדבריך) *delectable cõme une piece de põme de grenade.*[25]

    This is a pedantic and plodding translation, but it makes an honest effort to be accurate, word for word. Generally, Olivétan maintains the autonomy of the Old Testament with regard to the New. Identifications with Jesus are merely an additional dimension of the Hebrew text, but not its essence much less its sole *raison d'être*. He is not yet interested in Bible criticism or comparative mythology nor the conflicts of natural science with the miracles attested in the Bible. As one should have expected, he was a man of his time.

3. Sébastien Châteillon

Source: S. CHATEILLON: *La Genèse 1555* (ed. J. Chaurand / N. Gueunier / C. Skupien Dekens, with the collaboration of M. Engammare; Geneva: Droz 2003); on *La Bible ...*, see the general Bibliography above, p. 553.
    Studies: H. R. GUGGISBERG, *Sebastian Castallio, Humanist und Verteidiger der religiösen Toleranz im konfessionellen Zeitalter* (Göttingen: Vandenhoeck & Ruprecht 1997); F. BUISSON, *Sébastien Castellion. Sa vie et son œuvre (1515–1563). Etudes sur les origines du christianisme libéral français* (Paris: Hachette 1891); N. GUEUNIER, "Une Bible française méconnue, Sébastian Castellion (1555)", *Esprit* (2001) 693–95; idem, "La Genèse de Castellion et la langue-source", in: S. CASTELLION, *La Genèse 1555* (Geneva: Droz 2003) 11–37; C. SKUPIEN DEKENS, "Castellion et la langue cible", ibid. 39–67; J. CHAURAND, "Castellion et la langue cible. Le lexique", ibid. 69–91; M. ENGAMMARE, "L'illustration de la Genèse", ibid. 93–112.

Like Olivétan's Bible, Sébastien Châteillon's is a translation from the Hebrew[26] and, necessarily, from the *massoretic* text. He, too, numbers the Psalms according to the *massoretic* system, but he introduces the apocryphal Prayer of Manasseh after 2 Chr 33:13, and translates the other books that the Catholics consider canonical but which Jews and some Protestants regard as apocryphal, Tobit, Judith, Ben-Sira and the Wisdom of Solomon, and he adds the first two books of Maccabees and then, in a smaller type-face, Josephus Flavius's *Antiquities* xiii.15-xviii.3 (the "Testimonium Flavium") to bridge the gap between the Old Testament canon and the New. Rather than being a book of revelations, his Bible is very 'protestant', a sacred history. Châteillon is no more a partisan of the *massoretic* text than he is of the Jewish canon.

    In Psalm 22, he still translates כרו, *Car les chiens m'environnent: une bricade de garnemens m'assiege, qui m'ont percé mains et pieds*, rather than the more standard but less comprehensible *massoretic* כארי, without, however, identifying this verse as a prophecy of Jesus' crucifixion. R. Simon claimed

---

[25] מדברך is traditionally derived from דבר, 'speech', but מדבר, 'wilderness', from the Ugaritic and Akkadian, yields a suggestive metonymy. See HAL, s.v. Cf. Lysistrata 89 for a similar metonymy.
    [26] Gueunier, Une Bible française méconnue (2001); Guggisberg, Sebastian Castallio (1997); Buisson, Sébastien Castellion. Sa vie et son œuvre (1891).

that, in his Latin translation of the Bible, Châteillon had corrected the Hebrew text according to the canons of textual criticism,[27] and he approved, but we have not found good examples, only a few expansions of texts, like the one concerning sexual congress with a menstruating woman to be cited *infra*, where Châteillon requires the woman to have informed her partner for him to be deemed sinful, which is not in the Hebrew text (והיא גלתה את מקור דמיה, Lev 20:18, which assumes that she was a willing accomplice to her partner's impudicity but not that a declaration of impurity be a necessary condition for his guilt).

We have not found more interest in Bible criticism in Châteillon than in Olivétan and possibly even less, because we have not noticed marginal references to variants in the Hebrew text, but he is intentionally writing a less pedantic translation than Olivétan's, avoiding Latinate and Greek French.

He writes, for example, *arriere-femme* (Judges 20) for *concubine*, *avantpeau* ("*forgé sur le mot aleman, vorhaut*"), *rogné* and *empellé* (all three in Genesis 17) for *prépuce*, *circoncis* and *incirconcis*, respectively, and *appaisoire* rather than *propitiatoire* for כפרת, and *flamage* or *brûlage*, *sacrifice pour la prospérité*, *defaute* and *deforfaitte* for the עולה, שלמים, חטאת and אשם sacrifices (see his *Déclaration de certains mots*, at the end of his Bible). He uses the French forms of Hebrew proper nouns rather than Olivétan's transliterations: *Isaac* for *Isahak*, *Iudah* for *Iehudah* and *Moïse* for *Moseh*. He does not call attention any more than Olivétan had done to the Leviticus citation identified in 2 Chr 36:21 as a prophecy of Jeremiah, and he disguises the problem of בעבר הירדן in Deut 1:1 by translating *deça le Iordan*. On the other hand, he occasionally spots doublets, for example Isa 7:2 and Exod 15:2, but more often does not, as in Ps 68:2 and 8–9 which are identical to Num 10:35 and to Judg 5:4–5, respectively. This was to be a translation for the "imbéciles" and not a treatise on the composition and transmission of the biblical text, so there was no reason to annotate exhaustively much less to draw explicit conclusions.

Like Olivétan, Châteillon translates אלהים as *Dieu* or *dieu*, even when the verb agreement is with a plural.

So is the case in Gen 20:13: *E quãd Dieu me fit déloger de chés mõ pere*, and Gen 35:7, *à cause que Dieu s'y étoit montré*, thus hiding the traces of a premonotheistic conception of god (but see also Gen 1:26: *Faisons hõme a notr'image, semblable a nous*). יהוה אלהים of Genesis 2 and elsewhere is translated *le Seigneur Dieu*, as it is in Olivétan, while יהוה alone tends to be translated *le Seigneur*, as in Gen 28:13, or *Iova*, his spelling of Olivétan's transliteration, *Jehovah*, as in Exod 6:1. For אל שדי (Gen 48:3 and Exod 6:2), he again follows the Vulgate and Olivétan to render the expression *tout puissant*. Exod 3:14 comes out: *Ie serai qui serai: Tu diras ainsi aux Enfans d'Israel (dit-il) SERAI m'envoye a vous. Tu diras aux Enfans d'Israel (dit encore Dieu a Moyse) que IOVA le Dieu de leurs peres ... t'envoye a eux.*

Châteillon is still less insistent than Olivétan on translating and commenting on the Old Testament as a prophecy and prototype of the New.

The famous prophecy about the עלמה who will bear a man child (Isa 7:14) comes out: *Saches qu'il y a une fille enceinte, laquelle enfantera un fils et le nommera Emmanuel*, with marginal cross references to Luke and Matthew but no explicit identification of the *fille* in question with Mary. Where the word occurs again, Cant 1:3 (in plural), he again translates *les filles* but in Gen 24:43, Exod 2:8 and Prov 30:19, he translates *garse*, a feminine of *garçon* which has not been retained in polite French, *Il y a trois ou quatre choses qui surmontēt ma portée et lêquelles ie n'entend pas: la trace de l'aigle en l'aer; la trace d'un serpent par dessus une Pierre: la trace d'une nef parmi la mer: e la trace d'un homme en une garse. Telle êt la côtume d'une femme adultere: elle mange e se torche la bouche, puis dit qu'elle n'a point cõmis de vilenie.* Another passage that confirms that *garse* had no virginal connotations for Châteillon is Judges 19, where the Levite's פילגש is also a *garse*. The אל גבור of Isa 9:5 is rendered: *Car un enfant nous nait, un fis nous êt donné, qui porte seigneurie sur ses épaules, qui a nom Merveilleux conseillier: Dieu puissant: Pere de iamais: Prince de paix*, with a general identifica-

---

[27] *Histoire critique* (1685) 326.

tion with Christ, rather than with Jesus, whose divinity he neither seeks to exclude from this verse nor to mitigate. However the translations of Isaiah 11–12 and Psalm 110 are not explicitly messianic except for a general marginal identification of the subject of Isaiah 11 as Christ, and the inevitable marginal cross references to the New Testament. In Isaiah 53 he decodes the metaphorical language, *Des liens e du iugement il a été mené [a savoir a la mort] e qui diroit [qu'il soit fis de Dieu, veu qu'il êt le plus méprisé du monde] son lignage?* In the margin of Isaiah 35 he adds, *Les payēs viē-dront a Christ.* He may be asserting in some of these cases that these are indeed messianic prophecies without asserting that it is Jesus to whom they refer, but that may be reading him too precisely. This is not to suggest that Châteillon was a closet free-thinker, merely that he does not choose to use his translation to determine a ubiquitous apologetic reading of the Old Testament. This is confirmed by the Preface where he admits to identifying certain prophecies with Jesus but prefers to leave explorations of the "spiritual sense" of other prophecies to more gifted interpreters. In the notes at the end of the second volume of his Bible, he decodes Isaiah 7–9 and Psalm 90, upon which he had not commented in the translation itself, as referring to Jesus.

Châteillon's approach to myth in the Bible is not consistent, but he tends to reduce it to the realm of the (more or less) natural phenomena.

התנינם הגדלים of Gen 1:21 are mere *grans poissonars*. בני האלהים of Gen 6:2 become *les grans seigneurs* and, despite the obvious etymology, the נפלים of v. 4 become *les preux*, which follows the Jewish tradition (cf. Bereshith Rabbah and Rashi, Nahmanides, Ibn Ezra, Shmuel ben Meir, etc. who sought to exclude the Christian mythology-theology of autonomous angels that had to be vanquished by God) and, like Olivétan, he avoids any suggestion of a revolt of the angels and their subsequent fall.

In Gen 3:24 God bars the entrance to Eden with the *cherubim* (plural) and the flaming and revolving sword, which in Châteillon's translation loses its definite article, *Il logea devers le levãt du vergier d'Eden, les Cherubins, et une flamboyante épee, brandissante, pour garder l'entrée de l'arbre de vie*, and with it its mythological status as a special sword endowed with autonomous power. *Behemoth* in Job 40:15 is an elephant. The two *leviathans* of Isa 27:1 are identified with kinds of snake, as though they were not unique beasts, *Alors le Seigñr a tout son dur, grand e puissant glaive, punira Leviathan serpent long comm'une perche, e Leviathan serpent tortu, et tuera le poissonar qui êt en mer*, while *leviathan* is a whale in Job 40:25 and Ps 74:13–14, where תנין, too, is a banal beast, *Tu mipartis la mer par ta puissance, e brisas les têtes des poissonars [Egytiēs] es eaux. Tu écartelas les têtes de la baleine [Pharaon]....* Elsewhere as well he identifies the subjects of prophecies: Ps 110:6, *Il assomera la tête qui tient grand pays [l'empire de Rome]*. The strange beasts of Isa 13:21 and 34:11, 13–14 are not terribly demonic either, ... *ains y coucheront les Sylvains* (ציים), *e les faunes* (אחים) *rēplirõt leurs maisons, e y habiterõt les autruches* (בנות יענה), *e y sauteront les Luittõs* (שעירים), *les hibous* (איים) *chanterõt en ses châteaux, e les dragons* (תנים) *en ses plaisans palais* and, adding two plurals to harmonize his text, *E les ibes* (קאת) *e herissons* (קפד) *s'en saisiront, e y habiteront, les cheveches* (וינשוף) *e corbeaux* (ערב) *e étendra sur elle le cordeau de deshabitacion, e la pesera es balances de sauvageté ... e croitront épines* (סירים) *en ses châteaux, e chardons* (קמוש) *e aubepins* (וחוח) *en ses forteresses: elle sera repaire de dragons* (תנים) *e demeure d'autruches* (לבנות יענה). *Les Sylvains* (ציים) *rencontreront les Faunes* (איים) *e les Luittons* (שעיר) *se hucheront l'un l'autre : voire les Faées* (לילית) *s'y logeront.* Hellel ben Shahar of Isa 14:12 is a fallen star that is not identified with Lucifer, *Comment es-tu trêbuché du ciel, ô étoille iournalle, fils de l'aube, abbatu a terre?* The רפאים of v. 9 are translated by a classical equivalent which is perhaps too specific but at least remains in the mythological scale, *L'enfer de lá bas, effrayé de ta venue e arrivée, remue les Titanes pour toi*, and elsewhere by one form or other of 'death' while the שעירים of Lev 17:7, which Olivétan had rendered *diables*, are merely *satyres*, borrowed from Greek legend, mild mythology in preference to dualistic theology.

Objects that are specific to the Bible tend to be naturalized or explained.

The אהל מועד, 'tabernacle' in standard translations, becomes the *pavillon des oracles*, צבא השמים becomes *l'arroi celeste* (2 Kgs 23:4). Sometimes he reduces terms that his archaeology could not define with certitude. Thus אשרה becomes *bois de devociõ* (Deut 16:21), and בתי הקדשים become "bordeaux" (also 2 Kgs 23:6 and 7). The gnomic Gen 36:24,

הוא ענה אשר מצא את הימם במדבר

comes out, as in Olivétan, ... *lequel Ana trouva [la facon de faire engendrer les mulets] les mulets es bois, en paissant les ânes de Sibeon son pere*, but his marginal note (inserted here into the quotation) follows Ibn Ezra in imagining what natural phenomenon Ana discovered.

Châteillon's vocabulary is very sixteenth-century French and sometimes no longer familiar.

The חגורות, which Adam and Eve sewed to cover their nakedness (Gen 3:7) are *brayes*, and Noah's nakedness which Shem and Yepheth covered (Gen 9:23) is *la vergoigne de leur pere* as is ערות אביו of the incest prohibitions of Leviticus 18 and 20:11. A stream (נחל) is a *bié*. The wealth that Abraham acquired before migrating to Canaan (Gen 12:5) is *chevance*. He uses *tettin* (Cant 4:10, *Tes tettins sōt beaucoup plus iolis, ma sœur mon épouse: tes tettins sont beaucoup plus beaux que vin* ... and elsewhere) where Olivétan had used *mamelle* which was to become standard in polite seventeenth-century French – de Sacy will use the word without compunction – while *tettin* would be reserved for animals.[28] A glance at the Huguet *Dictionnaire de la langue française du seizième siècle*[29] shows that all these words, as well as *brebiette* (Cant 6:6) were well known in Châteillon's time. But others, for instance *deâtre* (false god) and *poissonar* (marine monster), that he admits inventing, do not appear in that very complete dictionary, while *brunette*, at least as he uses it, does not either, which shows that his linguistic inventions, unlike Rabelais's, were not adopted.

Regarding sex, Châteillon can be direct though not crude. In Gen 38:9 *Onan quand il vouloit avoir la compagnie de la femme de son frere, se corrompit a terre*, like Olivétan's translation, and, v. 15, Judah mistakes the disguised Tamar for a *putain* and propositions her (v. 16): *Veus-tu que i'aye ta compagnie? ... E il lui bailla [son ruben et son bâton] e eut affair'avec elle e lengrossa.* Cant 5:4 is as close to a description of sexual union as one finds in Scripture, but Châteillon's translation is no more explicit than the Hebrew:

> *J'ai dépouillé ma chemise, cōment la vêtirai-ie? J'ai lave mes pieds, comment les suillerai-ie? Mon ami a mis sa main par un pertuis, de quoi i'ai eu le cueur émeu, que ie me suis levee pour ouvrir a mon ami: dont i'ai senti couler par mes doits de la myrre, qui passoit par les trous du verroil. J'ai bien ouvert a mon ami, mais mon ami s'étoit retiré, e a son parler j'ai été pâmée ....*

Another passage that might have lent itself to a pornographic imagination comes out as chastely as it had in Olivétan's translation, *Tes levres sont cōm'un rubē d'écarlatte : ton parler plaisāt* (Cant 4:3).

Châteillon can also translate euphemistically, as in Lev 20:18: *E si un hōme qui couche avec une fēme qui a ses fleurs* [אשה דוה]*, e qu'il ait affaire a elle, e ouvre le flux d'elle, e q[ue]lle l'ait averti du flux de sō sang, qu'ils soiēt tous les deux raclés d'entre leurs gēs.* Châteillon can be vigorous, *N'envilaine point ta fille en en faisāt une putain* (Lev 19:29) or delightfully inventive, *Tes dents ressemblēt a un troupeau de brebiettes* [הרחלים]*, qui viennēt tout frais d'être lavées* (Cant 6:6). He has a fine ear for the music of the language: Cant 1:5, *Vrai êt que ie suis brunette* [שחורה]*; mais ie suis autant jolie, filles de Jérusalem* is rather witty in its translation of the conjunction ו as *mais autant*, which is justified by the context, and its use of *brunette*; which had three different senses: a delicate woolen fabric, a kind of flower or a kind of bird, for a dark complectioned girl, Cant 7:7, *O q[ue] tu es belle, o q[ue] tu es iolie, ma mignonne par amour* is lyrical, while Isa 58:1, *Crie a bon gousier, sans t'épargner : hausse ta voix comme*

---

[28] See Littré, s. v.
[29] Paris 1925.

d'une trompette … is heroic, and 54:11, *O souffreteuse, tempêtée, déconsolée, sache que ie coucherai tes pierres en margarites, e te fondrai en saphirs* … pathetic. The episode of Balaam's talkative ass (Num 22:28–30) is eloquent in Châteillon's French:

> *Adonc le Seigneur ouvrit la bouche de l'ânesse, dont elle dit a Balaam: Que t'ai-ie fait que tu m'as battue dêia trois fois? E Balaam dit a l'ânesse: c'êt pourtant que tu te truffes de moi. E pleût a Dieu q[ue] i'eusse un'épée: car ie te tueroi tout a cêt'heure. Et l'ânesse dit a Balaam : Ne sui-ie pas tõ ânesse, laquelle tu as toute ta vie chevauchée iusqu'a present? Ai-ie accôtume de te fair'ainsi? Nenni dit il.*[30]

Sayce cites the translation of Ps 104:3–4 as an illustration that Châteillon was "capable of rising to the greatness of his task and of attaining true poetic quality",[31] and we heartily agree.

Finally, Châteillon's translation is less word-for-word slavish than Olivétan's. He will gloss his text when necessary for comprehension without indicating that he has added a word or two. He sometimes encloses a few words in parentheses, as in Exod 6:1 and Gen 36:24, cited above, and he translates conjunctions according to context, as for instance the כי in Exod 13:17 as *qui étoit le plus court* which is neither unreasonable nor unfaithful to the original though a concessive, "even though it was shorter" would make still more sense. He is aware of the difficulty of translating the names of plants, animals and articles of clothing but takes a stab at it anyway because he has warned his readers in the "Avertissement touchant cête translacion":

> *E quand i'écri que ie n'entend pas un tel passage, ou un tel, ie ne veux pas pourtant donner a entendre que i'entende bien tous les autres: ains veux dire que és autres i'y voi quelque peu, e en ceux lá ie n'y voi goutte: e le fai aussi afin qu'ê quelques tels passages on ne se fie pas trop en ma translacion. Toute-fois ie ne mõtre pas partout ce que ie n'entend pas: car ce seroit une chose infinie (4v°).*

This explains the precision with which he permits himself to identify the beasts in Isaiah 34, or the fabrics in Esth 1:6 , *Lá y avoit de voiles de taffetas, e de fin lin, e de vermeil, étêdus a tout des cordes de lin e de pourpre, q[ui] passoi[e]nt par des poulies d'argêt lêquelles voiles étoĩt pêdues en colõnes de marbre. Les couches etoĩt d'or e d'argêt et l'aire de porphire, de marbre, de pierre tralvisãte, e de pierre de feu*, where any modern translator would be more prudent. It would be interesting to see to what extent Olivétan's orthodox revisers profited from Châteillon's intelligent work.

4. Louis-Isaac Le Maistre de Sacy

Studies: M. DE CERTEAU, "L'idée de traduction de la Bible au XVIIIᵉ siècle: Sacy et Simon", *RSR* 66 (1978) 73–92; G. DELASSAULT, *Le Maistre de Sacy et son temps* (Paris 1957); B. MUNTEANU, "Port-Royal et la stylistique de la traduction", *Actes du VIIᵉ congrès de l'Association internationale des études françaises* (Paris 1955) 151–72; H. MESCHONIC, "Traduire le goût, c'est la guerre du rythme", *L'Infini* 76 (2001) 25–60.

---

[30] The *pleût a Dieu* is not in the Hebrew לו יש חרב בידי כי עתה הרגתיך, Num 22:29.
[31] French Versions (1976) 120.

With Louis-Isaac Le Maistre de Sacy (1613–84)[32] we are in the world of post-Tridentine Catholic orthodoxy and "le classicisme", a very particular literary style reflecting the language and self-conscious values of the French court and aristocracy, both of which exercised very strong constraints upon him. The word 'constraint' suggests an unwilling author struggling to free himself, and that is surely not his case. He recognized three different vertices for a translation: fidelity, defined as attachment to the letter of the source text, which did not imply for him, as it tended to imply for Olivétan, word-to-word translation, comprehensibility and clarity, and beauty and the graces of the target language.[33] All good translators recognize these three objectives, though the position of a translation within the triangle that those vertices determine varies with the translator's intentions and skill. When translating the Bible, de Sacy tried to tip the balance towards fidelity to the text, at least relative to his practice when he translated pagan texts, where he had tipped the scale towards the literary idiom of his target language. MUNTEANU quotes an example from de Sacy's translation of Cicero where he makes the Roman orator speak like a seventeenth-century marquis. Despite his good intentions, de Sacy's Bible translation is still more ideological than literal, calculated to re-enforce piety and apologetics rather than to explore the philology of the Hebrew and, for the New Testament, Greek texts underlying the Vulgate. Even the Old Testament part of de Sacy's Bible is completely Christ-centred, Church-centred and Trinitarian. He never seems to have asked himself whether the ancient authors he was translating could have imagined the theology he projected onto their words and phrases. His Old Testament is thus oracular and even sibylline, in the sense that its authors are not assumed to have necessarily understood the profound meaning of what they were inspired to pronounce or write, rather than prophecy and admonition addressed to the historical Israel, as it had been for the Jewish commentators, or testimony to a sacred history, as it had been for Olivétan, Châteillon and for Huguenots more generally. DE CERTEAU compares de Sacy and Richard Simon as translators, and argues implicitly that de Sacy should not be held up to a high standard of philological accuracy because "he aimed at the meaning of the biblical authors", which is to say "the Spirit of God", defined for him by the Fathers, whereas Simon, who also translated from the Vulgate, so that Church goers might understand the text in liturgical use, but added remarks that admitted the primordial value of the underlying Greek, aimed at "the meaning of texts", which is to say "their literary and semantic organization".[34] Rather than emerging from the literal sense of biblical texts, the "geography" of de Sacy's faith, DE CERTEAU further asserts, is circumscribed by the oral and prophetic tradition of Church teaching, and we have found no reason to qualify this description. In view of this idiosyncratic approach to the Bible, which de Sacy shared with his Port-Royal collaborators, their apparently democratic insistence on Bible reading by the

---

[32] De Certeau, L'idée de traduction de la Bible (1978) 73–92, and Sayce, French Versions (1976) 348–49.
[33] See Munteanu, Port-Royal et la stylistique de la traduction (1955) 151–72.
[34] De Certeau, L'idée de traduction de la Bible (1978) 80.

laity must be construed as only superficially akin to the Protestant practice, because the daily Bible reading that Pasquier Quesnel and his fellow Jansenists urged upon the laity was exclusively a coded reading that permitted them little latitude in the way they might understand and appreciate the Bible. Whether this is an adequate apology for the translator's liberties with the biblical text which will be demonstrated here is for theologians to decide, but it will become clear that from the point of view of biblical philology, de Sacy had more to answer for than Olivétan and Châteillon who did their best to represent faithfully the most ancient and authentic text available to them.

There are no introductions to or résumés of the chapters of de Sacy's Old Testament except for the Psalms, very few notes at the bottom of the page, and those that are there are printed in an extremely small type-face and very rarely cite their authorities. We have used the volumes in the Mazarine Library in Paris, two of which are first editions and the remainder are 1690s editions which seem to be faithful to the pattern of the first edition. Subsequent editions were revised and should be consulted with great caution if the objective is to study de Sacy's understanding of Bible. If the notes in the Paris 1704 edition are faithful reflections of de Sacy's readings, which seems to be the case,[35] we may deduce that he drew upon the relatively literalist but still strictly orthodox seventeenth-century Catholic interpreters anthologized by Jean de La Haye[36] who included Cajetan, Estius, Menochius, Gagnius and Serrarius. We have not noticed, in that 1704 edition, nor in the 1690s editions, references to Jesuit interpreters like Jacques Bonfrère, whom Richard Simon admired because their more humanistic theory of biblical inspiration permitted them to approach Bible criticism. De Sacy added to this relatively literalist tradition edifying interpretations drawn from Augustine and other Fathers who made no pretence of interpreting the letter of the biblical texts. Again judging from the 1704 edition's notes it seems that de Sacy took the little he knew about the Hebrew text from François Vatable's "annotations", notes taken during Vatable's lectures as the first Royal Professor of Hebrew (1530 to 1547), published in Robert Estienne's 1545 Latin Bible and reissued in subsequent, more orthodox Bibles. The problem of translation of the many difficult Old Testament verses was thus reduced, first by de Sacy's choice of translating the Vulgate, that had been identified by the Council of Trent in 1546 as the sole authentic biblical text, which already represented Jerome's choices of a clear sense for most texts, and then by a choice of edifying interpretations with no pretensions to explaining difficult words and syntactical structures when the Vulgate was still not sufficiently clear or edifying. By comparison, Calmet's *Commentaire littéral*, which would provoke the amusement of Voltaire, Mme du Châtelet and other eighteenth-century *philosophes*, is a model of scholarly ambition and rigor. Each chapter in de Sacy is followed by an *explication* of the *sens littéral* and

---

[35] The "explication" of Judg 18:30–31 in the 1690s series of exemplars, mentions Estius (Willem van Est) who figures very frequently in the notes of the Paris 1704 edition, which confirms that he was one of the commentators upon whom de Sacy relied.

[36] *Biblia magna commentariorum literalium* (Paris 1643) 5v in-folio, and *Biblia maxima versionum ex linguis orientalibus ... et eius expositione literali ...* (Paris 1660) 19v in-folio.

then by a second *explication* of the *sens spirituel*, which implies that, for him, they were distinct, although in view of the generosity of his conception of the *sens littéral*. That that distinction is no longer entirely clear is confirmed by his practice of merging his two *explications* for relatively uninteresting chapters. These *explications* further determine how the biblical text should be understood, and de Sacy's translation was apparently not meant to be read alone, without their qualifications.

The clarity and comprehensibility that de Sacy sought had, as one of their elements, total consistency with Catholic doctrine and apologetics. The result was that in his hands, the Old Testament lost its autonomy and consequently its Jewish character, contrary to Chédozeau's claim,[37] that de Sacy does not "evacuate" the Old Testament of its most obvious meanings.

Isaiah 54, for example, which, to a literal-minded reader, might seem to be a prophecy of consolation addressed to Israel, is summarized according to Augustine's interpretation as

> *Le Prophete donc dit, que l'Eglise ... aura plus d'enfans que la Synagogue qui avoit pris Dieu pour son Seigneur & pour son Epoux, en se soumettant a la loy qu'il luy avoit donnée. Car les Juifs ayāt crucifié ce meme Messie qui leur avoit esté promis & qu'ils attendoient depuis si longtemp, l'Eglise que Jésus-Christ a choisie pour son Epouse & qu'il a remplie de son Esprit l'a fait connoistre & adorer dans toute la terre* (*Sens littéral*, Isa 54:1).

Gen 1:26, instead of being a faint echo of some early moment in Jewish religious history when its eventual monotheism had not yet been entirely consolidated, is for him a proof of the Trinitarian quality of God:

> *Les mêmes saints Docteurs remarquent aussi avec raison que ces paroles:* Faisons l'homme à nostre image, *montrent clairement la pluralité des personnes de la sainte Trinité, le Pere parlant au Fils & au Saint-Esprit; & ils ajoûtent que ce qui est dit ensuite,* Et Dieu crea l'homme à son image, *marque encore que ces trois personnes ne sont qu'un seul Dieu* (*Sens littéral*, ad loc.).

One rather expects the translation of Song of Songs to be very euphemistic, but not at all. It is surprisingly honest and literal, but that is compensated by very extensive *explications* which completely purge the text of its bucolic primary sense, which de Sacy regards as unthinkable because it is contrary to the Patristic exegetical tradition, and transform it into a coded account of the relations of Jesus and his Church, ...*le vray sens littéral de ce saint Cantique regarde l'union toute divine de Jésus-Christ & de l'Eglise, de l'Epoux par excellence avec l'épouse* ... (*Sens littéral et spirituel*, Cant 1:1), and thus the דדיך of Cant 1:2 are *vos mamelles*, which represent the maternal love of Jesus-Christ for his Church, and the rest follows that venerable pattern. Asking whether the eighth-century Isaiah, or the sixth-century Deutero-Isaiah or the still later authors of Canticles could have imagined symmetric institutions like *l'Eglise* and *la Synagogue* and an eschatological Messiah's love of the one in preference to the other is surely the wrong question. De Sacy has narrowed the scope of Bible to the point where Israel has lost its national identity; Moses, David and the prophets are no longer individuals through whose experiences and actions God revealed an ethical and religious message to the Jews and through them to the world, but figures of Jesus and the Church, so why expect greater fidelity to the primary sense of Canticles?

De Sacy defends the correctness of the Vulgate with respect to the Hebrew as, for instance, in Judg 17:1, and still prefers it even when he admits that the Hebrew text is better, for instance as regards the break between chapters 4 and 5 of the Song of Songs: *Il semble qu'il eust esté plus naturel de suivre l'Hebreu en*

---

[37] See Bogaert, *Les Bibles* (1991) 150.

cet endroit ...; he did not realize that, while the division of the text into verses is a Jewish legacy, the division into chapters was adopted by the Jews in the 1517 Venice folio Bible from Christian sources. There must be examples that we have not yet identified that extend to the Old Testament Simon's complaints that de Sacy chose his New Testament text eclectically.[38] Even when the Vulgate was quite impossible, he follows it, especially if it suggested a christological sense.

In Genesis 49:11, for example, he writes: *Il liera son ânon à la vigne, il liera, ô mon fils, son ânesse à la vigne*, though he does not make the referent of *ô mon fils* explicit in the explication of the *sens littéral* (ad loc.). This is a bit strange because the christological implications of verses are almost always made explicit, for instance in Gen 3:1 and 15, where Eve is Mary, her descendants are Jesus, and the snake is Satan, or Genesis 49:8–12, where שלה, *shilo*, is *Celui qui doit estre envoyé* because *cette prophetie, selon le consentement des plus savans Interpretes, enferme certainement le temps de la venue du Messie, comme la plûpart des Hebreux le reconnoissent aussi bien que la paraphrase chaldaïque* (*Sens littéral*, Gen 49:10), or the summary of Psalm 22, *Le titre de ce Pseaume s'entend proprement de la resurrection de Jésus-Christ, qui arrive le matin, & qui fut l'effet de l'assistance toute puissance de Dieu, qui tire son corps du fond du tombeau* .... Sometimes an identification, like that of the עלמה who is to conceive and bear a man-child in Isa 7:14 with Mary, is too obvious for him and for his readers to assert. In this case he does not think it necessary to explain why that word means "virgin" in this chapter but not elsewhere in the Bible.

More interesting are the notes that reflect doubts about the authenticity of certain verses. Though de Sacy makes no comment on 2 Chr 36:22, nor on several Pentateuch verses like ויררדף עד דן (Gen 14:14) and והכנעני אז בארץ (Gen 12:6), the Ibn Ezra/Spinoza repertoire of post-Mosaic verses,[39] he cannot avoid Deut 1:1, where it is said that Moses spoke בעבר הירדן, "across the Jordan", defined as the land of Moab, which is indeed "across the Jordan" from the west bank where Moses is not supposed to have entered. De Sacy simply ignores the problem: בעבר הירדן is translated to refer to the other side of the Jordan without reflection upon the side from which the author is writing.

> *Voici les paroles que Moïse dit à tout le peuple d'Israel au deça du Jourdain* (cf. Deut 3:5 : *les Israelites étant en deça du Jourdain*, and 3:8: *Nous nous rendîmes donc maîtres en ce tems-là du païs des deux rois des Amorrhéens, qui étoient au-deça du Jourdain*),
> and the note to Deut 1:1 is: *On l'a [trans Iordanum] traduit au-deça; parce que Moïse & les Israelites n'ayant point encore passé le Jourdain, le pays où ils étoient se doit dire être au deça, à l'égard du pays de Canaan qui étoit au-delà de ce fleuve.*

For other evidently anachronistic verses de Sacy dismisses the problem with *ad hoc* solutions rather than a coherent critical approach.

> *Mais les plus habiles [interpretes] conviennent, ou que l'on ne doit pas avoir d'égard à ces paroles* [בימים ההם אין מלך בישראל], *comme ayant été ajoutées, & ne se trouvant ni dans l'Hébreu [sic !] ni dans les Septantes, ou que si l'on veut y avoir égard, elles doivent s'expliquer d'une maniere plus générale ...* (*Sens littéral*, Judg 17:1[6]).
> *Quelques Interpretes croyent que ces paroles* [ואלה המלכים אשר מלכו בארץ אדום לפני מלך מלך לבני ישראל] *ont pû estre ajoûtées par celuy qui a recueilli les livres de Moïse. D'autres, que Moïse les a pû dire par esprit de prophétie, sachant fort bien que les Israélites auroient un jour un Roy, comme il paroist par quelques autres endroits de ses livres* (*Sens littéral*, Gen 36:31).

The history of Micah's altar and its capture by the Danites, Judges 17 and 18, posed a more complex problem because de Sacy had to harmonize three elements: the testimony that the Israelites were faithful to Yahweh during

---

[38] *Histoire critique des versions du Nouveau Testament* (Rotterdam: Reinier Leers 1690) 397.
[39] See the commentary of Abraham ibn Ezra on Deut 1:2, and Baruch Spinoza, *Tractatus theologico-politicus*, Ch. 8.

Joshua's lifetime (Josh 24:31) which requires a date well after Joshua's death, the priest Jonathan's genealogy as described in the Vulgate, which identifies him as a grandson of Moses, which requires a relatively early date, and an unattested exile of the tribe of Dan much earlier than its ultimate exile of the tribe of Dan by Sennacherib in 722 BCE, and the tradition that the book of Judges was written by Samuel or some near contemporary.

> *Quant à ce que l'Ecriture ajoûte, que Jonathan & ses fils furent Prêtres dans la Tribu de Dan jusqu'au jour de leur captivité; quelques-uns entendent par cette captivité celle des dix Tribus d'Israel, qui arriva sous les roys des Assyriens. Mais il n'y a nulle vray-semblance que cette Tribu de Dan ait persévéré si long-tems dans l'idolatrie … Ainsi tous les autres Interpretes soûtiennent avec beaucoup plus de fondement, que par cette capitivité dont il est parlé icy, on doit entendre plûtôt celle qu'on vit arriver du tems du Grand-Prêtre Heli, lorsque l'Arche étant enlevée par les Philistins, il y eut sans doute beaucoup de peuples de cette Tribu de Dan qui furent aussi emmenez captifs … (Sens littéral, Judg 18:30).*

For the Cyrus prophecy of Isa 44:28 he notes: *Il est remarquable que Dieu parlant par la bouche d'Isaïe appelle Cyrus par son nom & prédit icy les grandes choses qu'il devoit faire prés de deux cent ans avant qu'il fust né (Sens littéral, Isa 45:1),* which clearly admits that the anachronistic verse is a problem. For the Psalm 137, he treats the verses 1–6 without scruple as the lament of the exiled Jews of 586, but he regards the remaining verses, quite arbitrarily, as David's prophecy. Only once have we found a frank admission of post-Mosaic verses in the Pentateuch, Deut 34:5–6:

> *On voit aisément que Moïse n'a pû écrire lui-même ce qui regardoit sa mort & sa sépulture. Et c'est sans raison que les impies veulent abuser de cet endroit pour rejetter tout le Pentateuque, puisque tous les interpretes conviennent que cette fin a été depuis ajoûtée, ou par Josué, ou par le Grand prestre Eleazar.*

In other words, the rudimentary observations that had motivated the Bible criticism of Louis Cappel, Hobbes, Spinoza and Richard Simon – they must be the *impies* to whom he was referring – may be ignored or interpreted or translated away or, *in extremis*, admitted, but he was aware of these analyses and they are often implicit in his explications.

Textual problems must be very obvious for him to notice. The discontinuity of Isa 56:8 with 56:9–57:2, and the disorder of Zech 4:5 and 6, where 11–14 and 10b should be interposed, do not suggest themselves to him. He interprets those chapters as though there were no problems of continuity.

Fundamentally, de Sacy is not interested in the meaning of words as he implicitly admits in the equivalences he establishes without any philological justification, such as for the word שאל, which he translates in Gen 37:35 by an obvious metonymy as: *je pleurai toûjours jusqu'à ce que je descende avec mon fils dans le tombeau*, which does not make its meaning, and thus the ancient Israelite idea of what follows death, precise, while in Prov 30:16 he translates the same word as "enfer", which carries a heavy theological burden for Christian readers.

The famous עלמה of Isa 7:14 occurs as well in Prov 30:19–20, where de Sacy translates it: *la voie de l'homme dans sa jeunesse. Telle est la voie de la femme adultere, qui après avoir mangé s'essuie la bouche, & dit: Je n'ai point fait de mal.* Of course this word, like so many others, may be susceptible of more than one translation, but his note: *Heb. Viam viri in Virgine. Ce que quelques-uns rapportent à l'incarnation de Jésus-Christ au ventre de la sainte vierge*, is clearly absurd since it asserts that

עלמה has only one sense, which is in fact inappropriate here and does not correspond to his own translation. Referring to interpreters who considered the cynical adulteress of v. 20 to be a prefiguration of the *sainte vierge* shows that anthologizing Catholic exegesis was so important to de Sacy, that he would even contradict his own translation, which is adequate for this verse, not to speak of the sense of this verse.

The *explications littérales* are interesting in other regards, too. When the biblical text is scientifically wrong, de Sacy cannot help but note it and, of course, try to explain away the problem. Concerning Gen 1:16, he is aware of a scientific problem: *Quoiqu'il y ait plusieurs étoilles plus grandes que la lune, parce que Moïse parle aux hommes d'une maniere humaine, & que nous voyons que la lune nous éclaire sans comparaison davantage durant la nuit que toutes les étoiles ensemble … (Sens littéral).* Gen 7:8, that recounts how Noah introduced into his ark a pair of every sort of beast and seven pairs of the pure beasts, but does not specify marine life, confirms de Sacy's scruples about how Noah could have cared for fish in his cramped ark: *Il parle de ce qui vit sur la terre, pour le distinguer de ce qui vit dans les eaux, étant inutile de conserver dans l'arche les poissons & plusieurs oiseaux qui vivent dans l'eau.* Given the choice between scientific plausibility and the letter of the text, it is clear that de Sacy's loyalty is to the latter. He summarizes the objections to Joshua's miracle at Gibeon,

> *Quelques-uns n'ont pû se persuader qu'un si grand prodige soit arrivé effectivement; & envisageant sans doute cette occasion d'une bataille ordinaire comme une cause trop légére pour un tel miracle qui alloit renverser tout l'ordre de la nature, ils se sont imaginez que ni le Soleil ni la Lune ne s'étoient point arrêtez, mais qu'ils avoient seulement paru s'arrêter,*

and then rejects those objections,

> *Mais cette explication est insoûtenable, comme très forcée, & visiblement contraire au texte sacré de l'Ecriture. … C'est le sentiment unanime de tous les Péres … Quoique nous envisagions, dit saint Augustin, tous les prodiges, comme étant contre nature, il est certain néanmoins qu'ils ne le sont pas. Car comment pourroit être contre la nature ce qui se fait par la volonté de Dieu … (Sens littéral, Josh 10:12).*

Aldous Huxley remarked that moral discourse is nothing but a systematic application of bad words, and de Sacy does it even more enthusiastically than Leviticus in Jerome's translation: *Vous ne vous approcherez point de la femme de votre prochain, & vous ne vous soüillerez point par cette alliance honteuse & illégitime* (Lev 18:20). When the Bible seems to approve an act or a speech that de Sacy could no longer countenance, he cannot help but express his scandal. Regarding Judg 19:24 he writes:

> *J'ai une fille vierge, & cet homme a sa concubine, je vous les amenerai & vous les aurez pour satisfaire votre passion: je vous prie seulement de ne pas commettre à l'égard d'un homme ce crime détestable contre la nature,* he comments, *Ce vieillard n'avoit pas droit de prostituer sa fille, non plus ce Levite sa femme, on ne peut regarder leur action comme une action juste et légitime,*

and then refers to Augustine. He is very uncomfortable with the ordeal of the wife suspected of adultery, but not because of its magical quality, and explains it as a concession:

> *Cette ordonnance paroît avoir été faite, selon la remarque d'un savant théologien, à cause de la dureté des Juifs, qui auroient pû s'emporter jusqu'à tuer leurs femmes, à moins que Dieu n'eût arrêté un si grand mal par ce remede extraordinaire, qui étoit un miracle continuel de sa bonté envers ce peuple (Sens littéral et spirituel, Num 5:14).*

His morality is grievously offended by Lemekh, Gen 4:19: *Les anciens Peres ont condamné dans Lamech cette polygamie, c'est-à-dire cette pluralité de femmes qu'il introduisit contre la premiere loi que Dieu donna au premier homme dans le Paradis. La polygamie a esté permise après le déluge* ... (*Sens littéral*, Gen 4:19), and by divorce: *Jésus-Christ déclare que cette ordonnance de Moïse étoit plutôt une permission accordée à la dureté du cœur juif qu'un précepte donné au peuple de Dieu. Marc 10.5. Elle tendait à empêcher un plus grand mal, qui étoit la haine & le meurtre des premieres femmes* (*Sens littéral*, Deut 24:1).

De Sacy has no general approach to biblical mythology that we have been able to identify.

The שעירים of Lev 17:7 and the שדים of Deut 32:17 are both translated *démons*: *& ainsi ils n'immoleront plus à l'avenir leurs hosties aux demons, auxquels ils s'abandonnoient dans leurs fornications*,
   and *au lieu d'offrir leur sacrifices à Dieu, ils les ont offerts aux démons: à des dieux nouveaux, à des dieux qui jusqu'alors leur avoient été inconnus & que leurs peres n'avoient jamais révérés*,
   respectively. Noteworthy here is the word *hostie*, with its very Catholic resonance, in the place of the neutral Hebrew, זבחיהם, which one could even translate "their butcheries" because זבח and טבח come from the same palæo-Hebrew word, and, analogously, he translates the entirely banal כוס as *calice* in Isa 51:17. He has some idea that comparative folklore has been used to suggest that the Bible was inspired in certain passages by pagan legends, and, to judge from Genesis 9:28–29, *Sens littéral*, he prefers to reverse the direction of the borrowing, like the "comparatist" school of Gerard Vossius and Pierre-Daniel Huet, and to consider the Bible the primitive text that the gentiles had copied and deformed.

But despite that, he does not recognize archetypes of pagan legend like the triumph of the celestial gods over the sea and its monsters: Ps 74:13–14: *C'est vous qui avez affermi la mer par vostre puissance, & brisé les têtes des dragons dans le fond des eaux. C'est vous qui avez écrasé les têtes du grand dragon: vous l'avez donné en nourriture aux peuples d'Ethiopie*. The translation of ראשי תנינים and ראשי לויתן as *têtes de dragons*, which is at least the right idea, was inherited from the Vulgate, *draco*, but de Sacy's decoding hides the mythology in a figurative interpretation, *Celuy qu'il appelle en particulier le dragon, qui dans la langue originale est nommé, le grand dragon, ou le prince des dragons, & des monstres de la mer, signifie icy le roy d'Egypte, Pharaon*, and see v. 14 where the 'sea' is the very particular Red Sea, the 'dragons' are the Egyptians, and their head which is to be broken is *leur orgueil*. In Isa 13:21–22 he translates ציים *bestes sauvages*, but then mentions real and mythological ones in the same verse, *Mais les bestes sauvages s'y retireront. Ses maisons seront remplies de dragons, les autruches y viendront habiter, & les satyres y feront leurs danses. Les hibous hurlent à l'envie l'un de l'autre dans ses maisons superbes, & les cruelles sirennes habiteront dans ses palais de délices.* התנינם הגדלים of Gen 1:21, surely marine monsters, come out as merely *grands poissons*, and Gen 6:2–4 is partially rationalized: *Les enfans de Dieu voïant que les filles des hommes étoient belles, prirent pour leurs femmes celles d'entr'elles qui leur avoient plû. ... Or il y avoit des geans sur la terre en ce tems-là. Car depuis que les enfans de Dieu eurent épousé les filles des hommes, il en sortit des enfans qui furent des hommes puissants* [נפלים] *& fameux dans le siècle*, which is close to the Vulgate and not very different from Olivétan and Châteillon. In fact, de Sacy denies that these בני האלהים are the angels that revolted and were cast down from heaven because this *opinion si fausse, en elle-même, [est] si injurieuse à la sainteté de ces purs esprits*.

A comparison of the above quotations and many other verses with both the Hebrew and the Vulgate shows that de Sacy added words quite freely, and not always in italics. In Deut 32:2 he changed an active voice to the passive voice, a common liberty in his translation, and then added qualifying clauses to explain metaphors:

Que les véritez que j'enseigne entrent dans les ames comme l'eau dans la terre, que mes paroles les penetrent comme la rosée, comme la pluie qui se répand sur les plantes, & comme les gouttes de l'eau du ciel qui tombent sur l'herbe qui ne commence qu'à pousser.

In fact, de Sacy does not restrict his explanations to the notes but introduces them into the body of his translation.

Thus Onan *empêchoit par une action exécrable qu'elle ne devint mere* (Gen 38:9). His translation is replete with periphrases. Where Châteillon and the Hebrew were content to say that Judah mistook his former daughter-in-law for a *putain* (זונה), de Sacy's translation renders her a *femme de mauvaise vie* and *une certaine femme* [קדשה] *qui étoit assise dans ce carrefour* (v. 21). Sometimes he developes Jerome's Latin: *Qui croiroit qu'on auroit jamais pû dire à Abraham, que Sara nourriroit de son lait un fils* for just plain "nursed sons" (Gen 21:7). He explains: *Juda l'ayant vûë, s'imagina que c'étoit une femme de mauvaise vie, parce qu'elle s'étoit couvert le visage de peur d'être reconnuë* (Gen 38:15), where the final clause appears in the Latin but not in the Hebrew, and embroiders the story of Dinah like a novelist: *Son cœur demeura fortement attaché à cette fille; & la voyant triste, il tâcha de la gagner par ses caresses* (Gen 34:3, where Olivétan had *[il] parloit cordialement avec la fille*, which is a delightful rendering of [וידבר על לב הנערה]). Where the Vulgate is concise and dispenses with a verb in Jacob's blessing of Ruben, *tu fortitudo mea … prior in donis, major in imperio* (Gen 49:3), de Sacy writes a novel: *Vous deviez estre ma force, & vous estes devenu la principale cause de ma douleur: Vous deviez estre le plus favorisé dans les dons, & le plus grand en autorité & en commandement*, translating a single Latin noun, *imperio*, by two prepositional phrases, or follows the Vulgate when Jerome invents a bit: *C'est cet Ana qui a trouvé des eaux chaudes* [הימם] *dans la solitude lorqu'il conduisait les ânes de Sebeon son pere* (Gen 36:24). Simon also criticized de Sacy's embroideries and periphrases in his New Testament translation as unnecessary for rendering the direct diction of the Gospels.[40] This was the judgement of a contemporary who was a better judge of their common language and literary idiom than any twenty first-century critic can hope to be.

De Sacy's Bible is much more prudish than the Hebrew.

Sexual congress becomes marriage, as when Loth's daughters worry that *il n'est demeuré aucun homme sur la terre qui nous puisse épouser selon la coûtume de tous les païs* (Gen 19:31), *dormons avec luy [leur pere]* rather than *couchons avec lui* (v. 32). There is a sexual suggestion in the word מצחק which Sacy suppresses: *[Ishmael] joüoit avec Isaac* (Gen 21:9, and cf. Gen 36:8 and Exod 32:6 where that word has sexual connotations) and *ce qui arrive d'ordinaire aux femmes avoit cessé à Sara* (Gen 18:11) is periphrastic. Menstruation is clearly a phenomenon to be disguised: *Vous ne vous approcherez point d'une femme qui souffre ce qui arrive tous les mois, & vous ne découvrirez point en elle ce qui n'est pas pur* (Lev 18:19) and *Si un homme s'approche d'une femme qui souffre alors l'accident du sexe, ou s'il découvre ce que l'honnêteté auroit du cacher, ou si la femme se laisse voir en cet état, …* (Lev 18:20) even though the Pentateuch had no scruples about describing it by a transparent euphemism. Homosexual unions and bestiality are described even more periphrastically in Lev 18:22: *Vous ne commettrez point cette abomination exécrable qui se sert d'un homme comme si c'étoit une femme*, and *Si quelqu'un abuse* [dormierit] *d'un homme comme si c'étoit une femme …*" (Lev 20:13), and *Vous ne vous approcherez d'aucune beste, & vous ne vous soüillerez point avec elle. La femme ne se prostituera point aussi en cette maniere à une bête, parce que c'est un crime abominable* (Lev 20:13) are nearly hysterical. He can, however, mention breasts in his translation, Isa 66:11: *Afin que vous succiez & que vous tiriez de ses mamelles le lait de ses consolations, & que vous trouviez une abondance de délices dans la gloire qui l'environne de toutes parts.*

Isaiah's rhetoric sometimes emerges with the sweep of the Hebrew, for example 66:1: *Voici ce que dit le Seigneur: Le ciel est mon trône, & la terre est mon marche-pied. Quelle maison me bastirez-vous, & où me donnerez-vous un lieu de repos*, but the last verb is one too many and de Sacy refused to decode the metonymy, מנוחתי. Bogaert describes the literary effect quite damningly: *Sacy est désuet, lourd et souvent à cent lieues de la sensibilité nouvelle*,[41] and Meschonic is still more brutal: *La Bible de Sacy n'est, à mes oreilles, nullement ce qu'est la traduction de Galland pour les Mille et une nuits, un chef-d'œuvre. Je n'y lis qu'un discours terne, sans rythme ni prosodie, un document de la langue de son temps.*[42]

---

[40] *Histoire critique des versions du Nouveau Testament* (1690) 404–08.
[41] Bogaert, Les Bibles (1991) 195.
[42] Meschonic, Traduire le goût (2001) 44.

However, much of his attack upon the de Sacy translation is misguided. He reproaches it for not following the analysis of the Hebrew text coded in the conjunctive and disjunctive cantilations, but that is absurd since de Sacy made no claim to be translating the Hebrew. The appropriate criticism is that he is unfaithful to the syntax, concision and music of Jerome's Latin.

It is hard to escape the impression that much of the French Enlightenment's antagonism directed towards the Bible came as a result of reading it in de Sacy's prissy, endlessly explicative and ineluctably periphrastic French. His French was nowhere so appropriate to his subject as were Racine's and Pascal's, whose style suited their endless psychological analysis and argumentation, to theirs. His periphrases, euphemisms and explanations did not represent the Bible as the primitive document that a more historically minded age expected to find and wanted to deplore. The conjugation of his explications and his translation created a thoroughly Christianized and Patristic Old Testament that satisfied seventeenth-century Jansenist piety but not the eighteenth-century philosophers who had liberated themselves from the Fathers if not entirely from Christianity, and wanted to read a more authentically Jewish Bible which some of them, like Newton, thought still contained valid prophecies and secret meanings. In some ways, the Paris 1704 edition with its still more doctrinaire notes – syntheses of the *explications* which had sometimes offered a variety of Patristic interpretations from which the pious reader might choose those which satisfied him, and which implied that the literal, as de Sacy imagined it, and the spiritual were equally valid – and summaries of chapters with their frequent references to the seventeenth-century Catholic interpreters made de Sacy's defects even more visible. For all their weaknesses, Olivétan and Châteillon were trying to put into French what was intrinsic to the Bible, while de Sacy betrayed that objective, imposing upon it what for most readers could only have been extrinsic material even though it was, for him and his like-minded colleagues, by hypothesis, identical to the sense of the Bible, whatever its words might express directly.

CHAPTER TWENTY-THREE

Scriptural Interpretation among Radical Reformers

By HANS-JÜRGEN GOERTZ, Hamburg

Sources: S. BRÄUER (ed.), "Die beiden Briefe des Grebel-Kreises an Thomas Müntzer vom 5. September 1524", *Mennonitische Geschichtsblätter* 57 (2000) 147–74; H. BUSZELLO, *Der deutsche Bauernkrieg von 1525 als politische Bewegung mit besonderer Berücksichtigung der Anonymen Flugschrift* An die Versamlung Gemayner Pawerschafft (Berlin 1969; Text: 150–92).

General works: G. FRANZ, *Der deutsche Bauernkrieg* (10th edn.; Darmstadt 1975); B. LOHSE, *Martin Luther. Eine Einführung in sein Leben und sein Werk* (München 1981); J. M. STAYER / H.-J. GOERTZ (eds.), *Radikalität und Dissent im 16. Jahrhundert / Radicalism and Dissent in the Sixteenth Century* (Berlin 2002); G. H. WILLIAMS, *Radical Reformation* (3rd edn.; Kirksville, MO 1992).

Special abbreviations:
CS = Corpus Schwenckfeldianorum (see Sect. 4);
FB = E. FREYS / H. BARGE, "Verzeichnis ..." (see Sect. 1);
Fiche = Microfiche-edition (see Sect. 1);
MSB = Müntzer, *Schriften und Briefe* (see Sect. 2);
TQ = Quellen zur Geschichte der Täufer (see Sect. 4).

'Scripture and Tradition' – this coupling was subjected to a trenchant critique by Martin Luther. To be precise, the significance of this connection was not a precondition but a consequence of the Reformation's understanding of Scripture, which found its classic formulation in the watchword *scriptura sola*. "Only in the course of the conflict between Luther and Rome", wrote B. LOHSE, "did the sharp opposition between Scripture and tradition emerge, which was to dominate opinion for a long period".[1] Scripture became the only source of divine knowledge and the single norm for the Christian life. In the hands of lay people it also became the sole criterion according to which the condition of Christendom could be measured. The pope in Rome and the priest in the village were equally accountable to Scripture. Once the theology of Luther spread from the lecture room of Wittenberg University among the wider public, *scriptura sola* became a battle cry and weapon at the disposal of many.

Not only the followers of the Reformers stood under the impression of *scriptura sola* but also those sympathizers who soon parted company with them – above all, Andreas Bodenstein von Karlstadt, Thomas Müntzer, the Anabaptists, Spiritualists and Antitrinitarians, but also the rebellious peasants of 1525, who thoroughly justified their radical demands from Scripture, in what has been referred to as "sacred jurisprudence".[2] Even the magistrates of imperial cities applied *scriptura sola*, so as to impose a religious lowest common de-

---

[1] Lohse, Martin Luther (1981) 161.
[2] Buszello, Der deutsche Bauernkrieg von 1525 (1969) 157, 177 pass.

nominator upon both supporters of the Old Faith and of Reform, and in this way to suppress their fractiousness. Very quickly this scriptural principle extended beyond exegesis and became the norm of public affairs in general. For instance, those erstwhile followers of Ulrich Zwingli who were headed for a break with him, and who had already given up on Luther, nevertheless called on *scriptura sola*, when they wrote to Thomas Müntzer in September 1524, that there was more than enough wisdom and counsel in Scripture in order to decide how "to teach, govern, instruct and edify everyone, of whatever condition".[3]

The general Reformation principle of *scriptura sola* focused people's attention more than ever before on the reading of Holy Scripture. "Each peasant household", it was said in a contemporary report from Switzerland, "is a school where people can develop the highest skill, the reading of the Old and New Testament".[4] This concentration on Scripture, however, resulted in extremely pluriform approaches to Scripture. The Reformation formula of a Bible which interpreted itself (*sui ipsius interpres*) did not produce uniformity in the understanding of particular Scriptural texts. On the contrary, since the papal authority of interpretation was destroyed and no longer recognized, each lay person felt entitled to give Scripture the sense that he or she read from it. The *scriptura sola* principle became the foundation of a pluralistic understanding of Scripture. So it came about that the Reformers reproached the "schismatics" with a false approach to Scripture, while on their side the radicals perceived the Reformers as damnable "scribes" or "new popes". The radicals, too, approached Holy Scripture in various ways: some, moved by the Holy Spirit, gave the Bible a spiritualist interpretation, while others, stressing obedient discipleship of Christ, gave it a legalistic reading. In most cases their approach to Scripture oscillated between these extremes in the most diverse ways.[5]

1. Karlstadt: Letter and Spirit

Sources: ANDREAS BODENSTEIN VON KARLSTADT: *Welche bucher biblisch seint* (Wittenberg 1521); *Auslegung und Lewterung etzlicher heyligenn geschrifften* (see E. FREYS / H. BARGE, "Verzeichnis der gedruckten Schriften des Andreas Bodenstein von Karlstadt", *Zentralblatt für das Bibliothekswesen* [abbrev.: FB] 21 (1904) 153–79, 209–43, 305–31; FB Nr. 129); *Von geweychtem wasser vn(n) saltz. Doct. Andreas Carlstadt wider denn vnordienten Gardian Franciscus Seyler*, in: H.-J. KÖHLER (ed.), *Flugschriften des frühen 16. Jahrhunderts 1501–1530* (Microfiche-edition [abbrev.: Fiche]; Zug / Switzerland 1978; Fiche 1123, Nr. 2866); ANDREE CAROLSTATINI doctoris et archidiaconi Wittenbergensis: *CCCLXX: et apologeticae Conclusiones pro sacris literis & Vuittenburgen(n). ita editae ut & lectoribus profuturae sint* (Wittenberg 1518; FB Nr. 3).

Special studies: M. BRECHT, "Andreas Bodenstein von Karlstadt, Martin Luther und der Kanon der Heiligen Schrift", in: U. BUBENHEIMER / S. OEHMIG (eds.), *Querdenker der Reformation – Andreas Bodenstein von Karlstadt und seine frühe Wirkung* (Würzburg 2001) 135–50; U. BUBENHEIMER, *Consonantia Theologiae et Iurisprudentiae. Andreas Bodenstein von Karlstadt als Theologe und Jurist zwischen Scholastik und Reformation* (Tübingen 1977); idem, "Scandalum et ius divinum. Theolo-

---

[3] Bräuer, Die beiden Briefe des Grebel-Kreises (2000) 160.
[4] Cit. in: Franz, Der deutsche Bauernkrieg (1975) 87 f.
[5] Williams, Radical Reformation (1992).

gische und rechtstheologische Probleme der ersten reformatorischen Innovationen in Wittenberg 1521/22", *Zeitschrift der Savigny-Stiftung für Rechtsgeschichte*, Kanonistische Abteilung 102 (1985) 147–214; H.-P. Hasse, *Karlstadt und Tauler. Untersuchungen zur Kreuzestheologie* (Gütersloh 1993); E. Kähler, *Karlstadt und Augustin. Der Kommentar des Andreas Bodenstein von Karlstadt zu Augustins Schrift* De spiritu et litera (Halle 1957); J.-M. Kruse, "Karlstadt als Wittenberger Theologe. Überlegungen zu einer pluralen Darstellungsweise der frühen Reformation", *Mennonitische Geschichtsblätter* 57 (2000) 7–30; R. J. Sider, *Andreas Bodenstein von Karlstadt. The Development of his Thought 1517–1525* (Leiden 1974); S. Todt, "Äußeres und Inneres Wort in den frühen Flugschriften des Andreas Bodenstein von Karlstadt – Das Bild vom Laien", in: Bubenheimer / Oehmig, Querdenker (2001) 111–34; C. Windhorst, *Täuferisches Taufverständnis. Balthasar Hubmaiers Lehre zwischen traditioneller und reformatorischer Theologie* (Leiden 1976).

Andreas Bodenstein von Karlstadt (1486–1541) was a Reformer of the first hour. A theologian and jurist, he belonged to the academics at Wittenberg University who developed the common project of searching for ways to renew theology and Church.[6] As early as 1518/19 Martin Luther and Philip Melanchthon arrived at the insight that there was no other criterion for the validity of an interpretation of Scripture than Scripture itself. Karlstadt only came to the same conclusion in 1520, although he wrote in defense of the Reformation ideas of Luther as early as his *Apologeticae Conclusiones pro sacris literis* (1518). Even before Luther, he asserted that ecumenical councils could err, and that Scripture had higher authority than they. Ulrich Bubenheimer is of the view that Karlstadt was at first more deferential to papal authority, granting the pope the right to interpret unclear passages of Scripture definitively, while conversely Luther granted councils the right to make authoritative pronouncements about Scripture but denied this competence to the pope.[7] Clear texts of Scripture were in need of no external exegetical authority.

Karlstadt changed his standpoint when he found his name on the papal bull threatening Luther with excommunication. Now, in *De canonicis scripturis libellus* (August 1520) he also turned against the pope. He accused the pope of heresy, contested the scriptural legitimacy of papal pronouncements and declared that the threat of excommunication had no biblical foundation. He identified Holy Scripture with divine law – the *ius divinum* or *ius biblicum* – and set this law against the canon law of the pope. 'Scripture and Tradition' gave way to 'Scripture against Tradition'. Now the exclusivity of Scripture was asserted with its far-reaching consequences: anti-papal, anticlerical and anti-canonist. This identification of the Bible with the *ius divinum* or *ius biblicum* obviously brought legalistic tendencies into Karlstadt's understanding of Scripture. Bubenheimer wrote of an "unconditional biblicism".[8] Karlstadt treated Holy Scripture like a book of law.

This legalism undergirded Karlstadt's arguments against the abuses in Christendom. Likewise it leveled the distinction between the Old and New Testaments – indeed, led to the application of Old Testament ordinances to

---

[6] Kruse, Karlstadt als Wittenberger Theologe (2000) 7–30. Cf. also Bubenheimer, Consonantia Theologiae (1977) 159.

[7] Andree Carolstatini, *Conclusiones* (1518); Bubenheimer, Consonantia Theologiae (1977) 158, 160.

[8] Bubenheimer, Consonantia Theologiae (1977) 175.

his own surroundings. Already in 1519 Karlstadt reflected on the canonicity of the books of the Bible, and undertook to determine precisely the boundaries and the inner structure of the canon. The Old and New Testaments were divided into three categories which determined their degree of authority: the books with definite authorship, those with indefinite authorship, and those whose authorship was in dispute. The canonical books of these three kinds were distinguished from the apocryphal books. The decisive criterion of canonicity was the approval of the Church, but also the presence of "Christ in the Scripture".[9] This could be found in the New Testament, above all in the four Gospels and Acts, but also in the Pauline Epistles. In this way the preeminence of the New Testament over the Old Testament could be established. Old Testament Scripture, too, should be read, to the extent that these books "picture Christ, with his suffering, with his power, with his kindness, with his holiness, and place him before the eyes of the reader".[10] It is unmistakably clear that the "abolition of images" received its justification from the Decalogue, and that the new rules for religious and temporal life that followed the Wittenberg Movement of 1521/22 were based on the laws of the Bible.[11]

But Karlstadt did not limit himself to this legalistic application of Scripture. Even before he adopted the principle of *scriptura sola* Karlstadt had written of the spiritual quality of Scripture. From the time that he studied Augustine and wrote a commentary on *De spiritu et litera* (1517) he distinguished between the outer and the inner Word, between the letters of Holy Scripture and the spirit.[12] This two-fold understanding of the Word was strengthened by his reception of mystical ideas from the *Predigten* of Johannes Tauler and the *Theologia Deutsch*.[13] Medieval mysticism with its conception of the passive reception of the Spirit seems to have provided him with the ideas and the language to express the Reformation's principle of *sola gratia*. Mystical influence was particularly clear in Karlstadt's *Missive von der allerhochsten tugend gelassenheit* (1520). Karlstadt now had no doubt that it is the Spirit of God that rules in Scripture and that opens it to the reader – the Spirit alone. This Spirit is the kernel of Scripture; the letter is merely its outer shell. In its outer form the Scripture is unable to convey faith. It kills and does not make alive: "But each and all of these Holy Scriptures kill people, in that they forbid sin and show Christ but do not help people. Hence the sinner must find his death in Scriptures, if he seeks other help in them than the visible manifestation of the divine will and of our insufficiencies. For the letters without divine mercy hold the

---

[9] Karlstadt, *Welche bucher biblisch seint* (1521) Cij.

[10] Ibid. Cij.

[11] Bubenheimer, *Scandalum et ius divinum* (1985) 147–214.

[12] Kähler, Karlstadt und Augustin (1957) 28f: *In Karlstadts Thesen ist nur noch die spiritualistische Tendenz wirksam: das Gesetz tötet nicht deshalb, weil es Gottes richtende Heiligkeit bezeugt, sondern weil es toter Buchstabe ist, der erst des lebenden Geistes bedarf, um zu seiner eigentlichen Bestimmung zu gelangen.*

[13] Bubenheimer, Consonantia Theologiae (1977) 178–85; Sider, Karlstadt (1974) 180, 204, 206–11. On Karlstadt's reception of the medieval mysticism see recently also Hasse, Karlstadt (1993).

wicked prisoner".[14] The Scripture holds the law before people's eyes and speaks to their conscience, but God "works in it through the mysterious infusion of willingness".[15] Here Karlstadt situates himself in the tradition of late medieval Augustinian spiritualism, which assumes an "ontological barrier"[16] between *signa* and *res*, between the letter and the divine Spirit. It can be broken through only by the Spirit in the interior being of the person. Not the council, not the pope, but the lay person seized by the Spirit of God is the proper judge in the exegesis of Scripture. That does not mean, however, that the lay person stands above Scripture; rather, Scripture herself is "queen, ruler and judge, who holds sway over all",[17] not as letter but as pneumatic power.

Scripture is not rendered ineffective in this way – on the contrary, it becomes a sharp weapon in the battle against the clergy: "It is said drastically about Holy Scripture that it destroys human traditions, spits them out, tears out their eyes, exorcises their brain, and finally casts them out of the city like a rotting corpse, so that no one unwisely profanes himself on them".[18] Scripture becomes a tool for the laity through their reading to free themselves from dependency on the clergy and gradually to find their way to faith: "All lay people should learn the word of God every day, either read the Bible themselves or have it read to them, so as to salt their sacrifice, their lives and their customs with the salt of genuine wisdom".[19] The Scripture as law leads to the Spirit, because the Spirit is its author and lives within it. Using reception theory, SABINE TODT has shown that Karlstadt used the Holy Scripture sometimes pneumatologically, sometimes literally, depending on the readership to whom he was addressing himself.[20] Nevertheless, the tension between Scripture and Spirit was maintained. His pneumatological accent did not abandon the *scriptura sola*, just as his literal exegesis did not disavow the spiritual character of Scripture.

In order to qualify the laity to use the Bible, Karlstadt made use of the pneumatological schema of outer and inner Word. In order to undertake the reordering of ecclesiastical and social life, he employed Scripture as *nova lex* – the Old Testament as well as the New. The Old Testament, particularly Deuteronomy, lent itself better to his juristic thinking than the New Testament. It was not "the Saxon Spiegel of the Jews", as it was for Luther; hence it was not without validity for his own present. After all, the old Law was explicitly confirmed by Jesus. What separated Luther and Karlstadt from each other was the biblical-dialectical manner of thinking of the former and the juristic-mystical approach of the latter. It was Karlstadt's understanding of Scripture that stood

---

[14] Karlstadt, *Auslegung und Lewterung etzlicher heyligenn geschrifften von 1519* (FB Nr. 129), D iv; Hasse, Karlstadt (1993) 101 f.

[15] Kähler, Karlstadt und Augustin (1957) 23* (*73. These: "Deus" autem "intrensecus occulta inspiratione" "velle"*; cf. Augustin, *De concept. et gratia cc. 6,9* ML 44, 911).

[16] Cf. Windhorst, Taufverständnis (1976) 195.

[17] Cit. in: Brecht, Karlstadt (2001) 137 (FB Nr. 34, §§ 2–4).

[18] Ibid. 137 f. (FB Nr. 34, §§ 7–12).

[19] Karlstadt, *Von geweychtem wasser vn(n) saltz* (1978) C v, 23–26; Bubenheimer, Consonantia Theologiae (1977) 155.

[20] Todt, Äußeres und Inneres Wort (2001) 130–34.

behind the radical innovations of the Wittenberg Movement. It was of use to him later, after he served as deacon in the Grossmünster in Zurich (1530–34), when he assumed a professorate in Old Testament at Basle (1534–41) and searched for ways to bring an Evangelical law into being.[21] In this manner he finally left behind his phase as a radical Reformer in the first stage of the Reformation.

2. Müntzer: "Living Word" and "Dead Thing"

Sources and translations: T. MÜNTZER: *Schriften und Briefe. Kritische Gesamtausgabe* [MSB] (ed. G. Franz; Gütersloh 1968); *Collected Works of Thomas Müntzer* (ed. P. Matheson; Edinburgh 1988). – M. LUTHER, *Eyn brieff an die Fürsten zu Sachsen von dem auffrürischen geyst* (1524) and PH. MELANCHTHON, *Die Histori Thome Muntzers / des anfanges der Döringischen uffrur / sehr nutzlich zu lesen,* in: L. FISCHER (ed.), *Die lutherischen Pamphlete gegen Thomas Müntzer* (Tübingen 1976) 1–12, 27–42.

Special studies: H. BÖHMER, "Thomas Müntzer und das Jüngste Deutschland", in: idem, *Gesammelte Aufsätze* (Gotha 1927) 187–222; R. DISMER, *Geschichte, Glaube, Revolution. Zur Schriftauslegung Thomas Müntzers* (Theol. Diss. Hamburg 1974); W. ELLIGER, *Thomas Müntzer. Leben und Werk* (Göttingen ²1976); idem, "Thomas Müntzer und das Alte Testament", *Wort und Geschichte* (FS K. Elliger; Neukirchen-Vluyn 1973) 57–64; H. GERDES, *Luthers Streit mit den Schwärmern um das rechte Verständnis des Gesetzes Mose* (Göttingen 1955); H.-J. GOERTZ, "'Lebendiges Wort' und 'totes Ding'. Zum Schriftverständnis Thomas Müntzers im Prager Manifest", *ARefG* 67 (1976) 153–78; idem, "Zu Thomas Müntzers Geistverständnis", in: S. BRÄUER / H. JUNGHANS (eds.), *Der Theologe Thomas Müntzer. Untersuchungen zu seiner Entwicklung und Lehre* (Göttingen 1989) 84–99; H. JUNGHANS, "Thomas Müntzer als Wittenberger Theologe", in: Bräuer / Junghans (eds.), Der Theologe Thomas Müntzer (1989) 258–82; G. MARON, "Thomas Müntzer als Theologe des Gerichts. Das 'Urteil' – ein Schlüsselbegriff seines Denkens", *ZKG* 83,2 (1972) 195–225; R. SCHWARZ, "Thomas Müntzers hermeneutisches Prinzip der Schriftvergleichung", Lutherjahrbuch 56 (1989) 11–25.

"He wants to abolish the Scripture and the word of God's mouth, and get rid of the sacraments of baptism and the altar":[22] So Luther denounced the "rebellious spirit" of Allstedt in an open letter to the Electoral court at Weimar. Neither of these accusations was true; the one was as false as the other. Neither did Thomas Müntzer (c. 1489–1525) abandon baptism and the Lord's Supper, nor did he reject the Scripture and the verbal word of God. On the contrary, he insisted upon hearing God's voice in the abyss of the soul, where salvation continually repeated itself: there was no more dependable witness than "the living speech of God that the Father speaks to the Son in the human heart".[23] Only in this way does Scripture receive a voice: "I affirm and swear by the living God: for whoever does not hear it from God's mouth, Bible and Babble is nothing else than a dead thing".[24] Müntzer has no intention to devalue Scripture; what he wants to do is to validate its pneumatic character. He does not want to pray to a dumb but to a speaking God.[25] However, as he saw

---

[21] Bubenheimer, Consonantia Theologiae (1977) 251–80.
[22] Luther, *Eyn brieff an die Fürsten* (1976) 8.
[23] Müntzer, *Schriften und Briefe* [MSB], 498.
[24] Ibid. 501.
[25] Ibid. 505; cf. 511 (Latin vers.)

it, the Scripture does not lead to the reception of the divine word – which he understood to be Luther's opinion. It was the other way around, the experience of the Spirit of God opens up the Scripture.

What Müntzer implied in the *Prague Manifesto* (1521) he confirmed in the *Ausgedrückten Entblößung* (1524). Here Müntzer rejects the notion that "one should not begin in the spirit of Christ but the Scripture should provide faith".[26] Here we doubtless hear an echo of his earlier quarrel in Zwickau with Sylvius Egranus, who thought that the divine Spirit ceased to manifest itself after the age of the Apostles, and who undertook to understand Scripture by philological means alone, hence without the aid of the Spirit. Müntzer thought he detected a similar attitude in Luther, when Luther replaced what he said, writing on the *Magnificat* (1520/21), that salvation was granted "without intermediaries",[27] by reference to the promises of Scripture. Indeed, Müntzer's view was the complete opposite; and he expressed his ideas in the most drastic terms when he wrote that even someone who had never heard or read the Bible throughout his life could still have a "true faith", just as the Apostles and writers of the Gospels could produce their writings without any written models whatever, so long as they had a full awareness of the Holy Spirit.[28] Here, of course, he is not speaking of the general rule but of the exception. Hence we can understand that at the beginning of his Sermon to the Princes Müntzer can only conceive of a renewal of Christendom as a time when the elect "occupy themselves daily with the Bible in singing, reading and preaching".[29] Thus he is not contradicting himself. His concern was not to exercise himself daily in the "dead thing", but in the scriptural word that was filled with the divine Spirit. With it Müntzer justified his reform of ritual in Allstedt. For him, like Karlstadt, daily exercise in it focused people on "the arrival of faith", and finally led to a "future Reformation".[30] Here Scripture has an anagogical function – like the worship service generally – which gradually initiates people into the secrets of God and strengthens the "fear of God" among the elect. With reference to the letter, which kills, and the spirit, which brings life (2 Corinthians 3), Müntzer, like Karlstadt before him, went back to Augustine's *De spiritu et litera* and combined it with ideas drawn from late medieval mysticism. Scripture turns against anyone who tries to derive consolation from it without being prepared to expose himself to suffering. It becomes a demanding and destroying law. It kills. This effect of Scripture, too, is denied by the priests. In their hands it is a "dead thing". Müntzer involved Scripture not only in his teaching of word and spirit, as was inferred by the mystical tradition, he included it in the salvation process in general.[31] Correct understanding of Holy Scripture is identical with the speaking of God, or the birth of his Son in the "abyss of the soul". In the *Prague Manifesto* Müntzer complained that the

---

[26] Ibid. 279.
[27] Luther, WA 7, 546 (German trans. and commentary on Magnificat, 1520 and 1521).
[28] MSB, 277.
[29] Ibid. 242.
[30] Ibid. 281 (*ankunfft des glaubens*), 255 (*zukünfftige reformation*).
[31] Ibid. 218, 224; ibid. 499; ibid. 501 (*todt ding*); Goertz, "Lebendiges Wort" und "totes Ding" (1976) 160f, 167.

priests had closed up the Scriptures, because God "in his own person" was not permitted to speak with human beings. He continued with an image from the Parable of the Sower (Matthew 10): "When the seed falls on good soil, that is in the hearts that are full of the fear of God, that is the paper and parchment upon which God writes the genuine Holy Scripture, not with ink but with his living finger – this is the Scripture to which the external Bible bears witness".[32] Here Müntzer not only describes the genuine Holy Scripture – the interiorizing of the external is typical for him; here he also indicates the significance that the external Scripture has for him. It is not the revelation of God which brings salvation; nevertheless it is the "witness" to the salvation-bringing manner in which God relates to human beings. It lets them know what they had to watch for if they awaited the "arrival of faith", were afflicted with great sorrow, and the divine word took form within them: "For the act of God must be witnessed to in the Holy Scriptures through a thorough comparison of all the words which stand clearly written in both Testaments".[33] The "act of God" is the perception of the speaking God in the "abyss of the soul".

This function of Scripture has the effect that Müntzer's writings and letters teem with biblical references, both to particular texts and to whole chapters (e. g., Daniel 2, Luke 1). From the reservoir of the Bible he draws his arguments ("proven with truth from the Scripture"[34]) for critique of clergy and temporal rulers. From it he takes instructions on how to deal with the "priests of Baal" and the "godless". With its apocalyptic scenarios Scripture helps him to read the signs of his own time, and to trust the promise that "the people will become free and God alone will rule over them".[35]

Melanchthon referred to Müntzer as a man who "was learned in Holy Scripture", although he added immediately that he "did not remain on the Scriptural path".[36] Luther warned about the fanatic breathing murderer, who, with his affinity for the Old Testament, was in the course of hurling the world into an apocalyptic fiasco.

Later HEINRICH BÖHMER termed him an Old Testament "murder prophet"; for WALTER ELLIGER he was an Old Testament "servant of God", for GOTTFRIED MARON a "prophet of judgment"; and HAYO GERDES found in Müntzer a legalistic exegesis of the Old Testament that tended towards a restoration of the Mosaic law which affected his entire understanding of Scripture.[37] ROLF DISMER tried to characterize Müntzer as a "Scriptural theologian" and HELMAR JUNGHANS described him as a representative of a Wittenberg strain of early Reformation biblical humanism. DISMER took issue with the notion of Müntzer's particular affinity for the Old Testament, and showed that his references to the New Testament were just as numerous.[38]

---

[32] MSB, 498.

[33] Ibid. 228.

[34] Ibid. 396.

[35] Ibid. 343.

[36] Melanchthon, *Die Histori Thome Muntzers* (1976) 28.

[37] Böhmer, Thomas Müntzer und das Jüngste Deutschland (1927) 209 pass.; Elliger, Thomas Müntzer. Leben und Werk (1976); idem, Thomas Müntzer und das Alte Testament (1973) 57, 44; Maron, Thomas Müntzer als Theologe des Gerichts (1972) 195–225; Gerdes, Luthers Streit (1955) 76 ff.

[38] Dismer, Geschichte (1974) 180, 231 pass.; Junghans, Thomas Müntzer als Wittenberger Theologe (1989) 258–82.

But DISMER's idea that Scripture was the source of the structure of Müntzer's theology is problematic. In the center stood, as DISMER suggests, the deuteronomistic conception of history, with its idea of the restoration of the people of Israel; and he conceived of the history of decline of the Church of Rome as a summons to revolutionary reconstruction of Christendom. It is certainly correct to call attention to Müntzer's intensive knowledge of the Bible, as well as his efforts to support his own arguments with proofs from the Bible. Nevertheless, since the biblical material is seldom clear, the question has to be asked whether tradition and situation do not provide the direction in which scriptural proofs are sought and to which the words of the Bible are applied as decisive arguments, and whether tradition and situation do not put their stamp on the content of biblical texts. The language of mysticism is not a secondary element in the work of Müntzer, it incorporates an element which in a contextual, not a "fragmentary manner"[39] – one text produces the next, one figure of speech the next – lends its voice to Scripture. Müntzer warned against calling upon isolated Bible texts. He wanted them compared with each other, also with a look at what was contradictory, so as to understand the whole; and he proposed that in the worship service the Scripture should be read by chapters, so that members of the congregation would have the opportunity to form their own judgments about the meaning of biblical texts in context. Likewise, in the Bible figures appeared with whom the spiritually driven person – above all, Müntzer himself – could identify: Elijah, Daniel, Jeremiah, John the Baptist. Finally, he used the Bible as a criterion for deciding about the truth of dreams which contain revelations but which could also be insinuations of the devil. When these dreams were not in harmony with Scripture they were to be rejected.

Müntzer occupied himself intensively with the problem of the decay of authority in his time. In the mystical tradition he found a stimulus to build anew the authority which determined how people should properly occupy themselves with Scripture. In this way he challenged both clerical and temporal authority, and set the Spirit-filled, Scripture-reading lay person against them. That changed all relationships. In the place of the fear of creatures, the dependence of people on things, created beings and powers, there came the fear of God, placing people in a new relation to their Creator, the creatures and powers.[40]

3. Anabaptists: Between Biblicism and Spiritualism

Sources and translations: S. BRÄUER (ed.), Die beiden Briefe des Grebel-Kreises (2000; s. above); *Quellen zur Geschichte der Täufer in der Schweiz* I. *Zürich* (ed. L. von Muralt / W. Schmid; Zürich 1952); L. HARDER (ed.), *The Sources of Swiss Anabaptism. The Grebel Letters and Related Documents* (Scottdale, PA 1985); W. KLAASSEN (ed.), *Anabaptism in Outline: Selected Primary Sources* (Scottdale, PA 1981). – HANS DENCK: *Schriften* I–III (ed. G. Baring / W. Fellmann; Gütersloh, I 1955, II

---

[39] MSB, 209.
[40] Goertz, Zu Thomas Müntzers Geistverständnis (1989) 95 f.

1956, III 1960). – MELCHIOR HOFFMAN: *Das freudenreiche zeucknus vam warren friderichen ewigen evangelion, 1532*, in: F. O. ZUR LINDEN (ed.), *Melchior Hoffmann, ein Prophet der Wiedertäufer* (Haarlem 1885); *Dat eerste Capitel des Evangelisten St. Mattheus, 1528. Vorrede*, in: K. DEPPERMANN, *Melchior Hoffman* (Göttingen 1979) 346. – HANS HUT: *Von dem geheimnis der tauf, baide des zaichens und des wesens, ein anfang eines rechten warhaftigen christlichen lebens*, in: L. MÜLLER (ed.), *Glaubenszeugnisse oberdeutscher Taufgesinnter* I (Leipzig 1938) 12–28; *Ein christlicher underricht, wie göttliche geschrift vergleicht und geurtailt solle werden*, in: Müller, Glaubenszeugnisse (1938) 28–37. – PILGRAM MARPECK: *Verantwortung über Casparn Schwenckfelds Iudicium* (s.l., s.a.), in: J. LOSERTH (ed.), *Pilgram Marpecks Antwort auf Kaspar Schwenckfelds Beurteilung des Buches der Bundesbezeugung von 1542* (Wien / Leipzig 1929); *Vermanung auch gantz klarer gründtlicher un(d) unwidersprechlicher bericht zu warer Christlicher ewigbestendiger pundtsvereynigung* (s.l., s.a.), see CHR. HEGE (ed.), "Pilgram Marpecks Vermahnung. Ein wiedergefundenes Buch", in: *Gedenkschrift zum 400-jährigen Jubiläum der Mennoniten oder Taufgesinnten 1525–1925* (Ludwigshafen 1925) 177–281; *Testamenterleütterung, Erleutterung durch ausszug auss Heiliger Biblischer schrifft / tail und gegentail / sampt ainstails angehangen beireden (...)* (c. 1550). Preface, in: W. KLASSEN / W. KLAASSEN (eds.), *The Writings of Pilgram Marpeck* (Kitchener, Ont. / Scottdale, PA 1978). – MENNO SIMONS: *Dat fundament des christelycken leer door Menno Simons op dat aldercorste geschreven 1539/40* (ed. H. W. Meihuizen; Den Haag 1967). – U. STADLER: *Vom lebendigen Wort und geschriebenen*, in: Müller, Glaubenszeugnisse I (1938) 212–28. – L. SCHIEMER: *Etlich Schöne Epistel und Fürneme Articl des Glaubens*, in: Müller, Glaubenszeugnisse I (1938) 44–58. – BALTHASAR HUBMAIER: *Schriften* (ed. G. Westin / T. Bergsten; Gütersloh 1962). – BERNHARD ROTHMANN: *Von der Verborgenheit der Schrift des Reiches Christi*, in: idem, *Die Schriften* (bearb. von Robert Stupperich; Münster 1970).

Special studies: G. BARING, "Die 'Wormser Propheten', eine vorlutherische evangelische Prophetenübersetzung aus dem Jahre 1527", ARefG 31 (1934) 23–41; C. BAUMAN, *Gewaltlosigkeit im Täufertum. Eine Untersuchung zur theologischen Ethik des oberdeutschen Täufertums der Reformationszeit* (Leiden 1968) 125–70; idem (ed.), *The Spiritual Legacy of Hans Denck. Interpretation and Translation of Key Texts* (Leiden 1991); N. BLOUGH, *Christologie Anabaptiste. Pilgram Marpeck et l'humanité du Christ* (Genève 1984); C. BORNHÄUSER, *Leben und Lehre Menno Simons'. Ein Kampf um das Fundament des Glaubens (etwa 1496–1561)* (BGLRK 35; Neukirchen-Vluyn 1973); K. DEPPERMANN, *Melchior Hoffman. Soziale Unruhen und apokalyptische Visionen im Zeitalter der Reformation* (Göttingen 1979); H. FAST, "Hans Krüsis Büchlein über Glauben und Taufe", Zwing. XI,7 (1962) 456–75; idem, *Heinrich Bullinger und die Täufer. Ein Beitrag zur Historiographie und Theologie des 16. Jahrhunderts* (Weierhof/Pfalz 1959); G. GERNER, *Der Gebrauch der Heiligen Schrift in der süddeutschen Täuferbewegung* (Theol. Diss.; Heidelberg 1973); H.-J. GOERTZ, *Die Täufer. Geschichte und Deutung* (München ²1988. ET: *The Anabaptists* [London / New York 1996]); T. HIMMIGHÖFER, *Die Zürcher Bibel bis zum Tode Zwinglis (1531). Darstellung und Bibliographie* (Mainz 1995); R. C. HOLLAND, *The Hermeneutics of Peter Riedeman (1506–1556)* (Basel 1970); P. KAWERAU, *Melchior Hoffman als religiöser Denker* (Haarlem 1954); J. J. KIWIET, *Pilgram Marpeck. Ein Führer in der Täuferbewegung der Reformationszeit* (Kassel 1958); W. KLASSEN, *Covenant and Community. The Life, Writings and Hermeneutics of Pilgram Marpeck* (Grand Rapids 1968); R. KLÖTZER, *Die Täuferherrschaft von Münster. Stadtreformation und Welterneuerung* (Münster 1992); W. O. PACKULL, *Hutterite Beginnings. Communitarian Experiments during the Reformation* (Baltimore / London 1995); J. D. REMPEL, *The Lord's Supper in Anabaptism. A Study in the Christology of Balthasar Hubmaier, Pilgram Marpeck, and Dirk Philips* (Waterloo, Ont. 1993); J. D. ROTH, "Harmonizing the Scriptures: Swiss Brethren understandings of the relationship between the Old and New Testament during the last half of the sixteenth century", in: W. O. PACKULL / G. L. DIPPLE (eds.), *Radical Reformation Studies. Essays presented to James Stayer* (Aldershot 1999) 35–52; H. POETTCKER, *The Hermeneutics of Menno Simons* (Princeton 1961); G. SEEBASS, *Müntzers Erbe. Werk, Leben und Theologie des Hans Hut (1527)* (Gütersloh 2002); J. R. SEILING, "Solae (Quae?) Scripturae: Anabaptists and the Apocrypha", MennQR 80 (2006) 5–34; J. STAYER / K. DEPPERMANN / W. O. PACKULL, "From Monogenesis to Polygenesis: The Historical Discussion of Anabaptist Origins", MennQR 49 (1975) 83–121; A. STRÜBIND, *Eifriger als Zwingli. Die frühe Täuferbewegung in der Schweiz* (Berlin 2003); W. SWARTLEY, *Essays on Biblical Interpretations: Anabaptist-Mennonite Perspectives* (Elkhart, IN 1984); S. TODT, *Kleruskritik, Frömmigkeit und Kommunikation in Worms im Mittelalter und in der Reformationszeit* (Stuttgart 2005); G. WAITE, *David Joris and Dutch Anabaptism 1524–1543* (Waterloo, Ont. 1990); CHR. WINDHORST, *Täuferisches Taufverständnis. Balthasar Hubmaiers Lehre zwischen traditioneller und reformatorischer Theologie* (Leiden

1976); F. J. Wray, "The Vermanung of 1542 and Rothmann's 'Bekenntnisse'", *ARefG* 47 (1956) 243–51; J. H. Yoder, *Täufertum und Reformation im Gespräch. Dogmengeschichtliche Untersuchung der frühen Gespräche zwischen Schweizerischen Täufern und Reformatoren* (Zürich 1968); S. Zijlstra, *Om de ware gemeente en de oude gronden. Geschiedenis van de dopersen in de Nederlanden 1531–1675* (Hilversum 2000).

Anabaptism was not a unified movement. In current scholarship not only are Anabaptist variants discussed, which emerged in the course of painful internal disagreements, but polygenetic origins of Anabaptism have been discovered. Anabaptism basically arose from three starting points: Switzerland, south and central Germany, and north Germany and the Netherlands.[41] In each of these regions Anabaptists understood Scripture somewhat differently, and used it differently from the others, even though sometimes similar or common approaches are observable.

3.1. The Anabaptists in Switzerland

In Zurich and St. Gallen, as early as 1522, followers of the Reformers Ulrich Zwingli and Johannes Kessler antagonized defenders of the Old Faith by instituting Bible reading circles for the laity. Members of these groups – in Zurich even their leader, the bookseller Andreas Castelberger – soon turned up among the Anabaptists. The humanist educated patrician's son Konrad Grebel (c. 1498–1526) made himself a rallying point for these "proto-Anabaptists" after the second Zurich Reformation disputation of October 1523 on the mass and religious images. In his famous letter to Thomas Müntzer of September 1524 he expressed the opinion that the preachers of the Reformation had indeed directed them on the road to the Gospel, but the word of the preachers was not in harmony with the word of God. They only became conscious of this error when they took the Bible into their own hands, and prayed to God that they "might be led out of the destruction of all godly order and away from human abominations, so as to come into the true faith and practice of God".[42] Thus the breakthrough to Reformation was tightly connected with the reading of Holy Scripture, and *scriptura sola* became the source of religious renewal.

This experience of the Scripture must have been so profound that the future Anabaptists reacted allergically when, in their opinion, someone mixed the divine word with the human, or undertook to add to, or remove something from, the word of God. Only that had legitimacy which was commanded in Scripture; whatever was not taught with "clear words and examples" should be forbidden.[43] Nowhere in Scripture was it written that Jesus commanded that small children should be baptized, hence infant baptism must be rejected and believers' baptism reintroduced.[44] As the Grebel letter already indicated, the future Anabaptists no longer accepted the exegetical authority of the preachers

---

[41] Stayer / Deppermann / Packull, From Monogenesis to Polygenesis (1975) 83–121.
[42] Bräuer, Die beiden Briefe des Grebel-Kreises (2000) 153.
[43] Ibid. 154 f.
[44] Quellen zur Geschichte der Täufer in der Schweiz I (1952) 24.

of the Reformation. They wanted to discover the meaning of Scripture in discussions among themselves; hence they became "a hermeneutic community with ongoing congregational conversations based on the vernacular Scriptures".[45] This was, indeed, the ideal of a new congregational order rather than something that was realized in practice; nevertheless, it does show how seriously the Anabaptists took the Reformation watchword of the priesthood of all believers.

Zwingli justified infant baptism with the Old Testament practice, according to which the children were initiated into the covenant of God through circumcision. In their demand for believers' baptism the Anabaptists called upon the New Testament, in which there was no mention of infant baptism. The opposing fronts began to harden. W. O. PACKULL in this context introduces an interesting observation into the discussion of the Zurich Anabaptists' understanding of Scripture. He suggests that possibly the preference that they had for the New, as opposed to the Old Testament, could be connected with the fact that at first only the vernacular New Testament was available to them (since 1522, and particularly since 1524), and their understanding of Scripture crystallized out of concrete application to this part of the Bible.[46] The more strongly the Anabaptists were persecuted, the more the hope disappeared on both sides that the dispute about the interpretation of Scripture could be settled.

Living under persecution, the Anabaptists were obliged to arm themselves with the Holy Scripture against persecutors, judges and executioners. Thus ordinary Anabaptists acquired a knowledge of the Bible that often astonished their opponents. In any case, the stereotypical repetition of the same Bible texts sometimes suggests that it was not intensive Bible study that gave them the appearance of being so well read, but frequently only the reading of concordance-like collections of pertinent texts, such as Hans Krüsi's concordance with the headings "faith" and "baptism" which originated with Konrad Grebel.[47] In this way the ordinary Anabaptists were equipped with biblical arguments, not only to answer their prosecutors in court, but also to participate in internal congregational discussions.

The disputations that took place between Anabaptists and Reformed – e.g., Bern 1531, Zofingen 1532, Bern 1538, Pfeddersheim 1557 and Frankenthal 1571 – regularly failed because the Anabaptists were compelled at the start, before other issues were discussed, to accept the Old as well as the New Testament as the norm by which divergent opinions could be judged. The Anabaptists objected that in the Old Testament God's will for his people was still partly concealed, and was fully revealed only in the New Testament. The Reformed insisted on their side upon the unity of God's salvific action in the old and new covenants, and they would not permit a separation between the Old and the New Testament.[48] The watchword of *scriptura sola* thus not only united the Reformation's supporters, at least not for long; it divided them as well.

---

[45] Packull, Hutterite Beginnings (1995) 16.
[46] Ibid. 16–20.
[47] Fast, Hans Krüsis Büchlein (1962) 456–75.
[48] Fast, Heinrich Bullinger und die Täufer (1959) 157.

Recently JOHN D. ROTH has noted that, outside the major disputations with the Reformed pastors, the Anabaptists gave full respect to the Old Testament, and the reproof that they rejected the Old Testament was unjust. In concordances, letters, songs and devotional literature they supplemented arguments and examples from the New Testament with Old Testament material in the course of defending or explaining their religious life.[49] Moreover, the Anabaptists also could reach back to the traditional approach to Scripture and interpret the Old Testament in a figurative or allegorical manner. For instance, Noah's Ark, not circumcision, was interpreted as the prefiguration of saving baptism. So the Anabaptists took the Old Testament seriously, "without denying the fundamental discontinuity in human history which was marked by the Incarnation of Jesus Christ".[50]

3.2. The Anabaptists in Central and Southern Germany

Central and south German Anabaptism was stamped above all by Hans Hut (c. 1490–1527), an associate of Thomas Müntzer in the days of revolution. Important roles were also played by Hans Denck (c. 1500–27), schoolmaster at St. Sebald in Nuremberg, and Balthasar Hubmaier (1485–1528), Anabaptist Reformer of Waldshut on Lake Constance. Finally, mention must also be made of Pilgram Marpeck (c. 1495–1556), who assembled a loose circle of Anabaptists and came into critical discussions with the Swiss Brethren on one side and Caspar von Schwenckfeld on the other. There were points of contact among these Anabaptists, but nevertheless each had his own profile, so that in this wide region – extending to the Tyrol and Moravia – a heterogeneous Anabaptism emerged.

Hans Hut was deeply influenced by the mystical soteriology that had been propagated by Müntzer. For him, too, Holy Scripture was not the revelation of God that brings salvation, but rather the "witness" that shows the way on which a human being can come to faith. First, Scripture testifies to the "gospel of all creatures", which shows the person how he can read the divine plan of salvation from the created world, the "book of all creatures", and how much he has fallen into dependency on creatures and turned away from his Creator.[51] Second, Scripture points to suffering, "through which the person turns away from the creatures and towards the Creator".[52] The necessity of suffering has already been described in the book of nature. And, third, Scripture reports of the "perfection" into which the person is led by the Holy Spirit.[53] This soteriological function of Scripture is the foundation of the biblicism that has

---

[49] Roth, Harmonizing the Scriptures (1999) 38.
[50] Ibid. 51f.
[51] Hut, *Von dem geheimnis der tauf* (1938) 14 pass. (*zeuknus*), 15 (*evangelion aller creatur*); cf. 33 (*die creatur aller güete anstatt des schöpfers stellen*); Seebass, Müntzers Erbe (2002) 400–12; Hut, *Ein christlicher underricht* (1938) 29. On the scriptural understanding see Gerner, Gebrauch der Heiligen Schrift (1973).
[52] Hut, *Ein christlicher underricht* (1938) 29.
[53] Ibid. 29.

been observed in Hut. On the other hand, the disciple of Müntzer remains under the influence of the radical spiritualism of his teacher. The Scripture opens itself only to the person seized by the Spirit of God; in itself it is nothing but a "counterfeited sign or witness of the inner or eternal or living word", as Hut's follower, Ulrich Stadler (d. 1540), wrote in *Vom lebendigen wort und geschriebenen*.[54] Hans Denck wrote in a similar way, expressing himself in a manner that had more authentic roots in the mystical tradition (e.g., the *Theologia Deutsch*) than the ideas of Hut. "Whoever does not have the Spirit and presumes to find him in the Scripture, seeks light and finds darkness, seeks life and finds sheer death, not only in the Old Testament but also in the New; that is the reason the most learned always take most offense at the truth, for they suppose that their understanding, which they have so cleverly and delicately extracted from the Holy Scripture, will not fail them."[55] The confrontation of spirit and letter brings with it the consequence that the Old and New Testaments are welded into a unity. For Hut there is no distinction between Moses, the prophets, the authors of the Gospels and the Apostles. Consequently, the general apocalyptic tone can be joined with the militancy of the Mosaic law and express itself in a summons to the destruction of the godless. In this manner the Scripture applies not only to the process of the salvation of individuals, but also expresses itself in the external world. The threats of the last judgment, the proclamation of the great division of the sheep and the goats, the transfer of power from the godless to the elect, touch the structure of society, just as they stamp the social form of the Anabaptist movement. These views draw their imagery and their justification from the Bible.

The authority of the Old Testament was, to be sure, weakened by Hut's follower Leonhard Schiemer (d. 1528), who took the position that everything in the Old Testament was also to be found in the New Testament. Nevertheless, in drawing the Old Testament into the New Testament, he conceded that the caesura between the two had been leveled.[56] The Spirit confronts the whole Scripture: the Old and New Testaments serve it equally.

With an order patterned on the divine Trinity (the "gospel of all creatures" corresponds to the Creator God, suffering to the Son, and the life of the Christians to the Holy Spirit) all the contradictions in Scripture dissolve themselves for Hut. The individual Bible texts are compared with each other, with the objective of assigning each to its function in the salvation process, after which they are combined into a harmonious whole. For a layman, Hut demonstrated astonishing systematizing power in this way of applying himself to Scripture in his tract *Ein christlicher underricht* (1527).[57] To assist his memory in this work with Scripture, moreover, he assembled a concordance with numerous Bible texts which served as support for his basic ideas. Once more, this underscores the importance he assigned to Scripture despite his mystical-spiritualist orientation. Denck stated that directly: "Holy Scriptures I hold above

---

[54] Stadler, *Vom lebendigen Wort* (1938) 212.
[55] Denck, Schriften II (1956) 59.
[56] Schiemer, *Etlich Schöne Epistel* (1938) 45.
[57] Hut, *Ein christlicher underricht* (1938) 28.

all".[58] That would also be the reason why Denck joined the project of Ludwig Hätzer, and together with him produced a translation of the Old Testament prophets in dialogue with Jewish scholars in Worms. The "Worms Prophets" first appeared in 1527; further editions followed soon afterwards. This translation, recently described as a "work of high philological worth", had strong influence in matters of detail upon both the later Luther translation of the prophets and that of the Zurich Bible, although it was rejected in general because of its spiritualistic tendencies.[59] After the death of Denck in 1527, Hätzer went on to translate apocryphal books in 1528, undisturbed by the pertinent questions of Old Testament canonicity – first Baruch 6, the Epistula Jeremiae, and then other apocryphal books.

Balthasar Hubmaier placed a still greater value on Scripture: in Waldshut, in the region of the Peasants' War in southwest Germany, and in Nikolsburg in Moravia. Among the Anabaptists he was a man of learning, once professor beside John Eck at Ingolstadt University, able to dispute with theological competence against the foundations of scholasticism and against Ulrich Zwingli's understanding of Scripture. For Hubmaier the exegesis of Scripture was very intimately connected with the problem of infant baptism, or the foundation of believers' baptism.[60] He rejected infant baptism because there was no instance of it in Holy Scripture. He rejected each and every exegetical "trick" that might be used to make infant baptism appear to be scriptural after all. For him Scripture was "bright", "clear", "pure", and "simple".[61] The command only to baptize persons who had perceived the word of repentance and turned to God in faith was clear and was to be followed unconditionally. CHR. WINDHORST has shown that Hubmaier, in his stubbornly conducted controversy with Zwingli, was incapable of maintaining a "simple" Scriptural proof of believers' baptism, but that he allowed himself to be pressured into a legalistic approach to Scripture. In the course of this controversy he also decided for the dominance of the New Testament. He rejected the Old Testament arguments of Zwingli for infant baptism, in that he denied "analogies to New Testament ceremonies" in the Old Testament, "since God himself got rid of [Old Testament ceremonies]".[62] In this way he tried to remain loyal to the Reformation principle that "the church is built upon the word, not the word upon the church".[63] The correct understanding of baptism and Church for Hubmaier was dependent on the understanding of Scripture. His endorsement of Scripture and proper exegesis could hardly be surpassed when he writes against Zwingli: "Or we will not cease to cry against you: Word, word, word, Scripture, Scripture, Scripture"; and he continued to appeal to Zwingli's conscience: "You know, Zwingli, that the Holy Scripture is such a complete, complex, genuine, infallible, eternal and immortal speech that not the smallest letter or syllable can be

---

[58] Denck, Schriften II (1956) 106.
[59] Most recently: Himmighöfer, Die Zürcher Bibel (1995) 296–341. On its printing history, see Baring, Die "Wormser Propheten" (1934) 23–41. See also Todt, Kleruskritik (2005) 297–320.
[60] Windhorst, Taufverständnis (1976).
[61] Hubmaier, Schriften (1962) 120 f.
[62] Windhorst, Taufverständnis (1976) 106 f.; Hubmaier, Schriften (1962) 174.
[63] Hubmaier, Schriften (1962) 177.

subtracted from it or changed".[64] This confession hardly gives space for a balance between letter and spirit, such as was maintained to some extent by Hut, and even more by Denck. For his part, however, Hubmaier writes of an external "drawing" to salvation by the Scripture, and of an inner such process by the Spirit. The two processes work together. The Spirit gives the word life within the person; but the word must be heard in order to be quickened. Fundamentally Hubmaier tried to avoid a dualism of Scripture and Spirit. He did not go so far as to assume that faith, even without Scripture, only through the work of the Spirit, could take shape within human beings. Rather, he tried to think through the unity of Scripture and Spirit.

Originally stimulated by the spirit of Hut's Anabaptism, the Strasbourg and Augsburg water construction engineer, Pilgram Marpeck, developed a scriptural understanding of his own that he situated between spiritualism and biblicism. He distinguished himself from the dominance of Spirit as taught by Jacob Kautz, Johannes Bünderlin and Caspar von Schwenckfeld. However, he also opposed the allegedly spiritless scriptural understanding of the Wittenberg Reformers, as well as the legalistic, biblicistic community of goods of the Hutterites, and also the Swiss Brethren, who, from his standpoint, were in the process of destroying their own congregations with a legalistic application of the ban (Matthew 18). On the one hand, he stressed the work of the Holy Spirit, which created faith and opened up the Scriptures; on the other, he insisted that the divine Spirit makes use of the word of Scripture in order to exercise its influence on human beings. The Holy Spirit gives the decisive witness to the human spirit, but as a "co-witness" the Scriptures assist it.[65] Here a certain affinity to Lutheran positions is evident. Scripture is a product of Spirit; hence Spirit and Scripture form an indivisible unity. For Marpeck this unity is ultimately founded in the Incarnation of Christ. The Incarnation is also in his view the foundation of the "co-witness" of the external form of the sacraments and of the visible Church.[66] In this manner Marpeck discovered a middle way between spiritualism and biblicism.[67]

Marpeck also took a mediating position in the battle over the correct understanding of the Old and New Testament. Against the Strasbourg Reformers he objected that it was false to preach the Gospel before the Law. He insisted upon the order of succession of Law and Gospel, but at the same time accepted a caesura between the two Testaments. The Old Testament Law had only a preparatory function for faith, and only referred to the history which began anew with Jesus Christ. The promises of the Old Testament find their fulfillment, hence also their end, in the New Testament. In this way Marpeck can decisively reject the Reformers' recourse to the Old Testament, with which above all they justified infant baptism. Hence as early as his Strasbourg confession of 1531 he cites the New Testament substantially more than the Old Testament. JAN J. KIEWIT enumerated 350 New Testament citations, as compared

---

[64] Ibid. 206, 210.
[65] Marpeck, *Verantwortung* (1929) 112 pass.
[66] Cf. Rempel, *The Lord's Supper* (1993) 120f.
[67] Cf. Goertz, *Die Täufer* (1988) 62f.

to only 50 from the Old Testament.[68] Marpeck had no sympathy for a literal realization of an Old Testament theocracy in his own time, as was horribly apparent in the Anabaptist rule in Münster. This did not hinder him, however, from publishing Bernhard Rothmann's early tract, *Bekenntnisse van beyden Sacramenten* (1533), under the title *Vermanung auch gantz klarer / gründlicher und unwidersprechlicher bericht zu warer Christlicher ewigbestendiger puntss vereynigung* (c. 1542), albeit without naming the Münsterite author.[69] In this way Marpeck separated himself from the practice of making the Old Testament an apocalyptic instrument, whether it was done in the Dutch Anabaptism or in Hut's Anabaptism. At the same time he opposed the claim that the Church was only the true Church when it practiced community of goods in the manner of Acts 2.

After his expulsion from Strasbourg Marpeck, with associates, wrote extensively on the relation of the two Testaments, above all in the two-part *Antwort auf Kaspar Schwenckfelds Beurteilung des Buches der Bundesbezeugung von 1542* (1544) and in the *Testamentserleuterung*. The latter work, a sort of concordance, was written by Marpeck together with like-minded authors; it was conceived between 1544 and 1550 in a controversy with Lutheran theologians.[70] The *Testamentserleuterung* brought together 125 chapters of Old and New Testament texts, ordered under particular theological concepts. It referred particular Old Testament promises to the New Testament. Beyond that, exegetical differences from the Lutheran theologians were often pointed out. The chapters of this concordance, thematically ordered, amounted to a sort of manual on the authors' controversies with the Reformers. For example, they treated individual faith, the Holy Spirit and its gifts, the congregation, the temporal rulers, and finally explained the relationship of the Old and New Testaments from a christological standpoint. The occasion for the composition of the *Testamentserleuterung* was to clarify precisely the relationship between the two Testaments, and to outline it more sharply than did the Lutherans.[71] Since this concordance was compiled between the first and second parts of the *Verantwortung*, it is to be read above all in the context of the controversy of Marpeck and his close associates with Schwenckfeld.[72]

The scriptural understanding of Marpeck and his associates is not representative of south German Anabaptism, and it must not be retroactively stylized as the purest form of Anabaptist scriptural understanding. With the likeminded persons whom he gathered around him, and in the so-called *Kunstbuch*, which contains some of the reflections of the group, Marpeck created a

---

[68] Kiwiet, Pilgram Marpeck (1958) 71f.

[69] Wray, The Vermanung (1956) 243–51.

[70] The compilation of the *Testamentserleuterung*, as well as the creative editing of writings of Rothmann, Schwenckfeld, and even Luther, by Marpeck and associates like Leopold Scharnschlager, indicate Marpeck's unique role among early Anabaptists as a sort of compiler-editor – hence the later writings that appeared under his name were not so much individual creations as products of group activity. Cf. Wray, The Vermanung (1956) 74–81; Blough, Christologie Anabaptiste (1984).

[71] (Marpeck), *Testamenterleütterung* (c. 1550). On the composition of the *Testamentserläuterung*, cf. Loserth, Antwort (1929) 38–48.

[72] Klassen / Klaassen, The Writings of Pilgram Marpeck (1978) 555.

distinctive form of Anabaptism, which however disbanded after a short period.

3.3. *The Anabaptists in Northern Germany and the Netherlands*

There was also a fundamental spiritualistic element in the Anabaptism of north Germany and the Netherlands, which was founded by the furrier Melchior Hoffman (c. 1500–43). Already in his Lutheran period Hoffman was of the view that there was a hidden meaning beneath the letters of Holy Scripture, and that it disclosed itself only to those who were led by the divine Spirit. In his Commentary on Daniel 12 (1526) Hoffman focused on the figures of the four Evangelists and developed what KLAUS DEPPERMANN correctly described as an allegorical division of the Bible:

In the Old Testament the "figures" of the lion and the calf were dominant. The lion refers to the letters of the Mosaic law; and the calf – clumsy and laughable in its gait – refers to the Old Testament's sometimes coarse and laughable symbols and pre-figurations of the later fulfillment of the history of salvation. The New Testament is dominated by the "human face" – an image of the parables of Jesus, so accessible to human thought – and the "eagle" – the symbol for the unveiled Spirit of God.[73]

This Spirit should be searched for in the three other forms of the divine word, for the word of God as a whole is permeated with it, and it serves the purpose of leading human beings by degrees to the knowledge of the Spirit of God. The human being himself is incapable of reaching the level of the eagle. "Just as no bird can surpass an eagle in flight, no human spirit can surpass the clear, pure, bright word."[74] This was Hoffman's manner of appropriating the Reformation's discovery of the justification of the sinner *sola gratia*.

Hoffman further developed this understanding of Scripture in his Anabaptist period. Now also he sought to convey the spiritual content of Holy Scripture from the literal text. The typological and allegorical methods of exegesis assisted him in this purpose. He connected biblical persons or events with each other, e.g., Melchizedek with Christ or the Patriarchs Abraham, Isaac and Jacob with the Holy Trinity (typology); or he unveiled the secret meaning of a past event or a biblical figure, e.g., the ladder of Jacob upon which the elect attain heaven is referred to Christ,[75] or he connected a biblical figure or event with a person or event in the present, e.g., the dragon of the Apocalypse signifies Emperor Charles V (allegory). Hoffman combined the typological and allegorical methods of exegesis into what he referred to as the "figurative" interpretation of Holy Scripture.[76] In the "figure" the Spirit hides itself; and through the interpretation of the "figure" the Spirit reveals itself. This is the reason why, despite his spiritualistic point of departure, Hoffman was more

---

[73] So Deppermann, Melchior Hoffman (1979) 59.

[74] Hoffman, *Dat eerste Capitel des Evangelisten St. Mattheus*, 1528, cit. from the preface, in: Kawerau, Melchior Hoffman (1954) 35; detailed discussion of his scriptural understanding, 31–45.

[75] Ibid. 35.

[76] Deppermann, Melchior Hoffman (1979) 213 f.

interested in exegetical work than were Hut and Denck, and accordingly wrote detailed commentaries, like those on the Revelation of John (1530) and Paul's Epistle to the Romans (1533). On the other hand, only the Spirit or the person seized by the divine Spirit could open up the meaning of the "figure". The "figure" in itself did not disclose its meaning. Without the Spirit it was nothing but empty letter. With the help of an arbitrary hermeneutical circle Hoffman had bound letter and spirit together into an indivisible unity and arrived at a solution similar to that of Marpeck.

At the same time figurative exegesis provided that salvation history was interpreted as a not yet completed history moving towards its end in the Last Judgment, which made possible an apocalyptic diagnosis of contemporary events. Hoffman did not submit himself to arbitrary visions of the future, rather he applied the biblical prophecies of the Old and New Testaments – often driven by his wayward imagination – to the generally perceptible events of his own time. In this way, from figurative scriptural exegesis the apocalyptic model of the Anabaptist rule in Münster came into being. The "cloven hoof", finally, became a hermeneutical metaphor for Hoffman; its meaning was the observation that "all God's words are doubled or twofold, the one against the other".[77] In this he saw himself called, like Hut and Denck, to resolve spiritually or mediate the occasional contradictions between biblical texts, so as to arrive at a "clear" interpretation of Scripture. For the relation of the two Testaments to each other that meant that they should neither be sharply divided from each other nor drawn together into a single holy text. Since the Old Testament pre-figurations are fulfilled in the New Testament, the Testaments remain divided as distinct stages of the history of salvation, and nevertheless are connected to each other. They represent the progress of divine revelation: from appearance to essence, from shadow to light.

Melchior Hoffman's understanding of history had a deep effect upon the branch of Anabaptism created by him. It was, however, also changed and applied to new needs. Bernhard Rothmann (c. 1495–1535), the "royal orator" at Münster, repressed the figurative-spiritualistic exegesis of Old Testament texts, and stressed the analogies between Old Testament institutions and the theocratic institutions in his present. Obviously he feared a spiritualistic evaporation of the new institutions in Münster that had been justified with reference to the Old Testament (kingdom, polygamy, iconoclasm). The letter of Holy Scripture, which helps a person to attain insight about salvation history in the past, now and in the future, as long as he is ready to follow the will of God, weighs more heavily here than does the Spirit. David Joris (1501/02–56) reacted in the opposite way. He stressed the effectiveness of the Spirit more strongly than did Hoffman, and accepted the consequent devaluation of the New Testament. Again more one-sidedly than Hoffman, he connected the effect of the Spirit chiefly with the salvation process in the human mind.[78] In the

---

[77] Hoffman, *Das freudenreiche zeucknus* (1885) 430.
[78] On Bernhard Rothmann, cf. Klötzer, Die Täuferherrschaft (1992) 170–73 (on his tract *Von der Verborgenheit der Schrift des Reiches Christi* [1535], see ibid. 298–372); on David Joris, cf. Waite, David Joris (1990) 90–94; cf. also Zijlstra, Om de ware gemeente (2000) 162: *Melchior*

spiritualization of Scripture, sacraments, and Church or kingdom of God, he saw a chance to form a bridge between the disagreements among the Anabaptists after the collapse of Anabaptist rule in Münster in 1535, and an opportunity to validate his claim to leadership in Melchiorite Anabaptism.

Menno Simons (1496–1561), the Catholic priest from Frisia who crossed over to Anabaptism, also basically followed the trail of Melchiorite understanding of Scripture: He interpreted the Old Testament "figuratively" and focused all promises on Jesus Christ. What was foretold in the old covenant was fulfilled in the new. In any case, he avoided the "arbitrary profusion of figurative scriptural interpretation"[79] and had an essentially paraenetic understanding of the Old Testament: as a warning against the overstepping of God's commandments and as an exhortation to live a better life from now on. Above all, Menno Simons distinguished himself from Rothmann, for whom the Old Testament was not entirely fulfilled in the New Testament but was in the process of fulfilling itself in the present and near future: in the Anabaptist kingdom of Münster at the end of days. As was usual in Melchiorite Anabaptism, Menno proposed a tripartite division of the history of salvation; but he accented the periodization differently: for him there was a time before the law, a time under the law, and a time of grace, which was granted in Jesus Christ. Thereafter there was nothing new to await. In this way the New Testament became the center of scriptural understanding, and the normative power of the Old Testament, as it was asserted at Münster, was broken. And, other than for David Joris, for Menno the time of the Holy Spirit was not a time of its own but the time of the grace of Jesus Christ. Jesus Christ was the "foundation of faith" (1 Cor 3:11) who was not to be excelled. In this manner Menno thought that the aberrations of Münsterite Anabaptism could best be corrected, and the dispersed Anabaptists could be assembled into a peaceful congregation, freed from apocalyptic violence.

Throughout his life Menno Simons maintained the Melchiorite conviction that the Spirit opens up the Scripture. Nevertheless, the christological focus of his thought had the consequence that under increasing pressure he came to identify the word of Christ with the New Testament. Scripture became a firm support. Whoever transgressed against the letters of Scripture was in the wrong. CHR. BORNHÄUSER writes perceptively: "Verbally the Christocentric understanding of Scripture was indeed maintained, but in reality it was to a great extent given up in favor of a rigid, legalistic 'It is written'".[80] Above all in the controversy with the Reformed preachers, Menno declared the entire Scripture, which is "written for instruction, admonition and punishment", to be the only plumb-line "with which a Christian life must be measured and ruled".[81] At first Menno Simons did insist that Scripture, now so strongly placed in the center, must be understood spiritually, but his later writings on the Incarnation

---

Hoffman had immers niet zozeer de letter verworpen ten faveure van de Geest, zoals Joris deed, maar een systeem uitgedacht warin voor letter én Geest een plaats was.

[79] Bornhäuser, Leben und Lehre Menno Simons' (1973) 47 f.

[80] Ibid. 56.

[81] Simons, *Dat fundament des christelycken leer* (1967) 106.

of Christ and on congregational discipline "do not breathe the spirit of Christ but the spirit of legalism and dogmatism".[82] It is difficult to explain how this kind of treatment of Scripture could have developed. Perhaps Menno had concluded that in an oppressed situation he could win his battle only with the weapons of his opponents: He must engage only logically, obediently and precisely with the Spirit which for all time has been given its tangible form in Scripture.

4. The Spiritualists: Spirit and Scripture

Sources: S. FRANCK / J. CAMPANUS, *Quellen zur Geschichte der Täufer* [abbr. TQ], *Elsaß* I. *Stadt Straßburg 1522–1532* (Gütersloh 1959) 301–25; *Corpus Schwenckfeldianorum* [abbr. CS] I–XIX (Leipzig 1907–61), IV, 414–43, 519–64; XII, 417–541.
   Studies: C. DEJUNG, *Wahrheit und Häresie. Untersuchungen zur Geschichtsphilosophie bei Sebastian Franck* (Zürich 1980); G. MARON, *Individualismus und Gemeinschaft bei Caspar Schwenckfeld. Seine Theologie, dargestellt mit besonderer Ausrichtung auf seinen Kirchenbegriff* (Stuttgart 1961); R. E. MCLAUGHLIN, *Caspar Schwenckfeld. Reluctant Radical. His Life to 1540* (New Haven / London 1986); D. H. SHANTZ, *Crautwald and Erasmus. A Study in Humanism and Radical Reform in Sixteenth Century Silesia* (Baden-Baden 1992); G. SEEBASS, "Das Verständnis des Alten Testaments bei Caspar Schwenckfeld von Ossig", in: idem, *Die Reformation und ihre Außenseiter. Gesammelte Aufsätze und Vorträge* (Göttingen 1997) 336–49.

The Silesian nobleman Caspar von Schwenckfeld (1489–1561) was at first a follower of Martin Luther. As early as 1520 he assembled like-minded persons and initiated church reforms in the Duchy of Liegnitz. He soon came to the opinion, however, that the Wittenbergers' teaching of justification was ill-suited to achieve moral improvement in the population at large.[83] Likewise the new understanding of the Lord's Supper seems to have disappointed his expectations. So, in 1525 he began to develop his own spiritualistic theology, which had the objective of tying justification and sanctification more closely together than hitherto; he conceived of the Lord's Supper as an interiorized element in the economy of salvation and undertook to intensify the religious instruction and holiness of life of the congregation members. The Holy Scripture assumed a key role in this theology, which explains why Schwenckfeld in his literary work touched on the understanding and use of Scripture with unusual frequency. The two writings that he published in Strasbourg after being exiled from Liegnitz (1529) are of particular importance: *Unterschied des Alten und Neuen Testaments, der Figur und Wahrheit* (1531) and *Sendschreiben an die Straßburger Brüder* (1532). Later he published *Von Alten und Neuen Testament, ein kleines Bedenken* (1540), *Von der heiligen Schrift* (1551), and the *Summarium der Bibel* (1556).[84]

---

   [82] Bornhäuser, ibid. 60.
   [83] McLaughlin, Schwenckfeld (1986) 61f, 104.
   [84] CS IV, 414–43, 519–64; CS XII, 417–541; CS XV, 11–15. Schwenckfeld's interest in scriptural exegesis is, on questions of Christology and eucharistic theology, also evident in his use of the exegetical work of Valentin Krautwald, the humanist educated and spiritualist canon at Liegnitz (1524–37). Cf. Shantz, Crautwald (1992).

Throughout his life Schwenckfeld stood on the foundation of the Reformation principle of *scriptura sola*. Already in Liegnitz he opposed the tendency, which he viewed with alarm, to sacrifice the life-giving power of the divine word by sacramentalizing or materializing it, as if it had the capacity to bring salvation by itself.[85] So Schwenckfeld distinguished between the letters of Scripture and the divine word – entirely in a spiritualistic manner.

Taken by itself Scripture is nothing other than the dead letter, from which salvation is not to be expected. In order to have a beneficial effect on the process of sanctifying the individual person and Christendom, it must be opened and animated by the Holy Spirit. If someone wanted to derive his faith from Scripture, it would be a human work, not a work of God. So it turns out that only and solely the spiritualization of Scripture serves the purpose of realizing the Reformation's understanding of the justification of the sinner *sola gratia* and *sola fide*. Schwenckfeld believed that he had correctly understood the Reformation's message, so it was difficult for him to grasp why the Wittenbergers rejected him and forced him to leave Silesia. Indeed, he had quite consciously fastened upon the early, mystically oriented statements of Luther. His reference to Abraham, who was for Luther, too, an example of justification by faith, shows how close he regarded the connection of Scripture and justification: "Abraham, the model and example of our justification, had faith in God, not in the preached word (for at that time there were no preachers, and not even the law), and that was reckoned to him as justification".[86] Here we have less a form of philosophic thinking – e.g., Platonism, which was the godfather for the path into spiritualism – but rather an expression of the fear that the Lutheran justification teaching itself could suffer damage in the course of the Reformation. This explains the Reformation pathos of Schwenckfeld.

In the sphere of this spiritualistic understanding of Scripture the relation of the Old and the New Testament played a special role. The relation of the Testaments became a problem for Schwenckfeld in the controversy over Reformation sacramental understanding. GOTTFRIED SEEBASS has recently written on this topic.[87] Both Luther and Zwingli drew on the Old Testament in their controversies on baptism and the Lord's Supper. Luther demonstrated the necessity of visible signs with Old Testament examples; and Zwingli discovered in Jewish circumcision and the Passover feast clear correspondences with baptism and the Lord's Supper of the New Testament. Against this practice, Schwenckfeld objected that there are enough texts in the New Testament that refer to the fulfillment of the Old Testament in the New. Besides that, he opposed the opinion that faith is transmitted through external promises. However, Schwenckfeld was entirely receptive to a spiritual, figurative interpretation of biblical conceptions; he desired a logical, christological interpretation of the Old Testament. His distinction from the Reformers resided in the fact that he

---

[85] McLaughlin, Schwenckfeld (1986) 79: "The fundamental task of the church was to teach the word, not merely proclaim it".

[86] CS II, 594: *Abraham typus & exemplum nostra iustificationis, credidit deo, non verbo predicatio (nondum enim erant predicatores, neque lex) et reputatem est ei ad iusticiam.*

[87] Seebass, Das Verständnis des Alten Testaments (1997) 336–49.

"allowed himself to be fully guided by his spiritualism and referred all the statements of both Testaments concerning externals to the inner, spiritual, salvific event in Christ".[88] On the level of the external letter both Testaments move together. On the level of the divine word that works in the human mind and opens up the Scripture, the Testaments distinguish themselves from each other. "Everything that was external in the Old Testament – the promise, the mediator, the people of the covenant, the sign of the covenant, the temple, the ceremonies, the priesthood, the obedience – is internal in the New Testament".[89] The content of the New Testament, as opened by the Spirit of God, is dominant. It also rules the understanding of the Old Testament. The Old Testament is christologically and spiritually interpreted, not to the degree that the two Testaments grow together into a unity, but in such a way that the ordinances of the Old Testament remain limited to the old covenant and receive no function as forerunner for the ordinances of the new covenant.

GOTTFRIED MARON asserts that Schwenckfeld's teachings are not nourished "from the fountains of Holy Scripture", "but from the writings of the mystics and his own imagination".[90] However, an appraisal of this kind is misplaced. It comes from a point of view that does not really take seriously the Reformation's pluralistic exegesis of the Scriptures, but finds the standard of Reformation theology in Luther's scriptural interpretation alone.

Besides Schwenckfeld, Sebastian Franck (1499–1542) must be numbered in the Spiritualist camp, as is the case with Johannes Bünderlin, Christian Entfelder and Dirck Volkertszoon Coornhert. It is impossible to draw precise boundaries for this group. Karlstadt, Müntzer, Denck, Hoffman and Joris might also be labeled Spiritualists. Franck was a free spirit who cannot be assigned to any ecclesiastical tradition whatever. In Franck's letter to Johannes Campanus – a figure who might be classified a Spiritualist or an Antitrinitarian – he expressed himself candidly about his beliefs, praised the Anabaptist and Spiritualist Johannes Bünderlin, and warned against those who draw their faith from Scripture: "I refer to those who fold forth the falsified word from the pulpit to the common folk (...). They preach without any fruit because they are not sent from God, but vomit out the word according to the letter only, soiled with human filth, not according to the divine meaning".[91] Franck, too, as was already reported of Schwenckfeld, wanted to bring the Reformation's "righteousness by faith" into effect with the spiritualization of the word. Scripture is not a divine revelation but only a "witness" for the conscience. It testifies and accompanies on the path to faith but it does not bestow faith. "The Scripture and the human being are able to give only a witness to other people and brothers in faith, but to teach nothing godly".[92] The secret of Scripture can be grasped only by those who are taught by God. That is Spiritualism in the purest form.

---

[88] Ibid. 340.
[89] Ibid. 347.
[90] Maron, Individualismus und Gemeinschaft (1961) 81.
[91] Sebastian Franck to Johannes Campanus, TQ, Elsaß I, 320 f.
[92] Ibid. 319 f.

Sebastian Franck made the meaning of Scripture dependent on the working of the Spirit of God in the mind of a person. In this respect he was hardly different from many others who had derived their spiritualistic tendencies either from late medieval Augustinianism or from the mystical tradition. Beyond that, he introduced the argument about the historicity of Scripture into the discussion and added it to the spiritualism that he had adopted.[93] The New Testament distinguished itself from the Old in the sense that it expressed the divine message under the conditions of another period. Logically extended, that means that the New Testament, too, is biblical testimony from and for its time. The Wittenberg Reformers were criticized for not applying this contextual understanding and for mixing the Testaments with each other: "They [the Church Fathers] mingle the New Testament with the Old, just as their descendants do today; and when they have nothing with which to defend their cause, they immediately run to their empty pots, that is, to the Old Testament; and from it they prove war, oath, government, violence of the rulers, tithes, priesthood, and praise them all and impose all these things on Christ against his will".[94] In this way they give all power to the letter of Scripture, a letter that kills and does not make alive, as Franck cites from 2 Cor 3:6.[95]

The reference to the historicity of the revelation of God limits the significance of the Scripture. It also opens the sphere of history for efforts toward the knowledge of God. It is no accident that the *Chronica* or *Zeytbuoch* of Franck became the *Geschychtbibel* (1531). Not only the Holy Scripture but history, too, was read as a testimony of the work of God, as a "living Bible" – it should be stressed, as a witness and not as a revelation which brings about faith. History is ultimately observed from the vantage of the divine spirit that works in the human being. In history, first and above, all the cruelties and mistakes of human beings are on display, as well as the longing of all for a change in the evil conditions, and last but not least the acts of God with humanity. The will of God is unchangeable;[96] though changeable is the form in which this will is manifested on earth: differently in the Old than in the New Testament, and differently again in the present. From this it follows, finally, that any theology, no matter how convincingly formulated, is provisional. The final word has not been spoken with the Reformation, not even with Franck's own theology.[97] The insight into the historicity of the biblical writings and of one's own theology constitutes the radicalism of Franck's Reformation initiative: *theologia semper reformanda est* ("theology must constantly be reformed") – also and exactly in the radical movements of the Reformation.

---

[93] Dejung, Wahrheit und Häresie (1980) 188–93.
[94] TQ, Elsaß I, 308.
[95] TQ, Elsaß I, 323 (*todtschlagender buchstab*).
[96] TQ, Elsaß I 314: *Es wirt aber gott bey seiner weise bleiben, besonder im newen testament, solang die welt steht.*
[97] TQ, Elsaß I, 324: *Denn all ding hat sein zeit.*

5. Antitrinitarians and Paracelsus:
on the Way to Historical-critical Exegesis

Sources: S. Castellio: *De Arte Dubitandi et Confidendi Ignorandi et Sciendi* (ed. Elisabeth Feist Hirsch; Leiden 1981). – Theophrast von Hohenheim genannt Paracelsus: *Sämtliche Werke* (ed. K. Sudhoff; München / Berlin 1922–33), 1. Abt., Vol. XI, *Schriftwerke aus den Jahren 1537–41* (1928).

   Studies and reference works: J. Friedman, "Michael Servet", TRE 31 (2000) 173–76; idem, *Michael Servetus. A Case Study in Total Heresy* (Geneva 1978); H. R. Guggisberg, *Sebastian Castellio im Urteil seiner Nachwelt vom Späthumanismus bis zur Aufklärung* (Basel / Stuttgart 1956); H. Rudolph, "Paracelsus", TRE 25 (1995) 699–705; V. Urban, "Sozzini / Sozinianer", TRE 31 (2000) 598–604.

Exegesis of Scripture is a pertinent topic when considering Paracelsus and Antitrinitarians, since Paracelsus and various Antitrinitarians wrote numerous commentaries on Scripture. Paracelsus, Theophrast Bombastus von Hohenheim (1493/94–1541), for example, published sixteen commentaries on biblical writings. Moreover, it is suspected that he wrote additional manuscript commentaries which have not survived. Paracelsus was a medical doctor who pioneered new medical practices based on experience and popular traditions, but he called himself a "doctor of the Holy Scriptures". The originality of these figures lay less in a special approach to Scripture than in their distinctive viewpoints about God, human nature, ecclesiology, nature, reason and knowledge; hence for purpose of brevity their less striking understanding of Scripture will here receive only cursory attention.

   Michael Servetus (b. around 1511), burned at the stake in Geneva in 1553 because he denied the Trinity and criticized infant baptism, made only a small contribution to biblical exegesis, unless we accept the view of his modern biographer, Jerome Friedman, that his antitrinitarian doctrine gave an important impetus to modern historical-critical exegesis.[98] Servetus surveyed the Old Testament's names for God and came to the conclusion that God manifested himself under changing names throughout history, corresponding to the changing human possibilities of comprehension from age to age. In this sense the divine names in the New Testament – God the Father, the Son (Christ), and the Holy Spirit – are changing representations of one and the same God. The Trinitarian teaching only arose later as a concession to the mathematical differentiation of the Greek way of thinking, and amounted to a misunderstanding of biblical modalism. In this way Servetus leveled the gap between the Old and New Testaments. Jesus Christ was for him the last link in a chain of progressive revelation in which the struggle between God and Satan was continued, and the human being, with the help of the Holy Spirit and his own moral striving, was put in a position to be deified. Viewed in this way, Antitrinitarianism was not only rationalistic but biblically grounded, in any case under the premise that, through critical exegesis drawing from Jewish and Hermetic tra-

---

[98] Friedman, Michael Servet (2000) 173; cf. idem, Michael Servetus (1978).

ditions, the images of God can be comprehended in their actual historical content.

The emphasis on biblical criticism is still stronger in the case of Sebastian Castellio / Chatillon (1515–63). He criticized the narrow, dogmatic scriptural understanding of the Reformers, which had led to so many quarrels, and made no secret of his view that some New Testament teachings, e.g., on baptism, the Lord's Supper and predestination, could no longer be accepted. Likewise, the accounts in the synoptic Gospels were full of contradictions. In his tract *De Arte Dubitandi et Confidendi Ignorandi et Sciendi* (1563), teachings of the Reformers are called into doubt and their claim to general validity shattered.[99] Laelius Socinus / Lelio Sozzini (1525–62) had a stronger interest in biblical exegesis. His nephew, Faustus Socinus / Fausto Sozzini (1539–1604), indebted to his uncle, began his publishing career with *Explicatio initii primi capitis Evangelii Johannis* (1562) and followed with a treatise *De S. Scripturae autoritate* (c. 1580). VACLAW URBAN characterizes the occupation of Fausto Sozzini with the Scripture as a "literal interpretation of the Bible".[100] Among the Socinians and Antitrinitarians the spiritualistic interest in the tension between spirit and Scripture no longer played a role, but it still determined the structure of their argument. Indeed, the spirit was no longer detected in the letter, but the letter was interpreted according to the standard of reason or common sense.

The exegetical creativity of Paracelsus did not continue through all stages of his work. The spritualistic trait of his early period ("What I have spoken has come from the Holy Spirit; hence it is the gospel") gradually dissipated and gave place to a quasi-rationalist manner of interpretation oriented to the "light of nature".[101] The experience of nature comes from God, just like the Holy Scriptures; God "is the supreme writer in all things, the first, the highest, of all our texts".[102] Experience opens up not only nature and the whole cosmic context, but also history and Scripture. All spheres of knowledge are grasped and bound together through the medium of salvific, apocalyptic and natural experience. Paracelsus opened horizons beyond which the still unanticipated developments of modernity would appear.

***

The scriptural understanding of the radical Reformers is anything but unified. Common to all is a front erected against the teaching authority of the Pope and against the major Reformers. However, as for the concrete use of Scripture and in justification of the ways they used Scripture, their emphasis varied between biblicism, spiritualism and numerous mixtures of spirit, letter and early modern reason.

Translated by James M. Stayer

---

[99] Castellio, *De Arte Dubitandi* (1981) 3. Cf. also Chap. 22, Sect. 3, in this volume.
[100] Urban, Sozzini / Sozinianer (2000) 599. Cf. also Chap. 32, Sect. 2, in the present volume.
[101] Rudolph, Paracelsus (1995) 702.
[102] Paracelsus, *Sämtliche Werke*, Part 1, Vol. XI, 173 (cit. in: Rudolph, ibid. 702).

CHAPTER TWENTY-FOUR

Further Development of Reformation Hermeneutics

By BERNT T. OFTESTAD, Oslo

General works: A. ADAM, *Dogmengeschichte 2. Mittelalter und Reformationszeit* (Gütersloh: Güters-sloher Verlagshaus 1972); C. ANDRESEN (ed.), *Handbuch der Dogmen- und Theologiegeschichte 2. Die Lehrentwicklung im Rahmen der Konfessionalität* (Göttingen: Vandenhoeck & Ruprecht 1980); T. JOHANSSON, *Reformationens hovudfrågor* (1999) [see below, Sect. 3]; J. PELIKAN, *The Christian Tradition. A History of the Development of Doctrine 4. Reformation of Church and Dogma (1300–1700)* (Chicago / London: University of Chicago Press 1984); R. D. PREUS, *The theology of post-reformation Lutheranism* 1–2 (St. Louis: Concordia 1970–72); H. GRAF REVENTLOW, *Epochen der Bibelauslegung IV. Von der Aufklärung bis zum 20. Jahrhundert* (München: Beck 2001); O. RITSCHL, *Dogmengeschichte des Protestantismus. Grundlagen und Grundzüge der theologischen Gedanken- und Lehrbildung in den protestantischen Kirchen* 1 (Leipzig: Hinrichs'sche Buchhandlung 1908); H. SCHEIBLE (ed.), *Die Anfänge der reformatorischen Geschichtsschreibung. Melanchthon, Sleidan, Flacius und die Magdeburger Zenturien* (Gütersloh: Gütersloher Verlagshaus 1966); R. SEEBERG, *Lehrbuch der Dogmengeschichte 4/2. Die Fortbildung der reformatorischen Lehre und die gegenreformatorische Lehre* (1920; repr. Darmstadt: Wiss. Buchgesellschaft 1975); N. P. TANNER SJ (ed.), *Decrees of the Ecumenical Councils* II (London: Sheed & Ward / Washington: Georgetown UP 1990); P. TSCHACKERT, *Die Entstehung der lutherischen und der reformierten Kirchenlehre samt ihren innerpro-testantischen Gegensätzen* (Göttingen: Vandenhoeck & Ruprecht 1909); K. WEIMAR, *Historische Einleitung zur literaturwissenschaftlichen Hermeneutik* (Tübingen: Mohr 1975).

1. Introduction

Sola Scriptura became one of the most central and efficacious catchwords of the reforming movement of the sixteenth century. Emphasising the authority of Scripture the Reformers attacked the Catholic Church, demanding her ec-clesial doctrinal authorities, the bishops, the council and the Pope, had to be subjected to the Scripture. The reformation principle of Scripture was deeply anchored in the Protestant concept of revelation, salvation and anthropology. The second generation of reforming theologians, who began their academic carrier around 1550, found that the theological and political conditions had gravely changed since the reforming movement began. In 1545 the Council in Trent was constituted and began its negotiations, certainly without any repre-sentatives from the Protestant Churches in Germany. One of the urgent pro-blems the council had to face was the precise definition of the authority of Scripture in the Church. In its first decree the council condemned the Protes-tant principle of *sola Scriptura*. Confirming and demonstrating the fundamental gap between the Catholic and Protestant churches, the council formulated as catholic doctrine, that the revelation, "the whole truth of salvation and rule of conduct (…) are contained in written books and in unwritten traditions". The council venerated "with a like feeling of piety and reverence all the books" of the Bible, "as well as the traditions concerning both faith and conduct (...)". Consequently, the revelation could be apprehended from two different sources, but the inner relation between them the council did not precisely determine.[1] Although the Catholic Church was theologically and spiritually consolidated by the Council of Trent and was enabled to strengthen inner reform, including an offensive against the Protestant movements, during the fifties the political position of the Protestants was decisively improved. The diet in Augsburg 1555 established equal status for Lutheran and Catholic princes, including their respective subjects, in the German *Reich*. In this way, Lutheran Churches gained a new and a safer legal position. But the theological and doctrinal conflicts between Catholicism and Protestantism continued. In some senses the doctrinal decisions of Trent intensified the antagonism.

Two of the most learned theologians of the second Lutheran generation, Matthias Flacius Illyricus (1520–75) and Martin Chemnitz (1522–86) accepted the challenge from Trent, mainly presented by the recently founded *Jesuit Order* (*Societas Iesu*). The contributions of Flacius and Chemnitz especially to the theology of Scripture and the methodology of interpretation not only influenced the actual polemical situation, but also laid the foundations for the later Lutheran orthodoxy, especially its concept of Scriptural authority and the theoretical premises of biblical interpretation.

Chemnitz was a student of Melanchthon and deeply influenced by the great teacher's theology. Although his theological framework was evidently Melanchthonian, he did not join the 'Philipistic' wing of Protestantism, on the contrary he defended the Lutheran doctrine of the sacrament and the classical Lutheran Christology against various forms of heresy. As one of the men behind the last Lutheran confession, *Formula Concordiae* (1577), he was regarded as one of the foremost Protestant leaders, holding the honorary name, "the second Martin". Flacius was a more radical character. His deepest commitment was to remain faithful to the heritage of the Reformer. He was fully in accordance with this theology when, in the forties, he attacked the plan of the Emperor – and the Lutheran acceptance of it – to establish an ecclesiastical unity in Germany, based on theological compromises and administered by imperial power undermining the freedom of the Gospel. Later on he developed his anthropology and ended up in a heretical position concerning original sin.

Both Flacius and Chemnitz put in a lot of work as ecclesiastical historians – first and foremost to establish a foundation for their criticism of Catholicism and to justify the stabilization of the Reformation.[2] With regard to personal attitude and career Chemnitz and Flacius were very different. Flacius died poor and fatigued in Frankfurt a. M., persecuted for his deviant doctrine of anthropology. Chemnitz ended his days as a widely esteemed superintendent in Brunswick.

---

[1] Cf. Tanner, Decrees II (1990) 663 f.
[2] Cf. Scheible, Geschichtsschreibung (1966); Johansson, Reformationens hovudfrågor (1999).

2. The Hermeneutics of Matthias Flacius Illyricus

Sources: Matthias Flacius Illyricus: *De vocabulo fidei et aliis qvibvsdam vocabilis, explicatio vera & utilis, sumta ex fontibus Ebraicis* (Vitebergae 1549); *De voce et re fidei, contra pharisaicum hypocritarum fermentum* (Basileae 1555); *Clavis Scripturae Sacrae sev de Sermone sacrarum literarum* I-III (1567; Basileae 1628); *Glossa compendiaria M. Matthiae Flacij Illyrici Albonensis in Novum Testamentum* (Basileae 1570).

Studies: J. Baur, *Matthias Flacius Illyricus, 1575–1975* (Schriftenreihe des Regensburger Osteuropainstituts 2; Regensburg 1975); W. Dilthey, "Die Entstehung der Hermeneutik", *Gesammelte Schriften* V (Leipzig / Berlin: Teubner 1924) 332–38; H.-G. Gadamer, "Logik oder Rhetorik", *Archiv für Begriffsgeschichte* XX (1976) 7–16; idem, *Rhetorik und Hermeneutik* (Göttingen: Vandenhoeck & Ruprecht 1976); L. Geldsetzer, "Foreword and Introduction to Matthias Flacius Illyricus, *De ratione cognoscendi Sacras literas / Über den Erkenntnisgrund der Hl. Schrift*" (Instrumenta Philosophica, Series Hermeneutica III; Düsseldorf: Stern Verlag 1968); idem, "Matthias Flacius Illyricus und die wissenschaftstheoretische Begründung der protestantischen Philosophie", in: Matesic, Matthias Flacius Illyricus – Leben und Werk (1993; see below) 199–223; B. Hägglund, "Førkantiansk hermeneutik", in: *Nåd och sanning. Församlingsfakulteten 10 år* (Göteborg: Församlingsförlaget 2003) 73–86; L. Haikola, *Gesetz und Evangelium bei Matthias Flacius* (STL 1; Lund: Gleerup 1952); R. Keller, *Der Schlüssel der Schrift. Die Lehre vom Wort Gottes bei Matthias Flacius Illyricus* (AGTL NF 5; Hannover: Lutherisches Verlagshaus 1984); I. Kordić, *Matthias Flacius Illyricus und sein Beitrag zur Entwicklung der Hermeneutik als des verstehenden Zugangs zur Wirklichkeit und zu ihrem Niederschlag im Text* (Diss. Freiburg 1987); J. Matesic (ed.), *Matthias Flacius Illyricus – Leben und Werk* (Südosteuropa-Studien 53; München: Südosteuropa-Gesellschaft 1993); M. Mirković, *Matija Vlačić Ilirik* (Zagreb 1960; with Croatian bibliography); G. Moldaenke, *Schriftverständnis und Schriftdeutung im Zeitalter der Reformation* (Stuttgart: Kohlhammer 1936); O. K. Olson, "Flacius Illyricus, Matthias (1520–1575)", TRE 11 (1983) 206–14; W. Preger, *Matthias Flacius und seine Zeit* 1–2 (Erlangen: Bläsing 1859/61); H. Scheible (ed.), *Die Anfänge der reformatorischen Geschichtsschreibung* (1966) [see above, *General works*]; K. A. Schwartz, *Die theologische Hermeneutik des Matthias Flacius* (Diss. München 1933).

Matthias Flacius Illyricus / Matija Vlačić (1520–75) was born in Bosnia. Sixteen years-old he went to study in Venice. In 1540 he transferred to Tübingen and then to Wittenberg, where he obtained a Master's Degree in Greek and Hebrew languages in 1543. In Wittenberg he came under the influence of Martin Luther. In 1544 he was made professor of Hebrew at Wittenberg. His first work, *De vocabulo fidei*, published in 1549, is a linguistic interpretation of the definition of faith, based on the Hebrew language.[3] In 1567 working as a teacher of the Hebrew and Greek languages in Regensburg, he published his book *Clavis Scripturae sacrae*, which remains his most important work.

Flacius was a philologist and interpreter. His understanding of the Old Testament elucidates the principles he regards as necessary for an adequate interpretation of the Bible. In his *Clavis Scripturae sacrae* his theology of revelation and his hermeneutical rules were topics thoroughly clarified and developed. Today his reflections on the methodology of textual interpretation and the hermeneutical rules he introduced, are regarded as an anticipation of the manner of thinking in modern hermeneutics.[4]

The Flacian theology of Scripture has two characteristics, firstly, the

---

[3] It became a supplement in the work *De voce et re fidei* (1555).
[4] Cf. Dilthey, Die Entstehung der Hermeneutik (1924) 332–38; Gadamer, Rhetorik und Hermeneutik (1976).

authority of the Bible is based on cognitive principles dependant on his concept of revelation and the history of salvation. Secondly, in order to grasp the biblical revelation in an adequate and congenial way, Flacius formulated a set of hermeneutical rules. In the most recent discussions about the theology of Flacius an issue of wider relevance has been brought up: Did Flacius succeed in integrating his dogmatic identification of the Bible as a medium of revelation with his general hermeneutical rules for interpretation of the biblical text?[5] The question is not a narrow historical problem, because the relation between normative dogmatics and a more 'neutral' hermeneutics is fundamental in the modern theology. Flacius, confronted with the Catholic challenge, found it urgent to show that Scripture could be interpreted independent of ecclesiastical texts and authorities, in some sense in a 'neutral' way. Because the principle of *sola Scriptura* could appear evident and adequate, when his hermeneutical rules were taken into account and used in the interpretation of the Bible, his dogmatic theology would also be self-evident simply because of the principle of *sola Scriptura*, itself a genuine reformation principle.

An essential point in every theological conception of Scripture is the understanding of the Old Testament as an integrated part of the canon. In the Lutheran tradition the doctrine of justification was regarded as the right paradigm for an adequate interpretation of the biblical texts. The *law* and *gospel*- and the *promise* and *fulfilment*-relation determined its structure, which are the fundamental basis when the relationship between the Old and the New Testaments are be understood. The promises of the Messiah are fulfilled in the new covenant by the incarnation of the Son of God in Jesus Christ, his messianic mission, suffering, death and resurrection, which is the aim of the history of revelation.

To identify the function of the law in the new covenant (the natural and the Mosaic) became a problem for Protestant theology. In the Protestant-Catholic confrontation the function of the law came forward as one of the main topics. Loyal to the original traditions from the Reformer, Flacius took up the paradigm of Law and Gospel and laid it down as the fundamental premise for his dogmatic understanding of Scripture in general, and the Old Testament in particular.

In a traditional way Flacius connected law and gospel to the biblical concept of covenant. The covenants of respectively law and gospel have always been present in the history of mankind, mutually dependant on each other.[6] As natural law (*lex naturae*) the law prevailed in the period from Adam until Moses, but in fallen humanity in an obscure way. An aspect of the Mosaic covenant, established at Sinai, was the exceptional insight in the law, including the religious commandments, which was given to the Jewish people, but remained unknown in the pagan world.[7]

How did Flacius interpret the relation between law and gospel? This is an

---

[5] Cf. Geldsetzer, Foreword and Introduction (1968) 19; Weimar, Historische Einleitung (1975) 39, 126; Kordić, Matthias Flacius Illyricus (1987) 28 ff.

[6] *Novum testamentum Filii Dei* (1570) 5.

[7] Cf. Haikola, Gesetz und Evangelium (1952) 195 f.

important question when we try to characterize his understanding of the Old Testament.

Obeying the law, was the first way to salvation, but because of sin the law appeared powerless, unable to produce a new spiritual life in man. Therefore, the gospel was revealed as another possibility of salvation, which also gave the law a new function, as a servant of the gospel, becoming a teacher of the humankind towards faith in the gospel. In this perspective the law turned out to be the primary, since the gospel was later revealed. But in another perspective, which was important for Flacius as well, the gospel is prior and fundamental to the law, being originally revealed to Adam and Eve soon after the Fall and repeated to Abraham as a prototype messianic promise at the beginning of the history of salvation. In the final analysis there are only two covenants in the history of salvation, the Mosaic and the messianic, the last one fulfilled in *testamentum Christi*. In this perspective the gospel is fundamental to the law, because it is the fulfilment of the law. The gospel endows the law with a new function in the history of revelation, impossible to grasp from the law itself.[8] On these premises Flacius developed his theology of Scripture, which is the principle feature of his method for obtaining an adequate theological understanding.

In accordance with the Lutheran tradition Flacius asserted that the only way to reach an adequate understanding of the whole Scripture is to grasp the right concept of Law and Gospel, their *concordia & discrimen*, which is thoroughly outlined in the Pauline theology. Not until in the New Testament and the final realisation of salvation for mankind in Christ was such understanding of the structure of revelation possible. Faith in Christ lifted the "veil" from the eyes of the Jews. And everyone, Jews and pagans as well, have such a veil preventing them from the right understanding of Scripture, as long as they live in unbelief.[9] Faith in the gospel is the right foundation of a theology of Scripture, and the personal insight for an appropriate understanding of the Bible as well as the basic hermeneutical condition of its interpretation. In this way Flacius represented a kind of *Theologia regenitorum*.[10]

Lack of understanding depends not only on the blindness of man, but also on the wisdom of God, because he has revealed his mysteries in a process beginning with a vague impression and ending with a clearer one. Flacius ascertains that revelation is imbedded in a developing process, beginning in the Old Testament and completed in the New. But even the believers in the new covenant do not recognize the revelation completely, because God has spoken in metaphors, so that nobody has the spiritual capacity to apprehend all the divine mysteries. At last, when we have gained eternal salvation, we can achieve the full understanding of the mysterious God, at that time we shall see Christ "face to face". In the meantime, under the conditions of this world we are like an embryo in its mother's womb, satisfied although it does not see the sun. Nevertheless, Flacius claims, the new theology of the Reformation has brought

---

[8] *Clavis* II/1, 5; II/6, 606–18.
[9] Ibid. *Clavis* II/1, 6.
[10] Ibid.

to light a deeper insight concerning the revelation, since the Reformation has disguised and driven Antichrist out, for the Reformers the pope and the Catholic Church.[11]

Flacius' principle theology of Scripture was cognitively structured, concentrated on the question of revelation: How can we recognize and understand the divine mysteries of salvation described in the Bible? The same problem was discussed by Luther, and his solution was the doctrine of *claritas Scripturae*, "clearity of Scripture". God in Christ was revealed in history, his words and deeds and his saving life, death and resurrection are evidently recognized in Scripture, when read and heard in accordance with its plain texts. The *speculatio majestatis* typical for the medieval scholasticism, would lead astray, the only way to the merciful God present in Christ is the Word of God in the biblical texts. The Flacian theology of Scripture and hermeneutics must be understood as an attempt typical of the second generation of Lutheran theologians to continue the tradition from the Reformer. As the Reformer, Flacius rejected the competence of the philosophy (*speculatio majestatis*) in the field of theology,[12] and in accordance with Luther he concentrated on Scripture as the one and only source of revelation, but in order to grasp the content of revelation we have to interpret the "difficult" (unclear) texts of the Bible. There is a difference between Luther and Flacius on this point. While Luther regards the scriptural revelation of the gospel as evident in itself, since the Scripture interprets itself and in this way creates the faith in the hearts of men, the cognitive problem is the starting point by Flacius, and his intention is by practicing his methodological rules to *demonstrate* the "clearity" of Scripture. If we have the right key (*clavis*), the appropriate remedies, then the biblical texts can be interpreted with convincing evidence. God himself has provided adequate means at our disposal.[13]

Flacius introduced his methodological-hermeneutical program with a presentation of what can prevent an adequate comprehension of the meaning of the biblical texts. Our own thoughts and conventional ideas are ascribed to Scripture. The most central religious concepts of sin, justification, faith, grace, flesh and spirit are interpreted in terms drawn from Aristotelian philosophy. In this way we distort the meaning of the biblical texts. In accordance with the Lutheran anthropology he emphasizes that the nature of man is not only incompetent at comprehending what belongs to God, but finds the divine truth silly and scandalous.[14] Not only do the human foolishness and incompetence obscure the meaning of the texts, but so also does human corruption. It is obvious that the contemporary controversial theological situation provided the context when Flacius characterized the various forms of misinterpretations of the Bible. The core of Protestant anti-Catholicism was the allegation that the Catholic Church misread the biblical texts and words and misinterpreted the

---

[11] Ibid.
[12] Cf. Kordić, Matthias Flacius Illyricus (1987) 1–28.
[13] *Clavis* II/1, 6.
[14] Ibid. 1 ff.

doctrine of Scripture, not only because of unsatisfactory insight, but also as a result of an evil delusion.

Flacius' attempt to synthesise a dogmatic concept of revelation and scriptural authority with a hermeneutical view of the scriptural texts is expressed when he developed the necessary religious requirement for an adequate interpretation of Scripture. One after the other Flacius mentioned the religious "remedia" necessary to handle the difficult problem of interpretation. Firstly, it is required that we seek God, the Holy Trinity, and foremost the Holy Spirit, who will guide us to the whole truth so that we can be taught by God. The fundamental basis for a true and right interpretation is in other words a Trinitarian belief in God and faith in salvation, shaping spiritual experience. Consequently, he also underlined spiritual meditation and prayers. These ideas are summoned up in the demand that the Bible must be interpreted in accordance with the concept of *analogia fidei*.[15] The interpretation of Holy Scripture is all in all a practical matter; theology and ethics are intimately connected. For Flacius it was extremely important to stress the practical dimension of theology, a consequence of his doctrine of Justification by Faith Alone, and manifest in his radical understanding of freedom in Christ.

The Holy Spirit is the author of the Bible. This statement includes a pneumatological qualification of Holy Scripture as well as characterisation of it as text. The Holy Spirit speaks to us and teaches us by the medium of the biblical texts, but since the Holy Spirit is mentioned as an *author*, the Scripture must also be regarded a composition of literary documents and can and ought to be treated in accordance with it. The pneumatological and the literal aspects of the Bible are integrated, because the spiritual message is linguistically given and can be philologically and stylistically analysed. Last but not least, the Spirit is not only the author of Scripture but its interpreter as well. The Spirit leads us to truth and writes the words of Scripture in our hearts. The interpretation of Scripture cannot be a task for human rationality alone, but has to be interpreted in the light of the Spirit and by means of faith.[16]

In the light of the literary characterization of the biblical texts it is natural for Flacius to reflect on language as a medium for understanding. Flacius considered language from two angles. It is a symbol and a representation, which refers to concrete case circumstances. At the same time language provides the spectacles we wear, which make it possible for us to consider and understand reality. The natural consequence of such a 'philosophy of language' is the thorough philological analysis of the biblical texts when the intention is to take hold of the central and structural content of Scripture: the divine revelation or – as Flacius often puts it – *doctrina coelestis*. Naturally, Flacius emphasised especially philological examination, because old languages remain obscure to present-day people, and one of the greatest difficulties is to understand the

---

[15] Ibid. 6–7; 12: *Omnia igitur, quae de scripturâ, aut ex Scripturâ, dicuntur, debent esse consona praedicatae Cathechesticae summae, aut articulis fidei.* Concerning the analogia, cf. Kordić, Matthias Flacius Illyricus (1987) 102–33.

[16] *Spiritus S. est autor simul, & explicator Scripturae. Ipsius est, nos ducere in omnem veritatem: Ioh. 16.13. Ipsius est, Scripturam cordi nostro inscribere: Ier. 31.v. 33"*, Clavis II/1, 8.

mentality and way of life of past cultures.[17] A philological analysis of the texts will not be sufficient; we have to uncover the linguistic style and way of expression characteristic of ancient texts. Therefore, Flacius recommends a rhetorical analysis of the biblical texts, which is absolutely necessary and appropriate when these texts are to be interpreted, because the Bible is filled with metaphors, parables, allegories, typology etc.[18] The hermeneutical method of humanism, as Erasmus introduced it, was an integral part of the Flacian theology of Scripture.[19] As an outstanding expert on Hebrew language he declared that the language of the Old Testament is particularly rich in metaphors. Therefore it is very difficult to understand, simply because these metaphors are usually integral to it. The words: "The Hand of the Lord touched me" are an anthropomorph metaphor applied to God, but at the same time "the Hand" stands for an action by God, i.e. his punishment.[20] There are difficulties in understanding Hebrew grammar too. Flacius discussed in detail some of the philological problems of the Hebrew texts and demonstrated how difficult their interpretation is, in particular from a rhetorical point of view. Remarkable is his awareness of the historical distance between the original context of the biblical texts and his own cultural situation. Places, conventions and conceptual imagery, to which the texts refer and which give meaning to metaphors and comparisons, are unknown to us today. In addition, we find many general formulations in the biblical texts – both in the Old and the New Testament – which the unskilled easily can misinterpret. According to Flacius this is what the Catholic theologians have done, when they referred to Matt 16:19 as the argument for the hierarchical structure of the Church and the papal authority.

In his opus magnum, *Clavis Scripturae sacrae*, philological and rhetorical analyses claim a considerable space. The first part of the book is a biblical dictionary; in the second part we find an elucidation of the roles of metaphors, tropes and Old Testamenther forms of stylistic imagery in the biblical texts. But the intention of Flacius differs from the traditional humanistic evaluation of the figurative expressions as the most appropriate medium of communication of Christian wisdom, instead he promotes the fundamental premise of the Reformation: the Christian revelation must be outlined from the biblical texts interpreted in accordance with their straightforward meaning; the *sensus historicus*, based on the philological-grammatical analysis of Scripture, is the cognitive basis for perceiving revelation. In this way Flacius attended to the Lutheran idea of *perspicuitas Scripturae*.

If Protestant theology is to be able to protect the doctrine of *sola Scriptura* against Catholic attacks, then it needs a method of textual interpretation which not only prevents a breach of the hermeneutical horizon, but proves adequate and realistic to delimit the structure of interpretation to the Scripture alone. In this perspective the function of Flacius' hermeneutical methodology was a reasoned legitimizing of the doctrine of *sola Scriptura*. This is the end his

---

[17] Ibid. 2–6.
[18] Ibid.
[19] Cf. Keller, Der Schlüssel der Schrift (1984) 172–76.
[20] *Clavis* II/1, 3.

famous rules of interpretation are to serve. Consequently, it is very important that these rules are *externae & generales*, that means, their character has to be hermeneutical and not dogmatic.[21]

If we want to understand a book or another presentation, it is necessary first of all to grasp the *aim* of the work. This is the first of Flacius' rules. His next recommendation is to summarize briefly the principal content, the "summa" or the "head" of the work. We have thereafter to clarify the disposition. In this context Flacius refers to the human body as an analogy. The literal work has its head, breast, arms and legs. If we can grasp the organic disposition and construction of the work, we will obtain an understanding of how the different parts are related to each other within the entire literary body, understanding how they function in relation to each other in the context of the literary structure. In this way we can discover the inner harmony of the work, which it is our task to interpret, and above all we can realize how its individual parts and branches are related to the "head". This insight must be written down as a synopsis or table. If the interpreter keeps to these four rules in an adequate and correct way, he has developed a foundation for a right and precise concept of the work. He is able to understand the individual parts in the perspective of its central ideas. And he can realize how the different parts and aspects support and confirm the fundamental aim of the work.

Flacius' concern was to give the hermeneutical process a rational and effective structure and purpose. We do not go astray because of a false understanding of the individual parts, since the different aspects have to be interpreted from the totality of the work. At the same time it will be necessary to analyse the individual *loci*, if the totality is to be conceptualised.[22] In the literary analysis all means and methods which God has put at our disposal, must be employed. In Flacius' 'formcritical' investigation he asks for *scopus* and *genus*, and he seeks to determine if the text is a *narratio* or a *doctrina*, a *consolatio* or an *objurgatio*, perhaps *descriptio* or *oratio*.[23] When the *genus* is clear, the content of the text must be determined in accordance with the rules valid for this particular *genus*. In order to interpret the individual *loci* grammatical and dialectical analysis must be used. Finally, the interpreter must formulate the content of the text in his own words. Flacius named it a kind of "anatomical record", a "skeleton" expressing the meaning of the text.[24]

The core of Flacius' hermeneutical rules was the idea that the parts are to be interpreted from the totality, and the totality by means of the individual parts. He applied this method in his interpretation of the Bible, even when he interpreted individual biblical books and small paragraphs.[25] This was for Flacius a methodological consequence of the Protestant theology of Scripture, a practi-

---

[21] Ibid. 22.

[22] Ibid. 22f.

[23] Ibid. 23–25.

[24] Ibid. 24.

[25] *Ibi igitur accurate expendas, quale illud corpus sit; quomodo omnia ea membra complectatur: quave ratione, illa tota membra aut partes ad effeciendum hoc unum corpus, conveniant: quænam sit, singulorum membrorum, vel inter sese, vel etiam cum toto corpore ac praesertim cum capite ipso, convenientia, harmonia, ac proportio.* Ibid. 22.

cal documentation of the legitimacy of Protestantism, its idea of the supreme authority of Holy Writ, its *sufficientia*, based on clarity and evidence.

The Flacian hermeneutic has two fundamental premises: Although there are great impediments to an adequate understanding of the biblical texts, partly in the text itself and partly in our own spirit, nevertheless Scripture is in reality harmonious and consistent, given by God as a book, whose message is intelligible. By means of general philological and hermeneutical methods its content can be evidently outlined for everyone. Although faith is a necessary personal presupposition for the theologian, the meaning of the biblical text is comprehensible in general. But Flacius does not assert any "open" or relativistic hermeneutic, he takes the objective meaning of the truth for granted. "The truth is everywhere, but first of all in the theology, (...). Not without reason Christ instructs the Apostles and all pious men to adhere to his word" (John 14:21, 23; 17:6 and 8).[26]

The Word of God is true. This is the principal thing in Holy Writ. And this contention does not require any evidence. Our words, ascertained Moses and the prophets, are the Words of God. Through them God has spoken. Therefore, their words and books (about the creation, the fall of man and the messianic promises) are altogether truthful, confirmed by the history of the old covenant, notably the miracles during the "exodus" from Egypt and the capture of the Holy Land, and the protection of Israel during the time of trouble. All these prove that the books of the Old Testament originate from God. The New Testament presupposes that the prophetic description of the promised Messiah is true. Furthermore, in the New Testament we learn that all that the prophets wrote about the Messiah, are fulfilled in Jesus. Eyewitnesses – Apostles and other people – have confirmed it. In this way the Old Testament is proved to be the true word of God.

What God says or bears witness to, is really true. In the New Testament the voice of God the Father loudly testifies what Jesus proclaims in his public speeches (Matt 3:17; 17:5; John 12:28). Consequently, what Jesus and his Apostles say and teach, is absolute truth. Flacius draws the conclusion, that the central doctrines of the Old and the New Testament are the most adequate presupposition to understand Holy Writ, because Scripture and Scripture alone is the true Word of God, the textual expression of *doctrina coelestis*.[27] In this way, Flacius connected his dogmatic view with his hermeneutic, and gave his general rules of interpretation a theological function. *Doctrina coelestis*, which is developed and has proved its truth during the history of salvation, has to be interpreted on its own prepositions *and* by relevant and general hermeneutical methods for interpretation of texts.

---

[26] Ibid. 19.
[27] Ibid. 9 f.

3. Martin Chemnitz and his Focus on the 'Scriptural' Character of Theology

Sources: MARTIN CHEMNITZ: *Theologiae Jesuitarum praecipua capita* (Lipsiae 1562); *Examen Concilii Tridentini (1566–1573)* (ed. Ed. Preuss; Berolini 1861); *Enchiridion in qvo praecipvis capitibus doctrinae coelestis…* (1577) (Lipsiae 1601); *Loci theologici. Quibus et loci communes D. Philip Melanchthonis explicantur* I–III (1589) (Witebergae 1623); *Harmonia evangelica, conscripta a reverendo et clarissimo viro domini Martino Chemnitio…* (Francofurti 1593); *Postilla oder außlegung der Evangelien, welche auff die sontage, auch die fürnembste fest- und aposteltage in der gemeine Gottes abgelesen und erkläret werden* (1593) (Magdeburg 1594).

Studies: P. J. REHTMEYER, *Historiae ecclesiasticae inclytae urbis Brunsvigae oder Der berühmten Stadt Braunschweig Kirchen-Historia* III (Braunschweig 1710); H. HACHFELD, *Martin Chemnitz nach seinem Leben und Wirken, insbesondere nach seinem Verhältnisse zum Tridentinum* (Leipzig: Breitkopf und Härtel 1867); F. E. KOLDEWEY, "Johannes Monheim und die Kölner. Der Streit zwischen Jesuitismus und Protestantismus", *ZWTh* 42 (1899) 106–38; R. MUMM, *Die Polemik des Martin Chemnitz gegen das Konzil von Trient* (Naumburg a. S.: Lippert 1905); G. NOTH, *Grundzüge der Theologie des Martin Chemnitz* (Diss. Erlangen 1930); B. LOSSNER, *Martin Chemnitz and his locus De sacra Scripturae against Roman errors* (St. Louis 1947); A. L. OLSON, *Scripture and Tradition in the Theology of Martin Chemnitz* (Cambridge, MA 1965); E. F. KLUG, *From Luther to Chemnitz. On Scripture and the Word* (Grand Rapids: Eerdmanns 1971); W. A. JÜNKE (ed.), *Der zweite Martin der Lutherischen Kirche. Festschrift zum 400. Todestag von Martin Chemnitz* (Braunschweig 1986; bibliography by T. Mahlmann); B. T. OFTESTAD, "Traditio und Norma – Hauptzüge der Schriftauffassung bei Martin Chemnitz", in: Jünke, Der zweite Martin (1986) 172–91; idem, "Harmonia Evangelica. Die Evangelienharmonie von Martin Chemnitz – theologische Ziele und methodologische Voraussetzungen", *StTh* 45 (1991) 57–74; M. ROENSCH, "Die kontroverstheologische Bedeutung des Examen Concilii Tridentini von Martin Chemnitz", in: Jünke, Der zweite Martin (1986) 190–200; B. HÄGGLUND, "Glaubensregel und Tradition nach Martin Chemnitz", *Tragende Tradition. Festschrift für Martin Seils zum 65. Geburtstag* (ed. A. Freund / U. Kern / A. Radler; Frankfurt a. M.: Lang 1992) 75–80; J. A. O. PREUS, *The second Martin. The Life and Theology of Martin Chemnitz* (St. Louis: Concordia 1994); J. D. HEISER, "The Use of Ireneus's Adversus Hareses in Martin Chemnitz's Loci Theologici", *Logia. A Journal of Lutheran Theology* 8 (1998) 19–31; T. JOHANSSON, *Reformationens hovudfrågor och arvet från Augustinus. En studie i Martin Chemnitz' Augustinusreception* (Göteborg: Församlingsförlaget 1999); T. MAHLMANN, "Chemnitz, Martin (1522–1586)", TRE 7 (1981) 714–21.

As one of the dominating Lutheran theologians during the last decades of the sixteenth century Martin Chemnitz (1522–86) was intensively preoccupied with the challenge from the current Catholic theology. His most important contribution to the actual interconfessional debate was his opus magnum, *Examen Concilii Tridentini*. His analysis of the doctrinal decisions in Trent determined the future Protestant opinion of Catholicism; in addition, he gave rational grounds for the idea of *sola Scriptura*, which was later on developed in Lutheran orthodoxy. In his *Harmonia evangelica* (1593) he made an apologetic attempt to defend the historical reliability of the narratives in the Gospels.[28] While Flacius tried to demonstrate that the ecclesiastical traditions were superfluous for the interpretation of the Bible, Chemnitz, on the other hand, concentrated on the problem of the trustworthy cognition of the divine revelation.

In the introduction to the *Formula Concordiae* – Chemnitz was one of the originators behind that confession – we find a concise formulation of the main

---

[28] Cf. Oftestad, Harmonia Evangelica (1991) 57–74.

points of the Lutheran concept of Scripture: The Holy Writ is the "only rule and guideline" when doctrines and teachers (*omnia dogmata omnesque doctores*) have to be examined.[29] No authoritative ecclesiastical text is above the Bible. The original Lutheranism did not harbour theological or philosophical animosity against the tradition. Luther and Melanchthon as well underlined that the Lutheran doctrines did not deviate from the Trinitarian and Christological dogmas. Confronted with the Jesuitical offensive in Germany the task was not only to document the continuity between Reformation and the old Church, but also to protect the exclusive authority of Scripture. One of the arguments in the polemic of the Jesuits was the assertion that Scripture was obscure and therefore insufficient as the only source of revelation.[30] In his book *Theologia Jesuitarum praecupia capita* and in his great work, *Examen Concilii Tridentini*, Chemnitz positively developed and argued in favour of his apprehension of Scripture.

Called "the second Martin" Chemnitz emphasised what he conceived as the genuine Lutheran tradition. But he worked out his ideas of Scripture as authority from another viewpoint than that of the Reformer. How far he substantially continued Luther's theology of Scripture, is disputed.[31] In his *Enchiridion* he raised the question: What is the Word of God? In his answer he does not refer to the Bible, but to the historical acts of revelation.[32] The revelation takes place *in* history, and the creation is the beginning of its process within history. Chemnitz regarded Scripture in the perspective of a soteriological finality. In this way the Old Testament as evidence of the revelation in the old covenant takes on a particular significance for Chemnitz. At the beginning of history God unveils his secret existence and lets his light shine over the world. His *essence* and *will* are revealed in history. And the medium for his revelation is his Word, manifested by means of human language and confirmed by miracles, which implies that revelation was adapted to human presuppositions.[33] Revelation is the fundamental truth of God, given at the beginning of world-history. But it has as well its own history, by Chemnitz characterized by the concept of *traditio*. Within the framework of *traditio* Scripture has its function, and here Chemnitz finds the reason why Scripture is the necessary and unique source of revelation.

When Chemnitz applied the concept of *doctrina coelestis*[34] he signalised the importance of the cognitive question. The human situation after the fall of man is above all marked by spiritual ignorance. But humanity is in addition a victim under the dominance of satanic powers, even human ability to comprehend the Word of God is perverted, and natural man refuses the wisdom of God. The reason is evident. The spirit of this world stands against the Holy Spirit. The consequence is that the *doctrina coelestis* has been continuously fal-

---

[29] Cf. *Die Bekenntnisschriften der evangelisch-lutherischen Kirche* (Göttingen: Vandenhoeck & Ruprecht 1959) 767 f.
[30] Cf. Koldeway, Johannes Monheim und die Kölner (1899) 106–38.
[31] Cf. Losner, Martin Chemnitz (1947); Olson, Scripture and Tradition (1965).
[32] *Enchiridion* 43.
[33] *Examen* 8B; *Enchiridion* 43; *Loci* I 234A.
[34] *Examen* 8Bff.; *Loci* I 9.

sified and obscured. In order to secure the Protestant view against Catholic attacks, Chemnitz referred to human spiritual weakness and satanic power. There are no formal or institutional guarantees against perversion of the pure doctrine, neither the pope nor the council. They both can be, and have been, subordinated to spiritual corruption, and they have in a fatal way falsified the Word of God. In the perspective of Chemnitz the Catholic Church had perverted the genuine Christian *tradition*.[35]

The *doctrina coelestis* is delivered through the history of salvation. But the blindness of man, satanic lies and the ungodliness of the world threaten the tradition of the divine doctrine. When the doctrine is delivered by oral tradition, it is particularly vulnerable, it is easily falsified and distorted. During the period between Adam and Moses the tradition was only oral, and decay took place, the oral tradition was misinterpreted and partly changed. But God protected it against the worst deviation. It was the will of God that the tradition of *doctrina coelestis* should avoid corruption. In consequence He determined that oral tradition alone is unsuitable and too vulnerable when doctrine is preserved in history. Chemnitz regarded the revelation of the Law at Sinai as an intervention from God to institute a new "method" of preserving the divine doctrine. In a miraculous way God himself wrote down the Law on stone tablets. It was no coincidence, but had a revelatory signification: God pointed out that his revelation should be preserved for the future by a scriptural tradition, which was the only way to secure its content against misinterpretation and deviation. Oral tradition by itself had failed; the only trustworthy "method" was the written fixation of the revelation. On Sinai God "sanctified" with signs and miracles the written text as the only adequate medium of tradition. In this way he initiated Holy Writ in the story of salvation. Consequently, the written tradition has to take precedence over the oral.[36]

In accordance with the cultural development from the late Middle Ages, for instance the reception of the written Roman law and the invention of the art of printing, Chemnitz prescribed the written form of revelation as the prerequisite for a true theological understanding. In this way he developed a general basis for the Lutheran principle of Scripture, later taken over by Lutheran orthodoxy and in a sophisticated way reflected in the theory of verbal inspiration. But the actual horizon for Chemnitz was naturally the conflict with the Council of Trent and its doctrine of Scripture and oral tradition and the Church as the only legitimate interpreter of the revelation. When the council looked at the oral tradition as a specific and independent source of revelation, it neglected the obvious demand for cognitive reliability and left the revelation open to deviation and corruption.

Emphasizing the written text Chemnitz also had another theological opponent in mind. At that time there was a living Jewish (talmudic) theology partially based on oral tradition reputedly from Moses. When Chemnitz argued that the written text was miraculously instituted at Sinai, he undermined the spiritual authority of the oral and esoteric kabbalistic traditions. As far as this

---

[35] *Examen* 8A-9A; *Enchiridion* 44–47; *Loci* I 19–23.
[36] *Theologia* 5B; *Examen* 8A-9A; 10A-11B; *Loci* III 234.

type of polemic was relevant in Germany at that time, he gained an advantage in his confrontation with Trent. In this perspective, Catholicism and Judaism were two of a kind.[37]

Lutheran orthodoxy sought to explain the record of revelation in Holy Writ by formulating the theory of verbal inspiration. Such a theory is not to be found in Chemnitz. But the linguistic form of the revelation of the divine reality he is fully aware of. The history of revelation shows that the authentic language of revelation is Hebrew, he contends. When God first spoke to humankind he used Hebrew language. The essential content of revelation knowable at the beginning of history, was revealed in Hebrew. Consequently, the Old Testament occupies a special position in the history of revelation.[38]

The central and decisive event in the history of salvation is the incarnation of the Son of God, his suffering, death, and resurrection. The promise of salvation by grace fulfilled in Christ is the *materia* of the revelation. This message is not only in the New Testament, already the first parents of mankind received it (Gen 3:15). Although the history of revelation is a process beginning in the Old Testament its substance is unchanged from the original revelation immediately after the fall of man (from divine grace) until its definite realization in the new covenant. Chemnitz determined the relation between *materia* and process in this way: The original, essential and permanent aspects of the biblical revelation were developed and "repeated" in the old covenant, and then were brought to fulfilment in the salvation through Christ. The unity of the two Testaments is important; at the same time Chemnitz recognized the *propria* of the Testaments. The *proprium* of the Old Testament is the messianic promise, whereas in the New Testament the promise is fulfilled.[39]

In the theological conflicts between the Protestant and the Catholic camps Protestant theologians considered the problem of tradition, oral as well as written, as particularly urgent. In *Examen* Chemnitz discussed the topic with great energy and delineated various types of tradition.[40] The *Apostolic* tradition, firstly in an oral form, is naturally the most central in the Church. Little by little it was written down and carried on in the Church as Holy Writ. Chemnitz took over the concept of the apostolate from the Primitive Church, firstly formulated by the Church Father *Ireneus*.[41] Only the doctrine committed by the Apostles is true and genuine, because the Lord himself gave the Apostles the authority to interpret and pass on his doctrine to the later Church. The Apostles are the "authorized" tradents, and they received a special spiritual qualification for their task. Their authority had a pneumatological basis.[42] The doctrine and the apostolic preaching were in danger of being distorted and corrupted. That is why the Apostles let their doctrine be re-

---

[37] *Examen* 13B-15B.
[38] *Examen* 61A-65B; *Postilla* 132f.
[39] *Loci* I 9; II 228-234; III 93-94; 96ff.
[40] *Examen* 69A-99B.
[41] *Examen* 19Bf.
[42] Ibid. 18A.

corded. They were shepherds for the Church; in this way they secured the true and authentic tradition.[43]

For Chemnitz the divine authorizing of the holy text at Sinai serves as a typical model for the recording of the apostolic doctrine in the new covenant. But at Sinai great miracles occurred, when God revealed himself in a theophany. An analogous incident in the new covenant is the Apostolic Council in Jerusalem (Acts 15), which confirms that the authority of the Apostles in the Church is given by God, because the council in Jerusalem was directly guided by the Holy Spirit. Accordingly the Apostles could introduce their decision with the words: "The Holy Spirit and we have decided..." (Acts 15:28). God appointed a group of persons to formulate the revealed "divine doctrine", and a miracle confirmed this choice, so that nobody could deny that their scriptures were the Word of God.[44] The scriptures in the New Testament are authoritative, because they represent a trustworthy tradition of apostolic doctrine. Nevertheless, Chemnitz had in addition a pneumatical argument for the authority of Scripture: The Holy Writ is inspired by the Holy Spirit (2 Tim 3:16; 2 Pet 1:21).[45]

Although Chemnitz had a polemical anti-Catholic horizon, he did not assert a mere biblical fundamentalism. Emphasising the tradition, the act of the Holy Spirit and the apostolate with Chemnitz the Church – especially the *ecclesia primitiva* – is assigned an important role in his concept of the authority of Scripture. The *ecclesia primitiva* received the revelation, but she was passive and receptive, the Church had no productive function in this respect. From another point of view she was nevertheless active – in her own way – she confirmed that Scripture had a divine origin and was the Word of God.[46] Although Chemnitz' theology of Scripture had ecclesiological aspects, it brought him no closer to the Catholic position. With him the Church is no spiritual sphere for a living, productive tradition, guided and defined by the ecclesial ministry. Only the ecclesiastical testimony from the first Church is carried on in the history, because she had the unique opportunity of witnessing the genesis of Holy Writ. But the first Church did not endow the Scripture its authority. The authority of the Scripture is anchored in the Scripture itself, its apostolic origin.[47]

In his theology of Scripture Chemnitz developed the Reformers' doctrine of *sola Scriptura*, its exclusive authority and cognitive clarity. But his starting point was the cognitive question: How can we find the most reliable source of revelation? His argument in favour of the written tradition of *doctrina coelestis* was in its substance general and rational, although the reasons were found in revelatory biblical narratives (the delivery of the Ten Commandments at Sinai and the Apostolic Council in Jerusalem).

---

[43] Ibid. 19B; 26B; 42A; 44A.
[44] Ibid. 22B; 44A; 54A.
[45] Ibid.
[46] Ibid. 56A-57A.
[47] Ibid. 54B-61B.

Chapter Twenty-five

Catholic Old Testament Interpretation in the Reformation and Early Confessional Eras

By Jared Wicks, University Heights, OH

General works: V. Baroni, *Le Contre-Réforme devant la Bible* (Lausanne 1943; repr. Geneva: Slatkine 1986); G. Bedouelle / B. Roussel (eds.), *Le temps des Réformes et la Bible* (BTT 5; Paris: Beauchesne 1989); R. Bireley, *The Refashioning of Catholicism, 1450–1700* (Houndsmills / London: Macmillan 1999); R. Fabris, *Galileo Galilei e gli orientamenti esegetici del suo tempo* (Vatican City: Pontificia Academia Scientiarum 1986); J. W. O'Malley (ed.), *Catholicism in Early Modern Europe: a Guide to Research* (Reformation Guides to Research 2; St. Louis: Center for Reformation Research 1988); idem, *Trent and All That. Renaming Catholicism in the Early Modern Era* (Cambridge, MA / London: Harvard UP 2000).

Bibliographies: *Archivo teologico granadino*, Bolétin de historia della Teología (1500–1800), annual; K. Reinhardt, *Bibelkommentare spanischer Autoren (1500–1700)* 1–2 (Medievalia et Humanistica 5; Madrid: CSIC 1990, 1999).

This chapter treats the works of sixteenth-century Catholic Old Testament commentators along with analysis of directives given by the Council of Trent and the founding documents of the Jesuit order, which gave Catholic biblical study its profile in the post-Reformation, 'confessional' era. The creative commentaries of Cardinal Cajetan preceded Trent, but then remained outside the post-Tridentine mainstream, as the chapter will illustrate from selected authors in its final section.

The terms 'counter reformation' and 'catholic reform' are not used, since neither captures the main intentions of sixteenth-century Catholic work on the Old Testament, which aimed to raise the cultural level of the Latinate elite, improve preaching, and promote a spirituality animated by a new Christian reception of the Scriptures of Israel.[1]

1. The Old Testament Interpretation of Tommaso de Vio, Cardinal Cajetan

Works: Cajetan's commentaries on the Psalms, Pentateuch, Joshua to Esther, and Job-Proverbs-Qoheleth-Isaiah 1–3, were printed sporadically, beginning in 1530, at Venice, Lyon, and Paris. A century later, the Dominicans of Madrid published them together in *Thomae de Vio, Cardinalis Cajetani, opera omnia quotquot in Sacrae Scripturae expositiones reperiuntur* 1–3 (Lyon 1639; on microfiche, Leiden: IDC 1987; reprint offered by Olms, Hildesheim).

---

[1] On the many-sided question of nomenclature, see O'Malley, Trent and All That (2000).

Studies: A. ALLGEIER, "Les commentaires de Cajétan sur les Psaumes. Contribution à l'histoire de l'exégèse avant le Concile de Trente", *RThom* 17 (1934–35) 410–43; T. A. COLLINS, "The Cajetan Controversy", *AEcR* 128 (1953) 90–100; idem., "Cardinal Cajetan's Fundamental Biblical Principles", *CBQ* 17 (1955) 363–78; J. F. GRONER, *Kardinal Cajetan. Eine Gestalt aus der Reformationszeit* (Fribourg: Société Philosophique / Louvain: Nauwelaerts 1951); A. F. VON GUNTEN, "La contribution des "Hébreux" à l'oeuvre exégétique de Cajétan", *Histoire de l'exégèse au XVIe siècle* (ed. O. Fatio / P. Fraenkel; Geneva: Droz 1978) 46–83; U. HORST, "Der Streit um die hl. Schrift zwischen Kardinal Cajetan und Ambrosius Catharinus", *Wahrheit und Verkündigung* (ed. L. Scheffczyk e.a.; München: Schöningh 1967) 1, 551–77; M. O'CONNOR, "Exegesis, Doctrine and Reform in the Biblical Commentaries of Cardinal Cajetan (1469–1534)" (D. Phil. thesis, Oxford 1997, accessible in the Bodleian Library); J. WICKS, "Thomas de Vio, Cajetan (1469–1534)", *The Reformation Theologians* (ed. C. Lindberg; Oxford / Malden, MA: Blackwell 2002) 269–83; S. M. ZARB, "La dottrina del Gaetano intorno al canone biblico", *Il Cardinale Tommaso de Vio Gaetano nel quarto centenario della sua morte* (Suppl. to *Rivista di filosofia neo-scolastico*; Milan: Vita e pensiero 1935) 103–26.

Tommaso de Vio (1469–1534), known as *Caietanus* from his birthplace Gaeta, took up biblical studies in his mid-fifties after influential philosophical and theological writing, governance of his Dominican order, and service as papal legate to the German Empire (1518–19) and Hungary (1523–24).[2] Upon returning to Rome in 1524, he turned to biblical studies encouraged by Pope Clement VII.[3]

1.1. *Cajetan's Interpretive Work*

Three years of sustained work led to Cajetan's Psalter-commentary and then, after studies from 1527 into 1529 on the New Testament, he took up the Pentateuch (1529–31), Joshua to Esther (1531–32), Job (1532–33), and Proverbs and Qoheleth (1533–34). He began Isaiah in 1534, but died before completing Isaiah 3.[4]

Cajetan held firmly the principle of *Hebraica veritas* and gave new Latin translations of all the Psalms, of Genesis 1–3, and of other selected passages, as more accurate renderings than given in the Vulgate. He did not learn Hebrew himself but for the Psalter employed two linguistic assistants knowledgeable in Hebrew and surrounded himself with recent Hebrew-based Latin translations, such as those by Felice de Prato,[5] Agostino Giustiniani,[6] and Sanctes Pagninus.[7] Cajetan added to the Vulgate of each Psalm a more accurate version based on consultation over rendering the original and then ex-

---

[2] On Cajetan's life and thought, see Wicks, Thomas de Vio (2002).

[3] F. VON GUNTEN connects Clement's encouragement to his little-known commissioning in the mid-1520s of six Jewish and six Christian scholars to produce a Latin Old Testament more faithful than the Vulgate to the Hebrew original; La contribution des «Hébreux» (1978) 60–62.

[4] Cajetan regularly noted the date of completion at the end of each commentary.

[5] *Psalterium ex Hebraeo diligentissime ad verbum fere translatum* (Venice 1515).

[6] *Psalterium hebraicum, graecum, arabicum et chaldaicum cum tribus latinis interpretationibus et glossis* (Genoa 1516).

[7] *Psalterium Tetraglottum* (on Psalms 1–29; Rome, before the death in 1521 of its sponsor, Pope Leo X).

plained the latter text. Later he added corrected readings to important Vulgate verses, as on Exod 3:14: "Iuxta Hebraeum habetur *Ero, qui ero*".[8] Cajetan saw versions as interpretations but in his work, "It is Moses' text, not that of his interpreter, which we are to expound".[9]

Concentrating on the literal sense, Cajetan made no significant use of patristic or medieval interpretations. In presenting his Psalter commentary to Clement VII, he noted that commentaries then circulating privileged various "mystical" senses, but neglected the literal sense, the importance of which he would measure by the frequency with which Psalms are recited in the Church.[10] Cajetan took figurative expressions as part of the literal sense, explaining on Gen 3:1 that the 'serpent' is a metaphorical reference to the Devil.[11] When Prov 30:16 spoke of the insatiability of Sheol, a barren womb, the earth, and fire, he reluctantly admitted a mystical sense in the text, since no prophetic or moral teaching was evident.[12] He knew that the New Testament applied texts according to mystical senses, e. g., Exod 12:46 in John 19:36, on not breaking the legs of the paschal lamb, but this was "in fulfillment of Scripture" and while intended by the inspiring Holy Spirit it is no model for human interpreters.[13]

Cajetan knew that a single-minded exposition of the literal sense was innovative in his day but he urged readers of his Pentateuch commentary not to rush to judgments of error. He may well diverge from other "doctors" but his readings deserve serious consideration if they are consonant with the text's original form and do not clash with the rest of Scripture or Church doctrine.[14] Grounding this option for the literal sense was the principle that the Bible gives no truth necessary for salvation only in an allegorical or other spiritual manner, but such a truth must be elsewhere manifest as the literal sense of a text.[15] As a Thomist Cajetan held that faith rests on what God revealed to the Apostles and Prophets, precisely those who wrote the canonical Scriptures.[16]

---

[8] *Opera omnia* (1639) 1, 158.

[9] Ibid. 1, facing p. 1 (Preface, Pentateuch commentary). Cajetan admitted not rendering the Psalms word-for-word, because Hebrew and Latin were so different regarding cases of nouns and tenses and moods of verbs.

[10] CAJETAN, *Psalmi Davidici ad hebraicam veritatem castigati et iuxta sensum quem literalem dicunt enarrati* (Venice: Iunta 1530), facing fol. 1r. Cajetan's dedicatory letters to Clement VII were not published in the Lyon biblical *Opera omnia* (1639). Cajetan's Dominican confrere, Sanctes Pagninus, published an exhaustive dictionary of the "mystical" (allegorical, symbolic) meaning of over 700 *realia* of the Bible: *Isagogae ad sacras literas ... eiusdem Isagogae ad mysticos sacrae scripturae sensus* (Lyon: Iustus 1536).

[11] *Opera omnia* (1639) 1, 24.

[12] Ibid. 3, 593.

[13] Ibid. 4, 420. Also Paul's application in Eph 4:8 of Ps 68:18, was "mystical" since literally the Psalm is about God's power working efficaciously in Israel; ibid. 5, 233.

[14] Ibid. 1, facing p. 1.

[15] Thomas Aquinas, *Summa Theologiae*, I, 1, 10, which Cajetan explicitly restated in his *Summa* commentary, adding that if one's search for the literal meaning proved inconclusive, the Church's teaching authority could give certainty about it; in: Aquinas, *Opera omnia* 4 (Leonine ed.; Rome 1888) 25 f. However, Cajetan's biblical commentaries contain no appeals to ecclesial determinations of textual meaning.

[16] Aquinas, *Summa Theologiae*, I, 1, 8 ad 2.

For the Psalter, Cajetan described his interpretive method at some length.[17] Beyond giving a new Hebrew-based version of each verse, he held that each Psalm had a single topic. David was guided by divine wisdom "ordering all things *suaviter*" (Wis 8:1) and so his Psalms do not shift thematically as they unfold their subject. To determine this topic, the biblical titles give initial guidance. Where titles are lacking, recourse is had to the New Testament, which may indicate Psalms concerning the Messiah, as when Matt 22:43f cites Ps 110:1. A third step is to apply the "apostolic rule" given by Peter (Acts 2:34) and Paul (Acts 13:35f), where Psalm verses not verified of David are taken as messianic. Thus if one verse goes beyond David, the whole Psalm must be prophetic utterance either in the person of Jesus the Messiah or descriptive of his coming, encounter with rejection, resurrection, or glorious return as judge. On this basis Cajetan expounds thirty-two Psalms as messianic.[18] When the content does not go beyond David's life, it is literally David's inspired prayer, reflection, teaching, or invitation to worship, as in over ninety Psalms, for which Cajetan finds in fifty-eight cases a definite setting in the Davidic cycle of 1 Samuel 16 to 1 Kings 2 or 1 Chronicles 11–29.[19]

Cajetan's Pentateuch commentary begins by interpreting the plural *Elohim* in Gen 1:1 as not referring to the Trinity but to the divine Lordship of the Creator of all things in their good order and the Judge of all human actions. In Exod 20:2 the term refers to God ruling "in judgment and justice".[20] A recurrent theme is God's care of human beings, noted against philosophers whose First Mover exercises no providence over human lives. Cajetan's biblical work shows little concern with Lutheranism which is at times said to have motivated his turn to Scripture.[21] But he brings out the Bible's opposition to a naturalistic worldview excluding creation, providence, and human immortality. The danger to faith comes from popularized forms of Averroistic Aristotelianism which Cajetan knew well from his early teaching in Padua.[22]

Cajetan sees Gen 2:4b–3:24 going back over the prior creation account so Moses may treat difficulties left by it and fill in lacunae. He wrote metaphorically, not historically, in Gen 2:21–22, on the creation of Eve from the rib of Adam, to show that having a wife diminishes the *robur* of a man, but also to bring out the social likeness between husband and wife, in which the latter is neither superior nor servant, but a "collateral" of her husband. Although Eve gave in when tempted, Gen 3:15 indicates that many women of holiness will show enmity to the serpent by their faith, hope, chastity, liberality and mercy.[23]

Cajetan sees the transition from Numbers to Deuteronomy as a shift from the mandates Moses

---

[17] Ibid. 3, 1–5.

[18] Eight others (Psalms 42, 43, 76, 77, 79, 80, 126, 137) are prophecies of events to come in Israel's unfolding history, while four (Psalms 44, 45, 46, 47) are spoken in the name of the apostolic church. Psalm 48 and Psalm 87 are prophecies of the spiritual Jerusalem, our future dwelling. On Psalm 21, the messianic interpretation is backed by earlier Jewish reading, as attested in the Targum, about which Cajetan's assistants or Pagninus's *Psalterium tetraglottum* would have informed him.

[19] This contrasts with options to find Christ in every psalm, e.g., by Lefèvre d'Etaples, in his *Quincuplex Psalterium* (1509). See G. BEDOUELLE, *Le* Quincuplex Psalterium *de Lefèvre d'Etaples. Une guide de lecture* (Geneva: Droz 1979) 134–64. Also, M. Luther, in the *Dictata super Psalterium* (1513–15), wrote programmatically: *Omnis prophetia et omnis propheta de Christo domino debet intelligi, nisi ubi manifestis verbis appareat de alio loqui*, WA 55/1, 6–8. Luther's norm was reversed by Cajetan, who understood a majority of the Psalms as David's own inspired prayer or teaching and as such models for Christians.

[20] *Opera omnia* (1639) 1, 1–2 and 205.

[21] In Exod 29:44 Aaron's consecration for priesthood is a special divine action in which present-day "heretics" should see a foreshadowing of priestly ordination in the Christian economy, *Opera omnia* (1639) 1, 246. The diabolical Leviathan, in Job 41, has teeth which shred the good, which prompts Cajetan to mention the Lutheran schism, divisive of a nation and so breaking down public order with much *peccandi licentia*, ibid. 2, 551.

[22] The "haughty eyes" of Prov 6:17 can well refer to those who exceed their own limited *ingenia* by denying divine providential punishment or reward of human actions and the immortality of the soul, *Opera omnia* (1639) 3, 522. The questions of Prov 30:4 are answered by the *scientia sanctorum*, based on God as creator and providential governor of the heavens, ibid. 3, 590 f.

[23] Ibid. 1, 22f and 29.

received from God to what Moses "as *doctor*" gives as inspired teaching.[24] Deut 6:5 expounds the first commandment, in which 'heart' stands for the will, 'soul' for bodily life, and 'strength' is in Hebrew equivalent to the adverb *valde*, indicating that the love-command totally excludes anything contrary to love of God from every part of one's being. But this prompted Cajetan to look ahead from this Mosaic precept to the Pauline "grace of the Holy Spirit animating love and faith" already foreseen in Jeremiah 31.[25]

Treating the historical books from Joshua to Esther, Cajetan ascribed the Book of Ruth to an unknown author who wrote after David had become king, to complete the royal genealogy. But the book is so clear as to need little interpretation.[26] The wording of 2 Sam 23:2: "The Spirit of the Lord speaks by me", accounts for inspiration, which links the human author with the principal author, namely God speaking by his Spirit in David. What follows are sayings of David uttered under inspiration, and like Peter's words on the day of Pentecost, the inspired speech is then set down in writing.[27]

The Book of Job attracted Cajetan by its disputation vindicating divine providence regarding human beings and their actions. Authorial anonymity raises the question of Job's entry into the canon but a reasonable solution is to take it as a work of Moses, as Cajetan proposes in his Preface.[28] Job not only witnesses to faith in God's judgment of individuals but in 3:11–16, speaking of the "rest" he could have had with kings and princes, he presupposes that the human soul lives on beyond death to pass to another mode of life, which posits a tenet of faith against philosophical views, e. g., of Pietro Pomponazzi, then circulating in Italy.[29] Job 19:25a, corrected from the Hebrew as "I have known (*scivi*) that my Redeemer is alive (*vivum*)", deserves to be incised in stone, for Job here confesses faith in the messianic redeemer and future resurrection. Saying "*my* Redeemer" expresses Job's hope of being released from servitude to bodily corruption, in which his fidelity is now being tested.[30]

At the end of a relatively brief exposition of Qoheleth, Cajetan admitted not being able to grasp the literal meaning of the Song of Solomon, as he also admitted for the Book of Revelation in the New Testament, and so he passed on to interpreting the prophets, but he covered only Isaiah 1–3 before his death. Isa 1:1, by referring to Judah and Jerusalem, occasioned the declaration that the "principal intention of the book is to treat the mystery of the Messiah" who was born in Judah and in Jerusalem met death to redeem the world, rose from the dead and ascended into heaven, and gave the first-fruits of the Holy Spirit to the Church.[31] In Isa 2:2–4, the "mountain" is metaphorically, but literally, the Messiah who is the one foundation of God's house (1 Cor 3:11), whose elevation will come by his miracles and his obedience even to being raised on the cross to die.[32] The law going out from Zion (Isa 2:3b) is the new law of the Spirit by which from Christ's disciples a new people is born, as the Gospel goes out to the whole world from Jerusalem.

1.2. Cajetan's Hebrew Canon

In July 1532, Cajetan's commentary on the historical books reached Est 10:3, occasioning a declaration of principle on the canonical books of the Christian Old Testament. Cajetan will not expound the rest of Esther, nor treat Judith, Tobit, 1–2 Maccabees, Wisdom, or Sirach, which Jerome placed among the

---

[24] Ibid. 1, 429.

[25] Ibid. 1, 444f.

[26] Ibid. 2, 72.

[27] Ibid. 2, 169.

[28] Ibid. 2, 401.

[29] Ibid. 2, 411. In Job 7:7, Job is begging God to be mindful that his soul will not return to our present bodily life but will be punished or rewarded upon death and then be raised to a spiritual life quite different from present existence, ibid. 2, 427.

[30] Ibid. 2, 468f.

[31] Ibid. 3, 635.

[32] Ibid. 3, 641.

Apocrypha. If this disturbs a reader who knows canonical lists including these books, he should realize that Church councils and other teachers are to be interpreted according to the boundary (*limes*) set by Jerome. Accordingly, the just-mentioned books do not furnish firm grounds for the content of faith. They may, however, be taken as normative for the edification of believers' lives. With such a distinction, one can interpret the canon as it was specified by Augustine in Bk. II of *De doctrina christiana*, by the provincial councils of Carthage and Laodicaea, by Popes Innocent and Gelasius, and by the Council of Florence under Pope Eugenius IV.[33]

This statement on the canon concluded an exposition that Cajetan dedicated to Pope Clement VII. The dedicatory letter expresses the Latin Church's indebtedness to "the divine Jerome", both for his notes on Scripture, and for his discerning separation of canonical from non-canonical books. The latter contribution was significant for Jewish-Christian relations, since it frees Christians from Jewish accusations of fashioning books not present in their canon.[34] While Cajetan was convinced that portions of the Hebrew Bible were literally prophetic of the Christian economy, he held that the Christian Old Testament was meant to coincide with the Bible of his Jewish contemporaries. On this basis Jews and Christians could collaborate in textual and interpretive work.

1.3. A Critical Reception of Cajetan's Commentaries

Cajetan's biblical scholarship raised suspicions of error. After a first edition in Venice in 1530, Cajetan's Psalter commentary was printed in Paris in 1532, along with his New Testament commentaries, and the Parisian Theology Faculty soon heard a denunciation of errors in these works. The Faculty prepared a list of errors for censure, but Pope Clement VII intervened to stop the action against Cajetan. The Faculty composed letters to the Pope and to Cajetan, with an attached list of twenty-four errors found in his works, which were confirmed on May 15, 1533 and sent to Rome.[35] But copies circulated, even reaching Wittenberg, where the list was printed in 1534, with a seven-page polemical postscript by Luther against the Parisians' attachment to the Vulgate and their blindness in the face of Cajetan's insights into the New Testament.[36]

---

[33] Ibid. 2, 400. ZARB holds that for Cajetan authority on the canon was not Jerome's personal endowment, but rested on his witness to traditions concerning authorship, since Cajetan's ultimate canonical criterion was Mosaic, Davidic, Prophetic, or Apostolic authorship, La dottrina del Gaetano (1935) 106–18. While this is plausible, one looks in vain in Cajetan's works for such an interpretation of his appeals to Jerome.

[34] Dedication, not given in the *Opera omnia* (1639), vol. 2, but standing at the beginning of *Reverendissimi Domini Thomae de Vio Caietani Cardinalis Santi Xysti: in omnes authenticos veteris testamenti historiales libros, commentarii* (Paris: Jean Roigny 1546).

[35] *Registre des procès-verbaux de la Faculté de Théologie de l'Université de Paris de janvier 1524 à novembre 1533* (ed. J. K. Farge; Paris: Aux Amateurs de livres 1990) 266f, 276–78, 281–83, 293. M.-H. LAURENT gave excerpts from the same minutes of the Faculty's meetings in: "Quelques documents des Archives Vaticanes", R Thom 17 (special issue on Cajetan; 1934–35) 50–148, at 122–26, adding the twenty-four censured propositions on 126–29.

[36] *Epistola Theologorum Parisiensium ad Cardinalem Coetanum [sic] reprehensoria* (Wittenberg: N. Schirlentz 1534), from which WA 60, 123–30 gives Luther's text, charging that binding Chris-

Sixteen of the Parisian censures concerned positions in Cajetan's New Testament commentaries, but his criticisms of the Vulgate also drew fire, especially the Psalter commentary where his goal was to expound the genuine text and not interpretations infiltrated into the Vulgate of common usage.[37]

Johann Dietenberger sent from Mainz a copy of the Parisian propositions to Cajetan and asked for clarification. Cajetan claimed that the extracts were ascribing to him views he did not hold and they failed to acknowledge the backing he had from Jerome on the canon. Cajetan said that his insistence on translating from the original language was twisted into a denial that the Vulgate gave the Church a true text of Scripture.[38]

An energetic opponent from his own Dominican order, Ambrosius Catharinus Politi, treated Cajetan's option for the Hebrew Canon in a critical barrage against Cajetan's biblical work.[39] Two false principles underlay Cajetan's position: first, that Jerome, a fallible individual, was the normative voice, and, second, that works of uncertain authorship were doubtfully canonical. Against Cajetan, there stands the Church, which authoritatively received the further books both in the fifth century through Popes Innocent and Gelasius and more recently under Pope Eugenius IV in the *Bull of Union* with the Copts at the Council of Florence (1442). In addition, these books are valuable for the grounds they give regarding doctrines contested by the Reformation, such as human free choice (Sir 15:11–17) and purgatory (2 Macc 12:39–45).[40] In exegesis, Catharinus detects "judaizing" in Cajetan's neglect of the "mystical" sense. Cajetan was also wrong to hold that Psalms literally about David could not also be messianic and concern Jesus.[41] On Genesis, Cajetan's non-trinitarian interpretation of *Elohim* was a mistaken departure from mainstream Catholic teachers, while his parabolic account of the creation of Eve struck at the foundations of the faith.[42]

Catharinus was no minor adversary, for he was sent in 1545 by Pope Paul III as papal theologian to the Council of Trent. A rejection of Cajetan's view of the canon was formulated in a more orderly manner by Melchior Cano in the premier work of early modern Catholic theological methodology, which also treated as misguided Cajetan's independence from the patristic and medieval tradition of interpretation.[43]

These polemics against Cajetan anticipate changes in sixteenth-century Catholic biblical study, as it will move from Renaissance creativity and high evaluation of original sources to work within narrower confines marked out by tradition and authority. A century and a half passed before Cajetan's commentaries were treated appreciatively by Richard Simon.[44]

---

tians to the Vulgate infringed on Christian freedom. Still, philology and grammar should not become lord and judge over theology and the transmitted faith, WA 60, 130.

[37] Quelques documents (ed. Laurent; 1934–35) 128f.

[38] Cajetan, *Responsionum ad quosdam articulos nomine Theologorum Parsiensium editos, ad magistrum Ioannem studii Moguntini Regentem missus*, in: Cajetan, *Opuscula omnia* (Lyon 1581) 298f. Also in *Registre des Conclusions de la Faculté de Théologie de l'Université de Paris* 2 (ed. J. K. Farge; Paris: Klincksieck 1994) 426–34.

[39] *Annotationes in Commentaria Caietani denuo multo locupletiores et castigatiores redditae* (Lyon: M. Bonhomme 1542, in octavo), a 586-page hostile march through numerous works by Cajetan. An earlier version of these *Annotationes* came out in 1535. On this dispute, see Horst, Der Streit um die hl. Schrift (1967).

[40] Catharinus, *Annotationes in Commentaria Caietani* (1542) 13f, 33–43.

[41] Ibid. 18–20, 57, 64f.

[42] Ibid. 264f, 63f.

[43] *De locis theologicis* (Salamanca 1563), II, 11,4.13.27; VII, 3.11–31, reprinted thirty times down to the Rome edition in 1890 of Cano's *Opera*.

[44] *Histoire critique du Vieux Testament* (Rotterdam: Renier Leers 1685) 319f, 419–21.

2. The Decrees of the Council of Trent on the Old Testament Canon, the Vulgate and Biblical Interpretation

Sources: *Concilium Tridentinum, Diariorum, Actorum, Epistularum, Tractatuum nova collectio*, 13 vols. in 19 (ed. S. Merkle e.a. for the Görresgesellschaft; Freiburg: Herder 1901–2001); *Conciliorum oecumenicorum Decreta* (ed. G. Alberigo e.a.; Freiburg: Herder 1962) 633–775; *Decrees of the Ecumenical Councils* (ed. N. P. Tanner; London: Sheed & Ward / Washington DC: Georgetown UP 1990), 2, 657–799; *Enchiridion Biblicum. Documenti della Chiesa sulla Sacra Scrittura* (bilingual edn.; Bologna: Dehoniane 1993).

Studies: G. ALBERIGO, "The Council of Trent", *Catholicism in Early Modern Europe* (ed. O'Malley; 1988) 211–26; *Concilium Tridentinum* (ed. R. Bäumer; WdF 313; Darmstadt: Wiss. Buchgesellschaft 1979); H. JEDIN, *Geschichte des Konzils von Trient, 2. Die erste Trienter Tagungsperiode 1545/47* (Freiburg: Herder 1957) 42–103; A. VACCARI, "Esegesi ed esegeti al Concilio di Trento", *Bib.* 27 (1946) 320–37.

In three working periods, 1545–47, 1551–52, and 1562–63, the Council of Trent created a body of doctrine and disciplinary prescriptions which shaped modern Catholicism. Drawing selectively on works of theologians who had for a quarter-century opposed the Reformation, the Council formulated teaching on original sin, grace and justification, the mass, and the seven sacraments. It did not treat the nature of the Church, which left ecclesiology to later theologians, such as Robert Bellarmine (1542–1621), with his influential emphasis on the visible, institutional church. Trent also drew on existing reform-proposals citing pastoral deficiencies and abuses, as it formulated thirteen decrees of reform of ecclesiastical practice.

We feature here the decrees approved at Trent on April 8, 1546: (1) the reception of the canon of biblical books and certain "unwritten traditions" coming from Jesus or his Apostles, and (2) the adoption of the Latin Vulgate as "authentic" for public use, leading to regulative norms on interpreting the Bible and making it available by printing. The former document specified the sources of the Council's subsequent doctrinal clarifications, while the latter initiated the series of reform-decrees on preaching, worship, and pastoral care. A further section will treat the reform-decree of June 17, 1546, on establishing biblical lectureships in major churches and on preaching.

2.1. Trent's Reception of the Canon and Apostolic Traditions

Studies: G. BEDOUELLE, "Le canon de l'Ancien Testament dans le perspective du Concile de Trente", *Le canon de l'Ancient Testament* (ed. J.-D. Kaestli / O. Wermelinger; Genève: Labor et Fides 1984) 253–82; P. DUNCKER, "The Canon of the Old Testament at the Council of Trent", *CBQ* 15 (1953) 277–99; I. JERICÓ BERMEJO, "El canon de la Sagrada Escritura ante y después de Trento. Dos exposiciones en la escuela de Salamanca: B. Carranza y P. de Sotomajor", *Studium* (Madrid) 34 (1994) 223–74; A. MAICHLE, *Der Kanon der biblischen Bücher und das Konzil von Trient. Eine quellenmässige Darstellung* (FThSt 33; Freiburg: Herder 1929).

The agenda at Trent prescribed the preparation of doctrinal and reform decrees in tandem, and thus the Council worked from February into early April

1546 on drafting a doctrinal clarification on Scripture and tradition and norms to remedy abuses in biblical-based preaching and teaching.

The biblical canon came first, since doubts had been raised about the status of certain books, not only by Cajetan, but especially by the Protestants. A definition of the canon led to treatment of "traditions", that is, revealed teachings not written down but first implanted in the hearts of Jesus' Apostles and in time clarified in the Church, especially by previous councils. Scripture and the apostolic traditions were to be the foundation on which the Council would base its further work of teaching and reform.[45]

> Trent's work on the canon was prepared by Catholics in debate with the Reformation, for example, by the insistence of Johann Cochlaeus and Johann Eck on the authoritative role of the Church in ascertaining which books truly belonged to the canon.[46] In 1532 Johann Dietenberger, O.P., laid out the problematic by first giving three early Christian canons listing only the twenty-two books of the Hebrew canon, but then testimonies to the larger canon from Augustine, John Damascene, Pope Innocent I, and the Council of Carthage (397).[47] Of importance for deliberations at Trent was the work of Alfonso de Castro, O.F.M., who argued that the larger canon emerged as a development under God's enlightenment, especially in the conciliar decrees by which the Church is inerrantly guided.[48] Shortly before the Council, a Louvain theologian, John Driedo, treated the catalogues of biblical books, concluding that while the Christian Old Testament does add a "fourth order", beyond the Pentateuch, Prophets, and Hebrew Writings, nonetheless all four are "divine Scriptures" known by tradition and received in the Church, as attested by the Third Council of Carthage (397).[49]

At Trent initial deliberations led to agreement to "receive purely and simply" as the authentic biblical books those listed by the Council of Florence in its *Bull of Union* of 1442 with the Coptic Church of Egypt.[50] This inclusive canon (with Tobit, Judith, Wisdom, Sirach, Baruch, and 1–2 Maccabees) was taken to be a recent confirmation of a millennial tradition which some saw as having such authority that Trent should not even discuss arguments justifying the broader Old Testament canon. But others felt such a discussion was necessary, not to question an earlier Council's position, but to prepare bishops and tea-

---

[45] Letter of Feb. 7–8 from the presiding Legates, Cardinals Del Monte, Cervini, and Pole, to Cardinal Alessandro Farnese in Rome, who headed a commission serving as liaison between the Council and Pope Paul III, in: Concilium Tridentinum, 10, 373 f.

[46] J. Cochlaeus, *De autoritate ecclesiae et scripturae* (Rome 1524), on the normativity of Augustine and the Church over Jerome and the Jews. J. Eck, *Enchiridion locorum communium adversus Lutherum et alios hostes ecclesiae* (Landshut: Weyssenberger 1525; repr. c. 115 times by 1575; ed. P. Fraenkel; CCath 34; Münster: Aschendorff 1979), 27f, 81–83, 187, 261f, with the last two passages treating 1–2 Maccabees as giving a basis for venerating saints and praying for the souls in purgatory.

[47] *Phimostomus scripturariorum* (Cologne: Quentel 1532; ed. E. Iserloh e.a.; CCath 38; Münster: Aschendorff 1985) 97–114.

[48] *Adversus omnes haereses* (Cologne: A. Birckmann 1539) 4r-6v. The work was printed nine times before the Council opened in Trent.

[49] *De ecclesiasticis scripturis et dogmatibus* (Louvain: B. Gavius 1543) 1r-26v.

[50] Concilium Tridentinum, 1, 30f; 5, 7–9, recording the discussion of Feb. 12, 1546. The Florentine canon is given in: Conciliorum oecumenicorum Decreta (1962), 548; Decrees (1990) 1, 572; and Enchiridion Biblicum (1993) no. 47. Catharinus had cited Florence against Cajetan, but no appeal to its authority had been made by anti-Protestant controversialists in their defense of the Catholic canon.

chers to meet objections and to instruct others. But no agreed set of reasons emerged to ground the canon Trent intended to formally receive.[51]

Trent did not intend to receive Scripture alone, but also the "unwritten traditions" of the Apostles (e. g., 2 Thess 2:15). The Decree of April 8, 1546, states that the Gospel of Christ, prophetically prepared and then proclaimed, is the one source of all saving truth and guidance for practice, but later ages find this truth and guidance "in written books and in unwritten traditions", with the latter being specified (1) as originating with Jesus himself or the Holy Spirit's instruction of the Apostles and (2) as transmitted in unbroken succession to the Church today.[52] Trent's text leaves open whether the traditions only interpret Scripture or whether they also add doctrines and practices beyond Scripture. It left space for divergent conceptions of the relation between Scripture and Tradition, which was creatively reformulated by the Second Vatican Council in its Constitution on Divine Revelation, *Dei Verbum* (1965).[53]

At Trent the question arose whether within the Church's Old Testament canon one might make a qualitative distinction between the books grounding doctrines of faith and additional books, outside the Hebrew canon, giving only guidance for life. An exponent of this view at Trent was Girolamo Seripando, Master General of the Augustinian order, but no wider backing emerged for his inner-canonical distinction between the *canon fidei* and the *canon morum*.[54] The conciliar position remained that of leaving this issue open, just as it had come to the Council.[55] The Council's basic concern was to remove all doubt about the outer limits of the body of inspired and inerrant books received from Israel by the Church.

The Tridentine Old Testament canon, proclaimed on April 8, 1546, is a sober listing, without supporting argument and without internal differentiation, of the books to be received "as sacred and canonical". The decree speaks of "these entire books and all their parts, as they have been read in the Catholic Church, and as contained in the old Latin Vulgate edition", which thus includes not only Tobit, Judith, Wisdom, Sirach, Baruch, and 1–2 Maccabees, but also certain "parts", that is, additions to Esther, insertions into Daniel 3 of the Prayer of Azariah and the Song of the Three Young Men, and Daniel 13–14 on Susanna, on Daniel's triumph over the Babylonian idols, Bel and the dragon, and his survival in the den of lions.[56]

This specification of the canon, however, left an ample field for further cla-

---

[51] Two treatises composed at Trent set out arguments for the canonicity of the disputed books: G. Calvi [Franciscan Master General], *Apologia pro libris canonicis*, and A.Pasquali [bishop of Mottola], *De libris canonicis*, in: Concilium Tridentinum, 12, 473–83; 506–09.

[52] Concilium oecumenicorum Decreta (1962), 639; Decrees (1990) 2, 663; Enchiridion Biblicum (1993) no. 57.

[53] Y. CONGAR, *La tradition et les traditions. Essai historique* (Paris: Fayard 1960); J. R. GEISELMANN, *Die Heilige Schrift und die Tradition* (Freiburg: Herder 1962); J. WICKS, "Tradition", *Catholicisme hier, aujourd'hui, demain* 15 (Paris: Beauchesne 1997) 185–99.

[54] The acta have preserved a position-paper based on patristic and conciliar sources: G. Seripando, *De libris sacrae scripturae*, in: Concilium Tridentinum, 12, 483–88.

[55] Concilium Tridentinum, 1, 31; 5, 7; and 10, 382.

[56] Concilium oecumenicorum Decreta (1962) 639f; Decrees (1990) 2, 663f; Enchiridion Biblicum (1993) nos. 58–60.

rification regarding the biblical texts to be used, and how to rightly interpret biblical history and teaching.

2.2. Trent's Decree on the "Authenticity" of the Vulgate

Studies: A. ALLGEIER, "'Haec vetus et vulgata editio'. Neue wort- und begriffsgeschichtliche Beiträge zur Bibel auf dem Tridentinum", *Bib.* 29 (1948) 353–90; R. DRAGUET, "Le maître louvaniste Driedo inspirateur du Décret de Trente sur la Vulgate", *Miscellanea historica in honorem Alberti de Meyer* (Leuven: Universiteitsbibliotheek 1946) 836–54; A. GARCIA-MORENO, "Reflexiones en torno a la Sessión IV de Trento", *La Bibbia "Vulgata" dalle origini ai nostri giorni* (ed. T. Stramare; CBLa 16; Rome: Abbazia San Girolamo / Vatican City: Libreria Vaticana 1987) 40–60; J.-M. VOSTÉ, "La Volgata al Concilio di Trento", *Bib.* 27 (1946) 301–19.

To initiate preparation of Trent's first reform decree, one of the few French bishops at the first period, Antoine Filhol, of Aix, offered on March 1, 1546, a list of abuses in the use of Scripture and of corresponding reforms.[57] First, the differences between the Latin translations of the Bible now circulating cause confusion. Linguistic and theological experts should produce a corrected version, in line with Jerome's Vulgate but improving it where necessary. Second, norms for interpretation conformed to the *sensus catholicus* are needed to prevent twisting the meaning of biblical texts.[58] Third, restrictions are needed regarding the printing of Bibles, imposing pre-censorship of any explanatory annotations. Also vernacular versions–if allowed–must first be examined to insure their fidelity to the corrected Latin Bible. Fourth, the Council should lay down more stringent norms on qualifications for preachers and on the content of their sermons.

In the same meeting, Bishop Tommaso Caselli, O.P., spoke to the issue of multiple Latin versions in a manner that proved decisive, calling for the designation of one translation as authoritative on doctrine, which should be a corrected version of the Vulgate, to be approved because of its long service in transmitting the faith of the Church.[59] The commission on abuses and remedial measures submitted a draft formulation to the Council on March 17. First, confusion should be reduced by receiving only one Latin version as authentic, that is, authoritative, in the public sphere of the Church. But the Septuagint retains its authority and other Latin versions can help one understand the Vulgate.[60] Second, the Vulgate should be revised to give the Catholic world a "pure and genuine" edition. The Pope should undertake the work, while also commissioning corrected Greek and Hebrew biblical texts.[61]

---

[57] Concilium Tridentinum, 5, 22–24; 1, 500–02.

[58] Bishop Tommaso Campeggio, one time legate to England and Germany, saw improper use of Scripture in the Reformers' citing of texts to show the abusive character of communion under one form, of clerical celibacy, and of fasting laws; see Concilium Tridentinum, 5, 24–25; 1, 502–04.

[59] Concilium Tridentinum, 5, 27, n. 2. Caselli also called for outlawing sermons on obscure and curious questions often based on allegorical readings, ibid. 5, 26.

[60] Concilium Tridentinum, 5, 29. R. Draguet, Le maître louvaniste Driedo (1946), showed the dependence of this formulation on Driedo, De ecclesiasticis scripturis (1535), II, 1, who defended the Vulgate, not as inspired or inerrant, but as having long served the integral transmission of the faith. Its obscure and inadequate renderings do not support any heresy nor do they destroy the overall validity of the translation for public use.

[61] Concilium Tridentinum, 5, 29; 1, 37 (noting the manuscript resources of the Vatican Li-

Cardinal Pedro Pacheco of Jaen, spokesman at Trent for Emperor Charles V, called in question the omission, from the list of abuses, of vernacular Bible translations, which have been prohibited in Spain since the time of Ferdinand and Isabella. But Cardinal Madruzzo of Trent responded that vernacular Bibles should never be judged "abuses". This clash revealed sharp divisions between national groups over a topic on which consensus would never be reached.[62]

On April 1 and 3 Council members voiced their views on the draft decree and the status of the Vulgate drew attention, with Card. Pacheco and others holding it to be inconsistent to declare the Vulgate authoritative, while (1) acknowledging, and not rejecting, the Septuagint and other Latin versions and (2) implying defects in the received translation, which has to be correct if it is accepted as authentic. An attempted clarification of the draft left many unconvinced and a majority followed Pacheco's option for one version only in public use without mention of others whether in Latin or in the original languages.[63] The legatine presidents reported to Rome that the Council also preferred not to speak openly of needed corrections of the very Bible it was declaring "authentic" but to ask the Pope to have prepared a corrected Vulgate and then editions of the Greek and Hebrew originals.[64] Therefore Trent's second decree of April 8, 1546, looking to regulate practice in the Church, begins by declaring that among the Latin versions of the Bible then circulating, only the Vulgate, which has proved itself over the centuries, is henceforth the official text for public use in lectures, disputations, and sermons.[65]

But the decree made only indirect mention of revising the Vulgate and this attracted immediate notice. At Trent, Giovanni Consiglio, O.F.M., wrote on recourse to original-language texts as the only way to have the revised Bible needed to meet the desire of the Council.[66] In Rome, sharp criticism was leveled against the Vulgate-decree, as the Council's presidents heard in letters arriving two weeks after they had presided over its formal adoption. Both the liaison commission headed by Card. Farnese and cardinals in consistory with the Pope voiced consternation over a text that left the Vulgate isolated from

---

brary). – Analysis of the two further abuses, on interpretation and printing of Scripture, will come in our following section.

[62] Concilium Tridentinum, 1, 37; 5, 30 f. The Legates had their secretary, A. Massarelli, try to convince Pacheco of the prudence of not treating vernacular translations, which while outlawed in Spain and France are promoted in Germany, Italy, and Poland; see Concilium Tridentinum, 1, 518 f. But Pacheco repeated his opposition in the assemblies of April 1 and 3. – Treatises extant from Trent mirror the division, cf. Concilium Tridentinum, 12, 512; 516f (arguments contrary), 528–36 (arguments favorable). On the clash, cf. F. Cavallera, "La Bible en langue vulgaire au Concile de Trente", *Mélanges E. Podechard* (Lyon: Facultés Catholiques 1945) 37–56, and R. E. McNally, "The Council of Trent and Vernacular Bibles", *TS* 27 (1966) 204–27.

[63] Concilium Tridentinum, 1, 41–44; 5, 58–67. On correcting the Vulgate, presiding Legate del Monte suggested that a commission of the Council should gather *codices* and quickly produce the emended Vulgate henceforth to be considered authentic, ibid. 5, 65.

[64] Letter of April 26, 1546, to Cardinal Farnese; Concilium Tridentinum, 10, 471.

[65] Conciliorum Oecumenicorum Decreta (1962) 640; Decrees (1990) 2, 644; Enchiridion Biblicum (1993) no. 61. Vosté shows this applied only to the Latin Church and that the reason, centuries-long usage, indicates that no claim is made for the Vulgate's technical superiority, La Volgata al Concilio di Trento (1946), 309–12. Allgeier points out that in 1546 the term 'Vulgate' was still indeterminate in its reference to older Latin texts, Haec vetus et vulgata editio (1948).

[66] Concilium Tridentinum, 12, 537 f.

the Hebrew and Greek original texts and only implied a needed work of correcting, no easy task, the many inaccuracies of the Vulgate.[67]

The Legates answered that the Council indeed wanted the Vulgate revised to give the Church a Bible closer to the original texts, but had judged it prudent not to say this directly, to avoid giving a target for attack by opponents of the Roman Church. The decree rested on a conviction that the Vulgate was a trustworthy text that underlay Church teaching and had never led to heresy.[68] But Roman dissatisfaction remained, at least for a time, over a decree judged to need correction, for example, to avoid condemning those who diverge from the Vulgate when its text does not render well the Hebrew or Greek original.[69]

2.3. Trent on Interpretation and Diffusion of Scripture

On March 1, Archbishop Filhol's catalogue of abuses said that "many twist the testimonies … of Sacred Scripture into perverse senses", while other bishops mentioned recondite allegories in preaching and use of Scripture in Reformation attacks on Catholic practice. From this starting-point Trent turned to formulating norms of biblical interpretation.

As with the canon, the Council drew upon previous work. The Fifth Lateran Council had in 1516 censured preachers for biblical interpretations alien to the Gospel and ordered all to adhere to Scripture itself and to the views of approved teachers.[70] In 1528 the French Provincial Council of Sens reproached untraditional and heretical corruptions of Scripture's genuine meaning, against which the Holy Spirit has given guidelines through the Fathers and Church Councils. When disputes arise over the content of faith, the Church has the infallible authority to discern the *sensus catholicus* and thus rule out heretical interpretations.[71] Countering Luther's contention that Scripture should be *sui ipsius interpres*,[72] Bishop John Fisher argued that difficult passages make Scripture the source of disputes and errors, not of interpretations which settle controversies. Also, the Church has a normative interpretive tradition in the Fathers and General Councils. Further, when Scripture gives rise to disputes over doctrine, the See of Peter is the "judge of controversies" to which recourse must be had.[73]

---

[67] Letters to the Legates: Concilium Tridentinum, 10, 462 (A. Farnese); 463 (B. Maffeo, secretary of the Pope); 891 (G. B. Cervini, contact in Rome of Legate M. Cervini), and 939 (G. Sirleto, confidant of Cervini). These were written in Rome a few days after copies of the decree arrived from Trent and initial evaluations began circulating.

[68] Concilium Tridentinum, 10, 467f (Cervini to Maffeo, April 24, 1546) and 470f (Legates to Farnese, April 26).

[69] Cardinal Farnese to the Legates, May 29, in a letter also correcting their idea that a revised Vulgate could be rapidly produced; Concilium Tridentinum, 10, 507.

[70] Decree *Supernae maiestatis praesidio*, 19 December 1516, in: Concilium oecumenicorum decreta (1962) 610–14, and Decrees (1990) 1, 634–37.

[71] *Sacrorum Conciliorum nova et amplissima Collectio*, 35 (ed. J. D. Mansi; Paris: Welter 1902) 1164; Enchiridion Biblicum (1993) nos. 52–54. On these councils: W. Brandmüller, "Die Lehre der Konzilien über die rechte Schriftinterpretation bis zum 1. Vaticanum", *Annuarium Historiae Conciliorum* 19 (1987) 13–61, at 27–32; English: *CHR* 73 (1987) 523–40.

[72] Preface to *Assertio omnium articulorum* (1521), WA 7, 97. On this, see W. Mostert, "Scriptura sacra sui ipsius interpres: Bemerkungen zum Verständnis der Heiligen Schrift durch Luther", LuJ 46 (1979) 60–96.

[73] Proem of "ten truths" in: *Assertionis luteranae confutatio* (1523), in: *Ioannis Fisheri Opera* (Würzburg: Fleischmann 1597; repr. Farnsborough: Gregg 1967) 279–96. J. Dietenberger devel-

At Trent the commission on reform branded abusive the interpretation of Scripture idiosyncratically in matters of faith and discipline relevant to Christian doctrine. The remedy is to set down binding norms of interpretation.[74] The commission's proposal found a positive echo and remained substantially what the Council adopted in the second paragraph of its reform Decree of April 8, 1546.[75] The Council addressed biblical interpretation in order "to control those of unbalanced character" who, relying on their own abilities, twist the meaning of Scripture to fit their own purposes.[76] The decree applies to a specific area, namely, that of faith and instruction on practice relevant to Christian doctrine. There was no need then to speak on questions of narrative historicity.[77] Interpretations are not to range freely according to individual lights but to remain within the bounds of the perennial and present meaning of Scripture held by the Church and they must not go counter to positions of patristic consensus. Trent gave a negative norm, laying down limits within which interpreters were to work. But shortly after the Council, in 1564, Pope Pius IV issued an obligatory Profession of Faith, in which one accepts the Bible positively as grasped by the *sensus Ecclesiae*.[78] Furthermore, interpretations are subject to judgment, for it is the Church's role to discern in doctrinal matters between interpretations in harmony with or in dissonance from its understanding of the meaning of the Bible.[79] For post-Tridentine Catholic Old Testament interpreters, the Council's reference to patristic positions will prove influential, leading away from Cajetan's focus on the literal sense and instead toward spiritual interpretation, the recovery of messianic foreshadowings, and possibilities of multiple meanings.[80]

The initial catalogue of abuses named in the fourth place the unauthorized

---

oped arguments for Scripture interpretation conformed to the Fathers and Councils, *Phimostomos Scripturariorum* (1532), Chs. I-V.

[74] Concilium Tridentinum, 5, 29 (the third abuse listed on March 17, 1546).

[75] Concilium oecumenicorum Decreta (1962) 640 (2nd paragraph, beginning *Praeterea* ...); Decrees (1990) 2, 644; Enchiridion Biblicum (1993) no. 62.

[76] BRANDMÜLLER, whose analysis we follow, finds here less an anti-Lutheran intent than an effort to curtail humanist frivolity and apocalyptic exaltation, see Die Lehre der Konzilien (1987) 34 f.

[77] However, *res fidei et morum* are not "matters of faith and morals" since in sixteenth-century parlance, *mores* referred to the traditions of Church life and Christian practice; cf. P. F. FRANSEN, "A Short History of the Meaning of the Formula «fides et mores»", *Louvain Studies* 7 (1978) 270–301.

[78] Enchiridion Biblicum (1993) no. 73; also Brandmüller, Die Lehre der Konzilien (1987) 37. The First Vatican Council (1870) also speaks affirmatively, namely, that in doctrinal matters the perennial *sensus ecclesiae* is to be taken as the true meaning of Scripture, *Dogmatic Consitution on the Catholic Faith*, ch. II, par. 4. Concilium oecumenicorum Decreta (1962) 782; Decrees (1990) 2, 806; Enchiridion Biblicum (1993) no. 78.

[79] A late draft had said that interpretation is by the Church alone, but this was changed at the behest of Card. Pacheco, who saw bishops and doctors of theology working together in interpretation; Concilium Tridentinum, 1, 42f; 5, 59. – In the Decree, the Church does not furnish interpretations, but instead evaluates the validity of interpretations being offered.

[80] Luis de León in 1581 acknowledged the dogmatic role of the literal sense and encouraged moderation in allegorical readings, but took from the Fathers the primacy of the spiritual sense in interpreting the Old Testament, *Tractatus de sensibus Sacrae Scripturae* (ed. O. Garcia de la Fuente; in Fray Luis's *Opera* 9, *Reportata Theologica*, ed. J. Rodriguez Diez; El Escorial: Ediciones Escurialenses 1996) 619–60, at 657 ff.

printing of Bibles, often with explanatory notes, and of biblical expositions which combine views received by the Church with views not received. Consequently Trent's reform-decree of April 8, 1546, after authenticating the Vulgate and giving norms of interpretation, continued with restrictive measures on printing. The revised Vulgate, along with all other religious books, must have prior approval of the printer's local bishop. Books by members of religious orders must first be examined by the order's superiors. Such approval must appear in the book's opening pages. In any case, anonymous religious books are prohibited. As Fifth Lateran had decreed, those who offend in these matters are subject to fines and even excommunication.[81]

2.4. Biblical Lectureships and Preaching

Studies: A. ALLGEIER, "Das Konzil von Trient und das theologische Studium", HJ 52 (1932) 313–39; H. JEDIN, *Geschichte des Konzils von Trient* 2 (Freiburg: Herder 1957) 82–103; L. B. PASCOE, "The Council of Trent and Bible Study: Humanism and Scripture", *CHR* 52 (1966–67) 18–38.

The first listing of abuses by Archbishop Filhol had included the need to reform preaching on Holy Scripture, a point seconded by others, but Cardinal Cervini's remarks that day went deeper by calling abusive the way most theologians learn Scripture from passages cited in scholastic treatises and not from the Bible itself.[82] By April 5, the commission on abuses had ready a draft on institutionalizing biblical instruction and on bishops' and pastors' obligations to preach regularly, avoiding recondite topics while treating Scripture itself in accord with the faith of the Church and patristic interpretation.[83] But there was no time to develop this text as a second part of the reform-decree adopted on April 8, 1546. Thus, this application to church practice was detached from its logical place and treated in the reform decree adopted June 17, 1546.[84]

The draft moved through revisions during two months.[85] The Decree treats instruction on the Bible in eight points, to avoid neglecting the "heavenly

---

[81] Concilium oecumenicorum Decreta (1962) 640f; Decrees (1990) 2, 644f; Enchiridion Biblicum (1993) no. 63. Fifth Lateran had prescribed pre-censorship on May 4, 1515. Subsequently, Pope Paul IV, *Index of Prohibited Books* (1559), following the Louvain Index of 1546, forbade any use of numerous Latin Bibles published between 1522 and 1555 in Antwerp, Strasbourg, Basel, Lyon, Paris, and Venice. *Index de Rome 1559, 1559, 1564 (Index des Livres interdites*, ed. J. M. De Bujanda, 8; Sherbrooke: Éditions de l'Université / Geneva: Droz 1990) 307–25. These Bibles, however, were not named in the *Index of the Council of Trent* authorized by Pope Pius IV in 1564, which gave instead Rules, drafted at Trent, giving bishops scope to permit trustworthy individuals to use such Bibles to help understand the Vulgate text, ibid. 814f. On the latter Index, see D. DE PABLO MAROTO, "El Índice de libros prohibitos en el Concilio de Trento", *Revista española de teología* 36 (1976) 39–64.

[82] Concilium Tridentinum, 5, 23; 1, 500–06, esp. 506 (Cervini).

[83] Concilium Tridentinum, 5, 72–75.

[84] Allgeier, Das Konzil (1932), 320f, sees the separation as weakening the force of the reform-decree of April 8. The June decree on lectureships and preaching is in fact little known, since it is not printed in manual-editions of Church documents relevant to theology.

[85] Concilium Tridentinum 5, 105–08 (April 13), 122–25 (May 1), 125–27 (May 7–10), and 226–28 (June 15). The initial drafts began by affirming that Christian instruction should offer everyone Scripture as daily bread, but this gave way to a simpler incipit.

treasure of the sacred books that the Holy Spirit ... has bestowed on us".[86]
Where church-sponsored theological lectureships exist, bishops are to have
the incumbents expound Scripture. In other major churches, in monastic and
mendicant houses, and in public schools, positions are to be established for
lectures on Scripture, under the supervision of the bishop or religious superior.
In poorer churches a teacher of grammar must be installed to prepare students
to move on to study Scripture. The Decree continues on preaching the Gospel
as the chief task of bishops and parish pastors, with provision for episcopal
supervision of preaching in the dioceses. However, in the drafting process, a
lengthy paragraph was dropped that ruled out contentious and speculative sermons and prescribed that preachers offer the pure content of Scripture to the
people.

Trent's June 1546 decree on lectureships and preaching represented the
high-water-mark of biblical humanist influence on charting the path of Catholic renewal. In Trent's later decrees on doctrine, the role of Scripture waned,
while scholastic theologians made valued contributions. The biblical lectureships were in time marginalized by the reform-decree of July 15, 1563, which
made only cursory reference to biblical studies in its influential prescription
that bishops should found seminaries for the formation of their clergy.

3. The Status of the Vulgate

Studies: B. EMMI, "Il decreto tridentino sulla Vulgata nei commenti della prima polemica protes-
tantico-cattolica", *Angelicum* 30 (1953) 107–30; 228–72; H. HÖPFL, *Beiträge zur Geschichte der
Sixto-Klementischen Vulgata* (Biblische Studien 18,1–3; Freiburg: Herder 1913); U. HORST, "Der
Streit um die Autorität der Vulgata: zur Rezeption des Trienter Schriftdekrets in Spanien", *Revista
da Universidade de Coimbra* 29 (1983) 157–252; idem, "Melchior Cano und Domenico Bañez über
die Autorität der Vulgata. Zur Deutung des Trienter Vulgatadekrets", *MThZ* 51 (2000) 331–51; S.
MUÑOZ IGLESIAS, "El decreto tridentino sobre la Vulgata y su interpretación por los teólogos del si-
glo XVI", *EstB* 5 (1946) 137–69; H. QUENTIN, *Mémoire sur l'établissement du texte de la Vulgate*
(CBLa 6; Rome: Desclée / Paris: Gabalda 1922).

In the mid-sixteenth century, most Latin Bibles gave the text established from
Parisian medieval manuscripts in the thirteenth century. Some editions introduced textual modifications from other medieval manuscripts and some had
given marginal variants from the same sources.[87] But in 1524–27 Card. Cajetan
drew on three Latin Psalters newly translated from the Hebrew and commented on his own Hebrew-based version.[88] The Dominican Hebraist Sanctes
Pagninus brought out a complete Latin Bible in 1528, newly translating the
Old Testament from the original, the first such Christian Bible since Jerome.[89]

---

[86] Conciliorum oecumenicorum Decreta (1962) 643–45; Decrees (1990) 2, 667–69; Enchiridion
Biblicum (1993) nos. 65–72.

[87] Quentin, Mémoire sur l'établissement du texte de la Vulgate (1922) 75–120, notes the minor
advances in the 1511 Venice Vulgate of Albert de Castello, the minimal textual progress of the Latin text in the Complutensian Polyglot, and the characteristics of the Parisian Vulgates of Robert
Estienne (1528–46).

[88] See above, nn. 5–7 and 10, in this chapter.

[89] *Biblia. Habes in hoc libro ... utriusque instrumenti novam translationem aeditam a ... Sancte*

Pagninus' Pentateuch was interpreted by a Portuguese Dominican, Jeronimo Oleaster.[90] Another Hebrew-based Latin Old Testament was the work of a Benedictine abbot present at Trent, Isidore Clarius.[91] But his introduction and annotations proved upsetting and the work was forbidden by Pope Paul IV's *Index* of 1559.[92]

This, then, was the context of Trent's concern to declare the traditional Vulgate as alone "authentic" for public liturgical and scholastic use. But the Decree was open to different interpretations. The Council theologian A. de Vega gave a strict reading in 1548, that is, that Trent did not approve faulty Vulgate texts, but looked instead to their correction while holding the received text to be free from dogmatic errors.[93] But this witness to the *intentio auctorum* of the Decree contrasted with an influential reading by M. Cano that found in the *sensus textus* that, while recourse to the original Hebrew and Greek might heighten one's literary appreciation of the Latin text, this was not strictly necessary for knowing the biblical message.[94]

Lecturing in Salamanca in 1569, the Augustinian Luis de León extended A. de Vega's interpretation, first, by arguing for the reliability of the Hebrew texts of the Scriptures of Israel then available and, second, by a strict construction of Trent's Vulgate-Decree as compatible both with present use of alternate readings and then with a thorough revision, based on the Hebrew and Greek originals, to improve the current Latin Bible.[95] But others extended Cano's views to the point of making the Vulgate text an inerrant foundation of Catholic doctrine, leading to the denunciation in late 1571 of Luis de León and two Salamancan Hebraists before the Inquisition.[96] In prison from

---

pagnino lucensi (Lyon: F. Turchi & D. Bert 1528), with a prefatory Presentation to Pope Clement VII. A subsequent edition was corrected by Pagninus (Lyon 1542), followed by a printing of his Latin Old Testament with modifications by F. Vatable in R. Estienne's Geneva Bible of 1556–57, a Basle edition in 1564, and Plantin editions edited by B. Aldas Montano (e. g. Antwerp 1572, and in 5 vols., Leyden 1608–13). Pagninus's Hebrew grammar preceded his Old Testament, *Hebraicas Institutiones* (Lyon 1526), and there followed his often reprinted Hebrew-Latin dictionary, *Thesaurus linguae sanctae* (Lyon: Gryphius 1529), and his *Isagogae* (Lyon: Iustus 1536), already mentioned in n. 10, above, in this chapter. On Pagninus, see T. M. CENTI, "L'attività litteraria di Santi Pagnini (1470 -1536) nel campo delle scienze bibliche", *AFP* 15 (1945) 5–51.

[90] *Commentaria in Mose Pentateuchum iuxta M. Santis Pagnini, quibus Hebraica veritas exactissime explicatur* (Lisbon 1556, Antwerp 1569, Lyon 1586 & 1589).

[91] *Vulgata editio Novi et Veteris Testamenti* (Venice 1542). On Clarius, see the entry by R. AUBERT, in: *Dictionnaire d'Histoire et de Géographie Ecclésiastiques* 26 (1997) 192–93.

[92] Clarius was suspect for drawing on the former Franciscan now Protestant, Sebastian Münster, *Biblia hebraica* (Basle 1534/35). M. Cano accused Clarius of disseminating doubts and confusion in *De locis* (1563), II, 13, 22. Following the norms of the Tridentine Index deputation, Clarius brought out a revision: *Biblia sacrosancta veteris ac novi Testamenti* (Venice: Iunta 1564).

[93] *De iustificatione doctrina universa* (Venice 1548; repr. Ridgewood, NJ: Gregg 1964) 2, 691 f. A. de Vega had heard from Card. Legate Cervini that the Decree did not prohibit work from the original languages to bring the Vulgate more in line with the inspired meaning of Scripture.

[94] *De locis* (1563) II, 13–15.

[95] *Tractatus de fide*, in: *Mag. Luysi Legionensis Opera* 5 (Salamanca: Episcopali Calatravae Collegio 1893) 259–68 (Hebrew texts), 298–319 (the Vulgate and Trent), 327–37 (the status of the Vulgate, concluding that a new Latin Bible could well give the original Scripture "more meaningfully and exactly" than does the Vulgate). In Latin and Castillian, in: I. Jericó Bermejo, *Fray Luis de León. La teología sobre el artículo y el dogma de fe (1568)* (Pensamiento 2; Madrid: Editorial Revista Agustiniana 1997) 337–90.

[96] A. ALCALÁ (ed.), *Proceso inquisitorial de Fray Luis de León* (Valladolid: Junta de Castilla y León 1991) 3–13. On L. de León's fellow-suspect, who died in the prison of the Inquisition, see F. DOMÍNGUEZ REBOIRAS, *Gaspar de Grajal. Frühneuzeitliche Bibelwissenschaft im Streit mit Universität und Inquisition* (RGST 140; Münster: Aschendorff 1998).

1572 to 1576, L. de León defended his positions on the Vulgate as coherent with Trent, for example, by appeal to the views of J. Driedo and A. de Vega and insisting on the difference between holding Vulgate passages to be badly translated, as he did, and saying that they teach error.[97] L. de León was acquitted, but this did not signal a decisive victory for a strict construction of the "authenticity" of the Vulgate in the Church. The Spanish quarrel reached Louvain where R. Bellarmine reported that some held the Vulgate wholly adequate in conveying biblical meanings as well as did the original manuscripts. But others take Trent as ruling only on public reading, while vindicating the Vulgate as orthodox but not claiming it to be perfect.[98]

Stirred to action by disputes over the Antwerp Polyglot's inclusion of a Hebrew-based translation, the Roman Congregation of the Council, overseeing the implementation of Trent, stated in January 1576 that, beyond its doctrine, the Vulgate text was sacrosanct and no sentence, word, or syllable was to be changed. Differences found in the original texts may serve interpretation but not any change in public use of the sacred text.[99]

Trent's Vulgate Decree, in its third paragraph regulating printing, spoke of the Vulgate being printed "after thorough revision". Emperor Charles V immediately commissioned the Louvain Theology Faculty to prepare such a revised Latin Bible, which came out in November 1547 under the editorship of Jan Henten.[100] The text came from the Estienne Parisian edition of 1540, moderately revised in the light of some twenty Latin medieval biblical manuscripts.

In Rome, under Popes Pius IV (1559–65), Pius V (1565–72), and Gregory XIII (1572–85), work on the mandated Vulgate-revision gave way to other projects, such as the *Catechismus Romanus* (1566), a reformed Breviary (1568) and Missal (1570), a revised *Corpus Iuris Canonici* (1582), and work from 1578 to 1587 on an edition of the Septuagint. Vulgate commissions did work in 1561 and 1569–72, but were impeded both by lack of systematic collations of manuscripts and by internal divisions between those attached to the Latin Scripture long in use and others open to text-critical change. The second commission received collations of variants in twelve Latin manuscripts available at the Benedictine Badia of Florence and from thirty-four manuscripts of the Abbey of Monte Cassino.[101]

---

[97] Alcalá, Proceso inquisitorial (1991) 25, 247–74 (on 249, the difference between poor translation and teaching error), 501–44 (detailed defense), and 643–51 (concluding judgments).

[98] R. Bellarmine, Letter of April 1, 1575, to Cardinal Sirleto in Rome, in: X.-M. Le Bachelet, *Bellarmin et la Bible Sixto-Clémentine* (ETH 3; Paris: Beauchesne 1911) 104. Bellarmine goes on to ask (1) whether Jewish scholars have changed the Hebrew text to suppress messianic meanings, (2) whether there is a reliable version of the Septuagint, and (3) whether Trent meant to canonize the longer Greek text of the Book of Esther.

[99] Text in: Höpfl, Beiträge zur Geschichte der Sixto-Klementischen Vulgata (1913), 35. B. Rekers has "Cardinal" R. Bellarmine presiding at the Congregation, *Benito Arias Montano (1527–1598)* (London / Leiden 1972) 61. But Bellarmine was in Louvain until mid-1576 and only became a Cardinal in 1599. – A theologian like Domingo Bañez, O.P., could in 1584 envision good in an approved revision of the Vulgate but Gregory of Valencia, S.J., professor 1575–92 in Ingolstadt, held that "authenticity" placed the Vulgate in a category above the allegedly pristine Hebrew and Greek texts. See Horst, Melchior Cano and Dominicus Bañez (2000) 341–51.

[100] On the Louvain Vulgate editions, see Quentin, Mémoire sur l'établissement du texte de la Vulgate (1922) 128–46, with an excerpt of the Index of Prohibited Books of 1546, issued as an Imperial Edict, outlawing twenty-two recently printed Latin Bibles. On this Index and Bibles, see *Index de l'Université de Louvain 1546, 1550, 1558* (ed. J. M. De Bujanda; *Index des livres interdits* 2; Sherbrooke: Éditions de l'Université / Geneva: Droz 1986) 46, 106–30, 408–12.

[101] On the work in 1561, see Höpfl, Beiträge zur Geschichte der Sixto-Klementischen Vulgata (1913) 60–76. On the second commission, Höpfl, Beiträge (1913) 77–101, and Quentin, Mémoire (1922) 148–68. The latter offers examples of the Monte Cassino collations of Genesis 18 and Ruth 2, describes the work of April-September 1569 on revising Genesis and Exodus, and gives a list of emendations of Genesis proposed by one of the consultors.

One man, Cardinal Guglielmo Sirleto, worked steadily to prepare a revised Vulgate by filling the margins of his 1547 Louvain Bible with variants he found in later Latin Fathers, old Missals and Psalters, and manuscripts in Rome such as the tenth-century *Codex S. Mariae Rotundae* and the ninth-century *Codex Paulinus*.[102] After his death in 1585, Sirleto's work was a major source for the Commission formed by Pope Sixtus V (1585–90) in November 1586 under Cardinal Marcantonio Carafa. By order of the Pope, the early eighth-century *Codex Amiatinus* was delivered to the Commission and variants were collected in Spain from the tenth-century *Codex Legionensis II* and the eighth-century *Codex Toletanus*. The Carafa Commission entered the many variants in the margins of a 1583 Plantin folio copy of the Vulgate, adding to those printed there by the Louvain editor Luc de Bruges. The aim was not a new translation from the original languages but a critical revision of Jerome's Latin Bible drawn from codices judged representative of his pristine text.[103]

But Sixtus V reserved to himself the decision on emendations and in late 1588, when Card. Carafa submitted the results of the commission's work, the Pope rejected the proposed changes. With his own two assistants, Sixtus set to work emending another Louvain Bible of 1583, introducing rarely the proposals of the Carafa Commission, but mostly his own changes, especially in orthography, punctuation, and verse-division. By July 1589 the Sixtine Old Testament was being printed and in May 1590, copies of the Sixtine Vulgate were distributed to the Cardinals, sold in Rome, and sent to Catholic heads-of-state.[104] The volume included the notorious bull *Aeternus ille*, explaining Sixtus's purpose of preserving formulations long received in the Church. The Bull outlined sound text-critical procedures, which Sixtus had had no time to follow, and it went on to declare the new edition to be the Vulgate received by the Council of Trent and so henceforth the only authentic Latin Bible for use in the Church.[105]

The members of the Carafa Commission muted their outrage until Sixtus V died on August 27, 1590, when sales of the new Vulgate were halted. Under Gregory XIV (1590–1591), a new Commission began correcting the Sixtine edition, working rapidly to produce the Vulgate then published under Pope Clement VIII (1592–1605) in November 1592. The new Sixto-Clementine edition is corrected as Sixtus is said to have seen necessary in his last days. The revision makes some use of the critical work of the Commission of 1586–88, but it remains substantially the text of Sixtus V and the Louvain Vulgate, stemming from a thirteenth-century Latin biblical text.[106]

However, the prefaces prepared under Pope Clement VIII do not declare

---

[102] See Höpfl, Beiträge (1913) 114f, and Quentin, Mémoire (1922) 168f, where the latter shows that Sirleto did not in fact receive from Tuscany the *Amiatinus* variants for which he had asked. On Sirleto, see G. DENZLER, *Kardinal Guglielmo Sirleto* (MThS.H 17; Munich: Hueber 1964).

[103] HÖPFL describes the Commission's work in Beiträge (1913) 128–40, with its recommended emendations of Joshua 2, Genesis 1 and 50. Appendix I gives all the changes proposed for Proverbs (Beiträge, 240–77). Quentin, Mémoire (1922) 170–80, adds examples of the corrections proposed for Exodus 2, Ruth, and Genesis 42–50.

[104] On Sixtus's revision, see Höpfl, Beiträge (1913) 140–53, with a synoptic presentation on Proverbs (Louvain / Sirleto / Carafa Commission / Sixtus) 240–77. Also, Quentin, Mémoire (1922) 181–92.

[105] Text in: P. M. BAUMGARTEN, *Die Vulgata Sixtina von 1590 und ihre Einführungsbulle* (ATA 3/2; Münster: Aschendorff 1911) 40–64.

[106] On the production of the "Sixto-Clementine" Vulgate, see Höpfl, Beiträge (1913) 158–86, with a synoptic presentation of its emendations of Proverbs, 278–91; also, Quentin, Mémoire

the 1592 edition to be the authentic Vulgate of the Tridentine Decree of 1546.[107] But papal reticence did not prevent the multiplication of apologetic defenses of it as the normative and inerrant Bible of the Catholic Church, even to rendering unnecessary any scholarly recourse to the Hebrew and Greek originals. In 1610 J. de Mariana carefully set forth the problematic, with recourse to A. de Vega.[108] But only in the twentieth century has the valid text-critical work of the 1586–88 Vulgate Commission been taken up again on a fresh basis, while the *Sixto-Clementina* remained the norm, for example, in Roman Catholic liturgical texts. Even into the early twentieth century it was also taken to be regulative of the vernacular translations of Scripture authorized for Catholic use.[109]

4. Biblical Studies in the Early Jesuit Order

Sources: Constitutiones Societatis Iesu et Normae complementariae (Rome: Curia Generalis Societatis Iesu 1995), translated, e.g., as *The Constitutions of the Society of Jesus and Their Complementary Norms* (St. Louis: Institute of Jesuit Sources 1996); *Monumenta Paedagogica Societatis Iesu*, 7 vols. (*Monumenta Historica Societatis Iesu* 92, 107–08, 124, 129, 140–41; ed. L. Lukács; Rome: Institutum Historicum S.I. 1965–92).

Bibliographies: C. SOMMERVOGEL e.a., *Bibliothèque de la Compagnie de Jésus*, 12 vols. (Brussels: Schepens / Paris: Picard 1890-1932); L. POLGÀR, *Bibliographie sur l'histoire de la Compagnie de Jésus, 1901-1980*, 3 vols. in 6 (Rome: Institutum Historicum Societatis Iesu 1981-90, continued annually in *Archivum Historicum Societatis Iesu*).

Studies: W. V. BANGERT, *A History of the Society of Jesus* (St. Louis: Institute of Jesuit Sources, 2nd edn. 1986); A. BEA, "La Compagnia di Gesù e gli studi biblici", *La Compagnia di Gesù e le scienze sacre* (AnGr 29; Rome: Università Gregoriana 1942) 115-43; M. GILBERT, "Biblia sagrada", *Diccionario historíco de la Compañia de Jesús* (eds. C. O'Neill / J. M. Domínguez; Rome: Institutum Historicum S.I. / Madrid: Universidad Pont. Comillas 2001) 1, 437-43; J. W. O'MALLEY, *The First Jesuits* (Cambridge, MA: Harvard UP 1993).

The first Jesuits were an international band of ten priests gathered around Ignatius Loyola in the 1530s while studying in Paris. Pope Paul III approved them in 1540 as a new order dedicated to "helping souls" by word and sacrament, spiritual guidance, and instructing youth in Christian doctrine. A decade later, Pope Julius III confirmed the growing order, adding to their ministries the defense of the faith and giving the public lectures mandated by the Council of Trent in June 1546.[110] For the latter, Diego Lainez composed a short trea-

---

(1922) 192–201, with the emendations of Genesis 18 and 40–50. Editions correcting printers' mistakes came out in 1593 and 1598.

[107] Robert Bellarmine contributed to the preface, after working on the rapidly revised text of the 1592 edition; see X.-M. LE BACHELET, *Bellarmin et la Bible Sixto-Clementine* (ETH 3; Paris: Beauchesne 1911) 35–53, which also gives Bellarmine's proposal, implemented by Clement VIII, of reacquiring all copies of the 1590 Sixtine Vulgate and having them destroyed (54–60).

[108] *Pro editione vulgata*, in: *Tractatus VII* (Cologne: Hieratus 1610) 33–126, citing Vega on p. 99, and while admitting the Vulgate's faults, also warning that the available Hebrew and Greek texts are not perfect.

[109] The Sixto-Clementine Latin Bible ceased to be the official Scripture of the Catholic Church with the promulgation of the *Nova Vulgata* by Pope John Paul II, 25 April 1979.

[110] Constitutiones (1995) 3 f.

tise on interpreting Scripture as offering biblical doctrine, based on the literal sense as confirmed in the Church, so that the hearers may grow in love of God and neighbor, while imitating the virtues presented in the biblical text.[111]

The Jesuit founding documents are silent on schools but in 1548 Loyola sent men to Messina when asked to open a college. The order quickly realized the potential of education for promoting the well-being of Church and society and when the founder died in 1556 Jesuits were operating over thirty schools and by 1600 some three hundred. Messina was the pilot-project, following and adapting the curriculum and pedagogy known from Paris. Latin grammar, literature, and rhetoric were fundamental with young students advancing to Greek and Hebrew. The first classes on Scripture were given by Jerónimo Nadal to which he added public biblical lectures in Messina's Cathedral.[112] Some early Jesuit schools, such as the Roman College (founded 1551) added higher studies in philosophy and theology for younger recruits to the order and other candidates for the priesthood. Theology began with two years studying the *Summa* of Aquinas with biblical classes then held daily during two further years while continuing the *Summa*.

Thus Jesuit biblical studies rest on languages and the humanities, philosophy, and systematic theology. Jesuit expositors of Scripture are theologians; their students learn the Bible's theological, moral, and spiritual doctrine. Loyola drafted the order's constitutions, including planned formation of new members. The prescribed study of biblical languages has a Tridentine note, namely, thereby to defend the Church's Vulgate version. Theology, both scholastic and positive (patristic, conciliar), should precede or accompany biblical study.[113]

The impact of Jesuits on Catholic life owed much to their following designs refined on the basis of experience. For the schools, Loyola's basic sketch and the programs of Messina and the Roman College gave initial guidance.[114] In time a comprehensive codification took shape, after drafts and feedback from the schools, in the *Ratio studiorum* of 1599, which consists in thirty sets of rules for those in Jesuit governance, school administration and teaching. The provincial superior should select Scripture teachers expert in languages and theology who can teach Hebrew and speak well (*in eloquentia versatos*).[115] The biblical professors should focus on the literal sense, setting it forth so as to confirm faith and morality. The Vulgate is the basis of instruction but one should also gain light from the original texts and ancient versions, while taking account of relevant Church teaching and respectfully drawing on the Fathers. Scripture calls for disciplined exposition, avoiding recondite questions and not

---

[111] "Documenta ad bene interpretandas scripturas", *Disputationes Tridentiniae* 1–2 (ed. H. Grisar; Innsbruck: Rauch 1886) 2, 501–05.

[112] O'Malley, First Jesuits (1993) 200–42; G. Codina Mir, *Aux sources de la pédagogie des Jésuites. Le "modus parisiensis"* (Bibliotheca Instituti Historici S.I. 28; Rome: Institutum Historicum 1968) 256–336.

[113] Constitutiones (1995) nos. 366–68.

[114] Constitutiones (1995) nos. 446–509. Monumenta Paedagogica, 1, 93–106 (Coudret, Messina, 1551), 133–63 (Nadal, 1552) and 163–85 (Olave, on higher studies in Rome, 1553).

[115] Monumenta Paedagogica, 5, 357 f.

straying into intricate argumentation. But like all Jesuit professors at this level, the biblicist aims at forming students by his teaching and example as dedicated and virtuous Christians.[116] Later, in 1687, a legislative assembly of the order reaffirmed the priority of biblical studies, to assure the *sacra eruditio* necessary to Jesuit ministries. Such scriptural learning, in a felicitous phrase, should be "the very soul of theology".[117]

In the order's first century, some Jesuits published major Old Testament work.[118] Others made contributions valued in their day, such as the Bavarian G. Mayr, whose Hebrew textbook saw ten printings.[119] G. de Zamora of Seville produced a complete concordance of the Vulgate.[120] The Portuguese Emanuel Sá, teaching at the Roman College 1556-72, explained terms of the whole Bible.[121] Juan de Mariana, controversial historian of Spain and political theorist, also treated all of Scripture.[122] The Italian G. S. Menochio drew on the Fathers on the whole Bible in a work used over three centuries.[123]

F. de Ribera, professor of Scripture at Salamanca 1575-91, set forth the minor prophets from different perspectives.[124] J. de Prado, teacher at Cordoba, began a minute treatment of Ezechiel, completed by G. B. Villalpando.[125] J. de Pineda of Seville treated Job in an often reprinted work.[126] The productive Würzburg and Mainz professor, N. Serarius, explained the deuterocanonical

---

[116] Monumenta Paedagogica, 5, 383-85 (Rules of the Professor of Scripture and of Hebrew); also, 380-83 (Rules of All Professors of the Advanced Faculties). The 1599 Rules for teachers of Bible simplify drafts circulated in 1586 (ibid. 43-47, 163-66) and 1591 (267-69).

[117] General Congregation XIII, Decree 15, in: *Institutum Societatis Iesu* (Florence: S. Conceptio 1895), 2, 408. That Scripture study should animate theology was repeated by Pope Leo XIII in his 1893 encyclical, *Providentissimus Deus* (Enchiridion Biblicum, no. 114) and by the Second Vatican Council in its Constitution on Revelation, *Dei Verbum*, no. 24. J. M. LERA, "Sacrae paginae studium sit velut anima sacrae theologiae (Notas sobre el origen y procedencia de este frase)", *Miscellanea Comillias* 41 (1983) 409-22.

[118] The following section will treat Juan Maldanato, Benito Perera, and Robert Bellarmine. On these and the other Jesuit authors mentioned here, see entries in *Diccionario histórico de la Compañía de Jesús*, 4 vols. (ed. C. O'Neill / J. M. Domínguez; Rome: Institutum Historicum S.I. / Madrid: Universidad Pont. Comillas 2001). Their commentaries are evaluated in Bk. III of R. Simon, Histoire critique du Vieux Testament (1685).

[119] *Institutiones linguae hebraicae* (Augsburg: Mangium 1616), adding an exercise on translating the book of Jonah.

[120] *Sacrorum Bibliorum Concordantiae* (pp. 1177; Rome: Zannetti 1627).

[121] *Notationes in totam Scripturam Sacram* (Mainz: Kinckius 1610, and 7 further printings; in microfiche, Leiden: IDC 1987).

[122] *Scholia in Vetus et Novum Testamentum* (Paris: Sonnius 1620). The comments of Sá and Mariana were given in *Biblia Sacra Vulgatae editionis* 1-2 (Antwerp: Plantin-Moretus 1624). On Mariana's evaluation, for the Inquisition, of the Antwerp Polyglot, see Rekers, Benito Arias Montano (1972) 62-64, and on the Vulgate, above, at n. 108.

[123] *Brevis Explicatio sensus literalis totius s. Scripturae ex optimis quibusque Auctoribus per Epitomen collecta* (Cologne: Kinchius 1630, repr. in Latin in Antwerp, Lyon, Paris, and Venice; in French with printings 1825-1872).

[124] In Librum Duodecim prophetarum Commentarii, sensum eorundem ... historicum & moralem, persaepe etiam allegoricum complectentes (Salamanca: Ferdinandus 1587, repr. at Rome, Cologne, Paris, Brescia, and Douai). On the clash between Mariana's Hebraicism and Ribera's option for the Christian Fathers, see F. ASCENSIO, "Encuentro bíblico entre Juan de Mariana y Francisco de Ribera", EstB 27 (1968) 129-52.

[125] *In Ezechielem Explanationes et Apparatus Urbis ac Templi Hierosolymitani, Commentariis et Imaginibus illustratus* 1-3 (Rome: Zannetti 1596-1604).

[126] *Commentariorum in Iob libri tredecim, adiuncta singulis capitibus sua paraphrase* (Seville: Colegío D. Ermenegildi 1598-1602, repr. in Cologne, Venice, Antwerp, Mainz, and Paris). On the author: A. GARCÍA-MORENO, "Juan de Pineda y el libro di Job", EstB 35 (1976) 23-47, 165-85, and E. OLIVARES, "Juan de Pineda S.I. (1557-1637). Biografía, Escritos, Bibliografía", *Archivo teologico granadino* 51 (1988) 5-133. For Pineda Job 9:6 showed Copernicanism to be false, against D. Zuñiga's reconciliation of heliocentrism with such a text.

books, Judges and Ruth, and the life of Joshua.[127] Comments, exhaustively informative for their time, on the historical and prophetic books and on Job and Canticle were the work of G. Sánchez, professor 1607-28 in Murcia and Alcalá.[128]

5. Post-Tridentine Biblical Commentators

Catholic writing on the Old Testament in the half-century after the Council of Trent varied in methods and aims, from philological scholarship, through defensive argument, to spiritual edification. This section reviews the work of six such Catholic scholars.

5.1. Sixtus of Siena

Source: *Bibliotheca sancta* (Venice: Franciscus Senensis 1566; repr. Lyon / Frankfurt 1575, Cologne 1586, 1626, Lyon 1591, Paris 1610, Naples 1742; microfiche of Lyon 1575 edition, Leiden: IDC 1988).
Studies: A. DEL COL, "Note sull'eterodossia di fra Sisto da Siena. I suoi rapporti con Orazio Brunetto e un gruppo veneziano di 'spirituali'", *Collectanea Franciscanea* 47 (1977) 27-64; J. W. MONTGOMERY, "Sixtus of Siena and Roman Catholic Biblical Scholarlship in the Reformation Period", *ARefG* 54 (1963) 214-34; F. PARENTE, "Alcune osservazioni preliminari per una biografia di Sisto Senese. Fu realmente Sisto un ebreo convertito?", *Italia Judaica* (Pubblicazioni degli Archivi di Stato, Saggi 6; Roma 1986) 211-31; J. QUETIF / J. ECHARD, *Scriptores Ordinis Praedicatorum* 2 (Paris: Ballard & Simars 1721) 206-08.

Obscurity shrouds the early years of the author of the prototype manual of biblical introduction, Sixtus of Siena / Sisto da Siena (1520-1569). It is stated, but remains doubtful, that he was Jewish by birth and early education, becoming Christian as an adolescent. He called Ambrosius Catharinus his first *praeceptor*, but the latter was in France during Sixtus's formative years. Sixtus was first a Franciscan preacher who in Venice had contacts with a circle of heterodox exponents of spiritual reform. After preaching in Naples in 1552, he was accused of heresy, convicted, and condemned to death. But the Inquisition Commissioner M. Ghislieri, O.P., brought him to recant and transfer to the Dominican order, with affiliation to the friary of Genoa, where Sixtus concentrated on biblical studies and preaching until his death in 1569, with one foray into inquisitorial suppression of rabbinical books at Cremona in 1559.

Sixtus's works included *Sophias Monotessaron*, a harmony of Proverbs, Qohelet, Sirach, and Wisdom; also, sermons on Genesis 1, on Job 1-3, and

---

[127] *In sacros divinorum Bibliorum libros, Tobiam, Iudith, Esther, Machabaeos, Commentarius* (Mainz: Lippius 1599); *Iudices et Ruth explanati* (Mainz: Lippius 1609); *Iosue, ab utero ad ipsum usque tumulum, e Moysi Exodo, Levitico, Numeris, Deuteronomio & e proprio ipsius libro, ac Paralipomenis... explanatus* 1-2 (Mainz: Albini 1609-10).

[128] *In Isaiam prophetam commentarii cum paraphasi* (Lyon: Cardon 1615); *In Danielem Prophetam commentarii cum paraphrase* (pp. 1050; Lyon: Cardon 1619). Sommervogel, Bibliothèque, 7, 523-26, gives entries on nine commentaries by Sánchez, published at Lyon and Antwerp 1615-28.

Psalms 1 and 50. But his only extant work is *Bibliotheca sancta*, a trove of information and corrective elucidations of the whole Christian Bible. Sixtus laments that a Catholic reading of Scripture is impeded by tendentious translations, prefaces and glosses which twist the meaning of patristic commentaries, and by Bibles lacking the deuterocanonical books. One remedy is the *Bibliotheca*, which may seem to offer an excess of information but the author justifies this to inform and orient beginners.

Book I classifies the biblical books, with Sixtus's terminological proposal of 'protocanonical', 'deuterocanonical', and 'apocryphal' works.[129] Book II catalogues alphabetically all writings and writers mentioned in the Bible (e.g. Cyrus, Henoch, Jezabel), adding the sixty-three tractates of the Talmud. Sixtus claims originality for Book III, an analysis of interpretive methods, working from generic categories of 'historical' and 'mystical' to indicate over thirty specific approaches of patristic and scholastic authors. A concluding overview, in verse, suggests the Catholic turn to tradition by naming Jerome as outstanding for biblical history, Origen and Ambrose for allegorical and anagogical readings, John Chrysostom and Pope Gregory for moralizing, Augustine for light on obscure passages, and Nicholas of Lyra as helpful for those beginning their biblical studies.[130] Book IV presents all "Catholic expositors" and their biblical works to date, from the Septuagint translators, Philo, and Josephus, through the fathers and scholastics, down to Sanctes Pagninus, Cajetan, Catharinus, Driedo, Foreiro, and Sixtus himself. He adds a short catalogue of thirty-six rabbinical authors, whose works he had burned, along with copies of the Talmud, at Cremona.[131] In Book V Sixtus goes through the Scriptures of Israel to list and correct 264 mistaken interpretations found in the authors just presented, for example, on Genesis, fourteen misleading Septuagint translations, ten errors of Philo, and nine of Origen. On the Hebrew Bible, the *Bibliotheca* notes seven erroneous views of Cajetan, taken from Catharinus, to which Sixtus adds his own dislike of Cajetan's whole Psalter commentary because there can hardly ever finds Christ.[132] On the remission and 'covering' of sins in Ps 31:1 (Vg), Sixtus censures Augustine for supporting the pessimistic view of humans now espoused by Luther and Calvin.[133] The syllabus of errors continues on the New Testament in Book VI (mistaken views of Catholics) and Book VII (heresies old and new), before ending the *Bibliotheca* in Book VIII with thirteen heresies that question the validity for Christians of Israel's Scriptures whether as a whole, in particular books (especially the deuterocanonicals), or in the Vulgate translation. After a dense argument in defense of the Church's Latin version, Sixtus's final lines cite Trent's decree on the authenticity of the Vulgate.

The encyclopedic *Bibliotheca* of Sixtus of Siena comes with extensive indices of biblical passages, Catholic authors, heretics, and notable topics treated.

5.2. Francisco Foreiro

Source: *Iesaiae prophetae vetus & nova ex Hebraico versio, Cum commentario* (Venice: Zileto 1563; Antwerp: Nuntius 1567).[134]

Studies: R. DE ALDEMA ROLO, "Foreiro, Francisco", *Dictionnaire d'histoire et de géographie ecclésiastiques* 17 (1971), 1030–32; J. NUNES CARREIRA, *Filologia e crítica de Isaías no comentário de Francisco Foreiro* (Coimbra 1974).

---

[129] *Bibliotheca sancta* (Lyon: Pesnot 1575 / Leiden: IDC 1988) 1, 13–14.
[130] Ibid. 1, 209.
[131] Ibid. 1, 485–487.
[132] Ibid. 2, 59–60 (Censure no. 157).
[133] Ibid. 2, 62 (Censure no. 167).
[134] Repr. in *Critici Sacri* (ed. J. Pearson / A. Scattergood e.a.; London 1660, Frankfurt 1695, Amsterdam: Boom / Utrecht: de Water 1698), 4, 14–756, with comments of others; also, in: *Scripturae sacrae Cursus completus* (ed. J.-P. Migne; Paris: Migne 1840) 18, 799–1644. The reprints omit Foreiro's Preface and new Latin translation of Isaiah.

As a youth Francisco Foreiro (1523–1581) was sponsored by the King of Portugal for studies in Paris. Back in Portugal, he entered the Dominicans (profession, 1540) and in 1555 became preacher to the royal court. Sent by King Sebastian, he took an active part at Trent 1562–63, serving as secretary of the commission preparing the Index of Prohibited Books promulgated by Pope Pius IV in 1564. After the Council Foreiro was a principal redactor of the *Catechismus Romanus* (1566).[135] Again in Portugal, he served in various posts in his order until death in 1581. Among his works, only the Isaiah commentary survives, while expositions of the other prophets, Job, Psalms, and the Wisdom books are lost.

Foreiro composed his Isaiah commentary in Portugal and brought it to Trent for publication in Venice. It gives his own translation to render Hebrew terms precisely but expounds the Vulgate text, which the commentary repeatedly defends as conveying the sense of verses even if terms are imprecise. The whole Hebrew Bible is the principal interpretive resource, as Foreiro amasses other passages which illuminate Isaiah's wording. Patristic interpretations play no role. Textual observations arise with some frequency, as Foreiro gives accounts of variants and rejects some rabbinical readings and vocalizations.[136]

This commentary recognizes large literary blocks, e.g., ch. 1 as the *argumentum* of the whole, chs. 1–39 as *orationes invectivae* with interspersed messianic promises, and chs. 40–66, where the prophet dons the mantle of an evangelist to speak more openly than before about redemption by Christ. Foreiro repeatedly criticizes "judaizing" interpretations, without naming the culprits who see texts relating primarily to events prior to messianic times. Elucidating messianic texts, he draws on New Testament passages on redemption, evangelization, the Church assembled from Jews and Gentiles, and spiritual endowments given those graced in Christ.

Foreiro's commentary saw only one reprint, but Cornelius à Lapide gave many passages.[137] Its philological concentration and eschewing of the Fathers resonated weakly with the exegetical preferences of the Catholic confessional age.

5.3. Andreas Masius

Sources: *Josuae imperatoris historia illustrata et explicata ab Andrea Masio* (Antwerp: Plantin 1574);[138] *Annotationes in Deuteronomium* (capp. 17–34), in: *Critici sacri* (1698), 2/1, 113–286; Moses bar Kepa, *De paradiso commentarius* (tr. from Syriac by A. Masius; Antwerp: Plantin 1569);[139] M. Lossen (ed.), *Briefe von Andreas Masius und seinen Freunden* (Leipzig: A. Dürr 1886).

Studies: H. de Vocht, "Andreas Masius", *Miscellanea Giovanni Mercati*, 4 (StT 124; Vatican City: Biblioteca Apostolica Vaticana 1946) 425–41; T.-J. Lamy, "Maes (André)", *Biographie nationale de Belgique* 13 (Brussels: Bruylant 1884) 120–25.

---

[135] P. Rodríguez / R. Lanzetti, *El Catechismo Romano. Fuentes y historia del texto y de la redacción* (Pamplona: Universidad de Navarra 1982) 100–06.

[136] J. Nunez Carreira lists 57 proposals by Foreiro of emendations of the Hebrew text, Filologia e crítica de Isaías (1974) 131–33.

[137] J. Nunez Carreira, ibid. 187–210, surveys various appreciations of Foreiro's commentary.

[138] Reprinted, giving commentary and textual notes, in: Critici Sacri (1698) 2, 3–553, and with Masius's Hebrew-based version and commentary in Migne, Sacrae Scripturae Cursus Completus (1839) 7, 851–1126; 8, 9–458.

[139] See HBOT 1/2 (2000) 562, n. 2. Masius's translation is in Critici Sacri (1698), 1/2, 387–496, and PG 111, 481–608.

The lay scholar, Andreas Masius / Maes (1514–1573), was born at Lennik near Brussels and excelled at the Louvain Collegium trilingue. Serving Johann de Weze, Bishop of Constance, he visited Italy 1544–46 and then as councillor of Duke William of Cleves was again in Rome 1551–52, where meeting a priest from Mesopotamia led to his study of Syriac. Masius prepared the Syriac-Latin dictionary and Syriac grammar of the Antwerp polyglot.[140] Settling at Zevenaar near Arnhem, he carried on a erudite correspondence and pursued scholarly biblical studies. His notes on Deuteronomy mainly treat variations between the Hebrew, Greek, and Syriac texts but expand to commentary on Deuteronomy 31–33.

Masius's great Joshua commentary, published shortly after he died, offers the Hebrew with a Latin version and, on facing pages, the Greek text with its own Latin translation, with both texts marked by asterisks and obelisks to indicate variants, which text-critical annotations then explain. The Vulgate ranges across the lower portion of both pages. After the ample exposition of the Vulgate text, six indices cover topics, places, Hebrew terms, biblical texts, and the Hebrew books Masius has used.

Masius holds that Ezra composed Joshua from annals preserved in archives, which accounts for some breaks in the narrative. His authorities include classical authors, especially Zenophon, Pliny, and Strabo, but he constantly cites rabbinical opinion, along with Josephus and Maimonides. Masius cites Church Fathers with moderation. From Justin and Augustine he takes over 'anagogical' readings on Joshua as a type of the Messiah and Rahab as prefiguring gentile Christians. But he cuts short such accounts to return to his preferred philological work and questions of history and geography. The conduct of Joshua, a zealous and observant leader, occasions admonitions for the readers on their arrogance, spiritual lethargy, and neglect of prayer.

On Josh 10:12–14, the commentary examines views on how long the sun stood still, but concludes by urging one to marvel at the power of Joshua's prayer for longer light to complete his victory. The campaign mentioned in Josh 22:12 raises the question of applying coercion to vindicate true religion in Masius's own day, which he can admit against the malicious, while lamenting inquisitorial cruelty in treating ordinary people misled into deviant forms of piety. References in Joshua to rites and monuments occasioned Masius's laments over present-day iconoclasm and recent polemic against traditional ceremonies. On Joshua 12 he moved from the barrenness of post-conquest Canaan, due to Israel's ingratitude, to mention the Reformation's rejection of Church authority, leading to decline in piety, the subversion of dogma, and even to bad weather, poor harvests, and inflated prices.

However, contemporary applications are incidental to the scholarly project of A. Masius, whose philological acumen, literary sensitivity, and broad learning combined to produce a work in which R. Simon could recognize authentic critical study and a sensitive understanding of biblical ways of expression.[141]

---

[140] See Ch. 30, below.
[141] Histoire critique du vieux Testament (1685) 444, 462.

5.4. Juan Maldonado

Sources: *Commentarii in Prophetas IIII: Ieremiam, Baruch, Ezechielem & Danielem. Accessit expositio Psalmi CIX* (Paris: Cardon 1610; Tournai 1611, Mainz 1611); *Commentarii in praecipuos Sacrae Scripturae locos Veteris Testamenti* (Paris: Cramoisy 1643); "De constitutione theologiae" (1570; ed. J. I. Tellechea), in: *Scriptorium Victoriense* 1 (1954) 226–55; "De ratione theologiae docendae" (1573), Monumenta Paedagogica Societatis Iesu, 4, 186–96.

Bibliographies: Reinhardt, Bibelkommentare spanischer Autoren 2 (1999) 9–20; Sommervogel, Bibliothèque de la Compagnie de Jésus, 5, 403–12.

Studies: J. CABALLERO, "Apuntes biograficas", in: J. Maldonado, *Comentarios a los cuatro Evangelios* 1 (Madrid: Biblioteca de autores cristianos 1950) 1–43; J. M. PRAT, *Maldonat et l'Université de Paris au XVIᵉ siècle* (Paris: Julien 1856; repr. Aalen 1969); H. GRAF REVENTLOW, *Epochen der Bibelauslegung*, III. *Renaissance, Reformation, Humanismus* (Munich: Beck 1997), 201–11; P. SCHMITT, *Le réforme catholique. Le combat de Maldonat* (ThH 74; Paris: Beauchesne 1985); J. I. TELLECHEA, "Metodología teológica de Maldonado", *Scriptorium Victoriense*, 1 (1954) 184–255; idem, "Maldonado, Juan", in: Diccionario historico de la Compagñia de Jésus 3 (2001) 2484–85.

After his education in languages, philosophy, and Thomist theology at Salamanca 1547–1558, Juan Maldonado (1533–1583) became a Jesuit in 1562. At the order's College of Clermont in Paris, he taught 1563–76 a new-style "positive" theology drawn from biblical and patristic sources.[142] The hostility of the Gallican theologians of the Sorbonne and influential Calvinists occasioned suspension of his lectures and retirement to Bourges for study and writing. Called to Rome in 1581 for the Jesuit General Congregation, Maldonado stayed to work on the order's *Ratio Studiorum* and the papal-sponsored edition of the Septuagint, but he died before either project was completed.

Maldonado's best known work is his ample commentary on the Gospels (Pont-à-Mousson 1596–97, repr. into the nineteenth century), but he left Old Testament comments in manuscripts which were edited by Jesuit confreres and published in 1610 and 1643. Maldonado's commentary on Ps 109 (110) was reworked from public lectures of 1576.[143] The Psalm is christological, from patristic precedents, especially against Arian subordination of the divine Son to the Father. Calvinist positions are also rebutted, e. g., on God's "right hand" as a placement preventing Christ's eucharistic presence. On Ps 109:3 (Vg) Maldonado defended the accuracy of the Vulgate, as being close to the Septuagint, which Justin and Epiphanius said agreed with the Hebrew text of their day.

Maldonado treated the major prophets in texts-for-study based on the Vulgate.[144] He states the topic of each chapter briefly but then philology predominates to show relations of terms to Hebrew or Greek originals, to rabbinic readings, to Greek versions, and to recent Hebrew-based Latin translations. Some shortcomings of the Vulgate are noted but it is mostly found better. For Baruch and Daniel 13–14, canonical authority is argued from citations and references in early Church Fathers. The order of passages is not historical, for later editors combined prophecies from different contexts without concern for chronology. Messianic readings occur on Jeremiah and Ezechiel but do not predominate, whereas half the chapters of Isaiah look beyond the historical

---

[142] He set forth his method in *De constitutione theologiae* (1570, ed. Tellechea).

[143] *Commentarii in Prophetas* (1610) 768–829; *Commentarii in praecipuos locos* (1643) 779–810.

[144] On Jeremiah, Lamentations, Baruch, Ezekiel, Daniel, in: *Commentarii in Prophetas* (1610) 1–767; on Isaiah, in: *Commentarii in praecipuos locos* (1643) 190–352.

setting to Christ, the Gospel, and the call of all peoples to the Church. On Ezechiel, Maldonado admits the difficulty of explaining the four visions of Ezekiel 1, Gog and Magog in 38:2, and the restored city and Temple of 40–48, and after surveying opinion does not reach clear solutions. But the "waters" of 47:12 indicate the "sense of the Church", a source of life for those who draw upon its understanding of Scripture.[145] Beyond Isaiah Maldonado's commentaries published in 1643 vary notably, from brief notes on the Hebrew of the Psalms to a christological and ecclesial reading of the Canticle.[146]

Maldonado never taught Scripture but did compose rules of exegetical method, submitted for the Jesuit *Ratio* in 1573: Attend first to textual variants and then to translations. Be wary of rabbinical readings based on pointing which may affect the sense. Aim at culling the literal sense of difficult passages, focusing on "our" Vulgate. Collate similar passages with attention to their Hebrew and Greek originals, before noting whether a dogma of faith is involved and whether heretics have argued from the passage. Make applications to moral life, but with minimal use of allegory, scholastic subtleties, and homiletics. Let the two Testaments illumine each other.[147]

5.5. Benito Perera

Sources: *Commentariorum in Danielem Prophetam Libri sexdecim* (Rome: Ferrarius 1587); *Commentariorum et dissertationum in Genesim tomus I-IV* (Rome: Ferrarius 1591–1599); *Primus tomus selectarum disputationum in Sacram Scripturam, continens super libro Exodii centum triginta septem Disputationes* (Ingolstadt: Sartorius 1601); "De ratione interpretandi S. Scripturam in gymnasiis nostrae Societatis", Monumenta Paedagogica Societatis Iesu, 7, 122–26.

Bibliographies: Reinhardt, Bibelkommentare spanischer Autoren 2 (1999) 177–83; Sommervogel, Bibliothèque de la Compagnie de Jésus, 6, 499–507.

Study: F. DE P. SOLA, "Perera, Benito", Diccionario historico de la Compagñia de Jésus 3 (2001) 3088–89.

The Spanish Jesuit Benito Perera (Pereira, Pereyra) (1535–1610) studied and taught at the Collegio Romano from 1553 to the end of his life. His early philosophy lectures (1558–1567) were judged to be infected with the naturalist thought of Averroes, but his view of mathematics as not scientific by Aristotelian criteria influenced later Jesuit opponents of the new method of Galileo.[148] Perera's move from philosophy to teaching Scripture led to erudite commentaries, several still in manuscript.[149]

---

[145] *Commentarii in Prophetas* (1610) 589; *Commentarii in praecipuos locos* (1643) 679.

[146] *Commentarii in praecipuos locos* (1643) 1–100 (Psalms), 101–46 (Proverbs), 147–64 (Qoheleth), 165–80 (Canticle), 181–89 (Wisdom 1–4).

[147] *De ratione theologiae docendae* (1573), Monumenta Paedagogica, 4, 193f.

[148] Perera's commentary on *De anima* of Aristotle, *De communibus omnium rerum naturalium principiis et affectionibus*, first published as *Physicorum sive de principiis rerum naturalium libri XV*, saw 13 editions 1562–1618; cf. G. C. GIACOBBE, "Un Gesuita progressista nella 'Quaestio de certitudine mathematicarum' rinascimentale", *Physis* 19 (1977) 51–86. On the censure of his philosophical positions see M. SCADUTO, *L'epoca di Giacomo Lainez 1556–65* 2 (Storia della Compagnia di Gesù in Italia, 4; Rome: Civiltà cattolica 1974) 282–88. On Perera and opposition to Galileo cf. W. A. WALLACE, "The Problem of Apodictic Proof in Early Seventeenth-Century Mechanics", *Galileo, the Jesuits and the Medieval Aristotle* (Variorum Collected Studies; Aldershot: Ashgate 1991), Study VII, 79–81.

[149] Reinhardt, Bibelkommentare spanischer Autoren 2 (1999) 177–82, lists unpublished works

In his Daniel commentary, Perera's dedicatory epistle to Cardinal Carafa lavishly praises Scripture for its divine dignity and efficacy. Daniel is an obscure work which however when explained shows the work of divine providence, offers evidence for Christianity, and strengthens believers to face trials and persecutions. The explanations emerge from extensive reviews of positions of Roman classical authors, of Philo and Josephus, and of the Christian Fathers.

Christology comes to the fore on Dan 2:45, the stone cut by no human hand; on 3:91 (Vg), the fourth figure in the furnace; on 7:8, the little horn; and on 7:13f, the one like a son of man. Dan 9:24 (Vg: *et impleatur visio et propheta*) occasioned a listing of Old Testament passages sketching the messianic coming, life, death, and resurrection of Jesus. Perera is concerned with chronology, e.g., in his 40-page excursus on the "seventy weeks" of Dan 9:24. He also expounded extensively the canticle of the three young men (3:26–45 Vg) as the exultant praise of those who find God in his creatures, with a concluding reference to the Church's liturgical adaptation of the conclusion of the canticle.

Perera gave three lecture-courses on Genesis, leading to his four-volume commentary (printed 8 times, 1591–1622). Perera accepts additions of phrases long after Moses by editors shaping a better ordered text. Textual differences between the Hebrew and the Vulgate are mentioned only rarely. The literal sense of narratives holds primacy of place, which Perera vindicates against Philo, Augustine, and Cajetan on the six-day sequence of creation and against Cajetan on the creation of Eve from Adam's rib. Occasional offerings of allegorical and tropological applications are relatively short, after elucidation of the history. Previous commentators are massively present throughout the commentary, often in generous citations taken not only from the Christian Fathers but also medieval authors such as Bernard of Clairvaux, Hugh of St. Victor, Bonaventure and Aquinas, along with more recent authors like Cajetan, Catharinus, and A. Masius.

Because so many learned predecessors have treated Genesis, Perera cautions against stubbornly holding to a personal interpretation. But he also adds a point cited by Galileo, namely, that regarding the cosmos one should not assert as biblical doctrine any view contrary to the evidence of the human sciences.[150] Perera's doctrinal concerns led to a refutation of astrology (on Gen 1:14), based on human free choice.[151] He treated expansively how all humans bear God's image and likeness (Gen 1:27) both in intelligence and freedom and in their dominion over other creatures. Little space is devoted to refuting Reformation positions, with an exception on pervasive human sin (Gen

---

on Psalms, Jonah, the Gospels, Mary Magdalene, and the Passion of Jesus. In published New Testament works, Perera expounded John, Romans, and Revelation.

[150] R. Fabris, Galileo Galilei e gli orientamenti esegetici del suo tempo (1986), 29–33. R. J. BLACKWELL, *Galileo, Bellarmine, and the Bible* (Notre Dame, IN: Univ. of Notre Dame Press 1991) 20–22.

[151] Contemporary with vol. 1 on Genesis was *Adversus fallaces et superstitiosas artes, id est, De magia, de observatione somniorum, de divininatione astrologica libri III* (Ingolstadt 1591).

6:5). Perera turns often to positive issues, like the geography of Paradise and its rivers, the wood and shape of Noah's ark, and the chronology resulting from the genealogies of Genesis 5 and 10.[152]

Commenting on Exodus, Perera expounded chapters 1–15, in 137 studies of terms and events needing explanation. Only twenty of these move on from the literal sense to end with a "mystical" application to the Church or the believer, usually by citing Augustine, Gregory of Nyssa, or the monastic theologian Rupert of Deutz.

5.6. Robert Bellarmine

Sources: *Institutiones Linguae hebraicae* (Rome: Zanetti 1578); *De Verbo Dei scripto et non scripto* (Prima controversia generalis), in: *Disputationes de controversiis Christianae Fidei* 1 (Ingolstadt: D. Sartroius 1586), in: *Opera omnia* 1–12 (Paris: Vivès 1870–1876) 1, 67–213; *In omnes Psalmos dilucida explanatio* (Rome: B. Zanetti 1611), critical edition, *Explanatio in Psalmos* 1–2 (ed. R. Glados; Rome: Pont. Universitas Gregoriana 1931–32).

Bibliographies: Sommervogel, Bibliothèque de la Compagnie de Jésus, 1, 1151–1254; 8, 1797–1807; A. MANCIA, "Bibliografia sistematica e commentata degli studi sull'opera bellarminiana dal 1900 al 1990", in: *Roberto Bellarmino Archivescovo di Capua* 1–2 (Capua: Archidiocesi e Istituto di scienze religiose 1990) 2, 805–72.

Studies: R. J. BLACKWELL, *Galileo, Bellarmine, and the Bible* (Notre Dame, IN: Univ. of Notre Dame Press 1991); J. BRODRICK, *Robert Bellarmine, Saint and Scholar* (Westminster, MD: Newman 1961); P. FRAENKEL, "Le débat entre Martin Chemnitz et Robert Bellarmine sur les livres deutéro-canoniques et la place du Siracide", *Le canon de l'Ancient Testament* (ed. J.-D. Kaestli / O. Wermelinger; Genève: Labor et Fides 1984) 283–312; G. GALEOTA, "Bellarmini, Roberto", TRE 5 (1980) 525–31; idem, "Bellarmino, Roberto", Diccionario historico de la Compagñia de Jésus 1 (2001) 387–90; J. R. GEISELMANN, *Die heilige Schrift und die Tradition* (Freiburg: Herder 1962) 184–221; R. W. RICHTIGELS, "The Pattern of Controversy in a Counter-Reformation Classic: the *Controversies* of Robert Bellarmine", *Sixteenth Century Journal* 11 (1980) 3–15.

Robert Bellarmine (1542–1621), born in Montepulciano in Tuscany, became a Jesuit in 1560. After studies in Rome and Padua, he went to Louvain for preaching and teaching on the *Summa* of Aquinas (1569–1576). Pope Gregory XIII had him called to Rome to teach controversial theology at the Collegio Romano (1576–1587), from which came his *De controversiis*, the standard Catholic defense of doctrines disputed by the Reformation. The popes drew Bellarmine into service as doctrinal advisor and Cardinal (1599). His writings included the preface to the Clementine Vulgate of 1592, a catalogue of ecclesiastical authors, various defenses, e.g., of the Jubilee indulgence of 1600 and Pope Paul V's 1606 interdict against Venice, works against King James I of Britain over the divine origin of royal authority, an often translated catechism, a Psalms commentary, and works of spiritual edification, e.g., on knowing God through creatures and the "art of dying well".

Bellarmine taught himself Hebrew and drew on this experience in his *Institutiones* (1578) to help others. Editions after 1580 add a grammatical exercise on Psalm 34 and some after 1585 have a Hebrew-Latin dictionary. Not a Hebraist of high caliber, Bellarmine's pedagogy led to his self-help manual seeing twenty printings during his lifetime. The *Controversies*, first published 1586–90, treat fifteen topics beginning with Scripture and moving through ecclesiology, the papacy, councils, and the sacraments to the human person as fallen

---

[152] Gen 1:16f, on the stars, occasioned a reference to C. Clavius, a principal architect of the calendar reform of 1582, suggesting a source of Perera's interest in chronology.

but restored to life in grace.[153] Bellarmine gives over 7100 references to and citations of his adversaries, with the chapters on the Catholic canon of Scripture
responding to Calvin, M. Chemnitz (the *Examen* of Trent's canon-decree),
the Magdeburg *Centuries*, and the biblical prefaces of Luther and Zwingli.

Bellarmine knows of early doubts over the standing of the deuterocanonical
books, but he argues for the legitimacy of the resolution by late fourth-century
councils. This resembled the earlier gradual specification of the New Testament canon and rested on good testimonies, on the coherence of these books
with undoubted Scripture, and on the *sensus* or *gustus* of the Christian people.
Bellarmine clarifies the accuracy of the Bible in Hebrew (substantially incor-
rupt) and the Septuagint (corrupt in places, since different from the Hebrew).
He wards off objections to the Vulgate by arguing from its service over 1000
years as the basis of preaching and teaching the faith, from the respect shown
it from Augustine through the medieval doctors, and from it being the Bible of
the Latin Church centered in the See of Peter. On thirteen Old Testament Vulgate passages charged by Chemnitz as misleading, Bellarmine offers linguistic-
theological rebuttals and then defends thirteen passages of the Latin Psalter
against Calvin's charges of inaccuracy.[154]

The issue of normative interpretation is central to Bellarmine's biblical controversy.[155] Scripture is not sufficiently clear in itself to "terminate" controversies over teaching. Bellarmine omits mention of the Church Fathers as interpretive guides, but argues at length for there being a public "judge of controversies" endowed with the same Spirit that inspired the Bible, so as to make
this judge normative in resolving disputes over biblical doctrine. The Spirit
may well be given to individuals but it is certainly present in a Council of
bishops confirmed by the Pope. For this Bellarmine marshals arguments beginning with a foreshadowing in Israel, in Moses' and the priests' solving of cases
(Exodus 18, Deuteronomy 17), and finding support in the New Testament in
the office of Peter and the Apostles. Each century shows the established custom of seeking an ecclesial resolution of disputes, as do texts from early popes
and fifteen Fathers of the Church. Rational arguments give support and then
seventeen objections, mainly from texts on interior divine instruction, are
shown not to undercut the existence in the Church of a teaching office empow-
ered to settle controversies over the meaning of Scripture.

Bellarmine composed his Psalter commentary in snatches of free time after
becoming Cardinal.[156] He regularly compares his Vulgate text with the Hebrew and Septuagint. Textual work raised Bellarmine's esteem for the Greek
version as a witness to the Hebrew text before it was pointed by the Rabbis.
Patristic authors clarify questions raised by variants and Augustine at times
justifies a christological reading. David's historical vicissitudes serve interpre-

---

[153] Sommervogel, Bibliothèque, 1, 1156–80; 8, 1797–98, lists full and partial printings, along
with the responses of Protestant anti-bellarminists to the *De controversiis*.

[154] *De Verbo Dei*, II, 12–13; *Opera omnia 1* (1870) 143–50.

[155] *De Verbo Dei*, III; *Opera omnia 1* (1870) 167–93.

[156] The 1931–32 edition lists thirty-one printings by 1776 and six more in the nineteenth century. The English translation (Dublin 1866) omits Bellarmine's detailed textual clarifications.

tation but more important is his being a type of the Messiah. For the Spirit who inspired David the Prophet, the principal intent is to set forth Christ and the Church. Reformation controversy is all but absent from this commentary. Bellarmine shows no concern with reform of the Church, as he instructs on sin and repentance, patience amid trials, and trust in God, all within the economy culminating in the Messiah, his Church, and his graced members.

Late in life, Bellarmine conveyed to Galileo the 1616 Holy Office censure of works on Copernican heliocentrism.[157] The year before, he assessed the new cosmology, responding to P. A. Foscarini's efforts to reconcile it with Scripture.[158] For Bellarmine, the new view was not proven and it is contrary to the Church Fathers' interpretation of Scripture (Genesis, Psalms, Qoheleth, Joshua). The topic itself is not a matter of faith but still the inspired word taken literally seems to resolve it. A demonstration of the earth's movement is for Bellarmine highly unlikely but if once given, it would call forth new biblical interpretation and admission of our imperfect understanding to date of the relevant texts.

Bellarmine's strict Thomist criteria of proof joined a patristic consensus, here serving as "judge of controversies", to prevail over possibilities opened by B. Perera's principles and Galileo's argument from Augustine and Thomas on the common-sense discourse of the Bible for human salvation. Bellarmine's verdict attests to a Catholic commitment to the Bible as an all-embracing source of knowledge, which for a time obscured the role of evidence and reasoned argument in reading nature, the "other book" of God's revelation.

---

[157] See Ch. 27, below.

[158] Letter of 12 April 1615; *Le Opere di Galileo Galilei* (ed. A. Favero; Florence: Barbera 1890–1909), 12, 171f; in English in: M. A. FINOCCHIARO, *The Galileo Affair. A Documentary History* (Berkeley, CA: Univ. of California Press 1989) 67f. See R. J. Blackwell, Galileo, Bellarmine, and the Bible (1991) 104–07, and R. FELDHAY, *Galileo and the Church. Political Inquisition or Critical Dialogue* (Cambridge: Cambridge UP 1995) 232–39. Blackwell relates how Galileo and Foscarini appealed to B. Perera on not reading Scripture as contrary to scientific conclusions.

CHAPTER TWENTY-SIX

The Educational System during the Confessional Age

By ULRICH KÖPF, Tübingen

Sources: Sacrorum conciliorum nova et amplissima collectio 1–53 (ed. J. D. Mansi; Firenze 1759–1827; quoted: Mansi); *Enchiridion symbolorum, definitionum et declarationum de rebus fidei et morum* (ed. H. Denzinger / A. Schönmetzer; Barcelona / Freiburg im Br. / Roma [36]1976; quoted: DS); *Conciliorum Oecumenicorum Decreta* (ed. J. Alberigo e.a.; Bologna [3]1983; quoted: COD); *Urkundenbuch der Universität Wittenberg* 1 *[1502–1611]* (ed. W. Friedensburg; Geschichtsquellen der Provinz Sachsen und des Freistaates Anhalt NS 3; Magdeburg 1926; quoted: Urk. 1).

General literature (in chronological order): M. H. CURTIS, *Oxford and Cambridge in Transition 1558–1642* (Oxford 1959); *Los monjes y los estudios. IV Semana de estudios monasticos Poblet 1961* (Poblet 1963); H. KEARNEY, *Scholars and Gentlemen. Universities and Society in Pre-Industrial Britain 1500–1700* (London 1970); *Universität und Gelehrtenstand 1400–1800* (ed. H. Rössler / G. Franz; Deutsche Führungsschichten in der Neuzeit 4; Limburg / Lahn 1970); *Stadt und Universität im Mittelalter und in der frühen Neuzeit* (ed. E. Maschke / J. Sydow; Stadt in der Geschichte 3; Sigmaringen 1977); *Beiträge zu Problemen deutscher Universitätsgründungen der frühen Neuzeit* (ed. P. Baumgart / N. Hammerstein; Wolfenbütteler Forschungen 4; Nendeln 1978); *Università, Accademie e Società scientifiche in Italia e in Germania dal Cinquecento al Settecento* (ed. L. Boehm / E. Raimondi; Annali dell'Istituto storico italo-germanico Quaderno 9; Bologna 1981); *Histoire des Universités en France* (ed. J. Verger; Toulouse 1986); *The History of the University of Oxford* (Gen. ed. T. H. Aston), III. *The Collegiate University* (ed. J. McConica; Oxford 1986), IV. *Seventeenth-Century Oxford* (ed. N. Tyacke; Oxford 1997); *Handbuch der Geschichte des Bayerischen Bildungswesens* 1. *Geschichte der Schule in Bayern. Von den Anfängen bis 1800* (ed. M. Liedtke; Bad Heilbrunn/Obb. 1991); R. STICHWEH, *Der frühmoderne Staat und die europäische Universität* (Frankfurt/M. 1991); *Stadt und Universität* (ed. H. Duchhardt; Städteforschung A/33; Köln e.a. 1993); A. SCHINDLING, *Bildung und Wissenschaft in der frühen Neuzeit* (Enzyklopädie deutscher Geschichte 30; München 1994); *Universität und Aufklärung* (ed. N. Hammerstein; Das achtzehnte Jahrhundert. Supplementa 3; Göttingen 1995); *Handbuch der deutschen Bildungsgeschichte*, 1. *15. bis 17. Jahrhundert* (ed. N. Hammerstein; München 1996); V. MORGAN / C. BROOKE, *A History of the University of Cambridge* II. *1546–1750* (Cambridge 2004).

Special abbreviations (see above):
COD = *Conciliorum Oecumenicorum Decreta*
DS = *Enchiridion symbolorum* etc. (ed. H. Denzinger e.a.)
Mansi = *Sacrorum conciliorum nova et amplissima collectio* 1–53 (ed. J. D. Mansi)
Urk. 1 = *Urkundenbuch der Universität Wittenberg* 1 (1502–1611)

1. The Importance of the Confessional Age for the Educational System

The result of the Reformation was not, as the Reformers had intended, a uniform, reformed Church at least in the occident, but an additional and definitive splitting of the western Christian world in a plurality of Churches each with its own confessional character. In this break up late mediaeval trends of

national Churches also took effect. But far beyond this effect a religious pluralism emerged dominating the whole of modern Christianity. Thus the influence of the old Church dependent on Rome was very much restricted. The
Catholic (i.e., the "Common") Church, which hitherto had dominated the
whole of western Christianity, now became the particular Roman Catholic
Church. In the non-European mission territories (especially in Latin America)
it gained a substantial strengthening. Among the newly grown Protestant
Churches in the German Empire first the Lutherans (i.e., the adherents of the
Confessio Augustana) were acknowledged besides the Roman Catholic Church
by imperial law in the Augsburg Religious Peace of 1555.[1] The "Reformed"
Churches spread from Switzerland and after 1555 took root in territories and
cities of the Empire in a process today called the "Second Reformation" by Reformation scholars.[2] They received an acknowledgement in imperial laws not
before the Westphalian Peace of 1648. The English National Church (Anglican Church) was separated from Rome by Henry VIII in 1534, but developed
only in the course of more than hundred years into a true Protestant Church.
Whilst Calvinist ideas on the one hand spread across France and the Netherlands as far as Scotland (1560 Reformed state Church), on the other hand in
Eastern Middle Europe and Eastern Europe, Lutheran state churches were
formed in the countries around the Baltic Sea (1525 Prussia; 1536 Denmark,
Norway; 1544 Sweden). In homogeneous Protestant Churches anabaptists
and other Protestant dissidents were prosecuted and banished. They managed
to survive at first in territories with mixed confessions and later on emigrated
especially to North America.

The religious splitting of Western Christianity was effected chiefly by confessionalization.[3] This started with the formation of confessions, which began
not later than at the Augsburg Reichstag in 1530 (formulation of Protestant
confessions: *Confessio Augustana, Confessio Tetrapolitana*, Zwingli's *Fidei ratio*) and ended in a penetration of the whole social and cultural life by a confessional character. In the area under the influence of the Wittenberg Reformation Martin Luther, already in his lifetime, had become an ecclesiastical and
theological authority. After long controversies about his legacy, in 1577 the
Formula concordiae was worked out as the definitive confession of the Lutherans. In 1580 it was united together with the *Confessio Augustana* and other
texts in the *Liber Concordiae*.[4] The Reformed Churches, in contrast, produced
many different confessions, among them some consensus papers, too, but only

---

[1] Text in: *Reformationszeit 1495–1555* (ed. U. Köpf; Deutsche Geschichte in Quellen und Darstellung 3; Stuttgart 2001) 471–87.
[2] *Die reformierte Konfessionalisierung in Deutschland – Das Problem der "Zweiten Reformation"*
(ed. H. Schilling; SVRG 195; Gütersloh 1986).
[3] *Die lutherische Konfessionalisierung in Deutschland* (ed. H.-C. Rublack; SVRG 197; Gütersloh
1992); *Die katholische Konfessionalisierung* (ed. W. Reinhard / H. Schilling; SVRG 198; Gütersloh
1995); *Interkonfessionalität – Transkonfessionalität – binnenkonfessionelle Pluralität. Neue Forschungen zur Konfessionalisierungsthese* (ed. K. von Greyerz / M. Jakubowski-Tiessen / T. Kaufmann /
H. Lehmann; SVRG 201; Gütersloh 2003).
[4] *Bekenntnisschriften der evangelisch-lutherischen Kirche* (ed. Deutscher Evangelischer
Kirchenausschuß; Göttingen 1930 [12]1999).

of a limited validity. The formation of Reformed confessions never was entirely completed.[5]

The Roman Catholic Church responded to the reforming claims, that had grown over decades, and to the challenge of the Protestant Reformation by the Council of Trent (1545–63).[6] With its decrees on *peccatum originale*,[7] justification[8] and the seven sacraments[9] it completed the doctrinal development of the Middle Ages on these fields with a tendency that was decidedly anti-reforming. For Catholic exegesis a set of decisions directed against the principle *sola scriptura* and the humanistic-reforming demand for a return to Holy Scripture in its original form, became fundamental: the decisions to acknowledge the ecclesiastical tradition in addition to the Scripture as an equivalent source, and to declare that the Old Testament, including the Apocrypha, is canonical and that the Latin translation of the Vulgate is the obligatory version of the Bible.[10] The *Professio fidei Tridentinae*, published by Paul IV on 13 November 1564, summarizes the most important doctrines in an oath, that had to be taken by every clergyman.[11]

The entire educational system was confessionally influenced in a very distinct way. The institutions of education from the elementary school to the universities were penetrated by the confessional characteristics of their governing political entities (territories and, in the German Empire, also imperial cities), and its staff were obliged to profess the confessions that in addition to the Holy Scripture had become doctrinal authorities. Moreover, in the age of confessionalism erudition and education were influenced by the differences of the confessions. Only Enlightenment and Pietism mitigated this contrast, although they did not yet do away with the confessional shaping of the educational system. For Roman Catholicism the decrees of the Tridentinum have remained permanently valid.

2. Reformation of Education in Roman Catholicism

2.1. The Reforming Work of the Council of Trent[12]

One of the greatest grievances in the mediaeval Church had been the lack of education of the clergy, which had often been deplored, but never been eliminated.[13] For the first time the Reformation fought successfully against this de-

---

[5] *Bekenntnisschriften der reformierten Kirche* (ed. E. F. K. Müller; Leipzig 1903).
[6] H. Jedin, *Geschichte des Konzils von Trient* 1–4 (Freiburg/Br. 1950–75; 1, ³1977).
[7] COD 665–67.
[8] COD 671–81.
[9] COD 684–86, 693–98, 703–13, 726–28, 732–37, 741–44, 753–59.
[10] COD 663–65.
[11] DS 425–427 (no. 1862–1870).
[12] J. A. O'Donahue, *Tridentine Seminary Legislation. Its Sources and Its Formation* (BETL 9; Louvain 1957); H. Tüchle, "Das Seminardekret des Trienter Konzils und Formen seiner geschichtlichen Verwirklichung", *TQ* 144 (1964) 12–30; K. M. Comerford, "Italian Tridentine Diocesan Seminaries: A Historiographical Study", *SCJ* 29 (1998) 999–1022.

fect. From its beginning it created a growing number of humanistically educated clergymen. Their model was a challenge to the reforming aspirations in the Catholic Church; but for a long time most attempts for a general improvement in clerical education remained fruitless. Only the Council of Trent gave the basis for a remedy.

At the fifth session of 17 June 1546 a decree *super lectione et praedicatione* was ratified. Resuming a demand of the *Lateranum* IV (1215)[14] it was decided, that prebendaries or holders of another *stipendium pro lectoribus sacrae scripturae* should be obliged to explain Scripture – if necessary, the explanation was to be done by a qualified substitute. Where such prebends were missing, they should be established. Churches with small revenues should engage at least one teacher of grammar, who had to prepare the clergy and other pupils for the study of the Bible. All prelates were obliged to preach about the Gospel.[15] But newly repeated reforming efforts later on showed that these claims had for a long time remained unfulfilled. First successes in creating new institutions of education were achieved by the *Societas Iesu* in establishing *Collegia* (see 2.2). At a London synod in 1556 Cardinal Reginald Pole (1500–58), Archbishop of Canterbury during the reign of Queen Mary since 1556, ordered that episcopal seminaries for boys ought to be established in order to prepare for a clerical career.[16] The Council resumed the subject, however, only much later and on 15 July 1563 published among the reform decrees in addition to the doctrine of the *sacramentum ordinis* one decree on the education of future clergymen.[17] It demanded that each episcopal church was to establish a college, which was to be a *seminarium* ('nursery garden', in German: *Pflanzschule*) for the clergy.[18] To enforce clerical discipline its pupils had to wear the tonsure from the beginning; the Holy Scripture had to be one of the main subjects of learning.[19] These colleges were simply ecclesiastical institutions; universities were not mentioned in this decree.[20]

2.2. The Jesuit Order

Sources: Ratio Studiorum et Institutiones Scholasticae Societatis Jesu Tom. 1. *Ab anno 1541 ad annum 1599*; 2. *Ratio studiorum ann. 1586. 1599. 1832* (ed. G. M. Pachtler; Monumenta Germaniae Paedagogica 2, 5; Berlin 1887; quoted: Pachtler 1, 2); *Ratio atque Institutio Studiorum Societatis Iesu (1586 1591 1599)* (ed. L. Lukács; Monumenta Paedagogica Societatis Iesu. Nova editio penitus retractata 5 = Monumenta Historica Societatis Iesu 129; Roma 1986; quoted: Lukács); *Ratio Studiorum. Édition bilingue latin-français* (ed. A. Demoustier e.a.; Paris 1997).

---

[13] F. W. Oediger, *Über die Bildung der Geistlichen im späten Mittelalter* (STGMA 2; Leiden / Köln 1953).

[14] Constitutio 11 (COD 240).

[15] COD 667–70.

[16] Decretum 11 (Mansi 33, 1029–1031); cf. Pole to Cardinal Morone, in: *Calendar of State Papers. Venetian Series* 6,1 (ed. R. Brown; London 1894) 347–50.

[17] Canon 18 *Cum adolescentium aetas* (COD 750–53).

[18] Ibid. 751,2f: *ita ut hoc collegium Dei ministrorum perpetuum seminarium sit.*

[19] Ibid. 751,3–9.

[20] The fact, that this did not express an aversion towards universities, is especially stressed by S. Merkle, *Das Konzil von Trient und die Universitäten* (Würzburg 1905).

Studies: A. P. FARRELL, *The Jesuit Code of Liberal Education* (Milwaukee 1938); G. CODINA MIR, *Aux sources de la pédagogie des Jésuites. Le "modus Parisiensis"* (Bibliotheca Instituti Historici S.I. 28; Roma 1968); *Les Jésuites à la Renaissance. Système éducatif et production du savoir* (ed. L. Giard; Paris 1993); *I Gesuiti e la Ratio Studiorum* (ed. M. Hinz e.a.; Europa delle Corti. Centro studi sulle società di antico regime. Biblioteca del Cinquecento 113; Roma 2004).

Special abbreviations (see above):
Lukács = *Ratio atque Institutio Studiorum Societatis Iesu* (ed. L. Lukács)
Pachtler = *Ratio Studiorum et Institutiones Scholasticae Societatis Jesu* (ed. G. M. Pachtler)

The most important part in the renewal of Roman Catholic education matters after the Reformation was played by the *Societas Iesu*, which was founded by Ignatius of Loyola (1491–1556) and approved of as an order in 1540 by Pope Paul III. It was a community of regular clergymen, who were destined for preaching and ministry, mission and education, and soon also became engaged in fighting against the Protestant heretics.[21] From the very beginning studies and education were a part of their duties. "The Jesuits were the first religious order in the Catholic Church to undertake formal education as a major ministry. They became a 'teaching order'."[22] Soon after their arrival at Rome in 1537 Diego Laínez and Pierre Favre had taught theology at the university, and rapidly the teaching work of the Jesuits extended to other countries. For students of the order early on *collegia* were founded – at first as mere dormitories without formal connection with the university. About 1544 there were already seven such colleges at the universities of Paris, Louvain, Cologne, Padua, Alcalá, Valencia and – the largest, because it was promoted by the king of Portugal – Coimbra.[23] Inevitably the *collegia* soon became places of study, which within a short time were opened to external students, too. In 1548 at the request of the city at Messina a first open *collegium* was established, in 1549 another in Palermo, and subsequently many more in other cities. In 1551 the *Collegium Romanum* as the central institution for studies in the order was opened together with a domicile. In 1552 the *Collegium Germanicum* as hostel for students from Germany and Northern and Eastern Europe followed.[24] For the archdiocese of Rome Pope Pius IV already in 1564, one year after the Trent seminary decree, had established the *Seminarium Romanum*. Since 1573 the *Germanicum* became a model for other national *collegia* at Rome. Besides, the Jesuits in all Roman-Catholic countries founded many schools and colleges, some of them later on being turned into universities by the granting of privileges, others integrated into universities. Moreover, the Jesuits took over existing universities.[25]

---

[21] J. W. O'MALLEY, *The First Jesuits* (Cambridge, MA / London 1993).
[22] Ibid. 15.
[23] Ibid. 202.
[24] A. STEINHUBER, *Geschichte des Kollegium Germanikum et Hungarikum in Rom* I-II (Freiburg/ Br. ²1906); P. SCHMIDT, *Das Collegium Germanicum in Rom und die Germaniker: Zur Funktion eines römischen Ausländerseminars (1552–1914)* (Bibliothek des Deutschen Historischen Instituts in Rom 56; Tübingen 1984).
[25] An exemplary study for Germany: K. HENGST, *Jesuiten an Universitäten und Jesuitenuniversitäten. Zur Geschichte der Universitäten in der Oberdeutschen und Rheinischen Provinz der Gesellschaft Jesu im Zeitalter der konfessionellen Auseinandersetzung* (Quellen und Forschungen aus dem Gebiet der Geschichte, NF 2; Paderborn e.a. 1981).

The *Societas Iesu*, however, was not only effective by its institutions of education, but just as much by the way, in which it gave life to these institutions. Already in the *Constitutiones* drafted between 1540 and 1550 Ignatius had inserted sketchy regulations for the education of the members of the order.[26] In the practice of their teaching the Jesuits soon understood the necessity of a detailed curriculum. Since the fifties of the sixteenth century they made efforts to create their own school regulations.[27] The completion of a comprehensive schedule of studies *(Ratio studiorum)* took a long time from the first draft, which was sent to the provinces by General Claudius Aquaviva in 1586, but was not initially successful,[28] until the fully developed version from 1599 was accepted by the order.[29] The curriculum, which focused on theology, was composed of three levels. The lowest level, the *Gymnasium*, comprised five classes: three classes of grammar *(infima – media – suprema classis)*, leading from the basics to the full knowledge of Latin and Greek, were followed by the *Classis humanitatis*, which consisted of an introduction to literature, and the *Classis Rhetoricae*, which provided the training for a perfect active mastering of languages *(eloquentia)*.[30] The middle level of the programme offered the study of philosophy (according to Aristotle) for at least three years: in the first year logic, theory of science and the principles of natural science, in the second year physics and other parts of natural sciences, in the third year most of all psychology and metaphysics.[31] In addition, particular professors taught in the second class mathematics[32] and in the third class moral philosophy.[33] The educational accomplishment was reached by a quadrennial study of theology, which consisted of two parallel branches: the study of scholastic theology according to the doctrine of Thomas Aquinas (i.e., based on his *Summa theologiae)*[34] and the study of Holy Scripture based on the Vulgate, but consulting the original Hebrew and Greek text.[35] A special professor was appointed for Hebrew; he had to connect teaching the language with explaining the Old Testament.[36] Besides, professors of the Bible as well as those of scholastic theology were ordered to enter into controversies with heretics *(controversiae)* and in moral questions *(casus conscientiae)* only so far as necessary.[37] Already in the first draft of the *Ratio studiorum* from 1586 we find lectures on controversialist theology for the *ultramontanes* and on casuistry.[38] The arrangement of 1599 contains a particular section with directions for the professor of casuis-

---

[26] Constitutionum pars IV: *De iis, qui in Societate retinentur, instruendis in litteris et aliis, quae ad proximos juvandos conferunt*, in: Pachtler 1, 8–69.
[27] Cf. the drafts in: Pachtler 1, 152–54; 155–72.
[28] Pachtler 2, 25–222; Lukács 1–162.
[29] Ratio atque Institutio Studiorum Societatis Iesu: Pachtler 2, 234–481; Lukács 355–454.
[30] Pachtler 2, 378–448; Lukács 416–42.
[31] Pachtler 2, 328–50; Lukács 397–402.
[32] Pachtler 2, 256; 348–50; Lukács 362; 402.
[33] Pachtler 2, 344–46; Lukács 401f.
[34] Pachtler 2, 300–19; Lukács 366–94.
[35] Pachtler 2, 294–98; Lukács 383–85.
[36] Pachtler 2, 298–300; Lukács 385.
[37] Pachtler 2, 298 no. 16; 306 no. 9 §§ 2, 4; Lukács 384 no. 16; 387f no. 9 §§ 2, 4.
[38] Pachtler 2, 115–18; 118–24; Lukács 85–88; 88–93.

try.[39] Because the Jesuits opened their educational establishments to external students, too, in catholic countries they soon obtained an important influence on the whole educational system, which continued until the suspension of the Order by Pope Clemens XIV in 1773.

3. Institutions of Education and Erudition

Under the influence of Humanism and even more of the Reformation the institutions of higher education important for the history of theology in general and for the history of exegesis in particular were multiplied and differentiated. In the area of Roman Catholicism, on the one hand, the mediaeval complete universities with four faculties and full graduation rights remained. In theology apart from old universities like Paris[40] during the sixteenth century two universities with young theological faculties, that had not been impaired by the Reformation, became prominent: Salamanca in Spain, where the theological faculty with four chairs[41] was founded only in 1416 by Pope Benedictus XIII (Pedro de Luna) and reached its summit in the first half of the sixteenth century;[42] and Coimbra, where the university was firmly established in 1537 with at first three theological chairs, but the number of theological staff was extended in the following decades.[43] To the existing institutions new catholic full universities with four faculties and full papal and imperial privileges were added (in the Empire esp. Würzburg 1582 and Innsbruck 1668, first dominated by Jesuits), and completely privileged Jesuit *Collegia*, too, without juridical and medical faculties.[44] In the first German foundation of the Counterreformation, Dillingen, which was privileged by the Emperor in 1553, ten years later the Jesuits prevailed over the original draft of a university with four faculties.[45]

---

[39] Pachtler 2, 322–28; Lukács 395 f.

[40] J. K. Farge, *Orthodoxy and Reform in Early Reformation France. The Faculty of Theology of Paris, 1500–1543* (SMRT 32; Leiden 1985).

[41] Two at the university, one each at the Dominican and the Franciscan monastery.

[42] A. M. Rodríguez Cruz, *Historia de la Universidad de Salamanca* (Salamanca 1990); J. Barrientos García, "La Escuela de Salamanca: desarrollo y caracteres", in: *Semitica, Escurialensia, Augustiniana. Homenaje a Fray Luciano Rubio, OSA* (727–65) = La Ciudad de Dios 208 (1995) 1041–79; F. Domínguez Reboiras, "Die Schule von Salamanca. Eine kritische Ortsbestimmung", in: *Von der Suche nach Gott. Helmut Riedlinger zum 75. Geburtstag* (ed. M. Schmidt / F. Domínguez Reboiras; Mystik in Geschichte und Gegenwart I,15; Stuttgart-Bad Cannstatt 1998) 463–87.

[43] M. A. Rodrigues, *Chronologia Historiae Vniversitatis Conimbrigensis* (Coimbra 1998); idem, *A Cátedra de Sagrada Escritura na Universidade de Coimbra. Primeiro Século (1537–1640)* (Coimbra 1974); idem, *A Cátedra de Sagrada Escritura na Universidade de Coimbra de 1640 a 1910* (Coimbra 1974).

[44] The *Constitutiones* explicitly renounce these two subjects: *Medicinae et Legum studium ut a Nostro Instituto magis remotum, in Universitatibus Societatis vel non tractabitur, vel saltem Societas per se id oneris non suscipiet* (ch. 12 no. 4; Pachtler 1, 54). – For the relation of collegium and university of the Jesuits cf. E. Schubert, "Zur Typologie gegenreformatorischer Universitätsgründungen: Jesuiten in Fulda, Würzburg, Ingolstadt und Dillingen", in: Universität und Gelehrtenstand (1970) 85–105.

[45] L. Boehm, "'Usus Dilingae' – Modell oder Ärgernis? Eine Besinnung auf die Bedeutung der ehemaligen Universität Dillingen als Glückwunsch zum ersten Jubiläum der Universität Augs-

In the area of Protestantism, on the other hand, there were the traditional full universities, which had been won for the Reformation, as well as new Protestant universities and Reformed High Schools, which were not, or were only later on, endowed with graduation rights: after Marburg (above Ch. 16; sect. 4.1) the foundations of sovereigns as Jena (since 1548/58), Helmstedt (1576–1810), Herborn (Reformed, 1584–1817), Gießen (since 1606), Rinteln (1619/20–1809), Duisburg (Reformed, 1655–1818), Kiel (since 1665) and the municipal foundations Strasbourg and Altdorf (above Ch. 16; sect. 5). Frequently a part of the education in the *artes* was withdrawn from the universities and transferred to pre-universitarian schools. By the enlargement and deepening of these disciplines in a humanistic direction these schools became very important for theology, and by learned teachers, at the same time, they turned into important places of theological research and education. The transition between the different institutions often developed in an indistinct and more or less organic way, which becomes obvious by the fact that many schools which originally were founded as an academic *gymnasium* or *collegium* later on became universities, when they were enlarged and received privileges (e. g., Jena,[46] originally founded in 1548 as *Gymnasium academicum* with two chairs for theology and philology, soon enlarged by law and medicine, continued as university since 1558 after having received privileges in 1557 by Emperor Ferdinand I). The name of the institution, however, is only of limited validity concerning its state, since under the influence of Humanism in addition to the ancient terms *universitas, studium generale (universale), universitas studii generalis* and the like, the Greek terms *gymnasium* and *academia* had become usual for full universities, too.[47] On the other hand, the standard of erudition was independent of privileges. Thus, in the Reformed Netherlands Leiden (1575),[48] Groningen (1612)[49] and Utrecht (1634/36)[50] were highly respected full universities with four faculties, but without privileges; their degrees, however, were commonly acknowleged. Moreover, in the different institutions learned professors of philology and theology worked as biblical exegetes.

In the Catholic area during the confessional age the studies of the *religiosi*

---

burg", in: *Probleme der Integration Ostschwabens in den bayerischen Staat. Bayern und Wittelsbach in Ostschwaben* (ed. P. Fried; Augsburger Beiträge zur Landesgeschichte Bayerisch-Schwabens 2; Sigmaringen 1982) 245–67.

[46] K. HEUSSI, *Geschichte der Theologischen Fakultät zu Jena* (Darstellungen zur Geschichte der Universität Jena 1; Weimar 1954); E. MASCHKE, *Universität Jena* (Mitteldeutsche Hochschulen 6; Köln / Graz 1969); *Dokumente zur Frühgeschichte der Universität Jena 1548 bis 1558* (ed. J. Bauer e.a.; Quellen und Beiträge zur Geschichte der Universität Jena 3,1; Weimar / Jena 2003).

[47] Cf. the decree of foundation by Maximilian I for Wittenberg university dating from 1502 (Urk. 1 [1926] 1f): *ut [...] studium generale sive universitatem aut gymnasium in civitate Wittenberg [...] institueremus;* and others. In the *Rotulus doctorum* the terms *academia Vitembergensis* and *gymnasium nostrum* appear equivalently (ibid. 14), in the statutes of 1508 the expression *Gymnasium nostrum litteratorium* at the side of *universitas nostra Vittenburgensis* and similar terms (ibid. 18, 20).

[48] H. L. CLOTZ, *Hochschule für Holland. Die Universität Leiden im Spannungsfeld zwischen Provinz, Stadt und Kirche, 1575–1619* (Contubernium 48; Stuttgart 1998).

[49] *Gedenkboek ter gelegenheit van het 350-jarig bestaan der Rijks-Universiteit te Groningen* (ed. E. Visser; Universitas Groningana MCMXIV-MCMLXIV, 1; Groningen 1964).

[50] H. JAMIN, *Kennis als opdracht: De Universiteit Utrecht 1636–2001* (Utrecht 2001).

were also continued undiminished. The Council of Trent had ordered that the ancient monasteries and the houses of the other *religiosi* were to take care of the *lectio sacrae scripturae* as much as possible.[51] For clergymen among the *religiosi* higher education had become obligatory, in any case, since the Council. Moreover, now to an increasing extent new communities of men and especially of women emerged, who devoted themselves to education and therefore needed a particular training,[52] at first the Order of Saint Ursula, founded by Angela Merici (c. 1470–1540) in 1535,[53] or the Institute of the Blessed Virgin Mary (in German: *Englische Fräulein*), founded by Mary Ward (1585–1645).[54] The mendicants continuously pursued theological studies in their *studia generalia* and *particularia*. At the same time, studies powerfully revived within the Benedictine monasticism – competing with the Jesuits as well.[55] In 1563 the Council of Trent had ordered, by recourse to Lateranum IV, that all exempt monasteries had to unite into *congregationes*.[56] As a result of this direction, a number of Benedictine congregations were formed, some of which also became important in the field of learning. The most outstanding was the French congregation of the Maurists, existing since 1618 and named for St. Maurus, which after a slow decline since about 1750 perished due to the French Revolution.[57] In its six provinces this congregation created houses for studies with chairs for Greek and Hebrew. Part of its extensive philological, editorial and historical studies were biblical studies, too (especially Bernard de Montfaucon, 1655–1741, and Pierre Sabatier, 1682–1742).[58] For the German speaking monasteries the Benedictine University of Salzburg became fundamental; it had developed from a gymnasium founded in 1617 *(Institutum litterarium Salisburgense)*, was opened in 1622 with theological and philosophical faculties and enlarged in 1624 by canon law and in 1652 by a faculty of law.[59] In addi-

---

[51] Sessio V (1546), Decretum 2, § 4 f. (COD 668,35–41).

[52] *Les religieuses enseignantes: XVI-XX siècles* (Actes de la quatrième rencontre d'histoire religieuse; Angers 1981).

[53] A. CONRAD, *Mit Klugheit, Mut und Zuversicht. Angela Merici und die Ursulinen* (Mainz ²2003).

[54] H. PETERS, *Mary Ward. Ihre Persönlichkeit und ihr Institut* (Innsbruck / Wien 1991).

[55] For monks in general cf. Los monjes (1963); for Benedictines cf. D. JULIA, "Les Bénédictins et l'enseignement aux XVIIe et XVIIIe siècles", in: *Sous la règle de Saint Benoît. Structures monastiques et sociétés en France du moyen âge à l'époque moderne* (Centre de Recherches d'histoire et de philologie V. Hautes études médiévales et modernes 47; Genève 1982; 345–400).

[56] Sessio XXV *Decretum de regularibus et monialibus* c. 8 (COD 779).

[57] D. KNOWLES, "The Maurists", in: idem, *Great Historical Enterprises. Problems in Monastic History* (London e.a. 1963) 33–62; F. VANDENBROUCKE, "L'esprit des études dans la Congrégation de Saint-Maur", in: Los monjes (1963) 457–501; P.GASNAULT, "Les travaux d'érudition des Mauristes au XVIIIe siècle", in: *Historische Forschung im 18. Jahrhundert* (ed. K. Hammer / J. Voss; Pariser Historische Studien 13; Bonn 1976) 102–21; Y. CHAUSSY, *Les Bénédictins de St-Maur* 1–2 (Paris 1989–91).

[58] B. de Montfaucon, *Hexaplorum Origenis quae supersunt* 1–2 (Paris 1713); P. Sabatier, *Bibliorum sacrorum latinae versiones antiquae seu vetus Italica* 1–3 (Reims 1743–49). *Studies: Bernard Dom de Montfaucon. Actes du Colloque de Carcassonne 1996* (ed. D.-O. Hurel / R. Rosé; Bibliothèque Bénédictine 4; Saint-Wandrille-Rançon 1998).

[59] V. REDLICH, "Die Salzburger Benediktiner-Universität als Kulturerscheinung", in: *Benediktinisches Mönchtum in Österreich* (Wien 1949) 79–97; *Universität Salzburg 1622–1962–1972. Festschrift* (ed. Akademischer Senat der Universität Salzburg; Salzburg 1972).

tion to the university, some Benedictine abbeys developed into centres of learned studies since the seventeenth, especially in the eighteenth century: Göttweig, Melk, Kremsmünster (with notable equipment for natural sciences), St. Blasien and others.[60] To ensure the continuity of their learned enterprises, the single monasteries took care to establish manifold mutual and outward connections. Especially during the eighteenth century they strove to organize their studies into the projects of academies,[61] a fact which must be seen in connection with the great European academy movement.[62]

In this movement which was typical of the seventeenth and eighteenth centuries, the humanistic institution of the Italian academies continued to be active.[63] Furthermore the academy became an alternative to the university and had a certain affinity to the monastic *conventus*. Typical examples for this were the *Accademia della Crusca*, founded at Florence in 1584, which took care of philological and literary studies, and the *Accademia dei Lincei*, established in 1603 at Rome, a community of natural scientists. The idea of the academy was realized in France already during the sixteenth century,[64] in the seventeenth century by German *Sprachgesellschaften* (Language Societies) or by the *Académie Française* (1635), in the historically and archaelogically orientated *Académie des Inscriptions et Belles Lettres* (1661), in the scientifically and medicinally interested *Academia Naturae Curiosorum* (1652, since 1687 Imperial Academy "Leopoldina"), the "Royal Society of London for the Promotion of Natural

---

[60] L. Hammermayer, "Die Forschungszentren der deutschen Benediktiner und ihre Vorhaben", in: *Historische Forschung im 18. Jahrhundert* (ed. K. Hammer / J. Voss; Pariser Historische Studien 13; Bonn 1976) 122–91.

[61] Ibid., esp. 153–64.

[62] L. Hammermayer, "Akademiebewegung und Wissenschaftsorganisation", in: *Wissenschaftspolitik in Mittel- und Osteuropa. Wissenschaftliche Gesellschaften, Akademien und Hochschulen im 18. und beginnenden 19. Jahrhundert* (ed. E. Amburger e.a.; Studien zur Geschichte der Kulturbeziehungen in Mittel- und Osteuropa 3; Berlin 1976) 1–84; *Der Akademiegedanke im 17. und 18. Jahrhundert* (ed. F. Hartmann / R. Vierhaus; Wolfenbütteler Forschungen 3; Bremen / Wolfenbüttel 1977); J. Voss, "Die Akademie als Organisationsträger der Wissenschaften im 18. Jahrhundert", *HZ* 231 (1980) 43–74; *Università, Accademie e Società scientifiche in Italia e in Germania dal Cinquecento al Settecento* (ed. L. Boehm / E. Raimondi; Annali dell'Istituto storico italo-germanico. Quaderno 9; Bologna 1981); J. Voss, "Akademien und Gelehrte Gesellschaften", in: *Aufklärungsgesellschaften* (ed. H. Reinalter; Schriftenreihe der Internationalen Forschungsstelle "Demokratische Bewegungen in Mitteleuropa 1770–1850" 10; Frankfurt/Main e.a. 1993) 19–38; *Europäische Sozietätsbewegung und demokratische Tradition. Die europäischen Akademien der Frühen Neuzeit zwischen Frührenaissance und Spätaufklärung* 1–2 (ed. K. Garber / H. Wismann; Frühe Neuzeit 26–27; Tübingen 1996).

[63] Cf. above Ch. 6, 2.3; moreover, M. Plaisance, "Une première affirmation de la politique culturelle de Côme Ier: la transformation de l'Académie des 'Humidi' en Académie Florentine (1540–1542)", in: A. Rochon e.a., *Les écrivains et le pouvoir en Italie à l'époque de la Renaissance* [1.] (Centre de recherche sur la Renaissance italienne 2; Paris 1973) 361–438; idem, "Culture et politique à Florence de 1542 à 1551: Lasca et les *Humidi* aux prises avec l'Académie Florentine", in: ibid. [2.] (Centre de recherche sur la Renaissance italienne 3; Paris 1974) 149–242; R. S. Samuels, "Benedetto Varchi, the *Accademia degli Infiammati*, and the Origins of the Italian Academic Movement", *Renaissance Quarterly* 29 (1976) 599–633; F. Waquet, "Moderne Gelehrsamkeit und traditionelle Organisation. Die gelehrten Akademien im Italien der Frühaufklärung", in: Europäische Sozietätsbewegung (1996; above n. 52) 1, 271–83.

[64] F. A. Yates, *The French Academies of the Sixteenth Century* (London 1947); Europäische Sozietätsbewegung (1996; above n. 52) 1, 285–509: "III. Das nationale Paradigma: Frankreich".

Knowledge" (1660)[65] and other institutions for research. In the eighteenth century there appeared new academies all over Europe, which propagated the spirit of Enlightenment.

4. Theological Studies

The development of theological erudition in modern times is distinguished by a progressive differentiation of theology into diverse disciplines. The Middle Ages knew only two methods of treating theological subjects: the commenting on traditional texts (especially Bible, Sentences of Peter Lombard) in lectures and the discussion of single problems (*quaestiones*) in the disputation. The collection of topics and its discussion in the Sentence lecture (until the beginning of the fourteenth century in the *Summa*, too) made it possible to present dogmatics and ethics in a systematical arrangement. In Catholic countries since the early sixteenth century the Sentences as a textbook of dogmatics and ethics were gradually replaced by Thomas Aquinas' *Summa theologiae*. At the beginnings of the Wittenberg and Zurich Reformation for some years theological instruction was restricted to the exposition of the Bible. But already in 1521 Melanchthon by his *Loci communes* introduced a new dogmatic and ethical handbook. The lecture about these *Loci* at Lutheran faculties resulted in the discipline "dogmatics". Not until Georg Calixt's *Epitome theologiae moralis* (1634) was a theological ethics as an autonomous theological discipline (besides philosophical ethics) separated from dogmatics. In the curricula of Protestant theological faculties at first the exegesis of Scripture dominated, which was considered as the essence of theology. It was based on the principles of *sola scriptura* and of the inspiration of the Bible, which was regarded as a consistent whole. Already in the statutes dating from the time of the Reformation, however, a distinction was made between the exposition of the Old and New Testaments because of their different languages. Later on the integration of a discipline called *controversiae* into the theological curriculum reinforced the weight of sytematic work; at some faculties during the Confessional Age controversialist theology became the most esteemed theological chair. This discipline was maintained as "Polemics" up to the nineteenth century. As a fourth discipline Church History was introduced into theological teaching at the end of the sixteenth century (first lectures 1583 in Frankfurt/Oder), on a permanent basis not before the middle of the seventeenth century (first chair in Helmstedt in 1650). Until the late eighteenth century, however, in most cases it was only handled pragmatically (i.e., as a mere collection of examples), not as a critical and basic part of theology. Although the peculiar methods of exegetical, systematic and practical studies were recognized increasingly, in the description of theological chairs the diverse tasks of the single disciplines remained connected with one another until the nineteenth century. In addition

---

[65] W. WEISS, "»An Attempt, which all Ages had despair'd of«. Das Selbstverständnis der Royal Society im 17. Jahrhundert", in: Europäische Sozietätsbewegung (1996; above n. 62) 1, 669–88.

to the lecture the disputation was continued, too, as a main form of education.[66]

The differentiating and specializing of theological disciplines was also reflected by the curricula and the literature informing students of convenient studies. Luther and Melanchthon already had given instructions for studying theology, which contained both intellectual work and religious practice.[67] The Reformer's advices inspired a vast Protestant literature on the study of theology. The most important author of such instructions in the transition to the Confessional Age was David Chytraeus (1530–1600), professor in Rostock.[68] Others followed during the seventeenth century; the best known of them is Johann Gerhard (1582–1637).[69] Johann Franz Buddeus (1667–1729) composed a late example of extensive treatment of the study of theology, containing an encyclopedic presentation of the theological disciplines (including the *propaedeumata theologica*).[70]

5. The Ending of the Confessional Age
by Enlightenment and Pietism

The end of the confessional age in the German Empire was brought about by the Westphalian Peace of 1648. This treaty of peace ended the Thirty Years' Confessional War and gave to the Reformed as well as to the Roman Catholics and Lutherans a legitimation by laws of the Empire within the limits of the *ius reformandi* of the sovereigns. True common tolerance did not yet exist; the institutions of education, too, remained obligated to their confessions. But by the end of the confessional struggle the mental and religious climate was changed. Two movements, which were related, although in a different way accentuated, caused deep changes. On the one hand, a movement of piety spread across the whole of Europe and all confessions and reached from Spanish and French catholic mysticism by way of British Puritanism and the Dutch yearning after *precysheyt* (correctness) to German Pietism. On the other hand, an intellectual movement similarly spread over Europe, which from a broad early modern rationalism (René Descartes and others) led to the Enlightenment.

Enlightenment and Pietism in like manner were interested in the problems

---

[66] Cf., e.g., K. G. Appold, *Orthodoxie als Konsensbildung. Das theologische Disputationswesen an der Universität Wittenberg zwischen 1570 und 1710* (BHTh 127; Tübingen 2004).

[67] R. Mau, "Programme und Praxis des Theologiestudiums im 17. und 18. Jahrhundert", in: Theologische Versuche 11 (1979) 71–91; O. Bayer, "Oratio, Meditation, Tentatio. Eine Besinnung auf Luthers Theologieverständnis", in: LuJ 55 (1988) 7–59; M. Nieden, "Wittenberger Anweisungen zum Theologiestudium", in: *Die Theologische Fakultät Wittenberg 1502 bis 1602* (ed. I. Dingel / G. Wartenberg; Leucorea-Studien 5; Leipzig 2002) 133–53.

[68] T. Kaufmann, *Universität und lutherische Konfessionalisierung. Die Rostocker Theologieprofessoren und ihr Beitrag zur theologischen Bildung und kirchlichen Gestaltung im Herzogtum Mecklenburg zwischen 1550 und 1675* (QFRG 66; Gütersloh 1997) 253–318.

[69] J. Gerhard, *Isagoge historico-theologica ad theologiam universam singulasque eius partes* (Leipzig 1727).

[70] J. F. Buddeus, *Methodus studii theologici / Publicis praelectionibus in Academia Jenensi Anno 1617 exposita* (Jena 1620 e.a.).

of education and developed new theories and methods of study. Both movements refused learning as a mere acknowledgement and reception of doctrines
and demanded personal appropriation and attention to utility. As for the curriculum, both prefered knowledge of the exact and historical sciences to a mere
philological and logical study of texts. But within the context of this common
attitude they differed. The Pietism as a religious movement like the Reformers
and many orthodox theologians, too, stressed the cultivation of piety in the
study of theology.[71] Especially influential were the ideas that Philipp Jacob
Spener (1635–1705) published in his *Pia desideria* (1675)[72] and in his letters
and counsels later on collected.[73] His criticism of the traditional education of
clergymen concerns especially the controversialist theology and the method of
disputation. In his proposals he connects the central exegetical studies with a
personal application of the text to the theologian, intending a practice of puri-
fication and sanctification of life. Spener's ideas were seized and continued by
Hermann August Francke (1663–1727), professor at the university and founder of important social and educational institutions in Halle. On the basis of
his *Collegium paraeneticum*[74] he published several writings on the study of
theology.[75] Despite its predominant practical interests the Pietism has also
merits in the field of learned biblical studies, e.g., by Johann Albrecht Bengel
(1687–1752).

The Enlightenment as a cultural and intellectual movement continued the
tendencies of European humanism. Its pedagogy, indeed, had generally pragmatic aims, and its common ideal was the advancement of morality. But, as its
name expresses, it meant also liberation from obscurity and mental immatur-
ity, i.e., the advancement of independent and critical thinking. Therefore it intended education to a critical attitude in all fields – including the areas of religion with ecclesiastical as well as biblical traditions. The key-word 'free-thinkers' was created about the end of the seventeenth century for English Deists
and picked up by John Toland (1670–1722) and Anthony Collins (1676–
1729).[76] The English Deists in theology started an unprejudiced discussion of
inconsistencies and disagreements within the Bible, some of which had been
observed already by the theologians of the Ancient Church, but had hitherto
not often been openly admitted and discussed.[77] The ideas of Deism were introduced into Germany especially via Hamburg. Here Hermann Samuel Reim-

---

[71] C.-W. KANG, *Frömmigkeit und Gelehrsamkeit. Die Reform des Theologiestudiums im lutherischen Pietismus des 17. und frühen 18. Jahrhunderts* (Kirchengeschichtliche Monographien 7;
Gießen 2001).

[72] Ph. J. Spener, *Pia desideria* (ed. K. Aland; Kleine Texte für Vorlesungen und Übungen 170;
Berlin ³1964).

[73] Ph. J. Spener, *Consilia et judicia theologica latina; Opus posthumum, ex ejusdem litteris Singulari industria ac fide collectum* (Frankfurt/Main 1709), pars 1, 198–303, caput 2, articulus 1: *De studiis academicis*.

[74] Published in A. H. Francke, *Lectiones paraeneticae* (1–7; Halle 1726–36).

[75] Esp. A. H. Francke, *Timotheus Zum Fürbilde Allen Theologiae Studiosis dargestellet* (Halle
1695); idem, *Idea Studiosi Theologiae* (Halle 1712) (new edition in: A. H. Francke, *Werke in Auswahl* [ed. E. Peschke; Witten 1969] 154–201).

[76] E.g., A. Collins, *A Discourse of Free-thinking* (London 1713).

[77] E.g., T. Woolston, *Six discourses on the miracles of Our Saviour* (London 1727–29).

arus (1694–1768) composed a work of biblical criticism never printed during his lifetime.[78] When Gotthold Ephraim Lessing (1729–1781) in 1774–78 published pieces of Reimarus' manuscripts as "Fragments by an unknown writer", he caused a vehement controversy. By the works mentioned, along with many others, the thinkers of the Enlightenment initiated a historical and critical view of the Holy Scripture which was more than mere textual or philological criticism. Scholars of this movement also published works on the study of theology as a kind of advanced education.[79]

Enlightenment and Pietism not only created many new ideas in pedagogy, but also changed institutions and methods of education. They not only brought extensive reforms of existing universities, especially in Catholic territories,[80] but also gave rise to some important new ones. In Protestant Germany, in 1694 Halle university was founded by elector Frederick III (since 1701 King Frederick I) as a central Lutheran[81] state-university of Brandenburg-Prussia.[82] By the appointment of August Hermann Francke (and of Christian Thomasius, too) Halle at first became a stronghold of Pietism[83] (reaching its height in the ejection of the philosopher Christian Wolff in 1723), whose dominance was suddenly ended by King Frederick II the Great (in 1740 after his accession to the throne Wolff immediately returned). Since 1740 the Enlightenment dominated in Halle. But already in 1737 the foundation of the well endowed Göttingen University (under king George II of Great Britain, at the same time Elector George August of Hannover) created a new reform institution in the spirit of the Enlightenment, which soon surpassed Halle in its importance.[84] Especially in Halle and Göttingen University the new ideas, that were to overcome confessionalism, were comprehensively effective.

---

[78] First complete edition: H. S. Reimarus, *Apologie oder Schutzschrift für die vernünftigen Verehrer Gottes* 1–2 (ed. G. Alexander; Frankfurt/Main 1972).

[79] E.g., J. L. von Mosheim, *Kurze Anweisung, die Gottesgelahrtheit vernünftig zu erlernen, in akademischen Vorlesungen vorgetragen* (ed. C. E. von Windheim; Helmstädt 1756; ²1763); J. S. Semler, *Versuch einer nähern Anleitung zu nützlichem Fleisse in der ganzen Gottesgelersamkeit für angehende Studiosos Theologiä* (Halle 1757).

[80] Cf., e.g., R. HAASS, *Die geistige Haltung der katholischen Universitäten Deutschlands im 18. Jahrhundert* (Freiburg/Br. 1952); N. HAMMERSTEIN, *Aufklärung und katholisches Reich. Untersuchungen zur Universitätsreform und Politik katholischer Territorien des Heiligen Römischen Reichs deutscher Nation im 18. Jahrhundert* (Historische Forschungen 12; Berlin 1977).

[81] Frankfurt/Oder was Reformed since 1613.

[82] *Aufklärung und Erneuerung. Beiträge zur Geschichte der Universität Halle im ersten Jahrhundert ihres Bestehens (1694–1806)* (ed. G. Jerouschek; Hanau e.a. 1994); *Martin-Luther-Universität: von der Gründung bis zur Neugestaltung nach zwei Diktaturen* (ed. G. Berg / H.-H. Hartwich; Opladen 1994); *Reformation und Neuzeit. 300 Jahre Theologie in Halle* (ed. U. Schnelle; Berlin / New York 1994).

[83] Cf. U. STRÄTER, "Aufklärung und Pietismus – das Beispiel Halle", in: Universitäten und Aufklärung (1995), 49–61.

[84] G. VON SELLE, *Die Georg-August-Universität zu Göttingen 1737–1937* (Göttingen 1937); *Zur geistigen Situation der Zeit der Göttinger Universitätsgründung 1737* (ed. J. von Stackelberg; Göttinger Universitätsschriften A 12; Göttingen 1988); *Theologie in Göttingen* (ed. B. Moeller; Göttinger Universitätsschriften A 1; Göttingen 1987).

C.

Scriptural Interpretation between Orthodoxy
and Rationalism and the Establishing
of a Historical-Critical Study of the Hebrew Bible /
Old Testament in the Seventeenth
and Eighteenth Centuries

On the Threshold of a New Age: Expanding Horizons as the Broader Context of Scriptural Interpretation

By CHARLOTTE METHUEN, Oxford

General literature: W. B. ASHWORTH, Jr., "Catholicism and Early Modern Science", in: Lindberg / Numbers, God and Nature (1986 [see below]) 136–66; J. H. BROOKE, *Science and Religion: Some Historical Perspectives* (Cambridge: Cambridge UP 1991); J. H. BROOKE / M. J. OSLER / J. v. d. MEER (eds.), *Science in Theistic Contexts: Cognitive Dimensions* (*Osiris*, Second series, vol. 16; Chicago: University of Chicago Press for the History of Science Society 2001); J. E. FORCE / R. H. POPKIN, *Books of Nature and Scripture: Recent Essays on Natural Philosophy, Theology, and Biblical Criticism in the Netherlands of Spinoza's Time and the British Isles of Newton's Time* (International Archives of the History of Ideas 139; Dordrecht: Kluwer 1994); P. HARRISON, *The Bible, Protestantism, and the Rise of Natural Science* (Cambridge: Cambridge UP 1998); K. J. HOWELL, *God's Two Books: Copernican Cosmology and Biblical Interpretation in Early Modern Science* (Notre Dame: Notre Dame UP 2002); A. KOYRÉ, *The Astronomical Revolution: Copernicus – Kepler – Borelli* (London: Methuen 1973); D. C. LINDBERG / R. L. NUMBERS (eds.), *God and Nature. Historical Essays on the Encounter between Christianity and Science* (Berkeley / Los Angeles / London: University of California Press 1986); D. C. LINDBERG / R. S. WESTMAN (eds.), *Reappraisals of the Scientific Revolution* (Cambridge: Cambridge UP 1990); J. v. d. MEER (ed.), *Interpreting Nature and Scripture* (Leiden: Brill forthcoming); C. METHUEN, *Kepler's Tübingen* (Aldershot: Ashgate 1998); eadem, "'This comet or new star': theology and the interpretation of the nova of 1572", in: *Perspectives on Science* 5 (1997) 499–515; M. MULSOW, "Gundling vs. Buddeus: Competing Models of the History of Philosophy", in: D. R. KELLEY, *History and the Disciplines: The Reclassification of Knowledge in Early Modern Europe* (Rochester, NY: University of Rochester Press 1997) 103–25; S. PUMFREY / P. ROSSI / M. SLAWINSKI (eds.), *Science, Culture and Popular Belief in Renaissance Europe* (Manchester / New York: Manchester UP 1991); R. S. WESTMAN, "The Copernicans and the Churches", in: Lindberg / Numbers, God and Nature (1986) 76–113.

Special abbreviation:
KGW = *Johannes Kepler Gesammelte Werke* [s. Sect. 3.2]

1. The Medieval World View

From the twelfth century onwards, the medieval world view was dominated by the natural philosophy and cosmology presented in the works of Aristotle and Pseudo-Aristotle, which offered a comprehensive explication of the nature and constitution of the cosmos and its contents. Perhaps inevitably, the focus on Aristotelian philosophy led to tensions between natural philosophy and theology, particularly in areas where Aristotle was recognised as deviating from Scripture. In 1277 this resulted in the condemnation of 219 philosophical propositions which were held to run counter to the teachings of theology.

Although the condemnation discouraged certain trends in philosophical speculation, it did little to lessen the influence of Aristotelian philosophy, for "the
219 condemned errors were without apparent order, repetitious, and even contradictory".[1] With a few exceptions, such as the infinite universe proposed by
Nicholas of Cusa, by the end of the fifteenth century the standard world view
had come to be Aristotelian.

Aristotelian cosmology was dominated by the sphere, regarded as mathematically perfect. The earth, known to be approximately spherical, lay at the centre of a system of concentric spheres in which the seven planets of the geocentric universe (the moon, Mercury, Venus, the sun, Mars, Saturn and Jupiter) moved, and which in turn were surrounded by the sphere of the fixed
stars. Aristotle taught that the heavens or supralunar region were of a different
substance to the sublunar sphere which surrounded the earth, and which was
constituted from four elements, an ascending hierarchy of earth, water, air
and fire, which were subject to change and decay. The heavens, on the other
hand, were composed of a perfect 'quintessence' (fifth essence) within which
no change could take place; their spherical form and the constant, circular motion of the heavenly bodies were seen as a corollary of their perfection. Aristotelian science believed the regular, circular motion of the heavens to exert a
strong influence upon the irregular motion of the sublunar elements, including
those which made up the human body. This causal link between the heavens
and the sublunar sphere formed the basis for the analogy frequently drawn between the macrocosmos (the universe) and the microcosmos (the human
body); it meant that astrology had an important medical application.

Aristotelian physics was concerned with discovering the nature and causes
of the universe and its constituent parts. It was recognised, however, that it
had certain limitations. For instance, the movements of the planets as observed
by astronomers did not accord with Aristotelian cosmology. Thus, whilst planetary positions, and particularly conjunctions, could be predicted with some
accuracy according to the astronomical theories of Ptolemy, who had postulated a complicated system of epicycles (circular motion around a centre which
itself moves in a circle), Ptolemy's theories were not easily reconciled with the
spheres of Aristotelian cosmology, generally being regarded as inferior to it.[2]
A number of theories were put forward to account for the relationship between
the physical – Aristotelian – and mathematical or astronomical – Ptolemaic –
explications of the universe. These centred on the nature of the spheres: did
they actually exist as some kind of crystal, or should they, like Ptolemy's
mathematical calculations, be understood simply as conceptual constructions?[3]

---

[1] E. Grant, "Science and Theology in the Middle Ages", in: Lindberg / Numbers, God and
Nature (1986) 49–75, here 54.

[2] For the ancient theory of "saving the appearances", see J. Mittelstrass, "'Phaenomena bene
fundata': from 'saving the appearances' to the mechanisation of the world picture", in: R. R. Bol-
gar (ed.), Classical Influences on Western Thought: 1650–1870 (Cambridge: Cambridge UP 1977)
39–59.

[3] See, for instance, E. Grant, "Celestial perfection from the Middle Ages to the late seventeenth century", in: M. J. Osler / P. L. Farber (eds.), Religion, Science and Worldview: Essays in
honor of Richard S. Westfall (Cambridge: Cambridge UP 1985) 137–62.

By the sixteenth century, these and similar questions had come to be included in biblical lectures on Genesis.[4]

Medieval scholars were well aware that the Aristotelian and pseudo-Aristotelian works about the natural world were far from comprehensive in their descriptions of species. In their reception of the Aristotelian corpus, Albertus Magnus and others expanded the catalogues of animals to include accurate information about creatures unknown to Aristotle and to express scepticism about fabulous beasts and marvellous behaviours, although they showed little concern as to whether the resulting catalogues of animals or descriptions of the natural world did in fact offer an accurate description of the world.[5] Moreover, during the fifteenth and sixteenth centuries, the medieval approach to understanding the natural world and of the relationship between the world and the ancient texts which described it began to change. It is certainly no coincidence that this period also gave rise to the Reformation, with its radical shifts in the understanding of authority, and, although it would be simplistic to suggest a direct causal link between the Protestant Reformation and the establishment of the new sciences,[6] parallels between the two movements were observed even by contemporaries. A number of seventeenth-century students of nature came to see the changing status of nature and of methods of understanding as a reformation which was parallel to the Protestant Reformation. Thus the English herbalist Thomas Culpeper spoke of the need for the pope in Philosophy (Aristotle) "to be dethroned along with the other Pope", whilst the Paracelsian Robert Bostocke referred to Copernicus and Paracelsus as the Luther and Calvin of natural philosophy.[7] Despite these contemporary analogies, the relationship between the Reformation and the changes in the understanding of the natural world which gave rise to the new natural sciences and their empirical methodology was not a simple one. Nevertheless, changes to the methods used to understand and interpret both classical, and perhaps especially biblical, texts do seem to be related to the development of new ways of observing and interpreting the natural world. Long seen as the *liber naturae*, or Book of Nature, a source of divine revelation which complemented the *liber scripturae*, the Book of Scripture, or Holy Scripture, this second of God's two books came to the fore during the sixteenth and seventeenth centuries. This article traces the shift in the relationship between the two books through the work of a number of significant figures in the development of the new sciences, discussing the challenges posed by new discoveries, observations and theories

---

[4] As can be seen from the lectures on Genesis given by Jakob Heerbrand at the University of Tübingen in the later sixteenth century (J. HEERBRAND, *In Genesin* – student's lecture notes, Archive of the University of Tübingen, MS number Mc36). It is apparent that Heerbrand discussed the constitution of the spheres in considering God's creative work on the second and fourth days, although the state of the manuscript unfortunately makes it impossible to say what his opinion was.

[5] Harrison, Bible, Protestantism (1998) 64–69.

[6] Brooke points to the difficulties implicit to such a hypothesis: Brooke, Science and Religion (1991) 82–116.

[7] Harrison, Bible, Protestantism (1998) 104–06.

both to the accepted world view and to the reading and understanding of Scripture.

2. Copernicus, Comets, and Voyages of Discovery: A New Heaven, a New World and a New World View

2.1. Voyages of Discovery and the Expansion of the Natural World

It had already become clear during the Middle Ages that the descriptions of the flora and fauna of the natural world found in the classical texts contained errors, which were sometimes exacerbated by mistakes made in the transmission or translation of texts. By the beginning of the early modern period, awareness of these textual problems was growing. Initially, as P. HARRISON has shown, scholarly attention centred on the errors in textual transmission which could be identified by means of methods of textual criticism developed by Renaissance humanists. Applied to texts about the animal world, these showed mistakes in received texts, exposed translators' misunderstandings, and revealed cases where later interpreters had conflated passages referring to different species to produce descriptions of imaginary beasts or strange combinations of behaviours.[8] Some of these had been given credence through the apparent witness of biblical texts, but a more exact study of Hebrew terminology and of rabbinic sources also reduced the number of fantastic beasts supposedly testified to by the Old Testament.[9] In tandem with the attempt to establish the accuracy of ancient texts and the consequent discovery of these textual corrections went an increasing interest in the application of the methods used by ancient authors to gather their information which led to a shift of focus away from "a mere rehearsal of findings [of the classical authors]" to the adoption of these methods. As a result, local species (especially of plants) began to be catalogued and new observations (for instance of the human body) started to be recorded.[10] The dissemination of this new knowledge was made easier by the advent of printing which made possible the accurate reproduction of botanical and anatomical drawings.[11] K. REEDS estimates that by 1623 the catalogue of 600 plants described by ancient authors had grown to approximately 6000.[12]

Central to the extending of natural historical knowledge were the voyages of discovery which took Europeans to new lands, confronting them with previously unknown animals, vegetables, and minerals, with previously unknown diseases (such as syphilis), and with peoples with different customs and societies. As a result of these voyages, the map of the world expanded to take in re-

---

[8] Ibid. 70, 76f.
[9] Ibid. 75–77.
[10] Ibid. 70, 81f.
[11] Ibid. 82.
[12] K. REEDS, "Renaissance Humanism and Botany", *Annals of Science* 33 (1976) 519–43, here 540.

gions unknown or unexplored by ancient authors. Not only were people discovered to be living in regions close to the equator claimed by Aristotle to be
uninhabitable because too hot,[13] but regions believed by philosophers such as
Augustine and Lactantius to be mythical were found to exist.[14] The voyages of
discovery thus resulted in new knowledge which contradicted ancient authorities or brought them into conflict against each other,[15] and they also revealed
significant gaps in the knowledge of the natural world displayed by classical
authors. It gradually began to be realised that classical scholarship was based
primarily upon the species of plants and animals encountered in and around
the Mediterranean, and was therefore limited, "while for us the whole world is
open", as George Ent put it in 1615: knowledge was not "exhausted by the first
ages of the world" but was constantly expanding.[16]

2.2. Comets and the Critique of Aristotelian Cosmology

At the same time that questions were being raised about classical knowledge of
plants and animals, Aristotle's understanding of the world was being brought
into question on another front, through criticism of his cosmology. Towards
the end of the sixteenth century, new observations of a number of celestial
phenomena, including a nova (new star) in 1572, and comets in 1577–78 and
1581 convinced some astronomers that these phenomena must be supralunar,
and not sublunar, as Aristotelian cosmology indicated they must be.[17] One of
the astronomers to draw this conclusion was Michael Maestlin, initially pastor
in Backnang, in Württemberg, and subsequently Professor of Mathematics
and Astronomy at the University of Tübingen and the teacher of Johannes Kepler. Fully aware of the audacity of his conclusions with their implicit criticism
of Aristotle's cosmology, Maestlin drew upon a higher authority to justify his
observations: the Bible. Referring to the Old Testament wisdom tradition, he
explained that all people were commanded by God to praise the works of the
Creator, and that such praise included taking precise observations in order to
discover just how the created world functioned rather than relying on the reports of others. The knowledge gained through precise observations of the
heavens was knowledge to the glory of God; it would enable the correction of

---

[13] See, for instance, M. MAESTLIN, *Epitome astronomiae, qua brevi explicatione omnia, tam ad spaericam quam theoricam eius partem pertinentia* (Heidelberg: Jacob Mylius 1582) 161. Cf. also Harrison, Bible, Protestantism (1998) 70, 82–84, and K. A. VOGEL, "Das Problem der relativen Lage von Erd- und Wassersphäre im Mittelalter und die kosmographische Revolution", *Mitteilungen der Österreichischen Gesellschaft für Wissenschaftsgeschichte* 13 (1993) 103–44.

[14] Howell, God's Two Books (2002) 150.

[15] For instance, that the tropics were inhabited had been claimed by Ptolemy and Avicenna but denied by Aristotle.

[16] Dedication letter in: W. HARVEY, *Anatomical Exercises on the Generation of Animals* (tr. R. Willis; Dedication; Chicago: Encyclopedia Britannica 1951) 329, cited in Harrison, Bible, Protestantism (1998) 83.

[17] For a range of approaches to the nova, see Methuen, This comet or new star (1997); and cf. also the responses to the comet of 1577/78 discussed in C. D. HELLMAN, *The Comet of 1577: Its Place in the History of Science* (New York: Columbia UP 1944).

the mistaken theories put forward by ancient authors.[18] Maestlin thus appealed to Scripture to justify his criticism of Aristotle's cosmology. Other observers of the nova of 1572, such as Casper Peucer, realised that it was above the moon but preferred to retain their faith in Aristotelian physics, explaining their conclusions by reference to special providence: God had chosen in this case to overrule the normal (Aristotelian) rules governing the cosmos and to introduce supralunar change by placing a new star in the heavens.[19] It was generally agreed that Scripture showed that God had chosen to communicate with the world through heavenly phenomena in the past (the use of the star to mark Jesus' birth at Bethlehem) and would do so again in the future (as witnessed by the dominical warning that signs and portents in the heavens would precede the end of the world, cf. Luke 21:11). Indeed, many observers interpreted the 1572 nova as a certain sign that the end of the world was about to come.[20]

Whether regarded as exceptions to a general rule, or as demonstrations of the fallibility of received understandings of physics, the interpretation – and thus the observation – of such phenomena could relatively easily be justified from a literal reading of Scripture. This provided a higher authority which could justify the revision of the Aristotelian world view according to new, more accurate, observations. By the late sixteenth century, with the full support of biblical interpretation, the heavens and the natural world, rather than texts by classical philosophers, were beginning to be taken as the test of accuracy and with it of truth.

2.3. Nicolaus Copernicus, the Copernican Hypothesis and Problems of Biblical Interpretation

Sources: N. COPERNICUS: *Complete Works* (London: Macmillan 1972–1985); *De revolutionibus* (ed. H. M. Nobis / B. Sticker; Hildesheim: Gerstenberg Verlag 1984).
   Literature: J. DOBRZYCKI, *The Reception of Copernicus' Heliocentric Theory* (Dordrecht: Reidel 1972); J. HÜBNER, "Kopernikus, Nikolaus (1473–1543)", TRE 19 (1990) 591–95; R. S. WESTMAN (ed.), *The Copernican Achievement* (Berkeley: University of California Press 1976).

The discovery of new kinds of plants and animals, or the observational placing of comets and novae above the moon could relatively easily be justified biblically, for they in no way contradicted the biblical world view. The situation was very different with the heliocentric theory propounded by Nicolaus Copernicus (1473–1543), which presented a fundamental challenge to the geocentric world view. The Copernican hypothesis was generally perceived to create problems not only for Aristotelian cosmology, but also for the biblical world view. At the same time, it was held to contradict common sense, for

---

   [18] Maestlin developed these arguments in the preface to his considerations of the comets of 1577/78 and 1581, as discussed in Methuen, Kepler's Tübingen (1998) 171–77.
   [19] Methuen, This comet or new star (1997) 508–11, and cf. C. METHUEN, "Special providence and sixteenth-century astronomical observation: some preliminary reflections", *Early Science and Medicine* 4 (1999) 108–11.
   [20] Methuen, This comet or new star (1997) 504–06, 512 f.

from principles of dynamics it seemed obvious that the earth could not possibly be moving with the velocity required by the heliocentric theory. Therefore,
and precisely because the study of the natural world was believed to be biblically justified, the Copernican theory required of its sixteenth-century and seventeenth-century proponents that they in some way reconciled it to the biblical text, that is, that they responded to those who regarded the theory as illegitimate because of its perceived contradictions to certain scriptural passages.
For this reason, issues of scriptural interpretation became an important factor
in the reception of the Copernican theory.[21]

The heliocentric theory had been known (although generally not accepted)
since its proposal by Aristarchus in Antiquity. It was revived by Copernicus in
a treatise *Commentariolus*, completed in 1514, of which manuscript copies circulated throughout Europe. Although he continued to refine his ideas, it was
not until 1543, the year of his death, that *De revolutionibus*, the summation of
his life's work, was finally published in Lutheran Nuremberg, with the support
and encouragement of Georg Joachim Rheticus, mathematician at the University of Wittenberg.[22] During the latter part of the sixteenth century, Copernicus' hypothesis began to be taken seriously by some astronomers, although it
was not to become widely accepted until much later.[23]

Copernicus' principal thesis was that the earth is a planet which revolves on
its own axis as it orbits a motionless sun placed slightly off the centre of the
sphere of the universe. His theory accounted for all known celestial phenomena as accurately as had the best Ptolemaic theories and offered a better explanation of the annual cycle, which had been reproduced in, but not explained
by, Ptolemy's theories. However, Copernicus' theory was not significantly simpler, for in an attempt to preserve the Aristotelian principle that celestial motion must be circular, he was forced to introduce complex systems of epicycles.
Moreover, although Copernicus' theory offered a systematic explanation of
observed celestial phenomena, it could not be proved by application of the observational techniques and technologies available to astronomers in the late
sixteenth century.[24]

It is not entirely clear whether Copernicus believed his theory to present the
true ordering and motion of the universe or not. The anonymous preface to *De
revolutionibus*, written almost certainly by Andreas Osiander, presented Copernicus' work as a mathematical hypothesis which "saved the appearances" as
well if not better than Ptolemy's calculations had done, but which made no
claims in the realm of physics, and thus did not claim to be a true representation of the universe. In this reading, Copernicus is essentially understood to
leave intact the Aristotelian cosmology of a system of concentric spheres
centred on the earth whilst offering a mathematical explanation for the motion

---

[21] See especially Howell, God's Two Books (2002), to which work I am greatly indebted for
what follows.
[22] See, for instance, Westman, The Copernicans and the Churches (1986) esp. 76–81.
[23] For the reception of Copernicanism, see, for instance, Dobrzycki, Reception (1972), and
Westman, Copernican Achievement (1976).
[24] See e. g., Westman, The Copernicans and the Churches (1986) 79 f.

of the planets and for other astronomical phenomena.[25] Although the preface most probably did not represent Copernicus' understanding of what he had done, it did allow those who had fundamental objections to his theory to justify the use of his tables of observations and predictions of planetary positions.[26] To suggest that Copernicus' theory was simply a mathematical construction which accounted for observations and which enabled more accurate predictions was to make no claims about the actual order of the planets and could therefore be deemed to leave Aristotelian cosmology untouched. Those who took this approach had no need to account for passages in Scripture which apparently supported a geocentric theory.

The situation for those who accepted the Copernican hypothesis and believed it to offer an accurate and true portrayal of the universe was rather different. R. S. WESTMAN has summarised the range of problems which faced those whom he terms "pre-Galilean Copernicans":

> First, their central premise had the status of an assumed, unproven and (to most people) absurd proposition. Second, whatever probability it possessed was drawn primarily from consequences in a lower discipline (geometry). Third, even granting the legitimacy of arguing for equivalent predictive accuracy with Ptolemy, the practical derivation of Copernicus' numerical parameters was highly problematic. Fourth, the Copernican system flagrantly contradicted a fundamental dictum of a higher discipline, physics – namely, that a simple body can only have one motion proper to it – for the earth both orbited the sun and rotated on its axis. And finally, it appeared to conflict with the interpretations of another higher discipline, biblical theology – in particular, the literal exegesis of certain passages in the Old Testament.[27]

Biblical passages which were held to be contradicted by Copernicanism included Ps 93:1 ("He has established the world; it shall never be moved"), Eccl 1:5 ("The sun rises and the sun goes down") and Josh 10:13 ("The sun stopped in midheaven and did not hurry to set for about a whole day"), all of which apparently supported the theory that the earth did not move.[28] Opponents of the Copernican hypothesis could and did cite these passages in order to accuse the theory's proponents of contravening Scripture, an accusation to which most felt required to respond by providing some kind of hermeneutical justification for their revised understanding of the universe. They did so by means of a variety of arguments, most of which drew upon the doctrine of accommodation, that is, the understanding that the Bible is written in such language as can be understood by the people to whom it is directed, but also, and increasingly, with the recognition that the writings of Scripture were themselves historical texts. The interpretative consequences of Copernicanism not only set the precedent for the reconciliation of Scripture with the empirical observation of the

---

[25] For Osiander, see Howell, God's Two Books (2002) 44–48, and cf. also R. S. WESTMAN, "The Astronomer's Role in the Sixteenth Century: Some Preliminary Considerations", *History of Science* 23 (1980) 105–47.

[26] Howell, God's Two Books (2002) 44–48.

[27] Westman, The Copernicans and the Churches (1986) 80.

[28] The conviction that the earth did not move did not necessarily imply the acceptance of Aristotelian/Ptolomaic geocentrism. Tycho Brahe's conviction that the earth must be immobile led him to develop the theory of geoheliocentrism, in which the moon and the sun move around the earth, while the other planets move around the sun. For Brahe's use of Scripture, see Howell, God's Two Books (2002) 73–108.

natural world, as J. HÜBNER has suggested,[29] but reflect the shifting relationship between the books of nature and of Scripture.

3. A New Astronomy, its Interpretative Consequences and the Reaction of the Church

3.1. Melanchthon, Rheticus and Peucer: Responses to Copernicus in Wittenberg

Sources: R. HOOYKAAS, G. J. Rheticus's Treatise on the Holy Scripture and the Motion of the Earth, with translation, annotations, commentary and additional chapters on Ramus-Rheticus and the development of the problem before 1650 (Verhandelingen der Koninklijke Nederlandse Akademie van Wetenschappen, Afd. Letterkunde, Nieuwe Reeks, Deel 124; Amsterdam: North Holland Publishing Company 1984) [cited: Hooykaas, Rheticus's Treatise (1984a)]. – PH. MELANCHTHON: Initia doctrinae physicae (1549), in: CR 13, 180–412.

Literature: D. BELLUCCI, Science de la Nature et Réformation. La physique au service de la Réforme dans l'enseignement de Philippe Mélanchthon (Rome: Edizioni Vivere 1998); G. FRANK, Die theologische Philosophie Philipp Melanchthons (1497–1560) (EThSt 67; Leipzig: Benno 1995); R. HOOYKAAS, "Rheticus's Treatise on Holy Scripture and the Motion of the Earth", Journal of the History of Astronomy 15 (1984) 77–80 [cited: Hooykaas, Rheticus's Treatise (1984b)]; S. KUSUKAWA, The Transformation of Natural Philosophy: The Case of Philip Melanchthon (Ideas in Context; Cambridge: Cambridge UP 1995); R. S. WESTMAN, "The Melanchthon Circle, Rheticus, and the Wittenberg Interpretation of the Copernican theory", Isis 66 (1975) 164–93.

R. S. WESTMAN has argued that one of the most important centres for the reception of the Copernican theory was Wittenberg and in particular the circles around the Reformer, Philip Melanchthon.[30] Indeed, Melanchthon's thought seems to have been at the root of a willingness in many Lutheran circles to embrace new departures in questions of anatomy, natural philosophy and astronomy,[31] for although Melanchthon himself was neither a mathematician nor an astronomer, he was convinced that the careful study of the natural world could and did yield an understanding of the divine order according to which it had been created. The understanding of the natural world would in turn lead to an understanding of God's will for the ordering of the world in general and of society in particular.[32] Physics, or natural philosophy could thus be regarded as providing a kind of blueprint for ethics or moral theology.

Despite his promotion of the mathematical sciences and his belief that understanding of the natural world must be based on observations, and although his interest in astrology, which he regarded as a part of physics, meant that he was enthusiastic in his praise of Copernicus' astronomical tables, Melanchthon

---

[29] Hübner, Die Theologie Johannes Keplers (1975) 210.
[30] See, for instance, Westman, Melanchthon Circle (1975).
[31] For Melanchthon's natural philosophy, see Kusukawa, Transformation (1995), and cf. also Bellucci, Science de la Nature (1998), and Frank, Theologische Philosophie (1995).
[32] As discussed in C. METHUEN, "The Role of the Heavens in the Thought of Philip Melanchthon", JHI 57 (1996) 385–403.

was not a proponent of Copernican heliocentricity.[33] His reservations about
the heliocentric theory were based not only on arguments drawn from natural
philosophy but also on biblical passages. Thus, discussing the question *Quis
est motus mundi?* in his textbook of natural philosophy, he cites the testimony
of Aristotle, but also that of the Psalmist, who, he says, taught the movement
of the sun (Ps 19:4–6) and the stability of the earth (Ps 93:1).[34] HOWELL believes that an important hermeneutic principle based on the clarity of biblical
texts is here at stake for Melanchthon: these readings, he suggests, "must not
be understood as naive literalism. ... Melanchthon stressed the clarity of the
Bible on this and other divisive issues because biblical perspicuity was the
foundation of his hermeneutics".[35] For Melanchthon, the Bible is the supreme
arbiter of the one truth, so that, although "there are many things in the
church's teachings which cannot be explained without physics",[36] it is also necessary that "philosophy be united to heavenly considerations" by the consultation of divine authority on obscure matters.[37]

A rather different approach was taken by Georg Joachim Rheticus. Rheticus, who had supported the publication of *De revolutionibus*, was convinced
that Copernicus' theory should be understood as the physical truth. It was thus
necessary for him to explain its apparent contradiction of certain biblical texts.
To do so, he seems to have invoked the principle of adoption. In an anonymous *Treatise on Holy Scripture*, which has been convincingly attributed to
Rheticus by REIJER HOOYKAAS,[38] hermeneutical principles derived from Augustine are applied in order to absolve the Copernican hypothesis from any apparent contradiction to Scripture.[39] The author distinguished between texts which
reveal a deeper theological (often redemptive) meaning, such as accounts of
creation, and those which simply represent the common perceptions of the
world and modes of speech employed by biblical writers. The interpreter must
seek to understand the theological purpose of a text, and not expect scriptural
texts to present the knowledge of astronomy or natural philosophy. However,
although he was adamant that the Bible is not a book of natural philosophy,
Rheticus did conclude that once the motion of the earth has been demonstrated it is possible to find hints of it in Scripture. Although he was not always
entirely consistent in his treatment of texts, his conclusion was clear: Scripture

---

[33] For Melanchthon's reception of Copernicus, see Methuen, Kepler's Tübingen (1998) 91–95,
and further literature cited there. For Melanchthon's understanding of astrology, see Methuen,
Kepler's Tübingen (1998), 76–86; cf also Kusukawa, Transformation (1995) 124–49, and W.-D.
MÜLLER-JAHNCKE, "Melanchthon und die Astrologie – Theoretisches und Mantisches", in: G.
FRANK / S. RHEIN (eds.), *Melanchthon und die Naturwissenschaften seiner Zeit* (Melanchthon-
Schriften der Stadt Bretten 4; Sigmaringen: Thorbecke 1998) 123–35.
[34] Melanchthon, Initia (1549) 217; cf. Howell, God's Two Books (2002) 53.
[35] Howell, God's Two Books (2002) 53.
[36] Melancthon, Initia (1549) 192.
[37] Ibid. 216.
[38] Hooykaas, Rheticus's Treatise (1984a); cf. also Hooykaas, Rheticus's Treatise (1984b). His
arguments for Rheticus' authorship are summarised in Howell, God's Two Books (2002) 57–60.
[39] For the following, see Hooykaas, Rheticus's Treatise (1984a), and Hooykaas, Rheticus's
Treatise (1984b), discussed in Howell, God's Two Books (2002) 60–67.

cannot be regarded as providing decisive arguments in questions of natural philosophy.

In his realism, Rheticus was, however, an exception amongst the Wittenberg proponents of Copernicus, who tended to follow in the footsteps of Osiander and to interpret Copernicus' work as a mathematical construct which allowed the appearances to be saved. Of the remaining members of the "Melanchthon circle", the most important was the Reformer's son-in-law, Caspar Peucer, who did much to consolidate and institutionalise an instrumentalist interpretation of Copernicus within German universities.[40] A physician by training, Peucer also taught astronomy at Wittenberg, recommending that his students should consult Copernicus' *De revolutionibus* as well as Ptolemaic works such as Peurbach's *Theoricae novae planetarum*. Peucer was also a talented observational astronomer. While he remained committed to a strongly Aristotelian cosmology, he was also prepared to acknowledge the possibility of God's intervention to produce phenomena which were not in accordance with physics. As noted above, when his observations of the nova of 1572 placed it above not only the moon but all the other planets as well, Peucer concluded that he had observed a new star, placed in the heavens by God in an event of special providence which overrode the order of Aristotelian physics and which pointed to the great significance of this star, suggesting that it might be one of the portents of the approaching end of the world as prophesied in Luke's Gospel.[41]

Peucer's interpretation of his observations was shaped by his belief that the Bible could yield important knowledge of cosmology. This sometimes required him to read text against text. In the course of his correspondence with Tycho Brahe, Peucer agreed with Brahe that the comparison of the heavens to a "mirror of worked iron" in Job 37:18 did not in fact imply that the heavens or the celestial spheres were hard like steel (an interpretation endorsed by the Vulgate's translation of the Hebrew *chazaq* with *solidissimi*), but should in fact be taken to refer to the "solidity and firmness of constancy" of the heavens and all that is in them.[42] On the other hand, Peucer remained convinced not only of the Aristotelian distinction between the sublunar and supralunar or celestial regions, but also that there was a further, supracelestial region of waters "above the firmament" in which the eternal light of God could be found. This conviction he derived from scriptural references to the floodgates of heaven (Gen 8:2) and the dark waters of the skies (Ps 18:11), and from the Hebrew word *shamayim*, 'heaven', which he regarded as being derived from *sham* ('there') and *mayim* ('water').[43] Rejecting this interpretation, Brahe was adamant that Peucer should not attempt to use the Bible as the source for a cosmology: cosmology must be based upon astronomy, physics (natural philosophy) and chemical correspondences.[44] In Brahe's view, the Bible should not – indeed, could not – be read as a textbook of natural philosophy.

---

[40] Westman, Melanchthon circle (1975) 178. For Peucer's life and work, see ibid. 178–81.
[41] Methuen, This comet or new star (1997) 510f.
[42] Howell, God's Two Books (2002) 103.
[43] Ibid. 105.
[44] Ibid. 106.

3.2. *Johannes Kepler: Priest of the Book of Nature*

Sources: J. KEPLER: *Johannes Kepler Gesammelte Werke*, currently 21 vols. (Munich: C. H. Beck 1937–2002) [abbr. KGW]; *Mysterium Cosmographicum* (1596), in: KGW 8, 5–128; *Astronomia Nova* (1609), in: KGW 3.

Literature: J. HÜBNER, *Die Theologie Johannes Keplers zwischen Orthodoxie und Naturwissenschaft* (BHTh 50; Tübingen: Mohr Siebeck 1975); H. KARPP, "Der Beitrag Keplers und Galileis zum neuzeitlichen Schriftverständnis", *ZThK* 67 (1970) 40–55.

Johannes Kepler (1571–1630) is best known for his discovery of the three laws determining planetary motion. His work, although not widely influential during his lifetime, was rediscovered in the late seventeenth century and was highly significant for the theories of motion derived by Isaac Newton.[45] Moving during his lifetime from an animistic theory of the universe, in which the planets were understood to be self-propelling entities, perhaps even with some kind of soul, to a physical theory, which understood the planets to be moved by an external force,[46] Kepler's cosmology took a major step towards breaking down the long-established distinction between physics, which in Aristotelian thought pertained to causes, and astronomy, which was seen as previously offering mathematical "hypotheses" as opposed to an actual portrayal of the physical place and motion of the planets.

In his first work, the *Mysterium Cosmographicum* of 1596, Kepler explained the distances between the planets as predicted in the Copernican theory by their relationship to the radial lengths of spheres drawn around a cluster of the five perfect solids. In Kepler's eyes the correlation between these ratios clearly showed the hand of the divine creator who, in Kepler's view, had used the building blocks of geometry in designing the universe. For Kepler, the remarkable correlation could be taken as *a priori* proof that the Copernican structure of the universe does indeed represent the physical truth. It was theologically founded, for Kepler understood the sphere as an image of the Trinity, reflecting the deepest essence of the Creator God, and thus as archetypal for the universe. Although this meant that, unlike Nicholas of Cusa, he believed the universe to be finite, he drew upon and developed Cusa's understanding of the relationship between the Trinity and a sphere. Cusa had drawn an analogy between God the Father as the centre, God the Son as the radius and the Holy Ghost as the surface of a sphere.[47] Kepler saw the sphere as the archetype of the Trinity, comparing the fixed sphere of the stars, the sun and the ether between them to the Son, the Father and the Spirit.[48] Despite Kepler's later discovery that planetary orbits are elliptical, the perfection of the sphere remained central to his cosmology and to the theology that underlay it. That the physical explanation is bound up with the theological is to be expected, since for Kepler to observe the true structure of the heavens is to interpret the *liber*

---

[45] See, for instance, Koyré, The Astronomical Revolution (1973) 362–64.

[46] Ibid. 185–279.

[47] Nicholas of Cusa, *De docta ignorantia* (Hamburg: Meiner 2002), I.9–10.

[48] Kepler to Maestlin, 3.10.1595, letter 23, KGW 13, 71, and cf. Hübner, Die Theologie Johannes Keplers (1975) 188 f.

naturae as created by God, so that his role may be understood as that of a *sacerdos libri naturae* ("priest of the Book of Nature").[49] Educated in the theological faculty of the University of Tübingen, Kepler's initial ambition had been to be a pastor, and he was initially disappointed to be sent as a teacher of mathematics to Graz in 1594. As an astronomer and mathematician, however, he came to understand himself as a "priest of the Book of Nature" and was profoundly convinced that the work of interpreting the heavens and the revealing of their physical truth, praise and glory could be offered to God.[50] HOWELL suggests that this interest is revealed by the title of Kepler's first work: by his use of the term "cosmographicum" Kepler emphasises that the work would consider physical descriptions and causes in its contemplation of the universe, "this most glorious temple of God", while the term "mysterium" alludes to the almost sacramental nature of the presence of God in the created world.[51]

Like his teacher Maestlin before him, Kepler appeals to the Psalms in order to justify his seeking the "clearer voice of God" through the study of the heavens. Maestlin had recognised that although the Bible commands the observation of the heavens, the fundamental principles, or hypotheses, of astronomy cannot actually be found in Scripture, but have to be derived from mathematics and physics.[52] For this reason Scripture could never offer a truly accurate description of the heavens: biblical texts are not written in the language of the heavens, which is mathematics. Taking up the Lutheran distinction between the Law and the Gospel, Kepler elaborates on Maestlin's comment, making a clear distinction between the Bible – which speaks the language of the Gospel, of faith, and perhaps of ethics – and the language of natural philosophy and astronomy. In doing so, Kepler demonstrates a clear understanding of the historicity of the Bible and its nature as a collection of historical writings.

Kepler is well aware that the Psalms do not portray a Copernican cosmology, but argues that this is to be expected since Copernican cosmology was not known at the time that they were composed. When references to the movement of the sun appear, Kepler argues, this represents the use of the language of everyday life and its perceptions, rather than the language of astronomers or philosophers. In such passages, God or the Holy Spirit, as first author of Scripture, has accommodated the reality of the natural world to the knowledge of the people of the time.[53] That Joshua asks that the sun be held back when asking for the day to be extended represents accurately what people see; it would be unreasonable to expect Joshua to pause to take account of questions of astronomy or optics when phrasing his prayer.[54] Similarly, in Kepler's opinion, the Psalmist of Psalm 19, writing of the movement of the sun, really be-

---

[49] See, for example, Kepler to Herwart von Hohenberg, 26.3.1598, letter 91, KGW 13, 193.

[50] For Kepler's use of the Bible, see Howell, God's Two Books (2002) 109–135; Karpp, Beitrag, 42–47; Hübner, Die Theologie Johannes Keplers (1975), esp. 210–29.

[51] Howell, God's Two Books (2002) 112–114.

[52] See, for instance, Maestlin, *Epitome astronomiae*, fol. *6ᵛ, discussed in Methuen, Kepler's Tübingen (1998) 155 f.

[53] Howell, God's Two Books (2002) 120; Karpp, Beitrag (1970) 45 f.

[54] Hübner, Die Theologie Johannes Keplers (1975) 225.

lieved that the sun moved. However, the issue at stake in Psalm 19 is not the movement or otherwise of the sun, but the experience of God and the spread of the Gospel: the language used here is not that of astronomy or natural philosophy, but that of poetry, so that the reference to the movement of the sun is allegorical, in Kepler's view intended to express the extent of the Gospel.[55] Somewhat along the lines of Rheticus, Kepler distinguished between the theological intention of a text and its formulation. Kepler's reading of Psalm 19 revealed his conviction that the divine intention of a text cannot necessarily be equated with words of the text itself.

In understanding Scripture in this way, Kepler clearly understands it to be made up of texts which arise from a particular historical context as well as transmitting divine revelation. That he also regards the biblical texts within the scriptural corpus to be historically related to one another and in part dependent upon one another can be seen from his exegesis of Psalm 104 in his *Astronomia Nova* of 1609. HOWELL shows that far from taking Psalm 104 to be essentially a disputation in natural philosophy, as did some of his contemporaries, Kepler interprets it as a doxological commentary on the creation story in Genesis 1. Thus, rather than seeing it as a commentary on the natural world, Kepler shows Psalm 104 to be a commentary on another text.[56] What is important for Kepler is the discipline of proper reading. HOWELL concludes:

> The divine intention must be discerned in both books in order to arrive at their proper meaning, and since intention can only be judged rightly by examining the language employed, the reader must know thoroughly the language of each book. For the heavens – whose language was mathematics – and for Scripture – whose characteristic mode of discourse was ordinary human language – interpretation crucially depended on knowing the relation between the vocabulary and the referents. Kepler had no doubt that geometrical constructs had a one-to-one correspondence with the physical referents in the universe, but the language of Scripture, like all human language, was imprecise and indirect.[57]

Thus, although Kepler remained convinced of the absolute authority of Scripture in matters of grace and salvation, he also drew attention to the fallibility of its language in matters unrelated to salvation.

That Kepler was not always at one with the Lutheran Church in Württemberg may come as no surprise. However, it was not Kepler's cosmology or his understanding of the Bible which caused him trouble – although these did elicit critical reactions[58] – but his theology of the Eucharist. As a schoolboy, even before he began his studies of theology at the university of Tübingen, Kepler had come to hold a doctrine of the Eucharist which was significantly closer to Calvinist than to Lutheran teaching.[59] As a result he felt himself unable to sign the Lutheran *Formula Concordiae*, both because he did not accept its teaching on the Eucharist and because he refused to declare Calvinist teachings anathema. Since assent to the *Formula Concordiae* was required of all pastors and teachers in Württemberg, Kepler's refusal to sign it cost him his chance of a

---

[55] Ibid. 222–26.
[56] Howell, God's Two Books (2002) 119–25.
[57] Ibid. 124 f.
[58] See, for instance, Hübner, Die Theologie Johannes Keplers (1975) 286–90.
[59] Ibid. 29–44.

post at the University of Tübingen, and it eventually led to his exclusion from the Eucharist by Daniel Hitzler, Lutheran pastor in Linz from 1611, although Kepler continued to receive the Eucharist from other Lutheran pastors.[60]

3.3. The Universe of Giordano Bruno

Sources: G. Bruno: Opera latine conscripta (3 vols. in 8 parts; ed. F. Fiorentino; Naples / Florence: Tocco e.a. 1879–91; facsimile edition, Stuttgart-Bad Canstatt: Fromann 1962); Opere complete (Roma: Lexis 1999; CD-ROM electronic edition); Le opere italiane I-II (ed. P. de Lagarde; Göttingen: Dieterich 1888). – A. Mercati, Il sommario del processo di Giordano Bruno con appendice di documenta sull'eresia e l'inquizatione a Moden nelo secolo XVI (Vatican State: Biblioteca Apostolica Vaticana 1942; repr. 1988).
    Literature: M. A. Granada, Cosmología, teología y religíon en la obra en el proceso de Giordano Bruno (Barcelona: Barcelona UP 2001); B. Ulianich, "Bruno, Giordano (1548–1600)", TRE 7 (1981) 242–46; F. A. Yates, Giordano Bruno and the Hermetic Tradition (Chicago: University of Chicago Press 1964; repr. 1991).

Johannes Kepler was excluded from the Eucharist by Hitzler on account of his views on the Eucharist. Giordano Bruno (1548–1600) achieved condemnation both by Lutherans in Wittenberg and by Calvinists in Geneva for his views before being imprisoned in Rome in 1592 and subsequently burnt there on 17 February 1600. However, although Bruno's cosmological views were far from not orthodox, in his case, as in that of Kepler, it was not so much his cosmology which was at the root of his condemnation, but his theological ideas, and particularly his rejection of the incarnation, which was rooted in his Hermetic beliefs.[61] Bruno derived his theological convictions from a wide range of sources, including Marsilio Ficino and Giovanni Pico della Mirandola, who brought together the writings of Hermes Trismegistus and the Neoplatonism of Pseudo-Dionysius (both erroneously presumed ancient) with Jewish kabbalist theories, as well as Averroes and classical philosophy. He understood the Egyptian religion, represented by Hermes, to be the prisca theologica, prior to – and more authoritative than – the religion of Moses. The attributes of Power, Wisdom and Goodness were equated in his ideas with mens, intellectus and amor, but he was reluctant to recognise in the Hermetic intellectus the second person of the Trinity. The cross he understood to be also a sacred sign of the Egyptian religion.

In developing a metaphysical cosmology in conjunction with these beliefs, Bruno wove together several philosophical strands. Beginning from the assumption that every aspect of the universe is a shadow or a vestige of divinity, he developed a cosmology in which natural philosophical structures mirrored his theological assumptions. For instance, the metaphysical minimum (the

---

[60] Ibid. 30–33.
[61] For the following, see the documents in Mercati, Sommario (1942), discussed by Yates, Bruno (1991) esp. 350–54; cf. also Brooke, Science and Religion (1991) 39f, 73 f. For the debate about Yates's focus on the influence of the Hermetic Tradition, see, for instance, B. Copenaver, "Natural Magic, Hermeticism, and Occultism in Early Modern Science", in: Lindberg / Westman, Reappraisals (1990) 261–301.

One, God) is related to the mathematical minimum (the point) and the natural philosophical minimum (the atom).[62] Similarly, his conviction, drawn from Nicholas of Cusa, that the universe must be infinite was rooted in his belief that an infinite divine power would not have created a finite universe and that the immensity and perfection of God required God's creation of real, rather than hypothetical, infinite worlds. Copernican cosmology fitted into this infinite universe by offering a model for a planetary system which could be seen as extending to infinity; like Kepler, Bruno was attracted by the placing of the sun at the centre (although, unlike Kepler, he was happy to contemplate an infinite number of suns), but he was also convinced of the importance of the earth's movement as representing its potential for renewal and change.[63] This truth is deeper than a mathematical assertion: for Bruno, suggests F. YATES, "the Copernican sun heralds the full sunrise of the ancient and true philosophy after its age-long burial in dark caverns", leading to a truth which is "neither orthodox Catholic nor orthodox Protestant; it is Egyptian truth, magical truth".[64] Bruno's cosmology was associated with a rejection of many aspects of Aristotelianism, including Aristotle's ordering of the elements, which he criticised as a logical, rather than a natural conception,[65] and arguing that all matter, including the heavenly bodies and the "waters" of the universe, was formed from the elements.[66]

Both Bruno's espousal of an infinite universe in connection with Copernicanism and his rejection of Aristotelianism resulted from his conviction that he had access to the true knowledge that had been suppressed by "false Mercuries", of which he saw Christianity as being one. His belief that true religion is not Christian but the preserve of the philosophers, and pre-eminently Egyptian and pre-Mosaic, meant that, unlike Christian Hermeticists such as Paracelsus, who wrote extensive scriptural commentaries, Bruno had little interest in seeking to reconcile his beliefs with the Bible. In *La cena de la ceneri*, in which he defended Copernicus's theory of the movement of the earth against theological criticism, he argued that the Scriptures, and with them Christian religion, are for the uneducated, whose knowledge is limited to what is experienced by the senses, and not for the wise minority.[67] Knowledge of Copernican theory and the recognition of the infinite universe must also be restricted to this minority, since the uneducated are incapable of attaining the necessary intellectual understanding. Such knowledge would have a disastrous effect on morality and behaviour (as evidenced, for Bruno, by the civic unrest which followed the Reformation).[68] Bruno relied on his status as one to whom the truth had been revealed to interpret the revelations of the divine represented in the infinite universe and its infinite worlds, so that, for instance, the waters over

---

[62] Ulianich, Bruno (1981) 243.

[63] For Bruno's cosmology and his adoption of Copernicus, see Yates, Bruno (1991) 235–49.

[64] Ibid. 238 f.

[65] Ibid. 251.

[66] M. A. GRANADA, "Giordano Bruno, la Biblia y la religión: las agues sobre el firmamento y la union con Dios", in: Granada, Cosmología (2001) 212.

[67] Granada, Giordano Bruno 203 f.

[68] Granada, Giordano Bruno 207 f.

the firmament become a natural allegory of the way in which the wise soul achieves union with God.[69] As a necessary condition for this project, he demanded complete freedom of thought – a demand which was conceded by no church of the time and which eventually cost him his life.[70]

Although Bruno, like Kepler, was deeply influenced by Platonism, Bruno's interests were far less mathematical, and he conceived of thought as a way of reaching intuitive knowledge of that revelation and thus of God.[71] Bruno's ideas were later to attract considerable interest,[72] in part at least because his cosmology was understood as a precursor to more modern hypotheses about the structure of the universe. However, just as Bruno was no scriptural interpreter, he was very far from being a modern rationalist. His ideas demonstrate most clearly the complex and creative interactions of not only philosophical and mathematical but also magical and iatro-chemical ideas during the later sixteenth and seventeenth centuries which informed the work not only of Bruno, Paracelsus and Kepler, but of many later thinkers, including the alchemically inclined Isaac Newton.

3.4. Galileo Galilei: Quantifiable Physics and Cosmology

Sources: GALILEO GALILEI: *Opere di Galileo Galilei: edizione nazionale* (20 vols.; ed. A. Favaro; Florence: Le Monnier 1890–1909; repr. Florence: Barbera 1964–68); *Dialog über die beiden hauptsächlichsten Weltsysteme, das ptolemäische und das kopernikanische* (tr. Emil Straus; Leipzig: Teubner 1891; facs. repr. Stuttgart: Teubner / Darmstadt: Wissenschaftliche Buchgesellschaft 1982); *Dialogue concerning the two chief world systems, Ptolemaic and Copernican* (tr. Stillman Darke; Berkeley: University of California Press [2]1967); "Letter to the Grand Duchess Christina", ET in: Blackwell, *Galileo, Bellarmine and the Bible* (1991) 217–51; *Sidereus nuncius or the sidereal messenger* (tr. with introd., conclusion, and notes by Albert von Helden; Chicago: Univ. of Chicago Press 1989); selection of sources online at: http://www.liberliber.it/biblioteca/g/galilei/index.htm.
Literature: E. BELLONE, *Galileo Galilei: Leben und Werk eines unruhigen Geistes* (Heidelberg: Spektrum-der-Wiss.-Verl.-Ges. [2]2002); R. J. BLACKWELL, *Galileo, Bellarmine and the Bible* (Notre Dame: University of Notre Dame Press 1991); W. CARROLL, "Galileo and the Interpretation of the Bible", *Science Education* 8 (1999) 151–87; E. McMULLIN, *Galieo, Man of Science* (New York: Basic Books 1967; repr. Princeton, NJ: Scholar's Bookshelf 1988); idem, "Galileo on Science and Scripture", in: P. MACHAMER (ed.), *The Cambridge Companion to Galileo* (Cambridge: Cambridge UP 1998) 217–347; P. REDONDI, *Galileo Heretic* (London: Allen Lane The Penguin Press 1987); H.-W. SCHÜTT, "Galilei, Galileo (1564–1642)", TRE 12 (1984) 14–17; W. A. WALLACE, *Galileo and his sources: The heritage of the Collegio Romano in Galileo's science* (Princeton, NJ: Princeton UP 1984).

Unlike the speculative thought of Giordano Bruno, the interests of Galileo (1564–1642) centred on observation: both of astronomical phenomena and of physical motion. He investigated flotation, adding significantly to Archimedean hydrostatics; he studied the motion of falling objects, of objects moving on an inclined plane and also of the pendulum. Like Kepler, he recognised that the Aristotelian distinction between mathematics and physics must be rejected

---

[69] Granada, Giordano Bruno 209–19.
[70] Condert, Newton and the Rosicrucian Enlightenment (1999) 22.
[71] Yates, Bruno (1991) 249.
[72] Ulianich, Bruno (1981) 244 f.

if motion was to be understood. He also carried out important astronomical observations, constructing telescopes which revealed to him the moons of Jupiter, the phases of Venus and sun spots and their motion, on which basis he postulated the rotation of the sun. An advocate of the Copernican system by 1597, he sought to prove the double motion of the earth, as postulated by the Copernican system, by means of a discussion of tides, and published these theories in 1613. Later that year he expounded his views on the relationship between the Bible and natural philosophy in a letter to the Benedictine monk, Benedetto Castelli, and was denounced to the Holy Office in Rome.[73] In 1615, a letter addressed to the General of the Carmelite Order was published by a priest of the order, Paolo Antonio Foscarini, in which Foscarini argued that "the opinion of the Pythagoreans and of Copernicus about the mobility of the earth and the stability of the sun and the new Pythagorean system of the world … agrees with, and is reconciled with, the passages of Sacred Scripture and the theological propositions which are commonly adduced against it".[74] This treatise was condemned by the Congregation of the Index on 5 March 1616.[75] A month earlier, Copernicanism had been indicted as false and clearly contrary to Scripture,[76] and later that year Galileo was instructed by the Pope, via Cardinal Bellarmine to abandon his commitment to heliocentrism, although he was not forced to recant.[77] Focusing his interest on mechanics and the criticism of Aristotelian physics for a time, Galileo went on to compose a cosmological work, the *Dialogues*, completed by 1630, but not allowed to be published until 1632. However, its sale was soon forbidden and in 1633 Galileo was called to trial. In June 1633, Galileo recanted his "error" but was placed under house arrest for the rest of his life.

Galileo's condemnation by the Catholic Church was rooted in questions of biblical interpretation which were associated with his espousal of Copernicanism. This contrasts with the condemnation of Bruno, but in many ways both Bruno and Galileo were victims of the Catholic Church's reaction to the Reformation and its need for clarification and control, a context in which deviation from the defined norm, not only in theological questions but also in issues of cosmology and natural philosophy, was no longer to be either tolerated or ignored.[78] Galileo's astronomical views were held to put him in opposition to the teaching of the Church in the interpretation of certain biblical passages. These were questions for which the Church, drawing support from the Fathers, had declared herself to be the arbiter, for instance by the decrees of the Fourth Session of the Council of Trent (8 April 1546) concerning the Ca-

---

[73] There are many accounts of the proceedings against Galileo; for a detailed study focusing on the hermeneutical issues, see Blackwell, Galileo, Bellarmine and the Bible (1991).

[74] This is the title of Foscarini's treatise, cited in Blackwell, Galileo, Bellarmine and the Bible (1991) 88. For a detailed discussion, see ibid. 87–110; an English translation is given in ibid. 217–51.

[75] Ibid. 110.

[76] Ibid. 111–25.

[77] Ibid. 125–29.

[78] P. Dear, "The Church and the New Philosophy", in: Pumfrey / Rossi / Slawinski, Science, Culture and Popular Belief (1991) 119–39, here 122.

non of Scripture and its interpretation. The second paragraph of the second decree stated that

> in matters of faith and morals [*in rebus fidei et mores*] pertaining to the understanding of Christian doctrine, no-one relying on their own judgement and distorting the Holy Scriptures according to their own ideas shall dare to interpret them contrary to the sense which the Church gives them, for it is up to the Church to judge the true sense and meaning of Scripture. Nor is it permitted to hold interpretations contrary to the unanimous agreement of the Fathers, even though such interpretations should at no time be published.[79]

Whilst the Council of Trent was not directly concerned with questions of natural philosophy, in Galileo's case, and in relation to heliocentrism generally, because the new ideas were deemed by the hierarchy of the Church to contradict accepted understanding of Scripture, the controversy was played out in hermeneutics.

Galileo expounded his views on the interpretation of Scripture in a letter to Castelli, written in 1613, which he expanded early in 1615 to form a lengthier discussion addressed to the Grand Duchess Christina.[80] In it, Galileo draws upon principles of biblical interpretation put forward in Augustine's *De Genesi ad litteram* and generally accepted by the Catholic Church in order to counter the theological objections to his natural philosophy and cosmology. In the treatise, Galileo develops three stages of argument, each of which he draws from Augustine.[81] His first step closely follows Augustine's argument that Scripture should not be relied upon as a source of knowledge about cosmological problems such as the shape of the heavens. Following Augustine, Galileo argues that Scripture's primary purpose is to instruct believer in matters of faith and morals.[82] However, in matters of natural philosophy which have been proved, Scripture must be interpreted in terms of that sure knowledge. This is Galileo's second argument, again following Augustine.[83] His use of it, in circumstances in which the cosmological proposition he wished to defend had not been proved, may reflect his expectation that he would be able to prove the truth of the Copernican hypothesis by means of his arguments from tides.[84] Thirdly, Galileo suggests that the Ptolemaic system is not in fact the best explanation of all the cosmological inferences in the Bible. Thus, he argues that if the sun is understood to rotate on its own axis at the centre of the universe, and if it may be assumed that the influence of the sun's rotation causes the planets to move around it, then the planets will stop moving if the sun stops moving and Josh 10:13 can in fact be taken literally: the sun stopped

---

[79] Blackwell, Galileo, Bellarmine and the Bible (1991) 5–14, esp. 11f; cf. also Howell, God's Two Books (2002) 182–86.

[80] For a more detailed discussion of Galileo's hermeneutics, see besides Blackwell, Galileo, Bellarmine and the Bible (1991), Carroll, Galileo and the Interpretation of the Bible (1999), McMullin, Galileo on Science and Scripture (1998). Galileo's arguments are summarised in Howell, God's Two Books (2002) 186–96.

[81] For the relationship of these arguments to Augustine's *De Genesi ad litteram*, see Howell, God's Two Books (2002) 186–93.

[82] Howell, God's Two Books (2002) 188–89.

[83] Ibid. 189–91; cf. Carroll, Galileo and the Interpretation of the Bible (1999) 165–66.

[84] Carroll, Galileo and the Interpretation of the Bible (1999) 166.

moving, in consequence of which the whole system stopped, and the day was lengthened.[85]

HOWELL notes that Galileo's arguments function on different levels or in response to different arguments and suggests that the order is not incidental. Galileo's preferred method was the first: he wished to distinguish clearly between theological questions, subject to and of biblical hermeneutics, and questions of natural philosophy, for which Scripture could not be seen as authoritative. However, if someone were to insist that Scripture in some way pertained to the understanding of the natural world, then it should be recognised that demonstrated philosophical truths could be used to give a better interpretation of biblical texts, which was not necessarily literal. But if it were insisted that the interpretation must be literal, it could be shown by the third stage of argument that a literal understanding of the text was in any case not contradicted.[86] In arguing thus, Galileo sought to confound the theological and hermeneutical objections of his opponents by appealing to just the arguments and principles of biblical interpretation which they themselves advocated.[87] The hermeneutical responses to the reception of the Copernican hypothesis made it very clear that the issues at stake could not be decided simply by invoking the *sensus literalis* of any given scriptural passage, for this was what all sides of the debate claimed to be doing.

4. A New Science: The Mechanical Philosophy

As has been seen above, the adoption of the Copernican hypothesis as a real description of the universe was associated with a critique of Aristotelian physics and the blurring of the distinction between natural philosophy and astronomy. Although Aristotelian philosophy and natural philosophy remained influential until well into the seventeenth century and beyond,[88] Aristotelian natural philosophy came under strong attack from two directions: the Paracelsian world view, and the so-called mechanistic philosophy, propounded by René Descartes. Deeply anchored in a biblical tradition, Paracelsus (Theophrast of Hohenheim) developed "a new system of medicine, self-consciously designed ... to undermine classical medicine on the basis of premises derived from the Bible",[89] the so-called iatro-chemical medicine which was rooted in alchemy and which was to be strongly influential on the development of chem-

---

[85] Howell, God's Two Books (2002) 191.

[86] Ibid. 192–203.

[87] See esp. Carroll, Galileo and the Interpretation of the Bible (1999), 173–75, but cf. also Howell, God's Two Books (2002) 198f, 204–07.

[88] The enormous range of editions of Aristotle printed during the seventeenth century has been documented by C. H. LOHR, *Latin Aristotle Commentaries: II Renaissance Authors* (Florence: Olschki 1988).

[89] As defined by C. WEBSTER, "Puritanism, Separatism, and Science", in: Lindberg / Numbers, God and Nature (1986) 192–217, here 205. For Paracelsus, see C. WEBSTER, *From Paracelsus to Newton: magic and the making of modern science: the Eddington memorial lectures delivered at Cambridge University November 1980* (Cambridge: Cambridge UP 1982), and O. P. GRELL (ed.), *Paracelsus: the man and his reputation, his ideas and their transformation* (SHCT 85; Leiden: Brill 1998).

istry during the seventeenth century. Descartes, on the other hand, offered a new, mathematically based way of understanding the structure of the world and disdained the suggestion that nature might point a path to God.[90] Descartes' ideas inevitably produced a theological spin-off, for instance in the work of the radically empiricist Pierre Gassendi, who produced a Christianised version of Epicurean philosophy which he offered as a metaphysical foundation for the new science,[91] or in the *Pensées* of Blaise Pascal, who distanced himself from natural theology, arguing that theology and science appeal to different authorities.[92] Moreover, the Catholic Church's efforts to eradicate magic led to the denunciation of alchemy and chemical medicine.[93] In England, however, the work of thinkers such as Robert Boyle and Isaac Newton arose out of the controversies between these two approaches.

4.1. Robert Boyle

Sources: R. BOYLE: *The Christian Virtuoso: Showing, that by being addicted to Experimental Philosophy, a man is rather assisted then indisposed to be a good Christian* (London: printed by Edward Jones for John Taylor 1690).
    Literature: M. J. OSLER, "The intellectual sources of Robert Boyle's philosophy of Nature: Gassendi's voluntarism, and Boyle's physico-theological project", in: R. KROLL / R. ASHCROFT / P. ZAGORIN (eds.), *Philosophy, Science and Religion in England 1640–1700* (Cambridge: Cambridge UP 1992) 178–98.

Robert Boyle (1627–91) was one of the most significant proponents of the mechanical philosophy in England. Appealing to a corpuscular theory of matter, Boyle sought to show that all physical (i.e., not spiritual) phenomena can be explained in terms of matter and motion, and thus to extend the principles of mechanical philosophy to encompass not only astronomical, mechanical and optical phenomena, to which they had been applied by Descartes, but also the chemical phenomena he observed. As was the case for most mechanical philosophers, Boyle felt compelled not only to define the philosophical and experimental support for his theories, but to show that his approach did not lead inevitably to atheism. Boyle himself was deeply worried by atheism, and seems to have planned a work on this theme which was never published.[94] His published work includes several treatises considering the relationship between faith and natural philosophy, including *The Christian Virtuoso: Showing, that by being addicted to Experimental Philosophy, a man is rather assisted then indisposed to be a good Christian* (1690). Here Boyle argued that the study of nature, rather than fostering atheism, "reveals God's aims in the creation, and it

---

[90] As argued by Ashworth, Catholicism and Early Modern Science (1986) 139f.
[91] For Gassendi, see Ashworth, Catholicism and Early Modern Science (1986) 141f, and cf. also Osler, Intellectual Sources (1992) 179–82.
[92] See, for instance, J. MIEL, *Pascal and Theology* (Baltimore / London: Johns Hopkins Press 1969); P. STOLZ, *Gotteserkenntnis bei Blaise Pascal* (Frankfurt am Main: Peter Lang 2001).
[93] Ashworth, Catholicism and Early Modern Science (1986) 150f.
[94] M. HUNTER, "Science and Heterodoxy: An Early Modern Problem reconsidered", in: Lindberg / Westman, Reappraisals (1990) 437–60, here 439.

renders visible the divine attributes, God's power, wisdom, and goodness", although he was also at pains to emphasise that the knowledge of God acquired through natural is not complete, but must be supplemented by scriptural revelation.[95]

Boyle's position was founded on his voluntarist understanding of God's interaction with the natural world. Boyle believed God to be "the free establisher of the laws of motion, whose general concourse is necessary to the conservation and efficacy of every physical agent"; these laws are as they are because they were created that way by God, and God is always free to intervene to change the action of these laws (for instance to prevent Daniel's companions from being burned in the fiery furnace).[96] Because God created the world and established its laws, the study of nature must inevitably lead to knowledge of God, but this knowledge is incomplete and must be supplemented by the reading of Scripture, for only in Scripture is the working of God revealed, and some theological knowledge, such as the existence of the soul, can only be learned from Scripture.

M. OSLER has argued that Boyle's philosophy of nature, and in particular his conviction that matter had a corpuscular structure was rooted in his voluntarism: instead of needing Aristotelian elements or Paracelsian principles, Boyle's physics made it possible for God to determine the accidents, and thus the characteristics, of particular bodies directly. Boyle's method of determining the interactions of corpuscular bodies was strongly empirical. He believed similarly that knowledge of God – and hence doctrine – could only be derived from experience of some kind reflected on by reason.[97] The relationship between reason and faith, rooted in his conviction that it was not necessary to forego reason in order to believe, was of great importance to Boyle. He understood the truths of faith to be based on Scripture interpreted in the light of right reason, so that "there is not any thing in the Christian religion, that does really contradict any principle of right reason; if the principle be found, and the article rightly proposed, and duly grounded on Scripture, well interpreted".[98] In order to avoid conflict between propositions of natural philosophy and religious tenets, it was essential to be clear about the source of different propositions. Boyle thus proposed a fairly clear distinction between Scripture and natural philosophy, with theological insights being drawn from both.

4.2. Isaac Newton

Sources: ISAAC NEWTON: *The Correspondence of Isaac Newton* (Cambridge: Cambridge UP 1959-); *Chronology of Ancient Kingdoms Amended* (London 1728); *The Mathematical Papers of Isaac Newton* (Cambridge: Cambridge UP 1967-); *Theological, alchemical and administrative writings in manuscript* (online at http://www.newtonproject.ic.ac.uk [in progress]).
Literature: J. A. I. CHAMPION, "'Acceptable to inquisitive men': some Simonian contexts for New-

---

[95] Osler, Intellectual Sources (1992) 184 f. (quote on 184).
[96] Ibid. 185.
[97] Ibid. 186 f.
[98] Ibid. 190 f.

ton's biblical criticism, 1680–1692", in: Force / Popkin, Newton and Religion (1999) 77–96; A. CONDERT, "Newton and the Rosicrucian Enlightenment", in: Force / Popkin, Newton and Religion (1999) 17–43; J. E. FORCE / R. H. POPKIN (eds.), *Essays on the context, nature, and influence of Isaac Newton's theology* (Dordrecht: Kluwer 1990); iidem, *Newton and Religion: Context, Nature and Influence* (Dordrecht / Boston / London: Kluwer 1999); S. HUTTON, "More, Newton, and the Language of Biblical Prophecy", in: Force / Popkin, Books of Nature and Scripture (1994) 39–53; eadem, "The Seven Trumpets and the Seven Vials: Apocalypticism and Christology in Newton's Theological Writings", in: Force / Popkin, Newton and Religion (1999) 165–78; R. ILIFFE, "'Making a shew': apocalyptic hermeneutics and Christian idolatry in the work of Isaac Newton and Henry More", in: Force / Popkin, Books of Nature and Scripture (1994) 55–98; K. J. KNOESPEL, "Interpretative Strategies in Newton's *Theologiae gentiles*", in: Force / Popkin, Newton and Religion (1999) 179–202; F. E. MANCEL, *The Religion of Isaac Newton* (Oxford: Clarendon Press 1974); R. MARKLEY, "Newton, Corruption, and the Tradition of Universal History", in: Force / Popkin, Newton and Religion (1999) 121–43; R. H. POPKIN, "Newton as a Bible Scholar", in: Force / Popkin, Essays on Newton's Theology (1990) 103–18.

Isaac Newton (1643–1727) is probably the best known and most influential of all English natural philosophers. It was he who developed the theory of gravitation and established principles of mechanics which provided a coherent explanation of motion of all bodies, dealing a final death blow to the Aristotelian distinction between the sub- and supralunar spheres. Newton also did important mathematical work, including the development of calculus (concurrently with Leibniz), and showed important properties of light. But although Newton's work was long viewed as exemplary for modern science, his *Principia Mathematica* and his *Optics* are in many ways as much religious as scientific works, and his avowed intention was the provision of empirical evidence of divine Providence.[99] Indeed, like Bruno, Newton felt that he had been blessed with a special gift for interpreting God's word in both the "Book of Scripture" and the "Book of Nature",[100] and that the natural world better able to reveal aspects of the divine than the corrupted text of Scripture.[101] Here Newton departs from the assumptions of those who viewed the biblical, revealed text of Scripture as somehow coherent and unassailable in itself, and thus as guaranteeing the coherency of the natural world.[102] For Newton, the *liber naturae* and *liber scripturae* must both be read and understood if God's world and God's providence were properly to be revealed. The reading and understanding of the structure of nature could serve as a measure for the reading and understanding of Scripture, but the two were bound together. Natural philosophy (including alchemical experiments), scriptural interpretation and history were all part of the complex enquiry into the deepest structures of the world created by God.[103]

It is perhaps not surprising that in his scriptural interpretation Newton brought to bear the empirical methodology which formed the foundation of his scientific understanding. Like Kepler, Newton was highly conscious of the biblical text as historical, but unlike Kepler, for Newton this included the rea-

---

[99] Condert, Newton and the Rosicrucian Enlightenment (1999) 39.
[100] Ibid. 41
[101] Ibid. 41, and cf. Markley, Newton, Corruption (1999) 134f.
[102] Markley, Newton, Corruption (1999) 135.
[103] Ibid. 137, and cf. Knoespel, Interpretative Strategies (1999) 186f, 190.

lisation that the text itself had been altered over time. One of Newton's primary interests was to understand the true religion of the children of Israel before it became corrupted by the worship of false gods.[104] His *Chronology of Ancient Kingdoms Amended*, published in London 1728, employs newly discovered scientific findings to evaluate the historical status of the Bible. Using description of the positions of the stars to calculate the dates of significant events, Newton concluded that the events of the Bible took place before the earliest events in Greek or Egyptian history, and that Scripture therefore offered a more accurate historical account than did Greek, Phoenician, Babylonian or Egyptian records.[105] In an unpublished historical treatise, *Of the Church*, Newton argued that the unity of a simple creed of faith had been infected and corrupted by the development of the Church, by its association with the state of Rome, and by the intrusion of questions of metaphysics, Platonism, and the Kabbalah.[106] Nevertheless, he remained convinced that, despite the problems and errors of its transmission, the text of Scripture had retained a divinely revealed prophetic message,[107] and this he set out to find. This quest lay behind his deep interest in the prophetic and apocalyptic tradition, focusing on the book of Daniel and the Revelation of St John the Divine.[108]

Newton's methodology of biblical interpretation and his understanding of prophecy were influenced by – but deviated from – the millenarian thought of Joseph Mede.[109] He tended always towards the literal reading of a text, distrusting allegory as an appeal "to human imagination or human authority rather than to Scripture".[110] Prophecy, however, was for the eyes of the elect only, and not accessible be means of philosophical reason. Its meaning must be arrived at by means of the rigorous comparison of Scripture with Scripture, so that, HUTTON suggests, he treats prophecies "as if [they] were some kind of divine algebra the values (meanings) of whose symbols can only be deduced by comparing the occurrences of a particular symbol".[111] Since in Newton's view prophecy makes use of "the vocabulary of the natural world which represents not nature but human affairs",[112] he saw science and the study of biblical prophecy as two important and related ways of comprehending God's message: progress in understanding the natural world and the prophetic books indicated that God was "opening the seals" and revealing human destiny.[113]

In his discussions of the New Testament, POPKIN has suggested, "Newton's chief concern was to argue to the primacy of the book of Revelation and to point out the deliberate alteration of New Testament texts by wicked charac-

---

[104] Knoespel, Interpretative Strategies (1999) 192.
[105] Popkin, Bible Scholar (1990) 111.
[106] M. GOLDISCH, "Newton's *Of the Church*: Its Contents and Implications", in: Force / Popkin, Newton and Religion (1999) 145–64, here 148 f.
[107] Popkin, Bible Scholar (1990) 107.
[108] Ibid., and cf. also Hutton, Seven Trumpets (1999), and Iliffe, Making a Shew (1994).
[109] See, for instance, Hutton, More, Newton (1994) and Iliffe, Making a Shew (1994).
[110] Hutton, More, Newton (1994) 46 f.
[111] Ibid. 48 f; quote on 49.
[112] Ibid. 49.
[113] Popkin, Bible Scholar (1990) 114.

ters such as St Athanasius",[114] that is, to reveal the full extent of what he understood to be the corruption of Trinitarianism.[115] To this end, he devoted much effort to tracing the changes and Trinitarian adaptations made to 1 John 5:7 and 1 Tim 3:16, both frequently cited as offering evidence that the doctrine of the Trinity was scriptural, and to establishing the earlier, non-Trinitarian texts. Newton sought out and collated as many editions and manuscripts as were available to him: correspondence between Locke and Newton shows them exchanging opinions and interpretations of difficult and controversial passages and of recently discovered manuscript versions of Scripture.[116] This work was prepared for publication but never published during his lifetime. Newton also undertook a historical examination of the literary history of the text of Scripture, including challenges to the work of Erasmus and Theodore Beza.[117] Both Locke and Newton were closely in touch with and influenced by Richard Simon, an important figure in continental biblical criticism,[118] and it was in part the public reception of Simon's works which persuaded Newton not to publish his own.

5. The Broadening of the Historiographical Perspective

The developments traced in this article affected not only natural philosophers and theologians, but many other disciplines: a similar development can be observed in the writing of history, which moved away from a chronology determined by biblical history to one derived from other sources and information. As for natural history, voyages of discovery extended European's understanding of history, for the voyagers encountered peoples with very different pasts, whom sixteenth-century scholars sometimes sought to draw into one, biblically centred narrative. The Reformation also played a role in the changing nature of history: for instance, the demand that it be determined which saints had actually lived promoted an understanding of history as a discipline which sought to establish what had been, rather than the recounting of tales about the past.[119] With the Enlightenment came an awareness of the a-historicity of the Fall, and with it the perception that humankind was not constantly deteriorating from pre-lapsarian perfection. Instead, it began to be believed that humankind was not only capable of shaping the culture and world within which it lived, but also constantly developing.[120] Edmund Halley's efforts to investigate the earth's history independently of scriptural authority, and his re-

---

[114] Ibid. 107.
[115] For the "Corrupters Ancient and Modern" as perceived by Newton, see Mancel, Religion of Isaac Newton (1974) 53–79.
[116] Champion, Acceptable to inquisitive men (1999) 79.
[117] Ibid. 82.
[118] Ibid. 83, and cf. also Popkin, Bible Scholar (1990) 103–06. Newton may also have read Spinoza: ibid.
[119] For this process, see for instance, S. Ditchfield, *Liturgy, sanctity and history in Tridentine Italy: Pietro Maria Campi and the preservation of the particular* (Cambridge: Cambridge UP 1995).
[120] See, for instance, Mulsow, Gundling vs. Buddeus (1997).

sulting suggestion that the earth might not be eternal,[121] show the way in which astronomical interests and historical interests could be closely related. But the process was interlinked: the questions could not have been asked had not scriptural interpretation and understandings of biblical authority already shifted and changed to take account of earlier observations.

The congruence of the interest in textual questions raised by Humanism with the new discoveries which came about through the development of empirical science brought about a fundamental change in the relationship between the "Book of Nature" and the "Book of Scripture" and in turn led to a radical reinterpretation of the relative authority of God's two books. Still viewed in the late sixteenth century as the measure against which philosophical truth must be measured, by the end of the seventeenth century the Bible had no direct role to play in judging the results of the empirical work of natural philosophers, however significant it might be to them in their religious lives. Just as the voyages of discovery had revealed the historical context of ancient philosophical texts, and thus their limitations, so too astronomical observations and scientific discoveries had emphasised the historicity of the Bible, and thus its inability to speak the language of the new science. Not only were new strategies of biblical interpretation called for in the face of these discoveries, but a whole new understanding of the nature of the Bible and of its place – and indeed that of religion – in defining knowledge.

---

[121] Brooke, Science and Religion (1991) 80.

CHAPTER TWENTY-EIGHT

The Development of the Reformation Legacy: Hermeneutics and Interpretation of the Sacred Scripture in the Age of Orthodoxy

By Johann Anselm Steiger, Hamburg

Sources: H. ALTING: *METHODUS THEOLOGIAE DIDACTICAE, Perpetuis S. Scripturae testimoniis explicata & confirmata* ... (Amsterdam: Janssonius 1650). – ANONYMUS [J. J. MÜLLER]: *De imposturis religionum (De tribus impostoribus). Von den Betrügereyen der Religionen* (Philosophische Clandestina der deutschen Aufklärung I,6; ed. W. Schröder; Stuttgart-Bad Cannstatt: frommann-holzboog 1999). – J. AVENARIUS: ספר השרשים *HOC EST, LIBER RADICVM SEV LEXICON EBRAICVM* ... (Wittenberg: Crato 1568). – S. J. BAUMGARTEN: *Auslegung des Evangelii St. Johannis* (ed. J. S. Semler; Halle/S.: Gebauer 1762); *Evangelische Glaubenslehre* I-III (Halle/S.: Gebauer 1759–60); *Theologische Lehrsätze von den Grundwarheiten der christlichen Lehre* ... (ed. A. F. Büsching; Halle/S.: Waisenhaus 1747); *Unterricht von Auslegung der heiligen Schrift* ... (Dritte vermehrte Auflage; Halle/S.: Gebauer 1751). – M. BECANUS: *MANUALE CONTROVERSIARUM* ... (Passau: Manfre 1727 [orig.: Würzburg: Volmar & Dalius 1623]). – *Die Bekenntnisschriften der evangelisch-lutherischen Kirche. Herausgegeben im Gedenkjahr der Augsburgischen Konfession 1930* (Göttingen: Vandenhoeck & Ruprecht ²1952; abbr. BSLK); *Die Bekenntnisschriften der reformierten Kirche* (ed. E. F. K. Müller; Leipzig: Deichert 1903; abbr. BSRK). – R. BELLARMIN: *DISPVTATIONES* ... *DE CONTROVERSIIS CHRISTIANAE FIDEI* ... I-IV (Ingolstadt: Sartorius 1601). – TH. BEZA: *CONFESSIO CHRISTIANAE FIDEI, ET EIVSDEM COLLATIO CUM PAPISTICIS HAERESIBVS* (s.l.: Bonnefoy 1560); *IN HISTORIAM PASSIONIS ET SEPVLTVRAE DOMINI NOstri Iesu Christi* ... (s.l.: Le Preux 1592). – *Bibliotheca Gerhardina. Rekonstruktion der Gelehrten- und Leihbibliothek Johann Gerhards (1582–1637) und seines Sohnes Johann Ernst Gerhard (1621–1668)* (Doctrina et Pietas I,9; ed. J. A. Steiger; Stuttgart-Bad Cannstatt: frommann-holzboog 2002). – W. BIDEMBACH: *Passio Christi EX HISTORIA IOSEPHI ALLEgoricè Tractata* ... (Tübingen: Gruppenbach 1599). – TH. BRUNNER: *Tobias 1569* (Nachdrucke deutscher Literatur des 17. Jahrhunderts; ed. W. F. Michael / D. Reeves; Bern: Lang 1978). – H. BÜNTING: *ITINERARIVM SACRAE SCRIPTVRAE. Das ist/ Ein Reisebuch/ Vber die gantze heilige Schrifft* ... I-III (Helmstedt: Lucius 1582); H. BULLINGER: *RATIO STVDIORVM, SIVE De institutione eorum, qui studia literarum sequuntur, libellus aureus* ... (Zürich: Wolphius 1594). – J. BUXTORF the Elder: *EPITOME RADICUM HEBRAICARUM ET CHALDAICARUM* ... (Basel: Waldkirch 1607); *LEXICON HEBRAICUM ET CHALDAICUM* ... (Basel: Waldkirch 1615); *PRAECEPTIONES GRAMMATICAE DE Lingua Hebraea* ... (Basel: Waldkirch 1605); *THESAURUS GRAMMATICUS LINGUAE SANCTAE Hebraeae* ... (Basel: Waldkirch 1609). – J. BUXTORF the Younger: *TRACTATUS DE PUNCTORUM VOCALIUM, ET ACCENTUUM, IN LIBRIS VETERIS TESTAMENTI HEbraicis, ORIGINE, ANTIQUITATE, & Authoritate: Oppositus ARCANO PUNCTATIONIS LUDOVICI CAPPELLI* (Basel: König 1648). – A. CALOV: *BIBLIA* ... *ILLUSTRATA* ... *Editio secunda* I-IV (Dresden / Leipzig: Zimmermann 1719 [orig.: Frankfurt/Main: Wust 1672–1676]); *CRITICUS SACER BIBLICUS De Sacrae Scripturae autoritate, Canone, lingvâ originali, fontium puritate, ac versionibus praecipuis, imprimis verò Vulgatâ Latinâ, & Graecâ LXX. Interpretum* ... *Altera vice, sed seorsim editus* ... (Wittenberg: Borckard 1673); *PAEDIA THEOLOGICA DE METHODO STUDII THEOLOGICI PIE, DEXTRE, FELICITER TRACTANDI* ... (Wittenberg: Hartmann 1652). – J. CAPPELLUS, *COMMENTARII ET NOTAE CRITICAE IN VETUS TESTA-*

MENTUM. Accessere ... OBSERVATIONES IN EOSDEM LIBROS. Item ... ARCANUM PUNCTATIONIS auctius & emendatius ... (Amsterdam: Wolfgang 1689); [L. Cappellus]: סוד הניקוד הנגלה *HOC EST ARCANVM PVNCTATIONIS REVELATVM. SIVE De Punctorum Vocalium & Accentuum apud Hebraeos vera & germana Antiquitate, Diatriba* (ed. Th. Erpenius; Leiden: Maire 1624). – Johann Benedikt Carpzov: *HISTORIA CRITICA VETERIS TESTAMENTI AUTORE RICHARDO SIMONE PRESBYTERO Congregationis Oratoriae Parisiis edita, ORATIONE INAUGURALI discussa* (Leipzig: Grossius 1684). – Johann Gottlob Carpzov: *Critica Sacra VETERIS TESTAMENTI, PARTE I. CIRCA TEXTVM ORIGINALEM, II. CIRCA VERSIONES, III. CIRCA PSEVDO-CRITICAM GVIL. WHISTONI, SOLICITA, DENVO RECOGNITA, HINC INDE AVCTA ET INDICIBVS NECESSARIIS INSTRVCTA, SECVNDA VICE EDITA* (Leipzig: Martinus 1748); *Censuren vnd Bedencken Von Theologischen Faculteten vnd Doctoren Zu Wittenberg/ Königsberg/ Jehna/ Helmstädt Vber M. HERMANNI RATHMANNI ... außgegangenen Büchern ...* (Jena: Birckner & Weidner 1626). – J. Clericus: *ARS CRITICA, IN QUA AD STUDIA Linguarum Latinae, Graecae, & Hebraicae via munitur; Veterumque emendandorum, & Spuriorum Scriptorum à Genuinis dignoscendorum ratio traditur* I-II (Amsterdam: Gallet 1697). – J. Cocceius: *CENTUM QUINQUAGINTA PSALMI ET EXTREMA VERBA DAVIDIS, CUM COMMENTARIO* (Leiden: Elzevir 1660); *SANCTAE SCRIPTVRAE POTENTIA DEMONSTRATA* (Leiden: Elzevir 1655). – A. Collins: *A DISCOURSE OF THE GROUNDS and REASONS OF THE CHRISTIAN RELIGION ...* (London: s.n. 1724); *THE SCHEME OF Literal PROPHECY CONSIDERED ...* (London: s.n. 1727). – D. Cramer: *SCHOLAE PROPHETICAE, SECVNDA CLASSIS ...* (Hamburg: Froben 1607). – L. Crocius: *Disputationes DE VERBO DEI, OPPOSITAE ROB. BELLARMINI ERRORIBUS* (Hanau: Willerius & Le Clercq 1614). – J. K. Dannhauer: *HERMENEVTICA SACRA SIVE METHODUS exponendarum S. Literarum proposita & vindicata* (Straßburg: Städel 1654); *IDEA BONI INTERPRETIS ET MALITIOSI CALUMNIATORIS QUAE OBSCURITATE DISPULSA, VERUM SENSUM à falso discernere in omnibus auctorum scriptis ac orationibus docet, & plenè respondet ad quaestionem Unde scis hunc esse sensum non alium? ...* (Straßburg: Glaser 1630); *Idea boni interpretis et malitiosi calumniatoris* (Straßburg: Stadel 1652; repr., ed. W. Sparn, Hildesheim: Olms-Weidmann 2004). – S. Deyling: *OBSERVATIONVM SACRARVM, PARS PRIMA, IN QVA MVLTA SCRIPTVRAE VETERIS AC NOVI TESTAMENTI DVBIA VEXATA SOLVVNTVR, LOCA DIFFICILIORA EX ANTIQVITATE, ET VARIAE DOCTRINAE APPARATV, ILLVSTRANTVR, ATQVE AB AVDACI RECENTIORVM CRITICORVM DEPRAVATIONE SOLIDE VINDICANTVR ...* (EDITIO ALTERA; Leipzig: Lanckisch ²1720 [orig.: Leipzig: Lanckisch 1708–15]). – C. Dieterich: *Das Buch der Weißheit Salomons In unterschiedenen Predigen erkläret und außgelegt/ darinn so wol allerhand gemeine Lehren/ als auch mancherley sonderbare Theologische/ Ethische/ Politische/ Physische/ Elementarische Materien ... begriffen werden ...* I (Ulm: Saur 1627). – L. de Dieu: *CRITICA SACRA, sive Animadversiones In loca quaedam difficiliora VETERIS ET NOVI TESTAMENTI* (Editio nova ...; Amsterdam: Borstius 1693). – J. M. Dilherr: "Oratio tertia De Linguae Ebraeae praestantia", in: idem, *ICARVS ACADEMICVS ...* (Nürnberg: Endter 1643) F 1v-G 3r. – J. A. Eisenmenger: *Entdecktes Judenthum/ Oder Gründlicher und Wahrhaffter Bericht/ Welchergestalt Die verstockte Juden die Hochheilige Drey=Einigkeit/ GOtt Vater/ Sohn und Heil. Geist/ erschrecklicher Weise lästern und verunehren/ die Heil. Mutter Christi verschmähen/ das Neue Testament/ die Evangelisten und Aposteln/ die Christliche Religion spöttisch durchziehen/ und die gantze Christenheit auff das äusserste verachten und versuchen ...* I-II (Königsberg: s.n. 1711). – N. Erich: *SYLVVLA SENTENTIARVM, EXEMPLORVM, HISTORIARVM, SImilitudinùm, Facetiarum, Partim ex Reuerendi Viri, D. MARTINI LVTHERI, ac PHILIPPI MELANCHTHONIS cùm priuatis tùm publicis relationibus ...* (Frankfurt/Main: Fabricius & Feyrabend 1566). – C. Finck: *CLAVIS SCRIPTURAE SACRAE SIVE DE RATIONE SCRUTANDI, LEGENDI, INTELLIGENDI, INTERPRETANDi, tractandi, aestimandi, memoriâ facilè comprehendendi universam Scripturam sacram, LIBRI SEX* (Jena: Steinmann 1618). – M. Flacius: *CLAVIS SCRIPTVRAE S. seu de Sermone Sacrarum literarum* I-II (Basel: Episcopius 1580). – J. Forster: *Dictionarium Hebraicum ...* (Basel: Froben & Episcopius 1557). – A. H. Francke, *PRAELECTIONES HERMENEVTICAE, AD VIAM DEXTRE INDAGANDI ET EXPONENDI SENSVM SCRIPTVRAE S. THEOLOGIAE STVDIOSIS OSTENDENDAM ...* (Halle/S.: Orphanotropheus 1717). – W. Franzius: *TRACTATUS THEOLOGICUS Novus & Perspicuus, De INTERPRETATIONE SACRARUM SCRIPTURARUM MAXIME LEGITIMA ...* (Wittenberg: Seelfisch 1619). – J. Gerhard: *COMMENTARIUS SUPER EPISTOLAM AD EBRAEOS ...* (Jena: Härtel 1641); *COMMENTARIUS Super*

GENESIN ... (Jena: Steinmann 1637); *Erklährung der Historien des Leidens vnnd Sterbens vnsers HErrn Christi Jesu nach den vier Evangelisten* (Doctrina et Pietas I,6: ed. J. A. Steiger; Stuttgart-Bad Cannstatt: frommann-holzboog 2002); *Loci theologici* ... I-XXII (ed. F. Cotta; Tübingen: Cotta 1767–89); *Meditationes Sacrae (1606/7), lateinisch-deutsch* (1–2, Doctrina et Pietas I,3; ed. J. A. Steiger; Stuttgart-Bad Cannstatt: frommann-holzboog 2000); *METHODUS STUDII THEOLOGICI* ... (Jena: Steinmann 1620); *POSTILLA SALOMONAEA* ... I-II (Jena: Sengenwald ²1652 [orig.: Jena: Steinmann 1631]); *Sämtliche Leichenpredigten nebst Johann Majors Leichenrede auf Gerhard* (Doctrina et Pietas I,10; ed. J. A. Steiger; Stuttgart-Bad Cannstatt: frommann-holzboog 2001); *Tractatus de Legitima SCRIPTURAE SACRAE INTERPRETATIONE* ... (Jena: Steinmann 1610); *Von der Natur, Krafft vndt Wirckung des geoffenbahrten, gepredigten vndt geschriebenen Worts Gottes* (manuscript; Forschungsbibliothek Gotha, Chart. A 88, 113–152); *Von der Natur, Krafft vndt Wirckung des geoffenbarten vndt geschriebenen Wortes Gottes* (manuscript; Forschungsbibliothek Gotha, Chart. A 88, 159–239). – M. GEYER: *COMMENTARIUS IN PSALMOS DAVIDIS, Fontium Ebraeorum mentem, & vim vocum Phrasiumque Sacrarum, sensumque adeo genuinum, adductis copiose locis parallelis, collatis etiam, ubi opus, Versionibus Interpretumque sententiis, & enodatis difficultatibus Grammaticis cum cura eruens. EDITIO NOVISSIMA* ... (Amsterdam: Blaeu 1695 [orig.: Dresden: Bergen 1668]). – S. GLASSIUS: *Bericht von dem Studio Theologico, wie solches von einem künfftigen Prediger füglich und mit nuzen getrieben werden möge*, in: J. A. Steiger, "Die Rezeption der rabbinischen Tradition im Luthertum (Johann Gerhard, Salomo Glassius u. a.) und im Theologiestudium des 17. Jahrhunderts. Mit einer Edition des universitären Studienplanes von Glassius und einer Bibliographie der von ihm konzipierten Studentenbibliothek", in: *Das Berliner Modell der Mittleren Deutschen Literatur. Beiträge zur Tagung Kloster Zinna 29.9.–01.10.1997* (Chloe 33; ed. C. Caemmerer / W. Delabar / J. Jungmayr / K. Kiesant; Amsterdam: Rodopi 2000) 191–252, here: 222–32; *Christlicher Glaubens=Grund. Das ist/ Deutliche Ausführung/ daß allein die H. Schrifft der Christlichen Lehr/ Glaubens und Lebens/ waares principium, vester Grund/ sichere Regel/ und unbetriegliche Richtschnur* ... (Nürnberg: Endter 1654); *CHRISTOLOGIA MOSAICA, ex prioribus Capitibus Geneseos, ut & CHRISTOLOGIA DAVIDICA, ex Ps. CX. conscripta* ... (Jena: Steinmann 1678); *PHILOLOGIA SACRA* ... (Frankfurt/Main / Leipzig: Gleditsch 1713 [orig.: Jena: Steinmann 1623–36]). – C. GOLDTWURM: *Die Fürnemsten/ schöne vnd Tröstliche Allegorie vnnd Geystliche Bedeutunge/ des Ersten Buchs Moysi* ... (Frankfurt/Main: Jacobus 1552). – H. GROTIUS, *ANNOTATIONES IN LIBROS EVANGELIORVM* ... (Amsterdam: Blaeu 1641); *ANNOTATIONES IN VETVS TESTAMENTUM* ... (ed. J. L. Vogel; Halle/S.: Curt 1775–76 [orig.: 1644]); *Hebraica Biblia, latina planeque noua SEBAST. MVNSTERI TRALATIONE [!], POST OMNEIS [!] OMnium hactenus ubiuis gentium aeditiones euulgata, & quoad fieri potuit, hebraicae ueritati conformata: adiectis insuper è Rabinorum commentarijs annotationibus haud poenitendis, pulchrè & uoces ambiguas, & obscuriora quaeque loca elucidantibus* (Basel: Isengrin & Petri 1546). – A. GRYPHIUS: *Gesamtausgabe der deutschsprachigen Werke* I-VIII (ed. M. Szyrocki / H. Powell; Tübingen: Niemeyer 1963–72). – CH. HELWIG: *Compendium HEBRAEAE GRAMMATICAE* ... (Gießen: Chemlin 1613). – H. HEPPE, *Die Dogmatik der evangelisch-reformierten Kirche. Dargestellt und aus den Quellen belegt* (ed. E. Bizer; Neukirchen: Neukirchener 1958). – V. HERBERGER: *MAGNALIA DEI, DE IESV scripturae nucleo & medulla. Die grossen Thaten GOttes* ... I-XII (Leipzig: Schürer 1607–18). – J. HERTEL: *ALLEGOriarum, typorum, ET EXEMPLORVM Veteris & noui Testamenti Libri duo* ... (Basel: Oporinus 1561). – J. H. HOTTINGER: *Christenlicher/ vnpartheyischer Wägweyser* ... I-III (Zürich: Hamberger 1647–49); *THESAURUS PHILOLOGICUS, Seu CLAVIS SCRIPTURAE* ... (Zürich: Bodmer 1649). – J. HÜLSEMANN: *METHODUS CONCIONANDI, auctior edita. Cui accesserunt Ejusdem Autoris METHODUS STUDII THEOLogici* ... (Wittenberg: Berger 1638). – L. HÜTTER, *Compendium locorum theologicorum ex Scripturis Sacris et libro concordiae* (Doctrina et Pietas II,3; ed. J. A. Steiger; Stuttgart-Bad Cannstatt: frommann-holzboog 2006); idem, "Consilium ... De Studio Theologico rectè inchoando feliciterque continuando", in: J. Hülsemann, *METHODUS CONCIONANDI, auctior edita* (1638) 338–59; idem, *Loci Communes Theologici* ... (Wittenberg: Fincelius & Seelfisch 1661). – A. HYPERIUS: *De rectè formando Theologiae studio, libri IIII* (Basel: Oporinus 1556); *DE SACRAE Scripturae LectioNE AC MEDITATIONE QVOtidiana* ... *Libri II* (Basel: Oporinianus 1569 [orig.: Basel: Oporinus 1561]); *Ein trewer vnd Christlicher Rath. Wie man die Heilige Schrifft teglich lesen vnd betrachten soll* (Mühlhausen: Schmidt 1562). – F. JUNIUS: *SACRORVM PARALLELORVM LIBRI TRES: ID EST, COMPARATIO locorum Scripturae sacrae, qui ex Testamento vetere in Novo adducuntur* ... (Heidelberg: Commelinus 1588). – J. F. KÖNIG: *Theologia positiva acroamatica (Rostock 1664)* (ed. A. Stegmann;

Tübingen: Mohr 2006); [Lehre], *Der reinen/ wahren/ Evangelischen Kirchen/ vnd vngeänderter Augspurgischer Confession zugethaner THEOLOGEN Wiederholete richtige/ gründliche/ vnd vnwiderlegliche Lehr/ Von der heiligen Schrifft/ Oder dem heiligen geoffenbarten Wort Gottes/ was dasselbe seiner Natur vnd Eigenschafft nach sey/ vnd daß es die Krafft vnd Vermögen zu erleuchten/ zu bekehren/ vnd selig zu machen warhafftig vor/ vnd in dem Gebrauch/ in vnd bey sich habe* … (Leipzig: Goetze & Schürer 1629). – E. Leigh: *CRITICA SACRA, Id est, OBSERVATIONES Philologico-Theologicae, In omnes RADICES vel Primitivas voces Hebraeas VETERIS TESTAMENTI* … (tr. H. a Middoch; Gotha: Boetius 1696); *CRITICA SACRA: OR, Philologicall and Theologicall OBSERVATIONS UPON ALL THE GREEK WORDS OF THE NEW TESTAMENT, In order Alphabeticall* … *The second Edition* … (London: Underhill 1646 [orig.: London: Young 1639]). – Th. Ch. Lilienthal: *Die gute Sache der in der heiligen Schrift alten und neuen Testaments enthaltenen Göttlichen Offenbarung, wider die Feinde derselben erwiesen und gerettet* I-XVI (Königsberg: Hartung 1750–82). – V. E. Löscher: *PRAENOTIONES THEOLOGICAE CONTRA NATVRALISTARVM ET FANATICORVM OMNE GENVS* … *EDITIO QVARTA EMENDATA* … (Wittenberg: Hannaverus 1728); [idem], *Unschuldige Nachrichten von Alten und Neuen Theologischen Sachen* … (Leipzig: Grosse 1702–03). – A. Lucas: *Ein schöne vnd tröstliche Comoedia* … *wie Abraham seinen Son Jsaac/ aus Gottes befelh/ zum Brandopffer opffern solte* … (Leipzig: Guenter 1551). – J. Mathesius: *PASSIONALE Mathesij, Das ist/ CHristliche vnnd andechtige Erklerung vnd Außlegung des Zwey vnd Zwantzigsten Psalms/ vnd Drey vnd Funfftzigsten Capitels des Propheten Esaiae* … (Leipzig: Beyer 1587). – J. Meelführer: *CLAVIS sanctae seu Hebraeae linguae* … (Nürnberg: Halbmayer 1628). – B. Meisner: "BREVIS INSTRUCTIO DE LEctione Biblicâ & Locis Communibus" [1614], in: J. Hülsemann, *METHODUS CONCIONANDI, auctior edita* (1638) 379–92. – H. Mencelius: "Vorrede", in: B. Gernhard, *LehreBuch/ Himlischer Weisheit/ fur allerley Stende/ aus den vier Edlen Büchern Salomonis/ vnd Jhesu Syrachs* … (Eisleben: Gaubisch 1575). – B. Mentzer (Praes.) / A. Bodenius (Disp.): *TERTIA Disputatio Theologica & Scholastica, De vero sacrae scripturae sensu & interpretatione: OPPOSITA TERTIO CAPITI LIBELLI PISTORIANI, QUI INSCRIBITUR: Wegweiser für alle verführete Christen/ etc.* (Marburg: Egenolph 1600). – M. Merian: *ICONES BIBLICAE Praecipuas Sacrae Scripturae Historias eleganter & graphicè repraesentantes* … I-II (Frankfurt/Main: De Bry 1625). – J. Morinus: מסורת הברית *EXERCITATIONES BIBLICAE DE HEBRAEI GRAECIQVE TEXTVS sinceritate, germana LXXII. Interpretum translatione dignoscenda, illius cum Vulgata conciliatione, & iuxta Iudaeos diuina integritate; totiusque Rabbinicae antiquitatis, operis Masorethici aera, explicatione, & censura* (Paris: Vitray 1633). – J. Müller: *JUDAISMUS oder Jüdenthumb/ Das ist/ Außführlicher Bericht von des Jüdischen Volckes Vnglauben/ Blindheit vnd Verstockung/ Darinne Sie wider die Prophetischen Weissagungen/ von der Zukunfft/ Person vnd Ampt Messiae/ insonderheit wider des HErrn JEsu von Nazareth wahre GOttheit/ Gebuhrt von einer Jungfrawen* … *streiten* … (Hamburg: Härtel 1644). – J. Narhamer: *Historia Jobs* (Arbeiten zur Mittleren Deutschen Literatur und Sprache 12; ed. B. Könneker / W. F. Michael; Bern: Lang 1983). – J. Olearius: *Methodus STUDII THEOLOGICI* … (Halle: Mylius 1664). – M. Opitz, *Gesammelte Werke. Kritische Ausgabe* (vol. 4/1; Bibliothek des literarischen Vereins in Stuttgart 312; ed. G. Schulz-Behrend; Stuttgart: Hiersemann 1989). – L. Osiander: *DE STVDIIS PRIVATIS RECTE INSTITVENDIS Admonitio* … (Tübingen: Gruppenbach 1591). – Sanctes Pagninus: אוצר לשון הקדש *HOC EST, THESAVRVS LINGUAE SANCTAE* … (Lyon: Gryphius 1529). – D. Pareus: *DISCEPTATIO EPISTOLARIS JOANNIS MAGIRI JESUITAE CONCIONATORIS: ET DAVIDIS PAREI CHRISTIANI THEOLOGI. DE AVTHORITATE DIvina & Canonica S. Scripturarum: deque absoluta Ecclesiae infallibilitate* (Heidelberg: Voegelin 1604); *OPERVM THEOLOGICORVM Tomus I [-II]* (Frankfurt/Main: Rosa 1628). – A. Pfeiffer: *HERMENEVTICA SACRA, sive LUCULENTA SUCCINCTA TRACTATIO, De LEGITIMA INTERPRETATIONE SACRARUM LITERARUM* (Dresden: Huebner 1684). – A. Pfeilschmidt: *Esther 1555* (ed. B. Könneker / W. F. Michael; Arbeiten zur Mittleren Deutschen Literatur und Sprache 16; Bern: Lang 1986). – M. Pflacher: *ANALYSIS TYPICA Omnium cùm veteris, tum noui Testamenti Librorum Historicorum: ad intelligendam rerum seriem, & memoriam iuuandam accommodata* … (Basel: Waldkirch 1606). – A. P. von Polansdorf: *EXEGESIS ANALYTICA Illustrium aliquot vaticiniorum veteris Testamenti DE INCARNATIONE, PASSIONE, MORTE ET RESVRRECTIONE DOMINI NOSTRI JESU CHRISTI* … (Basel: Waldkirch 1608). – H. Rahtmann: *JESU CHRISTI. Deß Königs aller Könige vnd HERRN aller Herren GNADENREJCH* … (Danzig: Huenefeldt 1621); *Wolgegründetes Bedencken. Was Von deß D. Conradi dieterichs seinen SchwarmFragen/ darinnen er vom Schwenckfeldianismo/ betreffend das Beschriebene vnd gepredigte*

Wort Gottes/ handelt/ vnd desselbigen andere beschüldiget/ zuhalten sey ... (Lüneburg: Stern 1623). – J. J. RAMBACH: *Erläuterung über seine eigene INSTITVTIONES HERMENEVTICAE SACRAE* ... (Gießen: Krieger 1738); *INSTITVTIONES HERMENEUTICAE SACRAE VARIIS OBSERVATIONIBVS COPIOSISSIMISQVE EXEMPLIS BIBLICIS ILLVSTRATAE* (Jena: Hartung 1752 [orig.: Jena: Hartung 1723]). – A. REUDEN: *Jsagoge Biblica BIBLIORUM SACRORUM COMPLECTENS VOCABULUM, DEFINITIONEM, CAUSAS, EFFECTUM, Subjecta, Adjuncta, & commendationem, certitudinem, rationem docendi & discendi, atque Pugnantia* (Hamburg: Moller 1601). – J. RIST: *Neues Musikalisches Seelenparadis/ Jn sich begreiffend Die allerfürtreflichste Sprüche der heiligen Schrifft/ Alten Testaments/ Jn gantz Lehr= vnd Trostreichen Liederen und HertzensAndachten* ... (Lüneburg: Stern 1660). – A. RIVETUS: *ISAGOGE SEV Introductio generalis, ad Scripturam Sacram Veteris & Novi Testamenti* ... (Leiden: Commelinus 1627). – M. SACHSE: *IOSEPH TYPICVS. Drey vnd Zwantzig Sehr schöne lehr vnnd Trostreiche Allegorien vnd Vergleichungen Josephs mit dem Herrn Jesu Christo* ... (Leipzig: Beyer 1596). – J. SAUBERT: *GEJSTLJCHE GEMAELDE Vber die Sonn= vnd hohe Festtägliche EVANGELJA Sambt etlichen andern Predigten Aus den Sprüchwörtern Salomonis/ den Propheten/ vnd Episteln deß H. Apostels Pauli* ... (Nürnberg: Endter 1652). – V. SCHINDLER: *LEXICON PENTAGLOTTON, Hebraicum, Chaldaicum, Syriacum, Talmudico-Rabbinicum, & Arabicum* ... (Hanau: Rulandius 1612). – V. SCHMUCK: *Bibelbüchlin. Deutsche Monsticha auff alle vnd jgliche Capitel aller Bücher heiliger Schrifft* ... (Leipzig: Lantzenberger 1600). – B. SELLIUS / H. JANSEN / P. van der BORCHT: *EMBLEMATA SACRA, è praecipuis vtriusque Testamenti historiis concinnata* (Leiden: Plantinus 1593). – N. SELNECKER: *NOTATIO* ... *De studio sacrae Theologiae, & de ratione discendi doctrinam coelestem* (Leipzig: Rhamba 1579). – J. SIMLER: *EXODVS IN EXODVM VEL Secundum Librum Mosis* ... *Commentarij* (Zürich: Froschoverus 1584). – J. STRACK: *Das Ander Buch des heiligen Propheten vnd Mannes Gottes Exodus genant* ... (Kassel: Wessel 1621). – J. TARNOW: *In Prophetam JONAM COMMENTARIUS* ... (Rostock: Hallervord 1626). – C. VITRINGA: *COMMENTARIUS IN LIBRUM PROPHETIARUM JESAIAE* ... *PARS PRIOR [– POSTERIOR]* (Herborn: Andreae 1715/1722 [orig.: Leeuwarden: Halma 1714/1720]). – G. VOETIUS: *EXERCITIA ET BIBLIOTHECA, Studiosi Theologiae* ... *Editio Secunda* ... (Utrecht: a Waesberge 1651 [orig.: Utrecht: Strick 1644]). – H. WELLER: *RATIO Formandi Studij THEOLOGICI. ITEM: De modo & RaTIONE CONcionandi* (Nürnberg: Neuber & Montanus 1565). – S. WERENFELS: *OPUSCULA THEOLOGICA, PHILOSOPHICA ET PHILOLOGICA. EDITIO TERTIA* ... (Leiden / Leeuwarden: Le Mair & de Chalmot 1777 [orig.: Basel: Mechel]). – G. WICELIUS: "Oratio in laudem linguae Ebraicae", in: J. M. Dilherr, *ICARVS ACADEMICVS* ... (Nürnberg: Endter 1643) G 3v–I 2v. – J. WOLLEB: *COMPENDIVM THEOLOGIAE CHRISTIANAE* ... (Amsterdam: Blaeu 1633).

Bibliographies: P. BESODNERUS, *Bibliotheca Theologica, Hoc est, INDEX BIBLIORVM PRAECIPVORVM, EORUNDEMQUE INTERPRETUM, HEBRAEORUM, GRAECORUM, ET LATINORUM, TAM VETERUM, QVAM RECENTIum, in certas classes ita digestorum, ut primo intuitu apparere possit, qui in numero Rabbinorum, Patrum, Lutheranorum, Pontificiorum, aut Cinglio-Calvinianorum contineantur* (Frankfurt/Oder: Thieme 1608); G. DRAUD, *BIBLIOTHECA CLASSICA, Sive Catalogus Officinalis* ... (Frankfurt/Main: Oster 1625); M. LIPENIUS, *BIBLIOTHECA REALIS THEOLOGICA OMNIVM MATERIARVM, RERUM ET TITULORUM* ... I–II (Frankfurt/Main: Friedrich 1685; repr. Hildesheim / New York: Olms 1973); [VD16], *Verzeichnis der im deutschen Sprachbereich erschienenen Drucke des XVI. Jahrhunderts* 1–22 (Stuttgart: Hiersemann 1983–95); [VD17], *Das Verzeichnis der im deutschen Sprachraum erschienenen Drucke des 17. Jahrhunderts* (www.vd17.de); J. CHR. WOLF, *BIBLIOTHECA HEBRAEA, Sive NOTITIA TVM AVCTORVM HEBR. CVJVSCVNQVE AETATIS, TVM SCRIPTORVM, QVAE VEL HEBRAICE PRIMVM EXARATA VEL AB ALIIS CONVERSA SVNT, AD NOSTRAM AETATEM DEDVCTA* I–IV (Hamburg / Leipzig: Liebezeit 1715-33).

General works: L. DIESTEL, *Geschichte des Alten Testaments in der christlichen Kirche* (Jena: Mauke 1869; repr. Leipzig: Zentralantiquariat der DDR 1981); H.-J. KRAUS, *Geschichte der historisch-kritischen Erforschung des Alten Testaments von der Reformation bis zur Gegenwart* (Neukirchen: Neukirchner 1956; ³1982); G. W. MEYER, *Geschichte der Schrifterklärung seit der Wiederherstellung der Wissenschaften* I–V (Göttingen: Röwer 1802–09); H. GRAF REVENTLOW, *Epochen der Bibelauslegung* III. *Renaissance, Reformation, Humanismus* (München: Beck 1997); IV. *Von der Aufklärung bis zum 20. Jahrhundert* (2001).

Special studies: H. AARSLEFF, "The Rise and Decline of Adam and his Ursprache in Seventeenth-Century Thought", *The Language of Adam. Die Sprache Adams* (Wolfenbütteler Forschungen 84;

ed. A. P. Coudert; Wiesbaden: Harrassowitz 1999) 277–95; W. ALEXANDER, *Hermeneutica Generalis. Zur Konzeption und Entwicklung der allgemeinen Verstehenslehre im 17. und 18. Jahrhundert* (Stuttgart: M & P Verlag 1993); N. BACK, "'Die alten Hebreer haben recht und wol gesagt …'. Johann Gerhard und die jüdische Schriftauslegung", *Von Luther zu Bach* (ed. R. Steiger; Sinzig: Studio 1999) 179–86; J. BAUR, "Flacius – Radikale Theologie", *Matthias Flacius Illyricus 1575–1975* (Schriftenreihe des Regensburger Osteuropainstituts 2; Regensburg 1975) 37–49; S. G. BURNETT, *From Christian Hebraism to Jewish Studies. Johannes Buxtorf (1564–1629) and Hebrew Learning in the Seventeenth Century* (SHCT 68; Leiden: Brill 1996); P. BÜHLER, "L'herméneutique de Johann Conrad Dannhauer", in: *La logique herméneutique du XVIIe siècle. J. C. Dannhauer et J. Clauberg* (ed. J.-C. Gens; Paris: Le Cercle Herméneutique Ed. 2006) 69–91; L. DANNEBERG, "Kontroverstheologie, Schriftauslegung und Logik als 'donum Dei'", in: *Kulturgeschichte Preußens königlich polnischen Anteils* (Frühe Neuzeit 103; ed. S. Beckmann / K. Garber; Tübingen: Niemeyer 2005) 479–582; idem, "Siegmund Jacob Baumgartens biblische Hermeneutik", *Unzeitgemäße Hermeneutik. Verstehen und Interpretation im Denken der Aufklärung* (ed. Axel Bühler; Frankfurt/Main: Klostermann 1994), 88–157; M. VON ENGELHARDT, "Der Rahtmannische Streit", *ZHTh* NF 18 (1854) 43–131; P. FRAENKEL, "Le débat entre Martin Chemnitz et Robert Bellarmin sur les livres deutérocanoniques et la place du Siracide", *Le Canon de l'Ancien Testament. Sa formation et son histoire* (ed. J.-D. Kaestli e.a.; Genève: Labor et Fides 1984) 283–312; H.-G. GADAMER, "Rhetorik und Hermeneutik" (1976), in: idem, *Hermeneutik II. Wahrheit und Methode* (Tübingen: Mohr 1986) 276–91; R. H. GRÜTZMACHER, *Wort und Geist. Eine historische und dogmatische Untersuchung* (Leipzig: Deichert 1902); B. HÄGGLUND, *Die Heilige Schrift und ihre Deutung in der Theologie Johann Gerhards. Eine Untersuchung über das altlutherische Schriftverständnis* (Lund: Gleerup 1951); idem, "Die Theologie des Wortes bei Johann Gerhard", *KuD* 29 (1983) 272–83; idem, "Vorkantianische Hermeneutik", in: *KuD* 52 (2006) 165–81; H. HALVERSCHEID, *Lumen Spiritus prius quam Scriptura intellecta. Hermann Rahtmanns Kritik am lutherischen Schriftprinzip* (Diss. Marburg 1971); P. HERBERS, *Die hermeneutische Lehre Johann Jakob Rambachs* (Diss. Heidelberg 1952); G. HOFFMANN, "Lutherische Schriftauslegung im 17. Jahrhundert, dargestellt am Beispiel Abraham Calovs", *Das Wort und die Wörter* (ed. H. Balz / S. Schulz; Stuttgart: Kohlhammer 1973) 127–42; V. JUNG, *Das Ganze der Heiligen Schrift. Hermeneutik und Schriftauslegung bei Abraham Calov* (Calwer Theologische Monographien B 18; Stuttgart: Calwer 1999); R. KIRSTE, *Das Zeugnis des Geistes und das Zeugnis der Schrift. Das testimonium spiritus sancti internum als hermeneutisch-polemischer Zentralbegriff bei Johann Gerhard in der Auseinandersetzung mit Robert Bellarmins Schriftverständnis* (GTA 6; Göttingen: Vandenhoeck & Ruprecht 1976); M. I. KLAUBER, *Between Reformed Scholasticism and Pan-Protestantism. Jean-Alphonse Turretin (1671–1737) and Enlightened Orthodoxy at the Academy of Geneva* (Selinsgrove: Susquehanna UP 1994); W. P. KLEIN, "Die ursprüngliche Einheit der Sprachen in der philologisch-grammatischen Sicht der frühen Neuzeit", *The Language of Adam. Die Sprache Adams* (Wolfenbütteler Forschungen 84; ed. A. P. Coudert; Wiesbaden: Harrassowitz 1999) 25–56; H. C. KNUTH, *Zur Auslegungsgeschichte von Psalm 6* (BGBE 11; Tübingen: Mohr 1971); E. KOCH, "Die 'Himlische Philosophia des heiligen Geistes'. Zur Bedeutung alttestamentlicher Spruchweisheit im Luthertum des 16. und 17. Jahrhunderts", *ThLZ* 115 (1990) 706–20; R. KOLB, "Sixteenth-Century Lutheran Commentary on Genesis and the Genesis Commentary of Martin Luther", in: idem, *Luther's Heirs Define His Legacy. Studies on Lutheran Confessionalization* (Collected Studies Series 539; Aldershot: Variorum 1996) 243–58; G. KRAUSE, *Andreas Gerhard Hyperius. Leben – Bilder – Schriften* (BHTh 56; Tübingen: Mohr 1977); D. LERCH, *Isaaks Opferung christlich gedeutet. Eine auslegungsgeschichtliche Untersuchung* (BHTh 12; Tübingen: Mohr 1950); E. MÜHLENBERG, "Schriftauslegung III. Kirchengeschichtlich", *TRE* 30 (1999) 472–88; B. T. OFTESTAD, "Traditio und Norma. Hauptzüge der Schriftauffassung bei Martin Chemnitz", *Der zweite Martin der Lutherischen Kirche* (ed. W. Jünke; Braunschweig: s.n. 1986) 172–89; A. L. OLSEN, "The Hermeneutical Vision of Martin Chemnitz. The Role of Scripture and Tradition in the Teaching Church", *Augustine, the Harvest, and Theology (1300–1650)* (ed. K. Hagen; Leiden: Brill 1990) 314–32; L. PERLITT, "Hoc libro maxime fides docetur. Deuteronomium 1,19–46 bei Martin Luther und Johann Gerhard", *NZSTh* 32 (1990) 105–12; C. H. RATSCHOW, *Lutherische Dogmatik zwischen Reformation und Aufklärung* 1–2 (Gütersloh: Mohn 1964/1966); H. GRAF REVENTLOW, *Bibelautorität und Geist der Moderne. Die Bedeutung des Bibelverständnisses für die geistesgeschichtliche und politische Entwicklung in England bis zur Aufklärung* (FKDG 30; Göttingen: Vandenhoeck & Ruprecht 1980; ET: London: SCM 1984); idem, "Bibelexegese als Aufklärung. Die Bibel im Denken des Johannes Clericus (1657–1736)", *Historische Kritik und bib-*

lischer Kanon in der deutschen Aufklärung (Wolfenbütteler Forschungen 41; ed. H. Graf Reventlow / W. Sparn / J. Woodbridge; Wiesbaden: Harrassowitz 1988) 1–19; idem, "Wurzeln der modernen Bibelkritik", in: *Historische Kritik und biblischer Kanon* (1988) 47–63; M. SCHLOEMANN, *Siegmund Jacob Baumgarten. System und Geschichte in der Theologie des Überganges zum Neuprotestantismus* (FKDG 26; Göttingen: Vandenhoeck & Ruprecht 1974); idem, "Wegbereiter wider Willen. Siegmund Jacob Baumgarten und die historisch-kritische Bibelforschung", in: *Historische Kritik und biblischer Kanon* (1988) 149–55; W. SCHMIDT-BIGGEMANN, "Die katholische Tradition. Bellarmins biblische Hermeneutik", in: idem, *Apokalypse und Philologie. Wissensgeschichte und Weltentwürfe in der Frühen Neuzeit* (ed. A. Hallacker / B. Bayer; Berliner Mittelalter- und Frühneuzeitforschung 2; Göttingen: Vandenhoeck & Ruprecht 2006) 53–78; G. SCHNEDERMANN, *Die Controverse des Ludovicus Cappellus mit den Buxtorfen über das Alter der hebräischen Punctation. Ein Beitrag zur Geschichte des Studiums der Hebräischen Sprache* (Leipzig: Schnedermann 1878); K. SCHOLDER, *Ursprünge und Probleme der Bibelkritik im 17. Jahrhundert. Ein Beitrag zur Entstehung der historisch-kritischen Theologie* (FGLP 10,33; München: Kaiser 1966); R. SDZUJ, *Historische Studien zur Interpretationsmethodologie der frühen Neuzeit* (Epistemata, Reihe Literaturwissenschaft 209; Würzburg: Königshausen & Neumann 1997); G. SEEBASS, "Zum Verständnis des Alten Testaments bei Caspar Schwenckfeld von Ossig", in: idem, *Die Reformation und ihre Außenseiter. Gesammelte Aufsätze und Vorträge* (Göttingen: Vandenhoeck & Ruprecht 1997) 336–49; R. SMEND, "Der ältere Buxtorf", *ThZ* 53 (1997) 109–17; idem, "Spätorthodoxe Antikritik. Zum Werk des Johann Gottlob Carpzov", *Historische Kritik und biblischer Kanon* (1988) 127–37; J. A. STEIGER, "'Das Wort sie sollen lassen stahn …'. Die Auseinandersetzung Johann Gerhards und der lutherischen Orthodoxie mit dem Danziger Pfarrer Hermann Rahtmann und deren abendmahlstheologische und christologische Implikate", *ZThK* 95 (1998) 338–65; idem, "Die Rezeption der rabbinischen Tradition im Luthertum (Johann Gerhard, Salomo Glassius u.a.) und im Theologiestudium des 17. Jahrhunderts. Mit einer Edition des universitären Studienplanes von Glassius und einer Bibliographie der von ihm konzipierten Studentenbibliothek", *Das Berliner Modell der Mittleren Deutschen Literatur* (Chloe 33; ed. C. Caemmerer / W. Delabar / J. Jungmayr / K. Kiesant; Amsterdam: Rodopi 2000) 191–252; idem, *Johann Gerhard (1582–1637). Studien zu Theologie und Frömmigkeit des Kirchenvaters der lutherischen Orthodoxie* (Doctrina et Pietas I,1; Stuttgart-Bad Cannstatt: frommann-holzboog 1997); idem, "Johann Gerhards biblische Exzerptbücher. Zwei Autographen-Funde und die Suche nach mehr", *ZKG* 110 (1999) 247–50; idem, *Melancholie, Diätetik und Trost. Konzepte der Melancholie-Therapie im 16. und 17. Jahrhundert* (Heidelberg: Manutius 1996); idem, "Zu Gott gegen Gott. Oder: Die Kunst, gegen Gott zu glauben. Isaaks Opferung (Gen 22) bei Luther, im Luthertum der Barockzeit, in der Epoche der Aufklärung und im 19. Jahrhundert", in: *Isaaks Opferung (Gen 22) in den Konfessionen und Medien der Frühen Neuzeit* (ed. idem / Ulrich Heinen; AKG 101; Berlin / New York: de Gruyter 2006) 185–237; J. WALLMANN, "Straßburger lutherische Orthodoxie im 17. Jahrhundert. Johann Conrad Dannhauer. Versuch einer Annäherung", *RHPhR* 68 (1988) 55–71.

1. The Age of Protestant Orthodoxy

1.1. Observations on the History of Research

For a long time Protestant Orthodoxy was ignored by scholarship, reflecting a deep-seated disesteem with a long history. Orthodoxy was regarded as lifeless, fossilised and one-sidedly doctrinaire. At times it was reproached for having betrayed the heritage of the Reformation by slipping back into the Middle Ages. The renewed reception of Aristotelian-stamped scholasticism, as well as threads of the mystical tradition, were believed to have distorted and concealed the message of God offering salvation to sinful humanity and the preaching of justification by faith alone. This was also thought to have had fatal consequences for biblical exegesis, since a "living, historical understanding of the Bible" (*lebendig-geschichtliches Verständnis der Bibel*)[1] was thereby made impossible. Even today such judgements of Protestant Orthodoxy are often still found in encyclopaedias, textbooks and elsewhere. They have their origin in a view of history formed by Radical Pietism. In his *Unpartheiische Kirchen- und Ketzerhistorie* (1699–1700), Gottfried Arnold had overturned the traditional interest in the work of Church history, sometimes traced back to Flacius: Church history, in Arnold's view, is not synonymous with the history of doctrine held as Orthodox at any given time and the teachings which opposed it, since the true, Spirit-endowed Church is not found in the externally organised institution. Rather the *ecclesia vera* exists outside external polity. The true Church of the Spirit is represented by the heretics, who once suffered, or still endure, various persecutions on the part of the *babylonische Mauerkirche*.

Arnold's pietistic-polemical attack on Orthodoxy had sweeping effect: it marked Orthodoxy as dead, obstinately doctrinaire and concerned with *theologia polemica* (controversial theology), as well as blind in matters of piety.[2] The tendentious establishment of this assessment had already been called attention to by the late-Orthodox Lutheran theologian Ernst Salomo Cyprian (1673–1745) – Arnold, Johann Konrad Dippel and Christian Thomasius "turned the words Orthodoxy and Orthodox ... into pejorative criticisms"[3], according to Cyprian. However, this did not prevent the following generations of scholars from accepting and furthering the caricature of a dead Orthodoxy. It is noteworthy that the assertion of obfuscatory Orthodoxy links together various theological schools and parties as sharing a *consensus communis* even though they could not be any more contrary. In the context of the Revivalist Movement, August Tholuck charged Orthodoxy with having paved the way for enlightened rationalism, which he strongly rejected. Theological Liberalism, which advanced under the banner of promoting Kant's philosophical criticism of metaphysics and of applying it to the Reformation tradition, objected especially to the renewed reception of Aristotelianism and to the early modern Protestant scholastic philosophy. It also criticised the elements of mysticism within Protestantism, which it traced back to Roman Catholicism (ALBRECHT and OTTO RITSCHL). On the one hand WINFRIED ZELLER deserves credit for having moved Orthodoxy back to centre stage by focusing on the history of piety. On the other hand he has furthered the old arguments against it by his assertion that Orthodoxy produced a crisis of piety.[4] Recently the German philologist HANS-GEORG KEMPER has renewed the familiar *cliché*.[5]

Not until recent years has a line of scholarship emerged, in recourse to older positions, such as, for example, that of HANS LEUBE,[6] which can claim to regard Protestant Orthodoxy as a valid academic subject in its own right. An important impetus for this change of tack has been provided by theological research into the work of J. S. Bach,[7] works on German philology in the lit-

---

[1] Reventlow, Wurzeln (1988) 63. Cf. Kraus, Geschichte (1956) 29, 33.

[2] H. LEUBE, *Die Reformideen in der deutschen lutherischen Kirche zur Zeit der Orthodoxie* (Leipzig: Dörffling & Franke 1924) 4ff; M. MATTHIAS, "Orthodoxie I", TRE 25 (1995) 464–85, here: 467.

[3] E. S. CYPRIAN, *Vernünfftige Warnung für dem Jrrthum von Gleichgültigkeit derer Gottesdienste, oder Religionen ...* (Gotha: Reyher ²1744) 120. Cf. idem, *Allgemeine Anmerckungen über Gottfried Arnolds Kirchen= und Ketzer= Historie ...* (Frankfurt/Main / Leipzig: Pfotenhauer ³1701).

[4] W. ZELLER, "Protestantische Frömmigkeit im 17. Jahrhundert", in: idem, *Theologie und Frömmigkeit. Gesammelte Aufsätze* (MThSt 8; ed. B. Jaspert; Marburg: Elwert 1971) 85–116.

[5] H.-G. KEMPER, *Deutsche Lyrik der frühen Neuzeit* (Tübingen: Niemeyer 1987-), vol. 2, 9, 171 ff. and vol. 3, 4.

[6] See n. 2 above.

[7] *Theologische Bachforschung heute. Dokumentation und Bibliographie der Internationalen Arbeitsgemeinschaft für theologische Bachforschung* (ed. R. Steiger; Glienicke: Galda & Wilch 1998); R.

erary-theological field,[8] as well as by research into Pietism. However, as far as the latter is concerned, it increasingly became apparent that regarding the piety of Orthodoxy simply as the 'prehistory' of Pietism both falls short of the subject under research and restricts the view of it.

Although important partial results have been reached regarding research into Orthodoxy in recent years, substantial work remains to be done. This includes the task of producing critical editions of texts from the period which, apart from the writings of Johann Gerhard, has yet to be taken in hand. A more broadly based initiative, with the aim of researching Reformed Orthodoxy, does not yet appear to emerge.[9] Quite a lot of attention has been paid to Orthodox dogmatics, and thereby to the systematic-theological work of Orthodox theologians. A certain balance to this one-sidedness can be discerned in that, in recent years, the theology of Lutheran Orthodox piety and meditation has been studied with increasing intensity.[10]

Meanwhile the broad field of the history of scriptural exegesis in the age of Orthodoxy remains almost completely untouched. Indeed in recent years the intensive debate, led particularly by historical and church-historical scholarship over the confessional partisanship of Orthodoxy research, has provided many impulses. However, the discussion about confessional preferences has had a rather paralysing effect on the exploration of Scripture interpretation in this period. This deficit is all the greater, since according to Orthodox view the Holy Scripture is the sole and exclusive basis of faith and therefore its exegesis must be the starting point and the goal of theological scholarship.

In view of this state of affairs it can be seen as a matter of course that the following remarks 1. dispense with perpetuating false assessments largely based on ignorance of the original sources; 2. are rendered more complex because results of research concerning Orthodox exegesis (especially of the Old Testament) are almost non-existent; 3. as a study of individual cases cannot

---

STEIGER, *Gnadengegenwart. Johann Sebastian Bach im Kontext lutherischer Orthodoxie und Frömmigkeit* (Doctrina et Pietas II,2; Stuttgart-Bad Cannstatt: frommann-holzboog 2002).

[8] To name just two: H.-H. KRUMMACHER, *Der junge Gryphius und die Tradition. Studien zu den Perikopensonetten und Passionsliedern* (München: Fink 1976); E. TRUNZ, *Johann Matthäus Meyfart. Theologe und Schriftsteller in der Zeit des Dreißigjährigen Krieges* (München: Beck 1987).

[9] Cf. however C. STROHM, *Ethik im frühen Calvinismus. Humanistische Einflüsse, philosophische, juristische und theologische Argumentationen sowie mentalitätsgeschichtliche Aspekte am Beispiel des Calvin-Schülers Lambertus Danaeus* (AKG 65; Berlin: de Gruyter 1996).

[10] E. AXMACHER, *Praxis Evangeliorum. Theologie und Frömmigkeit bei Martin Moller (1547–1606)* (FKDG 43; Göttingen: Vandenhoeck & Ruprecht 1989); idem, *Johann Arndt und Paul Gerhardt. Studien zur Theologie, Frömmigkeit und geistlichen Dichtung des 17. Jahrhunderts* (Mainzer hymnologische Studien 3; Tübingen / Basel: Francke 2001); T. KOCH, *Johann Habermanns "Betbüchlein" im Zusammenhang seiner Theologie. Eine Studie zur Gebetsliteratur und zur Theologie des Luthertums im 16. Jahrhundert* (BHTh 117; Tübingen: Mohr 2001); M. MATTHIAS, *Theologie und Konfession. Der Beitrag von Aegidius Hunnius (1550–1603) zur Entstehung einer lutherischen Religionskultur* (Leipzig: Evangelische Verlagsanstalt 2004); J. A. STEIGER, *Gerhard* (1997); A. M. STEINMEIER-KLEINHEMPEL, *"Von Gott kompt mir ein Frewdenschein". Die Einheit Gottes und des Menschen in Philipp Nicolais "FrewdenSpiegel deß ewigen Lebens"* (EHS.T 430; Frankfurt/Main: Lang 1991); U. STRÄTER, *Meditation und Kirchenreform in der lutherischen Kirche des 17. Jahrhunderts* (BHTh 91; Tübingen: Mohr 1995); J. WALLMANN, *Theologie und Frömmigkeit im Zeitalter des Barock* (Tübingen: Mohr 1995).

serve as a substitute for a handbook, which has so far not been composed; 4. are preliminary results, gained from original sources, and provide only a few perspectives for future research. In any case, however, one conclusion with regard to future research into the Post-Reformation history of interpretation is inescapable: to discard the claim that serious scholarly (that is, historical) exegesis only became scientifically critical in the age of the Enlightenment. The biblical erudition of previous ages is then held to contain, at best, only occasional glimpses which anticipate the modern goal of research. Such a view, represented, for example, by GOTTLOB WILHELM MEYER in the nineteenth century and, similarly, by HANS-JOACHIM KRAUS and HENNING GRAF REVENTLOW[11] in the twentieth, distorts the true facts. In reality the results of the so-called 'pre-critical' exegesis (not only of Protestantism) are phenomena *sui generis* and, as such, merit proper appraisal. This, nevertheless, is hindered if the research is directed, by prior intention, to look for signs of the dawning of modernity in past eras and, with this, to trace the prehistory of one's own way of thinking.

1.2. Orthodoxy – the Age of Developing Protestant Fundamentals

As we have noted, since Gottfried Arnold the history of Orthodoxy has been described as one of decline. In pursuing a carefully balanced investigation of the post-Reformation period it would certainly be more appropriate to turn this premise round. In many respects the Reformation only reached its goal in the seventeenth century. Striving to fulfil the claim of the Reformation to be built on old foundations, this age performed a vast extent of receptive as well as productive work. A list should include the adaptation of classical pagan learning, especially Aristotelian philosophy, rhetoric and poetics, dietetics and medicine, etc., besides their application to theological doctrine.

The application of neo-Aristotelian philosophy was not simply essential, insofar as theology was in need of a foundation in the philosophy of science. The "return of metaphysics" (*Wiederkehr der Metaphysik*)[12] was therefore necessary for the theological, and especially exegetical, work produced during the period of the Reformation for the following reasons: 1. to be able to describe and summarise this work methodically; 2. to make exegesis teachable and adaptable for educational service in secondary schools and universities; 3. to render the theology of the Reformers open to debate, i.e., it was necessary to participate in theological controversy with particular regard to post-Tridentine, particularly Jesuit, teaching methods. The same may hold true with regard to logic, which ensured that the processes of learning and discourse, not least in disputation exercises in secondary schools and universities, received a clear methodological framework and foundation. The Latin school system,[13] which – as is widely recognised – largely bears the mark of Melanchthon, served an important role in this area.

---

[11] See n. 1 above. Clearly, however, REVENTLOW's view becomes more differentiated. Certainly he furthers the assertion of the diminishment and fossilization of the Reformation heritage by Orthodoxy, but he does grant the Orthodox exegesis attractive philological features and an orientation concerned with piety (cf. Reventlow, Epochen 3, 1997, 229–33).

[12] W. SPARN, *Wiederkehr der Metaphysik. Die ontologische Frage in der lutherischen Theologie des frühen 17. Jahrhunderts* (CThM B 4; Stuttgart: Calwer 1976).

[13] *Quellen zur Geschichte des kirchlichen Unterrichts in der evangelischen Kirche Deutschlands zwischen 1530 und 1600* 1-2 (ed. J. M. Reu; Gütersloh: Bertelsmann 1904–1935). F. PAULSEN,

Since the last third of the sixteenth century mainly Lutheran theologians had been concerned with taking up and studying the mystical treasures of devotional literature, such as those of [Ps]-Augustine, [Ps]-Anselm and [Ps]-Bernard. As we follow carefully this process of reception from the perspective of traditional critical methodology, it becomes clear that the inheritance of medieval piety goes hand in hand with its transformation defined by the Reformation doctrines of justification and reconciliation and, most notably, by Luther's discourse on the *commercium* between Christ and the believer. Moreover the *unio mystica* is consequently located in the Lord's Supper and the *fides* is emphasised as the unifying factor. The medieval mystical texts also enjoyed great popularity among Roman Catholics, yet they were reworked in such a way that, as a rule, they did not contradict the official teaching of the Church. All the same, the two developing confessions had a common language and tradition which formed an important basis for inter-confessional discourse. This may also be said concerning the reception of neo-Aristotelianism. The formulation of the Reformation teaching with the help of the scholastic material definitions, and not least the representation of the individual *loci* according to the scheme of the four *causae*, served the consolidation of *doctrina* and also its inner confirmation. Along with this an important precondition was created for it, describing the common ground shared with other confessions open to formal description on the one hand, but on the other hand also pointing out its differences, thereby to allowing them to be recognised as contestable. In brief, the controversial theological discourse between Johann Gerhard and Robert Bellarmine, for example, would never have achieved such a high standard of reflection and (on both sides) such well defined clarity if an elucidation of prolegomena to methodology and philosophy of science had not been previously established.

An additional aspect of the highly stratified lines of reception within Orthodoxy involves rhetoric. Here also a conjunction of reception and a productive new definition is characteristic. The first aim was to provide access to ancient rhetorical education in the form of textbooks. Melanchthon, in particular, achieved fundamentally significant results in this regard, as well as Gerhard Johann Vossius (1577-1649) among others. In addition to the practical application of good speaking skills within academic instruction, rhetoric was also tailored to the needs of homiletics. In recourse to patristic examples (Jerome, Augustine, the Venerable Bede, etc.) the literary style of the biblical texts was described with the help of the ancient pagan categories of rhetoric. The aim of this work was, on the one hand, to describe the biblical forms of speech, but also on the other to show how this rhetoric could be made fruitful in preaching in the context of worship. The result was a new academic discipline: the *rhetorica sacra*.[14] It became increasingly concerned with the question of how rhetoric, with regard to discourse in German, could be exercised not only in the academic context, but particularly in the framework of practical homiletics (Caspar Goldtwurm [1524-59], Johann Matthäus Meyfart [1590-1642], *et al.*). After that it was also demonstrated how pagan rhetorical traditions are useful for learning to imitate the language of the Bible in the sense of *mimesis* and, in this way, to find language oneself. The baroque homiletic rhetoricians regarded ancient rhetoric *per analogiam fidei* and reformulated it from canonical Scripture.

The study of Patristics with a Protestant stance and responsible as theological discipline was first established in the sixteenth century but was only completed in the seventeenth.[15] It is well known that humanist scholars provided a multitude of editions of ancient, patristic and other original texts. However, the fact requires closer investigation that the era of Orthodoxy was also an age of editing: a flood of patristic, rabbinical, medieval and Reformation texts were made available and became known. The study of the biblical texts for exegesis, alongside concern with the history of their interpretation, was not pursued separately but in conjunction with each other. The theologians working in the wake of the Reformation were concerned to show the far-reaching agreement of their theology with that of early Christianity and the ancient Church. To be sure, this often led to an eclectic and sometimes harmonising reception of the patristic tradition. At the same time,

---

Geschichte des gelehrten Unterrichts auf den deutschen Schulen und Universitäten vom Ausgang des Mittelalters bis zur Gegenwart. Mit besonderer Rücksicht auf den klassischen Unterricht (Berlin / Leipzig: de Gruyter ³1919-1921).

[14] J. A. STEIGER, "Rhetorica sacra seu biblica. Johann Matthäus Meyfart (1590-1642) und die Defizite der heutigen rhetorischen Homiletik", *ZThK* 92 (1995) 517-58.

[15] *Die Patristik in der Bibelexegese des 16. Jahrhunderts* (Wolfenbütteler Forschungen 85; ed. D. C. Steinmetz; Wiesbaden: Harrassowitz 1999).

however, it should not be overlooked that the Fathers of the Church are always measured against the Holy Scripture. For this reason interpretations which contradict each other are not simply placed side by side, but in many cases are themselves subjected to critical evaluation. Accordingly, the exegesis of Scripture was not to be measured against a history of interpretation, taken as normative. Rather, Scripture became the touchstone for all exegetical conclusions, past and current.

Luther's hermeneutics, applied by the Reformer himself, but not described in a systematic fashion, was brought to completion in a newly established scientific subject area – the *hermeneutica sacra* (Glassius, Dannhauer, *et al.*). Not to be left out at this point are the achievements regarding the adoption of rabbinical treasures in the history of interpretation as well as the introduction of Oriental Studies as an academic discipline (Theodoricus Hackspan, Hiob Ludolf, Johann Ernst Gerhard, *et al.*). The foundations of this had long been established before the spirit of the Enlightenment brought about a return to it and sought to build on it. Moreover, it is not far off the mark to assert that, just at the time of the strongest confessional distinctions, the respective opponents were most willing to work painstakingly through each others' arguments, to immerse themselves into the respective way of thinking and also to treat each other as worthy of detailed critique. The *theologia polemica* of the Baroque era, which was then eagerly pursued, paid very careful attention to the literary works of the opponents in a manner that has seldom been the case again in later ages.

Viewed thus, the era of Orthodoxy constitutes a period of high achievement for Protestantism, within which it was able to work through the heritage of the Reformation, and thereby to maintain its success by making it teachable, accessible and amenable to systematic formulation. During the course of the Reformation, the rapid sequence of events meant that Luther and his followers rarely had time to set down fresh approaches fully and systematically. This is not to say that, in the sixteenth century, there was not already an impressively broad movement of consolidation. The contrary was, in fact, the case. Admittedly, the seventeenth century was anything but peaceful. Nevertheless, it then became possible to take the necessary time and concentration for the work of organisation and consolidation with a view to establishing the intellectual penetration of what was new. This, of course, claimed to be based on what was old.

We must add to this point that the era of Orthodoxy is marked by a great radiation of faith and piety into the cultural sphere. This is true whether it was in the form of devotional literature not directly tied to the Church (e.g. Andreas Gryphius, Martin Opitz, Simon Dach), vocal sacred music (Heinrich Schütz, Johann Sebastian Bach, *et al.*), religious theatre, funerary culture, fine arts, or architecture. Here we can rightly speak of a cultivation of Christian faith and the establishment of a culture of faith which was possibly unique, yet typical of the age. The more this culture of faith is described in all its stratification and richness, the more the claim of the liberal-theological position loses its foundation. Such a thesis regarded the disintegration of the supposed early Protestant 'monoculture' as a necessary qualification for the possibility of establishing a culture[16] stamped by the Christian spirit, that is by its secularised aspects. Yet to speak of a 'monoculture' of the seventeenth century displays ignorance of the great variety of these cultures of faith. According to TROELTSCH, secularised Christian faith defines human culture first and foremost ethically-socially and politically. However, among religious poets and orators, writers of libretti and artists grounded in Lutheran Orthodoxy, it is not a surrogate of faith, but rather faith itself which is active in creating such cultural works. This distinction should be considered and studied in greater detail. The result may be that a clear distinction between Culture Protestantism and the culture of

---

[16] E. TROELTSCH, "Luther, der Protestantismus und die moderne Welt", in: idem, *Gesammelte Schriften* 4. *Aufsätze zur Geistesgeschichte und Religionssoziologie* (Tübingen: Mohr 1925) 202–54, here: 209, and idem, "Das Verhältnis des Protestantismus zur Kultur", ibid. 191–202, here: 198 f.

Protestantism is necessary. The permeation of the entire life in the light of faith is especially reflected in Neo-Latin occasional poetry, which has not been appreciated even in rudiments, particularly not from a theological perspective. This poetry was in the form of epitaphs, epicedia, congratulatory and dedicatory poems etc., as well as in the heterogeneous types of public oration made outside an ecclesiastical setting. The latter are found, for example, in funeral or burial orations which are in some respects the religiously motivated secular counterparts of the funeral sermon.

Not enough effort has yet been expended to make it possible to describe the seventeenth century as a marriage between learning (*eruditio*) and a reconciled co-operation of erudition and education on the one hand and a culture of faith on the other. At the beginning of the eighteenth century, however, matters already stood differently. The strong impulses towards integration outlined above are already lacking in late Orthodoxy. Although Pietism assumed the heritage of Orthodox piety, adding to it and changing it, Pietism increasingly (especially after Spener) objected to Orthodox educational ideals and to the involvement of Christianity in wider cultural pursuits. The Enlightenment, in contrast, embraced the educational ideal in an innovative fashion but more or less turned strongly against the central tenets of biblical Reformation faith. The era of Reformation would accordingly have ended at the moment when the two poles which Orthodoxy had been able to keep together in a balanced tension more strongly began to drift apart. These were the poles of doctrine and piety, learning (*eruditio*) and the praxis of faith, inwardness and world, Christian faith and pagan antiquity, Athens and Jerusalem, Reformation and Humanism. In reality the actual interpenetration of Renaissance and Christianity, which TROELTSCH regarded as taking place in the period of the Enlightenment,[17] already occurred in the Baroque era.

2. The Word of God and *scriptura sacra*.
The Divine Inspiration of Scripture

According to both the Orthodox Lutheran as well as Calvinistic hermeneutics, the Holy Scripture (*scriptura sacra*) is the *verbum Dei* set in written form by the biblical writers. In biblical times, God chose to reveal himself directly to the Patriarchs, Prophets, Evangelists and Apostles within the framework of a *revelatio immediata*. He now makes himself known to human beings by means of the Holy Scripture, which means by way of a *revelatio mediata*. Because in the Orthodox view there is no other independent source of revelation apart from Scripture, all theological thought, speech, writing and activity is to be grounded on Scripture alone. In the course of the academic theoretical consolidation of theology, the principle of *Sola Scriptura* upheld by the Reformers was further refined to the effect that Scripture was spoken of as the absolutely irreplaceable canon. It was spoken of as the *fundamentum ecclesiae* (Hütter[18]), the basis of faith, as well as the sole *principium*[19] of theology. Johannes Wolleb (1586–1629), for example writes: *Nullum igitur aliud Theologiae principium, quam Verbum Dei scriptum agnoscimus.*[20] Salomo Glassius (1593–1656) entitled his handbook in German on hermeneutics as follows: *Christlicher Glaubens=*

---

[17] E. TROELTSCH, "Renaissance und Reformation", ibid. 261–96, here: 292.

[18] Hütter, *Loci* (1661) 24. Cf. idem, *Compendium* (2006) 36.

[19] Gerhard, *Methodus* (1620) 141, calls Scripture *unicum ac proprium Theologiae principium*. König, *Theologia* (2006) 28, speaks of the *principium cognoscendi*.

[20] Wolleb, *Compendium* (1633) 2.

*Grund. Das ist/ Deutliche Ausführung/ daß allein die H. Schrifft der Christlichen
Lehr/ Glaubens und Lebens/ waares principium, vester Grund/ sichere Regel/
und unbetriegliche Richtschnur … sey.* This was biblically justified with, among
other passages, 1 Cor 3:11, according to which Christ, the *Verbum aeternum*
(John 1:1), is the sole basis of the *ecclesia* and of the Christian faith.

Johann Gerhard (1582–1637), like many others, identifies the words of Scripture with those of
the Holy Spirit (*Verba Scripturae sunt verba Spiritus S.*[21]) and in connection to 2 Tim 3:16 speaks
of the *theopneustia* of Scripture, which originates in the teaching that the Trinitarian God, as the
true *auctor*, bestowed the biblical *scribentes* with the Holy Spirit. Prophets, Evangelists and Apostles are therefore *Spiritus sancti amanuenses*,[22] "secretaries of the Holy Spirit". Calvinist theologians taught something analogous. According to Andreas Rivetus (1572–1651), God is the author
of Scripture, while the writers can be called *autores* only *per quandam catachresim.* Actually they are
calami Dei, vel amanuenses. But even these designations are misrepresentative, since after all, secretaries deserve to be described as *autores secundarij.*[23] The critical function is clearly discernible
here, which this hermeneutics has concerning the Roman Catholic (especially the Tridentine) understanding, as well as to the spiritualistic view. The *Spiritus S[ancti] mens* can only be recognised
through the Holy Scripture. That is to say that no teaching office is required to reveal the meaning
inspired by the Holy Spirit on the basis of the *traditio ecclesiae.* At the same time the view represented, for instance, by Thomas Müntzer, Valentin Weigel and Caspar Schwenckfeld was ruled
out, the result of which was that a preceding inner, immediate endowment of the Spirit is needed
before Scripture can be properly interpreted. Ultimately, the concern of Orthodox hermeneutics is
to emphasise the vitality of Scripture. This goes back to the fact that it is the Holy Spirit who gives
life (John 6:63) by communicating himself to humans through the medium of Scripture, instils faith
in the hearers of the biblical message (Rom 10:17: *fides ex auditu*), in this way quickens them spiritually and leads them to eternal life. The Reformation-ecclesiological understanding is reflected
here in hermeneutical perspective, according to which every Christian stands directly *coram Deo*
and needs no intercession other than that of the one mediator (*intercessor*) Christ alone (1 Tim
2:5). Scripture, and with it the sermon in accordance with the Gospel, as well as the Sacraments
(Baptism and the Lord's Supper) administered according to their institution, are the only *media salutis.* For this reason, there is no need for that kind of a Church which (mis)understands itself as
an institution mediating salvation, nor even a teaching office which reserves for itself the correct interpretation of Scripture. The *pontificii* on the other hand, according to Gerhard, not only improperly separate the Holy Spirit from Scripture, but in addition suppose that the presumedly dead
biblical letter must firstly be endued with the Spirit of the Church, by means of the exegetical work
which is the duty of the priests and the Pope.[24] David Pareus (1548–1622) in his correspondence
with Johannes Magirus (d. 1609) reproaches the Roman Church for operating an inadmissible circular argument: *scripturae enim vobis sunt infallibiles propter Ecclesiam: Ecclesia vobis est infallibilis
propter scripturas.*[25]

Especially in the Lutheran sphere, while less in the Calvinist, the definition
of theology was marked chiefly as a practical discipline. Gerhard calls theology *doctrina practica.*[26] It deals not only with knowledge and discernment, but
foremost with leading sinful people, i.e., those separated from God, to faith
and thus to salvation through use of the means of salvation (*media salutis*). For
this reason, the theological discipline is closely related to the medical. For the

---

[21] Gerhard, *Tractatus* (1610) 13.
[22] Ibid. 15.
[23] Rivetus, *Isagoge* (1627) 15.
[24] Gerhard, *Tractatus* (1610) 29f: *1. Spiritus sancti sententiam à verbis Scripturae separant … 2.
Scripturam constituunt literam mortuam spiritu Ecclesiae animandam.*
[25] Pareus, *Disceptatio* (1604) 59.
[26] Gerhard, *Meditationes* (2000) I, 3.

latter can neither stop at the diagnosis. Rather, the aim of the medical profession is either to preserve health, or – in case of illness – to restore it.[27] Hence, Gerhard's outline of a *theologia medicinalis* defines *Gottesgelahrtheit* ("theology") as a *medicina spiritualis* (*Seelenarznei* ["medicine of the soul"]) and this stands in a long pastoral tradition going back to the early Church, which is supported, among other passages, by Exod 15:26, Isa 53:4 and Matt 9:12.[28] In accordance with the understanding of the Reformers and their followers, the *medicina spiritualis* is now centred around the Holy Scripture as the basis of all faith and comfort so that the Bible appears as the only *apotheca* of the soul, to be made abundant use of – regarding exegesis, catechetics, homiletics, meditation and piety.

Following the Orthodox definition, theology is not a purely speculative science, but rather a practical one to the highest degree,[29] because it deals with the question of how a person can be cured of the condition of sin through God's action, when in faith he partakes of the *iustificatio* through the *imputatio* of the righteousness of Christ, which is alien to him. Theology as *scientia practica* has the task of teaching people that which is necessary to know in order to gain eternal life and salvation. From this, Gerhard develops the concept of *habitus* θεόσδοτος.[30] To be a theologian, it is not enough simply to acquire the necessary philological, exegetical, historical and dogmatic knowledge of the subject, though this is also indispensable. Becoming a theologian in the true sense is only possible by centring all activities around *meditatio* – i.e., around the ever-new reading and interpretation of the Holy Scripture. Only here does a person abandon himself to God's speech and only here does the person discover that to speak of and about God is not possible until one has first been endued with comfort by God; through this the teaching is also made part of the *experientia fidei* as well as the living practice of *pietas*. According to Aristotle, a *habitus* (a ἕξις) is acquired through discernment and practice. Thus, a fair judge must not only have discernment in what is right and proper, he must also administer justice in a fair manner. Gerhard takes up the concept of *habitus*, but he gives it a new meaning: theology is a *habitus*, however, one that cannot be acquired, only given from outside by God himself. Genuine Bible study develops from *tentatio*, because only the situation of being tempted guarantees that one experiences the efficacy (*efficacia*) of the Word of God, the first Comforter. For this reason, it is not surprising that more than once Gerhard not only repeats Luther's dictum that *oratio*, *meditatio* and *tentatio* make a theologian,[31] but even formulates it in the manner of a methodology.[32]

The Orthodox understanding of inspiration has been widely and sharply rejected by contemporary theology. The doctrine of inspiration has been held to be an undiscerning belief in miracles, to exclude the literary individuality of the biblical authors, to devalue them to "unconscious breakthrough points of the Word of God"[33] and to be responsible for the misuse of the Bible as a seemingly uncontradicted quarry of diverse *dicta probantia*. Yet, on closer inspection, it becomes clear that assessments such as these cannot claim for them-

---

[27] Ibid.
[28] Cf. J. A. Steiger, *Medizinische Theologie. Christus medicus und theologia medicinalis bei Martin Luther und im Luthertum der Barockzeit* (SHCT 104; Leiden: Brill 2005).
[29] Gerhard, *Loci* (1767-) II, 4: *Postremam hanc sententiam reliquis praeferimus, eamque veritati magis consentaneam judicamus, cum finis theologiae ultimus non sit nuda* γνῶσις, *sed* πρᾶξις *ac proinde omnia, quae in theologia traduntur, ad* πρᾶξιν *spectent.*
[30] Ibid. 13.
[31] Luther, WA 50, 659.
[32] Gerhard, *Methodus* (1620) 13f, and Gerhard, *Loci* (1767-) II, 7.
[33] Kraus, Geschichte (1956) 76: *selbstlose[n] Durchgangspunkte[n] des Wortes Gottes.*

selves a sound knowledge of the sources. This is evident already with Matthias Flacius[34] who, starting from 2 Tim 3:16, considers the inspiration of the biblical authors by the Holy Ghost to be indisputable: the doctrine of inspiration by no means results in the different sections of biblical texts being harmonised with each other contrary to the philological and stylistic data. To be sure, Flacius is convinced that there is a harmony and *cohaerentia*[35] of the biblical writings. However, this harmony is not to be confused with a monotony, but it rather resembles musical polyphony, which thrives on the diversity of the individual voices. For this reason even, e.g., Hieronymus Mencelius (1517–90) could say: "The heart rejoices when in a delightful Musica many harmonies blend into one another. Much more is it so with the most beautiful Musica of the Holy Spirit".[36]

Flacius' *Clavis Scripturae Sacrae* shows that from the outset the fundamental hermeneutical work of Lutheranism was embedded in making ancient rhetorical education fruitful for the sake of the interpretation of Scripture. In the *DE STYLO SACRARUM LITERARUM TRACTATUS*,[37] for instance, Flacius painstakingly analyses the very distinct literary-rhetorical strategies applied by Paul and John. He points out, among other things, that the letters of Paul frequently employ the stylistic device of emphasis, while the dialectical skill of Paul is evident, in intellectual and linguistic respects, in the course of the refutation of his opponents.[38] John's style, however, is characterised by many epexegeses (e.g., John 1:8). In addition, according to Flacius, John uses many antitheses (*nati ex Deo, nati ex hominibus: credentes in Christum, incredulis*, etc.) and clarifies his message by often speaking *affirmatiuè & negatiuè* (*Confessus est, non negauit* [John 1:20], *Omnia per ipsum facta sunt, & sine ipso factum est nihil* [John 1:3]).[39] Glassius also analyses the styles of John and Paul[40] and stresses that the literary *stylus* utilised in the biblical texts is by no means *uniformis*.[41] He reports that for Melanchthon the Psalter attests a nearness to Attic Greek and that for Luther the diction of Solomon's writings acknowledges a nearness to the *genus grande*. This shows: the doctrine of verbal inspiration does not prevent analysis of the individuality of the writers and the characteristics of their styles – on the contrary. This is also manifest, e.g., in the sermons of Orthodox theologians, in which precisely the stylistic, rhetori-

---

[34] O. K. OLSON, "Flacius", TRE 11 (1983) 206–14. Cf. zur *Clavis* R. KELLER, *Der Schlüssel zur Schrift. Die Lehre vom Wort Gottes bei Matthias Flacius Illyricus* (AGTL NF 5; Hannover: Lutherisches Verlagshaus 1984); B. J. DIEBNER, "Matthias Flacius Illyricus. Zur Hermeneutik der Melanchthon-Schule", *Melanchthon in seinen Schülern* (Wolfenbütteler Forschungen 73; ed. H. Scheible; Wiesbaden: Harrassowitz 1997) 157–81; Reventlow, Epochen 4 (2001) 11–21; O. K. OLSON, *Matthias Flacius and the Survival of Luther's Reform* (Wolfenbütteler Abhandlungen zur Renaissanceforschung 20; Wiesbaden: Harrassowitz 2002).

[35] Flacius, *Clavis* (1580) I, 105: *Sacra scriptura cohaeret sibi tota. Chrysost. in Marc. Homil. 4.*

[36] *Wenn in einer lieblichen Musica viel Concordantiae in einander gehen/ erfrewet es das Hertze. Viel mehr wird es diese aller schönste Musica des heiligen Geistes thun.* Mencelius, Vorrede (1575) a 1r.

[37] Flacius, *Clavis* (1580) I, 261 ff.

[38] Ibid. 290.

[39] Ibid. 301.

[40] Glassius, *Philologia* (1713) 338–46.

[41] Ibid. 279.

cal features of biblical texts are frequently raised as a matter of consideration.[42]

Near the end of the Orthodox era, Johann Jakob Rambach (1693–1735) pursues the interaction of divine operation of the Spirit and its human impact on the biblical texts even further, when he pays particularly close attention to the emotional states of the writers. In one respect, Rambach is relying here on Flacius, Glassius, et al. Furthermore, he is clearly dependent on August Hermann Francke's *Praelectiones hermeneuticae*,[43] which is where Francke formulates the *REGVLA GENE-RALIS: Cognitio Affectum est necessarium sanae & accuratae interpretationis adminiculum*.[44] According to Francke, the *animus* and *intimus sensus* of the biblical writers and *dramatis personae* only reveal themselves to that person who pays attention to the emotional situation of the respective speaker in the Bible.[45] In order to be able to redeem this maxim, Francke develops a *pathologia sacra*,[46] contrasting natural-sinful emotions with spiritual ones which mark those who are born again. The former are the expression of interest in and love of the world, judged reprehensible by Francke, while the latter are forms of articulation of the love of God.[47] From this follows Francke's assertion that only the born again person can rightly apply the *pathologia sacra* to the Holy Scripture and can comprehend the emotional situation of the *personae biblicae*.[48]

An innovation with Rambach might therefore lie in the fact that – more strongly than the earlier Lutheran hermeneutics – he teaches the reader to examine closely the emotional situation of the biblical characters. As this is rarely readily apparent, but rather is hidden in the texts, certain methodical steps are needed to be able to bring it to light.[49] To cite an example, the observation of the said *res* belongs to this. Thus it becomes clear, e. g., in the rhetorical-emotional analysis of Isa 9:5, that the joy of Isaiah is reflected in his words, although this itself is not made the theme of the text. Yet the *circumstantiae temporis* must also be kept in mind. In Jeremiah's Lamentations the emotional state of *tristitia* prevails not least on the basis of the circumstances of the time.[50] According to Rambach, the Holy Spirit has not only accommodated to the linguistic *ingenium*, but also to the emotional state of the writer.[51] For the work of interpretation this means concretely that the emotional situation from which the writing flows is to be kept in mind. From this perspective, Rambach, e. g., criticises Luther's translation of Job 32:10, 18, which the Reformer is held to have translated incorrectly because of insufficient attention to the emotional state.[52] In spite of Francke's influence, Rambach does not adopt his opinion that being converted is *conditio sine qua non* for the proper attention to the emotional state, as to the correct interpretation of Scripture.

The appreciation of the various *ingenia* of the biblical writers is nothing typically Lutheran. Rivetus, for example, shows that the Holy Spirit employed

---

[42] Nachwort, in: Gerhard, Leichenpredigten (2001) 343–45.

[43] Francke, *Praelectiones* (1717).

[44] Ibid. 193.

[45] Ibid. 192.

[46] Ibid. 229.

[47] Ibid. 231 f.

[48] Ibid. 239: *In affectibus cognoscendis solus recte versatur regenitus, & quidem ita, vt in consideratione Textus Sacri probe secernat affectum ipsius Scriptoris sacri, affectum eius, ad quem scribitur, affectum illius, de quo sermo est, nec non affectum, qui ipsi Deo tribuitur.*

[49] Ibid. 130.

[50] Ibid. 134.

[51] Rambach, *Erläuterung* (1738) 378f: *Der heilige Geist hat sich in negotio* θεοπνευστίας *accommodiret nach der natürlichen Beschaffenheit seiner Werckzeuge, und auch so gar nach ihrem natürlichen Temperament. Daher hat er ihre Affecten in der inspiration nicht eingeschläfert und aller activität beraubet; sondern vielmehr dieselben excitiret und geheiliget.*

[52] Ibid. 375. *Wenn dieser Elihu z.E. zu dem Hiob spricht Job. 32. 10. Höre mir zu, Hiob, ich will meine Kunst auch sehen lassen. Wie odieus klinget das? welches nur herkommt aus der unrichtigen consideration derer Affecten, da ihn Lutherus sich vorgestellet als einen Prahler. Jm Ebräischen hingegen heists:* אחוה דעי *indicabo sententiam meam, ich wil meine Meynung auch anzeigen, wie ich die Sache ansehe.*

the highly varied skills of *amanuenses* and thereby also different writing styles, adapting himself to them in the manner of an *attemperatio*.[53] The dialectics of verbal inspiration and the ensured literary individuality was no longer maintained by Jean Le Clerc / Johannes Clericus. In his view, the activity of the Holy Spirit is limited to a non-verbal inspiration [Realinspiration][54] and the authors' activities are self-actuating. The opinion held in the research literature, according to which only negating the doctrine of verbal inspiration makes possible the analysis of the human literary production of the biblical writers,[55] nevertheless reveals itself as incorrect.

How prominent the Orthodox comparison of the literary diversity of the biblical writings with musical polyphony was, is evident in the fact that it was employed also by the Calvinists, for instance, by Heinrich Alting (1583–1644). In his opinion, the Holy Spirit inspired the writers *tum res tum verba*,[56] besides even those things already known to the writers, so that no error would arise. Nevertheless, the writers put down words in different styles, which is due to God condescending to the respective styles of the writers concerned, i.e., he accommodates himself to them. This results in the formation of a harmony of different voices – as in an orchestra. *Qua etiam in* συγκατα-βάσει *Deus suae authoritatis & Majestatis rationem ita habuit, ut in diversitate styli uniformis gravitas, & Deo digna Majestas deprehendatur, atque variante licet stylo, at stylo expressa eadem, unum os omnium quae dicta sunt, videri possit. Planè ut in Organo Musico substantia Cantici, Harmoniae, toni una est, fistulis autem aliis acutioribus, obtusioribus aliis spiritus, qui tibias inflat, accommodat.*[57]

This shows that on both the Lutheran as well as the Reformed side, a form of thought was decisive within the theory of accommodation which cannot be understood without its ultimately Christological background: as Christ relinquishes his true divinity and takes on the form of a servant (Phil 2:7), so also the third person of the Trinity takes himself to the level of human speech. Notwithstanding, a fine, though essential, distinction between Lutheran and Calvinist pneumatology remains to be observed, which also has consequences for hermeneutics. Following in Luther's line, his heirs stress the attachment of the Spirit to the *verbum externum*, or, to the *litera*. Accordingly, the inner, faith-endowing virtue of the Spirit results from the external Word when this is preached or read. Indeed, the Calvinist doctrinal position is also far removed from any Spiritualism and Spirit-Flesh-Dualism. On the other hand – and this has parallels both in the doctrine of God as well as in Christology – the followers of Calvin more strongly emphasise the freedom of the Spirit, and in doing so abide by the principle *finitum non capax infiniti*. Thus it is said of the virtue of the Spirit that it joins itself to the *verbum externum*, but is in no case bound to the same. Interpreting Rom 10:17, Pareus, for instance, expresses this parallelism of the external activity of the Word and the internal activity of

---

[53] Rivetus, *Isagoge* (1627) 15: *Ita Sp. Sanctus autor singularis scripturarum, diversis ingenijs & stylis hominum usus est, quibus se attemperavit, quorum alij eloquentia pollebant magis, alij minus, omnium tamen stylum sanctificavit & direxit, ut unam & eandem veritatis doctrinam, etsi variantibus verbis, exponerent.*

[54] Reventlow, Bibelexegese (1988) 17.

[55] Reventlow, Wurzeln (1988) 51–53; Reventlow, Bibelexegese (1988) 17; Kraus, Geschichte (1956) 74 f.

[56] Alting, *Methodus* (1650) 32.

[57] Ibid. 33.

the Spirit with the words: *EX AUDITU EST) hoc est, per auditum externum verbi, operante intus spiritu Dei, fides in cordibus electorum generatur.*[58]

Ultimately then, in Calvinist doctrine formation, not only the doctrine of God, but also pneumatology and with it the biblical hermeneutics are marked by the *theologumenon* of the *immutabilitas Dei*, while the Lutheran theologians are more strongly guided by the *theologumenon* of the Incarnation.

This fact is also evident in the practice of interpreting Scripture, for instance, in the varying exegeses of Exod 32:14 and Jonah 3:10. In both passages it is recounted that God relented from his plan of judgement in view of human repentance. According to the Calvinist reading (e.g., of Josias Simler[59] [1530–76] and Johannes Strack[60] [1553–1612] in conjunction with Oecolampadius), this passage is to be understood only figuratively, since the decrees of God are unchangeable: here God is spoken of anthropopathically (ἀνθρωποπάθως), therefore not *proprie*. Certainly, the Lutheran commentators likewise frequently advance the category of anthropopathy. Nevertheless, the predominant view here is that the repentance of the sinner, who believes and takes refuge in God's *promissio*, in fact has the power to bring about a change even in the merciful God. For this reason, Johannes Tarnow (1586–1629), for instance, differentiates between the divine essence, which is *immutabilis*, and his *decreta*, which are changeable, in so far as they have distinct *conditiones* in view which are changing. *Decreta Dei conditionalia possunt, conditione mutatà, mutari, cum tamen ipse semper sit immutabilis.*[61]

The theory of inspiration cannot be deemed miraculous; rather, it first has to be valued itself as the result of the exegesis of a whole string of biblical statements (2 Tim 3:16; 2 Pet 1:20, *et al.*). To this the circumstance may be added that the biblical writers are by no means removed from the human sphere through inspiration – in any case, they are no further separated from it than those who engage with the biblical texts by reading, i.e., meditating them. As with the writers, for whom the presentation by the Spirit was the *conditio sine qua non* for the writing process, so with the readers, for whom precisely the same inspiration is prerequisite for a truly effective reading of Scripture.[62] With this, Gerhard (citing Scaliger) bases his argument philosophically on the Aristotelian-epistemological principle that if knowledge aims at succeeding, there must be a *inter intellectum cognoscentem & rem cognoscendam adaequatio.*[63] He combines this principle with the biblical-Pauline understanding that the communication of God with human beings is one of the divine spirit with the human spirit (Rom 8:16). For this reason, Gerhard recommends speaking a prayer before Bible reading in order to receive the Holy Spirit, rather like a period of incubation. In this, he supposes – differently from the spiritualists – that the Spirit communicates himself to humans in prayer only because the prayer reflects on biblical texts. The fact is: the doctrine of inspiration is not only most closely connected with the theory and practice of prayer, but concretely motivates to the exercise of piety. Inspiration and illumination of the

---

[58] Pareus, *Opera* II (1628) 239.

[59] Simler, *Exodus* (1584) 157v.

[60] Strack, *Ander Buch* (1621) 391. Strack cites Simler, yet without indicating this work as a reference.

[61] Tarnow, *In Prophetam Jonam* (1626) 112.

[62] Ratschow, Dogmatik I (1964) 99.

[63] Gerhard, *Tractatus* (1610) 32.

reader are the prerequisites for the truly effective, instructive and comforting exegesis of the Bible,[64] which was put down in writing by the inspired writers. *Haec Spiritus sancti collustratio necessaria est ad totam Scripturam & quamlibet ejus partem Salutariter cognoscendam & interpretandam.*[65] The inspiration of the writers is seen as no different in quality from that of the readers. The distinction lies only in that the former have received the Spirit *immediate*, while the latter have partaken of the Spirit *mediate* – i.e., through mediation of Scripture.

Despite all rather far-reaching agreement concerning the high esteem of Scripture as the starting point and goal of all theology, the specific differences between the Lutheran and Calvinist perceptions may not be overlooked. Of course, the Reformed theologians also speak of the faith-endowing and thus saving virtue of the Spirit through the Holy Scripture. It is clear, however, that the Calvinist dogmaticians teach – unlike the Lutheran universal salvation – that the purpose and goal (*finis*) of Scripture is above all the *gloria Dei*, and secondarily, the *salus electorum*.[66] This ensures that the doctrine of theological principles does conflict with the doctrine of double predestination, which it is part of. This circumstance also marks the Calvinist exegesis of Rom 10:17: the Word of God, thus Pareus, brings about faith through the sermon, but exclusively in the *electi*.[67]

3. The Clarification of the Relationship of *scriptura sacra* and the Holy Spirit in the Course of the Rahtmann Controversy

The fact that the Holy Scripture is the Word of God, according to Orthodox hermeneutics, in no way signifies an unreflected identification of either. Particularly Lutheran high Orthodoxy was obliged by the dispute with Spiritualism to clarify and further develop the doctrine of theological principles. Incentive for this was offered by Hermann Rahtmann (1585–1628), a pastor in Danzig and spiritualistic recipient of the theology of Johann Arndt (1555–1621). The Rahtmann Controversy lasted from 1621 to 1630.[68]

The Holy Scripture, following Rahtmann, is not identical with the eternal Word of the Father.[69] On the contrary, there is a fundamental distinction between the external written Word and the divine-internal Word inspired by the

---

[64] The alternative formulated by Mühlenberg, Schriftauslegung (1999) 485 ("for this reason not the inspiration of the interpreter, but rather his philological will was presupposed") is nonsensical.

[65] Gerhard, *Tractatus* (1610) 34.

[66] Crocius, *Disputationes* (1614) 27.

[67] Pareus, *Opera* II (1628) 239.

[68] Steiger, Das Wort (1998); Engelhardt, Der Rahtmannische Streit (1854); Grützmacher, Wort (1902); Halverscheid, Lumen (1971); Hägglund, Theologie (1983).

[69] Rahtmann, *Gnadenreich* (1621) a 1v.

Spirit, which the prophets and Apostles kept for themselves in writing down what was revealed directly to them, because it could not be contained in letters.[70] According to Rahtmann, there can be no discussion of the Spirit being bound to the letters of the Bible or to the verbal Word of the sermon. Formulated positively, in his Spirit-Scripture-Dualism Rahtmann has in mind the safeguarding of the freedom and sovereignty of the Spirit and ultimately his divinity. Following the principle that a thing can only be known by its equal, it is Rahtmann's conviction that the divine will and the message of the Gospel cannot be known from the act of reading the Bible, unless the Holy Spirit assists by joining the reader in a supplementary action and unlocks understanding of the Scripture.[71]

Although Rahtmann's understanding of Scripture betrays influences of a rather strong spiritualistic interpretation of Arndt, as well as of Schwenckfeld and Weigel, it also resembles very much the doctrine of the Lord's Supper of Calvin and his followers. Rahtmann's doctrine of scripture and Calvin's theology of the Lord's Supper are ultimately based on the same fundamental idea. With the aim of safeguarding the divine transcendence and freedom, Calvin had also taught that it is impossible for Christ to be truly bodily present in bread and wine, because since the ascension, his body sits at the right hand of God. For this reason, Christ's presence in the Sacrament of the Altar cannot be understood as a real presence, but rather only as a spiritual presence. According to this teaching, the Holy Spirit assists by joining the external elements of bread and wine in representing Christ in an analogous manner to his bodily presence.[72] To be sure, the Orthodox theologians knew of the differences between the positions of Rahtmann and Calvin. That the Orthodox also pursued an anti-Calvinist controversial theology in the conflict with Rahtmann had its cause not least of all in Rahtmann's thought, definitely displaying a kinship with Calvinism, which he had come into contact with in Danzig. In addition, Rahtmann occasionally refers to the writings of Beza and Pareus.

Rahtmann compares the Holy Scripture to a signpost, which shows the way, but cannot cause the traveller to proceed along it.[73] For this reason, according to Rahtmann, the Bible as the external Word, is only a *signum*. The *res signata* – the faith-endowing and salutary message – still lies in the internal Word, only to be grasped and appropriated on the strength of the illumination of the Holy Spirit.[74] However, following Rahtmann, this *illuminatio*, in contradiction to the Lutheran view, cannot be effected by the reading and preaching of biblical texts. Rather, it must already be present beforehand, or, as the case may be, have been originated outside any association with the written or preached Word.

Rahtmann made his way, at the very least, towards the spiritualism of Karlstadt, Weigel, Schwenckfeld and Jakob Böhme,[75] which teaches in a radical way that the mortifying letters of the Bible can only be interpreted correctly after the internal illumination of the heart by the Spirit has occurred. Yet, in their polemical identification of Rahtmann's position with that of the spiritualists, the Orthodox frequently, but not always,[76] understand too little that Rahtmann differs fundamentally from the spiritualists and even thoroughly criticises them.[77] Thus Rahtmann, unlike

---

[70] Ibid. a 4r/v.

[71] Ibid. b 3r.

[72] J. CALVIN, *Institutio Christianae Religionis 1559*, IV, 17, 3, *Opera Selecta* 5 (ed. P. Barth / W. Niesel; München: Kaiser ²1962) 344 f.

[73] Rahtmann, *Gnadenreich* (1621) b 1r, and idem, *Wolgegründetes Bedencken* (1623) 22 f.

[74] Rahtmann, *Gnadenreich* (1621) a 4v.

[75] Ibid. b 4r/v.

[76] The Königsberg Gutachten (dated March 22, 1624) in: *Censuren* (1626) 67–85, here: 71, makes a stronger distinction here.

[77] The Jena Censur of December 16, 1623, in: *Censuren* (1626) 86–191, here: 136; *Lehre* (1629) 4 and 116, where Rahtmann's doctrine is called *der newe Schwenckfeldische Schwarm*. On Rahtmann's distancing from Schwenckfeld, cf. Rahtmann, *Wolgegründetes Bedencken* (1623) 77 ff.

Schwenckfeld, for instance, at first cleaves to the idea that the beginning of knowledge and of faith is laid by the Holy Scripture as the initial kindling,[78] and the Bible has far more to bring about in the salvation process than a confirmation of the previous direct illumination in a person's heart.

The Orthodox side fundamentally objected to Rahtmann's remarks. Rahtmann's heterodox statements affected the doctrine of scripture and thus the most important fundamental article of Reformation theology. Rahtmann had called into question the canonicity of the Holy Scripture.[79] Frequently, the Orthodox advance the argument against Rahtmann that he divests the Holy Scripture of its greatest honour and sacredness and that he ultimately regards it as any other piece of writing.[80] Here already, modernity and enlightenment rationalism are dawning in that Rahtmann wishes to subject the Bible to no other hermeneutical principle than that applicable to any other literary composition.

Yet, the Orthodox hermeneutics surpassed Rahtmann's in its ability to reflect and, for this reason, was also ultimately more modern in a permanent sense. It is striking that starting from the biblical-hermeneutical horizon, the Orthodox also reflect on general hermeneutical questions. In the course of this they observed, for example, that the individual letters can be viewed at best as mere outward phenomena. Still, word combinations, sentences and entire texts are not merely *verba externa*, but have been conferred by the spirit of the respective author and grant the reader insight into it.[81] The soundness of the Orthodox hermeneutics, which considers the dialectics of interior and exterior, is proven precisely on the basis of non-biblical literature. There is no static subject-object scheme here which separates the perceiving from the perceived. Instead, the insight brings itself to bear here that in the process of understanding, this very diastasis is reconciled and a communion of author and reader is established.

Rahtmann was of the opinion that the Spirit is limited in his divine freedom when he is imagined to be bound to the Word. Against this, the Orthodox maintained that true divine freedom lies in the fact that God is free to commit himself to a qualified freedom through binding and thus into a covenant. Consequently then, this is also an indication of the freedom of God – of the Holy Spirit – to bind himself to Scripture. The Orthodox sought to prevail over Rahtmann's rationalistic Spirit-Flesh- and Subject-Object-Dualism through Christological reflection: when divine and human nature, the everlasting and the mortal, omnipotence and powerlessness come together in Christ in one person, how much more this must hold true for the Holy Spirit. He must be preached as someone who is capable of incarnation – and that means capable of concretisation and verbalisation – in the *verbum externum*. As Christ subsists in two natures and is fully man and God at the same time, so the divinity

---

[78] Rahtmann, *Gnadenreich* (1621) b 3r/v. Later, nevertheless, this aspect recedes in Rahtmann, which Halverscheid indicates, in: Lumen (1971) 174 f.
[79] *Lehre* (1629) 19, and Gerhard, *Natur*, 230v.
[80] The Jena Censur, in: *Censuren* (1626) 117.
[81] Ibid. 108 ff.

of the Spirit also takes external form precisely in that he articulates himself by means of human speech, which is at the same time the Word of God itself.

Gerhard already develops these thoughts in the first draft of his work *Von der Natur* and with it probably started a process of reflection, which is also found documented in the detailed report of the Leipzig theologians' convent (1631). In the same way as from an anthropological perspective, the body and soul of a person form an inseparable unity, and in Christology, the human and divine nature belong together in Christ, so it holds true, with respect to the hermeneutics of God's Word, that the external letter and the Spirit working internally can clearly be distinguished but cannot be separated from one another.[82]

According to the Orthodox, the Bible is an *ens concretum*. The external Word and Spirit-given meaning, *signum* and *res signata* form in the Holy Scripture just as inseparable a unity as the divine and human nature in Christ.[83] Scripture, therefore, is *signum* in the utmost imaginable sense: *signum efficax*, a speech-event which calls creation out of nothing (Gen 1:3), a word that says what it does and does what it says, a word that does not return to God void (Isa 55:11). The *verbum* of God is a temporal verb (*Zeitwort*) and thus a word issued in time and for this reason must be a human word. Yet, as such it is at the same time an action word, therefore divine (Ps 33:9). In this it becomes evident how much the Orthodox allowed the theology of the Lord's Supper to grow into hermeneutics in the course of the Rahtmann controversy by making sacramental-theological categories fruitful within the doctrine of Scripture. The elements of the Lord's Supper are also not only signs of something that would not be administered and communicated with them. Rather, they are also *signa exhibitiva* and administer the signified *res* – namely faith, forgiveness of sins and salvation – since the promise of the Word of God is present together with the signs and in the Word the Logos himself is truly present (*realpräsent*).[84]

The hermeneutical operational consequences of reflection on the Lord's Supper theology is also evident in the Orthodox teaching – in line with the genuinely Lutheran understanding of the Lord's Supper according to which Christ's body and blood are present in, with and under bread and wine – that "the meaning, intention and counsel of God" are "with and in the external words".[85] This is not to be misunderstood to the effect that the decrees and intentions of God are contained *localiter* in the Word. Rather, the *verbum externum* is the only certain and certainty-giving medium through which the pronouncements of God are articulated. Here was revived very forcefully what Luther says in connection to Gabriel Biel, concerning the manner of Christ's presence in the Lord's Supper: that Christ is not present *localiter* in the elements, like beer in a keg, but rather *diffinitive*.[86] Christ is present in the Supper just as the view is in all places at the same time, which it looks through or over, or the voice of a preacher, which is audible in many ears at the same time.[87] Saying that God's *Meinung* ("intention") is in the letters "is not then to be understood as though the intention of God is in the external words, like a salve in a tin, or rye, wheat, barley, or oats in a sack, by no means; rather *quoad significationem passivam*, that is so that according to and through God's ordinance, his will and intention is given to us to understand through the external literal words and is revealed".[88]

---

[82] Gerhard, *Von der Natur*, 122r/v.

[83] Lehre (1629) 14.

[84] Ibid. 33.

[85] Ibid. 16: *Verstandt/ Meynung vnd Rhat Gottes* [are] *mit vnd bey denen eusserlichen Worten.*

[86] M. Luther, *Studienausgabe* 1–6 (ed. H.-U. Delius; Berlin: Evangelische Verlagsanstalt 1979–99), here: 4 (1986) 87 f.

[87] Luther, Studienausgabe 4 (1986) 90, 98 f.

[88] Lehre (1629) 21f: [it is] *nicht also zu verstehen/ als ob die Meynung Gottes in den eusserlichen Worten were/ wie etwa eine Salbe in einer Büchsen: Oder Korn/ Weitz/ Gersten/ Habern in einem Sack: Keines Weges: Sondern quoad significationem passivam, das ist/ dergestalt/ daß nach vnd durch Gottes Verordnung/ sein Will vnd Meynung vns durch die eusserlichen buchstäbischen Wörter zu verstehen gegeben/ vnd geoffenbaret werde.* Cf. Gerhard, *Von der Natur*, 125r.

The *Christus praesens* becomes manifest and is present not only in the Supper, but also in the biblical Word. This is based first and foremost in the fact that sermon and sacrament are interrelated with one another in the sermon being *sacramentum audibile* and the sacraments *verba visibilia*. Thus, the Supper is itself word-event and sermon of the Words of Institution. But as in Luther's view, the blessings of salvation administered through the Sacrament of the Altar can also be grasped outside the sacramental action in the *manducatio spiritualis*; something similar, so say the Orthodox, applies to the Holy Scripture.[89] According to the Orthodox view, the Holy Scripture is not a mere signpost in Rahtmann's sense, but rather a guiding, enlightening authority (Ps 119:105 and 2 Pet 1:19) and thus nothing less than the way itself.[90] Certainly, a distinction must be made between the essential Word of God on the one hand and the testimony and the written record of that Word through the verbally-inspired biblical writers on the other, just as between the mere letters and the Spirit. Yet Spirit and letter still stand in a mutually interpreting relationship of exchange. And in no way is the *dynamis* of the Spirit such that it would have to join the Word in a separate act from outside. On the contrary, the Spirit conveys himself through the activity of the biblical Word, the preaching of which creates faith. For this reason, in the Orthodox view, the Spirit is also inherent in the Word *extra usum*.[91]

The doctrine of the inspiration of the Holy Scripture also outside its application is consequently a result of Christological reflection seeking to prevent a Nestorian approach of a Christology of separation, as advocated by Andreas Osiander the Elder (1496–1552), from being transferred to the determination of the relationship of letters and the Spirit. It is important to keep this context in mind in order to understand the Orthodox concern. For this reason, it is not wise to first isolate the *extra-usum* thesis and then renounce it as Orthodox abstrusity. This is what KARL BARTH did,[92] for example, without noticing that precisely what he was criticising had ultimately constituted the preliminary work for his own doctrine of scripture not only historically but also factually.

Contrary to Rahtmann's separation of the external and internal Word, the Orthodox hermeneutic concept defines God's Word as one, yet of manifold form. There are distinctions among the Word that Christ has brought along from the bosom of the Father, the Word that was impressed in the hearts of the Apostles and prophets by the Holy Spirit, the Word that the biblical writers carried on and expressed in writing, and the Word that is read today in the Bible, heard in the sermon and is believed. Although these four forms of

---

[89] Lehre (1629) 235: *Es ist Christus ... in der heiligen Schrifft/ respectu exhibitionis & applicationis: daß er vns in der Schrifft/ vnd durch die Schrifft fürgetragen vnd gegeben wird: Dann dahin gehet die Geistliche Niessung des HErrn JEsu Christi/ ausser dem Abendmal/ vnd ohne das Abendmal/ daß vns in der Schrifft/ gleichsam als in GOTtes Schüssel/ das Lämblin GOTtes JEsus Christus mit allen seinen Wolthaten ... täglich fürgesetzet vnd dargereichet wird.*

[90] Ibid. 61.

[91] Ibid. 61: *Diese Krafft wird dem Worte Gottes auch nicht erst von aussen zu= vnd beygefüget/ sondern es hat das Wort diese jnnerliche Krafft in vnd bey sich/ seiner Natur nach/ auch vor allem Gebrauch/ vnd ausser allem Gebrauch/ das ist/ ehe es noch von den Menschen gelesen vnd betrachtet wird/ ob es schon die thätliche Wirckung nicht ehe verrichtet in den Menschen/ bis es gelesen vnd betrachtet wird.* Dannhauer rejected the *extra-usum* doctrine; cf. Jung, Schrift (1999) 100f.

[92] K. BARTH, *Kirchliche Dogmatik* I/1 (Zürich: Evangelischer Verlag ⁶1952) 113.

God's Word should be differentiated, they must not be separated from one another.[93]

In the light of arguably the most significant Protestant dogmatic concept of the twentieth century, this hermeneutical concept is of greatest importance. KARL BARTH transferred the dialectics of the doctrine of the trinity (*una substantia, tres personae*) to the qualification of the relationship of the revealed, written and proclaimed Word.[94] Of course, according to BARTH, these three forms of God's Word must be distinguished, yet at the same time it still must be noted that we just cannot encounter the outgoing Word other than in the shape of the testimony by the biblical writers and in the form of the sermon.[95] BARTH was aware that in doing this he was concurring with the genuine Reformation understanding, in particular with Heinrich Bullinger's maxim: *Praedicatio verbi Dei est verbum Dei*.[96] What BARTH evidently did not know, however, is the fact that he was teaching nothing new – on the contrary, with his differentiation of the various forms of the one divine word he was following Lutheran Orthodoxy closely. The original version of the aforementioned document drafted by Gerhard for the Leipzig theologians' convent bore the title: *Von der Natur, Krafft vndt Wirckung des geoffenbahrten, gepredigten vndt geschriebenen Worts Gottes* ("On the Nature, Efficacy and Effect of the revealed, preached and written Word of God").[97] With that Gerhard even employs almost the same terminology of which BARTH will later make use.

It is also noteworthy that BARTH, who believed he might congratulate himself on not having to choose between the historical-critical method and the doctrine of verbal inspiration of Orthodoxy, unwittingly arrived at a conclusion in the doctrine of scripture near-identical with the one intimately connected to exactly this doctrine of inspiration which he viewed so critically.

4. The *affectiones scripturae sacrae*

According to Orthodox understanding, the Holy Scripture is defined as distinct from other literary works by a series of specific attributes. Its pertinent attributes are: *auctoritas, perspicuitas* (*claritas*) and *perfectio* (*sufficientia*).

The *auctoritas* of Scripture results from its *causa efficiens*, which is God. The authority of Scripture is based then on God's authorship.[98] For this reason, Scripture alone is the starting point and goal of theology and consequently the foundation of doctrine, of the sermon, of piety, etc. Consistently, Scripture is the Canon, the *norma normans* of doctrine and the supreme judge with regard to the arbitration of contested points of doctrine (*perspicua, sufficiens, & omnium controversiarum canon & norma*[99]) and *unica regula et norma* in the judgement of all "dogmata" and "doctores",[100] as the *Formula Concordiae* says.

---

[93] Jena Censur, in: *Censuren* (1626) 131. Here the distinction is made concerning the Word, *so Christus aus dem Schoß des Vaters gebracht/ vnd bey sich behalten/ das ander daß die Aposteln in jhr Hertz gepreget/ das dritte daß sie Schrifftlich begrieffen vnd vns tradiret, das vierdte daß wir hören vnd gläuben*. If anyone would wish to separate them, this would be *eine wunderseltzame Theologiam geben/ bey welcher man nimmermehr zur Gewißheit kommen köndte*.

[94] Barth, ibid. § 4. Regarding his reflections on the theology of Trinity, cf. ibid. 124 f.

[95] Cf. ibid. 124.

[96] BSRK 171,10 (*Confessio helvetica posterior I*).

[97] *Von der Natur, Krafft vndt Wirckung des geoffenbahrten, gepredigten vndt geschriebenen Worts Gottes*; Gerhard, *Von der Natur*, 113r.

[98] Gerhard, *Loci* 2 (1767-) 36; Hottinger, *Wägweyser* I (1647) 17.

[99] Finck, *Clavis* (1618) 52.

[100] BSLK 767, 15–17 (*Formula Concordiae*, Epitome).

Faith results from the sermon on biblical texts (Rom 10:17). Hence, the Church is subject to Scripture as *creatura verbi*, on account of which the equal ranking of Scripture and tradition in Roman Catholicism is to be rejected. At the same time it follows from this that neither a teaching office nor a council may be set over the Church. *Ecclesia nata est ex verbo Dei, non autem verbum Dei ex Ecclesia. Ergo verbum Dei non est Ecclesiae subjectum, sed Ecclesia verbo.*[101]

The triune God, however, is not only *Scripturae autor*,[102] rather also its first and greatest interpreter. For this reason Gerhard can say, the Holy Spirit is *Summus & authenticus Scripturae Interpres*.[103] Ambrosius Reuden (1543-1615) calls the Spirit *interpres internus ... qui nos per verbum intùs docet*.[104] Here Luther's programmatic hermeneutical thought comes to bear that Scripture is its own interpreter (*scriptura sacra sui ipsius interpres*).[105] This is sharpened to the effect that the Scripture authenticates itself and thus is αὐτόπιστος.[106] This in no way means that there is an automatism of interpretation. In fact, intensive hermeneutical work and philological competence are necessary in order to be able to experience the self-interpreting dynamism of Scripture. The Roman Catholic argument clutches at straws when it claims that the Protestant doctrine of scripture is nonsensical, because if Scripture were actually plain and clear, Lutherans would not have needed to write so many Bible commentaries.[107] To develop a philological-hermeneutical methodology in order to interpret the Scripture through and from Scripture itself (*Scripturas debemus interpretari per Scripturas*[108]), was therefore an urgent goal of both Lutheran as well as Calvinist exegesis.[109] This exegesis was pursued within the new disciplines of *Hermeneutica sacra* and *Philologia sacra* amongst others (see below). Ultimately, hermeneutics aim to pursue the intertextual monologue of the biblical texts – and that is to say the communication of the Holy Spirit with himself – in order then to be able to enter into this communication. Consequently, the Orthodox understanding of the *autopistia* of Scripture is not an unbending dogma. Rather, it reflects the experience, gained in the course of exegetical work, that the Holy Spirit causes and promotes understanding of Scripture. This is to say, the Spirit makes known perspectives of exegesis – not in that he joins Scripture as something secondary, but in that he himself acts in and through it. The model for the *interpretatio scripturae per scripturam* is the hermeneutics which Christ himself uses, particularly within the account of the Temptation (Matt 4:1-11) in the course of the dispute with the Devil: *Christus ipse Matth. 4. in congressu cum Diabolo Scripturam per Scripturam explicat, quod ipsum fecêre Evangelistae & Apostoli.*[110]

The *auctoritas* of Scripture is recognisable in the following external characteristics (*criteria externa*): by its *Miranda antiquitas, Doctrinae & rerum Majestas, Praeceptorum intemerata Sanctitas, Sermonis simplicis venerandae gravitas, Exacta harmonia & conformitas, Prophetiarum de rebus futuris dignitas, Complementi Prophetiarum veritas, Miraculorum ... divinitas, Historiarum quarundam singularitas, Propagationis doctrinae claritas, ipsa in persuadendo & permovendo efficacitas, Martyrum obsignationis dignitas, poenarum in hostes contumaces atro-*

---

[101] Mentzer, *Tertia Disputatio* (1600) L 2r. Cf. BSLK 767,25-768,7 (*Formula Concordiae*, Epitome).

[102] Glassius, *Philologia* (1713) 265.

[103] Gerhard, *Tractatus* (1610) 47.

[104] Reuden, *Isagoge* (1601) N 2r.

[105] Luther, WA 7, 97.

[106] Gerhard, *Loci* 2 (1767-) 36.

[107] Bellarmin, *Disputationes* (1601) I, 163. Cf. Schmidt-Biggemann (2006).

[108] Franzius, *Tractatus* (1619) a 3r. Cf. Finck, *Clavis* (1618) 52: *Scriptura per Scripturam est explicanda*. Cf. Glassius, *Glaubens=Grund* (1654) 265: *Die H. Schrifft muß aus ihr selbst erkläret/ nicht aber der Verstand von aussen hinein gebracht werden*.

[109] BSRK 101,16-18 (*Confessio helvetica prior* II). Cf. Heppe-Bizer, *Dogmatik* (1958) 29.

[110] Finck, *Clavis* (1618) 52.

citas.[111] Only a part of these arguments seek to be rationally and empirically comprehended, for instance, if the age of Scripture or its stylistic importance is advanced. The remaining *criteria* are qualified by already presupposing the *fides*, or by being formulated from the experience of faith (*experientia fidei*). This is the case, for instance, when the efficacy of Scripture is depicted as penetration of hearts according to Luke 24:32. For this reason, concerning their rational-argumentative strength, the aforementioned external criteria are granted a purely minor relevance. However, the *auctoritas* of Scripture truly brings itself to bear only on the basis of the internal witness of the Holy Spirit (*testimonium internum Spiritus Sancti*) in the hearts of believers or of those coming to faith. Glassius calls this *die innerliche Vberzeugung des H. Geistes* ("the internal persuasion of the Holy Spirit").[112] Glassius defined the driving force of the Holy Spirit (Rom 8:14) as *persuasio*, and in doing this employs a rhetorical category, making it fruitful for biblical hermeneutics.

In addition, Scripture is marked by *claritas* or *perspicuitas*. The biblical *loci classici* with respect to this are Pss 19:9; 109:105; Prov 6:23; 2 Pet 1:19.[113] Accordingly, the divine message is clear and intelligible from the biblical texts not only to a special religious elite, but to all Christians, if they possess the necessary competences which have to be mediated and practised catechetically and homiletically. This understanding is levelled at the Roman Catholic view of things, according to which Scripture is obscure in many places and for this reason remains so to the common man for whom independent Bible reading is too taxing, as long as the teaching office does not authoritatively determine the guiding principles of interpretation. Following Roman doctrine, from the *obscuritas* of Scripture results the necessity to interpret it in compliance with the *traditio* and *auctoritas* of the Church, which is also in possession of the *verbum non scriptum*.[114] When the Orthodox describe Scripture as clear, they do not lose sight of the fact that there are texts that are difficult or impossible to understand. The reason for the non-interpretability is not firstly seen as the fault of the biblical texts, but rather is sought in the interpreter's *obscuritas* of understanding, or of the heart. In this way – at times in connection to Luther's work *De servo arbitrio*[115] – a distinction is made between an *obscuritas interna* (of the heart and mind) and an *obscuritas externa* (of the biblical *verbum*). To the blind even the brightest sun is obscure.[116] This means: in the process of reading, the *epiphenomenon* of the sinfulness of humans, chiefly the darkening of human reason, can be relied on hindering the penetrating understanding of Scripture. One the one hand, Scripture is the sole medium that can bring about faith. On the other, faith, and with it the enlightening of reason, is the prerequisite of truly being able to decipher Scripture. Out of these dialectics, as well as out of the *claritas* of Scripture, which at times is frustrated by moments of

---

[111] Glassius, *Glaubens=Grund* (1654) 33–36.
[112] *Die innerliche Vberzeugung des H. Geistes.* Ibid. 43.
[113] Gerhard, *Tractatus* (1610) 38.
[114] Bellarmin, *Disputationes* (1601) I, 201ff; Becanus, *Manuale* (1727) 112f.
[115] Thus Finck, *Clavis* (1618) 40, refers to *De servo arbitrio* at length and formulates: *Alia est Scripturae S. sive perspicuitas sive obscuritas interna, alia externa.*
[116] Dannhauer, *Hermeneutica* (1654) 51: *Sol clarissimus obscurus est caeco.*

obscuritas, the reader of the Holy Scripture is not able to escape. According to Gerhard, the *perspicuitas* of Scripture does not only lie in the fact that the meaning of the biblical texts is evident to the one inspired by the Spirit, but also in that the Scripture has a *vis illuminativa*. The *illuminatio* of reason darkened by sin thus is achieved by the divine Word testified to in Scripture. *Sicut lux naturalis pellit tenebras; ita per Scripturae lucem intellectus nostri spirituales tenebrae illuminantur*.[117] However, in distinction from the spiritualistic view, the Spirit is not directly irradiated to the reader of Scripture. Rather, the *illuminatio* occurs in reading, meditating on and searching in the Scripture itself (*in Scripturis, & per Scripturas, lux illa Spiritus sancti quaerenda & impetranda*).[118] With respect to the *obscuritas* this means: only with the help of clear Scripture and of the "enlightenment" of human reason through faith, which in turn Scripture establishes, can the dark passages of the biblical text be deciphered. This deciphering takes place methodically within the *collatio*, the intertextual reading of biblical texts. The obscure texts should be enlightened by the clear ones, from which the *regula* or, as the case may be, the *analogia fidei* is taken: *Dicta obscuriora debent explicari per clariora*.[119] In doing this, Orthodoxy follows a suggestion which Irenaeus, Augustine,[120] *et al.*, had already given in the context of the early Church. A prototypical example of such con- and inter-textual exegesis of a text which at first appeared to be obscure is offered in Luther's account of his Reformation discovery.[121] It is based on his wrestling with the interpretation of Rom 1:17 in the light of Hab 2:4 and the recognition that the issue here is not the *iustitia Dei activa*, but rather the *iustitia passiva*, through which God makes the sinner righteous.

A prominent difference between the Lutheran and the Calvinist analysis of the *claritas scripturae* is discernible in the following: certainly the Lutherans are also of the opinion that the Old Testament is to be read consequently from the New and then appears in the correct light. For this reason, foreshadowings (*umbrae*) in the Old Testament are often spoken of, especially in typological exegesis. Yet, the Lutheran interpretation of Scripture is sustained by the certainty that all the Old Testament texts talk about Christ as the centre of the entire Scripture – and of course, in full *claritas*. The message of Christ is a "clavis", which deciphers the prophetic texts.[122] An instance of a biblical model of such a deciphering is the exegesis used by the Risen One on the way to Emmaus, in which he unlocked the understanding of the Old Testament to his companions (Luke 24:27). To some extent, the Lutherans conferred the doctrine of the bodily ubiquity of Christ to their hermeneutics. Already Luther was of the opinion that everything in the Old Testament was to be interpreted towards Christ, the centre of Scripture. And if this were not possible *prophetice*, then it would have to happen *typice* or *allegorice*.[123] A result of this is that exegesis aims at tracking down Christ, the *viva vox euangelii*, everywhere in the Old Testament. This is the reason why according to Lutheran understanding there is no gradation with respect to the *claritas* of both Testaments. One and the same clarity is inherent in the Old Testament and in the New.

---

[117] Gerhard, *Tractatus* (1610) 37.
[118] Ibid. 37.
[119] Finck, *Clavis* (1618) 57.
[120] Ibid. Finck refers to: Augustine, *De doctr. Chr.* II, 9.
[121] Luther, WA 54,185 f.
[122] Dannhauer, *Hermeneutica* (1654) 51.
[123] Luther, WA 20, 354; 15, 413.

In the Calvinist sphere, matters are considerably different. Johannes Cocceius (1603–69) is of importance for the history of theology, above all for his approach to federal theology.[124] His theology, oriented eschatologically towards the history of salvation, is based on the distinction between the covenant of works established in paradise and the covenant of grace set up in five stages (the Fall into sin, the Protoevangelium [Gen 3:15], Incarnation, Death and Resurrection of the flesh). Cocceius' concept of federal theology defines his view of the relationship between the Old and New Testament, as is reflected in his widely ignored, yet rich biblical exegeses. In his interpretation of Ps 119:105, Cocceius distinguishes the clarity of both Testaments by saying: *Veteris Testamenti verbum habet lucem suam, Novi Testamenti majorem.*[125] The greater extent of *claritas* of the New Testament is based on the fact that the writings of the New Covenant contain the Word of Christ, who appeared in the flesh. According to Cocceius, both Testaments are equal in rank because they are inspired by the Holy Spirit to the same extent. Yet the Old Testament is subordinate to the New in that the latter not only treats the Logos-become-flesh in a shadowing-prophetic way, but has the proclamation of the Logos as its subject. There is assent between both confessions that both Testaments are equally inspired by the Spirit. However, by way of a combination of John 1:1 and Heb 1:1f, the Lutherans move into the centre of their intertestamentary interpretation of Scripture the idea that Christ explicates himself as Logos ubiquitously already in the *logoi* of the Old Testament – precisely in the sense of 1 Cor 10:4. On the Calvinist side meanwhile – Beza may serve as an example here[126] – it is not first and foremost Christ becoming incarnate in both Testaments who holds both parts of the Canon together, but rather the Third Person of the Trinity working here as there.

Pareus also sees a gradation in the value of the two Testaments, which is clear from his exegesis of Heb 1:1. Of course, the *congruentia* of the Testaments lies in the fact that the author of both is God.[127] The diction of both Testaments differs in that in the Old Testament not Christ, but only the prophets speak as God's legates, who are not *authores doctrinae.*[128] Christ, however, is not only *legatus*, but *author ipse doctrinae.*[129] As a result, Pareus considers the Old Testament obscure, as long as it is not enlightened by the New Testament.[130] According to Lutheran hermeneutics, it is true that the Old Testament is also deciphered by the New Testament. However, it is Christ himself who speaks in the *sensus literalis* of the Old Testament *promissiones*, though prophetically. Yet according to Pareus, not Christ speaks through the prophets, but rather the Holy Spirit going out from him as from the Father.[131] For this reason, thus Pareus, not only is the content of the New Testament clearer than that of the Old Testament, but in the end could stand even without the Old Testament. On the other hand, the conjunction of Old and New Testament message ensures that this can be proclaimed *efficacius.*[132]

---

[124] W. J. van Asselt, *The federal theology of Johannes Cocceius (1603–1669)* (SHCT 100; Leiden: Brill 2001); H. Faulenbach, *Weg und Ziel der Erkenntnis Christi. Eine Untersuchung zur Theologie des Johannes Coccejus* (BGLRK 36; Neukirchen-Vluyn: Neukirchener 1973); G. Schrenk, *Gottesreich und Bund im älteren Protestantismus, vornehmlich bei Johannes Coccejus. Zugleich ein Beitrag zur Geschichte des Pietismus und der heilsgeschichtlichen Theologie* (BFChrT II/5; Gütersloh: Bertelsmann 1923).

[125] Cocceius, *Psalmi* (1660) 504.

[126] Beza, *Confessio* (1560) 99: *Ita igitur Spiritus sanctus, per Euangelii praedicationem, vulnus sanat quod praedicatio Legis aperuit & deterius effecit: ità, inquam, Spiritus sanctus per Euangelii praedicatione in nobis creat Dei donum, cuius ea vis est vt statim in Iesu Christo apprehendat quicquid ad salutem requiritur, sicut anteà demonstrauimus.*

[127] Pareus, *Opera* II (1628) 833.

[128] Ibid.

[129] Ibid.

[130] Ibid. 969.

[131] Ibid. 1032f: *Spiritus Christi fuit & loquutus est in Prophetis. Illustre testimonium Deitatis tum Christi, tum Spiritus Sancti. Dedit enim Christus Prophetis Spiritum suum ... Spiritus sanctus author oraculorum in Prophetis.*

[132] Ibid. 468: *Praeterea vtilis & necessaria est lectio scripturae propheticae propter eosdem effectus cum doctrina Apostolica. Vtraque enim nos vocat ad poenitentiam & fidem: vtraque nos manu ducit ad Christum. Ac licet doctrina Apostolica id faciat proprius & clarius, quam illa, atque etiam sine illa: tamen multo id facit efficacius cum illa coniuncta.*

When one compares Pareus' exposition of Heb 1:1 with that of Gerhard, the following differences become apparent: according to Gerhard, both Testaments also have one and the same author (*unum & eundem autorem*).[133] Yet, the coherence of the Testaments is founded in the fact that in the New Testament God speaks through the incarnate Logos. It is one and the same Logos, Christ himself, who speaks in the New Testament as *logos ensarkos* and had previously spoken as *logos asarkos* through the prophets in the Old Testament.[134] If, according to Pareus, the New Testament message could ultimately manage without the Old Testament, then according to Gerhard it is the reverse: on the basis of Acts 26:22 and Luke 16:28 it is without doubt that already the Old Testament taken by itself owns the full *perfectio* and thus contains everything that is necessary to know in order to receive the *salus aeterna*.[135] Yet precisely because this is the case, both Testaments are inseparably connected to each other. *Etiamsi apostoli plura scripserint, ea tamen non esse diversa ab iis, quae in vet. test. continentur. In vet. test. novum latet, in novo vetus patet; illud Christum exhibendum promittit, hoc Christum exhibitum ostendit.*[136]

Precisely this difference is reflected in the way that Ps 22:2 is interpreted by Lutheran and Calvinist theologians. According to Lutheran understanding, the suffering Christ himself speaks in Ps 22 through the prophetically preaching mouth of David, who is inspired by the Holy Spirit.[137] Theodor Beza (1519–1605), who also awaits discovery yet as a Bible commentator,[138] says on the contrary that Christ in Matt 27:46 makes use of the words that David spoke in a situation of far less *tentatio*.[139] According to Beza, the Crucified One cites the wealth of tradition of Jewish piety, which, however, actually only fits the exceptional situation of Good Friday partially. A parallel to this may be discovered in the following: the Lutherans understand Isaiah 53 as one of the most important key texts in deciphering the accounts of the Passion of Christ.[140] This was taken to the extent that Daniel Cramer (1568–1637) says with Jerome that in Isaiah 53 not a prophet speaks, but rather an Evangelist.[141] Certainly in Beza's exposition of the Passion story Isaiah 53 plays a minor role.[142]

In the Lutheran view, the factor establishing the unity of the Testaments is Christ presenting himself ubiquitously, even sacramentally in both. Yet according to the Calvinist idea, the factor is the unity of the covenant, or, as the case may be, the activity of the Spirit in both Testaments. The christologically motivated definition of the unity of the Testaments is made concrete on the

---

[133] Gerhard, *Commentarius Super Epistolam* (1641) 19.

[134] Ibid. 19, where Gerhard says, *quod Deus Pater novissimis temporibus corporali ore & voce per Filium incarnatum in N. T. locutus sit, qui antea per Prophetas in Vet. Test. locutus fuerat.*

[135] Gerhard, *Loci* (1767-) I, 15: *Ergo in Mose & prophetis omne consilium Dei de salute nostra est propositum.*

[136] Ibid. 15.

[137] Mathesius, *Passionale* (1587) 4r, who states, *das Dauid in diesem Psalm nicht ist ein fürbilde der Leiden vnnd Todesangst vnnd kampff des HERRN Christi ... Sondern dieser Psalm ist schlechts ... von Dauid auff das Leiden/ Creutz/ Todt/ Aufferstehung vnnd Reich des HERRN Christi gemacht.*

[138] This can be seen, among others, in W. Kickel, *Vernunft und Offenbarung bei Theodor Beza. Zum Problem des Verhältnisses von Theologie, Philosophie und Staat* (BGLRK 25; Neukirchen: Neukirchener 1967). Aside from the fact that Kickel adopts the theory of Orthodoxy as a symptom of decay, for example with reference to Troeltsch, and assigning it to Beza, a further weakness in this work lies in it paying hardly any consideration to Beza's activity as a Bible commentator and preacher.

[139] Beza, *In Historiam Passionis* (1592) 816: *Obiter autem magna inaequalitas hac in parte inter figuram & veritatem est obseruanda. Nam Dauidis hunc Psalmum scribentis afflictissimus & calamitosissimus status, infinitis partibus erat inferior passionibus quas in Cruce Christus patiebatur, siue causam, siue mensuram, siue etiam effecta consideremus.* Apparently, this interpretation is in any case not representative for the Calvinist interpretation history of Psalm 22, since Cocceius, *Psalmi* (1660) 113, calls Psalm 22 *Oratio Christi patientis*.

[140] Cf. for example, Gerhard, *Erklährung* (2002) 26, where Gerhard calls Isaiah 53 a *Schlüssel die Geheimnis des Leidens Christi zu eröffnen* ("key to unlock the secrets of the Passion of Christ").

[141] Cramer, *Schola* (1607) 280.

[142] Beza, *In Historiam Passionis* (1592).

Lutheran side in their hermeneutical equality. In contrast, the Calvinist, federal-theological unity of the *foedus* based on the Third Article results in the inferior valuation of the Old Testament.

Thus the Calvinist differentiation of the various degrees of the *claritas* of both Testaments also has its place within the reflections on the covenant (*foedus*) of God. It is a greater concern to the Reformed dogmaticians than to the Lutherans to emphasise the unity of the *foedus Dei* in both Testaments. There is only one covenant, yet there are distinct *administrationes* of it. This unity is based – thus Wolleb – in the fact that there is only one "Testator", namely Christ. The *foedus* is administered differently in that the Old Covenant is limited temporally and locally, i.e., to Israel, while the New Covenant is eternal and affects the entire world. A further distinction concerns the *claritas*: the divine *promissiones* are proclaimed more clearly (*clarius*) in the New Testament than in the Old.[143]

Consensus exists between the Lutheran and Calvinist doctrine of principles with respect to the *perfectio* and *sufficientia* of Scripture (2 Tim 3:16). The Roman Catholic equal ranking of Scripture and tradition, as well as the view that the Word of God becomes only truly efficacious through the Church's interpretation of Scripture and then through the function of the Church as mediating salvation, was rejected by both parties. Following Glassius, Scripture is perfect because it contains everything that is *zur Erlangung des ewigen Lebens nötig* ("necessary for the attainment of eternal life"). Scripture presents the *Artickel des Glaubens* ("articles of faith") in such a way, *daß wir ... völliger Weise darinnen unterrichtet werden* ("that we are instructed in a complete manner").[144] Wolleb formulates: *S. Scriptura ad salutem perfecta est.*[145] Cocceius expressed his view similarly, starting with 2 Tim 3:16: *Nostra thesis est: Scriptura utilis est ad docendum, quicquid scitu ad salutem necessarium; & quidem potenter.*[146] Meanwhile, the fact that the Gospels, taking passages like John 20:30 and 21:25, do not include all statements and sermons of Christ or reports about all the miracles he did, cannot – as the Roman Catholic theologians do[147] – be used for the argument against the *perfectio* and for the necessity of the *traditio non scripta*. For this is not the object and claim of the biblical books, to offer complete verbatims and chronicles, rather it is chiefly this: to instruct people in the faith so that they receive salvation (cf. John 20:31). And concerning this object, according to Cocceius, Scripture is sufficient.[148]

In genuine Orthodox view, Scripture is therefore perfect in that it contains all the necessary knowledge in the sense of a canon and a guiding principle that is necessary to know for the attainment of salvation. The doctrine of the *perfectio* of Scripture is thought of as strictly soteriological.[149] Hence, König counts the *perfectio* with the *affectiones scripturae primariae*, while he names the *integ-*

---

[143] Wolleb, *Compendium* (1633) 108.
[144] Glassius, *Glaubens=Grund* (1654) 117 (*daß wir von denselbigen Stücken völliger Weise darinnen unterrichtet werden*).
[145] Wolleb, *Compendium* (1633) 6.
[146] Cocceius, *Potentia* (1655) 203.
[147] Bellarmin, *Disputationes* 1 (1601) 216.
[148] Cocceius, *Potentia* (1655) 249: *Scopus scribendorum librorum sacrorum non est is, ut in iis omnium miraculorum catalogus extaret, vel etiam omnes omnino sermones Christi verbotenus repeterentur, sed ut fides in D. Jesum Christum filium Dei adstrueretur & ut in fide illius salutem adipiscamini.*
[149] Ratschow, *Dogmatik* I (1964) 117.

ritas of the biblical Canon, of the individual biblical books and the inventory of letters under the *affectiones secundariae*.[150] Certainly the Orthodox theologians also assign to Scripture an authenticity with respect to the presentation of historical dates and real facts. However, this by no means constitutes the *perfectio* of Scripture. In the course of the rise of the Enlightenment spirit, the increasingly strong criticism of the Bible supposed to the contrary, through text-critical questioning of the *integritas* of Scripture, through the exhibition of historical contradictions and similar things, so as to be able to declare the *imperfectio* of Scripture. In reaction to this on the Orthodox side, now for apologetic reasons, there is an increasing confusion of the *perfectio ad salutem* with a general, even abstract *perfectio* and inerrancy of Scripture in every respect, particularly with regard to historical and scientific dates. In this way, the *integritas*, originally classified as secondary argument, became a primary one, even a synonym of the *perfectio*, assuming that the former could only be 'saved' by proving the latter.

5. Methodical Instructions to the Exegesis of Scripture – Philological *eruditio* and Meditative *pietas*

Lutheran and Calvinist theologians alike have developed methodologies of Scripture reading and exegesis in a considerable abundance of writings, be it in academic orations, in study instructions, or elsewhere.[151] All these treatises advise placing Scripture reading at the centre not only of university study, but also of the official duties of pastor or university teacher. This is often grounded biblically on John 5:39 and thus with Jesus' call, *Scrutari Scripturas*.[152] True Scripture reading is rereading, which has to be continuously engaged with. Therefore, August Pfeiffer (1640–98) says that a theologian must be "industrius" *in crebra lectione & relectione Scripturarum*.[153] Here the high esteem of Scripture within the work economy of theologians is made concrete. Scripture is to be read daily and, of course, – as most school councils made plain – in several lessons, which should be dispersed throughout the day.

Hieronymus Weller (1499–1572) advises reading passages from the Psalter and the Gospels early in the morning, to take up the prophets and the Pauline epistles in the forenoon and to study the Old Testament pericopes in the afternoon. Weller distributes work on the other theological disciplines as well as the *artes* to the intervals.[154] Balthasar Meisner (1587–1626) recommends advancing the cursory readings of the Bible in German in the morning and repeating the same in the eve-

---

[150] König, *Theologia* (2006) 36; Ratschow, Dogmatik I (1964) 101.

[151] M. Brecht, "Theologiestudium II", TRE 33 (2002) 354–58. The article, in its passages on Orthodoxy, remains rather colourless and does not consider more recent literature. At the least should be added: R. Mau, "Programme und Praxis des Theologiestudiums im 17. und 18. Jahrhundert", *Theologische Versuche* 11 (1979) 71–91; Steiger, Gerhard (1997) 143–55; Steiger, Rezeption (2000). Cf. M. Nieden, *Die Erfindung des Theologen. Wittenberger Anweisungen zum Theologiestudium im Zeitalter von Reformation und Konfessionalisierung* (Tübingen: Mohr 2006).

[152] Pfeiffer, *Hermeneutica* (1684) 87.

[153] Ibid.

[154] Weller, *Ratio* (1565) a 2v/3r.

ning, yet in the remaining time he suggests pursuing the *lectio accurata* of selected texts chiefly from the prophets or apostolic epistles. This more thorough reading must take place *in linguâ Originali vel Hebraicâ vel Graecâ*. The reader should submit the text in question to an exhaustive logical, rhetorical and philological analysis. With the aid of dictionaries and concordances he should decipher uncertain passages by application of related Bible texts and take into consideration the history of interpretation in the form of commentaries.[155] In this it is apparent what a central role exegesis came to play in the Orthodox curriculum. The common bias, among others propagated by Tholuck,[156] that Orthodox theologians had put dogmatics in the place of concrete Scripture interpretation, shows itself to be unfounded. In addition, Meisner gives pragmatic instructions for always using the same copy of the respective edition of the Bible, *cùm variatio exemplarium vehementer turbet memoriam*.[157]

Leonhart Hütter (1563–1616) called the "lectio S. Bibliorum" *initium & finis*[158] of the entire study of theology and gave the recommendation to thoroughly read one chapter or at most two every morning, to analyse it and collate it in its German, Latin and Hebrew or Greek wording. In addition, he urges his students to arrange three excerpt books in octavo format. In the first, core passages of Scripture should be recorded which are useful for the establishment of the articles of faith and for the comfort of troubled consciences. In the second, the summaries of individual chapters of the Bible and other reading selections are to be noted, while the third excerpt book should contain *loci communes*. With the help particularly of the second entry book, over time a portable library is produced, which allows to observe official duties when en route or when for some other reasons no library is available. Hütter's student Johann Gerhard apparently acted upon these recommendations zealously and at a later time transmitted it in modified form to his own students. Gerhard advises them to draw up excerpt books for exegetical work. These books should assign several pages for every chapter of the Bible. Thus the possibility is given of taking notes during the reading of the Holy Scripture as well as the Church Fathers and other authors.[159] In this way it is ensured that, in time, a treasury of biblical-theological reading selections is produced, a *eruditionis Theologicae thesaurus*,[160] which offers rich material both for the study of theology and for the future profession. This thesaurus ought to be expanded not only in study, but *per totam hominis vitam*.[161]

According to the Orthodox view, the study of the Holy Scripture ultimately requires two things: *eruditio* and *pietas*. Following Pfeiffer, the ideal is the "interpres πολυμαθής",[162] who has profound knowledge of languages, but is also at home in the remaining *artes*, especially in rhetoric and logic. Knowledge of the *disciplinae reales*[163] must be added, that is, in metaphysics, physics, ethics, politics, geography, chronology and history. The original foundation of all theological activity, according to Gerhard, is the study of the Bible. From it arises piety and learning. The *Sincerum pietatis studium*[164] is the starting point and goal of the study of theology and embraces the entire life of a theologian. Accordingly, Gerhard in a way uses Luther's famous formulation that *oratio*, *meditatio* and *tentatio* make a theologian[165] as a heading to his "Metho-

---

[155] Meisner, *Instructio* (1638) 381 f.
[156] F. Uhlhorn, *Geschichte der deutsch-lutherischen Kirche* I–II (Leipzig: Dörffling & Franke 1911) I, 135.
[157] Meisner, *Instructio* (1638) 379.
[158] Hütter, *Consilium* (1638) 339.
[159] Gerhard, *Methodus* (1620) 158. Cf. Steiger, Exzerptbücher.
[160] Gerhard, *Methodus* (1620) 159.
[161] Ibid.
[162] Pfeiffer, *Hermeneutica* (1684) 73.
[163] Ibid. 174 ff.
[164] Gerhard, *Methodus* (1620) 14.
[165] Luther, WA 50,659.

dus".[166] In addition to the exercise of piety, Gerhard includes the necessary solemnity and prayer: *1. Rectae intentionis debitum. 2. Sincerum pietatis studium. 3. Devotae orationis officium.*[167]

In the five years of study devised by Gerhard, the focal points of the learning endeavour are respectively exegesis, dogmatics, homiletics, Church history or controversial theology. Still, there is the study of the Bible, the steadily renewed, cursory and exhaustive Bible readings, running through the entire curriculum like a red thread. *POst seriam Dei invocationem nullum est studii Theologici adminiculum magis necessarium & utile, quam diligens & assidua Scripturae sacrae lectio.*[168] Piety, for Gerhard, is not a private passing phenomenon of theological activity. Quite on the contrary, *pietas* and *lectio scripturae sacrae* are the starting points for all further theological endeavours. For this reason, devotional Bible reading and rigorous philological work are distinct but form a unity for Gerhard. *Docta pietas* and *pia eruditio* are the two goals of study that cannot be torn from each other.

Knowledge of the three holy languages – according to Luther, the scabbards in which the sword of the Holy Spirit is fixed[169] – is indispensable in Gerhard's view, yet the Hebrew language receiving the highest position. After all, it is Hebrew from which all other languages originate only after the building of the Tower of Babel. Hebrew is – as Flacius also says[170] – the mother and *matrix* of all other languages and with that the first and most important communication medium of God.[171]

According to the Orthodox view, theological existence is, so to speak, from beginning to end a *lectio continua* of biblical texts, and for this reason also *tentatio perpetua*. The *tentatio* is not an undesirable disturbance. Rather, the *tentatio*, as alienation from God, is the motivation for theological study. For only the *tentatio* is able to draw stale, theoretical knowledge out of its abstraction and let it become an appropriated knowledge – appropriated because it has undergone suffering: μάθος and πάθος belong together. Only the occupation with the divine Word brings *tentatio*, and only *tentatio* teaches to listen to God's Word (Isa 28:19). Only those who read the Bible seeking comfort because they are tempted and perceive the *efficacia consolatoria scripturae sacrae* coming to effect in themselves, only they truly read the Bible in its real sense. In this respect, the triad of *oratio, meditatio, tentatio* is a matter of a circular rotation, or, as Reuden says, of a "gradatio": *Credens tentatur, tentatus orat, orans liberatur, liberatus agit gratias.*[172] This cycle cannot come to a standstill, because 1. it belongs to the very nature of faith continually to be tempted, and 2. the encounter with the *verbum Dei* in one respect evokes the *tentatio*, but at the same time Scripture represents the sole efficient spiritual basis of consolation.

Exegetical learning and living piety belong closely together also in the Calvi-

---

[166] Gerhard, *Methodus* (1620) 13: *Lutherus in praefation. tom. I. oper. Germ. Jen. ex Ps. 119. colligit tria studii Theologici requisita videlicet Orationem, Meditationem et Tentationem.* Cf. Gerhard, *Loci* (1767-) II, 7a.

[167] Gerhard, *Methodus* (1620) 14.

[168] Ibid. 140.

[169] Luther, WA 15, 38.

[170] Flacius, *Clavis* (1580) I, 383, calls the Hebrew language *lingua aliarum omnium mater.* Cf. on the subject Klein, Einheit (1999), as well as Aarsleff, Rise (1999).

[171] Gerhard, *Methodus* (1620) 41.

[172] Reuden, *Isagoge* (1601) S 8r.

nist view. It is noteworthy, though, that on the Reformed side, it is first in the so-called *Nadere Reformatie* that the alignment of exegesis toward the *pietas* is increasingly taken into view. For example, according to Voetius, the "Praxis pietatis" should embrace the entire course of study. Voetius therefore urges those studying not only to transfer the study of Scripture into the practice of prayer, but in addition to occupy themselves with meditative literature. Aside from the medieval authors (Bernhard, Tauler, *et al.*), Voetius lists as relevant also Lutherans, for instance Martin Moller (1547–1606) and Gerhard.[173] In as far as this exegetical methodology, aiming at *meditatio* and *pietas*, is concerned, Voetius by no means stood alone within the Reformed arena. Already Heinrich Bullinger demanded that the occupation with the Scripture should be *non tam lectio ... quàm ad Deum pia oratio.*[174]

> Exegesis – this is the Protestant consensus, which in turn had humanistic roots – must be concerned with the biblical texts in their original languages. Neither the reading of the Septuagint nor the Vulgate can replace these efforts. With this, Protestant hermeneutics contradicts Roman dogmatics, which takes the Vulgate to be the canonical "versio", because it is approved by the Church.[175] Nevertheless, – and this is often overlooked – Protestant Orthodoxy was characterised by a high esteem for the Vulgate, which is not only continually present in exegetical and dogmatic work, but among other things also produced a linguistically strongly marked Latin meditation literature.[176] Important in the use of the Vulgate, however, was the frequent suggestion to do this in a critical manner. Thus, Caspar Finck (1578–1631) recommended the utilisation of the edition by Andreas Osiander the Younger (1562–1617) or those of the Spanish orientalist Arias Montanus (1527–98), who became famous by the publication of the Antwerp Polyglot. These editions of texts, according to Finck, call the reader's attention to the "discrepantiae" of the Vulgate text in comparison to the respective original texts by annotation.[177]

6. The Interest of Orthodox Theologians in the Rabbinical History of Interpretation

The view is widespread that only in recent times and with a developing Jewish-Christian dialogue an awareness has emerged on the Christian side of a double *Wirkungsgeschichte* of the Old Testament: a Jewish and a Christian one. It is said, however, that formerly Christians had no interest in the Jewish interpretation of the Old Testament developing parallel to their own and at most had acquired knowledge of Hebrew from the Jews.[178] Nevertheless, this view is in-

---

[173] Voetius, Exercitia (1651) 176. On Voetius, cf. F. A. VAN LIEBURG, *De Nadere Reformatie in Utrecht ten tijde van Voetius. Sporen in de gereformeerde kerkeraadsacta* (Rotterdam: Lindenberg 1989); J. A. VAN RULER, *The crisis of causality. Voetius and Descartes on God, nature and change* (SIH 66; Leiden: Brill 1995).

[174] Bullinger, Ratio (1594) 23r.

[175] Becanus, Manuale (1727) 4.

[176] J. A. STEIGER, *Nachwort*, Gerhard, Meditationes (2000) 625–765, here: 678.

[177] Finck, Clavis (1618) 11.

[178] R. RENDTORFF, "Rabbinische Exegese und moderne christliche Bibelauslegung", in: idem, *Kanon und Theologie. Vorarbeiten zu einer Theologie des Alten Testaments* (Neukirchen-Vluyn: Neukirchener 1991) 15–22, here: 15.

correct considering the history of interpretation, since Protestant Orthodoxy had a very vital interest in the Jewish interpretation of Scripture.[179] When regarding Orthodox exegetical literature, it is astonishing how often it explicitly refers to the rabbinical tradition. Johann Gerhard's exposition of the Old Testament, for instance, took place in a continuous dialogue with Jewish exegesis. Gerhard drew his knowledge of the resulting history of the Old Testament in the Jewish domain from his own study of the relevant rabbinical sources, which can be seen among other things by Gerhard frequently citing the Rabbis in Hebrew and including Latin translations.

How intensive Gerhard's studies in the Judaistic field were, is also made obvious from the catalogue of his library.[180] Gerhard pursued his study of the Targumim with the help of a Latin translation of the Targum with commentary, made available by the Strasbourg Hebraist and Old Testament scholar Paulus Fagius (1504–49).[181] Yet, Gerhard also possessed an edition of the Pentateuch that offered the commentaries of Rashi, *et al.*, printed with the texts of the three Targumim,[182] as well as various Hebrew Bibles, dictionaries, concordances and grammars.

There is scarcely a modern Christian Genesis commentary that pursues such an intensive discourse with the Jewish expositions as the commentary on Genesis by Gerhard.[183] Gerhard's Judaistic interest was not an isolated case. In his writings, Johann Matthäus Meyfart also showed consideration for expositions of Jewish origin.

The Reformation brought with it a high esteem for the Hebrew Old Testament. This is reflected, for example, in Gerhard's discussion of Genesis 11, the account of the building of the Tower of Babel. Gerhard here refers to the biblical Hebrew as the matrix of all other languages and thus the mother tongue of a theologian: *Magna est Hebraeae linguae dignitas, quòd sit omnium antiquissima & reliquarum omnium matrix.*[184] Before God confused the language of the proud human race, and before the alienation of humans from God became concretised after the building of the Babylonian tower when they met as strangers in different languages, there had only been one language, namely the divine Hebrew. Yet the position of the Hebrew language did not only have to do

---

[179] The examination of these facts has not yet progressed very far. Cf. however G. MÜLLER, "Antisemitismus VI", TRE 3 (1978) 143–55, here: 149f; idem, "Christlich-jüdisches Religionsgespräch im Zeitalter der protestantischen Orthodoxie. Die Auseinandersetzung Johann Müllers mit Rabbi Isaak Trokis 'Hizzuk Emuna'", *Glaube, Geist, Geschichte* (ed. G. Müller / W. Zeller; Leiden: Brill 1967) 513–24; idem, "Der Judenarzt im Urteil lutherisch-orthodoxer Theologen 1642–1644", *KALIMA NA DINI. Studien zu Afrikanistik, Missionswissenschaft, Religionswissenschaft* (ed. H.-J. Greschat / H. Jungraithmayr; Stuttgart: Evangelischer Missionsverlag 1969) 370–76.

[180] This catalogue shows a subject heading "Biblia Ebraea, et Chaldaica" (Bibliotheca Gerhardina, 39), a rubric "Lexica et Concordantiae Ebraea et chald." (334f) as well as a classification "Catalogus Librorum Ebraeorum". Among other things, Gerhard possessed and used the Hebrew-Latin "Hebraica Biblia" (1546), annotated with rabbinical commentaries by the Basel Hebraist Sebastian Münster (1489–1552) – the first of its kind. In addition, an edition of the five books of Moses (Pentateuch) also with rabbinical commentary and the Jewish festival scrolls (Megilloth) are likewise found in Gerhard's library.

[181] Bibliotheca Gerhardina (2002) 40.

[182] Ibid. 337: חמשה חומשי תורה h. e. *Pentateuchus Ebraeus cum Comment. Perpetuis* רשי *sive R. Salomonis Jarchi ac triplici Targhum, sc. Onkelosij, Jonathanis Ben Uziel ac Hierosolymitano In 8t. maj*, published in Basel by Conrad Waldkirch.

[183] Reventlow, Epochen 4 (2001) 11–21, in his portrait on Gerhard's exegesis, gets along without mentioning even one of his numerous commentaries.

[184] Gerhard, *Commentarius super Genesin* (1637) 271.

with its *antiquitas*. Rather, singular *puritas* and *elegantia* – as Carpzov indicated – are suited to the language of God.[185]

On the Reformed side, Andreas Hyperius (1511–64) particularly praised the *dignitas* of Hebrew and referred to the careful learning of the language in which God first articulated his will as indispensable.[186] According to Johann Heinrich Hottinger (1620–67),[187] learning is perfected in the study of Hebrew, in the grammar of the language of God. *Homine Grammaticae Hebraeae perito doctius nihil est. Optimus Grammaticus Hebraeus, optimus Theologus. Scriptura non potest intelligi Theologicè, nisi priùs intelligatur Grammaticè.*[188] Considered thus, philology is not a useful auxiliary science to theology, but theology *is* philological science – is itself *philologia sacra*. It is apparent here that the appreciation of the biblical *litera* by the Reformers and the consequent alignment of theology to the *sensus literalis* leads to an impressive high esteem for the Hebrew language, which Hottinger also calls the "mater" of all other languages.[189] However, it is clear that early modern Hebrew studies had an even broader rooting, namely in the effort of humanist scholars for the original language. Hottinger, for instance, particularly emphasised in what an intensive manner Johannes Reuchlin (1455–1522) had contributed to the *Literarum Hebraicarum restauratio*.[190] Consequently, within Orthodox-Hebrew scholarship Reformation and humanistic heritage coincide. The professionalisation of Christian Hebrew studies undertaken by humanists like Giovanni Pico della Mirandola (1463–94), Reuchlin, Fagius, *et al.*, was theologically processed and made fruitful for the hermeneutics of the Holy Scripture.

The study of the Hebrew language and of the original text of the Old Testament played a central role in Orthodox curricula. As a resource for the study of Hebrew, Gerhard recommended to his students the grammars by Johann Meelführer,[191] Christoph Helwig[192] and Johannes Buxtorf[193] as well as dictionaries by Sanctes Pagninus,[194] Johannes Förster,[195] Johannes Avenarius[196] and Buxtorf.[197] Gerhard called special attention to the *Lexicon Pentaglotton, Hebraicum, Chaldaicum, Syriacum, Talmudico Rabinicum & Arabicum Schindleri*.[198] Differing from Wilhelm Gesenius' Hebrew dictionary, Schindler always cites Talmudic and rabbinical authorities and lists lexemes found only in these sources and not in biblical Hebrew. Gesenius, in contrast, cites parallels from every possible Semitic language, but not from post-biblical Hebrew – an implicit lexicographical anti-Judaism.

---

[185] Carpzov, *Critica* (1748) 198: *Haec itaque lingua, non antiquitate modo sua; puritate, copia, & elegantia, sed divina cumprimis, ad coelestia mysteria cum hominibus communicanda, consecratione & destinatione, unde sanctitatis eidem character accedit, ceteris omnibus praeripit palmam.*

[186] Cf. e.g., Hyperius, *De rectè formando* (1556) 61 f.

[187] H. STEINER, *Der Zürcher Professor Johann Heinrich Hottinger in Heidelberg 1655–1661* (Zürich: Schulthess 1886); G. A. BENRATH, *Reformierte Kirchengeschichtsschreibung an der Universität Heidelberg im 16. und 17. Jahrhundert* (Speyer: Verein für Pfälzische Kirchengeschichte 1963).

[188] Hottinger, *Thesaurus* (1649))(4r.

[189] Ibid.)()(2v.

[190] Ibid.)(3v.

[191] Meelführer, *Clavis* (1628).

[192] Helwig, *Compendium* (1613).

[193] Buxtorf the Elder, *Praeceptiones* (1605); Buxtorf the Elder, *Thesaurus* (1609).

[194] Sanctes Pagninus, *Thesaurus* (1529).

[195] Förster, *Dictionarium* (1557).

[196] Avenarius, *Lexicon Hebraicum* (1568).

[197] Buxtorf the Elder, *Epitome* (1607); Buxtorf the Elder, *Lexicon Hebraicum* (1615).

[198] Gerhard, *Methodus* (1620) 56; Schindler, *Lexicon* (1612).

The knowledge of Chaldean (i.e., Aramaic) and Syrian is necessary, according to Gerhard, in order to be able to read the respective passages of the Old Testament, to occupy oneself with the Targumim, to understand the Aramaic expressions of the New Testament and to be able to become acquainted with the Bible commentaries of the Rabbis.[199] The education in Aramaic and Syrian should then enable students of theology to be able to make themselves thoroughly acquainted not only with the Biblia Hebraica, but also with the early Jewish tradition of interpretation. In this respect, Gerhard's curriculum was not an isolated case. In his *Oratio in laudem linguae Ebraicae*,[200] Georg Wicelius (1501–73) sang the praises not only of the Hebrew language, but also reflected on its relationship to Aramaic and Syrian. Johann Michael Dilherr (1604–69), who reprinted Wicelius' oration, also held a panegyric oration on the Hebrew language and recommended the intensive study of the same with the remark that no translation can truly be in a position to render the biblical Hebrew text in its multiplicity of meaning. Hebrew, according to Dilherr, is the language of God himself. For this reason he equated the effort connected with learning this language to a *Gottesdienst (cultus Dei)*.[201] The necessity of knowing the Hebrew language is the result of, among other things, the fact that the Hebrew lexemes frequently include meaning in a contracted manner to such an extent that an adequate translation is not at all possible. An example: *In versione Veteris Testamenti Latina saepè occurit vox misereri. At illa voci substituitur Ebraicae* רחם *quae multò plus significat; quàm misereri. Nativa enim ejus significatio notat, si ita, salva Latinitate, loqui liceat, inviscerare aliquem, intimo commiserationis adfectu amplecti, quo videlicet matrix solet concipere, complecti, fovere, alere, tueri, & conservare foetum.*[202]

The Orthodox professionalisation of Old Testament scholarship is not only found in the area of Hebrew studies. Rather, this process took place alongside a similar professionalisation in the field of rabbinical studies. In his *Philologia Sacra*, Glassius exchanged intensively with Jewish hermeneutics. He took up, among other things, the Jewish Kabbalah in the development of the doctrine of *sensus spiritualis seu mysticus*,[203] and introduced the view held not only by Rabbi Abraham ibn Esra (1089–1164) that each biblical text makes possible 70 different interpretations.[204] In addition, Glassius wrote a *Christologia Mosaica*, which interprets Genesis typologically to Christ and at the same time is concerned with Jewish hermeneutics. Thus the Rabbis are cited with the view *non esse in lege unicam literulam, à quâ non magni suspensi sint (doctrinarum, seu sapientiae divinae) montes.*[205] Glassius further quotes a succession of authorities from the early Christian Church tradition (Chrysostom, Basil, Jerome) in order to show that the foundation of Jewish and Christian hermeneutics newly come to light by the Reformation are similar, because both sides are guided by the canonicity of the Holy Scripture. How important a role Jewish education played for Glassius becomes evident also in his study plan, transmitted in his own hand-writing.[206]

The *Hermeneutica Sacra* by Johann Konrad Dannhauer (1603–66)[207] also sees an important common interest of Jewish and Orthodox Lutheran hermeneutics in the recognition that there is

---

[199] Ibid. 62f.
[200] Wicelius, *Oratio* (1643).
[201] Dilherr, *Oratio* (1643) F 2v.
[202] Ibid. F 4r.
[203] Glassius, *Philologia* (1713) 302–12. Here is found a minutely crafted chapter betraying a great knowledge of Jewish sources: *De Rabbinorum allegoriis, quae Cabbala dicuntur.*
[204] Ibid. 259.
[205] Glassius, *Christologia* (1678) a 2r.
[206] Glassius, *Bericht.*
[207] Cf. Alexander (1993), Sdzuj (1997) and Bühler (2006).

nothing superfluous in the holy texts. Citing the *Zohar*, the principal work of the Spanish Kabbalah attributed to the Rabbi Simeon ben Jochai (second century), Dannhauer says: *Non est ullum verbum frustraneum (in scriptura scilicet) aut si est, vel esse videtur ex vobis est ([id] est [ex] vestra coecitate & ignorantia) in Zohar scribit R. Simeon: ... Non est ullum verbum aut unica litera in lege, in qua non sint mysteria sublimia & pretiosa.*[208]

Later Johann Hülsemann (1602-61) and Johann Olearius (1611-84) emphasised the necessity of the mastery of the Semitic languages in their curricula and listed study aids.[209] Nicolaus Selnecker (1530-92) described it as grace that *sacros libros Hebraicè, Chaldaicè, Syriacè, AEthiopicè, Graecè, Latinè, & Germanicè, sine omni difficultate & molestia comparare, habere, cognoscere, & conferre possumus.*[210]

It is noteworthy that Calvinist theologians also held the knowledge of the rabbinical tradition to be urgently necessary, particularly with regard to the interpretation of the Old Testament. For example, Voetius presents students with an opulent reading plan, when he recommends the following works: *commentaria Kimchi, Jarchi, Aben Esra, in Hoseam, Jachiadae in Danielem ... tractatus aliquot Maymonidae nunc hebraicè & latine editos; tractatus aliquot Talmudicos, ut Middot Sanhedrin, Bava Kama, Joma; partes aliquot grammaticae Kimchi, logicae R. Simeon, physicae R. Aben Tibhon; sphaerae R. Eliae Orientalis; chronici majoris & minoris hebraeorum.*[211] Rivetus puts forward rabbinical-hermeneutical principles, for example, when he emphasises that according to the view of the Rabbis, it amounts to a perversion of the Word of God when one does not keep in view the context of the text to be interpreted in each case.[212] Ludovicus de Dieu (1590-1642),[213] Johann Heinrich Heidegger (1633-98) and Hottinger – to name only a few – conversed intensively with rabbinical authors in their respective commentaries and biblical-philological writings.

However, not all Orthodox theologians agreed upon the purpose of the discourse with the Jewish tradition. Lukas Osiander the Elder (1534-1604) was of the opinion that it is a waste of time and lamp oil to read rabbinical writings and that the knowledge of biblical Hebrew is sufficient.[214]

Although Luther had warned against an all too searching occupation with the Rabbis, it is evident with the majority of Orthodox theologians: in the seventeenth century, the high esteem of the Old Testament as the *viva vox euangelii* originating in Luther increasingly amalgamated with Christian Hebrew studies founded by humanists such as Pico della Mirandola and Reuchlin. Gerhard's exposition of the Holy Scripture therefore takes place in a continuous discourse with Jewish exegesis. Most of Gerhard's numerous references to the Jewish tradition are of a positive and affirmative character. Precisely because there is a fundamental difference of opinion between Jews and Christians concerning the question whether Jesus is the promised Messiah or not, Gerhard is free also to elaborate on the Jewish-Christian consensus. That Gen 49:11 talks about the Messiah is evident, according to Gerhard, *ex Rabbinor-*

---

[208] Dannhauer, *Hermeneutica* (1654) 134f.

[209] Hülsemann, *Methodus* (1638) 229f, and Olearius, *Methodus* (1664) 52-54, 203.

[210] Selnecker, *Notatio* (1579) 139.

[211] Voetius, *Exercitia* (1651) 166.

[212] Rivetus, *Isagoge* (1627) 262: *Qua de re apud Ebraeos extat communis regula, qui non advertit quod supra & infra in scriptoribus scribitur, is pervertit verba Dei viventis.*

[213] Cf. de Dieu, *Critica* (1693).

[214] Osiander, *De Studiis* (1591) 21: *In Hebraea lingua satis fuerit, si quis Hebraea Biblia intelligat: etiamsi hoc studio non omnes Ecclesiae Ministri onerandi videntur. Qui verò in id incumbunt, vt Rabinorum commentarios hebraeos intelligant, oleum & operam perdunt. Nam & barbarißimè scribunt, stylo ex varijs linguis, & quidem corruptis, consarcinato, & in explicatione sacrae Scripturae non magis Lectori prosunt, quàm si ab homine caeco viam sibi monstrari Theologiae studiosus peteret. Quare Theologus ingenium & laborem in alijs studijs multò melius collocare poterit.*

um & Christianorum Interpretum consensione.[215] Citing Rabbi Kahana, Gerhard shows that this passage has also been interpreted on the Jewish side to point to the Messiah with reference to the promises of the Messiah in Zech 9:9 and Isaiah 53.[216] Gerhard concludes: *Ergò per Siloh hic intelligendus est Messias, ut patet 1. ex praedicatis sequentibus, quae nemini, nisi Messiae congruunt. 2. Ex Chaldaicis versionibus … 3. Ex confessione veterum Rabbinorum.*[217]

Gerhard's enquiry into the rabbinical tradition frequently followed grammatical, philological and text-critical interests. Also, he readily consulted the Rabbis for explanation of historical circumstances and biblical institutions and customs. Yet at the same time it is evident that Gerhard also had a genuine theological-hermeneutical interest in the Jewish tradition.[218] According to Gerhard, the fundamental basis of Jewish and Christian faith, despite all their differences, consists in the fact that they have a common text and for this reason Jews and Christians construct a community of interpretation in the reading of the writings of the old covenant. In Gerhard's view, Christian exegesis has to respect, e. g., that in the Song of Songs the relationship of YHWH to the people first chosen by him is first and foremost. The Christian reading, which sees the relationship of God to the Church mirrored in the union of the bridegroom and bride, by no means contradicts the previously mentioned interpretation. Gerhard's form-historical interest in the Song is amazingly intensive. He attempts, in a form-critical manner, to define the literary *genus* of the Song and shows consideration for Jewish cultural history, referring to the fact that it was customary in Israel to compose bridal songs (*Brautlieder*) on the occasion of weddings.[219] Hence, Gerhard assumes a profane context for development of the Song. He does not hesitate to characterise the Song as originally a secular poem that in later times was explained spiritually, first on the Jewish and then also on the Christian side, and received its position in the Canon as a *spirituale Epithalamium, ein geistliches Brautlied.*[220] The mystical-allegorical interpretation of the Song – and in this Gerhard is in agreement with the Rabbis – was thus the prerequisite interpretative condition for the canonisation of an originally secular bridal song.

Gerhard's hermeneutics followed Luther, who describes the Bible as *sui ipsius interpres.* Gerhard knows that this manner of exegesis which searches for the most possible *dicta parallela* in order to interpret the Holy Scripture from itself is closely related to the rabbinical practice of interpretation. Despite all disagreement over the question of whether the Messiah was manifested in Christ or not, Gerhard is aware that Jews and Christians together await the revealing of eschatological salvation. Gerhard is accordingly not of the opinion that only a single interpretation of a biblical text is possible, rather he regards a text as the sum of its possible interpretations; similar to the Jewish tradition, Gerhard for this reason frequently places various possibilities of exegesis side by side.

However, matters appear to stand differently in the period of later Orthodoxy. Here the voices warning with Luther against a close consideration of rabbinical exegesis multiply once again. According to Pfeiffer, the Rabbis contribute nothing to actual textual interpretation (*nil sani afferunt*)[221] and are to be consulted at best with regard to philology. Abraham Calov (1612–86) considers knowledge of Aramaic with a view to the Targumim, if not unnecessary,

---

[215] Gerhard, *Commentarius super Genesin* (1637) 844.
[216] Ibid.
[217] Ibid. 841.
[218] On the other hand, it is improper to assert, *daß Hebraismen dem Hineingeheimnissen des eigenen theologischen Standpunktes dienten* ("that Hebraisms served the internal mysteries of his own theological point of view"); cf. Mühlenberg, Schriftauslegung (1999) 484.
[219] Cf. Gerhard, *Postilla Salomonaea* (1652) I, t 1r.
[220] Ibid. m 1v.
[221] Pfeiffer, *Hermeneutica* (1684) 89.

then at least less important.[222] Still stronger are Calov's reservations against the Talmudic tradition. Only such scholars should deal with it who pursue the *refutatio Judaeorum* and have specialised in it.[223] Calov places the positive reception, i. e., the reception founded on the Jewish-Christian commonalties of the rabbinical tradition, firmly in the background. This noteworthy shift with Calov, in comparison to Gerhard, Glassius and the other high Orthodox theologians, was certainly not accidental. It may perhaps be traced back to the fact that Calov's most prominent opponent, Hugo Grotius (1583–1645) legitimises his consistently antichristologically-aligned exegesis of the Old Testament with the help of rabbinical authorities. Thus it is not surprising that Calov, in enumerating the causes of misguided interpretation, lists also the *Ebraeorum nimia veneratio.*[224]

In addition, there was still another facet of Orthodox interest in the rabbinical tradition. Johannes Müller (1598–1672), the main Hamburg pastor, indeed also advises occupying oneself with rabbinical theology. However, the predominant motive for this was to plan and set going the most effective conversion of the Jews possible.[225] Here interest in Rabbinism becomes mixed up with a brusque anti-Judaism. Müller does not have a theological or hermeneutical interest in the Jewish tradition in the sense of common interpretation efforts of Jews and Christians. Rather – and in this he is in agreement with several decidedly enlightened theologians[226] – he is able to appreciate the Talmudim at the most as reference books which could be helpful in the exegesis of the Old Testament and the clarification of historical facts and other institutions and customs.[227] In agreement, Müller takes up the sharpest anti-Semitic remarks of Luther from his late writings on the Jews. He cites Luther with the words: "Apart from the devil, a Christian has no more bitter and powerful enemy than a proper Jew".[228] Müller likewise perpetuates the old ritual murder charge.[229] He considers Luther's demand that Jews should only be allowed to live in pens *nicht vnbillich* ("not unreasonable").[230] It is already clear from the comparison of the motives for the study of rabbinical theology in Gerhard, Glassius, *et al.* on the one side and Müller on the other, as well as from the heterogeneous statements on the relations with Jews in social and political life, how varied the position of Orthodox theologians was on the question of the Jews.

Meanwhile, on the side of Reformed Late Orthodoxy, it was Johann Andreas Eisenmenger (1654–1704) who left behind an unsightly anti-Semitic monument. He also views the benefit of the study of Jewish sources by Christians mainly for a successful mission to the Jews.[231] Eisenmenger's decisive interest with his Judaistic studies, in the course of which he also fostered personal contact with Jews, was continually the disparagement of Judaism. Eisenmenger discards the Pauline dialectic, according to which the Jews are God's chosen people and have also remained such, although they stand under divine judgement. If a Jew says he is a member of the people chosen by God, then according to Eisenmenger, this is only expression of the *Hochmuth* ("pride") of the Jews and their *grossen Ruhmredigkeit* ("great vaingloriousness")[232] as well as their *irrigen Wahn[s]/ daß sie heilige*

---

[222] Calov, *Paedia* (1652) 97.
[223] Ibid. 98: *Utilis tamen est aliqva horum notitia Theologis Professoribus, qvi in refutatione Judaismi occupantur, cùm Thalmud summae sit autoritatis apud Judaeos, eorumque mysteria exhibeat.*
[224] Calov, *Biblia* (1719) I, 16.
[225] Müller, *Judaismus* (1644) 59.
[226] Steiger, Rezeption (2000) 240.
[227] Müller, *Judaismus* (1644) 40.
[228] Ibid. 1386: *Ein Christ habe nechst dem Teufel keinen bittern vnd hefftigern Feind/ denn einen rechten Jüden.*
[229] Ibid.
[230] Ibid. 1395.
[231] Eisenmenger, *Judenthum* (1711) II, 992.
[232] Ibid. I, 568.

Leute seyn ("false delusion that they are holy people").[233] Since Eisenmenger has not grasped the Pauline dialectic of Romans 9–11 and therefore cannot think of election and judgement as one, he is certain that the Jewish consciousness of being an elect people is mere presumptuousness.[234]

7. Typological and Allegorical Exegesis of the Old Testament. Intertestamentary Hermeneutics

Looking at the history of Lutheran biblical exegesis in the Post-Reformation period, a veritable flood of sources devoted to the typological-allegorical interpretation of the Old Testament as well as to natural subjects and similar things can be found. Common to all of them is the conviction that whoever speaks of the Old Testament as *viva vox euangelii*, must also put this into effect hermeneutically in the practice of interpretation. Thus were produced a multitude of writings which are concerned with allegorical and typological exegesis and continuously cite Luther as the founder of a hermeneutics of the intercontextuality of both Testaments. The consideration of this tradition[235] is necessary, especially since quite often it is alleged that Luther's students had in principle distanced themselves from typological and allegorical exegesis.[236]

Encouraged by Luther, Caspar Goldtwurm exposited Genesis typologically quite early (1552). It is – according to Goldtwurm following Luther – "dangerous to treat every case and occasion as allegory",[237] thus to pursue allegorical exegesis without hermeneutical guidelines, as is seen not least of all among the Anabaptists. Rather, the formulation of a *regula fidei* is needed beforehand, which may only be taken from the literal sense of the Holy Scripture, in order that sound spiritual interpretations may then be found *per analogiam fidei* (Rom 12:7). Forced allegorisations, yet, are to be rejected, as well as the displacement of the literal sense of the Bible connected with this. Only keeping sight of the conformity of Scripture as a criterion in the spiritual-metaphorical interpretation of the Bible can prevent exegesis from becoming eisegesis.[238] In particular, Augustine, Jerome, Hilary, Ambrose and above all Origen – according to Goldtwurm – employed allegory *zu überflüssig* ("to excess").[239]

However, the true allegorical-typological art of interpretation is in the service of *explicatio textus*, *consolatio* and *delectatio* (*hilaritas*) of the addressee.[240]

---

[233] Ibid. 573.

[234] Ibid. 568.

[235] An important impulse is given by H. REINITZER, "'Da sperret man den leuten das maul auff'. Beiträge zur protestantischen Naturallegorese im 16. Jahrhundert", Wolfenbütteler Beiträge 7 (1987) 27–56. On the Lutheran exegesis of Genesis, cf. Kolb (1996).

[236] Interpreting the Lutheran theologians of the second half of the sixteenth and beginning of the seventeenth century as recipients and students of Luther, taking seriously their own claim, it is hardly possible to say: *An seinen Schülern hat sich Luthers Stellung zur Allegorese dahin ausgewirkt, daß sie die Allegorese nicht gebrauchten*, G. EBELING, *Evangelische Evangelienauslegung. Eine Untersuchung zu Luthers Hermeneutik* (Tübingen: Mohr ³1991) 89. Similarly also M. BRECHT, "Zur Typologie in Luthers Schriftauslegung", in: idem, *Ausgewählte Aufsätze 1. Reformation* (Stuttgart: Calwer 1995) 134–47, here: 145.

[237] Goldtwurm, *Allegorie* (1552) B 4r: *gefärlich Allegorias nach aller sachen gelegenheit zu tractieren*.

[238] Ibid.

[239] Ibid. C 1v.

[240] Ibid. C 1r.

The material standard for the invention of the spiritual sensus of the Holy Scripture is the way in which Scripture forms allegories itself. Accordingly, it is first of all necessary to examine how the New Testament spiritually explains the Old in conversation in order then to carry on this manner of exegesis mimetically.[241] As an example, Goldtwurm designates the allegorical image of baptism in the Flood in 1 Pet 3:20f, the parallelisation of Christ raised on the cross with the bronze serpent (Num 21:8f) in John 3:14, as well as the description of Jesus as the rock that accompanied the people of Israel through the wilderness (1 Cor 10:4). From these biblical examples all other spiritual interpretations proceed; they ought "to be a model for us, how and in what way we should treat and direct our allegories".[242]

Luther's allegorical and typological interpretation of Scripture concerned with biblical *exempla*[243] was a central starting point for the growing interest in this form of exegesis within biblical scholarship of the second half of the sixteenth century. This is made clear by a compilation published in 1561 of relevant passages from Luther's writings made available by Jacob Hertel (1536–64). In his preface, Hertel names, with Luther, the *sensus literalis* the substance and foundation of faith and of theology. It alone can bestow true comfort in the predicament of *tentatio*.[244] Nevertheless, Luther, whose maxim it was to remain with the literal sense as long as possible, regarded allegorical interpretation as permissible where it was a matter of finding rhetorical ornamentation.[245] Of course, allegorical interpretation has no role within the formulations of doctrine, as Augustine had already known: *FIGVRA NIHIL PROBAT*.[246] A similar work was compiled by Nikolaus Erich (d. 1584).[247]

Another example of the increased interest of Lutheran Orthodoxy in typological interpretation, particularly of the story of Joseph, comes from Michael Sachse (1542–1618).[248] Luther had himself initiated an undertaking of this exegetical task in his sermons on Genesis 37–50, in which he did not interpret all sections typologically-spiritually towards Christ.[249] In his preface, Sachse indicates that an application of the Reformation *solus Christus* to the hermeneutics of the Holy Scripture makes it unquestioningly necessary to search for prefigurements of the Christ-event in the Old Testament, especially since Jesus himself called for diligent searching in the Scripture (John 5:39) in this way.[250]

If the Holy Scripture is inspired by the Holy Spirit not only in what relates to its macrostructure, but also to its microstructure, then the inspiration of every text as *praesentia Christi* – since the Spirit indeed proceeds in like manner from the Father and the Son – can and must be made exegetically vivid. For this reason it is Sachse's intention "that I for my part, in all passages, stories

---

[241] Ibid.

[242] Ibid. C 1v: [they ought] *vnns ein fürbildt sein/ wie vnnd in was gestalt/ wir vnsere Allegorias tractieren vnd füren sollen.*

[243] J. A. STEIGER, "Martin Luthers allegorisch-figürliche Auslegung der Heiligen Schrift", *ZKG* 110 (1999) 331–51.

[244] Hertel, *Allegoriae* (1561) a 3v/4r.

[245] Ibid. a 5r/v.

[246] Ibid. a 5v.

[247] Erich, *Sylvula* (1566).

[248] Sachse, *Joseph Typicus* (1596).

[249] Luther, WA 24, 667.

[250] Sachse, *Joseph Typicus* (1596) a 2v.

and types of the Old Testament, may discover and identify Christ".[251] Sachse sees the particular excellence of the story of Joseph in that it, as no other Old Testament account, portrays the life and suffering of Christ as in a mirror.[252] The story of Joseph in a way offers a contextual collection of typology that is unrivalled in the Old Testament.

Like Sachse, Wilhelm Bidembach (1538–72) also devoted himself to the typological exegesis of the story of Joseph in sermons. According to Bidembach, the Old Testament is full of manifest and more hidden prophetic references to the passion of Christ.[253] In particular, it is advantageous to read the story of Joseph's suffering intertextually with that of Jesus' Passion. It is Bidembach's aim that the hearers of the sermon "may view the old Passion as though it were painted with new colours".[254] In this quotation it is evident that the typological hermeneutics stands in the service of what Luther called *fürbilden* ("to model"), which in addition to hearing always conveys a visual sense to the addressees. The spiritual interpretation of Old Testament texts seeks to [re-]open eyes for the New Testament, which interrelates the visual meaning to the act of hearing. In this sense, the Old Testament is the picture book illustrating the New Testament and an originator of a figurative rhetoric that is accomplished audiovisually.

Johann Gerhard gives detailed attention to the theme of typological and allegorical exegesis most of all in his *Loci*.[255] Gerhard, who – taking up a parable from Luther[256] – calls the Old Testament types *fasciae, quibus Christus involutus*,[257] makes a clear conceptual distinction between allegory and type. Typological exegesis brings the facts narrated in the Old Testament into a relationship with New Testament texts and therein is more strongly impacted contextually. Allegorical interpretation, on the other hand, takes individual Old Testament images and motifs for the purpose of interpreting them as prefigurements of New Testament realities.[258] Allegorical interpretation thus deals more freely with the text to be interpreted. Still, one and the same text can be interpreted both typologically as well as allegorically.[259] According to Gerhard, a typological reading sees the prefigurement of Christ's struggle with the devil in the story of David's struggle with Goliath (1 Sam 17:23ff); however, an allegorical reading sees the struggle of the flesh with the Spirit.[260]

The greatest attention, thus Gerhard, must be paid – and in this he is in complete agreement with Luther – to presenting above all the *sensus literalis*. From this basis alone can the systematic-theological, ethical, pastoral and controversial-theological work experience its material foundation and the filling of its contents. Here neither the allegorical[261] nor the typological interpretation has anything to offer.[262] Or with the words of the principle formulated by

---

[251] Ibid. a 7r: *das ich für meine Person inn allen Sprüchen/ Geschichten vnd Typis des Alten Testaments/ Christum finden vnd erkennen möchte.*
[252] Ibid.
[253] Bidembach, *Passio Christi* (1599) 7.
[254] Ibid. 8: *anderst nichts dann den alten Passion/ als ob der gleichsam mit newen farben gemaalet/ anschawen mögen.*
[255] Hägglund, Heilige Schrift (1951), esp. 229–41.
[256] Luther, WA 10/I/1,15.
[257] Gerhard, *Loci* (1767-) III, 365b.
[258] Ibid. I, 69a.
[259] Ibid.
[260] Ibid.
[261] Ibid.: *In praeceptis moralibus, promissionibus, comminationibus, & tractationibus dogmatum nullae sunt quaerendae allegoriae.*
[262] Ibid.

Finck: *Theologia allegorica non est argumentativa.*[263] However, if the fundamental theological-dogmatic work is carried out, then it does not mean, according to Gerhard, that one may venture fancy-free on a metaphorical interpretation of the Holy Scripture. Rather, in order to find a guiding principle, it
must be first discovered how allegorical exegesis is used within biblical texts
themselves. The exegete who wishes to learn the art of spiritual interpretation
must first of all go to school in the Holy Spirit as source of all interpretation in
accordance with Scripture. There allegorical exegesis is to be practised, where
it is to be found in Scripture itself.[264] Both these principles should ensure that
the *analogia fidei* is taken into account in every spiritual interpretation. Allegorical exegesis is thus based on the literal sense of other biblical texts. Moreover, it is to be observed that Christ – in the sense of Luther's concentration on
those pericopes focussing on Christ (*was Christum treibet*)[265] – is the *scopus totius scripturae*: *Ergo illius officium, illius beneficia, illius regnum potissimum in allegoriis sunt explicanda.*[266] Precisely this moved Flacius to entitle his hermeneutics *Clavis Scripturae Sacrae* and to identify the key to the textual world of the
Bible as a whole, and to that of the Old Testament in particular, with the Person of Christ. Only Christ, the Word of God, opens up the clasp of the book
that without him is locked with seven seals (*solus ille aperit librum clausum*).[267]

The spiritual interpretation can nevertheless also become a necessity, when
– according to Gerhard in consensus with Luther and Andreas Hyperius[268] –
there exists a *necessitas exponendi per allegoriam*, thus a Bible text is in opposition to the *regula fidei* or is grammatically nonsensical.[269]

Gerhard designates the sermon (and here above all the Exordium) as the place where this kind
of exegesis – used moderately, i.e., in brief excurses,[270] – has its traditional and legitimate place.
Allegorical interpretations *delectant, excitant, taedium auferunt.*[271] The spiritual interpretation of
Scripture is not concerned mainly with *docere* and *movere*, but rather with the *delectare*. Of course,
this does not mean that the mystical interpretation does not also teach and move. It certainly does,
since the point is to find a biblical hermeneutics completely integrating both parts of the Canon
and to exercise this hermeneutics with the help of allegorical interpretation. In doing so, the addressees are meant to be moved emotionally. However, mystical exegesis is dependent on the doctrine first being raised and founded in a manner establishing certainty from the literal sense of the
biblical text. Only then can it be adorned homiletically-rhetorically and allegorically.[272]

The spiritual interpretation of the Old Testament does not result in levelling both parts of the
Canon. Rather, in comparing type with antitype it is precisely the understanding of the *differentia
specifica* in the Holy Scriptures of the old covenant which is sharpened. This illustrates Gerhard's

---

[263] Finck, *Clavis* (1618) 53.

[264] Gerhard, *Loci* (1767-) I, 69a: *Si ipse Spiritus sanctus in scripturis aliquid typice vel allegorice
interpretatur, ibi tuto sequimur allegoriam, possumus enim esse certi, Spiritum sanctum ad illam respex-
isse.*

[265] Luther, WA.DB 7, 385. Cf. H. BORNKAMM, *Luther und das Alte Testament* (Tübingen: Mohr
1948) 128.

[266] Gerhard, *Loci* (1767-) I, 69b.

[267] Flacius, *Clavis* (1580) I, b 2r.

[268] Gerhard apparently refers, without citing a point of reference, to Hyperius, *De Sacrae
Scripturae lectione* (1569) 250.

[269] Gerhard, *Loci* (1767-) I, 70a.

[270] Ibid.

[271] Ibid. 69b.

[272] Ibid.

indication of the fact that as in the Adam-Christ parallels (Rom 5:12ff; 1 Cor 15:21f) each typology is qualified to be spoken of, *tum* τυπικῶς & *modo consentaneo ... tum* ἀντιθετικῶς & *modo dissentaneo.*[273] For example, as far as the Pauline parallelisation of Adam and Christ is concerned, the supralapsarian aspect represents a *collatio*, yet an *oppositio* under an infralapsarian view.[274] That means that precisely through the intertestamentary comparison, the otherness of the *typos* is also appreciated in regard to the *antitypos*. In other words, only through the mystical interpretation of the actualisation of the *typos*, those aspects of many Old Testament texts also receive a new (at times prophetic) significance, which cannot be made fruitful directly for the *collatio Veteris et Novi Testamenti*.

An essential characteristic of Gerhard's typological exegeses lies in the aspect of exceeding. What once happened in the earthly-physical existence is announced in prophetic prospective as a spiritual *recapitulatio* in the sense of a promise. History is exceeded by the eschata. Nevertheless, it remains to be observed that the depth of Gerhard's interpretation of Scripture cannot be fathomed with the help of typological and allegorical methodologies if (post-)enlightenment models of promise and fulfilment are applied as criteria in an anachronistic manner. The latter are mostly inspired by the rationalist idea that a *promissio* is, so to speak, mathematically paid off by the fulfilment of the promise. Gerhard, however, is of the view that type and antitype mutually put each other in perspective and interpret each other reciprocally. Looked upon from the antitype, the type accrues a surplus of meaning, which has a lasting relevance precisely for the reason that the final fulfilment of the *promissio* eschatologically is still yet to come. In addition, the type has its unmistakable hermeneutical plus in the fact that in it – for instance, in the coming to peace of the people of Israel after the annexation of territory or in the successful deliverance from enslavement in Egypt – the fulfilment of the promises can be viewed. Yet, the fulfilment, as far as the spiritual antitype is concerned, must still be believed contrary to empirical evidence. Israel has already been delivered from Pharaoh's oppression, while believers still need to pray for deliverance from sin, death and devil and must hope for the same.

In his *Philologia Sacra*, Glassius provided a full treatment of typology and allegory. Glassius was clearly concerned with expanding the hermeneutical approach of his teacher Gerhard and to systematise it more strongly. Like Gerhard, Glassius also spoke of a *sensus mysticus*, including the allegorical, typological and parabolic senses. *Estque in universum triplex: ALLEGORICUS, TYPICUS, PARABOLICUS.*[275] In order to distinguish the three from one another in terms of definition, Glassius offered the following definitions which have become classic: *Allegoricus est, quando historia Scripturae vere gesta ad mysterium quoddam, sive spiritualem doctrinam, ex intentione Spiritus sancti refertur. Typicus est, quando sub externis factis seu propheticis visionibus res occultae, sive praesentes sive futurae, figurantur, & praesertim, quando res gestae V. T. praesignificant seu adumbrant res gestas N. T. Parabolicus est, quando res aliqua ut gesta narratur, & ad aliud spirituale designandum refertur.*[276]

The *sensus mysticus* has its deepest hermeneutical basis in the fact that the merciful God takes upon himself the weakness and comprehension of human beings and reveals himself in humanly intelligible images and narratives. God in Christ gives up his Godhead in order to reveal himself in this *kenosis* as God incarnate (Phil 2:7). Something similar holds true for the first Person of the Trinity, who condescends, takes on a συγκατάβασις and gives himself to be re-

---

[273] Ibid. III, 365b.
[274] Ibid.
[275] Glassius, *Philologia* (1713) 406.
[276] Ibid.

cognised within this process of accommodation – already in the old covenant – in images and prefigurements of the forthcoming divine condescendence in Christ.[277] In this respect, God's anthropopathy and anthropomorphy in the Old Testament have a Christological and hermeneutical relevance. In this may lie an essential difference from the Calvinist understanding of Scripture: according to that, the passages that speak anthropopathically of God are to be understood figuratively.[278] However, according to Glassius, God's speaking and action carry the merciful mark of anthropopathy – *essentialiter*.

That God made himself known through types, allegories and parables in human speech, parables and stories adapted to simile is considered by Glassius as a lasting attribute of his *revelatio*. In this respect, this hermeneutics of accommodation, conceived from the Christological condescendence, differs fundamentally from the one that was to emerge in the context of Enlightenment theology. For here the accommodation is defined as a purely transitory and paedagogically motivated act of the biblical writers, who showed consideration above all for Jewish *Vorstellungen* ("notions") and for such irreconcilable with reason (as, for instance, ritual sacrifice and vicarious substitution). The widespread premise was that historical truth and its lasting effect could only be ascertained by subtracting the accommodations as circumstantial appearances, in order then to be able to catch sight of the supertemporal-rational, usually ethical core.

On the one hand, Glassius referred to the fact that there is more to be found in the New Testament antitype than in the type, since it is indeed often a question of a spiritual-eschatological fulfilment of something prefigured with the help of fleshly-external events. *Plus est saepe in antitypo, quam in typo figuratum est.*[279] Yet, on the other hand, the opposite also holds true that the type includes more than simply that which finds its fulfilment in the New Testament. *Plus est saepe in typo, quam in antitypo.*[280] The type thus has a prototypical relevance. For the New Testament antitype can really only be understood, when it is 1. always collated anew with the type and thus is meditated in a true sense; and 2. a real collation can only occur when the otherness and antitypology of the otherwise typical text is realised and preserved.

Like Luther and Gerhard, Glassius is also convinced that a person can only learn the mystical interpretation of Scripture if he allows himself to be introduced into this methodology by Scripture itself. However, what is novel is that Glassius makes more precise terminological distinctions and thus contributes to the methodological clarification of this matter. For this reason, Glassius differentiates explicitly and in a specific nomenclature between those allegories and types which Scripture itself provides and those that are brought into this category by the interpreter.[281] Glassius also develops an analogous distinction regarding the types. Concerning the "inborn" types (*typi innati*) of Scripture he differentiates those that are used *expresse & explicite*[282] from those that are found *tacite & implicite*.[283] To the first group belongs, for instance, the parallel of the Prophet Jonah, who was in the belly of the whale for three days, with Christ, who rose on the third day (Matt

---

[277] Ibid.: *Fundamentum ejus est DEI* συγκατάβασις *quam* ἀνθρωποπάθειαν *etiam vocant; quia enim DEUS in Scriptura sacra cum misellis agit hominibus, igitur saepius ipsis* συγκαταβαίνει *seu condescendit, & ad captum ipsorum se accommodans, sub involucris rerum humanarum mysteria sua coelestia proponit.*

[278] See above p. 709.

[279] Glassius, *Philologia* (1713) 467.

[280] Ibid. 466.

[281] Ibid. 410.

[282] Ibid. 458.

[283] Ibid.

12:39f). The latter group includes Rom 3:25 where Paul refers to Exod 25:17 and other Old Testament texts likewise mentioning the ἱλαστήριον, without explicitly indicating the text referred to.

Moreover, it is noteworthy that Glassius by no means knew only one such Old Testament typology that points across into the New Testament. Apart from the reference of both parts of the Canon to one another, he also examines closely the pictorial and symbolic language as an essential characteristic of the Old Testament style. Thus in the enumeration of the various *genera typorum*, Glassius first lists the currently so-called prophetic sign acts. *Actiones prophetiarum typicae sunt, quando iis, quae exterius divino mandato Prophetae peragebant, ... mysticum aliquod & occultum adumbratur.*[284] Among his examples, Glassius cites Isaiah's nakedness (Isa 20:2ff) and the judgement of God prefigured by it. Only after that Glassius treats *De visionibus Propheticis ac typicis*[285] and *De typo historiae & ejus prima divisione.*[286]

Among Calvinist exegetes there was a basic conformity with the Lutherans concerning the interpretation of the Old Testament in light of the New Testament. This pertained not only to the pre-eminent position of the *sensus literalis* before the *sensus mysticus* and to the application of the latter in the course of the illustration of the *doctrina*. According to Bullinger, allegorical interpretation of Scripture must be in conformity with Scripture, thus harmonising with the literal sense of other texts: *Curabis ante omnia, vt Allegoria tua cum alijs scripturae locis componi queat.*[287] Rivetus calls the literal sense *sensus praecipuus*[288] and the mystical *sensus secundarius*. Then a distinction must be made between the allegories and types that Christ and the Apostles used and the others. According to Rivetus, the latter do not have the same relevance as the former, because they are not certain to such an extent.[289] Yet, dogmata can only be deduced from the literal sense. Ludwig Crocius spoke – as Gerhard – of the *unus sensus* of Scripture (*verus ac legitimus S. scripturarum sensus est duntaxat unus, videlicet grammaticus sive literalis & historicus*).[290] That is to say that the allegorical, tropological and anagogical sense cannot be held as equal to the literal, because 1. from the mystical *sensus* no fundamental theological arguments can be formulated, 2. it is uncertain whether the mystical interpretation is in agreement with the intention of the Holy Spirit (and with that the *mens auctoris*), 3. the mystical interpretation originates in the human *ingenium* and 4. mystical interpretations sometimes contradict each other. This is in accordance with the Lutheran position. On the intertestamentary deciphering of both parts of the Canon, the tradition in the wake of the Genevan Reformation, like the Lutheran, expended a lot of trouble. To mention only a few scholars: Franciscus Junius (1545–1602), Mose Pflacher (1548?–89) and Amandus Polanus von Polansdorf (1561–1610).[291] It is clear that differences from Lutheran exegesis appear and that this has its origin in different systematic-theological assessments.[292] To become acquainted with the more specific char-

---

[284] Ibid. 451.
[285] Ibid. 453 ff.
[286] Ibid. 458 ff.
[287] Bullinger, *Ratio* (1594) 37v.
[288] Rivetus, *Isagoge* (1627) 231.
[289] Ibid. 231 f.
[290] Crocius, *Disputationes* (1614) 90.
[291] Junius, *Sacrorum Parallelorum libri tres* (1588); Pflacher, *Analysis* (1606); Polanus, *Exegesis* (1608).
[292] See above p. 718–20.

acteristics, however, a detailed investigation of the history of interpretation is needed.

The Arminian Hugo Grotius established a completely different hermeneutical procedure. He interprets the Old Testament to a large extent without consideration for the inner-biblical relationship established by the New Testament texts. In Isaiah 53, he does not see Christ portrayed as the servant of God, but rather Jeremiah.[293] At most, a hidden-mystical reading of Isaiah 53 can establish something christologically relevant out of this. In Gen 1:26, a trinitarian-theological interpretation is definitely incorrect according to Grotius,[294] while Gen 49:11 cannot be interpreted other than referring to the Messiah, since the Targumim and the majority of Rabbis do this.[295] Grotius has been regarded as one of those who pointed a way to modern exegesis in that they used and promoted grammatical-historical interpretation. Without doubt, this is correct, for Grotius was eager to inquire first of all about the historical situation *behind* the Old Testament text. Yet, on the other hand – and this was pointed out not least of all by Campegius Vitringa (1659–1722) – Grotius in this way lost sight of the fact that both Testaments are intended to be read in their mutually illuminating intertextuality. For this reason, Vitringa sought a middle way between Grotius on the one hand and traditional exegesis on the other. Therefore, Vitringa lingered – and this is seen clearly in his influential Isaiah commentary – as long as possible with the grammatical and historical analysis of the text in question, yet aimed to find a perspective motivated by the New Testament quasi in a second reading. First comes the careful analysis *in quo tempore figenda sit scena prophetiae*.[296] Despite all kinship with Grotius regarding the premise that the historical sense must be lingered with as long as possible, Vitringa is nevertheless of the view that the prophetic texts are treated too forcefully by Grotius: Grotius leads the reader away from Christ, breaks up the unity of the Old and New Testament and in this way reiterates the error of Marcion under different conditions.[297] According to Vitringa, this contradicts the intention of the New Testament writers (John 1:46; Acts 10:43; Acts 3:24; 1 Pet 1:10f; Luke 24:27), who held the view that in many passages the prophets speak literally of Christ. The balance of Vitringa's approach to the Old Testament prophets is evident for example in his interpretation of Isaiah 40. Vitringa first interprets this text without the context of the New Testament and says that the Prophet opens *fontes purae & liquidae consolationis*,[298] while he looks ahead to the *Manifestatio REGNI DEI sive MESSIAE in Mundo*.[299] Isaiah 40 refers so strongly to Israel's situation in exile that this pericope must be interpreted first and foremost out of this concrete context. For this reason, Isaiah 40 can also be properly understood without mystical-typological exegesis.[300] Yet – and Vitringa does not conceal this – the entire Christian exegetical tradition since the early Church to Calvin and to the present day is of the opinion that in Isaiah 40 at the very least *umbrae* of the redemption brought by Christ are found – above all, because the preaching of John the Baptist made use of Isaiah 40 (Matt 3:3). However, regarding the promise of Immanuel (Isa 7:14), Vitringa sees finally no other possibility, than to favour that interpretation, which is asserted by the New Testament in Matt 1:22f. Otherwise, the sense of the text would have to remain in darkness. Adopting the classical exegesis of this passage, Vitringa recognises in the name 'Immanuel' a summary of the Chalcedonian two-natures-doctrine, a *symbolum arctissimae & unitissimae conjunctionis Dei cum hominibus, sive cum natura humana*.[301]

---

[293] Grotius, *Annotationes in VT* (1775–76) II, 101.

[294] Ibid. I, 3.

[295] Ibid. 52: *Onkelos, Ionathan, Hierosolymitanus, Paraphrastae, Thalmudici, Beresith Rabba, Rabbi Salomo, Echa Rabthi: omnes Messiam hic indicari consentiunt.*

[296] Vitringa, *Commentarius* (1715/22) I, 9.

[297] Ibid. I, 16: *Illorum quoque vaticinia sic tractat, ut in illis etiam locis, in quibus imago Christi Jesu certissimis lineis pingitur, lectorem à JESU Domino nostro abducat, idque pro virili agat, ut ne credant alii, Prophetas directe de Domino nostro vaticinatos esse; haud fere aliter acsi Marcionis aliqua recoqueretur haeresis, qui ex alia hypothesi Messiam Prophetarum à nostro Jesu diversum statuebat.*

[298] Ibid. II, 409.

[299] Ibid. 408.

[300] Ibid. 411.

[301] Ibid. I, 219.

On the Lutheran side, Calov was the one who most intensively grappled with Grotius' exegesis critically. His comprehensive, four-volume *Biblia Illustrata* (1672–76), a commentary on all the books of the Holy Scripture, served alongside the greatest scholarly safeguard of Orthodox exegesis of the day, above all in the argument with Grotius.[302] Against Grotius' assertion that the general point in Gen 3:15 is simply the enmity between human beings and serpents as well as the hostility of humans among themselves, Calov argues that (not the *sensus allegoricus*, but rather) the *literae* of the Protoevangelium speak of Christ. Passing a sentence of judgement on the serpent used by Satan (in a way as a mask), God preaches to the fallen protoplasts, who have first heard the judgement on them, the Gospel *in nuce* (Gen 3:15), from which – with Luther – *omnes credentes usque ad novissimum diem*[303] gather hope and live.[304] The Protoevangelium centres on Christ, who breaks the power of Satan, conquering death, sin and hell. Calov by no means aims primarily at understanding the Old Testament from the situation of proclamation produced by the New Testament; the Old Testament is not simply overlaid with the New. Rather, it was Calov's claim to decode the inherit *sensus* of the Old Testament texts, in that he reads the prophecies in such a way that they decipher themselves on the basis of their fulfilments.[305] Grotius – and this is also the opinion of critical exegesis – proceeds from the premise that the historical situation behind the biblical texts has to be measured in order to be able to understand the Bible from the contexts going beyond. Calov, on the other hand, presupposed that the biblical texts themselves create a situation of their own, precisely that of biblical proclamation, which, among other things, becomes concrete in the inner-biblical plausibility of the Old and New Testament. However, this does not mean that the historical *realia* of the Old Testament texts can be treated lightly.

8. *Hermeneutica Sacra* and *Philologia Sacra*

The Lutheranism of the seventeenth century in particular produced a series of fundamental and widely received hermeneutical works. They are all methodologies that seek to open up manifold interpretative approaches to the Holy Scripture. Yet, conversely, they are nothing other than methodologically reflected outcomes of previously practised exegesis. It is evident, in any case, that the hour of the birth of hermeneutical scholarship occurred in the time of the development of the Orthodox *Hermeneutica Sacra*. The differentiation of the hermeneutics as a prominent element of philosophical discipline, manifested especially in post-Enlightenment time and not least of all connected

---

[302] Cf. Jung, Schrift (1999) 129–226.
[303] Calov, *Biblia* (1719) I, 247.
[304] Cf. Jung, Schrift (1999) 190–96.
[305] Cf. ibid. 186.

with the names of Schleiermacher and Dilthey, had it roots within Orthodox Protestantism.[306]

The Orthodox hermeneutical treatment of the Holy Scripture reflects its uniqueness. Every philological activity is motivated by love for the Word. The *Philologia Sacra*, however, is moved by love for the Word of God, which for this reason is all the greater, because the biblical texts are special and exceptional cases of the history of literature. For this *verbum* alone teaches heavenly wisdom and imparts eternal life. Love for biblical *literae* is a mirror of the love that the believer has toward God, because it is he who first loved human beings (1 John 4:19). This is the foundation of the philology of faith. The philological precision, the intensity and the energy that was also put exactly in the interpretation of the Old Testament is a consequence of the search for the paths of faith. With Herberger's words: "If we want to find the Lord Jesus in the Bible, we may not read it superficially ... But we have to search all *plica*, all corners and folds and we may not pass by any word without special recognition".[307]

Seen this way, it is not too far-fetched to assert that the high esteem of the biblical *litera* as divinely inspired led to a still more thorough intensification of philological and hermeneutical endeavours and that the early modern professionalisation of philology with all its thrusts of innovation (also and precisely influencing the "profane" sector) ultimately would not be thinkable at all without the competencies and sensibilities handed down and practised in the course of scholarship on Scripture. And conversely, it may be said that philology and grammar were ultimately the leading theological sciences within Orthodoxy, if it is true that the biblical *litera* is the bearer of the Word of God. For this reason Glassius says: *Quanto eris melior Grammaticus, tanto melior Theologus.*[308]

Yet, the common conviction that Orthodoxy discarded the rigorous philological alignment of theology coined by Humanism and that only in Pietism was philology recalled again, testifies to ignorance of the Orthodox exegetical literature. Reventlow lists Johann Albrecht Bengel's *Gnomon* as a prominent source thought to document the Pietistic rediscovery of philology.[309] However, if one compares the *Gnomon* with any Orthodox commentary, it quickly becomes evident that Bengel's philological area of interest was by no means as pronounced as was the case within Orthodoxy. Orthodoxy was not stamped by a one-sidedness in the sense of an overexertion of doctrine and certainly not at all by a diastasis of doctrine and philology. Rather, the reverse holds true: here, philological, dogmatic and practically concerned approaches to the biblical texts have a uniquely well-balanced relationship to each other. This allows both Lutheran and Calvinist exegetes to limit themselves in not a few commentaries completely to the investigations of the *sensus literalis* from the original language, without taking consideration of practical applicability. Examples of such a procedure are the Psalms commentary of the Wittenberg theologian Martin Geyer (1580–1631) and that from the pen of Cocceius. The interpretation, according to which philological exegesis starts detaching itself from the (practical-)theological[310] only in the period of the early Enlightenment, requires a distinction here. Comparing the Lutheran and Calvinist commentary literature, different points of accent are revealed. Whereas the latter is inclined more frequently to stick to philological analysis, the Lutherans most strongly keep in view the predictability of the texts concerned in the sense of the *usus* formulated in 2 Tim 3:16.

---

[306] Olson, Survival (2002) 15 f. Cf. Gadamer (1976) 277 f.

[307] Herberger, *Magnalia* 5 (1616) B 4r: *Wollen wir den HErrn Jesum in der Bibel finden/ so müssen wir sie nicht von oben vberhin lesen ... Sondern wir müssen fleissig alle plicas, alle winckel vnd falden durchsuchen/ vnd kein wort ohn besondere betrachtung vberhüpffen.*

[308] Glassius, *Philologia* (1713) 11.

[309] Reventlow, Wurzeln (1988) 51.

[310] Reventlow, Bibelexegese (1988) 10f, and W. Sparn, "Vernünftiges Christentum", *Wissenschaften im Zeitalter der Aufklärung* (ed. R. Vierhaus; Göttingen: Vandenhoeck & Ruprecht 1985) 18–57, here: 26.

The frequently advanced assertion that Orthodox exegesis shows little or no consideration for the historical situation of the text to be interpreted is unfounded. Rather, it is a common property of Orthodox hermeneutics first of all to emphasise the situation of the text in various respects. According to Franzius, the *antecedentia & consequentia*,[311] i.e., the micro- and macro-contexts of the text under interpretation must be kept in view. Then the addressees must be inquired after and afterwards who speaks when about what: *tria diligenter consideranda sunt, Tempus, quando scriptum est, quod dicitur: Persona, quae dicit, vel per quam, aut de qua dicitur: & Res, propter quam, aut de qua scribitur.*[312] Time and again it is described as indispensable in the analysis of a biblical text to clarify the individual lexemes and phrases with the help of dictionaries, to consider the languages most closely related to Hebrew in the process, to consult the Talmudim as interpretation aids and to analyse *dicta parallela* in order to get to the root of difficult grammatical circumstances. Added to this is the clarification of institutions and customs, of the realia – not only the historical, but also the geographical, moral and cultural settings.

Rambach summarises the rules recommended and utilised by the Orthodox in order to survey the historical circumstances in which a text speaks, in the following manner: in the *exegetica euolutio circumstantiarum*[313] the speaker must first of all be inquired about, and then the *obiectum orationis*, i.e., about the *persona ad quam, vel de qua sermo est.*[314] Both the historical as well as the rhetorical arrangement of the circumstances then need to be attended to. *Porro cogitandum est de tempore, tum illo, in quo sermo editus est, tum illo, de quo sermo agit.*[315] The geographical identification of the place in which the related events occurred is also part of this. Not least of all, the *occasio* must be observed, which was the reason for the composition of a work.[316]

According to Flacius, one should read the Holy Scripture – this is the biblical-philological principle – *summa diligentia*,[317] since God himself has commanded, *ut sacras Literas exactissimè cognoscamus.* When Flacius formulates as a principle that it is necessary, *Scripturam summa diligentia legere, scrutari, meditarique die ac nocte*,[318] he takes up along with this, among other things, Ps 1:2 and John 5:39, and indicates that the reading instructions appropriate for the Bible are to be found in the Bible itself. The *Hermeneutica Sacra* accordingly is not focused first of all on finding a methodology, which then would be used in a second move on the Bible. Rather, to develop this methodology is in itself an assignment, which can only be carried out when dealing exegetically with Scripture. As Scripture is to be interpreted from Scripture and the role of the only authentic interpreter belongs to the Holy Spirit, this also holds true regarding the hermeneutics: no interpreter, translator, or expounder is necessary, who must be joined as a third party to the text and recipient. Rather a

---

[311] Franzius, *Tractatus* (1619) b 3v. Cf. Finck: *Clavis* (1618) 54; Glassius, *Glaubensgrund* (1654) 109; Rivetus, *Isagoge* (1627) 262.

[312] Franzius, *Tractatus* (1619) b 3v.

[313] Rambach, *Institutiones* (1752) 108.

[314] Ibid. 113.

[315] Ibid. 116.

[316] Ibid. 120.

[317] Flacius, *Clavis* (1580) 391.

[318] Ibid. 392.

hermeneutics is required that is developed from the text to be explained itself, so that Scripture can explain itself.

Hermeneutics is first of all the science that deals with the interpretation of texts. For this reason Dannhauer says, *Finem Hermenevticae esse verum orationis sensum exponere aque falso vindicare.*[319] It is noteworthy that the first handbooks that sought to give a summary of the *Hermeneutica Sacra*, short dispensed with a terse self-definition of this branch of the discipline. Still, Pfeiffer offers the following definition: *HERMENEVTICA SACRA est habitus mentis practicus sacer, cujus opera homo de intentione Spiritus Sancti dubius per media appropriata perducitur ad verum textus sacri sensum eruendum & exprimendum, in DEI gloriam, Ecclesiae aedificationem, nec non desideratam ipsius interpretis* ἀσφάλειαν *& certitudinem.*[320] The most important objective of the *Hermeneutica Sacra* is in the sense of the *finis ultimus* 1. the advancement of the *Gloria DEI* through focus on the Word of God, and 2. the *salus hominis aeterna*, which can solely be found in the encounter with Scripture. *Finis subordinatus* is 1. *proximi aedificatio per Sensus Sacrae Scripturae declarationem 1. Cor. XII. 7. 10;* and 2. – with regard to the reading subject – *veri Scripturae sensus investigatio & certificatio.*[321]

Rambach condensed the results of the hermeneutical-theoretical discourse within Lutheranism – in the manner of a summary which needed to be defended against early-Enlightenment criticism. According to Rambach, the *Hermeneutica Sacra* centres on the interpretation of the Holy Scripture. *Hermeneutica sacra, si vocis originem spectes, est facultas, diuinas scripturas interpretandi.*[322] However, this science is not reserved for academic theology. Rather, it concerns all Christians. For this reason, Rambach described the *Hermeneutica Sacra* as *facultas practica, qua homo christianus, bona mente, & obuiis bonae mentis adminiculis instructus, ac spiritus sancti lumine adiutus, scripturae sensum, ex ipsa scriptura, ad suam vtilitatem ac salutem scrutatur.*[323]

Thus the *Hermeneutica Sacra* motivates practice in two different ways: on the one hand, it seeks to be the methodological ground of scholarly exegetical work and to be used in the biblical-philological and systematic-theologically motivated interpretation of Scripture. On the other hand, however, the *Hermeneutica Sacra* must also seek a way to be able to impart itself in fundamentals to all Christians, who in the same way are obliged to interpret Scripture, or who have to pass judgement on the exegesis brought forward by pastors. Because of this backdrop, it is no coincidence that often precisely those authors who wrote scholarly hermeneutical compendia made the results of their work available also in the German language, in order to broaden the circle of addressees and to find a hearing outside of the circle of experts and scholars (Hyperius, Glassius, Rambach).

---

[319] Dannhauer, *Idea* (1630) 12.
[320] Pfeiffer, *Hermeneutica* (1684) 1.
[321] Ibid. 7.
[322] Rambach, *Institutiones* (1752) 1.
[323] Ibid. 2.

9. The Multifaceted Richness of the Orthodox Exposition of the Old Testament

When studying the sources of Protestant Orthodoxy more closely than is commonly the case, it is soon observable that dogmatics and the *theologica polemica* by no means were the only fields of theological concern in this period. The vitality of exegetical theology is apparent in a veritable flood of commentaries on individual biblical books, but also in the multitude of series of disputation theses, which often deal with a certain biblical work.[324] LUDWIG DIESTEL introduced into the world the legend over 130 years ago[325] that the Old Testament found attention above all in Reformed circles, while it was pushed aside in Lutheranism (among other things on the erroneous presumption that only pericopes from the NT ought to be used for sermons in general).[326] This allegation, which has often been repeated, is entirely misguided. The Old Testament was present in Lutheran worship, for instance in the Psalm introit, but also in the exordia of sermons on the New Testament texts assigned by the pericope series. Moreover, not only did Calvinist preachers – following the usus of the *lectio continua* – preach on entire biblical books, but the Lutherans did also, especially in the sermons for services throughout the week. For instance, Herberger's famous *Magnalia Dei*, an exposition of Genesis to Judges, are built on those as well as Vincentius Schmuck's (1565–1628) homiletical exegesis of Genesis and Exodus in eight volumes. It is striking what degree of attention is given to wisdom and apocryphal literature within extensive sermon series, but also in occasional sermons.[327] As paradoxical as it may sound: abridging the Canon of the Vulgate and relegating several writings to the apocrypha, Luther created the provision for a previously hardly existent revaluation especially of the Book of Sirach and of Wisdom. This is the case, for example, with Conrad Dieterich (1575–1639), who expounded the Wisdom of Solomon verse by verse in sermons. The *sapientia secularis*, according to Dieterich, is to be highly esteemed, most of all because the Holy Spirit has taken it up and perfected it in the manner of heavenly philosophy. In addition, the Book of Sirach found broad attention, especially within a guidebook genre for the heads of family (the *Hausväterliteratur*) (Caspar Huberinus, Johannes Mathesius, Herberger, *et al.*). Old Testament wisdom literature was understood as a connecting link between the message of the Holy Scripture on the one hand and the ancient pagan tradition on the other hand – for instance, of the medicine of Claudius Galenus and of dietetics. This can be demonstrated,

---

[324] Dannhauer, who gave decisive impulse to hermeneutics, yet wrote not a single Bible commentary, is the absolute exception here in comparison with other prominent Lutheran theologians of the seventeenth century. Cf. Wallmann, Dannhauer (1988).

[325] Cf. E. Koch, Philosophia (1990) 706.

[326] Diestel, Geschichte (1867) 313: *An Stelle der alttestam. Lectionen trat der Katechismus und nur die zehn Gebote wurden aus dem A. T. gelesen und erläutert; die Einführung der alten Perikopen* that an den meisten Orten das Uebrige, um einen umfangreicheren Gebrauch des A. T. zu verbannen. More differentiated in this respect is A. NIEBERGALL, "Die Geschichte der christlichen Predigt", *Leiturgia* 2 (ed. K. F. Müller; Kassel: Stauda 1955) 181–353, here: 271.

[327] Cf. E. Koch, Philosophia (1990).

among other things, in the manner in which Orthodox theologians (at times based on Sirach 38) developed both spiritual as well as medical-dietary strategies in order to overcome melancholy.[328] By reading the Old Testament wisdom and ancient pagan tradition synoptically, a new material ethic emerged in this era which made intensive use of the wealth of knowledge handed down in order to give practical suggestions for daily life. The exposition of Sirach by Johannes Mathesius (1504–65), for example, is a handbook in ethics, an advice manual, a book of solace and reference work for everyday questions all in one. Here it is evident how the evangelical proclamation was concrete in the sense of help and management for daily life. Through instruction in school, the epigrammatic wisdom of the Old Testament and intertestamentary period was taught.[329]

How great an importance the Holy Scripture and the Old Testament in particular had in the life circumstances of individuals can only be sketched here. Not only do the inscriptions on houses (*Hausinschriften*)[330] play a significant role here (Ps 127:1 is one of the highlights), but also the citation of passages of comfort from the Old Testament (Job 19:25; Ps 73:25f; Wis 3:1, *et al.*) on epitaphs and coffins. The programmatics of the evangelical use of the Old Testament within the framework of funeral culture and of the *ars moriendi* is illustrated, for instance, by the rich inscription of the sarcophagus of Posthumus Reuß (1572–1635).[331] The compilation of *dicta biblica* and hymn stanzas selected for his sarcophagus in connection with Martin Moller's *Manuale de praeparatione ad mortem* (1593) served Heinrich Schütz (1585–1672) as a pattern for his *Musicalische Exequien*. In addition, the Old Testament core passages already mentioned were chosen remarkably often as the basis for funeral sermons (*Leichenpredigten*).

Other facets of the vitality of the Old Testament are demonstrated in religious theatre in schools, which readily referred to Old Testament and apocryphal narrative material – among others to Genesis 22 (Andreas Lucas),[332] Job (Johann Narhamer), Tobit (Thomas Brunner), Esther (Andreas Pfeilschmidt) – but also in religious poetry, not least in psalmic poetry.[333] In his sonnets, epigrams and odes, Andreas Gryphius (1616–64) treats not only the New Testament pericopes for Sundays, but also uses Old Testament texts and transforms the treatment of them within the exegetical literature in poetic form. Gryphius' approach to the subject of *vanitas* has its focus in Qoh 1:2, while the eschatological visions of the *Kirchhofgedanken* circle around Psalm 90, Ezekiel 37, Matthew 24f and other apocalyptic-biblical texts. Referring to that, Gryphius thus underpins his conviction that *Wolredenheit* and *Dichtkunst*[334] have a right of domicile in the Church: the Psalms, which are poems themselves, but also the songs of Miriam (Exod 15:20f), Hannah (1 Sam 2:1–10) and Jonah (Jonah 2) legitimise religious poetry and at the same time act as poetic-rhetorical models. *Das Hohelied Salomonis* by Martin Opitz (1597–1639), a poetic adaptation of the Canticum, also adopts – as the preface shows[335] – conclusions of the history of interpretation of the Canticum and reflects on the same in the medium of poetic speech. In contrast, in his *Neues Musikalisches Seelenparadis*, Johann Rist (1607–67) fashions hymns from central core passages of the

---

[328] Steiger, Melancholie (1996).

[329] E. Koch, Philosophia (1990) 709f.

[330] D. MACK, *Drei Patrizierhäuser in Braunschweigs Gördelingerstraße – ihre Inschriften im Wandel von drei Jahrhunderten* (Braunschweig: Waisenhaus 1982); H. SCHÜTTE, *Hildesheimer Hausinschriften und der figürliche Schmuck Hildesheimer Fachwerkhäuser* (Hildesheim: Borgmeyer 1920).

[331] R. STEIGER, "'Der Gerechten Seelen Sind In Gottes Hand'. Der Sarg des Heinrich Posthumus Reuss als Zeugnis lutherischer ars moriendi", *Diesseits- und Jenseitsvorstellungen im 17. Jahrhundert* (ed. I. Stein; Jena: Quartus 1996) 189–212.

[332] Steiger, Zu Gott (2006) 209.

[333] H. GALLE, "Psalmendichtung", *Literaturlexikon* 14 (ed. W. Killy; Gütersloh: Bertelsmann 1993) 235f.

[334] Gryphius, Gesamtausgabe 2 (1964) 98.

[335] Opitz, Werke 4/1 (1989) 13–15.

Old Testament and establishes a correspondence between the meditation of Old Testament texts and congregational singing. Rist's objective was, among other things, to defend the Old Testament and its canonicity against early rationalist criticism,[336] as expounded, for instance, in the tractate *De tribus magnis impostoribus*.[337] According to Rist and also the Nürnberg Pegnitz shepherd (*Pegnitzschäfer*) Johannes Klaj (c. 1616–56), *poiesis* is a process in which the poet draws from the Holy Scripture as from a fountain and imitates the flow of biblical speech.[338] By the poet's repeating the language of God and becoming active creatively, the restitution of the *imago Dei* takes place. Through the *fides poetica*, in which the eschatological hymn of praise is now already audible, and through religious-poetic creativity God creates a new creature.

The Orthodox efforts to open up the textual worlds of the Holy Scripture for educational purposes were also exceptionally broad. For example, Schmuck published a *Bibelbüchlein* (1600), which he designated as *Biblidion*.[339] For each chapter of the Bible, Schmuck presents a brief mnemonic and reproduces principal passages. The narrative texts are illustrated with the help of woodcuts. As plainly as the booklet is furnished, it is nevertheless a testimony to the relationship of Lutheran biblical hermeneutics with the *ars memorativa* and also to the iconography that likewise has a mnemotechnical-catechetical relevance. Yet, the Old Testament was not only interpreted in printed media and on the stage. Consideration must also be given to the reception of the Old Testament within ecclesiastical art reaching as far as religious emblemism (e. g., Daniel Cramer[340]) including its influence on homiletics (Johannes Saubert[341]) and Bible illustrations.[342] The media of word and picture entered into a communication that intensifies meditation. Pieter van der Borcht (ca. 1535–1608) in the *Emblemata Sacra* (1593) and Matthäus Merian Sen. (1593–1651) in the *Icones biblicae* (1625) offered examples of a series of copper etchings very close to the *historiae* of both Testaments.

Additionally worthy of careful investigation are the various resources for the study of the Holy Scripture, which the age of Orthodoxy produced. To be listed here are not only concordances to the different editions of texts, but an abundance of sources that treat biblical chronology, geography, animal kingdom, etc., from the perspective of the entire biblical *fides*. To name but one prominent example here the *Itinerarium Sacrae Scripturae* of Heinrich Bünting (1545–1606) takes the reader along on a virtual journey through the Holy Land and the world of the biblical text in one.

It is impossible here to give an overview of the various Bible editions that were used or produced in the era of Orthodoxy. However, we should at least mention the *Herborner Bibelwerk* that Johannes Piscator (1546–1625) made available in the years 1602–04 by commission of his ruler.[343] It

---

[336] Rist, *Seelenparadis* (1660) b 7r.

[337] On this tractate, circulating (as a phantom?) throughout the Early Modern period and to the present day not identifiable, let alone datable, cf. the introduction on the edition of: [Anonym], *De tribus impostoribus* (1999) 7–40.

[338] Ibid. d 2r: *Jhr himlische Tichter ... wollet ihr dem Himmel von Tage zu Tage noch mehr gleich und ähnlich werden/ so entschlaget euch/ so viel nur immer müglich/ aller weltlichen Eitelkeiten/ netzet eure Federn in den Ströhmen/ welche aus dem Paradys Gottes fliessen/ und schreibet dem Schöpfer zu Ehren/ und zu Erbauung seiner Kirchen nur solche Bücher/ welche nach dem Himmel schmekken.*

[339] Schmuck, *Bibelbüchlein* (1600))(7v.

[340] S. MÖDERSHEIM, *"Domini Doctrina Coronat"*. *Die geistliche Emblematik Daniel Cramers* (Mikrokosmos 38; Frankfurt/Main: Lang 1994).

[341] Saubert, *Geistliche Gemälde* (1652).

[342] K. A. KNAPPE, "Bibelillustrationen", TRE 6 (1980) 131–60, here 154f.

[343] F. L. Bos, *Johann Piscator. Ein Beitrag zur Geschichte der reformierten Theologie* (Kampen: Kok 1932).

is important as the first newly-translated post-Luther German Bible. In various appendices this *opus magnum* included, among other things, treatises on biblical chronology and the monetary system. Piscator claims to translate the text more faithfully than Luther. The style of the translation also makes it plain that Piscator sought to provide support for Calvinist doctrine (in distinction from the Lutheran doctrine). Of great importance were the subsequent debates between Lutheran and Calvinist theologians over the theological tendency of Piscator's translation and over translational-hermeneutical questions.

On the Lutheran side, the *Kurfürsten-Bibel*,[344] which was also named the *Nürnberger Bibelwerk* after its place of printing, should be mentioned. First printed in 1641, the *Kurfürsten-Bibel* appeared in fourteen impressions. Ernst von Sachsen-Gotha-Altenburg (1601–75), with the sobriquet *der Fromme* ("the Pious"), had initiated this large project and secured the most prominent Lutheran theologians of the time (Gerhard, Glassius, J. Major, J. M. Dilherr, *et al.*) as collaborators. This is an edition of the Bible presenting the entire text of the Luther-Bible along with numerous supplements and illustrates these in the form of brief explanatory comments inserted into the text. The overall direction of this project was first occupied by Gerhard and after his death by his student Glassius.

10. *Critica Sacra*

Around the middle of the seventeenth century, a new literary-theological genre emerged: the *Critica Sacra*. In such or similarly titled works the results of early modern textual criticism were introduced with the objective of disputing the infallibility of the biblical text and of explaining its historical development. But the wording of the title *Critica Sacra* was also used on the Orthodox side in order to be involved apologetically for the purposes of counter-criticisms and to defend the canonical position of the Bible.

However, the first work with this title is by Edward Leigh (1602–71) and is a Greek dictionary of the New Testament (1639). The *Critica Sacra* thus has a lexicographical-philological origin. In his *Critica Sacra* of the Old Testament published in 1641, Leigh was interested in explaining the diversity of meaning of the Hebrew language and the different possibilities of translation of the Hebrew lexemes. Leigh does not question every single Hebrew word regarding its meaning, *sed solas Radices, seu voces primitivas, quae ... constituunt numerum 1500.*[345] The first *Critica* with programmatic textual-critical interests was that from the pen of Louis Cappel / Ludovicus Cappellus (1585–1658) and was printed in 1650. Already here, textual criticism emancipated itself clearly from the traditional Protestant doctrine of scripture.

A protracted controversy developed in the first third of the seventeenth century over the pointing of the Hebrew Bible. The Lutheran, like the Calvinist tradition, assumed that the divinely inspired Word definitely cannot comprise only the consonantal text. The vocalisation must also be

---

[344] On the *Kurfürstenbibel*, cf. R.-D. Jahn, *Die Weimarer ernestinische Kurfürstenbibel und Dilherr-Bibel des Endter-Verlags in Nürnberg (1641–1788). Versuch einer vollständigen Chronologie und Bibliographie* (Odenthal: Selbstverlag 1986); H. Oertel, "Die Frankfurter Feyerabend-Bibeln und die Nürnberger Endter-Bibeln", Mitteilungen des Vereins für Geschichte der Stadt Nürnberg 70 (1983) 75–116.

[345] Leigh, *Critica* (1696) b 2r.

given by the Spirit, otherwise the sensus of Scripture would not be certain. Flacius is of the opinion that already Adam knew the system of Hebrew vocalisation and that all Old Testament writers used it.[346] Jesus' statement in Matt 5:18 – that neither jot nor tittle will pass from the Law – is seen by Flacius as a central biblical argument advanced time and again in the subsequent period .[347]

Already in the first third of the seventeenth century, Orthodoxy saw itself confronted with an opposition which had doubts about the *antiquitas* and with it also the inspired character of the vocalisation of the Old Testament. The controversy had begun when Elias Levita (1469–1549)[348] attempted to prove that the pointing of the Hebrew Old Testament dated from post-Talmudic times and had been concocted by the Masoretes. This aroused the opposition of Johannes Buxtorf the Elder (1564–1629).[349] As a result, Louis Cappel set about refuting Buxtorf's defense of the originality of the pointing.[350] In this undertaking he found the support of Thomas Erpenius (1584–1624), who furnished Cappel's anonymously published work *Arcanum punctationis revelatum* (1624) with a preface and had it printed. Cappel made his argument not only with the help of the rabbinical tradition (Ibn Esra, David Qimhi, *et al.*), but to support his thesis he analysed, among other things, Josephus' and Philo's method of citation. *Ketib* and *Qere* as well as the collation of the Targumim with the Hebrew Old Testament supplied him with additional arguments.[351] He arrives at the conclusion, *Puncta ista Hebraica à Masorethis esse excogitata, & textui sacro addita circa Christi annum 500. aut saltem post 400.*[352]

One of the authors who most vehemently opposed Cappel was Johannes Buxtorf the Younger (1599–1664). To start with, he summarises five different views regarding the age of the vocalisation of the Hebrew Old Testament and with this takes into consideration various rabbinical and Talmudic source materials.[353] Buxtorf's goal is to argue the *antiquitas* of the pointing. As for his knowledge of this, Buxtorf was in no way inferior to his opponent Cappel. Yet, the theological interest very clearly becomes evident in spite of all historical arguments, when Buxtorf, quoting his father, indicates that the certainty of the Old Testament text depends precisely on the vocalisation. If this were not the case, then the Old Testament, on the basis of the uncertainty emerging in consequence, could by no means be the final authority on questions of doctrine.[354] In brief: the inspired nature of the Old Testament, and together with it its canonicity, stands and falls with the vocalisation, for *Vocales sunt animae dictionum & vocum, quae eas vivificant.*[355]

---

[346] Flacius, *Clavis* (1580) 364: *Mea est igitur sententia, Vocales, seu (ut vocant) puncta unà cum consonantibus iam olim (fortasse ad ipsomet Adamo) inuenta, omnesque sacrarum Literarum scriptores integrè, dilucideque scripsisse, non solùm consonantibus, sed & uocalibus.*

[347] Ibid. 365.

[348] See below p. 753.

[349] On Buxtorf the Elder, cf. Burnett, Christian Hebraism (1996), and his essay, Ch. 31, in the present volume; Smend, Buxtorf (1997).

[350] Cf. Schnedermann, Controverse (1878).

[351] G. W. Meyer, Geschichte (1802-) III, 275.

[352] Cappellus, *Arcanum* (1624) 312.

[353] Buxtorf the Younger, *Tractatus* (1648) 2. According to Buxtorf, some think that the vocalization was not commonly used until the termination of the Talmud, while others maintain that the pointing was a product of the eleventh century. On the other hand, others assert, *Puncta jam ante Mosen, imò ab Adamo, unà cum Literis, inventa & excogitate fuisse.* Another thesis claims that God revealed the pointing to the prophet Moses on Sinai, however, this fell into oblivion and was first recalled again by Ezra. Another variety of this view lies in the following hypothesis: how Scripture should be read was revealed to Moses on Sinai and subsequently was handed down orally. But from Ezra comes the discovery of the *Puncta & Accentus* as well as their establishment in writing.

[354] Ibid. 419. If the pointing dates from a later period and is not divine, then *incertitudo ubique erit maxima, unâ voce, propter unum etiam punctum mutatum, in alium sensum transeunte: tunc textus nudis literis constans, erit instar cerae in diversas formas mutabilis: tunc in tantis litibus Judex superior erit nullus, ac proinde Sacrae Scripturae V. Testamenti Canon quoque nullus, qui controversarum interpretationum sit mensura & terminus.*

[355] Ibid.

Nevertheless, despite this exchange of blows the controversial matter still remained unsettled. It rather advanced to a true slow burner. The positions in dispute became the distinguishing feature of a position either aligned with the critics, or the Orthodox. Even Louis Cappel's grandson Jacobus (1639–1722) took pains to once again broadly present and sharpen the argumentation of his grandfather.[356]

Jean Morin / Johannes Morinus (1591–1659) invigorated the discussions with a traditional-critical thesis that doubted the *integritas* of the Old Testament. In his view, the Hebrew text of the Old Testament was certainly not deliberately falsified, nevertheless, through the careless work and "incuria"[357] of the copyists it was garbled to such an extent that it does not represent an authentic basis. The Greek text of the New Testament is worse still since it, in addition, had been altered by early Christian heretics. For this reason, Morin recommended that preference should be given to the ecclesiastically approved text of the Vulgate. Morin's traditional-critical work was motivated by Roman Catholic dogmatics. He seeks to establish historically that the Vulgate deserves the highest position. According to Leigh, the Vulgate is not to be corrected from the Greek and Hebrew codices, but, conversely, these must be emended on the basis of the Vulgate.[358]

The *Critica Sacra* (1650) by Louis Cappel is most often named as the first work of biblical criticism not marked by partiality. Unlike Morin, Cappel is not anxious to undermine the *auctoritas* of Scripture by way of criticism. Nor, on the other hand, did he share the convictions of the increasingly apologetic Orthodox anti-criticism, which believed that the canonicity of Scripture can be maintained only by denying or smoothing out the textual- and traditional-critical facts. In his extensive folio volume, which contains the fruits of decades of long research, Cappel explains that the text of the Hebrew Old Testament is certainly unreliable in several places due to circumstances of textual transmission. Yet, by no means can the conclusion be drawn from this that Scripture does not possess *auctoritas*. Cappel's results were also sobering regarding the prospect of using the Septuagint or the Vulgate as a reliable starting position for the critical judgement of the Hebrew Old Testament. Alongside the analysis of *Ketib* and *Qere*, the comparison of the Hebrew text with early translations, the Talmudim, rabbinical writings and the Masorah, Cappel took great pains to interpret critically the Old Testament citations in the New Testament.

As the "pioneer of modern biblical criticism", Richard Simon (1638–93), whose chief work was the *Histoire critique du Vieux Testament* (1678), must not be passed over.[359] Simon is regarded, in comparison with Cappel, as a still more deeply penetrating source authority, especially with respect to biblical manuscripts. Yet, by no means was Simon's concern defined only by the fervour of the historical explorer, rather by his biblical-critical studies he tried to find arguments that would make it possible to upset the credibility of Scripture with a thoroughly anti-Protestant motive.[360] The Pentateuch, according to Simon, cannot be attributed to Moses. Rather, it was written by public scribes, who were engaged as redactors of the older written tradition. Not a few Lutherans – for instance, Johann Benedikt Carpzov (1639–99)[361] and Salomon Deyling (1677–1755)[362] – reacted to Simon by attempting to demonstrate that the Pentateuch must indeed be attributed to Moses.

---

[356] J. Cappellus, *Commentarii* (1689) 703: *Is in libro quem de Masorâ scripsit, quaestionem hanc movet, atque adeò definit. Stauit nimirum, non à Mose, aliisve Veteris Testamenti scriptoribus* θεοπνεύστοις, *esse hoc vocalium & accentuum Apiculos, sed à Masorethis fuisse excogitatos & consonantibus additos, aliquantò post absolutum Talmud.*

[357] Morinus, *Exercitationes* (1633) 121.

[358] Ibid. 45.

[359] *Pionier der modernen Bibelkritik*, so F. STUMMER, *Die Bedeutung Richard Simons für die Pentateuchkritik* (ATA III/4; Münster: Aschendorff 1912).

[360] Reventlow, Bibelexegese (1988) 12.

[361] Cf. e.g., Carpzov, *Historia* (1684) 12f. Simon's thesis that Genesis to 2 Kings had been compiled by Ezra *è variis Scriptoribus* (ibid. 13), amounted to the assertion, according to Simon, *Scripturam esse erroneam, mendosam, truncatam, adulteratam, & autoritatem vulgô ejus divinam neqvicqvam jactari.*

[362] Deyling, *Observationes* (1720) 7–19: *DE MOSE, PENTATEUCHI AUCTORE.*

The developments in the area of early biblical criticism, only barely outlined above,[363] were heterogeneous in the highest degree and produced a considerable amount of Orthodox reaction. One of the most prominent was the *Hermeneutica Sacra* of the late-Orthodox Lutheran theologian August Pfeiffer. In his view, the pointing of the Old Testament text belongs to the original textual work inspired by the Spirit. The assertion of Simon and his predecessors that the pointing dates from a later time was dismissed by Pfeiffer; instead he held fast to the *Textus V. T. integritas.* To assume, as Simon does, that knowledge about the correct vocalisation had been transmitted through the oral tradition, Pfeiffer maintained as impossible.[364] The integrity of both the consonantal text and the pointing, according to Pfeiffer, is a result of the *DEI pro suo verbo providentia* (in conformity with Matt 5:18) and from the *stupenda diligentia,*[365] with which the Holy Scriptures has been passed down through the centuries. *Ketib* and *Qere*, meanwhile, are not indicative of corruptions in the text but rather of the fact that there were *variae lectiones* in less reliable codices.[366]

Already before Pfeiffer, Calov[367] had entered the discussion and in his *Criticus Sacer Biblicus* (1673) subjected the theses of Morin and Cappel to a critical analysis. Among other things, Calov concerned himself with the thesis that the vowel symbols are not as old as the consonantal text while vocalisation was fixed and was transmitted through oral tradition.[368] If this were the case, then, in a manner fatal to matters of faith, there would be dependency on the *traditio humana*, which however is never able to establish certainty: *ea traditio … humana erit, & ita dubia, & fallibilis: Proinde fidem divinam fundare non poterit.*[369] If the theses regarding the later supplementation of the vocalisation were true, then this would mean that the Rabbis, respectively the Masoretes, first established the *perspicuitas* and *perfectio* of Scripture,[370] which however, according to Calov, is impossible. Together with both Buxtorfs, Calov maintains the thesis that the pointed text of the Old Testament has been transmitted unaltered since the time of Ezra. Notwithstanding, Calov acknowledged that individual manuscripts can be imperfect, but suggested that they can be corrected by more precise transmission.[371]

Jean Le Clerc / Johannes Clericus (1657–1736)[372] produced a foundational work for Old Testament textual criticism: the *Ars critica*, published in Amsterdam in 1697. He describes in great detail different circumstances on the basis of which corruptions in the text can arise. They can – to name only a few – be traced back to *LIBRARIORUM incuriâ, aut imperitiâ.*[373] Anyone who has ever transcribed something, thus Johannes Clericus, knows that mistakes can occur. However,

---

[363] See, further, some of the following chapters of the present volume, esp. 29, 31 and 34.
[364] Pfeiffer, *Hermeneutica* (1684) 7.
[365] Ibid. 21.
[366] Ibid. 23.
[367] On Calov as an exegete, cf. Hoffmann, Schriftauslegung (1973); Reventlow, Epochen 3 (1997) 225–33; Jung, Schrift (1999).
[368] Calov, *Criticus* (1673) 92.
[369] Ibid. 93.
[370] Ibid. 128 f.
[371] Reventlow, Epochen 3 (1997) 228.
[372] M. C. Pitassi, *Entre croire et savoir. Le problème de la méthode critique chez Jean Le Clerc* (Kerkhistorische bijdragen 14; Leiden: Brill 1987).
[373] Clericus, *Ars* (1697) II, 6.

FALSARII must be considered who have intentionally falsified the texts.[374] Errors can also originate *ex imperitia Dictantis*,[375] or be the result of the *MALA Dictantis pronuntiatio*,[376] for instance, when marginalia are mistakenly interpolated into the text.[377] Le Clerc's methodical instructions how to emend were very constructive in regard to textual-critical scholarship. Thus, emendations should not depart too far from the oldest manuscripts. In order to be able to find appropriate emendations, the textual critic must have first empathetically familiarised himself with the writing style and the world of ideas of the author concerned. This applies not only to textual criticism, but should also be observed as a general hermeneutical principle. According to Le Clerc, obscure passages of the Bible become clear – in distinction from the Orthodox view – neither by way of a collation of related *loci* of Scripture nor by attention to the *analogia fidei*. On the contrary, the attempt must be made to reconstruct the historical situation from which the text was written and be able to trace the intention of the author. The outcome of Le Clerc's biblical criticism with regard to the doctrine of scripture is: Scripture is clear and sufficient, however only relating to that which is essential to religion, ultimately consisting of two things: "the first is to tell us where the greatest happiness is found, after which we strive naturally, and the second is to show us the means to attain it".[378] He abandoned the doctrine of verbal inspiration and replaced it with the theory that the Spirit suggested to the biblical authors the sense of what to write, but entrusted to them to fix this in writing in their own literary-linguistic style.

A sensation was caused by the theses of the student of Newton, William Whiston (1667–1752), who vehemently questioned the reliability of the transmission of the biblical texts, but did so rather in apologetic interests. Whiston built on the premise that the Apostles had quoted philologically correctly – and certainly, without exception, from the Septuagint. However, since that time, both the Hebrew as well as the Greek text of the Old Testament had been corrupted. The differences between the Old Testament quotes in the New Testament and the modern textual versions of the Old result from this. According to Whiston, this hangs together with the Jews deliberately altering the textual form of the Old Testament in the second century after Christ due to their opposition to early Christianity, not least of all in order to undermine the argumentation of the Evangelists and Apostles, if not to make it ridiculous. The Jews are said to have passed on to Origen a copy of the Septuagint larded with textual corruptions, who would have transferred them into the Hexapla. In the fourth century, thus Whiston, the Jews then disseminated corrupt textual versions of the Hebrew Old Testament among Christians. The goal of Whiston's textual critical work was to restore the true, original text and to show that the predictions of the prophets are in fact literally fulfilled.[379] As sources for his reconstruction efforts Whiston referred to the Codex Samaritanus, Philo and Josephus, translations of the Septuagint to other languages, the Talmudim and above all to Aquila, Theodotion and Symmachus.

It must not be overlooked that Whiston's critical examination of the Old Testament citations in the New Testament was an expression of a hermeneutical development which can be observed on the part of Orthodoxy gradually aligning itself with rationalist and enlightenment principles. The more Orthodoxy saw itself exposed to rational-historically arguing criticism, the more strongly it attempted to provide proof of the credibility of the Bible by arguing with the fulfilment of prophecies of the Old Testament in the New. To be sure, original Orthodoxy was of the view that the fulfilment of the *promissiones* only makes itself accessible to faith. But now, above all, the passages in the Gospels which refer to Old Testament *promissiones* and present these as fulfilled from the experience of faith, were highly stylised as proofs of prophecy and were claimed as to be open to rational examination. Despite all counter-criticism directed towards the enlightened theologians trusting in reason, this type of Orthodoxy was itself already a child of the age of reason. This scheme, claiming to be rational, without fail had to cause a reaction. Accordingly the deist An-

---

[374] Ibid. 18.
[375] Ibid. 43.
[376] Ibid. 85.
[377] Ibid. 117.
[378] Quote according to Reventlow, Bibelexegese (1988) 13: *das eine ist, uns zu sagen, wo sich das höchste Glück befindet, nach dem wir natürlicherweise streben, und das andere, uns die Mittel zu zeigen, dahin zu gelangen.*
[379] Reventlow, Bibelautorität (1980) 599.

thony Collins (1676–1729) attacked this methodology.[380] He also designated the proofs of prophecy as "direct proofs"[381] and assigned to them a greater persuasive power than to the miracles.
But Collins endeavours to show that all the Old Testament prophecies were already fulfilled within
the Old Testament and frequently bases his argument on the exegesis of Grotius. Thus, following
Collins, Isa 7:14 refers to Isaiah's own son, not to Christ. The Evangelists meanwhile, according
to Collins, show proofs of prophecy, yet in doing so do not make use of the Old Testament's literal
sense, but rather pursue typological-allegorical exegesis. However, this scheme, which is absolutely
foreign to Collins among other things on account of his affinity to the epistemology of John Locke,
is inconclusive; it is rather to be understood as an accommodation to the exegetical usage in the
time of the Apostles.[382] Collins was opposed, for instance, by Thomas Woolston (1670–1733). He
agrees with Whiston and his thesis that the New Testament passages on fulfilled prophecies represent central arguments for the Christian faith. However, in distinction from Whiston, Woolston favours the allegorical-typological methodology rejected by the former.[383] Yet, the rationalistic procedure however was common to both.

Among the Lutherans, Johann Gottlob Carpzov (1679–1767)[384] in particular grappled intensively with Whiston's theses. The third section of Carpzov's
Critica Sacra is completely reserved for the refutation of Whiston. In detailed
fashion, Carpzov submits the Old Testament citations in the New Testament,
analysed by Whiston, to a renewed examination in order to harmonise them
with their Old Testament models. Whiston, according to Carpzov, disputes
the *integritas* of the Old Testament by asserting that the text of the Old Testament as it is used today is thoroughly different from the one Christ and the
Apostles worked with.[385] With this Whiston supposes that Christ and the
Apostles always cited exactly and transmitted an older stage of development of
the text.[386] Carpzov disputes this premise and explains that in fact divergences
can be found in individual formulations, but by no means must this also necessarily result in an alteration of the *sensus*. In spite of all the display of learning
in Carpzov's *Critica*, his work is a testimony to late Orthodoxy's increasing
entanglement in apologetics. As a result the delineation of the fundamental
guiding principles of biblical hermeneutics becomes less significant in comparison with high Orthodoxy. Instead a hermeneutical system presumed to be familiar and elaborated was increasingly defended against the critics, without
sufficiently taking into account that the position which they wanted to defend
needed to be delineated anew constantly. Or, stated differently, apologetics
within late Orthodoxy ranked above fundamental hermeneutical work.

Rambach, likewise, favours the thesis that Ezra discovered the vowel signs which are commonly
used today and, enlightened by the Spirit of God, conferred on the Old Testament its pointing. He
takes this to be *die gemeinste Meynung der Jüden*, which he assumes also to be held by Reuchlin,
Flacius, Gerhard, Glassius, Cocceius, Buxtorf, Hottinger, Lightfoot, *et al.*[387] Meanwhile, the opinion of Elias Levita, according to which the *Iudaei Tibernienses*[388] had discovered the pointing,
was said to have been met with rejection among Jews. Rambach insists on pointing out that the

---

[380] Collins, *Discourse* (1724).
[381] Collins, *Scheme* (1727) 329.
[382] Reventlow, Bibelautorität (1980) 601 f.
[383] Ibid. 611.
[384] Smend, Antikritik (1988).
[385] Carpzov, *Critica* (1748) 793.
[386] Ibid. 854.
[387] Rambach, *Erläuterung* (1738) 112.
[388] Ibid.

Orthodox view of things – in contrast to that of the *critici* – is in agreement with that of the majority of the Rabbis.

In order to bolster up the thesis of the *antiquitas* of the pointing, Rambach, among other things, advances the argument that without pointing many passages would be simply incomprehensible.[389] Moreover, the Masorah is assumed by Rambach to include comments on peculiar pointing,[390] thus it must have existed previously. However, the chief argument for Rambach is also drawn from the doctrine of Scripture. The pointing must be old, "because perfection, clarity and certainty of the sense of the Scripture depend for the greatest part on the punctuation so that by the absence of the pointing the sense of the Scripture becomes uncertain and ambiguous; whereas it receives its certainty through the pointing."[391] Against the argument that on the basis of the Septuagint there were apparently various understandings with regard to the correct vocalization and thus there was not yet an established pointing at the time of the development of the Septuagint, Pfeiffer raises the following objection: "However, the old interpreters not only made mistakes concerning certain vowels but also concerning certain consonants and entire words, they even frequently substituted other consonants. Does it follow from this that no other consonants were written in their codices? Not at all."[392]

11. Peculiarities of the Dealing with Scripture within Rational Orthodoxy

Orthodoxy, Pietism and Enlightenment were not eras superseding one another. Rather in the sense of an unsimultaneous simultaneity they moved side by side for quite a long time and intermingled to some extent. That the Orthodox argumentation changed in the course of the warding off of authors critical of the Bible or dogma, becomes apparent not only in Orthodox counter-criticism, but for instance also in Valentin Ernst Löscher (1673–1749). To be sure, Löscher vehemently dismisses the early deistic reduction of the theological contents to the *ideae innatae*, as championed by Herbert of Cherbury (1582/3–1648). According to Löscher, Cherbury's rational theology amounts to the fact that he *schändlich vernichtet* ("disgracefully eradicated") God's revelation in Law and Gospel.[393] Yet, at the same time, Löscher is of the view that the knowledge of human beings about the existence of God is given by nature, a fact about which one cannot be deceived – it is a *praenotio*. Löscher substantiated this for example with Rom 1:19 and 2:14.[394] The radicality of the Pauline view that even though there is a natural knowledge of God among the heathens, yet they are inexcusable because they have neither worshipped God

---

[389] Ibid. 114.

[390] Ibid. 115.

[391] Ibid. 117: *Weil perfectio, perspicuitas & certitudo sensus scripturae grösten theils ad adscriptis punctis oder von der punctation dependiret, so daß durch die Abwesenheit derer punctorum der sensus scripturae incertus & ambiguus gemacht wird; da er hingegen per adscripta puncta vocalia seine certitudinem bekommt.*

[392] Ibid. 119: *Aber es haben die alten interpretes, z.E. die LXX. nicht nur oft quoad vocales, sondern auch quoad consonantes und in gantzen Wörtern gefehlet, sie haben oft andre consonantes substituiret ... Folget denn daraus, daß auch keine consonantes in ihren codicibus gestanden? Keinesweges.*

[393] Löscher, *Unschuldige Nachrichten* (1702) 904.

[394] Löscher, *Praenotiones* (1728) 8 f.

nor obeyed his commandments, is clearly toned down by Löscher. For this reason, the high Orthodox doctrine, according to which the *cognitio Dei naturalis* in no case is able to establish certainty, also recedes into the background with Löscher.

Cherbury knows five natural fundamental truths, which Löscher reports as follows: "1. There is one highest God, 2. whom one must worship, 3. and to such worship belongs chiefly a virtuous life; 4. one must repent of sins committed; 5. after this life there is also a reward of good and a punishment of evil".[395] Löscher does deny that these *notiones communes* are sufficient to gain salvation. Nevertheless, he was convinced that the metaphysics of the natural knowledge of God presents an irrefutable argument against the scepticism of Thomas Hobbes and John Locke. For this reason, according to Löscher, it is incorrect to reduce Christian doctrine to the natural knowledge of God, as do the deists and also the Cartesian Hermann Alexander Roëll (1653–1718). Yet, in the same way, it would be misguided to criticise the doctrine of the *notiones communes* as radically as does Roëll's antagonist Gerard de Vries (1648–1705).[396] Löscher does not tire of repeatedly coming to the defense of the canonicity and fundamental importance of the Holy Scripture. Yet in apologetic interests and in refuting scepticism and the empiricism of an Anglo-Saxon stamp, Löscher granted a higher status to the natural knowledge of God than high Orthodox theology had done. Considered externally, this had no consequences for the doctrine of Scripture as canon and norm. However, when studying Löscher's argumentation more closely, it is apparent that he is inclined to list in the first position in apologetic interests the arguments which he deems rationally applicable. Biblical texts are not seldom cited only in a second set of arguments – advanced in a way as illustrations from the Canon. Ultimately this procedure however contradicts the hermeneutical principle of the normativeness of the *scriptura sacra*. For this reason, a certain tension results between the canonical value of the Holy Scripture maintained by Löscher and the actual use that he makes of it.

An amalgamation of Orthodoxy with methodologies and philosophical propositions imbued with the ideas of the early Enlightenment can clearly be exemplified in Lutheranism, especially with Siegmund Jakob Baumgarten (1706–57),[397] the teacher of Johann Salomo Semler. Baumgarten essentially adhered to Orthodox doctrine, yet dismissed Aristotelianism and puts in its place the *more geometrico* methodology of the Halle philosopher Christian Wolff (1679–1754). Baumgarten transfers Wolff's method, which strives for mathematical precision, to theology and is anxious to prove the Orthodox truths of faith rationally and "demonstrably", as he often says.

In this way, a significance previously not present (not even in Luther!) was assigned to the accounts of miracles in the Bible. They were now understood as rational attestations and proofs not only of the Messiahship of Jesus, but also of his divinity.[398] A similar rationalistic shift in accent is evident in the manner in which Baumgarten treated Old Testament prophecies. They are stylised as proofs of prophecy with the help of the New Testament cognisance of their fulfilment which are, from a rational point of view, indisputable. Thus the *criteria externa*, which only had a secondary importance in high Orthodoxy,[399] were promoted as irrefutable arguments. According to the

---

[395] *1. Es sey ein höchster GOtt/ 2. denselben müste man verehren 3. und zu solcher Verehrung gehöre vornemlich ein tugendhafftes Leben/ 4. man müsse die begangenen Sünden bereuen/ 5. es sey auch nach diesen [!] Leben eine Belohnung des Guten/ und Bestraffung des Bösen.* Löscher, *Unschuldige Nachrichten* (1702) 902.

[396] Ibid. 1078.

[397] Cf. Schloemann, Baumgarten (1974), and Schloemann, Wegbereiter (1988), and Danneberg (1994).

[398] Baumgarten, *Auslegung* (1762) 211 (on John 4:48–50): *Dergleichen Zeichen und Wunderwerke sind allerdings ein richtiger Beweis und hinlänglicher Grund der Ueberzeugung von dem Meßia ... gewesen.*

[399] See above p. 716 f.

understanding of the original Orthodox hermeneutics, the *experientia fidei* is capable of describing the effectiveness of Scripture. However, the fact that such assertions of the believer are plausible only in the ears of those who share this very experience was always considered. Yet, Baumgarten raises a person's coming into faith, like prophecies and miracles, to the rank of proof, when he says that the divinity of Scripture can be proven *aus der eigenen Erfarung* ("from one's own experience"),[400] without reflecting in the process that such an argumentation – precisely for the non-believer – cannot be convincing *eo ipso*.

This kind of rationalisation of Orthodoxy is also reflected in Baumgarten's discussion of the doctrine of Scripture. It is fully in line with high Orthodoxy, as regards *theopneustia*,[401] *autopistia* and the necessity to perform exegesis of Scripture from Scripture.[402] However, Baumgarten departs from the Lutheran tradition when, in addition, he designates Scripture as the source from which "all doctrines of the faith and truths belonging to the *ordo salutis*" can be made "demonstrable and comprehensible".[403] "The scientific character of theology is now suspended – as hanging by a thread – by the divinity of the Bible fully justified by reason."[404] Likewise, Baumgarten sharpens the doctrine of inspiration. He takes up the emphasis often found already in late Orthodox theology that the Holy Spirit also once again inspired the biblical writers with what was already known to them,[405] in order to make mistakes impossible. Yet, Baumgarten emphasises in addition that the stylistic-rhetorical design of the biblical texts is traced simply and solely to the Spirit. The original Orthodox appreciation of the human *ingenium*, already found with Flacius, and the rhetorical-literary capabilities of the writers, to which the Holy Spirit accommodated himself, are placed in the background by Baumgarten. Certainly, he also makes reference to the theory of accommodation,[406] and with its help explains the "undeniable diversity of the writing style of the different men of God in the divine inspiration common to all".[407] It seems clear, however, that Baumgarten *in actu* of the exposition of Scripture made less use than the high Orthodox exegetes of the possibilities that the *rhetorica (sacra)* keeps in readiness for the analysis of the stylistic characteristics of the biblical writers. Incidentally, this fact might have its parallels in Pietism, which was characterised strongly by Spener's criticism of rhetoric,[408] and which was reflected not only – in comparison with Orthodoxy – in a more dispassionate sermon praxis, but also in exegetical methodology.

---

[400] Baumgarten, *Theologische Lehrsätze* (1747) 299.

[401] Baumgarten, *Glaubenslehre* (1759–60) III, 17.

[402] Baumgarten, *Unterricht* (1751) 9.

[403] Baumgarten, *Glaubenslehre* (1759–60) III, 23: *alle Glaubenslehren und zur Heilsordnung gehörige Warheiten* [can be made] *erweislich und begreiflich*.

[404] *An der vernünftig begründeten Göttlichkeit der Bibel hängt jetzt – wie an einem seidenen Faden – die Wissenschaftlichkeit der Theologie*; Schloemann, Wegbereiter (1988) 150.

[405] Baumgarten, ibid. III, 33.

[406] Baumgarten, *Unterricht* (1751) 45: *die götliche Eingebung [hat] sich in der Wahl der Vorstellungen und Ausdrucke nach der Männer GOttes gewönlichen Art zu dencken und zu reden aufs möglichste gerichtet*.

[407] Baumgarten, ibid. 45: *unleugbare Verschiedenheit der Schreibart verschiedener Männer GOttes bey der allen gemeinen götlichen Eingebung*.

[408] P. J. SPENER, *Pia Desideria* (ed. K. Aland; Kleine Texte für Vorlesungen und Übungen 170; Berlin: de Gruyter ²1955) 79.

Conversion, according to Baumgarten, cannot be regarded as a prerequisite of apt interpretation of Scripture.[409] Here, Baumgarten distances himself from a hermeneutical principle of Francke, who is of the view that only those who have experienced the event of the *conversio* can correctly interpret the Bible.[410] Yet, on the other hand, Baumgarten's treatment of Scripture is related to that of Francke, as Baumgarten also pursues a psychologisation of exegesis. Francke advises the affective situation of the text to be interpreted.[411] Thus, according to Baumgarten, it must also be inquired, "whether the person speaking was in a strong sensual agitation or emotional state, and what kind it actually was".[412] For this reason it is necessary that the expositor "is well-informed" with respect to "psychological truths of quality, difference, mixture, origin and characteristics of sensual agitation".[413]

Certainly, the most detailed apologetic, rational-Orthodox refutation in German of the Enlightenment's biblical and dogmatic criticism came from the Königsberg theologian Theodor Christoph Lilienthal (1717–81). His work was published in sixteen parts between 1750–68 under the title: *Die gute Sache der in der heiligen Schrift alten und neuen Testaments enthaltenen Göttlichen Offenbarung, wider die Feinde derselben erwiesen und gerettet.* In great detail it takes on the so-called naturalists, particularly those associated with English Deism (Herbert of Cherbury, Matthew Tindal, *et al.*), but also with Spinoza, Hobbes and many others, in order to prove "that in Holy Scripture nothing false and contrary to reason is found".[414] That which according to Orthodox belief cannot be comprehended by reason, but surpasses *ratio*, wrenches it out from its *incurvatio in se* and causes it to become new, namely the supernatural revelation of God, is proved rationally by Lilienthal. According to high Orthodox doctrine, the content of the *revelatio specialis* of God is, after the fall into sin, not only *supra*, but also *contra rationem*.[415] Lilienthal, however, sees no discrepancies at all between reason and revelation. From this originates the fundamentalism within the Scriptural exegesis of this enlightened Orthodoxy.

Against the argument by Jacques Masse (that is: Simon Tyssot de Patot[416]) that there can be no physical resurrection, because not all humans could find room on the earth, Lilienthal advances the following estimation (*more geometrico!*): since the time of creation, 180 billion people have lived on the earth. Since a person takes up 2 *Quadratschuh*[417] (square feet) in a standing position, a surface area of 360 billion square feet is required. However, since the surface area of the *terra firma* all together amounts to 3,096 million square miles, the earth must *noch 4550mal so lange stehen*

---

[409] Baumgarten, *Unterricht* (1751) 19: *[Es] kan ein unbekerter sowol als ein bekerter den richtigen Verstand der heiligen Schrift einsehen; zumal da der Einflus götlicher Warheiten in den Willen der Menschen auch bey den Wirckungen der zuvorkommenden und bearbeitenden Gnade GOttes stat findet: so wie im Gegentheil ein bekerter sowol als ein unbekerter in Auslegung der heiligen Schrift irren kan".*

[410] See above, p. 707.

[411] See above, p. 707.

[412] Baumgarten, *Unterricht* (1751) 43f: *ob die redende Person in einer starcken sinlichen Gemütsbewegung oder Affect gestanden, und was vor eine es eigentlich gewesen.*

[413] Ibid. 58f: [that the expositor] *der psychologischen Warheiten von Beschaffenheit, Unterschied, Mischung, Ursprung und Kenzeichen der sinlichen Gemütsbewegungen kündig ist.*

[414] Lilienthal, *Die gute Sache* (1750-) I/II, 337: *daß in der heiligen Schrift nichts falsches und widersinnisches gefunden werde.*

[415] Gerhard, *Loci* II (1767-) 372.

[416] S. Tyssot de Patot, *LA VIE, Les avantures, & le VOYAGE DE GROENLAND Du Révérend PERE CORDELIER PIERRE DE MESANGE* I-II (Amsterdam: Roger 1720).

[417] Lilienthal, *Die gute Sache* (1750-) I/II, 327.

("still exist 4550 times as long as it has"),[418] i.e., 27.3 million years, before space runs short for the resurrected. Here reason stands against reason. Orthodoxy itself thus unintentionally took the course towards the emancipation of reason from *revelatio*, as it would be adopted within Neology and Rationalism.

On the Calvinist side, a fusion of Orthodox heritage and Enlightenment mentality increasingly occurred in the eighteenth century. This is evident, for instance, in the *Orthodoxie libérale* and its chief representatives, the three Swiss professors of theology Johann Alphons Turretin[419] (1671–1737), Samuel Werenfels (1657–1740) and Jean-Frédéric Ostervald (1663–1747).

In a different way from that on the Lutheran side, the intermixture of Orthodoxy and Enlightenment principles has far-reaching consequences. Werenfels, who publicly exposes the Orthodox tendency for quarrelling and attributes it to poor moral standards (above all to *superbia*), strives (similarly to Turretin[420]) for the union of the Protestant confessions on the basis of the fundamental articles of the Christian faith. Werenfels dismisses the doctrine of inspiration. Following Werenfels, God revealed himself to the biblical writers *per sanum rationis usum*[421] and directed them in such a manner that they wrote down nothing that contradicted this revelation. As a result Werenfels is inclined to restrict the canonicity of the Bible to the area of ethics and therefore emphasises its *certitudo moralis*.[422] He rejected the interpretation of *scriptura per scripturam* as an inadmissable *petitio principii* in a logical sense.[423] How much Werenfels pushes rational premises into the foreground, is apparent in the fact that he apostrophises the miracles as proofs of the existence of God,[424] favours the cosmological argument for the existence of God and, in addition, considers the divinity of Scripture to be psychologically demonstrable. According to Werenfels, from the works of creation God can be shown to be its *opifex*. At the same time it also holds true: *ita ex diligenti lectione & consideratione Scripturae probari potest esse Deum hujus libri auctorem.*[425]

Translated by Gerhard Bode and Anja Hill-Zenk

---

[418] Ibid.
[419] Cf. Klauber, Turretin (1994).
[420] Cf. ibid. 143–64.
[421] Werenfels, *Opuscula* II (1772) 345.
[422] Ibid. 333.
[423] Ibid. 343.
[424] Ibid. 277.
[425] Ibid. 278.

CHAPTER TWENTY-NINE

The Catholic Counterpart and Response to the Protestant Orthodoxy

By Pierre Gibert, Paris

Sources and general works: G. Bedouelle / B. Roussel (eds.), *Le temps des Réformes et la Bible* (BTT 5; Paris 1989); J.-R. Armogathe (ed.), *Le Grand Siècle et la Bible* (BTT 6; Paris 1989); M. Paquot, *Mémoires pour servir à l'histoire littéraire des dix-sept provinces des Pays-Bas, de la Principauté de Liège et de quelques contrées voisines* (18 vols.; Louvain 1763–70); R. Simon, *Histoire critique du Vieux Testament* (Rotterdam 1685); S. L. Greenslade (ed.), *The West from the Reformation to the Present Day* (CHB 3; Cambridge 1963); J. Astruc, *Conjectures sur les Mémoires originaux dont il paraît que Moïse s'est servi pour composer le livre de la Genèse* (Brussels [Paris?] 1753; repr. with introd. and notes by P. Gibert; Paris 1999).

To speak of a controversy between Catholics and Protestants on the nature and status of the Bible in the first half of the seventeenth century, is first of all to evaluate the reception in both camps of the – normally unchallenged – literal meaning, regardless of extra qualifications (like spiritual, mystical, christological). Consequently, it is also to grasp the question of the debate on authority: does Scripture have authority *per se*? If not, by what other authority could it be guaranteed? This debate not only involved the opposition between the Protestant *sola Scriptura*, guaranteed by *divina claritas*, and the Catholic distinction between Scripture and Tradition, the latter embracing or integrating the former; the authors mentioned in this article, despite certain oversimplifications of their opponents' positions, showed a certain complexity that distinguished them and, paradoxically, revealed a move towards these same opponents – by reason of an increasingly critical study of the biblical text.[1]

1. Jacques Bonfrère

Sources: C. Sommervogel, S.J., *Bibliothèque de la Compagnie de Jésus* 1 (Brussels / Paris 1890), cols. 1713–15; M. Paquot, *Mémoires pour servir à l'histoire littéraire des dix-sept provinces des Pays-Bas* XI (Louvain 1768).

---

[1] These authors, therefore, differ significantly from the controversialist François Véron (1577–1649), pastor of Charenton, near Paris, who appeared as the anti-Protestant polemicist *par excellence* and whose *œuvre* consisted of 202 titles! His Protestant 'counterpart' was minister Charles Drelincourt (1595–1669).

The Jesuit Jacques Bonfrère, alias Bonfrerius, was born in Dinant, then part of the Principality of Liège, on 12 April 1573. He entered the Society of Jesus in 1592 and spent most of his life in the city of Douai where in 1617 he became a doctor in theology at the University and started to teach philosophy and scholastic theology at the theological College of Anchin. However, he dedicated himself above all to the teaching of Holy Scripture. He was a prolific commentator, and he wrote a commentary on each of the 'historical books' of the Old Testament except for the book of Esther. As for the New Testament, he dealt with the Gospels, the Acts of the Apostles and Saint Paul's letters.

Being a hard intellectual worker he also showed an aptitude for government and management, which probably explains why in 1630 he became Rector of the Scots' College, which at the time was a unit in a significant institution. This College (or Seminary) was part of a series of foundations that, alongside the Scot's Colleges in Paris and Rome, were the products of John Lesley, Catholic bishop of Rosse, Scotland, concerned with training priests for the priesthood. Before becoming a bishop, J. Lesley was a faithful supporter of Mary Stuart, and her ambassador to England in 1571. At one time, he was imprisoned by Queen Elizabeth.

The fact that Bonfrère was appointed Rector of this College doubtless underlines the atmosphere among the Catholics in Northern France at that time, a region that appeared both as a haven for Catholics persecuted in Great Britain and as a center of Counter-Reformation activity. Was Bonfrère's position sufficient to label him an anti-Protestant polemicist? Whatever his personal feelings and the atmosphere of the College at the time, it would probably be going too far to consider him so. First and foremost, he was a biblical scholar of his time, concentrating principally on the plain sense of the text, i.e., its literal meaning. His exegesis belonged to the intellectual and academic context of the time. Richard Simon, for example, did not overlook this, despite his own strong polemical streak, he never referred to this characteristic of Bonfrère when he mentioned him several decades later. In fact, the allusions and certain arguments of Bonfrère, concerning Luther and Protestantism in general, belonged to the "refutations" that are so typical of Catholic theologians of that time. Richard Simon, despite his sympathy for some Protestant commentators, unashamedly used these arguments, in part to defend his own positions against his opponents in the Catholic party. Bonfrère, whilst he was in the process of commenting on the Book of Psalms, went blind and was obliged to retire from teaching. He died in Tournai on 9 May 1642, ceasing his work at Psalm 34.

What should be retained from his considerable work, part of which is lost, due to the 1643 fire that broke out in the printing house which held the ready-to-be-distributed copies of his commentaries on the Books of Kings (1 and 2 Samuel and 1 and 2 Kings) and Paralipomenes (1 and 2 Chronicles)? Before treating the text in which he expressed his positions and beliefs on Scripture in general, it may be noted that, as an heir to the intellectual traditions of sixteenth century Humanists, he was committed to the literal meaning of the text, although, as we shall see later on, he did not shy away from qualifying the text according to precise theological perspectives. Therefore, some forty years later, Richard Simon, though a harsh critic of the literal meaning of the text and despite some reserves, arbitrarily rallied him to his own flag: "the Prolegomena [*Praeloquia*] that Bonfrerius has composed on the Bible deserve to be read, although they have not attained the perfection that we seek. [He] nonetheless has an adequate grasp of the subject he was dealing with, and in addition, [he] shows... considerable judgment...".[2]

---

[2] *Histoire critique* (1685) 455–56.

Secondly, it should be noted that, although he was well-versed in Latin and Greek, he was quite weak in Hebrew which he nonetheless taught. Once again, Simon, while acknowledging his merits in matters of the Septuagint and the Vulgate "to give them a more correct meaning", affirmed that he "would have done even better if he had a marginally better knowledge of Oriental languages...".[3] This marked his research orientations in biblical matters, and led him to take a particular interest in the Septuagint and Vulgate, from which he drew certain conclusions regarding the composition of the biblical books and corpus. We, therefore, are inclined to believe that his distance from the Hebrew text of the Old Testament and his interest for the two translations mentioned is to be related more to the state of his knowledge and competence than to a more or less forced obedience to decrees of the Council of Trent on the 'authority' of the Vulgate.

1625 saw the publishing of his commentary on the Pentateuch that opens with *Praeloquia* whose ambition is underlined by the title and especially the final "rules": viz. to introduce the reader into a good understanding not only of the Pentateuch, but also the whole Scripture – in other words: *In Totam Scripturam Sacram Praeloquia*. Divided into twenty-one chapters, it is by its length alone a weighty introduction that ends in a set of forty-six rules explicitly labeled *Regulae vel Canones ad totius Sacrae Scripturae intelligentiam perutiles*.

Among these twenty-one chapters dominated by a pedagogical and didactic demand that reviews each book of the Old and New Testament, our concern here only relates to those that implicitly or explicitly reveal any points of friction between Catholics and Protestants. It is hardly surprising, therefore, that the chapters dealing with the number of canonical books (Chap. III), the opacity of Scripture (Chap. IX) and the authority of the Vulgate (Chap. XV) are the most overt ones as regards his positions and the positions of the Catholic Church – which should not lead to an omission of his conception of literal meaning, *inter alia*.

Although he did not immediately state any opposing position which would force him to restate an orthodox one, we can hardly overlook, in the context of the day, the background to his appeal to the authority of the Church to establish and guarantee the list of canonical books received both as sacred Scripture and the actual Word of God:

> Firstly, note this: although in the present case, canon and authenticity meet together, since these books only receive their authority from the Church following the Canon and the list itself, and since the Church, when it makes a list thereof, declares that it receives these books as Holy Scripture and true Word of God, nevertheless, the term 'authority' extends further. Indeed, a text can receive authority from the Church, regardless of any Canon or catalogue of many documents being established. Therefore, we will show later that a version of the Bible can justly be declared authentic or non-authentic, without being canonical. Indeed, no list or canon of the different versions is guaranteed by the Church, but there is nonetheless one that is approved, and for that reason is said to be 'authoritative'; the others, whether rejected by the Church or unapproved without being rejected, are not called 'authoritative' (III, section V).

---

[3] Ibid. 422.

The Hebrew canon, although dependent on the Synagogue, only has value insofar as the Church, established by Christ and inspired by the Holy Spirit, acknowledges such value (III, section VI).

In practically all the chapters of the *Praeloquia*, there is a recurring insistence on the links between the Church, Christ, and the Holy Spirit, regarding the nature or status of the Scripture.

Bonfrère progressively examined the "canonical books whose canonical authority" is tainted by doubt (Chap. VI). After examining the books of Esther, Tobit and Judith, the book of Wisdom and Sirach, Baruch and Maccabees, and, in the New Testament, the letters of James and Jude, the second letter of Peter, the second and third letters of John and Revelation, he dwelled on certain disputed passages of the book of Daniel, the final chapter of Mark, the episode of the sweating of blood in Luke and the adulterous woman in John. In general, his statements were erudite and started by referring to the oldest states of the manuscripts or versions. But in examining various standpoints since the patristic era, he established a continuity between the Samaritans and Sadducees (*in veteri Synagoga haeretici*) and a series of "heretics" whose heirs are clearly pointed to: Châteillon (or Casteillon), Beza and Luther:

> All these "heretics" have been imitated remarkably by new shoots from Hell: Sébastien Châteillon, according to the testimony of Beza, rejects the Song of Solomon as an impure and obscene song. Luther, in his "Table Talk", considers the book of Job as a tale and jeers at the book of Ecclesiastes. Almost all the heretics of our time globally reject the books that have not found their place in the Hebrew canon (IV, section I).

It is true that on the subject of the New Testament, where he also argued vehemently against the Lutheran position on the letter of James or the second or third letters of John, he referred to Erasmus.

The chapter entitled *De obscuritate Scripturae sacrae* (Chap. IX) even starts its first section with Luther's name strategically placed in the first line:

> In Scripture, there is no obscurity, no difficulty, but only a perfect clarity, that is what Luther in his book *De servo arbitrio* and most heretics of our day pretend; subsequently, everything in Scripture is accessible and open to shoemakers, stone-cutters, craftsmen, good-wives, shepherds and idiots (and they would even add, jesters and madmen) (IX, section I).

From the strict point of view of exegetical history and the passage between the sixteenth and seventeenth centuries, this chapter of Bonfrère, in a way, went beyond a doctrinal perspective. Consistent with the philosophy of Descartes which was then spreading throughout the Netherlands, thanks in large part to Spinoza, this was the time when readers increasingly discovered difficulties, "irreconcilable conflicts" and a lack of order that became ever harder to ignore. It led, notwithstanding the Libertines of the early seventeenth century and any outstanding controversies, to a collective reckoning of these difficulties by Catholics, Protestants, and even certain Jews. In this regard, it is of particular interest to examine Bonfrère's approach.

Placing himself under the patronage of Saint Jerome, Bonfrère acknowledges the difficulties of a grammatical nature, but especially the fact that the Bible is meant to be explained and commented. Saint Peter himself, as he recalls, recognized certain difficulties in reading Saint Paul's letters… However, he notes that Luther made use of a purely doctrinal stratagem: by eliminating the letter of James or the books of Maccabees. His first motivation was to cast aside any item that opposed his own way of seeing, whether regarding the relation between works and faith, his "false doctrine of Justification" or his rejection of the dogma of purgatory, prayers for the dead, etc. (section III).

In fact, Bonfrère remarks that opacity is linked to the very will of the Holy Spirit (section V), for which he gives four reasons:

> Firstly, so that Scripture should not be despised: indeed, any art, science or knowledge that contains some difficulty and is accessible only to few, becomes valuable: and so on and so forth for all the rest...
>
> Secondly, so that [Scripture] may offer men an honorable occupation and enable the exercising of their mind, through conversations, writings and commentaries. The Holy Spirit seems to have had this in view: to grant us a very abundant crop of these exercises with a great merit for us, for no occupation is more honorable than that which is exercised in these sublime mysteries of our faith, in seeking the divine will and his most holy commandments in these matters so necessary to our salvation, in these matters which are so worthy of a Christian man.
>
> Thirdly, and also importantly, to increase the pleasure in dealing with such Scripture, so that we may be more constrained and more touched by our reason. Those who train in this holy study feel a transparent and pure voluptuousness more than one would believe. And to be honest, it often occurs that we delight much more in the [truths] that we have discovered by our study and our work, that they touch our spirit and that we love them like our own children.
>
> Fourthly, so that the [truths] contained in Scripture may be inlaid more solidly in our spirits and remain set there. Indeed, the obscure passages are often read over and over again and examined with a more careful meditation. Consequently, another benefit arises that, in becoming aware of our weakness to understand Scripture, we grow in humility, our pride decreases and we turn to God through prayers to obtain light (section IV).

Obviously, in this instance, Bonfrère blends various arguments, while exhorting the reader to a kind of humility, in that the intelligence finds itself overcome by the very object of consideration, and all the more so when it fails to establish immediacy in its approach to Scripture: the authority of the Church and the tradition of the Fathers (section X) are reliable for him in a quest that is more religious than critical.

One can suggest that the two chapters on the 'authority' of the Vulgate (Chap. XV) and the Septuagint (Chap. XVI) manifest both the doctrinal positions of Bonfrère and his competency of preference. As regards the Vulgate with which – for reasons of "Catholic doctrine" – he deals before the Septuagint, Bonfrère took a position of defense as regards its 'authority' and 'authenticity'. The impact of the Reformation, to which the Council of Trent responded, was an obvious motivation here. The Protestant position, illustrated by Calvin, Munster *et simili farinae arrosores musculi*, as well as Luther, is certainly not developed at length, although it was sufficient in a time where challenging it had become a commonplace in Catholic thinking and would remain so until the end of the nineteenth century.

The arguments which he used here are mainly those of 'venerability' and 'authority', the former argument being illustrated not only by the quality of the work of St. Jerome, but also by the recognition it received among the Fathers and until the Middle Ages, while the latter argument obviously relates to the decrees of the Council of Trent, which proclaimed the Vulgate 'authentic', whereby it contains nothing against faith and mores (sections II and III).

Naturally, this version is not free of difficulties, but for Bonfrère, the "heretics", and in particular Calvin, were wrong in insisting on such details that do not require in any manner recourse to the Hebrew text alone (section IV). In a manner of speaking, the defense of the Vulgate is reinforced in the chapter on the Septuagint (Chap. XVI), in respect of which Bonfrère naturally invoked the 'authority' of the authors of the New Testament and the Greek Fathers for whom it was 'the Bible'. Obviously comfortable on this issue, this chapter is not especially relevant here.

Although Chap. XX, entitled *De sacrae Scripturae interpretatione, ejusque variis sensibus*, revisits the four medieval meanings (sections IV and V), it is in fact a direct legacy of the sixteenth century, its criticism of the four meanings and its defense of the literal meaning in the sense promoted by Lefèvre d'Etaples and Erasmus, among others. In this instance, Bonfrère typically belonged to the immediately pre-critical era that started in the second half of the seventeenth century, with Richard Simon in particular. More especially in the legacy of the sixteenth century, the literal meaning for Bonfrère is consistently 'mystical': "It is customary, here and there, to attribute a double meaning to Scripture: the literal meaning, which is also called the historical meaning, and the mystical meaning that some call spiritual meaning, and others, figurative meaning" (section I). But he immediately adds: "This distinction of meanings is rejected and condemned by a great number of heretics of our time, along with Luther, since they only recognize the literal meaning" (ibid.). The repeated phrase "against the heretics" obviously ignores the development of Luther on this point and how liberating it was in the late fifteenth and early sixteenth century to claim a return to the literal meaning alone, whether on behalf of the Humanists or the early Reformers.

As for the fourty-six *Regulae vel Canones* that end these *Praeloquia*, we underline a certain tension in the text, typical, in our opinion, of the early seventeenth century, and which is already shared by Protestants and Catholics, beyond any differences and antagonisms. In a way, this tension prefigures the oncoming coalescing of opponents over the same questions and answers, whether in Saumur with Louis Cappel, in Geneva with Jean Le Clerc, in Amsterdam with Baruch de Spinoza or in Paris with Richard Simon.

The literal meaning progressively occupied the place which made it almost mandatory for study, even if that entailed questioning the work of the Holy Spirit and the sacred character of Scripture.

Canon I. After the interpretation given by the Church or the consensus of the Holy Fathers, nothing is as helpful for discovering the literal meaning than to compare the passage whose meaning we are searching with the passages which precede or follow it; and, if all is in agreement, that is the literal meaning; and where all the elements are in accordance, the most true and original meaning is to be found. And if all the elements [also] accord with a different meaning, then either both meanings can be the literal meaning, as equally intended by the Holy Spirit in an immediate and primary manner, or one in a primary and the other in some secondary manner, by the mediation of the first meaning which it completes, as I have shown above when we dealt with the literal meaning. With the mystical meanings, it is not in the least necessary to compare them with what precedes or follows, as with the literal meaning; it is sufficient that this meaning should arise from the passage itself and not seem to be distorted or torn out arbitrarily; the more it is grounded in the letter, the more it is worthy and the higher the probability that it was intended by the Holy Spirit.

Obviously, Bonfrère did not dispute any more or less with the Protestants than with Catholic commentators of the Bible of his time. He thus hinted at the fact that the apparent complexity in the very approach to Scripture would be overcome. A few decades later, at the level of research attained by him, the polemic dimension could only be secondary, and as a result, diminish and lose its edge.

2. Cornelius a Lapide

Sources / studies: M. PAQUOT, *Mémoires pour servir à l'histoire littéraire des dix-sept provinces des Pays-Bas* VII (Louvain 1766); V. CARRAUD, "Descartes et la Bible", in: Armogathe (ed.), *Le Grand Siècle et la Bible* (1989) 277–91.
  Bibliography: C. SOMMERVOGEL, S.J., *Bibliothèque de la Compagnie de Jésus* IV (Brussels / Paris 1893) cols. 1511–26.

With Cornelius a Lapide (1566?-1637), we remain in the circle of the Jesuit commentators, even if this circle is made wider for him due to the repeated references to him until the nineteenth century in the Society of Jesus, but also due to the fact that he was an advisor to Descartes. Did he really belong to the anti-Protestant controversialists? Should not his work rather be viewed as a promotion of the 'Catholic orthodoxy' in his general theory of the Bible and above all the way of introducing it?

Like Jacques Bonfrère, Cornelius Cornelissen van den Steen – whose Latin name is Cornelius Cornelii a Lapide and whose French name is Corneille de la Pierre – was born in the Principality of Liège, in Bocholt, "circa 1566".[4] He studied in the Three-Crowns College in Cologne where he graduated as Master of Arts in 1584. Although we do not know what he did until 1592, we do know that he joined the Society of Jesus on 8 July of this year. In the Society, he taught Holy Scripture and Hebrew, which he did for twenty years before joining the Roman College where he continued this same task for another twenty years. He died in Rome in his seventies, in that same College, on 12 March 1637.

In the context of a study on polemics, two episodes from his youth may be mentioned, whose consequences are ultimately unknown: On the eight of September 1592, during a visit to Montaigu for confessions and preaching on the feast of the Nativity of the Blessed Virgin Mary, he was strongly threatened and "on the verge of being slaughtered by a group of the Dutch cavalry", according to Paquot.[5] Then, in 1608, "he and his colleague, Fr. Adrian Mangot, took part in the Conferences held in Antwerp between these two Jesuits and two ministers from Rotterdam, François Landsberghen and his son Samuel; but the outcome of this dispute is unknown".[6] These two facts reflect the state of affairs of the time, a mixture of war-like events and debates or 'disputes', in the academic sense, between the proponents of both confessions, Catholic and Protestant.

Opinions vary on his especially prolific output, including a commentary on the entire Bible, omitting the book of Job and the Psalms. Unusually, in this instance, Richard Simon is particularly oblique, quite different from his attitude towards Fr. Morin:

The comments of Cornelius a Lapide also have this deficiency [of mixing Commentaries of the Bible with erudition and questions far from their text]; but this author nonetheless states, from

---

[4] Paquot, *Mémoires* 7 (1766) 335.
[5] Ibid. 366.
[6] Ibid. 336.

the very start of his work, that he will be brief and will gather in a few words that which others have already noted at length.[7]

He then goes on by establishing his own methodological requirements: "I know that this sort of Commentary which is full of erudition pleases many a person and especially preachers; *but they cannot be to the taste of wise persons who want each thing to be dealt with separately and in its place*".[8] Paquot seems to deal with him, finally, by noting characteristics and making more or less sincere recommendations:

> Many flaws have been pointed out in these Commentaries. The style of the author is overly scholastic and heavy, although quite understandable. He does not have sufficient knowledge of Greek and Hebrew; he does not seem to understand the other Oriental languages; and the variations that he finds between the old versions are often only due to the different way of translating into Latin words which had the same meaning in Ethiopian, Persian, Arabic, etc. as in Greek or Hebrew.

However, "it would be very wrong to classify Fr. a Lapide as a bad commentator on the basis of the preceding flaws. There is much that is good in his works, and one can make great use of them, provided one is discerning. A Protestant did not hesitate to prefer them to the synopsis of Polus…".[9] In fact, Lapide appears to be more clearly than Bonfrère a member of the so-called "Republic of Letters", established in the seventeenth century and which despite controversies, polemics and even actual violence allowed sufficiently free and honest spirits of the day to cross confessional barriers, especially as regards biblical studies – which, admittedly, became easier in the second half of the century, despite the Revocation, in France, of the Edict of Nantes in 1685.

How should one appreciate this sizeable work that marks a sort of transition between the humanist heritage of the sixteenth century, memories of the patristic and medieval tradition, and a predominant concern for the literal meaning, yet, which is pre-critical compared to the demands of Simon and Spinoza? What are the effects of the other, Protestant perspective, for this Catholic whose life was largely lived in Rome?

More than his fellow Catholic, Bonfrère, Lapide seems concerned with a major preoccupation of the seventeenth century for rationality and the relations between the Bible, philosophy and science. The first lines of his magnum opus are typical, opening naturally on a commentary of Genesis (1616). In these pages of general introduction entitled *Prooemium et enconium S. Scripturae*, he refers to the "famous theologian of the Egyptians", Hermes Trismegistos, whose statement can be traced back to Psalm 19:

> This famous Egyptian theologian Mercury, Trismegistos according to the opinion of the Pagans, when he reflected at length how he could best describe the universe, he finally came to this conclusion: "The Universe", he says, "is the book of the divinity and this visible world is the mirror of divine realities", precisely in the book where he had taught his own theology with a broad commentary. "*The heavens*, indeed, *are telling the glory of God and the firmament pro-*

---

[7] *Histoire critique* (1685) 423.
[8] Ibid., the italics are my own.
[9] Paquot, *Mémoires* 7 (1766) 343–44, 346.

claims his handiwork; and *from the greatness and beauty of created things comes a corresponding perception of their Creator, and his might and eternal and* invisible *divinity*".[10]

Above all, "Cornelius a Lapide expands on the world viewed as a book... Nonetheless, this book remains imperfect and obscure and cannot teach us anything beyond the limits of nature".[11]

In fact, Lapide gave expression here to what became a significant part of the seventeenth century's concern: grasping or establishing a coherence in the order of knowledge within the context of a certain need for rationality and harmonization between the contributions of a new approach of the universe, a new philosophy and the realities of faith, especially the teachings of the Bible. He thus established Canon 2 of his principles for reading the Pentateuch:

> Philosophy and physics should adapt to Holy Scripture and the Word of God, since He is the source of all that is number, order and mode of nature, says Saint Augustine. Conversely, Holy Scripture itself should not be twisted to adapt to the opinions of philosophers, or the light and dictatorship of [the sciences] of nature.[12]

This is the heart of the inquiring that implied Descartes' contributions and his dialogue with Comenius and which may have led the author of the *Discours de la Méthode* to consult Lapide, directly or through his work. We should mention here the complete misunderstanding, not only between the future bishop of the Moravian brothers and Descartes (despite the admiration of Comenius for the French philosopher), but also regarding the Bible by Descartes. As has been pointed out, "the Cartesian metaphysics of Descartes, or rather, his simple presentation in the form of a dedication to the theologians of the Sorbonne, only quote Scripture in order to legitimate the possibility of managing without it".[13]

It is significant that Lapide took an open perspective with a view to the integration of the biblical data in the knowledge of his time. Did he oppose Protestants, or did he suggest a "doctrine" of Bible reading that could lead one to believe so? Nothing explicit can be found in this *Proemium* that would allow one to make such an assertion, in contrast to Bonfrère's *Praeloquia*. For that matter, can he be deemed indifferent to, or absolutely ignorant of, another perception and reception of the Bible?

> If from the start of the *Proemium*, Lapide did not challenge the fact that God expresses himself in the very letter of the Holy Scriptures, he nonetheless established the famous parallel of the "two tables", i.e., the tables of the Scripture and of the Eucharist, based on a series of patristic references. Throughout his argument, he did not merely pose this set of references as a sort of "proof" of his position. However, he never pretended to oppose explicitly any position whatsoever, contenting himself to adduce the information and confirmations he presented. He thus established a kind of legitimization and comprehension of Scripture on the basis of an on-going tradition which, without granting a definitive God-given authority, assures the interest one should invest in the text.

Whatever may be inferred from this process, the fundamental principle of his commentary remains: to stick to the text and its historical meaning, with a view to the fact that any potential mystical meaning would be immediately

---

[10] *Commentaria in Pentateuchum Mosis, Ultima editio aucta et recognita* (1714) 1.
[11] J.-R. Armogathe, "Etudier", in: Le Grand Siècle (1989) 30.
[12] *Commentaria* (1714) 24.
[13] Carraud, Descartes et la Bible (1989) 277.

linked to such a historical meaning. He, therefore, approached both the Fathers and the medieval authors to confirm the primacy of this historical meaning, even if he did not want to hold strictly to the letter of the text or wander off in allegory. In this regard, his effort to determine a set of rules to read and study Scripture in his *Canones*, to structure his commentary of the Pentateuch, manifested his concern to grasp the variety of literary conventions and, hence, the literary types that the reader must recognize in the writing habits of Moses and, therefore, the Hebrews.

Once again, if Lapide did not lead us to critical exegesis in the strict sense as fundamentally established by Simon, he moved in that direction and revealed an expectation of that order. This may be seen as the sign of his distancing himself from any obsessive controversy with the Protestants, and even when his tone very obviously relates to Catholic orthodoxy in a certain understanding of tradition, nothing in him opposed the "Republic of Letters" that, some forty or fifty years later, would lead Simon to contemplate an ecumenical translation of the Bible with Protestant ministers in Geneva.

3. Jean Morin

Sources / studies: P. AUVRAY, "Jean Morin", *RB* 66 (1959) 396–414; R. SIMON, *Histoire critique du Vieux Testament* (Rotterdam 1685).

"A fine theologian lost in the field of biblical criticism", such is the conclusion reached by PAUL AUVRAY in 1959 regarding the work of Jean Morin (1591–1659).[14] To support this conclusion, AUVRAY appealed to the judgment of Richard Simon, certain insights of Morin himself, and the conclusions available to potential students of his specifically theological work. Does this mean that from this theological perspective, J. Morin is situated in the context of a history of anti-Protestant controversy? Nothing seems less certain, but since his biblical work is significant, it will serve our purpose here.

Jean Morin was born in Blois, France, into a Protestant family of tradesmen. It is very likely that his first studies of Latin and Greek in the Protestant stronghold of La Rochelle and, even more, his further studies in Leiden (philosophy, law, Hebrew and theology) indicate a strong sense of belonging to the Protestant community. However, it seems that the disputes that were then held in that Dutch city between Arminians and Gomarians contributed to shaking his Protestant faith. In Paris in 1613, he converted to Catholicism and entered the Oratory in 1618 and became a priest in 1619.

His intense life as an editor and his visits of varying lengths in England and Rome, not to mention certain responsibilities as superior of the Oratorians, cannot hide his undoubtedly shy and discreet temper and his tendency to bold affirmation when he had to defend his point of view. Despite the negative – and *a posteriori* – judgments of Richard Simon, whose incapacity for compliments is notorious, Jean Morin's discretion, unselfishness and passion for work are above suspicion. He died on 28 February 1659, on the verge of a new era of the history of biblical text studies. He certainly contributed to these, in particular by his concern for textual criticism, even if Richard Simon was later to go much further in literary and historical criticism.

Whatever the importance of his theological work, we can only note here the advances of J. Morin in the field of biblical exegesis. Even then, we will seek to

---

[14] Auvray, Jean Morin (1959) 414.

highlight those items that either mark an exceptional originality or a doctrinal undertaking which, as we will see, is not distinct from the confrontation with other interpretations of the Bible, whether Protestant or Jewish and rabbinical. Indeed, beyond his first two works – a set of texts on Church history and law published in Paris in 1626 and a poorly written "History of the Deliverance of the Christian Church by the Emperor Constantine..." published in 1630 – the work that really launched him was an order by the Assembly of the Clergy in 1626 which directly placed him in charge of the publication of an edition of the Septuagint.

Before evaluating this work and its implications, we need to place it in a perspective that is characterized by more than mere differences in doctrinal positions. Indeed, here, as in many other biblical fields, the seventeenth century is heir to the sixteenth century tradition of erudition and everything implied by the quest for the double *veritas* of the text, *graeca* and *hebraica*. Whatever the doctrinal implications, this double quest inaugurated a search for texts, a history of texts and manuscripts, and especially editions, that really began what we can call, in this context, modernity.

Staying with the precise context in which J. Morin wrote his first exegetical work, let us recall that during the same first third of the seventeenth century, a new edition of the polyglot Bible was being prepared in Paris, edited by Michel Le Jay.[15] This was a project of Cardinal du Perron and Jacques du Thou. Morin was invited to take part in this enterprise in 1628, given the interest and competence shown by the request of the Assembly of the Clergy and his work that same year 1628 in publishing three large volumes of his *Vetus Testamentum secundum LXX, et ex auctoritate Sixti V pont. Max. editum, cum scholiis Romanae editionis in singula capita distributis. Omnia de exemplari romano fidelissime et studiosissime expressa.*

The originality of J. Morin is probably not manifest in most of this edition, even though it does not immediately merit the heavy criticism it received – posthumously, predictably – from Richard Simon, in particular for engaging the reader in "an infinity of contradictions".[16] In fact, as AUVRAY notices, "the work is not original: the Greek only reproduces the edition of Sixtus V (Rome 1587), while the Latin is the version of Fl. Nobilius, published in Rome in 1588, which was the first attempt to reconstitute the *Vetus Latina* on the basis of patristic quotations".[17]

As in Bonfrère's *Praeloquia*, it is in the lengthy preface that Morin reveals his personality and expresses convictions regarding the authority of the Septuagint which he upheld until the end of his life. He was not content merely to establish this authority in the name of the tradition of the Fathers or even of the New Testament, he also brought a new argument to support his conviction, viz. the reference to the Samaritan Pentateuch.

---

[15] On the Paris Polyglot, see the next essay in the present volume, Chap. 30, sect. 2, by A. SCHENKER.

[16] *Histoire critique* (1685) 466.

[17] Auvray, Jean Morin (1959) 400.

In this perspective, then, Morin took advantage of a new datum, the recent acquisition by the library of the Oratory of rue Saint-Honoré of a manuscript purchased in Damascus in 1616 by Pietro della Valle. Not only did the proximity of this text enable him to become familiar with it and use it extensively, but also to engage in a study of the writings of the Samaritans, doubtless with some errors, but also with an eagerness to establish his 'great idea': "to exalt the Greek Bible at the expense of the Massoretic text, and to that end, to rely on the Samaritan Pentateuch".[18]

In the context of the time, such a position was unexpected, and even shocking, including for Catholics in favor of the Hebrew version, and all the more so for the Protestants who were predominantly marked by the *veritas hebraica* of the text and the canon since Luther. Such a position could only be received in a spirit of controversy. "This is where the secret of his success most probably lies", comments P. AUVRAY. Without reducing Morin's career to the foregoing position and his incessant demonstration of it, since – as mentioned above – he remained a theologian, even though he became lost in the fields of biblical criticism, nevertheless, this same position should not be minimized, especially as, in the aftermath of this edition of the Septuagint, other works kept Morin on the path he trod until two years before his death.

Thus, Morin found himself engaged in the aforementioned project of editing a new polyglot Bible, on the suggestion of Fr. de Bérulle. Quite naturally, the edition and addition of the Samaritan Pentateuch were handed over to him. As early as 1628, his correspondence with Jerome Alexander the Younger[19] enabled him to enter the debate on the subject of the Samaritans' writings, and then discover that two other texts of that Pentateuch existed in Rome, one in the Vatican Library, and the other probably in the hands of Pietro della Valle (1586–1652). The latter was an Aramaic translation in Samaritan script. Although it is to Morin's credit to have ensured publication of the principal edition of this Pentateuch in 1632, one can nevertheless question the quality of his work and the positions taken therein, partly expressed in four dissertations, which fired controversies rather that tempering them.

These controversies only increased with Morin's three books, which sought both to answer his opponents and justify his position. The first of these books, published in 1631, was the *Exercitationes ecclesiasticae in utrumque Samaritanorum pentateuchum, de illorum religione et moribus, de antiquitis Hebraeorum litteris et siclis.*[20] It was followed in 1633 by the *Exercitationes biblicae de hebraei graecique textus sinceritate, germana LXXII interpretum translatione dignoscenda, illius cum Vulgata conciliatione et juxta judaeos divina integritate totiusque rabbinicae antiquitatis et operis masorethici aera, explicatione, censura.*[21]

In this second book, Morin announced in the first part, or Exercitatio I,

---

[18] Auvray, ibid. 401.

[19] See *Antiquitates Ecclesiae Orientalis… Dissertationibus Epistolicis enucleatae* (Londini 1682), Epist. IV to X.

[20] "Ecclesiastical research on one and the other Pentateuch of the Samaritans, their religion and mores, the writings and riches of the ancient Hebrews".

[21] "Biblical research on the necessity to discern the authenticity of the Hebrew text and Greek text, thanks to the authentic translation of the seventy-two interpreters, on the reconciliation of

what his purpose was, and labeled it unambiguously: *In Catholicorum, anti-quorum et neotericorum, nec non Haereticorum de codicum Hebraïcorum sinceri-tate sententiam.*[22] Using the words of Tertullian, he addressed himself to the new heretics, i.e., the Protestants, whose references, restricted to the Hebrew Bible only, do not repose solely on a concern with originality, but also reject the only place of conservation of authentic texts, the Catholic Church.

> Here, reader, consider with awe the Spirit of God, perfectly present to His Church, who walks with a sure foot through all obscurities, difficulties and entanglements. Despite the ignorance due to the gross negligence of the rabbis, the monstrous and shameful corruption of the Jewish books, even when the heretics disdainfully attacked these passages with pompous eloquence, never was the Church brought to rewrite or alter a version that it had used alone for nearly eleven hundred years, to bring it to the norms and rules of the Hebrew text. It would have been the highest injustice to reject and drive the Catholic Church – as if it questioned itself – back to those who have been its fiercest enemies for so many centuries so that they would teach her the truth, when she is confirmed and set up by the Holy Spirit as the column and foundation of Truth.[23]

In short, "Let us therefore seek the Words of God in the Church, let us receive them from the Church, let us withdraw them and gather them, not from the hands of strangers, or even worse, enemies, but from the treasures and ar-chives of the Church".

Finally, in 1639, Morin published his *Diatribe elenctica de sinceritate hebraei graecique textus dignoscenda, adversus insanas quorumdam hereticorum calum-nias. Accedunt appendix in qua nonnula divinitatis et incarnationis Iesu-Chisti Domini nostri illustrissima testimonia in hebraeo textu nunc corrupta talmudis et rabinorum antiquorum authoritate restituuntur, et animadversiones in censuram ad Samaritanorum Pentateuchum.*[24] The second part of this title marks expli-citly change in Morin's positions and reflections on his relation to the Samari-tan Pentateuch and the Septuagint, albeit that he had already defended these ideas. Indeed, the question was not only the issue of the reduction of the authenticity of Scripture due to the exclusive *veritas hebraica* defended by the Protestants, but also the issue of the quasi-material authenticity of the text by reason of the alleged corruption which it was deemed to have suffered on be-half of the Jews and especially Rabbis because of their hatred of Christ and Christians, and therefore, with a view to preventing Scripture from being used in favor of the divinity of Jesus.

His succeeding work seemed to neglect biblical issues for nearly twenty years, but one should note that in addition to not abandoning his ideas, he ac-tually confirmed them in his last work, published two years before his death, in 1657. This is entitled *Opuscula hebraeo-semetica, 1° Grammatica samaritana*

---

this translation with the Vulgate, its divine integrity according to the Jews and its explanation and its examination at the time of all rabbinical antiquity and the works of the Massorah".

[22] *Exercitationes biblicae* (1633) 1–13.

[23] Ibid. 11.

[24] "Convincing discussion on the discernment between the faithfulness of the Hebrew text and the Greek text, against the mad slanders of certain heretics. Attached thereto, an Appendix in which certain very famous passages on the divinity and incarnation of Our Lord Jesus Christ cur-rently corrupted in the Hebrew text under the influence of the Talmud and ancient Rabbis, and cri-tical remarks on the Samaritans' Pentateuch".

cui cunjuncta est dissertatio de literis Hebraeorum vocalibus et earum usu. 2° Ad-notationes in translationem Pentateuchi hebraei samariticam. 3° De samariticis Legis sectionibus colis, periodis, aliisque notulis. 4° Quae veterum grammaticorum de punctorum autoribus sententia. 5° Variae lectiones ex antiquis textus hebraeo-samaritani codicibus collectae... 6° Lexicon samaritanum omnes dictiones difficiles explicans.[25]

Although, from the start of his long career, Morin somewhat downplayed his ideas on the specificity of the 'Samaritan language' and admitted that "at most, it is but a mere dialect of classical Aramaic", one should not overlook the general perspective of the work: "with a deceptively serene air, the bulk of the work is devoted to disparaging the vowel-marks and other corruptions introduced by the rabbis in Hebrew writing".[26] While accepting that this is quite commonplace, AUVRAY also discerns a "questionable apologetic", even if, ultimately, a year before his death, Morin re-edited his *Exercitationes biblicae* under the title *Exercitationum biblicarum de hebraei graecique textus sinceritate...* In this he relies on contributions of Jewish authors, and shows, according to Richard Simon, a prodigious erudition with regard to Jewish books.

More specifically, the judgment of the author of the *Histoire Critique du Vieux Testament* can help us appreciate the work of Morin, despite his relentless attacks against this work. He says: "No one has written more on biblical criticism, nor with more erudition, than Fr. Morin, of the Oratory. Since he has today a great number of followers who follow his opinions blindly and without having examined them thoroughly, it is fitting that we examine them in greater detail...".

Beginning with his first publications, "he worked on his ambition... to undermine, as far as possible, the present Hebrew text in order to augment the value of the Septuagint version and the Hebrew Pentateuch of the Samaritans. He argued that the Hebrew text of the Jews was corrupt in most of the places where it differs from the Greek version of the Septuagint, the Hebrew copy of the Samaritans and even the Vulgate. He thought that in so doing, he was doing the Church a great service by defending by all possible means the ancient versions it had approved by a long use. But he may not have been aware that the Church, in authorizing the old version of the Septuagint and the new translation by St. Jerome, never pretended to condemn the Hebrew text, nor did it accuse the Jews of having corrupted it".[27]

With regard to the apologetic of Morin and his criticism of both Protestants and Jews, Simon's reaction may be said to mark definitively the evolution of a state of mind. "Therefore, Fr. Morin's opinion should be tempered, where, under the pretence of defending the authority of old translations received by a long use in the Church, he has done everything possible to destroy the authority of the Hebrew text as the Jews have given it to us. There is a necessary intermediate position between this position and that of the Protestants he is fighting, whereby justice will be meted out to Jews and Christians, to Catholic doctors and the wisest Protestants, who never pretended that the Hebrew copies of today were flawless. If one should submit entirely, as suggested by Fr. Morin, to the Greek version of the Septuagint because the Church and the Apostles approved it, and yet the same Apostles did not deem useful to produce a new one, why was St. Jerome's new translation received so favorably, which Fr. Morin also alleges one should adhere to because the same Church

---

[25] "Hebrew-Semitic booklets, 1° Samaritan Grammar, to which is attached a dissertation on the Hebrew vowels and their usage. 2° Remarks on the Samaritan translation of the Hebrew Pentateuch. 3° On the Samaritan section of the Law, its divisions, its periods and other remarks. 4° The view of the ancient grammarians on the authors of punctuation (or vocalization). 5° Variant readings gathered in the ancient manuscripts of the Hebrew-Samaritan codices... 6° Samaritan lexicon giving an explanation of all difficult expressions".

[26] Auvray, *RB* 66 (1959) 405.

[27] *Histoire Critique* (1685) 464.

deems it absolutely flawless?... Hence, Fr. Morin's system cannot be defended without falling into an infinity of contradictions".[28]

One can accept that both Fr. Morin's position and his polemics against the Protestants and especially against the Jews show that his arguments are so entwined that they mutually contradict each other or become inconsistent. AUV-RAY's judgment on Fr. Morin's getting lost in biblical criticism has already been mentioned, whereas several of his works prove the temper of a real theologian rather than an exegete. Nonetheless, it would be far-fetched and even perhaps out-of-date to reduce Fr. Morin's exegetical work to a polemical game, despite the narrowness of his positions and the often questionable character of his apologetic.

There is a letter by him to the Protestant scholar Louis Cappel, dated 11 March 1647, which is mainly motivated by the answer to a previous letter:

> A few days ago, your honorable son delivered a letter to me on your behalf, in which you thank me for some favors I had done for you: there was no need to thank me in that respect, as two quite strong considerations encouraged me to do what I did, one being the truth you defend in the position shown in your writings, the other being your own merit and renown that you have justly acquired for yourself among those whose profession is letters; as for the rest of what you ask me, I shall always do it with affection and sincerity whenever the occasion occurs.[29]

In his long, erudite letter wherein Morin confirmed his positions on the Septuagint and the Massoretic text, he shared his ideas and information with someone with whom he knew he shared certain convictions and certain theoretical positions. But what should be remembered is the expression used here by Morin concerning those "whose profession is letters". Regardless of his first anti-Protestant intentions, which only belonged to the commonplace opinions of Catholic apologetic of the time, his approach to texts and his attachment to languages showed a spirit that we would attribute to a critical and scientific mind. In that sense, he is not as far from Richard Simon as might appear, a position which Simon himself did not definitively challenge.

Any researcher in biblical science who shared his ideas and opinions demonstrating a certain rigor would thereby be recognized by Morin as a respectable colleague, even if he were Protestant. And even with regard to Judaism, as mentioned above, he also became able at the end of his life to appraise the positive contribution made by Jewish authors.

*

As we mentioned regarding Bonfrère and Lapide, an actual "Republic of Letters" was established in the first half of the seventeenth century. This 'republic' was capable of transcending differences of confession with the still vivid memories of the wars of religion and in an immediate context where polemic and sometimes acts of persecution or war, in France and England especially, marked the relations between these confessions and the civil power.

Although Richard Simon has been evoked on several occasions, notwith-

---

[28] Ibid. 465 f.
[29] *Antiquitates Ecclesiae Orientalis...* (Londini 1682) Epist. LXXII, p. 399.

standing his controversial exaggerations, we should note the extent to which the author of the *Histoire Critique du Vieux Testament* took his forebears into account in the research he was undertaking. He showed considerable respect towards them, but especially as he definitively marked a point of no-return in biblical criticism. At that time, i.e., the last third of the seventeenth century, the doctrinal quarrels, in particular between Protestants and Catholics, in the biblical field at least, began to diminish, even if Simon himself defended his critical positions by asserting that they could not reinforce the Catholic doctrine of Tradition that integrates the constitution of the Scriptures. The issue was no longer doctrine in the strict sense. Nor was it only textual criticism; the issue was a double evaluation of literal meaning and historical questions.

Altogether, the three authors that we have examined show that they distanced themselves from anti-Protestant polemic, by adhering to shared opinions that soon only survived in theology as such. The controversy continued to diminish until it disappeared completely in the eighteenth century in the exchanges between biblical scholars of both confessions, and from one nation to another, as shown, e.g., in 1753, by the success of *Conjectures on Genesis* by Jean Astruc,[30] in Germany, Sweden and France alike, with Catholic and Protestant alike, with the risk that in the nineteenth century and the beginning of the twentieth, the new Catholic exegetes fell under strong suspicion by the authorities of their own Church. Not only was a "Republic of Letters" established, but even more so a scientific community took its place. As far as can be established, the authors that have been examined are already witnesses of such a community – naturally, within the limits of their time and their own intelligence, since none of them really is what one could call a 'great mind'. In this regard, it was necessary to wait for people like Spinoza and Richard Simon, but also, and that is the law of culture, another era, even if such a new era should not forget what it owes to its predecessor, viz. the first half of the seventeenth century, and the authors that graced it by their works, notwithstanding their limits.[31]

---

[30] Cf. the recent reprint: *Conjectures sur la Genèse*. Introduction et notes de Pierre Gibert (Paris 1999).

[31] The text has been translated by Nicolas Steeves and the Latin citations by Louis Neyrand and William Fennelly.

CHAPTER THIRTY

The Polyglot Bibles of Antwerp, Paris and London: 1568–1658

By ADRIAN SCHENKER, Fribourg, CH

Bibliography (see also the Bibliography of Chap. 12 above): J.-R. ARMOGATHE (ed.), *Le grand siècle et la Bible* (BTT 6; Paris: Beauchesne 1989); M. BAILLET, "Samaritains: manuscrits", DBS XI (1991) 881–83; V. BARON, *La contre-réforme devant la Bible. La question biblique* (Lausanne 1943; repr. Genève: Slatkine 1986); M. BATAILLON, *Erasme et l'Espagne* (Nouvelle éd. en trois volumes; Travaux d'humanisme et de renaissance 250; Genève: Droz 1991) 1, 781–87; 2, 311–15 (notes); G. BEDOUELLE / B. ROUSSEL (eds.), *Le temps des Réformes et la Bible* (BTT 5; Paris: Beauchesne 1989); S. BERGER, *La Bible au XVIe siècle. Etude sur les origines de la critique biblique* (Paris 1879; repr. Genève: Droz 1969); A. BERTHOLET (B. J. ROBERTS), "Polyglotten", RGG 5 (³1961) 447–48; T. H. DARLOW / H. F. MOULE, *Historical Catalogue of the Printed Editions of Holy Scripture...II. Polyglots and Languages other than English* (London: The British and Foreign Bible Society 1911; repr. Cambridge, MA: Maurizio Martino-Publisher, s.a.); W. A. COPINGER, *The Bible and Its Transmission Being an Historical and Bibliographical View...* (London: Henry Sotheran 1897; repr. Leipzig: Zentralantiquariat 1972); L. DEQUEKER / F. GISTELINCK, *Biblia vulgata Lovaniensis 1547–1574* (Leuven: Bibliotheek van de Faculteit der Godgeleerdheid 1989); N. FERNÁNDEZ MARCOS / E. FERNÁNDEZ TEJERO (eds.), *Biblia y Humanismo. Textos, talantes y controversias del siglo XVI español* (Madrid: FUE 1997); N. FERNÁNDEZ MARCOS, "El tratado *De arcano sermone* de Arias Montano", in: idem / eadem, Biblia y Humanismo (1997) 177–84; idem, "La edición de textos bíblicos en España", in: idem / eadem, Biblia y Humanismo (1997) 261–73; idem, "La polémica entorno a la Biblia Regia de Arias Montano", in: idem / eadem, Biblia y Humanismo (1997) 229–38; N. FERNÁNDEZ MARCOS / E. FERNÁNDEZ TEJERO, "De '*Elteqeh* a *Hita*: Arias Montano, traductor de topónimos", in: E. ROMERO (ed.), *Estudios en memoria de José Luis Lacave Riaño* (Madrid: CSIC 2002) 255–64; E. FERNÁNDEZ TEJERO, "Benedicti Ariae Montani ... *De Mazzoreth ratione atque vsv*", in: Fernández Marcos / Fernández Tejero, Biblia y Humanismo (1997) 155–60; E. FERNÁNDEZ TEJERO, "Cipriano de la Huerga, Luis de León y Benito Arias Montano: Tres Hombres, tres talantes", in: L. GÓMEZ CANSECO (ed.), *Anatomía del Humanismo: Benito Arias Montano 1598–1998* (Huelva 1998) 181–200; A. VON GALL, *Der hebräische Pentateuch der Samaritaner* (Giessen: A. Töpelmann 1918); S. L. GREENSLADE (ed.), *The West from the Reformation to the Present Day* (CHB 3; Cambridge: UP 1963); S. KESSLER MESGUICH, "Les hébraïsants chrétiens", BTT 6 (1989) 83–95; J. LE LONG, *Bibliotheca Sacra in binos syllabos distincta, quorum prior qui iam tertio auctior prodit, omnes sive textus sacri sive Versionum ejusdem ... Editiones ... exhibet* 1 (Paris 1723) 1–47; J. E. MANGENOT, "Polyglottes", DB 5 (1912) 513–29; E. NESTLE (E. REUSS), "Polyglottenbibeln", RE 15 (³1904) 528–35; G. MOROCHO GAYO, "Felipe II: las ediciones liturgicas y la *Biblia Real*", *La Ciudad de Dios* 211 (1998) 813–82; F. PEREZ CASTRO, "La 'Biblia regia' de Arias Montano, monumento de ecumenismo humanista en la España del siglo XVI", in: F. PEREZ CASTRO / L. VOET, *La Biblia Políglota de Amberes* (Madrid: FUE 1973) 11–34; idem, "Biblias Políglotas", Gran Enciclopedia Rialp 2 (Madrid: FUE 1979) 178–85; K. REINHARDT, *Bibelkommentare spanischer Autoren (1500–1700)* I-II (Madrid: CSIC 1990, 1999); B. REKERS, *Benito Arias Montano (1527–1598)* (SWI 33; London: Warburg Institute University of London / Leiden: Brill 1972) 45–69; E. REUSS, "Polyglottenbibeln", RE 12 (1860) 20–28; A. ROEDIGER, *De origine et indole Arabicae Librorum V.T. Historicorum Interpretationis libri duo* (Halle: Libraria Kuemmeliana 1829) 66–70; J.-P. ROTHSCHILD, "Autour du Pentateuque samaritain. Voyageurs, enthousiastes et savants", BTT 6 (1989) 61–74; B. ROUSSEL, "Recueil du savoir: la 'Polyglotte d'Anvers'", BTT 5 (1989) 262–69; A.

SCHENKER, "Der alttestamentliche Text der vier grossen Polyglottenbibeln nach dem heutigen Stand der Forschung", *ThRv* 90 (1994) 177–88; idem, "Polyglottenbibeln", TRE 27 (1997) 22–25; R. SIMON, *Histoire critique du Vieux Testament* (Nouvelle édition, et qui est la première imprimée sur la copie de Paris …; Rotterdam: chez Reinier Leers 1685; repr. Genève: Droz 1971) 514–22; CH. F. SCHNURRER, "De Pentateucho arabico Polyglotto", in: idem, *Dissertationes philologicae-criticae* (Gotha: Ettinger 1790) 191–238, 501–04; M. V. SPOTTORNO, "The Textual Significance of Spanish Polyglot Bibles", *Sef.* 62 (2002) 375–92; M. VAN DURME, "Granvelle e Plantin", *Estudios dedicados a Menéndez y Pidal* 7,1 (Madrid: CSIC 1957) 225–73, esp. 239–45; L. VOET, "La Bible polyglotte d'Anvers et Benedictus Arias Montanus. L'histoire de la plus grande entreprise scripturaire et typographique du XVIe siècle", in: F. PEREZ CASTRO / L. VOET, *La Biblia políglota* (Madrid: FUE 1973) 35–53; J. C. WOLF, *Bibliothecae Hebraeae P. II. quae praeter historiam Scripturae Sacrae Veteris Instrumenti, codicumque eius, tum editorum tum mss. tradit notitiam…* (Hamburg: Felginer 1721; repr. Bologna: Forni editore 1967) 332–64.

1. The Antwerp Polyglot Bible 1568–72

Since the Complutensian polyglot Bible had become scarce (a certain number of copies were lost in a shipwreck between Spain and Italy)[1] and expensive, the French printer Christophe Plantin (1520–1598), who wanted to serve the "Christian republic" through his printing press nourished as early as in the mid-sixties of the sixteenth century the idea of a reprint of the famous polyglot Bible of Alcalá.

Plantin (Plantinus) was born in Tours (France) at about 1520 and came to Antwerp towards 1548–49 as a bookbinder. In 1555 he installed there his own printer's shop. By means of the capital of the Protestant Van Bomberghen family it developed soon into the most important printing house in the Netherlands and beyond.[2] Because of his ties with Protestants favorable to the insurrection of 1566 against the Spanish government of the Netherlands Plantin feared for his person and his enterprise. That is why he looked for mighty protectors at home and in Spain. He happened to become acquainted with the influential secretary of Philip II, Gabriel de Zayas, who had lived in the Netherlands in 1555–59. Entering in epistolary relations with him in 1566, he at once propounded to him his plan of a new edition of the *Complutensis* of which he had produced sample sheets for the fair of Frankfort 1566. In 1567 de Zayas reported to Plantin that the king himself was much interested. Philip provided the sum of 12.000 fl, which he later increased up to 21.500 fl. In return Plantin had to furnish to the king, once the work completed, 13 copies printed on vellum and 129 copies on paper, while Philip II granted him in return the monopoly of all liturgical books to be printed for Spain according to the norms of the Council of Trent.[3] 1568 the king appointed as chief editor a theologian and humanist which Plantin did not know yet personally, Benito (Benedictus) Arias Montano (1527–98).[4] Montano, a learned Orientalist, 1562–63 expert at

---

[1] Fernández Tejero, Benedicti Ariae Montani (1997) 156.
[2] Voet, Bible polyglotte d'Anvers (1973) 36–37.
[3] Ibid. 40–41, 52–53.
[4] Reinhardt, Bibelkommentare (1990) 30–42; Rekers, Arias Montano (1972).

the council of Trent, had been appointed chaplain to the king in 1566. 1576–
78 he was librarian at the Escorial. His preference went towards a simple
Christian faith based on Scripture, free of scholastic theology and mighty
Church structures, close to the ideals of the *familia charitatis* in Flanders which
was dear to the French Orientalist Guillaume Postel. Montano was charged by
the king with several diplomatic missions as well. He possibly inspired Philip
II to act as a Maecenas for the planned polyglot Bible.[5] Plantin and Montano
became close friends during their co-operation in Antwerp, 1568–72.

The Bible whose title runs as follows: *Biblia sacra Hebraice, Chaldaice,
Graece, Latine*, is in eight volumes in folio, which needed only four years to be
printed between 17th May 1568 (date when Arias Montano arrived in Antwerp) and 9th June 1572 in Plantin's printing office.[6] The edition consisted of
1200 copies. Because of war events, it had to be composed twice, a first set of
600 copies before June 1572, the second set not until 1573.[7] Arias Montano
had outstanding Orientalists as collaborators: François Raphelengien (Raphe-
lengius, van Ravelingen), Plantin's son-in-law, who reviewed the Bible of
Sanctes (Santes, Xantes) Pagninus (1470–1541)[8], reproduced in volume 6 of
the *Biblia Regia*, an edition of the original Bible texts with an interlinear Latin
translation, first published in Lyons 1527;[9] he was assisted in his review by his
teacher Guillaume Postel (1510–81). Arias Montano had first projected to replace the Vulgate by the translation of Pagninus, but Philipp II insisted on the
printing of the Vulgate in the same way as it had been presented in the Complutensian Polyglot, because of the outstanding authority of Jerome's translation in the Latin church.[10] Therefore Montano decided to devote a separate
volume to the translation of Pagninus. Another scholar contributing to the
Biblia Regia was the Frenchman Guy Lefèvre de la Boderie (Fabricius Boder-
ianus) (1541–98) with his brother Nicolas (1550–1613). Raphelengien, the
brothers de la Boderie and Postel had already prepared the Syriac New Testament before 1568.[11] Andrew Maes (Andreas Masius) (1514–81) played an important role for the Targums because he had rediscovered by chance in Rome
the Targum Jonathan of the historical and prophetic books which Alfonso de
Zamora had compiled in view of its edition in the Complutension Polyglot,
where they had been discarded, however, by a decision of Cisneros.[12]

Augustin Hunnaeus, Cornelius Reyner of Gouda, the Jesuit Jan Willems
(Jan Harlem) (Harlemius), divines of the University of Louvain, simulta-

---

[5] Bataillon, Erasme (1991) 783.

[6] Voet, Bible polyglotte d'Anvers (1973) 41, 45–46.

[7] Ibid. 45–46. This is the explanation of small differences between certain copies of this Polyglot.

[8] On Sanctes Pagninus see the essay by A. VANDERJAGT, Chap. 7, Sect. 5.2, of this volume.

[9] This Bible (OT and NT) was reprinted by Robert Estienne (Stephanus) in Geneva 1557 and
Paris 1577 and by Plantin in 1564, 1569, 1584, 1588, cf. Copinger, Bible (1897) 255, besides Plantin's printing of it in the Antwerp Polyglot. It was the first Bible with verse numbers which all modern verse numbering is based upon.

[10] Spottorno, Spanish Polyglot Bibles (2002) 389.

[11] Ibid. 388.

[12] Ibid. 381.

neously acted as censors of the new Bible and advisors to Arias Montano.[13] Henri Perrenot Cardinal Granvella (1517–86), Archbishop of Malines and counselor of Margareth of Parma, vice-regent of the Netherlands, had compiled manuscripts in Rome for the polyglot Bible, and Cardinal Guglielmo Sirleto (1514–85), Frans Lucas van Brugge (Lucas Brugensis; François Luc) (1549–1619), divine of Louvain, and others assisted Montano as well in his editorial task. But Arias Montano checked himself every page of the Bible. The papal approval was granted by pope Gregory XIII in 1572 against strong opposition on the part of adversaries of the humanistic and linguistic approach of the *Biblia Regia*. The *apparatus sacer* was placed in the *Index librorum prohibitorum* of 1607 and 1612.[14]

The first goal of the *Biblia Regia* was an improved and enlarged reedition of the Complutensian Bible. The comprehensive apparatus of volumes 7 and 8 of the *Biblia Regia* shows that the didactic purpose of Cisneros was maintained and enlarged by Arias Montano. The Antwerp Polyglot was to be not only a compendium of the original texts, but also of biblical learning. Volumes 1–4 are devoted to the Old Testament: Pentateuch, Joshua-2 Chronicles, Ezra-Sirach, Prophets (Jeremiah with Lamentations, Baruch, Epistle of Jeremiah; Daniel with the Greek additions in Daniel 3 and Daniel 13–14), 1-2 Maccabees (Greek text with a new Latin translation and Vulgate), and 3 Maccabees in Greek with Latin translation. The texts are displayed on both pages. On the left hand page the MT occupies the first (or exterior) column while the Vulgate is printed as the second or inward column of the same page. The right hand page is arranged in two columns as well. The outward (right) column containing the Septuagint faces its Latin translation, printed in italics as the inward (left) column. The Targums are set in much smaller types. Their vocalized text is to be found at the bottom of the left hand page while its Latin translation is facing it on the right hand page. These Latin translations are due to Alfonso de Zamora[15] and were revised by Arias Montano. There is no Targum for 1-2 Chronicles, Ezra-Nehemiah, Daniel. In the display of the Aramaic text, the traditional paragraph division (*petuhot, setumot*) is observed. The whole Old Testament reads from left to right in the way of occidental books. This was the case in the Complutensian Polyglot as well. In the section of the deuterocanonical (apocryphal) books and additions of Daniel and Esther each page is divided in three columns with, from left to right, Vulgate, Septuagint, Latin translation of the latter. As for the *Oratio Manasse* at the end of 2 Chronicles and for 3-4 Ezra after Ezra-Nehemiah, they are printed in Latin only. No *masorah*, neither for the MT nor for Targum Onkelos, is printed. However, in the apparatus, vol. 7 and 8, Arias Montano composed an explanatory chapter on it: *De varia in Hebraicis libris lectione ac de Mazzoreth ratione atque usu*. The vowel and accent signs (*te'amim*), however, are reproduced in the MT. Vol. 5

---

[13] Copinger, Bible (1897) 232. They participated in the critical edition of the Vulgate in Louvain 1574, prepared by Frans Lucas of Brugge.
[14] Fernández Tejero / Fernández Marcos, Polemica (1997) 229–33; Reinhardt, Bibelkommentare I (1990) 34.
[15] Reinhardt, Bibelkommentare II (1999) 416–17.

is devoted to the New Testament in Syriac, Greek and Latin. The unvocalized
Syriac text is placed on the left hand page in the first or exterior (left) column
of the page while its Latin translation occupies the second or inward (right)
column of that same page. On the right hand page, the Greek text is placed in
the exterior (right) column while the Vulgate is facing it in the inward (or left)
column of that page. At the bottom of both the left and right hand pages, in
the very same place corresponding to the Targums in the Old Testament parts
of the Polyglot, there is a vocalized Syriac text in Hebrew characters with Hebrew vowel points. This device allows the readers unfamiliar with unvocalized
Syriac texts to read these aloud and in a correct way. The privileged place of
the Syriac text in the first column of the double page, which reads from left to
right, seems to suggest a ranking of the texts, i.e. the Syriac first because closest to the original form of Jesus' words, the Latin and Greek texts being both
translations. The Syriac New Testament in the *Biblia Regia* ist the *editio princeps.*

Volumes 7 and 8 contain the *apparatus sacer.*[16] Since they were printed without explicit volume number one volume may be quoted for the other. Moreover, the order of the treaties differs in various copies. One part of the *apparatus* is devoted to philological and linguistic matters, such as a Hebrew grammar by Raphelengien, an abridged edition of Pagninus's Hebrew *Thesaurus*,
an Aramaic grammar with an Aramaic-Syriac dictionary by Guy Lefèvre,
Maes' *Peculium Syrorum* (grammar and dictionary), a Greek grammar and
dictionary together with a selection of Aramaic readings discarded from the
Targums printed in the *Biblia Regia*, and a text-critical commentary of the
Targum, all that being the work of Raphelengien. The other volume is a biblical encyclopedia, composed largely by Arias Montano himself: *Liber Joseph,
sive de arcano sermone* (an hermeneutical treatise drawing heavily on Jewish exegesis),[17] a special dictionary of Hebrew verbs, on weights and measures, biblical geography, the tribes of Israel, the allotment of the Promised Land, the
tent of covenant and the priestly garments, the city of Jerusalem, biblical
chronology, a biblical index, the list of canonical books of the Council of
Carthago 400 A.D., Hebrew, Aramaic, Greek and Latin proper names,[18] variants and *masorah* of the Masoretic text. Other authors, such as Guillén Can-
tero, Sirleto, Guy Lefèvre contributed text-critical matters to the Greek Old
Testament and New Testament and to the Vulgate.[19] This encyclopedia was
separately published anew 1593 in Leiden with the title: *Antiquitates Judai-
cae.*[20]

The Hebrew Bible texts were taken over from the *Complutensis*, provided
with vowel points and accents (*te'amim*) and revised according to the two first
rabbinic Bibles of Felix Pratensis (1516–17) and Jacob b. Hayyim (1524–25).

---

[16] Reinhardt, Bibelkommentare I (1990) 34, 37–38; Fernández Marcos / Fernández Tejero,
Biblia y Humanismo (1997) 155–91.
[17] Fernández Marcos, El tratado (1997).
[18] Such lists of proper names already occur in the Complutensian polyglot Bible. For Arias
Montano see Fernández Marcos, 'Elteqeh (2002).
[19] Schenker, Polyglottenbibeln (1994) 182–83.
[20] Roussel, Recueil du savoir (1989) 269.

The text of Targum Onkelos and its Latin translation correspond equally to the text of the Complutensian Polyglot, the Aramaic text in the Antwerp Polyglot being however vocalized. The Targums of the historical and prophetical books (Targum Jonathan) and of most of the Hagiographa were new in the *Biblia Regia*. Arias Montano could make use of the edition prepared by Alfonso de Zamora for the Cisneros Bible (see above). Arias Montano added the vowel points and the division in sections and translated part of these Targums into Latin where the translation did not yet exist. The Greek text of the Old Testament reprints that of the Complutensis. For the New Testament its text makes use of the editions of Robert Estienne (Stephanus) (themselves relying on Erasmus' and the Complutensian editions) and of the New Testament of the Bible of Alcalá.[21] The Vulgate, Old Testament and New Testament, reproduces the text of the Complutensian Bible, but in a revised form, according to the observations of Arias Montanus' advisors of the University of Louvain, authors of the *Biblia Vulgata Lovaniensis* (1574).[22]

2. The Paris Polyglot Bible 1628–45

Some fifty years after the Antwerp polyglot Bible, the need was felt in France of a new edition of it. Among the persons who thought of such a project were Cardinal Jacques-Davy Duperron (1556-1618), Jacques Auguste de Thou (Thuanus) (1553-1617), the librarian of the king, and the French ambassador at Istanbul, François Savary de Brèves (1560-1628). Finally, the initiative to publish the work was taken, however, by an enthusiastic private person, lawyer at the parliament of Paris, Guy Michel Le Jay (Jajus) who alone assumed the huge expenses of the whole enterprise. He was to ruin himself with this undertaking. Cardinal Richelieu wished to take the project under his high protection when it was already well underway. Le Jay, however, declined the offer. Le Jay had no scholar as scientific director of the editorial task.[23]

The whole Bible consists of 9 volumes in large in-folio format (imperial in-folio). Volumes 1-6 are divided in two parts. The printer was Antoine Vitray (Vitré) in Paris. The biblical books did not appear in print according to their biblical order. Some of the volumes bear no date. The title of this polyglot Bible reads: *Biblia 1. Hebraica, 2. Samaritana, 3. Chaldaica, 4. Graeca, 5. Syriaca, 6. Latina, 7. Arabica. Quibus textus originales totius Scripturae Sacrae quorum pars in editione Complutensi, deinde Antverpiensi Regiis sumptibus exstat, nunc integri, ex manuscriptis toto ferè orbe quaesitis exemplaribus, exhibentur. Lutetiae Parisiorum, excudebat Antonius Vitray Regis, Reginae Regentis, & Cleri Gallicani Typographus, 1629-1645.* This Bible was approved by the Assembly of the Gallican Clergy on 24 January 1636.

---

[21] Nestle, Polyglottenbibeln (1904) 532.
[22] Dequeker / Gistelink, Biblia Vulgata Lovaniensis (1989) 23, 27; see also above.
[23] Copinger, Bible (1897) 47–48; Darlow / Moule, Catalogue (1911) 20–22; Nestle, Polyglottenbibeln (1904) 532; Mangenot, Polyglottes (1912) 520–22; Rothschild, Pentateuque samaritain (1989) 63–74; Schenker, Polyglottenbibeln (1994) 183–85.

The collaborators and editors were the following scholars: for the Syriac and Arabic parts the Lebanese Maronites Gabriel Sionita (1577–1648) and Joannes Hesronita had been engaged by Duperron and de Thou since 1614 in order to prepare the Syriac texts for the Old Testament and the Arabic version of the whole Bible, as well as the Latin translations of these texts. Hesronita is the author of the Latin translation of the Arabic Pentateuch. Another Lebanese Maronite, Ibrahim al-Haqilani (Abraham Ecchellensis) (1605–64) joined the work for one year during which he translated the Arabic book of Ruth. The Oratorian Jean Morin, from Blois (1591–1659), a convert from Protestantism, realised the edition of the Samaritan Pentateuch together with the Samaritan Targum. It was Cardinal Bérulle who gave the advice to publish these two texts in their entirety, not only as variants at the bottom of the Masoretic text, as it was first planned. The Samaritan texts appear in the Paris Polyglot without variant readings. Morin published these separately in Paris 1657. Other editors and collaborators were Philippe Aquinas (ca 1575–1650), a convert from Judaism with his former name Yehuda Mordekai of Carpentras (corrector of Hebrew and Aramaic in 1635), two divines of the Sorbonne: Jérôme Parent and Godefroy Hermant (1617–90), further Jean Aubert and Jean Tarin.

The aim of this Bible was to complete what had still been lacking in the two previous polyglot editions (Old Testament in Syriac, the Samaritan Pentateuch and Targum, the Arabic Bible) and, at the same time, to serve an apologetic purpose, i.e., to prove the superior quality of the Vulgate. The scholarly level of such a perspective did not match that of the *Biblia Regia*. At the same time, no *apparatus* was included. Thus the Paris Polyglot restricts itself to the biblical texts without linguistic or historical helps and without further text-critical materials. The scholarly importance of the Paris polyglot Bible is based on its first edition of the Samaritan Pentateuch with its Samaritan Targum, the *editio princeps* of the Old Testament in Syriac and of the whole Bible in Arabic.

Volumes 1–4 reproduce the first four volumes of the Antwerp Polyglot in the same disposition. Vol. 5 contains the New Testament (printed in 1630 and 1633). Its display and text are like that of the Antwerp polyglot Bible in the upper part of the page while, at the bottom of the double page, the Arabic text appears on the left hand and its Latin translation on the right. Volumes 6–9 contain the Samaritan, Syriac and Arabic texts of the Old Testament.

Vol. 6 Pentateuch: Peshitta with Latin translation on the left hand page, Arabic text with Latin translation in front of it on the right hand page, both occupying the upper part of the page. At the bottom of it, both the Samaritan Pentateuch and its Targum on the left hand page, the Targum being placed in the first or left hand column of the page, while the Samaritan Hebrew Pentateuch occupies the right side of the same page. Does this surprising display suggest that the editor, Jean Morin, considered the Samaritan Targum, wich he calls *textus Samaritanus*, to be original, while the Hebrew Samaritan Pentateuch, *textus Hebraeo-Samaritanus* was deemed to be a translation? On the right hand page, at the bottom, one Latin translation faces the two Samaritan texts of the opposite (left hand) page. Further, vol. 7, printed 1642: Joshua-2 Chronicles in the same display of the Syriac on the left and Arabic on the right hand page with their translations; vol. 8 (1635): Ezra-Sirach (3–4 Ezra, additions to Esther, Judith, Tobit, additions to Daniel do not occur); vol. 9 contains Isaiah-Malachi (additions to Daniel only in Arabic), 1 Maccabees-2 Maccabees only in Arabic, however, instead of 2 Maccabees in its canonical form, the Book of Josippon (*Megillat Antiochos*) is printed in Arabic.

The texts are as follows: the Masoretic text, the Targums, the Septuagint and the Vulgate are borrowed from the *Biblia Regia*. As for the Septuagint, surprisingly the editors did not choose the more official Sixto-Clementine edition of Rome 1586–87, nor the new edition of it prepared by Jean Morin 1628 in Paris. The Latin translations of all these versions stem from the Antwerp Polyglot as well. It surprises still more that the Paris Polyglot preferred the Vulgate of the *Biblia Regia* to the official Clementine edition, Rome 1592, although this edition had been declared compulsory for the Catholic Church by Pope Clemens VIII.

The Samaritan Pentateuch of the Paris Polyglot is the *editio princeps*. It is mainly based on a manuscript of the fourteenth century, now in the Bibliothèque Nationale, that Pietro della Valle had purchased 1616 in Damascus, and which was given by Harley de Sancy 1642 to the Oratorians of Paris (manuscript B of the edition of A. Frh. von Gall). But other manuscripts were made use of as well. The Samaritan Targum was also printed for the first time in this polyglot Bible, from another manuscript in possession of della Valle. Thus the Old Testament of the Peshitta and in Arabic were the first printed editions of these texts. The manuscripts which served as sources for the editors are known and exist still in Paris.

The guiding principles of the edition of this polyglot Bible are explained in a short preface in vol. 1: the Samaritan text is considered to be older than the Masoretic text which came about in the time of Ezra; the Targums are significant because of their messianic passages and as clues for obscure phrases in the Hebrew text; the Peshitta of the Old Testament goes back to king Solomon's time, and that of the New Testament to the time of the Apostles; Job and Mark were originally written in Syriac; the Arabic Bible is to be dated into the fourth century. Moreover, the old versions prove the outstanding quality of the Vulgate.

3. The Polyglot Bible of London 1653–57(58)

This Bible consists of six volumes in-folio. Its full title runs as follows: *S.S. BIBLIA Polyglotta Complectentia Textus Originales Hebraicos cum Pent. Samarit: Chaldaicos Graecos. Versionumque Antiquarum Samarit. Graec. Sept. Chaldaic. Syriacae. Lat. Vulg. Arabicae. Aethiopic. Persicae Quicquid comparari poterat. Ex M.SS. Antiquiss: undique conquisitis optimisque Exemplaribus impressis summa fide collatis. Edidit Brianus Waltonius. S.T.D.* It was published in London 1653–58 (although the printed date on the front page is 1657).[24] It is the largest Polyglot Bible as far as the number of texts and versions assembled therein is concerned. It is the most widely used polyglot Bible until today. It

---

[24] Copinger, Bible (1897) 49–50; Darlow / Moule, Catalogue (1911) 23–26; Nestle, Polyglottenbibeln (1904) 532f; Mangenot, Polyglottes (1912) 522–24; Schenker, Polyglottenbibeln (1994) 185–88; Kessler Mesguich, Hébraïsants (1989) 91f.

contains a large number of introductions and text-critical materials which continue the idea of an organon for students of Holy Scripture present at the very origin of printed polyglot Bible editions. That is why the Lexicon hepta-glotton of Edmund Castell in two volumes, London 1669, was conceived as a supplement for this Bible and as the linguistic achievement of the London Polyglot.

Its editor, Brian (Bryan) Walton (c. 1600–61), bishop of Chester in 1660, prepared his polyglot Bible since 1645, encouraged by the learned archbishop of Armagh, James Ussher (1561–1656). The London Polyglot Bible, by the way, was the first book to have been sold to subscribers to the whole work before its realization.

He had a large staff of collaborators at his disposition: Edmund Castell (Castellus) (1606–85), professor of Arabic in Cambridge, was responsible for the Samaritan, Syriac, Arabic, Ethiopic texts, Samuel Clarke (Clericus) (1623–69), librarian of the Bodleian, preparing the Masoretic text, the Targum and translating the Persian Gospels into Latin, Thomas Greaves (Gravius) (1612–76), Alexander Huish (Huyssius) (c. 1594–1668) in charge of the Septuagint, Vulgate and of the collation of the Alexandrinus, Thomas Hyde (Hydius) (1636–1703), co-operating as a student and transcribing the Persian Pentateuch of the Constantinople polyglot Bible of 1546 from Hebrew into Arabic characters, corrector of the Syriac, Arabic, Persian portions, John Lightfoot (1602–1675), revisor of the Samaritan Pentateuch, Dudley Loftus (1609–95), Edward Pococke (1604–91), Herbert Thorndike (1598–1672) and other collaborators.

This polyglot Bible edition was to complete and to improve the preceding editions of Antwerp and Paris. All texts used by Jews, Samaritans and old Christian Churches (except Coptic, Armenian and Georgian) were presented in a practical display, together with collections of variant readings and other textual informations and a dictionary of seven languages. Thus it became the most complete of all polyglot Bibles.

The first volume (1653) corresponds to an introduction into the Holy Scripture, valuable until today (table of contents, preface by Walton, treatises on chronology by Louis Capelle [1585–1658] and Lightfoot, numismatics by Edward Brerewood and Walton, weights and measures, Hebrew idiomatic expressions, geography of the Holy Land by Lightfoot and Jacques Bonfrère [1573–1642] etc., prolegomena on the texts and versions of the Bible by Walton). Then follows the Pentateuch, presented in 13 separate sections, from left to right on the double page of the open book: on the left hand page Masoretic text of the Sixth Rabbinic Bible of Buxtorf (Basel 1618–19) with the interlinear Latin translation of Sanctes Pagninus borrowed from the Antwerp polyglot Bible, Vulgate (Clementine editions of 1592, 1593 and 1598), Septuagint of the Sixto-clementine edition of 1628 by Jean Morin with the Latin translation of Peter Morinus (1531–1608) and the variant readings of codex Alexandrinus, at the bottom the Syriac version of the Paris Polyglot with the Latin translation of Sionita, but corrected by Walton. On the right hand page Targum Onkelos according to the Bible edition of Buxtorf with a Latin translation, the Samaritan Pentateuch with a Latin translation as well, the Samaritan text being that of the polyglot Bible of Paris, finally the Samaritan Targum with a partial Latin translation for passages where the Hebrew and Aramaic Samaritan texts differ. At the bottom of the page the Arabic Pentateuch taken over from the Paris Polyglot with Latin translation.

Vol. 2 (1655) Joshua – 2 Chronicles, Ezra-Nehemiah, Esther. It has the same display, instead of Targum Onkelos Targum Jonathan. Chronicles, Ezra-Nehemiah are without Targum (of course, no Samaritan texts).

Vol. 3 (1656) Hagiographa, prophets. For Psalms and Canticles the Ethiopic text is added, reproducing the edition of Psalms, Hymns, Prayers, Canticles, by Johannes Potken, Rome 1513 (first ever printed Ethiopic text).[25] For Esther in Syriac, Walton and his co-editors supplied the Syriac text on the base of Syriac manuscripts in England.

Vol. 4 (1657) Apocryphal or Deuterocanonical books. These books were furnished as fascicles and could be bound at the places the buyer of the whole Bible would prefer. In addition to the Deuterocanonical books, received as canonical by the Roman-catholic Church, there were included: 1 (3) Ezra; 4 Ezra in the Vulgate; Tobit with two Latin translations by Paul Fagius (1504–49) and Sebastian Münster (1484–1552); 3 Maccabees; instead of 2 Maccabees in Arabic there is an Arabic translation of Josippon (from the Paris Polyglot). Several apocryphal books which did not occur in Syriac in the Paris polyglot Bible were added in Syriac in the London Polyglot. In the same volume are placed the Targum Pseudo-Jonathan and the Targum Jerushalmi (*Fragmententargum*) and the Persian Pentateuch, all three with a Latin rendering. The Persian Pentateuch was that of the polyglot Pentateuch of Constantinople of 1546 and 1547.[26]

Vol. 5 contains the New Testament. The Greek text is that of the Paris 1550 edition of Estienne (the folio edition, called *Regia*), which corresponds to the fifth edition of Erasmus from 1535. The Latin interlinear translation is that of Arias Montano. The variants of codex Alexandrinus are added. On the left hand page there are placed, in the Gospels, in addition to the Greek, the Syriac and Persian texts, while the Vulgate, the Arabic, the Ethiopic and the Persian occupy the right hand page. In the rest of the New Testament the Persian text is not given.

Vol. 6 is textcritical in nature since it offers a large number of various collations and annotations. Among the authors of these textual and exegetical materials are, in addition to the contributors already mentioned above, Frans Lucas from Bruges (1549–1619), Hugo Grotius (1583–1643), Patrick Young (Junius) (1584–1652), Petrus Morinus (1531–1608), who is erroneously quoted, however, as Flaminius Nobilius from Lucca, and many others. Moreover, this volume contains the indexes and various useful lists, e. g. Ketiv-Qere, *hillufim* between Ben-Asher and Ben-Naftali, the reading sections of the Pentateuch (*parashyot*) and of the former and later prophets (*haftarot*) and others.

The London Polyglot Bible remained until today a much used source for Bible texts, especially for the Samaritan and Syriac texts. The quality of these texts of course depends on that of their sources. Moreover, its systematic translation of all presented texts gave the reader a key to the use of all these,

---

[25] Cf. Joh. Potken, *Psalterium in quatuor linguis, Hebraea, Graeca, Chaldaea, Latina...*(Cologne 1518; in reality, the third language is not Aramaic, but Ethiopic).

[26] On the two Jewish polyglot Pentateuch editions of Constantinople of 1546 and 1547 cf. Mangenot, Polyglottes (1912) 524.

even though he might have no first hand knowledge of some of the languages. This added a supplementary pedagogical value to the whole work. These philological and pedagogical qualities may explain why no new polyglot edition of the same scale was to be attempted after the publication of this large edition, at least until the *Biblia Polyglotta Matritensia* in the middle of the twentieth century. But this polyglot Bible corresponds to another conception than the first four Polyglots of the sixteenth and seventeenth centuries.[27] Beyond the limits of this chapter on the four large Polyglots several small or manual polyglot editions of the Bible might be mentioned, produced from the sixteenth century until today. At least one deserves a brief mention: *Biblia Sacra quadrilingua ... accurante M. Christiano Reineccio...*, 1–3 (Lipsiae: sumtibus Haeredum Lanckisianorum 1750–51 = vol. 1–2; 1747 = vol. 3 New Testament) because of the quality of its texts in Hebrew, Greek, Latin, Syriac and German.[28] Richard Simon had made plans for a full polyglot Bible which was never realized.[29]

---

[27] Fernández Marcos, Textos bíblicos (1997) 265–73.

[28] Darlow / Moule, Catalogue (1911) 27 f. For many other smaller polyglot Bibles cf. Copinger, Bible (1897) 50–52; Nestle, Polyglottenbibeln (1904) 533–35; Darlow / Moule, Catalogue (1911) 1–36

[29] For a good description of the principal other polyglot Bibles cf. Mangenot, Polyglottes (1912) 524–29.

CHAPTER THIRTY-ONE

Later Christian Hebraists

By STEPHEN G. BURNETT, Lincoln, NE

Sources: JOHANNES BUXTORF the Elder: *Tiberias sive commentarius Masorethicus* (Basel: Ludwig König 1620); *Lexicon chaldaicum talmudicum et rabbinicum* (ed. Johannes Buxtorf the Younger; Basel:
Ludwig König 1639). – JOHANNES BUXTORF the Younger: *Anticritica: seu vindiciae veritatis Hebraicae* (Basel: L. König haeredes 1653). – LOUIS CAPPEL, *Arcanum punctationis revelatum. sive de punctorum vocalium & accentuum apud Hebraeos vero & germana antiquitate, diatriba* (Leiden: Johannes
Maire 1624; Basel UB); *Critica Sacra* (Paris: S. Cramoisy 1650). – CHARLES F. HOUBIGANT, *Biblia
critica cum notis criticis* (Paris 1753–1754); *Notae criticae in universos Veteris Testamenti libros*
(Frankfurt/Main: Varrentrapp Filium & Wenner 1777). – THOMAS ERPENIUS: "Thomas Erpenius
(1584–1624) on the Value of the Arabic Language" (tr. Robert Jones), *Manuscripts of the Middle
East* 1 (1986) 15–25. – JACOB BEN HAYYIM IBN ADONIAH: *Introduction to the Rabbinical Bible, He-
brew and English* (ed. and tr. Chr. D. Ginsburg; London: Longmans, Green, Reader & Dyer
²1867; repr. New York: KTAV 1968). – BENJAMIN KENNICOTT: *The State of the Printed Hebrew
Considered: A Dissertation in Two Parts* (Oxford: Clements and Fletcher 1753); *The Ten Annual
Accounts of the Collation of Hebrew MSS of the Old Testament. Begun in 1760 and compleated in
1769* (Oxford: Fletcher and Prince 1770); *Vetus Testamentum Hebraicum cum variis lectionibus*
(Oxford: Clarendon 1776–80). – ELIAS LEVITA / ELIYAHU ASHKENAZI: מסורת המסורת / *Masoreth
ha-Masoreth* (Venice 1538; ed. Chr. D. Ginsburg; London 1867; repr. New York: KTAV 1968). –
JOHANN HEINRICH MICHAELIS, *Biblia Hebraica ex aliqvot manvscriptis et complvribvs impressis codicibus…recensita… Accedvnt loca Scriptvrae parallela…brevesqve adnotationes* I-II (Halle: Orphano-
tropei 1720). – AZARIAH DE ROSSI: *Me'or Enayim The Light of the Eyes* (tr. Joanna Weinberg; YJS
31; New Haven: Yale UP 2001). – GIOVANNI BERNARDO DE ROSSI: *Variae lectiones Veteris Testamenti* I-IV (Parma: Ex Regio Typographeo 1784–88). – ALBERT SCHULTENS: *Oratio de linguae Arabicae
antiquissima origine intima ac sororia cum lingua Hebraicae affinitate, nullisque seculis praeflorate puritate* (Franeker, Excudit Gulielmus Coulon, Illustr. Frisiae Ordd. Academiae Typogr. Ordinar.
1729); *Vetus et regia via Hebraïzandi* (Leiden: Johannes Luzac 1738); *Opera minora* (Leiden /
Leeuwarden: J. Le Mair & H. A. de Chalmot 1769). – RICHARD SIMON: *Histoire critique du Vieux
Testament* (Paris 1678, Amsterdam 1680; repr. Frankfurt/Main: Minerva 1967). – JOHANN CHRIS-
TOPH WOLF, *Bibliotheca Hebraea, sive notitia tum auctorum Hebraeorum cujuscunque aetatis, tum
scriptorum quae vel Hebraice primum exarata vel ab aliis conversa sunt* I-IV (Hamburg / Leipzig:
Christian Liebzeit 1715–33).

General works: D. BARTHÉLEMY, *Critique textuelle de l'Ancien Testament*, 1. *Josué, Juges, Ruth, Samuel, Rois, Chroniques, Esdras, Néhémie, Esther* (OBO 50/1; Fribourg: Éditions Universitaires /
Göttingen: Vandenhoeck & Ruprecht 1982); E. BREUER, *The Limits of Enlightenment: Jews, Germans and the Eighteenth Century Study of Scripture* (Cambridge, MA / London: Harvard UP
1996); SH. BRISMAN, *A History and Guide to Jewish Bibliography* (Cincinnati / New York: Hebrew
Union College Press / KTAV 1977); J. BRUGMAN, "Arabic Scholarship", in: *Leiden University in
the Seventeenth Century: An Exchange of Learning* (ed. Th. H. Linsingh Scheurleer / G. H. M.
Posthumus Meyjes; Leiden: Brill 1975) 203–15; S. G. BURNETT, *From Christian Hebraism to Jewish
Studies: Johannes Buxtorf (1564–1629) and Hebrew Learning in the Seventeenth-Century* (SHCT
68; Leiden: Brill 1996); idem, "Christian Hebrew Printing in the Sixteenth Century: Printers, Hu-
manism and the Impact of the Reformation", *Helm.* 51 (2000) 13–42; T. DARLOW / H. F. MOULE,
*Historical Catalogue of the Printed Editions of Holy Scripture in the Library of the British and Foreign
Bible Society* 2. *Languages other than English: Greek to OPA* (London: The Bible House 1903); M.

FEINGOLD, "Oriental Studies", in: *The History of Oxford University*, 4. *Seventeenth-Century Oxford* (ed. N. Tyacke; Oxford: Clarendon Press 1997) 449–503; J. FRIEDMAN, *The Most Ancient Testimony: Sixteenth-Century Christian-Hebraica in the Age of Renaissance Nostalgia* (Athens, OH: Ohio UP 1983); J. FÜCK, *Die arabischen Studien in Europa bis in den Anfang des 20. Jahrhunderts* (Leipzig: Otto Harrassowitz 1955); M. GOSHEN-GOTTSTEIN, "Hebrew Biblical Manuscripts: Their History and their Place in the HUBP Edition", *Bib.* 48 (1967) 243–90; idem, "The Textual Criticism of the Old Testament: Rise, Decline, Rebirth", *JBL* 102 (1983) 365–99; A. HAMILTON, "Arabic Studies in the Netherlands in the Sixteenth and Seventeenth Centuries", in: *Philologia Arabica. Arabische studiën en drukken in de Nederlanden in de 16de en 17de eeuw* (Antwerp: Museum Plantin-Moretus 1986) xciv–cxxxi; P. E. KAHLE, *The Cairo Geniza* (2nd edn.; Oxford: Blackwell 1959); J. KALTNER, *The Use of Arabic in Biblical Hebrew Lexicography* (CBQ.MS 28; Washington, DC: Catholic Biblical Association of America 1996); A. L. KATCHEN, *Christian Hebraists and Dutch Rabbis. Seventeenth Century Apologetics and the Study of Maimonides'* Mishne Torah (Cambridge, MA: Harvard UP 1984); E. KAUTZSCH, *Johannes Buxtorf der Ältere* (Basel: C. Detloff 1879); F. LAPLANCHE, *L'Écriture, Le Sacré et L'Histoire: Érudits et Politiques Protestants devant la Bible en France au XVIIe siècle* (Studies of the Institute of Intellectual Relations between the West-European Countries in the Seventeenth Century 12; Amsterdam: APA-Holland UP 1986); F. E. MANUEL, *The Broken Staff: Judaism through Christian Eyes* (Cambridge, MA: Harvard UP 1992); W. McKANE, "Benjamin Kennicott: An Eighteenth-Century Researcher", *JTS* NS 28/2 (1977) 445–64; P. N. MILLER, "The 'Antiquarianization' of Biblical Scholarship and the London Polyglot Bible (1653–57)", *JHI* 62 (2001) 463–82; idem, "Making the Paris Polyglot Bible: Humanism and Orientalism in the Early Seventeenth Century", in: *Die europäische Gelehrtenrepublik im Zeitalter des Konfessionalismus / The European Republic of Letters in the Age of Confessionalism* (ed. H. Jaumann; Wolfenbütteler Forschungen 96; Wiesbaden: Harrassowitz 2001) 59–85; idem, "A Philologist, a traveler, and an antiquary rediscover the Samaritans in Seventeenth Century Paris, Rome, and Aix: Jean Morin, Pietro della Valle and N.-C. Fabri de Peiresc", in: *Die Praktiken der Gelehrsamkeit in der Frühen Neuzeit* (ed. H. Zedelmaier / M. Mulsow; Tübingen: Niemeyer 2001) 123–46; F. MÜHLAU, "Albert Schultens und seine Bedeutung für die hebräische Sprachwissenschaft", *Zeitschrift für die gesammte lutherische Theologie und Kirche* 31 (1870) 1–21; J. NAT, *De Studie van de Oostersche Talen in Nederland in de 18e en de 19e Eeuw* (Purmerend: J. Muusses 1929); PH. DE ROBERT, "La naissance des Etudes Samaritaines en Europe aux XVIe et XVIIe siècles", in: *Études samaritaines Pentateuque et Targum exégèse et philologie, chroniques* (communications présentées à la table ronde internationale: "Les manuscrits samaritains. Problèmes et méthodes", Paris 1985; ed. J.-P. Rothschild / G. D. Sixdenier; Louvain: Peeters 1988) 15–26; B. J. ROBERTS, *The Old Testament Text and Versions. The Hebrew Text in Transmission and the History of the Ancient Versions* (Cardiff: University of Wales Press 1951); D. B. RUDERMAN, *Jewish Enlightenment in an English Key: Anglo-Jewry's Construction of Modern Jewish Thought* (Princeton / Oxford: Princeton UP 2000); B. E. SCHWARZBACH, "Les éditions de la Bible hébraïque au xvie siècle et la création du texte massorétique", in: *La Bible imprimée dans l'Europe moderne* (ed. B. E. Schwarzbach; Paris: BNF 1999) 16–67; E. Tov, *The Text-Critical Use of the Septuagint in Biblical Research* (2nd rev. edn.; Jerusalem: Simor 1997); idem, *Textual Criticism of the Hebrew Bible* (2nd rev. edn.; Minneapolis: Fortress / Assen: Van Gorcum 2001); P. T. VAN ROODEN, *Theology, Biblical Scholarship and Rabbinical Studies in the Seventeenth Century: Constantijn L'Empereur (1591–1648) Professor of Hebrew and Theology at Leiden* (Studies in the History of Leiden University 6; Leiden: Brill 1989); F. P. VAN STAM, *The Controversy over the Theology of Saumur, 1635–1650. Disrupting Debates among the Huguenots in Complicated Circumstances* (Studies of the Institute Pierre Bayle, Nijmegen, 19; Amsterdam: APA-Holland UP 1988); TH. WILLI, "Hebraica veritas in Basel. Christliche Hebraistik aus jüdischen Quellen", in: *Congress Volume Basel 2001* (ed. A. Lemaire; VTSup 92; Leiden: Brill 2002) 375–97.

Christian Hebrew scholarship as an academic discipline was born during the sixteenth century. The founding of chairs of Hebrew language at European universities, the emergence of Hebrew presses to supply the needs of Christian customers, the willingness of some Jewish experts to instruct Christian pupils, and above all the humanist motivation for a return to the sources of the Christian faith together made Hebrew education possible for greater numbers of

Christian scholars than ever before.[1] The majority of these scholars had only a smattering of Hebrew, and those such as Conrad Pellican, and Paul Fagius who could read and understand the Targums and medieval Jewish Bible commentaries were relatively rare. The second edition of the Biblia rabbinica of Bomberg, *Mikra'ot gedolot* (1524–25), contained enough texts and aids to more than meet the needs of most Christian Hebraists, and parts of it such as the Masorah remained a closed book to them.

Over the next two centuries, several remarkable Hebraists developed the conceptual tools to evaluate the received Hebrew Bible text both as a document with a transmission history and a text whose language could also be evaluated in light of other Semitic languages. The two Buxtorfs, father and son, provided the intellectual foundation for these developments by producing scholarly aids in the form of grammars and dictionaries of Hebrew of far higher quality than had been available previously, and above all by publishing a Latin language manual to introduce Christian students to the intricacies of the Masorah. Thanks to his exposure to Arabic, Louis Cappel could conceive of a Semitic language that did not require vowel points to be read and understood. By the end of his career Cappel provided trenchant arguments demonstrating that the paratextual elements of the masoretic text (including its vocalization) could not have been written by the original biblical authors, and therefore only the consonantal text was canonical. Albert Schultens, also a student of Arabic, revolutionized the practice of comparing Hebrew with other Semitic languages by proposing that Hebrew and Arabic were "twin sister" languages, both descendents of the primordial language. By the end of the eighteenth century, Benjamin Kennicott and Giovanni de Rossi would explore the Hebrew Bible manuscript tradition through Europe-wide surveys of biblical manuscripts and by publishing summaries of textual variations present in over a thousand manuscripts and printed Hebrew Bibles. These philological breakthroughs when taken together resulted in the birth of both textual criticism and comparative philology as sub disciplines of biblical studies.

1. The Buxtorfs of Basel

Johannes Buxtorf the Elder (1564–1629) and his equally talented son Johannes Buxtorf the Younger (1599–1664) dominated Hebrew scholarship in their own times and throughout the seventeenth century. Their influence upon biblical scholarship would continue for centuries after their death. EMIL KAUTZSCH, during his inaugural lecture as professor of Old Testament at the University of Basel, praised a number of Buxtorf's works and recommended them to his hearers since he himself used them in his own scholarship.[2]

According to one scholarly witticism the two Buxtorfs were as much alike as two eggs, and they indeed shared many of the same responsibilities and per-

---

[1] Burnett, Christian Hebrew Printing in the Sixteenth Century (2000) 13–42.
[2] Kautzsch, Johannes Buxtorf der Ältere (1879) 7–9.

spectives.[3] Both were professors of Hebrew at the University of Basel, holding the chair in succession from 1591–1664, both were firmly convinced of the value of Jewish biblical scholarship for Christian concerns, and both were involved in scholarly controversies with Louis Cappel over the transmission and integrity of the Hebrew Bible text. The elder Buxtorf wrote works related to Hebrew studies in four different areas: grammars, lexicons and manuals for students and experts, works devoted to the Hebrew Bible text, a bibliography of Jewish books, and books on Jews and Judaism. Apart from his Talmudic lexicon, Buxtorf's grammatical and lexical works can best be characterized as incremental improvements over their predecessors, and because of their obvious quality they were frequently reprinted.[4] Significantly, Buxtorf the Elder did not know Arabic and never made a serious effort to learn it, but focused all of his attention on the resources of Jewish scholarship for understanding obscure linguistic features of the Hebrew Bible text.[5]

The elder Buxtorf's works relating to the biblical text itself were fundamental contributions to biblical scholarship since no Christian scholar before him was so concerned with the work of the Masoretes, especially the vocalization of the biblical text, "paratextual elements" and the masoretic apparatus.[6] As a companion volume to the *Biblia rabbinica* Buxtorf published *Tiberias* (1620), the first comprehensive guide to the masoretic apparatus ever written for a non-Jewish audience. Buxtorf devoted the first part of the book to an historical account of the composition of the Masorah, together with a refutation of Elias Levita's post-talmudic dating of the vowel points and Masorah in his *Masoret ha-Masoret* (1538). He provided the generally accepted argument for the position that the vowel points dated from the biblical age, no later than the "Great Synagogue" of Ezra, Nehemiah and their fellow contemporary prophets. Buxtorf based his position largely upon evidence drawn from Jewish tradition, including arguments advanced by Jacob ben Hayyim in his introduction to the rabbinical Bible (1524–25) and by Azariah de Rossi in *Me'or Enayim / The Light of the Eyes.*[7] He was especially impressed with the witness of the kabbalistic literature to the antiquity of the vowel points, not knowing that both *Bahir* and the *Zohar* dated from the period after the Masoretes. By affirming the prophetic origin of the pointed text Buxtorf argued that the vowel points were a part of the canonical biblical text, thus protecting the clarity of biblical revelation. The remainder of the book was a Latin guide to the Masorah, its parts (parva, marginalis, magna), its abbreviations, Qere-Ketib, and so on.[8] Buxtorf's *Tiberias* was an indispensable guidebook for the technical study and evaluation of not only printed Bibles, but also of biblical manuscripts. Ironically, the book also provided Louis Cappel with the information and insights that were essential for his refutation first of the antiquity of the vowel points in

---

[3] *Non ovum ovo similius, quam Buxtorfius pater et filius*, ibid. 18, n. 3.
[4] Kautzsch, ibid.
[5] Burnett, Christian Hebraism (1996) 127.
[6] Tov, Textual Criticism (2001) 23, 49–67.
[7] Ben Hayyim, Introduction to the Rabbinical Bible (1867); Azariah de Rossi, The Light of the Eyes (2001) 699–709.
[8] Burnett, Christian Hebraism (1996) 216–28.

Arcanum punctationis revelatum (1624) and later for his book on textual criticism *Critica sacra* (1650).

The younger Buxtorf had already established himself as a Hebraist of note, even before the death of his father. He published his first book, a lexicon of Syriac, in 1622. By the late 1620's the younger Buxtorf was working closely with his father, preparing several of his books for reprinting. When the elder Buxtorf died in 1629, the younger Buxtorf took upon himself the responsibility of completing his father's unfinished works, first his Bible concordance (1632) and then ultimately his *Lexicon chaldaicum talmudicum et rabbinicum* (1639–40). The last of these works is justly the elder Buxtorf's most celebrated book. Apart from honoring his father's memory and legacy, Buxtorf the Younger made his own mark in Hebrew studies. He translated both Maimonides' *The Guide of the Perplexed* (1629), and Judah Halevi's *Kuzari* (1660) from medieval Hebrew translations into Latin. He also made extensive use of Jewish biblical commentaries in his teaching and in the disputations he conducted, especially those of Isaac Abarbanel.[9] Buxtorf the Younger is best remembered, however, as the upholder of his father's position on the age of the vowel points and the overall integrity of the Hebrew text in his decade long scholarly battle with Louis Cappel.

2. Louis Cappel and the Birth of Textual Criticism

Perhaps the most important new insight into the biblical text gained by Christian Hebraists in the seventeenth century, was that the Hebrew Bible text had a transmission history and that it was subject to the same kinds of textual corruption as secular texts. Some Hebraists also came to believe that the Hebrew language itself had experienced change over time and had to be analyzed by comparison with other Semitic languages in order to be understood properly. Both of these insights grew out of the work of Joseph Scaliger and Thomas Erpenius, professors at the University of Leiden in the early seventeenth century.[10] Their insights would be refined further by other scholars who either taught or studied in Leiden, Paris and at Oxford over the course of the next century. In these three places biblical and Semitic language scholarship reached what PETER MILLER has termed a "critical mass of erudition", comprising scholars who were well versed in "oriental" languages, well-stocked libraries, and specialized printing facilities, all of which were supported financially by well-disposed patrons.[11] Louis Cappel, who studied Arabic and Hebrew at both Oxford and Leiden, was one of the first Christian Hebraists to apply these new philological and textual approaches to biblical studies.

Cappel was one of the central figures in early modern biblical scholarship, yet he has still not been the subject of a scholarly biography. He is best known

---

[9] On Abarbanel see E. LAWEE in Chap. 8 of the present volume.
[10] Brugman. Arabic Scholarship (1975) 203–15.
[11] Miller, Making the Paris Polyglot Bible (2001) 85.

for two books, already mentioned, *Arcanum punctationis revelatum* (1624), which was published at the very beginning of his career, and *Critica sacra* (1650), published less than a decade before his death. Cappel wrote *Arcanum* (which he published anonymously) to be a direct refutation of Buxtorf's position on the age of the vowel points. As Levita had done a century earlier,[12] Cappel adduced arguments both from history and philology to support his point of view. He pointed out that Jews had always used unvocalized texts in synagogue worship and that the vowel points themselves were never mentioned in Jewish literature before the Talmud. His principal arguments against the antiquity of the vowel points, however, were philological ones. He believed that many passages in the Septuagint could only be explained if the translators had used an unvocalized Hebrew text as their *Vorlage*. Cappel argued that the testimony of the versions, the Church Fathers, and the Targums could not be left out of consideration when studying the history of the biblical text. Yet he did not believe that the Hebrew Bible text had become less authoritative as a result of his findings. By employing what LAPLANCHE called the "principle of totality", considering the individual words of Scripture in their context, Cappel argued that almost any biblical text could be understood.[13]

The book caused an immediate stir within scholarly circles throughout Europe. Buxtorf apparently planned to write his refutation but died before he could do so.[14] The "battle over the vowel points", however, would not break out in earnest until more than a decade later.

Cappel did not acknowledge publicly that he had written *Arcanum* until 1643, but by this time he was involved in a far more serious conflict with Buxtorf the Younger over his book *Critica sacra*. The latter book was the fruit of thirty-six years of labor in which Cappel sought to resolve discrepancies within the received Hebrew Bible text itself. He analyzed textual variations not only between the Hebrew Bible and the ancient translations (as well as the Samaritan Pentateuch), but also internal biblical quotations, whether of the Hebrew Bible quoting itself (such as Jeremiah 52, quoting 2 Kings 25) or in New Testament quotations of the Old. Cappel concluded from textual variations in internal biblical quotations that such differences in wording did not prevent both forms of the text from being sacred scripture. He concluded that the state of preservation of the Hebrew Bible text was adequate for purposes of theology. An absolutely pristine text would have required that God preserve it through a succession of miracles, something he clearly did not do.[15]

The bulk of *Critica sacra* was devoted to the study of specific kinds of textual corruption, including those attested to within the masoretic apparatus itself (such as Qere-Ketib), and those adduced through comparison with the versions. Cappel's categories of textual transmission errors were often identical

---

[12] *Masoret ha-Masoreth* (1538/1968) 121–31.
[13] Cappel, *Arcanum punctationis revelatum* (1624) 289. See also Laplanche, L'Écriture (1986) 234.
[14] Feingold, Oriental Studies (1997) 457; Burnett, Christian Hebraism (1996) 237.
[15] Cappel, *Critica sacra* (1650) 51.

to those that contemporary scholars observe. When comparing the Hebrew and Septuagint texts Cappel considered the possibility of differences in word division, additions to the text, haplography and dittography, and misreadings or metathesis of individual consonants.[16] He was also prepared to offer conjectural emendations of the biblical text when he felt that other possibilities had been tried.[17] In the final chapter of the book Cappel noted that after he had come to his conclusions about textual criticism of the Hebrew Bible, he read Henri Estienne's *Castigationes in Marci Tullii Ciceronis locos quamplurimos* (1557). He was astonished by how closely his discussion of biblical transmission errors paralleled errors found in manuscripts of Cicero.[18]

Critica sacra caused a storm of scholarly controversy even before its publication. Cappel sought a publisher for his work for over a decade, because there were few Hebrew printers anywhere in Europe who had enough type, learned personnel and experience with so large and complicated a book, and because his findings were theologically controversial.[19] Buxtorf the Younger responded to Cappel's views in *Dissertatio de literarum Hebraea genuina antiquitate* (1643), *Tractatus de punctorum* (1648), and finally *Anticritica* (1653).[20] Cappel's *Critica Sacra* was ultimately published only with help from Jean Morin and Marin Mersenne, who were well-connected Catholic scholars. Morin himself edited the work slightly to bring Cappel's conclusions more closely in line with his own.

Cappel's conclusions in *Critica Sacra* were accepted by some of his scholarly contemporaries, but the book faced stiff theological opposition, particularly from Protestant scholars. Many Reformed theologians held Cappel's scholarship suspect, in part because he and several of his colleagues at Saumur had been involved in controversies throughout the 1640s with Dutch and Swiss theologians over a number of other theological issues. In England, by contrast, Cappel's conclusions were accepted by many scholars, including Brian Walton, editor of the London Polyglot.[21] Lutheran theologians and Hebraists by and large supported Buxtorf's position. Catholic scholars too were divided, some such as Valerin de Flavigny supporting the Buxtorfs,[22] while Morin vigorously backed Cappel. It would be another hundred years before Cappel's conclusions would be widely accepted among Protestant scholars, and even then they would continue to stir controversy, as the reception of Kennicott's work illustrates.

GOSHEN-GOTTSTEIN asserted that Cappel's greatest achievement as a textual critic was his use of systematic textual comparisons, juxtaposing the Hebrew text and the versions and then reconstructing "retroverted" readings. He argued that the other great breakthrough in the textual study of the Hebrew Bible during the early modern period came when Albert Schultens proposed a ra-

---

[16] Tov, The Text-Critical Use of the Septuagint (1997) 117, 127, 132–34; see also Laplanche, L'Écriture (1986) 231.

[17] Cappel, *Critica Saçra* (1650) 424f.

[18] Cf. Laplanche, L'Écriture (1986) 242.

[19] Buxtorf the Elder faced much the technical same problem when he sought a printer for his Hebrew Bible concordance; see Burnett, Christian Hebraism (1996) 196f. On Cappel's theological difficulties, see Laplanche, L'Écriture (1986) 224–27.

[20] Van Stam, The Controversy over the Theology of Saumur, 1635–1650 (1988) 259f.

[21] Miller, The "Antiquarianization" of Biblical Scholarship (2001) 476.

[22] Professor of Hebrew at the College Royal (1640–47). Laplanche, L'Écriture (1986) 874, n. 123.

tionale for analyzing biblical Hebrew by comparing it with other Semitic languages, and by providing rules for such systematic comparisons.[23]

3. Albert Schultens and Comparative Semitic Philology

Albert Schultens (1686–1750) has sometimes been called the father of comparative Semitic philology.[24] He was born in Groningen, and studied at Groningen (1700), Leiden (1706), and Utrecht (1707).[25] While he was still a student at Groningen he published *Dissertatio theologico-philologica de utilitate linguae Arabicae in interpretanda sacra lingua* (1706), a disputation whose thesis would establish his reputation as an iconoclast and Hebraist of the first order. In this work Schultens provided 35 instances of "dark places" (fifteen of them from the book of Job alone) where the interpreter could profitably compare the Hebrew wording with Arabic cognates.[26]

Schultens' argument for the practical value of using cognate Semitic languages to shed light on obscure biblical Hebrew words and expressions had long been well accepted within the Protestant world. In his inaugural lecture as Professor of Arabic at Leiden in 1621, Thomas Erpenius stated that "[Hebrew] is susceptible of so much illumination from Arabic, both with regard to expression and to figures of speech, and the meaning, origin and etymology of words as to deserve a book in itself".[27] By the mid-seventeenth century a number of important reference works had been published, including Erpenius' *Grammatica Arabica* (1613), Jacob Golius' *Lexicon Arabico-Latinum* (1653), and Edmund Castell's *Lexicon heptaglotton* (1669), which simplified the work of comparison.[28] Schultens himself named Castell, Louis de Dieu, Edward Pocock, and Johann Heinrich Hottinger among others as his predecessors in using Semitic languages to illuminate the features of biblical Hebrew.[29]

The controversial part of Schultens' disputation was his theoretical discussion of the linguistic relationship between Hebrew and other Semitic languages. He argued that classical Arabic, Aramaic, Syriac, and Ethiopic were daughter languages of Hebrew, even "dialects". They were as closely related to Hebrew as Aeolic, Ionic and Attic Greek were to each other. The basis of his assertion is perhaps best described as a "pseudo-historicist construction".[30] Of the descendents of Eber, Abraham passed pure Hebrew on to his descendents, and Jerah son of Joktan did the same to the tribes of South Arabia (Gen 10:21–29). Ishmael, son of Abraham, was father of the tribes of northern Arabia, and thus the tribes of northern and southern Arabia were in a position to know and to preserve true Hebrew.[31]

---

[23] Goshen-Gottstein, The Textual Criticism of the Old Testament (1983) 373–78.
[24] On Schultens's career, see Nat, De Studie van de Oostersche Talen (1929) 37–68, Fück, Die arabischen Studien (1955) 105–07, and Hamilton, Arabic Studies (1986) CVII-CVIII.
[25] Mühlau, Albert Schultens und seine Bedeutung für die hebr. Sprachwissenschaft (1870) 2 f.
[26] Schultens, *Dissertatio theologico-philologica*, in: *Opera minora* (1769) 489–510.
[27] Thomas Erpenius (1584–1624) on the Value of the Arabic Language (1986) 20.
[28] Hamilton, Arabic Studies (1986) CI-CIV.
[29] Schultens, *Dissertatio theologico-philologica* (1769) 490, 493.
[30] Goshen-Gottstein, Textual Criticism (1983) 378; see also Fück, Die arabischen Studien (1955) 105 f.
[31] Schultens, *Dissertatio theologico-philologica* (1769) 492.

In providing this 'historical' rationale for comparative Semitic philology, Schultens was reacting consciously to the anti-philological views of Jacques Gousset, whose massive *Commentarii linguae Ebraicae* (1702) Schultens had recently read. Gousset wished to retreat completely from historical or philological study of the Hebrew Bible. He argued that the analogy of faith was adequate for resolving obscure passages in the Bible, without recourse to either Arabic or Syriac. He wrote in the introduction to the Commentarii:

> I doubt that God has arranged matters so that we have to learn so many languages in order that we, and his people may understand him. After all, she [the Hebrew language] is the mother of those languages. She takes neither words nor sounds from them, nor learned to speak from them. It is the source, and therefore it flows with purer waters. For this reason I rarely refer to them and not as a favor to the Hebrew language, but to them, that I might shed light upon them through Hebrew.[32]

Schultens would later mockingly compare Gousset's position to that of Johann Forster, a sixteenth century Lutheran scholar who rejected the use of Jewish Hebrew scholarship in favor of using New Testament Greek to explicate biblical Hebrew.[33]

By 1729, Schultens had modified his position on the relationship between the Semitic languages, asserting that Hebrew and Arabic were actually "twin sisters" linguistically, both descended from a now lost mother Semitic language. He went on to argue that Arabic actually retained more of this original language than did biblical Hebrew because the tribes of South Arabia were far more geographically isolated and did not experience national destruction and exile as the Israelites had.[34] Both versions of his thesis, however, stressed the close relationship between Arabic and Hebrew (whether mother-daughter or sister-sister) and Jerah son of Joktan as the link between the two. Schultens' linkage of the family descent of biblical personalities and linguistic relationships suggests that for all his radicalism, he like Cappel remained fairly conservative in his theological outlook. Biblical history, like biblical dogma, guided his philological and exegetical thinking.

Schultens began his teaching career as a professor of Hebrew at the University of Franeker. He was called to Leiden in 1729, and ultimately held two professorships there, Oriental Languages and Old Testament Antiquities, until his death in 1750. While teaching at Leiden, he published extensively in the fields of comparative Semitic philology, both theoretical and practical, biblical commentary, and Arabic studies. For Schultens, the three fields were mutually interrelated.

---

[32] *Nec crediderim Deum ut a populo suo nobisque intelligeretur, onerare nos tot Linguis discendis voluisse. Denique illa* (sc. *lingua Hebraea*) *mater est istarum, nec ab iis verba vocesque desumpsit, aut fari didicit. Fons est, et purioribus proinde aquis fluit. Hinc evenit ut illas raro attingam, idque non in Linguae Ebraicae gratiam, sed ipsarum, ut ipsas per eam illustrem,* quoted by Nat, Studien (1929) 34. On Gousset, see DBF 7, 824.

[33] Schultens, *Vetus et regia via Hebraïzandi* (1738; I consulted the München: Bayerische SB exemplar) 9. On Forster, see Friedman, The Most Ancient Testimony (1983) 170.

[34] *Linguae Arabicae, praecelsae illius Arboris, Originem antiquissimam, intimam ac sororiam cum Hebraea Lingua consanguintatem, nullaque temporum injuria praefloratam puritatem, qua idem illud generosum, vegetum antiquum, adhucdum spirat, quod ortus primigenius, ac quodammodo Paradisiacus, ei inspiravit, penitentissimisque ejus radicibus inseminavit,* Schultens, *Oratio de linguae Arabicae antiquissima origine* (1729) 5. On the long preservation of pure "Hebrew" among the Arabs, see ibid. 22–28. Cf. Nat, Studien (1929) 47.

In two series of disputations, *Origines Hebraeae sive Hebraeae linguae anti-quissima natura et indoles ex Arabiae penetralibus revocata* I-II (1724–38) and his book *Vetus et regia via Hebraïzandi* (1738), Schultens provided an extensive discussion of his reasons for linking Hebrew and Arabic so closely, as well as a critique of those, such as Jacques Gousset, who favored a "metaphysical" approach to Hebrew as opposed to his "historical" and philological method. Schultens also published his own grammar of biblical Hebrew *Institutiones ad fundamenta linguae Hebraea* (1737), and *De Defectibus hodiernis linguae Hebraeae* (1731). He further wrote two massive commentaries on the books of Job (1737) and Proverbs (1748) in which he made extensive use of Arabic to elucidate obscure Hebrew expressions. Finally, Schultens contributed to the field of Arabic language. He reprinted Erpenius' Arabic grammar with an extensive appendix on the relationship between Hebrew and Arabic roots, and he published a number of Arabic texts, notably in *Monumenta vetustiora Arabiae* (1740).[35]

Schultens' linguistic scholarship did not go unchallenged either in the Netherlands or elsewhere. Antonius Driessen, a theologian who taught in Groningen, publicly questioned Schultens's use of Arabic to explain Hebrew grammar in *Dissertatio de veris causis et auxiliis interpretandi linguam hebraeam biblicam* and in *Considerationes ad novam versionem libri Jobi*. Taco Hajo van den Honert, a Leiden theologian, defended the conventional position that Hebrew was older than Arabic in *De lingua primaeva*. For his part Schultens contemptuously accused them of "Hebrew biblical fanaticism", and he devoted portions of *Vetus et regia via Hebraïzandi* (1739) to refuting their works.[36] But it was Schultens' Arabic scholarship that would provoke the most searching criticism of his life's work.

Johann Jacob Reiske (1716–74) was a one-time student of Schultens who objected to his old teacher's co-opting of Arabic language and literature to serve theological interests. When Schultens reprinted Erpenius' Arabic grammar and his Proverbs commentary, both in 1748, Reiske responded with two harsh reviews in the journal *Nova acta eruditorum* (1748 and 1749).[37] He was especially critical of Schultens' misuse of etymologies. Schultens, for his part, published two long (140 and 131 page) pamphlets in the form of letters to the editor, in order to rebut Reiske's criticisms.[38] Schultens' reputation had been based upon his work on the relationship between Arabic and Hebrew, and Reiske's criticism had attacked the very essence of his scholarly contribution.

Schultens' insight that Hebrew and the other Semitic languages are historically related, and even that they are siblings in the same linguistic family, was a fundamental contribution to scholarship. GOSHEN-GOTTSTEIN argued that Schultens provided, albeit on tenuous historical grounds, a framework that ultimately made modern textual criticism possible since it allowed for both comparative philological analysis and also retroversion of the Hebrew text used by translators of the versions.[39] Schultens' scholarship has been harshly criticized by Arabic specialists such as FÜCK. Yet many of his insights and suggestions, whether acknowledged or not, have found their way into biblical commentaries. While Schultens has been derided as a "hyperarabist", scholars continue

---

[35] Nat, Studien (1929) 49, and Fück, Die arabischen Studien (1955) 106, n.275.
[36] Nat, ibid. 53; Mühlau, Schultens (1870) 11.
[37] Fück, Die arabischen Studien (1955) 118.
[38] Ibid. 117f; Nat, Studien (1929) 62f.
[39] Goshen-Gottstein, Textual Criticism (1983) 377f.

to pursue his goal to make principled use of the Arabic language to illuminate Hebrew words, phrases, and expressions.[40]

4. Benjamin Kennicott and Giovanni de Rossi and the Search for the True Hebrew Bible Text

Before 1600, Christian Hebraists devoted little attention to manuscripts of the Hebrew Bible. The editors of the Complutensian Polyglot Bible (1514–17) had consulted seven biblical manuscripts when preparing the text for publication, but few Hebraists would follow their example until the editing of the Paris Polyglot over a century later.[41] A number of practical and theoretical barriers discouraged scholars from consulting biblical manuscripts directly. First, Christian scholars had access to a fairly limited selection of manuscripts. Johann Reuchlin owned a manuscript codex of the entire Hebrew Bible, but in this as in so many other ways he was exceptional. Some noble and ecclesiastical libraries, such as the Palatine Library in Heidelberg and the Protestant minister's library in Erfurt, held biblical (or Masorah) manuscripts, and a few sought to acquire new manuscripts. In the early decades of the seventeenth century Achille Harlay de Saucy, the French ambassador to the Ottoman empire, assembled an enormously important manuscript collection, including a copy of the Samaritan Pentateuch, which he donated to the Paris library of the Oratorian order in 1628.[42] Second, if some libraries owned biblical manuscripts, most Hebraists did not know where the best collections were located. The pioneers of Hebrew bibliography, including Johann Buxtorf the Elder and the Younger, Bishop Jean Plantavit de la Pause, and Johann Heinrich Hottinger, were more interested in listing printed Jewish books and Hebrew Bibles in their works rather than manuscripts of any kind.[43] A third barrier to the study of biblical manuscripts was the lack of a Latin language guide to the features of the biblical text. Buxtorf's *Tiberias* (1620) more than met this need, but it and later works published by the younger Buxtorf may have had the effect of discouraging the use of biblical manuscripts. The Buxtorfs argued that it made no difference whether scholars used printed Bibles or biblical manuscripts, since the ancient copies are the same as the modern ones, both preserved through the Masora. In *Anticritica* (1653), the younger Buxtorf went so far as to argue, as paraphrased by Kennicott, that where the "versions differ from the present Hebrew, the cause must be either that they translated periphrastically or improperly at first, or that their Versions have been since corrupted: since there are no traces in any MS, not the least mention, memory or

---

[40] Kaltner, The Use of Arabic in Biblical Hebrew Lexicography (1996) 5.
[41] Kahle, The Cairo Geniza (1959) 125.
[42] De Robert, La naissance des Études Samaritaines en Europe (1988) 23 f.
[43] Brisman, A History and Guide to Jewish Bibliography (1977) 3–8. On Buxtorf, see Burnett, Christian Hebraism (1996) 157–67.

remainder of such variations in the Hebrew copies, as are expressed in those ancient versions".[44]

The text-critical labors of Jean Morin and Louis Cappel were crucially important for spurring scholars to seek out and use Hebrew biblical manuscripts in order to "restore" and "purify" the Hebrew Bible text. In a rather delicate balancing act, Morin argued as early as 1628, that while the masoretic Hebrew Bible text contained many corrupt readings, the versions and the Samaritan Pentateuch bore witness to a purer pre-masoretic Hebrew Bible text. By introducing the Samaritan Pentateuch into the debate over the reliability of the masoretic text, Morin not only demonstrated that not all Hebrew biblical texts agreed with each other, but also that in places the Samaritan Pentateuch agreed with the Septuagint against the masoretic text. The Septuagint and other early translations were therefore worthy of greater respect as textual witnesses.[45] For Kennicott and de Rossi, two of the intellectual heirs of Morin and Cappel, the search for the true Hebrew Bible text would use masoretic manuscripts, but would focus upon identifying the consonantal text.

The text-critical work of Benjamin Kennicott and Giovanni de Rossi represented an important new approach in the study of the Hebrew Bible text. Kennicott organized both the first census of hundreds of biblical manuscripts and a systematic collation of variant readings found within them. De Rossi built upon Kennicott's foundation, collating still more manuscripts and publishing his findings in a somewhat different format. Both scholars were far more ambitious than any of their predecessors, whether in the field of bibliography or the use of biblical manuscripts to emend or comment upon the masoretic Hebrew Bible text.

The pioneering bibliographical work of Johann Christoph Wolf played an important part in fostering the work of Kennicott, de Rossi and modern masoretic studies. Wolf was professor of Oriental languages and literature at the Hamburg gymnasium, and is best known for his four volume *Bibliotheca Hebraea* (1715–43). His bibliography contained 2.231 author entries and a further 784 entries for books written anonymously. In addition to the previously published bibliographies of the Buxtorfs, Bartolocci and Shabbetai Bass, Wolf made extensive use of the Oppenheimer collection, then kept in Hannover. Unlike his predecessors, however, he set out to write a bibliography of *Hebraica* rather than Judaica, and included not only Hebrew books written by Christians, but an extensive discussion of biblical manuscripts in Hebrew. He provided a census of manuscripts and their locations, mentioning not only manuscripts held in German libraries such as Codex Reuchlinianus and the three Erfurt Codices, but also those found in Florence, Paris, in the Bodleian Library, and in other major libraries.[46] Wolf described 36 dated biblical manuscripts and a further 175 undated manuscripts, including several Torah scrolls from Amsterdam synagogues. He also described thirteen manuscripts of the Samaritan Pentateuch.[47] His survey of biblical manuscripts was unprecedented in scope, identifying 224 biblical manuscripts, but it was far from comprehensive. His achievement would soon be eclipsed by the impressive work of Benjamin Kennicott.

Among Christian biblical scholars, only a few of Kennicott's predecessors consulted biblical manuscripts when editing biblical texts for publication. Ri-

---

    [44] Summarized by Kennicott, The State of the Printed Hebrew Considered (1753) 281 f. Cf. Buxtorf, *Anticritica* (1653) 70–73, 90, passim.
    [45] Miller, A Philologist, a traveler, and an antiquary rediscover the Samaritans (2001) 125f, 137; and idem, Making the Paris Polyglot (2001) 76.
    [46] Wolf, *Bibliotheca Hebraea* I–IV (1715–33), II, 293–321.
    [47] Ibid. 425.

chard Simon planned to edit a polyglot Bible and his *Histoire critique* contains a good deal of theoretical reflection on nature of the masoretic text and its transmission history. In Chaps. 21–22 he even provided guidance on identifying the best masoretic manuscripts for use in text-critical study.[48] The Bible editions of Johann Heinrich Michaelis (1668–1738) and Charles-François Houbigant (1686–1783) serve to illustrate the revolutionary character of Kennicott's project. Michaelis edited a new printing of the Hebrew Bible in 1720, which was ultimately based upon the Ben Hayyim text, using nineteen printed Bibles and five manuscripts from the Erfurt ministerial library.[49] Houbigant's edition was in its own way more ambitious than Michaelis had been. In his *Biblia critica cum notis criticis* (1743–54), he printed the unvocalized text of van der Hooght's 1705 edition of the Hebrew Bible, together with a critical apparatus with notes drawn from twelve masoretic Hebrew manuscripts and one Samaritan Pentateuch manuscript. Most of the manuscripts he consulted were in the Oratorian library collection and a further three were from the Royal Library in Paris. Houbigant used his manuscript evidence, however, to support readings present in the versions rather than systematically.[50] Michaelis and Houbigant both made only limited use of the variants that they found in biblical manuscripts, and they had only a few manuscripts to work with, all of them held in local libraries.

Benjamin Kennicott must be numbered among the greatest academic entrepreneurs in the history of biblical studies. He was educated at Oxford where he received his Bachelor of Arts degree in 1747, and then became a fellow of Exeter College, a position he held until 1771. He received the Doctor of Divinity degree from Oxford in 1761 and became a Fellow of the Royal Society in 1764, and ultimately he was appointed a Canon of Christ Church College in 1770, a position he held until his death in 1783.[51]

Kennicott first made his mark in the academic world at large by publishing *The State of the Printed Hebrew Considered: A Dissertation in Two Parts* (1753), in which he compared the text of 1 Chronicles 11 with 2 Samuel 5 and 23. Building upon the work of Cappel, Kennicott concluded that the received Hebrew Bible text had suffered significant textual corruption and that a return to the manuscripts was necessary in order to restore the pristine purity of the text. In 1758, when the Delegates of Oxford Press "requested the several Professors to recommend to them such works as they thought would be most acceptable to the public and which it would be most honourable for them to encourage the publication of", Kennicott suggested that they publish a collation of all Hebrew manuscripts of the Old Testament held by the Bodleian Library.[52] In the end Kennicott conceived of an even more ambitious project, a ten year long campaign to analyze all of the Hebrew Bible manuscripts in the

---

[48] Simon, Histoire critique du Vieux Testament (1678 / 1967) 91–126; Schwarzbach, Les éditions de la Bible hébraïque (1999) 61.

[49] Michaelis, *Biblia Hebraica* (1720) 4f; cf. Breuer, Limits (1996) 92–95.

[50] Houbigant, *Notae criticae* (1777) lxiii-lxxxi. See also Breuer, Limits (1996) 86f, and Barthélemy, Critique textuelle 1 (1982) 25*-28*.

[51] McKane, Benjamin Kennicott (1977) 445.

[52] Ibid. 446.

British Isles and a selection of those found in libraries on the Continent. He funded this effort by annual subscription, and published annual reports to chart the progress of the project.[53]

In his report for 1761, Kennicott reprinted the Latin instructions for collating manuscripts, which he sent to his foreign correspondents.[54] Like Houbigant, he was concerned only to identify the consonantal Hebrew text and he too used the Bible printing edited by E. van der Hooght (1705) as his base text and standard of comparison.[55] Kennicott described his own work pattern as follows: a reader was to read the consonants of the van der Hooght text one by one, while he and another assistant would follow along in the manuscript, marking each and every variation from the consonants.[56] He specifically asked his correspondents to note additions and omissions, transpositions, variations (which included Qere-Ketib, alternative word divisions and spelling variations), and confusions over letters such as *daleth* and *resh*.[57] Kennicott focused his own efforts on the 144 manuscripts preserved in British libraries (as well as early printed Hebrew Bibles) and on manuscripts lent to him for the task by foreign owners. He only traveled abroad once, to work in the libraries of Paris during the summer of 1767. Since Kennicott's apparatus in his *Vetus Testamentum Hebraicum* (1776–80) contained references to 615 biblical manuscripts and 52 printings of the entire Hebrew Bible or parts of the Bible, the success of his venture lay to a large extent in the hands of his foreign correspondents and patrons.[58]

Kennicott's accounts of his foreign collaborators and patrons, and their successes and setbacks still makes exciting reading centuries later. He enlisted the support of fellow scholars, English diplomats, noblemen and merchants, foreign royalty and nobles and even several Catholic cardinals to implement his project. Occasionally foreign libraries such as the Escorial Library in Madrid were willing to send manuscripts to England, so that Kennicott could examine them personally.[59] Most of the time, however, he had to rely upon foreign colleagues, following the instructions that he sent them, to collate manuscripts for him. Paul Jacob Bruns was ultimately responsible for collating almost half of the manuscripts in Kennicott's survey.[60] The most important centers of activity were Rome, Florence, and Paris, and Kennicott's reports of the cooperation he received from dignitaries and scholars in these places there were full of praise. At other times, as happened in Bern, he related how his colleagues gained access to manuscripts only after the intervention of local English diplomats.[61] On occasion Kennicott failed to gain access at all to manuscripts, as when he tried to arrange for an examination of the Aleppo Codex.[62]

Kennicott, as noted, published the results of his massive survey in his *Vetus Testamentum Hebraicum* (1776–1780). For each book of the Bible he printed

---

[53] Kennicott, The Ten Annual Accounts of the Collation of Hebrew MSS (1770). The base text was a descendent of Jacob ben Hayyim's *Mikra'ot gedolot* (1524–1525). See Roberts, The Old Testament Text and Versions (1951) 89.

[54] Kennicot, Ten Annual Accounts (1770) 35–43.

[55] Darlow / Moule, Historical Catalogue of the Printed Editions of Holy Scripture (1903) 718.

[56] McKane, Kennicott (1977) 451.

[57] Ibid. 451, and Kennicot, Ten Annual Accounts (1770) 36–40.

[58] Roberts, Old Testament Text and Versions (1951) 77.

[59] Kennicot, Ten Annual Accounts (1770) 60 (1763 report).

[60] McKane, Kennicott (1977) 448, and ADB 3, 450f.

[61] Kennicot, Ten Annual Accounts (1770) 75 (1764).

[62] Ibid. 76 (1764).

the unpointed consonantal text of the van der Hooght edition, and listed variations from that text at the foot of the page together with the numbers of the manuscripts where the variation could be found. In the Pentateuch Kennicott printed variants from the Samaritan Pentateuch using the text printed in the London Polyglot Bible, with its own list of manuscript variants noted separately.[63] At the end of each biblical book Kennicott provided a list of the manuscripts (by identifying number) that he consulted in creating the textual apparatus for the book. He did not publish the key for identifying number with manuscript until 1780, which evoked harsh criticism from many of his readers.

By the time that Kennicott finally published the key to manuscripts in volume 2 of his *Vetus Testamentum*, both the strengths and the weaknesses of his method had begun to emerge. He had sought to collate variations in the consonantal Hebrew text, and systematically done so in his own part of the massive project (Kenn. Mss 1–144). But he admitted that his co-worker Bruns had only partially collated the manuscripts that he had studied, rather than reporting on all of the variants.[64] Kennicott also collated a number of printed Hebrew Bibles or individual Bible books, whose variants were given equal authority within his apparatus (especially Kenn. Mss 255–300). Some of his "witnesses" were fragmentary, including biblical quotations from Jewish prayer books and halakhic works, masoretic lists of variants, and even collations of biblical manuscripts published by other scholars such as Michaelis.[65] While Kennicott had amassed an astounding number of textual variants, his textual witnesses were for the most part not fully analyzed even by his own standards.

Kennicott's *Vetus Testamentum Hebraicum* met with a very mixed response when it was published. Even before the first volume appeared Ignatius Dumay, a former assistant of Kennicott himself, had published an attack on his former employer in 1770, accusing him of both sloppy scholarship and using error-ridden Hebrew manuscripts.[66] Fellow scholars on the Continent, notably Johann David Michaelis and his one-time co-worker Bruns, also harshly criticized him.[67] At the other end of the theological spectrum, Kennicott's work was roundly criticized by conservative English churchmen.[68] Interestingly, his quest to discover the true Hebrew Bible text (the consonantal text) also evoked criticism from some Jewish scholars, most famously from Moses Mendelssohn. Kennicott's search for the true Hebrew consonantal text was necessarily a rejection of the received masoretic text, its vocalization and paratextual elements being seen as rabbinic additions to the text, which they were.[69]

Kennicott's pioneering survey of Hebrew biblical manuscripts and his impressive harvest of variants from them and from printed Bibles inspired his

---

[63] See Schwarzbach, Les éditions (1999) 66, for a photograph illustrating Kennicott's layout.

[64] BENJAMIN KENNICOTT, *Dissertatio generalis in Vetus Testamentum Hebraicum cum variis lectionibus ex codicibus manuscriptis et impressis*, in: *Vetus Testamentum Hebraicum* (1780) 70 (separately paginated).

[65] Kenn. nos. 669, 684 were both taken from articles by JOHANN DAVID MICHAELIS in his *Orientalische und exegetische Bibliothek*, parts 2, 4, and 6 (1772–1774). Kennicott, *Dissertatio*, 108f. (Mss 669, 684).

[66] Ruderman, Jewish Enlightenment (2000) 49–54.

[67] Barthélemy, Critique textuelle 1 (1982) 34*-37*.

[68] Ruderman, Jewish Enlightenment (2000) 32–44.

[69] Ibid. 23–56, and Breuer, Limits (1996) 121–24.

younger contemporary Giovanni Bernardo de Rossi to expand and improve upon his work. De Rossi was appointed Professor of Hebrew at the newly founded University of Parma in 1770, and was one of the most diligent collectors of Hebraica of his day. His own textual apparatus would list 413 biblical manuscripts and 159 printed Bibles from his own library.[70] Kennicott had been aware of De Rossi's collection, but had not made any effort to collate his manuscripts.

In early 1782, less than two years after Kennicott's collection was finally published, De Rossi published a prospectus outlining his plans for his more audacious text-critical project. His proposed four volume *Variae lectiones Veteris Testamenti* would incorporate references from over 1200 sources. These included Bible manuscripts and editions reflected in Kennicott's apparatus, together with sources from his own library, other manuscripts from the continent and another 16 manuscripts of the Samaritan Pentateuch. In addition, De Rossi's work would include references to the Septuagint, Vulgate, the Targums and other ancient versions, and even some reference to the biblical pointing on occasion.

De Rossi's four-volume collection appeared between 1784 and 1786, and he published a fifth supplementary volume in 1793. He included a list of the manuscripts and printed Bibles he consulted in the first volume, and lists of newly discovered sources in subsequent volumes. Unlike Kennicott, he did not include a complete Hebrew Bible text, but only discussions of individual variants that occurred within individual biblical books arranged in verse order. His textual notes in their own way are just as diffuse and uncritical as Kennicott's were. For example, in Num 1:20 he discussed a variant, gave its Latin translation, and then a dizzying number of manuscript references, noting its occurrence in Kennicott's manuscripts and his own, the Targum and several Jewish authors. In his note to a variant in Num 1:42 De Rossi referred to the Samaritan Targum, to the Septuagint, to the Vulgate, and to the Arabic, to a version of the Targum and to Houbigant's critical notes.[71] De Rossi's collation was not only a guide to the Hebrew consonantal text, but a work of textual criticism.

De Rossi's *Variae lectiones* received even greater praise than Kennicott's work, most notably from Johann David Michaelis. Yet in some respects De Rossi's work proved to be a dead end for textual criticism. Johann Gottfried Eichhorn noted that the Hebrew manuscript tradition was of no help in resolving the most difficult text-critical problems. While Kennicott and De Rossi noted the existence of a plethora of textual variations, neither scholar attempted to evaluate the quality of the medieval manuscripts that they collated, counting rather than 'weighing' the value of the textual witnesses in their works. Goshen-Gottstein concluded "almost all our evidence from medieval [biblical] manuscripts would be explicable as a secondary development from a common archetype and practically all of it as belonging to one rescension".[72]

While Kennicott and De Rossi continue to occupy a small place within the field of textual criticism, particularly in the apparatus of the various editions

---

[70] Barthélemy, Critique textuelle 1 (1982) *38.
[71] De Rossi, *Variae lectiones Veteris Testamenti* 2 (1785) 1.
[72] Goshen-Gottstein, Hebrew Biblical Manuscripts (1967) 277f, 285f.

of the *Biblia Hebraica*, they are seldom cited in the literature.[73] Their quest for the true Hebrew Bible text provided them not with a path back to the autographs, but to the Masoretic type of Hebrew text, which became the predominant form of the biblical text after 100 CE.[74]

5. Conclusion

Christian Hebraists of the seventeenth and eighteenth centuries were largely conservative in their outlook. For all of their importance in the development of biblical studies, Louis Cappel, Albert Schultens and even Benjamin Kennicott were all unrepresentative of their peers. The Hebraist contemporaries of Cappel and Schultens, and even to some extent Kennicott, criticized them not only for their audacity as would-be improvers of the holy text, but also on scholarly grounds, usually citing one or both of the Buxtorfs. Most Christian Hebraists of this era were theologians by training who looked to Jewish literature as a means to satisfy theological concerns, and whose primary interest was interpretation of the biblical text.[75] Yet it would be unfair to consign the Buxtorfs and the many scholars within Lutheran and Reformed Orthodoxy who employed a form of comparative Semitics during this period to what MANUEL termed the "cemetery of Baroque learning".[76] If Cappel, Schultens and Kennicott all sought to understand the biblical text as an historical artifact whose wording and language had experienced changes over time, they had all been educated in the intricacies of the traditional Hebrew Bible text and the biblical languages by the Buxtorfs and their successors, and they built their new critiques partially upon insights gleaned from such works. Despite the claims of their detractors, Cappel, Schultens and Kennicott all maintained a fairly conservative view of the biblical text. They believed that although the present copies of the Hebrew Bible were either corrupt textually or imperfectly understood for a lack of proper comparison with Arabic or other Semitic languages, the biblical autographs themselves had been both perspicuous and without error. Christian Hebraists of this era focused upon the received text and its linguistic features, creating a philological apparatus of reference works that would serve biblical scholars until well into the nineteenth century.[77]

Acknowledgements: I wish to thank the special collections staff at the University of Wisconsin-Madison, the Center for Advanced Judaic Studies Library at the University of Pennsylvania, and the Bavarian State Library in Munich for making available the source materials for this article.

---

[73] Both the Kennicott and De Rossi collations reflect only a fraction of the total available biblical manuscripts in their apparatus. Tov noted that over 2700 dated Hebrew biblical manuscripts, dating from before 1540, are extant; see his Textual Criticism (2001) 23.

[74] Goshen-Gottstein, Hebrew Biblical Manuscripts (1967) 247. More recently, Tov, Textual Criticism (2001) 37–39.

[75] Van Rooden, Theology, Biblical Scholarship and Rabbinical Studies (1989) 12, 183.

[76] Manuel, The Broken Staff (1992) 68.

[77] Van Rooden, Theology, Biblical Scholarship and Rabbinical Stuidies (1989) 11.

Chapter Thirty-two

Growing Tension between Church Doctrines and Critical Exegesis of the Old Testament

By H. J. M. Nellen, The Hague

General works: L. Diestel, *Geschichte des Alten Testamentes in der christlichen Kirche* (Jena 1869; facsimile repr. Leipzig 1981); H.-J. Kraus, *Geschichte der historisch-kritischen Erforschung des Alten Testaments* (Neukirchen-Vluyn ³1982) 1–76; Fr. Laplanche, "Débats et combats autour de la Bible dans l'orthodoxie réformée", *Le Grand Siècle et la Bible* (BTT 6; Paris 1989) 117–40; idem, *L'Écriture, le sacré et l'histoire: érudits et politiques protestants devant la Bible en France au XVIIe siècle* (Études de l'Institut de recherches des relations intellectuelles entre les pays de l'Europe occidentale au XVIIe siècle 12; Amsterdam / Maarssen e.a. 1986); idem, *La Bible en France entre mythe et critique (XVIe-XIXe siècle)* (L'évolution de l'humanité; Paris 1994); J. Le Brun, "Das Entstehen der historischen Kritik im Bereich der religiösen Wissenschaften im 17. Jahrhundert", *TThZ* 89 (1980) 100–17; J. C. H. Lebram, "Ein Streit um die Hebräische Bibel und die Septuaginta", *Leiden University in the Seventeenth Century. An Exchange of Learning* (ed. Th. H. Lunsingh Scheurleer / G. H. M. Posthumus Meyjes; Leiden 1975) 21–63; R. H. Popkin, *The History of Scepticism from Erasmus to Spinoza* (Berkeley e.a. ³1979); idem, "Cartesianism and biblical criticism", *Problems of Cartesianism* (ed. Th. M. Lennon e.a.; Kingston, Montreal 1982) 61–81; H. Graf Reventlow, *Renaissance, Reformation, Humanismus*, in: idem, *Epochen der Bibelauslegung* III (München 1997); idem, "Wurzeln der modernen Bibelkritik", *Historische Kritik und biblischer Kanon in der deutschen Aufklärung* (ed. H. Graf Reventlow e.a.; Wolfenbütteler Forschungen 41; Wiesbaden 1988) 47–63; P. T. van Rooden, *Theology, Biblical Scholarship and Rabbinical Studies in the Seventeenth Century. Constantijn L'Empereur (1591–1648), Professor of Hebrew and Theology at Leiden* (Studies in the History of Leiden University 6; Leiden e.a. 1989); K. Scholder, *Ursprünge und Probleme der Bibelkritik im 17. Jahrhundert. Ein Beitrag zur Entstehung der historisch-kritischen Theologie* (FGLP X/33; München 1966).

1. Introduction

The agitated polemics surrounding the explanation of the Bible in the first half of the seventeenth century had roots stretching way back into history. Under the influence of the Reformation, more attention was paid to the Bible as an object of study. Against the *sola scriptura* of the Reformation, the Counter-Reformation stressed the importance of Tradition in interpretation. Thus many polemics originated from confessional differences and must in this way be seen as a legacy of the sixteenth century. Confessional dissension manifested itself in disastrous wars of religion and encouraged the revival of counter-movements, such as scepticism, which undermined the vision of the Bible as the sacrosanct basis of Christian beliefs. Furthermore, the ideals of Renaissance and Humanism stimulated a rational approach, conducive to the philological study of the text. Roman Catholic apologists were the first to avail themselves of the results of this kind of research: they pointed at the deficiencies in the transmission of the text so as to undermine the Protestant view of the Bible as a divine source with a self-evident status. Before long, the opposite camp reacted. In general, the controversy led to a thorough examination of the text and the history of the Bible.

In this immense and complex area of tension, Faustus Socinus, Hugo Grotius, Isaac de La Peyrère and René Descartes played a role as exegetes of the Old Testament. Their work accelerated the demolition of the doctrine of literal inspiration as an undisputable foundation for the Christian faith. A second analogy is to be found in the fact that these scholars studied the Bible outside the frame of an established Church or a university; their non-conformist opinions could only evolve and flourish in a kind of isolation. Of course, the negative reception of their research reinforced this isolation, although it has to be said that Faustus Socinus established his own denomination, while René Descartes and Hugo Grotius found encouragement in the relations they maintained in the scholarly world, whereas Isaac de La Peyrère eventually took refuge in the Roman Catholic Church after having renounced, albeit only nominally, his heretical convictions.

A third similarity lies in the fact that these four exegetes regarded the Old Testament as a secondary field of research: their exegetical work derived from objectives that went far beyond a satisfactory explication of the Old Testament. Socinus for example wanted to justify his Antitrinitarianism. And although Grotius divulged his annotations on the Old Testament in an independent publication, this work resulted from his lifelong study of the New Testament, which in its turn was entirely subordinated to his struggle for the unity of the Christian Churches. La Peyrère studied the Old Testament to confirm an eschatology in which the Jewish people were assigned a leading role. Descartes, in his turn, touched upon passages from the Old Testament to illustrate his view of the relationship between theology and philosophy.

2. Faustus Socinus

Sources: FAUSTUS SOCINUS: "De Sacrae Scripturae auctoritate libellus", "Lectiones sacrae ... quibus auctoritas Sacrarum Literarum praesertim Novi Foederis asseritur, opus imperfectum", and "Praelectiones theologicae ...", *Opera omnia in duos tomos distincta. Quorum prior continet eius opera exegetica et didactica* ... (Bibliotheca Fratrum Polonorum quos unitarios vocant [BFP] 1, Irenopoli [= Amsterdam], post annum Domini 1656 [= c. 1668]) 265–80, 287–322, 535–600; *Catechesis ecclesiarum quae in regno Poloniae et Magno Ducatu Lithuaniae ... affirmant neminem alium praeter patrem domini nostri Iesu Christi esse illum unum Deum Israelis...*(Racoviae 1609).

Bibliographies: CHR. SANDIUS, *Bibliotheca anti-trinitariorum* ... (Freistadii 1684; facsimile repr. Biblioteka Pisarzy Reformacyjnych 6; Varsoviae 1967); *Bibliographia Sociniana. A Bibliographical Reference Tool for the Study of Dutch Socinianism and Antitrinitarianism* (ed. Ph. Knijff e.a.; Hilversum / Amsterdam 2004).

General works: G. A. BENRATH, "Antitrinitarier", TRE 3 (1978) 168–74; D. CANTIMORI, *Italienische Haeretiker der Spätrenaissance* (Basel 1949); L. DIESTEL, "Die socinianische Anschauung vom Alten Testamente in ihrer geschichtlichen und theologischen Bedeutung", *JDTh* 7 (1862) 709–77; A. JOBERT, *De Luther à Mohila. La Pologne dans la crise de la chrétienté 1517–1648* (Collection historique de l'Institut d'études slaves 21; Paris 1974); ST. KOT, "Le mouvement antitrinitaire au XVIe et au XVIIe siècle", *HeR* 4 (1937) 16–58, 109–56; idem, *Socinianism in Poland. The Social and Po-litical Ideas of the Polish Antitrinitarians in the Sixteenth and Seventeenth Centuries* (Boston 1957); W. J. Kühler, *Het Socinianisme in Nederland* (Leiden 1912; facsimile repr. Leeuwarden 1980); Zb. Ogonowski, "Faustus Socinus 1539–1604", *Shapers of Religious Traditions in Germany, Switzer-land, and Poland, 1560–1600* (ed. J. Raitt; New Haven / London 1981) 195–209; J.-P. Osier, "Faust Socin et la Bible", *Le Grand Siècle et la Bible* (BTT 6; Paris 1989) 643–65; G. Pioli, *Fausto Socino. Vita-opere-fortuna. Contributo alla storia del liberalismo religioso moderno* (Guanda 1952); W. Urban, "Sozzini/Sozinianer", TRE 31 (2000) 598–604; E. Wenneker, "Fausto Sozini" and "Lelio Sozini", BBKL 10 (Herzberg 1995) 849–59; E. M. Wilbur, *A History of Unitarianism: Soci-nianism and Its Antecedents* (Cambridge, MA 1946); G. H. Williams, *The Polish Brethren. Docu-mentation of the History and Thought of Unitarianism in the Polish-Lithuanian Commonwealth and in the Diaspora, 1601–1685* I-II (HThS 30; Missoula, MT 1980); idem, *The Radical Reformation* (Sixteenth Century Essays and Studies 15; Kirksville, MO ³1992); *Reformation und Frühaufklärung in Polen. Studien über den Sozinianismus und seinen Einfluß auf das westeuropäische Denken im 17. Jahrhundert* (ed. P. Wrzecionko; Kirche im Osten 14; Göttingen 1977).

Special abbreviation (see above):
BFP = Bibliotheca Fratrum Polonorum quos unitarios vocant

In the second half of the sixteenth century, many Italian theologians who re-fused to agree with the traditional Christian dogma of the Trinity, succeeded in finding a safe haven in Poland and Transylvania. Among these Antitrinitar-ians, it was Faustus Socinus / Fausto Sozzini (1539–1604) who exerted the greatest influence in (and afterwards outside) the Polish territory.

The self-taught Socinus, born into an affluent and distinguished family in Siena, elaborated the theological ideas of his uncle Laelius Socinus / Lelio Sozzini (1525–62), whose personal archive he had acquired. In 1579, after a short stay in Koloszvár (Cluj or Klausenburg in Transylvania), he settled in Poland. Although adhering to different views on baptism, he developed many activities in the Ecclesia Minor, the community of the so-called Polish Brethren, a liberal and variegated movement with Raków in Little-Poland as its centre, after its secession from the Reformed Churches in Poland (Ecclesia Maior) in the period 1562–65.[1] In due course a rationalistic Antitri-nitarianism prevailed in the Ecclesia Minor which, after Socinus acquired great authority there, came to be known as Socinianism. At Kraków in 1580 Socinus embarked on a treatise, which he first wrote in his native language and afterwards translated into Latin: *De Sacrae Scripturae auctori-tate*. Published in 1588 under the pseudonym Dominicus Lopez S.J. in the fictitious 'Hispalis' (Am-sterdam instead of Sevilla?) by a printer named L. Ferrerius, the work was the outcome of huma-nistic Bible research in the vein of Lorenzo Valla.[2] Its approach might be characterized as rational and dogmatically liberal, with arguments mainly based on historical grounds. For the description of Socinus' ideas on the Bible, the Old Testament in particular, *De Sacrae Scripturae auctoritate* of-fers a starting point.[3]

---

[1] Kot, Le mouvement antitrinitaire (1937) 33–36; Williams, The Radical Reformation (1992) 991–1061, esp. 1048–50.

[2] Williams, The Radical Reformation (1992) 1162, n. 60. Copies of the Latin edition 1588 (*De Sacrae Scripturae auctoritate, opusculum temporibus his nostris utilissimum …*) in Paris, BNF, shelf number Rés. P-A-19, and in Tilburg, Catholic University Brabant, shelf number TFH A 4675. Cf. Sandius (1967) 66f; here the edition has been attributed to the Amsterdam printer and publisher Cornelius Nicolai (Claesz). Later editions are Steinfurt 1611 (ed. Conradus Vorstius; BNF, shelf number D2–3714), and Racoviae 1611, as might be inferred from a dedication ("Racoviae, Calend. April, anno 1611") printed in BFP I, 265. Furthermore, there is a French translation, published in 1592, and Dutch translations from [1622–1623] (Amsterdam, University Library Pfl. C. p. 16; The Hague, Royal Library pflt 3497; 560 D 20; 938 G 13) and 1666 (The Hague, Royal Library 199 C 11: 4). See also *Bibliographia Sociniana*, nos. 2118 and 2130–2133.

[3] On *De Sacrae Scripturae auctoritate* (BFP I, 265–80), see Pioli, Fausto Socino (1952) 91–118, and Heering, Hugo de Groot (1992) 117–36 [see sect. 3 below].

Socinus had no doubts about the divine origin of the Bible,[4] but he refused to take sides with the Roman Catholic Church, where the authority of the Bible was founded on Tradition and ecclesiastical authority. He also refused to accept the Protestant doctrine of the internal testimony of the Holy Spirit, preferring to advocate a 'naturalistic' solution which, in his opinion, would enable him to convince not only Christians, but wavering believers and convinced atheists alike. Everyone who accepted the truth of the Christian faith but questioned the authority of the Bible would shrug off his doubts once he considered the plausibility of divine revelation.[5] Everyone who doubted the truth of Christianity would eventually acknowledge its superiority by comparing its precepts (*praecepta*) and promises (*promissa*) with those of other religions.[6] To convince outright non-believers, Socinus again produced rational arguments,[7] but he also admitted that they could not be sufficient, because articles of faith were not self-evident.[8] According to Socinus, human responsibility was decisive. It was man's duty to consider precepts and promises in Revelation in order to make choices between good and evil, virtue and wickedness, and eternal life and definite non-existence. Socinian soteriology did not stress divine mercy. Instead, human free will had to decide the individual whether or not to pledge himself to Christian ethics.

In *De Sacrae Scripturae auctoritate* Socinus first came up with a rational argumentation for the plausibility of the New Testament message. He examined the books of the New Testament, making use of such criteria as reliability, authenticity, textual integrity and the absence of external contradictory evidence. Next, he stated that the Old Testament books in the Hebrew canon were generally accepted at the time of Christ and the Apostles, and for that reason had to be considered trustworthy. And although Moses had described events that had taken place long before his own time, he deserved absolute credibility as God's confidant. In the past the text of the Old Testament had not been corrupted in such a way as to impair its essential message. Errors might have crept in incidentally, but these would be detectable, or else unimportant. The possibility of deliberate omissions and adaptations had to be excluded because the Jews had left many passages on the Messiah untouched, passages that were now interpreted as predictions of the coming of Christ.[9]

Socinus particularly emphasized man's natural reason (*humana ratio*) as a means to investigate the Bible. In doing so, he supposed that this *ratio* would not lead to conclusions which were contrary to the Bible, since he precluded *a priori* a fundamental antinomy between divine revelation and human reason.

---

[4] On Socinus' acceptance of the divine origin of the Bible, see *De Sacrae Scripturae auctoritate* and *Praelectiones theologicae*, BFP I, 272f, 278B and 537–39. Cf. Osier, Faust Socin et la Bible (1989) 658–65; Ogonowski, Faustus Socinus (1981) 205–07. The last author, in particular, offers a clear outline of Socinus' doctrine.

[5] *De Sacrae Scripturae auctoritate*, BFP I, 265–71.

[6] Ibid. 271–73, esp. 272A.

[7] Ibid. 273–75.

[8] Ibid. 279B–80.

[9] Ibid. 270B–71B. Socinus' knowledge of the Hebrew language was very superficial; cf. Osier, Faust Socin (1989) 646, n. 13, referring to BFP II, 171A: ... *ego* ... *Hebraicae linguae admodum rudis*.

In this way he made reason a reliable tool to explain the Bible, but he also stated that reason was not capable of knowing God; natural knowledge of God was impossible. Therefore, the only thing to do was to accept the religion revealed by God in the Bible. Ideally, this would not cause any insurmountable problems: guided by reason, the believer had to study the Holy Scriptures and to clarify any obscure passages from what was obvious and transparent. Thus, by means of an independent examination, he could lay the foundation of an impeccable moral attitude. Socinus rejected the possibility of a natural religion merely founded on reasonable insights, arguing that many peoples had no notion of the supernatural, something that had become apparent from the exploration of recently discovered areas like Brazil.

On the basis of a rigid distinction between reason and belief, Socinus renewed exegesis by stripping it of all dogmatic, scholastic frills, which he saw as superstitious additions. He tried to promote a literal exegesis, following the dictates of common sense. Inspired by the results of humanistic research, he saw human history as a gradual ascension towards salvation. By putting emphasis on historical development, he detached the Old Testament from the New or at least created a sharp distinction between the two documents. According to Socinus and other, like-minded theologians, the Old Testament was of limited importance, because salvation was announced here only vaguely, in blurred notions. Were the promises in the Old Testament not meant exclusively for the Jewish people and did they not serve earthly purposes only? By bringing full clarity to the question of how to attain the bliss of heavenly salvation, the New Testament had made the Old superfluous. Reading the Old Testament could be useful, but it was not necessary.[10] Whereas orthodox Protestant exegetes explained the Old Testament in a Christological sense, thus expressing their conviction that the essence of the Christian doctrine of salvation was recorded in the Old, the Socinians rejected the view that the Old Testament already contained the full truth: they even denied that any Christian dogma might have an independent basis in the Old Testament alone. The immortality of the Soul, for example, and eternal life in the hereafter, had been alluded to only in a metaphorical sense (*mystice*). The *umbra* of the Old Testament had been pushed aside by the *veritas* of the New, as is also attested by the Socinian explanation of the passages on the coming of the Messiah. Socinus, for his part, opposed pushing a Christological interpretation so far that it violated the historical context. He preferred to relate predictions to contemporary Jewish history, to end up with Christ only in the second place. Very often citations from the Old in the New Testament attested to a similarity between events, and not to events being identical. And some citations were, in addition to their original literal meaning, imbued with an allegorical, obscure or mystical purport, which did not become apparent until fulfilment had taken place.[11] In this way, by undermining or even dissolving the unity of the two

---

[10] See *De Sacrae Scripturae auctoritate*, BFP I, 271B and 278B. Cf. Diestel in a thorough article on the Socinian exegesis of the Old Testament, Die socinianische Anschauung, JDTh 7 (1862) 709–77, esp. 733–38.

[11] *Lectiones sacrae*, BFP I, 291–96, esp. 291A; cf. BFP I, 267B, 385B-86A and 507. See also

Testaments, Socinus was following the precepts of humanist criticism, as developed by exegetes like Lorenzo Valla and Desiderius Erasmus.

Socinus had an optimistic view of the relationship between God and mankind, as is shown by his denial of essential articles of faith, such as original sin and atonement through Christ's death on the cross. Even before Adam's fall, man had been mortal. The sin committed by Adam was an independent, individual deed, which did not affect his nature, let alone his offspring. Therefore, it could not prevent mankind from obtaining heavenly happiness. After Adam, man had indeed lapsed further and further away into sinfulness. Yet he continued to have a free choice between good and evil. As may be clear from this view of man's road to salvation, redemption from Adam's sin was no longer necessary to Socinus. He considered the reconciliation rendered possible by Christ's crucifixion as an unnecessary, irrational and exegetically indefensible addition to Christian doctrine. Much more important than Christ's death was his resurrection, which was meant to encourage the believer to lead a virtuous life. Since man was mortal, he returned to dust after his death. God, however, had promised resurrection and eternal life to those who lived according to his rules. In this respect, Christ had set a shining example. All in all, Socinus preferred ethical values to sharply defined dogmas.

Socinus became famous for his criticism of the traditional doctrine of the Trinity. In the eyes of Socinus, Christ was a human being, but as *homo divinus* he held a position above humanity. After his resurrection, he resided next to God the Father in heaven. Socinus stressed the significance of Christ's three offices of prophet, priest and king; he particularly dwelled upon the prophetical task. After having been baptized, Christ had spent forty days in the desert. In this period he had ascended into heaven for an initiation into the divine mysteries (on the basis of John 3:13; 6:38; 6:62 and 8:28ff). Here Socinus detected a parallel with Moses, who was given the Ten Commandments on Mount Sinai and stayed forty days and nights with the Lord, neither eating nor drinking (Exod 34:28).

In 1605, disciples of Socinus, probably led by Valentinus Smalcius, published the Racovian Catechism[12] on the basis of the preliminary work of their teacher. The title of the first part reads: *De Scriptura Sacra*. By demonstrating the reliability, sufficiency and transparency of the Scriptures, the Catechism summarizes the gist of *De Sacrae Scripturae auctoritate*.[13]

After Socinus' death, the circle of Polish Socinians went through a remarkable development, which led to a further confirmation of the rational and moral elements in their doctrines. The theologian and exegete Johannes Crellius

---

Diestel, Die socinianische Anschauung (1862) 741–44. Socinus' exegesis is not quite consistent, however. Let us take for example Isa 7:14 ("A young woman is with child ..."), cited in Matt 1:23. According to Socinus this prediction refers to Immanuel, Isaiah's son in the first place. Nevertheless, if the proper sense of the words would be taken into account (*si proprietas verborum spectetur*) it would be first and for all (*praecipue ac potissimum*) Jesus who is meant.

[12] Williams, The Polish Brethren I (1980) 180–92, 205–45. A Polish version appeared in 1605, a German one, prepared by Smalcius, in 1608 and 1612, a Latin one by Jerome Moskorzowski (Moscorovius) in 1609 (The Hague, Royal Library, shelf number 1175 G 35).

[13] *Catechesis* 1–17.

founded his proof for the existence of God on nature and mankind's consent (*consensus gentium*), this of course in evident disagreement with the teachings of Socinus. Thus rationalism more and more came to prevail in a system that, under the guidance of Socinus, had had an unwavering balance or at least recognized a clear distinction between reason and faith. This rationalism also came to the fore in the debate on the doctrine of Atonement, an article of faith on which Socinianism continued to challenge traditional Christianity with great cogency. In this field Crellius engaged in a polemic with the Dutch humanist Hugo Grotius, who had tried to refute the Socinian point of view. Grotius condemned Socinianism as such, but he refused to ostracize its adherents. For in *De veritate*, his apologetic introduction to Christian beliefs from 1627, he tacitly made use of arguments taken from Socinus' *De Sacrae Scripturae auctoritate*.[14]

3. Hugo Grotius

Sources: HUGO GROTIUS: *Defensio fidei catholicae de satisfactione Christi adversus Faustum Socinum Senensem* (ed. E. Rabbie; ET: H. Mulder; Hugo Grotius, *Opera theologica* 1; Assen / Maastricht 1990); *De iure belli ac pacis libri tres*... (ed. B. J. A. de Kanter-Van Hettinga Tromp; Leiden 1939; facsimile repr. with *annotationes novae*, ed. R. Feenstra e.a.; Aalen 1993); *Opera omnia theologica, in tres tomos divisa*... (Amstelaedami 1679; facsimile repr. Stuttgart / Bad Cannstatt 1972); *Briefwisseling van Hugo Grotius* I-XVII (ed. P. C. Molhuysen / B. L. Meulenbroek / P. P. Witkam / H. J. M. Nellen / C. M. Ridderikhoff; Rijks Geschiedkundige Publicatiën, Grote Serie; 's-Gravenhage 1928-2001); *Correspondance intégrale d'André Rivet et de Claude Sarrau 1641-1650* I-III (ed. H. Bots / P. Leroy; Publications de l'Institut de recherches des relations intellectuelles entre les pays de l'Europe occidentale au XVIIe siècle; Amsterdam 1978-82).

Bibliographies: J. TER MEULEN / P. J. J. DIERMANSE, *Bibliographie des écrits imprimés de Hugo Grotius* (La Haye 1950; facsimile repr. Zutphen 1995); iidem, *Bibliographie des écrits sur Hugo Grotius imprimés au XVIIe siècle* (La Haye 1961); H. J. M. NELLEN / E. RABBIE, "Hugo Grotius as a Theologian: a Bibliography (ca. 1840-1993)", *Hugo Grotius Theologian. Essays in Honour of G. H. M. Posthumus Meyjes* (ed. H. J. M. Nellen / E. Rabbie; SHCT 55; Leiden e.a. 1994) 219-45.

General works: A. H. HAENTJENS, *Hugo de Groot als godsdienstig denker* (Amsterdam 1946); J.-P. HEERING, *Hugo de Groot als apologeet van de christelijke godsdienst. Een onderzoek van zijn geschrift* De veritate religionis christianae *(1640)* ('s-Gravenhage 1992; ET: SHCT 111; Leiden e.a. 2004); H. J. DE JONGE, "Hugo Grotius: exégète du Nouveau Testament", *The World of Hugo Grotius (1583-1645). Proceedings of the International Colloquium... Rotterdam 6-9 April 1983* (Amsterdam / Maarssen 1984) 97-115; idem, "Grotius' view of the Gospels and the Evangelists", *Hugo Grotius Theologian. Essays in Honour of G. H. M. Posthumus Meyjes* (1994 [see above]) 65-74; FR. LAPLANCHE, *L'évidence du Dieu chrétien. Religion, culture et société dans l'apologétique protestante de la France classique (1576-1670)* (Strasbourg 1983); idem, "Grotius et les religions du paganisme dans les *Annotationes in Vetus Testamentum*", *Hugo Grotius Theologian. Essays in Honour of G. H. M. Posthumus Meyjes* (1994 [see above]) 53-63; A. KUENEN, "Hugo de Groot als uitlegger van het Oude Verbond", *Verslagen en mededeelingen der Koninklijke Akademie van Wetenschappen, Afd. Letterkunde*, 2ᵉ reeks, 12 (1883) 301-32 (German tr. in: idem, *Gesammelte Abhandlungen zur biblischen Wissenschaft*; Freiburg i.B. / Leipzig 1894, 161-85); M. H. DE LANG, "Excurs IV, Hugo Grotius", *De opkomst van de historische en literaire kritiek in de synoptische beschouwing van de Evangeliën van Calvijn (1555) tot Griesbach (1774)* (Leiden 1993) 125-35; H. J. M. NELLEN, "In Strict Confidence: Grotius' Correspondence with his Socinian Friends", *Self-presentation and Social*

---

[14] See Van Rooden / Wesselius, The Early Enlightenment and Judaism (1987) 151f; Heering, Hugo de Groot (1992) 118f; and cf. the next section below.

Identification. The Rhetoric and Pragmatics of Letter Writing in Early Modern Times (ed. T. van Houdt e.a.; Supplementa humanistica Lovaniensia 18; Louvain 2002) 227–45; E. RABBIE, "Hugo Grotius and Judaism", *Hugo Grotius Theologian. Essays in Honour of G. H. M. Posthumus Meyjes* (1994 [see above]) 99–120; H. GRAF REVENTLOW, "Humanistic Exegesis: the Famous Hugo Grotius", *Creative Biblical Exegesis. Christian and Jewish Hermeneutics through the Centuries* (ed. B. Uffenheimer / H. Graf Reventlow; JSOTSup 59; Sheffield 1988) 175–91 (French tr. in: *Le Grand Siècle et la Bible*, BTT 6; 1989, 141–54); P. T. VAN ROODEN / J. W. WESSELIUS, "The early Enlightenment and Judaism: the «civil dispute» between Philippus van Limborch and Isaac Orobio de Castro (1687)", *Studia Rosenthaliana* 21 (1987) 140–53; A. W. ROSENBERG, "Hugo Grotius as Hebraist", *Studia Rosenthaliana* 12 (1978) 62–90; R. VERMIJ, *The Calvinist Copernicans. The Reception of the New Astronomy in the Dutch Republic, 1575–1750* (History of Science and Scholarship in the Netherlands 1; Amsterdam 2002).

The humanist Hugo Grotius / Huigh de Groot (1583–1645), born in Delft, became famous as a theoretician in natural law and the law of nations. Up to 1618, he made a lightning career in Holland, the most prominent province of the Dutch Republic. The Advocate of Holland, Johan van Oldenbarnevelt, was at the head of the liberal Protestant class of regents who strove after governmental supremacy in ecclesiastical affairs and tolerance in respect of Arminianism. With the removal of Oldenbarnevelt in 1618–1619 Grotius' role as his chief assistant was over. After his escape from Loevestein Castle in 1621, he fled to France. For the time being he stayed here as a private citizen; after 1634 he held the honourable position of Swedish ambassador at the French court. By then relations with his homeland were irreparably broken.

During his years in Holland, Grotius had already developed remedies to restore the disturbed relationship between Church and State. In doing so, he became deeply absorbed in theology and exegesis. Many years later, in 1644, the printing house of Sébastien Cramoisy in Paris published his *Annotata ad Vetus Testamentum*. The presentation of this extensive work was seriously delayed, as Cramoisy had to wait for a privilege. Chancellor Pierre Séguier refused to collaborate, on the pretext that in France no royal privilege could be granted to theological publications by dissidents. But there were already two doctors of the Sorbonne, Claude Hemeré and Jean de Launoy, who had approved the book. Cramoisy's main worry was that he would suffer financial loss if competitors in the Republic published cheap and unauthorized reprints.[15] The publication of Grotius' commentary was related to another, even greater enterprise, namely the edition of the annotations on the New Testament, published in three big volumes in the years 1641, 1646 and 1650 in Amsterdam and Paris.[16]

In order to assess the significance of Grotius' exegesis more attention has to be paid to his intentions. Contrary to many contemporary exegetes, who used the Bible only to underpin and corroborate their own established confessions, Grotius was keen to avoid having any specific confessional conviction interfering with his exegesis. His idea was to promote the unity of the Christian

---

[15] *Corr. intégrale d'André Rivet et de Claude Sarrau* II, 264f, 361, 393f and 429, letters of 7 May, 26 August, 1 October and 12 November 1644; *Briefw. van Hugo Grotius* XV, nos. 7017 and 7018, to Willem de Groot, 27 August 1644. In December 1644, Grotius' brother Willem de Groot unexpectedly announced that Cramoisy had eventually been given a royal privilege. At that time, Grotius did not know about this government decision. See *Briefw. van Hugo Grotius* XVI, nos. 7179 and 7199, letters of 5 and 17 December 1644.

[16] A prolific commentary on Exodus 20, based on the text of the Septuagint, was published independently (*Explicatio Decalogi ut Graece exstat*; Amstelodami 1640), as well as an appendix to the first part of the annotations to the New Testament (Amsterdam 1641). Afterwards this commentary was reprinted in its proper place in the annotations on the Old Testament in Grotius, *Opera omnia theologica* I, 34–51.

Churches in the spirit of the Early Christian Church, when such unity, according to him at least, still existed. In his annotations on the Bible he aimed at a correct understanding of oral and scriptural tradition in those early centuries. In blatant contravention of Reformed doctrine he emphasized the importance of oral tradition as a supplement to, but on the same level as, written sources.[17] The Holy Scriptures, together with the works of the early Fathers and conciliar decrees, had to yield information that would permit a limited number of essential dogmas to be laid down and, furthermore, rules to be established for everyday church practice. To a large extent Grotius' view of religion was ethically determined: the central commandment was to love one's neighbour. It is apparent not only from his annotations on the New Testament but also from his exegesis of the Old Testament that his highest ideal was to promote peace among Christians.

Apart from a short notice to the reader, the *Annotata ad Vetus Testamentum* do not provide us with any general information on the exegetical methods that had been applied. Hence other sources must be consulted in order to describe Grotius' view of the Old Testament, in particular *De iure belli ac pacis* (1625) and *De veritate* (1627). In his preface to the *Annotata ad Vetus Testamentum* the author not only mentioned his annotations to the Gospels (1641), but also *De iure belli ac pacis* and *De veritate* as works he had constantly been referring to. So the reader was supposed to understand that through the years Grotius had not changed his views fundamentally. From these last two works it became obvious that Grotius had adopted a positive attitude towards Jews and Judaism. According to sect. 48 of the *Prolegomena* in *De iure belli ac pacis*, the New Testament did not make the Old Testament superfluous. Furthermore, the laws in the Old Testament should not be identified with natural law, since many precepts in the Old Testament resulted from the free will of God. This positive divine law was never in conflict with the law of nature. The New Testament reproduced and extended the moral teachings of the Old. Here, too, Grotius distinguished natural law from the moral perfection that was recommended to Christians in the New Testament (sect. 50). In his *Prolegomena* Grotius also refers to the usefulness of Hebrew writers in interpreting the books of the Old Testament (sect. 49).

In *De veritate*, a plea for moderate, latitudinarian Christian beliefs, Grotius based the reliability of the New Testament partly on arguments he had tacitly taken from Socinus. He also followed Socinus in his defence of the reliability of the Old Testament. Unlike Socinus, however, he assigned an autonomous value to the Old Testament and therefore devoted more effort to this, referring to the long tradition of the Jewish faith, the credibility of Moses and the abundance of gentile witnesses who corroborated the truth of Moses' books. Like Socinus, he rejected the possibility of significant textual corruption.[18]

---

[17] Grotius, *Opera omnia theologica* III, 647f, 673f and 723–26, with observations made to refute the Calvinist minister André Rivet.

[18] On Grotius' relationship with Socinianism, see Heering, Hugo de Groot (1992) 117–36, 195–213; Nellen, In Strict Confidence (2002) 227–45, and the introduction to Hugo Grotius, *Defensio fidei catholicae de satisfactione Christi* (ed. E. Rabbie).

Grotius' positive attitude towards Judaism can clearly be traced in his exegesis. He based his commentary on the text of the Vulgate which, in his opinion, did not contain any dogmatic anomalies and also attested to great erudition. Again and again, however, he returned to the original Hebrew text. He also consulted the Septuagint and other translations as well, for example two recent ones, the Zurich Bible ('Tigurina')[19] and the translation by Franciscus Junius and Immanuel Tremellius ('Tremelliana').[20] As he informed his readership, he had furthermore made frequent use of great commentaries like those written by St Jerome, St John Chrysostom and also some contemporary exegetes, amongst whom he expressly mentioned the French Hebraist François Vatable, his own teacher Franciscus Junius and the Jesuit Giovanni Stefano Menochio. Grotius was very short and to the point, passing over long passages and not going into the overall structure of the books of the Bible; his chief aim was to clarify obscurities by means of detailed observations so as to facilitate the uninterrupted reading of the text.

To study the Bible, Grotius wanted to make use of the results of modern philological research. He was convinced that, in spite of a reliable transmission, the text of the Bible was marred by many errors and impurities, which required improvement. As a philologist he therefore stipulated a certain liberty to bring up textual variants for discussion. Studying the text in its original form and confronting it with early translations would enable him to achieve a better understanding of the Bible. Unlike many theologians he was prepared to compare textual variants, even at the risk of conclusions that would undermine traditional exegesis. He also left room for conflicting opinions. But it could not be helped that a philologist operating in this way was bound to irritate orthodox theologians, who swore by dogmatic certainty and abhorred any textual adaptation whatsoever. In their view, this procedure might be applied to classical sources, but never to the Bible with its sacrosanct status.[21] In his philological approach Grotius was not alone. At the time, research into the transmission

---

[19] Grotius referred to the translation made by Leo Jud(ae), which was carried on by Theodorus Bibliander and Petrus Cholinus, with editions in Zurich 1543, Zurich 1544, Paris 1545, Salamanca 1586 and Hanau 1605. See TH. H. DARLOW / H. F. MOULE, *Historical Catalogue of the Printed Editions of Holy Scripture in the Library of the British and Foreign Bible Society* I–II (London 1903–11), nos. 6124, 6126, 6127, 6176 and 6193.

[20] The translation by Immanuel Tremellius and Franciscus Junius, Frankfort on the Main 1577–1579, or one of the subsequent editions, for instance Hanau 1603. See DARLOW / MOULE, *Historical Catalogue of the Printed Editions of Holy Scripture*, nos. 6165 and 6192; L. D. PETIT, *Bibliographische lijst der werken van de Leidsche hoogleeraren* ... (Leiden 1894) 41 no. 5 and 43 no. 5m; Grotius, *Defensio fidei catholicae de satisfactione Christi* (ed. E. Rabbie) 56f; *Briefw. van Hugo Grotius* I, no. 498, to G. J. Vossius, 12 January 1617 (556, n. 1). In any case, Grotius made use of a bilingual edition of the Old Testament in five volumes, "ex officina Plantiniana Raphelengii" ([Leiden] 1613), as appears from a reference (in an auction catalogue) to Grotius' autograph annotations in a copy of this edition, which later came into the possession of Isaac Vossius. Cf. L. FUKS / R. G. FUKS-MANSFELD, *Hebrew Typography in the Northern Netherlands 1585–1815* ... I (Leiden 1984) 28f, no. 23; A. E. C. SIMONI, *Catalogue of Books from the Low Countries 1601–1621 in the British Library* (London 1990) 58f, 63, 67; F. F. BLOK, *Contributions to the History of Isaac Vossius's Library* (Verhandelingen der Koninklijke Nederlandse Akademie van Wetenschappen, afd. Letterkunde, nieuwe reeks 83; Amsterdam / London 1974) 38, nos. 14–15, and De Jonge, Hugo Grotius: exégète du Nouveau Testament (1984) 108, n. 27.

[21] Van Rooden, Theology, Biblical Scholarship and Rabbinical Studies (1989) 145, n. 188.

of the Hebrew text had found its most devoted scholar in Louis Cappel, professor at the Calvinist Academy in Saumur. Grotius was well acquainted with Cappel's works and helpfully supported plans for the publication of his pioneering study *Critica sacra*.[22] Grotius' occupation with the Hebrew text did not go very far, however, as he believed that the Old Testament text had not been corrupted systematically in the Jewish tradition.

Furthermore it is important to emphasize that Grotius not only worked as a philologist, but as a historian as well. He wanted to place the books of the Bible within the context of the days of their origin. He therefore paid much attention to external pagan, Jewish and early Christian sources, which shed light on the text of the Bible. He remained inside the boundaries of the Greco-Latin, Mediterranean world. In this way he prevented contemporary, seventeenth-century dogmatic conventions from dominating his interpretation. The same neutral thrust also characterizes his exegesis of the Old Testament. In the *lectori* preceding his annotations he stated that he had dwelled upon the meaning and background of the Old Testament commandments on the basis of the old Jewish masters. Grotius' knowledge of these sources has been much discussed in recent decades. Although it is beyond any doubt that he knew biblical Hebrew reasonably well, he initially did not have a thorough knowledge of post-biblical Jewish literature. A change took place in the years 1620–45, when he studied the Mishnah, the Talmud, and Jewish commentaries on the Old Testament and other rabbinical treatises, those by Maimonides in particular. VAN ROODEN has pointed out, however, that for his exegesis Grotius mainly used bilingual editions which were published at the time by Christian Hebraists, and that his knowledge of the original and often obscure sources remained rather limited.[23] In his commentary on Lev 7:16, for instance, Grotius explained the difference between a votive and a free will offering with a reference to *Ma'asseh Korbanot*, part of Maimonides' *Mishneh Torah*, but this wisdom is second-hand, because it stems from a bilingual edition of the Mishnah treatise *Baba Qamma* by Constantijn L'Empereur (Leiden 1637). According to VAN ROODEN, the bulk of Grotius' references to rabbinical literature in his annotations on Genesis, Exodus and Leviticus can be retraced directly to the works of authors like Paulus Fagius, Sebastian Münster, François Vatable, Johannes Drusius, Sixtinus ab Amama, Johannes Buxtorf the Younger (editor of *Doctor perplexorum*, Basel 1629, written by Maimonides), Menasseh ben Israel (*Conciliator*, Francofurti 1633) and, last but not least, Constantijn L'Em-

---

[22] Laplanche, L'Écriture (1986) 224–29; *Briefw. van Hugo Grotius* VI, no. 2313, Grotius to L. Cappel, 13 October 1635; ibid., X, no. 4330, Cappel to Grotius, 10 October 1639. These letters establish conclusive proof of Grotius' positive judgement on ... *Arcanum punctationis revelatum sive de punctorum vocalium et accentuum apud Hebraeos vera et germana antiquitate diatriba* (anonymously published in Leiden 1624) and *Ludovici Capelli Critica Sacra sive de variis quae in sacris Veteris Testamenti libris occurrunt lectionibus libri sex*. The last work, which was due to appear in Paris in 1650, has a preface in which Cappel mentions Grotius as one of the scholars who had favoured publication: *Praefatio ad lectorem* (p. ẽiiij^r), dated 24 December 1649.

[23] Van Rooden, Theology (1989) 144f, and n.186. Cf. Rabbie, Hugo Grotius and Judaism (1994) 103.

pereur. So Grotius borrowed his 'eruditio rabbinica' from specialists,[24] but that does not alter the fact that his exegesis was aimed to a large extent at a confrontation of biblical texts with pagan, Jewish and early Christian sources.

As a rule, Grotius searched for explanations by clarifying the historical context. From this starting point he arrived at an exegesis that loosened the ties between the two Testaments. As a humanist he was focused on the literal meaning of the text. He rejected the idea that the Old Testament prophecies were fulfilled in a way that would have been meaningless to a contemporary audience. In his opinion there was a "splendid coherence" between biblical prophecies and events described in the books of the prophets.[25] Anyone who neglected this coherence read the Bible wrongly. In Isa 7:14, for example, Immanuel was a symbolic name given to one of Isaiah's sons. Isaiah 53 must be interpreted as a prophecy of the suffering of Jeremiah. Jer 23:5 and Ezek 34:23 and 37:22, containing predictions concerning the righteous Branch sprung from David's line, the one shepherd and the king of Israel, all referred to Zerubbabel, leader of the tribe of Judah at the time of the return from the Babylonian Captivity. In this way Grotius' exegesis of the Old Testament stayed within the domain of the history of Israel. Only in the second instance did he express views on a metaphorical, figurative and more elevated explanation referring to Christ. He did, however, accept the idea that Christ's activities had been predicted in the Old Testament and therefore refused to separate one Testament from the other. Time and again he referred to a *sensus sublimior, altior, abstrusior* or *mysticus*, as against a *sensus historicus, primus* or *apertus*. Illustrative examples are the explanations of Pss 2:1; 22 (21):1; 45 (44); Isa 11:3; 53:1[26] and Zech 9:9. It might also be relevant here to mention Grotius' brief, but very informative commentary on the Song of Songs; by referring to authors like Theocritus, Catullus and Horace he managed to shed clear light on the sexual allusions in this poem. Notwithstanding, Solomon had enriched the Song of Songs, a colloquy with his Egyptian bride, with allegories of God's love for Israel. In Grotius' view, this love could be seen as a 'typus', prefiguring Christ's love for the Church.

Against the traditional interpretation of the Bible as a consistent, homogeneous message regarding man's salvation, Grotius preferred to persist in a historical approach and stressed the peculiar character of the Old Testament in comparison with the New Testament. In this respect he was clearly influenced by Socinian exegesis. In order to characterize the interdependence of the Old

---

[24] See also Blok, Contributions (1974) 34–43, no. 11, with a reference to Grotius' handwritten marginalia in copies of works by L'Empereur and Menasseh ben Israel.

[25] See the *Lectori*, in the *Annotata ad Vetus Testamentum* (*Opera omnia theologica* I, p. [3*4ʳ]): *In Prophetiis plurimum posui operae, ut singulas ad respondentes ipsis historias referrem … In hac parte locos nonnullos, quos veteres ad Christum et Evangelii tempora retulere, retuli ad historias aevo Prophetarum propiores, sed quae tamen involutam habent Christi et Evangelicorum temporum figuram. Feci autem hoc, quod ni id fieret, viderem male cohaerere verborum rerumque apud Prophetas seriem, quae caeteroqui pulcherrima est. Et talia quidem loca nobis Christianis Dei consilium patefaciunt, qui non per verba tantum, sed et per res nobis Messiam et beneficia per ipsum exhibenda adumbraverit.*

[26] Grotius, *Opera omnia theologica* I, 323B, explaining the distinctive features (*notae*) of the servant of the Lord in Isa 53:1ff: *Hae notae in Jeremiam quidem congruunt prius, sed potius sublimiusque, saepe et magis 'katà léxin' [secundum verba] in Christum.*

and New Testaments he applied, according to VAN ROODEN, four hermeneutical theories. These all came down to a loosening of the ties between the Testaments.[27] The first one, referred to above, was based on the concept of typology. Grotius described the literal meaning of certain events in the history of Israel and then explained how these events showed a particular God-given structure which denoted other events, for instance events in the life of Christ. But in
Grotius' exegesis this second, typological meaning lost all concrete value; it
was no more than a vague theological justification or adumbration of the redemption by Christ. Grotius' second approach was based on the assumption
that the evangelists and Apostles only referred to the Old Testament to illustrate what was generally believed and accepted. Thus citations from the Old
Testament had an additional function subordinate to Christ's miracles and
teaching. This vision implied that only confirmed believers would accept that
the structure of Old Testament history foreshadowed Christ's activities. In the
third place, Grotius adhered to the idea that certain passages conveyed another secret, mystical meaning, revealed by Christ and thereafter preserved in
the Church. Finally, there was a fourth, historical method: at the time, some
passages in the Old Testament had been understood by everyone in a messianic sense and had therefore been used as evidence by the evangelists and Apostles, thus complying with a communis opinio instead of expressly confirming
certain prophecies in the Old Testament.[28] The conclusion must be that it was
Grotius who made the indirect, typological meaning not only vague, but also
mystic and esoteric. In all four cases his method lacked clear, theological conceptions. He wanted to offer solutions to the problems created by his objective, historical and principally unbiased exegesis. In all four cases his exegesis
resulted in the curtailment of the authority of the New Testament as a guideline for the interpretation of the Old Testament. This approach had its limitations, however. As H. J. DE JONGE has noted, Grotius sometimes allowed his
theological convictions to interfere with his historicizing explanations.[29] He
explained certain passages on divine mercy in an Arminian sense, for example.

It goes without saying that Grotius' exegetical method, which was focused
on the historical context, did not dovetail with the dogma of literal inspiration.
Grotius accepted literal inspiration, but he did introduce a thorough differentiation. If the text expressly mentioned divine inspiration, it was a crime to
deny it. This, after all, was the way in which the prophets had been inspired,
as well as the predictions in the Apocalypse and those of the Apostles; furthermore, Christ's sayings in the New Testament had a divine origin. On the other
hand, Grotius did not accept an inspirational origin for the historical books
and moral wisdom of the Old Testament. Ezra and the evangelist Luke had
not acted as prophets, but had based themselves on the reports of reliable wit-

---

[27] Van Rooden, Theology (1989) 142–48; a short characterization in: Van Rooden / Wesselius, Early Enlightenment and Judaism (1987) 149–52.
[28] A fine example of Grotius' typological explanation is to be found in his commentary on Luke
24:27. See also his annotations to Matt 1:22; 1 Cor 10:1 and Gal 4:24.
[29] De Jonge, Hugo Grotius: exégète (1984) 112 f.

nesses; it was therefore wrong to interpret their words as divinely inspired.[30] So Grotius opposed traditional claims to the truth of the Bible by basing its authority on rational arguments: where inspiration was not expressly attested to, reliability had to be judged by the credibility of the biblical authors and their informants. In his opinion, this credibility was corroborated by the miracles these authors had performed or by the miracles that had been observed near their graves. The optimism Grotius demonstrated in adhering to such arguments is remarkable, since he must have realized that a trueborn sceptic would make short work of it. This naivety shows that Grotius was a representative of a late humanistic tradition which supported a historical approach to the Bible, but was loath to enforce a drastic and irreversible break with orthodoxy.[31]

The fact that Grotius must be seen as a key figure in a period of transition can be illustrated by his view of miracles. Although he attributed an essential meaning to miracles in his apologetic work *De veritate*, he sometimes could not resist the temptation to minimize the role of miracles in his Old Testament commentary. Jewish exegetes, who reasoned away the differences in the two versions of the Ten Commandments in Exodus 20 and Deuteronomy 5, by assuming a simultaneous and fully identical announcement, found no favour in his eyes. As he wrote laconically, there were so many miracles described in the Bible that it was senseless to add any new ones.[32] Although modern mechanistic cosmology did not influence Grotius greatly, he nevertheless wanted to restrict the domain of the supernatural. In his commentary on Josh 10:13, "Stand still, O Sun in Gibeon ...", he referred to the Flemish exegete Andreas Masius. In a detailed commentary,[33] Masius had gone into the exegesis of Maimonides and other Hebrew authors who tried to give a natural explanation for the miraculous story of sun and moon having been halted in their course. Whereas Masius rejected such a line of reasoning,[34] Grotius followed the Jewish authorities. In the passage "The sun stayed in mid heaven and made no haste to set for almost a whole day", the words "for almost a whole day" (*spatio unius diei*) should be understood as a long summer's day. The poetic phrasing of the text conveyed the idea of a miracle, as if the sun had waited until the enemy had been destroyed. As a matter of fact, the passage was only meant to indicate that the Israelites had chased the enemy as long as the light of the sun

---

[30] Grotius, *Opera omnia theologica* III, 722B-3A, with informative polemical observations addressed to arch-enemy André Rivet. As if he regretted having gone too far, Grotius concluded his argument with a tactical retreat: *Longe ergo aliter acti Prophetae, aliter Lucas: cuius tamen tam pium consilium Spiritui Sancto potest adscribi. Haec ipsa veritas est, non blasphemia.*

[31] Laplanche, L'Écriture (1986) 334–39. On Grotius' view of divine inspiration and miracles, see also De Lang, Excurs IV, Hugo Grotius (1993) 125–35, and the studies, mentioned there, of H. J. de Jonge.

[32] Laplanche, L'Écriture (1986) 335, n. 34, with a reference to Grotius, *Opera omnia theologica* I, 35B: *Satis multa sunt in sacris historiis miracula, ut nova extra necessitatem nullique usui comminisci nihil sit opus.*

[33] Andreas Masius, *Josuae imperatoris historia illustrata atque explicata* (Antwerp 1574) 48f and (second pagination) 184–90. See further Chap. 25.5.3 in this volume.

[34] Masius, *Josuae imperatoris historia illustrata* 190 (second pagination): *Universus enim sacrorum verborum tenor rem novam atque inusitatam prae se fert.*

or the moon had allowed them to do so. This explanation was confirmed by Heb 11:30, which did record the fall of Jericho but not a much greater miracle such as the interruption of the sun's course. God had complied with Joshua's call by investing his people with invincible vigour and courage. Having thus reduced the miracle to an allegorical phrase, Grotius concludes his annotation by stating that God obviously had the power to bring heavenly bodies to a standstill, or even to create, in a cloud above the horizon, a reflection of the sun after it had set.[35]

This sceptical attitude towards the supernatural must have affected Grotius' view of biblical prophecies. As has been pointed out, he continually looked for a primary historical fulfilment, only to wind up with Christ in the second place. Nevertheless, he mentioned the fulfilment in Christ time and again. Why is it then that his exegesis aroused such bitter resistance? The reason must be that Grotius, following in Socinus' footsteps, dismantled the exegetical authority of the New Testament over the Old Testament and in this way criticized or undermined traditional christological exegesis in many places. To many orthodox Lutherans and Calvinists of the seventeenth century Grotius was a dangerous innovator, who claimed too much freedom in treating the text. He suggested textual emendations, drew up historical explanations and in this way trespassed upon the territory of the theologians, who availed themselves of the Bible as a collection of probative statements (*dicta probantia*) to endorse their dogmatic points of view. He was also blamed for an overestimation of external sources, in particular those written by Jewish exegetes. The greatest reproach, however, concerned his alleged Judaism: for the benefit of the Jews, Grotius had stripped the Old Testament of its most important christological pieces of evidence. The prominent Calvinistic theologian André Rivet was convinced that Grotius was 'judaizing'. In a diatribe against Grotius' explanation of Isaiah 53, he called the annotations to the Old Testament *annotata Iudaico-Sociniana* and accused the author of conspiring with the enemies of Christianity.[36]

To a certain extent Rivet's indignation is understandable. Grotius left the beaten tracks by stating that the Old Testament was in the first place about the history and laws of the Jews and had to be seen as a book that had been written by the Jews for the Jews. In his standard work DIESTEL contends that in Grotius' exegesis the typological explanations were only meant to anticipate critical reactions from the orthodox side. This supposition is based on a mistaken assumption of insincerity in Grotius' motives.[37] VAN ROODEN[38] empha-

---

[35] Grotius, *Opera omnia theologica* I, 106A. Cf. Kraus, Geschichte (1982) 39, and Vermij, The Calvinist Copernicans (2002) 245 f.

[36] A. Rivet, ... *Operum theologicorum quae Latine edidit tomus alter* ... (Roterodami 1652) 813f, cited in Rabbie, Hugo Grotius and Judaism (1994) 99f, n. 3 and *Corr. intégrale d'André Rivet et de Claude Sarrau* II, 431f, n. 6.

[37] *Dem aufmerksamen Leser aber kann es unmöglich entgehen, dass diese allegorischen Wendungen niemals die eigentliche Meinung des Grotius ausdrücken, dass sie seiner wissensch[af]tlichen Ansicht als etwas Fremdes gegenüberstehen; über den Vorwurf einer hermeneutischen Inkonsequenz hätte der kluge Staatsmann vielsagend gelächelt, ohne ihn abzuwehren. Der mystische Sinn war offenbar für ihn eine nothwendige Concession an den Zeitgeist, nicht als ob er seine wahre Ansicht hätte verhüllen wollen,*

sized the historicism in Grotius' exegesis, which created many new problems instead of solving old ones and therefore aroused great annoyance in the orthodox camp. This appears, for instance, from a letter of Johannes Buxtorf the Younger to André Rivet, dated 1 September 1644: it says that critics like Grotius caused great damage to the Christian belief; they took pride in their far-fetched arguments, aroused many controversies and in this way favoured the enemies of the true religion. Grotius would have answered this reproach with a shrug: for a long time the established Christian religions had been involved in an internal struggle; they were constantly locked in battle with one another, neglecting the very principle of their doctrine. In his annotations, he stated, he had refused to indulge in the partisanship that divided Christianity. He had even granted to the Jews what was reasonable, without disparaging Christian doctrine in any respect whatsoever.[39]

Rivet suspected Grotius of making common cause with Socinianism. Nevertheless he was mistaken, since Grotius always distanced himself from this heterodox doctrine. He remained within the dogmatic limits set by the Early Christian Church. This became apparent again when he read the writings of Isaac de La Peyrère. He rejected La Peyrère's thesis of the pre-adamites without any reservation, undoubtedly because this thesis undermined the universality of original sin.

4. Isaac de La Peyrère[40]

Sources: ISAAC DE LA PEYRÈRE: *Du rappel des Juifs* (s.l. 1643); *Praeadamitae sive Exercitatio super versibus duodecimo, decimotertio et decimoquarto capitis quinti epistolae D. Pauli ad Romanos, quibus inducuntur primi homines ante Adamum conditi* ([Amsterdam] 1655); *Correspondance du P. Marin Mersenne, religieux minime* I-XVII (ed. P. Tannery / C. de Waard e.a.; Paris 1932–88).

Reference works: K. GRÜNWALDT, "Isaac de la Peyrère", BBKL 4 (Herzberg 1992) 1145–55; J.-P. LOBIES, "Isaac de La Peyrère", DBF 19 (Paris 1995) 851f.

General works: A. GRAFTON, "Isaac La Peyrère and the Old Testament", *Defenders of the Text. The Traditions of Scholarship in an Age of Science, 1450–1800* (Cambridge, MA / London 1991) 204–13; 307f; R. PINTARD, *Le libertinage érudit dans la première moitié du XVIIᵉ siècle* (Paris 1943); R. H. POPKIN, *Isaac La Peyrère (1596–1676). His Life, Work and Influence* (SIH 1; Leiden e.a. 1987); E. QUENNEHEN, "Lapeyrère, la Chine et la chronologie biblique", La Lettre clandestine 9 (2000) 243–55; I. ROBINSON, "Isaac de la Peyrère and the Recall of the Jews", *Jewish Social Studies* 40 (1978) 117–30; L. STRAUSS, "Isaac de La Peyrère", *Die Religionskritik Spinozas als Grundlage seiner Bibelwissenschaft (Gesammelte Schriften* I, ed. H. Meier; Stuttgart / Weimar ²2001) 97–125; M. YARDENI, "La religion de La Peyrère et «le Rappel des Juifs»", *RHPhR* 51 (1971) 245–59.

Isaac de La Peyrère (1596–1676) – or, Lapeyrère, as he referred to himself in his writings – studied the Old and New Testament like an amateur theologian.

---

sondern weil er ihn als kirchlich nothwendig betrachtet haben mag. See Diestel, Geschichte (1869/ 1981) 430–32; the citation on 431.

[38] Van Rooden, Theology (1989) 48, n.201.

[39] *Briefw. van Hugo Grotius* XVI, no. 7120, to N. Rigault, 31 October 1644: *Illud vere testor optima fide me haec tractasse, nec quicquam dedisse studio aut odio earum partium quae christianitatem nunc dividunt, quin et iudaeis concessisse me quae ratione niti videbantur, in quibus tamen nihil est quod christianae religionis laedat dogmata.*

[40] I am greatly indebted to Dr. Elisabeth Quennehen, of Paris, for her remarks on this section.

According to Richard Simon,[41] he had no knowledge at all of Hebrew and Greek, but this statement does not hold up in the face of the philological remarks in La Peyrère's most famous works, *Du rappel des Juifs* and the *Praeadamitae*. As is also evident from his autograph papers, he read and wrote Greek reasonably well. On the other hand, his knowledge of Hebrew was in all probability only second-hand and very rudimentary. Basing himself on Paul's Epistle to the Romans, chapter XI in particular, La Peyrère proposed an exegesis that was completely subservient to his eschatological convictions. He foresaw a world empire, soon to be expected, in which a vital role was reserved for the Jewish people. But the Jewish people could only fulfil this role if the Christian and Jewish religions merged. In La Peyrère's view, the Scriptures offered no justification for any distinction whatsoever between the two religions. To La Peyrère, the Old Testament was essentially the announcement or adumbration (*la figure*) of the New Testament. Therefore, the New Testament had to determine the interpretation of the Old, as far as man's salvation was concerned.

Isaac de La Peyrère originated from a Protestant family of some renown in Bordeaux, where he practiced law. Later on, he was a member of the household of the Condé family and served Henry II and Louis II de Bourbon, Princes of Condé, as secretary, diplomatic agent and librarian. He is still well known for his geographical descriptions of Greenland and Iceland, but in his own eyes his messianistic studies were his main aim in life. According to La Peyrère, Christians disregarded the Jewish mission in the Holy Scriptures.

In 1643 he anonymously published *Du rappel des Juifs*, containing his first statement on the central role of the Jewish people in attaining salvation.[42] After Christ's first advent, described in the Gospels, a second coming was due. With this second coming the promise of the Jewish Messiah would be fulfilled. But before the Jews adhered to the cause of this common Messiah, Christianity had to be freed from all superfluous elements which had been added to it from time immemorial. All gentiles would be converted to Christianity, while Christians would cease internal strife and restore unity. God would call Jews as well as Christians, eventually bringing about the unification of humanity in one religion. La Peyrère proposed to make the Christian belief acceptable to the Jewish people by adapting and simplifying it, in accordance with the ideal of the Early Christian Church; Jews and Christians had to practise this religion in churches without statues. La Peyrère speaks of "new temples devoted to the conversion of Jews and Pagans alike".[43] This statement did not, however, prevent him from arguing that existing church buildings had to remain intact.[44] Baptism and the Eucharist would be the only important sacraments in a puri-

---

[41] Popkin, Isaac La Peyrère (1987) 42, referring to Richard Simon, *Lettres choisies* II (Amsterdam 1730) 30, letter to Z. S., 1688: *Il ne savoit ni Grec ni Hebreu, et cependant il se mêloit de donner de nouveaux sens à plusieurs passages de la Bible.*

[42] Pintard (*Le libertinage*, 423 and 642) mentions a manuscript in the Condé papers at Chantilly, the fruit of La Peyrère's endeavours, at an advanced age, to rewrite this book. This manuscript, one of the versions of the tract *Des Juifs élus, rejetés et rappelés*, is an autograph dating from 1673.

[43] La Peyrère, *Du rappel des Juifs* V, 358–60.

[44] Ibid. 365.

fied religion, reduced to belief in Christ and his resurrection from the dead. La Peyrère referred to Rom 10:19: to be saved, man should bear witness to the Lord Jesus and believe in his heart that God had raised Him from death.[45] He also argued that man's soul and body were both capable of resurrection and immortality.[46]

La Peyrère had a precise scheme in mind: the Jews would come together in France, accept Christianity and return to the Holy Land, led by the King of France. Then the Messianic Age would begin, in which Jesus would rule the world together with the King of France and the Jewish Christians acting as prime movers. The French King was given his pivotal role partly on the basis of v. 8 of Psalm 45 (44); here the Hebrew text was corrupt, owing to a transposition of vowels: instead of "oil of joy", La Peyrère preferred to read "oil of lilies".[47] It will be clear that the messianic ideas of La Peyrère not only attest to a rich imaginative power, but also to a remarkable latitudinarianism. Differences between the Jewish and Christian creeds were so minimal that in the view of the author agreement would be easy to reach. The central concepts 'Son of God' and 'God-Man' were both recorded in the Old Testament. Isaiah 53 testified to a pure form of Christianity.[48] The Jews subscribed to this passage and could therefore be seen as near-Christians. Apart from that, the author also supposed that the Jews could achieve salvation without fully understanding the mystery of the incarnation of Christ. This applied a fortiori to the 7000 elected Jews mentioned by Paul in Rom 11:4, quoting 1 Kgs 19:18.[49]

This vision of the future, a combination of messianism, philosemitism and French nationalism, may have been inspired by the ecclesiastical unionism that was promoted for a while by the mighty prelate and principal minister to Louis XIII, Cardinal Richelieu.[50] But La Peyrère was reluctant to join in and play along with contemporary developments in Church and State. He also refused to indulge in predictions in respect of the coming of the thousand-year reign or the Antichrist. Yet, his phantasms were so bizarre that they must have filled even seventeenth-century readers with utter amazement. Undeterred by the scepticism of his critics, however, he continued on the road he had chosen. As the final piece of his doctrine had now been revealed, he decided to underpin it theoretically. To this end he elaborated his thesis on the pre-adamites, which

---

[45] Ibid. 305.

[46] La Peyrère, *Du rappel des Juifs* II, 64f and IV, 237.

[47] *Susan* ('lily') instead of *sasun* ('joy'). Nevertheless, La Peyrère wished to maintain the phrase "oil of joy" in Heb 1:9 as a testimony to Christ's unction in a spiritual, non-material sense; see *Du rappel des Juifs*, 114–39, especially 132f. Cf. *Corr. du P. Marin Mersenne* XIII, 157, letter by Martinus Ruarus to Mersenne, 20 June 1644. In arguing for this transposition of vowels, La Peyrère does not show any knowledge whatsoever of the theories developed by Louis Cappel on the late origin of the vocalisation of the Hebrew text. From the *Réponse de Lapeyrere aux calumnies de des Marais, ministre de Groningue* (p. 34), however, it becomes clear that Cappel showed him the manuscript of the *Critica sacra* several years before it came from the press in 1650. Autograph copies of the *Réponse* are preserved in Chantilly and Dôle.

[48] Popkin, Isaac La Peyrère (1987) 56f.

[49] Ibid. 55f.

[50] *Corr. du P. Marin Mersenne* XII, 339, letter by Jacques de Valois to Mersenne, 11 October 1643.

shed light on the election of the Jews and thus paved the way for the unification of mankind. Instead of a universal history, he believed that the Old Testament simply related the history of the Jewish people, beginning with Adam.
Beside the Bible itself, other sources, for instance gentile chronologies, had to
be taken into account, because they yielded conclusive evidence that other human beings inhabited the world at the same time as and before Adam. La Peyrère's greatest originality lies in having stressed the reliability of this extra-Biblical historical documentation.

La Peyrère gave voice to his ideas from the beginning of 1642 onwards. He
even handed over his manuscript on the pre-adamites to Cardinal Richelieu,
who promptly vetoed its publication. In the following years hordes of scholars
were given access to the work, among them the learned Hugo Grotius, who
unreservedly disapproved of it.[51] Finally, in the summer of 1655, the book appeared in Holland with a title page that did not show the name of the author
or publisher: *Praeadamitae sive Exercitatio super versibus duodecimo, decimotertio et decimoquarto capitis quinti epistolae D. Pauli ad Romanos, quibus inducuntur primi homines ante Adamum conditi*. Next, with a special title page and pagination, came the *Systema theologicum ex praeadamitarum hypothesi pars prima*
(1655). The publication soon proved to be a real bestseller, to judge from the
rapid succession in which the new editions came.[52] On 24th November 1655,
the States of Holland condemned the book; the States-General and the Court
of Holland and Zeeland joined in with their own proclamations on 26 November.

This energetic response on the part of the authorities is understandable. It
was useless for La Peyrère to state in the preface to the *Systema* that he would
withdraw any pronouncements detracting from the Bible and the essential articles of faith. The doctrine of the pre-adamites was heretical and even offensive
to the extent that only a naive mind, fully preoccupied with his phantasms,
would be capable of introducing it with such recklessness. La Peyrère took
Rom 5:12–14 as his point of departure; from this passage, as he firmly believed, it could be inferred that Adam was the arch-father of the Jews, but not
of whole mankind:

> Mark what follows. It was through one man that sin entered the world, and through sin death,
> and thus death pervaded the whole human race, inasmuch as all men have sinned. For sin was
> already in the world before there was law, though in the absence of law no reckoning is kept of
> sin. But death held sway from Adam to Moses, even over those who had not sinned as Adam
> did, by disobeying a direct command – and Adam foreshadows the Man who was to come.

The argument based on this passage ran as follows: Paul referred to the Law
imposed upon humanity, that is the Law given by God to Adam, and not, as
was generally believed, the Law given to Moses, which only applied to the

---

[51] H. Grotius, *De origine gentium Americanarum dissertatio altera* (Paris 1643) 15.

[52] The Short-Title Catalogue Netherlands (STCN) gives four Dutch editions, three by Elzevier, one by Janssonius. Popkin, Isaac La Peyrère (1987) 14, mentions five 5 editions, 3 from the
Netherlands, 1 from Basle, 1 of which the origin is unidentified, furthermore an English translation from 1656, and a Dutch one from 1661. Research by E. QUENNEHEN has made clear that already before November 1655 at least three of the four identified editions (in 4°, in 12°, in 8° by Elzevier, in 12° by Janssonius) had been put on the market.

Jewish people.[53] Paul then stated that even before this Law, the world was in-
fested with sin, which however had not been taken into account: "... in the absence of law no reckoning is kept of sin". According to La Peyrère, these last
words should definitely not be applied to the time from Adam till Moses, since
death was the punishment for sin and Adam had actually been punished with
death for having disobeyed God's command not to eat of the Tree of Knowledge. This death, to be sure, should be seen as a spiritual, legal death, in view
of the fact that natural death had always existed. Besides, Adam continued to
live until he reached the age of 930 years.[54] Therefore Rom 5:13 ("For sin was
already in the world ...") could only refer to those people living at the same
time as and before Adam. La Peyrère compared this passage with Gen 1:26–31
and 2:5–25, which he explained in a peculiar way: first God had created man
in his natural state, but this human race had degenerated. Afterwards, in a second act of creation, God took dust from the earth to create Adam and this human being, initially immortal like God in a spiritual, legal sense, had become
the ancestor of the Jews. Adam was the father of all mankind only in so far as
he had brought original sin into the world. La Peyrère paid much attention to
this original sin. He made a sharp distinction between the sin committed by
Adam and natural corruption to which mankind had already been subjected
before Adam. Original sin must be understood in a spiritual sense, *mystice*; it
affected the whole of mankind before and after Adam, until the mystical atonement of sin by the sacrifice of Christ. After this, man was relieved from his
spiritual, legal death, resulting from Adam's sin. On the other hand, his natural wickedness and corruption, entailing a natural death, would exist until the
end of time, when Christ's second resurrection would bring ultimate salvation.[55]

   To La Peyrère's contemporaries, the pre-adamite theory must have seemed
a far-fetched and dubious line of argument, but nevertheless the exegete created a furore, as he provided a wide reading public with solutions to a range of
practical exegetical problems which until then had been swept under the car-
pet. How could Adam, Eve and their children have laid their hands on so
many ingenious tools and weapons? Who was Cain afraid of after he had mur-
dered his brother? Where did the wife of Cain come from?[56] Moreover, pre-
adamite doctrine made it possible to fit biblical history into the framework of
a universal human history. In this way justice could be done to many facts recorded in pagan chronologies or revealed by recent ethnographical research in
newly discovered areas.

   This did not alter the fact, however, that the exegesis clashed with orthodox
Christian doctrine. Although La Peyrère enjoyed the protection of Louis II,
the Great Condé, and although he had published his book as an anonymous

---

[53] La Peyrère, *Praeadamitae sive Exercitatio*, c. 1; *Systema theologicum* I, c. 1.
[54] La Peyrère, *Systema theologicum* I, c. 3; V, c. 3.
[55] La Peyrère, *Systema theologicum* V, c. 5 and 6.
[56] Gen 4:1–17. Cf. *Corr. du P. Marin Mersenne* XV, 98f, where Mersenne, in a letter of 15 February 1647 to André Rivet, writes: *Il est vray que si cette hypothese de plusieurs hommes independans
d'Adam se pouvoit admettre, il semble que plusieurs lieux de l'Ecriture soient plus faciles à estre enten-
dus ... Mais il y a certains inconveniens en ceste hypothese qu'il me seroit trop long de reporter.*

Protestant in a Protestant country, he soon fell into the hands of the authorities after his return to the Spanish Netherlands, where his patron had settled: in February 1656 he was arrested. It was only by arranging his conversion to Roman Catholicism and by issuing an official denunciation of the theories laid down in the book that his protector managed to get him out of prison. La Peyrère stayed in the service of the Condé family, but also entered the Oratorian Order as a lay member.

By publishing his book La Peyrère managed to draw attention to the universality and the historical accuracy of the Bible as matters of discussion. This reckless innovator attracted wide interest and as such made an important contribution to the history of exegesis. Consequently, the Bible lost much credibility as far as its traditional value for the revelation of Christianity was concerned. La Peyrère had undermined the authority of Moses as the author of the Pentateuch and intermediary between God and mankind. If Moses had not been the author of the Pentateuch, others with less authority and lacking direct divine inspiration, must be credited with the authorship. La Peyrère acknowledged divine inspiration, but at the same time he indicated that the text had been liable to corruption due to scribal errors. He pointed at inconsistencies and absurdities such as the passage in which Moses described his own death. He saw the Bible as a conglomerate of texts coming from different sources, with a defective transmission and a specific target group, the Jewish people: a history of the world was not given here. Furthermore, he felt it incumbent on him to rationalize the miracles described in the Bible and reduce them to more manageable proportions; the Flood had just been a local event. Due to his exegetical remarks, the Bible was seen more and more as a profane, historical document with a specific Jewish character. If, as La Peyrère stated, the Old Testament was only concerned with the history of Judaism, one was permitted to wonder if the destiny of the Jews really had a universal meaning. This was enough to undermine the monopoly of a biblical worldview in Christian historiography. In the long run, it was due to the audacity of freethinkers like La Peyrère that other histories of salvation were put on a par with Christian Messianism.

La Peyrère recognized the danger and hoped to avert it by according the Jews a leading role in his eschatology. On the basis of (quite rudimentary) historical and ethnographic material regarding areas like Egypt, the Near East, China, America, Greenland and the Southland, he produced adequate and groundbreaking, though completely heterodox answers to questions that were raised in erudite circles. The polygenism developed by La Peyrère not only gave a simple explanation for the origin of America's inhabitants, but also for racial differences such as the *"couleur des nègres"*. For a long period of time, his theories offered many a freethinker and deist enough material to develop his own ideas. La Peyrère's far-reaching influence is demonstrated by the negative reception of his ideas in many reactions and refutations. According to POPKIN, one of his biographers, La Peyrère also influenced Richard Simon and Baruch de Spinoza (who possessed a copy of the *Praeadamitae*): Simon leant heavily on La Peyrère for his view of Moses' authorship of the Pentateuch, but at the same time he thought himself superior to this occasional exegete. Spinoza in his turn made use of elements from La Peyrère's criticism of the Bible for his *Tractatus Theologico-Politicus*.[57]

Aside from the fact that La Peyrère's exegesis showed the hand of the dilettante, his controversial convictions stimulated new ways to interpret the Bible. In this field, however, he was only an enthusiastic amateur. The same can be said of René Descartes, who preferred to leave the study of the Holy Scriptures to professional theologians. For his own personal sake, Descartes' only desire was to put an end to the encroachments of theology and science on each other's territory.

5. René Descartes / Cartesius

Sources: Oeuvres de Descartes I-XII (ed. Ch. Adam / P. Tannery; rev. edition; Paris 1964–76; facsimile repr. Paris 1973–78); *René Descartes et Martin Schoock. La querelle d'Utrecht* (ed. Th. Verbeek; preface by J.-L. Marion; Paris 1988).
General works: V. CARRAUD, "Les références scripturaires du corpus cartésien", Bulletin Cartésien XVIII, Liminaire II, *Archives de Philosophie* 53/1 (1990) 11–21; idem, "Descartes et l'Écriture sainte", in: *L'Écriture sainte au temps de Spinoza et dans le système spinoziste* (Groupe de recherches spinozistes. Travaux et documents 4; Paris 1992) 41–70 (previously published in: *Le Grand Siècle et la Bible*, BTT 6; 1989, 277–91); H. GOUHIER, *La pensée religieuse de Descartes* (Études de philosophie médiévale 6; Paris 1972); W. HÜBENER, "Descartes, René (1596–1650)", TRE VIII (1981) 499–510; G. RODIS-LEWIS, "René Descartes", in: *Die Philosophie des 17. Jahrhunderts 2/1 (Grundriss der Geschichte der Philosophie, Frankreich und Niederlande*, ed. J.-P. Schobinger; Basel 1993) 273–348.

Although Descartes was well read in the Bible, he did not devote himself to the exegesis of the Old Testament systematically. He preferred to develop a philosophy that has exerted great influence on the sacrosanct position of theology.

René Descartes / Cartesius (1596–1650) was born in La Haye (Touraine) and studied at the Jesuit college of La Flèche. Afterwards he read law at the University of Poitiers (1615–16). From 1629 onwards, he lived mainly in the Dutch Republic, where he hoped to find the tranquillity necessary to put his philosophical ideas into writing.

In his works Descartes did not cite the Bible very often. Sometimes his citations just had a rhetorical meaning, sometimes he commented on citations his adversaries had brought up, but of his own accord he hardly ever referred to the Bible and in these rare cases the exegetical gain is modest. What is more, the citations are not essential or even necessary to understand the line of his reasoning. All in all, in his oeuvre about fifty precise biblical references have been located.[58]

The problematical relationship of Bible, religion and science was discussed in the *Regulae ad directionem ingenii*, written in the 1620's, in the *Traité de la Divinité* (this treatise has not been preserved) and in the *Notae in Programma quoddam sub finem anni 1647 in Belgio editum cum hoc titulo: Explicatio mentis humanae* (Amsterdam 1648). From this material it can be inferred that Des-

---

[57] Popkin, Isaac La Peyrère (1987) 80–88. The relation of La Peyrère to Thomas Hobbes is unclear; there is no evidence attesting to personal contact. Cf. Thomas Hobbes, *The Correspondence* (ed. N. Malcolm; The Clarendon Edition of the Works of Thomas Hobbes, 6 and 7; Oxford 1994) I, 212–16; Popkin, Isaac La Peyrère (1987) 72.
[58] A useful survey in Carraud, Les références scripturaires du corpus cartésien (1990) 11–21.

cartes found himself in a difficult position. He refused, or was reluctant, to bring up the divine origin of Holy Scriptures for discussion. What he aimed at in the first place was to demarcate the authority of the Bible by means of an ingenious system of distinctions. In *Regula* III[59] the philosopher compared revealed truths with truths that could be ascertained in a rational way only, by making use of human *intuitus* and *deductio*. Revealed truths concerned obscure matters, but in spite of their incomprehensibility their certainty was beyond any doubt. This had to be so, because any knowledge of things from this category resulted from the *actio voluntatis et non ingenii*. With this phrase Descartes referred to human faith (*fides*) as a supernatural principle, leading to a certitude superior to any rational knowledge. Between these categories he made a distinction, though not a strict separation, since he concluded his argument by stating that, if faith had its foundation in the human intellect, that foundation could also successfully be subjected to an examination by *intuitio* and *deductio*. As he said, he hoped to be able to demonstrate this one day.

Later on, Descartes refined this distinction in his *Notae in Programma*.[60] He dwelled on the relationship between reason (philosophy) and revelation (theology) and now distinguished three independent categories: in the first place revealed dogmas like those on Trinity and Incarnation; secondly matters of faith which could be verified by reason, such as the existence of God and the relation between body and soul; and lastly, problems which could only be solved by human reason, such as the square of the circle and the fabrication of gold by chemical means. It was very important to maintain a rigorous separation between the first and third category. According to Descartes, the Bible was abused if one tried to deduce facts from it that pertained to the third category. For the same reason it was not permitted to underpin the truth of the Bible with arguments taken from the third category. It was the second category in particular that drew Descartes' attention, since he was convinced that, in this middle area, he might establish irrefutable metaphysical arguments with respect to such matters as the existence of God or the relation between body and soul.

In Descartes' view, metaphysics came down to a rational kind of theology. He fully accepted the divine authority of the Bible,[61] but as a philosopher, he also defended the autonomy of reason, assuming that reason and belief could not lead to contradictory truths. Thus he began his treatise, called *Monde*, in good spirits, hoping to reconcile his philosophy, in particular his physical theories, with the book of Genesis. His philosophy offered a better explanation than exegetical studies in Aristotelian vein had yielded so far, he optimistically stated in a letter presumed to date from 1641.[62] The work was never finished, but other writers continued along the same lines. The attempt to harmonize

---

[59] *Oeuvres de Descartes* X, 366–70.

[60] *Oeuvres de Descartes* VIII-2, 353 f.

[61] Cf. *Oeuvres de Descartes* VIII-1, 14–16, 39 (= *Principia philosophiae*, Amsterdam 1644: 1, 25; 1, 28; 1, 76).

[62] *Oeuvres de Descartes* IV, 698, 3–14, and 715. The recipient of this letter is also uncertain; perhaps it was William Boswell.

Genesis with his physics sheds new light on Descartes' view of the Bible. In general, he wanted to interpret the Bible in accordance with its literal meaning. Such an interpretation was incumbent on the philosopher, while the metaphorical explanation (which could be allegorical, tropological or anagogical) was theologian territory. This metaphorical explanation had to be applied to the Song of Songs and the Apocalypse, for instance. In his struggle for a literal and detailed explanation, however, Descartes came up against a wall of insurmountable problems, for instance in Gen 1:4, on the separation of light and dark.[63] Although Descartes' enterprise came to a standstill after 1644, he stuck to the general axiom that a literal explanation by the philosopher-physicist was feasible. By drawing attention to the necessity of a literal explanation he sided with Robert Bellarmine, Benito Perera, Cornelius a Lapide (Van den Steen) and Guilielmus Estius (Van Est). The first three were Jesuits and all four became known as exegetes who, between 1590 and 1640, promoted the search for the literal sense of the Holy Scriptures against the metaphorical explanation then in use. In order to assess this literal meaning, Descartes for some time even tried to learn Hebrew, but these studies did not occupy him very long.[64]

The problems ensuing from a literal explanation could be solved, according to Descartes, if the exegete took the aim of the Bible into consideration. In his view, the books of the Bible were written for simple-hearted souls trying to achieve salvation. The language of the Bible was appropriate for this aim. Therefore it would only be wrong to look for physical theses or a detailed cosmology. Like Bellarmine, Descartes distinguished matters under discussion in the Bible from the way these matters were treated. If a literal explanation were to lead to problems, they could be avoided or solved by looking at the style of speech. Descartes also followed Bellarmine in the relation between reason and belief. He attached great value to the arbitrational authority of the Catholic Church, that is to say, he was prepared to comply with the decisions of the Council of Trent. There, it was stated that Tradition and Councils, as explained by the Church, must determine the interpretation of the Bible. Repeatedly the French philosopher affirmed that, in sacral matters, he wanted to act prudently and with reserve, knowing all too well that he lacked the divine assistance necessary for an independent exegesis.[65]

Descartes strove to establish a scientific explanation of the literal text of the Bible, but abhorred a symbolic explanation, which consequently had to serve as a basis for a physical system. Well aware as he was of the danger of mixing up different categories, Descartes stuck to his distinction between physical research and exegesis. In this respect his reservation towards Johan Amos Comenius (1592–1670) is illustrative. Comenius based his physics on the Bible, while Descartes held on to his idea of the necessity of a clear separation and so gave up the old medieval theme of the two books (Bible and Nature). Physical truths did not serve to acquire heavenly bliss and should therefore not be ex-

---

[63] *Oeuvres de Descartes* X, 218, 15–18, and 686.
[64] *Oeuvres de Descartes* IV, 700 f.
[65] Carraud, Descartes et l'Ecriture Sainte (1992) 58–60. My characterization of Descartes' knowledge of the Bible is based on this article.

tracted from the Bible. Since he eventually did not succeed in harmonizing his physics with the book of Genesis, Descartes will also have distanced himself from an exegete like Marin Mersenne (1588–1648), who wanted to find in Genesis all the results of modern physical research. In an attempt to confirm its authority, Mersenne turned the explanation of the literal meaning into a scientific commentary heedless of the fact, however, that in doing so he was seriously undermining the Bible as a source of divine revelation.

Descartes supposed that reason and belief were consistent. In his view, theology and philosophy were separate territories; there was also a middle territory, where reason and faith overlapped and complemented each other. By explaining the relationship between reason and faith in this way, Descartes was following a tradition originating with Thomas Aquinas.

6. Conclusion

In the second half of the seventeenth century biblical studies that were not associated with a specific confession gained ground quickly. The authority of traditional dogmas such as divine inspiration, and the sufficiency and the transparency of the Bible crumbled away. The conviction that the Word of God had been preserved in one sacral, perfect source gave way to the awareness of a complicated transmission in a plurality of texts each of which had their own value. The exclusive claim to the truth exerted by the Christian doctrine of salvation was gradually undermined. Inevitably, though with great difficulty, modern science gained an autonomous status vis-à-vis scholastic theology. Before long, the same development occurred in other fields of knowledge, such as philology and history; the increasing knowledge of languages, institutions, law, geography and history resulted in an attack on the position of the Judeo-Christian tradition, which slowly lost its aura of uniqueness and inviolability. A new age dawned. It is in this development that the four scholars discussed above played an important role.

CHAPTER THIRTY-THREE

The Bible Hermeneutics of Baruch de Spinoza

By STEVEN NADLER, Madison, WI

Sources: BENEDICTUS / BARUCH DE SPINOZA: *Spinoza Opera* 1–5 (ed. C. Gebhardt; Heidelberg: Carl Winters Universitätsverlag 1972–87 [abbr. G]); *Ethics*, in: *The Collected Works of Spinoza* 1 (ed. and tr. E. Curley; Princeton: Princeton UP 1984); *Theological-Political Treatise* (ed. and tr. S. Shirley; Indianapolis: Hackett Publishing 1998 [abbr. S]). – ABRAHAM IBN EZRA: *Commentary on the Torah* (ed. A. Wiesner; Jerusalem 1976). – THOMAS HOBBES: *Leviathan* (ed. E. Curley; Indianapolis: Hackett Publishing 1994). – MOSES MAIMONIDES: *Guide of the Perplexed* 1–2 (tr. Sh. Pines; Chicago: UP 1963).

General works: E. CURLEY, "Notes on a Neglected Masterpiece: Spinoza and the Science of Hermeneutics", in: G. HUNTER (ed.), *Spinoza: The Enduring Questions* (Toronto: UP 1994); J. FORCE / R. H. POPKIN (eds.), *The Books of Nature and Scripture* (Dordrecht: Kluwer 1994); J. ISRAEL, *Radical Enlightenment: Philosophy and the Making of Modernity, 1650–1750* (Oxford: UP 2001); N. K. LEVENE, *Spinoza's Revelation: Religion, Democracy, and Reason* (Cambridge: UP 2004); Z. LEVY, *Baruch or Benedict: On Some Jewish Aspects of Spinoza's Philosophy* (New York / Bern: Peter Lang 1989); S. NADLER, *Spinoza's Heresy: Immortality and the Jewish Mind* (Oxford: UP 2002); idem, *Spinoza: A Life* (Cambridge / New York: Cambridge UP 1999); R. H. POPKIN, "Spinoza and La Peyrère", in: R. W. SHAHAN / J. I. BIRO (eds.), *Spinoza: New Perspectives* (Norman, OK: Oklahoma UP 1978); idem, "Spinoza and Samuel Fisher", *Philosophia* 15 (1985) 219–36; idem, "Some New Light on the Roots of Spinoza's Science of Bible Study", in: M. GRENE / D. NAILS (eds.), *Spinoza and the Sciences* (Dordrecht: Reidel 1986); idem, "Spinoza and Bible Scholarship", in: D. GARRET (ed.), *The Cambridge Companion to Spinoza* (Cambridge: UP 1996); J. S. PREUS, *Spinoza and the Irrelevance of Biblical Authority* (Cambridge: UP 2001); S. B. SMITH, *Spinoza, Liberalism and the Question of Jewish Identity* (New Haven: Yale UP 1997); L. STRAUSS, *Spinoza's Critique of Religion* (New York: Schocken Books 1965); TH. VERBEEK, *Spinoza's Theologico-political Treatise: Exploring 'the Will of God'* (Hampshire: Ashgate 2003); S. ZAC, *Spinoza et l'interprétation de l'écriture* (Paris: Presses Universitaires de France 1965).

Special abbreviations:
G = *Spinoza Opera* 1–5 (ed. C. Gebhardt, 1972–87)
S = *Theological-Political Treatise* (ed. and tr. S. Shirley, 1998)
TTP = *Tractatus Theologico-Politicus*

Baruch (or Benedictus) de Spinoza (1632–77) was, without question, the most radical (and vilified) philosopher of his time.[1] In his philosophical masterpiece, the *Ethica* (not published until after his death), he propounded an extremely naturalistic conception of God, one which identifies God with *Substantia*, that is, with the most general and fundamental active principles of Nature; denies the personal immortality of the soul, and offers a neo-Stoic conception of human happiness. The public furor over his views, however, began with the anonymous publication in 1670 of his 'scandalous' *Tractatus Theologico-Politicus* [TTP]. Among other things, Spinoza insists in the TTP that the belief in

---

[1] See Israel, Radical Enlightenment (2001).

divine miracles, understood as supernatural exceptions to the ordinary course of nature, is based simply on an ignorance of nature's necessary causal operations; that most sectarian religions are, in fact, simply organized superstition, and that ecclesiastics succeed in wielding power over the hearts and minds of ordinary people by preying on their most basic hopes and fears. In the work, Spinoza makes a special effort at providing a naturalistic reduction of the doctrines, texts, traditions and history of the Jewish people. He denies that there was any theologically, metaphysically or morally interesting sense in which the ancient Hebrews were 'elected', and argues that Jewish religious law (which, he adds, needs to be distinguished from the true and universal moral law) was a convention of political expediency for only a limited period of time and thus is no longer valid and binding upon contemporary Jews.

It was Spinoza's extraordinary views on the status and interpretation of Hebrew Scripture, however, that earned him the deep and lasting enmity of his critics, Jews and Gentiles alike. And there are good reasons for thinking that when, in 1656 and before he had published anything, the young Spinoza was put under a ban (or *cherem*) by the Amsterdam Portuguese-Jewish community in which he had been born and raised, among his "horrendous deeds and abominable heresies" were his views on the Bible.[2]

Spinoza's account of Hebrew Scripture, found in chapters seven through ten of the TTP, constitutes, without question, the most radical and (to his contemporaries) offensive theses of the work. To be sure, others before Spinoza had suggested that Moses was not the author of the entire Pentateuch. But no one had taken that claim to the extreme limit that Spinoza did, arguing for it with such boldness and learning and at such length. Nor had anyone before Spinoza been willing to draw from it the conclusions about the meaning and interpretation of Scripture that Spinoza drew.

Spinoza's discussion of Scripture takes place in the broader political context of his argument for a liberal, tolerant secular state, one in which the freedom to philosophize is defended against attempts to make it conform to so-called religious truth. With respect to the contemporary Dutch scene, Spinoza's immediate intention is to undercut the political power exercised in the Republic of the Netherlands by ecclesiastic authorities. For it is the "excessive authority and egotism of preachers", he tells one of his correspondents, which most threatens the freedom "to say what we think".[3] The key to diminishing the undue influence of the clergy, who justify their abuses by appealing to the holiness of a certain book as the word of God, is to demonstrate the true nature of Scripture and its message, and eliminate the "superstitious adornments" of popular religion. By naturalizing Scripture, Spinoza hopes to redirect the authority invested in it from the words on the page to a simple moral principle; and by formulating what he takes to be the proper method of interpreting Scripture, he seeks to encourage his readers to examine it anew and find therein the doctrines of the "true religion". Only then will people be able to delimit

---

[2] For a discussion of Spinoza's *cherem* and the reasons behind it, see Nadler, Spinoza (1999), Chap. 6; and idem, Spinoza's Heresy (2002).
[3] Letter 30, to Oldenburg, G IV.166.

exactly what needs to be done to show proper respect for God and obtain blessedness.

Spinoza denies that Scripture is literally of divine origin and that Moses (either as God's amanuensis or on his own) wrote all, or even most of the Torah. Much of the evidence he brings forward for this thesis was not unfamiliar to Bible scholars, and had been used before to argue against Moses' comprehensive authorship, most famously by Abraham ibn Ezra in the twelfth century.[4] Spinoza begins by summarizing what he takes to be Ibn Ezra's argument, which he breaks down into six basic points: 1. Moses could not have written the preface to Deuteronomy, since he never crossed the Jordan River; 2. We are told that the book that Moses did actually write was produced on the circumference of a single alter (Deuteronomy 27), and was thus much shorter than the Pentateuch; 3. The words of Deut 31:9 ("And Moses wrote the Law") cannot be ascribed to Moses himself, but rather to another writer narrating the deeds of Moses; 4. Scripture often speaks of the time when "the Canaanite was then in the land" (Gen 12:6), indicating that it was written some time after the Canaanites had been driven from their territory (and, thus, after the death of Moses); 5. In the Torah, Mount Moriah is called 'the Mount of God'(Gen 22:14), a name it acquired only after the building of the Temple; 6. Certain narrative elements (e. g., in Deuteronomy 3, where we are told that "Only Og, king of Bashan, remained as the sole survivor of the giants. Behold, his bedstead was a bedstead of iron, the bedstead that is now in Rabbah of the children of Ammon ...") establish that the writer lived long after the time of the events about which he is speaking.

Ibn Ezra had been arguing for a very limited claim, namely, that Moses, while still the author of the Pentateuch, could not have written every single line of the work. Spinoza adds his own points to extend the scope of Ibn Ezra's case: 1. Not only is Moses consistently spoken of in the third person, but the writer also "bears witness" to many details concerning him; 2. The history narrates not only the death, burial and mourning of Moses, but also compares him to all the prophets that came after him; 3. Many places are referred to not by the names that they bore in Moses' time but by names that they acquired much later; 4. The narrative of events often continues beyond the death of Moses. All of these points, which can be used to highlight many texts and passages that could not have been written by Moses, "makes it clear beyond a shadow of a doubt" that the writings commonly referred to as "the Five Books of Moses" were, in fact, written by someone who lived many generations after Moses.[5]

Moses did, Spinoza grants, compose some books of history and of law, and remnants of those long lost writings can be found in the Pentateuch. But the Torah as we have it, as well as other books of the Hebrew Bible (such as Joshua, Judges, Ruth, Samuel and Kings) were written neither by the individuals whose names they bear nor by any person appearing in them. Spinoza argues that these were, in fact, all composed by a single historian living many

---

[4] Cf. U. Simon, "Abraham ibn Ezra", HBOT I/2 (2000) 377–87.
[5] TTP VIII, G III.118–122; S 109–112.

generations after the events narrated, and that this was most likely Ezra. It was the post-exilic leader who took the many writings that had come down to him and began weaving them into a single (but not seamless) narrative. Ezra's work was later completed and supplemented by the editorial labors of others. What we now possess, then, is nothing but a compilation of human literature, and a rather mismanaged, haphazard and "mutilated" one at that.

> If one merely observes that all the contents of these five books, histories and precepts, are set forth with no distinction or order and with no regard to chronology, and that frequently the same story is repeated, with variations, it will readily be recognised that all these materials were collected indiscriminately and stored together with a view to examining them and arranging them more conveniently at some later time. And not only the contents of these five books but the other histories in the remaining seven books right down to the destruction of the city were compiled in the same way.[6]

As for the books of the Prophets (*Nevi'im*), they are of even later provenance, compiled (or "heaped together", in Spinoza's view) from a variety of sources by chroniclers or scribes from the Second Temple period. The compilers were eclectic in their sources and selective in what they included. The result is a fragmentary and often unrepresentative collection. "The writers of these books did not collect the prophecies of all who prophesied, nor all the prophecies of those prophets whom we do possess." Canonization of all of these writings into Scripture occurred only in the second century BCE, when the Pharisees selected a number of texts from a multitude of others. Because the process of transmission was a historical one, involving the conveyance of writings of human origin over a long period of time through numerous scribes and redactors, and because the decision to include some books but not others was made by ordinary, fallible human beings, there are good reasons for believing that a significant portion of the extant text of the "Old Testament" is, relative to its original texts, corrupt.

Spinoza was working within a well-known tradition. Ibn Ezra was only the first to argue that Moses was not the author of every word of the Pentateuch. His discussion of Deuteronomy 33 in his commentary on the Pentateuch, in which he claims that Moses could not have written the account of his own death, was taken up by many later thinkers (including Martin Luther) who had no intention of arguing that Moses did not write almost all of the Torah.

Things began to get more complex in Spinoza's own era, however. The English philosopher Thomas Hobbes insists in his *Leviathan* (1651) – which Spinoza clearly studied very closely – that a good deal of the content of the five books attributed to Moses was actually written long after his time, though he agrees that Moses did indeed compose much of what appears in them, namely, "all that which he is there said to have written".[7] Mid-seventeenth-century Amsterdam was itself home to a number of controversial writers who took this line of thought into even more unorthodox terrain. Isaac de la Peyrère, for example, was a French Calvinist – and, by the end of his life, Catholic – millen-

---

   [6] TTP IX, G III.131; S 121.
   [7] *Leviathan*, Book III, Chap. 33; cf. also Chap. 35, by H. GRAF REVENTLOW, in the present volume.

arian and the author of a book on the existence of human beings before Adam, the *Pre-Adamitae*. La Peyrère questioned not only the Mosaic authorship of the entire Pentateuch, but also the reliability of the transmission process and, hence, the accuracy (relative to the "real" Bible, truly representing the word of God) of the Biblical texts now in our possession.[8] In 1660, Samuel Fisher, the Quaker leader in Amsterdam, published *The Rustic's Alarm to the Rabbies*. Scripture, Fisher insisted, is a historical document, a text written by human beings, and therefore should not be confused with the Word of God, which is ahistorical and eternal. Moses' contribution was simply to begin the process of writing down God's message. Fisher cast doubt on the authenticity of what now passes for Holy Scripture. The books that we have are, in fact, copies of copies of copies, and so on, all of which passed through numerous hands. During this transmission process, alterations and omissions must have crept into the texts, which now are fairly corrupt. Spinoza could not read English, but his possible personal connection with Fisher in the late 1650s in Amsterdam could explain any influence that Fisher's views might have had on him.[9]

Despite these precedents, denying the *general* Mosaic authorship of the Torah was still an exceedingly unorthodox view. Spinoza noted that "the author [of the Pentateuch] is almost universally believed to be Moses", and he knew that rejecting that dogma would earn an author the condemnation of religious authorities. But there was nothing original, by 1670, in claiming that Moses did not write all (or even most) of the Torah, nor in suggesting that Scripture was composed by human beings and transmitted through a fallible historical process. Spinoza's radical and innovative claim was to argue that this holds great significance for how Scripture is to be read and interpreted. He was dismayed by the way in which Scripture itself was worshiped, by the reverence accorded to the words on the page rather than to the moral message they conveyed. If the Bible is an historical and thus natural document, then it should be treated like any other work of nature. The study of Scripture, or biblical hermeneutics, should therefore proceed as the study of nature, or natural science proceeds: by gathering and rationally evaluating empirical data, that is, by examining the "book" itself for its general principles.

> I hold that the method of interpreting Scripture is no different from the method of interpreting Nature, and is in fact in complete accord with it. For the method of interpreting Nature consists essentially in composing a detailed study of Nature from which, as being the source of our assured data, we can deduce the definitions of the things of Nature. Now in exactly the same way the task of Scriptural interpretation requires us to make a straightforward study of Scripture, and from this, as the source of our fixed data and principles, to deduce by logical inference the meaning of the authors of Scripture. In this way – that is, by allowing no other principles or data for the interpretation of Scripture and study of its contents except those that can be gathered only from Scripture itself and from a historical study of Scripture – steady progress can be made without any danger of error, and one can deal with matters that surpass our understanding with no less confidence than those matters that are known to us by the natural light of reason.[10]

---

[8] Cf. the discussion by H. NELLEN, Chap. 32.4 in the present volume.

[9] See Popkin, Spinoza and Samuel Fisher (1985). For a discussion of Spinoza's Bible scholarship and its precedents, see Popkin, Spinoza and Bible Scholarship (1996).

[10] TTP VII, G III.98; S 89.

Just as the knowledge of nature must be sought from nature alone, so must the knowledge of Scripture – an apprehension of its authors' intended meaning – be sought from Scripture alone. In natural science, we seek to learn, through both deduction from self-evident, *a priori* principles and induction from observation and a close examination of Nature itself, "those features that are most universal and common to" all natural things. In the case of bodies, this means the nature of extension and motion and rest and the laws "which Nature always observes and through which she constantly acts". We then advance from these general principles to more particular features of nature and the explanation of specific phenomena. Likewise, with respect to Scripture, we must try to discover, through the reading and analysis of Scripture alone, without appealing to any authority or criteria external to the text, what its most general claims are.

> We must first seek … that which is most universal and forms the basis and foundation of all Scripture; in short, that which is commended in Scripture by all the prophets as doctrine most eternal and most profitable for all mankind. For example, that God exists, one alone and omnipotent, who alone should be worshiped, who cares for all, who loves above all others those who worship him and love their neighbors as themselves.

Then, after having acquired a proper understanding of these "universal doctrines of Scripture", we can proceed to "other matters which are of less universal import but affect our ordinary daily life, and which flow from the universal doctrine like rivulets from their source. Such are all the specific eternal actions of true virtue which need a particular occasion for their exercise".[11] If there is anything about these matters that appears ambiguous or obscure, or if any contradictions appear in what Scripture seems to teach from one passage to the next, then further investigation into the text, its language, its writers and their times is required (much as one, in the face of a natural phenomenon difficult to explain, would simply further one's investigations into the causes in nature that are suspected of producing similar phenomena).

It follows that the implementation of the method to discover the meaning of Scripture, to learn what the authors of Scripture intended to teach, requires a number of linguistic, textual and historical skills. The first step is a knowledge of the language in which Scripture is written and which its authors spoke, Hebrew. This is essential to making any headway into the possible meanings of a passage. Second, the "pronouncements" made in each book of Scripture should be collected and organized by subject; ambiguous and contradictory statements should be noted. Finally, one who would understand Scripture needs to learn about "the circumstances relevant to all the extant books of the prophets, giving the life, character and pursuits of the author of every book".[12] Apprehending the meaning of a writer's work requires knowing who that writer was and what kind of life he led (even going so far as to try to learn about his temperament, beliefs and "prejudices"), what audience he was writing for, and what was the occasion for and purpose of his writing. Moreover, since the transmission of the original composition was a historical process, one needs to

---

[11] TTP VII, G III.102–03; S 93.
[12] TTP VII, G III.101; S 92.

know what happened to each book (including its initial reception), how many versions there were and what the variants are, who admitted it into the final canon and on what criterion, and how all the books of Scripture were ultimately united into a single work.

One consequence of Spinoza's views is that the interpretation of Scripture is, at least in principle, open and accessible to any person endowed with intelligence and who is able and willing to acquire the necessary skills. To be sure, a sophisticated understanding of Scripture is not readily apprehended by the untrained layperson, but then neither does it require supernatural gifts ("the divine light") or even deep philosophical study. Spinoza insists that his method of interpreting Scripture "requires only the aid of natural reason", along with some very specialized linguistic and scholarly abilities. There is no need for lengthy and complex commentaries or ordained intermediaries such as priests, rabbis or pastors. "Since the supreme authority for the interpretation of Scripture is vested in each individual, the rule that governs interpretation must be nothing other than the natural light that is common to all, and not any supernatural right, nor any external authority."[13]

There are, of course, numerous obstacles standing in the way of even the most well-trained of scholars who seek to discover the meaning of prophetic writings. Spinoza points, first of all, to the fragmentary contemporary knowledge of the Hebrew language. "The men of old who used the Hebrew language have left to posterity no information concerning the basic principles and study of this language … [W]e possess from them nothing at all, neither dictionary nor grammar nor text-book on rhetoric."[14] Words for many objects have been forgotten, and the meanings of many words lost. Moreover, even when the meanings of words are known, we often lack a knowledge of the idiom and modes of speech that would allow us to make sense of an obscure passage. There are also inherent obscurities in the Hebrew alphabet, vocabulary and grammar; for example, letters that look the same (such as *resh* and *dalet*), ambiguities in the parts of speech (e. g., the *waw* can be conjunctive or disjunctive), and the lack of a clear and precise tense system among the verbs. In addition to these linguistic problems, there is the sheer difficulty of accurately reconstructing the history surrounding such ancient writings. About most of Scripture's authors we either have no knowledge whatsoever or only partial and dubious information. All of these difficulties, Spinoza concludes, are "so grave that I have no hesitation in affirming that in many instances we either do not know the true meaning of Scripture or we can do no more than make conjecture".[15] But this applies only to those communications from the prophets that go beyond "normal comprehension", including "mysterious symbols and narratives that exceed all human belief". On the other hand, propositions that are evident to intellectual apprehension, and especially the true moral doctrines that Scripture conveys, are accessible by means of Spinoza's "historical method of study"; and the basic message of Scripture is evident even to the

---

[13] TTP VII, G III.117; S 107.
[14] TTP VII, G III.106; S 97.
[15] TTP VII, G III.111; S 101.

most unlearned of readers. "The teachings of true piety are expressed in quite ordinary language, and being directed to the generality of people they are therefore straightforward and easy to understand ... We can understand the meaning of Scripture with confidence in matters relating to salvation and necessary to blessedness."[16]

Spinoza's account of the interpretation of Scripture is a direct attack on Maimonides's approach in the *Guide of the Perplexed*,[17] as well as on the line of rationalist exegetes before him (such as Saadiah Gaon and Ibn Ezra). Maimonides had argued that deciphering the meaning of Scripture is a matter of seeing what is "approved by" reason. Because Scripture is the Word of God, and thus the work of an omniscient and necessarily veracious author, its intended meaning must be consistent with demonstrable truth. In other words, what Scripture says must be what is true. Therefore, if some passage, when read literally, cannot possibly be accepted by reason as true, then the literal meaning must be rejected in favor of a figurative one. For example, the Bible speaks, on occasion, of divine body parts. But reason tells us that an eternal, perfect God must be immaterial and therefore does not have a body. Therefore, any references in Scripture to God's feet or hands must be read metaphorically.[18] On the other hand, because reason cannot demonstrate with certainty that the world is eternal (contrary to what some Aristotelians had insisted), there is no justification for reading the Bible's account of creation figuratively.

For Spinoza, this type of exegesis is illegitimate in so far as it goes beyond Scripture itself – to an external standard of rationality or truth – in order to interpret Scripture. "The question as to whether Moses did or did not believe that God is fire must in no wise be decided by the rationality or irrationality of the belief, but solely from other pronouncements of Moses."[19] There must, in other words, be a distinction between the meaning of Scripture, which is what one is after when interpreting it, and what is philosophically or historically true.

> The point at issue is merely the meaning of the texts, not their truth. I would go further: in seeking the meaning of Scripture we should take every precaution against the undue influence, not only of our own prejudices, but of our faculty of reason in so far as that is based on the principles of natural cognition. In order to avoid confusion between true meaning and truth of fact, the former must be sought simply from linguistic usage, or from a process of reasoning that looks to no other basis than Scripture.[20]

Much of what Scripture relates is not, in fact, true, no more so than what is related by any other work of human literature. And if what Scripture states does happen to be true, it is not, *pace* Maimonides, *necessarily* the case that what it states is true. In one of his typically bold statements, Spinoza insists that "to understand Scripture and the mind of the prophets is by no means the same

---

[16] TTP XII, G III.111; S 101.
[17] Cf. the discussion by S. KLEIN-BRASLAVY, HBOT I/2 (2000) 311–20.
[18] See *Guide of the Perplexed* II.25.
[19] TTP VII, G III.100–01; S 91.
[20] TTP VII, G III.100; S 91.

thing as to understand the mind of God, that is, to understand truth itself".[21] Scripture is not by its nature a source of knowledge, least of all true knowledge about God, the heavens or even human nature (although it *is* a source of knowledge about what its writers believed on these matters). It is not, in other words, philosophy or science, and therefore the principles of reason, the touchstone of truth, must not serve as our guide in interpreting Scripture. The moral message of Scripture – that one should love God above all, and one's neighbor as oneself – does, indeed, agree with reason in the sense that our rational faculties approve of it. But *that* Scripture teaches such a message can be discovered only through the "historical" method.

When, then, is a figurative or metaphorical reading of a passage from Scripture called for, if not when that passage conflicts with rationally demonstrated truth? Only when a literal reading is in clear violation of "the basic principles derived from the study of Scripture", that is, only when a literal reading stands in the way of clarifying the intentions or beliefs of the author. The question, then, is not whether God is, in metaphysical truth, fire or susceptible to passions such as anger and jealousy, but whether or not a particular prophet believed these things and intended to convey that message through his writings. And we can only answer this question by examining those writings themselves, as well as the circumstances of their composition. Now Moses (assuming him to be the author) proclaims in the Torah that God has no resemblance to visible things, and yet he also likens God to fire. One needs to inquire, then, as to which of these passages needs to be read metaphorically, regardless of the rationality or irrationality of the belief that would consequently be attributed to the prophet. If linguistic usage suggests that the word 'fire' does not have anything besides a literal meaning, then the other passages that say that God has no resemblance to things in heaven or on the earth need to be read figuratively.

One needs to keep in mind, then, that the purpose of Scripture is not to communicate speculative truth, but to compel obedience. The narratives of the Torah and other writings of the Hebrew Bible – the events they relate about God, human beings, and nature – are a reflection of the beliefs, values, preconceptions and purposes of their authors and especially what they presumed would most appeal to their audience. The prophets, distinguished from ordinary people by their particularly active and vivid imaginations, adopted various literary devices to convey a simple moral and religious message and to inspire readers to obey it. The truth of the resulting propositions and stories is irrelevant to this goal, and indeed to the value of Scripture itself.

In response to the accusation that he has robbed Scripture of its authority and that, on his view, "the Word of God is faulty, mutilated, adulterated and inconsistent", Spinoza insists that, on the contrary, he has restored the true luster and original utility of the work. "A thing is called sacred and divine when its purpose is to foster piety and religion, and it is sacred only for as long as men use it in a religious way ... So Scripture likewise is sacred, and its words

---

[21] TTP XII, G III.163; S 154.

divine, only as long as it moves men to devotion towards God."[22] If a book succeeds in inspiring piety and showing people the way to salvation, then there is nothing corrupt about it. And if an account of Scripture and its interpretation forestalls the idolatrous worship of mere paper and ink and turns people towards genuine devotion to God, then, Spinoza believes, it has made an important contribution to dispelling superstition and to the propagation of true religion.

---

[22] TTP XII, G III.160; S 150.

CHAPTER THIRTY-FOUR

Early Old Testament Critics in the Roman Catholic Church – Focussing on the Pentateuch

By JOHN W. ROGERSON, Sheffield

Sources: RICHARD SIMON: *Histoire critique du Vieux Testament* (Paris 1678, Amsterdam 1680, Rotterdam ²1685); *Réponse au livre intitulé Sentiments de quelques Theologiens de Hollande sur l'Histoire Critique du Vieux Testament* (Rotterdam 1686); *De l'inspiration des Livres Sacrez (sic). Avec une Réponse au livre intitulé Defense des Sentiments de quelques Theologiens de Hollande sur l'Histoire Critique du Vieux Testament* (Rotterdam 1699, but dated 15 November 1686). – AUGUST CALMET: *Commentaire littéral sur tous les livres de l'Ancien et du Nouveau Testament* (Paris 1707–16); *Dissertations qui peuvent servir de prolégomènes de l'Ecriture Sainte, Revûës, corrigées, considérablement augmentées, et mises dans un ordre méthodique* (Paris 1720); *Dictionnaire Historique, critique, chronologique, géographique et littéral de la Bible* (Paris 1721, Geneva ²1730, incorporating the *Supplement* 1727). – JEAN ASTRUC: *Conjectures sur les Mémoires originaux dont il paraît que Moïse s'est servi pour composer le livre de la Genèse, avec des Remarques qui appuient ou qui eclaircissent ces Conjectures* (Brussels 1753; repr. *Conjectures sur la Genèse*. Introduction et notes de Pierre Gibert; Paris 1999). – CHARLES FRANÇOIS HOUBIGANT: *Racines Hebraiques sans points-voyelles ou Dictionaire Hebraique par racines, Où sont expliquez, suivant les Anciens et Nouveaux Interpretes, touts les Mots Hebreux et Caldaïques du Texte Original des Livres Saints* [whole title *sic*] (Paris 1732); *Biblia Hebraica cum notis criticis et versione Latina ad notas criticis facta.* Tomes I-IV (Paris 1753).

General works: C. HOUTMAN, *Inleiding in de Pentateuch* (Kampen 1980) 52–56; A. WESTPHAL, *Les sources du Pentateuque. Étude de critique et d'histoire* I. *Le problème littéraire* (Paris 1888) 101–15; F. DECONINCK-BROSSARD, "England and France in the Eighteenth Century", *Reading the Text. Biblical Criticism and Literary Theory* (ed. S. Prickett; Oxford 1991) 136–81.

Special studies and reference works: P. AUVRAY, *Richard Simon 1638-1712: Étude bio-bibliographique avec des textes inédits* (Paris 1974); F. GORMAN JR, "Simon, Richard (1638-1712)", DBI K-Z (1999) 468–70; W. MCKANE, "RICHARD SIMON", in: idem, *Selected Christian Hebraists* (Cambridge 1989) 111–50; H. GRAF REVENTLOW, "Richard Simon und seine Bedeutung für die kritische Erforschung der Bibel", *Historische Kritik in der Theologie. Beiträge zu ihrer Geschichte* (ed. Georg Schwaiger; Göttingen 1980) 11–36; idem, "Richard Simon", *Klassiker der Theologie* II (ed. Heinrich Fries / Georg Kretschmar; Munich 1983) 9–21; J. STEINMANN, *Richard Simon et des origines de l'exégèse biblique* (Bruges 1960); J. WOODBRIDGE, "Richard Simon's Reaction to Spinoza's 'Tractatus Theologico-Politicus'", *Spinoza in der Frühzeit seiner religiösen Wirkung* (ed. Karlfried Gründer / Wilhelm Schmidt-Biggemann; Heidelberg 1984) 201–26; idem, "German Responses to the Biblical Critic Richard Simon: From Leibniz to J. S. Semler", *Historische Kritik und biblischer Kanon in der deutschen Aufklärung* (ed. H. Graf Reventlow e.a.; Wolfenbütteler Forschungen 41; Wiesbaden 1988) 65–87; idem, "Richard Simon le 'père de la critique biblique'", BTT 6 (Paris 1989) 193–206; J. GERTZ, "Astruc, Jean", RGG⁴ (1999) 863–64; J. H. HAYES, "Astruc, Jean (1684-1766)", DBI A-J (1999) 83; idem, "Calmet, Dom Augustin", ibid. 158–59; B. E. SCHWARZBACH, "Dom Augustin Calmet. Man of the Enlightenment Despite Himself", *ARelG* 3 (2001) 135–48; idem, "Dom Augustin Calmet: Homme des Lumières malgré lui", *Dix-Huitième Siècle* 34 (2002) 451–63.

1. Richard Simon

Richard Simon (1638–1712) is at once a fascinating and elusive character. Estimates of his motivation and of his subsequent influence vary wildly. Was he a *strenger Rationalist* who was *bemüht, ohne Rücksicht auf die geltende Lehrtradition die Entstehung des Alten Testaments kritisch zu erarbeiten*,[1] or was he a faithful member of the Roman Catholic Church?[2] In what sense was his *Histoire critique du Vieux Testament* a work, *das in der Geschichte unsrer Disciplin* [sic] *epochemachende Bedeutung hat?*[3]

The facts of his life are relatively simple. Born in Dieppe on 13 May 1638, Simon studied Hebrew, Syriac and Arabic at the Sorbonne, before becoming an Oratorian novice in 1662. The years of his novitiate were spent in the study of Jewish, Catholic and Protestant biblical scholarship. Following his ordination to the priesthood in Paris in 1670, he published various works on the Eastern churches, Jewish ceremonies, and Islam and became associated with a project for a new French translation of the Bible. The publication of his *Histoire critique* in 1678 brought tragic consequences, mainly because of its view that large parts of the Pentateuch were written by public scribes rather than by Moses. Bishop Jacques-Bénigne Bossuet, to whom was entrusted the education of the son of Louis XIV, ordered the book to be confiscated, and on 21 May 1678 Simon was expelled from the Oratory. He removed to take up pastoral work in Bolleville, in Normandy, from where he later defended his writings under the title of Le Prieur de Bolleville. The notoriety afforded to the book by its confiscation led to its republication in Amsterdam in 1680 and, in France, in a Latin translation in 1681. An English translation appeared in London in 1682 and was followed by an enlarged French edition published in Rotterdam in 1685. Simon continued to publish scholarly works, principally on the text and interpretation of the New Testament and to answer critics of his views on the Old Testament, up to his death on 11 April 1712. After his death, his work continued to provoke opposition. With the emergence of Protestant German historical criticism towards the end of the eighteenth century Simon was claimed as a pioneer of biblical criticism, a verdict that has endured, sometimes in exaggerated form.

It could be argued that disputes about Simon's motivation and theological beliefs are irrelevant to the fact that he made certain critical proposals about the Old Testament, and that later scholarship took these proposals up and enlarged upon them. Such an opinion is tenable only if a history of biblical scholarship concerns itself with 'results' divorced from the complex situations that give rise to them. The aims of historical enquiry are not served by such oversimplification. In what follows, it will be maintained that Simon was a loyal member of his Church, who sought to meet contemporary attacks upon the authority of the Bible by appealing to the writings of the Church Fathers and the decisions of the Councils. That this involved him in relying on statements in the Fathers that did not suit the prevailing Catholic orthodoxy in France as represented, for example, by Bossuet, inevitably brought him into conflict with his superiors. In several ways, Simon is similar to William Robertson Smith who was dismissed from his position in the Free Church College in Aberdeen

---

[1] H.-J. Kraus, *Geschichte der historisch-kritischen Erforschung des Alten Testaments* (Neukirchen-Vluyn ²1969) 65.

[2] Auvray, Richard Simon (1974) 170–72.

[3] E. Riehm, *Einleitung in das Alte Testament* I (Halle 1889) 23.

in 1881 for trying to defend the Bible and Christian faith in ways that did not suit the prevailing orthodoxies.[4]

Simon was roughly contemporary with Benedict Spinoza (1632–77), whose *Tractatus Theologico-Politicus*, published in 1670, and building upon Jewish forebears such as Abraham ibn Ezra (1089–1164), attributed much of the Pentateuch and other books to Ezra, writing in the post-exilic period. This amounted to an attack upon traditional views of authorship and inspiration of the Bible, and Simon's purpose was to defend the Bible against Spinoza. However, Simon was aware that some of the claims of Spinoza could also be found in the Fathers of the Church. Theodoret (c. 393 – c. 466), Bishop of Cyprus, had written of the quotation from the Book of Jashar in Josh 10:13, that it had a different author from the rest of the material and had been taken from another book.[5] In his introduction to the books of Kings, Theodoret had drawn attention to the various sources mentioned in Kings and Chronicles as providing the information upon which the biblical writers had based their work.[6] Closer to Simon's own time, the Belgian scholar Andreas du Mas / Masius (1514–73) had written a commentary on Joshua in which he proposed that Ezra, alone or helped by others, had compiled the books of Joshua, Judges and Kings from records that had been preserved, and that the Pentateuch had been subjected to various forms of editing and explanation long after the time of Moses.[7]

What had caused outrage in Simon's *Histoire critique* was his suggestion that considerable parts of the Pentateuch were the work of what he called 'public writers'. However, in the light of what had been proposed by Theodoret and Masius, Simon's proposal that the historical parts of the Pentateuch had been written by 'public writers', while the laws were written by Moses himself was not so startlingly innovative. Indeed, Simon's view was in some ways more conservative, in that he asserted that the 'public writers' lived in the time of Moses and did their work on his orders. Thus, the Pentateuch could truly be called the work of Moses. An implication was that the 'public writers' continued to function in the generations following Moses, and that they were responsible for many changes and additions to the Bible, as well as the composition or editing of other biblical books, making use of records that were collected and preserved in the registries of the nation.

Simon was accused by Catholics and Protestants alike of undermining the

---

[4] J. W. ROGERSON, *The Bible and Criticism in Victorian Britain. Profiles of F. D. Maurice and William Robertson Smith* (JSOTSup 201; Sheffield 1995).

[5] Theodoret, *Quaest. In Josue*, in: Migne, PLG 80, 475: Δηλον τοινυν καντευθεν, ως αλλος τις των μεταγενεστερων την βιβλον ταυτην συνεγραψε, λαβων εξ ετερας βιβλον τας αφορμας.

[6] Theodoret, *Quest. In I Reg.*, Migne, PLG 80, 529.

[7] Andreas Masius, *Iosuae Imperatoris Historia illustrata atque explicata* (Antwerp 1574) 2 (of commentary): *Mihi certè ea est opinio, ut putem, Esdram, sive solum, sine unà cum aequilibus, insigni pietati et eruditione viris, coelisti spiritu afflatum, non solùm hunc Iosuae, verum etiam Iudicum, Regum, alios, quos in sacris, ut vocant, Bibliis legimus libros, ex diversis annabilis apud Ecclesiam Dei conservatis compilasse; in eumq. ordinem, qui iam olim habetur, redegisse atque disposuisse. Quin ipsum etiam Mosis opus, quod vocant πεντάτευχον, longo post Mosen tempore, interiectis saltem, hîc, illic, verborum, et sententiarum clausulis, veluti sarcitum, atque omnino explicatius redditum esse, coniecturae bonae afferri facilè possunt;* Simon, *Histoire critique*, Bk. 1, Ch. 1.

inspiration and authority of the Bible. That this was not a necessary conclusion can be seen from the Puritan commentator Matthew Poole, whose biblical credentials were hardly in doubt. In his contemporary *Commentary on the Holy Bible* of 1685, he was happy to ascribe passages such as Num 12:3 to "some succeeding prophet" without this, in his view, disparaging "the authority of Holy Scriptures, seeing it is all written by one hand, though divers pens be used by it".[8] Presumably it was the large number of passages that Simon attributed to authors other than Moses (all the historical parts of the Pentateuch) that his opponents found objectionable.

Simon's defence of his appeal to 'public writers' was set out in two works: his reply to objections from certain Dutch theologians, and his treatise on the inspiration of Scripture.[9] Jean le Clerc, the main author of the *Sentiments de quelques Theologiens de Hollande* had argued that there was no reference to scribes or writers in the Pentateuch. Simon's reply distinguished between prophets who predicted the future and prophets who were called 'writers' by the Hebrews. Evidence for the latter could be found in passages such as 1 Chron 29:29, where the acts of David were said to be written in the chronicles of Nathan the prophet (Hebr. *nabi'*) and Gad the seer. Further, the books of Joshua to 2 Kings, consisting largely of history, were designated 'former prophets' in the Hebrew canon of Scripture, while in the Targums the Hebrew *nabi'* was often rendered as *saphra'* meaning 'scribe'.[10] In the treatise on inspiration, Simon claimed a special status for Hebrew scribes, as opposed to the scribes of other nations. While all scribes worked in similar ways, God accorded the privilege of inerrancy to those of the Hebrews.[11] In any case, the letters of Paul were not disregarded because Tertius had written down the letter to the Romans (Rom 16:22) nor did Jeremiah's use of Baruch as a scribe affect the status of his book. Simon also quoted Augustine to the effect that everything that Aaron did was on the authority of Moses.[12]

Another charge brought against Simon was that he questioned the inspiration of the Bible by accepting that 'public writers' had abbreviated their sources when incorporating them into the Bible, and that their methods of working were responsible for repetitions and even the incorrect ordering of events in the narratives. This was probably one of the most serious objections to Simon's position from a traditional point of view. In outlining his view that public writers had made additions to the text, he had questioned whether one writer would have presented the creation of humans twice in Genesis 1–2. He had drawn attention to the differences of style in the Pentateuch, where language was sometimes curt and sometimes prolix even though such devices were not demanded by the subject matter. He had argued that the story of the Flood was confused, and that if it had had one author it would have been shorter

---

[8]   M. Poole, *A Commentary on the Holy Bible* I (1685) 286.

[9]   Simon, *Réponse au livre intitulé Sentiments* (1686); *De l'inspiration des Livres Sacrez* (1699).

[10] Simon, *Réponse*, 57–70.

[11] Simon, *De l'inspiration*, 20: *Dieu leur avoit accordé ce privilege, qu'ils ne pouvoient pas errer.*

[12] Simon, *De l'inspiration*, 27. The quotation from Augustine's *Quaest. In Exod.* reads: *Quod Aaron fecit Moysi potius tribuendum est, quia per Moysem Deus jubebat quae faceret Aaron; et in Moyse autoritas, in illo autem ministerium fuit.*

and more succinct.[13] The charge of abbreviating was easily met, since it was accepted in the Roman Catholic Church that the Gospel of Mark was essentially an abridgement of Matthew. Did this mean that Mark was not inspired? If editorial processes had led to repetitions and the disorder of events, this did not mean that inaccuracies had crept in. The public writers had made no errors while working within the constraints of their time and place. They could not be dismissed for working within their human limitations. Jerome had remarked adversely on the Hebrew style of Jeremiah and Amos, while the Greek Fathers had found fault with Paul's Greek. They had not called into question the inspiration of these writings.[14]

To sum up the matter so far, Simon was not a rationalist bent on questioning received beliefs on the authorship and authority of the Bible. Simon was concerned to defend the Bible from attacks upon it by thinkers such as Spinoza.[15] He realised, however, that this could only be done intelligently, by meeting objections half way, and by showing that valid points made by detractors of the Bible could be interpreted differently. If, in the process, he stressed the human, practical side of the nature of the inspiration of the Bible, he was not so much innovating as drawing out what was already implicit in Christian and Jewish tradition. At the same time, it has to be granted that his critical observations prepared the ground for later literary and source criticism. However, it is necessary to consider another important point of Simon's motivation, his defence of Catholic as opposed to Protestant principles of biblical interpretation.

Chapters 13 to 16 of Book 3 of the *Histoire Critique* deal with the hermeneutics of biblical interpretation, and Simon makes his own position clear by aligning himself with Luther's opponent, Cardinal Thomas de Vio Cajetan (1469–1534). Cajetan is praised for paying attention to the Hebrew text of the Old Testament and for advocating a literal interpretation of the Bible. Simon claimed that Cajetan (and, by implication, Simon himself) is following Augustine's rules of interpretation in *De doctrina Christiana*. A long section is then devoted to the influential Protestant work, the *Clavis Scripturae Sacrae* of Matthias Flacius (Illyricus) published in 1567.[16] The fifty-one reasons given by Flacius for difficulties in the Bible illustrate Simon's point that biblical interpretation is not a straightforward matter of reading the text literally, while the rules proposed by Flacius only duplicate what had already been said by the Fathers. Flacius's appeal to the Protestant rule of faith is further confirmation of Simon's belief that a rule of faith is necessary for a Christian understanding of the Bible. The most devastating part of Simon's argument occurs in Ch.16, where he discusses the Socinians, and points out that while Protestants and Socinians maintain that the meaning of the Bible is clear, they disagree fundamentally about this meaning. Simon implies that if one is to follow the Protestant line consistently, one has to finish up as a Socinian. Protestants can only

---

[13] Simon, *Histoire critique*, Bk. 1, Ch. 5.
[14] Simon, *De l'inspiration*, 38f, 49.
[15] See further ibid. 43 ff.
[16] See further Ch. 24, by B. T. OFTESTAD, in the present volume.

oppose Socinianism by appealing to a rule of faith, something that they then criticise Catholics for doing.

There are, then, good hermeneutical grounds for allowing the Catholic Church to have the ultimate authority in interpreting the Bible; but Simon is also led to this position by other considerations, and especially the fact that no autographs of the biblical writings exist. Christian tradition, both Catholic and Protestant, had tried to deal with this fact in various ways. Augustine believed that the Septuagint was an inspired and inerrant Christian version of the Old Testament. Some Protestant confessions of faith required belief in the divine inspiration of the Masoretic Hebrew text, including the vowel points. A mediating position, in the preface to Brian Walton's *London Polyglot*, acknowledged errors in the extant versions of the Bible, but invoked the working of divine providence to ensure that extant versions were not misleading to faith.

Simon's vast knowledge of biblical versions and manuscripts convinced him that these positions were untenable. It was necessary to proceed critically and rationally, as one would do in trying to establish the best text of any writing; and in this task there were noticeable forerunners such as Origen, Jerome and the unpublished *Correctorium Sorbonicum* which was used by Robert Etienne in his edition of the Latin Bible. Simon's proposals for a new translation of the Bible based upon scholarly attempts to achieve the best possible text were startlingly modern, and are as yet partially unfulfilled. Simon argued that there was a need for a published Hebrew text which, while based upon the Masoretic text, was willing to depart from it both in consonants and vowels, if other Hebrew manuscripts or the versions provided good reasons for doing so. In translating the Hebrew, scholars should not use the Grammar and Dictionary of Qimhi uncritically (nor those of Buxtorf who depended upon Qimhi). The evidence of Origen's *Hexapla* was that the pronunciation of Hebrew in the third century CE was not exactly the same as that of the Masoretes. Any translator into a modern language needed to consult the customs of the Levant for possible light on obscure Hebrew words, should indicate to readers by way of notes where the meaning of the original was uncertain, and should provide a dictionary of difficult and obscure words, their different possible translations, and why a particular rendering had been preferred in the translation. Information should also be given about the geography, chronology and genealogies contained in the Bible.

Before I conclude, it is necessary to mention Johann Salomo Semler's contention that Simon had destroyed the idea that Catholic faith was founded upon the unified tradition of the Church Fathers.[17] This observation fails to recognise the extent to which Catholic tradition has been characterised by vigorous discussion and dispute among religious orders and competing philosophies and theologies. Simon may have fallen foul of ecclesiastical authority as

---

[17] See G. HORNIG, *Die Anfänge der historisch-kritischen Theologie. Johann Salomo Semlers Schriftverständnis und seine Stellung zu Luther* (FSThR 8; Göttingen 1961) 186.

represented by Bishop Bossuet, but his appeal to tradition in the persons of Jerome, Augustine and Cajetan, to name but some, certainly did not undermine it or destroy it.

Simon was certainly a man ahead of his time, combining great learning with a sharp intellect and a fundamental honesty. If the integrity of the Bible and Christian faith were to be defended against a Spinoza, the only possible method was by way of an honest recognition of difficulties inherent in the Bible, and of the imperfect state of existing translations, and editions of the Hebrew text and versions. The decree of the Council of Trent, that the Vulgate was the version best suited to supporting traditional Christian belief and practice, did two things in Simon's view. It provided a secure foundation for Christian interpretation of the Old Testament, while opening up the possibility of the critical investigation of its textual history and composition processes. Such critical investigation could not impugn its inspiration or authority. That Simon's work was rejected by his Church, seized upon by sceptics at the time,[18] and later greeted as a warrant for critical investigation unfettered by doctrinal commitment, was hardly his fault. That he was capable of being misunderstood in so many ways is perhaps an indication of his originality.

2. Augustin Calmet

In contrast to Simon, Augustin Calmet aroused no great controversy and made little impact on the history of biblical criticism; yet his voluminous writings abound with critical observations, and anyone taking his work seriously could never have concluded that biblical interpretation was a simple matter of reading the text.

Born on 26 February 1672 in Ménil-la-Horgne, he entered the Benedictine order in 1689, having received his schooling in the local Benedictine college. His extensive studies enabled him to begin work in 1698 on a commentary on the Bible, assisted by other members of his community. It was published in twenty-six volumes between 1707 and 1716. This gave the Latin text of the Bible with a translation and commentary in French. It was later accompanied by a volume of dissertations which were extracted from the commentary, and which put together Calmet's critical introductions to the books of the Bible.[19] The commentary was followed by Calmet's best-known work (it was translated into Latin, German and English), his Dictionary of the Bible.[20] From 1718 to 1723 Calmet was (temporary) abbot of S. Léopold, Nancy, and in 1728 he became abbot of Senones, where he died on 25 October 1757.

In referring to Simon, Calmet touched upon the latter's text-critical views, not his literary-critical views and he was certainly much more traditional than Simon. In one regard, however, Calmet echoed Simon in asserting the importance of criticism in matters that did not affect faith and morals, namely, lit-

---

[18] See Woodbridge, German Responses (1988).

[19] Calmet, *Dissertations qui peuvent servir de prolégomenes de l'Ecriture Sainte* (1720).

[20] Calmet, *Dictionnaire Historique* (1721). The second edition, to which reference is made, was published in Geneva in 1730 and incorporates the *Supplement* published in 1727.

erary criticism, geography, chronology, natural history, architecture and customs, and that any expert in these fields could be consulted.[21]

On the literary criticism of the Pentateuch, Calmet assigned the work to
Moses, while allowing that passages such as Gen 12:6; Num 21:14; Deut 1:1;
3:8; 3:14; 11:30 (where the writer is on the wrong side of the river Jordan!)
and 34:5–8 (the death of Moses) were later additions.[22] However, such additions were light, did not alter the sense, and served to clarify the passages in
which they appeared.[23] Calmet's treatment of Deuteronomy, however, seems
to have advanced critically beyond this position. Deuteronomy was a collection and abridgement of the laws distributed throughout Exodus, Leviticus
and Numbers. The additions in Deuteronomy (not, at this point, specified by
Calmet) arose from the fact that this book was copied more than the other
books of the Pentateuch, in line with the command in Deut 17:18. Scribes
working in, or close to, the times of David had substituted better-known for
unknown names, and had added sentences to clarify the meaning of the text.[24]
This proposal is reminiscent of Simon's 'public writers' theory, though with
less radical implications. Regarding the writing activity of Moses, Calmet believed that Genesis was composed during the last two years of the wilderness
wanderings. This accounted for anachronisms, such as the occurrence of the
divine name Jehovah in Genesis before Exod 6:3, and the distinction between
clean and unclean animals in the story of the Flood (Gen 7:2–3). For the accounts of the creation of the world and the patriarchs, Moses depended on
oral testimony going back to Adam. Noah knew the sons and grandsons of
Adam, Abraham knew those of Noah, and so on to the time of Moses.[25] The
admission of the anachronistic use of the divine name Jehovah in Genesis is interesting, because it implies that Moses could be inaccurate. The same implication arises from Calmet's statement that the events recorded in the Pentateuch
were not necessarily in the correct order.[26]

Calmet's critical observations were not, of course, confined to the Pentateuch, but before these other views are outlined, two other matters concerning
the Pentateuch will be considered, textual criticism and 'scientific' problems.
Calmet's stress upon the importance of studying the Old Testament in Hebrew
can be illustrated from his appendix to the *Dictionnaire* which contained a literal (etymological) rendering of the Hebrew, Aramaic and Greek names occurring in the Bible, many of the derivations being quite bizarre from a modern standpoint. The Masoretic text was not sacrosanct, however, and in nu-

---

[21] Calmet, *Dictionnaire*, I, iii: *on peut consulter et suivre les Sçavans* [sic], *même ceux qui ne sont pas dans la Communion de l'Eglise Catholique.*
[22] Calmet, *Dissertations*, 16.
[23] Calmet, *Dictionnaire*, II, 308.
[24] Calmet, *Dissertations* 52: *Les Ecrivains substituérent quelquefois des noms connus à ceux qui n'étoient plus de leur tems* [sic], *et suppléerent quelques périodes, où ils jugérent qu'elles étoient néces- saires pour l'éclairissement du Texte.*
[25] Calmet, ibid. 24f. However, in his article on the Ark of Noah, in *Dictionnaire*, I, 281, Cal- met says that Noah probably knew of the distinction between clean and unclean animals.
[26] Calmet, ibid. 18.

merous places the readings of the Samaritan Pentateuch were superior, especially where they agreed with the Septuagint.[27]

A notable feature of Calmet's *Dictionnaire* is its honest and fair-minded discussions of passages that raised 'scientific' difficulties for contemporary readers. An excellent example of this is his article "Déluge" in the *Dictionnaire*.[28]
An honest statement of difficulties (e.g. if everything died [Gen 7:21] where
did the dove get the olive leaf from, what about animals known only in remote
places, and how did Noah get to them to bring them into the ark?) was followed by a long discussion of Isaac Vossius's *Dissertatio de Vera Aetate Mundi*
(1659). Calmet did not agree with its conclusions, but having pointed out that
this Protestant work did not, in the opinion of the Roman Catholic censors,
undermine faith or morals, he defended the right of scholars to seek varying
solutions to problems of this sort and left it to readers to accept Vossius if they
wished. Among Calmet's own answers were that trees could survive being inundated (hence the olive leaf) and that there were fewer species of animals in
Noah's days so that he did not need to get any from remote places. Typical similar discussions concern the reversal of the shadow on Ahab's sundial (2 Kgs
20:8–11)[29] and the sun standing still in Josh 10:13.[30] This kind of material
must have contributed to the rise of biblical criticism simply by drawing attention to the difficulties that had been pointed out in the biblical narratives.

Returning to Calmet's other critical views, he did not accept that David was
responsible for the composition of all the Psalms, and disagreed with Bishop
Bossuet, who believed that all the Psalm titles were inspired. The variants in
the Septuagint and Peshitta showed that this was not so, as did the omission
of the titles from the Psalms as used in the daily Offices of the Church. On the
other hand, Calmet did not reject their information out of hand, and although
his final view of the composition of the Psalms remained unclear, he cited the
view of some of the Fathers that Ezra was the sole, or principal, author of the
collections of Psalms.[31] The Masoretic text of the Psalms was not faultless.
The reference to the Passion of Christ was missing in Ps 21:17 (MT 22:17)
and in the acrostic Psalms the *'ain* was lacking in Ps 36:28 (MT 37:28) and
the *nun* in Ps 144:13–14 (MT 145:13–14).[32]

On the prophetic books, he disagreed with Jerome's view that the order of
the Minor Prophets indicated their relative dates. This was not the case with
Jonah and Amos, while Joel probably prophesied after the fall of Samaria.[33]
His view of Amos was that his first prophecies, in chronological order, were
those of Ch. 7. The mention of Tekoa did not mean that Amos was born there.

---

[27] Calmet, ibid. 24. Examples include Gen 2:4; 7:2; 19:19; 20:2; 23:16; 24:14; 49:10–11;
50:26; Exod 1:2; 4:2.
[28] Calmet, *Dictionnaire*, II, 215–26.
[29] Calmet, *Dissertations*, II, 2: 201–15.
[30] Calmet, ibid. 105–19.
[31] Calmet, *Dictionnaire*, II, 719–27, *Dissertations*, 183–221.
[32] Calmet, *Dissertations*, 225.
[33] Calmet, *Dissertations* I, 380, *Dictionnaire* II, 785.

He was probably a native of the northern kingdom, Israel, who retired to Te-koa following his expulsion from Bethel.[34]

A short account can in no way give an indication of the astonishing breadth of Calmet's work, nor its detail. It ranged over every aspect of biblical inter-pretation from textual criticism to hermeneutics. It was a mine of information on subjects such as the geography, chronology, customs and natural history of the Bible. It faced up honestly to any difficulty that had been advanced against the biblical text; and it was written in a spirit of fairness and generosity to op-ponents. That it should have served as the standard Dictionary of the Bible for a hundred and fifty years is no wonder, and even if it did not mediate ad-vanced critical results to its users, it pointed out difficulties with great honesty and clarity and indicated that serious biblical interpretation required a great deal of learning and sophistication.

3. Jean Astruc

It was the fate of Jean Astruc (1684–1766) to compose a work whose intention was to defend the integrity of the Bible, but which succeeded in opening the way to the modern literary-critical analysis of the Pentateuch.

Born on 19 March 1684 in Sauve, Languedoc, the son of a pastor who wavered between Protes-tantism and Catholicism,[35] Astruc became a renowned physician. He held chairs in medicine in Toulouse, Montpellier and Paris, and became a consulting physician to the Polish king August II and to the French king Louis XV. His main work, *Conjectures sur les Mémoires originaux dont il paraît que Moïse s'est servi pour composer le Livre de la Genèse, avec des Remarques qui appuient ou qui eclaircissent ces Conjectures* appeared anonymously in Brussels in 1753, and was the result of re-searches carried out while at the Polish and French courts.

Astruc accepted that scholars before him, such as Hobbes, Spinoza and Le Clerc, had demonstrated the lack of literary unity in Genesis. What he did not accept was that these findings disproved the traditional view that Moses had been the author of Genesis, with the further implication that the book's integ-rity was thereby impugned. Astruc squared the circle by arguing that Genesis consisted of a number of documents that had been available to Moses, and which gave information about events before Moses's time. These documents ran from the beginning of Genesis to the beginning of Exodus, after which the material was composed by Moses himself. Astruc maintained that these docu-ments could be reconstructed from the text of Genesis, and accordingly he set them out in four columns, using the text of the 1610 Geneva Bible. One of the chief criteria for dividing the sources was the occurrence of the divine names Jehovah and Elohim.

---

[34] Calmet, *Dictionnaire* I, 177 f.
[35] The authorities are agreed that Astruc's Hugenot father converted to Catholicism after the revocation of the Edict of Nantes in 1685. J. C. GERTZ (RGG[4], I, 863) says that he returned to Pro-testantism before his death.

Column A, the document which used the name Elohim, and which was on the left-hand side, consisted of the following passages: Gen 1:1–2:3; 5; 6:9–22; 7:6–10, 19, 22, 24; 8:1–19; 9:1–10, 12, 16, 17, 28, 29;[36] 11:10–26; 17:3–27; 20:1–17; 21:2–32; 22:1–10; 23; 25:1–11; 30:1–23; 31:4–47, 51, 55; 32:1–2, 24–32; 33:1–16; 35:1–27; 37; 40; 41; 42; 43; 44; 45; 46; 47; 48; 49:29–33; 50; Exodus 1–2. Column B, the document which used the name Jehovah, and which was on the right-hand side, consisted of Genesis 2:4–4:26; 6:1–8; 7:1–5, 11–18, 21, 24; 8:20–22; 9:11, 13–15, 18–27; 10; 11:1–9, 27–32; 12; 13; 15; 16; 17:1–2; 18; 19; 20:18; 21:1, 33–34; 22:11–19; 24; 25:19–34; 26; 27; 28:1–5, 10–22; 29; 30:24–43; 31:1–3, 48–50; 32:3–23; 33:17–20; 38; 39; 49:1–29. Column C, printed to the right of Column A, consisted of Gen 7:20, 23–24; 34[37]. Column D contained eight fragments possibly obtained from neighbouring peoples: 1 (Genesis 14) war of five cities, 2 (Gen 19:30–38) Lot and his daughters, 3 (Gen 22:20–24) family of Nahor, 4 (Gen 25:1–4, 12–18) genealogy of Ishmael and the sons of Keturah, 5 (Genesis 34) rape of Dinah, 6 (Gen 26:34–35; 28:9; 36:1–8) marriages of Esau, 7 (Gen 36:9–19) descendants of Esau, 8 (Gen 36:20–31) descendants of Seir the Horite.

A typical problem that this proposal could solve was the question whether Abraham died before or after the marriage of Isaac and the birth of his sons. The biblical chronology gave a straightforward answer to this question. Abraham was aged 100 when Isaac was born (Gen 21:5), and Isaac was aged 40 when he married (Gen 25:20) and 60 when his sons Esau and Jacob were born (Gen 25:26). Since Abraham lived to the age of 175 (Gen 25:7) he must have been alive on the occasions of his son's marriage and the birth of his children. However, Genesis 24 pictures an aged Abraham making provision before his death for Isaac's marriage within his wider kin group, and there is no account of Abraham meeting his future daughter-in-law. Further, the opening of Genesis 25 lists the descendants of Abraham by his wife Keturah, but mentions Isaac without reference to his wife or family. The narrative of Chs. 24–25 lacks unity and raises the question whether or not Abraham lived to see his son Isaac married, and with children. Astruc's division of the accounts into documents dealt with the problem by assuming that Gen 25:19–26, the record of Abraham's descendants by Isaac and Rebecca and of the birth of Esau and Jacob, followed on from the end of Ch. 24. Document B, to which the account belonged, was coherent in itself, and the charge that literary unity was lacking could be dismissed.

However, there was a heavy price to pay for this approach, because Astruc had to concede that Genesis in its extant form was not the work of Moses, even if Moses was responsible for all the material that made up Genesis. By whom the documents had been combined was not stated by Astruc. Although his theory did not necessarily entail that the different documents were the work of several authors in addition to, or to the exclusion of, Moses – Eichhorn, for example, used the documentary theory to defend the Mosaic authorship of the Pentateuch – it opened the door to such views. What Astruc had shown in his attempt to vindicate the Mosaic authorship of Genesis was that its literary sources could be separated and reconstructed using criteria such as the occurrence of the divine names Jehovah and Elohim. This paved the way for a major advance in the critical study of the Old Testament.

---

[36] Gen 9:28–29 could belong either to A or B.
[37] See also under Column D.

4. Charles François Houbigant

In 1753, the year of the appearance of Astruc's *Conjectures*, a four-volume folio edition of the Old Testament and Apocrypha was published in Paris[38] under the name of C. F. Houbigant (1686–1784).[39] Vol. I contained an Introduction of 190 pages in Latin which set out the author's views on the state of the
Massoretic text, his reasons for distrusting it and its vowel points, and his reasons for preferring the Samaritan Pentateuch for the first five books of the Bible. The main part of the Introduction was devoted to classifying the mistakes
that, in his opinion, had crept into the Massoretic text, and to laying down
principles for correcting them, including conjectural emendation. The text of
the Hebrew Bible was given without vowel points and followed the edition
published in 1705 by Van der-Hooght; for the Pentateuch it gave the readings
of the Samaritan in the margin, where they differed from the MT. For the
books of the Apocrypha a Latin or Greek text was given, as appropriate, and
opposite the Hebrew, Latin or Greek was Houbigant's own translation into
Latin. Extensive notes in Latin not only on the text and translation, but on critical matters followed each chapter. At the end of each volume, magnificent indexes detailed verses in which the text had been emended, and gave the Massoretic text and the emendation. A rough count suggests that Houbigant proposed around five thousand alterations to the MT, but while many were based
upon readings in the ancient versions, not a few were purely conjectural.

The author of this astonishing achievement of scholarship was born in Paris in 1686 and entered the Oratory there at the age of eighteen. After teaching in Juilly, Marseilles and Soissons he
was called by his superiors to work at the Church of Saint Magloire in Paris. Here, as a result of
his labours in the church, he suffered the complete loss of his hearing, after which he seems to have
devoted himself to scholarship. He adopted the system of vocalising Hebrew advocated by François Masclef (d. 1728) and in 1732 he published a work entitled *Racines Hebraiques sans points-
voyelles* in which he attacked the Massoretic text and its vowel points and appended a dictionary
of Hebrew verbs and their meanings.[40] All the principles of his later *Biblia Hebraica* were contained in this work. In the years that remained until his death in Paris, possibly on 31 October
1784, apart from reissues of sections of the *Biblia Hebraica*, Houbigant's main publication was a
critical examination of a French psalter prepared by the friars of the Capuchin order.

Houbigant's views on the composition of the books of the Bible were thoroughly traditionalist, but in one respect he was a radical critic, and that was in
his attitude to the Massoretic text. On the assumption that the text of the Bible
must make grammatical and historical sense, Houbigant regarded any deviation from that norm as evidence for corruption that had crept into the text in
the course of its transmission. It was the task of biblical scholarship to correct
such mistakes, and Houbigant undertook this work with energy, skill and in-

---

[38] Houbigant, *Biblia Hebraica cum notis criticis* (1753). Some authorities give 1747–53 as the
dates of publication, but the copy that I consulted in Aberdeen gave the date of each of the four volumes as 1753, and this is also the information given in the British Library Catalogue.
[39] Houbigant's dates are not completely secure. He may have been born a year earlier and died
a year later. See A.-M.-P. INGOLD (ed.), *Essai de bibliographie oratorienne* (Paris 1880–82) 62 f.
[40] Houbigant, *Racines Hebraiques sans points-voyelles* (1732).

genuity. His corrections included not only grammatical, but also what today would be called historical-critical matters. For example, the fact that the total length of the years of the reigns of the kings of Judah and Israel in the books of Kings did not add up to the same number was evidence of corruption, and Houbigant lengthened the reign of Zechariah son of Jeroboam by ten years (cf. 2 Kgs 15:8) and that of Pekah from twenty to thirty years (cf. 2 Kgs 15:27) in order to make the figures agree.[41] In discussing Isa 7:17, Houbigant argued that the words 'the king of Assyria' were a marginal gloss because they could not be satisfactorily explained in their context – a position that has come to be widely accepted in modern scholarship.[42] A sampling of his five thousand or so proposed alterations to the Massoretic text suggests that many of them have become commonplace in commentaries and critical editions of the Hebrew Bible.[43]

Whereas Astruc's *Conjectures* of 1753 has become a celebrated work, albeit not for the reasons that its author intended, Houbigant has passed into an undeserved obscurity. The main reason for this is that he allied himself with those who distrusted the Massoretic text at a time when it was still regarded in some quarters as divinely inspired. Houbigant also adopted the method of reading Hebrew that followed not the Massoretic vocalisation, but the system developed by François Masclef in his *Grammaire Hébraïque* of 1716. This made two assumptions, first, that a Hebrew consonant should be pronounced together with the vowel of its name, i.e. *beth* should be pronounced bé, gimel as gi, *dalet* as da etc.; second, that there were six written vowels in Hebrew, *aleph* pronounced 'a', *he* pronounced 'e', *vav* pronounced 'i', *het* pronounced 'u', *yod* pronounced 'ai' (as in 'raison' in French) and ᶜ*ayn* pronounced 'â'.[44]

Contemporaries were sharply divided over Houbigant's work. Scholars such as Robert Lowth, Benjamin Kennicott and Alexander Geddes valued it highly.[45] E. F. K. Rosenmüller questioned his competence as a linguist and accused him of exaggerating the extent of the corruptions in the Massoretic text.[46] The verdict that was passed down in the history of scholarship, if refer-

---

[41] Houbigant, *Biblia Hebraica*, II, xliv.

[42] Houbigant, ibid. IV, 20.

[43] See my article, "Charles François Houbigant (1686–1784). His Background, Work and Importance for Lowth", in: J. JARICK (ed.), *Sacred Conjectures. The Context and Legacy of Robert Lowth and Jean Astruc* (Library of Hebrew Bible / Old Testament Studies 457; New York / London: T&T Clark International 2007).

[44] Houbigant, *Racines*, lxxv-lxxvi. See also James Robertson, *Clavis Pentateuchi, sive Analysis omnium vocum hebraicarum suo ordine in Pentateucho Moseos occurentium. Una cum Versione Latina et Anglica* (Edinburgh 1770) 80f.

[45] See Alexander Geddes, *Prospectus of a New Translation of the Holy Bible from corrected Texts of the Originals, compared with the Ancient Versions, with Various Readings, Explanatory Notes and Critical Observations* (London 1786) 81: "Nothing can exceed the purity, simplicity, perspicuity and energy of his translation; and if he has not always been equally happy in his conjectural emendation of the text, it cannot be denied that he has, at least, carried away the palm from all those who preceded him in the same career. The clamors [sic] that have been raised against him are the clamors of illiberal ignorance, or of partiality to a system which he had turned into ridicule. While his mode of interpreting is approved by a Lowth, a Kennicott, a Michaelis and a Starck, the barkings of inferior critics will not much injure him".

[46] E. F. K. Rosenmüller, *Handbuch für die Literatur der biblischen Kritik und Exegese* (Göttingen 1797) 500.

ence was indeed made to Houbigant at all, was that his work was marred by excessive enthusiasm for the Samaritan version of the Pentateuch, and by his wild conjectures. This was undeserved, as a comparison of his conjectures with modern commentaries and critical editions of the Hebrew Bible makes clear. From the standpoint of contemporary scholarship it is evident that his admirers were closer to the truth than his detractors.

CHAPTER THIRTY-FIVE

English Deism and Anti-Deist Apologetic

By Henning Graf Reventlow, Bochum

General and reference works: T. Bautz (ed.), *Biographisch-Bibliographisches Kirchenlexikon* [BBKL] (Hamm e.a. 1975-); D. Berman, *A History of Atheism in Britain: from Hobbes to Russell* (London / New York 1988); P. Byrne, *Natural Religion and the Nature of Religion. The Legacy of Deism* (London / New York 1989); P. Byrne / G. Hornig / D. A. Pailin / K. S. Walters, "Deismus", RGG⁴ II (1999) 614–23; A. Champion, *The Pillars of Priestcraft Shaken: the Church of England and its Enemies, 1660–1730* (Cambridge 1992); W. L. Rowe, "Deism", REncPh 2 (1998) 853–56; G. Gawlick, "Deismus", HWP 2 (1972) 44–47; idem, "Epikur bei den Deisten", in: G. Paganini / E. Tortarolo (eds.), *Der Garten und die Moderne. Epikureische Moral und Politik vom Humanismus bis zur Aufklärung* (Stuttgart-Bad Cannstatt 2004) 323–39; E. Feil, "Die Deisten als Gegner der Trinität. Zur ursprünglichen Bedeutung und speziellen Verwendung des Begriffs 'Deistae' für die Sozinianer", *ABG* 33 (1990) 115–24; idem, "Déisme", DEurLum (1997) 314–16 = "Deism", Enc-Enl A-L (Chicago e.a. 2001) 361–64; J. H. Hayes (ed.), *Dictionary of Biblical Interpretation* [DBI] A-J, K-Z (Nashville 1999); J. A. Herrick: *The Radical Rhetoric of the English Deists: The Discourse of Skepticism, 1680–1750* (Columbia, SC 1997); M. C. Jacob, *The Radical Enlightenment: Pantheists, Freemasons and Republicans* (London e.a. 1981); G. V. Lechler, *Geschichte des Englischen Deismus* (Stuttgart / Tübingen 1841; repr. with Introduction and Bibliography, ed. G. Gawlick; Hildesheim 1965); J. Leland, *A View of the Principal Deistical Writers that have Appeared in England in the last and present century; with Observations upon them* 1–2 (London 1754; ⁵1766); J. MacKinnon Robertson, *A History of Freethought: ancient and modern to the period of the French Revolution*, I-II (London ⁴1936; repr. London 1969); J. Orr, *English Deism. Its Roots and Its Fruits* (Grand Rapids, MI 1934); D. A. Pailin, "Rational Religion in England from Herbert of Cherbury to William Paley", in: S. Gilley / W. J. Sheils (eds.), *A History of Religion in Britain: Practice and Belief from Pre-Roman Times to the Present* (Oxford 1994) 211–33; H. Graf Reventlow, *The Authority of the Bible and the Rise of the Modern World* (tr. J. Bowden; London 1984 / Philadelphia 1985); idem, *Epochen der Bibelauslegung* 4 (Munich 2001; ET in prep; to appear 2008); idem, "Freidenkertum (Deismus) und Apologetik", in: H. Holzhey / V. Murdoch (eds.), *Die Philosophie des 18. Jahrhunderts* (F. Ueberweg [ed.], *Grundriss der Geschichte der Philosophie* 4) 1. *Grossbritannien und Nordamerika.* Niederlande (Basel 2004) 177–245; L. Stephen, *History of English Thought in the Eighteenth Century* I-II (London 1876, ²1881, ³1902; repr. New York & Burlingame 1962; Bristol 1991); R. N. Stromberg, *Religious Liberalism in Eighteenth-century England* (Oxford 1954); C. Taylor, *Sources of the Self. The Making of the Modern Identity* (Cambridge 1989); W. H. Trapnell, *The Treatment of Christian Doctrine by Philosophers of the Natural Light from Descartes to Berkeley* (Oxford 1988); J. A. Trinius, *Freydenker-Lexicon, oder Einleitung in die Geschichte der neuern Freygeister, ihrer Schriften, und deren Widerlegungen* (Leipzig / Bernburg 1759; erste Zugabe 1765, anon. reprint of both parts: premessa di Franco Venturi; Torino 1960); E. Troeltsch, "Der Deismus" (1898), in: idem, *Aufsätze zur Geistesgeschichte und Religionssoziologie. Gesammelte Schriften* IV (ed. H. Baron; Tübingen 1925; repr. Aalen 1962 and 1966) 429–87; J. Yolton e.a. (eds.): *The Dictionary of Eighteenth-century British Philosophers* I-II (Bristol 1999).

1. Origins of Deism.
The Impact of Philosophical, Ecclesiastical and Theological Currents That Were Influential on Basic Convictions of the English Deists

Sources: W. CHILLINGWORTH, *The Religion of Protestants. A Safe Way to Salvation* (Oxford 1638; several later editions); A. A. COOPER, Third Earl of SHAFTESBURY, Standard Edition, vols. I,1.2; II,1.2 (Stuttgart-Bad Canstatt 1981–98). – W. H. FRERE / C. E. DOUGLAS (eds.), *Puritan Manifestoes* (London 1907; repr. 1954); T. HALYBURTON, *Natural Religion Insufficient and Revealed Necessary to Man's Happiness in the Present State ...* (Edinburgh 1714; repr. 1798). – T. HOBBES, *Leviathan or the matter, form and power of a commonwealth ecclesiastical and civil* (ed. W. Molesworth; *The English Works of Thomas Hobbes now first collected and edited* 1; London 1839; repr. Aalen 1962, 1966); *Leviathan* (ed. M. Oackeshott; Oxford 1946); *Leviathan* (ed. J. C. A. Gaskin; New York 1996). – R. HOOKER, *Of the Lawes of Ecclesiastical Polity* (The Folger Library Edition of the Works of Richard Hooker; vol. 1, ed. G. Edelen; vol. 2, ed. W. S. Hill; Cambridge, MA / London 1977). – J. LOCKE, *An Essay Concerning Human Understanding. In Four Books* (London 1690; [5]1706; ed. P. H. Nidditsch; Oxford 1975, = P. H. NIDDITSCH [ed.], *The Clarendon Edition of the Works of John Locke* 1); *The Reasonableness of Christianity, as deliver'd in the Scriptures*, in: *The Works of John Locke* 7 (repr. Aalen 1963). – A. PEEL / L. H. CARLSON (eds.), *Elizabethan Nonconformist Texts* 1-6 (London 1951-70). – J. WILKINS, *Of the Principles and Duties of Natural Religion* (London 1675; [2]1693, repr. New York / London 1969).

Studies: M. AYERS, "Locke, John (1632-1704)", in: J. Locke, *Works* 5 (London / New York 1998) 665–87; S. J. BARNETT, *Idol Temples and Crafty Priests: The Origin of Enlightenment Anticlericalism* (New York / Basingstoke 1999); P. COLLINS, "Puritanismus, I. In Grossbritannien", TRE 28 (1997) 8–25 (bibl. 24–25); S. GREAN, *Shaftesbury's Philosophy of Religion and Ethics. A Study in Enthusiasm* (Athens, OH 1967); G. HILLERDAL, *Reason and Revelation in Richard Hooker* (AUL NF 1, vol. 54,7; Lund 1962); W. J. T. KIRBY, *The Theology of Richard Hooker in the Context of the Magisterial Reformation* (SRTH NS 5; Princeton, NJ 2000; cf. "Select Bibliography", 59–63); D. BAKER-SMITH, "Glaube, Vernunft, Erleuchtung", in: J. P. SCHOBINGER (ed.), *Die Philosophie des 17. Jahrhunderts* (F. UEBERWEG [ed.], *Grundriss der Geschichte der Philosophie* 3), *Die Philosophie des 17. Jahrhunderts 3. England* (Basel 1988) 35–89 (§ 2, "Der Kreis von Tew", 39–54); E. G. JACOBY / J. BERNHARDT / F. TRICAUD, "Hobbes und sein Umkreis", in: ibid., ch. 3, 91–177; "Locke und die Auseinandersetzungen über sein Denken", ibid., ch. 9, 605–758 (§ 29, R. BRAND, ibid. "John Locke", 607–713); D. McNAUGHTON, "Shaftesbury, third Earl of (Antony Ashley Cooper: 1671–1713)", in: J. W. YOLTON e.a. (eds.), *Dictionary of Eighteenth-Century British Philosophers* 2 (Bristol 1999) 781–88; J. R. MILTON, "Chillingworth, William (1602-44)", REncPh 2 (1998) 307–09; S. I. MINTZ, *The Hunting of Leviathan. Seventeenth-century Reactions to the Materialism and Moral Philosophy of Thomas Hobbes* (Cambridge 1962); R. R. ORR, *Reason and Authority. The Thought of William Chillingworth* (Oxford 1967); D. A. PAILIN, "Natürliche Religion II. Theologie und Religionsphilosophie vom 17. Jh. bis zur Gegenwart", TRE 24 (1994) 78–85; R. VOITLE, *The Third Earl of Shaftesbury* (Baron Rouge, LA 1984); P. B. WOOD, "John Wilkins", in: Schobinger, Grundriss der Geschichte der Philosophie 3 (1988; see above) 430–34, 499–500 (bibl.).

'Deism', according to E. TROELTSCH's famous statement, is "the religious philosophy of Enlightenment".[1] But it had different roots. Already the original meaning of the name is debated. Whereas G. GAWLICK[2] describes the Deists as people "who did not want either to be atheists or adherents of an inherited belief in revelation, but stopped with a confession of natural religion", E. FEIL[3]

---

[1] *Religionsphilosophie der Aufklärung*: Troeltsch, Der Deismus (1898 / 1925) 429.
[2] Gawlick, Deismus (1972) 44f; similarly idem, Epikur bei den Deisten (2004) 323.
[3] Feil, Deisten (1990) 115–24

regards 'deism' as originally a term for Socianianism in the sense of an antitrinitarian movement. Already in the sixteenth century, an underground movement, especially in France and Italy, might themselves have used the label or been vilified by it.[4] A direct connection with Deism in England is not evident.

For England since the Reformation, which stopped halfway, the existence of a broad humanistic and rationalistic movement is characteristic. Recently W. T. J. Kirby[5] has shown that already Richard Hooker (c. 1554–1600), the leading theologian of the much later so-called Anglican Church during the Elizabethan Settlement, inherited the dualism between natural and revealed theology from the magisterial Reformation of M. Luther, J. Calvin, H. Bullinger.

Bullinger was the most influential continental theologian in England besides Beza. It is well known that especially the Reformed theologians shared the rational and moral approach of the scholastics. At first Aristotelianism was the philosophical basis,[6] but even the move to other systems did not change the general character of this thinking. According to S. J. Barnett,[7] the Enlightenment anticlericalism, which also stamped the polemics of the Deistic writers against "priestcraft", was a widespread tendency operative since the Reformation. Puritanism[8] as a radical movement inside the Church also overstated an anti-cultic trait observable already in the 'left wing' of the Reformation, denying Melanchthon's conviction shared by the main Church that outer cultic forms are *adiaphora* – not important for the Gospel proclaimed in the Church. The opposition became first visible, when Bishop Hooper (d. 1555) refused to be consecrated in his bishop's vestment, and lead to a long lasting strife in the Church, continuing until the Revolution under O. Cromwell, the period of the Commonwealth, and the restoration of 1660. This was a movement against the episcopal rule of the Church and its ceremonies (represented by Archbishop W. Laud, 1573–1645), not against the clergy as such. It originated with the militant anti-Catholic propaganda that characterised the situation in the Church of England since Henry VIII (1509–47) claimed the supremacy over the Church in 1534. The fear of a forced return to Catholicism was always alive, strengthened by the experience under the 'bloody' queen Mary (1553–58), the attempt of an invasion of England by the Spanish Armada in 1588 and becoming actual again when the catholic Stuart King James II (1685–88) ascended the throne. Polemics against the catholic clergy headed by the Pope could easily have been extended to the official Protestant Church, in which also wealth, venal offices and absentee of benefice-holders gave ground for protest. But the polemic against "priestcraft" was less directed against these concrete grievances and instead had an ideological character, repeated again and again in a stereotyped manner.

Another aspect was rational thinking. This was not the business of the masses, but was cultivated in élitist circles. Well known is the circle of Great Tew, which gathered around Lucius Cary, Lord Falkland (c. 1610–43) on his estate before the outbreak of the civil war. It is remarkable for its intellectual climate, embracing a mild rationalistic attitude. Of its members, two are especially important: John Hales (1584–1646) and William Chillingworth (1602–44). Chillingworth's famous work, *The Religion of Protestants A Safe Way to Salvation*, is the fruit of his controversy with the Catholic author T. Matthew

---

[4] Cf. besides P. Viret, quoted in: Lechler, Geschichte des Englischen Deismus (1965), Vorwort, VIII-X, also the text of 1576 mentioned by Feil, Deisten (1990) 117, and Halyburton, *Natural Religion Insufficient* (1714 / 1798) 19 f.

[5] Kirby, The Theology of Richard Hooker (2000).

[6] Hillerdal, Reason and Revelation in Richard Hooker (1962), esp. 24f, mentions Thomistic influence on Hooker.

[7] Barnett, Idol Temples and Crafty Priests (1999).

[8] Cf. Collins, Puritanismus (1997) 8–25.

(1577–1655), who in the anonymous tract *Charity Mistaken*[9] defended the standpoint that salvation was not attainable outside the visible community of the Roman Church. Chillingworth's reply is stamped by his rational scepticism: The Roman Church claims infallibility, but the possession of absolute truth cannot be trusted before all the premises upon which it is built can be rationally proven as true. Thus, the assertion of Rome that its pretensions have a biblical basis is based on a circular argument by adding that only the Church can interpret the Bible accurately. More freedom is conceded: God's unrestricted goodness assesses the weakness of mortals and does not demand more than what human rational capacity is able to understand in the Bible and human conduct can strive to fulfil. Salvation is gained by searching for it. Reason is the means by which the Bible, though being the source of truth, can be evaluated. In this sense Chillingworth's famous statement must be understood: "The BIBLE, I say, the BIBLE only is the religion of Protestants!".[10] Although the Bible is "God's Word" and has "sufficient certainty" to be the basis of true faith[11], everybody has to judge for himself what is the correct interpretation. The thinking individual has the last word. Chillingworth partakes also in the typical humanist moralism. Chillingworth's book in spite of all its structural weaknesses exerted a large influence in the future and passed through several new editions as far as the nineteenth century.

Thomas Hobbes (1588–1679) is rightly regarded in histories of exegesis as an early representative of Biblical criticism. He developed his theory of government in the first parts of his *Leviathan* by using a rational method (*more geometrico*). His critical observations on the Old Testament were just a by-product of his main aim, to give reasons for a Christian Commonwealth,[12] though he regarded the Bible as very important for a proof of his political arguments. Several observations prevent taking him as an influential precursor of the Deists:[13] 1. He was a stout defender of a state Church ruled by a central governor (an absolute king or theoretically even a democratic regiment). 2. Being denounced by his enemies as an atheist (and forced to fly to the Continent during the Commonwealth) he suffered even in his old age a continuous defamation and was forbidden to publish any more.[14] His theories were not discussed in a

---

[9] s.l. 1630

[10] Chillingworth, *The Religion of Protestants* (1638), ch. VI, 56.

[11] Ibid.

[12] Already by his contemporaries Hobbes was accused of being an atheist. Though using a materialistic approach, he rightly refused this accusation. Modern historians not seldom disregard his interest in the Church and the Bible, treating him exclusively as a political theorist. See, however, H. Graf Reventlow, The Authority of the Bible (1984 / 1985) 194–222; idem, Epochen der Bibelauslegung 4 (2001) 39–57.

[13] F. TRICAUD, "Thomas Hobbes. Wirkungsgeschichte", in: Schobinger, Grundriss 3. England (1988) 160–77, 167, does not dare to say more than "It is *possible* that Hobbes's work influenced Deism and Freethinking to a certain degree" (*In England hat das Werk von Hobbes in der ersten Hälfte des 18. Jahrhunderts wahrscheinlich einen gewissen Einfluß auf den Deismus und das Freidenkertum ausgeübt*).

[14] On the reception of Hobbes' legacy in England cf. F. TRICAUD, "Die Jagd auf Leviathan", in: Schobinger, Grundriss (1988), ch. 3 "Hobbes und sein Umkreis" (91–177), *Wirkungsgeschichte*, 160–63.

positive sense[15] but much later, because his name was proscribed for a long time.

In contrast to Hobbes, J. Locke deserves to be mentioned as the thinker whose theory of knowledge, especially in his *Essay Concerning Human Understanding*, offered a methodological basis for the inherent value system from which the Deists started.[16] His repudiation of innate ideas and his empiricist approach from experience allowed standpoints seemingly independent from orthodox tradition. J. Toland considered himself a pupil of Locke, though the latter refused to receive him after his book *Christianity not Mysterious* had appeared.[17] Locke himself in his late work *The Reasonableness of Christianity*,[18] on the basis of his own study of the Bible, defended a standpoint between the orthodox dogma of original sin inherited from Adam and a strict moral freedom: The basis of morality can be found in the life and wisdom of Jesus and his moral teachings. In falling short of these rules, everybody becomes guilty by his own deeds, but can receive pardon through belief in Christ. At the end of his life, Locke personally kept his trust in the authority of the Bible, but in his rationalism and moralism he prepared the tools for overturning this authority.

An important trend in the period was a stress on natural religion. As the term is ambiguous and has several aspects,[19] different parties could use the idea. It could be an important basis for objections against revealed religion, but also an argument of its defence by Christian apologists. It is important to see that natural scientists in the second half of the seventeenth century were mostly Christian believers. One famous example is Robert Boyle (1627-91), the "devout naturalist",[20] who defended the theory of the "two books", through which God speaks: Nature and Holy Scripture, and was also the sponsor of the "Boyle Lectures".[21] Not accidentally J. Wilkins (1614-1672), among the founders of the Royal Society (1662) and one of their first secretaries, was the author of the apologetic book *Of the Principles and Duties of Natural Religion* (1674).

The third Earl of Shaftesbury (1671-1713), already a contemporary of the Deists,[22] contributed also to the discussion. The humanist heritage stamps his thinking. As a youth he wrote two notebooks of reflections drawn largely from the Stoic philosophers Epictetus and Marcus Aurelius, the *Philosophical Regimen*.[23] His interest in ethics he shared with other humanists. He is famous for his theory of a "moral sense", which, however, is not just a feeling, but has a rational basis. To

---

[15] Polemic *against* Hobbes was quite common in the second half of the seventeenth century and still later (cf. Mintz, The Hunting of Leviathan, 1962).

[16] Taylor, Sources of the Self (1989), even speaks about Locke's "Deism", thought he states: "Locke has still not gone all the way towards this Deism", ibid. 247.

[17] See sect. 3.1. below.

[18] *The Works of John Locke* 7 (1823/ 1963).

[19] Cf. Pailin, Natürliche Religion (1994) 80–85.

[20] Cf. M. S. FISHER, *Robert Boyle. Devout Naturalist* (Philadelphia 1945); cf. also H. D. RACK, "Boyle, Robert (1627–1691)", TRE 7 (1981) 101–04; P. B. WOOD, "Robert Boyle", in: Schobinger, Grundriss (1988) 395–407.

[21] See below 870–71.

[22] J. Toland was among his friends. Some writers even regard himself as a Deist.

[23] B. RAND, *The Life, Unpublished Letters and Philosophical Regimen of Anthony, Earl of Shaftesbury* (London / New York 1900).

develop this capacity, mankind does not need a divine inspiration or grace and forgiveness. There is a divine order in nature, and following the natural laws is enough for a life according to the will of God. His view of beauty inherent in the order of the world made him one of the fathers of aesthetics and romanticism. Recently J. A. HERRICK[24] pointed to Shaftesbury's theory of ridicule[25] as important for the rhetoric of several Deists.[26]

R. E. STROMBERG remarks that it would be a "mistake of thinking that all the criticisms of Christianity brought forward in the eighteenth century were new".[27] He reminds us of P. Pomponazzi (1462–1525) and his Stoic and Epicurean sources, and of Averroism in the Middle Ages "holding reason capable of full religious truth".[28] The pre-history of Deism goes further back than is normally accepted. It is a battle in the long underground war between the classic heritage of European culture and the Christian message.

Thus, the way for the deistic movement was partly prepared, but its distinctive features remained to emerge. The political conditions for their representatives to present their opinions to the public were unfavourable during the Civil War and the period of the Commonwealth (1640–1660) and some decades thereafter. The situation changed with the Glorious Revolution in 1689. From then onwards, freedom of the press prevailed and the old censorship under the Stuart kings and during the Commonwealth did not return. This allowed the deist authors to express their private opinion more openly, though not without restrictions.

2. Edward Lord Herbert of Cherbury – the First English Deist?

Sources: E. HERBERT LORD CHERBURY: *De veritate. Prout Distinguitur a Revelatione, a Verisimile, a Possibile, et a Falso* ([Paris] 1624; ³London 1645; repr. of the 3rd edn. ed. G. Gawlick; Stuttgart-Bad Cannstatt 1966); *De causis errorum* (London 1645; repr. [together with *De veritate*] ed. G. Gawlick; Stuttgart-Bad Cannstatt 1966); *De Religione Gentilium Errorumque apud eos Causis* (Amsterdam 1663; repr. ed. G. Gawlick; Stuttgart-Bad Cannstatt 1967); *A Dialogue Between a Tutor and His Pupil* (London 1768; repr. ed. G. Gawlick; Stuttgart-Bad Cannstatt 1971).

Studies: R. D. BEDFORD, *The Defence of Truth. Herbert of Cherbury and the Seventeenth Century* (Manchester 1979); S. HUTTON, "Lord Herbert of Cherbury and the Cambridge Platonists", in: S. BROWN (ed.), *British Philosophy and the Age of Enlightenment* (Routledge History of Philosophy V; London / New York 1996) 20–42; D. A. PAILIN, "Herbert of Cherbury and the Deists", *ET* 94 (1982/3) 196–200; idem, "Herbert von Cherbury, Edward (1583?-1648)", TRE 15 (1986) 62–66; idem, "Herbert von Cherbury", in: J.-P. Schobinger (ed.), *Grundriss der Geschichte der Philosophie. Die Philosophie des 17. Jahrhunderts, 3. England,* 1. Halbband (Basel 1988) 224–39, 284–85; M. M. ROSSI, *La vita, le opere, i tempi di Edoardo Herbert di Cherbury* 1–3 (Florence 1947); M. SECKLER, "Aufklärung und Offenbarung", in: CGG 21 (1980) 5–78; C. STROPPEL, *Edward Herbert von Cherbury. Wahrheit – Religion – Freiheit* (TSTP 20; Tübingen 2000).

---

[24] J. A. HERRICK, *The Radical Rhetoric of the English Deists. The Discourse of Skepticism, 1680–1750* (Columbia, SC 1997) esp. 53 f.

[25] Especially in Shaftesbury's *Letter Concerning Enthusiasm* (1708), in: *Standard Edition* I,1 (1981) 302–75, and in the tract *Sensus Communis, or an Essay on Wit and Humour* (1709), in: Standard Edition I,3 (1992). Cf. already S. GREAN, *Shaftesbury's Philosophy of Religion and Ethics. A Study in Enthusiasm* (Athens, OH 1967) 120–34.

[26] His judgement is impaired, however, by regarding Deism as an atheistic movement. We will see that this is not the case, except perhaps with some radical outsiders. Taylor, Sources of Self (1989) 266, rightly stresses "the force of these deist vows as religious beliefs".

[27] Stromberg, Religious Liberalism (1954) 32.

[28] Ibid.

Since T. Halyburton in 1714[29] and J. Leland in 1754[30] called Herbert of Cherbury (1582/3–1648) the initiator of Deism in England, he has often been characterised as the "father of Deism".[31] Recent scholarship[32] has noted more and
more that this label is not correct. Herbert lived a hundred years earlier than
the mainstream of Deism. Connections to the movement are not visible – some
uncertain allusions of Charles Blount (1654–93) excepted. D. A. PAILIN finds
in his thinking motifs of Renaissance Humanism (especially Neo-Stoicism)
mixed with those of the early Enligthenment[33] and characterises him with
some caution as "a liberal theologian in the sense of the 17th century".[34] M.
SECKLER declares: "Herbert's work has a key-position in the revelation-criti-
cism of the Enlightenment".[35] His student C. STROPPEL[36] even calls him an
"advocate for freedom of conscience and religion". We will see if this judgement is correct.

Herbert was born in March 1582 (old style) as son of a landowner. After studies in Oxford and
London from 1596 to c. 1604 and travels through France 1608–09 he served as officer during a
campaign to Jülich (1610) and later in the Netherlands under the Prince of Orange. A second journey brought him to Rome and Padua, where he studied with C. Cremonini, an Averroist Aristotelian. From 1619–24 (with a short interruption) he was (as it seems, a skilled) British ambassador in
Paris. Fallen into disgrace with the king (James I) for uncertain reasons, he returned to England.
He was created Irish Pair of Castle Island (1624) and Baronet of Cherbury (1629). In 1632 he became a member of the War Council. Permanent attempts at rehabilitation with the king (Charles I)
– including a History of Henry VIII[37] – and repeated pleas for having his expenses refunded failed.
In the Civil War he tried to remain neutral to preserve his possessions, though his sons fought in
the royal army. When parliamentary troupes arrived in 1644, he opened Montgomery Castle to
them, for the same reasons. The parliament granted him a pension and he spent the rest of his life
mostly in London, where he died in 1648.

Herbert was no theologian, but a philosopher. His main work *De veritate*
contains predominantly a theory of knowledge. Finally Herbert arrived at the
"Common notions regarding religion".[38] These are the following: [1.] "There
is an uppermost divine being"; [2.] "This uppermost divine being must be venerated"; [3.] "Virtue combined with piety are the most important parts of divine service"; [4.] "Sins and crimes whatever must be expiated by atonement";
[5.] "There is reward and punishment after this life". These statements were
neither revolutionary nor new: Clearly they belonged to the standard rules of

---

[29] Halyburton, Natural Religion (1714 / 1798).
[30] J. Leland, A View of the Principal Deistical Writers that have Appeared in England in the
last and present century; with Observations upon them I-II (London 1754; ⁵1766), vol. I, 23.
[31] Until recently, the present writer shared this opinion, cf. Reventlow, Freidenkertum (2004)
179 (the chapter was written in 1993); but convincing arguments speak against this classification.
[32] Pailin, Herbert of Cherbury and the Deists (1982/3) 196–200; cf. also idem, Herbert von
Cherbury, Edward (1986) 65; idem, Herbert von Cherbury (1988) 224–39, 284 f.
[33] "In the person of Herbert of Cherbury Renaissance lifestyle and tendencies of Enlightenment are combined to a paradox unity" (*In der Person Herberts von Cherbury verbinden sich Lebens-
formen der Renaissance und Tendenzen der Aufklärung zu einer paradoxen Einheit*), Pailin, Herbert
von Cherbury (1988) 231.
[34] Ibid. 235.
[35] Seckler, Aufklärung und Offenbarung (1980) 41.
[36] Stroppel, Edward Herbert von Cherbury (2000), ch. 8, superscription, 497.
[37] *The Life and Raigne of King Henry the Eight* (London 1649; several reprints).
[38] Herbert Lord Cherbury, *De veritate* (1645 / 1966) 208–22.

neo-stoicism. Remarkably Herbert also acknowledged the existence of revelation.[39] In contrast to human truths founded on our faculties, the fundament of
revealed truths consists in the authority of the revealer.[40] In a certain way,
Herbert was a conservative thinker, starting from humanist tradition.

The main points in Herbert's other tracts on religion are a consequence of his basic position. In
his *De religione laici* Herbert suggests that the traveller who comes in contact with foreign religions
in remote parts of the world – this was the period of the voyages of discovery – should judge about
their truth according to the "universal Church truths".[41] They are valid everywhere, because they
are "inscribed from heaven in the heart itself"[42] and should be followed as long as they do not contradict reason. Herbert has been applauded as the founder of the science of comparative religion.[43]
This leads to considerations about the value of historical narrations, including the Bible. Herbert
remarks that not all parts of the Bible could be regarded as God's word, "because the words of
criminals, of women [!], of beasts, even of the Devil are delivered in the Holy Scripture".[44] There
is also a difference between miracles, prophecies, rites, sacrament, ceremonies and religious cult of
the Hebrews and "love, fear of God, charity, penitence, and the hope of a better life".[45] It is clear
what Herbert regarded as essential. And he was convinced that even a layman is able to decide
where true religion can be found using these measures. But he was also prepared to accept the exterior cultic forms as illustrations and confirmations of interior piety.[46] He was no radical!

His basic definition of religion allowed him also to find true believers in all
religions. This was not completely new, because in humanist tradition a theory
existed about the philosophers of classic antiquity as Socrates, Plato etc., who
had already found the truth without revelation. Now, after so many peoples in
foreign continents had been discovered that never could have been reached by
the Gospel – should they without personal guilt be excluded from salvation?
How could this be reconciled with God's comprehensive providence? In *De religione Gentilium*[47] Herbert therefore[48] extended his principles to the heathen-
ish peoples of his time. His solution to the problem is that it is the fault of the
priests that Christian theologians in Antiquity and in the present could rightly
accuse the heathen of worshipping false gods by means of an erroneous and
idolatrous cult. At first only one God was venerated. But later "the cunning
species of priests crept in (I believe), who not being satisfied by having one
God in this universe, thought it useful for them to add other gods to this highest Divine being".[49] Here again the typical anti-priestly attitude becomes visible that belongs to the heritage of Humanism. The ancients believed they were

---

[39] Ibid. 226.
[40] Ibid.
[41] *De Religione Laici*, in: *De veritate* (1645 / 1966) 129: *Catholicas Ecclesiae Veritates*.
[42] Ibid.
[43] Especially by Stroppel, Edward Herbert von Cherbury (2000).
[44] *De veritate*, 135: *Quum ut Consceleratorum, Mulierum, Bestiarum, quin & ipsius Diaboli verba
in S.S. tradita, mittantur.*
[45] Ibid.
[46] Ibid. – He is also reported to have prayed himself twice a day.
[47] *De religione Gentilium* (1663 / 1967).
[48] Cf. ibid. 1.
[49] Ibid. 1: … *callidum (puto) irrepsit Sacerdotum genus, qui haud satis habentes unum tantum in
hac rerum universitate constitui Deum, è re suâ esse putaverant, ut alois huic summo Numini adjunger-
ent Deos.* This is the theory of an original monotheism, popular in the period. We find it also with
G. J. Vossius, *De Theologia Gentili et Physiologia Christiana, sive de Origine ac Progressu Idolatriae*
(Amsterdam 1642).

saved by a virtuous life: In ch. XV[50] Herbert has a list of terms such as "virtue", "piety", "concord", "peace" etc., by which a life can be characterised that is pleasing to God. Herbert did not publish this book during his lifetime. Though he had not mentioned the clergy of the Church of England, he was surely afraid of the reactions to be expected from the official theologians. Nevertheless, this was not yet the aggressive polemics of the later Deists.

3. Prominent Deistic Authors and the Bible

3.1. John Toland

Sources: Anon. [JOHN TOLAND]: Christianity not Mysterious; or a Treatise shewing, That there is nothing in the Gospel contrary to Reason, nor above it: And that no Christian Doctrine can be properly call'd a Mystery (London 1696; repr. ed. G. Gawlick; Stuttgart-Bad Cannstatt 1964; ed. J. V. Price; Bristol 1999; London [2]1696; repr. London 1995); Nazarenus, or, Jewish, Gentile and Mahometan Christianity. With an Appendix (London 1718; [2]1718; ed. J. Champion [detailed introduction, 1–106] ; Oxford 1999); (pseudon.: Janus Junius Eoganesius), Pantheisticon, sive formula celebrandae sodalitatis Socraticae ... (Cosmopoli [London] 1720; ET: Pantheisticon; or, the Form of celebrating the Socratic-Society ...; London 1751; repr. New York 1976).

Studies and reference articles: D. BERMAN, "Enlightenment and Counter-Enlightenment in Irish Philosophy", AGPh 64 (1982) 148–65; S. H. DANIEL, John Toland: his Methods, Manners and Mind (Kingston, Montreal 1984); R. R. EVANS, Pantheisticon, The Career of John Toland (New York 1991); C. GIUNTINI, Toland e i liberi pensatori dell' 700 (Florence 1974); eadem, Panteismo e ideologia repubblicana: John Toland (1670-1722) (Bologna 1979); F. HEINEMANN, "John Toland and the Age of Reason", APh 4 (1950) 35–66; M. IOFRIDA, La filosofia di John Toland: Spinozismo, scienza e religione nella cultura europea fra '600 e '700 (Milano 1983); R. E. SULLIVAN, John Toland and the Deist Controversy: A study in adaptations (Cambridge, MA / London 1982); K.-G. WESSELING, "John Toland (1670-1722) et la crise de la conscience européenne", RSyn 116,2-3 (1995). "Toland, John", BBKL XII (1997) 267–86 (K.-G. Wesseling); BB 6 (1763) 3965–77; DNB 46 (1898) 438–42 (L. Stephen).

John Toland (1670–1722), born an Irish Catholic, possibly the natural son of a priest, soon converted to Protestantism. He concluded his study of liberal arts in Glasgow and Edinburgh with the promotion to MA. During studies in Holland (Leiden and Utrecht) 1692–93 he made the acquaintance of the Arminian professors J. le Clerc / Clericus and P. van Limborch. Returning to England, he was unwilling to accept ordination to clerical office. In London, later in Oxford he lived by literary work undertaken for different patrons and frequented republican circles.

In 1696 he published his work Christianity not Mysterious, first anonymously, but shortly afterwards with a second edition under his own name. The book placed him under suspicion. During a stay in Ireland – possibly on a secret political mission – he was officially prosecuted. The Irish House of Commons ordered his book to be burnt publicly by the hangman. When in 1698 he published a Life of Milton,[51] in which he uttered his conviction that not all the Scriptures published under the names of Christ or the Apostles were genuine, he was forced to flee to Holland. But Clericus and van Limborch (like Locke) kept their distance from him. In 1700 the Convocation of the Church

---

[50] De religione Gentilium (1663 / 1967) 184–218.
[51] Cf. also his Amyntor, or a Defense of Milton's Life (1699).

of England condemned his book *Christianity not Mysterious*, but the liberal Bishops in the House of Lords refused leave to prosecute him.

Toland's personal relations with the influential Tory Secretary of State R. Harley (later Earl of Oxford; 1661-1724) and his book *Anglia libera* (1701) gave him the opportunity for a political mission to Hanover in 1701. He was member of a delegation, which brought a document about the succession of the Welf family on the British throne to the electress Sophie (1630-1714). But when Queen Anne (1702-14) succeeded first, he fell into disgrace. Privately he returned to Germany, first to Hanover, where he discussed metaphysical problems with G. W. Leibniz (1646-1716), then to Berlin, to Queen Sophie Charlotte of Prussia (1668-1705), a lady with philosophical interests, to whom he sent his *Letters to Serena*. After the accession of King George I, the beginning of a long rule of the Whigs, his situation became hopeless. Plagued by ill health and financial difficulties he sought to keep his head above water as a political and theological writer. In this period he wrote i.a. his *Pantheisticon* (1720), in which he described the rites of a Pantheistic club, to which he seems to have belonged.

In our context, Toland's first work *Christianity not Mysterious* is the most important. First, it must be said that this book is in no way an antichristian work. G. GAWLICK, in his introduction remarks: "In Christianity not mysterious Toland presupposed the truth of Christian revelation instead of questioning it or even denying it".[52] Toland even affirms: "I demonstrate the Verity of Divine Revelation against Atheists and all Enemies of reveal'd Religion". But he has a methodical demand: In his "Preface"[53] he declares, reasonable creatures should not use anything else than their God-given reason to judge about articles of religion. He contrasts "the plain convincing Instructions of Christ"[54] to "the intricate ineffectual Declamations of the Scribes", their "wild Speculations" to the sound judgement of the "Vulgar", "the Poor".[55] The credo of the Enlightenment is "that the true Religion must necessarily be reasonable and intelligible".[56]

In the first part of his book (*Of Reason*, 7-22), he develops his understanding of reason completely in the sense of Locke. Knowledge consists in the identity or non-identity between ideas. These ideas are perceived either immediately by intuition or mediated by the senses on the way of "intermediate ideas". Toland also acknowledges authority: either human authority or "Moral Certitude",[57] or God's authority in Divine revelation. It "is the Manifestation of Truth by Truth itself, to whom it is impossible to lie".[58] On the other hand, it is just a "Means of Information" (14; cf. 37f; 146). "I believe nothing purely upon his word without Evidence in the things themselves."[59]

This is the theme of Part II (23–66), in which Toland tries to show "That the Doctrines of the Gospel are not contrary to Reason", more exactly the "common notions".[60] The scale is here the same: There is no "different Rule to be follow'd in the Interpretation of Scripture from what is

---

[52] Toland, *Christianity not Mysterious* (1964), Introduction, 11*. Cf. Toland, ibid., Preface, XXVI: "In the following Discourse … the Divinity of the New Testament is taken for granted".

[53] Ibid. III-XXX.

[54] Cf. also "I am … of the Lord Jesus Christ, who alone is the Author and Finisher of my Faith", ibid. XXVII.

[55] Ibid. XIX-XXI.

[56] Ibid. XXVII.

[57] Ibid. 15: "as when I believe an intelligible Relation made by my Friend, because I have no Reason to suspect his Veracity, nor he any Interest to deceive me".

[58] Ibid. 16; cf. the quotation of Num 23:19, p. 33.

[59] Ibid. 38.

[60] Ibid. 23.

common to all other Books".[61] "The New Testament (if it be indeed Divine) must consequently agree with Natural Reason, and our own ordinary Idea's [sic!]".[62] Much in Scripture would not fulfil these conditions, if it could not be figuratively interpreted: "that God is subject to Passions, is the Author of Sin, that Christ is a Rock, was actually guilty of and defil'd with our Transgressions…".[63]

The importance of Scripture is above all that it delivers additional information, on which human reason cannot get hold of itself. God alone as creator can inform about the creation, about the last judgement. This, however, has to be clear and possible, insofar as it is subject to examination by reason. The commandment to stone false prophets (Deut 13:1–3) and Deut 18:21f – the truth of a prophecy is confirmed when it takes place – are proof texts. Toland even acknowledges the miracles of Jesus as proofs for the divinity of his teaching.[64] This is far from the miracle-criticism of the later Enlightenment.

In Part III (67–173) Toland seeks to show that in the Gospel "nothing mysterious or above Reason" is contained. The examples taken from classical Antiquity hide the typical anti-priestly bias: It was the "cunning Priests" who by their rituals and the feigned mysteries seduced the people. "Superstition" is the catchword appearing in this context, behind which a sharp criticism of the present Church officials is concealed. "Mystery" is "a thing intelligible of itself, but so vail'd by others, that it could not be known without special Revelation".[65] In the New Testament, such is contained – but, once revealed, it is no mystery any more. This will be checked in the New Testament itself.[66] "Now since by Revelation Men are not endu'd with any new Faculties, it follows that God should lose his end in speaking to them, if what he said did not agree with their common Notions". "Faith or Perswasion must necessarily consist of two Parts, Knowledge and Assent".[67] Fact cannot be known without revelation, but what is revealed must pass the check of reason. Also miracles are not excepted: Because contradiction is the same as impossible, the "miraculous Action therefore must be something in itself intelligible and possible".[68] "No miracle then is contrary to Reason."[69] Ethics is the other main theme of Enlightenment. Jesus is the prototype of a moralist: He "preached the purest morals … So having stripp'd the truth of all those external Types and Ceremonies … he rendered it easy and obvious to the meanest Capacities".[70]

Toland did not yet know historical criticism of the Bible, but he formulated already characteristic approaches and ideas for later criticism of the Bible, including the focus on the New Testament. In a way, his ideology has links with the Puritans on one side, and the Latitudinarians on the other.

Toland's position is debated. If we regard *Christianity not Mysterious* as his most important work, the label 'deist' as one who denies revelation, cannot be adequate for him. If we recognise this work as a radical version of the Latitudinarian position, it is striking that it met with so much opposition in his time.

---

[61] Ibid. 49.
[62] Ibid. 46. Cf. also 32: "But if we believe the *Scripture* to be Divine, not upon its own bare Assertion, but … from the Evidence of the things contain'd therein… what is this but to prove it by *Reason*?"
[63] Ibid. 34.
[64] Ibid. 46–49.
[65] Ibid. 72.
[66] Ibid. 90.
[67] Ibid. 133.
[68] Ibid. 150.
[69] Ibid. 151.
[70] Ibid. 158.

His *Pantheisticon* seems to differ totally from this attitude. But the discrepancy between the pantheistic topic of this work and a basic Christian attitude cannot be explained as an inner development, because in the comparatively late *Nazarenus* Toland's Christian background seems to be unchanged. In this work Toland affirms that two groups existed: in early Christianity the Jewish Christians or "Nazarenes"[71] and the Gentile Christians. Only a duality between his religious and philosophical thinking (and a Freemason-like praxis) can explain the riddle.

3.2. Anthony Collins

Sources: A. Collins: *A Discourse of Free-Thinking, Occasion'd by The Rise and Growth of a Sect call'd Free-thinkers* (London 1713; anon. repr. with German transl., ed. G. Gawlick; Stuttgart-Bad Cannstatt 1965; another repr. New York 1984; repr. also in: D. Berman [ed.], *Atheism in Britain* I [Bristol 1996]); *A Discourse of the Grounds and Reasons of the Christian Religion. In two parts ...* (London 1724; several new editions 1724–1741). Correspondence between Collins and Locke, in: E. S. De Beer (ed.), *The Correspondence of John Locke* VII-VIII (Oxford 1982–89).

Studies and reference articles: D. Berman, "Anthony Collins and the Question of Atheism in the Early Part of the Eighteenth Century", *Proceedings of the Royal Irish Academy* LXXV, Sect. C, No. 5 (Dublin 1975) 85–102; J. O'Higgins, *Anthony Collins: The Man and His Work* (The Hague 1970); U. Horstmann, *Die Geschichte der Gedankenfreiheit in England. Am Beispiel von Anthony Collins: A Discourse of Free-Thinking* (Meisenheim / Glan 1980); P. Taranto, *Du déisme à l'athéisme: la libre-pensée d'Anthony Collins* (Paris 2000). – DBI A-J (1999) 206 (D. Berman); DNB 11 (1887) 363f (L. Stephen).

Anthony Collins was born in 1676 as the son of a well-to-do landowner in Heston, Middlesex. He studied at Eton and Cambridge, followed by Law at the Middle Temple in London, but passed no examination. As a man living in a comfortable financial situation[72] he was more independent then the rest of the Deists. 67 preserved letters witness to his friendly relationship to Locke. Though author of publications that rendered him ill-famed as a freethinker, it seems that he did not suffer from persecution. Politically he sympathized with the Whig party. Above all, he was engaged in the local politics of Essex. In his manor he collected one of the largest private libraries in England. Officially he showed himself a loyal member of the Church of England; he attended regularly its services. He died in 1729.

Collins became famous for his *Discourse of Free-Thinking* (1713).[73] Here he is evidently concerned with the right of freethinking independent of any given authority and on any possible theme. He quickly turns to his opponents, whom he has in view, the priests,[74] and the object of their central concern, the Bible.[75] The meaning of those scriptures which are regarded as holy[76] is a main

---

[71] According to Acts 24:5; cf. *Nazarenus* (1718 / 1999) 26. For the discussion about the importance of this work cf. Reventlow, Authority (1984) 574, n. 149.

[72] He married in 1698 the daughter of a banker, but his wife died already 1703 after having born four children. A second marriage in 1724 remained childless.

[73] He defines it: "By Free-Thinking I mean, The Use of the Understanding in endeavouring to find out the Meaning of any Proposition whatsoever, in considering the nature of the Evidence of or against it, and in judging of it according to the seeming Force or Weakness of the Evidence", *Free-Thinking* (1713 / 1965) 5.

[74] Ibid. 8

[75] Ibid. 10.

[76] Ibid. 32

subject for an independent examination. One is refused the right to think in this sphere by the "enemies of freethinking", the priests.

Collins justifies the duty of freethinking by seven arguments.[77] The last states as a consequence: "The Conduct of the Priests ... makes Free-Thinking on the Nature and Attributes of God, on the Authority of the Scriptures, and on the sense of Scriptures, unavoidable".[78] Collins discusses extensively the different opinions of the priests of various religions over the extent and nature of their sacred scriptures, and within the Christian Churches and sects over the extent and nature of the canon,[79] and over the meaning of Scripture. Here he refers both to text-critical problems and the obscurities of its content and problems of interpretation.[80] Some protestant theologians are accused of damaging the cause of Protestantism over against the Papists by drawing attention to the numerous textual variants in the New Testament.[81] It is not so easy to define Collins' own attitude to Scripture. Was his intention to preserve "this pure text" intact in branding as doubtful the scientific investigations of the theologians as being lamentable consequences of the doubtful behaviour of "the priests" and to point to private judgement of each individual layman as the way to rescue an authentic scriptural authority? This was taken by his critics to be a tacit rejection of Christianity in general. More probably, considering his positive judgement of the Gospel,[82] this was in line with the humanist and rationalist tradition from the Puritans on one side to the Deists on the other. From his frequent references to Chillingworth and other intellectual forebears, which he himself provides,[83] he continued to value the Bible, especially the New Testament.[84]

A second treatise that is important in our context is Collins' *Discourse of the Grounds and Reasons of the Christian Religion*. This is a response to W. Whiston's apologetic work *An Essay Towards Restoring the True Text of the Old Testament* (1722). In the second section Collins presents a lengthy criticism of Whiston's arguments. In the first section he joins in the actual discussion of the significance of Old Testament prophecy for Christian faith. Collins declares that the only touchstone for the truth of Christianity is that the prophecies of the Old Testament are fulfilled in Jesus. In the New Testament the predictions from the Old are used by the Apostles as the main argument for the truth of Christianity. According to Collins there are no other solid arguments; if this particular does not hold water, then Christianity has no just foundation. He then checks five exemplary proof texts from the Old Testament in the Gospel of Matthew (Matt 1:22f; 2:15; 2:23; 11:4; 13:14) and shows that they are used in a typological ("mystical" or "allegorical") sense; he claims to have tested this by all the prophecies quoted by the Apostles.[85] For Collins, however, as for Whiston, there is only one legitimate fulfilment, the literal one. If

---

[77] Among them the catchphrase "superstition", third argument, ibid. 35 ff.

[78] Ibid. 46. This is followed by an extended passage on no less than ten instances of their conduct. A whole series of them is concerned with Scripture.

[79] Ibid. 58, 52–56.

[80] Ibid. 57–61.

[81] Ibid. 88 ff. Here Collins refers to JOHN MILL's critical edition of the text of the New Testament (*Novum Testamentum* [1707]), adopting the arguments of D. WHITBY, *Examen Variantum Lectionum Johannis Millii S.T.P. in Novum Testamentum* (1710).

[82] "The Design of the Gospel was, by preaching, to set all Men upon Free-Thinking". Sixth Argument, Collins, *Free-Thinking* (1713 / 1965) 44.

[83] Ibid. 121 ff. O'Higgins, Anthony Collins (1970) 92, thinks of the ancestors of freethinking mentioned by Collins, which go from Socrates, Plato and Aristotle through Cicero, Seneca and Solomon to Bacon, Hobbes and Tillotson.

[84] "He still had links with what he considered to be the Prostestant idea", O'Higgins, ibid. 84.

[85] A. Collins, *A Discourse of the Grounds and Reasons* (1724) 44.

it can be shown that this already took place in the Old Testament period, the claim of Christianity to a second fulfilment by Jesus is clearly refuted. For instance, on Isa 7:14 he comes to the conclusion that the promised child is Isaiah's own son.[86] O'HIGGINS has pointed out that for exegetical conclusions of this kind Collins bases his work on that of the Dutch Arminians, especially H. Grotius.[87] But this is a misunderstanding: Grotius and his followers had assumed that some prophecies were literally fulfilled in Jesus; others were first fulfilled in Old Testament times, but this did not exclude a second typological fulfilment in Christ.

Is there now no basis for Christianity? One must conclude that Collins at the time when he wrote this book was an open opponent of Christianity. But he never expressed such a conclusion in his book and remained a practising member of the Church of England.[88] The problem can hardly be solved in this form, but for the men of this time, as today, there were evidently different levels of awareness, between which contradictions were not excluded. Positively it can be said that the move against New Testament Christianity was the expression of a high estimate of the Old Testament. This was the heritage of a Puritan standpoint at its strongest. The Lockean epistemology made the old way of connecting the testaments impossible, but the escape into a historical view of development was not yet in sight.

3.3. Matthew Tindal

Sources: M. TINDAL: Christianity as Old as the Creation: or, the Gospel, a Republication of the Religion of Nature (London 1730; repr. ed. and intr. by G. Gawlick; Stuttgart-Bad Cannstatt 1967; other reprints: New York 1978; repr. with a new Introduction, by J. V. Price; History of British Deism; London 1995).
Reference articles: BB 6 (1763) 3960–65; DNB 46 (1898) 403–05; BBKL XII (1997) 156–59 (Chr. Schmitt); "Tindal, Matthew (1655–1733)", DBI K-Z (1999) 576–77 (F. Watson).

Matthew Tindal (1653/57[?]-1733) was in his seventies when he published the work that made him famous: Christianity as Old as the Creation: or, the Gospel, a Republication of the Religion of Nature (1730).

Born as son of a parson in Devonshire, educated in the High Church spirit, he pursued his studies in Oxford. In1678 he was elected law fellow in the All Souls College. For a short time he converted to Catholicism, but annulled his conversion soon. In 1685 he was promoted Doctor of Civil Law and worked as lawyer. After the Revolution of 1688 he was consulted by ministers of the Whig government and the court in problems of international law. For pamphlets in which he advocated the position of the Whigs and the Low Church, he received from the government an annual allowance of 200 £.

Christianity as Old as the Creation has been called "the Bible of Deism"[89] and is a sort of compendium, containing the most important features of the deistic concept of religion. It has the form of a dialogue between two persons:

---

[86] Ibid. 43 ff.
[87] O'Higgins, Anthony Collins (1970) 156 ff.
[88] Ibid. 171 ff.
[89] P. SKELTON, Ophiomaches: or, Deism revealed I-II (London 1749), II, 344.

A, speaker of Tindals's own convictions, and B, who with moderate objections keeps the discussion running. All in all, the work is unclear and often redundant. Tindal's main thesis is the assumption of the existence of a natural religion, which holds for all men and is adequate for everyone. Tindal defines it as "the Belief of the Existence of a God, and the Sense and Practice of those Duties, which result from the Knowledge, we, by our Reason, have of him, and his perfections".[90] It is based on the law of nature, which for its part is none other than "the Relation between Things, and the Fitness resulting from thence".[91] It can be recognised by all men, because it corresponds to their own rational nature. Religion is strictly connected with morality; it is "the practice of Morality in Obedience to the Will of God".[92] This morality is clearly eudemonistic: God as an infinitely happy, all-wise Being can give to his creatures only commandments which are to their advantage.[93]

Because this religion (morality) corresponds to the nature of God and at the same time to the nature of things and the rational nature of men, it can also be known directly. It is distinct from outward revelation only by the way in which it is communicated. "The one being the Internal, as the Other the External Revelation of the same Unchangeable Will of a Being, who is alike at all times infinitely Wise and Good".[94] Reason is the organ of this inner revelation; this is the heritage, which combines rationalism with the Spiritualist ancestry. Natural religion contains everything that man needs to know about God's will for his salvation.[95] An external revelation can at best confirm what men would know by themselves if they only used their reason rightly. However, Tindal concedes (as Locke and Shaftesbury did) that in practice people do not always live up to this ideal. This is the foundation for his central thesis (which resembles totally the arguments of the Latitudinarian apologists): Christianity is not a new religion, but is the new proclamation of the law, which has been valid from the beginning and is given with human nature itself.[96] It is the "Republication of the Religion of Nature".[97] Tindal does not want to say that the Christian revelation is superfluous. It could this be in an ideal situation. According to Tindal's conviction (which, however, he hints at rather than express clearly)[98] it fulfils an important role. A "Republication" or "Restoration" of natural religion calls men's attention to the natural, which in reality they have continually failed to follow purely, because from time immemorial they have fallen victim to superstition by following a positive religion. All external cultic practices are superstition.[99] They can only detract from true religion, which consists only in ethical knowledge and moral action.

The consequences of this system were particularly evident in the sphere of understanding the Bible. Tindal devotes a whole, very detailed chapter to the role of the Bible, in which a number of ideas are repeated several times.[100] Also here he regards natural religion as the only binding form. Holy Scripture – and this he takes for granted – can be significant only in respect of the divine commandments, which are contained in it. The definition of religion, which is

---

[90] Tindal, *Christianity* (1730 / 1967) 23.
[91] Ibid. 30.
[92] Ibid. 298.
[93] Ibid. 230.
[94] Ibid. 3; cf. 125.
[95] Ibid. 357; cf. 394.
[96] Ibid. 4.
[97] Gawlick, in: Tindal, *Christianity* (1730 / 1967), *Einleitung*, 14*f, points out that Tindal here took up a formula of the Latitudinarian T. Sherlock and made it more radical.
[98] Cf. Gawlick, ibid. 28*f.
[99] Here Tindal takes up the old Humanist and Puritan classifications.
[100] Tindal, *Christianity* (1730 / 1967), ch. XIII, 232–352.

exclusively identified with morality, does not allow anything else.[101] To a God who is alone metaphysically defined, no personal relations are possible. Also an unbridgeable abyss opens up towards a religion which has become historical and which by nature rests on tradition. A special problem is the question of the moral integrity of the persons responsible for the first dissemination of this historical religion plays a considerable role. As recipients of revelation they deserve trust only if they were personally of unexceptionable morality, so that they themselves were not deceived and did not deceive others.[102] A short survey from Abraham to Paul[103] shows that the best known biblical figures were anything but infallible men. In addition there is the reference to tradition generally: the more indirect a witness, the less convincing he is.[104]

A basic problem also is the biblical image of God in its contrast to the metaphysical conception of God. The freedom of God in the Bible cannot be reconciled with the eternal changelessness of the supreme Being.[105] The same is the case with statements like God swearing, getting angry, repenting, and the many anthropomorphic descriptions of God (God having hands, legs etc.).[106] For the uncertainty of biblical tradition stand the countless textual variants in the New Testament,[107] not to mention the differences of opinion in interpreting the content.[108] It is above all the Old Testament, in which offences of this kind accumulate. The cruel actions of the Jews towards the Canaanites are referred to with particular abhorrence, the way, in which they exterminated them along with their children (a command of God cannot justify this action if it does not agree with the law of nature).[109] In accordance with humanist tradition Tindal therefore gives to the New Testament predominance over the Old.[110] But he is far from accepting New Testament precepts as binding like the Puritans. His reservations about the New Testament are striking. Thus, the Apostles (and Jesus himself, as is indicated) were mistaken in their expectation of the imminent return of Christ. If not in this, could they then be inspired in other less central things?[111] This leads to a fixed rule of interpretation, with which to avoid all difficulties: "to admit all for divine Scripture, that tends to the Honour of God, and the Good of Man; and nothing which does not".[112]

---

[101] Cf. ibid. 278f: "Is not the Foundation of all Religion, the believing there's only one self-existent Being, to whom all others owe their Being, and their Continuance in Being? And is it not certain, ... that he did not create Mankind to supply any Wants of his own; or give them Rules for their Conduct, but to oblige them to act for their common Good?"

[102] Ibid. 243.

[103] Ibid. 243–45, 263–65.

[104] Ibid. 294. Not for the first time, Tindal here quotes Locke.

[105] "that an arbitrary will, which might change every Moment, wou'd govern all Things?", ibid. 247.

[106] Ibid. 250ff.

[107] Ibid. 24f (where Tindal quotes the famous Bentley, to have a witness above suspicion).

[108] Ibid. 322f.

[109] Ibid. 278.

[110] "And if there's a Contrast between the Spirit of the Old, and the Spirit of the New Testament, ought not we Christians to stick to the latter...?", ibid. 269.

[111] Ibid. 262.

[112] Ibid. 328.

Evidently this rule means the agreement of the relevant commands with the law of nature.

All in all, though Tindal sets out to demonstrate the parallel in content between the religion of nature and the Christian revelation, his work has in fact demonstrated precisely the opposite. The Old Testament is ruled out from the start, because neither its God nor its human beings are adequate to the moral claim. This negative verdict is good humanist tradition. But even the New Testament does not pass the test. Much of its content is offensive, and the process of tradition doubtful. Thus, what appeared central to the early humanists and the Puritans, the commands of the Gospels and Jesus' own commandments, need interpretation. They fall under the verdict of being the kind of authority from which in fact he seeks to free mankind. So we might concede that subjectively it was Tindal's intention to salvage revealed religion. What he actually effected, was the contrary. Ultimately he has shown that revealed religion is superfluous, as the religion of nature is enough for human salvation, and is so much more easily accessible to man.

3.4. Thomas Morgan

Sources: T. MORGAN: *The Moral Philosopher*, I. *In A Dialogue Between Philalethes a Christian Deist, And Theophanes a Christian Jew* etc. (London 1737; 2nd rev. ed.; London 1738; repr. with introd. J. V. Price; Bristol 1999); II. *Being A Farther Vindication Of Moral Truth and Reason* (London 1739); III. *Superstition and Tyranny Inconsistent with Theocracy* (London 1740). Reprint of all three volumes [vol. I, 2nd ed.] (ed. G. Gawlick; Stuttgart-Bad Cannstatt 1969).

General and reference works: J. VAN DEN BERG, "Thomas Morgan versus William Warburton. A Conflict the other Way round", *JEH* 42 (1991) 8–85; C. G. JÖCHER, *Historiae controversiarum a Thoma Morgano excititarum primas lineas ducit* (Lipsiae 1745). "Morgan, Thomas", BBKL VI (1993) 117–19 (Chr. Schmitt); "Morgan, Thomas", *Dictionary of Eighteenth-Century British Philosophers* 2 (1999) 641–44.

Thomas Morgan was born 1680. About his early years few details are known. He is said to have been of Welsh origin and to have been living as a farmer's son in the County of Somerset, when John Moore (c. 1642–1717), a Dissenter parson, cared for his education. He then was himself a Dissenter pastor in Somerset, and from 1716 onwards, after his Presbyterian ordination, pastor in Marlborough, Wiltshire. But soon he seems to have changed his mind. Formerly of orthodox conviction, he was dismissed shortly after 1720 from his office for his offensive opinions. He then studied Medical sciences and called himself since 1726 Doctor of Medicine. He died in January 1743.

Morgan has become known by his main work in three volumes *The Moral Philosopher*, in which, on the basis of ethical rationalism, he denies the authority of the Old Testament. Already in the Preface of Vol. I[113] he declares that it is "the moral Truth, Reason, or Fitness of Things" which alone can demonstrate that a doctrine comes from God and is part of the true religion.[114] Accordingly, it is "the moral Truth, Reason and Fitness of Actions … founded in the natural and necessary Relations of Persons and Things, antecedent to any

---

[113] Morgan, *The Moral Philosopher* I (1737) VIII.

[114] Adopting a formulation of S. Clarke (*Letter to Eusebius*, in: Morgan, *Moral Philosopher* II, Appendix, 28).

positive Will or Law".[115] "Moral philosophy" – used by Morgan for the title of his work that appeared first anonymously – means for him "the knowledge of God, Providence, and Human Nature".[116] The justification of morality is its prime goal. His world-view is not mechanical: Morgan stresses the constant presence and the direct activity of God in his creation.[117] This shows his relationship to Clarke, and behind him, Newton.[118] Another trait is Morgan's hedonistic ethics (which he learnt from Clarke and which goes back to the French Neo-Epicureanistic school around Gassendi). It is one of the starting points for Morgan's criticism of the Mosaic Law, that its sanctions extend only to temporal things, "none of its Rewards or Punishments relating to any future State, or extending themselves beyond this life".[119] The inner tensions between absolute and eudemonistic morality which produce an apologetic stamped by ethical rationalism, but incorporating elements from the Christian tradition, also recur in Morgan.

Morgan also assigns Christian revelation a necessary role. Though natural religion is principally sufficient for man's salvation, in practice it has disseminated so much obscurity and ignorance in the world that the teaching of Jesus was very necessary to put its authentic principles in a true light again.[120] Nevertheless, "Natural and revealed Religion are essentially and subjectively the same, and they can only be distinguished by the different Ways or Means of conveying the same truth to the mind".[121] The morality of the Gospel is none other than that of the pagan philosophers like Plato, Cicero and Plutarch, though these men were not inspired, "wrought no miracles, and did not pretend to be Prophets".[122] Following Tindal, Morgan can then term Christianity the "restoration", "revival",[123] or even the "best rendering"[124] of the religion of nature.

Morgan's special contribution on this basis is his total rejection of the Old Testament as part of the Christian Bible. The battlefield was the problem of the typological view that regarded the event of Christ as predicted in the Old Testament. This view had already lost its credibility since Anthony Collins[125] had argued that the assertion that Christ had been foretold in the Old Testa-

---

[115] Ibid. I, VIII.

[116] Ibid. I, 282.

[117] Already Lechler, Geschichte (1841 / 1965) 371f, remarked this; cf. also ibid., Gawlick, Einleitung, 14*ff. Cf. the prayer of Morgan's "Christian Deist" to the creator and governor of the world: Morgan, Moral Philosopher I (1737) 426f. In another context (I, 183–92), where he argues that the difference between the opinion that the world, once created, can continue going on without any supreme governor of the world who preserves its existence, and the opposite opinion that reckons with such a divine supervisor, is the borderline between Atheists and Christian Deists.

[118] This was Newton's religious conviction which he resolutely defended against Leibniz, cf. D. KUBRIN, "Newton and the Cyclical Cosmos: Providence and the Mechanical Philosophy", JHI 28 (1967) 325–46.

[119] Morgan, Moral Philosopher I (1737) 27; cf. 169, 179.

[120] Ibid. I, 144f; cf. II, 22f.

[121] As Morgan stresses again in the preface to III (1740) III.

[122] Ibid. III, 151.

[123] Ibid. I, 392.

[124] Ibid. I, 439.

[125] A. Collins, The Scheme of Literal Prophecy considered … (London / Den Haag 1726).

ment was untenable on a literal understanding of the book. If one could write off the Old Testament as testimony to a pre-Christian religion, Christianity could still be defended, albeit as a pedagogical means to the moral illumination of mankind. But for Morgan it was a principal judgement on the insight that almost everything in the Old Testament is irreconcilable with the principle of "moral truth".

Morgan rejects the Mosaic Law in its two forms of ceremonial and moral law. There was already a consensus that the ceremonial law is to be regarded as abdicated by the Gospel. But Morgan does not even allow a typological significance to it.[126] He criticises the ceremonial law for having favoured the priesthood as greedy eaters through meaningless sacrifices,[127] using the Levites as examples of his anticlericalism. He includes everything that contradicts the pure moral religion: the sacraments of baptism and Eucharist. He allows baptism merely as proselyte baptism. In rejecting infant baptism he follows old Spiritualist tradition. Dogmatic statements which stand in the way of a purely legal retribution of human deeds at the last judgement, like the doctrine of the vicarious righteousness of Christ he rejects as "the corrupt dregs of Judaism".[128] Prophecy, at least in its original intention, is excepted from the critical judgement: the prophets studied above all "Moral Philosophy, or the Knowledge of God, Providence and human Nature".[129] The claim that the prophets proclaimed morality[130] and attacked rites and the priesthood[131] has remained significant for ethical and rationalistic exegesis and the understanding of the prophets down to the present day. Though Morgan seems to be well instructed in the exegetical science of his time, as many details show, historical events for him can never be the basis of faith;[132] this, because he reduces Christianity to the teaching of Christ, which he understands as moral law.[133]

4. Apologetic Authors

We restrict ourselves to dealing with two prominent authors who in a special manner fought against deism: Samuel Clarke and William Warburton. We select these two writers out of numerous others because their works are especially important in the history of Bible understanding.

Rational apologetics originated in the wake of I. Newton and the new science. The new plan of the world detected by Newton found its organised expression in the foundation of the British Society (1662) by a group of natural scholars, among whom besides W. Whiston especially Robert Boyle (1627–

---

[126] Morgan, *Moral Philosopher* I, 42–47.
[127] Ibid. I, 125–28.
[128] Ibid. I, 198 f.
[129] Ibid. I, 282.
[130] Ibid. I, 284.
[131] Ibid. II (1739) 162.
[132] Ibid. I, 411.
[133] Ibid. I, 167: "our Christian Prophet, who is the only Legislator in Matters of Religion".

91), the "devout naturalist"[134] was active. Shortly before his death he laid down in a codicil to his testament that the rent of one of his houses in London should be used for eight sermons, in which a theologian should defend the truth of the Christian religion against atheists, Deists, heathen, Jews and Mohammedans. Among the lecturers of the first period (the sermons were in fact popular lectures) was Samuel Clarke.

4.1. Samuel Clarke

Sources: SAMUEL CLARKE: *The Works of Samuel Clarke, D.D.* I-IV (ed. B. Hoadly; London 1738–42; repr. Bristol 1999); *A Demonstration of the Being and Attributes of God … Being the Substance of Eight SERMONS Preach'd at the Cathedral Church of St. Paul, in the Year 1704 at the Lecture Founded by the Honourable ROBERT BOYLE Esq.* (London 1705); *A Discourse Concerning the Unchangeable Obligations of Natural Religion and the Truth and Certainty of the Christian Revelation. Being Eight SERMONS Preach'd at the Cathedral Church of St Paul, in the Year 1705, at the Lecture Founded by the Honourable ROBERT BOYLE Esq.* (London 1706); both works repr. together in one volume (Stuttgart-Bad Cannstatt 1964). – G. BURNET (ed.), *A Defence of Natural and Revealed Religion: Being an abridgement of the Sermons Preached at the Lecture Founded by Robert Boyle* (Dublin 1737; repr. with Introd. by A. Pyle, Preface by A. P. F. Sell; Philosophy and Christian Thought in Britain, 1770–1900; Bristol 2000).

Studies and reference articles: R. ATTFIELD, "Clarke, Collins, and Compounds", *JHP* 15 (1977) 45–54; J. P. FERGUSON, *The Philosophy of Dr. Samuel Clarke and its Critics* (New York 1974); idem, *An 18th Century heretic: Dr. Samuel Clarke* (Kineton 1976); "Clarke, Samuel (1675–1729)", *Dictionary of Eighteenth-Century British Philosophers* (Bristol 1999) 202–08 (C. Brown); "Clarke, Samuel (1675–1729)", TRE 8 (1981) 90–92 (D. A. Pailin).

Samuel Clarke (1675–1729), born in Norwich as son of an alderman and Member of Parliament, was educated at Caius College in Cambridge and became Junior Fellow there in 1696. After a period of publications on Newton's theories and other physical works and as a classical scholar he was ordained in 1698 and J. Moore, bishop of Norwich, called him to be his chaplain. Using Moore's comprehensive library, he began writing theological books. But he became famous by the lectures (sermons) he held when invited to be Boyle lecturer for the years 1704 and 1705.

The influence of Newton's theories on theology can best be seen in Clarke's Boyle lectures. They were held under the titles *A Demonstration of the Being and Attributes of God* for 1704 and *A Discourse Concerning the Unchangeable Obligations of Natural Religion and the Truth and Certainty of the Christian Revelation* for 1705, published each in the respective following year, but conceived of as a connected whole. Each lecture begins with a thesis ("proposition") that Clarke explains in what follows. Clarke wants to develop his ethics consistently from his natural philosophy and his doctrine of God. But his attempt to reconcile the legacies of Christianity and Antiquity on the basis of a mechanistic and dynamic view of the world leads to a fatal dualism. In the *Demonstration* Clarke, on one hand, tries to argue that God is free and the present ordering of the world is created by his arbitrary decrees, and as such bears witness to the existence of its creator. On the other hand, in "Proposition XII" he concludes from the principle that as *suprema causa*, God must be a being of infinite goodness, righteous-

---

[134] On him cf. i.a. H. D. RACK, "Boyle, Robert (1627–1691)", TRE 7 (1981) 101–04; R. S. WESTFALL, *Science and Religion in 17th Century England* (New Haven 1958).

ness and truth,[135] that his action must necessarily always be determined by what corresponds with these criteria on any given occasion.[136] This is an internal contradiction in the Newtonian system. As Clarke has spoken before about God's unlimited freedom, he comes in the context of a mechanical view of the world order into an antinomy, which he cannot overcome.

The *Discourse*, his lecture series of 1705, develops his system of ethics. Here we meet with the same lack of balance between two basic presuppositions which conflict with one another. Clarke's basic thesis on ethics follows first of all directly from the considerations which appear at the end of the *Demonstration*: "The same consequent Fitness or Unfitness … with regard to which, the Will of God always and necessarily does determine itself, to choose to act only what is agreeable to Justice, Equity, Goodness and Truth, in order to the Welfare of the whole Universe … ought likewise constantly to determine the Wills of all subordinate rational Beings, to govern all their Actions by the same Rules, for the good of the Publick …".[137]

It is known that in this argument Clarke is influenced by the natural law approach of R. Cumberland,[138] who similarly stresses the ordered structure of the cosmos, and assigns to the laws of moral action their place in the ordering of the whole. The same Stoic heritage plays a decisive role in Clarke, strengthened through the Newtonian world-view with its cosmological ideas of order. But in the following "Proposition III" Clarke states: "That the same eternal moral Obligations, which are of themselves incumbent indeed on all rational Creatures, antecedent to any respect of particular Rewards and Punishments; must yet certainly and necessarily be attended with Rewards and Punishments".[139] At this point Clarke sees the limitations of human moral existence, feelings, which provoke irrational behaviour, and arrives at the distinction between a "primary" and a "secondary" moral obligation. The doctrine of rewards and punishments to be expected in a "future state"[140] is a traditionally Christian heritage, but represents a complete break with the approach, which has been followed hitherto. The Christian doctrine of original sin[141] allows Clarke to criticise the Stoic doctrine that virtue is a reward in itself.[142] But by stopping here and not following Shaftesbury on the way to an autonomous ethic, Clarke remains at the halfway stage.

Clarke also introduces a theory of miracles, in which he follows Newton's dynamic cosmology: since God's normal guidance of the world, as a constant overcoming of the inertia of the matter, represents continuing divine action, even miracle is not impossible in itself. It is in fact harder to achieve than the normal divine action. But it is merely a "work effected in a manner unusual, by the interposition either of God himself, or of some Intelligent Agent superiour to Man, for the Proof or Evidence of some particular Doctrine, or in attestation to the Authority of some particular Person".[143]

From Clarke's Boyle lectures one can recognise the forced situation in which

---

[135] Clarke, *Demonstration of the Being and Attributes of God* (1705) 233 = *Works* (1738 / 1978) II, 571.
[136] *Demonstration* (1705) 247 = *Works* II, 574.
[137] *Discourse* (1706) 45f = *Works* II, 612.
[138] R. Cumberland, *De legibus naturae disquisitio philosophica* (1672).
[139] S. Clarke, *Discourse*, Table of Contents, unpaginated.
[140] "Proposition IV", Clarke, *Discourse*, 160–207 = *Works* II, 643–52.
[141] Cf. Clarke, *Discourse*, Table of Contents and Margin Title, 165 = *Works* II, 644.
[142] Clarke, *Discourse* 178 = *Works* II, 645–48.
[143] Clarke, *Discourse*, 367 = *Works* II, 701.

rationalistic apologetics found itself in this period. It could not overcome the intrinsic contradiction between the philosophical approach, which it also wanted to follow, and traditional Christian doctrines, which it sought to defend. As natural religion was an integral part of this system, at best it could approve of revelation as a necessary pedagogical expedient. It was in the position of making the principles of morality more accessible to the weakened reason of the average person, even though such a person should have been able to recognise these rules.

4.2. William Warburton

Sources: W. Warburton: *The Works* I-VII (ed. R. Hurd; London 1788-94; London ²1860; repr. Hildesheim / New York 1980); contains also R. Hurd, "Some Account of the Life, Writings, and Character of the Author", in: Vol. I, 1-141.

Studies and reference articles (selected): H. Graf Reventlow, Freidenkertum (2004) 177-245 [see Gen. Bibl. above]; S. Taylor, "William Warburton and the Alliance of Church and State", *JEH* 43 (1992) 271-86; J. van den Berg, "Thomas Morgan versus William Warburton: A Conflict the Other Way Round", *JEH* 42 (1991) 82-85; A. W. Watson, *Warburton and the Warburtonians: A Study in some Eighteenth-Century Controversies* (London 1932); J. S. Watson, *The Life of William Warburton* (London 1863). "Warburton, William", BBKL XIII (1998) 350-53 (Chr. Schmidt); "Warburton, William (1698-1779)", DBI K-Z (1999) 622 (D. D. Wallace, Jr.).

William Warburton was born in 1698 in Newark (Nottinghamshire) as son of a town writer. After having studied with a solicitor he worked as such in his hometown from 1719. Nevertheless, his interests were focused on theology. By self-taught studies he acquired the knowledge afforded for being ordained deacon in 1723 and priest in 1727. Afterwards he officiated in several rural parishes of the Church of England. In 1738 he became preacher at the court of the Prince of Wales, in 1728 of the (juridical) Society of Lincoln=s Inn in London, in 1753 he became Dean of Gloucester Cathedral. In 1754 he was promoted Doctor of Theology; in 1757 he moved to the same office in Bristol, and in 1759 he became bishop of Gloucester. He died there in 1779.

Warburton was a prolific writer. To mention just the most characteristic of his works: *The Alliance between Church and State, or the Necessity and Equity of an Established Religion* etc (1736)[144] is a classical apology of the Constitution of the Church of England as an ordered co-operation of Church and state for the welfare of both institutions.[145] The course of sermons preached before the Society of Lincoln's Inn under the general title *The Principles of Natural and Revealed Religion*[146] expounds the typical Latitudinarian theology, laying the stress on the moral side of belief.

But Warburton's fame rests on his best known magnum opus, *The Divine Legation of Moses Demonstrated on the Principles of a Religious Deist, from the Omission of the Doctrine of a Future State of Rewards and Punishments in the Jewish Dispensation* I-II (1737/38).[147] It is also the most important contribu-

---

[144] Warburton, *Works* IV, 1-331.

[145] For occasion and details of the discussion cf. Taylor, Warburton and the Alliance of Church and State, *JEH* 43 (1992) 271-86. Cf. also Reventlow, Freidenkertum (2004) 232.

[146] Warburton, *Works* V, 1-203.

[147] Warburton, *Works* I-III; the title was later shortened, ending with the word "Demonstrated". Cf. also the essay of William McKane in the present volume, Ch. 40, sections 1-2.

tion of Anti-deist apologetic to our topic. In the Preface to the first edition of
Books I–III of his work in 1738 he declares as his design "to prove the DI-
VINE ORIGIN OF THE JEWISH RELIGION".[148] The full title already announces the – for his readers rather paradoxical – arguments he intends to develop. He also mentions the reason for writing a "defence of Moses", namely
"from observing a notion to have spread very much of late, even amongst many
who would be thought Christians, that the truth of Christianity is independent
of the Jewish dispensation".[149] In contrast to this error Warburton in 1754 is
convinced to have reached his aim: "I shall strengthen one foundation of
Christianity".[150]

The thesis proposed by G. V. Lechler,[151] and repeated by numerous followers,[152] that Warburton replied directly to Thomas Morgan's *Moral Philosopher* must be abandoned.[153] Instead with a touch of irony he dedicated his
work in 1738 to the whole community of Freethinkers.[154] Using in his approach the distinction made by the apologists between "external" and "internal" evidence,[155] Warburton states his main thesis: The "Jewish dispensation",
mediated by Moses, is divine, because it did not know of a future state.

He argues as follows (Book I): Civil society is not able to punish disobedience and reward obedience sufficiently, specially as regards moral duties. Therefore it needs a religion that teaches a
providential reward for the good and punishment for the evil. Using the form of syllogism, he concludes: "Whatsoever Religion and Society have no future state for their support, must be supported
by an extraordinary Providence. The Jewish Religion and Society had no future state for their support: Therefore, the Jewish Religion and Society were supported by an extraordinary Providence".[156] Warburton in the following tries to support his thesis that the doctrine of a future state
is "the only support of Religion under the present and ordinary dispensations of providence" and
"NECESSARY to the well-being of Society",[157] by showing "that there never was, in any time or
place, a civilized People (the Jewish only excepted) who did not found their Religion on this doctrine".[158] In a discussion with P. Bayle, who had argued[159] that also an atheist could live a virtuous
life,[160] Warburton goes on to affirm that neither "moral sense" nor natural discernment is enough
to serve as a basis for morality: a superior will, the will of God, is needed to impose obligation to
moral action.[161]

---

[148] *Works* I, XLIII.
[149] *Works* I, 49. Warburton ascribes this belief especially to the Socinians, in whose conception
even "the knowledge of the Old Testament is not absolutely necessary", ibid. It may be remarked
that this position is still alive in spite of many recent arguments against it.
[150] "Dedication to a New Edition ... 1754", *Works* I, III.
[151] Lechler, Geschichte (1841 / 1965) 388.
[152] Among whom also the present author (The Authority of the Bible [1984] 396).
[153] van den Berg, Thomas Morgan versus William Warburton (1991) 82–85. Warburton despised Morgan too much to deign him to confute him.
[154] Warburton, "Dedication to the First Edition of Books I. II. III. in 1738", *Works* I, V-XLII.
[155] *Divine Legation*, Book I, sect. I, *Works* I, 45–48. By "internal evidence" Warburton means
the "interior marks of truth" in revealed religion, to which belongs the observation he chooses as
his starting point.
[156] Ibid., *Works* 1, 51.
[157] Ibid., sect. II, *Works* 1, 66.
[158] Ibid.
[159] In his *Pensées diverses Ecrites à un Docteur de Sorbonne A l'occasion de la Comete Qui parut ou
mois de Décembre M.DC.Lxxx*, § CXXXIII, in: *Oeuvres Diverses* III (The Hague 1727; repr. Hildesheim 1966) 86 f.
[160] *Divine Legation*, Book I, sect.4, *Works* I, 74–97.
[161] *Divine Legation*, Book I, sect.4, *Works* I, 76 f.

Book II[162] shows in detail that all founders of states therefore pretended to have established them on the basis of a divine revelation. Besides they disseminated the doctrine of providence, connected with the belief in a future retribution, which they communicated through mysteries to the imagination of their peoples. In Book III[163] he also maintains that the philosophers of classical Antiquity (whose schools are described with a wealth of scholarly learning) regarded belief in a future life – even if not sharing this belief themselves – to be crucial for the existence of civil society.

In Book IV-VI[164] Warburton arrives at the central thesis of his work. As a result of his overview of the formation and philosophy of pagan states he sets out a desperate situation. An invented doctrine of a future retribution could not be sufficient for true morality, and the wisest philosophers such as Socrates openly confessed their ignorance. "There only remains ... the general tradition of God's early revelation of his will to mankind, as delivered in Scripture".[165] Now the figure of Moses comes to the fore. But first Warburton describes the high age of ancient Egypt[166] and its state of learning. One insight is especially very remarkable: By comparing them with old Mexican picture-writing and Chinese letters Warburton detects that the ancient Egyptian hieroglyphs were originally not symbolic mystical signs, as believed in his period. They were a sort of writing, developed from the earlier picture-writing to be used as means of normal communication.[167] He is rightly proud to state: "Thus we have brought down the general history of writing ... from a PICTURE to a LETTER".[168] But Egypt was also full of superstition. The laws given by Moses, including the rituals, "were instituted, partly in compliance to their prejudices, and partly in opposition to those superstitions".[169] This is no objection against their divine origin.[170] On the contrary: The "circumstances of Moses' Egyptian learning and the laws he instituted in compliance to and in opposition to Egyptian superstitions, are a strong confirmation of the divinity of his mission".[171]

Paradoxically, however, the main reason for the divine legation of Moses is "that the doctrine of a future state of rewards and punishments is not to be found in, nor did make part of, the mosaic dispensation".[172] After the long way of learned observations on Ancient Egypt Warburton comes to his aim in Book V of his work. The summary[173] shows his arguments: Whereas in modern societies law and morality is split, punishments and rewards accordingly on two levels: the mundane reality and the eschatological future, Israel was a theocracy.[174] Because this theocracy existed in the Here and Now, only one level of retribution existed. That this theocracy had such a long duration[175] in spite of the lack of future rewards and punishments, shows "that is must be administered by an extraordinary *Providence*".[176]

---

[162] *Works* I, 127–336.
[163] *Works* II, 1–213.
[164] *Works*, II.
[165] *Divine Legation*, Book IV, sect. I, *Works* II, 339 f.
[166] Ibid., *Works* II, 354–65. This observation was important in a time when the common opinion still believed that the Bible was the oldest book of the world, Israel the most ancient people, and that the other peoples, including the Egyptians, had borrowed from the Israelites (cf. also Book IV, sect. VI, *Works* I, 588).
[167] *Divine Legation*, Book IV, sect. IV, in: *Works*, vol. II, 387–417.
[168] Ibid. II, 403.
[169] Ibid. II, 565.
[170] Ibid. II, 602.
[171] Ibid. II, 642.
[172] Ibid., sect. II, *Works* II, 347.
[173] Cf. the "Contents", *Works* III, V–VI.
[174] Ibid., Book V, sect. II, *Works* III, 16–69.
[175] Ibid., sect. III, *Works*, III, 69–98.
[176] "Contents", *Works*, III, VI.

CHAPTER THIRTY-SIX

Early Rationalism and Biblical Criticism on the Continent

By Christoph Bultmann, Erfurt

General works: Dictionary of Biblical Interpretation [DBI] A-J, K-Z (ed. J. H. Hayes; Nashville 1999); *Le Grand Siècle et la Bible* (ed. J.-R. Armogathe; BTT 6; Paris 1989); *Le siècle des Lumières et la Bible* (ed. Y. Belaval / D. Bourel; BTT 7; Paris 1986); W. BAIRD, *History of New Testament Research* 1 (Minneapolis 1992); C. BULTMANN, *Die biblische Urgeschichte in der Aufklärung* (Tübingen 1999); P. BYRNE, *Natural Religion and the Nature of Religion* (London 1989); C. HOUTMAN, *Der Pentateuch. Die Geschichte seiner Erforschung neben einer Auswertung* (Kampen 1994 [Dutch original 1980]); H. GRAF REVENTLOW, *The Authority of the Bible and the Rise of the Modern World* (London 1984; orig.: *Bibelautorität und Geist der Moderne*; Göttingen 1980); idem, *Epochen der Bibelauslegung* 4 (München 2001); *Historische Kritik und biblischer Kanon in der deutschen Aufklärung* (ed. H. Graf Reventlow / W. Sparn / J. Woodbridge; Wiesbaden 1988); *Geschichte der Hermeneutik und die Methode der textinterpretierenden Disziplinen* (ed. J. Schönert / F. Vollhardt; Berlin 2005); J. SHEEHAN, *The Enlightenment Bible. Translation, Scholarship, Culture* (Princeton 2005).

1. Introduction[1]

Studies: L. DANNEBERG, "Ezechiel Spanheim's Dispute with Richard Simon. On the Biblical Philology at the End of the 17th Century", *The Berlin Refuge 1680-1780. Learning and Science in European Context* (ed. S. Pott / M. Mulsow / L. Danneberg; Leiden 2003) 49-88; J. LE BRUN, "Richard Simon", DBS 12 (1996) 556-86; idem, "Das Entstehen der historischen Kritik im Bereich der religiösen Wissenschaften im 17. Jahrhundert", *TTZ* 89 (1980) 100-17; F. LAPLANCHE, *La Bible en France entre mythe et critique. XVIe-XIXe siècle* (Paris 1994); S. MÜLLER, *Kritik und Theologie. Christliche Glaubens- und Schrifthermeneutik nach Richard Simon* (St. Ottilien 2004); M. C. PITASSI, *Entre Croire et Savoir. Le problème de la méthode critique chez Jean Le Clerc* (Leiden 1987; extensive bibl.); R. H. POPKIN, "Some Aspects of Jewish-Christian Theological Interchanges in Holland and England 1640-1700", *Jewish-Christian Relations in the Seventeenth Century* (ed. J. van den Berg / E. van der Wall; Dordrecht 1988) 3-32; C. POULOUIN, *Le Temps des origines. L'Eden, le Déluge et 'les temps reculés' de Pascal à l'Encyclopédie* (Paris 1998); H. GRAF REVENTLOW, "Bibelexegese als Aufklärung. Die Bibel im Denken des Johannes Clericus (1657-1736)", in: *Historische Kritik und biblischer Kanon* (1988) 1-19; B. E. SCHWARZBACH, "Les sources rabbiniques de la critique biblique de Richard Simon", BTT 6 (1989) 207-231; idem, "Dom Augustin Calmet. Man of the Enlightenment Despite Himself", *ARelG* 3 (2001) 135-48; M. S. SEGUIN, *Science et religion dans la pensée française du XVIIIe siècle. Le mythe du Déluge universel* (Paris 2001); R. SMEND, "Spätorthodoxe Antikritik. Zum Werk des Johann Gottlob Carpzov", in: *Historische Kritik und biblischer Kanon*

---

[1] I would like to thank Professor B. E. Schwarzbach (Paris), Professor F. Vollhardt (Munich) and Professor H. B. Nisbet (Cambridge) for their valuable comments on earlier versions of this chapter, especially the sections on Voltaire and on Lessing respectively. The responsibility for the format and the emphasis of this presentation rests with the author.

(1988) 127–37 (also in: idem, *Epochen der Bibelkritik* [München 1991] 33–42); G. G. STROUMSA, "Richard Simon: From Philology to Comparatism", *ARelG* 3 (2001) 89–107 (extensive bibl.); idem, "John Spencer and the Roots of Idolatry", *HR* 40 (2001) 1–23.

By the end of the seventeenth century a substantial body of erudite commentary on the Bible had accumulated in all Christian denominations. To name only a few works, Brian Walton's *Biblia Sacra Polyglotta* and its prolegomena and appendices (1657) provided a new foundation for the study of text-critical issues, and John Pearson's cumulative edition of *Critici Sacri* (1660 and subsequent editions) provided a rich resource for the study of philological issues. In particular, the work made Hugo Grotius's critical *Annotationes* on the Bible (1644) more widely available, and permitted them to become an influential point of reference in subsequent biblical criticism despite the vigorous criticism, for example, by the Lutheran theologian Abraham Calov in his *Biblia Illustrata* (1672–76). In a different form, the material was again presented by Matthew Poole in his *Synopsis Criticorum* (1669–76 and subsequent editions). In 1678, Richard Simon (1638–1712) published an extensive review of previous scholarship as the third part of his *Histoire Critique du Vieux Testament* (1678, suppressed and burnt, but republished in 1685). Simon also set the tone for subsequent biblical criticism when, in the first part of this work, he put forward the idea of "official scribes" (*écrivains publics*) – and poets – who had composed and revised the books of the Old Testament. Even if in the preface to his book Simon rejected a suggestion by Henry Holden (1596–1662, in his *Divinae fidei analysis* of 1652) that the notion of divine inspiration of biblical texts could be limited to points of doctrine only, the idea of such *écrivains publics* prepared the ground for further critical investigation, thus accentuating the challenge which Spinoza's *Tractatus Theologico-Politicus* (1670) posed for the study of the Bible.

In the context of the 1680s – which also saw the publication of John Locke's *Letter concerning Toleration* – the state of biblical studies is conveniently documented in a book by Jean Le Clerc (1657–1736), published in response to Simon's tome. In Le Clerc's *Sentimens de quelques Théologiens de Hollande sur l'histoire critique du Vieux Testament* (1685), biblical criticism is presented in the form of a conversation amongst scholars (*savants*) who consider the possibilities and the probabilities of certain scholarly judgments and hypotheses, with the author himself posing as a correspondent who reports to the reader in letters about these debates. The participants discuss ideas about biblical writers and the formation of the canon irrespective of denominational loyalties and "without prejudice". They extend the scope of historical criticism to include the question of an author's intention and the situation in which he wrote (6–7):

> *Faire l'Histoire d'un Livre n'est pas simplement dire quand [et] par qui il a été fait [...]. Il faut encore nous découvrir, si cela se peut, dans quel dessein l'Auteur l'a composé, quelle occasion lui a fait prendre la plume, [et] à quelles opinions, ou à quels évenemens, il peut faire allusion dans cet Ouvrage, sur tout lors qu'il ne s'agit pas d'un livre qui contienne des réflexions générales, ou des veritez éternelles, qui sont les mêmes dans tous les Siècles, [et] parmi tous les peuples du monde.*

The hermeneutical principle is illustrated by a reference to André Dacier's commentary on Horace (1681–89), while John Spencer's study of the ceremonial laws of the Pentateuch (*Dissertatio de Urim [et] Thummim* [on Deut 33:8], 1669, followed by *De Legibus Hebraeorum Ritualibus et earum rationibus*, 1685) is quoted as a model of a proper scholarly approach to the biblical documents. One consequence of Le Clerc's attempt at giving a sharper profile to a historical hermeneutics is his rejection of the expectation that the Bible should offer an outline of universal history and his consequent criticism of Isaac de La Peyrère's hypothesis about Pre-adamites (*Praeadamitae* and *Systema Theologicum*, 1655). In letters 6–9 of the *Sentimens*, conjectures about the authors of the Pentateuch and other biblical books are considered, and the view emerges that the Pentateuch might have been composed from older traditions by a priest or priests in Bethel in the late seventh century who would have had some first-hand knowledge of Mesopotamian geography and culture but who would also have known the law code which Hilkiah discovered in the Jerusalem temple (based on 2 Kgs 17:27–28 in combination with 2 Kgs 22:3–8 [129]).

The liberal, though occasionally confessionalist, scholarly discussion of critical issues also has an apologetic side to it. To relate biblical texts to the 'design' and 'situation' of their authors and thus to admit certain limitations of the texts is seen by Le Clerc as a way to counter critical attacks on the Bible by 'deists' or 'atheists' or 'libertins'. This apologetic undercurrent in his work grows even stronger in his commentary on the Pentateuch (1693–96). Le Clerc not only reverts, in his introductory dissertations, to the traditional view of a Mosaic authorship of the Pentateuch (allowing, after a careful discussion of a list of doubtful verses, for a few later additions), but also, in his running glosses on the text, defends biblical miracles and biblical morality. For example, Le Clerc explains that in their exodus from Egypt the three million Israelites (a calculation based on Exod 12:37) might well have crossed the narrow Red Sea given that they were marching in a wide phalanx (on Exodus 12–14 and *Dissertatio de Maris Idumaei Trajectione* in the appendix). The logical gap at Exod 7:22 is filled in with a remark that the water had returned to its original state before the Egyptian magi imitated Moses' action. The notion of a 'ban' in the stories about the conquest of land east of the river Jordan under Moses is given a theological explanation stating that the Israelites did not act as enemies of the inhabitants but as ministers of divine justice (*Sed Israëlitae non hostes agebant, verùm, ut dici, divinae justitiae ministros* [on Deut 2:34; cf. on Num 21:2]). Scholarly as it is, an 'erudite' commentary does not necessarily mean a 'critical' commentary.

The line of biblical studies which runs as it were from the authors of the annotations collected in the *Critici Sacri* to Le Clerc's commentaries continues with Augustin Calmet's (1672–1752) commentaries which started to appear in 1707. This monumental work shows a similar synthesis of philological and classical, as well as patristic, erudition and theological apologetics. A survey of the considerable amount of exegetical works which were available to the student of the Bible in the early eighteenth century can be found in Johann Gottlob Carpzov's *Introductio ad libros canonicos bibliorum Veteris Testamenti omnes* (1714–21). Carpzov deals with many points of critical detail even if he consistently advocates traditional views regarding the authorship of the biblical books and their relevance for the Christian faith.

The development of critical scholarship of the Bible in universities, colleges and monastic orders or by independent scholars in the early modern period is the subject of previous chapters of the present volume. However, it is important to note that Reimarus and Voltaire (and Lessing more with regard to the New Testament) were familiar with the contemporary state of biblical scholarship which was easily accessible through the major commentaries. In many places their criticisms read like a refutation of the kind of apologetics which characterize those erudite works. With Reimarus and Voltaire the ideal conversation of Le Clerc's *Sentimens* takes on a more aggressive tone, and their provocative observations and arguments only secondarily filter through into the scholarly tradition of biblical studies. The conversational ideal is to a certain degree revived in Lessing's edition of fragments of Reimarus's work and his subsequent polemical pamphlets.

2. Hermann Samuel Reimarus

Sources: H. S. REIMARUS: *Kleine gelehrte Schriften* (ed. W. Schmidt-Biggemann; Göttingen 1994); *Vindicatio dictorum Veteris Testamenti in Novo allegatorum* (ed. P. Stemmer; Göttingen 1983); *Johann Adolf Hoffmanns Neue Erklärung des Buchs Hiob* (Hamburg 1734); *Die vornehmsten Wahrheiten der natürlichen Religion* (1754; microfiche edn.: *Bibliothek der deutschen Literatur* [München: Saur 1990–99]; ed. G. Gawlick, Göttingen 1985); *Vernunftlehre* (1756; microfiche edn. ibid.; ed. F. Lötzsch, München 1979); *Allgemeine Betrachtungen über die Triebe der Thiere* (1762; microfiche edn. ibid.; ed. J. von Kempski, Göttingen 1982); *Apologie oder Schutzschrift für die vernünftigen Verehrer Gottes* (ed. G. Alexander; Frankfurt 1972); *Fragments* (ed. C. H. Talbert; Philadelphia 1970, ²1985); *Übrige noch ungedruckte Werke des Wolfenbüttlischen Fragmentisten. Ein Nachlaß von G. E. Lessing* ([Berlin] 1787; microfiche edn. ibid.); [idem, *Fragments of the 'Apologie'*, ed. G. E. Lessing] in: G. E. LESSING, *Werke und Briefe* (ed. W. Barner e.a.; vol. 8, ed. A. Schilson, Frankfurt 1989; vol. 9, ed. K. Bohnen / A. Schilson, Frankfurt 1993). – J. C. DÖDERLEIN, *Fragmente und Antifragmente* 1–2 (Nürnberg 1778/79; microfiche edn. ibid.).

Studies: C. BULTMANN, "Langweiliges Wissen. Die Wahrheiten des Hermann Samuel Reimarus", *Religion und Aufklärung* (ed. A. Beutel / V. Leppin; Leipzig 2004) 81–91; G. FREUND, *Theologie im Widerspruch. Die Lessing-Goeze-Kontroverse* (Stuttgart 1989); U. GOLDENBAUM, "Der Skandal der Wertheimer Bibel", *Appell an das Publikum. Die öffentliche Debatte in der deutschen Aufklärung 1687–1796* (ed. U. Goldenbaum; Berlin 2004) I, 175–508; R. A. HARRISVILLE / W. SUNDBERG, *The Bible in Modern Culture* (Grand Rapids ²2002) 46–61; H. HÜBNER, "Die 'orthodoxe' hermeneutica sacra des Hermann Samuel Reimarus", *Die Hermeneutik im Zeitalter der Aufklärung* (ed. M. Beetz / G. Cacciatore; Köln 2000) 99–111; H. GRAF REVENTLOW, "Das Arsenal der Bibelkritik des Reimarus: Die Auslegung der Bibel, insbesondere des Alten Testaments, bei den englischen Deisten", *Hermann Samuel Reimarus (1694–1768) ein 'bekannter Unbekannter' der Aufklärung in Hamburg* ([no ed.]; Joachim Jungius-Gesellschaft der Wissenschaften; Göttingen 1973) 44–65 (and other contributions to this volume); U. RÜTERSWÖRDEN, "Das Alte Testament im Kontext der Naturkunde. Reimarus – und gegenwärtige Versuche", *Gott und Mensch im Dialog* (ed. M. Witte; Berlin 2004) II, 899–917; W. SCHMIDT-BIGGEMANN, "Die destruktive Potenz philosophischer Apologetik oder der Verlust des biblischen Kredits bei Hermann Samuel Reimarus", in: *Historische Kritik und biblischer Kanon* (1988) 193–204; idem, "Erbauliche versus rationale Hermeneutik. Hermann Samuel Reimarus' Bearbeitung von Johann Adolf Hoffmanns 'Neue Erklärung des Buchs Hiob'", *Hermann Samuel Reimarus 1694–1786* [recte 1768] (ed. W. Walter, Göttingen 1998) 23–52; W. SCHRÖDER, *Ursprünge des Atheismus* (Stuttgart / Bad Cannstatt 1998); A. SCHWEITZER, *Geschichte der Leben-Jesu-Forschung* (Tübingen [1906]/1913, ⁶1951) 13–26; P. S. SPALDING, *Seize the book, jail the author: Johann Lorenz Schmidt and censorship in eighteenth-century Germany* (West Lafayette, IN 1998); P. STEMMER, *Weissagung und Kritik. Eine Studie zur Hermeneutik bei Hermann Samuel Reimarus* (Göttingen 1983).

Hermann Samuel Reimarus (1694–1768) is often regarded as the *bête noire* in eighteenth-century biblical studies. His work in the philosophy of religion led him to a radical rejection of the Bible as a document reflecting a divine revelation. It is not easy to situate Reimarus in the distant world of eighteenth-century atheism and orthodoxy, scholarly discovery and learning, theoretical philosophy and political philosophy, religious controversy and religious persecution. He shared his contemporaries' preoccupation with the universality of religious belief and the plausibility of a rational religion, or more specifically, of a physico-theology.[2] His reliance on reason as the foundation of a natural religion made the acceptance of a historically contingent scriptural tradition difficult for him, and his philosophical understanding of the attributes of God was not compatible with an appreciation of numerous details of the biblical texts. Reimarus's thought proceeded in clear alternatives according to the fundamental logical tenet that of two contradictory assumptions only one could be true. Any critique of Reimarus's rationalism ought to make clear what exactly is wrong with his understanding of human reason and the way it operates.[3] In order to understand his antithesis between rational religion and biblical revelation one also needs to be aware of the predominant understanding of the Bible amongst his contemporaries most of whom saw the Bible as a single, unified body of divinely revealed truths.[4]

Reimarus did not embark on a career at a German university. Instead, he worked for forty years from 1728 in the college-like, academic Gymnasium in his home town of Hamburg, where his teaching included oriental languages, i.e., Hebrew, and biblical antiquities based on textbooks like Conrad Iken's *Antiquitates Hebraicae* (1732, [4]1764). He had himself been a student at this gymnasium where the philologist and bibliographer Johann Albert Fabricius (1668–1736) and the Hebraist Johann Christoph Wolf (1683–1739) had been his teachers. From there, Reimarus went to the University of Jena in 1714, where he studied with the philosopher and theologian Johann Franz Buddeus (1667–1729), and then moved on to the University of Wittenberg, where he presented a dissertation in four parts on questions of Hebrew lexicography. He was admitted to the Faculty of Philosophy with a dissertation on Machiavellian political attitudes before Machiavelli's *Il Principe* of 1532.[5] One wonders how far this study of Machiavellianism may have influenced his understanding of history generally, and, more particularly, his later characterizations of the moral corruption of Israelite and Judean rulers as well as the political intentions of Jesus and the Apostles. In 1720, Reimarus left Wittenberg to visit the libraries of Leiden and Oxford and, at the suggestion of J. A. Fabricius, produced an edition and Latin translation of two orations by the Byzantine theologian, Matthaios Kamariotes (d. 1490), refuting the Neo-Platonic philosophy of religion of Georgios Gemistos Pletho (c. 1360–1452).[6] It is again an open question what impact on his understanding of Christianity his work on this theological controversy may have had. Other works from this period show that his philosophical interests ranged from metaphysics to moral philosophy.[7]

In 1731, Reimarus delivered a series of lectures on Old Testament prophecy, *Vindicatio dictorum Veteris Testamenti in Novo allegatorum*,[8] in which he takes

---

[2] See Byrne, Natural Religion (1989); Freund, Theologie im Widerspruch (1989).

[3] See the articles by Schmidt-Biggemann (1988; 1998).

[4] One of the most authoritative presentations of this view in the early eighteenth century was Johann Gottlob Carpzov's *Introductio ad libros canonicos bibliorum Veteris Testamenti omnes* (1714–21, [4]1757).

[5] Repr. in: *Kleine gelehrte Schriften* (ed. Schmidt-Biggemann; 1994, 69–130; not, however, the philological dissertations); for further details of the biography see the introduction to this volume.

[6] See the respective entries in the *Oxford Dictionary of Byzantium* (New York 1991).

[7] Repr. in: *Kleine gelehrte Schriften* (1994) 131–298.

a traditional approach to the supposed interconnection between the Old and New Testaments. He accepts the concept of a specific Christian hermeneutics of the Bible, a *hermeneutica sacra*, which allows the Christian reader of the Old Testament to discover the 'true' meaning of prophetic utterances from pre-Christian antiquity. Within the framework of this concept, Old Testament prophecy could then function as one of the two pillars on which any demonstration of the truth of the Christian religion would rely (the other being the reports about miracles in the Old and New Testaments). These lectures represent an attempt to respond to the reservations of Hugo Grotius (1583–1645) about the application of Old Testament oracles to Jesus Christ, and to answer the claim of Anthony Collins (1676–1729) that only an assumed – and doubtful – special figurative sense of Old Testament prophecies would allow the reader to understand these texts as prophetic predictions of the coming of Christ (*A discourse of the grounds and reasons of the Christian religion*, 1724; *The scheme of literal prophecy considered*, 1726). However, Reimarus was fighting for a cause which he was soon to abandon.

The most substantial work on the Old Testament published by Reimarus during his lifetime is a commentary on the book of Job (1734).[9] It is a massive tome, half of which contains the pious annotations to the text of the erudite Hamburg dilettante and translator of Cicero's *De officiis*, Johann Adolf Hoffmann (1676–1731). Reimarus's contribution is based on the relevant works by A. Schultens (1708), H. B. Starke (1717), J. H. Michaelis (1720), and J. Le Clerc (1731). Due to his philological interests there is a new emphasis on the text as a document from remote antiquity. While, for Reimarus, the *book* of Job dates from the reign of David and Solomon, he argues that the historical *figure* of Job was genealogically linked to Uz, son of Nahor (based on Job 1:1 and Gen 22:20–21). The religious thought of the book is therefore seen to reflect ideas which are independent of the divine promises to Abraham and the divine law transmitted to Moses.[10] Historical imagination thus leads Reimarus to establish a point of reference within Scripture itself for a kind of religious belief which is not grounded in a particular revelation.[11]

The fate of Johann Lorenz Schmidt (1702–49)[12] who suffered persecution in Germany after the publication of his annotated translation of the Pentateuch in 1735 may have been one reason why Reimarus began to write an apology for a purely rational form of worship of God. A manuscript of about 1735, *Gedanken von der Freiheit eines vernünftigen Gottesdienstes*, shows the original plan of an encyclopaedic work in six parts,[13] ranging from a philosophical definition of human reason, an outline of a natural religion according to rational principles and an investigation of the concept of

---

[8]   Edited from the manuscript and discussed by Stemmer (1983).

[9]   See Schmidt-Biggemann, Erbauliche versus rationale Hermeneutik (1998).

[10]   See sections III, 8; VI, 1; VIII, 2 of the introduction.

[11]   The context for this critical and hermeneutical move is the preoccupation with physico-theology amongst intellectuals in Hamburg at the time when J. A. Fabricius sponsored a translation of William Derham's (1657–1735) *Physico-Theology* (1713; French transl. 1726; German transl. 1730) and B. H. Brockes wrote an extensive body of poetry on human delight in the ubiquitous traces of the creator God.

[12]   See Spalding (1998); Goldenbaum (2004).

[13]   Repr. in: *Kleine gelehrte Schriften* (1994) 427–30. The thrust of the work may have been inspired by Spinoza's *Tractatus Theologico-Politicus*.

a divine revelation as a way to salvation for all humankind, through biblical issues – notably the question whether the Old Testament prophets had in fact claimed to teach a religion for salvation, whether Jesus had intended to introduce a new religion and whether the Apostles had invented a different religion from the one which Jesus had taught – to a discussion of the question of divine attributes, of immortality, and of christology as well as of the two main arguments for demonstrating the truth of the Christian religion, i.e., biblical prophecies and miracles. A concluding chapter was to offer observations on the style of the biblical writings and the formation of the canon, and the epilogue would have been a hortatory "address to all Christian rulers and in particular the Protestant ones". The work was obviously intended to function as an appeal for toleration and equal rights for those who were and those who were not able to overcome their doubts regarding the truth of the biblical revelation. In a study of Reimarus's biblical criticism this wider framework should not be neglected.

While the full work never saw the light of day, Reimarus published a highly acclaimed outline of natural religion (*Die vornehmsten Wahrheiten der natürlichen Religion*, 1754), a critique of the logical operations of reason (*Vernunftlehre*, 1756) and a book on zoology from the perspective of physico-theology (*Über die Triebe der Thiere [...]*, 1760). The readers of these books were not supposed to notice that their author advocated the sufficiency of a rational religious faith. His rejection of biblical revelation and biblical authority became part of the intellectual and theological debate only when Gotthold Ephraim Lessing published selected sections of the vast manuscript – the so-called *Wolfenbüttel Fragments* – after the author had died. It is not entirely clear what stage of the long process of composition and revision of the manuscript between the 1730s and 1760s is represented by Lessing's source.[14]

Following Lessing's lead in reading Reimarus, the first point to note is that Reimarus understood the historical Jesus to have been a teacher of the universal and rational principles of a moral religion. Thus in the first 'fragment' (1774), on the toleration of deists, Reimarus states that the "pure teaching of Christ" was a rational, practical religion (116, cf. 178) in which the understanding of virtue was derived from "sound reason" and the "natural law" as its only sources (120).[15] Reimarus refers to the seventeenth-century apostate and reconvert Uriel Acosta (1585–1640) for the idea that, in Judaism, a kind of religion used to be acknowledged which was exclusively based on "sound reason" and "natural law", and that it was this religion which had been the religion of all Patriarchs from Noah to Abraham (123). He claims that this kind of natural religion is also supposed in the Mosaic legislation on aliens (*gērîm*) as well as in Solomon's prayer in 1 Kings 8 (124f). Thus biblical traditions are not disputed as long as they can be seen to be in harmony with a concept of natural religion. In this sense Reimarus finds the key to Old Testament hermeneutics in Matt 22:37–40 where Jesus summarizes "all the law and the prophets" in a synthesis of Deut 6:5 and Lev 19:18.[16] In contrast to this, any more particular assertions are dismissed as merely historical beliefs. This applies to the second component of Jesus' teaching, i.e., his failed messianic expectations, as well as to the representation of the history of Israel in the Old Testament.

---

[14] The original publication was in a journal of the Wolfenbüttel library in 1774 and 1777, followed by a further volume in 1778. The remaining parts of one manuscript version were published in 1787, a further edition of a full manuscript in 1972. The *Wolfenbüttel Fragments* of 1774, 1777 and 1778 now in vols. 8–9 of the Frankfurt edition of Lessing's Works (see bibliography above).

[15] Unless otherwise indicated, page numbers in the text refer to vol. 8 of the Frankfurt edition of Lessing's Works. The approximative translations are my own.

[16] *Apologie* II (1972) 30.

In his publication of 1777, Lessing arranged a sequence of five treatises which starts with a defence of human reason, continues with a discussion of the practical impossibility of a divine revelation to humankind following its dispersion throughout the world, and concludes with a demonstration that the Old Testament does not stand up to critical scrutiny with regard to the criterion of historical truthfulness or to that of conformity with necessary notions of natural religion. The series is completed with a rejection of the New Testament accounts of the resurrection of Jesus and, in 1778, with Reimarus's interpretation of Jesus as a political figure in first-century Judaism.

Old Testament interpretation plays a role in the first treatise with regard to a central aspect of the doctrine of original sin. The question is whether Genesis 1–3 first shows human beings in their full perfection, with the story of the fall then revealing a corruption of their natural faculties, and of human reason in particular. Opposing such an understanding of Genesis 1–3, Reimarus suggests an interpretation according to which it was Adam and Eve's fault not to have employed their rational faculties in order to subdue their passions. He accepts the idea of a limitation of human reason, but not the idea of its corruption. Reason, he claims, "seems to have come from the hand of the creator directly and from its beginning with the same essential limits which it now has" (187). On philosophical grounds as well as on the authority of Moses, Reimarus thus rejects the traditional doctrine of a corruption of human nature.

In his second treatise, Reimarus makes the possibility of rational assent to any claims of revelation the condition for a divine revelation, and develops two arguments. First, in consequence of the divine attributes of wisdom and benevolence which can be discovered in natural religion, God must not set any conditions for the salvation of human beings which it would be impossible for them to meet. Since no particular revelation could be communicated to every single member of the human family, it cannot be claimed that belief in a particular revelation was necessary for salvation (235).[17] Second, if there were to be a divine revelation, it would need to exhibit unambiguous marks of its revelatory character. Its historical content would be judged by the standard of credibility, its scientific content by the standard of rationality, and its religious content would need to be consistent in itself as well as with the truths of rational religion. "One single untruth which runs counter to plain experience, or to history, or to sound reason, or to undisputable principles, or to the rules of common decency, is enough to dismiss a book as a divine revelation" (231). In addition, the revelatory character of a certain book would have to be demonstrated by fulfilled predictions and by miracles (232–33).

In his third and fourth treatises, Reimarus shows that the Old Testament collapses when such criteria are applied to it. The first test: The story of the exodus of three million people (a calculation based on Exod 12:37) and their crossing of the Red Sea during one night is in his view an account of a miracle which is in itself impossible. The story therefore does not stand up to the criterion of historical credibility nor even to that of logical possibility of the

---

[17] For the background of this debate cf., e.g., Spinoza, *Tractatus Theologico-Politicus*, chap. 13, or clandestine manuscripts like *Examen de la religion* (first printed in 1745, German transl. by J. L. Schmidt 1747; see Schröder, Ursprünge [1998] 468–71). I owe these references to B. E. Schwarzbach.

event. The second test: The teaching of Moses and other Old Testament writers (e.g., in Reimarus's reading, at Gen 2:9 and 3:22; 2 Sam 14:14; Ps 6:5–6 [ET 4–5]; 16:9–11; Job 7:6–10; 14:7–12; 19:25–27; Qoh 3:18–21) does not include the idea of immortality or life after death. The Old Testament therefore does not satisfy the criterion of coherence with the truths of natural religion.

As a biblical critic, Reimarus recommends a principle according to which a reader of the Bible should try to study the text itself without any preconceived theological convictions. He insists that there is a wide gap between the biblical writings and the several doctrinal systems which have been based on them (224). However, what applies to theology does not apply to philosophy, and, for Reimarus, the ideas of a rational natural religion do have a distinctive function in biblical hermeneutics. A further aspect of his position as a biblical critic is the ideal of erudition: textual criticism, philology, historical knowledge about the times, manners, and opinions of the ancient writers are requisite for any competent study of the Bible (227, 233). The attribution of the individual documents to their assumed authors is a relevant issue as is the formation of the canon (225f). As a historian, Reimarus shows particular expertise in first-century CE matters which may, in part, be explained by his extensive work on a full-scale critical edition (1750/52) of the *Roman History* of Cassius Dio (c. 150–235). His view of the history of Israel is mainly determined by the Deuteronomists' polemics against apostasy on the one hand and Ezra's institution of education in the Torah on the other (203, 225, 272).

The series of 'fragments' on reason, revelation, and the critique of the Bible published by Lessing is not greatly enriched by those sections of the manuscript which Lessing did not publish. The book of 1787 contains extended chapters on the moral character of the protagonists of Israel's history, and throughout the text a line of argument is pursued which is well known from the work of Matthew Tindal and others. Reimarus applies the criterion of moral demands of the natural law to the narrative traditions in Genesis – 2 Kings as well as 1–2 Chronicles only to conclude that from Noah through to Josiah, none of the Patriarchs, leaders, and rulers of Israel stands up to this standard and that therefore none of them can be considered an agent of divine revelation.[18] Although his study is driven by a kind of philosophical concern, it includes a number of repellent anti-Jewish comments.[19]

Reimarus's rejection of the Bible is occasionally counterbalanced by glimpses of certain truths of natural religion within the Bible when he mentions, for example, that there are some reflections of what is essential to religion in Moses' Decalogue, that there are some magnificent poems among David's Psalms, and that the prophets also appealed to true monotheism and the natural law.[20] The pre-eminence of the ritual law in the Pentateuch, the em-

---

[18] Basically, it reminds the reader of Horace's review of Homer's *Iliad* in *Epistles* I.2: *seditione, dolis, scelere atque libidine et ira / Iliacos intra muros peccatur et extra* (lines 15–16).

[19] E.g., Reimarus (1787) 37–39, 318–32; with variations in Reimarus (1972) 262–65, 671–79. Cf. already in the *Wolfenbüttel Fragments*, 229.

[20] The references are to Reimarus (1972) 690, 706, 718 respectively.

phasis on the political fate of Israel in the historical and the prophetic books, and not least the lack of a doctrine of immortality in Old Testament writings remain objections which he feels himself unable to overcome. As far as the Christian faith is concerned, Reimarus, following Anthony Collins, does not accept the hermeneutical concept of allegorical predictions and prefigurations of Christian truths in the Old Testament. Old Testament prophecy, ritual, and history do not point towards Jesus Christ, and Genesis 1–3 does not provide a foundation for a belief in a "spiritual saviour" (*geistlicher Erlöser*).

On a more technical level, Reimarus offers a view of Israel's history in three main stages. The time of the monarchy is seen as a continuous history of idolatry and of conflicts between priests or prophets and kings.[21] The time of the Babylonian captivity is seen as a period of cultural exchange,[22] that was followed by a period of religious education based on the Pentateuch which has continued since the time of Ezra.[23] As far as Israel's sacred texts are concerned, Reimarus accepts the idea of a short Mosaic book of the law, comprising some material in Exodus 20–23 and Deuteronomy 27–28 and possibly Deuteronomy 32,[24] and attributes the composition of the Pentateuch to Ezra, and the composition of the historical and prophetic books to Ezra's contemporaries.[25] He sees the formation of the biblical canon as a prolonged process which had not even come to an end at the time of the New Testament writers.[26] Although Reimarus offers a fairly consistent picture of the historical development, the methodological grounds for his critical acceptance of certain biblical data in these studies are not always clear.

3. Voltaire

Sources: VOLTAIRE: *Voltaire électronique* (Cambridge: Chadwyck-Healey / Oxford: Voltaire Foundation 1998; in part based on the Moland edition, in part on the Oxford edition); *Œuvres complètes de Voltaire* (ed. L. Moland; Paris 1877–85; abbr. *Œuvres*); *Œuvres complètes de Voltaire / Complete works of Voltaire* (ed. U. Kölving e.a.; Geneva / Oxford 1968-; abbr. OC); *Correspondence and related documents* (ed. T. Besterman; Oxford 1968–77); *Mélanges* (ed. J. van den Heuvel; Bibliothèque de la Pleiade; Paris 1961). – H. ST JOHN VISCOUNT BOLINGBROKE: *Letters on the Study and Use of History* (London 1752, and reprints and translations; also in: *Historical Works*, ed. I. Kramnick; Chicago 1972); *Works* (London 1754, and reprints). – J. F. W. JERUSALEM, *Betrachtungen über die vornehmsten Wahrheiten der Religion* 1–3 (Braunschweig 1768–79).

Bibliographies: Bibliographie analytique des écrits relatifs à Voltaire 1966-1990 (ed. F. A. Spear; Oxford 1992); "Bibliographie de la littérature française. XVIᵉ-XXᵉ siècles" (annually in: *Révue d'Histoire littéraire de la France*).

Studies: A. AGES, "Voltaire, Calmet and the Old Testament", SVEC [see below] 41 (1966) 87–187; F. BESSIRE, "Voltaire lecteur de dom Calmet", SVEC 284 (1991) 139–77; idem, *La Bible dans la correspondence de Voltaire*, SVEC 367 (1999); T. BESTERMAN, *Voltaire* (Chicago ³1976); L. BIANCHI, "Religion et superstition dans le *Traité sur la tolérance*: notes en marge du chapitre XX", Combats (1997) [see below] 519-26; TH. E. D. BRAUN, "La présentation positive du déisme dans des œuvres de fiction", Combats (1997) 173–79; C. BULTMANN, "Dichtung und Weisheit der Blütezeit. Zum Salomobild im 18. Jahrhundert", *Ideales Königtum. Studien zu David und Salomo* (ed. R. LUX; Leipzig 2005) 153–74; E. S. Christianson, "Voltaire's 'Précis' of Ecclesiastes: a case study in the Bible's afterlife", *Journal for the Study of the Old Testament* 29 (2005) 455–484; M.-H. COTONI, "Vol-

---

[21] Ibid. 624–71.
[22] *Wolfenbüttel Fragments*, 272–5; Reimarus (1972) 805–08.
[23] Reimarus (1972) 687, 914–21.
[24] Ibid. 844–49, 914 f.
[25] Ibid. 687, 873, 898–900, 918–21.
[26] Ibid. 828–31.

taire, Rousseau, Diderot", *Le Siècle des Lumières et la Bible* (ed. Y. Belaval / D. Bourel; BTT 7; Paris 1986) 779–803; eadem, "Voltaire et l'Ecclésiaste", *Hommage à Claude Faisant* (Nice 1991) 163–74; eadem, "La référence à la Bible dans les *Lettres philosophiques* de Voltaire", *Revue d'histoire littéraire de la France* 92 (1992) 198–209; eadem, "Présence de la Bible dans la correspondence de Voltaire", SVEC 319 (1994) 357–98; eadem, "Voltaire lit la Bible", *Voltaire en son temps* 4 (Oxford 1994) 214–29 (bibl. 435–37); eadem, "Histoire et polémique dans la critique biblique de Voltaire: le *Dictionnaire philosophique*", *Raison présente* (Special issue; 1994) 27–47; eadem, "Les personnages bibliques dans le *Dictionnaire philosophique* de Voltaire", *Revue d'histoire littéraire de la France* 95 (1995) 151–64; eadem, "Les clausules des articles du *Dictionnaire philosophique*", Combats (1997) 365–76; J. HÄSELER, "Voltaire vu par Formey et ses amis, ou éléments d'une histoire de la réception de Voltaire en Prusse", Combats (1997) 969–75; H. A. KORFF, *Voltaire im literarischen Deutschland des XVIII. Jahrhunderts* (Heidelberg 1917); J. P. LEE, "The publication of the Sermon des cinquante: was Voltaire jealous of Rousseau?", Combats (1997) 687–94; J. LEIGH, "Bazin, Bazing and interpretations of history", Combats (1997) 303–09; S. LEROUX, "Un Dieu rémunérateur et vengeur comme fondement-garantie de la morale: de la philosophie de Newton à la morale de Voltaire", Combats (1997) 739–50; A. McKENNA, "La diffusion clandestine des œuvres de Voltaire: un exemple", Combats (1997) 455–65; idem, "Réflexions sur un recueil de manuscrits philosophiques clandestins", *De bonne main. La communication manuscrite au XVIIIe siècle* (ed. F. Moureau; Paris / Oxford 1993) 51–57; P. MALANDAIN, "Le travail intertextuel de l'écriture dans les *Lettres philosophiques*", Combats (1997) 285–301; C. MERVAUD, "Avant l'orage: l'été de 1752", *Voltaire en son temps* 3 (1991) 83–102; R. POMEAU, *La religion de Voltaire* (Paris ²1969); idem e.a., *Voltaire en son temps* 1–5 (Oxford 1985–94); L. RÉTAT, "Renan, Voltaire et l'intelligence de la Bible", *Le Siècle de Voltaire. Hommage à René Pomeau* (ed. C. Mervaud / S. Menant; Oxford 1987) II, 747–59; B. E. SCHWARZBACH, *Voltaire's Old Testament Criticism* (Geneva 1971); idem, "Voltaire et les Huguenots de Berlin: Formey et Isaac de Beausobre", *Voltaire und Deutschland* (ed. P. Brockmeier / R. Desné / J. Voss; Stuttgart 1979) 103–18; idem, "Coincé entre Pluche et Lucrèce: Voltaire et la théologie naturelle", SVEC 192 (1980) 1072–84; idem, "Voltaire et ses inversions des 'mythes et origines' juives par une haute critique biblique", *Primitivisme et mythes des origines dans la France des Lumières 1680-1820* (ed. C. Grell / C. Michel; Paris 1989) 135–51; idem, "Une légende en quête d'un manuscrit: le *Commentaire sur la Bible* de Mme Du Châtelet", *De bonne main. La communication manuscrite au XVIIIe siècle* (ed. F. Moureau; Paris 1993) 97–116; idem, "La critique biblique dans les *Examens de la Bible* et dans certains autres traités clandestins", *La lettre clandestine* 4 (1995) 69–86; idem, "Voltaire et les Juifs: bilan et plaidoyer", SVEC 358 (1998) 27–91; idem, "Les études bibliques à Cirey", *Cirey dans la vie intellectuelle. La réception de Newton en France* (ed. F. de Gandt; SVEC 2001,11) 26–54; idem, "Dom Augustin Calmet. Man of the Enlightenment Despite Himself", *ARelG* 3 (ed. J. Assmann e.a.; München / Leipzig 2001) 135–48; A. U. SOMMER, "Kritisch-moralische exempla-Historie im Zeitalter der Aufklärung: Viscount Bolingbroke als Geschichtsphilosoph", *Saeculum* 53 (2002) 269–310; J. VON STACKELBERG, "Voltaires Geschichtsphilosophie: La philosophie de l'histoire", in: idem, *Über Voltaire* (München 1998) 45–57; Y. TOUCHEFEU, *L'antiquité et le christianisme dans la pensée de Jean-Jacques Rousseau* (SVEC 372; 1999).

Special abbreviations (see above):
Combats (1997) = *Voltaire et ses combats* (ed. U. Kölving / C. Mervaud; Oxford 1997)
OC = *Œuvres complètes de Voltaire* (ed. U. Kölving e.a.; 1968-)
Œuvres = *Œuvres complètes de Voltaire* (ed. L. Moland; 1877–85)
SVEC = *Studies on Voltaire and the Eighteenth Century* (Oxford)

Biblical criticism in Voltaire (1694–1778, born François-Marie Arouet) is a central element in his polemics against disfigurations of God in traditional religions. Voltaire is an ardent supporter of the idea of a natural religion, i.e., a religion which would have its focus exclusively on the – preferably silent – worship of a supreme creator god and on morality. The philosopher who adores God (*le philosophe adorateur d'un dieu*) represents the ideal type of a human being who does not deny that there is a transcendent dimension to human life. Where Voltaire mentions this character, he may be offering something like an idealized self-portrait. However, when he turns his attention to the Bible, this philosopher finds it abound with ridiculous absurdities and repugnant immoralities. As far as the Old Testament / Hebrew Bible is concerned, Voltaire's biblical criticism is impregnated with a distinctly anti-Jewish tone, and his writings ought to be approached from a critical perspective of intellectual history. Furthermore, the reader needs to be aware of the fact that throughout his œuvre, Voltaire's anti-Jewish arguments are anti-biblical arguments and vice versa, and that Voltaire sees a significant dependence of the New Testament on the Old Testament, a continuity as it were between Jesus Christ and his ancestor David. This line of tradition is understood to continue into Voltaire's own present, since for him the thought of the theologians and reformers of the Christian Church, in all their diversity, is linked to those biblical disfigurations of God, and this would equally be the case with Jewish religious beliefs. Voltaire's biblical criticism is one aspect of his struggle against religious fanaticism and persecution. This struggle in turn includes strong condemnations of any persecution of the Jews as is clear, for example, from the *Sermon du Rabbin Akib* (1761).[27]

Stylistically, Voltaire's critique of the Bible shows all the ingenuity and energy of his rhetoric and wit. As B. E. Schwarzbach has pointed out in his comprehensive study of Voltaire's Old Testament criticism of the 1760s and 1770s, "Voltaire assumes the guise of a rabbi, a doctor of theology, several quakerish ministers of Deism, an *honnête homme*, an *abbé*, a Spanish student of theology, a British milord, and the collective person of four royal chaplains. He poses as his own friend ... and as the nephew of *l'Abbé* Bazin ... Like a latter day psalmist, Voltaire seems to declare: let all who have breath and wit praise God and denounce the unworthy muddle imposed upon them in His name."[28] Reading, for argument's sake, the Bible literally and historically, Voltaire telescopes the narrative tradition of the Old Testament into grotesque panoramas of cruelty and lechery. What originated as sharp and perceptive provocations, designed to challenge the biblical hermeneutics of Roman Catholic as well as Protestant theologians, turns into excessive elaborations in the literary forms of, for example, dictionary articles, a treatise on universal history, a play, a tale, a biblical commentary of sorts.[29] One factor which contributed to this development was the execution in Catholic France of the Huguenot merchant Jean Calas in Toulouse in 1762 following which Voltaire embarked on a sustained campaign against what he generally saw as Christian superstitions founded upon claims to a biblical revelation.[30]

In order to provide a general idea about Voltaire's place within the history of Old Testament interpretation it will be best to concentrate on his terse references to the Bible in the context of his writings on natural religion around

---

[27] References will be given on the basis of the Moland edition (*Œuvres*) and the volume edited by van den Heuvel (*Mélanges*). Where available, the number of the volume in the new *Œuvres complètes* (ed. by Kölving e.a.; abbr. OC) will be added. *Œuvres* 24, 277–84; *Mélanges* 447–54; see Schwarzbach, Voltaire et les Juifs (1998).

[28] Schwarzbach, Voltaire's OT Criticism (1971) 16.

[29] *Dictionnaire philosophique* (1764/65/67) [OC 35–36] and *Questions sur l'encyclopédie* (1770/72) in: *Œuvres* 17–20; *La philosophie de l'histoire* (1765) [OC 59] and *Défense de mon oncle* (1767) [OC 64] in: *Œuvres* 11, 3–156 and 26, 367–433; *Saül* (1763) in: *Œuvres* 5, 569–611; *Le Taureau blanc* (1774) in: *Œuvres* 21, 483–512; *La Bible enfin expliquée* (1776) in: *Œuvres* 30, 1–316.

[30] See for all biographical aspects Bestermann, Voltaire (1976); Pomeau, Voltaire en son temps 1–5 (1985–1994). For an analysis of the theological and exegetical writings of Voltaire see the relevant sections in these biographies and especially Pomeau, La religion de Voltaire (1969); Schwarzbach, Voltaire's OT Criticism (1971), and the articles by Cotoni.

1750, especially since the more elaborate later publications, and notably his critical historical intuitions, have been exhaustively studied in Schwarzbach's monograph.[31] The writings in question date from a period from 1750 to 1753 when Voltaire lived at the court of Frederick the Great in Berlin and Potsdam and thus found himself in a milieu characterized by the conservatism of Lutherans and Calvinists on the one side, and the attractions of atheism as represented by Julien Offray de La Mettrie (1709–51) on the other. During this period, Voltaire published a *Défense de Milord Bolingbroke* (1752, reprinted in the journal *Bibliothèque raisonnée* in 1753[32]), composed a *Poème sur la religion naturelle* (1752, published in 1756 under the title *Poème sur la loi naturelle* and in conjunction with a *Poème sur le désastre de Lisbonne*) and wrote a *Sermon des cinquante* (circulated in manuscript after 1752, published in 1762).[33]

Voltaire had known Henry Saint-John Viscount Bolingbroke (1678–1751) for many years and was already familiar with his ideas when his *Letters on the study and use of history* appeared in 1752.[34] Although the biblical tradition is only one among many issues addressed in this work, Bolingbroke clearly states his view that the Bible contains no source materials for universal history, and that the traditional scholarly endeavour of harmonizing 'profane' with 'sacred' history was futile. Thus he concludes his discussion of ancient history with the observation that "these sacred books do not aim, in any part of them, at any thing like universal chronology and history. They contain a very imperfect account of the Israelites themselves [...]". "We have therefore neither in profane nor in sacred authors such authentic, clear, distinct, and full accounts of the originals of ancient nations, and of the great events of those ages that are commonly called the first ages, as deserve to go by the name of history [...]". Bolingbroke wanted to reverse a scholarly convention which in his view had started with Julius Africanus, Eusebius, and Georgios Syncellos who "corrupted the waters". As far as the authority of the Bible is concerned, he refers to a quotation from Henry Holden (1652) in Richard Simon's preface to the *Histoire critique du Vieux Testament* (1678/85) which suggests that divine inspiration in a strict sense was restricted to foundational doctrinal aspects of the Christian faith only.[35] In response to attacks on the author which followed the publication of the *Letters*, Voltaire publicly insisted on the significance of Bolingbroke's critical reflections.[36] For this purpose he assumed the persona of "Le docteur Goodnatur'd Wellwisher,

---

[31] The writings of the early 1750s were no entirely new departure in Voltaire's thought. His critique of the Christian – biblical and ecclesiastical – tradition and his philosophical interest in the concept of natural religion or 'theism' can be traced back at least to a poem of 1722 (*Œuvres* 9, 357–364; see Pomeau, Voltaire en son temps 1, 150–64). A considerable amount of relevant material can be found in his early plays, notably the hugely successful *Zaïre* of 1732, as well as in his *Lettres philosophiques* of 1733/34 (*Œuvres* 2, 531–618; 22, 75–187; *Mélanges* 1–133; see Pomeau, La religion de Voltaire [1969], and the relevant articles by Braun and Cotoni).

[32] Within the cultural atmosphere of the time, the anonymous reprint of the *Défense* in the *Bibliothèque raisonnée* tied in, e.g., with this journal's previous notices about Bolingbroke and his critics, with a favourable review of Voltaire's *Le siècle de Louis XIV*, and with an article about Thomas Sherlock's reply to Anthony Collins's critique of Genesis 3 in issues of 1751 and 1752. The journal helped the text which may be considered the most focussed statement of Voltaire's theological views to a wider circulation.

[33] The *Défense* in: *Œuvres* 23, 547–54; the *Poèmes* in: *Œuvres* 9, 433–80; *Mélanges* 271–87 and 301–09; the *Sermon* in: *Œuvres* 24, 437–54; *Mélanges* 253–70. For the secondary literature see n. 30 and Lee, Publication of the Sermon des cinquante (1997).

[34] French transl. 1752, German transl. 1758; the work was known in manuscript to some readers since 1738.

[35] The references are to *Letters* (1752) 113, 115, 7, 92, in the edition of 1972: 47f, 5, 39, respectively.

[36] In his apologetic writings, J. F. W. Jerusalem in turn emphasized the link between Bolingbroke's and Voltaire's criticism.

Chapelain du comte de Chesterfield" (not in the *Bibliothèque raisonnée*) who gives sober and judicious advice to Protestant hotheads fighting against all adherents of deism. One of the stylistic features of this text, therefore, is an ironic use of the first-person plural.

In the *Défense* (23, 547–54), Voltaire's view of the Old Testament and biblical criticism is firmly rooted in his representation of deism. According to Voltaire, deists worship one single god, they inculcate virtue, they respect political authority, and they consider all human beings as their brothers and sisters. Their moral teaching is "pure" and related to the "great principle" of a monotheistic creed. In this belief they are united with Jews, Muslims, disciples of Confucius and with ancient philosophers like Socrates, Plato, Cicero and Marcus Aurelius. Voltaire's "Chapelain" not only opposes all persecution but also all defamation of any such believers. This understanding of deism is then linked to the Old Testament: *Un déiste est un homme qui est de la religion d'Adam, de Sem* [*sic* for Seth], *de Noé*.[37] As far as the Old Testament is accepted as presenting a picture of earliest human history, it leaves room for deism as the natural or original religion. However, what adherents of deism do not accept is that they should take the one "step" from the religion of Noah to that of Abraham which would then directly lead on to that of Moses, of Christ, of the Catholic Church, and of the confusing multitude of reformers (even including George Fox, the founder of quakerism). This biblical and ecclesiastical line of tradition which in theory could function as a "thread" in the "great labyrinth" of history remains an alternative to the religious convictions of a deist, and Voltaire's comments on the biblical tradition are designed to show that it is no valid alternative.

Voltaire's reference to Adam, Seth, and Noah does not imply his acceptance of the biblical primeval history. In his *Défense* this becomes clear when he addresses the issue of miracles in the Pentateuch. The serpent of Genesis 3 is just as much a funny curiosity as is the donkey of Numbers 22. The familiar critique of biblical miracles is evoked through a reference to the stories about Moses in Egypt which are exemplified by Exod 7:14–21, and for further complication with a reference to the successes of the Egyptian magicians according to Exod 7:22. A second familiar point is the critique of biblical morality which is, however, of secondary importance in the *Défense* where only brief allusion is made to David's and Solomon's harems (2 Sam 3:2–5; 6:13–16; 1 Kgs 11:1–3). The discussion of biblical miracles aims at provoking the reader by a complete dissociation of 'faith' from 'reason', and by a definition of 'faith' as being nothing but the credulous assent to historical traditions.[38] More specifically, Voltaire defends Bolingbroke's scholarly approach to the biblical text as that of a reader who is an expert in history and philosophy, who keeps what is dogmatic in religion separate from what is historical, and who modestly limits his investigations to the historical side. This side, he claims, is open to inquiry by any learned person (*la partie historique, soumise à l'examen de tous les savants*)

---

[37] The name of 'Sem' must be a slip of the pen for 'Seth' here; cf. *Profession de foi des théistes* (1768), *Œuvres* 27, 55–74, 72, or the *Examen important de Milord Bolingbroke* (1767) [OC 62], *Œuvres* 26, 195–306, 299; *Mélanges* 1019–1117, 1116.

[38] Cf. the article "Foi. II", *Dictionnaire philosophique* (see n. 29).

and can be examined following established rules of criticism (*les règles de la critique profane*). In this sense, the Pentateuch can be summoned as it were before the court of reason alone (*au tribunal seul de la raison*). Finally, he insists that the scholarly issue of the question of authorship of the Pentateuch must be considered independent of any judgment about Bolingbroke's personal life-style which some of his opponents tried to denigrate. On the basis of such principles, not only the miracles but also the chronology and geography of the Pentateuchal narratives can be questioned. Voltaire dismisses a suggested analogy between the *Iliad* as a composition by Homer and the *Pentateuch* as a composition by Moses on the grounds of anachronisms in the latter work. Thus he sees no rational basis for asserting a Mosaic authorship of the Pentateuch. Voltaire traces Bolingbroke's critique back to Simon's view that the Pentateuch was composed and supplemented by priests in a later period of Israel's history on the basis of some earlier Mosaic traditions.

What emerges from this apology for Bolingbroke in the *Défense* is the idea of a historically contingent origin of the Pentateuch which in turn would corroborate a deist's reluctance to take the "step" from natural religion to the religion "of Abraham, of Moses, of the Messiah". Voltaire puts his seal of irony on the discussion when he states, *Il suffit qu'on croie en ces livres avec une foi humble et soumise, sans qu'on sache précisément quel est l'auteur à qui Dieu seul les a visiblement inspirés pour confondre la raison.* The philosophical context for his interest in the Pentateuch is indicated by a positive mention of several Enlightenment thinkers,[39] while on the other hand, he rejects the appeal by Bolingbroke's opponents to such popular apologetic works as Jacques Abbadie's (1654–1727) *Traité de la vérité de la religion chrétienne* (1684/89 and many later editions and translations), or Claude François Houtteville's (1686–1742) *La religion chrétienne prouvée par les faits* (1722).[40] As the public character of his controversy with Protestants in Berlin demonstrates, Voltaire obviously does not regard biblical criticism to be a merely academic exercise.[41]

The paradigmatic synthesis of a philosophy of religion and biblical criticism in the *Défense* is a by-product of the more elaborate *Poème sur la loi naturelle* and *Sermon des cinquante*. The *Poème* (9, 441–60) proclaims a universal moral law as one aspect of a world which owes its origin to a creator god. While Voltaire dismisses metaphysical debates about a *creatio ex nihilo* or about the nature of the soul, he defends his understanding of a natural law against philosophical critics. The *Poème* reveals the variety of deism to which Voltaire subscribed and which functions as the standard against which he measures the

---

[39] Voltaire mentions Pierre Bayle (1647–1706) and Shaftesbury (1671–1713) and expresses his admiration for Alexander Pope (1688–1744), notably this poet's *Essay on Man* (1733/34; this will change in the *Poème sur le désastre de Lisbonne* of 1756). In his *Poème sur la loi naturelle* (III, 85–90) he adds the names of, for example, Gottfried Wilhelm Leibniz (1646–1716), John Locke (1632–1704), Isaac Newton (1643–1727), and Joseph Addison (1672–1719) to this list.

[40] In *Le Taureau blanc*, Pharaoh's daughter, an ardent reader of John Locke's *Essay concerning human understanding*, is also tired of the works of Abbadie and Houtteville: *Œuvres* 21, 483–512, 505 f.

[41] Voltaire directly hints at the corruption among the Christian clergy and at the rise of deism in Prussian society.

biblical tradition. The following lines may demonstrate the force of his beliefs
(I, 39–41.45–46.49–51.84–86):

> ... Je ne puis ignorer ce qu'ordonna mon maître;
> Il m'a donné sa loi, puisqu'il m'a donné l'être.
> Sans doute il a parlé; mais c'est à l'univers ...
> La morale uniforme en tout temps, en tout lieu,
> À des siècles sans fin parle au nom de ce Dieu. ...
> Le bon sens la reçoit; et les remords vengeurs,
> Nés de la conscience, en sont les défenseurs;
> Leur redoutable voix partout se fait entendre. ...
> Le ciel fit la vertu; l'homme en fit l'apparence.
> Il peut la revêtir d'imposture et d'erreur,
> Il ne peut la changer; son juge est dans son cœur.

Voltaire assigns to all positive religions only a limited value in comparison with
this fundamental natural religion (II, 21–22; III, 1–2):

> ... Usages, intérêts, cultes, lois, tout diffère.
> Qu'on soit juste, il suffit; le reste est arbitraire. ...
>
> L'univers est un temple où siège l'Éternel.
> Là chaque homme à son gré veut bâtir un autel. ...

He accepts no justification for religious controversy and persecution, and in
this context even refers to the biblical idea of the human being as created in
the image of God (III, 80). For the religious situation in post-Reformation
Europe he offers the following explanation (III, 37–40):

> ... C'est que de la nature on étouffa la voix;
> C'est qu'à sa loi sacrée on ajouta des lois;
> C'est que l'homme, amoureux de son sot esclavage,
> Fit, dans ses préjugés, Dieu même à son image. ...

The philosophical concept of the *Poème* shows in fact striking parallels with J.
Abbadie's apologetic treatise (esp. Sect. II, chs. V-IX). However, where Abbadie finds such 'prejudices' in paganism only and tries to prove that the Bible is
a repository of a divine revelation, Voltaire applies the notion of 'prejudice' to
the Bible itself. The *Sermon des cinquante* (24, 437–54) consequently offers a
devastating critique of the Old and New Testament. While in principle the biblical tradition might be honoured as one example of an 'arbitrary' form of religious worship, Voltaire only sees it as a document of superstition, and condemns it on the two counts of contradiction to the universal moral law and
contradiction to historical plausibility (*C'est sous ce double aspect de perversité et
de fausseté que nous examinerons ... les livres des Hébreux et de ceux qui leur ont
succédé*).[42] In the *Sermon* as in many publications of the following 25 years,
biblical criticism predominantly has the form of an enumeration of outrageous
or ridiculous scenes in the Bible. Voltaire constructs in the *Sermon* a paraphrase of the biblical story-line from the time of the creation to the age of David (as the ancestor of Jesus) in which he relentlessly highlights points such as
Gen 20:2 and 26:2; 25:31–34 and 30:3–13; 34:25–29 and 47:13–21; Exod

---

[42] *Œuvres* 24, 439; *Mélanges* 254.

32:26–29 and Num 25:9 (1 Cor 10:8); Lev 27:29 and Judg 11:39; Num 31:17–18 and 31:32–35; Deut 2:34 and 20:16; Josh 6:16–21 and Judg 12:5–6; 3:12–30 and 1 Sam 8:7–8; 14:24–46 and 15:7–33; 25:4–42 and 27: 8–11; 2 Samuel 11 and 24; finally 2 Kgs 2:23–24: in telescoping such elements of biblical narratives into one single picture, he demonstrates the moral deficiencies of the historical characters. A similar procedure is followed under the rubric of lack of credibility when Voltaire alludes to passages such as Gen 1:14–19 after 1:3–5; Gen 2:18–23 after 1:27; the stories of Genesis 3 and 6–8; Gen 32:23–33; 41:37–57; Exod 7:14–22; 8:1–3; 8:12–14; Exod 12:29 and 14:19–29; Num 5:11–31 and Deut 8:2–4; Joshua 6 and 10; 1 Sam 28:13–14 and 2 Kgs 20:8–11; finally 2 Kgs 2:11 and Dan 3:19–27. The extensive survey of miraculous stories is designed to demonstrate the unreliability of the ancient scribes. Through a critique of prophetic traditions, such as those in Isaiah 7–8 or Ezekiel 1–4, Voltaire rejects Jewish and Christian ideas about prophetic predictions of the coming of a Messiah, and through a critique of contradictory or miraculous stories in the Gospels, he extends his attacks to include the New Testament as well. The narrator of Mark 5:9–13 and 11:12–14 does not fare any better than the narrator of Judg 15:4–5 and 15:15–17. Despite the occasional remark about oriental taste and oriental customs, Voltaire seems to argue that a rational and literal reading of the Bible must lead to the discovery of a grotesque comedy of human passion and delusion. In conclusion, he emphasizes that there can be no biblical alternative to natural religion.[43]

The *Sermon* can be considered the culminating point of a tradition of clandestine manuscripts about biblical issues and of the polemics of critics such as Anthony Collins (1676-1729) and Matthew Tindal (1657-1733) and their followers.[44] There is no reason to assume that Voltaire had any positive intention to stimulate the scholarly investigation of the world of the ancient biblical scribes or to advance reflections on biblical hermeneutics. Even if in his subsequent writings on biblical matters he shows a considerable awareness of more specific points of criticism, these writings are hardly anything but repetitive variations on a set theme. Amongst them, the play *Saül* (1763) exaggerates the grotesque even more than the *Sermon*, the numerous articles on biblical persons or themes in the *Dictionnaire philosophique* (1764, revised and enlarged 1765/67/69) and the *Questions sur l'Encyclopédie* (1770-72, enlarged 1774) appear as thought-provoking fragments, the discussion of biblical history in *La Philosophie de l'histoire par feu l'Abbé Bazin* (1765; from 1769 as an introduction to the *Essai sur les mœurs*; followed by a sequel, *Défense de mon oncle*, i.e., the "late Abbé Bazin", in 1767) emphasizes the argument concerning universal history, the *Examen important de Milord Bolingbroke ou le tombeau du fanatisme* (1767; possibly based on earlier manuscript materials) adopts a somewhat analytical style, the *Dieu et les hommes* (1769) sets biblical criticism in the context of a history of religion, the *Taureau blanc* (1774) offers a parody of biblical narratives, and *La Bible enfin expliquée* (1776) rehearses all critical points almost in a chapter-by-chapter gloss on Genesis-2 Kings (including Ruth; with a brief glance also at Tobit, Judith, Ezra, Esther, Daniel, Ezekiel, Hosea, Jonah, Maccabees, and some brief chapters on Jewish political parties at the time of Herod, and on the New Testament Gospels).[45] Voltaire's detailed observations on the Old Testament and his response to the work of contemporaries in this series of writings cannot be summarized here.[46]

---

[43] In the final section (§ 53) of *La Philosophie de l'histoire*, however, the Decalogue is used to illustrate 'natural law': *Œuvres* 11,155.

[44] See Reventlow, The Authority of the Bible (1984).

[45] See the references in the notes above. *Dieu et les hommes* in: *Œuvres* 28, 129-248.

[46] See Schwarzbach, Voltaire's OT Criticism (1971), chap. 3; Houtman, Pentateuch (1980/1994) § 30.

Another aspect of Voltaire's biblical criticism are two poetic compositions based on Qohelet and the Song of Songs (*Précis de l'Ecclésiaste*, 1759; *Précis du Cantique des cantiques*, 1759).[47] Voltaire – following Grotius – considers both these biblical books to be post-Solomonic writings. He shows a positive interest in Qohelet as a work of philosophy, and in the Song of Songs as a charming document of human affection as it was shaped within the world of oriental manners. He takes verses such as Qoh 11:9 and 12:13 as an opportunity to anchor his religious convictions in a poetic paraphrase of ancient Judaean philosophy (lines 173–80). However, in a *Lettre de M. Eratou à M. Clocpitre* (1761) – as well as in his article "Salomon" in the *Dictionnaire philosophique* (1764/65)[48] – he expresses reservations about *ce qui pouvait paraître d'une métaphysique trop dure* in Qohelet which almost amount to a retraction of his poetic *Précis*. Notable is not least Voltaire's reference to Old Testament prophecy in comments on Jer (7:22 and) 27:6; 38:17 in the *Traité sur la tolérance à l'occasion de la mort du Jean Calas* (1762), which are again undermined by comments in the *Examen* on Jeremiah as having been bribed by the Babylonians.[49]

An unexpected note of appreciation rings in Voltaire's review of *De Sacra Poesi Hebraeorum* of Robert Lowth (1710–87).[50] Voltaire shows himself impressed by Lowth's decision to follow in his study of Hebrew poetry "the principles which critics have applied to that of the Greek and Romans", he quotes from Horace and Vergil, and mentions Lowth's suggestion that Isaiah, Jeremiah, and Ezekiel might be compared to Homer, Simonides, and Aischylos respectively. He praises the poetic beauty and force of lines such as Cant 2:10–13 or Isa 30:26; 60:19–20 while finding fault with the imagery in Psalm 114:4 and Isa 24:23. However, where Voltaire addresses Lowth's essential ideas about the sublime in Hebrew poetry, he immediately puts the emphasis on the use of sublime imagery in biblical representations of the anger of God. The majestic imagery of Ps 104:3–4 is eclipsed for this reader by the frightful imagery of Jer 4:23–26. Finally, while Voltaire accepts the common view that poetry was the original kind of language for literary compositions in the early ages of human history, he criticizes Lowth for not having provided a lecture on *la voix naïve de la nature* in the patriarchal narratives and the book of Ruth.[51]

Seen against the background of Abbadie's influential apologetic treatise, Voltaire may be regarded from his early years as a religious apologist who simply did not follow Abbadie's apology of and admiration for the Bible and refused to take the one "step" beyond natural religion of which he writes in the *Défense*. Voltaire's biblical criticism represents a challenge for biblical hermeneutics, but it lacks a sense for religious language, and the biblical language in particular.

---

[47] *Œuvres* 9, 481–506, including the *Lettre de M. Eratou à M. Clocpitre* (1761).

[48] *Œuvres* 20, 381–90.

[49] *Œuvres* 25, 13–118, 75f; *Mélanges* 563–650, 606, 610; and *Œuvres* 26, 218; *Mélanges* 1028.

[50] Review of the 2nd edition 1763, reviewed in the *Gazette Litteraire*, 1764, in: *Œuvres* 25, 201–08.

[51] One wonders whether Voltaire's biblical criticism would have taken a different turn if he had had the freedom to review the Hebrew classics in the same way as Senator Pococurante reviews Greek and Roman classics in *Candide* (1759, chap. 25 [*Œuvres* 21, 137–218]).

4. Gotthold Ephraim Lessing

Sources: G. E. LESSING: *Werke und Briefe* 1–12 (in 13 vols.; ed. W. Barner e.a.; Frankfurt 1985–2003; esp. vol. 8, ed. A. Schilson; Frankfurt 1989; vol. 9, ed. K. Bohnen / A. Schilson; Frankfurt 1993; vol. 10, ed. A. Schilson / A. Schmitt; Frankfurt 2001; includes extensive commentary and bibl.); *Philosophical and Theological Writings* (tr. H. B. Nisbet; Cambridge 2005); *Lessing's Theological Writings* (tr. H. Chadwick; London 1956); *Nathan the Wise, Minna von Barnhelm, and other plays and writings* (ed. P. Demetz; New York 1991); [G. E. LESSING], *Des Herrn von Voltaire kleinere historische Schriften* (Rostock 1752; microfiche edn.: *Bibliothek der deutschen Literatur* [München: Saur, 1990–99]); *G. E. Lessings Schriften* (Berlin 1753–55; microfiche edn. ibid.); *Gotthold Ephraim Leßings theologischer Nachlaß* (ed. K. G. Lessing; Berlin 1784; microfiche edn. ibid.); *Gotthold Ephraim Lessings Leben, nebst seinem noch übrigen litterarischen Nachlasse* (ed. K. G. Lessing; Berlin 1793–95; microfiche edn. ibid.; repr. Hildesheim 1998).

Bibliographies: W. BARNER e.a., *Lessing. Epoche, Werk, Wirkung* (Tübingen [6]1998); S. SEIFERT, *Lessing-Bibliographie* (Berlin / Weimar 1973); D. KUHLES, *Lessing-Bibliographie 1971–1985* (Berlin / Weimar 1988); *Lessing Yearbook* (ed. for the Lessing Society; Göttingen / Detroit, MI 1969–).

Studies: A Companion to the Works of Lessing (ed. B. Fischer / T. C. Fox; Rochester, NY 2005); H. E. ALLISON, Lessing and the Enlightenment: His Philosophy of Religion and its Relation to Eighteenth-Century Thought (Ann Arbor 1966); O. F. BEST, "Noch einmal: Vernunft und Offenbarung. Überlegungen zu Lessings 'Berührung' mit der Tradition des mystischen Rationalismus", *Lessing Yearbook* 12 (1980) 123–56; H. M. BLOCK, "Confrontations of Voltaire in 18th-century Germany: Lessing, Herder, Goethe", *Voltaire et ses combats* (ed. U. Kölving / C. Mervaud; Oxford 1997) 1165–71; K. BOHNEN, *Geist und Buchstabe. Zum Prinzip des kritischen Verfahrens in Lessings literarästhetischen und theologischen Schriften* (Köln 1974); idem, "Leidens-Bewältigungen. Der Lessing-Goeze-Disput im Horizont der Hermeneutik von 'Geist' und 'Buchstabe'", *Verspätete Orthodoxie. Über D. Johann Melchior Goeze (1717–1786)* (ed. H. Reinitzer / W. Sparn; Wiesbaden 1989) 179–96; M. BOLLACHER, *Lessing: Vernunft und Geschichte. Untersuchungen zum Problem religiöser Aufklärung in den Spätschriften* (Tübingen 1978); C. BULTMANN, "Bewunderung oder Entzauberung? Johann Gottfried Herders Blick auf Mose", *Johann Gottfried Herder. Aspekte seines Lebenswerkes* (ed. M. Keßler / V. Leppin; Berlin 2005) 15–28; J. DESCH, "Lessings 'poetische' Antwort auf die Reimarusfragmente", *Hermann Samuel Reimarus (1694–1768) ein "bekannter Unbekannter" der Aufklärung in Hamburg* ([no ed.]; Joachim Jungius-Gesellschaft der Wissenschaften; Göttingen 1973) 75–95; V. C. DÖRR, "Offenbarung, Vernunft, und 'fähigere Individuen'. Die positiven Religionen in Lessings *Erziehung des Menschengeschlechts*", *Lessing Yearbook* 26 (1994) 29–54; K. EIBL, "Lauter Bilder und Gleichnisse. Lessings religionsphilosophische Begründung der Poesie", *DVfLG* 59 (1985) 224–52; M. FICK, *Lessing-Handbuch. Leben – Werk – Wirkung* (Stuttgart 2000; 2nd rev. edn. 2004); G. FREUND, *Theologie im Widerspruch: Die Lessing-Goeze-Kontroverse* (Stuttgart 1989); K. S. GUTHKE, "Die Geburt des *Nathan* aus dem Geist der Reimarus-Fragmente", Lessing Yearbook / Jahrbuch 36 (2004/2005) 13–49; C. HEBLER, *Lessing-Studien* (Bern 1862); S. HERRMANN, "G. E. Lessings 'Erziehung des Menschengeschlechts' – eine kleine 'Biblische Theologie'?", *Theologie und Aufklärung* (ed. W. E. Müller / H. H. R. Schulz; Würzburg 1992) 76–88; B. LOHSE, "Johann Melchior Goeze als Theologe des 18. Jahrhunderts", *Johann Melchior Goeze 1717–1786* (ed. H. Reinitzer; Hamburg 1987) 40–56; J. VON LÜPKE, *Wege der Weisheit. Studien zu Lessings Theologiekritik* (Göttingen 1989); D. MÜLLER NIELABA, *Die Wendung zum Bessern. Zur Aufklärung der Toleranz in Gotthold Ephraim Lessings* Nathan der Weise (Würzburg 2000); *Neues zur Lessing-Forschung* (ed. E. J. Engel / C. Ritterhoff; Tübingen 1998); H. B. NISBET, "The Rationalisation of the Holy Trinity from Lessing to Hegel", *Lessing Yearbook* 31 (1999) 65–89; idem, "Lessing, *Nathan der Weise*: A Landmark in the History of Tolerance", *Landmarks in German Drama* (ed. P. Hutchinson; Frankfurt 2002) 11–29; G. PONS, *Gotthold Ephraïm Lessing et le Christianisme* (Paris 1964); idem, "Lessings Auseinandersetzung mit der Apologetik", *ZThK* 77 (1980) 381–411; H. GRAF REVENTLOW, "Zwischen Rationalismus und Spiritualismus: Lessings biblisches Dilemma", *Mille Anni Sicut Dies Hesterna. Studia in Honorem Kalle Kasemaa* (ed. M. Lepajõe / A. Gross; Tartu 2003) 257–71; J. RICHES, "Lessing's Change of Mind", *JTS* 29 (1978) 121–36; idem, "Lessing as Editor of Reimarus' Apologie", *Studia Biblica* (JSNTSup 2; Sheffield 1980) 247–54; A. SCHILSON, *Geschichte im Horizont der Vorsehung. G. E. Lessings Beitrag zu einer Theologie der*

Geschichte (Mainz 1974); idem, "Offenbarung und Geschichte bei J. M. Goeze und G. E. Lessing. Hinweise zu einer offenbarungstheologischen Neuorientierung", *Verspätete Orthodoxie. Über D. Johann Melchior Goeze (1717–1786)* (ed. H. Reinitzer / W. Sparn; Wiesbaden 1989) 87–119; idem, [editor's introductions to] *G. E. Lessing, Werke und Briefe* 8–10 (Frankfurt 1989/1993/2001; incl. bibl.); E. Schmidt, *Lessing. Geschichte seines Lebens und seiner Schriften* 1–2 (Berlin 1884–92, ⁴1923; repr. Hildesheim 1983); J. Schneider, *Lessings Stellung zur Theologie vor der Herausgabe der Wolfenbüttler Fragmente* ('s-Gravenhage 1953); R. Smend, "Lessing und die Bibelwissenschaft", VTSup 29 (1978) 298–319 (also in: idem, *Epochen der Bibelkritik* [München 1991] 74–92); idem, "Lessings Nachlaßfragmente zum Alten Testament", NAWG.PH 1979, 93–103 (repr. in: *Epochen der Bibelkritik* [1991] 93–103); W. Sparn, "Vernünftiges Christentum. Über die geschichtliche Aufgabe der theologischen Aufklärung im 18. Jahrhundert in Deutschland", *Wissenschaften im Zeitalter der Aufklärung* (ed. R. Vierhaus; Göttingen 1985) 18–57; *Streitkultur. Strategien des Überzeugens im Werk Lessings* (ed. W. Mauser / G. Sasse; Tübingen 1993); I. Strohschneider-Kohrs, *Vernunft als Weisheit. Studien zum späten Lessing* (Tübingen 1991); eadem, "Lessings Hiob-Deutungen im Kontext des 18. Jahrhunderts", *Edith-Stein-Jahrbuch* (2002) 255–68; G. Vallée, *Soundings in G. E. Lessing's Philosophy of Religion* (Lanham 2000); F. Vollhardt, *Selbstliebe und Geselligkeit* (Tübingen 2001); idem, "Kritik der Apologetik. Ein vergessener Zugang zum Werk G. E. Lessings", *Prägnanter Moment* (ed. P.-A. Alt / A. Košenina / H. Reinhardt / W. Riedel; Würzburg 2002) 29–47; idem, "Lessings Lektüre", *Euphorion* 100 (2006) 359–93; B. A. Wagner, "Voltaires kleinere historische Schriften, übersetzt von Lessing", *Lessing-Forschungen nebst Nachträgen* (Berlin 1881) 3–58; P. Wellnitz (ed.), *G. E. Lessings Nathan der Weise [und] Die Erziehung des Menschengeschlechts* (Strasbourg 2000); T. Yasukata, *Lessing's Philosophy of Religion and the German Enlightenment* (Oxford / New York 2002).

Gotthold Ephraim Lessing (1729–81) was an independent critic and poet who, after changing activities and employment became the librarian to the Duke of Braunschweig-Wolfenbüttel in 1770.[52]

Lessing was the son of a Lutheran minister in Kamenz, Saxony, received a good education in classics at the University of Leipzig and graduated from the University of Wittenberg in 1752. Lessing became one of the leading figures of the Enlightenment in mid-eighteenth-century Germany. He contributed as a reviewer to numerous literary journals, notably the *Berlinische Privilegierte Zeitung* in the early 1750s and the wide-ranging *Briefe, die neueste Litteratur betreffend* in 1759–65. He translated a volume of Voltaire's minor historical writings in 1751, wrote a number of successful plays, and published an edition of his collected writings as early in his career as 1753–55. He engaged in a critical attack on a new German translation of the odes of Horace and defended his favourite Roman poet against insensitive literary criticism.[53] An attentive observer of contemporary debates in aesthetics, philosophy, and theology, Lessing already occupied himself with theological issues in the 1750s and 1760s.[54] During three years at the theatre in Hamburg from 1767–1770, Lessing met the disputatious minister and head of the Lutheran clergy in Hamburg J. M. Goeze (1717–86) as well as the son and daughter of the erudite classical and biblical scholar H. S. Reimarus (1694–1768). The great spectacle of a public controversy about biblical hermeneutics between Lessing and Goeze in 1777/78 had a prehistory of personal acquaintance and mutual respect of its protagonists. Only after an act of ducal censorship had put an end to this controversy, did Lessing compose the play *Nathan der Weise* (1779) as a dramatic statement of his theological opinions and a forceful exhortation to tolerance between Islam, Judaism, and Christianity.[55]

---

[52] For biographical questions, Schmidt, Lessing (repr. 1983), may usefully be consulted, see esp. 193–216 on early encounters with Voltaire. A new biography of Lessing by H. B. Nisbet is due to appear in the near future.

[53] *Werke* 2, 705–09; 3, 105–46 on the translation by S. G. Lange; 3, 158–97: 'Rettungen des Horaz' (of 1754).

[54] See, e.g., his discussion of a comparison between religions in his vindication and critique of Geronimo Cardano (1501–76) of 1754 in *Werke* 3, 198–223; and early manuscripts in *Werke* 2, 403–07; 5/1, 399–445.

[55] The many sources for this play include not least Voltaire's *Zaïre* of 1732 and the portrait of

In some early manuscripts on philosophical and theological issues, Lessing already demonstrates his awareness of the contemporary debates about natural religion and the problem of the particular character of the biblical tradition.[56] However, he shows less interest in the Old Testament than in the New Testament and the historical development of the Christian religion. In general, Lessing is concerned with what he regards as a misappropriation in his time of the basic principle of Lutheran theology according to which the Bible must be regarded as the unique and only source of a faith which leads to salvation (*sola scriptura*). He opposes apologetic attempts at equating biblical revelation with historical inerrancy and at demonstrating a perfect consistency of the biblical tradition with itself, with the course of history, and with a universalist ethics. In this situation, Reimarus's challenge to the biblical tradition, notably the narrative traditions of the Old and New Testament, is welcome material for a critique of a peculiar eighteenth-century biblicism or 'bibliolatry'.

The main 'fragments' from Reimarus's manuscript were published in a journal of the Wolfenbüttel library in 1777 (see above, sect. 2). While the second of these 'fragments' offers an analysis of the general probability, or rather improbability, of a divine revelation in Israel or any other particular people in antiquity, the third and fourth 'fragments' focus on the Old Testament: Lessing employs Reimarus's analysis of the Israelites' crossing of the Red Sea in the exodus from Egypt (Exod 12:37–38; 14:20–29) as an example of questioning a biblical miracle, and Reimarus's analysis of the absence in the Old Testament of the idea of immortality as an example of discussing a doctrinal deficiency. In the ensuing debate, Lessing in particular reasserts some of Reimarus's observations on the New Testament Gospels in a treatise *Eine Duplik* of 1778, and publishes a further 'fragment' on Jesus's failed political messianism and the disciples' transmogrification of his teaching into a doctrine of a spiritual salvation (*Von dem Zwecke Jesu und seiner Jünger*, 1778). As far as the Old Testament is concerned, Lessing's pronouncements are largely confined to the *Gegensätze des Herausgebers* (*Counter-propositions of the editor*) in the publication of 1777, which includes the first part of *Die Erziehung des Menschengeschlechts* (*The education of the human race*), and general statements on biblical hermeneutics in *Über den Beweis des Geistes und der Kraft* (*On the proof of the spirit and of power*), in *Eine Duplik* (*A rejoinder*), in *Eine Parabel* (*A parable*), and, most importantly, in the *Axiomata* (*Axioms*), all of these published in 1777 and 1778 and followed by the full publication of the *Erziehung* in 1780.[57]

Saladin in his Minor historical writings which Lessing translated in 1751 (see *Werke* 2, 311–30, 924–54; 9, 1157–59).

[56] "Über die Entstehung der geoffenbarten Religion"; "Von der Art und Weise der Fortpflanzung und Ausbreitung der christlichen Religion" (*Werke* 5/1, 423–25 [tr. in Nisbet (2005) 35–36]; 426–45).

[57] The page numbers in the following paragraphs refer to the edition of these texts in *Werke* 8–10, and, where preceded by 'tr.', to Nisbet's translation in *Philosophical and Theological Writings* (2005): *Gegensätze* together with the first part of the *Erziehung* (8, 312–50; tr. 61–82, 218–31), *Beweis* (8, 437–45; tr. 83–88), the relevant introduction to *Eine Duplik* (8, 506–23; tr. 95–109), *Eine Parabel* (9, 39–52; tr. 110–19), *Axiomata* (9, 53–89; tr. 120–47), *Nathan der Weise* (9, 483–627 [tr. in Demetz (1991) 173–275]), the full text of *Erziehung* (10, 73–99; tr. 217–40). All quotations are from Nisbet's translation. – Further pamphlets against J. M. Goeze are in vol. 9. On two short

In the *Axiomata*, a substantial hermeneutical treatise, Lessing elaborates on the series of theses which, in the introduction to his *Gegensätze*, served as his 'general answer' to Reimarus's biblical criticism. Fundamental to this answer is a distinction between the Bible and religion. While Lessing's understanding of natural religion, of a rational religion, and of the Christian faith cannot be discussed here in any detail,[58] the following main points may be noted (expressed as they are with regard to Christianity and its sacred Scriptures including the New Testament):

> ... the Bible is not religion. ... the Bible obviously contains more than what pertains to religion ... Religion also existed before there was a Bible. Christianity existed before the evangelists and apostles wrote about it. ... The religion is not true because the evangelists and apostles taught it; on the contrary, they taught it because it is true. The written records must be explained by its inner truth, and none of the written records can give it any inner truth if it does not already have it (8, 312f; tr. 63).

Lessing's distinction between 'the religion' and the text, between the 'spirit' of a religion and the process of the formation of a canon of written documents would obviously apply to the Old Testament as much as to the New Testament. More specifically, the contemporary debate centred on the historical traditions in the Bible.[59]

While it is the New Testament Gospels which figure most prominently in the Lessingian controversies, a number of observations can be made, and inferences drawn, with regard to the Old Testament, notably the Pentateuch (which Lessing seems to read from a pre-critical point of view as far as questions of authorship, sources and composition are concerned). The particular significance of the Pentateuch in this context may be due to the following reasons: 1) In the story of the creation in Genesis 1, God is presented as the universal creator god. This idea is resumed in the Decalogue in Exodus 20, where the prohibition of images indicates a further depening of religious understanding.[60] 2) In the Torah, including the Decalogue, the issue of ethics is addressed. However, since Lessing is mainly concerned with the debate about immortality, it is more the hortatory motive clauses in Old Testament law which come into view.[61] 3) The Pentateuch tells the story about the foundational period of Israel's history and thus inspires a diachronic model of studying religious ideas, based on the concept of an 'educational' process. While the first two points are directly related to the main tenets of eighteenth-century philosophy of religion, i.e., a universal deity and a moral law, the third pre-

---

manuscripts on Isaac (8, 617–18) and on Hilkiah (cf. 10, 917), see Smend, Nachlaßfragmente (1979/1991).

[58] Cf., e.g., *Werke und Briefe*, 8, 319, 342; 10, 95; and see Pons (1964), Nisbet (1999), and Schilson in *Werke und Briefe* 8–10. It should be noted, however, that the debate about 'natural religion' goes back to humanistic ideas which came to fruition not least in the writings of Herbert of Cherbury (*De veritate*, 1624; *De religione laici*, 1645; *De religione gentilium*, posthumously 1663); see Byrne (1989).

[59] Cf. the explicit references to "the historical books of the Bible" in: *Werke*, 9, 65 (tr. 218), and to David's "Cherethites and Pelethites" [2 Sam 8:18 etc.] in: ibid. 9, 59 (tr. 124). However, the discussion mainly refers to the Gospels.

[60] See, of course, also Deuteronomy 4–5, and cf. *Erziehung*, § 39.

[61] Cf. *Erziehung*, §§ 16–17, 23, 48.

sents a challenge to the understanding of the relationship between the course of history and a religious faith.

Responding to Reimarus's critique of the exodus tradition, Lessing attacks a certain popular strand within Protestant orthodoxy.[62] He directs his polemics against theologians who are neither sufficiently devout simply to accept a miracle as a miracle, nor sufficiently critical to dismiss the account of a miracle on the grounds of its improbability. Thus the controversy revolves around the use in Christian apologetics of arguments from history (8, 324–28, 519; tr. 72–75, 105f). Lessing draws a distinction between historical truths, and the kind of certainty attainable with regard to historical truth claims, on the one hand, and the truth of a religion on the other hand. This point is further explained in the *Beweis*, where the apologetic strategy of demonstrating claims to religious truth through references to (scriptural) prophecies and miracles is rejected. According to Lessing, metaphysical and moral ideas, and correspondingly ideas about God, belong to one class of truths, persuasions about historical events to another class of truths (8, 443; tr. 87). From the point of view of a philosophy of religion he concludes: "If no historical truth can be demonstrated, then nothing can be demonstrated *by means* of historical truths. That is: *contingent truths of history can never become the proof of necessary truths of reason*" (8, 441; tr. 85). Speaking in the imagery of the *Beweis*, there is a 'great chasm' (the proverbial *garstige breite Graben*, "the broad and ugly ditch") between these two classes of truth (8, 443; tr. 87); speaking in the imagery of the *Duplik*, the supposed historical truth of (scriptural) predictions and miracles can only be regarded as the 'scaffolding' for the construction of the 'building' which is the Christian religion.

> The scaffolding is dismantled as soon as the building is finished. Anyone who thinks he can demonstrate the excellence of the building from the dismantled scaffolding … must have little interest in that building. … I would not … allow this prejudice concerning the scaffolding to deter me in the least from judging the building itself by the recognised rules of good architecture (8, 519; tr. 105).

Lessing feels no need to dispute biblical predictions and miracles which once served their function in a remote past[63] since in an age of Enlightenment the emphasis has changed and religious truth has become an issue for a philosophy of religion. Thus, in the *Beweis*, he concludes that the religious "teachings themselves" must be the ground for any assent and commitment to such teachings (8, 444; tr. 87), and, in the *Parabel*, suggests the notion of an "inner feeling for the essential truths of religion" which he sees located in the human "heart" (9, 47; tr. 115). In the *Axiomata*, Lessing confirms and further explains his view that true acceptance of (the Christian) religious truth would rest on philosophical grounds, i.e., on a recognition of the religious ideas in question as being the ideas most worthy of God, as well as on existential grounds, i.e.,

---

[62] Lessing saw the Wittenberg theologian Abraham Calov (1612–1686) as the main instigator of this doctrinal movement, cf. the *Axiomata* (9, 60–63; tr. 125–27). On Calov see Chap. 28 in this volume.

[63] Cf. *Erziehung*, § 22.

on a sense of satisfaction and comfort gained through them.[64] There ought to be a clear distinction between the 'religion' and the 'history of [this] religion', since all understanding of history can only lead to a kind or degree of certainty which would be irrelevant for a religious conviction (9, 84f; tr. 144).

A second point which Lessing takes up from Reimarus's writings is the doctrine of immortality which he sees linked to the issue of Old Testament ethics. In eighteenth-century philosophy of religion, the notion of immortality was regarded to be a basic notion of natural religion, and through the work of William Warburton it had come to play a prominent role for Christian apologetics of the Bible.[65] While Reimarus claimed that the absence of this notion was a serious deficiency of the Old Testament, notably the Pentateuch, and concluded that this would prove the futility of any claims to divine revelation raised with regard to this literary tradition, Lessing offers a different explanation. For him, the absence of this notion from the texts is due to the specific historical situation of the period of their origin. Lessing argues that any revelatory utterances would generally have been accommodated to their audience and context at the time when they were first made.[66] He also objects to Reimarus that precisely because the latter employed an aspect of natural religion as the criterion for his judgment, claims to revelation could neither be proved nor disproved by it.[67] Lessing therefore proceeds to a discussion of the biblical tradition in the light of an even more fundamental theme (which admittedly is also a theme of natural religion), namely that of the unity of God or monotheism.[68] This results in a picture of ancient Israel and its sacred writings which is mainly informed by the – predominantly deuteronomistic – idea of recurring phases of apostasy in Israel (cf. Judg 2:11f etc.) and rests on a positive view of Israel's cultural development in the Persian period (cf. Ezra 1; 7).[69]

The development of monotheism in Israel is of pivotal significance for Lessing's discussion of the biblical tradition. Notwithstanding his high estimation of the assumedly rational Persian religion, he accepts as a historical fact that within the context of Graeco-Roman antiquity Judaism (or rather the Judaeo-Christian tradition) was the religious force which eventually overcame polytheism.[70] How then was the transition achieved from the worship of a national deity, however powerful this may have looked, to the worship of 'God'? Lessing refers to Israel's encounter with the Persian religion at the time of the exile. The alleged historical development is then explained in terms of reason

[64] For the former of these two aspects see *Werke* 9, 83; tr. 143; cf. 9, 69; tr. 131; for the latter *Werke* 9, 83.87; tr. 143, 145; cf. in *Nathan* III/1: ibid. 9, 543; Demetz (1991) 222.

[65] *The Divine Legation of Moses demonstrated on the Principles of a Religious Deist* (1738/41, and many later, revised editions), cf. *Erziehung*, §§ 24–25. Cf. the fourth 'fragment' from Reimarus, esp. 8, 247–48; and for Reimarus's philosophical discussion of the issue of immortality his *Die vornehmsten Wahrheiten der natürlichen Religion*, esp. chs. 8–10.

[66] *Erziehung*, §§ 17, 23. A kind of secular proof-text for the hermeneutically important idea of accommodation is a quotation by Solon in Plutarch's *Solon* 15.2 (*Axiomata*: 9, 84; tr. 143).

[67] *Gegensätze*: 8, 330f; tr. 77f.

[68] *Gegensätze*: ibid.; *Erziehung*, §§ 1–15, 18–21, 34–40.

[69] In points of detail, Lessing's historical ideas about Israel's encounter with the Persians (and Chaldeans) are not entirely clear, cf. *Erziehung*, §§ 35, 39, 42.

[70] Cf. *Erziehung*, §§ 7–8, 18, 40, and – for a subsequent 'educational' step – §§ 54–56; *Gegensätze*: 8, 348; tr. 80.

and revelation: In his revelation, God allows Israel to pass through several stages of a limited understanding of God, however, this people of revelation then encounters the Persians as a people of reason who have already arrived at a more advanced stage of religious insight, and 'reason' now comes to illuminate 'revelation'.[71] As a result of this historical development – or educational process – Israel in Lessing's view became the people of monotheism *par excellence.*[72]

Lessing seems to remain ambivalent about the role of Moses and the Mosaic writings according to this scheme: On the one hand, Moses did not convey to the people the true notion of God;[73] on the other hand, this notion could be discovered in the writings of Moses as well as other Old Testament writers once the idea of a monotheistic faith had been adopted from the Persians.[74] Thus the Old Testament appears to be a truly significant religious tradition which, following the hermeneutical principles discussed in the *Axiomata* (9, 69, 79; tr. 132, 139f), should be studied for its "inner truth".

The theological and philosophical question of a universal creator god is combined in the *Erziehung* with the problem of ethics and notably that of the motivation of moral behaviour. At the centre of this debate is the question of immortality. This is the context for Lessing's remarks on the Old Testament as a "primer" or "elementary textbook",[75] on rabbinical hermeneutics as exceeding the limitations of the biblical text (§§ 51–52), and on the New Testament as a second, better "primer" (§§ 64–69, 86). The background for this discussion is a general critique of religious doctrines of reward and punishment – be it in this life, be it in a future life – and the ideal of a greater "purity of heart" as the true motivational force behind moral behaviour. While to some extent this ideal might even be traced back to biblical roots (cf., e.g., Ps 24:4; 51,12; Matt 5:8), Lessing presents it in a visionary tone as an ideal of Enlightenment moral philosophy.[76] Since his focus is on the question of immortality, he does, however, not engage more fully in a discussion of Old Testament ethics. It would also be tempting to speculate about the exegesis Lessing might have offered, for instance, of Mic 6:8.

Most of the issues which concern Lessing with regard to the Old Testament also reverberate in his 'dramatic poem' *Nathan the Wise* of 1779. As Nathan,

---

[71] *Erziehung*, §§ 11–15, 34–39. The tension between § 4 and § 20 (and 34–39) cannot be discussed here. Lessing does not fully succeed in compensating for his rejection of the idea of (a lasting significance of) a *prisca theologia* in §§ 6–7. A further issue would be his allusion in § 39 to contemporary ideas about 'Sabeism' which had come to play a prominent role not least through G. J. Vossius's (1577–1649) work in comparative religion (*De theologia gentili, et physiologia christiana; sive de origine ac progressu idololatriae*, 1642/1668).

[72] Cf. *Erziehung*, §§ 18, 21.

[73] *Gegensätze*: 8, 330; tr. 77; *Erziehung*, §§ 11–12.

[74] *Gegensätze*: ibid.; *Erziehung*, § 39.

[75] *Erziehung*, §§ 26–27, 47, 50, 53.

[76] *Erziehung*, §§ 80, 85. On Enlightenment moral discourses based on the concept of natural law, see Vollhardt, Selbstliebe (2001), esp. 254–60 on Lessing. Cf. also David Hume's analysis of the 'practical consequences of natural religion' in his *Enquiry concerning Human Understanding* (1748), sect. XI, as well as his *Enquiry concerning the Principles of Morals* (1751).

the Jew, explains to Saladin, the Muslim, historical truth can only be accepted in good faith, i.e., through an act of confidence.[77] Such truth, therefore, may serve a function for continuing an established line of tradition and for shaping the identity of a particular religious community, however, it cannot be demonstrated. Any attempt at demonstrating the truth of a particular positive religion is bound to fail – thus the judge in Nathan's *Ringparabel* pronounces on objectifiable grounds his 'verdict': "Your rings are false, all three. The genuine ring / No doubt got lost. …".[78] However, in Nathan's version of the story about a father and his three sons who lived "in the East" in primordial times,[79] the judge also functions as Lessing's mouthpiece for his 'advice' to follow the principles of natural religion, i.e., moral behaviour and devout worship:

> … Let each aspire / To emulate his father's unbeguiled, / Unprejudiced affection! Let each strive / To match the rest in bringing to the fore / The magic of the opal in his ring! / Assist that power with all humility, / With benefaction, hearty peacefulness, / And with profound submission to God's will![80]

The sense of belonging to a particular religious community which is characterized by its historical tradition must not turn into "prejudice", since such partiality would subvert the religious ideal of morality or "uncorrupted love".

Within the context of his dramatic poem,[81] Lessing thus confirms his understanding of the religious idea of election (the election of Israel) which in a dialogue between Nathan, the Jew, and the Templar, the Christian, he had put in the perspective of a shared ground of humanity.[82] In the same vein the figure of Moses is set into new light: The historical circumstances under which Moses received the divine law on Mount Sinai are denied any importance so that it can be said of Moses as of any other human being: "He stood [be]fore God wherever he stood".[83] Finally, the idea of a 'promised' land is turned into that of a promising land which is praised because the experience of this land leads to a renunciation of previously held religious prejudices.[84]

The purpose of Lessing's theological polemics is to recover an essentially philosophical religion from an apologetic and exegetical tradition which is primarily focussed on a close literal interpretation of historical accounts in the Bible, including predictions and miracles. In his view, medieval Aristotelianism was less detrimental to Christian theology than is the scripturalism or bibliolatry of late Calovian Protestantism.[85] Even the most elaborate investigations of historical truths offer no point of transition to religious truth or, in Lessing's imagery, no bridge across "the broad and ugly ditch". While in retrospect one

---

[77] III/7: 9, 557; Demetz 233.
[78] III/7: 9, 559; Demetz 234.
[79] 9, 555; Demetz 231; the allusion is to Gen 11:2.
[80] III/7: 9, 559; Demetz 235.
[81] It has persuasively been argued that the figure of Job served, to a certain extent, as Lessing's model for Nathan, notably in IV/7; see Strohschneider-Kohrs (1991) 62–101 and (2002).
[82] II/5: 9, 532f; Demetz 213f.
[83] III/2: 9, 546; Demetz 224.
[84] III/8: 9, 563; Demetz 237.
[85] *Duplik*: 8, 519; tr. 105; *Parabel*: 9, 50; tr. 118.

would acknowledge Lessing's challenge to clarify the status of historical arguments in biblical exegesis, his engagement with the Old Testament prophetic and wisdom literature is limited. Lessing did not explore, from his philosophical point of view, whether Old Testament writers had already grasped more of the 'spirit' of religion than just the doctrine of monotheism.

Chapter Thirty-seven

Scriptural Understanding and Interpretation in Pietism

By Johannes Wallmann, Berlin

Sources: J. A. Bengel: *Gnomon Novi Testamenti in quo ex nativa verborum vi simplicitas, profunditas, concinnitas, salubritas sensuum coelestium indicatur* (Tübingen 1742). – Ph. J. Spener: *Pia Desideria* (Frankfurt am Main 1675; Kleine Texte, ed. K. Aland, 170; Berlin 1940); *Das nötige und nützliche Lesen der Heiligen Schrift* (Frankfurt a. M. / Leipzig 1695). – A. H. Francke: *Einfältiger Unterricht, wie man die H. Schrifft zu seiner wahren Erbauung lesen solle* (Halle 1694); *Observationes biblicae* (Halle 1695); *Kurtzer Auszug aus der Einleitung zur Lesung der H. Schrifft* (Halle 1698); *Christus der Kern Heiliger Schrifft oder Einfältige Anweisung, wie man Christus als den Kern der gantzen heil. Schrifft recht suchen, finden, schmäcken und damit seine Seele nähren, sättigen und zum ewigen Leben erhalten solle* (Halle 1702); *Praelectiones hermeneuticae* (Halle 1717). – J. J. Rambach: *Institutiones Hermeneuticae Sacrae* (Jena 1723). – N. L. Graf Zinzendorf: *Hauptschriften* (Hildesheim 1962-; repr.).

Studies: K. Aland (ed.), *Pietismus und Bibel* (AGP 9; Witten 1970); idem, "Bibel und Bibeltext bei August Hermann Francke und Johann Albrecht Bengel", in: Pietismus und Bibel (1970) 59–88; M. Brecht (ed.), *Geschichte des Pietismus 1. Der Pietismus vom siebzehnten bis zum frühen achtzehnten Jahrhundert* (Göttingen 1993); idem / K. Deppermann, *Geschichte des Pietismus 2. Der Pietismus im achtzehnten Jahrhundert* (Göttingen 1995); idem, "Johann Albrecht Bengel und die Bibelauslegung", in: idem, *Ausgewählte Aufsätze 2. Pietismus* (Stuttgart 1997) 251–408; A. Deppermann, *Johann Jakob Schütz und die Anfänge des Pietismus* (Tübingen 2002); L. Diestel, *Geschichte des Alten Testamentes in der christlichen Kirche* (Jena 1869; ND Leipzig 1981) 409–19; K. Dose, *Die Bedeutung der Schrift für Zinzendorfs Denken und Handeln* (Diss. theol. Bonn 1971); E. Hirsch, *Geschichte der neuern evangelischen Theologie im Zusammenhang mit den allgemeinen Bewegungen des europäischen Denkens* 2 (Göttingen 1951); M. Hofmann, *Theologie und Exegese der Berleburger Bibel (1726–42)* (BFChTh 39; Gütersloh 1937); B. Köster, *Die Lutherbibel im frühen Pietismus* (TAzB 1; Bielefeld 1984); H.-J. Kraus, *Geschichte der historisch-kritischen Erforschung des Alten Testaments* (Neukirchen-Vluyn ²1969); E. Ludwig, *Schriftverständnis und Schriftauslegung bei Johann Albrecht Bengel* (*BWKG*, Sonderheft 9; Stuttgart 1952); G. Mälzer, *Johann Albrecht Bengel. Leben und Werk* (Stuttgart 1970); E. Peschke, "Die Heilige Schrift", in: idem, *Studien zur Theologie August Hermann Franckes* II (Berlin 1966) 13–126; idem, "August Hermann Francke und die Bibel", in: Aland, Pietismus und Bibel (1970) 59–88; E. Peterson, "Das Problem der Bibelauslegung im Pietismus des 18. Jahrhunderts", *ZSTh* 1 (1923) 468–81; O. Podczeck, "Die Arbeit am Alten Testament in Halle zu Zeit des Pietismus", *WZH.GS* VII.5 (Halle 1958) 1059–78; K. H. Rengstorf, "Johann Heinrich Michaelis und seine *Biblia Hebraica* von 1720", in: N. Hinske (ed.), *Zentren der Aufklärung* I. Halle (Wolfenbütteler Studien zur Aufklärung 15; Heidelberg 1989) 15–64; H. Graf Reventlow, "Die Bibel in Pietismus und deutscher Aufklärung", in: idem, *Epochen der Bibelauslegung* IV (München 2001) 126–226; M. Schmidt, "Philipp Jakob Spener und die Bibel", in: Pietismus und Bibel (1970) 9–58; H. Schneider, "Der radikale Pietismus im 17. Jahrhundert", in: Brecht, Geschichte des Pietismus 1 (1993) 391–437; idem, "Der radikale Pietismus im 18. Jahrhundert", in: Brecht / Deppermann, Geschichte des Pietismus 2 (1995) 107–97; H.-J. Schrader, *Literaturproduktion und Büchermarkt des radikalen Pietismus* (Göttingen 1989); H. Stroh, "Hermeneutik im Pietismus", *ZThK* 74 (1977) 38–57; J. Wallmann, *Philipp Jakob Spener und die Anfänge des Pietismus* (Tübingen ²1986); idem, *Der Pietismus* (KIG O 1; Göttingen 1989 = UTB 2598, Göttingen 2005); idem, "Was ist Pietismus?" (Pietismus und Neuzeit 20; Göttingen 1994) 11–27; idem, "Vom Katechismuschristentum zum Bibelchristentum. Zum Bibelverständnis im Pietismus", in: R. Ziegert (ed.), *Die Zukunft des Schriftprinzips* (Stuttgart 1994) 30–56; P. Zimmerling, "Zinzendorfs Schriftverständnis im Spannungsfeld der Geistesströmungen seiner Zeit", *Unitas Fratrum* 25 (1989) 69–103; H.-J. Zobel, "Die Hebraisten an der Universität zu Wittenberg (1502–1817)", *WZH.GS* VII.6 (Halle 1958) 1173–86.

1. Roots of Pietism

Pietism of the late seventeenth and eighteenth centuries was the largest religious renewal movement in Continental Protestantism since the Reformation. Both in the lands of Reformed theology as well as of the Lutheran confession, this movement superseded the immediate post-Reformation era of the old Protestant Orthodoxy. Five constitutive elements set Pietism apart from Orthodoxy and gave it its specific character: (i) the priority of a godly life over pure doctrine with the stress moving from justification to sanctification (the Piety movement); (ii) the central importance of Bible reading (the Scripture movement); (iii) the encouragement and gathering of the Godly for closer community (the Fellowship movement); (iv) the practice of the universal priesthood (the Laity movement); and (v) the hope for better times before the Last Day (the Kingdom of God movement).

As opposed to Orthodoxy, Pietism was, at first, in step with the Enlightenment, although later they visibly went in different directions (e. g., the expulsion of Christian Wolff from the Pietist city of Halle). Pietism set itself apart from the Enlightenment by its stress on human sinfulness and by its interpretation of the Bible. Firmly holding on to Orthodoxy's doctrine of the verbal inspiration of Scripture, the movement thoroughly rejected the historical-critical method in biblical exegesis.

The roots of Pietism are many and varied. Partly, it was nothing more than a development of the basic principles inherited from Luther and the Reformation (the central place of the Bible, the universal priesthood). Partly, its impetus sprang from mystical Spiritualism and the practice of an internalized piety demanded by John Arndt (*Vier Bücher von wahrem Christenthumb / Four Books on True Christianity*, 1605–10). The renewal literature of English Puritanism (Lewis Bayly, Daniel Dyke) promoted self-assessment and world-renouncing ascetic practices. In addition, Pietism would take over English Puritanism's chiliastic eschatology, with its expectation of the imminent coming of the Kingdom of God.

Pietism began in 1670 at Frankfurt am Main when Philipp Jakob Spener formed his first *Collegium pietatis*. Five years later he published the book which laid out the new movement's objectives, *Pia Desideria*. After the unrest over the new movement at Leipzig in 1689–90, Pietism spread like wildfire to many Protestant areas. Founded in 1694, the University of Halle on the Saale was for many decades the center of Pietism. Through its ambassadors Halle Pietism expanded well beyond German-speaking lands – to Scandinavia, to the Baltic and Eastern Europe, including Russia, and even to overseas missionary enterprises in India and North America. The golden age of Pietism lasted for a good fifty years. In Germany, it held sway up to 1740, when the reign of

Frederick II of Prussia began. From then on, the Enlightenment took over the leading role in German cultural life, deeply impacting even the Church and its theology.

The most important theologian for German reformed Pietism was Friedrich Adolf Lampe (1683–1729), pastor and professor at the academic Gymnasium in Bremen and adjunct professor at Utrecht. Lampe's theology was biblical theology. His chief work, *The Secret of the Covenant of Grace, to the glory of the great Covenant God* (*Geheimnis des Gnaden-Bunds*; 1712–19, six volumes), was not a biblical commentary with a continuous explication of the text, but rather a systematic handbook of scriptural doctrine. For the Reformers the Bible was, above all else, the Word of God to us, which we must hear. For the Pietist exegete of Scripture, the Bible was at the same time the revelation of God's plan for Salvation History. Although often mysteriously encoded, his plan for the future could be deciphered through biblical research, especially in the books of the prophets and the prophecies of the Book of Revelation. Making good use of the Federal theology of Johannes Cocceius, Lampe developed a comprehensive picture of Salvation History. God was a covenant God, seeking fellowship with humanity through a covenant. With this notion of covenant as an organizing principle, all of history, from Creation to Judgment Day, could be grasped as a continuously unfolding plan with several distinct phases: the time of the covenant of works in the Garden of Eden, after the Fall and the establishment of the Covenant of Grace whose provisions were then manifested through a series of dispensations, beginning first with the period from the promise given to Adam through Moses, then from the Mosaic Law to Christ, and finally from Christ to the end of the World. Since Lampe fixed the previous periods of Church History as well as the future of the Church (i.e., the millennium) according to the promises and prophecies of the Bible, he was able to decipher "The Secret of the Divine Covenant of Grace". With the wide dissemination of his work, through numerous editions and its translation into Dutch, Lampe contributed greatly to the movement's emerging theology. As a result, the theology of God's Word characteristic of the Reformation was in Pietism reinvigorated through a theology of Salvation History, even as it was in some ways replaced by it. Although derived from reformed Federal theology, this Salvation History perspective not only left its mark on Reformed Pietism's biblical interpretation but also crossed over and deeply affected Lutheran Pietism as well (Johann Albrecht Bengel).

Since Pietism had its main strength and most important representatives in the lands of the Lutheran Confession, what follows will focus on them.

2. The Pietism of Philipp Jakob Spener and August Hermann Francke: Their Promotion of Biblical Studies

2.1. Philipp Jakob Spener

The founder of Lutheran Pietism, Philipp Jakob Spener (1635–1705) served as pastor and *Senior* of the Lutheran *Predigerministerium* in Frankfurt am Main from 1666 to 1686. In 1686 he became the chief court preacher in Dresden, and from 1691 to his death in 1705 Spener was the provost of Berlin's St. Nicholas Church and counsellor to the consistory. During his studies in Strasbourg, Johann Conrad Dannhauer (1603–66) trained him in the theological system of Lutheran Orthodoxy, from whose teachings, except in matters of eschatology, he never wanted to depart for the remainder of his life. He also received a foundational education in biblical exegesis from the important biblical theologian Sebastian Schmidt (1617–96). In addition, he took instruction in the Talmud and rabbinical writings, first privately with an Alsatian Jew, then through a course in Basel with Johann Buxtorf the Younger (1599–1664). Buxtorf had defended Lutheran Orthodoxy's doctrine of biblical inspiration, as well as the authenticity of the Hebrew vowels, from the critique of Louis Cappel and the first stirrings of the historical-critical method. Spener formed a close relationship with Buxtorf and remained his lifelong disciple. Thus, his rejection of Orthodoxy's formalism and its use of Aristotelian philosophy did not lead him to reject Orthodoxy's doctrine of verbal inspiration.

Pietism and Verbal Inspiration. Lutheran Orthodoxy since Johann Gerhard went beyond the Reformers, when they developed their doctrine of the Holy Scriptures as a principle, that is, that the Bible had all the characteristics which belonged to the Aristotelian understanding of an academic principle. For according to Aristotle, a principle came first and was undivided. It was true, beyond every criticism, self-attesting, unassailable and needing no evidence for support. Spener's critique of the Aristotelianism of Orthodoxy's theology, a throwback to Luther and the Bible, did not lead to a diminution of the orthodox view that Scripture was verbally inspired, a development which would have opened a new way for a freer scriptural interpretation, as was characteristic of Luther. Spener adhered to the orthodox teaching of the Holy Scriptures as the verbally inspired, inerrant principle for theology, and after discarding its Aristotelian intellectual presuppositions, Spener continued to maintain the doctrine in a more rigorous and more fundamentalist manner. He considered the suggestion that there could be errors in the Bible to be a dangerous notion to be thoroughly rejected. Throughout his life Spener was committed to the traditional orthodox doctrine which he had received from his teacher Johann Conrad Dannhauer, namely, that not only the concepts, but also the Words of Holy Scripture had been given by the Holy Spirit:

> θεοπνευστίαν sacrorum auctorum absit, ut ego ullo modo infirmem; potius verbi Praeceptoris mei agnosco sacras literas a coelesti procedere Spiritu inspirante ... ne vel in puncto erraret Scriptor ... Ita non res solum, sed ipsa verba quoque divinae revelationi vel inspirationi tribuo.[1]

Allowing a larger roll for the individuality of the biblical authors, Spener simply taught that the Holy Spirit adapted itself to the confines of their capacities. In so doing, he developed the orthodox doctrine of inspiration further in the

---

[1] Ph. J. Spener, *Consilia et Iudicia theologica latina* 1 (Frankfurt a. M. 1711) 46.

direction of the theory of accommodation. As a result of Spener's adherence to
the orthodox doctrine of verbal inspiration, his authority made the use of the
historical-critical method and every form of biblical criticism impossible for
Pietism. Nikolaus Ludwig Graf von Zinzendorf represented an outsider's position in Pietism, when he asserted: "Scripture has so many mistakes, as scarcely
any other book" (*Litany of the Wounds*). Indeed, he saw in the human errors
of the biblical authors (e.g., Josh 10:12f) a profound sign of the Bible's divinity.[2]

During Spener's tenure in Frankfurt am Main, the Lutheran Pietist Movement began. Preaching a sharp message of repentance, Spener rebuked the citizens of the wealth trading center for a mere external, dead, routine Christianity which lacked a living faith. Instead, he called for them to develop an inner,
true and active Christian life. Although unrest arose amongst the citizens as a
result, a small, gradually growing group of serious Christians gathered around
Spener. For their edification in 1670 he established an exercise of piety, the
Collegium pietatis. In the beginning, they read and discussed religious literature. However, after some years, they put aside the works of human authors
and concentrated solely on Scripture. The laity were also permitted to take
part in interpreting the Bible for edification. The Frankfurt *Collegium pietatis*
became the model for edifying gatherings as a supplement to public worship
services. These conventicles quickly arose in many places and were the chief
characteristic of the Pietist movement. When opponents attempted to suppress
Pietism, they did so through a government ban on these meetings.

In 1675 Spener published his *Pia Desidera*, a program for reform in the
Lutheran Church. According to this program only doctrine was pure and intact there. The life of the members was corrupt. All estates of German society
(the authorities, the preachers, the congregations) lacked true Christianity and
living faith. The first and defining proposal of the reform program called for
"bringing about a richer experience of God's Word among us", thus making
Pietism a Bible movement. The other proposals flowed from this fundamental
aim: (i) the realization of the universal priesthood of all believers; (ii) a shift of
emphasis from the theory of Christianity to its praxis; (iii) the limiting of confessional polemics; (iv) the reform of theological studies; (v) and the directing
of preaching towards the inner person.

Spener justified his chief proposal – to bring about a richer experience of
God's Word among us – on the grounds that the Lutheran Church's lectionary
system meant that only parts of the Bible were made known during worship
services. Yet, the laity needed to be familiar with all of the Bible. Hence, they
had to come to know Scripture through both private and public Bible reading
as well as through the establishment of edifying bible studies in addition to
public worship. These study groups needed to be directed by the pastor but
with the right of the laity to make contributions (*Collegia pietatis*).

Tota Scriptura. Luther and Lutheran Orthodoxy had called the Catechism
the laypeople's Bible, for daily Bible reading by simple Christians was not re-

---

[2] N. L. von Zinzendorf, *Declaration über die Frage: Ob in der heiligen Schrift einige Fehler vor-
kommen können* (Unitätsarchiv Herrnhut R. 18. A. 9. 98).

quired. Recognizing the increasing literacy rate, Spener demanded a biblical Christianity, not the Church's customary catechetical Christianity. The Catechism was downgraded to a preparation and guide for independent Bible reading. Scripture was "a letter from our Heavenly Father to all his children",[3] a gift not exclusively for theologians and some Christians but something to be read by every believer. Of course, Spener adhered to the Reformation principle of *sola Scriptura*, which he saw as defining the common ground he had with Reformed theologians against the Catholic Church's commitment to tradition. Yet he augmented and completed *sola Scriptura* through the Pietist commitment to *tota Scriptura*, all the Holy Scriptures. In Spener's wake, the most popular genre of Pietist literature focused on providing instruction in how to read the Bible properly.[4] Pietism also promoted the printing and the wide distribution of the Scriptures. Previously, the cost of their production had been expensive, but due to the efforts of Canstein's Bible Institute, founded in Halle in 1710, Bibles became so cheap that every Christian household had a copy.

Spener's motto, *tota Scriptura*, led to a much wider knowledge of the Old Testament, although at the same time its status remained clearly behind that of the New Testament. Herein lies a difference between Lutheran Pietism and that of the Reformed and the Anglo-Saxon Churches, which valued the Old Testament so highly as to draw the names for their children from it. Like Luther himself, Lutheran Orthodoxy put the main emphasis of biblical interpretation on the Old Testament. Sebastian Schmidt, Spener's teacher in Strasbourg, made a commentary on almost all of the Old Testament. Johann Arndt devoted his extremely thick book of sermons to the Psalter. Spener seldom preached on individual verses from Psalms, mostly for special occasions (funeral sermons). In the long row of volumes that Spener's collected sermons require, homilies on Old Testament texts are lacking. Among a wide number of Pietists, the Song of Solomon was highly esteemed as the love language of Jesus the bridegroom to the believing Soul. Yet Spener remained sceptical. He considered the Song of Songs to be the most difficult biblical book of all and admitted his inability to expound it.[5] He himself wanted the traditional interpretation of the Bridegroom and the Bride as Christ and the Church.

For Spener, *tota Scriptura* steered attention away from the Gospels to the Epistles and to the life of the first Christians, not to the Old Testament. Consequently, in his numerous sermon volumes Spener presented a virtually complete exposition of the New Testament letters, in particular the epistles of Paul and John, and herein lies his importance for the history of biblical interpretation. He gave only a small number of sermons on the penitential prayer of the Prophet Daniel (Ch. 9). As Spener admitted in later years: "I have done nothing or only a little with the Old Testament, which I do not understand".[6]

---

[3] Ph. J. Spener, *Das Geistliche Priestertum* (Frankfurt a. M. 1677), Frage 29.

[4] Ph. J. Spener, *Das nötige und nützliche Lesen der Heiligen Schrift* (Frankfurt a. M. / Leipzig 1695); A. H. Francke, *Einleitung zur Lesung der H. Schrifft* (Halle 1694); idem, *Einfältiger Unterricht, wie man die H. Schrifft zu seiner Erbauung lesen solle* (Halle 1694).

[5] Spener, *Predigten über Johann Arndts Wahres Christentum* II (Frankfurt a. M. 1711) 158.

[6] *Der Briefwechsel Carl Hildebrand von Cansteins mit August Hermann Francke* (Berlin / New York 1972) 696.

When Spener demanded more Bible reading in *Pia Desideria*, he added: "but particularly the New Testament".[7] A. H. Francke initially followed Spener's instructions for Bible reading.[8] Whereas Orthodoxy had given instructions on how the whole Bible could be read through one or more times in a year, Spener's advice followed a different pattern. After an initial general reading of the whole Bible, at the second time one should, at first, carry out a thorough reading of only the Pentateuch, then carefully read through all of the New Testament. After having finished going through the New Testament, one should carry on once again reading only a portion of the Old Testament before returning to the New, etc. Consequently, the New Testament would be read through five times, as opposed to only twice for the Old Testament.[9] To the charge that the Pietists despised the Old Testament and only recommended the New,[10] Spener answered:

> It is true that we recommend the New Testament ... I also do not deny that we greatly prefer the New to the Old and always ask that the New be read more often than the Old. We also believe we have sufficient reason for this. For, what was in the Old as pictures and shadows, is in the New as light and truth. Because of its greater simplicity and clarity as well as its greater application, the New Testament is worthy of us turning to it.[11]

Promise and Fulfillment. Spener considered the magnificent promises of the prophets to be the most important part of the Old Testament. He agreed with Luther and Lutheran Orthodoxy that the Old Testament must be interpreted christologically and that the prophets pointed to Christ and his coming kingdom. Yet Spener doubted that the messianic promises of the Old Testament had already been completely fulfilled in Christ, just as he also thought that the prophecies of the Book of Revelation had not all come to pass in the course of Church history. *Pia Desideria* based its reform program on a future optimism, namely, Spener's "Hope for better times", which looked for the fulfillment of those biblical promises not yet realized. The Church should expect still better times before the Last Day, since the conversion of Israel (Rom 11:25f; Hos 3:4f) and the Fall of Babylon, i. e., a greater decline in the papacy (Revelation 18, 19), was still to come.[12] Spener clearly and unmistakably criticized Luther's understanding of the biblical prophets. Luther was good on the Apostle Paul, but poor on the prophets. Instead, Spener adopted the biblical interpretation of the federal theologian Johannes Cocceius which was free from dogmatic premises. Only in his last years did Spener study the Old Testament intensively. In his late work against the Socinians, *Defense of evidence for*

---

[7] *Pia Desideria* 54, 29f.

[8] A. H. Francke, *Einleitung zur Lesung der H. Schrifft/ Insonderheit Des Neuen Testaments* (Halle 1694).

[9] Cf. Spener's "Forward" in the 1694 and 1699 editions of the Bible.

[10] *Novum Testamentum commendari, spreto Veteri, quod fanaticorum esset proprium, inde etiam factum, ut per vos N.T. solitarie fuerit exscriptum*, Ph. J. Spener, *Frankfurter Briefe* 3, No. 61, p. 551 f. [13.8.1677]. Also A. H. Francke defended himself against the "new accusation of rejecting the Old Testament", *Observationes Biblicae* (1695), cited from A. H. Francke, *Werke in Auswahl* (Berlin 1962) 262.

[11] *Frankfurter Briefe*, ibid. 556–61.

[12] In later years Spener also included the thousand year reign of Revelation 20 among his future expectations.

the eternal divinity of our Lord Jesus Christ (Vertheidigung des Zeugnüsses von der ewigen Gottheit unsers Herrn Jesu Christi, published posthumously at Frankfurt a. M. in 1706), he went to great pains to save the messianic prophecies of the Old Testament from the Socinian critique.

2.2. *August Hermann Francke*

Spener's most important student was August Hermann Francke (1663–1726). Although theologically dependent on Spener, Francke surpassed him in drive and in the ability to get things done. Originally intending an academic career, he received a stipend from the Schabbel Foundation of Lübeck which enabled him to pursue a thorough theological education at the universities of Kiel and Leipzig, thus equipping him for an academic position. He studied Hebrew with Esdras Edzard in Hamburg and in 1685 he received his MA at Leipzig for submitting a dissertation on Hebrew Grammar (*Dissertatio Philologica de Grammatica Hebraica*, 1685).

The following year in Leipzig, 1686, Francke and a university classmate named Paul Anton founded the *Collegium philobiblicum*, a study group of eight MAs who met on Sundays to practice philological exegesis. At each meeting, a passage from the Old and New Testaments in the original languages would be interpreted and jointly discussed. In the beginning the purpose was purely academic. Spener, who at this time was court preacher in Dresden, sought, through letters and a personal visit to Leipzig, to influence the *Collegium philobiblicum* to align themselves with his pietist ideas on reform, namely, placing more emphasis on personal renewal and giving the New Testament priority over the Old.

In order to further his education in Old Testament exegesis, Francke decided to study in Lüneburg with Caspar Hermann Sandhagen, a former student of Sebastian Schmidt. During his stay there in the Fall of 1687, Francke experienced a conversion which completely changed his life. Breaking with his customary multifaceted scholarship, he returned to Leipzig and no longer held lectures on the Old Testament, but only on the New. At the same time, he reorganized the *Collegium philobiblicum*, abandoning its previous emphasis on scholarly learning and stressing instead biblical interpretation for personal renewal. The friends of Francke soon established other *collegia* besides the *Collegium philobiblicum*, where students and townspeople read the Bible for inner renewal. Thus, the pietist method of biblical interpretation spread beyond academic circles into the city itself. Disquiet and conflict with the university followed, finally culminating in the expulsion of the Pietists from Leipzig. The word 'Pietist' was first coined in Leipzig, and the assessment of Joachim Feller, the Professor of Rhetoric in Leipzig, is well-known: "What is a Pietist? Someone who studies God's Word and, in his own opinion, also leads a holy life".

Francke was briefly parish pastor in Erfurt, where he worked for a better Bible knowledge through distributing inexpensive editions of the New Testament. Then in 1691 he was called to be professor of Oriental languages in the newly established University of Halle and, at the same time, to be a parish pastor in Glaucha near Halle. Here in 1694 Francke founded the orphanage which would become the nucleus of an expanding complex of schools and business enterprises in front of the city gates. Henceforth, the leadership of his institutions would require the greater part of his energies. In 1699 Francke was called to the theological faculty. He irritated the adherents of Lutheran Orthodoxy with his *Observationes biblicae* (Halle 1695), a commentary which used a philological approach to the meaning of words in order to improve numerous passages in Luther's translation of the Bible. Afterwards, he concentrated on instructing the growing number of students who were coming to Halle in the right understanding of the Bible and its application to their spiritual edification. His lectures, in so far as they could be considered an academic treatment of the Bible, dealt with themes of the Old and New Testaments, mainly as introductions to individual biblical writings and as guides to biblical hermeneutics. While Lutheran Orthodoxy read the Bible for the doctrine it contained (*dicta probantia*), Francke highlighted the particular characteristics of the individual biblical authors. Here was his answer to the contemporary search for the hermeneutical key to understanding Scripture (*Commentatio de scopo librorum Veteris et Novi Testamenti*, Halle 1724). In addition to the prophets, for which he wrote a general introduction together with a sample interpretation of the Book of Jonah (*Introductio ad lectionem Prophetarum, I. Generalis, II. Specialis ad Lectionem Ionae, quae in reliquis exemplo esse possit*, Halle 1724), he devoted himself once again to the Psalms. After his death, his son Gotthilf August Francke edited an introduction to the Psalms, which was the elder Francke's most extensive work of biblical interpretation (*Introductio in Psalterium generalis et specialis*, Halle 1734; 1229 pages). The proof of the agreement between the Old and the New Testaments was important for him, since they both had the same total aim – Christ.

The Collegium Orientale. When Francke switched over to the theological faculty, Johann Heinrich Michaelis (1668–1738) became his successor as Professor for Oriental Languages, serving in this post until 1712, when he was accepted into the Faculty of Theology as well. Francke handed over to Michaelis the academic work on the Old Testament. In 1702 Francke founded the *Collegium Orientale Theologicum*. Twelve specially chosen theological students made up the membership of the college, which Francke wanted to expand later to about 50, although this plan was never fulfilled. While living and eating together under the supervision of the Professor for Oriental Languages and an assistant from the theological faculty, the members were to devote themselves to a thorough study of the Holy Scriptures. Besides Greek and Hebrew, each participant was to learn, at the very least, one further Oriental language, "Chaldean, Syriac, Aramaic, Arabic, Ethiopic, and Rabbinic Hebrew". Those more philologically gifted were to also learn modern languages, into which the Bible had been translated or should be translated. When Francke sought in aristocratic and merchant circles financial support for the orphanage and the needs of the poor, he also requested assistance for the Oriental Theological College as an institution primarily devoted to a more thoroughly academic study of the Bible.

Originally, the Oriental Theological College had nothing to do with the Halle mission to the Eastern Churches, even when, some time later, students where accepted from Greece. Under the leadership of Johann Heinrich Michaelis, the *Collegium Orientale* was for the first two decades of its existence almost exclusively pre-occupied with academic work on the Old Testament, seeking to complete the project that would in the end become Michaelis's life work – an edition of the Hebrew Bible with a reliable text and a thorough philological, historical and theological commentary. The chief co-workers on the project were his nephew, Christian Benedikt Michaelis (1680–1764), later Professor for Oriental Languages (after 1731, for Theology), and the young Johann Jakob Rambach (1693–1735), later Professor in Jena, Halle and, lastly, Giessen.

To produce the text for a Hebrew Bible, Michaelis obtained five manuscripts (from Erfurt) and nineteen printed editions of the Old Testament. By collating the textual tradition, with special attention to the Hebrew Bible edited by Daniel Ernst Jablonski (Berlin 1696), he sought to establish the most reliable text possible. He took great pains with the commentary, following in large measure the concordance method in philological matters and explaining the historical circumstances in which the biblical authors had written their texts. In the process he leaned heavily on rabbinic writers. For the theological commentary, Michaelis followed the hermeneutical instructions of Francke, namely, that under the "husk" of the literal sense, as established philologically and historically, Christ must be found as the "kernel" of Scripture.

Francke had estimated that the work would take five years, yet year after year its completion was delayed. In keeping with his favorable attitude toward Francke and the Halle institutions, the Prussian king granted a longer research sabbatical for Michaelis, so that in Berlin he could devote himself entirely to further work on the project. With five participants in the project already dead, Francke had been impatient for a long time, when after eighteen years the work finally appeared:

BIBLIA HEBRAICA, EX ALIQUOT MANUSCRIPTIS ET COMPLURIBUS IMPRESSIS CODICIBUS, ITEM MASORA TAM EDITA, QUAM MANUSCRIPTA, ALIISQUE HEBRAEORUM CRITICIS DILIGENTER RECENSITA, PRAETER NOVA LEMMATA TEXTUS. S. IN PENTATEUCHO, ACCEDUNT LOCA SCRIPTURAE PARALLELA, VERBALIA ET REALIA, BREVESQUE ADNOTATIONES, QUIBUS NUCLEUS GRAECAE LXX INTERPRETUM ET OO. VERSIONUM EXHIBETUR, DIFFICILES IN TEXTU DICTIONES ET PHRASES EXPLICANTUR, AC DUBIA RESOLVUNTUR, UT SUCCINCTI COMMENTARII VICEM PRAESTARE POSSINT. SINGULIS DENIQUE COLUMNIS SELECTAE VARIANTES LECTIONES SUBIICIUNTUR CURA AC STUDIO D. IO. HEINR. MICHAELIS. S.S. THEOL.& AC OO. LNGG. IN ACAD. FRIDE. P.P.ORD. ET EX PARTE OPERA SOCIORUM; UT PLURIBUS IN PRAEFATIONE DICETUR (Halle 1720).

The commentary was set as marginal glosses next to the Hebrew Text. In the end, these grew so numerous during the course of the work that they had to be printed in a very small, barely readable type. Therefore, beginning with the Psalms, Michaelis decided to publish the explanatory material as a separate work simultaneously with his Hebrew Bible. This three volume commentary was entitled:

UBERIORUM ADNOTATIONUM PHILOLOGICO-EXEGETICARUM IN HAGIOGRAPHOS VET. TESTAMENTI LIBROS (Halle 1720).

Together, the volumes contained almost 4000 pages of textual explanations. Johann Heinrich Michaelis wrote only a portion of these (Psalms, Job, Song of Songs, Ezra, I Chronicles), sharing the work with Christian Benedikt Michaelis (Proverbs, Lamentations, Daniel) and Johann Jakob Rambach (Ruth, Proverbs, Esther, Nehemiah, II Chronicles). Later, in hindsight Christian Benedikt Michaelis criticized the Hebrew Bible prepared by his uncle in Halle as inadequate for academic purposes. Although the scholarly outcome of the *Adnotationes* was more an accumulation of learning than an advancement in the academic study of the Scriptures, the biblical scholarship of Johann Heinrich Michaelis still remains as the most important contribution of Pietism in Halle to Old Testament studies.

3. The Bearing of Radical Pietism on Scriptural Interpretation

In addition to the Pietism which Spener and Francke founded as a renewal movement within Protestant Churches, early on a radical Pietism arose which distanced itself from the mainstream Churches. Denouncing them as corrupt like Babylon (Revelation 18), radical Pietists not infrequently separated from these Churches and formed their own communities, where they could belong to a "division-free", non-denominational Christianity. Adhering to a chiliastic reckoning of time, on many occasions they raised expectations that the beginning of the coming thousand-year Kingdom of God on earth was near. Johann Jakob Schütz (1640–90), a jurist from Frankfurt who was a close friend of Spener and a co-founder of the Frankfurt *Collegium pietatis*, was the first to take the conscious step to separate from the Lutheran Church. He can be considered as the founder of Radical Pietism in Lutheranism. He caused the works of mystics (Johann Tauler, among others) and chiliastic authors to be published. Criticizing Luther's translation of the Bible and ignoring the Church's confessions, he sought to find for himself in Holy Scripture a "denominationally-free" basis for faith. His *Rules for a Christian Life, or rather, Sayings drawn from the New Testament* (1677) furthered a Christianity based on the New Testament alone. The promises of the Old Testament referred only to earthly goods and did not concern Christians under the "New Covenant".[13] Because of his devaluation of the Old Testament, Schütz was early on suspected of Socianism.

Gottfried Arnold (1666–1714), author of *Non-sectarian History of the Church and of Heretics* (*Unparteyische Kirchen- und Ketzer-Historie*, Frankfurt a. M. 1729), maintained a largely negative critical distance from academic theology. After a year, he resigned his professorship in History at Giessen out of "loathing for the pompous, glory-seeking and overly intellectual nature of the academic life". Like Spener in his *Pia Desideria*, Arnold lamented in *History of the Church and Heretics* the fact that soon after the Reformation the study of the Bible was once again pulled through the sieve of dogmatic and po-

---

[13] Deppermann, Johann Jakob Schütz (2002) 171–80.

lemical theology, thus recreating a "scholastic theology". While Spener called for a "biblical theology", Arnold countered the prevailing scholastic theology with a "mystical theology".[14] This mystical theology, or secret divine learning, was something every Christian could obtain, although only a small number of true Christians actually did so. Its essence was humanity's conversation with God (or from God), and its aim was a mystical union with him. God's love, or the experience of God, assumed the role Protestants normally assigned to faith. This mystical theology had its source in God and was apprehended only through the Holy Spirit. Its basis and "wellspring" was the Bible, in which "Moses and the Prophets, but especially David in his Psalms and Solomon in his Song received from God the true, secret divine learning and have bequeathed it to us".[15] Only with reservation could Platonic philosophy be respected as a second source for mystical theology, for Plato mingled what he had learned about the beliefs of the Fathers from Jewish writings with pagan trifles.

With regard to biblical exposition, Arnold's theology followed the method of looking for the secret, mystical meaning lying underneath the husk of the literal sense. Yet, his scriptural interpretation was not so very allegorical. He kept largely to the literal sense of the text. Still, a right understanding of Holy Scripture required that attention be paid not only to the words of the biblical writer but also above all else to his affections and the moving of the reader to experience those same affections himself. Citing Ps 34:9, Arnold stressed the priority of "tasting" over "seeing". Among the books of the Old Testament, the Song of Solomon was the most important. Arnold called it "the *Summa* of secret divine doctrine".[16] Following Bernhard von Clairvaux, Arnold asserted: "In this bridal song it is necessary to reflect not upon the words, but upon the affections". When he wrote his own spiritual poem, he drew upon the Song of Solomon and the Wisdom of Solomon the most.[17] Other than his historical and edifying writings, Arnold did little exposition of the Bible. In sermons, he expounded passages from Genesis in the usual christological sense.[18]

Since Pietism generally, and radical Pietism in particular, kept its distance from Luther's Bible while seeking an unmediated access to Holy Scripture, numerous new translations and new editions of the Bible were produced. The largest portion of these were editions of the New Testament. Of those editions to include the Old Testament, the first was the *Biblia Pentapla* (1710–12), which was printed in the Duchy of Gottorf, a territory belonging to the Danish crown and, hence, lying immediately outside the jurisdiction of the imperial Book Censor:

---

[14] G. Arnold, *Historie und Beschreibung der Mystischen Theologie Oder Geheimen Gottesgelehrtheit* (Leipzig 1703).

[15] *Historie* (1703) 41.

[16] *Historie* (1703) 58.

[17] G. Arnold, "Poetische Lob- und Liebes-Sprüche von der Ewigen Weißheit, nach Anleitung des Hohenliedes Salomos", *Das Geheimniß Der Göttlichen Sophia oder Weißheit* (Leipzig 1700).

[18] G. Arnold, *Das Wahre Christenthum Altes Testaments im heilsamen Gebrauch der vornehmsten Sprüche aus dem Ersten Buch Mosis* (Frankfurt a. M. 1707).

BIBLIA PENTAPLA, That is: The Books of Holy Scripture of the Old and New Testaments /
According to the fivefold German interpretations I. of the Roman Catholics / by Caspar Ulenberg, Theol. Lic. II. Of the Lutherans Protestants / by Martin Luther, Theol. D. III. Of the Reformed Protestants / by Johann Piscator, Theol. Prof. IV. Of the Jews / on the Old Testament
/ by Joseph Atiae, and of the New / on the New Testament / by Joh. Henrich Reitzen. V. Of
the Dutch / according to the order of Lords Estate-General. Each with its own forward / and
parallels, together with short summaries and helpful tables. Printed and published by Hermann
Heinrich Holle, licensed book printer in Gottorf, the high principality of Holstein (Schiffbek
at Hamburg 1711).[19]

Its editor was Johann Otto Glüsing (c. 1676–1727), who was won over to radical Pietism as a theological student at Jena by the writings of Gottfried Arnold.
Earlier on he had spread the Pietist philosophy in Denmark and Norway and,
as a private tutor, held Pietist conventicles in Copenhagen and Christiana
(Oslo). Deported from Denmark in 1706, he established himself in Hamburg,
where he became the leading mind of the Angel Brotherhood, a group founded
by Johann Georg Gichtel which adhered to the theosophical ideas of Jakob
Böhme. By making possible the comparison of many translations, the aim of
the *Biblia Pentapla* was to improve the understanding of the meaning of the
words of Scripture. At the same time, it was the first application of radical
Pietism's characteristic "impartiality" to an edition of the Bible – impartiality
understood, however, not as historical objectivity but as standing above confessional considerations. The reader was to be able to learn the basis of each
religious group's beliefs which then could be tested. The *Pentapla* wanted to
further "a general, brotherly love and harmony" among the religious groups of
the day, including the Jews. It contained the translation by Caspar Ulenberg,
the so-called Mainz Bible, which was the most widely used translation in the
Roman Catholic Church, Martin Luther's translation, the reformed Bible of
Johann Piscator, and the Dutch State Bible. In addition to these, the "Jewish
translation" is especially noteworthy. Translated by Rabbi Joseph Josel from
Witzenhausen and printed by Joseph ben Abraham Athias in Amsterdam in
1670, this text served as the representative of German Jewish religious thought.
In the New Testament, its place was taken by the "new translation" of the ra-
dical Pietist Johann Henrich Reitz.

Quickly condemned by the Lutheran side as a poorly done piece of syncret-
ism, this "impartial" edition of the Bible ignored the Church canon and included an extraordinary number of non-canonical writings. In the New Testament, besides the Apocrypha and the Pseudepigrapha, the *Pentapla* also contained the Apostolic Fathers, as translated by Gottfried Arnold. In the Old
Testament Apocrypha, 3 and 4 Ezra and 3 Maccabees were included, although
it noted that 4 Ezra had nothing to do with Ezra, despite the fact that "these
days many inexperienced friends of prophetic writings hold to it excessively".
The book was written long after the Apostolic age and later than the Book of
Revelation, when "after the conclusion of the first period of spiritual richness"
it was often popular to make a pious forgery (*pia fraus*). However, with due

---

[19] Tübingen, Bibliothek Evangelisches Stift, q 319.

caution, one can read 4 Ezra as a commentary on the Book of Revelation, "without obligation, since the source itself is pure and clear".[20]

If the "mystical" understanding of the Bible was more a product of the Lutheran tradition, the "prophetic" interpretation of Scripture – with its interest in the chronology of Salvation History and the date for the beginning of the millennial kingdom – had its roots chiefly in the Reformed tradition. In his biblical studies the Reformed court preacher Konrad Brösske paid particular attention to the *Studium Chronologicum und Propheticum*. In this he followed the English chiliast Thomas Beverly, whose chronology Brösske translated, thus making the work widely known in German radical Pietist circles.[21] John Henrich Horch (1652–1729), was Professor of Theology at the Reformed academy in Herbon from 1690 until his removal in 1697. By founding a church of brotherly love, he became the father of Pietist separatism in Hesse. He, too, was influenced by English Chiliasm and focused his biblical investigations on understanding the "timeline" from the beginning of the world to its end.[22] Horch published an example of radical Pietist biblical scholarship:

> The Mystical and Prophetic Bible / That is, the whole of the Holy Scripture / of the Old and New Testaments / New and thoroughly improved / A complete explanation of the most noble Symbols and Prophecies / Especially of the Song of Solomon and the Revelation of Jesus Christ as well as its most noble doctrine / as is appropriate for these last days (Marburg 1712).

In the title we see the double emphasis that is characteristic of radical Pietism's biblical interpretation. Like Arnold, for Horch what mattered in scriptural exposition was extracting the mystical meaning. It would be found, when the exegesis "separates the hidden kernel from the husk of the letter" and "focuses everything on the inner man". As with Arnold, the Song of Solomon was for Horch the most important part of the Old Testament. Its interpretation should be "prophetic", since by carefully considering past and current events, "the timeline of Salvation History and the end-times character of the present should be discerned".[23]

Radical Pietism's most important work of biblical scholarship was the *Berleburg Bible*. Published in eight volumes from 1726 to 1742, four volumes were devoted to the Old Testament, with four for the New. The title of the first volume was

> The Holy Scripture of the Old and New Testaments / According to the original texts newly edited and translated: Together with some explanation of the literal meaning / As also of the most noble examples and prophecies of Christ and his kingdom /and at the same time of some doctrines which concern the state of the churches in our time in the last days; To all of which is further added an explanation which makes clear the inner state of the spiritual life / or the ways and workings of God in the soul for its purification, illumination and unification with him. Printed in Berlenburg in the year of our Savior Jesus Christ, the source of Holy Scripture, 1726.

---

[20] *Pentapla* (1711), Foward to the Old Testament.

[21] K. Brösske (ed.), Thomas Beverley, *Zeit-Register Mit denen Zeichen der Zeiten / Vom Anfange biß ans Ende der Welt. Wie beyde von Gott selbsten in seinem Worte geoffenbahret seynd* (Frankfurt a. M. [2]1697). Cf. Chr. Fende (ed.), *Verbesserung des Zeit-Registers, Herrn Thomas Beverleys* (s.l. 1729) [in the appendix of the first edition of J. A. Bengel, *Discipuli de Temporibus*].

[22] H. Horch, *Das A und O oder Zeitrechnung der gantzen H. Schrifft* (Leipzig 1697).

[23] Schneider, *Der radikale Pietismus im 18. Jahrhundert II* (1995) 121.

Berleburg was the seat of Count Casimir von Wittgenstein. Since he was one of the first to practice religious tolerance in his small western German territory, he welcomed and supported religious refugees from many lands. Consequently, Berleburg was a center for radical Pietist book production.[24] The chief editor of the Berleburg Bible was Johann Friedrich Haug (1680–1753), a man expelled from his native city of Strasbourg because of his Pietist activities. Besides him, however, many others worked together on this monumental Bible project. Among these contributors was occasionally (for II Timothy, Titus and Philemon) Johann Christian Edelmann (1698–1767), a scholar who would later leave radical Pietism behind and embrace the free-thinking characteristic of Spinoza and the Enlightenment.

Holding fast to Protestant Orthodoxy's doctrine of verbal inspiration, the Berleburg Bible adopted the conservative position on the question of the authorship of the Old Testament writings. As a result, Moses wrote the Pentateuch. His five books were "the oldest of all in the learned world" and the foundation of all scholarship.

> [N]ot only [were they] a well and a brief summary of all theology, so that neither the Prophets nor the apostles, nor even Christ himself either said or wrote something which was not derived from them and which therefore did not belong to an evangelical exposition and fulfillment of the same, but they were even the foundation of legal learning. Indeed, even for the introduction to medicine, they contribute considerable knowledge, describing the chief cause of all sickness and their classifications as well as remedies, as from the best doctors (Exod 15:36).

The Berleburg Bible made a universal claim: "Therefore, all reckoning of time must also begin with Moses". It tried very hard, then, to understand the historical circumstances in which the biblical authors had lived and written, as well as their personal fate. As a result, the Berleburg Bible pondered whether Solomon wrote his Song in youth or as a wiser, older man. For otherwise the key interpretative question – whether the Song of Solomon should be understood as a song about earthly love or mystical love – cannot be answered. Moreover, if Solomon had in mind his wife, the daughter of Pharaoh, when he wrote his Song, "it is still certain, that he must have written down this song through the leading of the Holy Spirit / ... he wanted to focus on the spiritual love of Christ". The Berleburg Bible strove to provide a fresh translation from the original languages which highlighted the literal sense. It did not despise scholarly commentary but made good use of academic biblical interpretation. From among Reformed scholars, first place was given to Johann Cocceius. Among the Lutherans, Abraham Calov, Johann Andreas Osiander and Sebastian Schmidt were cited. The secret, spiritual sense had to be extracted out from under the husk of the literal sense. Explanations of the mystical meaning took up most of the space and drew heavily on the mystical-quietist biblical expositions of Jeanne Marie de Guyon (*La Sainte Bible*, printed 1713–15).

---

[24] Schrader, Literaturproduktion (1989).

4. The Biblical Studies of Johann Albrecht Bengel

Johann Albrecht Bengel (1687–1752) is considered the most important Pietist exegete. As a youth, he grew up in radical Pietist circles. At the University of Tübingen, he received theological training in the spirit of a moderate Lutheran orthodoxy open to the intentions of Spener. During a period of study at the University of Halle, Bengel confirmed his affiliation with the Pietism of Spener and Francke. Although he also at this time became acquainted with A. H. Francke's worldwide projects, he held himself apart from the world-improving plans of the Halle Pietists. "These men can from time to time divide the brooklets of life and fruitfully spread them. I, however, look after the well-house."

The "well-house" for Bengel was his work on biblical text criticism. Already in his student days, he became captivated by the task, when he heard of the unreliability of the *Textus receptus* and of the many variants of the New Testament text. While a student at Tübingen, he had planned an edition of the Greek New Testament. During his visit to Halle, Johann Heinrich Michaelis had shown him his preliminary work on his edition of the Hebrew Bible. For twenty-eight years Bengel served as the Preceptor of the Cloister School, an educational institution for future theologians, in Denkendorf, a village by Stuttgart. Here Bengel had to take his students through the entire Greek New Testament in two-year cycles. In order to produce a reliable text, he began to compare manuscripts and printed copies that he had collected in Denkendorf, by borrowing them from afar, as J. H. Michaelis had done. After he announced the principles of his textual work in a forward to an edition of Chrysostom, his *Novum Testamentum Graecum* appeared in 1734 as a quarto with critical apparatus for the text:

Η ΚΑΙΝΗ ΔΙΑΘΗΚΗ. NOVUM TESTAMENTUM GRAECUM ita adornatum ut textus probatarum editionum medullam margo variantium lectionum in suas classes distributarum locorumque parallelorum delectum apparatus subiunctus criseos sacrae Millianae praesertim compendium, limam, supplementum ac fructum exhibeat inserviente Jo. Alberto Bengelio (Tübingen 1734; 884 pages, 4°).

Bengel consulted more manuscripts and printed editions than had J. H. Michaelis for the Halle *Biblia Hebraica*. However, Bengel could not keep up with the contemporary textual critic Johann Jakob Wettstein. Also, Bengel kept to the *Textus receptus* and referred to the variants only in the apparatus. Only the poor transmission history of the Book of Revelation compelled him in places to reconstruct the text. Still, Bengel's sifting and ordering of the variants made decided progress. With arduous effort, he separated the real variants from the very many accidental scribal errors. Then, he ordered the variants in five classes, according to the their quality:

(i) those considered original;
(ii) those uncertain, but preferable to the *Textus receptus*;
(iii) those considered to be of the same weight as the *Textus receptus*;
(iv) those less certain than the *Textus receptus*;
(v) those variants that should be dismissed.

Moreover, Bengel was successful in first grasping the overall picture of the surviving variants and assigning the individual manuscripts to text families, or "nations" in Bengel's words. Bengel divided the texts between an Asian nation and an African nation – a distinction which proved its worth during the course of subsequent research, since Johann Salomo Semler had to go one step further along this path and add a third textual family, the Western text. Bengel was also able to reduce the traditional rules of textual criticism through logic to a single consideration: *Proclivi scriptioni praestat ardua* ("the more understandable variant is the more difficult one to prefer"). Concerned to produce a reliable text which came as close as was possible to the original, verbally-inspired autograph, Bengel became the father of modern textual criticism.

Like J. H. Michaelis in his *Biblia Hebraica*, Bengel had originally wanted to add a continuous commentary to his critical edition of the text. He decided, however, to publish it separately, and this work became Bengel's most influential, being continually reprinted up to the present:

> GNOMON NOVI TESTAMENTI in quo ex nativa verborum vi simplicitas, profunditas, concinnitas, salubritas sensuum coelestium indicatur opera Jo. Alberti Bengelii (Tübingen 1742; XVII, 1208 pages).

The *Gnomon* ("Pointer") offered a new, verse by verse Latin translation and an ensuing exposition of all the New Testament writings. Careful observations on the biblical text, the use of the concordance method and concise historical explanations were combined with sound theological judgment and practical, edifying applications. Despite its artless format which resembles nothing so much as a file box of index cards, the *Gnomon*'s commentary displays an impressive inner unity, and for many generations it has proved its worth when Protestant pastors prepare their sermons. In the eighteenth century, John Wesley drew heavily on the *Gnomon* for a Bible commentary in English. In the nineteenth century, the *Gnomon* itself was translated into English. The latest German editions were Berlin 1960 and Stuttgart 1970.

Bengel's exegetical work was focused almost exclusively on the New Testament. Among his numerous publications on biblical theology, none is devoted to the Old Testament text, but many interpret the Book of Revelation. This final book of the Bible in his eyes was the most important, for here the Holy Spirit had spoken directly, unmediated through the witness of prophets and Apostles. Moreover, the Book of Revelation was the most important key for understanding Salvation History. With the help of Revelation, Bengel calculated the dates of Salvation History, from the coming of Christ to the Last. According to Bengel's reckoning, Jesus Christ would return to establish his millennial – for Bengel bis-millennial – reign, as prophesied in Revelation 20, in 1836.

As a coherent system of revealed, divine truth, the Bible, according to Bengel, contained the secrets of Salvation History, or, as Bengel expressed it, of the divine economy. For Bengel, this idea of 'economy' is the defining concept by which the Bible as a whole can be described, as well as the relationship of the New Testament to the Old. In keeping with Federal theology (J. Cocceius), Bengel rejected different divine covenants and did not differentiate between the Old Covenant and the New. The term 'covenant' (*berit*) was appropriate only for the covenant of Moses in the Old Testament. God had not made any new covenant in Christ. At this point, it is necessary to speak of the New Testament. Bengel, as a good Lutheran, stressed more strongly than Reformed Federal theology the difference between the Old and the New Testaments.

After completing his chronology of Salvation History from the coming of Christ to his return based on the writings of the New Testament, Bengel devoted himself to calculating the timeline from the creation of the world to the coming of Christ, based on the Old Testament. From the beginning he had intended to complete his New Testament chronology with one for the Old Testament. "When one considers the Old and New Testament together to be a single, inseparable document, only then is such a timeline first completed and concluded."[25] Bengel understood Salvation History as a timeline, which ran from creation to the end of the world on the Last Day. Bengel's efforts to determine the dates of Salvation History, which were so often written down in the Bible in coded language, and then from these dates to construct a comprehensive chronology of Salvation History was published in

> Ordo temporum a principio per periodos oeconomiae divinae historicas atque propheticas ad finem usque ita deductus ut tota series et quarumvis partium analogia sempiternae virtutis ac sapientiae cultoribus ex scriptura V. et N. T. tanquam uno revera documento proponatur (Stuttgart 1741).

By consulting dates from secular history, i.e., the 'pagan' chronologies of the ancient Orient and of the reigns of Roman emperors, but chiefly by examining details in the Bible, namely, a particular interpretation of Daniel's Seventy weeks, Bengel in the end was able to expand his timeline of Salvation History to become a comprehensive chronology of world history:

> The World-Ages in which is proven the scriptural timeline and the seventy weeks along with other important texts and saving doctrines are examined (1746).

Using the same Salvation-History method he had employed in his exegesis of the Book of Revelation, Bengel examined the entire Old Testament, looking for its underlying chronological framework. He determined the year of creation, even Autumn as the season in which the world was made. He established chronologically all the people of the Old Testament who were of particular importance as well as the Old Testament's important events. Together with his timeline derived from the Book of Revelation, Bengel produced a biblical chronology for the world which depicted its whole history, from its creation to its end.[26]

> From the beginning of the first book of Moses to end of the Book of Revelation many epochs are reported and indeed not without reason. When viewed separately, they often appear to be meaningless and contemptible. However, when taken together, according to the instructions which lie in Scripture itself, there is a universal and coherent timeline, proportioned into parts, designed according to divine wisdom and having an inestimable importance and usefulness.

Bengel's Salvation-History chronology is the most extreme consequence of Pietism's continuing to hold to Orthodoxy's doctrine of inspiration. When the

---

[25] J. A. Bengel, *Welt-Alter darin die schriftmässige Zeiten-Linie bewiesen und die siebenzig Wochen samt andern wichtigen Texten und heilsamen Lehren erörtert werden* (Esslingen 1746) 3 [see the following text].

[26] Ibid. 374.

year 1836 passed without any noticeable indication of the second-coming of Christ as predicted by Bengel, the problems inherent in his calculations became evident to the Pietists. Although they continued to develop their theology of Salvation History, they did so without setting specific dates.

5. The Exegetical and Hermeneutical Significance of Pietism

When compared to the preceding old Protestant Orthodoxy and the parallel movement of the Enlightenment, Pietism's contribution to biblical scholarship appears negligible. In his *History of Old Testament in the Christian Church*, L. DIESTEL gave no separate account of Pietism, but included it in his description of exegesis in the Lutheran Church under the influence of Orthodoxy, from 1600–1750. In addition to Johann Gerhard, Abraham Calov and August Pfeiffer, at least ten pages were devoted to Pietism.[27] H.-J. KRAUS, in his *History of Historical-Critical Old Testament Research*, conceded merely a meager page to Pietism.[28] Although Pietists contributed hardly anything to the development of the historical-critical method, they promoted the study of the Bible, and their instructions as well as rules for reading and understanding Scripture played a role in the history of biblical hermeneutics.

DIESTEL argued that the Lutheran Church, by sticking to the lectionary for its Sunday preaching (to the Gospel and Epistle lessons) hindered an extensive use of the Old Testament, whereas the Reformed Church, by replacing the lectionary with a *lectio continua* of all the biblical books, gave greater room to the Old Testament.[29] DIESTEL's analysis, however, failed to take into account the customary weekday worship services in older Lutheranism which did expound the Old Testament.[30] It also overlooked the academic work done on the Old Testament by the theologians of Lutheran Orthodoxy. One of the three professorships in a theological faculty was reserved by statute for the exegesis of the Old Testament. Moreover, in the faculty of philosophy, there were professors for Hebrew, that is, Oriental languages.[31] The holders of chairs in Hebrew were considered without exception as trained theologians, many of whom would later exchange their position for one in theology. August Hermann Francke in Halle and Johann Heinrich May (1653–1719) in Giessen, the two most important teachers in higher education during the time of early Pietism, were first professors of Hebrew in the Faculty of Philosophy before they stepped up to a professorship in the theological faculty.

The philological work on the Old Testament, like the work on the Greek New Testament, was carried out in the philosophical faculty. The subject of hermeneutics was also a part of biblical philology (Salomon Glassius, *Philologia sacra*, 1623–36). Philosophy, especially Aristotelian logic and

---

[27] Diestel, Geschichte (1869/1981) 409–19.
[28] Kraus, Geschichte (²1969) 90f.
[29] Diestel, ibid. 313.
[30] E. KOCH, "'Die himlische Philosophia des heiligen Geistes'. Zur Bedeutung alttestamentlicher Spruchweisheit im Luthertum des 16. und 17. Jahrhunderts", *ThLZ* 115 (1990) 705.
[31] Zobel, Hebraisten (1958).

rhetoric, was used without difficulty in biblical interpretation. Although Luther was horrified by Aristotelian metaphysics, and Melanchthon excluded it from the academic canon, Aristotelianism was well received in Lutheran universities from 1600. Its increasingly high estimation as a fundamental academic discipline, which even had to be respected by theology, led many times to a low estimation of philology. In Helmstedt, Cornelius Martini taught that the one who mastered logic and metaphysics could in a moment understand the Bible.[32] Georg Calixt told a theological student immersed in his Hebrew studies, "it would not appear to be worth such trouble, to devote so much time and effort to grammar and vocabulary". It would be better for his proper understanding of biblical truth, if he concentrated more on philosophy, metaphysics and logic as the necessary aids.[33] Also Calixt's opponent, Johann Hülsemann (1602–61), thought it sufficient, if one was familiar with grammar and knew how to use a lexicon and concordance.[34] Now, one does not find Johann Conrad Dannhauer, Spener's teacher in Strasbourg, holding this low estimation of biblical philology, nor Abraham Calov in Wittenberg, who defended the Orthodox doctrine of verbal inspiration against Hugo Grotius in his *Biblia illustrata* (1672). Still, both were staunch followers of Aristotelian scholastic metaphysics and very far from questioning its use in theology.

Pietism was the first to criticize Aristotelian philosophy, indeed the first to deny the importance of philosophy in general for theology and biblical studies. In *Pia Desideria* Philipp Jakob Spener had demanded that in the place of *theologia scholastica*, which Luther had thrown out the front door but which had been brought back in through the rear door, proper biblical theology should be established.[35] "But this kind of *theologica scholastica* has arisen, since we began to depart from Scripture and its simplicity and mix theology with philosophy."[36]

In *De impedimentis studii theologici* (1590), originally a forward to Spener's rendering of Johann Conrad Donnhauer's doctrinal teaching into tables, but later printed many times separately, Spener made concrete proposals for bringing about the reform of theology and theological education he had demanded in *Pia Desideria*.[37] In the place of Aristotelian philosophy, whose metaphysical terminology blocked access to the Bible, a modern, more eclectic philosophy should emerge. Nevertheless, philosophy was not necessary for understanding the Bible. "Even without philosophy, theology can become something marvelous and most useful to the church."[38] The only thing necessary was to study the biblical languages of Greek and Hebrew, so that one would be familiar with the text in the form in which the Holy Spirit gave it to the biblical writers. Spener did not reject the use of philosophy for understanding the Bible. It was his desideratum to base the exegesis of Scripture on a biblical philosophy as well as biblical philology. Spener regretted that ancient Jewish philosophy was unknown to us, and wished that the concepts behind the sayings of Moses, David, Solomon, and the prophets would be discovered, so that Aristotelian philosophy could be replaced with a "*philosophia Judaica*" or a "*philosophia sacra*". Had the many writings of King Solomon (1 Kgs 4:32f)

---

[32] *Allgemeines Gelehrten-Lexicon* (ed. Chr. G. Jöcher) III (1751) 227.

[33] A. Tholuck, *Der Geist der lutherischen Theologen Wittenbergs* (Hamburg / Gotha 1852) 249.

[34] J. Hülsemann, *Methodus studii theologici* (1635), Paragraph 4 (see Tholuck, op. cit.).

[35] *Pia Desideria* (ed. Aland) 25, 21–24.

[36] Spener, *Die Evangelische Glaubens-Gerechtigkeit* (Frankfurt a. M. 1684) 143.

[37] Spener, *Consilia et Iudicia theologica latina* 1 (Frankfurt a. M. 1709) 200–39.

[38] Spener, *Theologische Bedenken* 4 (Halle 1702) 185.

been preserved, they could have been a great help in such a task, even if they had not shared the Bible's infallibility.[39] For a time, Spener pinned his hopes on the Kabbalah (Knorr von Rosenroth, *Kabbala denudata*, 1677/86). In the end, however, he did not believe this task could be accomplished in his days. The search for the *philosophia sacra* so desired by Spener was first taken up two generations later by Friedrich Christoph Oetinger (1702–1782), a Pietist from Württemberg and a student of Bengel. Still, when Oetinger lectured on the *philosophia sacra* which he had drawn out of the Bible, chiefly from Proverbs, he found little interest among the successors of August Hermann Francke, who, under Siegmund Jakob Baumgarten had just embraced the philosophy of Christian Wolff. Spener's rejection of biblical scholarship which employed terminology drawn from Greek thought and his desired goal of a pure biblical philosophy continued to have adherents into the nineteenth and twentieth centuries (Johann Tobias Beck, Adolf Schlatter).

Spener's reform program caused a complete reversal of the respective assessments of philology and philosophy as aids for studying the Bible. At the University of Halle, newly founded in 1694, August Hermann Francke and his friends took the critical suggestions of Spener's *De impedimentis studii theologici* and applied them thoroughly. Since the Bible was at the center of theology, exegetical theology was the most important theological discipline and was clearly preferred to all the other disciplines. Since all theological knowledge must come from the study of the Bible, philology was preferred over philosophy. Fundamental to the Pietist understanding of the Bible was Francke's distinction between the husk and the kernel of Holy Scripture. The husk consisted of everything that philosophy and historical scholarship could help establish as the *sensus litteralis* of Scripture. Like Spener, Francke also followed Luther's claim that *vera theologia est grammatica*. The Bible had only one meaning and that was the grammatical one. Like Lutheran Orthodoxy before him, Francke rejected medieval hermeneutics, with its call for a four-fold interpretation of Scripture. Francke cogently outlined the basic principles of his biblical hermeneutics in his book:

> MANDUCTIO AD LECTIONEM SCRIPTURAE SACRAE HISTORICAM, GRAMMATICAM, LOGICAM, EXEGETICAM, DOGMATICAM, PORISMATICAM ET PRACTICAM, una cum Additamentis regulas Hermeneuticas de affectibus, & enarrationes ac introductiones in aliquot Epistolas Paulinas complectentibus (Halle 1693).

According to Francke's instructions, there was a three-fold task required for understanding the husk of Scripture: (i) historical; (ii) grammatical; and (iii) logical. There was as well a four-fold task involved in understanding the kernel of the Bible: (i) exegetical; (ii) dogmatic; (iii) porismatic; and (iv) practical.

For Francke, the *Lectio historica* was a knowledge of the biblical writings in their entirety, acquired through a general reading and consisting of Bible content as well as a knowledge of *res externae* (manuscripts, editions, translations and variants). The *Lectio grammatica* concentrated on a more precise study of individual books or texts and required, above all else, a knowledge of the bib-

---

[39] Ibid. 3, 945; cf. *De impedimentis*, 212.

lical languages of Greek and Hebrew. The *Lectio logica* or *analytica*, the last remaining use of philosophy for biblical studies, sought to understand the structure and inner coherence of individual texts or books in Holy Scripture and to determine the aim of their principle theme. If, as in I Corinthians, they were many themes, then the *Lectio logica* was to discern their many aims. With regard to the historical books of the Old Testament, it was necessary to understand the individual stories. The same was true for the prophetic books. The Psalms were to be individually analyzed. Only after grasping the overall aim should one begin to examine an individual passage.

The historical, grammatical and analytical readings of the Bible created the necessary conditions for breaking the husk of Holy Scripture and so opening the way to understanding its kernel. The *Lectio exegetica* was the most important part of bible study, for it determined the *sensus litteralis*, the meaning of the words and ideas. The *sensus litteralis* was differentiated from the *sensus litterae* which had been established during the *Lectio grammatica*. On the authority of Luther, Francke explained that the *sensus litteralis* was also the true, theological meaning. For, with Luther and Lutheran Orthodoxy, Francke taught that the Holy Spirit had put only one literal meaning in every statement to be grasped. The unregenerate could comprehend this meaning with their natural understanding, but not its spiritual significance. As a result, such a person could only grasp the grammatical meaning, but not the conceptual meaning. Only the regenerate Christian could find Christ as the kernel of Scripture under the husk of the Old Testament. This was the hermeneutical consequence of the Pietist demand for a *theologia regenitorum*, which denied to the unregenerate not only any claim to be true theologians but also any ability to understand Holy Scripture correctly. Since the *Lectio dogmatica* was used to apprehend the true understanding of the divine nature and will which brought salvation, spiritual insight was indispensable, and the regenerate received it through the illumination of the Holy Spirit. The *Lectio porismatica* made theoretical or practical deductions (*porismata*) based on either a close reading of the grammatical sense or by comparing the text to other biblical passages. Francke would later de-emphasize the porismatic interpretation of Scripture which had been part of Spener's legacy,[40] although other Pietist theologians (J. J. Rambach, J. Lange) stressed it more strongly. According to Francke, the decisive endpoint for every exegesis was the *Lectio practica*, the application (*applicatio*) of the insights which had been garnered to the life of the individual or of his neighbor.

Francke had carefully retreated from Spener's higher estimation of the New Testament than of the Old, and, despite the differences, stressed more strongly the unity of both. The Holy Scriptures were an integrated whole, so that every individual passage could be consulted for the clarification of another. For Francke, the unity of the Old and New Testaments was such that the kernel of all Scripture was Christ. The Old Testament spoke of Christ not

---

[40] Peschke, Studien II (1966) 28.

only in the predictions of the prophets but also in its entirety. In 1701 Francke published a university program, *The Irenic Harmony between Moses, the Prophets and the Psalms, concerning the Resurrection of Christ.*[41] That the Old Testament spoke of Christ could not be proven by the literal or grammatical sense. Francke did not return to the doctrine of multiple meanings of Scripture, but he did teach that under the literal sense there was a still deeper meaning, which he called the *sensus mysticus*, that needed to be extracted. Only the regenerate Christian could find Christ, the kernel of Scripture, everywhere behind the husk of the Old Testament. Francke found widespread agreement in Pietism with the thesis that Christ was the kernel of the Holy Scripture, thus necessitating a strict Christological interpretation of the Old Testament. Nikolaus Ludwig Graf von Zinzendorf, founder of the Herrnhut Brethren community, examined the question, "Whether Jesus Christ is not the single, provable object of the Old Testament? Whether all the books of the Old Testament do not discuss him?".[42] Joachim Lange (1670–1744) was Professor in Halle and author of a voluminous number of biblical commentaries according to the principles of Halle Pietism.[43] He stressed that the chief result of his biblical studies was that he had

> very much more fully and wonderfully found in the Old Testament the basic principles and chief doctrines of revealed religion concerning the mystery of the Holy Trinity and therein those of the true divinity of Jesus Christ and of his role as mediator than was usually realized and presented.[44]

On account of their devaluation of the Old Testament, the first Pietists were suspected of being close to Socianism. Consequently, the Halle Pietists Rambach and Lange, with their Christological interpretation of the Old Testament, bore the main burden of the ultimately futile fight against the Socianian interpretation of Scripture which paved the way for the Enlightenment.

Lange was also the author of a hermeneutic.[45] The classic textbook for Pietist hermeneutics was, however, written by Johann Jakob Rambach: *Institutiones hermeneutica sacrae* (Halle 1724, [6]1764). In this work Rambach picked up the thread of Orthodoxy's hermeneutical tradition (M. Flacius, J. Gerhard, S. Glassius, J. C. Dannhauer) and developed it further in the spirit of the ideas of Francke and Spener. At the beginning of exegesis, and completely in line with Orthodoxy, Rambach recognized the *Analogia fidei* as the principle for

---

[41] A. H. Francke, *Harmonicum Mosis, Prophetarum et Psalmorum de resurrectione Christi* (Halle 1701). In German, see Francke, *Christus der Kern heiliger Schrifft* (Halle 1702) 466–92.

[42] N. L. Zinzendorf, *Peri Heautou, Reale Beylage IX: Der Evangelisch – Mährischen Kirchen – Diener Abgenöthigte Gewissens-Rüge* ... 125 [*Supplemental Volumes*, IV].

[43] 8 volumes, Halle-Leipzig 1726–38. The four volumes on the Old Testament have the titles: *Mosaisches Licht und Recht, Das ist Richtige und Erbauliche Erklärung der Fünff Bücher Mosis; Biblisch-Historisches Licht und Recht, Das ist Richtige und Erbauliche Erklärung der sämmtlichen Historischen Bücher; Davidisch-Salomonisches Licht und Recht, Das ist Richtige und Erbauliche Erklärung der geistreichen Psalmen Davids ... wie auch der lehrreichen Sprüche / auch des Predigers und des Hohenlieds Salomons; Prophetisches Licht und Recht, Das ist Richtige und Erbauliche Erklärung der Propheten.*

[44] J. Lange, *Biblisches Licht und Recht ... aus dem grösseren Bibelwerck in eine Erbauliche Hausbibel gezogen* (Leipzig 1743), Foreword, fol. 1r.

[45] J. Lange, *Hermeneutica sacra* (Halle 1733).

every interpretation of a biblical text.[46] Then came the enumeration of aids to understanding the genuine meaning of a passage of Scripture, a step essentially in agreement with A. H. Francke. At the end came the specifically Pietistic concern – the practical application of the exegetical meaning.[47] According to H.-G. GADAMER, Rambach's *Institutiones hermeneutica sacrae* had the merit of adding application (*applicatio*) to understanding (*intelligere*) and interpretation (*explicare*), thereby restoring the validity of the long suppressed "third aspect of the hermeneutical problem".[48] The most important contribution of Pietism to the history of hermeneutics may lie in "the recognition of application as an integrating component of every understanding".[49]

Translation: Ashley Null

---

[46] L.II, c. 1, *De analogia fidei, genuinae interpretationis principio.*
[47] L.IV, c. 3, *De sensus adplicatione porismatica et practica.*
[48] H.-G. GADAMER, *Wahrheit und Methode. Grundzüge einer philosophischen Hermeneutik* (Tübingen ³1972) 291.
[49] Ibid. 292.

Chapter Thirty-eight

Scriptural Interpretation in the English Literary Tradition

By Stephen Prickett, Waco, TX

(Baylor University)

General works: F. R. A. de Chateaubriand, *The Genius of Christianity, or The spirit and beauty of the Christian religion*, by Viscount de Chateaubriand (orig.: *Génie du christianisme*, 1802; tr. Ch. White; Baltimore 1856; repr. Baltimore / New York 1976); D. L. Jeffrey (ed.), *A Dictionary of Biblical Tradition in English Literature*, (Grand Rapids, MI: Eerdmans 1992); D. Jasper / S. Prickett (eds.), *The Bible and Literature: A Reader* (Oxford: Blackwell 1999); S. Prickett (ed.), *Reading the Text: Biblical Interpretation and Literary Theory* (Oxford: Blackwell 1991).

Each age reads the Bible in terms of its own dominant concerns and genres. Thus, in addition to a visual art that was almost exclusively religious, Anglo-Saxon and mediaeval England interpreted the Bible in poetry. From the verse of the late seventh century Caedmon, often seen as the first 'English' poet, through to Langland, Bible stories were experienced primarily in poetic terms. Though it would be untrue to say that there was no vision of the Bible as narrative – *Piers Ploughman*, like Dante's *Divine Comedy*, is a narrative poem – it did mean that, at a time when most people were unable to read the Bible for themselves, scripturally inspired writing tended to be lyrical and meditative. More popularly, biblical stories were also interpreted as drama – usually verse drama. The vast bulk of the mediaeval miracle and morality plays are lost – many were perhaps never written down – but what remains of what was already, by the fourteenth century, a powerful dramatic tradition is enough to demonstrate how the Bible had given rise to a new and most-unbiblical medium. If, as is commonly argued, the great flowering of the theatre in the sixteenth and early seventeenth centuries grew directly out of that dramatic tradition, it is also true to say that the Bible gave rise to the drama of Marlowe, Jonson, and Shakespeare. By the early eighteenth century we find the word 'drama' itself has come full circle, and is itself deployed as a metaphor of biblical action. The first recorded use of the word in this sense comes in a sermon preached by John Sharp, Archbishop of York, in 1714, when he speaks of the Bible as "the great drama and contrivances of God's providence". Sharp, we are told, was a great lover of poetry and the theatre, and was wont to say that the Bible and Shakespeare had made him archbishop.[1]

---

[1] G. Burnet, *History of his own Time* III (London 1725) 100.

Sharp, of course, was well-educated. Though by the beginning of the eighteenth century many households were literate, far fewer had had more than a minimum of schooling. Without easily accessible libraries, and where even the average literate home had only two or three books, reading was very restricted. Contemporary accounts suggest that after the Bible, the commonest books to be found were Milton's *Paradise Lost* and Bunyan's *Pilgrim's Progress*. As the century progressed, in nonconformist households these staples were often augmented by one or more of a number of hymn books containing metrical psalms and scriptural hymns by (among others) Isaac Watts and Charles Wesley.

1. John Milton

Sources: JOHN MILTON: *Complete Poetical Works* (ed. H. C. Beeching; Oxford: Oxford UP 1921). – WILLIAM BLAKE: *Complete Writings* (ed. Geoffrey Keynes; Oxford: Oxford UP 1966).
   Selected studies: DE CHATEAUBRIAND, *The Genius of Christianity* (1856, see above); W. EMPSON, *Milton's God* (Chatto 1965); C. S. LEWIS, *A Preface to Paradise Lost* (Oxford: Oxford UP 1967); H. F. FLETCHER, *Milton's Semitic Studies and Some Manifestations of Them in His Poetry* (Chicago 1926); A. D. NUTTALL, *The Alternative Trinity: Gnostic Heresy in Marlowe, Milton, and Blake* (Oxford: Oxford UP 1998); A. J. A. WALDOCK, *Paradise Lost and its Critics* (Gloucester, MA: P. Smith 1959).

Not surprisingly, in the mid-seventeenth century, when John Milton (1608–74) finally decided on a biblical theme for his epic ("long choosing, and beginning late" – he had earlier thought of the Arthurian cycle) the poem embraced both what we would now think of as drama *and* narrative. He was not, however, writing for an illiterate audience, to whom a single monolithic truth had to be conveyed through visual or poetic symbols, but for a Bible-literate Protestant public, created and informed by the 'technologized word' of the printing-press. But if the plot was better-known than ever before, its interpretation was more controversial. The mediaeval Catholic synthesis (real or imaginary) had now fractured into open and rancorous debate, not merely between Catholics and Protestants, but also between a multitude of fissiparous Protestant groups. Though living in an officially Protestant country, after the Restoration of Charles II in 1660, Milton was an identifiable member of a political and religious counter-culture. Like a communist in modern Eastern Europe, he represented a failed revolutionary ideology – one that had seized power and then lost popular support. If the literary genre was one constraining factor in Milton's biblical interpretation, the other was a sense of failure. Blindness was only one outward symbol of a frustration and marginalization that was at once personal and universal. The Fall, for him, was less a theoretical doctrine than an ever-present human reality.

   If this marginalization made Milton unusual among English poets, it also, ironically, brought him closer to the mood of the Hebrew narratives of the deracinated Adam, or the suicidal 'terrorist' Samson, than any of his contemporaries. Unlike the conventional triumphalist story of a Christianity which, despite human depravity, is ultimately victorious, the Old Testament from Genesis onwards records a see-saw of victory and defeat, with the latter finally predominant. Yet by, perhaps, an even stranger irony, Milton was able to imprint his own re-telling of the Genesis story of the Fall on English, and even European, consciousness so effectively that not merely did his version in many cases supplant the biblical one, but also so that within a hundred years his own heretical drama had imperceptibly become main-stream and seemingly orthodox.

So powerful, indeed, had his reputation become that, by the nineteenth century, Milton, the former rebel and yesterday's man, had been quietly reinstated as the great Christian poet. *Paradise Lost* was tacitly assumed as the type of the Christian epic, justifying the "ways of God to man". Few before the nineteenth century drew attention to the cracks, paradoxes, and contradictions that underlay its apparently monolithic biblical structure. Yet they are there for all to see, and the story of the transformation of myth to literature is in large measure, the story of how those problems were addressed.

Yet in theory Milton had no room to manoeuvre. As a deeply religious man, to him the Genesis story was sacrosanct. A poet might augment, but not alter the divinely-inspired Word of God. Yet what of the context of that Word? If the Hebrew universe of Genesis was essentially that of the Babylonians, nowhere is it explicit enough to contradict Milton, living in a post-Galilean world, who knew that the earth, like the seven other known planets, revolved around the sun. Milton's choice of a Ptolemaic system for his poem, in which both sun and moon circled around the earth, is the more extraordinary, since he knew that this represented *neither* the biblical universe, *nor* the real universe revealed by modern science. What it did give him, of course, was a universe where the earth was literally as well as symbolically at the centre of all things, and where, therefore, the events of Eden had a truly cosmic significance. Such choices illustrate very clearly how modern is our distinction between 'fact' and 'fiction' in biblical exegesis. Similarly, Milton had no hesitation in attributing words and motives to his characters for which there was no biblical justification – a convention so common that it is rarely questioned.[2] Truth, for Milton, was still poetic rather than literal.

Other gaps in the Genesis account had already been filled in by Jewish and Christian folklore and commentary. Thus the serpent was held to be Satan, a fallen angel, in disguise – and accordingly, much of *Paradise Lost* is devoted to telling Satan's story, rather than that of Adam and Eve. But on other questions – Why did Eve eat the forbidden fruit? Why should Adam support her? – the biblical account remains enigmatically silent. Central to all these problems is something entirely beyond the scope of the Old Testament, but which had, from Chaucer to Shakespeare, become increasingly central to English literature: the idea of 'character'. Though Milton may not have been aware of it when he began his epic, it was an idea that was to transform both the narrative and, more importantly, the *theology* of the Fall.

For CHATEAUBRIAND, one of the greatest Romantic admirers of Milton, and

---

[2] See A. D. NUTTALL, *Overheard by God: fiction and prayer in Herbert, Milton, Dante and St John* (London: Methuen 1980).

his finest French translator, this was evidence for the *literary* superiority of Christian civilization over its antecedents. Taking *Paradise Lost* as one his prime examples, he argues in *The Genius of Christianity* (1802) that Christianity had transformed the nature of European literature: "... by mingling with the affections of the soul, [it] has increased the resources of drama, whether in the epic or on the stage".[3] Only when Christianity replaced paganism was the modern European idea of character free to develop. It was 'a double religion': "Its teaching has reference to the nature of intellectual being, and also to our own nature: it makes the mysteries of the Divinity and the mysteries of the human heart go hand-in-hand; and, by removing the veil that conceals the true God, it also exhibits man just as he is. Such a religion must necessarily be more favourable to the delineation of *characters* than another which dives not into the secret of the passions. The fairer half of poetry, the dramatic, received no assistance from polytheism, for morals were separated from mythology".[4]

This new idea of literary character affects even that most difficult problem lurking almost unexamined in the briefer biblical narrative: *at what point* did the Fall actually occur? In Genesis there is little gap between temptation and deed, but by making his protagonists weigh the consequences, Milton raises the question of whether, by imagining the outcome, they had *already*, in effect, sinned. This certainly follows Jesus' insistence that contemplating adultery is tantamount to committing it. But Milton introduces a further complication. Milton's Eve is initially altruistic – she will help Adam. When having eaten, she brings the fruit to Adam, he, however, has no illusions about the outcome. Instead, without replying directly, he realistically surveys his options – including that of leaving her to her fate:

> Should God create another Eve, and I
> Another rib afford, yet loss of thee
> Would never from my heart: no, no ! I feel
> The link of nature draw me, flesh of flesh,
> Bone of my bone thou art, and from thy state
> Mine never shall be parted, bliss or woe.

As critics have subsequently noted, this is less a matter of sinning in thought before the action, than of *loyalty* afterwards.[5] Adam is standing by his wife. Although he knows the consequences, he also knows the worse those are, the more she will need him. This deliberate suffering with the sinner, of course, effectively narrows the traditional Christian contrast between Adam and Christ, the 'second Adam', who took human flesh and identified with humanity to redeem us from the sin of the original Adam. The difference is that Adam 'identified' with Eve by sinning *with* her, whereas Christ remained sinless. But as feminists may quickly observe, the effect of shifting Adam's motives only increases Eve's responsibility for human sin.

The Fall has two elements: first, an arbitrary prohibition. The tree is evi-

---

[3] de Chateaubriand, The Genius of Christianity (1856) 299.
[4] Ibid. 232.
[5] See E. SMITH, *Some versions of the Fall: the myth of the Fall in English Literature* (Pittsburgh: University of Pittsburgh Press 1973).

dently put there as a test. If not, why have it there at all? Secondly, it is "the tree of the knowledge of good and evil". In one sense this is simply circular: if we define 'evil' in terms of disobedience to God's (here, arbitrary) commands, then to eat of the fruit is, by definition, to 'know' evil, and, contrarywise, to 'know' the good lost. But this is a sense of 'good' and 'evil' that few but the strictest Calvinist would readily acknowledge. Milton was certainly a Calvinist of sorts, but was there more to the Fall than breaking an arbitrary taboo?

The problem is complicated by the explicitly sexual secondary meaning of the word 'knowledge' within the biblical narrative.[6] Without waiting, as Genesis does, for the expulsion from Eden before indulging in such 'knowledge', Milton makes sex the immediate consequence of the Fall – thus helping, incidentally, to pass any time between the eating of the fruit and the 'cool of the day' when God took his walk in the garden:[7]

> But that false fruit
> Far other operation first displayed,
> Carnal desire inflaming: he on Eve
> Began to cast lascivious eyes; she him
> As wantonly repaid; in lust they burn...
>
> Her hand he seized; and to a shady bank,
> Thick overhead with verdant roof embowered,
> He led her, nothing loath; flowers were the couch,
> Pansies and violets, and ashphodel,
> And hyacinth; earth's freshest, softest lap.
> There they their fill of love and love's disport
> Took largely, of their mutual guilt the seal,
> The solace of their sin; till dewey sleep
> Oppressed them, wearied with their amorous play.

This cross-linking of sex with the Fall has, of course, an inner logic within the literal story. Unfallen humanity, we must suppose, was destined to be immortal, and, therefore, having no need of reproduction, had also no need of sex. But for most humans sex has other pleasant and less functional uses. Milton is here, as so often, significantly ambiguous. On the one hand, he stresses that their dash into the undergrowth is 'lascivious', 'wanton', and 'lustful'; on the other hand, he also makes the whole exercise sound (to fallen ears) remarkably attractive. Certainly the effect of linking sex with the Fall, in both biblical and Miltonic versions, has been to suggest that there is an inherently 'fallen', if not downright evil, quality to sex. But Milton's own life (not to mention his treatise on Divorce) indicates a powerful sex-drive. He was not merely a political rebel, but a sexual one. His masque, *Comus*, is a debate about the nature of chastity, and though the Lady finally defeats Comus, the evil enchanter, his account of the joys of sex can rank with any love-poem in English.

But, of course, for Milton the Fall was not just a human event. For all the stress on justifying "the ways of God to man", Satan's story (and his character) are as important in *Paradise Lost* as that of Adam and Eve. William Blake's famous comment in *The Marriage of Heaven and Hell* (1783) that "Milton was of

---

6   See Gen 4:1 "And Adam knew Eve his wife; and she conceived ...".
7   *Paradise Lost* IX, 1011–16; 1037–45.

the Devil's party without knowing it" has been hotly debated ever since. For his entire life Milton had fought the principles of divine autocracy in the form of the Stuart monarchy, and it would be hardly surprising if he did not have some unacknowledged sympathy with the 'parliament' of the rebel angels.[8] Moreover at the heart of the extra-human Fall is a drama of character that is specifically not *Christian* at all. The reason for Satan's initial revolt is the *creation* of Jesus, the Son, whom Milton, for good reason usually calls the 'Messiah', rather than by name as the Second Person of the Trinity. There is good reason for this. Milton, of course, is not a Trinitarian in the normal sense. His Son is *not* co-eternal with the Father, but begotten by him at some later period. Not merely is he *not* co-eternal with the Father, however, he is *not even* co-eternal with the angelic host. It is Satan's rage at being so displaced by this latest of new-comers that leads eventually to his revolt and ejection from Heaven (Book V).

But there is another anomaly to Milton's God that is, if anything, more disquieting. So far from being the Jehovah of the Old Testament, Milton's God resembles Aristotle's 'unmoved mover'. Perfection, according to the Greek argument, is stasis – in effect, a condition of suspended animation. To act is to provoke change, so the syllogism runs, and any change acknowledges that the previous state was in some way less than perfect. Ergo, God is incapable of action. This, to modern ears, convoluted logic, is the reason why God, when faced by Satan's revolt, is limited to sending first two Archangels, and then (when Satan produces a military stand-off by his invention of gunpowder!) finally his Son. Divine omnipotence (if such it be) can only be manifested through the actions of the Messiah, who more resembles a hero from *The Lord of the Rings*, than the Jesus of the Gospels (Book VI).

Though some critics, such as C. S. Lewis, have detected a progressive degeneration in Satan's character between his first ejection from heaven in Books I and II of *Paradise Lost*, and the reptilian tempter (toad and serpent) in Books XV and X, for many readers there remains something inescapably heroic, if not admirable, in Satan's lonely Byronic struggle against hopeless odds in perverting human innocence – not without, one might add, a certain degree of co-operation from Adam and Eve. For most readers Milton's Satan has a fascinatingly tragic stature.

In lasting power and literary influence *Paradise Lost* is not merely one of the great poems of the English language, but of Europe. By the end of the eighteenth century it had been translated in Swedish, Dutch (twice), German (four times), Italian (four times), and Spanish. In France it was translated or read in the original so often that a school of imitators – known as the 'French Miltonians' – were one of the dominant schools of the eighteenth century. Perhaps the greatest French, and in some ways the ultimate romantic translation of Milton was that of Chateaubriand (1836).

But as we have seen, the question of its scriptural interpretation is more complex. Some have argued that such revisions were an inevitable result of

---

[8] See, for instance, Empson, Milton's God (1965); Lewis, Preface (1967); Waldock, Paradise Lost and its Critics (1959).

turning the barebones biblical narrative into a twelve-book epic, and so exposing contradictions and problems that were always inherent in the original myth. Moreover, it was only by blowing it up to such gigantic proportions, and so questioning the nature of God's prohibition on eating the forbidden fruit, the motivations of Adam, Eve and the serpent, that later generations could come to question the historical plausibility of the whole myth, and so open the way to higher criticism.[9] What is clear is that Milton had transformed a story previously understood as one of disobedience and divine punishment into a much more controversial debate over justice, motivation, and responsibility, while at the same time creating the impression that such a radical revision was both orthodox and mainstream in its doctrine.

2. *Pilgrim's Progress* of John Bunyan

Sources: JOHN BUNYAN: *Pilgrim's Progress from this World to that Which is to Come* (ed. J. B. Wharey; 2nd edn.; Oxford: Clarendon Press 1960).

Studies: E. AUERBACH, 'Figura' (tr. R. Mannheim), in: idem, *Scenes from the Drama of European Literature* (New York: Meridian 1959); B. E. BATSON, *'Grace Abounding' and the 'Pilgrim's Progress': an overview of literary studies* (New York: Garland 1988); 1960–87; A. MINNIS, *Mediaeval Theory of Authorship* (London: Scholars Press 1984); A. D. NUTTALL, *Two Concepts of Allegory: a study of Shakespeare's 'The Tempest' and the logic of allegorical expression* (London: Routledge 1967); *'Pilgrim's Progress': Critical and Historical Views* (ed. Vincent Newey; Liverpool: Liverpool UP 1980).

Exactly when the main line of English fiction passed over from verse to prose is more a matter of definition than dating, but most would put it in the early nineteenth century, and outside the scope of this volume. Nevertheless, the contrast between the self-consciously high-art of Milton's poetry and the no-less consciously vulgar and low-status prose of John Bunyan (1628–88) is important. Whereas Milton's models were Homer and Virgil, Bunyan's were popular contemporary pamphlets and broadsheets. Only in retrospect is it possible to see the degree to which Bunyan's vulgar masterpiece was a key point in the growth of English prose fiction.

In one respect, however, the classical tradition remained central. Though there is allegory in the Old Testament,[10] it is uncharacteristic. Only later, under Hellenistic influence, were Jewish commentators to use allegory to interpret, for instance, the Song of Solomon. For the new Hellenistic Christian communities scattered around the eastern Mediterranean much of the Hebrew canon involved Jewish rituals which had little or no relevance, and, in some cases, actually seemed to contradict the narratives, laws, and even ethical teachings of the New Testament. Allegory provided the perfect tool of appropriation. Soon the general claim that Christianity was the key to understanding the Hebrew Scriptures – the message of Philip to the Ethiopian in Acts 8 – was

---

[9] See Prickett, Reading the Text (1991), esp. Ch. 3 ("England and France in the Eighteenth Century", by F. Deconnink-Brossard) and Ch. 4 ("Romantics and Victorians: from Typology to Symbolism", by S. Prickett).

[10] See, for instance, Nathan's denunciation of David (2 Sam 12:1–15).

supported by an increasingly elaborate system of figurative and allegorical interpretation in which even pagan classical texts were given Christian readings. Thus Virgil's *Aeneid* was also read as an allegory of the Christian soul's journey through life.

In the process the idea of allegory (from the Greek *allegoria*) itself underwent considerable change. The new Christian sense differed from the classical sense of a fiction with another meaning – as in Aesop – in that what was believed to be the historical actuality of the story served to guarantee its inner spiritual meaning.[11] Even more important, allegorization of the canon further helped to prize stories loose from their original setting and to give them the possibility of universal significance. For ERICH AUERBACH this new Christian interpretative theory was an essential ingredient in its becoming a world religion.

> Figural interpretation changed the Old Testament from a book of laws and a history of the people of Israel into a series of figures of Christ and the Redemption – so Celtic and Germanic peoples, for example, could accept the Old Testament as part of the universal religion of salvation and a necessary component of the equally magnificent and universal vision of history conveyed to them along with this religion... Its integral, firmly teleological, view of history and the providential order of the world gave it the power to capture the imagination... of the convert nations. Figural interpretation was a fresh beginning and a rebirth of man's creative powers.[12]

In effect, the tool for the Christian appropriation of the Hebrew Scriptures had become that of the conversion of Europe. As AUERBACH also observes, this appropriation was accompanied by an outburst of creative energies – much of it devoted to increasingly ingenious biblical interpretations. By the Middle Ages even the literal meaning of Paul's epistles were secondary to figurative ones.

The effect of this, now almost-invisible, tradition upon the subsequent development of European literature can scarcely be over-estimated. Until almost the end of the eighteenth century the literal meaning of the Bible was only *one* among many ways of understanding it. Not merely did allegorical, figural, and typological modes of reading co-exist with the literal, but, because more universal, they were often given higher status. Moreover, such multi-levelled modes of reading the Bible also influenced the way other books were read. Allegorical levels in Dante's *Divine Comedy*, or the popular mediaeval love-story, *The Romance of the Rose*, were not optional extras, but a normal and integral part of what was expected from books. The tradition of descriptive names for characters, familiar to us from the mediaeval play, *Everyman*, continues in such characters as Sir Politick Would-Be, in Ben Johnson's *Volpone*, and runs through into the English novel. One thinks of Fielding's Squire Allworthy in *Tom Jones*, Pip in Dickens' *Great Expectations*, or even Mr. Chasuble in Wilde's *The Importance of Being Earnest*. Similarly, the idea of a primary literal meaning to a given text is an essentially modern one – dating, in effect,

---

[11] M. REEVES, "The Bible and Literary Authorship in the Middle Ages", in: Prickett, Reading the Text (1991) 17.

[12] Auerbach, Figura (1959) 28.

from the rise in status and popularity of the novel. *Pilgrim's Progress*, though certainly a popular low-status work, draws on a fifteen-hundred year-old allegorical tradition as venerable as anything in Milton. For Bunyan and his contemporaries, to be allegorical *was* to be biblical. Moreover, this was Christian allegory. Not merely is the name of the principal character 'Christian', but, by definition, he is a 'real' person – you, me, everyman. The reality of the Old Testament figures is both superseded and at the same time internalised, by putting the reader at the centre of the narrative. Yet to read *Pilgrim's Progress* simply in allegorical terms is to miss both its complexity and the source of its enduring popularity.

In classical allegory there is an immediate and complete correspondence between the 'deep' message and the 'surface' narrative. In his essay "Poetic Diction and Legal Fiction" OWEN BARFIELD designates these levels as A and B respectively.

> We feel that B, which is actually said, ought to be necessary, even inevitable in some way. It ought to be in some sense the best, if not the only way of expressing A satisfactorily. The mind should dwell on it as well as on A and thus the two should be somehow inevitably fused together into one simple meaning. But if A is too obvious and could be equally or almost as well expressed by other and more direct means, then the mind jumps straight to A, remains focused on it, and loses interest in B, which shrinks to a kind of dry and hollow husk.[13]

Most allegories, from Aesop's fables, to Jesus' parables, to Orwell's *Animal Farm*, entice the reader by suggesting that A is in some way secret – to be puzzled over, guessed at, or known only to initiates. In contrast, *Pilgrim's Progress* actually *invites* us to read B in terms of A.

> The names, Christian, Faithful, Vanity Fair, Doubting Castle, and so on, flaunt their allegorical status, and seemingly leave no room for debate over interpretation. Yet the real 'secret' here is that, against the odds, B comes to dominate A. Christian, Faithful, and Hopeful are not mere cardboard figures. They rapidly acquire personal attributes. We *want* to know what happens to them; how Christian escapes from the dungeons of the Giant despair; what happens when he crosses the river to the Celestial City. Even when, as in the case of Faithful's trial and martyrdom in Vanity Fair, the model appears to be the trial of Stephen in Acts 6–7, the biblical origin is overlaid by the immediacy of a corrupt English Court remarkably like that which eventually led to Bunyan's own twelve-year imprisonment in Bedford. Similarly the exchanges of Giant Despair and his wife have qualities more in common with Chaucer than with the Bible. There is, presumably, no philosophical or theological reason for Despair to be dominated by Diffidence. To reveal that domination in pillow-talk belongs more to the world of the mediaeval fabliaux than to Calvin's *Institutes*. In other words, just as in Milton, what began as animated theological concepts become characters with personal problems, motivations and development. To read the story, B, simply in terms of A is to miss the degree to which *Pilgrim's Progress* is better understood as a transitional work, anticipating the modern novel.

But Bunyan, of course, also draws on two other very ancient literary traditions: those of the dream and of the journey. Stories of dreams and visions are a central part of the Bible narrative. Both Isaiah and Ezekiel begin with visionary experiences, and the New Testament ends, of course, with Revelation, perhaps the most celebrated vision of all time. Many mediaeval poems use dreams

---

[13] O. BARFIELD, "Poetic Diction and Legal Fiction", in: *The Importance of Language* (ed. Max Black; Eaglewood Cliffs, NJ: Prentice-Hall 1962) 54.

(*The Pearl*) and even one of Shakespeare's plays is presented as a hoax dream (*The Taming of the Shrew*). The extended dream provides an alternative, parallel, reality in which the present can be de-familiarised, allegorised, or in some other way, presented in a new light. Thus Jacob's dream in Genesis 28 allows him to discover that *where he is*, on the run, sleeping rough with his head on a stone, is none other than the gate of heaven, with angels ascending and descending before him.

Thus even for a semi-literate readership, familiar with little more than the Bible, the idea of a dream taps into a rich vein of associative imagery. Bunyan's story becomes part of a long tradition of revelatory dreams in which the true nature of the contemporary world is divinely revealed. Similarly, it allows him to present his allegory as intersecting with the real world of his own time – but seeing people, as it were naked, with names that describe who they *truly* are, much as the unfallen language of Adam was supposed to have described things in their essences. Bunyan's constant repetition of phrases such as "and I saw in my dream..." reminds the reader of the privileged viewpoint of the narrator – at once able to speak first-hand of what is going on, yet able to describe scenes, such as Christian's entry to the Celestial City to which no normal author could have access.

The metaphor of a journey, like that of the dream, was, similarly, often used with allegory, most notably by Dante, but also by Spencer in *The Faerie Queene*. For them, as for many Christian writers before and since, the journey as an allegory of the soul's pilgrimage through life was an established literary and devotional trope. Unlike that other conventional metaphor of human life, the four seasons, the journey provides a model not of growth and eventual decay as in nature, but offers the potential for continuous development, from 'start' to 'finish'. Indeed, the metaphor of the journey with a goal – a pilgrimage – can itself be made a metaphor for divine grace *superseding* the law of nature in a Pauline sense.

As Paul was well aware, the Old Testament offers two such models, one, that of Abraham leaving Ur at God's command to journey to the Promised Land, is one of divine guidance; the other, that of the Children of Israel wandering in the desert for forty years, is of divine punishment. Part of Bunyan's skill in *Pilgrim's Progress* is to combine both models in a single narrative. From the first, it is clear to Christian that he has no abiding city here on earth – whether its inhabitants know it or not, he dwells in the City of Destruction, which will suffer the same fate as the cities of the plain, Sodom and Gomorrah. He has no choice but to set out on a journey. The difference between the pilgrims, Christian, Faithful, Hopeful, etc., and the people they encounter, Pliable, at the beginning, and Talkative, Money-Love, By-Ends, etc., on their journey, is that the latter are also travelling – but, like the wanderers in the desert, actually going nowhere.

There is also another group of characters who rather than going nowhere are fixtures: helpers, such the Porter and the Evangelist near the beginning, and later the four virgins, Discretion, Piety, Charity and Prudence; and those who would hinder – the fiend Apollyon, Giant Despair and his wife, Diffidence, and of course the whole motley crew in Vanity Fair. Their narrative function is, of course, to help or hinder the progress of the pilgrims, but their presence raises an important pro-

blem about the whole nature of allegory. As A. D. NUTTALL has pointed out,[14] there is always difficulty with allegorical characters named after absolutes: no one could (presumably) be more discreet
than Discretion, more charitable than Charity, etc. This is all right for some qualities, but pilgrims
should always beware of battles against someone called Courage or even Victory, because they are
unlikely to win. Bunyan cleverly sidesteps some of this problem by avoiding absolutes as opponents
– either with non-allegorical figures, such as Apollyon, or with names that suggest remediable internal qualities, like the robbers Mistrust, Guilt, and Little-Faith.

What is happening, in other words, is that two different kinds of allegorical
'characters' are emerging. One is, as it were, animated character-traits, personal qualities, good or bad, that must be encouraged or held in check; the other
is philosophical absolutes which the pilgrims encounter. Thus, in the Delectable Mountains, Christian and Hopeful (the former) encounter helpful shepherds, Knowledge and Experience (the latter). The other shepherds, Watchful
and Sincere, as their names suggest, seem both grammatically and structurally
misplaced – to match the first two their names should be nouns ('watchfulness'
and 'sincerity') and not adjectives, which are more common among the pilgrims. But the very confusion of grammatical categories suggests that so far
from being a carefully worked-out plan, the narrative itself is forcing Bunyan
in certain directions.

In short, what had begun in *Pilgrim's Progress* as three very stylised rhetorical tropes of contemporary Biblical exegesis – allegory, dream, and the metaphor of pilgrimage – are all in the process of being re-shaped into something
that, once again, begins to look much more like the modern novel, in which
character is destiny, and motivation is complex and internalised. That, in turn,
was to totally re-shape the reading of the Bible.[15]

With the growth of prose narrative and its new associated art-form, the so-
called 'novel', it comes as little surprise to find that by the end of the eighteenth
century the Bible was being read almost as if it were a contemporary work of
fiction – not so much in the sense that people questioned its truth (though
some were prepared to do just that) but in the wake of Milton and Bunyan
even devotional readers looked at biblical stories in terms of plot, character,
or motivation, rather than in the typological ways that had once been normal.
In one of his numerous ironic asides to the reader in *Tom Jones*, Fielding warns
that we must not be too hasty in our judgements of the plot, because, unlike
him, we are not the creator, and can have no sense of the whole picture that
will be eventually revealed. This oblique reference to himself as a Calvinistic
God is less blasphemous than prophetic. Here, for instance, is precisely the
same argument, in reverse, only a few years from a popular biblical commentary on the Old Testament:

> The Books that follow, as far as the BOOK OF ESTHER, are called the HISTORICAL
> BOOKS. The Histories they contain differ from all the other histories that ever were written,
> for they give an account of the ways of GOD; and explain *why* GOD *protected and rewarded*
> some persons and nations, and *why* he *punished* others; also, *what led* particular persons men-

---

    [14] Nuttall, Two Concepts of Allegory (1967).
    [15] See STEPHEN PRICKETT, *Origins of Narrative: the Romantic Appropriation of the Bible* (Cam-
bridge: Cambridge UP 1996).

tioned in Scripture to *do* certain things for which they were approved or condemned; whereas writers who compose histories in a common way, without being *inspired of God*, can only form guesses and conjectures concerning God's dealings with mankind, neither can they know what passed in the hearts of those they write about; such knowledge as this, belongs to *God* alone, whose ways are *unsearchable and past finding out*, and *to whom all hearts are open, all desires known*![16]

It is only a comparatively short step from regarding God as the supreme novelist, to reading the Bible as 'literature' in an aesthetic sense, though (as German Romantics, such as Schleiermacher were to show) this could enhance rather than detract from its devotional meaning. Meanwhile, lyric poets and hymnwriters were showing the way to quite different methods of reading the Bible.

3. Scriptural Interpretation in Hymns: George Herbert, Isaac Watts and Charles Wesley

Sources: ISAAC WATTS: *Hymns and Spiritual Songs* (London 1709); *Horae Lyricae* I–III (London 1706–09, 6th edn. 1731). – CHARLES WESLEY: *Short Hymns on Select Passages of Holy Scripture* (London 1796); *An Annotated Anthology of Hymns* (ed. J. R. Watson; Oxford: Oxford UP 2002).
Studies: I. BRADLEY, *Abide with Me: The World of Victorian Hymns* (London: SCM Press 1997); B. MANNING, *The Hymns of Wesley and Watts* (London: Epworth Press 1942); J. R. WATSON, *The English Hymn: a critical and historical study* (Oxford: Oxford UP 1997).

Congregational singing was central to the new Protestant orders of service that replaced the Mass. In Continental Europe many of the Reformers had also been poets and composers. Luther and, later, Zinzendorf, wrote some of the great hymns of German Protestantism. The Churches of Knox, in Scotland, and Henry VIII in England had been less fortunate, and despite the adherence of some of the finest poets in the language during the century after the Reformation, including Donne, Herbert, Marvell and Milton, English-speaking Protestantism relied almost exclusively on metrical versions of the Psalms – particularly the popular versions of Thomas Sternhold (c. 1500–49) and John Hopkins (d. 1570). But as THOMAS FULLER has remarked, Sternhold and Hopkins were "men whose piety was better than their poetry, and they had drunk more of Jordan than of Helicon".[17]

Not all poets of English Puritanism were of Milton's stature. The first English Hymn Book, *Hymns and Spiritual Songs* (1641) was by George Wither (1588–1667). During the Civil War as a major in the Parliamentary forces, he was taken prisoner, and was about to be hanged until Sir John Denham, another poet, serving the Royalist army, intervened, arguing that: "his Majesty really must not hang George Wither, for so long as Wither lived no one would account himself the worst poet in England". Wither was spared, but it was not until the early eighteenth century, with the publication of the first collection of

---

[16] Mrs TRIMMER, *Help to the Unlearned in the Study of the Holy Scriptures* (Sec. edn. 1806) iii.
[17] See J. OTTENHOFF, "Recent Studies In Metrical Psalms", *English Literary Renaissance* 33 (2003) 252–75.

hymns by Isaac Watts (1674–1748), also entitled *Hymns and Spiritual Songs* (1707–09) that the transition from congregational psalm-singing to hymn-singing was really achieved.

In his lifetime Watts is said to have produced over 6.000 hymns, of which the greatest still rank among the best-known of all time. "Our God, our help in ages past", "Before Jehovah's awful throne", "Jesus shall reign where'er the sun", "When I survey the wondrous cross", or "Come, let us join our cheerful song", are all widely reproduced and sung today. Yet though almost all his hymns are closely based on identifiable passages of Scripture, for the most part they amplify and paraphrase rather than interpret those texts. There are, of course, two good reasons for this. The first is the nonconformist belief that Scripture needed no intermediary or interpretation: "God is his own inter-preter/And he will make it plain".[18] The second is the perhaps less-conscious assumption that hymns should be essentially expressive rather than explora-tory. They expressed the communal emotions of the congregation: repentance, hope, joy, grief – even doubt and fear – but, unlike devotional verse, they rarely offer new theological metaphors or what A. FARRER has called "a rebirth of images".[19] Watts's images are commonly a careful patchwork of biblical re-ference in terms that every member of a congregation might recognise. Thus his famous paraphrase of Psalm 90, "Our God, our help in ages past" immedi-ately links Old with New Testament:

> Like flowery fields the nations stand
> Pleas'd with the morning light;
> The flowers beneath the mower's hand
> Lie with'ring ere 'tis night.

Perhaps the nearest Watts comes to originality are in the lines from "When I survey the wondrous cross". Here the blood of love mixes with the tears of sor-row in Christ's death,

> See from his head, his hands, his feet
> Sorrow and love flow mingled down!
> Did e'er such love and sorrow meet,
> Or thorns compose so rich a crown?

Yet though there is an almost metaphysical *frisson* in the sheer physicality of the image, neither paradox changes our perception of Christ's Passion – nor was it intended to do so. Similarly, Watts's view of Creation and humanity in the Great Chain of Being is entirely conventional.

> Lord, what is worthless man,
> That thou shouldst love him so?
> Next to thine angels he is placed,
> And lord of all below.
>
> Thine honours crown his head,
> While beasts, like slaves, obey;

---

[18] William Cowper, "God Moves in a Mysterious Way" (1744) lines 23/4.
[19] A. FARRER, *A Rebirth of Images: the Making of St John's Apocalypse* (London: Dacre Press 1944).

> And birds that cut the air with wings,
> And fish that cleave the sea.
>
> How rich thy bounties are!
> And wondrous are thy ways:
> Of dust and worms thy power can frame
> A monument of praise.

If we compare this with, say, George Herbert (1593–1638), writing almost a century before, we find already far bolder and more complex images. Here, for instance, he explores in more compressed metaphors the Creation story that was to so fascinate Milton only a few years later.

> When God at first made man,
> Having a glass of blessings standing by,
> "Let us", said he, "pour on him all we can.
> Let the world's riches, which dispersed lie,
> Contract into a span".

There is nothing un-biblical about Herbert's image – indeed, it is directly based on the Hebrew ceremonial anointing found throughout the Old Testament as a symbol of God's election – but we are in a much more creative world of poetic metaphor. 'Contract' at this period was still used primarily in its legal sense, especially in marriages, and the word 'riches' in the line above might imply a dowry – even a wedding-present from God. But, at the same time, the word 'dispersed' reminds us of the other meaning of 'contract': 'to reduce in size by drawing together'. This was in fact a very *new* meaning of the word in the early seventeenth century, and Herbert is clearly making a pun between the older sense, which implied the Hebrew 'Law', and the new, suggesting perhaps the New Covenant, in which Christ, as the Second Adam, might draw things finally together where the first Adam had failed.

The 'span' into which the contraction is made is, of course, a biblical unit of measurement: an outstretched hand from the tip of the thumb to the little finger (conventionally taken as nine inches or 22.8 cm). From this comes the obvious metaphor: a small measure of space or time. As a sub-text to this is a sixteenth-century use of the word as a rope or cable by which a ship was moored – the more relevant in view of the poem's title: *The Pulley*. The riches of the world, which had originally led man away from God and into sin, can now be reinterpreted under the New Covenant, and drawing together in the little space of a human life may eventually bind mankind back to God.

Just over two hundred years later, in 1746, Charles Wesley (1707–88) who – unusually for the time – knew Herbert well, returned to this image in one of his greatest Christmas hymns:

> Let earth and heaven combine,
> Angels and men agree,
> To praise in songs divine
> The incarnate Deity,
> Our God contracted to a span,
> Incomprehensibly made man.[20]

---

[20] *Nativity Hymns* (1749).

The reference to Herbert is obvious, but for the riches of the world Wesley has substituted those of God himself. Man is not now turning *to* God; God is turning *into* man. In the Incarnation, the boundless and infinite is 'incomprehensibly' reduced to the quantifiable and tiny. The primary meaning of 'span' is still the allotted extent of human life, but its linear form is not ignored: the length of a tiny new-born baby has become the unit by which all creation must be measured. But in the century since Herbert the word 'span' had acquired other meanings. New in Wesley's time (1725) was its use for bridges: here the arch linking earth and heaven in new unity – in the words of a later stanza, "Widest extremes to join". Older Christian metaphors, such as the Pope as 'supreme Pontiff', are superseded (or 'abridged'). For the Arminian Wesley, *all* may now have access to God through Christ.

Similarly the word 'contracted' had changed. Though, as we have seen, the idea of the New Covenant is never absent from Herbert's poem, for Wesley it is central. By his own 'contract', God is committed to this new 'span'. This shift in theological emphasis is reinforced by the new, early eighteenth-century meaning of 'contracted' as 'restricted' (1710). The Incarnation is a self-imposed restriction on divinity. No wonder that the making of God into man is 'incomprehensible' – both in its modern sense of 'not to be understood' and in the still-current older meaning of 'not to be grasped', either physically (even by the span of an outstretched hand) nor figuratively, 'not to be contained within limits'. The original meaning of 'span', the verb, is 'to grasp' in a sense that corresponds precisely with the physical sense of 'comprehend' – as in John 1:5.[21] Thus, Jesus, the 'incarnate Deity', is the shining of the light that could neither be understood nor extinguished. The syntax of the penultimate line is now deeply ambiguous. Is 'made' active or passive? Is Jesus merely allowing himself to be made man, and, through 'contracted' obedience making true man for the first time (the doctrine of the Second Adam) or is he, by the Incarnation, actively 'making' mankind afresh?

Behind such a question lies another important linguistic development. As late as the mid-seventeenth century there was no substantive distinction made between 'compelled' and 'obliged'.[22] It would not, therefore, have been possible for Herbert to raise the question implied by Wesley as to whether the 'contract' *compelled* God to a course of action under the old dispensation of 'law', or whether he acted from the inner moral freedom of the new. Absurd as such a question might be about God, what it foreshadows, of course, is the immanent collapse of the whole system of legal imagery that had been such an integral part of theology from Paul to Calvin. Once this distinction between outer and inner motivation had become part of common speech it was difficult for the legalism of either the Covenant or the Ransom theory of the Atonement to retain its old force.

Herbert and, to an even greater extent, Charles Wesley *think* theologically. Like all great artists, they alter perception so that the reader (or, in the latter case, the singing congregation) sees and experiences the world differently. For Milton and Watts alike the mediaeval hierarchy of angels, men, and animals persists in divinely ordered stasis. Though Archangels in *Paradise Lost* hold what amounts to seminars for our unfallen ancestors, there is little that could be called cooperation. Unlike both Milton and Watts, Wesley has no Calvinistic leanings. Humanity may be fallen, but it is capable of symbolising the Incarnation through art, if not grasping its full mysteries intellectually. He probably believed in angels as literally as Watts, but he is less interested in hierar-

---

[21] "the light shineth in darkness and the darkness comprehended it not".
[22] A fact which enabled Hobbes in *Leviathan* (1651) to maintain that there could be no such thing as guilt.

chy. The ways of God are as inscrutable to angels as to man, but the *whole* of creation joins in welcoming the Incarnation – a theme emphatically repeated in what is probably his best-known hymn, the carol "Hark the herald angels sing", where we are *all* urged to "join the triumph of the skies", proclaiming the birth of Christ in Bethlehem. The constraining legalism of the Old Dispensation has given way to the free cooperation of the New.

> Unsearchable the love
> That hath the Saviour brought;
> The grace is far above
> Or man or angel's thought:
> Suffice for us that God, we know,
> Our God, is manifest below.

Once again, the punch is in the last line (one repeated almost exactly at the end of stanza 4 – see below). The primary meaning of 'manifest' is, of course, 'shown', or 'made visible' – a sense that links it immediately with the Epiphany, when Jesus was 'shown' to the wise men. But other meanings lurk in a complex sub-text. A manifest is also the contents of a ship's cargo (harking back to the earlier idea of 'span' as a mooring rope). We do not know the full 'freight' that the Incarnation has brought to earth, but it is there to be unloaded by countless Christian generations – past, present (including Wesley himself) and to come. Finally, and almost crudely, the word can be split into component syllables: 'man', 'i', 'fest'. Man can henceforth be 'in festival' – rejoicing in what has been brought.

> He deigns in flesh to appear
> Widest extremes to join;
> To bring our vileness near
> And make us all divine:
> And we the life of God shall know,
> For God is manifest below.

Again hierarchy is swept aside. Though the 'widest extremes' (now bridged by the 'span' of Incarnation), may bring home as never before the 'vileness' of our condition, that is only the prelude to making us 'all divine'. Since all value is untimely derived from God, angels and men, whatever their differences in capacity or moral status, 'combine' in equality at least before Him. A new democratic theology is being born that would, in the course of the next century, make it impossible to defend not merely social and political rank as part of a divinely ordered social structure, but even slavery itself – Charles Wesley, like his brother, John, had been to Georgia, then one of the centres of the slave-trade, and had not liked what he had seen.

  In the process, the biblical idea of the Creation has been re-read not merely in the light of the Incarnation, but in the light of eighteen hundred years of Christian tradition. As much a child of the Enlightenment as an evangelical, Wesley would not have been as aware as the next generation of the historical difference between the biblical world and his own – the rhetoric of the Methodist revival stresses personal immediacy rather than distance – but there is nevertheless a fundamental difference between the world of the early seventeenth century, and that of the late eighteenth. Herbert is still in touch with the mythological world of the Bible in a way that Wesley could not be – like Milton, Herbert belonged to a world where man still occupied the centre stage as of right. Between them and Wesley stand Newton and Locke, and the whole imaginative shift of key encapsulated by the phrase the 'scientific revolution'. For Wesley the Incarnation is no less miraculous than for Herbert, but because the physical universe had expanded and achieved a different kind of reality for the eighteenth century, the nature of a 'miracle' had also changed. Herbert would never have claimed to have understood either the Creation or the Incarnation, but he would not (I think) have described it as 'incomprehensible'. In the post-Newtonian universe the gap between humanity and nature was more consciously mysterious; the 'widest extremes' to be spanned had grown wider.

Not all Wesley's writing is of this poetic and prophetic intensity, nor was he alone in raising many of these issues, but his writing was one stream contributing to a steady shift in the climate of late eighteenth-century thought and feeling. The anti-slavery movement was itself only part of a wider change in sensibility (a word that had itself then only just appeared in the language) that we call 'romanticism'. Similar movements were to occur at almost the same time in Germany and France, but Wesley was at least one reason why English romanticism was to be both more socially engaged, and more biblically based than the corresponding Continental movements.[23]

---

[23] It is significant that whereas 'reactionary' Britain abolished the slave trade in 1807, the French Revolutionary National Assembly had committed itself to keeping slavery. See S. Prickett, *Romanticism & Religion: the tradition of Coleridge and Wordsworth in the Victorian Church* (Cambridge: Cambridge UP 1976), and idem, Origins of Narrative (1996).

CHAPTER THIRTY-NINE

Hermeneutics in Hasidism

By Moshe Idel, Jerusalem

Sources: '*Or ha-'Emet* (Zhitomir; repr. Benei Beraq 1967); Aharon Kohen of Apta, '*Or ha-Ganuz le-Tzaddiqim* (Zolkiew 1800); Zeev Wolf of Zhitomir, '*Or ha-Me'ir* (Perizek 1815); *Maggid Devarav Le-Ya'aqov* (ed. R. Schatz-Uffenheimer; Jerusalem: The Magnes Press 1976); Dov Baer of Medzerich, '*Or Torah* (Jerusalem 1968); Isaac Aizik Haver, '*Or Torah* (pr. in: '*Amudei ha-Torah;* ed. Shmuel Mayevski; Jerusalem 1971); *Botzina' di-Nehora'* (repr. 1985); *Degel Mahaneh Ephrayyim* (Jerusalem 1995); Levi Isaac, '*Imrei Tzaddiqim* (Zhitomir 1900); *Liqqutei Moharan* (Benei Berak 1972); *Liqqutei Torah* (Benei Beraq 1983); *Liqqutim Yeqarim* (Jerusalem 1981); Menahem Mendel of Rimanov, '*Ilana' de-Hayyei* (Pietrkov 1908); *Sefer Yakhin w-Vo'az* (Ostraha 1795); Jacob Kaidaner, *Sippurim Nora'im* (ed. G. Nigal; Jerusalem 1992); *Qedushat Levi* (Jerusalem 1993); Aharon ha-Levi Horowitz of Zhitomir, *Toledot 'Aharon* (Lemberg 1985).

Studies: A. GREEN, *Tormented Master: A Life of Rabbi Nahman of Bratslav* ([1979] New York: Schocken Books 1981); idem, "The Zaddik as Axis Mundi in Later Judaism", *JAAR* 45 (1977) 327–47; A. Y. HESCHEL, *The Theology of Ancient Theology* (London: Soncino 1962; Heb.); M. IDEL, *Hasidism: Between Ecstasy and Magic* (Albany: SUNY Press 1995); idem, "*Deus sive Natura*, the Metamorphosis of a Dictum from Maimonides to Spinoza", in: *Maimonides and the Sciences* (ed. S. Cohen / H. Levine; Dordrecht: Kluwer Academic Publishers 2000); idem, "From the 'Hidden Light' to the 'Light within the Torah': A Chapter in the Phenomenology of Jewish Mysticism", *On Light, Migvvan De'ot beYisrael* 11 (2002) 46–60 (Heb.); idem, *Absorbing Perfections: Kabbalah and Interpretation* (New Haven: Yale UP 2002); idem, "White Letters: From R. Levi Isaac of Berditchev's Views to Modern Hermeneutics", *Modern Judaism* 26 (2006) 168–92; *In the Praise of the Baal Shem Tov* (tr. Dan ben Amos / J. R. Mintz; Northvale: Aroson 1993); HAYYIM LIEBERMAN, '*Ohel RaHeL* (New York 1980; Heb.); A. RAPOPORT-ALBERT, "God and the Zaddik as the two Focal Points of Hasidic Worship", *History of Religions* 18 (1979) 296–325; R. SCHATZ-UFFENHEIMER, "Hasidism as Mysticism", *Quietistic Elements in Eighteenth Century Hasidic Thought* (Jerusalem: Magnes Press / Princeton: Princeton UP 1993); G. SCHOLEM, *On the Kabbalah and its Symbolism* (tr. R. Manheim; New York: Schocken Books 1969); J. WEISS, "Talmud-Torah le-Shitat R. Israel Besht", in: *Essays Presented to the Chief Rabbi Israel Brodie Israel* (London 1967).

1. From the Oral Community to Written Documents

Hasidism is a revivalist religious movement that started in the regions of Ukraine in the mid-eighteenth century. A paramount popular movement based upon verbal communication, and basically dependent upon the vernacular, Yiddish, no book authored by a Hasidic master has been printed or even written during the first generation of this movement. This is no doubt part of a preference of the oral contact over the written literature. Indeed in a later Hasidic legend, this oral propensity has been put in relief in connection with the founder of the movement R. Israel Ba'al Shem Tov, known by the acronym *ha-Besht*:

> There was a man who wrote down the Torah [= teaching] of the Besht that he heard from him. Once the Besht saw a demon walking and holding a book in his hand. He said to him: "What is the book that you hold in your hand?" He answered him: "This is the book that you have written". The Besht then understood that there was a person who was writing down his Torah. He gathered all his followers and asked them: "Who among you is writing down my Torah?" The man admitted it and he brought the manuscript to the Besht. The Besht examined it and said: "There is not even a single word here that is mine".[1]

However, since 1780, when the first Hasidic book was printed, numerous Hasidic books started to appear in print, and through some decades, Hasidism generated a huge printed literature. Most of those books are sermons delivered in the vernacular but printed in Hebrew, following the pattern of commentaries on the pericopes of the Pentateuch. Hundreds and hundreds of collections of sermons have been published since 1780, imposing Hasidic literature as one of the most productive forms of Jewish creativity in the eighteenth and nineteenth centuries. Thus, though elaborating on the oral teaching of the Besht, the formal focus of the literature are the verses of the Bible, radically reinterpreted. This transition from the centrality of oral preaching to printed texts has first to do with competition over the status of the different disciples of the Besht. Later on, it expresses the need of the Hasidic leader to display his knowledge, not only to his immediate followers, but also in a more classical manner, by addressing a wider audience in Hebrew. Thereby he could compete with other seminal figures in earlier forms of Judaism, who also interpreted the Bible.

2. Exegetical Grids in Hasidism

Hasidic exegesis differs dramatically from most of the Kabbalistic schools that preceded it. Symbolic exegesis based upon the importance of a theosophical understanding of divinity was relegated to the margin. This means that resort to the various nuances of Hebrew words of the Bible as reflecting the characteristics of the ten divine powers, the *sefirot*, or the Lurianic divine countenances, the *partzufin*, was greatly attenuated. In lieu of the tenfold structure, the Hasidic masters conspicuously preferred binary types of oppositions that in their view shape the discourse of the sacred texts: body versus soul, the righteous and the multitude, *gadelut*, grandeur involved in the spiritual state of the mystic, versus *qatenut*, smallness of the spiritual state, God versus nature, study of texts versus devotion, the world of speech versus the world of thought, etc. Often the Hasidic teachers imposed these types of binary relationship upon biblical and Talmudic material, emphasizing the moral and devotional aspects of religion, rather than the theological. By its anthropocentric emphasis, the Hasidic master became much less interested in the Bible as a reflection of the inner and dynamic life of God, than in the understanding of the text as referring to the inner spiritual development of the mystic. From this point of view, Hasidism was closer to the metaphorical approach of the ec-

---

[1] In the Praise of the Baal Shem Tov (1993) 179.

static brand of Kabbalah, which also emphasized the paramount importance of inner transformation.[2]

3. The Divinity within and between the Torah-Letters or Represented by Them

A major development in Jewish mysticism that culminated in Hasidism is the vision of the Torah-text as a direct, non-semantic representation of God. According to a teaching of the Great Maggid:

> He [God], blessed be He, concentrated Himself into the Torah; therefore, when someone speaks on issues of Torah or prayer, let him do it with all his power, since by it [i.e. the utterance] he united himself with Him, blessed be He, since all his power is in the pronounced letter, and He, blessed be He, dwells in the pronounced letter.[3]

The mystical implication of the divine presence within letters will be dealt with below. Here it is important to highlight the sharp formulation of the process of concentration of the divine within letters as part of a cosmogonic event. Moreover, the power mentioned here implies a certain proportion between the loudness of the sound and the amount of divine presence that may enter such a linguistic container. On the other hand, elsewhere in his book he asserts that

> The Torah in its entirety is collected from [the deeds of] righteous men, from Adam, and the forefathers, and Moses, who caused the dwelling of the *Shekhinah* on their deeds, and this is the complete Torah. However, the luminosity of the essence has not been revealed yet, until the Messiah will come and they will understand the luminosity of His essence. And this is the new Torah that goes forth from me, whose meaning is "From My essence".[4]

The Great Maggid argues that the revealed Torah deals with human deeds, and their interaction with the divine. The forefather had been able to cause the descent of the divine presence here below. However, the divine essence in itself is not expounded in the Torah that recounts their deeds, perfect as it is. The luminosity, the new Torah and the divine essence are explicitly related to each other. It is not a new text that is revealed but the depths of the canonical document already in the possession of the Jews. The view that the white letters are the esoteric aspect of the revealed Torah, which consists of the black letters is found in many earlier sources. One of his followers, R. Levi Isaac of Berditchev, was reported to have said:

> We can see by the eye of our intellect why in the Torah handed down to us one letter should not touch the other. The matter is that also the whiteness constitutes letters but we do not know

---

[2] See Idel, Hasidism (1995) 227–38.

[3] 'Or ha-'Emet, fols. 15b–17a. Cp. also Aharon Kohen of Apta, 'Or ha-Ganuz le-Tzaddiqim (1800), fol. 30ab. On other aspects of this text and its context see Schatz-Uffenheimer, Hasidism as Mysticism (1993) 180–82. See also his disciple R. Zeev Wolf of Zhitomir, 'Or ha-Me'ir, fol. 240c, and cp. ibid. fol. 247cd. For the view that light is found in the letters see now Idel, From the 'Hidden Light' (2002) 46–60.

[4] Maggid Devarav Le-Ya'aqov (1976) 17–18. Cp. also the discussion of the same author, ibid. 201–03, and esp. 326; see also R. Aharon of Zhitomir's Toledot 'Aharon I (1985) fol. 5c, where an interesting passage on the forefathers is found. See further R. Dov Baer of Medzerich, 'Or Torah (1968) 47, where the phrase behirut ha-Torah, "the luminosity of the Torah", occurs.

how to read them as [we know] the blackness of the letters. But in the future God, blessed be He, will reveal to us even the whiteness of the Torah. Namely we will [then] understand the white letter in our Torah, and this is the meaning of "A new Torah will go forth from me" that it stands for the whiteness of the Torah, that all the sons of Israel will understand also the letters that are white in our Torah, which was delivered to Moses. But nowadays, the letters of whiteness are concealed from us. But in the Song of the Sea, when it has been said: "This is my Lord, I shall praise Him" [Exod 15:2], it is written in [the writings of] Isaac Luria that "their soul had fled when they heard the song of the angels" and God had opened their ear to hear etc., and this is the reason why the maidservant had seen on the sea [more than Ezekiel] – the whiteness of the letters, she saw what has not been seen etc., because the matter has been concealed until the advent of the Messiah.[5]

Moreover, according to a tradition found in the student of one of the main disciples of the Great Maggid, R. Shneur Zalman of Liady's follower R. Aharon ha-Levi of Staroselye, the 'new Torah' that has not been revealed at the time of creation, is revealed by the performance of the commandments and the study of the Torah in this world, and they will cause the revelation of the secrets of the acts of generation. This is quite a traditional view, that is, in principle, consonant to the Great Maggid's passage. In his own book R. Levi Isaac writes that

It is known that the letters of the Torah have the aspect of inner lights which are revealed according to the order of the emanation of the worlds. And the boundary of the white that encompasses the letters possesses the aspect of the encompassing lights, which are not revealed but are found in a hiddeness, in the aspect of the encompassing light. From this we may understand that also the white boundaries possess also the aspect of letters but they are hidden letters, higher than the revealed letters ... because the aspect of the whiteness which is [identical with] the hidden letters is derived from the revelation of the aspect of the revealed letters and that is the meaning of what has been written:[6] "The maidservant had seen on the [Red] Sea [more than what Ezekiel has seen]" because the revelation of the divinity was so great that even the maidservant was capable of understanding. This is the meaning of the verse "A new Torah will go forth from me": That in the future, when the revelation of the divinity and the Glory of God will be disclosed, and all men will see etc., it means that the revelation of the aspect of the encompassing and the revelation of the aspect of the whiteness, namely the white letters which encompass the revealed letters of the Torah, [will take place] this being the meaning of "A new Torah will go forth from me".[7][8]

Interestingly enough, the theory of the existence of the white letters had an impact on some philosophies of text in recent decades.[9]

An immediate follower of R. Levi Isaac, insists upon the light as divine presence within the Torah-letters:

even now, when a righteous person pronounces the letters in a state of devotion ... he unites the letters to the light of the Infinite ... and ascends higher than all the worlds to the place where

---

[5] *'Imrei Tzaddiqim* (1900) fol. 5b. Here a different translation of a larger portion of the discussion, which was already analyzed by Scholem, On the Kabbalah and its Symbolism (1969) 81–82, has been adduced.

[6] *Mekhilta'*, Beshalah, II. A list of mainly rabbinic sources dealing with this issue is found in Heschel, The Theology of Ancient Judaism, I (1962) 283–84.

[7] Isa 51:4.

[8] *Qedushat Levi* (1993) 327–28. Interestingly enough, this passage is closest to the presentation of one of the most learned among the Kabbalists belonging to the camp of the *Mitnaggedim*, R. Isaac Aizik Haver, *'Or Torah* (1971) 219–20.

[9] See Idel, White Letters: From R. Levi Isaac of Berditchev's Views to Modern Hermeneutics (forthcoming).

the letters are white and are not combined and then he can perform there whatever combination he wants.[10]

Much more graphic is the approach found in other Hasidic masters. R. Aharon Kohen of Apta, a late eighteenth century compiler of Hasidic traditions asserted that

> The name *'Eheyeh* shows His divinity which emanated and caused the emergence of everything, in order to announce His divinity which is announced by *'Eheyeh*. This is similar to someone who sees the form of the king, which is inscribed on a paper, and he very much enjoys seeing the form and its beauty. And whoever is [found in the state of] *qatenut ha-sekhel*, enjoys and delights in the inscribed form. But whoever has a wise heart says that because there is such a great joy which is derived from the inscribed form, I shall be more glad and I shall delight [more] from the light of the face of the king, namely when seeing the form of the king himself. Therewith he makes an effort to enter the palace of the king. Thus whoever is in [the state of] *qatenut ha-sekhel* is enjoying the study of the Torah or the prayer whose letters are the inscribed form of the king of the world... But whoever is [in the state of] *gadelut [ha-sekhel]* says that it is good to enjoy the light of the face of the king, namely he causes the adherence of his thought to the light of *'Ein Sof* which is found within the letters, by directing [his thought] that in each letter there are three hundreds and ten worlds, souls and divinity, and man has to integrate his soul in each and every one of the aspects etc.[11]

4. Atomization of the Text

What is also characteristic of Hasidic exegesis is a combination of the atomization of the biblical text, with both magical and mystical understandings of the verbal human activity related to ritual. Each of the individual letters of the biblical verses in their oral form were conceived not only as representing the divine as mentioned above but also as comprising the "divinity, the souls and the worlds" altogether. This maximalist understanding of individual letters is based upon the importance of an intimate relationship of the performer of the verbal activity with the vocal aspects of the letters. According to Hasidic masters, the efficacy of the verbal performance is independent of the understanding of the performed text. Letters are conceived of as consisting of an external aspect, understood as palace or box, within which the luminous, vital, spiritual of even divine aspect is present. Thus, the semantic aspects of the text are reduced in favor of a mystical event: cleaving to the divinity found within the sounds related to the liturgical or biblical texts on the one hand, and overlaid by the magical aspects involved in the fact that a supernal power is imagined to be inherent within, or attracted by the Hasidic masters, within the pronounced letters. Following some earlier Kabbalistic views, found in Moses Cordovero and his followers' theories, the semantic aspects of the classical texts are subor-

---

[10] R. Aharon ha-Levi Horowitz, *Toledot Aharon*, I, fol. 18c.
[11] R. Aharon Kohen of Apta, *'Or ha-Ganuz le-Tzaddiqiм*, col. 8, fol. 3ab. On this book see, e.g., Lieberman, *'Ohel RaHeL* (1980) 8–11.

dinated to the experiential moments. This approach is found already in R. Meir Harif Margoliot of Ostrog who may be the earliest and most widely quoted reported in the name of the founder of Hasidism, by one of his companions. The Besht is quoted to the effect that

> whoever prepares himself to study for its own sake, without any alien intention, as I was warned by my great teachers in matters of Torah and Hasidism, included [among them] being my friend, the Hasid and the Rabbi, who is the paragon of the generation, our teachers and Rabbi Israel the Besht, blessed be his memory, let his desirable intention concerning study for its own sake be to attach himself in holiness and purity to the letters, *in potentia* and *in actu*, in speech and in thought, [so that he will] link part of [his] [lower] soul, spirit, [higher] soul, *Hayah* and *Yehidah* to the holiness of the candle of the commandment and Torah, [to] the enlightening letters, which cause the emanation of the influx of lights and vitality, that are true and eternal.[12]

The issue of manipulating the letters is a central theme in Hasidism, and includes some magical aspects, as we learn, for example, from an early nineteenth century figure, R. Aharon of Zhitomir:

> Sometimes, the letters rule over man, and sometimes man rules over the letters. This means that when man utters speeches with power and devotion, the speeches then rule over him, because the light within the letters confers upon him vitality and delight so that he may utter speeches to the Creator, but this man cannot abolish anything bad, by performing other combinations [of letters]. But when someone utters speeches with devotion and brings all his power within the letters and cleaves to the light of the Infinite, blessed be He, that dwells within the letters, this person is higher than the letters and he combines letters as he likes … and he will be able to draw down the influx, the blessing and the good things.[13]

Thus, the sacred text is conceived of as divine since the divinity is immanent within its letters, a phenomenon that can be described as "linguistic immanence". The emphasis upon the role played by discrete linguistic units holds good also insofar as Hasidic interpretations were not interested in the larger context of a certain chapter, but refer more to single words or locutions found in a verse. Those units have been reified, by understanding the sounds produced by the worshiper as if being entities possessing some form of objective existence. This reification is evident in the most frequently recurring Hasidic pun, which comments upon the verse from Gen 6:16, "A window shall you make to the ark [= *teivah*]" as if the last word points to "word" another meaning of the Hebrew *teivah*. According to many Hasidic commentators, it is a linguistic rather than architectural building that Noah was commanded to make, and to enter. Someone should enter the word within which the divinity is dwelling.

The maximalization of the divine power and presence within the letters constituting the canonical discourse diminishes the importance of the semantic valence of the text. If for the main kabbalistic schools the assumption was that reference – namely the theosophical structure – is found outside the text, in Hasidism the divine is found either in the letters of the Bible, or between them, as we shall see below.

Following an older tradition the term *Teva'* – 'nature' – is interpreted as

---

[12] *Sefer Yakhin w-Vo'az* (1795) fol. 6bc. For a detailed analysis of this quote see Weiss, Talmud Torah (1967) 162–67, and Idel, From the 'Hidden Light' (2002) 47–49.
[13] *Toledot 'Aharon*, I, fol. 40ab.

pointing the divine name *'Elohim* (as both amount in gematria to 86);[14] when this external garment of reality is broken, someone may arrive at the core, represented by the Tetragrammaton, which is related to the light of the face of God. Therefore, the immanence is understood to relate to the most revered divine name, the Tetragrammaton, while the external aspects of reality are designated by the name *'Elohim*. The Tetragrammaton is related to the state of *Gadelut* while *'Elohim* to that of *Qatenut*, all this in a context related to the hiding of the face of God and its shining. There is a form of affinity between the hiding of God, which means some form of retraction and withdrawal, and a form of divine *Qatenut*, understood as the condition of man's attaining *Gadelut*. We may discern a shift from the manner in which the two terms have been used in Lurianic material and Hasidism. This shift is not so much a matter of a conceptual change, as claimed, neither it is a simple continuation of Lurianism in Hasidism, since only in the later type of thought do these two terms become part of a more comprehensive hermeneutical grid related to ritual performance. Simplifying the more complex theosophy of Luria, by disregarding for example the importance of the concept of *'Ibbur*, 'impregnation', that precedes *Qatenut*, Hasidic masters turned the two terms into a scheme that shapes the understanding of two main modes of worship. This is done in a manner that has no parallel in Lurianism, and it becomes an interpretive grid.

Again following many Kabbalists, Hasidic masters envisioned the Torah as made up of divine names, which means that the text and the author are identical. So, for example, R. Moses Hayyim Ephrayyim of Sudylkov, writes that

> How is it possible to take the Holy One, blessed be He, as if He will dwell upon man? It is by means of the Torah which is indeed the names of God, since He and His name are one unity, and when someone studies the Torah for the sake of God and in order to keep His commandments and he abstains from what is prohibited, and he pronounces the letters of the Torah, which are the names of God, by these [activities] he takes God indeed and it is as if the Divine Presence dwells upon him, as it is written: "in all places where I pronounce the name of God", which is the holy Torah, which is in its entirety His names, then "I will come unto thee and I will bless thee".[15]

Elsewhere in his book he writes that "since the Torah and God and Israel – all them are one unity only when they [namely Israel] study the Torah for its own sake [or name]. Then there is in her [i. e. the Torah] the power of God and she becomes the secret of emanation, to vivify and heal".[16]

The magical element is quite evident, and so is the mystical one. According to many Hasidic sources, the author, namely God, the text, namely the Torah, and the interpreter, are conceived to be one, an experience of mystical union grounded in the view that

> 'Man' is God, as the numerical value of the Tetragrammaton when spelled fully is forty five, like the value of Adam ('man'), and the Torah is [constituted] of 248 positive commandments and 365 interdictions... And when man studies Torah for its own sake, to keep it and perform it, then he brings all his limbs close to their source whence they originated and were generated,

---

[14] M. Idel, *Deus sive Natura*, The Metamorphosis of a Dictum from Maimonides to Spinoza (2000) 87–110.

[15] *Degel Mahaneh Ephrayyim* (1995) 108.

[16] Ibid. 93–94.

namely, to the Torah. Each of his limbs becomes a substratum of a particular commandment
pertinent to this particular limb, and he becomes identical with the Torah in a unification and a
complete union, like the unification of man and woman.[17]

There is a great amount of isomorphism between Torah, Man [in fact only Is-
rael] and God. By performing the Torah by means of a limb, a person attracts
a divine power upon it. How is this triple union imagined to take place according to other Hasidic masters?

5. Letters as Palaces and Light

A leitmotif of Hasidic understanding of the Torah-letters is the vision that
each of them is a palace. There are innumerable discussions illustrating this
view in Hasidism. So, for example R. Mordekhai of Chernobyl, a late eighteenth century Ukrainian master, offered an interesting view of letters as palaces where the King, God, is dwelling. He describes the letters of Torah and
prayer as monads:

> palaces for the revelation of the light of 'Eiyn Sof [= Infinity], blessed be He and blessed His
> Name, that is clothed within them. When someone studies the Torah and prays, then they [!]
> take them out of the secret places and their light is revealed here below... By the cleaving of
> man to the letters of the Torah and of the prayer, he draws down onto himself the revelation of
> the light of 'Eiyn Sof.[18]

Unlike the more conspicuously magical drawing of the influx within the letters, the letters were conceived also as palaces full of divine light from the very
beginning and the study is the way to extract that light and reach an experience
of union with the divine. Thus, in lieu of the talismanic view of the sounds in
the great majority of Hasidic texts, namely the capacity to bring down the
higher forces by uttering the letters, in some of the texts of R. Mordekhai of
Chernobyl it is only the passage of these forces from their hidden status within
the canonical texts to the performer.

The letters as containers are imagined to contain the divine light, and the
moment of illumination is, therefore, connected to penetrating the linguistic
palaces and enter there just as in the case of the ark-word. In the school of the
Great Maggid, in *Liqqutim Yeqarim*, the Besht is quoted as saying that

> a person who [orally] reads the Torah, and sees the lights of the letters [or sounds] which are
> in the Torah, even if he does not properly know the cantillation [of the biblical text], because
> of his reading with great love and with enthusiasm, God does not deal with him strictly even if
> he does not properly pronounce them [i.e. the cantillations].[19]

Also in this case, study is an oral activity whose final aim is to achieve union
with God. The light as divine dwelling in the Torah was understood as active

---

[17] Ibid. 242.
[18] *Liqqutei Torah* (1983) fol. 29d.
[19] *Liqqutim Yeqarim* (1981) fol. 1a; idem, *'Or ha-'Emet* (1967) fol. 83d. See Weiss, Talmud-
Torah (1967) 161 (Heb. part).

power that can be put in the service of man, and the Besht has been portrayed as using the text of the Torah for magical purposes. His grandson, R. Moses Hayyim Ephraim of Sudylkov wrote that

> by study and involvement with the Torah for its own sake [or name], he can vivify his soul and amend his 248 limbs and 365 sinews, [and] join himself [sic] to their root, and to the root of their root which are the Torah and the Tetragrammaton, blessed be He,... all of this is [achieved] by the study of Torah for its own sake [or name] and for the sake of asking from the letters themselves. And I heard the interpretation of the Besht ... from "the secret of God" that is in them, which ["the secret of God"] will help them [the students of Torah] to speak the letters with a firm interpretation "for its own sake".[20]

6. Hasidism and Strong Interpreters

The ascent of the importance of a strong personality as the center of religion, as it is the case of the Hasidic righteous, the *tzaddiq*, is certainly related to the vision that the righteous is also a strong interpreter. According to a later legend, reported in Jacob Kaidaner's *Sippurim Nora'im*, the Besht was given the authority from above to do whatever he wished with the letters of the Torah.[21] The view of R. Barukh of Medzibush, another grandson of the Besht, is that the Hasidic interpretations "Touch and [at the same time] do not touch" the text, because of the implicit assumption, that it is the effect of the divine spirit that informs the interpreter.[22] His brother, the author of *Degel Mahaneh Ephrayyim* speaks about the revelation of the secrets of the Torah by means of the divine spirit. Moreover, the above-mentioned R. Levi Isaac of Berdichev, indicates that the *tzaddiqim* "now have the power to interpret the Torah in the way they like",[23] even if in heaven this interpretation is not accepted. Another prominent Hasidic master, R. Menahem Mendel of Rimanov, argues in the introduction to his *'Ilana' de-Hayyei*, that if someone studies the Torah for its sake, he is allowed to introduce in the Torah his thoughts.[24]

On the other hand, the famous R. Nahman of Bratzlav, the great-grandson of the Besht, conceives the righteous of the generation, presumably he himself in his generation, as the pipeline through which interpretations are pouring into the world. In one of the most remarkable descriptions of the interpreter he writes:

> Know that there is a soul in the world through which all interpretations of the Torah are revealed... All interpreters of Torah receive [their words] from this soul... And when this soul falls from its rung, and its words become cold, it dies. When it dies, the interpretations that had come through it also disappear. Then all the interpreters are unable to find any meaning in the Torah... He who wants to interpret the Torah has to begin by drawing unto himself words as hot as burning coals. Speech comes out of the upper heart... The interpreter first has to pour out his words to God in prayer, seeking to arouse His mercies, so that the heart will open.

---

[20] *Degel Mahaneh Ephrayyim* (1995) 94.
[21] *Sippurim Nora'im* (ed. Gedalyah Nigal; 1992) 34.
[22] *Botzina' di-Nehora'* (1985) 73.
[23] *Pirqei 'Avot* (Jerusalem 1972) fol. 25b.
[24] Introduction, fol. 3a.

> Speech then flows from the heart, and interpretation of the Torah flows from that speech... On this heart are inscribed all the interpretations of the Torah.[25]

These statements prove, in their theoretical formulations, that the Hasidic masters were aware of the radical exegetical moves they implemented in their writings. They either project their thoughts into the divine text as if interpreting it, or they receive some form of revelation. In both cases, the exegetical enterprise is much less a matter of listening attentively to the specificity of the message found in a certain given text. The divinity of the text and the anthropology of the righteous person as a semi-divine being,[26] allowed radical forms of exegesis, hardly matched by postmodern hermeneutics. In several Hasidic discussions the sermons of the righteous were conceived as identical with Torah, as noted above, which should be fathomed and interpreted in seventy ways, just as the divine Torah.[27]

---

[25] *Liqqutei Moharan;* cp. the translation of Green, Tormented Master (1979/81) 200–01; see idem, The Zaddik as Axis Mundi in Later Judaism (1977) 341.

[26] See Rapoport-Albert, God and the Zaddik (1979) 296–325.

[27] See Idel, Absorbing Perfections: Kabbalah and Interpretation (2002) 470–81.

CHAPTER FORTY

Early Old Testament Critics in Great Britain

by WILLIAM McKANE †

(University of St Andrews)

General and special studies: C. BULTMANN, *Die biblische Urgeschichte in der Aufklärung: Johann Gott-fried Herders Interpretation der Genesis als Antwort auf die Religionskritik David Humes* (BHTh 110; Tübingen: Mohr Siebeck 1999); T. K. CHEYNE, *Founders of Old Testament Criticism* (London: Methuen 1893); J. DRURY (ed.), *Critics of the Bible 1724–1873* (Cambridge: Cambridge UP 1989); E. GIBBON, *Memoirs* (ed. G. B. Hill; London 1900); *Dictionary of National Biography* [DNB] (*Dictionary of National Biography* 1–66; ed. L. Stephen / S. Lee; London 1885–1901[and later editions]; rev. edn. *Oxford Dictionary of National Biography: from earliest times to the year 2000* 1–60; ed. H. C. G. Matthew / B. Harrison; Oxford: Oxford UP 2004); J. H. HAYES (ed.), *Dictionary of Biblical Interpretation* A-J, K-Z [DBI] (Nashville: Abingdon 1999); A. HERMAN, *The Scottish Enlightenment. The Scots Invention of the Modern World* (London: Harper Collins 2001); J. JARICK (ed.), *Sacred Conjectures: The Context and Legacy of Robert Lowth and Jean Astruc* (Library of Hebrew Bible / Old Testament Studies 457; New York / London: T & T Clark International 2007); D. S. KATZ, *God's Last Words. Reading the English Bible from the Reformation to Fundamentalism* (New Haven: Yale UP 2004); J. LAMB, *The Rhetoric of Suffering. Reading the Book of Job in the Eighteenth Century* (Oxford: Clarendon Press 1995); S. MANDELBROTE, "The English Bible and its Readers in the Eighteenth Century", in: I. RIVERS (ed.), *Books and the Readers in the Eighteenth Century. New Essays* (London: Continuum 2001); J. G. A. POCOCK, *Barbarism and Religion. The Enlightenment of Edward Gibbon 1737–1764* (Cambridge: Cambridge UP 2000); S. PRICKETT (ed.), *Reading the Text. Biblical Criticism and Literary Theory* (Oxford: Blackwell 1991); J. SHEEHAN, *The Enlightenment Bible. Translation. Scholarship. Culture* (Princeton: Princeton UP 2005); R. SMEND, "Lowth in Deutschland", in idem: *Epochen der Bibelkritik* (München: Kaiser 1991) 43–62; repr. in: idem, *Bibel und Wissenschaft* (Tübingen: Mohr Siebeck 2004) 51–70; L. STEPHEN, *History of English Thought in the Eighteenth Century* I-II (London ³1902); B. W. YOUNG, *Religion and Enlightenment in Eighteenth-Century England. Theological Debate from Locke to Burke* (Oxford: Clarendon Press 1998).

Special abbreviation (see above):
DNB = *Dictionary of National Biography* / *Oxford Dictionary of National Biography*

1. Introductory: Warburton and Lowth

The literary conflict between William Warburton (1698–1779) and Robert Lowth (1710–87), both eminent clerics of the Church of England, came to be celebrated as the most important public debate over the nature of the Bible and its teaching that erupted in Great Britain since the Reformation. After the fierce theological debates of the previous century, the declining interest in Deism and the concern to maintain a united national Church, this debate arose out of the claims of the Church to uphold an authoritative interpretation of the Bible over all manifestations of public dissent, whether from freethinkers, Catholics, Methodists or radical Christians. Such was the position defended by William Warburton, anxious to uphold a close alliance between Church and state. His major writing, *The Divine Legation of Moses*, that ran through several editions, used the example of the Old Testament in support of the right of the state to use its powers to suppress religious dissent. In the process of defending this claim, he argued that the book of Job was merely a late poetic allegory. Fiercely combative in literary manner and intent, Warburton, who had commenced his professional life as a lawyer, showed little restraint in defending his position, although he was not a Hebrew scholar.

His opponent and critic, against whom he waged a public campaign by correspondence, was Robert Lowth, who, after a decade as Professor of Poetry at Oxford, was appointed Bishop of Oxford in 1766, transferring to London in 1777. He was an excellent Hebrew scholar who had been taught by Thomas Hunt, an eminent Orientalist and Professor of Arabic and Hebrew in Oxford. Lowth was an Old Testament scholar,[1] whereas Warburton made his principal foray into the Old Testament with his *Divine Legation of Moses*, and it was because of this that their paths crossed.[2]

2. William Warburton and His Polemic Correspondence with Robert Lowth

Sources: W. WARBURTON: *Works* I-XII (ed. with a life of the author, by R. Hurd; London 1811); *The Divine Legation of Moses Demonstrated* (5th edn., London 1765; 10th edn., I-III, 1846; repr. I-IV, 1978); *The Second Part of a Literary Correspondence, between the Bishop of Gloucester and a late Professor of Oxford* (Oxford 1766).

Reference articles: on Warburton: DNB 57 (2004) 268-74 (B. W. YOUNG); DBI K-Z, 622 (D. D. WALLACE, JR.).

Special studies: M. C. BATTESTIN, *The Providence of Wit* (Oxford: Clarendon Press 1974) 197-200; A. W. EVANS, *Warburton and the Warburtonians* (Oxford 1932); J. LAMB, *The Rhetoric of Suffering* (1995 [see sect. 1]) 110-27; M. PATTISON, *Essays by the late Mark Pattison* 1-II (ed. H. Nettleship; Oxford: Clarendon Press 1889), esp. II, xiv, 119-76; S. TAYLOR, "William Warburton and the Alliance of Church and State", *JEH* 43 (1992) 271-86; J. SELBY WATSON, *The Life of William Warburton, DD, Lord Bishop of Gloucester, from 1760 to 1779, with Remarks on his Works* (London: Longmans 1863).

Warburton's *Divine Legation of Moses* is here the principal source of interest.[3] Warburton launches his enterprise with three propositions and two syllogisms.[4]

---

[1] For Warburton see esp. Young, Religion and Enlightenment (1998). For Lowth see esp. B. HEPWORTH, *Robert Lowth* (Boston 1996). The background to the debate is covered in detail in: Lamb, The Rhetoric of Suffering (1995), on the particular controversy with Robert Lowth see esp. 110-27. For its importance cf. also Sheehan, The Enlightenment Bible (2005) 148-81.

[2] For Warburton see also the essay of H. GRAF REVENTLOW in the present volume, Chap. 35, sect. 4.2.

[3] I am using the tenth edition of that book which was published in three volumes in London in 1846.

[4] *Divine Legation* I (1846) 112.

The three propositions are: 1.That to inculcate the doctrine of a future state of rewards and punishments, is necessary to the well-being of a civil society. 2. That all humankind, especially the most wise and learned nations of antiquity, have concurred in believing and teaching, that this doctrine was of such use to civil society. 3. That the doctrine of a future state of rewards and punishments is not to be found in, nor did make part of, the Mosaic dispensation.

The two syllogisms are: 1.Whatsoever religion and society have no future state for their support, must be supported by an extraordinary providence. The Jewish religion and society had no future state for their support: Therefore, the Jewish religion and society were supported by an extraordinary providence. 2.The ancient lawgivers universally believed that such a religion could be supported only by an extraordinary providence. Moses, an ancient lawgiver, versed in all the wisdom of Egypt, purposely instituted such a religion. Therefore, Moses believed his religion was supported by an extraordinary providence.

Warburton announces: "I have now at length gone through the first two propositions ... The next book (iv) begins with the proof of the third".[5] He creates the illusion of a rigorous logic, but he is more of an attorney with a penchant for paradoxes than he is a logician. He equates the Old Testament with the "Mosaic dispensation" and argues for a Mosaic theocracy as if it were an Old Testament theocracy. He defines the Mosaic theocracy as a unique system of civil law which is supported by a "special providence". Hence it is both civil law and a religion, but it is a religion which, unlike all other religions, is exclusively this-worldly and is not supported by a doctrine of rewards and punishments beyond this present world. Hence the dispensation of Moses is "of divine original"[6] and as both civil law and religion it is unique. Yet the Jews are not to bask in this aura of superiority, for "the omission of a future state in that dispensation evidently obliges them to look for a more perfect revelation of God's will"[7] [in Christianity]. So that instead of reaching the conclusion that the Mosaic dispensation is a system of civil law akin to other systems of civil law, Warburton elevates it into civil law which is a theocracy, both law and religion, which is "a divine original" and is unique among religions in that it is not supported by a belief in rewards and punishments beyond existence in this world.

The correspondence between Warburton and Lowth began in 1756 and Lowth wrote the first letter on September 9. It lasted until October 14, ending with two letters which are tolerably amicable, that of Lowth generous, though firm, and Warburton's less so, signalling a truce rather than a reconciliation. Apart from these final letters, Warburton wrote another one and Lowth two; the second (Warburton) and the third (Lowth) are the most informative of the five in respect of their dispute. In them Warburton gives three examples of where he has been badly done by in the *Praelectiones* of Lowth, and Lowth takes up his points. The controversy proceeded from observations made by

---

[5] Ibid. II, 49.
[6] Ibid. I, 112.
[7] Ibid. I, 111.

Lowth on the book of Job to which Warburton took exception and in which he discerned sly digs at opinions on Job which he had expressed in *The Divine Legation*. The issue arose, however, on the basis of Warburton's study, published earlier, on the relationship between Church and State[8] and the question whether religious dissent should be punished by the civil order in the manner that the Mosaic legislation made provision for the punishment of idolatry under the Jewish economy. That Lowth offered a different answer from that of Warburton, caused the latter to take offence.

That the Book of Job became the bone of contention in the letters of both Warburton and Lowth reflects the point that the former declared the Book of Job to be an allegory. Accordingly he argued that it did not seriously question the beneficence of the divine providential order in which the state fulfilled a necessary, if punitive, role for the suppression of the evil. He held that Job was a drama of a kind[9] which did not impugn the goodness of divine providence, whilst Lowth argued that it was not "just a drama" but "a mere dialogue"[10] and raised serious questions. Warburton asked why it should not be deemed an allegory, since it was generally supposed that the Song of Songs was an allegory.[11] His combative temperament urged him into sharp debate, despite his lack of knowledge of Hebrew, or biblical studies generally. He did not necessarily hold that Job was an allegory: he was wrangling, thirsting for an argument which had no point, and simply crossing swords with a "critical orthodoxy" in order to uphold his reputation as a major authority on all such questions. Lowth retorted: "If you deny Job to be an allegory, I see no ill consequence, it stands just where it did; but if you deny that the Song of Solomon is an allegory, you must exclude it from the canon of Holy Scripture, for it holds its place there by no other tenure".[12] JONATHAN LAMB explains Warburton's position: "In deciding to read Job as an allegory of the plight of the Jews after the Babylonian captivity Warburton was doing nothing new... What distinguished Warburton's choice of an allegorical reading was the size of his personal investment in it – no less than the whole argument of his life's work, *The Divine Legation of Moses Demonstrated* (1738–41)".[13]

This correspondence was published by Lowth in 1765 in a Letter which he wrote to Warburton, of which more below. I have not had access to this Letter, but the correspondence of 1756 also appears in the appendix of Warburton's *Works*[14] and I have read it there. The impression which I gather from it is that Lowth is the party who has been wronged. He writes engagingly in flowing, melodious English; it is a well of English undefiled. He is congenial and his style is relaxed, but he does not pander to Warburton or make any effort to sweeten his suspicious mind. The author who praised Warburton to the heavens in *The Delicacy of Friendship* did it at the expense of the commonwealth of learning and Lowth refers to him as having shown "more zeal than discretion, more malevolent wit than good sense in the performance, the manifest tendency of which is to sow strife and foment discord" (447). Lowth has no intention of imitating him. He is perplexed and cannot under-

---

8 *Alliance between Church and State* (1736).
9 Warburton, *Works* XII (1811) 449.
10 Ibid. 456.
11 Ibid. 450.
12 Ibid. 458.
13 Lamb, The Rhetoric of Suffering (1995) 112.
14 *Works* XII, 444–66; cf. the following references in the text.

stand why Warburton has come to the conclusion that he has made a veiled attack on his book. He remarks: "I cannot have misrepresented your particular notions, for I never intended to represent them at all, nor had I anything to do with them. In a word my lectures, and every expression of them, might have stood just as they do now, though your dissertation had never been written" (446f). The two men who had conveyed Warburton's displeasure to Lowth are praised by the former as "brethren" who had discharged a valuable office to whom he is obliged (448) and by Lowth as "our good friends" (444). Lowth continues (447): "I shall be offended at no man merely for differing from me in sentiment, much less on points so very doubtful on which no two persons out of all who examine and judge for themselves, either have agreed or probably will ever perfectly agree". His first letter to Warburton has a sting in its tail: "If you use me other than I deserve, your own character will suffer and not mine" (447). This is reinforced in his second letter to Warburton where he holds out the hand of friendship to him (462), but is adamant that he will not be bullied by an unreasonable man: "I should not have thought of setting forth my bravery [initiating the correspondence with Warburton], if I had not first been called a coward and accordingly looked upon as one who was to be awed by menaces" (460). Again: "I do but join with many other sincere well-wishers to you in regretting that you have not something more of toleration in literary matters: that you are so hasty in taking up your resentments and that you deal with such as differ from you in so severe and contemptuous a manner ... I am a true lover of peace and quietness, of mutual freedom, candour and benevolence. I detest and I despise the squabbles that are perpetually arising from the jealousy and the peevishness of the *genus irritabile Scriptorum*" (462). Warburton's first letter (Sept. 17) contrasts with the benevolent elegance and forthrightness of the first letter of Lowth. He is a nitpicker who cannot suffer disagreement with his own opinions and he is pedantic to boot. Worse, he sniffs suspiciously for snide attacks on what he has written which do not exist; he is ill-mannered and arrogant. In the letters which he wrote to Lowth in 1756 most of his complaints are either trivial or superfluous: he has misunderstood the passages in the *Praelectiones* to which he takes exception or he offers explanations of points he has made in the *Divine Legation* of which Lowth has no need. He is addicted to the delusion that what he has written is being attacked.

Hostilities are resumed by him in 1765 in the 4th edition of the *Divine Legation*[15] over the date which Lowth had assigned to the book of Job which Warburton jeered at, and the *coup de grâce* was administered by Lowth in the Letter to Warburton, already mentioned, in the same year. It was a pamphlet in which he exploited the considerable resources of his command of the English language, his effortless fluency and his polished irony. He described the *Divine Legation* as "Lord Peter's brown loaf containing inclusive all the necessaries of life". The informed view was that Lowth had the better of the controversy and had emerged triumphant from it. Gibbon has remarked that his victory "was clearly established by the silent confusion of Warburton and his slaves", that Lowth's Letter was "a pointed and polished epistle".[16] Warburton was unwilling to admit defeat and he wrote the first letter of a second series of letters between them, complaining that Lowth had published a private correspondence in his Letter of 1765. This was published as *The Second Part of a Literary Correspondence, between the Bishop of Gloucester and a late Professor of Oxford* (1766).

Nevertheless, despite Warburton's objectionable arrogance, his assumption of superiority and his tendency to sneer at Lowth, this difference over the date of Job is the only occasion where an opinion which he expresses has substance, although his contention that Ezra is the author is wide of the mark[17] and Lowth had rejected it out of hand.[18] This combination, making a real contribution to Old Testament scholarship and displaying arrogant rudeness in doing it, is a genuine paradox, unlike the quirky paradoxes of Warburton. Yet, the forthrightness of literary debate in the eighteenth century should be

---

[15] Warburton (1765) 409–20.
[16] Gibbon, *Memoirs* (1900) 179.
[17] Warburton, *Divine Legation* V (1765) 416.
[18] Ibid. 415–16.

borne in mind and Lowth was able to take care of himself. "The book of Job", he had said , "savours of Antiquity and those who cannot relish it, have as depraved a taste as Father Harduis who could not distinguish partridges from horseflesh".[19] Warburton is equally uncomplimentary with his remark concerning the reviewer who had asked Lowth (then Bishop of London) a question on one of his Sermons, Lowth's answer to which gave rise to Warburton's outburst in 1765. The question was whether the Jewish economy was unique in the circumstance that idolatry was punished by a civil magistrate. The answer given by Lowth assumed that the book of Job was set in the patriarchal age and conflicted with a principal conclusion drawn by Warburton who remarks: "But a little more civility at parting would not have been amiss, for he (the reviewer) who did not spare the Bishop would certainly demolish the Professor should he take it into his head to examine the *Praelectiones*".[20]

In his first letter to Warburton in the correspondence of 1756 Lowth had said of the book of Job that it was "the most ancient extant, it had no relations with the affairs of the Israelites: it was neither allegorical nor properly dramatic".[21] The Rabbis, though the book of Job was located in the third part of the Hebrew canon, had held that Job lived in the time of Moses, an opinion which, as may be gathered from the above citation, Lowth did not hold. The Vulgate places it at the head of a sub-list named *libri didactici* which also included (among other books) Psalms, Proverbs and Ecclesiastes, all wisdom books and all in the third division of the Hebrew canon. The precedence given to Job may be an indication that it was thought to be the earliest of these books. It is understandable that it was taken to reflect conditions of life in a patriarchal age; the opinions of modern scholarship are far from unanimous about its origins, but a prominent view is that the Prologue and the Epilogue are prose folk-tales which have been used to bracket the poetry of the Dialogue and that the book of Job is late, post-exilic, Israelite theological wisdom, the most dogmatic book in the wisdom literature.

3. Robert Lowth

Sources and translations: R. LOWTH: *De sacra poesi Hebraeorum praelectiones academiae Oxonii habitae...* (Oxford 1753; German edn. with notes by J. D. Michaelis, I-II; Göttingen 1758-61); *Lectures on the Sacred Poetry of the Hebrews* I-II (tr. from Latin by G. Gregory and S. Henley; London 1787); *A Letter to the Right Reverend Author of the Divine Legation of Moses ... by a Late Professor in the University of Oxford* (Oxford 1765); *A Larger Confutation of Bishop Hare's System of Hebrew Metre* (London 1766); *Isaiah: A New Translation, with a Preliminary Dissertation and Notes, Critical, Philological and Explanatory* I-II (London 1778; 2nd edn. 1779); *Sermons and Other Remains of Robert Lowth* (ed. P. Hall; London 1834). – B. KENNICOTT, *Two Dissertations* (Oxford 1753, 1759); idem (ed.), *Vetus testamentum Hebraicum cum variis lectionibus* I-II (Oxford 1776, 1780).

Reference articles: on Lowth: DNB 34 (2004) 613-16 (S. Mandelbrote); DBI K-Z, 89-90 (R. R. Marks); on Kennicott: DNB 31 (2004) 294-96 (N. Aston); DBI K-Z, 19-20 (W. McKane).

Special studies: R. S. CRIPPS, "Two British Interpreters of the Old Testament: Robert Lowth

---

[19] Ibid. 417.
[20] Ibid. 420.
[21] Warburton, *Works* XII, 445.

(1710–1787) and S. Lee (1783–1852)", *BJRL* 35 (1952/53) 385–404; B. HEPWORTH, *Robert Lowth* (Boston 1978); J. JEBB, *Sacred Literature: Comprising a Review of the Principles of Composition Laid down by the Late Robert Lowth … in his Praelectiones and Isaiah* (London 1820); T. M. JOHNSTON, *Neo-Classical Background of Robert Lowth's Lectures on the Sacred Poetry of the Hebrews* (Diss. Duke University 1938); J. KUGEL, *The Idea of Biblical Poetry: Parallelism and Its History* (New Haven / London 1981) 274–86; R. LOWTH, Jr., *Memoirs of the Life and Writings of the Late Right Reverend Robert Lowth* (1787); W. MCKANE, "Benjamin Kennicott: An Eighteenth-Century Researcher", *JTS* 28 (1977) 446–64; S. PRICKETT, *Words and the Word: Language, Poetics and Biblical Interpetation* (Cambridge: Cambridge UP 1986) 105–23; F. REHKOPF, "Der 'Parallelismus' im Neuen Testament. Versuch einer Sprachregelung", *ZNW* 71 (1980) 46–57; J. SHEEHAN, *The Enlightenment Bible* (Princeton 2005; see Gen. Bibl. above) 148–81; D. S. KATZ, "The Hutchinsonians and Hebraic Fundamentalism in Eighteenth-Century England", in: *Sceptics, Millenarians and Jews* (FS R. H. Popkin; ed. D. S. Katz / J. J. Israel; Leiden: Brill 1990) 237–55; idem, God's Last Words (2004) 204–11; R. SMEND, "Lowth in Deutschland", in: idem, *Epochen der Bibelkritik* (BEvTh 109, München: Kaiser 1991) 43–62 (repr. in: idem, *Bibel und Wissenschaft. Historische Aufsätze* [Tübingen: Mohr Siebeck 2004] 51–70); L. TANNENBAUM, *Biblical Tradition in Blake's Early Prophecies: The Great Code of Art* (Princeton, NJ: Princeton UP 1982) 8–54.

Among the scholarly achievements of Robert Lowth (1710–87) his *De sacra poesi Hebraeorum praelectiones*, published in 1753, was a pioneer work in modern biblical studies.[22] Sacred poetry is, according to him, amenable to criticism from which is learned both the origin of the art and how to estimate its excellence.[23] Sacred poetry was the first and peculiar office of poetry to commend to the Almighty the prayers and thanksgivings of his creatures, to celebrate his praises, to display to mankind the mysteries of the divine will and to predict future events, the last and noblest of all its employments. This is a value judgement that theological poetry is the noblest of all the employments of poetry which Lowth considers to be compatible with his resolve to hold literary criticism and theology apart, not to transgress into the domain of the latter.[24]

He observes that there is hardly any real knowledge of the metre of Hebrew versification. Some vestiges are discernible and a few observations of a general nature can be made. On the other hand, the style of Hebrew poetry gives ample scope for discussion: it possesses not only the principal excellences which are common to poetry, but many which are proper and peculiar to itself. Lowth comments on the dangers of wandering too much at large in the ample field of poetry and the impudent breaking in to the boundaries of theology.[25]

He returns to the metre of Hebrew poetry.[26] The real quantity, the rhythm or modulation, seem from the present state of the language to be altogether unknown and even to admit of no examination by human art and industry. The loss of metre is connected with the loss of a representation of vowels in the writing of Hebrew,[27] since number, quantity and accent cannot be ascertained without a perfect pronunciation of the language. The poems in the He-

---

[22] Citing Lowth's *Praelectiones* the pagination of the English translation of his Latin by Gregory and Henley, *Lectures* I-II (1787) is used.
[23] *Lectures* I, 46.
[24] Ibid. 47.
[25] Ibid. 53.
[26] Ibid. 55–71.
[27] Ibid. 65; Lowth, *Isaiah* (1778) viii, ix.

brew Bible are mostly couplets, though sometimes of greater length.[28] The metres are neither complex nor capable of much variety, but rather simple, grave, temperate; less adapted to fluency than dignity and force.

A poem translated literally from Hebrew into the prose of any other language will, while the same form of sentences remain, still retain, even in respect of versification, much of its native dignity and a faint appearance of versification, but a Hebrew poem cannot be translated into Greek or Latin without a loss of its genuine elegance and peculiar beauty. The result of translation is something very unlike the original in kind and form.[29]

Lowth mentions specimens of early Hebrew poetry, the execration of Noah on Ham who was the "father of Canaan" and the blessing of Shem (Gen 9:25–26). He alludes to the inspired benedictions of the Patriarchs, Isaac (Gen 27:27–29) and Jacob (Gen 48:15–16, 20) [also Jacob's address to his sons, 49:1–27], all of the same kind. It is highly probable that they were extant from before the time of Moses and were afterwards committed to writing by the inspired historian, exactly as he had received them from his ancestors.[30] Lowth thus takes account not only of poetic books in the Hebrew Bible, but of snatches of poetry and longer pieces in prose books, the Pentateuch and Judges, such as the Song of Moses (Exod 15:1–18) and the Song of Deborah (Judg 5:1–31). Also three sayings from Numbers (21:15, 17–18, 27–30) and the visionary oracles of Balaam (Numbers 23 and 24) who pronounced in the parabolic style.[31]

The proverb (or the parable) is didactic poetry; the words of the wise and their dark sayings (Prov 1:6b), on the other hand, are "truly poetical". The parabolic and sententious style is a general description of poetry; a more exact tally of the "constitutional principles" is a division into the sententious, the figurative and the sublime. The value of poetry is enhanced when it deals with mystery, when it is visionary and prophetic, when it explores the height and the depths. Parable and mystery are two types of sentential (didactic) poetry and of those mystery is the more poetic. It is didactic poetry adorned with all the more splendid colouring of language magnificently divine in the sentiments, animated by the most pathetic expression, and diversified and embellished by figurative diction and poetical imagery. Such are the productions of the prophets.[32] The sententious style is then the primary characteristic of Hebrew poetry; even poetry which is highly figurative and infinitely sublime has a didactic form.[33] Hebrew poetry is concise, it has brevity and simplicity and yet it is repetitive. Lowth alludes to synonymous and antithetic parallelism, but he does not use this terminology. He refers to sentences which are parallel to each other, which express the same or a similar, and often a contrary sentiment in

---

[28] Ibid. 68.
[29] Ibid. 72 f.
[30] Ibid. 91.
[31] Ibid. 91–96.
[32] Ibid. 97 f.
[33] Ibid. 98 f.

the same form of words.[34] He deals with parallelism at greater length, synonymous, antithetic and synthetic, in Isaiah.[35]

The figurative style[36] consists of metaphor, allegory, simile and personification (*prosapoeia*). Metaphor has four principal sources: nature (120–43), common life (144–66), sacred topics (167–83) and sacred history (184–203). Allegory, a kind of metaphor, is given special treatment (214–49), then simile
(250–79) and personification (280–301). Lowth moves on to a consideration of
sublimity in general and sublimity of expression in particular (302–45) and
then to the sublimity of passion (346–64), where the first volume comes to an
end.

Further comments may be made on Lowth's divisions of figurative language.
It is language in which one or more images or words are substitutes in the
room of others, or even introduced by way of illustration on the principle of
resemblance. The resemblance if it be only imitated and confined to a few
words is called a metaphor; if the figure is continued, it is called an allegory. If
it be directly expressed by comparing ideas together and by the insertion of
any words expressive of likeness ('like' or 'as'), it is called simile or comparison.[37] Personification occurs when a character and person is assigned even to
things inanimate or fictitious, or when a fictitious speech is attributed to a real
personage. These are the principal kinds of figurative language in Hebrew poetry.[38]

Lowth deals with obscurities of figures of speech: difficulties and inconve-
niences must necessarily occur. There is, therefore, great danger, lest viewing
them from an improper situation, and rashly estimating all things from our
own standard, we form an erroneous judgement.[39] But error does not only
spring from our modernity and their antiquity, from a failure of literary appreciation. It is also related to their linguistic obscurity and to the corruption of
the Hebrew text which lies before us. This is a significant if incomplete admission by Lowth, because lexicography, philology and text-criticism, of which
Lowth says very little in his *Praelectiones*, are necessary to make sense of these
obscurities as well as the sensitive appreciation of their poetic content which
Lowth displays. He has a point in holding that of the cluster of images which
the human mind collects from all nature and from itself, from its emotions and
operations, the least clear and evident are those explained by reason and argument. That may be so: poetry in all its expressions does not have its origin in
reason and argument,[40] but these are needed to elucidate an ancient text,
which swarms with difficulties, before the wealth of its literary assets can be
appreciated. That Lowth is fully aware of this is demonstrated at length in his
Isaiah, but his virtual silence on this aspect of the problem in the *Praelectiones*

---

[34] Ibid. 100.
[35] Lowth, *Isaiah* (1778) xi–xxvii.
[36] *Lectures* I, 103–19; cf. the following references in the text.
[37] Ibid. 106.
[38] Ibid. 107 f.
[39] Ibid. 113.
[40] Ibid. 117–18.

is striking. He knows that literary elegance will not compensate for lack of ac-curacy in a translation of the poetry of the Hebrew Bible.[41]

He resumes the topic that the more evident and distinct of the sources of po-etry are the impressions made by external objects on the senses and that the most vivid and clear of these are perceived by the eye. The images which are furnished by the senses depict the obscure by the more manifest, the subtle by the more substantial. As far as simplicity is the object of poetry it pursues those ideas which are the most familiar and the most evident, which are so abundant that they serve the purpose of ornament as well as that of illustration.[42]

Lowth was a Hebraist and a professor of poetry, an unusual combination which makes a mark on his Hebrew scholarship. His power of literary appre-ciation and analysis are those of a professor of poetry, but his literary criticism was founded on a thorough knowledge of the Hebrew language and the He-brew Bible. He was a Hebrew scholar of international stature, perhaps more acknowledged to be such in Germany rather than England.[43] The impression which has to be registered concerning the *Praelectiones* is not that Lowth made too much of a knowledge of Hebrew which he did not have, but that he dis-played too little of the formidable knowledge of it which he had in his literary criticism of the poetry of the Hebrew Bible. There is doubtless a reason for the absence of any reference to lexicography and criticism of the Hebrew text as fundamental equipment of a Hebraist.

His silence on the basic preliminaries which have to be gone through before the task of appreciating the poetry of the Hebrew Bible can proceed is then a deliberate decision, perhaps partly attributable to his absorption in the subject of Hebrew poetry, partly to the nature of the lectures which he had to deliver to an audience among which were non-Hebraists, but neither of these explana-tions are adequate. The accuracy of our translation of the poetry of the He-brew Bible into another language is the first step in the textual criticism of it and that Lowth is well aware of this is evident from his commentary on Isaiah,[44] but he would certainly have added that the poetry which is trans-lated, despite our ignorance of its metre and the absence of rhyme, must be displayed as poetry and set out in a manner which clearly distinguishes it from prose. This is the practice of modern editions of the Biblia Hebraica (both BHK and BHS) as well as in RSV, NEB and REB.

What is it then that accounts for Lowth's different practice in the *Praelec-tiones* as compared with that of his commentary on Isaiah? It has been suggested to me by ANNA CULLHED that he may have been loathe to combine his account of sacred biblical poetry with such technical matters as text criticism and lexicogra-phy out of a conviction that he could not do it without damaging the impression he wished to convey of the elevated rank of that poetry.[45] In that case it would

---

[41] Lowth, *Isaiah*, lii.

[42] Lowth, *Lectures* I, 117 ff.

[43] Cf. R. Smend, Lowth in Deutschland (1991) 43–62 (= 2004, 51–70).

[44] Lowth, *Isaiah*, lii.

[45] Cf. further the contribution of Dr. A. CULLHED in the Volume of the Conference (held at Ox-ford, April 2003) on "Sacred Conjectures. The Context and Legacy of Robert Lowth and Jean As-truc" (ed. by J. Jarick; see the Bibl. above).

be because he had poetry in his soul that he refrained form exhibiting his Hebrew learning; but another explanation would be that when he lectured on the poetry of the Hebrew Bible, the theological doctrine that Holy Scripture was the inspired word of God still exercised a strong influence on him.

In that case Sacred Poetry would not only be for Lowth a sublime human expression of the being of God, as all poetry revealed the highest reaches of the mind and the most delicate and exalted insights and feelings, but also an inspired revelation of the Word of God. Lowth published the *Praelectiones* in 1753 and the commentary on Isaiah in 1778, and Kennicott published his edition of the Hebrew Bible without vocalization and Massora, based on Hebrew manuscripts which had been collected and scrutinized, in the years 1760–1769.[46] For this task he employed van der Hooght's vocalized Hebrew Bible.[47]

It is possible that Lowth changed his theological stance between 1753 and 1778 and was won over to the new textual criticism which suspected the Massoretic vocalization, though this was a change which could not be reconciled with the original form of his belief in the inerrancy of Old Testament Scripture. A. Geddes,[48] however, is persuaded that there was an inconsistency between Kennicott's textual criticism and his theology, and the same could be the case with Lowth. Kennicott's own description of his Old Testament theology confirms that this gulf indeed existed: the inerrant Hebrew Bible was now the one that was restored by Kennicott's collations whose aim was to recover in a consonantal text the original texts of the biblical authors.[49] The inerrancy of the Hebrew Bible may have rested on the same assumption in Lowth's *Isaiah*, published in 1778, where he acknowledged receipt of collations and variations in the book of Isaiah sent to him by Kennicott, who also sent him the printed book as soon as it was finished at the press. Lowth says that he had used these collations and had benefited from them.[50] In *Isaiah* Lowth is, without a shadow of doubt, an accomplished Old Testament scholar, displaying in his preliminary dissertation (i-lxxiv) a mastery of the lexicographical, text-critical and literary-critical skills which are the foundation of his translation of Isaiah (174 pages) and adding a lengthy commentary (283 pages) to it. He is aware of the necessity of translating the best Hebrew text available and of the importance of Kennicott's enterprise and the ancient versions in this connection. He notices that some books of the Old Testament are generally supposed to have been written in verse, but that the prophetic books are not included among them. Both the Jews and Jerome concluded that the prophetic books were written in prose and one of Lowth's aims is to demonstrate that the book of Isaiah is, principally, metrical, no different in that respect from Job, Psalms and Proverbs.[51]

---

[46] *Vetus Testamentum Hebraicum cum variis lectionibus* I-II (Oxford 1776, 1780).

[47] E. van der Hooght, *Biblia Hebraica* (Amsterdam 1705).

[48] See further sect. 4 below.

[49] On Kennicott cf. McKane, Benjamin Kennicott (1977) 458. In his *Biblia Hebraica cum notis criticis et versione Latina ad notas criticis facta* (Paris 1753) C. F. Houbigant also employs a consonantal text. Further on Houbigant see Chap. 34.4 by J. W. ROGERSON in the present volume.

[50] Lowth, *Isaiah*, lxix; also lxxi.

[51] Ibid. ii-iii.

In *Isaiah* Lowth lauds the textual work of both J. D. Michaelis (1717–91) and B. Kennicott. He expresses his indebtedness to Michaelis[52] for his edition of the Hebrew Bible (Halle, 1726) and salutes him as "an excellent person, an illustrious monument of learning, judgement and indefatigable industry". Michaelis supplied notes on Lowth's *Praelectiones* which are printed in the Göttingen edition of that work (1770) and in the English translation of Gregory.

Finally, the contents of Gregory's English translation of Volume II of the *Praelectiones* may be summarized as follows: It deals with the poetic books in the Hebrew Bible and with pieces of poetry in the prose books. It examines first the characteristics of prophetic poetry (24–83) and this is followed by a consideration of the peculiar character of the poetry of each of the prophets (84–120); the Hebrew elegy (121–61); didactic poetry, Psalms, Proverbs and the Lamentations of Jeremiah (162–87); the Hebrew Ode, Psalms, Song of Moses and the Song of Deborah (188–210); the mixed style of the Hebrew Ode (211–68), the Hymn (269–86); dramatic poetry, Song of Solomon is not "a regular drama" but an allegory (277–34); the Poem of Job is "not a perfect drama" (386–405); the manners, sentiments and style of the book of Job (406–35).[53]

4. Alexander Geddes

Sources: A. GEDDES: *Idea of a New English Edition of the Holy Bible for the Use of Roman Catholics in Great Britain and Ireland* (London 1782); *Prospectus of a New Translation of the Holy Bible ...* (London 1786); *A Letter to the Right Reverend the Lord Bishop of London ...* (London 1787); *The Holy Bible Faithfully Translated ...* I (Genesis-Joshua; London 1792); II (Judges-Ruth; London 1797); *Proposals for printing by subscription a New Translation of the Holy Bible ...* (London 1788); *Dr. Geddes's General Answer to the Queries, Counsils and Criticisms ...* (London 1790); *Critical Remarks on the Hebrew Scriptures corresponding with a New Translation of the Bible ...* I (London 1800).

Reference articles: on Geddes: DNB 21 (1890) 98–101 (Thompson Cooper); DBI A-J, 434–35 (R. C. Fuller).

Special studies: S. BULLOUGH, "British Interpreters: Alexander Geddes", *ScrB* 14 (1984) 26–30; Cheyne, Founders (1893; see Gen. Bibl. above) 4–12; R. C. FULLER, *Alexander Geddes, 1737–1802: A Pioneer of Biblical Criticism* (Historic Texts and Interpreters in Biblical Scholarship 3; Sheffield: Almond 1984); W. JOHNSTONE (ed.), *The Bible and the Enlightenment: A Case Study: Dr. Alexander Geddes 1737–1802* (The Proceedings of the Bicentenary Geddes Conference held at the University of Aberdeen, 1–4 April 2002; London / New York: T&T Clark Intern. 2004); W. McKANE, "Alexander Geddes", in: idem, *Selected Christian Hebraists* (Cambridge: Cambridge UP 1989) 151–90; J. W. ROGERSON, *Old Testament Criticism in the Nineteenth Century: England and Germany* (London: SPCK 1984) 154–57; idem, "Was Geddes a 'Fragmenist'?", in (see above): The Bible and the Enlightenment (2004) 157–67; B. E. SCHWARZBACH, "Geddes in France", in: The Bible and the Enlightenment (2004) 78–118.

Alexander Geddes, born 1737, died in 1802, 23 years later than Warburton and 18 years later than Lowth, but at an earlier age than both. Warburton died at 81, Lowth at 75 and Geddes at 65. He came out of a farming community and hailed from a part of north-east Scotland which was only lightly touched by the Reformation, though the piety of his Roman Catholic home bore some resemblance to Scottish Presbyterian piety of the period in so far as it would

---

[52] Ibid. lxix.
[53] Lowth, *Lectures* II (1787) 24–435.

appear to have been founded on the King James Version of the Bible: "Although my parents were Roman Catholics", wrote Geddes, "they were not bigots and the Bible was the principal book in their scanty library".[54] It would be difficult to exaggerate the effect on Geddes exercised by the intellectual and cultural influences he absorbed during his six years at the Scots College in Paris (1758–64). Scottish Roman Catholic bishops had nursed a long-standing dissatisfaction with the Scots College in Paris and Bishop Hay, of whom Geddes was subsequently to fall foul, was prominent in these representations. The theological education which Geddes received in Paris seems to have been of another kind from its elementary stage in Scotland and his scholarly inclinations were aroused by it. He was himself well connected with the upper echelons of Scottish Catholicism. He corresponded regularly with his cousin, Bishop Geddes of Edinburgh, with whom he shared his early education, certainly up to 1791,[55] and one letter closes with an expression of his awareness that the path of criticism on which he was set might not commend itself to the Roman Catholic Church, that his future ecclesiastical standing was touched with uncertainty.

When he returned to Scotland from Paris his priestly duties were fulfilled as a chaplain to the Earl and Countess of Traquair at Traquair House in Peebles (1764–68) and then he had pastoral responsibilities as priest in his calf country, the north-east of Scotland. There is evidence that between 1764 and 1780 he still retained the common touch, but it was already evident that he was not made to be a country priest. He was a welcome guest in the houses of the nobility, mostly Episcopalians, and without this, and conversations with professors of the University of Aberdeen, his situation would hardly have been tolerable. That University acknowledged the merit of his translation of *Select Satires of Horace* (1779) by conferring on him the degree of Doctor of Laws *honoris causa* in May 1780.

When he left Auchenalrig for London in 1780, it was the beginning of the end of his life as a practising Roman Catholic priest, though his disenchantment with that Church and his alienation from it proceeded by stages and after Easter 1782 "he gave up all ministerial functions and seldom officiated".[56] He found a patron in Lord Petre, a patronage which was continued by his son, and with their financial help he continued his work in preparing a new translation of the Hebrew Bible into English. He had embarked on this with the needs of the Roman Catholic Church particularly in mind as is evident from his publication in 1782.[57] He was proposing a replacement of the Rheims-Douai version, not a new translation from Hebrew and Greek, but a revision of its translation from the Vulgate. He now abandoned that plan and no trace of a distinctively Roman Catholic scheme appears in the *Prospectus*, of 1786, where the "vulgar version" to which Geddes refers is the King James Version.[58]

---

[54] Geddes, *Dr. Geddes's General Answer* (1790) 2.
[55] Fuller, Geddes (1984) 160–62; see further Schwarzbach, Geddes in France (2004) 106–18.
[56] DNB 21, 99.
[57] Geddes, *Idea of a New English Edition of the Holy Bible* (1782).
[58] Geddes, *Prospectus of a New Translation* (1786) 95.

The Douai version of 1609 is described as "literal and barbarous".[59] The notion of translating from a Latin translation of the Hebrew into English is now dismissed as unscholarly and unreasonable.[60]

Such ecclesiastical connections as appear in the *Prospectus* link Geddes with the Church of England, but he is essentially a scholar giving birth to what he hopes will be a literary success. Like Lowth he had a high regard for the variants of the text of the Hebrew Bible which had been collated by Benjamin Kennicott from mediaeval Hebrew manuscripts, and considered that they had opened up a new door to the study of the Hebrew Bible. Kennicott died in 1783, so that it was only in the early period of his residence in London that Geddes had the benefit of his friendship, encouragement and influence, but he remembered him fondly for anticipating that he would need advice and assistance, and regretted that he had so few opportunities of benefiting from his conversation.[61] Geddes reserved a crescendo of praise and deference for Lowth in *A Letter*, of 1787, in which he thanks him for past assistance and asks him to peruse a draft of his translation of the Hebrew Bible into English.[62] Lowth received this draft and made a general, favourable response without entering into the detailed criticism which Geddes had asked for.

Geddes rarely ventures into open disagreement with the work of these Anglican scholars whose work he notices and acclaims. He parts company with Lowth, Blayney and Newcombe on the question whether 'Jehovah' should appear in an English translation of the Hebrew Bible. His disagreement with Lowth[63] about how the poetry of the Hebrew Bible should set out in an English translation does not amount to very much. He accepts that the difference between Hebrew prose and Hebrew poetry must be marked in an English translation. Lowth, for his part, admits that the metre of Hebrew poetry is lost, that it has no rhyme, and his efforts to restore it are limited to the length of its lines and the scope of its stanzas. Geddes argues for the "sober garb of a measured prose" and "a plain prose-like version" for the poetry.[64]

The publication of a consonantal text of the Hebrew Bible without points and Massorah by Kennicott and De Rossi[65] was a signal that the time of bondage to the Massoretic vocalization had come to an end and that a new era in the textual criticism of the Hebrew Bible had been inaugurated. Advances in the fundamental criticism of the text were to be made by collecting large numbers of mediaeval manuscripts (Kennicott and De Rossi), and so purifying the consonantal text. This would furnish a scientific foundation for a critical text of the Hebrew Bible and would replace the former reliance on Massoretic scholarship. Such were the expectations and aims of this new enterprise.

Geddes entered whole-heartedly on this programme. He argued that flawed translations have issued from the bad Hebrew text which was translated, and

---

[59] Ibid. 110.
[60] Ibid. 107.
[61] Ibid. 143 ff.
[62] Geddes, *A Letter* (1787) 72 f.
[63] Ibid. 45.
[64] Ibid. 45 ff.
[65] J. B. de Rossi, *Variae lectiones Veteris Testamenti* I-IV (Parma 1784–88).

he contrasted the critical attitude to the text of the Hebrew Bible with the pains which have been taken with classical texts.[66] He deplored the attention paid to the Massoretic text and the Massorah in Christian circles of learning, and asserted that most of those engaged in Bible translation for the last three hundred years "have voluntarily put out their own eyes and allowed themselves to be led by the worst of guides".[67] The anti-Jewish trend of this new textual criticism was already present in a milder form in Lowth and Kennicott, but the form of Kennicott's *Vetus Testamentum Hebraicum* I–II (1776 and 1780), leaves no room for the operation of a theological tendency, and his theological convictions, which are evident in his *Dissertations* (1753 and 1759) did not encroach on it.

Geddes envisaged the outcome of Kennicott's collation in different terms from Kennicott himself. He regarded Kennicott's theology as a kind of biblical fundamentalism which is a disease of Protestantism. He accepted the thesis of Massoretic corruption, but he also had in mind[68] an accidental contamination to which all ancient documents are subject and from which the Hebrew Bible is not exempt: "That waters which have rolled for ages through a thousand different soils and channels should still be as pure and untainted as when they issued from their primitive source, would be far less wonderful than that the Hebrew Scriptures should have remained in their first integrity".[69] Geddes was not disposed to a belief in miracles, and he did not share Kennicott's concern that the Hebrew Bible should be recovered perfectly – as God had given it. This was a biblicism foreign to the Catholic texture of his mind, and he observes that belief in an "immaculate original" is not yet universally exploded.[70] His strategy was rather to reassure the reader to whom the very idea of a better Hebrew text is disturbing, because his supposition had been that a perfect Hebrew text had always existed. It is enough to be assured that the present Hebrew text is essentially the same as its original. Whatever changes it has undergone, whether from design or accident, are not such as to damage its authority as a genuine record.[71]

There are indications that Geddes viewed the Hebrew *Vorlage* of the Septuagint as, in general, a more original Hebrew text than that of the Hebrew Bible. He noticed that there are citations in Josephus which disagree with our extant Hebrew text and agree with the Septuagint. He supposed that Josephus would not have tolerated this state of affairs in his work and that these discrepancies between the Hebrew and the Greek texts did not exist in his time: "The only fair conclusion we can draw from his disagreeing with our present Hebrew text, where he agrees with the Septuagint, is that our present Hebrew text and his Hebrew text were not the same".[72] His assumption was that where Josephus appears to prefer the Greek text to the Hebrew one, the reason is

---

[66] Geddes, *Prospectus* (1786) 2.
[67] Ibid. 6, 63.
[68] Ibid. 6.
[69] Ibid. 15.
[70] Ibid. 123.
[71] Ibid. 16.
[72] Ibid. 54 f.

that our present Hebrew text is corrupt. Geddes was also influenced by the consideration that the Hebrew text, when it was translated into Greek, must have been nearer the original than the extant text of the Hebrew Bible: "It was excellently translated into Greek, at a period when the copies must have been much less perfect than they afterwards became: this translation we have entire, though not uncorrupted".[73]

It is an easy step from this to Geddes's criticism of Jerome's *Hebraica veritas* and to his perception of the role of the Vulgate in the textual criticism of the Hebrew Bible. On Jerome he says: "The greatest imperfection of St. Jerome's version arises from too great a confidence in his Jewish guides and from his being prepossest with an idea that the Hebrew copies were then absolutely faultless. This leads him to blame the Septuagint in many places where they are not blameable and where they read and render better than he".[74] He perceived, however, a reconciliation of Catholic and Protestant critical scholarship with extremists on both sides yielding to a more balanced criticism, and this tends to pull the argument in a direction the reverse of that indicated by his remarks on the *Hebraica veritas*: "The Catholics are less insistent on the purity of the Vulgate and Protestants as readily acknowledge that the present Hebrew text is not so untainted a source as was long believed".[75] Hence Geddes combined a perception that the Hebrew *Vorlage* of the Septuagint is often better than Jerome's *Hebraica veritas* with another that the *Hebraica veritas* of Jerome's Vulgate is sometimes better than the extant Hebrew text. It is because of the latter persuasion that he can assign a function to the Vulgate in the textual criticism of the Hebrew Bible.

As he passed from textual criticism to the problems of translation Geddes touched on the lexicography of biblical Hebrew, remarking that the ascertaining of the meaning of a word is often as difficult as the discerning a true reading of the Hebrew text.[76] He directs attention to the lexicographical problems created by the antiquity of Hebrew, the smallness of the corpus, the high proportions of rare words and the hapax legomena encountered. There is a need for a wide range of ancillary, extra linguistic learning to complete the process of understanding the literature of an ancient society in which there are "references to monuments that no longer exist" and "frequent allusions to facts that are not recorded or barely hinted".[77]

Reflections on the smallness of the corpus of biblical Hebrew, "The whole text together makes but an ordinary volume",[78] and on the other obstacles to lexicographical elucidation which it presents, lead to a recognition of the need to have access to the resources of a comparative Semitic philology and a warning against too heavy a reliance on etymology: "The best lexicons are yet very imperfect; the significance of many words is extremely dubious and their ety-

---

[73] Geddes, *Holy Bible* I (1792) 20.
[74] Geddes, *Prospectus* (1786) 48.
[75] Ibid. 52.
[76] Ibid. 61 f.
[77] Ibid. 62.
[78] Ibid. 72.

mology very often equivocal. Hence he who aspires at but a competent knowledge of it [biblical Hebrew] must frequently have recourse to the other Oriental dialects".[79] Comparative Semitic philology has recently been a preoccupation of lexicographers and the words of Geddes have a modern ring. It is not so clear that he is seizing on the fallacy of 'etymologizing' as it has been perceived in recent times, that he is balancing the etymology of a word against its use in different contexts.

Geddes was not clearly pushing in this direction and his praise of "uniformity" in translation might be thought to give a reverse indication. He had a point in complaining of the lack of uniformity[80] in English translations of the Hebrew Bible in so far as he is attacking different renderings of the same Hebrew word which arise solely from a failure in overall superintendence and produce an unnecessary unevenness. This is a tiresome task of revision, but Geddes is right to insist that it must not be neglected, as he alleges it was in the case of the King James Version. It arises, according to Geddes, from the "committee" character of the translation and was not overcome by the members "assembled for this purpose". He continues: "When we consider that they were only nine months about this revision, much less for a reduction of its stile to the same colour and complexion".[81] In so far as "uniformity" simply demands that a Hebrew word should be translated by the same English word throughout, if there is no reason for deviation, its achievement requires good organization and meticulous thoroughness, but, otherwise, it is not a complex matter. When the examples of "uniformity" in Geddes's *Letter* to Lowth are examined,[82] it becomes evident that it is not this simple kind of uniformity that exercises him, that, on occasions, he is pressing for a uniformity which betrays his lack of sensitivity as a translator.

Geddes could ill afford to have lost Lowth and Kennicott and the bad effect which it had on the coolness of his scholarship and the reasonableness of his temper is evident in the second volume of his translation of the Hebrew Bible into English (1797) and in his *Critical Remarks* (1800). Already in the first of these there is evidence of a lack of composure, of an inner turmoil which is producing deterioration and of a tendency to rant, an example of which is his anticipation of a fury of dissent and denunciation in response to his statement that he cannot reconcile the veracity of the Pentateuch with "the divine legation of Moses".[83] The contrast between this tirade and the scholarly proposals of the *Prospectus*, the precise discussion of translation problems in the *Letter* to Lowth, or the moderate tone of the preface to the first volume of *The Holy Bible* (1792), is striking. This anxiety and inner disquiet arose from a continuation of his work beyond the stage of textual criticism and translation, his entanglement with questions about the historical accuracy of sections of the Hebrew Bible and its "inspiration". In his earlier books Geddes had been occu-

---

[79] Ibid. 139.
[80] Geddes, *A Letter* (1787) 5–14.
[81] Geddes, *Prospectus* (1786) 94.
[82] Geddes, *A Letter* (1787) 9 ff.
[83] Geddes, *The Holy Bible* II (1797) iv.

pied with critical considerations preparatory to translation: textual criticism, the Massoretic text, the ancient versions, the lexicography of biblical Hebrew and translational problems of principle and detail. His criticism had been focused on the Hebrew text, Hebrew manuscripts and the ancient versions, though it had extended into higher criticism with his early form of the Fragment Hypothesis of the Pentateuch.[84] The Roman Catholic Church moved against him, prohibiting his work to the faithful, and Geddes was suspended from all ecclesiastical functions soon after the publication of the first first volume of *The Holy Bible* (1792).

Geddes had ventured into a different kind of biblical criticism, less precise than textual criticism or translation, and more contentious. Even so, if he had limited himself to higher criticism and not attempted to construct a new religion out of it, he might have retained a scholarly calm which he had lost by 1797. His higher criticism interacted with an adventurous theology. When one reads the preface in his *Critical Remarks*, it becomes evident that Geddes is as cut off from Anglicanism or Presbyterianism as he is from Roman Catholicism, that he has no longer any regard for the historical creeds of Christianity. His sense of isolation and rejection must have contributed to the darkness of his mood and to his imperious sweeping away of all forms of institutional Christianity. He was now nursing an élitist hope of a gathering of thoughtful Christians from all sects to embrace a new Christianity in a temple of reason, where only religious belief recommended by reason would have currency.

Geddes was not content to assert that a critical study of the Hebrew Bible resembles the study of any other collection of ancient documents; that it is a function of humanist scholarship, a department of biblical science, unfettered by religious restrictions. He extended the range of his criticism beyond a humanist scholarship and endeavoured to create a rational religion. His rationalism was too narrow to make sense of Christianity and he ended up with his intellectual élite in circumstances hardly less absurd than those attaching to a dogmatic predestinarianism. The principal flaw in his new religion was that few could jump over the hurdle he erected and many were excluded from the "genuine religion" which was conducive to human happiness.

---

[84] Rogerson, Old Testament Criticism (1984) 154–57; see now, however, idem, Was Geddes a 'Fragmentist?', in: The Bible and the Enlightenment (2004) 157–67.

CHAPTER FORTY-ONE

Early Old Testament Critics on the Continent

By JOHN SANDYS-WUNSCH, Victoria, BC

General works on the period: K. ANER, *Die Theologie der Lessingzeit* (Halle: Niemeyer 1929); H. W. FREI, The Eclipse of Biblical Narrative (New Haven / London: Yale UP 1974); E. HIRSCH, *Geschichte der neuern evangelischen Theologie* 1–5 (Gütersloh: Gütersloher Verlagshaus Gerd Mohn ³1964); J. I. ISRAEL, *Radical Enlightenment* (Oxford: Oxford UP 2001); H.-J. KRAUS, *Geschichte der historisch-kritischen Erforschung des Alten Testaments* (rev. edn.; Neukirchen-Vluyn: Neukirchener Verlag ³1982); J. KIRCHNER, *Das Deutsche Zeitschriftenwesen: Seine Geschichte und seine Probleme*, Teil I (Wiesbaden: Otto Harrassowitz ²1958); F. PAULSEN, *Geschichte des gelehrten Unterrichts* (Leipzig: von Veit ³1919); J. SANDYS-WUNSCH, *What Have They Done to the Bible? A History of Modern Biblical Interpretation* (Collegeville, MN: Liturgical Press 2005).

1. Introduction

Campegius Vitringa (1659–1722), Johann August Ernesti (1707–1781) and Johann David Michaelis (1717–1791) illustrate the ways in which the new Enlightenment ideas of philosophy, language and world history affected scholars who claimed orthodoxy for themselves but who were not insensitive to the claims of discoveries and approaches in biblical scholarship.

Vitringa was a scholar's scholar, formally in that he usually published in Latin, substantially in his painstaking attention to detail and his superb knowledge of biblical languages. Unlike his contemporary Jean Le Clerc (1657–1736), Vitringa did not enter into the wider public debate by participating in the emerging learned journals. Ernesti was basically a philologist in the Renaissance tradition, interested in the scholarly examination of the meaning of words and grammar. His sense of Latin style attracted admiration and he wrote elegant, even ironic German as editor of perhaps the most important theological journal of the period. Michaelis had much wider interests than either Vitringa or Ernesti and played a prominent role in learned societies and public debate. While he was a competent scholar in oriental languages, he permitted himself the dangerous luxury of straying beyond his own field into areas such as dogmatics and biblical translation where his work aroused less enthusiasm. While not altogether a popularizer in the modern sense of the term, he tended to write more often in German than Latin with an eye for the new reading public whose growing importance and influence is reflected in the numbers of periodicals that sprang up in Germany and elsewhere in the eighteenth century.[1] An indication of his interest in assuming a 'trendy' mantle is shown in his early work *Von der Verpflichtung der Menschen die Wahrheit zu reden*[2] where he puts his profession as the fashionable *Professor von Weltweisheit* rather than the more formal title of Professor of Philosophy.

2. Campegius Vitringa

Sources: Major works of VITRINGA on the Old Testament: *Sacrarum observationum* (also *Observationum sacrarum*; various editions marked by increasing contents from 1689–1726); *De synagoga vetere libri tres* (Franequerae 1696; 2nd edn. Leovardiae 1726; ET [partial]: *The Synagogue and the Church*, London 1842); *Commentarius in librum prophetiarum Jesaiae* (Herbornae Nassaviorum 1715, 1722; Leovardiae 1724; Basel 1732; Harlingen 1734); *De decem-viris otiosis, ad sacra necessaria* (Franequeræ 1687); *Commentarii ad librum prophetiarum Zachariae* (Leovardiae 1734). - JoHANNES COCCEJUS / JUAN BAUTISTA VILLALPANDO / CAMPEGIUS VITRINGA: *Naeder ondersoeck van het rechte verstand van den Tempel die den propheet Ezechiel gesien en beschreven heeft in sijn laetste gesichte* (Amsterdam 1691); *Hypotyposis historiae et chronologiae sacrae ... Accedit typus doctrinae propheticae* (Leovardiae 1716, 1722; ET [partial]: "On the Interpretation of Prophecy", *The Investigator* 4 [1834–35] 153–76). - *Geographia sacra Primum* edita opera Daniel Godofredi Werner (Jenae 1723).

General works: B. S. CHILDS, "Hermeneutical Reflections on C. Vitringa, Eighteenth-century interpreter of Isaiah", *In Search of True Wisdom* (ed. Edward Ball; Sheffield: JSOT 1999) 89–98; E. VAN DER WALL, "Between Grotius and Coccejus. The 'Theologia Prophetica' of Campegius Vitringa (1659–1722)", in: *Hugo Grotius Theologian: Essays in Honour of G. H. M. Posthumus Meyjes* (ed. Henk J. M. Nellen / Henk and Edwin Rabbie; Leiden: Brill 1994) 195–215; K. M: WITTEVEEN, "Campegius Vitringa und die Prophetische Theologie", *Reformiertes Erbe: Festschrift für Gottfried W. Locher zu seinem 80. Geburtstag* (ed. H. A. Oberman e.a.; Zürich: Theologischer Verlag 1993) 343–59.

Campegius Vitringa (1659–1722) – to be distinguished from his son Campegius Vitringa (1698–1723) – studied at Franeker and then at Leiden under Herman Witsius (1636–1708). He took a teaching position at Franeker which he never left. His interests extended beyond biblical exegesis to church history, dogmatics, archeology, and homiletics, but he is best known for his great commentary on Isaiah.

2.1. The Influence of the New Importance Attributed to History

In his early work *De confusione linguarum* which is an extensive discussion of the Tower of Babel story, Vitringa shows the influence of one important new direction in European thought, namely the rising perception of the significance of history as a factor to be considered in the discussion of books and ideas. From the mid-seventeenth century there had been a growing sense both of the importance of history in the shaping of human thought and the need to investigate historical statements critically rather than making somewhat hazy gener-

---

[1] See Kirchner, Das Deutsche Zeitschriftenwesen (1958).
[2] Göttingen 1750.

alisations about epochs in the past.[3] In this early work Vitringa addressed two issues that go far beyond lists of dates and genealogies, namely Moses' possible use of pre-existing documents and the origin of languages.

Now the theory of the composite origins of the Pentateuch was not a new idea; hinted at by Andreas Karlstadt (Carlstadt), argued by Andreas Masius, and incorporated into Pererius' great Genesis commentary; the arguments were well known to scholars by the beginning of the seventeenth century. However, it was more radical writers such as La Peyrère, Hobbes, and Spinoza who espoused this viewpoint in the mid-seventeenth century, but by the time of *De confusione linguarum* Richard Simon and Jean Le Clerc had reintroduced the debate into scholarly circles. Clearly Vitringa despite his conservatism was impressed and he even mentioned Masius who had argued that the Pentateuch had been re-edited after Moses. Vitringa did not discuss Masius' ideas in detail, but it is clear he was susceptible to arguments from historical probability to the point where he showed a relative freedom from the strict theory of inspiration endorsed by Protestant Orthodoxy. This not altogether original detour into less conservative ways was to earn Vitringa the mild regrets of V. E. Loescher and the admiring endorsement of J. C. Edelmann who classed him, perhaps too optimistically, amongst those who broke with biblical literalism.[4]

Vitringa rejected the interpretation that the Tower of Babel story is about the historical origins of different languages; rather what was meant was that God effected misunderstandings whose origin was personal rather than linguistic. While it is clear he was dependent here upon Samuel Bochart's *Pheleg* and Le Clerc's *Genesis*, the reason why he finds their arguments compelling was his knowledge of how language works and how it develops. Vitringa was obviously not convinced that languages suddenly just happen; instead he saw new languages emerging as groups of humans move away from each other and arriving eventually at different languages as changes make mutual comprehension impossible. The appeal behind his position is to natural historical process rather than sudden divine intervention. While some of his explanations of the derivations of particular languages are no longer convincing, his instincts were modern.

2.2. Vitringa and Cocceius' Federal Theology

Vitringa's acceptance of the importance of historical process was to affect his conservative interpretation of prophecy in two respects even if it did not overthrow it completely. In order to understand what Vitringa did that was new, it

---

[3] It was at this time that serious attention began to be paid to treating not just the truth of philosophy but also its history and development. Thomas Stanley's *History of Philosophy* appeared in 1656–60. Even the history of scholarship began to be scrutinized with Gottlieb Stolle's *Anleitung zur Historie der Gelahrtheit* (1724) which went through several editions in the first part of the eighteenth century. Stolle also produced studies on the history of theology and law.

[4] See V. E. Loescher, *Unschuldige Nachrichten* (Leipzig 1712) 39–41, and J. C. Edelmann, *Moses mit aufgedecktem Angesichte* (Freyburg 1740) 1: 58.

is necessary to understand the great gulf that exists between modern scholar-ship and the view of prophecy that was common to most scholars at the outset of the eighteenth century. In the past hundred years or so it has been common if not universal to interpret the prophets of the Bible as 'forthtellers' rather than 'foretellers' and to see their role as either teachers of morality or as social commentators and reformers. Furthermore, a distinction is often made be-tween prophecy and apocalyptic, usually to the disadvantage of the latter. In the seventeenth and eighteenth centuries, however, the basic function of pro-phets was seen as the foretelling of future events, whether immediate or far off. Furthermore the Book of Revelation in the New Testament was seen as a prophetic work similar in nature but greater in scope than prophecy in the Old Testament. This remained Vitringa's basic position from which he did not wa-ver, but his sense of history was to modify it both with regard to Cocceius' fed-eral theology and to his own approach in his Isaiah commentary.

The obvious future reference of biblical prophecy had been given a new force in Protestant dogmatics by Cocceius in the seventeenth century whose federal theology represented a departure from older orthodoxy that treated the Bible as a pool of proof texts to the view of the Bible as a book that pre-sented the shape of history as a series of events leading to the introduction of the Kingdom of God. The prophets contained the evidence for this system of *Heilsgeschichte.* This viewpoint was influential in Calvinist circles, but even Lutheran theologians were attracted to it. On the other hand, Hugo Grotius had put forward a very different view which discounted the longer range impli-cations of biblical prophecy, confining it to foretelling or commenting on mat-ters in the immediate times of the prophets, even to the point of interpreting the "suffering servant" in Isaiah as a description of Jeremiah rather than as a prophecy of Christ and rejecting any notion that the prophets foresaw events such as the defeat of the Spanish Armada. Vitringa's teacher Witsius had modified this viewpoint and Vitringa made further adjustments in his attempt to combine the views of Cocceius with those of Grotius who had insisted on a strong realistic biblical exegesis.[5]

Witsius had already modified Cocceius' ideas to make them fit better into the orthodox Protestant dogmatic schema. Vitringa went further in his modifi-cation of federal theology. In his preface to the reader in his Isaiah commen-tary he shows he is conscious of trying to steer a middle course between Coc-ceius' theology which tended to find in the prophets foreshadowings of various epochs throughout world history up to the present and beyond, and Grotius' more realistic, literal reading of the Old Testament.[6] While Vitringa was un-willing to abandon the possibility that a biblical prophecy might refer to hap-penings at a much later time, his sense of what actually happened at a point in history made him suspect that no one would have been interested in events that were to happen long after their own day. This meant that the oracles of the

---

[5] For an excellent discussion of Vitringa's relation to Cocceius and Grotius, see Witteveen, Ca-pegius Vitringa und die Prophetische Theologie (1993) 343–59.

[6] The oft-repeated saying is that in the interpretation of the Old Testament whereas Cocceius found Christ described everywhere, Grotius found Christ nowhere.

Hebrew prophets had to refer at least to happenings in their own periods even if wider implications were also to be found.[7] A new point of tension had been introduced into orthodox Protestant scholarship.

2.3. New Departures in the Isaiah Commentary

Vitringa's outstanding achievement was his great Isaiah commentary published in two folio volumes (1, 1713; 2, 1722). The first impression it gives is not only its size but its quality; obviously a labour of love – it took him thirty years to complete it; it must be one of the most thorough Isaiah commentaries ever written. Its very format is indicative of the care that went into the book, for indexes of subjects covered and Hebrew words discussed are provided for each volume and the quality of the printing and production is superb. The work is characterized by careful attention to details of grammar and the meaning of words in context and various views on the meaning of the text are carefully discussed.

More important in the development of biblical scholarship was Vitringa's emphasis on Isaiah as a book written at a particular period of history before it is interpreted as a source of doctrine. He devoted a prolegomena to the sort of subjects that are found in better modern commentaries, namely our knowledge of the author, his style of writing, the times in which he lived, the reason for the book's place in the canon, and an analysis of its argument. In other words, in place of a series of proof texts for dogmatics, the book of Isaiah becomes a work written by a man in a particular period of history. Vitringa suggested it is even possible that editorial work can be seen, the first sentence of Isaiah was originally a genuine saying of the prophet but was then used by later disciples as the introduction to all the prophet's work. Vitringa breaks chapters down into collections of individual oracles and often his decisions are tenable today. He discusses the meanings of words by considering their historical context in a manner that was to earn the praise of Ernesti himself. Obviously many of the judgements in the work have been made obsolete by more recent discoveries, but Vitringa himself was aware of the fragmentary nature of his information about the history of the period and recognized how the discovery of further information about biblical times would change scholarship's viewpoint on prophecy.

The change of tone that underlies this commentary can be seen by comparing Vitringa's commentary with that of Hector Pintus (1526[?]-84) which Vitringa referred to on a regular basis.[8] Pintus' work has a two dimensional feel to it; in its explanations of passages in Isaiah Pintus jumps around the whole Bible in search of explanations of passages without any apparent feeling of in-

---

[7] This concern is similar to the debate in England between William Whiston, *The Accomplishment of Scripture Prophecies* (London 1708) who argued that a prophet's oracle could only refer to one thing, and Samuel White, *Commentary on the Prophet Isaiah* (London 1709) who defended the view that more than one future event could be found in a prophetic saying.

[8] Hector Pintus, *In Esaiam prophetam commentaria* (Lugduni [Louvain] 1567).

congruity; for him the Bible is a flat, almost undifferentiated surface of which one part is much the same as another without reference to date, place, or circumstance.

Vitringa's influence in Old Testament interpretation was considerable for his Isaiah commentary served as a quarry for commentators for some time to come. His other works consisted of a re-edited and ever growing number of smaller works on the Tower of Babel, the Kabbalah (whose neo-Platonic origins he was aware of), a commentary on the Apocalypse, a study of Israelite institutions, and two commentaries left unfinished and published after his death. More recently Vitringa's hermeneutical method has attracted the attention of BREVARD CHILDS who argues that it still has relevance to the discussion about canonical criticism.[9]

In short, Vitringa was, as the German proverb has it, *ein zwei Seelen Mensch*, that is a good scholar caught between two worlds. On one hand, his temperament was conservative and he was reluctant to waver from Orthodoxy. On the other hand, he was too honest to ignore the evidence from within the Bible and from sources outside it that would suggest it is no longer sufficient to assert the *theopneustia* of the Bible in the traditional manner; what is to be said has to be proved in the face of criticism. The *modus vivendi* Vitringa worked out was not to endure even though he has some modern admirers; however, the philological acumen and historical sense of his particular observations meant his commentary was to endure as a reference for scholars for some time to come.

3. Johann August Ernesti

Sources: J. A. ERNESTI: *Institutio interpretis Novi Testamenti* (Leiden 1761; editions later than the third, 1775, ed. by C. F. Ammon; ET: *Elements of interpretation*, tr. Moses Stuart; Andover 1827; and *Principles of Biblical interpretation*, tr. Charles H. Terrot; *The Biblical Cabinet* 1,4; Edinburgh 1832/33); *Neue Theologische Bibliothek* (1760–70); *Neueste Theologische Bibliothek* (1771–75); *Opuscula oratoria* (Lugduni batavorum [Leiden] 1762; [2]1767); *Opuscula philologica critica* (Lugduni batavorum 1764; [2]1776); *Opuscula theologica* (Lipsiae [Leipzig] 1773; [2]1792).

Bibliographies: Leipziger Universitäts-Program auf den wohlseligen Herrn D/ Ernesti (Uebersetzt von M. Carl Gottfried Küttner; Frankfurt / Leipzig 1782); A. WESTERMANN, *Memoriam Ioannis Augusti Ernesti* (Leipzig 1846).

General works: B. F. SCHMIEDER, *Ernestiana* (Halle 1782), *Allgemeine Deutsche Bibliothek* 55 (1783) 15–39; W. A. TELLER, *Des Herrn Joh. August Ernesti ... Verdienst um die Theologie und die Religion* (Berlin 1783; Zusätze hierzu von Johann Salomo Semler, 1783); E. F. K. ROSENMÜLLER, *Handbuch für die Literatur der biblischen Kritik und Exegese* 3 (1799) 151–56; G. HEINRICI, "Ernesti Johann August", *Hauck's Realenzyklopedia* V, 469ff; W. PHILIPP, "Ernesti, Johann August", RGG[3] II, 600–01. See also ANER, FREI, HIRSCH, KRAUS and PAULSEN above.

Johann August Ernesti (1707–81) studied mathematics, philosophy, and theology at Wittenberg where one of his teachers was Wernsdorf.[10] He moved to Leipzig to be a private tutor but soon was given a position at the Thomasschule where he eventually became rector. Overlapping his work

---

[9] Childs, Hermeneutical Reflections on C. Vitringa (1999) 89–98.

[10] I am indebted to Dr. Friedrich Christoph Ilgner of the University of Leipzig for an electronic communication about Ernesti's attitude to Scripture, but my views in this article should not necessarily be attributed to Dr. Ilgner. His thesis *Die neutestamentliche Auslegungslehre des Johann August*

at the Thomasschule Ernesti began lecturing at the University of Leipzig where he remained for the rest of his career. As was the custom of the day he began in the Faculty of litterarum humaniorum where he lectured on the Latin classics but eventually he transferred to the theological faculty. He is best remembered in popular history either as the assertive young administrator at the Thomasschule who had a quarrel with J. S. Bach or as the dull university professor whose dry lectures were part of the sorrows of young Goethe.

In his *Kirchen und Ketzer Almanach* C. F. Bahrdt, the Falstaff of Enlightenment theology, praised Ernesti's knowledge, especially of philology, and concluded that only two weaknesses prevented him from being the greatest German theologian of his era, namely his disinterest in philosophy and his lack of taste in evaluating literature.[11] Bahrdt praised Ernesti as a teacher, pointing out that the best students went to Ernesti, the others went to his rival Crusius, perhaps an ironic reflection on himself by Bahrdt who had been at Leipzig but where he was a pupil of Crusius and not Ernesti. Bahrdt's tribute to Ernesti's teaching ability was confirmed by similar elogies by others after Ernesti's death.

A classicist as much as a biblical scholar, and without any serious publications on the Hebrew Bible, Ernesti is important for the history of Old Testament studies for his writings on the theory of interpretation and for his excellent editing of a leading theological journal. His introduction to the hermeneutics of the New Testament, *Institutio interpretis Novi Testamenti* (1761), was translated twice into English (along with notes from German scholars who had edited the work), and the book's influence in both England and The United States was considerable. In this work Ernesti concentrated on how one discovers the meanings of words in the context where they occur, taking into account both the style of the author and the general context in which they would have been used. For example he argues that it is inappropriate to interpret the word 'servant' in the Epistle to the Romans in the way the word is used in the Justinian code; rather the background for its meaning in Paul is to be found in the document common to Paul and his readers, namely the Old Testament in its Septuagint version.[12] While Ernesti has little to say about the Old Testament, it is clear that the use of historical background would also apply to determining the meaning of words in the Old Testament, and it is a discussion of his principles in one of his smaller works that Ernesti praises Vitringa's Isaiah commentary as a model to follow.[13]

Ernesti's approach to the Bible and how to interpret it was conditioned by his negative reaction to the growing esteem given to the new philosophy where it was thought possible to combine the certainty of mathematics with the usefulness of moral suasion and reasonable behaviour.[14] Ernesti's dissention from

---

Ernesti (1707–1781). Ein Beitrag zur Erforschung der Aufklärungshermeneutik (Diss. theol. Univ. Leipzig 2002) will be published soon.

[11] [Carl/Karl Friedrich Bahrdt], *Kirchen und Ketzer Almanach, zweyte quinquiennium* (Gihon: Kasimir Lange 1787) 53.

[12] Surprisingly, Ernesti paid little attention to the problem of texts, a weakness found in his work generally including his editions of Latin authors.

[13] *De vanitate philosophantium in interpretatione librorum s[acrorum]*, 235, 238.

[14] Wolf gave rise to the fashion of doing theology "by the mathematical method" by which was

this point of view is expressed in his *De vanitate philosophantium in interpreta-tione librorum s[acrorum]* – "the futility of philosophizing in the interpreting the Bible". There were three different targets Ernesti had in mind in attacking philosophically based exegesis. The first was the new "popular" approach found most notably in Christian Wolf but also in Ernesti's colleague at Leipzig C. A. Crusius whose own direction is best shown in his *Anweisung vernünftig zu leben*. Ernesti's second target was Spinoza's friend Ludowijk Meyer who had published his *Philosophia scripturae interpres* in 1666 in which he argued, perhaps a little naively, that since an exact and universally convincing interpre-tation of Scripture was impossible, it made more sense to use Descartes' philo-sophy as the guide to the meaning of Scripture. Ernesti's third target included writers such as Spinoza, Toland, Tindal, and Morgan who each in his own way went beyond philosophy as a key to biblical exegesis to philosophy as a better guide to true religion than the Bible.

Ernesti opposed this new tradition with an older one, a tradition that went back to Renaissance humanists such as Erasmus and Camerarius for whom the determination of the meaning of words was paramount in theology.[15] The ba-sis for this approach was the assumption that since divine revelation is neces-sary for human beings whereas philosophy is not, it follows that it is in the careful interpretation of Scripture that truth is to be found. This meant that an appropriate method must be worked out. In his *Oratio de institutis criticorum in studiis theologiae imitandis*, Ernesti praised *critica sacra* in the older sense of the careful investigation of the meaning of the words of the Bible. He included an interesting autobiographical passage which discusses his early dedication to theology and how he studied the classical non-biblical authors in order to un-derstand the meaning of the Bible better. His disdain for what he considered the superficial approach of the latest philosophically tinged exegesis is clear in his approval of the advice of Grotius: *Lege veteres…, sperne recentiores* – "read the older …, spurn the newer", as well as in his vigorous attack on the then fashionable Le Clerc who in Ernesti's opinion, *e quolibet quidlibet fecit* – "finds anything anywhere at all", thanks to his inadequate knowledge of language.[16]

At the outset of *De vanitate* Ernesti addressed himself particularly to those who were discouraged by the difficulties of interpreting the New Testament and other old books by the proper means of grammatical investigation. It is important nonetheless to carry on with this, for this is the only way to sure and certain knowledge of Christian doctrine. It is possible that Ernesti had in mind the attitude of Crusius who in his *Anweisung vernünftig zu leben* says specifically of the duties of rational faith: *Sie werden in der geoffenbahrten Theologie vorausgesetzet, und man kann sie nirgends als in der Moralphilosophie*

---

meant by a method whose approach yielded results as secure in theology as the results of mathe-matics.

[15] It is interesting that in his edition of Lodewijk [also Ludweg and Louis] Meyer's *Philosophia scripturae Interpres* Semler included as a counterbalance to Meyer's exclusively philosophical ap-proach, Camerarius' *De forma orationis scriptorum, et aliis quibusdam consideratione non indignis* whose conclusion was: *Grammatica & Litterarum nostras est doctrina, altior atque sublimior, & quaer-enda & inuenienda alibi,* 287.

[16] *Oratio de institutis criticorum in studiis theologiae imitandis,* 46.

suchen – "they are presupposed in revealed theology and one can find them only in moral philosophy".[17] Ernesti implied that the charm of such a use of philosophy to interpret the Bible is that it makes things easy for the lazy, but its drawback is that people have gone off the track in doctrine thanks to its method. Ernesti made the point in detail that trying to introduce philosophical doctrines into biblical terminology is incorrect and while he does not mention Crusius by name, he cites two glaring examples of this practice in A. F. Hofmann, a deceased philosopher on whom Crusius had heaped great praise.[18]

Another influence in biblical interpretation was the federalist doctrine that originated with Cocceius that Scripture was a guide to past and coming history divided into various epochs. This pattern which was imposed upon the Bible as much as derived from it, existed in various version through Witsius, Vitringa, and once again Crusius in his function as theologian rather than philosopher. With this approach Ernesti had no patience for it meant applying a preconceived pattern to exegesis instead of allowing conclusions to come from careful exegesis based on grammar and idiom.

But while Ernesti accepted the inspiration of the Bible, he did not see it as an undifferentiated text. In his review of Semler's work on the canon, Ernesti rejected Semler's criterion that books that were purely history were not to be seen as important.[19] However, Ernesti was also quite clear that much of what was in the Old Testament was no longer of significance for the Christian Church for it came from the days of the theocracy which preceded the preaching of the kingdom of God. Ironically, while Ernesti had been seen by some as weaker than Semler in matters of history, and indeed he did not discuss them in detail, nonetheless he had a higher opinion than Semler of the importance of history for the self-understanding of a people and consequently the importance of having an accurate history for the establishment of Israel's religion.

Ernesti's textbook on hermeneutics exercised a wide influence, especially in editions made by others which balanced his concentration on grammar and language alone. Two different translations were made into English and they influenced the education of theological students throughout the nineteenth century. Ernesti's reviews in the *Neue Theologische Bibliothek* and its successor *Die Neueste Theologische Bibliothek* performed a useful function in their day, for his work was informed by great erudition and his tone was sympathetic even when he was critical, although he could occasionally permit himself an ironic remark.

Ernesti then was a conservative, but an extraordinarily learned one. In his attitude to the current thought of his day he was in fact reactionary, but then one has to ask who now remembers Ernesti's rival the modish Crusius? His direct contribution to biblical studies was his re-emphasis on the philological

---

[17] *Anweisung vernünftig zu leben* (1744), *Vorrede*, not numbered, fourteenth and fifteenth side from beginning (C. A. Crusius, Die philosophischen Hauptwerke 1; repr. Hildesheim: Olms 1969).

[18] Crusius, *Vorrede*, 20th side from the beginning.

[19] Review of part two of Semler's *Abhandlung von freyer Untersuchung des Canon*, in: *Neueste Theologische Bibliothek* 20 (1772) 429–44, esp. 441–44.

acuity of the Renaissance scholars to which he added a sharper sense of the importance of time and context. His indirect contribution lay in his work as an educator and in his balanced review of new ideas not only in biblical studies but in theology and religion generally.

4. Johann David Michaelis

Sources: J. D. MICHAELIS: *Dissertatio de punctuorum hebraicorum antiquitate, sub examen vocans argumenta adversariorum contra punctorum antiquitatem* (Halle / Magdeburg 1739); *Hebräische Grammatik nebst einem Anhange von gründlicher Erkentniss derselben* (Halle 1745, 1753, 1778); *Commentatio de mente et ratione legis mosaicae usuram prohibentis* (Erfurt 1746); *Commentatio prior ad leges divinas de poena homicidii* (Göttingen 1747); *Commentatio posterior* (Göttingen 1750); *Verpflichtung der Menschen die Wahrheit zu reden und zeiget zugleich an, wie er künftig seine Arbeit auf der Georg-Augustus-Universität einzurichten gedencke* (Gottingen 1750; [includes description of the courses M. planned to teach]); *Berurtheilung der Mittel: welche man anwendet, die ausgestorbene hebäische Sprache zu verstehen* (Göttingen 1757); *Essai physique sur l'heure des marées dans la mer rouge comparée avec l'heure du passage des hébreux* (Göttingen 1758); *De l'influence des opinions sur le langage, et du langage sur les opinions* (Breme [Bremen] 1762); *Abhandlung von der syrischen Sprache, und ihrem Gebrauch nebst dem ersten Theil einer syrischen Chrestomathie* (Göttingen 1772); *Vermischte Schriften* (Frankfurt am Main 1766); *Roberti Lowth A.M. Collegii novi Socii & Poeticae Publici Praelectoris de Sacra Poesia Hebraeorum Praelectione Academiae Oxoniae habitae. Subiicitur Metricae Harianae brevis confutatio & Oratio Crewiana. Notas & epimetra adiecit I.D.M. …* (Pars Prior, Göttingen 1758; Pars Posterior, 1761; ET: *Lectures on the sacred poetry of the Hebrews*; tr. Gregory; London 1787); *Fragen an eine Gesellschaft gelehrter Männer …* (Frankfurt a. M. 1762); *Specilegium geographiae Hebraeorum exterae post Bochartum* (Göttingen 1769, 1780); *Deutsche Übersetzung des Alten Testaments, mit Anmerkungen für Ungelehrte* (Göttingen 1769–82); *Übersetzung des Neuen Testaments* (Göttingen 1790–92); *Mosaisches Recht* (Frankfurt a. M. 1770; Reutlingen* ²1788–93; ET: *Commentaries on the laws of Moses*; tr. Alexander Smith; London 1814); *Lebensbeschreibung, von ihm selbst abgefaßt und mit Anmerkungen herausgegeben von J. W. Hassencamp. Nebst Bemerkungen über dessen litterarischen Character von Eichhorn, Schulz und dem Eulogium von Heyne* (Rinteln / Leipzig 1793). – For a more complete bibliography see the article "Michaelis" at WWW.BAUTZ.DE.

General works: J. G. EICHHORN, *Johann David Michaelis, Einige Bemerkungen über seinen literarischen Charakter* (s.l. 1791); D. GUTZEN, "Bemerkugen zur Bibelübersetzung des Johann David Michaelis, *Was Dolmetschen für Kunst und Erbeit sey*", *Vestigia Bibliae* 4 (1982) 71–78; TH. HANSEN, *Arabia Felix* (tr. J. & K. McFarlane; London 1964); G. HASSLER, *Sprachtheorien der Aufklärung: zur Rolle der Sprache im Erkenntnisprozess* (Berlin 1984); A.-R. LÖWENBRÜCK, "Johann David Michaelis et les débuts de la critique biblique", in: *Le siècle des Lumières et la Bible* (BTT 7; 1986) 113–28, eadem, "Johann David Michaeli's Verdienst um die philologisch-historische Bibelkritik", in: H. GRAF REVENTLOW e.a., *Historische Kritik und biblischer Kanon in der deutschen Aufklärung* (Wolfenbütteler Forschungen 41; Wiesbaden 1988) 157–70; J. C. O'FLAHERTY, The quarrel of reason with itself (Columbia, SC: Camden House cr. 1988); J. MEYER, "Geschichte der Göttinger theologische[n] Fakultät", *ZGNKG* 42 (1937) 7–107, esp. 28ff, 43, 98; J. W. ROGERSON, Old Testament Criticism in the Nineteenth Century. England and Germany (London 1985) 162ff, 167ff; idem, "Michaelis, John David (1717–1791)", HHMBI (1998) 343–46; R. SMEND, "Aufgeklärte Bemühung um das Gesetz. Johann David Michaelis' 'Mosaisches Recht'", in: H.-G. GEYER e.a. (eds.), *"Wenn nicht jetzt, wann dann?" Aufsätze für Hans-Joachim Kraus zum 65. Geburtstag* (Neukirchen-Vluyn 1983) 129–39 (repr. in: idem, *Epochen der Bibelkritik*, BevTh 109; München 1991, 63–73); idem, "Johann David Michaelis und Johann Gottfried Eichhorn – zwei Orientalisten am Rande der Theologie", in: B. MOELLER (ed.), *Theologie in Göttingen. Eine Vorlesungsreihe* (Göttingen: Vandenhoeck & Ruprecht 1987) 58–81; idem, "Johann David Michaelis. 1717–1791", in: idem, *Deutsche Alttestamentler in drei Jahrhunderten* (Göttingen: Vandenhoeck & Ruprecht 1989) 13–24; W. WIEFEL, "Michaelis, Johann David (1717–1791)", TRE 23 (1992) 712–14.

Johann David Michaelis (1717–91), one of the more exciting theologians of the eighteenth century, was one of the glories of the new university of Göttingen. Goethe in *Dichtung und Wahrheit* tells how he originally wanted to go to Göttingen because of the fame of Heyne, Michaelis and others but he had to settle for Leipzig in deference to his father's strong opinions on the subject. Michaelis' personal attributes have attracted critical comment. C. F. BAHRDT began his entry on Michaelis with: "Louis d'ors; it is raining Louis d'ors". Whether Michaelis was as avaricious as he is painted, there is no doubt that the by eighteenth century standards magnificent house he owned, still extant today in Göttingen, is a reminder that not all professors died poor. He was also criticised for taking advantage of his non-clerical state to wear a sword to class and to make remarks of a scandalous nature on a frequent basis. To be fair to Michaelis he was ready to admit that his judgments could be wrong and that new ideas could force him to reconsider old opinions. His personal autobiography is both an interesting description of how under English influence Michaelis weaned himself away from the Pietist Orthodoxy of his family and also an illustration of a new note that occurred frequently in other writings of his day, namely the growing sense in Protestant Germany of how much had been achieved in theology in the course of the eighteenth century.

Michaelis was trained as a semitic philologist. He began his instruction from his father, but under the influence of Albert Schultens he recognized the semitic languages as a family and throughout his life published grammars, dictionaries and other aids to the learning of Hebrew, Arabic, Syriac. While philology might have been his greatest competence, Michaelis was not content to be only a linguist; his philosophical bent led him to theorize about language and his prize essay on language for the Berlin Academy made him famous over Europe, thanks to its early translation into French. To be fair, Michaelis was not the only person discussing language and a work like James Harris' *Hermes*[20] shows how the debate had begun before Michaelis' work. Michaelis divided his essay into three parts to show how the opinions of nations influenced the form of their languages, how this could be a useful, and then how it could be hurtful to clear communication. One example of the dangers of imprecise words in a language was the Hebrew word *reagh* [רֵעַ] which could mean either a 'friend' or someone with whom one has something to clear up. Because of this ambiguity the Jews disputed over the love of one's neighbour and Jesus had to show what Moses meant. Had Moses written in German rather than Hebrew, concluded Michaelis, this would never have happened.[21] Here was a distinct advance over seventeenth century theories of language which saw it as purely communicative and where the possibility of universal symbols might permit communication amongst nations. Leibniz had based his project for a

---

[20] James H. Harris, *Hermes or a Philosophical Inquiry concerning Language and Universal Grammar* (London 1751).

[21] Michaelis, *De l'influence des opinions sur le langage* (1762) 97. The French translation of Michaelis' essay contains additional material from Michaelis and represents a fuller exposition of his thought. Michaelis also discusses in the section on the unfavorable influence of language on knowledge misunderstandings of the nature of 'dew' and 'manna' coming from the linguistic expression that had both of them falling from heaven when in fact neither did, 106–10.

universal language on the model of geometry; Michaelis' pattern was derived from botany, in particular the development of classification that had taken place in the eighteenth century. Michaelis postulated a direct connection between the awareness of things in the world and the number of words available for such descriptions. Michaelis has to be credited with seeing the weakness in Leibniz's hope of a universal symbolic language – his point was that words have too many overtones to be reduced to figures; but one also has to wonder whether Michaelis had a very subtle understanding of the nature of poetry when he can say that its function is to be a stimulant for its hearers to study plant classification.[22]

Michaelis included some remarks about how Israelite attitudes were enshrined in the picturesque idioms of Hebrew, an observation which fitted in with his tendency to find natural or linguistic explanations for miracles in the Old Testament. However his principle contribution to the understanding of non-factual forms of discourse was his enthusiastic editing of Lowth's lectures on the sacred poetry of the Hebrews which led to Michaelis' notes making their way into the English translation of the work.

However, Michaelis' concerns ranged far beyond the study of language; many of his contributions to Old Testament studies sprang from his concern to bring the discussion of the Old Testament out of the remote world of abstruse, abstract theological works written in Latin into the general arena of popular discussion.[23] It is often pointed out in discussions of his work that his aim was apologetic, and sometimes this is meant more as a criticism than a recommendation. However Michaelis is described as an interpreter his efforts may be seen as more positive, for he aimed both to understand the Bible from the standpoint provided by the new thought of his day and to make the Bible more generally understood by explaining the differences between the thought world of the Bible and the new Europe that was emerging.

His almost equally well known work was his *Mosaisches Recht*, a study of the Mosaic law.[24] In this work Michaelis lanced a boil that had troubled Europe for hundreds of years, namely how normative for a Christian country is the law code of the Old Testament? In the sixteenth and seventeenth centuries there had been a series of works on the subject of the Hebrew or Jewish "reipublic", in which standards or bad examples for the present day were pointed out; even the second half of Spinoza's *Tractatus Theologico-Politicus* can be seen as a radical variation on this theme. What Michaelis did was to argue that Old Testament law was not binding on Christians, but that it should be studied for evidence about law in general. Here the shadow of Montesquieu is invoked at the beginning of the work. Michaelis' preferred explanation of Old Testament ordinances was to explain them in terms of human culture rather than divine command. For example instead of seeing the lists of clean and unclean animals as God's will working in peculiar ways, Michaelis saw the origin of dietary prescriptions in a more prosaic cultural conditioning. He argued

---

[22] Ibid. 84.
[23] This is similar to Calmet's intention in writing his great biblical commentary.
[24] See Smend, Aufgeklärte Bemühung um das Gesetz (1983) 129–39.

that just as in Europe the French eat horsemeat with gusto whereas Germans would be horrified at the thought, Israel elevated its own dietary preferences to commandments of its God in order to distinguish itself from its neighbours.

Furthermore, Michaelis was blessed with an almost Baconian sense of practical investigation; there was some question whether the body of the camel met the demands for a clean (i.e., edible) animal; Michaelis heard of a German prince who had a camel in his private zoo so he wrote to a friend of his to arrange an examination of the camel's hoofs to see whether they were cloven or not. It was this sort of pragmatic interest that led to his idea for what was to be the first scientific expedition to the Near East. Obviously, Europeans had been travelling in the orient for hundred of years, but their efforts, to the extent they did not concern trade and diplomacy, were concentrated on learning languages, acquiring manuscripts, or in the case of the more generalized traveller, bringing back personal observations and impressions which were recorded in accounts of their travels for the general reading public.

While much had been discovered, Michaelis proposed an expedition to gather background material for the study of the Bible in a systematic, scientific matter. It was to be made up of specialists chosen for the task who were to be given a series of questions set out by Michaelis to serve as a basis for their work and to provide a framework for the report they were to bring back. So interested were learned circles in Europe that when the French occupied Göttingen during the Seven Years' War, Thierry specifically instructed the occupation authorities not to do anything to interfere with the progress of Michaelis' expedition.[25] The expedition eventually set out in 1761, but only one of its members survived to return. However, the one survivor, Carsten Niebuhr, brought back a great deal of material including accurate transcriptions of Egyptian and Assyrian inscriptions which were to prove useful in the process of deciphering ancient languages in the nineteenth century.

Michaelis wrote a very successful introduction to the New Testament which went through several editions and was eventually translated into English by Herbert Marsh who had been a student in Göttingen and was able to work his way through Michaelis' awkward German. Michaelis set out his plans for a parallel Old Testament introduction but in the event this work did not appear until much later by which time it was already out of date in comparison with the work of Eichhorn and only one volume was published.

Michaelis' major weakness was his unwillingness to think in terms of sources rather than personalities as possible explanations for problems in explaining texts. For example both in his treatment of the Mosaic laws and his criticism of the Fragmentist's attack on the Old Testament, Michaelis cast his discussion in terms of why Moses personally made certain decisions about the sources he used or the laws he laid down. Michaelis was not able to recognize the existence of substantial blocks of disparate material within the Pentateuch although the matter had been discussed for two hundred years before him and more recently by H. B. Witter and J. Astruc. One is tempted to see Michaelis'

---

[25] That is, if one can believe Michaelis' statement in his autobiography.

person of Moses as the counterpart to the historical Jesus who was singled out
as the replacement for Christology from the eighteenth century on. Yet in fairness to Michaelis he cannot be described as hidebound. In his writings on the
Fragmentist he freely admits that there were some matters which he had to recognize as puzzling and while he feels he has solved the puzzle, he is honest
enough to state that he could be wrong.

All in all, Michaelis was a major figure in the development of biblical exegesis in the eighteenth century, important as much for his awareness of a general public beyond the confines of the academy as for his serious exegetical
work. In his own time his prodigious energy and wide interests helped to make
the educated public aware of developments within biblical exegesis and the
study of religion. Thanks to Herbert Marsh's translation of some of his works
into English Michaelis had an on-going influence in the Anglo-Saxon world,
possibly because Marsh's English was clearer and more pleasing than Michaelis' German, a situation not unknown in the case of some other German works
done into English. Michaelis then was a lively and wide ranging mind, moderately well informed, and occupying the middle ground between competence
and genius.

Chapter Forty-two

Historical Criticism of the Old Testament Canon

By John H. Hayes, Atlanta, GA

1. Early Canon Criticism

General works: R. A. Bohlmann, *The Criteria of Biblical Canonicity in Sixteenth Century Lutheran, Roman Catholic, and Reformed Theology* (diss., Yale University 1968); A. C. Cochrane, *Reformed Confessions of the Sixteenth Century* (Philadelphia, PA: Westminster Press 1966); K. A. Credner, *Zur Geschichte des Kanons* (Halle: Verlag der Buchhandlung des Waisenhauses 1847); T. H. Darlow / H. F. Moule, *Historical Catalogue of the Printed Editions of Holy Scripture in the Library of the British and Foreign Bible Society* (2 vols. in 4; London: The British and Foreign Bible Society 1903–11); B. A. Gerrish, "Biblical Authority and the Continental Reformation", *SJT* 10 (1957) 337–60; W. Grimm, *Kurzgefasste Geschichte der lutherischen Bibelübersetzung* (Jena: Hermann Costenoble 1884); H. H. Howorth, "The Origin and Authority of the Biblical Canon in the Anglican Church", *JTS* 8 (1906–07) 1–40; idem, "The Origin and Authority of the Biblical Canon According to the Continental Reformers: I. Luther and Karlstadt", *JTS* 8 (1906–07) 321–65; idem, "The Origin and Authority of the Biblical Canon According to the Continental Reformers: II. Luther, Zwingli, Lefèvre, and Calvin", *JTS* 9 (1907–08) 188–230; idem, "The Canon of the Bible Among the Later Reformers", *JTS* 10 (1908–09) 183–232; E. F. A. Klug, *From Luther to Chemnitz: On Scripture and the Word* (Grand Rapids, MI: Eerdmans 1971); J. Leipoldt, *Geschichte des neutestamentlichen Kanons* 1–2 (Leipzig: Hinrichs 1907–08); J. Lenhart, "Protestant Latin Bibles of the Reformation from 1520–1570", *CBQ* 8 (1946) 416–32; A. F. Loisy, *Histoire du canon de l'Ancien Testament* (Paris: Letouzey et Anê 1890); J. A. O. Preus, "The New Testament Canon in the Lutheran Dogmaticians", *The Springfielder* 25 (1961) 8–33; J. M. Reu, *Luther's German Bible: An Historical Presentation Together with a Collection of Sources* (Columbus, OH: The Lutheran Book Concern 1934); E. Reuss, *Die Geschichte der heiligen Schriften Neuen Testaments* (Brunswick: Schwetschke 1842), = *History of the Sacred Scriptures of the New Testament* 1–2 (Boston, MA: Houghton, Mifflin 1842); idem, *Histoire du Canon des Saintes Écritures dans l'Eglise chrétienne* (Strasbourg: Treuttel et Wurtz² 1863) = *History of the Canon of the Holy Scriptures* (Edinburgh: J. Gemmell 1884); Ph. Schaff, *The Creeds of Christendom with a History and Critical Notes* 1–3 (New York: Harper & Brothers 1877, ³1881); K. A. Strand, *Reformation Bibles in the Crossfire* (Ann Arbor, MI: Ann Arbor Publishers 1961); idem, *Catholic German Bibles of the Reformation Era: The Versions of Emser, Dietenberger, Eck, and Others* (Naples, FL: Ann Arbor Publications 1982); H. Volz, "Luthers Stellung zu den Apokryphen des Alten Testaments", *Jahrbuch der Luther-Gesellschaft* 26 (1959) 93–108; B. F. Westcott, *The Bible in the Church: A Popular Account of the Collection and Reception of the Holy Scriptures in the Christian Church* (London: Macmillan 1864).

In the sixteenth century, the canon of the Bible became one of the most controversial issues of the time. Prior to this period, some differences of opinion existed in the Church over the extent of the canon, the canonicity of certain books, and whether different degrees of authority should be assigned to different works, but generally opinion followed the positions established in the

Decretum Gelasianum from the early Middle Ages.[1] In conjunction with the Council of Florence (4 February 1441) Pope Eugenius IV had provided a list of biblical books identical with what would be approved at the Council of Trent (8 April 1546).

Uneasiness about the appearance of certain works in the canon was expressed by some Catholic scholars at the time, especially those influenced by humanism. Cardinal Francisco Ximénes de Cisneros (1436–1517) in one of the prologues to the Complutensian Polyglot (III.b),[2] noted that the Old Testament books not found in Hebrew, which were printed in the polyglot only in the Vulgate Latin and Greek (with an interlinear Latin translation), stood outside the canon and were received by the Church only for the edification of the people rather than for confirming the authority of the Church's teachings. Erasmus (1466/69–1536), in the annotations to his *Novum Instrumentum* (1516), noted the doubts raised about the New Testament *antilegomena*. In his edition of Jerome (1525), he wrote that the Church certainly does not wish the books of Judith, Tobit, and Wisdom to have the same weight as the Pentateuch. In his Exposition of the Creed (1533), he provided a list of canonical Old Testament books (omitting Esther) and declared that "Wisdom, Ecclesiasticus, Tobit, Judith, Esther, and the additions to Daniel have been received into ecclesiastical use. Whether, however, the Church receives them as possessing the same authority as the others the spirit of the Church must know".[3]

Sanctes Pagninus (1466–1541)[4] began working on a Latin translation of the Bible in about 1493 which was published in its entirety in 1528.[5] Several features of this work are noteworthy. It was the first 'modern' translation of the entire Bible made from the Hebrew and Greek texts and the first with numbered verses throughout (Pagninus's numbering of the verses of the New Testament, however, did not become standard). The apocryphal books (Tobit, Judith, Wisdom, Ecclesiasticus, Baruch, 1–2 Maccabees) were printed here in a new Latin translation for the first time but were separated from the other Old Testament books indicating Pagninus's view of their subordinate nature.

Cardinal Cajetan / Tommaso de Vio (1469–1534), at the conclusion of his commentary on all the authentic historical books of the Old Testament (1531–32) which ended with the book of Esther, wrote: "In this place we close our commentaries on the historical books of the Old Testament, for the remaining books (Judith, Tobit, Maccabees 1–2) are reckoned by St. Jerome without the canonical books and placed among the Apocrypha together with Wisdom and Ecclesiasticus.... Nor must you be disturbed by the strangeness of the fact, if you shall anywhere find those books reckoned among the canonical books, either in the Sacred Councils or in the Sacred Doctors. For the language of Councils and Doctors must alike be revised by the judgment of Jerome".[6]

---

[1] Credner, Geschichte des Kanons (1847) 148–290, provides a thorough examination of the decretals. See also E. VON DOBSCHÜTZ, *Das Decretum Gelasianum de libris recipiendis et non recipiendis* (TU 38/4; Leipzig: Hinrichs 1912).

[2] See further Chap. 12, sect. 2, by A. SCHENKER, in the present volume.

[3] Quoted in Westcott, Bible in the Church (1864) 252 f. See Humphrey Hody, *De Bibliorum textibus originalibus, versionibus Graecis, et Latina Vulgata* I–IV (Oxonii: E Theatro Sheldoniano 1705) 644–64, and John Cosin, *A Scholastical History of the Canon of Holy Scripture* (London: T. Garthwait 1657); both supply a collection of early testimonies about the contents of the canon and illustrate how the issues were viewed in the seventeenth century, although the latter from a decidedly biased Protestant viewpoint.

[4] See further Chap. 7, sect. 5.2, by A. VANDERJAGT, in the present volume.

[5] Darlow and Moule, 2/2. 925–26, #6108

[6] Translation from Westcott, Bible in the Church (1864) 253f; see Bohlmann, Criteria (1968) 85–98. Both Erasmus and Cajetan were later condemned by the Theological Faculty at the Univer-

In 1520, Karlstadt published two works which constitute the first systematic defense of what might be called the Protestant canon. The first, *De canonicis scripturis libellus*,[7] appeared in August (*Anno 1520. die vero 18. Mensis Augusti*) and the second, *Welche bucher Biblisch seint*,[8] in November (*Sontag nach aller-heiligen* 1520). The German was a much shortened version of the material in the Latin. These works were not only a defense of the idea of absolute biblical authority in theological matters but also Karlstadt's exposition of his views of the biblical canon over against the accepted views of the Catholic Church and those of his fellow Reformer Luther. He divided the contents of the Old Testament into three orders of descending authority or dignity: (1) the Pentateuch, (2) the Prophets, Joshua – Malachi, with Ruth associated with Joshua, and (3) Job, Psalms, Proverbs, Ecclesiastes, Song of Songs, Daniel, 1–2 Chronicles, Ezra and Nehemiah, and Esther. Of the third group he wrote: *Düet ordnung diesser bucher behelt die niderste stad seint aber doch sunder allen zweyssel Biblisch.* Similarly, the writings of the New Testament were divided into three categories or orders: (1) the four Gospels with the Acts of the Apostles,[9] (2) thirteen epistles of Paul plus 1 Peter and 1 John, and (3) Hebrews, James, 2 Peter, 2–3 John (*Duae seniores, presbyteri*), Jude, and Apocalypse (*Johannis des Theologen*). These latter seven books include the five controverted writings (*antilegomena*) noted by Eusebius (*Hist. eccl.* 3.25.3–4): James, Jude, 2 Peter, and 2 and 3 John.

In §§113–14 of *De canonicis*, Karlstadt summarized his views on the so-called Old Testament apocryphal books. On Wisdom, Ecclesiasticus, Judith, Tobit, and 1–2 Maccabees he wrote: *Hi sunt apocryphi, i. e. extra canonem hebraeorum, tamen agiographi*; the third order of the Old Testament had also been designated Hagiographa. Of 1–2 Esdras, Baruch, Prayer of Manasseh, a good part of the third chapter of Daniel, and the two last chapters of Daniel, he wrote: *Hi libri sunt plane apocryphi, virgis censoriis animadvertendi.* In §118, he made clear that he did not consider these works canonical nor authoritative: "What they contain is not to be despised at once, and still …it is not right that a Christian should relieve much less slake his thirst with them. The springs which are far from all suspicion must be sought which can have no poison in them; that is, before all things the best books must be read, those which are canonical beyond all controversy; after-

---

sity of Paris. The condemned propositions of Cajetan were first published by Lutherans, in 1534. On Cajetan, see TH. A. COLLINS, "The Cajetan Controversy", *AER* 128 (1953) 90–100; idem, "Cardinal Cajetan's Fundamental Biblical Principles", *CBQ* 17 (1955) 363–78, and M. O'CON-NOR, "A Neglected Facet of Cardinal Cajetan: Biblical Reform in High Renaissance Rome", in: R. GRIFFITHS (ed.), *The Bible in the Renaissance: Essays on Bible Commentary and Translation in the Fifteenth and Sixteenth Centuries* (St. Andrews Studies in Reformation History; Aldershot / Burlington, VT: Ashgate 2001) 71–94; cf. further Chap. 25, sect. 1, by J. WICKS, in the present volume. On the fifteenth- and sixteenth-century recovery of Jerome, see E. F. RICE, Jr., *Saint Jerome in the Renaissance* (Baltimore, MD: Johns Hopkins UP 1985); for Jerome's influence on sixteenth-century decisions about the canon, see H. H. HOWORTH, "The Influence of St. Jerome on the Canon of the Western Church", *JTS* 10 (1908–09) 481–96; 11 (1909–10) 321–47; and 13 (1911–12) 1–18.

[7] (Wittenbergae: Ioannem Viridi Montanum). This work is extremely rare but has been reprinted in Credner, Geschichte des Kanons (1847) 316–412, with Credner's introduction (291–315) and annotations. The following paragraph references are those of Credner.

[8] (Wittenberg: Melchior Lotter). The book was also printed in the same year with the title *Weliche Biecher Biblisch seind* (Augsburg: Melchior Ramminger 1520) and in the following year with the title *Welche bücher heilig und Biblisch seind* (Basel: Adam Petri 1521).

[9] In the charts in §165 of *De canonicis*, Acts is omitted (but see §124) but is included in the charts of *Welche bucher*.

wards if there should be leisure, it is allowed to peruse the controverted books, provided that you compare and collate the non-canonical books with those which are truly canonical".[10] Near the end of his work *Welche bucher*, Karlstadt provided a list of *Apocryphen altes und newes* which includes all the above works but adds "the last chapter of Mark"[11] and Paul's epistle to the Laodiceans. In *De canonicis*, he refers to other gospels (§§141–42) mentioned by the ancients but places none of these into the category of apocrypha. He also noted some of the Old Testament pseudepigrapha. Karlstadt was familiar with and quoted much of the patristic evidence regarding the canon, especially Augustine and Jerome whom he played off against one another.

Luther's conclusions and judgments on the canon were much more theologically and subjectively based than those of Karlstadt.[12] As early as July, 1519, Luther had declared the book of 2 Maccabees non-canonical or non-scriptural even though in the Bible, in his debates with Johann Eck (1486–1543) over the doctrine of purgatory and the sale of indulgences, and also had had harsh things to say about the Epistle of James.[13] The latter led to controversy with Karlstadt (§§90–91 of the latter's *De canonicis* are understood as his attack on Luther's position without naming him). In his September Testament of 1522,[14] his translation of the New Testament, Luther provided a short introduction, "which are the best and finest books of the New Testament". In this he declared that John's Gospel, St. Paul's Letters, especially Romans, and the first Epistle of Peter are "the true kernel and marrow of all the books".

In regard to these, "the foremost books", Luther noted that "in them you do not find many works and miracles of Christ described, but you do find depicted in masterly fashion how faith in Christ overcomes sin, death, and hell and gives life, righteousness, and salvation. This is the real nature of the gospel.... If I had to do without one or the other – either the works or the preaching of Christ – I would rather do without the works....John writes very little about the works of Christ....John's Gospel is the one, fine, true, and chief gospel, and is far, far to be preferred over the other three and placed high above them. So, too, the epistles of St. Paul and St. Peter far surpass the other three gospels.... In a word St. John's Gospel and his first epistle, St. Paul's epistles, especially Romans, Galatians, and Ephesians, and St. Peter's first epistle are the books that show you Christ and teach you all that is necessary and salvatory for you to know, even if you were never to see or hear any other book or doctrine. Therefore, St. James' epistle is really an epistle of straw, compared to

---

[10] Translation from Westcott, Bible in the Church (1864) 267–68. See also Bohlmann, Criteria (1968) 78–85.

[11] Here he refers to Mark 16:9–20 and bases his opinion on textual considerations. His discussion of the Gospel of Mark can be found in §§ 129–32 where he refers to Erasmus's scholia on Mark.

[12] Karlstadt was willing to grant limited recognition to the Church's role in ratifying Scripture's status. In § 91, on the Epistle of James, he wrote: "Why if you allow the Jews to stamp books with authority by receiving them, do you refuse to grant as much power to the Churches of Christ, since the Church is not less than the Synagogue?"; translation from Westcott, Bible in the Church (1864) 268.

[13] In his *Resolutions* of 1519 and *Babylonian Captivity* of 1520; see Reu, Luther's German Bible (1934) 176; Bohlmann, Criteria (1968) 112f.

[14] See Darlow and Moule, 2/1. 486–87, #4188.

these others, for it has nothing of the nature of the gospel about it".[15] For Luther then those works which most clearly present the Gospel as he understood it are the finest works in the New Testament. This distinction between the books led to what would be later designated "the canon within the canon" (but not by Luther himself).

In Luther's list of books in the New Testament, twenty-three are numbered, then, following a blank line, and without numbers, are listed Hebrews, James, Jude, and Revelation.[16] This provides another of Luther's distinctions among the books of the New Testament. In the preface to Hebrews, Luther wrote: "Up to this point we have had the true and certain chief books of the New Testament. The four which follow have from ancient times had a different reputation".[17] In his prefaces to these four works, he not only noted the questions about their apostolic origin and canonicity raised by the ancients but also passed negative subjective judgment upon the works. On Revelation he wrote: "I stick to the books which present Christ to me clearly and purely".[18] In the prefaces to James and Revelation, he suggested that persons could make up their own minds about the matter and the books' usage. Luther did not isolate the other three *antilegomena* (2 Peter and 2 and 3 John) as did Karlstadt. In his prefaces to these books no reference is made to the fact that they constituted disputed books.

Between 1522 when the September Testament was published and 1534 when the entire Luther's Bible made its appearance, Luther translated and published translations of a number of books of the Old Testament and "Apocrypha". When the Pentateuch appeared in 1523, it contained a numbered list of Old Testament books and, separated from them, an untitled unnumbered list of apocryphal works (Tobit, Judith, Baruch, Esdras, Wisdom, Ecclesiasticus, and Maccabees). When his complete Bible appeared in 1534,[19] two blank pages separated the book of Malachi from the Apocrypha which had its own title page: *Apocrypha. Das sind Bücher so nicht der heiligen Schrift gleichgehalten: und doch nützlich und gut zu lesen sind. I. Judith. II. Sapientia. III. Tobias. IIII. Syrach. V. Baruch. VI. Maccabeorum. VII. Stücke jnn Esther. VIII. Stücke jnn Daniel.* This ordering of these books is unique being found neither in Septuagint nor Vulgate texts. In his preface to these works, Luther discussed earlier opinions about them and evaluated their content. Luther included the Prayer of Manasseh[20] but did not list it in the table of contents or on the special apocryphal title page nor did he provide it with a preface. Only of 2 Maccabees does he say: "it is proper that this second book should be thrown out, even though it contains some good things".[21] Again, he frequently recommended that readers form their own opinions about the writings.

None of the major Lutheran confessions contained a list of the canonical

---

[15] LW 35. 361–62.

[16] The practice of placing these books at the end of the New Testament was followed in the early English translations, Tyndale's (1525), Coverdale's (1535, who placed Baruch following Jeremiah), Matthew's (Tyndale's completed by John Rogers, 1537), and Taverner's (1539), and by subsequent Lutheran German Bibles. According to Reu, the last German Bible to leave them unnumbered was published in 1689 (Luther's German Bible, 1934, 176). The English "Great Bible" (1539) abandoned Luther's canon and reverted to the older order of the Vulgate.

[17] LW 35. 394.

[18] LW 35. 399.

[19] See Darlow and Moule, 2/1. 492–93, #4199.

[20] See WA DB, 12. 528–32.

[21] LW 35. 353.

books of the Bible although in them emphasis is placed on doctrine being derived "from the Holy Scriptures and pure Word of God" (preface to the Augsburg Confession of 1530).[22] This ambiguity or open-endness about the canon,
inherited from Luther, is frequently reflected in sixteenth-century Lutheran
writings. In his 1555 work *De methodis libri duo*, the Scandinavian Lutheran
theologian Niels Hemmingsen (1513-1600), for example, describes the books
of the New Testament – Gospels, Acts, twenty-one Epistles, and the Apocalypse – but then comments: "All these books of the New Testament are in the
canon except Second Peter, Second and Third John, the Epistles of James and
Jude along with the Apocalypse. Some also place the Epistle to the Hebrews
outside the canon".[23] Here one finds the assertion that writings could be found
in the Bible but not be canonical (authoritative).

The Reformed or Calvinistic branch of Protestantism reached a consensus
on the canon with less dispute than the Lutherans. In Olivétan's 1535 French
Bible,[24] the Apocrypha is described as the books found in the Vulgate translation but not found in Hebrew or Chaldee, and Jerome is called upon as the
authority for such a distinction. The first edition (1536) of Calvin's *Institutes*
contained no *locus* on Scripture. Beginning with the second edition (1539), the
role of Scripture was spelled out fully (*Institutes* I vii-xiv). According to Calvin,
the authority of the Scriptures is not derived from the Church but vice versa.
The Scriptures were given by God through the inspiration of the Holy Spirit;
they are self-authenticating; and the same Spirit who spoke through the writers speaks to the faithful reader, confirming their divine origin.

None of the Reformers produced any systematic defense for inclusion of the
Old Testament Apocrypha within the Bible even if in a subordinate position.
Luther's "useful and good to read" was hardly a rationale. Theoretically the
Protestant Reformers could have omitted them entirely; probably public opinion and the books' appearance in the Vulgate made it impossible to exclude
them totally. The various editions of the Bible produced in the first half of the
sixteenth century varied considerably with regard to which of the apocryphal
books were included. The Weimar Bible (1644) contained, for the first time
among Lutheran Bibles, Third and Fourth Esdras and Third Maccabees. The
Catholic Bible edited by the Dominican Johann Dietenberger (1534) continued Paul's Epistle to the Laodiceans.[25]

At its fourth session (8 April 1546), the Council of Trent, after considerable
debate with various opinions,[26] issued its decree on tradition and the canon of
Sacred Scripture declaring that the "Gospel, which was initially promised by

---

[22] See R. A. BOHLMANN, *Principles of Biblical Interpretation in the Lutheran Confessions* (St. Louis, MO: Concordia Publishing House 1968).
[23] P. 124. See K. HAGEN, "*De Exegetica Methodo*': Niels Hemmingsen's *De Methodis* (1555)", in: *The Bible in the Sixteenth Century* (Duke Monographs in Medieval and Renaissance Studies 11; ed. David C. Steinmetz; Durham, NC: Duke UP 1990) 181-96; quotation from p. 188. Subsequent Lutheran theologians often referred to the *antilegomena* as the New Testament apocrypha or *cano-nici secundi*; see Howorth, *JTS* 10 (1908-09) 194-96, and Bohlmann, Criteria (1968) 249-68.
[24] See Darlow and Moule, 2/1. 882-85, #3710.
[25] See Darlow and Moule, 2/1. 493, #4200.
[26] On the debate, especially over whether degrees of authority should be assigned to different books, see A. MAICHLE, *Der Kanon der biblischen Bücher und das Konzil von Trent* (FThSt 33; Frei-

the prophets in the Sacred Scriptures, was first promulgated by Our Lord Jesus Christ, Son of God, by his own mouth, who then commanded His Apostles to preach it to all creatures as the source both of all saving truth and of moral rules... these truths and rules are contained in the written books and in the unwritten traditions...". The decree then provided a list of the sacred books: "The true books" in the Old Testament include "Tobit, Judith...Wisdom, Ecclesiasticus...Jeremiah with Baruch...and two books of the Maccabees". No differentiation was made between the books previously known as ecclesiastical or apocryphal and the remainder. The listing was followed by an anathema: "If there be anyone who will not accept these books as sacred and canonical, both as wholes and in all their parts, as they have been customarily read in the Catholic Church, and as contained in the old Latin Vulgate edition, and who knowingly and deliberately rejects the above-mentioned traditions, let him be anathema". The text proceeds to declare "that the old Latin Vulgate edition, which has been approved for use in the Church for so many centuries, is to be taken as authentic in public lectures, disputations, sermons, and expositions...".[27]

In spite of the declaration of the council, some Catholics continued to describe the contents of the Bible in slightly different terms, assigning them to different categories. This would indicate that the Council of Trent was understood to have held a similar view which went unexpressed in the decree. In his *Bibliotheca Sancta* (1566), Sixtus of Siena / Sisto da Siena (1520–1569),[28] a Jewish convert to Catholicism, categorized the various biblical writings into three classes: a first order or protocanonical, a second order or deuterocanonical (formerly designated ecclesiastical), and a third order or apocryphal. To the first class belong those writings universally recognized and accepted. To the second order, "those which were not generally known till a late period", belonged those works on which there had not been universal agreement or about which there were problems: Esther, Tobit, Judith, Baruch, Epistle of Jeremiah, Wisdom of Solomon, Ecclesiasticus, the song of Azariah, the hymn of the three young men, the history of Bel, 1 and 2 Maccabees, *Marci caput ultimum* [Mark 16:9–20], *Lucae historia de Sudore Christi sanguineo, & apparitione Angeli* [Luke 22:43–44], *Ioannis historia de muliere adultera* [John 7:53–8:11], Hebrews, James, 2 Peter, 2 and 3 John, Jude, and the Johannine Apocalypse. To the category of Apocrypha are assigned *1. Libri secundi Paralipomenon Accessio, 2. Esdras liber tertius, 3. Esdras liber quartus, 4. Libri Esther Appendix, 5. Libri Iob Appendix, 6. Psalterii Auctarium, 7. Libri Ecclesiastici Additamentum, 8. Lamentationum Ieremiae Praefatiuncula, 9. Maccabaeorum liber tertius,* and *10. Maccabaeorum liber quartus.* Of the apocryphal writings he noted that these were those which "the Fathers of the Church did not venture to decide whether their authors were inspired by the Holy Spirit and therefore forbid them to be alleged for the support of doctrines or for public reading but allowed them to be read only privately".[29] The distinction between proto- and deuterocanonical was one of "cognition and time, not of authority, certitude, or worth, for both orders received their excellency and majesty from the same Holy Spirit".[30]

---

burg 1929); P. G. DUNCKER, "The Canon of the Old Testament at the Council of Trent", *CBQ* 15 (1953) 277–99; and Bohlmann, Criteria (1968) 177–207.

[27] Translation taken from R. J. BLACKWELL, *Galileo, Bellarmine, and the Bible* (Notre Dame, IN: University of Notre Dame Press 1991) 181–84.

[28] See further Chap. 25, sect. 5.1, by J. WICKS, in the present volume.

[29] *Bibliotheca Sancta ex praecipuis catholicae ecclesiae autoribus collecta, et in octo libros digesta* 1–2 (Venetiis: Franciscum Franciscium Senensem 1566). In the 1574–75 edition, the apocryphal materials are discussed in 1.65–74. On Sixtus, see Bohlmann, Criteria (1968) 220–24, and J. W. MONTGOMERY, "Sixtus of Sienna and Roman Catholic Biblical Scholarship in the Reformation Period", *ARefG* 54 (1963) 214–34.

[30] Translation from Bohlmann, Criteria (1968) 222.

Following the Decree of Trent, most non-Lutheran Protestant confessions included lists of the canonical books: the 1559 Gallican Confession (art. 3) which notes that "we know these books to be canonical, and the sure rules of our faith, not so much by the common accord and consent of the Church, as by the testimony and inward illumination of the Holy Spirit" (art. 4); the 1561 Belgic Confession which also lists the Old Testament Apocrypha (art. 4–6); and the 1562 Thirty-Nine Articles of the Church of England (art. 6 lists the apocryphal Old Testament books). When the Westminster Confession was approved in 1647, the Puritan opposition to the Apocrypha was so strong that no list of these works was provided in the specification of the books of the Bible (art. 2). They were severely circumscribed in importance: "The books commonly called Apocrypha, not being of divine inspiration, are no part of the Canon of the Scripture; and therefore are of no authority in the Church of God, nor to be any otherwise approved, or made use of, than other human writings" (art. 3).[31]

One of the early Reformers, Sebastian Castellio / Castallion / Sébastien Châteillon (1515–63),[32] argued for the decanonization of the Song of Songs on the grounds that it was a purely human book which dealt with earthly emotions. Calvin opposed his view of the book as "a lascivious and obscene poem, in which Solomon has described his shameless love affairs".[33] According to Calvin, the issue of the book's canonicity was one of the reasons Castellio was forced to leave Geneva in 1544.

Protestants devoted much energy attacking the Council of Trent and its decisions. In the year following its decree on the Bible and tradition, Calvin replied in his *Acta Synodi Tridentinae. Cum Antidoto*.[34] From a theological perspective, he denounced the idea that the Church could determine the content of Scripture; the inner witness of the Spirit not ecclesiastical judgment assures the divinity and authority of the canonical writings. He appealed to the practice of the primitive Church and the New Testament authors, and the testimony of Rufinus, Jerome, and others, and the style and phraseology of the apocryphal books to argue for their subordinate and limited place in the Church.[35] Even Augustine, he said, illustrates that the matter of their canonicity was still undecided in his day. Reformed theologians constantly rehearsed the same arguments.

---

[31] See S. TH. MURPHY, *The Doctrine of Scripture in the Westminster Assembly* (diss., Drew University 1984).

[32] See further Chap. 22, sect. 1 and 3, by B. E. SCHWARZBACH, in the present volume.

[33] Quoted in H. H. ROWLEY, "The Interpretation of the Song of Songs", in: idem, *The Servant of the Lord and Other Essays on the Old Testament* (London: Lutterworth Press 1952) 187–234, quotation from p. 207. Castellio's view on the content of the book was also later shared by Grotius, Le Clerc, and William Whiston.

[34] "Acts of the Council of Trent with the Antidote", in his *Tracts and Treatises in Defense of the Reformed Faith*, annotated by Thomas F. Torrance (Grand Rapids, MI: Eerdmans 1958) 3, 17–188.

[35] See W. NEUSER, "Calvins Stellung zu den Apokryphen des Alten Testmentes", in: *Text – Wort – Glaube* (ed. Martin Brecht; Berlin: Walter de Gruyter 1980) 298–323.

The most influential Lutheran attack on Trent and the Catholic canon was *Examen Concilii Tridentini* (1578) by Martin Chemnitz (1522–86).[36] A complete section is devoted to the canon. His arguments against the apocrypha as authoritative, inspired Scripture emphasized primarily the testimony of primitive tradition, both as to the books' usage and the recognition of their inspiration. "Sufficiently sure, firm, and harmonious testimonies of their authority" do not exist.[37]

During the years of the English Revolution (1640–60), there occurred for the first time in history a full-blown democratization of biblical interpretation. State censorship ended, pamphlet literature abounded, suppressed groups gave vent to long pent-up thought and feeling, many of the uneducated became biblical interpreters, and the Bible even became the object of ridicule in a manner that foreshadowed the writings of Voltaire (1694–1778) and Thomas Paine (1737–1809). Radical thought flourished and radical groups like the Ranters, Diggers, Levellers, Fifth Monarchists, Quakers, and Muggletonians espoused their political and religious viewpoints as part of the social mix.[38] The most sophisticated and influential spokesman among these radicals was Samuel Fisher (1605–65), an Oxford educated minister who successively became a Presbyterian, a Baptist, and eventually a Quaker.[39] After the Restoration of the monarchy in 1660, Fisher spent much of his last years in prison.

Fisher's most significant work was composed as an attack upon the university and the learned by a country rustic.[40] This repetitive polemical work filled with endless alliteration was directed against a number of divines, the most prominent being the Puritan John Owen (1616–83) who had served as vice-chancellor of Oxford University under Cromwell. Owen, an ardent opponent of the Quakers, in 1659 wrote a volume that not only attacked Brian Walton (c. 1600–61) and the London Polyglot but also defended a rigid orthodox view of the Bible as the inspired Word of God as well as the antiquity of the Hebrew vowel points.[41]

---

[36] *Examination of the Council of Trent* 1–4 (St. Louis, MO: Concordia Publishing House 1971–86). See further Chap. 24, sect. 3, by B. T. Oftestad, in the present volume.

[37] For continued debate over the Old Testament canon with a focus on the Council of Trent, see H. J. Sieben, "Die Krontroverse zwischen Bossuet und Leibniz über den alttestamentlichen Kanons des Konzils von Trient", *Zum Problem des biblischen Kanons* (JBTh 3; Neukirchen-Vluyn: Neukirchener Verlag 1988) 201–14.

[38] This radical element in English society has been explored in numerous works by Christopher Hill; see his *The World Turned Upside Down: Radical Ideas During the English Revolution* (London: Maurice Temple Smith 1972), and *The English Bible and the Seventeenth-Century Revolution* (London: Allan Lane The Penguin Press 1993). See also J. Redwood, *Reason, Ridicule and Religion: The Age of Enlightenment in England, 1660–1750* (London: Thames and Hudson 1976), and N. Smith, *Perfection Proclaimed: Language and Literature in English Radical Religion, 1640–60* (Oxford: Clarendon Press 1989).

[39] For Fisher's possible influences on Spinoza, see R. H. Popkin, "Spinoza and Samuel Fisher", *Philosophia. Philosophical Quarterly of Israel* 15 (1985) 219–36. No full treatment of Fisher exists; see J. S. Preus, "The Bible and Religion in the Century of Genius: Part II: The Rise and Fall of the Bible", *Religion* 28 (1998) 15–27.

[40] *Rusticus ad Academicos in Exercitationibus, Expostulatoriis, Apologeticis Quatuor. The Rustick's Alarm to the Rabbies; or, the Country Correcting the University and Clergy...* (London: Robert Wilson 1660), repr. in his collected works, *The Testimony of Truth Exalted by the Collected Labours of...Samuel Fisher Who Died a Prisoner for the Testimony of Jesus and Word of God, anno 1665* (London: s.l. 1679).

[41] *Of the Divine Originall Authority, Self-evidencing Light, and Powers of the Scriptures. With an Answer to the Enquiry, How We know the Scriptures to be the Word of God? Also, A Vindication of the Purity and Integrity of the Hebrew and Greek Texts...* (London: Henry Hall 1659). On the vowel

Fisher was well acquainted with all phases of contemporary biblical scholarship and knowledgeable about rabbinic materials, Hebrew inscriptions on coins, and ancient versions including the Samaritan. Fisher made a frontal assault on what would later come to be called bibliolatry. He noted that no original autographs of the biblical books existed but only transcripts, human copies of copies, thus there is no infallible Bible just as there is no infallible Church.

For Fisher, the creation of the canon was an act of humans, not a divine creation (436),[42] its closure was a human action (269), and what was in the canon was as much the product of accident as of divine purpose; some of Paul's letters just happened to be preserved while others were inadvertently lost. The letter to the Laodiceans might be as legitimate as any others (281). The Old Testament apocryphal books were used by New Testament writers and thus should not be thrown out (267). The idea that biblical authors wrote through inspiration is not their claim but an idea imposed upon them (420). The view that the Spirit inspired the words of the text and then inspires the reader merely has the Spirit reading its own letters. The view that Scripture is the Word of God is itself unscriptural (250). The Bible is not the word of God (411); the word of God is that "written of, and not the writing of it" (413), the truth that is in it (199). This "original truth" was before the "texts were ever talked on" (278). The bare letter is not the word (562). Like other Quakers, Fisher stressed the role of the "inner light" and personal illumination: "Christ and his inward light, living word, and life giving spirit" (247). What counted was the light within not the letter without (660). This light enlightened every person (see John 1:9, a favorite Quaker text) and was universal, preexisting the writing of the Bible (696). Fisher was not a Deist arguing for natural religion; the "light", even in its approximation to right reason (670), was not natural (603).

Fisher's arguments thus had three thrusts: (1) The Bible was certainly not the book that orthodox Christianity claimed. Rather than the inspired, infallible word of God, it was a work "much mistranscribed, much more mistranslated, most infinitely misinterpreted". (2) It must be rescued from the religious establishment of "prelatical and presbyterian pontificalibus, parochial preferments and excrementitious university excellencies". (3) Illuminated understanding must be applied by the laity to find the word of God in the Bible.[43] It was left to Spinoza, however, to argue many of Fisher's ideas in a more dispassionate and rational form.[44]

The publication of ancient non-biblical texts produced several challenges to the exclusivity of the biblical canon early in the eighteenth century. In 1698, John Toland (1670–1722) published *The Life of John Milton* in which he sought to disprove the view that King Charles I had written the work *Eikon Basilike*. Just as people had been mistaken about the authenticity of this work, so also, they might be mistaken about the authenticity of New Testament writings. A year later he

---

points controversy and Owen's role in the debate, see B. Pick, "The Vowel-Points Controversy in the XVI. and XVII. Centuries", *Hebraica* (= *American Journal of Semitic Languages and Literature*) 8 (1891–92) 150–73.

[42] Page references are to Fisher's collected works.

[43] On English efforts to control the popular reading of the Bible, see V. Strudwick, "English Fears of Social Disintegration and Modes of Control, 1533–1611", in: The Bible in the Renaissance (2001) 133–49.

[44] See R. H. Popkin, "Spinoza and Bible Scholarship", in: *The Cambridge Companion to Spinoza* (ed. Don Garrett; Cambridge: Cambridge UP 1996) 383–407. The arguments of Spinoza in chapter twelve of the *Tractatus Theologico-Politicus* parallel closely the main arguments of Fisher; compare the list of Spinoza's outlined ideas in: D. L. Dungan, *A History of the Synoptic Problem: The Canon, the Text, the Composition, and the Interpretation of the Gospels* (Anchor Bible Reference Library; New York: Doubleday 1999) 242–46, with Fisher's views noted above.

published, *Amyntor; or, a Defence of Milton's Life*,[45] in which he provided a catalogue of books mentioned and/or quoted by the Church Fathers "truly or falsely ascribed to Jesus Christ, his Apostles, and other eminent persons" which Toland argued might have as much right to canonical status as the currently received books. In his *Nazarenus; or Jewish, Gentile, and Mohametan Christianity*,[46] among other things, he claimed to have recovered the original gospel of Jesus in the recently found *Gospel of Barnabas*. Toland argued that if this were the case, then the accepted canon of the New Testament was clearly flawed.[47]

Collections of such ancient writings noted by Toland were published by the classical scholar and father-in-law of H. S. Reimarus, Johann Albert Fabricius (1688–1736), in his *Codex apocryphus Novi Testamenti* (2 vols., 1703, enlarged to 3 vols., 1719) and *Codex pseudepigraphus Veteris Testamenti* (1713). These collections made available such works for the first time in an accessible form. The question of the relationship of these texts to the biblical books and their status in the early Jewish and Christian communities presented issues that would eventually impinge on the issue of canonicity.[48]

A further matter relative to the Hebrew canon was proposed in 1719 by Francis Lee (1661–1719). In his completion of an edition of the Septuagint based on Codex Alexandrinus by Johannes Ernst Grabe (1666–1711), Lee proposed that ancient Judaism had actually possessed two different canons of Scripture.[49] The normal Hebrew Bible had been that accepted by Palestinian Jews whereas the longer, septuagintal canon was the authorized Bible sanctioned by the Alexandrian sanhedrin in Egypt. This view, later widely accepted, called into great question the belief that the early Church had inherited a definitive canon of Scripture from Judaism identical with the Hebrew Bible.

2. The New Canon Criticism of Johann Salomo Semler

Sources: JOHANN SALOMO SEMLER: "Historische Einleitung in die Dogmatische Gottesgelehrsamkeit von ihrem Ursprung und ihrer Beschaffenheit bis auf unsere Zeiten", in: S. J. BAUMGARTEN, *Evangelische Glaubenslehre* I–III (ed. J. S. Semler; Halle: Johann Justinus Gebauer 1759-60) I, 34–138; II, 4–161; III, 4–148; *Vorbereitung zur theologischen Hermeneutik* I–IV (Halle: Carl Hermann Hemmerde 1760-69); *Umständliche Untersuchung der dämonischen Leute oder so genannten Besessenen* (Halle: Johann Justinus Gebauer 1762, [2]1776); *Apparatus ad liberalem Novi Testamenti interpretationen* (Halle: Caroli Hermmani Hemmerde 1767); *Abhandlung von freier Untersuchung des*

---

[45] (London: John Darby 1699), repr. in: *John Toland: A Collection of Several Pieces* 1-2 (New York: Garland Publishing 1977) 1, 350–403. See Dungan, History of the Synoptic Problem (1999) 287–90.

[46] *Nazarenus, or, Jewish, Gentile, and Mohometan Christianity: Containing the History of the Ancient Gospel of Barnabas*...(London: J. Brotherton, J. Roberts, and A. Dodd 1718).

[47] On the responses to Toland, see B. M. METZGER, *The Canon of the New Testament: Its Origin, Development, and Significance* (Oxford: Clarendon Press 1987) 12–14.

[48] A young Welsh nonconformist minister, Jeremiah Jones (1693-1724), provided an English translation of the New Testament apocryphal documents in his widely used and posthumously published *A New and Full Method of Settling the Canonical Authority of the New Testament* 1-3 (London: J. Clark and R. Hett 1726-27).

[49] *Vetus Testamentum juxta LXX interpretes* 1-2 (Oxonii: E Theatro Sheldoniano 1707-20). Lee's discussion is in the Prolegomena to vol. 2, chap. I, propositio XXIV, §§ 75-77, pp. g-g3.

Canon I-IV (Halle: Carl Hermann Hemmerde 1771–75); 2nd edn. of vol. 1, 1776 = Heinz Scheible (ed.), Johann Salomo Semler, *Abhandlung von freier Untersuchung des Canon* (Texte zur Kirchen- und Theologiegeschichte 5; Gütersloh: Gerd Mohn 1967); *Apparatus ad liberalem Veteris Testamenti interpretationen* (Halle: Caroli Hermmani Hemmerde 1773); *Apparatus ad libros symbolicos ecclesiae Lutheranae* (Halle: Caroli Hermmanni Hemmerde 1775); *Beantwortung der Fragmente eines Ungenannten* (Halle: Erziehungsinstitut 1779, [2]1780); *Das Bahrdtische Glaubensbekenntnis* (Erlangen: Erziehungsinstitut 1779); *Lebensbeschreibung von ihm selbst abgefasst* I-II (Halle: Schwetschke 1781–82), *Neuer Versuch die gemeinnüzige Auslegung und Anwendung des neuen Testaments zu befördern* (Halle: Carl Hermann Hemmerde 1786); *Zur Revision der kirchlichen Hermeneutik und Dogmatik* (Halle: 1788); *D. Joh. Salomo Semlers letztes Glaubensbekenntnis über natürliche und christliche Religion* (ed. C. G. Schutz; Königsberg: Friedrich Nicolovius 1792).

General works: W. Baird, *History of New Testament Research: Volume One: From Deism to Tübingen* (Minneapolis, MN: Fortress Press 1992) 117–27, 174–77; H. Donner, "Gesichtspunkte zur Auflösung des klassischen Kanonsbegriffes bei Johann Salomo Semler", in: *Fides et communicatio* (FS Martin Doerne; ed. D. Rössler e.a.; Göttingen: Vandenhoeck & Ruprecht 1970) 56–68; Johann Gottfried Eichhorn, "Johann Salomo Semler, geb. am 18ten Dec. 1725, gest. am 14ten März 1791", *Allgemeine Bibliothek der biblischen Litteratur 5* (1793) 1–202; H. W. Frei, *The Eclipse of Biblical Narrative: A Study in Eighteenth and Nineteenth Century Hermeneutics* (New Haven, CN: Yale UP 1974); Chr. Frey, "Semlers Glaubensbekenntnis", in: *Theologie und Aufklärung* (FS Gottfried Hornig; ed. W. E. Miller / H. H. Schulz; Würzburg: Königshausen und Neumann 1992) 165–78; P. Gastrow, *Joh. Salomo Semler in seiner Bedeutung für die Theologie mit besonderer Berücksichtigung seines Streites mit G. E. Lessing* (Giessen: Alfred Töpelmann 1905); E. Hirsch, *Geschichte der neuern evangelischen Theologie* 1-5 (Gütersloh: Gerd Mohn 1960) 4, 48–89; H. Hoffman, *Die Theologie Semlers* (Leipzig: Dieterich 1905); G. Hornig, *Die Anfänge der historisch-kritischen Theologie. Johann Salomo Semlers Schriftverständnis und seine Stellung zu Luther* (FSThR 8; Göttingen: Vandenhoeck & Ruprecht 1961); idem, *Johann Salomo Semler. Studien zu Leben und Werk des Hallenser Aufklärungstheologen* (Hallesche Beiträge zur europäischen Aufklärung 2; Tübingen: Niemeyer 1996); F. Huber, *Johann Salomo Semler, seine Bedeutung für die Theologie, sein Streit mit Gotthold Ephraim Lessing* (Berlin: Trenkel 1906); O. Kaiser, "Johann Salomo Semler als Bahnbrecher der modernen Bibelwissenschaft", in: *Textgemäss. Aufsätze und Beiträge zur Hermeneutik des Alten Testaments* (FS Ernst Würthwein; ed. A. H. Gunneweg / Otto Kaiser; Göttingen: Vandenhoeck & Ruprecht 1979) 59–74, = *Von der Gegenwartsbedeutung des Alten Testaments. Gesammelte Studien zur Hermeneutik und Redaktionsgeschichte* (ed. V. Fritz e.a.; Göttingen: Vandenhoeck & Ruprecht 1984) 79–94; H.-J. Kraus, *Geschichte der historisch-kritischen Erforschung des Alten Testaments* (Neukirchen-Vluyn: Neukirchener Verlag [3]1982) 103–13; W. G. Kümmel, *The New Testament: The History of the Investigation of Its Problems* (Nashville, TN: Abingdon Press 1972) 62–69; A. Lüder, *Historie und Dogmatik. Ein Beitrag zur Genese und Entfaltung von Johann Salomo Semlers Verständnis des Alten Testaments* (BZAW 233; Berlin / New York: de Gruyter 1995); J. C. O'Neill, *The Bible's Authority: A Portrait Gallery of Thinkers from Lessing to Bultmann* (Edinburgh: T & T Clark 1991) 39–53; T. Rendtorff, *Church and Theology: The Systematic Function of the Church Concept in Modern Theology* (Philadelphia, PA: Westminster Press 1976) 28–58; H. Graf Reventlow, *Epochen der Bibelauslegung IV. Von der Aufklärung bis zum 20. Jahrhundert* (Munich: Beck 2001) 175–89; D. Ritschl, "Johann Salomo Semler: The Rise of the Historical-Critical Method in Eighteenth-Century Theology on the Continent", *Introduction to Modernity: A Symposium on Eighteenth-Century Thought* (ed. R. Mollenauer; Austin, TX: University of Texas Press 1965) 107–33; H. Rollmann, "Semler, Johann Salomo (1725–1791)", in: *Historical Handbook of Major Biblical Interpreters* (ed. Donald K. McKim; Downers Grove, IL / Leicester: InterVarsity Press 1998) 355–59; H. H. R. Schulz, *Johann Salomo Semlers Wesenbestimmung des Christentums. Ein Beitrag zur Erforschung der Theologie Semlers* (Würzburg: Königshausen und Neumann 1988); H. Strathmann, "Die Krisis des Kanons der Kirche. Joh. Gerhards und Joh. Sal. Semlers Erbe", *ThBl* 20 (1941) 295–310 = *Das Neue Testament als Kanon. Dokumentation und kritische Analyse zur gegenwärtigen Diskussion* (ed. E. Käsemann; Göttingen: Vandenboeck & Ruprecht 1970) 41–61; J. Stroup, "Protestant Church Historians in the German Enlightenment", in: *Aufklärung und Geschichte. Studien zur deutschen Geschichtswissenschaft im 18. Jahrhundert* (Veröffentlichungen des Max-Planck-Institutes für Geschichte 81; ed. H. E. Bodeker e.a.; Göttingen: Vandenhoeck & Ruprecht 1986) 169–92; L. M. Vogelsang, *Stability and Transgression: Studies in Canon Formation* (diss., Yale University 1996) 126–73.

Johann Salomo Semler (1725-91), the son of a Lutheran minister who was also an avid book collector, was born in Saalfeld, Thuringia, on 18 December 1725. His mother was a strongly religious person and highly influential on her son. Semler was reared in and deeply imprinted by a strongly pietistic environment. As a precocious lad he had access to an excellent library and quickly mastered Latin, Greek, and Hebrew. From 1743 to 1750, he studied at the University of Halle working in classical philology, history, logic, mathematics, and theology. He was greatly influenced by Siegmund Jacob Baumgarten (1706-57) who taught at Halle from 1734 until his death. Semler became Baumgarten's protégé, took his evening meals at the professor's home where he met such figures as Voltaire and Wolff, and no doubt became acquainted with the thought of Alexander Gottlieb Baumgarten (1714-62), Siegmund's younger brother, a pioneer in the study of aesthetics, who has been called "Wolff's most brilliant disciple".[50] The older Baumgarten was a polymath who worked to achieve new and more scientific (*wissenschaftliche*) approaches to Church history, theology, and hermeneutics.[51]

Semler completed his work at Halle in 1750 with a thesis in which he defended the authenticity of the Johannine Comma (1 John 5:7) against the English Arian William Whiston (1667-1752), a position which he later rescinded. After working for a newspaper in Coburg for a year, he moved to the University of Altdorf as professor of German history and Latin poetry and then in 1752 returned to Halle where he taught until his death. Semler played a leading role in the life of the university serving in important administrative posts and aiding in the reorganization of theological studies.

His voluminous writings[52] cover an enormously wide range of topics, even including works on entomology, the Rosicrucians, the healing effects of *Luftsalzwasser*, alchemy, and Latin handbooks for youth. He wrote paraphrases with notes of Romans (1769), 1 Corinthians (1770), Gospel of John (1771-72), 2 Corinthians (1776), Galatians (1779), Hebrews (1779), James (1781), 1 Peter (1783), 2 Peter (1784), and 1 John (1792). He was responsible for publishing editions of, comments on, or translations of works by numerous authors in addition to those of A. and S. Baumgarten: Hesychius (1749), Cicero (1749), Isidore (1750), Ptolemy (1750), Livy (1750), Elias Levita (1754, 1772), Montfaucon (1757), the Centuriators of Magdeburg (1757-60), Johann von Ferreras (1757-62), Christian Waldburg (1759, 1760), Friedrich Eberhard Boysen (1760), Daniel Neal (1762), Johann Jacob Wettstein (1764, 1756), Albert Schultens (1769), Tertullian (1770-76), F. A. Stroth (1771), Johann Sleidans (1771-73), Samuel Clarke (1774), Pelagius (1775), Hugh Farmer (1776, 1783), Ludwig Meyer (1776), Richard Simon (1776-80), Erasmus (1777, 1782), Arthur Ashby Sykes (1778), Balthasar Bekker (1781-82), Lord Barrington (1783), Johann Kiddel (1783), Thomas Townsen (1783-84), Robert Fludd (1785), Johann Conrad Müller (1786), and Nicholas of Cusa (1787).

Semler worked in an age which witnessed the confluence of several streams of thought and he drank deeply from all of them. There was, first of all, the movement toward the universalization of hermeneutical methodology. In the

---

[50] P. H. REILL, *The German Enlightenment and the Rise of Historicism* (Berkeley, CA: University of California Press 1975) 60, see 59-65. Semler later spoke of hermeneutics as aesthetics (*Beantwortung der Fragmente eines Ungenanten*, 2nd edn., 290) and reissued with a preface one of A. G. Baumgarten's works (1773).
[51] Semler, who described himself as a mere midget compared to Baumgarten, assisted in the latter's study, *Christliches Concordienbuch* (1747), in his review journals, and edited numerous of his works after Baumgarten's early death. On Baumgarten, see M. SCHOLEMANN, *Siegmund Jacob Baumgarten. System und Geschichte in der Theologie des Überganges zum Neuprotestantismus* (FKDG 26; Göttingen: Vandenhoeck & Ruprecht 1974), and idem, "Wegbereiter wider Willen. Siegmund Jacob Baumgarten und die historisch-kritische Bibelforschung", in: *Historische Kritik und biblischer Kanon in der deutschen Aufklärung* (Wolfenbütteler Forschungen 41; ed. H. Graf Reventlow e.a.; Wiesbaden: Otto Harrassowitz 1988) 149-55.
[52] Hornig, Studien (1996), lists 250 works, some multi-volume.

second edition of his work on universal hermeneutics, an older contemporary, Hermann von der Hardt (1660–1746), wrote that interpretation is "the most difficult of all endeavors, the light of the past, the path to all learning, the vehicle of the sciences, the spice of civil tranquility, the bulwark of Church and state, the remedy of ignorance, the refuge of the truth, and the acme of the disciplines".[53] This exaggerated claim gives expression to the widespread nature of the contemporary discussion on hermeneutics. The first half of the eighteenth century witnessed for the first time the full integration of history and historical perspectives into the mainstream of hermeneutical work.[54] The application of general hermeneutics to biblical study, already achieved in a disorganized fashion among English Deists often influenced by Spinoza,[55] resulted in the Bible's loss of its exceptionalism and thus the view that the Bible was unique among literary works thereby necessitating a special hermeneutic. The following conclusions were a consequence: (1) The Bible should be read and studied like any other book. Individual biblical books or groupings of books must be read on their own, not filtered through the Bible as a whole or through Church/Synagogue tradition. (2) The Bible is a book of antiquity separated from the present both chronologically and conceptually. (3) A biblical text is the product of a human author(s) living in a particular time and place. (4) The form and content of a text reflect and are intelligible only in the light of the author's conceptions, intentions, beliefs, and worldview, which are conditioned by the time and context of the original writers' and readers' environment and thought world. (5) The causes and nature of events in the Bible must be understood in terms of historical analogy; what was possible to occur in biblical times must be possible in the present and vice versa.

Secondly, Semler lived in an age that witnessed the real internationalization of biblical scholarship. Although the older informal but self-conscious Republic of Letters had provided communication between the international learned of all disciplines,[56] this did not compare with the new accessibility of scholarship. Two examples can illustrate this internationalism. First, in an effort to bring continental scholarship abreast of that in England, a multivolume work was produced as a running biblical commentary drawing entirely upon English authors. The work appeared in French, Dutch, and German, the latter being

---

[53] *Universalis exegeseos elementa pro omnis generis veteribus scriptis, sacris et exteris, recte legendis ac digne interpretandis* (Helmstedt: s.l. 1708) 19; translated in: M. ERMATH, "Hermeneutics and History: The Fork in Hermes' Path through the 18th Century", in: Aufklärung und Geschichte (1986) 193.

[54] See Reill, The German Enlightenment (1975). On the role of Johann Martin Chladenius (1710–59), a contemporary and probable acquaintance of Semler, see Ermath, Hermeneutics and History (1986) 206–21 as well as J. GRONDIN, *Einführung in die philosophische Hermeneutik* (Darmstadt: Wiss. Buchgesellschaft 1991).

[55] See P. BYRNE, *Natural Religion and the Nature of Religion: The Legacy of Deism* (London: Routledge1989), and J. C. WEINSHEIMER, *Eighteenth-Century Hermeneutics: Philosophy of Interpretation in England from Locke to Burke* (New Haven, CT: Yale UP 1993).

[56] For a description of the "members" of this group, although probably with some over extension of its membership, see J.-P. NICERON, *Mémoires pour servir à l'histoire des hommes illustres dans la Republique des Lettres, avec un catologue raisonné des leurs ouvrages* (43 vols. in 44; Paris: Briasson 1727–45).

translated with expansions from either the French or Dutch.[57] The German edition, later referred to as *das englische Bibelwerk*, was the most expansive edition and included material drawn from a wide variety of English sources ranging from the annotations on the Bible attributed to the Westminster divines[58] to the writings of Isaac Newton (1642-1727) but none from deistic authors. The editors of the German edition were Romanus Teller (1703-50), Johann Augustin Dietelmair (1717-85), Baumgarten, and Jacob Brucker (1721-90). A second example of the internationalization of scholarship is reflected in the monthly journal work of Baumgarten who reviewed practically all contemporary and classical writings in all phases of theological and biblical studies.[59] His reviews helped introduce deistic thought into Germany. Baumgarten like Semler was responsible for editions and/or translations of numerous works into German.[60]

A third factor in Semler's environment was a strong emphasis on reason and rationality in both the understanding and practice of religion and in biblical studies in particular. The role of reason in religion, of course, had been a permanent issue for centuries but had reached a radical stage at the end of the seventeenth century. Cartesian philosophy, Lockian empiricism, and deistic natural religion as well as Socinian theology had all contributed to the debate. In Semler's student days, Halle was not only a center for Pietism but also where the mathematician-philosopher Christian Wolff (1679-1754), after his triumphant return from exile (imposed 8 November, 1723) on 6 December, 1740, expounded his version of a rational, mathematical form of philosophy and theology. On the occasion of the Frankfurt Fair, 17-24 April 1735, Johann Lorenz Schmidt (1702-49), offered for sale his handsomely produced and expensive 1040 page translation of the Pentateuch with notes (the so-called "Wertheim Bible"). As a Wolffian devotee, Schmidt had hoped to present to

---

[57] *La Sainte Bible, ou, Le Vieux et le Nouveau Testament: avec un commentaire litteral composé de notes choisie & tirées de divers auteurs anglois* (6 vols. in 11; Le Haye: Pierre Paupie 1742-77); *Verklaring van de gehelle Heilige Schrift, door eenigen van de voornaamste Engelsche Godgeleerden* (tr. and introd. by J. van den Honert; 17 vols. in 18; Amsterdam: Isaak Tirion & Jacobus Loveringh 1740-57); *Die Heilige Schrift des Alten und Neuen Testaments, nebst einer vollständigen Erklärung derselben, welche aus den auserlesensten Anmerkungen verschiedener Engländischen Schriftsteller* (19 vols.; Leipzig: Bernhard Christoph Breitkopf 1749-70). The first two volumes of the German edition were based on the French; the remaining volumes were based on the Dutch.

[58] *Annotations upon all the Books of the Old and New Testament Wherein the Text is Explained, Doubts Resolved, Scriptures Paralleled, and Various Readings Observed by the Joynt Labour of Certain Learned Divines* (London: J. Legatt and J. Raworth 1645; 2nd edn. greatly enlarged, 2 vols., London: J. Legatt, 1651; 3rd edn. 1658).

[59] The reviews were published in his *Nachrichten von einer Hallischen Bibliothek* (8 vols.; 1748-51) and *Nachrichten von merkwürdigen Büchern* (12 vols.; 1752-58; both series published in Halle by Johann Justinus Gebauer). The final volume in the second series, an index volume published after Baumgarten's death, contains a six page preface by Semler.

[60] See M. B. PRICE / L. M. PRICE, *The Publication of English Humaniora in Germany in the Eighteenth Century* (University of California Publications in Modern Philology 44, Berkeley, CA: University of California Press 1955) which supplies a bibliographical survey. See also B. FABIAN, "English Books and Their Eighteenth-Century German Readers", in: P. KORSHIN (ed.), *The Widening Circle: Essays on the Circulation of Literature in Eighteenth-Century Europe* (Haney Foundation Series 20; Philadelphia, PA: University of Pennsylvania Press 1976) 117-96. Unfortunately, Fabian completely ignored Baumgarten.

the German educated class a work of biblical translation and interpretation that drew upon rational principles and modern thought. His work met with strong opposition and eventual censorship.[61] Throughout his career, Semler, like many others, wrestled with the issues of faith and reason, revelation and natural thought.[62]

A fourth characteristic of Semler's time was the increased emphasis on the subjectivity of religious faith and experience and its concomitant stress on individualism, toleration, and human freedom. Semler, like so many other Germans in the eighteenth century (Christian Thomasius, Johann David Michaelis, Gotthold Ephraim Lessing, and Immanuel Kant), had deep roots in Pietism, which like rationalism strongly emphasized subjectivity and the authority of the individual. This emphasis on subjectivity, however, had roots more diverse than mere Pietism and rationalism. As early as 1660, the English Quaker Samuel Fisher had written that the inner light claimed by Quakers was "not against, but according to right reason; for they are synonymous".[63] This subjectivity found expression in the 1675 *Confession of the Society of Friends, commonly called Quakers*[64] which elevated the illumination of the Spirit to the individual above the authority of the Scriptures which were demoted to a secondary role subordinate to the inward testimony of the Spirit.[65]

Above all else, Semler was an historian and not just a Church historian. For several years, he worked on a project begun by Baumgarten, namely, to produce a universal history in German based on the English *Universal History* which had begun to appear in sections in 1730 and was subsequently translated into French and German.[66] Semler made contributions to the *Algemeine Welthistorie* from 1747 to 1766. Semler's work on the Bible and the Church's and individuals' expressions of Christian faith (his theological studies) were basically historical in orientation and outlook.[67]

The historical character of the writings of the Bible, for Semler, encompassed everything, from the language in which revelation was given to the

---

[61] For a discussion of the work, its background, and impact, see P. S. Spalding, *Seize the Book, Jail the Author: Johann Lorenz Schmidt and Censorship in Eighteenth-Century Germany* (West Lafayette, IN: Purdue UP 1998), and H. Ehmer, "Die Wertheimer Bibel. Der Versuch einer rationalistischen Bibelübersetzung", *Jahrbuch der hessischen kirchengeschichtlichen Vereinigung* 43 (1992) 289–312. Schmidt later translated into German Matthew Tindal's *Christianity as Old as Creation* (1741) and Spinoza's *Ethics* (1744) as well as other works.

[62] The Racovian Catechism of 1609 had declared that without right reason "we could neither perceive with certainty the authority of the sacred writings, understand their contents, discriminate one thing from another, nor apply them to practical purpose" (I, ii).

[63] *Rusticus ad Academicos*, book IV, 178.

[64] See Schaff, The Creeds of Christendom 3 (1881) 789–98.

[65] It was not fortuitous that Bruno Bauer (1809–82) included a section on Semler in his *Einfluss des englischen Quäkertums auf die deutsche Cultur und auf das englisch-russische Project einer Weltkirche* (Berlin: Eugen Grosser 1878) 127–58.

[66] *An Universal History from the Earliest Account of Time to the Present* (23 vols.; London: Printed for J. Batley and others 1736–65). For the publishing history, see G. Abbattista, "The Business of Paternoster Row: The Publication of the *Universal History* (1736–65)", *Publishing History* 17 (1985) 5–50. Supplements to the work continued to be published for years. Semler's "Remarks on the Egyptian History, in the First Part of the Universal History" was published in 1760.

[67] Semler remarked in his autobiography that his early interest in general history contributed to his study of Church history; see his Lebensbeschreibung 1 (1781) 208–10.

authors, to the writing of the individual biblical books, and to the process of canonization. Semler was well acquainted with the work of earlier scholars who had already clearly demonstrated that the manuscripts and texts of both testaments had a long and complicated history. He wrote articles, for example, on the massoretic vowel points (1754, 1758), annotated a German edition of Levita's *Massoreth Hammassoreth* (1772), and supplied notes to three volumes of Simon's works on the New Testament text and translations (1776–80).[68] He was himself a contributor to the textual criticism of the New Testament arguing that in the fourth century, there were at least three families of textual archetypes, the Eastern (associated with Antioch and Constantinople), the Western (in North Africa), and the Alexandrian (associated with Origen).[69]

According to Semler, the very language used in the production of the original biblical texts, like all language, was historically conditioned and based on the rationality of the authors.[70] No new, non-human language was employed when God wanted to teach humans certain important matters since this would have required the introduction of a completely new set of signs and concepts. Normal human rationality was involved as well as the natural universal principles of all knowledge which had not been obliterated by the Fall. Any special revelation would not have contradicted general natural revelation or knowledge which humans possessed through the natural powers of understanding and reason. Thus, scholarly interpretation must be based on historical-grammatical considerations.[71] Of this interpretation, Semler wrote: "The most important thing, in short, in hermeneutical skill depends upon one's knowing the Bible's use of language properly and precisely, as well as distinguishing and representing to oneself the historical circumstances of a biblical discourse, and on one's being able to speak today of those matters in such a way as the changed times and circumstances of our fellow-men demand.... All the rest of hermeneutics can be reduced to these two things".[72] Understanding the historical circumstances required one to recognize that "all biblical writings, like all

---

[68] See J. D. WOODBRIDGE, "German Responses to the Biblical Critic Richard Simon: from Leibniz to J. S. Semler", in: Historische Kritik und biblischer Kanon (1988) 65–87.

[69] See Kümmel, The New Testament (1972) 66f, and B. M. METZGER, *Chapters in the History of New Testament Textual Criticism* (New Testament Tools and Studies 4; Leiden: Brill 1963) 15. Semler supplied a preface (III–XXIV) and an appendix (583–686) to the reissue of J. J. Wettstein's *Prolegomena in Novum Testamentum* in 1764. He was apparently the first to speak of "recensions" of the text.

[70] See "Historische Einleitung", in Baumgarten, *Evangelische Glaubenslehre* 1 (1759) 35–40.

[71] In the late 1660s, debate had raged over the 1666 work *Philosophia sacrae scripturae interpres* by Ludwig Meyer (1629–81), an Amsterdam physician and intellectual friend of Spinoza who advocated the use of non-sectarian philosophy rather than Church tradition and/or dogmatic theology in interpreting Scripture. See J. S. PREUS, "A Hidden Opponent in Spinoza's *Tractatus*", HTR 88 (1995) 361–88. Meyer's liberal opponents, Ludwig Wolzogen (1633–90) and Lambert van Velthuysen (1622–85) argued that common usage of language (*usus loquendi*) should be the rule in biblical interpretation which should be concerned with meaning not truth. In 1776, Semler reissued Meyer's work with a preface (pp. III–XIV) in which he agreed with Wolzogen. For the controversy over Meyer's work, see J. S. PREUS, *Spinoza and the Irrelevance of Biblical Authority* (Cambridge: Cambridge UP 2001). Meyer's work is available in a modern French translation: *La Philosophie interprète de l'écriture sainte* (Collection "Horizons"; tr. with notes by J. Lagrée / P.-F. Moreau; Paris: Intertextes 1988).

[72] *Vorbereitung*, 1, 160–61; transl. from Frei, The Eclipse of Biblical Narrative (1974) 247.

other books by rational authors, consist of written dialogues (*Reden*) which were originally set down for particular readers, in a particular country, at a particular time, and, despite any other general usefulness, for a particular occasion".[73] The biblical books, therefore, were not written for a universal application, for all times and places.

Semler spoke of how the biblical writers and even Jesus expressed their thoughts and the essence of their teachings in the thought forms and language of their historical circumstances. In describing this historical conditionality, he employed the concept of "accommodation" or "condescension".[74] To speak of God's accommodation of revelation to the limitations of human understanding had been common throughout Jewish and Christian history.[75] In the Enlightenment and for Semler, however, the theory took on new emphasis. The concept was used not only to explain the nature of biblical materials and views but also to conclude that certain factors and characteristics in the biblical text did not constitute authentic instruction, for example, for Semler the eschatological elements in the teaching of Jesus and the apocalyptic thought of the book of Revelation. In such cases, Jesus and the New Testament writers were accommodating themselves and their thoughts to the concepts current at the time.

In order to understand Jesus and the rise of the Christian religion, Semler explored the multifaceted world of pre-Christian Judaism arguing that it was necessary to understand "the actual ideas of the contemporaries of Christ and the Apostles". He distinguished two major pre-Christian Jewish movements, the Hellenic and the Hebraic, existing in tension and each with sub-sects. Each interpreted the Hebrew Bible in its own way; the former (Alexandrian Jews, Essenes, and others) tended toward allegorization and universalization of the text and its content while the latter (Pharisees, Sadducees, and others) employed a more literal, restricted interpretation. These two streams in tension continued in the early Church and found expression, on the one hand, in the particularistic, Judaic circles associated with the early Jerusalem Church, Peter, James, and Jude, and, on the other hand, in the universalism of Pauline

---

[73] "Historische Einleitung" 1 (1759) 35; transl. from O'Neill, The Bible's Authority (1991) 43.

[74] Early in his career, in 1759, Semler became involved in the case of Anna Elizabeth Lohmann, a twenty-two year old woman from the village of Kemberg near Wittenberg. The woman was "possessed" by an evil spirit and three angels; see J. BLACKWELL, "Controlling the Demonic: Johann Salomo Semler and the Possessions of Anna Elizabeth Lohmann (1759)", in: *Impure Reason: Dialectic of Enlightenment in Germany* (ed. W. D. Wilson / R. C. Holub; Detroit, MI: Wayne State UP 1993) 425–42. Semler wrote three works on this case in 1759–60, denying the existence of demons and demon possession. This issue and the appearance of demonic possession in the New Testament occupied his attention for years leading to three additional books (in 1762 [²1776], 1767, and 1779) and the translation into German with Semler's notations of works by the English dissenting minister Hugh Farmer (1714–87) who denied the reality of demon possession and argued that Jesus and his Apostles did not believe in demons but, although knowing better, accommodated themselves to vulgar opinions. See the reissue of the German translation with Semler's preface and annotations of Farmer's *Briefe an D. Worthington über die Dämonischen in den Evangelien* (with an introd. by Dirk Fleischer; Wissen und Kritik 20; Waltrop: Harmut Spenner 2000). The appearance of *Bezauberte Welt* (*The Bewitched World*, orig. published in 1691) by Balthasar Bekker (1636–98) in three volumes with Semler's prefaces and annotations (1781–82) supported Semler's position since Bekker denied the world-view supportive of witchcraft, the devil, and magic.

[75] See S. D. BENIN, *The Footprints of God: Divine Accommodation in Jewish and Christian Thought* (Albany, NY: State University of New York Press 1993).

and Gentile circles.[76] The majority of the writings of the New Testament manifest the influence of either one or the other of these strands, in images drawn
from the real world of the writers' and readers' conditions of life and traditional forms of thought.

In spite of Jesus' and Paul's use of time and place conditioned thought forms
they were able to convey the central message of Christianity. All the early
Apostles had been instructed in the true spiritual message of Jesus but this was
overshadowed by the external forms in which it was encoded. For Semler there
was never a period of pure primitive Christianity nor a pure expression of
Christianity valid for all times, places, and people.

In expressing his views, Semler drew upon a number of distinctions, most all
of which reflected his differentiation between form and spirit: public and private, theology and religion, philosophy and theology, community and individual, external and internal, interpretation and application, capable-thoughtful
and incapable-unthoughtful readers, and Sacred Scripture and Word of God.
All forms, though indispensable, and whether dogmas, confessions, canons,
rituals, or whatever manifestation, were thoroughly historically conditioned
and could become a hindrance to the spirit and to the universal moral drive toward greater realization of faith in Christ if they proved stifling to the latter.

In his work on the canon, especially in his famous four-volume *Abhandlung
von freier Untersuchung des Canon* (1771-75), Semler argued, first of all, that
the biblical canon, like all products of human consciousness, reflects and was
conditioned by historical and local conditions. Secondly, the biblical canon
cannot be identified with the "Word of God" as was claimed by the orthodox
theologians of the time. Thirdly, different writings in the Bible reflected in different degrees the "Word of God", if at all.

Semler noted that differing collections of sacred books or canons had existed even among Palestinian and non-Palestinian Jews and even among the
Palestinian Jews themselves (Samaritans, Pharisees, and Sadducees) as well as
differing approaches to their interpretations. The Christian New Testament
developed over a period of centuries. The early Church had no canon but came
to possess a number of writings which were read in public worship and used in
instruction. What texts were read varied and included works such as Sirach,
Wisdom of Solomon, Tobit, Clement, martyr legends and so on. If one could
speak of a canon during this early period, then one would have to call it an
open canon.[77] The Church gradually complied a collection of writings to give

---

[76] The view of two strands (Peterine and Pauline) in early Christianity had already been pur-
posed by John Toland (1670–1722) in his *Amyntor, or, a Defense of Milton's Life* (London: John
Darby 1699) and by Thomas Morgan (1680–1743) in his *The Moral Philosopher: In a Dialogue between Philalethes a Christian Deist, and Theophanes a Christian Jew* (4 vols.; London: Printed for
the author 1737–41); see 1, 349–54.

[77] In vol. III (1–189) of the *Abhandlung von freier Untersuchung des Canon*, Semler incorporated material from *Historie de l'église depuis Jésus Christ jusqu'à présent* (1699) by Jacques Basnage
(1653–1723) who had argued that during the first three centuries of the Church the canon was
open and each Church could choose to use or ignore books. The Apocalypse in the eastern
Churches Basnage offered as a prime example.

expression to its unity which was sanctioned by the Church by the end of the fourth and the beginning of the fifth century.

Highly relevant to his studies of the canon was Semler's distinction between Scripture and Word of God.[78] While orthodox Christianity of the time identified Scripture with the Word of God (*scriptura sacra est verbum dei*), Semler argued that Scripture contains the Word of God.[79] Whereas the biblical books were written for particular times, persons, and places, the Word of God was for all humans, in all times and places (*Worte Gottes, das alle Menschen in allen Zeiten weise macht zur Seligkeit*[80]). Although Semler does not, and according to his position really could not, spell out in detail the content of the Word of God in the Holy Scriptures,[81] he refers to this distinction throughout his writings. He described the Word of God in terms of universal moral (spiritual) truth, salvific living knowledge, and so on. The Word of God, however, was revelation and dependent upon the teachings and story of Jesus.[82]

The Word of God was not considered present everywhere or throughout Scripture. Like Luther, Semler gave highest honor to the Gospel of John and the epistles of Paul (especially Romans). Some portions of Scripture were devoid of the Word of God. As examples, with different listings in various places, Semler noted most of the books of the Hebrew Bible although he recognized that these still had value for the Jewish community.[83] He considered Judaism to be a less universal religion than Christianity.

In his stress on tolerance and the right of individuals to their own private religion, Semler argued that readers could and should make their own judgments about the value of Scripture or portions thereof.[84] Individuals should really

---

[78] See Hornig, Anfänge (1961) 84–115; idem, Johann Salomo Semler (1996) 237–39; and Vogelsang, Stability and Transgression (1996), esp. 127–36, 146–51.

[79] Hornig traces Semler's distinction back to Luther and Melanchthon but Semler does not explicitly attribute his concept to the Reformers. The idea of the Word of God as distinct from the Bible was a pervasive concept among Enthusiasts such as Samuel Fisher.

[80] *Abhandlung* [2]I (1776) 60. Semler is probably here alluding to Rom1:16–17; see Vogelsang, Stability and Transgression (1996) 148.

[81] Eichhorn already noted Semler's lack of specificity on certain matters; see *Allgemeine Bibliothek* 5 (1793) 89.

[82] In the famous cases of Carl Friedrich Bahrdt (1741–92), who was denied a university position because of his unorthodox theology, and the publication of the Fragments of the deceased Deist Hermann Samuel Reimarus (1694–1768), Semler affirmed the necessity of divine revelation and argued that Jesus proclaimed and founded a revolutionary, universal religion based on moral grounds and a spiritual kingdom.

[83] He refers to the books of Ruth, Esther, Ezra, Nehemiah, and Chronicles (I, [2]1776, 27), the historical books with their accounts of the past of a particular people (ibid. 28, 35), and genealogical lists (ibid. 36). More reflective of universal concerns and of the word of God were books like the Psalms, Proverbs, Ecclesiastes, and Job (ibid. 42), and the latter prophets (ibid. 63). Semler used terms like "fable" and "mythology" in describing portions of the Old Testament; see CHR. HARTLICH / W. SACHS, *Der Ursprung des Mythosbegriffes in der modernen Bibelwissenschaft* (Schriften der Studiengemeinschaft der Evangelischen Akademien 2; Tübingen: Mohr 1952) 165–68.

[84] See Hornig, Johann Salomo Semler (1996) 180–94, and Vogelsang, Stability and Transgression (1996) 159–66. Semler was very much interested in personal biographies. Between 1759 and 1770, he supervised the publication of and wrote prefaces for 6 volumes (5 through 10) in the series *Samlung von merkwürdigen Lebensbeschreibungen*, begun by Baumgarten, and in his own autobiography (1781–82) frequently illustrated how personal religion played a role in life.

create there own canons of Scripture. They should read the text and in so doing find the Word of God here and there and feel no guilt about considering much of what they read as irrelevant, uninspired and uninspiring. The Word of God, however, was outside and beyond criticism.

Chapter Forty-three

Jewish Study of the Bible
Before and During the Jewish Enlightenment

By Edward Breuer, Jerusalem

Sources: S. Asaf: Mekorot le-Toldot ha-Hinukh be-Yisrael (Tel Aviv: Dvir 1954). – Judah Leib ben Ze'ev: Mavo' el Mikra'ē Kodesh (Vienna 1810). – Solomon Dubno / Moses Mendelssohn: 'Alim Litrufah (Amsterdam 1778; repr. in: Gesammelte Schriften. Jubiläumsausgabe; ed. F. Bamberger e.a. [Stuttgart: Friedrich Frommann 1971–2001] 14, 1972, 321–68). – S. Hanau: Binyan Shelomoh (Frankfurt 1708); Tzohar ha-Teivah (Berlin 1733). – Moses Mendelssohn: Sefer Megillat Kohelet (Berlin 1770; repr. in: Gesammelte Schriften. Jubiläumsausgabe [see above] 14, 145–207); Sefer Netivot ha-Shalom (Berlin 1780–83; repr. in: Gesammelte Schriften. Jubiläumsausgabe [see above], vols. 15–18). – N. Wessely: Divrē Shalom ve-Emet (Berlin 1782); Gan Na'ul (Amsterdam 1755–56). – A. Worms: Seyag la-Torah (Frankfurt 1766).

Studies: A. Altmann, Moses Mendelssohn: A Biographical Study (Philadelphia: Jewish Publication Society 1973); E. Breuer, "Naphtali Herz Wessely and the Cultural Dislocations of an Eighteenth-Century Maskil", in: S. Feiner / D. Sorkin (eds.), New Perspectives on the Haskalah (London: Littman 2001) 27–47; idem, The Limits of Enlightenment: Jews, Germans, and the Eighteenth-Century Study of Scripture (Cambridge, MA: Harvard University Center for Jewish Studies 1996); J. Harris, How Do We Know This? Midrash and the Fragmentation of Modern Judaism (Albany: State University of New York 1995); E. Levenson, Moses Mendelssohn's Understanding of Logico-Grammatical and Literary Construction in the Pentateuch: A Study of his German Translation and Hebrew Commentary (The Biur) (Brandeis University diss. 1972); S. Lowenstein, "The Readership of Mendelssohn's Bible Translation", HUCA 53 (1982) 179–213; P. Sandler, Ha-Biur la Torah shel Moshe Mendelson ve-Si'ato (Jerusalem: Reuven Mas 1940); D. Sorkin, Moses Mendelssohn and the Religious Enlightenment (Berkeley: University of California Press 1996); W. Weinberg, "Language Questions Relating to Moses Mendelssohn's Pentateuch Translation", HUCA 55 (1984) 197–242.

1. Introduction

The eighteenth century represented the beginning of a new chapter in the history of Jewish biblical interpretation, one which would impact significantly on the ways in which Jews would come to study and think about the Hebrew Bible. These developments, which sprouted from the Jewish communities of Central Europe, reflected a new flourish of Jewish cultural activity and a process of acculturation that brought Jews into greater contact with European ideas and scholarship. While this exposure to European culture resulted in the absorption and internalization of some of the exegetical trends of the Enlightenment, it also elicited a Jewish reaction that sought to preserve the distinct modes of rabbinic and medieval traditions of interpretation.

Before turning to these eighteenth-century developments, it is important to appreciate the nature of Jewish Bible study in the centuries preceding these changes. Sixteenth and seventeenth-century European Jewry was clearly suffused with an intense interest in Scripture, but the quality of the scholarly contribution paled in comparison with the attainments of medieval exegetes. One reason for this was the place of biblical scholarship in the Jewish culture of early modern Europe. There was a pronounced ambivalence, if not indifference, toward serious attention to the Hebrew Bible, with the study of the Talmud and the legal codes being given intellectual and spiritual primacy, while the study of the Bible was relegated to an honored but distinctly secondary position.[1] Scholars of this era produced hundreds of Bible commentaries and supercommentaries, but the vast majority of these texts were unoriginal and highly dependent upon earlier scholarship. For the most part, these texts were uninterested in the philological and grammatical exegesis of medieval French and Spanish scholars, and turned instead to homiletic modes of interpretation or to the time-honored tradition of carefully parsing Rashi's commentary to the Pentateuch. Early modern rabbinic leaders recognized the general lack of pedagogic and scholarly interest in serious Bible study and complained about it regularly, but to no avail.[2]

The few commentaries and supercommentaries that did make lasting and important contributions to the Jewish study of the Hebrew Bible reflected these very cultural patterns. R. Judah b. Betzalel Loew of Prague (1525–1609), for example, complained openly about the neglect of disciplined textual study of the Hebrew Bible.[3] However, his primary contribution to the study of the Pentateuch, *Gur 'Aryeh*, was a supercommentary to Rashi that was ultimately more concerned with this medieval scholar's use of rabbinic sources than with the biblical text itself. This was true also of other, mostly Eastern European scholars who also penned substantial supercommentaries to Rashi: R. Mordechai Jaffe's *Levush ha-'Orah* (1604), R. David b. Samuel Ha-Levi's *Divrē David – Turē Zahav* (1689), and R. Shabbetai Bass' *Siphtē Hakhamim* (1680). Perhaps the most influential new commentary to the Pentateuch, R. Ephraim Luntshitz' *Keli Yakar* (1602), was a thoroughly homiletic work that was generally unconcerned with textual or linguistic questions pertaining to the Hebrew Bible.

One interesting exception to this general pattern was the culture of the Italian-Jewish communities, which had always maintained the traditions of medieval Spain more assiduously than their brethren north and east of the Alps. Of particular note were the Masoretic works of Menahem di Lonzano (1550–1624) and Yedidyah Norzi (1560–1616), both of whom attempted to address

---

[1] On the relationship and tension between the study of rabbinical literature and other scholarly pursuits, see I. Twersky, "Talmudists, Philosophers, Kabbalists: The Quest for Spirituality in the Sixteenth Century", in: B. Cooperman (ed.), *Jewish Thought in the Sixteenth Century* (Cambridge, MA: Harvard UP 1983) 431–44; and idem, "Law and Spirituality in the Seventeenth Century: A Case Study in R. Yair Hayyim Bachrach", in: I. Twersky / B. Septimus (eds.), *Jewish Thought in the Seventeenth Century* (Cambridge, MA: Harvard UP 1987) 447–67; and J. Elbaum, *Petihut ve-Histagrut* (Jerusalem: Magnes Press 1990) 72–81.

[2] This reality is amply illustrated in the sources gathered in Asaf, *Mekorot* I (1954) 43 ff.

[3] See his *Gur 'Aryeh* to Deut 6:7.

various discrepancies between extant Torah scrolls and the classical Masoretic codices. Theirs were clearly pre-critical works that focused on *plene* and defective spellings and issues of vocalization and accentuation, with the stated aim of producing first rate copies of the MT for liturgical purposes.[4]

It is important to note, in this regard, that although a number of Jews in Western Europe were aware of the growing Christian sophistication in the study of the Hebrew Bible, Jewish scholars of the seventeenth century nowhere engaged the critical questions being raised by leading Christian Hebraists. The disparate writings of scholars such as Louis Cappel, Isaac de La Peyrère, and Richard Simon were directly or indirectly known to a small handful of mostly Dutch Jews who had regular contact with their scholarly Christian peers, but these Jews either remained oblivious to the far-reaching nature of the new critical scholarship or simply chose to ignore them.[5] Interestingly, the same was true of the Jewish reaction to the textual issues raised in Baruch Spinoza's *Theologico-Political Treatise* (1670); this work simply had no impact on the Jewish study of the Hebrew Bible until at least a century after it was published. As we shall see, it was only late in the eighteenth century that Jews began to acknowledge and respond to the initial advances of early biblical criticism.

2. The Study of the Hebrew Bible in the Eighteenth Century

The early modern European attitudes towards the Bible began to change at the beginning of the eighteenth century, with a renewed interest in the medieval exegetes of France, Provence, and Spain. The *peshat*-oriented commentary of R. Samuel b. Meir (Rashbam), which had remained in manuscript and not widely known or appreciated, was published for the first time in 1705.[6] Within a few decades the first supercommentary to this work appeared, and from this point onward the commentary of Rashbam came to be included among the classics of medieval Jewish exegesis.[7] Although the exegetical and grammatical writings of scholars such as R. David Qimhi (Radak) and Abraham ibn Ezra had been frequently published, they appear to have garnered some new attention. In 1765 Aaron Gumpertz produced a commentary to Ibn Ezra on the

---

[4] Lonzano's *'Or Torah* was published as part of his *Shtē Yadot* (Venice 1618) and reprinted four times by the mid-eighteenth century. Norzi's *Minhat Shai* was originally titled *Goder Peretz*, but was not published until 1742–44 in Mantua.

[5] These Jews included Menasseh b. Israel (1604–57), Isaac Cardoso (d. 1683) and Isaac Orobio de Castro (d. 1687). See Phillippus Van Limborch, *De Veritate Religionis Christianae* (1687), and Isaac Cardoso, *Las Excelencias de los Hebreos* (1679). To the degree that these Jewish writers responded to questions surrounding the reliability of the Hebrew text of the Bible, they did so as a continuation of earlier Christian polemical claims regarding Jewish textual corruption, and not in recognition of a nascent scholarly discourse.

[6] *Hamishah Humshē Torah...* (Berlin 1705), with the commentary of Rashbam appearing alongside the MT and other classical commentaries. This manuscript of Rashbam's commentary came from the important collection of R. David Oppenheimer.

[7] This first commentary to Rashbam was Solomon Zalman Ashkenazi, *Keren Shmuel* (Frankfurt/Oder 1727). Rashbam's commentary was also included in another Pentateuch published in Amsterdam, 1764.

Five Scrolls,[8] and in 1780–82, Yehiel Hillel Altschuler completed the two-part commentary of his father, R. David Altschuler, to the Prophets and Hagiographa. These parallel commentaries, *Metzudat Tzion* (which rendered each verse according to its contextual *peshat*) and *Metzudat David* (which focused on philology), drew heavily on R. David Qimhi and other commentators who developed *peshat* approaches, and Altschuler referred to himself as an anthologist rather than as an exegete.[9] His commentaries did not develop new approaches nor offer many original readings, but they did demonstrate a serious reengagement with medieval *peshat* exegesis. It should also be noted that while this renewed interest anticipated and prepared the ground for the later revival of Jewish Bible study, the publication of the commentaries and supercommentaries enumerated here emerged from within traditional Jewish society.

Hand in hand with this reengagement with medieval exegesis was the new attention being devoted to the study of biblical grammar. Solomon Hanau (1687–1746), a native of Frankfurt am Main who also lived for a time in Amsterdam and other Western European cities, joined other scholars in complaining bitterly about the neglect of Hebrew and its detrimental effect on the study of the Hebrew Bible. Hanau fully recognized that part of the problem was the stultifying effect of the deference paid to the authority of medieval scholarship.[10] He set out, therefore, to deal afresh with irregularities and grammatical difficulties that had not been adequately addressed in earlier writings. Towards this end, he attempted to offer some new ideas regarding a number of technical-linguistic issues, clearly treating biblical Hebrew as an open and dynamic subject of inquiry.[11] In his *Tzohar ha-Tevah*, Hanau forcefully insisted that the Sages of late Antiquity had fully internalized the grammatical and philological nuances of the Hebrew language, and that their interpretation of Scripture therefore represented an extraordinarily perspicacious reading of the Hebrew Bible. As such, in his desire to justify the importance of Hebrew grammar and philology, Hanau linked its study to the cultural primacy of rabbinic learning by broadly suggesting that a disciplined mastery of grammar would shed significant light upon the interpretative stratagems employed in midrashic literature.[12] Although there were eighteenth-century scholars who strongly denied the real substantive connections between *peshuto shel mikra* and rabbinic teachings, Hanau's view, as we shall see, would significantly shape the views of the early contributors to the Jewish Enlightenment.[13]

While Hanau appeared to be aware of at least some developments in contemporary Christian scholarship, his work did not engage the critical issues

---

[8] *Megalleh Sod (Hamburg 1765).*

[9] Altschuler's commentaries were published in Livorno, 1780–82, with each biblical book published with a separate title page reading simply *Sefer... im shenē perushim.*

[10] See Hanau, *Binyan Shelomoh* and *Tzohar ha-Tevah*, introductions.

[11] One such example is the idea of the intermediate *shewa*, with which Hanau tried to explain why in certain instances the *bgdkpt* consonants remained without a dagesh even following what would have appeared to have been a *shewa na*. See W. CHOMSKY, *David Kimhi's Hebrew Grammar (Mikhlol)* (New York: Bloch 1952) 18, 39–40.

[12] See Hanau, *Tzohar ha-Tevah*, introduction.

[13] In juxtaposition to Hanau, see I. ZAMOSC, *Netzah Yisrael* (Frankfurt/Oder 1741) 1b; and see Harris, How Do We Know This? (1995) 138–40.

that were now becoming an increasingly important feature of the European study of the Hebrew Bible.[14] In fact, the first Jewish response to the growing development of critical scholarship came from a slightly younger contemporary, the physician Asher Anshel Worms of Frankfurt (1695–1769). In 1766, he published a treatise on the Masorah, *Seyag la-Torah*, in which he insisted that the Hebrew Bible had been preserved "without any alterations and changes, as if they were given today at Sinai". He apparently penned Hebrew and Latin treatises – no longer extant, to the best of our knowledge – in which he claimed to respond to the work of Louis Cappel, Brian Walton and Matthew Hiller, among others.[15] *Seyag la-Torah* itself, however, did not address specific critical claims being raised against the MT. He simply stressed the fact that the early medieval Masoretes had merely transmitted and preserved a truly ancient text, and that the Hebrew Bible had not been subject to the kinds of textual corruptions that plagued other ancient texts. He was quick to applaud those Christian scholars who continued to support the authority and integrity of the MT, and warned that "no man should raise his hand to emend anything in Scripture" without the guidance of the traditional Masorah.[16]

3. The Early Haskalah and Bible Study

The most important development in the Jewish study of the Hebrew Bible in the eighteenth century was the emergence of the German Haskalah, the Jewish Enlightenment that was centered primarily in the Prussian cities of Berlin and Königsberg. As part of their effort to promote the integration of Jews into European society, the *Maskilim*, as the proponents of this group came to be known, set out on an ambitious program of cultural revival. Highly attuned to the achievements of contemporary German culture and sensitive to the perceived deficiencies of Jewish education and scholarship, the Maskilim were attracted by the literary-aesthetic sophistication of the German and European Enlightenments, and they sought to infuse Jewish Bible study with the same textual sensibilities. At the same time, embarrassed by the state of biblical scholarship within their own communities, they wanted to showcase the wealth of inherited textual traditions and advance the study of Scripture in distinctly Jewish terms. In so doing, the Maskilim sought to infuse biblical scholarship with the spirit of creativity and originality that characterized the work of their medieval forerunners.

The earliest articulations of these new cultural perspectives were found in the writings of Moses Mendelssohn (1729–86) and Naftali Hirz Wessely (1725–1805). Mendelssohn had been born in the provincial Prussian town of

---

[14] Hanau's familiarity with at least some Christian scholarship was suggested by ARON DOTAN in his prolegomena to W. WICKES, *Two Treatises on the Accentuation of the Old Testament* (New York: Ktav 1970) xi-xii; and by I. YEIVIN, *Introduction to the Tiberian Masorah* (tr. E. J. Revell; Missoula: Scholars Press 1980) 162, 168 f.

[15] Worms, *Seyag la-Torah* (1766) 20b.

[16] Ibid. 10b, 19a.

Dessau, but moved to Berlin in his youth. By the time he had reached adulthood, he had mastered traditional rabbinic texts as well as the European world
of philosophy and literature, and he ultimately came to be regarded as one of
the most important German thinkers of his age. In addition, Mendelssohn was
an outspoken champion of Jewish civic equality and the abolition of all discri-
minatory social and economic measures directed at Jews. Finally, by word and
deed, Mendelssohn was an early and forceful exponent of Jewish cultural revival, and his writings became a touchstone for generations of Maskilim. Wessely, a native of Hamburg who later lived in Amsterdam, Copenhagen and
Berlin, participated far less in the European world of ideas, but he was a passionate and untiring scholar who devoted his adult life to the advancement of
Hebrew literature, including the study of the Hebrew Bible.

In *Kohelet Mussar*, Mendelssohn's early attempt at publishing a Hebrew
journal patterned on the English moralistic weeklies, he called for a revival of
Hebrew language study, clearly linking the issues of language and Bible
study.[17] In 1765–66, Wessely, who had studied briefly with Hanau, published
a thick two-volume work titled *Gan Na'ul*, which was intended to be the first
of a series of studies on Hebrew language, and which gave expression to his
life-long desire to demonstrate its poetic richness and subtlety. *Gan Na'ul* focused on the issue of the apparent synonymity of Hebrew verbs and nouns,
and it was Wessely's first attempt at pointing the way towards the full modern
appreciation of its literary possibilities. This work also returned time and again
to another idea, namely that a careful analysis of Hebrew roots would simultaneously shed light upon the astute and exacting textual insights of rabbinic
and midrashic exegesis. The Sages of Antiquity, he argued, "knew the principles of the language, and understood the purity of its refined expressions; they
built their statements and midrashim on the trusted principles which were
made known to them".[18] This statement clearly represented a strategic grafting
of traditionalist preoccupations with rabbinic literature onto a new-found desire to effect a real linguistic and literary revival. Wessely was apparently cog-
nizant of European scholars and others who were questioning the authenticity
and integrity of rabbinic traditions, including their interpretations of Scripture. In his mind, an effective defense of these traditions had everything to do
with a proper understanding of the ancient traditions of biblical exegesis.

> When these matters become clear to us, then we understand with our discerning eye the hidden
> words of our Sages – the masters of the legal traditions who received the explanations of the
> commandments and teachings; how their words agree with the prefect *peshat* such that each
> and every phrase written in the Torah will be reliable testimony to their tradition that they re-
> ceived from mouth to mouth.[19]

It appears, then, that hand in hand with the early efforts on the part of Wessely to effect a cultural renaissance came a defensive desire to protect ancient
Jewish traditions against perceived European challenges.

---

[17] *Kohelet Mussar* was published in the mid to late 1750s; see Mendelssohn, Gesammelte
Schriften 14 (1972) 3–5.
[18] Wessely, *Gan Na'ul*, I, 20a; see also 8b, 10a.
[19] Ibid. 3b.

A few years later, Mendelssohn published *Sefer Megillat Kohelet*, an introduction and commentary to Ecclesiastes which was intended to combine his biblical and philosophical interests. His introduction began by invoking the medieval Hebrew acronym for the fourfold interpretation of Scripture, PaRDeS, although it became immediately clear that for him, questions concerning Jewish scriptural exegesis revolved around *peshat* and *derash*, the plain sense and the rabbinic interpretations of the Hebrew Bible. Taking the value of the *peshat* approach for granted, Mendelssohn's introduction concerned itself with the hermeneutical problem of how one could justify the rabbinic predilection for multiple interpretations alongside the literal or contextual meaning represented by *peshat*. Mendelssohn, in effect, was asking how, from a linguistic and logical point of view, one could sustain the Jewish penchant for reading Scripture as a polysemous text.[20]

Addressing this problem, Mendelssohn offered a careful formulation of the interpretative underpinnings of both *peshat* and *derash*, a formulation that drew upon elements of medieval Spanish literary sensibilities and the rabbinic predilections of early modern Europe. Mendelssohn understood *peshat* to be the readily apparent and intended level of meaning intrinsic to all discourse, prophetic no less than prosaic. "The meaning that follows the continuity and flow of the words, stated without any additions or deletions, is called the primary meaning, and the explication of this meaning is called *peshat*... The manner of *peshat* or the primary meaning is to pay attention to the sense and not the words."[21] At this level of meaning, word choices were made solely for aesthetic or rhetorical purposes, "without giving particular meaning or deliberate substance to every variation in speech".[22] This was the level according to which Mendelssohn interpreted Ecclesiastes, for he found his predecessors explaining this difficult biblical book verse by verse, without regard to the contextual flow of the verses.[23]

The fact that Mendelssohn's notion of *peshat* disregarded certain kinds of textual subtlety and variation was calibrated to leave room for another, parallel level of meaning, namely *derash*. The basis for *derash* was the self-conscious desire on the part of a prophet – or any speaker or writer for that matter – to choose his words with precision and care.

> He weighs the meaning of each and every word judiciously and without any dilatation (*harhavah*) [of speech]. Then he uses a word or phrase of particular connotation – not another similar to it in grammar and meaning, nor [one chosen] by accident and chance or [because of] some stylistic flourish – in order to hint and teach a particular idea that he does not want, or cannot be, explicitly explained... This desired detail is like a second meaning... [and] the explication of this second meaning is called *derush*.[24]

As with *peshat*, meaning and intentionality were one. When reader or listener took note of the intended message and understood specific linguistic choices

---

[20] *Sefer Megillat Kohelet*, in: Mendelssohn, Gesammelte Schriften 14 (1972) 148 ff.
[21] Ibid. 148.
[22] Ibid. 149.
[23] Ibid. 153.
[24] Ibid. 149. Mendelssohn here consistently utilized the term *derush* rather than *derash*.

to be necessary but ultimately arbitrary, this was *peshat*; but when the reader or listener paid attention to the particular choice of words, metaphors and other literary features, the arbitrary is rendered purposeful, and one interprets in a fashion referred to as *derash*. For Mendelssohn, this distinction was as simple as it was universal, since the notion of multilayered meaning was not a function of prophetic speech, but necessarily enmeshed in all language.

Despite Mendelssohn's embrace of European culture and his substantial contributions to its philosophical and literary discourse, these exegetical writings embraced traditional Jewish sensibilities even while they sought to find new grounds upon which to articulate its hermeneutics. This same conservatism was operative, albeit privately, with regard to his evaluation of the growing European predilection for critical scholarship. Commenting upon what he saw as the hasty use of textual emendations, Mendelssohn was unimpressed and dismissive. "I do not know where this audacity will end. Here too, however, one has to allow fashion to run its course for as long as it has the lure of novelty. People eventually lose their taste for it, and then the time comes to lead them back to the path of sound reason."[25] Soon after, he again commented privately that critical scholars "treat Scripture in a far too arbitrary manner; they permit themselves liberties with it which modest critics do not even permit themselves with respect to common writers".[26]

During these decades, Wessely gave expression to yet another aspect of the maskilic revival of Bible study when he published his *Sefer Hokhmat Shelomo*, a Hebrew reconstruction of the apocryphal Wisdom of Solomon.[27] Believing this text to be a Solomonic piece that had been lost to medieval and modern Jews, he translated this work from European vernaculars into biblical Hebrew, thereby restoring it – or so he believed – back to its original form. Although European Bible scholars disputed the Solomonic origin of the text, some did accept the notion that the ancient Greek versions were translated from some Hebrew original. As such, Wessely's work paralled that of no less a scholar than Robert Lowth, who also attempted to reconstruct the Hebrew original.

Mendelssohn and Wessely were two individuals working independently, but by the early 1780s their vision of cultural renewal began to attract others, and their writings ultimately served as the central texts of the early Haskalah. In 1782, Wessely wrote *Divrē Shalom ve-'Emet* in response to Joseph II's *Toleranzpatent*, the Hapsburg edict that sought to ease restrictions against Jews and effect some degree of integration into their communities. The *Toleranzpatent* called for Jewish schools to include a modicum of general education in their curriculum, and Wessely seized upon this development to call for broad reforms in Jewish education. Among other problems, Wessely complained about the fact that Jews were proficient in neither Hebrew nor German, and that the imprecision and coarseness of language that pervaded Jewish society was an impediment to the proper study of the Hebrew Bible. Teachers had no appre-

---

[25] Mendelssohn, Gesammelte Schriften 12,2 (1976) 33.
[26] Ibid. 42.
[27] Sefer Hokhmat Shelomo (Berlin 1780). Wessely also penned an extensive commentary to this work titled *Ruaḥ Ḥen*.

ciation for Hebrew grammar, nor had they mastered the refined qualities of the language. A part of his call for thorough educational reform, Wessely moved Bible study to the center of Jewish elementary education, and insisted that Scripture had to be taught in a bilingual framework, such that the teacher could effectively translate all words and idioms into a native language. Wessely's *Divrē Shalom ve-Emet* served as a manifesto for the Haskalah, and his ideas regarding the centrality of Bible study within a rejuvenated Jewish educational system became the touchstone for an entire generation of Maskilim.

The biblical interests of the Haskalah were also evident in the Hebrew journal *Ha-Me'assef*, dedicated to the dissemination and promotion of the Jewish Enlightenment throughout Europe.[28] Founded by a group of young Jewish writers and teachers in Königsberg, the journal sought to encourage a wide range of contemporary Hebrew writing, from current events to biographies of great medieval Jews to belles letters. The study of Bible and Hebrew language, however, remained a central concern, and towards this end the editors included numerous essays on biblical synonyms, the relationship of biblical and Mishnaic Hebrew, and other related subjects. Perhaps most importantly, *Ha-Me'assef* somewhat inadvertently drew attention to the divergent approaches of Maskilim and critical scholars to problems regarding the reliability of the MT. In order to stimulate biblical scholarship among Jews, the editors of *Ha-Me'assef* had invited submissions on specific biblical passages that were deemed challenging or problematic. In the very first volume, one such query regarding two verses in Proverbs elicited over forty submissions, all of which set out to solve the exegetical problem at hand by assuming the textual integrity of the Hebrew Bible. At least one of the Jewish respondents was self-consciously aware of the differences in Jewish and European scholarly perspectives, and let his displeasure be known: "Upon seeing [what Christian scholars wrote] I was astonished, for they distorted the words and changed the reading and the vocalization... If their ways are correct in their own eyes, they are not correct for us Jews...".[29] This maskilic journal, moreover, also attracted a note from the German Bible scholar and Semiticist Bernhard Köhler, who cited evidence of textual corruption and proposed an emendation of the verses in Proverbs.[30] Writing on behalf of the editors, Isaac Euchel (1756–1804) responded by articulating what would be the late-eighteenth-century Jewish view of the burgeoning fields of biblical criticism. He argued that European scholars took far too many liberties with the biblical text, and that they did so in an undisciplined fashion that rarely offered satisfactory solutions to the difficulties at hand.[31]

---

[28] The biblical interests of this journal were laid out in its prospectus, titled *Nahal ha-Besor*, which appeared in 1783 and was generally bound with volume 1 of *Ha-Me'assef*; see p. 2.

[29] *Ha-Me'assef* I (1784) 71 f.

[30] His comments were published in a German language supplement to HA-ME'ASSEF titled *Erste Zugabe zu der Hebräischen Monatschrift dem Semler* (1784) 10 f.

[31] Ibid. 12–14.

4. Moses Mendelssohn and His New Edition of the Pentateuch

In 1778, Mendelssohn and Solomon Dubno (1738–1813) circulated a prospectus titled *'Alim Litrufah* announcing their intention to publish a new edition of the Pentateuch. This project included a German translation rendered in fine *hochdeutsch* by Mendelssohn, accompanied by a Hebrew commentary designed to elucidate the translation and to anthologize and synthesize the fruits of medieval Jewish *peshat* exegesis. This commentary, popularly known as the *Bi'ur*, was to be written mainly by Dubno, and was to be accompanied by a separate set of notes concerning the MT called *Tikkun Sopherim* which aimed at correcting errors of orthography, vocalization and accentuation that had crept into many printed version of the Hebrew Bible. By the time this project was published as *Sefer Netivot ha-Shalom* between 1780 and 1783 it had undergone a number of changes. At some point Mendelssohn realized that the *Bi'ur* was too ambitious for Dubno to complete alone, and he decided to write the commentary to Exodus himself while enlisting Wessely to contribute the commentary to Leviticus. Shortly thereafter Dubno left Berlin and the project, and Mendelssohn turned to two younger Maskilim to contribute the commentary to Numbers and Deuteronomy.[32]

In many ways, *Sefer Netivot ha-Shalom* incorporated the enlightened and traditionalist elements within the German Haskalah. In the most general terms, the publication of this work underscored the Haskalah's rejection of the traditionally narrow Jewish preoccupation with rabbinic literature. The German translation, which was presented in Hebrew script, replaced not only the traditional Aramaic version of Onkelos, but also the early modern Yiddish translations that the Maskilim viewed as crude and primitive. The Hebrew commentary, for its part, exhibited a strong commitment to the textual and contextual qualities of the text, and Mendelssohn and the other contributors offered eighteenth-century readers a reading of the Hebrew Bible that was thoroughly committed to *peshuto shel mikra'*. Their aim was to reawaken the Jewish study of grammar and Scripture in order to illustrate the true sophistication of Jewish exegetical traditions.

One of the novel literary features of Mendelssohn's commentary, for example, was his attention to biblical poetry. Drawing upon Robert Lowth's ideas regarding biblical parallelism, Mendelssohn pointed out that biblical poetry was neither metrical nor given to rhyme, and that by eschewing these poetic modes biblical poetry could focus upon "excellence of meaning and thought", rather than "sensual pleasure and the delight enjoyed by the ear".[33] For Mendelssohn, there was an important confluence of form and purpose. The use of parallelism, with different phrases of poetic verses either reinforcing each other or standing in juxtaposition or even opposition, was in his view the best means of conveying ideas in a clear and straightforward manner. This ren-

---

[32] This edition of the Hebrew Bible was reprinted dozens of times between 1783 and the 1860's. It is also now reprinted in Mendelssohn, Gesammelte Schriften, vols. 15,2–18.

[33] *Biur*, introduction to Exodus 15; see Mendelssohn, Gesammelte Schriften 16 (1990) 127, 134.

dered biblical poetry superior to that of other nations, and in the context of his maskilic vision, Mendelssohn wanted Jews to fully appreciate their biblical heritage rather than being swept up with the contemporary – and in his view inferior – fashions of European poetry.

This same matrix of attitudes towards Jewish traditions and contemporary culture shaped *Sefer Netivot ha-Shalom* in two fundamental ways, namely, in Mendelssohn's defense of the MT and in his justification of rabbinic exegesis. Mendelssohn's private reservations regarding text-critical scholarship were explicitly raised in his lengthy introduction to this Bible. In offering a justification of this new translation of the Pentateuch, Mendelssohn emphasized the need for a contemporary version that would serve the social and linguistic needs of late eighteenth-century German Jewry. He appreciatively noted that Christian scholars had gone out of their way to retranslate Scripture "in accordance with the needs of the time, the suitability of the language, and a refined style".[34] This was true in his generation as well, but given the shifting cultural realities, there was one significant effect: in the absence of a good German translation of the Hebrew Bible produced by Jewish scholars, Jews too were drawn to Christians editions.

> However, that path which many of our nation have followed, is full of snares and stumbling blocks… For Christian translators – who do not have the traditions of our Sages, and who do not heed the words of the Masorah, not even accepting the vowel points and accents that we have – liken the words of the Torah to a broken wall. Everyone goes out against [the Masorah] and does with it as he pleases; they add and delete and change the divine Torah. [This affects] not only the vocalization and the accents, but sometimes even letters and words (for who will stop their vanity?) in according to what they think and feel. As a result, they occasionally do not read what is written in the Torah, but that which occurs to them.[35]

Mendelssohn, to be sure, conceded that Christian scholars had no reason to remain beholden to the MT, given that the Hebrew Bible served them with a different set of religious needs. From a Jewish perspective, however, the emendations offered by European scholars were to be viewed as capricious and arbitrary, and any translation based on them had to be rejected. Rabbinic traditions of interpretation, after all, were formally anchored in the precise lettering and vocalization of the Hebrew Bible, and the slightest change to the text would ostensibly appear to undermine this ancient structure.

> For us, the Torah is an inheritance… Our Sages decreed for us the Masorah and erected a fence for the Torah and for the commandments… We should not move from their straight path… [to follow] the conjectures and deliberations of a grammarian or editor drawn from his own mind. We do not live from the mouth [of such an emendator], but from that which our trustworthy masters of the Masorah transmitted to us.[36]

In Mendelssohn's mind, at least, the legal traditions of Judaism made it imperative for him to maintain the authority and integrity of the MT.

Much of the introduction, in fact, was given over to an extended discussion of Jewish sources regarding the original language and script of the Hebrew Bi-

---

[34] Mendelssohn, Gesammelte Schriften 15,1 (1990) 39.
[35] Ibid.
[36] Ibid. 39 f.

ble, as well as the issues relating to the authenticity and antiquity of the vowel points and accentuation. On all these questions, Mendelssohn adhered to traditional rabbinic views and rejected modern critical assertions. Mendelssohn did, on occasion, make use of contemporary European scholarship, as for example with regard to the question of the relative authority of the Samaritan and Masoretic versions, but this was done in support of his conservative position.[37] All in all, this introduction underscored the fact that on issues relating to the Hebrew Bible, his faithful adherence to traditional Jewish positions set him apart from his enlightened German contemporaries. Conversely, the only late eighteenth-century scholars he could cite in support of his traditional views were orthodox or evangelical Protestants who hardly shared his enlightened commitments and ideals.

Mendelssohn's translation, then, hewed faithfully to the MT and offered his Jewish readers a version that would support the rabbinic edifice that was built upon its every nuance and detail. In *Sefer Megillat Kohelet*, he had laid out an hermeneutical understanding whereby the text could simultaneously include both the *peshat* and various rabbinic midrashim. A German translation, however, would seemingly resist or be impervious to the precise content of such multivalence, and Mendelssohn addressed this problem by restating the hermeneutical principles articulated earlier.

> Anywhere that the *peshat* is distinct but complementary to the *derash*, [and] not opposed to it – the Scriptural verse does not lose its plain meaning, and the *derashah* is maintained. For then, the plain sense of Scripture is the primary and essential meaning, and the *derashah* is the second intended meaning… If the translator rendering a passage into another language cannot incorporate the two meanings together, and cannot conceal the second meaning in the shadow of the primary meaning as is the case in the language before him, then he must choose the primary and plain sense … and leave the *derashah* to one who understands the book being translated. However, if the approach which appears to us to be the plain sense of Scripture contradicts and opposes the received *derash* transmitted to us from the Sages… then we are obligated to follow the approach of the *derash* and to translate Scripture accordingly.[38]

Mendelssohn's translation, then, remained fully sensitive not only to the integrity of the MT, but to the need to translate in complete accordance with the needs of inherited rabbinic traditions.

Along these lines, the commentary to the Hebrew Bible also combined its interests in reawakening the serious Jewish study of Scripture with a deep appreciation for rabbinic traditions of interpretation. On one level the mandate of the commentary was to explicate the interpretive choices made by the German translation, but the *Bi'ur* also went to great lengths to discuss different exegetical approaches culled from the leading medieval commentators to the Hebrew Bible: Rashi, Rashbam, Ibn Ezra, Qimhi, and Ramban.[39] Beyond this, however, the *Bi'ur*, particularly the commentaries to Genesis, Exodus, and Leviticus, drew upon the hermeneutical foundations laid out in Mendelssohn's *Sefer Megillat Kohelet*, and utilized this new work as an extended study of the relationship of *peshat* and rabbinic midrash. This eighteenth-century

---

[37] Ibid. 28.
[38] Ibid. 40 f.
[39] Ibid. 40.

commentary, in fact, contained a great deal of material drawn from rabbinic literature and lengthy analyses of their medieval handling, with the aim of demonstrating the textual perspicacity and precision of the Sages' reading of the Hebrew Bible. A few examples drawn from Genesis 12 and Exodus 21 will illustrate these manifold interests of the commentary.

In Gen 12:1, "And the Lord said to Abram: Go forth (*lekh lekha*) from your native land...", the phrase *lekh lekha*, combining a prepositional pronoun and verbal imperative, had been the subject of much medieval discussion. On the one hand, Spanish exegetes took the phrase to be idiomatic and eschewed any attempt to read extra meaning into the addition of the prepositional pronoun. Rashi, on the other hand, apparently drew upon a passage from the Talmud and read the word *lekha* as a superfluous addition that indicated that God was telling Abram to go forth for his "own benefit and good", for only by uprooting himself would he merit having children and become the father of a great nation. Mendelssohn's translation, for its part, tried to capture – albeit imperfectly – something of the Hebrew phrase by rendering the passage as *zieh hinweg aus deinem Lande*. Dubno's commentary, however, addressed the question of what to do with the phrase *lekh lekha*, rejecting the Spanish criticism of Rashi and defending the rabbinic textual sensibility that spawned Rashi's comment.

> If you look very carefully [at the words], you will often find that in its implied [meaning] there is a sense of need and fulfillment with regard to the one being addressed in the expression – that his wants and desires will be granted... Even the verse "the rain is over and gone (*halakh lô*)" [Cant 2:11] has something of this meaning, for it is a poetic expression, as if the rain... could be at one with its nature, which is its want and desire and its fulfillment. And for this [reason], Rashi also explained our verse "*lekh lekha*, for your benefit and good etc.".[40]

The *Bi'ur* thus demonstrated how the rabbinic sense of the superfluous *lekha* was based upon a precise consideration of language, one that Rashi alone had grasped.

A few verses later, the *Bi'ur* again set out to explain a midrashic interpretation of Scripture on the basis of good Hebrew philology. Like their rabbinic and medieval predecessors, these maskilic exegetes had to explain just what was meant by the verb *'asū* in Gen 12:5: "And Abram took Sarai his wife, and Lot his brother's son, and all the wealth they had amassed, and the persons they had gotten (*'asher 'asū*) in Haran...". The question was how to make sense of this apparently unidiomatic phrase in which persons or souls were 'made'. In a midrashic reading of this passage, one Sage suggested that the phrase be read as a reference to conversion, since "anyone who draws an idolater near and converts him, it is as if he created him".[41] Rashi's comment alluded to this rabbinic reading, but this medieval exegete also demonstrated lexically that the verb *'asah* could also mean 'to acquire', and that a *peshat* reading of the verse would therefore refer to Abraham's acquisition of servants. Drawing upon the work of Qimhi, Dubno set forth a parallel textual basis for the rabbinic interpretation.

---

[40] Ibid. 15,2 (1990) 105.
[41] *Gen. Rab.* § 39:14.

Our Sages explained this verse regarding the persons that they converted and returned to belief in God... According to this, the meaning of *'asū* was like the verse "It is the Lord that made (*'asah*) Moses and Aaron" [1 Sam 12:6] – he made them great and taught them. The German translation rendered the verse in a language that implies both [*peshat* and midrashic] meanings.[42]

Once again, Dubno and Mendelssohn were able to maintain the textual veracity of both *peshat* and *derash*.

Mendelssohn offered much the same kind of exegesis in his own commentary to Exodus. Here, however, the legal nature of the material demanded a more clearly delineated application of the hermeneutical principles laid down in the introduction.

Exegetically, the plain sense of Scripture may stand in a complementary relationship with the traditions of our Sages, but cannot contradict them with regard to strictures and laws. This is because it is possible that things that are complementary can both be true, while with regard to things that contradict, if one of them is true, the second is necessarily false. Thus, in every instance that the apparent meaning of the plain sense of Scripture seems to contradict a tradition of our Sages concerning strictures or laws, the exegete is obligated to completely abandon the approach of *peshat* and to follow the path of true tradition, or to effect some compromise, if he is able to do so successfully.[43]

In a number of instances, Mendelssohn indeed tried to offer such textual support for *midrash Halakhah*. In Exod 21:6, for example, the Bible refers to the rite by which a Hebrew slave could relinquish his freedom even after the requisite six years of servitude have passed: "Then his master shall bring him unto the judges, and shall bring him to the door or unto the doorpost; and his master shall bore his ear through with an awl". The problem appearing fairly early in rabbinic literature was that a repetition of this law in Deut 15:17 stated simply that the master should "take an awl, and thrust it through his ear and into the door". The *Mekhilta* suggested that the verse in Deuteronomy had the effect of limiting the act to the use of a door (but not a doorpost), while the verse in Exodus included the doorpost only to indicate the proper physical position of the door (i. e., it had to be standing up). None of the medieval exegetes attempted to harmonize the plain sense of the verse with its rabbinic reading, tacitly acknowledging that the interpretative gap between them could not be closed. For Mendelssohn, however, the solution was plain:

The Sages have taught that it is not proper to bore the ear upon a doorpost, as it is written "[and you shall] thrust it through his ear and into the door" [Deut 15:17] – in a door and not a doorpost. The reason [the verse in Exodus] had "or unto the doorpost" [was to teach] that they should bring him to the place where the door was attached to the doorpost; the door should not be lying on the ground, but rather upright next to the doorpost... the verse is speaking only of bringing him near... to the place of the door or the doorpost.[44]

The rabbinic interpretation thus never abandoned the *peshat* meaning of Scripture. The verse in Exodus referred only to where the Hebrew slave was to be brought, and to the fact that the door was to be positioned according to its

---

[42] Mendelssohn, Gesammelte Schriften 15,2 (1990) 107. The German translation read: *wie auch die Seelen, die sie zu Haran erworben.*

[43] *Bi'ur*, introduction to Exodus 21; ibid. 16, 198 f.

[44] Ibid. 201.

function; the verse in Deuteronomy alone addressed the particular detail of the object against which his ear was to be pierced.

Wessely's commentary to Leviticus applied a related though distinct hermeneutic to the same set of textual concerns. Wessely had long been interested in Leviticus and its rabbinic commentaries, and he brought with him a well-developed approach to its interpretation. In his introduction to this section of *Sefer Netivot ha-Shalom*, Wessely drew upon his earlier writing in *Gan Na'ul* and insisted that he would embrace both the textual plain sense and the vast amount of rabbinic material apparently derived from its verses.

> If the way to effect a bridge between the peshat and the midrash – which appear to be far from one another – is narrow, I said there is hope only if God favors me to understand clearly the meaning of the roots (*hora'at ha-shorashim*); if we reflect upon them, it will become clear that the words of the midrash are nothing but the depths of the peshat, and distant matters will be made close.[45]

Like Mendelssohn and Dubno, Wessely was fully committed to demonstrating the textual basis of the rabbinic interpretations of Scripture, largely on the basis of his philological analysis. Indeed, more than any other section of the *Bi'ur*, the commentary to Leviticus contained a great quantity of rabbinic literature, and Wessely clearly expended considerable energy and originality towards this end. Unlike the other maskilic exegetes, Wessely appeared to collapse the distinction of *peshat* and rabbinic midrash. While Mendelssohn endeavored to formulate the relationship of *peshat* and *derash* as two complementary, equally veracious, but different levels of interpretation, Wessely's notion of the "depths of peshat", was meant to suggest that at its core, the rabbinic reading actually *was* the *peshat*.

In practice, Wessely's efforts to demonstrate the textual basis for midrash paralleled those found in Genesis and Exodus. In describing the role of the High Priest in the ritual of the Day of Atonement and the ceremonial casting of the lots upon two he-goats, Lev 16:10 calls for the 'release' of one of the animals into the desert: "The goat upon which the lot fell for Azazel shall be set alive before the Lord to make atonement over him, to send him away (*leshalah 'oto*) for Azazel into the wilderness". Although the Biblical verse did not indicate whether the he-goat was to be merely released or sent to its death, the rabbinic reading of this verse affirmed the latter. Wessely was able to explicate the rabbinic reading with reference to v. 22 later in the same chapter: "And the goat shall bear upon it all their iniquities unto a land which is cut off, and he shall send (*ve-shilah*) the goat in the wilderness". Since the goat, in the context of the earlier verses, was already in the wilderness, it could not be read as indicating that the goat should be sent *to* the wilderness. Wessely drew upon his study of synonyms and pointed out that the word *shilah* in both verses had to be read as a directive to 'let the goat go' in the sense of dispatching him from life: "For this is one of the meanings of this root, a complete letting go from life unto death".[46] Wessely buttressed his argument by citing further lexical

---

[45] Ibid. 17 (1990) 4.
[46] Ibid. 235.

evidence, namely, that a sword is also called a *shelah*, precisely because of its function.

5. Other Contributors to the Haskalah

The maskilic effort to bring about a revival of Hebrew Bible study found success in a number of different areas. Throughout the 1780s and 1790s, the journal *Ha-Me'assef* continued to carry essays on Biblical Hebrew as well as exegetical pieces on passages deemed difficult or challenging. At the end of the eighteenth and beginning of the nineteenth centuries, there appeared a number of supercommentaries to the *Bi'ur*, including one by Herz Homberg (1749–1841), who had also contributed part of the *Bi'ur* to Deuteronomy.[47] There also continued to be a maskilic interest in Apocryphal literature, and at the end of the eighteenth century, Judah Leib ben Ze'ev (1764–1811) published reconstructed Hebrew versions of The Wisdom of Ben Sira and Judith.[48] Finally, the cultural predilections of the Haskalah and its particular interests in Hebrew and Bible study were also taken up by a number of important scholars not directly identified with this movement. Solomon Pappenheim (1740–1814), a rabbinic court judge in Breslau, wrote a multi-volume study of Hebrew synonyms somewhat paralleling the work of Wessely, while Wolf Heidenheim (1757–1832), an important publisher and editor of traditional liturgical texts, penned a series of commentaries on the Masorah and a supercommentary to Rashi.[49]

After Mendelssohn's death in 1786 there was considerable interest in 'completing' the project by extending the German translation and Hebrew commentary to cover the other nineteen books of the traditional Hebrew Bible. In the early 1790s, Meir Obernik (1764–1805) and Samuel Detmold (1765–1830) oversaw the publication of such a work under the title *Minhah Hadashah*.[50] While Obernik and Detmold produced the translations and commentaries to many of the prophetic books themselves, this work also incorporated the earlier work of Maskilim such as Mendelssohn (Psalms, Ecclesiastes), Isaac Euchel (Proverbs) and others. The *Bi'ur* to these Biblical books was far less ambitious than the commentaries to the Pentateuch discussed above, and they tended to offer the reader a relatively spare *peshat*-oriented reading of the text. This completed Tanakh went through many editions and proved to be quite popular across Central Europe.

---

[47] His supercommentary was published as Ha-Korem, and appeared in a number of editions of *Sefer Netivot ha-Shalom*.

[48] *Hokhmat Yehoshua ben Sira* (Breslau 1798); and *Megillat Yehudit* (Vienna 1799). These texts were reconstructed by Ben Ze'ev from the Aramaic (Syriac) text included in Brian Walton's *Biblia Polyglotta* (London 1657).

[49] S. Pappenheim, *Yeri'ot Shelomoh* (Dyhernfurt 1784); W. Heidenheim, *Mishpete ha-Ta'amim* (Rödelheim 1808), and idem, *Humash 'Ein ha-Sofer* (Rödelheim 1818)

[50] Vienna 1792–93.

Perhaps the most important post-Mendelssohnian development in the study of the Hebrew Bible was Judah Leib ben Ze'ev's *Mavo' el Mikra'ē Kodesh.*[51] This text, which was comprised of introductory essays to the books of the Prophets and Hagiographa, sought to elicit the distinct historical and literary features of each individual Biblical book. Ben Ze'ev, a prolific contributor to the German Haskalah, drew heavily on the contemporary German writings of Johann Gottfried Eichhorn (1752–1827), effectively introducing Jewish readers to the early fruits of modern critical scholarship. This Maskil, however, was sensitive to the fact that modern historical judgements regarding chronology and authorship would conflict with traditional views, and he sought to allow for new critical perspectives:

> It is the obligation of one who inquires after something and attempts to discern the truth from among divergent opinions to render his heart free and his thoughts clear; nothing should sway him nor should he unduly favor anything, fear should not alarm him, and the pressure of men should not weigh upon him to force him to decide a matter against reason and in opposition to proper judgment... in [all] deliberations, truth must be the aim of his intentions.[52]

Beyond this, he utilized arguments marshaled in Azariah de Rossi's *Me'or 'Enayim* to revive earlier distinctions between rabbinic Halakhah and rabbinic Aggadah, the latter being of significantly lesser authority and entirely subject to critical and independent analyses.[53]

In the body of the work, Ben-Ze'ev tried to strike a balanced approach. On the on hand, he openly embraced the contemporary skepticism regarding the integrity of the book of Isaiah, and supporting the notion of Deutero-Isaiah.[54] Ben Ze'ev was no doubt encouraged by a similar inclination on the part of medievals such as Ibn Ezra, but there is little doubt regarding the contemporary nature of his presentation. On the other hand, he attempted to give rabbinic traditions their due, even if, at times, this was done in rather unconvincing terms. With regard to the story of David and Goliath, for example, Ben-Ze'ev clearly shared the contemporary critical view that the story appears to have been unnaturally inserted into 1 Samuel 17 at some point after the book's composition. And yet, he ended the discussion by weakly asserting that Jews had to accept the received text and address the myriad of narrative problems emanating from this pericope within the bounds of tradition.[55] Clearly wary of traditionalist reactions to his work, Ben-Ze'ev wanted to signal his readers that there was ample room to question the presumptive authority of Jewish traditions with regard to the study of the Hebrew Bible.

While the Haskalah clearly succeeded in opening up Jewish culture to European ideas and movements, the nineteenth-century inheritors of this cultural movement remained cautious with regard to the developments of European biblical scholarship, and internalized it only in modest and measured degrees.

---

[51] *Mavo' el Mikra'ē Kodesh* (Vienna 1810).

[52] *Hakdamah kelalit*, 3 [unpaginated in text].

[53] Ibid. 4–5. For further discussion, including Ben Ze'ev's evident plagiarisms, see E. BREUER, "(Re)Creating Traditions of Language and Texts: The Haskalah and Cultural Continuity", *Modern Judaism* 16 (1996) 174–78.

[54] *Mavo'*, 29b–30b.

[55] Ibid. 11a–13a.

Following Ben Ze'ev, critical notions regarding the text, its editing and its historical context were raised only with regard to the non-Pentateuchal books of the Hebrew Bible, and largely where medieval scholars had either opened the door to such notions or where there existed sufficient ambiguity to allow for new ideas. As the Haskalah spread from Prussia into Galicia and Italy, for example, various scholars sought to reinvigorate Hebrew Bible study through their writings, including contributions to maskilic journals such as *Bikkurei ha-Ittim* and *Kerem Hemed.* In his *Moreh Nebukhe ha-Zeman*, published posthumously in 1851, Nachman Krochmal (1785–1840) accepted the late dating of sections of Isaiah, Ecclesiastes, and Psalms, and argued that such critical awareness was already evident in rabbinic literature.[56] His contemporary Solomon Rappoport (1790–1867) similarly included critical ideas regarding the books of Isaiah and Psalms in his writings, as did the Italian scholar Isaac Samuel Reggio (1784–1855).[57]

The immediate legacy of the Haskalah, finally, was conservative in another respect as well. The explication of midrashic exegesis offered in the writings of Mendelssohn, Wessely, and Dubno, served the traditionalist exegetes of the early nineteenth century in their defense of rabbinic traditions. Facing the determined effort of reform-minded Jews to change the religious norms of Jewish life, rabbinic leaders who sought to maintain their inherited traditions did so by extending the maskilic notion that a proper textual understanding of the Hebrew Bible gave ample support to its ancient rabbinic interpretations. Some of the most important and original exegetical contributions of the nineteenth century, including those of J. Mecklenburg's *Ha-Ketab ve-ha-Kabbalah* and the combined biblical and rabbinic commentaries of Meir Leibush b. Yehiel Michael (Malbim), were thus shaped in part by the exegetical beginnings of the Haskalah.

---

[56] *Moreh Nebukhe ha-Zeman* (ed. S. Rawidowicz; Waltham: Ararat Press 1961) 114, 140–57.

[57] These later maskilic figures and their biblical scholarship is discussed in Harris, How Do We Know This? (1995) 156 ff.

Chapter Forty-four

Towards the End of the 'Century of Enlightenment': Established Shift from *Sacra Scriptura* to Literary Documents and Religion of the People of Israel

By Henning Graf Reventlow, Bochum

1. The French Revolution of 1789 – a Symptom of a New Political and Cultural Situation

Sources: J. Mallet du Pan, *Mémoires et correspondance pour servir à l'histoire de la Révolution française* (ed. A. Sayous; Paris 1851); J. M. Roberts / J. Hardman / R. C. Cobb (eds.), *French Revolution Documents* 1–2 (Oxford 1966–1973); Institute of French Studies, Univ. of Southwestern Lousiana (ed.), *Annals of the French Revolution* 1– (Lafayette, LA 1978-).

General works: 1 a. On the History of the French Revolution: D. Andress, *The Terror: Civil War in the French Revolution* (London 2005); A. Aulard, *Histoire politique de la Révolution française* (Paris 1901; ⁶1926, repr. Aalen 1977); K. M. Baker (ed.), *The French Revolution and the Creation of Modern Political Culture*, Vol. 1. *The Political Culture of the Old Regime* (Oxford 1987); Vol. 4. *The Terror* (Oxford 1994); T. W. C. Blanning, *The French Revolution: Class War or Culture Clash?* (Studies in European History; Houndsmills, Basingstoke / New York 1987, ²1998); idem (ed.), *The Rise and Fall of the French Revolution* (Chicago 1996); J. F. Bosher, *The French Revolution* (New York 1988; London 1989): T. Carlyle, *The French Revolution: a History* I–III ([1839] Centenary edn.; London 1974); U. Dierse, "Menschenrechte und Bürgerpflichten in der französischen Aufklärung und Revolution", in: K. Wegmann / W. Ommerborn / H. Roetz (eds.), *Menschenrechte: Rechte und Pflichten in Ost und West* (Münster 2001) 161–83; W. Doyle, *The Oxford History of the French Revolution* (Oxford 1989); B. Faÿ, *L'Esprit révolutionnaire en France et aux États Unies à la fin du XVIIIᵉ siècle* (Paris 1925); idem, *La Grande Révolution* (Paris 1959); F. Furet / D. Richet, *La Révolution française* 1–2 (Paris 1965, ²1973); F. Furet, *Penser la Revolution française* (Bibliothèque des histoires; Paris 1978; several repr.), ET: *Interpreting the French revolution* (Cambridge e.a. 1981; several repr.); idem, *La Révolution: De Turgot à Jules Ferry (1770–1880)* (Histoire de France Hachette; Paris 1988), ET: *Revolutionary France 1770–1880* (A History of France 4, Oxford 1992, paperback 1995); F. Furet / M. Osouf (eds.), *Dictionnaire critique de la Révolution Française* (Paris 1988), ET: *A Critical Dictionary of the French Revolution* (Cambridge 1989); F. Furet, *La révolution française en débat* (Paris 1999); P. R. Hanson (ed.), *Historical Dictionary of the French Revolution* (Lanham, MD e.a. 2004); J. Jaurès, *Histoire socialiste de la Révolution française* 1–4 (Paris 1901–04; repr. in 6 vols., Paris 1968–73); G. Jellinek, *Die Erklärung der Menschen- und Bürgerrechte. Ein Beitrag zur modernen Verfassungsgeschichte* (Leipzig 1895; ⁴1927; repr. Schutterwald/Baden 1996); also in: R. Schnur (ed.), *Zur Geschichte der Erklärung der Menschenrechte* (WdF XI; Darmstadt 1964) 1–77; S. L. Kaplan, *Farewell, Revolution. The Historian's Feud. France 1789/1989* (lthaca, NY 1995); A. Köhn, *Die französische Revolution* (Stuttgart 1999); W. Kruse, *Die Französische Revolution* (Paderborn e.a. 2005); G. Lefebvre, *Quatre-Vingt-Neuf* (Paris 1939; repr. 1970), ET: *The Coming of the French Revolution* ([1947] repr. New York 1957); idem, *La révolution française* (Paris ³1963), ET: *The French Revolution* 1–2 (London 1964/1965); C. Lucas (ed.), *The French Revolution and the Creation of Modern Political*

Culture 2. *The Political Culture of the French Revolution* (Oxford 1988); J. MICHELET, *Histoire de la Révolution française* 1–7 (Paris 1847–53, many repr.); éd. établie et commentée par G. Walter (Bibliothèque de la Pléiade, 2 vols.; Paris 1952), ET: *The French Revolution from 1789–1815* (New York 1939); F. A. MIGNET, *Histoire de la Révolution française depuis 1789 jusque'en 1814*, 1–2 (Paris 1824; many repr.); R. R. PALMER, *The Age of the Democratic Revolution. A Political History of Europe and America, 1760–1800*, 1. *The Challenge*, 2. *The Struggle* (Princeton, NJ 1959/1964); R. REICHARDT (ed.), *PLOETZ. Die französische Revolution* (Würzburg 1988); G. RUDÉ, *Revolutionary Europe* (Meridian Books; Cleveland 1964; The Fontana History of Europe, London 1965; [12]1974; Blackwell Classic Histories of Europe, Oxford [2]2000); G. SALVEMINI, *LA RIVOLUZIONE FRANCESE* (1788–1792) ([1905], Opere II/1; Milano [3]1968); E. SCHMITT, *Einführung in die Geschichte der französischen Revolution* (München 1976; E. SCHULIN, *Die französische Revolution* (Munich 1988); A. SOBOUL, *La Révolution française* (Paris 1988); U. THAMER, *Die Französische Revolution* (Beck'sche Reihe 2347; München [2]2006); M. VOVELLE, *Breve storia della Rivoluzione francese* (Roma 1979) = German tr. *Die französische Revolution: soziale Bewegung und Umbruch der Mentalitäten* (Frankfurt/ Main 1985).
1 b. On the Origins and the Importance of the French Revolution: K. M. BAKER, *Inventing the French Revolution. Essays on French Political Culture in the Eighteenth Century* (Ideas in Context; Cambridge 1990; repr. 1994); P. R CAMPBELL (ed.). *The Origins of the French Revolution* (Basingstoke e.a. 2005); J. CENSER, "Commenting the Third Century of Debate", *AHR* 4 (1989) 1309–1325; R. CHARTIER, *Les origines culturelles de la Révolution française* (Paris 1990); A. COBBAN, *Aspects of the French Revolution* (London 1968); idem, *The Social Interpretation of the French Revolution* (Cambridge 1964; repr. 1965); idem, "The Myth of the French Revolution" (1954), = idem, *Aspects* (1968) 90–111; R. DARNTON, *The Business of Enlightenment. A Publishing History of the Encyclopédie, 1775–1800* (Cambridge, MA 1979); idem, *Édition et sédition. L'univers de la littérature clandestine au XVIIIe siècle* (Paris 1991); idem, "The Forbidden Books of Pre-Revolutionary France", in: C. Lucas (ed.), *Rewriting* (1991, see below) 1–32; idem, *The Literary Underground of the Old Regime* (Cambridge, MA 1982); P. J. DAVIES, *The Debates on the French Revolution* (Manchester 2006); W. DOYLE, *Origins of the French Revolution* (Oxford 1980; [3]1999); J. C. JONES (ed.), *The French Revolution in Perspective* (Renaissance and Modern Studies 33; Nottingham 1989); P. M. JONES, *Reform and Revolution in France: the Politics of Transition* (Cambridge 1995); T. E. KAISER, "This Strange Offspring of Philosophy: Recent Historiographical Problems in Relating the Enlightenment to the French Revolution", *French Historical Studies* 15 (1987/88) 549–62; G. KATES (ed.), *The French Revolution: recent debates and new controversies* (New York, NY e.a. [2]2006); F. KLÖVEKORN, *Die Entstehung der Erklärung der Menschen- und Bürgerrechte* (HS XC; Berlin 1911; repr. Vaduz 1965); C. LUCAS (ed.), *Rewriting the French Revolution* (Oxford 1989; repr. 1991); D. MORNET, *Les Origines intellectuelles de la Révolution française 1715–1787* (Paris 1933; repr. 1967); E. QUINET, *La Révolution, précedée de la critique de la révolution* (Paris 1865; repr. Paris 1987), = idem, *Oeuvres complètes* (Paris 1895–1910; repr. Genève 1989/90) 18–20; R. REICHARDT / E. SCHMITT, "Die Französische Revolution. Umbruch oder Kontinuität?", *ZHF* 7 (1980) 257–320; S.-J. SAMWER, *Die französische Erklärung der Menschen- und Bürgerrechte von 1789/91* (Hamburg 1970); J. SANDWEG, *Rationales Naturrecht als revolutionäre Praxis* (Berlin 1972); J. SHOVLIN, *The Political Economy of Virtue: luxury, patriotism, and the origins of the French Revolution* (Ithaca, N.Y. 2006); A. SOBOUL, *Comprendre la révolution: problemes politiques* (Paris 1981), ET: *Understanding the French Revolution* (London 1988); B. STONE, *The Genesis of the French Revolution: A Global-Historical Interpretation* (Cambridge 1994); idem, *Reinterpreting the French Revolution: a Global-historical Perspective* (Cambridge, U.K. / New York 2002); G. V. TAYLOR, "Noncapitalist Wealth and the Origins of the French Revolution", *AHR* 72 (1966/67) 469–96; N. TEMPLE, *The Road to 1789. From Reform to Revolution in France* (Cardiff 1992); A. DE TOCQUEVILLE, *L'Ancien Régime et la Révolution* (Paris 1856), = idem, *Oeuvres complètes*. Ed. définitive, 2/1 (ed. J. P. Mayer; Paris [9]1951); M. VOVELLE, "La Révolution française: mutation ou crise des valeurs?", in: idem, *Idéologies et mentalités* (Paris 1982) 293–320; idem, *La mentalité revolutionnaire. Societé et mentalités sous la Révolution française* (Paris 1985, [2]1988).
1 c. Religious Aspects: J. MCMANNERS, *The French Revolution and the Church* (Church History Outlines 4; New York 1969); A. MELLOR, *Histoire de l'anticléricalisme français* (Paris 1966; [2]1978); D. C. MILLER, "A.-G. Camus and the Civil Constitution of the Clergy", *CHR* 76 (1990) 481–505; F. R. NECHELES, "The Constitutional Church, 1794–1802: An Essay in Voluntarism", *Proceedings of the Consortium on Revolutionary Europe 1974* (Gainsville, FL 1974) 80–90; M. OSOUF, *Festivals*

and the French Revolution (Cambridge, MA / London 1988); B. PLONGERON, *Conscience religieuse en Révolution. Regards sur l'historiographie religieuse de la Révolution française* (Paris 1969); B. C. POLAND, *French Protestantism and the French Revolution: A Study in Church and State. Thought and Religion. 1685–1815* (Princeton, NJ 1957); D. K. VANKLEY, *Les origines religieuses de la Révolution française: 1560 -1791* (Paris 2002), ET: (A. Spiess) *The Religious Origins of the French Revolution: from Calvin to the Civil Constitution* (New Haven, CT e.a. 2002).

1 d. The Impact of the Revolution: M. AGULHON, *Marianne au combat: l'imagerie et la symbolique républicaine de 1789 à 1880* (Paris 1979), ET: *Marianne into Battle: Republican Imagery and Symbolism in France. 1789–1880* (Cambridge 1981); idem, *Le XIXe siècle et la Révolution française* (Paris 1992); H. AHRENDT, *On Revolution* (New York 1963; ²1965; repr. 1985); C. ALBRECHT, art. "Revolution I. Neuzeit", TRE 29 (1998) 109–26; B. BAUER, *Deutschland und die französische Revolution* [2.] Fortsetzung: 1. Abt.: *Deutschland während der französischen Revolution*, and 3. Abt. *Geschichte der Politik, Kultur und Aufklärung des achtzehnten Jahrhunderts* (Charlottenburg [Berlin] 1844; repr. Aalen 1965); E. BEHLER, *Unendliche Perfektibilität. Europäische Romantik und Französische Revolution* (Paderborn 1989); I. BERLIN, "The Counter-Enlightenment", DHJ 2 (New York 1973) 110–12, = idem, *Against the Current* (ed. H. Harry; London 1979) 1–24; E. BÖDEKER, "Zur Rezeption der französischen Menschen- und Bürgerrechtserklärung von 1789/1791 in der deutschen Aufklärungsgesellschaft", in: G. BIRTSCH (ed.), *Grund- und Freiheitsrechte im Wandel von Gesellschaft und Geschichte* (Göttingen 1981) 258–86; M. BOUCHER, *La révolution de 1789 vue par les écrivains allemands contemporains: Klopstock, Wieland, Herder, Schiller, Kant, Fichte, Goethe* (Etudes de littérature étrangère et comparée 30; Paris 1954); R. BRINKMANN e.a., *Deutsche Literatur und französische Revolution. Sieben Studien* (Göttingen 1974); E. BURKE, *Reflections on the Revolution in France* (1790; critical edn. ed. J. C. D. CLARK; Stanford, CA 2001), esp. "Introduction", 23–112; J. G. A. POCOCK (ed.), *Reflections on the Revolution in France* (Indianopolis, IN 1987), esp. "Editor's Introduction", VII–XLVIII; idem, *Further Reflections on the Revolution in France* (ed. D. E. RITSCHIE; Indianapolis, IN 1992); K. CARPENTER, *The French Émigrés in Europe and the Struggle against Revolution 1789–1814* (Basingstoke e.a. 2002); A. COBBAN (ed.), *The Debate on the French Revolution. 1789–1800* (The British Political Tradition 2; London ²1960); idem, *Edmund Burke and the Revolt against the Eighteenth Century* (London ²1962); H. T. DICKINSON, *British Radicalism and the French Revolution 1789–1815* (Oxford 1985); idem (ed.), *Britain and the French Revolution* (Houndsmills, Basingstoke / London 1989); idem, "Popular Conservatism and Militant Loyalism 1789–1815", in: idem, *Britain and the French Revolution* (1989)103–25; J. DROZ, *L'Allemagne et la Revolution* (Paris 1949); F. DUMONT, "La déclaration des droits de l'Homme et du Citoyen en Allemagne", *Annales historiques de la Révolution française* 50 (1978) 220–45; K. EPSTEIN, *The Genesis of German Conservatism* (Princeton, NJ 1966); F. FEHER (ed.), "The French Revolution and the Birth of Modernity", *Social Research* 56 (1989) 1–293, esp. idem, "Introduction", 3–4; G.-L. FINK, "La littérature allemande face à la Révolution française (1789–1800). Littérature et politique, libertés et contraintes", in: Voss (ed.), Deutschland und die französische Revolution (1983; see below) 249–300; F. FURET / M. OSOUF (eds.) *The French Revolution and the Creation of Modern Political Culture* III. *The Transformation of Political Culture 1789–1848* (Oxford 1989); C. GANTET / B. STRUCK, *Revolution, Krieg und Verflechtung 1789 bis 1815* (WBG Deutsch-Französische Geschichte; V; Darmstadt 2006); M. GILLI (ed.), "Le Mouvement révolutionnaire allemand à la fin du dix-huitième siècle", *Annales historiques de la Révolution française* F 2, 56 (No. 255-56, 1984); J. GODECHOT, "L'expansion de la déclaration des droits de l'Homme de 1789 dans le monde", *Annales historiques de la Révolution française* F 2, 50 (1978) 201–13; J. GÖRRES, *Teutschland und die Revolution* (Coblenz 1819, = idem, *Gesammelte Schriften*, ed. W. Schellberg; 13, ed. G. Wohlers; Köln 1929) 35–143; H. GÜNTHER, *Die französische Revolution. Berichte und Deutungen deutscher Schriftsteller und Historiker* [commented reader] (Bibliothek der Geschichte und Politik 12, ed. R. Koselleck / H. Günther; Frankfurt a. M. 1985); idem, art. "Revolution", HWP 8 (1992) 957–73; J. HABERMAS, "Hegels Kritik der Französischen Revolution", in: idem, *Theorie und Praxis. Sozialphilosophische Studien* (Neuwied / Berlin 1963, ⁴1971, = Suhrkamp Taschenbuch, Frankfurt a. M. 1978) 128–47; K. HAMMER, "Deutsche Revolutionsreisende in Paris", in: Voss (ed.), Deutschland und die französische Revolution (1983; see below), 26–42; I. HAMPSHER-MONK (ed.), *The Impact of the French Revolution: texts from Britain in the 1790s* (Cambridge Readings in the History of Political Thought; Cambridge e.a. 2005); A. HERZIG / I. STEPHAN / H. E. WINTER (eds.), *"Sie und nicht wir". Die französische Revolution und ihre Auswirkung auf Norddeutschland und das Reich*, I/ 1. *Norddeutschland*, 1/2 *Das Reich* (Hamburg 1989); J. L. HIGH, *Schillers Rebellionskonzept und die*

Französische Revolution (Studies in German Language and Literature 35 (Lewiston, N.Y. 2004); I. KANT, *Der Streit der Fakultäten* (1798; see below); E. KENNEDY, *A Cultural History of the French Revolution* (New Haven, CN / London 1989); A. KUHN, *Freiheit, Gleichheit, Brüderlichkeit. Debatten um die französische Revolution in Deutschland* (Hannover 1989); G. KURZ, *Deutschland und die französische Revolution* (Bonn 1989); J. LEFEBVRE, *La Révolution française vue par les allemands* (Lyon 1987); H. MEIXNER, "Politische Aspekte der Frühromantik", in: S. VIETTA (ed.), *Die literarische Frühromantik* (Kleine Vandenhoeck-Reihe 1488; Göttingen 1983) 180-91; F. G. NAUEN, *Revolution, Idealism and Human Freedom: Schelling. Hölderlin and Hegel and the Crisis of Early Idealism* (International Archives of the History of Ideas / Archives internationales d'histoire des idées 45; The Hague 1971); E. NAUJOKS, *Die französische Revolution und Europa, 1789-1799* (Stuttgart e.a. 1969); C. NICOLET, *L'idée républicaine en France (1789-1924). Essai d'histoire critique* (Paris 1982; ²1994, 1995); NOVALIS (F. von Hardenberg), "Die Christenheit oder Europa", in: idem, *Schriften* (ed. R. Samuel / P. Kluckhohn / H.-J. Mahl / G. Schulz e. a.; Stuttgart 1960-88) 3 (²1968, ³1983) 495-524; R. SAMUEL, "Einleitung", ibid. 497-506; I. A. PELCZYNSKI (ed.), *Hegel's Political Philosophy: Problems and Perspectives* (Cambridge 1971); ST. PRICKETT, *England and the French Revolution* (Oxford 1989); J. RITTER, *Hegel und die französische Revolution* (Arbeitsgemeinschaft für Forschung des Landes Nordrhein-Westfalen. Geisteswissenschaften, H. 63; Köln / Opladen 1957), = idem, *Metaphysik und Politik – Studien zu Aristoteles und Hegel* (Frankfurt a. M. 1969) 183-255; F. SCHLEGEL, "Über das Studium der griechischen Poesie", in: *Kritische Friedrich-Schlegel-Ausgabe* (ed. E. Behler, 1/1; Paderborn e.a. 1979) 217-367; idem, "Versuch über den Begriff des Republikanismus, veranlaßt durch die Kantische Schrift zum ewigen Frieden", in: *Kritische Ausgabe 7. Studien zur Geschichte und Politik* (Paderborn 1966) 11-25; T. SCHIEDER, "Das Problem der Revolution im 19. Jahrhundert": *HZ* 170 (1950) 233-71; G. SCHULZ, *Die deutsche Literatur zwischen Französischer Revolution und Restauration. Erster Teil: Das Zeitalter der französischen Revolution 1789-1806* (München 1983, ²2000); S. SKALWEIT, *Edmund Burke und Frankreich* (Köln 1956); T. SKOCPOL, "Reconsidering the French Revolution in World-Historical Perspective", in: F. FEHER (ed.), French Revolution (1989) 53-70; S. B. SMITH, "Hegel and the French Revolution: An Epitaph for Republicanism", in: Feher (ed.), French Revolution (1989) 233-61; T. STAMMEN / F. EBERLE (eds.), *Deutschland und die französische Revolution: 1789-1806* (Darmstadt 1988); L. VON STEIN, *Geschichte der sozialen Bewegung in Frankreich von 1789 bis auf unsere Tage 1. Der Begriff Gesellschaft und die soziale Geschichte der Französischen Revolution bis zum Jahre 1830* (Leipzig 1850; repr. München 1921; Hildesheim 1959); A. STEM, *Der Einfluß der französischen Revolution auf das deutsche Geistesleben* (Stuttgart / Berlin 1928); I. STEPHAN, "Faszination und Abwehr. Französische Revolution und Deutsche Literatur", in: Schoch e.a. (eds.), Freiheit, Gleichheit, Brüderlichkeit (1989) 99-106; J. STEVENSON, "Popular Radicalism and Popular Protest", in: Dickinson (ed.), Britain and the French Revolution (1989) 61-81; H. U. THAMER, "Aufbruch in die Moderne. Französische Revolution und politisch-sozialer Wandel in Deutschland", in: M. Schoch e.a. (eds.), Freiheit, Gleichheit, Brüderlichkeit (1989) 59ff; C. TRAGER (ed.), *Die französische Revolution im Spiegel der deutschen Literatur* (Frankfurt a. M. / Leipzig 1975; Köln ³1989); R. VIERHAUS, "«Sie und nicht wir». Deutsche Urteile über die französische Revolution", in: Voss (ed.), Deutschland und die französische Revolution (1983; see below) 1-15; U. VOGEL, *Konservative Kritik an der bürgerlichen Revolution. August Wilhelm Rehberg* (Darmstadt / Neuwied 1972); M. VOVELLE, *L'image de la Révolution française* (Communications presentées lors du Congres Mondial pour le Bicentenaire de la Révolution, Sorbonne, Paris, 6-12 juillet 1989, 1-4; Paris 1990); J. Voss (ed.), *Deutschland und die französische Revolution. 17. Deutsch-Französisches Historikerkolloquium des Deutschen Historischen Instituts Paris* (Beih. d. Francia, 12; München e.a. 1983); I. WALLERSTEIN, "The French Revolution as a World-Historical Event", in: FEHER (ed.), French Revolution (1989) 33-52; C. M. WIELAND, *Aufsätze über die Französische Revolution* (Warendorf 2004); W. D. WILSON (ed.), *Goethes Weimar und die Französische Revolution: Dokumente der Krisenjahre* (Köln e.a. 2004).

The French Revolution broke into the world of the eighteenth century as a totally unexpected event. Two revolutions had shaken Britain in the seventeenth century, but at the end they had modified, but not totally altered a traditionally constitutional monarchy. Only the new democratic constitution of the United States after the independence of the American colonies from Britain

(1776/1783) offered an alternative model to the structures of the old continent, in which the absolute rule of princes in nearly all countries had absolved the traditional estate-system. In France *le roi de soleil* Louis XIV (1643–1714) was the prototype of the absolute ruler; he suppressed the last remains of parliamentary influence on the local level. The General Estates had not been called together since 1614!

The long-enduring discussion among historians about the origins of the French Revolution, beginning with judgements of the contemporaries, has continued to the present time. The marxist position (J. JAURÈS, G. LEFEBVRE, A. MATHIEZ, A. SOBOUL e.a.) regarded the revolution as the rise of the capitalist bourgeois class against feudalism. A. COBBAN first attacked this "Myth of the French Revolution".[1] He showed that the bourgeois members in the National Assembly of 1789 were no capitalists, but partly themselves possessed those 'feudal' rights and incomes in the countryside that traditionally belonged to the nobility.[2] The on-going discussion in its so-called 'revisionist' phase showed that the economic conditions were not decisive for the outbreak of the revolution.[3] Also the *sans-culottes* were not the instigators of the revolution. The poorer masses could be incited by their economic situation to public uproar in the course of the events, but they did not initiate the movement to constitutionalism. Also the deep-rooted prejudice regarding the *Old Regime* as immovable and unable to accommodate reforms had to be revised: Only his sudden and unexpected death by smallpox impeded Louis XV (1715–1774) to complete his intended thoroughgoing reforms, and even the government of Louis XVI had started reforms since 1787.[4] Besides, he was not the stupid weakling that he has been accused of being. Taken together, structural conditions were not decisive for the outbreak of the revolution. The course of events depended on a singular political situation: Louis XVI in 1788 was forced by a severe financial state crisis, caused by the expenses for the colonial wars against Britain, to convene the General Estates. From this moment on the development became progressively worse and from phase to phase by an inner automatism, ending after the re-constitution of the General Estates as "National Assembly" (later "Constitutional Assembly"), the new constitution, the deposition of Louis XVI in October 1792 and the declaration of France as a republic, the death sentence against the king and his execution in January 1793, with the assumption of power by the Jacobins and the period of terror (1793/94).

How far was the French Revolution as an historical event a symptom of a New Cultural and Political Situation? A response to this question can only be given if, according to a 'post-revisionist' tendency in most recent research, aspects of intellectual history are integrated into political ones. Thus, the quest has a twofold aspect:

First, how far did intellectual influences contribute to the outbreak of the French Revolution? A direct impact of the French *philosophes* (as Voltaire, Diderot, Rousseau) can be dismissed, because the generation of the famous French Enlightenment philosophers had passed away years before. Thus, their impact upon the political development was restricted.[5] Certainly the clandestine diffusion of forbidden books was made effective by an underground sys-

---

[1] Cobban, Myth (1954), in: Aspects (1968) 90–111. Cf. Cobban's other contributions, bibliography, above. – The best short overview over the discussion is given by Doyle, Origins (1999) 3–41; cf. also Censer, Third Century of Debate (1989) 1309–25, and the critical review of the French *Historikerstreit* by Kaplan, Farewell, Revolution (1995).

[2] Similarly, later Taylor, Noncapitalist Wealth (1966/67) 469–96.

[3] Cf. Furet, Penser la Revolution (1978); ET: Interpreting the French Revolution (1981); K. M. Baker, Inventing the French Revolution (1994), "Introduction", 1–11.

[4] Cf. Jones, Reform and Revolution (1995).

[5] Cf. Doyle, Origins (1999) 82; Kaiser, Strange Offspring (1987/88).

tem of distribution.[6] Rousseau's *Contrat social* (1762), however, was only known in restricted circles. A change of outlook in France during the revolution can be observed – French scholars as M. Vovelle made this clear.[7]

However, the best-known event in the Revolution, the *Declaration of Human and Civil Rights*, had a prehistory outside France.[8] It was instigated by a motion in the National Assembly of the marquis M.-J. de Lafayette (1757–1834), a French noble man who had fought as general in the American War of Independence.[9] Lafayette had already drafted the formulations about Human and Civil Rights in the *American Declaration of Independence* in July 1776, which in a similar version by Thomas Jefferson (1743–1826) was part of the constitution of the state of Virginia, proclaimed in June of the same year. Jefferson, 1784–89 ambassador ("resident") of the United States in Paris,[10] was like Lafayette a convinced advocate of natural rights and natural religion. Important also was Thomas Paine (1737–1809).[11] Born English, he wrote in America 1776 his pamphlets for the revolution, the enormously popular *Common Sense* and *The American Crisis*.[12] In 1787 he returned to England. As a self-made man he had studied the works of the Deist Bolingbroke[13] and the enlightened economist Adam Smith (1723–90). As ambassador in Paris (1789–90), he supported the revolution. His best known work, *The Rights of Man* (1791/92),[14] is the most radical declaration of Human Rights. In 1792 he was nominated Honorary French Citizen and elected member of the Constitutional Assembly. G. JELLINEK has been first to observe[15] that the possible indirect influence of the *philosophes* on the ideology of the Revolution can be neglected compared with the direct participation of American Deists in the formulations of the revolutionary constitution.[16]

The second field of research is the impression made by the outbreak and further developments of the French Revolution upon foreign spectators.[17] In its own country, the revolution, on one hand, had a political extension, which reached beyond the crucial period 1789–94 and the following period of the rule of the *Directorium* (1795–99) and the Napoleonic time (1799–1815) far

---

[6] Cf. Damton's contributions in the bibliography above.

[7] Vovelle, *Breve storia* (1979); idem, *Mentalité revolutionnaire* (1988).

[8] On their origins, cf. Samwer, Erklärung der Menschen- und Bürgerrechte (1970).

[9] On Lafayette, cf. P. BUCKMAN, *Lafayette. A Biography* (New York e.a 1977); L. GOTTSCHALK/ M. REICHENTHAL-MADDOX, *Lafayette in the French Revolution* 1–2 (Chicago 1969/1973); L. KRAMER, *Lafayette in Two Worlds: Public Cultures and Personal Identities in an Age of Revolution* (Chapel Hill e.a. 1996); E. TAILLEMITE, *La Fayette* (Paris 1989).

[10] Cf. W. H. ADAMS, *The Paris Years of Thomans Jefferson* (New Haven e.a. 1997); N. FOUCHÉ, *Benjamin Franklin et Thomas Jefferson. Aux sources de l'amitie franco-amaericaine. 1776–1808* (Paris 2000); A. JAYNE, *Jefferson's Declaration of Independence: Origins, Philosophy and Theology* (Lexington 1998); C. C. O'BRIEN, *The Long Affair: Thomas Jefferson and the French Revolution. 1785–1800* (London 1996); D. S. BROWN, *Thomas Jefferson: a Biographical Companion* (Santa Barbara 1998); C. B. SANFORD, *The Religious Life of Thomas Jefferson* (Charlottesville 1984).

[11] On Paine, cf. i.a. D. F. HAWKE, *Paine* (New York 1974, repr. 1992, with bibl.).

[12] Modern editions: T. PAINE, *Rights of Man* (Introduction by M. Foot; Everyman's Library; London 1994); idem, *Rights of Man, Common Sense, and Other Political Writings* (ed. with an Introduction of M. Philp; The World's Classics, Oxford 1995).

[13] Henry St. John, Viscount Bolingbroke (1678–1751), one of the last representatives of the earlier English school of Deism.

[14] Against Burke, see below.

[15] Jellinek, Erklärung, in: Schnur, Zur Geschichte (1964) 1–77. Cf. also Faÿ, Esprit revolutionnaire (1925); Dierse, Menschenrechte (2001).

[16] On the relationship between the two revolutions, cf. also P. HIGGONET, *Sister Republics. The Origins of French and American Republicanism* (Cambridge, MA / London 1988); P. RAYNAUD, art. "American Revolution", in: Furet / Osouf, Critical Dictionary (1989) 593–603; Sandweg, Rationales Naturrecht (1972) 24–81.

[17] A comprehensive world-wide overview in: Vovelle, L'image II, III (1990).

into the nineteenth century. Not until 1883 was the republican state form established as a final solution. As a symbol of the French nation the revolution became a "myth",[18] though the social conditions had not so much changed after the revolution as one might have expected – the depressed situation of the Church excepted[19] – even if the official rank of the nobility and the feudal rights of the two first estates had been abolished.[20] Even until today the Revolution and its slogan "freedom, equality, fraternity" remained in France the event that is kept sacred as a symbol of French identity.[21] On the other hand, a centralised administration was a permanent result of the Revolution.

In Britain, the situation was different. Similar to Germany, some poets[22] first welcomed enthusiastically the revolution. But there was just a small and short-lived politically progressive group in the country, most of them nonconformists.[23] The conditions were not favourable for such a movement, because Britain had already passed through its revolution in the seventeenth century, in which the execution of a king (Charles I, 1649), a republican system (the "Commonwealth" under Oliver Cromwell, 1651–59), ending in a total breakdown, the restoration of the monarchy (1660) and the "Glorious Revolution" of 1688 had followed upon one another. A balance of power in a constitutional monarchy was the result of this development. On the other hand, the existence of a widespread loyalist movement in the country[24] explains the enormous success of Edmund Burke's (1729–97), a Whig politician's (!), *Reflections on the Revolution in France*.[25] He wrote before the later terror could have been foreseen, but already announced that the Revolution would end in an autocratic regime, as actually happened with Napoleon's rule. What he achieved was to defend an unwritten, but very stable British constitution.

In Spain, the system of a Catholic nationalism, based on the dominance of the Church, prevented any infection by revolutionary initiatives from abroad. Also Italy, split up in numerous territories, though not untouched by revolutionary upheavals and for a period totally re-structured by the Napoleonic conquest, returned after 1815 to the former order.[26] It remained a country stamped by a traditional Catholicism, though a vehement anti-clericalism was growing in the underground, to break out later in the century.

In Germany, centre of intellectual development in the nineteenth century, and on which research has focused for about eighty years,[27] the reaction was the heaviest. When the first news about the events in France reached Germany – a country split up in countless small territories and

---

[18] This was also shown by the installation of a chair specialised on the French Revolution in 1891 at the Sorbonne – the first professor being A. Aulard (1849–1928).

[19] But the total separation between Church and State did not become final until 1905!

[20] Blanning, Class War (1998) 53, states that the French nobles lost "a number of honorific privileges", but "were offered limitless opportunities for political and material advancement", especially because many of them were men of means and education. Already Napoleon filled the upper ranks in army and administration to a high degree by members of the old noble families.

[21] Cf. Agulhon, Marianne au combat (1971), ET: Marianne into Battle (1981); idem, XIXe siècle (1992); Nicolet, Idée republicaine (1995); idem, Republique (1982; ²1994, 1995); for further titles cf. Nicolet, *Idée* (1995), "Postface", 509, n. 2.

[22] W. Blake (1757–1827), S. T. Coleridge (1772–1834) and W. Wordsworth (1770–1850).

[23] Cf. S. Lynd, *Intellectual Origins of American Radicalism* (London 1968) 24–42; Dickinson, British Radicalism (1985); Stevenson, Popular Radicalism (1989). The event which made the greatest public impression was the sermon given in the Old Jewry Chapel in London in November 1789 by the unitarian preacher Richard Price entitled "The Love of our Country", which induced Burke to write his book, on which see below.

[24] Cf. Dickinson, Popular Conservatismn (1989); idem, French Revolution and Counter-Revolution (1989).

[25] First published in 1790. Cf. the critical editions by O'Brien (1986) and Clark (1973, 2001), esp. the introductions. – On Burke cf. also Cobban, Burke (1962); Skalweit, Burke (1956); Furet / Osouf (eds.), Revolution and Creation (1989), III, I "Burke or Why a Revolution?", 3–114.

[26] The occupation of the Venetian territory by Austria excepted.

[27] Cf. the works and collections in the Bibliography above, part. 2.

a few bigger regional states – the academic youth: poets and intellectuals welcomed the expected liberation from a system they regarded as antiquated and the beginning of a new age.[28] Several German and English "Freedom tourists"[29] travelled to Paris, to become eyewitnesses of the Revolution. But most adherents of the revolution were soon disappointed or terrified by its further course, especially the violence that followed the moderate beginning and later the Napoleonic wars. Critics of the revolution like A. W. Rehberg[30] and F. Gentz[31] reached a growing audience. The revolutionary ideology vanished more and more.[32]

Was there a new cultural and political situation? The whole period from 1789 to 1815, taken together, brought such a change,[33] though the Congress of Vienna in 1815 had restored officially the old order in Europe, followed by a long period of restoration under the leadership of Prince K. W. Metternich (1773–1859). Stable in spite of the disturbance by the bourgeois revolution of 1830 in France, this order was preserved until the European revolution of 1848. Most thoroughgoing were the changes in Germany. The end of the *Roman Empire of the German Nation* sealed in 1805, was final. Many small territories had lost their independence and were united to middle size states. The secularization of 1803 had brought the end of ecclesiastical territories and the expropriation of monasteries. The imperial dignity was not restored (until 1871). *Der Deutsche Bund* ("The German Federation") was further just a loose form of co-operation between the German states.

Also the cultural situation had changed to a high degree. The century of Enlightenment was closed, and though rationalism was still kept alive by some authors,[34] new movements of thought and feeling had left their traces on the intellectual scene. It was not just the proclamation of the theory of freedom in the revolutionary constitution, but also the attempt at realising the rule of rea-

---

[28] Best known is a group of students in the Tübingen Stift, to which F. Hölderlin (1770–1843), G. W. F. Hegel (1770–1831) and F. Schlegel (1772–1829) belonged. They believed to be witnesses of the birth of a new world-order with the official proclamation of *Freedom, Equality and Brotherhood*, an order uniting mankind in an all-embracing peace. A similar feeling of freedom characterised F. Schiller's (1759–1805) early period as a poet and writer of revolutionary dramas like *Don Carlos* and *Die Räuber* (1781) and his famous *Ode an die Freude (Alle Menschen werden Brüder...)*.

[29] Germans as J. H. Campe (later a conservative writer) and G. Forster, member of the Jacobine Club in Mainz. English travellers were H. M. Williams and Mary Wollstonecraft, well known as one of the first fighters for the emancipation also of women.

[30] A. REHBERG, *Sämmtliche Schriften* 1–2, 4 (Hannover 1828–31; vol. 3 not published); idem, *Untersuchungen über die französische Revolution* (2 vols. in one; Hannover 1793); French transl. and introd. by L. K. SOSOE, preface by A. Renaut (Recherches sur la Revolution Française. Bibliothèque des textes philosophiques; Paris 1998).

[31] F. (VON) GENTZ, *Ueber den Ursprung und Charakter des Krieges gegen die Französische Revolution* (Berlin 1801; repr. in: G. KRONENBITTER [ed.], *Gesammelte Schriften* 1, Hildesheim e.a. 1997); idem, *Von dem politischen Zustande von Europa vor und nach der französischen Revolution* (Berlin 1801; repr. in Ges. Schriften 2, Hildesheim e.a. 1997); idem, *The Origin and Principles of the American Revolution, Compared with the Origins and Principles of the French Revolution* (Philadelphia, PA 1800).

[32] Already in 1794 the territories on the left side of the Rhine, which had declared their unification with France in order to participate in the Revolution, saw their intention betrayed by the advancing French forces, which had no other aim than to extend their power. Even the Jacobite republic of Mainz remained a short intermezzo (1792/93). Cf. Gilli, Mouvement révolutionnaire allemand (1984) 7–23.

[33] Cf. F. DUMONT, "Wirkungen auf Deutschland und Europa", in: Reichardt, PLOETZ (1988) 264–84.

[34] As H. G. E. Paulus.

son in the concrete society, even by force, by Robespierre and his followers during the Jacobin period, that motivated these speculations.

Idealism was the most immediate heir to Enlightenment. Its first prominent representative, J. G. Fichte (1762–1814),[35] who published an anonymous pamphlet on the Revolution,[36] built his system on Kant's understanding of freedom, rendering it more concrete as a bundle of personal rights on the paradigm of the Revolution. Hegel's position in relation to the Revolution is debated. J. RITTER sees Hegel's philosophy in the wake of the Revolution: … *es gibt keine zweite Philosophie, die so sehr und bis in ihre innersten Antriebe hinein Philosophie der Revolution ist wie die Hegels.*[37] J. HABERMAS modified this thesis by stating that Hegel made the Revolution the principle of his philosophy as a form of exorcism of its danger.[38] Whatever the motive – Hegel's philosophy is an innovation by placing freedom as the central abstract idea into dialectic with necessity, the idea of right into dialectic with freedom as a title of the individual, realising his being human. But Hegel's thinking is also stamped by his negative experience of the Revolution, which proved unable to create a stable order. Thus, the aim of carrying justice into effect is not yet accomplished. It is world-history that has the task of realising the rule of reason in the state.[39] The *Weltgeist*[40] is the moving power, driving history forwards to the accomplishment of right.

Speculation on history was not new,[41] but its central role in Hegel's thinking prefigured the importance of the topic for the nineteenth century. It was also significant that Hegel acknowledged the subjective character of any picture of history that an individual thinker can form. A positivistic form of *historicism*, characterised by the claim of objectivity as intended by L. (von) Ranke (1795–1886)[42] – cf. his famous utterance *zeigen, wie es eigentlich gewesen*[43] – seems to be a regression compared with Hegel's modern hermeneutic insight in this aspect.

---

[35] On Fichte, cf. recently G. MECKENSTOCK, art. "Fichte, Johann Gottlieb", in: *Biographische Enzyklopädie deutschsprachiger Philosophen* (ed. B. Jahn; Munich 2001) 114–15.

[36] *Beitrag zur Berichtigung der Urtheile des Publikums über die französische Revolution*, Erster Theil (1793/94; 2nd part never published), in: *J. G. Fichte-Gesamtausgabe der Bayerischen Akademie der Wissenschaften*, 1,1 (Stuttgart-Bad Cannstatt 1964) 193–296. Cf. also idem (anonymous), *Zurückforderung der Denkfreiheit von den Fürsten Europas, die sie bisher unterdrückten*, ibid. 167–92.

[37] Ritter, Hegel (1957) 15 / idem, Metaphysik (1969) 192.

[38] *Hegel feiert die Revolution, weil er sie fürchtet*: Habermas, Hegels Kritik, in: Theorie und Praxis (1978) 128.

[39] Cf. G. W. F. HEGEL, *Grundlinien der Philosophie des Rechts* (Werke in zwanzig Bänden. Theorie Werkausgabe; Frankfurt a. M. 1970, repr. 1980) §§ 341–60. – On Hegel's theories of freedom, the individual and the state, cf. also Pelczynski, Hegel's Political Philosophy (1971).

[40] § 352; Hegel speaks also about *den allgemeinen Geist* ("common spirit"), § 341.

[41] Not casually Hegel alludes in § 343 to G. E. Lessing's *Erziehung des Menschengeschlechtes*.

[42] On him, cf. W. HARDTWIG, art. "Ranke", in: TRE 28 (1997) 133–38 (bibl.).

[43] L. RANKE, *Geschichten der romanischen und germanischen Völker von 1494 bis 1514*, in: *Sämtliche Werke* 33 (Leipzig 1874), *Vorrede der ersten Ausgabe, Oktober 1824*, VII. The perseverance of this methodical presupposition is shown by J. RÜSEN's essay, *Von der Aufklärung zum Historismus. Idealtypische Perspektiven eines Strukturwandels*, in: H. W. BLANKE / J. RÜSEN (eds.), *Von der Aufklärung zum Historismus. Zum Strukturwandel des historischen Denkens* (Paderborn e.a. 1984) 15–57.

Another movement characteristic for the period was early Romanticism. It cannot be directly derived from the French Revolution, because it was a reaction of feeling and aesthetics against the rationalism of Enlightenment.[44] The first representatives of Romanticism, after the initial enthusiasm for the Revolution and the following disappointment, shifted the idea of perfectibility to the field of literature.[45]

The Enlightenment idea of progress was kept, but the Romanticists doubted whether the Revolution had contributed to it. Thus, F. Schlegel's speech *Über das Studium der griechischen Poesie*[46] awaits an "aesthetic revolution" as the end of a development in which the progressive cultivation of humankind is the motivating force. Novalis (F. von Hardenberg),[47] writing in the papal interregnum at the end of 1799,[48] draws in his speech *Die Christenheit oder Europa*[49] the utopian picture of a new golden age in whole Europe, an age of peace and freedom, fed by the religious heritage of a renewed Christendom, as it flourished in the Middle Ages. This "second reformation" of a "secular Protestantism"[50] will, by passing through a period of anarchism,[51] be the birthplace of a new spiritual universal "church", whose prodigies are already visible in Germany.[52] English Romanticism – the so-called *Lake School* – experienced in a similar way the expectation of a new age.[53]

Indirectly by its universal missionary pretension the Revolution strengthened the reaction of the German historical school in stressing the peculiarity of national history. The 'national awakening' in Europe was not completely new at the beginning of the nineteenth century, but it was intensified by the heir of the Revolution, Napoleon, through his military subjugation of Europe. But it also reacted upon earlier understandings of history. The objectivity intended by Ranke wanted to purify historical research from using history as an educational example. But also the evolutionist historical thinking characteristic for the nineteenth century must be regarded as an aspect of historicism. In its

---

[44] Though the Enlightenment knew also already an aesthetic aspect, cf. Meixner, Politische Aspekte (1983) 182.

[45] On the following, cf. Behler, Unendliche Perfektibilität (1989); R. BRINKMANN, "Deutsche Frühromantik und französische Revolution", in: idem e.a., Deutsche Literatur (1974) 172–91.

[46] Kritische Ausgabe 1,1 (1979) 224, 262, 269–70, 356. Cf. also the fragment *Versuch über den Begriff des Republikanismus*, in: Kritische Ausgabe 7, in which Schlegel formulates directly political aims: democracy, an universal republic, a real community on the basis of common morality. There is no break between Enlightenment and Romanticism!

[47] On Novalis, cf. recently H. UERLINGS, *Novalis* (Reclam Universal-Bibliothek 17612 Stuttgart 1998; bibl.); idem, *Friedrich von Hardenberg, genannt Novalis. Werk und Forschung* (Stuttgart 1991; comprehensive bibl.).

[48] Pope Pius VI (1775–99) had died in French captivity, the election of a successor was not to be expected.

[49] The original title was "Europa", cf. letter to F. Schlegel, Schriften 4 (1975) 317. The work was not printed before 1826.

[50] Schriften 3, 517–18.

[51] *Wahrhafte Anarchie ist das Zeugungselement der Religion*, ibid. 517.

[52] Ibid. 524. This utopia is spiritualistic in the Romantic sense, an awakening of science and culture (518), not the restoration of Middle Ages Catholicism, regarded by Novalis as come to an end. – H. KURZKE, *Romantik and Konservatismus. Das »politische« Werk Friedrich von Hardenbergs (Novalis)* (Literaturgeschichte und Literaturkritik; Munich 1983) shows that Novalis's intention is transcendentalist, which the conservative interpretation fails to understand.

[53] Cf. W. Wordsworth's impressions from his voyage through France: W. J. B. OWEN (ed.), *The Fourteen-Book Prelude* (Ithaca / London 1985), Books IX-XI, 1 79–231. Prickett, England and the French Revolution (1989), gives an overview of the reactions on the French Revolution in England.

vision revolutions were seen as a returning move needed for the next step in human progress.[54]

One aspect of the impact of the French Revolution remains: The formulation of a constitution by its protagonists had the consequence that other states did the same in the following century. Very early J. Görres protested against the restoration, claiming democratic rights for the people.[55] In his opinion, the Revolution had accelerated the slow development of centuries in a few years.[56] The Declaration of Human and Civil Rights in the French Constitution had the consequence that in most European constitutions a similar catalogue of subjective rights of the individual was introduced.[57] In recent years, under American influence, it has become the ideology of the western world. And, as H. ARENDT has remarked,[58] the combination of the idea of freedom with the experience of a new beginning indicates a shift in political thinking, which distinguishes modernity from earlier periods. "Rights, liberty and the fatherland" in the place of the old sacral values[59] – the Revolution brought an important step into secularism. However, I. BERLIN's last words on the Revolution are a counter-stroke: "The failure of the French Revolution to bring about the greater portion of its declared ends marks the end of the French Enlightenment as a movement and a system".[60] The result remains ambiguous.

2. Immanuel Kant – the Impact of his Philosophy on Biblical Hermeneutics

Sources: I. KANT: *Der Streit der Fakultäten* (1798; ed. K. Vorländer, in: *Kant's gesammelte Schriften*; ed. Königlich Preußische Akademie der Wissenschaft [abbr. AA]; Berlin 1900-) = *Kants Werke* (Akademie-Textausgabe [abbr. Werke]) VII (Berlin 1968) 1–116; *Werke* I-VI (ed. W. Weischedel [abbr. WW]; Wiesbaden / Darmstadt 1956-64) VI, 261–393; *Muthmaßlicher Anfang der Menschengeschichte* (1786), AA VIII, 107–24 = WW VI, 83–102; *Die Religion innerhalb der Grenzen der bloßen Vernunft* (1793), AA VI, 1–202 = WW IV, 645–879; other editions: *Die Religion innerhalb der Grenzen der bloßen Vernunft* (ed. K. Vorländer; Einleitung: "Die Religionsphilosophie im Gesamtwerk Kants"; PhB 45; Hamburg [8]1956, repr. 1961); *Der Streit der Fakultäten* (ed. K. Reich; PhB 252; Hamburg 1959); *Kant's Briefwechsel* II (1789–94), AA 11 (Berlin / Leipzig [2]1922); *Kant's Briefwechsel* IV (Anmerkungen und Register), AA 13 (Berlin / Leipzig 1922); cf. also N. HINSKE / W. WEISCHEDEL, *Kant-Seitenkonkordanz*, WW 7 (Darmstadt 1970). – C. W. FLÜGGE, *Versuch einer historisch-kritischen Darstellung des bisherigen Einflusses der Kantischen Philosophie auf Zweige der wissenschaftlichen und praktischen Theologie* 1-2 (Hannover 1796/98; repr. 1 vol. Hildesheim / New York 1982). – J. W. SCHMID, *Ueber christliche Religion, deren Beschaffenheit*

---

[54] Cf. J. BURCKHARDT, *Weltgeschichtliche Betrachtungen* (1905; repr. Munich 2000; new critical edn. by P. Ganz; Munich 1982); cf. Schieder, Problem der Revolution (1950). – The judgement of K. Marx (1818–83), founder of the Communist ideology, about the French Revolution was divided. On one hand, it moved him to his theory of the revolutionary development of mankind, on the other hand, he regarded it as a misguided and unsuccessful undertaking.

[55] Görres, Teutschland (1819/1929).

[56] Ibid. 81.

[57] This was already stressed by Jellinek, Erklärung, in: Schnur, Zur Geschichte (1964) 2.

[58] H. Arendt, On Revolution (1985) 29.

[59] Cf. Osouf, Festivals (1988) 282.

[60] Berlin, Counter-Enlightenment (1973) 24.

und zweckmäßige Behandlung als Volkslehre und Wissenschaft für das gegenwärtige Zeitalter (Jena 1797).

Bibliography: Kant-Bibliographie 1945- (founded by R. Malter; ed. M. Ruffing [*Kant-Studien;* currently]).

General works: P. ADDINAL, "Immanuel Kant", in: idem, *Philosophy and Biblical Interpretation. A study in nineteenth-century conflict* (Cambridge 1991) 217-61; S. AJZENSTAT, "Liberalism between Nature and Culture: Kant's Exegesis of Genesis 2-6", in: K. I. Parker (ed.), *Liberal Democracy and the Bible* (Lewinston, NY e.a. 1992) 129-54; G. D'ALESSANDRO, "L'interpretazione kantiana dei testi biblici e i suoi critici": *Studi kantiani* 8 (1995) 57-85; O. BAYER, "Vernunftautorität und Bibelkritik in der Kontroverse zwischen Johann Georg Hamann und Immanuel Kant", in: H. Graf Reventlow (ed.), *Historische Kritik und biblischer Kanon in der deutschen Aufklärung* (Wolfenbütteler Forschungen 41, Wolfenbüttel 1988) 21-46; L. BELLATALIA, "All'origine dell'Università moderna. «Il conflitto delle facoltà» di Kant", *Studi kantiani* 10 (1997) 81-93; G. J. BOHATEC, *Die Religionsphilosophie Kants in der "Religion innerhalb der Grenzen der bloßen Vernunft". Mit besonderer Berücksichtigung ihrer theologisch-dogmatischen Quellen* (Hamburg 1938; repr. Hildesheim 1966); R. BRANDT, "Zum »Streit der Fakultaten«", in: R. Brandt / W. Stark (eds.), *Neue Autographen und Dokumente zu Kant: Leben. Schriften und Vorlesungen* (*Kant-Forschungen* 1, Hamburg 1987) 31-78; J.-L. BRUCH, *La philosophie religieuse de Kant* (Analyse et raison, 1, Paris 1968); E. COLOMBO, "Kant e l'esegesi biblica", *Rivista teologica di Lugano* 3 (1998) 601-10; H. D'AVIAU DE TERNAY, "Kant et la Bible. Des traces aux frontières", in: Y. Belaval / D. Bourel (eds.), *Le siècle des Lumières et la Bible* (BTT 7; Paris 1986) 823-35; W. DÜSING, "Die Interpretation des Sündenfalls bei Herder, Kant und Schiller", B. POSCHMANN (ed.), *Bückeburger Gespräche über Johann Gottfried Herder 1988* (Schaumburger Studien 49, Rinteln 1989) 227-44; A. EDGAR, "Kant's Two Interpretations of Genesis", in: *Literature and Theology: an interdisciplinary journal of theory, criticism and culture* 6 (1992) 280-90; E. L. FACKENHEIM, "Kant's Concept of History", *Kant-Studien* 48 (1956/57) 381-98; O. KAISER, "Eichhorn und Kant", in: *Das ferne und nahe Wort* (FS L. Rost, BZAW 105; Berlin 1967) 114-23 = in: idem, *Von der Gegenwartsbedeutung des Alten Testaments. Gesammelte Studien* (Göttingen 1984) 61-70; idem, "Kants Anweisung zur Auslegung der Bibel. Ein Beitrag zur Geschichte der Hermeneutik", in: *Glaube. Geist. Geschichte* (FS E. Benz; Leiden 1967) 75-90 = *NZSTh* 11 (1969) 126-138 = in: idem, *Von der Gegenwartsbedeutung* (1984) 47-60; E. KATZER, "Kants Prinzipien der Bibelauslegung", *Kant-Studien* 18 (1913) 97-128; M. KUEHN, *Kant. A Biography* (Cambridge 2001); A. LAMACCHIA, "Le fonti teologico-positive nella filosofia della religione di Kant", *Annali della Facoltà di Lettere e Filosofia* [di Bari] 10 (1965) 143-83; idem, *La filosofia della religione in Kant. 1. Dal dogmatismo teologico al teismo morale (1755-1783)* (Manduria 1969); I. MANCINI, *Kant e la teologia* (Orizonte Filosofico, Assisi 1975); O. MERK, *Biblische Theologie des Neuen Testaments in ihrer Anfangszeit* (MThSt 9, Marburg 1972); G. L. PETRONE, *L'ancella della ragione. Le origine di Der Streit der Fakultäten di Kant* (Napoli 1997); N. PIRILLO (ed.), *Kant e la filosofia della religione* 1-2 (Brescia 1996); W. SCHMIDT-BIGGEMANN, "Geschichte der Erbsünde in der Aufklärung. Philosophiegeschichtliche Mutmaßungen", in: idem, *Theodizee und Tatsachen. Das philosophische Profil der deutschen Aufklärung* (Frankfurt a. M. 1988) 88-116; A. WARDA, "Der Streit um den Streit der Fakultaten", *Kant-Studien* 23 (1918) 385-405; A. WINTER, *Der andere Kant. Zur philosophischen Theologie Immanuel Kants* (Hildesheim 2000), esp. "Theologiegeschichtliche und literarische Hintergründe der Religionsphilosophie Kants", 425-76 = in: F. RICKEN / F. MARTY (eds.), *Kant über Religion* (Münchner philosophische Studien, NF 7, Stuttgart 1992) 17-51.

Special abbreviations (see above):
AA = *Kant's gesammelte Schriften* (1900-)
Werke = *Kants Werke* (Akademie-Textausgabe)
WW = *Werke* I-VI (ed. W. Weischedel)

When Immanuel Kant (1724–1804) published his book *Die Religion innerhalb der Grenzen der bloßen Vernunft*[61] he entered, after his three Critiques, a completely new field of research. Though he himself had planned this step ear-

---

[61] Königsberg [1]1793, [2]1794.

lier,[62] and in his *Criticism of Practical Reason* had already indicated his approach in the definition of 'religion' as "perception of all duties as divine commandments",[63] for his readership it was rather a surprise. The beginning with the First Part *Von der Einwohnung des bösen Prinzips neben dem Guten: oder aber das radikale Böse in der menschlichen Natur* ("About the inhabitancy of the evil principle besides the good, or about the radical Evil in human nature"), even if published in advance,[64] seemed unusual for the critical philosopher. At the first look it differed from common Enlightenment optimism and appeared more like a relic of orthodox dogmatic.[65] However, the christological starting-point for Part Two – though the use of Christology as such seems to be a second indication of a traditional heritage – already shows that Kant did not desert his earlier approach. For him humankind in its total moral perfection is the intention of the divine decree and the end of creation.[66] Jesus Christ as the only human being pleasant in God's eyes, descended from heaven, represents the idea of a humankind of the same moral integrity. *Zu diesem Ideal der moralischen Vollkommenheit, d. i. dem Urbilde der sittlichen Gesinnung ... uns zu erheben, ist allgemeine Menschenpflicht.*[67] Also this utterance, in which Kant describes Christ as *the* moral example, is typical for the view common in Enlightenment thinking. In regarding morality as the genuine content of religion, Kant is the most consequent representative of this ideology. The same can be said about his anticlericalism, expressed in his distinction in Part Four between *Dienst* and *Afterdienst*,[68] or 'religion' and 'priestcraft' – an expression already used by the English Deists. Part Three is the most important in our context. It describes under the heading *Der Sieg des guten Prinzips über das böse und die Gründung eines Reichs Gottes auf Erden* the development from an ethical state of nature (the war of everybody against one another[69]) to an ethical polity, i. e. a "people of God", ruled by moral laws.[70]

Kant distinguishes between this ideal, to be imagined just as an "invisible church", and the real, visible church, founded upon an historical faith. Because religion consists in regarding God as legislator of our duties,[71] one has to distinguish between "statutory" and moral laws. The first, consisting in outer forms is needed, but secondary, human, and cannot be regarded as divine order. They are morally indifferent.[72] But because getting hold of something visible belongs to the natural needs of humans, a historical church-faith is una-

---

[62] Cf. his letter of May 1793 to C. F. Stäudlin, AA XI, 429–30.

[63] *Erkenntnis aller Pflichten als göttlicher Gebote*, AA V = Werke V,129 = WW IV, 261. The same sentence is repeated in "Religion", AA VI = Werke VI, 1 53 = WW IV, 822.

[64] In the *Berlinischen Monatsschrift* 1792, 323–85.

[65] It has been regarded as the impact of Kant's early youth, in which the influence of his Pietist mother was dominant.

[66] Religion", AA VI, 60 = Werke VI, 60 = WW IV, 712 = PhB 45, 63.

[67] Ibid.

[68] "Service" and "wrong service".

[69] Already with T. Hobbes, *Leviathan*, I, 13, this is not a primeval period of history, but a theoretical model.

[70] AA VI = Werke, VI, 99 = WW IV, 758.

[71] AA VI = Werke, VI, 103 = WW IV, 763.

[72] Again we meet with the already humanist theory of *indifferentia*.

voidable. It is not possible without a Holy Scripture. A Bible exists as the foundation of Christian faith. But it would be insufficient if it would just establish the statutory church-faith. The real problem is how to pass to the "pure religious faith".[73]

Kant develops his hermeneutic considerations in § 3, VI under the heading "The Church-faith has as its highest interpreter the pure religious faith".[74] He reckons with a gradual shift from church-faith to pure religious faith. As the first is founded on the Holy Scriptures, a *durchgängige Deutung derselben zu einem Sinn, der mit den allgemeinen praktischen Regeln einer reinen Vernunftreligion zusammenstimmt* ("a thoroughgoing interpretation of them to a sense that is in accordance with the common practical rules of a pure religion of reason") is afforded.[75] The literal sense in many cases does not contain anything of morality, sometimes even might have a contrary effect.[76] In these cases Kant suggests one should use a forced interpretation, which indeed could be far removed from the historical sense of the text.[77] Calling to his support the well known verse 2 Tim 3:16, he stresses the character of Holy Scripture as (moral) teaching and sees his program in the wake of allegorical explanation to be found in all world religions from the Homer-interpretation of the Ancients to Indians (*Veda*), Muslims, Jews and Christians. Another form of interpretation is the work of the *Schriftgelehrte* ('scriptural scholar'). His office is, however, subordinated, as he has just the task of searching the Scriptures as historical documents for their credibility. It is the condition for their use as documents of church-faith, which cannot be neglected as the people's faith.

The second occasion for Kant to speak about the role of the Bible was his essay *Der Streit der Fakultäten*.[78]

Written in 1793/94 (originally in three parts), it was not published until 1798. In his *Vorrede* Kant explains the reason:[79] The edict on religion by the Prussian minister J. C. Wöllner (1732–1800) had introduced a severe censorship on publications in the field, and king Frederick William II (ruled 1786-97), annoyed by Kant's essay on Religion, in an order of cabinet had prohibited him from any further utterance in the matter.

Kant's remarks on biblical hermeneutics in this work are similar to the ones in his essay on Religion, but in a way more elaborated. In an *Anhang* ('annex') at the end of the treatise on the dispute

---

[73] This dualism can be found already with J. S. Semler, on whom Kant obviously depends, though he does not mention Semler's name and does not quote him at all. – For a recent summary on Semler cf. Reventlow, Epochen IV (2001) 175–89.

[74] AA VI = Werke, VI, 109–14 = WW IV, 770.

[75] AA VI = Werke, VI, 110 = WW IV, 771.

[76] Kant mentions in a footnote AA VI, 110 (WW IV, 771) as example the ill-famed "Psalm of avenge", Ps 59:11–16.

[77] *Diese Auslegung mag uns selbst in Ansehung des Textes (der Offenbarung) oft gezwungen scheinen, oft es auch wirklich sein, und doch muß sie ... einer solchen [morally indifferent or contrasting] buchstäblichen vorgezogen werden*, AA VI = Werke VI, 110 = WW IV, 771.

[78] AA VII = Werke VII, 1–116 = WW VI, 261–393. Cf. Brandt, Zum »Streit der Fakultäten« (1987).

[79] Kant printed the correspondence in his *Vorrede*, AA VII = Werke VII, 6–10. Cf. also the fragment E 73, in: R. Reicke (ed.), *Lose Blätter aus Kants Nachlass* 2 (Königsberg 1895) 250–53 (= AA XXXIII, 423–25) 253: *Mein Buch ist keine Rede ans Volk denn dazu ist es viel zu gelehrt und unverständlich sondern an die Facultäten um wie weit die Rechte der biblisch theologischen im Verhältnis auf die philosophisch theol[og]ischen gehen auszumachen weil beyde in Harmonie sollen gebracht werden.*

between the Philosophical and the Theological Faculty Kant distinguishes between two sorts of exegesis: The "authentic" – which has to be adequate to the literal sense of the author – and the moral – which he also calls "doctrinal".[80] The first is related to a statutory, messianic (mosaic-messianic and evangelical-messianic) history-faith, founded upon an old and new covenant of humanity with God.[81] It would be the most effective guide for the temporal and eternal welfare of man and citizen, if it could be authenticated as God's word. But this is not the case: How can a human being know that God is speaking to him? There is only the negative proof: Whatever is against the moral law, cannot be a word of God. And there are such passages in the Bible: In Kant's eyes, the most striking example is the story in Genesis 22.[82] All concerning the spirit of the Scriptures (the moral side) authenticates itself; the letter (the statutory) does not need an authentication, because it belongs just to the accessories of the Bible. For: *der Glaube an einen bloßen Geschichtssatz ist todt an ihm selber.*[83] The Bible has an educational value, for it gave the *Ausübung der Religion in der bürgerlichen Gesellschaft eine Form,*[84] had an catechizing and homiletic effect on people's heart and serves for a while as text of a systematic doctrine of faith. Insofar, as an historic document, it should be the subject of exegetical endeavours. But one day it even might become superfluous.

Several years earlier, Kant already delivered an example of this sort of exegesis in his essay *Muthmaßlicher Anfang der Menschengeschichte,*[85] an interpretation of Genesis 2–6, in which he used the biblical text for developing a theory of the history of humankind. Without trying an exact exegesis of the passage, but in the manner of a "pleasure trip",[86] Kant follows the episodes related in the chapters – which he regards as historical – explaining them as consequent steps in a development. The way leads from the original state, in which man was guided by instinct (described as the voice of God in the story Gen 3:1–3) to eat some fruits, to avoid others, over the waking up of reason, stirring up other desires against instinct (3:6) and thus opening the door to a freely chosen way of life. This, though the "fall" as such was absolutely an evil, if one regards its immediate results. For the individual it was a "loss", but for humankind a "gain".[87] The step was unavoidable on the way of humankind to progress. The fig leaf (3:7) indicates the next advance, by which the humans reach a sublimation of sexual desires. With the third step of reason (3:13–19) the man and his wife learn to look into the future: a future carrying with it toil and sorrow and at the end the pre-knowledge of death – an ability which distinguishes humans from animals. The fourth and last insight is testified in 3:21:

---

[80] AA VII = Werke VII, 66–67 = WW VI, 336–38.

[81] AA VII = Werke VII, 61–62 = WW VI, 330–31.

[82] AA VII = Werke, note on p. 63 = WW VI, 333: Abraham should have answered upon the divine voice: *Daß ich meinen guten Sohn nicht tödten solle, ist ganz gewiß; daß aber du, der du mir erscheinst, Gott sei, davon bin ich nicht gewiß und kann es auch nicht werden.* Cf. also H. ROSENAU, "Die Erzählung von Abrahams Opfer (Gen 22) und ihre Deutung bei Kant, Kierkegaard und Schelling", *NZSTh* 27 (1985) 251–61.

[83] AA VII = Werke VII, 66 = WW VI, 337. This reminds of G. E. Lessing's famous sentence: *Zufällige Geschichtswahrheiten können der Beweis von notwendigen Vernunftswahrheiten nie werden*: "Über den Beweis des Geistes und der Kraft", *Werke* 8 (ed. H. G. Göpfert; Munich / Darmstadt 1979) 12. Lessing's influence on Kant is visible in his whole approach to the Bible.

[84] AA VII = Werke VII, 64 = WW VI, 333–34.

[85] (1786). AA VIII = Werke VIII, 107–24 = WW VI, 83–102; ET: E. L. FACKENHEIM, I. Kant, On History (ed. L. W. Beck; Indianapolis, IN 1963) 53–68. Cf. esp. Ajzenstat, Liberalism (1992); Edgar, Two Interpretations (1992).

[86] AA VIII = Werke VIII, 109 = WW VI, 85.

[87] AA VIII, 115 = WW 6, 92–93.

Man learns that he is *eigentlich der Zweck der Natur* ("the purpose of nature"),[88] he can use the sheep and take its furrow for himself. This includes the restrictions he owes from now on his fellow man, which will be of equal rights as pre-condition for human society, and even with "higher beings" (3:22)[89]. This means also the dismissal out of the protection of nature into the state of freedom.

In the following part of his essay, which consists of a note (*Anmerkung*, 115–18) and a concluding summary, Kant reflects the course of history as culture. He sees it as a history of gradual progress, passing through long periods of always impending war and other evils caused by humans, but developing to a better end. This is secularised philosophy of history – God's part in the story is eliminated – it turns the original sense of the story upside down – the story of the Fall becomes the history of progress – and as such it could correctly be criticised as allegory by the first readers. It shows how an ideology can dominate the interpretation of the Bible. In this case it is the philosopher who feels free to implant his speculation into the text – in the way of allegory. He was aware of the fact, as we saw.

However, Kant later abandoned his speculations on the course of history. In his *Religion innerhalb der Grenzen der bloßen Vernunft* (Religion within the Limits of Reason Alone) he defines radical Evil anthropologically as an inclination to Evil in human nature, which cannot be derived historically from the first parents. Instead every evil deed originates with the free will of the agent.[90]

Was Kant also influential in the history of biblical hermeneutics? It is not surprising that Kant's theory of moral exegesis in *Die Religion* III, 6 called forth the protest of leading biblical scholars of the period.[91] One of the first was J. G. Eichhorn.[92] In the fashionable form of a letter to a fictitious adherent of Kant's hermeneutics, who predicts the approaching end of historic-critical exegesis, he characterises Kant's program of a moral exegesis as a relapse into an antiquated allegorical method, looking back to the development of allegorical interpretation from the hellenistic Homer-exegesis and the allegorising of the Jews on Moses (as he sees it) onwards. Eichhorn expects better auspices for the future of historical-critical exegesis (see below). If, however, a philosophical school tries to harmonise its doctrines with an ancient author, his interpretation will be highly endangered! As an example he mentions Leibniz, who tried to prove the eternity of hell-punishments and the Lutheran dogma of the Eucharist by his philosophy.[93]

J. P. Gabler in his re-editing of Eichhorn's *Urgeschichte*[94] (see below) has an ambivalent judgement about Kant's exegesis of the primeval story, which he reckons among the allegoric interpretations. He therefore does not approve of it as correct historical-critical exegesis. He comes to the

---

[88] AA VIII = Werke VIII, 114 = WW VI, 91.

[89] Ibid.

[90] AA VI = Werke VI, 40 f. = WW IV, 689–90. On the difference between the two interpretations of the early chapters of Genesis in 1786 and 1793, cf. Edgar, Two Interpretations (1992).

[91] A contemporary report of the reactions in Flügge, Versuch (1796/98 resp. 1982); cf. the list of critics and adherers of Kant's hermeneutics, 167–70; also Kant, *Briefwechsel* IV (AA 13, Berlin and Leipzig 1922), no. 619, 361–363.

[92] J. G. EICHHORN, "Briefe die biblische Exegese betreffend", *Allgemeine Bibliothek der biblischen Literatur* 5 (1793/4) 203–53.

[93] Ibid. 214–15.

[94] J. G. EICHHORN, *Urgeschichte* 2,1 (ed. J. P. Gabler; Altdorf / Nürnberg 1792) 423–45, esp. 444–45. On Gabler's discussion with Kant, cf. Merk, Biblische Theologie (1972) 58–69.

conclusion: *Die wahre Erklärung der Urgeschichte hat demnach durch die Kantische Darstellung sicher nicht gewonnen; und als Auslegung der Mosaischen Urkunde hat sie sehr geringes Verdienst ... Aber als philosophische Entwicklung der successiven Fortschritte der menschlichen Vernunft hat sie unläugbar großen Werth.*[95] Gabler, as an enlightened theologian, also believed in the progress of human reason, and so did the young professor in Erlangen, soon in Göttingen, C. F. Ammon (1766–1850).[96] He welcomed enthusiastically in a private letter to Kant[97] the publication of the latter's hermeneutics, which confirmed, as he said, his favoured idea about "historical and common sense of the Holy Books". He even built his *Entwurf einer reinen biblischen Theologie* (Erlangen 1792) upon a Kantian philosophical basis.[98] But he met with sharp criticism from the side of Gabler,[99] who accused him of "Kantiolatry" and induced him to renounce in the second edition of his work expressly any use of Kantianism for a Biblical Theology.[100] The professor of theology in Jena Johann Wilhelm Schmid (1744–1798) tried to found the Christian Religion on the moral teaching of Jesus combined with Kant's philosophical morality.[101] As he died shortly later, we do not know whether he would have preserved his opinion also in the nineteenth century.

Undoubtedly Kant's epistemology and his moralism upheld an enormous influence on philosophical thinking in the following period – as far as the revival in Neo-Kantianism – and also on public opinion. Undisputed is also his less overt influence on protestant theology in the nineteenth century.[102] However, undoubtedly his impact on Biblical hermeneutics and exegesis in a strict sense remained minimal. The basic conflict between historical-critical exegesis, which he had attempted to place in the second tier, and a philosophical approach had been won by the first. Hegelianism would have a similar fate. What can be said, however, is that the idea of progress and a linear development in history held the field throughout the following century. That also rationalism (and in its wake supranaturalism) was inaugurated by Kant's *Critiques*, as sometimes is asserted, seems unfounded, because it was a form of thinking typical for Enlightenment on a broader scale, which we meet already with the English Deists in the beginning of the eighteenth century. Kant was the heir of rationalism and the executor of its heritage. His fame is founded on the fact that he pursued it to its last consequences. There was no further way ahead.

---

[95] Earlier in the book (*Urgeschichte* 11,2, XIV-XV) he formulates even sharper, that from Kant's hermeneutics, *wenn sie herrschend werden sollte (wofür [wovor] uns Gott in Gnaden bewahren wolle!) dem gelehrten Studium der Bibel weit mehr Unheil drohet, als alle alten nach Kirchendogmatik zugeschnittenen Hermeneutiken.*

[96] On him, cf. JOHANN DIETRICH SCHMIDT, *Die theologischen Wandlungen des Christoph Friedrich von Ammon: Ein Beitrag zur Frage des legitimen Gebrauches philosophischer Begriffe in der Christologie* (Theol. diss. [dactylogr.] Erlangen 1953).

[97] Nr. 619 (8.3.1794): AA 11, 493 f.

[98] Cf. Merk, Biblische Theologie (1972) 82–85.

[99] Advertisement of his *Urgeschichte* 11,2: *Neue nürnbergische gelehrte Zeitung* 1794, 121–136.

[100] C. F. VON AMMON, *Biblische Theologie*, 1 (Erlangen ²1801), Vorrede, XIII.

[101] *Ueber christliche Religion. deren Beschaffenheit und zweckmäßige Behandlung als Volkslehre und Wissenschaft für das gegenwärtige Zeitalter* (Jena 1797).

[102] Cf. e.a. Bot, *Kant.* Addinal, *Philosophy*, 217–61, however, denied – with regret – a dominating influence of the Kantian philosophy on British religious thought in the period.

3. Johann Gottfried Herder – Theologian, Promoter of Humanity, Historian

Sources: J. G. HERDER: *Sämtliche Werke* [abbr. SWS] (ed. B. Suphan e.a.; Berlin 1877–1913, repr. Hildesheim 1967–68); *Werke in zehn Bänden* [abbr. FA] (ed. M. Bollacher e.a.; Frankfurt a. M. 1985–2000); *Briefwechsel 1-7* (ed. W. Ziesemer / A. Henkel; Wiesbaden e.a. 1955–79); *Briefe. Gesamtausgabe 1763–1803 1-10* (ed. W. Dobbek / G. Arnold; Weimar 1984–96); separate ET: *Reflections on the Philosophy of the History of Mankind* (Abridged and with an Intr. by F. E. Manuel; Chicago / London 1968); *Sprachphilosophie: ausgewählte Schriften* (ed. E. Heintel; PhB 574; Hamburg 2005).

Bibliographies: G. GÜNTHER / A. A. VOLGINA / S. SEIFERT (eds.), *Herder-Bibliographie* (Berlin and Weimar 1978); *Herder-Bibliographie 1977–1992* (ed. D. Kuhles; Stuttgart and Weimar 1994).

General and special works:[103] H. ADLER, *Die Prägnanz des Dunklen. Gnoseologie-Ästhetik-Geschichtsphilosophie bei Johann Gottfried Herder* (Studien zum Achtzehnten Jahrhundert 13, Hamburg 1990); W. DOBBEK, *Herders Humanitätsidee als Ausdruck seines Weltbildes und seiner Persönlichkeit* (Braunschweig 1949); *Bückeburger Gespräche 1971* (ed. J. G. Maltusch; Schaumburger Studien 33; Bückeburg 1973), containing esp. H. D. IRMSCHER, "Grundzüge der Hermeneutik Herders", 17–57, H.-J. KRAUS, "Herders alttestamentliche Forschungen", 59–76; H. B. NISBET, "Zur Revision des Herder-Bildes im Lichte der neueren Forschung", 101–18; *Bückeburger Gespräche über Johann Gottfried Herder 1975* (ed. J. G. Maltusch; Schaumburger Studien 37; Rinteln 1976), containing esp. H. D. IRMSCHER, "Grundfragen der Geschichtsphilosophie Herders bis 1774", 10–32; *Bückeburger Gespräche über Johann Gottfried Herder 1979* (ed. B. Poschmann; Schaumburger Studien 41; Rinteln 1980), containing esp. J. G. ROGERSON, "Herders Bückeburger «Bekehrung»", 17–30; *Bückeburger Gespräche über Johann Gottfried Herder 1988* (Rinteln 1989), containing esp.: G. ARNOLD, "Das Schaffhauser Urmanuskript der »Ältesten Urkunde des Menschengeschlechts« und sein Verhältnis zur Druckfassung", 50–63; C. BULTMANN, "Herder als Schüler des Philologen Michaelis", 64–80; G. VOM HOFE, "Herders »Hieroglyphen«-Poetik", 190–209; S.-A. JØRGENSEN, "«wenn Sie wüssten, wie ich Sie buchstabiere»: Herder als Dolmetscher Hamanns in der «Aeltesten Urkunde»", 98–107; F. W. R. KANTZENBACH, "Die «Aelteste Urkunde des Menschengeschlechts» – Herders Schrift im theologiegeschichtlichen Zusammenhang", 292–320; T. MARKWORTH, "Zur Selbstdarstellung Herders in den ersten Bückeburger Jahren", 81–97; T. NAMOWICZ, "Anthropologie und Geschichtsphilosophie in Herders «Aeltester Urkunde» in ihrem Verhältnis zum Menschenbild des Sturm und Drang", 245–67; C. BULTMANN, *Die biblische Urgeschichte in der Aufklärung. Johann Gottfried Herders Interpretation der Genesis als Antwort auf die Religionskritik David Humes* (Tübingen 1999); M. BUNGE, "Herder's Historical View of Religion and the Study of Religion in the Nineteenth Century and Today", in: W. KOEPKE (ed.), *Johann Gottfried Herder. Academic Disciplines and the Pursuit of Knowledge* (Columbia, SC 1996) 232–43; U. CILLIEN, *Johann Gottfried Herder – Christlicher Humanismus* (Düsseldorf 1972); R. T. CLARK, *Herder. His Life and Thought* (Berkeley / Los Angeles 1955); H. W. FREI, *The Eclipse of Biblical Narrative. A Study in Eighteenth Century Hermeneutics* (New Haven, CN 1974; repr. 1977, 1978, 1980); G. FÜRST, *Sprache als metaphorischer Prozeß. Johann Gottfried Herders Theorie der Sprache* (Tübinger Theologische Studien 31, Mainz 1988); H.-G. GADAMER, "Herder und die geschichtliche Welt", Nachwort, in: JOHANN GOTTFRIED HERDER, *Auch eine Philosophie der Geschichte zur Bildung der Menschheit* (Frankfurt a. M. 1967) 146–77 = idem, *Kleine Schriften III. Idee und Sprache* (Tübingen 1972) 101–17; U. GAIER, *Herders Sprachphilosophie und Erkenntniskritik* (Problemata 118; Stuttgart-Bad Cannstatt 1988); R. HAYM, *Herder nach seinem Leben und seinen Werken 1-2* (Berlin 1877–85, repr. Berlin 1954; Osnabrück 1978); M. HEINZ, *Sensualistischer Idealismus. Untersuchungen zur Erkenntnistheorie des jungen Herder (1763–1778)* (Studien zum 18. Jahrhundert 17; Hamburg 1994); J. HEISE, *Johann Gottfried Herder zur Einführung* (Hamburg 1998; ²2006); A. HERZ, *Dunkler Spiegel – helles Dasein. Natur, Geschichte, Kunst im Werk Johann Gottfried Herders* (Heidelberg 1996); F. JAEGER / J. RÜSEN, *Geschichte des Historismus. Eine Einführung*

---

[103] In selection. R. SMEND, Bückeburger Gespräche 1988 (1989) 1, speaks of a *allmählich uferlosen Literatur über Johann Gottfried Herder.*

(Munich 1992); D. W. JÖNS, *Begriff und Problem der historischen Zeit bei Johann Gottfried Herder* (Göteborger Germanistische Forschungen 2; Göteborg 1956); F. W. KANTZENBACH, *Johann Gottfried Herder in Selbstzeugnissen und Bilddokumenten* (Rowohlts Monographien; Hamburg 1970); M. KESSLER / V. LEPPIN (eds.), *Johann Gottfried Herder: Aspekte seines Lebenswerkes* (AKG 92; Berlin / New York 2005); H.-J. KRAUS, *Geschichte der historisch-kritischen Erforschung des Alten Testaments* (Neukirchen-Vluyn 1956; ³1983 [⁴1988]); A. LÖCHTE, *Johann Gottfried Herder: Kulturtheorie und Humanitätsidee der "Ideen", "Humanitätsbriefe" und "Adrastea"* (Epistemata. Reihe Literaturwissenschaft 540; Würzburg 2005); F. MEINECKE, *Die Entstehung des Historismus*. Werke 3 (Munich 1959); E. A. MENZE, "Religion as the »Yardstick of Reason« and the »Primary Disposition of Humankind« in Herder's Ideen", in: *Vom Selbstdenken. Aufklärung und Aufklärungskritik in Herders »Ideen zur Philosophie der Geschichte der Menschheit«* (ed. R. Otto / J. H. Zammito; Heidelberg 2001) 37–47; M. METZGER, *Die Paradieseserzählung. Die Geschichte ihrer Auslegung von J. Clericus bis W. L. M. de Wette* (Bonn 1959); H. MEYER, "Überlegungen zu Herders Metaphern für Geschichte", ABG 25 (1981) 88–114; K. MUELLER-VOLMER (ed.), *Herder Today. Contributions from the International Herder Conference Nov. 5–8, 1987, Stanford, California* (Berlin / New York 1990), containing esp. H. MUELLER-SIEVERS, "»Gott als Schriftsteller«. Herder and the Hermeneutie Tradition", 319–30; P. PFAFF, "Hieroglyphische Historie. Zu Herders Auch eine Philosophie der Geschichte zur Bildung der Menschheit", Euphorion 77 (1983) 407–18; A. RECKERMANN, *Sprache und Metaphysik. Zur Kritik der sprachlichen Vernunft bei Herder und Humboldt* (Munich 1979); H. GRAF REVENTLOW, *Epochen* IV (Munich 2001) 189–200; G. SAUDER (ed.), *Johann Gottfried Herder 1744–1803* (Hamburg 1987), containing esp. G. VOM HOFE, "«Weitstrahlsinnige» Ur-Kunde. Zur Eigenart und Begründung des Historismus beim jungen Herder", 364–82; M. MAURER, "Die Geschichtsphilosophie des jungen Herder in ihrem Verhältnis zur Aufklärung", 141–55; H. SCHNUR, *Schleiermachers Hermeneutik und ihre Vorgeschichte im 18. Jahrhundert. Studien zur Bibelauslegung, zu Hamann, Herder und F. Schlegel* (Stuttgart / Weimar 1994); W. SCHOTTROFF, "«Offenbarung Gottes ist Morgenroth, Aufgang der Frühlingssonne fürs Menschengeschlecht». Johann Gottfried Herder und die biblische Urgeschichte", in: J. EBACH / R. FABER (eds.), *Bibel und Literatur* (Munich 1995) 259–76; H. C. SEEBA, "Geschichte als Dichtung. Herders Beitrag zur Ästhetisierung der Geschichtsschreibung", Storia della storiografia 8 (1985) 50–72; R. SIMON, *Das Gedächtnis der Interpretation. Gedächtnistheorie als Fundament für Hermeneutik, Ästhetik und Interpretation bei Johann Gottfried Herder* (Studien zum achtzehnten Jahrhundert 23; Hamburg 1998); R. SMEND, *Epochen der Bibelkritik* (Gesammelte Studien 3; BevTh 109; Munich 1991); idem, *Deutsche Alttestamentler in drei Jahrhunderten* (Göttingen 1989); C. TAYLOR, "The Importance of Herder", in: E. and A. MARGALIT (eds.), *Isaiah Berlin. A Celebration* (Chicago / London 1991) 40–63; T. WILLI, *Herders Beitrag zum Verstehen des Alten Testaments* (BGBH 8; Tübingen 1971); idem, "Die Metamorphose der Bibelwissenschaft in Herders Umgang mit dem Alten Testament", in: M. BOLLACHER (ed.), *Johann Gottfried Herder. Geschichte und Kultur* (Würzburg 1994) 239–56; M. ZAREMBA, *Johann Gottfried Herder: Prediger der Humanität. Eine Biografie* (Köln e.a. 2002); T. ZIPPERT, *Bildung durch Offenbarung. Das Offenbarungsverständnis des jungen Herder als Grundmotiv seines theologisch-philosophisch-literarischen Lebenswerks* (MThSt 39; Marburg 1994); *Herder-Gedenken: Interdisziplinäre Beiträge anlässlich des 200. Todestages von Johann Gottfried Herder Frankfurt/Main 18. 12. 2003* (ed. W.-L. Federlin; Frankfurt/Main e.a. 2005).

Special abbreviations (see above):
FA = *Werke in zehn Bänden* (ed. M. Bollacher e.a.)
SWS = *Sämtliche Werke* (ed. B. Suphan e.a.)

Johann Gottfried Herder (1744–1803) through all his life in his official positions was a pastor and leading churchman. Recently he has been detected anew in what he was – in the centre of his thinking – a theologian. The erroneous common opinion that regarded him mainly as a man of letters, an aesthete, a theorist of history, however, is not without foundation, because all this belonged to the reach of his interests. In his extensive engagement in the intellectual problems of his time, he was a first-rate universalist.

For his importance in the history of biblical interpretation, one has to include several aspects of his thinking. That he tried his new approach on biblical texts is not unexpected, as the Bible in the eighteenth century still retained its central role for the discussion of different topics. During his life he wrote on Old and New Testament texts. One main engagement of his was in Hebrew poetry, which he treated in several essays. But it must not be isolated, as often done, because he dealt with it in the interest of revelation. We will show this in following his exegesis of the first chapters of Genesis. Thus, it is rooted in his hermeneutical efforts, closely connected with the problems of understanding in general. Other aspects are his philosophy of language, which he started early in his career, closely related to his aesthetic theory of knowledge. It cannot be completely divided from his philosophy of history. He also was engaged in the promotion of humanity,[104] though calling him a humanist would be a mistake. At this point he participated in the ideals of Enlightenment. The fact that these themes are closely interconnected renders a comprehensive understanding of Herder's system extremely complicated. The earlier view, which distinguished between different periods in Herder's convictions – an early affinity to Enlightenment, followed by a "conversion" in Bückeburg and a later return to idealism in Weimar – had to be abandoned.[105] The difficulties become more troublesome by Herder's impressionistic-emphatic style, in which he is one of the most prominent representatives of the *Sturm und Drang* movement, though in his intentions he clearly differed from its anthropology.[106]

The influences, which stamped Herder's world-view, go back to the years of his academic studies in Königsberg (1762–64). There Herder attended the lectures of the pre-critical Kant, who acquainted his hearers also with Alexander Gottlieb Baumgarten (1714–62), the founder of Aesthetics as a methodology of knowledge besides rational thinking,[107] and with Rousseau. As important was presumably his theological teacher, the nearly forgotten T. C. Lilienthal (1717–1782),[108] who, though being orthodox in his dogmatic, in his lectures on hermeneutics referred to S. J. Baumgarten (1706–57), who allowed to human experience of salvation-truths a place *besides* the Bible. J. G. Hamann (1730–88), with whom he remained in lifelong friendly contact after their first meeting in Königsberg, was important for Herder's aesthetic approach to language – by Hamann's thesis about poetry as the original language of humankind in his *Aesthetica in nuce* (Summary of Aesthetics) – and history, though he did not share Hamann's Lutheran belief in justification by Jesus Christ's sacrifice on the cross and the "condescendence" of God in Jesus Christ in the incarnation.[109] Especially G. W. Leibniz (1646–1716) – his main work *Nouveaux essais*, published posthumously in 1765, he read in Riga – by his doctrine of *monads* as bearers of a dynamic power and the world as "pre-stabilised harmony" was important for some of his basic principles.

---

[104] Cf. especially the *Briefe zur Beförderung der Humanität*, FA 7.

[105] Cf. esp. Rogerson, Bekehrung (1980). According to Zippert, Bildung (1994) 215, Herder's awareness of his office is important for the shift. Markworth, Selbstdarstellung (1989) 89–90, however, speaks about an "existential crisis" and a change in Herder's concept of providence at this time.

[106] Cf. Namowicz, Anthropology (1989).

[107] Extracts of his *Aestetica* in the Latin-German edition (ed. H. R. Schweizer), A. G. Baumgarten, *Theoretische Aesthetik. Die grundlegenden Abschnitte aus der "Aesthetica" (1750–58)* (Hamburg 1983). More recently also the impact of British empirism (Locke and Berkeley) on Herder's aesthetics has been stressed; cf. esp. Clark, Herder (1955) 217–31; Nisbet, Revision (1973) 105–07.

[108] Herder recommends his apologetic work *Die gute Sache der Offenbarung* (Königsberg 1760) to the readers of his *Briefe, das Studium der Theologie betreffend*, 4th letter, FA 9/1, 179, as an "ocean of scholarship".

[109] Cf. Jørgensen, «Wenn Sie wüßten» (1989) 98–107.

Focussing our attention on Herder's contributions to the interpretation of the Bible, we have to keep in our memory that his observations on the Bible were always connected with his other fields of interest. Already during Herder's sojourn in Riga (1764–69) he wrote a manuscript on the Biblical primeval narrative (Genesis 1–11), which for a long time had disappeared and remained unprinted until 1993: *Über die ersten Urkunden des menschlichen Geschlechts. Einige Anmerkungen* (the so-called "Schaffhausener Urmanuskript"; FA 5, 9–178).[110] Fragments containing considerations about the material from a little later, and partially printed after Herder's death, are available under the title *Fragmente zu einer «Archäologie des Morgenlandes»* (SWS VI, 1–129), together with a collection of material from the years 1771–1772 under the headline: *Unterhaltungen und Briefe über die ältesten Urkunden* (131–192). The essay in FA 5 contains already the thesis – known from J. J. Astruc[111] – that for writing the primeval history Moses used old documents, already existing in written form. These were written on the basis of still more ancient poetic traditions. "They are from the time of traditions, and then everything became poetical" (FA 5, 26). Here we also first meet with the statement that was to become famous from his later works: Because the orthodox doctrine of verbal inspiration was "enthusiastic" in Herder's eyes – "God is thinking without words, without symbols", "in the Bible everything is completely human ... By a human spirit every written thought was produced" (FA 5, 29). This does not diminish the divine origin of the primeval story, because "the author was a holy person, building on the holy tradition ... originating from God's teaching the human beings" (FA 5, 35). This pre-supposition, by which Herder got rid of the traditional dogmatic restrictions, he repeated later in his *Briefe, das Studium der Theologie betreffend* (1780–81; FA 9/1, 139–607). He writes in the first letter: *Menschlich muß man die Bibel lesen, denn sie ist ein Buch durch Menschen für Menschen geschrieben* ("As [a] human [document] one has to read the Bible, because it is a book written by human beings for human beings ..."; FA 9/1, 145). Thereby opening the way to a historical exegesis of the Bible, he nevertheless speaks again about the "divine book" (ibid.). In his fragments to an *Archäologie des Morgenlandes* he is engaged again with the creation narrative (Gen 1:1–2:4). His starting point here is language; more exactly the thesis known already from the Church Fathers (Origen, Jerome, Augustine), that Hebrew is the original language of humankind. Herder extends this thesis to the language of all oriental peoples (the *Morgenländer*).

The topic 'language'[112] was basic for Herder's thinking, especially after he had responded to the prize competition of the Royal Academy in Berlin 1769 with the essay: *Über den Ursprung der Sprache* (SWS 5, 1–147). In this he attempted to show that the origin of language is not di-

---

[110] Cf. the commentary of the editor R. Smend, ibid. 1328–56; Arnold, Schaffhauser Urmanuskript (1989) 50–63; Bultmann, Herder als Schüler (1989); idem, Urgeschichte in der Aufklärung (1999) 39–48.

[111] See, further, Ch. 34, sect. 3, in this volume. It is debated whether Herder knew his book, at least at that time.

[112] Cf. Fürst, Sprache als metaphorischer Prozeß (1988).

vine,[113] not brutish, but specifically human, and the exact origin of language is to be sought with reflection, which invented language.[114] In the fragments *Ueber die neuere deutsche Litteratur. Eine Beilage zu den Briefen, die neueste Litteratur betreffend* (1766/67; SWS 1,131–531) he had already developed his theory about the different ages of language: In its childhood *ihre Sprache spricht für Auge und Ohr, für Sinne und Leidenschaften* ("speaks for eye and ear, for senses and passions"; SWS I, 152). In the period of youth its fierceness was mitigated, but it remained *sinnlich und reich an kühnen Bildern* ("sensual and wealthy with bold metaphors"). It was "the period of poets". The adult language was characterised by prose (SWS I, 154). The old age of language is a time of decline: *Das hohe Alter weiß statt Schönheit blos von Richtigkeit* ("Instead of beauty the old age knows only about correctness"; SWS I, 155). Important also is his theory of knowledge, in which he connects language, aesthetics and philosophy of history to a philosophy of experience as an alternative model to Kant's philosophy of transcendence. Recent research (H. ADLER, H. D. IRMSCHER; M. HEINZ, A. RECKERMANN e.a.) rehabilitated Herder in his approach.[115]

According to Herder we must be sensitive to the original language of humankind in order to understand the greatness of such an "original text" as the creation narrative in its "simplicity". *So trete man in die Zeiten zurück, da der uralte Morgenländer ("oriental man") noch sein Weltall würklich innerhalb dieser großen blauen Halbkugel und also zwischen Erd' und Himmel fühlte* (SWS VI, 4; cf. 34). In order to understand and interpret a work of the remote past we have to place ourselves in the mental state of its author, his public, his nation and at least into the intention of this his piece. Feeling is the way of understanding,[116] because as a human written document it is poetry. Nevertheless a historical distance remains.

However, the text speaks above all about man as creature and therefore as in the image of God. He is image because of his freedom, being able to act, to speak and to be educated – this quality even affects his corporal existence. The way to theology leads through anthropology. Nevertheless man is also an animal (SWS VI, 25–28, cf. 54–55). The insight "into the nature of things, into the plan of nature", which God granted to man with the creation (SWS VI, 88) is not effected by reason, but by feeling, perceiving in the work of art, the Creator as the artist.

In 1774 Herder published his completed work *Aelteste Urkunde des Menschengeschlechts*. In spite of its effusive, aphoristic style[117] a concrete plan becomes visible, and Herder introduces himself as thoroughly informed about the exegetical knowledge of his time. After having criticised the existing "schools" (natural science blaming the worldview of the primeval story, philo-

---

[113] Thus the orthodox opinion of J. P. SÜSSMILCH, *Beweis. daß der Ursprung der menschlichen Sprache göttlich sey* (Berlin 1766); cf. SWS 5, 10.

[114] SWS 5, 35–36. On the role of language with Herder, cf. Reckermann, Sprache (1979); Gaier, Sprachphilosophie (1988).

[115] Cf. Herz, Dunkler Spiegel (1996) 45–68. Remarkable is the reference to an analogous approach with L. WITTGENSTEIN's *Philosophische Untersuchungen* (Frankfurt a. M. 1967) 53. Taylor, Importance of Herder (1991), stresses the holistic aspect in Herder's theory of language.

[116] On this theory of knowledge, by which he presents an alternative to the rationalism of Enlightenment, represented by Kant, cf. Heinz, Sensualistischer Idealismus (1994). She also treats (81–108) the fragments of 1769: *Grundsätze der Philosophie* and *Zum Sinn des Gefühls* ("Basic Rules of Philosophy" and "About the Sense of Feeling"), in which Herder explains his approach.

[117] Haym, Herder, 1 (1885) 555, calls the first three parts a "monstrum horrendum". Kantzenbach, Herder (1970) 69, doubts because of the style and the *Unzahl gesuchter Hypothesen* in the essay the solidity of Herder's scholarship.

sophic cosmology, mystic-theosophic and metaphysic ideas about Divinity), he begins with securing the sense of the most important terms "of the Orient" (FA 5, 200). The pre-supposition is that the *Morgenländer* ("oriental man") connects sensual observations with feeling, for instance when observing the firmament and the surrounding earth as a totality. Thereby he receives *das ganze Weltall in seiner Seele* (FA 5, 201). He comprehends the earth as a symbol of solidity, enduring in eternity, or he feels that the cosmos was a dark abyss before the creation, upon which the Spirit of God descended. "Heaven and earth" is an example for the parallelism, which Herder had learned from R. Lowth.[118] When God says: "Let there be light – and there was light" (Gen 1:3), Herder meditates extensively about "God's appearance in nature" (FA 5, 205). On Gen 1:26–27, speaking about God's decision to create human beings, he observes that after the closing words in v. 25: "and God saw that it was good", the usual benediction does not follow. The creation is waiting upon God's counsel: *Wo ist sinnlicher Zweck des Allen? – Einheit?* (FA 5, 230). This break prepares for the creation of man in the image of God. Only in this way is the unity of creation achieved. The image of God is visible in the beauty of human soul and body, but central are the deeds of men as the "imitation of God" (FA 5, 232–33). This explanation deserves to be taken in earnest even in present discussions on the sense of the 'image'! Herder does not overlook that the reality differs from the ideal: *Städtische, zum Staub gebückte Menschen, denen das Bild Gottes freilich oft nichts ist, als Katechismusfrage* (FA 5, 233). But the ideal remains as incitement for life.

Important is Herder's description of revelation: The "most ancient wonderful revelation of God" can still be felt every morning when observing the transition from darkness to dawn (FA 5, 239–41). The feeling of God's presence arises out of the *Morgengemälde* (FA 5, 244). God's power fills the whole nature – this was an idea already of the young Herder: *Gott erfüllt den Raum … durch seine Kraft* (unpublished fragment, SWS 32, 228). But it is more than feeling: In a separate chapter (FA V, 246–257) Herder speaks about *Unterricht unter der Morgenröte*. It is important to see how Herder repudiates the predominant opinion that God reveals himself only in nature. Instead the rising dawn is for the *lebenden Naturmenschen* the *figure* (*Bild*), in which the *Morgenlektion Gottes* occurs (FA 5, 248). This is God's *Lehrmethode* (ibid.) for *das Menschengeschlecht in seiner Kindheit* (FA 5, 250). The education of humankind belonged to the standard ideas of Enlightenment – but Herder adds the catchword "revelation". Herder completes these important statements by a chapter on the seven-days-scheme, leading to the sabbath (FA 5, 282–292). This chapter is framed by remarks on his use of the word "hieroglyph". Writing in a period before the Egyptian hieroglyphs were deciphered, the word meant for him a mysterious sign (FA 5, 267–82), woven into the texture of the world (FA 5, 316). He believes to have detected such a hieroglyph in the structure of the seven-days work of the creation-story, as the *erste Schriftversuch*

---

[118] See, further, Ch. 40, sect. 3, in this volume.

Gottes mit dem Menschen (FA 5, 276). Upon a unity follows a differentiation, then a renewed unity, followed by a duality and the closing unity: *Laß zuerst, mein Leser, alles Außerwesentliche … aus, rücke die simplen nackten Bilder selbst, wie sie folgen, näher zusammen, was siehest du? … Gemälde der Morgenröthe* (FA 5, 239)

	Licht	
Himmelshöhe		Erdniedere
	Lichter	
Himmels-		Erdgeschöpfe

Sabbat*
(*FA 5, 271)[119]

Also man as the image of God is a "hieroglyph of the creation" (FA 5, 292–94): *Mensch, Bild Gottes! und selbst das sichtbare Nachbild und Hieroglyphe der Schöpfung* (FA 5, 292). *Der Mensch mit Haupt, Händ' und Füßen und dem Zusammenhangenden des Körpers Vorbild der Ersten Hieroglyphe!* (FA 5, 293). He also repeats now publicly his opinion that Moses adopted the creation narrative – *die älteste Urkunde des Menschengeschlechtes*, which originally belonged to all religions – in Egypt, but not from the Egyptians (FA 5, 313–14). This he attempts to show by a detailed comparative history of religions, starting with Egypt, but including Phoenicia, early Greek philosophy etc. He denies to contemporary egyptologists as W. Warburton (1698–1779)[120] their early insight that the hieroglyphs were ancient Egypt's priest- and inscription-letters. Instead, in his opinion, the hieroglyphic figure belongs in the background of the whole Egyptian system of deities.[121] Before cuneiform and hieroglyphic texts could be read, Herder was forced to use exclusively hellenistie material (as Manetho) and the Church Fathers. It was not sufficient for gaining an adequate picture of the ancient cultures. But methodically he was a pioneer in the field.

In the second volume, published in 1776, Herder comments on Gen 2:4–25, which he understands as an introduction to the following "garden-story" in Genesis 3. Momentous for later research[122] is Herder's innovative definition of the primeval stories as *heilige Sagen der Vorwelt* (headline on p. 491). He also revises an older opinion and regards the stories as history (FA 5, 566). In the explanation of the Fall, Herder now sees more clearly and dwells upon the consequences of the original sin for Eve and Adam (FA 5, 589–94). Retaliation for Eve's sin: bearing with pains, becoming a house-wife. Adam drudging in the field, burdened by sorrow and toil. Both on the way to being buried beneath the soil (FA 5,551–52, quoting Job 7:1; 14:1). In between a naturalistic explanation: The consequence of eating from the fruit of the tree of know-

---

[119] For the background, cf. Pfaff, Hieroglyphische Historie (1983); Simon, Gedächtnis (1998).

[120] The Divine Legislation of Moses Demonstrated 1–2 (London 1738–41; repr. New York 1978 [British Philosophers and Theologians of the 17th and 18th Century]).

[121] Cf. esp. his letter to Merck, 15.10.1770, *Briefe*, II (ed. Dobbek / Arnold) 261.

[122] H. Gunkel, see HBOT III (in prep.). For the moment, cf. Reventlow, Epochen IV (2001) 327–46.

ledge: the sense of shame, opening Adam's and Eve's eyes for their nakedness, marks the transition to puberty. But Herder also arrives at an enlightened vision of progress: Residence in Eden could no longer continue further since *eine gewisse Entwicklung der Menschlichen Fähigkeiten und Empfindungen da war*, so that this situation *nicht Unter-, sondern Über- und Fortgang des Menschengeschlechts im Plane Gottes gewesen* (FA 5, 604). On the other hand, the snake is the symbol of the harmful *Aufklärer: Ihr Aufklärer, ihr Verfeiner der Menschheit; allerdings habt ihr aufgeklärt und verfeinet, aber daß wir – uns nackt finden* (FA 5, 554). Some traits remind us of Kant's exegesis of the chapters, but the emphasis is totally different.[123]

All in all, Herder's main intention was to refute by a sort of apologetic the rationalistic criticism of the Bible, even though keeping his distance from Orthodoxy. After a shorter discussion of Genesis 4–6 the work ends as a fragment.

Herder's decision in this early essay, which he abandoned later,[124] to value the primeval stories as history – at the first glance following orthodox opinion – is important for his views. It places Gen 1–11 at the beginning of an ongoing history, on which he also develops his own opinion.

We have to cast a glance on his most original contribution to the philosophy of history, *Auch eine Philosophie zur Geschichte der Menschheit* (1774; FA 4, 9–107).[125] In the typical style of *Sturm und Drang* Herder guides his readers through the ages. He wrote this book against Voltaire's (pseudonymous) sceptic-pessimistic *Philosophie de l'histoire* (1765). In this the author describes history as a sequence of ruins. But he wrote as much against the enlightened optimistic expectation of a continual progress in the history of humankind. The curtain of the stage opens for a look at the first couple. Two metaphorical pictures[126] structure the whole: The first is the picture of a tree. *Der Keim fällt in die Erde und erstirbt* (FA 5,11) – an obvious allusion to John 12:24 – and becomes, in analogy to an embryo formed hidden in his mother's womb, the origin of a big tree stretching out many boughs. The cedar – again a biblical picture (cf. Ezek 17:22–24; 31:3–9) – is a symbol of humankind, spread out in the world in many peoples. The other picture, structuring the course of history in analogy to the life of an individual, is the succession of ages. On the time of "childhood", by Herder identified with the period of the Patriarchs, follows "boyhood" (*Knabenalter*), the age of Ancient Egypt and the Phoenicians. Ancient Greece is "youth" (*Jünglingszeit*), represented by the noble Greek young man, a period of freedom and the development of poetry and fine arts. The period of Roman rule, in which all the peoples were forced under one yoke and their national character destroyed (FA 4, 31), is the period of adult manhood. It is easy to see that again a Biblical text (the four kingdoms of Daniel 2) stands in the background. Herder's critics asked whether he regarded the times since the fall of the Roman Empire as the period of senility, but he did not intend to cover the whole history by the analogy. He also refused to see history as unbroken progress: The different ages are independent of one another, each possessing its special character and worth. That does not mean that they are not interrelated. Thus, Greek art, idealised by J. J. Winckelmann (1717–1768), has been influenced by Egyptian art etc. It has been argued[127] that Herder's view of historical development follows a "secularised" typological scheme. This presupposes the expectation of an ongoing progress in history. Herder in fact perceives a goal in the history of humankind: the *Bildung der Menschheit*, as indicated in the headline of his essay and repeated at its

---

[123] Cf. also Herz, Dunkler Spiegel (1996) 246–52.
[124] In *Ideen zur Philosophie der Geschichte der Menschheit* (1784–91; FA 6) the whole construction is different, and a view of the cosmos has replaced the Bible as basis.
[125] Cf. recently Simon, Gedächtnis (1998) 110–145; Maurer, Geschichtsphilosophie (1987).
[126] On Herder's metaphoric from nature cf. Meyer, Metaphern für Geschichte (1981).
[127] Cf. Malsch, Hamanns Bibeltypologie (1979) 93–114; cf. however, also the discussion, 114–116.

end.[128] He speaks also about a *Vorsehung* acting behind the scene.[129] But there he sees also his own present time as a period full of darker sides; there is no unbroken progress.

Herder's special sympathy is devoted to the first age (FA 4, 14):

> *Das Hirtenleben im schönsten Klima der Welt ..., die ruhige und zugleich wandernde Lebensart der väterlichen Patriarchenhütte, mit allem was sie gibt und dem Auge entziehet... welch ein erwählter Garten Gottes zur Erziehung der ersten, zartesten Menschengewächse! Siehe diesen Mann voll Kraft und Gefühl Gottes, aber so innig fühlend, als hier der Saft im Baum treibt ... Die ganze Welt rings-um, voll Segen Gottes: eine große, mutige Familie des Allvaters. ... Mensch, Mann, Weib, Vater, Mutter, Sohn, Erbe, Priester Gottes, Regent und Hausvater, für alle Jahrtausende sollt er da gebildet werden!*

The picture of the ancestor Adam, surrounded by his large family of several generations, depends on the longevity of the Patriarchs, which Herder is prepared to accept on the basis of the biblical numbers (FA 4, 12). In Herder's eyes this is the ideal past: *ewig wird Patriarchengegend und Patriarchenzeit das goldne Zeitalter der kindlichen Menschheit bleiben* (FA 4, 14-15). On the other hand, Herder (FA 4, 41-42) also partakes in the optimistic expectation of Enlightenment that the development of humankind is going on in spite of setbacks and interruptions like a stream flowing to the sea or like a growing tree to a goal. Herder stresses that every age has its own value (FA 4, 41), but there is continuity between them, *fortgehende Entwicklung, Schauplatz einer leitenden Absicht auf Erden!... Schauplatz der Gottheit* (FA 4, 42).[130] This tendency is strengthened in the *Ideen*: There Herder speaks about man as *der erste Freigelassene der Schöpfung* (FA 6, 145-46), he is gifted with reason and freedom, and there is a rising development in nature from stone via plants and animals to man (FA 6, 1 66). In his *Ideen*, perhaps under Goethe's influence, Herder calls the goal "humanity". But his understanding of the term is different. Whether Herder's concept of humanity with MALSCH[131] can be regarded as a form of secularisation, is debated. Already DOBBEK remarked, *daß Herders Humanitätsidee wesentlich vom Religiösen her zu verstehen, und darum mehr mystisch als aufklärerisch ist*,[132] which MENZE recently confirms.[133] Also in the *Ideen* Herder utters his conviction: *Religion [ist] die höchste Humanität des Menschen* (FA 6, 160) and speaks about creation and the human soul as *ein lebendiges, wirkendes Etwas, in dem der Schöpfer selbst gegenwärtig ist, in dem sich seine Gotteskraft einwohnend offenbaret* (FA 6, 68-69). Herder even declared: *Im Grunde enthält das Buch nichts als das Resultat des 1ten Theils der Urkunde nur auf anderen Wegen.*[134]

Connected with this picture of history is the much-debated question whether Herder can be regarded as the father of historicism. This thesis, pronounced by W. DILTHEY,[135] R. STADELMANN,[136] F. MEINECKE[137] e.a.,[138] recently has been debated on the basis of the perspectivity of Herder's historical view (which always connects the present generation to tradition in a form of application[139]) and the metaphoric of his language.[140] M. HEINZ[141] states: *daß die Wahrnehmung der Bückeburger*

---

[128] FA 4, 107.

[129] The term stands at a prominent place, ibid.

[130] There is a split between Herder's *totalen Invididualisierung der Geschichte*, which allows no connection between the periods, and his conviction that God guides history, cf. Irmscher, Hermeneutik Herders (1973) 26-27.

[131] Cf. also Ruprecht, Humanität (1980).

[132] Dobbek, Hurnanitätsidee (1949) 99.

[133] Menze, Religion (2001) 38.

[134] *Briefe* 5 (ed. Dobbek / Arnold) 43. For details cf. recently Menze, ibid.

[135] *Die Einbildungskraft des Dichters*, *Gesammelte Schriften* VI (Stuttgart ⁴1962) 120.

[136] Der historische Sinn (1928).

[137] Historismus 3 (²1959) 355-410. For him the two *Grundgedanken* of historicism (369) are first to be met with Herder.

[138] Cf. i.a. Jaeger / Rüsen, Geschichte des Historismus (1992) 25-26; also some essays in Bollacher, Geschichte und Kultur (1994).

[139] Cf. Jöns, Historische Zeit (1956) 82-98; Bunge, Herder's Historical View (1994).

[140] Cf. Irmscher, Grundzüge der Hermeneutik (1973), esp. 36-57; Seeba, Geschichte als Dichtung (1985); already Gadamer, *Nachwort* to his edition of *Auch eine Philosophie* (FA 4, 146-177), = idem, Kleine Schriften III (1972) 101-17; vom Hofe, »Weitstrahlsinnige« Ur-Kunde (1987), who stresses the importance of Herder's *Aelteste Urkunde* for his view of history.

Geschichtsphilosophie aus der Perspektive des Historismus eine einseitige Rezeptionsweise darstellt, die das eigentliche Fundament von Herders Geschichtsdenken verdeckt.

The anthropological approach leads Herder also in his translation and comment on the Song of Songs: *Lieder der Liebe* (FA 3, 431–521). Herder explains the Song in contrast to the traditional allegorical explanation of the biblical book with Jews and Christians in the verbal sense as a collection of Solomon's love-songs, arranged according to the growth of the king's love. Love is the main theme.[142] This understanding, also adopted by Eichhorn, who even denied Solomon's authorship, has been acknowledged by modem critical exegesis.

The best-known of Herder's books on the Bible and, though a fragment, also the longest: *Vom Geist der hebräischen Poesie* can rightly be regarded as a re-writing of the *Aelteste Urkunde*.[143] It is also an answer to Lowth.[144] Herder's main intention in the two volumes, the first of which is written in the form of a dialogue, is to describe the Hebrew poetic texts of the period before the Israelite kingdom, among which he numbers in volume 2 Job, Genesis 49, Deuteronomy 33 and especially the work of Moses. Volume 1 describes Israel's cosmology in "the most ancient tradition of this people" and "the basic ideas of their poetry and religion from the legends of the fathers" (FA 5, 927). The material is mixed – there is also a passage on the prophets (FA 5, 993–1017) and the Psalms (FA 5, 1189–1282). The theological intention also of this work – often neglected – becomes visible through the connections to the earlier writing. The misunderstanding that fondness for the Hebrew language was the main reason for writing these books induced H.-J. KRAUS[145] to subsume Hamann (!) and Herder under the headline "Hebrew Humanism". Hebrew was the language of the Bible, *therefore* a holy language, and worthy of the most intense study for a lover of languages. That it was regarded as the oldest language of the world was common opinion in the period.

How important the Bible was for Herder's theology, can be seen in his *Briefe, das Studium der Theologie betreffend*. Not only that the first letter begins with the sentence: *Es bleibt dabei, … das beste Studium der Gottesgelehrsamkeit ist Studium der Bibel* (FA 9/1, 145), but also the first 24 letters are dedicated to the Old and New Testament. Herder concludes this part with a statement on the Bible: *Sie ist der Grund des Glaubens für jeden Christen, nicht bloß für den Theologen* (FA 9/1, 367). Though he also skips over central theological aspects in the Bible under the influence of the theological climate of his time, he remains among the ones who mostly stimulated its study in the following period.

---

[141] Historismus oder Metaphysik? (1994) 85.
[142] H. Mueller-Sievers, «Gott als Schriftsteller» (1990) 326–30, sees Herder's hermeneutics at this point on the transition from biblical to secular hermeneuties, but without sufficient reason.
[143] Cf. Bultmann, Urgeschichte (1999) 16.
[144] Cf. FA 5, 663.
[145] Geschichte (³1983) 114. Cf. also Fürst, Sprache (1988) 135, e.a. – Also christening Herder a "Christian Humanist" (Cillien, Christlicher Humanismus, 1972) is inadequate.

4. Johann Gottfried Eichhorn – His *Einleitung in das Alte Testament* as a 'Summa' of the New 'Higher Criticism'

Sources: J. G. EICHHORN: *Briefe die biblische Exegese betreffend: Allgemeine Bibliothek der biblischen Literatur* 5 (1793/94) 203–53; *Urgeschichte: Repertorium für biblische und morgenländische Literatur* IV (1779) 129–256 (new edn. ed. J. P. Gabler; 1; 2,1.2; Altdorf / Nürnberg 1790–93); *Ueber Mosis Nachrichten von der Noachischen Flut. I. Buch Mose VI-VII-VIII-IX: Repertorium für biblische und morgenländische Literatur* V (1779) 185–216; *Einleitung in das Alte Testament* 1–3 (Leipzig 1780–83); 1–5 (Göttingen [4]1823–24); *Introduction to the Study of the Old Testament. A Fragment* ("Printed for private circulation"; London 1888); *Einleitung in das Neue Testament,* 4 parts in 5 vols. (Leipzig 1804–27); *Einleitung in die apokryphischen Schriften des Alten Testaments* (Leipzig 1795); *Die hebräischen Propheten* 1–3 (Göttingen 1816–19).

General works and studies: G. D'ALESSANDRO, *L'illuminismo dimenticato: Johann Gottfried Eichhorn (1752–1827) e il suo tempo* (La cultura storica 7; Napoli 2000); L. DIESTEL, *Geschichte des Alten Testamentes in der christlichen Kirche* (Jena 1869; repr. Leipzig 1981; see index); H. EWALD, "Ueber die wissenschaftliche Wirksamkeit der ehemaligen Göttingenschen Lehrer J. D. Michaelis, J. G. Eichhorn, Th. Chr.Tychsen", *Jahrbücher der biblischen Wissenschaft* I (1849) 26–34; C. HARTLICH / W. SACHS, *Der Ursprung des Mythosbegriffs in der modernen Bibelwissenschaft* (Tübingen 1952); K. HEUSSI, *Geschichte der theologischen Fakultät Jena* (Weimar 1954); O. KAISER, "Eichhorn und Kant" (see sect. 2 above); H.-J. KRAUS, *Geschichte* (see sect. 3 above) 131–51; W. G. KÜMMEL, *Das Neue Testament. Geschichte der Erforschung seiner Probleme* (München 1958, [2]1970); K. LEDER, *Universität Altdorf. Zur Theologie der Aufklärung in Franken. Die theologische Fakultat in Altdorf 1750–1809* (Nürnberg 1965); O. MERK, *Biblische Theologie* (see sect. 2 above); J. PUSCHMANN, *Alttestamentliche Auslegung und geschichtliches Denken bei Semler, Herder, Eichhorn, Schleiermacher und unter besonderer Berücksichtigung de Wette's* (Diss. Hamburg 1959 [manuscript]); REVENTLOW, *Epochen* IV (2001) 209–26; J. W. ROGERSON, *Myth in Old Testament Interpretation,* (BZAW 134; Berlin / New York 1974), Ch. 1, 1–15; E. SEHMSDORF, *Die Prophetenauslegung bei J. G. Eichhorn* (Göttingen 1971); R. SMEND, "Johann Gottfried Eichhorn", in: B. MÖLLER (ed.), *Theologie in Göttingen* (Göttingen 1987) 71–81, = idem, *Deutsche Alttestamentler in drei Jahrhunderten* (Göttingen 1989) 25–37; H.-J. ZOBEL, art. "Eichhorn, Johann Gottfried (1752–1827)", TRE 9 (1982) 369–71.

We met already Johann Gottfried Eichhorn (1752–1827) as a protagonist of historical-critical exegesis in his *Briefen,* arguing against Kant.[146] Eichhorn, after a short period as Professor of Oriental Languages in Jena, became 1778 and was to the end of his life Professor of Philosophy in Göttingen. He was a genuine universalist. His numerous volumes on world-history, history of culture and literature show his broad education. Though written in a fluent style, they are today almost forgotten. His speciality was, however, the Bible, and his abiding importance lies in its interpretation.

During his study in Göttingen Eichhorn was besides the historian A. L. Schlözer mainly a student of the orientalist J. D. Michaelis (1717–91) and the classical philologist C. G. Heyne (1729–1812). From the latter he learned the interpretation of myths, which Heyne explained as the characteristic form of expression of primitive mankind, who was not yet capable of abstract thinking.[147] Eichhorn used this theory for his early interpretation of the biblical primeval story (Genesis 1–3). Published in 1779, it still lacked a theoretical reflection about its method, which his pupil J. Ph. Gabler (see the next section) later added in his commented edition (1790–93).

---

[146] See sect. 2 above.

[147] Some of his essays are collected in V. Verra, *Mito, revelazione e filosofia in J. G. Herder e nel suo tempo* (Milano 1966).

But his principal contribution to the historical-critical exegesis of the OT consists of his *Einleitung in das Alte Testament* (1780–83) (Introduction to the Study of the Old Testament). The word *Einleitung* (Introduction) being old,[148] was first used as a technical term by J. D. Michaelis, *Einleitung in die göttlichen Schriften des Neuen Bundes* I (Göttingen 1750; [3]1788). It received its modern form in connection with historical-critical exegesis not earlier than with Eichhorn. For an adequate assessment of its importance it has to be kept in mind that critical exegesis was still at the time of its appearance a young science. The precursors treated in this volume: Grotius, de La Peyrère, R. Simon, Astruc, Clericus, were isolated figures. Semler's main interests lay in another field. As a biblical historian Eichhorn quite early developed a methodological approach, in which the historical circumstances in the background of a passage, chapter or book were to determine whether it could be attributed to the particular author to whom tradition ascribed it or not.

Above all Eichhorn was the first to extend his critical observations, even though unevenly, upon the whole Old Testament. He structured his work into two main parts: I. The General Introduction. In this part Eichhorn writes about the Scriptures of the Old Testament as a whole, their origin, edition, collection, genuineness and canonicity. His main approach becomes visible already on the first pages, in which he speaks about the fact that of the four oldest peoples of the world (Egyptians, Chaldeans, Phoenicians, Hebrews) three have disappeared without leaving behind any remains of their literature save pitiable fragments.[149] *Von diesen hingegen ist eine ganze Bibliothek der wichtigsten und so alter Schriftsteller noch ietzt vorhanden.*[150] Its most recent author is an approximate contemporary of Herodotus, the father of Greek history! In the same library are poets, prophets and history writers! Who will not ask: Are these books actually works of remote antiquity? What happened to them on their long journey through history?

In defining his task in this way, Eichhorn presents himself as an historian of literature. Theological questions he mostly neglects. His general idea about the composition of the Old Testament books (§ 2; 1, 5–6) is that not all of them came to us as one piece from the hand of their authors. Sometimes the authors themselves, later disciples or collectors put fragmented parts together. The lack of chronological order in the book of Isaiah and the twofold redaction in the book of Jeremiah are to be explained by this procedure. David's songs now occur in different parts of the Psalter.

How were the ancient texts preserved until after the Babylonian exile? (§ 3; I, 7–8) Eichhorn develops the hypothesis of a national library founded by Moses, the basis of which was established by the Pentateuch, which he ordered to be deposited beside the Ark of the Covenant (Deut 31:9.26). Whether also other pre-exilic books were put down there, is uncertain, because "history remains silent".[151] Moses' writings (laws) must have existed in more than one copy, because King Jehoshaphat had installed officials teaching the law in the cities of Judah (2 Chr 17:[9]). Of Jeremiah's prophecies at least two copies ex-

---

[148] It is derived from the title of the work of the monk Adrianus (ca. 440) Εἰσαγωγὴ εἰς τὰς θείας γραφάς.

[149] This seemed to be the case before the grandiose excavations of the Andent Near Eastern capitals in the nineteenth century.

[150] *Einleitung*[1] 1, I, 3.

[151] Here Eichhorn quotes R. Simon, *Histoire critique du Vieux Testament* (Rotterdam 1678, [2]1685 [repr. Frankfurt a. M. 1967], ET 1682).

isted, one in Chaldaea (Dan 9:2), the other presumably in Egypt, where the author lived at the end of his life. In postexilic times (§ 5; I, 11–13) the remains of the earlier scriptures were collected, more recent ones added until the period of Ezra and Nehemiah, in which the OT received its final shape. Eichhorn's careful judgement becomes visible in his remarks regarding the legend of the "Great Synagogue": "Should not here, as generally with legends, a true fact stand in the background...? I do not decide anything, but I cannot declare a tradition untrue, for which the conditions of the period, the situation of the Jews and the intentions of the founders of the new state in Palestine speak so loudly".[152] Upon the question whether all the authors of the Old Testament can be called prophets (§ 9) Eichhorn replies that not all of them were taught by divine teaching.

> When for instance the writers of history are writing the history of their time, they record things, which were known to them at any case as contemporaries. When they were describing what happened in earlier periods, they drew from sources that already existed. ... Thus, if one wants to subsume all the authors of the OT under the name of prophets, one ... will expose the single books to thousand doubts that will at last render the whole OT uncertain.[153]

The scriptures of the Old Testament, however, are genuine, not written by an impostor. The difference of style between them excludes this accusation.[154] Eichhorn detects a gradual decline of language from early to later texts.[155] He regards all the books of the Old Testament as genuine in the sense that they are written in a style fitting to the period they are ascribed to and by authors acquainted with its circumstances.[156] Because of the varying borderlines of the canon[157] Eichhorn selects the situation of Jesus and his Apostles as the basis for its definition.

> The rest of Vol. I and the first part of Vol. II are dedicated to the problems of "lower" introduction: The history of the text, translations, editions etc. In the Prolegomena to Vol. II Eichhorn stresses that he had worked alone on these problems, but had done so on the basis of what he had learned from J. D. Michaelis on biblical texts and from Heyne on classical texts. Comparisons with observations regarding classical authors recur throughout the volumes.

The second part of the Introduction into the single books of the Old Testament[158] deals first at length with the Pentateuch. Eichhorn defends the great antiquity of the book.[159] Methodically he begins with a positive judgement: "Is it appropriate for a scholar simply for *a priori* reasons to doubt about the genuineness of a monument [*Denkmahl*] of antiquity?"[160]

---

[152] *Einleitung*[1], I, 13.

[153] Ibid. 20–21.

[154] An insinuation known since the famous book *De tribus impostoribus, Anno MDIIC*; modern edition by G. Bartsch (Berlin 1960).

[155] *Einleitung*[1], I, 26. The late texts are full of Chaldaeisms [Aramaisms].

[156] Ibid. 29.

[157] Ibid. 1, I, 30–40.

[158] *Einleitung*[1] 1, II, 247–628.

[159] Characteristically he mentions Homer as an early parallel, ibid. 1, II, 250.

[160] Ibid. 1, II, 253. "If they neither by their content, or by other characteristic traces are postdated to a later century, as they attribute to themselves or tradition assigns to them, a critical scholar should not allow himself to doubt about their own witness or that of the tradition otherwise he is a despicable pettifogger and no more a historical scholar."

Eichhorn regards the Pentateuch as older than all the other books of the Old Testament. He argues from the apparently archaic language and numerous quotations (Sodom and Gomorrah e.a.) in other parts of the Old Testament. The author cannot be later as Moses, because the laws have been added to and actualised from time to time.[161] With the division of the kingdom the northern part had only the Pentateuch as Holy Scripture. In the book of Chronicles many hints show that they were used in Judah. Ezra cannot be the author, because his language is much inferior.[162] "Only a man like Moses can be author of these books."[163]

In the following Eichhorn mentions some scholars, among them J. Astruc,[164] who already distinguished between two sources in the Creation Story. He works out the distinction more carefully and now follows the sources in Genesis 1–11, the one characterised by the name for God "Jehovah",[165] the other "Elohim". Both are written by different authors and older than Moses. Both probably used still older documents (as Gen 2:4–3:24, distinguishable by the combination Jehovah Elohim). Moses (or a predecessor) probably worked the two sources together, preserving the whole material except for repetitions. The gain of the new insights lies for Eichhorn in the field of history: The historian can compare both sources and single out details. But the task of separating both threads from one another is difficult, because they are not preserved in the original order. In the following, Eichhorn praises the genuineness of different parts of Genesis as a document painting the childhood of the world, for instance the Patriarchal Stories dwelling upon the home-life of herdsmen with their herds. The difference between these stories and episodes in the life of David or Solomon is emphasised. Herder's influence can be felt in these and the following enthusiastic remarks. The usual objections to anachronisms are listed and refuted.

For Exodus-Numeri Eichhorn thinks that the books are composed of single "articles", which have been connected by the collectors with inserted stories. They are not Moses' work,[166] but approved by him and therefore authentic. Deut 1:1–31:29 are written by Moses himself, "the last word of the people's father and leader".[167] The last chapters are a supplement; ch. 34 from a later hand.

The books of Samuel and Kings were completed in the beginning of the Babylonian exile, but came together gradually with contributions from different times. The sources are mostly old and trustworthy, though some pieces (i.a. 1 Sam 17:11–32) are interpolated. 1 Kings 12–2 Kings 17 show the spirit of *one* author ("epitomator").

Eichhorn seeks the origin of prophecy in the ability of reason to divine the future from the course of nature and later the normal consequences of moral

---

[161] Ibid. 1, II, 263–64.

[162] "In Moses – the language clear, noble, charming; in Ezra unclear, rough, plane, tiring", ibid. l, II, 269.

[163] § 415, headline, ibid. 1, II, 290.

[164] It is debated whether Eichhom is dependent on Astrue for distinguishing between two Pentateuchal sources; cf. i.a. Smend, Alttestamentler (1989) 31.

[165] The usual reading for the Tetragrammaton in the period.

[166] Eichhorn presumes Moses might nevertheless be their author, ibid. 429f, but remains irresolute in the question.

[167] Ibid. II, 422.

actions.[168] The hearers, not yet accustomed "to penetrate into the real causes of things ... believed to perceive in those utterances the co-operation of a divinity".[169] Being fond of the power as representatives of the divinity over kings and peoples, the prophets spoke enthusiastically and like poets. Moses could not avoid a compromise with prophecy in Israel, but tried to limit the danger of seduction by laws (Deut 18:15–22). Thus, the Hebrew prophets became wise men, distinguished by reason and experience, pious men, zealots for truth, virtue and religion. They were also representatives of the mosaic laws, which they repeated, explained and applied.

"But Moses could not do more than gradually suppress the rough sensuality of his nation by a heavy burden of external rituals ... and offerings." His successors [the prophets] showed the people groaning under the burden, "how they could throw them totally away, and by an improved mind could make all offerings ... superfluous".[170] Eichhorn presents himself again as a genuine representative of Enlightenment! He also states that the oracles of the prophets follow for their mostly rather general announcements a simple form: "Fortune and happiness changes to misfortune and grief, misfortune and grief to fortune and happiness".[171] Numerous poetic forms are used, symbols and visions, but with late prophets like Ezekiel, Daniel and Zechariah flowering periods of language give way to worn out pictures. Eichhorn detects also connections between the life-conditions of the individual prophet and his language: "The priest would always have temple and altar ... before his eyes; the herdsman (like Amos) would always wander around on fields and near brooks and with herds".[172] He reckons with written manuscripts of the oracles as the basis for the collections we have now.

From the general observation that the contents of certain oracles do not fit the traditional age of a prophet Eichhorn arrives at the conclusion that they might be later additions. If it is allowed to an expert in the classics to find such pieces in the ancient literature,

> why should a critical examiner of the OT not follow the same path of giving back to every age what belongs to it, of removing later additions from older works, and after this procedure be allowed to acquiesce in the genuineness of those pieces, which can belong to the respective author for inner reasons?[173]

Eichhorn follows this path with the book of Isaiah. He comes to the conclusion that according to his insights "oracles from very different periods and totally different prophets are collected under his name, and linked together like single nameless pearls strung on a long cord".[174] Thus, for example Isa 16:14, an addition to Isaiah 15–16, cannot be Isaianic, for Moab was not totally destroyed three years after Isaiah's death.[175] Differences in language and colour

---

168 Ibid. 2–6.
169 Ibid. III, 5.
170 Ibid. III, 24.
171 Ibid. III, 27.
172 Ibid. III, 37.
173 Ibid. III, 69.
174 Ibid. III, 77.
175 Ibid.

are more important: Thus Isaiah 24–27 differ remarkably from genuine Isaianic utterances, and the accumulation of infinitives in Isaiah 58–59 is strange to his language.[176] If the book of Isaiah is examined according to the same rules as anonymous classical works, it can be shown for several passages, "that neither contents nor language ... correspond to the period of the kings, under whom Isaiah flourished, and that his early oracles are mixed with more recent ones of other prophets".[177] Above all, Isaiah 40–52 cannot be written before the Babylonian exile, because Babylon is consistently the scene in very concrete details, and the prophet speaks to fellow-exiles who are despairing at the delay of their return. If Isaiah were the author, how could he forget the prophetic habit of making circumstances of their own time the starting-point?

Isa 21:1–10 describes the conquest of Babylon by Cyrus in all details. Isaiah 23 contains many recent expressions. Isaiah 36–39 are an excerpt from the Book of Kings. Therefore all the following chapters must be later. The result is clear: "Our Isaiah received his present form no earlier than after the Babylonian exile".[178] At first smaller collections of Isaianic oracles existed. Economic reasons (to fill out unused space on the parchment rolls) led to the addition of pieces from other prophets.[179]

About other prophetic books, Eichhorn is less critical. The "lack of order" in the book of Jeremiah he explains by the thesis that Jeremiah had his prophecies written on single smaller or bigger rolls. The different form of the book in MT and in the Septuagint shows that two editions must have existed already before the first century CE. But the whole book, except Jeremiah 52, is Jeremianic. The miracles in Jonah (especially the three-days sojourn of the prophet in the belly of the fish) become understandable in a folk-story. The story in its written form is late, but depends on older tradition. On the book of Zechariah, Eichhorn's position differs from his judgements on the book of Isaiah. He notices the striking change in subject and style from ch. 9 onwards, but finally arrives at a solution "to the advantage of the tradition":[180] The difference in style can be caused by the change of subjects. *Maśśā'* in 9:1; 12:1 can be added. If the dates in the first part are lacking in the second, this is explicable: The first part is related to the life of the prophet, in the second he is looking into a distant future. The difference from the treatment of the book of Isaiah shows that Eichhorn still lacks a fixed methodical procedure.

Space does not allow to dwell upon Eichhorn's statements on Psalms and Proverbs. Job in his opinion is "the most ancient work of poetry from the whole of antiquity", a theodicy.[181] It is poetry, not historical truth, fiction or the revision of an older story. It surprises that no allusion to Abraham, Isaac and Jacob can be found; Moses and his constitution seem to be completely unknown to the author. For an early date of the book before Moses above all speaks the language and the picture of God not as absolute king, but simply as a busy father of the family and emir. Either the author is not a Hebrew, or he wrote before Moses. The Song of Songs, on the contrary,

---

[176] Ibid. III, 79–80.
[177] Ibid. III, 83.
[178] Ibid. III, 97.
[179] Again parallels in the works of classic authors, which were filled up with secondary pieces, are the model, ibid. III, 105.
[180] Ibid. 415.
[181] Ibid. III, 599.

is the latest of the poetical books. Eichhorn refutes all allegorical interpretations, but also the understanding as wedding song. "Nothing is more contrary to the customs of the orient than all that is presupposed with these hypotheses." Thus, a bride would never dance before the guests. She would be silent and veiled.[182] Correctly he states: "The book cannot be anything else but a collection of several sensations of love in separate songs, idylls, singing-matches".[183]

Looking back on the whole, one has to consider that Eichhorn's is a pioneer work. Methodically it is still uneven and was readily overtaken by its critical successors. On the other hand, Eichhorn's propensity to give the tradition the first word before seeking for radical solutions should be remembered in the present situation, in which literary criticism of the Bible not seldom becomes a destructive operation. Eichhorn's main interest lies in the fields of history and philology. Besides, a sense for aesthetics connects him with Herder (since his early *Urgeschichte*). In the fourth edition of his *Einleitung* he held mostly to his position with only slight modifications, though the development of research in the meantime in many points had overtaken him.[184]

From a modern standpoint we may criticise that Eichhorn in many aspects still followed traditional opinions. When the fourth edition appeared he was already outstripped by the next generation of critical scholars like de Wette. But already H. Ewald defended Eichhorn against such reproaches.[185] Eichhorn himself was conscious of his role; he wrote already in the prologue to the first edition:

> *In dieser Schrift ... wage ich den ersten Versuch, nicht eine Lüke ganz auszufüllen, sondern einem alten Bedürfnis einigermaßen abzuhelfen. Haben durch meine Bearbeitung dunkle Materien an Licht, verworrene an Deutlichkeit, ungewisse an Gewißheit auch nur einiges gewonnen; wird mein Versuch andere zu ähnlichen aufmuntern, und ihnen dabei, auch nur als erste Grundlage, nützlich seyn ... Morgenröthe muß vor dem Tage hergehen; warum nicht auch vor dem der biblischen Kritik?*[186]

5. Johann Philipp Gabler
and the New Discipline of a 'Biblical Theology'

Sources: J. P. GABLER: *De iusto discrimine theologiae biblicae et dogmaticae regundisque recte utriusque finibus*, in: T. A. / J. G. GABLER (eds.), *D. Johann Philipp Gablers kleinere theologische Schriften 2. Opuscula academica* (Ulm 1831, repr. s. l. s.a. [Munich 1980]) 179–98; ET: *On the Proper Distinction between Biblical and Dogmatic Theology and the Specific Objectives of Each*, in: J. SANDYS-WUNSCH / L. ELDREDGE, *SJT* 33, 134–44 (see below); German tr.: O. Merk, Biblische *Theologie* [see sect. 2 above] 273–84, repr. in: *Das Problem der Theologie des Neuen Testaments* (ed. G. Streck-

---

[182] Ibid. III, 690.
[183] Ibid. III, 691.
[184] Visible for example in W. L. M. DE WETTE, *Lehrbuch der historisch-kritischen Einleitung in die Bibel Alten und Neuen Testaments* (Berlin 1817–26).
[185] *Allein wo er zurück war, darin war er doch noch mit der ganzen zeit zurück ... Es ist unbillig einen übrigens arbeitsamen edles wollenden mann nach etwas anderm zu schäzen als nach der seite seiner thätigkeit worin er wirklich ... eine lücke ausfüllte und den nachfolgern nuzen schaffte*, Jahrbücher der Biblischen Wissenschaft 1 (1848) 30–31.
[186] *Einleitung*[1], I. Prologue (no headline, no page numbers). Cf. also Vol. II, Prologue: "Whether I worked successfully [*glüklich*] or unsuccessfully, is not yet decided".

er; WdF CCCLXVII; Darmstadt 1975) 31–44; (ed.), *Joh. G. Eichhorns Urgeschichte* [see sect. 4 above]; *Neuer Versuch über die Mosaische Schöpfungsgeschichte aus der höhern Kritik. Ein Nachtrag zum ersten Theil seiner Ausgabe der Eichhorn'schen Urgeschichte* (Altdorf / Nürnberg 1795). – G. T. ZACHARIÄ, *Biblische Theologie. oder Untersuchung des biblischen Grundes der vornehmsten theologischen Lehren* 1–5 (Göttingen 1771–86).

General literature and studies: H. BOERS, *What is New Testament Theology?* (Guides to Biblical Scholarship, NT series; Philadelphia 1979) 23–38; C. D. VON CÖLLN, *Biblische Theologie* 1 (Leipzig 1836); H.-J. DOHMEIER, *Die Grundzüge der Theologie Johann Philipp Gablers* (diss. theol. Münster 1976); K. HAACKER, "Biblische Theologie und historische Kritik" [review of O. Merk, see above], *Theologische Beiträge* 8 (1977) 223–26; C. HARTLICH / W. SACHS, *Ursprung* [see sect. 4 above]; G. F. HASEL, "The Relationship between Biblical Theology and Systematic Theology", *Trinity Journal* NS 5 (1984) 113–27; HENNEBERG, "Johann Philipp Gabler", in: *Neuer Nekrolog der Deutschen* (ed. Friedrich August Schmidt; Weimar, Ilmenau) 4 (1826) 80–92; R. P. KNIERIM, "On Gabler", in: idem, *The Task of Old Testament Theology: Substance, Method and Cases* (Grand Rapids / Cambridge 1995) 495–556; H.-J. KRAUS, *Biblische Theologie* [see sect. 3 above] 52–59; W. G. KÜMMEL, *Das Neue Testament* (see above) 115–24, ET: *The New Testament: A History of the Interpretation of its Problems* (Nashville, TN 1972) 98–100; O. MERK, *Biblische Theologie* [see sect. 2 above]; R. MORGAN, "Gabler's Bicentenary", *Expository Times* 98 (1987) 164–68; K.-W. NIEBUHR / C. BÖTTRICH (eds.), Johann Philipp Gabler (1753–1826) zum 250. Geburtstag (Leipzig 2003 [C. Böttrich, Bibliographie Johann Philipp Gabler, 172–200]); B. C. OLLENBURGER, "Biblical Theology: Situating the Discipline", in: *Understanding the Word* (FS B. W. Anderson, ed. J. T. Butler / E. W. Conrad / B. C. Ollenburger; JSOTSup 37; Sheffield 1986) 37–62; K. LEDER, *Universität Altdorf. Zur Theologie der Aufklärung in Franken. Die theologische Fakultät in Altdorf 1750–1809* (Schriftenreihe der altnürnberger Landschaft 14; Nürnberg 1965) 273–312; H. GRAF REVENTLOW, *Epochen* IV (2001) 209–26; idem, *Hauptprobleme der alttestamentlichen Theologie im 20. Jahrhundert* (EdF 173; Darmstadt 1982), = ET: *Problems of Old Testament Theology in the Twentieth Century* (London 1985); M. SÆBØ, "Johann Philipp Gablers Bedeutung für die Biblische Theologie", *ZAW* 99 (1987) 1–16, = in: idem, *On the Way to Canon. Creative Tradition History in the Old Testament* (JSOTSup 191; Sheffield 1998) 310–26; idem, "Der Weg der Biblischen Theologie von Gabler zu von Rad", in: P. HANSON / B. JANOWSKI / M. WELKER (eds.), *Biblische Theologie. Beiträge des Symposiums "Das Alte Testament und die Kultur der Moderne" anlässlich des 100. Geburtstags Gerhard von Rads (1901–1971), Heidelberg, 18.–21. Oktober 2001* (Altes Testament und Moderne 14; Münster 2005) 1–25; J. SANDYS-WUNSCH/ L. ELDREDGE, "J. P. Gabler and the Distinction between Biblical and Dogmatic Theology: Translation, Commentary and Discussion of His Originality", *SJT* 33 (1980) 133–44, = B. C. OLLENBURGER / E. A. MARTENS / G. F. HASEL (eds.), *The Flowering of Old Testament Theology: A Reader in Twentieth-century Old Testament Theology* (Sources for Biblical and Theological Study 1; Winona Lake, IN 1992) 489–502; W. SCHRÖTER, *Erinnerungen an Johann Philipp Gabler* (Jena 1827); R. SMEND, "Johann Philipp Gablers Begründung der biblischen Theologie", *EvTh* 22 (1962) 345–57, = idem, *Epochen der Bibelkritik* [see sect. 3 above] 104–16; L. T. STUCKENBRUCK, "Johann Philipp Gabler and the Delineation of Biblical Theology", *SJT* 52 (1999) 139–57; G. H. WITTENBERG, "Johann Philipp Gabler and the Consequences: In Search of a New Paradigm for Old Testament Theology", OTE N.S. 7 (1994) 103–28.

In common opinion, Johann Philipp Gabler (1753–1826) is regarded as one of, if not *the* founding father of Biblical Theology. This assumption has a certain validity, but is not the whole truth. K. LEDER's statement: "Gabler war kein Systematiker"[187] is misleading insofar as Gabler's main interest was on the field of systematic (dogmatic) theology, not of exegesis[188] – though he de-

---

[187] Who gave as reason that Gabler did not develop a closed theological system and never wrote a bigger scholarly work, Universität Altdorf (1965) 279. The second remark is not correct, if one looks on the lengthy *Introduction* to the re-edition of the second part of Eichhorn's *Urgeschichte*, which appeared as a separate volume II, 1 (Altdorf / Nürnberg 1792).

[188] The remarks in Reventlow, Problems (1985) 3f, have to be revised.

livered a mostly overlooked historical-critical study on the creation story.[189] This is already visible in the way, in which he framed the re-edition of his teacher Eichhorn's *Urgeschichte* (see the preceding section) by a lengthy Introduction and detailed comments. There he applied the theory of myth, which he had studied with Heyne, *in extenso* on Eichhorn's comparatively short reflections about the biblical creation-story.[190] One can ask whether this four-volume accomplishment was perhaps as representative for the so-called "mythical school", his most important contribution to the history of biblical exegesis. But in our context the much-discussed problem of Gabler's role in the development of a new discipline, Biblical Theology, should be in the centre of our considerations.

The first observation, which to some degree qualifies Gabler's importance for the issue, is the fact that already A. F. Büsching (1724–93), in the context of the Enlightenment, contended against the ruling scholastic theological system. He sought a self-contained Biblical Theology composed exclusively from the Scriptures.[191] More important is the four-volume work of G. T. Zachariä, *Biblische Theologie*, whom Gabler himself mentions as user of the term (*De justo discrimine*, 192–93; ET 144). O. Merk[192] shows, however, that central aspects of Zachariä's work also had an important impact on Gabler. This concerned especially Zachariä's intention to distil out of the whole canon trans-historical truths – independently from the differing opinions of the biblical authors – which could be used for an alternative system of confirming dogmatic statements, aside from the traditional method of *dicta probantia*.

Second, the usual isolated quotation of the best-known sentence in Gabler's inaugural address:

> *Est vero theologia biblica e genere historico, tradens, quid scriptores sacri de rebus diuinis senserint; theologia contra dogmatica e genere didactico, docens, quid theologus quisque ... ratione super rebus diuinis philosophetur* ("There is truly a biblical theology, of historical origin, conveying what the holy writers felt about divine matters; on the other hand, there is a dogmatic theology, of didactic origin, teaching what each theologian philosophises rationally about divine things").[193]

gives the false impression that Gabler wanted to define Biblical Theology as a historical-critical enterprise in the modern sense of the word.[194] But actually the definition cannot be used as an argument in the present-day discussion on the nature of the discipline. As the context shows, Gabler understood history in the manner typical for the Enlightenment: What is historical is a period of the past that can be characterised as a stage in the development of human knowledge and opinions. We met this understanding already with Herder's

---

[189] *Neuer Versuch* (1795).

[190] Cf. Reventlow, Epochen IV (2001) 216–19.

[191] A. F. Büsching, *Dissertatio inauguralis exhibens epitomen theologiae e solis literis sacris concinnatae* (Gottingae 1756); idem, *Epitome Theologiae e solis literis sacris concinnatae* (Lemgoviae 1757); idem, *Gedanken von der Beschaffenheit und dem Vorzug der biblisch-dogmatischen Theologie vor der scholastischen* (Lemgo 1758). Cf. Merk, Biblische Theologie (1972) 21.

[192] Ibid. 24–27.

[193] *Opuscula*, 183–84; ET 137.

[194] On this misinterpretation, cf. Ollenburger, Situating the Discipline (1985) 38. According to Ollenburger, W. Wrede was the first to have understood Gabler in this way.

and Eichhorn's christening the primeval period "childhood" of humanity, in which also language and feeling was "childish". The task for the modern scholar consists in grasping the meaning of ancient documents (*Urkunden*) by reason or *Einfühlung* in the period's worldview and way of thinking.

Gabler's main interest[195] is not focused on defining the methods of a historical-critical biblical theology. His starting point is the disharmony in theological opinions, which also leads to a sectarian splintering off of parties in the Church. As a remedy he seeks a foundation of unity in the Bible, especially the New Testament, which all members of the Christian community acknowledge as the source of "all true knowledge of the Christian religion" (179f; ET 134). Important for him is the distinction between religion and theology (which J. S. Semler first postulated). Religion is[196] *doctrina divina in scripturis tradita; docens, quid quisque Christianus et scire et credere et facere debeat ad tenendam huius et futurae vitae felicitatem* ("religion is passed on by the doctrine in the Scriptures, teaching what each Christian ought to know and believe and to do in order to secure happiness in this life and in the life to come"; 182; ET 136). In this Gabler is a typical "neologian": In the wake of the Enlightenment thinking religion is for him a form of doctrine, restricted to the means of reaching the aim of earthly and eternal happiness by knowing, believing and doing. Thus, it can and must be simple and easy to understand, opening the way to happiness[197] to every Christian. Neologian he is in holding fast to the Bible as an infallible source of truth.[198] Dogmatic theology, on the other side, after Semler is individualised as *quod theologus quisque ... super rebus diuinis philosophetur.* Gabler deplores the consequences and seeks to heal the loss of unity on all three levels: religion, Christian community and dogmatic theology by a return to the Bible as the basis of all-comprising truth.

But even the Bible cannot be treated as a unity any more. Gabler does not close his eyes to the darker side of the Scriptures and its different origins, which also have been caused by the deplorable fact that many interpreters introduced their own intentions into the Scriptures. Nevertheless, even the basis of a comprehensive theological interpretation of the canon (a term Gabler characteristically does not use) is destroyed in the formulation: *quod scriptores sacri de rebus diuinis senserint.* Also in the Bible we have to do with the personal opinions ("feelings") of individual writers.

These presuppositions and the intention of regaining a trustworthy basis for a revised dogmatic theology determine the rules of the projected Biblical

---

[195] Knierim, On Gabler (1995) 496–505, gives an overview over the different interpretations.

[196] Gabler quotes (*Opuscula* 182; ET 136) as the most recent utterance C. C. TITTMANN's (1744–1820) *Programma de discrimine theologiae et religionis* (Wittenberg 1782).

[197] Characteristic is the shift in terminology from "salvation" to "happiness" in the vocabulary from Orthodoxy to Enlightenment.

[198] He even can see himself as a believing Lutheran – as for instance also Semler did – cf. his utterance in the *Vorrede* to his re-edition of Eichhorn's *Urgeschichte* (XVIII): ... *ich bin nur auf die symbolischen Bücher [confession] unserer Evangelisch-Lutherischen Kirche verpflichtet.* However, regarding him as a believing Lutheran according to the theology of the Reformation would be misleading.

Theology. The first step has to be that the interpreter carefully gathers the "sacred ideas" (185; ET 138–39), using also the traditional method of comparison between different passages. The difference of periods – especially the higher value of the New Testament compared with the Old – does not allow us to place them in the same category. Because divine inspiration could not destroy "a holy man's own native intelligence and his natural way of knowing things" (186; ET 139), Gabler thinks it convenient to skip the theme of inspiration at this stage of interpretation, where it is important to find out what these men felt (186; the ET fails at this place). Thus, the authors, who are teaching the old doctrine, which Paul calls πτωχὰ στοιχεῖα (Gal 4:9), are on a lower level than the New Testament writers. There is also a remark on the genres (dicendi genera: historicum, didacticum, poeticum) that have to be distinguished. Gabler proceeds in counting down the authors from the Patriarchs[199] to the prophets, including also the apocryphal books, in the New Testament selecting Jesus, Paul, John, and James. He also suggests that one may include the apocryphal books. After the interpretation of the relevant passages follows "the careful comparison of the ideas of all the sacred authors among themselves" (187; ET 140). Gabler stresses the difficulties with this enterprise, especially the ambiguity of the sense of terms, partly as the result of a longer development of their use, the danger of introducing new dogmas the authors never could have thought about. But seemingly Gabler here trusts in the methods of the new historical-critical research, in which he was to show his competence some years later in the now forgotten distinctive interpretation of the creation story.[200] Later he would repeatedly speak about the "historical-philological" method.[201] Mixing ideas of different times should be avoided in any case. But the main goal remains untouched by these problems: Finding the common ideas that can be used for the purpose of dogmatic theology. After the opinions of the biblical authors have been collected, digested and referred to universal notions,[202] "one should investigate with great diligence which opinions have to do with the unchanging compendium[203] of Christian doctrine and therefore directly pertain to us, and which are said only to men of some particular era and doctrine" (191). As examples of the second kind Gabler mentions the Mosaic rites, abrogated by Jesus Christ, "or Paul's advice about women veiling themselves in church" (191; ET 142). Also in the NT "we must diligently investigate ... what was said as an accommodation to the ideas and the needs of the first Christians and what was said in reference to the unchanging

---

[199] The Patriarchs are classified as writers like Moses, David, Solomon – the ET, 140, is again not correct.

[200] Neuer Versuch (1795).

[201] Cf. Merk, Biblische Theologie (1972) 90–91.

[202] Gabler adopted the term, and also reason as criterion, from the philosopher and New Testament scholar S. F. N. Morus (1736–92). For Gabler's rationalism, cf. his remarks quoted by Merk, Biblische Theologie (1972) 105, n. 311. On Morus, cf. also Knierim, Task (1995) 534–36. For criticism of its use by Gabler, ibid. 548–50.

[203] ET "testament" is an inadequate translation of lat. formula, which can mean the essence of Christian doctrine, as formulated i.a. in the symbolic books.

idea of the doctrine of salvation; ... what in the sayings of the Apostles is truly divine, and what perchance merely human" (ibid.; ET 143). The idea of accommodation is a typical argument of neologian apologetics against antichristian rationalism ("naturalism"), explaining why the words of Jesus and the Apostles presupposed an out of date worldview.

After all these passages have been checked carefully "by exegetical observation only" (192; ET 143), the passages which are "truly divine", "appropriate to the Christian religion of all times", or the *dicta classica* will be singled out (ibid.). As *dicta classica* is an equivalent for the orthodox dogmatic prooftexts (*dicta probantia*) – though gained the other way round – it is noteworthy that Gabler's arguments at this point remain in the vocabulary of orthodox theology. The result is to be the foundation for a "biblical theology in the stricter sense of the word", a formulation, which Gabler claims to have adopted from Zachariä.[204] At least since 1802[205] he calls it a "*pure* biblical theology", that means: purified from ideas entailed by the times. The "un-falsified" original meaning of the biblical author he now calls "*true* biblical theology".[206] Thus we arrive at two stages of Biblical Theology, the second of which already mediates between exegesis and dogmatics. Thus, if MERK is right,[207] Gabler actually cannot be called the "father" of Biblical theology,[208] because he intended to use the results of the historical exegesis of the Bible for dogmatic purposes. According to him we owe this merit to G. L. Bauer (1755–1806),[209] a rationalistic theologian, who saw in the reconstruction of historical facts by historical-critical exegesis a goal in its own right and shared the enlightened theory of the development of humankind step by step.[210]

In the context of the inaugural address another formulation is remarkable: For dogmatic theology Gabler demands "that we then teach accurately the harmony of divine dogmatics and the principles of human reason" (193; ET 144). Here Gabler presents himself as a genuine *Aufklärer*.[211] The impression, which his contempories had of him, that he is partly self-contradictory and wavering in his thinking, actually is typical for the neologians, who tried in vain to reconcile reason and belief, confessional tradition and modernity. His engagement as an influential editor of consecutive theological journals[212]

---

[204] MERK's German translation (281) is correct; the criticism in ET (144, n. 1) is based on a misunderstanding of the sentence.

[205] Cf. Merk, Biblische Theologie (1972) 97. But cf. already the formulation in the inaugural address (191; ET 142).

[206] Cf. Merk, ibid. 98.

[207] Merk, ibid. 202. Cf. also K. Haacker's critical remarks on Merk's position: Review (1977).

[208] Sæbø, Gabler (1987/1998), at the end of his careful arguments, arrives at the opposite conclusion. It is a question of evaluation.

[209] Author i.a. of *Theologie des Alten Testaments oder Abriß der religiösen Begriffe der alten Hebräer...* (Leipzig 1896); *Biblische Theologie des Neuen Testaments* 1–4 (Leipzig 1800–02).

[210] Cf. Merk, ibid. 157–63. A Biblical Theology of both testaments then becomes impossible, a position supported by MERK himself.

[211] Cf. also his elaborate statement on his position, quoted by Dohmeier, Grundzüge (1976) 88.

[212] *Neuestes theologisches Journal*, 1798–1801; *Journal für theologische Literatur*, 1801–03; *Journal für auserlesene theologische Literatur*, 1805–11.

shows him in the role of a (nearly) impartial moderator between different theological positions.[213] However, personally he remained an adherer of the idea of progress.[214] Also in the field of Biblical Theology his position is not consequent. Nevertheless, criticising Gabler is all too easy, if we consider the unsolved problems which still burden the program of a Biblical Theology.

---

[213] Cf. Dohmeier, ibid. 49–52.
[214] Dohmeier, ibid. 53.

Contributors

Abbreviations

Indexes
Names / Topics / References

Contributors

EDWARD BREUER (b. 1960), Adjunct Lecturer of Jewish History, the Hebrew University of Jerusalem. Selected publications: "Haskalah and Scripture in Mendelssohn's Early Writings", *Zion* 59 (1994) 445–63 [Heb.]; *The Limits of Enlightenment: Jews, Germans, and the Eighteenth-Century Study of Scripture* (Cambridge, MA 1996); "Early Modern and Modern Interpretation of the Bible", in: *The Jewish Study Bible* (ed. M. Brettler / A. Berlin; Oxford 2003) 1900–08.

CHRISTOPH BULTMANN (b. 1961), Professor of Biblical Studies, University of Erfurt, Germany. Selected publications: *Die biblische Urgeschichte in der Aufklärung. Johann Gottfried Herders Interpretation der Genesis als Antwort auf die Religionskritik David Humes* (Tübingen 1999); "Bibliotheken der Geschichte: Diodorus Siculus und das Alte Testament", in: *Vergegenwärtigung des Alten Testaments. Beiträge zur biblischen Hermeneutik* (ed. C. Bultmann / W. Dietrich / C. Levin; Göttingen 2002) 242–56; "What Do We Mean when We Talk about '(Late) Enlightenment Biblical Criticism'?", in: *The Bible and the Enlightenment* (ed. W. Johnstone; London 2004) 119–34.

STEPHEN G. BURNETT (b. 1956), Associate Professor of Classics and Religious Studies, and of History, University of Nebraska, Lincoln, NE. Selected publications: *From Christian Hebraism to Jewish Studies: Johannes Buxtorf (1564–1629) and Hebrew Learning in the Seventeenth-Century* (Leiden 1996); *Jews, Judaism and the Reformation in Sixteenth Century Germany* (ed. D. P. Bell / S. G. Burnett; Leiden 2006); "Reassessing the Basel-Wittenberg Conflict: Dimensions of the Reformation-Era Discussion of Hebrew Scholarship", in: *Hebraica Veritas? Christian Hebraists and the Study of Judaism in Early Modern Europe* (ed. A. P. Coudert / J. S. Shoulsen; Philadelphia 2004) 181–201; "Spokesmen for Judaism: Medieval Jewish Polemicists and their Christian Readers in the Reformation Era", in: *Reuchlin und seine Erben. Forscher, Denker, Ideologen und Spinner* (ed. P. Schaefer / I. Wandrey; Stuttgart 2005) 41–51; "Dialogue of the Deaf: Hebrew Pedagogy and Anti-Jewish Polemic in Sebastian Münster's *Messiahs of the Christians and the Jews* (1529/39)", *ARefG* 91 (2000) 168–90.

EUAN K. CAMERON (b. 1958), Henry Luce III Professor of Reformation Church History and Academic Dean, Union Theological Seminary, New York. Selected publications: *The European Reformation* (Oxford 1991); *Waldenses: Rejections of Holy Church in Medieval Europe* (Oxford 2000); *Interpreting Christian History* (Oxford 2005).

JEREMY CATTO (b. 1939), Fellow of Oriel College, University of Oxford. Selected publications: *History of the University of Oxford*, vol. 1 (Oxford 1984), vol. 2 (Oxford 1992).

TROND BERG ERIKSEN (b. 1945), Professor of History of Ideas, University of Oslo. Selected publications: *Bios Theoretikos. Notes on Aristotle's Eth. Nic. X, 6–8* (Oslo 1976); *Reisen gjennom helvete. Dantes Inferno* (Oslo 1993); *Augustin. Det urolige hjerte* (Oslo 2000).

G. R. EVANS (b. 1944), PhD, LittD, DLitt, Professor of Medieval Theology and Intellectual History, Emerita, University of Cambridge. Selected publications: *The Language and Logic of the Bible: the Road to Reformation* 1–2 (Cambridge 1985); *The*

Thought of Gregory the Great (Cambridge 1986); *Anselm* (London 1989 / 2002); *Problems of Authority in the Reformation Debates* (Cambridge 1994); *The Church and the Churches: toward an Ecumenical Ecclesiology* (Cambridge 1994); *The Medieval Theologians* (Oxford 2001); *John Wyclif: Myth and Reality* (Oxford 2005).

SEYMOUR FELDMAN (b. 1932), Professor of Philosophy, Emeritus, Rutgers University, New Brunswick, NJ. Selected publications: *The Wars of the Lord of Levi ben Gershom (Gersonides)* 1–3 (transl. and notes; Philadelphia 1984, 1988, 1999); *Philosophy in a Time of Crisis: Don Isaac Abravanel – Defender of the Faith* (London 2003); "Platonic Cosmologies in the Dialoghi d'Amore of Leone Ebreo (Judah Abravanel)", *Viator* 36 (2005) 557–82.

PIERRE GIBERT (b. 1936), Professor of the Old Testament, Emeritus, Faculty of Theology, Lyon, France; Editor-in-Chief of *Recherches de Science Religieuse*. Selected publications: *Une théorie de la légende. H. Gunkel et les légendes de la Bible* (Paris 1979); *Bible, mythes et récits de commencement* (Paris 1986); *Vérité historique et esprit historien. L'historien biblique de Gédéon face à Hérodote* (Paris 1990); *L'espérance de Caïn. La violence dans la Bible* (Paris 2002).

HANS-JÜRGEN GOERTZ (b. 1937), Professor; recently retired from the Institut für Sozial- und Wirtschaftsgeschichte, University of Hamburg. Selected publications: *Die Täufer. Geschichte und Deutung* (Munich [2]1988); *Thomas Müntzer. Mystiker, Apokalyptiker, Revolutionär* (Munich 1989); *Deutschland 1500–1648. Eine zertrennte Welt* (Paderborn 2004).

JOHN H. HAYES (b. 1934), Franklin N. Parker Professor of Old Testament, Candler School of Theology, Emory University, Atlanta, GA. Selected publications: *Introduction to the Bible* (Philadelphia 1971); (editor), *Dictionary of Biblical Interpretation* (two vols.) A-J, K-Z (Nashville 1999); (co-author), *A History of Ancient Israel and Judah* (2nd edn.; Louisville 2006).

ROBERT GERALD HOBBS (b. 1941), Professor of Church History & Music, Emeritus, Vancouver School of Theology, Vancouver, BC, Canada. Selected publications: "Martin Bucer on Psalm 22: a study in the application of rabbinic exegesis by a Christian Hebraist", *Histoire de l'exégèse au XVIe siècle* (EPH 34; Geneva 1978) 144–63; "Conrad Pellican and the Psalms: the ambivalent legacy of a pioneer Hebraist", *RRRev* 1 (1999) 72–99; "<Quam apposite religioni sit musica> Martin Bucer and music in the liturgy", *RRRev* 6/2 (2004) 155–78; "Martin Bucer, the Jews and Judaism", in: S. BURNETT / D. BELL (eds.), *Jews, Judaism and the Reformation in Sixteenth-Century Germany* (Leiden 2006) 137–69.

MOSHE IDEL (b. 1947), Max Cooper Professor of Jewish Thought, the Hebrew University of Jerusalem. Selected publications: *Kabbalah: New Perspectives* (New Haven, CT 1988); *Perakim be-kabbalah nevuit* (Jerusalem 1990); *Golem: Magical and Mystical Traditions on the Artificial Anthropoid* (Albany 1990); *Hasidism: Between Ecstasy and Magic* (Albany 1995); *Messianic Mystics* (New Haven, CT 1998); *Absorbing Perfections: Kabbalah and Interpretation* (New Haven, CT 2002); *Kabbalah and Eros* (New Haven, CT 2005).

ULRICH KÖPF (b. 1941), Professor of Church History and Director of Institut für Spätmittelalter und Reformation, University of Tübingen. Selected publications: *Die Anfänge der theologischen Wissenschaftstheorie im 13. Jahrhundert* (BHTh 49; Tübingen 1974); *Religiöse Erfahrung in der Theologie Bernards von Clairvaux* (BHTh 61; Tübingen 1980); (Editor and author), *Historisch-kritische Geschichtsbetrachtung. Ferdinand Christian Baur und seine Schüler* (Contubernium 40; Sigmaringen 1994); (Editor and author), *Deutsche Geschichte in Quellen und Darstellung, 3. Reformationszeit 1495–1555* (Stuttgart 2001); (Editor and author), *Theologen des Mittelalters* (Darmstadt 2002).

Eric Lawee (b. 1963), Associate Professor of Humanities, York University, Toronto, Canada. Selected publications: *Isaac Abarbanel's Stance Toward Tradition: Defense, Dissent, and Dialogue* (Albany 2001); "Graven Images, Astromagical Cherubs, Mosaic Miracles: A Fifteenth-Century Curial-Rabbinic Exchange", *Speculum* 81 (2006) 754–95.

Natalio Fernández Marcos (b. 1940), Research Professor, Consejo Superior de Investigaciones Científicas (CSIC), Madrid. Selected publications: (with Emilia Fernández Tejero), *Biblia y Humanismo. Textos, talantes y controversias del siglo XVI español* (Madrid 1997); *Introducción a las versiones griegas del la Biblia* (Madrid 1998; 2nd edition translated into English, Leiden e.a. 2000, and into Italian, Brescia 2000); (with J. R. Busto Saiz), *El texto antioqueno de la Biblia griega* I-III (Madrid 1989–1996); (with M. V. Spottorno and J. M. Cañas), *Índice griego-hebreo del texto antioqueno en los libros históricos* I-II (Madrid 2005); *Liber Iudicum*, in: *Biblia Hebraica Quinta* (Stuttgart [forthcoming]).

William McKane (1921–2004) was Professor of Hebrew and Oriental Languages at St Andrews University. Selected publications: *Prophets and Wise Men* (London 1965); *Proverbs: A New Approach* (London 1970); *A Critical and Exegetical Commentary on Jeremiah* 1-2 (Edinburgh 1986; 1996); *Selected Christian Hebraists* (Cambridge 1989); *A Late Harvest. Reflections on the Old Testament* (Edinburgh 1997); *Micah. Introduction and Commentary* (Edinburgh 1998).

Sophie Kessler Mesguich (b. 1957), Professor of Hebrew language and linguistics, Université de Paris-3 Sorbonne nouvelle. Selected publications: "Les hébraïsants chrétiens", in: *Le Grand Siècle et la Bible* (BTT 6; Paris 1989) 83–95; *Les études hébraïques en France, de François Tissard à Richard Simon (1508–1680). Grammaires et enseignement* (Dr. thesis, Université de Paris-8, 1994); *La langue des sages, matériaux pour une étude linguistique de l'hébreu de la Mishna* (Paris / Louvain 2002); "L'enseignement de l'hébreu et de l'araméen par les premiers lecteurs royaux (1530–1560)", in: *Histoire du Collège de France 1. La création 1530–1560* (ed. A Tuilier; Paris 2006) 257–82.

Charlotte Methuen (b. 1964), Departmental Lecturer in Ecclesiastical History, Faculty of Theology, University of Oxford. Selected publications: "'This comet or new star': theology and the interpretation of the nova of 1572", *Perspectives on Science* 5 (1997) 499–515; *Kepler's Tübingen: Stimulus to a Theological Mathematics* (Aldershot 1998); "Special providence and sixteenth-century astronomical observation: some preliminary reflections", *Early Science and Medicine* 4 (1999) 99–113; "Time human or time divine: Theological aspects in opposing the Gregorian Calendar Reform", *Reformation and Renaissance Review* 3/1-2 (2001) 36–50; "Zur Bedeutung der Mathematik für die Theologie Philip Melanchthons", in: Stefan Rhein / Günther Frank (eds.), *Melanchthon und die Naturwissenschaften seiner Zeit* (Melanchthon-Schriften der Stadt Bretten 4; Sigmaringen 1998) 85–103, [Engl. "The role of the heavens in the theology of Philip Melanchthon", *Journal for the History of Ideas* 57 (1996) 385–403; repr. in: Michael L. LaBlanc (ed.), *Literature Criticism from 1400 to 1800*, vol. 90 (Farmington Hills, MI 2003) 116–27].

Steven M. Nadler (b. 1958), Professor of Philosophy, University of Wisconsin-Madison. Selected publications: *Spinoza: A Life* (Cambridge 1999); *Spinoza's Heresy: Immortality and the Jewish Mind* (Oxford 2002); *Spinoza's Ethics: An Introduction* (Cambridge 2006).

Henk J. M. Nellen (b. 1949), Dr. Senior researcher, Huygens Institute of the Royal Netherlands Academy of Arts and Sciences. Selected publications: (in collaboration with C. M. Ridderikhoff), *Briefwisseling van Hugo Grotius*, Rijks Geschiedkundige Publicatiën, Grote serie, vols. XIII (1642), XIV (1643), XV (January-September

1644), XVI (October 1644-August 1645), XVII, Supplement (1583–1645) (The Hague 1990–2001); (in collaboration with S. Surdèl), "Short but not sweet: the career of Gisbertus Longolius (1507–1543), headmaster of the Latin School in Deventer and Professor at the University of Cologne", *Lias* 32-1 (2005) 3–22; "The correspondence of Hugo Grotius", in: *Les grands intermédiaires culturels de la République des Lettres. Etudes de réseaux de correspondances du XVIe au XVIIIe siècles* (ed. Chr. Berkvens-Stevelinck e.a.; Paris 2005) 127–64; *Papieren betrekkingen. Zevenentwintig brieven uit de vroegmoderne tijd* (ed. P. G. Hoftijzer / O. S. Lankhorst / H. J. M. Nellen; Nijmegen 2005).

Bernt Torvild Oftestad (b. 1942), Professor of Church History, Norwegian School of Theology, Oslo. Selected publications: "Harmonia Evangelica. Die Evangelienharmonie von Martin Chemnitz – theologische Ziele und methodologische Voraussetzungen", *Studia theologica* 45 (1991) 57–74; "Lehre, die das Herz bewegt. Das Predigtparadigma Martin Chemnitz", *ARefG* 80 (1989) 125–53; "Traditio und Norma – Hauptzüge der Schriftauffassung bei Martin Chemnitz", in: *Der zweite Martin der Lutherischen Kirche. Festschrift zum 400. Todestag von Martin Chemnitz* (ed. W. A. Jüncke; Braunschweig 1986) 172–90.

Peter Opitz (b. 1957), *Oberassistent* at the Institute for Swiss Reformation, University of Zurich. Selected publications: *Calvins theologische Hermeneutik* (Neukirchen-Vluyn: Neukirchener Verlag 1994); *Calvin im Kontext der Schweizer Reformation* (Zürich: Theologischer Verlag 2003); (editor), *Heinrich Bullinger als Theologe* (Zürich: Theologischer Verlag 2004).

Stephen Prickett (b. 1939), Regius Professor at the University of Glasgow, Emeritus, and Margaret Root Brown Professor for Browning Studies and Victorian Poetry and Director of the Armstrong Browning Library, at Baylor University, Waco, TX. Selected publications: *Coleridge and Wordsworth: the Poetry of Growth* (Cambridge 1970); *Romanticism and Religion: The Tradition of Coleridge and Wordsworth in the Victorian Church* (Cambridge 1976); *Words and the Word: Language, Poetics and Biblical Interpretation* (Cambridge 1986); *Origins of Narrative: the Romantic Appropriation of the Bible* (Cambridge 1996); *Narrative, Science and Religion: Fundamentalism versus Irony, 1700–1999* (Cambridge 2002).

Siegfried Raeder (1929–2006) was Professor of Church History at the Evang.-Theol. Faculty, University of Tübingen. Selected publications: *Das Hebräische bei Luther untersucht bis zum Ende der ersten Psalmenvorlesung* (Tübingen 1961); *Die Benutzung des masoretischen Textes bei Luther in der Zeit zwischen der ersten und zweiten Psalmenvorlesung (1515–1518)* (Tübingen 1967); *Grammatica Theologica. Studien zu Luthers Operationes in Psalmos* (Tübingen 1977); *Der Islam und das Christentum. Eine historische und theologische Einführung* (2nd rev. and enlarg. edition; Neukirchen-Vluyn 2003); *Antworten auf den Islam. Texte christlicher Autoren vom 8. Jahrhundert bis zur Gegenwart* (zusammengestellt, eingeleitet und erläutert von Siegfried Raeder; Neukirchen-Vluyn 2006).

Tarald Rasmussen (b. 1949), Professor of Church History at the Faculty of Theology, University of Oslo. Selected publications: *Inimici ecclesiae. Das ekklesiologische Feindbild in Luthers Dictata super Psalterium (1513–1515) im Horizont der theologischen Tradition* (Studies in Medieval and Reformation Thought XLIV; Leiden 1989); "Jacob Perez of Valencia's 'Tractatus contra Judeos' (1484) in the light of the Medieval anti-Judaic Traditions", in: *Augustine, The harvest, and theology (1300–1650): Essays dedicated to Heiko Augustinus Oberman in honor of his sixtieth birthday* (ed. Kenneth Hagen; Leiden 1990) 41–59; (with Nils Gilje), *Tankeliv i den lutherske stat, 1537–1814. Norsk idéhistorie 2* (Oslo 2002).

HENNING GRAF REVENTLOW (b. 1929), Emeritus Professor of Old Testament, Faculty of Protestant Theology, University of the Ruhr, Bochum. Selected publications: *Das Amt des Propheten bei Amos* (Göttingen 1962); *Bibelautorität und Geist der Moderne* (Göttingen 1980; ET: *The Authority of the Bible and the Rise of the Modern World*, London / Philadelphia 1984); *Gebet im Alten Testament* (Stuttgart 1986); *Hauptprobleme der alttestamentlichen Theologie im 20. Jahrhundert* (EdF 173; Darmstadt 1982; ET: *Problems of Old Testament Theology in the Twentieth Century*, London 1985); *Hauptprobleme der Biblischen Theologie im 20. Jahrhundert* (EdF 203; Darmstadt 1983; ET: *Problems of Biblical Theology in the Twentieth Century*, London 1986); *Epochen der Bibelauslegung* I-IV (Munich 1990-2001; Engl. transl. in preparation); *Die Propheten Haggai, Sacharja und Maleachi* (ATD 25,2; Göttingen 1993); (editor, with W. FARMER), *Biblical Studies and the Shifting of Paradigms, 1850-1914* (Sheffield 1995).

RICHARD REX (b. 1961), Reader in Reformation History, Tutor and Director of Studies in History, Fellow of Queens' College, University of Cambridge. Selected publications: *The Lollards* (Basingstoke 2002); *Henry VIII and the English Reformation* (2nd edn.; Basingstoke 2006); (editor), *A Reformation Rhetoric: Thomas Swynnerton's The Tropes and Figures of Scripture* (Cambridge 1999).

J. W. ROGERSON (b. 1935), DD, DD h.c., Dr.theol. h.c., Professor of Biblical Studies, Emeritus, University of Sheffield. Selected publications: "Bibelwissenschaft I/2", TRE 6 (1980) 346-61; *Old Testament Criticism in the Nineteenth Century. England and Germany* (London 1984); "The Old Testament", in: J. ROGERSON / C. ROWLAND / B. LINDARS, *The Study and Use of the Bible* (Basingstoke 1988) 1-150; *W. M. L. de Wette, Founder of Modern Biblical Criticism. An Intellectual Biography* (Sheffield 1992); *The Bible and Criticism in Victorian Britain. Profiles of F. D. Maurice and William Robertson Smith* (Sheffield 1995); (editor), *The Oxford Illustrated History of the Bible* (Oxford 2001).

ERIKA RUMMEL (b. 1942), Professor of History, Emerita, Wilfrid Laurier University, Waterloo, Ont., Canada. Selected publications: *The Humanist - Scholastic Debate in the Renaissance and Reformation* (Cambridge, MA 1995); *The Confessionalization of Humanism in Reformation Germany* (New York 2000); *Erasmus* (London 2004).

MAGNE SÆBØ (b. 1929), Professor of Old Testament Theology, Emeritus, Norwegian School of Theology, Oslo. Selected publications: *Sacharja 9-14. Untersuchungen von Text und Form* (WMANT 34; Neukirchen-Vluyn 1969); *On the Way to Canon. Creative Tradition History in the Old Testament* (JSOTSup 191; Sheffield 1998); (editor), *Esther*, in: *Biblia Hebraica quinta editione*, 18 (Stuttgart 2004); "Zur neueren Interpretationsgeschichte des Alten Testaments", *ThLZ* 130 (2005) 1033-44.

JOHN SANDYS-WUNSCH (b. 1936), former President Thorneloe University and Professor of Religious Studies; Associate Fellow, Centre for Studies in Religion and Society, University of Victoria, Canada. Selected publications: *What Have They Done to the Bible? A History of Modern Biblical Interpretation* (Collegeville MN, 2005); (with L. ELDREDGE), "J. P. Gabler and the Distinction between Biblical and Dogmatic Theology: Translation, Commentary and Discussion of His Originality", *Scottish Journal of Theology* 33 (1980) 133-44.

ADRIAN SCHENKER (b. 1939), Professor of Old Testament, Emeritus, University of Fribourg, Switzerland. Editor-in-Chief of *Biblia Hebraica quinta editione*. Selected publications: *Septante et texte massorétique dans l'histoire la plus ancienne du texte de 1 Rois 2-14* (Paris 2000); *Älteste Textgeschichte der Königsbücher. Die hebräische Vorlage der ursprünglichen Septuaginta als älteste Textform der Königsbücher* (Freiburg, CH / Göttingen 2004); *Das Neue am neuen Bund und das Alte am alten. Jer 31 in der hebräischen und griechischen Bibel* (Göttingen 2006).

BERTRAM SCHWARZBACH (b. 1940), Dr. Selected publications: on Enlightenment iconoclasm, the "clandestin manuscripts", Voltaire's Bible studies, Huguenot politics, the
study of Hebrew in eighteenth-century France, collecting Hebrew books in pre-Revolutionary France, and studies of the religious philosophy of Yeshayahu Leibowitz.
Edited Voltaire's *Collection d'anciens évangiles* for the *Complete Works of Voltaire*
(*Les oeuvres complètes de Voltaire* 69; Paris 1994); one of the editors of the *Dictionnaire philosophique* (vols. 35–36; Paris 1994); preparing the critical edition of Voltaire's *La Bible enfin expliquée*; (editor of) Mme du Châtelet's *Examens de la Bible*
(Paris 2006).

OSKAR SKARSAUNE (b. 1946), Professor of Church History, Norwegian School of Theology, Oslo. Selected publications: *The Proof from Prophecy. A Study in Justin Martyr's
Proof-Text Tradition: Text-Type, Provenance, Thological Profile* (NovTSup LVI; Lei-
den 1987); *Incarnation. Myth or Fact?* (Concordia Scholarship Today; St. Louis
1991); *In the Shadow of the Temple: Jewish Influences on Early Christianity* (Downers
Grove, IL 2002); *We Have Found the Messiah: Jewish Believers in Jesus in Antiquity*
(Mishkan 45; Jerusalem 2005); (editor), *Jewish Believers in Jesus: The Early Centuries*
(Peabody, MA 2006).

LESLEY SMITH, Fellow and Tutor in Politics and Senior Tutor, Harris Manchester Col-
lege, Oxford University. Selected publications: *Medieval Exegesis in Translation:
Commentaries on the Book of Ruth* (Kalamazoo, MI 1996; repr. 2000); (editor, with
P. D. W. KREY), *Nicholas of Lyra: the Senses of Scripture* (Leiden 2000); *Masters of the
Sacred Page: Theology in the Latin West to 1274* (The Medieval Book, 2; Notre
Dame, IN 2001); (with JANE H. M. TAYLOR), *Women and the Book in the Middle Ages*
1–3 (1–2, Woodbridge 1995; 3, London / Toronto 1996).

JOHANN ANSELM STEIGER (b. 1967), Professor of Church History, University of Hamburg, Selected publications: *Melancholie, Diätetik und Trost* (Heidelberg 1996); *Johann Gerhard (1582–1637). Studien zu Theologie und Frömmigkeit des Kirchenvaters
der lutherischen Orthodoxie* (Stuttgart 1997); *Fünf Zentralthemen der Theologie
Luthers und seiner Erben* (Leiden 2002); *Medizinische Theologie. Christus medicus und
theologia medicinalis bei Martin Luther und im Luthertum der Barockzeit* (Leiden
2005).

EMILIA FERNÁNDEZ TEJERO (b. 1942), Research Professor, Consejo Superior de Investigaciones Científicas (CSIC), Madrid. Selected publications: (with NATALIO FERNÁN-
DEZ-MARCOS), *Biblia y Humanismo. Textos, talantes y controversias del siglo XVI español* (Madrid 1997); *La masora magna del Códice de Profetas de El Cairo* (Madrid
1995); *El Cantar más bello*. Cantar de los cantares de Salomón (3rd edition; Madrid
1998); *Las masoras del libro de Génesis*. Códice M1 de la Universidad Complutense de
Madrid (Madrid 2004); "¿Esposa o *Perfecta casada*? Dos personajes femeninos en la
exégesis de Fray Luis de León", *III Simposio Bíblico Español* (Valencia / Lisboa
1991).

ARJO VANDERJAGT (b. 1948), Professor of the History of Ideas, University of Groningen. General editor of Brill's Studies in Intellectual History. Selected publications:
Rodolphus Agricola Phrisius (1444–1485) (ed. F. Akkerman / A. J. Vanderjagt; Leiden
1988); *Northern Humanism in European Context, 1469–1625* (ed. F. Akkerman / G.
C. Huisman / A. J. Vanderjagt; Leiden 1993); *Wessel Gansfort (1419–1489) and
Northern Humanism* (ed. F. Akkerman / A. J. Vanderjagt / A. H. van der Laan; Leiden 1999); "Expropriating the past. Tradition and Innovation in the use of texts in
fifteenth-century Burgundy", *Tradition and Innovation in an Era of Change / Tradition und Innovation im Übergang zur Frühen Neuzeit* (ed. R. Suntrup / J. R. Veenstra;
Frankfurt am Main 2001) 177–201; "Mediating the Bible: Three approaches. The
cases of Giannozzo Manetti (1396–1459), Wessel Gansfort (1419–1489) and Sanctes

Pagninus (1470–1536)", *Cultural Mediators. Artist and Writers at the Crossroads of Tradition, Innovation and Reception in the Low Countries and Italy 1450–1650* (ed. A. de Vries; Leuven 2007, forthcoming).

JOHANNES WALLMANN (b. 1930), Professor of Church History, Emeritus, University of the Ruhr, Bochum, and *Honorarprofessor* of Church History, Humboldt University Berlin. Selected publications: *Der Theologiebegriff bei Johann Gerhard und Georg Calixt* (Tübingen 1961); *Philipp Jakob Spener und die Anfänge des Pietismus* (2nd edition; Tübingen 1986); *Theologie und Frömmigkeit im Zeitalter des Barock* (Tübingen 1995); *Der Pietismus* (Göttingen 2005); *Kirchengeschichte Deutschlands seit der Reformation* (6th edition; Tübingen 2006).

HENRY WANSBROUGH (b. 1934), Master of St Benet's Hall, Emeritus, Oxford. Selected publications: (editor), *New Jerusalem Bible* (London 1985); *The Passion and Death of Jesus* (London 2003); *The Story of the Bible* (London 2006).

JARED WICKS (b. 1929), Professor of Theology, John Carroll University, University Heights, Ohio. Selected publications: *Cajetan und die Anfänge der Reformation* (Münster 1983); *Luther's Reform. Studies on Conversion and the Church* (Mainz 1992).

Abbreviations

1. General and Non-literary Abbreviations

Abt.	Abteilung	Lat.	Latin
ad loc.	ad locum	LXX	Septuagint
Arab.	Arabic	MA	Middle Ages / Mittelalter /
b.	babli; ben / bar; born		Moyen Age
BCE	before Common Era	MT	Mas(s)oretic Text
BH	Biblia Hebraica	Ms(s)/ms(s)	manuscript(s)
Bk.	Book	NF	Neue Folge
BN(F)	Bibliothèque Nationale (Fran-	n(n).	note(s)
	çaise)	no(s).	number(s)
c.	circa / around	NS	New Series
CE	Common Era	NT	New Testament
cf.	confer, compare	obv.	obverse
ch./chap(s).	chapter(s)	OG	Old Greek
CNRS	Centre National de la Re-	OS	Old Series
	cherche Scientifique	OT	Old Testament
col(s).	column(s)	P	Peshitta
cr.	copyright	pass.	passim
CSIC	Consejo Superior de Investi-	p(p).	page(s)
	gaciones Científicas	Pl(s).	plate(s)
d.	died	pl.	plural
Diss.	Dissertation	Q	Qumran
e.a.	et alia/i	q(q).	quaestio(nes)
e.c.	exempli causa	q.v.	quod vide
ed(s).	editor(s) / edited by	r	recto (cf. v)
edn.	edition	ref(s).	reference(s)
ET	English translation	repr.	reprint(ed)
f(f)	following unit(s) / page(s)	rev.	revised
fol.	folio	RV	Revised Version
FS	Festschrift	s. a.	sine anno
FUE	Fundación universitaria espa-	sect(s).	section(s)
	ñola (Madrid)	s.l.	sine loco
G	Greek version	sg.	singular
HB	Hebrew Bible	s.v.	sub voce
Heb.	Hebrew	Syr.	Syriac
hgg.	herausgegeben	TaNaK	*Tora Nebi'im Ketubim*
i.a.	inter alia		('Law, Prophets, Writings'),
i.e.	id est		acronym for Hebrew Bible
ibid.	ibidem	Tg(s)	Targum(s)
j.	jeruschalmi (cf. y.)	tr.	translated / translatio

UP	University Press	VL	Vetus Latina
v	verso	vol(s).	volume(s)
v(v).	verse(s)	vs.	versus
var.	variant	y.	yerushalmi (cf. j.)
Vg	Vulgate		

2. Acronyms of Cited Rabbis

Besht	Rabbi Israel Ba'al Shem Tov (or, the / ha-Besht; see HBOT II, Ch. 39)
Malbim	Rabbi Meir Leibush / Loeb ben Yehiel Michael (see HBOT II, Ch. 43)
Radak	Rabbi David Qimhi (Kimhi) (see HBOT I/2, Ch. 33.3.3)
Ralbag	Rabbi Levi ben Gershom / Gersonides (see HBOT II, Ch. 2.2)
Rambam	Rabbi Moses ben Maimon / Maimonides (see HBOT I/2, Ch. 31.3.5)
Ramban	Rabbi Moses ben Nahman / Nahmanides (see HBOT I/2, Ch. 33.4)
Rambeman	Rabbi Moses Mendelssohn (see HBOT II, Ch. 43)
Rasad	Rabbi Saadiah Gaon (see HBOT I/2, Ch. 25.3)
Rashbam	Rabbi Samuel ben Meir (see HBOT II, Ch. 43)
Rashi	Rabbi Solomon Yishaqi (ben Isaac) (see HBOT I/2, Ch. 32.5)

3. Abbreviations of Periodicals, Yearbooks, Reference Works and Series

Abbreviations of periodicals and book titles are in italic

AAug	Analecta Augustiniana
AAWG.PH	Abhandlungen der Akademie der Wissenschaften in Göttingen, Philologisch-historische Klasse
ABD	*Anchor Bible Dictionary*
ABG	*Archiv für Begriffsgeschichte*
ACi	*Analecta Cisterciensia*
ADB	*Allgemeine Deutsche Biographie*
AER/AEcR	*American Ecclesiastical Review*
AFH	*Archivum Franciscanum historicum*
AFP	*Archivum Fratrum Praedicatorum*
AGP	Arbeiten zur Geschichte des Pietismus
AGPh	*Archiv für Geschichte der Philosophie (und Soziologie)*
AGTL	Arbeiten zur Geschichte und Theologie des Luthertums
AHR	*American Historical Review*
AJS	*American Journal of Sociology*
AKG	Arbeiten zur Kirchengeschichte
AKuG	*Archiv für Kulturgeschichte*
AnGr	Analecta Gregoriana
AÖG	*Archiv für österreichische Geschichte*
APh	*Archiv für Philosophie*
ARefG	*Archiv für Reformationsgeschichte*
ARelG	*Archiv für Religionsgeschichte*
ASGW.PH.	*Abhandlungen der Sächsischen Gesellschaft der Wissenschaften, Philologisch-historische Klasse*

ATA	Alttestamentliche Abhandlungen
AUL	Acta Universitatis Lundensis
AWA	Archiv zur Weimarer Ausgabe
BAC	Biblioteca de Autores Cristianos
BB	Biographia Britannica
BBAur	Bibliotheca bibliographica Aureliana
BBKL	*Biographisch-bibliographisches Kirchenlexikon* (Bautz)
BETL	Bibliotheca Ephemeridum Theologicarum Lovaniensium
BevTh	Beiträge zur evangelischen Theologie
BFChrTh	Beiträge zur Förderung christlicher Theologie
BGBE	Beiträge zur Geschichte der biblischen Exegese
BGBH	Beiträge zur Geschichte der biblischen Hermeneutik
BGLRK	Beiträge zur Geschichte und Lehre der Reformierten Kirche
BGPhMA	Beiträge zur Geschichte der Philosophie und Theologie des Mittelalters
BHK	*Biblia Hebraica* (ed. R. Kittel)
BHR	Bibliothèque d'humanisme et renaissance
BHRef	Bibliotheca humanistica et reformatorica
BHS	*Biblia Hebraica Stuttgartensia* (ed. K. Elliger / W. Rudolph)
BHTh	Beiträge zur historischen Theologie
Bib.	*Biblica*
BiblThom	Bibliothèque Thomiste
BJRL	*Bulletin of the John Rylands University Library of Manchester*
BMS	*Berlinische Monatsschrift*
BNYPL	*Bulletin of the New York Public Library*
BRHE	Bibliothèque de la Revue d'histoire ecclésiastique
BSHPF	*Bulletin de la société de l'histoire du protestantisme français*
BSLK	*Die Bekenntnisschriften der evangelisch-lutherischen Kirche*
BSRK	*Die Bekenntnisschriften der reformierten Kirche*
BTT	*Bible de tous les temps*
BWKG	*Blätter für Württembergische Kirchengeschichte*
CBLa	Collectanea Biblica Latina
CBQ	*Catholic Biblical Quarterly*
CCath	Corpus Catholicum
CCL/CCSL	Corpus Christianrum, series latina
CGG	*Christlicher Glaube in moderner Gesellschaft*
CH	*Church History*
CHB	*The Cambridge History of the Bible*
CHR	*Catholic Historical Review*
CHRP	*The Cambridge History of Renaissance Philosophy*
CR	Corpus Reformatorum
CSEL	Corpus scriptorum ecclesiasticorum Latinorum
CThM	Calwer theologische Monographien
CTJ	*Calvin Theological Journal*
CUP	*Chartularium Universitatis Parisiensis*
DB	*Dictionnaire de la Bible*
DBI	*A Dictionary of Biblical Interpretation* (ed. R. J. Coggins / J. L. Houlden)
DBInt	*Dictionary of Biblical Interpretation*, A-J, K-Z (ed. J. H. Hayes)
DBF	*Dictionnaire de Biographie Française*
DBS	*Dictionnaire de la Bible. Supplément*
DEurLum	*Dictionnaire européen des Lumières*
DHEE	Diccionario de Historia Eclesiástica de España
DHI	*Dictionary of the History of Ideas* (New York 1968–73)

DNB	*Dictionary of National Biography* (London 1885–1901) / *Oxford Dictionary of National Biography* (Oxford 2004)
DS	*Enchiridion symbolorum* ... (ed. Denzinger / Schönmetzer)
DVfLG	*Deutsche Vierteljahrschrift für Literaturwissenschaft und Geistesgeschichte*
EcR	*The Ecclesiastical Review*
EdF	Erträge der Forschung
EHPhR	Études d'histoire et de philosophie religieuses
EHS.T	Europäische Hochschulschriften. Reihe 23: Theologie
EncEnl	*Encyclopedia of Enlightenmemnt*
EncJud	*Encyclopaedia Judaica*
EncPh	*Encyclopedia of Philosophy*
EncRen	*Encyclopedia of the Renaissance*
EPH	*Études de philologie et d'histoire*
EPhM	*Études de philosophie médiévale*
ERSY	Erasmus of Rotterdam Society Yearbook
EstB	Estudios Bíblicos
ET	*Expository Times*
ETH	Études de théologie historique
EthSt	Erfurter theologische Studien
ETR	Études théologiques et religieuses
FGLP	Forschungen zur Geschichte und Lehre des Protestantismus
FKDG	Forschungen zur Kirchen- und Dogmengeschichte
FSThR	Forschungen zur systematischen Theologie und Religionsphilosophie
FThSt	Freiburger theologische Studien
FuF	*Forschungen und Fortschritte*
GTA	Göttinger theologische Arbeiten
GuG	*Geschichte und Gesellschaft*
HAL	*Hebräisches und Aramäisches Lexikon zum Alten Testament*
HBOT	*Hebrew Bible / Old Testament* (ed. M. Saeboe)
HDTG	*Handbuch der Dogmen- und Theologiegeschichte* (ed. C. Andresen)
HeR	*Humanisme et Renaissance*
Helm.	*Helmantica*
HHMBI	*Historical Handbook of Major Biblical Interpreters* (ed. D. K. McKim)
HHS	Harvard Historical Studies
HKG	*Handbuch der Kirchengeschichte* (ed. G. Krüger)
HThS	Harvard Theological Studies
HJ	Historisches Jahrbuch
HR	*History of Religions*
HS	Historische Studien
HTR	*Harvard Theological Review*
HUCA	Hebrew Union College Annual
HUTh	Hermeneutische Untersuchungen zur Theologie
HWP	*Historisches Wörterbuch der Philosophie*
HZ	*Historische Zeitschrift*
IDC	Inter Documentation Company
IliffRev	*Iliff Review*
Int.	*Interpretation*
JA	*Journal Asiatique*
JAAR	*Journal of the American Academy of Religion*
JBTh	Jahrbuch für Biblische Theologie
JDTh	Jahrbücher für deutsche Theologie

JE	*Jewish Encyclopaedia*
JEH	*Journal of Ecclesiastical History*
JHI	*Journal of the History of Ideas*
JHP	*Journal of the History of Philosophy*
JJS	*Journal of Jewish Studies*
JJTP	*The Journal of Jewish Thought and Philosophy*
JMRS	*Journal of Medieval and Renaissance Studies*
JRH	*The Journal of Religious History*
JSNTSup	Journal for the Study of the New Testament. Supplement Series
JSOTSup	Journal for the Study of the Old Testament. Supplement Series
JTS	*Journal of Theological Studies*
JQR	*Jewish Quarterly Review*
KIG	*Kirche in ihrer Geschichte*
LCL	Loeb Classical Library
LM	Lexikon des Mittelalters
LuJ	Luther-Jahrbuch
LuthQ	*Lutheran Quarterly*
LW	Luther's Works
MeH(M)	*Medievalia et Humanistica* (Madrid)
MF	Miscellanea francescana
MGH	Monumenta Germaniæ historica
MGMA	Monographien zur Geschichte des Mittelalters
MGWJ	*Monatsschrift für Geschichte und Wissenschaft des Judentums*
MennQR	*Mennonite Quarterly Review*
MQR	*Methodist Quarterly Review*
MRTS	Medieval & Renaissance Texts & Studies
MSU	Mitteilungen des Septuaginta-Unternehmens der Gesellschaft/Akademie der Wissenschaften in Göttingen
MThS.H	Münchener theologische Studien. Historische Abteilung
MThSt	Marburger theologische Studien
MThZ	*Münchener theologische Zeitschrift*
NAWG	Nachrichten der Akademie der Wissenschaften in Göttingen
NEB	*New English Bible*
NZSTh	*Neue Zeitschrift für systematische Theologie*
OBO	Orbis Biblicus et Orientalis
OEncRef	*Oxford Encyclopedia of the Reformation*
OTE	Old Testamnent Essays
PAAJR	Proceedings of the American Academy for Jewish Research
PaThSt	Paderborner theologische Studien
PhB	Philosophische Bibliothek
PhJ	Philosophisches Jahrbuch der Görres-Gesellschaft
PIASH	Proceedings of the Israel Academy of Sciences and Humanities
PIEM	Publications de l'Institut d'études médiévales
PL	Patrologiae cursus completus. Series Latina (ed. J.-P. Migne)
PThM	Pittsburgh Theological Monographs
QDGR	Quellen und Darstellungen aus der Geschichte des Reformationsjahrhunderts
QFRG	Quellen und Forschungen zur Reformationsgeschichte
QGPRK	Quellen zur Geschichte des Papsttums und des römischen Katholizismus
RBén	*Revue bénédictine de critique, d'histoire et de litterature religieuses*
RE	*Realencyclopädie für protestantische Theologie und Kirche*
REB	*Revised English Bible*
REncPh	*Routledge Encyclopedia of Philosophy*

RFE	*Revista de Filología Española*
REJ	*Revue des études juives*
RevSR	*Revue des sciences religieuses*
RGG³/RGG⁴	*Religion in Geschichte und Gegenwart* (3. resp. 4. Auflage)
RGST	Reformationsgeschichtliche Studien und Texte
RHE	*Revue d'histoire ecclésiastique*
RHPhR	*Revue d'histoire et de philosophie religieuses*
RKZ	*Reformierte Kirchenzeitung*
RoC	Records of Civilization. Sources and Studies
RRRev	*Reformation and Renaissance Review*
RSR	Recherches de science religieuse
RSV	*Revised Standard Version*
RSyn	*Revue de synthèse*
RT(h)AM	*Recherches de théologie ancienne et médiévale*
RThom	*Revue Thomiste*
RThPh	*Revue de théologie et de philosophie*
Saec.	*Saeculum*
SBLMS	Society of Biblical Literature. Masoretic Studies
SBLMT	Society of Biblical Literature. Masoretic Texts
SC	Sources chrétiennes
SCES	Sixteenth Century Essays and Studies
SCJ	*Sixteenth Century Journal*
ScrB	*Scripture Bulletin*
Sef.	*Sefarad*
SHAW	Sitzungsberichte der Heidelberger Akademie der Wissenschaften
SHCT	Studies in the History of Christian Thought
SIH	Studies in Intellectual History
SJT	*Scottish Journal of Theology*
SMRT	Studies in Medieval and Reformation Thought
Spec.	*Speculum*
SRTH	Studies in Reformed Theology and History
SSL	Spicilegium Sacrum Lovaniense
StGen	*Studium generale*
STGMA	Studien und Texte zur Geistesgeschichte des Mittelalters
StPB	Studia post-biblica
SThZ	*Schweizerische Theologische Zeitschrift*
STL	Studia theologica Lundensia
STPIMS	Studies and Texts. Pontifical Institute of Mediaeval Studies (Toronto)
StT	Studi e Testi. Biblioteca apostolica Vaticana
StTh	*Studia Theologica*
SVRG	Schriften des Vereins für Reformationsgeschichte
SWI	Studies of the Warburg Institute
TAzB	Texte und Arbeiten zur Bibel
TCBS	*Transactions of the Cambridge Bibliographical Society*
ThBl	*Theologische Blätter*
ThH	*Théologie historique*
ThLZ	*Theologische Literaturzeitung*
ThPh	*Theologie und Philosophie*
ThQ	*Theologische Quartalschrift*
THR	Travaux d'humanisme et renaissance
ThRv	*Theologische Revue*
TRE	*Theologische Realenzyklopädie*

TThZ	*Trierer theologische Zeitschrift*
ThZ	*Theologische Zeitschrift*
TS	Theological Studies (Woodstock, MD)
TSTP	Tübinger Studien zur Theologie und Philosophie
TU	Texte und Untersuchungen zur Geschichte der altkirchlichen Literatur
UJE	*The Universal Jewish Encyclopedia*
VB	*Vestigia Bibliae*
VC	*Vigiliae Christianae*
VIEG	Veröffentlichungen des Instituts für europäische Geschichte Mainz
VT	*Vetus Testamentum*
VTSup	Vetus Testamentum. Supplements
VVPfKG	Veröffentlichungen des Vereins für pfälzische Kirchengeschichte
VuF	*Verkündigung und Forschung*
WA	*Weimarana. Weimarer Ausgabe der Werke Martin Luthers*
WA.DB	*Weimarana. Deutsche Bibel*
WdF	Wege der Forschung
WMANT	Wissenschaftliche Monographien zum Alten und Neuen Testament
WTJ	*Westminster Theological Journal*
WZH.GS	*Wissenschaftliche Zeitschrift der Martin-Luther-Universität Halle-Wittenberg. Gesellschafts- und Sprachwissenschaften*
YJS	Yale Judaica Series
ZAW	*Zeitschrift für die alttestamentliche Wissenschaft*
ZBRG	Zürcher Beiträge zur Reformationsgeschichte
ZGNKG	*Zeitschrift der Gesellschaft für niedersächsische Kirchengeschichte*
ZHF	*Zeitschrift für historische Forschung*
ZHTh	*Zeitschrift für historische Theologie*
ZKG	*Zeitschrift für Kirchengeschichte*
ZNW	*Zeitschrift für die neutestamentliche Wissenschaft*
ZSTh	*Zeitschrift für systematische Theologie*
ZThK	*Zeitschrift für Theologie und Kirche*
ZRGG	*Zeitschrift für Religions- und Geistesgeschichte*
Zwing.	Zwingliana. Mitteilungen / Beiträge zur Geschichte Zwinglis, der Reformation und des Protestantismus in der Schweiz
ZWTh	*Zeitschrift für wissenschaftliche Theologie*

Indexes

Names/Topics/References

Names

1. Historical Names

(there may be minor differences in the spelling of the names)

2. Modern Authors

Topics

References

1. Bible

2. Apocrypha and Pseudoepigrapha

3. Hellenistic-Jewish Literature

4. Greek and Latin Authors

5. Ancient Jewish Sources

6. Early Jewish Authors
(including the Middle Ages)

7. Early Christian Authors
(including the Middle Ages)

De utilitate credendi
PL 42 68–69   225

Quaest. In Exod.
840

Bonacursus
Libellus contra Catharos
303
PL204, 777   303
PL204, 779–82 303
PL204, 784   303

Chrysostom
Homilies against the Jews
173

Eusebius
Hist. eccl.
3.25.3–4   987

Hugo Cardinalis / Hugo of St. Cher
51
Textus Bibliae cum Postilla
363

Postilla in totam bibliam
50–51, 57, 60–62

Textus Bibliae
368

Ireneus
Adversus haereses
612
IV 4,2   438

Isidore of Seville
Allegoriae quaedam scripturae sacrae
PL 83, 105   428

Jerome / Hieronymus
Opera omnia
261

Ad Pammachium
CSEL 54, 508, 9–13
(ep. 57, ch. 5)   404
CSEL 55, 275, 19–21
(ep. 106, ch. 55) 404

Appendici huic inest Quadruplex Psalterium
459

De Hebraica Veritate
171, 188, 968

Epistulae
363

Iuxta Septuaginta
171

Psalterium Hebraicum
374, 401–02, 485, 493,
502, 506

Quadruplex Psalterium
459

Moses bar Kepa
De paradiso commentarius
641

Origen
Hexapla
842

Peter Comestor
Historia Scholastica
57, 515

Peter Lombard
Sentences
50, 134, 316, 349, 353,
365–66, 397, 517, 532,
659
IV 17, 3   427
IV 18, 6   427

Priscian / Priscianus Caesariensis
Institutiones grammaticae
XVII   260

Pseudo-Dionysius
Mystical Theology
108–09

Tertullian
Praescr.
13   434

Theodoret
Quaest. In I Reg.
PLG 80, 529   839

Quaest. In Josue
PLG 80, 475   839

8. Jewish Authors Since the Renaissance
(including Spinoza)

Alantansi, Eliezer ben
Latter prophets
279

Torah
281

Altschuler, David / Altschuler Yehiel
  Hillel
Metzudat David
1009

Metzudat Tzion
1009

Anatoli, Jacob
Malmad ha-talmidim
10   198

Arama, Isaac ben Moses
'Aqedat yiṣḥaq
1,1v   199
5,89r   200

Asaf, S.
Mekorot le-Toldot ha-Hinukh be-Yisrael
1006
I, 43dff   1007

Ashkenazi, Solomon Zalman
Keren Shmuel
1008

Baer, Dov of Medzerich
'Or Torah
943
47   945

Bomberg, Daniel
Miqraoth gedoloth
458, 767

Arragel de Guadalajara, Mosés
Biblia de Alba
232

Cardoso, Isaac
Las Excelencias de los Hebreos
1008

Crescas, Hasdai
Or Adonai / The Light of the Lord
64

Sec. Treatise, First
Principle   71

David ben Solomon ibn Yacha
Kav w-Naki
283

Detmold, Samuel & Obernik, Meir
Minhah Hadashah
1021

Dubno, Solomon
Litrufah
1006, 1015

Sefer Netivot ha-Shalom (Bi'ur)
1015–18, 1020–1021
intr. Ex. 15   1015
intr. Ex. 21   1019

Tikkun Sopherim
1015

Edelmann, J.C.
Moses mit aufgedecktem Angesichte
1:58   973

Gersonides / Levi ben Gershom
*Perush al ha-Torah/Commentary on the
  Pentateuch*
64, 66–69, 72–75

Genesis
64, 72–74
Introduction   74
2a (Venice)   66
2c (Venice)   67
9c (Venice)   73
9d-10a (Venice) 68
14b-16d (Venice) 69
16d (Venice)   67
18d (Venice)   68
27a (Venice)   71
28b (Venice)   67
28d (Venice)   71
188d (Venice)   72
191a (Venice)   72
1–2 (Jerusalem) 66
3 (Jerusalem)   67
22 (Jerusalem)   73
26 (Jerusalem)   68

9. Authors in a Christian Context Since the Renaissance

(including philosophers)

Arnold, Gottfried
Das Geheimniß Der Göttlichen Sophia oder Weißheit
913

Das Wahre Christenthum Altes Testament
913

Historie und Beschreibung der Mystischen Theologie
41 913
58 913

Unpartheiische Kirchen- und Ketzerhistorie
698, 912

Ashton-Cooper, Antony, Third Earl of Shaftesbury
Letter Concerning Enthusiasm
Standard Edition I, 1 302–75 856

Philosophical Regimen
855

Sensus Communis
Standard Edition I, 3 856

Astruc, Jean
Conjectures sur la Genèse
773

Conjectures sur les Memoires
837, 846, 848–49

Avenarius, J.
Liber radicum seu lexicon ebraicum
691, 727

Bahrdt, Carl Friedrich
Kirchen und Ketzer Almanach
53 977

Bale, John
Scriptorum illustrium
512, 517

Basnage, Jacques
Histoire de l'église depuis Jésus Christ
1003

Bauer, G. L.
Biblische Theologie des Neuen Testaments
1062

Theologie des Alten Testaments
1062

Baumgarten, Alexander Gottlieb
Theoretische Aesthetik
1043

Baumgarten, Siegmund Jacob
Auslegung des Evangelii St. Johannis
691
211 754

Christliche Concordienbuch
997

Evangelische Glaubenslehre I-III
691
I, 34–138 995
I, 35–40 1001
II, 4–161 995
III, 4–148 995
III, 17 755
III, 23 755
III, 33 755

Nachrichten von einer Hallischen Bibliothek
999

Nachrichten von merkwürdigen Büchern
999

Sammlung von merkwürdigen Lebensbeschreibungen
1004

Theologische Lehrsätze
691
299 755

Unterricht von Auslegung der heiligen Schrift
691
9 755
19 756
43f 756
45 755

II, 571   871
II, 574   871
II, 612   871
II, 643–52   871
II, 644   871
II, 645–48   871
II, 701   871

A Defence of Natural and Revealed Reli-
    gion
               870

A Demonstration of the Being and Attri-
    butes of God
               870
230   871
247   871

A Discourse Concerning the Unchangeable
    Obligations of Natural Religion
               870–71
45f   871
160–207   871
178   871
367   871

Clericus, Johannes / le Clerc, Jean
Ars critica
               692, 750
II, 6   751
II, 18   751
II, 43   751
II, 85   751
II, 117   751

Dissertatio de Maris Idumaei Trajectione
               877

Genesis
               973

Sentiments de quelques theologiens
               840, 878
6–7   876
6–9   877

Cocceius, Johannes
Centum quinquaginta Psalmi
               692
113   720
504   719

Sanctae Scripturae Potentia
               692
203   721
249   721

Cochlaeus, Johann
De autoritate ecclesiae et scripturae
               625

Colet, John
Handbook of the Cristian Soldier
               217

Two Treatises on the Hierarchies of Diony-
    sius
106   530
154–57   530

Collins, Anthony
A Discourse of Free-thinking
               661, 862
5   862
8   862
10   862
32   862
35ff   863
44   863
46   863
52–56   863
57–61   863
58   863
88ff   863
121ff   863

A Discourse of the Grounds and Reasons of
    the Christian Religion
               692, 752, 862–63, 880
43ff   864
44   863

The Scheme of Literal Prophecy
               692, 880
329   752

Copernicus, Nicolaus
Complete Works
               670

Commentariolus
               671, 674

Hamann, J. G.
Aesthetica in nuce
1043

Hardenberg, Albert
Vita Wesseli Groningensis
160, 162–63
**[1v]   162
**3r–v   162

Hardenberg, F. von (Novalis)
Die Christenheit oder Europa
1033

Hardt, Hermann von der
Universalis exegeseos elementa
998

Harley, R.
Anglia libera
860

Harris, James H.
Hermes
981

Haye, Jean de La
Biblia magna commentariorum literalium
568

Biblia maxima versionum
568

Haymo of Halberstadt
In omnes psalmos explanatio
218

Hegel, G. W. F.
Grundlinien der Philosophie des Rechts
§§ 341–60   1032
§ 341   1032
§ 343   1032
§ 352   1032

Heinrich of Friemar
De decem praeceptis
150

Helwig, Ch.
Compendium Hebreae grammaticae
693, 727

Hemmingsen, Niels
De methodis libri duo
990

Henry VIII of England
Assertio Septem Sacramentorum
546

Herberger, V.
Magnalia Dei
    693, 744
5, B 4r   741

Herbert, Edward of Cherbury
A Dialogue Between a Tutor and His Pupil
856

De causis errorum
856

De Religione Gentilium Errorumque
    856, 858, 896
1   858
184–218   859

De veritate
    856–57, 896
129   858
135   858
208–22   857
226   858

Herder, Johann Gottfried
Sämtliche Werke (SWS)
    1041
1, 131–531   1045
I, 152   1045
I, 154   1045
I, 155   1045
VI, 1–129   1044
VI, 4   1045
VI, 25–28   1045
VI, 34   1045
VI, 54–55   1045
VI, 88   1045
VI, 131–92   1044
32, 228   1046

Werke in zehn Bänden (FA)
    1041
3, 431–521   1050

Die Schmalkaldischen Artikel
WA 50,
225 25–225,5   438

Ein deutsch Theologia
WA 1, 375–79,
LW 31, 73–76   341

Eine Predigt, daß man Kinder zur Schulen halten solle
WA 30II,
508–88   349

Ein Sendbrief vom Dolmetschen
                400
Aland,
no. 161   400
WA 30II,
632–46.694   400
WA 30II,
636, 18–20   398

Eine Unterricht, wie sich Christen in Mose sollen shicken
                385
Aland,
no. 520   385
AWA 17II,
516   385
WA 16,
363–93. 651   385
371, 13   385
373, 15–18   385
376, 13   386
381, 9   386
391, 7–8.10   386
389, 10–13   386
WA 24,
2–16, 739   385

Epistola Theologorum Parisiensium
WA 60,
123–30   622

Eyn brieff an die Fürsten zu Sachsen von dem auffrürischen geyst
                581
8   581

First Lecture on the Psalms
                348

Luthers Vorreden zur Bibel
                363, 382
31–46   382
32   382
33   382
34   383
34f   382
35   383
36   383
37   383
38   384
41   384
41f   384
42   384
43   386
43f   386
45   397
47   386
47f   386–87
51–55   387
52   87
53f   387
59–62   387
59   387
61   388
62   388
66–74   388
66   388
67   388
70   388
70f   389
71   389
72   389
75–80   389
77   389
78   389
79   389
79–80   390
80–83   390
81   390
82   390
83f   390
84–91   390
84   390
85   390
86   390
87   391
89   391
91–104   391
92   382
93   391

Enarratio brevis concionum libri Salomonis
495

Explicatio Proverbiorum Salomonis
495, 507, 511

Initia doctrinae physicae
342, 673
192   674
216–17   674

In obscuriora aliquot capita Geneseos
495

In Psalmos aliquot Davidicos
493, 507, 511

Interpretatio aliquot Psalmorum
493

Loci communes (1521)
499
CR 21, 81;
LCC 19, 19   506

Loci communes (1555)
501

Loci communes
487, 489–90, 496, 659
CR 21, 59–230 353
CR 21, 195;
LCC 19, 122–23 503

Nova Scholia
494

PAROIMIAI sive Proverbia Salomonis
494, 531

Salomonis Sententiae
494

Melville, Andrew
Scholastica diatriba de rebus divinis
527

Menochio, Giovanni Stefano
Brevis Explicatio
638

Mentzer, B. / Bodenius, A.
Tertia Disputatio Theologica
694
L 2r   716

Merian, M.
Icones Biblicae
694, 746

Meyer, Ludowijk
Philosophia scripturae interpres
978, 1001

Michael of Hungary
Sermones Michaelis de ungaria
337

Michaelis, Johann David
Abhandlung von der syrischen Sprache
980

Berurtheilung der Mittel
980

Commentaries on the laws of Moses (ET of
Mosaisches Recht)
980

Commentatio de mente et ratione
980

Commentatio posterior
980

Commentatio prior ad leges
980

De l'influence des opinons sur le langage
980
84   982
97   981
106–110   981

Deutsche Übersetzung des Alten Testament
980

Dissertatio de punctuorum hebraicum
980

Essai physique sur l'heure des marées
980

Pace, Richard
Praefatio in Ecclesiasten
522

Pagninus, Sanctes
Biblia... Habes in hoc libro prudens
270, 632
pref. 468

Biblia Veteris ac Novi Testamenti
536

Catena Argentea in Pentateuchum
186

Hebraicarum Institutionum libri IIII
268

Hebraicas Institutiones
633

Isagoge ad sacras literas Liber unicus
179, 186–87, 619, 633

Liber Psalmorum Hebraice
179, 187–88

Psalterium Tetraglottum
618, 620

Thesaurus linguae sanctae
179, 186, 188, 440, 555,
633, 694, 727, 778
col. 1821 188

Veteris et Novi Testamenti Nova Translatio
186

Paine, Thomas
Common Sense
1029

The American Crisis
1029

Rights of Man
1029

Paquot, M.
Mémoires
758, 764

335	764
336	764
343–44	765
346	765
366	764

Pareus, D.
Opera

II, 239	709–10
II, 833	719
II, 969	719
II, 1032f	719
II, 468	719

Operum Theologicorum
694

Disceptatio epistolaris Joannis
694
59 704

Pascal, B.
Pensées et opuscules
43, 685

Le Mémorial
43

Pasquali, A.
De libris canonicis

12	626
473–83	626
506–09	626

Patot, Simon Tyssot de
La vie I-II
756

Paul / Pablo of Burgos
Additiones
51, 232, 368, 507

Scrutinium scripturarum contra perfidiam iudaerorum
232

Paulus Venetus / Paul of Venice
Logica Magna
106

Reuchlin, Johannes
Sämtliche Werke 1–12
    254

Augenspiegel
    262

De accentibus et orthographia linguae hebraicae
    258

De arte cabalistica
        98, 257–58, 264, 363,
369,   521

De rudimentis hebraicis
        98, 144, 258–59, 264,
        337, 363, 368, 374, 397,
        414, 543, 555
Preface, 3   257, 259
1   369
123   369
231   507
557   260
582   261
585   401
615   260
621   259, 368

In Septem Psalmos poenitentiales
        261, 363, 369, 374, 507
7   404

De Verbo mirifico
        258, 262–64, 363, 369

Lexicon hebraicum et in Hebraeorum grammaticen
        261

Tutsch Missive
        262

Vocabularius Breviloquus
        256

Reuden, A.
Jsagoge Biblica
        695
N 2r   716
S 8r   724

Rheticus, Georg Joachim
Treatise on Holy Scripture
        674

Rist, Johann
De tribus magnis impostoribus
        746
d 2r   746
7–40   746

Neues Musikalisches Seelenparadis
        695, 745
b 7r   746

Rivetus, Andreas
Correspondance... d'André Rivet et de Claude Sarrau
        808
II, 264f   809
II, 361   809
II, 393f   809
II, 429   809
II, 431f, n.6   816

Isagoge
        695
15   704, 708
231f   738
231   738
262   729, 742

Operum theologicorum
813f   816

Robert of Gloucester
Gesta Regum
RS. 90.i.278   538

Robertson, James
Clavis Pentateuchi
80f   849

Rolle, Richard
Psalter
        539

Rosenmüller, E. F. K.
Handbuch für die Literatur der biblischen Kritik und Exegese
3, 151–56   976
500   849